The Bill James Handbook 2010

Baseball Info Solutions

www.baseballinfosolutions.com

Published by ACTA Sports

A Division of ACTA Publications

Cover by Tom A. Wright

Cover Photos by Samara Pearlstein

First Edition: November 2009

Published by:
ACTA Sports, a division of ACTA Publications
5559 W. Howard Street, Skokie, IL 60077
(800) 397-2282
www.actasports.com www.actapublications.com

ISBN: 978-0-87946-407-3
ISSN: 1940-8668

Printed in the United States of America

Table of Contents

Dedication

This book is dedicated to my wife, Carol, and children, particularly Kateri and Jimmy who still live with us at home. They have always been supportive and understanding of the occasional odd hours or last minute road trips that come up during baseball season, or the necessity of planning vacations, etc. around my schedule. It is greatly appreciated.

Jim Swavely

Acknowledgements

Two years ago this section summarized each person's contributions in comparison to a star baseball player. This year, we'll do the same with characters from baseball movies.

John Dewan should need no introduction at this point. He gets to be Roy Hobbs.

Bill James, while not involved in the day-to-day goings on is largely responsible for much of what BIS has come to be. He earns the role of "The Voice" from *Field of Dreams*.

Damon Lichtenwalner is Jake Taylor, the team's silent leader. He does the behind-the-scenes programming and database maintenance that keeps BIS running.

Jon Vrecsics and Jim Swavely run the minor league operation. Jon is Steve Nebraska from *The Scout*, because if anyone could perform the BIS equivalent of throwing a perfect game, it might be him. Jim is "Al", the head angel in *Angels in the Outfield*. (Al gets his name from the American League umpire's hat he wears.) Jim's a former umpire himself and a veteran scorer who knows how to explain all of the quirky rules and intricate scoring decisions that come up.

Matt Lorenzo is Crash Davis. In addition to his regular scoring and programming responsibilities, he's the veteran who passes along sage advice like "Don't think; it can only hurt the ballclub." OK, Matt doesn't actually say that, but the comparison is still valid.

Todd Radcliffe is Chet "The Rocket" Stedman. His years of scouting experience come in handy as a baseball tutor.

Dan Casey, Annemarie Stella and Austin Diamond do the heavy lifting as the Operations crew. Dan is Lou Collins, the experienced middle of the order run producer. Annemarie, the lone female, is Dottie Hinson—the star hitter that holds the team together. Austin turns on a good fastball like Pedro Cerrano, the difference being that Austin can recognize every other pitch too.

Jeff Spoljaric is the programmer who designs various software applications for the company. Jeff can be Henry Rowengartner, because you can't have a baseball movie character list without the *Rookie of the Year*. Like young Henry, Jeff's playing career was also derailed by arm injuries.

Pat Quinn is Archibald "Moonlight" Graham. In the past year Pat decided to hang up his spikes and move on to other things, but he still occasionally emerges from the past to make big contributions.

Ben Jedlovec and Rob Burckhard are the new faces at BIS, brought in to help with the wide array of research projects and analysis that the company is known for. Ben, the youngest BIS employee, is Ebby Calvin "Nuke" LaLoosh. Rob is Willie Mays Hayes because, well, he wanted to be.

The 2010 Video Scout crew includes Anthony Aloisi, Steve Altstadt, Joe Barbera, Coulson Barbiche, Bryan Bernsdorf, Dedan Brozino, Ken Hoffman, David Ireland, Tim Kay, Jake Lunemann, Brian Matthews, Mike McDonald, Bobby Muller, Mike Piekarski, Brandon Roesler, Jarrett Simpson, Craig Williams and Mike Wolverton. Also, a special thanks goes to Steve Goodfriend.

Our remote video crew consists of Brian Dewberry-Jones, David Dick, Don Masi, Al Melchior, John Menna, Gus Papadopoulos, Theo Papadopoulos, Harold Richter, Bob Routier, Wayne Sit and John Wagner. They play the role of Al Percolo, surveying baseball games far away.

Greg Pierce, Andrew Yankech, Charles Fiore, Donna Ryding, Mary Eggert, and Brendan Gaughan from ACTA Publications do an excellent job broadcasting BIS publications to a wider audience, much like Bob Uecker does for the Indians in *Major League*.

Thanks to our friends and helpers with a connection to the baseball industry: Greg Ambrosius, Andy Andres, Jeff Barton, Matthew Berry, Jim Callis, Mike Canter, Doug Dennis, Jeff Erickson, Peter Gammons, Steve Goldstein, Jason Grey, Durward Hamil, Joel Kammeyer, Peter Kreutzer, Michael Lehrer, Gene McCaffrey, Deric McKamey, Sig Mejdal, Bob Meyerhoff, Mike Murphy, Patrick Newman, Rob Neyer, Mat Olkin, Scott Pianowski, Mike Phillips, David Pinto, Joe Posnanski, Nate Ravitz, Hal Richman, Steve Ruskowski, Greg Rybarczyk, Mike Salfino, Peter Schoenke, Ron Shandler, Joe Sheehan, John Sickels, Dave Studenmund, Tom Tango, Sam Walker, Mark Watson, Rick Wilton, Rick Wolf, Trace Wood and Todd Zola.

And finally, Steve Moyer is Lou Brown, Morris Buttermaker, Jimmy Dugan, or Joe Riggans (take your pick). Somehow, he manages to get this group to produce a book every October. "It's a miracle."

Sincerely,

Ben Jedlovec
Research Analyst
Baseball Info Solutions

Introduction

It felt as if the season didn't quite know how to begin—or how to end.

Pitchers and catchers hadn't even reported to spring training before New York Yankee All-Star third basemen Alex Rodriguez admitted to having used steroids over a three-year period earlier in his career. It looked as if baseball fans might spend another season arguing over who cheated and who didn't—and whether or not the use of performance enhancing drugs (PEDs) could really be called cheating at all.

Even the start of a new baseball season provided only fleeting escape. Less than two weeks into April, the tragic death of pitching prospect Nick Adenhart rocked the Los Angeles Angels of Anaheim. Baseball mourned. Four days later, the Philadelphia Phillies, looking to defend their 2008 World Championship, lost beloved broadcaster Harry Kalas. Both teams would wear black patches—34 and HK respectively—for the remainder of the season.

When May 7 rolled around and Los Angeles Dodger outfielder Manny Ramirez was served with a 50-game suspension for violating MLB's drug policy, many fans found it hard to care. Baseball had rarely seemed less like a game.

But by the time the ivy turned green at Wrigley, the season began to take shape. Despite its inauspicious beginnings, 2009 had some great storylines brewing, if fans could just be patient.

In the National League Central, the St. Louis Cardinals used spit and elbow grease to assemble a division-winning roster, helped by the return of former Cy Young Award Winner Chris Carpenter, the mid-season acquisition of Matt Holliday, and Albert Pujols, the 2008 and likely 2009 MVP Award winner. The Dodgers shrugged off the absence of Ramirez and claimed the NL West crown, while in the East, the Phillies cruised to their third division title in as many years. The Wild Card provided the only real drama in the National League, as the Colorado Rockies held off a late-season charge from the Atlanta Braves to clinch on October 1.

In the American League East, the Yankees finally began to click under second-year manager Joe Girardi and became MLB's only 100-win team. They easily outdistanced their division rival, the Boston Red Sox, who, despite some PED scandals of their own, claimed the Wild Card. In the West, the Angels were slow out of the gate but moved into first place by mid-July and were never seriously challenged again.

And then there was Detroit, where the unemployment rate hit 28.9% in mid-summer. The Tigers took possession of first place in the AL Central on May 16 and held a seven-game lead as late as September 7. But Joe Mauer and the Minnesota Twins had other ideas.

The Twins, having just lost 2007 AL MVP Justin Morneau for the year, won 16 of their last 20 games to end the regular season tied with the Tigers for first place. For the third time in as many seasons, MLB needed an extra day to decide a division winner. The one-

1

game tiebreaker, held in the soon-to-be dismantled Metrodome, went twelve seesaw innings. It was as if the regular season wouldn't let go. Until Twins pinch hitter Alexi Casilla smacked a bouncing ball off the Metrodome carpet to score Carlos Gomez from second base and send the Twins off to face the Yankees in New York twenty-one hours later in the ALDS.

It was a thrilling finish for a season that saw so many memorable individual performances. Kansas City's Zack Greinke reeled off 24 consecutive scoreless innings pitched to start the season, extending his overall streak to 38. He would go on to win 16 games with a 2.16 ERA for the 65-win Royals. Seattle Mariners outfielder Ichiro Suzuki set the record for most consecutive seasons with 200 hits (9) and, for what it's worth, finally got himself ejected from a game for the first time in his professional career (including his years in Japan).

The San Francisco Giants' Jonathan Sanchez threw a no-hitter against the San Diego Padres on July 10. Chicago White Sox pitcher Mark Buehrle joined the immortals by hurling a perfect game against the Tampa Bay Rays on July 23. Also immortalized in the same game on U.S. Cellular Field's left-center field wall was Sox defensive replacement DeWayne Wise, who stole a ninth-inning home run off the bat of Gabe Kapler to preserve the 18th perfect game in MLB history in what forever will be known on the Southside as "The Catch."

So how does this all play out in the 2010 edition of the Handbook? Instant replay is a little more than a year old, and we have enough data to present our brand new Instant Replay History, showing each time instant replay has been used, what the ruling on the field was, and how the umpires ruled after viewing the video. Also new this year is Pinch Hitting Analysis, where we examine who's best and worst at coming off the bench in a pinch. Park Indices have been updated to include the new Yankee Stadium and Citi Field. And, as always, we present John Dewan's annual Fielding Bible Awards—exclusive to the Handbook. Inevitably, despite our best efforts, it seems that every year we have some Errata, and these will be available beginning February 1, 2010 at www.baseballinfosolutions.com.

RIP Nick Adenhart, Dom DiMaggio, Harry Kalas, et al. It's a game after all. But it's the greatest game.

LC Fiore
ACTA Sports

2009 Team Statistics

Sometimes it's fun to go back and look at some teams that maybe took us by surprise a little bit. The Florida Marlins have a nasty habit of doing this every sixth season.

The 1997 Marlins finished over .500 for the first time and won 92 games, the Wild Card, their first playoff berth, and the World Series. They followed their first title with five consecutive losing seasons, but bounced back in 2003 with a 91-win season and another Wild Card berth and world championship.

Here we are, six seasons later, watching the Marlins finish in second place again with their third best win total in the 17-year history of their franchise.

In the next few pages, major league teams are evaluated in aggregate against every other team in baseball. For example, you can see that the month of May was not kind to the Fighting Fish. If the Marlins had gone 15-14 that month, they would have beaten out the Rockies for the Wild Card and probably won the World Series, if history is any guide.

Similarly, if you want to know how many times the Milwaukee Brewers beat the Cincinnati Reds; how many games the Oakland A's won on turf; or how many home runs the Baltimore Orioles allowed, it's all here. Did you know that there were exactly four non-interleague season series sweeps, and the Rockies were responsible for three of them?

2009 American League Standings

Overall

EAST Team	W-L	Pct	GB	D1	LD1	LLd
New York Yankees	103-59	.636	0.0	92	10/6	10.5
Boston Red Sox*	95-67	.586	8.0	54	7/20	5.0
Tampa Bay Rays	84-78	.519	19.0	0	-	0.0
Toronto Blue Jays	75-87	.463	28.0	42	5/23	3.5
Baltimore Orioles	64-98	.395	39.0	3	4/14	0.5

CENTRAL Team	W-L	Pct	GB	D1	LD1	LLd
Minnesota Twins	87-76	.534	0.0	8	10/6	1.0
Detroit Tigers	86-77	.528	1.0	164	10/5	7.0
Chicago White Sox	79-83	.488	7.5	11	5/1	0.5
Cleveland Indians	65-97	.401	21.5	1	4/6	0.0
Kansas City Royals	65-97	.401	21.5	24	5/9	3.0

WEST Team	W-L	Pct	GB	D1	LD1	LLd
Los Angeles Angels	97-65	.599	0.0	102	10/6	10.0
Texas Rangers	87-75	.537	10.0	64	7/10	5.5
Seattle Mariners	85-77	.525	12.0	26	5/5	3.5
Oakland Athletics	75-87	.463	22.0	0	-	0.0

* Clinched Wild Card Birth on 9/29. Division Clinch Dates: New York 9/27, Los Angeles 9/28, Minnesota 10/6.
D1 = Number of days a team had at least a share of first place of their division; LD1 = Last date the team had at least a share of first place; LLd = The largest number of games that a team led their division

East Division

Tm	Home	Road	East	Cent	West	NL	LHS	RHS	Day	Night	Grass	Turf	1-Rn	5+Rn	XInn	April	May	June	July	Aug	S/O	Pre	Post
NYY	57-24	46-35	45-27	25-9	23-15	10-8	36-18	67-41	34-22	69-37	89-52	14-7	22-16	32-19	7-3	12-10	17-11	15-11	18-9	21-7	20-11	51-37	52-22
Bos	56-25	39-42	45-27	26-12	13-21	11-7	30-25	65-42	25-21	70-46	85-55	10-12	22-17	34-16	4-6	14-8	15-14	18-8	13-12	16-12	19-13	54-34	41-33
TB	52-29	32-49	40-32	19-20	12-21	13-5	30-30	54-48	25-24	59-54	25-44	59-34	20-25	26-22	6-3	9-14	16-14	19-7	12-12	15-12	13-19	48-41	36-37
Tor	44-37	31-50	26-46	23-15	19-15	7-11	22-28	53-59	31-29	44-58	27-41	48-46	21-28	29-21	7-13	15-9	14-15	12-14	8-16	10-16	16-17	44-46	31-41
Bal	39-42	25-56	24-48	17-20	12-23	11-7	24-37	40-61	17-27	47-71	59-82	5-16	17-22	18-26	5-7	9-13	14-15	12-14	9-16	10-20	10-20	40-48	24-50

Central Division

Tm	Home	Road	East	Cent	West	NL	LHS	RHS	Day	Night	Grass	Turf	1-Rn	5+Rn	XInn	April	May	June	July	Aug	S/O	Pre	Post
Min	49-33	38-43	10-22	46-27	19-21	12-6	28-32	59-44	27-33	60-43	35-39	52-37	24-20	24-21	7-7	11-11	14-16	15-12	12-12	14-14	21-11	45-44	42-32
Det	51-30	35-47	15-21	39-34	22-14	10-8	29-20	57-57	33-26	53-51	80-66	6-11	28-22	17-23	6-5	11-10	17-11	15-13	10-14	16-13	17-16	48-39	38-38
CWS	43-38	36-45	18-21	34-38	15-18	12-6	25-24	54-59	27-34	52-49	74-71	5-12	19-27	23-25	4-6	11-10	13-15	15-13	14-13	11-17	15-15	45-43	34-40
Cle	35-46	30-51	19-21	30-42	11-21	5-13	17-23	48-74	24-34	41-63	58-86	7-11	19-21	20-25	4-8	8-14	14-16	9-18	12-12	15-12	7-25	35-54	30-43
KC	33-48	32-49	14-25	32-40	11-22	8-10	20-36	45-61	22-32	43-65	59-84	6-13	16-25	18-41	6-3	12-10	11-17	10-16	7-19	10-19	15-16	37-51	28-46

West Division

Tm	Home	Road	East	Cent	West	NL	LHS	RHS	Day	Night	Grass	Turf	1-Rn	5+Rn	XInn	April	May	June	July	Aug	S/O	Pre	Post
LAA	49-32	48-33	26-17	27-17	30-27	14-4	34-14	63-51	34-14	63-51	90-57	7-8	27-17	29-17	6-4	9-12	16-12	17-9	19-7	17-12	19-13	49-37	48-28
Tex	48-33	39-42	27-20	21-19	30-27	9-9	29-27	58-48	20-21	67-54	84-69	3-6	19-18	28-26	6-4	10-11	20-9	11-15	17-8	14-15	15-17	48-39	39-36
Sea	48-33	37-44	21-19	22-25	31-26	11-7	28-30	57-47	26-20	59-57	80-69	5-8	35-20	18-24	9-7	13-9	11-18	15-10	14-13	15-14	17-13	46-42	39-35
Oak	40-41	35-46	21-23	26-17	23-34	5-13	19-31	56-56	25-27	50-60	68-81	7-6	15-23	27-23	3-10	8-11	11-18	13-15	12-14	14-15	17-14	37-49	38-38

Team vs. Team Breakdown

Team	NYY	Bos	TB	Tor	Bal	Min	Det	CWS	KC	Cle	LAA	Tex	Sea	Oak
New York Yankees	-	9	11	12	13	7	5	4	4	5	5	5	6	7
Boston Red Sox	9	-	9	11	16	4	6	4	5	7	4	2	2	5
Tampa Bay Rays	7	9	-	14	10	3	2	2	9	3	2	3	3	4
Toronto Blue Jays	6	7	4	-	9	5	5	6	3	4	4	5	4	6
Baltimore Orioles	5	2	8	9	-	3	3	5	4	2	2	5	4	1
Minnesota Twins	0	2	3	3	2	-	12	12	12	10	4	6	5	4
Detroit Tigers	1	1	5	3	5	7	-	9	9	14	5	7	5	5
Chicago White Sox	3	4	6	1	4	6	9	-	9	10	5	2	4	4
Cleveland Indians	3	2	5	4	5	8	4	8	10	-	2	1	6	2
Kansas City Royals	2	3	1	4	4	6	9	9	-	8	1	3	5	2
Los Angeles Angels	5	5	4	4	8	6	4	4	9	4	-	8	10	12
Texas Rangers	4	7	6	5	5	4	2	4	3	8	11	-	11	8
Seattle Mariners	4	4	5	3	5	5	4	5	4	4	9	8	-	14
Oakland Athletics	2	5	6	3	5	6	4	5	6	5	7	11	5	-

2009 National League Standings

Overall

EAST							CENTRAL							WEST						
Team	W-L	Pct	GB	D1	LD1	LLd	Team	W-L	Pct	GB	D1	LD1	LLd	Team	W-L	Pct	GB	D1	LD1	LLd
Philadelphia Phillies	93-69	.574	0.0	143	10/6	8.5	St Louis Cardinals	91-71	.562	0.0	135	10/6	11.5	Los Angeles Dodgers	95-67	.586	0.0	177	10/6	9.5
Florida Marlins	87-75	.537	6.0	29	5/4	5.0	Chicago Cubs	83-78	.516	7.5	16	8/6	0.5	Colorado Rockies*	92-70	.568	3.0	3	4/10	0.5
Atlanta Braves	86-76	.531	7.0	6	4/13	1.0	Milwaukee Brewers	80-82	.494	11.0	44	7/4	3.0	San Francisco Giants	88-74	.543	7.0	2	4/9	0.5
New York Mets	70-92	.432	23.0	13	5/29	2.0	Cincinnati Reds	78-84	.481	13.0	1	5/13	0.0	San Diego Padres	75-87	.463	20.0	8	4/18	1.0
Washington Nationals	59-103	.364	34.0	0	-	0.0	Houston Astros	74-88	.457	17.0	1	4/7	0.0	Arizona Diamondbacks	70-92	.432	25.0	1	4/6	0.0
							Pittsburgh Pirates	62-99	.385	28.5	3	4/8	0.0							

* Clinched Wild Card Birth on 10/1. Division Clinch Dates: St Louis 9/26, Philadelphia 9/30, Los Angeles 10/3.
D1 = Number of days a team had at least a share of first place of their division; LD1 = Last date the team had at least a share of first place; LLd = The largest number of games that a team led their division

East Division

Tm	AT		VERSUS						CONDITIONS				GAME			MONTHLY						ALL-STAR	
	Home	Road	East	Cent	West	AL	LHS	RHS	Day	Night	Grass	Turf	1-Rn	5+Rn	XInn	April	May	June	July	Aug	S/O	Pre	Post
Phi	45-36	48-33	44-28	23-16	20-15	0-12	29-16	64-53	28-17	65-52	90-66	3-3	24-21	28-21	11-5	11-9	17-11	11-15	20-7	16-11	18-16	48-38	45-31
Fla	43-38	44-37	42-30	18-21	17-16	10-8	29-22	58-53	22-22	65-53	84-72	3-3	30-20	20-19	7-7	14-8	9-20	17-11	14-10	14-14	19-12	46-44	41-31
Atl	40-41	46-35	41-31	20-20	18-17	7-8	31-22	55-61	24-21	62-55	00-70	0-0	27-25	29-14	9-7	10-11	15-14	11-15	16-11	17-11	17-14	43-45	43-31
NYM	41-40	29-52	28-44	22-17	14-21	5-10	10-27	54-65	30-25	40-67	70-92	0-0	19-24	15-22	4-7	9-12	19-9	9-18	12-14	10-19	11-20	42-46	28-47
Was	33-48	26-55	25-47	10-27	11-18	7-11	10-23	49-80	22-26	37-77	59-100	0-3	22-24	14-29	6-9	5-16	9-20	9-17	9-18	14-15	13-17	26-61	33-42

Central Division

Tm	AT		VERSUS						CONDITIONS				GAME			MONTHLY						ALL-STAR	
	Home	Road	East	Cent	West	AL	LHS	RHS	Day	Night	Grass	Turf	1-Rn	5+Rn	XInn	April	May	June	July	Aug	S/O	Pre	Post
StL	46-35	45-36	17-16	46-34	19-15	9-6	28-21	63-50	28-30	63-41	91-71	0-0	24-21	29-20	5-6	16-7	13-14	12-17	16-11	20-6	14-16	49-42	42-29
ChC	46-34	37-44	15-17	47-32	15-20	6-9	16-16	67-62	23-31	57-51	83-79	0-0	20-23	16-24	9-7	10-11	15-13	11-14	18-9	11-17	18-14	45-43	35-39
Mil	40-41	40-41	19-15	42-37	14-20	5-10	21-18	59-64	23-31	57-51	80-79	0-3	20-23	16-24	8-5	12-10	18-10	12-15	9-17	13-14	16-16	42-45	38-37
Cin	40-41	38-43	16-19	46-34	10-22	6-9	19-25	59-59	23-29	55-55	77-82	1-2	19-20	23-19	8-7	11-10	15-13	11-15	8-19	13-16	20-11	42-45	36-39
Hou	44-37	30-51	16-17	31-47	21-15	6-9	17-21	57-67	24-23	50-65	72-87	2-1	24-23	20-32	3-7	9-13	11-16	16-11	15-12	12-16	11-20	44-44	30-44
Pit	40-41	22-58	18-16	24-52	12-24	8-7	18-26	44-73	17-38	45-61	61-97	1-2	12-22	17-28	2-9	11-10	11-18	14-13	8-17	9-19	9-22	38-50	24-49

West Division

Tm	AT		VERSUS						CONDITIONS				GAME			MONTHLY						ALL-STAR	
	Home	Road	East	Cent	West	AL	LHS	RHS	Day	Night	Grass	Turf	1-Rn	5+Rn	XInn	April	May	June	July	Aug	S/O	Pre	Post
LAD	50-31	45-36	18-13	22-19	46-28	9-9	27-20	68-47	27-17	68-50	95-67	0-0	28-22	30-13	12-9	15-8	20-9	14-12	15-10	14-15	17-13	56-32	39-35
Col	51-30	41-40	17-16	31-11	33-39	11-4	27-26	65-44	31-23	61-47	92-70	0-0	23-20	27-18	4-5	8-12	12-17	21-7	15-11	16-12	20-11	47-41	45-29
SF	52-29	36-45	19-16	22-18	38-34	9-6	23-21	65-53	29-24	59-50	88-74	0-0	21-22	21-18	9-7	10-10	15-11	17-10	14-13	16-14	18-11	49-39	39-35
SD	42-39	33-48	16-16	21-22	33-39	5-10	26-29	49-58	18-27	57-60	75-87	0-0	23-18	10-32	10-7	11-11	14-14	9-17	8-20	15-14	18-11	36-52	39-35
Ari	36-45	34-47	15-19	20-21	30-42	5-10	17-30	53-62	18-28	52-64	70-92	0-0	20-27	19-27	10-5	9-13	13-16	9-17	14-12	15-14	10-20	38-51	32-41

Team vs. Team Breakdown

	EAST					CENTRAL						WEST				
	Phi	Fla	Atl	NYM	Was	StL	ChC	Mil	Cin	Hou	Pit	LAD	Col	SF	SD	Ari
Philadelphia Phillies	-	9	8	12	15	4	5	3	5	2	4	3	4	3	5	5
Florida Marlins	9	-	10	11	12	3	3	3	3	4	2	3	4	3	4	3
Atlanta Braves	10	8	-	13	10	4	4	3	3	3	3	4	4	3	3	4
New York Mets	6	7	5	-	10	4	3	3	4	5	4	1	4	5	2	2
Washington Nationals	3	6	8	8	-	1	2	3	4	3	3	2	0	2	2	5
St Louis Cardinals	1	3	2	5	6	-	10	9	8	9	10	5	1	3	6	4
Chicago Cubs	1	4	2	3	5	6	-	10	10	11	10	3	2	4	4	2
Milwaukee Brewers	4	4	3	3	5	9	7	-	7	10	9	3	0	4	2	5
Cincinnati Reds	2	3	6	2	3	8	5	8	-	12	13	1	0	3	1	5
Houston Astros	6	3	3	1	3	6	6	5	4	-	10	4	5	2	6	4
Pittsburgh Pirates	2	4	4	3	5	5	4	5	5	5	-	3	3	2	3	1
Los Angeles Dodgers	4	3	3	5	3	5	5	3	5	3	4	-	14	11	10	11
Colorado Rockies	2	2	4	3	6	6	4	6	7	2	6	4	-	8	10	11
San Francisco Giants	4	4	4	3	4	4	2	5	3	4	4	7	10	-	8	13
San Diego Padres	2	2	3	5	4	1	5	4	6	1	4	8	8	10	-	7
Arizona Diamondbacks	1	5	3	5	1	2	4	2	1	5	6	7	7	5	11	-

American League Batting

Tm	G	AB	H	2B	3B	HR	(Hm	Rd)	TB	R	RBI	TBB	IBB	SO	HBP	SH	SF	ShO	SB	CS	SB%	GDP	LOB	Avg	OBP	Slg
NYY	162	5660	1604	325	21	244	(136	108)	2703	915	881	663	35	1014	54	31	39	5	111	28	.80	144	1238	.283	.362	.478
LAA	162	5622	1604	293	33	173	(90	83)	2482	883	841	547	32	1054	41	43	52	6	148	63	.70	128	1134	.285	.350	.441
Bos	162	5543	1495	335	25	212	(114	98)	2516	872	822	659	39	1120	70	19	51	7	126	39	.76	137	1210	.270	.352	.454
Min	163	5608	1539	271	40	172	(96	76)	2406	817	770	585	46	1021	45	51	57	4	85	32	.73	147	1185	.274	.345	.429
TB	162	5462	1434	297	36	199	(103	96)	2400	803	765	642	36	1229	49	25	45	7	194	61	.76	104	1151	.263	.343	.439
Tor	162	5696	1516	339	13	209	(104	105)	2508	798	766	548	23	1028	45	24	49	5	73	23	.76	130	1195	.266	.333	.440
Tex	162	5526	1436	296	27	224	(122	102)	2458	784	748	472	23	1253	37	40	51	13	149	36	.81	97	1059	.260	.320	.445
Cle	162	5568	1468	314	28	161	(66	95)	2321	773	730	582	20	1211	81	39	50	11	84	31	.73	140	1198	.264	.339	.417
Oak	162	5584	1464	307	21	135	(71	64)	2218	759	723	527	16	1046	50	31	54	9	133	48	.73	130	1130	.262	.328	.397
Det	163	5540	1443	245	35	183	(92	91)	2307	743	718	540	30	1114	61	53	59	6	72	33	.69	131	1159	.260	.331	.416
Bal	162	5618	1508	307	19	160	(96	64)	2333	741	708	517	25	1013	39	13	46	10	76	37	.67	131	1160	.268	.332	.415
CWS	162	5463	1410	246	20	184	(103	81)	2248	724	695	534	25	1022	62	34	39	13	113	49	.70	139	1086	.258	.329	.411
KC	162	5532	1432	276	51	144	(65	79)	2242	686	657	457	20	1091	42	38	32	10	88	29	.75	136	1090	.259	.318	.405
Sea	162	5543	1430	280	19	160	(76	84)	2228	640	613	421	39	1093	49	56	44	10	89	33	.73	124	1121	.258	.314	.402
AL	1135	77965	20783	4131	388	2560	(1334	1226)	33370	10938	10437	7694	409	15309	725	497	648	116	1541	542	.74	1818	16116	.267	.336	.428

American League Pitching

Tm	G	CG	Rel	IP	BFP	H	R	ER	HR	SH	SF	HB	TBB	IBB	SO	WP	Bk	W	L	Pct.	ShO	Sv-Op	Hld	OAvg	OOBP	OSlg	ERA
Sea	162	4	410	1452.2	6159	1359	692	625	172	33	51	43	534	13	1043	61	5	85	77	.525	10	49-77	82	.247	.316	.394	3.87
CWS	162	4	415	1439.2	6155	1438	732	663	169	46	47	41	507	41	1119	55	5	79	83	.488	11	36-54	55	.261	.325	.414	4.14
Bos	162	8	463	1436.2	6283	1494	736	695	167	43	48	68	530	24	1230	42	5	95	67	.586	11	45-73	77	.267	.335	.422	4.35
Tex	162	8	436	1434.2	6172	1432	740	698	171	28	35	70	531	14	1016	45	8	87	75	.537	11	45-58	77	.260	.331	.416	4.38
Det	163	4	439	1447.0	6240	1449	745	690	182	43	47	41	594	42	1102	48	6	86	77	.528	9	42-66	67	.263	.336	.422	4.29
NYY	162	3	461	1450.0	6247	1386	753	687	181	28	49	71	574	28	1260	66	5	103	59	.636	8	51-66	74	.251	.327	.408	4.26
TB	162	3	510	1427.1	6146	1421	754	686	183	25	36	46	515	22	1125	46	5	84	78	.519	5	41-63	79	.257	.324	.417	4.33
LAA	162	9	434	1445.0	6252	1513	761	715	180	52	54	58	523	35	1062	67	2	97	65	.599	13	51-70	79	.272	.338	.432	4.45
Oak	162	2	488	1447.1	6243	1486	761	685	156	33	47	36	523	30	1124	43	2	75	87	.463	10	38-50	68	.265	.329	.413	4.26
Min	163	4	480	1453.0	6274	1542	765	726	185	38	49	58	466	20	1052	43	3	87	76	.534	7	48-64	82	.272	.341	.431	4.50
Tor	162	10	445	1451.0	6281	1509	771	720	181	25	49	58	551	26	1181	43	4	75	87	.463	10	25-41	50	.270	.339	.434	4.47
KC	162	10	426	1426.0	6265	1486	842	765	166	35	45	51	600	28	1153	89	6	65	97	.401	9	34-56	50	.269	.343	.422	4.83
Cle	162	5	445	1434.0	6359	1486	865	806	183	44	55	45	598	31	986	49	7	65	97	.401	6	25-43	49	.280	.351	.443	5.06
Bal	162	2	484	1429.0	6359	1633	876	817	218	35	51	51	546	45	933	31	7	64	98	.395	3	31-53	61	.288	.353	.476	5.15
AL	1135	76	6336	20173.1	87430	20718	10793	9978	2494	508	663	737	7592	399	15386	728	70	1147	1123	.505	123	557-820	945	.266	.334	.425	4.45

American League Fielding

Team	G	Inn	PO	Ast	OFAst	E	(Throw	Field)	TC	DP	GDP	SB	CS	SB%	CPkof	PPkof	PB	UER	UERA	FPct
Toronto	162	1451.0	4353	1740	27	76	(44	32)	6169	168	143	89	46	.66	4	3	13	51	0.32	.988
Minnesota	163	1453.0	4359	1565	19	76	(32	44)	6000	135	115	107	32	.77	0	7	16	39	0.24	.987
Boston	162	1436.2	4310	1453	29	82	(43	39)	5845	120	96	151	23	.87	0	1	10	41	0.26	.986
Los Angeles	162	1445.0	4335	1623	26	85	(36	49)	6043	174	155	128	39	.77	1	3	11	46	0.29	.986
New York	162	1450.0	4350	1493	15	86	(43	43)	5929	131	110	125	52	.71	2	5	11	66	0.41	.985
Detroit	163	1447.0	4341	1616	30	88	(48	40)	6045	164	140	88	50	.64	2	3	15	55	0.34	.985
Baltimore	162	1429.0	4287	1663	36	90	(46	44)	6040	151	132	119	33	.78	0	6	8	59	0.37	.985
Cleveland	162	1434.0	4302	1651	26	97	(40	57)	6050	170	149	111	33	.77	0	2	10	59	0.37	.984
Tampa Bay	162	1427.1	4282	1511	28	98	(51	47)	5891	135	114	90	28	.76	1	2	7	68	0.43	.983
Oakland	162	1447.1	4342	1592	28	105	(48	57)	6039	154	129	92	38	.71	1	3	5	76	0.47	.983
Seattle	162	1452.2	4358	1525	22	105	(42	63)	5988	150	128	67	44	.60	4	5	16	67	0.42	.982
Texas	162	1434.2	4304	1603	29	106	(54	52)	6013	168	136	99	43	.70	0	3	9	42	0.26	.982
Chicago	162	1439.2	4319	1669	32	113	(46	67)	6101	158	131	132	42	.76	1	10	8	69	0.43	.981
Kansas City	162	1426.0	4278	1569	34	116	(60	56)	5963	160	130	114	39	.75	1	6	14	77	0.49	.981
American League	1135	20173.1	60520	22273	381	1323	(633	690)	84116	2138	1808	1512	542	.74	17	59	153	815	0.36	.984

National League Batting

							BATTING														BASERUNNING					PERCENTAGES		
Tm	G	AB	H	2B	3B	HR	(Hm	Rd)	TB	R	RBI	TBB	IBB	SO	HBP	SH	SF	ShO		SB	CS	SB%	GDP	LOB	Avg	OBP	Slg
Phi	162	5578	1439	312	35	224	(108	116)	2493	820	788	589	47	1155	71	55	45	7		119	28	.81	90	1192	.258	.334	.447
Col	162	5398	1408	300	50	190	(98	92)	2378	804	760	660	40	1277	47	76	60	9		106	55	.66	112	1147	.261	.343	.441
Mil	162	5510	1447	281	37	182	(100	82)	2348	785	757	610	44	1231	71	58	47	8		68	37	.65	129	1203	.263	.341	.426
LAD	162	5592	1511	278	39	145	(70	75)	2302	780	739	607	76	1068	63	78	44	8		116	48	.71	141	1224	.270	.346	.412
Fla	162	5572	1493	296	25	159	(86	73)	2316	772	727	568	46	1226	63	70	39	8		75	35	.68	110	1216	.268	.340	.416
Atl	162	5539	1459	300	20	149	(69	80)	2246	735	700	602	54	1064	52	95	47	11		58	26	.69	142	1223	.263	.339	.405
StL	162	5465	1436	294	29	160	(66	94)	2268	730	694	528	73	1041	61	68	43	10		75	31	.71	128	1152	.263	.332	.415
Ari	162	5565	1408	307	45	173	(87	86)	2324	720	686	571	47	1298	37	54	41	10		102	40	.72	94	1173	.253	.324	.418
Was	162	5493	1416	271	30	158	(76	80)	2231	710	685	617	39	1208	56	64	42	7		73	40	.65	133	1223	.258	.337	.406
ChC	161	5486	1398	293	29	161	(82	79)	2232	707	678	592	44	1185	59	65	42	12		56	34	.62	134	1209	.255	.332	.407
Cin	162	5462	1349	280	25	158	(94	64)	2153	673	637	531	37	1129	53	100	41	6		96	40	.71	103	1131	.247	.318	.394
NYM	162	5453	1472	295	49	95	(49	46)	2150	671	631	568	49	928	36	88	55	11		122	44	.73	144	1083	.270	.335	.394
SF	162	5493	1411	275	43	122	(65	57)	2138	657	612	392	41	1158	50	67	55	10		78	28	.74	115	1080	.257	.309	.389
Hou	162	5436	1415	270	32	142	(78	64)	2175	643	616	448	37	990	43	66	45	13		113	44	.72	153	1080	.260	.319	.400
SD	162	5425	1315	265	31	141	(61	80)	2065	638	605	586	52	1182	57	74	36	10		82	29	.74	131	1168	.242	.321	.381
Pit	161	5417	1364	289	34	125	(75	50)	2096	636	612	499	44	1142	46	60	36	17		90	32	.74	124	1124	.252	.318	.387
NL	1295	87884	22741	4606	561	2482	(1264	1218)	35915	11481	10927	8926	770	18282	865	1138	718	157		1429	591	.71	1983	18728	.259	.331	.409

National League Pitching

									WHAT THEY GAVE UP										THE RESULTS							
HOW MUCH THEY PITCHED																											
Tm	G	CG	Rel	IP	BFP	H	R	ER	HR	SH	SF	HB	TBB	IBB	SO	WP	Bk	W	l.	Pct.	ShO	Sv-Op	Hld	OAvg	OOBP	OSlg	ERA
LAD	162	1	526	1473.1	6182	1265	611	558	127	75	38	57	584	68	1272	76	2	95	67	.586	9	44-70	77	.233	.312	.361	3.41
SF	162	11	457	1446.0	6103	1268	611	571	140	67	41	41	584	49	1302	71	3	88	74	.643	10	41-58	70	.236	.314	.372	3.55
StL	162	8	481	1440.2	6007	1407	640	586	123	70	44	53	460	23	1049	41	3	91	71	.562	72	43-57	72	.258	.319	.386	3.66
Atl	162	3	488	1462.2	6208	1399	641	581	119	86	34	49	530	59	1232	40	6	86	76	.531	10	30-50	71	.254	.323	.390	3.57
ChC	161	3	480	1445.1	6177	1020	072	616	160	87	43	59	586	46	1272	60	6	83	78	.516	8	40-58	75	.246	.324	.391	3.84
Phi	162	8	459	1455.2	6263	1479	709	673	189	60	46	75	489	31	1153	28	2	93	69	.574	9	44-66	81	.265	.329	.427	4.16
Col	162	5	484	1438.1	6171	1427	715	675	141	74	56	46	528	51	1154	48	5	92	70	.568	7	45-61	73	.261	.328	.405	4.22
Cin	162	6	478	1458.1	6253	1420	723	677	188	61	42	65	577	36	1069	45	1	78	84	.481	12	41-53	80	.258	.333	.418	4.18
NYM	162	3	511	1426.0	6284	1452	757	705	158	71	49	55	616	60	1031	41	10	70	92	.432	12	39-60	75	.264	.342	.418	4.45
Fla	162	5	530	1446.1	6299	1425	766	690	160	77	42	45	601	60	1248	59	6	87	75	.537	5	45-69	93	.257	.333	.408	4.29
Pit	161	5	456	1418.1	6144	1491	768	723	152	73	53	47	563	37	919	52	3	62	99	.385	7	28-45	62	.276	.346	.442	4.59
SD	162	2	527	1450.2	6273	1422	769	704	167	60	45	45	603	58	1187	52	8	75	87	.463	9	45-68	92	.258	.333	.406	4.37
Hou	162	5	497	1430.0	6237	1521	770	722	176	74	45	50	546	56	1144	43	4	74	88	.457	10	39-65	83	.275	.344	.440	4.54
Ari	162	4	483	1447.2	6267	1470	782	711	168	59	39	53	525	27	1158	79	2	70	92	.432	12	36-55	46	.263	.330	.419	4.42
Mil	162	1	512	1435.0	6352	1498	818	770	207	55	41	65	607	60	1104	61	1	80	82	.494	8	44-66	89	.268	.345	.450	4.83
Was	162	6	532	1421.1	6349	1533	874	791	173	78	45	48	620	59	911	74	5	59	103	.364	3	33-50	82	.276	.352	.450	5.00
NL	1295	76	7901	23098.2	99640	22806	11026	10753	2548	1127	703	853	9028	780	18205	872	68	1283	1307	.495	150	645-968	1201	.259	.332	.412	4.19

National League Fielding

								Fielding											
Team	G	Inn	PO	Ast	OFAst	E	(Throw | Field)	TC	DP	GDP	SB	CS	SB%	CPkof	PPkof	PB	UER	UERA	FPct
Pittsburgh	161	1418.1	4255	1766	45	73	37	36	6094	171	138	107	43	.71	1	8	13	45	0.29	.988
Philadelphia	162	1455.2	4367	1557	34	76	28	48	6000	132	107	95	37	.72	0	2	10	36	0.22	.987
Houston	162	1430.0	4290	1719	37	78	31	47	6087	161	142	65	29	.69	1	4	11	48	0.30	.987
Los Angeles	162	1473.1	4420	1594	25	83	36	47	6097	134	110	89	39	.70	2	4	5	53	0.32	.986
Colorado	162	1438.1	4315	1765	28	87	40	47	6167	146	119	115	27	.81	3	7	6	40	0.25	.986
Cincinnati	162	1458.1	4375	1596	37	89	38	51	6060	161	135	79	47	.63	5	5	4	46	0.28	.985
San Francisco	162	1446.0	4338	1511	28	88	39	49	5937	138	112	107	42	.72	2	0	9	40	0.25	.985
St Louis	162	1440.2	4322	1855	21	96	36	60	6273	167	147	44	28	.61	10	2	5	54	0.34	.985
Atlanta	162	1462.2	4388	1714	25	96	36	60	6198	159	138	97	46	.68	1	4	12	60	0.37	.985
San Diego	162	1450.2	4352	1566	25	94	44	50	6012	146	119	100	42	.70	0	4	12	65	0.40	.984
New York	162	1426.0	4278	1557	27	97	41	56	5932	134	116	66	34	.66	0	2	7	52	0.33	.984
Milwaukee	162	1435.0	4305	1590	19	98	45	53	5993	149	135	82	21	.80	2	5	6	48	0.30	.984
Chicago	161	1445.1	4336	1573	24	105	42	63	6014	144	119	89	43	.67	2	4	5	56	0.35	.983
Florida	162	1446.1	4339	1469	18	106	56	60	5914	129	114	129	42	.75	1	1	8	76	0.47	.982
Arizona	162	1446.1	4343	1606	22	124	63	61	6073	133	116	105	33	.76	1	5	8	71	0.44	.980
Washington	162	1424.1	4273	1742	31	143	63	80	6158	155	126	89	38	.70	0	3	9	83	0.52	.977
National League	1295	23098.2	69296	26180	446	1533	675	858	97009	2359	1993	1458	591	.71	31	60	130	873	0.34	.984

Team Efficiency Summary

Bill James

The Team Efficiency Summary (below) measures the effectiveness with which a team puts the pieces of wins—the parts of wins; the elements of wins—together into whole wins.

Hits, walks, stolen bases, double plays. . .these may be seen as small pieces of wins.

If a team has 11 hits and four walks in a game but scores only two runs, that's inefficient. If a team gets three hits and two walks but scores four runs, that's efficient.

If a team plays a double header and wins the first game 26 to 0 but loses the second game 4 to 2, that's extremely inefficient. They outscored their opponents 28 to 4 in the double-header, but split the games. From the standpoint of the other team, it's highly efficient.

The team efficiency summary (below) looks at a team's efficiency in three ways—Hitting Efficiency, Pitching Efficiency, and Run Efficiency. Hitting efficiency means getting the most runs you can out of your hits and walks and home runs. Pitching efficiency means giving up the fewest runs you can, based on your hits and walks and home runs (and doubles and triples and stuff. . .I'm abbreviating, but the formulas that underlie the analysis are anything but brief.) Run efficiency means winning as many games as you can based on the number of runs you score and allow. The charts below look at these things one at a time, and then put them all together.

The most efficient team in baseball is usually the Los Angeles Angels—anyway it was in 2009, and it was in 2008, and it has been in other years. The Angels do little things so well that they are consistently able to grind five or ten more wins a year out of their team than what one would think was available. We don't really understand how they do this, to be frank, but since they do it every year, we know it's not luck. Saying that they "do the little things well" is just a way of covering for the fact that we don't actually know how they do it.

The least efficient team was the Washington Nationals, and there is a difference between "inefficient" and "bad". If you look at the category performance of the two teams—at the pieces of wins, at the team batting average and the batting average allowed and the home runs and the home runs allowed—the Washington Nationals appear to be just as good as the Houston Astros. Each team could have been expected to win about 70 games. The Astros, however, were quite efficient, thus winning about 74 games, whereas the Nationals were dreadfully inefficient, winning only 59.

Teams bounce up and down in these rankings, and there is a lot of pure luck which is included under the heading "efficiency". If it wasn't for the Angels, we might think it was all luck. There are a couple of parts of the Angels' success that we do understand. For one thing, they run the bases extremely well. They picked up about 96 bases last year, or about 20 runs, just by running the bases better than an average team. Twenty-two of those bases are "stolen base gain", but 74 of them are bases gained by things like going first-to-third on a single or tagging up and advancing. That helps a lot. The Angels in 2009 had 221 "Manufactured Runs", by far the most of any major league team. Second, they usually have a good bullpen, which means that they can put a good pitcher on the mound when the game is close. Even in 2009, when they didn't have a really good bullpen, they also didn't have a really bad bullpen. Those things help to make a team "efficient", as we are using the term.

2008 American League Team Efficiency Summary

	RC	Runs	Hit Eff	Exp RA	RA	Pit Eff	Exp Wins	Wins	Runs Eff	Eff Wins	Wins	Overall Eff
Los Angeles Angels	864	883	102	770	761	101	93	97	104	90	97	107
Seattle Mariners	683	640	94	687	692	99	75	85	114	81	85	106
Detroit Tigers	756	743	98	756	745	102	81	86	106	81	86	106
Boston Red Sox	879	872	99	764	736	104	95	95	100	92	95	103
Texas Rangers	777	784	101	736	740	99	86	87	102	85	87	102
Minnesota Twins	825	817	99	773	765	101	87	87	100	87	87	100
New York Yankees	970	915	94	730	753	97	97	103	107	103	103	100
Chicago White Sox	729	724	99	722	732	99	80	79	99	82	79	97
Baltimore Orioles	761	741	97	894	876	102	68	64	95	68	64	94
Oakland Athletics	728	759	104	732	761	96	81	75	93	81	75	93
Kansas City Royals	698	686	98	801	842	95	65	65	101	70	65	93
Tampa Bay Rays	831	803	97	729	754	97	86	84	98	91	84	92
Toronto Blue Jays	818	798	97	772	771	100	84	75	90	86	75	87
Cleveland Indians	783	773	99	839	865	97	72	65	90	75	65	86

2008 National League Team Efficiency Summary

	RC	Runs	Hit Eff	Exp RA	RA	Pit Eff	Exp Wins	Wins	Runs Eff	Eff Wins	Wins	Overall Eff
Houston Astros	673	643	96	775	770	101	67	74	111	70	74	106
Cincinnati Reds	684	673	98	741	723	103	75	78	104	75	78	105
San Diego Padres	662	638	96	735	769	96	66	75	114	73	75	103
Milwaukee Brewers	795	785	99	830	818	101	78	80	103	78	80	103
Philadelphia Phillies	839	820	98	747	709	105	93	93	100	90	93	103
San Francisco Giants	652	657	101	617	611	101	87	88	101	86	88	103
Florida Marlins	790	772	98	739	766	97	82	87	107	86	87	101
St Louis Cardinals	742	730	98	636	640	99	92	91	99	93	91	97
Colorado Rockies	813	804	99	685	715	96	90	92	102	95	92	97
Chicago Cubs	729	707	97	681	672	101	85	83	98	86	83	97
Los Angeles Dodgers	797	780	98	599	611	98	100	95	95	103	95	92
Atlanta Braves	757	735	97	644	641	101	92	86	93	94	86	92
New York Mets	721	671	93	760	757	100	71	70	98	77	70	91
Arizona Diamondbacks	751	720	96	766	782	98	74	70	94	79	70	88
Pittsburgh Pirates	659	636	96	747	768	97	65	62	95	71	62	88
Washington Nationals	748	710	95	855	874	98	64	59	92	70	59	84

The Fielding Bible Awards 2009

John Dewan

We had two of the closest races in the history of the Fielding Bible Awards this year. They centered around the keystone sack. Aaron Hill, Dustin Pedroia and Chase Utley had 76, 76 and 73 points respectively in the battle for the Second Base award. We had to go to the tie-breaker procedure, and Aaron Hill came out on top for his second Fielding Bible Award. At shortstop, Jack Wilson and Troy Tulowitzki waged war defensively, and Wilson came out on top by just one vote.

Joining Hill as repeat winners are: Albert Pujols (four wins in four years of the award), Carl Crawford (his third), Yadier Molina (his third also), Ichiro (two) and Franklin Gutierrez (his second, this one for center field after claiming last year's right field award). First-time winners are Mark Buehrle, Ryan Zimmerman, and Wilson.

Here's a short refresher course on how the awards are determined: We asked our panel of ten experts to rank 10 players at each position on a scale from one to ten. We then use the same voting technique as the Major League Baseball MVP voting. A first place vote gets 10 points, second place 9 points, third place 8 points, etc. Total up the points for each player and the player with the most points wins the award. A perfect score is 100.

One important distinction that differentiates our award from most other baseball awards, including the Gold Gloves, is that we only have one winner for all of Major League

Baseball, instead of separate winners for each league. We also name the winners in left, right and center fields, instead of lumping all outfielders together (which has given an unfair advantage to center fielders in the Gold Glove voting). Our intention is to continue to stand up and say, "This is the best fielder at this position in the major leagues last season."

Here are the Fielding Bible Awards for the 2009 season:

First Base – Albert Pujols, St. Louis

What's left to say? Four Fielding Bible Awards in four years. When Pujols first came up I envisioned him as what Miguel Cabrera is now: a great hitter struggling to find a position he can play well defensively. Albert played left field (not so well). He played right field (not so well). He played third base (not so well). Then he discovered first base and has been the best in baseball, both offensively and defensively, ever since.

Second Base – Aaron Hill, Toronto

It's the second Fielding Bible Award for Hill (he won the 2007 award), and it didn't come easily. The regular voting by the panel ended in a tie between Hill and Dustin Pedroia at 76 points with Chase Utley just three behind. For the second time in the history of the award, we went to the tie-breaker. The first tie-breaker rule is based on the player with the most first-place votes. Hill wins because he had four first-place votes from our ten panelists to only one for Pedroia.

Third Base – Ryan Zimmerman, Washington

Third base is a very strong, deep defensive poistion in baseball right now. I would be comfortable with any of the top nine guys in our voting winning The Fielding Bible Award—or the Gold Glove award, for that matter—this year. Ryan Zimmerman has broken out of the pack in my estimation, however, by becoming the Defensive Runs Saved leader at third base over the last three years. His first Fielding Bible Award is well deserved. The rest of the best: Adrian Beltre, Chone Figgins, Evan Longoria, Scott Rolen, Brandon Inge, Pedro Feliz, Jack Hannahan and Joe Crede.

Shortstop – Jack Wilson, Pittsburgh and Seattle

Wilson won't win a Gold Glove this year. Just like Mark Teixeira didn't win one last year. He split time between leagues, and the Gold Glove voters don't know which league to put him in. Not so with The Fielding Bible Awards. Jack Wilson was the best shortstop in baseball last year. Period. We don't care which league he played in. He led all shortstops in Run Saved by a wide margin (27 runs saved to Brendan Ryan's 19) and has taken over the MLB lead for most Runs Saved over the last three years (51). Mr. Wilson is the Fielding Bible Award winner at shortstop for 2009.

Left Field – Carl Crawford, Tampa Bay

He's baaack! Again. Crawford wins his third award. The only year of our tour that he didn't win was two years ago (2007), when he came in a close second to Eric Byrnes. This year was no contest. No player has ever won with a perfect record (10 first place votes from 10 panelists), but Carl came as close as possible with nine first places and one second. That's 99 points. (The best previously was 98 points by Adam Everett at shortstop in 2006.) If Crawford doesn't win his first Gold Glove this year, I'm going to throw up.

Center Field – Franklin Gutierrez, Seattle

What a story. Gutierrez excelled defensively for two years playing right field for Cleveland. He led all right-fielders in plus/minus in each of 2007 and 2008, despite playing less than 100 games each year. Seattle put a huge emphasis on defense in 2009, and Franklin came through for them with another Fielding Bible Award, this time in center field. His 31 runs saved tied him with Chone Figgins for the most in baseball last year. For outfielders, Carl Crawford's 23 runs saved was second best to Gutierrez. The Seattle Mariners finished the 2009 season as the best defensive team in baseball, with 109 runs saved as a team.

Right Field – Ichiro Suzuki, Seattle

Ichiro was no small part of Seattle's defensive success as well. He saved 11 runs defensively, and our voters rewarded him with his second Fielding Bible Award. His first was in 2006. Hunter Pence gave him a run for his money, however, as Ichiro finished with 93 points to Hunter's 84. Suzuki was named first on five ballots to three for Pence.

Catcher – Yadier Molina, St. Louis

Yadier was the third "most popular" vote getter in 2009. He was named first on eight ballots, finishing with 96 points. Everyone knows about Molina's incredible throwing arm. Well, maybe not the eight guys he picked off this year (the most by any catcher—next most was four). But one thing that hasn't been measured until recently is a catcher's ability to prevent bad pitches from getting past him, allowing baserunners to move up. We measured this stat this year and shared it with our voters. No surprise, Yadier is one of the best. Here are the top five bad-pitch-blocking catchers from 2009:

Catcher	Made Blocks	Missed Blocks	Catcher Block Percentage
Jason Varitek, Boston	374	16	95.9
Carlos Ruiz, Philadelphia	271	12	95.8
Yadier Molina, St. Louis	564	29	95.1
Rod Barajas, Toronto	374	20	94.9
Kurt Suzuki, Oakland	506	30	94.4

Pitcher – Mark Buehrle, Chicago White Sox

In *The Fielding Bible—Volume II*, we put some extra time into analyzing pitcher defense. It's not only pitchers' ability to field their position that counts defensively. It's their ability to hold runners that matters in an important way as well. In Buehrle's case, he has it all. His plus/minus figure of +9 was tops among pitchers in 2009, but his ability to hold runners is legendary. In the last four years he's allowed a total of 15 stolen bases. His catchers have managed to catch five potential thieves in that time period. But even more importantly, when Mark throws over to first, the results are devastating for baserunners. Sixteen times in those same four years, he's thrown over to first and the runner broke for second and was thrown out. That's a Pitcher Caught Stealing (PCS) in our scorebook. Not only that, 14 more times Buehrle nabbed a baserunner at the base as he tried to get back. That's a Pitcher Pickoff (PPO), for those of you scoring at home. In total, 15 stolen bases against him (an average of just under four per year) and 35 guys thrown out (an average of almost nine per year). Not too shabby.

Background of the Fielding Bible Awards

While *The Fielding Bible* and *The Fielding Bible—Volume II* put a lot of emphasis on the numbers, especially Defensive Runs Saved and the Plus-Minus system, I feel that visual observation and subjective judgment are still very important parts of determining the best defensive players. Also, I think people have a right to know who is voting and all the players they are voting for. Therefore, in setting up the Fielding Bible Awards, we took the following steps:

1. *We appointed a panel of experts to vote.* We have a panel of ten experts plus three "tie-breaker" ballots. (See below.)

2. *We rate everybody in one group.* The Gold Glove vote is divided into National League and American League. We make ours different by putting everybody together. Besides, is playing shortstop in the American League one thing and playing shortstop in the National League a different thing, or are they really very much the same thing? This year is a great example of this rule. Without it, Jack Wilson wins nada. With it, he's the best fielding shortstop in baseball. We want to say who the best fielder was at each position last year in Major League Baseball, period. So we have a single ballot. (You're welcome, Jack.)

3. *We use a ten-man ballot and a ten-point scale.* We use a ten-man ballot (I'm referring to the players listed, not the panel of experts). Then we give ten points for first place, nine points for second place, etc, down to one point for tenth place. We feel strongly that a ten-man ballot with weighted positions leads to more accurate outcomes.

4. *We defined the list of candidates.* Only players who actually were regulars at the position are candidates. This eliminates the possibility of a vote going to somebody who wasn't really playing the position.

5. *We are publishing the balloting.* We summarize the voting at each position, clearly identifying whom everybody voted for. Publishing the actual vote totals encourages the voters to take their votes more seriously. Also, we feel the public will have more respect for the voting if they have more insight into the process.

There is something cool about having 10 experts and a 10-man ballot and a 10-point scale, because that gives each position 100 possible points. If all 10 voters place one player first on their ballot, he scores 100. That hasn't happened yet (although this year we came as close as possible with Carl Crawford's 99 points).

Here are the tie-breaker rules (which came into play in our very first year and did so again this year). They are applied one at a time until we have a winner:
1. Most first-place votes wins.
2. Count the tie-breaker ballots, highest point tally wins.

3. Award goes to player with the higher plus/minus rating.

Ballots were due on the Tuesday after the end of the regular season. Here is this year's panel:

Since you have this book, you probably know **Bill James**, a baseball writer and analyst published for more than thirty years. Bill is the Senior Baseball Operations Advisor for the Boston Red Sox.

The **BIS Video Scouts** at Baseball Info Solutions (BIS) study every game of the season, multiple times, charting a huge list of valuable game details.

The man who created Strat-O-Matic Baseball, **Hal Richman**, continues to lead his company's annual in-depth analysis of each player's season. Hal cautions SOM players that his voting on this ballot may or may not reflect the eventual 2009 fielding ratings for players in his game. Ballots were due prior to the completion of his annual research effort to evaluate player defense.

Named the best sports columnist in America by the Associated Press Sports Editors in 2003 and 2005, **Joe Posnanski** is a Senior Writer at *Sports Illustrated* and occasional columnist for the *Kansas City Star*.

For over twenty years, BIS owner **John Dewan** has collected, analyzed, and published in-depth baseball statistics and analysis. He wrote *The Fielding Bible* in 2006 and *The Fielding Bible—Volume II* in 2009.

Mat Olkin is a sabermetrics consultant to major league teams and has studied, analyzed, and written about baseball players for almost fifteen years.

Peter Gammons serves as a studio analyst on ESPN's *Baseball Tonight* and *Baseball Today*. He also provides "Diamond Notes" and other reports for *SportsCenter*. Gammons has been a senior writer for *ESPN The Magazine* since December 1999 and contributes to ESPN.com.

Rob Neyer writes baseball for ESPN.com and appears regularly on ESPN radio and ESPNews.

Todd Radcliffe is Lead Video Scout at Baseball Info Solutions and brings 15 years of Major League Baseball scouting experience to the panel.

The **Tom Tango Fan Poll** represents the results of a poll taken at the website, Tango on Baseball (Tangotiger.net). Besides hosting the website, Tom writes research articles devoted to sabermetrics.

Our three tie-breakers are **Steve Moyer**, president of Baseball Info Solutions, **Dan Casey**, veteran Video Scout at BIS, and **Dave Studenmund**, one of the founders of Hardballtimes.com and *The Hardball Times Baseball Annual*.

The Fielding Bible Awards

Below we show the final point tally for The Fielding Bible Awards in the 2009 season. We asked a panel of experts to complete a ten-man ballot ranking players from 1 to 10 based on the defensive abilities. We show the ranks in the tables below. We then awarded points in the same way as Major League Baseball's MVP voting: ten points for a first place vote, nine for second, etc., down to one point for tenth place. We cover all nine positions, looking at only their fielding work for the 2009 season. Non-pitchers are only eligible if they played at least 500 innings. Pitchers require a minimum of 100 innings pitched.

First Basemen

First Basemen	Bill James	BIS Video Scouts	Hal Richman	Joe Posnanski	John Dewan	Mat Olkin	Peter Gammons	Rob Neyer	Tango Fan Poll	Todd Radcliffe	Total Points
Albert Pujols	2	1	2	2	1	1	1	1	1	3	95
Kevin Youkilis	3	3	4	4	4	4	3	2	6	5	72
Adrian Gonzalez	1	2	3	1	2	3		3	4	9	71
Mark Teixeira	4	7	1	5	7	5	2	6	2	4	67
Casey Kotchman	7	4	5	6	3	9	5	5	9	2	55
Lyle Overbay	5	5	9		6	6		10	8	1	38
Kendry Morales		9		3		2	4	8		6	34
Travis Ishikawa	9	6			8		7	4	3		29
James Loney	8	8	7	8		7		9		7	23
Derrek Lee		10	8	7	5		10		7		19

Others receiving points: Daniel Murphy 18, Todd Helton 16, Chris Davis 3, Justin Morneau 3, Adam LaRoche 2, Carlos Pena 2, Lance Berkman 1, Miguel Cabrera 1, Paul Konerko 1

Second Basemen

Second Basemen	Bill James	BIS Video Scouts	Hal Richman	Joe Posnanski	John Dewan	Mat Olkin	Peter Gammons	Rob Neyer	Tango Fan Poll	Todd Radcliffe	Total Points
Aaron Hill	1	1	4	2	1	2	7	8	7	1	76
Dustin Pedroia	2	4	3	6	4	4	3	1	5	2	76
Chase Utley	3	3	9	1	2	3	6	2	4	4	73
Ian Kinsler	4	2		3	3	1	2	6		3	64
Orlando Hudson	9	5	1	7	7	7	5		3	8	47
Placido Polanco	5	9		4	5	5	8	4	6	6	47
Brandon Phillips	8		2	8	9	6		7	1	10	37
Clint Barmes	10	8	6	5	10	9	1	5	9		36
Ben Zobrist		6		10	6		4	3		5	32
Mark Ellis			5	9	8			9	2		22

Others receiving points: Howie Kendrick 8, Robinson Cano 8, Ryan Roberts 5, Akinori Iwamura 4, Brian Roberts 4, Jamey Carroll 4, Maicer Izturis 3, Jose Lopez 2, Jayson Nix 1, Kaz Matsui 1

Third Basemen

Third Basemen	Bill James	BIS Video Scouts	Hal Richman	Joe Posnanski	John Dewan	Mat Olkin	Peter Gammons	Rob Neyer	Tango Fan Poll	Todd Radcliffe	Total Points
Ryan Zimmerman	4	2	3	1	1	6	1	1	6	1	84
Adrian Beltre	2	5	1	4	2	4	5	4	1	6	76
Chone Figgins	3	1		3	3	2	2	3	5	2	75
Evan Longoria	1	3	4	2	5	1	9	2	4	4	75
Scott Rolen	5	4	2	5	4	7	4	5	2	3	69
Brandon Inge	9	9	7	6	7	5	3	6	3	8	47
Pedro Feliz	6	7	6	7	9	3		8	8	9	36
Jack Hannahan		6	5		6	9	8	10	10	7	27
Joe Crede	7	8	8	8	8			7	9	10	23
Casey Blake			9	10	8	6					11

Others receiving points: Kevin Kouzmanoff 10, Ian Stewart 6, Andy LaRoche 5, Bill Hall 3, David Wright 2, Mark Reynolds 1

Shortstops

Shortstops	Bill James	BIS Video Scouts	Hal Richman	Joe Posnanski	John Dewan	Mat Olkin	Peter Gammons	Rob Neyer	Tango Fan Poll	Todd Radcliffe	Total Points
Jack Wilson	1	1	2	1	1	4	3	1	6	4	86
Troy Tulowitzki	2	2	1	4	2	3	1	5	3	2	85
Elvis Andrus	4	3	10	2	5	2	2	2	1	10	69
Brendan Ryan	9	4		5	4	1	5	4	4	1	62
Yunel Escobar	3	6	4		6	5	7	9		6	42
Cesar Izturis	0	8	9	6	3	8		3	8	7	39
Marco Scutaro		5		8	8	6	4	7		5	34
Jimmy Rollins			3		9				5	3	24
Adam Everett			6	3	7			8			20
Paul Janish	7	7	7	10		10		10	9	8	20

Others receiving points: Jason Barlett 19, Erick Aybar 15, Stephen Drew 13, J.J. Hardy 6, Rafael Furcal 5, Asdrubal Cabrera 4, Derek Jeter 3, Hanley Ramirez 3, Alex Gonzalez 1

Left Fielders

Left Fielders	Bill James	BIS Video Scouts	Hal Richman	Joe Posnanski	John Dewan	Mat Olkin	Peter Gammons	Rob Neyer	Tango Fan Poll	Todd Radcliffe	Total Points
Carl Crawford	1	1	1	1	1	1	1	1	2	1	99
Nyjer Morgan	7	2	2	4	3	0	5	2	1	6	72
David DeJesus	5	5	3	3	7	2	4	5	4	4	68
Juan Rivera	3	3		2	2	5	3	3		2	65
Matt Holliday	2	4	0	5	4	3	2	1	10	3	64
Laynce Nix	8	8		7	5	7	10	6		8	29
Juan Pierre	4	9	6			10		7	7	10	24
Seth Smith	6	6			9	8		8		5	24
Chris Dickerson			5				6		3		19
Jason Bay		10	8			4				9	13
Scott Hairston		7			6					7	13

Others receiving points: Josh Anderson 9, David Murphy 8, Scott Podsednik 8, Chase Headley 6, Ryan Braun 6, Raul Ibanez 5, Ryan Spilborghs 5, Carlos Lee 3, Gerardo Parra 3, Fred Lewis 2, Johnny Damon 2, Ryan Raburn 2, Wladimir Balentien 1

Center Fielders

Center Fielders	Bill James	BIS Video Scouts	Hal Richman	Joe Posnanski	John Dewan	Mat Olkin	Peter Gammons	Rob Neyer	Tango Fan Poll	Todd Radcliffe	Total Points
Franklin Gutierrez	2	1	3	1	1	1	1	1	1	1	97
Carlos Gomez	8	2	10	2	2	2	2	4	9	2	67
Curtis Granderson	3	4		3	3	3	4	8		3	57
Rajai Davis	4	5		8	5	7		2		4	42
Michael Bourn		3			4		3	3	2		40
Tony Gwynn	6	7		4	10	4	6	6			34
Mike Cameron	9		6		7	6	7	5	6		31
Carlos Beltran	10		2	5			8		3	8	30
Torii Hunter			1	10		10	5	9		6	25
Chris Young	1	6			9			7			21
Grady Sizemore	5	10	5	9						5	21

Others receiving points: Colby Rasmus 14, Shane Victorino 14, Matt Kemp 12, B.J. Upton 11, Brett Gardner 10, Josh Hamilton 6, Denard Span 5, Willy Taveras 4, Aaron Rowand 3, Vernon Wells 3, Adam Jones 2, Andrew McCutchen 1

Right Fielders

Right Fielders	Bill James	BIS Video Scouts	Hal Richman	Joe Posnanski	John Dewan	Mat Olkin	Peter Gammons	Rob Neyer	Tango Fan Poll	Todd Radcliffe	Total Points
Ichiro Suzuki	2	2	1	1	2	1	4	2	1	1	93
Hunter Pence	1	1	4	4	1	2	5	3	3	2	84
Ryan Sweeney	3	3	8		4	3	3	1		3	60
Justin Upton		6		3		4	2	5	5		41
Nelson Cruz	8	5	10	2	10	6	8	4		5	41
Ryan Church	7	4	6	8	6		7	8		4	38
Jayson Werth			9	7	3	9	1		6	9	33
J.D. Drew	4		7	5			9			6	24
Nick Markakis	5		2				10		4		23
Randy Winn					5	5		6	10	7	22

Others receiving points: Jay Bruce 21, Will Venable 12, Alex Rios 10, Jeff Francouer 10, Nick Swisher 10, Shin-Soo Choo 7, Corey Hart 5, Jeremy Hermida 5, Gabe Gross 3, Gabe Kapler 3, Nate Schierholtz 3, Brandon Moss 1, Ryan Ludwick 1

Catchers

Catchers	Bill James	BIS Video Scouts	Hal Richman	Joe Posnanski	John Dewan	Mat Olkin	Peter Gammons	Rob Neyer	Tango Fan Poll	Todd Radcliffe	Total Points
Yadier Molina	4	1	1	1	1	1	1	1	1	2	96
Gerald Laird	8	2	5	2	2	2	3	2	3	1	80
Joe Mauer	2	3	2	3	10	4	2	6	2	6	70
Russell Martin	3	5	3	5	3		8	3	10	4	55
Kurt Suzuki		8	7	4	5	7	4	4	5	7	48
Carlos Ruiz		10	9		4	3	6	5	7	3	41
Jeff Mathis	1	7	4		6	6	9	9			35
Koyie Hill	7	4			9	5		8	9	5	30
Rob Johnson	6	6		8		9				9	17
Rod Barajas	5			7	8					8	16

Others receiving points: Jason Varitek 10, Ivan Rodriguez 9, Miguel Montero 9, Ryan Hanigan 7, Bengie Molina 5, Mike Napoli 5, Brian McCann 4, Jason Kendall 4, Matt Wieters 3, Chris Iannetta 2, Dioner Navarro 2, A.J. Pierzynski 1, Kelly Shoppach 1

Pitchers

Pitchers	Bill James	BIS Video Scouts	Hal Richman	Joe Posnanski	John Dewan	Mat Olkin	Peter Gammons	Rob Neyer	Tango Fan Poll	Todd Radcliffe	Total Points
Mark Buehrle		1	4	1	1	1	2	1	1	1	86
Zack Greinke	1	3	8	7	9	3	1	7	6	4	61
Johan Santana	6	7	1		6	2	3	8	9	6	51
Joel Pineiro		4	10	4	5		4	2	4	5	50
Brad Bergesen	2	2		5	7		10	5	7		39
Jon Garland	10	9	9	3	2			4	3		37
Aaron Cook		8	3		3			3	2		36
Jason Marquis	8	6	2	2			7				30
Zach Duke		10	6	10	4	9	8	6	5		30
Roy Oswalt	5					5				7	16

Others receiving points: Felix Hernandez 14, Josh Geer 14, Carlos Zambrano 12, Javier Vazquez 11, Cole Hamels 9, Chris Carpenter 8, Jon Lester 7, Aaron Laffey 6, Ryan Dempster 6, Livan Hernandez 5, Barry Zito 4, Kenshin Kawakami 4, John Lannan 3, Adam Wainwright 2, Andy Pettitte 2, Brian Bannister 2, Randy Wolf 2, Clayton Kershaw 1, Jeff Suppan 1, Jarrod Washburn 1

Runs Saved and Plus/Minus Leaders

For several years we've listed the Plus/Minus leaders and trailers in this section. The Plus/Minus System is a way to evaluate defensive range by measuring how often defenders turn grounders and fly balls into outs. A number greater than zero (plus "+") is above average. Below zero (minus "-") is below average.

In *The Fielding Bible—Volume II*, we combined Plus/Minus with our analysis of bunts, double plays, outfield arms, catchers' earned runs, catchers' stolen bases allowed, pitchers' stolen bases allowed, and home run saving catches. The end result is Defensive Runs Saved (or Runs Saved for short), which we've added to this year's *Handbook* to give you a more complete evaluation of defensive ability.

Please see the Glossary (or www.fieldingbible.com) for a more complete description of Plus/Minus and Runs Saved.

A few observations:

The three-year leaders clearly identify the best defensive players in baseball. Take a look at the top five at each position on the 3-Year Runs Saved and Plus/Minus Leaderboards and you get an excellent idea of the best defenders at each position.

Seven out of the eight 2009 Plus/Minus leaders also led their position in Runs Saved. The exception was right field, where Hunter Pence's arm carried him past Ichiro Suzuki for the top Runs Saved total.

Five winners of a 2009 "Runs Saved Crown" (the highest Runs Saved total) also won the Fielding Bible Award at their position: Albert Pujols, Jack Wilson, Carl Crawford, Franklin Gutierrez, and Mark Buehrle.

The Seattle Mariners had the best Runs Saved team total in baseball and featured three positional Runs Saved leaders: Rob Johnson, Jack Wilson, and Franklin Gutierrez.

Despite never winning a Gold Glove or a Fielding Bible Award, Chase Utley has the best Runs Saved and Plus/Minus totals over the past three seasons. Add his stellar defense at a premium defensive position to his annual 30 home runs, .300 average, .395 on-base percentage, and .530 slugging percentage and you have one of the most valuable players in baseball. Teammates Jimmy Rollins and Ryan Howard have won MVPs, but the real Phillies star gets far less attention than he deserves.

Infield Runs Saved Leaders

First Basemen 3-Year Leaders		Second Basemen 3-Year Leaders		Third Basemen 3-Year Leaders		Shortstops 3-Year Leaders	
Pujols,Albert	56	Utley,Chase	61	Zimmerman,Ryan	53	Wilson,Jack	51
Kotchman,Casey	35	Ellis,Mark	41	Beltre,Adrian	51	Tulowitzki,Troy	41
Youkilis,Kevin	22	Hill,Aaron	38	Rolen,Scott	38	Vizquel,Omar	28
Overbay,Lyle	17	Polanco,Placido	29	Figgins,Chone	38	Escobar,Yunel	26
Teixeira,Mark	15	Kinsler,Ian	23	Feliz,Pedro	34	Izturis,Cesar	25
Votto,Joey	15	Pedroia,Dustin	22	Crede,Joe	30	Scutaro,Marco	21
Helton,Todd	14	Phillips,Brandon	20	Hannahan,Jack	30	Hardy,J.J.	20
Berkman,Lance	13	Hudson,Orlando	18	Inge,Brandon	26	Everett,Adam	20
Barton,Daric	10	Cano,Robinson	16	Longoria,Evan	26	McDonald,John	20
Gonzalez,Adrian	8	Barmes,Clint	16	Glaus,Troy	12	Rollins,Jimmy	19

First Basemen 3-Year Trailers		Second Basemen 3-Year Trailers		Third Basemen 3-Year Trailers		Shortstops 3-Year Trailers	
Jacobs,Mike	-26	Castillo,Luis	-30	Encarnacion,Edwin	-37	Betancourt,Yuniesky	-39
Fielder,Prince	-22	Uggla,Dan	-19	Atkins,Garrett	-33	Jeter,Derek	-31
Giambi,Jason	-17	Casilla,Alexi	-16	Fields,Josh	-24	Harris,Brendan	-28
Millar,Kevin	-12	Lopez,Felipe	-15	Wigginton,Ty	-20	Cabrera,Orlando	-25
Huff,Aubrey	-10	DeRosa,Mark	-12	Reynolds,Mark	-20	Lugo,Julio	-23
Delgado,Carlos	-9	Callaspo,Alberto	-11	Young,Michael	-18	Ramirez,Hanley	-22

First Basemen 2009 Leaders		Second Basemen 2009 Leaders		Third Basemen 2009 Leaders		Shortstops 2009 Leaders	
Pujols,Albert	12	Kinsler,Ian	23	Figgins,Chone	31	Wilson,Jack	27
Gonzalez,Adrian	11	Hill,Aaron	19	Zimmerman,Ryan	22	Ryan,Brendan	19
Murphy,Daniel	11	Zobrist,Ben	18	Beltre,Adrian	22	Andrus,Elvis	14
Ishikawa,Travis	10	Utley,Chase	13	Longoria,Evan	17	Escobar,Yunel	13
Youkilis,Kevin	10	Pedroia,Dustin	12	Rolen,Scott	15	Scutaro,Marco	12
Kotchman,Casey	8	Barmes,Clint	9	Hannahan,Jack	13	Janish,Paul	11
Morales,Kendry	6	Cano,Robinson	7	Crede,Joe	12	Izturis,Cesar	10
Garko,Ryan	5	Polanco,Placido	7	Inge,Brandon	8	Tulowitzki,Troy	9
Loney,James	3	Kendrick,Howie	7	Blake,Casey	8	Furcal,Rafael	8
Lee,Derrek	3	Izturis,Maicer	6	LaRoche,Andy	7	Drew,Stephen	8

First Basemen 2009 Trailers		Second Basemen 2009 Trailers		Third Basemen 2009 Trailers		Shortstops 2009 Trailers	
Dunn,Adam	-18	Casilla,Alexi	-12	Lowell,Mike	-18	Cabrera,Orlando	-33
Giambi,Jason	-7	Callaspo,Alberto	-11	Young,Michael	-18	Betancourt,Yuniesky	-19
Huff,Aubrey	-7	Castillo,Luis	-11	Wright,David	-13	Tejada,Miguel	-16
Cantu,Jorge	-7	Getz,Chris	-8	Teahen,Mark	-11	Pennington,Cliff	-10
Johnson,Nick	-7	Schumaker,Skip	-8	DeRosa,Mark	-9	Renteria,Edgar	-10
Pena,Carlos	-6	Uggla,Dan	-8	McGehee,Casey	-8	Cabrera,Everth	-9

Outfield Runs Saved Leaders

Left Fielders 3-Year Leaders		Center Fielders 3-Year Leaders		Right Fielders 3-Year Leaders	
Crawford,Carl	38	Beltran,Carlos	35	Rios,Alex	33
Harris,Willie	26	Gutierrez,Franklin	34	Winn,Randy	32
Rivera,Juan	23	Gomez,Carlos	33	Pence,Hunter	31
Holliday,Matt	22	Amezaga,Alfredo	27	Suzuki,Ichiro	26
Hairston,Scott	20	Granderson,Curtis	24	Francoeur,Jeff	25
Byrnes,Eric	19	Jones,Adam	20	Werth,Jayson	25
Soriano,Alfonso	17	Davis,Rajai	20	Markakis,Nick	20
Damon,Johnny	9	Crisp,Coco	19	Church,Ryan	19
Lewis,Fred	9	Bourn,Michael	18	Upton,Justin	18
Podsednik,Scott	9	Patterson,Corey	17	Ludwick,Ryan	18

Left Fielders 3-Year Trailers		Center Fielders 3-Year Trailers		Right Fielders 3-Year Trailers	
Dunn,Adam	-34	McLouth,Nate	-22	Dye,Jermaine	-45
Ramirez,Manny	-24	Wells,Vernon	-20	Hawpe,Brad	-42
Young,Delmon	-19	Matthews Jr.,Gary	-15	Guillen,Jose	-18
Burrell,Pat	-18	DeJesus,David	-8	Griffey Jr.,Ken	-14
Ibanez,Raul	-17	Milledge,Lastings	-7	Abreu,Bobby	-11
Bay,Jason	-17	Ellsbury,Jacoby	-7	Giles,Brian	-9

Left Fielders 2009 Leaders		Center Fielders 2009 Leaders		Right Fielders 2009 Leaders	
Crawford,Carl	24	Gutierrez,Franklin	31	Pence,Hunter	19
Rivera,Juan	23	Granderson,Curtis	15	Sweeney,Ryan	15
Holliday,Matt	14	Morgan,Nyjer	15	Church,Ryan	14
Morgan,Nyjer	8	Gomez,Carlos	14	Suzuki,Ichiro	11
Nix,Laynce	8	Davis,Rajai	12	Cruz,Nelson	11
Span,Denard	8	Bourn,Michael	11	Upton,Justin	11
Hairston,Scott	7	Gwynn,Tony	11	Bruce,Jay	11
DeJesus,David	5	Gardner,Brett	9	Winn,Randy	11
Smith,Seth	5	Hamilton,Josh	9	Werth,Jayson	10
Balentien,Wladimir	5	Pagan,Angel	8	Moss,Brandon	9

Left Fielders 2009 Trailers		Center Fielders 2009 Trailers		Right Fielders 2009 Trailers	
Coghlan,Chris	-16	Fowler,Dexter	-14	Guillen,Jose	-17
Braun,Ryan	-15	Wells,Vernon	-13	Giles,Brian	-15
Quentin,Carlos	-10	Ellsbury,Jacoby	-9	Dye,Jermaine	-12
Lind,Adam	-8	McCutchen,Andrew	-8	Hawpe,Brad	-9
Young,Delmon	-8	Harris,Willie	-6	Bradley,Milton	-7
Ramirez,Manny	-7	Victorino,Shane	-6	Cuddyer,Michael	-6

Pitcher/Catcher Runs Saved Leaders

Pitchers 3-Year Leaders		Catchers 3-Year Leaders	
Buehrle,Mark	20	Molina,Yadier	22
Cook,Aaron	16	Laird,Gerald	18
Garland,Jon	14	Martin,Russell	13
Duke,Zach	13	Ross,David	12
Pineiro,Joel	12	Mauer,Joe	11
Arroyo,Bronson	10	Kendall,Jason	10
Vazquez,Javier	10	Barajas,Rod	10
Litsch,Jesse	10	Rodriguez,Ivan	9
Santana,Johan	10	Ruiz,Carlos	8
Greinke,Zack	10	Mathis,Jeff	7

Pitchers 3-Year Trailers		Catchers 3-Year Trailers	
Cabrera,Daniel	-20	Posada,Jorge	-23
Contreras,Jose	-13	Buck,John	-20
Young,Chris	-12	Napoli,Mike	-16
Lincecum,Tim	-12	Martinez,Victor	-11
Jackson,Edwin	-11	Bard,Josh	-9
Penny,Brad	-11	Zaun,Gregg	-8

Pitchers 2009 Leaders		Catchers 2009 Leaders	
Buehrle,Mark	11	Johnson,Rob	8
Bergesen,Brad	6	Hill,Koyie	7
Pineiro,Joel	5	Montero,Miguel	6
Duke,Zach	5	Laird,Gerald	5
Carrasco,D.J.	5	Martin,Russell	5
Geer,Josh	5	Mathis,Jeff	4
Marquis,Jason	4	Paulino,Ronny	4
Cook,Aaron	4	Molina,Yadier	4
Garland,Jon	4	Ruiz,Carlos	4
Wolf,Randy	4	Saltalamacchia,J	4

Pitchers 2009 Trailers		Catchers 2009 Trailers	
Penny,Brad	-7	Martinez,Victor	-12
Contreras,Jose	-5	Posada,Jorge	-11
Wells,Randy	-5	Molina,Bengie	-9
Lowe,Derek	-5	Kendall,Jason	-8
Lincecum,Tim	-5	Baker,John	-8
Jackson,Edwin	-4		

Infield Plus/Minus Leaders

First Basemen 3-Year Leaders		Second Basemen 3-Year Leaders		Third Basemen 3-Year Leaders		Shortstops 3-Year Leaders	
Pujols,Albert	+71	Utley,Chase	+82	Beltre,Adrian	+66	Wilson,Jack	+58
Kotchman,Casey	+48	Ellis,Mark	+44	Zimmerman,Ryan	+59	Tulowitzki,Troy	+50
Overbay,Lyle	+34	Hill,Aaron	+40	Rolen,Scott	+50	Escobar,Yunel	+37
Youkilis,Kevin	+30	Phillips,Brandon	+27	Figgins,Chone	+48	Izturis,Cesar	+33
Teixeira,Mark	+19	Polanco,Placido	+26	Crede,Joe	+41	Vizquel,Omar	+33
Votto,Joey	+17	Hudson,Orlando	+24	Feliz,Pedro	+39	Hardy,J.J.	+30
Berkman,Lance	+15	Pedroia,Dustin	+22	Hannahan,Jack	+39	Scutaro,Marco	+29
Barton,Daric	+15	Barmes,Clint	+18	Inge,Brandon	+36	McDonald,John	+28
Helton,Todd	+14	Kinsler,Ian	+16	Longoria,Evan	+32	Rollins,Jimmy	+27
Pena,Carlos	+13	Fontenot,Mike	+12	Glaus,Troy	+15	Bartlett,Jason	+27

First Basemen 3-Year Trailers		Second Basemen 3-Year Trailers		Third Basemen 3-Year Trailers		Shortstops 3-Year Trailers	
Jacobs,Mike	-34	Castillo,Luis	-28	Encarnacion,Edwin	-46	Betancourt,Yuniesky	-56
Fielder,Prince	-25	Uggla,Dan	-28	Atkins,Garrett	-41	Jeter,Derek	-40
Giambi,Jason	-24	Casilla,Alexi	-24	Fields,Josh	-32	Cabrera,Orlando	-37
Delgado,Carlos	-17	Callaspo,Alberto	-23	Reynolds,Mark	-26	Harris,Brendan	-36
Huff,Aubrey	-14	Lopez,Felipe	-21	Wigginton,Ty	-24	Ramirez,Hanley	-29
Millar,Kevin	-12	Roberts,Brian	-14	Young,Michael	-22	Lugo,Julio	-22

First Basemen 2009 Leaders		Second Basemen 2009 Leaders		Third Basemen 2009 Leaders		Shortstops 2009 Leaders	
Pujols,Albert	+14	Kinsler,Ian	+24	Figgins,Chone	+40	Wilson,Jack	+32
Murphy,Daniel	+14	Zobrist,Ben	+23	Zimmerman,Ryan	+28	Ryan,Brendan	+24
Youkilis,Kevin	+14	Hill,Aaron	+20	Beltre,Adrian	+27	Escobar,Yunel	+17
Ishikawa,Travis	+12	Utley,Chase	+14	Rolen,Scott	+22	Scutaro,Marco	+16
Gonzalez,Adrian	+11	Pedroia,Dustin	+12	Longoria,Evan	+21	Andrus,Elvis	+15
Overbay,Lyle	+10	Barmes,Clint	+10	Hannahan,Jack	+18	Izturis,Cesar	+14
Kotchman,Casey	+10	Cano,Robinson	+8	Crede,Joe	+17	Janish,Paul	+13
Morales,Kendry	+9	Hudson,Orlando	+8	Inge,Brandon	+13	Tulowitzki,Troy	+11
Garko,Ryan	+5	Carroll,Jamey	+6	Blake,Casey	+8	Drew,Stephen	+10
Loney,James	+4	Kendrick,Howie	+5	Kouzmanoff,Kevin	+8	Bartlett,Jason	+10

First Basemen 2009 Trailers		Second Basemen 2009 Trailers		Third Basemen 2009 Trailers		Shortstops 2009 Trailers	
Dunn,Adam	-24	Callaspo,Alberto	-19	Lowell,Mike	-23	Cabrera,Orlando	-40
Johnson,Nick	-14	Casilla,Alexi	-16	Young,Michael	-22	Betancourt,Yuniesky	-27
Giambi,Jason	-10	Schumaker,Skip	-14	Wright,David	-15	Tejada,Miguel	-21
Huff,Aubrey	-10	Uggla,Dan	-13	Teahen,Mark	-12	Pennington,Cliff	-14
Cantu,Jorge	-10	Castillo,Luis	-11	DeRosa,Mark	-12	Cabrera,Everth	-12
Butler,Billy	-7	Getz,Chris	-10	Sandoval,Pablo	-12	Renteria,Edgar	-10

Outfield Plus/Minus Leaders

Left Fielders 3-Year Leaders		Center Fielders 3-Year Leaders		Right Fielders 3-Year Leaders	
Crawford,Carl	+55	Beltran,Carlos	+52	Winn,Randy	+38
Harris,Willie	+45	Gomez,Carlos	+49	Suzuki,Ichiro	+34
Byrnes,Eric	+36	Gutierrez,Franklin	+41	Church,Ryan	+26
Holliday,Matt	+32	Crisp,Coco	+37	Cruz,Nelson	+23
Hairston,Scott	+23	Young,Chris	+28	Rios,Alex	+21
Rivera,Juan	+23	Amezaga,Alfredo	+28	Upton,Justin	+19
Pierre,Juan	+13	Granderson,Curtis	+26	Swisher,Nick	+17
Podsednik,Scott	+11	Cameron,Mike	+19	Pence,Hunter	+15
Damon,Johnny	+10	Bourn,Michael	+18	Hermida,Jeremy	+15
Headley,Chase	+8	Davis,Rajai	+17	Fukudome,Kosuke	+14

Left Fielders 3-Year Trailers		Center Fielders 3-Year Trailers		Right Fielders 3-Year Trailers	
Ibanez,Raul	-53	McLouth,Nate	-43	Dye,Jermaine	-81
Dunn,Adam	-51	Wells,Vernon	-40	Hawpe,Brad	-67
Burrell,Pat	-46	Matthews Jr.,Gary	-33	Abreu,Bobby	-52
Ramirez,Manny	-39	Cabrera,Melky	-27	Cuddyer,Michael	-46
Bay,Jason	-39	Kotsay,Mark	-25	Guillen,Jose	-43
Young,Delmon	-37	Ankiel,Rick	-22	Griffey Jr.,Ken	-25

Left Fielders 2009 Leaders		Center Fielders 2009 Leaders		Right Fielders 2009 Leaders	
Crawford,Carl	+32	Gutierrez,Franklin	+43	Suzuki,Ichiro	+21
Rivera,Juan	+26	Gwynn,Tony	+23	Sweeney,Ryan	+20
Holliday,Matt	+19	Granderson,Curtis	+17	Church,Ryan	+17
Smith,Seth	+13	Gomez,Carlos	+17	Pence,Hunter	+16
Morgan,Nyjer	+12	Morgan,Nyjer	+15	Upton,Justin	+13
Span,Denard	+11	Davis,Rajai	+14	Cruz,Nelson	+12
Nix,Laynce	+10	Hamilton,Josh	+12	Venable,Will	+12
Hairston,Scott	+9	Gardner,Brett	+11	Drew,J.D.	+11
Pierre,Juan	+8	Young,Chris	+10	Swisher,Nick	+11
Podsednik,Scott	+5	Bourn,Michael	+9	Winn,Randy	+10

Left Fielders 2009 Trailers		Center Fielders 2009 Trailers		Right Fielders 2009 Trailers	
Braun,Ryan	-31	Wells,Vernon	-30	Dye,Jermaine	-28
Coghlan,Chris	-29	Fowler,Dexter	-25	Guillen,Jose	-25
Quentin,Carlos	-20	Victorino,Shane	-24	Giles,Brian	-19
Reimold,Nolan	-15	Jones,Adam	-20	Abreu,Bobby	-18
Lee,Carlos	-14	McCutchen,Andrew	-17	Markakis,Nick	-17
Young,Delmon	-12	Fukudome,Kosuke	-15	Cuddyer,Michael	-16

Pitcher Plus/Minus Leaders

**Pitchers
3-Year Leaders**

Marquis,Jason	+13
Cook,Aaron	+12
Garland,Jon	+12
Buehrle,Mark	+11
Pineiro,Joel	+11
Litsch,Jesse	+11
Duke,Zach	+9
Vazquez,Javier	+9
Webb,Brandon	+8
Hernandez,Livan	+8

**Pitchers
3-Year Trailers**

Cabrera,Daniel	-17
Jackson,Edwin	-11
Kazmir,Scott	-10
Lee,Cliff	-10
Penny,Brad	-10
Johnson,Randy	-8

**Pitchers
2009 Leaders**

Buehrle,Mark	+9
Bergesen,Brad	+7
Marquis,Jason	+6
Garland,Jon	+5
Geer,Josh	+5
Pineiro,Joel	+4
Wolf,Randy	+4
Haren,Dan	+4
Carrasco,D.J.	+4
Zito,Barry	+4

**Pitchers
2009 Trailers**

Lowe,Derek	-7
Carpenter,Chris	-6
Richard,Clayton	-5
Penny,Brad	-5
Wells,Randy	-5
West,Sean	-4

Career Register

The Career Register includes complete career statistics through the 2009 season for every major league player who played in 2009. We included thirty-two bonus players as well, guys who missed the entire 2009 season, for example Justin Duchscherer and Ben Sheets, or potential foreign imports such as Ryota Igarashi and Hisanori Takahashi.

For players who have appeared in fewer than three major league seasons, we included their full minor league statistics. For those players with three or more years in the big leagues who also spent time in the minor leagues in 2009 (for example, if they had a rehab assignment) we included only their 2009 minor league statistics—indicated by an asterisk. Those players who split time between the majors and the minors last season but have fewer than three years of major league experience will still have their full minor league stats included.

If a player led the league in a particular category, that register total will appear in boldface.

The Register also features Runs Created (RC) for hitters and Component ERA (ERC) for pitchers, in addition to the more traditional statistics. Developed by Bill James, Runs Created is a method of measuring every facet of a hitter's strengths and weaknesses, combining those factors into one number, indicative of a player's production. Component ERA estimates what a pitcher's ERA should have been based upon his raw pitching statistics and gives us a good indication of whether or not a pitcher actually deserved his ERA. An explanation of Bill's most-current formulas for both RC and ERC can be found in the Baseball Glossary at the end of the Handbook.

A player's total career numbers in the postseason appear on one line above his total regular season career numbers. Note that because we work hard to bring you this publication before November 1, career postseason records are only updated through the 2008 World Series.

It's been an entire year since our last edition, so here's a little refresher:

Age is seasonal as of June 30, 2010.

For pitchers, BFP is Batters Facing Pitcher; TBB is Total Bases on Balls (or, Total Walks, intentional and unintentional); OP is Save Opportunities; Hld is Holds.

For varying levels of Class-A ball, we have used "A+" to indicate High A and "A-" to indicate Low A.

Finally, Bill James decided four years ago that we should start referring to all incarnations of the Los Angeles Angels of Anaheim as LAA. He cited the Philadelphia Blue Jays of 1943 and 1944 as a historical example of a very temporary team name being forgotten and eventually assimilated into the name they were called going forward: the Phillies.

David Aardsma

Pitches: R **Bats:** R **Pos:** RP-73   **Ht:** 6'4" **Wt:** 205 **Born:** 12/27/1981 **Age:** 28

		HOW MUCH HE PITCHED					WHAT HE GAVE UP												THE RESULTS						
Year Team	Lg	G	GS	CG	GF	IP	BFP	H	R	ER	HR	SH	SF	HB	TBB	IBB	SO	WP	Bk	W	L	Pct	Sh	Sv-Op Hld	ERC	ERA
2004 SF	NL	11	0	0	5	10.2	61	20	8	8	1	0	2	2	10	0	5	0	0	1	0	1.000	0	0-1 1	13.38	6.75
2006 ChC	NL	45	0	0	9	53.0	225	41	25	24	9	1	3	1	28	0	49	1	0	3	0	1.000	0	0-0 5	3.88	4.08
2007 CWS	AL	25	0	0	7	32.1	151	39	24	23	4	2	1	1	17	3	36	2	0	2	1	.667	0	0-3 5	5.93	6.40
2008 Bos	AL	47	0	0	7	48.2	228	49	32	30	4	3	2	5	35	2	49	3	0	4	2	.667	0	0-1 4	5.63	5.55
2009 Sea	AL	73	0	0	53	71.1	296	49	23	20	4	2	1	0	34	3	80	2	0	3	6	.333	0	38-42 6	2.34	2.52
5 ML YEARS		201	0	0	81	216.0	961	198	112	105	22	8	8	9	124	8	219	8	0	13	9	.591	0	38-47 19	4.39	4.38

Bobby Abreu

Bats: L **Throws:** R **Pos:** RF-126; DH-14; LF-10; PH-2   **Ht:** 6'0" **Wt:** 210 **Born:** 3/11/1974 **Age:** 36

							BATTING													BASERUNNING				AVERAGES		
Year Team	Lg	G	AB	H	2B	3B	HR	(Hm	Rd)	TB	R	RBI	RC	TBB	IBB	SO	HBP	SH	SF	SB	CS	SB%	GDP	Avg	OBP	Slg
1996 Hou	NL	15	22	5	1	0	0	(0	0)	6	1	1	1	2	0	3	0	0	0	0	0	-	1	.227	.292	.273
1997 Hou	NL	59	188	47	10	2	3	(3	0)	70	22	26	25	21	0	48	1	0	0	7	2	.78	0	.250	.329	.372
1998 Phi	NL	151	497	155	29	6	17	(10	7)	247	68	74	101	84	14	133	0	4	4	19	10	.66	6	.312	.409	.497
1999 Phi	NL	152	546	183	35	11	20	(13	7)	300	118	93	131	109	8	113	3	0	4	27	9	.75	13	.335	.446	.549
2000 Phi	NL	154	576	182	42	10	25	(14	11)	319	103	79	130	100	9	116	1	0	3	28	8	.78	12	.316	.416	.554
2001 Phi	NL	162	588	170	48	4	31	(13	18)	319	118	110	125	106	11	137	1	0	9	36	14	.72	13	.289	.393	.543
2002 Phi	NL	157	572	176	50	6	20	(8	12)	298	102	85	112	104	9	117	3	0	6	31	12	.72	11	.308	.413	.521
2003 Phi	NL	158	577	173	35	1	20	(11	9)	270	99	101	120	109	13	126	2	0	7	22	9	.71	13	.300	.409	.468
2004 Phi	NL	159	574	173	47	1	30	(13	17)	312	118	105	139	127	10	116	5	0	7	40	5	.89	5	.301	.428	.544
2005 Phi	NL	162	588	168	37	1	24	(15	9)	279	104	102	116	117	15	134	6	0	8	31	9	.78	7	.286	.405	.474
2006 2 Tms		156	548	163	41	2	15	(8	7)	253	98	107	123	124	6	138	3	2	9	30	6	.83	13	.297	.424	.462
2007 NYY	AL	158	605	171	40	5	16	(10	6)	269	123	101	101	84	0	115	3	0	1	25	8	.76	11	.283	.369	.445
2008 NYY	AL	156	609	180	39	4	20	(14	6)	287	100	100	108	73	2	109	1	0	1	22	11	.67	14	.296	.371	.471
2009 LAA	AL	152	563	165	29	3	15	(7	8)	245	96	103	109	94	7	113	1	0	9	30	8	.79	15	.293	.390	.435
06 Phi	NL	98	339	94	25	2	8	(5	3)	147	61	65	76	91	5	86	2	0	6	20	4	.83	8	.277	.427	.434
06 NYY	AL	58	209	69	16	0	7	(3	4)	106	37	42	47	33	1	52	1	2	3	10	2	.83	5	.330	.419	.507
Postseason		11	33	10	2	0	1	(1	0)	15	3	6	6	4	0	7	0	0	0	2	0	1.00	0	.303	.378	.455
14 ML YEARS		1951	7053	2111	483	56	256	(139	117)	3474	1270	1187	1441	1254	104	1518	30	6	74	348	111	.76	134	.299	.404	.493

Tony Abreu

Bats: B **Throws:** R **Pos:** PH-4; 2B-1; 3B-1   **Ht:** 5'9" **Wt:** 200 **Born:** 11/13/1984 **Age:** 25

							BATTING													BASERUNNING				AVERAGES		
Year Team	Lg	G	AB	H	2B	3B	HR	(Hm	Rd)	TB	R	RBI	RC	TBB	IBB	SO	HBP	SH	SF	SB	CS	SB%	GDP	Avg	OBP	Slg
2003 Ddgrs	R	45	163	48	7	5	0	(-	-)	65	30	20	24	11	1	24	5	0	3	9	3	.75	3	.294	.358	.399
2003 VeroB	A+	3	10	0	0	0	0	(-	-)	0	0	0	0	1	0	2	0	0	0	0	0	-	0	.000	.091	.000
2004 Clmbs	A	104	359	108	21	8	8	(-	-)	169	50	54	54	8	0	59	7	6	3	16	12	.57	5	.301	.326	.471
2004 VeroB	A+	11	43	18	3	1	0	(-	-)	23	8	3	9	1	0	8	1	1	1	4	1	.80	1	.419	.435	.535
2005 VeroB	A+	96	394	129	23	7	4	(-	-)	178	54	43	62	15	1	56	5	3	4	14	10	.58	9	.327	.356	.452
2005 Jaxnvl	AA	24	96	24	3	2	0	(-	-)	31	10	9	8	4	0	21	1	0	1	0	2	.00	2	.250	.284	.323
2006 Jaxnvl	AA	118	457	131	24	3	6	(-	-)	179	66	55	65	33	2	69	9	4	6	9	4	.69	15	.287	.343	.392
2007 LsVgs	AAA	54	234	83	22	5	2	(-	-)	121	48	18	48	14	1	34	4	0	1	5	0	1.00	3	.355	.399	.517
2009 Chatt	AA	23	89	26	4	1	0	(-	-)	32	11	5	8	1	0	12	0	0	0	2	0	.00	2	.292	.300	.360
2009 Albq	AAA	54	218	77	18	3	11	(-	-)	134	36	48	49	12	2	37	1	2	3	3	1	.75	3	.353	.385	.615
2007 LAD	NL	59	166	45	14	1	2	(0	2)	67	19	17	18	7	1	21	3	0	2	0	0	-	5	.271	.309	.404
2009 LAD	NL	6	8	2	0	0	0	(0	0)	2	0	1	2	3	0	2	0	0	0	0	1	.00	0	.250	.455	.250
2 ML YEARS		65	174	47	14	1	2	(0	2)	69	19	18	20	10	1	23	3	0	2	0	1	.00	5	.270	.317	.397

Winston Abreu

Pitches: R **Bats:** R **Pos:** RP-5   **Ht:** 6'2" **Wt:** 170 **Born:** 4/5/1977 **Age:** 33

				HOW MUCH HE PITCHED						WHAT HE GAVE UP											THE RESULTS				
Year Team	Lg	G	GS	CG	GF	IP	BFP	H	R	ER	HR	SH	SF	HB	TBB	IBB	SO	WP	Bk	W	L	Pct	Sh	Sv-Op Hld	ERC	ERA
2009 Drhm*	AAA	37	0	0	26	51.0	189	23	11	11	4	0	0	5	16	0	77	2	0	3	1	.750	0	15-- -	1.21	1.94
2006 Bal	AL	7	0	0	2	8.0	42	10	10	9	1	0	1	1	6	1	6	0	0	0	0	-	0	0-0 0	7.17	10.13
2007 Was	NL	26	0	0	3	30.1	133	37	21	20	7	1	1	0	9	1	26	2	1	0	1	.000	0	0-1 3	5.90	5.93
2009 2 Tms		5	0	0	1	6.0	32	10	8	7	2	0	0	1	4	0	6	0	0	0	0	-	0	0-0 0	12.70	10.50
09 TB	AL	2	0	0	1	3.2	15	3	1	1	0	0	0	0	2	0	3	0	0	0	0	-	0	0-0 0	3.10	2.45
09 Cle	AL	3	0	0	0	2.1	17	7	7	6	2	0	0	1	2	0	3	0	0	0	0	-	0	0-0 0	32.08	23.14
3 ML YEARS		38	0	0	6	44.1	207	57	39	36	10	1	2	2	19	2	38	2	1	0	1	.000	0	0-1 3	6.99	7.31

Jeremy Accardo

Pitches: R **Bats:** R **Pos:** RP-26   **Ht:** 6'1" **Wt:** 192 **Born:** 12/8/1981 **Age:** 28

				HOW MUCH HE PITCHED						WHAT HE GAVE UP											THE RESULTS				
Year Team	Lg	G	GS	CG	GF	IP	BFP	H	R	ER	HR	SH	SF	HB	TBB	IBB	SO	WP	Bk	W	L	Pct	Sh	Sv-Op Hld	ERC	ERA
2009 LsVgs*	AAA	27	0	0	22	30.0	130	32	11	10	1	1	1	1	8	0	27	0	0	2	1	.667	0	13-- -	3.53	3.00
2005 SF	NL	28	0	0	7	29.2	124	26	13	13	2	1	1	1	9	1	16	1	0	1	5	.167	0	0-1 4	2.87	3.94
2006 2 Tms		65	0	0	27	69.0	297	76	42	41	7	1	4	1	20	5	54	4	0	2	4	.333	0	3-8 10	4.17	5.35
2007 Tor	AL	64	0	0	48	67.1	275	51	19	16	4	0	1	2	24	2	57	0	1	4	4	.500	0	30-35 2	2.44	2.14
2008 Tor	AL	16	0	0	6	12.1	56	15	10	9	1	0	1	1	4	2	5	1	0	0	3	.000	0	4-6 2	4.88	6.57
2009 Tor	AL	26	0	0	5	24.2	107	23	8	7	2	0	2	2	17	1	18	0	0	0	0	-	0	1-1 4	5.26	5.26
06 SF	NL	38	0	0	16	40.1	170	38	23	22	2	0	4	1	11	3	40	2	0	1	3	.250	0	3-6 8	2.88	4.91
06 Tor	AL	27	0	0	11	28.2	127	38	19	19	5	1	0	0	9	2	14	2	1	1	1	.500	0	0-2 2	6.25	5.97
5 ML YEARS		199	0	0	93	203.0	859	191	92	86	16	2	9	7	74	11	150	6	2	7	16	.304	0	38-51 22	3.53	3.81

Alfredo Aceves

Pitches: R Bats: R Pos: RP-42; SP-1   **Ht:** 6'3" **Wt:** 220 **Born:** 12/8/1902 **Age:** 27

Year	Team	Lg	G	GS	CG	GF	IP	BFP	H	R	ER	HR	SH	SF	HB	TBB	IBB	SO	WP	Bk	W	L	Pct	Sh	Sv-Op	Hld	ERC	ERA
2008	Tampa	A+	8	8	0	0	47.0	179	32	16	11	1	0	0	1	8	0	37	2	0	4	1	.800	0	0- -	-	1.42	2.11
2008	Trnton	AA	7	7	1	0	50.0	184	37	10	10	3	4	0	0	6	0	35	1	0	2	2	.500	1	0- -	-	1.64	1.80
2008	S-WB	AAA	10	8	0	1	43.2	186	42	21	20	6	1	3	1	13	0	42	0	0	2	3	.400	0	0- -	-	3.75	4.12
2009	S-WB	AAA	4	4	0	0	23.2	98	18	11	10	3	1	2	1	5	0	18	0	1	2	0	1.000	0	0- -	-	2.31	3.80
2008	NYY	AL	6	4	0	1	30.0	120	25	8	8	4	0	0	0	10	0	16	1	0	1	0	1.000	0	0-0	0	3.23	2.40
2009	NYY	AL	43	1	0	10	84.0	337	69	36	33	10	1	2	5	16	2	69	0	0	10	1	.909	0	1-2	5	2.65	3.54
	2 ML YEARS		49	5	0	11	114.0	457	94	44	41	14	1	2	5	26	2	85	1	0	11	1	.917	0	1-2	5	2.80	3.24

Manny Acosta

Pitches: R Bats: B Pos: RP-36   **Ht:** 6'4" **Wt:** 170 **Born:** 5/1/1981 **Age:** 29

Year	Team	Lg	G	GS	CG	GF	IP	BFP	H	R	ER	HR	SH	SF	HB	TBB	IBB	SO	WP	Bk	W	L	Pct	Sh	Sv-Op	Hld	ERC	ERA
2009	Gwnntt*	AAA	18	0	0	7	27.1	113	21	8	8	4	0	0	0	13	0	25	2	0	1	3	.250	0	2- -	-	3.45	2.63
2007	Atl	NL	21	0	0	5	23.2	93	13	6	6	2	0	0	0	14	1	22	1	0	1	1	.500	0	0-0	4	2.39	2.28
2008	Atl	NL	46	0	0	22	53.0	226	48	25	21	7	4	1	1	26	5	31	5	0	3	5	.375	0	3-5	4	4.12	3.57
2009	Atl	NL	36	0	0	17	37.1	174	45	19	18	4	3	0	2	19	2	32	3	0	1	1	.500	0	0-0	2	5.90	4.34
	3 ML YEARS		103	0	0	44	114.0	493	106	50	45	13	7	1	3	59	8	85	9	0	5	7	.417	0	3-5	10	4.29	3.55

Mike Adams

Pitches: R Bats: R Pos: RP-37   **Ht:** 6'5" **Wt:** 204 **Born:** 7/29/1978 **Age:** 31

Year	Team	Lg	G	GS	CG	GF	IP	BFP	H	R	ER	HR	SH	SF	HB	TBB	IBB	SO	WP	Bk	W	L	Pct	Sh	Sv-Op	Hld	ERC	ERA
2009	SnAnt	AA	4	1	0	0	4.0	16	3	1	1	1	0	0	0	2	0	6	0	0	1	0	1.000	0	0- -	-	4.30	2.25
2009	Portlnd	AAA	4	0	0	0	5.0	19	4	3	3	1	0	0	0	1	0	9	0	0	0	0	-	0	0- -	-	2.95	5.40
2004	Mil	NL	46	0	0	11	53.0	226	60	21	20	5	5	2	2	14	2	39	2	0	2	3	.400	0	0-5	12	3.22	3.40
2005	Mil	NL	13	0	0	7	13.1	61	12	4	4	2	0	0	0	10	1	14	1	0	0	1	.000	0	1-2	2	5.12	2.70
2006	Mil	NL	2	0	0	0	2.1	13	4	3	3	1	0	0	0	2	0	1	0	0	0	0	-	0	0-0	0	13.74	11.57
2008	SD	NL	54	0	0	11	65.1	259	49	18	18	7	2	3	0	19	2	74	0	0	2	3	.400	0	0-2	10	2.38	2.48
2009	SD	NL	37	0	0	5	37.0	136	14	9	3	1	2	0	0	8	1	43	1	0	0	0	-	0	0-1	15	0.65	0.73
	5 ML YEARS		152	0	0	36	171.0	694	129	55	48	16	9	5	2	53	6	173	4	0	4	7	.364	0	1-10	39	2.38	2.53

Russ Adams

Bats: L Throws: R Pos: LF-5; DH-2; PH-2   **Ht:** 6'1" **Wt:** 197 **Born:** 8/30/1980 **Age:** 29

										BATTING													BASERUNNING				AVERAGES		
Year	Team	Lg	G	AB	H	2B	3B	HR	(Hm	Rd)	TB	R	RBI	RC	TBB	IBB	SO	HBP	SH	SF	SB	CS	SB%	GDP	Avg	OBP	Slg
2009	LsVgs*	AAA	24	72	23	7	2	1	(-	-)	37	15	9	13	5	0	17	1	0	2	0	0	-	0	.319	.363	.514
2009	Portlnd*	AAA	36	135	36	7	1	1	(-	-)	48	16	12	16	14	0	16	0	1	1	2	2	.50	5	.267	.333	.356
2004	Tor	AL	22	72	22	2	1	4	(1	3)	38	10	10	11	5	0	5	1	0	0	1	0	1.00	3	.306	.359	.528
2005	Tor	AL	139	481	123	27	5	8	(5	3)	184	68	63	66	50	1	57	3	3	8	11	2	.85	5	.256	.325	.383
2006	Tor	AL	90	251	55	14	1	3	(2	1)	80	31	28	23	22	0	41	1	3	3	1	2	.33	5	.219	.282	.319
2007	Tor	AL	27	60	14	3	0	2	(2	0)	23	14	12	9	7	1	14	0	2	0	2	1	.67	1	.233	.313	.383
2009	Tor	AL	8	20	4	0	0	0	(0	0)	4	2	0	0	1	0	1	0	0	0	0	0	-	0	.200	.238	.200
	5 ML YEARS		286	884	218	46	7	17	(10	7)	329	125	113	109	85	2	118	5	8	11	15	5	.75	14	.247	.313	.372

Nick Adenhart

Pitches: R Bats: R Pos: SP-1   **Ht:** 6'3" **Wt:** 200 **Born:** 8/24/1986

Year	Team	Lg	G	GS	CG	GF	IP	BFP	H	R	ER	HR	SH	SF	HB	TBB	IBB	SO	WP	Bk	W	L	Pct	Sh	Sv-Op	Hld	ERC	ERA
2005	Angels	R	13	12	1	0	44.0	192	39	26	18	0	3	2	4	24	0	52	3	1	2	3	.400	0	0- -	-	3.67	3.68
2005	Orem	R+	1	1	0	0	6.0	21	3	1	0	0	0	0	0	0	0	7	0	0	1	0	1.000	0	0- -	-	0.54	0.00
2006	CRpds	A	16	16	1	0	106.0	423	84	33	23	2	1	2	3	26	0	99	17	1	10	2	.833	0	0- -	-	2.05	1.95
2006	RCuca	A+	9	9	0	0	52.1	219	51	23	22	1	1	1	3	16	0	46	2	1	5	2	.714	0	0- -	-	3.29	3.78
2007	Ark	AA	26	26	0	0	153.0	669	158	72	62	7	6	3	17	65	1	116	13	0	10	8	.556	0	0- -	-	4.48	3.65
2008	Salt Lk	AAA	26	26	0	0	145.1	655	173	99	93	15	4	7	3	75	0	110	9	5	9	13	.409	0	0- -	-	5.93	5.76
2008	LAA	AL	3	3	0	0	12.0	63	18	12	12	0	0	0	0	13	0	4	2	0	1	0	1.000	0	0-0	0	9.55	9.00
2009	LAA	AL	1	1	0	0	6.0	27	7	0	0	0	0	0	0	3	0	5	1	0	0	0	-	0	0-0	0	4.72	0.00
	2 ML YEARS		4	4	0	0	18.0	90	25	12	12	0	0	0	0	16	0	9	3	0	1	0	1.000	0	0-0	0	7.84	6.00

Jeremy Affeldt

Pitches: L Bats: L Pos: RP-74   **Ht:** 6'5" **Wt:** 226 **Born:** 6/6/1979 **Age:** 31

Year	Team	Lg	G	GS	CG	GF	IP	BFP	H	R	ER	HR	SH	SF	HB	TBB	IBB	SO	WP	Bk	W	L	Pct	Sh	Sv-Op	Hld	ERC	ERA
2002	KC	AL	34	7	0	4	77.2	353	85	41	40	8	2	1	3	37	4	67	5	2	3	4	.429	0	0-1	1	4.97	4.64
2003	KC	AL	36	18	0	5	126.0	533	126	58	55	12	2	5	5	38	1	98	2	2	7	6	.538	0	4-4	3	3.82	3.93
2004	KC	AL	38	8	0	26	76.1	344	91	49	42	6	4	4	3	32	2	49	4	3	3	4	.429	0	13-17	6	5.26	4.95
2005	KC	AL	49	0	0	13	49.2	232	56	35	29	3	0	1	0	29	2	39	5	0	0	2	.000	0	0-0	12	5.08	5.26
2006	2 Tms		54	9	0	12	97.1	448	102	74	67	13	4	4	2	55	3	48	2	0	8	8	.500	0	1-3	5	5.21	6.20
2007	Col	NL	75	0	0	11	59.0	253	47	26	23	3	3	6	3	33	9	46	6	1	4	3	.571	0	0-4	9	3.19	3.51
2008	Cin	NL	74	0	0	20	78.1	335	78	36	29	9	7	0	4	25	0	80	6	0	1	1	.500	0	0-1	5	3.98	3.33
2009	SF	NL	74	0	0	8	62.1	248	42	14	12	3	0	1	0	31	3	55	5	0	2	2	.500	0	0-0	33	2.61	1.73

Year	Team	Lg	G	GS	CG	GF	IP	BFP	H	R	ER	HR	SH	SF	HB	TBB	IBB	SO	WP	Bk	W	L	Pct	Sh	Sv-Op	Hld	ERC	ERA
06	KC	AL	27	9	0	3	70.0	320	71	51	46	9	3	3	1	42	0	28	2	0	4	6	.400	0	0-0	2	5.18	5.91
06	Col	NL	27	0	0	9	27.1	128	31	23	21	4	1	1	1	13	3	20	0	0	4	2	.667	0	1-3	3	5.29	6.91
	Postseason		7	0	0	0	5.1	19	3	1	1	1	0	0	0	1	0	4	0	0	0	0	-	0	0-0	2	1.70	1.69
	8 ML YEARS		434	42	0	99	626.2	2746	627	333	297	57	22	22	22	280	24	482	35	8	28	30	.483	0	18-30	68	4.28	4.27

Jonathan Albaladejo

Pitches: R Bats: R Pos: RP-32 **Ht: 6'5" Wt: 260 Born: 10/30/1982 Age: 27**

Year	Team	Lg	G	GS	CG	GF	IP	BFP	H	R	ER	HR	SH	SF	HB	TBB	IBB	SO	WP	Bk	W	L	Pct	Sh	Sv-Op	Hld	ERC	ERA
2009	S-WB*	AAA	27	0	0	22	36.0	136	25	8	7	4	0	1	0	3	0	26	1	0	3	0	1.000	0	11--	-	1.52	1.75
2007	Was	NL	14	0	0	1	14.1	51	7	3	3	1	0	1	0	2	0	12	0	0	1	1	.500	0	0-1	2	1.10	1.88
2008	NYY	AL	7	0	0	2	13.2	58	15	6	6	1	1	0	0	6	0	13	0	0	0	1	.000	0	0-0	1	4.82	3.95
2009	NYY	AL	32	0	0	5	34.1	158	41	23	20	6	1	4	3	16	2	21	0	0	5	1	.833	0	0-1	1	6.41	5.24
	3 ML YEARS		53	0	0	8	62.1	267	63	32	29	8	2	5	4	24	2	46	0	0	6	3	.667	0	0-2	4	4.58	4.19

Matt Albers

Pitches: R Bats: L Pos: RP-56 **Ht: 6'0" Wt: 205 Born: 1/20/1983 Age: 27**

Year	Team	Lg	G	GS	CG	GF	IP	BFP	H	R	ER	HR	SH	SF	HB	TBB	IBB	SO	WP	Bk	W	L	Pct	Sh	Sv-Op	Hld	ERC	ERA
2009	Norfolk*	AAA	10	0	0	1	12.2	63	19	11	8	1	0	0	0	5	0	12	2	0	1	0	1.000	0	0--	-	6.60	5.68
2006	Hou	NL	4	2	0	0	15.0	66	17	10	10	1	2	0	0	7	0	11	0	0	0	2	.000	0	0-0	0	4.97	6.00
2007	Hou	NL	31	18	0	2	110.2	508	127	77	72	18	6	8	7	50	6	71	7	0	4	11	.267	0	0-0	0	5.76	5.86
2008	Bal	AL	28	3	0	5	49.0	208	43	21	19	4	1	3	2	22	1	26	1	0	3	3	.500	0	0-2	6	3.62	3.49
2009	Bal	AL	56	0	0	13	67.0	309	80	43	41	3	5	2	2	36	3	49	3	0	3	6	.333	0	0-4	10	5.41	5.51
	4 ML YEARS		119	23	0	20	241.2	1091	267	151	142	26	14	13	11	115	10	157	11	0	10	22	.313	0	0-6	16	5.16	5.29

Eliezer Alfonzo

Bats: R Throws: R Pos: C-30; PH-7; PR-1 **Ht: 5'11" Wt: 218 Born: 2/7/1979 Age: 31**

Year	Team	Lg	G	AB	H	2B	3B	HR	(Hm	Rd)	TB	R	RBI	RC	TBB	IBB	SO	HBP	SH	SF	SB	CS	SB%	GDP	Avg	OBP	Slg
2009	Portlnd*	AAA	55	204	63	11	0	14	(-	-)	116	27	36	39	7	2	51	4	1	3	1	0	1.00	2	.309	.339	.569
2006	SF	NL	87	286	76	17	2	12	(3	9)	133	27	39	36	9	7	74	7	4	3	1	0	1.00	10	.266	.302	.465
2007	SF	NL	26	64	16	2	1	1	(1	0)	23	5	6	5	2	2	23	1	0	0	2	2	.00	2	.250	.284	.359
2008	SF	NL	5	11	1	0	0	0	(0	0)	1	0	1	0	0	0	4	0	0	0	0	0	-	2	.091	.091	.091
2009	SD	NL	37	114	20	3	0	2	(1	1)	29	6	8	4	3	0	34	0	0	0	0	0	-	0	.175	.197	.254
	4 ML YEARS		155	475	113	22	3	15	(5	10)	186	38	54	45	14	9	135	8	4	3	1	2	.33	14	.238	.270	.392

Brandon Allen

Bats: L Throws: R Pos: 1B-32; PH-1 **Ht: 6'2" Wt: 235 Born: 2/12/1986 Age: 24**

Year	Team	Lg	G	AB	H	2B	3B	HR	(Hm	Rd)	TB	R	RBI	RC	TBB	IBB	SO	HBP	SH	SF	SB	CS	SB%	GDP	Avg	OBP	Slg
2004	Bristol	R+	58	185	38	9	1	3	(-	-)	58	17	23	16	16	1	60	4	0	2	2	3	.40	3	.205	.280	.314
2005	Gr Falls	R+	66	231	61	11	2	11	(-	-)	109	41	42	41	32	3	69	7	0	3	7	5	.58	7	.264	.366	.472
2006	Knapol	A	109	395	84	17	2	15	(-	-)	150	36	68	39	22	0	126	3	3	4	6	4	.60	8	.213	.257	.380
2007	Knapol	A	129	516	146	39	5	18	(-	-)	249	84	93	84	39	3	124	4	0	2	7	4	.64	4	.283	.337	.483
2008	WinSa	A+	89	319	89	26	4	15	(-	-)	168	57	44	64	41	2	83	6	0	0	14	3	.82	6	.279	.372	.527
2008	Brham	AA	41	153	42	6	2	14	(-	-)	94	30	32	33	19	0	41	1	0	0	3	1	.75	1	.275	.358	.614
2009	Brham	AA	62	241	70	12	3	7	(-	-)	109	39	35	41	30	3	47	2	0	1	1	2	.33	2	.290	.372	.452
2009	Charltt	AAA	15	61	16	4	0	1	(-	-)	23	6	8	5	0	0	13	0	0	0	0	0	-	0	.262	.262	.377
2009	Reno	AAA	38	145	47	8	1	12	(-	-)	93	33	32	37	20	1	25	2	0	0	6	0	1.00	4	.324	.413	.641
2009	Ari	NL	32	104	21	7	0	4	(1	3)	40	13	14	12	12	2	40	0	0	0	0	0	-	4	.202	.284	.385

Alfredo Amezaga

Bats: B Throws: R Pos: CF-15; PH-9; SS-5; RF-3; LF-2; PR-1 **Ht: 5'10" Wt: 182 Born: 1/16/1978 Age: 32**

Year	Team	Lg	G	AB	H	2B	3B	HR	(Hm	Rd)	TB	R	RBI	RC	TBB	IBB	SO	HBP	SH	SF	SB	CS	SB%	GDP	Avg	OBP	Slg
2009	Jupiter*	A+	3	9	3	0	0	0	(-	-)	3	0	1	1	2	0	1	0	0	0	0	0	-	0	.333	.455	.333
2002	LAA	AL	12	13	7	2	0	0	(0	0)	9	3	2	6	0	0	1	0	0	0	1	0	1.00	1	.538	.538	.692
2003	LAA	AL	37	105	22	3	2	2	(0	2)	35	15	7	7	9	0	23	1	5	0	2	2	.50	2	.210	.278	.333
2004	LAA	AL	73	93	15	2	0	0	(0	0)	23	12	11	5	3	0	24	3	6	0	3	2	.60	2	.161	.212	.247
2005	2 Tms	NL	5	6	1	0	0	0	(0	0)	1	2	0	0	1	0	0	0	0	0	1	0	1.00	0	.167	.286	.167
2006	Fla	NL	132	334	87	9	3	3	(0	3)	111	42	19	32	30	4	46	3	7	1	20	12	.63	5	.260	.332	.332
2007	Fla	NL	133	400	105	14	9	2	(1	1)	143	46	30	38	35	0	52	4	4	5	13	7	.65	4	.263	.324	.358
2008	Fla	NL	125	311	82	13	5	3	(2	1)	114	41	32	37	19	1	47	3	4	0	8	2	.80	6	.264	.312	.367
2009	Fla	NL	27	69	15	3	0	0	(0	0)	18	6	5	3	5	2	16	0	0	1	1	1	.50	0	.217	.267	.261
05	Col	NL	2	3	1	0	0	0	(0	0)	1	1	0	0	1	0	0	0	0	0	0	0	-	0	.333	.333	.333
05	Pit	NL	3	3	0	0	0	0	(0	0)	0	1	0	0	0	0	0	0	0	0	1	0	1.00	0	.000	.250	.000
	Postseason		2	2	0	0	0	0	(0	0)	0	1	0	0	0	0	2	0	1	0	0	0	-	0	.000	.000	.000
	8 ML YEARS		544	1331	334	46	19	12	(3	9)	454	167	106	128	105	7	209	14	26	7	49	26	.65	20	.251	.311	.341

Brett Anderson

Pitches: L Bats: L Pos: SP-30
Ht: 6'4" Wt: 215 Born: 2/1/1988 Age: 22

Year	Team	Lg	G	GS	CG	GF	IP	BFP	H	R	ER	HR	SH	SF	HB	TBB	IBB	SO	WP	Bk	W	L	Pct	Sh	Sv-Op	Hld	ERC	ERA
2007	Sbend	A	14	14	0	0	81.1	326	76	26	20	3	3	5	2	10	0	85	6	0	8	4	.667	0	0--	-	2.40	2.21
2007	Visalia	A+	9	9	0	0	39.0	174	50	23	21	6	1	0	1	11	0	40	1	2	3	3	.500	0	0--	-	5.79	4.85
2008	Stcktn	A+	14	13	0	0	74.0	311	68	35	34	5	1	2	4	18	0	80	5	1	9	4	.692	0	0--	-	2.98	4.14
2008	Mdland	AA	6	6	0	0	31.0	125	27	10	9	3	0	0	1	9	0	38	0	1	2	1	.667	0	0--	-	3.14	2.61
2009	Oak	AL	30	30	1	0	175.1	735	180	94	79	20	4	4	3	45	1	150	0	1	11	11	.500	1	0-0	0	3.84	4.06

Brian Anderson

Bats: R Throws: R Pos: CF-67; RF-17; PH-10; PR-7; LF-4
Ht: 6'2" Wt: 215 Born: 3/11/1982 Age: 28

Year	Team	Lg	G	AB	H	2B	3B	HR	(Hm	Rd)	TB	R	RBI	RC	TBB	IBB	SO	HBP	SH	SF	SB	CS	SB%	GDP	Avg	OBP	Slg
2009	Charltt*	AAA	11	43	12	1	1	2	(-	-)	21	6	5	6	2	0	16	0	1	0	1	0	1.00	2	.279	.311	.488
2009	Pwtckt*	AAA	24	80	16	4	0	4	(-	-)	32	9	8	8	7	0	22	2	1	0	0	2	.00	2	.200	.281	.400
2005	CWS	AL	13	34	6	1	0	2	(0	2)	13	3	3	2	0	0	12	0	1	0	1	0	1.00	2	.176	.176	.382
2006	CWS	AL	134	365	82	23	1	8	(7	1)	131	46	33	32	30	2	90	5	2	3	4	7	.36	3	.225	.290	.359
2007	CWS	AL	13	17	2	1	0	0	(0	0)	3	3	0	0	2	0	7	0	0	0	0	0	-	2	.118	.211	.176
2008	CWS	AL	109	181	42	13	0	8	(5	3)	79	24	26	21	10	0	45	0	2	0	5	1	.83	2	.232	.272	.436
2009	2 Tms	AL	86	202	49	9	0	4	(3	1)	70	32	18	21	23	0	54	3	2	1	3	6	.33	6	.243	.328	.347
09	CWS	AL	65	185	44	9	0	2	(2	0)	59	25	13	19	20	0	49	3	2	0	3	6	.33	4	.238	.322	.319
09	Bos	AL	21	17	5	0	0	2	(1	1)	11	7	5	2	3	0	5	0	0	1	0	0	-	2	.294	.381	.647
	Postseason		3	5	0	0	0	0	(0	0)	0	1	0	0	0	0	4	0	1	0	1	0	1.00	0	.000	.000	.000
	5 ML YEARS		355	799	181	47	1	22	(15	7)	296	108	80	76	65	2	208	8	7	4	13	14	.48	15	.227	.290	.370

Garret Anderson

Bats: L Throws: L Pos: LF-124; PH-11; DH-1
Ht: 6'3" Wt: 225 Born: 6/30/1972 Age: 38

Year	Team	Lg	G	AB	H	2B	3B	HR	(Hm	Rd)	TB	R	RBI	RC	TBB	IBB	SO	HBP	SH	SF	SB	CS	SB%	GDP	Avg	OBP	Slg
1994	LAA	AL	5	13	5	0	0	0	(0	0)	5	0	1	2	0	0	2	0	0	0	0	0	-	0	.385	.385	.385
1995	LAA	AL	106	374	120	19	1	16	(7	9)	189	50	69	63	19	4	65	1	2	4	6	2	.76	0	.321	.352	.505
1996	LAA	AL	150	607	173	33	2	12	(5	6)	240	79	72	68	27	5	84	0	5	3	7	9	.44	22	.285	.314	.405
1997	LAA	AL	154	624	189	36	3	8	(5	3)	255	76	92	80	30	6	70	2	1	6	10	4	.71	20	.303	.334	.409
1998	LAA	AL	156	622	183	41	7	16	(4	11)	283	62	79	88	29	8	80	1	3	3	8	3	.73	13	.294	.325	.455
1999	LAA	AL	157	620	188	36	2	21	(10	11)	291	88	80	92	34	8	81	0	0	6	3	4	.43	15	.303	.338	.469
2000	LAA	AL	159	647	185	40	3	35	(20	15)	336	92	117	95	24	5	87	0	1	9	7	6	.54	21	.286	.307	.519
2001	LAA	AL	161	672	194	39	2	28	(13	15)	321	83	123	97	27	4	100	0	0	5	13	6	.68	12	.289	.314	.478
2002	LAA	Al	158	638	195	56	3	29	(13	16)	344	93	123	108	30	11	80	0	4	6	6	4	.60	11	.306	.332	.539
2003	LAA	AL	159	638	201	49	4	29	(12	17)	345	80	116	114	31	10	83	0	0	4	6	3	.67	15	.315	.345	.541
2004	LAA	AL	112	442	133	20	1	14	(4	10)	197	57	75	70	29	6	75	1	0	3	2	1	.67	3	.301	.343	.446
2005	LAA	AL	142	575	163	34	1	17	(5	12)	250	68	96	82	23	8	84	0	1	5	1	1	.50	13	.283	.308	.435
2006	LAA	AL	141	543	152	28	2	17	(8	9)	235	63	85	75	38	11	95	0	0	7	1	0	1.00	8	.280	.323	.433
2007	LAA	AL	108	417	124	31	1	16	(11	5)	205	67	80	65	27	9	54	0	0	0	1	0	1.00	8	.297	.338	.492
2008	LAA	Al	145	557	160	27	3	15	(9	6)	241	80	84	86	29	6	77	1	0	6	7	4	.64	11	.293	.325	.433
2009	Atl	NL	135	496	133	27	0	13	(8	5)	199	52	61	50	27	2	73	2	0	9	1	0	1.00	11	.268	.303	.401
	Postseason		36	147	36	5	1	5	(2	3)	58	17	22	14	5	0	20	0	0	2	0	1	.00	2	.245	.266	.395
	16 ML YEARS		2148	8485	2501	516	35	285	(136	149)	3942	1076	1353	1235	424	103	1190	8	12	85	79	47	.63	191	.295	.326	.465

Josh Anderson

Bats: L Throws: R Pos: LF-49; CF-32; RF-29; PR-17; PH-12; DH-5
Ht: 6'2" Wt: 195 Born: 8/10/1982 Age: 27

Year	Team	Lg	G	AB	H	2B	3B	HR	(Hm	Rd)	TB	R	RBI	RC	TBB	IBB	SO	HBP	SH	SF	SB	CS	SB%	GDP	Avg	OBP	Slg
2007	Hou	NL	21	67	24	3	0	0	(0	0)	27	10	11	13	5	0	6	2	0	1	1	1	.50	0	.358	.413	.403
2008	Atl	NL	40	136	40	7	1	3	(0	3)	58	21	12	19	8	2	33	1	1	0	10	1	.91	1	.294	.338	.426
2009	2 Tms	AL	118	283	68	7	4	1	(0	1)	86	42	24	28	13	0	43	1	1	0	25	5	.83	7	.240	.276	.304
09	Det	AL	74	165	40	4	4	0	(0	0)	52	22	16	18	8	0	22	1	1	0	13	2	.87	4	.242	.282	.315
09	KC	AL	44	118	28	3	0	1	(0	0)	34	20	8	10	5	0	21	0	0	0	12	3	.80	3	.237	.268	.288
	3 ML YEARS		179	486	132	17	5	4	(0	4)	171	73	47	60	26	2	82	4	2	1	36	7	.84	8	.272	.313	.352

Marlon Anderson

Bats: L Throws: R Pos: PH-4
Ht: 5'11" Wt: 200 Born: 1/6/1974 Age: 36

Year	Team	Lg	G	AB	H	2B	3B	HR	(Hm	Rd)	TB	R	RBI	RC	TBB	IBB	SO	HBP	SH	SF	SB	CS	SB%	GDP	Avg	OBP	Slg
1998	Phi	NL	17	43	14	3	0	1	(1	0)	20	4	4	7	1	0	6	0	0	1	2	0	1.00	0	.326	.333	.465
1999	Phi	NL	129	452	114	26	4	5	(4	1)	163	48	54	49	24	1	61	2	4	2	13	2	.87	6	.252	.292	.361
2000	Phi	NL	41	162	37	8	1	1	(1	0)	50	10	15	12	12	0	22	0	0	5	2	2	.50	5	.228	.282	.309
2001	Phi	NL	147	522	153	30	2	11	(7	4)	220	69	61	72	35	5	74	2	10	5	8	5	.62	12	.293	.337	.421
2002	Phi	NL	145	539	139	30	6	8	(4	4)	205	64	48	53	42	14	71	5	2	4	5	1	.83	16	.258	.315	.380
2003	TB	AL	145	482	130	27	3	6	(2	4)	181	59	67	70	41	5	60	3	4	5	19	3	.86	6	.270	.328	.376
2004	StL	NL	113	253	60	12	0	8	(2	6)	96	31	28	23	12	1	38	1	0	5	6	2	.75	5	.237	.269	.379
2005	NYM	NL	123	235	62	9	0	7	(3	4)	92	31	19	23	18	0	45	1	1	2	6	1	.86	2	.264	.316	.391
2006	2 Tms	NL	134	279	83	16	4	12	(4	8)	143	43	38	42	25	1	49	1	4	3	4	6	.40	4	.297	.354	.513
2007	2 Tms	NL	66	95	28	7	0	3	(2	1)	44	17	27	17	8	1	17	0	1	2	4	1	.80	2	.295	.343	.463
2008	NYM	NL	87	138	29	6	0	1	(0	1)	38	16	10	4	9	0	27	0	2	0	1	0	1.00	0	.210	.255	.275
2009	NYM	NL	4	4	0	0	0	0	(0	0)	0	0	0	0	0	0	1	0	0	0	0	0	-	0	.000	.000	.000
06	Was	NL	109	215	59	13	2	5	(0	5)	91	31	23	28	18	1	41	1	3	2	2	4	.33	1	.274	.331	.423
06	LAD	NL	25	64	24	3	2	7	(4	3)	52	12	15	14	7	0	8	0	1	1	2	2	.50	3	.375	.431	.813

Year	Team	Lg	G	AB	H	2B	3B	HR	(Hm	Rd)	TB	R	RBI	RC	TBB	IBB	SO	HBP	SH	SF	SB	CS	SB%	GDP	Avg	OBP	Slg
07	LAD	NL	23	26	6	0	0	0	(0	0)	6	3	2	2	3	0	5	0	0	0	1	0	1.00	0	.231	.310	.231
07	NYM	NL	43	69	22	7	0	3	(2	1)	38	14	25	15	5	1	12	0	1	2	3	1	.75	2	.319	.355	.551
	Postseason		15	25	6	3	0	0	(0	0)	9	3	1	2	1	0	3	1	0	0	0	0	-	0	.240	.296	.360
	12 ML YEARS		1151	3204	849	174	20	63	(30	33)	1252	392	371	372	227	28	471	15	31	31	71	24	.75	60	.265	.314	.391

Robert Andino

Bats: R **Throws:** R **Pos:** SS-62; 2B-8; PR-6; PH-5; 3B-2; LF-1; CF-1; DH-1   **Ht:** 6'0" **Wt:** 195 **Born:** 4/25/1984 **Age:** 26

Year	Team	Lg	G	AB	H	2B	3B	HR	(Hm	Rd)	TB	R	RBI	RC	TBB	IBB	SO	HBP	SH	SF	SB	CS	SB%	GDP	Avg	OBP	Slg
2005	Fla	NL	17	44	7	4	0	0	(0	0)	11	4	1	1	5	1	8	0	1	0	1	0	1.00	2	.159	.245	.250
2006	Fla	NL	11	24	4	1	0	0	(0	0)	5	0	2	0	1	0	6	0	1	2	1	0	1.00	0	.167	.185	.208
2007	Fla	NL	7	13	5	1	0	0	(0	0)	6	0	0	1	0	0	2	0	0	0	0	0	-	0	.385	.385	.462
2008	Fla	NL	44	63	13	2	0	2	(1	1)	21	7	9	7	4	0	23	0	1	0	0	0	-	1	.206	.254	.333
2009	Bal	AL	78	198	44	7	0	2	(1	1)	57	31	10	11	15	1	47	0	0	2	3	3	.50	6	.222	.274	.288
	5 ML YEARS		157	342	73	15	0	4	(2	2)	100	42	22	20	25	2	86	0	3	4	5	3	.63	9	.213	.264	.292

Elvis Andrus

Bats: R **Throws:** R **Pos:** SS-145; PH-1   **Ht:** 6'0" **Wt:** 185 **Born:** 8/26/1988 **Age:** 21

Year	Team	Lg	G	AB	H	2B	3B	HR	(Hm	Rd)	TB	R	RBI	RC	TBB	IBB	SO	HBP	SH	SF	SB	CS	SB%	GDP	Avg	OBP	Slg
2005	Braves	R	46	166	49	6	1	3	(-	-)	66	26	20	26	19	0	28	4	0	2	7	4	.64	1	.295	.377	.398
2005	Danvle	R+	6	18	5	1	0	0	(-	-)	6	3	1	3	4	0	4	0	0	0	1	0	1.00	0	.278	.409	.333
2006	Rome	A	111	437	116	25	4	3	(-	-)	158	67	50	52	36	1	91	2	2	1	23	15	.61	8	.265	.324	.362
2007	MrtlBh	A+	99	385	94	20	3	3	(-	-)	129	59	37	48	44	0	88	6	3	2	25	7	.78	8	.244	.330	.335
2007	Bkrsfld	A+	27	110	33	2	0	2	(-	-)	41	19	12	15	10	0	19	2	1	0	15	8	.65	2	.300	.369	.373
2008	Frisco	AA	118	482	142	19	2	4	(-	-)	177	82	65	70	38	0	91	6	3	6	54	16	.77	17	.295	.350	.367
2009	Tex	AL	145	480	128	17	8	6	(3	3)	179	72	40	65	40	0	77	6	12	3	33	6	.85	4	.267	.329	.373

Rick Ankiel

Bats: L **Throws:** L **Pos:** CF-66; RF-27; PH-26; LF-25   **Ht:** 6'1" **Wt:** 210 **Born:** 7/19/1979 **Age:** 30

Year	Team	Lg	G	AB	H	2B	3B	HR	(Hm	Rd)	TB	R	RBI	RC	TBB	IBB	SO	HBP	SH	SF	SB	CS	SB%	GDP	Avg	OBP	Slg
1999	StL	NL	9	10	1	0	0	0	(0	0)	1	0	0	0	0	0	3	0	1	0	0	0	-	0	.100	.100	.100
2000	StL	NL	33	68	17	1	1	2	(2	0)	26	8	9	0	4	0	20	0	1	0	0	0	-	1	.250	.292	.382
2001	StL	NL	6	8	0	0	0	0	(0	0)	0	1	0	0	1	0	5	0	1	0	0	0	-	0	.000	.111	.000
2004	StL	NL	5	1	0	0	0	0	(0	0)	0	0	0	0	1	0	1	0	0	0	0	0	-	0	.000	.500	.000
2007	StL	NL	47	172	49	8	1	11	(9	2)	92	31	39	32	13	0	41	0	1	4	1	0	1.00	3	.285	.328	.535
2008	StL	NL	120	413	109	21	2	25	(11	14)	209	65	71	60	42	3	100	5	0	3	2	1	.67	8	.264	.337	.506
2009	StL	NL	122	372	86	21	2	11	(4	7)	144	50	38	32	26	4	99	3	0	3	4	3	.57	5	.231	.285	.387
	Postseason		3	1	0	0	0	0	(0	0)	0	0	0	0	0	0	0	0	0	0	0	0	-	0	.000	.000	.000
	7 ML YEARS		342	1044	262	51	6	49	(26	23)	472	155	157	124	87	7	269	8	4	10	7	4	.64	17	.251	.311	.452

Greg Aquino

Pitches: R **Bats:** R **Pos:** RP-10   **Ht:** 6'1" **Wt:** 190 **Born:** 1/11/1978 **Age:** 32

			HOW MUCH HE PITCHED					WHAT HE GAVE UP											THE RESULTS						
Year	Team	Lg	G	GS	CG	GF	IP	BFP	H	R	ER	HR	SH	SF	HB	TBB	IBB	SO	WP	Bk	W	L	Pct	Sh	Sv-Op	Hld	ERC	ERA
2009	Clmbs*	AAA	30	1	0	26	31.2	137	26	15	11	3	1	3	0	15	1	27	4	1	1	2	.333	0	16- --	-	3.20	3.13
2004	Ari	NL	34	0	0	26	35.1	147	24	15	12	4	2	2	2	17	2	26	4	0	0	2	.000	0	16-19	1	2.87	3.06
2005	Ari	NL	35	0	0	11	31.1	155	42	29	27	7	1	1	4	17	1	34	2	1	0	1	.000	0	1-3	3	8.22	7.76
2006	Ari	NL	42	0	0	12	48.1	220	54	27	24	8	1	0	4	24	2	51	2	0	2	0	1.000	0	0-0	2	5.99	4.47
2007	Mil	NL	15	0	0	8	14.0	59	13	9	7	2	1	0	0	5	1	12	2	0	0	1	.000	0	0-2	2	4.69	4.50
2008	Bal	AL	9	0	0	5	9.1	54	17	13	13	1	1	1	2	9	0	9	0	0	0	0	-	0	0-0	0	13.24	12.54
2009	Cle	AL	10	0	0	3	16.0	74	13	8	8	1	0	2	0	15	3	11	3	0	1	2	.333	0	0-0	1	4.48	4.50
	6 ML YEARS		145	0	0	65	154.1	709	163	101	91	23	6	6	12	87	9	143	13	1	3	6	.333	0	17-24	9	5.66	5.31

Alberto Arias

Pitches: R **Bats:** R **Pos:** RP-42   **Ht:** 5'11" **Wt:** 155 **Born:** 10/14/1983 **Age:** 26

			HOW MUCH HE PITCHED					WHAT HE GAVE UP											THE RESULTS						
Year	Team	Lg	G	GS	CG	GF	IP	BFP	H	R	ER	HR	SH	SF	HB	TBB	IBB	SO	WP	Bk	W	L	Pct	Sh	Sv-Op	Hld	ERC	ERA
2009	RdRck*	AAA	4	3	0	0	16.1	71	14	9	7	1	1	1	0	10	0	15	0	0	2	2	.500	0	0- --	-	3.85	3.86
2007	Col	NL	6	0	0	0	7.1	32	8	4	4	1	1	0	0	5	0	3	0	0	1	0	1.000	0	0-1	0	6.51	4.91
2008	2 Tms	NL	15	2	0	4	21.2	95	23	10	10	1	0	0	2	10	0	13	1	0	1	1	.500	0	0-0	0	4.77	4.15
2009	Hou	NL	42	0	0	12	45.2	209	49	21	17	1	3	1	6	19	4	39	5	0	2	1	.667	0	0-2	9	4.25	3.35
08	Col	NL	12	0	0	4	13.2	56	12	4	4	1	0	0	1	4	0	5	1	0	0	0	-	0	0-0	0	3.17	2.63
08	Hou	NL	3	2	0	0	8.0	39	11	6	6	0	0	0	1	6	0	8	0	0	1	1	.500	0	0-0	0	7.85	6.75
	3 ML YEARS		63	2	0	16	74.2	336	80	35	31	3	4	1	8	34	4	55	6	0	4	2	.667	0	0-3	9	4.60	3.74

Joaquin Arias

Bats: R Throws: R Pos: 2B-2; 3B-1   Ht: 6'1" Wt: 165 Born: 9/21/1984 Age: 25

Year	Team	Lg	G	AB	H	2B	3B	HR	(Hm	Rd)	TB	R	RBI	RC	TBB	IBB	SO	HBP	SH	SF	SB	CS	SB%	GDP	Avg	OBP	Slg
2009	Okla*	AAA	118	504	134	15	3	5	(-	-)	170	63	52	55	20	0	47	3	5	5	24	3	.89	17	.266	.295	.337
2006	Tex	AL	6	11	6	1	0	0	(0	0)	7	4	1	3	1	0	0	0	0	0	0	1	1.00	0	.545	.583	.636
2008	Tex	AL	32	110	32	7	3	0	(0	0)	45	15	9	15	7	0	12	2	1	0	4	1	.80	4	.291	.345	.409
2009	Tex	AL	3	8	0	0	0	0	(0	0)	0	0	0	0	0	0	3	0	1	0	0	0	-	0	.000	.000	.000
3 ML YEARS			41	129	38	8	3	0	(0	0)	52	19	10	18	8	0	15	2	2	0	4	2	.67	4	.295	.345	.403

Jose Arredondo

Pitches: R Bats: R Pos: RP-43   Ht: 6'0" Wt: 175 Born: 3/12/1984 Age: 26

Year	Team	Lg	G	GS	CG	GF	IP	BFP	H	R	ER	HR	SH	SF	HB	TBB	IBB	SO	WP	Bk	W	L	Pct	Sh	Sv-Op	Hld	ERC	ERA
2004	Angels	R	8	0	0	4	12.1	56	14	10	4	1	1	0	1	4	0	14	2	0	0	0	-	0	1--	-	4.61	2.92
2005	Ark	AA	5	0	0	3	5.1	22	5	2	2	0	0	0	0	4	0	4	1	0	0	0	-	0	0--	-	4.84	3.38
2005	Orem	R+	15	13	0	0	68.2	295	76	34	32	4	1	1	6	20	0	60	6	0	5	0	1.000	0	0--	-	4.39	4.19
2006	RCuca	A+	15	15	0	0	90.0	360	62	28	23	4	1	5	6	35	0	115	6	0	5	6	.455	0	0--	-	2.36	2.30
2006	Ark	AA	11	11	1	0	60.2	280	80	47	44	8	2	3	1	22	0	48	6	0	2	3	.400	1	0--	-	6.09	6.53
2007	Ark	AA	23	0	0	18	25.0	102	16	10	7	2	1	2	0	12	0	28	1	0	0	1	.000	0	10--	-	2.35	2.52
2007	Salt Lk	AAA	2	0	0	1	3.0	13	2	1	1	0	1	1	0	2	0	1	0	0	0	0	-	0	0--	-	2.54	3.00
2008	Salt Lk	AAA	15	0	0	15	17.0	66	12	4	4	2	1	1	1	4	0	15	1	0	1	1	.500	0	10--	-	2.32	2.12
2009	Salt Lk	AAA	19	0	0	11	20.2	88	13	7	5	1	2	1	2	14	1	24	1	0	1	1	.500	0	1--	-	3.08	2.18
2008	LAA	AL	52	0	0	10	61.0	244	42	15	11	3	0	0	1	22	0	55	1	0	10	2	.833	0	0-7	16	2.08	1.62
2009	LAA	AL	43	0	0	15	45.0	202	47	30	30	6	3	1	0	23	2	47	5	1	2	3	.400	0	0-1	16	4.91	6.00
Postseason			3	0	0	1	3.2	15	2	0	0	0	0	0	0	2	0	4	0	0	0	0	-	0	0-0	0	1.65	0.00
2 ML YEARS			95	0	0	25	106.0	446	89	45	41	9	3	1	1	45	2	102	6	1	12	5	.706	0	0-8	32	3.19	3.48

Bronson Arroyo

Pitches: R Bats: R Pos: SP-33   Ht: 6'4" Wt: 194 Born: 2/24/1977 Age: 33

Year	Team	Lg	G	GS	CG	GF	IP	BFP	H	R	ER	HR	SH	SF	HB	TBB	IBB	SO	WP	Bk	W	L	Pct	Sh	Sv-Op	Hld	ERC	ERA
2000	Pit	NL	20	12	0	1	71.2	338	80	61	51	10	5	2	4	30	6	50	3	1	2	6	.250	0	0-0	0	6.18	6.40
2001	Pit	NL	24	13	1	1	88.1	390	99	54	50	12	4	6	4	34	6	39	4	1	5	7	.417	0	0-0	2	5.09	5.09
2002	Pit	NL	9	4	0	1	27.0	123	30	14	12	1	1	1	0	15	3	22	0	0	2	1	.667	0	0-0	1	4.64	4.00
2003	Bos	AL	6	0	0	2	17.1	66	10	5	4	0	0	0	1	4	2	14	0	0	0	0	-	0	1-1	0	1.14	2.08
2004	Bos	AL	32	29	0	0	178.2	764	171	99	80	17	5	4	20	47	3	142	5	0	10	9	.526	0	0-0	0	3.65	4.03
2005	Bos	AL	35	32	0	1	205.1	878	213	116	103	22	4	4	14	54	3	100	5	1	14	10	.583	0	0-0	0	4.04	4.51
2006	Cin	NL	35	35	3	0	240.2	992	222	98	88	31	9	2	5	64	7	184	6	0	14	11	.560	1	0-0	0	3.37	3.29
2007	Cin	NL	34	34	1	0	210.2	921	232	109	99	28	10	7	13	63	6	156	4	0	9	15	.375	0	0-0	0	4.68	4.23
2008	Cin	NL	34	34	1	0	200.0	871	219	116	106	29	13	6	6	68	2	163	6	0	15	11	.577	0	0-0	0	4.83	4.77
2009	Cin	NL	33	33	3	0	220.1	923	214	101	94	31	9	5	9	65	6	127	1	0	15	13	.536	2	0-0	0	3.94	3.84
Postseason			10	2	0	3	17.0	80	19	14	14	5	0	0	2	9	0	20	0	0	0	0	-	0	0-0	2	7.30	7.41
10 ML YEARS			262	226	9	6	1460.0	6266	1498	773	687	181	60	37	76	450	44	997	34	3	86	83	.509	3	1-1	3	4.19	4.23

Jose Ascanio

Pitches: R Bats: R Pos: RP-16   Ht: 6'0" Wt: 170 Born: 5/2/1985 Age: 25

Year	Team	Lg	G	GS	CG	GF	IP	BFP	H	R	ER	HR	SH	SF	HB	TBB	IBB	SO	WP	Bk	W	L	Pct	Sh	Sv-Op	Hld	ERC	ERA
2009	Iowa*	AAA	12	12	0	0	51.1	219	47	23	18	1	4	1	6	18	0	47	1	0	2	4	.333	0	0--	-	3.33	3.16
2009	Indy*	AAA	1	1	0	0	6.2	26	6	2	2	1	0	0	0	1	0	9	0	0	1	0	1.000	0	0--	-	2.97	2.70
2007	Atl	NL	13	0	0	6	16.0	74	17	11	9	3	1	0	0	6	2	13	0	0	1	1	.500	0	0-0	0	4.43	5.06
2008	ChC	NL	6	0	0	1	5.2	30	8	5	5	1	1	1	1	4	1	3	0	0	0	0	-	0	0-0	0	8.81	7.94
2009	2 Tms	NL	16	0	0	5	18.0	86	22	8	8	1	2	2	3	9	2	20	1	0	0	2	.000	0	0-0	1	5.89	4.00
09	ChC	NL	14	0	0	4	15.1	73	18	6	6	1	1	0	2	9	2	18	1	0	0	1	.000	0	0-0	1	5.87	3.52
09	Pit	NL	2	0	0	1	2.2	13	4	2	2	0	1	2	1	0	0	2	0	0	0	1	.000	0	0-0	1	5.97	6.75
3 ML YEARS			35	0	0	12	39.2	190	47	24	22	5	4	3	4	19	5	36	1	0	1	3	.250	0	0-0	1	5.69	4.99

Garrett Atkins

Bats: R Throws: R Pos: 3B-78; PH-29; 1B-28; DH-5   Ht: 6'3" Wt: 215 Born: 12/12/1979 Age: 30

Year	Team	Lg	G	AB	H	2B	3B	HR	(Hm	Rd)	TB	R	RBI	RC	TBB	IBB	SO	HBP	SH	SF	SB	CS	SB%	GDP	Avg	OBP	Slg
2003	Col	NL	25	69	11	2	0	0	(0	0)	13	6	4	2	3	0	14	1	0	0	0	0	-	1	.159	.205	.188
2004	Col	NL	15	28	10	2	0	1	(1	0)	15	3	8	8	4	0	3	0	0	1	0	0	-	0	.357	.424	.536
2005	Col	NL	138	519	149	31	1	13	(9	4)	221	62	89	74	45	1	72	6	0	4	0	2	.00	18	.287	.347	.426
2006	Col	NL	157	602	198	48	1	29	(15	14)	335	117	120	129	79	6	76	7	0	7	4	0	1.00	24	.329	.409	.556
2007	Col	NL	157	605	182	35	1	25	(10	15)	294	83	111	106	67	3	96	2	0	10	3	1	.75	16	.301	.367	.486
2008	Col	NL	155	611	175	32	3	21	(9	12)	276	86	99	76	40	0	100	3	0	10	1	1	.50	20	.286	.328	.452
2009	Col	NL	126	354	80	12	1	9	(4	5)	121	37	48	44	41	2	58	2	0	2	0	0	-	6	.226	.308	.342
Postseason			11	40	7	3	0	1	(1	0)	13	6	3	4	5	1	5	1	0	0	0	0	-	0	.175	.283	.325
7 ML YEARS			773	2788	805	162	7	98	(48	50)	1275	394	479	439	279	12	419	20	0	34	8	4	.67	87	.289	.354	.457

Mitch Atkins

Pitches: R **Bats:** R **Pos:** RP-2   **Ht:** 6'3" **Wt:** 230 **Born:** 10/1/1985 **Age:** 24

Year	Team	Lg	G	GS	CG	GF	IP	BFP	H	R	ER	HR	SH	SF	HB	TBB	IBB	SO	WP	Bk	W	L	Pct	Sh	Sv-Op	Hld	ERC	ERA
2004	Cubs	R	10	8	0	0	29.2	146	42	33	26	0	0	2	4	14	0	20	8	1	2	2	.500	0	0--	-	6.55	7.89
2005	Boise	A-	15	15	0	0	73.1	337	85	45	41	8	4	2	9	30	0	59	6	4	3	6	.333	0	0--	-	5.60	5.03
2006	Peoria	A	25	25	0	0	138.1	570	110	47	37	10	1	6	3	53	0	127	4	3	13	4	.765	0	0--	-	2.83	2.41
2007	Dytona	A+	20	20	1	0	115.0	467	99	51	40	14	3	4	8	31	0	88	2	1	8	7	.533	0	0--	-	3.29	3.13
2007	Tenn	AA	7	4	0	0	26.0	119	30	18	16	5	2	0	2	11	0	18	2	0	1	1	.500	0	0--	-	6.07	5.54
2008	Tenn	AA	18	18	0	0	110.0	462	107	58	46	14	2	1	3	27	0	88	1	1	9	6	.600	0	0--	-	3.58	3.76
2008	Iowa	AAA	10	10	0	0	54.1	234	48	29	27	11	1	3	4	23	0	44	0	0	8	1	.889	0	0--	-	4.52	4.47
2009	Iowa	AAA	27	27	1	0	146.1	656	164	113	107	26	6	9	11	52	1	127	3	3	8	12	.400	0	0--	-	5.43	6.58
2009	ChC	NL	2	0	0	1	2.0	7	1	0	0	0	0	0	0	0	0	0	0	0	0	0	-	0	0-0	0	0.54	0.00

Michael Aubrey

Bats: L **Throws:** L **Pos:** 1B-25; PH-5; DH-2   **Ht:** 6'0" **Wt:** 195 **Born:** 4/15/1982 **Age:** 28

Year	Team	Lg	G	AB	H	2B	3B	HR	(Hm	Rd)	TB	R	RBI	RC	TBB	IBB	SO	HBP	SH	SF	SB	CS	SB%	GDP	Avg	OBP	Slg
2003	Lk Cty	A	38	138	48	13	0	5	(-	-)	76	22	19	30	14	0	22	1	0	1	0	0	-	2	.348	.409	.551
2004	Knstn	A	60	218	74	14	1	10	(-	-)	120	34	60	52	27	1	26	12	0	1	3	1	.75	4	.339	.438	.550
2004	Akron	AA	38	134	35	7	0	5	(-	-)	57	13	22	21	15	0	18	3	0	4	0	0	-	3	.261	.340	.425
2005	Akron	AA	28	106	30	5	1	4	(-	-)	49	17	20	17	7	2	18	3	0	3	1	0	1.00	3	.283	.336	.462
2006	Knstn	A+	8	28	8	3	0	2	(-	-)	17	8	10	7	5	0	5	2	0	1	0	0	-	0	.286	.417	.607
2006	Akron	AA	6	26	7	2	0	1	(-	-)	12	3	2	4	2	0	4	1	0	0	0	0	-	0	.269	.345	.462
2007	Knstn	A+	13	50	20	5	0	5	(-	-)	40	15	11	17	6	0	7	3	0	0	0	0	-	0	.400	.492	.800
2007	Akron	AA	54	207	51	11	0	7	(-	-)	83	22	34	25	11	1	35	3	0	2	0	0	-	5	.246	.291	.401
2008	Akron	AA	25	103	29	10	1	2	(-	-)	47	14	16	16	8	1	12	0	0	1	0	0	-	2	.282	.330	.456
2008	Buffalo	AAA	72	285	80	18	0	7	(-	-)	119	29	37	40	16	5	40	5	1	2	0	0	-	5	.281	.328	.418
2009	Clmbs	AAA	57	212	62	16	1	5	(-	-)	95	27	29	31	9	2	25	2	1	4	1	1	.50	4	.292	.322	.448
2009	Norfolk	AAA	44	164	47	13	0	3	(-	-)	69	14	23	23	11	3	13	0	0	4	1	1	.50	3	.287	.324	.421
2008	Cle	AL	15	45	9	0	0	2	(0	2)	15	2	3	1	5	0	5	0	0	0	0	0	-	2	.200	.280	.333
2009	Bal	AL	31	90	26	7	0	4	(2	2)	45	12	14	14	5	0	10	0	0	0	0	0	-	2	.289	.326	.500
	2 ML YEARS		46	135	35	7	0	6	(2	4)	60	14	17	15	10	0	15	0	0	0	0	0	-	4	.259	.310	.444

Bryan Augenstein

Pitches: R **Bats:** R **Pos:** RP-5; SP-2   **Ht:** 6'6" **Wt:** 232 **Born:** 7/11/1986 **Age:** 23

Year	Team	Lg	G	GS	CG	GF	IP	BFP	H	R	ER	HR	SH	SF	HB	TBB	IBB	SO	WP	Bk	W	L	Pct	Sh	Sv-Op	Hld	ERC	ERA
2007	Msoula	R+	10	2	0	4	21.1	92	20	13	8	2	2	1	2	7	0	16	2	0	0	2	.000	0	0--	-	3.73	3.38
2008	Sbend	A	13	13	0	0	87.1	337	73	21	21	2	1	1	0	9	1	69	0	0	5	1	.833	0	0--	-	1.72	2.16
2008	Visalia	A+	9	9	0	0	44.0	188	57	26	19	5	2	1	1	5	0	30	1	0	2	4	.333	0	0--	-	4.87	3.89
2009	Mobile	AA	9	9	0	0	45.2	165	27	5	5	0	0	0	0	8	0	36	0	0	5	0	1.000	0	0--	-	1.09	0.99
2009	Reno	AAA	8	7	0	0	36.0	155	43	23	22	2	1	2	1	7	0	29	1	0	2	5	.286	0	0--	-	4.16	5.50
2009	Ari	NL	7	2	0	2	17.0	81	23	16	15	2	2	2	2	6	2	6	0	0	0	1	.000	0	0-0	0	6.32	7.94

Rich Aurilia

Bats: R **Throws:** R **Pos:** PH-30; 1B-22; 3B-13; DH-1; PR-1   **Ht:** 6'1" **Wt:** 199 **Born:** 9/2/1971 **Age:** 38

Year	Team	Lg	G	AB	H	2B	3B	HR	(Hm	Rd)	TB	R	RBI	RC	TBB	IBB	SO	HBP	SH	SF	SB	CS	SB%	GDP	Avg	OBP	Slg
2009	Fresno*	AAA	2	7	1	0	0	1	(-	-)	4	1	2	1	1	0	0	0	0	0	0	0	-	1	.143	.250	.571
2009	SnJos*	A+	3	10	1	0	0	1	(-	-)	4	1	2	1	2	0	1	1	0	0	0	0	-	0	.100	.308	.400
1995	SF	NL	9	19	9	3	0	2	(0	2)	18	4	4	7	1	0	2	0	1	1	1	0	1.00	1	.474	.476	.947
1996	SF	NL	105	318	76	7	1	3	(1	2)	94	27	26	29	25	2	52	1	6	2	4	1	.80	1	.239	.295	.296
1997	SF	NL	46	102	28	8	0	5	(1	4)	51	16	19	16	8	0	15	0	1	2	1	1	.50	3	.275	.321	.500
1998	SF	NL	122	413	110	27	2	9	(5	4)	168	54	49	54	31	3	62	2	5	2	3	3	.50	3	.266	.319	.407
1999	SF	NL	152	558	157	23	1	22	(9	13)	248	68	80	79	43	3	71	5	3	5	2	3	.40	16	.281	.336	.444
2000	SF	NL	141	509	138	24	2	20	(12	8)	226	67	79	74	54	2	90	0	4	4	1	2	.33	15	.271	.339	.444
2001	SF	NL	156	636	**206**	37	5	37	(15	22)	364	114	97	124	47	2	83	0	3	3	1	3	.25	14	.324	.369	.572
2002	SF	NL	133	538	138	35	2	15	(4	11)	222	76	61	61	37	0	90	4	3	7	1	2	.33	15	.257	.305	.413
2003	SF	NL	129	505	140	26	1	13	(6	7)	207	65	58	56	36	0	82	1	0	3	2	2	.50	18	.277	.325	.410
2004	2 Tms		124	399	98	21	2	6	(3	3)	141	49	44	39	37	1	71	4	7	3	1	0	1.00	12	.246	.314	.353
2005	Cin	NL	114	426	120	23	2	14	(11	3)	189	61	68	70	37	2	67	1	1	3	2	0	1.00	8	.282	.338	.444
2006	Cin	NL	122	440	132	25	1	23	(13	10)	228	61	70	72	34	1	51	2	2	4	3	0	1.00	10	.300	.349	.518
2007	SF	NL	99	329	83	19	2	5	(2	3)	121	40	33	33	22	1	45	4	0	3	0	0	-	8	.252	.304	.368
2008	SF	NL	140	407	115	21	1	10	(5	5)	168	33	52	51	30	4	56	1	0	2	1	1	.50	11	.283	.332	.413
2009	SF	NL	60	122	26	2	0	2	(2	0)	34	10	16	4	8	1	24	0	0	3	0	0	-	5	.213	.256	.279
04	Sea	AL	73	261	63	13	0	4	(2	2)	88	27	28	25	22	1	43	2	6	1	1	0	1.00	10	.241	.304	.337
04	SD	NL	51	138	35	8	2	2	(1	1)	53	22	16	14	15	0	28	2	1	2	0	0	-	2	.254	.331	.384
	Postseason		25	98	22	6	0	6	(3	3)	46	17	18	14	7	0	22	1	3	1	0	0	-	0	.224	.280	.469
	15 ML YEARS		1652	5721	1576	301	22	186	(89	97)	2479	745	756	769	450	22	861	24	36	47	23	18	.56	140	.275	.328	.433

Brad Ausmus

Bats: R Throws: R Pos: C-30; PH-6; PR-2   Ht: 5'11" Wt: 190 Born: 4/14/1969 Age: 41

Year	Team	Lg	G	AB	H	2B	3B	HR	(Hm	Rd)	TB	R	RBI	RC	TBB	IBB	SO	HBP	SH	SF	SB	CS	SB%	GDP	Avg	OBP	Slg
1993	SD	NL	49	160	41	8	1	5	(4	1)	66	18	12	19	6	0	28	0	0	0	2	0	1.00	2	.256	.283	.413
1994	SD	NL	101	327	82	12	1	7	(6	1)	117	45	24	36	30	12	63	1	6	2	5	1	.83	8	.251	.314	.358
1995	SD	NL	103	328	96	16	4	5	(2	3)	135	44	34	49	31	3	56	2	4	4	16	5	.76	6	.293	.353	.412
1996	2 Tms		125	375	83	16	0	5	(2	3)	114	46	35	32	39	1	72	5	6	2	4	8	.33	8	.221	.302	.304
1997	Hou	NL	130	425	113	25	1	4	(1	3)	152	45	44	51	38	4	78	3	6	6	14	6	.70	8	.266	.326	.358
1998	Hou	NL	128	412	111	10	4	6	(2	4)	147	62	45	51	53	11	60	3	3	1	10	3	.77	18	.269	.356	.357
1999	Det	AL	127	458	126	25	6	9	(5	4)	190	62	54	69	51	0	71	14	3	1	12	9	.57	11	.275	.365	.415
2000	Det	AL	150	523	139	25	3	7	(3	4)	191	75	51	68	69	0	79	6	4	2	11	5	.69	19	.266	.357	.365
2001	Hou	NL	128	422	98	23	4	5	(4	1)	144	45	34	38	30	0	64	1	6	2	4	1	.80	13	.232	.284	.341
2002	Hou	NL	130	447	115	19	3	6	(4	2)	158	57	50	44	38	3	71	6	2	3	2	3	.40	30	.257	.322	.353
2003	Hou	NL	143	450	103	12	2	4	(1	3)	131	43	47	44	46	1	66	4	4	5	5	3	.63	8	.229	.303	.291
2004	Hou	NL	129	403	100	14	1	5	(2	3)	131	38	31	34	33	11	56	2	7	3	2	2	.50	13	.248	.306	.325
2005	Hou	NL	134	387	100	19	0	3	(1	2)	128	35	47	42	51	8	48	5	7	1	5	3	.63	17	.258	.351	.331
2006	Hou	NL	139	439	101	16	1	2	(1	1)	125	37	39	36	45	2	71	6	9	3	3	1	.75	21	.230	.308	.285
2007	Hou	NL	117	349	82	16	3	3	(2	1)	113	38	25	28	37	3	74	6	4	1	6	1	.86	11	.235	.318	.324
2008	Hou	NL	81	216	47	8	0	3	(1	2)	64	15	24	25	25	3	41	2	6	1	0	2	.00	4	.218	.303	.296
2009	LAD	NL	36	95	28	4	0	1	(0	1)	35	9	9	13	5	0	21	2	5	0	1	0	1.00	1	.295	.343	.368
96	SD	NL	50	149	27	4	0	1	(0	1)	34	16	13	6	13	0	27	3	1	0	1	4	.20	4	.181	.261	.228
96	Det	AL	75	226	56	12	0	4	(2	2)	80	30	22	26	26	1	45	2	5	2	3	4	.43	4	.248	.328	.354
	Postseason		35	106	26	5	0	3	(2	1)	40	12	7	8	9	3	29	1	2	1	1	0	1.00	5	.245	.308	.377
	17 ML YEARS		1950	6216	1565	268	34	80	(42	38)	2141	714	605	679	627	68	1019	68	82	37	102	53	.66	198	.252	.325	.344

Alex Avila

Bats: L Throws: R Pos: C-25; PH-7   Ht: 5'11" Wt: 210 Born: 1/29/1987 Age: 23

Year	Team	Lg	G	AB	H	2B	3B	HR	(Hm	Rd)	TB	R	RBI	RC	TBB	IBB	SO	HBP	SH	SF	SB	CS	SB%	GDP	Avg	OBP	Slg
2008	WMich	A	58	213	65	14	0	1	(-	-)	82	21	22	33	27	0	41	1	1	2	0	1	.00	8	.305	.383	.385
2009	Erie	AA	93	329	87	23	1	12	(-	-)	148	52	55	57	52	2	77	1	3	2	2	1	.67	4	.264	.365	.450
2009	Det	AL	29	61	17	4	0	5	(4	1)	36	9	14	12	10	0	18	0	0	1	0	0	-	0	.279	.375	.590

Mike Aviles

Bats: R Throws: R Pos: SS-34; 3B-2; DH-1; PH-1; PR-1   Ht: 5'9" Wt: 203 Born: 3/13/1981 Age: 29

Year	Team	Lg	G	AB	H	2B	3B	HR	(Hm	Rd)	TB	R	RBI	RC	TBB	IBB	SO	HBP	SH	SF	SB	CS	SB%	GDP	Avg	OBP	Slg
2003	Royals	R	52	212	77	19	5	6	(-	-)	124	51	39	48	13	0	28	5	2	5	11	5	.69	2	.363	.404	.585
2004	Wilmg	A+	126	463	139	40	4	6	(-	-)	205	66	69	73	39	2	57	1	1	6	2	5	.29	8	.300	.352	.443
2005	Wichta	AA	133	521	146	33	6	14	(-	-)	233	79	80	76	30	1	64	1	2	5	12	6	.67	16	.280	.318	.447
2006	Omha	AAA	129	469	125	21	3	8	(-	-)	176	52	47	57	28	1	49	2	0	3	14	5	.74	14	.267	.309	.375
2007	Omha	AAA	133	538	159	27	6	17	(-	-)	249	78	77	83	30	0	59	2	5	6	5	5	.50	24	.296	.332	.463
2008	Omha	AAA	51	214	72	21	6	10	(-	-)	135	42	42	48	11	0	23	1	0	1	3	0	1.00	4	.336	.370	.631
2008	KC	AL	102	419	136	27	4	10	(4	6)	201	68	51	62	18	4	58	2	0	2	8	3	.73	12	.325	.354	.480
2009	KC	AL	36	120	22	3	1	1	(1	0)	30	10	8	4	4	0	26	0	2	1	1	0	1.00	3	.183	.208	.250
	2 ML YEARS		138	539	158	30	5	11	(5	6)	231	78	59	66	22	4	84	2	2	3	9	3	.75	15	.293	.322	.429

John Axford

Pitches: R Bats: R Pos: RP-7   Ht: 6'5" Wt: 195 Born: 4/1/1983 Age: 27

Year	Team	Lg	G	GS	CG	GF	IP	BFP	H	R	ER	HR	SH	SF	HB	TBB	IBB	SO	WP	Bk	W	L	Pct	Sh	Sv-Op	Hld	ERC	ERA
2007	Tampa	A+	5	0	0	2	11.1	45	6	5	3	2	1	0	0	7	0	15	3	0	0	0	-	0	2--	-	3.00	2.38
2007	S-WB	AAA	1	0	0	1	0.2	5	2	1	1	0	0	0	0	1	0	1	1	0	0	0	-	0	0--	-	22.07	13.50
2007	CtnSC	A	13	5	0	3	26.2	129	29	20	13	2	1	1	0	22	0	21	7	0	0	3	.000	0	0--	-	6.06	4.39
2007	StIsInd	A-	8	0	0	5	24.1	102	13	8	6	0	1	0	1	15	1	30	3	0	1	1	.500	0	2--	-	1.85	2.22
2008	BrvdCt	A+	26	14	0	1	95.0	433	86	58	48	5	2	3	5	73	0	89	12	0	5	10	.333	0	0--	-	4.89	4.55
2009	BrvdCt	A+	19	0	0	4	27.2	110	14	5	5	0	1	0	0	16	1	43	1	0	4	1	.800	0	0--	-	1.60	1.63
2009	Hntsvl	AA	4	0	0	1	7.2	33	7	3	3	1	1	0	1	3	0	9	0	0	0	0	-	0	1--	-	4.33	3.52
2009	Nashv	AAA	22	0	0	11	33.0	138	23	13	13	2	1	1	0	19	1	37	2	0	5	0	1.000	0	0--	-	2.81	3.55
2009	Mil	NL	7	0	0	6	7.2	34	5	3	3	0	0	0	0	6	1	9	1	0	0	0	-	0	1-1	0	2.62	3.52

Luis Ayala

Pitches: R Bats: R Pos: RP-38   Ht: 6'2" Wt: 190 Born: 1/12/1978 Age: 32

Year	Team	Lg	G	GS	CG	GF	IP	BFP	H	R	ER	HR	SH	SF	HB	TBB	IBB	SO	WP	Bk	W	L	Pct	Sh	Sv-Op	Hld	ERC	ERA
2009	NewOr*	AAA	9	0	0	6	10.0	38	4	0	0	0	0	0	0	3	0	10	0	0	0	0	-	0	4--	-	0.76	0.00
2003	Mon	NL	65	0	0	24	71.0	288	65	24	23	8	3	1	5	13	3	46	1	0	10	3	.769	0	5-8	19	3.11	2.92
2004	Mon	NL	81	0	0	28	90.1	367	92	30	27	6	2	2	5	15	2	63	3	1	6	12	.333	0	2-7	21	3.32	2.69
2005	Was	NL	68	0	0	18	71.0	293	75	23	21	7	8	3	6	14	4	40	0	0	8	7	.533	0	1-3	22	3.95	2.66
2007	Was	NL	44	0	0	11	42.1	181	43	16	15	5	3	4	1	12	0	28	1	0	2	2	.500	0	1-2	6	3.88	3.19
2008	2 Tms	NL	81	0	0	25	75.2	335	86	53	48	9	4	3	4	24	4	50	1	0	2	10	.167	0	9-15	19	4.76	5.71
2009	2 Tms	NL	38	0	0	13	40.0	180	50	28	25	5	3	2	4	14	3	28	0	0	1	5	.167	0	0-4	3	5.94	5.63
08	Was	NL	62	0	0	12	57.2	257	63	41	37	6	4	2	4	22	4	36	1	0	1	8	.111	0	0-4	19	4.70	5.77
08	NYM	NL	19	0	0	13	18.0	78	23	12	11	3	0	1	0	2	0	14	0	0	1	2	.333	0	9-11	0	4.91	5.50
09	Min	AL	28	0	0	11	32.1	138	38	18	15	4	1	2	3	8	0	21	0	0	1	2	.333	0	0-3	1	5.21	4.18
09	Fla	NL	10	0	0	2	7.2	42	12	10	10	1	2	0	1	6	3	7	0	0	0	3	.000	0	0-1	2	9.04	11.74
	6 ML YEARS		377	0	0	119	390.1	1644	411	177	159	40	23	15	25	92	16	255	6	1	29	39	.426	0	18-39	90	3.98	3.67

Erick Aybar

Bats: B **Throws:** R **Pos:** SS-136; PH-1 **Ht:** 5'10" **Wt:** 170 **Born:** 1/14/1984 **Age:** 26

								BATTING													BASERUNNING				AVERAGES		
Year	Team	Lg	G	AB	H	2B	3B	HR	(Hm	Rd)	TB	R	RBI	RC	TBB	IBB	SO	HBP	SH	SF	SB	CS	SB%	GDP	Avg	OBP	Slg
2006	LAA	AL	34	40	10	1	1	0	(0	0)	13	5	2	4	0	0	8	0	0	0	1	0	1.00	1	.250	.250	.325
2007	LAA	AL	79	194	46	5	1	1	(0	1)	56	18	19	16	10	0	32	2	3	2	4	4	.50	8	.237	.279	.289
2008	LAA	AL	98	346	96	18	5	3	(2	1)	133	53	39	49	14	0	45	5	9	1	7	2	.78	2	.277	.314	.384
2009	LAA	AL	137	504	157	23	9	5	(2	3)	213	70	58	73	30	1	54	5	12	5	14	7	.67	9	.312	.353	.423
	Postseason		5	19	2	0	0	0	(0	0)	2	0	1	0	0	0	2	0	0	0	0	0	-	0	.105	.105	.105
	4 ML YEARS		348	1084	309	47	16	9	(4	5)	415	146	118	142	54	1	139	12	24	8	26	13	.67	20	.285	.324	.383

Willy Aybar

Bats: B **Throws:** R **Pos:** 1B-31; 2B-28; PH-26; DH-21; 3B-18 **Ht:** 5'11" **Wt:** 205 **Born:** 3/9/1983 **Age:** 27

								BATTING													BASERUNNING				AVERAGES		
Year	Team	Lg	G	AB	H	2B	3B	HR	(Hm	Rd)	TB	R	RBI	RC	TBB	IBB	SO	HBP	SH	SF	SB	CS	SB%	GDP	Avg	OBP	Slg
2005	LAD	NL	26	86	28	8	0	1	(0	1)	39	12	10	21	18	0	11	1	0	0	3	1	.75	0	.326	.448	.453
2006	2 Tms	NL	79	243	68	18	0	4	(3	1)	98	32	30	33	28	0	36	4	3	0	1	2	.33	7	.280	.364	.403
2008	TB	AL	95	324	82	17	2	10	(4	6)	133	33	33	32	32	3	44	4	1	1	2	2	.50	7	.253	.327	.410
2009	TB	AL	105	296	75	12	0	12	(8	4)	123	38	41	39	34	2	54	2	1	3	1	0	1.00	4	.253	.331	.416
06	LAD	NL	43	128	32	12	0	3	(2	1)	53	15	22	19	18	0	17	3	2	0	1	0	1.00	5	.250	.356	.414
06	Atl	NL	36	115	36	6	0	1	(1	0)	45	17	8	14	10	0	19	1	1	0	0	2	.00	2	.313	.373	.391
	Postseason		14	34	12	2	0	2	(1	1)	20	5	7	9	1	0	6	0	1	1	0	0	-	0	.353	.361	.588
	4 ML YEARS		305	949	253	55	2	27	(15	12)	393	115	114	125	112	5	145	11	5	4	7	5	.58	18	.267	.349	.414

Brandon Backe

Pitches: R **Bats:** R **Pos:** RP-4; SP-1 **Ht:** 6'0" **Wt:** 195 **Born:** 4/5/1978 **Age:** 32

			HOW MUCH HE PITCHED							WHAT HE GAVE UP											THE RESULTS						
Year	Team	Lg	G	GS	CG	GF	IP	BFP	H	R	ER	HR	SH	SF	HB	TBB	IBB	SO	WP	Bk	W	L	Pct	Sh	Sv-Op	Hld	ERC	ERA
2009	RdRck*	AAA	2	2	0	0	10.0	45	13	5	5	0	1	0	0	3	0	4	0	0	0	1	.000	0	0--	-	4.62	4.50
2009	CpChr*	AA	4	4	0	0	26.0	98	18	4	4	0	0	1	0	7	0	17	0	0	3	0	1.000	0	0--	-	1.59	1.38
2002	TB	AL	9	0	0	4	13.0	61	15	10	10	3	0	0	2	7	0	6	0	0	0	0	-	0	0-0	0	7.37	6.92
2003	TB	AL	28	0	0	8	44.2	192	40	28	27	6	2	1	2	25	1	36	3	0	1	1	.500	0	0-0	5	4.64	5.44
2004	Hou	NL	33	9	0	8	67.0	293	75	33	32	10	5	1	1	27	4	54	1	0	5	3	.625	0	0-0	0	5.18	4.30
2005	Hou	NL	26	25	1	0	149.1	653	151	82	79	19	7	1	4	67	1	97	5	2	10	8	.556	1	0-0	0	4.65	4.76
2006	Hou	NL	8	8	0	0	43.0	189	43	18	18	4	1	2	3	18	0	19	2	0	3	2	.600	0	0-0	0	4.37	3.77
2007	Hou	NL	5	5	0	0	28.2	123	27	13	12	4	0	1	2	11	0	11	0	0	3	1	.750	0	0-0	0	4.26	3.77
2008	Hou	NL	31	31	0	0	166.2	756	202	114	**112**	36	4	2	4	77	2	127	2	0	9	14	.391	0	0-0	0	6.67	6.05
2009	Hou	NL	5	1	0	3	13.0	65	21	15	15	5	0	1	0	6	1	10	2	0	0	0	-	0	0-0	0	10.50	10.38
	Postseason		7	6	0	0	36.2	145	24	12	12	3	0	2	3	12	1	32	1	0	1	0	1.000	0	0-0	0	2.21	2.95
	8 ML YEARS		145	79	1	23	525.1	2332	574	313	305	87	19	9	18	238	9	360	15	2	31	29	.517	1	0-0	8	5.49	5.23

Burke Badenhop

Pitches: R **Bats:** R **Pos:** RP-33; SP-2 **Ht:** 6'5" **Wt:** 204 **Born:** 2/8/1983 **Age:** 27

			HOW MUCH HE PITCHED							WHAT HE GAVE UP											THE RESULTS						
Year	Team	Lg	G	GS	CG	GF	IP	BFP	H	R	ER	HR	SH	SF	HB	TBB	IBB	SO	WP	Bk	W	L	Pct	Sh	Sv-Op	Hld	ERC	ERA
2005	Oneont	A-	14	14	1	0	77.0	321	69	32	25	0	2	0	3	26	0	55	2	0	6	4	.600	1	0--	-	2.77	2.92
2006	WMich	A	27	27	3	0	171.0	702	170	59	54	6	0	2	14	31	0	124	6	0	14	3	.824	0	0--	-	3.14	2.84
2007	Lkland	A+	23	23	1	0	135.1	570	130	61	47	5	4	3	11	34	0	78	2	1	10	6	.625	1	0--	-	3.17	3.13
2007	Erie	AA	3	3	2	0	18.2	68	8	3	3	1	0	1	1	3	0	12	0	0	2	0	1.000	0	0--	-	0.87	1.45
2008	Carlina	AA	1	1	0	0	6.1	25	6	1	0	0	0	0	0	0	0	3	0	0	1	0	1.000	0	0--	-	1.73	0.00
2008	Mrlns	R	1	1	0	0	3.0	10	1	0	0	0	0	0	0	0	0	2	0	0	0	0	-	0	0--	-	0.25	0.00
2009	NewOr	AAA	2	2	0	0	9.1	47	14	7	7	0	0	0	2	4	0	6	0	0	0	1	.000	0	0--	-	7.24	6.75
2009	Mrlns	R	2	2	0	0	3.0	14	2	3	0	0	1	0	1	0	0	4	0	0	0	1	.000	0	0--	-	1.35	0.00
2009	Jupiter	A+	2	2	0	0	8.0	29	2	1	0	0	0	0	0	1	0	8	0	0	0	0	-	0	0--	-	0.24	0.00
2008	Fla	NL	13	8	0	2	47.1	218	55	34	32	7	2	2	3	21	1	35	2	0	2	3	.400	0	0-0	0	5.74	6.08
2009	Fla	NL	35	2	0	7	72.0	303	71	32	30	5	3	2	1	24	4	57	1	0	7	4	.636	0	0-1	2	3.53	3.75
	2 ML YEARS		48	10	0	9	119.1	521	126	66	62	12	5	4	4	45	5	92	3	0	9	7	.563	0	0-1	2	4.37	4.68

Danys Baez

Pitches: R **Bats:** R **Pos:** RP-59 **Ht:** 6'1" **Wt:** 233 **Born:** 9/10/1977 **Age:** 32

			HOW MUCH HE PITCHED							WHAT HE GAVE UP											THE RESULTS						
Year	Team	Lg	G	GS	CG	GF	IP	BFP	H	R	ER	HR	SH	SF	HB	TBB	IBB	SO	WP	Bk	W	L	Pct	Sh	Sv-Op	Hld	ERC	ERA
2001	Cle	AL	43	0	0	8	50.1	202	34	22	14	5	0	1	3	20	4	52	3	0	5	3	.625	0	0-1	14	2.51	2.50
2002	Cle	AL	39	26	1	9	165.1	726	160	84	81	14	2	8	9	82	5	130	6	1	10	11	.476	0	6-8	0	4.35	4.41
2003	Cle	AL	73	0	0	46	75.2	318	65	36	32	9	6	1	4	23	0	66	5	0	2	9	.182	0	25-35	5	3.22	3.81
2004	TB	AL	62	0	0	59	68.0	295	60	31	27	6	5	1	7	29	4	52	3	1	4	4	.500	0	30-33	1	3.73	3.57
2005	TB	AL	67	0	0	64	72.1	308	66	27	23	7	4	2	2	30	0	51	0	0	5	4	.556	0	41-49	0	3.74	2.86
2006	2 Tms	NL	57	0	0	28	59.2	257	60	35	30	3	4	5	7	17	3	39	3	0	5	6	.455	0	9-17	12	3.69	4.53
2007	Bal	AL	53	0	0	25	50.1	233	50	36	36	8	3	1	7	29	5	29	0	0	0	6	.000	0	3-5	14	5.56	6.44
2009	Bal	AL	59	0	0	9	71.2	295	59	36	32	8	0	2	5	22	3	40	2	1	4	6	.400	0	0-2	15	3.06	4.02
06	LAD	NL	46	0	0	27	49.2	213	53	29	24	3	4	5	6	11	2	29	3	0	5	5	.500	0	9-16	6	3.90	4.35
06	Atl	NL	11	0	0	1	10.0	44	7	6	6	0	0	0	1	6	1	10	0	0	0	1	.000	0	0-1	6	2.64	5.40
	Postseason		3	0	0	2	3.2	15	4	1	1	0	0	0	0	0	0	6	0	0	0	0	-	0	0-0	0	2.36	2.45
	8 ML YEARS		453	26	1	248	613.1	2634	554	307	275	60	24	21	44	252	24	459	22	3	35	49	.417	0	114-150	61	3.79	4.04

Andrew Bailey

Pitches: R Bats: R Pos: RP-68   Ht: 6'3" Wt: 234 Born: 5/31/1984 Age: 26

Year	Team	Lg	G	GS	CG	GF	IP	BFP	H	R	ER	HR	SH	SF	HB	TBB	IBB	SO	WP	Bk	W	L	Pct	Sh	Sv-Op	Hld	ERC	ERA
2006	Vancvr	A-	13	10	0	0	58.0	237	39	20	13	2	3	2	3	20	0	53	2	0	2	5	.286	0	0--	-	1.93	2.02
2007	Kane	A	11	10	1	1	51.0	218	42	25	19	6	1	0	3	22	1	74	2	0	1	4	.200	0	0--	-	3.51	3.35
2007	Stcktn	A+	11	11	0	0	66.0	280	56	31	28	8	1	4	9	31	1	72	0	0	3	4	.429	0	0--	-	4.33	3.82
2007	Scrmto	AAA	1	1	0	0	8.0	28	3	1	1	0	1	0	1	1	0	4	0	0	1	0	1.000	0	0--	-	0.47	1.13
2008	Mdland	AA	38	15	0	7	111.1	489	99	63	53	13	6	5	6	57	1	112	6	0	5	9	.357	0	0--	-	4.18	4.28
2009	Oak	AL	68	0	0	54	83.1	323	49	17	17	5	3	2	0	24	3	91	6	0	6	3	.667	0	26-30	2	1.44	1.84

Homer Bailey

Pitches: R Bats: R Pos: SP-20   Ht: 6'3" Wt: 210 Born: 5/3/1986 Age: 24

Year	Team	Lg	G	GS	CG	GF	IP	BFP	H	R	ER	HR	SH	SF	HB	TBB	IBB	SO	WP	Bk	W	L	Pct	Sh	Sv-Op	Hld	ERC	ERA
2009	Lsvlle*	AAA	14	14	2	0	89.2	379	87	33	27	10	3	1	4	27	1	82	1	0	8	5	.615	1	0--	-	3.77	2.71
2007	Cin	NL	9	9	0	0	45.1	205	43	32	29	3	1	6	3	28	1	28	1	1	4	2	.667	0	0-0	0	4.61	5.76
2008	Cin	NL	8	8	0	0	36.1	180	59	36	32	8	5	2	0	17	1	18	4	1	0	6	.000	0	0-0	0	9.31	7.93
2009	Cin	NL	20	20	0	0	113.1	496	115	61	57	12	4	4	3	52	1	86	6	0	8	5	.615	0	0-0	0	4.56	4.53
	3 ML YEARS		37	37	0	0	195.0	881	217	129	118	23	10	12	6	97	3	132	11	2	12	13	.480	0	0-0	0	5.38	5.45

Jeff Bailey

Bats: R Throws: R Pos: 1B-23; LF-2; PR-2; RF-1; PH-1   Ht: 6'2" Wt: 200 Born: 11/26/1978 Age: 31

Year	Team	Lg	G	AB	H	2B	3B	HR	(Hm	Rd)	TB	R	RBI	RC	TBB	IBB	SO	HBP	SH	SF	SB	CS	SB%	GDP	Avg	OBP	Slg
2009	Pwtckt*	AAA	63	229	60	7	0	10	(-	-)	97	34	27	30	35	0	51	3	0	4	2	0	1.00	6	.262	.362	.424
2007	Bos	AL	3	9	1	0	0	0	(0	1)	4	1	1	0	0	0	1	0	0	0	0	0	-	0	.111	.111	.444
2008	Bos	AL	27	50	14	1	1	2	(2	0)	23	10	6	8	0	1	17	0	0	0	0	0	-	2	.280	.390	.460
2009	Bos	AL	26	77	16	3	2	3	(1	2)	32	14	9	9	10	0	21	4	0	0	0	0	-	5	.208	.330	.416
	3 ML YEARS		56	136	31	4	3	6	(3	3)	59	25	16	17	19	1	39	4	0	0	0	0	-	7	.228	.340	.434

Jeff Baker

Bats: R Throws: R Pos: 2B-52, 3B-20; PH-16; 1B-3   Ht: 6'2" Wt: 210 Born: 6/21/1981 Age: 29

Year	Team	Lg	G	AB	H	2B	3B	HR	(Hm	Rd)	TB	R	RBI	RC	TBB	IBB	SO	HBP	SH	SF	SB	CS	SB%	GDP	Avg	OBP	Slg
2009	Mdest*	A+	2	5	2	1	0	0	(-	-)	3	1	1	1	1	0	1	0	0	0	0	0	-	1	.400	.500	.600
2009	ColSpr*	AAA	7	23	5	2	0	1	(-	-)	10	3	1	3	4	0	3	0	0	0	0	0	-	1	.217	.333	.435
2005	Col	NL	12	38	8	4	0	1	(1	0)	15	6	4	4	5	0	12	0	0	0	0	0	-	1	.211	.302	.395
2006	Col	NL	18	57	21	7	2	5	(4	1)	47	13	21	17	1	0	14	0	0	0	2	0	1.00	0	.368	.379	.825
2007	Col	NL	85	144	32	2	2	4	(4	0)	50	17	12	8	13	1	40	2	0	0	0	0	-	7	.222	.296	.347
2008	Col	NL	104	299	80	22	1	12	(8	4)	140	55	48	40	26	2	85	1	1	6	4	0	1.00	6	.268	.322	.468
2009	2 Tms	NL	81	226	65	15	2	4	(3	1)	96	27	24	28	18	0	53	2	0	2	1	0	1.00	8	.288	.343	.425
09	Col	NL	12	23	3	0	1	0	(0	0)	5	0	0	0	1	0	7	0	0	0	1	0	1.00	3	.130	.167	.217
09	Chc	NL	69	203	62	15	1	4	(3	1)	91	27	21	28	17	0	46	2	0	2	0	0	-	5	.305	.362	.448
	Postseason		4	4	2	0	0	0	(0	0)	2	0	1	1	0	0	1	0	0	0	0	0	-	0	.500	.500	.500
	5 ML YEARS		300	764	206	50	7	26	(20	6)	348	118	109	97	63	3	204	5	1	8	7	0	1.00	21	.270	.326	.455

John Baker

Bats: L Throws: R Pos: C-105; PH-10   Ht: 6'1" Wt: 228 Born: 1/20/1981 Age: 29

Year	Team	Lg	G	AB	H	2B	3B	HR	(Hm	Rd)	TB	R	RBI	RC	TBB	IBB	SO	HBP	SH	SF	SB	CS	SB%	GDP	Avg	OBP	Slg
2002	Vancvr	A-	39	115	27	5	0	1	(-	-)	35	15	13	17	22	0	37	7	0	0	2	1	1.00	3	.235	.389	.304
2003	Kane	A	82	304	94	23	2	6	(-	-)	139	42	49	61	47	2	77	10	0	4	1	0	1.00	4	.309	.414	.457
2003	Mdland	AA	43	150	36	3	0	1	(-	-)	42	16	21	14	14	0	46	4	0	3	0	0	-	2	.240	.316	.280
2004	Mdland	AA	117	439	123	32	5	15	(-	-)	210	67	78	76	37	2	94	17	0	5	1	2	.33	16	.280	.355	.478
2004	Scrmto	AAA	14	49	17	3	0	0	(-	-)	20	11	10	8	6	1	23	1	0	0	0	0	-	0	.347	.429	.408
2005	Scrmto	AAA	103	346	81	24	3	5	(-	-)	126	43	41	40	30	0	90	4	7	0	1	0	1.00	5	.234	.303	.364
2006	Scrmto	AAA	83	293	80	19	1	4	(-	-)	113	49	38	45	40	1	77	2	2	3	6	0	1.00	10	.273	.361	.386
2007	Albq	AAA	89	270	77	15	0	8	(-	-)	116	35	41	43	28	1	58	4	0	1	2	0	1.00	7	.285	.360	.430
2008	Albq	AAA	35	193	62	14	1	6	(-	-)	96	35	31	38	24	0	34	2	0	2	1	2	.33	2	.321	.398	.497
2008	Fla	NL	61	197	59	14	0	5	(3	2)	88	32	32	36	30	4	48	2	1	3	0	0	-	6	.299	.392	.447
2009	Fla	NL	112	373	101	25	0	9	(3	6)	153	59	50	54	41	5	89	5	2	2	0	0	-	10	.271	.349	.410
	2 ML YEARS		173	570	160	39	0	14	(6	8)	241	91	82	90	71	9	137	7	3	5	0	0	-	16	.281	.364	.423

Scott Baker

Pitches: R Bats: R Pos: SP-33   Ht: 6'4" Wt: 220 Born: 9/19/1981 Age: 28

Year	Team	Lg	G	GS	CG	GF	IP	BFP	H	R	ER	HR	SH	SF	HB	TBB	IBB	SO	WP	Bk	W	L	Pct	Sh	Sv-Op	Hld	ERC	ERA
2005	Min	AL	10	9	0	0	53.2	217	48	21	20	5	2	2	0	14	0	32	0	0	3	3	.500	0	0-0	1	2.97	3.35
2006	Min	AL	16	16	0	0	83.1	377	114	63	59	17	2	4	3	16	1	62	0	0	5	8	.385	0	0-0	0	6.26	6.37
2007	Min	AL	24	23	2	0	143.2	606	162	70	68	15	6	2	5	29	4	102	0	0	9	9	.500	1	0-0	0	4.19	4.26
2008	Min	AL	28	28	0	0	172.1	703	161	66	66	20	2	3	3	42	2	141	6	0	11	4	.733	0	0-0	0	3.31	3.45
2009	Min	AL	33	33	1	0	200.0	828	190	99	97	28	1	6	4	48	1	162	4	0	15	9	.625	1	0-0	0	3.51	4.37
	5 ML YEARS		111	109	3	0	653.0	2731	675	319	310	85	13	17	15	149	8	499	10	0	43	33	.566	2	0-0	2	3.88	4.27

Paul Bako

Bats: L **Throws:** R **Pos:** C-42; PH-3   **Ht:** 6'3" **Wt:** 210 **Born:** 6/20/1972 **Age:** 38

Year	Team	Lg	G	AB	H	2B	3B	HR	(Hm	Rd)	TB	R	RBI	RC	TBB	IBB	SO	HBP	SH	SF	SB	CS	SB%	GDP	Avg	OBP	Slg
2009	Rdng*	AA	10	42	15	1	0	0	(-	-)	16	5	10	5	1	0	8	0	0	0	0	0	-	2	.357	.372	.381
1998	Det	AL	96	305	83	12	1	3	(2	1)	106	23	30	34	23	4	82	0	1	4	1	1	.50	3	.272	.319	.348
1999	Hou	NL	73	215	55	14	1	2	(2	0)	77	16	17	26	26	3	57	0	3	3	1	1	.50	4	.256	.332	.358
2000	3 Tms	NL	81	221	50	10	1	2	(2	0)	68	18	20	20	27	10	64	1	1	1	0	0	-	6	.226	.312	.308
2001	Atl	NL	61	137	29	10	1	2	(0	2)	47	19	15	15	20	2	34	0	0	0	1	0	1.00	4	.212	.312	.343
2002	Mil	NL	87	234	55	8	1	4	(2	2)	77	24	20	20	20	3	46	0	3	0	0	2	.00	4	.235	.295	.329
2003	ChC	NL	70	188	43	13	3	0	(0	0)	62	19	17	21	22	3	47	1	1	1	0	1	.00	2	.229	.311	.330
2004	ChC	NL	49	138	28	8	0	1	(1	0)	39	13	10	11	15	3	29	2	1	1	1	0	1.00	4	.203	.288	.283
2005	LAD	NL	13	40	10	2	0	0	(0	0)	12	1	4	6	7	1	12	0	0	0	0	0	-	0	.250	.362	.300
2006	KC	AL	56	153	32	3	0	0	(0	0)	35	7	10	9	11	0	46	0	2	1	0	0	-	3	.209	.261	.229
2007	Bal	AL	60	156	32	3	1	1	(0	1)	40	13	8	6	15	1	50	1	1	1	0	1	.00	4	.205	.277	.256
2008	Cin	NL	99	299	65	11	2	6	(2	4)	98	30	35	28	34	5	90	1	3	1	0	2	.00	9	.217	.299	.328
2009	Phi	NL	44	116	26	4	0	3	(1	2)	39	12	9	10	13	2	32	1	0	0	1	0	.00	2	.224	.308	.336
00	Hou	NL	1	2	0	0	0	0	(0	0)	0	0	0	0	0	0	1	0	0	0	0	0	-	0	.000	.000	.000
00	Fla	NL	56	161	39	6	1	0	(0	0)	47	10	14	16	22	7	48	1	1	1	0	0	-	4	.242	.335	.292
00	Atl	NL	24	58	11	4	0	2	(2	0)	21	8	6	4	5	3	15	0	0	0	0	0	-	2	.190	.254	.362
	Postseason		17	31	6	2	0	1	(1	0)	11	5	5	3	4	0	10	0	1	0	0	0	-	0	.194	.286	.355
	12 ML YEARS		789	2202	508	98	11	24	(12	12)	700	195	195	206	233	36	589	7	16	13	4	9	.31	44	.231	.305	.318

Rocco Baldelli

Bats: R **Throws:** R **Pos:** RF-35; PH-17; CF-8; DH-5; LF-2; 3B-1   **Ht:** 6'4" **Wt:** 200 **Born:** 9/25/1981 **Age:** 28

Year	Team	Lg	G	AB	H	2B	3B	HR	(Hm	Rd)	TB	R	RBI	RC	TBB	IBB	SO	HBP	SH	SF	SB	CS	SB%	GDP	Avg	OBP	Slg
2009	Pwtckt*	AAA	4	13	1	0	0	0	(-	-)	1	1	1	0	0	0	5	1	0	1	0	0	-	0	.077	.133	.077
2003	TB	AL	156	637	184	32	8	11	(2	9)	265	89	78	77	30	4	128	8	3	6	27	10	.73	10	.289	.326	.416
2004	TB	AL	136	518	145	27	3	16	(6	10)	226	79	74	70	30	2	88	8	3	6	17	4	.81	12	.280	.326	.436
2006	TB	AL	92	364	110	24	6	16	(6	10)	194	59	57	65	14	1	70	7	0	2	10	1	.91	2	.302	.339	.533
2007	TB	AL	35	137	28	6	0	5	(4	1)	49	16	12	14	9	1	35	3	1	0	4	1	.80	1	.204	.268	.358
2008	TB	AL	28	80	21	5	0	4	(0	4)	38	12	13	11	7	0	25	3	0	0	0	0	-	1	.263	.344	.475
2009	Bos	AL	62	150	38	4	1	7	(2	5)	65	23	23	17	11	0	37	2	0	1	1	0	1.00	6	.253	.311	.433
	Postseason		8	20	4	0	0	2	(0	2)	10	4	6	5	3	0	5	0	0	0	0	0	-	0	.200	.304	.500
	6 ML YEARS		509	1886	526	98	18	59	(20	39)	837	278	257	254	101	8	383	31	7	15	59	16	.79	32	.279	.324	.444

John Bale

Pitches: L **Bats:** L **Pos:** RP-43   **Ht:** 6'4" **Wt:** 203 **Born:** 5/22/1974 **Age:** 36

			HOW MUCH HE PITCHED						WHAT HE GAVE UP										THE RESULTS						
Year	Team	Lg	G	GS	CG	GF	IP	BFP	H	R	ER	HR	SH	SF	HB	TBB	IBB	SO	WP	Bk	W	L	Pct	Sh	Sv-Op	Hld	ERC	ERA
2009	NWArk*	AA	6	0	0	0	6.2	25	4	2	1	0	0	0	0	1	0	5	0	0	0	0	-	0	0--	-	1.02	1.35
1999	Tor	AL	1	0	0	0	2.0	10	2	3	3	1	0	0	0	2	0	4	0	0	0	0	-	0	0-0	0	9.87	13.50
2000	Tor	AL	2	0	0	0	3.2	22	5	7	6	1	0	1	2	3	0	6	0	0	0	0	-	0	0-0	0	11.52	14.73
2001	Bal	AL	14	0	0	3	26.2	113	18	14	9	2	0	2	1	17	0	21	1	0	1	0	1.000	0	0-0	2	3.21	3.04
2003	Cin	NL	10	9	0	0	46.1	195	50	24	23	7	1	2	2	12	2	37	1	0	1	2	.333	0	0-0	0	4.52	4.47
2007	KC	AL	26	0	0	5	40.0	179	45	18	18	1	3	3	1	17	2	42	2	0	1	1	.500	0	0-1	5	4.32	4.05
2008	KC	AL	13	3	0	1	26.2	110	29	13	13	1	3	2	0	6	0	14	1	0	0	3	.000	0	0-0	2	3.54	4.39
2009	KC	AL	43	0	0	12	28.1	136	34	19	18	3	0	2	1	18	2	24	2	0	0	1	.000	0	1-5	10	6.23	5.72
	7 ML YEARS		109	12	0	21	173.2	765	183	98	90	16	7	12	7	75	6	148	7	0	3	7	.300	0	1-6	19	4.58	4.66

Wladimir Balentien

Bats: R **Throws:** R **Pos:** LF-61; RF-22; PH-13; PR-5; DH-3   **Ht:** 6'2" **Wt:** 218 **Born:** 7/2/1984 **Age:** 25

Year	Team	Lg	G	AB	H	2B	3B	HR	(Hm	Rd)	TB	R	RBI	RC	TBB	IBB	SO	HBP	SH	SF	SB	CS	SB%	GDP	Avg	OBP	Slg
2007	Sea	AL	3	3	2	1	0	1	(1	0)	6	1	4	1	0	0	0	0	0	1	0	0	-	0	.667	.500	2.000
2008	Sea	AL	71	243	49	13	0	7	(3	4)	83	23	24	17	16	1	79	0	0	1	0	1	.00	12	.202	.250	.342
2009	2 Tms		96	265	62	17	1	7	(5	2)	102	30	24	28	28	1	70	0	0	2	2	1	.67	3	.234	.305	.385
09	Sea	AL	56	155	33	10	0	4	(2	2)	55	18	13	12	13	1	43	0	0	2	1	0	1.00	2	.213	.271	.355
09	Cin	NL	40	110	29	7	1	3	(3	0)	47	12	11	16	15	0	27	0	0	0	1	1	.50	1	.264	.352	.427
	3 ML YEARS		170	511	113	31	1	15	(9	6)	191	54	52	46	44	2	149	0	0	4	2	2	.50	15	.221	.281	.374

Collin Balester

Pitches: R **Bats:** R **Pos:** SP-7   **Ht:** 6'5" **Wt:** 199 **Born:** 6/6/1986 **Age:** 24

			HOW MUCH HE PITCHED						WHAT HE GAVE UP										THE RESULTS						
Year	Team	Lg	G	GS	CG	GF	IP	BFP	H	R	ER	HR	SH	SF	HB	TBB	IBB	SO	WP	Bk	W	L	Pct	Sh	Sv-Op	Hld	ERC	ERA
2004	Expos	R	5	4	0	1	24.2	101	20	8	6	0	1	1	1	5	1	21	4	0	1	2	.333	0	0--	-	1.80	2.19
2005	Savann	A	24	23	1	0	125.0	521	105	62	51	11	1	0	6	42	0	95	4	1	8	6	.571	0	0--	-	3.06	3.67
2006	Ptomc	A+	23	22	0	0	117.2	518	126	71	64	8	12	3	8	53	0	87	12	0	4	5	.444	0	0--	-	4.90	4.90
2006	Hrsbrg	AA	3	3	0	0	19.2	77	15	5	4	0	2	2	2	6	1	10	2	0	1	0	1.000	0	0--	-	2.27	1.83
2007	Hrsbrg	AA	17	17	0	0	98.2	423	103	44	41	9	5	2	5	25	0	77	5	0	2	7	.222	0	0--	-	3.85	3.74
2007	Clmbs	AAA	10	10	0	0	51.2	226	49	27	24	3	3	5	3	23	2	40	2	1	2	3	.400	0	0--	-	3.80	4.18
2008	Clmbs	AAA	15	15	0	0	78.2	332	79	37	35	14	2	3	4	23	0	64	4	0	9	3	.750	0	0--	-	4.46	4.00
2009	Syrcse	AAA	20	20	0	0	107.1	474	120	58	53	5	3	5	6	37	3	71	6	1	7	10	.412	0	0--	-	4.88	4.44
2008	Was	NL	15	15	0	0	80.0	358	92	53	49	12	2	3	6	28	1	50	4	0	3	7	.300	0	0-0	0	5.40	5.51
2009	Was	NL	7	7	0	0	30.1	135	34	24	23	10	0	0	0	14	0	20	0	0	1	4	.200	0	0-0	0	6.85	6.82
	2 ML YEARS		22	22	0	0	110.1	493	126	77	72	22	2	3	6	42	1	70	4	0	4	11	.267	0	0-0	0	5.80	5.87

Grant Balfour

Pitches: R Bats: R Pos: RP-73 Ht: 6'2" Wt: 105 Born: 12/30/1977 Age: 32

		HOW MUCH HE PITCHED						WHAT HE GAVE UP											THE RESULTS						
Year Team	Lg	G	GS	CG	GF	IP	BFP	H	R	ER	HR	SH	SF	HB	TBB	IBB	SO	WP	Bk	W	L	Pct	Sh	Sv-Op	Hld	ERC	ERA
2001 Min	AL	2	0	0	1	2.2	14	3	4	4	2	1	1	0	3	0	2	0	0	0	0	-	0	0-0	0	13.78	13.50
2003 Min	AL	17	1	0	6	26.0	115	23	12	12	4	2	1	0	14	2	30	0	0	1	0	1.000	0	0-1	1	4.14	4.15
2004 Min	AL	36	0	0	14	39.1	172	35	19	19	4	2	0	2	21	1	42	3	0	4	1	.800	0	0-1	4	4.16	4.35
2007 2 Tms		25	0	0	8	24.2	121	30	21	21	2	2	3	1	20	0	30	0	0	1	2	.333	0	0-0	1	7.15	7.66
2008 TB	AL	51	0	0	12	58.1	224	28	10	10	3	1	3	0	24	1	82	2	0	6	2	.750	0	4-5	14	1.38	1.54
2009 TB	AL	73	0	0	15	67.1	289	59	38	36	6	1	2	2	33	0	69	1	0	5	4	.556	0	4-9	18	3.79	4.81
07 Mil		3	0	0	2	2.2	18	4	6	6	1	1	0	1	4	0	3	0	0	0	2	.000	0	0-0	0	15.83	20.25
07 TB		22	0	0	6	22.0	103	26	15	15	1	1	3	0	16	0	27	0	0	1	0	1.000	0	0-0	1	6.19	6.14
Postseason		12	0	0	2	11.1	53	11	6	6	2	1	0	1	8	3	9	1	0	0	0	-	0	0-0	2	5.59	4.76
6 ML YEARS		204	1	0	56	218.1	935	178	104	102	21	9	10	5	115	4	255	6	0	17	9	.654	0	8-16	38	3.58	4.20

Josh Banks

Pitches: R Bats: R Pos: SP-3; RP-3 Ht: 6'3" Wt: 215 Born: 7/18/1982 Age: 27

		HOW MUCH HE PITCHED						WHAT HE GAVE UP											THE RESULTS						
Year Team	Lg	G	GS	CG	GF	IP	BFP	H	R	ER	HR	SH	SF	HB	TBB	IBB	SO	WP	Bk	W	L	Pct	Sh	Sv-Op	Hld	ERC	ERA
2009 Portlnd*	AAA	26	17	0	2	125.0	519	120	52	48	6	7	4	2	36	2	95	5	1	7	7	.500	0	0- -	-	3.14	3.46
2007 Tor	AL	3	1	0	1	7.1	35	11	6	6	1	0	1	0	2	0	2	0	0	0	0	-	0	0-0	0	6.66	7.36
2008 SD	NL	17	14	1	1	85.1	372	94	47	45	12	8	4	3	32	5	43	0	0	3	6	.333	0	0-0	0	4.97	4.75
2009 SD	NL	6	3	0	0	22.2	100	30	18	18	6	2	2	1	4	1	9	1	0	1	1	.500	0	0-0	0	6.45	7.15
3 ML YEARS		26	18	1	2	115.1	507	135	71	69	19	10	7	4	38	6	54	1	0	4	7	.364	0	0-0	0	5.36	5.38

Brian Bannister

Pitches: R Bats: R Pos: SP-26 Ht: 6'2" Wt: 217 Born: 2/28/1981 Age: 29

		HOW MUCH HE PITCHED						WHAT HE GAVE UP											THE RESULTS						
Year Team	Lg	G	GS	CG	GF	IP	BFP	H	R	ER	HR	SH	SF	HB	TBB	IBB	SO	WP	Bk	W	L	Pct	Sh	Sv-Op	Hld	ERC	ERA
2009 Omha*	AAA	3	3	0	0	13.0	51	12	5	5	1	0	0	0	1	0	8	1	1	0	1	.000	0	0- -	-	2.34	3.46
2006 NYM	NL	8	6	0	1	38.0	171	34	18	18	4	1	4	2	22	2	19	2	0	2	1	.667	0	0-0	0	4.27	4.26
2007 KC	AL	27	27	1	0	165.0	683	156	76	71	16	5	2	4	44	4	77	4	0	12	9	.571	0	0-0	0	3.36	3.87
2008 KC	AL	32	32	1	0	182.2	811	215	127	117	20	0	10	7	36	1	113	7	1	9	16	.360	0	0-0	0	5.34	5.76
2009 KC	AL	26	20	0	0	154.0	688	161	94	81	15	3	10	4	50	4	98	12	2	7	12	.368	0	0-0	0	4.04	4.70
4 ML YEARS		93	91	2	1	539.2	2333	666	315	287	63	9	28	19	174	8	307	25	3	30	38	.441	0	0-0	0	4.27	4.79

Rod Barajas

Bats: R Throws: R Pos: C-120; PH-6 Ht: 6'2" Wt: 250 Born: 9/5/1975 Age: 34

		BATTING																				BASERUNNING				AVERAGES		
Year Team	Lg	G	AB	H	2B	3B	HR	(Hm	Rd)	TB	R	RBI	RC	TBB	IBB	SO	HBP	SH	SF	SB	CS	SB%	GDP	Avg	OBP	Slg
1999 Ari	NL	5	16	4	1	0	1	(1	0)	8	3	3	2	1	0	1	0	1	0	0	0	-	0	.250	.294	.500
2000 Ari	NL	5	13	3	0	0	1	(1	0)	6	1	3	1	0	0	4	0	0	0	0	0	-	0	.231	.231	.462
2001 Ari	NL	51	106	17	3	0	3	(2	1)	29	0	0	4	4	0	26	0	0	0	0	0	-	0	.160	.191	.274
2002 Ari	NL	70	154	36	10	0	3	(1	2)	55	12	23	15	10	4	25	3	2	3	1	0	1.00	4	.234	.288	.357
2003 Ari	NL	80	220	48	15	0	3	(3	0)	72	19	28	19	14	7	43	1	1	3	0	0	-	6	.218	.265	.327
2004 Tex	AL	108	358	89	26	1	15	(8	7)	162	50	58	43	13	0	63	3	8	7	0	1	.00	3	.249	.276	.453
2005 Tex	AL	120	410	104	24	0	21	(7	14)	191	53	60	56	26	0	70	6	4	3	0	0	-	6	.254	.306	.466
2006 Tex	AL	97	344	88	20	0	11	(6	5)	141	49	44	36	17	0	51	4	5	1	0	0	-	9	.256	.298	.410
2007 Phi	NL	48	122	28	8	0	4	(1	3)	48	16	10	12	21	3	24	2	1	0	0	1	.00	5	.230	.352	.393
2008 Tor	AL	104	349	87	23	0	11	(4	7)	143	44	49	37	17	0	61	7	0	4	0	0	-	9	.249	.294	.410
2009 Tor	AL	125	429	97	19	0	19	(8	11)	173	43	71	50	20	2	76	1	3	7	1	0	1.00	4	.226	.258	.403
Postseason		5	9	3	0	0	2	(0	2)	9	2	2	2	0	0	1	0	0	0	0	0	-	0	.333	.333	1.000
11 ML YEARS		813	2521	601	149	1	92	(42	50)	1028	299	355	275	143	16	444	27	25	28	2	2	.50	46	.238	.284	.408

Daniel Bard

Pitches: R Bats: R Pos: RP-49 Ht: 6'4" Wt: 200 Born: 6/25/1985 Age: 25

		HOW MUCH HE PITCHED						WHAT HE GAVE UP											THE RESULTS						
Year Team	Lg	G	GS	CG	GF	IP	BFP	H	R	ER	HR	SH	SF	HB	TBB	IBB	SO	WP	Bk	W	L	Pct	Sh	Sv-Op	Hld	ERC	ERA
2007 Lancst	A+	5	5	0	0	13.1	86	21	23	15	2	2	1	1	22	0	9	5	0	0	2	.000	0	0- -	-	13.68	10.13
2007 Grnville	A	17	17	0	0	61.2	289	55	49	44	3	1	5	7	56	0	38	22	1	3	5	.375	0	0- -	-	5.64	6.42
2008 Grnville	A	15	0	0	3	28.0	100	12	2	2	1	0	0	3	4	0	43	0	0	1	0	1.000	0	0- -	-	0.91	0.64
2008 Portlnd	AA	31	0	0	14	49.2	203	30	14	11	3	1	0	3	26	0	64	9	0	4	1	.800	0	7- -	-	2.45	1.99
2009 Pwtckt	AAA	11	0	0	8	16.0	58	6	2	2	2	0	0	1	5	0	29	0	0	1	0	1.000	0	6- -	-	1.30	1.13
2009 Bos	AL	49	0	0	12	49.1	212	41	24	20	5	4	3	3	22	3	63	1	1	2	2	.500	0	1-4	13	3.43	3.65

Josh Bard

Bats: B Throws: R Pos: C-79; PH-15 Ht: 6'3" Wt: 225 Born: 3/30/1978 Age: 32

		BATTING																				BASERUNNING				AVERAGES		
Year Team	Lg	G	AB	H	2B	3B	HR	(Hm	Rd)	TB	R	RBI	RC	TBB	IBB	SO	HBP	SH	SF	SB	CS	SB%	GDP	Avg	OBP	Slg
2009 Syrcse*	AAA	13	40	7	1	0	0	(-	-)	8	2	1	1	4	0	10	0	0	0	0	0	-	1	.175	.250	.200
2002 Cle	AL	24	90	20	5	0	3	(2	1)	34	9	12	7	4	0	13	0	1	0	0	0	-	6	.222	.255	.378
2003 Cle	AL	91	303	74	13	1	8	(5	3)	113	25	36	34	22	1	53	0	1	3	0	2	.00	9	.244	.293	.373
2004 Cle	AL	7	19	8	2	0	1	(1	0)	13	5	4	6	3	0	0	0	0	1	0	0	-	0	.421	.478	.684
2005 Cle	AL	34	83	16	4	0	1	(0	1)	23	6	9	8	9	0	11	0	1	2	0	0	-	2	.193	.266	.277
2006 2 Tms		100	249	83	20	0	9	(5	4)	130	30	40	44	30	1	42	1	2	2	1	0	1.00	8	.333	.404	.522
2007 SD	NL	118	389	111	27	2	5	(4	1)	157	42	51	65	50	7	58	0	1	3	0	1	.00	16	.285	.364	.404

41

Year Team	Lg	G	AB	H	2B	3B	HR	(Hm	Rd)	TB	R	RBI	RC	TBB	IBB	SO	HBP	SH	SF	SB	CS	SB%	GDP	Avg	OBP	Slg
2008 SD	NL	57	178	36	9	0	1	(0	1)	48	11	16	13	18	2	25	1	1	0	0	0	-	5	.202	.279	.270
2009 Was	NL	90	274	63	18	0	6	(4	2)	99	20	31	27	24	1	50	1	1	1	0	1	.00	5	.230	.293	.361
06 Bos	AL	7	18	5	1	0	0	(0	0)	6	2	0	2	3	0	3	0	0	0	0	0	-	0	.278	.381	.333
06 SD	NL	93	231	78	19	0	9	(5	4)	124	28	40	42	27	1	39	1	2	2	1	0	1.00	9	.338	.406	.537
Postseason		3	7	1	0	0	0	(0	0)	1	0	0	0	1	0	2	1	0	0	0	0	-	0	.143	.333	.143
8 ML YEARS		521	1585	411	98	3	34	(21	13)	617	148	199	204	160	12	252	3	8	12	1	4	.20	52	.259	.326	.389

Brian Barden

Bats: R **Throws:** R **Pos:** 3B-46; PH-13; SS-4; 2B-1   **Ht:** 5'11" **Wt:** 200 **Born:** 4/2/1981 **Age:** 29

Year Team	Lg	G	AB	H	2B	3B	HR	(Hm	Rd)	TB	R	RBI	RC	TBB	IBB	SO	HBP	SH	SF	SB	CS	SB%	GDP	Avg	OBP	Slg
2009 Memp*	AAA	61	187	50	11	0	4	(-	-)	73	26	28	23	10	1	44	4	4	1	1	1	.50	7	.267	.317	.390
2007 2 Tms	NL	23	35	6	1	0	0	(0	0)	7	6	0	1	2	0	7	0	0	0	0	0	-	2	.171	.216	.200
2008 StL	NL	9	9	2	0	0	0	(0	0)	2	0	1	0	0	0	4	0	1	0	0	0	-	0	.222	.222	.222
2009 StL	NL	52	103	24	3	0	4	(1	3)	39	13	10	8	6	0	21	2	2	1	0	0	-	3	.233	.286	.379
07 Ari	NL	8	12	1	0	0	0	(0	0)	1	0	0	0	0	0	3	0	0	0	0	0	-	0	.083	.083	.083
07 StL	NL	15	23	5	1	0	0	(0	0)	6	6	0	1	2	0	4	0	0	0	0	0	-	2	.217	.280	.261
3 ML YEARS		84	147	32	4	0	4	(1	3)	48	19	11	9	8	0	32	2	3	1	0	0	-	5	.218	.266	.327

Josh Barfield

Bats: R **Throws:** R **Pos:** 2B-8; PR-8; PH-2; LF-1; DH-1   **Ht:** 6'0" **Wt:** 190 **Born:** 12/17/1982 **Age:** 27

Year Team	Lg	G	AB	H	2B	3B	HR	(Hm	Rd)	TB	R	RBI	RC	TBB	IBB	SO	HBP	SH	SF	SB	CS	SB%	GDP	Avg	OBP	Slg
2009 Clmbs*	AAA	73	305	77	15	0	3	(-	-)	101	27	35	27	8	0	48	1	2	3	5	3	.63	6	.252	.271	.331
2006 SD	NL	150	539	151	32	3	13	(6	7)	228	72	58	69	30	7	81	2	2	5	21	5	.81	8	.280	.318	.423
2007 Cle	AL	130	420	102	19	3	3	(2	1)	136	53	50	42	14	0	90	3	3	4	14	5	.74	3	.243	.270	.324
2008 Cle	AL	12	33	6	1	0	0	(0	0)	7	3	2	1	0	0	10	0	0	0	0	0	-	0	.182	.182	.212
2009 Cle	AL	17	20	8	1	0	0	(0	0)	9	5	2	4	0	0	7	0	0	0	0	1	.00	0	.400	.400	.450
Postseason		5	8	2	1	0	0	(0	0)	3	0	0	1	1	0	2	0	0	0	1	0	1.00	0	.250	.333	.375
4 ML YEARS		309	1012	267	53	6	16	(8	8)	380	133	112	116	44	7	188	5	5	9	35	11	.76	11	.264	.295	.375

Kevin Barker

Bats: L **Throws:** L **Pos:** PH-27; 1B-6   **Ht:** 6'2" **Wt:** 195 **Born:** 7/26/1975 **Age:** 34

Year Team	Lg	G	AB	H	2B	3B	HR	(Hm	Rd)	TB	R	RBI	RC	TBB	IBB	SO	HBP	SH	SF	SB	CS	SB%	GDP	Avg	OBP	Slg
2009 Lsvlle*	AAA	101	354	101	22	3	22	(-	-)	195	58	69	75	54	6	80	2	0	7	1	1	.50	10	.285	.376	.551
1999 Mil	NL	38	117	33	3	0	3	(1	2)	45	13	23	16	9	1	19	0	0	1	1	0	1.00	1	.282	.331	.385
2000 Mil	NL	40	100	22	5	0	2	(0	2)	33	14	9	14	20	0	21	1	0	1	1	0	1.00	1	.220	.352	.330
2002 SD	NL	7	19	3	0	0	0	(0	0)	3	0	0	0	1	0	6	0	0	0	1	0	1.00	0	.158	.200	.158
2006 Tor	AL	12	17	4	1	0	1	(0	1)	8	3	1	0	1	0	10	0	0	0	0	0	-	0	.235	.278	.471
2009 Cin	NL	29	32	9	3	0	0	(0	0)	12	2	3	4	3	1	9	0	0	1	0	0	-	2	.281	.333	.375
5 ML YEARS		126	285	71	12	0	6	(1	5)	101	32	36	34	34	2	65	1	0	3	3	0	1.00	4	.249	.328	.354

Clint Barmes

Bats: R **Throws:** R **Pos:** 2B-139; SS-16; PH-4; PR-1   **Ht:** 6'1" **Wt:** 210 **Born:** 3/6/1979 **Age:** 31

Year Team	Lg	G	AB	H	2B	3B	HR	(Hm	Rd)	TB	R	RBI	RC	TBB	IBB	SO	HBP	SH	SF	SB	CS	SB%	GDP	Avg	OBP	Slg
2003 Col	NL	12	25	8	2	0	0	(0	0)	10	2	2	3	0	0	10	2	0	1	0	0	-	0	.320	.357	.400
2004 Col	NL	20	71	20	3	1	2	(0	2)	31	14	10	12	3	0	10	1	2	0	0	1	.00	2	.282	.320	.437
2005 Col	NL	81	350	101	19	1	10	(7	3)	152	55	46	49	16	1	36	6	4	1	6	4	.60	4	.289	.330	.434
2006 Col	NL	131	478	105	26	4	7	(3	4)	160	57	56	47	22	6	72	9	19	7	5	4	.56	2	.220	.264	.335
2007 Col	NL	27	37	8	3	0	0	(0	0)	11	5	1	1	1	1	13	0	0	1	0	0	-	1	.216	.237	.297
2008 Col	NL	107	393	114	25	6	11	(8	3)	184	47	44	54	17	0	69	2	4	1	13	4	.76	9	.290	.322	.468
2009 Col	NL	154	550	135	32	3	23	(13	10)	242	69	76	63	31	2	121	10	6	7	12	10	.55	6	.245	.294	.440
7 ML YEARS		532	1904	491	110	15	53	(31	22)	790	249	235	229	90	10	331	30	36	17	36	23	.61	24	.258	.299	.415

Michael Barrett

Bats: R **Throws:** R **Pos:** C-7   **Ht:** 6'3" **Wt:** 210 **Born:** 10/22/1976 **Age:** 33

Year Team	Lg	G	AB	H	2B	3B	HR	(Hm	Rd)	TB	R	RBI	RC	TBB	IBB	SO	HBP	SH	SF	SB	CS	SB%	GDP	Avg	OBP	Slg
2009 Dnedin*	A+	3	8	1	0	0	0	(-	-)	1	1	0	0	1	0	1	0	0	0	0	1	.00	0	.125	.222	.125
2009 LsVgs*	AAA	7	26	6	2	0	0	(-	-)	8	2	5	2	1	0	5	0	1	0	0	0	-	2	.231	.259	.308
1998 Mon	NL	8	23	7	2	0	1	(0	1)	12	3	2	5	3	0	6	1	0	0	0	0	-	0	.304	.407	.522
1999 Mon	NL	126	433	127	32	3	8	(5	3)	189	53	52	59	32	4	39	3	0	1	0	2	.00	18	.293	.345	.436
2000 Mon	NL	89	271	58	15	1	1	(0	1)	78	28	22	19	23	5	35	1	1	1	0	1	.00	7	.214	.277	.288
2001 Mon	NL	132	472	118	33	2	6	(3	3)	173	42	38	46	25	2	54	2	4	3	2	1	.67	14	.250	.289	.367
2002 Mon	NL	117	376	99	20	1	12	(4	8)	157	41	49	49	40	7	65	1	6	5	6	3	.67	14	.263	.332	.418
2003 Mon	NL	70	226	47	9	2	10	(5	5)	90	33	30	25	21	7	37	2	2	1	0	0	-	6	.208	.280	.398
2004 ChC	NL	134	456	131	32	6	16	(9	7)	223	55	65	67	33	4	64	5	4	8	1	4	.20	13	.287	.337	.489
2005 ChC	NL	133	424	117	32	3	16	(9	7)	203	48	61	67	40	3	61	7	2	4	0	3	.00	7	.276	.345	.479
2006 ChC	NL	107	375	115	25	3	16	(9	7)	194	54	53	58	33	2	41	5	2	3	0	1	.00	12	.307	.368	.517
2007 2 Tms	NL	101	344	84	17	0	9	(6	3)	128	29	41	29	19	3	57	0	0	2	2	2	.50	10	.244	.281	.372
2008 SD	NL	30	94	19	3	0	2	(2	0)	28	9	9	7	9	0	16	1	1	2	0	0	-	4	.202	.274	.298

			BATTING																	BASERUNNING				AVERAGES		
Year	Team	Lg	G	AB	H	2B	3B	HR	(Hm Rd)	TB	R	RBI	RC	TBB	IBB	SO	HBP	SH	SF	SB	CS	SB%	GDP	Avg	OBP	Slg
2009	Tor	AL	7	18	3	0	0	1	(0 1)	6	3	2	1	1	1	5	0	0	0	0	0	-	0	.167	.211	.333
07	ChC	NL	57	211	54	9	0	9	(6 3)	90	23	29	22	17	3	36	0	0	3	2	2	.50	5	.256	.307	.427
07	SD	NL	44	133	30	8	0	0	(0 0)	38	6	12	7	2	0	21	0	0	1	0	0	-	5	.226	.235	.286
12 ML YEARS			1054	3512	925	220	21	98	(52 46)	1481	398	424	432	279	38	480	28	22	32	11	17	.39	105	.263	.320	.422

Jason Bartlett

Bats: R **Throws:** R **Pos:** SS-134; DH-3   **Ht:** 6'0" **Wt:** 190 **Born:** 10/30/1979 **Age:** 30

			BATTING																	BASERUNNING				AVERAGES		
Year	Team	Lg	G	AB	H	2B	3B	HR	(Hm Rd)	TB	R	RBI	RC	TBB	IBB	SO	HBP	SH	SF	SB	CS	SB%	GDP	Avg	OBP	Slg
2009	Charltt*	A+	3	11	5	0	1	0	(- -)	7	2	0	3	2	0	2	0	0	0	0	1	.00	0	.455	.538	.636
2004	Min	AL	8	12	1	0	0	0	(0 0)	1	2	1	1	1	0	1	0	1	0	0	1	.00	0	.083	.154	.083
2005	Min	AL	74	224	54	10	1	3	(2 1)	75	33	16	22	21	0	37	4	2	1	4	0	1.00	6	.241	.316	.335
2006	Min	AL	99	333	103	18	2	2	(0 2)	131	44	32	50	22	1	46	11	1	5	10	5	.67	8	.309	.367	.393
2007	Min	AL	140	510	135	20	7	5	(2 3)	184	75	43	65	50	3	73	8	0	2	23	3	.88	3	.265	.339	.361
2008	TB	AL	128	454	130	25	3	1	(1 0)	164	48	37	56	22	1	69	9	5	4	20	6	.77	9	.286	.329	.361
2009	TB	AL	137	500	160	29	7	14	(3 11)	245	90	66	97	54	2	89	5	4	4	30	7	.81	5	.320	.389	.490
Postseason			19	62	15	2	1	1	(1 0)	22	8	3	5	4	0	12	2	1	0	2	0	1.00	2	.242	.309	.355
6 ML YEARS			586	2033	583	102	20	25	(8 17)	800	292	195	291	170	7	315	37	13	16	89	21	.81	36	.287	.350	.394

Brian Barton

Bats: R **Throws:** R **Pos:** RF-1; PR-1   **Ht:** 6'3" **Wt:** 190 **Born:** 4/25/1982 **Age:** 28

			BATTING																	BASERUNNING				AVERAGES		
Year	Team	Lg	G	AB	H	2B	3B	HR	(Hm Rd)	TB	R	RBI	RC	TBB	IBB	SO	HBP	SH	SF	SB	CS	SB%	GDP	Avg	OBP	Slg
2005	Lk Cty	A	35	133	55	14	1	4	(- -)	83	31	32	40	18	1	21	8	0	1	7	2	.78	5	.414	.508	.624
2005	Knstn	A+	64	223	61	15	6	3	(- -)	97	42	32	42	34	2	57	15	1	0	13	8	.62	6	.274	.404	.436
2006	Knstn	A+	82	295	91	16	3	13	(- -)	152	66	57	00	39	2	83	16	3	6	26	3	.90	3	.308	.410	.515
2006	Akron	AA	42	151	53	5	0	6	(- -)	78	32	26	32	10	2	26	5	0	2	15	5	.75	3	.351	.415	.503
2007	Akron	AA	106	389	122	18	2	9	(- -)	171	56	59	76	41	2	99	28	2	1	21	9	.70	8	.314	.416	.440
2007	Buffalo	AAA	25	87	23	3	0	1	(- -)	29	9	7	10	7	0	18	2	0	0	1	1	.50	4	.264	.333	.333
2008	Mcmp	AAA	19	73	19	2	2	3	(- -)	34	12	11	11	9	0	23	2	0	2	1	4	.20	1	.260	.349	.466
2009	Mcmp	AAA	10	28	3	0	0	0	(- -)	3	2	1	0	4	0	9	0	0	0	0	3	.00	4	.107	.210	.107
2009	Gwnltt	AAA	114	369	98	17	4	7	(- -)	144	47	40	55	45	2	101	7	2	3	17	7	.71	7	.266	.354	.390
2008	StL	NL	82	153	41	9	2	2	(1 1)	60	23	13	19	19	0	39	2	4	1	3	1	.75	5	.268	.354	.392
2009	Atl	NL	1	0	0	0	0	0	(0 0)	0	0	0	0	0	0	0	0	0	0	0	1	.00	0	-	-	-
2 ML YEARS			83	153	41	9	2	2	(1 1)	60	23	13	19	19	0	39	2	4	1	3	2	.60	5	.268	.354	.392

Daric Barton

Bats: L **Throws:** R **Pos:** 1B-51; PH-2; PR-1   **Ht:** 6'0" **Wt:** 218 **Born:** 8/16/1985 **Age:** 24

			BATTING																	BASERUNNING				AVERAGES		
Year	Team	Lg	G	AB	H	2B	3B	HR	(Hm Rd)	TB	R	RBI	RC	TBB	IBB	SO	HBP	SH	SF	SB	CS	SB%	GDP	Avg	OBP	Slg
2009	Scrmto*	AAA	70	253	66	21	1	9	(- -)	116	48	48	49	45	2	43	9	2	4	1	0	1.00	2	.261	.386	.458
2009	As*	R	6	18	5	1	0	1	(- -)	9	3	3	4	8	0	4	0	0	0	0	0	-	0	.278	.458	.500
2009	Stcktn*	A+	1	4	0	0	0	0	(- -)	0	0	0	0	0	0	0	0	0	0	0	0	-	0	.000	.000	.000
2007	Oak	AL	18	72	25	9	0	4	(2 2)	46	16	8	14	10	0	11	1	0	1	0	1	.00	2	.347	.429	.639
2008	Oak	AL	140	446	101	17	5	9	(1 8)	155	59	47	56	65	5	99	3	6	3	2	1	.67	6	.226	.327	.348
2009	Oak	AL	54	160	43	12	1	3	(2 1)	66	31	24	28	26	0	25	2	1	3	0	2	.00	1	.269	.372	.413
3 ML YEARS			212	678	169	38	6	16	(5 11)	267	106	79	98	101	5	135	6	7	7	3	3	.50	9	.249	.348	.394

Brian Bass

Pitches: R **Bats:** R **Pos:** RP-48   **Ht:** 6'2" **Wt:** 215 **Born:** 1/6/1982 **Age:** 28

			HOW MUCH HE PITCHED						WHAT HE GAVE UP											THE RESULTS						
Year	Team	Lg	G	GS	CG	GF	IP	BFP	H	R	ER	HR	SH	SF	HB	TBB	IBB	SO	WP	Bk	W	L	Pct	Sh	Sv-Op	Hld	ERC	ERA
2000	Royals	R	12	9	0	0	44.0	200	36	27	19	0	1	1	9	18	0	44	10	0	3	5	.375	0	0--	-	3.01	3.89
2000	CtnWV	A	1	1	0	0	4.0	18	6	3	3	0	0	0	0	1	0	1	0	0	0	0	-	0	0--	-	4.47	6.75
2001	Burlgtn	A	26	26	1	0	139.1	613	138	82	72	16	3	5	15	53	0	75	14	1	3	10	.231	1	0--	-	4.46	4.65
2002	Burlgtn	A	20	20	1	0	110.1	456	103	57	47	8	1	3	2	31	0	60	9	0	5	7	.417	0	0--	-	3.16	3.83
2003	Wilmg	A+	26	26	2	0	152.1	625	129	59	48	7	5	7	7	43	1	119	7	0	9	8	.529	0	0--	-	2.63	2.84
2004	Wichta	AA	10	10	0	0	36.1	179	53	30	30	4	3	0	3	22	0	20	1	0	0	4	.000	0	0--	-	8.40	7.43
2004	Royals	R	5	5	0	0	17.2	73	17	6	5	0	0	0	1	3	0	23	2	0	1	0	1.000	0	0--	-	2.55	2.55
2005	Wichta	AA	27	27	0	0	165.0	713	185	106	96	14	4	8	3	53	0	102	10	0	12	8	.600	0	0--	-	4.46	5.24
2006	Omha	AAA	7	7	0	0	32.0	158	49	35	27	7	0	1	2	14	0	11	4	1	1	5	.167	0	0--	-	8.79	7.59
2006	Wichta	AA	6	5	1	0	27.0	117	29	14	12	2	0	0	3	6	0	18	3	0	4	1	.800	0	0--	-	4.02	4.00
2006	Royals	R	3	3	-	0	12.0	51	15	7	6	0	-	-	1	0	0	9	0	0	1	1	.500	-	0--	-	3.51	4.50
2007	Roch	AAA	37	10	1	12	103.1	424	96	45	40	8	0	4	5	24	2	80	5	0	7	3	.700	1	1--	-	3.08	3.48
2008	Roch	AAA	2	2	0	0	9.0	40	8	5	4	1	0	1	0	4	0	6	0	0	1	0	1.000	0	0--	-	4.05	4.00
2008	2 Tms	AL	49	4	0	14	89.1	388	98	55	48	12	1	1	5	31	4	45	6	0	4	4	.500	0	1-2	3	4.89	4.84
2009	Bal	AL	48	0	0	13	86.1	400	106	52	47	11	3	2	5	44	5	54	6	0	5	3	.625	0	0-0	1	6.30	4.90
08	Min	AL	44	0	0	14	68.1	303	84	42	37	11	0	1	3	22	3	32	4	0	3	4	.429	0	1-2	3	5.74	4.87
08	Bal	AL	5	4	0	0	21.0	85	14	13	11	1	1	0	2	9	1	13	2	0	1	0	1.000	0	0-0	0	2.42	4.71
2 ML YEARS			97	4	0	27	175.2	788	204	107	95	23	4	3	10	75	9	99	12	0	9	7	.563	0	1-2	4	5.58	4.87

Antonio Bastardo

Pitches: L **Bats:** R **Pos:** SP-5; RP-1   **Ht:** 5'11" **Wt:** 194 **Born:** 9/21/1985 **Age:** 24

Year	Team	Lg	G	GS	CG	GF	IP	BFP	H	R	ER	HR	SH	SF	HB	TBB	IBB	SO	WP	Bk	W	L	Pct	Sh	Sv-Op	Hld	ERC	ERA
2006	Phillies	R	9	2	0	2	23.0	106	20	16	10	1	0	1	0	14	0	27	3	3	1	2	.333	0	0- -	-	3.53	3.91
2007	Lakwd	A	15	15	0	0	91.2	382	63	23	19	3	1	2	4	42	0	98	12	3	9	0	1.000	0	0- -	-	2.34	1.87
2007	Clrwtr	A+	1	1	0	0	5.0	24	5	4	4	0	0	1	0	3	0	12	1	0	1	0	1.000	0	0- -	-	3.80	7.20
2008	Clrwtr	A+	5	5	0	0	30.2	120	20	4	4	2	0	0	1	10	0	47	0	1	2	0	1.000	0	0- -	-	1.97	1.17
2008	Rdng	AA	14	14	0	0	67.0	291	56	35	28	13	1	1	1	37	0	62	3	2	1	5	.167	0	0- -	-	4.46	3.76
2009	Rdng	AA	11	5	0	5	36.0	134	22	7	7	1	2	0	2	7	0	41	0	0	2	2	.500	0	3- -	-	1.39	1.75
2009	LV	AAA	2	2	0	0	13.0	50	11	3	3	1	0	0	0	3	0	12	0	0	1	0	1.000	0	0- -	-	2.62	2.08
2009	Phillies	R	3	2	0	0	4.1	19	2	1	0	0	0	0	2	2	0	3	1	0	0	0	-	0	0- -	-	2.37	0.00
2009	Clrwtr	A+	1	0	0	0	1.0	6	4	3	3	0	0	1	0	0	0	0	0	0	0	0	-	0	0- -	-	26.25	27.00
2009	Phi	NL	6	5	0	0	23.2	106	26	18	17	4	0	0	2	9	0	19	0	0	2	3	.400	0	0-0	0	5.41	6.46

Aaron Bates

Bats: R **Throws:** R **Pos:** 1B-5; PR-2   **Ht:** 6'4" **Wt:** 232 **Born:** 3/10/1984 **Age:** 26

Year	Team	Lg	G	AB	H	2B	3B	HR	(Hm	Rd)	TB	R	RBI	RC	TBB	IBB	SO	HBP	SH	SF	SB	CS	SB%	GDP	Avg	OBP	Slg
2006	Lowell	A-	27	100	36	8	0	3	(-	-)	53	17	14	23	9	0	21	6	0	2	2	1	.67	1	.360	.436	.530
2006	Grnville	A	43	152	41	7	0	4	(-	-)	60	13	16	22	17	0	26	3	0	2	0	0	-	3	.270	.351	.395
2007	Lancst	A+	98	373	124	21	2	24	(-	-)	221	89	88	100	69	1	83	19	0	4	0	1	.00	9	.332	.456	.592
2007	Portlnd	AA	27	91	18	9	0	4	(-	-)	39	16	13	14	17	0	29	4	0	0	0	0	-	2	.198	.348	.429
2008	Portlnd	AA	123	454	126	29	2	11	(-	-)	192	61	68	75	50	2	112	17	0	5	0	0	-	13	.278	.367	.423
2009	Portlnd	AA	52	206	70	13	0	7	(-	-)	104	41	39	42	17	0	49	7	0	2	1	0	1.00	4	.340	.405	.505
2009	Pwtckt	AAA	76	272	58	10	0	5	(-	-)	83	28	18	25	22	1	59	6	0	2	0	0	-	12	.213	.285	.305
2009	Bos	AL	5	11	4	2	0	0	(0	0)	6	2	2	2	1	0	4	0	0	0	0	0	-	0	.364	.417	.545

Miguel Batista

Pitches: R **Bats:** R **Pos:** RP-56   **Ht:** 6'1" **Wt:** 208 **Born:** 2/19/1971 **Age:** 39

Year	Team	Lg	G	GS	CG	GF	IP	BFP	H	R	ER	HR	SH	SF	HB	TBB	IBB	SO	WP	Bk	W	L	Pct	Sh	Sv-Op	Hld	ERC	ERA
1992	Pit	NL	1	0	0	1	2.0	13	4	2	2	1	0	0	0	3	0	1	0	0	0	0	-	0	0-0	0	20.26	9.00
1996	Fla	NL	9	0	0	4	11.1	49	9	8	7	0	3	0	0	7	2	6	1	0	0	0	-	0	0-0	0	2.77	5.56
1997	ChC	NL	11	6	0	2	36.1	168	36	24	23	4	4	4	1	24	2	27	2	0	0	5	.000	0	0-0	0	5.09	5.70
1998	Mon	NL	56	13	0	12	135.0	598	141	66	66	12	7	5	6	65	7	92	6	1	3	5	.375	0	0-3	3	4.70	3.80
1999	Mon	NL	39	17	2	3	134.2	606	146	88	73	10	8	11	7	58	2	95	6	0	8	7	.533	1	1-1	3	4.62	4.88
2000	2 Tms		18	9	0	2	65.1	310	85	68	62	19	1	2	2	37	2	37	4	0	2	7	.222	0	0-2	0	8.37	8.54
2001	Ari	NL	48	18	0	6	139.1	581	113	57	53	13	9	3	10	60	2	90	6	0	11	8	.579	0	0-0	4	3.43	3.36
2002	Ari	NL	36	29	1	2	184.2	790	172	99	88	12	5	8	6	70	3	112	9	2	8	9	.471	0	0-0	2	3.45	4.29
2003	Ari	NL	36	29	2	5	193.1	822	197	85	76	13	10	6	8	60	3	142	7	0	10	9	.526	1	0-0	0	3.77	3.54
2004	Tor	AL	38	31	2	7	198.2	867	206	115	106	22	7	6	3	96	1	104	12	0	10	13	.435	1	5-5	0	4.84	4.80
2005	Tor	AL	71	0	0	62	74.2	331	80	39	34	9	2	2	2	27	5	54	3	0	5	8	.385	0	31-39	0	4.39	4.10
2006	Ari	NL	34	33	3	0	206.1	910	231	116	105	18	12	5	6	84	5	110	14	1	11	8	.579	1	0-0	0	4.82	4.58
2007	Sea	AL	33	32	0	0	193.0	860	209	101	92	18	5	5	8	85	3	133	15	2	16	11	.593	0	0-0	0	4.81	4.29
2008	Sea	AL	44	20	0	9	115.0	556	135	89	80	19	3	11	6	79	6	73	5	0	4	14	.222	0	1-4	4	6.92	6.26
2009	Sea	AL	56	0	0	18	71.1	326	79	37	32	7	4	1	2	39	1	52	4	0	7	4	.636	0	1-5	14	5.37	4.04
00	Mon	NL	4	0	0	0	8.1	49	19	14	13	2	1	1	2	3	0	7	0	0	0	1	.000	0	0-2	0	14.73	14.04
00	KC	AL	14	9	0	2	57.0	261	66	54	49	17	0	1	0	34	2	30	4	0	2	6	.250	0	0-0	0	7.50	7.74
	Postseason		7	4	0	1	25.1	104	18	10	10	3	3	0	1	11	0	14	1	0	1	2	.333	0	0-0	0	2.94	3.55
	15 ML YEARS		530	237	10	133	1761.0	7787	1843	994	889	177	80	69	67	794	44	1128	94	6	95	108	.468	4	39-56	27	4.67	4.54

Denny Bautista

Pitches: R **Bats:** R **Pos:** RP-14   **Ht:** 6'5" **Wt:** 195 **Born:** 8/23/1980 **Age:** 29

Year	Team	Lg	G	GS	CG	GF	IP	BFP	H	R	ER	HR	SH	SF	HB	TBB	IBB	SO	WP	Bk	W	L	Pct	Sh	Sv-Op	Hld	ERC	ERA
2009	Indy*	AAA	36	0	0	13	48.0	233	54	29	26	2	2	4	3	34	1	58	2	0	2	3	.400	0	1- -	-	5.69	4.88
2004	2 Tms	AL	7	5	0	0	29.2	142	44	28	28	3	0	1	3	13	1	19	3	2	0	4	.000	0	0-0	0	7.76	8.49
2005	KC	AL	7	7	0	0	35.2	160	36	23	23	2	1	1	2	17	0	23	3	0	2	2	.500	0	0-0	0	4.27	5.80
2006	2 Tms		12	8	0	3	41.2	194	47	34	26	5	1	2	4	21	0	27	5	0	3	3	.500	0	0-0	0	5.75	5.62
2007	Col	NL	9	1	0	2	8.2	48	18	12	12	0	1	0	1	4	0	8	0	0	2	1	.667	0	0-0	2	10.84	12.46
2008	2 Tms		51	0	0	8	60.1	271	61	35	35	6	2	4	2	42	2	44	4	0	4	4	.500	0	0-1	10	5.58	5.22
2009	Pit	NL	14	0	0	4	13.2	61	15	8	8	1	1	3	1	7	0	15	3	0	1	1	.500	0	0-1	1	5.32	5.27
04	Bal	AL	2	0	0	0	2.0	15	6	8	8	1	0	1	1	2	0	1	1	0	0	0	-	0	0-0	0	28.67	36.00
04	KC	AL	5	5	0	0	27.2	127	38	20	20	2	0	0	2	11	1	18	2	2	0	4	.000	0	0-0	0	6.50	6.51
06	KC	AL	8	7	0	0	35.0	161	38	24	22	5	1	2	4	17	0	22	5	0	0	2	.000	0	0-0	0	5.70	5.66
06	Col	NL	4	1	0	3	6.2	33	9	10	4	0	0	0	0	4	0	5	0	0	1	0	.000	0	0-0	0	5.98	5.40
08	Det	AL	16	0	0	3	19.0	83	15	7	7	1	1	2	1	14	0	10	1	0	0	1	.000	0	0-0	3	4.42	3.32
08	Pit	NL	35	0	0	5	41.1	188	46	28	28	5	1	3	0	28	2	34	3	0	4	3	.571	0	0-1	7	6.14	6.10
	6 ML YEARS		100	21	0	17	189.2	876	221	140	132	17	6	11	13	104	3	136	18	2	9	15	.375	0	0-2	13	5.89	6.26

Jose Bautista

Bats: R Throws: R Pos: LF-42; RF-36; 3B-26; PH-8; CF-6; PR-4; DH-2   Ht: 6'0" Wt: 195 Born: 10/19/1980 Age: 29

Year	Team	Lg	G	AB	H	2B	3B	HR	(Hm	Rd)	TB	R	RBI	RC	TBB	IBB	SO	HBP	SH	SF	SB	CS	SB%	GDP	Avg	OBP	Slg
2004	4 Tms		64	88	18	3	0	0	(0	0)	21	6	2	2	7	0	40	0	1	0	0	1	.00	1	.205	.263	.239
2005	Pit	NL	11	28	4	1	0	0	(0	0)	5	3	1	0	3	0	7	0	0	0	1	0	1.00	2	.143	.226	.179
2006	Pit	NL	117	400	94	20	3	16	(11	5)	168	58	51	55	46	2	110	16	3	4	2	4	.33	12	.235	.335	.420
2007	Pit	NL	142	532	135	36	2	15	(8	7)	220	75	63	71	68	1	101	4	4	6	6	3	.67	16	.254	.339	.414
2008	2 Tms		128	370	88	17	0	15	(5	10)	150	45	54	43	40	5	91	2	8	4	1	1	.50	12	.238	.313	.405
2009	Tor	AL	113	336	79	13	3	13	(5	8)	137	54	40	42	56	1	85	4	6	2	4	0	1.00	9	.235	.349	.408
04	Bal	AL	16	11	3	0	0	0	(0	0)	3	3	0	1	1	0	3	0	0	0	0	0	-	0	.273	.333	.273
04	TB	AL	12	12	2	0	0	0	(0	0)	2	1	1	0	3	0	7	0	0	0	0	1	.00	0	.167	.333	.167
04	KC	AL	13	25	5	1	0	0	(0	0)	6	1	1	0	1	0	12	0	0	0	0	0	-	0	.200	.231	.240
04	Pit	NL	23	40	8	2	0	0	(0	0)	10	1	0	1	2	0	18	0	1	0	0	0	-	1	.200	.238	.250
08	Pit	NL	107	314	76	15	0	12	(3	9)	127	38	44	39	38	4	77	2	6	3	1	1	.50	10	.242	.325	.404
08	Tor	AL	21	56	12	2	0	3	(2	1)	23	7	10	4	2	1	14	0	2	1	0	0	-	2	.214	.237	.411
6 ML YEARS			575	1754	418	90	8	59	(29	30)	701	241	211	213	220	9	434	26	22	16	14	9	.61	52	.238	.329	.400

Jason Bay

Bats: R Throws: R Pos: LF-150; DH-1   Ht: 6'2" Wt: 205 Born: 9/20/1978 Age: 31

Year	Team	Lg	G	AB	H	2B	3B	HR	(Hm	Rd)	TB	R	RBI	RC	TBB	IBB	SO	HBP	SH	SF	SB	CS	SB%	GDP	Avg	OBP	Slg
2003	2 Tms	NL	30	87	25	7	1	4	(2	2)	46	15	14	19	19	0	29	1	0	0	3	1	.75	0	.287	.421	.529
2004	Pit	NL	120	411	116	24	4	26	(15	11)	226	61	82	75	41	2	129	10	5	5	4	6	.40	9	.282	.358	.550
2005	Pit	NL	162	599	183	44	6	32	(9	23)	335	110	101	128	95	9	142	6	0	7	21	1	.95	12	.306	.402	.559
2006	Pit	NL	159	570	163	29	3	35	(13	22)	303	101	109	103	102	9	156	8	0	9	11	2	.85	15	.286	.396	.532
2007	Pit	NL	145	538	133	25	2	21	(7	14)	225	78	84	74	59	3	141	9	0	8	4	1	.80	8	.247	.327	.418
2008	2 Tms		155	577	165	35	4	31	(18	13)	301	111	101	104	81	4	137	4	0	8	10	0	1.00	7	.286	.373	.522
2009	Bos	AL	151	531	142	29	3	36	(15	21)	285	103	119	122	94	4	162	5	0	4	13	3	.81	9	.267	.384	.537
03	SD	NL	3	8	2	1	0	1	(0	1)	6	2	2	2	1	0	1	1	0	0	0	0	-	0	.250	.400	.750
03	Pit	NL	27	79	23	6	1	3	(2	1)	40	13	12	17	18	0	28	0	0	0	3	1	.75	0	.291	.423	.506
08	Pit	NL	106	393	111	23	2	22	(15	7)	204	72	64	73	59	2	86	2	0	5	7	0	1.00	3	.282	.375	.519
08	Bos	AL	49	184	54	12	2	9	(3	6)	97	39	37	31	22	2	51	2	0	3	3	0	1.00	4	.293	.370	.527
Postseason			11	41	14	3	0	3	(0	3)	26	6	9	10	9	1	12	1	0	0	0	0	-	0	.341	.471	.634
7 ML YEARS			922	3313	927	193	23	185	(79	106)	1721	579	610	625	491	31	896	47	5	41	66	14	.83	60	.280	.376	.519

Yorman Bazardo

Pitches: R Bats: R Pos: SP-6; RP-4   Ht: 6'2" Wt: 220 Born: 7/11/1984 Age: 25

Year	Team	Lg	G	GS	CG	GF	IP	BFP	H	R	ER	HR	SH	SF	HB	TBB	IBB	SO	WP	Bk	W	L	Pct	Sh	Sv-Op	Hld	ERC	ERA
2009	RdRck*	AAA	23	20	3	0	135.0	542	121	61	48	15	8	0	6	32	0	80	4	1	9	6	.600	1	0--	-	3.22	3.20
2005	Fla	NL	1	0	0	0	1.2	12	5	5	4	0	0	0	0	2	0	2	1	0	0	0	-	0	0-0	0	20.56	21.60
2007	Det	AL	11	2	0	6	23.2	96	19	7	6	2	0	1	3	5	0	15	1	0	2	1	.667	0	0-0	1	2.71	2.28
2008	Det	AL	3	0	0	3	3.0	20	7	8	8	0	0	1	0	5	0	3	0	0	0	0	-	0	0-0	0	17.66	24.00
2009	Hou	NL	10	6	0	3	32.0	154	37	31	28	2	4	2	1	22	0	17	0	1	1	3	.250	0	0-0	0	5.92	7.88
4 ML YEARS			25	8	0	12	60.1	282	68	51	46	4	4	4	4	34	1	37	2	1	3	4	.429	0	0-0	1	5.41	6.86

Josh Beckett

Pitches: R Bats: R Pos: SP-32   Ht: 6'5" Wt: 222 Born: 5/15/1980 Age: 30

Year	Team	Lg	G	GS	CG	GF	IP	BFP	H	R	ER	HR	SH	SF	HB	TBB	IBB	SO	WP	Bk	W	L	Pct	Sh	Sv-Op	Hld	ERC	ERA
2001	Fla	NL	4	4	0	0	24.0	99	14	9	4	3	0	0	1	11	0	24	1	0	2	2	.500	0	0-0	0	2.36	1.50
2002	Fla	NL	23	21	0	0	107.2	454	93	56	49	13	5	3	1	44	2	113	5	0	6	7	.462	0	0-0	0	3.50	4.10
2003	Fla	NL	24	23	0	1	142.0	601	132	54	48	9	5	1	2	56	4	152	6	1	9	8	.529	1	0-0	0	3.44	3.04
2004	Fla	NL	26	26	1	0	156.2	654	137	72	66	16	9	3	6	54	3	152	5	0	9	9	.500	1	0-0	0	3.32	3.79
2005	Fla	NL	29	29	2	0	178.2	729	153	75	67	14	8	2	7	58	2	166	5	0	15	8	.652	1	0-0	0	3.06	3.38
2006	Bos	AL	33	33	0	0	204.2	869	191	120	114	36	2	3	10	74	1	158	11	1	16	11	.593	0	0-0	0	4.28	5.01
2007	Bos	AL	30	30	1	0	200.2	822	189	76	73	17	3	2	5	40	0	194	3	0	20	7	.741	0	0-0	0	2.99	3.27
2008	Bos	AL	27	27	1	0	174.1	725	173	80	78	18	4	3	9	34	1	172	5	0	12	10	.545	0	0-0	0	3.45	4.03
2009	Bos	AL	32	32	4	0	212.1	883	198	99	91	25	5	5	7	55	1	199	3	1	17	6	.739	2	0-0	0	3.39	3.86
Postseason			13	12	3	0	87.0	339	62	28	28	11	2	0	3	20	1	96	3	0	7	2	.778	3	0-0	0	2.25	2.90
9 ML YEARS			228	225	9	1	1401.0	5836	1280	641	590	151	41	22	48	426	14	1330	44	3	106	68	.609	4	0-0	0	3.41	3.79

Gordon Beckham

Bats: R Throws: R Pos: 3B-102; PR-1   Ht: 6'0" Wt: 190 Born: 9/16/1986 Age: 23

Year	Team	Lg	G	AB	H	2B	3B	HR	(Hm	Rd)	TB	R	RBI	RC	TBB	IBB	SO	HBP	SH	SF	SB	CS	SB%	GDP	Avg	OBP	Slg
2008	Knapol	A	14	58	18	2	0	3	(-	-)	29	11	8	10	5	0	7	0	0	0	0	1	.00	1	.310	.365	.500
2009	Brham	AA	38	147	44	17	0	4	(-	-)	73	23	22	27	14	1	24	2	2	1	1	0	1.00	4	.299	.366	.497
2009	Charltt	AAA	7	28	13	6	0	0	(-	-)	19	6	3	7	0	0	2	0	1	1	1	0	1.00	0	.464	.448	.679
2009	CWS	AL	103	378	102	28	1	14	(4	10)	174	58	63	60	41	0	65	6	1	4	7	4	.64	10	.270	.347	.460

Erik Bedard

Pitches: L **Bats:** L **Pos:** SP-15　　　　**Ht:** 6'1" **Wt:** 200 **Born:** 3/5/1979 **Age:** 31

Year	Team	Lg	G	GS	CG	GF	IP	BFP	H	R	ER	HR	SH	SF	HB	TBB	IBB	SO	WP	Bk	W	L	Pct	Sh	Sv-Op	Hld	ERC	ERA
2002	Bal	AL	2	0	0	0	0.2	4	2	1	1	0	0	0	0	0	0	1	0	0	0	0	-	0	0-0	0	14.52	13.50
2004	Bal	AL	27	26	0	0	137.1	633	149	83	70	13	0	4	7	71	1	121	7	2	6	10	.375	0	0-0	0	5.11	4.59
2005	Bal	AL	24	24	0	0	141.2	606	139	66	63	10	3	6	5	57	1	125	4	1	6	8	.429	0	0-0	0	3.95	4.00
2006	Bal	AL	33	33	0	0	196.1	844	196	92	82	16	4	4	5	69	0	171	6	0	15	11	.577	0	0-0	0	3.83	3.76
2007	Bal	AL	28	28	1	0	182.0	733	141	66	64	19	2	4	5	57	0	221	3	0	13	5	.722	1	0-0	0	**2.71**	3.16
2008	Sea	AL	15	15	0	0	81.0	347	70	34	33	9	1	2	4	37	0	72	3	0	6	4	.600	0	0-0	0	3.82	3.67
2009	Sea	AL	15	15	0	0	83.0	348	65	29	26	8	2	1	4	34	0	90	2	0	5	3	.625	0	0-0	0	3.08	2.82
	7 ML YEARS		144	141	1	0	822.0	3515	762	375	339	75	14	21	30	325	2	801	25	3	51	41	.554	1	0-0	0	3.73	3.71

Joe Beimel

Pitches: L **Bats:** L **Pos:** RP-71　　　　**Ht:** 6'3" **Wt:** 215 **Born:** 4/19/1977 **Age:** 33

Year	Team	Lg	G	GS	CG	GF	IP	BFP	H	R	ER	HR	SH	SF	HB	TBB	IBB	SO	WP	Bk	W	L	Pct	Sh	Sv-Op	Hld	ERC	ERA
2009	Ptomc*	A+	1	1	0	0	1.0	9	7	5	5	0	0	0	0	0	0	0	0	0	0	0	-	0	0- -	-	54.17	45.00
2001	Pit	NL	42	15	0	9	115.1	511	131	72	67	12	3	1	6	49	4	58	3	0	7	11	.389	0	0-0	0	5.24	5.23
2002	Pit	NL	53	8	0	8	85.1	389	88	49	44	9	7	3	4	45	12	53	2	0	2	5	.286	0	0-1	5	4.68	4.64
2003	Pit	NL	69	0	0	11	62.1	276	69	35	35	7	3	5	4	33	6	42	0	1	1	3	.250	0	0-5	12	5.62	5.05
2004	Min	AL	3	0	0	0	1.2	15	8	8	8	1	0	0	0	2	0	2	0	0	0	0	-	0	0-0	0	44.44	43.20
2005	TB	AL	7	0	0	3	11.0	51	15	4	4	1	0	0	0	4	1	3	1	0	0	0	-	0	0-0	0	5.80	3.27
2006	LAD	NL	62	0	0	10	70.0	295	70	26	23	7	4	3	0	21	3	30	6	1	2	1	.667	0	2-2	10	3.62	2.96
2007	LAD	NL	83	0	0	10	67.1	281	63	30	29	1	5	2	1	24	6	39	3	2	4	2	.667	0	1-1	16	2.93	3.88
2008	LAD	NL	71	0	0	10	49.0	214	50	11	11	0	1	4	3	21	4	32	1	1	5	1	.833	0	0-0	12	3.70	2.02
2009	2 Tms	NL	71	0	0	26	55.1	240	57	24	22	5	4	6	1	19	5	35	4	1	1	6	.143	0	1-6	13	3.84	3.58
09	Was	NL	45	0	0	19	39.2	172	38	17	15	3	2	4	1	15	4	24	2	1	1	5	.167	0	1-5	10	3.46	3.40
09	Col	NL	26	0	0	7	15.2	68	19	7	7	2	2	2	0	4	1	11	2	0	0	1	.000	0	0-1	3	4.84	4.02
	Postseason		3	0	0	0	0.2	4	0	0	0	0	0	0	0	2	0	0	0	0	0	0	-	0	0-0	0	7.00	0.00
	9 ML YEARS		461	23	0	87	517.1	2272	551	259	243	43	27	24	19	218	41	294	20	6	22	29	.431	0	4-15	68	4.45	4.23

Ronald Belisario

Pitches: R **Bats:** R **Pos:** RP-69　　　　**Ht:** 6'3" **Wt:** 237 **Born:** 12/31/1982 **Age:** 27

Year	Team	Lg	G	GS	CG	GF	IP	BFP	H	R	ER	HR	SH	SF	HB	TBB	IBB	SO	WP	Bk	W	L	Pct	Sh	Sv-Op	Hld	ERC	ERA
2001	Mrlns	R	13	10	1	0	73.0	309	62	29	19	4	4	3	11	20	0	54	8	1	4	6	.400	1	0- -	-	3.02	2.34
2002	Kane	A	23	22	1	0	140.1	619	131	67	54	4	5	5	21	56	0	98	13	4	6	5	.545	0	0- -	-	3.73	3.46
2003	Grnsbr	A	10	8	1	1	48.0	207	41	23	16	3	1	1	8	18	0	45	2	0	5	1	.833	0	0- -	-	3.55	3.00
2003	Jupiter	A+	6	4	0	2	18.1	82	20	10	10	0	1	0	1	8	0	13	0	0	1	2	.333	0	0- -	-	4.19	4.91
2004	Carlina	AA	15	15	0	0	73.0	331	75	52	45	10	9	4	6	43	3	58	7	2	3	5	.375	0	0- -	-	5.63	5.55
2004	Mrlns	R	2	0	0	0	2.0	6	1	0	0	0	0	0	0	0	0	2	0	0	0	0	-	0	0- -	-	0.63	0.00
2004	Jupiter	A+	6	0	0	1	8.2	34	2	1	0	0	0	0	1	6	0	7	0	0	1	1	.500	0	1- -	-	1.27	0.00
2007	Lynbrg	A+	19	0	0	9	34.1	153	38	18	17	5	3	1	1	13	0	19	2	0	0	3	.000	0	4- -	-	5.01	4.46
2007	Altna	AA	18	0	0	6	24.2	114	23	11	9	4	1	2	3	14	0	21	4	0	1	0	1.000	0	0- -	-	5.20	3.28
2008	Altna	AA	38	0	0	21	57.0	254	63	31	30	5	4	2	3	25	3	36	2	0	4	4	.500	0	9- -	-	4.90	4.74
2009	InldEm	A+	2	2	0	0	2.0	9	2	0	0	0	0	0	0	1	0	3	0	0	0	0	-	0	0- -	-	3.63	0.00
2009	LAD	NL	69	0	0	13	70.2	299	52	21	16	4	3	2	6	29	7	64	4	0	4	3	.571	0	0-7	12	2.54	2.04

Matt Belisle

Pitches: R **Bats:** R **Pos:** RP-24　　　　**Ht:** 6'4" **Wt:** 231 **Born:** 6/6/1980 **Age:** 30

Year	Team	Lg	G	GS	CG	GF	IP	BFP	H	R	ER	HR	SH	SF	HB	TBB	IBB	SO	WP	Bk	W	L	Pct	Sh	Sv-Op	Hld	ERC	ERA
2009	ColSpr*	AAA	33	4	0	17	58.1	237	58	20	20	2	0	2	0	15	1	47	1	1	1	1	.500	0	9- -	-	3.12	3.09
2003	Cin	NL	6	0	0	2	8.2	39	10	5	5	1	2	1	1	2	0	6	0	0	1	1	.500	0	0-1	0	4.73	5.19
2005	Cin	NL	60	5	0	17	85.2	382	101	49	42	11	4	2	6	26	6	59	3	0	4	8	.333	0	1-4	8	5.08	4.41
2006	Cin	NL	30	2	0	5	40.0	180	43	18	16	5	1	2	3	19	1	26	3	0	2	0	1.000	0	0-1	0	5.29	3.60
2007	Cin	NL	30	30	1	0	177.2	771	212	111	105	26	7	9	7	43	4	125	6	1	8	9	.471	0	0-0	0	5.05	5.32
2008	Cin	NL	6	6	0	0	29.2	142	47	24	24	4	1	2	0	6	0	14	2	0	1	4	.200	0	0-0	0	6.87	7.28
2009	Col	NL	24	0	0	6	31.0	133	35	21	19	6	0	2	1	5	1	22	1	0	3	1	.750	0	0-0	1	4.50	5.52
	6 ML YEARS		156	43	1	30	372.2	1647	448	231	211	53	15	18	18	101	12	252	15	1	19	23	.452	0	1-6	9	5.17	5.10

Heath Bell

Pitches: R **Bats:** R **Pos:** RP-68　　　　**Ht:** 6'3" **Wt:** 250 **Born:** 9/29/1977 **Age:** 32

Year	Team	Lg	G	GS	CG	GF	IP	BFP	H	R	ER	HR	SH	SF	HB	TBB	IBB	SO	WP	Bk	W	L	Pct	Sh	Sv-Op	Hld	ERC	ERA
2004	NYM	NL	17	0	0	2	24.1	94	22	9	9	5	1	0	0	6	0	27	0	0	0	2	.000	0	0-1	1	3.86	3.33
2005	NYM	NL	42	0	0	12	46.2	206	56	30	29	3	4	0	1	13	3	43	0	1	1	3	.250	0	0-0	4	4.42	5.59
2006	NYM	NL	22	0	0	6	37.0	166	51	25	21	6	1	0	0	11	2	35	1	0	0	0	-	0	0-0	0	6.40	5.11
2007	SD	NL	81	0	0	16	93.2	363	60	21	21	3	4	1	2	30	1	102	4	0	6	4	.600	0	2-6	34	1.67	2.02
2008	SD	NL	74	0	0	8	78.0	324	66	31	31	5	3	2	3	28	4	71	2	0	6	6	.500	0	0-7	23	2.93	3.58
2009	SD	NL	68	0	0	59	69.2	278	54	21	21	3	0	0	0	24	1	79	4	0	6	4	.600	0	**42-48**	0	2.36	2.71
	6 ML YEARS		304	0	0	103	349.1	1431	309	137	132	25	13	3	6	112	11	357	11	1	19	19	.500	0	44-62	62	3.02	3.40

Trevor Bell

Pitches: R **Bats:** L **Pos:** SP-4; RP-4   **Ht:** 6'2" **Wt:** 185 **Born:** 10/12/1986 **Age:** 23

				HOW MUCH HE PITCHED				WHAT HE GAVE UP										THE RESULTS							
Year	Team	Lg	G	GS	CG	GF	IP	BFP	H	R	ER	HR	SH	SF	HB	TBB	IBB	SO	WP	Bk	W	L	Pct	Sh	Sv-Op	Hld	ERC	ERA
2005	Angels	R	4	4	0	0	8.0	38	10	4	4	0	1	1	1	3	0	7	1	0	0	0	-	0	0--	-	5.00	4.50
2006	Orem	R+	16	16	0	0	82.1	337	82	35	32	8	1	2	5	15	0	53	4	1	4	2	.667	0	0--	-	3.49	3.50
2007	CRpds	A	21	21	0	0	115.1	499	136	64	53	8	1	7	3	23	0	90	6	1	8	4	.667	0	0--	-	4.15	4.14
2008	RCuca	A+	3	2	1	0	100.1	441	106	60	47	8	9	2	4	39	2	80	5	2	1	0	1.000	0	0--	-	4.32	4.22
2008	CRpds	A	3	2	1	0	17.0	61	13	4	4	0	0	1	0	4	0	13	0	2	1	0	1.000	0	0--	-	1.91	2.12
2009	Ark	AA	11	11	0	0	68.2	281	54	24	17	1	3	1	2	20	0	51	2	0	4	3	.571	0	0--	-	2.10	2.23
2009	Salt Lk	AAA	11	11	2	0	71.1	286	67	27	25	5	0	1	2	15	1	38	0	0	3	4	.429	2	0--	-	3.00	3.15
2009	LAA	AL	8	4	0	1	20.1	110	40	25	22	3	0	2	0	11	2	14	1	0	1	2	.333	0	0-0	0	11.15	9.74

Ronnie Belliard

Bats: R **Throws:** R **Pos:** 2B-60; PH-39; 1B-15; 3B-12; PR-1   **Ht:** 5'10" **Wt:** 212 **Born:** 4/7/1975 **Age:** 35

						BATTING															BASERUNNING				AVERAGES		
Year	Team	Lg	G	AB	H	2B	3B	HR	(Hm	Rd)	TB	R	RBI	RC	TBB	IBB	SO	HBP	SH	SF		SB	CS	SB%	GDP	Avg	OBP	Slg
1998	Mil	NL	8	5	1	0	0	0	(0	0)	1	1	0	0	0	0	0	0	0	0		0	0	-	0	.200	.200	.200
1999	Mil	NL	124	457	135	29	4	8	(5	3)	196	60	58	72	64	0	59	0	6	4		4	5	.44	16	.295	.379	.429
2000	Mil	NL	152	571	150	30	9	8	(4	4)	222	83	54	81	82	4	84	3	4	7		7	5	.58	12	.263	.354	.389
2001	Mil	NL	101	364	96	30	3	11	(7	4)	165	69	36	56	35	2	65	5	4	2		5	2	.71	5	.264	.335	.453
2002	Mil	NL	104	289	61	13	0	3	(0	3)	83	30	26	15	18	0	46	1	6	3		2	3	.40	9	.211	.257	.287
2003	Col	NL	116	447	124	31	2	8	(6	2)	183	73	50	71	49	0	71	2	6	1		7	2	.78	7	.277	.351	.409
2004	Cle	AL	152	599	169	48	1	12	(4	8)	255	78	70	87	60	5	98	2	0	2		3	2	.60	18	.282	.348	.426
2005	Cle	AL	145	536	152	36	1	17	(7	10)	241	71	78	71	35	0	72	1	8	7		2	2	.50	17	.284	.325	.450
2006	2 Tms		147	544	148	30	1	13	(5	8)	219	63	67	62	36	2	81	5	3	2		2	3	.40	17	.272	.322	.403
2007	Was	NL	147	511	148	35	1	11	(5	6)	218	57	58	64	34	1	72	1	6	5		3	0	1.00	12	.290	.332	.427
2008	Was	NL	96	296	85	22	0	11	(7	4)	140	37	40	53	37	1	58	3	1	0		3	2	.60	6	.287	.372	.473
2009	2 Tms		110	264	73	14	1	10	(6	5)	119	39	39	34	20	0	56	0	1	2		3	0	1.00	10	.277	.326	.451
06	Cle	AL	93	350	102	21	0	8	(3	5)	147	43	44	47	21	0	45	4	2	2		2	0	1.00	8	.291	.337	.420
06	Stl	NL	54	194	46	9	1	5	(2	3)	72	20	23	15	15	2	36	1	1	0		0	3	.00	9	.237	.295	.371
09	Was	NL	86	187	46	7	1	5	(2	3)	70	26	22	18	14	0	40	0	1	2		2	0	1.00	7	.246	.296	.374
09	LAD	NL	24	77	27	7	0	5	(3	2)	49	13	17	16	6	0	16	0	0	0		1	0	1.00	3	.351	.398	.636
	Postseason		14	50	12	1	0	0	(0	0)	13	2	4	5	3	1	6	1	1	0		1	0	1.00	1	.240	.296	.260
	12 ML YEARS		1402	4883	1342	318	23	112	(55	57)	2042	661	582	666	470	15	762	23	45	35		41	26	.61	129	.275	.339	.418

Edwin Bellorin

Bats: R **Throws:** R **Pos:** C-2   **Ht:** 5'9" **Wt:** 225 **Born:** 2/21/1982 **Age:** 28

						BATTING															BASERUNNING				AVERAGES		
Year	Team	Lg	G	AB	H	2B	3B	HR	(Hm	Rd)	TB	R	RBI	RC	TBB	IBB	SO	HBP	SH	SF		SB	CS	SB%	GDP	Avg	OBP	Slg
2009	ColSpr*	AAA	57	202	56	10	1	1	(-	-)	71	15	28	22	9	0	18	1	2	2		0	2	.00	11	.277	.308	.351
2007	Col	NL	3	2	0	0	0	0	(0	0)	0	0	0	0	0	0	0	0	0	0		0	0	-	0	.000	.000	.000
2008	Col	NL	3	3	1	0	0	0	(0	0)	1	0	0	0	0	0	0	0	0	0		0	0	-	0	.333	.333	.333
2009	Col	NL	2	8	2	0	0	0	(0	0)	2	1	0	2	1	1	1	0	0	0		0	0	-	0	.250	.333	.250
	3 ML YEARS		8	13	3	0	0	0	(0	0)	3	1	0	2	1	1	1	0	0	0		0	0	-	1	.231	.286	.231

Carlos Beltran

Bats: B **Throws:** R **Pos:** CF-77; DH-3; PH-1   **Ht:** 6'1" **Wt:** 199 **Born:** 4/24/1977 **Age:** 33

						BATTING															BASERUNNING				AVERAGES		
Year	Team	Lg	G	AB	H	2B	3B	HR	(Hm	Rd)	TB	R	RBI	RC	TBB	IBB	SO	HBP	SH	SF		SB	CS	SB%	GDP	Avg	OBP	Slg
1998	KC	AL	14	58	16	5	3	0	(0	0)	27	12	7	9	3	0	12	1	0	1		3	0	1.00	2	.276	.317	.466
1999	KC	AL	156	663	194	27	7	22	(12	10)	301	112	108	100	46	2	123	4	0	10		27	8	.77	17	.293	.337	.454
2000	KC	AL	98	372	92	15	4	7	(4	3)	136	49	44	43	35	2	69	0	2	4		13	0	1.00	12	.247	.309	.366
2001	KC	AL	155	617	189	32	12	24	(7	17)	317	106	101	118	52	2	120	5	1	5		31	1	.97	7	.306	.362	.514
2002	KC	AL	162	637	174	44	7	29	(19	10)	319	114	105	117	71	1	135	4	3	7		35	7	.83	12	.273	.346	.501
2003	KC	AL	141	521	160	14	10	26	(10	16)	272	102	100	117	72	4	81	2	0	7		41	4	.91	8	.307	.389	.522
2004	2 Tms		159	599	160	36	9	38	(15	23)	328	121	104	124	92	10	101	3	3	7		42	3	.93	8	.267	.367	.548
2005	NYM	NL	151	582	155	34	2	16	(6	10)	241	83	78	88	56	5	96	2	4	6		17	6	.74	9	.266	.330	.414
2006	NYM	NL	140	510	140	38	1	41	(15	26)	303	127	116	121	95	6	99	4	1	7		18	3	.86	6	.275	.388	.594
2007	NYM	NL	144	554	153	33	3	33	(11	22)	291	93	112	97	69	10	111	2	1	10		23	2	.92	8	.276	.353	.525
2008	NYM	NL	161	606	172	40	5	27	(14	13)	303	116	112	116	92	13	96	1	1	6		25	3	.89	11	.284	.376	.500
2009	NYM	NL	81	308	100	22	1	10	(3	7)	154	50	48	54	47	10	43	1	0	1		11	1	.92	9	.325	.415	.500
04	KC	AL	69	266	74	19	2	15	(8	7)	142	51	51	57	37	7	44	2	1	3		14	3	.82	4	.278	.367	.534
04	Hou	NL	90	333	86	17	7	23	(7	16)	186	70	53	67	55	3	57	1	2	4		28	0	1.00	4	.258	.368	.559
	Postseason		22	82	30	4	0	11	(4	7)	67	31	19	26	18	1	13	1	0	0		8	0	1.00	1	.366	.485	.817
	12 ML YEARS		1562	6027	1705	340	64	273	(116	157)	2992	1085	1035	1104	730	65	1086	33	16	71		286	38	.88	109	.283	.360	.496

Adrian Beltre

Bats: R **Throws:** R **Pos:** 3B-111; DH-1   **Ht:** 5'11" **Wt:** 222 **Born:** 4/7/1979 **Age:** 31

						BATTING															BASERUNNING				AVERAGES		
Year	Team	Lg	G	AB	H	2B	3B	HR	(Hm	Rd)	TB	R	RBI	RC	TBB	IBB	SO	HBP	SH	SF		SB	CS	SB%	GDP	Avg	OBP	Slg
1998	LAD	NL	77	195	42	9	0	7	(5	2)	72	18	22	20	14	0	37	3	2	0		3	1	.75	4	.215	.278	.369
1999	LAD	NL	152	538	148	27	5	15	(6	9)	230	84	67	84	61	12	105	6	4	5		18	7	.72	4	.275	.352	.428
2000	LAD	NL	138	510	148	30	2	20	(7	13)	242	71	85	85	56	2	80	2	3	4		12	5	.71	13	.290	.360	.475
2001	LAD	NL	126	475	126	22	4	13	(4	9)	195	59	60	60	28	1	82	5	2	5		13	4	.76	9	.265	.310	.453
2002	LAD	NL	159	587	151	26	5	21	(7	14)	250	70	75	74	37	4	96	4	1	6		7	5	.58	17	.257	.303	.426
2003	LAD	NL	158	559	134	30	2	23	(13	10)	237	50	80	66	37	4	103	5	1	6		2	2	.50	13	.240	.290	.424
2004	LAD	NL	156	598	200	32	0	48	(23	25)	376	104	121	120	53	9	87	2	0	4		7	2	.78	15	.334	.388	.629

							BATTING																	BASERUNNING				AVERAGES		
Year	Team	Lg	G	AB	H	2B	3B	HR	(Hm	Rd)	TB	R	RBI	RC	TBB	IBB	SO	HBP	SH	SF		SB	CS	SB%	GDP	Avg	OBP	Slg
2005	Sea	AL	156	603	154	36	1	19	(7	12)	249	69	87	75	38	6	108	5	0	4		3	1	.75	15	.255	.303	.413
2006	Sea	AL	156	620	166	39	4	25	(16	9)	288	88	89	85	47	4	118	10	1	3		11	5	.69	15	.268	.328	.465
2007	Sea	AL	149	595	164	41	2	26	(11	15)	287	87	99	79	38	2	104	2	0	4		14	2	.88	18	.276	.319	.482
2008	Sea	AL	143	556	148	29	1	25	(10	15)	254	74	77	71	50	10	90	2	0	4		8	2	.80	11	.266	.327	.457
2009	Sea	AL	111	449	119	27	0	8	(4	4)	170	54	44	48	19	1	74	7	0	2		13	2	.87	19	.265	.304	.379
	Postseason		4	15	4	0	0	0	(0	0)	4	1	1	1	0	0	3	0	0	1		0	0	-	0	.267	.250	.267
	12 ML YEARS		1681	6285	1700	348	26	250	(113	137)	2850	828	906	867	478	55	1084	53	14	47		111	38	.74	153	.270	.325	.453

Jeff Bennett

Pitches: R Bats: R Pos: RP-44

Ht: 6'3" Wt: 200 Born: 6/10/1980 Age: 30

			HOW MUCH HE PITCHED						WHAT HE GAVE UP											THE RESULTS							
Year	Team	Lg	G	GS	CG	GF	IP	BFP	H	R	ER	HR	SH	SF	HB	TBB	IBB	SO	WP	Bk	W	L	Pct	Sh	Sv-Op	Hld	ERC	ERA
2009	Gwnntt*	AAA	2	2	0	0	2.0	12	5	4	4	0	0	1	0	1	0	0	1	0	0	1	.000	0	0- -	-	13.27	18.00
2009	Drham*	AAA	3	3	0	0	11.1	52	14	6	6	1	2	0	5	0	8	0	0	1	0	1.000	0	0- -	-	5.50	4.76
2004	Mil	NL	60	0	0	20	71.1	316	78	43	38	12	2	5	2	26	2	45	6	0	1	5	.167	0	0-1	8	4.98	4.79
2007	Atl	NL	3	2	0	0	13.0	57	14	5	5	3	1	1	0	3	1	14	1	0	2	1	.667	0	0-0	0	4.41	3.46
2008	Atl	NL	72	4	0	12	97.1	419	86	44	40	5	6	5	7	47	6	68	5	0	3	7	.300	0	3-4	15	3.62	3.70
2009	2 Tms		44	0	0	14	46.2	233	66	27	26	4	4	2	4	32	4	27	1	0	2	4	.333	0	0-0	2	8.00	5.01
09	Atl	NL	33	0	0	8	34.0	163	42	13	12	2	4	2	3	21	4	23	1	0	2	4	.333	0	0-0	2	6.19	3.18
09	TB	AL	11	0	0	6	12.2	70	24	14	14	2	0	0	1	11	0	4	0	0	0	0	-	0	0-0	0	13.48	9.95
	4 ML YEARS		179	6	0	46	228.1	1025	244	119	109	24	13	13	108	13	154	13	0	8	17	.320	0	3-5	25	4.94	4.30

Joaquin Benoit

Pitches: R Bats: R Pos: P

Ht: 6'3" Wt: 220 Born: 7/26/1977 Age: 32

			HOW MUCH HE PITCHED						WHAT HE GAVE UP											THE RESULTS							
Year	Team	Lg	G	GS	CG	GF	IP	BFP	H	R	ER	HR	SH	SF	HB	TBB	IBB	SO	WP	Bk	W	L	Pct	Sh	Sv-Op	Hld	ERC	ERA
2001	Tex	AL	1	1	0	0	5.0	26	8	6	6	3	0	1	0	3	0	4	0	0	0	0	-	0	0-0	0	13.11	10.80
2002	Tex	AL	17	13	0	2	84.2	405	91	51	50	6	4	3	5	58	2	59	7	0	4	5	.444	0	1-1	0	5.52	5.31
2003	Tex	AL	25	17	0	1	105.0	462	99	67	64	23	1	4	3	51	0	87	3	1	8	5	.615	0	0-0	0	5.03	5.49
2004	Tex	AL	28	15	0	4	103.0	456	113	67	65	19	2	10	4	31	0	95	3	0	3	5	.375	0	0-0	0	5.10	5.68
2005	Tex	AL	32	9	0	6	87.0	369	69	39	36	9	2	1	2	38	0	78	1	0	4	4	.500	0	0-0	5	3.15	3.72
2006	Tex	AL	56	0	0	7	79.2	347	68	49	43	5	0	3	3	38	4	85	3	0	1	1	.500	0	0-2	7	3.30	4.86
2007	Tex	AL	70	0	0	22	82.0	337	68	28	26	6	3	2	2	28	2	87	3	0	7	4	.636	0	6-13	19	2.83	2.85
2008	Tex	AL	44	0	0	8	45.0	209	40	28	25	6	2	0	0	35	2	43	3	0	3	2	.600	0	1-4	13	5.02	5.00
	8 ML YEARS		273	55	0	48	591.1	2611	556	335	315	77	14	24	23	282	10	538	23	1	30	26	.536	0	8-20	44	4.33	4.79

Kris Benson

Pitches: R Bats: R Pos: RP-6; SP-2

Ht: 6'4" Wt: 205 Born: 11/7/1974 Age: 35

			HOW MUCH HE PITCHED						WHAT HE GAVE UP											THE RESULTS							
Year	Team	Lg	G	GS	CG	GF	IP	BFP	H	R	ER	HR	SH	SF	HB	TBB	IBB	SO	WP	Bk	W	L	Pct	Sh	Sv-Op	Hld	ERC	ERA
2009	Frisco*	AA	1	1	0	0	5.0	21	5	3	3	1	0	0	1	1	0	4	0	0	0	1	.000	0	0- -	-	4.93	5.40
2009	Okla*	AAA	11	10	1	0	68.2	302	78	45	40	5	2	1	2	23	0	49	3	0	4	5	.444	0	0- -	-	4.51	5.24
1999	Pit	NL	31	31	2	0	196.2	840	184	105	89	16	6	7	6	83	5	139	2	1	11	14	.440	0	0-0	0	3.78	4.07
2000	Pit	NL	32	32	2	0	217.2	936	206	104	93	24	7	6	10	86	5	184	5	0	10	12	.455	1	0-0	0	3.97	3.85
2002	Pit	NL	25	25	0	0	130.1	576	152	76	68	18	5	3	5	50	8	79	3	1	9	6	.600	0	0-0	0	5.31	4.70
2003	Pit	NL	18	18	0	0	105.0	475	127	67	58	14	3	4	1	36	4	68	7	0	5	9	.357	0	0-0	0	5.20	4.97
2004	2 Tms		31	31	1	0	200.1	854	202	106	96	15	8	6	10	61	8	134	5	0	12	12	.500	1	0-0	0	3.71	4.31
2005	NYM	NL	28	28	0	0	174.1	737	171	86	80	24	5	3	4	49	5	95	4	0	10	8	.556	0	0-0	0	3.78	4.13
2006	Bal	AL	30	30	3	0	183.0	781	199	105	99	33	9	13	7	58	2	88	6	0	11	12	.478	0	0-0	0	5.06	4.82
2009	Tex	AL	8	2	0	2	22.1	114	33	23	21	6	0	2	3	12	0	11	0	0	1	1	.500	0	0-0	0	9.61	8.46
04	Pit	NL	20	20	0	0	132.1	564	137	69	62	7	7	4	6	44	5	83	2	0	8	8	.500	0	0-0	0	3.84	4.22
04	NYM	NL	11	11	1	0	68.0	290	65	37	34	8	1	2	4	17	3	51	3	0	4	4	.500	1	0-0	0	3.45	4.50
	8 ML YEARS		203	197	8	2	1229.2	5313	1274	672	603	150	43	44	44	435	37	798	32	2	69	74	.483	2	0-0	0	4.36	4.41

Justin Berg

Pitches: R Bats: R Pos: RP-11

Ht: 6'3" Wt: 230 Born: 6/7/1984 Age: 26

			HOW MUCH HE PITCHED						WHAT HE GAVE UP											THE RESULTS							
Year	Team	Lg	G	GS	CG	GF	IP	BFP	H	R	ER	HR	SH	SF	HB	TBB	IBB	SO	WP	Bk	W	L	Pct	Sh	Sv-Op	Hld	ERC	ERA
2004	Yanks	R	15	1	0	4	30.2	147	40	22	20	3	0	3	3	15	0	29	3	0	3	2	.600	0	1- -	-	6.63	5.87
2005	StIsInd	A-	15	9	0	2	58.2	238	48	26	23	3	2	0	4	20	0	52	0	2	6	2	.750	0	0- -	-	2.89	3.53
2005	Peoria	A	2	1	0	0	6.2	32	9	7	7	0	0	1	0	6	0	3	2	0	0	0	-	0	0- -	-	7.93	9.45
2006	Dytona	A+	24	24	0	0	115.0	525	126	67	56	4	4	4	10	53	0	82	19	0	7	7	.500	0	0- -	-	4.67	4.38
2007	Tenn	AA	27	26	0	0	140.0	629	157	88	76	4	9	1	14	69	3	69	15	0	7	7	.500	0	0- -	-	5.08	4.89
2008	Tenn	AA	5	5	0	0	28.1	127	29	14	11	1	1	1	4	11	0	10	1	0	0	3	.000	0	0- -	-	4.20	3.49
2008	Iowa	AAA	27	16	0	2	90.1	400	91	64	57	11	6	1	7	48	0	49	8	0	4	6	.400	0	0- -	-	5.23	5.68
2009	Iowa	AAA	37	0	0	8	55.2	238	41	17	15	2	3	0	6	29	2	35	4	0	6	2	.750	0	0- -	-	3.01	2.43
2009	ChC	NL	11	0	0	6	12.0	46	10	1	1	0	1	0	0	1	0	7	0	1	0	0	-	0	0-0	0	1.58	0.75

Brad Bergesen

Pitches: R **Bats:** L **Pos:** SP-19   **Ht:** 6'2" **Wt:** 215 **Born:** 9/25/1985 **Age:** 24

Year	Team	Lg	G	GS	CG	GF	IP	BFP	H	R	ER	HR	SH	SF	HB	TBB	IBB	SO	WP	Bk	W	L	Pct	Sh	Sv-Op	Hld	ERC	ERA
2004	Bluefld	R+	5	0	0	0	5.2	27	7	5	5	1	0	0	0	3	1	6	0	0	0	0	-	0	0--	-	6.14	7.94
2005	Abrdn	A	15	15	0	0	71.0	311	89	45	38	5	2	5	1	14	0	54	3	0	1	3	.250	0	0--	-	4.53	4.82
2006	Dlmrva	A	18	14	1	3	86.1	370	97	44	41	6	1	4	9	10	0	49	5	0	5	4	.556	0	0--	-	3.81	4.27
2007	Dlmrva	A	15	15	1	0	94.1	377	75	30	23	3	2	0	7	17	0	73	2	1	7	3	.700	0	0--	-	2.06	2.19
2007	Frdrck	A+	10	10	1	0	56.1	256	78	38	36	4	1	4	7	9	0	35	3	1	3	6	.333	0	0--	-	5.65	5.75
2008	Frdrck	A+	4	3	0	0	17.1	73	15	6	4	2	0	0	1	6	0	15	0	0	1	1	.500	0	0--	-	3.44	2.08
2008	Bowie	AA	24	23	3	0	148.0	603	143	59	53	11	3	4	3	27	0	72	5	0	15	6	.714	2	0--	-	2.99	3.22
2009	Norfolk	AAA	2	2	0	0	11.0	45	6	4	3	0	1	0	2	3	0	9	0	0	1	1	.500	0	0--	-	1.43	2.45
2009	Bal	AL	19	19	1	0	123.1	519	126	52	47	11	3	4	5	32	4	65	2	0	7	5	.583	0	0-0	0	3.70	3.43

Jason Bergmann

Pitches: R **Bats:** R **Pos:** RP-56   **Ht:** 6'3" **Wt:** 222 **Born:** 9/25/1981 **Age:** 28

Year	Team	Lg	G	GS	CG	GF	IP	BFP	H	R	ER	HR	SH	SF	HB	TBB	IBB	SO	WP	Bk	W	L	Pct	Sh	Sv-Op	Hld	ERC	ERA
2009	Syrcse*	AAA	19	0	0	7	23.1	94	18	3	3	1	0	0	1	8	0	15	2	1	1	1	.500	0	2--	-	2.50	1.16
2005	Was	NL	15	1	0	4	19.2	85	14	6	6	1	1	1	2	11	1	21	0	0	2	0	1.000	0	0-0	1	3.05	2.75
2006	Was	NL	29	6	0	7	64.2	303	81	49	48	12	6	4	6	27	6	54	3	0	0	2	.000	0	0-0	1	6.50	6.68
2007	Was	NL	21	21	0	0	115.1	480	99	59	57	18	6	1	2	42	1	86	4	0	6	6	.500	0	0-0	0	3.59	4.45
2008	Was	NL	30	22	1	1	139.2	614	153	94	79	25	9	8	1	47	2	96	2	0	2	11	.154	0	0-0	0	4.88	5.09
2009	Was	NL	56	0	0	6	48.0	213	50	28	24	7	5	0	3	25	7	40	3	0	2	4	.333	0	0-1	10	5.26	4.50
	5 ML YEARS		151	50	1	18	387.1	1695	397	236	214	63	27	14	14	152	17	297	12	0	12	23	.343	0	0-1	12	4.69	4.97

Jason Berken

Pitches: R **Bats:** R **Pos:** SP-24   **Ht:** 6'0" **Wt:** 210 **Born:** 11/27/1983 **Age:** 26

Year	Team	Lg	G	GS	CG	GF	IP	BFP	H	R	ER	HR	SH	SF	HB	TBB	IBB	SO	WP	Bk	W	L	Pct	Sh	Sv-Op	Hld	ERC	ERA
2006	Abrdn	A-	9	8	0	0	45.0	178	39	20	14	4	1	3	2	5	0	46	1	0	1	4	.200	0	0--	-	2.40	2.80
2007	Frdrck	A+	27	26	2	1	151.0	650	160	90	76	12	3	7	6	49	0	124	4	0	9	9	.500	1	0--	-	4.15	4.53
2008	Bowie	AA	26	25	2	0	145.2	611	141	69	58	9	4	7	8	38	0	125	5	0	12	4	.750	1	0--	-	3.32	3.58
2009	Bowie	AA	2	2	0	0	8.0	34	4	5	5	1	0	0	1	6	0	8	0	0	1	1	.500	0	0--	-	3.38	5.63
2009	Norfolk	AAA	5	5	0	0	25.2	98	19	3	3	1	2	0	0	6	0	16	0	0	5	0	1.000	0	0--	-	1.86	1.05
2009	Bal	AL	24	24	0	0	119.2	560	164	92	87	19	3	5	6	44	2	66	0	1	6	12	.333	0	0-0	0	6.81	6.54

Lance Berkman

Bats: B **Throws:** L **Pos:** 1B-131; PH-5   **Ht:** 6'1" **Wt:** 220 **Born:** 2/10/1976 **Age:** 34

Year	Team	Lg	G	AB	H	2B	3B	HR	(Hm	Rd)	TB	R	RBI	RC	TBB	IBB	SO	HBP	SH	SF	SB	CS	SB%	GDP	Avg	OBP	Slg
1999	Hou	NL	34	93	22	2	0	4	(2	2)	36	10	15	12	12	0	21	0	0	1	5	1	.83	2	.237	.321	.387
2000	Hou	NL	114	353	105	28	1	21	(10	11)	198	76	67	76	58	1	73	1	0	7	6	2	.75	6	.297	.388	.561
2001	Hou	NL	156	577	191	55	5	34	(13	21)	358	110	126	144	92	5	121	13	0	6	7	9	.44	8	.331	.430	.620
2002	Hou	NL	158	578	169	35	2	42	(20	22)	334	106	128	130	107	20	118	4	0	3	8	4	.67	10	.292	.405	.578
2003	Hou	NL	153	538	155	35	6	25	(11	14)	277	110	93	115	107	13	108	9	1	3	5	3	.63	10	.288	.412	.515
2004	Hou	NL	160	544	172	40	3	30	(8	22)	308	104	106	126	127	14	101	10	0	6	9	7	.56	10	.316	.450	.500
2005	Hou	NL	132	468	137	34	1	24	(13	11)	245	76	82	88	91	12	72	4	0	2	4	1	.80	18	.293	.411	.524
2006	Hou	NI	152	636	169	29	0	45	(24	21)	333	95	136	130	98	22	106	4	0	8	3	2	.60	11	.315	.420	.621
2007	Hou	NL	153	561	156	24	2	34	(13	21)	286	95	102	105	94	11	125	8	0	5	7	3	.70	11	.278	.386	.510
2008	Hou	NL	159	554	173	46	4	29	(16	13)	314	114	106	129	99	18	108	7	0	5	18	4	.82	13	.312	.420	.567
2009	Hou	NL	136	460	126	31	1	25	(14	11)	234	73	80	83	97	14	98	1	0	4	7	4	.64	13	.274	.399	.509
	Postseason		29	106	34	8	0	6	(4	2)	60	18	26	27	20	5	26	1	0	2	2	1	.67	4	.321	.426	.566
	11 ML YEARS		1507	5262	1575	359	25	313	(144	169)	2923	969	1041	1146	980	130	1051	61	1	50	79	40	.66	112	.299	.412	.555

Roger Bernadina

Bats: L **Throws:** L **Pos:** LF-1; CF-1; RF-1   **Ht:** 6'2" **Wt:** 198 **Born:** 6/12/1984 **Age:** 26

Year	Team	Lg	G	AB	H	2B	3B	HR	(Hm	Rd)	TB	R	RBI	RC	TBB	IBB	SO	HBP	SH	SF	SB	CS	SB%	GDP	Avg	OBP	Slg
2002	Expos	R	57	196	54	7	0	3	(-	-)	70	22	18	26	19	0	25	4	0	2	1	0	1.00	2	.276	.348	.357
2003	Savann	A	77	278	66	12	3	4	(-	-)	96	36	39	30	19	1	53	4	3	4	11	4	.73	3	.237	.292	.345
2004	Savann	A	129	450	107	24	7	7	(-	-)	166	67	66	66	40	1	113	11	1	6	24	2	.92	7	.238	.338	.369
2005	Savann	A	122	417	97	15	3	12	(-	-)	154	64	54	66	75	0	92	7	2	4	35	8	.81	9	.233	.356	.369
2006	Ptomc	A+	123	434	117	19	3	6	(-	-)	160	60	42	63	56	1	98	4	6	4	28	11	.72	4	.270	.355	.369
2007	Hrsbrg	AA	97	371	100	15	2	6	(-	-)	137	58	36	52	38	0	80	2	3	1	40	13	.75	9	.270	.340	.369
2007	Clmbs	AAA	13	42	7	3	0	0	(-	-)	10	6	1	3	9	0	11	1	1	0	0	1	.00	0	.167	.327	.238
2008	Hrsbrg	AA	73	266	86	11	7	5	(-	-)	126	47	38	52	31	0	64	2	4	0	26	9	.74	4	.323	.398	.474
2008	Clmbs	AAA	47	191	67	13	3	4	(-	-)	98	33	16	40	16	0	37	1	7	0	15	2	.88	4	.351	.404	.513
2009	Syrcse	AAA	5	18	3	0	0	0	(-	-)	3	1	0	1	4	0	5	0	1	0	1	0	1.00	0	.167	.318	.167
2009	Nats	R	2	4	1	0	0	0	(-	-)	1	0	0	0	1	0	0	0	0	0	0	0	-	0	.250	.250	.250
2008	Was	NL	26	76	16	1	1	0	(0	0)	19	10	2	4	9	0	21	0	1	0	4	3	.57	3	.211	.294	.250
2009	Was	NL	3	4	1	1	0	0	(0	0)	2	1	0	1	1	0	1	0	0	0	1	0	1.00	0	.250	.400	.500
	2 ML YEARS		29	80	17	2	1	0	(0	0)	21	11	2	5	10	0	22	0	1	0	5	3	.63	3	.213	.300	.263

Angel Berroa

Bats: R **Throws:** R **Pos:** 3B-16; SS-8; PH-7; PR-7; DH-3   **Ht:** 6'0" **Wt:** 195 **Born:** 1/27/1978 **Age:** 32

Year	Team	Lg	G	AB	H	2B	3B	HR	(Hm	Rd)	TB	R	RBI	RC	TBB	IBB	SO	HBP	SH	SF	SB	CS	SB%	GDP	Avg	OBP	Slg
2009	S-WB*	AAA	14	57	18	4	0	2	(-	-)	28	7	13	9	4	0	7	1	0	1	0	2	.00	4	.316	.365	.491
2009	Buffalo*	AAA	2	8	2	0	0	0	(-	-)	2	0	1	0	0	0	2	0	0	0	0	0	-	1	.250	.250	.250
2009	Bklyn*	A-	2	8	2	0	0	0	(-	-)	2	2	1	0	1	0	1	0	0	0	1	0	1.00	1	.250	.333	.250
2001	KC	AL	15	53	16	2	0	0	(0	0)	18	8	4	6	3	0	10	0	0	0	2	0	1.00	1	.302	.339	.340
2002	KC	AL	20	75	17	7	1	0	(0	0)	26	8	5	8	7	1	10	1	0	0	3	0	1.00	1	.227	.301	.347
2003	KC	AL	158	567	163	28	7	17	(6	11)	256	92	73	82	29	3	100	18	13	8	21	5	.81	13	.287	.338	.451
2004	KC	AL	134	512	134	27	6	8	(3	5)	197	72	43	62	23	0	87	12	5	2	14	8	.64	10	.262	.308	.385
2005	KC	AL	159	608	164	21	5	11	(6	5)	228	68	55	68	18	3	108	14	10	2	7	5	.58	13	.270	.305	.375
2006	KC	AL	132	474	111	18	1	9	(6	3)	158	45	54	32	14	1	88	3	9	3	3	1	.75	21	.234	.259	.333
2007	KC	AL	9	11	1	0	0	0	(0	0)	1	0	1	0	0	0	4	1	1	0	0	1	.00	1	.091	.167	.091
2008	LAD	NL	84	226	52	13	1	1	(1	0)	70	26	16	14	20	4	41	4	6	0	0	0	-	13	.230	.304	.310
2009	2 Tms		35	49	7	2	0	0	(0	0)	9	10	3	2	3	1	12	1	2	0	0	0	-	2	.143	.208	.184
09	NYY	AL	21	22	3	1	0	0	(0	0)	4	6	1	0	0	0	6	1	1	0	0	0	-	1	.136	.174	.182
09	NYM	NL	14	27	4	1	0	0	(0	0)	5	4	2	2	3	1	6	0	1	0	0	0	-	1	.148	.233	.185
	Postseason		5	2	1	0	0	0	(0	0)	1	0	0	1	0	0	0	0	1	0	0	0	-	0	.500	.500	.500
9 ML YEARS			746	2575	665	118	21	46	(22	24)	963	329	254	274	117	13	460	54	46	15	50	20	.71	76	.258	.303	.374

Rafael Betancourt

Pitches: R **Bats:** R **Pos:** RP-61   **Ht:** 6'2" **Wt:** 200 **Born:** 4/29/1975 **Age:** 35

Year	Team	Lg	G	GS	CG	GF	IP	BFP	H	R	ER	HR	SH	SF	HB	TBB	IBB	SO	WP	Bk	W	L	Pct	Sh	Sv-Op	Hld	ERC	ERA
2009	Clmbs*	AAA	3	0	0	0	3.1	11	0	0	0	0	0	0	0	1	0	4	0	0	1	0	1.000	0	0- -	0	0.10	0.00
2003	Cle	AL	33	0	0	13	38.0	154	27	11	9	5	1	1	1	13	2	36	1	0	2	2	.500	0	1-3	4	2.54	2.13
2004	Cle	AL	68	0	0	21	66.2	286	71	32	29	7	1	2	0	18	6	76	5	1	5	6	.455	0	4-11	12	3.77	3.92
2005	Cle	AL	54	0	0	12	67.2	272	57	23	21	5	1	0	1	17	2	73	0	0	4	3	.571	0	1-3	10	2.49	2.79
2006	Cle	AL	50	0	0	17	56.2	231	52	25	24	7	2	2	0	11	5	48	0	0	3	4	.429	0	3-6	7	2.84	3.81
2007	Cle	AL	68	0	0	15	79.1	289	51	13	13	4	0	2	0	9	3	80	0	0	5	1	.833	0	3-6	31	1.24	1.47
2008	Cle	AL	69	0	0	20	71.0	309	76	41	40	11	4	5	0	25	5	64	2	0	3	4	.429	0	4-8	12	4.53	5.07
2009	2 Tms		61	0	0	10	56.0	227	42	20	17	4	2	4	0	20	5	61	0	0	4	3	.571	0	2-6	20	2.30	2.73
09	Cle	AL	29	0	0	7	30.2	129	25	15	12	3	1	2	0	15	4	32	0	0	1	2	.333	0	1-3	8	3.21	3.52
09	Col	NL	32	0	0	3	25.1	98	17	5	5	1	1	2	0	5	1	29	0	0	3	1	.750	0	1-3	12	1.42	1.78
	Postseason		7	0	0	2	10.0	39	7	7	6	1	1	1	0	1	1	9	0	0	0	0	-	0	0-0	2	1.42	5.40
7 ML YEARS			403	0	0	108	435.1	1768	376	165	153	43	11	16	1	113	28	438	8	1	26	23	.531	0	18-43	96	2.72	3.16

Yuniesky Betancourt

Bats: R **Throws:** R **Pos:** SS-133; PH-1   **Ht:** 5'10" **Wt:** 195 **Born:** 1/31/1982 **Age:** 28

Year	Team	Lg	G	AB	H	2B	3B	HR	(Hm	Rd)	TB	R	RBI	RC	TBB	IBB	SO	HBP	SH	SF	SB	CS	SB%	GDP	Avg	OBP	Slg
2009	Tacom*	AAA	1	2	1	1	0	0	(-	-)	2	0	1	0	0	0	0	0	0	0	0	0	-	0	.500	.500	1.000
2009	NWArk*	AA	3	13	2	0	0	0	(-	-)	5	2	1	0	0	0	1	0	0	0	0	0	-	0	.154	.154	.385
2005	Sea	AL	60	211	54	11	5	1	(1	0)	78	24	15	21	11	0	24	2	2	2	1	3	.25	2	.256	.296	.370
2006	Sea	AL	157	558	161	28	6	8	(2	6)	225	68	47	60	17	0	54	1	7	1	11	8	.58	10	.289	.310	.403
2007	Sea	AL	155	536	155	38	2	9	(6	3)	224	72	67	73	15	3	48	1	3	4	5	4	.56	10	.289	.308	.418
2008	Sea	AL	153	559	156	36	3	7	(3	4)	219	66	51	53	17	0	42	2	6	6	4	4	.50	23	.279	.300	.392
2009	2 Tms	AL	134	470	115	20	6	6	(2	4)	165	40	49	41	21	0	44	0	11	6	3	3	.50	17	.245	.274	.351
09	Sea	AL	63	224	56	10	1	2	(1	1)	74	15	22	19	10	0	18	0	8	3	3	1	.75	9	.250	.278	.330
09	KC	AL	71	246	59	10	5	4	(1	3)	91	25	27	22	11	0	26	0	3	3	0	2	.00	8	.240	.269	.370
5 ML YEARS			659	2334	641	133	22	31	(14	17)	911	270	229	248	81	3	212	6	29	19	24	22	.52	62	.275	.298	.390

Wilson Betemit

Bats: B **Throws:** R **Pos:** PH-8; 1B-7; 3B-6; DH-1   **Ht:** 6'3" **Wt:** 230 **Born:** 11/2/1981 **Age:** 28

Year	Team	Lg	G	AB	H	2B	3B	HR	(Hm	Rd)	TB	R	RBI	RC	TBB	IBB	SO	HBP	SH	SF	SB	CS	SB%	GDP	Avg	OBP	Slg
2009	Charltt*	AAA	72	261	63	19	0	11	(-	-)	115	36	49	35	21	2	73	0	0	4	2	0	1.00	10	.241	.294	.441
2001	Atl	NL	8	3	0	0	0	0	(0	0)	0	1	0	0	2	0	3	0	0	0	1	0	1.00	0	.000	.400	.000
2004	Atl	NL	22	47	8	0	0	0	(0	0)	8	2	3	0	4	0	16	0	0	1	0	1	.00	0	.170	.231	.170
2005	Atl	NL	115	246	75	12	4	4	(0	4)	107	36	20	36	22	4	55	0	4	2	1	3	.25	5	.305	.359	.435
2006	2 Tms	NL	143	373	98	23	0	18	(7	11)	175	49	53	52	36	6	102	0	1	2	3	1	.75	11	.263	.326	.469
2007	2 Tms		121	240	55	12	0	14	(8	6)	109	33	50	42	38	0	82	1	2	3	0	0	-	2	.229	.333	.454
2008	NYY	AL	87	189	50	13	0	6	(5	1)	81	24	25	17	6	0	56	1	1	1	0	1	.00	7	.265	.289	.429
2009	CWS	AL	20	45	9	5	0	0	(0	0)	14	2	3	5	0	0	13	0	0	0	0	0	-	2	.200	.280	.311
06	Atl	NL	88	199	56	16	0	9	(3	6)	99	30	29	35	19	3	57	0	1	0	2	1	.67	4	.281	.344	.497
06	LAD	NL	55	174	42	7	0	9	(4	5)	76	19	24	17	17	3	45	0	0	2	1	0	1.00	7	.241	.306	.437
07	Atl	NL	84	156	36	8	0	10	(6	4)	74	22	26	26	32	0	49	1	0	3	0	0	-	1	.231	.359	.474
07	NYY	AL	37	84	19	4	0	4	(2	2)	35	11	24	16	6	0	33	0	2	0	0	0	-	1	.226	.278	.417
	Postseason		6	10	5	1	0	1	(0	1)	9	3	1	2	2	1	2	0	0	0	0	0	-	0	.500	.583	.900
7 ML YEARS			516	1143	295	65	4	42	(20	22)	494	147	154	150	113	10	327	2	8	9	5	6	.45	27	.258	.324	.432

Chad Billingsley

Pitches: R Bats: R Pos: SP-32; RP-1 **Ht: 6'1" Wt: 245 Born: 7/29/1984 Age: 25**

Year	Team	Lg	G	GS	CG	GF	IP	BFP	H	R	ER	HR	SH	SF	HB	TBB	IBB	SO	WP	Bk	W	L	Pct	Sh	Sv-Op	Hld	ERC	ERA
2006	LAD	NL	18	16	0	0	90.0	403	92	43	38	7	4	0	3	58	3	59	5	0	7	4	.636	0	0-0	0	5.22	3.80
2007	LAD	NL	43	20	1	6	147.0	623	131	56	54	15	9	3	3	64	3	141	5	0	12	5	.706	0	0-1	3	3.70	3.31
2008	LAD	NL	35	32	1	1	200.2	859	188	76	70	14	8	5	8	80	6	201	10	0	16	10	.615	1	0-0	1	3.62	3.14
2009	LAD	NL	33	32	0	0	196.1	823	173	94	88	17	9	11	7	86	7	179	14	0	12	11	.522	0	0-0	0	3.63	4.03
Postseason			5	3	0	0	13.2	64	18	12	11	1	0	0	0	8	2	19	2	0	1	2	.333	0	0-0	0	6.37	7.24
4 ML YEARS			129	100	2	7	634.0	2708	584	269	250	53	30	19	21	288	19	580	34	0	47	30	.610	1	0-1	4	3.86	3.55

Brian Bixler

Bats: R Throws: R Pos: SS-10, 2B-5; PH-2; PR-2; CF-1 **Ht: 6'1" Wt: 195 Born: 10/22/1982 Age: 27**

Year	Team	Lg	G	AB	H	2B	3B	HR	(Hm	Rd)	TB	R	RBI	RC	TBB	IBB	SO	HBP	SH	SF	SB	CS	SB%	GDP	Avg	OBP	Slg
2004	Wmspt	A-	59	228	63	7	4	0	(-	-)	78	40	21	27	15	0	51	2	1	4	14	5	.74	3	.276	.321	.342
2005	Hkry	A	126	502	141	23	2	9	(-	-)	195	74	50	70	38	0	134	11	3	3	21	10	.68	5	.281	.343	.388
2006	Lynbrg	A+	73	267	81	16	2	5	(-	-)	116	46	33	50	35	1	58	9	6	0	18	7	.72	2	.303	.402	.434
2006	Altna	AA	60	226	68	13	1	3	(-	-)	92	36	19	35	16	0	57	7	2	2	6	2	.75	2	.301	.363	.407
2007	Indy	AAA	129	475	130	23	10	5	(-	-)	188	77	51	78	53	1	131	18	10	0	28	4	.88	6	.274	.368	.396
2008	Indy	AAA	86	321	90	8	5	7	(-	-)	129	44	36	48	27	0	107	7	6	3	23	7	.77	4	.280	.346	.402
2009	Indy	AAA	108	403	110	23	8	9	(-	-)	176	71	43	63	35	0	128	7	5	1	13	3	.81	4	.273	.341	.437
2008	Pit	NL	50	108	17	2	1	0	(0	0)	21	16	2	2	6	2	36	4	2	0	1	0	1.00	1	.157	.229	.194
2009	Pit	NL	18	44	10	5	0	0	(0	0)	15	5	3	3	2	0	26	0	0	1	1	0	1.00	0	.227	.261	.341
2 ML YEARS			68	152	27	7	1	0	(0	0)	36	21	5	5	8	2	62	4	2	0	2	0	1.00	1	.178	.238	.237

Nick Blackburn

Pitches: R Bats: R Pos: SP-33 **Ht: 6'4" Wt: 227 Born: 2/24/1982 Age: 28**

Year	Team	Lg	G	GS	CG	GF	IP	BFP	H	R	ER	HR	SH	SF	HB	TBB	IBB	SO	WP	Bk	W	L	Pct	Sh	Sv-Op	Hld	ERC	ERA
2007	Min	AL	6	0	0	3	11.2	54	19	12	10	2	0	0	0	2	0	8	0	0	0	2	.000	0	0-1	1	7.61	7.71
2008	Min	AL	33	33	0	0	193.1	823	224	102	87	23	5	4	7	39	4	96	2	0	11	11	.500	0	0-0	0	4.40	4.05
2009	Min	AL	33	33	3	0	205.2	882	240	103	92	25	5	6	0	41	1	98	0	0	11	11	.500	0	0-0	0	4.42	4.03
3 ML YEARS			72	66	0	0	410.2	1760	483	217	189	50	10	9	10	82	5	202	4	0	22	24	.478	0	0-1	1	4.53	4.14

Casey Blake

Bats: R Throws: R Pos: 3B-134; PH-6; 1B-2; LF-2 **Ht: 6'2" Wt: 204 Born: 8/23/1973 Age: 36**

Year	Team	Lg	G	AB	H	2B	3B	HR	(Hm	Rd)	TB	R	RBI	RC	TBB	IBB	SO	HBP	SH	SF	SB	CS	SB%	GDP	Avg	OBP	Slg
1999	Tor	AL	14	39	10	2	0	1	(0	1)	15	6	1	4	2	0	7	0	0	0	0	0	-	1	.256	.293	.385
2000	Min	AL	7	16	3	2	0	0	(0	0)	5	1	1	2	3	0	7	1	0	1	0	0	-	1	.188	.333	.313
2001	2 Tms	AL	19	37	9	1	0	1	(0	1)	13	3	4	5	4	1	12	0	0	0	3	0	1.00	0	.243	.317	.351
2002	Min	AL	9	20	4	1	0	0	(0	0)	5	2	1	1	2	0	7	0	0	0	0	0	-	0	.200	.273	.250
2003	Cle	AL	152	557	143	35	0	17	(2	15)	229	80	67	68	38	1	109	10	8	8	7	9	.44	11	.257	.312	.411
2004	Cle	AL	152	587	159	36	3	28	(13	15)	285	93	88	88	68	2	139	9	1	3	5	8	.38	19	.271	.354	.486
2005	Cle	AL	147	523	126	32	1	23	(7	16)	229	72	58	53	43	3	116	10	2	5	4	5	.44	9	.241	.308	.438
2006	Cle	AL	109	401	113	20	1	19	(9	10)	192	63	68	62	45	5	93	4	1	5	6	0	1.00	11	.282	.356	.479
2007	Cle	AL	156	588	159	36	4	18	(11	7)	257	81	78	69	54	2	123	10	5	5	4	5	.44	14	.270	.339	.437
2008	2 Tms	AL	152	536	147	36	1	21	(6	15)	248	71	81	85	49	11	120	11	1	4	3	0	1.00	12	.274	.345	.463
2009	LAD	NL	139	485	136	25	6	18	(7	11)	227	84	79	76	63	8	116	6	1	10	3	4	.43	12	.280	.363	.468
01	Min	AL	13	22	7	1	0	0	(0	0)	8	1	2	4	3	1	8	0	0	0	1	0	1.00	0	.318	.400	.364
01	Bal	AL	6	15	2	0	0	1	(0	1)	5	2	2	1	1	0	4	0	0	0	2	0	1.00	0	.133	.188	.333
08	Cle	AL	94	325	94	24	0	11	(1	10)	151	46	58	64	33	6	68	7	1	2	2	0	1.00	3	.289	.365	.465
08	LAD	NL	58	211	53	12	1	10	(5	5)	97	25	23	21	16	5	52	4	0	2	1	0	1.00	9	.251	.313	.460
Postseason			19	73	19	3	0	2	(2	0)	28	9	8	8	3	1	17	1	1	0	0	0	-	1	.260	.299	.384
11 ML YEARS			1056	3789	1009	226	16	146	(55	91)	1705	556	526	513	371	33	849	61	19	41	35	31	.53	90	.266	.338	.450

Hank Blalock

Bats: L Throws: R Pos: 1B-66; DH-50; PH-7; 3B-1 **Ht: 6'1" Wt: 200 Born: 11/21/1980 Age: 29**

Year	Team	Lg	G	AB	H	2B	3B	HR	(Hm	Rd)	TB	R	RBI	RC	TBB	IBB	SO	HBP	SH	SF	SB	CS	SB%	GDP	Avg	OBP	Slg
2002	Tex	AL	49	147	31	8	0	3	(2	1)	48	16	17	15	20	1	43	1	2	2	0	0	-	2	.211	.306	.327
2003	Tex	AL	143	567	170	33	3	29	(18	11)	296	89	90	90	44	1	97	1	0	3	2	3	.40	16	.300	.350	.522
2004	Tex	AL	159	624	172	38	3	32	(16	16)	312	107	110	119	75	7	149	6	0	8	2	2	.50	13	.276	.355	.500
2005	Tex	AL	161	647	170	34	0	25	(20	5)	279	80	92	86	51	1	132	3	0	4	1	0	1.00	16	.263	.318	.431
2006	Tex	AL	152	591	157	26	3	16	(8	8)	237	76	89	87	51	6	98	2	0	2	1	0	1.00	15	.266	.325	.401
2007	Tex	AL	58	208	61	16	3	10	(7	3)	113	32	33	38	21	1	38	1	0	2	4	1	.80	8	.293	.358	.543
2008	Tex	AL	65	258	74	19	1	12	(6	6)	131	37	38	36	19	3	40	2	0	2	1	0	1.00	16	.287	.338	.508
2009	Tex	AL	123	462	108	21	4	25	(13	12)	212	62	66	54	26	2	108	3	0	4	2	0	1.00	6	.234	.277	.459
8 ML YEARS			910	3504	943	195	17	152	(90	62)	1628	499	535	525	307	22	705	19	2	27	13	6	.68	86	.269	.329	.465

Andres Blanco

Bats: B **Throws:** R **Pos:** 2B-40; SS-15; PH-7   **Ht:** 5'10" **Wt:** 190 **Born:** 4/11/1984 **Age:** 26

Year Team	Lg	G	AB	H	2B	3B	HR	(Hm	Rd)	TB	R	RBI	RC	TBB	IBB	SO	HBP	SH	SF	SB	CS	SB%	GDP	Avg	OBP	Slg
2009 Iowa*	AAA	64	230	70	17	2	6	(-	-)	109	30	29	40	17	1	28	3	3	5	6	1	.86	9	.304	.353	.474
2004 KC	AL	19	60	19	2	2	0	(0	0)	25	9	5	12	5	0	6	1	1	0	1	2	.33	0	.317	.379	.417
2005 KC	AL	26	79	17	0	1	0	(0	0)	19	6	5	3	0	0	5	1	4	2	0	1	.00	3	.215	.220	.241
2006 KC	AL	33	87	21	4	1	0	(0	0)	27	9	9	9	5	0	14	1	3	0	0	1	.00	2	.241	.290	.310
2009 ChC	NL	53	123	31	8	0	1	(1	0)	42	15	12	9	8	3	14	1	6	0	0	2	.00	4	.252	.303	.341
4 ML YEARS		131	349	88	14	4	1	(1	0)	113	39	31	33	18	3	39	4	14	2	1	6	.14	9	.252	.295	.324

Gregor Blanco

Bats: L **Throws:** L **Pos:** CF-9; PH-8; PR-5; LF-3; RF-2   **Ht:** 5'11" **Wt:** 170 **Born:** 12/24/1983 **Age:** 26

Year Team	Lg	G	AB	H	2B	3B	HR	(Hm	Rd)	TB	R	RBI	RC	TBB	IBB	SO	HBP	SH	SF	SB	CS	SB%	GDP	Avg	OBP	Slg
2002 Macon	A	132	468	127	14	9	7	(-	-)	180	87	36	81	85	0	120	9	6	2	40	16	.71	2	.271	.392	.385
2003 MrtlBh	A+	126	461	125	19	7	5	(-	-)	173	66	36	67	54	0	114	8	3	1	34	16	.68	4	.271	.357	.375
2004 MrtlBh	A+	119	436	116	17	9	8	(-	-)	175	73	41	64	47	4	114	3	6	3	25	9	.74	5	.266	.339	.401
2005 Missi	AA	123	401	101	11	12	6	(-	-)	154	64	35	64	74	2	124	2	7	3	26	12	.68	7	.252	.369	.384
2006 Missi	AA	66	251	72	16	3	0	(-	-)	94	45	9	42	43	0	57	3	5	0	17	6	.74	3	.287	.397	.375
2006 Rchmd	AAA	73	269	79	12	1	0	(-	-)	93	43	19	43	52	1	53	0	6	0	14	9	.61	3	.294	.408	.346
2007 Rchmd	AAA	124	464	131	18	5	3	(-	-)	168	81	35	66	63	0	85	2	14	2	23	18	.56	5	.282	.369	.362
2009 Gwnntt	AAA	90	333	76	9	1	2	(-	-)	93	54	30	36	50	0	70	1	7	6	10	3	.77	6	.228	.326	.279
2008 Atl	NL	144	430	108	14	4	1	(0	1)	133	52	38	60	74	2	99	6	6	3	13	5	.72	3	.251	.366	.309
2009 Atl	NL	24	43	8	0	1	0	(0	0)	10	5	1	2	4	0	9	0	1	0	2	0	1.00	1	.186	.255	.233
2 ML YEARS		168	473	116	14	5	1	(0	1)	143	57	39	62	78	2	108	6	7	3	15	5	.75	4	.245	.357	.302

Henry Blanco

Bats: R **Throws:** R **Pos:** C-60; PH-6; 3B-1   **Ht:** 5'11" **Wt:** 220 **Born:** 8/29/1971 **Age:** 38

Year Team	Lg	G	AB	H	2B	3B	HR	(Hm	Rd)	TB	R	RBI	RC	TBB	IBB	SO	HBP	SH	SF	SB	CS	SB%	GDP	Avg	OBP	Slg
1997 LAD	NL	3	5	2	0	0	1	(0	1)	5	1	1	2	0	0	1	0	0	0	0	0	-	0	.400	.400	1.000
1999 Col	NL	88	263	61	12	3	6	(3	3)	97	30	28	32	34	1	38	1	3	2	1	1	.50	0	.232	.320	.369
2000 Mil	NL	93	284	67	24	0	7	(3	4)	112	29	31	33	36	6	60	0	0	4	0	3	.00	9	.236	.318	.394
2001 Mil	NL	104	314	66	18	3	6	(4	2)	108	33	31	30	34	6	72	2	5	2	3	1	.75	10	.210	.290	.344
2002 Atl	NL	81	221	45	9	1	6	(4	2)	74	17	22	15	20	5	51	1	2	5	0	2	.00	5	.204	.267	.335
2003 Atl	NL	55	151	30	8	0	1	(1	0)	41	11	13	13	10	2	21	1	3	1	0	0	-	3	.199	.252	.272
2004 Min	AL	114	315	65	19	1	10	(4	6)	116	36	37	25	21	0	56	3	11	3	0	3	.00	8	.206	.260	.368
2005 ChC	NL	54	161	39	6	0	6	(2	4)	63	16	25	17	11	1	24	0	4	2	0	0	-	4	.242	.287	.391
2006 ChC	NL	74	241	64	15	2	6	(2	4)	101	23	37	26	14	1	38	0	4	2	0	0	-	8	.266	.304	.419
2007 ChC	NL	22	54	9	3	0	0	(0	0)	12	3	4	2	2	0	12	0	1	1	0	0	-	0	.167	.193	.222
2008 ChC	NL	58	120	35	3	0	3	(2	1)	47	15	12	11	6	1	22	0	2	0	0	0	-	4	.292	.325	.392
2009 SD	NL	67	204	48	12	0	6	(4	2)	78	21	16	20	26	2	50	0	1	1	0	0	-	5	.235	.320	.382
Postseason		6	14	3	0	0	1	(1	0)	6	1	2	0	0	0	4	0	1	1	0	0	-	1	.214	.200	.429
12 ML YEARS		813	2333	531	129	10	58	(28	30)	854	235	257	226	214	25	445	8	36	23	4	10	.29	62	.228	.292	.366

Kyle Blanks

Bats: R **Throws:** R **Pos:** RF-22; LF-18; 1B-8; PH-8; DH-2; PR-1   **Ht:** 6'6" **Wt:** 285 **Born:** 9/11/1986 **Age:** 23

Year Team	Lg	G	AB	H	2B	3B	HR	(Hm	Rd)	TB	R	RBI	RC	TBB	IBB	SO	HBP	SH	SF	SB	CS	SB%	GDP	Avg	OBP	Slg
2005 Padres	R	48	164	49	10	1	7	(-	-)	82	33	30	36	25	3	49	10	0	1	3	1	.75	3	.299	.420	.500
2006 FtWyn	A	86	308	90	20	0	10	(-	-)	140	41	52	56	36	2	79	11	0	4	2	0	1.00	6	.292	.382	.455
2007 Lk Els	A+	119	465	140	31	4	24	(-	-)	251	94	100	97	44	1	98	18	0	4	11	2	.85	12	.301	.380	.540
2008 SnAnt	AA	132	492	160	23	5	20	(-	-)	253	75	107	102	51	0	90	17	0	5	5	4	.56	16	.325	.404	.514
2009 Portlnd	AAA	66	233	66	9	1	12	(-	-)	113	35	38	46	39	0	63	5	0	3	0	0	-	3	.283	.393	.485
2009 SD	NL	54	148	37	9	0	10	(6	4)	76	24	22	21	18	1	55	6	0	0	1	1	.50	4	.250	.355	.514

Joe Blanton

Pitches: R **Bats:** R **Pos:** SP-31   **Ht:** 6'3" **Wt:** 252 **Born:** 12/11/1980 **Age:** 29

Year Team	Lg	G	GS	CG	GF	IP	BFP	H	R	ER	HR	SH	SF	HB	TBB	IBB	SO	WP	Bk	W	L	Pct	Sh	Sv-Op	Hld	ERC	ERA
2004 Oak	AL	3	0	0	1	8.0	30	6	5	5	1	0	0	0	2	0	6	0	0	0	0	-	0	0-0	0	2.52	5.63
2005 Oak	AL	33	33	2	0	201.1	835	178	86	79	23	2	7	5	67	3	116	4	2	12	12	.500	0	0-0	0	3.37	3.53
2006 Oak	AL	32	31	1	0	194.1	856	241	111	104	17	3	9	5	58	4	107	3	0	16	12	.571	1	0-0	0	5.09	4.82
2007 Oak	AL	34	34	3	0	230.0	950	240	106	101	16	5	8	4	60	4	140	3	1	14	10	.583	1	0-0	0	3.30	3.95
2008 2 Tms		33	33	0	0	197.2	855	211	110	103	22	2	4	4	66	3	111	2	0	9	12	.429	0	0-0	0	4.33	4.69
2009 Phi	NL	31	31	0	0	195.1	837	198	89	88	30	11	4	8	59	4	163	7	0	12	8	.600	0	0-0	0	4.25	4.05
08 Oak	AL	20	20	0	0	127.0	550	145	74	70	12	1	2	1	35	3	62	1	0	5	12	.294	0	0-0	0	4.33	4.96
08 Phi	NL	13	13	0	0	70.2	305	66	36	33	10	1	2	3	31	0	49	1	0	4	0	1.000	0	0-0	0	4.33	4.20
Postseason		4	3	0	1	19.0	80	16	6	6	3	0	0	1	8	2	20	0	0	2	0	1.000	0	0-0	0	3.75	2.84
6 ML YEARS		166	162	6	1	1026.2	4363	1074	507	480	109	23	32	26	292	18	643	19	3	63	54	.538	2	0-0	0	4.01	4.21

Jerry Blevins

Pitches: L Bats: L Pos: RP-20   Ht: 6'6" Wt: 181 Born: 9/6/1983 Age: 26

		HOW MUCH HE PITCHED						WHAT HE GAVE UP											THE RESULTS						
Year	Team	Lg	G	GS	CG	GF	IP	BFP	H	R	ER	HR	SH	SF	HB	TBB	IBB	SO	WP	Bk	W	L	Pct	Sh	Sv-Op	Hld	ERC	ERA
2009	Scrmto*	AAA	45	0	0	13	63.1	272	65	28	27	5	9	1	4	18	4	62	3	0	5	3	.625	0	2- -	-	3.75	3.84
2007	Oak	AL	6	0	0	1	4.2	25	8	6	5	1	0	0	0	2	0	3	0	0	0	1	.000	0	0-0	-	9.08	9.64
2008	Oak	AL	36	0	0	8	37.2	156	32	14	13	2	0	1	3	13	2	35	0	0	1	3	.250	0	0-1	5	3.00	3.11
2009	Oak	AL	20	0	0	5	22.1	90	19	12	12	2	0	1	0	6	1	23	0	0	0	0	.---	0	0-0	0	2.68	4.84
	3 ML YEARS		62	0	0	14	64.2	271	59	32	30	5	0	2	3	21	3	61	0	0	1	4	.200	0	0-1	5	3.27	4.18

Willie Bloomquist

Bats: R Throws: R Pos: RF-61;SS-38;CF-22;2B-14;PH-11;LF-9;PR-4;1B-3;3B-3;DH-1   Ht: 5'11" Wt: 195 Born: 11/27/1977 Age: 32

					BATTING															BASERUNNING				AVERAGES		
Year	Team	Lg	G	AB	H	2B	3B	HR	(Hm	Rd)	TB	R	RBI	RC	TBB	IBB	SO	HBP	SH	SF	SB	CS	SB%	GDP	Avg	OBP	Slg
2002	Sea	AL	12	33	15	4	0	0	(0	0)	19	11	7	10	5	0	2	0	0	0	3	1	.75	0	.455	.526	.576
2003	Sea	AL	89	196	49	7	2	1	(1	0)	63	30	14	18	19	1	39	1	2	2	4	1	.80	6	.250	.317	.321
2004	Sea	AL	93	188	46	10	0	2	(0	2)	62	27	18	18	10	0	48	0	3	0	13	2	.87	2	.245	.283	.330
2005	Sea	AL	82	249	64	15	2	0	(0	0)	83	27	22	26	11	0	38	1	4	2	14	1	.93	5	.257	.289	.333
2006	Sea	AL	102	251	62	6	2	1	(0	1)	75	36	15	27	24	0	40	4	2	2	16	3	.84	3	.247	.320	.299
2007	Sea	AL	91	173	48	3	0	2	(1	1)	57	28	13	16	10	0	35	1	4	0	7	5	.58	7	.277	.321	.329
2008	Sea	AL	71	165	46	1	0	0	(0	0)	47	32	9	24	25	1	29	1	1	0	14	3	.82	1	.279	.377	.285
2009	KC	AL	125	434	115	11	8	4	(0	4)	154	52	29	45	27	1	73	1	4	2	25	6	.81	7	.265	.308	.355
	8 ML YEARS		665	1689	445	57	14	10	(2	8)	560	243	127	184	131	3	304	9	20	8	96	22	.81	31	.263	.318	.332

Geoff Blum

Bats: B Throws: R Pos: 3B-102; PH-14; 1B-10; SS-1   Ht: 6'3" Wt: 205 Born: 4/26/1973 Age: 37

					BATTING															BASERUNNING				AVERAGES		
Year	Team	Lg	G	AB	H	2B	3B	HR	(Hm	Rd)	TB	R	RBI	RC	TBB	IBB	SO	HBP	SH	SF	SB	CS	SB%	GDP	Avg	OBP	Slg
2009	RdRck*	AAA	2	7	1	1	0	0	(-	-)	2	0	1	0	0	0	1	0	0	0	0	0	-	0	.143	.143	.286
1999	Mon	NL	45	133	32	7	2	8	(0	8)	67	21	18	22	17	3	25	0	3	0	1	0	1.00	3	.241	.327	.504
2000	Mon	NL	124	343	97	20	2	11	(5	6)	154	40	45	50	26	2	60	3	3	4	1	4	.20	4	.283	.335	.449
2001	Mon	NL	148	453	107	25	0	9	(6	3)	159	57	50	49	43	8	94	10	3	5	9	5	.64	12	.236	.313	.351
2002	Hou	NL	130	368	104	20	4	10	(6	4)	162	45	52	62	49	5	70	1	1	2	2	0	1.00	8	.283	.367	.440
2003	Hou	NL	123	420	110	19	0	10	(6	4)	159	51	52	40	20	1	50	2	2	6	0	0	-	15	.262	.293	.379
2004	TB	AL	112	339	73	21	0	8	(2	6)	118	38	35	29	24	1	58	0	4	2	2	3	.40	4	.215	.266	.348
2005	2 Tms		109	319	73	15	2	6	(1	5)	110	32	25	27	28	0	43	3	0	1	3	3	.50	6	.229	.296	.345
2006	SD	NL	109	276	70	17	1	4	(0	4)	101	27	34	26	17	1	51	0	2	5	0	1	.00	5	.254	.293	.366
2007	SD	NL	122	330	83	21	1	5	(1	4)	121	34	33	38	32	4	52	2	3	3	0	0	-	10	.252	.319	.367
2008	Hou	NL	114	325	78	14	1	14	(6	8)	136	36	53	42	21	2	54	3	0	7	1	2	.33	5	.240	.287	.418
2009	Hou	NL	120	381	94	14	1	10	(4	6)	140	34	49	39	33	4	61	7	0	6	0	1	.00	9	.247	.314	.367
05	SD	NL	78	224	54	13	1	5	(1	4)	84	26	22	23	24	0	28	3	0	1	3	2	.60	5	.241	.321	.375
05	CWS	AL	31	95	19	2	1	1	(0	1)	26	6	3	4	4	0	15	0	0	0	0	1	.00	1	.200	.232	.274
	Postseason		6	10	2	1	0	1	(0	1)	6	1	2	1	4	1	1	0	0	1	0	0	-	1	.200	.400	.600
	11 ML YEARS		1256	3687	921	193	14	95	(37	58)	1427	415	446	424	310	31	610	31	21	39	19	19	.50	81	.250	.310	.387

Brandon Boggs

Bats: B Throws: R Pos: LF-3; CF-3; PH-3   Ht: 5'11" Wt: 205 Born: 1/9/1983 Age: 27

					BATTING															BASERUNNING				AVERAGES		
Year	Team	Lg	G	AB	H	2B	3B	HR	(Hm	Rd)	TB	R	RBI	RC	TBB	IBB	SO	HBP	SH	SF	SB	CS	SB%	GDP	Avg	OBP	Slg
2004	Spkane	A-	45	149	35	11	0	3	(-	-)	55	27	19	24	29	0	43	5	1	2	6	2	.75	5	.235	.373	.369
2005	Clinton	A	85	309	76	16	2	13	(-	-)	135	54	51	51	50	1	69	2	0	2	14	6	.70	3	.246	.353	.437
2006	Bkrsfld	A+	78	284	74	20	4	8	(-	-)	126	48	37	47	40	1	63	1	0	2	13	4	.76	3	.261	.352	.444
2007	Bkrsfld	A+	26	92	23	9	1	4	(-	-)	46	17	17	17	14	0	28	2	0	0	5	1	.83	0	.250	.361	.500
2007	Frisco	AA	104	354	94	21	4	19	(-	-)	180	69	55	73	70	5	103	1	0	4	11	4	.73	3	.266	.385	.508
2008	Okla	AAA	18	68	21	4	3	0	(-	-)	31	12	6	11	7	0	20	0	0	1	1	1	.50	0	.309	.368	.456
2009	Okla	AAA	93	332	89	15	2	8	(-	-)	132	45	47	56	59	2	98	3	1	3	9	2	.82	4	.268	.380	.398
2008	Tex	AL	101	283	64	17	4	8	(6	2)	113	30	41	37	44	1	93	3	1	3	3	2	.60	3	.226	.333	.399
2009	Tex	AL	9	17	1	1	0	0	(0	0)	2	0	0	0	1	0	8	0	0	0	0	0	-	0	.059	.111	.118
	2 ML YEARS		110	300	65	18	4	8	(6	2)	115	30	41	37	45	1	101	3	1	3	3	2	.60	3	.217	.322	.383

Mitchell Boggs

Pitches: R Bats: R Pos: SP-9; RP-7   Ht: 6'4" Wt: 215 Born: 2/15/1984 Age: 26

			HOW MUCH HE PITCHED						WHAT HE GAVE UP											THE RESULTS						
Year	Team	Lg	G	GS	CG	GF	IP	BFP	H	R	ER	HR	SH	SF	HB	TBB	IBB	SO	WP	Bk	W	L	Pct	Sh	Sv-Op	Hld	ERC	ERA
2005	NewJrs	A-	15	14	0	0	71.2	315	77	38	31	5	1	1	5	24	0	61	4	0	4	4	.500	0	0- -	-	4.28	3.89
2006	PlmBh	A+	27	27	1	0	145.0	634	153	69	55	7	4	6	8	51	0	126	9	0	10	6	.625	1	0- -	-	4.03	3.41
2007	Sprgfld	AA	26	26	0	0	152.1	688	167	86	65	15	8	8	10	62	2	117	7	0	11	7	.611	0	0- -	-	4.82	3.84
2008	Memp	AAA	21	21	1	0	125.1	508	107	52	48	11	4	1	2	46	0	81	10	1	9	3	.750	0	0- -	-	3.24	3.45
2009	Memp	AAA	14	14	0	0	76.1	346	90	45	41	8	3	0	4	32	1	58	5	0	6	4	.600	0	0- -	-	5.44	4.83
2008	StL	NL	8	6	0	1	34.0	164	42	29	28	5	1	1	2	22	0	13	2	0	3	2	.600	0	0-0	0	7.17	7.41
2009	StL	NL	16	9	0	2	58.0	268	71	28	27	3	1	2	4	33	0	46	4	1	2	3	.400	0	0-0	1	6.15	4.19
	2 ML YEARS		24	15	0	2	92.0	432	113	57	55	8	2	3	6	55	0	59	6	1	5	5	.500	0	0-0	1	6.53	5.38

Jeremy Bonderman

Pitches: R **Bats:** R **Pos:** RP-7; SP-1   **Ht:** 6'2" **Wt:** 220 **Born:** 10/28/1982 **Age:** 27

			HOW MUCH HE PITCHED					WHAT HE GAVE UP									THE RESULTS						
Year	Team	Lg	G	GS	CG	GF	IP	BFP	H	R	ER	HR	SH	SF	HB	TBB	IBB	SO	WP	Bk	W	L	Pct	Sh	Sv-Op	Hld	ERC	ERA
2009 WMich*	A	1	1	0	0	7.0	27	6	2	2	0	0	0	0	1	0	4	0	0	1	0	1.000	0	0--	-	1.86	2.57
2009 Toledo*	AAA	14	3	0	2	34.0	147	40	17	16	4	1	0	1	7	0	26	4	0	1	4	.200	0	1--	-	4.53	4.24
2003 Det	AL	33	28	0	0	162.0	727	193	118	100	23	3	6	4	58	2	108	12	2	6	19	.240	0	0-0	0	5.39	5.56
2004 Det	AL	33	32	2	0	184.0	793	168	101	100	24	10	5	10	73	5	168	7	0	11	13	.458	2	0-0	0	3.93	4.89
2005 Det	AL	29	29	4	0	189.0	801	199	101	96	21	3	3	4	57	0	145	5	1	14	13	.519	0	0-0	0	4.20	4.57
2006 Det	AL	34	34	0	0	214.0	903	214	104	97	18	3	6	3	64	7	202	3	1	14	8	.636	0	0-0	0	3.58	4.08
2007 Det	AL	28	28	0	0	174.1	753	193	105	97	23	2	4	4	48	6	145	12	1	11	9	.550	0	0-0	0	4.44	5.01
2008 Det	AL	12	12	0	0	71.1	319	75	39	34	9	2	3	3	36	2	44	1	0	3	4	.429	0	0-0	0	5.14	4.29
2009 Det	AL	8	1	0	1	10.1	53	16	10	10	4	0	0	1	8	0	5	0	0	0	1	.000	0	0-0	0	12.87	8.71
Postseason		3	3	0	0	20.1	84	17	7	7	1	1	0	0	7	1	11	1	0	1	0	1.000	0	0-0	0	2.58	3.10
7 ML YEARS		177	164	6	1	1005.0	4349	1058	578	534	122	23	27	29	344	22	817	40	5	59	67	.468	2	0-0	0	4.38	4.78

Emilio Bonifacio

Bats: B **Throws:** R **Pos:** 3B-86; SS-20; CF-11; PR-8; 2B-7; PH-7; LF-6   **Ht:** 5'11" **Wt:** 195 **Born:** 4/23/1985 **Age:** 25

						BATTING															BASERUNNING			AVERAGES		
Year	Team	Lg	G	AB	H	2B	3B	HR	(Hm	Rd)	TB	R	RBI	RC	TBB	IBB	SO	HBP	SH	SF	SB	CS	SB%	GDP	Avg	OBP	Slg
2007 Ari	NL	11	23	5	1	0	0	(0	0)	6	2	2	4	4	0	3	0	0	0	0	1	.00	0	.217	.333	.261
2008 2 Tms	NL	49	169	41	6	5	0	(0	0)	57	29	14	16	14	0	46	0	0	3	7	4	.64	2	.243	.296	.337
2009 Fla	NL	127	461	116	11	6	1	(1	0)	142	72	27	41	34	0	95	2	8	4	21	9	.70	5	.252	.303	.308
08 Ari	NL	8	12	2	1	0	0	(0	0)	3	3	2	1	0	0	5	0	0	0	1	0	1.00	0	.167	.167	.250
08 Was	NL	41	157	39	5	5	0	(0	0)	54	26	12	15	14	0	41	0	0	3	6	4	.60	2	.248	.305	.344
3 ML YEARS		187	653	162	18	11	1	(1	0)	205	103	43	61	52	0	144	2	8	7	28	14	.67	7	.248	.303	.314

Eddie Bonine

Pitches: R **Bats:** R **Pos:** RP-6; SP-4   **Ht:** 6'5" **Wt:** 220 **Born:** 6/6/1981 **Age:** 29

			HOW MUCH HE PITCHED					WHAT HE GAVE UP									THE RESULTS								
Year	Team	Lg	G	GS	CG	GF	IP	BFP	H	R	ER	HR	SH	SF	HB	TBB	IBB	SO	WP	Bk	W	L	Pct	Sh	Sv-Op	Hld	ERC	ERA
2003 Eugene	A-	31	0	0	26	33.1	143	32	15	14	2	1	1	3	10	0	33	1	0	1	2	.333	0	14--	-	3.51	3.78
2004 FtWyn	A	5	5	0	0	27.1	109	25	11	6	2	1	0	0	3	0	31	0	0	2	1	.667	0	0--	-	2.36	1.98
2004 Lk Els	A+	21	21	0	0	112.1	492	121	82	68	12	7	9	8	39	0	96	12	0	5	10	.333	0	0--	-	4.66	5.45
2005 Lk Els	A+	36	10	0	7	104.1	494	142	88	75	14	3	5	4	42	0	77	8	0	5	6	.455	0	0--	-	6.62	6.47
2005 Portlnd	AAA	1	0	0	0	2.0	7	0	0	0	0	0	0	0	0	0	5	0	0	1	0	1.000	0	0--	-	0.00	0.00
2006 Lkland	A+	41	11	0	13	106.1	450	108	62	47	9	2	4	5	27	0	83	8	1	4	4	.500	0	1--	-	3.67	3.98
2006 Erie	AA	1	1	0	0	6.0	26	8	6	6	3	0	0	1	0	0	2	0	0	1	0	1.000	0	0--	-	8.18	9.00
2007 Erie	AA	25	25	2	0	154.2	643	159	77	67	13	5	2	11	24	1	73	11	2	14	5	.737	0	0--	-	3.45	3.90
2007 Toledo	AAA	1	1	0	0	8.0	31	7	2	2	0	0	0	0	1	0	4	1	0	1	0	1.000	0	0--	-	1.87	2.25
2008 Toledo	AAA	17	17	1	0	106.1	440	107	53	49	10	6	3	5	18	0	69	3	0	12	4	.750	0	0--	-	3.36	4.15
2008 Erie	AA	1	1	0	0	3.2	17	4	2	1	0	0	0	1	2	0	1	0	0	0	1	.000	0	0--	-	5.65	2.45
2009 Toledo	AAA	17	17	1	0	102.0	423	112	54	49	9	2	1	4	16	2	51	1	0	4	5	.444	0	0--	-	3.77	4.32
2008 Det	AL	5	5	0	0	26.2	117	36	19	16	3	1	1	2	5	0	9	0	0	2	1	.667	0	0-0	0	5.82	5.40
2009 Det	AL	10	4	0	2	34.1	145	40	19	17	7	0	2	1	12	1	19	0	0	1	1	.500	0	0-0	0	6.00	4.46
2 ML YEARS		15	9	0	2	61.0	262	76	38	33	10	1	3	3	17	1	28	0	0	3	2	.600	0	0-0	0	5.93	4.87

Boof Bonser

Pitches: R **Bats:** R **Pos:** P   **Ht:** 6'4" **Wt:** 245 **Born:** 10/14/1981 **Age:** 28

			HOW MUCH HE PITCHED					WHAT HE GAVE UP									THE RESULTS								
Year	Team	Lg	G	GS	CG	GF	IP	BFP	H	R	ER	HR	SH	SF	HB	TBB	IBB	SO	WP	Bk	W	L	Pct	Sh	Sv-Op	Hld	ERC	ERA
2009 FtMyrs*	A+	1	0	0	0	1.0	4	0	0	0	0	0	0	0	1	0	1	0	0	0	0	-	0	0--	-	0.95	0.00
2006 Min	AL	18	18	0	0	100.1	419	104	50	47	18	2	2	1	24	0	84	2	0	7	6	.538	0	0-0	0	4.25	4.22
2007 Min	AL	31	30	0	0	173.0	772	199	108	98	27	4	3	5	65	4	136	3	1	8	12	.400	0	0-0	0	5.33	5.10
2008 Min	AL	47	12	0	9	118.1	532	139	87	78	16	3	4	1	36	1	97	6	1	3	7	.300	0	0-2	2	4.84	5.93
Postseason		1	1	0	0	6.0	25	7	2	2	0	0	0	0	1	0	3	0	0	0	0	-	0	0-0	0	3.46	3.00
3 ML YEARS		96	60	0	9	391.2	1723	442	245	223	61	9	9	7	125	5	317	11	2	18	25	.419	0	0-2	2	4.90	5.12

Aaron Boone

Bats: R **Throws:** R **Pos:** PH-8; 1B-2; 3B-1   **Ht:** 6'3" **Wt:** 206 **Born:** 3/9/1973 **Age:** 37

						BATTING															BASERUNNING			AVERAGES		
Year	Team	Lg	G	AB	H	2B	3B	HR	(Hm	Rd)	TB	R	RBI	RC	TBB	IBB	SO	HBP	SH	SF	SB	CS	SB%	GDP	Avg	OBP	Slg
2009 CpChr*	AA	7	15	3	1	0	0	(-	-)	4	2	1	1	3	0	3	0	0	0	0	0	-	0	.200	.333	.267
2009 RdRck*	AAA	4	11	1	0	0	0	(-	-)	1	1	0	0	0	0	1	0	0	0	0	0	-	0	.091	.091	.091
1997 Cin	NL	16	49	12	1	0	0	(0	0)	13	5	5	3	2	0	5	0	1	0	1	0	1.00	1	.245	.275	.265
1998 Cin	NL	58	181	51	13	2	2	(2	0)	74	24	28	27	15	1	36	5	3	2	6	1	.86	3	.282	.350	.409
1999 Cin	NL	139	472	132	26	5	14	(7	7)	210	56	72	70	30	2	79	8	5	5	17	6	.74	6	.280	.330	.445
2000 Cin	NL	84	291	83	18	0	12	(5	7)	137	44	43	50	24	1	52	10	2	4	6	1	.86	5	.285	.356	.471
2001 Cin	NL	103	381	112	26	2	14	(10	4)	184	54	62	63	29	1	71	8	3	6	6	3	.67	9	.294	.351	.483
2002 Cin	NL	162	606	146	38	2	26	(14	12)	266	83	87	83	56	4	111	10	9	4	32	8	.80	9	.241	.314	.439
2003 2 Tms	NL	160	592	158	32	3	24	(13	11)	268	92	96	89	46	2	104	8	6	2	23	3	.88	13	.267	.327	.453
2005 Cle	AL	143	511	124	19	1	16	(5	11)	193	61	60	52	35	3	92	9	4	6	9	3	.75	16	.243	.299	.378
2006 Cle	AL	104	354	89	19	1	7	(1	6)	131	50	46	46	27	1	62	6	4	1	5	4	.56	4	.251	.314	.370
2007 Fla	NL	69	189	54	11	0	6	(1	4)	83	20	27	28	32	2	41	13	1	4	2	0	1.00	6	.286	.388	.423
2008 Was	NL	104	232	56	13	1	6	(4	2)	89	23	28	22	18	1	52	2	1	2	1	0	1.00	8	.241	.299	.384
2009 Hou	NL	10	13	0	0	0	0	(0	0)	0	0	0	0	1	0	2	1	0	0	0	0	-	0	.000	.071	.000

Year	Team	Lg	G	AB	H	2B	3B	HR	(Hm	Rd)	TB	R	RBI	RC	TBB	IBB	SO	HBP	SH	SF	SB	CS	SB%	GDP	Avg	OBP	Slg
03	Cin	NL	106	403	110	19	3	18	(10	8)	180	61	05	65	35	2	74	5	3	0	15	3	.83	6	.273	.339	.469
03	NYY	AL	54	189	48	13	0	6	(3	3)	79	31	31	24	11	0	30	3	3	0	8	0	1.00	7	.254	.302	.418
	Postseason		17	53	9	1	0	2	(1	1)	16	4	4	2	1	0	15	1	2	1	2	1	.67	0	.170	.196	.302
	12 ML YEARS		1152	3871	1017	216	17	126	(62	64)	1645	519	555	537	303	20	707	80	39	36	107	30	.78	74	.263	.326	.425

Chris Bootcheck

Pitches: R Bats: R Pos: RP-13 **Ht: 6'5" Wt: 210 Born: 10/24/1978 Age: 31**

Year	Team	Lg	G	GS	CG	GF	IP	BFP	H	R	ER	HR	SH	SF	HB	TBB	IBB	SO	WP	Bk	W	L	Pct	Sh	Sv-Op	Hld	ERC	ERA
2009	Indy*	AAA	40	0	0	32	42.2	170	40	16	16	1	0	1	1	7	0	55	0	0	3	2	.600	0	20- -	-	2.51	3.38
2003	LAA	AL	4	1	0	2	10.1	53	16	13	11	5	0	0	0	6	0	7	0	0	0	1	.000	0	0-0	0	11.53	9.58
2005	LAA	AL	5	2	0	1	18.2	79	19	7	7	1	0	1	0	4	1	8	1	0	0	1	.000	0	1-1	0	3.00	3.38
2006	LAA	AL	7	0	0	5	10.1	54	16	12	12	3	1	0	0	9	0	7	1	0	0	1	.000	0	0-0	0	11.63	10.45
2007	LAA	AL	51	0	0	17	77.1	331	81	43	41	7	2	4	5	24	3	56	6	1	3	3	.500	0	0-1	4	4.16	4.77
2008	LAA	AL	10	0	0	4	16.0	90	30	18	18	2	0	0	0	12	0	14	2	0	0	1	.000	0	0 0	1	11.28	10.13
2009	Pit	NL	13	0	0	3	14.2	70	16	18	18	1	3	1	1	9	0	13	0	0	0	0	-	0	0 0	1	5.35	11.05
	6 ML YEARS		90	3	0	32	147.1	677	178	111	107	19	6	6	6	64	4	105	10	1	3	7	.300	0	1-2	6	5.75	6.54

Julio Borbon

Bats: L Throws: L Pos: DH-23; LF-16; CF-4; PH-4; PR-3 **Ht: 6'1" Wt: 180 Born: 2/20/1986 Age: 24**

Year	Team	Lg	G	AB	H	2B	3B	HR	(Hm	Rd)	TB	R	RBI	RC	TBB	IBB	SO	HBP	SH	SF	SB	CS	SB%	GDP	Avg	OBP	Slg
2007	Spkane	A-	7	29	5	0	0	0	(-	-)	5	1	2	0	2	0	3	0	0	0	3	1	.75	1	.172	.226	.172
2007	Rngrs	R	2	8	2	1	0	0	(-	-)	3	0	0	0	1	0	1	0	0	0	0	1	.00	0	.250	.333	.375
2008	Bkrsfld	A+	66	291	89	20	0	2	(-	-)	115	47	36	45	15	0	30	4	2	2	36	7	.84	4	.306	.346	.395
2008	Frisco	AA	60	265	86	12	2	5	(-	-)	117	40	22	40	14	0	32	4	6	1	17	11	.61	3	.337	.380	.459
2009	Okla	AAA	96	407	126	12	7	2	(-	-)	158	71	35	64	33	2	40	7	8	2	25	7	.78	7	.310	.370	.388
2009	Tex	AL	46	157	49	4	0	4	(2	2)	65	30	20	27	15	0	28	1	6	0	19	4	.83	3	.312	.376	.414

Jason Bourgeois

Bats: R Throws: R Pos: PH-16; RF-6; LF-1; PR-1 **Ht: 5'9" Wt: 190 Born: 1/4/1982 Age: 28**

Year	Team	Lg	G	AB	H	2B	3B	HR	(Hm	Rd)	TB	R	RBI	RC	TBB	IBB	SO	HBP	SH	SF	SB	CS	SB%	GDP	Avg	OBP	Slg
2000	Rngrs	R	24	88	21	4	0	0	(-	-)	25	18	6	11	14	0	15	2	2	0	9	2	.82	0	.239	.356	.284
2001	Pulaski	R+	62	251	78	12	2	7	(-	-)	115	60	34	47	26	0	47	6	0	1	21	7	.75	3	.311	.387	.458
2002	Savann	A	127	522	133	21	5	8	(-	-)	188	72	49	64	40	1	66	11	8	5	22	11	.67	5	.255	.318	.360
2002	Charltt	A+	9	27	5	1	0	0	(-	-)	6	5	4	1	2	0	4	0	0	1	1	1	.50	0	.185	.233	.222
2003	Stcktn	A+	69	277	91	22	3	4	(-	-)	131	75	34	58	36	0	33	7	3	2	16	3	.84	4	.329	.416	.473
2003	Frisco	AA	55	202	51	5	4	4	(-	-)	76	28	21	46	16	0	45	2	4	2	3	1	.75	4	.252	.308	.376
2004	Frisco	AA	138	530	135	19	7	2	(-	-)	174	73	58	60	44	0	81	3	2	4	30	10	.75	8	.255	.313	.328
2005	Rchmd	AAA	119	388	93	20	2	2	(-	-)	123	33	16	39	31	1	57	4	3	2	8	5	.62	3	.240	.301	.317
2006	SnAnt	AA	107	411	114	22	7	4	(-	-)	162	65	38	50	37	0	66	3	4	5	23	7	.77	6	.277	.338	.394
2007	Brham	AA	43	162	48	10	3	2	(-	-)	70	25	20	28	16	0	20	1	2	3	15	3	.83	0	.296	.357	.432
2007	Charltt	AAA	84	338	105	18	3	7	(-	-)	150	51	34	68	29	1	49	3	3	1	23	6	.79	5	.311	.309	.444
2008	Charltt	AAA	127	510	146	23	5	9	(-	-)	206	83	48	73	33	0	65	5	9	2	30	11	.73	9	.286	.335	.404
2009	Nashv	AAA	105	424	134	18	6	2	(-	-)	170	61	41	66	22	0	40	4	2	2	36	7	.84	7	.316	.354	.401
2008	CWS	AL	6	3	1	1	0	0	(0	0)	2	0	0	0	0	0	0	0	0	0	0	0	-	0	.333	.333	.667
2009	Mil	NL	24	37	7	0	0	1	(1	0)	10	6	3	1	3	0	7	0	0	0	3	0	1.00	2	.189	.250	.270
	2 ML YEARS		30	40	8	1	0	1	(1	0)	12	6	3	1	3	0	7	0	0	0	3	0	1.00	2	.200	.256	.300

Michael Bourn

Bats: L Throws: R Pos: CF-154; PH-2; PR-2 **Ht: 5'11" Wt: 180 Born: 12/27/1982 Age: 27**

Year	Team	Lg	G	AB	H	2B	3B	HR	(Hm	Rd)	TB	R	RBI	RC	TBB	IBB	SO	HBP	SH	SF	SB	CS	SB%	GDP	Avg	OBP	Slg
2006	Phi	NL	17	8	1	0	0	0	(0	0)	1	2	0	0	1	0	3	0	2	0	1	2	.33	0	.125	.222	.125
2007	Phi	NL	105	119	33	3	3	1	(1	0)	45	29	6	19	13	2	21	0	1	0	18	1	.95	1	.277	.348	.378
2008	Hou	NL	138	467	107	10	4	5	(3	2)	140	57	29	43	37	0	111	2	7	1	41	10	.80	3	.229	.288	.300
2009	Hou	NL	157	606	173	27	12	3	(2	1)	233	97	35	94	63	1	140	2	5	2	61	12	.84	1	.285	.354	.384
	Postseason		2	1	0	0	0	0	(0	0)	0	0	0	0	0	0	0	0	0	0	0	0	-	0	.000	.000	.000
	4 ML YEARS		417	1200	314	40	19	9	(6	3)	419	185	70	156	114	3	275	4	15	3	121	25	.83	5	.262	.327	.349

Michael Bowden

Pitches: R Bats: R Pos: RP-7; SP-1 **Ht: 6'3" Wt: 215 Born: 9/9/1986 Age: 23**

Year	Team	Lg	G	GS	CG	GF	IP	BFP	H	R	ER	HR	SH	SF	HB	TBB	IBB	SO	WP	Bk	W	L	Pct	Sh	Sv-Op	Hld	ERC	ERA
2005	RedSx	R	4	2	0	0	6.0	26	4	0	0	0	1	0	0	4	0	10	0	0	1	0	1.000	0	0- -	-	2.54	0.00
2006	Grnville	R	24	24	0	0	107.2	443	91	50	42	9	2	1	2	31	0	118	9	0	9	6	.600	0	0- -	-	2.77	3.51
2006	Wilmg	A+	1	1	0	0	5.0	25	9	5	5	0	0	1	0	1	0	3	1	0	0	0	-	0	0- -	-	7.08	9.00
2007	Lancst	A+	8	8	0	0	46.0	176	35	10	7	1	2	1	0	8	0	46	2	0	2	0	1.000	0	0- -	-	1.65	1.37
2007	Portlnd	AA	19	19	1	0	96.2	418	105	54	46	9	1	4	4	33	0	81	3	1	8	6	.571	0	0- -	-	4.50	4.28
2008	Portlnd	AA	19	19	0	0	104.1	403	72	31	27	5	3	1	0	24	0	101	3	0	9	4	.692	0	0- -	-	1.63	2.33
2008	Pwtckt	AAA	7	6	0	1	40.0	161	40	16	15	5	3	0	0	5	0	29	0	0		3	.000	0	0- -	-	3.19	3.38

Year Team	Lg	HOW MUCH HE PITCHED						WHAT HE GAVE UP												THE RESULTS							
		G	GS	CG	GF	IP	BFP	H	R	ER	HR	SH	SF	HB	TBB	IBB	SO	WP	Bk	W	L	Pct	Sh	Sv-Op	Hld	ERC	ERA
2009 Pwtckt	AAA	24	24	0	0	126.1	517	106	47	44	11	3	2	1	47	0	88	5	0	4	6	.400	0	0--	-	3.09	3.13
2008 Bos	AL	1	1	0	0	5.0	22	7	2	2	0	0	0	0	1	0	3	0	0	1	0	1.000	0	0-0	-	4.92	3.60
2009 Bos	AL	8	1	0	3	16.0	75	23	17	17	3	0	0	0	6	0	12	3	0	1	1	.500	0	0-0	1	7.35	9.56
2 ML YEARS		9	2	0	3	21.0	97	30	19	19	3	0	0	0	7	0	15	3	0	2	1	.667	0	0-0	1	6.76	8.14

John Bowker

Bats: L **Throws:** L **Pos:** LF-13; PH-11; RF-5; 1B-4   **Ht:** 6'2" **Wt:** 200 **Born:** 7/8/1983 **Age:** 26

Year Team	Lg	BATTING																					BASERUNNING				AVERAGES		
		G	AB	H	2B	3B	HR	(Hm	Rd)	TB	R	RBI	RC	TBB	IBB	SO	HBP	SH	SF				SB	CS	SB%	GDP	Avg	OBP	Slg
2004 Giants	R	10	43	22	7	1	2	(-	-)	37	14	11	17	7	0	11	0	0	0				1	0	1.00	1	.512	.580	.860
2004 SlmKzr	A-	31	127	41	9	2	4	(-	-)	66	23	16	25	8	2	25	6	0	0				1	0	1.00	5	.323	.390	.520
2005 SnJos	A+	121	464	124	27	1	13	(-	-)	192	66	67	62	36	0	108	3	2	8				3	7	.30	14	.267	.319	.414
2006 SnJos	A+	112	462	131	32	6	7	(-	-)	196	61	66	68	37	3	100	2	7	3				6	3	.67	12	.284	.337	.424
2006 Fresno	AAA	2	4	2	0	0	0	(-	-)	2	0	0	0	0	0	0	0	0	0				0	0	-	0	.500	.500	.500
2007 Conn	AA	139	522	160	35	6	22	(-	-)	273	79	90	98	41	1	103	12	0	12				3	7	.30	17	.307	.363	.523
2008 Fresno	AAA	23	93	22	3	1	2	(-	-)	33	13	9	10	7	0	23	2	0	0				2	0	1.00	1	.237	.304	.355
2009 Fresno	AAA	104	366	125	22	4	21	(-	-)	218	82	83	97	74	7	64	4	0	6				10	6	.63	6	.342	.451	.596
2008 SF	NL	111	326	83	14	3	10	(6	4)	133	31	43	41	19	1	74	3	0	2				1	1	.50	7	.255	.300	.408
2009 SF	NL	31	67	13	2	2	2	(2	0)	25	7	7	4	4	0	18	1	0	1				1	0	1.00	0	.194	.247	.373
2 ML YEARS		142	393	96	16	5	12	(8	4)	158	38	50	45	23	1	92	4	0	3				2	1	.67	7	.244	.291	.402

Blaine Boyer

Pitches: R **Bats:** R **Pos:** RP-48   **Ht:** 6'3" **Wt:** 215 **Born:** 7/11/1981 **Age:** 28

Year Team	Lg	HOW MUCH HE PITCHED						WHAT HE GAVE UP												THE RESULTS							
		G	GS	CG	GF	IP	BFP	H	R	ER	HR	SH	SF	HB	TBB	IBB	SO	WP	Bk	W	L	Pct	Sh	Sv-Op	Hld	ERC	ERA
2005 Atl	NL	43	0	0	5	37.2	158	32	13	13	1	1	1	2	17	0	33	2	0	4	2	.667	0	0-2	9	3.21	3.11
2006 Atl	NL	2	0	0	2	0.2	7	4	3	3	0	0	0	0	1	0	0	0	0	0	0	-	0	0-0	1	47.92	40.50
2007 Atl	NL	5	0	0	2	5.1	26	10	3	2	0	1	0	0	1	1	3	2	0	0	0	-	0	0-0	1	7.41	3.38
2008 Atl	NL	76	0	0	18	72.0	313	73	51	47	10	3	4	2	25	4	67	2	0	2	6	.250	0	1-5	14	4.19	5.88
2009 3 Tms	NL	48	0	0	21	54.2	241	56	36	25	1	4	1	5	20	0	29	2	0	0	2	.000	0	0-0	4	3.81	4.12
09 Atl	NL	3	0	0	1	1.1	11	3	6	6	0	0	0	1	3	0	2	0	0	0	1	.000	0	0-0	0	23.46	40.50
09 StL	NL	15	0	0	4	16.1	70	14	10	8	1	3	0	1	5	0	9	0	0	0	0	-	0	0-2	2	2.82	4.41
09 Ari	NL	30	0	0	16	37.0	160	39	20	11	0	1	1	3	12	0	18	2	0	0	1	.000	0	0-0	2	3.71	2.68
5 ML YEARS		174	0	0	46	170.1	745	175	106	90	12	9	6	9	64	5	132	8	0	6	10	.375	0	1-7	29	4.06	4.76

Dallas Braden

Pitches: L **Bats:** L **Pos:** SP-22   **Ht:** 6'1" **Wt:** 198 **Born:** 8/13/1983 **Age:** 26

Year Team	Lg	HOW MUCH HE PITCHED						WHAT HE GAVE UP												THE RESULTS							
		G	GS	CG	GF	IP	BFP	H	R	ER	HR	SH	SF	HB	TBB	IBB	SO	WP	Bk	W	L	Pct	Sh	Sv-Op	Hld	ERC	ERA
2007 Oak	AL	20	14	0	1	72.1	332	91	59	54	9	4	0	2	26	1	55	6	1	1	8	.111	0	0-0	1	5.63	6.72
2008 Oak	AL	19	10	0	7	71.2	301	77	36	33	8	1	2	2	25	2	41	0	1	5	4	.556	0	0-0	0	4.63	4.14
2009 Oak	AL	22	22	0	0	136.2	589	144	63	59	9	4	4	2	42	2	81	1	0	8	9	.471	0	0-0	0	3.78	3.89
3 ML YEARS		61	46	0	8	280.2	1222	312	158	146	26	9	6	6	93	5	177	7	2	14	21	.400	0	0-0	1	4.45	4.68

Chad Bradford

Pitches: R **Bats:** R **Pos:** RP-20   **Ht:** 6'5" **Wt:** 215 **Born:** 9/14/1974 **Age:** 35

Year Team	Lg	HOW MUCH HE PITCHED						WHAT HE GAVE UP												THE RESULTS							
		G	GS	CG	GF	IP	BFP	H	R	ER	HR	SH	SF	HB	TBB	IBB	SO	WP	Bk	W	L	Pct	Sh	Sv-Op	Hld	ERC	ERA
2009 Charltt*	A+	6	0	0	0	6.0	21	4	0	0	0	0	0	0	0	0	5	0	0	1	0	1.000	0	0--	-	0.96	0.00
2009 Mont*	AA	2	0	0	0	2.0	10	3	1	1	0	0	0	1	1	0	2	0	0	0	0	-	0	0--	-	9.50	4.50
2009 Drham*	AAA	4	0	0	0	4.2	22	7	3	3	0	0	1	0	1	0	2	0	0	1	0	1.000	0	0--	-	5.32	5.79
1998 CWS	AL	29	0	0	8	30.2	125	27	16	11	0	0	0	0	7	0	11	1	1	2	1	.667	0	1-3	9	2.16	3.23
1999 CWS	AL	3	0	0	0	3.2	24	9	8	8	1	0	0	0	5	0	0	1	0	0	0	-	0	0-0	0	21.34	19.64
2000 CWS	AL	12	0	0	5	13.2	52	13	4	3	0	0	0	0	1	1	9	0	0	1	0	1.000	0	0-0	2	2.01	1.98
2001 Oak	AL	35	0	0	19	36.2	154	41	12	11	6	1	0	1	6	0	34	0	0	2	1	.667	0	1-4	4	4.36	2.70
2002 Oak	AL	75	0	0	14	75.1	311	73	29	26	2	2	2	5	14	5	56	0	1	4	2	.667	0	2-5	24	2.77	3.11
2003 Oak	AL	72	0	0	12	77.0	322	67	28	26	7	1	0	7	30	9	62	0	1	7	4	.636	0	2-5	23	3.50	3.04
2004 Oak	AL	68	0	0	16	59.0	251	51	32	29	5	3	1	5	24	9	34	0	0	5	7	.417	0	1-4	14	3.35	4.42
2005 Bos	AL	31	0	0	2	23.1	104	29	10	10	1	3	1	3	4	1	10	2	0	1	1	.667	0	0-1	8	4.54	3.86
2006 NYM	NL	70	0	0	15	62.0	252	59	22	20	1	4	3	0	13	4	45	0	0	4	2	.667	0	2-3	10	2.48	2.90
2007 Bal	AL	78	0	0	14	64.2	289	77	28	24	1	4	1	6	16	3	29	0	0	4	7	.364	0	2-7	19	4.16	3.34
2008 2 Tms	AL	68	0	0	9	59.1	241	59	20	14	3	3	5	2	15	6	17	0	0	4	3	.571	0	0-2	21	3.24	2.12
2009 TB	AL	20	0	0	1	10.1	55	22	5	5	1	0	2	0	2	1	6	0	0	1	0	1.000	0	0-1	1	9.92	4.35
08 Bal	AL	47	0	0	5	40.1	160	41	17	11	2	3	2	1	7	3	13	0	0	3	3	.500	0	0-1	16	3.09	2.45
08 TB	AL	21	0	0	4	19.0	81	18	3	3	1	0	3	1	8	3	4	0	0	1	0	1.000	0	0-1	5	3.53	1.42
Postseason		24	0	0	2	23.1	88	18	1	1	0	0	0	2	6	3	13	0	0	0	0	-	0	0-1	2	2.05	0.39
12 ML YEARS		561	0	0	115	515.2	2180	527	214	187	28	21	15	29	137	39	313	4	3	36	28	.563	0	11-35	136	3.48	3.26

Milton Bradley

Bats: B **Throws:** R **Pos:** RF-109; PH-15; CF-1   **Ht:** 6'0" **Wt:** 225 **Born:** 4/15/1978 **Age:** 32

							BATTING													BASERUNNING				AVERAGES		
Year	Team	Lg	G	AB	H	2B	3B	HR	(Hm | Rd)	TB	R	RBI	RC	TBB	IBB	SO	HBP	SH	SF	SB	CS	SB%	GDP	Avg	OBP	Slg
2000	Mon	NL	42	154	34	8	1	2	(1 | 1)	50	20	15	14	14	0	32	1	1	1	2	1	.67	3	.221	.288	.325
2001	2 Tms		77	238	53	17	3	1	(0 | 1)	79	22	19	21	21	0	65	1	2	0	8	5	.62	7	.223	.288	.332
2002	Cle	AL	98	325	81	18	3	9	(4 | 5)	132	48	38	40	32	2	58	0	1	0	6	3	.67	12	.249	.317	.406
2003	Cle	AL	101	377	121	34	2	10	(4 | 6)	189	61	56	77	64	8	73	5	0	5	17	7	.71	10	.321	.421	.501
2004	LAD	NL	141	516	138	24	0	19	(8 | 11)	219	72	67	77	71	3	123	6	3	1	15	11	.58	12	.267	.362	.424
2005	LAD	NL	75	283	82	14	1	13	(6 | 7)	137	49	38	40	25	1	47	2	4	1	6	1	.86	6	.290	.350	.484
2006	Oak	AL	96	351	97	14	2	14	(7 | 7)	157	53	52	60	51	1	65	2	0	1	10	2	.83	13	.276	.370	.447
2007	2 Tms		61	209	64	9	1	13	(7 | 6)	114	37	37	42	31	3	41	3	0	1	5	2	.71	5	.306	.402	.545
2008	Tex	AL	126	414	133	32	1	22	(16 | 6)	233	78	77	90	80	13	112	9	0	6	5	3	.63	10	.321	.436	.563
2009	ChC	NL	124	393	101	17	1	12	(9 | 3)	156	61	40	56	66	4	95	11	2	1	2	3	.40	10	.257	.378	.397
01	Mon	NL	67	220	49	16	3	1	(0 | 1)	74	19	19	20	19	0	62	1	2	0	7	4	.64	6	.223	.288	.336
01	Cle	AL	10	18	4	1	0	0	(0 | 0)	5	3	0	1	2	0	3	0	0	0	1	1	.50	1	.222	.300	.278
07	Oak	AL	19	65	19	4	0	2	(1 | 1)	29	6	7	10	8	1	14	1	0	1	2	1	.67	2	.292	.373	.446
07	SD	NL	42	144	45	5	1	11	(6 | 5)	85	31	30	32	23	2	27	2	0	0	3	1	.75	3	.313	.414	.590
	Postseason		11	42	13	3	0	4	(3 | 1)	28	6	8	7	5	0	5	0	0	0	2	0	1.00	3	.310	.383	.667
	10 ML YEARS		941	3260	904	187	15	115	(62 | 53)	1466	501	439	510	455	35	711	40	13	17	76	38	.67	88	.277	.371	.450

Michael Brantley

Bats: L **Throws:** L **Pos:** CF-20; LF-8; PH-2   **Ht:** 6'2" **Wt:** 200 **Born:** 5/15/1987 **Age:** 23

							BATTING													BASERUNNING				AVERAGES		
Year	Team	Lg	G	AB	H	2B	3B	HR	(Hm | Rd)	TB	R	RBI	RC	TBB	IBB	SO	HBP	SH	SF	SB	CS	SB%	GDP	Avg	OBP	Slg
2005	Brewrs	R	44	173	60	3	1	0	(- | -)	65	34	19	31	22	0	13	2	4	0	14	5	.74	2	.347	.426	.376
2005	Helena	R+	10	34	11	2	0	0	(| -)	13	8	3	6	6	0	4	0	0	0	2	0	1.00	0	.324	.425	.382
2006	WV	A-	108	360	108	10	2	0	(| -)	122	47	42	60	61	0	51	4	6	5	24	7	.77	5	.300	.402	.339
2007	WV	A	56	218	73	15	1	2	(- | -)	96	41	33	43	31	0	22	1	1	4	18	6	.75	3	.335	.413	.440
2007	Hntsvl	AA	59	187	47	6	1	0	(- | -)	55	28	21	24	29	1	25	1	5	1	16	3	.84	8	.251	.353	.294
2008	Hntsvl	AA	108	420	134	17	2	4	(- | -)	167	80	40	73	50	5	27	4	3	2	28	8	.78	6	.319	.395	.398
2009	Clmbs	AAA	116	457	122	21	2	6	(- | -)	165	80	37	70	59	1	48	1	8	3	46	5	.90	7	.267	.350	.361
2009	Cle	AL	28	112	35	4	0	0	(0 | 0)	39	10	11	16	8	0	19	0	1	0	4	4	.50	3	.313	.358	.348

Russell Branyan

Bats: L **Throws:** R **Pos:** 1B-116   **Ht:** 6'3" **Wt:** 230 **Born:** 12/19/1975 **Age:** 34

							BATTING													BASERUNNING				AVERAGES		
Year	Team	Lg	G	AB	H	2B	3B	HR	(Hm | Rd)	TB	R	RBI	RC	TBB	IBB	SO	HBP	SH	SF	SB	CS	SB%	GDP	Avg	OBP	Slg
1998	Cle	AL	1	4	0	0	0	0	(0 | 0)	0	0	0	0	0	0	2	0	0	0	0	0	-	0	.000	.000	.000
1999	Cle	AL	11	38	8	2	0	1	(0 | 1)	13	4	6	4	3	0	19	1	0	0	0	0	-	0	.211	.286	.342
2000	Cle	AL	67	193	46	7	2	16	(13 | 3)	105	32	38	34	22	1	76	4	0	1	0	0	-	2	.238	.327	.544
2001	Cle	AL	113	315	73	16	2	20	(11 | 9)	153	48	54	50	38	1	132	3	0	5	1	1	.50	2	.232	.316	.486
2002	2 Tms		134	378	86	13	1	24	(5 | 19)	173	50	56	49	51	3	151	2	0	4	4	3	.57	5	.228	.320	.458
2003	Cin	NL	74	176	38	12	0	9	(7 | 2)	77	22	26	23	27	0	69	1	0	1	0	0	-	1	.216	.322	.438
2004	Mil	NL	51	158	37	11	1	11	(8 | 3)	83	21	27	23	20	0	68	2	0	2	1	0	1.00	1	.234	.324	.525
2005	Mil	NL	85	202	52	11	0	12	(3 | 9)	99	23	31	38	39	10	80	0	1	0	1	0	1.00	3	.257	.378	.490
2006	2 Tms		91	241	55	11	0	18	(9 | 9)	120	37	36	34	34	1	89	3	1	3	2	0	1.00	1	.228	.327	.498
2007	3 Tms	NL	89	163	32	5	1	10	(6 | 4)	69	22	26	25	28	1	69	2	0	1	1	0	1.00	2	.196	.320	.423
2008	Mil	NL	50	132	33	8	0	12	(7 | 5)	77	24	20	22	19	4	42	0	0	1	1	0	1.00	1	.250	.342	.583
2009	Sea	AL	116	431	108	21	1	31	(16 | 15)	224	64	76	69	58	6	149	9	1	6	2	0	1.00	6	.251	.347	.520
02	Cle	AL	50	161	33	4	0	8	(1 | 7)	61	16	17	14	17	0	65	0	0	2	1	2	.33	3	.205	.278	.379
02	Cin	NL	84	217	53	9	1	16	(4 | 12)	112	34	39	35	34	3	86	2	0	2	3	1	.75	2	.244	.349	.516
06	TB	AL	64	169	34	10	0	12	(7 | 5)	80	23	27	22	19	0	62	2	1	2	2	0	1.00	1	.201	.286	.473
06	SD	NL	27	72	21	1	0	6	(2 | 4)	40	14	9	12	15	1	27	1	0	1	0	0	-	0	.292	.416	.556
07	SD	NL	61	122	24	5	1	7	(5 | 2)	52	16	19	18	21	1	48	2	0	1	1	0	1.00	1	.197	.322	.426
07	Phi	NL	7	9	2	0	0	2	(0 | 2)	8	2	5	2	0	0	6	0	0	0	0	0	-	0	.222	.222	.889
07	StL	NL	21	32	6	0	0	1	(1 | 0)	9	4	2	3	7	0	15	0	0	0	0	0	-	1	.188	.333	.281
	Postseason		6	16	4	1	1	0	(0 | 0)	7	2	3	1	1	0	6	0	0	0	0	0	-	0	.250	.294	.438
	12 ML YEARS		882	2431	568	117	8	164	(87 | 77)	1193	347	396	369	339	27	946	27	3	24	13	4	.76	23	.234	.331	.491

Ryan Braun

Bats: R **Throws:** R **Pos:** LF-158; PH-2   **Ht:** 6'1" **Wt:** 200 **Born:** 11/17/1983 **Age:** 26

							BATTING													BASERUNNING				AVERAGES		
Year	Team	Lg	G	AB	H	2B	3B	HR	(Hm | Rd)	TB	R	RBI	RC	TBB	IBB	SO	HBP	SH	SF	SB	CS	SB%	GDP	Avg	OBP	Slg
2007	Mil	NL	113	451	146	26	6	34	(17 | 17)	286	91	97	94	29	1	112	7	0	5	15	5	.75	13	.324	.370	.634
2008	Mil	NL	151	611	174	39	7	37	(23 | 14)	338	92	106	100	42	4	129	6	0	4	14	4	.78	13	.285	.335	.553
2009	Mil	NL	158	635	203	39	6	32	(15 | 17)	350	113	114	133	57	1	121	13	0	3	20	6	.77	7	.320	.386	.551
	Postseason		4	16	5	2	0	0	(0 | 0)	7	0	2	2	0	0	4	0	0	1	0	0	-	0	.313	.294	.438
	3 ML YEARS		422	1697	523	104	19	103	(55 | 48)	974	296	317	327	128	6	362	26	0	12	49	15	.77	33	.308	.363	.574

Bill Bray

Pitches: L **Bats:** L **Pos:** P   **Ht:** 6'3" **Wt:** 222 **Born:** 6/5/1983 **Age:** 27

			HOW MUCH HE PITCHED						WHAT HE GAVE UP											THE RESULTS					
Year	Team	Lg	G	GS	CG	GF	IP	BFP	H	R	ER	HR	SH	SF	HB	TBB	IBB	SO	WP	Bk	W	L	Pct	Sh	Sv-Op	Hld	ERC	ERA
2009	Lsvlle*	AAA	3	0	0	1	5.0	18	2	0	0	0	0	0	0	1	0	6	0	0	0	0	-	0	0--	-	0.63	0.00
2006	2 Tms	NL	48	0	0	10	50.2	223	57	27	23	5	2	1	1	18	3	39	0	0	3	2	.600	0	2-3	3	4.58	4.09
2007	Cin	NL	19	0	0	5	14.1	63	16	10	10	1	0	1	0	5	1	14	0	0	3	3	.500	0	1-1	3	4.16	6.28

Year	Team	Lg	G	GS	CG	GF	IP	BFP	H	R	ER	HR	SH	SF	HB	TBB	IBB	SO	WP	Bk	W	L	Pct	Sh	Sv-Op	Hld	ERC	ERA
2008	Cin	NL	63	0	0	11	47.0	215	50	19	15	4	3	1	1	24	5	54	2	0	2	2	.500	0	0-4	9	4.57	2.87
06	Was	NL	19	0	0	4	23.0	100	24	11	10	2	1	1	1	9	2	16	0	0	1	1	.500	0	0-0	1	4.25	3.91
06	Cin	NL	29	0	0	6	27.2	123	33	16	13	3	1	0	0	9	1	23	0	0	2	1	.667	0	2-3	2	4.85	4.23
3 ML YEARS			130	0	0	26	112.0	501	123	56	48	10	5	3	2	47	9	107	2	0	8	7	.533	0	3-8	15	4.52	3.86

Craig Breslow

Pitches: L Bats: L Pos: RP-77   Ht: 6'1" Wt: 181 Born: 8/8/1980 Age: 29

Year	Team	Lg	G	GS	CG	GF	IP	BFP	H	R	ER	HR	SH	SF	HB	TBB	IBB	SO	WP	Bk	W	L	Pct	Sh	Sv-Op	Hld	ERC	ERA
2005	SD	AL	14	0	0	3	16.1	78	15	6	4	1	0	1	1	13	0	14	1	0	0	0	-	0	0-0	1	4.98	2.20
2006	Bos	AL	13	0	0	3	12.0	55	12	5	5	0	0	2	1	6	1	12	2	1	0	2	.000	0	0-0	3	3.78	3.75
2008	2 Tms	AL	49	0	0	13	47.0	189	34	12	10	1	2	0	0	19	2	39	4	1	0	2	.000	0	1-2	5	2.12	1.91
2009	2 Tms	AL	77	0	0	9	69.2	281	48	31	26	8	4	1	3	29	0	55	3	1	8	7	.533	0	0-2	15	2.79	3.36
08	Cle	AL	7	0	0	3	8.1	40	10	3	3	1	0	0	0	5	0	7	0	0	0	0	-	0	0-0	0	6.09	3.24
08	Min	AL	42	0	0	10	38.2	149	24	9	7	0	2	0	0	14	2	32	4	1	0	2	.000	0	1-2	5	1.49	1.63
09	Min	AL	17	0	0	5	14.1	64	11	11	10	3	2	0	1	11	0	11	3	0	1	2	.333	0	0-0	2	5.38	6.28
09	Oak	AL	60	0	0	4	55.1	217	37	20	16	5	2	1	2	18	0	44	0	1	7	5	.583	0	0-2	13	2.21	2.60
4 ML YEARS			153	0	0	28	145.0	603	109	54	45	10	6	4	5	67	3	120	10	3	8	11	.421	0	1-4	24	2.88	2.79

Reid Brignac

Bats: L Throws: R Pos: SS-28; PH-4; 2B-3; PR-1   Ht: 6'3" Wt: 195 Born: 1/16/1986 Age: 24

Year	Team	Lg	G	AB	H	2B	3B	HR	(Hm	Rd)	TB	R	RBI	RC	TBB	IBB	SO	HBP	SH	SF	SB	CS	SB%	GDP	Avg	OBP	Slg
2004	Princtn	R+	25	97	35	4	2	1	(-	-)	46	16	25	19	9	0	10	1	0	2	2	1	.67	2	.361	.413	.474
2004	CtnSC	A	3	14	7	1	0	0	(-	-)	8	3	5	3	1	0	2	0	0	0	0	0	-	0	.500	.533	.571
2005	SWMch	A	127	512	135	29	2	15	(-	-)	213	77	61	69	40	0	131	4	4	5	5	5	.50	5	.264	.319	.416
2006	Visalia	A+	100	411	134	26	3	21	(-	-)	229	82	83	85	35	0	82	4	2	3	12	6	.67	6	.326	.382	.557
2006	Mont	AA	28	110	33	6	2	3	(-	-)	52	18	16	19	7	0	31	3	0	1	3	0	1.00	1	.300	.355	.473
2007	Mont	AA	133	527	137	30	5	17	(-	-)	228	91	81	80	55	3	94	3	1	10	15	5	.75	11	.260	.328	.433
2008	Drham	AAA	97	352	88	26	2	9	(-	-)	145	43	43	45	25	2	93	2	1	6	5	2	.71	10	.250	.299	.412
2009	Drham	AAA	96	415	117	28	2	8	(-	-)	173	51	44	57	27	0	69	3	3	5	5	5	.50	7	.282	.327	.417
2008	TB	AL	4	10	0	0	0	0	(0	0)	0	1	0	1	0	1	5	0	0	0	0	0	-	0	.000	.091	.000
2009	TB	AL	31	90	25	8	2	1	(0	1)	40	10	6	10	3	0	20	0	0	0	2	2	.50	1	.278	.301	.444
2 ML YEARS			35	100	25	8	2	1	(0	1)	40	11	6	10	4	0	25	0	0	0	2	2	.50	1	.250	.279	.400

Lance Broadway

Pitches: R Bats: R Pos: RP-16   Ht: 6'3" Wt: 195 Born: 8/20/1983 Age: 26

Year	Team	Lg	G	GS	CG	GF	IP	BFP	H	R	ER	HR	SH	SF	HB	TBB	IBB	SO	WP	Bk	W	L	Pct	Sh	Sv-Op	Hld	ERC	ERA
2009	Charltt*	AAA	3	3	0	0	16.0	72	18	11	10	2	0	0	2	4	1	15	2	0	0	2	.000	0	0--	-	4.65	5.63
2009	Buffalo*	AAA	16	14	1	1	84.2	383	101	63	59	6	6	2	4	34	0	40	9	0	5	7	.417	0	0--	-	5.18	6.27
2007	CWS	AL	4	1	0	1	10.1	41	5	2	1	0	0	0	0	5	0	14	0	0	1	1	.500	0	0-0	0	1.34	0.87
2008	CWS	AL	7	1	0	4	14.0	66	20	11	11	4	0	0	0	5	1	7	0	0	1	0	1.000	0	0-0	0	7.80	7.07
2009	2 Tms	AL	16	0	0	8	30.2	143	38	21	20	0	0	2	0	15	1	18	0	0	0	1	.000	0	0-0	0	4.91	5.87
09	CWS	AL	8	0	0	5	16.0	76	19	10	9	0	0	1	0	9	1	9	0	0	0	1	.000	0	0-0	0	4.77	5.06
09	NYM	NL	8	0	0	3	14.2	67	19	11	11	0	0	1	0	6	0	9	0	0	0	0	-	0	0-0	0	5.07	6.75
3 ML YEARS			27	2	0	13	55.0	250	63	34	32	4	0	3	0	25	2	39	0	0	2	2	.500	0	0-0	0	4.80	5.24

Doug Brocail

Pitches: R Bats: L Pos: RP-20   Ht: 6'5" Wt: 250 Born: 5/16/1967 Age: 43

Year	Team	Lg	G	GS	CG	GF	IP	BFP	H	R	ER	HR	SH	SF	HB	TBB	IBB	SO	WP	Bk	W	L	Pct	Sh	Sv-Op	Hld	ERC	ERA
2009	RdRck*	AAA	7	0	0	0	7.0	30	8	5	4	0	0	0	1	2	0	3	1	0	0	1	.000	0	0--	-	4.44	5.14
2009	CpChr*	AA	2	0	0	0	2.0	8	2	0	0	0	0	0	0	0	0	1	0	0	1	0	1.000	0	0--	-	1.95	0.00
1992	SD	NL	3	3	0	0	14.0	64	17	10	10	2	2	0	0	5	0	15	0	0	0	0	-	0	0-0	0	5.33	6.43
1993	SD	NL	24	24	0	0	128.1	571	143	75	65	16	10	8	4	42	4	70	4	1	4	13	.235	0	0-0	0	4.60	4.56
1994	SD	NL	12	0	0	4	17.0	78	21	13	11	1	1	1	2	5	3	11	1	1	0	0	-	0	0-1	0	4.79	5.82
1995	Hou	NL	36	7	0	12	77.1	339	87	40	36	10	1	1	4	22	2	39	1	1	6	4	.600	0	1-1	0	4.68	4.19
1996	Hou	NL	23	4	0	4	53.0	231	58	30	27	7	3	2	2	23	1	34	0	0	1	5	.167	0	0-0	1	5.26	4.58
1997	Det	AL	61	4	0	20	78.0	332	74	31	28	10	1	3	3	36	4	60	6	0	3	4	.429	0	2-9	16	4.42	3.23
1998	Det	AL	60	0	0	24	62.2	247	47	23	19	2	2	3	1	18	3	55	6	0	5	2	.714	0	0-1	11	1.99	2.73
1999	Det	AL	70	0	0	22	82.0	326	60	23	23	7	4	2	4	25	1	78	4	1	4	4	.500	0	2-4	23	2.43	2.52
2000	Det	AL	49	0	0	10	50.2	221	57	25	23	5	3	3	1	14	2	41	1	1	5	4	.556	0	0-5	19	4.25	4.09
2004	Tex	AL	43	0	0	14	52.1	232	54	29	24	2	4	2	5	20	1	43	2	1	4	1	.800	0	1-1	4	4.05	4.13
2005	Tex	AL	61	0	0	13	73.1	344	90	48	45	2	3	4	4	34	3	61	4	0	5	3	.625	0	1-4	5	5.15	5.52
2006	SD	NL	25	0	0	6	28.1	119	27	16	15	1	3	1	0	8	2	19	1	0	2	2	.500	0	0-0	0	2.80	4.76
2007	SD	NL	67	0	0	16	76.2	319	66	33	26	8	2	1	2	24	3	43	2	0	5	1	.833	0	0-0	10	3.03	3.05
2008	Hou	NL	72	0	0	21	68.2	286	63	30	30	8	1	1	3	21	5	64	1	1	7	5	.583	0	2-5	22	3.45	3.93
2009	Hou	NL	20	0	0	9	17.2	84	21	9	9	4	1	2	0	13	0	9	0	0	1	0	1.000	0	0-1	3	7.79	4.58
15 ML YEARS			626	42	0	175	880.0	3793	885	436	391	85	41	34	35	310	34	642	33	7	52	48	.520	0	9-32	114	3.98	4.00

Dusty Brown

Bats: R Throws: R Pos: C-6   Ht: 6'0" Wt: 180 Born: 6/19/1982 Age: 28

								BATTING													BASERUNNING				AVERAGES		
Year	Team	Lg	G	AB	H	2B	3B	HR	(Hm	Rd)	TB	R	RBI	RC	TBB	IBB	SO	HBP	SH	SF	SB	CS	SB%	GDP	Avg	OBP	Slg
2001	RedSx	R	36	126	32	5	4	0	(-	-)	45	15	14	12	7	0	24	0	0	2	1	2	.33	3	.254	.289	.357
2002	RedSx	R	45	159	51	12	2	1	(-	-)	70	28	20	30	23	1	24	0	0	1	11	4	.73	1	.321	.404	.440
2002	Lowell	A-	21	78	22	3	1	0	(-	-)	27	12	12	11	8	0	20	3	1	0	1	0	1.00	0	.282	.371	.346
2003	Augsta	A	87	285	75	17	6	2	(-	-)	110	27	41	44	37	2	69	7	1	3	7	1	.88	4	.263	.358	.386
2004	Srsota	A+	38	118	27	3	0	1	(-	-)	33	11	8	12	15	1	28	1	0	0	2	0	1.00	0	.229	.321	.280
2005	Wilmg	A+	62	219	56	12	0	8	(-	-)	92	32	36	34	31	0	52	1	0	2	1	1	.50	7	.256	.348	.420
2005	RedSx	R	6	18	4	1	0	0	(-	-)	5	3	3	2	4	0	2	0	0	0	0	0	-	2	.222	.364	.278
2006	PortInd	AA	85	295	66	17	0	5	(-	-)	98	32	40	29	24	0	65	3	4	5	2	1	.67	5	.224	.284	.332
2007	PortInd	AA	69	254	68	16	2	9	(-	-)	115	43	43	40	28	0	64	2	0	1	0	0	-	7	.268	.344	.453
2007	Pwtckt	AAA	8	27	5	2	0	0	(-	-)	7	1	3	1	2	0	10	0	0	0	0	0	-	0	.185	.241	.259
2008	Pwtckt	AAA	84	297	86	14	2	12	(-	-)	140	39	55	55	40	1	81	6	0	7	0	0	-	7	.290	.377	.471
2009	Pwtckt	AAA	86	295	78	13	0	2	(-	-)	97	22	23	36	37	0	74	0	0	1	0	0	-	0	.264	.345	.329
2009	Bos	AL	6	3	1	0	0	1	(1	0)	4	1	1	1	1	0	0	0	0	0	0	0	-	0	.333	.500	1.333

Emil Brown

Bats: R Throws: R Pos: PH-2; RF-1   Ht: 6'2" Wt: 210 Born: 12/29/1974 Age: 35

								BATTING													BASERUNNING				AVERAGES		
Year	Team	Lg	G	AB	H	2B	3B	HR	(Hm	Rd)	TB	R	RBI	RC	TBB	IBB	SO	HBP	SH	SF	SB	CS	SB%	GDP	Avg	OBP	Slg
2009	Portlnd*	AAA	41	146	38	13	0	4	(-	-)	63	22	22	22	19	0	27	1	0	2	2	2	.50	6	.260	.345	.432
2009	Buffalo*	AAA	34	125	32	7	0	2	(-	-)	45	14	13	12	6	0	29	1	0	0	0	3	.00	1	.256	.295	.360
1997	Pit	NL	66	95	17	2	1	2	(1	1)	27	16	6	9	10	1	32	7	0	0	5	1	.83	1	.179	.304	.284
1998	Pit	NL	13	39	10	1	0	0	(0	0)	11	2	3	3	1	0	11	1	0	0	0	0	-	0	.256	.293	.282
1999	Pit	NL	6	14	2	1	0	0	(0	0)	3	0	0	0	0	0	3	0	0	0	0	0	-	0	.143	.143	.214
2000	Pit	NL	50	119	26	5	0	3	(2	1)	40	13	18	11	11	0	34	3	1	1	3	1	.75	3	.218	.299	.336
2001	2 Tms	NL	74	137	26	4	1	3	(2	1)	41	21	13	12	16	1	10	2	0	0	12	4	.75	2	.190	.284	.299
2005	KC	AL	150	545	156	31	5	17	(8	9)	248	75	86	91	48	1	108	8	1	7	10	1	.91	14	.286	.349	.455
2006	KC	AL	147	527	151	41	2	15	(6	9)	241	77	81	79	59	3	95	5	0	10	6	3	.67	15	.287	.358	.457
2007	KC	AL	113	366	94	13	1	6	(1	5)	127	44	62	49	24	2	71	1	0	6	12	2	.86	7	.257	.300	.347
2008	Oak	AL	117	402	98	14	2	13	(6	7)	155	48	59	44	27	2	65	5	0	4	4	2	.67	16	.244	.297	.386
2009	NYM	NL	3	5	1	0	0	0	(0	0)	1	0	0	0	0	1	0	0	0	0	0	0	-	1	.200	.333	.200
01	Pit	NL	61	123	25	4	1	0	(2	1)	40	18	13	12	15	1	42	2	0	0	10	4	.71	2	.203	.300	.325
01	SD	NL	13	14	1	0	0	0	(0	0)	1	3	0	0	1	0	7	0	0	0	2	0	1.00	0	.071	.133	.071
	10 ML YEARS		739	2240	581	112	12	59	(26	33)	894	296	326	298	197	10	468	32	2	28	52	14	.79	59	.258	.323	.398

Jonathan Broxton

Pitches: R Bats: R Pos: RP-73   Ht: 6'4" Wt: 294 Born: 6/16/1984 Age: 26

			HOW MUCH HE PITCHED					WHAT HE GAVE UP											THE RESULTS						
Year	Team	Lg	G	GS	CG	GF	IP	BFP	H	R	ER	HR	SH	SF	HB	TBB	IBB	SO	WP	Bk	W	L	Pct	Sh	Sv-Op	Hld	ERC	ERA
2005	LAD	NL	14	0	0	5	13.2	68	13	11	9	0	0	2	1	12	2	22	2	0	1	0	1.000	0	0-1	1	4.65	5.93
2006	LAD	NL	68	0	0	20	76.1	320	61	25	22	7	3	1	1	33	6	97	7	0	4	1	.800	0	3-7	12	2.07	2.60
2007	LAD	NL	83	0	0	18	82.0	004	69	30	26	6	0	1	1	25	3	99	4	0	4	4	.500	0	2-8	32	2.71	2.85
2008	LAD	NL	70	0	0	32	69.0	285	54	24	24	2	3	3	3	27	5	88	3	0	3	5	.375	0	14-22	13	2.48	3.13
2009	LAD	NL	73	0	0	58	76.0	300	44	24	22	4	0	3	1	29	1	114	2	0	7	2	.778	0	36-42	6	1.65	2.61
	Postseason		7	0	0	5	7.2	36	8	4	4	1	0	0	0	5	0	10	0	0	0	1	.000	0	1-2	0	5.45	4.70
	5 ML YEARS		308	0	0	133	317.0	1307	241	119	103	19	6	10	7	126	17	420	18	0	19	12	.613	0	66 80	59	2.53	2.92

Jay Bruce

Bats: L Throws: L Pos: RF-98; PH-4; PR-1   Ht: 6'3" Wt: 225 Born: 4/3/1987 Age: 23

								BATTING													BASERUNNING				AVERAGES		
Year	Team	Lg	G	AB	H	2B	3B	HR	(Hm	Rd)	TB	R	RBI	RC	TBB	IBB	SO	HBP	SH	SF	SB	CS	SB%	GDP	Avg	OBP	Slg
2005	Reds	R	37	122	33	9	2	5	(-	-)	61	29	25	19	11	0	31	1	0	2	4	6	.40	2	.270	.331	.500
2005	Billings	R+	17	70	18	2	0	4	(-	-)	32	16	13	11	11	0	22	0	0	0	2	2	.50	2	.257	.358	.457
2006	Dayton	A	117	444	129	42	5	16	(-	-)	229	69	81	82	44	4	106	4	0	6	19	9	.68	7	.291	.355	.516
2007	Srsota	A+	67	268	87	27	5	11	(-	-)	157	49	49	57	24	2	67	2	0	4	4	4	.50	4	.325	.379	.586
2007	Chatt	AA	16	66	22	7	1	4	(-	-)	43	10	15	16	8	0	20	0	0	0	2	1	.67	0	.333	.405	.652
2007	Lsvlle	AAA	50	187	57	12	2	11	(-	-)	106	28	25	36	15	1	48	1	0	1	2	2	.50	1	.305	.358	.567
2008	Lsvlle	AAA	49	184	67	9	5	10	(-	-)	116	34	37	44	12	4	45	0	0	5	8	1	.89	4	.364	.393	.630
2009	Lsvlle	AAA	5	18	5	0	0	0	(-	-)	5	3	0	2	2	0	3	0	0	0	2	0	1.00	0	.278	.350	.278
2008	Cin	NL	108	413	105	17	1	21	(13	8)	187	63	52	49	33	4	110	4	0	2	4	6	.40	8	.254	.314	.453
2009	Cin	NL	101	345	77	15	2	22	(13	9)	162	47	58	47	38	2	75	2	1	1	3	3	.50	5	.223	.303	.470
	2 ML YEARS		209	758	182	32	3	43	(26	17)	349	110	110	96	71	3	185	6	1	3	7	9	.44	13	.240	.309	.460

Brian Bruney

Pitches: R Bats: R Pos: RP-44   Ht: 6'3" Wt: 235 Born: 2/17/1982 Age: 28

			HOW MUCH HE PITCHED					WHAT HE GAVE UP											THE RESULTS						
Year	Team	Lg	G	GS	CG	GF	IP	BFP	H	R	ER	HR	SH	SF	HB	TBB	IBB	SO	WP	Bk	W	L	Pct	Sh	Sv-Op	Hld	ERC	ERA
2009	S-WB*	AAA	1	1	0	0	1.0	5	2	1	1	0	0	0	0	1	0	0	0	0	0	0	-	0	0- -	-	7.48	9.00
2009	Trntn*	AA	1	1	0	0	1.0	3	0	0	0	0	0	0	0	0	0	0	0	0	0	0	-	0	0- -	-	0.00	0.00
2004	Ari	NL	30	0	0	14	31.1	135	20	16	15	2	1	0	1	27	5	34	2	0	3	4	.429	0	0-1	3	3.54	4.31
2005	Ari	NL	47	0	0	21	46.0	230	56	39	38	6	2	1	5	35	2	51	2	0	1	3	.250	0	12-16	4	7.48	7.43
2006	NYY	AL	19	0	0	2	20.2	90	14	2	2	1	0	0	1	15	0	25	2	0	1	1	.500	0	0-0	4	3.37	0.87
2007	NYY	AL	58	0	0	16	50.0	228	44	28	26	5	1	6	3	37	2	39	4	0	3	2	.600	0	0-2	6	4.92	4.68

Year	Team	Lg		HOW MUCH HE PITCHED						WHAT HE GAVE UP											THE RESULTS					
			G	GS	CG	GF	IP	BFP	H	R	ER	HR	SH	SF	HB	TBB	IBB	SO	WP	Bk	W	L	Pct	Sh	Sv-Op Hld	ERC	ERA
2008	NYY	AL	32	1	0	5	34.1	137	18	7	7	2	0	2	1	16	0	33	1	0	3	0	1.000	0	1-2 12	1.75	1.83
2009	NYY	AL	44	0	0	6	39.0	175	36	17	17	6	2	1	1	23	3	36	2	0	5	0	1.000	0	0-1 14	4.71	3.92
	Postseason		3	0	0	1	2.2	9	1	1	1	1	0	1	0	0	0	4	0	0	0	0	-	0	0-0 0	1.00	3.38
	6 ML YEARS		230	1	0	64	221.1	995	188	109	105	22	6	10	12	153	12	218	13	0	16	10	.615	0	13-22 43	4.48	4.27

Eric Bruntlett

Bats: R Throws: R Pos: PH-31; 2B-13; PR-12; SS-9; 3B-7; RF-5; LF-4; 1B-2; CF-1   Ht: 6'0" Wt: 200 Born: 3/29/1978 Age: 32

Year	Team	Lg				BATTING																BASERUNNING				AVERAGES		
			G	AB	H	2B	3B	HR	(Hm	Rd)	TB	R	RBI	RC	TBB	IBB	SO	HBP	SH	SF	SB	CS	SB%	GDP	Avg	OBP	Slg
2003	Hou	NL	31	54	14	3	0	1	(1	0)	20	3	4	5	0	0	10	0	1	1	0	0	-	1	.259	.255	.370
2004	Hou	NL	45	52	13	2	0	4	(3	1)	27	14	8	9	7	0	13	0	0	2	4	0	1.00	4	.250	.328	.519
2005	Hou	NL	91	109	24	5	2	4	(2	2)	45	19	14	12	10	0	25	1	1	0	7	2	.78	4	.220	.292	.413
2006	Hou	NL	73	119	33	8	0	0	(0	0)	41	11	10	15	13	1	21	1	2	1	3	1	.75	2	.277	.351	.345
2007	Hou	NL	80	138	34	5	0	0	(0	0)	39	16	14	19	20	1	27	1	6	0	6	3	.67	1	.246	.346	.283
2008	Phi	NL	120	212	46	9	1	2	(1	1)	63	37	15	18	21	3	35	3	2	0	9	2	.82	7	.217	.297	.297
2009	Phi	NL	72	105	18	7	0	0	(0	0)	25	15	7	4	5	0	26	3	2	3	2	0	1.00	1	.171	.224	.238
	Postseason		28	16	3	0	0	1	(0	1)	6	4	1	2	2	0	5	1	1	0	1	1	.50	1	.188	.316	.375
	7 ML YEARS		512	789	182	39	3	11	(7	4)	260	115	72	82	76	5	157	9	14	7	31	8	.79	17	.231	.303	.330

Clay Buchholz

Pitches: R Bats: L Pos: SP-16   Ht: 6'3" Wt: 190 Born: 8/14/1984 Age: 25

Year	Team	Lg		HOW MUCH HE PITCHED						WHAT HE GAVE UP											THE RESULTS					
			G	GS	CG	GF	IP	BFP	H	R	ER	HR	SH	SF	HB	TBB	IBB	SO	WP	Bk	W	L	Pct	Sh	Sv-Op Hld	ERC	ERA
2009	Pwtckt*	AAA	17	16	1	0	99.0	387	67	30	26	7	1	0	0	30	0	89	4	1	7	2	.778	1	0- - -	1.92	2.36
2007	Bos	AL	4	3	1	0	22.2	88	14	6	4	0	0	1	1	10	0	22	0	0	3	1	.750	1	0-0 0	1.90	1.59
2008	Bos	AL	16	15	1	0	76.0	357	93	63	57	11	0	3	2	41	1	72	2	1	2	9	.182	0	0-0 0	6.40	6.75
2009	Bos	AL	16	16	0	0	92.0	399	91	44	43	13	2	3	2	36	1	68	1	0	7	4	.636	0	0-0 0	4.31	4.21
	3 ML YEARS		36	34	2	0	190.2	844	198	113	104	24	2	7	5	87	2	162	3	1	12	14	.462	1	0-0 0	4.80	4.91

Taylor Buchholz

Pitches: R Bats: R Pos: P   Ht: 6'4" Wt: 220 Born: 10/13/1981 Age: 28

Year	Team	Lg		HOW MUCH HE PITCHED						WHAT HE GAVE UP											THE RESULTS					
			G	GS	CG	GF	IP	BFP	H	R	ER	HR	SH	SF	HB	TBB	IBB	SO	WP	Bk	W	L	Pct	Sh	Sv-Op Hld	ERC	ERA
2006	Hou	NL	22	19	1	1	113.0	479	107	80	74	21	5	6	3	34	4	77	5	0	6	10	.375	1	0-0 0	3.97	5.89
2007	Col	NL	41	8	0	6	93.2	396	105	47	44	8	5	5	2	20	4	61	3	1	6	5	.545	0	0-0 0	3.97	4.23
2008	Col	NL	63	0	0	19	66.1	263	45	23	16	5	2	2	2	18	2	56	5	1	6	6	.500	0	1-3 21	1.87	2.17
	3 ML YEARS		126	27	1	26	273.0	1138	257	150	134	34	12	13	7	72	10	194	13	2	18	21	.462	1	1-3 22	3.42	4.42

John Buck

Bats: R Throws: R Pos: C-46; DH-11; PH-6   Ht: 6'3" Wt: 230 Born: 7/7/1980 Age: 29

Year	Team	Lg				BATTING																BASERUNNING				AVERAGES		
			G	AB	H	2B	3B	HR	(Hm	Rd)	TB	R	RBI	RC	TBB	IBB	SO	HBP	SH	SF	SB	CS	SB%	GDP	Avg	OBP	Slg
2009	Omha*	AAA	7	27	7	1	0	2	(-	-)	14	3	4	3	0	0	7	0	0	0	0	0	-	1	.259	.259	.519
2004	KC	AL	71	238	56	9	0	12	(6	6)	101	36	30	26	15	0	79	0	4	1	1	1	.50	4	.235	.280	.424
2005	KC	AL	118	401	97	21	1	12	(3	9)	156	40	47	43	23	2	94	3	1	2	2	2	.50	9	.242	.287	.389
2006	KC	AL	114	371	91	21	1	11	(6	5)	147	37	50	43	26	2	84	7	4	1	0	2	.00	7	.245	.306	.396
2007	KC	AL	113	347	77	18	0	18	(6	12)	149	41	48	37	36	0	92	10	0	6	0	1	.00	11	.222	.308	.429
2008	KC	AL	109	370	83	23	1	9	(4	5)	135	48	48	42	38	2	96	6	0	4	0	3	.00	12	.224	.304	.365
2009	KC	AL	59	186	46	12	4	8	(3	5)	90	16	36	30	13	0	55	1	1	1	1	1	.50	2	.247	.299	.484
	6 ML YEARS		584	1913	450	104	7	70	(28	42)	778	218	259	221	151	6	500	27	10	15	4	10	.29	47	.235	.298	.407

Travis Buck

Bats: L Throws: R Pos: RF-28; PH-6; LF-5   Ht: 6'2" Wt: 229 Born: 11/18/1983 Age: 26

Year	Team	Lg				BATTING																BASERUNNING				AVERAGES		
			G	AB	H	2B	3B	HR	(Hm	Rd)	TB	R	RBI	RC	TBB	IBB	SO	HBP	SH	SF	SB	CS	SB%	GDP	Avg	OBP	Slg
2009	Scrmto*	AAA	62	232	63	13	3	5	(-	-)	97	37	29	36	23	1	44	5	2	4	3	1	.75	2	.272	.345	.418
2007	Oak	AL	82	285	82	22	5	7	(3	4)	135	41	34	48	39	2	66	4	2	4	4	1	.80	9	.288	.377	.474
2008	Oak	AL	38	155	35	9	1	7	(3	4)	67	16	25	22	11	0	38	4	0	2	1	0	1.00	2	.226	.291	.432
2009	Oak	AL	36	105	23	3	0	3	(2	1)	35	11	10	10	10	0	20	0	0	0	1	1	.50	0	.219	.287	.333
	3 ML YEARS		156	545	140	34	6	17	(8	9)	237	68	69	80	60	2	124	8	2	6	6	2	.75	11	.257	.336	.435

Billy Buckner

Pitches: R Bats: R Pos: SP-13; RP-3   Ht: 6'2" Wt: 215 Born: 8/27/1983 Age: 26

Year	Team	Lg		HOW MUCH HE PITCHED						WHAT HE GAVE UP											THE RESULTS					
			G	GS	CG	GF	IP	BFP	H	R	ER	HR	SH	SF	HB	TBB	IBB	SO	WP	Bk	W	L	Pct	Sh	Sv-Op Hld	ERC	ERA
2009	Reno*	AAA	18	16	1	1	103.0	436	91	41	38	5	6	4	1	45	1	96	13	0	9	3	.750	1	0- - -	3.26	3.32
2007	KC	AL	7	5	0	1	34.0	143	37	20	20	5	0	1	0	16	0	17	0	0	1	2	.333	0	0-0 0	5.57	5.29
2008	Ari	NL	10	0	0	5	14.0	59	16	5	5	3	0	0	1	4	1	11	2	0	1	0	1.000	0	0-0 0	5.72	3.21
2009	Ari	NL	16	13	0	0	77.1	342	94	57	55	12	2	1	3	29	0	64	6	0	4	6	.400	0	0-0 0	5.97	6.40
	3 ML YEARS		33	18	0	6	125.1	544	147	82	80	20	2	2	4	49	1	92	8	0	6	8	.429	0	0-0 0	5.83	5.74

Ryan Budde

Bats: R Throws: R Pos: C-2; DH-1; PR-1 Ht: 5'11" Wt: 210 Born: 8/15/1979 Age: 30

						BATTING																		BASERUNNING				AVERAGES		
Year	Team	Lg	G	AB	H	2B	3B	HR	(Hm	Rd)	TB	R	RBI	RC	TBB	IBB	SO	HBP	SH	SF		SB	CS	SB%	GDP		Avg	OBP	Slg
2009	Salt Lk*	AAA	83	273	63	16	1	7	(-	-)	102	32	31	33	31	0	73	1	1	1		1	1	.50	6		.231	.310	.374
2007	LAA	AL	12	18	3	1	0	0	(0	0)	4	0	1	0	0	0	6	0	0	0		0	0	-	1		.167	.167	.222
2008	LAA	AL	8	2	0	0	0	0	(0	0)	0	0	0	0	0	0	0	0	1	0		0	0	-	1		.000	.000	.000
2009	LAA	AL	3	3	0	0	0	0	(0	0)	0	0	0	0	0	0	2	0	0	0		0	0	-	0		.000	.000	.000
3 ML YEARS			23	23	3	1	0	0	(0	0)	4	0	1	0	0	0	8	0	1	0		0	0	-	2		.130	.130	.174

Mark Buehrle

Pitches: L Bats: L Pos: SP-33 Ht: 6'2" Wt: 230 Born: 3/23/1979 Age: 31

			HOW MUCH HE PITCHED						WHAT HE GAVE UP													THE RESULTS								
Year	Team	Lg	G	GS	CG	GF	IP	BFP	H	R	ER	HR	SH	SF	HB	TBB	IBB	SO	WP	Bk	W	L	Pct	Sh	Sv-Op	Hld	ERC	ERA
2000	CWS	AL	28	3	0	6	51.1	225	55	27	24	5	1	0	3	19	1	37	0	0	4	1	.800	0	0-2	3	4.56	4.21
2001	CWS	AL	32	32	4	0	221.1	805	188	89	81	24	9	4	8	48	2	126	1	5	16	8	.667	2	0-0	0	2.79	3.29
2002	CWS	AL	34	34	5	0	239.0	984	236	102	95	25	9	3	3	61	7	134	6	1	19	12	.613	2	0-0	0	3.53	3.58
2003	CWS	AL	35	35	2	0	230.1	978	250	124	106	22	7	7	5	61	2	119	1	0	14	14	.500	0	0-0	0	4.10	4.14
2004	CWS	AL	35	35	4	0	245.1	1016	257	119	106	33	4	6	8	51	2	165	0	0	16	10	.615	1	0-0	0	4.00	3.89
2005	CWS	AL	33	33	3	0	236.2	971	240	99	82	20	7	4	4	40	4	149	2	2	16	8	.667	1	0-0	0	3.21	3.12
2006	CWS	AL	32	32	1	0	204.0	876	247	124	113	36	6	7	6	48	5	98	0	1	12	13	.480	0	0-0	0	5.37	4.99
2007	CWS	AL	30	30	3	0	201.0	835	208	86	81	22	7	5	5	45	5	115	1	0	10	9	.526	1	0-0	0	3.75	3.63
2008	CWS	AL	34	34	1	0	218.2	918	240	106	92	22	2	6	5	52	4	140	4	0	15	12	.556	0	0-0	0	4.12	3.79
2009	CWS	AL	33	33	1	0	213.1	874	222	97	91	27	11	7	5	45	3	105	2	1	13	10	.565	1	0-0	0	3.91	3.84
Postseason			6	4	1	2	30.2	124	32	14	14	3	2	1	1	1	1	16	0	0	2	1	.667	0	1-1	0	2.95	4.11
10 ML YEARS			326	301	24	6	2061.0	8562	2143	973	871	236	63	49	52	470	35	1188	17	10	135	97	.582	8	0-2	3	3.85	3.80

Jason Bulger

Pitches: R Bats: R Pos: RP-64 Ht: 6'4" Wt: 210 Born: 12/6/1978 Age: 31

			HOW MUCH HE PITCHED						WHAT HE GAVE UP													THE RESULTS								
Year	Team	Lg	G	GS	CG	GF	IP	BFP	H	R	ER	HR	SH	SF	HB	TBB	IBB	SO	WP	Bk	W	L	Pct	Sh	Sv-Op	Hld	ERC	ERA
2005	Ari	NL	9	0	0	5	10.0	48	14	6	6	1	1	0	0	5	1	9	0	0	1	0	1.000	0	0-0	0	6.08	5.40
2006	LAA	AL	2	0	0	1	1.2	9	1	3	1	0	0	0	0	3	0	1	1	0	0	0	-	0	0-0	0	6.15	16.20
2007	LAA	AL	6	0	0	4	6.1	25	5	2	2	0	0	0	0	3	0	8	1	0	0	0	-	0	0-0	0	2.74	2.84
2008	LAA	AL	14	0	0	7	16.0	73	15	13	13	3	0	0	2	9	0	20	0	0	0	0	-	0	0-0	0	5.50	7.31
2009	LAA	AL	64	0	0	20	65.2	262	46	26	26	7	5	4	1	30	1	68	5	0	6	1	.857	0	1-4	9	2.88	3.56
5 ML YEARS			95	0	0	37	99.2	417	81	50	50	11	6	4	3	50	2	106	7	0	7	1	.875	0	1-4	9	3.67	4.52

Bryan Bullington

Pitches: R Bats: R Pos: RP-4 Ht: 6'4" Wt: 220 Born: 9/30/1980 Age: 29

			HOW MUCH HE PITCHED						WHAT HE GAVE UP													THE RESULTS								
Year	Team	Lg	G	GS	CG	GF	IP	BFP	H	R	ER	HR	SH	SF	HB	TBB	IBB	SO	WP	Bk	W	L	Pct	Sh	Sv-Op	Hld	ERC	ERA
2009	LsVgs*	AAA	28	0	0	8	38.1	162	42	21	15	2	1	1	2	7	1	43	2	0	3	1	.750	0	3--	-	3.60	3.52
2005	Pit	NL	1	0	0	0	1.1	7	1	2	2	0	0	1	1	1	0	1	0	0	0	0	-	0	0-0	0	5.91	13.50
2007	Pit	NL	5	3	0	0	17.0	76	24	11	10	3	1	0	0	5	0	7	1	0	0	3	.000	0	0-0	0	6.90	5.29
2008	Clc	AL	3	2	0	0	14.2	60	15	9	8	4	0	1	1	2	0	12	1	0	0	2	.000	0	0-0	0	4.63	4.91
2009	Tor	AL	4	0	0	3	6.0	31	7	2	2	0	1	0	0	6	1	5	0	0	0	0	-	0	0-0	0	6.12	3.00
4 ML YEARS			13	5	0	3	39.0	174	47	24	22	7	2	3	2	14	1	25	2	0	0	5	.000	0	0-0	0	5.96	5.08

Madison Bumgarner

Pitches: L Bats: R Pos: RP-3; SP-1 Ht: 6'4" Wt: 215 Born: 8/1/1989 Age: 20

			HOW MUCH HE PITCHED						WHAT HE GAVE UP													THE RESULTS								
Year	Team	Lg	G	GS	CG	GF	IP	BFP	H	R	ER	HR	SH	SF	HB	TBB	IBB	SO	WP	Bk	W	L	Pct	Sh	Sv-Op	Hld	ERC	ERA
2008	Augsta	A	24	24	1	0	142.2	548	111	28	23	3	3	4	5	21	0	164	3	2	15	3	.833	1	0--	-	1.74	1.45
2009	SnJos	A+	5	5	0	0	24.1	100	20	10	4	0	0	2	2	4	0	23	0	0	3	1	.750	0	0--	-	1.91	1.48
2009	Conn	AA	20	19	1	0	107.0	421	80	28	23	6	2	3	3	30	1	69	4	0	9	1	.900	0	0--	-	2.19	1.93
2009	SF	NL	4	1	0	1	10.0	40	8	2	2	1	1	0	3	1	0	10	0	0	0	0	-	0	0-0	0	3.14	1.80

Chris Burke

Bats: R Throws: R Pos: SS-25; PH-8; 3B-2; 2B-1 Ht: 5'11" Wt: 195 Born: 3/11/1980 Age: 30

						BATTING																		BASERUNNING				AVERAGES		
Year	Team	Lg	G	AB	H	2B	3B	HR	(Hm	Rd)	TB	R	RBI	RC	TBB	IBB	SO	HBP	SH	SF		SB	CS	SB%	GDP		Avg	OBP	Slg
2009	Tacom*	AAA	10	38	9	2	0	1	(-	-)	14	7	3	5	7	1	11	0	0	0		2	1	.67	1		.237	.356	.368
2009	Gwnntt*	AAA	73	274	78	19	2	3	(-	-)	110	39	32	42	22	2	46	7	4	2		13	2	.87	9		.285	.351	.401
2004	Hou	NL	17	17	1	0	0	0	(0	0)	1	2	0	0	3	0	3	0	0	0		0	0	-	0		.059	.200	.059
2005	Hou	NL	108	318	79	19	2	5	(2	3)	117	49	26	35	23	0	62	6	9	3		11	6	.65	7		.248	.309	.368
2006	Hou	NL	123	366	101	23	1	9	(3	6)	153	58	40	49	27	0	77	14	4	2		11	1	.92	6		.276	.347	.418
2007	Hou	NL	111	319	73	19	2	6	(3	3)	114	39	28	33	27	1	52	8	8	1		9	3	.75	10		.229	.304	.357
2008	Ari	NL	86	165	32	5	1	2	(0	2)	45	20	12	14	27	8	33	2	2	3		5	0	1.00	2		.194	.310	.273
2000	SD	NL	32	82	17	5	0	1	(0	1)	25	8	5	4	6	0	16	1	0	0		4	1	.80	1		.207	.270	.305
Postseason			13	28	8	1	1	2	(1	1)	17	7	4	6	4	0	3	0	1	0		2	0	1.00	0		.286	.375	.607
6 ML YEARS			477	1267	303	71	6	23	(8	15)	455	176	111	135	113	9	243	31	23	9		40	11	.78	26		.239	.315	.359

Greg Burke

Pitches: R Bats: R Pos: RP-48   Ht: 6'4" Wt: 216 Born: 9/21/1982 Age: 27

			HOW MUCH HE PITCHED						WHAT HE GAVE UP													THE RESULTS							
Year	Team	Lg	G	GS	CG	GF	IP	BFP	H	R	ER	HR	SH	SF	HB	TBB	IBB	SO	WP	Bk	W	L	Pct	Sh	Sv-Op	Hld	ERC	ERA
2006	Lk Els	A+	12	0	0	5	18.2	81	24	14	12	1	1	0	1	5	0	9	0	0	2	1	.667	0	0- -	-	5.26	5.79
2006	FtWyn	A	24	17	0	2	120.2	500	130	58	48	8	8	3	3	14	0	87	2	0	6	5	.545	0	0- -	-	3.26	3.58
2007	Lk Els	A+	51	9	0	11	96.1	423	105	60	56	11	3	3	3	28	2	67	7	0	4	4	.500	0	0- -	-	4.26	5.23
2008	SnAnt	AA	59	1	0	36	84.1	343	76	26	21	7	5	0	2	17	1	92	1	0	2	7	.222	0	23- -	-	2.75	2.24
2009	Portlnd	AAA	13	0	0	13	16.0	59	8	4	4	1	0	0	0	4	0	14	2	0	3	0	1.000	0	7- -	-	1.17	2.25
2009	SD	NL	48	0	0	13	45.2	204	48	23	21	4	3	0	1	23	5	33	3	0	3	3	.500	0	0-2	10	4.59	4.14

Jamie Burke

Bats: R Throws: R Pos: C-18; 1B-1   Ht: 6'0" Wt: 225 Born: 9/24/1971 Age: 38

								BATTING													BASERUNNING				AVERAGES		
Year	Team	Lg	G	AB	H	2B	3B	HR	(Hm	Rd)	TB	R	RBI	RC	TBB	IBB	SO	HBP	SH	SF	SB	CS	SB%	GDP	Avg	OBP	Slg
2009	Tacom*	AAA	22	81	23	7	0	0	(-	-)	30	7	11	10	5	0	12	0	0	1	0	0	-	4	.284	.322	.370
2001	LAA	AL	9	5	1	0	0	0	(0	0)	1	1	0	0	0	0	2	0	0	0	0	0	-	0	.200	.200	.200
2003	CWS	AL	6	8	3	0	0	0	(0	0)	3	0	2	2	0	0	0	0	0	0	0	0	-	0	.375	.375	.375
2004	CWS	AL	57	120	40	9	0	0	(0	0)	49	22	15	21	10	0	13	1	1	1	0	0	-	3	.333	.386	.408
2005	CWS	AL	1	1	0	0	0	0	(0	0)	0	0	0	0	0	0	0	0	0	0	0	0	-	0	.000	.000	.000
2007	Sea	AL	50	113	34	8	0	1	(1	0)	45	19	12	16	7	0	17	4	5	0	0	1	.00	2	.301	.363	.398
2008	Sea	AL	48	92	24	3	0	1	(0	1)	30	10	8	9	5	0	7	1	1	1	0	1	.00	3	.261	.303	.326
2009	2 Tms		19	51	6	0	0	1	(1	0)	9	1	2	0	3	0	18	0	1	1	0	0	-	2	.118	.164	.176
09	Sea	AL	13	41	5	0	0	1	(1	0)	8	1	1	0	2	0	13	0	0	0	0	0	-	2	.122	.163	.195
09	Was	NL	6	10	1	0	0	0	(0	0)	1	0	1	0	1	0	5	0	1	1	0	0	-	0	.100	.167	.100
7 ML YEARS			190	390	108	20	0	3	(2	1)	137	53	39	48	25	0	57	6	8	3	0	2	.00	10	.277	.328	.351

A.J. Burnett

Pitches: R Bats: R Pos: SP-33   Ht: 6'4" Wt: 230 Born: 1/3/1977 Age: 33

						HOW MUCH HE PITCHED			WHAT HE GAVE UP												THE RESULTS							
Year	Team	Lg	G	GS	CG	GF	IP	BFP	H	R	ER	HR	SH	SF	HB	TBB	IBB	SO	WP	Bk	W	L	Pct	Sh	Sv-Op	Hld	ERC	ERA
1999	Fla	NL	7	7	0	0	41.1	182	37	23	16	3	1	3	0	25	2	33	0	0	4	2	.667	0	0-0	0	4.00	3.48
2000	Fla	NL	13	13	0	0	82.2	364	80	46	44	8	6	3	2	44	3	57	2	0	3	7	.300	0	0-0	0	4.45	4.79
2001	Fla	NL	27	27	2	0	173.1	733	145	82	78	20	6	8	7	83	3	128	7	1	11	12	.478	1	0-0	0	3.76	4.05
2002	Fla	NL	31	29	7	0	204.1	844	153	84	75	12	9	4	9	90	5	203	14	0	12	9	.571	5	0-1	0	2.77	3.30
2003	Fla	NL	4	4	0	0	23.0	106	18	13	12	2	1	1	2	18	2	21	2	0	2	0	.000	0	0-0	0	4.36	4.70
2004	Fla	NL	20	19	1	0	120.0	490	102	50	49	9	3	3	4	38	0	113	7	0	7	6	.538	2	0-0	0	2.95	3.68
2005	Fla	NL	32	32	4	0	209.0	873	184	97	80	12	7	5	7	79	1	198	12	0	12	12	.500	2	0-0	0	3.20	3.44
2006	Tor	AL	21	21	2	0	135.2	577	138	67	60	14	4	3	8	39	3	118	6	1	10	8	.556	1	0-0	0	3.97	3.98
2007	Tor	AL	25	25	2	0	165.2	691	131	74	69	23	0	2	12	66	2	176	5	0	10	8	.556	0	0-0	0	3.47	3.75
2008	Tor	AL	35	34	1	1	221.1	957	211	109	100	19	8	5	9	86	2	231	11	2	18	10	.643	0	0-0	0	3.78	4.07
2009	NYY	AL	33	33	1	0	207.0	896	193	99	93	25	2	5	10	97	0	195	17	1	13	9	.591	0	0-0	0	4.34	4.04
11 ML YEARS			248	244	20	1	1583.1	6713	1392	744	676	147	48	42	70	665	23	1473	83	5	100	85	.541	9	0-1	0	3.61	3.84

Sean Burnett

Pitches: L Bats: L Pos: RP-71   Ht: 6'1" Wt: 200 Born: 9/17/1982 Age: 27

						HOW MUCH HE PITCHED			WHAT HE GAVE UP												THE RESULTS							
Year	Team	Lg	G	GS	CG	GF	IP	BFP	H	R	ER	HR	SH	SF	HB	TBB	IBB	SO	WP	Bk	W	L	Pct	Sh	Sv-Op	Hld	ERC	ERA
2004	Pit	NL	13	13	1	0	71.2	318	86	41	40	9	2	1	1	28	2	30	2	0	5	5	.500	1	0-0	0	5.49	5.02
2008	Pit	NL	58	0	0	16	56.2	253	57	31	30	7	4	3	2	34	3	42	4	0	1	1	.500	0	0-0	8	5.23	4.76
2009	2 Tms	NL	71	0	0	8	57.2	237	36	21	20	6	6	1	3	28	8	43	4	0	2	3	.400	0	1-3	11	2.43	3.12
09	Pit	NL	38	0	0	7	32.1	133	22	12	11	3	4	1	3	15	4	23	2	0	1	2	.333	0	1-2	6	2.77	3.06
09	Was	NL	33	0	0	1	25.1	104	14	9	9	3	2	0	0	13	4	20	2	0	1	1	.500	0	0-1	5	2.02	3.20
3 ML YEARS			142	13	1	24	186.0	808	179	93	90	22	12	5	6	90	13	115	10	0	8	9	.471	1	1-3	19	4.38	4.35

Mike Burns

Pitches: R Bats: R Pos: SP-8; RP-7   Ht: 6'0" Wt: 185 Born: 7/14/1978 Age: 31

						HOW MUCH HE PITCHED			WHAT HE GAVE UP												THE RESULTS							
Year	Team	Lg	G	GS	CG	GF	IP	BFP	H	R	ER	HR	SH	SF	HB	TBB	IBB	SO	WP	Bk	W	L	Pct	Sh	Sv-Op	Hld	ERC	ERA
2009	Nashv*	AAA	14	14	2	0	92.2	379	89	32	27	9	2	4	4	16	0	63	3	0	8	3	.727	1	0- -	-	3.00	2.62
2005	Hou	NL	27	0	0	10	31.0	136	29	18	17	6	1	0	5	8	1	20	1	0	0	0	-	0	0-0	1	4.26	4.94
2006	2 Tms	NL	18	0	0	6	21.0	104	40	17	17	2	1	2	2	4	2	16	1	0	0	0	-	0	0-0	1	9.26	7.29
2009	Mil	NL	15	8	0	4	51.2	227	60	36	33	10	1	4	1	17	2	39	1	0	3	5	.375	0	0-0	0	5.45	5.75
06	Cin	NL	11	0	0	2	13.1	70	30	13	13	2	1	0	2	3	1	9	1	0	0	0	-	0	0-0	1	13.15	8.78
06	Bos	AL	7	0	0	4	7.2	34	10	4	4	0	0	2	0	1	1	7	0	0	0	0	-	0	0-0	0	3.68	4.70
3 ML YEARS			60	8	0	20	103.2	467	129	71	67	18	3	6	8	29	5	75	3	0	3	5	.375	0	0-0	2	5.80	5.82

Pat Burrell

Bats: R Throws: R Pos: DH-112; PH-9; LF-1; RF-1   Ht: 6'4" Wt: 235 Born: 10/10/1976 Age: 33

								BATTING													BASERUNNING				AVERAGES		
Year	Team	Lg	G	AB	H	2B	3B	HR	(Hm	Rd)	TB	R	RBI	RC	TBB	IBB	SO	HBP	SH	SF	SB	CS	SB%	GDP	Avg	OBP	Slg
2009	Mont*	AA	2	9	1	0	0	0	(-	-)	1	1	0	0	1	0	4	0	0	0	0	0	-	5	.111	.200	.111
2009	Charltt*	A+	1	4	0	0	0	0	(-	-)	0	0	0	0	0	0	2	0	0	0	0	0	-	0	.000	.000	.000
2000	Phi	NL	111	408	106	27	1	18	(7	11)	189	57	79	69	63	2	139	1	0	2	0	0	-	5	.260	.359	.463
2001	Phi	NL	155	539	139	29	2	27	(10	17)	253	70	89	86	70	7	162	5	0	4	2	1	.67	12	.258	.346	.469
2002	Phi	NL	157	586	165	39	2	37	(18	19)	319	96	116	104	89	9	153	3	0	6	1	0	1.00	16	.282	.376	.544

Year Team	Lg	G	AB	H	2B	3B	HR	(Hm	Rd)	TD	R	RBI	RC	TBB	IBB	SO	HBP	SH	SF	SB	CS	SB%	GDP	Avg	OBP	Slg
2003 Phi	NL	146	522	109	31	4	21	(9	12)	211	57	64	57	72	2	142	4	0	1	0	0	-	18	.209	.309	.404
2004 Phi	NL	127	448	115	17	0	24	(14	10)	204	66	84	72	78	7	130	2	0	6	2	0	1.00	10	.257	.365	.455
2005 Phi	NL	154	562	158	27	1	32	(20	12)	283	78	117	109	99	6	160	3	0	5	0	0	-	12	.281	.389	.504
2006 Phi	NL	144	462	119	24	1	29	(12	17)	232	80	95	81	98	5	131	3	0	4	0	0	-	11	.258	.388	.502
2007 Phi	NL	155	472	121	26	0	30	(16	14)	237	77	97	98	114	1	120	4	0	8	0	0	-	10	.256	.400	.502
2008 Phi	NL	157	536	134	33	3	33	(12	21)	272	74	86	93	102	8	136	1	0	6	0	0	-	10	.250	.367	.507
2009 TB	AL	122	412	91	16	1	14	(8	6)	151	45	64	52	57	2	119	2	0	5	0	0	1.00	6	.221	.315	.367
Postseason		17	55	12	1	0	4	(2	2)	25	4	9	6	10	0	16	0	0	0	0	0	-	2	.218	.338	.455
10 ML YEARS		1428	4947	1257	269	15	265	(126	139)	2351	700	891	821	842	49	1392	28	0	47	7	1	.88	110	.254	.363	.475

Brian Burres

Pitches: L Bats: L Pos: SP-2　　　　　　Ht: 6'1" Wt: 181 Born: 4/8/1981 Age: 29

Year Team	Lg	G	GS	CG	GF	IP	BFP	H	R	ER	HR	SH	SF	HB	TBB	IBB	SO	WP	Bk	W	L	Pct	Sh	Sv-Op Hld	ERC	ERA
2009 LsVgs*	AAA	19	17	1	0	107.2	472	121	68	57	11	2	5	3	30	0	84	2	1	6	7	.462	1	0- - -	4.36	4.76
2006 Bal	AL	11	0	0	2	8.0	31	6	2	2	1	0	0	0	1	0	6	0	0	0	0	-	0	0-0 4	1.91	2.25
2007 Bal	AL	37	17	0	9	121.0	559	140	81	80	14	2	0	5	66	1	96	8	0	6	8	.429	0	0-0 0	5.89	5.95
2008 Bal	AL	31	22	0	1	129.2	596	165	90	87	17	1	8	6	50	2	63	3	1	7	10	.412	0	0-1 0	6.03	6.04
2009 Tor	AL	2	2	0	0	6.1	37	12	12	10	0	0	0	0	5	0	4	0	0	0	2	.000	0	0-0 0	10.02	14.21
4 ML YEARS		81	41	0	12	265.0	1223	323	185	179	32	3	8	11	122	3	169	11	1	13	20	.394	0	0-1 4	5.92	6.08

Emmanuel Burriss

Bats: B Throws: R Pos: 2B-61; PR-2　　　　　　Ht: 6'0" Wt: 189 Born: 1/17/1985 Age: 25

Year Team	Lg	G	AB	H	2B	3B	HR	(Hm	Rd)	TB	R	RBI	RC	TBB	IBB	SO	HBP	SH	SF	SB	CS	SB%	GDP	Avg	OBP	Slg
2006 OlmKz*	A	65	254	78	8	2	1	(-	-)	93	50	27	42	27	1	22	6	4	2	35	11	.76	2	.307	.384	.366
2007 OlnDS	A*	36	139	23	2	0	0	(-	-)	25	23	8	7	12	0	20	2	4	3	17	3	.85	2	.165	.237	.180
2007 Augsta	A	89	365	117	14	4	0	(-	-)	139	64	38	59	28	0	49	5	4	3	51	15	.77	3	.321	.374	.381
2008 Fresno	AAA	14	62	16	1	1	0	(-	-)	19	6	6	4	2	0	6	0	0	0	2	2	.50	0	.258	.281	.306
2009 Fresno	AAA	17	71	19	2	1	1	(-	-)	26	9	7	8	3	0	4	2	0	1	6	2	.75	1	.268	.312	.300
2008 SF	NL	95	240	68	6	1	1	(0	1)	79	37	10	22	23	1	24	5	5	1	13	5	.72	7	.283	.357	.329
2009 SF	NL	61	202	48	6	0	0	(0	0)	54	18	13	15	14	1	34	2	1	1	11	4	.73	3	.238	.292	.267
2 ML YEARS		156	442	116	12	1	1	(0	1)	133	55	31	37	37	2	58	7	6	2	24	9	.73	10	.262	.328	.301

Jared Burton

Pitches: R Bats: R Pos: RP-53　　　　　　Ht: 6'5" Wt: 228 Born: 6/2/1981 Age: 29

Year Team	Lg	G	GS	CG	GF	IP	BFP	H	R	ER	HR	SH	SF	HB	TBB	IBB	SO	WP	Bk	W	L	Pct	Sh	Sv-Op Hld	ERC	ERA
2009 Lsvlle*	AAA	10	0	0	4	11.0	44	8	1	1	0	0	0	0	3	0	10	0	0	3	0	1.000	0	0- - -	1.63	0.82
2009 Dayton	A	1	0	0	0	1.0	4	1	0	0	0	0	0	0	0	0	3	0	0	1	0	1.000	0	0- - -	1.95	0.00
2007 Cin	NL	47	0	0	12	43.0	176	28	15	12	2	1	1	2	22	4	36	3	1	4	2	.667	0	0-3 11	2.37	2.51
2008 Cin	NL	54	0	0	12	58.2	257	56	24	21	6	2	3	2	25	3	58	2	1	5	1	.833	0	0-2 11	3.93	3.22
2009 Cin	NL	53	0	0	13	59.1	265	61	30	29	5	3	1	4	23	6	45	2	0	1	0	1.000	0	0-0 7	4.08	4.40
3 ML YEARS		154	0	0	37	161.0	698	145	69	62	13	6	5	8	70	13	139	7	2	10	3	.769	0	0-5 29	3.55	3.47

Brian Buscher

Bats: L Throws: R Pos: 3B-25; PH-22; 1B-13; DH-5　　　　　　Ht: 6'0" Wt: 222 Born: 4/18/1981 Age: 29

Year Team	Lg	G	AB	H	2B	3B	HR	(Hm	Rd)	TB	R	RBI	RC	TBB	IBB	SO	HBP	SH	SF	SB	CS	SB%	GDP	Avg	OBP	Slg
2009 Roch*	AAA	23	78	14	0	0	1	(-	-)	17	6	2	4	11	0	20	0	0	0	0	1	.00	2	.179	.281	.218
2007 Min	AL	33	82	20	1	0	2	(0	2)	27	8	10	8	10	0	16	0	1	1	1	0	1.00	2	.244	.323	.329
2008 Min	AL	70	218	64	9	0	4	(2	2)	85	29	47	36	19	0	42	0	0	7	0	2	.00	6	.294	.340	.390
2009 Min	AL	61	136	32	3	1	2	(2	0)	43	14	12	22	24	0	35	3	0	1	0	0	-	3	.235	.360	.316
3 ML YEARS		164	436	116	13	1	8	(4	4)	155	51	69	66	53	0	93	3	1	9	1	2	.33	11	.266	.343	.356

David Bush

Pitches: R Bats: R Pos: SP-21; RP-1　　　　　　Ht: 6'2" Wt: 204 Born: 11/9/1979 Age: 30

Year Team	Lg	G	GS	CG	GF	IP	BFP	H	R	ER	HR	SH	SF	HB	TBB	IBB	SO	WP	Bk	W	L	Pct	Sh	Sv-Op Hld	ERC	ERA
2009 Wisc*	A	2	2	0	0	7.2	28	4	1	0	0	0	0	1	1	0	9	0	0	0	0	-	0	0- - -	0.79	0.00
2009 Hntsvl*	AA	2	2	0	0	6.1	29	7	7	7	0	1	0	1	5	0	4	0	0	0	2	.000	0	0- - -	6.56	9.95
2004 Tor	AL	16	16	1	0	97.2	412	95	47	40	11	4	4	6	25	2	64	3	0	5	4	.556	1	0-0 0	3.65	3.69
2005 Tor	AL	25	24	2	1	136.1	575	142	73	68	20	3	2	13	29	3	75	2	0	5	11	.313	0	0-0 0	4.28	4.49
2006 Mil	NL	34	32	3	0	210.0	869	201	111	103	26	9	6	18	38	2	166	6	0	12	11	.522	2	0-0 1	3.47	4.41
2007 Mil	NL	33	31	0	2	186.1	810	217	106	106	27	6	2	11	44	1	134	1	0	12	10	.545	0	0-0 0	4.93	5.12
2008 Mil	NL	31	29	0	0	185.0	763	163	92	86	29	4	3	10	48	3	109	2	1	9	10	.474	0	0-0 0	3.44	4.18
2009 Mil	NL	22	21	0	0	114.1	508	131	84	81	19	6	5	15	37	2	89	2	0	5	9	.357	0	0-0 0	5.70	6.38
Postseason		1	1	0	0	5.1	21	5	1	1	0	0	0	0	0	0	3	0	0	1	0	1.000	0	0-0 0	1.68	1.69
6 ML YEARS		161	153	6	3	929.2	3937	949	517	484	132	32	22	73	221	13	637	18	1	48	55	.466	3	0-0 1	4.15	4.69

Billy Butler

Bats: R **Throws:** R **Pos:** 1B-145; DH-11; PH-4   **Ht:** 6'2" **Wt:** 240 **Born:** 4/18/1986 **Age:** 24

Year	Team	Lg	G	AB	H	2B	3B	HR	(Hm	Rd)	TB	R	RBI	RC	TBB	IBB	SO	HBP	SH	SF	SB	CS	SB%	GDP	Avg	OBP	Slg
2007	KC	AL	92	329	96	23	2	8	(5	3)	147	38	52	50	27	5	55	2	0	2	0	0	-	8	.292	.347	.447
2008	KC	AL	124	443	122	22	0	11	(4	7)	177	44	55	57	33	0	57	0	0	2	0	1	.00	23	.275	.324	.400
2009	KC	AL	159	608	183	51	1	21	(16	5)	299	78	93	99	58	3	103	2	0	4	1	0	1.00	20	.301	.362	.492
	3 ML YEARS		375	1380	401	96	3	40	(25	15)	623	160	200	206	118	8	215	4	0	8	1	1	.50	51	.291	.346	.451

Josh Butler

Pitches: R **Bats:** R **Pos:** RP-3   **Ht:** 6'5" **Wt:** 195 **Born:** 12/11/1984 **Age:** 25

Year	Team	Lg	G	GS	CG	GF	IP	BFP	H	R	ER	HR	SH	SF	HB	TBB	IBB	SO	WP	Bk	W	L	Pct	Sh	Sv-Op	Hld	ERC	ERA
2006	HudVal	A-	5	2	0	1	13.1	58	13	9	8	0	1	1	0	7	0	12	2	0	0	3	.000	0	0--	-	3.73	5.40
2007	Clmbs	A	13	13	0	0	78.0	310	63	25	20	3	1	2	6	20	0	54	5	0	5	1	.833	0	0--	-	2.50	2.31
2007	VeroB	A+	10	9	1	0	49.1	216	51	31	27	9	1	2	5	21	0	34	6	0	4	3	.571	1	0--	-	5.52	4.93
2008	VeroB	A+	3	3	0	0	17.0	74	18	13	12	1	0	0	2	5	0	10	0	0	0	2	.000	0	0--	-	4.17	6.35
2008	BrvdCt	A+	20	20	0	0	82.1	371	86	53	49	10	0	4	10	40	0	63	8	0	2	8	.200	0	0--	-	5.39	5.36
2009	BrvdCt	A+	9	9	0	0	51.0	216	44	16	14	0	1	1	4	23	1	32	1	0	6	0	1.000	0	0--	-	3.14	2.47
2009	Nashv	AAA	3	3	0	0	15.0	61	15	6	6	2	1	2	1	0	0	15	3	0	1	1	.500	0	0--	-	3.57	3.60
2009	Hntsvl	AA	8	8	0	0	41.0	171	37	17	13	2	1	0	3	13	1	33	2	0	2	1	.667	0	0--	-	3.16	2.85
2009	Brewrs	R	4	3	0	0	11.1	54	15	6	6	0	0	0	0	6	0	16	0	0	0	1	.000	0	0--	-	6.13	4.76
2009	Mil	NL	3	0	0	0	4.0	27	7	4	4	0	0	1	1	6	0	3	2	0	0	0	-	0	0-0	0	13.14	9.00

Marlon Byrd

Bats: R **Throws:** R **Pos:** CF-105; LF-36; RF-6; PH-2   **Ht:** 6'0" **Wt:** 245 **Born:** 8/30/1977 **Age:** 32

Year	Team	Lg	G	AB	H	2B	3B	HR	(Hm	Rd)	TB	R	RBI	RC	TBB	IBB	SO	HBP	SH	SF	SB	CS	SB%	GDP	Avg	OBP	Slg
2002	Phi	NL	10	35	8	2	0	1	(1	0)	13	2	1	0	1	0	8	0	0	0	0	2	.00	0	.229	.250	.371
2003	Phi	NL	135	495	150	28	4	7	(3	4)	207	86	45	72	44	3	94	7	4	3	11	1	.92	8	.303	.366	.418
2004	Phi	NL	106	346	79	13	2	5	(3	2)	111	48	33	35	22	1	68	7	2	1	2	2	.50	10	.228	.287	.321
2005	2 Tms	NL	79	229	61	15	2	2	(0	2)	86	20	26	30	19	1	50	2	5	4	5	1	.83	5	.266	.323	.376
2006	Was	NL	78	197	44	8	1	5	(1	4)	69	28	18	18	22	1	47	6	1	2	3	3	.50	6	.223	.317	.350
2007	Tex	AL	109	414	127	17	8	10	(4	6)	190	60	70	70	29	3	88	5	0	6	5	3	.63	9	.307	.355	.459
2008	Tex	AL	122	403	120	28	4	10	(7	3)	186	70	53	63	46	3	62	9	2	2	7	2	.78	10	.298	.380	.462
2009	Tex	AL	146	547	155	43	2	20	(14	6)	262	66	89	91	32	2	98	10	0	**10**	8	4	.67	11	.283	.329	.479
05	Phi	NL	5	13	4	0	0	0	(0	0)	4	0	0	2	1	0	3	1	0	0	0	0	-	0	.308	.400	.308
05	Was	NL	74	216	57	15	2	2	(0	2)	82	20	26	28	18	1	47	1	5	4	5	1	.83	5	.264	.318	.380
	8 ML YEARS		785	2666	744	154	23	60	(33	27)	1124	380	335	377	215	14	515	46	14	28	41	18	.69	59	.279	.340	.422

Paul Byrd

Pitches: R **Bats:** R **Pos:** SP-6; RP-1   **Ht:** 6'1" **Wt:** 190 **Born:** 12/3/1970 **Age:** 39

Year	Team	Lg	G	GS	CG	GF	IP	BFP	H	R	ER	HR	SH	SF	HB	TBB	IBB	SO	WP	Bk	W	L	Pct	Sh	Sv-Op	Hld	ERC	ERA
2009	RedSx*	R	2	2	0	0	7.0	33	10	8	4	1	0	0	1	0	0	3	1	0	0	1	.000	0	0--	-	5.51	5.14
2009	Pwtckt*	AAA	2	2	0	0	11.0	44	9	4	4	1	1	0	1	1	0	7	0	0	0	1	.000	0	0--	-	2.23	3.27
1995	NYM	NL	17	0	0	6	22.0	91	18	6	5	1	0	2	1	7	1	26	1	2	2	0	1.000	0	0-0	3	2.53	2.05
1996	NYM	NL	38	0	0	14	46.2	204	48	22	22	7	1	1	0	21	4	31	3	0	1	2	.333	0	0-2	3	4.67	4.24
1997	Atl	NL	31	4	0	9	53.0	236	47	34	31	6	2	2	4	28	4	37	3	1	4	4	.500	0	0-0	1	4.15	5.26
1998	2 Tms	NL	9	8	2	0	57.0	233	45	19	17	6	2	1	0	18	1	39	2	0	5	2	.714	1	0-0	0	2.62	2.68
1999	Phi	NL	32	32	1	0	199.2	872	205	119	102	34	5	6	**17**	70	2	106	11	3	15	11	.577	0	0-0	0	4.87	4.60
2000	Phi	NL	17	15	0	0	83.0	371	89	67	60	17	3	1	3	35	2	53	1	0	2	9	.182	0	0-0	0	5.42	6.51
2001	2 Tms	NL	19	16	1	1	103.1	444	120	54	51	12	4	6	2	26	1	52	2	0	6	7	.462	0	0-0	0	4.62	4.44
2002	KC	AL	33	33	7	0	228.1	935	224	111	99	36	2	13	7	38	1	129	3	1	17	11	.607	2	0-0	0	3.55	3.90
2004	Atl	NL	19	19	0	0	114.1	482	123	57	50	18	3	3	2	19	0	79	1	0	8	7	.533	0	0-0	0	3.98	3.94
2005	LAA	AL	31	31	2	0	204.1	842	216	95	85	22	7	7	7	28	1	102	1	0	12	11	.522	1	0-0	0	3.56	3.74
2006	Cle	AL	31	31	1	0	179.0	805	232	120	97	26	1	6	6	38	3	88	2	0	10	9	.526	0	0-0	0	5.40	4.88
2007	Cle	AL	31	31	2	0	192.1	835	239	107	98	27	4	4	6	28	3	88	5	0	15	8	.652	**2**	0-0	0	4.80	4.59
2008	2 Tms	AL	30	30	1	0	180.0	761	204	96	92	**31**	4	4	7	34	0	82	0	0	11	12	.478	0	0-0	0	4.70	4.60
2009	Bos	AL	7	6	0	0	34.0	155	47	22	22	4	1	0	1	11	0	11	0	0	1	3	.250	0	0-0	0	6.22	5.82
98	Atl	NL	1	0	0	0	2.0	11	4	3	3	0	0	0	0	1	0	1	0	0	0	0	-	0	0-0	0	9.72	13.50
98	Phi	NL	8	8	2	0	55.0	222	41	16	14	6	2	1	0	17	1	38	2	0	5	2	.714	1	0-0	0	2.41	2.29
01	Phi	NL	3	1	0	1	10.0	45	10	9	9	1	2	2	1	4	0	3	1	0	0	1	.000	0	0-0	0	4.36	8.10
01	KC	AL	16	15	1	0	93.1	399	110	45	42	11	2	4	1	22	1	49	1	0	6	6	.500	0	0-0	0	4.65	4.05
08	Cle	AL	22	22	1	0	131.0	553	146	70	66	23	3	4	5	24	0	56	0	0	7	10	.412	0	0-0	0	4.56	4.53
08	Bos	AL	8	8	0	0	49.0	208	58	26	26	8	1	0	2	10	0	26	0	0	4	2	.667	0	0-0	0	5.07	4.78
	Postseason		8	5	0	2	33.1	152	44	20	20	8	2	1	2	9	1	15	0	0	3	1	.750	0	0-0	0	6.70	5.40
	14 ML YEARS		345	256	17	30	1697.0	7266	1857	929	831	247	39	57	62	401	23	923	35	7	109	96	.532	6	0-2	7	4.39	4.41

Tim Byrdak

Pitches: L **Bats:** L **Pos:** RP-76   **Ht:** 5'11" **Wt:** 196 **Born:** 10/31/1973 **Age:** 36

Year	Team	Lg	G	GS	CG	GF	IP	BFP	H	R	ER	HR	SH	SF	HB	TBB	IBB	SO	WP	Bk	W	L	Pct	Sh	Sv-Op	Hld	ERC	ERA
1998	KC	AL	3	0	0	0	1.2	9	5	1	1	0	0	0	0	0	1	0	0	0	0	-	0	0-0	0	23.52	5.40
1999	KC	AL	33	0	0	5	24.2	128	32	24	21	5	3	0	1	20	2	17	3	1	0	3	.000	0	1-4	10	8.29	7.66
2000	KC	AL	12	0	0	1	6.1	34	11	8	8	3	0	0	0	4	0	8	1	0	0	1	.000	0	0-2	3	13.14	11.37
2005	Bal	AL	41	0	0	3	26.2	131	27	14	12	1	2	1	1	21	1	31	5	0	0	1	.000	0	1-1	11	5.04	4.05
2006	Bal	AL	16	0	0	2	7.0	42	14	10	10	2	2	0	0	8	1	2	1	0	1	0	1.000	0	0-0	3	15.90	12.86

Year	Team	Lg	G	GS	CG	GF	IP	BFP	H	R	ER	HR	SH	SF	HB	TBB	IBB	SO	WP	Bk	W	l	Pct	Sh	Sv-Op	Hld	ERC	ERA
2007	Det	AL	39	0	0	3	45.0	199	38	23	16	3	2	5	1	26	4	49	3	0	3	0	1.000	0	1-2	8	3.53	3.20
2008	Hou	NL	59	0	0	9	55.1	237	45	24	24	10	2	1	2	29	2	47	0	0	2	1	.667	0	0-0	8	4.18	3.90
2009	Hou	NL	76	0	0	8	61.1	261	39	23	22	10	0	3	3	36	0	58	2	0	1	2	.333	0	0-2	9	3.38	3.23
	8 ML YEARS		279	0	0	31	228.0	1041	211	127	114	35	11	10	8	144	10	213	15	1	7	8	.467	0	3-11	52	4.96	4.50

Eric Byrnes

Bats: R **Throws:** R **Pos:** LF-49; PH-25; CF-6; RF-5; DH-3; PR-1   **Ht:** 6'2" **Wt:** 215 **Born:** 2/16/1976 **Age:** 34

Year	Team	Lg	G	AB	H	2B	3B	HR	(Hm	Rd)	TB	R	RBI	RC	TBB	IBB	SO	HBP	SH	SF	SB	CS	SB%	GDP	Avg	OBP	Slg
2009	Reno*	AAA	16	68	19	7	1	2	(-	-)	34	14	0	11	5	0	4	1	0	1	1	0	1.00	0	.279	.333	.500
2000	Oak	AL	10	10	3	0	0	0	(0	0)	3	5	0	1	0	0	1	1	0	0	2	1	.67	0	.300	.364	.300
2001	Oak	AL	19	38	9	1	0	3	(1	2)	19	9	5	7	4	0	6	1	0	0	1	0	1.00	0	.237	.326	.500
2002	Oak	AL	90	94	23	4	2	3	(2	1)	40	24	11	10	4	0	17	3	1	2	3	0	1.00	3	.245	.291	.426
2003	Oak	AL	121	414	109	27	9	12	(7	5)	190	64	51	68	42	4	71	2	0	2	10	2	.83	3	.263	.333	.459
2004	Oak	AL	143	569	161	39	3	20	(10	10)	266	91	73	87	46	0	111	12	0	5	17	1	.94	11	.283	.347	.467
2005	3 Tms		126	412	93	24	3	10	(5	5)	153	49	40	41	32	0	71	8	3	1	7	2	.78	7	.226	.294	.371
2006	Ari	NL	143	562	150	37	3	26	(12	14)	271	82	79	78	34	2	88	5	2	3	25	3	.89	12	.267	.313	.482
2007	Ari	NL	160	626	179	30	8	21	(11	10)	288	103	83	103	57	5	98	10	1	4	50	7	.88	12	.286	.353	.460
2008	Ari	NL	52	206	43	13	1	6	(3	3)	76	28	23	19	16	0	36	2	0	0	4	4	.50	5	.209	.272	.369
2009	Ari	NL	84	239	54	14	1	8	(4	4)	94	26	31	24	12	0	30	3	2	1	9	3	.75	4	.226	.270	.393
05	Oak	AL	59	192	51	15	2	7	(3	4)	91	30	24	29	14	0	27	7	1	1	2	2	.50	1	.266	.336	.474
05	Col	NL	15	53	10	2	0	0	(0	0)	12	2	5	4	7	0	11	0	0	0	2	0	1.00	1	.189	.283	.226
06	Bal	AL	52	167	32	7	1	3	(2	1)	50	17	11	8	11	0	33	1	2	0	3	0	1.00	5	.192	.246	.299
	Postseason		16	45	12	2	1	1	(0	1)	19	3	7	3	2	0	14	0	0	0	2	0	1.00	0	.267	.298	.422
	10 ML YEARS		948	3170	824	189	30	109	(56	53)	1400	481	396	438	247	11	529	47	9	19	128	23	.85	57	.260	.321	.442

Andrubal Cabrera

Bats: B **Throws:** R **Pos:** SS 101; 2D-20; PH-3   **Ht:** 6'0" **Wt:** 170 **Born:** 11/13/1985 **Age:** 24

Year	Team	Lg	G	AB	H	2B	3B	HR	(Hm	Rd)	TB	R	RBI	RC	TBB	IBB	SO	HBP	SH	SF	SB	CS	SB%	GDP	Avg	OBP	Slg
2009	Akron*	AA	4	16	4	1	0	0	(-	-)	5	5	0	2	1	0	2	1	0	0	2	0	1.00	0	.260	.333	.313
2007	Cle	AL	45	159	45	9	2	3	(1	2)	67	30	22	27	17	0	29	2	5	3	0	-	-	7	.283	.354	.421
2008	Cle	AL	114	352	91	20	0	6	(5	1)	129	48	47	48	46	2	77	4	11	5	4	4	.50	3	.259	.346	.366
2009	Cle	AL	131	523	161	42	4	6	(4	2)	229	81	68	81	44	1	89	1	10	3	17	4	.81	13	.308	.361	.438
	Postseason		11	46	10	0	0	1	(1	0)	13	5	6	5	2	0	12	0	3	1	0	0	-	2	.217	.245	.283
	3 ML YEARS		290	1034	297	71	6	15	(10	5)	425	159	137	156	107	3	195	7	26	11	21	8	.72	28	.287	.355	.411

Daniel Cabrera

Pitches: R **Bats:** R **Pos:** SP-9; RP-6   **Ht:** 6'9" **Wt:** 258 **Born:** 5/28/1981 **Age:** 29

Year	Team	Lg	G	GS	CG	GF	IP	BFP	H	R	ER	HR	SH	SF	HB	TBB	IBB	SO	WP	Bk	W	L	Pct	Sh	Sv-Op	Hld	ERC	ERA
2009	Reno*	AAA	4	4	0	0	14.2	67	15	10	10	1	1	2	1	10	0	11	1	0	0	1	.000	0	0--	-	5.48	6.14
2004	Bal	AL	28	27	1	1	147.2	662	145	85	82	14	4	7	2	89	2	76	12	0	12	8	.600	1	1-1	0	4.79	5.00
2005	Bal	AL	29	29	0	0	161.1	716	144	92	81	14	2	3	11	87	2	157	9	1	10	13	.435	0	0-0	0	4.13	4.52
2006	Bal	AL	26	26	2	0	148.0	662	130	82	78	11	5	8	5	104	1	157	17	1	9	10	.474	1	0-0	0	4.55	4.74
2007	Bal	AL	34	34	1	0	204.1	922	207	133	126	25	13	5	15	108	6	166	7	2	9	18	.333	0	0-0	0	5.08	5.55
2008	Bal	AL	30	30	2	0	180.0	821	199	109	105	24	5	12	18	90	5	95	15	2	8	10	.444	0	0-0	0	5.77	5.25
2009	2 Tms	NL	15	9	0	4	51.0	258	59	47	34	4	3	4	2	42	1	23	11	0	0	6	.000	0	0-0	0	6.68	6.00
09	Was	NL	9	8	0	0	40.0	207	48	39	26	4	3	2	2	35	1	16	10	0	0	5	.000	0	0-0	0	7.16	5.85
09	Ari	NL	6	1	0	4	11.0	51	11	8	8	0	0	2	0	7	0	7	1	0	0	1	.000	0	0-0	0	5.00	6.55
	6 ML YEARS		162	155	6	5	892.1	4041	884	548	506	92	32	37	55	520	17	674	71	6	48	65	.425	2	1-1	0	4.99	5.10

Everth Cabrera

Bats: B **Throws:** R **Pos:** SS-102; PH-1; PR-1   **Ht:** 5'10" **Wt:** 176 **Born:** 11/17/1986 **Age:** 23

Year	Team	Lg	G	AB	H	2B	3B	HR	(Hm	Rd)	TB	R	RBI	RC	TBB	IBB	SO	HBP	SH	SF	SB	CS	SB%	GDP	Avg	OBP	Slg
2006	Casper	R+	54	185	47	4	2	0	(-	-)	55	30	14	26	37	1	45	2	3	1	18	7	.72	0	.254	.382	.297
2007	Mdest	A+	4	15	4	0	1	0	(-	-)	6	3	2	3	2	0	7	2	1	0	1	0	1.00	0	.267	.421	.400
2007	TriCity	A-	42	150	45	8	3	1	(-	-)	62	29	23	30	27	2	24	8	1	0	12	5	.71	1	.300	.432	.413
2008	Ashvll	A	121	479	136	25	6	6	(-	-)	191	80	38	81	51	2	101	8	10	2	73	16	.82	6	.284	.361	.399
2009	Lk Els	A+	7	23	9	1	1	0	(-	-)	12	7	4	5	5	0	2	0	0	0	4	3	.57	0	.391	.500	.522
2009	Portlnd	AAA	7	27	9	2	0	0	(-	-)	11	5	0	4	1	0	6	1	0	0	1	0	1.00	0	.333	.379	.407
2009	SD	NL	103	377	96	18	8	2	(1	1)	136	59	31	48	46	5	88	5	8	2	25	8	.76	3	.255	.342	.361

Fernando Cabrera

Pitches: R **Bats:** R **Pos:** RP-6   **Ht:** 6'4" **Wt:** 225 **Born:** 11/16/1981 **Age:** 28

Year	Team	Lg	G	GS	CG	GF	IP	BFP	H	R	ER	HR	SH	SF	HB	TBB	IBB	SO	WP	Bk	W	L	Pct	Sh	Sv-Op	Hld	ERC	ERA
2009	Pwtckt*	AAA	43	0	0	33	52.2	220	40	11	10	3	2	5	1	22	4	51	4	0	0	3	.000	0	22--	-	2.43	1.71
2004	Cle	AL	4	0	0	2	5.1	20	3	3	2	0	0	1	0	1	0	6	0	0	0	0	-	0	0-0	0	0.99	3.38
2005	Cle	AL	15	0	0	6	30.2	124	24	7	5	1	0	0	0	11	1	29	1	1	2	1	.667	0	0-0	1	2.33	1.47
2006	Cle	AL	51	0	0	20	60.2	256	53	36	35	12	1	4	1	32	2	71	5	0	3	5	.500	0	0-4	6	4.72	5.19
2007	2 Tms	AL	33	0	0	13	43.2	207	50	36	34	9	0	2	0	31	3	48	2	0	1	2	.333	0	1-1	1	6.98	7.21
2008	Bal	AL	22	0	0	8	28.1	132	32	18	17	7	4	2	0	17	2	31	3	0	2	1	.667	0	0-1	0	7.24	5.40

Year	Team	Lg	G	GS	CG	GF	IP	BFP	H	R	ER	HR	SH	SF	HB	TBB	IBB	SO	WP	Bk	W	L	Pct	Sh	Sv-Op	Hld	ERC	ERA
2009	Bos	AL	6	0	0	3	5.1	28	7	5	5	0	0	0	1	4	1	8	0	0	0	0	-	0	0-0	1	6.71	8.44
07	Cle	AL	24	0	0	9	33.2	157	38	22	21	7	0	2	0	22	3	39	1	0	1	2	.333	0	0-0	1	6.61	5.61
07	Bal	AL	9	0	0	4	10.0	50	12	14	14	2	0	0	0	9	0	9	1	0	0	0	-	0	1-1	0	8.26	12.60
6 ML YEARS			131	0	0	52	174.0	767	169	105	99	31	1	9	2	96	9	193	11	1	8	7	.533	0	1-6	9	5.10	5.12

Melky Cabrera

Bats: B **Throws:** L **Pos:** CF-103; RF-48; LF-40; PH-7; PR-2; DH-1   **Ht:** 5'11" **Wt:** 200 **Born:** 8/11/1984 **Age:** 25

Year	Team	Lg	G	AB	H	2B	3B	HR	(Hm	Rd)	TB	R	RBI	RC	TBB	IBB	SO	HBP	SH	SF	SB	CS	SB%	GDP	Avg	OBP	Slg
2005	NYY	AL	6	19	4	0	0	0	(0	0)	4	1	0	0	0	0	2	0	0	0	0	0	-	0	.211	.211	.211
2006	NYY	AL	130	460	129	26	2	7	(3	4)	180	75	50	68	56	3	59	2	5	1	12	5	.71	9	.280	.360	.391
2007	NYY	AL	150	545	149	24	8	8	(4	4)	213	66	73	70	43	0	68	5	10	9	13	5	.72	14	.273	.327	.391
2008	NYY	AL	129	414	103	12	1	8	(4	4)	141	42	37	37	29	5	58	3	4	3	9	2	.82	11	.249	.301	.341
2009	NYY	AL	154	485	133	28	1	13	(9	4)	202	66	68	69	43	4	59	4	4	4	10	2	.83	15	.274	.336	.416
Postseason			6	19	3	0	0	1	(0	1)	6	2	2	1	0	0	1	0	0	0	0	0	-	0	.158	.158	.316
5 ML YEARS			569	1923	518	90	12	36	(20	16)	740	250	228	244	171	12	246	14	23	17	44	14	.76	49	.269	.331	.385

Miguel Cabrera

Bats: R **Throws:** R **Pos:** 1B-153; DH-6; PH-1   **Ht:** 6'4" **Wt:** 240 **Born:** 4/18/1983 **Age:** 27

Year	Team	Lg	G	AB	H	2B	3B	HR	(Hm	Rd)	TB	R	RBI	RC	TBB	IBB	SO	HBP	SH	SF	SB	CS	SB%	GDP	Avg	OBP	Slg
2003	Fla	NL	87	314	84	21	3	12	(7	5)	147	39	62	51	25	3	84	2	4	1	0	2	.00	12	.268	.325	.468
2004	Fla	NL	160	603	177	31	1	33	(14	19)	309	101	112	92	68	5	148	6	0	8	5	2	.71	20	.294	.366	.512
2005	Fla	NL	158	613	198	43	2	33	(11	22)	344	106	116	108	64	12	125	2	0	6	1	0	1.00	20	.323	.385	.561
2006	Fla	NL	158	576	195	50	2	26	(15	11)	327	112	114	132	86	27	108	10	0	4	9	6	.60	18	.339	.430	.568
2007	Fla	NL	157	588	188	38	2	34	(19	15)	332	91	119	122	79	23	127	5	1	7	2	1	.67	17	.320	.401	.565
2008	Det	AL	160	616	180	36	2	37	(19	18)	331	85	127	109	56	6	126	3	0	9	1	0	1.00	14	.292	.349	.537
2009	Det	AL	160	611	198	34	0	34	(19	15)	334	96	103	114	68	14	107	5	0	1	6	2	.75	22	.324	.396	.547
Postseason			17	68	18	2	0	4	(1	3)	32	11	12	9	4	0	19	1	1	0	0	0	-	2	.265	.315	.471
7 ML YEARS			1040	3921	1220	253	12	209	(104	105)	2124	630	753	728	446	90	825	33	5	36	24	13	.65	125	.311	.383	.542

Orlando Cabrera

Bats: R **Throws:** R **Pos:** SS-158; PH-1; PR-1   **Ht:** 5'9" **Wt:** 185 **Born:** 11/2/1974 **Age:** 35

Year	Team	Lg	G	AB	H	2B	3B	HR	(Hm	Rd)	TB	R	RBI	RC	TBB	IBB	SO	HBP	SH	SF	SB	CS	SB%	GDP	Avg	OBP	Slg
1997	Mon	NL	16	18	4	0	0	0	(0	0)	4	4	2	0	1	0	3	0	1	0	1	2	.33	1	.222	.263	.222
1998	Mon	NL	79	261	73	16	5	3	(2	1)	108	44	22	34	18	1	27	0	5	1	6	2	.75	6	.280	.325	.414
1999	Mon	NL	104	382	97	23	5	8	(6	2)	154	48	39	42	18	4	38	3	4	0	2	2	.50	9	.254	.293	.403
2000	Mon	NL	125	422	100	25	1	13	(7	6)	166	47	55	43	25	3	28	1	3	3	4	4	.50	12	.237	.279	.393
2001	Mon	NL	162	626	173	41	6	14	(7	7)	268	64	96	85	43	5	54	4	4	7	19	7	.73	15	.276	.324	.428
2002	Mon	NL	153	563	148	43	1	7	(3	4)	214	64	56	61	48	4	53	2	9	4	25	7	.78	16	.263	.321	.380
2003	Mon	NL	162	626	186	47	2	17	(8	9)	288	95	80	92	52	3	64	1	3	9	24	2	.92	18	.297	.347	.460
2004	2 Tms		161	618	163	38	3	10	(2	8)	237	74	62	67	39	0	54	3	3	10	16	4	.80	16	.264	.306	.383
2005	LAA	AL	141	540	139	28	3	8	(2	6)	197	70	57	61	38	4	50	3	4	2	21	2	.91	10	.257	.309	.365
2006	LAA	AL	153	607	171	45	1	9	(3	6)	245	95	72	77	51	0	58	3	4	11	27	3	.90	12	.282	.335	.404
2007	LAA	AL	155	638	192	35	1	8	(3	5)	253	101	86	95	44	0	64	5	3	11	20	4	.83	12	.301	.345	.397
2008	CWS	AL	161	661	186	33	1	8	(5	3)	245	93	57	83	56	1	71	1	3	9	19	6	.76	16	.281	.334	.371
2009	2 Tms	AL	160	656	186	36	3	9	(3	6)	255	83	77	74	36	1	71	0	6	10	13	4	.76	22	.284	.316	.389
04	Mon	NL	103	390	96	19	2	4	(1	3)	131	41	31	37	28	0	31	2	2	3	12	3	.80	12	.246	.298	.336
04	Bos	AL	58	228	67	19	1	6	(1	5)	106	33	31	30	11	0	23	1	1	7	4	1	.80	4	.294	.320	.465
09	Oak	AL	101	414	116	23	0	4	(0	4)	151	41	41	48	25	1	39	0	5	4	11	4	.73	13	.280	.318	.365
09	Min	AL	59	242	70	13	3	5	(3	2)	104	42	36	26	11	0	32	0	1	6	2	0	1.00	9	.289	.313	.430
Postseason			31	128	31	8	0	1	(1	0)	42	14	18	15	9	0	15	2	0	1	1	0	1.00	1	.242	.300	.328
13 ML YEARS			1732	6618	1818	410	32	114	(51	63)	2634	882	761	814	469	26	635	26	51	77	197	49	.80	165	.275	.322	.398

Trevor Cahill

Pitches: R **Bats:** R **Pos:** SP-32   **Ht:** 6'3" **Wt:** 211 **Born:** 3/1/1988 **Age:** 22

Year	Team	Lg	G	GS	CG	GF	IP	BFP	H	R	ER	HR	SH	SF	HB	TBB	IBB	SO	WP	Bk	W	L	Pct	Sh	Sv-Op	Hld	ERC	ERA
2006	As	R	4	4	0	0	9.0	36	2	4	3	0	0	1	0	7	0	11	3	0	0	0	-	0	0- -	-	1.15	3.00
2007	Kane	A	20	19	0	0	105.1	437	85	38	32	3	1	1	9	40	1	117	8	0	11	4	.733	0	0- -	-	2.82	2.73
2008	Stcktn	A+	14	13	0	0	87.1	344	52	29	27	3	6	0	8	31	0	103	9	0	5	4	.556	0	0- -	-	1.82	2.78
2008	Mdland	AA	7	6	0	0	37.0	151	24	15	9	2	1	2	3	19	0	33	3	0	6	1	.857	0	0- -	-	2.70	2.19
2009	Oak	AL	32	32	0	0	178.2	773	185	99	92	27	4	7	4	72	1	90	5	0	10	13	.435	0	0-0	0	4.79	4.63

Matt Cain

Pitches: R **Bats:** R **Pos:** SP-33   **Ht:** 6'3" **Wt:** 246 **Born:** 10/1/1984 **Age:** 25

Year	Team	Lg	G	GS	CG	GF	IP	BFP	H	R	ER	HR	SH	SF	HB	TBB	IBB	SO	WP	Bk	W	L	Pct	Sh	Sv-Op	Hld	ERC	ERA
2005	SF	NL	7	7	1	0	46.1	181	24	12	12	4	2	1	0	19	1	30	1	0	2	1	.667	0	0-0	0	1.61	2.33
2006	SF	NL	32	31	1	1	190.2	818	157	93	88	18	11	6	6	87	1	179	9	2	13	12	.520	1	0-0	0	3.35	4.15
2007	SF	NL	32	32	1	0	200.0	832	173	84	81	14	8	5	5	79	3	163	12	0	7	16	.304	0	0-0	0	3.23	3.65
2008	SF	NL	34	34	1	0	217.2	933	206	95	91	19	7	7	7	91	9	186	7	2	8	14	.364	1	0-0	0	3.84	3.76
2009	SF	NL	33	33	4	0	217.2	886	184	73	70	22	10	6	3	73	6	171	9	0	14	8	.636	0	0-0	0	3.06	2.89
5 ML YEARS			138	137	8	1	872.1	3650	744	357	342	77	38	25	21	349	20	729	38	4	44	51	.463	2	0-0	0	3.27	3.53

Miguel Cairo

Bats: R Throws: R Pos: PH-19; 2B-5; SS-3; 3B-1; PR-1   Ht: 6'1" Wt: 210 Born: 5/4/1974 Age: 36

Year	Team	Lg	G	AB	H	2B	3B	HR	(Hm	Rd)	TB	R	RBI	RC	TBB	IBB	SO	HBP	SH	SF	SB	CS	SB%	GDP	Avg	OBP	Slg
2009	LV*	AAA	78	296	85	12	2	5	(-	-)	116	44	33	39	15	1	40	2	1	1	8	1	.89	6	.287	.325	.392
1996	Tor	AL	9	27	6	2	0	0	(0	0)	8	5	1	2	2	0	9	1	0	0	0	0	-	1	.222	.300	.296
1997	ChC	NL	16	29	7	1	0	0	(0	0)	8	7	1	3	2	0	3	1	0	0	0	0	-	0	.241	.313	.276
1998	TB	AL	150	515	138	26	5	5	(3	2)	189	49	46	58	24	0	44	6	11	2	19	8	.70	9	.268	.307	.367
1999	TB	AL	120	465	137	15	5	3	(1	2)	171	61	36	57	24	0	46	7	7	5	22	7	.76	13	.295	.335	.368
2000	TB	AL	119	375	98	18	2	1	(0	1)	123	49	34	42	29	0	34	2	6	5	28	7	.80	7	.261	.314	.328
2001	2 Tms	NL	93	156	46	8	1	3	(2	1)	65	25	16	23	18	1	23	0	7	1	2	1	.67	4	.295	.366	.417
2002	StL	NL	108	184	46	9	2	2	(1	1)	65	28	23	19	13	2	36	3	6	2	1	1	.50	5	.250	.307	.353
2003	StL	NL	92	261	64	15	2	5	(2	3)	08	41	32	25	13	1	30	6	3	7	4	1	.80	6	.245	.289	.375
2004	NYY	AL	122	360	105	17	5	6	(4	2)	150	48	42	50	18	1	49	14	12	4	11	3	.79	7	.292	.346	.417
2005	NYM	NL	100	327	82	18	0	2	(1	1)	106	31	19	29	19	2	31	4	12	5	13	3	.81	5	.251	.296	.324
2006	NYY	AL	81	222	53	12	3	0	(0	0)	71	28	30	26	13	0	31	1	5	3	13	1	.93	4	.239	.280	.320
2007	2 Tms	NL	82	174	44	9	2	0	(0	0)	57	20	15	21	11	1	24	2	5	1	10	2	.83	3	.253	.303	.328
2008	Sea	AL	108	221	55	14	2	0	(0	0)	73	34	23	26	18	0	32	4	6	1	5	2	.71	6	.249	.316	.330
2009	Phi	NL	27	45	12	2	1	1	(1	0)	19	6	2	2	0	0	4	1	1	0	0	0	-	1	.267	.283	.422
01	ChC	NL	66	123	35	3	1	2	(1	1)	46	20	9	17	16	1	21	0	7	1	2	1	.67	3	.285	.364	.374
01	StL	NL	27	33	11	5	0	1	(1	0)	19	5	7	6	2	0	2	0	0	0	0	0	-	1	.333	.371	.576
07	NYY	AL	54	107	27	7	0	0	(0	0)	34	12	10	12	8	1	19	1	4	1	8	1	.89	3	.252	.308	.318
07	StL	NL	28	67	17	2	2	0	(0	0)	23	8	5	9	3	0	5	1	1	0	2	1	.67	0	.254	.296	.343
	Postseason		19	61	20	5	0	1	(1	0)	28	11	6	9	4	0	12	5	2	0	2	1	.67	0	.328	.414	.459
	14 ML YEARS		1227	3361	893	166	30	28	(15	13)	1203	432	320	383	204	8	396	52	81	36	128	36	.78	71	.266	.315	.358

Kiko Calero

Pitches: R Bats: R Pos: RP-67   Ht: 6'1" Wt: 205 Born: 1/9/1975 Age: 35

Year	Team	Lg	G	GS	CG	GF	IP	BFP	H	R	ER	HR	SH	SF	HB	TBB	IBB	SO	WP	Bk	W	L	Pct	Sh	Sv-Op	Hld	ERC	ERA
2009	Jupiter*	A+	2	0	0	0	2.0	6	0	0	0	0	0	0	0	0	0	1	0	0	0	0	-	0	0--	-	0.00	0.00
2003	StL	NL	26	1	0	7	38.1	162	29	12	12	5	1	3	1	20	2	51	3	1	1	1	.500	0	1-4	1	3.44	2.82
2004	StL	NL	41	0	0	4	45.1	168	27	14	14	5	4	0	1	10	1	47	1	0	3	1	.750	0	2-3	12	1.62	2.78
2005	Oak	AL	58	0	0	15	55.2	229	45	20	20	6	1	1	1	18	2	52	2	0	4	1	.800	0	1-2	12	2.80	3.23
2006	Oak	AL	70	0	0	17	58.0	241	50	22	22	4	0	1	0	24	3	67	1	0	3	2	.600	0	2-5	23	3.13	3.41
2007	Oak	AL	46	0	0	6	40.2	185	46	26	26	3	0	5	2	21	2	31	1	0	1	5	.167	0	1-4	9	5.26	5.75
2008	Oak	AL	5	0	0	3	4.2	20	3	3	3	0	0	0	0	3	0	7	0	0	0	0	-	0	0-0	0	2.35	3.86
2009	Fla	NL	67	0	0	15	60.0	239	36	13	13	1	4	4	1	30	4	69	2	0	2	2	.500	0	0-5	12	1.87	1.95
	Postseason		12	0	0	1	12.1	55	13	5	5	1	0	0	1	7	0	11	0	0	1	0	1.000	0	0-1	2	5.41	3.65
	7 ML YEARS		313	1	0	67	302.2	1244	236	110	109	24	10	14	6	126	14	324	10	1	14	12	.538	0	7-23	69	2.86	3.24

Alberto Callaspo

Bats: B Throws: R Pos: 2B-146; 3B-14; PH-2; SS-1   Ht: 5'9" Wt: 180 Born: 4/19/1983 Age: 27

Year	Team	Lg	G	AB	H	2B	3B	HR	(Hm	Rd)	TB	R	RBI	RC	TBB	IBB	SO	HBP	SH	SF	SB	CS	SB%	GDP	Avg	OBP	Slg
2006	Ari	NL	23	42	10	1	1	0	(0	0)	13	2	6	5	4	0	6	0	0	1	0	1	.00	0	.238	.298	.310
2007	Ari	NL	56	144	31	8	0	0	(0	0)	39	10	7	7	8	0	14	1	1	1	1	1	.50	8	.215	.265	.271
2008	KC	AL	74	213	65	8	3	0	(0	0)	79	21	16	25	19	0	14	0	1	1	2	1	.67	6	.305	.361	.371
2009	KC	AL	155	576	173	41	8	11	(6	5)	263	79	73	90	52	4	51	1	0	5	2	1	.67	15	.300	.356	.457
	Postseason		2	2	0	0	0	0	(0	0)	0	0	0	0	0	0	0	0	0	0	0	0	-	0	.000	.000	.000
	4 ML YEARS		308	975	279	58	12	11	(6	5)	394	112	102	127	84	4	85	2	2	8	5	4	.56	29	.286	.341	.404

Kevin Cameron

Pitches: R Bats: R Pos: RP-11   Ht: 6'1" Wt: 191 Born: 12/15/1979 Age: 30

Year	Team	Lg	G	GS	CG	GF	IP	BFP	H	R	ER	HR	SH	SF	HB	TBB	IBB	SO	WP	Bk	W	L	Pct	Sh	Sv-Op	Hld	ERC	ERA
2009	As*	R	1	1	0	0	1.0	3	0	0	0	0	0	0	0	0	0	2	0	0	0	0	-	0	0--	-	0.00	0.00
2009	Scrmto*	AAA	10	0	0	6	13.0	55	7	5	4	0	0	0	0	11	0	14	1	0	2	1	.667	0	1--	-	2.61	2.77
2007	SD	NL	48	0	0	20	58.0	263	55	24	18	0	4	2	0	36	5	50	2	0	2	0	1.000	0	0-0	1	3.67	2.79
2008	SD	NL	10	0	0	4	10.0	46	10	9	4	0	1	1	0	6	2	5	0	0	0	0	-	0	0-0	0	3.64	3.60
2009	Oak	AL	11	0	0	4	18.1	74	15	7	7	1	0	0	0	6	0	15	0	0	0	0	-	0	1-1	1	2.58	3.44
	3 ML YEARS		69	0	0	28	86.1	383	80	40	29	1	5	3	0	48	7	70	2	0	2	0	1.000	0	1-1	2	3.44	3.02

Mike Cameron

Bats: R Throws: R Pos: CF-147; PH-3   Ht: 6'2" Wt: 205 Born: 1/8/1973 Age: 37

Year	Team	Lg	G	AB	H	2B	3B	HR	(Hm	Rd)	TB	R	RBI	RC	TBB	IBB	SO	HBP	SH	SF	SB	CS	SB%	GDP	Avg	OBP	Slg
1995	CWS	AL	28	38	7	2	0	1	(0	1)	12	4	2	3	3	0	15	0	3	0	0	0	-	0	.184	.244	.316
1996	CWS	AL	11	11	1	0	0	0	(0	0)	1	1	0	0	1	0	3	0	0	0	1	0	.00	0	.091	.167	.091
1997	CWS	AL	116	379	98	18	3	14	(10	4)	164	63	55	63	55	1	105	5	2	5	23	2	.92	8	.259	.356	.433
1998	CWS	AL	141	396	83	16	5	8	(5	3)	133	53	43	39	37	0	101	6	1	3	27	11	.71	6	.210	.285	.336
1999	Cin	NL	146	542	139	34	9	21	(12	9)	254	93	66	96	80	2	145	6	1	3	38	12	.76	4	.256	.357	.469
2000	Sea	AL	155	543	145	28	4	19	(5	14)	238	96	78	91	78	0	133	9	7	6	24	7	.77	10	.267	.365	.438
2001	Sea	AL	150	540	144	30	5	25	(7	18)	259	99	110	96	69	3	155	10	1	13	34	5	.87	13	.267	.353	.480
2002	Sea	AL	158	545	130	26	5	25	(7	18)	241	84	80	78	79	7	176	7	4	5	31	8	.79	8	.239	.340	.442
2003	Sea	AL	147	534	135	31	5	18	(11	7)	230	74	76	80	70	1	137	5	1	2	17	7	.71	13	.253	.344	.431
2004	NYM	NL	140	493	114	30	1	30	(11	19)	236	76	76	70	57	2	143	8	1	3	22	6	.79	5	.231	.319	.479
2005	NYM	NL	76	308	84	23	2	12	(7	5)	147	47	39	52	29	0	85	4	1	1	13	1	.93	5	.273	.342	.477

Year Team	Lg	G	AB	H	2B	3B	HR	(Hm	Rd)	TB	R	RBI	RC	TBB	IBB	SO	HBP	SH	SF	SB	CS	SB%	GDP	Avg	OBP	Slg
2006 SD	NL	141	552	148	34	9	22	(11	11)	266	88	83	98	71	2	142	6	0	5	25	9	.74	8	.268	.355	.482
2007 SD	NL	151	571	138	33	6	21	(10	11)	246	88	78	83	67	1	160	8	2	3	18	5	.78	9	.242	.328	.431
2008 Mil	NL	120	444	108	25	2	25	(7	18)	212	69	70	70	54	1	142	6	1	3	17	5	.77	4	.243	.331	.477
2009 Mil	NL	149	544	136	32	3	24	(14	10)	246	78	70	75	75	3	156	4	0	5	7	3	.70	12	.250	.342	.452
Postseason		27	92	16	6	0	1	(1	0)	25	14	7	7	14	0	29	4	2	0	3	1	.75	2	.174	.309	.272
15 ML YEARS		1829	6440	1610	362	59	265	(117	148)	2885	1013	926	994	825	19	1798	84	29	57	296	82	.78	105	.250	.340	.448

Shawn Camp

Pitches: R **Bats:** R **Pos:** RP-59   **Ht:** 6'0" **Wt:** 204 **Born:** 11/18/1975 **Age:** 34

Year Team	Lg	G	GS	CG	GF	IP	BFP	H	R	ER	HR	SH	SF	HB	TBB	IBB	SO	WP	Bk	W	L	Pct	Sh	Sv-Op	Hld	ERC	ERA
2004 KC	AL	42	0	0	12	66.2	286	74	37	29	10	2	3	5	16	1	51	2	1	2	2	.500	0	2-3	5	4.74	3.92
2005 KC	AL	29	0	0	7	49.0	228	69	40	35	4	0	3	4	13	3	28	3	0	1	4	.200	0	0-2	0	6.00	6.43
2006 TB	AL	75	0	0	15	75.0	328	93	43	39	9	2	3	7	19	3	53	4	0	7	4	.636	0	4-6	12	5.48	4.68
2007 TB	AL	50	0	0	8	40.0	198	63	33	32	7	5	1	3	18	6	36	2	0	0	3	.000	0	0-2	11	8.59	7.20
2008 Tor	AL	40	0	0	16	39.1	166	40	18	18	2	0	1	2	11	3	31	0	0	3	1	.750	0	0-0	7	3.47	4.12
2009 Tor	AL	59	0	0	17	79.2	333	73	36	31	7	1	1	4	29	4	58	0	0	2	6	.250	0	1-1	6	3.57	3.50
6 ML YEARS		295	0	0	75	349.2	1539	412	207	184	39	10	12	25	106	20	257	11	1	15	20	.429	0	7-14	41	5.05	4.74

Jorge Campillo

Pitches: R **Bats:** R **Pos:** RP-5   **Ht:** 6'1" **Wt:** 225 **Born:** 8/10/1978 **Age:** 31

Year Team	Lg	G	GS	CG	GF	IP	BFP	H	R	ER	HR	SH	SF	HB	TBB	IBB	SO	WP	Bk	W	L	Pct	Sh	Sv-Op	Hld	ERC	ERA
2009 Missi*	AA	1	1	0	0	2.0	8	1	0	0	0	0	0	0	1	0	2	0	0	0	0	-	0	0--	-	1.41	0.00
2009 Gwnntt*	AAA	1	0	0	1	3.0	13	4	2	2	1	0	0	0	0	0	1	1	0	0	0	-	0	1--	-	5.82	6.00
2005 Sea	AL	2	1	0	1	2.0	9	1	0	0	0	0	0	0	1	0	1	0	0	0	0	-	0	0-0	0	1.26	0.00
2006 Sea	AL	1	0	0	0	2.1	11	4	4	4	0	0	0	0	0	0	1	0	0	0	0	-	0	0-0	0	5.71	15.43
2007 Sea	AL	5	0	0	2	13.1	63	18	12	10	2	1	1	1	6	0	9	0	0	0	0	-	0	0-0	0	7.18	6.75
2008 Atl	NL	39	25	1	3	158.2	655	158	74	69	18	9	5	1	38	2	107	2	0	8	7	.533	0	0-0	4	3.55	3.91
2009 Atl	NL	5	0	0	4	4.1	21	7	3	2	0	0	0	0	3	0	3	0	0	1	0	1.000	0	0-1	0	8.83	4.15
5 ML YEARS		52	26	1	10	180.2	759	188	93	85	20	10	6	2	48	2	121	2	0	9	7	.563	0	0-1	4	3.90	4.23

Robinson Cancel

Bats: R **Throws:** R **Pos:** PH-1   **Ht:** 6'0" **Wt:** 239 **Born:** 5/4/1976 **Age:** 34

Year Team	Lg	G	AB	H	2B	3B	HR	(Hm	Rd)	TB	R	RBI	RC	TBB	IBB	SO	HBP	SH	SF	SB	CS	SB%	GDP	Avg	OBP	Slg
2009 Buffalo*	AAA	77	258	64	12	2	2	(-	-)	86	25	16	27	18	0	29	1	3	2	7	3	.70	10	.248	.297	.333
1999 Mil	NL	15	44	8	2	0	0	(	)	10	5	5	2	2	0	12	1	1	0	0	0	-	0	.182	.234	.227
2008 NYM	NL	27	49	12	2	0	1	(1	0)	17	5	5	3	3	0	6	0	1	0	1	2	.33	0	.245	.288	.347
2009 NYM	NL	1	1	0	0	0	0	(0	0)	0	0	0	0	0	0	0	0	0	0	0	0	-	0	.000	.000	.000
3 ML YEARS		43	94	20	4	0	1	(1	0)	27	10	10	5	5	0	18	1	2	0	1	2	.33	0	.213	.260	.287

Barbaro Canizares

Bats: R **Throws:** R **Pos:** 1B-5   **Ht:** 6'3" **Wt:** 240 **Born:** 11/21/1979 **Age:** 30

Year Team	Lg	G	AB	H	2B	3B	HR	(Hm	Rd)	TB	R	RBI	RC	TBB	IBB	SO	HBP	SH	SF	SB	CS	SB%	GDP	Avg	OBP	Slg
2006 MrtlBh	A+	6	21	8	0	0	1	(-	-)	11	3	1	4	1	0	3	0	0	0	1	0	1.00	0	.381	.409	.524
2006 Missi	AA	78	279	84	18	1	4	(-	-)	116	33	33	44	28	0	44	2	0	3	0	0	-	14	.301	.365	.416
2007 Rchmd	AAA	49	163	56	13	1	3	(-	-)	80	24	34	31	12	1	28	3	0	4	0	0	-	4	.344	.390	.491
2007 Braves	R	4	11	6	0	0	1	(-	-)	9	1	2	5	4	0	1	0	0	0	0	0	-	2	.545	.667	.818
2008 Rchmd	AAA	134	504	151	28	0	13	(-	-)	218	56	67	79	43	1	69	1	0	5	1	0	1.00	18	.300	.353	.433
2009 Gwnntt	AAA	130	506	149	31	2	12	(-	-)	220	55	79	84	52	4	67	7	0	4	2	2	.50	18	.294	.366	.435
2009 Atl	NL	5	21	4	1	0	0	(0	0)	5	1	0	0	0	0	6	0	0	0	0	0	-	0	.190	.190	.238

Robinson Cano

Bats: L **Throws:** R **Pos:** 2B-161; PH-2   **Ht:** 6'0" **Wt:** 205 **Born:** 10/22/1982 **Age:** 27

Year Team	Lg	G	AB	H	2B	3B	HR	(Hm	Rd)	TB	R	RBI	RC	TBB	IBB	SO	HBP	SH	SF	SB	CS	SB%	GDP	Avg	OBP	Slg
2005 NYY	AL	132	522	155	34	4	14	(5	9)	239	78	62	59	16	1	68	3	7	3	1	3	.25	16	.297	.320	.458
2006 NYY	AL	122	482	165	41	1	15	(9	6)	253	62	78	74	18	3	54	2	1	5	5	2	.71	19	.342	.365	.525
2007 NYY	AL	160	617	189	41	7	19	(10	9)	301	93	97	94	39	5	85	8	1	4	4	5	.44	19	.306	.353	.488
2008 NYY	AL	159	597	162	35	3	14	(7	7)	245	70	72	64	26	3	65	5	1	5	2	4	.33	18	.271	.305	.410
2009 NYY	AL	161	637	204	48	2	25	(14	11)	331	103	85	79	30	2	63	3	0	4	5	7	.42	22	.320	.352	.520
Postseason		13	49	12	4	0	2	(1	1)	22	6	8	5	3	0	6	0	0	0	0	2	.00	2	.245	.288	.449
5 ML YEARS		734	2855	875	199	17	87	(45	42)	1369	406	394	370	129	14	335	21	10	21	17	21	.45	94	.306	.339	.480

Jorge Cantu

Bats: R **Throws:** R **Pos:** 1B-111; 3B-45; DH-7; PH-5   **Ht:** 6'3" **Wt:** 207 **Born:** 1/30/1982 **Age:** 28

								BATTING												BASERUNNING				AVERAGES		
Year	Team	Lg	G	AB	H	2B	3B	HR	(Hm | Rd)	TB	R	RBI	RC	TBB	IBB	SO	HBP	SH	SF	SB	CS	SB%	GDP	Avg	OBP	Slg
2004	TB	AL	50	173	52	20	1	2	(0 | 2)	80	25	17	22	9	0	44	2	0	1	0	0	-	5	.301	.341	.462
2005	TB	AL	150	598	171	40	1	28	(16 | 12)	297	73	117	88	19	1	83	6	0	7	1	0	1.00	24	.286	.311	.497
2006	TB	AL	107	413	103	18	2	14	(7 | 7)	167	40	62	42	26	2	91	3	0	6	1	1	.50	16	.249	.295	.404
2007	2 Tms		52	115	29	9	0	1	(0 | 1)	41	12	13	12	12	0	26	3	0	3	0	0	-	6	.252	.331	.357
2008	Fla	NL	155	628	174	41	0	29	(18 | 11)	302	92	95	89	40	6	111	10	0	7	6	2	.75	15	.277	.327	.481
2009	Fla	NL	149	585	169	42	0	16	(8 | 8)	259	67	100	85	47	4	81	6	0	5	3	1	.75	15	.289	.345	.443
07	TB	AL	25	58	12	1	0	0	(0 | 0)	13	4	4	3	5	0	16	1	0	1	0	0	-	3	.207	.277	.224
07	Cin	NL	27	57	17	8	0	1	(0 | 1)	28	8	9	9	7	0	10	2	0	2	0	0	-	3	.298	.382	.491
	6 ML YEARS		663	2512	698	170	4	90	(49 | 41)	1146	309	404	338	153	13	436	30	0	29	11	4	.73	81	.278	.323	.456

Matt Capps

Pitches: R **Bats:** R **Pos:** RP-57   **Ht:** 6'2" **Wt:** 245 **Born:** 9/3/1983 **Age:** 26

			HOW MUCH HE PITCHED						WHAT HE GAVE UP											THE RESULTS						
Year	Team	Lg	G	GS	CG	GF	IP	BFP	H	R	ER	HR	SH	SF	HB	TBB	IBB	SO	WP	Bk	W	L	Pct	Sh	Sv-Op	Hld	ERC	ERA
2005	Pit	NL	4	0	0	0	4.0	16	5	2	2	0	0	0	1	0	0	3	0	0	0	0	-	0	0-0	0	4.62	4.50
2006	Pit	NL	85	0	0	15	80.2	329	81	37	34	12	8	2	3	12	5	56	4	0	9	1	.900	0	1-10	13	3.52	3.79
2007	Pit	NL	76	0	0	47	79.0	315	64	22	20	5	3	2	3	16	10	64	1	0	4	7	.364	0	18-21	15	2.10	2.28
2008	Pit	NL	49	0	0	39	53.2	211	47	20	18	5	2	0	2	5	0	39	0	0	2	3	.400	0	21-26	0	2.39	3.02
2009	Pit	NL	57	0	0	50	54.1	251	73	36	35	10	2	4	3	17	3	46	0	0	4	8	.333	0	27-32	1	6.53	5.80
	5 ML YEARS		271	0	0	151	271.2	1122	270	117	109	32	15	8	12	50	18	208	5	0	19	19	.500	0	67-89	29	3.40	3.61

Esmailin Caridad

Pitches: R **Bats:** R **Pos:** RP-14   **Ht:** 5'10" **Wt:** 193 **Born:** 10/20/1983 **Age:** 26

			HOW MUCH HE PITCHED						WHAT HE GAVE UP											THE RESULTS						
Year	Team	Lg	G	GS	CG	GF	IP	BFP	H	R	ER	HR	SH	SF	HB	TBB	IBB	SO	WP	Bk	W	L	Pct	Sh	Sv-Op	Hld	ERC	ERA
2008	Dytona	A+	14	13	0	0	69.1	279	64	35	34	3	2	4	2	17	0	38	1	0	8	4	.600	0	0--	-	2.89	4.41
2008	Tenn	AA	14	14	0	0	82.2	337	67	31	29	15	6	1	2	21	0	60	1	1	7	3	.700	0	0--	-	3.06	3.16
2009	Iowa	AAA	25	25	0	0	131.2	578	139	71	61	17	11	5	3	46	4	114	2	1	5	10	.333	0	0		4.00	4.17
2009	ChC	NL	14	0	0	7	19.1	71	16	4	3	0	0	0	3	3	0	17	0	0	1	0	1.000	0	0-0	2	2.10	1.40

Luke Carlin

Bats: B **Throws:** R **Pos:** PH-6; C-4   **Ht:** 5'11" **Wt:** 185 **Born:** 12/20/1980 **Age:** 29

								BATTING												BASERUNNING				AVERAGES		
Year	Team	Lg	G	AB	H	2B	3B	HR	(Hm	Rd)	TB	R	RBI	RC	TBB	IBB	SO	HBP	SH	SF	SB	CS	SB%	GDP	Avg	OBP	Slg
2002	Oneonta	A-	45	150	34	5	2	0	(-	-)	43	23	10	19	34	0	28	1	1	1	0	2	.00	2	.227	.371	.287
2003	FtWyn	A	17	50	12	0	0	0	(-	-)	12	2	4	3	4	0	11	0	0	0	0	1	.00	2	.240	.296	.240
2003	Eugene	A-	28	100	25	7	0	0	(-	-)	32	14	7	12	14	0	25	2	0	0	1	0	1.00	2	.250	.353	.320
2004	Lk Els	A+	37	107	28	7	0	1	(-	-)	38	12	12	12	10	0	19	0	0	2	0	1	.00	0	.262	.319	.355
2004	FtWyn	A	27	99	21	6	3	0	(-	-)	33	10	12	10	11	0	23	0	0	1	1	0	1.00	1	.212	.288	.333
2005	Mobile	AA	87	229	60	8	1	2	(-	-)	76	24	25	30	35	3	46	1	1	1	4	3	.57	4	.262	.361	.332
2006	Mobile	AA	2	5	0	0	0	0	(-	-)	0	0	0	0	0	0	1	0	0	0	0	0	-	0	.000	.000	.000
2006	Portlnd	AAA	73	244	65	14	1	4	(-	-)	93	27	29	41	49	0	54	2	1	1	0	0	-	7	.266	.392	.381
2007	Portlnd	AAA	98	300	66	20	2	0	(-	-)	90	35	17	32	47	2	77	0	6	0	0	3	.00	9	.220	.326	.300
2008	Portlnd	AAA	31	88	23	3	0	4	(-	-)	38	12	19	16	19	0	27	2	0	2	0	0	-	1	.261	.396	.432
2009	Reno	AAA	72	237	76	17	0	7	(-	-)	114	45	35	50	45	0	55	1	1	1	5	4	.56	2	.321	.430	.481
2008	SD	NL	36	94	14	3	1	1	(0	1)	22	12	6	2	10	0	34	1	0	0	0	0	-	3	.149	.238	.234
2009	Ari	NL	10	18	3	0	0	0	(0	0)	3	3	1	2	3	0	3	0	0	0	0	0	-	0	.167	.286	.167
	2 ML YEARS		46	112	17	3	1	1	(0	1)	25	15	7	4	13	0	37	1	0	0	0	0	-	3	.152	.246	.223

Jesse Carlson

Pitches: L **Bats:** L **Pos:** RP-73   **Ht:** 6'1" **Wt:** 160 **Born:** 12/31/1980 **Age:** 29

			HOW MUCH HE PITCHED						WHAT HE GAVE UP											THE RESULTS						
Year	Team	Lg	G	GS	CG	GF	IP	BFP	H	R	ER	HR	SH	SF	HB	TBB	IBB	SO	WP	Bk	W	L	Pct	Sh	Sv-Op	Hld	ERC	ERA
2002	Oneont	A-	19	0	0	4	38.0	143	19	8	7	1	2	0	1	10	0	47	1	1	2	2	.500	0	0--	-	1.11	1.66
2003	Lxngtn	A	53	0	0	27	63.1	241	37	11	11	2	3	0	2	16	3	84	1	0	3	0	1.000	0	13--	-	1.33	1.56
2004	RdRck	AA	41	0	0	19	55.1	248	57	33	31	5	0	0	4	21	3	51	2	0	5	0	1.000	0	1--	-	4.18	5.04
2005	Syrcse	AAA	22	0	0	6	18.2	93	26	10	10	4	1	0	5	7	1	17	0	0	1	1	.500	0	0--	-	8.30	4.82
2005	NHam	AA	39	0	0	14	40.0	150	28	8	8	2	1	1	3	5	0	43	0	1	2	2	.500	0	5--	-	1.65	1.80
2006	Frisco	AA	43	0	0	17	58.0	263	65	39	30	7	3	0	5	18	4	45	0	0	6	5	.545	0	3--	-	4.65	4.66
2006	Okla	AAA	10	0	0	2	11.0	42	6	0	0	0	0	2	0	4	0	5	0	0	0	0	-	0	0--	-	1.31	0.00
2007	NHam	AA	58	0	0	25	70.1	304	77	39	38	4	6	1	3	18	0	81	0	1	8	2	.800	0	6--	-	3.74	4.86
2008	Syrcse	AAA	2	0	0	1	3.2	13	1	0	0	0	1	0	0	0	0	2	1	0	0	0	-	0	0--	-	0.47	0.00
2008	Tor	AL	69	0	0	10	60.0	237	41	16	15	6	1	3	3	21	7	55	2	1	7	2	.778	0	2-2	19	2.32	2.25
2009	Tor	AL	73	0	0	12	67.2	291	67	37	35	7	2	5	3	21	3	51	2	1	1	6	.143	0	0-3	12	3.75	4.66
	2 ML YEARS		142	0	0	22	127.2	528	108	53	50	13	3	8	6	42	10	106	4	2	8	8	.500	0	2-5	31	3.06	3.52

Buddy Carlyle

Pitches: R **Bats:** L **Pos:** RP-16 **Ht:** 6'3" **Wt:** 210 **Born:** 12/21/1977 **Age:** 32

Year	Team	Lg	G	GS	CG	GF	IP	BFP	H	R	ER	HR	SH	SF	HB	TBB	IBB	SO	WP	Bk	W	L	Pct	Sh	Sv-Op	Hld	ERC	ERA
2009	Rome*	A	1	1	0	0	2.0	6	1	0	0	0	0	0	1	0	0	1	0	0	0	0	-	0	0--	-	1.96	0.00
2009	Gwnntt*	AAA	12	1	0	1	15.1	59	13	3	3	0	0	0	1	1	0	23	0	2	3	1	.750	0	0--	-	1.77	1.76
1999	SD	NL	7	7	0	0	37.2	162	36	28	25	7	1	2	2	17	0	29	1	0	1	3	.250	0	0-0	0	4.95	5.97
2000	SD	NL	4	0	0	2	3.0	18	6	7	7	0	0	0	0	3	0	2	0	0	0	0	-	0	0-0	0	12.01	21.00
2005	LAD	NL	10	0	0	2	14.0	62	16	13	13	4	2	0	1	4	0	13	0	0	0	0	-	0	0-1	0	6.07	8.36
2007	Atl	NL	22	20	0	1	107.0	462	117	67	62	19	11	5	2	32	8	74	3	0	8	7	.533	0	0-0	0	4.71	5.21
2008	Atl	NL	45	0	0	5	62.2	259	52	26	25	5	4	0	1	26	6	59	4	1	2	0	1.000	0	0-0	3	3.03	3.59
2009	Atl	NL	16	0	0	7	21.1	107	35	23	21	5	2	1	0	12	4	12	2	0	0	1	.000	0	0-0	2	9.78	8.86
	6 ML YEARS		104	27	0	17	245.2	1070	262	164	153	40	20	8	6	94	18	189	10	1	11	11	.500	0	0-1	2	4.85	5.61

Fausto Carmona

Pitches: R **Bats:** R **Pos:** SP-24 **Ht:** 6'4" **Wt:** 230 **Born:** 12/7/1983 **Age:** 26

Year	Team	Lg	G	GS	CG	GF	IP	BFP	H	R	ER	HR	SH	SF	HB	TBB	IBB	SO	WP	Bk	W	L	Pct	Sh	Sv-Op	Hld	ERC	ERA
2009	Lk Cty*	A	1	1	0	0	6.1	21	1	0	0	0	0	0	0	1	0	7	0	0	1	0	1.000	0	0--	-	0.17	0.00
2009	Akron*	AA	1	1	1	0	7.0	24	4	1	1	1	0	0	0	0	0	5	0	0	1	0	1.000	0	0--	-	1.11	1.29
2009	Clmbs*	AAA	5	5	0	0	33.0	140	32	13	13	5	1	2	3	6	0	27	1	0	1	3	.250	0	0--	-	3.67	3.55
2006	Cle	AL	38	7	0	12	74.2	340	88	46	45	9	2	4	7	31	3	58	3	1	1	10	.091	0	0-3	10	5.69	5.42
2007	Cle	AL	32	32	2	0	215.0	879	199	78	73	16	2	4	11	61	2	137	5	1	19	8	.704	1	0-0	0	3.32	3.06
2008	Cle	AL	22	22	1	0	120.2	549	126	80	73	7	1	4	9	70	0	58	8	1	8	7	.533	1	0-0	0	5.07	5.44
2009	Cle	AL	24	24	0	0	125.1	596	151	97	88	16	4	2	8	70	0	79	5	1	5	12	.294	0	0-0	0	6.38	6.32
	Postseason		3	3	0	0	15.0	66	13	12	12	2	0	0	0	11	0	12	0	0	0	1	.000	0	0-0	0	5.02	7.20
	4 ML YEARS		116	85	3	12	535.2	2364	564	301	279	48	9	14	35	232	5	332	21	4	33	37	.471	2	0-3	10	4.72	4.69

Mike Carp

Bats: L **Throws:** R **Pos:** 1B-16; PH-6 **Ht:** 6'2" **Wt:** 215 **Born:** 6/30/1986 **Age:** 24

Year	Team	Lg	G	AB	H	2B	3B	HR	(Hm	Rd)	TB	R	RBI	RC	TBB	IBB	SO	HBP	SH	SF	SB	CS	SB%	GDP	Avg	OBP	Slg
2004	Mets	R	57	191	51	12	0	4	(-	-)	75	30	26	28	22	3	51	5	0	0	2	1	.67	1	.267	.358	.393
2005	Hgrstn	A	89	313	78	12	1	19	(-	-)	149	49	63	56	35	3	96	21	1	5	2	2	.50	2	.249	.358	.476
2006	StLuci	A	137	491	141	27	1	17	(-	-)	221	69	88	88	51	5	107	25	0	6	2	1	.67	13	.287	.379	.450
2007	Bnghtn	AA	97	359	90	16	0	11	(-	-)	139	55	48	50	39	1	75	10	0	4	2	1	.67	13	.251	.337	.387
2007	StLuci	A+	1	4	1	0	0	0	(-	-)	1	0	0	0	0	0	0	0	0	0	0	0	-	0	.250	.250	.250
2008	Bnghtn	AA	134	478	143	29	1	17	(-	-)	225	67	72	94	79	5	88	6	0	3	1	2	.33	14	.299	.403	.471
2009	Tacom	AAA	110	413	112	25	1	15	(-	-)	184	66	64	73	58	1	99	12	1	6	0	1	.00	10	.271	.372	.446
2009	Sea	AL	21	54	17	3	1	1	(1	0)	25	7	5	8	8	0	10	2	0	1	0	0	-	1	.315	.415	.463

Chris Carpenter

Pitches: R **Bats:** R **Pos:** SP-28 **Ht:** 6'6" **Wt:** 230 **Born:** 4/27/1975 **Age:** 35

Year	Team	Lg	G	GS	CG	GF	IP	BFP	H	R	ER	HR	SH	SF	HB	TBB	IBB	SO	WP	Bk	W	L	Pct	Sh	Sv-Op	Hld	ERC	ERA
1997	Tor	AL	14	13	1	1	81.1	374	108	55	46	7	1	2	2	37	0	55	7	1	3	7	.300	1	0-0	0	6.38	5.09
1998	Tor	AL	33	24	1	4	175.0	742	177	97	85	18	4	5	5	61	1	136	5	0	12	7	.632	1	0-0	0	4.12	4.37
1999	Tor	AL	24	24	4	0	150.0	663	177	81	73	16	4	6	3	48	1	106	9	1	9	8	.529	1	0-0	0	4.90	4.38
2000	Tor	AL	34	27	2	1	175.1	795	204	130	122	30	3	1	5	83	1	113	3	0	10	12	.455	0	0-0	0	6.04	6.26
2001	Tor	AL	34	34	3	0	215.2	930	229	112	98	29	3	1	16	75	5	157	5	0	11	11	.500	2	0-0	0	4.82	4.09
2002	Tor	AL	13	13	1	0	73.1	327	89	45	43	11	1	4	4	27	0	45	3	0	4	5	.444	0	0-0	0	5.91	5.28
2004	StL	NL	28	28	1	0	182.0	746	169	75	70	24	6	3	8	38	2	152	4	0	15	5	.750	0	0-0	0	3.32	3.46
2005	StL	NL	33	33	7	0	241.2	953	204	82	76	18	7	7	3	51	0	213	5	0	21	5	.808	4	0-0	0	2.49	2.83
2006	StL	NL	32	32	5	0	221.2	896	194	81	76	21	12	4	10	43	3	184	3	0	15	8	.652	3	0-0	0	2.75	3.09
2007	StL	NL	1	1	0	0	6.0	29	9	5	5	0	1	0	1	1	0	3	0	0	0	1	.000	0	0-0	0	5.80	7.50
2008	StL	NL	4	3	0	0	15.1	63	16	5	3	0	2	1	0	4	0	7	0	0	1	1	.500	0	0-0	0	3.19	1.76
2009	StL	NL	28	28	3	0	192.2	750	156	49	48	7	10	4	7	38	1	144	1	0	17	4	.810	1	0-0	0	2.14	2.24
	Postseason		8	8	0	0	53.1	215	45	16	15	5	6	1	2	15	0	35	1	0	5	1	.833	0	0-0	0	2.94	2.53
	12 ML YEARS		278	260	28	6	1730.0	7268	1732	817	745	181	54	38	64	506	14	1315	45	2	117	74	.613	13	0-0	0	3.87	3.88

Drew Carpenter

Pitches: R **Bats:** R **Pos:** RP-2; SP-1 **Ht:** 6'3" **Wt:** 225 **Born:** 5/18/1985 **Age:** 25

Year	Team	Lg	G	GS	CG	GF	IP	BFP	H	R	ER	HR	SH	SF	HB	TBB	IBB	SO	WP	Bk	W	L	Pct	Sh	Sv-Op	Hld	ERC	ERA
2006	Phillies	R	2	1	0	1	3.0	10	2	0	0	0	0	0	0	0	0	4	0	0	0	0	-	0	0--	-	1.01	0.00
2006	Batvia	A-	3	3	0	0	11.2	46	10	1	1	0	0	1	0	5	0	12	1	0	0	0	-	0	0--	-	3.34	0.77
2007	Clrwtr	A+	27	24	3	1	163.0	682	150	65	58	16	2	4	3	53	1	116	1	0	17	6	.739	2	1--	-	3.41	3.20
2008	Rdng	AA	16	16	0	0	93.2	417	114	68	59	13	8	2	3	30	1	69	3	0	6	8	.429	0	0--	-	5.44	5.67
2008	Clrwtr	A+	8	8	2	0	52.1	207	44	17	17	2	3	1	1	9	2	32	0	0	3	3	.500	1	0--	-	2.07	2.92
2008	LV	AAA	1	1	0	0	7.0	29	6	2	2	1	0	0	1	3	0	5	1	0	0	1	.000	0	0--	-	4.49	2.57
2009	LV	AAA	25	24	0	0	156.0	655	162	67	58	18	5	4	1	47	2	120	5	0	11	6	.647	0	0--	-	4.08	3.35
2008	Phi	NL	1	0	0	1	1.0	5	1	0	0	0	0	0	0	1	1	1	0	0	0	0	-	0	0-0	0	3.46	0.00
2009	Phi	NL	3	1	0	0	5.2	32	11	7	7	1	1	0	1	4	0	5	0	0	1	0	1.000	0	0-0	0	13.36	11.12
	2 ML YEARS		4	1	0	1	6.2	37	12	7	7	1	2	0	1	5	1	6	0	0	1	0	1.000	0	0-0	0	11.69	9.45

Carlos Carrasco

Pitches: R Bats: R Pos: SP-5   Ht: 6'3" Wt: 215 Born: 3/21/1987 Age: 23

Year	Team	Lg	G	GS	CG	GF	IP	BFP	H	R	ER	HR	SH	SF	HB	TBB	IBB	SO	WP	Bk	W	L	Pct	Sh	Sv-Op	Hld	ERC	ERA
2004	Phillies	R	11	8	0	0	48.0	212	53	23	19	2	0	2	3	15	0	34	2	0	5	4	.556	0	0- -	-	4.10	3.56
2005	Lakwd	A	13	13	1	0	62.2	297	78	50	49	11	0	2	9	28	0	46	1	1	1	7	.125	0	0- -	-	6.93	7.04
2005	Batvia	A-	4	4	0	0	15.1	82	29	25	23	8	0	1	2	5	0	12	3	1	0	3	.000	0	0- -	-	13.83	13.50
2005	Phillies	R	2	2	0	0	5.0	20	3	1	1	0	0	0	2	1	0	2	0	1	0	0	-	0	0- -	-	2.16	1.80
2006	Lakwd	A	26	26	2	0	159.1	643	103	50	40	6	2	1	9	65	0	159	12	2	12	6	.667	0	0- -	-	2.10	2.26
2007	Clrwtr	A+	12	12	1	0	69.2	277	49	22	22	8	2	1	6	22	0	53	2	0	6	2	.750	1	0- -	-	2.67	2.84
2007	Rdng	AA	14	13	1	0	70.1	321	65	42	38	9	3	4	5	46	0	49	0	2	6	4	.600	1	0- -	-	5.13	4.86
2008	Rdng	AA	20	19	1	0	114.2	485	108	58	55	13	1	4	6	45	1	109	8	1	7	7	.500	0	0- -	-	4.08	4.32
2008	LV	AAA	6	6	0	0	36.2	163	36	15	7	1	0	1	1	13	0	46	2	1	2	2	.500	0	0- -	-	3.24	1.72
2009	LV	AAA	20	20	0	0	114.2	501	118	73	66	14	4	2	7	38	0	112	3	0	6	9	.400	0	0- -	-	4.32	5.18
2009	Clmbs	AAA	6	6	0	0	42.1	166	31	18	15	3	0	1	0	7	0	36	2	0	5	1	.833	0	0- -	-	1.67	3.19
2009	Cle	AL	5	5	0	0	22.1	112	40	23	22	6	0	1	0	11	1	11	0	1	0	4	.000	0	0-0	0	11.36	8.87

D.J. Carrasco

Pitches: R Bats: R Pos: RP-48, SP-1   Ht: 6'3" Wt: 220 Born: 4/12/1977 Age: 33

Year	Team	Lg	G	GS	CG	GF	IP	BFP	H	R	ER	HR	SH	SF	HB	TBB	IBB	SO	WP	Bk	W	L	Pct	Sh	Sv-Op	Hld	ERC	ERA
2003	KC	AL	50	2	0	21	80.1	355	82	44	43	8	1	4	7	40	4	57	6	0	6	5	.545	0	2-5	6	4.94	4.82
2004	KC	AL	30	0	0	11	35.1	163	41	22	19	5	1	3	3	15	3	22	2	0	2	2	.500	0	0-3	4	5.56	4.84
2005	KC	AL	21	20	1	0	114.2	511	129	67	61	11	3	5	6	51	2	49	7	3	6	8	.429	0	0-0	0	5.20	4.79
2008	CWS	AL	31	0	0	6	38.2	158	30	17	17	2	1	1	5	14	1	30	0	0	1	0	1.000	0	0-1	7	2.94	3.96
2009	CWS	AL	49	1	0	11	93.1	405	103	42	39	5	2	4	2	29	4	62	3	0	5	1	.833	0	0-1	0	3.98	3.76
5 ML YEARS			181	23	1	49	362.1	1592	385	192	179	31	8	15	23	149	14	220	18	3	20	16	.556	0	2-10	17	4.60	4.45

Cesar Carrillo

Pitches: R Bats: R Pos: SP-3   Ht: 6'3" Wt: 172 Born: 4/29/1984 Age: 26

Year	Team	Lg	G	GS	CG	GF	IP	BFP	H	R	ER	HR	SH	SF	HB	TBB	IBB	SO	WP	Bk	W	L	Pct	Sh	Sv-Op	Hld	ERC	ERA
2005	Lk Els	A+	7	7	0	0	25.2	120	20	21	20	0	0	1	3	9	0	20	1	0	1	2	.333	0	0- -	-	5.28	7.01
2005	Mobile	AA	5	5	0	0	30.2	122	23	11	11	2	1	0	1	7	0	35	1	0	4	0	1.000	0	0- -	-	2.05	3.23
2006	Mobile	AA	9	9	0	0	50.2	209	45	23	17	5	1	1	4	15	0	43	0	1	1	3	.250	0	0- -	-	3.42	3.02
2006	Portlnd	AAA	1	1	0	0	2.2	13	2	2	2	0	0	0	1	3	0	1	0	0	0	0	-	0	0- -	-	6.41	6.75
2007	Portlnd	AAA	5	5	0	0	16.2	81	22	16	16	2	0	1	1	14	0	8	0	0	0	2	.000	0	0- -	-	9.37	8.62
2008	Lk Els	A+	15	14	0	0	57.1	272	69	43	38	6	4	3	3	33	0	32	4	1	3	5	.375	0	0- -	-	6.22	5.97
2009	SnAnt	AA	20	20	0	0	121.0	501	115	61	57	10	3	4	9	37	0	57	4	2	8	4	.667	0	0- -	-	3.71	4.24
2009	Portlnd	AAA	5	5	0	0	29.1	131	37	19	18	2	1	0	1	9	0	26	2	1	0	3	.000	0	0- -	-	5.14	5.52
2009	SD	NL	3	3	0	0	10.1	60	16	15	15	4	0	0	2	12	2	4	1	0	1	2	.333	0	0-0	0	14.40	13.06

Brett Carroll

Bats: R Throws: R Pos: RF-60, PH-26; LF-15; PR-5; CF-2   Ht: 6'0" Wt: 210 Born: 10/3/1982 Age: 27

Year	Team	Lg	G	AB	H	2B	3B	HR	(Hm	Rd)	TB	R	RBI	RC	TBB	IBB	SO	HBP	SH	SF	SB	CS	SB%	GDP	Avg	OBP	Slg
2009	NewOr*	AAA	27	103	24	3	1	5	(-	-)	44	16	12	13	8	0	23	1	0	0	0	1	.00	2	.233	.295	.427
2007	Fla	NL	23	49	9	1	0	0	(0	0)	10	10	2	0	3	0	15	0	1	0	0	0	-	0	.184	.231	.204
2008	Fla	NL	26	17	1	0	1	0	(0	0)	3	5	1	0	1	0	6	0	0	0	0	0	-	0	.059	.111	.176
2009	Fla	NL	92	141	33	8	2	3	(1	2)	54	18	18	20	11	1	33	4	1	1	0	0	-	2	.234	.306	.383
3 ML YEARS			141	207	43	9	3	3	(1	2)	67	33	21	20	15	1	54	4	2	1	0	0	-	3	.208	.273	.324

Jamey Carroll

Bats: R Throws: R Pos: 2B-56; 3B-23; PH-11; RF-6; LF-4; DH-2; PR-2   Ht: 5'9" Wt: 170 Born: 2/18/1974 Age: 36

Year	Team	Lg	G	AB	H	2B	3B	HR	(Hm	Rd)	TB	R	RBI	RC	TBB	IBB	SO	HBP	SH	SF	SB	CS	SB%	GDP	Avg	OBP	Slg
2009	Clmbs*	AAA	3	11	3	1	0	0	(-	-)	4	2	0	1	0	0	3	0	0	0	0	0	-	1	.273	.273	.364
2002	Mon	NL	16	71	22	5	3	1	(1	0)	36	16	6	12	4	0	12	0	4	0	1	0	1.00	1	.310	.347	.507
2003	Mon	NL	105	227	59	10	1	1	(1	0)	74	31	10	18	19	0	39	3	9	2	5	2	.71	10	.260	.323	.326
2004	Mon	NL	102	218	63	14	2	0	(0	0)	81	36	16	28	32	1	21	1	2	3	5	1	.83	3	.289	.378	.372
2005	Was	NL	113	303	76	8	1	0	(0	0)	86	44	22	38	34	1	55	5	13	3	3	4	.43	2	.251	.333	.284
2006	Col	NL	136	463	139	23	5	5	(2	3)	187	84	36	65	56	1	66	3	9	3	10	12	.45	10	.300	.377	.404
2007	Col	NL	108	227	51	9	1	2	(1	1)	68	45	22	24	28	1	34	4	6	3	6	2	.75	2	.225	.317	.300
2008	Cle	AL	113	347	96	13	4	1	(0	1)	120	60	36	48	34	0	65	9	10	2	7	3	.70	2	.277	.355	.346
2009	Cle	AL	93	315	87	10	2	2	(0	2)	107	53	26	43	36	0	63	3	3	1	4	2	.67	8	.276	.355	.340
Postaeason			4	2	0	0	0	0	(0	0)	0	0	0	0	1	0	0	0	0	0	0	0	-	0	.000	.333	.000
8 ML YEARS			786	2171	593	92	19	12	(5	7)	759	369	174	276	243	4	355	28	56	17	41	26	.61	38	.273	.351	.350

Matt Carson

Bats: R Throws: R Pos: RF-8; LF-1; DH-1; PH-1   Ht: 6'2" Wt: 200 Born: 7/1/1981 Age: 28

Year	Team	Lg	G	AB	H	2B	3B	HR	(Hm	Rd)	TB	R	RBI	RC	TBB	IBB	SO	HBP	SH	SF	SB	CS	SB%	GDP	Avg	OBP	Slg
2002	StsIsnd	A-	48	177	36	8	4	1	(-	-)	55	19	11	15	11	1	48	4	0	1	4	1	.80	6	.203	.264	.311
2003	Btl Crk	A	119	432	112	20	1	11	(-	-)	167	61	52	57	37	3	100	6	0	7	1	1	.50	5	.259	.322	.387
2004	Tampa	A+	37	129	22	7	0	3	(-	-)	38	16	17	7	6	1	33	1	1	0	2	1	.67	2	.171	.213	.295
2004	Btl Crk	A	95	381	116	23	2	12	(-	-)	179	59	58	65	22	0	78	9	0	2	21	7	.75	4	.304	.355	.470

Year	Team	Lg	G	AB	H	2B	3B	HR	(Hm	Rd)	TB	R	RBI	RC	TBB	IBB	SO	HBP	SH	SF	SB	CS	SB%	GDP	Avg	OBP	Slg
2005	Tampa	A+	84	321	81	14	3	8	(-	-)	125	43	39	45	31	0	68	8	0	4	10	2	.83	6	.252	.330	.389
2005	Trntn	AA	28	99	19	5	0	1	(-	-)	27	10	5	3	0	0	25	2	2	0	2	3	.40	2	.192	.208	.273
2006	Tampa	A+	40	136	33	4	1	8	(-	-)	63	15	21	23	21	1	31	2	3	3	5	3	.63	4	.243	.346	.463
2006	Trntn	AA	29	86	22	8	1	2	(-	-)	38	10	9	11	4	0	25	2	5	0	0	0	-	2	.256	.304	.442
2007	Trntn	AA	129	471	117	24	3	16	(-	-)	195	72	76	64	33	0	109	9	2	6	9	0	1.00	13	.248	.306	.414
2008	Trntn	AA	27	112	31	7	4	5	(-	-)	61	17	26	20	9	1	20	0	1	0	1	1	.50	2	.277	.331	.545
2008	S-WB	AAA	84	305	88	10	6	10	(-	-)	140	53	38	50	21	3	63	8	2	3	10	3	.77	8	.289	.347	.459
2009	Scrmto	AAA	118	440	116	29	3	25	(-	-)	226	68	77	77	38	1	94	6	4	5	15	4	.79	6	.264	.327	.514
2009	Oak	AL	10	21	6	0	0	1	(1	0)	9	1	5	4	0	0	7	0	0	1	0	0	-	0	.286	.273	.429

Chris Carter

Bats: L Throws: L Pos: PH-3; RF-1   **Ht: 6'0" Wt: 230 Born: 9/16/1982 Age: 27**

Year	Team	Lg	G	AB	H	2B	3B	HR	(Hm	Rd)	TB	R	RBI	RC	TBB	IBB	SO	HBP	SH	SF	SB	CS	SB%	GDP	Avg	OBP	Slg
2004	Yakima	A-	70	256	86	15	1	15	(-	-)	148	47	63	63	46	1	34	1	0	1	2	3	.40	7	.336	.438	.578
2005	Lancst	A+	103	412	122	26	2	21	(-	-)	215	71	85	81	46	4	66	6	0	6	0	0	-	12	.296	.370	.522
2005	Tenn	AA	36	128	38	4	0	10	(-	-)	72	21	30	27	19	4	11	3	0	1	0	3	.00	1	.297	.397	.563
2006	Tucsn	AAA	136	509	153	30	3	19	(-	-)	246	87	97	100	78	4	69	1	0	6	10	4	.71	14	.301	.395	.483
2007	Tucsn	AAA	126	501	162	39	3	18	(-	-)	261	73	84	100	50	4	68	2	0	6	1	0	1.00	19	.323	.383	.521
2007	Pwtckt	AAA	12	47	11	1	0	1	(-	-)	15	6	4	4	4	0	7	1	0	0	0	0	-	1	.234	.308	.319
2008	Pwtckt	AAA	121	470	141	25	2	24	(-	-)	242	65	81	87	41	6	84	4	0	7	0	0	-	10	.300	.356	.515
2009	Pwtckt	AAA	116	428	126	25	0	16	(-	-)	199	50	61	73	42	8	63	3	0	5	1	0	1.00	16	.294	.358	.465
2008	Bos	AL	9	18	6	0	0	0	(0	0)	6	5	3	2	2	0	5	0	0	0	0	0	-	0	.333	.400	.333
2009	Bos	AL	4	5	0	0	0	0	(0	0)	0	0	1	0	0	0	4	0	0	0	0	0	-	0	.000	.000	.000
	2 ML YEARS		13	23	6	0	0	0	(0	0)	6	5	4	2	2	0	9	0	0	1	0	0	-	0	.261	.308	.261

Kevin Cash

Bats: R Throws: R Pos: C-10   **Ht: 6'0" Wt: 200 Born: 12/6/1977 Age: 32**

Year	Team	Lg	G	AB	H	2B	3B	HR	(Hm	Rd)	TB	R	RBI	RC	TBB	IBB	SO	HBP	SH	SF	SB	CS	SB%	GDP	Avg	OBP	Slg
2009	S-WB	AAA	23	68	15	1	0	2	(-	-)	22	7	9	7	9	0	23	0	0	0	0	0	-	4	.221	.312	.324
2002	Tor	AL	7	14	2	0	0	0	(0	0)	2	1	0	0	1	0	4	0	0	0	0	0	-	1	.143	.200	.143
2003	Tor	AL	34	106	15	3	0	1	(1	0)	21	10	8	0	4	0	22	1	5	1	0	0	-	6	.142	.179	.198
2004	Tor	AL	60	181	35	9	0	4	(2	2)	56	18	21	11	10	0	59	4	0	2	0	0	-	3	.193	.249	.309
2005	TB	AL	13	31	5	1	0	2	(1	1)	12	4	2	0	1	0	13	1	0	0	0	0	-	3	.161	.212	.387
2007	Bos	AL	12	27	3	1	0	0	(0	0)	4	2	4	1	4	0	13	1	0	1	0	0	-	2	.111	.242	.148
2008	Bos	AL	61	142	32	7	0	3	(3	0)	48	11	15	11	18	1	50	0	0	2	0	0	-	6	.225	.309	.338
2009	NYY	AL	10	26	6	2	0	0	(0	0)	8	1	3	2	0	0	5	1	0	1	0	0	-	2	.231	.250	.308
	Postseason		4	3	1	0	0	1	(1	0)	4	1	1	0	0	0	1	0	0	0	0	0	-	0	.333	.333	1.333
	7 ML YEARS		197	527	98	23	0	10	(7	3)	151	47	53	25	38	1	166	8	5	7	0	0	-	22	.186	.248	.287

Alexi Casilla

Bats: B Throws: R Pos: 2B-72; PR-11; DH-4; SS-2; PH-1   **Ht: 5'9" Wt: 178 Born: 7/20/1984 Age: 25**

Year	Team	Lg	G	AB	H	2B	3B	HR	(Hm	Rd)	TB	R	RBI	RC	TBB	IBB	SO	HBP	SH	SF	SB	CS	SB%	GDP	Avg	OBP	Slg
2009	Roch*	AAA	40	156	53	3	4	2	(-	-)	70	21	17	26	11	0	23	0	2	2	9	6	.60	2	.340	.379	.449
2006	Min	AL	9	4	1	0	0	0	(0	0)	1	1	0	1	2	0	1	0	0	0	0	0	-	0	.250	.250	.250
2007	Min	AL	56	189	42	5	1	0	(0	0)	49	15	9	11	9	0	29	0	5	1	11	1	.92	5	.222	.256	.259
2008	Min	AL	98	385	108	15	0	7	(2	5)	144	58	50	50	31	0	45	2	13	6	7	2	.78	8	.281	.333	.374
2009	Min	AL	80	228	46	7	3	0	(0	0)	59	25	17	20	22	0	36	3	2	1	11	0	1.00	6	.202	.280	.259
	4 ML YEARS		243	806	197	27	4	7	(2	5)	253	99	76	82	64	0	111	5	20	8	29	3	.91	19	.244	.301	.314

Santiago Casilla

Pitches: R Bats: R Pos: RP-46   **Ht: 6'0" Wt: 202 Born: 7/25/1980 Age: 29**

Year	Team	Lg	G	GS	CG	GF	IP	BFP	H	R	ER	HR	SH	SF	HB	TBB	IBB	SO	WP	Bk	W	L	Pct	Sh	Sv-Op	Hld	ERC	ERA
2009	Stcktn*	A+	1	1	0	0	1.0	3	0	0	0	0	0	0	0	0	0	0	0	0	0	0	-	0	0--	-	0.00	0.00
2009	Scrmto*	AAA	1	1	0	0	1.0	3	0	0	0	0	0	0	0	0	0	0	0	0	0	0	-	0	0--	-	0.00	0.00
2004	Oak	AL	4	0	0	2	5.2	32	5	8	8	3	0	0	1	9	0	5	0	0	0	0	-	0	0-0	0	13.22	12.71
2005	Oak	AL	3	0	0	3	3.0	12	2	1	1	0	0	0	0	1	0	1	1	0	0	0	-	0	0-0	0	1.57	3.00
2006	Oak	AL	2	0	0	1	2.1	10	2	3	3	0	0	0	0	2	0	2	0	0	0	0	-	0	0-0	0	4.61	11.57
2007	Oak	AL	46	0	0	10	50.2	219	43	25	25	6	0	3	1	23	6	52	5	0	3	1	.750	0	2-5	12	4.44	4.44
2008	Oak	AL	51	0	0	9	50.1	229	60	22	22	5	3	2	3	20	2	43	6	0	2	1	.667	0	2-3	7	5.34	3.93
2009	Oak	AL	46	0	0	15	48.1	233	61	36	32	6	1	3	3	25	3	35	5	0	1	2	.333	0	0-0	5	6.32	5.96
	6 ML YEARS		152	0	0	40	160.1	735	173	95	91	20	4	8	8	80	11	138	17	0	6	4	.600	0	4-8	24	5.13	5.11

Alberto Castillo

Pitches: L Bats: L Pos: RP-20   **Ht: 6'3" Wt: 220 Born: 7/5/1975 Age: 34**

Year	Team	Lg	G	GS	CG	GF	IP	BFP	H	R	ER	HR	SH	SF	HB	TBB	IBB	SO	WP	Bk	W	L	Pct	Sh	Sv-Op	Hld	ERC	ERA
1994	Everett	A-	6	0	0	2	5.1	24	7	4	4	1	0	0	0	1	0	8	0	0	0	0	-	0	0--	-	5.53	6.75
1996	Bllghm	A-	9	7	0	1	24.0	102	20	5	5	2	0	0	3	12	0	18	2	1	3	0	1.000	0	0--	-	4.02	1.88
1997	SnJos	A+	18	1	0	8	33.2	162	41	26	21	2	2	2	4	15	0	30	7	0	2	2	.500	0	0--	-	5.51	5.61
1998	Tampa	A+	12	0	0	3	11.1	75	14	17	17	2	1	2	3	25	1	11	5	2	0	0	-	0	0--	-	15.29	13.50
1998	Grnsbr	A	5	0	0	3	9.2	48	8	6	4	0	0	0	0	14	0	13	2	0	0	0	-	0	0--	-	6.60	3.72

Year	Team	Lg	G	GS	CG	GF	IP	BFP	H	R	ER	HR	SH	SF	HB	TBB	IBB	SO	WP	Bk	W	L	Pct	Sh	Sv-Op	Hld	ERC	ERA
1999	Schbrg	IND	17	16	2	1	97.0	432	97	57	46	9	3	1	8	47	0	70	17	0	7	5	.583	0	0--	-	4.70	4.27
2000	Schbrg	IND	17	17	2	0	102.0	454	107	60	52	10	2	1	5	49	0	77	12	0	7	7	.500	0	0--	-	4.89	4.59
2002	Newark	IND	28	0	0	15	49.2	195	37	19	18	7	1	1	1	15	0	42	3	0	2	2	.500	0	5--	-	2.76	3.26
2003	Newark	IND	28	15	2	7	114.2	507	112	61	56	13	11	5	7	49	7	98	5	1	7	8	.467	0	1--	-	4.23	4.40
2006	RdWar	IND	16	8	0	1	59.1	277	74	42	35	6	0	6	5	28	2	32	8	0	4	3	.571	0	1--	-	6.16	5.31
2007	RdWar	IND	18	0	0	5	33.0	134	28	12	11	1	3	0	2	8	1	38	1	0	3	2	.600	0	0--	-	2.44	3.00
2007	Cam	IND	28	1	0	11	35.0	136	24	10	9	2	1	0	2	7	0	31	2	1	2	0	1.000	0	4--	-	1.73	2.31
2008	Norfolk	AAA	19	0	0	6	26.1	103	16	6	6	2	0	0	4	6	0	26	0	0	3	1	.750	0	1--	-	1.89	2.05
2009	Norfolk	AAA	50	0	0	31	52.0	222	49	23	16	2	0	3	6	17	2	54	0	0	2	3	.400	0	13--	-	3.45	2.77
2008	Bal	AL	28	0	0	5	26.0	121	27	11	11	3	0	0	7	10	0	23	1	0	1	0	1.000	0	0-1	0	5.36	3.81
2009	Bal	AL	20	0	0	4	12.0	49	12	4	3	0	1	0	1	4	1	8	0	0	0	0	-	0	0-0	5	3.51	2.25
	2 ML YEARS		48	0	0	9	38.0	170	39	15	14	3	1	0	8	14	1	31	1	0	1	0	1.000	0	0-1	5	4.76	3.32

Luis Castillo

Bats: B **Throws:** R **Pos:** 2B-137; PH-7   **Ht:** 5'11" **Wt:** 197 **Born:** 9/12/1975 **Age:** 34

												BATTING										BASERUNNING				AVERAGES		
Year	Team	Lg	G	AB	H	2B	3B	HR	(Hm	Rd)	TB	R	RBI	RC	TBB	IBB	SO	HBP	SH	SF	SB	CS	SB%	GDP	Avg	OBP	Slg
1996	Fla	NL	41	164	43	2	1	1	(0	1)	50	26	8	19	14	0	46	0	2	0	17	4	.81	0	.262	.320	.305
1997	Fla	NL	75	263	63	8	0	0	(0	0)	71	27	8	21	27	0	53	0	1	0	16	10	.62	6	.240	.310	.270
1998	Fla	NL	44	153	31	3	2	1	(0	1)	41	21	10	14	22	0	33	1	1	0	3	0	1.00	1	.203	.307	.268
1999	Fla	NL	128	487	147	23	4	0	(0	0)	178	76	28	78	67	0	85	0	6	3	50	17	.75	3	.302	.384	.366
2000	Fla	NL	136	539	180	17	3	2	(1	1)	209	101	17	105	70	0	86	0	9	0	62	22	.74	11	.334	.418	.388
2001	Fla	NL	134	537	141	16	10	2	(1	1)	183	76	45	67	67	0	90	1	4	3	33	16	.67	6	.263	.344	.341
2002	Fla	NL	146	606	185	18	5	2	(0	2)	219	86	39	84	55	4	76	2	4	1	48	15	.76	7	.305	.364	.361
2003	Fla	NL	152	595	187	19	6	6	(2	4)	236	99	39	87	63	0	60	2	15	1	21	19	.53	7	.314	.381	.397
2004	Fla	NL	160	564	164	12	7	2	(1	1)	196	91	47	84	75	2	68	1	5	4	21	4	.84	15	.291	.373	.348
2005	Fla	NL	122	439	132	12	4	4	(0	4)	164	72	30	61	65	1	32	1	18	1	10	7	.59	11	.301	.391	.374
2006	Min	AL	142	584	173	22	6	3	(0	6)	216	84	49	80	56	0	58	1	9	2	25	11	.69	14	.296	.358	.370
2007	2 Tms		135	548	165	19	5	1	(0	1)	197	91	38	76	53	0	45	0	12	2	19	6	.76	5	.301	.362	.359
2008	NYM	NL	87	298	73	7	1	3	(2	1)	91	46	28	40	50	2	35	2	7	2	17	2	.89	13	.245	.355	.305
2009	NYM	NL	142	486	147	12	3	1	(1	0)	168	77	40	70	69	3	58	1	19	5	20	6	.77	15	.302	.387	.346
07	Min	AL	85	349	106	11	3	0	(0	0)	123	54	18	45	29	0	28	0	5	1	9	4	.69	3	.304	.356	.352
07	NYM	NL	50	199	59	8	2	1	(0	1)	74	37	20	31	24	0	17	0	7	1	10	2	.83	2	.296	.371	.372
	Postseason		20	82	18	4	0	0	(0	0)	22	6	4	6	11	0	15	0	2	0	3	2	.60	0	.220	.312	.268
	14 ML YEARS		1634	6263	1831	190	57	28	(11	17)	2219	973	426	876	761	12	825	12	112	24	362	139	.72	114	.292	.369	.354

Wilkin Castillo

Bats: B **Throws:** R **Pos:** PH-3; PR-1   **Ht:** 6'0" **Wt:** 200 **Born:** 6/1/1984 **Age:** 26

												BATTING										BASERUNNING				AVERAGES		
Year	Team	Lg	G	AB	H	2B	3B	HR	(Hm	Rd)	TB	R	RBI	RC	TBB	IBB	SO	HBP	SH	SF	SB	CS	SB%	GDP	Avg	OBP	Slg
2004	Msoula	R+	63	243	66	13	5	4	(-	-)	101	32	32	32	8	1	40	7	4	5	5	2	.71	1	.272	.308	.416
2004	Tucsn	AAA	6	20	3	1	0	0	(-	-)	4	2	2	1	3	0	3	0	1	0	0	0	-	0	.150	.261	.200
2005	Sbend	A	113	411	124	21	3	6	(-	-)	169	65	53	59	26	0	38	4	16	4	9	9	.50	11	.302	.346	.411
2006	Lancst	A+	56	200	57	10	1	3	(-	-)	78	25	19	27	13	0	24	1	2	2	9	2	.82	6	.285	.329	.390
2006	Tucsn	AAA	6	21	5	1	0	1	(-	-)	9	3	4	2	0	0	8	1	0	0	1	0	1.00	0	.238	.273	.429
2006	Tenn	AA	27	76	19	3	0	0	(-	-)	22	7	5	8	6	1	10	2	2	2	1	0	1.00	1	.250	.314	.289
2007	Mobilo	AA	109	410	124	30	3	6	(-	-)	178	50	46	58	17	1	62	3	16	3	18	14	.56	5	.302	.333	.434
2008	Tucsn	AAA	104	386	98	18	2	6	(-	-)	138	40	47	44	24	2	54	6	6	3	4	1	.80	10	.254	.305	.358
2008	Lsvlle	AAA	11	42	8	0	0	0	(-	-)	8	2	0	0	1	0	5	0	0	0	1	2	.33	0	.190	.209	.190
2009	Lsvlle	AAA	37	122	27	5	1	2	(-	-)	40	12	7	9	1	0	20	1	3	0	1	3	.75	3	.221	.234	.328
2008	Cin	NL	18	32	9	1	0	0	(0	0)	10	6	1	3	1	0	5	0	1	0	0	0	-	0	.281	.303	.313
2009	Cin	NL	4	3	2	0	0	0	(0	0)	2	0	1	1	0	0	0	0	0	0	0	0	-	0	.667	.667	.667
	2 ML YEARS		22	35	11	1	0	0	(0	0)	12	6	2	4	1	0	5	0	1	0	0	0	-	0	.314	.333	.343

Juan Castro

Bats: R **Throws:** R **Pos:** SS-28; 2B-20; 3B-8; PR-7; PH-6; LF-2   **Ht:** 5'11" **Wt:** 190 **Born:** 6/20/1972 **Age:** 38

												BATTING										BASERUNNING				AVERAGES		
Year	Team	Lg	G	AB	H	2B	3B	HR	(Hm	Rd)	TB	R	RBI	RC	TBB	IBB	SO	HBP	SH	SF	SB	CS	SB%	GDP	Avg	OBP	Slg
2009	Albq*	AAA	3	11	2	0	0	0	(-	-)	2	1	0	0	0	0	3	0	0	0	0	0	-	1	.182	.182	.182
1995	LAD	NL	11	4	1	0	0	0	(0	0)	1	0	0	1	1	0	1	0	0	0	0	0	-	0	.250	.400	.250
1996	LAD	NL	70	132	26	5	3	0	(0	0)	37	16	5	8	10	0	27	0	4	0	1	0	1.00	3	.197	.254	.280
1997	LAD	NL	40	75	11	3	1	0	(0	0)	16	3	4	2	7	1	20	0	2	0	0	0	-	0	.147	.220	.213
1998	LAD	NL	89	220	43	7	0	2	(0	2)	56	25	14	12	15	0	37	0	9	2	0	0	-	5	.195	.245	.255
1999	LAD	NL	2	1	0	0	0	0	(0	0)	0	0	0	0	0	0	1	0	0	0	0	0	-	0	.000	.000	.000
2000	Cin	NL	82	224	54	12	2	4	(1	3)	82	20	23	20	14	1	33	0	4	2	0	2	.00	9	.241	.283	.366
2001	Cin	NL	96	242	54	10	0	3	(0	3)	73	27	13	16	13	2	50	0	4	2	0	0	-	9	.223	.261	.302
2002	Cin	NL	54	82	18	3	0	2	(0	2)	27	5	11	11	7	0	18	0	1	1	0	0	-	0	.220	.278	.329
2003	Cin	NL	113	320	81	14	1	9	(4	5)	124	28	33	36	18	1	58	0	7	3	2	3	.40	7	.253	.290	.388
2004	Cin	NL	111	299	73	21	2	5	(3	2)	113	36	26	26	14	1	51	0	2	1	1	0	1.00	11	.244	.277	.378
2005	Cin	AL	97	272	70	18	1	5	(2	3)	105	27	33	28	9	1	39	0	9	2	1	0	1.00	8	.257	.279	.386
2006	2 Tms		104	251	63	10	3	3	(1	2)	88	18	28	26	11	0	36	0	1	1	1	2	.33	6	.251	.281	.351
2007	Cin	NL	54	89	16	5	0	0	(0	0)	21	5	5	2	4	0	21	0	0	0	0	0	-	2	.180	.211	.236
2008	2 Tms		61	161	31	6	0	2	(1	1)	43	16	16	7	11	0	26	1	2	2	0	0	-	9	.193	.246	.267
2009	LAD	NL	57	112	31	4	0	1	(0	1)	38	18	9	11	6	1	25	0	2	1	0	0	-	0	.277	.311	.339
06	Min	AL	50	156	36	5	2	1	(1	0)	48	10	14	11	6	0	23	0	1	1	1	1	.50	6	.231	.258	.308
06	Cin	NL	54	95	27	5	1	2	(2	0)	40	8	14	15	5	0	13	0	0	0	0	1	.00	0	.284	.320	.421

Year Team	Lg	G	AB	H	2B	3B	HR	(Hm	Rd)	TB	R	RBI	RC	TBB	IBB	SO	HBP	SH	SF	SB	CS	SB%	GDP	Avg	OBP	Slg
08 Cin	NL	7	10	0	0	0	0	(0	0)	0	1	0	0	1	0	0	0	0	0	0	0	-	0	.000	.091	.000
08 Bal	AL	54	151	31	6	0	2	(0	2)	43	15	16	7	10	0	26	1	2	2	0	0	-	9	.205	.256	.285
Postseason		2	5	1	1	0	0	(0	0)	2	0	1	0	1	0	1	0	0	0	0	0	-	0	.200	.333	.400
15 ML YEARS		1041	2484	572	118	13	36	(13	23)	824	244	220	206	140	8	443	1	50	19	5	8	.38	72	.230	.270	.332

Ramon Castro

Bats: R **Throws:** R **Pos:** C-52; PH-5; DH-1   **Ht:** 6'3" **Wt:** 246 **Born:** 3/1/1976 **Age:** 34

Year Team	Lg	G	AB	H	2B	3B	HR	(Hm	Rd)	TB	R	RBI	RC	TBB	IBB	SO	HBP	SH	SF	SB	CS	SB%	GDP	Avg	OBP	Slg
1999 Fla	NL	24	67	12	4	0	2	(0	2)	22	4	4	6	10	3	14	0	0	1	0	0	-	1	.179	.282	.328
2000 Fla	NL	50	138	33	4	0	2	(0	2)	43	10	14	14	16	7	36	1	0	2	0	0	-	1	.239	.318	.312
2001 Fla	NL	7	11	2	0	0	0	(0	0)	2	0	1	0	1	0	1	0	0	0	0	0	-	0	.182	.250	.182
2002 Fla	NL	54	101	24	4	0	6	(4	2)	46	11	18	14	14	3	24	0	1	3	0	0	-	4	.238	.322	.455
2003 Fla	NL	40	53	15	2	0	5	(4	1)	32	6	8	8	4	0	11	0	0	0	0	0	-	0	.283	.333	.604
2004 Fla	NL	32	96	13	3	0	3	(0	3)	25	9	8	4	11	2	30	1	0	0	0	0	-	1	.135	.231	.260
2005 NYM	NL	99	209	51	16	0	8	(5	3)	91	26	41	30	25	2	58	0	3	3	1	0	1.00	7	.244	.321	.435
2006 NYM	NL	40	126	30	7	0	4	(1	3)	49	13	12	11	15	2	40	1	1	1	0	0	-	2	.238	.322	.389
2007 NYM	NL	52	144	41	6	0	11	(3	8)	80	24	31	23	10	0	39	1	0	2	0	0	-	1	.285	.331	.556
2008 NYM	NL	52	143	35	7	0	7	(5	2)	63	15	24	23	13	2	34	1	0	0	0	0	-	2	.245	.312	.441
2009 2 Tms	NL	57	155	34	8	0	7	(2	5)	63	13	25	18	16	1	39	0	0	0	0	0	-	4	.219	.292	.406
09 NYM	NL	26	79	20	5	0	3	(1	2)	34	5	13	9	8	1	16	0	0	0	0	0	-	3	.253	.322	.430
09 CWS	AL	31	76	14	3	0	4	(1	3)	29	8	12	9	8	0	23	0	0	0	0	0	-	1	.184	.262	.382
11 ML YEARS		507	1243	290	61	0	55	(24	31)	516	131	186	151	135	22	326	5	5	12	1	0	1.00	23	.233	.308	.415

Frank Catalanotto

Bats: L **Throws:** R **Pos:** PH-40; RF-31; LF-7; 2B-3   **Ht:** 6'0" **Wt:** 205 **Born:** 4/27/1974 **Age:** 36

Year Team	Lg	G	AB	H	2B	3B	HR	(Hm	Rd)	TB	R	RBI	RC	TBB	IBB	SO	HBP	SH	SF	SB	CS	SB%	GDP	Avg	OBP	Slg
2009 Hntsvl*	AA	3	12	3	2	0	0	(-	-)	5	2	3	1	2	0	0	0	0	0	0	0	-	0	.250	.357	.417
1997 Det	AL	13	26	8	2	0	0	(0	0)	10	2	3	4	3	0	7	0	0	0	0	0	-	0	.308	.379	.385
1998 Det	AL	89	213	60	13	2	6	(3	3)	95	23	25	30	12	1	39	4	0	5	3	2	.60	4	.282	.325	.446
1999 Det	AL	100	286	79	19	0	11	(6	5)	131	41	35	42	15	1	49	9	0	5	3	4	.43	4	.276	.327	.458
2000 Tex	AL	103	282	82	13	2	10	(6	4)	129	55	42	49	33	0	36	6	3	2	6	2	.75	5	.291	.375	.457
2001 Tex	AL	133	463	153	31	5	11	(4	7)	227	77	54	88	39	3	55	8	1	1	15	5	.75	5	.330	.391	.490
2002 Tex	AL	68	212	57	16	6	3	(2	1)	94	42	23	39	25	0	27	8	3	2	9	5	.64	3	.269	.364	.443
2003 Tor	AL	133	489	146	34	6	13	(7	6)	231	83	59	84	35	1	62	6	2	3	2	2	.50	9	.299	.351	.472
2004 Tor	AL	75	249	73	19	1	1	(1	0)	97	27	26	34	17	1	33	4	1	3	1	0	1.00	7	.293	.344	.390
2005 Tor	AL	130	419	126	29	5	8	(3	5)	189	56	59	80	37	0	53	10	4	5	1	3	.25	11	.301	.367	.451
2006 Tor	AL	128	437	131	36	2	7	(2	5)	192	56	56	72	52	0	37	4	2	4	1	3	.25	11	.300	.376	.439
2007 Tex	AL	103	331	86	20	4	11	(9	2)	147	54	44	51	28	0	37	11	6	1	2	1	.67	6	.260	.337	.444
2008 Tex	AL	88	248	68	23	1	2	(1	1)	99	28	21	30	20	0	29	6	3	1	1	1	.50	6	.274	.342	.399
2009 Mil	NL	77	144	40	6	3	1	(1	0)	55	18	9	18	14	5	23	2	0	2	2	0	1.00	2	.278	.346	.382
13 ML YEARS		1240	3799	1109	261	37	84	(44	40)	1696	560	456	621	330	12	487	78	25	34	45	27	.63	71	.292	.358	.446

Brett Cecil

Pitches: L **Bats:** R **Pos:** SP-17; RP-1   **Ht:** 6'1" **Wt:** 235 **Born:** 7/2/1986 **Age:** 23

Year Team	Lg	G	GS	CG	GF	IP	BFP	H	R	ER	HR	SH	SF	HB	TBB	IBB	SO	WP	Bk	W	L	Pct	Sh	Sv-Op	Hld	ERC	ERA
2007 Auburn	A-	14	13	0	0	49.2	197	36	10	7	1	0	0	3	11	0	56	0	0	1	0	1.000	0	0- -	-	1.76	1.27
2008 Dnedin	A+	4	4	0	0	10.1	38	6	2	2	1	0	0	0	2	0	11	0	0	0	0	-	0	0- -	-	1.41	1.74
2008 NHam	AA	18	18	0	0	77.2	324	66	24	22	4	3	2	5	23	0	87	2	0	6	2	.750	0	0- -	-	2.77	2.55
2008 Syrcse	AAA	6	6	0	0	30.2	135	28	17	14	1	1	0	0	16	0	31	2	0	2	3	.400	0	0- -	-	3.52	4.11
2009 LsVgs	AAA	9	9	1	0	49.0	219	53	37	31	2	2	1	3	19	0	32	1	0	1	5	.167	0	0- -	-	4.25	5.69
2009 Tor	AL	18	17	0	1	93.1	422	116	59	55	17	0	2	5	38	0	69	0	0	7	4	.636	0	0-0	0	6.53	5.30

Ronny Cedeno

Bats: R **Throws:** R **Pos:** SS-82; 2B-13; LF-7; PH-6; 3B-2; PR-2   **Ht:** 6'0" **Wt:** 180 **Born:** 2/2/1983 **Age:** 27

Year Team	Lg	G	AB	H	2B	3B	HR	(Hm	Rd)	TB	R	RBI	RC	TBB	IBB	SO	HBP	SH	SF	SB	CS	SB%	GDP	Avg	OBP	Slg
2005 ChC	NL	41	80	24	3	0	1	(0	1)	30	13	6	11	5	1	11	2	2	0	1	0	1.00	4	.300	.356	.375
2006 ChC	NL	151	534	131	18	7	6	(4	2)	181	51	41	41	17	4	109	3	15	3	8	8	.50	10	.245	.271	.339
2007 ChC	NL	38	74	15	2	0	4	(2	2)	29	6	13	8	3	0	18	0	2	1	2	1	.67	0	.203	.231	.392
2008 ChC	NL	99	216	58	12	0	2	(2	0)	76	36	28	23	18	2	41	1	1	0	4	1	.80	6	.269	.328	.352
2009 2 Tms	NL	105	341	71	8	3	10	(7	3)	115	32	38	29	19	3	79	3	13	0	5	2	.71	9	.208	.256	.337
09 Sea	AL	59	186	31	4	2	5	(2	3)	54	15	17	7	10	1	50	1	9	0	3	2	.60	6	.167	.213	.290
09 Pit	NL	46	155	40	4	1	5	(5	0)	61	17	21	22	9	2	29	2	4	0	2	0	1.00	3	.258	.307	.394
Postseason		3	0	0	0	0	0	(0	0)	0	0	0	0	0	0	0	0	0	0	1	0	1.00	0	-	-	-
5 ML YEARS		434	1245	299	43	10	23	(15	8)	431	138	126	112	62	10	258	9	33	4	20	12	.63	29	.240	.280	.346

Francisco Cervelli

Bats: R Throws: R Pos: C-40; PH-1; PR-1   Ht: 6'1" Wt: 210 Born: 3/6/1986 Age: 24

BATTING / BASERUNNING / AVERAGES

Year Team	Lg	G	AB	H	2B	3B	HR	(Hm	Rd)	TB	R	RBI	RC	TBB	IBB	SO	HBP	SH	SF	SB	CS	SB%	GDP	Avg	OBP	Slg
2005 Yanks	R	24	58	11	2	0	1	(--	--)	16	10	9	5	8	0	13	2	0	2	1	0	1.00	0	.190	.300	.276
2006 StsIsInd	A-	42	136	42	10	0	2	(--	--)	58	21	16	24	13	1	30	7	1	0	0	0	--	4	.309	.397	.426
2007 Tampa	A+	89	290	81	24	2	2	(--	--)	115	34	32	48	36	0	59	16	4	2	4	3	.57	8	.279	.387	.397
2008 Tampa	A+	3	10	3	0	0	0	(--	--)	3	2	1	1	0	0	3	1	0	0	0	0	--	0	.300	.364	.300
2008 Yanks	R	3	8	2	1	0	0	(--	--)	3	0	0	0	0	0	1	0	0	0	0	0	--	0	.250	.250	.375
2008 Trntn	AA	21	73	23	5	0	0	(--	--)	28	8	8	13	11	0	14	4	0	0	0	0	--	3	.315	.432	.384
2009 Trntn	AA	16	58	11	1	0	2	(--	--)	18	8	7	4	6	0	13	0	0	0	0	0	--	1	.190	.266	.310
2009 S-WB	AAA	21	69	19	5	0	1	(--	--)	27	7	7	8	3	0	13	1	1	1	0	2	.00	3	.275	.311	.391
2009 Yanks	R	2	6	1	0	0	0	(--	--)	1	1	0	0	1	0	0	0	0	0	0	0	--	1	.167	.286	.167
2008 NYY	AL	3	5	0	0	0	0	(0	0)	0	0	0	0	0	0	3	0	0	0	0	0	--	1	.000	.000	.000
2009 NYY	AL	42	94	28	4	0	1	(0	1)	35	13	11	11	2	0	11	0	4	1	0	3	.00	1	.298	.309	.372
2 ML YEARS		45	99	28	4	0	1	(0	1)	35	13	11	11	2	0	14	0	4	1	0	3	.00	2	.283	.294	.354

Jhoulys Chacin

Pitches: R Bats: R Pos: RP-8; SP-1   Ht: 6'3" Wt: 200 Born: 1/7/1988 Age: 22

HOW MUCH HE PITCHED / WHAT HE GAVE UP / THE RESULTS

Year Team	Lg	G	GS	CG	GF	IP	BFP	H	R	ER	HR	SH	SF	HB	TBB	IBB	SO	WP	Bk	W	L	Pct	Sh	Sv-Op	Hld	ERC	ERA
2007 Casper	R+	16	16	0	0	92.0	380	85	45	32	5	5	4	2	26	0	77	6	0	6	5	.545	0	0--	-	3.01	3.13
2008 Ashvll	A	16	16	2	0	111.1	447	82	30	23	3	3	2	12	30	0	98	8	0	10	1	.909	0	0--	-	2.19	1.86
2008 Mdest	A+	12	12	0	0	59.2	264	61	20	17	3	1	0	4	12	0	62	4	0	8	2	.800	0	0--	-	3.15	2.56
2009 Tulsa	AA	18	18	1	0	103.1	431	87	45	36	10	4	1	7	35	0	86	5	0	8	6	.571	0	0--	-	3.22	3.14
2009 ColSpr	AAA	4	4	0	0	14.1	64	11	7	6	2	1	0	0	13	0	11	0	1	1	2	.333	0	0--	-	5.20	3.77
2009 Col	NL	9	1	0	3	11.0	48	6	6	6	1	1	0	0	11	0	13	2	0	0	1	.000	0	0-0	0	3.87	4.01

Joba Chamberlain

Pitches: R Bats: R Pos: SP-31; RP-1   Ht: 6'2" Wt: 230 Born: 9/23/1985 Age: 24

HOW MUCH HE PITCHED / WHAT HE GAVE UP / THE RESULTS

Year Team	Lg	G	GS	CG	GF	IP	BFP	H	R	ER	HR	SH	SF	HB	TBB	IBB	SO	WP	Bk	W	L	Pct	Sh	Sv-Op	Hld	ERC	ERA
2007 NYY	AL	19	0	0	3	24.0	91	12	2	1	1	1	0	1	6	0	34	1	0	2	0	1.000	0	1-1	8	1.16	0.38
2008 NYY	AL	42	12	0	5	100.1	417	87	32	29	5	2	1	2	39	3	118	4	2	4	3	.571	0	0-1	19	3.04	2.60
2009 NYY	AL	32	31	0	0	157.1	709	167	94	83	21	6	5	12	76	2	133	5	2	9	6	.600	0	0-0	0	5.32	4.75
Postseason		2	0	0	0	3.2	17	3	2	2	0	1	0	1	3	0	4	2	0	0	0	-	0	0-1	0	5.09	4.91
3 ML YEARS		93	43	0	8	281.2	1217	266	128	113	27	9	6	15	121	5	285	10	4	15	9	.625	0	1-2	27	4.05	3.61

Endy Chavez

Bats: L Throws: L Pos: LF-40; CF-8; PR-8; RF-4; DH-4; PH-1   Ht: 6'0" Wt: 170 Born: 2/7/1978 Age: 32

BATTING / BASERUNNING / AVERAGES

Year Team	Lg	G	AB	H	2B	3B	HR	(Hm	Rd)	TB	R	RBI	RC	TBB	IBB	SO	HBP	SH	SF	SB	CS	SB%	GDP	Avg	OBP	Slg
2001 KC	AL	29	77	16	2	0	0	(0	0)	18	4	5	2	3	0	8	0	0	0	0	2	.00	3	.208	.238	.234
2002 Mon	NL	36	125	37	8	5	1	(0	1)	58	20	9	14	5	0	16	0	7	1	3	5	.38	0	.296	.321	.464
2003 Mon	NL	141	483	121	25	5	5	(4	1)	171	66	47	56	31	3	59	0	9	3	18	7	.72	7	.251	.294	.354
2004 Mon	NL	132	502	139	20	6	5	(4	1)	186	65	34	56	30	0	40	1	12	2	32	7	.82	6	.277	.318	.371
2005 2 tms	NL	98	116	25	4	3	0	(0	0)	35	19	11	8	7	0	14	0	7	0	2	2	.50	3	.216	.260	.302
2006 NYM	NL	133	353	108	22	5	4	(2	2)	152	48	42	54	24	3	44	0	11	2	12	3	.80	7	.306	.348	.431
2007 NYM	NL	71	150	43	7	2	1	(1	0)	57	20	17	20	9	0	16	0	5	1	5	2	.71	5	.287	.325	.380
2008 NYM	NL	133	270	72	10	2	1	(1	0)	89	30	12	21	17	3	22	0	9	2	6	1	.86	6	.267	.308	.330
2009 Sea	AL	54	161	44	3	1	2	(1	1)	55	17	13	15	14	1	22	0	5	2	9	1	.90	4	.273	.328	.342
05 Was	NL	7	9	2	1	0	0	(0	0)	3	2	1	1	3	0	1	0	0	0	0	1	.00	1	.222	.417	.333
05 Phi	NL	91	107	23	3	3	0	(0	0)	32	17	10	7	4	0	13	0	7	0	2	1	.67	2	.215	.243	.299
Postseason		10	35	8	2	0	0	(0	0)	10	2	0	0	0	0	1	0	0	0	0	0	-	1	.229	.229	.286
9 ML YEARS		827	2237	605	101	29	19	(13	6)	821	289	190	246	140	10	241	1	65	13	87	30	.74	41	.270	.312	.367

Eric Chavez

Bats: L Throws: R Pos: 3B-8   Ht: 6'1" Wt: 220 Born: 12/7/1977 Age: 32

BATTING / BASERUNNING / AVERAGES

Year Team	Lg	G	AB	H	2B	3B	HR	(Hm	Rd)	TB	R	RBI	RC	TBB	IBB	SO	HBP	SH	SF	SB	CS	SB%	GDP	Avg	OBP	Slg
1998 Oak	AL	16	45	14	4	1	0	(0	0)	20	6	6	7	3	1	5	0	0	0	1	1	.50	1	.311	.354	.444
1999 Oak	AL	115	356	88	21	2	13	(8	5)	152	47	50	50	46	4	56	0	0	0	1	1	.50	7	.247	.333	.427
2000 Oak	AL	153	501	139	23	4	26	(15	11)	248	89	86	86	62	8	94	1	0	5	2	2	.50	9	.277	.355	.495
2001 Oak	AL	151	552	159	43	0	32	(14	18)	298	91	114	99	41	9	99	4	0	7	8	2	.80	7	.288	.338	.540
2002 Oak	AL	153	585	161	31	3	34	(17	17)	300	87	109	103	65	13	119	1	0	2	8	3	.73	8	.275	.348	.513
2003 Oak	AL	156	588	166	39	5	29	(12	17)	302	94	101	97	62	10	89	1	0	3	8	3	.73	14	.282	.350	.514
2004 Oak	AL	125	475	131	20	0	29	(15	14)	238	87	77	84	95	10	99	3	0	4	6	3	.67	21	.276	.397	.501
2005 Oak	AL	160	625	168	40	1	27	(15	12)	291	92	101	95	58	4	129	2	0	9	6	0	1.00	19	.269	.329	.466
2006 Oak	AL	137	485	117	24	2	22	(8	14)	211	74	72	70	84	6	100	1	0	6	3	0	1.00	19	.241	.351	.435
2007 Oak	AL	90	341	82	21	2	15	(10	5)	152	43	46	38	34	2	76	0	0	4	4	2	.67	9	.240	.306	.446
2008 Oak	AL	23	89	22	7	0	2	(1	1)	35	10	14	14	6	0	18	0	0	0	0	0	-	2	.247	.295	.393
2009 Oak	AL	8	30	3	1	0	0	(0	0)	4	0	1	0	1	0	7	0	0	0	0	0	-	0	.100	.129	.133
Postseason		27	108	24	7	0	3	(3	0)	40	11	12	12	7	2	22	0	0	0	1	0	1.00	2	.222	.270	.370
12 ML YEARS		1287	4672	1250	274	20	229	(115	114)	2251	720	777	743	557	67	891	13	0	40	47	17	.73	106	.268	.345	.482

Jesse Chavez

Pitches: R **Bats:** R **Pos:** RP-73

Ht: 6'2" **Wt:** 170 **Born:** 8/21/1983 **Age:** 26

Year	Team	Lg	HOW MUCH HE PITCHED						WHAT HE GAVE UP												THE RESULTS							
			G	GS	CG	GF	IP	BFP	H	R	ER	HR	SH	SF	HB	TBB	IBB	SO	WP	Bk	W	L	Pct	Sh	Sv-Op	Hld	ERC	ERA
2003	Spkane	A-	17	8	0	1	55.1	259	63	30	28	5	0	1	7	31	0	48	4	0	2	2	.500	0	1--	-	6.03	4.55
2004	Clinton	A	27	22	0	1	123.0	537	148	75	64	8	7	9	3	35	1	96	4	0	6	10	.375	0	0--	-	4.65	4.68
2005	Bkrsfld	A+	11	0	0	5	24.1	97	16	6	6	2	0	0	0	9	0	31	1	0	0	0	-	0	2--	-	2.09	2.22
2005	Frisco	AA	30	0	0	7	56.0	253	71	43	36	10	1	3	2	25	2	27	8	1	4	3	.571	0	1--	-	6.77	5.79
2006	Frisco	AA	38	0	0	22	59.0	256	54	33	29	5	4	2	2	28	3	70	7	0	2	5	.286	0	4--	-	3.83	4.42
2006	Indy	AAA	12	0	0	1	17.0	77	18	9	8	0	1	1	0	9	1	15	0	0	2	1	.667	0	0--	-	4.00	4.24
2006	Okla	AAA	1	0	0	1	2.0	9	3	1	1	0	0	0	0	0	0	3	0	0	0	0	-	0	0--	-	4.47	4.50
2007	Indy	AAA	46	1	0	12	80.1	349	94	41	35	4	1	5	1	18	2	65	3	0	3	3	.500	0	2--	-	3.95	3.92
2008	Indy	AAA	51	0	0	27	68.2	283	58	30	29	8	2	2	0	22	4	70	6	0	2	6	.250	0	14--	-	2.94	3.80
2008	Pit	NL	15	0	0	0	15.0	74	20	11	11	2	3	1	0	9	2	16	2	0	1	0	1.000	0	0-2	0	6.76	6.60
2009	Pit	NL	73	0	0	24	67.1	286	69	33	30	11	1	1	1	22	3	47	5	0	1	4	.200	0	0-4	15	4.39	4.01
	2 ML YEARS		88	0	0	30	82.1	360	89	44	41	13	4	2	1	31	5	63	7	0	1	5	.167	0	0-6	15	4.81	4.48

Raul Chavez

Bats: R **Throws:** R **Pos:** C-51; PR-1

Ht: 5'11" **Wt:** 225 **Born:** 3/18/1973 **Age:** 37

Year	Team	Lg	BATTING																			BASERUNNING				AVERAGES		
			G	AB	H	2B	3B	HR	(Hm	Rd)	TB	R	RBI	RC	TBB	IBB	SO	HBP	SH	SF	SB	CS	SB%	GDP	Avg	OBP	Slg
2009	LsVgs*	AAA	2	7	1	0	0	0	(-	-)	1	0	0	0	0	0	0	0	0	0	0	0	-	0	.143	.143	.143
1996	Mon	NL	4	5	1	0	0	0	(0	0)	1	1	0	0	1	0	1	0	0	0	1	0	1.00	1	.200	.333	.200
1997	Mon	NL	13	26	7	0	0	0	(0	0)	7	0	2	2	0	0	5	0	0	1	1	0	1.00	0	.269	.259	.269
1998	Sea	AL	1	1	0	0	0	0	(0	0)	0	0	0	0	0	0	0	0	0	0	0	0	-	0	.000	.000	.000
2000	Hou	NL	14	43	11	2	0	1	(0	1)	16	3	5	3	3	2	6	0	0	1	0	0	-	5	.256	.298	.372
2002	Hou	NL	2	4	1	0	0	0	(0	0)	2	1	0	1	1	0	0	1	0	0	0	0	-	0	.250	.500	.500
2003	Hou	NL	19	37	10	1	1	1	(0	1)	16	5	4	4	1	0	6	0	0	0	0	0	-	3	.270	.289	.432
2004	Hou	NL	64	162	34	8	0	0	(0	0)	42	9	23	10	10	3	38	0	4	0	0	1	.00	9	.210	.256	.259
2005	Hou	NL	37	99	17	3	0	2	(1	1)	26	6	6	2	4	0	18	1	0	1	0	1	1.00	5	.172	.210	.263
2006	Bal	AL	16	28	5	0	0	0	(0	0)	5	1	0	0	1	0	4	0	0	0	0	0	-	0	.179	.207	.179
2008	Pit	NL	42	116	30	4	0	1	(1	0)	37	12	10	12	4	1	14	1	0	1	0	0	-	2	.259	.287	.319
2009	Tor	AL	51	159	41	8	0	2	(1	1)	55	10	15	15	6	0	23	0	3	0	1	1	.50	4	.258	.285	.346
	Postseason		5	10	4	0	0	1	(0	1)	7	1	2	3	1	0	1	0	1	0	0	0	-	0	.400	.455	.700
	11 ML YEARS		263	680	157	27	1	7	(3	4)	207	48	65	49	31	6	115	3	7	4	4	2	.67	29	.231	.266	.304

Bruce Chen

Pitches: L **Bats:** L **Pos:** SP-9; RP-8

Ht: 6'1" **Wt:** 215 **Born:** 6/19/1977 **Age:** 33

Year	Team	Lg	HOW MUCH HE PITCHED						WHAT HE GAVE UP												THE RESULTS							
			G	GS	CG	GF	IP	BFP	H	R	ER	HR	SH	SF	HB	TBB	IBB	SO	WP	Bk	W	L	Pct	Sh	Sv-Op	Hld	ERC	ERA
2009	Omha*	AAA	14	13	3	0	82.0	323	57	33	31	8	2	3	4	23	0	69	0	0	4	2	.667	3	0--	-	2.25	3.40
1998	Atl	NL	4	4	0	0	20.1	91	23	9	9	3	1	0	1	9	1	17	0	0	2	0	1.000	0	0-0	0	5.55	3.98
1999	Atl	NL	16	7	0	3	51.0	214	38	32	31	11	1	1	2	27	3	45	0	0	2	2	.500	0	0-0	0	4.07	5.47
2000	2 Tms	NL	37	15	0	4	134.0	559	116	54	49	18	8	3	2	46	4	112	4	1	7	4	.636	0	0-0	0	3.35	3.29
2001	2 Tms	NL	27	27	0	4	146.0	634	146	90	79	29	4	7	1	59	4	126	5	0	7	7	.500	0	0-0	0	4.75	4.87
2002	3 Tms	NL	55	6	0	9	77.2	360	85	53	48	16	2	3	2	43	5	80	4	0	2	5	.286	0	0-0	4	5.99	5.56
2003	2 Tms	NL	16	2	0	4	24.1	110	26	16	15	6	3	3	2	10	1	20	0	0	1	1	1.000	0	0-0	1	5.81	5.55
2004	Bal	AL	8	7	1	0	47.2	196	39	19	16	7	2	1	0	16	0	32	0	0	2	1	.667	0	0-0	0	3.13	3.02
2005	Bal	AL	34	32	1	0	197.1	832	187	94	84	33	3	3	9	63	0	133	2	1	13	10	.565	0	0-0	0	4.12	3.83
2006	Bal	AL	40	12	0	16	98.2	453	137	81	76	28	3	5	0	35	3	70	1	0	0	7	.000	0	0-0	1	7.73	6.93
2007	Tex	AL	5	0	0	3	10.0	46	11	11	8	3	0	0	0	6	1	7	0	0	0	0	-	0	0-0	0	6.90	7.20
2009	KC	AL	17	9	0	4	62.1	279	74	42	40	12	2	2	4	25	3	45	4	0	1	6	.143	0	0-0	0	6.18	5.78
00	Atl	NL	22	0	0	4	39.2	176	35	15	11	4	3	2	1	19	2	32	0	1	4	0	1.000	0	0-0	0	3.62	2.50
00	Phi	NL	15	15	0	0	94.1	383	81	39	38	14	5	1	1	27	2	80	4	0	3	4	.429	0	0-0	0	3.22	3.63
01	Phi	NL	16	16	0	0	86.1	381	90	53	48	19	2	4	1	31	4	79	2	0	4	5	.444	0	0-0	0	4.87	5.00
01	NYM	NL	11	11	0	0	59.2	253	56	37	31	10	2	3	0	28	0	47	3	0	3	2	.600	0	0-0	0	4.58	4.68
02	NYM	NL	1	0	0	0	0.2	3	1	0	0	0	0	0	0	0	0	0	0	0	0	0	-	0	0-0	0	4.47	6.00
02	Mon	NL	15	5	0	4	37.1	179	47	29	29	9	0	0	1	23	3	43	3	0	2	3	.400	0	0-0	0	7.69	6.99
02	Cin	NL	39	1	0	5	39.2	178	37	24	19	7	2	3	1	20	2	37	1	0	0	2	.000	0	0-0	4	4.55	4.31
03	Hou	NL	11	0	0	2	12.0	60	14	8	8	2	3	2	2	8	1	8	0	0	0	0	-	0	0-0	1	7.11	6.00
03	Bos	AL	5	2	0	2	12.1	50	12	8	7	4	0	1	0	2	0	12	0	0	0	1	.000	0	0-0	0	4.40	5.11
	11 ML YEARS		259	121	2	43	869.1	3774	882	501	455	166	29	28	23	339	25	687	20	2	36	43	.456	0	0-0	6	4.83	4.71

Matt Chico

Pitches: L **Bats:** L **Pos:** P

Ht: 5'11" **Wt:** 219 **Born:** 6/10/1983 **Age:** 27

Year	Team	Lg	HOW MUCH HE PITCHED						WHAT HE GAVE UP												THE RESULTS							
			G	GS	CG	GF	IP	BFP	H	R	ER	HR	SH	SF	HB	TBB	IBB	SO	WP	Bk	W	L	Pct	Sh	Sv-Op	Hld	ERC	ERA
2003	Yakima	A-	17	13	0	0	71.1	309	75	28	28	4	3	2	5	25	1	71	9	1	7	4	.636	0	0--	-	4.15	3.53
2004	Sbend	A	14	14	2	0	87.2	344	59	26	25	9	2	1	3	27	0	89	5	0	8	5	.615	1	0--	-	2.22	2.57
2004	ElPaso	AA	14	12	0	0	62.1	300	82	53	40	7	3	5	2	36	1	59	7	1	3	7	.300	0	0--	-	6.91	5.78
2005	Tenn	AA	10	10	0	0	52.2	246	75	44	36	8	5	4	2	15	1	35	2	2	1	7	.125	0	0--	-	6.62	6.15
2005	Lancst	A+	18	18	0	0	110.0	462	101	50	46	13	0	5	3	39	0	102	4	1	7	2	.778	0	0--	-	3.70	3.76
2006	Lancst	A+	10	10	0	0	50.1	215	48	25	21	5	1	1	1	11	0	49	4	0	3	4	.429	0	0--	-	3.06	3.75
2006	Tenn	AA	13	13	0	0	81.0	319	62	22	20	6	1	2	0	21	0	63	8	1	7	2	.778	0	0--	-	2.21	2.22
2006	Hrsbrg	AA	4	4	0	0	22.0	98	28	9	8	3	0	0	2	8	0	13	3	1	2	0	1.000	0	0--	-	6.45	6.00
2007	Clmbs	AAA	2	2	0	0	11.0	44	9	4	4	1	0	0	0	5	0	7	0	0	1	1	.500	0	0--	-	3.42	3.27
2008	Clmbs	AAA	1	1	0	0	4.0	20	7	4	4	0	1	0	0	2	0	1	3	0	0	0	-	0	0--	-	8.49	9.00
2009	Hgrstn	A	3	3	0	0	11.0	43	11	3	3	2	0	0	1	0	0	8	1	0	0	0	-	0	0--	-	3.49	2.45

			HOW MUCH HE PITCHED						WHAT HE GAVE UP											THE RESULTS							
Year	Team	Lg	G	GS	CG	GF	IP	BFP	H	R	ER	HR	SH	SF	HB	TBB	IBB	SO	WP	Bk	W	L	Pct	Sh	Sv-Op	Hld	ERC	ERA
2009	Hrsbrg	AA	12	12	0	0	50.1	222	54	27	24	2	2	1	0	28	0	36	4	0	2	4	.333	0	0- -	-	4.78	4.29
2007	Was	NL	31	31	0	0	167.0	747	183	96	86	26	6	10	5	74	3	94	7	0	7	9	.438	0	0-0	0	5.31	4.63
2008	Was	NL	11	8	0	0	48.0	219	63	34	33	10	4	2	1	17	1	31	1	0	0	6	.000	0	0-0	0	6.67	6.19
	2 ML YEARS		42	39	0	0	215.0	966	246	130	119	36	10	12	6	91	4	125	8	0	7	15	.318	0	0-0	0	5.61	4.98

Randy Choate

Pitches: L Bats: L Pos: RP-61   **Ht: 6'1" Wt: 200 Born: 9/5/1975 Age: 34**

			HOW MUCH HE PITCHED						WHAT HE GAVE UP											THE RESULTS							
Year	Team	Lg	G	GS	CG	GF	IP	BFP	H	R	ER	HR	SH	SF	HB	TBB	IBB	SO	WP	Bk	W	L	Pct	Sh	Sv-Op	Hld	ERC	ERA
2009	Drham*	AAA	21	0	0	2	19.1	83	16	8	8	0	0	0	0	9	1	15	1	0	3	0	1.000	0	0- -	-	2.57	3.72
2000	NYY	AL	22	0	0	6	17.0	75	14	10	9	3	0	1	1	8	0	12	1	0	0	1	.000	0	0-0	2	3.99	4.76
2001	NYY	AL	37	0	0	13	48.1	207	34	21	18	0	2	1	9	27	2	35	3	0	3	1	.750	0	0-0	3	3.03	3.35
2002	NYY	AL	18	0	0	11	22.1	101	18	18	15	1	0	0	3	15	0	17	3	0	0	0	-	0	0-0	0	4.13	6.04
2003	NYY	AL	5	0	0	2	3.2	16	7	3	3	0	0	0	0	1	0	0	0	0	0	0	-	0	0-0	0	9.72	7.36
2004	Ari	NL	74	0	0	17	50.2	232	52	26	26	1	0	4	5	28	11	49	1	1	2	4	.333	0	0-2	11	4.18	4.62
2005	Ari	NL	8	0	0	1	7.0	35	8	7	7	0	0	0	1	5	1	4	1	0	0	0	-	0	0-0	2	5.48	9.00
2006	Ari	NL	30	0	0	3	16.0	75	21	9	7	0	0	0	3	3	0	12	0	0	0	1	.000	0	0-0	5	4.87	3.94
2007	Ari	NL	2	0	0	1	0.0	3	3	0	0	0	0	0	0	0	0	0	0	0	0	0	-	0	0-0	0	-	-
2009	TB	AL	61	0	0	13	36.1	142	28	15	14	4	0	0	0	11	3	28	0	0	1	0	1.000	0	5-5	9	2.54	3.47
	Postseason		4	0	0	0	5.1	27	7	5	2	0				2	1	4	0	0	0	0	-	0	0-0	0	4.15	3.38
	9 ML YEARS		257	0	0	65	201.1	886	185	109	99	9	2	6	22	98	17	157	9	1	6	7	.462	0	5-7	32	3.85	4.43

Shin-Soo Choo

Bats: L Throws: L Pos: RF-124; LF-20; DH-12; PH-3; CF-1   **Ht: 5'11" Wt: 200 Born: 7/13/1982 Age: 27**

			BATTING														BASERUNNING				AVERAGES		
Year	Team	Lg	G	AB	H	2B	3B	HR	(Hm | Rd)	TB	R	RBI	RC	TBB	IBB	SO	HBP	SH	SF	SB	CS	SB%	GDP	Avg	OBP	Slg
2005	Sea	AL	10	18	1	0	0	0	(0 | 0)	1	1	1	0	3	0	4	0	0	0	0	0	-	0	.056	.190	.056
2006	2 Tms	AL	49	157	44	12	3	3	(2 | 1)	71	23	22	24	18	2	50	2	1	1	5	3	.63	3	.280	.360	.452
2007	Cle	AL	6	17	5	0	0	0	(0 | 0)	5	5	5	3	2	1	5	0	0	1	0	1	.00	0	.294	.350	.294
2008	Cle	AL	94	317	98	28	3	14	(10 | 4)	174	68	66	72	44	4	78	5	0	4	4	3	.57	5	.309	.397	.549
2009	Cle	AL	156	583	175	38	6	20	(11 | 9)	285	87	86	111	78	5	151	17	0	7	21	2	.91	9	.300	.394	.489
06	Sea	AL	4	11	1	1	0	0	(0 | 0)	2	0	0	0	0	0	4	1	0	0	0	0	-	1	.091	.167	.182
06	Cle	AL	45	146	43	11	3	3	(2 | 1)	69	23	22	24	18	2	46	1	1	1	5	3	.63	2	.295	.373	.473
	5 ML YEARS		315	1092	323	78	12	37	(23 | 14)	536	184	180	210	145	12	288	24	1	13	30	9	.77	17	.296	.386	.491

Vinnie Chulk

Pitches: R Bats: R Pos: RP-8   **Ht: 6'2" Wt: 195 Born: 12/19/1978 Age: 31**

			HOW MUCH HE PITCHED						WHAT HE GAVE UP											THE RESULTS							
Year	Team	Lg	G	GS	CG	GF	IP	BFP	H	R	ER	HR	SH	SF	HB	TBB	IBB	SO	WP	Bk	W	L	Pct	Sh	Sv-Op	Hld	ERC	ERA
2009	Clmbs*	AAA	18	0	0	9	21.2	91	22	7	5	0	3	1	0	7	0	16	1	0	1	0	1.000	0	4- -	-	3.21	2.08
2003	Tor	AL	3	0	0	2	5.1	25	6	3	3	0	0	0	0	3	0	2	0	0	0	0	-	0	0-1	0	4.53	5.06
2004	Tor	AL	47	0	0	10	56.0	248	59	30	29	6	1	1	1	27	1	44	2	0	1	3	.250	0	2-5	13	4.83	4.66
2005	Tor	AL	62	0	0	10	72.0	301	68	33	31	9	3	4	1	26	3	39	5	0	0	1	.000	0	0 1	13	3.83	3.88
2006	2 Tms	AL	48	0	0	13	46.1	205	46	29	27	6	0	2	3	20	2	43	4	0	1	3	.250	0	0-2	6	4.53	5.24
2007	SF	NL	57	0	0	15	53.0	222	53	22	21	3	1	4	2	14	2	41	2	0	5	4	.556	0	0-2	3	3.37	3.57
2008	SF	NL	27	0	0	9	31.2	139	33	18	17	6	1	1	2	8	2	16	1	0	0	3	.000	0	0-2	2	4.36	4.83
2009	Cle	AL	8	0	0	3	12.0	55	10	6	5	1	2	0	0	10	0	4	0	0	0	1	.000	0	0-1	0	4.68	3.75
06	Tor	AL	20	0	0	8	24.0	107	29	16	14	4	0	1	2	5	0	18	1	0	1	0	1.000	0	0-1	1	5.25	5.25
06	SF	NL	28	0	0	5	22.1	98	17	13	13	2	0	1	1	15	2	25	3	0	0	3	.000	0	0-1	5	3.74	5.24
	7 ML YEARS		252	0	0	62	276.1	1195	275	141	133	31	8	12	9	108	10	189	14	0	7	15	.318	0	2-14	43	4.17	4.33

Ryan Church

Bats: L Throws: L Pos: RF-86; CF-23; PH-10; PR-2   **Ht: 6'2" Wt: 218 Born: 10/14/1978 Age: 31**

			BATTING														BASERUNNING				AVERAGES		
Year	Team	Lg	G	AB	H	2B	3B	HR	(Hm | Rd)	TB	R	RBI	RC	TBB	IBB	SO	HBP	SH	SF	SB	CS	SB%	GDP	Avg	OBP	Slg
2004	Mon	NL	30	63	11	1	0	1	(0 | 1)	15	6	6	2	7	1	16	0	1	0	0	0	-	3	.175	.257	.238
2005	Was	NL	102	268	77	15	3	9	(5 | 4)	125	41	42	34	24	0	70	5	1	3	3	2	.60	6	.287	.353	.466
2006	Was	NL	71	196	54	17	1	10	(6 | 4)	103	22	35	36	26	0	60	3	3	2	6	1	.86	4	.276	.366	.526
2007	Was	NL	144	470	128	43	1	15	(5 | 10)	210	57	70	70	49	4	107	8	0	3	3	2	.60	12	.272	.349	.464
2008	NYM	NL	90	319	88	14	1	12	(6 | 6)	140	54	49	46	33	3	83	3	1	3	2	3	.40	9	.276	.346	.439
2009	2 Tms	NL	111	359	98	28	0	4	(2 | 2)	138	46	40	40	33	6	58	3	2	2	6	2	.75	11	.273	.338	.384
09	NYM	NL	67	232	65	16	0	2	(1 | 1)	87	26	22	22	17	4	36	2	2	2	6	2	.75	7	.280	.332	.375
09	Atl	NL	44	127	33	12	0	2	(1 | 1)	51	20	18	18	16	2	22	1	0	0	0	0	-	4	.260	.347	.402
	6 ML YEARS		548	1675	456	118	6	51	(24 | 27)	739	226	242	228	172	14	394	22	8	13	20	10	.67	45	.272	.345	.441

Alex Cintron

Bats: B Throws: R Pos: PH-18; 2B-2; SS-2   **Ht: 6'2" Wt: 211 Born: 12/17/1978 Age: 31**

			BATTING														BASERUNNING				AVERAGES		
Year	Team	Lg	G	AB	H	2B	3B	HR	(Hm | Rd)	TB	R	RBI	RC	TBB	IBB	SO	HBP	SH	SF	SB	CS	SB%	GDP	Avg	OBP	Slg
2009	Syrcse*	AAA	5	18	9	1	0	0	(- | -)	10	2	3	4	0	0	1	0	0	1	0	0	-	0	.500	.474	.556
2009	Ms*	R	3	6	2	1	0	0	(- | -)	3	1	0	1	2	0	1	0	0	0	1	0	1.00	0	.333	.500	.500
2009	Tacom*	AAA	30	113	28	4	1	2	(- | -)	40	8	9	10	2	0	18	0	3	0	2	0	1.00	5	.248	.261	.354
2001	Ari	NL	8	7	2	0	1	0	(0 | 0)	4	0	0	1	0	0	0	0	0	0	0	0	-	0	.286	.286	.571
2002	Ari	NL	38	75	16	6	0	0	(0 | 0)	22	11	4	5	12	2	13	0	3	0	0	0	-	2	.213	.322	.293
2003	Ari	NL	117	448	142	26	6	13	(6 | 7)	219	70	51	70	29	0	33	2	5	3	2	3	.40	7	.317	.359	.489

Year	Team	Lg		BATTING																			BASERUNNING				AVERAGES		
			G	AB	H	2B	3B	HR	(Hm	Rd)	TB	R	RBI	RC	TBB	IBB	SO	HBP	SH	SF	SB	CS	SB%	GDP	Avg	OBP	Slg
2004	Ari	NL	154	564	148	31	7	4	(1	3)	205	56	49	59	31	2	59	2	12	4	3	3	.50	11	.262	.301	.363
2005	Ari	NL	122	330	90	19	2	8	(5	3)	137	36	48	35	12	3	33	1	2	3	1	2	.33	8	.273	.298	.415
2006	CWS	AL	91	288	82	10	3	5	(3	2)	113	35	41	33	10	0	35	2	1	3	10	3	.77	10	.285	.310	.392
2007	CWS	AL	68	185	45	7	1	2	(1	1)	60	23	19	21	9	1	35	1	0	1	2	1	.67	5	.243	.281	.324
2008	Bal	AL	61	133	38	5	1	1	(1	0)	48	12	10	14	7	0	15	0	4	0	0	2	.00	5	.286	.321	.361
2009	Was	NL	21	26	2	0	0	0	(0	0)	2	1	0	0	2	0	7	0	0	0	0	0	-	1	.077	.143	.077
	Postseason		2	0	0	0	0	0	(0	0)	0	0	0	0	0	0	0	0	0	0	0	0	-	0	.-	-	-
	9 ML YEARS		680	2056	565	104	21	33	(17	16)	810	244	222	238	112	8	230	8	27	14	18	14	.56	49	.275	.313	.394

Anthony Claggett

Pitches: R **Bats:** B **Pos:** RP-3

Ht: 6'3" **Wt:** 195 **Born:** 7/15/1984 **Age:** 25

Year	Team	Lg		HOW MUCH HE PITCHED						WHAT HE GAVE UP											THE RESULTS						
			G	GS	CG	GF	IP	BFP	H	R	ER	HR	SH	SF	HB	TBB	IBB	SO	WP	Bk	W	L	Pct	Sh	Sv-Op	Hld	ERC	ERA
2005	Oneont	A-	21	0	0	16	22.1	103	23	10	10	1	2	2	2	12	0	25	7	0	0	1	.000	0	7--	-	4.65	4.03
2006	WMich	A	51	0	0	30	59.1	224	35	7	6	0	3	0	0	20	0	58	0	0	7	2	.778	0	14--	-	1.40	0.91
2006	Toledo	AAA	1	0	0	0	1.0	6	1	0	0	0	0	0	0	1	0	2	0	0	0	0	-	0	0--	-	4.47	0.00
2007	Tampa	A+	32	16	0	8	112.1	475	119	51	46	7	4	4	1	31	1	76	9	1	9	8	.529	0	2--	-	3.70	3.69
2007	S-WB	AAA	1	1	0	0	5.0	22	5	3	3	1	0	0	1	1	0	1	0	0	0	0	-	0	0--	-	4.68	5.40
2008	Tampa	A+	1	0	0	1	3.0	10	4	1	1	0	0	0	0	0	0	3	0	0	0	0	-	0	0--	-	4.80	3.00
2008	Trntn	AA	28	0	0	14	57.2	250	51	15	14	1	3	0	1	29	2	53	2	0	3	2	.600	0	9--	-	3.24	2.18
2009	S-WB	AAA	39	5	0	17	82.0	347	78	32	28	6	1	1	3	32	2	43	3	1	7	7	.500	0	4--	-	3.74	3.07
2009	2 Tms		3	0	0	2	3.2	28	13	11	11	3	0	0	0	4	0	3	1	0	0	0	-	0	0-0	0	35.34	27.00
09	NYY	AL	2	0	0	1	2.2	23	11	10	10	2	0	0	0	4	0	3	1	0	0	0	-	0	0-0	0	42.17	33.75
09	Pit	NL	1	0	0	1	1.0	5	2	1	1	1	0	0	0	0	0	0	0	0	0	0	-	0	0-0	0	16.28	9.00

Tony Clark

Bats: B **Throws:** R **Pos:** 1B-21; PH-20

Ht: 6'7" **Wt:** 245 **Born:** 6/15/1972 **Age:** 38

Year	Team	Lg		BATTING																			BASERUNNING				AVERAGES		
			G	AB	H	2B	3B	HR	(Hm	Rd)	TB	R	RBI	RC	TBB	IBB	SO	HBP	SH	SF	SB	CS	SB%	GDP	Avg	OBP	Slg
2009	Reno*	AAA	7	25	4	1	0	1	(-	-)	8	1	2	2	5	0	4	0	0	0	0	0	-	0	.160	.300	.320
1995	Det	AL	27	101	24	5	1	3	(0	3)	40	10	11	11	8	0	30	0	0	0	0	0	-	2	.238	.294	.396
1996	Det	AL	100	376	94	14	0	27	(17	10)	189	56	72	55	29	1	127	0	0	6	0	1	.00	7	.250	.299	.503
1997	Det	AL	159	580	160	28	3	32	(18	14)	290	105	117	107	93	13	144	3	0	5	1	3	.25	11	.276	.376	.500
1998	Det	AL	157	602	175	37	0	34	(18	16)	314	84	103	107	63	5	128	3	0	5	3	3	.50	16	.291	.358	.522
1999	Det	AL	143	536	150	29	0	31	(12	19)	272	74	99	94	64	7	133	6	0	3	2	1	.67	14	.280	.361	.507
2000	Det	AL	60	208	57	14	0	13	(6	7)	110	32	37	35	24	2	51	0	0	0	0	0	-	10	.274	.349	.529
2001	Det	AL	126	428	123	29	3	16	(7	9)	206	67	75	74	62	10	108	1	0	6	0	1	.00	14	.287	.374	.481
2002	Bos	AL	90	275	57	12	1	3	(1	2)	80	25	29	19	21	0	57	1	0	1	0	0	-	11	.207	.265	.291
2003	NYM	NL	125	254	59	13	0	16	(9	7)	120	29	43	29	24	2	73	1	0	1	0	0	-	8	.232	.300	.472
2004	NYY	AL	106	253	56	12	0	16	(5	11)	116	37	49	37	26	3	92	2	0	2	0	0	-	6	.221	.297	.458
2005	Ari	NL	130	349	106	22	2	30	(19	11)	222	47	87	71	37	6	88	1	0	6	0	0	-	10	.304	.366	.636
2006	Ari	NL	79	132	26	4	0	6	(3	3)	48	13	16	10	13	2	40	2	0	0	0	0	-	5	.197	.279	.364
2007	Ari	NL	113	221	55	5	1	17	(14	3)	113	31	51	28	21	3	59	0	0	3	0	0	-	8	.249	.310	.511
2008	2 Tms	NL	108	151	34	5	0	3	(2	1)	48	12	24	20	31	1	55	1	0	1	0	0	-	8	.225	.359	.318
2009	Ari	NL	36	66	12	4	0	4	(4	0)	28	7	11	7	11	0	24	0	0	1	0	0	-	3	.182	.295	.424
08	SD	NL	70	88	21	3	0	1	(1	0)	27	5	11	13	19	0	32	0	0	0	0	0	-	2	.239	.374	.307
08	Ari	NL	38	63	13	2	0	2	(1	1)	21	7	13	7	12	1	23	1	0	1	0	0	-	6	.206	.338	.333
	Postseason		12	37	5	2	0	0	(0	0)	7	0	1	0	1	1	13	0	0	0	0	0	-	0	.135	.158	.189
	15 ML YEARS		1559	4532	1188	233	11	251	(135	116)	2196	629	824	704	527	55	1209	21	0	40	6	9	.40	133	.262	.339	.485

Tyler Clippard

Pitches: R **Bats:** R **Pos:** RP-41

Ht: 6'3" **Wt:** 200 **Born:** 2/14/1985 **Age:** 25

Year	Team	Lg		HOW MUCH HE PITCHED						WHAT HE GAVE UP											THE RESULTS						
			G	GS	CG	GF	IP	BFP	H	R	ER	HR	SH	SF	HB	TBB	IBB	SO	WP	Bk	W	L	Pct	Sh	Sv-Op	Hld	ERC	ERA
2009	Syrcse*	AAA	24	0	0	5	39.0	149	20	8	4	2	0	1	0	15	1	42	0	0	4	1	.800	0	1--	-	1.43	0.92
2007	NYY	AL	6	6	0	0	27.0	124	29	19	19	6	0	0	0	17	1	18	2	1	3	1	.750	0	0-0	-	6.37	6.33
2008	Was	NL	2	2	0	0	10.1	48	12	5	5	2	0	0	0	7	1	8	1	0	1	1	.500	0	0-0	0	6.90	4.35
2009	Was	NL	41	0	0	8	60.1	246	36	20	18	9	3	1	1	32	1	67	1	1	4	2	.667	0	0-1	3	2.79	2.69
	3 ML YEARS		49	8	0	8	97.2	418	77	44	42	17	3	1	1	56	3	93	4	2	8	4	.667	0	0-1	3	4.10	3.87

Todd Coffey

Pitches: R **Bats:** R **Pos:** RP-78

Ht: 6'4" **Wt:** 241 **Born:** 9/9/1980 **Age:** 29

Year	Team	Lg		HOW MUCH HE PITCHED						WHAT HE GAVE UP											THE RESULTS						
			G	GS	CG	GF	IP	BFP	H	R	ER	HR	SH	SF	HB	TBB	IBB	SO	WP	Bk	W	L	Pct	Sh	Sv-Op	Hld	ERC	ERA
2005	Cin	NL	57	0	0	14	58.0	265	84	33	29	5	3	2	5	11	2	26	1	0	4	1	.800	0	1-2	3	6.11	4.50
2006	Cin	NL	81	0	0	28	78.0	340	85	34	31	7	0	1	2	27	5	60	4	0	6	7	.462	0	8-12	15	4.29	3.58
2007	Cin	NL	58	0	0	8	51.0	242	70	36	33	12	1	0	5	19	4	43	4	0	2	1	.667	0	0-3	7	7.58	5.82
2008	2 Tms	NL	26	0	0	9	26.2	116	31	13	13	4	2	1	1	8	0	15	0	0	1	0	1.000	0	0-0	1	5.19	4.39
2009	Mil	NL	78	0	0	17	83.2	336	76	28	27	8	2	2	3	21	3	65	1	0	4	4	.500	0	2-6	27	3.16	2.90
08	Cin	NL	17	0	0	6	19.1	87	25	13	13	4	1	1	1	6	0	8	0	0	0	0	-	0	0-0	0	6.57	6.05
08	Mil	NL	9	0	0	3	7.1	29	6	0	0	0	1	0	0	2	0	7	0	0	1	0	1.000	0	0-0	1	2.09	0.00
	5 ML YEARS		300	0	0	76	297.1	1299	346	144	133	36	8	6	16	86	14	209	10	0	17	13	.567	0	11-23	53	4.91	4.03

Chris Coghlan

Bats: L **Throws:** R **Pos:** LF-123; PH-6; 2B-1　　　　　　　　　　**Ht:** 6'0" **Wt:** 190 **Born:** 6/18/1985 **Age:** 25

Year	Team	Lg	G	AB	H	2B	3B	HR	(Hm	Rd)	TB	R	RBI	RC	TBB	IBB	SO	HBP	SH	SF	SB	CS	SB%	GDP	Avg	OBP	Slg
2006	Mrlns	R	2	7	2	0	0	0	(-	-)	2	2	3	0	0	0	1	0	0	0	0	0	-	0	.286	.286	.286
2006	Jmstwn	A-	28	94	28	5	1	0	(-	-)	35	14	12	15	13	0	9	0	1	3	5	2	.71	1	.298	.373	.372
2007	Grnsbr	A	81	305	99	26	4	10	(-	-)	163	60	64	71	47	4	43	5	0	3	19	4	.83	1	.325	.419	.534
2007	Jupiter	A+	34	130	26	5	3	2	(-	-)	43	17	18	13	15	0	19	0	0	3	5	1	.83	4	.200	.277	.331
2008	Carlina	AA	132	483	144	32	5	7	(-	-)	207	83	74	90	67	1	65	12	2	1	34	10	.77	9	.298	.396	.429
2009	NewOr	AAA	25	96	33	9	1	3	(-	-)	53	21	22	23	12	0	10	1	0	1	9	1	.90	3	.344	.418	.552
2009	Fla	NL	128	504	162	31	6	9	(5	4)	232	84	47	91	53	2	77	4	3	1	8	5	.62	3	.321	.390	.460

Phil Coke

Pitches: L **Bats:** L **Pos:** RP-72　　　　　　　　　　**Ht:** 6'1" **Wt:** 210 **Born:** 7/19/1982 **Age:** 27

Year	Team	Lg	G	GS	CG	GF	IP	BFP	H	R	ER	HR	SH	SF	HB	TBB	IBB	SO	WP	Bk	W	L	Pct	Sh	Sv-Op	Hld	ERC	ERA
2003	Yanks	R	10	0	0	3	12.0	53	13	7	5	0	0	1	0	3	0	5	3	0	0	-	-	0	0--	-	3.11	3.75
2004	StIsInd	A-	3	1	0	1	8.0	35	9	6	6	1	0	0	0	3	0	7	2	0	0	0	-	0	0--	-	4.91	6.75
2004	Yanks	R	7	1	0	1	11.1	54	18	7	5	0	1	0	0	3	0	13	1	1	0	1	.000	0	0--	-	6.17	3.97
2005	CtnSC	A	24	18	0	0	103.0	459	122	67	62	11	3	3	2	34	0	68	5	1	8	11	.421	0	0--	-	4.95	5.42
2006	CtnSC	A	5	2	0	2	17.0	64	10	1	1	0	0	1	0	4	0	19	0	0	0	1	.000	0	1--	-	1.30	0.53
2006	Tampa	A+	22	18	1	1	110.0	470	101	52	44	6	7	3	2	35	0	88	6	0	5	7	.417	0	0--	-	3.00	3.60
2007	Tampa	A+	17	16	1	1	99.0	411	93	36	34	4	0	2	2	37	0	76	3	0	7	3	.700	1	0--	-	3.40	3.09
2008	Trntn	AA	23	20	1	1	118.1	484	105	39	33	7	4	1	0	39	1	115	1	0	9	4	.692	1	0--	-	2.96	2.51
2008	S-WB	AAA	14	1	0	1	17.1	76	19	11	9	0	0	1	0	5	0	22	1	0	2	2	.500	0	0--	-	3.38	4.67
2008	NYY	AL	12	0	0	0	14.2	52	8	1	1	0	0	0	0	2	0	14	1	0	1	0	1.000	0	0-0	5	0.89	0.61
2009	NYY	AL	72	0	0	13	60.0	238	44	34	30	10	1	5	1	20	4	49	7	0	4	3	.571	0	2-7	21	2.84	4.50
	2 ML YEARS		84	0	0	13	74.2	290	52	35	31	10	1	5	1	22	4	63	8	0	5	3	.625	0	2-7	26	2.34	3.74

Jesus Colome

Pitches: R **Bats:** R **Pos:** RP-21　　　　　　　　　　**Ht:** 6'2" **Wt:** 241 **Born:** 12/23/1977 **Age:** 32

Year	Team	Lg	G	GS	CG	GF	IP	BFP	H	R	ER	HR	SH	SF	HB	TBB	IBB	SO	WP	Bk	W	L	Pct	Sh	Sv-Op	Hld	ERC	ERA
2008	Syrcse	AAA	9	0	0	9	10.1	44	10	10	7	4	0	0	1	2	0	9	1	0	0	2	.000	0	3--	-	5.26	6.10
2009	Nashv*	AAA	7	0	0	4	7.0	27	3	0	0	0	0	0	0	2	0	11	1	0	1	0	1.000	0	2--	-	0.80	0.00
2001	TB	AL	30	0	0	9	48.2	209	37	22	18	8	2	2	2	25	4	31	2	0	2	3	.400	0	0-0	8	3.62	3.33
2002	TB	AL	32	0	0	15	41.1	204	56	41	38	6	4	1	2	33	5	33	5	0	2	7	.222	0	0-5	3	8.57	8.27
2003	TB	AL	54	0	0	24	74.0	334	69	37	37	9	2	4	3	46	5	69	7	0	3	7	.300	0	2-8	11	4.76	4.50
2004	TB	AL	33	0	0	9	41.1	169	28	16	15	4	5	0	1	18	1	40	1	1	2	2	.500	0	3-4	8	2.54	3.27
2005	TB	AL	36	0	0	18	45.1	212	54	29	23	7	1	0	2	18	3	28	5	0	2	3	.400	0	0-1	2	5.46	4.57
2006	TB	AL	1	0	0	0	0.1	2	0	1	1	0	0	0	0	1	0	0	0	0	0	0	-	0	0-0	0	7.00	27.00
2007	Was	NL	61	0	0	16	66.0	286	64	30	28	6	4	6	1	27	3	43	4	0	5	1	.833	0	1-4	12	3.83	3.82
2008	Was	NL	61	0	0	25	71.0	312	61	38	34	6	7	2	4	39	4	55	7	0	2	2	.500	0	0-2	1	3.86	4.31
2009	2 Tms	NL	21	0	0	8	21.1	103	34	18	18	2	1	1	1	6	1	15	3	2	1	1	.500	0	0-1	0	7.20	7.59
09	Was	NL	16	0	0	5	15.0	75	23	14	14	1	1	1	1	6	1	12	2	2	1	1	.500	0	0-1	0	7.00	8.40
09	Mil	NL	5	0	0	3	6.1	28	11	4	4	1	0	0	0	0	0	3	1	0	0	0	-	0	0-0	0	7.66	5.68
	9 ML YEARS		329	0	0	124	409.1	1831	403	232	212	48	26	16	16	213	26	314	34	3	19	26	.422	0	0-25	43	4.61	4.66

Bartolo Colon

Pitches: R **Bats:** R **Pos:** SP-12　　　　　　　　　　**Ht:** 5'11" **Wt:** 245 **Born:** 5/24/1973 **Age:** 37

Year	Team	Lg	G	GS	CG	GF	IP	BFP	H	R	ER	HR	SH	SF	HB	TBB	IBB	SO	WP	Bk	W	L	Pct	Sh	Sv-Op	Hld	ERC	ERA
2009	Charltt*	AAA	2	2	0	0	12.0	47	10	5	5	2	0	0	0	4	0	1	1	0	1	1	.500	0	0--	-	3.53	3.75
2009	Knapol*	A-	1	1	0	0	7.0	26	7	2	2	0	0	0	0	1	0	8	0	0	0	1	.000	0	0--	-	2.75	2.57
1997	Cle	AL	19	17	1	0	94.0	427	107	66	59	12	4	1	3	45	1	66	5	0	4	7	.364	0	0-0	0	5.53	5.65
1998	Cle	AL	31	31	6	0	204.0	883	205	91	84	15	10	2	3	79	5	158	4	0	14	9	.609	2	0-0	0	3.87	3.71
1999	Cle	AL	32	32	1	0	205.0	858	185	97	90	24	5	4	7	76	5	161	4	0	18	5	.783	1	0-0	0	3.68	3.95
2000	Cle	AL	30	30	2	0	188.0	807	163	86	81	21	2	3	4	98	4	212	4	0	15	8	.652	1	0-0	0	3.97	3.88
2001	Cle	AL	34	34	1	0	222.1	947	220	106	101	26	8	4	2	90	2	201	4	1	14	12	.538	0	0-0	0	4.24	4.09
2002	2 Tms		33	33	8	0	233.1	966	219	85	76	20	19	6	2	70	5	149	4	0	20	8	.714	3	0-0	0	3.29	2.93
2003	CWS	AL	34	34	9	0	242.0	984	223	107	104	30	5	8	5	67	3	173	8	3	15	13	.536	0	0-0	0	3.47	3.87
2004	LAA	AL	34	34	0	0	208.1	897	215	122	116	38	5	8	3	71	1	158	1	0	18	12	.600	0	0-0	0	4.64	5.01
2005	LAA	AL	33	33	2	0	222.2	906	215	93	86	26	9	4	3	43	0	157	2	1	21	8	.724	0	0-0	0	3.28	3.48
2006	LAA	AL	10	10	1	0	56.1	251	71	39	32	11	4	1	3	11	0	31	1	0	1	5	.167	1	0-0	0	5.61	5.11
2007	LAA	AL	19	18	0	0	99.1	453	132	74	70	15	4	3	5	29	1	76	1	0	6	8	.429	0	0-0	1	6.17	6.34
2008	Bos	AL	7	7	0	0	39.0	173	44	23	17	5	3	2	2	10	0	27	0	0	4	2	.667	0	0-0	0	4.53	3.92
2009	CWS	AL	12	12	0	0	62.1	276	69	42	29	13	4	3	2	21	3	38	1	0	3	6	.333	0	0-0	0	5.22	4.19
02	Cle	AL	16	16	4	0	116.1	467	104	37	33	11	6	3	2	31	1	75	3	0	10	4	.714	2	0-0	0	3.09	2.55
02	Mon	NL	17	17	4	0	117.0	499	115	48	43	9	13	3	0	39	4	74	1	0	10	4	.714	1	0-0	0	3.48	3.31
	Postseason		9	9	1	0	52.1	215	49	21	21	5	1	1	2	22	1	41	0	0	2	3	.400	0	0-0	0	4.01	3.61
	13 ML YEARS		328	325	31	0	2076.2	8828	2068	1031	945	256	82	49	44	710	30	1607	39	5	153	103	.598	8	0-0	1	4.07	4.10

Roman Colon

Pitches: R Bats: R Pos: RP-43　　　　　　　　　　　　　Ht: 6'6" Wt: 237 Born: 8/13/1979 Age: 30

		HOW MUCH HE PITCHED						WHAT HE GAVE UP												THE RESULTS						
Year Team	Lg	G	GS	CG	GF	IP	BFP	H	R	ER	HR	SH	SF	HB	TBB	IBB	SO	WP	Bk	W	L	Pct	Sh	Sv-Op	Hld	ERC	ERA
2009 Omha*	AAA	13	0	0	7	25.1	108	27	9	8	1	1	1	0	8	1	26	2	0	2	3	.400	0	2- -	-	3.64	2.84
2004 Atl	NL	18	0	0	7	19.0	82	18	9	7	0	1	2	0	8	1	15	0	1	2	1	.667	0	0-1	1	3.05	3.32
2005 2 Tms		35	7	0	7	69.1	306	82	45	43	17	2	3	0	21	1	47	4	1	2	6	.250	0	0-1	2	5.75	5.58
2006 Det	AL	20	1	0	4	38.2	170	46	21	21	6	1	2	1	14	2	25	6	0	2	0	1.000	0	1-1	3	5.56	4.89
2009 KC	AL	43	0	0	13	50.1	220	50	27	27	7	1	0	2	22	1	29	1	2	2	3	.400	0	0-3	6	4.60	4.83
05 Atl	NL	23	4	0	6	44.1	191	47	28	26	10	2	2	0	14	1	30	2	1	1	5	.167	0	0-0	2	4.90	5.28
05 Det	AL	12	3	0	1	25.0	115	35	17	17	7	0	1	0	7	0	17	2	0	1	1	.500	0	0-1	0	7.34	6.12
4 ML YEARS		116	8	0	31	177.1	778	196	102	98	30	5	7	3	65	5	116	11	3	8	10	.444	0	1-6	12	5.08	4.97

Tyler Colvin

Bats: L Throws: L Pos: CF-6　　　　　　　　　　　　　Ht: 6'3" Wt: 190 Born: 9/5/1985 Age: 24

		BATTING																	BASERUNNING				AVERAGES		
Year Team	Lg	G	AB	H	2B	3B	HR	(Hm Rd)	TB	R	RBI	RC	TBB	IBB	SO	HBP	SH	SF	SB	CS	SB%	GDP	Avg	OBP	Slg
2006 Boise	A-	64	265	71	12	6	11	(- -)	128	50	53	41	17	1	55	2	0	4	12	5	.71	3	.268	.313	.483
2007 Dytona	A+	63	245	75	24	3	7	(- -)	126	38	50	42	10	2	47	3	0	4	10	4	.71	3	.306	.336	.514
2007 Tenn	AA	62	247	72	11	2	9	(- -)	114	34	31	36	5	0	54	3	1	1	7	1	.88	5	.291	.313	.462
2008 Tenn	AA	137	540	138	27	11	14	(- -)	229	68	80	75	44	0	101	4	5	9	7	4	.64	7	.256	.312	.424
2009 Dytona	A+	32	112	28	5	2	1	(- -)	40	18	10	14	13	0	27	1	0	3	3	1	.75	8	.250	.326	.357
2009 Tenn	AA	84	307	92	13	7	14	(- -)	161	51	50	54	16	2	57	1	4	2	5	1	.83	3	.300	.334	.524
2009 ChC	NL	6	17	3	0	0	0	(0 0)	3	1	2	1	2	0	5	0	0	1	0	0	-	0	.176	.250	.176

Clay Condrey

Pitches: R Bats: R Pos: RP-45　　　　　　　　　　　　　Ht: 6'3" Wt: 223 Born: 11/19/1975 Age: 34

		HOW MUCH HE PITCHED						WHAT HE GAVE UP												THE RESULTS						
Year Team	Lg	G	GS	CG	GF	IP	BFP	H	R	ER	HR	SH	SF	HB	TBB	IBB	SO	WP	Bk	W	L	Pct	Sh	Sv-Op	Hld	ERC	ERA
2009 Phillies*	R	3	1	0	0	3.0	11	3	0	0	0	0	0	0	0	0	3	0	0	0	0	-	0	0- -	-	2.18	0.00
2009 Clrwtr*	A+	2	0	0	0	3.0	9	1	0	0	0	0	0	0	0	0	2	0	0	0	0	-	0	0- -	-	0.28	0.00
2002 SD	NL	9	3	0	2	26.2	106	20	7	5	1	2	2	2	8	1	16	1	1	1	2	.333	0	0-0	3	2.29	1.69
2003 SD	NL	9	6	0	0	34.0	168	43	32	32	7	3	0	3	21	4	25	0	0	1	2	.333	0	0-0	0	7.50	8.47
2006 Phi	NL	21	0	0	10	28.2	122	35	11	10	3	2	1	0	9	2	16	0	0	2	2	.500	0	0-1	1	5.14	3.14
2007 Phi	NL	39	0	0	14	50.0	228	61	30	28	4	1	3	5	16	3	27	1	0	5	0	1.000	0	2-2	2	5.14	5.04
2008 Phi	NL	56	0	0	30	69.0	303	85	26	25	6	1	0	2	19	8	34	1	0	3	4	.429	0	1-1	1	4.77	3.26
2009 Phi	NL	45	0	0	11	42.0	174	37	17	14	4	0	0	1	14	3	25	0	0	6	2	.750	0	1-2	7	3.14	3.00
Postseason		3	0	0	0	3.1	17	5	2	2	0	0	1	1	3	1	3	0	0	0	0	-	0	0-0	0	9.82	5.40
6 ML YEARS		179	9	0	67	250.1	1101	281	123	114	25	9	6	13	87	21	143	3	1	18	12	.600	0	4-6	14	4.66	4.10

Brooks Conrad

Bats: B Throws: R Pos: PH-19; 2B-11; PR-2; 3B-1　　　　　　　　Ht: 5'11" Wt: 190 Born: 1/16/1980 Age: 30

		BATTING																	BASERUNNING				AVERAGES		
Year Team	Lg	G	AB	H	2B	3B	HR	(Hm Rd)	TB	R	RBI	RC	TBB	IBB	SO	HBP	SH	SF	SB	CS	SB%	GDP	Avg	OBP	Slg
2001 Pittsfld	A-	65	232	65	16	5	4	(- -)	103	41	39	44	26	3	52	13	4	6	14	2	.88	1	.280	.375	.444
2002 Mich	A	133	499	143	25	14	14	(- -)	238	94	94	92	62	0	102	7	1	8	18	8	.69	2	.287	.368	.477
2003 Lxngtn	A	38	140	26	5	2	3	(- -)	44	20	11	14	17	0	25	3	1	0	7	1	.88	2	.186	.288	.314
2003 Salem	A+	99	345	98	24	3	11	(- -)	161	50	61	62	42	3	60	6	5	3	4	2	.67	7	.284	.369	.467
2004 RdRck	AA	129	480	139	38	6	13	(- -)	228	84	83	86	63	1	105	1	5	12	8	7	.53	8	.290	.365	.475
2005 RdRck	AAA	113	418	110	22	3	21	(- -)	201	84	58	73	52	3	104	4	5	4	12	3	.80	7	.263	.347	.481
2005 CpChr	AA	22	77	18	6	1	2	(- -)	32	13	11	14	16	1	15	1	0	0	8	0	1.00	1	.234	.372	.416
2006 RdRck	AAA	138	533	143	40	16	24	(- -)	287	101	94	99	54	2	134	4	1	8	15	6	.71	5	.268	.336	.538
2007 RdRck	AAA	139	533	116	36	3	22	(- -)	224	85	70	73	63	5	144	5	1	3	12	3	.80	4	.218	.305	.420
2008 Scrmto	AAA	117	465	113	29	5	28	(- -)	236	86	91	76	46	1	127	2	2	2	4	1	.80	5	.243	.313	.508
2009 Gwnntt	AAA	110	398	107	25	0	12	(- -)	168	66	64	67	53	5	108	7	2	9	13	1	.93	4	.269	.358	.422
2008 Oak	AL	6	19	3	1	0	0	(0 0)	4	0	2	1	0	0	9	0	0	0	0	0	-	1	.158	.158	.211
2009 Atl	NL	30	54	11	1	2	2	(0 2)	22	7	8	6	3	1	14	1	0	0	0	0	-	1	.204	.259	.407
2 ML YEARS		36	73	14	2	2	2	(0 2)	26	7	10	7	3	1	23	1	0	0	0	0	-	2	.192	.234	.356

Jose Contreras

Pitches: R Bats: R Pos: SP-23; RP-5　　　　　　　　　　　Ht: 6'4" Wt: 255 Born: 12/6/1971 Age: 38

		HOW MUCH HE PITCHED						WHAT HE GAVE UP												THE RESULTS						
Year Team	Lg	G	GS	CG	GF	IP	BFP	H	R	ER	HR	SH	SF	HB	TBB	IBB	SO	WP	Bk	W	L	Pct	Sh	Sv-Op	Hld	ERC	ERA
2009 Charltt*	AAA	5	5	1	0	33.1	134	19	12	10	2	0	0	2	16	0	27	3	0	3	1	.750	1	0- -	-	2.14	2.70
2003 NYY	AL	18	9	0	2	71.0	293	52	27	26	4	0	1	5	30	1	72	2	0	7	2	.778	0	0-1	1	2.71	3.30
2004 2 Tms	AL	31	31	0	0	170.1	758	166	114	104	31	3	6	8	84	1	150	17	0	13	9	.591	0	0-0	0	5.05	5.50
2005 CWS	AL	32	32	1	0	204.2	857	177	91	82	23	7	2	9	75	2	154	20	2	15	7	.682	0	0-0	0	3.46	3.61
2006 CWS	AL	30	30	1	0	196.0	833	194	101	93	20	2	8	10	55	4	134	16	0	13	9	.591	0	1-0	0	3.72	4.27
2007 CWS	AL	32	30	2	2	189.0	858	232	134	117	21	8	10	15	62	1	113	3	0	10	17	.370	2	0-0	0	5.49	5.57
2008 CWS	AL	20	20	1	0	121.0	522	130	64	61	12	4	2	3	35	0	70	6	0	7	6	.538	0	0-0	0	4.13	4.54
2009 2 Tms	AL	28	23	0	0	131.2	589	141	86	72	13	10	2	6	53	4	106	8	0	6	13	.316	0	0-1	1	4.55	4.92
04 NYY	AL	18	18	0	0	95.2	425	93	66	60	22	1	4	6	42	1	82	10	0	8	5	.615	0	0-0	0	5.18	5.64
04 CWS	AL	13	13	0	0	74.2	333	73	48	44	9	2	2	2	42	0	68	7	0	5	4	.556	0	0-0	0	4.87	5.30
09 CWS	AL	21	21	0	0	114.2	513	121	83	69	11	7	2	6	45	3	89	8	0	5	13	.278	0	0-0	0	4.41	5.42
09 Col	NL	7	2	0	0	17.0	76	20	3	3	2	3	0	0	8	1	17	0	0	1	0	1.000	0	0-1	1	5.51	1.59
Postseason		12	4	1	3	43.0	176	37	18	18	2	5	1	3	9	0	31	3	0	3	3	.500	0	0-1	2	2.52	3.77
7 ML YEARS		191	175	5	4	1083.2	4710	1092	617	555	124	34	31	56	394	13	799	72	2	71	63	.530	3	0-2	2	4.25	4.61

Aaron Cook

Pitches: R **Bats:** R **Pos:** SP-27   **Ht:** 6'3" **Wt:** 215 **Born:** 2/8/1979 **Age:** 31

Year	Team	Lg	G	GS	CG	GF	IP	BFP	H	R	ER	HR	SH	SF	HB	TBB	IBB	SO	WP	Bk	W	L	Pct	Sh	Sv-Op	Hld	ERC	ERA
2002	Col	NL	9	5	0	1	35.2	154	41	18	18	4	0	0	2	13	0	14	0	0	2	1	.667	0	0-0	1	5.31	4.54
2003	Col	NL	43	16	1	4	124.0	579	160	89	83	8	4	6	8	57	7	43	10	0	4	6	.400	0	0-0	1	5.95	6.02
2004	Col	NL	16	16	1	0	96.2	433	112	47	46	7	5	1	7	39	5	40	6	1	6	4	.600	0	0-0	0	5.05	4.28
2005	Col	NL	13	13	2	0	83.1	357	101	38	34	8	1	3	2	16	2	24	3	0	7	2	.778	0	0-0	0	4.53	3.67
2006	Col	NL	32	32	0	0	212.2	915	242	107	100	17	8	5	7	55	11	92	2	0	9	15	.375	0	0-0	0	4.23	4.23
2007	Col	NL	25	25	2	0	166.0	698	178	87	76	15	6	3	6	44	6	61	0	0	8	7	.533	0	0-0	0	4.05	4.12
2008	Col	NL	32	32	2	0	211.1	886	236	102	93	13	9	4	4	48	2	96	6	0	16	9	.640	1	0-0	0	3.92	3.96
2009	Col	NL	27	27	1	0	158.0	675	175	76	73	19	3	6	2	47	2	78	2	0	11	6	.647	1	0-0	0	4.51	4.16
	Postseason		1	1	0	0	6.0	23	6	3	3	1	0	0	0	0	0	2	0	0	0	1	.000	0	0-0	0	3.02	4.50
8 ML YEARS			197	166	9	5	1087.2	4697	1245	564	523	91	36	28	38	319	35	448	29	1	63	50	.558	2	0-0	2	4.50	4.33

Alex Cora

Bats: L **Throws:** R **Pos:** SS-56; 2B-19; PH-10; 1B-1; PR-1   **Ht:** 6'0" **Wt:** 200 **Born:** 10/18/1975 **Age:** 34

								BATTING													BASERUNNING				AVERAGES		
Year	Team	Lg	G	AB	H	2B	3B	HR	(Hm	Rd)	TB	R	RBI	RC	TBB	IBB	SO	HBP	SH	SF	SB	CS	SB%	GDP	Avg	OBP	Slg
2009	Buffalo*	AAA	3	14	3	1	0	0	(-	-)	4	0	0	0	0	0	0	0	0	0	0	0	-	1	.214	.214	.286
1998	LAD	NL	29	33	4	0	1	0	(0	0)	6	1	0	1	2	0	8	1	2	0	0	0	-	0	.121	.194	.182
1999	LAD	NL	11	30	5	1	0	0	(0	0)	6	2	3	0	0	0	4	1	0	0	0	0	-	1	.167	.194	.200
2000	LAD	NL	109	353	84	18	6	4	(2	2)	126	39	32	38	26	4	53	7	6	2	4	1	.80	6	.238	.302	.357
2001	LAD	NL	134	405	88	18	3	4	(2	2)	124	38	29	30	31	6	58	8	3	2	0	2	.00	16	.217	.285	.306
2002	LAD	NL	115	258	75	14	4	5	(4	1)	112	37	28	46	26	4	38	7	2	0	7	2	.78	3	.291	.371	.434
2003	LAD	NL	148	477	119	24	3	4	(3	1)	161	39	34	46	16	3	59	10	9	2	4	2	.07	5	.249	.287	.338
2004	LAD	NL	138	405	107	9	4	10	(4	6)	154	47	47	63	47	10	41	18	12	2	3	4	.43	9	.264	.364	.380
2005	2 Tms	AL	96	260	58	8	4	3	(1	2)	83	25	24	21	11	0	30	5	4	3	7	2	.78	6	.223	.275	.000
2006	Bos	AL	96	235	56	7	2	1	(1	0)	70	51	18	24	19	1	29	6	4	0	6	2	.76	4	.238	.312	.298
2007	Bos	AL	83	207	51	10	5	3	(0	3)	80	30	18	19	7	2	23	9	7	2	1	1	.50	5	.246	.298	.386
2008	Bos	AL	75	152	41	8	2	0	(0	0)	53	14	9	19	16	1	13	9	1	1	1	1	.50	3	.270	.371	.349
2009	NYM	NL	82	271	68	11	1	1	(0	0)	84	31	18	26	25	1	28	3	8	1	8	3	.73	2	.251	.320	.310
05	Cle	AL	49	146	30	5	2	1	(1	0)	42	11	8	9	5	0	18	4	1	1	6	0	1.00	1	.205	.250	.288
05	Bos	AL	47	104	28	3	2	2	(0	2)	41	14	16	12	6	0	12	1	0	2	1	2	.33	3	.260	.310	.394
	Postseason		10	20	4	1	1	0	(0	0)	7	2	1	1	1	0	5	1	1	0	0	0	-	2	.154	.214	.269
12 ML YEARS			1116	3076	756	128	35	35	(17	18)	1059	334	260	333	226	32	384	84	58	15	41	20	.67	60	.246	.313	.344

Roy Corcoran

Pitches: R **Bats:** R **Pos:** RP-16   **Ht:** 5'10" **Wt:** 185 **Born:** 5/11/1980 **Age:** 30

Year	Team	Lg	G	GS	CG	GF	IP	BFP	H	R	ER	HR	SH	SF	HB	TBB	IBB	SO	WP	Bk	W	L	Pct	Sh	Sv-Op	Hld	ERC	ERA
2009	Tacom*	AAA	3	0	0	0	3.0	13	3	1	0	0	0	0	0	0	0	2	0	0	1	0	1.000	0	0--	-	1.76	0.00
2009	RdRck*	AAA	13	1	0	1	19.2	87	24	12	9	0	0	2	1	7	0	11	0	0	0	0	-	0	0--	-	4.71	4.12
2003	Mon	NL	5	0	0	2	7.1	31	7	2	1	0	0	0	0	3	0	2	1	0	0	0	-	0	0-0	0	3.20	1.23
2004	Mon	NL	5	0	0	3	5.1	28	7	4	4	0	0	0	0	5	0	4	0	0	0	0	-	0	0-0	0	7.12	6.75
2006	Was	NL	6	0	0	2	5.2	34	12	8	7	1	0	1	0	4	0	6	0	0	0	1	.000	0	0-1	0	12.96	11.12
2008	Sea	AL	50	0	0	13	72.2	316	65	31	26	1	3	3	2	36	4	39	3	0	6	2	.750	0	3-6	8	3.24	3.22
2009	Sea	AL	16	0	0	2	19.0	91	25	13	13	2	1	2	1	17	0	6	0	0	2	0	1.000	0	0-1	0	9.04	6.16
5 ML YEARS			82	0	0	22	110.0	500	116	58	51	4	4	6	3	65	4	57	4	0	8	3	.727	0	3-8	10	4.71	4.17

Chad Cordero

Pitches: R **Bats:** R **Pos:** P   **Ht:** 6'0" **Wt:** 224 **Born:** 3/18/1982 **Age:** 28

Year	Team	Lg	G	GS	CG	GF	IP	BFP	H	R	ER	HR	SH	SF	HB	TBB	IBB	SO	WP	Bk	W	L	Pct	Sh	Sv-Op	Hld	ERC	ERA
2009	Ms*	R	6	6	0	0	6.2	33	10	5	5	0	0	0	0	3	0	8	1	0	0	1	.000	0	0--	-	6.27	6.75
2009	Everett*	A-	8	0	0	7	7.2	35	13	10	10	2	0	1	0	2	0	7	1	0	0	2	.000	0	1--	-	9.77	11.74
2003	Mon	NL	12	0	0	4	11.0	40	4	2	1	1	0	0	0	3	1	12	1	0	1	0	1.000	0	1-1	1	0.86	1.64
2004	Mon	NL	69	0	0	40	82.2	357	68	28	27	8	2	4	1	43	4	83	5	0	7	3	.700	0	14-18	8	3.47	2.94
2005	Was	NL	74	0	0	62	74.1	300	55	24	15	9	2	1	2	17	2	61	0	0	2	4	.333	0	47-54	0	2.22	1.82
2006	Was	NL	68	0	0	59	73.1	307	59	27	26	13	6	2	3	22	5	69	0	0	7	4	.636	0	29-33	0	3.10	3.19
2007	Was	NL	76	0	0	59	75.0	321	75	31	28	8	2	1	0	29	3	62	5	1	3	3	.500	0	37-46	1	4.02	3.36
2008	Was	NL	6	0	0	2	4.1	22	6	1	1	0	0	0	0	3	1	5	1	0	0	0	-	0	0-0	1	6.09	2.08
6 ML YEARS			305	0	0	226	320.2	1347	267	113	99	39	13	8	6	117	16	292	12	1	20	14	.588	0	128-152	11	3.12	2.78

Francisco Cordero

Pitches: R **Bats:** R **Pos:** RP-68   **Ht:** 6'3" **Wt:** 238 **Born:** 5/11/1975 **Age:** 35

Year	Team	Lg	G	GS	CG	GF	IP	BFP	H	R	ER	HR	SH	SF	HB	TBB	IBB	SO	WP	Bk	W	L	Pct	Sh	Sv-Op	Hld	ERC	ERA
1999	Det	AL	20	0	0	4	19.0	91	19	7	7	2	2	4	0	18	2	19	1	0	2	2	.500	0	0-0	6	6.19	3.32
2000	Tex	AL	56	0	0	13	77.1	365	87	51	46	11	2	6	4	48	3	49	7	0	1	2	.333	0	0-3	4	6.15	5.35
2001	Tex	AL	3	0	0	2	2.1	12	3	1	1	0	0	0	0	2	1	1	1	0	0	1	.000	0	0-0	1	5.73	3.86
2002	Tex	AL	39	0	0	25	45.1	177	33	12	9	2	0	0	2	13	1	41	1	0	2	0	1.000	0	10-12	5	2.11	1.79
2003	Tex	AL	73	0	0	36	82.2	352	70	33	27	4	3	4	2	38	6	90	1	0	5	8	.385	0	15-25	18	3.08	2.94
2004	Tex	AL	67	0	0	63	71.2	304	60	19	17	1	5	1	1	32	2	79	3	2	3	4	.429	0	49-54	0	2.78	2.13
2005	Tex	AL	69	0	0	60	69.0	302	61	28	26	5	4	3	4	30	2	79	0	0	3	1	.750	0	37-45	0	3.47	3.39
2006	2 Tms		77	0	0	47	75.1	322	69	32	31	7	3	5	3	32	2	84	4	0	10	5	.667	0	22-33	16	3.79	3.70
2007	Mil	NL	66	0	0	58	63.1	261	52	23	21	4	2	1	1	18	1	86	2	0	0	4	.000	0	44-51	0	2.45	2.98
2008	Cin	NL	72	0	0	63	70.1	307	61	28	26	6	3	3	3	30	5	78	3	0	5	4	.556	0	34-40	0	3.86	3.33

HOW MUCH HE PITCHED							WHAT HE GAVE UP												THE RESULTS							
Year	Team	Lg	G	GS	CG	GF	IP	BFP	H	R	ER	HR	SH	SF	HB	TBB	IBB	SO	WP	Bk	W	L	Pct	Sh	Sv-Op	Hld	ERC	ERA
2009	Cin	NL	68	0	0	59	66.2	276	58	21	16	2	3	4	0	30	2	58	3	0	2	6	.250	0	39-43	0	3.11	2.16
06	Tex	AL	49	0	0	21	48.2	210	49	27	26	5	1	5	3	16	1	54	0	0	7	4	.636	0	6-15	15	4.05	4.81
06	Mil	NL	28	0	0	26	26.2	112	20	5	5	2	2	0	0	16	1	30	1	0	3	1	.750	0	16-18	1	3.30	1.69
11 ML YEARS			610	0	0	430	643.0	2769	573	255	227	44	27	31	20	299	25	664	26	2	33	37	.471	0	250-306	46	3.55	3.18

Lance Cormier

Pitches: R **Bats:** R **Pos:** RP-53   **Ht:** 6'1" **Wt:** 200 **Born:** 8/19/1980 **Age:** 29

HOW MUCH HE PITCHED							WHAT HE GAVE UP												THE RESULTS							
Year	Team	Lg	G	GS	CG	GF	IP	BFP	H	R	ER	HR	SH	SF	HB	TBB	IBB	SO	WP	Bk	W	L	Pct	Sh	Sv-Op	Hld	ERC	ERA
2004	Ari	NL	17	5	0	3	45.1	218	62	42	41	13	2	3	2	25	2	24	2	1	1	4	.200	0	0-0	2	8.76	8.14
2005	Ari	NL	67	0	0	13	79.1	356	86	50	45	7	4	1	5	43	5	63	6	0	7	3	.700	0	0-1	13	5.30	5.11
2006	Atl	NL	29	9	0	5	73.2	333	90	44	40	8	1	4	2	39	7	43	2	0	4	5	.444	0	0-0	2	6.13	4.89
2007	Atl	NL	10	9	0	1	45.2	210	56	38	36	16	3	0	0	22	3	27	4	0	2	6	.250	0	0-0	0	7.66	7.09
2008	Bal	AL	45	1	0	10	71.2	319	78	36	32	4	1	3	1	34	3	46	2	1	3	3	.500	0	1-3	0	4.55	4.02
2009	TB	AL	53	0	0	11	77.1	331	75	31	28	6	2	2	1	25	2	36	3	1	3	3	.500	0	2-2	6	3.41	3.26
6 ML YEARS			221	24	0	43	393.0	1767	447	241	222	54	13	13	11	188	22	239	19	3	20	24	.455	0	3-6	23	5.55	5.08

Manny Corpas

Pitches: R **Bats:** R **Pos:** RP-35   **Ht:** 6'3" **Wt:** 170 **Born:** 12/3/1982 **Age:** 27

HOW MUCH HE PITCHED							WHAT HE GAVE UP												THE RESULTS							
Year	Team	Lg	G	GS	CG	GF	IP	BFP	H	R	ER	HR	SH	SF	HB	TBB	IBB	SO	WP	Bk	W	L	Pct	Sh	Sv-Op	Hld	ERC	ERA
2009	ColSpr*	AAA	3	0	0	0	2.2	10	2	0	0	0	0	0	0	1	0	3	0	0	0	0	-	0	0- -	-	2.27	0.00
2006	Col	NL	35	0	0	3	32.1	136	36	13	13	3	0	0	2	8	1	27	2	0	1	2	.333	0	0-0	7	4.39	3.62
2007	Col	NL	78	0	0	46	78.0	306	63	20	18	6	2	1	2	20	3	58	0	0	4	2	.667	0	19-22	16	2.51	2.08
2008	Col	NL	76	0	0	20	79.2	346	93	41	40	7	6	1	2	23	4	50	1	0	3	4	.429	0	4-13	19	4.55	4.52
2009	Col	NL	35	0	0	16	33.2	146	44	22	22	3	2	1	1	7	0	24	0	0	1	3	.250	0	1-3	7	5.24	5.88
Postseason			9	0	0	8	10.1	37	6	1	1	0	0	0	1	0	0	7	0	0	1	0	1.000	0	5-6	0	0.90	0.87
4 ML YEARS			224	0	0	85	223.2	934	236	96	93	19	10	3	7	58	8	159	3	0	9	11	.450	0	24-40	49	3.87	3.74

Carlos Corporan

Bats: B **Throws:** R **Pos:** C-1   **Ht:** 6'2" **Wt:** 218 **Born:** 1/7/1984 **Age:** 26

BATTING																			BASERUNNING				AVERAGES		
Year	Team	Lg	G	AB	H	2B	3B	HR	(Hm | Rd)	TB	R	RBI	RC	TBB	IBB	SO	HBP	SH	SF	SB	CS	SB%	GDP	Avg	OBP	Slg
2003	Brewrs	R	34	120	30	6	0	2	(- | -)	42	13	9	11	3	0	22	2	0	1	0	1	.00	5	.250	.278	.350
2003	Helena	R+	10	27	6	1	0	0	(- | -)	7	4	4	3	4	0	7	2	0	1	0	0	-	2	.222	.353	.259
2004	Beloit	A	63	197	45	7	2	1	(- | -)	59	20	16	14	7	0	65	3	3	4	1	3	.25	1	.228	.261	.299
2005	WV	A-	99	343	82	15	2	9	(- | -)	128	46	38	41	28	3	97	7	9	3	0	0	-	10	.239	.307	.373
2006	BrvdCt	A+	86	282	76	14	0	3	(- | -)	99	29	38	33	13	1	45	10	5	3	0	2	.00	8	.270	.321	.351
2006	Hntsvl	AA	3	9	3	0	0	0	(- | -)	3	2	1	0	0	0	3	0	0	0	0	0	-	1	.333	.333	.333
2007	BrvdCt	A+	23	80	29	8	0	3	(- | -)	46	11	19	17	2	0	9	3	3	0	0	1	.00	1	.363	.400	.575
2007	Hntsvl	AA	56	179	36	14	0	2	(- | -)	56	18	24	15	8	0	48	8	8	2	1	0	1.00	1	.201	.264	.313
2008	Hntsvl	AA	34	113	30	8	0	3	(- | -)	47	14	15	18	14	1	15	3	5	0	1	1	.50	0	.265	.362	.416
2008	Nashv	AAA	25	87	20	6	1	3	(- | -)	37	8	12	9	1	0	24	1	1	0	1	1	.50	2	.230	.244	.425
2009	Nashv	AAA	57	179	36	9	1	1	(- | -)	50	9	18	12	5	2	43	5	2	7	0	1	.00	6	.201	.250	.279
2009	BrvdCt	A+	14	46	12	1	0	0	(- | -)	13	1	6	3	1	0	10	1	0	0	0	0	-	0	.261	.292	.283
2009	Mil	NL	1	1	1	0	0	0	(0 | 0)	1	1	0	1	0	0	0	0	0	0	0	0	-	0	1.000	1.000	1.000

Kevin Correia

Pitches: R **Bats:** R **Pos:** SP-33   **Ht:** 6'3" **Wt:** 200 **Born:** 8/24/1980 **Age:** 29

HOW MUCH HE PITCHED							WHAT HE GAVE UP												THE RESULTS							
Year	Team	Lg	G	GS	CG	GF	IP	BFP	H	R	ER	HR	SH	SF	HB	TBB	IBB	SO	WP	Bk	W	L	Pct	Sh	Sv-Op	Hld	ERC	ERA
2003	SF	NL	10	7	0	1	39.1	173	41	16	16	6	1	4	4	18	1	28	2	0	3	1	.750	0	0-0	0	5.46	3.66
2004	SF	NL	12	1	0	5	19.0	92	25	20	17	3	3	3	1	10	0	14	0	0	0	1	.000	0	0-0	0	7.12	8.05
2005	SF	NL	16	11	0	1	58.1	264	61	31	30	12	5	1	4	31	2	44	2	0	2	5	.286	0	0-0	0	5.94	4.63
2006	SF	NL	48	0	0	9	69.2	295	64	27	27	5	1	4	3	22	0	57	0	0	2	0	1.000	0	0-1	10	3.25	3.49
2007	SF	NL	59	8	0	9	101.2	437	94	39	39	9	4	3	2	40	7	80	1	1	4	7	.364	0	0-3	12	3.48	3.45
2008	SF	NL	25	19	0	2	110.0	514	141	80	74	15	3	5	4	47	3	66	5	0	3	8	.273	0	0-0	0	6.19	6.05
2009	SD	NL	33	33	1	0	198.0	830	194	92	86	17	9	3	4	64	6	142	5	1	12	11	.522	1	0-0	0	3.64	3.91
7 ML YEARS			203	79	1	27	596.0	2605	620	305	289	67	26	20	22	232	19	431	15	2	26	33	.441	1	0-4	22	4.44	4.36

Chris Coste

Bats: R **Throws:** R **Pos:** C-55; PH-18; 1B-16; DH-3   **Ht:** 6'1" **Wt:** 211 **Born:** 2/4/1973 **Age:** 37

BATTING																			BASERUNNING				AVERAGES		
Year	Team	Lg	G	AB	H	2B	3B	HR	(Hm | Rd)	TB	R	RBI	RC	TBB	IBB	SO	HBP	SH	SF	SB	CS	SB%	GDP	Avg	OBP	Slg
2006	Phi	NL	65	198	65	14	0	7	(4 | 3)	100	25	32	36	10	1	31	5	0	0	0	0	-	6	.328	.376	.505
2007	Phi	NL	48	129	36	3	0	5	(5 | 0)	54	15	22	17	4	1	20	2	2	0	0	0	-	1	.279	.311	.419
2008	Phi	NL	98	274	72	17	0	9	(7 | 2)	116	28	36	37	16	1	51	10	3	2	0	1	.00	5	.263	.325	.423
2009	2 Tms	NL	88	205	46	13	0	2	(2 | 0)	65	15	18	16	22	1	55	1	1	1	0	0	-	5	.224	.301	.317
09	Phi	NL	45	102	25	8	0	2	(2 | 0)	39	12	8	10	14	1	27	1	1	0	0	0	-	2	.245	.342	.382
09	Hou	NL	43	103	21	5	0	0	(0 | 0)	26	3	10	6	8	0	28	0	0	1	0	0	-	3	.204	.259	.252
Postseason			3	6	1	0	0	0	(0 | 0)	1	0	0	1	0	0	0	0	0	0	0	0	-	0	.167	.167	.167
4 ML YEARS			299	806	219	47	0	23	(18 | 5)	335	83	108	106	52	4	157	18	6	3	0	1	.00	19	.272	.329	.416

Neal Cotts

Pitches: L **Bats**: L **Pos**: RP-19   **Ht**: 6'1" **Wt**: 200 **Born**: 3/25/1980 **Age**: 30

| | | | HOW MUCH HE PITCHED | | | | | | WHAT HE GAVE UP | | | | | | | | | | | THE RESULTS | | | | | | |
Year	Team	Lg	G	GS	CG	GF	IP	BFP	H	R	ER	HR	SH	SF	HB	TBB	IBB	SO	WP	Bk	W	L	Pct	Sh	Sv-Op	Hld	ERC	ERA
2009	Iowa*	AAA	12	0	0	4	12.2	51	7	4	4	1	0	0	1	6	0	11	1	0	1	1	.500	0	1--	-	2.21	2.84
2003	CWS	AL	4	4	0	0	13.1	69	15	12	12	1	1	0	0	17	0	10	0	0	1	1	.500	0	0-0	0	8.43	8.10
2004	CWS	AL	56	1	0	12	65.1	281	61	45	41	13	0	1	3	30	2	58	8	0	4	4	.500	0	0-2	4	4.84	5.65
2005	CWS	AL	69	0	0	10	60.1	248	38	15	13	1	0	3	4	29	5	58	3	0	4	0	1.000	0	0-2	13	2.03	1.94
2006	CWS	AL	70	0	0	14	54.0	251	64	33	31	12	3	1	3	24	6	43	3	0	1	2	.333	0	1-4	14	6.24	5.17
2007	ChC	NL	16	0	0	4	16.2	76	15	9	9	1	1	2	3	9	0	14	0	0	0	1	.000	0	0-0	2	4.41	4.86
2008	ChC	NL	50	0	0	7	35.2	160	38	18	17	7	3	0	1	13	2	43	3	0	0	2	.000	0	0-2	9	4.87	4.29
2009	ChC	NL	19	0	0	3	11.0	55	14	9	9	3	0	0	1	9	0	9	0	0	0	2	.000	0	0-1	2	9.64	7.36
	Postseason		8	0	0	3	4.0	16	2	0	0	0	0	0	0	2	0	5	0	0	1	0	1.000	0	0-0	2	1.41	0.00
	7 ML YEARS		284	5	0	50	256.1	1140	245	141	132	38	8	7	15	131	15	235	17	0	10	12	.455	0	1-11	44	4.74	4.63

Craig Counsell

Bats: L **Throws**: R **Pos**: 2B-50; 3B-44; SS-27; PH-25; PR-2   **Ht**: 6'0" **Wt**: 179 **Born**: 8/21/1970 **Age**: 39

| | | | | | | | | | BATTING | | | | | | | | | | | | BASERUNNING | | | | AVERAGES | | |
Year	Team	Lg	G	AB	H	2B	3B	HR	(Hm	Rd)	TB	R	RBI	RC	TBB	IBB	SO	HBP	SH	SF	SB	CS	SB%	GDP	Avg	OBP	Slg
1995	Col	NL	3	1	0	0	0	0	(0	0)	0	0	0	0	1	0	0	0	0	0	0	0	-	0	.000	.500	.000
1997	2 Tms	NL	52	164	49	9	2	1	(1	0)	65	20	16	24	18	2	17	3	3	1	1	1	.50	5	.299	.376	.396
1998	Fla	NL	107	335	84	19	5	4	(2	2)	125	43	40	48	51	7	47	4	8	1	3	0	1.00	5	.251	.355	.373
1999	2 Tms	NL	87	174	38	7	0	0	(0	0)	45	24	11	12	14	0	24	0	5	2	1	0	1.00	2	.218	.274	.259
2000	Ari	NL	67	152	48	8	1	2	(0	2)	64	23	11	25	20	0	18	2	1	1	3	3	.50	4	.316	.400	.421
2001	Ari	NL	141	458	126	22	3	4	(4	0)	166	76	38	61	61	3	76	2	6	6	8	4	.43	9	.275	.359	.362
2002	Ari	NL	112	436	123	22	1	2	(0	2)	153	63	51	65	45	3	52	1	4	3	7	5	.58	10	.282	.348	.351
2003	Ari	NL	89	303	71	6	3	3	(3	0)	92	40	21	29	41	0	32	2	3	2	11	4	.73	4	.234	.320	.304
2004	Mil	NL	140	473	114	19	6	2	(1	1)	149	59	23	48	59	9	88	5	5	3	17	4	.81	5	.241	.330	.315
2005	Ari	NL	160	578	148	34	4	9	(5	4)	217	95	42	80	70	4	69	8	2	4	26	7	.79	8	.256	.350	.375
2006	Ari	NL	105	372	95	14	4	4	(3	1)	129	58	30	45	31	0	47	9	2	1	15	8	.65	1	.255	.327	.347
2007	Mil	NL	122	282	62	12	2	3	(0	3)	87	31	24	29	41	4	47	3	6	2	4	2	.67	7	.220	.323	.309
2008	Mil	NL	110	248	56	14	1	1	(1	0)	75	31	14	26	46	1	42	5	1	2	3	1	.75	5	.226	.355	.302
2009	Mil	NL	130	404	115	22	8	4	(2	2)	165	61	39	57	42	0	54	6	3	4	3	4	.43	12	.285	.357	.408
97	Col	NL	1	0	0	0	0	0	(0	0)	0	0	0	0	0	0	0	0	0	0	0	0	-	0			
97	Fla	Nl	51	164	49	9	2	1	(1	0)	65	20	16	24	18	2	17	3	3	1	1	1	.50	5	.299	.376	.396
99	Fla	NL	37	66	10	1	0	0	(0	0)	11	4	2	1	5	0	10	0	2	0	0	0	-	1	.152	.211	.167
99	LAD	NL	50	108	28	6	0	0	(0	0)	34	20	9	11	9	0	14	0	3	2	1	0	1.00	1	.259	.311	.315
	Postseason		35	114	27	5	0	2	(1	1)	38	12	14	11	12	3	23	1	7	1	2	0	1.00	1	.237	.313	.333
	14 ML YEARS		1415	4380	1129	208	39	39	(22	17)	1532	612	360	549	548	33	613	50	49	32	100	47	.68	77	.258	.345	.350

Jesse Crain

Pitches: R **Bats**: R **Pos**: RP-56   **Ht**: 6'1" **Wt**: 215 **Born**: 7/5/1981 **Age**: 28

| | | | HOW MUCH HE PITCHED | | | | | | WHAT HE GAVE UP | | | | | | | | | | | THE RESULTS | | | | | | |
Year	Team	Lg	G	GS	CG	GF	IP	BFP	H	R	ER	HR	SH	SF	HB	TBB	IBB	SO	WP	Bk	W	L	Pct	Sh	Sv-Op	Hld	ERC	ERA
2009	Roch*	AAA	12	0	0	2	17.2	71	13	5	5	0	0	0	0	8	0	22	3	0	1	0	1.000	0	1--	-	2.30	2.55
2004	Min	AL	22	0	0	3	27.0	109	17	6	6	2	1	0	1	12	1	14	1	0	3	0	1.000	0	0-1	2	2.25	2.00
2005	Min	AL	75	0	0	17	79.2	326	61	28	24	6	9	3	5	29	7	25	2	0	12	5	.706	0	1-4	11	2.66	2.71
2006	Min	Al	68	0	0	24	76.2	325	79	31	30	6	1	2	2	18	2	60	1	0	4	5	.444	0	1-4	10	3.48	3.52
2007	Min	AL	18	0	0	5	16.1	71	19	16	10	4	0	1	1	4	0	10	0	1	1	2	.333	0	0-0	6	5.73	5.51
2008	Min	AL	66	0	0	14	62.2	268	62	29	25	6	0	2	1	24	3	50	2	0	5	4	.556	0	0-3	17	3.93	3.59
2009	Min	AL	56	0	0	15	51.2	230	48	28	27	3	3	3	5	27	3	43	1	1	7	4	.636	0	0-0	4	4.12	4.70
	Postseason		3	0	0	0	1.1	10	4	3	1	1	0	0	0	1	0	1	0	0	0	0	-	0	0-0	0	24.65	6.75
	6 ML YEARS		305	0	0	78	314.0	1329	286	138	122	27	14	11	15	114	16	202	7	2	32	20	.615	0	2-12	50	3.46	3.50

Carl Crawford

Bats: L **Throws**: L **Pos**: LF-154; PH-5; DH-1; PR-1   **Ht**: 6'2" **Wt**: 215 **Born**: 8/5/1981 **Age**: 28

| | | | | | | | | | BATTING | | | | | | | | | | | | BASERUNNING | | | | AVERAGES | | |
Year	Team	Lg	G	AB	H	2B	3B	HR	(Hm	Rd)	TB	R	RBI	RC	TBB	IBB	SO	HBP	SH	SF	SB	CS	SB%	GDP	Avg	OBP	Slg
2002	TB	AL	63	259	67	11	6	2	(1	1)	96	23	30	34	9	0	41	3	6	1	9	5	.64	0	.259	.290	.371
2003	TB	AL	151	630	177	18	9	5	(5	0)	228	80	54	80	26	4	102	1	1	3	55	10	.85	5	.281	.309	.362
2004	TB	AL	152	626	185	26	19	11	(6	5)	282	104	55	96	35	2	81	1	4	6	59	15	.80	2	.296	.331	.450
2005	TB	AL	156	644	194	33	15	15	(5	10)	302	101	81	102	27	1	84	5	5	6	46	8	.85	11	.301	.331	.469
2006	TB	AL	151	600	183	20	16	18	(7	11)	289	89	77	113	37	3	85	4	9	2	58	9	.87	8	.305	.348	.482
2007	TB	AL	143	584	184	37	9	11	(6	5)	272	93	80	97	32	5	112	5	1	2	50	10	.83	11	.315	.355	.466
2008	TB	AL	109	443	121	12	10	8	(3	5)	177	69	57	57	30	1	60	2	0	5	25	7	.78	10	.273	.319	.400
2009	TB	AL	156	606	185	28	8	15	(9	6)	274	96	68	91	51	1	99	8	2	5	60	16	.79	7	.305	.364	.452
	Postseason		16	62	18	3	1	2	(1	1)	29	8	8	11	3	0	10	1	0	0	7	0	1.00	0	.290	.333	.468
	8 ML YEARS		1081	4392	1296	185	92	85	(42	43)	1920	655	502	670	247	17	664	29	28	30	362	80	.82	54	.295	.335	.437

Joe Crede

Bats: R **Throws**: R **Pos**: 3B-84; DH-4; PH-3   **Ht**: 6'2" **Wt**: 230 **Born**: 4/26/1978 **Age**: 32

| | | | | | | | | | BATTING | | | | | | | | | | | | BASERUNNING | | | | AVERAGES | | |
Year	Team	Lg	G	AB	H	2B	3B	HR	(Hm	Rd)	TB	R	RBI	RC	TBB	IBB	SO	HBP	SH	SF	SB	CS	SB%	GDP	Avg	OBP	Slg
2000	CWS	AL	7	14	5	1	0	0	(0	0)	6	2	3	2	0	0	3	0	0	1	0	0	-	1	.357	.333	.429
2001	CWS	AL	17	50	11	1	1	0	(0	0)	14	1	7	4	3	0	11	1	0	1	1	0	1.00	1	.220	.273	.280
2002	CWS	AL	53	200	57	10	0	12	(7	5)	103	28	35	31	8	0	40	0	0	1	0	2	.00	1	.285	.311	.515
2003	CWS	AL	151	536	140	31	2	19	(11	8)	232	68	75	69	32	1	75	6	2	4	1	1	.50	11	.261	.308	.433
2004	CWS	AL	144	490	117	25	0	21	(12	9)	205	67	69	58	34	0	81	10	4	5	1	2	.33	14	.239	.299	.418

Year	Team	Lg	G	AB	H	2B	3B	HR	(Hm	Rd)	TB	R	RBI	RC	TBB	IBB	SO	HBP	SH	SF	SB	CS	SB%	GDP	Avg	OBP	Slg
2005	CWS	AL	132	432	109	21	0	22	(12	10)	196	54	62	62	25	3	66	8	2	4	1	1	.80	7	.252	.303	.454
2006	CWS	AL	150	544	154	31	0	30	(16	14)	275	76	94	84	28	1	58	7	0	7	0	2	.00	18	.283	.323	.506
2007	CWS	AL	47	167	36	5	0	4	(0	4)	53	13	22	18	10	0	24	0	0	1	0	1	.00	1	.216	.258	.317
2008	CWS	AL	97	335	83	18	1	17	(11	6)	154	41	55	45	30	0	45	4	0	4	0	3	.00	10	.248	.314	.460
2009	Min	AL	90	333	75	16	1	15	(10	5)	138	42	48	35	29	1	56	2	0	3	0	0	-	6	.225	.289	.414
	Postseason		12	45	13	3	0	4	(2	2)	28	6	11	9	2	0	6	1	1	1	0	1	.00	0	.289	.327	.622
	10 ML YEARS		888	3101	787	159	5	140	(79	61)	1376	392	470	408	199	6	459	38	8	31	4	12	.25	69	.254	.304	.444

Coco Crisp

Bats: B **Throws:** R **Pos:** CF-49   **Ht:** 6'0" **Wt:** 180 **Born:** 11/1/1979 **Age:** 30

Year	Team	Lg	G	AB	H	2B	3B	HR	(Hm	Rd)	TB	R	RBI	RC	TBB	IBB	SO	HBP	SH	SF	SB	CS	SB%	GDP	Avg	OBP	Slg
2002	Cle	AL	32	127	33	9	2	1	(1	0)	49	16	9	19	11	0	19	0	3	2	4	1	.80	0	.260	.314	.386
2003	Cle	AL	99	414	110	15	6	3	(3	0)	146	55	27	48	23	1	51	0	7	3	15	9	.63	4	.266	.302	.353
2004	Cle	AL	139	491	146	24	2	15	(8	7)	219	78	71	72	36	4	69	0	9	2	20	13	.61	8	.297	.344	.446
2005	Cle	AL	145	594	178	42	4	16	(4	12)	276	86	69	92	44	1	81	0	13	5	15	6	.71	7	.300	.345	.465
2006	Bos	AL	105	413	109	22	2	8	(4	4)	159	58	36	51	31	1	67	1	7	0	22	4	.85	5	.264	.317	.385
2007	Bos	AL	145	526	141	28	7	6	(1	5)	201	85	60	68	50	1	84	1	9	5	28	6	.82	12	.268	.330	.382
2008	Bos	AL	118	361	102	18	3	7	(1	6)	147	55	41	49	35	0	59	1	8	4	20	7	.74	6	.283	.344	.407
2009	KC	AL	49	180	41	8	5	3	(0	3)	68	30	14	25	29	1	23	1	4	1	13	2	.87	4	.228	.336	.378
	Postseason		20	57	16	3	0	0	(0	0)	19	7	3	6	6	0	12	0	0	0	3	0	1.00	3	.281	.349	.333
	8 ML YEARS		832	3106	860	166	31	59	(22	37)	1265	463	327	424	259	9	453	4	60	22	137	48	.74	46	.277	.331	.407

Bobby Crosby

Bats: R **Throws:** R **Pos:** 1B-54; 3B-42; PR-7; SS-6; 2B-5; PH-5; RF-1; DH-1   **Ht:** 6'3" **Wt:** 203 **Born:** 1/12/1980 **Age:** 30

Year	Team	Lg	G	AB	H	2B	3B	HR	(Hm	Rd)	TB	R	RBI	RC	TBB	IBB	SO	HBP	SH	SF	SB	CS	SB%	GDP	Avg	OBP	Slg
2003	Oak	AL	11	12	0	0	0	0	(0	0)	0	1	0	0	1	0	5	1	0	0	0	0	-	0	.000	.143	.000
2004	Oak	AL	151	545	130	34	1	22	(11	11)	232	70	64	60	58	0	141	9	5	6	7	3	.70	20	.239	.319	.426
2005	Oak	AL	84	333	92	25	4	9	(3	6)	152	66	38	47	35	0	54	1	1	1	0	0	-	10	.276	.346	.456
2006	Oak	AL	96	358	82	12	0	9	(3	6)	121	42	40	38	36	1	76	0	2	2	8	1	.89	11	.229	.298	.338
2007	Oak	AL	93	349	79	16	0	8	(7	1)	119	40	31	26	23	1	62	2	0	0	10	2	.83	11	.226	.278	.341
2008	Oak	AL	145	556	132	39	1	7	(2	5)	194	66	61	52	47	0	96	0	0	2	7	3	.70	18	.237	.296	.349
2009	Oak	AL	97	238	53	10	2	6	(2	4)	85	35	29	21	24	0	44	2	4	4	2	1	.67	7	.223	.295	.357
	7 ML YEARS		677	2391	568	136	8	61	(28	33)	903	320	263	244	224	2	478	15	12	15	34	10	.77	77	.238	.305	.378

Trevor Crowe

Bats: B **Throws:** R **Pos:** LF-32; CF-30; PR-7; RF-5; PH-2   **Ht:** 6'0" **Wt:** 190 **Born:** 11/17/1983 **Age:** 26

Year	Team	Lg	G	AB	H	2B	3B	HR	(Hm	Rd)	TB	R	RBI	RC	TBB	IBB	SO	HBP	SH	SF	SB	CS	SB%	GDP	Avg	OBP	Slg
2005	MhVlly	A-	12	51	13	2	1	1	(-	-)	20	9	6	7	6	0	8	1	0	0	4	3	.57	0	.255	.345	.392
2005	Lk Cty	A	44	178	46	8	2	0	(-	-)	58	18	23	20	18	1	25	1	0	2	7	5	.58	4	.258	.327	.326
2005	Akron	AA	3	10	1	0	0	0	(-	-)	1	1	0	0	0	0	3	0	0	0	0	0	-	0	.100	.100	.100
2006	Knstn	A+	60	219	72	15	2	4	(-	-)	103	51	31	53	48	0	46	2	1	3	29	6	.83	6	.329	.449	.470
2006	Lk Cty	A	2	5	0	0	0	0	(-	-)	0	0	0	0	0	0	1	0	0	0	0	0	-	0	.000	.000	.000
2006	Akron	AA	39	154	36	7	2	1	(-	-)	50	20	13	18	20	1	24	0	0	2	16	6	.73	6	.234	.318	.325
2007	Akron	AA	133	518	134	26	4	5	(-	-)	183	87	50	70	62	3	71	4	2	3	28	9	.76	15	.259	.341	.353
2008	Akron	AA	49	198	64	16	2	4	(-	-)	96	45	28	40	27	1	29	1	1	2	13	5	.72	3	.323	.404	.485
2008	Buffalo	AAA	35	146	40	12	2	5	(-	-)	71	25	13	25	15	1	43	2	1	0	5	2	.71	0	.274	.350	.486
2009	Clmbs	AAA	49	185	55	11	1	2	(-	-)	74	27	20	32	30	2	31	2	2	0	14	7	.67	5	.297	.401	.400
2009	Cle	AL	68	183	43	9	3	1	(0	1)	61	22	17	18	11	0	39	1	4	3	6	0	1.00	7	.235	.278	.333

Juan Cruz

Pitches: R **Bats:** R **Pos:** RP-46   **Ht:** 6'2" **Wt:** 165 **Born:** 10/15/1978 **Age:** 31

| | | | HOW MUCH HE PITCHED | | | | | | WHAT HE GAVE UP | | | | | | | | | | THE RESULTS | | | | | | |
Year	Team	Lg	G	GS	CG	GF	IP	BFP	H	R	ER	HR	SH	SF	HB	TBB	IBB	SO	WP	Bk	W	L	Pct	Sh	Sv-Op	Hld	ERC	ERA
2001	ChC	NL	8	8	0	0	44.2	185	40	16	16	4	2	0	2	17	1	39	0	0	3	1	.750	0	0-0	0	3.59	3.22
2002	ChC	NL	45	9	0	14	97.1	431	84	56	43	11	7	8	8	59	4	81	1	0	3	11	.214	0	1-4	3	4.49	3.98
2003	ChC	NL	25	6	0	3	61.0	284	66	44	41	7	7	2	7	28	0	65	4	0	2	7	.222	0	0-1	1	5.23	6.05
2004	Atl	NL	50	0	0	22	72.0	300	59	24	22	7	4	1	2	30	1	70	1	0	6	2	.750	0	0-0	2	3.25	2.75
2005	Oak	AL	28	0	0	14	32.2	159	38	33	27	5	0	2	4	22	4	34	3	0	0	3	.000	0	0-0	0	6.87	7.44
2006	Ari	NL	31	15	0	5	94.2	413	80	45	44	7	5	4	11	47	2	88	2	0	5	6	.455	0	0-0	0	3.82	4.18
2007	Ari	NL	53	0	0	15	61.0	262	45	28	21	7	2	2	5	32	3	87	1	2	6	1	.857	0	0-0	4	3.43	3.10
2008	Ari	NL	57	0	0	10	51.2	215	34	17	15	5	2	2	3	31	0	71	1	0	4	0	1.000	0	0-2	8	3.25	2.61
2009	KC	AL	46	0	0	18	50.1	219	46	34	32	6	1	1	1	29	1	38	6	0	3	4	.429	0	2-6	7	4.55	5.72
	Postseason		8	0	0	2	9.0	44	7	5	4	0	1	0	1	8	0	15	1	0	0	0	-	0	0-0	0	4.12	4.00
	9 ML YEARS		343	38	0	101	565.1	2468	492	297	261	59	30	20	43	295	16	573	19	2	32	35	.478	0	3-13	25	4.12	4.16

Luis Cruz

Bats: R **Throws:** R **Pos:** SS-17; 2B-5; PH-5   **Ht:** 6'1" **Wt:** 213 **Born:** 2/10/1984 **Age:** 26

								BATTING												BASERUNNING				AVERAGES		
Year	Team	Lg	G	AB	H	2B	3B	HR	(Hm | Rd)	TB	R	RBI	RC	TBB	IBB	SO	HBP	SH	SF	SB	CS	SB%	GDP	Avg	OBP	Slg
2001	RedSx	R	53	197	51	9	0	3	(- | -)	69	18	18	18	7	0	17	1	0	2	1	4	.20	8	.259	.285	.350
2002	Augsta	A	58	202	38	7	1	3	(- | -)	56	16	15	10	9	0	30	0	1	2	0	2	.00	6	.188	.221	.277
2002	RedSx	R	21	72	21	4	0	0	(- | -)	25	10	9	8	3	0	6	1	1	0	2	2	.50	1	.292	.329	.347
2003	FtWyn	A	129	481	111	24	1	8	(- | -)	161	55	53	47	30	1	55	5	5	8	2	2	.50	15	.231	.279	.335
2004	Lk Els	A+	124	512	142	35	3	8	(- | -)	207	75	72	64	24	1	56	3	6	6	3	7	.30	9	.277	.310	.404
2005	Mobile	AA	44	151	24	2	1	3	(- | -)	37	14	6	6	9	0	31	2	1	1	0	1	.00	7	.159	.215	.245
2006	Mobile	AA	130	499	130	35	3	12	(- | -)	207	65	65	64	29	1	62	2	5	4	8	4	.67	11	.261	.301	.415
2007	Portlnd	AAA	46	156	26	10	1	5	(- | -)	53	15	17	11	9	1	24	1	0	2	0	0	-	5	.167	.214	.340
2007	SnAnt	AA	69	238	60	10	0	4	(- | -)	82	24	10	25	13	2	20	2	0	3	3	0	1.00	5	.252	.293	.345
2008	Altna	AA	105	375	99	24	1	6	(- | -)	143	41	46	44	19	0	34	4	4	4	3	3	.50	7	.264	.303	.381
2008	Indy	AAA	32	120	39	10	0	3	(- | -)	58	19	15	18	3	1	14	1	3	0	2	4	.33	4	.325	.347	.483
2009	Indy	AAA	66	229	58	15	0	3	(- | -)	82	28	23	22	6	1	26	1	0	1	3	3	.50	5	.253	.274	.358
2008	Pit	NL	22	67	15	3	0	0	(0 | 0)	18	6	3	4	3	0	2	2	2	0	1	1	.50	3	.224	.278	.269
2009	Pit	NL	27	70	15	1	0	0	(0 | 0)	16	5	2	3	6	1	7	1	0	1	0	0	-	1	.214	.282	.229
	2 ML YEARS		49	137	30	4	0	0	(0 | 0)	34	11	5	7	9	1	9	3	2	1	1	1	.50	4	.219	.280	.248

Nelson Cruz

Bats: R **Throws:** R **Pos:** RF-120; DH-5; PH-4; LF-2   **Ht:** 6'3" **Wt:** 230 **Born:** 7/1/1980 **Age:** 29

								BATTING												BASERUNNING				AVERAGES		
Year	Team	Lg	G	AB	H	2B	3B	HR	(Hm | Rd)	TB	R	RBI	RC	TBB	IBB	SO	HBP	SH	SF	SB	CS	SB%	GDP	Avg	OBP	Slg
2009	Okla*	AAA	3	10	0	0	0	0	(- | -)	0	0	0	0	1	0	5	0	0	0	1	0	1.00	0	.000	.091	.000
2005	Mil	NL	8	5	1	1	0	0	(0 | 0)	2	1	0	1	2	0	0	0	0	0	0	0	-	0	.200	.429	.400
2006	Tex	AL	41	130	29	3	0	6	(3 | 3)	50	15	22	18	7	0	32	0	0	1	1	0	1.00	1	.223	.261	.385
2007	Tex	AL	96	307	72	16	2	9	(4 | 5)	118	35	34	32	21	1	87	2	1	1	2	4	.33	5	.235	.287	.384
2008	Tex	AL	31	115	38	8	1	7	(4 | 3)	70	19	20	33	17	2	28	1	0	0	3	1	.75	1	.330	.421	.609
2009	Tex	AL	128	462	120	21	1	33	(18 | 15)	242	75	76	72	49	8	118	2	0	2	20	4	.83	9	.260	.332	.524
	5 ML YEARS		304	1019	260	49	4	55	(29 | 26)	482	145	158	153	96	9	265	5	1	4	26	9	.74	16	.255	.321	.473

Michael Cuddyer

Bats: R **Throws:** R **Pos:** RF-117; 1B-34; CF-3; DH-3; PH-2; 2B-1   **Ht:** 6'2" **Wt:** 215 **Born:** 3/27/1979 **Age:** 31

								BATTING												BASERUNNING				AVERAGES		
Year	Team	Lg	G	AB	H	2B	3B	HR	(Hm | Rd)	TB	R	RBI	RC	TBB	IBB	SO	HBP	SH	SF	SB	CS	SB%	GDP	Avg	OBP	Slg
2001	Min	AL	8	18	4	2	0	0	(0 | 0)	6	1	1	2	2	0	6	0	0	0	1	0	1.00	1	.222	.300	.333
2002	Min	AL	41	112	29	7	0	4	(2 | 2)	48	12	13	14	8	0	30	1	1	1	2	0	1.00	3	.259	.311	.429
2003	Min	AL	35	102	25	1	3	4	(1 | 3)	44	14	8	10	12	0	19	0	0	0	1	1	.50	6	.245	.325	.431
2004	Min	AL	115	339	89	22	1	12	(8 | 4)	149	49	45	51	37	2	74	3	2	1	5	5	.50	8	.263	.339	.440
2005	Min	AL	126	422	111	25	3	12	(8 | 4)	178	55	42	43	41	5	93	3	1	3	3	4	.43	19	.263	.330	.422
2006	Min	AL	150	557	158	41	5	24	(15 | 9)	281	102	109	101	62	5	130	10	0	6	6	0	1.00	11	.284	.362	.504
2007	Min	AL	144	547	151	28	5	16	(8 | 8)	237	87	81	82	64	1	107	7	0	5	5	0	1.00	19	.276	.356	.433
2008	Min	AL	71	249	62	13	4	3	(1 | 2)	92	30	36	37	25	4	40	5	0	0	5	1	.83	7	.249	.330	.369
2009	Min	AL	153	588	162	34	7	32	(18 | 14)	306	93	94	89	54	3	118	6	0	2	6	1	.86	22	.276	.342	.520
	Postseason		16	49	17	1	1	1	(1 | 0)	23	4	5	2	4	1	12	0	0	0	0	2	.00	1	.347	.396	.469
	9 ML YEARS		843	2934	791	173	28	107	(61 | 46)	1341	443	429	429	305	20	617	35	4	18	34	12	.74	96	.270	.344	.457

Johnny Cueto

Pitches: R **Bats:** R **Pos:** SP-30   **Ht:** 5'10" **Wt:** 201 **Born:** 2/15/1986 **Age:** 24

				HOW MUCH HE PITCHED						WHAT HE GAVE UP										THE RESULTS						
Year	Team	Lg	G	GS	CG	GF	IP	BFP	H	R	ER	HR	SH	SF	HB	TBB	IBB	SO	WP	Bk	W	L	Pct	Sh	Sv-Op	Hld	ERC	ERA
2005	Reds	R	13	6	0	4	43.0	191	49	31	24	2	2	4	5	8	0	38	1	4	2	2	.500	0	1- -	-	3.99	5.02
2005	Srsota	A+	2	1	0	0	6.0	25	5	2	2	0	0	0	0	2	0	6	2	0	0	1	.000	0	0- -	-	2.26	3.00
2006	Dayton	A	14	14	2	0	76.1	292	52	22	22	5	1	0	4	15	0	82	1	0	8	1	.889	2	0- -	-	1.76	2.59
2006	Srsota	A+	12	12	1	0	61.2	255	48	25	24	6	1	1	6	23	0	61	3	3	7	2	.778	1	0- -	-	3.16	3.50
2007	Srsota	A+	14	14	1	0	78.1	332	72	34	29	3	2	2	5	21	0	72	0	2	4	5	.444	0	0- -	-	2.91	3.33
2007	Lsvlle	AAA	4	4	0	0	22.0	89	22	5	5	2	0	2	2	2	0	21	0	0	2	1	.667	0	0- -	-	3.23	2.05
2007	Chatt	AA	10	10	0	0	61.0	252	52	24	21	6	4	4	8	11	0	77	2	1	6	3	.667	0	0- -	-	2.91	3.10
2008	Cin	NL	31	31	0	0	174.0	769	178	101	93	29	9	5	14	68	1	158	6	1	9	14	.391	0	0-0	0	4.95	4.81
2009	Cin	NL	30	30	0	0	171.1	740	172	90	84	24	5	3	14	61	0	132	4	0	11	11	.500	0	0-0	0	4.57	4.41
	2 ML YEARS		61	61	0	0	345.1	1509	350	191	177	53	14	8	28	129	1	290	10	1	20	25	.444	0	0-0	0	4.76	4.61

Aaron Cunningham

Bats: R **Throws:** R **Pos:** RF-16; LF-9; PH-1; PR-1   **Ht:** 5'11" **Wt:** 203 **Born:** 4/24/1986 **Age:** 24

								BATTING												BASERUNNING				AVERAGES		
Year	Team	Lg	G	AB	H	2B	3B	HR	(Hm | Rd)	TB	R	RBI	RC	TBB	IBB	SO	HBP	SH	SF	SB	CS	SB%	GDP	Avg	OBP	Slg
2005	Bristol	R+	56	222	70	10	2	5	(- | -)	99	41	25	40	16	0	45	14	0	3	6	5	.55	3	.315	.392	.446
2005	Knapol	A-	10	26	3	0	0	0	(- | -)	3	7	2	0	3	0	7	0	0	0	1	0	1.00	0	.115	.207	.115
2006	Knapol	A	95	341	104	26	3	11	(- | -)	169	58	41	66	34	1	72	13	11	3	19	10	.66	4	.305	.386	.496
2007	WinSa	A+	67	252	74	12	5	8	(- | -)	120	51	37	49	34	0	39	4	8	8	22	8	.73	4	.294	.376	.476
2007	Visalia	A+	29	123	44	11	2	3	(- | -)	68	25	20	25	5	0	23	2	3	2	5	3	.63	2	.358	.386	.553
2007	Mobile	AA	31	118	34	8	3	5	(- | -)	63	25	20	21	12	0	27	2	0	0	1	3	.25	1	.288	.364	.534
2008	Mdland	AA	87	347	110	18	6	12	(- | -)	176	65	52	70	38	1	92	5	5	6	12	4	.75	3	.317	.386	.507
2008	Scrmto	AAA	20	76	29	5	0	5	(- | -)	49	21	14	21	11	0	16	1	0	1	3	1	.75	1	.382	.461	.645

BATTING

Year	Team	Lg	G	AB	H	2B	3B	HR	(Hm	Rd)	TB	R	RBI	RC	TBB	IBB	SO	HBP	SH	SF	SB	CS	SB%	GDP	Avg	OBP	Slg
2009	Scrmto	AAA	83	334	101	24	1	11	(-	-)	160	62	48	61	33	0	74	5	1	2	11	4	.73	5	.302	.372	.479
2008	Oak	AL	22	80	20	7	1	1	(1	0)	32	7	14	12	6	1	24	1	0	0	2	0	1.00	1	.250	.310	.400
2009	Oak	AL	23	53	8	2	0	1	(0	1)	13	6	6	3	3	0	16	1	0	0	0	0	-	3	.151	.211	.245
	2 ML YEARS		45	133	28	9	1	2	(1	1)	45	13	20	15	9	1	40	2	0	0	2	0	1.00	4	.211	.271	.338

Jack Cust

Bats: L **Throws:** R **Pos:** DH-96; RF-51; PH-3 **Ht:** 6'1" **Wt:** 240 **Born:** 1/7/1979 **Age:** 31

BATTING

Year	Team	Lg	G	AB	H	2B	3B	HR	(Hm	Rd)	TB	R	RBI	RC	TBB	IBB	SO	HBP	SH	SF	SB	CS	SB%	GDP	Avg	OBP	Slg
2001	Ari	NL	3	2	1	0	0	0	(0	0)	1	0	0	1	1	0	0	0	0	0	0	0	-	0	.500	.667	.500
2002	Col	NL	35	65	11	2	0	1	(0	1)	16	8	8	6	12	0	32	0	0	1	0	1	.00	3	.169	.295	.246
2003	Bal	AL	27	73	19	7	0	4	(2	2)	38	7	11	17	10	0	25	1	0	0	0	0	-	0	.260	.357	.521
2004	Bal	AL	1	1	0	0	0	0	(0	0)	0	0	0	0	0	0	1	0	0	0	0	0	-	0	.000	.000	.000
2006	SD	NL	4	3	1	0	0	0	(0	0)	1	1	0	0	0	0	1	0	0	0	0	0	-	0	.333	.333	.333
2007	Oak	AL	124	395	101	18	1	26	(14	12)	199	61	82	87	105	2	164	1	0	6	0	2	.00	6	.256	.408	.504
2008	Oak	AL	148	481	111	19	0	33	(20	13)	229	77	77	84	111	3	197	2	0	4	0	0	-	7	.231	.375	.476
2009	Oak	AL	149	513	123	16	0	25	(14	11)	214	88	70	83	93	5	185	2	0	4	4	1	.80	7	.240	.356	.417
	8 ML YEARS		491	1533	367	62	1	89	(50	39)	698	242	248	278	332	10	605	6	0	15	4	4	.50	23	.239	.374	.455

Matt Daley

Pitches: R **Bats:** R **Pos:** RP-57 **Ht:** 6'2" **Wt:** 175 **Born:** 6/23/1982 **Age:** 28

			HOW MUCH HE PITCHED					WHAT HE GAVE UP											THE RESULTS						
Year	Team	Lg	G	GS	CG	GF	IP	BFP	H	R	ER	HR	SH	SF	HB	TBB	IBB	SO	WP	Bk	W	L	Pct	Sh	Sv-Op Hld	ERC	ERA
2004	Casper	R+	21	0	0	7	30.1	131	31	19	16	3	0	0	4	5	1	30	1	0	2	1	.667	0	0- -	3.65	4.75
2005	Ashvll	A	45	0	0	21	82.1	349	90	46	35	10	2	3	12	16	0	49	5	0	8	2	.800	0	1- -	4.64	3.83
2006	Mdest	A+	51	0	0	27	68.2	298	70	27	24	3	0	3	4	20	0	79	3	0	4	3	.571	0	15- -	3.53	3.15
2006	Tulsa	AA	3	0	0	1	6.1	24	4	1	1	0	1	0	0	3	0	2	0	0	0	0	-	0	0- -	1.99	1.42
2007	Tulsa	AA	43	10	0	7	95.1	400	83	40	37	12	2	5	6	22	3	84	3	0	2	6	.250	0	0- -	3.00	3.49
2008	Tulsa	AA	3	0	0	0	4.0	18	5	1	1	0	0	0	0	1	0	4	0	0	0	0	-	0	0- -	4.05	2.25
2008	ColSpr	AAA	60	0	0	17	62.1	278	56	27	26	6	2	6	5	33	3	61	5	0	4	6	.400	0	1- -	4.17	3.75
2009	ColSpr	AAA	7	0	0	1	10.0	38	8	1	1	0	0	0	0	1	0	19	0	0	0	0	-	0	0- -	1.52	0.90
2009	Col	NL	57	0	0	15	51.0	211	43	24	24	6	2	3	2	18	2	55	0	0	1	1	.500	0	0-3 12	3.27	4.24

Johnny Damon

Bats: L **Throws:** L **Pos:** LF-133; PH-8; DH-4 **Ht:** 6'2" **Wt:** 205 **Born:** 11/5/1973 **Age:** 36

BATTING

Year	Team	Lg	G	AB	H	2B	3B	HR	(Hm	Rd)	TB	R	RBI	RC	TBB	IBB	SO	HBP	SH	SF	SB	CS	SB%	GDP	Avg	OBP	Slg
1995	KC	AL	47	188	53	11	5	3	(1	2)	83	32	23	29	12	0	22	1	2	3	7	0	1.00	2	.282	.324	.441
1996	KC	AL	145	517	140	22	5	6	(3	3)	190	61	50	64	31	3	64	3	10	5	25	5	.83	4	.271	.313	.368
1997	KC	AL	146	472	130	12	8	8	(3	5)	182	70	48	63	42	2	70	3	6	1	16	10	.62	3	.275	.338	.386
1998	KC	AL	161	642	178	30	10	18	(11	7)	282	104	66	98	58	4	84	4	3	3	26	12	.68	4	.277	.339	.439
1999	KC	AL	145	583	179	39	9	14	(5	9)	278	101	77	108	67	5	50	3	3	4	36	6	.86	13	.307	.379	.477
2000	KC	AL	159	655	214	42	10	16	(10	6)	324	136	88	129	65	4	60	1	8	12	46	9	.84	7	.327	.382	.495
2001	Oak	AL	155	644	165	34	4	9	(2	7)	234	108	49	79	61	1	70	5	5	4	27	12	.69	7	.256	.324	.363
2002	Bos	AL	154	623	178	34	11	14	(5	9)	276	118	63	101	65	5	70	6	3	5	31	6	.84	4	.286	.356	.443
2003	Bos	AL	145	608	166	32	6	12	(5	7)	246	103	67	92	68	4	74	2	6	6	30	6	.83	5	.273	.345	.405
2004	Bos	AL	150	621	189	35	6	20	(9	11)	296	123	94	115	76	1	71	2	0	3	19	8	.70	8	.304	.380	.477
2005	Bos	AL	148	624	197	35	6	10	(3	7)	274	117	75	105	53	3	69	2	0	9	18	1	.95	5	.316	.366	.439
2006	NYY	AL	149	593	169	35	5	24	(13	11)	286	115	80	99	67	1	85	4	2	5	25	10	.71	4	.285	.359	.482
2007	NYY	AL	141	533	144	27	2	12	(5	7)	211	93	63	84	66	1	79	2	1	3	27	3	.90	4	.270	.351	.396
2008	NYY	AL	143	555	168	27	5	17	(7	10)	256	95	71	109	64	0	82	1	2	1	29	8	.78	6	.303	.375	.461
2009	NYY	AL	143	550	155	36	3	24	(17	7)	269	107	82	97	71	1	98	2	2	1	12	0	1.00	5	.282	.365	.489
	Postseason		40	180	50	9	2	7	(3	4)	84	26	21	26	12	0	27	1	0	0	10	1	.91	5	.278	.326	.467
	15 ML YEARS		2131	8408	2425	451	95	207	(99	108)	3687	1483	996	1372	866	35	1048	41	53	65	374	96	.80	85	.288	.355	.439

John Danks

Pitches: L **Bats:** L **Pos:** SP-32 **Ht:** 6'1" **Wt:** 205 **Born:** 4/15/1985 **Age:** 25

			HOW MUCH HE PITCHED					WHAT HE GAVE UP											THE RESULTS						
Year	Team	Lg	G	GS	CG	GF	IP	BFP	H	R	ER	HR	SH	SF	HB	TBB	IBB	SO	WP	Bk	W	L	Pct	Sh	Sv-Op Hld	ERC	ERA
2007	CWS	AL	26	26	0	0	139.0	622	160	92	85	28	7	4	4	54	4	109	3	0	6	13	.316	0	0-0 0	5.73	5.50
2008	CWS	AL	33	33	0	0	195.0	804	182	74	72	15	2	2	4	57	1	159	7	0	12	9	.571	0	0-0 0	3.26	3.32
2009	CWS	AL	32	32	1	0	200.1	839	184	89	84	28	5	6	5	73	1	149	1	0	13	11	.542	0	0-0 0	3.89	3.77
	Postseason		1	1	0	0	6.2	30	7	3	3	1	0	0	0	3	0	7	0	0	1	0	1.000	0	0-0 0	4.81	4.05
	3 ML YEARS		91	91	1	0	534.1	2265	526	255	241	71	14	12	13	184	6	417	11	0	31	33	.484	0	0-0 0	4.11	4.06

Daniel Davidson

Pitches: L **Bats:** L **Pos:** RP-4 **Ht:** 6'4" **Wt:** 210 **Born:** 1/8/1981 **Age:** 29

			HOW MUCH HE PITCHED					WHAT HE GAVE UP											THE RESULTS						
Year	Team	Lg	G	GS	CG	GF	IP	BFP	H	R	ER	HR	SH	SF	HB	TBB	IBB	SO	WP	Bk	W	L	Pct	Sh	Sv-Op Hld	ERC	ERA
2003	Provo	R+	15	13	0	0	71.1	294	65	17	13	3	4	1	3	15	0	50	3	0	8	2	.800	0	0- -	2.65	1.64
2004	RCuca	A+	28	28	0	0	163.1	699	196	92	83	15	7	11	9	41	0	121	3	2	12	7	.632	0	0- -	4.94	4.57
2005	Ark	AA	28	26	1	0	154.1	681	178	93	80	22	5	4	5	45	0	110	6	1	13	5	.722	0	0- -	4.92	4.67
2006	Ark	AA	29	16	0	6	113.1	520	146	81	71	13	6	10	4	43	0	62	5	0	2	8	.200	0	0- -	5.96	5.64
2006	Salt Lk	AAA	4	4	1	0	23.1	105	32	16	15	3	0	0	0	6	0	17	1	0	2	3	.333	0	0- -	5.92	5.79
2007	Ark	AA	7	7	0	0	43.2	166	34	14	10	4	1	0	2	8	1	25	0	0	2	4	.333	0	0- -	2.32	2.06

Year	Team	Lg	G	GS	CG	GF	IP	BFP	H	R	ER	HR	SH	SF	HB	TBB	IBB	SO	WP	Bk	W	L	Pct	Sh	Sv-Op	Hld	ERC	ERA
2008	Ark	AA	20	6	0	3	46.0	186	35	15	15	3	2	0	5	15	2	44	4	0	1	0	1.000	0	0--	-	2.71	2.93
2008	Salt Lk	AAA	4	0	0	1	7.2	30	7	2	2	1	1	0	1	0	0	2	0	0	0	0	-	0	0--	-	2.83	2.35
2009	Salt Lk	AAA	45	0	0	6	50.1	239	66	44	41	12	5	2	7	24	2	46	2	0	2	3	.400	0	0--	-	8.10	7.33
2009	LAA	AL	4	0	0	1	1.2	11	3	1	1	0	0	0	0	3	1	0	0	0	0	0	-	0	0-0	0	12.61	5.40

Dave Davidson

Pitches: L **Bats:** L **Pos:** RP-1
Ht: 6'1" **Wt:** 200 **Born:** 4/23/1984 **Age:** 26

Year	Team	Lg	G	GS	CG	GF	IP	BFP	H	R	ER	HR	SH	SF	HB	TBB	IBB	SO	WP	Bk	W	L	Pct	Sh	Sv-Op	Hld	ERC	ERA
2003	Pirates	R	7	0	0	2	7.2	41	10	12	11	0	0	2	4	7	0	8	1	0	0	2	.000	0	0--	-	9.86	12.91
2004	Pirates	R	7	1	0	2	18.1	89	16	11	7	0	1	1	5	14	0	24	2	0	1	0	1.000	0	0--	-	4.94	3.44
2005	Hkry	A	10	2	0	3	19.1	96	16	22	21	4	1	0	3	21	0	23	5	0	1	2	.333	0	0--	-	7.41	9.78
2005	Wmspt	A-	5	4	0	0	17.0	72	14	7	6	0	0	0	2	8	0	23	2	0	1	1	.500	0	0--	-	3.19	3.18
2006	Hkry	A	27	0	0	2	56.0	229	39	18	12	2	1	3	4	21	0	72	5	0	2	1	.667	0	0--	-	2.24	1.93
2006	Lynbrg	A+	5	0	0	1	8.1	24	6	2	2	0	0	0	1	2	0	11	1	0	0	0	-	0	0--	-	2.83	2.16
2006	Altna	AA	10	1	0	3	11.2	53	8	4	3	0	0	0	0	10	1	13	0	1	1	1	.500	0	0--	-	3.10	2.31
2007	Altna	AA	39	0	0	10	59.2	254	45	30	29	3	2	3	4	30	2	55	5	1	3	1	.750	0	2--	-	2.98	4.37
2007	Indy	AAA	6	0	0	0	7.2	33	6	2	1	0	1	0	1	3	0	9	1	0	1	0	1.000	0	0--	-	2.62	1.17
2008	Altna	AA	35	0	0	7	64.2	279	58	27	24	3	3	2	4	36	1	51	6	2	4	2	.667	0	0--	-	4.03	3.34
2009	Indy	AAA	3	0	0	0	4.1	16	3	2	2	0	0	0	0	1	0	4	1	0	1	0	1.000	0	0--	-	1.52	4.15
2009	NewOr	AAA	10	0	0	2	10.2	48	7	5	3	0	2	2	3	4	0	14	0	0	0	0	-	0	0--	-	2.33	2.53
2007	Pit	NL	2	0	0	1	2.0	17	6	6	5	1	0	0	2	2	0	0	0	0	0	0	-	0	0-0	0	29.58	22.50
2009	Fla	NL	1	0	0	0	1.0	11	4	5	5	0	0	0	0	4	0	3	0	0	0	0	-	0	0-0	0	43.35	45.00
	2 ML YEARS		3	0	0	1	3.0	28	10	11	10	1	0	0	2	6	0	3	0	0	0	0	-	0	0-0	0	34.33	30.00

Kyle Davies

Pitches: R **Bats:** R **Pos:** SP-22
Ht: 6'2" **Wt:** 218 **Born:** 9/9/1983 **Age:** 26

Year	Team	Lg	G	GS	CG	GF	IP	BFP	H	R	ER	HR	SH	SF	HB	TBB	IBB	SO	WP	Bk	W	L	Pct	Sh	Sv-Op	Hld	ERC	ERA
2009	Omha*	AAA	8	8	0	0	46.1	195	47	19	11	3	1	2	0	14	0	44	7	0	4	2	.667	0	0--	-	3.56	2.14
2005	Atl	NL	21	14	0	2	87.2	403	98	51	40	8	3	0	1	49	5	62	1	0	7	6	.538	0	0-1	0	5.26	4.03
2006	Atl	NL	11	14	1	0	83.1	312	80	60	59	14	3	2	3	33	2	51	3	0	3	7	.300	0	0-0	0	8.33	8.38
2007	2 Tms		28	28	0	0	136.0	628	155	102	92	22	5	3	5	70	1	99	8	1	7	15	.318	0	0-0	0	5.90	6.09
2008	KC	AL	21	21	0	0	113.0	487	121	57	51	10	1	3	2	43	0	71	8	1	9	7	.563	0	0-0	0	4.46	4.06
2009	KC	AL	22	22	1	0	123.0	538	122	76	72	18	3	4	4	66	1	86	10	0	8	9	.471	0	0-0	0	5.16	5.27
07	Atl	NL	17	17	0	0	86.0	389	92	61	55	12	3	2	2	44	3	59	1	1	4	8	.333	0	0-0	0	5.24	5.76
07	KC	AL	11	11	0	0	50.0	239	63	41	37	10	2	1	3	26	1	40	7	0	3	7	.300	0	0-0	0	7.09	6.66
	5 ML YEARS		106	99	2	2	523.0	2368	586	346	322	72	15	12	15	261	10	360	30	2	34	44	.436	0	0-1	2	5.58	5.54

Chris Davis

Bats: L **Throws:** R **Pos:** 1B-100; 3B-11; DH-4; PH-2
Ht: 6'4" **Wt:** 235 **Born:** 3/17/1986 **Age:** 24

Year	Team	Lg	G	AB	H	2B	3B	HR	(Hm	Rd)	TB	R	RBI	RC	TBB	IBB	SO	HBP	SH	SF	SB	CS	SB%	GDP	Avg	OBP	Slg
2006	Spkane	A-	69	253	70	18	1	15	(-	-)	136	38	42	45	23	2	65	3	0	1	2	3	.40	4	.277	.343	.534
2007	Bkrsfld	A+	99	386	115	28	3	24	(-	-)	221	69	93	73	22	2	123	5	0	5	3	3	.50	8	.298	.340	.573
2007	Frisco	AA	30	109	32	7	0	12	(-	-)	75	21	25	26	13	1	27	1	0	1	0	0	-	0	.294	.371	.688
2008	Frisco	AA	40	186	62	14	0	13	(-	-)	115	43	42	42	13	2	44	1	0	2	5	1	.83	3	.333	.376	.618
2008	Okla	AAA	31	111	37	7	1	10	(-	-)	76	25	31	29	13	1	29	1	0	2	2	0	1.00	3	.333	.402	.685
2009	Okla	AAA	44	165	54	12	1	6	(-	-)	86	27	30	36	25	2	39	2	0	2	0	1	.00	7	.327	.418	.521
2008	Tex	AL	80	295	84	23	2	17	(8	9)	162	51	55	44	20	1	88	1	0	1	1	2	.33	5	.285	.331	.549
2009	Tex	AL	113	391	93	15	1	21	(11	10)	173	48	59	50	24	2	150	2	0	2	0	0	-	6	.238	.284	.442
	2 ML YEARS		193	686	177	38	3	38	(19	19)	335	99	114	94	44	3	238	3	0	3	1	2	.33	11	.258	.304	.488

Doug Davis

Pitches: L **Bats:** R **Pos:** SP-34
Ht: 6'4" **Wt:** 213 **Born:** 9/21/1975 **Age:** 34

Year	Team	Lg	G	GS	CG	GF	IP	BFP	H	R	ER	HR	SH	SF	HB	TBB	IBB	SO	WP	Bk	W	L	Pct	Sh	Sv-Op	Hld	ERC	ERA
1999	Tex	AL	2	0	0	0	2.2	20	12	10	10	3	0	0	0	3	0	3	0	0	0	0	-	0	0-0	0	41.42	33.75
2000	Tex	AL	30	13	1	4	98.2	450	109	61	59	14	6	4	3	58	3	66	5	1	7	6	.538	0	0-3	0	5.93	5.38
2001	Tex	AL	30	30	1	0	186.0	828	220	103	92	14	4	6	3	69	1	115	7	2	11	10	.524	0	0-0	0	4.90	4.45
2002	Tex	AL	10	10	1	0	59.2	262	67	36	33	7	3	3	2	22	0	28	2	2	3	5	.375	1	0-0	0	5.05	4.98
2003	3 Tms		21	20	1	0	109.1	491	123	55	49	16	6	2	1	51	1	62	7	0	7	8	.467	0	0-0	0	5.46	4.03
2004	Mil	NL	34	34	0	0	207.1	880	192	84	78	14	11	5	7	79	3	166	4	1	12	12	.500	0	0-0	0	3.49	3.30
2005	Mil	NL	35	35	2	0	222.2	946	196	103	95	20	12	2	4	93	5	208	3	2	11	11	.500	1	0-0	0	3.62	3.84
2006	Mil	NL	34	34	1	0	203.1	904	206	118	111	19	16	8	5	102	1	159	3	0	11	11	.500	1	0-0	0	4.59	4.91
2007	Ari	NL	33	33	0	0	192.2	862	211	100	91	21	10	2	5	95	7	144	10	1	13	12	.520	0	0-0	0	5.15	4.25
2008	Ari	NL	26	26	0	0	146.0	650	160	76	70	13	10	4	4	64	4	112	7	0	6	8	.429	0	0-0	0	4.77	4.32
2009	Ari	NL	34	34	0	0	203.1	889	203	101	93	25	15	6	4	103	1	146	12	1	9	14	.391	0	0-0	0	4.80	4.12
03	Tex	AL	1	1	0	0	3.0	17	4	4	4	2	0	0	0	4	0	2	0	0	0	0	-	0	0-0	0	15.81	12.00
03	Tor	AL	12	11	0	0	54.0	250	70	33	30	6	3	0	1	26	1	25	6	0	4	6	.400	0	0-0	0	6.39	5.00
03	Mil	NL	8	8	1	0	52.1	224	49	18	15	8	3	2	0	21	0	35	1	0	3	2	.600	0	0-0	0	4.06	2.58
	Postseason		2	2	0	0	10.2	50	10	6	5	1	1	1	0	8	0	13	0	0	1	0	1.000	0	0-0	0	4.94	4.22
	11 ML YEARS		289	269	7	4	1631.2	7182	1699	847	781	172	93	42	39	736	26	1209	60	10	90	97	.481	3	0-3	2	4.64	4.31

Rajai Davis

Bats: R **Throws:** R **Pos:** CF-113; PR-9; PH-8; RF-5; DH-2   **Ht:** 5'11" **Wt:** 195 **Born:** 10/19/1980 **Age:** 29

								BATTING												BASERUNNING				AVERAGES		
Year	Team	Lg	G	AB	H	2B	3B	HR	(Hm | Rd)	TB	R	RBI	RC	TBB	IBB	SO	HBP	SH	SF	SB	CS	SB%	GDP	Avg	OBP	Slg
2006	Pit	NL	20	14	2	1	0	0	(0 | 0)	3	1	0	0	2	0	3	0	1	0	1	3	.25	0	.143	.250	.214
2007	2 Tms	NL	75	190	53	11	2	1	(0 | 1)	71	32	9	26	21	1	28	4	3	1	22	6	.79	1	.279	.361	.374
2008	2 Tms		113	214	52	5	4	3	(0 | 3)	74	30	19	24	8	0	40	1	2	1	29	6	.83	1	.243	.272	.346
2009	Oak	AL	125	390	119	27	5	3	(1 | 2)	165	65	48	63	29	0	70	7	2	4	41	12	.77	12	.305	.360	.423
07	Pit	NL	24	48	13	2	1	0	(0 | 0)	17	6	2	6	7	0	3	0	1	1	5	2	.71	1	.271	.357	.354
07	SF	NL	51	142	40	9	1	1	(0 | 1)	54	26	7	20	14	1	25	4	2	0	17	4	.81	0	.282	.363	.380
08	SF	NL	12	18	1	0	0	0	(0 | 0)	1	2	0	0	1	0	6	0	0	0	4	0	1.00	0	.056	.105	.056
08	Oak	AL	101	196	51	5	4	3	(0 | 3)	73	28	19	24	7	0	34	1	2	1	25	6	.81	1	.260	.288	.372
	4 ML YEARS		333	808	226	44	11	7	(1 | 6)	313	128	76	113	60	1	141	12	8	6	93	27	.78	14	.280	.336	.387

Wade Davis

Pitches: R **Bats:** R **Pos:** SP-6   **Ht:** 6'5" **Wt:** 220 **Born:** 9/7/1985 **Age:** 24

			HOW MUCH HE PITCHED						WHAT HE GAVE UP											THE RESULTS						
Year	Team	Lg	G	GS	CG	GF	IP	BFP	H	R	ER	HR	SH	SF	HB	TBB	IBB	SO	WP	Bk	W	L	Pct	Sh	Sv-Op	Hld	ERC	ERA
2004	Princtn	R+	13	13	0	0	57.2	264	71	46	39	8	1	6	2	19	0	38	3	0	3	5	.375	0	0--	-	5.46	6.09
2005	HudVal	A-	15	15	0	0	86.0	353	75	35	26	5	4	0	5	23	0	97	3	0	7	4	.636	0	0--	-	2.85	2.72
2006	SWMch	A	27	27	1	0	146.0	608	124	61	49	5	0	5	8	64	0	165	4	1	7	12	.368	0	0--	-	3.24	3.02
2007	VeroB	A+	13	13	1	0	78.1	305	54	20	16	5	4	0	4	21	0	88	4	0	3	0	1.000	1	0--	-	2.02	1.84
2007	Mont	AA	14	14	0	0	80.0	340	74	37	28	3	4	5	4	30	0	81	5	0	7	3	.700	0	0--	-	3.34	3.15
2008	Mont	AA	19	19	0	0	107.2	455	104	49	46	7	3	2	9	42	1	81	4	0	9	6	.600	0	0--	-	4.03	3.85
2008	Drham	AAA	9	9	0	0	53.0	221	39	16	16	5	1	2	4	24	1	55	0	0	4	2	.667	0	0--	-	3.09	2.72
2009	Drham	AAA	28	28	0	0	158.2	673	139	71	60	14	2	4	6	60	1	140	7	0	10	8	.556	0	0--	-	3.34	3.40
2009	TB	AL	6	6	1	0	36.1	150	33	19	15	2	0	0	0	13	1	36	1	0	2	2	.500	1	0-0	0	3.12	3.72

Alejandro De Aza

Bats: L **Throws:** L **Pos:** PH-13; LF-6; CF-5; PR-4   **Ht:** 5'11" **Wt:** 189 **Born:** 4/11/1984 **Age:** 26

								BATTING												BASERUNNING				AVERAGES		
Year	Team	Lg	G	AB	H	2B	3B	HR	(Hm	Rd)	TB	R	RBI	RC	TBB	IBB	SO	HBP	SH	SF	SB	CS	SB%	GDP	Avg	OBP	Slg
2002	Ddgrs	R	38	128	29	6	1	1	(-	-)	40	27	14	18	22	0	17	2	2	1	16	2	.89	3	.227	.346	.313
2003	Ogden	R+	55	208	48	11	1	2	(-	-)	67	36	24	26	23	0	34	10	5	0	15	6	.71	2	.231	.336	.322
2004	Clmbs	A	102	341	87	17	2	4	(-	-)	120	63	45	46	38	1	54	10	3	1	24	10	.71	3	.255	.346	.352
2005	Jupiter	A+	123	472	135	24	9	3	(-	-)	186	75	37	75	58	3	87	8	11	5	34	17	.67	8	.286	.370	.394
2006	Carlina	AA	69	230	64	12	2	2	(-	-)	86	40	16	33	21	0	46	4	9	2	28	10	.74	5	.278	.346	.374
2006	Mrlns	R	7	24	11	1	0	0	(-	-)	12	7	4	6	4	0	2	0	0	0	3	2	.60	0	.458	.536	.500
2006	Jupiter	A+	2	7	1	0	1	0	(-	-)	3	1	0	0	0	0	2	0	1	0	1	0	1.00	0	.143	.143	.429
2007	Mrlns	R	4	9	6	2	0	0	(-	-)	8	2	1	4	2	0	1	1	0	0	2	2	.50	0	.667	.750	.889
2007	Jupiter	A+	2	8	4	1	1	0	(-	-)	7	1	0	2	1	0	1	0	0	0	1	0	1.00	0	.500	.556	.875
2007	Carlina	AA	5	20	7	2	0	2	(-	-)	15	7	3	5	3	0	2	0	0	0	0	0	-	0	.350	.435	.750
2009	NewOr	AAA	87	267	80	21	5	8	(-	-)	135	45	34	51	27	0	53	4	7	2	11	5	.69	5	.300	.370	.506
2007	Fla	NL	45	144	33	8	2	0	(0	0)	45	14	8	11	6	1	37	1	5	2	2	0	1.00	2	.229	.261	.313
2009	Fla	NL	22	20	5	1	0	0	(0	0)	6	6	3	4	5	0	5	0	1	1	0	0	-	0	.250	.385	.300
	2 ML YEARS		67	164	38	9	2	0	(0	0)	51	20	11	15	11	1	42	1	6	3	2	0	1.00	2	.232	.279	.311

Eulogio de la Cruz

Pitches: R **Bats:** R **Pos:** RP-3   **Ht:** 5'10" **Wt:** 215 **Born:** 3/12/1984 **Age:** 26

			HOW MUCH HE PITCHED						WHAT HE GAVE UP											THE RESULTS						
Year	Team	Lg	G	GS	CG	GF	IP	BFP	H	R	ER	HR	SH	SF	HB	TBB	IBB	SO	WP	Bk	W	L	Pct	Sh	Sv-Op	Hld	ERC	ERA
2009	Portlnd*	AAA	48	4	0	25	69.1	297	52	26	24	2	2	1	0	44	5	59	11	1	2	6	.250	0	9--	-	3.00	3.12
2007	Det	AL	6	0	0	4	6.2	32	10	8	5	1	0	0	0	4	1	5	3	0	0	0	-	0	0-0	0	8.47	6.75
2008	Fla	NL	6	1	0	1	9.0	53	15	20	18	2	1	1	0	11	0	4	1	0	0	0	-	0	0-0	0	13.08	18.00
2009	SD	NL	3	0	0	2	3.1	17	2	2	2	0	0	1	0	6	0	2	0	0	0	0	-	0	0-0	0	6.55	5.40
	3 ML YEARS		15	1	0	7	19.0	102	27	30	25	3	1	2	0	21	1	11	4	0	0	0	-	0	0-0	0	10.29	11.84

Jorge de la Rosa

Pitches: L **Bats:** L **Pos:** SP-32; RP-1   **Ht:** 6'1" **Wt:** 210 **Born:** 4/5/1981 **Age:** 29

			HOW MUCH HE PITCHED						WHAT HE GAVE UP											THE RESULTS						
Year	Team	Lg	G	GS	CG	GF	IP	BFP	H	R	ER	HR	SH	SF	HB	TBB	IBB	SO	WP	Bk	W	L	Pct	Sh	Sv-Op	Hld	ERC	ERA
2004	Mil	NL	5	5	0	0	22.2	113	29	20	16	1	1	3	1	14	0	5	3	0	0	3	.000	0	0-0	0	6.12	6.35
2005	Mil	NL	38	0	0	13	42.1	208	48	23	21	1	2	2	0	38	4	42	6	0	2	2	.500	0	0-2	5	6.04	4.46
2006	2 Tms		28	13	0	4	79.0	367	81	59	57	14	2	4	2	54	1	67	6	1	5	6	.455	0	0-0	1	6.05	6.49
2007	KC	AL	26	23	0	1	130.0	589	160	88	84	20	2	4	3	53	6	82	4	0	8	12	.400	0	0-0	0	5.93	5.82
2008	Col	NL	28	23	0	0	130.0	571	128	77	71	13	6	7	7	62	3	128	14	1	10	8	.556	0	0-0	0	4.50	4.92
2009	Col	NL	33	32	0	0	185.0	799	172	95	90	20	11	6	9	83	3	193	12	1	16	9	.640	0	0-0	0	4.11	4.38
06	Mil	NL	18	3	0	4	30.1	146	32	30	29	4	1	3	1	22	1	31	4	0	2	2	.500	0	0-0	1	5.90	8.60
06	KC	AL	10	10	0	0	48.2	221	49	29	28	10	1	1	1	32	0	36	2	1	3	4	.429	0	0-0	0	6.14	5.18
	6 ML YEARS		158	96	0	18	589.0	2647	618	362	339	69	24	26	22	304	17	517	45	4	41	40	.506	0	0-2	6	5.06	5.18

David DeJesus

Bats: L Throws: L Pos: LF-139; CF-3; RF-2; PH-1   Ht: 6'0" Wt: 190 Born: 12/20/1979 Age: 30

Year	Team	Lg	G	AB	H	2B	3B	HR	(Hm	Rd)	TB	R	RBI	RC	TBB	IBB	SO	HBP	SH	SF	SB	CS	SB%	GDP	Avg	OBP	Slg
2003	KC	AL	12	7	2	0	1	0	(0	0)	4	0	0	2	1	0	2	1	1	0	0	0	-	0	.286	.444	.571
2004	KC	AL	96	363	104	15	3	7	(2	5)	146	58	39	53	33	0	53	9	8	0	8	11	.42	6	.287	.360	.402
2005	KC	AL	122	461	135	31	6	9	(6	3)	205	69	56	77	42	1	76	9	5	6	5	5	.50	6	.293	.359	.445
2006	KC	AL	119	491	145	36	7	8	(4	4)	219	83	56	76	43	4	70	12	2	4	6	3	.67	10	.295	.364	.446
2007	KC	AL	157	605	157	29	9	7	(3	4)	225	101	58	87	64	7	83	23	7	4	10	4	.71	10	.260	.351	.372
2008	KC	AL	135	518	150	25	7	12	(6	6)	234	70	73	93	46	3	71	5	4	4	11	8	.58	10	.307	.366	.452
2009	KC	AL	144	558	157	28	9	13	(4	9)	242	74	71	83	51	0	87	8	5	5	4	9	.31	10	.281	.347	.434
7 ML YEARS			785	3003	859	164	42	56	(25	31)	1275	455	353	471	280	15	442	67	32	23	44	40	.52	52	.286	.358	.425

Manny Delcarmen

Pitches: R Bats: R Pos: RP-64   Ht: 6'2" Wt: 205 Born: 2/16/1982 Age: 28

Year	Team	Lg	G	GS	CG	GF	IP	BFP	H	R	ER	HR	SH	SF	HB	TBB	IBB	SO	WP	Bk	W	L	Pct	Sh	Sv-Op	Hld	ERC	ERA
2005	Bos	AL	10	0	0	2	9.0	41	8	3	3	0	0	0	1	7	0	9	0	0	0	0	-	0	0-0	0	4.68	3.00
2006	Bos	AL	50	0	0	11	53.1	243	68	32	30	2	3	1	2	17	2	45	0	0	2	0	1.000	0	0-4	14	4.90	5.06
2007	Bos	AL	44	0	0	5	44.0	176	28	11	10	4	2	2	2	17	1	41	0	0	0	0	-	0	1-2	11	2.23	2.05
2008	Bos	AL	73	0	0	16	74.1	307	55	28	27	5	4	4	3	28	1	72	0	0	1	2	.333	0	2-5	18	2.51	3.27
2009	Bos	AL	64	0	0	6	59.2	278	64	34	30	5	2	1	4	34	3	44	1	0	5	2	.714	0	0-3	6	5.16	4.53
Postseason			11	0	0	2	8.2	46	11	11	11	2	0	0	2	8	0	8	0	0	1	0	1.000	0	0-0	1	10.24	11.42
5 ML YEARS			241	0	0	40	240.1	1045	223	108	100	16	11	8	12	103	7	211	1	0	8	4	.667	0	3-14	49	3.66	3.74

Carlos Delgado

Bats: L Throws: R Pos: 1B-25; PH-1   Ht: 6'3" Wt: 246 Born: 6/25/1972 Age: 38

Year	Team	Lg	G	AB	H	2B	3B	HR	(Hm	Rd)	TB	R	RBI	RC	TBB	IBB	SO	HBP	SH	SF	SB	CS	SB%	GDP	Avg	OBP	Slg
1993	Tor	AL	2	1	0	0	0	0	(0	0)	0	0	0	0	1	0	0	0	0	0	0	0	-	0	.000	.500	.000
1994	Tor	AL	43	130	28	2	0	9	(5	4)	57	17	24	20	25	4	46	3	0	1	1	1	.50	5	.215	.352	.438
1995	Tor	AL	37	91	15	3	0	3	(2	1)	27	7	11	5	6	0	26	0	0	2	0	0	-	1	.165	.212	.297
1996	Tor	AL	138	400	132	28	2	25	(12	13)	239	68	92	83	58	2	139	9	0	8	0	0	-	13	.270	.353	.490
1997	Tor	AL	153	519	136	42	3	30	(17	13)	274	79	91	94	64	9	133	8	0	4	0	3	.00	6	.262	.350	.528
1998	Tor	AL	142	530	155	43	1	38	(20	18)	314	94	115	117	73	13	139	11	0	6	3	0	1.00	8	.292	.385	.592
1999	Tor	AL	152	573	156	39	0	44	(17	27)	327	113	134	121	86	7	141	15	0	7	1	1	.50	11	.272	.377	.571
2000	Tor	AL	162	569	196	57	1	41	(30	11)	378	115	137	164	123	18	104	15	0	4	0	1	.00	12	.344	.470	.664
2001	Tor	AL	162	574	160	31	1	39	(13	26)	310	102	102	126	111	22	136	16	0	3	3	0	1.00	9	.279	.408	.540
2002	Tor	AL	143	505	140	34	2	33	(17	16)	277	103	108	117	102	18	126	13	0	8	1	0	1.00	8	.277	.406	.549
2003	Tor	AL	161	570	172	38	1	42	(24	18)	338	117	145	146	109	23	137	19	0	7	0	0	-	9	.302	.426	.593
2004	Tor	AL	128	458	123	26	0	32	(18	14)	245	74	99	88	69	12	115	13	0	11	0	1	.00	11	.269	.372	.535
2005	Fla	NL	144	521	157	41	3	33	(16	17)	303	81	115	110	72	20	121	17	0	6	0	0	-	16	.301	.399	.582
2006	NYM	NL	144	524	139	30	2	38	(18	20)	287	89	114	101	74	11	120	10	0	10	0	0	-	12	.265	.361	.548
2007	NYM	NL	139	538	139	30	0	24	(9	15)	241	71	87	70	52	8	118	11	0	6	4	0	1.00	12	.258	.333	.448
2008	NYM	NL	159	598	162	32	1	38	(21	17)	310	96	115	104	72	19	124	8	0	8	1	1	.50	16	.271	.353	.518
2009	NYM	NL	26	94	28	7	1	4	(3	1)	49	15	23	19	12	0	20	4	0	2	0	0	-	3	.298	.393	.521
Postseason			10	37	13	3	0	4	(3	1)	28	8	11	10	6	0	6	0	0	0	0	0	-	0	.351	.442	.757
17 ML YEARS			2035	7283	2038	483	18	473	(242	231)	3976	1241	1512	1485	1109	186	1745	172	0	93	14	8	.64	152	.280	.383	.546

David Dellucci

Bats: L Throws: L Pos: DH-12; LF-7; PH-3   Ht: 5'11" Wt: 205 Born: 10/31/1973 Age: 36

Year	Team	Lg	G	AB	H	2B	3B	HR	(Hm	Rd)	TB	R	RBI	RC	TBB	IBB	SO	HBP	SH	SF	SB	CS	SB%	GDP	Avg	OBP	Slg
2009	Clmbs*	AAA	7	29	12	1	1	0	(-	-)	15	7	2	7	3	0	4	0	0	0	2	0	1.00	0	.414	.469	.517
2009	LsVgs*	AAA	16	63	20	6	0	3	(-	-)	35	10	9	13	6	0	18	1	0	1	1	0	1.00	1	.317	.380	.556
1997	Bal	AL	17	27	6	1	0	1	(0	1)	10	3	3	3	4	1	7	1	0	0	0	0	-	2	.222	.344	.370
1998	Ari	NL	124	416	108	19	12	5	(1	4)	166	43	51	51	33	2	103	3	0	1	3	5	.38	6	.260	.318	.399
1999	Ari	NL	63	109	43	7	1	1	(0	1)	55	27	15	24	11	0	24	3	0	0	2	0	1.00	3	.394	.463	.505
2000	Ari	NL	34	50	15	3	0	0	(0	0)	18	2	2	6	4	0	9	0	0	0	2	0	1.00	1	.300	.352	.360
2001	Ari	NL	115	217	60	10	2	10	(5	5)	104	28	40	36	22	4	52	2	0	0	2	1	.67	2	.276	.349	.479
2002	Ari	NL	97	229	56	11	2	7	(2	5)	92	34	29	26	28	5	55	1	0	3	2	4	.33	7	.245	.326	.402
2003	2 Tms		91	216	49	12	3	3	(3	0)	76	26	23	23	23	1	58	5	2	2	12	0	1.00	6	.227	.313	.352
2004	Tex	AL	107	331	80	13	1	17	(9	8)	146	59	61	61	47	3	88	5	1	3	9	4	.69	4	.242	.342	.441
2005	Tex	AL	128	435	109	17	5	29	(14	15)	223	97	65	81	76	0	121	5	0	2	5	3	.63	7	.251	.367	.513
2006	Phi	NL	132	264	77	14	5	13	(6	7)	140	41	39	43	28	0	62	6	0	3	1	3	.25	1	.292	.369	.530
2007	Cle	AL	56	178	41	11	2	4	(0	4)	68	25	20	18	17	2	40	1	0	3	2	1	.67	4	.230	.296	.382
2008	Cle	AL	113	336	80	19	2	11	(4	7)	136	41	47	41	24	1	76	11	0	4	3	2	.60	12	.238	.307	.405
2009	2 Tms		22	65	10	3	0	0	(0	0)	16	5	3	4	5	0	19	3	0	1	0	0	-	3	.185	.270	.246
03	Ari	NL	70	165	40	11	3	2	(2	0)	63	18	19	21	19	1	45	3	1	2	9	0	1.00	4	.242	.328	.382
03	NYY	AL	21	51	9	1	0	1	(1	0)	13	8	4	2	4	0	13	2	1	0	3	0	1.00	2	.176	.263	.255
09	Cle	AL	14	40	11	3	0	0	(0	0)	14	3	1	2	2	0	12	2	0	1	0	0	-	1	.275	.333	.350
09	Tor	AL	8	25	1	0	0	0	(0	0)	2	2	2	2	3	0	7	1	0	0	0	0	-	2	.040	.172	.080
Postseason			17	16	5	0	0	1	(0	1)	8	5	2	2	0	0	2	1	1	0	1	0	1.00	0	.313	.353	.500
13 ML YEARS			1099	2873	736	141	35	101	(44	57)	1250	431	398	410	322	20	714	46	3	22	41	25	.62	58	.256	.338	.435

Ryan Dempster

Pitches: R **Bats:** R **Pos:** SP-31   **Ht:** 6'2" **Wt:** 215 **Born:** 5/3/1977 **Age:** 33

			HOW MUCH HE PITCHED							WHAT HE GAVE UP												THE RESULTS							
Year	Team	Lg	G	GS	CG	GF	IP	BFP	H	R	ER	HR	SH	SF	HB	TBB	IBB	SO	WP	Bk	W	L	Pct	Sh	Sv-Op	Hld	ERC	ERA
1998	Fla	NL	14	11	0	1	54.2	272	72	47	43	6	5	6	9	38	1	35	5	0	1	5	.167	0	0-1	0	8.14	7.08
1999	Fla	NL	25	25	0	0	147.0	666	146	77	77	21	3	6	6	93	2	126	8	0	7	8	.467	0	0-0	0	5.49	4.71
2000	Fla	NL	33	33	2	0	226.1	974	210	102	92	30	4	5	5	97	7	209	4	0	14	10	.583	1	0-0	0	4.04	3.66
2001	Fla	NL	34	34	2	0	211.1	954	218	123	116	21	15	7	10	112	5	171	5	0	15	12	.556	1	0-0	0	4.91	4.94
2002	2 Tms	NL	33	33	4	0	209.0	915	228	127	125	28	9	6	10	93	2	153	2	0	10	13	.435	0	0-0	0	5.35	5.38
2003	Cin	NL	22	20	0	1	115.2	545	134	89	84	14	9	4	5	70	4	84	3	0	3	7	.300	0	0-0	0	6.11	6.54
2004	ChC	NL	23	0	0	8	20.2	93	16	9	9	1	1	0	2	13	0	18	1	0	1	1	.500	0	2-2	3	3.61	3.92
2005	ChC	NL	63	6	0	53	92.0	401	83	35	32	4	5	0	4	49	7	89	4	0	5	3	.625	0	33-35	1	3.69	3.13
2006	ChC	NL	74	0	0	64	75.0	342	77	47	40	5	5	4	3	36	3	67	6	0	1	9	.100	0	24-33	2	4.26	4.80
2007	ChC	NL	66	0	0	58	66.2	282	59	36	35	8	3	2	1	30	4	55	2	1	2	7	.222	0	28-31	0	3.77	4.73
2008	ChC	NL	33	33	1	0	206.2	856	174	75	68	14	4	3	7	76	1	187	5	0	17	6	.739	0	0-0	0	3.03	2.96
2009	ChC	NL	31	31	1	0	200.0	842	196	94	81	22	10	8	6	65	4	172	11	0	11	9	.550	1	0-0	0	3.87	3.65
02	Fla	NL	18	18	3	0	120.1	521	126	66	64	12	7	3	7	55	1	87	0	0	5	8	.385	0	0-0	0	4.95	4.79
02	Cin	NL	15	15	1	0	88.2	394	102	61	61	16	2	3	3	38	1	66	2	0	5	5	.500	0	0-0	0	5.90	6.19
	Postseason		2	1	0	1	5.2	27	4	4	4	1	0	0	0	7	0	4	0	0	0	1	.000	0	0-0	0	6.45	6.35
	12 ML YEARS		451	226	10	185	1625.0	7142	1613	861	802	174	73	51	68	772	40	1366	56	1	87	90	.492	3	87-102	5	4.53	4.44

Chris Denorfia

Bats: R **Throws:** R **Pos:** LF-1; CF-1; RF-1; PR-1   **Ht:** 6'0" **Wt:** 204 **Born:** 7/15/1980 **Age:** 29

						BATTING																BASERUNNING				AVERAGES		
Year	Team	Lg	G	AB	H	2B	3B	HR	(Hm	Rd)	TB	R	RBI	RC	TBB	IBB	SO	HBP	SH	SF	SB	CS	SB%	GDP	Avg	OBP	Slg
2009	Scrmto*	AAA	107	432	117	18	5	9	(-	-)	172	62	49	58	31	0	52	1	4	6	15	6	.71	16	.271	.317	.398
2005	Cin	NL	18	38	10	3	0	1	(1	0)	16	8	2	3	6	0	9	0	0	0	1	0	1.00	1	.263	.364	.421
2006	Cin	NL	49	106	30	6	0	1	(0	1)	39	14	7	13	11	1	21	1	2	0	1	1	.50	1	.283	.356	.368
2008	Oak	AL	29	62	18	3	0	1	(0	1)	24	10	9	9	6	0	16	1	2	0	2	0	1.00	3	.290	.362	.387
2009	Oak	AL	4	2	0	0	0	0	(0	0)	0	1	1	0	0	0	0	0	0	0	0	0	-	0	.000	.000	.000
	4 ML YEARS		100	208	58	12	0	3	(1	2)	79	33	19	25	23	1	46	2	4	0	4	1	.80	5	.279	.356	.380

Mark DeRosa

Bats: R **Throws:** R **Pos:** 3B-105; LF-18; 1B-10; RF-10; PH-5; 2B-2; DH-2   **Ht:** 6'1" **Wt:** 205 **Born:** 2/26/1975 **Age:** 35

						BATTING																BASERUNNING				AVERAGES		
Year	Team	Lg	G	AB	H	2B	3B	HR	(Hm	Rd)	TB	R	RBI	RC	TBB	IBB	SO	HBP	SH	SF	SB	CS	SB%	GDP	Avg	OBP	Slg
1998	Atl	NL	5	3	1	0	0	0	(0	0)	1	2	0	0	0	0	1	0	0	0	0	0	-	0	.333	.333	.333
1999	Atl	NL	7	8	0	0	0	0	(0	0)	0	0	0	0	0	0	2	0	0	0	0	0	-	0	.000	.000	.000
2000	Atl	NL	22	13	4	1	0	0	(0	0)	5	9	3	2	2	0	1	0	0	0	0	0	-	0	.308	.400	.385
2001	Atl	NL	66	164	47	8	0	3	(3	0)	64	27	20	22	12	6	19	5	1	2	2	1	.67	3	.287	.350	.390
2002	Atl	NL	72	212	63	9	2	5	(3	2)	91	24	23	27	12	3	24	3	2	3	2	3	.40	5	.297	.339	.429
2003	Atl	NL	103	266	70	14	0	6	(3	3)	102	40	22	28	16	0	49	5	0	1	1	0	1.00	6	.263	.316	.383
2004	Atl	NL	118	309	74	16	0	3	(0	3)	99	33	31	24	23	3	53	3	4	6	1	3	.25	6	.239	.293	.320
2005	Tex	AL	66	148	36	5	0	8	(7	1)	65	26	20	20	16	0	35	2	0	0	1	0	1.00	5	.243	.325	.439
2006	Tex	AL	136	520	154	40	2	13	(5	8)	237	78	74	78	44	1	102	6	0	2	4	4	.50	13	.296	.357	.456
2007	ChC	NL	149	502	147	28	3	10	(5	5)	211	64	72	76	58	2	93	7	3	4	1	2	.33	17	.293	.371	.420
2008	ChC	NL	149	505	144	30	3	21	(11	10)	243	103	87	95	69	0	106	9	2	8	6	0	1.00	9	.285	.376	.481
2009	2 Tms	NL	139	515	129	23	1	23	(11	12)	223	78	78	68	47	1	121	7	2	5	3	2	.60	11	.250	.319	.433
09	Cle	AL	71	278	75	13	0	13	(8	5)	127	47	50	45	29	1	63	3	1	3	1	1	.50	6	.270	.342	.457
09	StL	NL	68	237	54	10	1	10	(3	7)	96	31	28	23	18	0	58	4	1	2	2	1	.67	5	.228	.291	.405
	Postseason		19	40	14	5	1	1	(1	0)	24	7	9	6	4	0	6	1	0	0	0	0	-	2	.350	.422	.600
	12 ML YEARS		1032	3165	869	174	11	92	(48	44)	1341	484	430	440	299	16	606	47	14	31	21	15	.58	75	.275	.343	.424

Ian Desmond

Bats: R **Throws:** R **Pos:** SS-17; 2B-5; RF-1; PH-1   **Ht:** 6'2" **Wt:** 210 **Born:** 9/20/1985 **Age:** 24

						BATTING																BASERUNNING				AVERAGES		
Year	Team	Lg	G	AB	H	2B	3B	HR	(Hm	Rd)	TB	R	RBI	RC	TBB	IBB	SO	HBP	SH	SF	SB	CS	SB%	GDP	Avg	OBP	Slg
2004	Expos	R	55	216	49	11	0	1	(-	-)	63	28	27	18	10	0	40	4	2	2	13	3	.81	6	.227	.272	.292
2004	Vrmnt	A-	4	12	3	0	0	1	(-	-)	6	2	1	1	0	0	2	1	0	0	0	1	.00	2	.250	.308	.500
2005	Savann	A	73	296	73	10	2	4	(-	-)	99	37	23	31	13	0	60	6	4	1	20	6	.77	5	.247	.291	.334
2005	Ptomc	A+	55	219	56	13	3	3	(-	-)	84	37	15	29	21	0	53	2	5	1	13	6	.68	5	.256	.325	.384
2006	Hrsbrg	AA	37	121	22	4	1	0	(-	-)	28	8	3	5	5	0	35	0	6	0	4	1	.80	1	.182	.214	.231
2006	Ptomc	A+	92	365	89	20	2	9	(-	-)	140	50	45	46	29	0	79	9	2	3	14	8	.64	7	.244	.313	.384
2007	Ptomc	A+	129	458	121	30	4	13	(-	-)	198	69	45	76	57	0	99	11	6	4	27	11	.71	8	.264	.357	.432
2008	Hrsbrg	AA	90	323	81	14	0	12	(-	-)	131	42	44	43	31	4	78	2	6	2	12	8	.60	7	.251	.318	.406
2008	Nats	R	3	13	5	1	0	0	(-	-)	6	1	2	2	0	0	2	0	0	0	3	0	1.00	0	.385	.385	.462
2009	Hrsbrg	AA	42	170	52	12	1	6	(-	-)	84	29	18	32	16	2	40	2	1	0	13	4	.76	2	.306	.372	.494
2009	Syrcse	AAA	55	178	63	12	2	1	(-	-)	82	25	14	37	20	1	31	3	4	0	8	1	.89	5	.354	.428	.461
2009	Was	NL	21	82	23	7	2	4	(2	2)	46	9	12	10	5	0	14	0	1	1	1	0	1.00	2	.280	.318	.561

Elmer Dessens

Pitches: R **Bats:** R **Pos:** RP-28   **Ht:** 5'11" **Wt:** 200 **Born:** 1/13/1971 **Age:** 39

						HOW MUCH HE PITCHED							WHAT HE GAVE UP												THE RESULTS				
Year	Team	Lg	G	GS	CG	GF	IP	BFP	H	R	ER	HR	SH	SF	HB	TBB	IBB	SO	WP	Bk	W	L	Pct	Sh	Sv-Op	Hld	ERC	ERA
2009	Buffalo*	AAA	27	0	0	23	35.0	136	26	9	9	2	0	0	0	9	1	28	2	0	3	2	.600	0	11- -	-	1.98	2.31
1996	Pit	NL	15	3	0	1	25.0	112	40	23	23	2	3	1	0	4	0	13	0	0	0	2	.000	0	0-0	3	6.77	8.28
1997	Pit	NL	3	0	0	1	3.1	13	2	0	0	0	0	0	1	0	0	2	0	0	0	0		0	0-0	0	1.31	0.00
1998	Pit	NL	43	5	0	8	74.2	332	90	50	47	10	4	3	0	25	2	43	1	0	2	6	.250	0	0-1	6	5.19	5.67

90

Year	Team	Lg	G	GS	CG	GF	IP	BFP	H	R	ER	HR	SH	SF	HB	TBB	IBB	SO	WP	Bk	W	L	Pct	Sh	Sv-Op	Hld	ERC	ERA
			HOW MUCH HE PITCHED						**WHAT HE GAVE UP**												**THE RESULTS**							
2000	Cin	NL	40	16	1	6	147.1	640	170	73	70	10	12	7	3	43	7	85	4	0	11	5	.688	0	1-1	1	4.31	4.28
2001	Cin	NL	34	34	1	0	205.0	862	221	103	102	32	7	7	1	56	1	128	4	1	10	14	.417	1	0-0	0	4.49	4.48
2002	Cin	NL	30	30	0	0	178.0	737	173	70	60	24	7	1	7	49	8	93	3	1	7	8	.467	0	0-0	0	3.82	3.03
2003	Ari	NL	34	30	0	1	175.2	781	212	107	99	22	9	3	4	57	6	113	3	2	8	8	.500	0	0-0	0	5.19	5.07
2004	2 Tms	NL	50	10	0	9	105.0	468	123	61	52	15	4	3	1	31	4	73	2	0	2	6	.250	0	2-5	4	4.83	4.46
2005	LAD	NL	28	7	0	4	65.2	277	63	30	26	6	1	3	1	19	2	37	1	0	1	2	.333	0	0-0	1	3.35	3.56
2006	2 Tms	NL	62	0	0	12	77.0	334	86	43	39	8	5	1	1	22	8	52	3	0	5	8	.385	0	2-7	18	4.17	4.36
2007	2 Tms	NL	17	5	0	7	34.0	156	45	32	27	6	2	1	0	12	0	22	0	0	2	2	.500	0	0-0	0	6.37	7.15
2008	Atl	NL	4	0	0	1	4.0	26	10	10	10	1	0	2	0	4	0	2	0	0	0	1	.000	0	0-1	0	18.65	22.50
2009	NYM	NL	28	0	0	8	32.2	130	24	12	12	5	2	2	2	10	1	14	1	0	0	0	-	0	0-0	0	2.89	3.31
04	Ari	NL	38	9	0	7	85.1	386	107	54	45	11	4	3	1	23	4	55	2	0	1	6	.143	0	2-4	4	5.08	4.75
04	LAD	NL	12	1	0	2	19.2	82	16	7	7	4	0	0	0	8	0	18	0	0	1	0	1.000	0	0-1	0	3.74	3.20
06	KC	AL	43	0	0	10	54.0	234	63	31	27	4	3	1	1	13	6	36	2	0	5	7	.417	0	2-7	12	4.08	4.50
06	LAD	NL	19	0	0	2	23.0	100	23	12	12	4	2	0	0	9	2	16	1	0	0	1	.000	0	0-6		4.37	4.70
07	Mil	NL	12	0	0	7	15.0	69	24	16	11	3	0	1	0	3	0	12	0	0	1	1	.500	0	0-0	0	7.85	6.60
07	Col	NL	5	5	0	0	19.0	87	21	16	16	3	2	0	0	9	0	10	0	0	1	1	.500	0	0-0	0	5.29	7.58
Postseason			1	0	0	0	1.1	5	1	1	1	1	0	0	0	0	0	1	0	0	0	0	-	0	0-0	0	4.25	6.75
13 ML YEARS			388	140	2	58	1127.1	4868	1259	614	567	141	56	34	21	332	39	677	22	4	48	62	.436	1	5-15	33	4.53	4.53

Ross Detwiler

Pitches: L Bats: R Pos: SP-14; RP-1 Ht: 6'5" Wt: 174 Born: 3/6/1986 Age: 24

Year	Team	Lg	G	GS	CG	GF	IP	BFP	H	R	ER	HR	SH	SF	HB	TBB	IBB	SO	WP	Bk	W	L	Pct	Sh	Sv-Op	Hld	ERC	ERA
			HOW MUCH HE PITCHED						**WHAT HE GAVE UP**												**THE RESULTS**							
2007	Nats	R	4	4	0	0	12.0	50	11	3	3	1	0	0	2	3	0	15	0	0	0	0	-	0	0--	-	3.65	2.25
2007	Ptomc	A+	5	4	0	1	21.1	100	27	11	10	1	0	1	3	9	0	13	1	0	2	2	.500	0	0--	-	5.91	4.22
2008	Ptomc	A+	26	26	0	0	124.0	559	140	72	67	8	5	5	7	57	0	114	3	0	8	8	.500	0	0--	-	5.05	4.86
2009	Hrsbrg	AA	6	6	0	0	27.1	122	28	14	9	2	1	1	1	10	0	28	0	0	0	3	.000	0	0--	-	3.89	2.96
2009	Syrcse	AAA	10	10	0	0	49.1	220	55	28	17	2	0	1	0	20	0	42	0	0	4	2	.667	0	0--	-	4.40	3.10
2007	Was	NL	1	0	0	0	1.0	4	0	0	0	0	0	0	0	0	0	1	0	0	0	0	-	0	0-0	0	0.00	0.00
2009	Was	NL	15	14	1	0	75.2	341	87	43	42	3	4	1	2	33	3	43	4	0	1	6	.143	0	0 0	1	4.65	5.00
2 ML YEARS			16	14	1	1	76.2	345	87	43	42	3	4	1	2	33	3	44	4	0	1	6	.143	0	0 0	1	4.52	4.93

Joey Devine

Pitches: R Bats: R Pos: P Ht: 5'11" Wt: 205 Born: 9/19/1983 Age: 26

Year	Team	Lg	G	GS	CG	GF	IP	BFP	H	R	ER	HR	SH	SF	HR	TBB	IBB	SO	WP	Bk	W	L	Pct	Sh	Sv-Op	Hld	ERC	ERA
			HOW MUCH HE PITCHED						**WHAT HE GAVE UP**												**THE RESULTS**							
2005	Atl	NL	5	0	0	1	5.0	26	6	7	7	2	0	0	0	5	1	3	0	0	0	1	.000	0	0-0	1	9.97	12.60
2006	Atl	NL	10	0	0	1	6.1	36	8	7	7	1	0	1	0	9	1	10	4	1	0	0	-	0	0-1	0	11.11	9.95
2007	Atl	NL	10	0	0	5	8.1	39	7	1	1	0	1	1	0	8	2	7	1	0	0	1	1.000	0	0-0	0	4.08	1.08
2008	Oak	AL	42	0	0	10	45.2	170	23	7	3	0	1	0	1	15	2	49	0	0	6	1	.857	0	1-2	11	1.09	0.59
Postseason			3	0	0	1	1.2	10	3	2	2	1	0	0	1	1	1	3	0	0	0	1	.000	0	0-0	0	16.60	10.80
4 ML YEARS			67	0	0	17	65.1	271	44	22	18	3	2	2	1	37	6	69	5	1	7	2	.778	0	1-3	12	2.54	2.48

Blake DeWitt

Bats: L Throws: R Pos: PH-20; 3B-14; 2B-2; SS-2; PR-1 Ht: 5'11" Wt: 204 Born: 8/8/1985 Age: 24

Year	Team	Lg	G	AB	H	2B	3D	HR	(Hm	Rd)	TB	R	RBI	RC	TBB	IBB	SO	HBP	SH	SF	SB	CS	SB%	GDP	Avg	OBP	Slg
			BATTING																		**BASERUNNING**				**AVERAGES**		
2004	Ogden	R+	70	299	85	19	3	12	(-	-)	146	61	47	51	28	0	78	3	1	1	1	1	.50	6	.284	.350	.488
2005	Clmbs	A	120	481	136	31	3	11	(-	-)	206	61	65	70	34	0	79	4	0	3	0	1	.00	13	.283	.333	.428
2005	VeroB	A+	8	31	13	3	0	1	(-	-)	19	4	7	7	1	0	3	0	0	0	0	0	-	0	.419	.438	.613
2006	VeroB	A+	106	425	114	18	1	18	(-	-)	188	61	61	66	45	1	79	3	0	5	8	5	.62	8	.268	.339	.442
2006	Jaxnvl	AA	27	104	19	1	0	1	(-	-)	23	6	6	4	8	0	21	0	0	0	0	1	.00	4	.183	.241	.221
2007	InldEm	A+	83	339	101	29	2	8	(-	-)	158	48	46	53	20	0	42	1	0	1	2	3	.40	7	.298	.338	.466
2007	Jaxnvl	AA	45	178	50	13	1	6	(-	-)	83	20	20	25	7	0	26	0	0	1	0	1	.00	1	.281	.306	.466
2008	LsVgs	AAA	27	111	34	4	2	4	(-	-)	54	16	18	20	10	0	14	1	1	1	1	0	1.00	4	.306	.366	.486
2009	Albq	AAA	92	352	90	21	9	7	(-	-)	150	64	47	55	48	2	44	0	4	3	2	2	.50	8	.256	.349	.426
2008	LAD	NL	117	368	97	13	2	9	(5	4)	141	45	52	51	45	9	68	3	0	5	3	0	1.00	6	.264	.344	.383
2009	LAD	NL	31	49	10	3	0	2	(1	1)	19	4	4	1	3	0	7	0	0	1	0	0	-	2	.204	.245	.388
Postseason			8	24	4	2	1	0	(0	0)	8	2	6	0	1	0	6	0	0	1	0	0	-	3	.167	.192	.333
2 ML YEARS			148	417	107	16	2	11	(5	5)	160	49	56	52	48	9	75	3	0	6	3	0	1.00	8	.257	.333	.384

Matt Diaz

Bats: R Throws: R Pos: RF-66; LF-50; PH-18; CF-2; PR-2 Ht: 6'1" Wt: 215 Born: 3/3/1978 Age: 32

Year	Team	Lg	G	AB	H	2B	3B	HR	(Hm	Rd)	TB	R	RBI	RC	TBB	IBB	SO	HBP	SH	SF	SB	CS	SB%	GDP	Avg	OBP	Slg
			BATTING																		**BASERUNNING**				**AVERAGES**		
2003	TB	AL	4	9	1	0	0	0	(0	0)	1	2	0	0	1	0	3	0	0	0	0	0	-	0	.111	.200	.111
2004	TB	AL	10	21	4	1	1	1	(1	0)	10	3	3	2	1	0	6	2	0	0	0	0	-	0	.190	.292	.476
2005	KC	AL	34	89	25	4	2	1	(0	1)	36	7	9	11	4	0	15	2	1	1	0	1	.00	3	.281	.323	.404
2006	Atl	NL	124	297	97	15	4	7	(3	4)	141	37	32	40	11	3	49	9	1	4	5	5	.50	9	.327	.364	.475
2007	Atl	NL	135	358	121	21	0	12	(5	7)	178	44	45	53	16	3	63	4	1	5	4	0	1.00	8	.338	.368	.497
2008	Atl	NL	43	135	33	2	0	2	(0	2)	41	9	14	10	3	0	32	1	0	1	4	2	.67	4	.244	.264	.304
2009	Atl	NL	125	371	116	18	4	13	(4	9)	181	56	58	67	35	2	90	13	5	1	12	5	.71	14	.313	.390	.488
7 ML YEARS			475	1280	397	61	11	36	(15	21)	588	158	161	183	71	8	258	31	8	12	25	13	.66	38	.310	.358	.459

Robinzon Diaz

Bats: R **Throws:** R **Pos:** C-33; PH-8   **Ht:** 5'11" **Wt:** 220 **Born:** 9/19/1983 **Age:** 26

Year	Team	Lg	G	AB	H	2B	3B	HR	(Hm	Rd)	TB	R	RBI	RC	TBB	IBB	SO	HBP	SH	SF	SB	CS	SB%	GDP	Avg	OBP	Slg
2002	Dnedin	A+	10	25	3	0	0	0	(-	-)	3	3	1	0	1	0	4	0	1	1	0	0	-	0	.120	.148	.120
2002	MdHat	R+	58	192	57	9	0	0	(-	-)	66	29	20	23	13	1	19	1	0	0	7	4	.64	6	.297	.345	.344
2003	Pulaski	R+	48	182	68	20	2	1	(-	-)	95	33	44	36	10	1	14	3	0	4	1	4	.20	5	.374	.407	.522
2004	CtnWV	A	105	407	117	20	2	2	(-	-)	147	62	42	54	27	0	31	8	3	4	10	4	.71	17	.287	.341	.361
2005	Dnedin	A+	100	388	114	17	6	1	(-	-)	146	47	65	49	15	0	28	5	2	4	5	2	.71	11	.294	.325	.376
2006	Dnedin	A+	104	418	128	21	1	3	(-	-)	160	59	44	57	20	2	37	3	4	2	8	1	.89	20	.306	.341	.383
2007	NHam	AA	74	301	95	17	1	3	(-	-)	123	33	29	44	11	2	16	3	2	2	5	0	1.00	11	.316	.344	.409
2007	Syrcse	AAA	19	65	22	3	0	1	(-	-)	28	4	10	10	1	0	6	1	2	0	0	0	-	2	.338	.358	.431
2008	Syrcse	AAA	36	131	32	7	1	1	(-	-)	44	7	13	11	5	2	10	0	2	3	0	1	.00	5	.244	.266	.336
2008	B Jays	R	15	44	17	3	0	2	(-	-)	26	9	10	10	2	0	4	2	0	0	0	0	-	0	.386	.420	.591
2008	Dnedin	A+	6	25	8	1	0	1	(-	-)	12	3	3	3	0	0	0	0	0	0	0	0	-	1	.320	.320	.480
2008	Indy	AAA	5	14	5	0	1	0	(-	-)	7	0	3	1	0	0	0	0	0	0	1	2	.33	0	.357	.357	.500
2009	Indy	AAA	44	149	39	4	0	3	(-	-)	52	18	15	16	9	0	12	1	3	0	0	1	.00	4	.262	.308	.349
2008	2 Tms		3	10	3	0	0	0	(0	0)	3	0	1	2	0	0	2	0	0	0	1	0	1.00	0	.300	.300	.300
2009	Pit	NL	41	129	36	7	0	1	(0	1)	46	9	19	13	3	0	9	3	1	2	0	1	.00	5	.279	.307	.357
08	Tor	AL	1	4	0	0	0	0	(0	0)	0	0	0	0	0	0	1	0	0	0	0	0	-	0	.000	.000	.000
08	Pit	NL	2	6	3	0	0	0	(0	0)	3	0	1	2	0	0	1	0	0	0	1	0	1.00	0	.500	.500	.500
	2 ML YEARS		44	139	39	7	0	1	(0	1)	49	9	20	15	3	0	11	3	1	2	1	1	.50	5	.281	.306	.353

Chris Dickerson

Bats: L **Throws:** L **Pos:** LF-37; CF-27; PH-27; RF-20; PR-1   **Ht:** 6'3" **Wt:** 228 **Born:** 4/10/1982 **Age:** 28

Year	Team	Lg	G	AB	H	2B	3B	HR	(Hm	Rd)	TB	R	RBI	RC	TBB	IBB	SO	HBP	SH	SF	SB	CS	SB%	GDP	Avg	OBP	Slg
2003	Billings	R+	58	201	49	6	4	6	(-	-)	81	36	38	34	39	0	66	4	5	1	9	4	.69	0	.244	.376	.403
2004	Dayton	A	84	314	95	15	3	4	(-	-)	128	50	34	57	51	1	92	8	2	3	27	14	.66	1	.303	.410	.408
2004	Ptomc	A+	15	45	9	2	0	0	(-	-)	11	5	5	4	7	0	14	1	3	0	3	1	.75	1	.200	.321	.244
2005	Srsota	A+	119	436	103	17	7	11	(-	-)	167	68	43	61	53	2	124	6	7	3	19	3	.86	2	.236	.325	.383
2006	Chatt	AA	116	389	94	21	7	12	(-	-)	165	65	48	65	65	4	129	5	3	3	21	6	.78	2	.242	.355	.424
2007	Chatt	AA	30	114	31	4	1	1	(-	-)	40	11	11	14	7	1	31	2	0	0	7	2	.78	2	.272	.325	.351
2007	Lsvlle	AAA	104	354	92	11	6	13	(-	-)	154	58	44	61	52	4	131	5	3	2	23	5	.82	2	.260	.361	.435
2008	Lsvlle	AAA	97	349	100	16	9	11	(-	-)	167	65	53	69	54	2	102	3	5	3	26	7	.79	2	.287	.384	.479
2009	Lsvlle	AAA	4	12	3	0	0	0	(-	-)	3	2	1	2	3	0	4	0	0	0	2	0	1.00	0	.250	.400	.250
2008	Cin	NL	31	102	31	9	2	6	(4	2)	62	20	15	22	17	0	35	2	1	0	5	3	.63	0	.304	.413	.608
2009	Cin	NL	97	255	70	13	3	2	(0	2)	95	31	15	34	39	1	66	1	2	2	11	3	.79	3	.275	.370	.373
	2 ML YEARS		128	357	101	22	5	8	(4	4)	157	51	30	56	56	1	101	3	3	2	16	6	.73	3	.283	.383	.440

R.A. Dickey

Pitches: R **Bats:** R **Pos:** RP-34; SP-1   **Ht:** 6'2" **Wt:** 216 **Born:** 10/29/1974 **Age:** 35

Year	Team	Lg	G	GS	CG	GF	IP	BFP	H	R	ER	HR	SH	SF	HB	TBB	IBB	SO	WP	Bk	W	L	Pct	Sh	Sv-Op	Hld	ERC	ERA
2009	Roch*	AAA	5	5	1	0	33.1	146	39	20	19	1	1	0	5	9	1	18	4	0	2	1	.667	0	0- -	-	3.92	5.13
2001	Tex	AL	4	0	0	1	12.0	53	13	9	9	3	0	0	0	7	1	4	1	0	0	1	.000	0	0-0	0	6.57	6.75
2003	Tex	AL	38	13	1	6	116.2	513	135	68	66	16	4	3	5	38	5	94	5	2	9	8	.529	1	1-1	3	5.09	5.09
2004	Tex	AL	25	15	0	2	104.1	480	136	77	65	17	3	3	4	33	1	57	5	1	6	7	.462	0	1-1	0	6.08	5.61
2005	Tex	AL	9	4	0	2	29.2	134	29	23	22	4	0	1	2	17	0	15	2	0	1	2	.333	0	0-0	0	5.18	6.67
2006	Tex	AL	1	1	0	0	3.1	18	8	7	7	6	0	0	0	1	0	1	0	0	1	0	1.000	0	0-0	0	32.05	18.90
2008	Sea	AL	32	14	0	9	112.1	500	124	65	65	15	4	6	2	51	4	58	11	1	5	8	.385	0	0-0	0	5.19	5.21
2009	Min	AL	35	1	0	13	64.1	293	74	34	33	8	2	2	4	30	1	42	4	0	1	1	.500	0	0-0	1	5.66	4.62
	7 ML YEARS		144	48	1	33	442.2	1991	519	283	267	69	13	15	17	177	12	271	28	4	22	28	.440	1	2-2	4	5.63	5.43

Mark DiFelice

Pitches: R **Bats:** R **Pos:** RP-59   **Ht:** 6'2" **Wt:** 181 **Born:** 8/23/1976 **Age:** 33

Year	Team	Lg	G	GS	CG	GF	IP	BFP	H	R	ER	HR	SH	SF	HB	TBB	IBB	SO	WP	Bk	W	L	Pct	Sh	Sv-Op	Hld	ERC	ERA
1998	Portlnd	AA	15	13	0	2	81.2	343	83	45	30	6	1	2	3	11	0	62	3	1	4	6	.400	0	0- -	-	3.03	3.31
1999	Salem	A+	27	23	3	1	156.1	642	142	71	67	20	4	6	4	36	0	142	3	1	8	12	.400	0	0- -	-	3.19	3.86
2000	Carlina	AA	23	22	2	0	133.0	556	152	58	53	15	2	3	0	19	0	98	2	0	7	5	.583	0	0- -	-	3.96	3.59
2001	Carlina	AA	19	18	2	0	123.0	498	108	47	43	13	3	5	3	23	0	98	1	0	6	4	.600	1	0- -	-	2.73	3.15
2001	ColSpr	AAA	8	8	0	0	46.0	207	56	29	27	11	2	1	8	8	3	43	1	0	3	2	.600	0	0- -	-	6.02	5.28
2002	TriCity	A-	6	1	0	0	17.0	77	18	12	10	2	1	1	2	0	0	13	1	0	0	0	-	0	0- -	-	3.03	5.29
2002	Salem	A+	6	6	0	0	35.1	146	40	12	11	3	1	0	2	5	0	21	0	0	3	0	1.000	0	0- -	-	4.03	2.80
2003	Tulsa	AA	21	21	0	0	113.2	479	121	61	47	16	4	2	4	24	2	75	7	0	7	6	.538	0	0- -	-	4.09	3.72
2004	Ottawa	AAA	36	4	0	3	89.0	365	73	42	34	10	1	1	2	27	1	70	3	1	9	4	.692	0	1- -	-	2.88	3.44
2005	NewOr	AAA	14	2	0	0	31.0	148	39	35	28	10	3	3	1	13	1	21	1	0	1	2	.333	0	0- -	-	7.27	8.13
2005	Smrset	IND	14	11	1	1	75.2	297	72	26	26	11	1	1	1	8	0	53	1	1	7	4	.636	0	0- -	-	3.08	3.09
2006	Cam	IND	25	25	7	0	158.0	656	163	66	56	12	6	7	4	24	2	132	0	0	12	9	.571	2	0- -	-	3.19	3.19
2007	Hntsvl	AA	26	3	0	5	66.2	250	50	12	12	3	1	1	1	6	1	60	3	0	6	1	.857	0	0- -	-	1.54	1.62
2007	Nashv	AAA	10	10	0	0	58.0	229	45	21	20	6	2	3	3	9	0	63	1	0	4	2	.667	0	0- -	-	2.21	3.10
2008	Nashv	AAA	13	12	0	0	64.1	252	50	25	23	5	2	2	4	8	0	65	3	0	5	1	.833	0	0- -	-	2.01	3.22
2008	Mil	NL	15	0	0	5	19.0	78	17	7	6	4	0	0	0	4	0	20	1	0	1	0	1.000	0	0-0	0	3.39	2.84
2009	Mil	NL	59	0	0	9	51.2	219	49	21	21	6	3	0	1	15	6	48	1	0	4	1	.800	0	0-1	9	3.32	3.66
	2 ML YEARS		74	0	0	14	70.2	297	66	28	27	10	3	0	1	19	6	68	2	0	5	1	.833	0	0-1	10	3.35	3.44

Tim Dillard

Pitches: R Bats: R Pos: RP-2   Ht: 6'4" Wt: 223 Born: 7/19/1983 Age: 26

Year	Team	Lg	G	GS	CG	GF	IP	BFP	H	R	ER	HR	SH	SF	HB	TBB	IBB	SO	WP	Bk	W	L	Pct	Sh	Sv-Op	Hld	ERC	ERA
2003	Brewrs	R	11	4	0	3	35.2	154	36	19	15	1	1	1	9	5	0	32	1	0	1	2	.333	0	0--	-	3.58	3.79
2003	Helena	R+	3	0	0	1	5.0	22	5	0	0	0	0	0	0	2	0	6	2	0	0	0	-	0	0--	-	3.28	0.00
2004	Beloit	A	43	1	0	28	77.2	349	89	46	34	4	0	1	8	22	2	61	6	0	2	5	.286	0	10--	-	4.37	3.94
2005	BrvdCt	A+	28	28	5	0	185.1	740	150	64	51	9	5	7	13	31	0	128	13	0	12	10	.545	2	0--	-	2.17	2.48
2006	Hntsvl	AA	29	25	1	2	163.0	698	166	76	57	10	9	6	6	36	0	108	12	0	10	7	.588	1	0--	-	3.28	3.15
2007	Nashv	AAA	34	16	1	4	133.0	584	167	72	71	13	5	6	7	37	2	62	3	0	8	4	.667	0	0--	-	5.35	4.80
2008	Nashv	AAA	37	0	0	15	63.1	272	57	21	14	5	6	1	2	28	2	55	1	0	6	1	.857	0	2--	-	3.60	1.99
2009	Nashv	AAA	24	24	2	0	147.2	644	162	86	74	11	10	4	11	52	0	64	4	0	11	7	.611	1	0--	-	4.62	4.51
2008	Mil	NL	13	0	0	5	14.1	65	17	12	7	2	0	1	0	6	2	5	1	0	0	0	-	0	0-0	1	5.24	4.40
2009	Mil	NL	2	0	0	0	4.1	23	7	6	6	1	0	1	0	5	1	1	0	0	0	1	.000	0	0-1	0	12.99	12.46
	2 ML YEARS		15	0	0	5	18.2	80	24	18	13	3	0	2	0	11	3	6	1	0	0	1	.000	0	0-1	1	6.85	6.27

Joe Dillon

Bats: R Throws: R Pos: DH-8; PH-6; 3B-3; 2B-2; PR-2   Ht: 6'2" Wt: 214 Born: 8/2/1975 Age: 34

Year	Team	Lg	G	AB	H	2B	3B	HR	(Hm	Rd)	TB	R	RBI	RC	TBB	IBB	SO	HBP	SH	SF	SB	CS	SB%	GDP	Avg	OBP	Slg
2009	Drham*	AAA	35	123	30	5	0	2	(-	-)	41	18	13	17	14	0	17	6	0	4	4	0	1.00	1	.244	.340	.333
2005	Fla	NL	27	36	6	1	0	1	(1	0)	10	6	1	0	1	0	8	1	1	0	0	0	-	3	.167	.211	.278
2007	Mil	NL	39	76	26	8	2	0	(0	0)	38	12	10	13	5	0	14	1	0	0	0	0	-	2	.342	.390	.500
2008	Mil	NL	56	75	16	3	0	1	(0	1)	22	13	6	9	13	0	21	1	1	0	1	0	1.00	1	.213	.337	.293
2009	TB	AL	15	30	9	0	0	1	(1	0)	12	4	2	3	3	0	4	2	0	0	0	0	-	1	.300	.400	.400
	4 ML YEARS		137	217	57	12	2	3	(2	1)	82	35	19	25	22	0	47	5	2	0	1	0	1.00	7	.263	.344	.378

Lenny DiNardo

Pitches: L Bats: L Pos: SP-5   Ht: 6'2" Wt: 220 Born: 9/19/1979 Age: 30

Year	Team	Lg	G	GS	CG	GF	IP	BFP	H	R	ER	HR	SH	SF	HB	TBB	IBB	SO	WP	Bk	W	L	Pct	Sh	Sv-Op	Hld	ERC	ERA
2009	Omha*	AAA	29	24	0	3	151.2	621	139	61	56	5	8	6	5	38	0	127	3	1	10	5	.667	0	2--	-	2.77	3.32
2004	Bos	AL	22	0	0	6	27.2	130	34	17	13	1	1	1	2	12	1	21	1	0	0	0	-	0	0-0	0	5.17	4.23
2005	Bos	AL	8	1	0	3	14.2	62	13	6	3	1	1	1	0	5	1	15	1	0	0	1	.000	0	0-0	0	2.86	1.84
2006	Bos	AL	13	6	0	0	39.0	190	61	35	34	6	0	1	1	20	1	17	1	0	1	2	.333	0	0-0	1	8.80	7.85
2007	Oak	AL	35	20	0	9	131.1	555	136	74	60	13	7	6	3	50	2	59	2	0	8	10	.444	0	0-0	0	4.39	4.11
2008	Oak	AL	11	2	0	8	23.0	114	31	20	19	3	1	0	2	13	2	12	1	0	1	2	.333	0	0-0	0	7.21	7.43
2009	KC	AL	5	5	0	0	21.1	117	41	28	24	2	0	2	1	15	0	8	1	0	0	3	.000	0	0-0	0	11.70	10.13
	6 ML YEARS		94	34	0	26	257.0	1168	316	180	153	26	10	11	9	115	7	132	7	0	10	18	.357	0	0-0	1	5.80	5.36

Brent Dlugach

Bats: R Throws: R Pos: 3B-2; SS-2; DH-1; PR-1   Ht: 6'4" Wt: 200 Born: 3/3/1983 Age: 27

Year	Team	Lg	G	AB	H	2B	3B	HR	(Hm	Rd)	TB	R	RBI	RC	TBB	IBB	SO	HBP	SH	SF	SB	CS	SB%	GDP	Avg	OBP	Slg
2004	Oneont	A-	47	183	39	7	2	1	(-	-)	53	17	12	12	8	0	59	3	3	1	5	4	.56	4	.213	.250	.290
2005	WMich	A	124	488	138	26	5	5	(-	-)	189	55	61	62	19	0	121	7	4	4	13	5	.72	10	.283	.317	.387
2006	WMich	A+	125	465	119	24	6	5	(-	-)	170	51	52	51	27	0	144	2	9	1	13	8	.62	7	.256	.299	.360
2006	Toledo	AAA	3	9	1	0	0	0	(-	-)	1	0	0	0	0	0	3	0	0	0	0	0	-	0	.111	.111	.111
2007	Erie	AA	22	72	21	4	3	1	(-	-)	34	12	7	11	6	2	25	0	0	0	1	1	.50	0	.292	.346	.472
2008	Tigers	R	7	15	3	2	0	0	(-	-)	5	2	2	1	2	0	4	0	0	1	0	0	-	2	.200	.278	.333
2009	Toledo	AAA	125	466	137	36	4	9	(-	-)	208	58	59	74	39	3	137	3	4	5	5	3	.63	10	.294	.349	.446
2009	Det	AL	5	3	0	0	0	0	(0	0)	0	1	0	0	0	0	2	0	0	0	0	0	-	0	.000	.000	.000

Greg Dobbs

Bats: L Throws: R Pos: PH-66; 3B-16; LF-13; 1B-6; RF-2; DH-2   Ht: 6'1" Wt: 210 Born: 7/2/1978 Age: 31

Year	Team	Lg	G	AB	H	2B	3B	HR	(Hm	Rd)	TB	R	RBI	RC	TBB	IBB	SO	HBP	SH	SF	SB	CS	SB%	GDP	Avg	OBP	Slg
2004	Sea	AL	18	53	12	1	0	1	(1	0)	16	4	9	5	1	0	14	1	0	1	0	0	-	0	.226	.250	.302
2005	Sea	AL	59	142	35	7	1	1	(0	1)	47	8	20	16	9	3	25	0	1	2	1	0	1.00	4	.246	.288	.331
2006	Sea	AL	23	27	10	3	1	0	(0	0)	15	4	3	5	0	0	4	1	0	0	1	0	1.00	1	.370	.393	.556
2007	Phi	NL	142	324	88	20	4	10	(5	5)	146	45	55	42	29	4	67	1	0	4	3	0	1.00	7	.272	.330	.451
2008	Phi	NL	128	226	68	14	1	9	(3	6)	111	30	40	38	11	1	40	1	0	2	3	1	.75	4	.301	.333	.491
2009	Phi	NL	97	154	38	6	0	5	(3	2)	59	15	20	15	11	1	29	1	0	2	1	0	1.00	2	.247	.296	.383
	Postseason		11	17	7	1	0	0	(0	0)	8	2	0	2	3	2	5	0	0	0	0	0	-	0	.412	.500	.471
	6 ML YEARS		467	926	251	51	7	26	(12	14)	394	106	147	121	61	9	179	5	1	12	8	2	.80	17	.271	.316	.425

Freddy Dolsi

Pitches: R Bats: R Pos: RP-6   Ht: 6'0" Wt: 160 Born: 1/9/1983 Age: 27

Year	Team	Lg	G	GS	CG	GF	IP	BFP	H	R	ER	HR	SH	SF	HB	TBB	IBB	SO	WP	Bk	W	L	Pct	Sh	Sv-Op	Hld	ERC	ERA
2003	Tigers	R	8	2	0	0	23.0	114	27	20	12	1	1	1	2	12	0	19	3	1	1	1	.500	0	0--	-	5.13	4.70
2005	WMich	A	23	0	0	6	37.0	163	36	16	10	5	0	2	1	14	0	27	7	0	1	0	1.000	0	0--	-	4.07	2.43
2006	Lkland	A+	30	0	0	11	42.2	190	47	25	19	5	1	2	1	17	0	29	7	1	4	4	.500	0	1--	-	4.84	4.01
2007	Lkland	A+	48	0	0	42	51.2	222	52	24	20	3	3	4	3	17	3	44	3	1	5	3	.625	0	23--	-	3.67	3.48
2007	Erie	AA	1	0	0	1	1.0	5	1	0	0	0	0	0	0	1	0	0	0	0	0	0	-	0	0--	-	5.48	0.00
2008	Lkland	A+	9	0	0	8	7.1	34	7	5	5	1	0	0	2	3	0	11	0	1	0	1	.000	0	5--	-	5.10	6.14

			HOW MUCH HE PITCHED						WHAT HE GAVE UP												THE RESULTS							
Year	Team	Lg	G	GS	CG	GF	IP	BFP	H	R	ER	HR	SH	SF	HB	TBB	IBB	SO	WP	Bk	W	L	Pct	Sh	Sv-Op	Hld	ERC	ERA
2008	Erie	AA	3	0	0	3	3.0	10	1	0	0	0	0	0	0	1	0	1	0	0	0	0	-	0	2- -	-	0.75	0.00
2008	Toledo	AAA	4	0	0	1	9.0	33	5	1	1	0	0	0	0	3	0	7	1	0	0	0	-	0	1- -	-	1.32	1.00
2009	Toledo	AAA	39	0	0	28	51.2	223	49	27	22	2	1	1	5	19	1	31	4	0	4	3	.571	0	10- -	-	3.57	3.83
2008	Det	AL	42	0	0	13	47.2	218	50	21	21	3	0	0	3	28	5	29	4	1	1	5	.167	0	2-3	7	4.89	3.97
2009	Det	AL	6	0	0	5	10.2	47	13	6	2	0	0	1	0	4	0	3	0	0	1	0	1.000	0	0-1	0	4.56	1.69
2 ML YEARS			48	0	0	18	58.1	265	63	27	23	3	0	1	3	32	5	32	4	1	2	5	.286	0	2-4	7	4.83	3.55

Brendan Donnelly

Pitches: R **Bats:** R **Pos:** RP-30 **Ht:** 6'3" **Wt:** 240 **Born:** 7/4/1971 **Age:** 38

			HOW MUCH HE PITCHED						WHAT HE GAVE UP												THE RESULTS							
Year	Team	Lg	G	GS	CG	GF	IP	BFP	H	R	ER	HR	SH	SF	HB	TBB	IBB	SO	WP	Bk	W	L	Pct	Sh	Sv-Op	Hld	ERC	ERA
2009	RdRck*	AAA	24	0	0	12	25.2	102	21	6	5	0	3	1	1	7	0	23	2	0	2	0	1.000	0	6- -	-	2.23	1.75
2009	Jupiter*	A+	1	1	0	0	1.0	4	1	0	0	0	0	0	0	0	0	0	0	0	0	0	-	0	0- -	-	1.95	0.00
2002	LAA	AL	46	0	0	11	49.2	199	32	13	12	2	3	1	2	19	3	54	1	0	1	1	.500	0	1-3	13	1.89	2.17
2003	LAA	AL	63	0	0	15	74.0	307	55	14	13	2	3	1	4	24	1	79	1	0	2	2	.500	0	3-5	29	2.12	1.58
2004	LAA	AL	40	0	0	10	42.0	172	34	14	14	5	2	2	1	15	0	56	0	0	5	2	.714	0	0-0	5	3.12	3.00
2005	LAA	AL	66	0	0	14	65.1	271	60	30	27	9	3	1	2	19	3	53	3	0	9	3	.750	0	0-5	16	3.52	3.72
2006	LAA	AL	62	0	0	17	64.0	278	58	32	28	8	2	2	4	28	3	53	6	0	6	0	1.000	0	0-1	11	4.02	3.94
2007	Bos	AL	27	0	0	4	20.2	90	19	8	7	0	0	0	4	5	0	15	2	0	2	1	.667	0	0-0	8	3.00	3.05
2008	Cle	AL	15	0	0	3	13.2	69	20	13	13	2	0	2	0	10	0	8	0	0	1	0	1.000	0	0-0	4	8.84	8.56
2009	Fla	NL	30	0	0	9	25.1	104	22	8	5	1	2	0	1	9	1	25	1	1	3	0	1.000	0	2-2	9	2.94	1.78
Postseason			17	0	0	3	20.0	83	14	12	11	2	0	0	1	9	2	23	2	0	1	0	1.000	0	0-0	4	2.69	4.95
8 ML YEARS			349	0	0	83	354.2	1490	300	132	119	29	15	9	18	129	11	343	14	1	29	9	.763	0	6-16	95	3.11	3.02

Octavio Dotel

Pitches: R **Bats:** R **Pos:** RP-62 **Ht:** 6'0" **Wt:** 215 **Born:** 11/25/1973 **Age:** 36

			HOW MUCH HE PITCHED						WHAT HE GAVE UP												THE RESULTS							
Year	Team	Lg	G	GS	CG	GF	IP	BFP	H	R	ER	HR	SH	SF	HB	TBB	IBB	SO	WP	Bk	W	L	Pct	Sh	Sv-Op	Hld	ERC	ERA
1999	NYM	NL	19	14	0	1	85.1	368	69	52	51	12	3	5	6	49	1	85	3	2	8	3	.727	0	0-0	0	4.30	5.38
2000	Hou	NL	50	16	0	25	125.0	563	127	80	75	26	7	8	7	61	3	142	6	0	3	7	.300	0	16-23	0	5.47	5.40
2001	Hou	NL	61	4	0	20	105.0	438	79	35	31	5	2	2	2	47	2	145	4	0	7	5	.583	0	2-4	14	2.62	2.66
2002	Hou	NL	83	0	0	22	97.1	376	58	21	20	7	3	7	4	27	2	118	2	0	6	4	.600	0	6-10	11	1.61	1.85
2003	Hou	NL	76	0	0	13	87.0	346	53	25	24	9	2	1	3	31	2	97	2	0	6	4	.600	0	4-6	33	2.02	2.48
2004	2 Tms		77	0	0	70	85.1	356	68	38	35	13	4	2	4	33	7	122	4	1	6	6	.500	0	36-45	0	3.31	3.69
2005	Oak	AL	15	0	0	13	15.1	65	10	6	6	2	0	0	0	11	2	16	1	0	1	2	.333	0	7-11	0	3.44	3.52
2006	NYY	AL	14	0	0	7	10.0	59	18	13	12	2	0	1	0	11	1	7	3	0	0	0	-	0	0-0	1	12.97	10.80
2007	2 Tms		33	0	0	25	30.2	138	29	16	14	4	1	0	4	12	4	41	2	0	2	1	.667	0	11-15	1	4.12	4.11
2008	CWS	AL	72	0	0	10	67.0	288	52	34	28	12	4	0	5	29	3	92	4	0	4	4	.500	0	1-5	21	3.64	3.76
2009	CWS	AL	62	0	0	12	62.1	268	54	26	23	7	3	3	0	36	1	75	4	1	3	3	.500	0	0-3	16	4.14	3.32
04	Hou	NL	32	0	0	29	34.2	146	27	15	12	4	2	1	1	15	4	50	3	1	0	4	.000	0	14-17	0	3.01	3.12
04	Oak	NL	45	0	0	41	50.2	210	41	23	23	9	2	1	3	18	3	72	1	0	6	2	.750	0	22-28	0	3.52	4.09
07	KC	AL	24	0	0	22	23.0	108	24	11	10	3	1	0	4	11	4	29	2	0	2	1	.667	0	11-14	0	5.13	3.91
07	Atl	NL	9	0	0	3	7.2	30	5	5	4	1	0	0	0	1	0	12	0	0	0	0	-	0	0-1	1	1.51	4.70
Postseason			8	0	0	2	8.0	40	12	7	7	1	0	0	1	4	1	13	1	0	1	0	1.000	0	0-0	1	8.09	7.88
11 ML YEARS			562	34	0	218	770.1	3265	617	346	319	99	29	29	35	347	28	940	35	4	46	39	.541	0	83-122	117	3.48	3.73

Ryan Doumit

Bats: B **Throws:** R **Pos:** C-71; PH-3; RF-1 **Ht:** 6'1" **Wt:** 215 **Born:** 4/3/1981 **Age:** 29

			BATTING																			BASERUNNING				AVERAGES		
Year	Team	Lg	G	AB	H	2B	3B	HR	(Hm	Rd)	TB	R	RBI	RC	TBB	IBB	SO	HBP	SH	SF	SB	CS	SB%	GDP	Avg	OBP	Slg
2009	Pirates*	R	2	7	0	0	0	0	(-	-)	0	0	0	0	1	0	2	0	0	0	0	0	-	0	.000	.125	.000
2009	Indy*	AAA	5	17	2	0	0	0	(-	-)	2	1	0	0	1	0	3	0	0	0	0	0	-	0	.118	.167	.118
2005	Pit	NL	75	231	59	13	1	6	(4	2)	92	25	35	32	11	1	48	13	1	1	2	1	.67	5	.255	.324	.398
2006	Pit	NL	61	149	31	9	0	6	(3	3)	58	15	17	17	15	1	42	11	1	2	0	0	-	3	.208	.322	.389
2007	Pit	NL	83	252	69	19	2	9	(7	2)	119	33	32	34	22	2	59	4	0	1	1	2	.33	5	.274	.341	.472
2008	Pit	NL	116	431	137	34	0	15	(8	7)	216	71	69	79	23	4	55	6	0	5	2	2	.50	10	.318	.357	.501
2009	Pit	NL	75	280	70	16	0	10	(6	4)	116	31	38	26	20	6	49	1	0	3	4	0	1.00	12	.250	.299	.414
5 ML YEARS			410	1343	366	91	3	46	(28	18)	601	175	191	188	91	14	253	35	2	12	9	5	.64	35	.273	.332	.448

Matt Downs

Bats: R **Throws:** R **Pos:** 2B-17 **Ht:** 6'2" **Wt:** 190 **Born:** 3/19/1984 **Age:** 26

			BATTING																			BASERUNNING				AVERAGES		
Year	Team	Lg	G	AB	H	2B	3B	HR	(Hm	Rd)	TB	R	RBI	RC	TBB	IBB	SO	HBP	SH	SF	SB	CS	SB%	GDP	Avg	OBP	Slg
2006	Giants	R	46	168	52	16	4	0	(-	-)	76	34	29	31	17	0	9	3	3	5	6	1	.86	5	.310	.373	.452
2007	SlmKzr	A-	73	287	97	33	0	8	(-	-)	154	68	48	65	28	0	34	10	7	4	16	2	.89	5	.338	.410	.537
2008	SnJos	A+	109	437	133	30	1	17	(-	-)	216	74	75	78	34	0	57	5	7	6	24	13	.65	9	.304	.357	.494
2008	Fresno	AAA	22	86	21	5	0	3	(-	-)	35	10	7	11	4	1	10	3	0	1	1	0	1.00	2	.244	.298	.407
2009	Fresno	AAA	109	424	127	33	3	14	(-	-)	208	68	74	73	25	0	58	7	4	7	8	2	.80	6	.300	.343	.491
2009	SF*	NL	17	53	9	2	0	1	(0	1)	14	6	2	1	6	1	13	0	0	1	1	0	1.00	2	.170	.250	.264

Scott Downs

Pitches: L Bats: L Pos: RP-48   Ht: 6'2" Wt: 209 Born: 3/17/1976 Age: 34

Year	Team	Lg	G	GS	CG	GF	IP	BFP	H	R	ER	HR	SH	SF	HB	TBB	IBB	SO	WP	Bk	W	L	Pct	Sh	Sv-Op	Hld	ERC	ERA
2009	Dnedin*	A+	3	2	0	1	2.1	13	3	1	1	0	0	0	1	1	0	2	0	0	0	0	-	0	0--	-	6.07	3.86
2000	2 Tms	NL	19	19	0	0	97.0	442	122	62	57	13	2	4	5	40	1	63	1	0	4	3	.571	0	0-0	0	6.19	5.29
2003	Mon	NL	1	1	0	0	3.0	17	5	5	5	2	0	0	0	3	2	4	0	1	0	1	.000	0	0-0	0	15.01	15.00
2004	Mon	NL	12	12	1	0	63.0	284	79	47	36	9	2	1	3	23	2	38	2	0	3	6	.333	1	0-0	0	5.97	5.14
2005	Tor	AL	26	13	0	0	94.0	407	93	49	45	12	0	1	5	34	0	75	3	0	4	3	.571	0	0-0	0	4.25	4.31
2006	Tor	AL	59	5	0	13	77.0	327	73	38	35	9	1	1	2	30	6	61	7	0	6	2	.750	0	1-4	6	3.87	4.09
2007	Tor	AL	81	0	0	13	58.0	239	47	15	14	3	1	2	1	24	3	57	2	1	4	2	.667	0	1-4	24	2.81	2.17
2008	Tor	AL	66	0	0	14	70.2	290	54	15	14	3	5	0	4	27	7	57	3	0	0	3	.000	0	5-9	24	2.47	1.78
2009	Tor	AL	48	0	0	24	46.2	200	46	18	16	4	0	2	2	13	1	43	1	0	1	3	.250	0	9-13	10	3.50	3.09
00	ChC	NL	18	18	0	0	94.0	426	117	59	54	13	2	4	5	37	1	63	1	0	4	3	.571	0	0-0	0	5.17	5.00
00	Mon	NL	1	1	0	0	3.0	16	5	3	3	0	0	0	0	3	0	0	0	0	0	0	-	0	0-0	0	10.34	9.00
8 ML YEARS			312	50	1	64	509.1	2206	519	249	222	55	11	11	22	194	22	398	19	2	22	23	.489	1	16-30	64	4.28	3.92

J.D. Drew

Bats: L Throws: R Pos: RF-132; PH-9; DH-1   Ht: 6'1" Wt: 200 Born: 11/20/1975 Age: 34

Year	Team	Lg	G	AB	H	2B	3B	HR	(Hm	Rd)	TB	R	RBI	RC	TBB	IBB	SO	HBP	SH	SF	SB	CS	SB%	GDP	Avg	OBP	Slg
1998	StL	NL	14	36	15	3	1	5	(4	1)	35	9	13	12	4	0	10	0	0	1	0	0	-	4	.417	.463	.972
1999	StL	NL	104	368	89	16	6	13	(5	8)	156	72	39	58	50	0	77	6	3	3	19	3	.86	4	.242	.340	.424
2000	StL	NL	135	407	120	17	2	18	(11	7)	195	73	57	80	67	4	99	6	5	1	17	9	.65	3	.295	.401	.479
2001	StL	NL	109	375	121	18	5	27	(15	12)	230	73	73	92	57	4	75	4	3	4	13	3	.81	6	.323	.414	.613
2002	StL	NL	135	424	107	19	1	18	(9	9)	182	61	56	65	57	4	104	8	3	4	2	1	.80	4	.252	.349	.429
2003	StL	NL	100	287	83	13	3	15	(7	8)	147	60	42	58	36	0	48	3	2	0	2	2	.50	6	.289	.374	.512
2004	Atl	NL	145	518	158	28	8	31	(14	17)	295	118	93	121	118	2	116	5	1	3	12	3	.80	7	.305	.436	.569
2005	LAD	NL	72	252	72	12	1	15	(10	5)	131	10	36	48	51	3	50	5	0	3	1	1	.50	3	.286	.412	.520
2006	LAD	NL	146	494	140	34	6	20	(12	8)	246	84	100	92	89	8	106	4	1	6	2	3	.40	4	.283	.393	.498
2007	Bos	AL	140	466	126	30	4	11	(4	7)	197	84	64	64	79	10	100	1	0	6	4	2	.67	12	.270	.373	.423
2008	Bos	AL	109	368	103	23	4	19	(10	9)	191	79	64	72	79	5	80	4	0	5	4	1	.80	11	.280	.408	.519
2009	Bos	AL	137	452	126	30	4	24	(11	13)	236	84	68	81	82	5	109	3	1	1	2	6	.25	5	.279	.392	.522
Postseason			52	175	46	6	0	6	(3	3)	70	18	23	20	17	0	35	1	1	0	0	1	.79	4	.263	.336	.400
12 ML YEARS			1346	4447	1260	243	45	216	(112	104)	2241	852	705	848	769	45	974	49	19	37	84	35	.71	70	.283	.392	.504

Stephen Drew

Bats: L Throws: R Pos: SS-132; PH-5; DH-1   Ht: 6'0" Wt: 185 Born: 3/16/1983 Age: 27

Year	Team	Lg	G	AB	H	2B	3B	HR	(Hm	Rd)	TB	R	RBI	RC	TBB	IBB	SO	HBP	SH	SF	SB	CS	SB%	GDP	Avg	OBP	Slg
2009	Reno*	AAA	2	9	3	0	1	0	(-	-)	5	0	1	1	0	0	1	0	0	0	0	0	-	0	.333	.333	.556
2006	Ari	NL	59	209	66	13	7	5	(3	2)	108	27	23	31	14	4	50	0	2	1	2	0	1.00	1	.316	.357	.517
2007	Ari	NL	150	543	129	28	4	12	(6	6)	201	60	60	71	60	5	100	3	5	8	9	0	1.00	4	.238	.313	.370
2008	Ari	NL	152	611	178	44	11	21	(9	12)	307	91	67	97	41	8	109	1	2	7	0	0	.00	5	.291	.333	.502
2009	Ari	NL	135	533	109	29	12	12	(4	8)	228	71	65	76	49	7	87	1	5	7	5	1	.83	6	.261	.320	.428
Postseason			7	31	12	1	1	2	(1	1)	21	6	4	5	1	0	7	0	0	0	1	0	1.00	1	.387	.406	.677
4 ML YEARS			496	1896	512	114	34	50	(22	28)	844	249	215	275	164	22	346	5	15	23	16	4	.83	15	.270	.326	.445

Justin Duchscherer

Pitches: R Bats: R Pos: P   Ht: 6'2" Wt: 201 Born: 11/19/1977 Age: 32

Year	Team	Lg	G	GS	CG	GF	IP	BFP	H	R	ER	HR	SH	SF	HB	TBB	IBB	SO	WP	Bk	W	L	Pct	Sh	Sv-Op	Hld	ERC	ERA
2009	Stcktn*	A+	1	1	0	0	2.0	6	0	0	0	0	0	0	0	0	0	2	0	0	0	0	-	0	0--	-	0.00	0.00
2009	Scrmto*	AAA	1	1	0	0	4.0	15	2	0	0	0	0	0	0	1	0	3	0	0	0	0	-	0	0--	-	0.94	0.00
2009	As*	R	1	1	0	0	5.0	17	4	0	0	0	0	0	0	0	0	3	0	0	0	0	-	0	0--	-	1.42	0.00
2001	Tex	AL	5	2	0	1	14.2	76	24	20	20	5	0	0	4	4	0	11	1	0	1	1	.500	0	0-0	0	10.68	12.27
2003	Oak	AL	4	3	0	0	16.1	71	17	7	6	1	1	0	2	3	0	15	0	0	1	1	.500	0	0-0	0	3.58	3.31
2004	Oak	AL	53	0	0	18	96.1	398	85	37	35	13	7	1	5	32	6	59	1	1	7	6	.538	0	0-2	6	3.57	3.27
2005	Oak	AL	65	0	0	24	85.2	338	67	25	21	7	4	2	2	19	3	85	2	0	7	4	.636	0	5-7	10	2.23	2.21
2006	Oak	AL	53	0	0	17	55.2	224	52	18	18	4	1	0	1	9	0	51	3	0	2	1	.667	0	9-11	17	2.73	2.91
2007	Oak	AL	17	0	0	2	16.1	75	18	9	9	3	1	2	0	8	3	13	0	0	3	3	.500	0	0-2	5	5.22	4.96
2008	Oak	AL	22	22	1	0	141.2	557	107	45	40	11	1	4	8	34	2	95	1	0	10	8	.556	1	0-0	0	2.31	2.54
Postseason			2	0	0	0	4.0	13	1	1	1	0	0	0	0	0	0	4	0	0	0	0	-	0	0-0	2	0.46	2.25
7 ML YEARS			219	27	1	62	426.2	1739	370	161	149	44	15	9	22	109	14	329	8	1	31	24	.564	1	14-22	38	3.00	3.14

Brian Duensing

Pitches: L Bats: L Pos: RP-15; SP-9   Ht: 5'11" Wt: 195 Born: 2/22/1983 Age: 27

Year	Team	Lg	G	GS	CG	GF	IP	BFP	H	R	ER	HR	SH	SF	HB	TBB	IBB	SO	WP	Bk	W	L	Pct	Sh	Sv-Op	Hld	ERC	ERA
2005	Elizab	R+	12	9	0	0	50.1	215	49	19	13	4	1	1	0	16	0	55	6	0	4	3	.571	0	0--	-	3.41	2.32
2006	Beloit	A	11	11	0	0	70.1	291	68	26	23	3	7	4	1	14	0	55	1	0	2	3	.400	0	0--	-	2.79	2.94
2006	FtMyrs	A+	7	7	0	0	40.1	170	47	25	19	4	0	3	0	8	0	33	1	0	2	5	.286	0	0--	-	4.26	4.24
2006	NwBrit	AA	10	9	0	0	49.1	211	51	29	20	6	3	5	1	18	0	30	0	0	1	2	.333	0	0--	-	4.42	3.65
2007	NwBrit	AA	9	9	0	0	50.2	206	47	19	15	2	1	1	1	7	0	38	0	0	4	1	.800	0	0--	-	2.37	2.66
2007	Roch	AAA	19	19	3	0	116.2	483	115	54	42	13	2	6	5	30	0	86	1	0	11	5	.688	1	0--	-	3.75	3.24
2008	Roch	AAA	26	25	0	0	144.1	615	155	81	72	16	7	5	6	38	2	80	4	0	5	12	.294	0	0--	-	4.20	4.49
2009	Roch	AAA	13	13	0	0	75.1	321	87	40	39	2	2	6	2	19	2	44	2	0	4	6	.400	0	0--	-	3.97	4.66
2009	Min	AL	24	9	0	3	84.0	359	84	37	34	7	3	2	3	31	1	53	1	0	5	2	.714	0	0-0	1	4.00	3.64

Chris Duffy

Bats: L **Throws:** L **Pos:** PH-9; CF-5; LF-3; RF-2; PR-1   **Ht:** 5'9" **Wt:** 185 **Born:** 4/20/1980 **Age:** 30

Year	Team	Lg	BATTING																		BASERUNNING				AVERAGES		
			G	AB	H	2B	3B	HR	(Hm	Rd)	TB	R	RBI	RC	TBB	IBB	SO	HBP	SH	SF	SB	CS	SB%	GDP	Avg	OBP	Slg
2009	Nashv*	AAA	3	6	1	0	0	0	(-	-)	1	1	0	0	1	0	2	0	2	0	0	1	.00	0	.167	.286	.167
2005	Pit	NL	39	126	43	4	2	1	(0	1)	54	22	9	22	7	0	22	1	2	1	2	2	.50	1	.341	.385	.429
2006	Pit	NL	84	314	80	14	3	2	(0	2)	106	46	18	36	19	1	71	10	4	1	26	1	.96	1	.255	.317	.338
2007	Pit	NL	70	241	60	11	3	3	(1	2)	86	31	22	29	21	0	43	3	2	3	13	4	.76	2	.249	.313	.357
2009	Mil	NL	19	32	4	1	0	0	(0	0)	5	3	3	1	4	0	12	0	1	0	0	0	-	1	.125	.222	.156
	4 ML YEARS		212	713	187	30	8	6	(1	5)	251	102	52	88	51	1	148	15	8	4	41	7	.85	5	.262	.323	.352

Zach Duke

Pitches: L **Bats:** L **Pos:** SP-32   **Ht:** 6'2" **Wt:** 205 **Born:** 4/19/1983 **Age:** 27

Year	Team	Lg	HOW MUCH HE PITCHED						WHAT HE GAVE UP												THE RESULTS						
			G	GS	CG	GF	IP	BFP	H	R	ER	HR	SH	SF	HB	TBB	IBB	SO	WP	Bk	W	L	Pct	Sh	Sv-Op	Hld	ERC	ERA
2005	Pit	NL	14	14	0	0	84.2	341	79	20	17	3	3	1	2	23	2	58	1	0	8	2	.800	0	0-0	0	2.96	1.81
2006	Pit	NL	34	34	2	0	215.1	935	255	116	107	17	13	4	7	68	6	117	8	1	10	15	.400	1	0-0	0	4.82	4.47
2007	Pit	NL	20	19	0	0	107.1	482	161	74	66	14	2	4	3	25	2	41	0	1	3	8	.273	0	0-0	0	6.96	5.53
2008	Pit	NL	31	31	1	0	185.0	829	230	111	99	19	14	4	7	47	1	87	2	2	5	14	.263	1	0-0	0	4.99	4.82
2009	Pit	NL	32	32	3	0	213.0	891	231	101	96	23	18	10	3	49	0	106	2	1	11	16	.407	1	0-0	0	4.05	4.06
	5 ML YEARS		131	130	6	0	805.1	3478	956	422	385	76	50	23	22	212	11	409	13	5	37	55	.402	3	0-0	0	4.71	4.30

Elijah Dukes

Bats: R **Throws:** R **Pos:** RF-65; CF-35; PH-7; LF-5; PR-2   **Ht:** 6'1" **Wt:** 248 **Born:** 6/26/1984 **Age:** 26

Year	Team	Lg	BATTING																		BASERUNNING				AVERAGES		
			G	AB	H	2B	3B	HR	(Hm	Rd)	TB	R	RBI	RC	TBB	IBB	SO	HBP	SH	SF	SB	CS	SB%	GDP	Avg	OBP	Slg
2009	Hrsbrg*	AA	2	8	2	0	0	0	(-	-)	2	0	0	0	1	0	1	0	0	0	0	0	-	0	.250	.333	.250
2009	Syrcse*	AAA	20	68	19	8	0	3	(-	-)	36	8	10	14	9	1	9	3	0	0	5	1	.83	0	.279	.388	.529
2007	TB	AL	52	184	35	3	2	10	(4	6)	72	27	21	20	33	0	44	2	0	1	2	4	.33	6	.190	.318	.391
2008	Was	NL	81	276	73	16	2	13	(7	6)	132	48	44	46	50	1	79	6	0	2	13	4	.76	10	.264	.386	.478
2009	Was	NL	107	364	91	20	4	8	(6	2)	143	38	58	44	46	2	74	3	0	3	3	10	.23	8	.250	.337	.393
	3 ML YEARS		240	824	199	39	8	31	(17	14)	347	113	123	110	129	3	197	11	0	6	18	18	.50	24	.242	.349	.421

Phil Dumatrait

Pitches: L **Bats:** R **Pos:** RP-15   **Ht:** 6'2" **Wt:** 200 **Born:** 7/12/1981 **Age:** 28

Year	Team	Lg	HOW MUCH HE PITCHED						WHAT HE GAVE UP												THE RESULTS						
			G	GS	CG	GF	IP	BFP	H	R	ER	HR	SH	SF	HB	TBB	IBB	SO	WP	Bk	W	L	Pct	Sh	Sv-Op	Hld	ERC	ERA
2009	Pirates*	R	1	1	0	0	4.0	16	3	0	0	0	0	0	0	2	0	2	0	0	0	0	-	0	0--	-	2.58	0.00
2009	StCol*	A-	1	1	0	0	5.0	22	5	4	2	1	1	1	0	0	0	4	0	0	0	1	.000	0	0--	-	2.72	3.60
2009	Altna*	AA	1	1	0	0	4.0	21	9	5	5	0	0	0	1	0	0	4	0	0	0	1	.000	0	0--	-	10.81	11.25
2009	Indy*	AAA	4	2	0	0	15.0	65	16	11	7	2	0	0	0	4	0	5	0	0	0	2	.000	0	0--	-	4.05	4.20
2007	Cin	NL	6	6	0	0	18.0	104	39	30	30	6	2	2	1	12	0	9	0	0	0	4	.000	0	0-0	0	15.81	15.00
2008	Pit	NL	21	11	0	4	78.2	351	82	48	46	7	1	3	2	42	2	52	1	0	3	4	.429	0	0-0	0	4.87	5.26
2009	Pit	NL	15	0	0	2	13.0	64	13	11	10	4	0	1	0	11	0	7	0	0	0	2	.000	0	0-1	1	7.35	6.92
	3 ML YEARS		42	17	0	6	109.2	519	134	89	86	17	3	6	3	65	2	68	1	0	3	10	.231	0	0-1	1	6.73	7.06

Chris Duncan

Bats: L **Throws:** R **Pos:** LF-68; PH-15; 1B-6; DH-4   **Ht:** 6'5" **Wt:** 230 **Born:** 5/5/1981 **Age:** 29

Year	Team	Lg	BATTING																		BASERUNNING				AVERAGES		
			G	AB	H	2B	3B	HR	(Hm	Rd)	TB	R	RBI	RC	TBB	IBB	SO	HBP	SH	SF	SB	CS	SB%	GDP	Avg	OBP	Slg
2009	Pwtckt*	AAA	27	85	16	3	0	2	(1	1)	25	8	10	6	7	0	20	1	0	1	0	0	-	2	.188	.255	.294
2005	StL	NL	9	10	2	1	0	1	(1	0)	6	2	3	1	0	0	5	0	0	0	0	0	-	1	.200	.200	.600
2006	StL	NL	90	280	82	11	3	22	(9	13)	165	60	43	47	30	0	69	2	0	2	0	0	-	4	.293	.363	.589
2007	StL	NL	127	375	97	20	0	21	(8	13)	180	51	70	69	55	3	123	1	0	1	2	1	.67	4	.259	.354	.480
2008	StL	NL	76	222	55	8	0	6	(4	2)	81	26	27	27	34	3	52	0	0	1	2	1	.67	9	.248	.346	.365
2009	StL	NL	87	260	59	15	2	5	(2	3)	93	25	32	33	41	1	67	0	0	3	0	1	.00	6	.227	.329	.358
	Postseason		10	22	3	1	0	1	(1	0)	7	3	2	2	4	0	7	0	0	0	0	0	-	2	.136	.269	.318
	5 ML YEARS		389	1147	295	55	5	55	(24	31)	525	164	175	177	160	7	316	3	0	7	4	3	.57	24	.257	.348	.458

Shelley Duncan

Bats: R **Throws:** R **Pos:** RF-8; PH-3; PR-2; DH-1   **Ht:** 6'5" **Wt:** 225 **Born:** 9/29/1979 **Age:** 30

Year	Team	Lg	BATTING																		BASERUNNING				AVERAGES		
			G	AB	H	2B	3B	HR	(Hm	Rd)	TB	R	RBI	RC	TBB	IBB	SO	HBP	SH	SF	SB	CS	SB%	GDP	Avg	OBP	Slg
2009	S-WB*	AAA	123	452	125	30	1	30	(-	-)	247	85	99	93	64	2	94	6	0	5	2	0	1.00	3	.277	.370	.546
2007	NYY	AL	34	74	19	1	0	7	(6	1)	41	16	17	14	8	0	20	0	1	0	0	0	-	2	.257	.329	.554
2008	NYY	AL	23	57	10	3	0	1	(1	0)	16	7	6	4	7	0	13	0	0	1	0	0	-	1	.175	.262	.281
2009	NYY	AL	11	15	3	0	0	0	(0	0)	3	1	1	1	0	0	5	0	0	0	0	0	-	1	.200	.200	.200
	Postseason		3	4	2	0	0	0	(0	0)	2	1	0	1	0	0	1	0	0	0	0	0	-	0	.500	.500	.500
	3 ML YEARS		68	146	32	4	0	8	(7	1)	60	24	24	19	15	0	38	0	1	1	0	0	-	4	.219	.290	.411

Adam Dunn

Bats: L **Throws:** R **Pos:** 1B-67; LF-62; RF-22; DH-6; PH-4   **Ht:** 6'6" **Wt:** 287 **Born:** 11/9/1979 **Age:** 30

Year	Team	Lg	G	AB	H	2B	3B	HR	(Hm	Rd)	TB	R	RBI	RC	TBB	IBB	SO	HBP	SH	SF	SB	CS	SB%	GDP	Avg	OBP	Slg
2001	Cin	NL	66	244	64	18	1	19	(8	11)	141	54	43	51	38	2	74	4	0	1	4	2	.67	4	.262	.371	.578
2002	Cin	NL	158	535	133	28	2	26	(13	13)	243	84	71	96	128	13	170	9	1	3	19	9	.68	8	.249	.400	.454
2003	Cin	NL	116	381	82	12	1	27	(16	11)	177	70	57	61	74	8	126	10	0	4	8	2	.80	4	.215	.354	.465
2004	Cin	NL	161	568	151	34	0	46	(25	21)	323	105	102	108	108	11	195	5	0	0	6	1	.86	8	.266	.388	.569
2005	Cin	NL	160	543	134	35	2	40	(**26**	14)	293	107	101	112	114	14	168	12	0	2	4	2	.67	6	.247	.387	.540
2006	Cin	NL	160	561	131	24	0	40	(22	18)	275	99	92	96	112	12	194	6	1	3	7	0	1.00	8	.234	.365	.490
2007	Cin	NL	152	522	138	27	2	40	(19	21)	289	101	106	103	101	8	165	5	0	4	9	2	.82	12	.264	.386	.554
2008	2 Tms	NL	158	517	122	23	0	40	(21	19)	265	79	100	101	122	13	164	7	0	5	2	1	.67	7	.236	.386	.513
2009	Was	NL	159	546	146	29	0	38	(19	19)	289	81	105	100	116	10	177	4	0	2	0	1	.00	8	.267	.398	.529
08	Cin	NL	114	373	87	14	0	32	(16	16)	197	58	74	74	80	6	120	6	0	5	1	1	.50	4	.233	.373	.528
08	Ari	NL	44	144	35	9	0	8	(5	3)	68	21	26	27	42	7	44	1	0	0	1	0	1.00	3	.243	.417	.472
	9 ML YEARS		1290	4417	1101	230	8	316	(169	147)	2295	780	777	837	913	97	1433	62	2	23	59	20	.75	65	.249	.383	.520

Mike Dunn

Pitches: L **Bats:** L **Pos:** RP-4   **Ht:** 6'1" **Wt:** 195 **Born:** 5/23/1985 **Age:** 25

Year	Team	Lg	G	GS	CG	GF	IP	BFP	H	R	ER	HR	SH	SF	HB	TBB	IBB	SO	WP	Bk	W	L	Pct	Sh	Sv-Op	Hld	ERC	ERA
2006	Yanks	R	11	0	0	7	24.2	95	13	2	2	0	1	0	1	9	0	26	1	0	3	0	1.000	0	4--	-	1.33	0.73
2006	StIsInd	A-	3	0	0	0	6.1	31	3	6	4	0	0	0	0	7	0	7	2	0	0	0	-	0	0--	-	2.77	5.68
2007	CtnSC	A	27	27	0	0	144.2	597	136	69	55	14	3	8	3	45	0	138	10	0	12	5	.706	0	0--	-	3.52	3.42
2008	Tampa	A+	30	22	0	4	124.2	543	124	70	63	10	8	6	5	58	2	118	7	0	4	7	.364	0	1--	-	4.34	4.55
2008	Trntn	AA	1	0	0	0	1.2	7	1	0	0	0	0	0	0	1	0	2	0	0	1	0	1.000	0	0--	-	2.03	0.00
2009	Trntn	AA	26	0	0	6	53.1	230	41	23	22	3	2	0	2	32	2	76	0	0	3	3	.500	0	2--	-	3.35	3.71
2009	S-WB	AAA	12	0	0	2	20.0	90	17	5	5	1	0	1	1	14	0	23	1	0	1	0	1.000	0	0--	-	4.21	2.25
2009	NYY	AL	4	0	0	3	4.0	20	3	3	3	1	0	0	0	5	0	3	1	0	0	0	-	0	0-0	0	7.17	6.75

Luis Durango

Bats: B **Throws:** R **Pos:** PH-6; LF-1; CF-1; PR-1   **Ht:** 5'9" **Wt:** 158 **Born:** 4/23/1986 **Age:** 24

Year	Team	Lg	G	AB	H	2B	3B	HR	(Hm	Rd)	TB	R	RBI	RC	TBB	IBB	SO	HDP	SH	SF	SB	CS	SB%	GDP	Avg	OBP	Slg
2006	Padres	R	39	143	54	2	4	0	(-	-)	64	35	14	32	23	0	16	2	2	0	17	6	.74	2	.378	.470	.448
2007	Eugene	A-	69	300	110	6	8	2	(-	-)	138	60	32	58	29	2	32	1	3	2	17	10	.63	5	.367	.422	.460
2008	FtWyn	A	93	334	102	11	3	1	(-	-)	122	66	25	53	49	0	43	1	4	1	14	7	.67	9	.305	.395	.365
2008	Lk Els	A+	17	72	31	4	1	0	(-	-)	37	20	10	18	13	0	7	0	0	2	1	1	.50	0	.431	.506	.514
2009	SnAnt	AA	129	456	128	9	2	0	(-	-)	141	78	25	68	81	2	70	2	19	2	44	17	.72	7	.281	.390	.309
2009	SD	NL	9	11	6	0	0	0	(0	0)	6	3	0	3	2	0	2	0	1	0	2	1	.67	0	.545	.615	.545

Chad Durbin

Pitches: R **Bats:** R **Pos:** RP-59   **Ht:** 6'2" **Wt:** 222 **Born:** 12/3/1977 **Age:** 32

Year	Team	Lg	G	GS	CG	GF	IP	BFP	H	R	ER	HR	SH	SF	HB	TBB	IBB	SO	WP	Bk	W	L	Pct	Sh	Sv-Op	Hld	ERC	ERA
2009	Clrwtr*	A+	2	1	0	0	3.0	13	3	0	0	0	0	0	0	1	0	4	0	0	0	0	-	0	0--	-	3.05	0.00
2009	LV*	AAA	1	1	0	0	1.0	3	1	0	0	0	0	0	0	0	0	1	0	0	0	0	-	0	0--	-	2.79	0.00
1999	KC	AL	1	0	0	0	2.1	9	1	0	0	0	0	0	0	1	0	3	1	0	0	0	-	0	0-0	0	1.08	0.00
2000	KC	AL	16	16	0	0	72.1	349	91	71	66	14	1	3	0	43	1	37	7	0	2	5	.286	0	0-0	0	7.05	8.21
2001	KC	AL	29	29	2	0	179.0	777	201	109	98	26	2	7	11	58	0	95	6	0	9	16	.360	0	0-0	0	5.15	4.93
2002	KC	AL	2	2	0	0	8.1	43	13	11	11	3	0	1	0	4	0	5	0	0	1	0	1.000	0	0-0	0	10.58	11.88
2003	Cle	AL	3	1	0	0	8.2	45	18	12	7	2	0	0	0	3	0	8	2	0	0	1	.000	0	0-0	0	12.37	7.27
2004	2 Tms	AL	24	8	1	5	60.2	291	72	50	47	11	2	2	5	35	3	48	5	0	6	7	.462	0	0-0	1	6.75	6.97
2006	Det	AL	3	0	0	1	6.0	24	6	1	1	0	0	0	0	3	0	3	0	0	0	0	-	0	0-0	1	2.87	1.50
2007	Det	AL	36	19	0	7	127.2	561	133	71	67	21	1	7	8	49	4	66	2	0	8	7	.533	0	1-2	3	4.92	4.72
2008	Phi	NL	71	0	0	12	87.2	365	81	33	28	5	4	2	4	35	7	63	3	0	5	4	.556	0	1-7	17	3.51	2.87
2009	Phi	NL	59	0	0	15	69.2	314	56	38	34	8	3	3	7	47	2	62	2	0	2	2	.500	0	2-3	8	4.47	4.39
04	Cle	AL	17	8	1	5	51.1	239	63	40	38	10	0	2	4	24	3	38	3	0	5	6	.455	0	0-0	0	6.70	6.66
04	Min	AL	7	0	0	0	9.1	52	9	10	9	1	2	0	1	11	0	10	2	0	1	1	.500	0	0-0	1	6.92	8.68
	Postseason		6	0	0	0	3.1	21	7	2	1	1	0	0	1	3	0	3	0	0	0	0	-	0	0-0	2	17.12	2.70
	10 ML YEARS		244	75	3	40	622.1	2778	672	396	359	91	13	24	36	275	17	390	28	0	32	43	.427	0	4-12	29	5.26	5.19

Jermaine Dye

Bats: R **Throws:** R **Pos:** RF-133; DH-7; PH-1   **Ht:** 6'5" **Wt:** 245 **Born:** 1/28/1974 **Age:** 36

Year	Team	Lg	G	AB	H	2B	3B	HR	(Hm	Rd)	TB	R	RBI	RC	TBB	IBB	SO	HBP	SH	SF	SB	CS	SB%	GDP	Avg	OBP	Slg
1996	Atl	NL	98	292	82	16	0	12	(4	8)	134	32	37	36	8	0	67	3	0	3	1	4	.20	11	.281	.304	.459
1997	KC	AL	75	263	62	14	0	7	(3	4)	97	26	22	26	17	0	51	1	1	1	2	1	.67	6	.236	.284	.369
1998	KC	AL	60	214	50	5	1	5	(3	2)	72	24	23	17	11	2	46	1	0	4	2	2	.50	8	.234	.270	.336
1999	KC	AL	158	608	179	44	8	27	(15	12)	320	96	119	106	58	4	119	1	0	6	2	3	.40	17	.294	.354	.526
2000	KC	AL	157	601	193	41	2	33	(15	18)	337	107	118	125	69	6	99	3	0	6	0	1	.00	12	.321	.390	.561
2001	2 Tms	AL	158	599	169	31	4	26	(16	10)	286	91	106	99	57	6	112	7	1	11	9	1	.90	8	.282	.346	.467
2002	Oak	AL	131	488	123	27	1	24	(13	11)	224	74	86	70	52	2	108	10	0	5	2	0	1.00	15	.252	.333	.459
2003	Oak	AL	65	221	38	6	0	4	(3	1)	56	28	20	10	25	2	42	3	0	4	1	0	1.00	11	.172	.261	.253
2004	Oak	AL	137	532	141	29	4	23	(12	11)	247	87	80	69	49	4	128	4	0	5	4	2	.67	16	.265	.329	.464
2005	CWS	AL	145	529	145	29	2	31	(15	16)	271	74	86	80	39	3	99	9	0	2	11	4	.73	15	.274	.333	.512
2006	CWS	AL	146	539	170	27	3	44	(21	23)	335	103	120	116	59	4	118	6	0	7	3	1	.70	15	.315	.385	.622
2007	CWS	AL	138	508	129	34	0	28	(14	14)	247	68	78	67	45	2	107	4	0	4	2	1	.67	17	.254	.317	.486

97

Year	Team	Lg	G	AB	H	2B	3B	HR	(Hm	Rd)	TB	R	RBI	RC	TBB	IBB	SO	HBP	SH	SF	SB	CS	SB%	GDP	Avg	OBP	Slg
2008	CWS	AL	154	590	172	41	2	34	(18	16)	319	96	96	91	44	3	104	6	0	5	3	2	.60	18	.292	.344	.541
2009	CWS	AL	141	503	126	19	1	27	(15	12)	228	78	81	79	64	2	108	5	0	2	0	2	.00	15	.250	.340	.453
01	KC	AL	97	367	100	14	0	13	(8	5)	153	50	47	54	30	3	68	6	1	6	7	1	.88	2	.272	.333	.417
01	Oak	AL	61	232	69	17	1	13	(8	5)	127	41	59	45	27	3	44	1	0	5	2	0	1.00	6	.297	.366	.547
	Postseason		44	163	44	9	0	5	(2	3)	68	16	17	17	12	0	33	3	1	2	2	1	.67	2	.270	.328	.417
	14 ML YEARS		1763	6487	1779	363	25	325	(167	158)	3167	984	1072	991	597	40	1308	63	2	65	46	26	.64	184	.274	.338	.488

Adam Eaton

Pitches: R **Bats:** R **Pos:** SP-8; RP-4 **Ht:** 6'2" **Wt:** 216 **Born:** 11/23/1977 **Age:** 32

Year	Team	Lg	G	GS	CG	GF	IP	BFP	H	R	ER	HR	SH	SF	HB	TBB	IBB	SO	WP	Bk	W	L	Pct	Sh	Sv-Op	Hld	ERC	ERA
2009	ColSpr*	AAA	14	12	0	0	79.1	332	81	33	28	4	4	2	4	16	1	50	2	0	4	3	.571	0	0- -	-	3.27	3.18
2000	SD	NL	22	22	0	0	135.0	583	134	63	62	14	1	3	2	61	3	90	3	0	7	4	.636	0	0-0	0	4.34	4.13
2001	SD	NL	17	17	2	0	116.2	499	108	61	56	20	3	2	5	40	3	109	3	0	8	5	.615	0	0-0	0	4.01	4.32
2002	SD	NL	6	6	0	0	33.1	142	28	20	20	5	2	2	5	17	0	25	2	0	1	1	.500	0	0-0	0	4.28	5.40
2003	SD	NL	31	31	1	0	183.0	789	173	91	83	20	5	5	7	68	6	146	7	1	9	12	.429	0	0-0	0	3.78	4.08
2004	SD	NL	33	33	0	0	199.1	848	204	113	102	28	12	7	10	52	3	153	5	0	11	14	.440	0	0-0	0	4.10	4.61
2005	SD	NL	24	22	0	2	128.2	568	140	70	61	14	4	6	5	44	6	100	5	0	11	5	.688	0	0-0	0	4.44	4.27
2006	Tex	AL	13	13	0	0	65.0	291	78	38	37	11	1	1	4	24	0	43	0	0	7	4	.636	0	0-0	0	5.98	5.12
2007	Phi	NL	30	30	0	0	161.2	734	192	117	113	30	10	5	11	71	4	97	6	0	10	10	.500	0	0-0	0	6.33	6.29
2008	Phi	NL	21	19	0	0	107.0	478	131	71	69	15	3	2	6	44	5	57	2	0	4	8	.333	0	0-0	0	6.07	5.80
2009	2 Tms		12	8	0	2	49.0	235	65	44	44	10	1	1	0	27	3	35	2	0	3	5	.375	0	0-0	0	7.38	8.08
09	Bal	AL	8	8	0	0	41.0	194	56	39	39	9	0	1	0	19	1	28	1	0	2	5	.286	0	0-0	0	7.47	8.56
09	Col	NL	4	0	0	2	8.0	41	9	5	5	1	1	0	0	8	2	7	1	0	1	0	1.000	0	0-0	0	6.84	5.63
	10 ML YEARS		209	201	3	4	1178.2	5167	1253	688	647	167	42	34	52	448	33	855	35	1	71	68	.511	0	0-0	0	4.80	4.94

David Eckstein

Bats: R **Throws:** R **Pos:** 2B-131; PH-8 **Ht:** 5'7" **Wt:** 177 **Born:** 1/20/1975 **Age:** 35

Year	Team	Lg	G	AB	H	2B	3B	HR	(Hm	Rd)	TB	R	RBI	RC	TBB	IBB	SO	HBP	SH	SF	SB	CS	SB%	GDP	Avg	OBP	Slg
2001	LAA	AL	153	582	166	26	2	4	(3	1)	208	82	41	80	43	0	60	21	16	2	29	4	.88	11	.285	.355	.357
2002	LAA	AL	152	608	178	22	6	8	(3	5)	236	107	63	93	45	0	44	27	14	8	21	13	.62	7	.293	.363	.388
2003	LAA	AL	120	452	114	22	1	3	(1	2)	147	59	31	53	36	0	45	15	10	4	16	5	.76	9	.252	.325	.325
2004	LAA	AL	142	566	156	24	1	2	(2	0)	188	92	35	60	42	1	49	13	14	2	16	5	.76	11	.276	.339	.332
2005	StL	NL	158	630	185	26	7	8	(3	5)	249	90	61	103	58	0	44	13	8	4	11	8	.58	13	.294	.363	.395
2006	StL	NL	123	500	146	18	1	2	(0	2)	172	68	23	60	31	0	41	15	3	3	7	6	.54	7	.292	.350	.344
2007	StL	NL	117	434	134	23	0	3	(1	2)	166	58	31	55	24	0	22	12	7	7	10	1	.91	9	.309	.356	.382
2008	2 Tms		94	324	86	21	0	2	(2	0)	113	32	27	42	31	1	32	9	9	3	2	1	.67	7	.265	.343	.349
2009	SD	NL	136	503	131	27	2	2	(2	0)	168	64	51	62	39	1	46	9	13	4	3	1	.75	8	.260	.323	.334
08	Tor	AL	76	260	72	18	0	1	(1	0)	93	27	23	37	24	1	27	8	9	2	2	1	.67	6	.277	.354	.358
08	Ari	NL	18	64	14	3	0	1	(1	0)	20	5	4	5	7	0	5	1	0	1	0	0	-	1	.219	.301	.313
	Postseason		44	176	49	4	0	2	(1	1)	59	26	18	25	12	0	9	7	3	2	7	1	.88	2	.278	.345	.335
	9 ML YEARS		1195	4599	1296	209	20	34	(17	17)	1647	652	363	608	349	3	383	134	94	37	115	44	.72	82	.282	.348	.358

Jack Egbert

Pitches: R **Bats:** L **Pos:** RP-2 **Ht:** 6'3" **Wt:** 220 **Born:** 5/12/1983 **Age:** 27

Year	Team	Lg	G	GS	CG	GF	IP	BFP	H	R	ER	HR	SH	SF	HB	TBB	IBB	SO	WP	Bk	W	L	Pct	Sh	Sv-Op	Hld	ERC	ERA
2004	Gr Falls	R+	17	9	0	0	58.2	253	51	25	22	2	4	1	5	33	0	52	4	0	4	1	.800	0	0- -	-	3.93	3.38
2005	Knapol	A	30	24	4	1	147.0	610	127	66	51	5	4	2	16	48	0	107	10	0	10	5	.667	3	0- -	-	3.08	3.12
2006	WinSa	A+	25	25	0	0	140.2	588	131	57	46	2	3	2	5	46	0	120	2	0	9	8	.529	2	0- -	-	3.00	2.94
2006	Brham	AA	4	4	0	0	21.0	88	17	4	2	0	1	0	0	8	0	24	1	0	0	2	.000	0	0- -	-	2.30	0.86
2007	Brham	AA	28	28	0	0	161.2	654	138	63	55	3	3	1	10	44	0	165	6	0	12	8	.600	0	0- -	-	2.57	3.06
2008	Brham	AA	1	1	0	0	4.0	17	5	1	1	0	0	0	0	1	0	4	0	0	0	0	-	0	0- -	-	4.32	2.25
2008	Charltt	AAA	24	22	1	0	129.2	565	133	80	67	15	5	6	8	41	2	117	3	0	4	12	.250	1	0- -	-	4.17	4.65
2009	Charltt	AAA	30	18	0	2	108.2	497	132	73	61	13	3	3	7	33	1	79	3	0	6	11	.353	0	1- -	-	5.20	5.05
2009	CWS	AL	2	0	0	1	2.2	18	8	8	8	1	0	1	0	2	1	0	0	0	0	0	-	0	0-0	0	21.82	27.00

Mike Ekstrom

Pitches: R **Bats:** R **Pos:** RP-12 **Ht:** 5'11" **Wt:** 189 **Born:** 8/30/1983 **Age:** 26

Year	Team	Lg	G	GS	CG	GF	IP	BFP	H	R	ER	HR	SH	SF	HB	TBB	IBB	SO	WP	Bk	W	L	Pct	Sh	Sv-Op	Hld	ERC	ERA
2004	Eugene	A-	12	7	0	1	39.0	171	38	18	16	1	1	4	4	10	0	42	2	0	3	1	.750	0	0- -	-	3.14	3.69
2004	FtWyn	A	3	3	0	0	14.1	62	21	15	13	1	1	1	0	3	0	10	3	0	0	2	.000	0	0- -	-	6.14	8.16
2005	FtWyn	A	28	28	1	0	167.2	703	167	76	69	11	6	6	5	36	0	112	4	0	13	6	.684	1	0- -	-	3.19	3.70
2006	Lk Els	A+	14	14	1	0	82.1	335	76	32	21	2	3	1	7	21	0	68	3	0	7	4	.636	1	0- -	-	3.02	2.30
2006	Mobile	AA	14	14	3	0	84.1	360	87	46	36	2	4	2	2	19	3	49	5	0	3	7	.300	1	0- -	-	3.03	3.84
2007	SnAnt	AA	27	27	0	0	143.2	643	183	85	76	6	9	1	5	47	0	98	8	0	7	10	.412	0	0- -	-	5.12	4.76
2008	SnAnt	AA	41	15	0	10	108.0	496	137	68	55	14	3	2	8	34	2	101	4	0	11	8	.579	0	1- -	-	5.74	4.58
2009	Portlnd	AAA	42	1	0	7	62.1	240	44	12	12	2	1	3	1	16	0	43	2	0	4	2	.667	0	0- -	-	1.77	1.73
2008	SD	NL	8	0	0	0	9.2	47	14	8	8	2	0	0	0	7	1	6	0	0	0	2	.000	0	0-0	0	9.38	7.45
2009	SD	NL	12	0	0	5	18.1	83	21	14	13	3	0	2	1	8	0	19	2	0	0	0	-	0	0-0	0	5.80	6.38
	2 ML YEARS		20	0	0	6	28.0	130	35	22	21	5	0	2	1	15	1	25	2	0	0	2	.000	0	0-0	0	6.97	6.75

Scott Elbert

Pitches: L **Bats:** L **Pos:** RP-19   **Ht:** 6'1" **Wt:** 213 **Born:** 8/13/1985 **Age:** 24

			HOW MUCH HE PITCHED						WHAT HE GAVE UP												THE RESULTS						
Year	Team	Lg	G	GS	CG	GF	IP	BFP	H	R	ER	HR	SH	SF	HB	TBB	IBB	SO	WP	Bk	W	L	Pct	Sh	Sv-Op	Hld	ERC	ERA
2004	Ogden	R+	12	12	0	0	49.2	217	47	33	29	5	6	2	5	30	0	45	5	0	2	3	.400	0	0--	-	5.21	5.26
2005	Clmbs	A	25	24	1	0	115.0	482	83	37	34	8	0	5	4	57	0	128	5	0	8	5	.615	1	0--	-	2.86	2.66
2006	VeroB	A+	17	15	0	1	83.2	346	57	27	22	4	4	0	5	41	0	97	6	0	5	5	.500	0	0--	-	2.62	2.37
2006	Jaxnvl	AA	11	11	0	0	62.1	267	40	26	25	11	6	2	1	44	0	76	1	0	6	4	.600	0	0--	-	3.89	3.61
2007	Jaxnvl	AA	3	3	0	0	14.0	57	6	6	6	0	0	0	0	10	0	24	0	0	0	1	.000	0	0--	-	1.66	3.86
2008	Jaxnvl	AA	25	1	0	7	41.1	162	22	14	11	2	1	1	1	19	1	46	1	0	4	1	.800	0	0--	-	1.70	2.40
2009	Chatt	AA	12	11	0	0	62.1	276	59	32	27	5	1	2	5	30	0	87	2	0	2	3	.400	0	0--	-	4.25	3.90
2009	Albq	AAA	8	7	1	0	33.2	147	34	16	14	2	1	0	2	14	0	38	4	1	2	1	.667	1	0--	-	4.15	3.74
2008	LAD	NL	10	0	0	1	6.0	31	9	8	8	2	0	0	1	4	0	4	0	0	0	1	.000	0	0-0	2	11.46	12.00
2009	LAD	NL	19	0	0	3	19.2	83	19	11	11	4	1	0	0	7	0	21	1	0	2	0	1.000	0	0-0	3	4.45	5.03
	2 ML YEARS		29	0	0	4	25.2	114	28	19	19	6	1	0	1	11	0	29	1	0	2	1	.667	0	0-0	5	5.92	6.66

A.J. Ellis

Bats: R **Throws:** R **Pos:** C-7; PH-1   **Ht:** 6'2" **Wt:** 227 **Born:** 4/9/1981 **Age:** 29

							BATTING													BASERUNNING				AVERAGES		
Year	Team	Lg	G	AB	H	2B	3B	HR	(Hm	Rd)	TB	R	RBI	RC	TBB	IBB	SO	HBP	SH	SF	SB	CS	SB%	GDP	Avg	OBP	Slg
2003	SoGA	A	3	6	0	0	0	0	(-	-)	0	0	0	0	0	0	0	1	0	0	0	1	.00	0	.000	.143	.000
2004	VeroB	A+	40	114	25	4	0	2	(-	-)	35	15	22	15	24	0	20	1	1	1	1	0	1.00	2	.219	.357	.307
2005	VeroB	A+	57	176	45	8	0	3	(-	-)	62	27	22	23	22	0	26	0	1	1	1	3	.25	3	.256	.356	.352
2006	Jaxnvl	AA	82	252	63	9	1	0	(-	-)	74	34	21	36	53	2	53	3	3	3	2	0	1.00	3	.250	.383	.294
2007	Jaxnvl	AA	110	357	96	22	2	8	(-	-)	146	59	57	60	60	1	61	8	1	4	1	4	.20	12	.269	.382	.409
2008	LsVgs	AAA	84	274	88	17	4	4	(-	-)	125	44	59	58	50	0	44	8	2	3	0	2	.00	8	.321	.436	.456
2009	Albq	AAA	90	283	89	13	2	0	(-	-)	106	48	39	55	64	3	44	3	4	6	2	2	.50	11	.314	.438	.375
2008	LAD	NL	4	3	0	0	0	0	(0	0)	0	1	0	0	0	0	2	0	0	0	0	0	-	0	.000	.000	.000
2009	LAD	NL	8	10	1	0	0	0	(0	0)	1	0	1	0	0	0	1	0	0	0	0	0	-	0	.100	.100	.100
	2 ML YEARS		12	13	1	0	0	0	(0	0)	1	1	1	0	0	0	3	0	0	0	0	0	-	0	.077	.077	.077

Mark Ellis

Bats: R **Throws:** R **Pos:** 2B-105   **Ht:** 5'11" **Wt:** 193 **Born:** 6/6/1977 **Age:** 33

							BATTING													BASERUNNING				AVERAGES		
Year	Team	Lg	G	AB	H	2B	3B	HR	(Hm	Rd)	TB	R	RBI	RC	TBB	IBB	SO	HBP	SH	SF	SB	CS	SB%	GDP	Avg	OBP	Slg
2009	Stcktn*	A+	2	4	0	0	0	0	(-	-)	0	0	0	0	1	0	1	0	0	0	0	0	-	0	.000	.200	.000
2009	Scrmto*	AAA	8	33	6	1	0	0	(-	-)	7	2	3	0	0	0	2	0	0	0	0	0	-	2	.182	.182	.212
2002	Oak	AL	98	345	94	16	4	6	(6	0)	136	58	35	55	44	1	54	4	8	3	4	2	.67	3	.272	.359	.394
2003	Oak	AL	154	553	137	31	5	9	(7	2)	205	78	52	69	48	4	94	7	9	5	6	2	.75	7	.248	.313	.371
2005	Oak	AL	122	434	137	21	5	13	(5	8)	207	76	52	78	44	1	51	4	4	0	1	3	.25	10	.316	.384	.477
2006	Oak	AL	124	441	110	25	1	11	(7	4)	170	64	52	53	40	1	76	8	4	7	4	0	1.00	13	.249	.319	.385
2007	Oak	AL	150	583	161	33	3	19	(10	9)	257	84	76	76	44	1	94	10	2	3	9	4	.69	10	.276	.336	.441
2008	Oak	AL	117	442	103	20	3	12	(7	5)	165	55	41	54	53	2	65	5	5	2	14	2	.88	11	.233	.321	.373
2009	Oak	AL	105	377	99	23	0	10	(4	6)	152	52	61	54	23	1	54	2	3	6	10	0	.77	10	.263	.305	.403
	Postseason		12	43	11	2	0	1	(1	0)	16	3	4	6	5	0	11	1	0	0	0	0	-	0	.256	.347	.372
	7 ML YEARS		870	3175	841	169	21	80	(46	34)	1292	467	369	439	296	11	488	40	35	25	48	16	.75	64	.265	.333	.407

Jacoby Ellsbury

Bats: L **Throws:** L **Pos:** CF-153; PH-2   **Ht:** 6'1" **Wt:** 185 **Born:** 9/11/1983 **Age:** 26

							BATTING													BASERUNNING				AVERAGES		
Year	Team	Lg	G	AB	H	2B	3B	HR	(Hm	Rd)	TB	R	RBI	RC	TBB	IBB	SO	HBP	SH	SF	SB	CS	SB%	GDP	Avg	OBP	Slg
2007	Bos	AL	33	116	41	7	1	3	(3	0)	59	20	18	26	8	0	15	1	0	2	9	0	1.00	2	.353	.394	.509
2008	Bos	AL	145	554	155	22	7	9	(4	5)	218	98	47	71	44	2	80	7	4	3	50	11	.82	10	.280	.336	.394
2009	Bos	AL	153	624	188	27	10	8	(4	4)	259	94	60	97	49	3	74	6	6	6	70	12	.85	13	.301	.355	.415
	Postseason		19	57	15	7	0	0	(0	0)	22	10	11	10	6	1	8	0	0	1	5	1	.83	2	.263	.328	.386
	3 ML YEARS		331	1294	384	56	18	20	(11	9)	536	212	125	194	98	5	169	14	10	11	129	23	.85	25	.297	.350	.414

Alan Embree

Pitches: L **Bats:** L **Pos:** RP-36   **Ht:** 6'2" **Wt:** 202 **Born:** 1/23/1970 **Age:** 40

			HOW MUCH HE PITCHED						WHAT HE GAVE UP												THE RESULTS						
Year	Team	Lg	G	GS	CG	GF	IP	BFP	H	R	ER	HR	SH	SF	HB	TBB	IBB	SO	WP	Bk	W	L	Pct	Sh	Sv-Op	Hld	ERC	ERA
1992	Cle	AL	4	4	0	0	18.0	81	19	14	14	3	0	2	1	8	0	12	1	1	0	2	.000	0	0-0	0	5.25	7.00
1995	Cle	AL	23	0	0	8	24.2	111	23	16	14	2	2	2	0	16	0	23	1	0	3	2	.600	0	1-1	6	4.51	5.11
1996	Cle	AL	24	0	0	2	31.0	141	30	26	22	10	1	3	0	21	3	33	3	0	1	1	.500	0	0-0	1	6.58	6.39
1997	Atl	NL	66	0	0	15	46.0	190	36	13	13	1	4	1	2	20	2	45	3	1	3	1	.750	0	0-0	16	2.66	2.54
1998	2 Tms	NL	55	0	0	16	53.2	237	56	32	25	7	4	1	1	23	0	43	3	0	4	2	.667	0	1-3	12	4.71	4.19
1999	SF	NL	68	0	0	13	58.2	244	42	22	22	6	3	2	3	26	2	53	3	0	3	2	.600	0	0-3	22	2.86	3.38
2000	SF	NL	63	0	0	21	60.0	263	62	34	33	4	4	5	3	25	2	49	1	0	3	5	.375	0	2-5	9	4.24	4.95
2001	2 Tms	NL	61	0	0	17	54.0	245	65	47	44	14	0	6	3	17	2	59	3	0	1	4	.200	0	0-3	9	6.20	7.33
2002	2 Tms	NL	68	0	0	20	62.0	251	47	19	15	6	1	2	1	20	3	81	1	0	4	6	.400	0	2-7	18	2.48	2.18
2003	Bos	AL	65	0	0	15	55.0	221	49	26	26	5	0	2	0	16	3	45	0	0	4	1	.800	0	1-2	14	3.01	4.25
2004	Bos	AL	71	0	0	11	52.1	217	49	28	24	7	2	2	1	11	1	37	0	0	2	2	.500	0	0-1	20	3.21	4.13
2005	2 Tms	NL	67	0	0	15	52.0	231	62	47	44	10	3	3	2	14	3	38	1	1	2	5	.286	0	1-3	10	5.34	7.62
2006	SD	NL	73	0	0	11	52.1	221	50	21	19	4	2	3	0	15	2	53	0	0	4	3	.571	0	1-1	16	3.13	3.27
2007	Oak	AL	68	0	0	36	68.0	284	67	30	30	5	1	4	0	19	5	51	0	0	1	2	.333	0	17-21	16	3.24	3.97
2008	Oak	AL	70	0	0	11	61.2	270	59	36	34	8	2	3	2	30	5	57	2	0	2	5	.286	0	0-5	18	4.39	4.96
2009	Col	AL	36	0	0	6	24.2	111	28	18	16	3	2	0	1	12	2	12	2	0	2	2	.500	0	0-3	6	5.47	5.84
98	Atl	NL	20	0	0	5	18.2	87	23	14	9	2	1	1	0	10	0	19	0	0	1	0	1.000	0	0-1	6	6.06	4.34

Year	Team	Lg	G	GS	CG	GF	IP	BFP	H	R	ER	HR	SH	SF	HB	TBB	IBB	SO	WP	Bk	W	L	Pct	Sh	Sv-Op	Hld	ERC	ERA
98	Ari	NL	35	0	0	11	35.0	150	33	18	16	5	3	0	1	13	0	24	3	0	3	2	.600	0	1-2	6	4.03	4.11
01	SF	NL	22	0	0	7	20.0	106	34	26	25	7	0	3	2	10	2	25	1	0	0	2	.000	0	0-1	0	11.29	11.25
01	CWS	AL	39	0	0	10	34.0	139	31	21	19	7	0	3	1	7	0	34	2	0	1	2	.333	0	0-2	9	3.61	5.03
02	SD	NL	36	0	0	13	28.2	118	23	7	4	2	0	0	0	9	2	38	1	0	3	4	.429	0	0-2	10	2.38	1.26
02	Bos	AL	32	0	0	7	33.1	133	24	12	11	4	1	2	1	11	1	43	0	0	1	2	.333	0	2-5	8	2.56	2.97
05	Bos	AL	43	0	0	11	37.2	163	42	33	32	8	1	2	1	11	2	30	1	1	1	4	.200	0	1-3	4	5.14	7.65
05	NYY	AL	24	0	0	4	14.1	62	20	14	12	2	2	1	1	3	1	8	0	0	1	1	.500	0	0-0	6	5.85	7.53
Postseason			31	0	0	6	21.2	84	16	5	4	0	2	2	1	5	2	13	0	0	1	0	1.000	0	0-1	5	1.64	1.66
16 ML YEARS			882	4	0	217	774.0	3318	744	429	395	95	31	41	20	293	35	691	24	3	39	45	.464	0	25-57	193	3.95	4.59

Edwin Encarnacion

Bats: R **Throws:** R **Pos:** 3B-85   **Ht:** 6'2" **Wt:** 231 **Born:** 1/7/1983 **Age:** 27

Year	Team	Lg	G	AB	H	2B	3B	HR	(Hm	Rd)	TB	R	RBI	RC	TBB	IBB	SO	HBP	SH	SF	SB	CS	SB%	GDP	Avg	OBP	Slg
2009	Lsvlle*	AAA	11	37	10	1	0	2	(-	-)	17	5	8	7	8	0	6	0	0	0	0	0	-	1	.270	.400	.459
2005	Cin	NL	69	211	49	16	0	9	(3	6)	92	25	31	24	20	2	60	3	0	0	3	0	1.00	8	.232	.308	.436
2006	Cin	NL	117	406	112	33	1	15	(7	8)	192	60	72	66	41	3	78	13	0	3	6	3	.67	9	.276	.359	.473
2007	Cin	NL	139	502	145	25	1	16	(10	6)	220	66	76	86	39	4	86	14	0	1	8	1	.89	5	.289	.356	.438
2008	Cin	NL	146	506	127	26	1	26	(15	11)	236	75	68	72	61	1	102	10	0	5	1	0	1.00	13	.251	.340	.466
2009	2 Tms		85	293	66	11	2	13	(5	8)	120	35	39	37	37	0	67	5	0	3	2	1	.67	5	.225	.320	.410
09	Cin	NL	43	139	29	6	1	5	(3	2)	52	10	16	19	24	0	38	2	0	0	1	1	.50	3	.209	.333	.374
09	Tor	AL	42	154	37	5	1	8	(2	6)	68	25	23	18	13	0	29	3	0	3	1	0	1.00	2	.240	.306	.442
5 ML YEARS			556	1918	499	114	5	79	(40	39)	860	261	286	285	198	10	393	45	0	12	20	5	.80	40	.260	.341	.448

Darin Erstad

Bats: L **Throws:** L **Pos:** PH-73; LF-24; 1B-15; RF-4; CF-1; PR-1   **Ht:** 6'2" **Wt:** 220 **Born:** 6/4/1974 **Age:** 36

Year	Team	Lg	G	AB	H	2B	3B	HR	(Hm	Rd)	TB	R	RBI	RC	TBB	IBB	SO	HBP	SH	SF	SB	CS	SB%	GDP	Avg	OBP	Slg
2009	CpChr*	AA	2	9	3	2	0	0	(-	-)	5	1	1	1	0	0	2	0	0	0	0	0	-	1	.333	.333	.556
1996	LAA	AL	57	208	59	5	1	4	(1	3)	78	34	20	26	17	1	29	0	1	3	3	3	.50	3	.284	.333	.375
1997	LAA	AL	139	539	161	34	4	16	(8	8)	251	99	77	92	51	4	86	4	5	6	23	8	.74	5	.299	.360	.466
1998	LAA	AL	133	537	159	39	3	19	(9	10)	261	84	82	94	43	7	77	6	1	3	20	6	.77	2	.296	.353	.486
1999	LAA	AL	142	585	148	22	5	13	(7	6)	219	84	53	64	47	3	101	1	2	3	13	7	.65	16	.253	.308	.374
2000	LAA	AL	157	676	240	39	6	25	(11	14)	366	121	100	145	64	9	82	1	2	4	28	8	.78	8	.355	.409	.541
2001	LAA	AL	157	631	163	35	1	9	(3	6)	227	89	63	79	62	7	113	10	1	7	24	10	.71	8	.258	.331	.360
2002	LAA	AL	150	625	177	28	4	10	(2	8)	243	99	73	74	27	4	67	2	5	4	23	3	.88	9	.283	.313	.389
2003	LAA	AL	67	258	65	7	1	4	(1	3)	86	35	17	22	18	1	40	4	2	2	9	1	.90	5	.252	.309	.333
2004	LAA	AL	125	495	146	29	1	7	(3	4)	198	79	69	76	37	1	74	4	3	4	16	1	.94	9	.295	.346	.400
2005	LAA	AL	153	609	166	33	3	7	(4	3)	226	86	66	79	47	3	109	1	4	2	10	3	.77	8	.273	.325	.371
2006	LAA	AL	40	95	21	8	1	0	(0	0)	31	8	5	6	6	0	18	2	1	1	1	1	.50	2	.221	.279	.326
2007	CWS	AL	87	310	77	13	1	4	(2	2)	104	33	32	36	28	0	44	0	6	1	7	2	.78	4	.248	.310	.335
2008	Hou	NL	140	322	89	16	0	4	(2	2)	117	49	31	39	14	3	68	2	2	2	2	3	.40	3	.276	.309	.363
2009	Hou	NL	107	134	26	8	2	2	(1	1)	44	13	11	10	14	3	31	0	1	1	0	2	.00	2	.194	.268	.328
Postseason			29	118	40	9	0	3	(2	1)	58	18	12	17	5	0	17	1	2	1	4	0	1.00	3	.339	.368	.492
14 ML YEARS			1654	6024	1697	316	33	124	(54	70)	2451	913	699	842	475	46	939	37	36	43	179	58	.76	87	.282	.336	.407

Sergio Escalona

Pitches: L **Bats:** L **Pos:** RP-14   **Ht:** 6'0" **Wt:** 170 **Born:** 8/3/1984 **Age:** 25

Year	Team	Lg	G	GS	CG	GF	IP	BFP	H	R	ER	HR	SH	SF	HB	TBB	IBB	SO	WP	Bk	W	L	Pct	Sh	Sv-Op	Hld	ERC	ERA
2007	Clrwtr	A+	1	1	0	0	4.0	21	8	1	1	0	1	0	0	2	0	4	0	0	0	0	-	0	0--	-	10.21	2.25
2007	Wmspt	A-	7	7	0	0	27.1	128	32	26	23	2	0	1	2	19	0	26	2	0	2	2	.500	0	0--	-	6.58	7.57
2007	Lakwd	A	7	7	0	0	39.0	177	51	25	18	4	2	4	1	11	0	32	1	0	1	4	.200	0	0--	-	5.47	4.15
2008	Lakwd	A	28	0	0	8	44.2	181	36	18	17	1	1	1	0	18	1	60	5	0	5	1	.833	0	2--	-	2.58	3.43
2008	Rdng	AA	15	0	0	5	24.1	112	27	12	6	3	1	0	1	14	0	29	0	0	0	1	.000	0	1--	-	5.80	2.22
2009	Rdng	AA	32	0	0	22	40.2	168	31	12	8	1	2	0	3	14	1	38	3	0	2	1	.667	0	12--	-	2.35	1.77
2009	LV	AAA	15	1	0	9	19.2	89	21	15	13	4	0	1	1	8	1	15	3	1	0	2	.000	0	2--	-	5.26	5.95
2009	Phi	NL	14	0	0	4	13.2	60	12	7	7	0	0	2	3	5	1	10	1	0	1	0	1.000	0	0-0	2	3.24	4.61

Alcides Escobar

Bats: R **Throws:** R **Pos:** SS-37; PR-1   **Ht:** 6'1" **Wt:** 182 **Born:** 12/16/1986 **Age:** 23

Year	Team	Lg	G	AB	H	2B	3B	HR	(Hm	Rd)	TB	R	RBI	RC	TBB	IBB	SO	HBP	SH	SF	SB	CS	SB%	GDP	Avg	OBP	Slg
2004	Helena	R+	68	231	65	8	0	2	(-	-)	79	38	24	30	20	0	44	4	6	1	20	9	.69	6	.281	.348	.342
2005	WV	A-	127	520	141	25	8	2	(-	-)	188	80	36	60	20	0	90	7	11	4	30	13	.70	4	.271	.305	.362
2006	BrvdCt	A+	87	350	90	9	1	2	(-	-)	107	47	33	36	19	1	56	3	7	7	28	8	.78	4	.257	.296	.306
2007	BrvdCt	A+	63	268	87	8	3	0	(-	-)	101	37	25	29	7	0	35	3	2	3	18	10	.64	4	.325	.345	.377
2007	Hntsvl	AA	62	226	64	5	4	1	(-	-)	80	27	28	25	11	4	36	0	6	2	4	3	.57	6	.283	.314	.354
2008	Hntsvl	AA	131	547	180	25	5	8	(-	-)	239	95	76	92	31	0	82	3	9	7	35	8	.81	10	.329	.364	.437
2009	Nashv	AAA	109	430	128	24	6	4	(-	-)	176	76	34	69	32	2	65	5	19	1	42	10	.81	13	.298	.353	.409
2008	Mil	NL	9	4	2	0	0	0	(0	0)	2	2	0	0	0	0	1	0	0	0	0	0	-	0	.500	.500	.500
2009	Mil	NL	38	125	38	3	1	1	(0	1)	46	20	11	16	4	0	18	2	2	1	4	2	.67	0	.304	.333	.368
2 ML YEARS			47	129	40	3	1	1	(0	1)	48	22	11	16	4	0	19	2	2	1	4	2	.67	0	.310	.338	.372

Kelvim Escobar

Pitches: R Bats: R Pos: SP-1   Ht: 6'1" Wt: 230 Born: 4/11/1976 Age: 34

	HOW MUCH HE PITCHED						WHAT HE GAVE UP											THE RESULTS						
Year Team	Lg	G	GS	CG	GF	IP	BFP	H	R	ER	HR	SH	SF	HB	TBB	IBB	SO	WP	Bk	W	L	Pct	Sh	Sv-Op	Hld	ERC	ERA
2009 RCuca*	A+	2	2	0	0	10.2	36	2	1	0	0	0	0	1	1	0	12	0	0	0	0	-	0	0- -	-	0.24	0.00
2009 Salt Lk*	AAA	1	1	0	0	5.0	24	8	5	4	0	1	0	1	2	0	1	0	0	0	0	-	0	0- -	-	8.20	7.20
1997 Tor	AL	27	0	0	23	31.0	139	28	12	10	1	2	0	0	19	2	36	0	0	3	2	.600	0	14-17	1	3.68	2.90
1998 Tor	AL	22	10	0	2	79.2	342	72	37	33	5	0	3	0	35	0	72	0	0	7	3	.700	0	0-1	5	3.41	3.73
1999 Tor	AL	33	30	1	2	174.0	795	203	118	110	19	2	8	10	81	2	129	6	1	14	11	.560	0	0-0	0	5.62	5.69
2000 Tor	AL	43	24	3	8	180.0	794	186	108	107	26	5	4	3	85	3	142	4	0	10	15	.400	1	2-3	3	4.94	5.35
2001 Tor	AL	59	11	1	15	126.0	517	93	51	49	8	2	5	3	52	5	121	2	0	6	8	.429	1	0-0	13	2.54	3.50
2002 Tor	AL	76	0	0	68	78.0	355	75	39	37	10	1	0	5	44	6	85	4	0	5	7	.417	0	38-46	0	4.77	4.27
2003 Tor	AL	41	26	1	12	180.1	797	189	94	86	15	5	5	0	70	3	159	9	0	13	9	.591	1	4-5	0	4.53	4.29
2004 LAA	AL	33	33	0	0	208.1	878	192	91	91	21	3	6	7	76	2	191	9	0	11	12	.478	0	0-0	0	3.65	3.93
2005 LAA	AL	16	7	0	2	59.2	242	45	21	20	4	2	0	2	21	1	63	4	0	3	2	.600	0	1-1	2	2.51	3.02
2006 LAA	AL	30	30	1	0	189.1	789	192	93	76	17	6	3	4	50	2	147	7	0	11	14	.440	0	0-0	0	3.67	3.61
2007 LAA	AL	30	30	3	0	195.2	812	182	79	74	11	5	4	3	66	2	160	9	0	18	7	.720	1	0-0	0	3.25	3.40
2009 LAA	AL	1	1	0	0	5.0	23	4	2	2	0	0	1	1	4	0	5	0	0	0	1	.000	0	0 0	0	4.56	3.60
Postseason		8	2	0	2	19.2	92	15	12	8	2	0	2	0	17	2	24	2	0	1	2	.333	0	0 1	2	4.22	3.66
12 ML YEARS		411	202	10	132	1507.0	6483	1461	755	695	137	33	39	47	611	28	1310	54	1	101	91	.526	4	59-73	24	3.97	4.15

Yunel Escobar

Bats: R Throws: R Pos: SS-139; PH-2   Ht: 6'2" Wt: 200 Born: 11/2/1982 Age: 27

							BATTING												BASERUNNING				AVERAGES		
Year Team	Lg	G	AB	H	2B	3B	HR	(Hm	Rd)	TB	R	RBI	RC	TBB	IBB	SO	HBP	SH	SF	SB	CS	SB%	GDP	Avg	OBP	Slg
2007 Atl	NL	94	319	104	25	0	5	(3	2)	144	54	28	52	27	1	44	5	2	2	5	3	63	6	.326	.385	.451
2008 Atl	NL	136	514	148	24	2	10	(5	5)	206	71	60	70	59	4	62	5	7	2	2	5	29	24	.288	.366	.401
2009 Atl	NL	141	528	158	26	2	14	(7	7)	230	89	76	80	57	3	62	10	7	2	5	4	.56	21	.299	.377	.436
3 ML YEARS		371	1361	410	75	4	29	(15	14)	580	214	161	212	143	8	168	20	16	6	12	12	.50	51	.301	.375	.426

Johnny Estrada

Bats: B Throws: R Pos: C   Ht: 5'11" Wt: 254 Born: 6/27/1976 Age: 34

							BATTING												BASERUNNING				AVERAGES		
Year Team	Lg	G	AB	H	2B	3B	HR	(Hm	Rd)	TB	R	RBI	RC	TBB	IBB	SO	HBP	SH	SF	SB	CS	SB%	GDP	Avg	OBP	Slg
2001 Phi	NL	89	298	68	14	0	8	(7	1)	107	26	37	25	16	6	32	4	2	4	0	0	-	15	.228	.273	.359
2002 Phi	NL	10	17	2	1	0	0	(0	0)	3	0	2	0	2	1	2	0	0	0	0	0	-	0	.118	.211	.176
2003 Atl	NL	16	36	11	0	0	0	(0	0)	11	2	2	2	0	0	3	3	0	0	0	0	-	1	.306	.359	.306
2004 Atl	NL	134	462	145	36	0	9	(4	5)	208	56	76	78	39	7	66	11	1	4	0	0	-	18	.314	.378	.450
2005 Atl	NL	105	357	93	26	0	4	(2	2)	131	31	39	36	20	6	38	3	0	3	0	0	-	13	.261	.303	.367
2006 Ari	NL	115	414	125	26	0	11	(7	4)	184	43	71	59	13	7	40	7	1	8	0	0	-	17	.302	.328	.444
2007 Mil	NL	120	442	123	25	0	10	(3	7)	178	40	54	41	12	3	43	2	1	7	0	0	-	16	.278	.296	.403
2008 Was	NL	23	53	9	0	0	0	(0	0)	9	0	4	4	1	0	4	1	0	0	0	0	-	0	.170	.200	.170
Postseason		6	21	7	0	0	2	(1	1)	13	3	5	4	3	0	5	0	0	1	0	0	-	0	.333	.400	.619
8 ML YEARS		612	2079	576	129	0	42	(23	19)	831	198	285	245	103	30	228	31	5	26	0	0	-	80	.277	.317	.400

Marco Estrada

Pitches: R Bats: R Pos: RP-3; SP-1   Ht: 6'0" Wt: 197 Born: 7/5/1983 Age: 26

	HOW MUCH HE PITCHED						WHAT HE GAVE UP											THE RESULTS						
Year Team	Lg	G	GS	CG	GF	IP	DFP	H	R	ER	HR	SH	SF	HB	TBB	IBB	SO	WP	Bk	W	L	Pct	Sh	Sv-Op	Hld	ERC	ERA
2006 Nats	R	5	4	0	0	23.2	91	14	4	4	1	0	0	0	6	0	27	0	0	2	0	1.000	0	0- -	-	1.34	1.52
2006 Savann	A	8	8	0	0	37.0	166	44	23	23	6	1	1	4	14	0	29	2	0	1	4	.200	0	0- -	-	6.15	5.59
2007 Hgrstn	A	8	8	0	0	36.0	163	39	24	21	4	3	2	1	17	0	35	0	0	1	5	.167	0	0- -	-	4.98	5.25
2007 Ptomc	A+	11	11	0	0	58.1	249	67	32	32	7	1	1	0	17	0	54	0	1	5	3	.625	0	0- -	-	4.72	4.94
2007 Nats	R	4	4	0	0	11.1	57	19	6	4	1	0	1	1	3	0	13	0	0	0	0	-	0	0- -	-	7.74	3.18
2008 Hrsbrg	AA	13	13	1	0	74.1	314	62	27	22	5	1	1	2	32	1	67	0	0	6	3	.667	1	0- -	-	3.14	2.66
2008 Clmbs	AAA	12	12	0	0	65.1	281	73	28	26	3	0	2	4	21	1	52	0	1	3	3	.500	0	0- -	-	4.36	3.58
2009 Syrcse	AAA	27	25	0	0	136.1	560	133	61	55	10	2	3	1	33	2	98	5	2	9	5	.643	0	0- -	-	3.20	3.63
2008 Was	NL	11	0	0	3	12.2	63	17	13	11	4	0	0	2	5	1	10	0	0	0	0	-	0	0-1	3	8.13	7.82
2009 Was	NL	4	1	0	1	7.1	33	6	6	5	1	1	0	0	4	0	9	1	0	0	1	.000	0	0-0	0	3.67	6.14
2 ML YEARS		15	1	0	4	20.0	96	23	19	16	5	1	0	2	9	1	19	1	0	0	1	.000	0	0-1	3	6.37	7.20

Andre Ethier

Bats: L Throws: L Pos: RF-158; PH-6   Ht: 6'2" Wt: 210 Born: 4/10/1982 Age: 28

							BATTING												BASERUNNING				AVERAGES		
Year Team	Lg	G	AB	H	2B	3B	HR	(Hm	Rd)	TB	R	RBI	RC	TBB	IBB	SO	HBP	SH	SF	SB	CS	SB%	GDP	Avg	OBP	Slg
2006 LAD	NL	126	396	122	20	7	11	(9	2)	189	50	55	62	34	2	77	5	0	6	5	5	.50	11	.308	.365	.477
2007 LAD	NL	153	447	127	32	2	13	(8	5)	202	50	64	65	46	12	68	4	0	8	0	4	.00	10	.284	.350	.452
2008 LAD	NL	141	525	160	38	5	20	(10	10)	268	90	77	99	46	4	88	4	1	7	6	3	.67	6	.305	.375	.510
2009 LAD	NL	160	596	162	42	3	31	(22	9)	303	92	106	94	72	10	116	13	0	4	6	4	.60	19	.272	.361	.508
Postseason		10	33	6	1	0	0	(0	0)	7	6	0	2	5	0	10	0	0	0	0	0	-	1	.182	.289	.212
4 ML YEARS		580	1964	571	132	17	75	(49	26)	962	282	302	320	211	24	349	26	1	25	17	16	.52	46	.291	.363	.490

Nick Evans

Bats: R **Throws:** R **Pos:** PH-16; LF-10; 1B-5　　　　　**Ht:** 6'2" **Wt:** 219 **Born:** 1/30/1986 **Age:** 24

Year	Team	Lg	G	AB	H	2B	3B	HR	(Hm	Rd)	TB	R	RBI	RC	TBB	IBB	SO	HBP	SH	SF	SB	CS	SB%	GDP	Avg	OBP	Slg
2004	Mets	R	50	182	47	10	3	7	(-	-)	84	36	27	26	14	0	51	0	0	0	3	2	.60	3	.258	.311	.462
2005	Kngspt	R+	15	64	22	7	0	6	(-	-)	47	11	22	16	4	1	17	0	0	0	1	0	1.00	1	.344	.382	.734
2005	Bklyn	A-	57	226	57	11	3	6	(-	-)	92	30	33	28	17	1	34	0	0	2	0	1	.00	3	.252	.302	.407
2006	Hgrstn	A	137	511	130	33	3	15	(-	-)	214	55	67	72	45	3	99	6	0	3	2	0	1.00	17	.254	.320	.419
2007	StLuci	A+	103	378	108	25	1	15	(-	-)	180	65	54	71	53	4	64	3	2	4	3	0	1.00	10	.286	.374	.476
2008	Bnghtn	AA	75	296	92	18	7	14	(-	-)	166	52	53	59	26	1	64	1	0	3	2	1	.67	7	.311	.365	.561
2009	Buffalo	AAA	66	237	50	12	3	10	(-	-)	98	27	30	28	23	1	55	0	0	-	8	.211	.280	.414
2009	Bnghtn	AA	25	105	29	9	1	3	(-	-)	49	16	9	17	10	0	22	2	0	1.00	6	.276	.350	.467
2008	NYM	NL	50	109	28	10	0	2	(0	2)	44	18	9	10	7	2	24	1	0	2	0	0	-	1	.257	.303	.404
2009	NYM	NL	30	65	15	5	1	1	(1	0)	25	5	7	8	4	0	20	0	0	0	0	0	-	4	.231	.275	.385
	2 ML YEARS		80	174	43	15	1	3	(1	2)	69	23	16	18	11	2	44	1	0	2	0	0	-	5	.247	.293	.397

Terry Evans

Bats: R **Throws:** R **Pos:** RF-7; PR-4; DH-3; LF-2; CF-1　　　　　**Ht:** 6'3" **Wt:** 205 **Born:** 1/19/1982 **Age:** 28

Year	Team	Lg	G	AB	H	2B	3B	HR	(Hm	Rd)	TB	R	RBI	RC	TBB	IBB	SO	HBP	SH	SF	SB	CS	SB%	GDP	Avg	OBP	Slg
2002	JhsCty	R+	60	230	66	22	2	7	(-	-)	113	42	41	43	29	1	67	0	0	2	17	4	.81	5	.287	.364	.491
2003	Peoria	A	104	382	94	28	1	10	(-	-)	154	35	41	45	19	0	86	3	4	2	13	6	.68	8	.246	.286	.403
2004	Peoria	A	101	365	81	21	1	13	(-	-)	143	48	59	45	35	1	105	7	1	1	8	3	.73	7	.222	.301	.392
2004	PlmBh	A+	19	58	13	4	0	2	(-	-)	23	7	7	7	4	0	16	1	0	1	1	0	1.00	6	.224	.281	.397
2005	PlmBh	A+	114	385	85	16	1	8	(-	-)	127	34	47	37	29	1	110	7	1	3	12	6	.67	5	.221	.285	.330
2006	PlmBh	A+	60	238	74	10	1	15	(-	-)	131	43	45	51	20	0	50	4	0	1	21	1	.95	6	.311	.373	.550
2006	Sprgfld	AA	21	75	23	4	0	7	(-	-)	48	13	20	17	3	0	21	5	0	1	5	1	.83	0	.307	.369	.640
2006	Ark	AA	52	188	58	9	2	11	(-	-)	104	48	22	39	18	1	56	6	0	1	11	6	.65	4	.309	.385	.553
2007	Salt Lk	AAA	120	475	150	40	4	15	(-	-)	243	70	75	85	26	1	119	2	2	2	24	9	.73	6	.316	.352	.512
2008	Salt Lk	AAA	46	174	47	12	0	4	(-	-)	71	31	21	25	20	1	60	2	0	4	6	5	.55	4	.270	.345	.408
2008	Angels	R	4	12	5	2	0	1	(-	-)	10	5	2	4	2	0	2	0	0	0	0	0	-	0	.417	.500	.833
2009	Salt Lk	AAA	135	537	156	33	6	26	(-	-)	279	104	90	99	40	1	146	5	2	8	28	5	.85	7	.291	.341	.520
2007	LAA	AL	8	11	1	0	0	1	(1	0)	4	3	2	0	2	0	4	0	0	0	0	0	-	1	.091	.231	.364
2009	LAA	AL	11	7	2	0	0	0	(0	0)	2	2	1	1	0	0	2	0	0	0	0	0	-	0	.286	.286	.286
	2 ML YEARS		19	18	3	0	0	1	(1	0)	6	5	3	1	2	0	6	0	0	0	0	0	-	1	.167	.250	.333

Dana Eveland

Pitches: L **Bats:** L **Pos:** SP-9; RP-4　　　　　**Ht:** 6'1" **Wt:** 216 **Born:** 10/29/1983 **Age:** 26

			HOW MUCH HE PITCHED							WHAT HE GAVE UP										THE RESULTS						
Year	Team	Lg	G	GS	CG	GF	IP	BFP	H	R	ER	HR	SH	SF	HB	TBB	IBB	SO	WP	Bk	W	L	Pct	Sh	Sv-Op	Hld	ERC	ERA
2009	Scrmto*	AAA	21	21	0	0	124.0	548	133	79	68	12	4	1	5	51	0	92	8	0	8	6	.571	0	0- -	-	4.68	4.94
2005	Mil	NL	27	0	0	3	31.2	146	40	21	21	2	0	1	1	18	3	23	1	0	1	1	.500	0	1-2	7	6.16	5.97
2006	Mil	NL	9	5	0	1	27.2	141	39	25	25	4	1	1	5	16	2	32	2	0	0	3	.000	0	0-1	0	8.30	8.13
2007	Ari	NL	5	1	0	0	5.0	28	8	8	8	0	0	1	0	5	0	3	1	0	1	0	1.000	0	0-0	0	9.25	14.40
2008	Oak	AL	29	29	1	0	168.0	737	172	82	81	10	2	5	12	77	2	118	6	1	9	9	.500	0	0-0	0	4.47	4.34
2009	Oak	AL	13	9	0	2	44.0	221	70	39	35	4	1	2	0	26	1	22	2	0	2	4	.333	0	0-0	0	8.50	7.16
	5 ML YEARS		83	44	1	6	276.1	1273	329	175	170	20	4	10	18	142	8	198	12	1	13	17	.433	0	1-3	7	5.71	5.54

Adam Everett

Bats: R **Throws:** R **Pos:** SS-116; PR-4; PH-3　　　　　**Ht:** 6'0" **Wt:** 178 **Born:** 2/5/1977 **Age:** 33

Year	Team	Lg	G	AB	H	2B	3B	HR	(Hm	Rd)	TB	R	RBI	RC	TBB	IBB	SO	HBP	SH	SF	SB	CS	SB%	GDP	Avg	OBP	Slg
2001	Hou	NL	9	3	0	0	0	0	(0	0)	0	1	0	0	0	0	1	0	0	0	1	0	1.00	0	.000	.000	.000
2002	Hou	NL	40	88	17	3	0	0	(0	0)	20	11	4	6	12	1	19	1	2	0	3	0	1.00	1	.193	.297	.227
2003	Hou	NL	128	387	99	18	3	8	(5	3)	147	51	51	50	28	6	66	9	11	1	8	1	.89	7	.256	.320	.380
2004	Hou	NL	104	384	105	15	2	8	(5	3)	148	66	31	51	17	0	56	9	22	3	13	2	.87	4	.273	.317	.385
2005	Hou	NL	152	549	136	27	2	11	(7	4)	200	58	54	61	26	1	103	8	8	4	21	7	.75	5	.248	.290	.364
2006	Hou	NL	150	514	123	28	6	6	(2	4)	181	52	59	50	34	5	71	4	10	4	9	6	.60	5	.239	.290	.352
2007	Hou	NL	66	220	51	11	1	2	(1	1)	70	18	15	21	14	0	31	1	1	0	4	2	.67	3	.232	.281	.318
2008	Min	AL	48	127	27	6	1	2	(2	0)	41	19	20	15	12	1	15	1	6	4	0	0	-	3	.213	.278	.323
2009	Det	AL	118	345	82	21	0	3	(1	2)	112	43	44	34	22	0	61	4	15	4	5	2	.71	9	.238	.288	.325
	Postseason		19	53	11	1	1	0	(0	0)	14	5	3	1	2	0	9	0	2	1	0	1	.00	2	.208	.232	.264
	9 ML YEARS		815	2617	640	129	15	40	(23	17)	919	319	278	288	165	14	423	37	75	20	64	20	.76	34	.245	.297	.351

Tommy Everidge

Bats: R **Throws:** R **Pos:** 1B-21; DH-3; PH-1　　　　　**Ht:** 6'0" **Wt:** 244 **Born:** 4/20/1983 **Age:** 27

Year	Team	Lg	G	AB	H	2B	3B	HR	(Hm	Rd)	TB	R	RBI	RC	TBB	IBB	SO	HBP	SH	SF	SB	CS	SB%	GDP	Avg	OBP	Slg
2004	Vancvr	A-	74	291	80	13	1	6	(-	-)	113	42	52	39	23	0	72	4	1	3	0	0	-	4	.275	.333	.388
2005	Kane	A	114	365	102	26	3	14	(-	-)	176	59	66	69	56	1	73	1	0	8	1	0	1.00	10	.279	.370	.482
2006	Stcktn	A+	133	504	127	32	2	20	(-	-)	223	89	83	75	44	0	116	13	0	9	5	5	.50	13	.252	.323	.442
2007	Stcktn	A+	124	461	119	13	3	26	(-	-)	216	75	90	80	66	0	103	6	0	6	2	2	.50	13	.258	.354	.469
2007	Mdland	AA	10	36	13	4	0	0	(-	-)	17	7	4	6	2	0	5	0	0	0	0	0	-	1	.361	.395	.472
2008	Mdland	AA	137	535	149	34	0	22	(-	-)	249	89	116	90	55	2	134	7	0	14	0	0	-	16	.279	.345	.465
2009	Mdland	AA	55	229	70	18	0	8	(-	-)	112	41	53	42	28	0	34	0	0	1	0	1	.00	6	.306	.380	.489
2009	Scrmto	AAA	52	201	74	15	1	12	(-	-)	127	39	41	51	23	0	34	1	0	4	0	0	-	7	.368	.428	.632
2009	Oak	AL	24	85	19	6	0	2	(1	1)	31	13	7	4	8	1	17	2	1	1	0	0	-	6	.224	.302	.365

Scott Eyre

Pitches: L Bats: L Pos: RP-42   Ht: 6'1" Wt: 225 Born: 5/30/1972 Age: 38

Year	Team	Lg	G	GS	CG	GF	IP	BFP	H	R	ER	HR	SH	SF	HB	TBB	IBB	SO	WP	Bk	W	L	Pct	Sh	Sv-Op	Hld	ERC	ERA
2009	Rdng*	AA	2	1	0	0	1.2	11	4	1	1	1	0	0	0	2	0	3	0	0	0	0	-	0	0--	-	23.09	5.40
1997	CWS	AL	11	11	0	0	60.2	267	62	36	34	11	1	2	1	31	1	36	2	0	4	4	.500	0	0-0	0	5.37	5.04
1998	CWS	AL	33	17	0	10	107.0	491	114	78	64	24	2	3	2	64	0	73	7	0	3	8	.273	0	0-0	0	6.31	5.38
1999	CWS	AL	21	0	0	8	25.0	129	38	22	21	6	0	1	1	15	2	17	1	0	1	1	.500	0	0-0	1	9.23	7.56
2000	CWS	AL	13	1	0	3	19.0	93	29	15	14	3	0	2	1	12	0	16	0	0	1	1	.500	0	0-0	0	9.49	6.63
2001	Tor	AL	17	0	0	5	15.2	66	15	6	6	1	0	1	1	7	2	16	2	0	1	2	.333	0	2-3	3	3.96	3.45
2002	2 Tms		70	3	0	6	74.2	333	80	41	37	4	2	4	0	36	8	58	5	0	2	4	.333	0	1-3	20	4.26	4.46
2003	SF	NL	74	0	0	10	57.0	256	60	23	21	4	2	3	1	26	0	35	6	0	2	1	.667	0	1-3	20	4.37	3.32
2004	SF	NL	83	0	0	12	52.2	229	43	26	24	8	3	3	0	27	3	49	3	0	2	2	.500	0	1-5	23	3.67	4.10
2005	SF	NL	86	0	0	15	68.1	277	48	21	20	3	4	3	4	26	0	65	3	0	2	2	.500	0	0 2	32	2.32	2.63
2006	ChC	NL	74	0	0	15	61.1	266	61	25	23	11	2	4	0	30	4	73	6	0	1	3	.250	0	0-3	18	4.94	3.38
2007	ChC	NL	55	0	0	17	52.1	240	59	26	24	3	2	1	1	35	5	45	3	0	2	1	.667	0	0-4	5	5.61	4.13
2008	2 Tms	NL	38	0	0	3	25.2	106	23	12	12	2	0	2	2	7	2	32	1	0	5	0	1.000	0	0-2	8	3.09	4.21
2009	Phi	NL	42	0	0	3	30.0	128	22	6	5	3	2	2	1	16	0	22	2	0	2	1	.667	0	0-0	13	3.23	1.50
02	Tor	AL	49	3	0	3	63.1	283	69	37	35	4	2	4	0	29	7	51	4	0	2	4	.333	0	0-1	12	4.32	4.97
02	SF	NL	21	0	0	3	11.1	50	11	4	2	0	0	0	0	7	1	7	1	0	0	0	-	0	0-0	6	3.91	1.59
08	ChC	NL	19	0	0	1	11.1	53	15	9	9	1	0	2	1	4	1	14	1	0	2	0	1.000	0	0-1	4	5.86	7.15
08	Phi	NL	19	0	0	2	14.1	53	8	3	3	1	0	0	1	3	1	18	0	0	3	0	1.000	0	0-1	4	1.39	1.88
	Postseason		17	0	0	2	9.1	42	12	2	1	0	2	0	0	2	2	4	0	0	0	0	-	0	0-0	3	3.75	0.96
	13 ML YEARS		617	32	0	107	649.1	2881	654	337	305	83	20	31	15	332	27	537	41	0	28	30	.483	0	4-23	141	4.80	4.23

Willie Eyre

Pitches: R Bats: R Pos: RP-17   Ht: 6'2" Wt: 205 Born: 7/21/1978 Age: 31

Year	Team	Lg	G	GS	CG	GF	IP	BFP	H	R	ER	HR	SH	SF	HB	TBB	IBB	SO	WP	Bk	W	L	Pct	Sh	Sv-Op	Hld	ERC	ERA
2009	Okla*	AAA	19	2	0	5	34.1	134	24	8	8	1	2	2	1	12	2	26	1	1	0	0	-	0	2--	-	2.00	2.10
2006	Min	AL	42	0	0	20	61.0	275	75	36	35	8	1	3	6	22	4	26	4	0	1	0	1.000	0	0-0	0	6.07	5.31
2007	Tex	AL	33	2	0	10	68.0	307	78	42	39	8	5	1	1	32	4	42	5	0	4	6	.400	0	1-1	1	5.32	5.16
2009	Tex	AL	17	0	0	6	18.0	72	18	9	9	0	2	0	0	6	2	8	0	0	0	0	-	0	0-0	0	3.16	4.50
	3 ML YEARS		92	2	0	36	145.1	654	171	87	83	16	8	4	7	60	10	76	9	0	5	6	.455	0	1-1	1	5.34	5.14

Brian Falkenborg

Pitches: R Bats: R Pos: P   Ht: 6'7" Wt: 235 Born: 1/18/1978 Age: 32

Year	Team	Lg	G	GS	CG	GF	IP	BFP	H	R	ER	HR	SH	SF	HB	TBB	IBB	SO	WP	Bk	W	L	Pct	Sh	Sv-Op	Hld	ERC	ERA
2009	Fk Dai*	Jap	46	0	0	0	51.2	199	39	11	10	1	-	-	1	9	0	62	1	0	6	0	1.000	0	1--	-	1.66	1.74
1999	Bal	AL	2	0	0	0	3.0	12	2	0	0	0	0	0	0	2	0	1	0	0	0	0	-	0	0-0	0	2.79	0.00
2004	LAD	NL	6	0	0	1	14.1	73	19	14	12	2	2	0	3	9	0	11	1	0	1	0	1.000	0	0-0	0	8.19	7.53
2005	SD	NL	10	0	0	3	11.0	54	17	11	10	2	0	0	0	5	1	10	2	0	0	0	-	0	0-0	0	8.14	8.18
2006	StL	NL	5	0	0	0	6.1	25	5	2	2	0	1	0	1	0	0	5	0	0	0	1	.000	0	0-0	1	1.57	2.84
2007	StL	NL	16	0	0	2	18.2	84	22	10	10	2	0	0	1	8	0	16	1	0	0	1	.000	0	0-0	1	5.58	4.82
2008	2 Tms	NL	25	0	0	8	22.1	102	20	13	13	4	2	0	0	12	2	19	0	0	2	3	.400	0	0-1	1	6.11	5.24
08	LAD	NL	16	0	0	2	11.2	49	11	8	8	2	1	0	0	4	1	9	0	0	2	2	.500	0	0-1	1	3.89	6.17
08	SD	NL	9	0	0	6	10.2	53	15	5	5	2	1	0	0	8	1	10	0	0	0	1	.000	0	0-0	0	8.80	4.22
	6 ML YEARS		64	0	0	17	75.2	350	91	50	47	10	5	0	6	36	3	62	4	0	3	5	.375	0	0-1	2	6.05	5.59

Kyle Farnsworth

Pitches: R Bats: R Pos: RP-41   Ht: 6'4" Wt: 233 Born: 4/14/1976 Age: 34

Year	Team	Lg	G	GS	CG	GF	IP	BFP	H	R	ER	HR	SH	SF	HB	TBB	IBB	SO	WP	Bk	W	L	Pct	Sh	Sv-Op	Hld	ERC	ERA
2009	Omha*	AAA	2	1	0	0	2.0	6	0	0	0	0	0	0	0	0	0	2	0	0	0	0	-	0	0--	-	0.00	0.00
2009	NWArk*	AA	3	0	0	0	3.2	13	1	0	0	0	0	0	0	1	0	3	0	0	0	0	-	0	0--	-	0.47	0.00
1999	ChC	NL	27	21	1	1	130.0	579	140	80	73	28	6	2	3	52	1	70	7	1	5	9	.357	1	0-0	0	5.39	5.05
2000	ChC	NL	46	5	0	8	77.0	371	90	58	55	14	4	4	4	50	8	74	3	0	2	9	.182	0	1-6	6	6.72	6.43
2001	ChC	NL	76	0	0	24	82.0	339	65	26	25	8	2	2	1	29	2	107	2	2	4	6	.400	0	2-3	24	2.76	2.74
2002	ChC	NL	45	0	0	17	46.2	213	53	47	38	9	2	5	1	24	7	46	1	0	4	6	.400	0	1-7	6	5.89	7.33
2003	ChC	NL	77	0	0	13	76.1	312	53	31	28	6	4	1	0	36	1	92	6	0	3	2	.600	0	0-3	19	2.58	3.30
2004	ChC	NL	72	0	0	25	66.2	298	67	39	35	10	5	0	2	33	1	78	1	0	4	5	.444	0	0-4	18	4.91	4.73
2005	2 Tms		72	0	0	34	70.0	277	44	18	17	5	2	1	3	27	0	87	3	1	1	1	.500	0	16-18	19	2.12	2.19
2006	NYY	AL	72	0	0	24	66.0	289	62	34	32	8	3	2	1	28	3	75	5	1	3	6	.333	0	6-10	19	3.88	4.36
2007	NYY	AL	64	0	0	11	60.0	266	60	35	32	9	1	2	2	27	2	48	4	2	2	1	.667	0	0-3	15	4.67	4.80
2008	2 Tms	AL	61	0	0	11	60.1	261	70	32	30	15	3	1	1	22	4	61	1	1	2	3	.400	0	1-4	14	6.11	4.48
2009	KC	AL	41	0	0	18	37.1	168	43	22	19	3	1	2	1	14	2	42	2	0	2	5	.167	0	0-2	5	4.65	4.58
05	Det	AL	46	0	0	16	42.2	174	29	12	11	1	1	1	1	20	0	55	2	0	1	1	.500	0	6-8	15	2.26	2.32
05	Atl	NL	26	0	0	18	27.1	103	15	6	6	4	1	0	2	7	0	32	1	1	0	0	-	0	10-10	4	1.86	1.98
08	NYY	AL	45	0	0	6	44.1	185	43	18	18	11	3	1	1	17	3	43	1	1	1	2	.333	0	1-1	11	5.02	3.65
08	Det	AL	16	0	0	5	16.0	76	27	14	12	4	0	0	0	5	1	18	0	0	1	1	.500	0	0-3	3	9.43	6.75
	Postseason		13	0	0	3	14.0	58	11	9	9	2	1	1	0	5	2	16	0	0	0	0	-	0	0-0	2	2.78	5.79
	11 ML YEARS		653	26	1	186	772.1	3373	747	422	384	115	33	22	19	342	31	780	35	9	31	53	.369	1	27-60	145	4.42	4.47

Ryan Feierabend

Pitches: L Bats: L Pos: P　　　　　　　　　　　　Ht: 6'3" Wt: 228 Born: 8/22/1985 Age: 24

Year	Team	Lg	G	GS	CG	GF	IP	BFP	H	R	ER	HR	SH	SF	HB	TBB	IBB	SO	WP	Bk	W	L	Pct	Sh	Sv-Op	Hld	ERC	ERA
2006	Sea	AL	4	2	0	2	17.0	73	15	7	7	3	1	0	0	7	0	11	1	2	0	1	.000	0	0-0	0	3.91	3.71
2007	Sea	AL	13	9	0	0	49.1	236	73	44	44	10	0	2	4	23	2	27	3	0	1	6	.143	0	0-0	0	8.71	8.03
2008	Sea	AL	8	8	0	0	39.2	183	59	34	34	7	1	1	1	14	0	26	1	0	1	4	.200	0	0-0	0	7.83	7.71
3 ML YEARS			25	19	0	2	106.0	492	147	85	85	20	2	3	5	44	2	64	5	2	2	11	.154	0	0-0	0	7.54	7.22

Scott Feldman

Pitches: R Bats: L Pos: SP-31; RP-3　　　　　　　　Ht: 6'5" Wt: 210 Born: 2/7/1983 Age: 27

Year	Team	Lg	G	GS	CG	GF	IP	BFP	H	R	ER	HR	SH	SF	HB	TBB	IBB	SO	WP	Bk	W	L	Pct	Sh	Sv-Op	Hld	ERC	ERA
2005	Tex	AL	8	0	0	3	9.1	37	9	1	1	0	0	0	0	2	1	4	0	0	0	1	.000	0	0-1	1	2.48	0.96
2006	Tex	AL	36	0	0	5	41.1	175	42	19	18	4	2	1	4	10	0	30	0	0	0	2	.000	0	0-1	7	3.94	3.92
2007	Tex	AL	29	0	0	10	39.0	192	44	26	25	3	0	2	3	32	5	19	2	2	1	2	.333	0	0-0	0	6.40	5.77
2008	Tex	AL	28	25	0	2	151.1	651	161	103	89	22	1	9	10	56	2	74	4	2	6	8	.429	0	0-0	0	5.03	5.29
2009	Tex	AL	34	31	0	0	189.2	791	178	87	86	18	1	3	9	65	0	113	5	2	17	8	.680	0	0-0	0	3.74	4.08
5 ML YEARS			135	56	0	20	430.2	1846	434	236	219	47	4	15	26	165	8	240	11	6	24	21	.533	0	0-1	8	4.41	4.58

Pedro Feliciano

Pitches: L Bats: L Pos: RP-88　　　　　　　　　　　Ht: 5'10" Wt: 192 Born: 8/25/1976 Age: 33

Year	Team	Lg	G	GS	CG	GF	IP	BFP	H	R	ER	HR	SH	SF	HB	TBB	IBB	SO	WP	Bk	W	L	Pct	Sh	Sv-Op	Hld	ERC	ERA
2002	NYM	NL	6	0	0	3	6.0	26	9	5	5	0	0	0	0	1	0	4	0	0	0	0	-	0	0-0	0	5.56	7.50
2003	NYM	NL	23	0	0	8	48.1	218	52	21	18	5	0	1	3	21	3	43	3	1	0	0	-	0	0-0	4	4.77	3.35
2004	NYM	NL	22	0	0	3	18.1	82	14	12	11	2	1	1	1	12	0	14	1	0	1	1	.500	0	0-0	2	3.93	5.40
2006	NYM	NL	64	0	0	10	60.1	256	56	15	14	4	4	3	3	20	1	54	1	0	7	2	.778	0	0-3	10	3.34	2.09
2007	NYM	NL	78	0	0	12	64.0	275	47	26	22	3	2	2	5	31	4	61	1	1	2	2	.500	0	2-3	18	2.74	3.09
2008	NYM	NL	86	0	0	14	53.1	237	57	24	24	7	2	3	3	26	8	50	2	0	3	4	.429	0	2-4	21	5.11	4.05
2009	NYM	NL	88	0	0	11	59.1	242	51	25	20	7	2	1	0	18	4	59	2	1	6	4	.600	0	0-2	24	2.98	3.03
Postseason			6	0	0	0	4.2	18	2	1	1	0	0	0	0	2	0	3	1	0	1	0	1.000	0	0-1	1	1.92	1.93
7 ML YEARS			367	0	0	61	309.2	1336	286	128	114	28	11	11	15	129	20	285	10	3	19	13	.594	0	4-12	75	3.72	3.31

Neftali Feliz

Pitches: R Bats: R Pos: RP-20　　　　　　　　　　Ht: 6'3" Wt: 190 Born: 5/2/1988 Age: 22

Year	Team	Lg	G	GS	CG	GF	IP	BFP	H	R	ER	HR	SH	SF	HB	TBB	IBB	SO	WP	Bk	W	L	Pct	Sh	Sv-Op	Hld	ERC	ERA
2006	Braves	R	11	5	0	2	29.0	118	20	13	13	0	0	0	0	14	0	42	4	1	0	2	.000	0	2--	-	2.14	4.03
2007	Danvle	R+	8	7	0	0	27.1	107	18	8	6	0	0	1	0	12	0	28	0	0	2	0	1.000	0	0--	-	1.92	1.98
2007	Spkane	A-	8	1	0	0	15.0	71	13	8	6	2	1	0	1	12	0	27	2	0	0	2	.000	0	0--	-	5.30	3.60
2008	Clinton	A	17	17	0	0	82.0	324	55	25	23	2	3	2	6	28	0	106	5	1	6	3	.667	0	0--	-	2.01	2.52
2008	Frisco	AA	10	10	0	0	45.1	185	34	16	15	1	1	2	2	23	0	47	2	0	4	3	.571	0	0--	-	2.89	2.98
2009	Okla	AAA	25	13	0	6	77.1	323	69	36	30	2	0	3	3	30	0	75	4	1	4	6	.400	0	0--	-	3.13	3.49
2009	Tex	AL	20	0	0	3	31.0	117	13	6	6	2	1	0	3	8	0	39	0	0	1	0	1.000	0	2-3	9	1.14	1.74

Pedro Feliz

Bats: R Throws: R Pos: 3B-155; PH-6; SS-2　　　　　Ht: 6'1" Wt: 210 Born: 4/27/1975 Age: 35

Year	Team	Lg	G	AB	H	2B	3B	HR	(Hm	Rd)	TB	R	RBI	RC	TBB	IBB	SO	HBP	SH	SF	SB	CS	SB%	GDP	Avg	OBP	Slg
2000	SF	NL	8	7	2	0	0	0	(0	0)	2	1	0	1	0	0	1	0	0	0	0	0	-	0	.286	.286	.286
2001	SF	NL	94	220	50	9	1	7	(3	4)	82	23	22	20	10	2	50	2	3	3	2	1	.67	5	.227	.264	.373
2002	SF	NL	67	146	37	4	1	2	(1	1)	49	14	13	12	6	1	27	0	0	1	0	0	-	2	.253	.281	.336
2003	SF	NL	95	235	58	9	3	16	(6	10)	121	31	48	34	10	0	53	1	1	2	2	2	.50	7	.247	.278	.515
2004	SF	NL	144	503	139	33	3	22	(11	11)	244	72	84	56	23	1	85	0	0	5	5	2	.71	18	.276	.305	.485
2005	SF	NL	156	569	142	30	4	20	(10	10)	240	69	81	58	30	1	102	1	1	6	2	0	.00	20	.250	.295	.422
2006	SF	NL	160	603	147	35	5	22	(6	16)	258	75	98	71	33	4	112	1	1	6	1	1	.50	18	.244	.281	.428
2007	SF	NL	150	557	141	28	2	20	(8	12)	233	61	72	67	29	2	70	1	0	3	2	2	.50	15	.253	.290	.418
2008	Phi	NL	133	425	106	19	2	14	(8	6)	171	43	58	47	33	3	54	0	3	2	0	0	-	14	.249	.302	.402
2009	Phi	NL	158	580	154	30	2	12	(8	4)	224	62	82	77	35	3	68	3	2	5	0	1	.00	12	.266	.308	.386
Postseason			22	54	13	1	1	0	(0	0)	16	2	5	5	2	0	10	0	0	0	0	0	-	1	.241	.268	.296
10 ML YEARS			1165	3845	976	197	23	135	(61	74)	1624	451	558	443	217	17	622	9	11	33	12	11	.52	111	.254	.293	.422

Prince Fielder

Bats: L Throws: R Pos: 1B-162　　　　　　　　　　Ht: 5'11" Wt: 268 Born: 5/9/1984 Age: 26

Year	Team	Lg	G	AB	H	2B	3B	HR	(Hm	Rd)	TB	R	RBI	RC	TBB	IBB	SO	HBP	SH	SF	SB	CS	SB%	GDP	Avg	OBP	Slg
2005	Mil	NL	39	59	17	4	0	2	(2	0)	27	2	10	10	2	0	17	0	0	1	0	0	-	0	.288	.306	.458
2006	Mil	NL	157	569	154	35	1	28	(11	17)	275	82	81	84	59	5	125	12	0	8	7	2	.78	17	.271	.347	.483
2007	Mil	NL	158	573	165	35	2	50	(27	23)	354	109	119	125	90	21	121	14	0	4	2	2	.50	9	.288	.395	.618
2008	Mil	NL	159	588	162	30	2	34	(18	16)	298	86	102	105	84	19	134	12	0	10	3	2	.60	12	.276	.372	.507
2009	Mil	NL	162	591	177	35	3	46	(23	23)	356	103	141	134	110	21	138	9	0	9	2	3	.40	14	.299	.412	.602
Postseason			4	14	1	0	0	1	(1	0)	4	1	2	0	2	2	5	0	0	1	0	0	-	0	.071	.176	.286
5 ML YEARS			675	2380	675	139	8	160	(81	79)	1310	382	453	458	345	66	535	47	0	32	14	9	.61	52	.284	.381	.550

Josh Fields

Bats: R Throws: R Pos: 3B-49; 1B-17; PH-9; DH-8, PR-5   Ht: 6'2" Wt: 225 Born: 12/14/1982 Age: 27

Year	Team	Lg	G	AB	H	2B	3B	HR	(Hm	Rd)	TB	R	RBI	RC	TBB	IBB	SO	HBP	SH	SF	SB	CS	SB%	GDP	Avg	OBP	Slg
2009	Charltt*	AAA	27	98	26	5	0	5	(-	-)	46	15	13	16	13	0	22	1	2	0	1	2	.33	4	.265	.357	.469
2006	CWS	AL	11	20	3	2	0	1	(1	0)	8	4	2	1	5	0	8	0	0	0	0	0	-	0	.150	.320	.400
2007	CWS	AL	100	373	91	17	1	23	(15	8)	179	54	67	56	35	0	125	1	6	3	1	1	.50	11	.244	.308	.480
2008	CWS	AL	14	32	5	1	0	0	(0	0)	6	3	2	1	3	0	17	0	0	0	0	0	-	0	.156	.229	.188
2009	CWS	AL	79	239	53	5	2	7	(4	3)	83	29	30	22	25	0	76	2	2	0	2	3	.40	5	.222	.301	.347
	4 ML YEARS		204	664	152	25	3	31	(20	11)	276	90	101	80	68	0	226	3	8	3	3	4	.43	16	.229	.302	.416

Casey Fien

Pitches: R Bats: R Pos: RP-9   Ht: 6'2" Wt: 195 Born: 10/21/1983 Age: 26

Year	Team	Lg	G	GS	CG	GF	IP	BFP	H	R	ER	HR	SH	SF	HB	TBB	IBB	SO	WP	Bk	W	L	Pct	Sh	Sv-Op	Hld	ERC	ERA
2006	Oneont	A-	20	0	0	3	42.2	169	39	17	13	1	3	1	0	8	0	37	2	0	1	1	.500	0	1--	-	2.40	2.74
2007	WMich	A	39	0	0	21	61.0	253	55	28	21	4	2	1	3	10	0	77	0	1	6	1	.857	0	6--	-	2.55	3.10
2008	Erie	AA	40	0	0	33	45.2	183	38	16	15	5	2	1	0	12	3	42	2	0	3	3	.500	0	12--	-	2.65	2.96
2008	Toledo	AAA	12	0	0	4	15.0	62	14	4	4	2	0	0	1	4	0	17	1	0	2	0	1.000	0	1--	-	3.73	2.40
2009	Toledo	AAA	42	0	0	26	58.0	234	51	23	22	5	1	1	2	15	3	66	2	1	2	1	.667	0	14--	-	2.91	3.41
2009	Det	AL	9	0	0	5	11.1	53	13	11	10	2	0	2	0	6	0	9	0	0	0	1	.000	0	0-0	0	5.92	7.94

Alfredo Figaro

Pitches: R Bats: R Pos: SP-3; RP-2   Ht: 6'0" Wt: 173 Born: 7/7/1984 Age: 25

Year	Team	Lg	G	GS	CG	GF	IP	BFP	H	R	ER	HR	SH	SF	HB	TBB	IBB	SO	WP	Bk	W	L	Pct	Sh	Sv-Op	Hld	ERC	ERA
2006	Tigers	R	14	4	0	5	38.1	152	29	7	3	0	1	0	1	12	0	31	0	1	3	1	.750	0	1--	-	2.01	0.70
2007	Lkland	A+	5	4	0	0	22.2	99	26	15	12	1	0	1	3	6	0	6	3	0	0	2	.000	0	0--	-	4.22	4.76
2007	Oneont	A	11	11	0	0	53.1	231	56	23	20	1	0	2	5	16	0	40	3	2	4	2	.667	0	0--	-	3.76	3.38
2008	WMich	A	19	19	2	0	123.0	493	99	35	28	0	3	2	4	30	0	96	7	0	12	2	.857	2	0--	-	2.00	2.05
2008	Lkland	A+	6	5	1	0	29.1	133	37	22	16	2	1	0	1	12	1	23	3	0	5	0	.000	0	0--	-	5.55	4.91
2009	Erie	AA	16	11	0	1	80.0	326	67	36	32	8	3	1	1	23	2	69	2	0	6	3	.667	0	0--	-	2.79	3.60
2009	Det	AL	5	3	0	0	17.0	83	23	12	12	3	1	0	1	10	0	10	0	0	2	2	.500	0	0-0	0	7.94	6.35

Chone Figgins

Bats: B Throws: R Pos: 3B-154; 2B-2; DH-2, LF-1   Ht: 5'8" Wt: 180 Born: 1/22/1978 Age: 32

Year	Team	Lg	G	AB	H	2B	3B	HR	(Hm	Rd)	TB	R	RBI	RC	TBB	IBB	SO	HBP	SH	SF	SB	CS	SB%	GDP	Avg	OBP	Slg
2002	LAA	AL	15	12	2	1	0	0	(0	0)	3	6	1	0	0	0	5	0	0	0	2	1	.67	1	.167	.167	.250
2003	LAA	AL	71	240	71	9	4	0	(0	0)	88	34	27	39	20	0	38	0	6	4	13	7	.65	1	.296	.345	.367
2004	LAA	AL	148	577	171	22	17	5	(3	2)	242	83	60	93	49	0	94	0	10	4	34	13	.72	6	.296	.350	.419
2005	LAA	AL	158	642	186	25	10	8	(2	6)	255	113	57	94	64	1	101	0	9	5	62	17	.78	9	.290	.352	.397
2006	LAA	AL	155	604	161	23	8	9	(2	7)	227	93	62	84	66	1	100	2	5	7	52	18	.78	6	.267	.336	.376
2007	LAA	AL	115	442	146	24	6	3	(1	2)	191	81	58	88	51	0	81	0	2	8	41	12	.77	7	.330	.393	.432
2008	LAA	AL	116	453	125	14	1	1	(0	1)	144	72	22	59	62	3	80	3	2	0	34	13	.72	7	.276	.367	.318
2009	LAA	AL	150	615	183	30	7	5	(2	3)	242	114	54	110	101	0	114	1	8	4	42	17	.71	8	.298	.395	.393
	Postseason		26	87	18	5	2	0	(0	0)	27	10	5	5	2	0	26	1	2	0	4	1	.80	1	.207	.233	.310
	8 ML YEARS		936	3585	1045	148	53	31	(10	21)	1392	596	341	567	412	5	613	8	42	30	280	96	.74	45	.291	.363	.388

Nelson Figueroa

Pitches: R Bats: R Pos: SP-10; RP-6   Ht: 6'1" Wt: 180 Born: 5/18/1974 Age: 36

Year	Team	Lg	G	GS	CG	GF	IP	BFP	H	R	ER	HR	SH	SF	HB	TBB	IBB	SO	WP	Bk	W	L	Pct	Sh	Sv-Op	Hld	ERC	ERA
2009	Buffalo*	AAA	17	17	1	0	112.0	437	91	29	28	5	4	4	1	24	0	94	1	0	7	5	.583	1	0--	-	2.17	2.25
2000	Ari	NL	3	3	0	0	15.2	68	17	13	13	4	1	2	0	5	0	7	2	0	0	1	.000	0	0-0	0	5.31	7.47
2001	Phi	NL	19	13	0	1	89.0	393	95	40	39	8	4	0	7	37	3	61	2	0	4	5	.444	0	0-0	0	4.76	3.94
2002	Mil	NL	30	11	0	4	93.0	412	96	59	52	18	11	5	4	37	6	51	5	0	1	7	.125	0	0-0	1	4.94	5.03
2003	Pit	NL	12	3	0	1	35.1	146	28	13	13	8	2	2	2	13	2	23	2	0	2	1	.667	0	0-0	0	3.80	3.31
2004	Pit	NL	10	3	0	0	28.1	121	32	18	18	4	4	0	0	11	1	10	3	0	0	3	.000	0	0-0	0	5.21	5.72
2008	NYM	NL	16	6	0	2	45.1	211	48	26	23	3	2	1	2	26	1	36	0	0	3	3	.500	0	0-1	0	4.88	4.57
2009	NYM	NL	16	10	1	2	70.1	320	80	33	32	8	3	4	9	24	4	59	1	0	3	8	.273	1	0-0	0	5.09	4.09
	7 ML YEARS		106	49	1	10	377.0	1671	396	202	190	53	27	14	24	153	17	247	15	0	13	28	.317	1	0-1	1	4.85	4.54

Jeff Fiorentino

Bats: L Throws: R Pos: CF-14; LF-7; PH-5; RF-2; PR-1   Ht: 6'1" Wt: 185 Born: 4/14/1983 Age: 27

Year	Team	Lg	G	AB	H	2B	3B	HR	(Hm	Rd)	TB	R	RBI	RC	TBB	IBB	SO	HBP	SH	SF	SB	CS	SB%	GDP	Avg	OBP	Slg
2009	Bowie*	AA	7	23	2	1	0	0	(-	-)	3	1	0	0	3	0	4	0	0	0	2	0	1.00	0	.087	.192	.130
2009	Norfolk*	AAA	102	365	114	26	5	12	(-	-)	186	70	67	73	48	3	62	0	3	6	13	6	.68	2	.312	.387	.510
2005	Bal	AL	13	44	11	2	0	1	(1	0)	16	7	5	2	2	0	10	0	0	1	1	0	1.00	0	.250	.277	.364
2006	Bal	AL	19	39	10	2	0	0	(0	0)	12	8	7	6	7	0	3	1	2	1	1	0	1.00	1	.256	.375	.308
2008	Oak	AL	2	1	1	0	0	0	(0	0)	1	0	1	1	0	0	0	0	0	0	0	0	-	0	1.000	1.000	1.000
2009	Bal	AL	24	64	18	1	0	0	(0	0)	19	8	8	9	8	0	16	0	1	2	2	0	1.00	1	.281	.351	.297
	4 ML YEARS		58	148	40	5	0	1	(1	0)	48	23	21	18	17	0	29	1	3	4	4	0	1.00	2	.270	.341	.324

Carlos Fisher

Pitches: R **Bats:** R **Pos:** RP-39 **Ht:** 6'4" **Wt:** 225 **Born:** 2/22/1983 **Age:** 27

Year	Team	Lg	G	GS	CG	GF	IP	BFP	H	R	ER	HR	SH	SF	HB	TBB	IBB	SO	WP	Bk	W	L	Pct	Sh	Sv-Op Hld	ERC	ERA
2005	Billings	R+	15	8	0	1	53.2	235	56	30	25	3	0	2	5	19	0	45	3	0	4	4	.500	0	1- - -	4.20	4.19
2006	Dayton	A	27	27	0	0	150.0	609	133	53	46	5	4	1	5	38	0	122	6	0	12	5	.706	0	0- - -	2.65	2.76
2007	Srsota	A+	7	7	0	0	41.0	164	34	12	10	1	0	2	1	7	0	41	0	0	4	1	.800	0	0- - -	1.96	4.29
2007	Chatt	AA	21	21	0	0	113.1	502	127	61	54	11	7	7	10	42	0	94	9	0	5	9	.357	0	0- - -	5.04	4.29
2008	Chatt	AA	36	0	0	21	50.2	226	52	28	21	3	4	0	1	20	4	46	6	0	1	5	.167	0	8- - -	3.74	3.73
2008	Lsvlle	AAA	14	0	0	3	17.1	77	14	2	2	0	1	1	1	9	2	21	0	0	5	0	1.000	0	0- - -	2.70	1.04
2009	Lsvlle	AAA	13	0	0	6	18.0	69	11	4	4	0	1	0	1	4	0	21	2	0	2	0	1.000	0	2- - -	1.31	2.00
2009	Srsota	A+	2	0	0	1	2.0	9	1	0	0	0	0	0	0	2	0	2	0	0	0	0	-	0	0- - -	2.80	0.00
2009	Cin	NL	39	0	0	17	52.1	226	50	26	26	4	2	1	1	31	2	48	6	0	1	1	.500	0	0-1 2	4.58	4.47

Doug Fister

Pitches: R **Bats:** L **Pos:** SP-10; RP-1 **Ht:** 6'8" **Wt:** 193 **Born:** 2/4/1984 **Age:** 26

Year	Team	Lg	G	GS	CG	GF	IP	BFP	H	R	ER	HR	SH	SF	HB	TBB	IBB	SO	WP	Bk	W	L	Pct	Sh	Sv-Op Hld	ERC	ERA
2006	Everett	A-	20	4	0	13	40.0	167	35	18	10	2	2	0	1	11	0	35	2	1	3	5	.375	0	4- - -	2.65	2.25
2007	WTenn	AA	24	24	1	0	131.0	560	156	78	67	14	5	4	3	32	0	85	3	0	7	8	.467	0	0- - -	4.78	4.60
2008	WTenn	AA	31	23	0	5	134.1	602	155	95	81	12	2	8	11	45	0	104	4	2	6	14	.300	0	0- - -	4.93	5.43
2009	WTenn	AA	2	0	0	0	5.2	19	2	0	0	0	0	0	0	1	0	5	0	0	1	0	1.000	0	0- - -	0.53	0.00
2009	Tacom	AAA	22	17	0	1	106.1	458	132	51	46	10	5	4	5	11	0	79	4	1	6	4	.600	0	0- - -	4.39	3.89
2009	Sea	AL	11	10	0	1	61.0	256	63	29	28	11	0	0	2	15	0	36	1	0	3	4	.429	0	0-0 0	4.36	4.13

Jesus Flores

Bats: R **Throws:** R **Pos:** C-24; PH-6 **Ht:** 6'1" **Wt:** 229 **Born:** 10/26/1984 **Age:** 25

Year	Team	Lg	G	AB	H	2B	3B	HR	(Hm	Rd)	TB	R	RBI	RC	TBB	IBB	SO	HBP	SH	SF	SB	CS	SB%	GDP	Avg	OBP	Slg
2009	Hrsbrg*	AA	3	11	4	0	0	0	(-	-)	4	1	0	1	0	0	1	0	0	0	0	0	-	0	.364	.364	.364
2007	Was	NL	79	180	44	9	0	4	(1	3)	65	21	25	19	14	0	48	3	0	0	0	1	.00	5	.244	.310	.361
2008	Was	NL	90	301	77	18	1	8	(2	6)	121	23	59	45	15	1	78	4	0	4	0	1	.00	7	.256	.296	.402
2009	Was	NL	29	93	28	3	2	4	(0	4)	47	13	15	14	11	1	26	0	1	1	0	0	-	1	.301	.371	.505
	3 ML YEARS		198	574	149	30	3	16	(3	13)	233	57	99	78	40	2	152	7	1	5	0	2	.00	13	.260	.313	.406

Randy Flores

Pitches: L **Bats:** L **Pos:** RP-27 **Ht:** 6'0" **Wt:** 190 **Born:** 7/31/1975 **Age:** 34

Year	Team	Lg	G	GS	CG	GF	IP	BFP	H	R	ER	HR	SH	SF	HB	TBB	IBB	SO	WP	Bk	W	L	Pct	Sh	Sv-Op Hld	ERC	ERA
2009	ColSpr*	AAA	38	0	0	8	31.2	142	37	20	15	2	4	0	1	11	0	33	2	0	0	2	.000	0	0- - -	4.63	4.26
2002	2 Tms		28	2	0	9	29.0	140	40	26	24	7	2	2	3	16	3	14	4	0	0	2	.000	0	1-2 2	8.69	7.45
2004	StL	NL	9	1	0	3	14.0	57	13	3	3	0	1	1	3	3	1	7	0	0	1	0	1.000	0	0-0 0	3.15	1.93
2005	StL	NL	50	0	0	6	41.2	174	37	22	16	5	1	3	3	13	0	43	2	0	3	1	.750	0	1-3 11	3.55	3.46
2006	StL	NL	65	0	0	10	41.2	196	49	29	26	5	3	1	1	22	3	40	1	0	1	1	.500	0	0-1 18	5.64	5.62
2007	StL	NL	70	0	0	11	55.0	253	71	31	26	2	4	2	3	15	0	47	3	0	3	0	1.000	0	1-2 14	4.87	4.25
2008	StL	NL	43	0	0	3	25.2	131	34	16	15	2	0	2	1	20	3	17	1	0	1	0	1.000	0	1-3 14	7.23	5.26
2009	Col	NL	27	0	0	2	12.0	52	14	7	7	2	0	0	0	2	0	14	0	0	0	1	.000	0	0-0 10	4.43	5.25
02	Tex	AL	20	0	0	5	12.0	52	11	7	6	2	1	2	0	8	2	7	3	0	0	0	-	0	1-2 2	5.07	4.50
02	Col	AL	8	2	0	4	17.0	88	29	19	18	5	1	0	3	8	1	7	1	0	0	2	.000	0	0-0 0	11.52	9.53
	Postseason		12	0	0	0	9.0	34	7	1	1	0	0	0	0	2	0	7	0	0	1	0	1.000	0	0-0 3	2.45	1.00
	7 ML YEARS		292	3	0	44	219.0	1003	258	134	117	23	11	11	14	91	10	182	11	0	9	5	.643	0	4-11 69	5.35	4.81

Tyler Flowers

Bats: R **Throws:** R **Pos:** C-6; DH-2; PH-2 **Ht:** 6'4" **Wt:** 245 **Born:** 1/24/1986 **Age:** 24

Year	Team	Lg	G	AB	H	2B	3B	HR	(Hm	Rd)	TB	R	RBI	RC	TBB	IBB	SO	HBP	SH	SF	SB	CS	SB%	GDP	Avg	OBP	Slg
2006	Danvle	R+	34	129	36	9	0	5	(-	-)	60	24	16	23	16	0	30	4	0	1	0	0	-	1	.279	.373	.465
2007	Rome	A	106	389	116	34	2	12	(-	-)	190	65	70	72	49	1	74	3	0	4	3	4	.43	8	.298	.378	.488
2008	MrtlBh	A+	122	413	119	32	1	17	(-	-)	204	72	88	92	98	2	102	5	0	4	8	7	.53	8	.288	.427	.494
2009	Brham	AA	77	248	75	18	2	13	(-	-)	136	54	43	63	57	5	76	9	0	3	3	0	1.00	6	.302	.445	.548
2009	Charltt	AAA	31	105	30	10	0	2	(-	-)	46	13	13	17	10	0	32	3	1	0	0	0	-	4	.286	.364	.438
2009	CWS	AL	10	16	3	1	0	0	(0	0)	4	3	0	2	3	0	8	1	0	0	0	0	-	1	.188	.350	.250

Cliff Floyd

Bats: L **Throws:** R **Pos:** PH-8; DH-2 **Ht:** 6'4" **Wt:** 230 **Born:** 12/5/1972 **Age:** 37

Year	Team	Lg	G	AB	H	2B	3B	HR	(Hm	Rd)	TB	R	RBI	RC	TBB	IBB	SO	HBP	SH	SF	SB	CS	SB%	GDP	Avg	OBP	Slg
2009	Lk Els*	A+	7	21	4	1	0	0	(-	-)	5	0	0	0	1	0	2	0	0	0	0	0	-	1	.190	.227	.238
1993	Mon	NL	10	31	7	0	0	1	(0	1)	10	3	2	2	0	0	9	0	0	0	0	0	-	0	.226	.226	.323
1994	Mon	NL	100	334	94	19	4	4	(2	2)	133	43	41	46	24	0	63	3	2	3	10	3	.77	3	.281	.332	.398
1995	Mon	NL	29	69	9	1	0	1	(1	0)	13	6	8	2	7	0	22	1	0	0	3	0	1.00	1	.130	.221	.188
1996	Fla	NL	117	227	55	15	4	6	(3	3)	96	29	26	35	30	1	52	5	1	3	7	1	.88	3	.242	.340	.423
1997	Fla	NL	61	137	32	9	1	6	(2	4)	61	23	19	23	24	0	33	2	1	1	6	2	.75	3	.234	.354	.445
1998	Fla	NL	153	588	166	45	3	22	(10	12)	283	85	90	92	47	7	112	3	0	3	27	14	.66	10	.282	.337	.481
1999	Fla	NL	69	251	76	19	1	11	(4	7)	130	37	49	45	30	5	47	2	0	2	5	6	.45	8	.303	.379	.518
2000	Fla	NL	121	420	126	30	0	22	(13	9)	222	75	91	88	50	5	82	8	0	9	24	3	.89	4	.300	.378	.529

	BATTING																		BASERUNNING				AVERAGES		
Year Team	Lg	G	AB	H	2B	3B	HR	(Hm Rd)	TB	R	RBI	RC	TBB	IBB	SO	HBP	SH	SF	SB	CS	SB%	GDP	Avg	OBP	Slg
2001 Fla	NL	149	555	176	44	4	31	(16 15)	321	123	103	121	59	19	101	10	0	5	18	3	.86	9	.317	.390	.578
2002 3 Tms		146	520	150	43	0	28	(13 15)	277	86	79	92	76	19	106	10	0	3	15	5	.75	6	.288	.388	.533
2003 NYM	NL	108	365	106	25	2	18	(10 8)	189	57	68	69	51	2	66	3	0	6	3	0	1.00	10	.290	.376	.518
2004 NYM	NL	113	396	103	26	0	18	(7 11)	183	55	63	64	47	6	103	11	0	3	11	4	.73	8	.260	.352	.462
2005 NYM	NL	150	550	150	22	2	34	(21 13)	278	85	98	99	63	13	98	11	0	2	12	2	.86	5	.273	.358	.505
2006 NYM	NL	97	332	81	19	1	11	(5 6)	135	45	44	45	29	3	58	12	0	3	6	0	1.00	5	.244	.324	.407
2007 ChC	NL	108	282	80	10	1	9	(3 6)	119	40	45	43	35	5	47	5	0	0	0	0	--	6	.284	.373	.422
2008 TB	AL	80	246	66	13	0	11	(9 2)	112	32	39	36	28	2	58	5	0	5	1	0	1.00	4	.268	.349	.455
2009 SD	NL	10	16	2	0	0	0	(0 0)	2	0	0	0	1	0	7	0	0	0	0	0	--	0	.125	.176	.125
02 Fla	NL	84	296	85	20	0	18	(7 11)	159	49	57	64	58	18	68	7	0	1	10	5	.67	0	.287	.414	.537
02 Mon	NL	15	53	11	2	0	3	(3 0)	22	7	4	2	3	1	10	1	0	0	1	0	1.00	0	.208	.263	.415
02 Bos	AL	47	171	54	21	0	7	(3 4)	96	30	18	26	15	0	28	2	0	2	4	0	1.00	6	.316	.374	.561
Postseason		19	37	8	1	0	2	(2 0)	15	7	4	3	4	2	13	1	0	0	0	0	--	0	.216	.310	.405
17 ML YEARS		1621	5319	1479	340	23	233	(119 114)	2564	824	865	902	601	87	1064	91	4	48	148	43	.77	85	.278	.358	.482

Gavin Floyd

Pitches: R Bats: R Pos: SP-30   Ht: 6'5" Wt: 230 Born: 1/27/1983 Age: 27

	HOW MUCH HE PITCHED						WHAT HE GAVE UP												THE RESULTS						
Year Team	Lg	G	GS	CG	GF	IP	BFP	H	R	ER	HR	SH	SF	HB	TBB	IBB	SO	WP	Bk	W	L	Pct	Sh	Sv-Op	Hld	ERC	ERA
2004 Phi	NL	6	4	0	0	28.1	126	25	11	11	1	1	0	5	16	0	24	1	1	2	0	1.000	0	0-0	0	4.33	3.49
2005 Phi	NL	7	4	0	0	26.0	127	30	31	29	5	1	1	3	16	2	17	2	0	1	2	.333	0	0-0	0	6.82	10.04
2006 Phi	NL	11	11	1	0	54.1	264	70	48	44	14	2	5	3	32	3	34	2	0	4	3	.571	1	0-0	0	8.02	7.29
2007 CWS	AL	16	10	0	4	70.0	314	85	45	41	17	3	2	6	19	0	49	1	0	1	5	.167	0	0-0	0	6.22	5.27
2008 CWS	AL	33	33	1	0	206.1	878	190	107	88	30	7	5	9	70	6	145	9	0	17	8	.680	0	0-0	0	3.80	3.84
2009 CWS	AL	30	30	1	0	193.0	797	178	93	87	21	3	2	2	59	4	163	8	0	11	11	.500	0	0-0	0	3.38	4.06
Postseason		1	1	0	0	3.0	16	5	4	4	2	0	0	0	2	0	4	0	0	0	1	.000	0	0-0	0	14.65	12.00
6 ML YEARS		103	92	3	4	578.0	2506	578	335	300	88	16	16	28	212	15	432	23	1	36	29	.554	1	0-0	0	5.16	4.67

Josh Fogg

Pitches: R Bats: R Pos: RP-23; SP-1   Ht: 6'0" Wt: 205 Born: 12/13/1976 Age: 33

	HOW MUCH HE PITCHED						WHAT HE GAVE UP												THE RESULTS						
Year Team	Lg	G	GS	CG	GF	IP	BFP	H	R	ER	HR	SH	SF	HB	TBB	IBB	SO	WP	Bk	W	L	Pct	Sh	Sv-Op	Hld	ERC	ERA
2009 ColSpr*	AAA	8	8	0	0	40.1	177	44	26	26	8	3	2	0	17	2	16	3	0	3	1	.750	0	0--	-	5.37	5.80
2001 CWS	AL	11	0	0	4	13.1	53	10	3	3	0	0	1	1	3	1	17	0	0	0	0	--	0	0-0	2	1.73	2.03
2002 Pit	NL	33	33	0	0	194.1	832	199	102	94	28	6	3	8	69	12	113	2	0	12	12	.500	0	0-0	0	4.46	4.35
2003 Pit	NL	26	26	1	0	142.0	625	166	90	83	22	6	4	9	40	0	71	2	0	10	9	.526	0	0-0	0	5.25	5.26
2004 Pit	NL	32	32	0	0	178.1	770	193	98	92	17	9	6	8	66	8	82	4	1	11	10	.524	0	0-0	0	4.60	4.64
2005 Pit	NL	34	28	0	1	109.1	742	196	106	95	27	4	6	6	53	11	85	2	1	6	11	.353	0	0-0	0	5.13	5.05
2006 Col	NL	31	31	1	0	172.0	765	206	115	105	24	6	5	6	60	13	93	3	0	11	9	.550	1	0-0	0	5.36	5.49
2007 Col	NL	30	29	0	0	165.2	745	194	99	91	23	5	5	13	59	7	94	3	0	10	9	.526	0	0-0	0	5.44	4.94
2008 Cin	NL	22	14	0	3	78.1	362	97	69	66	17	6	2	6	27	1	45	1	0	2	7	.222	0	0-0	1	6.36	7.58
2009 Col	NL	24	1	0	9	45.2	187	32	20	19	7	1	3	1	20	1	27	3	0	0	2	.000	0	0-0	1	3.02	3.74
Postseason		3	2	0	0	10.2	49	18	7	7	1	0	0	0	3	1	6	0	0	2	1	.667	0	0-0	0	8.00	5.91
9 ML YEARS		243	194	2	17	1159.0	5081	1293	702	648	165	43	35	58	397	54	627	20	2	62	69	.473	1	0-0	4	4.97	5.03

Mike Fontenot

Bats: L Throws: R Pos: 2B-70; 3B-50; PH-20   Ht: 5'8" Wt: 170 Born: 6/9/1980 Age: 30

	BATTING																		BASERUNNING				AVERAGES		
Year Team	Lg	G	AB	H	2B	3B	HR	(Hm Rd)	TB	R	RBI	RC	TBB	IBB	SO	HBP	SH	SF	SB	CS	SB%	GDP	Avg	OBP	Slg
2005 ChC	NL	7	2	0	0	0	0	(0 0)	0	4	0	1	2	0	0	1	0	0	0	0	--	0	.000	.600	.000
2007 ChC	NL	86	234	65	12	4	3	(2 1)	94	32	29	26	22	0	43	0	1	3	5	4	.56	5	.278	.336	.402
2008 ChC	NL	119	243	74	22	1	9	(4 5)	125	42	40	49	34	2	51	3	3	1	2	0	1.00	1	.305	.395	.514
2009 ChC	NL	135	377	89	22	2	9	(3 6)	142	38	43	37	35	4	83	2	0	5	4	1	.80	7	.236	.301	.377
Postseason		5	8	2	0	0	0	(0 0)	2	0	0	0	0	0	1	0	0	0	0	0	--	0	.250	.250	.250
4 ML YEARS		347	856	228	56	7	21	(9 12)	361	116	112	113	93	6	177	6	4	9	11	5	.69	13	.266	.339	.422

Casey Fossum

Pitches: L Bats: L Pos: RP-3   Ht: 6'1" Wt: 160 Born: 1/6/1978 Age: 32

	HOW MUCH HE PITCHED						WHAT HE GAVE UP												THE RESULTS						
Year Team	Lg	G	GS	CG	GF	IP	BFP	H	R	ER	HR	SH	SF	HB	TBB	IBB	SO	WP	Bk	W	L	Pct	Sh	Sv-Op	Hld	ERC	ERA
2009 Buffalo*	AAA	2	2	0	0	11.0	38	5	1	1	0	0	0	0	5	0	12	2	0	0	0	-	0	0--	0	1.35	0.82
2009 S-WB*	AAA	10	10	0	0	50.2	214	50	24	19	7	1	2	1	16	0	43	4	0	3	3	.500	0	0--	-	4.03	3.38
2009 Iowa*	AAA	13	12	0	0	67.2	286	59	32	31	8	1	1	7	22	1	70	5	0	6	4	.600	0	0--	-	3.58	4.12
2001 Bos	AL	13	7	0	3	44.1	197	44	20	24	4	0	1	6	20	1	26	1	1	3	2	.600	0	0-0	0	4.70	4.87
2002 Bos	AL	43	12	0	13	106.2	461	113	56	41	12	2	4	4	30	0	101	3	0	5	4	.556	0	1-1	3	4.14	3.46
2003 Bos	AL	19	14	0	1	79.0	346	82	55	48	9	1	3	4	34	0	63	4	0	6	5	.545	0	1-1	0	4.77	5.47
2004 Ari	NL	27	27	0	0	142.0	652	171	111	105	31	8	4	10	63	5	117	4	2	4	15	.211	0	0-0	0	6.67	6.65
2005 TB	AL	36	25	0	1	162.2	725	170	100	89	21	3	5	18	60	3	128	8	1	8	12	.400	0	0-1	0	4.80	4.92
2006 TB	AL	25	25	0	0	130.0	594	136	89	77	18	2	3	12	63	3	88	4	1	6	6	.500	0	0-0	0	5.25	5.33
2007 TB	AL	40	10	0	7	76.0	364	109	71	65	15	2	7	6	27	1	53	3	0	5	8	.385	0	0-4	2	7.59	7.70
2008 Det	AL	31	0	0	9	41.1	179	44	26	26	4	0	0	3	18	1	28	1	0	3	1	.750	0	0-1	6	4.98	5.66
2009 NYM	NL	3	0	0	0	4.0	19	4	1	1	0	0	0	0	4	0	3	0	0	0	0	-	0	0-0	0	5.79	2.25
9 ML YEARS		237	120	0	35	786.0	3537	873	535	476	114	18	27	63	319	14	607	28	5	40	53	.430	0	2-8	11	5.37	5.45

Dexter Fowler

Bats: B **Throws:** R **Pos:** CF-127; PH-14; PR-7   **Ht:** 6'4" **Wt:** 185 **Born:** 3/22/1986 **Age:** 24

Year	Team	Lg	G	AB	H	2B	3B	HR	(Hm	Rd)	TB	R	RBI	RC	TBB	IBB	SO	HBP	SH	SF	SB	CS	SB%	GDP	Avg	OBP	Slg
2005	Casper	R+	62	220	60	10	4	4	(-	-)	90	43	23	35	27	1	73	2	3	0	18	6	.75	2	.273	.357	.409
2006	Ashvll	A	99	405	120	31	6	8	(-	-)	187	92	46	71	43	0	79	7	2	1	43	23	.65	8	.296	.373	.462
2007	Mdest	A+	65	245	67	7	5	2	(-	-)	90	43	23	40	44	0	64	7	2	1	20	11	.65	4	.273	.397	.367
2008	Tulsa	AA	108	421	141	31	9	9	(-	-)	217	92	64	96	65	4	89	8	8	3	20	8	.71	6	.335	.431	.515
2009	Tulsa	AA	3	10	4	2	0	0	(-	-)	6	3	3	3	3	0	3	0	0	0	1	0	1.00	1	.400	.538	.600
2008	Col	NL	13	26	4	0	0	0	(0	0)	4	3	0	0	1	0	5	1	0	0	0	1	.00	0	.154	.185	.154
2009	Col	NL	135	433	115	29	10	4	(2	2)	176	73	34	68	67	1	116	1	14	3	27	10	.73	4	.266	.363	.406
	2 ML YEARS		148	459	119	29	10	4	(2	2)	180	76	34	68	67	1	121	2	14	3	27	11	.71	4	.259	.354	.392

Chad Fox

Pitches: R **Bats:** R **Pos:** RP-2   **Ht:** 6'3" **Wt:** 215 **Born:** 9/3/1970 **Age:** 39

Year	Team	Lg	G	GS	CG	GF	IP	BFP	H	R	ER	HR	SH	SF	HB	TBB	IBB	SO	WP	Bk	W	L	Pct	Sh	Sv-Op	Hld	ERC	ERA
2009	Iowa*	AAA	11	0	0	6	11.1	44	8	3	2	0	2	1	0	3	0	10	1	0	1	0	1.000	0	2- -	-	1.58	1.59
1997	Atl	NL	30	0	0	8	27.1	120	24	12	10	4	0	0	0	16	0	28	4	0	0	1	.000	0	0-1	7	4.44	3.29
1998	Mil	NL	49	0	0	12	57.0	242	56	27	25	4	6	0	1	20	0	64	5	0	1	4	.200	0	0-2	20	3.66	3.95
1999	Mil	NL	6	0	0	2	6.2	36	11	8	8	1	0	0	1	4	0	12	1	1	0	0	-	0	0-0	1	9.96	10.80
2001	Mil	NL	65	0	0	9	66.2	287	44	16	14	6	2	1	5	36	7	80	5	1	5	2	.714	0	2-4	20	2.75	1.89
2002	Mil	NL	3	0	0	1	4.2	25	6	3	3	0	1	0	0	5	1	3	0	0	1	0	1.000	0	0-0	0	7.03	5.79
2003	2 Tms		38	0	0	13	43.1	198	35	16	15	3	5	5	1	31	4	46	6	0	3	3	.500	0	3-5	7	3.80	3.12
2004	Fla	NL	12	0	0	1	10.2	49	9	8	8	1	0	0	1	8	0	17	1	0	0	1	.000	0	0-2	5	4.88	6.75
2005	ChC	NL	11	0	0	4	8.0	38	8	6	6	2	0	1	0	8	0	11	0	0	0	0	-	0	1-1	3	8.11	6.75
2008	ChC	NL	3	0	0	1	3.1	14	2	2	2	1	1	0	0	3	0	1	1	0	0	1	.000	0	0-0	0	5.57	5.40
2009	ChC	NL	2	0	0	0	0.1	6	2	5	5	0	0	0	0	3	0	1	0	0	0	0	-	0	0-0	0	87.50	135.0
03	Bos	AL	17	0	0	10	18.0	93	19	10	9	2	2	1	1	17	2	19	1	0	1	2	.333	0	3-5	0	6.42	4.50
03	Fla	NL	21	0	0	3	25.1	105	16	6	6	1	3	4	0	14	2	27	5	0	2	1	.667	0	0-0	7	2.18	2.13
	Postseason		9	0	0	1	11.1	53	12	5	5	2	2	0	0	9	3	9	0	0	1	0	1.000	0	0-0	1	6.25	3.97
	10 ML YEARS		219	0	0	50	228.0	1015	197	103	96	22	15	7	9	134	12	262	24	2	10	12	.455	0	6-15	63	4.03	3.79

Jake Fox

Bats: R **Throws:** R **Pos:** PH-30; 3B-27; LF-23; 1B-7; C-3; RF-3; DH-3   **Ht:** 6'0" **Wt:** 210 **Born:** 7/20/1982 **Age:** 27

Year	Team	Lg	G	AB	H	2B	3B	HR	(Hm	Rd)	TB	R	RBI	RC	TBB	IBB	SO	HBP	SH	SF	SB	CS	SB%	GDP	Avg	OBP	Slg
2003	Cubs	R	15	50	12	5	0	1	(-	-)	20	4	6	6	5	0	14	1	0	0	0	1	.00	0	.240	.321	.400
2003	Lansng	A	29	100	26	8	0	5	(-	-)	49	13	12	16	8	0	19	3	0	1	2	1	.67	3	.260	.330	.490
2004	Lansng	A	97	366	105	19	3	14	(-	-)	172	49	55	57	17	0	75	8	2	2	2	1	.67	7	.287	.331	.470
2005	Dytona	A+	83	270	76	20	0	9	(-	-)	123	37	40	46	26	3	48	8	1	4	5	2	.71	8	.281	.357	.456
2006	Dytona	A+	66	249	78	15	1	16	(-	-)	143	45	61	55	27	3	49	6	1	8	4	1	.80	4	.313	.383	.574
2006	WTenn	AA	55	193	52	17	0	5	(-	-)	84	20	25	25	9	0	44	1	0	1	0	0	-	10	.269	.304	.435
2007	Tenn	AA	91	359	102	23	1	18	(-	-)	181	60	60	60	17	3	72	8	0	4	6	2	.75	8	.284	.327	.504
2007	Iowa	AAA	25	99	28	7	0	6	(-	-)	53	18	19	18	5	0	23	4	0	0	2	0	1.00	2	.283	.343	.535
2008	Iowa	AAA	29	117	26	10	1	6	(-	-)	56	17	26	14	2	0	31	1	0	0	3	0	1.00	3	.222	.242	.479
2008	Tenn	AA	105	388	119	28	1	25	(-	-)	224	76	79	89	46	2	73	17	0	8	4	2	.67	7	.307	.397	.577
2009	Iowa	AAA	45	164	67	14	3	17	(-	-)	138	44	53	59	21	1	31	8	0	1	2	1	.67	5	.409	.495	.841
2007	ChC	NL	7	14	2	2	0	0	(0	0)	4	3	1	1	1	0	2	0	0	0	0	0	-	1	.143	.200	.286
2009	ChC	NL	82	216	56	12	0	11	(4	7)	101	23	44	32	14	1	47	5	0	6	0	0	-	5	.259	.311	.468
	2 ML YEARS		89	230	58	14	0	11	(4	7)	105	26	45	33	15	1	49	5	0	6	0	0	-	6	.252	.305	.457

Jeff Francis

Pitches: L **Bats:** L **Pos:** P   **Ht:** 6'5" **Wt:** 205 **Born:** 1/8/1981 **Age:** 29

Year	Team	Lg	G	GS	CG	GF	IP	BFP	H	R	ER	HR	SH	SF	HB	TBB	IBB	SO	WP	Bk	W	L	Pct	Sh	Sv-Op	Hld	ERC	ERA
2004	Col	NL	7	7	0	0	36.2	164	42	22	21	8	2	1	1	13	1	32	2	0	3	2	.600	0	0-0	0	5.62	5.15
2005	Col	NL	33	33	0	0	183.2	828	228	119	116	26	6	10	8	70	5	128	2	0	14	12	.538	0	0-0	0	5.94	5.68
2006	Col	NL	32	32	1	0	199.0	843	187	101	92	18	7	7	13	69	15	117	0	0	13	11	.542	1	0-0	0	3.63	4.16
2007	Col	NL	34	34	1	0	215.1	922	234	103	101	25	7	4	7	63	7	165	1	1	17	9	.654	1	0-0	0	4.37	4.22
2008	Col	NL	24	24	0	0	143.2	636	164	84	80	21	6	4	3	49	4	94	0	0	4	10	.286	0	0-0	0	5.00	5.01
	Postseason		3	3	0	0	16.2	75	21	9	9	3	0	0	2	6	2	15	0	0	2	1	.667	0	0-0	0	6.57	4.86
	5 ML YEARS		130	130	2	0	778.1	3393	855	429	410	98	28	26	32	264	32	536	5	1	51	44	.537	2	0-0	0	4.71	4.74

Ben Francisco

Bats: R **Throws:** R **Pos:** LF-61; CF-40; RF-18; PH-17; DH-2; PR-2   **Ht:** 6'1" **Wt:** 190 **Born:** 10/23/1981 **Age:** 28

Year	Team	Lg	G	AB	H	2B	3B	HR	(Hm	Rd)	TB	R	RBI	RC	TBB	IBB	SO	HBP	SH	SF	SB	CS	SB%	GDP	Avg	OBP	Slg
2007	Cle	AL	25	62	17	5	0	3	(2	1)	31	10	12	6	3	0	19	0	0	1	0	2	.00	2	.274	.303	.500
2008	Cle	AL	121	447	119	32	0	15	(7	8)	196	65	54	57	40	0	86	6	2	4	4	3	.57	10	.266	.332	.438
2009	2 Tms		126	405	104	30	1	15	(6	9)	181	58	46	56	38	0	83	9	4	3	14	7	.67	12	.257	.332	.447
09	Cle	AL	89	308	77	21	1	10	(4	6)	130	48	33	43	33	0	59	8	4	2	13	3	.81	11	.250	.336	.422
09	Phi	NL	37	97	27	9	0	5	(2	3)	51	10	13	13	5	0	24	1	0	1	1	4	.20	1	.278	.317	.526
	3 ML YEARS		272	914	240	67	1	33	(15	18)	408	133	112	119	81	0	188	15	6	8	18	12	.60	24	.263	.330	.446

Frank Francisco

Pitches: R Bats: R Pos: RP-51   Ht: 6'3" Wt: 230 Born: 9/11/1979 Age: 30

Year Team	Lg	G	GS	CG	GF	IP	BFP	H	R	ER	HR	SH	SF	HD	TBB	IBB	SO	WP	Bk	W	L	Pct	Sh	Sv-Op	Hld	ERC	ERA
2009 Frisco*	AA	2	1	0	0	2.0	7	1	0	0	0	0	0	0	0	0	1	0	0	0	0	-	0	0--	-	0.54	0.00
2004 Tex	AL	45	0	0	7	51.1	216	36	19	19	4	2	1	3	28	2	60	4	1	5	1	.833	0	0-3	10	3.04	3.33
2006 Tex	AL	8	0	0	2	7.1	32	8	4	4	2	0	0	0	2	0	6	1	0	0	1	.000	0	0-0	2	5.17	4.91
2007 Tex	AL	59	0	0	16	59.1	268	57	33	30	3	6	1	2	38	4	49	8	0	1	1	.500	0	0-0	21	4.44	4.55
2008 Tex	AL	58	0	0	18	63.1	264	47	24	22	7	0	3	0	26	2	83	5	0	3	5	.375	0	5-11	12	2.70	3.13
2009 Tex	AL	51	0	0	42	49.1	203	40	21	21	6	0	0	1	15	1	57	3	0	2	3	.400	0	25-29	4	2.85	3.83
5 ML YEARS		221	0	0	85	230.2	983	188	101	96	22	8	5	6	109	9	255	21	1	11	11	.500	0	30-43	49	3.33	3.75

Juan Francisco

Bats: l Throws: R Pos: PH-11; 3D-4   Ht: 6'2" Wt: 180 Born: 6/24/1987 Age: 23

Year Team	Lg	G	AB	H	2B	3B	HR	(Hm	Rd)	TB	R	RBI	RC	TBB	IBB	SO	HBP	SH	SF	SB	CS	SB%	GDP	Avg	OBP	Slg
2006 Reds	R	45	182	51	14	0	3	(-	-)	74	24	30	23	6	1	35	1	0	1	2	0	1.00	6	.280	.305	.407
2006 Billings	R+	9	36	12	3	0	0	(-	-)	15	6	2	4	0	0	8	0	0	0	2	1	.67	2	.333	.333	.417
2007 Dayton	A	135	534	143	21	4	25	(-	-)	247	69	90	74	23	6	161	3	0	2	12	6	.67	14	.268	.301	.463
2008 Srsota	A+	127	516	143	34	5	23	(-	-)	256	71	92	77	19	5	123	2	0	4	1	2	.33	14	.277	.303	.496
2009 Carlina	AA	109	437	123	26	2	22	(-	-)	219	64	74	70	20	4	91	4	0	3	6	2	.75	7	.281	.317	.501
2009 Lsvlle	AAA	22	92	33	5	1	5	(-	-)	55	17	19	20	4	1	24	1	0	2	0	0	-	3	.359	.384	.598
2009 Cin	NL	14	21	9	1	0	1	(1	0)	13	4	7	6	3	0	7	1	0	0	0	0	-	0	.429	.520	.619

Jeff Francoeur

Bats: R Throws: R Pos: RF-154; PH-3   Ht: 6'4" Wt: 220 Born: 1/8/1984 Age: 26

Year Team	Lg	G	AB	H	2B	3B	HR	(Hm	Rd)	TB	R	RBI	RC	TBB	IBB	SO	HBP	SH	SF	SB	CS	SB%	GDP	Avg	OBP	Slg
2005 Atl	NL	70	257	77	20	1	14	(11	3)	141	41	45	50	11	3	58	4	0	2	3	2	.60	4	.300	.336	.549
2006 Atl	NL	162	651	169	24	6	29	(19	10)	292	83	103	91	23	6	132	9	0	3	1	6	.14	15	.260	.293	.449
2007 Atl	NL	162	642	188	40	0	19	(7	12)	285	84	105	97	42	5	129	5	0	7	5	2	.71	14	.293	.338	.444
2008 Atl	NL	155	599	143	33	3	11	(5	6)	215	70	71	49	39	5	111	10	0	4	0	1	.00	18	.239	.294	.359
2009 2 Tms	NL	157	593	166	32	4	15	(7	8)	251	72	76	60	23	0	92	0	1	9	6	4	.60	13	.280	.309	.423
09 Atl	NL	82	304	76	12	2	5	(3	2)	107	32	35	25	12	2	46	3	1	4	5	1	.83	10	.250	.282	.352
09 NYM	NL	75	289	90	20	2	10	(4	6)	144	40	41	34	11	3	46	3	0	5	1	3	.25	3	.311	.338	.498
Postseason		4	17	4	1	1	0	(0	0)	7	2	1	2	2	1	4	1	1	0	0	0	-	1	.235	.350	.412
5 ML YEARS		706	2742	743	149	14	88	(49	39)	1184	350	400	346	138	24	522	34	1	25	15	15	.50	64	.271	.311	.432

Kevin Frandsen

Bats: R Throws: R Pos: 2B-14; SS-7; PH-4   Ht: 6'0" Wt: 184 Born: 5/24/1982 Age: 28

Year Team	Lg	G	AB	H	2B	3B	HR	(Hm	Rd)	TB	R	RBI	RC	TBB	IBB	SO	HBP	SH	SF	SB	CS	SB%	GDP	Avg	OBP	Slg
2009 Fresno*	AAA	110	427	126	18	2	13	(-	-)	187	67	55	67	23	2	34	16	5	3	3	4	.43	11	.295	.352	.438
2006 SF	NL	41	93	20	4	0	2	(0	2)	30	12	7	7	3	0	14	6	0	0	0	1	.00	3	.215	.284	.323
2007 SF	NL	109	264	71	12	1	5	(1	4)	100	26	31	29	21	3	24	5	3	3	4	3	.57	17	.269	.331	.379
2008 SF	NL	1	1	0	0	0	0	(0	0)	0	0	0	0	0	0	0	0	0	0	0	0	-	0	.000	.000	.000
2009 SF	NL	23	50	7	2	0	0	(0	0)	9	3	1	0	3	0	4	1	0	0	0	0	-	2	.140	.204	.180
4 ML YEARS		174	408	98	18	1	7	(1	6)	139	41	39	36	27	3	42	12	3	3	4	4	.50	22	.240	.304	.341

Ryan Franklin

Pitches: R Bats: R Pos: RP-62   Ht: 6'3" Wt: 190 Born: 3/5/1973 Age: 37

Year Team	Lg	G	GS	CG	GF	IP	BFP	H	R	ER	HR	SH	SF	HB	TBB	IBB	SO	WP	Bk	W	L	Pct	Sh	Sv-Op	Hld	ERC	ERA
1999 Sea	AL	6	0	0	2	11.1	51	10	6	6	2	0	0	1	8	1	6	0	0	0	0	-	0	0-0	1	5.52	4.76
2001 Sea	AL	38	0	0	14	78.1	335	76	32	31	13	1	2	4	24	4	60	2	0	5	1	.833	0	0-1	5	4.08	3.56
2002 Sea	AL	41	12	0	10	118.2	495	117	62	53	14	5	5	5	22	1	65	0	0	7	5	.583	0	0-1	3	3.40	4.02
2003 Sea	AL	32	32	2	0	212.0	877	199	93	84	34	4	5	9	61	3	99	1	2	11	13	.458	1	0-0	0	3.90	3.57
2004 Sea	AL	32	32	2	0	200.1	870	224	116	109	33	2	11	10	61	1	104	0	3	4	16	.200	1	0-0	0	5.08	4.90
2005 Sea	AL	32	30	2	0	190.2	832	212	110	108	28	3	3	7	62	4	93	3	1	8	15	.348	1	0-0	0	4.89	5.10
2006 2 Tms	NL	66	0	0	19	77.1	343	86	42	39	13	2	2	4	33	10	43	2	0	6	7	.462	0	0-3	8	5.41	4.54
2007 StL	NL	69	0	0	8	80.0	317	70	28	27	8	2	2	3	11	0	44	2	0	4	4	.500	0	1-6	25	2.59	3.04
2008 StL	NL	74	0	0	39	78.2	346	86	34	31	10	2	2	3	30	4	51	3	0	6	6	.500	0	17-25	13	4.82	3.55
2009 StL	NL	62	0	0	54	61.0	250	49	13	13	2	0	2	1	24	3	44	1	0	4	3	.571	0	38-43	1	2.58	1.92
06 Phi	NL	46	0	0	13	53.0	233	59	28	27	10	0	1	4	17	4	25	1	0	1	5	.167	0	0-1	8	5.26	4.58
06 Cin	NL	20	0	0	6	24.1	110	27	14	12	3	2	1	0	16	6	18	1	0	5	2	.714	0	0-2	0	5.67	4.44
10 ML YEARS		452	106	6	146	1108.1	4716	1129	536	501	157	25	34	47	336	31	609	14	6	55	70	.440	3	56-79	56	4.23	4.07

Jason Frasor

Pitches: R Bats: R Pos: RP-61   Ht: 5'10" Wt: 175 Born: 8/9/1977 Age: 32

Year Team	Lg	G	GS	CG	GF	IP	BFP	H	R	ER	HR	SH	SF	HB	TBB	IBB	SO	WP	Bk	W	L	Pct	Sh	Sv-Op	Hld	ERC	ERA
2004 Tor	AL	63	0	0	37	68.1	299	64	31	31	4	3	3	2	36	3	54	4	2	4	6	.400	0	17-19	8	3.97	4.08
2005 Tor	AL	67	0	0	12	74.2	305	67	31	27	8	2	1	3	28	2	62	1	0	3	5	.375	0	1-3	15	3.72	3.25
2006 Tor	AL	51	0	0	12	50.0	215	47	24	24	8	0	3	2	17	1	51	3	0	3	2	.600	0	0-1	12	3.98	4.32

Year	Team	Lg	G	GS	CG	GF	IP	BFP	H	R	ER	HR	SH	SF	HB	TBB	IBB	SO	WP	Bk	W	L	Pct	Sh	Sv-Op	Hld	ERC	ERA
			HOW MUCH HE PITCHED						**WHAT HE GAVE UP**												**THE RESULTS**							
2007	Tor	AL	51	0	0	18	57.0	242	47	29	29	3	1	2	2	23	1	59	2	1	1	5	.167	0	3-6	4	2.88	4.58
2008	Tor	AL	49	0	0	21	47.1	208	36	23	22	4	0	2	1	32	4	42	6	0	1	2	.333	0	0-1	4	3.62	4.18
2009	Tor	AL	61	0	0	36	57.2	227	43	17	16	4	1	2	2	16	3	56	2	0	7	3	.700	0	11-14	4	2.22	2.50
6 ML YEARS			342	0	0	136	355.0	1496	304	155	149	31	7	13	12	152	14	324	18	3	19	23	.452	0	32-44	47	3.40	3.78

Ryan Freel

Bats: R **Throws:** R **Pos:** RF-14; 3B-9; LF-7; PH-6; CF-5; PR-5; 2B-3   **Ht:** 5'9" **Wt:** 180 **Born:** 3/8/1976 **Age:** 34

Year	Team	Lg	G	AB	H	2B	3B	HR	(Hm	Rd)	TB	R	RBI	RC	TBB	IBB	SO	HBP	SH	SF	SB	CS	SB%	GDP	Avg	OBP	Slg
			BATTING																		**BASERUNNING**				**AVERAGES**		
2009	Bowie*	AA	3	9	1	0	0	0	(-	-)	1	2	2	0	1	0	1	0	0	0	1	0	1.00	0	.111	.200	.111
2009	Iowa*	AAA	7	24	10	4	0	0	(-	-)	14	6	4	7	3	0	4	1	0	0	5	1	.83	0	.417	.500	.583
2009	Okla*	AAA	2	6	2	0	0	0	(-	-)	2	0	1	0	0	0	2	1	0	0	0	0	-	0	.333	.429	.333
2001	Tor	AL	9	22	6	1	0	0	(0	0)	7	1	3	3	1	0	4	1	0	0	2	1	.67	0	.273	.333	.318
2003	Cin	NL	43	137	39	6	1	4	(0	4)	59	23	12	17	9	1	13	4	2	1	9	4	.69	2	.285	.344	.431
2004	Cin	NL	143	505	140	21	8	3	(1	2)	186	74	28	73	67	0	88	12	8	0	37	10	.79	7	.277	.375	.368
2005	Cin	NL	103	369	100	19	3	4	(2	2)	137	69	21	55	51	0	59	8	3	0	36	10	.78	9	.271	.371	.371
2006	Cin	NL	132	454	123	30	2	8	(6	2)	181	67	27	59	57	0	98	9	3	0	37	11	.77	5	.271	.363	.399
2007	Cin	NL	75	277	68	13	3	3	(2	1)	96	44	16	31	18	0	47	7	2	0	15	8	.65	4	.245	.308	.347
2008	Cin	NL	48	131	39	8	0	0	(0	0)	47	17	10	19	8	0	18	1	2	1	6	4	.60	3	.298	.340	.359
2009	3 Tms		41	88	17	2	0	0	(0	0)	19	11	5	6	11	0	23	1	1	0	1	0	1.00	1	.193	.290	.216
09	Bal	AL	9	15	2	0	0	0	(0	0)	2	2	1	1	5	0	4	0	0	0	0	0	-	1	.133	.350	.133
09	ChC	NL	14	28	4	0	0	0	(0	0)	4	1	1	0	2	0	7	1	1	0	1	0	1.00	1	.143	.226	.143
09	KC	AL	18	45	11	2	0	0	(0	0)	13	8	3	5	4	0	12	0	0	0	0	0	-	0	.244	.306	.289
8 ML YEARS			594	1983	532	100	17	22	(11	11)	732	306	122	263	222	1	350	43	21	2	143	48	.75	31	.268	.354	.369

David Freese

Bats: R **Throws:** R **Pos:** PH-8; 3B-7; 1B-3; C-1   **Ht:** 6'2" **Wt:** 220 **Born:** 4/28/1983 **Age:** 27

Year	Team	Lg	G	AB	H	2B	3B	HR	(Hm	Rd)	TB	R	RBI	RC	TBB	IBB	SO	HBP	SH	SF	SB	CS	SB%	GDP	Avg	OBP	Slg
			BATTING																		**BASERUNNING**				**AVERAGES**		
2006	Eugene	A-	18	58	22	8	0	5	(-	-)	45	19	26	19	7	0	12	4	0	2	0	0	-	2	.379	.465	.776
2006	FtWyn	A	53	204	61	13	3	8	(-	-)	104	27	44	39	21	1	44	4	0	1	1	1	.50	2	.299	.374	.510
2007	Lk Els	A+	128	503	152	31	6	17	(-	-)	246	104	96	103	69	0	99	16	0	4	6	1	.86	11	.302	.400	.489
2008	Memp	AAA	131	464	142	29	3	26	(-	-)	255	83	91	91	39	0	111	3	0	4	5	2	.71	11	.306	.361	.550
2009	Memp	AAA	56	200	60	15	0	10	(-	-)	105	34	37	39	22	1	51	1	0	2	1	0	1.00	9	.300	.369	.525
2009	Cards	R	4	11	5	2	0	1	(-	-)	10	2	6	4	1	0	3	0	0	0	0	0	-	0	.455	.500	.909
2009	Sprgfld	AA	4	16	6	1	0	1	(-	-)	10	3	5	4	2	0	2	0	0	0	0	0	-	2	.375	.444	.625
2009	StL	NL	17	31	10	2	0	1	(0	1)	15	3	7	4	2	0	7	0	0	1	0	0	-	1	.323	.353	.484

Luke French

Pitches: L **Bats:** L **Pos:** SP-12; RP-3   **Ht:** 6'4" **Wt:** 220 **Born:** 9/13/1985 **Age:** 24

Year	Team	Lg	G	GS	CG	GF	IP	BFP	H	R	ER	HR	SH	SF	HB	TBB	IBB	SO	WP	Bk	W	L	Pct	Sh	Sv-Op	Hld	ERC	ERA
			HOW MUCH HE PITCHED						**WHAT HE GAVE UP**												**THE RESULTS**							
2004	Tigers	R	11	10	0	0	49.1	212	43	21	15	1	4	4	1	19	0	49	2	1	1	3	.250	0	0--	-	2.78	2.74
2005	Tigers	R	2	2	0	0	10.2	47	16	10	9	3	0	0	0	6	0	9	1	0	1	0	1.000	0	0--	-	6.68	7.59
2005	Lkland	A+	4	4	0	0	22.1	103	29	14	11	3	0	0	0	9	0	17	1	1	3	1	.750	0	0--	-	6.09	4.43
2005	WMich	A	6	6	0	0	34.2	159	42	23	21	4	2	1	1	14	0	24	7	0	1	2	.333	0	0--	-	5.50	5.45
2006	WMich	A	26	26	1	0	157.1	668	156	75	65	10	9	3	7	44	0	94	8	0	11	8	.579	1	0--	-	3.47	3.72
2007	Lkland	A+	27	27	0	0	149.0	654	172	94	67	10	2	8	5	47	1	93	5	0	5	14	.263	0	0--	-	4.51	4.05
2008	Erie	AA	27	26	3	0	170.0	745	195	92	76	16	5	7	6	60	1	88	10	0	9	11	.450	0	0--	-	4.88	4.02
2009	Toledo	AAA	13	13	1	0	81.2	328	71	32	27	6	5	3	1	20	0	72	1	0	4	4	.500	0	0--	-	2.71	2.98
2009	2 Tms	AL	15	12	0	2	67.1	312	87	45	39	11	0	5	2	28	1	42	3	0	4	5	.444	0	0-0	0	6.47	5.21
09	Det	AL	7	5	0	1	29.1	133	33	13	11	2	0	1	1	11	1	19	1	0	1	2	.333	0	0-0	0	4.41	3.38
09	Sea	AL	8	7	0	1	38.0	179	54	32	28	9	0	4	1	17	0	23	2	0	3	3	.500	0	0-0	0	8.24	6.63

Ernesto Frieri

Pitches: R **Bats:** R **Pos:** RP-2   **Ht:** 6'2" **Wt:** 190 **Born:** 7/19/1985 **Age:** 24

Year	Team	Lg	G	GS	CG	GF	IP	BFP	H	R	ER	HR	SH	SF	HB	TBB	IBB	SO	WP	Bk	W	L	Pct	Sh	Sv-Op	Hld	ERC	ERA
			HOW MUCH HE PITCHED						**WHAT HE GAVE UP**												**THE RESULTS**							
2005	Padres	R	17	5	0	5	46.1	187	21	7	6	0	1	0	4	29	0	59	2	1	7	1	.875	0	0--	-	1.79	1.17
2005	Lk Els	A+	2	0	0	0	3.1	14	3	1	1	1	0	0	0	1	0	3	0	0	0	0	-	0	0--	-	4.34	2.70
2006	FtWyn	A	1	0	0	0	1.0	8	1	4	1	0	0	0	0	5	0	1	0	0	0	0	-	0	0--	-	25.88	9.00
2006	Eugene	A-	27	1	0	10	37.2	158	31	18	16	3	2	3	4	15	0	38	2	0	3	3	.500	0	2--	-	3.42	3.82
2006	Lk Els	A+	2	0	0	0	6.0	28	8	4	4	0	0	2	0	3	0	4	0	0	0	0	-	0	0--	-	5.70	6.00
2007	FtWyn	A	40	0	0	4	64.2	262	48	19	19	4	2	5	2	23	1	65	1	0	1	2	.333	0	0--	-	2.42	2.64
2007	Lk Els	A+	13	1	0	6	21.2	78	11	3	3	1	0	1	0	6	0	27	1	0	1	0	1.000	0	1--	-	1.23	1.25
2008	Lk Els	A+	33	18	0	4	123.2	521	125	61	55	14	3	5	4	32	1	108	3	1	8	6	.571	0	0--	-	3.79	4.00
2008	Portlnd	AAA	1	1	0	0	6.0	23	2	1	1	0	1	0	0	2	0	7	1	0	1	0	1.000	0	0--	-	0.66	1.50
2008	SnAnt	AA	2	2	0	0	11.0	41	5	3	5	0	1	0	1	2	0	10	1	0	1	0	1.000	0	0--	-	2.80	4.09
2009	SnAnt	AA	27	26	0	0	140.1	602	125	61	56	13	4	5	4	62	1	118	6	0	10	9	.526	0	0--	-	3.67	3.59
2009	SD	NL	2	0	0	2	2.0	7	0	0	0	0	0	0	0	1	0	2	0	0	0	0	-	0	0-0	0	0.27	0.00

Brian Fuentes

Pitches: L **Bats:** L **Pos:** RP-65 **Ht:** 6'4" **Wt:** 230 **Born:** 8/9/1975 **Age:** 34

Year	Team	Lg	G	GS	CG	GF	IP	BFP	H	R	ER	HR	SH	SF	HB	TBB	IBB	SO	WP	Bk	W	L	Pct	Sh	Sv-Op	Hld	ERC	ERA
2001	Sea	AL	10	0	0	3	11.2	47	6	6	6	2	0	1	3	8	0	10	1	0	1	1	.500	0	0-1	1	4.39	4.63
2002	Col	NL	31	0	0	9	26.2	118	25	14	14	4	0	2	3	13	0	38	1	0	2	0	1.000	0	0-0	0	4.91	4.73
2003	Col	NL	75	0	0	23	75.1	320	64	24	23	7	0	3	6	34	2	82	2	1	3	3	.500	0	4-6	19	3.71	2.75
2004	Col	NL	47	0	0	12	44.2	201	46	30	28	5	7	0	4	19	6	48	3	0	2	4	.333	0	0-1	13	4.50	5.64
2005	Col	NL	78	0	0	55	74.1	321	59	25	24	6	5	1	10	34	4	91	8	0	2	5	.286	0	31-34	6	3.44	2.91
2006	Col	NL	66	0	0	58	65.1	274	50	25	25	8	2	1	6	26	4	73	6	0	3	4	.429	0	30-36	0	3.19	3.44
2007	Col	NL	64	0	0	38	61.1	255	46	26	21	6	1	1	7	23	0	56	2	0	3	5	.375	0	20-27	5	3.06	3.08
2008	Col	NL	67	0	0	48	62.2	256	47	22	19	3	3	1	1	22	1	82	1	0	1	5	.167	0	30-34	6	2.27	2.73
2009	LAA	AL	65	0	0	57	55.0	242	53	24	24	6	2	2	5	24	2	46	1	0	1	5	.167	0	**48-55**	0	4.37	3.93
	Postseason		10	0	0	0	9.2	47	14	7	7	2	0	0	0	5	0	11	1	0	1	0	1.000	0	0-0	3	8.22	6.52
	9 ML YEARS		503	0	0	303	477.0	2034	396	190	184	47	20	12	45	203	19	526	25	1	18	32	.360	0	163-194	53	3.53	3.47

Kosuke Fukudome

Bats: L **Throws:** R **Pos:** CF-113; RF-44; PH-10 **Ht:** 6'0" **Wt:** 187 **Born:** 4/26/1977 **Age:** 33

Year	Team	Lg	G	AB	H	2B	3B	HR	(Hm	Rd)	TB	R	RBI	RC	TBB	IBB	SO	HBP	SH	SF	SB	CS	SB%	GDP	Avg	OBP	Slg
1999	Chnchi	Jap	132	461	131	25	2	16	(-	-)	208	76	52	68	50	-	121	5	8	2	4	7	.36	3	.284	.359	.451
2000	Chnchi	Jap	97	316	80	18	2	13	(	-)	141	50	42	51	45	-	79	3	2	2	8	5	.62	5	.253	.350	.446
2001	Chnchi	Jap	120	375	94	22	2	15	(-	-)	165	51	56	62	56	-	90	4	4	3	8	4	.67	4	.251	.352	.440
2002	Chnchi	Jap	140	542	186	42	3	19	(-	-)	291	85	65	116	56	2	96	5	0	5	4	2	.67	4	.343	.406	.537
2003	Chnchi	Jap	140	528	165	30	11	34	(-	-)	319	107	96	125	78	1	118	4	1	6	10	5	.67	5	.313	.401	.604
2004	Chnchi	Jap	92	350	97	19	7	23	(-	-)	199	61	81	73	48	0	93	3	1	2	8	3	.73	3	.277	.367	.569
2005	Chnchi	Jap	142	515	169	39	6	28	(-	-)	304	102	103	128	93	3	128	1	0	3	13	5	.72	8	.328	.430	.590
2006	Chnchi	Jap	130	496	174	47	5	31	(-	-)	324	117	104	135	74	4	94	3	0	3	11	2	.85	4	.351	.438	.653
2007	Chnchi	Jap	81	269	79	22	0	13	(-	-)	140	64	48	67	60	2	60	0	0	4	3	2	.71	5	.294	.443	.520
2008	ChC	NL	150	501	129	25	3	10	(6	4)	190	79	58	77	81	9	104	1	2	5	12	4	.75	7	.257	.359	.379
2009	ChC	NL	146	499	129	38	5	11	(4	7)	210	79	54	76	93	3	112	3	3	5	6	10	.38	15	.259	.375	.421
	Postseason		3	10	1	0	0	0	(0	0)	1	0	0	0	0	0	4	0	0	0	0	0	-	0	.100	.100	.100
	2 ML YEARS		296	1000	258	63	8	21	(10	11)	400	158	112	153	174	12	216	4	5	10	18	14	.56	22	.258	.367	.400

Jeff Fulchino

Pitches: R **Bats:** R **Pos:** RP-61 **Ht:** 6'5" **Wt:** 252 **Born:** 11/26/1979 **Age:** 30

Year	Team	Lg	G	GS	CG	GF	IP	BFP	H	R	ER	HR	SH	SF	HB	TBB	IBB	SO	WP	Bk	W	L	Pct	Sh	Sv-Op	Hld	ERC	ERA
2000	RdRck*	AAA	2	1	0	0	4.0	17	3	3	3	0	0	0	0	2	0	3	0	0	0	0	-	0	0--	-	2.40	6.75
2006	Fla	NL	1	0	0	0	0.1	2	0	0	0	0	0	0	0	1	0	0	0	0	0	0	-	0	0-0	0	7.00	0.00
2008	KC	AL	12	0	0	1	14.0	72	21	15	14	2	0	1	1	8	0	12	1	0	0	1	.000	0	0-0	0	8.38	9.00
2009	Hou	NL	61	0	0	18	82.0	336	70	33	31	7	4	1	3	27	3	71	2	1	6	4	.600	0	0-3	12	3.05	3.40
	3 ML YEARS		74	0	0	25	96.1	410	91	48	45	9	4	2	4	36	3	83	3	1	6	5	.545	0	0-3	12	3.75	4.20

Sam Fuld

Bats: L **Throws:** L **Pos:** LF-29; CF-26; PH-16; PR-4; RF-2 **Ht:** 5'10" **Wt:** 185 **Born:** 11/20/1981 **Age:** 28

Year	Team	Lg	G	AB	H	2B	3B	HR	(Hm	Rd)	TB	R	RBI	RC	TBB	IBB	SO	HBP	SH	SF	SB	CS	SB%	GDP	Avg	OBP	Slg
2005	Peoria	A	125	443	133	32	6	5	(-	-)	192	82	37	75	50	0	44	7	4	4	18	11	.62	16	.300	.377	.433
2006	Dytona	A+	89	353	106	19	6	4	(-	-)	149	63	40	62	40	5	54	5	6	1	22	3	.88	6	.300	.378	.422
2007	Tenn	AA	90	335	97	23	2	2	(-	-)	130	56	27	54	41	1	38	5	8	3	11	3	.79	2	.290	.372	.388
2007	Iowa	AAA	14	52	14	4	1	1	(-	-)	23	13	2	10	9	0	5	2	0	0	2	0	1.00	1	.269	.397	.442
2008	Iowa	AAA	20	63	14	3	0	1	(-	-)	20	11	4	6	8	0	12	0	5	0	3	2	.60	3	.222	.310	.317
2008	Tenn	AA	85	339	92	16	3	5	(-	-)	129	48	48	50	50	2	40	3	1	4	7	8	.47	9	.271	.366	.381
2009	Iowa	AAA	84	328	93	17	10	2	(-	-)	136	62	33	54	38	1	24	1	1	2	23	5	.82	4	.284	.358	.415
2007	ChC	NL	14	6	0	0	0	0	(0	0)	0	3	0	0	3	0	3	0	0	0	0	0	-	0	.000	.333	.000
2009	ChC	NL	65	97	29	6	1	1	(1	0)	40	17	2	15	17	1	10	1	0	0	2	1	.67	1	.299	.409	.412
	2 ML YEARS		79	103	29	6	1	1	(1	0)	40	20	2	15	20	1	13	1	0	0	2	1	.67	1	.282	.403	.388

Rafael Furcal

Bats: B **Throws:** R **Pos:** SS-149; PH-9 **Ht:** 5'8" **Wt:** 187 **Born:** 10/24/1977 **Age:** 32

Year	Team	Lg	G	AB	H	2B	3B	HR	(Hm	Rd)	TB	R	RBI	RC	TBB	IBB	SO	HBP	SH	SF	SB	CS	SB%	GDP	Avg	OBP	Slg
2000	Atl	NL	131	455	134	20	4	4	(1	3)	174	87	37	78	73	0	80	3	9	2	40	14	.74	2	.295	.394	.382
2001	Atl	NL	79	324	89	19	0	4	(3	1)	120	39	30	41	24	1	56	1	4	2	22	6	.79	5	.275	.321	.370
2002	Atl	NL	154	636	175	31	8	8	(4	4)	246	95	47	80	43	0	114	3	9	2	27	15	.64	8	.275	.323	.387
2003	Atl	NL	156	664	194	35	**10**	15	(4	11)	294	130	61	107	60	2	76	3	4	3	25	2	**.93**	1	.292	.352	.443
2004	Atl	NL	143	563	157	24	5	14	(5	9)	233	103	59	82	58	4	71	1	5	5	29	6	.83	9	.279	.344	.414
2005	Atl	NL	154	616	175	31	11	12	(9	3)	264	100	58	98	62	3	78	1	5	5	46	10	.82	11	.284	.348	.429
2006	LAD	NL	159	654	196	32	9	15	(12	3)	291	113	63	110	73	3	98	1	3	5	37	13	.74	7	.300	.369	.445
2007	LAD	NL	138	581	157	23	6	6	(4	2)	206	87	47	65	55	3	68	1	2	3	25	6	.81	11	.270	.333	.355
2008	LAD	NL	36	143	51	12	2	5	(3	2)	82	34	16	33	20	0	17	1	0	0	8	3	.73	3	.357	.439	.573
2009	LAD	NL	150	613	165	28	5	9	(5	4)	230	92	47	73	61	2	89	1	3	2	12	6	.67	11	.269	.335	.375
	Postseason		33	137	32	1	2	3	(3	0)	46	23	10	18	21	1	21	1	4	0	11	2	.85	1	.234	.340	.336
	10 ML YEARS		1300	5249	1493	255	58	92	(50	42)	2140	880	465	767	529	18	747	16	45	32	271	81	.77	68	.284	.350	.408

Armando Gabino

Pitches: R Bats: R Pos: SP-1; RP-1　　　　Ht: 6'3" Wt: 210 Born: 8/31/1983 Age: 26

Year	Team	Lg	G	GS	CG	GF	IP	BFP	H	R	ER	HR	SH	SF	HB	TBB	IBB	SO	WP	Bk	W	L	Pct	Sh	Sv-Op	Hld	ERC	ERA
2004	Burlgtn	A	5	4	0	0	19.0	85	20	13	9	1	1	2	3	5	0	12	0	0	0	1	.000	0	0--	-	4.01	4.26
2005	Elizab	R+	17	3	0	1	30.0	152	45	28	27	7	1	0	6	12	0	23	7	0	1	2	.333	0	0--	-	9.07	8.10
2006	Elizab	R+	5	1	0	0	10.1	39	5	1	1	0	0	0	1	2	0	8	0	0	1	0	1.000	0	0--	-	0.97	0.87
2006	Beloit	A	16	0	0	6	30.1	123	29	15	14	4	4	1	2	5	0	20	2	0	2	3	.400	0	1--	-	3.44	4.15
2007	Beloit	A	12	0	0	4	22.0	85	18	2	2	1	1	0	1	4	0	16	0	0	1	0	1.000	0	0--	-	2.25	0.82
2007	FtMyrs	A+	26	0	0	15	37.0	151	27	17	13	1	1	1	0	15	0	25	1	0	2	2	.500	0	4--	-	2.21	3.16
2007	NwBrit	AA	10	0	0	4	16.0	68	12	4	0	0	1	1	0	8	0	14	1	0	2	0	1.000	0	4--	-	2.40	0.00
2008	NwBrit	AA	49	0	0	23	81.1	349	84	28	28	6	1	2	6	31	0	61	3	1	6	5	.545	0	3--	-	4.40	3.10
2009	Roch	AAA	38	7	1	12	98.0	390	80	34	32	7	3	6	5	24	1	64	3	0	6	4	.600	0	1--	-	2.57	2.94
2009	Min	AL	2	1	0	0	3.2	25	9	7	7	1	0	0	0	5	0	2	0	0	0	0	-	0	0-0	0	20.46	17.18

Armando Galarraga

Pitches: R Bats: R Pos: SP-25; RP-4　　　　Ht: 6'4" Wt: 180 Born: 1/15/1982 Age: 28

Year	Team	Lg	G	GS	CG	GF	IP	BFP	H	R	ER	HR	SH	SF	HB	TBB	IBB	SO	WP	Bk	W	L	Pct	Sh	Sv-Op	Hld	ERC	ERA
2007	Tex	AL	3	1	0	2	8.2	40	8	6	6	2	0	1	0	7	0	6	0	0	0	0	-	0	0-0	0	6.35	6.23
2008	Det	AL	30	28	0	0	178.2	746	152	83	74	28	2	4	6	61	2	126	6	0	13	7	.650	0	0-1	0	3.50	3.73
2009	Det	AL	29	25	0	1	143.2	642	158	93	90	24	1	11	6	67	1	95	1	0	6	10	.375	0	0-0	0	5.65	5.64
	3 ML YEARS		62	54	0	3	331.0	1428	318	182	170	54	3	16	12	135	3	227	7	0	19	17	.528	0	0-1	0	4.47	4.62

Sean Gallagher

Pitches: R Bats: R Pos: RP-12; SP-2　　　　Ht: 6'2" Wt: 235 Born: 12/30/1985 Age: 24

Year	Team	Lg	G	GS	CG	GF	IP	BFP	H	R	ER	HR	SH	SF	HB	TBB	IBB	SO	WP	Bk	W	L	Pct	Sh	Sv-Op	Hld	ERC	ERA
2009	Scrmto*	AAA	5	5	0	0	20.2	80	12	5	4	0	1	0	1	6	0	15	1	0	1	0	1.000	0	0--	-	1.34	1.74
2009	Portlnd*	AAA	1	1	0	0	1.0	6	3	3	3	1	0	0	0	0	0	1	0	0	1	0	1.000	0	0--	-	25.51	27.00
2007	ChC	NL	8	0	0	3	14.2	74	19	15	14	3	0	1	1	12	0	5	0	0	0	0	-	0	1-1	0	8.95	8.59
2008	2 Tms		23	21	0	1	115.1	522	118	73	66	13	3	6	6	58	2	103	2	0	5	7	.417	0	0-0	0	4.83	5.15
2009	2 Tms		14	2	0	5	19.2	96	26	16	13	1	1	1	2	12	1	14	1	0	3	2	.600	0	0-0	0	6.83	5.95
08	ChC	NL	12	10	0	1	58.2	256	58	31	29	6	2	1	4	22	1	49	2	0	3	4	.429	0	0-0	0	4.14	4.45
08	Oak	AL	11	11	0	0	56.2	266	60	42	37	7	1	5	2	36	1	54	0	0	2	3	.400	0	0-0	0	5.57	5.88
09	Oak	AL	6	2	0	3	14.1	71	21	16	13	1	1	1	2	7	0	10	1	0	1	2	.333	0	0-0	0	7.65	8.16
09	SD	NL	8	0	0	2	5.1	25	5	0	0	0	0	0	0	5	1	4	0	0	2	0	1.000	0	0-0	0	4.72	0.00
	3 ML YEARS		45	23	0	9	149.2	692	163	104	93	17	4	8	9	82	3	122	3	0	8	9	.471	0	1-1	0	5.46	5.59

Yovani Gallardo

Pitches: R Bats: R Pos: SP-30　　　　Ht: 6'2" Wt: 222 Born: 2/27/1986 Age: 24

Year	Team	Lg	G	GS	CG	GF	IP	BFP	H	R	ER	HR	SH	SF	HB	TBB	IBB	SO	WP	Bk	W	L	Pct	Sh	Sv-Op	Hld	ERC	ERA
2007	Mil	NL	20	17	0	1	110.1	466	103	48	45	8	4	3	2	37	2	101	3	0	9	5	.643	0	0-0	0	3.30	3.67
2008	Mil	NL	4	4	0	0	24.0	97	22	5	5	3	2	1	0	8	0	20	0	0	0	0	-	0	0-0	0	3.66	1.88
2009	Mil	NL	30	30	1	0	185.2	793	150	78	77	21	5	3	5	94	5	204	9	0	13	12	.520	0	0-0	0	3.57	3.73
	Postseason		2	1	0	0	7.0	30	4	3	0	0	1	0	0	5	1	4	0	0	0	1	.000	0	0-0	0	2.03	0.00
	3 ML YEARS		54	51	1	1	320.0	1356	275	131	127	32	11	7	7	139	7	325	12	0	22	17	.564	0	0-0	0	3.48	3.57

Mat Gamel

Bats: L Throws: R Pos: PH-29; 3B-27; DH-6　　　　Ht: 6'0" Wt: 200 Born: 7/26/1985 Age: 24

Year	Team	Lg	G	AB	H	2B	3B	HR	(Hm	Rd)	TB	R	RBI	RC	TBB	IBB	SO	HBP	SH	SF	SB	CS	SB%	GDP	Avg	OBP	Slg
2005	Helena	R+	50	199	65	15	2	5	(-	-)	99	34	37	36	12	1	49	4	0	1	7	4	.64	6	.327	.375	.497
2005	WV	A-	8	23	4	0	0	1	(-	-)	7	2	1	2	5	1	9	0	0	0	0	0	-	0	.174	.321	.304
2006	WV	A-	129	493	142	28	5	17	(-	-)	231	65	88	86	52	8	81	5	0	5	9	2	.82	7	.288	.359	.469
2007	BrvdCt	A+	128	466	140	37	8	9	(-	-)	220	78	60	86	58	9	98	3	2	5	14	7	.67	5	.300	.378	.472
2008	Hntsvl	AA	127	508	167	35	7	19	(-	-)	273	96	97	105	55	5	111	4	0	5	7	7	.50	8	.329	.395	.537
2008	Nashv	AAA	5	21	5	0	0	1	(-	-)	8	3	3	2	2	0	10	0	0	0	0	0	-	0	.238	.304	.381
2009	Nashv	AAA	75	273	76	18	1	11	(-	-)	129	42	48	49	38	9	89	3	1	5	1	0	1.00	4	.278	.367	.473
2008	Mil	NL	2	2	1	1	0	0	(0	0)	2	0	0	1	0	0	1	0	0	0	0	0	-	0	.500	.500	1.000
2009	Mil	NL	61	128	31	6	1	5	(4	1)	54	11	20	20	18	2	54	1	0	1	1	0	1.00	1	.242	.338	.422
	2 ML YEARS		63	130	32	7	1	5	(4	1)	56	11	20	21	18	2	55	1	0	1	1	0	1.00	1	.246	.340	.431

Victor Garate

Pitches: L Bats: L Pos: RP-4　　　　Ht: 6'2" Wt: 210 Born: 9/25/1984 Age: 25

Year	Team	Lg	G	GS	CG	GF	IP	BFP	H	R	ER	HR	SH	SF	HB	TBB	IBB	SO	WP	Bk	W	L	Pct	Sh	Sv-Op	Hld	ERC	ERA
2005	Grnsvle	R+	19	0	0	7	32.1	142	21	20	20	2	2	0	3	26	0	53	4	1	4	1	.800	0	0--	-	3.81	5.57
2006	TriCity	A-	21	0	0	17	39.1	157	14	6	4	2	0	3	8	21	0	59	5	2	4	0	1.000	0	8--	-	1.74	0.92
2007	Lxngtn	A	26	0	0	11	42.0	208	47	32	30	3	4	3	5	35	3	41	6	0	3	1	.750	0	1--	-	6.66	6.43
2007	TriCity	A-	17	0	0	6	32.2	138	31	15	12	4	1	0	2	7	0	45	1	0	3	1	.750	0	2--	-	3.39	3.31
2008	Gt Lks	A	17	12	0	2	77.2	317	61	22	16	4	0	2	3	28	0	103	3	1	6	3	.667	0	0--	-	2.64	1.85
2008	InldEm	A+	7	7	0	0	38.1	172	44	20	20	6	3	0	3	14	0	47	1	0	3	0	1.000	0	0--	-	5.55	4.70
2009	Chatt	AA	47	0	0	20	53.0	219	36	12	12	1	1	2	4	23	0	56	4	1	1	0	1.000	0	4--	-	2.26	2.04
2009	Was	NL	4	0	0	0	2.0	15	5	5	5	1	0	1	1	3	0	0	0	0	0	0	-	0	0-0	0	27.16	22.50

Freddy Garcia

Pitches: R **Bats:** R **Pos:** SP-9   **Ht:** 6'4" **Wt:** 260 **Born:** 6/10/1976 **Age:** 34

Year	Team	Lg	G	GS	CG	GF	IP	BFP	H	R	ER	HR	SH	SF	HB	TBB	IBB	SO	WP	Bk	W	L	Pct	Sh	Sv-Op	Hld	ERC	ERA
2009	Buffalo*	AAA	2	2	0	0	11.0	48	12	10	10	2	1	0	0	5	0	6	0	0	0	2	.000	0	0- -	-	5.55	8.18
2009	Knapol*	A	1	1	0	0	3.0	10	2	0	0	0	0	0	0	1	0	3	0	0	0	0	-	0	0- -	-	1.95	0.00
2009	Bristol*	A-	2	2	0	0	11.0	38	6	3	2	0	0	0	0	0	0	7	0	0	0	0	-	0	0- -	-	0.65	1.64
2009	Charltt*	AAA	1	1	0	0	6.0	25	8	2	2	1	0	0	0	0	0	9	1	0	0	1	.000	0	0- -	-	4.90	3.00
1999	Sea	AL	33	33	2	0	201.1	888	205	96	91	18	3	6	10	90	4	170	12	3	17	8	.680	1	0-0	0	4.46	4.07
2000	Sea	AL	21	20	0	0	124.1	538	112	62	54	16	6	1	2	64	4	79	4	2	9	5	.643	0	0-0	0	4.20	3.91
2001	Sea	AL	34	34	4	0	238.2	971	199	88	81	16	8	5	5	69	6	163	3	1	18	6	.750	3	0-0	0	2.61	3.05
2002	Sea	AL	34	34	1	0	223.2	955	227	110	109	30	4	8	6	63	3	181	7	1	16	10	.615	0	0-0	0	3.98	4.39
2003	Sea	AL	33	33	1	0	201.1	862	106	109	101	31	2	8	11	71	2	144	11	0	12	14	.462	0	0-0	0	4.33	4.51
2004	2 Tms		31	31	1	0	210.0	878	192	92	89	22	8	3	7	64	3	184	0	0	13	11	.542	0	0-0	0	3.37	3.81
2005	CWS	AL	33	33	2	0	228.0	943	225	102	98	26	5	5	3	60	2	146	20	1	14	8	.636	0	0-0	0	3.65	3.87
2006	CWS	AL	33	33	1	0	216.1	917	228	116	109	32	1	6	7	48	3	135	4	0	17	9	.654	0	0-0	0	4.09	4.53
2007	Phi	NL	11	11	0	0	58.0	264	74	39	38	12	4	3	5	19	3	50	5	0	1	5	.167	0	0-0	0	6.57	5.90
2008	Det		3	3	0	0	15.0	61	11	8	7	3	0	0	1	6	0	12	0	0	1	1	.500	0	0-0	0	3.61	4.20
2009	CWS	AL	9	9	0	0	56.0	229	56	27	27	4	0	1	0	12	0	37	2	0	3	4	.429	0	0-0	0	3.21	4.34
04	Sea	AL	15	15	1	0	107.0	446	96	39	38	8	4	1	2	32	1	82	5	0	4	7	.364	0	0-0	0	3.00	3.20
04	CWS	AL	16	16	0	0	103.0	432	96	53	51	14	4	2	5	32	2	102	3	0	9	4	.692	0	0-0	0	3.77	4.46
	Postseason		9	9	1	0	55.0	230	51	20	19	5	2	0	2	22	1	45	1	0	6	2	.750	0	0-0	0	3.82	3.11
11 ML YEARS			275	274	12	0	1772.2	7506	1725	849	804	210	41	46	57	566	30	1301	76	8	121	81	.599	4	0-0	0	3.84	4.08

Jaime Garcia

Pitches: L **Bats:** L **Pos:** P   **Ht:** 6'2" **Wt:** 200 **Born:** 7/8/1986 **Age:** 23

Year	Team	Lg	G	GS	CG	GF	IP	BFP	H	R	ER	HR	SH	SF	HB	TBB	IBB	SO	WP	Bk	W	L	Pct	Sh	Sv-Op	Hld	ERC	ERA
2006	Quad C	A	13	13	1	0	77.0	317	81	28	25	1	5	0	2	18	0	80	7	4	5	4	.556	0	0- -	-	2.25	2.90
2006	PlmBh	A+	12	12	0	0	77.1	319	84	33	33	3	2	1	1	16	0	51	5	5	5	4	.556	0	0- -	-	3.52	3.84
2007	Sprgfld	AA	18	18	0	0	103.1	440	93	47	43	14	10	3	3	45	1	97	13	1	5	9	.357	0	0- -	-	4.03	3.75
2008	Sprgfld	AA	6	6	1	0	35.0	145	26	10	8	1	0	2	0	16	0	41	1	0	3	2	.600	0	0- -	-	2.49	2.06
2008	Memp	AAA	13	12	0	0	71.0	310	74	41	35	6	4	3	3	26	0	59	9	3	4	4	.500	0	0- -	-	4.22	4.44
2009	Cards	R	2	2	0	0	4.0	17	4	2	2	0	0	0	0	1	0	3	1	0	0	1	.000	0	0- -	-	2.77	4.50
2009	PlmBh	A+	3	2	0	0	12.2	42	4	1	1	0	0	0	0	4	0	16	0	0	0	1	.000	0	0- -	-	0.68	0.71
2009	Memp	AAA	4	4	0	0	21.0	87	17	14	9	5	0	1	2	9	0	22	2	0	2	0	1.000	0	0- -	-	4.59	3.86
2008	StL	NL	10	1	0	4	16.0	69	14	10	10	4	0	0	1	8	0	8	3	0	1	1	.500	0	0-0	3	5.15	5.63

Nomar Garciaparra

Bats: R **Throws:** R **Pos:** PH-28; DH-20; 1B-16; 3B-6; PR-1   **Ht:** 6'0" **Wt:** 190 **Born:** 7/23/1973 **Age:** 36

Year	Team	Lg	G	AB	H	2B	3B	HR	(Hm	Rd)	TB	R	RBI	RC	TBB	IBB	SO	HBP	SH	SF	SB	CS	SB%	GDP	Avg	OBP	Slg
1996	Bos	AL	24	87	21	2	3	4	(3	1)	41	11	16	13	4	0	14	0	1	1	5	0	1.00	0	.241	.272	.471
1997	Bos	AL	153	684	209	44	11	30	(11	19)	365	122	98	122	35	2	92	6	2	7	22	9	.71	9	.306	.342	.534
1998	Bos	AL	143	604	195	37	8	35	(17	18)	353	111	122	117	33	1	62	8	0	7	12	6	.67	20	.323	.362	.584
1999	Bos	AL	135	532	190	42	4	27	(14	13)	321	103	104	125	51	7	39	8	0	4	14	3	.82	11	.357	.418	.603
2000	Bos	AL	140	529	197	51	3	21	(7	14)	317	104	96	127	61	20	50	2	0	7	5	2	.71	8	.372	.434	.599
2001	Bos	AL	21	83	24	3	0	4	(3	1)	39	13	8	13	7	0	9	1	0	0	1	0	1.00	1	.289	.352	.470
2002	Bos	AL	156	635	197	56	5	24	(10	14)	335	101	120	113	41	4	63	4	0	11	5	2	.71	17	.310	.352	.528
2003	Bos	AL	156	658	198	37	13	28	(18	10)	345	120	105	114	39	1	61	11	1	10	19	5	.79	10	.301	.345	.524
2004	2 Tms		81	321	99	21	3	9	(6	3)	153	52	41	53	24	2	30	6	1	2	4	1	.80	10	.308	.365	.477
2005	ChC	NL	62	230	65	12	0	9	(5	4)	104	28	30	30	12	0	24	2	0	3	0	0	-	6	.283	.320	.452
2006	LAD	NL	122	469	142	31	2	20	(9	11)	237	82	93	87	42	9	30	8	0	4	3	0	1.00	15	.303	.367	.505
2007	LAD	NL	121	431	122	17	0	7	(6	1)	160	39	59	60	31	5	41	0	0	4	3	1	.75	6	.283	.328	.371
2008	LAD	NL	55	163	43	9	0	8	(5	3)	76	24	28	20	15	2	11	1	0	2	1	1	.50	12	.264	.326	.466
2009	Oak	AL	65	160	45	8	0	3	(3	0)	62	17	16	15	8	1	28	0	0	1	2	0	1.00	4	.281	.314	.388
04	Bos	AL	38	156	50	7	3	5	(3	2)	78	24	21	26	8	2	16	4	0	1	2	0	1.00	4	.321	.367	.500
04	ChC	NL	43	165	49	14	0	4	(3	1)	75	28	20	27	16	0	14	2	1	1	2	1	.67	6	.297	.364	.455
	Postseason		32	112	36	7	1	7	(3	4)	66	16	24	20	12	4	18	1	0	2	2	0	1.00	3	.321	.386	.589
14 ML YEARS			1434	5586	1747	370	52	229	(117	112)	2908	927	936	1007	403	54	554	59	5	63	95	31	.75	129	.313	.361	.521

Brett Gardner

Bats: L **Throws:** L **Pos:** CF-99; PR-11; PH-6; DH-1   **Ht:** 5'10" **Wt:** 183 **Born:** 8/24/1983 **Age:** 26

Year	Team	Lg	G	AB	H	2B	3B	HR	(Hm	Rd)	TB	R	RBI	RC	TBB	IBB	SO	HBP	SH	SF	SB	CS	SB%	GDP	Avg	OBP	Slg
2005	StIsInd	A-	73	282	80	9	1	5	(-	-)	106	62	32	47	39	1	49	6	3	5	19	3	.86	4	.284	.377	.376
2006	Tampa	A+	63	232	75	12	5	0	(-	-)	97	46	22	48	43	0	51	2	1	0	30	7	.81	4	.323	.433	.418
2006	Trntn	AA	55	217	59	4	3	0	(-	-)	69	41	13	31	27	1	39	2	1	4	28	5	.85	1	.272	.352	.318
2007	Trntn	AA	54	203	61	14	5	0	(-	-)	85	43	17	38	33	0	32	0	1	4	18	4	.82	5	.300	.392	.419
2007	S-WB	AAA	45	181	47	4	3	1	(-	-)	60	37	9	25	21	0	43	2	3	0	21	3	.88	0	.260	.343	.331
2008	S-WB	AAA	94	341	101	12	11	3	(-	-)	144	68	32	70	70	2	76	1	11	3	37	9	.80	2	.296	.414	.422
2009	S-WB	AAA	4	11	1	0	0	0	(-	-)	1	3	0	1	5	0	1	0	0	0	3	0	1.00	0	.091	.375	.091
2008	NYY	AL	42	127	29	5	2	0	(0	0)	38	18	16	17	8	0	30	2	3	1	13	1	.93	0	.228	.283	.299
2009	NYY	AL	108	248	67	6	6	3	(1	2)	94	48	23	38	26	0	40	3	6	1	26	5	.84	3	.270	.345	.379
2 ML YEARS			150	375	96	11	8	3	(1	2)	132	66	39	55	34	0	70	5	9	2	39	6	.87	3	.256	.325	.352

Ryan Garko

Bats: R **Throws:** R **Pos:** 1B-84; PH-19; DH-11; LF-7; RF-5   **Ht:** 6'2" **Wt:** 225 **Born:** 1/2/1981 **Age:** 29

									BATTING												BASERUNNING				AVERAGES		
Year	Team	Lg	G	AB	H	2B	3B	HR	(Hm	Rd)	TB	R	RBI	RC	TBB	IBB	SO	HBP	SH	SF	SB	CS	SB%	GDP	Avg	OBP	Slg
2005	Cle	AL	1	1	0	0	0	0	(0	0)	0	0	0	0	0	0	1	0	0	0	0	0	-	0	.000	.000	.000
2006	Cle	AL	50	185	54	12	0	7	(4	3)	87	28	45	32	14	0	37	7	0	3	0	0	-	5	.292	.359	.470
2007	Cle	AL	138	484	140	29	1	21	(12	9)	234	62	61	71	34	1	94	20	0	3	0	1	.00	12	.289	.359	.483
2008	Cle	AL	141	495	135	21	1	14	(8	6)	200	61	90	81	45	1	86	15	0	8	0	0	-	10	.273	.346	.404
2009	2 Tms		118	354	95	13	1	13	(6	7)	149	39	51	58	29	1	50	13	2	2	0	0	-	8	.268	.344	.421
09	Cle	AL	78	239	68	10	0	11	(6	5)	111	29	39	43	20	1	40	10	2	2	0	0	-	6	.285	.362	.464
09	SF	NL	40	115	27	3	1	2	(0	2)	38	10	12	15	9	0	10	3	0	0	0	0	-	2	.235	.307	.330
	Postseason		9	35	11	2	1	1	(1	0)	18	7	5	6	1	0	6	3	0	0	0	0	-	1	.314	.385	.514
	5 ML YEARS		448	1519	424	75	3	55	(30	25)	670	190	247	242	122	3	268	55	2	16	0	1	.00	35	.279	.351	.441

Jon Garland

Pitches: R **Bats:** R **Pos:** SP-33   **Ht:** 6'6" **Wt:** 210 **Born:** 9/27/1979 **Age:** 30

			HOW MUCH HE PITCHED						WHAT HE GAVE UP											THE RESULTS							
Year	Team	Lg	G	GS	CG	GF	IP	BFP	H	R	ER	HR	SH	SF	HB	TBB	IBB	SO	WP	Bk	W	L	Pct	Sh	Sv-Op	Hld	ERC	ERA
2000	CWS	AL	15	13	0	1	69.2	324	82	55	50	10	0	2	1	40	0	42	4	0	4	8	.333	0	0-0	1	6.26	6.46
2001	CWS	AL	35	16	0	8	117.0	510	123	59	48	16	2	5	4	55	2	61	3	0	6	7	.462	0	1-1	2	5.16	3.69
2002	CWS	AL	33	33	1	0	192.2	827	188	109	98	23	3	4	9	83	1	112	5	0	12	12	.500	1	0-0	0	4.46	4.58
2003	CWS	AL	32	32	0	0	191.2	813	188	103	96	28	4	8	4	74	1	108	8	0	12	13	.480	0	0-0	0	4.38	4.51
2004	CWS	AL	34	33	1	0	217.0	923	223	125	118	34	9	5	4	76	2	113	3	0	12	11	.522	0	0-0	0	4.56	4.89
2005	CWS	AL	32	32	3	0	221.0	901	212	93	86	26	9	5	4	47	3	115	2	0	18	10	.643	3	0-0	0	3.39	3.50
2006	CWS	AL	33	32	1	0	211.1	900	247	112	106	26	5	8	6	41	4	112	4	0	18	7	.720	1	0-0	0	4.50	4.51
2007	CWS	AL	32	32	2	0	208.1	883	219	114	98	19	3	7	4	57	3	98	1	0	10	13	.435	1	0-0	0	3.87	4.23
2008	LAA	AL	32	32	1	0	196.2	864	237	116	107	23	8	8	8	59	4	90	4	0	14	8	.636	0	0-0	0	5.18	4.90
2009	2 Tms	NL	33	33	1	0	204.0	882	225	106	91	23	11	6	6	61	7	109	6	0	11	13	.458	0	0-0	0	4.42	4.01
09	Ari	NL	27	27	1	0	167.2	728	188	90	80	19	9	4	6	52	5	83	5	0	8	11	.421	0	0-0	0	4.63	4.29
09	LAD	NL	6	6	0	0	36.1	154	37	16	11	4	2	2	0	9	2	26	1	0	3	2	.600	0	0-0	0	3.51	2.72
	Postseason		2	2	1	0	16.0	58	11	6	4	2	2	0	0	3	0	11	0	0	1	0	1.000	0	0-0	0	2.00	2.25
	10 ML YEARS		311	288	10	9	1829.1	7827	1944	992	898	228	54	61	53	593	27	960	40	0	117	102	.534	6	1-1	3	4.45	4.42

Matt Garza

Pitches: R **Bats:** R **Pos:** SP-32   **Ht:** 6'4" **Wt:** 215 **Born:** 11/26/1983 **Age:** 26

			HOW MUCH HE PITCHED						WHAT HE GAVE UP											THE RESULTS							
Year	Team	Lg	G	GS	CG	GF	IP	BFP	H	R	ER	HR	SH	SF	HB	TBB	IBB	SO	WP	Bk	W	L	Pct	Sh	Sv-Op	Hld	ERC	ERA
2006	Min	AL	10	9	0	0	50.0	232	62	33	32	6	0	3	0	23	0	38	1	0	3	6	.333	0	0-0	0	5.82	5.76
2007	Min	AL	16	15	0	1	83.0	367	96	44	34	8	1	4	4	32	4	67	4	0	5	7	.417	0	0-0	0	5.08	3.69
2008	TB	AL	30	30	3	0	184.2	772	170	83	76	19	3	9	6	59	2	128	3	2	11	9	.550	2	0-0	0	3.47	3.70
2009	TB	AL	32	32	0	0	203.0	861	177	93	89	25	2	8	11	79	0	189	3	0	8	12	.400	0	0-0	0	3.69	3.95
	Postseason		4	4	0	0	25.0	107	21	11	11	4	0	1	1	12	0	25	2	0	2	1	.667	0	0-0	0	4.07	3.96
	4 ML YEARS		88	86	3	1	520.2	2232	505	253	231	58	6	24	21	193	6	422	11	2	27	34	.443	2	0-0	0	4.02	3.99

Joey Gathright

Bats: L **Throws:** R **Pos:** CF-15; PR-11; PH-10; LF-7; RF-2; DH-1   **Ht:** 5'10" **Wt:** 185 **Born:** 4/27/1981 **Age:** 29

									BATTING												BASERUNNING				AVERAGES		
Year	Team	Lg	G	AB	H	2B	3B	HR	(Hm	Rd)	TB	R	RBI	RC	TBB	IBB	SO	HBP	SH	SF	SB	CS	SB%	GDP	Avg	OBP	Slg
2009	Norfolk*	AAA	80	322	106	11	2	0	(-	-)	121	49	20	51	27	0	41	3	10	0	24	7	.77	10	.329	.386	.376
2009	Pwtckt*	AAA	3	10	2	0	0	0	(-	-)	2	1	0	0	0	0	1	0	1	0	0	1	.00	0	.200	.200	.200
2004	TB	AL	19	52	13	0	0	0	(0	0)	13	11	1	4	2	0	14	3	0	0	6	1	.86	2	.250	.316	.250
2005	TB	AL	76	203	56	7	3	0	(0	0)	69	29	13	22	10	0	39	2	3	0	20	5	.80	5	.276	.316	.340
2006	2 Tms	AL	134	383	91	12	3	1	(1	0)	112	59	41	46	42	0	75	7	9	4	22	9	.71	3	.238	.321	.292
2007	KC	AL	74	228	70	8	0	0	(0	0)	78	28	19	31	20	0	36	3	10	0	9	8	.53	2	.307	.371	.342
2008	KC	AL	105	279	71	3	1	0	(0	0)	76	41	22	31	20	0	40	4	10	2	21	4	.84	3	.254	.311	.272
2009	2 Tms		37	30	8	0	0	0	(0	0)	8	9	0	2	1	0	8	0	0	0	2	2	.50	2	.267	.313	.267
06	TB	AL	55	154	31	6	0	0	(0	0)	37	25	13	15	20	0	30	3	5	0	12	3	.80	1	.201	.305	.240
06	KC	AL	79	229	60	6	3	1	(1	0)	75	34	28	31	22	0	45	4	4	4	10	6	.63	2	.262	.332	.328
09	ChC	NL	20	14	3	0	0	0	(0	0)	3	2	0	1	1	0	6	0	0	0	1	2	.33	0	.214	.267	.214
09	Bos	AL	17	16	5	0	0	0	(0	0)	5	7	0	1	0	0	2	0	0	0	1	0	1.00	2	.313	.353	.313
	6 ML YEARS		445	1175	309	30	7	1	(1	0)	356	177	96	136	96	0	212	19	32	6	80	29	.73	17	.263	.327	.303

Chad Gaudin

Pitches: R **Bats:** R **Pos:** SP-25; RP-6   **Ht:** 5'10" **Wt:** 188 **Born:** 3/24/1983 **Age:** 27

			HOW MUCH HE PITCHED						WHAT HE GAVE UP											THE RESULTS							
Year	Team	Lg	G	GS	CG	GF	IP	BFP	H	R	ER	HR	SH	SF	HB	TBB	IBB	SO	WP	Bk	W	L	Pct	Sh	Sv-Op	Hld	ERC	ERA
2009	Portlnd*	AAA	2	2	0	0	8.2	31	4	0	0	0	0	0	0	2	0	10	1	0	0	0	-	0	0- -	-	0.84	0.00
2003	TB	AL	15	3	0	5	40.0	173	37	18	16	4	0	2	1	16	0	23	1	0	2	0	1.000	0	0-0	0	3.70	3.60
2004	TB	AL	26	4	0	5	42.2	201	59	27	23	4	2	4	4	16	4	30	0	0	1	2	.333	0	0-1	5	6.46	4.85
2005	Tor	AL	5	3	0	0	13.0	74	31	19	19	6	0	1	1	6	0	12	0	0	1	3	.250	0	0-0	0	18.35	13.15
2006	Oak	AL	55	0	0	13	64.0	276	51	24	22	3	0	3	1	42	2	36	2	2	4	2	.667	0	2-3	11	3.62	3.09
2007	Oak	AL	34	34	1	0	199.1	886	205	108	98	21	3	6	8	100	8	154	3	1	11	13	.458	0	0-0	0	4.80	4.42
2008	2 Tms		50	6	0	14	90.0	382	92	50	44	11	2	2	3	27	3	71	2	2	9	5	.643	0	0-1	4	4.06	4.40
2009	2 Tms		31	25	0	4	147.1	664	146	85	76	14	7	8	8	76	4	139	7	1	6	10	.375	0	0-0	0	4.56	4.64
08	Oak	AL	26	6	0	9	62.2	263	63	29	25	6	2	1	3	17	1	44	2	1	5	3	.625	0	0-0	2	3.78	3.59
08	ChC	NL	24	0	0	5	27.1	119	29	21	19	5	0	1	0	10	2	27	0	1	4	2	.667	0	0-1	2	4.74	6.26

Year Team	Lg	G	GS	CG	GF	IP	BFP	H	R	ER	HR	SH	SF	HB	TBB	IBB	SO	WP	Bk	W	L	Pct	Sh	Sv-Op	Hld	ERC	ERA
09 SD	NL	20	19	0	0	105.1	470	105	69	60	7	7	6	5	56	3	105	4	1	4	10	.286	0	0-0	0	4.41	5.13
09 NYY	AL	11	6	0	4	42.0	188	41	16	16	7	0	2	3	20	1	34	3	0	2	0	1.000	0	0-0	0	4.93	3.43
Postseason		3	0	0	0	3.1	15	2	0	0	0	1	0	0	3	1	1	0	0	0	0	-	0	0-0	0	2.46	0.00
7 ML YEARS		216	75	1	41	596.1	2656	621	331	298	63	14	26	26	283	21	465	15	6	34	35	.493	0	2-5	20	4.77	4.50

Geoff Geary

Pitches: R Bats: R Pos: RP-16 **Ht: 6'0" Wt: 180 Born: 8/26/1976 Age: 33**

Year Team	Lg	G	GS	CG	GF	IP	BFP	H	R	ER	HR	SH	SF	HB	TBB	IBB	SO	WP	Bk	W	L	Pct	Sh	Sv-Op	Hld	ERC	FRA
2009 RdRck*	AAA	26	0	0	14	40.0	181	53	23	22	4	4	2	0	11	5	26	0	0	1	3	.250	0	2--	-	5.19	4.95
2003 Phi	NL	5	0	0	2	6.0	28	8	3	3	1	0	1	0	3	0	3	0	0	0	0	-	0	0-0	0	5.70	4.50
2004 Phi	NL	33	0	0	16	44.2	200	52	29	27	8	1	2	3	16	3	30	2	1	1	0	1.000	0	0-0	0	5.63	5.44
2005 Phi	NL	40	0	0	12	58.0	247	54	29	24	5	2	4	1	21	4	42	3	0	2	1	.667	0	0-1	3	3.38	3.72
2006 Phi	NL	81	0	0	17	91.1	390	103	34	30	6	3	1	6	20	4	60	2	0	7	1	.875	0	1-4	15	4.07	2.96
2007 Phi	NL	57	0	0	10	67.1	296	72	44	33	8	5	3	9	25	6	38	3	0	3	2	.600	0	0-3	9	4.98	4.41
2008 Hou	NL	55	0	0	8	64.0	262	45	18	18	3	3	1	2	28	5	45	0	1	2	3	.400	0	0-2	12	2.32	2.53
2009 Hou	NL	16	0	0	3	20.0	97	30	19	18	4	2	0	1	10	1	12	2	0	1	3	.250	0	0-2	2	8.74	8.10
7 ML YEARS		287	0	0	68	351.1	1520	364	176	153	34	17	11	22	123	23	230	12	2	16	10	.615	0	1-12	41	4.23	3.92

Josh Geer

Pitches: R Bats: R Pos: SP-17; RP-2 **Ht: 6'3" Wt: 194 Born: 6/2/1983 Age: 27**

Year Team	Lg	G	GS	CG	GF	IP	BFP	H	R	ER	HR	SH	SF	HB	TBB	IBB	SO	WP	Bk	W	L	Pct	Sh	Sv-Op	Hld	ERC	ERA
2005 Eugene	A	7	6	0	0	31.2	131	35	13	13	5	2	1	1	4	0	13	1	0	3	1	.750	0	0--	-	4.14	3.69
2005 FtWyn	A	5	5	0	0	29.2	125	29	16	14	3	2	1	1	9	0	23	0	0	1	1	.500	0	0--	-	3.73	4.25
2006 FtWyn	A	12	11	1	0	73.2	305	70	27	25	3	5	1	3	13	0	46	2	0	6	2	.750	1	0--	-	3.14	3.10
2006 Lk Els	A+	15	15	0	0	89.0	392	116	60	49	7	4	2	3	16	0	56	3	2	7	4	.636	0	0--	-	4.92	4.96
2007 SnAnt	AA	26	26	2	0	171.1	699	163	67	61	9	12	2	11	27	1	102	7	0	16	6	.727	0	0--	-	2.84	3.20
2007 PortInd	AAA	1	1	0	0	6.0	23	6	2	2	0	0	1	0	1	0	6	1	0	1	0	1.000	0	0--	-	2.76	3.00
2008 PortInd	AAA	28	27	0	0	166.2	718	187	95	84	22	6	6	4	45	1	107	6	1	8	9	.471	0	0--	-	4.58	4.54
2009 PortInd	AAA	9	9	1	0	52.2	226	60	29	26	5	4	2	2	14	1	31	0	0	2	5	.900	0	0--	-	4.48	4.44
2008 SD	NL	5	5	0	0	27.0	117	29	8	8	2	0	0	0	9	2	16	0	0	2	1	.667	0	0-0	0	3.90	2.67
2009 SD	NL	19	17	0	0	102.2	438	116	73	68	27	3	5	4	23	0	54	0	0	1	7	.125	0	0-0	0	5.47	5.96
2 ML YEARS		24	22	0	0	129.2	555	145	81	76	29	3	5	4	32	2	70	0	0	3	8	.273	0	0-0	0	5.14	5.28

Craig Gentry

Bats: R Throws: R Pos: CF-7; PR-3; RF-2; DH-1 **Ht: 6'2" Wt: 190 Born: 11/29/1983 Age: 26**

Year Team	Lg	G	AB	H	2B	3B	HR	(Hm	Rd)	TB	R	RBI	RC	TBB	IBB	SO	HBP	SH	SF	SB	CS	SB%	GDP	Avg	OBP	Slg
2006 Spkane	A-	56	221	62	15	4	0	(-	-)	85	27	13	33	9	0	37	15	0	1	20	6	.77	2	.281	.350	.385
2007 Clinton	A	55	223	61	15	0	3	(-	-)	85	40	12	33	15	0	37	7	0	3	24	3	.89	5	.274	.335	.381
2007 Rngrs	R	3	11	3	0	0	0	(-	-)	3	4	1	1	1	0	3	1	0	0	2	0	1.00	0	.273	.385	.273
2007 Bkrsfld	A+	51	213	58	16	1	1	(-	-)	79	31	18	27	12	0	46	6	1	3	16	7	.70	4	.272	.325	.371
2008 Frisco	AA	76	301	83	17	0	4	(-	-)	112	43	33	39	17	2	55	11	3	4	15	8	.65	3	.276	.333	.372
2008 Okla	AAA	18	59	12	1	0	0	(-	-)	13	6	1	4	9	0	18	0	1	0	1	0	1.00	0	.203	.309	.220
2009 Frisco	AA	127	512	155	21	7	8	(-	-)	214	100	53	93	49	1	64	16	0	5	49	6	.89	4	.303	.378	.418
2009 Tex	AL	11	17	2	1	0	0	(0	0)	3	4	1	1	2	0	5	0	0	0	0	0	-	0	.118	.211	.176

Esteban German

Bats: R Throws: R Pos: 3B-10; 2B-6; PH-3; 1B-1; LF-1; PR-1 **Ht: 5'9" Wt: 195 Born: 1/26/1978 Age: 32**

Year Team	Lg	G	AB	H	2B	3B	HR	(Hm	Rd)	TB	R	RBI	RC	TBB	IBB	SO	HBP	SH	SF	SB	CS	SB%	GDP	Avg	OBP	Slg
2009 Okla*	AAA	105	389	124	15	5	4	(-	-)	161	63	59	78	65	0	63	8	2	8	35	9	.80	11	.319	.419	.414
2002 Oak	AL	9	35	7	0	0	0	(0	0)	7	4	0	2	4	0	11	1	0	0	1	0	1.00	0	.200	.300	.200
2003 Oak	AL	5	4	1	0	0	0	(0	0)	1	0	1	1	0	0	1	0	0	0	0	0	-	1	.250	.250	.250
2004 Oak	AL	31	60	15	1	1	0	(0	0)	18	9	7	8	4	0	13	0	1	0	1	0	1.00	1	.250	.297	.300
2005 Tex	AL	5	4	3	1	0	0	(0	0)	4	3	1	2	0	0	1	0	0	0	2	1	.750	0	.750	.750	1.000
2006 KC	AL	106	279	91	18	5	3	(2	1)	128	44	34	55	40	0	49	6	6	0	7	3	.70	8	.326	.422	.459
2007 KC	AL	121	348	92	15	6	4	(3	1)	131	49	37	48	43	0	60	5	6	3	11	7	.61	11	.264	.351	.376
2008 KC	AL	89	216	53	14	3	0	(0	0)	73	30	22	26	18	1	42	1	4	3	7	3	.70	5	.245	.303	.338
2009 Tex	AL	19	46	14	4	0	0	(0	0)	18	9	4	7	4	0	7	0	0	0	1	0	1.00	0	.304	.360	.391
8 ML YEARS		385	992	276	53	15	7	(5	2)	380	148	106	149	113	1	184	13	17	6	29	14	.67	26	.278	.358	.383

Jody Gerut

Bats: L Throws: L Pos: PH-59; CF-42; RF-37; LF-3; PR-1 **Ht: 6'0" Wt: 190 Born: 9/18/1977 Age: 32**

Year Team	Lg	G	AB	H	2B	3B	HR	(Hm	Rd)	TB	R	RBI	RC	TBB	IBB	SO	HBP	SH	SF	SB	CS	SB%	GDP	Avg	OBP	Slg
2003 Cle	AL	127	480	134	33	2	22	(13	9)	237	66	75	73	35	4	70	7	1	2	4	5	.44	13	.279	.336	.494
2004 Cle	AL	134	481	121	31	5	11	(3	8)	195	72	51	60	54	4	59	7	3	3	13	6	.68	9	.252	.334	.405
2005 3 Tms		59	170	43	11	1	1	(1	0)	59	15	14	18	20	1	20	0	1	1	1	1	.50	4	.253	.330	.347
2008 SD	NL	100	328	97	15	4	14	(4	10)	162	46	43	55	28	0	52	0	0	4	6	4	.60	1	.296	.351	.494
2009 2 Tms	NL	122	274	63	13	0	9	(3	6)	103	40	35	23	19	1	43	1	0	4	6	2	.75	8	.230	.279	.376
05 Cle	AL	44	138	38	9	1	1	(1	0)	52	12	12	17	18	1	14	0	0	1	1	1	.50	3	.275	.357	.377
05 ChC	NL	11	14	1	1	0	0	(0	0)	2	1	0	0	2	0	3	0	0	0	0	0	-	0	.071	.188	.143

Year	Team	Lg	G	AB	H	2B	3B	HR	(Hm	Rd)	TB	R	RBI	RC	TBB	IBB	SO	HBP	SH	SF	SB	CS	SB%	GDP	Avg	OBP	Slg
05	Pit	NL	4	18	4	1	0	0	(0	0)	5	2	2	1	0	0	3	0	0	0	0	0	-	1	.222	.222	.278
09	SD	NL	37	113	25	6	0	4	(-	4)	43	17	14	9	5	1	22	0	0	3	2	0	1.00	2	.221	.248	.381
09	Mil	NL	85	161	38	7	0	5	(3	2)	60	23	21	14	14	0	21	1	0	1	4	2	.67	6	.236	.299	.373
5 ML YEARS			542	1733	458	103	12	57	(24	33)	756	239	218	229	156	10	244	15	4	10	30	18	.63	35	.264	.329	.436

Sammy Gervacio

Pitches: R Bats: R Pos: RP-29   Ht: 6'0" Wt: 170 Born: 1/10/1985 Age: 25

			HOW MUCH HE PITCHED						WHAT HE GAVE UP											THE RESULTS							
Year	Team	Lg	G	GS	CG	GF	IP	BFP	H	R	ER	HR	SH	SF	HB	TBB	IBB	SO	WP	Bk	W	L	Pct	Sh	Sv-Op	Hld	ERC	ERA
2005	Grnsvle	R+	21	0	0	16	33.2	134	24	10	10	1	1	1	0	6	0	53	2	0	3	2	.600	0	8- -	-	1.46	2.67
2005	Lxngtn	A	5	0	0	2	9.1	33	4	1	1	0	0	0	0	1	0	11	1	2	1	0	1.000	0	0- -	-	0.55	0.96
2006	Lxngtn	A	47	0	0	28	83.2	340	58	28	24	8	5	4	8	28	0	89	2	0	7	5	.583	0	10- -	-	2.55	2.58
2007	Salem	A+	39	0	0	33	55.1	228	42	16	15	1	2	0	5	15	1	80	3	1	1	3	.250	0	18- -	-	2.09	2.44
2007	CpChr	AA	13	0	0	4	22.2	89	15	7	5	1	2	0	0	11	2	24	1	0	3	2	.600	0	0- -	-	2.25	1.99
2008	CpChr	AA	47	0	0	31	65.1	286	69	36	30	8	3	3	3	26	2	82	1	0	2	5	.286	0	5- -	-	4.71	4.13
2008	RdRck	AAA	3	0	0	0	8.0	34	6	2	2	0	0	1	1	3	0	14	0	0	1	0	1.000	0	0- -	-	2.40	2.25
2009	RdRck	AAA	39	0	0	11	52.1	224	43	30	28	5	4	3	3	21	4	58	3	3	2	2	.500	0	0- -	-	3.11	4.82
2009	Hou	NL	29	0	0	4	21.0	83	16	5	5	1	1	0	1	8	3	25	0	0	1	1	.500	0	0-1	6	2.50	2.14

Chris Getz

Bats: L Throws: R Pos: 2B-106; PH-2; PR-2   Ht: 6'0" Wt: 185 Born: 8/30/1983 Age: 26

			BATTING																		BASERUNNING				AVERAGES		
Year	Team	Lg	G	AB	H	2B	3B	HR	(Hm	Rd)	TB	R	RBI	RC	TBB	IBB	SO	HBP	SH	SF	SB	CS	SB%	GDP	Avg	OBP	Slg
2005	Gr Falls	R+	6	24	8	1	0	0	(-	-)	9	3	4	3	1	0	2	0	1	1	2	1	.67	0	.333	.346	.375
2005	Knapol	A	55	214	65	13	2	1	(-	-)	85	38	28	39	35	1	10	3	0	1	11	4	.73	5	.304	.407	.397
2006	Brham	AA	130	508	130	15	2	1	(-	-)	163	67	36	59	52	3	47	2	9	2	19	6	.76	10	.256	.326	.321
2007	Brham	AA	72	278	83	10	2	3	(-	-)	106	40	29	44	36	2	30	2	2	1	13	7	.65	4	.299	.382	.381
2008	Charltt	AAA	112	404	122	24	1	11	(-	-)	181	61	52	70	41	2	53	3	4	5	12	4	.75	5	.302	.366	.448
2009	Charltt	AAA	5	15	4	0	0	0	(-	-)	4	4	0	2	3	0	1	1	0	0	2	0	1.00	1	.267	.421	.267
2008	CWS	AL	10	7	2	0	0	0	(0	0)	2	2	1	1	0	0	1	0	0	0	1	1	.50	0	.286	.286	.286
2009	CWS	AL	107	375	98	18	4	2	(1	1)	130	49	31	47	30	1	54	6	1	3	25	2	.93	4	.261	.324	.347
2 ML YEARS			117	382	100	18	4	2	(1	1)	132	51	32	48	30	1	55	6	1	3	26	2	.90	4	.262	.323	.346

Jason Giambi

Bats: L Throws: R Pos: 1B-63; DH-22; PH-18   Ht: 6'3" Wt: 240 Born: 1/8/1971 Age: 39

			BATTING																		BASERUNNING				AVERAGES		
Year	Team	Lg	G	AB	H	2B	3B	HR	(Hm	Rd)	TB	R	RBI	RC	TBB	IBB	SO	HBP	SH	SF	SB	CS	SB%	GDP	Avg	OBP	Slg
2009	ColSpr*	AAA	6	18	8	1	0	2	(-	-)	15	4	4	7	6	0	3	0	0	0	0	1	.00	1	.444	.583	.833
1995	Oak	AL	54	176	45	7	0	6	(3	3)	70	27	25	27	28	0	31	3	1	2	2	1	.67	4	.256	.364	.398
1996	Oak	AL	140	536	156	40	1	20	(6	14)	258	84	79	88	51	3	95	5	1	5	0	1	.00	15	.291	.355	.481
1997	Oak	AL	142	519	152	41	2	20	(14	6)	257	66	81	91	55	3	89	6	0	8	0	1	.00	11	.293	.362	.495
1998	Oak	AL	153	562	166	28	0	27	(12	15)	275	92	110	103	81	7	102	5	0	9	2	2	.50	16	.295	.384	.489
1999	Oak	AL	158	575	181	36	1	33	(17	16)	318	115	123	132	105	6	106	7	0	8	1	1	.50	11	.315	.422	.553
2000	Oak	AL	152	510	170	29	1	43	(23	20)	330	108	137	152	137	6	96	9	0	8	2	0	1.00	9	.333	.476	.647
2001	Oak	AL	154	520	178	47	2	38	(27	11)	343	109	120	153	129	24	83	13	0	9	2	0	1.00	17	.342	.477	.660
2002	NYY	AL	155	560	176	34	1	41	(19	22)	335	120	122	139	109	4	112	15	0	5	2	2	.50	18	.314	.435	.598
2003	NYY	AL	156	535	134	25	0	41	(12	29)	282	97	107	120	129	9	140	21	0	5	2	1	.67	9	.250	.412	.527
2004	NYY	AL	80	264	55	9	0	12	(5	7)	100	33	40	42	47	1	62	8	0	3	0	1	.00	5	.208	.342	.379
2005	NYY	AL	139	417	113	14	0	32	(16	16)	223	74	87	102	108	5	109	19	0	1	0	0	-	7	.271	.440	.535
2006	NYY	AL	139	446	113	25	0	37	(20	17)	249	92	113	106	110	12	106	16	0	7	2	0	1.00	10	.253	.413	.558
2007	NYY	AL	83	254	60	8	0	14	(6	8)	110	31	39	41	40	2	66	8	0	1	1	0	1.00	1	.236	.356	.433
2008	NYY	AL	145	458	113	19	1	32	(16	16)	230	68	96	79	76	5	111	22	0	9	2	1	.67	6	.247	.373	.502
2009	2 Tms		102	293	59	14	0	13	(7	6)	112	43	51	44	57	1	80	7	0	2	0	0	-	6	.201	.343	.382
09	Oak	AL	83	269	52	13	0	11	(7	4)	98	39	40	36	50	1	72	7	0	2	0	0	-	0	.193	.332	.364
09	Col	NL	19	24	7	1	0	2	(0	2)	14	4	11	8	7	0	8	0	0	0	0	0	-	0	.292	.452	.583
Postseason			42	135	39	6	0	7	(5	2)	66	18	18	25	30	2	29	4	0	2	2	0	1.00	3	.289	.427	.489
15 ML YEARS			1952	6625	1871	376	9	409	(203	206)	3492	1159	1330	1419	1262	88	1388	164	2	82	18	11	.62	145	.282	.405	.527

Dan Giese

Pitches: R Bats: R Pos: RP-6; SP-1   Ht: 6'2" Wt: 200 Born: 5/19/1977 Age: 33

			HOW MUCH HE PITCHED						WHAT HE GAVE UP											THE RESULTS							
Year	Team	Lg	G	GS	CG	GF	IP	BFP	H	R	ER	HR	SH	SF	HB	TBB	IBB	SO	WP	Bk	W	L	Pct	Sh	Sv-Op	Hld	ERC	ERA
2009	Scrmto*	AAA	1	0	0	0	4.0	14	3	1	1	0	1	0	0	0	0	2	0	0	0	1	1.000	0	0- -	-	1.21	2.25
2007	SF	NL	8	0	0	3	9.1	37	8	5	5	4	1	0	0	2	0	7	0	0	0	2	.000	0	0-0	-	4.61	4.82
2008	NYY	AL	20	3	0	6	43.1	186	39	22	17	3	0	3	1	14	1	29	1	0	1	3	.250	0	0-0	0	2.98	3.53
2009	Oak	AL	7	1	0	2	22.0	94	22	13	13	5	0	1	0	9	1	11	0	0	0	3	.000	0	0-0	0	5.01	5.32
3 ML YEARS			35	4	0	11	74.2	317	69	40	35	12	1	4	1	25	2	47	1	0	1	8	.111	0	0-0	0	3.77	4.22

Brian Giles

Bats: L **Throws:** L **Pos:** RF-58; PH-5 **Ht:** 5'10" **Wt:** 205 **Born:** 1/20/1971 **Age:** 39

Year	Team	Lg	G	AB	H	2B	3B	HR	(Hm	Rd)	TB	R	RBI	RC	TBB	IBB	SO	HBP	SH	SF	SB	CS	SB%	GDP	Avg	OBP	Slg
1995	Cle	AL	6	9	5	0	0	1	(0	1)	8	6	3	3	0	0	1	0	0	0	0	0	-	0	.556	.556	.889
1996	Cle	AL	51	121	43	14	1	5	(2	3)	74	26	27	29	19	4	13	0	0	3	3	0	1.00	6	.355	.434	.612
1997	Cle	AL	130	377	101	15	3	17	(7	10)	173	62	61	66	63	2	50	1	3	7	13	3	.81	10	.268	.368	.459
1998	Cle	AL	112	350	94	19	0	16	(10	6)	161	56	66	66	73	8	75	3	1	3	10	5	.67	7	.269	.396	.460
1999	Pit	NL	141	521	164	33	3	39	(24	15)	320	109	115	127	95	7	80	3	0	8	6	2	.75	14	.315	.418	.614
2000	Pit	NL	156	559	176	37	7	35	(16	19)	332	111	123	139	114	13	69	7	0	8	6	0	1.00	6	.315	.432	.594
2001	Pit	NL	160	576	178	37	7	37	(18	19)	340	116	95	131	90	14	67	4	0	4	13	6	.68	10	.309	.404	.590
2002	Pit	NL	153	497	148	37	5	38	(15	23)	309	95	103	128	135	24	74	7	0	5	15	6	.71	10	.298	.450	.622
2003	2 Tms	NL	134	492	147	34	6	20	(12	8)	253	93	88	102	105	12	58	8	0	4	4	3	.57	12	.299	.427	.514
2004	SD	NL	159	609	173	33	7	23	(10	13)	289	97	94	99	89	6	80	4	0	9	10	3	.77	12	.284	.374	.475
2005	SD	NL	158	545	164	38	8	15	(6	9)	263	92	83	112	119	9	64	2	0	8	13	5	.72	14	.301	.423	.483
2006	SD	NL	158	604	159	37	1	14	(6	8)	240	87	83	95	104	6	60	5	0	4	9	4	.69	18	.263	.374	.397
2007	SD	NL	121	483	131	27	2	13	(1	12)	201	72	51	74	64	5	61	4	0	1	4	6	.40	8	.271	.361	.416
2008	SD	NL	147	559	171	40	4	12	(4	8)	255	81	63	92	87	2	52	2	0	5	2	2	.50	18	.306	.398	.456
2009	SD	NL	61	225	43	10	1	2	(1	1)	61	18	23	14	26	2	31	1	0	1	1	0	1.00	6	.191	.277	.271
03	Pit	NL	105	388	116	30	4	16	(10	6)	202	70	70	79	85	11	48	6	0	2	0	3	.00	8	.299	.430	.521
03	SD	NL	29	104	31	4	2	4	(2	2)	51	23	18	23	20	1	10	2	0	2	4	0	1.00	4	.298	.414	.490
	Postseason		29	77	16	6	0	0	(0	0)	22	4	4	6	11	0	21	1	0	1	1	1	.50	2	.208	.311	.286
	15 ML YEARS		1847	6527	1897	411	55	287	(132	155)	3279	1121	1078	1280	1103	114	835	51	4	70	109	45	.71	160	.291	.400	.502

Chris Gimenez

Bats: R **Throws:** R **Pos:** 1B-18; LF-14; C-8; RF-7; PR-2; PH-1 **Ht:** 6'2" **Wt:** 200 **Born:** 12/27/1982 **Age:** 27

Year	Team	Lg	G	AB	H	2B	3B	HR	(Hm	Rd)	TB	R	RBI	RC	TBB	IBB	SO	HBP	SH	SF	SB	CS	SB%	GDP	Avg	OBP	Slg
2004	MbVlly	A	71	260	79	22	0	10	(	)	131	40	38	58	30	1	62	24	1	1	2	2	.50	3	.300	.419	.527
2005	Lk Cty	A	112	384	90	24	1	13	(	-)	155	54	66	60	48	0	90	25	2	4	4	3	.57	4	.234	.354	.404
2006	Lk Cty	A	91	329	84	25	1	11	(-	-)	144	55	40	55	33	1	72	26	1	5	6	8	.43	8	.255	.364	.438
2007	Knstn	A+	83	269	76	14	1	20	(-	-)	152	56	54	63	50	0	55	8	2	3	3	2	.60	3	.283	.406	.565
2007	Akron	AA	30	113	25	6	0	6	(-	-)	49	20	12	14	9	0	31	1	0	0	1	0	1.00	1	.221	.285	.434
2008	Akron	AA	55	177	60	15	1	6	(-	-)	95	46	36	48	52	3	33	1	1	2	0	1	.00	7	.000	.407	.537
2008	Buffalo	AAA	54	106	63	0	1	3	(-	-)	73	23	19	28	23	1	60	4	3	4	2	1	.67	4	.272	.354	.374
2009	Clmbs	AAA	39	136	32	8	0	6	(-	-)	58	20	15	19	15	1	40	3	2	1	0	0	-	4	.235	.323	.426
2009	Cle	AL	45	111	16	2	0	3	(0	3)	27	12	7	3	17	0	36	0	1	1	1	1	.50	3	.144	.256	.243

Troy Glaus

Bats: R **Throws:** R **Pos:** 3B-8; PH-8; 1B-2 **Ht:** 6'5" **Wt:** 240 **Born:** 8/3/1976 **Age:** 33

Year	Team	Lg	G	AB	H	2B	3B	HR	(Hm	Rd)	TB	R	RBI	RC	TBB	IBB	SO	HBP	SH	SF	SB	CS	SB%	GDP	Avg	OBP	Slg
2009	PlmBh*	A+	6	25	5	1	0	0	(-	-)	6	2	4	1	1	0	6	0	0	0	0	0	-	1	.200	.231	.240
2009	Memp*	AAA	15	51	11	0	0	3	(-	-)	20	10	8	8	12	0	17	1	0	1	1	0	1.00	1	.216	.369	.392
2009	Sprgfld*	AA	3	9	2	0	0	0	(-	-)	2	1	2	1	3	0	1	0	0	0	0	0	-	1	.222	.417	.222
1998	LAA	AL	48	165	36	9	0	1	(0	1)	48	19	23	13	15	0	51	0	0	2	1	0	1.00	3	.218	.280	.291
1999	LAA	AL	154	551	132	29	0	29	(12	17)	240	85	79	84	71	1	143	6	0	3	5	1	.83	9	.240	.331	.450
2000	LAA	AL	159	563	160	37	1	47	(24	23)	340	120	102	129	112	6	163	2	0	1	14	11	.56	14	.284	.404	.604
2001	LAA	AL	161	588	147	38	2	41	(22	19)	312	100	108	114	107	7	158	6	0	7	10	3	.77	16	.250	.367	.531
2002	LAA	AL	156	569	142	24	1	30	(13	17)	258	99	111	100	88	4	144	6	0	8	10	3	.77	12	.250	.352	.453
2003	LAA	AL	91	319	79	17	2	16	(9	7)	148	53	50	48	46	4	73	1	0	1	7	2	.78	4	.248	.343	.464
2004	LAA	AL	58	207	52	11	1	18	(9	9)	119	47	42	41	31	3	52	3	0	1	2	3	.40	6	.251	.355	.575
2005	Ari	NL	149	538	139	29	1	37	(20	17)	281	78	97	87	84	2	145	7	0	5	4	2	.67	7	.258	.363	.522
2006	Tor	AL	153	540	136	27	0	38	(25	13)	277	105	104	84	86	6	134	3	0	5	3	2	.60	25	.252	.355	.513
2007	Tor	AL	115	385	101	19	1	20	(7	13)	182	60	62	65	61	2	102	5	0	5	0	1	.00	7	.262	.366	.473
2008	StL	NL	151	544	147	33	1	27	(13	14)	263	69	99	88	87	3	104	3	0	3	0	1	.00	14	.270	.372	.483
2009	StL	NL	14	29	5	2	0	0	(-	-)	7	2	2	2	3	0	8	0	0	0	0	0	-	1	.172	.250	.241
	Postseason		19	72	25	5	1	9	(4	5)	59	18	16	15	9	2	18	1	0	0	0	0	-	1	.347	.427	.819
	12 ML YEARS		1409	4998	1276	275	10	304	(154	150)	2483	837	879	855	791	38	1277	42	0	41	56	29	.66	122	.255	.359	.497

Ross Gload

Bats: L **Throws:** L **Pos:** PH-80; 1B-41; RF-10; LF-1; PR-1 **Ht:** 6'1" **Wt:** 190 **Born:** 4/5/1976 **Age:** 34

Year	Team	Lg	G	AB	H	2B	3B	HR	(Hm	Rd)	TB	R	RBI	RC	TBB	IBB	SO	HBP	SH	SF	SB	CS	SB%	GDP	Avg	OBP	Slg
2000	ChC	NL	18	31	6	0	1	1	(0	1)	11	4	3	3	3	0	10	0	0	1	0	0	-	1	.194	.257	.355
2002	Col	NL	26	31	8	1	0	1	(1	0)	12	4	4	3	3	0	7	0	0	0	0	0	-	0	.258	.324	.387
2004	CWS	AL	110	234	75	16	0	7	(3	4)	112	28	44	41	20	1	37	2	1	3	0	3	.00	11	.321	.375	.479
2005	CWS	AL	28	42	7	2	0	0	(0	0)	9	2	5	2	2	0	9	0	0	0	0	0	-	1	.167	.205	.214
2006	CWS	AL	77	156	51	8	2	3	(1	2)	72	22	18	24	6	0	15	1	3	1	6	0	1.00	3	.327	.354	.462
2007	KC	AL	102	320	92	22	3	7	(2	5)	141	37	51	45	16	2	39	2	0	8	2	2	.50	13	.288	.318	.441
2008	KC	AL	122	388	106	18	1	3	(2	1)	135	46	37	41	23	4	39	3	1	3	3	4	.43	12	.273	.317	.348
2009	Fla	NL	125	230	60	10	2	6	(3	3)	92	33	30	26	23	4	30	2	1	3	0	0	-	3	.261	.329	.400
	8 ML YEARS		608	1432	405	77	9	28	(12	16)	584	176	192	185	96	11	186	10	6	19	11	9	.55	44	.283	.328	.408

Jimmy Gobble

Pitches: L Bats: L Pos: RP-12   Ht: 6'3" Wt: 208 Born: 7/19/1981 Age: 28

Year	Team	Lg	G	GS	CG	GF	IP	BFP	H	R	ER	HR	SH	SF	HB	TBB	IBB	SO	WP	Bk	W	L	Pct	Sh	Sv-Op	Hld	ERC	ERA
2009	Charltt*	AAA	11	0	0	5	12.0	51	8	8	7	2	0	0	1	4	0	19	2	0	0	1	.000	0	1- -	-	2.62	5.25
2003	KC	AL	9	9	0	0	52.2	230	56	32	27	8	1	3	4	15	0	31	1	0	4	5	.444	0	0-0	0	4.61	4.61
2004	KC	AL	25	24	1	0	148.0	638	157	94	88	24	4	7	3	43	0	49	4	0	9	8	.529	0	0-0	0	4.47	5.35
2005	KC	AL	28	4	0	11	53.2	249	64	34	34	9	3	1	1	30	4	38	2	0	1	1	.500	0	0-0	4	6.39	5.70
2006	KC	AL	60	6	0	17	84.0	370	95	51	48	12	3	0	1	29	1	80	4	0	4	6	.400	0	2-4	11	4.93	5.14
2007	KC	AL	74	0	0	12	53.2	233	56	23	18	6	1	5	2	23	6	50	6	1	4	1	.800	0	1-3	16	4.56	3.02
2008	KC	AL	39	0	0	10	31.2	159	39	31	31	5	0	1	2	23	1	27	6	0	0	2	.000	0	1-2	4	7.36	8.81
2009	CWS	AL	12	0	0	3	12.0	59	14	10	10	3	0	0	2	7	1	10	2	0	0	0	-	0	0-0	0	7.46	7.50
	7 ML YEARS		247	43	1	53	435.2	1938	481	275	256	67	12	17	15	170	13	285	25	1	22	23	.489	0	4-9	35	5.10	5.29

Greg Golson

Bats: R Throws: R Pos: CF-1   Ht: 6'0" Wt: 190 Born: 9/17/1985 Age: 24

Year	Team	Lg	G	AB	H	2B	3B	HR	(Hm	Rd)	TB	R	RBI	RC	TBB	IBB	SO	HBP	SH	SF	SB	CS	SB%	GDP	Avg	OBP	Slg
2004	Phillies	R	47	183	54	8	5	1	(-	-)	75	34	22	28	10	0	54	5	1	2	12	2	.86	2	.295	.345	.410
2005	Lakwd	A	89	375	99	19	8	4	(-	-)	146	51	27	49	26	0	106	6	2	0	25	9	.74	4	.264	.322	.389
2006	Lakwd	A	93	387	85	15	4	7	(-	-)	129	56	31	35	19	1	107	2	8	3	23	7	.77	2	.220	.258	.333
2006	Clrwtr	A+	40	159	42	11	2	6	(-	-)	75	31	17	24	11	1	53	3	1	0	7	3	.70	3	.264	.324	.472
2007	Clrwtr	A+	99	418	119	27	3	12	(-	-)	188	66	52	63	21	2	124	4	2	4	25	8	.76	4	.285	.322	.450
2007	Rdng	AA	37	153	37	5	2	3	(-	-)	55	20	16	14	2	0	49	1	1	1	5	0	1.00	4	.242	.255	.359
2008	Rdng	AA	106	426	120	18	4	13	(-	-)	185	64	60	65	34	0	130	1	4	5	22	5	.81	3	.282	.333	.434
2009	Okla	AAA	123	457	118	17	8	2	(-	-)	157	46	40	51	29	0	114	0	8	6	20	4	.83	8	.258	.299	.344
2008	Phi	NL	6	6	0	0	0	0	(0	0)	0	2	0	0	0	0	4	0	0	0	1	0	1.00	0	.000	.000	.000
2009	Tex	AL	1	1	0	0	0	0	(0	0)	0	0	0	0	0	0	1	0	0	0	0	0	-	0	.000	.000	.000
	2 ML YEARS		7	7	0	0	0	0	(0	0)	0	2	0	0	0	0	5	0	0	0	1	0	1.00	0	.000	.000	.000

Jonny Gomes

Bats: R Throws: R Pos: LF-37; RF-34; PH-22; DH-9   Ht: 6'1" Wt: 225 Born: 11/22/1980 Age: 29

Year	Team	Lg	G	AB	H	2B	3B	HR	(Hm	Rd)	TB	R	RBI	RC	TBB	IBB	SO	HBP	SH	SF	SB	CS	SB%	GDP	Avg	OBP	Slg
2009	Lsvlle*	AAA	37	131	37	10	1	9	(-	-)	76	18	27	27	12	1	36	4	0	0	4	1	.80	2	.282	.361	.580
2003	TB	AL	8	15	2	1	0	0	(0	0)	3	1	0	0	0	0	6	1	0	0	0	0	-	0	.133	.188	.200
2004	TB	AL	5	14	1	0	0	0	(0	0)	1	0	1	0	1	0	6	0	0	0	0	0	-	0	.071	.133	.071
2005	TB	AL	101	348	98	13	6	21	(11	10)	186	61	54	62	39	1	113	14	1	5	9	5	.64	6	.282	.372	.534
2006	TB	AL	117	385	83	21	1	20	(7	13)	166	53	59	53	61	2	116	6	0	9	1	5	.17	10	.216	.325	.431
2007	TB	AL	107	348	85	20	2	17	(10	7)	160	48	49	47	35	1	126	7	0	4	12	4	.75	1	.244	.322	.460
2008	TB	AL	77	154	28	5	1	8	(2	6)	59	23	21	18	15	1	46	7	0	1	8	1	.89	1	.182	.282	.383
2009	Cin	NL	98	281	75	17	0	20	(11	9)	152	39	51	46	26	2	85	5	0	2	3	1	.75	8	.267	.338	.541
	7 ML YEARS		513	1545	372	77	10	86	(41	45)	727	225	235	226	177	7	498	40	1	21	33	16	.67	26	.241	.330	.471

Carlos Gomez

Bats: R Throws: R Pos: CF-132; PR-22; PH-2; DH-1   Ht: 6'4" Wt: 215 Born: 12/4/1985 Age: 24

Year	Team	Lg	G	AB	H	2B	3B	HR	(Hm	Rd)	TB	R	RBI	RC	TBB	IBB	SO	HBP	SH	SF	SB	CS	SB%	GDP	Avg	OBP	Slg
2007	NYM	NL	58	125	29	3	0	2	(1	1)	38	14	12	11	8	2	27	3	0	3	12	3	.80	0	.232	.288	.304
2008	Min	AL	153	577	149	24	7	7	(3	4)	208	79	59	66	25	0	142	7	3	2	33	11	.75	7	.258	.296	.360
2009	Min	AL	137	315	72	15	5	3	(1	2)	106	51	28	33	22	0	72	4	7	1	14	7	.67	1	.229	.287	.337
	3 ML YEARS		348	1017	250	42	12	12	(5	7)	352	144	99	110	55	2	241	14	10	6	59	21	.74	8	.246	.292	.346

Adrian Gonzalez

Bats: L Throws: L Pos: 1B-156; PH-3; DH-2   Ht: 6'2" Wt: 225 Born: 5/8/1982 Age: 28

Year	Team	Lg	G	AB	H	2B	3B	HR	(Hm	Rd)	TB	R	RBI	RC	TBB	IBB	SO	HBP	SH	SF	SB	CS	SB%	GDP	Avg	OBP	Slg
2004	Tex	AL	16	42	10	3	0	1	(1	0)	16	7	7	7	2	0	6	0	0	0	0	0	-	0	.238	.273	.381
2005	Tex	AL	43	150	34	7	1	6	(3	3)	61	17	17	13	10	2	37	0	0	2	0	0	-	3	.227	.272	.407
2006	SD	NL	156	570	173	38	1	24	(10	14)	285	83	82	82	52	9	113	3	1	5	0	1	.00	24	.304	.362	.500
2007	SD	NL	161	646	182	46	3	30	(10	20)	324	101	100	108	65	9	140	3	0	6	0	0	-	6	.282	.347	.502
2008	SD	NL	162	616	172	32	1	36	(14	22)	314	103	119	107	74	18	142	7	0	3	0	0	-	24	.279	.361	.510
2009	SD	NL	160	552	153	27	2	40	(12	28)	304	90	99	109	119	22	109	5	1	4	1	1	.50	23	.277	.407	.551
	Postseason		4	14	5	0	0	0	(0	0)	5	2	0	1	3	0	3	0	0	0	0	0	-	0	.357	.471	.357
	6 ML YEARS		698	2576	724	153	8	137	(50	87)	1304	401	424	426	322	60	547	18	2	20	1	2	.33	80	.281	.362	.506

Alberto Gonzalez

Bats: R Throws: R Pos: 2B-55; SS-41; PH-13; PR-5; 3B-3; DH-1   Ht: 5'10" Wt: 194 Born: 4/18/1983 Age: 27

Year	Team	Lg	G	AB	H	2B	3B	HR	(Hm	Rd)	TB	R	RBI	RC	TBB	IBB	SO	HBP	SH	SF	SB	CS	SB%	GDP	Avg	OBP	Slg
2009	Syrcse*	AAA	23	90	28	3	1	0	(-	-)	33	5	8	10	1	0	8	0	1	0	1	0	1.00	4	.311	.319	.367
2007	NYY	AL	12	14	1	0	0	0	(0	0)	1	3	1	0	1	0	1	0	0	0	0	1	.00	0	.071	.133	.071
2008	2 Tms		45	101	26	8	0	1	(0	1)	37	13	10	11	8	0	14	1	2	0	0	1	.00	6	.257	.318	.366

118

Year Team	Lg	G	AB	H	2B	3B	HR	(Hm Rd)	TB	R	RBI	RC	TBB	IBB	SO	HBP	SH	SF	SB	CS	SB%	GDP	Avg	OBP	Slg
2009 Was	NL	105	291	77	16	3	1	(1 0)	102	31	33	30	14	1	27	3	2	6	1	1	.50	8	.265	.299	.351
08 NYY	AL	28	52	9	2	0	0	(0 0)	11	4	1	0	4	0	8	0	2	0	0	0	-	4	.173	.232	.212
08 Was	NL	17	49	17	6	0	1	(0 1)	26	9	9	11	4	0	6	1	0	0	0	1	.00	2	.347	.407	.531
3 ML YEARS		162	406	104	24	3	2	(1 1)	140	47	44	41	23	1	42	4	4	6	1	3	.25	15	.256	.298	.345

Alex Gonzalez

Bats: R Throws: R Pos: SS-112　　　　**Ht: 5'11" Wt: 216 Born: 2/15/1977 Age: 33**

Year Team	Lg	G	AB	H	2B	3B	HR	(Hm Rd)	TB	R	RBI	RC	TBB	IBB	SO	HBP	SH	SF	SB	CS	SB%	GDP	Avg	OBP	Slg
2009 Lsvlle*	AAA	4	13	1	0	0	0	(- -)	1	1	1	0	2	0	1	0	0	0	0	0	-	2	.077	.200	.077
1998 Fla	NL	25	86	13	2	0	3	(1 2)	24	11	7	5	9	0	30	1	2	0	0	0	-	1	.151	.240	.279
1999 Fla	NL	136	560	155	28	8	14	(7 7)	241	81	59	69	15	0	113	12	1	3	3	5	.38	13	.277	.308	.430
2000 Fla	NL	109	385	77	17	4	7	(5 2)	123	35	42	26	13	0	77	2	5	2	7	1	.88	7	.200	.229	.319
2001 Fla	NL	145	515	129	36	1	9	(5 4)	194	57	48	56	30	6	107	10	3	3	2	2	.50	13	.250	.303	.377
2002 Fla	NL	42	151	34	7	1	2	(1 1)	49	15	18	14	12	1	32	4	3	2	3	1	.75	2	.225	.296	.325
2003 Fla	NL	150	528	135	33	6	18	(7 11)	234	52	77	67	33	13	106	13	3	5	0	4	.00	8	.256	.313	.443
2004 Fla	NL	159	561	130	30	3	23	(13 10)	235	67	79	58	27	9	126	4	3	4	3	1	.75	17	.232	.270	.419
2005 Fla	NL	130	435	115	30	0	5	(2 3)	160	45	45	47	31	10	81	5	4	3	5	3	.63	11	.264	.319	.368
2006 Bos	AL	111	388	99	24	2	9	(4 5)	154	48	50	40	22	1	67	5	7	7	1	0	1.00	6	.255	.299	.397
2007 Cin	NL	110	393	107	27	1	16	(8 8)	184	55	55	51	24	1	75	8	2	3	0	1	.00	13	.272	.325	.468
2009 2 Tms		112	391	93	22	0	8	(7 1)	139	42	41	40	20	4	65	4	10	4	2	1	.67	7	.238	.279	.355
09 Cin	NL	68	243	51	12	0	3	(2 1)	72	16	26	25	15	4	36	2	6	4	0	1	.00	3	.210	.258	.296
09 Bos	AL	44	148	42	10	0	5	(5 0)	67	26	15	15	5	0	29	2	4	0	2	0	1.00	4	.284	.316	.453
Postseason		17	62	10	4	0	1	(1 0)	17	6	6	2	1	0	16	0	1	0	0	1	.00	2	.161	.175	.274
11 ML YEARS		1229	4393	1087	256	26	114	(60 54)	1737	508	521	473	236	46	870	68	43	36	20	19	.58	99	.247	.294	.395

Andy Gonzalez

Bats: R Throws: R Pos: PH-8; SS-4; 3B-2; PR-1　　　　**Ht: 6'3" Wt: 205 Born: 12/15/1981 Age: 28**

Year Team	Lg	G	AB	H	2B	3B	HR	(Hm Rd)	TB	R	RBI	RC	TBB	IBB	SO	HBP	SH	SF	SB	CS	SB%	GDP	Avg	OBP	Slg
2009 NewOr*	AAA	102	352	91	11	0	8	( )	126	45	43	49	48	0	70	0	0	1	0	2	.00	12	.259	.351	.358
2007 CWS	AL	67	109	35	6	0	2	(1 1)	47	17	11	12	25	1	61	0	1	0	1	5	.17	4	.185	.280	.249
2008 Cle	AL	10	24	5	0	0	1	(1 0)	8	2	2	3	0	0	5	0	0	0	0	1	.00	1	.208	.367	.333
2009 Fla	NL	14	12	1	0	1	0	(0 0)	3	1	0	0	0	0	4	0	0	0	0	0	-	0	.083	.083	.250
3 ML YEARS		91	225	41	6	1	3	(2 1)	58	21	13	15	31	1	70	0	1	0	1	6	.14	5	.182	.281	.258

Carlos Gonzalez

Bats: L Throws: L Pos: LF-47; CF-43; PH-10; RF-8; PR-2　　　　**Ht: 6'1" Wt: 215 Born: 10/17/1985 Age: 24**

Year Team	Lg	G	AB	H	2B	3B	HR	(Hm Rd)	TB	R	RBI	RC	TBB	IBB	SO	HBP	SH	SF	SB	CS	SB%	GDP	Avg	OBP	Slg
2003 Msoula	R+	72	275	71	14	4	6	(- -)	111	45	25	35	16	1	61	5	0	3	12	7	.63	3	.258	.308	.404
2004 Sbend	A	14	51	14	4	0	1	(- -)	21	5	8	5	1	0	13	0	0	0	0	2	.00	0	.275	.288	.412
2004 Yakima	A-	73	300	82	15	2	9	(- -)	128	44	44	43	22	0	70	3	2	2	2	0	1.00	4	.273	.327	.427
2005 Sbend	A	120	515	158	20	6	18	(- -)	252	91	92	94	40	8	86	6	0	1	7	3	.70	12	.307	.371	.489
2006 Lancst	A+	104	403	121	35	4	21	(- -)	227	82	94	81	30	7	104	10	0	9	15	8	.65	6	.300	.356	.563
2006 Tenn	AA	18	61	13	6	0	2	(- -)	25	11	5	7	7	1	12	0	1	0	1	0	1.00	3	.213	.294	.410
2007 Mobile	AA	120	458	131	33	3	16	(-)	218	63	74	73	32	2	103	1	2	6	9	5	.64	7	.286	.330	.476
2007 Tucsn	AAA	10	42	13	5	0	1	(- -)	21	9	11	8	6	1	6	0	0	0	1	0	1.00	1	.310	.396	.500
2008 Scrmto	AAA	46	173	49	9	1	4	(- -)	72	23	28	25	16	3	35	0	0	0	1	1	.50	5	.283	.344	.416
2009 ColSpr	AAA	48	192	65	12	7	10	(- -)	121	43	59	48	22	2	32	5	3	1	6	3	.67	2	.339	.418	.630
2008 Oak	AL	85	302	73	22	1	4	(3 1)	109	31	26	30	13	1	81	0	0	4	4	1	.80	7	.242	.273	.361
2009 Col	NL	89	278	79	14	7	13	(7 6)	146	53	29	42	28	3	70	3	5	3	16	4	.80	3	.284	.353	.525
2 ML YEARS		174	580	152	36	8	17	(10 7)	255	84	55	72	41	4	151	3	6	3	20	5	.80	10	.262	.313	.440

Edgar Gonzalez

Pitches: R Bats: R Pos: RP-20; SP-6　　　　**Ht: 6'2" Wt: 210 Born: 2/23/1983 Age: 27**

	HOW MUCH HE PITCHED						WHAT HE GAVE UP										THE RESULTS						
Year Team	Lg	G	GS	CG	GF	IP	BFP	H	R	ER	HR	SH	SF	HB	TBB	IBB	SO	WP	Bk	W	L	Pct	Sh	Sv-Op	Hld	ERC	ERA
2009 Scrmto*	AAA	7	7	0	0	39.2	179	48	23	23	4	0	2	1	16	1	27	2	0	3	2	.600	0	0- -		5.40	5.22
2003 Ari	NL	9	2	0	1	18.1	85	28	10	10	3	1	1	0	7	2	14	2	0	2	1	.667	0	0-1	0	7.81	4.91
2004 Ari	NL	10	10	0	0	46.1	228	72	49	48	15	5	1	5	18	4	31	3	1	0	9	.000	0	0-0	0	9.78	9.32
2005 Ari	NL	1	0	0	0	0.1	5	2	4	1	0	0	0	0	2	0	1	1	0	0	0	-	0	0-0	0	124.7	108.0
2006 Ari	NL	11	5	0	1	42.2	182	45	20	20	7	4	1	3	9	0	28	2	0	3	4	.429	0	0-0	1	4.33	4.22
2007 Ari	NL	32	12	0	5	102.0	437	110	61	57	18	2	3	4	28	4	62	5	1	8	4	.667	0	0-0	0	4.67	5.03
2008 Ari	NL	17	6	0	3	48.0	221	58	34	32	8	4	1	3	21	2	32	4	0	1	3	.250	0	0-0	0	6.16	6.00
2009 Oak	AL	26	6	0	10	65.1	299	76	41	40	4	2	3	6	28	4	39	4	0	0	4	.000	0	0-0	0	5.09	5.51
7 ML YEARS		106	41	0	20	323.0	1457	391	219	211	56	18	10	21	113	16	207	21	2	14	25	.359	0	0-1	1	5.86	5.88

Edgar Gonzalez

Bats: R **Throws:** R **Pos:** PH-47; 2B-15; RF-14; 3B-5; 1B-2; LF-1; DH-1   **Ht:** 6'0" **Wt:** 182 **Born:** 6/14/1978 **Age:** 32

								BATTING													BASERUNNING				AVERAGES		
Year	Team	Lg	G	AB	H	2B	3B	HR	(Hm	Rd)	TB	R	RBI	RC	TBB	IBB	SO	HBP	SH	SF	SB	CS	SB%	GDP	Avg	OBP	Slg
2000	HudVal	A-	41	145	32	4	4	0	(-	-)	44	17	8	13	12	0	32	0	1	0	5	1	.83	3	.221	.280	.303
2000	Princtn	R+	20	63	17	3	3	0	(-	-)	26	6	8	12	13	0	14	1	1	0	4	1	.80	2	.270	.403	.413
2001	HudVal	A-	73	277	92	19	4	9	(-	-)	146	49	34	60	37	6	56	3	2	4	6	3	.67	5	.332	.411	.527
2002	CtnSC	A	134	447	123	28	1	8	(-	-)	177	68	62	73	74	3	75	4	1	7	21	14	.60	14	.275	.378	.396
2003	Bkrsfld	A+	100	349	104	34	3	6	(-	-)	162	51	62	63	45	0	82	5	1	5	8	7	.53	7	.298	.381	.464
2004	Frisco	AA	106	394	114	25	4	8	(-	-)	171	58	55	63	36	0	83	6	1	3	6	2	.75	12	.289	.355	.434
2005	Hrsbrg	AA	99	333	93	24	3	8	(-	-)	147	41	49	54	42	1	74	4	2	6	5	7	.42	6	.279	.361	.441
2005	NewOr	AAA	23	48	17	4	0	0	(-	-)	21	12	4	7	1	0	10	0	1	0	0	0	-	2	.354	.367	.438
2006	Jupiter	A+	21	75	22	8	0	2	(-	-)	36	10	10	11	6	0	18	0	1	1	1	3	.25	1	.293	.341	.480
2006	Carlina	AA	64	210	62	10	3	6	(-	-)	96	19	25	36	24	0	37	3	0	3	6	4	.60	7	.295	.371	.457
2006	Albq	AAA	46	143	56	10	1	5	(-	-)	83	29	36	37	20	1	32	4	1	2	1	1	.50	4	.392	.473	.580
2007	Memp	AAA	126	459	142	34	3	8	(-	-)	206	64	53	81	50	1	69	2	4	2	15	4	.79	13	.309	.378	.449
2008	Portlnd	AAA	27	82	24	1	0	4	(-	-)	37	10	12	14	12	0	12	2	0	1	4	.00	3	.293	.392	.451
2009	Lk Els	A+	5	14	4	1	0	1	(-	-)	8	2	3	2	1	0	6	0	0	0	0	1	.00	1	.286	.333	.571
2009	Portlnd	AAA	6	18	5	0	0	1	(-	-)	8	3	1	4	5	0	3	1	0	0	0	0	-	0	.278	.458	.444
2008	SD	NL	111	325	89	15	0	7	(2	5)	125	38	33	34	25	1	76	2	0	1	1	3	.25	11	.274	.329	.385
2009	SD	NL	82	153	33	8	2	4	(2	2)	57	16	18	12	11	0	36	3	0	2	1	2	.33	5	.216	.278	.373
	2 ML YEARS		193	478	122	23	2	11	(4	7)	182	54	51	46	36	1	112	5	0	3	2	5	.29	16	.255	.312	.381

Enrique Gonzalez

Pitches: R **Bats:** R **Pos:** RP-2   **Ht:** 5'10" **Wt:** 224 **Born:** 7/14/1982 **Age:** 27

			HOW MUCH HE PITCHED						WHAT HE GAVE UP											THE RESULTS						
Year	Team	Lg	G	GS	CG	GF	IP	BFP	H	R	ER	HR	SH	SF	HB	TBB	IBB	SO	WP	Bk	W	L	Pct	Sh	Sv-Op	Hld	ERC	ERA
2009	Pwtckt*	AAA	26	23	0	1	139.0	617	159	85	79	20	1	5	0	53	0	99	4	2	8	11	.421	0	0- -	-	5.14	5.12
2006	Ari	NL	22	18	0	1	106.1	462	114	71	67	14	7	3	4	34	0	66	1	0	3	7	.300	0	0-0	0	4.53	5.67
2007	Ari	NL	1	0	0	1	2.0	11	4	4	3	0	0	0	0	1	0	0	0	0	0	0	-	0	0-0	0	9.72	13.50
2008	SD	NL	4	0	0	3	3.1	15	4	4	4	0	0	0	0	2	0	1	0	0	1	0	1.000	0	0-1	0	5.47	10.80
2009	Bos	AL	2	0	0	2	3.2	18	5	2	2	1	0	0	0	2	0	1	0	0	0	0	-	0	0-0	0	8.17	4.91
	4 ML YEARS		29	18	0	7	115.1	506	127	81	76	15	7	3	4	39	0	68	1	0	4	7	.364	0	0-1	0	4.75	5.93

Gio Gonzalez

Pitches: L **Bats:** R **Pos:** SP-17; RP-3   **Ht:** 5'11" **Wt:** 197 **Born:** 9/19/1985 **Age:** 24

			HOW MUCH HE PITCHED						WHAT HE GAVE UP											THE RESULTS						
Year	Team	Lg	G	GS	CG	GF	IP	BFP	H	R	ER	HR	SH	SF	HB	TBB	IBB	SO	WP	Bk	W	L	Pct	Sh	Sv-Op	Hld	ERC	ERA
2004	Bristol	R+	7	6	0	0	24.0	94	17	8	6	0	0	0	8	0	36	4	1	1	2	.333	0	0- -	-	1.78	2.25
2004	Knapol	A-	6	6	0	0	32.2	147	30	13	11	1	2	1	0	13	0	27	1	1	1	1	.500	0	0- -	-	2.92	3.03
2005	Knapol	A-	11	10	0	0	57.2	231	36	16	12	3	0	1	2	22	0	84	2	3	5	3	.625	0	0- -	-	1.91	1.87
2005	WinSa	A+	13	13	0	0	73.1	297	61	33	29	5	2	1	1	25	0	79	2	3	8	3	.727	0	0- -	-	2.85	3.56
2006	Rdng	AA	27	27	1	0	154.2	684	140	88	80	24	4	5	8	81	2	166	9	2	7	12	.368	0	0- -	-	4.58	4.66
2007	Brhm	AA	27	27	0	0	150.0	611	116	57	53	10	9	5	2	57	1	185	5	2	9	7	.563	0	0- -	-	2.64	3.18
2008	Scrmto	AAA	23	22	1	0	123.0	524	106	65	58	12	3	3	2	61	1	128	5	0	8	7	.533	0	0- -	-	3.75	4.24
2009	Scrmto	AAA	12	12	0	0	61.0	256	42	21	17	5	2	1	3	34	2	71	6	0	4	1	.800	0	0- -	-	3.02	2.51
2008	Oak	AL	10	7	0	3	34.0	163	32	34	29	9	2	1	3	25	1	34	1	0	1	4	.200	0	0-0	0	6.54	7.68
2009	Oak	AL	20	17	0	0	98.2	455	113	68	63	14	2	3	1	56	2	109	2	0	6	7	.462	0	0-0	0	5.96	5.75
	2 ML YEARS		30	24	0	3	132.2	618	145	102	92	23	4	4	4	81	3	143	3	0	7	11	.389	0	0-0	0	6.11	6.24

Mike Gonzalez

Pitches: L **Bats:** R **Pos:** RP-80   **Ht:** 6'2" **Wt:** 213 **Born:** 5/23/1978 **Age:** 32

			HOW MUCH HE PITCHED						WHAT HE GAVE UP											THE RESULTS						
Year	Team	Lg	G	GS	CG	GF	IP	BFP	H	R	ER	HR	SH	SF	HB	TBB	IBB	SO	WP	Bk	W	L	Pct	Sh	Sv-Op	Hld	ERC	ERA
2003	Pit	NL	16	0	0	2	8.1	38	7	7	7	4	1	1	0	6	0	6	1	0	0	1	.000	0	0-0	3	7.18	7.56
2004	Pit	NL	47	0	0	12	43.1	169	32	7	6	2	3	0	1	6	0	55	4	0	3	1	.750	0	1-4	13	1.60	1.25
2005	Pit	NL	51	0	0	15	50.0	212	35	15	15	2	0	2	1	31	2	58	3	0	1	3	.250	0	3-3	15	2.90	2.70
2006	Pit	NL	54	0	0	47	54.0	234	42	13	13	1	3	1	2	31	2	64	0	0	3	4	.429	0	24-24	3	3.00	2.17
2007	Atl	NL	18	0	0	5	17.0	70	15	3	3	0	0	1	0	8	0	13	0	0	2	0	1.000	0	2-5	3	3.13	1.59
2008	Atl	NL	36	0	0	29	33.2	142	26	21	16	6	1	2	1	14	3	44	0	0	3	0	.000	0	14-16	3	3.33	4.28
2009	Atl	NL	80	0	0	29	74.1	315	56	28	20	7	6	1	7	33	8	90	5	0	5	4	.556	0	10-17	17	3.04	2.42
	7 ML YEARS		302	0	0	139	280.2	1180	213	94	80	22	14	8	12	129	15	330	13	0	14	16	.467	0	54-66	56	2.92	2.57

Alex Gordon

Bats: L **Throws:** R **Pos:** 3B-49   **Ht:** 6'1" **Wt:** 220 **Born:** 2/10/1984 **Age:** 26

								BATTING													BASERUNNING				AVERAGES		
Year	Team	Lg	G	AB	H	2B	3B	HR	(Hm	Rd)	TB	R	RBI	RC	TBB	IBB	SO	HBP	SH	SF	SB	CS	SB%	GDP	Avg	OBP	Slg
2009	Royals*	R	4	7	2	0	0	1	(-	-)	5	1	3	3	5	0	3	0	0	1	0	0	-	0	.286	.538	.714
2009	Omha*	AAA	18	67	21	4	1	2	(-	-)	33	17	10	15	13	2	16	3	0	2	0	0	-	0	.313	.435	.493
2009	NWArk*	AA	8	30	11	3	0	2	(-	-)	20	4	10	8	5	1	5	0	0	0	0	0	-	2	.367	.457	.667
2007	KC	AL	151	543	134	36	4	15	(8	7)	223	60	60	69	41	4	137	13	1	2	14	4	.78	12	.247	.314	.411
2008	KC	AL	134	493	128	35	1	16	(9	7)	213	72	59	71	66	5	120	6	1	5	9	2	.82	8	.260	.351	.432
2009	KC	AL	49	164	38	6	0	6	(2	4)	62	28	22	16	21	0	43	2	1	1	5	0	1.00	5	.232	.324	.378
	3 ML YEARS		334	1200	300	77	5	37	(19	18)	498	160	141	156	128	9	300	21	3	8	28	6	.82	25	.250	.331	.415

Tom Gordon

Pitches: R Bats: R Pos: RP-3   Ht: 5'10" Wt: 200 Born: 11/18/1967 Age: 42

Year	Team	Lg	G	GS	CG	GF	IP	BFP	H	R	ER	HR	SH	SF	HB	TBB	IBB	SO	WP	Bk	W	L	Pct	Sh	Sv-Op	Hld	ERC	ERA
2009	Reno*	AAA	11	1	0	2	9.2	59	19	14	12	0	3	0	0	14	0	4	2	0	0	0	-	0	0-0	2	14.57	11.17
2009	Visalia*	A+	1	0	0	0	1.0	6	1	1	1	0	0	0	0	2	0	1	0	0	0	0	-	0	0- -		9.51	9.00
1988	KC	AL	5	2	0	0	15.2	67	16	9	9	1	0	0	0	7	0	18	0	0	0	2	.000	0	0-0	2	4.22	5.17
1989	KC	AL	49	16	1	16	163.0	677	122	67	66	10	4	4	1	86	4	153	12	0	17	9	.654	1	1-7	3	2.97	3.64
1990	KC	AL	32	32	6	0	195.1	858	192	99	81	17	8	2	3	99	1	175	11	0	12	11	.522	1	0-0	0	4.37	3.73
1991	KC	AL	45	14	1	11	158.0	684	129	76	68	16	5	3	4	87	6	167	5	0	9	14	.391	0	1-4	4	3.67	3.87
1992	KC	AL	40	11	0	13	117.2	516	116	67	60	9	2	6	4	55	4	98	5	2	6	10	.375	0	0-2	0	4.17	4.59
1993	KC	AL	48	14	2	18	155.2	651	125	65	62	11	6	6	1	77	5	143	17	0	12	6	.667	0	1-6	2	3.18	3.58
1994	KC	AL	24	24	0	0	155.1	675	136	79	75	15	3	8	3	87	3	120	12	1	11	7	.611	0	0-0	0	4.04	4.35
1995	KC	AL	31	31	2	0	189.0	843	204	110	93	12	7	11	4	89	4	119	9	0	12	12	.500	0	0-0	0	4.59	4.43
1996	Bos	AL	34	34	4	0	215.2	998	249	143	134	28	2	11	4	105	5	171	6	1	12	9	.571	1	0-0	0	5.50	5.59
1997	Bos	AL	42	25	2	16	182.2	774	155	85	76	10	3	4	3	78	1	159	5	0	6	10	.375	1	11-13	0	3.08	3.74
1998	Bos	AL	73	0	0	69	79.1	317	55	24	24	2	2	2	0	25	1	78	9	0	7	4	.636	0	46-47	0	1.72	2.72
1999	Bos	AL	21	0	0	15	17.2	82	17	11	11	2	0	0	1	12	2	24	0	0	0	2	.000	0	11-13	1	5.04	5.60
2001	ChC	NL	47	0	0	40	45.1	187	32	18	17	4	0	0	1	16	1	67	2	0	1	2	.333	0	27-31	0	2.27	3.38
2002	2 Tms	NL	34	0	0	10	42.2	181	42	19	16	3	3	0	1	16	3	48	0	0	1	3	.250	0	0-0	6	3.71	3.38
2003	CWS	AL	66	0	0	35	74.0	310	57	29	26	4	4	3	4	31	3	91	5	0	7	6	.538	0	12-17	7	2.74	3.16
2004	NYY	AL	80	0	0	15	89.2	342	56	23	22	5	5	2	1	23	5	96	3	0	9	4	.692	0	4-10	36	1.50	2.21
2005	NYY	AL	79	0	0	17	80.2	324	59	25	23	8	1	3	0	29	4	69	1	1	5	4	.556	0	2-9	33	2.45	2.57
2006	Phl	NL	59	0	0	53	59.1	253	53	23	22	9	2	1	1	22	4	68	3	0	3	4	.429	0	34-39	0	3.62	3.34
2007	Phl	NL	44	0	0	11	40.0	170	40	21	21	7	1	2	2	13	0	32	1	0	3	2	.600	0	6-11	14	4.55	4.73
2008	Phl	NL	34	0	0	7	29.2	139	31	19	17	3	0	1	0	17	1	26	4	0	5	4	.556	0	2-3	14	4.77	5.16
2009	Ari	NL	3	0	0	1	1.2	10	3	4	4	0	0	0	0	3	0	0	2	0	0	1	.000	0	0-1	0	15.74	21.60
02	ChC	NL	19	0	0	7	23.2	104	27	12	9	1	1	0	1	10	1	31	0	0	1	1	.500	0	0-0	2	4.75	3.42
02	Hou	NL	15	0	0	3	19.0	77	15	7	7	2	2	0	0	6	2	17	0	0	0	2	.000	0	0-0	4	2.53	3.32
Postseason			21	0	0	6	21.2	100	24	18	17	6	0	1	2	9	1	19	3	0	0	1	.000	0	0-1	6	6.29	7.06
21 ML YEARS			890	203	19	217	2100.0	9080	1855	1010	927	178	58	69	38	977	57	1928	112	5	138	126	.523	4	168-213	122	3.05	3.90

Reid Gorecki

Bats: R Throws: R Pos: LF-22; PR-8; CF-5; RF-1   Ht: 6'1" Wt: 200 Born: 12/22/1980 Age: 29

Year	Team	Lg	G	AB	H	2B	3B	HR	(Hm	Rd)	TB	R	RBI	RC	TBB	IBB	SO	HBP	SH	SF	SB	CS	SB%	GDP	Avg	OBP	Slg
2002	NewJrs	A-	73	274	77	8	13	8	(-	-)	135	55	52	45	20	0	57	2	1	7	22	11	.67	2	.281	.327	.493
2003	Peoria	A	128	480	128	19	8	15	(-	-)	208	77	61	74	51	4	90	3	4	4	23	11	.68	5	.267	.338	.433
2004	PlmBh	A+	118	440	122	23	3	8	(-	-)	175	74	47	65	46	3	80	2	7	8	23	9	.72	9	.277	.343	.398
2004	Tenn	AA	7	25	8	3	0	0	(-	-)	11	1	1	4	2	0	3	0	0	0	1	0	1.00	4	.320	.370	.440
2005	Sprgfld	AA	46	159	29	6	0	3	(-	-)	44	12	16	11	18	0	38	0	4	1	1	3	.25	2	.182	.264	.277
2005	PlmBh	A+	64	234	67	18	2	6	(-	-)	107	38	41	44	32	1	55	3	2	4	24	7	.77	5	.286	.374	.457
2006	Sprgfld	AA	85	327	82	21	2	16	(-	-)	155	56	51	54	42	3	80	3	7	2	17	9	.65	9	.251	.340	.474
2006	Memp	AAA	21	74	12	4	0	1	(-	-)	19	7	9	7	9	0	21	1	1	2	3	3	.50	1	.162	.256	.257
2007	Sprgfld	AA	24	76	18	1	0	0	(-	-)	19	9	8	7	11	0	20	0	0	2	3	2	.60	2	.237	.333	.250
2007	Cards	R	10	32	10	5	0	0	(-	-)	15	7	5	6	4	0	4	0	0	0	4	0	1.00	1	.313	.389	.460
2008	Missi	AA	63	240	70	9	0	10	(-	-)	109	51	43	44	31	2	46	3	1	2	16	4	.80	8	.292	.377	.454
2008	Rchmd	AAA	4	13	7	0	0	0	(-	-)	7	2	1	3	2	0	4	0	0	0	1	1	.50	0	.538	.600	.538
2009	Gwnntt	AAA	107	371	106	27	6	9	(-	-)	172	57	49	62	34	2	73	5	3	3	14	7	.67	6	.286	.351	.464
2009	All	NL	31	25	5	0	0	0	(0	0)	5	6	3	2	1	0	12	0	0	1	1	0	1.00	0	.200	.222	.200

Tom Gorzelanny

Pitches: L Bats: L Pos: RP-15; SP-7   Ht: 6'2" Wt: 202 Born: 7/12/1982 Age: 27

Year	Team	Lg	G	GS	CG	GF	IP	BFP	H	R	ER	HR	SH	SF	HB	TBB	IBB	SO	WP	Bk	W	L	Pct	Sh	Sv-Op	Hld	ERC	ERA
2009	Indy*	AAA	15	15	0	0	87.0	358	73	31	24	3	2	2	4	30	0	85	3	0	4	3	.571	0	0- -	-	2.78	2.48
2005	Pit	NL	3	1	0	0	6.0	32	10	8	8	1	1	0	0	3	0	3	0	0	0	1	.000	0	0-0	0	8.76	12.00
2006	Pit	NL	11	11	0	0	61.2	267	50	29	26	3	7	4	4	31	2	40	3	0	2	5	.286	0	0-0	0	3.23	3.79
2007	Pit	NL	32	32	1	0	201.2	874	214	90	87	18	3	9	11	68	3	135	5	1	14	10	.583	1	0-0	0	4.31	3.88
2008	Pit	NL	21	21	0	0	105.1	490	120	79	78	20	3	6	1	70	0	67	5	1	6	9	.400	0	0-0	0	6.86	6.66
2009	2 Tms	NL	22	7	0	2	47.0	204	45	30	29	6	3	3	1	17	0	47	1	0	7	3	.700	0	0-1	2	3.88	5.55
09	Pit	NL	9	0	0	2	8.2	36	6	5	5	0	1	0	0	4	0	7	0	0	3	1	.750	0	0-1	1	2.02	5.19
09	ChC	NL	13	7	0	0	38.1	168	39	25	24	6	2	3	1	13	0	40	1	0	4	2	.667	0	0-0	1	4.33	5.63
5 ML YEARS			89	72	1	2	421.2	1867	439	236	228	48	17	22	17	189	5	292	14	2	29	28	.509	1	0-1	2	4.75	4.87

Mike Gosling

Pitches: L Bats: L Pos: RP-15   Ht: 6'2" Wt: 210 Born: 9/23/1980 Age: 29

Year	Team	Lg	G	GS	CG	GF	IP	BFP	H	R	ER	HR	SH	SF	HB	TBB	IBB	SO	WP	Bk	W	l	Pct	Sh	Sv-Op	Hld	ERC	ERA
2009	Roch*	AAA	21	0	0	9	35.0	153	33	17	17	2	0	0	2	17	0	43	1	0	7	1	.875	0	1- -	-	4.02	4.37
2009	Clmbs*	AAA	8	4	0	1	32.1	141	45	21	19	5	2	0	0	7	0	30	0	0	0	3	.000	0	0- -	-	6.26	5.29
2004	Ari	NL	6	4	0	0	25.1	112	26	13	13	5	2	0	2	13	1	14	2	0	1	1	.500	0	0-0	0	6.83	4.62
2005	Ari	NL	13	5	0	5	32.1	154	40	16	16	2	2	0	0	19	2	14	0	0	0	3	.000	0	0-0	0	5.74	4.45
2006	Cin	NL	1	0	0	0	1.1	7	1	2	2	1	0	0	1	1	0	1	0	0	0	0	-	0	0-0	0	12.98	13.50
2007	Cin	NL	23	0	0	7	33.0	164	42	22	18	5	2	1	1	28	8	32	1	0	2	0	1.000	0	0-1	0	7.81	4.91
2009	Cle	AL	15	0	0	7	25.0	114	30	15	14	5	0	0	0	11	1	13	0	0	0	0	-	0	0-0	0	6.09	5.04
5 ML YEARS			58	9	0	19	117.0	551	139	72	63	18	6	1	4	72	12	74	3	0	3	4	.429	0	0-1	0	6.50	4.85

John Grabow

Pitches: L Bats: L Pos: RP-75   Ht: 6'2" Wt: 205 Born: 11/4/1978 Age: 31

			HOW MUCH HE PITCHED						WHAT HE GAVE UP												THE RESULTS							
Year	Team	Lg	G	GS	CG	GF	IP	BFP	H	R	ER	HR	SH	SF	HB	TBB	IBB	SO	WP	Bk	W	L	Pct	Sh	Sv-Op	Hld	ERC	ERA
2003	Pit	NL	5	0	0	1	5.0	22	6	3	2	0	0	0	0	0	0	9	0	0	0	0	-	0	0-0	0	2.73	3.60
2004	Pit	NL	68	0	0	10	61.2	286	81	39	35	8	6	1	0	28	7	64	5	0	2	5	.286	0	1-7	11	6.21	5.11
2005	Pit	NL	63	0	0	8	52.0	222	46	31	28	6	2	0	2	25	2	42	1	0	2	3	.400	0	0-1	14	4.00	4.85
2006	Pit	NL	72	0	0	17	69.2	303	68	34	32	7	5	3	3	30	3	66	0	0	4	2	.667	0	0-2	11	4.17	4.13
2007	Pit	NL	63	0	0	14	51.2	228	56	27	26	6	4	2	1	19	2	42	3	0	3	2	.600	0	1-2	8	4.51	4.53
2008	Pit	NL	74	0	0	18	76.0	322	60	25	24	9	3	2	1	37	2	62	4	2	3	3	.667	0	4-8	16	3.37	2.84
2009	2 Tms	NL	75	0	0	12	72.1	314	62	28	27	5	1	4	3	40	3	57	1	0	3	0	1.000	0	0-2	23	3.76	3.36
09	Pit	NL	45	0	0	4	47.1	209	43	19	18	4	1	3	2	28	2	41	0	0	3	0	1.000	0	0-2	16	4.32	3.42
09	ChC	NL	30	0	0	8	25.0	105	19	9	9	1	0	1	1	12	1	16	1	0	0	0	-	0	0-0	7	2.77	3.24
7 ML YEARS			420	0	0	80	388.1	1697	379	187	174	41	21	12	10	179	19	342	14	2	20	15	.571	0	6-22	83	4.24	4.03

Tony Graffanino

Bats: R Throws: R Pos: 2B-4; 3B-3; PR-1   Ht: 6'1" Wt: 190 Born: 6/6/1972 Age: 38

			BATTING																			BASERUNNING				AVERAGES		
Year	Team	Lg	G	AB	H	2B	3B	HR	(Hm	Rd)	TB	R	RBI	RC	TBB	IBB	SO	HBP	SH	SF	SB	CS	SB%	GDP	Avg	OBP	Slg
2009	Clmbs*	AAA	69	261	69	24	0	6	(-	-)	111	39	40	36	17	0	46	3	0	5	3	0	1.00	0	.264	.311	.425
1996	Atl	NL	22	46	8	1	1	0	(0	0)	11	7	2	3	4	0	13	1	0	1	0	0	-	0	.174	.250	.239
1997	Atl	NL	104	186	48	9	1	8	(5	3)	83	33	20	29	26	1	46	1	3	5	6	4	.60	3	.258	.344	.446
1998	Atl	NL	105	289	61	14	1	5	(3	2)	92	32	22	22	24	0	68	2	1	1	1	4	.20	7	.211	.275	.318
1999	TB	AL	39	130	41	9	4	2	(0	2)	64	20	19	23	9	0	22	1	2	0	3	2	.60	1	.315	.364	.492
2000	2 Tms	AL	70	168	46	6	1	2	(1	1)	60	33	17	23	22	0	27	2	1	1	7	4	.64	2	.274	.363	.357
2001	CWS	AL	74	145	44	9	0	2	(1	1)	59	23	15	22	16	0	29	1	4	3	4	1	.80	4	.303	.370	.407
2002	CWS	AL	70	229	60	12	4	6	(4	2)	98	35	31	35	22	1	38	2	4	2	2	1	.67	2	.262	.329	.428
2003	CWS	AL	90	250	65	15	3	7	(4	3)	107	51	23	36	24	1	37	3	3	1	8	0	1.00	1	.260	.331	.428
2004	KC	AL	75	278	73	11	0	3	(0	3)	93	37	26	35	27	0	38	3	4	2	10	2	.83	5	.263	.332	.335
2005	2 Tms	AL	110	379	117	17	3	7	(4	3)	161	68	38	58	31	2	51	4	2	1	7	2	.78	14	.309	.366	.425
2006	2 Tms	AL	129	456	125	33	3	7	(3	4)	185	68	59	67	45	1	68	5	4	1	5	4	.56	10	.274	.345	.406
2007	Mil	NL	86	231	55	8	0	9	(7	2)	90	34	30	24	24	6	44	3	0	2	0	1	.00	7	.238	.315	.390
2009	Cle	AL	7	23	3	1	0	0	(0	0)	4	1	0	0	1	0	5	0	0	0	0	0	-	1	.130	.167	.174
00	TB	AL	13	20	6	1	0	0	(0	0)	7	8	1	2	1	0	2	1	0	0	0	0	-	1	.300	.364	.350
00	CWS	AL	57	148	40	5	1	2	(1	1)	53	25	16	21	21	0	25	1	1	1	7	4	.64	1	.270	.363	.358
05	KC	AL	59	191	57	5	2	3	(1	2)	75	29	18	32	22	1	28	2	2	0	3	1	.75	6	.298	.377	.393
05	Bos	AL	51	188	60	12	1	4	(3	1)	86	39	20	26	9	1	23	2	0	1	4	1	.80	8	.319	.355	.457
06	KC	AL	69	220	59	16	0	5	(2	3)	90	34	32	31	25	1	31	1	4	0	3	4	.43	4	.268	.346	.405
06	Mil	NL	60	236	66	17	3	2	(1	1)	95	34	27	36	20	0	37	4	0	1	2	0	1.00	6	.280	.345	.403
Postseason			15	26	6	4	0	0	(0	0)	10	3	1	4	4	1	5	0	1	0	0	0	-	1	.231	.333	.385
13 ML YEARS			981	2810	746	145	21	58	(32	26)	1107	442	302	377	275	12	486	28	28	20	53	25	.68	57	.265	.335	.394

Curtis Granderson

Bats: L Throws: R Pos: CF-160; PH-1; PR-1   Ht: 6'1" Wt: 185 Born: 3/16/1981 Age: 29

			BATTING																			BASERUNNING				AVERAGES		
Year	Team	Lg	G	AB	H	2B	3B	HR	(Hm	Rd)	TB	R	RBI	RC	TBB	IBB	SO	HBP	SH	SF	SB	CS	SB%	GDP	Avg	OBP	Slg
2004	Det	AL	9	25	6	1	1	0	(0	0)	9	2	0	2	3	0	8	0	0	0	0	0	-	-	.240	.321	.360
2005	Det	AL	47	162	44	6	3	8	(5	3)	80	18	20	26	10	0	43	0	2	0	1	1	.50	2	.272	.314	.494
2006	Det	AL	159	596	155	31	9	19	(7	12)	261	90	68	89	66	0	174	4	7	6	8	5	.62	4	.260	.335	.438
2007	Det	AL	158	612	185	38	23	23	(10	13)	338	122	74	106	52	3	141	5	5	2	26	1	.96	3	.302	.361	.552
2008	Det	AL	141	553	155	26	13	22	(11	11)	273	112	66	100	71	1	111	3	1	1	12	4	.75	7	.280	.365	.494
2009	Det	AL	160	631	157	23	8	30	(10	20)	286	91	71	92	72	4	141	2	3	2	20	6	.77	1	.249	.327	.453
Postseason			13	53	12	3	1	3	(1	2)	26	8	7	8	5	0	10	0	0	1	2	0	1.00	1	.226	.288	.491
6 ML YEARS			674	2579	702	125	57	102	(43	59)	1247	435	299	415	274	8	618	14	18	11	67	17	.80	18	.272	.344	.484

Jeff Gray

Pitches: R Bats: R Pos: RP-24   Ht: 6'3" Wt: 196 Born: 11/19/1981 Age: 28

			HOW MUCH HE PITCHED						WHAT HE GAVE UP												THE RESULTS							
Year	Team	Lg	G	GS	CG	GF	IP	BFP	H	R	ER	HR	SH	SF	HB	TBB	IBB	SO	WP	Bk	W	L	Pct	Sh	Sv-Op	Hld	ERC	ERA
2004	As	R	14	2	0	2	38.0	152	30	14	8	0	1	1	5	3	0	32	4	1	3	0	1.000	0	0--	-	1.69	1.89
2005	Vancvr	A-	12	11	0	0	46.2	183	33	16	13	0	4	0	1	5	0	24	4	1	4	2	.667	0	0--	-	1.24	2.51
2006	Kane	A	22	11	0	2	78.1	322	77	47	41	2	2	1	7	19	0	62	7	0	5	5	.500	0	0--	-	3.32	4.71
2006	Stcktn	A+	19	0	0	6	31.2	129	32	15	12	0	2	2	0	6	0	26	0	0	1	1	.500	0	1--	-	2.71	3.41
2007	Mdland	AA	8	0	0	8	12.1	44	7	1	0	0	1	0	1	2	0	12	0	0	2	0	1.000	0	3--	-	1.18	0.00
2007	Scrmto	AAA	46	0	0	31	55.0	239	58	27	25	2	1	1	3	22	4	45	2	2	2	4	.333	0	12--	-	4.07	4.09
2008	Scrmto	AAA	54	0	0	23	67.2	306	86	33	33	9	3	1	4	23	4	50	6	0	2	7	.222	0	4--	-	5.87	4.39
2009	Scrmto	AAA	37	0	0	31	41.0	158	30	8	7	2	0	0	2	6	1	22	1	0	2	2	.500	0	16--	-	1.68	1.54
2008	Oak	AL	5	0	0	2	4.2	24	8	4	4	1	0	0	1	0	4	0	0	0	0	0	-	0	0-0	-	9.48	7.71
2009	Oak	AL	24	0	0	11	26.1	116	30	12	11	3	2	0	2	4	1	19	0	0	0	1	.000	0	0-0	1	4.07	3.76
2 ML YEARS			29	0	0	13	31.0	140	38	16	15	4	2	0	3	5	1	23	0	0	0	1	.000	0	0-0	1	4.79	4.35

Andy Green

Bats: R Throws: R Pos: PH-4; 2B-1; 3B-1   Ht: 5'10" Wt: 178 Born: 7/7/1977 Age: 32

								BATTING											BASERUNNING				AVERAGES		
Year	Team	Lg	G	AB	H	2B	3B	HR	(Hm | Rd)	TB	R	RBI	RC	TBB	IBB	SO	HBP	SH	SF	SB	CS	SB%	GDP	Avg	OBP	Slg
2009	Buffalo*	AAA	50	174	45	7	1	4	(- | -)	66	24	20	23	18	0	32	1	5	1	3	0	1.00	2	.259	.330	.379
2009	Mets*	R	2	6	1	0	0	0	(- | -)	1	1	2	0	3	0	1	0	0	0	0	0	-	0	.167	.444	.167
2009	Bklyn*	A-	7	23	7	0	0	1	(- | -)	10	4	2	4	5	0	2	0	0	0	1	1	.50	0	.304	.429	.435
2004	Ari	NL	46	109	22	2	1	1	(1 | 0)	29	13	4	7	5	0	17	1	3	1	1	1	.50	2	.202	.241	.266
2005	Ari	NL	17	31	7	1	0	0	(0 | 0)	8	5	2	3	7	0	3	0	0	1	0	0	-	1	.226	.359	.258
2006	Ari	NL	73	86	16	4	0	1	(1 | 0)	23	15	6	7	13	0	20	0	3	0	1	0	1.00	0	.186	.293	.267
2009	NYM	NL	4	4	1	0	0	0	(0 | 0)	1	0	0	0	1	0	1	0	0	0	0	0	-	0	.250	.400	.250
4 ML YEARS			140	230	46	7	1	2	(2 | 0)	61	33	12	17	26	0	41	1	6	2	2	1	.67	3	.200	.282	.265

Nick Green

Bats: R Throws: R Pos: SS-81; 3B-9; PR-9; 2B-7; LF-3; DH-2; PH-2   Ht: 6'0" Wt: 178 Born: 9/10/1978 Age: 31

								BATTING											BASERUNNING				AVERAGES		
Year	Team	Lg	G	AB	H	2B	3B	HR	(Hm | Rd)	TB	R	RBI	RC	TBB	IBB	SO	HBP	SH	SF	SB	CS	SB%	GDP	Avg	OBP	Slg
2004	Atl	NL	95	264	72	15	3	3	(3 | 0)	102	40	26	36	12	1	63	4	8	2	1	2	.33	0	.273	.312	.386
2005	TB	AL	111	318	76	15	2	5	(2 | 3)	110	53	29	38	33	0	86	11	10	3	3	1	.75	5	.239	.329	.346
2006	2 Tms	AL	63	114	21	5	0	2	(1 | 1)	32	12	4	10	11	0	40	1	1	0	1	4	.20	2	.184	.262	.281
2007	Sea	AL	6	7	0	0	0	0	(0 | 0)	0	0	0	0	0	0	3	0	0	0	0	0	-	0	.000	.000	.000
2009	Bos	AL	103	276	65	18	0	6	(4 | 2)	101	35	35	28	20	1	69	8	2	3	1	4	.20	10	.236	.303	.366
06	TB	AL	17	39	3	0	0	0	(0 | 0)	3	4	0	0	6	0	11	0	0	0	0	3	.00	2	.077	.200	.077
06	NYY	AL	46	75	18	5	0	2	(1 | 1)	29	8	4	10	5	0	29	1	1	0	1	1	.50	0	.240	.296	.387
Postseason			2	0	0	0	0	0	(0 | 0)	0	0	0	0	0	0	0	0	0	0	0	0	-	0	-	-	-
5 ML YEARS			378	979	234	53	5	16	(10 | 6)	345	140	94	112	76	2	261	24	21	8	6	11	.35	17	.239	.307	.352

Sean Green

Pitches: R Bats: R Pos: RP-79   Ht: 6'6" Wt: 227 Born: 4/20/1979 Age: 31

			HOW MUCH HE PITCHED						WHAT HE GAVE UP										THE RESULTS						
Year	Team	Lg	G	GS	CG	GF	IP	BFP	H	R	ER	HR	SH	SF	HB	TBB	IBB	SO	WP	Bk	W	L	Pct	Sh	Sv-Op	Hld	ERC	ERA
2006	Sea	AL	24	0	0	11	32.0	139	34	16	16	2	1	1	2	13	1	15	2	0	0	0	-	0	0-1	3	4.47	4.50
2007	Sea	AL	64	0	0	10	68.0	304	77	31	29	2	1	6	0	34	0	93	2	0	5	2	.714	0	0-3	13	4.81	3.84
2008	Sea	AL	72	0	0	13	79.0	358	90	47	41	3	3	7	6	36	1	62	5	1	4	5	.444	0	1-4	17	4.09	4.67
2009	NYM	NL	79	0	0	19	69.2	316	64	37	35	5	4	0	9	36	5	54	8	1	1	4	.200	0	1-3	14	4.17	4.52
4 ML YEARS			239	0	0	53	248.2	1117	265	131	121	12	12	13	20	119	13	184	17	2	10	11	.476	0	2-11	47	4.35	4.38

Khalil Greene

Bats: R Throws: R Pos: PH-38; SS-30; 3B-16   Ht: 5'11" Wt: 186 Born: 10/21/1979 Age: 30

								BATTING											BASERUNNING				AVERAGES		
Year	Team	Lg	G	AB	H	2B	3B	HR	(Hm | Rd)	TB	R	RBI	RC	TBB	IBB	SO	HBP	SH	SF	SB	CS	SB%	GDP	Avg	OBP	Slg
2009	Memp*	AAA	15	55	19	3	0	4	(- | -)	34	9	10	11	2	0	4	0	0	0	0	0	-	1	.345	.368	.618
2009	Sprgfld*	AA	3	14	2	0	0	1	(- | -)	5	1	1	0	0	0	4	0	0	0	0	0	-	0	.143	.143	.357
2003	SD	NL	20	65	14	4	1	2	(0 | 2)	26	8	6	4	4	0	19	1	0	0	0	1	.00	3	.215	.271	.400
2004	SD	NL	139	484	132	31	4	15	(3	12)	216	67	65	73	53	10	94	8	1	8	2	.07	9	.273	.349	.446
2005	SD	NL	121	436	109	30	2	15	(6 | 9)	188	51	70	58	25	3	93	6	3	6	5	0	1.00	8	.250	.296	.431
2006	SD	NL	122	412	101	26	2	15	(6 | 9)	176	56	55	48	39	0	87	7	0	2	5	1	.83	15	.245	.320	.427
2007	SD	NL	153	611	155	44	3	27	(12 | 15)	286	80	97	77	32	3	128	5	0	11	4	0	1.00	12	.254	.291	.468
2008	SD	NL	105	389	83	15	2	10	(7 | 3)	132	30	35	26	22	1	100	5	0	7	5	1	.83	7	.213	.260	.339
2009	StL	NL	77	170	34	7	0	6	(1 | 5)	59	21	24	19	15	1	35	3	2	3	2	1	.67	5	.200	.272	.347
Postseason			6	14	4	2	0	0	(0 | 0)	6	2	1	1	1	0	4	0	0	1	0	0	-	0	.286	.313	.429
7 ML YEARS			737	2567	628	157	14	90	(35 | 55)	1083	322	352	305	190	18	556	35	6	37	25	6	.81	59	.245	.302	.422

Tyler Greene

Bats: R Throws: R Pos: SS-30; 3B-11; 2B-7; PH-7; PR-3; 1B-1; CF-1   Ht: 6'2" Wt: 190 Born: 8/17/1983 Age: 26

								BATTING											BASERUNNING				AVERAGES		
Year	Team	Lg	G	AB	H	2B	3B	HR	(Hm | Rd)	TB	R	RBI	RC	TBB	IBB	SO	HBP	SH	SF	SB	CS	SB%	GDP	Avg	OBP	Slg
2005	NewJrs	A-	35	138	36	12	0	1	(- | -)	51	28	18	21	15	1	37	5	0	1	13	1	.93	7	.261	.352	.370
2005	PlmBh	A+	20	85	23	4	0	2	(- | -)	33	17	5	12	5	0	28	2	0	0	6	0	1.00	1	.271	.326	.388
2006	PlmBh	A+	71	268	60	10	1	5	(- | -)	87	38	19	31	29	0	90	4	1	1	22	3	.88	7	.224	.308	.325
2006	QuadC	A	59	223	64	8	3	15	(- | -)	123	42	47	48	20	1	65	12	0	1	11	0	1.00	6	.287	.375	.552
2007	Sprgfld	AA	65	221	54	17	2	8	(- | -)	99	41	25	32	16	2	62	5	4	1	10	2	.83	3	.244	.309	.448
2008	Sprgfld	AA	97	374	97	15	4	16	(- | -)	168	62	41	53	22	1	99	5	4	3	14	6	.70	5	.259	.307	.449
2008	Memp	AAA	30	111	26	7	0	0	(- | -)	33	17	7	13	11	0	35	4	2	0	6	0	1.00	1	.234	.325	.297
2009	Memp	AAA	89	340	99	10	5	15	(- | -)	164	70	42	66	38	1	86	5	3	2	31	3	.91	7	.291	.369	.482
2009	StL	NL	48	108	24	5	0	2	(1 | 1)	35	9	7	6	4	0	32	3	1	0	3	0	1.00	2	.222	.270	.324

Luke Gregerson

Pitches: R Bats: L Pos: RP-72   Ht: 6'3" Wt: 200 Born: 5/14/1984 Age: 26

			HOW MUCH HE PITCHED						WHAT HE GAVE UP										THE RESULTS						
Year	Team	Lg	G	GS	CG	GF	IP	BFP	H	R	ER	HR	SH	SF	HB	TBB	IBB	SO	WP	Bk	W	L	Pct	Sh	Sv-Op	Hld	ERC	ERA
2006	JhsCty	R+	15	0	0	7	16.1	70	14	10	7	0	0	0	1	6	0	24	4	2	0	1	.000	0	5- -	-	2.67	3.86
2006	StCol	A-	12	0	0	10	15.2	66	9	5	3	0	1	1	0	9	0	22	5	0	6	1	.857	0	4- -	-	1.80	1.72

			HOW MUCH HE PITCHED							WHAT HE GAVE UP												THE RESULTS							
Year	Team	Lg	G	GS	CG	GF	IP	BFP	H	R	ER	HR	SH	SF	HB	TBB	IBB	SO	WP	Bk	W	L	Pct	Sh	Sv-Op	Hld	ERC	ERA
2007	PlmBh	A+	53	0	0	43	64.0	251	42	14	14	0	5	2	1	20	3	69	5	1	3	4	.429	0	29--	-	1.51	1.97
2007	Sprgfld	AA	1	0	0	1	1.0	4	1	0	0	0	0	0	0	0	0	3	0	0	0	0	-	0	0--	-	1.95	0.00
2008	Sprgfld	AA	57	0	0	29	75.1	312	62	32	28	6	3	0	3	26	5	78	5	1	7	6	.538	0	10--	-	2.83	3.35
2009	SD	NL	72	0	0	7	75.0	318	62	29	27	3	3	1	3	31	9	93	4	0	2	4	.333	0	1-7	27	2.72	3.24

Kevin Gregg

Pitches: R **Bats:** R **Pos:** RP-72   **Ht:** 6'6" **Wt:** 238 **Born:** 6/20/1978 **Age:** 32

			HOW MUCH HE PITCHED							WHAT HE GAVE UP												THE RESULTS							
Year	Team	Lg	G	GS	CG	GF	IP	BFP	H	R	ER	HR	SH	SF	HB	TBB	IBB	SO	WP	Bk	W	L	Pct	Sh	Sv-Op	Hld	ERC	ERA
2003	LAA	AL	5	3	0	0	24.2	97	18	9	9	3	0	0	1	8	0	14	0	0	2	0	1.000	0	0-0	0	2.74	3.28
2004	LAA	AL	55	0	0	23	87.2	377	86	43	41	6	4	5	3	28	3	84	13	1	5	2	.714	0	1-2	3	3.47	4.21
2005	LAA	AL	33	2	0	9	64.1	290	70	37	36	8	1	1	3	29	2	52	5	0	1	2	.333	0	0-1	1	5.08	5.04
2006	LAA	AL	32	3	0	12	78.1	341	88	41	36	10	0	3	2	21	0	71	6	0	3	4	.429	0	0-0	0	4.51	4.14
2007	Fla	NL	74	0	0	55	84.0	355	63	34	33	7	3	0	6	40	1	87	6	0	0	5	.000	0	32-36	6	3.15	3.54
2008	Fla	NL	72	0	0	59	68.2	296	51	30	26	3	3	1	4	37	4	58	7	0	7	8	.467	0	29-38	4	2.90	3.41
2009	ChC	NL	72	0	0	51	68.2	298	60	38	36	13	0	3	3	30	2	71	7	0	5	6	.455	0	23-30	1	4.19	4.72
Postseason			2	0	0	0	4.0	18	4	0	0	0	0	0	0	2	0	3	1	0	0	0	-	0	0-0	0	3.63	0.00
7 ML YEARS			343	8	0	209	476.1	2054	436	232	217	50	11	13	22	193	12	437	44	1	23	27	.460	0	85-107	15	3.77	4.10

Zack Greinke

Pitches: R **Bats:** R **Pos:** SP-33   **Ht:** 6'2" **Wt:** 192 **Born:** 10/21/1983 **Age:** 26

			HOW MUCH HE PITCHED							WHAT HE GAVE UP												THE RESULTS							
Year	Team	Lg	G	GS	CG	GF	IP	BFP	H	R	ER	HR	SH	SF	HB	TBB	IBB	SO	WP	Bk	W	L	Pct	Sh	Sv-Op	Hld	ERC	ERA
2004	KC	AL	24	24	0	0	145.0	599	143	64	64	26	3	2	8	26	3	100	1	1	8	11	.421	0	0-0	0	3.85	3.97
2005	KC	AL	33	33	2	0	183.0	829	233	125	118	23	4	4	13	53	0	114	4	2	5	17	.227	0	0-0	0	5.71	5.80
2006	KC	AL	3	0	0	1	6.1	28	7	3	3	1	0	0	0	3	2	5	0	0	1	0	1.000	0	0-0	0	4.93	4.26
2007	KC	AL	52	14	0	7	122.0	507	122	52	50	12	3	4	3	36	5	106	3	1	7	7	.500	0	1-1	12	3.77	3.69
2008	KC	AL	32	32	1	0	202.1	851	202	87	78	21	2	4	4	56	1	183	8	1	13	10	.565	0	0-0	0	3.68	3.47
2009	KC	AL	33	33	6	0	229.1	915	195	64	55	11	8	3	4	51	0	242	5	0	16	8	.667	3	0-0	0	**2.39**	**2.16**
6 ML YEARS			177	136	9	8	888.0	3729	902	395	368	94	20	17	32	225	11	750	21	5	50	53	.485	3	1-1	12	3.77	3.73

Ken Griffey Jr.

Bats: L **Throws:** L **Pos:** DH-94; PH-15; LF-8; RF-3   **Ht:** 6'3" **Wt:** 230 **Born:** 11/21/1969 **Age:** 40

			BATTING																		BASERUNNING				AVERAGES		
Year	Team	Lg	G	AB	H	2B	3B	HR	(Hm	Rd)	TB	R	RBI	RC	TBB	IBB	SO	HBP	SH	SF	SB	CS	SB%	GDP	Avg	OBP	Slg
1989	Sea	AL	127	455	120	23	0	16	(10	6)	191	61	61	64	44	8	83	2	1	4	16	7	.70	4	.264	.329	.420
1990	Sea	AL	155	597	179	28	7	22	(8	14)	287	91	80	101	63	12	81	2	0	4	16	11	.59	12	.300	.366	.481
1991	Sea	AL	154	548	179	42	1	22	(16	6)	289	76	100	112	71	21	82	1	4	9	18	6	.75	10	.327	.399	.527
1992	Sea	AL	142	565	174	39	4	27	(16	11)	302	83	103	102	44	15	67	5	0	3	10	5	.67	15	.308	.361	.535
1993	Sea	AL	156	582	180	38	3	45	(21	24)	359	113	109	137	96	25	91	6	0	7	17	9	.65	14	.309	.408	.617
1994	Sea	AL	111	433	140	24	4	40	(18	22)	292	94	90	107	56	19	73	2	0	2	11	3	.79	9	.323	.402	.674
1995	Sea	AL	72	260	67	7	0	17	(13	4)	125	52	42	49	52	6	53	0	0	2	4	2	.67	4	.258	.379	.481
1996	Sea	AL	140	545	165	26	2	49	(26	23)	342	125	140	131	78	13	104	7	1	7	16	1	.94	7	.303	.392	.628
1997	Sea	AL	157	608	185	34	3	56	(27	29)	393	125	147	142	76	23	121	8	0	12	15	4	.79	12	.304	.382	.646
1998	Sea	AL	161	633	180	33	3	56	(30	26)	387	120	146	136	76	11	121	7	0	4	20	5	.80	14	.284	.365	.611
1999	Sea	AL	160	606	173	26	3	48	(27	21)	349	123	134	132	91	17	108	7	0	2	24	7	.77	8	.285	.384	.576
2000	Cin	NL	145	520	141	22	3	40	(22	18)	289	100	118	111	94	17	117	9	0	8	6	4	.60	7	.271	.387	.556
2001	Cin	NL	111	364	104	20	2	22	(12	10)	194	57	65	69	44	6	72	4	1	4	2	0	1.00	6	.286	.365	.533
2002	Cin	NL	70	197	52	8	0	8	(4	4)	84	17	23	27	28	6	39	3	0	4	1	2	.33	6	.264	.358	.426
2003	Cin	NL	53	166	41	12	1	13	(5	8)	94	34	26	26	27	5	44	6	1	1	1	0	1.00	3	.247	.370	.566
2004	Cin	NL	83	300	76	18	0	20	(11	9)	154	49	60	56	44	3	67	2	0	2	1	0	1.00	3	.253	.351	.513
2005	Cin	NL	128	491	148	30	0	35	(15	20)	283	85	92	89	54	3	93	3	0	7	0	1	.00	9	.301	.369	.576
2006	Cin	NL	109	428	108	19	0	27	(14	13)	208	62	72	55	39	6	78	2	0	3	0	0	-	13	.252	.316	.486
2007	Cin	NL	144	528	146	24	1	30	(17	13)	262	78	93	87	85	14	99	1	0	9	6	1	.86	14	.277	.372	.496
2008	2 Tms		143	490	122	30	1	18	(8	10)	208	67	71	70	78	14	89	3	0	4	0	1	.00	13	.249	.353	.424
2009	Sea	AL	117	387	83	19	0	19	(13	6)	159	44	57	50	63	2	80	1	0	3	0	0	-	6	.214	.324	.411
08	Cin	NL	102	359	88	20	1	15	(7	8)	155	51	53	59	61	13	64	2	0	3	0	1	.00	7	.245	.355	.432
08	CWS	AL	41	131	34	10	0	3	(1	2)	53	16	18	20	17	1	25	1	0	1	0	0	-	6	.260	.347	.405
Postseason			18	69	20	2	0	6	(3	3)	40	12	11	15	8	1	16	1	0	1	5	1	.83	0	.290	.367	.580
21 ML YEARS			2638	9703	2763	522	38	630	(332	298)	5251	1656	1829	1862	1303	246	1762	81	8	101	184	69	.73	196	.285	.371	.541

Jason Grilli

Pitches: R **Bats:** R **Pos:** RP-52   **Ht:** 6'5" **Wt:** 225 **Born:** 11/11/1976 **Age:** 33

			HOW MUCH HE PITCHED							WHAT HE GAVE UP												THE RESULTS							
Year	Team	Lg	G	GS	CG	GF	IP	BFP	H	R	ER	HR	SH	SF	HB	TBB	IBB	SO	WP	Bk	W	L	Pct	Sh	Sv-Op	Hld	ERC	ERA
2009	Frisco*	AA	1	1	0	0	1.0	4	0	0	0	0	0	0	0	1	0	1	0	0	0	0	-	0	0--	-	0.95	0.00
2000	Fla	NL	1	1	0	0	6.2	35	11	4	4	0	2	0	2	2	0	3	0	0	1	0	1.000	0	0-0	0	7.84	5.40
2001	Fla	NL	6	5	0	1	26.2	115	30	18	18	6	1	2	0	11	0	17	0	0	2	2	.500	0	0-0	0	6.44	6.08
2004	CWS	AL	8	8	1	0	45.0	203	52	38	37	11	2	1	3	20	0	26	2	0	2	3	.400	0	0-0	0	6.67	7.40
2005	Det	AL	3	2	0	0	16.0	63	14	6	6	1	1	1	0	6	0	5	0	0	1	1	.500	0	0-0	0	3.27	3.38
2006	Det	AL	51	0	0	18	62.0	270	61	31	29	6	2	4	5	25	3	31	5	0	2	3	.400	0	0-0	9	4.23	4.21
2007	Det	AL	57	0	0	13	79.2	352	81	46	42	5	1	5	5	32	1	62	5	0	5	3	.625	0	0-2	11	4.09	4.74
2008	2 Tms		60	0	0	16	75.0	323	67	27	25	2	1	3	2	38	7	69	4	0	3	3	.500	0	1-2	4	3.34	3.00
2009	2 Tms		52	0	0	11	45.2	212	50	27	27	4	2	1	1	27	2	49	2	0	2	3	.400	0	1-1	7	5.25	5.32
08	Det	AL	9	0	0	4	13.2	59	12	5	5	1	0	0	1	7	1	10	1	0	0	1	.000	0	0-1	0	3.85	3.29
08	Col	NL	51	0	0	12	61.1	264	55	22	20	1	1	3	1	31	6	59	3	0	3	2	.600	0	1-1	4	3.23	2.93

Year	Team	Lg	G	GS	CG	GF	IP	BFP	H	R	ER	HR	SH	SF	HB	TBB	IBB	SO	WP	Bk	W	L	Pct	Sh	Sv-Op	Hld	ERC	ERA
09	Col	NL	22	0	0	6	19.1	99	29	13	13	2	1	1	0	13	2	22	2	0	0	1	.000	0	1-1	3	8.02	6.05
09	Tex	AL	30	0	0	5	26.1	113	21	14	14	2	1	0	1	14	0	27	0	0	2	2	.500	0	0 0	4	3.44	4.78
	Postseason		5	0	0	0	3.0	14	1	0	0	0	0	0	0	4	1	1	0	0	0	0	-	0	0-0	1	2.44	0.00
8 ML YEARS			238	16	1	59	356.2	1573	366	197	188	35	12	15	20	161	13	262	18	0	18	18	.500	0	2-5	31	4.60	4.74

Gabe Gross

Bats: L **Throws:** R **Pos:** RF-100; PH-32; DH-8; PR-2   **Ht:** 6'3" **Wt:** 220 **Born:** 10/21/1979 **Age:** 30

										BATTING												BASERUNNING				AVERAGES		
Year	Team	Lg	G	AB	H	2B	3B	HR	(Hm	Rd)	TB	R	RBI	RC	TBB	IBB	SO	HBP	SH	SF	SB	CS	SB%	GDP	Avg	OBP	Slg
2004	Tor	AL	44	129	27	4	0	3	(2	1)	40	18	16	15	19	0	31	0	0	0	2	2	.50	1	.209	.311	.310
2005	Tor	AL	40	92	23	4	1	1	(1	0)	32	11	7	11	10	0	21	0	0	0	1	1	.50	0	.250	.324	.348
2006	Mil	NL	117	208	57	15	0	9	(5	4)	99	42	38	42	36	3	60	2	3	3	1	0	1.00	3	.274	.382	.476
2007	Mil	NL	93	183	43	12	2	7	(4	3)	80	28	24	23	25	2	37	1	0	1	3	1	.75	1	.235	.329	.437
2008	2 Tms		143	345	82	16	3	13	(7	6)	143	46	40	46	50	0	82	2	0	2	4	2	.67	6	.238	.336	.414
2009	TB	AL	115	282	64	16	1	6	(2	4)	100	31	36	40	42	1	79	0	1	1	6	3	.67	2	.227	.326	.355
08	Mil	NL	16	43	9	3	0	0	(0	0)	12	6	2	6	10	0	7	0	0	1	2	0	1.00	0	.209	.352	.279
08	TB	AL	127	302	73	13	3	13	(7	6)	131	40	38	40	40	0	75	2	0	1	2	2	.50	6	.242	.333	.434
	Postseason		10	19	1	0	0	0	(0	0)	1	0	2	0	3	0	7	0	0	1	2	0	1.00	1	.053	.174	.053
6 ML YEARS			552	1239	296	67	7	39	(21	18)	494	176	161	177	182	6	310	5	4	7	17	9	.65	13	.239	.337	.399

Eddie Guardado

Pitches: L **Bats:** R **Pos:** RP-48   **Ht:** 6'0" **Wt:** 225 **Born:** 10/2/1970 **Age:** 39

Year	Team	Lg	G	GS	CG	GF	IP	BFP	H	R	ER	HR	SH	SF	HB	TBB	IBB	SO	WP	Bk	W	L	Pct	Sh	Sv-Op	Hld	ERC	ERA
1993	Min	AL	19	16	0	2	94.2	426	123	68	65	13	1	3	1	36	2	40	0	0	3	8	.273	0	0-0	0	6.18	6.18
1994	Min	AL	4	4	0	0	17.0	81	26	16	16	3	1	2	0	8	0	8	0	0	0	2	.000	0	0-0	0	7.01	8.47
1995	Min	AL	51	5	0	10	91.1	410	99	54	52	13	6	5	0	45	2	71	5	1	4	9	.308	0	2-5	5	5.20	5.12
1996	Min	AL	83	0	0	17	73.2	313	61	45	43	12	6	4	3	33	4	74	3	0	6	5	.545	0	4-7	18	3.81	5.25
1997	Min	AL	69	0	0	20	46.0	201	45	23	20	7	2	1	2	17	2	54	2	0	0	4	.000	0	1-1	13	4.23	3.91
1998	Min	AL	79	0	0	12	65.2	286	66	34	33	10	3	6	0	28	6	53	2	0	3	1	.750	0	0-4	16	4.42	4.52
1999	Min	AL	63	0	0	13	48.0	197	37	24	24	6	2	1	2	25	4	50	0	0	2	5	.286	0	2-4	13	3.03	4.50
2000	Min	AL	70	0	0	36	61.2	262	55	27	27	14	3	3	1	25	3	52	1	1	7	4	.636	0	9-11	8	4.34	3.94
2001	Min	AL	67	0	0	26	66.2	270	47	27	26	5	5	3	1	23	4	67	4	0	7	1	.875	0	12-14	14	2.13	3.51
2002	Min	AL	68	0	0	62	67.2	270	53	22	22	9	2	2	1	18	2	70	0	0	1	3	.250	0	45-51	0	2.66	2.93
2003	Min	AL	66	0	0	60	65.1	260	50	22	21	7	3	2	0	14	2	60	5	0	3	5	.375	0	41-46	0	2.14	2.89
2004	Sea	AL	41	0	0	35	45.1	176	31	14	14	8	0	1	1	14	0	45	0	0	2	2	.500	0	18-25	0	2.69	2.78
2005	Sea	AL	58	0	0	55	56.1	238	52	23	17	7	3	2	0	15	3	48	1	0	2	3	.400	0	36-41	0	3.12	2.72
2006	2 Tms	AL	43	0	0	26	37.0	166	44	10	16	10	3	1	1	13	2	39	0	0	1	3	.250	0	13-18	2	6.26	3.89
2007	Cin	NL	15	0	0	2	13.2	62	16	11	11	2	0	1	1	4	0	8	0	0	0	0	-	0	0-2	1	5.14	7.24
2008	2 Tms	AL	64	0	0	14	56.1	227	50	26	26	4	2	2	0	19	2	33	1	0	4	4	.500	0	4-5	25	3.09	4.15
2009	Tex	AL	48	0	0	11	38.1	166	39	21	19	8	3	0	2	16	1	20	1	0	1	2	.333	0	0-2	5	5.15	4.46
06	Sea	AL	28	0	0	15	23.0	108	29	14	14	8	3	0	0	11	1	22	0	0	1	3	.250	0	5-8	2	7.78	5.40
06	Cin	NL	15	0	0	11	14.0	58	15	5	2	2	0	1	1	2	1	17	0	0	0	0	-	0	8-10	0	3.98	1.29
08	Tex	AL	55	0	0	14	49.1	194	38	20	20	3	2	2	0	17	2	28	1	0	3	3	.500	0	4-4	23	2.45	3.65
08	Min	AL	9	0	0	0	7.0	33	12	6	6	1	0	0	0	2	0	5	0	0	1	1	.500	0	0-1	2	8.69	7.71
	Postseason		5	0	0	5	5.0	27	10	5	5	2	0	0	0	2	0	5	0	0	0	0	-	0	3-3	0	13.18	9.00
17 ML YEARS			908	25	0	401	944.2	4011	894	476	452	138	45	38	16	348	39	798	25	2	46	61	.430	0	187-235	122	3.97	4.31

Vladimir Guerrero

Bats: R **Throws:** R **Pos:** DH-93; PH-5; RF-2   **Ht:** 6'3" **Wt:** 235 **Born:** 2/9/1975 **Age:** 35

										BATTING												BASERUNNING				AVERAGES		
Year	Team	Lg	G	AB	H	2B	3B	HR	(Hm	Rd)	TB	R	RBI	RC	TBB	IBB	SO	HBP	SH	SF	SB	CS	SB%	GDP	Avg	OBP	Slg
2009	RCuca*	A+	2	6	3	2	0	0	(-	-)	5	2	2	2	0	0	1	0	0	0	0	0	-	0	.500	.500	.833
1996	Mon	NL	9	27	5	0	0	1	(0	1)	8	2	1	1	0	0	3	0	0	0	0	0	-	1	.185	.185	.296
1997	Mon	NL	90	325	98	22	2	11	(5	6)	157	44	40	51	19	2	39	7	0	3	3	4	.43	11	.302	.350	.483
1998	Mon	NL	159	623	202	37	7	38	(19	19)	367	108	109	124	42	13	95	7	0	5	11	9	.55	15	.324	.371	.589
1999	Mon	NL	160	610	193	37	5	42	(23	19)	366	102	131	127	55	14	62	7	0	2	14	7	.67	18	.316	.378	.600
2000	Mon	NL	154	571	197	28	11	44	(25	19)	379	101	123	137	58	23	74	8	0	4	9	10	.47	15	.345	.410	.664
2001	Mon	NL	159	599	184	45	4	34	(21	13)	339	107	108	116	60	24	88	9	0	3	37	16	.70	24	.307	.377	.566
2002	Mon	NL	161	614	206	37	2	39	(20	19)	364	106	111	123	84	32	70	6	0	5	40	20	.67	20	.336	.417	.593
2003	Mon	NL	112	394	130	20	3	25	(15	10)	231	71	79	83	63	22	53	6	0	4	9	5	.64	18	.330	.426	.586
2004	LAA	AL	156	612	206	39	2	39	(19	20)	366	124	126	122	52	14	74	8	0	8	15	3	.83	19	.337	.391	.598
2005	LAA	AL	141	520	165	29	2	32	(19	13)	294	95	108	108	61	26	48	8	0	5	13	1	.93	16	.317	.394	.565
2006	LAA	AL	156	607	200	34	1	33	(14	19)	335	92	116	109	50	25	68	4	0	9	15	5	.75	16	.329	.382	.552
2007	LAA	AL	150	574	186	45	1	27	(13	14)	314	89	125	127	71	28	62	9	0	6	2	3	.40	10	.324	.403	.547
2008	LAA	AL	143	541	164	31	3	27	(13	14)	282	85	91	96	51	16	77	4	0	4	5	3	.63	27	.303	.365	.521
2009	LAA	AL	100	383	113	16	1	15	(7	8)	176	59	50	51	19	3	56	4	0	1	2	1	.67	16	.295	.334	.460
	Postseason		20	75	18	1	0	1	(0	1)	22	8	7	8	9	2	8	2	0	0	2	1	.67	2	.240	.337	.293
14 ML YEARS			1850	7000	2249	420	44	407	(213	194)	3978	1185	1318	1375	685	242	869	87	0	54	175	87	.67	235	.321	.386	.568

Matt Guerrier

Pitches: R Bats: R Pos: RP-79 Ht: 6'3" Wt: 195 Born: 8/2/1978 Age: 31

			HOW MUCH HE PITCHED					WHAT HE GAVE UP										THE RESULTS							
Year	Team	Lg	G	GS	CG	GF	IP	BFP	H	R	ER	HR	SH	SF	HB	TBB	IBB	SO	WP	Bk	W	L	Pct	Sh	Sv-Op	Hld	ERC	ERA
2004	Min	AL	9	2	0	5	19.0	84	22	13	12	5	2	0	1	6	0	11	0	0	0	1	.000	0	0-0	0	6.10	5.68
2005	Min	AL	43	0	0	14	71.2	306	71	29	27	6	4	1	3	24	5	46	3	0	0	3	.000	0	0-0	1	3.71	3.39
2006	Min	AL	39	1	0	13	69.2	300	78	29	26	9	3	4	0	21	0	37	6	0	1	0	1.000	0	1-1	2	4.59	3.36
2007	Min	AL	73	0	0	16	88.0	351	71	23	23	9	0	3	5	21	1	68	6	0	2	4	.333	0	1-4	14	2.70	2.35
2008	Min	AL	76	0	0	15	76.1	344	84	47	44	12	1	1	0	37	9	59	2	0	6	9	.400	0	1-5	20	5.20	5.19
2009	Min	AL	79	0	0	15	76.1	304	58	23	20	10	3	1	4	16	2	47	6	0	5	1	.833	0	1-4	33	2.44	2.36
	Postseason		1	0	0	1	1.0	3	0	0	0	0	0	0	0	0	0	0	0	0	-	0	-	0	0-0	0	0.00	0.00
6 ML YEARS			319	3	0	78	401.0	1689	384	164	152	51	13	10	13	125	17	268	23	0	14	18	.438	0	4-14	70	3.75	3.41

Carlos Guillen

Bats: B Throws: R Pos: LF-42; DH-34; PH-4; 1B-2 Ht: 6'1" Wt: 213 Born: 9/30/1975 Age: 34

						BATTING													BASERUNNING				AVERAGES		
Year	Team	Lg	G	AB	H	2B	3B	HR	(Hm | Rd)	TB	R	RBI	RC	TBB	IBB	SO	HBP	SH	SF	SB	CS	SB%	GDP	Avg	OBP	Slg
2009	Lkland*	A+	5	12	3	1	0	0	(- | -)	4	3	0	2	4	0	3	0	0	0	0	0	-	0	.250	.438	.333
2009	Toledo*	AAA	2	7	4	0	0	0	(- | -)	4	2	1	2	2	0	1	0	0	0	0	0	-	0	.571	.667	.571
1998	Sea	AL	10	39	13	1	1	0	(0 | 0)	16	9	5	7	3	0	9	0	0	0	2	0	1.00	0	.333	.381	.410
1999	Sea	AL	5	19	3	0	0	1	(1 | 0)	6	2	3	1	1	0	6	0	1	0	0	0	-	1	.158	.200	.316
2000	Sea	AL	90	288	74	15	2	7	(3 | 4)	114	45	42	36	28	0	53	2	7	3	1	3	.25	6	.257	.324	.396
2001	Sea	AL	140	456	118	21	4	5	(2 | 3)	162	72	53	56	53	0	89	1	7	6	4	1	.80	9	.259	.333	.355
2002	Sea	AL	134	475	124	24	6	9	(4 | 5)	187	73	56	58	46	4	91	1	3	3	4	5	.44	8	.261	.326	.394
2003	Sea	AL	109	388	107	19	3	7	(4 | 3)	153	63	52	53	52	2	64	1	5	5	4	4	.50	12	.276	.359	.394
2004	Det	AL	136	522	166	37	10	20	(7 | 13)	283	97	97	98	52	3	87	2	3	4	12	5	.71	12	.318	.379	.542
2005	Det	AL	87	334	107	15	4	5	(3 | 2)	145	48	23	39	24	3	45	2	0	1	2	3	.40	9	.320	.368	.434
2006	Det	AL	153	543	174	41	5	19	(10 | 9)	282	100	85	106	71	10	87	4	0	4	20	9	.69	16	.320	.400	.519
2007	Det	AL	151	564	167	35	9	21	(12 | 9)	283	86	102	94	55	10	93	3	0	8	13	8	.62	14	.296	.357	.502
2008	Det	AL	113	420	120	29	2	10	(8 | 2)	183	68	54	65	60	3	67	3	2	4	9	3	.75	11	.286	.376	.436
2009	Det	AL	81	277	67	10	3	11	(6 | 5)	116	36	41	38	39	2	56	3	0	3	1	3	.25	7	.242	.339	.419
	Postseason		19	61	21	5	1	2	(0 | 2)	34	8	7	10	8	0	12	0	0	0	1	1	.50	2	.344	.420	.557
12 ML YEARS			1209	4325	1240	247	49	115	(60 | 55)	1930	699	613	651	484	37	747	22	28	41	72	44	.62	105	.287	.358	.446

Jose Guillen

Bats: R Throws: R Pos: RF-65; DH-11; LF-4; PH-3 Ht: 6'0" Wt: 195 Born: 5/17/1976 Age: 34

						BATTING													BASERUNNING				AVERAGES		
Year	Team	Lg	G	AB	H	2B	3B	HR	(Hm | Rd)	TB	R	RBI	RC	TBB	IBB	SO	HBP	SH	SF	SB	CS	SB%	GDP	Avg	OBP	Slg
1997	Pit	NL	143	498	133	20	5	14	(5 | 9)	205	58	70	56	17	0	88	8	0	3	1	2	.33	16	.267	.300	.412
1998	Pit	NL	153	573	153	38	2	14	(10 | 4)	237	60	84	68	21	0	100	6	1	4	3	5	.38	7	.267	.298	.414
1999	2 Tms		87	288	73	16	0	3	(1 | 2)	98	42	31	28	20	2	57	7	1	2	1	0	1.00	16	.253	.315	.340
2000	TB	AL	105	316	80	16	5	10	(5 | 5)	136	40	41	43	18	1	65	13	2	0	3	1	.75	6	.253	.320	.430
2001	TB	AL	41	135	37	5	0	3	(0 | 3)	51	14	11	15	6	2	26	3	0	1	2	3	.40	2	.274	.317	.378
2002	2 Tms	NL	85	240	57	7	0	8	(5 | 3)	88	25	31	16	14	1	43	3	1	1	4	5	.44	13	.238	.287	.367
2003	2 Tms		136	485	151	28	2	31	(14 | 17)	276	77	86	86	24	2	95	14	8	3	1	3	.25	16	.311	.359	.569
2004	LAA	AL	148	565	166	28	3	27	(13 | 14)	281	88	104	98	37	5	92	15	0	3	5	4	.56	14	.294	.352	.497
2005	Was	NL	148	551	156	32	2	24	(3 | 21)	264	81	76	72	31	6	102	19	1	9	1	1	.50	14	.283	.338	.479
2006	Was	NL	69	241	52	15	1	9	(4 | 5)	96	28	40	23	15	4	48	7	0	5	1	0	1.00	8	.216	.276	.398
2007	Sea	AL	153	593	172	28	2	23	(12 | 11)	273	84	99	90	41	2	118	15	0	5	5	1	.83	17	.290	.353	.460
2008	KC	AL	153	598	158	42	1	20	(8 | 12)	262	66	97	68	23	3	106	9	0	3	2	1	.67	23	.264	.300	.438
2009	KC	AL	81	281	68	8	0	9	(4 | 5)	103	30	40	33	22	1	50	8	0	1	1	0	1.00	13	.242	.314	.367
99	Pit	NL	40	120	32	6	0	1	(0 | 1)	41	18	18	12	10	1	21	0	1	1	1	0	1.00	7	.267	.321	.342
99	TB	AL	47	168	41	10	0	2	(1 | 1)	57	24	13	16	10	1	36	7	0	1	0	0	-	9	.244	.312	.339
02	Ari	NL	54	131	30	4	0	4	(3 | 1)	46	13	15	7	7	1	25	2	0	1	3	4	.43	7	.229	.277	.351
02	Cin	NL	31	109	27	3	0	4	(2 | 2)	42	12	16	9	7	0	18	1	1	0	1	1	.50	6	.248	.299	.385
03	Cin	NL	91	315	106	21	1	23	(10 | 13)	198	52	63	64	17	1	63	9	6	2	1	3	.25	8	.337	.385	.629
03	Oak	AL	45	170	45	7	1	8	(4 | 4)	78	25	23	22	7	1	32	5	2	1	0	0	-	8	.265	.311	.459
	Postseason		4	11	5	1	0	0	(0 | 0)	6	1	1	3	3	0	2	0	0	0	0	0	-	0	.455	.571	.545
13 ML YEARS			1502	5364	1456	283	23	195	(84 | 111)	2370	693	810	696	289	29	990	131	14	40	30	26	.54	165	.271	.322	.442

Jeremy Guthrie

Pitches: R Bats: R Pos: SP-33 Ht: 6'1" Wt: 196 Born: 4/8/1979 Age: 31

			HOW MUCH HE PITCHED					WHAT HE GAVE UP										THE RESULTS							
Year	Team	Lg	G	GS	CG	GF	IP	BFP	H	R	ER	HR	SH	SF	HB	TBB	IBB	SO	WP	Bk	W	L	Pct	Sh	Sv-Op	Hld	ERC	ERA
2004	Cle	AL	6	0	0	2	11.2	49	9	6	6	1	0	0	1	6	0	7	1	0	0	0	-	0	0-0	0	3.58	4.63
2005	Cle	AL	1	0	0	1	6.0	29	9	4	4	2	1	1	0	2	0	3	0	0	0	0	-	0	0-0	0	8.58	6.00
2006	Cle	AL	9	1	0	1	19.1	93	24	15	15	2	0	0	2	15	1	14	3	0	0	0	-	0	0-0	0	7.78	6.98
2007	Bal	AL	32	26	0	3	175.1	723	165	78	72	23	4	6	4	47	2	123	8	1	7	5	.583	0	0-1	0	3.55	3.70
2008	Bal	AL	30	30	1	0	190.2	796	176	82	77	24	2	2	7	58	2	120	3	0	10	12	.455	0	0-0	0	3.59	3.63
2009	Bal	AL	33	33	1	0	200.0	874	224	120	112	35	1	8	9	60	1	110	1	1	10	17	.370	0	0-0	0	5.08	5.04
6 ML YEARS			111	90	2	7	603.0	2564	607	305	286	87	8	17	23	188	6	377	16	2	27	34	.443	0	0-1	0	4.23	4.27

Franklin Gutierrez

Bats: R Throws: R Pos: CF-153   Ht: 6'2" Wt: 190 Born: 2/21/1983 Age: 27

								BATTING											BASERUNNING				AVERAGES		
Year	Team	Lg	G	AB	H	2B	3B	HR	(Hm | Rd)	TB	R	RBI	RC	TBB	IBB	SO	HBP	SH	SF	SB	CS	SB%	GDP	Avg	OBP	Slg
2005	Cle	AL	7	1	0	0	0	0	(0 | 0)	0	2	0	0	1	0	0	0	0	0	0	0	-	0	.000	.500	.000
2006	Cle	AL	43	136	37	9	0	1	(1 | 0)	49	21	8	12	3	0	28	0	2	0	0	0	-	4	.272	.288	.360
2007	Cle	AL	100	271	72	13	2	13	(10 | 3)	128	41	36	36	21	1	77	1	5	3	8	3	.73	7	.266	.318	.472
2008	Cle	AL	134	399	99	26	2	8	(6 | 2)	153	54	41	37	27	1	87	8	4	2	9	3	.75	10	.248	.307	.383
2009	Sea	AL	153	565	160	24	1	18	(7 | 11)	240	85	70	80	46	3	122	3	13	2	16	5	.76	14	.283	.339	.425
	Postseason		10	29	6	0	0	1	(0 | 1)	9	5	4	3	5	0	11	0	0	0	0	0	-	1	.207	.324	.310
5 ML YEARS			437	1372	368	72	5	40	(24 | 16)	570	203	155	165	98	5	314	12	24	7	33	11	.75	35	.268	.321	.415

Juan Gutierrez

Pitches: R Bats: R Pos: RP-65   Ht: 6'3" Wt: 210 Born: 7/14/1983 Age: 26

			HOW MUCH HE PITCHED						WHAT HE GAVE UP									THE RESULTS							
Year	Team	Lg	G	CS	CG	GF	IP	BFP	H	R	ER	HR	SH	SF	HB	TBB	IBB	SO	WP	Bk	W	L	Pct	Sh	Sv-Op	Hld	ERC	ERA
2003	Mrtnsvl	R+	16	3	0	4	34.0	162	42	22	18	2	1	4	5	13	1	30	7	1	1	2	.333	0	2--	-	5.45	4.76
2004	Grnsvle	R	13	13	0	0	65.2	294	74	31	27	4	3	2	7	30	0	59	6	0	8	2	.800	0	0--	-	5.29	3.70
2005	Lxngtn	A	22	21	1	1	120.2	505	106	55	43	10	2	6	10	43	0	100	7	2	9	5	.643	0	0--	-	3.49	3.21
2005	Salem	A+	3	2	0	0	12.0	51	10	4	4	1	0	0	0	8	0	9	0	0	1	1	.500	0	0--	-	4.23	3.00
2006	CpChr	AA	20	20	0	0	103.2	438	94	39	35	10	1	2	5	34	0	106	4	0	8	4	.667	0	0--	-	3.43	3.04
2007	RdRck	AAA	26	25	0	0	156.0	665	154	84	72	17	7	4	2	63	4	108	6	1	5	10	.333	0	0--	-	4.15	4.15
2008	Tucsn	AAA	25	22	0	0	116.2	537	152	94	79	11	3	7	5	44	1	87	5	1	5	11	.313	0	0--	-	5.89	6.09
2007	Hou	NL	7	3	0	1	21.1	93	25	14	14	3	0	3	0	6	2	16	1	0	1	1	.500	0	0-0	0	4.71	5.91
2009	Ari	NL	65	0	0	21	71.0	307	67	33	32	2	2	4	3	30	5	66	5	0	4	3	.571	0	9-10	7	3.38	4.06
2 ML YEARS			72	3	0	22	92.1	400	92	47	46	5	2	7	3	36	7	82	6	0	5	4	.556	0	9-10	7	3.68	4.40

Angel Guzman

Pitches: R Bats: R Pos: RP-55   Ht: 6'3" Wt: 200 Born: 12/14/1981 Age: 28

			HOW MUCH HE PITCHED						WHAT HE GAVE UP									THE RESULTS							
Year	Team	Lg	G	GS	CG	GF	IP	BFP	H	R	ER	HR	SH	SF	HB	TBB	IBB	SO	WP	Bk	W	L	Pct	Sh	Sv-Op	Hld	ERC	ERA
2009	Peoria*	A	1	1	0	0	1.0	3	0	0	0	0	0	0	0	0	0	2	0	0	0	0	-	0	0--	-	0.00	0.00
2009	Iowa*	AAA	1	1	0	0	1.1	6	1	0	0	0	0	0	0	1	0	1	0	0	0	0	-	0	0--	-	3.21	0.00
2006	ChC	NL	15	10	0	1	56.0	272	68	48	46	9	5	3	6	37	1	60	8	1	0	6	.000	0	0-0	0	7.41	7.39
2007	ChC	NL	12	3	0	3	30.1	128	32	12	12	2	1	1	2	9	0	26	3	0	0	1	.000	0	0-1	0	4.10	3.56
2008	ChC	NL	6	1	0	1	9.2	44	10	6	6	1	0	0	1	4	0	10	1	0	0	0	-	0	0-0	0	4.65	5.59
2009	ChC	NL	55	0	0	14	61.0	245	41	20	20	8	5	2	1	23	4	47	1	0	3	3	.500	0	1-1	15	2.44	2.95
4 ML YEARS			88	14	0	19	157.0	689	151	86	84	20	11	6	10	73	5	143	13	1	3	10	.231	0	1-2	15	4.53	4.82

Cristian Guzman

Bats: B Throws: R Pos: SS-117; PH-17; DH-2   Ht: 6'0" Wt: 211 Born: 3/21/1978 Age: 32

								BATTING											BASERUNNING				AVERAGES		
Year	Team	Lg	G	AB	H	2B	3B	HR	(Hm	Rd)	TB	R	RBI	RC	TBB	IBB	SO	HBP	SH	SF	SB	CS	SB%	GDP	Avg	OBP	Slg
1999	Mln	AL	131	420	95	12	3	1	(1	0)	116	47	26	29	22	0	90	3	7	4	9	7	.56	6	.226	.267	.276
2000	Mln	AL	156	631	156	25	20	8	(3	5)	245	89	54	76	46	1	101	2	7	4	28	10	.74	5	.247	.299	.388
2001	Mln	AL	118	493	149	28	14	10	(7	3)	235	80	51	79	21	0	78	5	8	0	25	8	.76	6	.302	.337	.477
2002	Mln	AL	148	623	170	31	6	9	(6	3)	240	80	59	63	17	2	79	2	8	6	12	13	.48	12	.273	.292	.385
2003	Mln	AL	143	534	143	15	14	3	(1	2)	195	78	53	62	30	0	79	5	12	4	18	9	.67	4	.268	.311	.365
2004	Mln	AL	145	576	158	31	4	8	(5	3)	221	84	46	66	30	4	64	1	13	4	10	5	.67	15	.274	.309	.384
2005	Was	NL	142	456	100	19	6	4	(0	4)	143	39	31	26	25	6	76	1	8	2	7	4	.64	12	.219	.260	.314
2007	Was	NL	46	174	57	6	6	2	(1	1)	81	31	14	30	15	1	21	1	0	2	2	0	1.00	1	.328	.380	.466
2008	Was	NL	138	579	183	35	5	9	(4	5)	255	77	55	84	23	1	57	5	1	4	6	5	.55	10	.316	.345	.440
2009	Was	NL	135	531	151	24	7	6	(0	1)	207	74	52	58	16	0	75	1	6	1	4	4	.50	9	.284	.306	.390
	Postseason		18	67	16	3	0	1	(0	1)	22	9	2	5	5	0	12	1	2	0	3	0	1.00	5	.239	.301	.328
10 ML YEARS			1302	5017	1362	226	85	60	(33	27)	1938	679	441	573	245	15	720	26	70	31	121	66	.65	80	.271	.307	.386

Freddy Guzman

Bats: B Throws: R Pos: PR-8; LF-5; RF-3; DH-1; PH-1   Ht: 5'10" Wt: 165 Born: 1/20/1981 Age: 29

								BATTING											BASERUNNING				AVERAGES		
Year	Team	Lg	G	AB	H	2B	3B	HR	(Hm	Rd)	TB	R	RBI	RC	TBB	IBB	SO	HBP	SH	SF	SB	CS	SB%	GDP	Avg	OBP	Slg
2009	Tacom*	AAA	13	42	9	2	1	0	(-	-)	13	5	3	3	2	0	5	0	0	1	4	2	.67	1	.214	.244	.310
2009	Pwtckt*	AAA	62	214	49	6	2	2	(-	-)	65	25	10	19	13	0	35	0	3	1	21	7	.75	5	.229	.272	.304
2009	Norfolk*	AAA	20	73	14	1	1	0	(-	-)	17	7	3	6	5	0	9	0	0	1	13	0	1.00	2	.192	.241	.233
2009	S-WB*	AAA	6	21	6	0	1	0	(-	-)	8	7	1	5	5	0	5	0	0	0	7	0	1.00	0	.286	.423	.381
2004	SD	NL	20	76	16	3	0	0	(0	0)	19	8	5	4	3	0	13	1	0	0	5	2	.71	0	.211	.250	.250
2006	Tex	AL	9	7	2	0	0	0	(0	0)	2	1	0	1	1	0	1	1	0	0	0	0	-	0	.286	.444	.286
2007	Tex	AL	8	6	1	0	0	1	(0	1)	4	2	1	1	0	0	2	0	0	0	0	1	.00	0	.167	.167	.667
2009	NYY	AL	10	6	1	0	0	0	(0	0)	1	2	1	0	0	0	1	0	0	1	4	1	.80	0	.167	.143	.167
4 ML YEARS			47	95	20	3	0	1	(0	1)	26	13	7	5	4	0	17	2	0	1	9	4	.69	0	.211	.255	.274

Jesus Guzman

Bats: R **Throws:** R **Pos:** PH-9; 1B-3; DH-1　　　　　　　**Ht:** 5'10" **Wt:** 190 **Born:** 6/14/1984 **Age:** 26

Year	Team	Lg	G	AB	H	2B	3B	HR	(Hm	Rd)	TB	R	RBI	RC	TBB	IBB	SO	HBP	SH	SF	SB	CS	SB%	GDP	Avg	OBP	Slg
2004	InldEm	A+	114	442	137	35	3	6	(-	-)	196	80	71	79	57	0	105	6	3	4	9	8	.53	6	.310	.393	.443
2005	SnAnt	AA	119	453	117	18	8	9	(-	-)	178	61	53	59	45	0	101	4	11	1	6	11	.35	10	.258	.330	.393
2006	SnAnt	AA	115	408	105	18	3	9	(-	-)	156	57	55	56	46	0	74	4	9	4	7	3	.70	12	.257	.335	.382
2007	Hi Dsrt	A+	130	518	156	38	5	25	(-	-)	279	102	112	102	50	1	85	8	6	3	3	3	.50	14	.301	.370	.539
2008	Scrmto	AAA	15	59	14	2	0	2	(-	-)	22	5	9	5	4	0	13	0	1	1	0	2	.00	2	.237	.281	.373
2008	Mdland	AA	80	341	124	21	2	14	(-	-)	191	57	76	76	33	4	56	0	1	1	5	2	.71	6	.364	.419	.560
2008	As	R	5	15	7	3	0	1	(-	-)	13	2	3	5	0	0	1	2	0	0	1	0	1.00	0	.467	.529	.867
2009	Fresno	AAA	116	452	145	26	5	16	(-	-)	229	75	71	86	37	2	82	7	1	3	0	2	.00	9	.321	.379	.507
2009	SF	NL	12	20	5	0	0	0	(0	0)	5	0	0	0	0	0	3	0	0	0	0	0	-	2	.250	.250	.250

Tony Gwynn

Bats: L **Throws:** R **Pos:** CF-102; PH-14; RF-11　　　　　　　**Ht:** 5'11" **Wt:** 193 **Born:** 10/4/1982 **Age:** 27

Year	Team	Lg	G	AB	H	2B	3B	HR	(Hm	Rd)	TB	R	RBI	RC	TBB	IBB	SO	HBP	SH	SF	SB	CS	SB%	GDP	Avg	OBP	Slg
2009	Nashv*	AAA	38	152	47	8	1	1	(-	-)	60	34	9	27	20	0	21	0	2	1	15	1	.94	2	.309	.387	.395
2006	Mil	NL	32	77	20	2	1	0	(0	0)	24	5	4	5	2	0	15	0	0	1	3	1	.75	2	.260	.275	.312
2007	Mil	NL	69	123	32	3	2	0	(0	0)	39	13	10	16	12	1	24	0	0	0	8	1	.89	0	.260	.326	.317
2008	Mil	NL	29	42	8	1	0	0	(0	0)	9	5	1	2	4	0	7	1	1	1	3	1	.75	1	.190	.271	.214
2009	SD	NL	119	393	106	11	6	2	(1	1)	135	59	21	48	48	2	65	2	5	3	11	7	.61	2	.270	.350	.344
	Postseason		3	3	1	0	0	0	(0	0)	1	0	0	0	0	0	1	0	0	0	0	0	-	0	.333	.333	.333
	4 ML YEARS		249	635	166	17	9	2	(1	1)	207	82	36	71	66	3	111	3	6	5	25	10	.71	5	.261	.331	.326

Eric Hacker

Pitches: R **Bats:** B **Pos:** RP-3　　　　　　　**Ht:** 6'1" **Wt:** 215 **Born:** 3/26/1983 **Age:** 27

Year	Team	Lg	G	GS	CG	GF	IP	BFP	H	R	ER	HR	SH	SF	HB	TBB	IBB	SO	WP	Bk	W	L	Pct	Sh	Sv-Op	Hld	ERC	ERA
2002	Yanks	R	3	0	0	0	3.2	15	2	0	0	0	1	0	1	1	0	2	0	0	0	0	-	0	0- -	-	1.65	0.00
2003	Yanks	R	7	5	0	1	28.1	114	25	9	9	1	0	0	0	7	0	26	1	0	3	2	.600	0	0- -	-	2.50	2.86
2003	StIsInd	A-	2	2	0	0	9.0	40	10	2	1	0	0	0	1	1	0	5	0	0	0	0	-	0	0- -	-	3.13	1.00
2005	CtnSC	A	10	10	1	0	62.0	238	49	14	11	0	0	0	0	14	0	40	0	0	5	2	.714	0	0- -	-	1.84	1.60
2007	CtnSC	A	17	17	0	0	95.0	379	89	34	27	5	1	2	7	18	0	54	4	1	9	2	.818	0	0- -	-	3.02	2.56
2007	Tampa	A+	9	7	0	0	38.1	178	52	28	26	3	2	1	3	14	1	22	0	0	3	3	.500	0	0- -	-	6.21	6.10
2007	S-WB	AAA	1	0	0	0	2.2	15	5	2	2	0	0	1	1	1	0	3	0	0	1	0	1.000	0	0- -	-	10.00	6.75
2008	Tampa	A+	9	9	0	0	53.0	197	38	14	11	1	0	1	2	9	1	31	0	1	2	2	.500	0	0- -	-	1.60	1.87
2008	Trntn	AA	17	17	0	0	91.1	375	83	33	28	3	3	4	5	28	1	84	4	1	7	4	.636	0	0- -	-	3.04	2.76
2009	Trntn	AA	3	3	0	0	15.1	67	16	10	7	0	1	1	0	7	0	8	2	1	1	1	.500	0	0- -	-	3.83	4.11
2009	S-WB	AAA	3	3	0	0	16.0	70	19	14	14	3	1	2	2	4	0	12	0	1	0	1	.000	0	0- -	-	5.85	7.88
2009	Indy	AAA	21	21	0	0	116.1	516	135	57	52	6	5	5	8	46	2	82	4	1	5	5	.500	0	0- -	-	4.95	4.02
2009	Pit	NL	3	0	0	2	3.0	14	4	2	2	0	0	0	0	2	0	1	0	0	0	0	-	0	0-0	0	6.62	6.00

Charlie Haeger

Pitches: R **Bats:** R **Pos:** SP-3; RP-3　　　　　　　**Ht:** 6'1" **Wt:** 211 **Born:** 9/19/1983 **Age:** 26

Year	Team	Lg	G	GS	CG	GF	IP	BFP	H	R	ER	HR	SH	SF	HB	TBB	IBB	SO	WP	Bk	W	L	Pct	Sh	Sv-Op	Hld	ERC	ERA
2009	Albq*	AAA	22	22	4	0	144.2	625	134	63	57	16	7	5	12	58	0	103	9	0	11	6	.647	0	0- -	-	4.07	3.55
2006	CWS	AL	7	1	0	4	18.1	79	12	10	7	0	0	0	0	13	0	19	0	0	1	1	.500	0	1-1	0	2.65	3.44
2007	CWS	AL	8	0	0	5	11.1	59	17	11	9	3	1	1	1	8	2	1	0	0	0	1	.000	0	0-0	1	10.02	7.15
2008	SD	NL	4	0	0	1	4.1	28	8	10	8	2	0	0	2	5	0	4	0	0	0	0	-	0	0-0	0	19.18	16.62
2009	LAD	NL	6	3	0	2	19.0	79	13	7	7	4	1	0	2	7	0	15	0	0	1	1	.500	0	0-0	0	3.31	3.32
	4 ML YEARS		25	4	0	12	53.0	245	50	38	31	9	2	1	5	33	2	39	0	0	2	3	.400	0	1-1	1	5.42	5.26

Travis Hafner

Bats: L **Throws:** R **Pos:** DH-88; PH-6　　　　　　　**Ht:** 6'3" **Wt:** 240 **Born:** 6/3/1977 **Age:** 33

Year	Team	Lg	G	AB	H	2B	3B	HR	(Hm	Rd)	TB	R	RBI	RC	TBB	IBB	SO	HBP	SH	SF	SB	CS	SB%	GDP	Avg	OBP	Slg
2009	Clmbs*	AAA	12	39	13	4	0	1	(-	-)	20	6	8	9	9	0	3	0	0	0	0	0	-	2	.333	.458	.513
2002	Tex	AL	23	62	15	4	1	1	(0	1)	24	6	6	7	8	1	15	0	0	0	0	1	.00	0	.242	.329	.387
2003	Cle	AL	91	291	74	19	3	14	(7	7)	141	35	40	42	22	2	81	10	0	1	2	1	.67	7	.254	.327	.485
2004	Cle	AL	140	482	150	41	3	28	(7	21)	281	96	109	103	68	7	111	17	0	6	3	2	.60	11	.311	.410	.583
2005	Cle	AL	137	486	148	42	0	33	(14	19)	289	94	108	115	79	7	123	9	0	4	0	0	-	9	.305	.408	.595
2006	Cle	AL	129	454	140	31	1	42	(21	21)	299	100	117	118	100	16	111	7	0	2	0	0	-	10	.308	.439	.659
2007	Cle	AL	152	545	145	25	2	24	(12	12)	246	80	100	94	102	17	115	7	0	5	1	1	.50	15	.266	.385	.451
2008	Cle	AL	57	198	39	10	0	5	(2	3)	64	21	24	21	27	6	55	5	0	3	1	1	.50	4	.197	.305	.323
2009	Cle	AL	94	338	92	19	0	16	(9	7)	159	46	49	49	41	6	67	3	0	1	0	0	-	7	.272	.355	.470
	Postseason		11	43	8	1	0	2	(1	1)	15	6	4	3	7	1	15	0	0	0	0	0	-	1	.186	.300	.349
	8 ML YEARS		823	2856	803	191	10	163	(72	91)	1503	478	553	549	447	62	678	58	0	22	7	6	.54	63	.281	.387	.526

Jerry Hairston

Bats: R **Throws**: R **Pos**: 3B-49; SS-42; LF-19; RF-14; 2B-12; PH-11; PR-8; CF-5; DH-2   **Ht**: 5'10" **Wt**: 190 **Born**: 5/29/1976 **Age**: 34

Year	Team	Lg	G	AB	H	2B	3B	HR	(Hm	Rd)	TB	R	RBI	RC	TBB	IBB	SO	HBP	SH	SF	SB	CS	SB%	GDP	Avg	OBP	Slg
1998	Bal	AL	6	7	0	0	0	0	(0	0)	0	2	0	0	0	0	1	0	0	0	0	0	-	0	.000	.000	.000
1999	Bal	AL	50	175	47	12	1	4	(1	3)	73	26	17	24	11	0	24	3	4	0	9	4	.69	2	.269	.323	.417
2000	Bal	AL	49	180	46	5	0	5	(2	3)	66	27	19	22	21	0	22	6	5	0	8	5	.62	8	.256	.353	.367
2001	Bal	AL	159	532	124	25	5	8	(5	3)	183	63	47	57	44	0	73	13	9	4	29	11	.73	12	.233	.305	.344
2002	Bal	AL	122	426	114	25	3	5	(2	3)	160	55	32	55	34	0	55	7	8	4	21	6	.78	5	.268	.329	.376
2003	Bal	AL	58	218	59	12	2	2	(1	1)	81	25	21	32	23	0	25	6	10	2	14	5	.74	8	.271	.353	.372
2004	Bal	AL	86	287	87	19	1	2	(0	2)	114	43	24	45	29	1	29	8	4	6	13	8	.62	3	.303	.378	.397
2005	ChC	NL	114	380	99	25	2	4	(3	1)	140	51	30	46	31	0	46	12	7	0	8	9	.47	5	.261	.336	.368
2006	2 Tms		101	170	35	6	1	0	(0	0)	43	25	10	0	13	2	34	2	7	0	5	2	.71	5	.206	.270	.253
2007	Tex	AL	73	159	30	7	0	3	(1	2)	46	22	16	12	11	0	24	3	7	4	5	1	.83	5	.189	.249	.289
2008	Cin	NL	80	261	85	20	2	6	(3	3)	127	47	36	52	23	0	36	3	8	2	15	3	.83	0	.326	.384	.487
2009	2 Tms		131	383	96	23	1	10	(8	2)	151	62	39	42	32	0	54	6	8	4	7	4	.64	3	.251	.315	.394
06	ChC	NL	38	82	17	3	0	0	(0	0)	20	8	4	5	4	2	14	1	5	0	3	0	1.00	1	.207	.253	.244
06	Tex	AL	63	88	18	3	1	0	(0	0)	23	17	6	4	9	0	20	1	2	0	2	2	.50	4	.205	.286	.261
09	Cin	NL	86	307	78	18	1	8	(6	2)	122	47	27	30	21	0	46	3	6	3	7	3	.70	2	.254	.305	.397
09	NYY	AL	45	76	18	5	0	2	(2	0)	29	15	12	12	11	0	8	3	2	1	0	1	.00	1	.237	.352	.382
	12 ML YEARS		1029	3178	822	179	18	49	(26	23)	1184	448	291	396	272	3	423	69	79	24	134	58	.70	56	.259	.328	.373

Scott Hairston

Bats: R **Throws**: R **Pos**: LF-60; CF-51; PH 8; DH-3; PR-1   **Ht**: 6'0" **Wt**: 196 **Born**: 5/25/1980 **Age**: 30

Year	Team	Lg	G	AB	H	2B	3B	HR	(Hm	Rd)	TB	R	RBI	RC	TBB	IBB	SO	HBP	SH	SF	SB	CS	SB%	GDP	Avg	OBP	Slg
2009	Lk Els*	A+	3	10	1	0	0	0	(-	-)	1	1	0	0	1	0	3	2	0	0	0	0	-	0	.100	.308	.100
2004	Ari	NL	101	330	84	15	6	13	(6	7)	150	39	20	32	21	0	80	1	2	1	3	3	.50	4	.248	.293	.442
2005	Ari	NL	15	20	2	1	0	0	(0	0)	3	0	0	0	0	0	8	0	0	0	0	0	-	1	.100	.100	.150
2006	Ari	NL	9	15	6	2	0	0	(0	0)	8	2	2	2	1	0	5	0	0	0	0	0	-	1	.400	.438	.533
2007	2 Tms	NL	107	263	64	18	2	11	(6	5)	119	37	36	36	26	0	55	1	3	1	2	0	1.00	4	.243	.313	.452
2008	SD	NL	112	326	81	18	3	17	(9	8)	156	42	31	43	28	2	84	3	3	2	3	1	.75	2	.248	.312	.479
2009	2 Tms		116	430	114	27	2	17	(9	8)	196	50	64	60	25	0	83	3	1	5	11	3	.79	9	.265	.307	.456
07	Ari	NL	76	176	39	13	1	3	(1	2)	63	21	16	19	19	0	37	1	3	0	2	0	1.00	4	.222	.291	.358
07	SD	NL	31	87	25	5	1	8	(5	3)	56	16	20	17	7	0	18	0	0	1	0	0	-	0	.287	.337	.644
09	SD	NL	56	197	59	14	1	10	(5	5)	105	26	29	35	17	0	45	1	1	0	8	1	.90	4	.300	.360	.533
09	Oak	AL	60	233	55	13	1	7	(4	3)	91	24	35	25	8	0	38	2	0	5	3	2	.60	5	.236	.262	.391
	6 ML YEARS		460	1393	351	81	13	58	(30	28)	632	170	162	173	101	2	321	8	9	9	19	7	.73	21	.252	.304	.454

Bill Hall

Bats: R **Throws**: R **Pos**: 3B-69; LF-22; RF-15; PH-7; 2B-3; CF-1   **Ht**: 6'0" **Wt**: 210 **Born**: 12/28/1979 **Age**: 30

Year	Team	Lg	G	AB	H	2B	3B	HR	(Hm	Rd)	TB	R	RBI	RC	TBB	IBB	SO	HBP	SH	SF	SB	CS	SB%	GDP	Avg	OBP	Slg
2009	Nashv*	AAA	4	14	4	1	0	1	(-	-)	8	1	4	2	1	0	4	0	0	0	1	0	1.00	1	.286	.333	.571
2002	Mil	NL	19	36	7	1	1	1	(0	1)	13	3	5	3	3	0	13	0	0	0	0	1	.00	1	.194	.256	.361
2003	Mil	NL	52	142	37	9	2	5	(2	3)	65	23	20	18	7	0	28	1	4	1	1	2	.33	5	.261	.298	.458
2004	Mil	NL	126	390	93	20	3	9	(5	4)	146	43	53	41	20	1	119	1	2	2	12	6	.67	4	.238	.276	.374
2005	Mil	NL	146	501	146	39	8	17	(12	5)	248	69	62	73	39	2	103	1	2	3	18	6	.75	11	.291	.342	.495
2006	Mil	NL	148	537	145	39	4	35	(18	17)	297	101	85	87	63	6	162	1	3	4	8	9	.47	12	.270	.345	.553
2007	Mil	NL	136	452	115	35	0	14	(10	4)	192	59	63	59	40	1	128	3	1	7	4	5	.44	9	.254	.315	.425
2008	Mil	NL	128	404	91	22	1	15	(10	5)	160	50	55	43	37	2	124	3	1	3	5	6	.45	4	.225	.293	.396
2009	2 Tms		110	334	67	20	1	8	(4	4)	113	32	36	23	27	0	120	0	0	4	2	2	.50	11	.201	.258	.338
09	Mil	NL	76	214	43	12	0	6	(3	3)	73	22	24	15	19	0	72	0	0	1	1	0	1.00	10	.201	.265	.341
09	Sea	AL	34	120	24	8	1	2	(1	1)	40	10	12	8	8	0	48	0	0	3	1	2	.33	1	.200	.244	.333
	Postseason		3	8	2	0	0	0	(0	0)	2	1	0	1	1	0	3	0	0	0	0	0	-	0	.250	.333	.250
	8 ML YEARS		865	2796	701	185	18	104	(61	43)	1234	380	379	347	236	12	797	10	13	24	50	37	.57	57	.251	.309	.441

Toby Hall

Bats: R **Throws**: R **Pos**: C   **Ht**: 6'2" **Wt**: 255 **Born**: 10/21/1975 **Age**: 34

Year	Team	Lg	G	AB	H	2B	3B	HR	(Hm	Rd)	TB	R	RBI	RC	TBB	IBB	SO	HBP	SH	SF	SB	CS	SB%	GDP	Avg	OBP	Slg
2000	TB	AL	4	12	2	0	0	1	(0	1)	5	1	1	1	0	0	0	0	0	0	0	0	-	0	.167	.231	.417
2001	TB	AL	49	188	56	16	0	4	(1	3)	84	28	30	25	4	0	16	3	0	1	2	2	.50	5	.298	.321	.447
2002	TB	AL	85	330	85	19	1	6	(2	4)	124	37	42	39	17	3	27	1	2	3	0	1	.00	14	.258	.293	.376
2003	TB	AL	130	463	117	23	0	12	(4	8)	176	50	47	45	23	4	40	7	0	5	0	1	.00	14	.253	.295	.380
2004	TB	AL	119	404	103	21	0	8	(6	2)	148	35	60	42	24	1	41	5	1	7	0	2	.00	20	.255	.300	.366
2005	TB	AL	135	432	124	20	0	5	(1	4)	159	28	48	46	10	1	39	5	3	7	0	0	-	15	.287	.315	.368
2006	2 Tms		85	278	72	17	0	8	(6	2)	113	17	31	25	10	4	22	2	0	4	0	2	.00	10	.259	.286	.406
2007	CWS	AL	38	116	24	4	0	0	(0	0)	28	8	3	3	3	0	12	0	0	1	0	0	-	2	.207	.225	.241
2008	CWS	AL	41	127	33	3	0	2	(2	0)	42	7	7	14	6	1	19	2	1	0	0	0	-	8	.260	.304	.331
06	TB	AL	64	221	51	13	0	8	(6	2)	88	15	23	18	8	2	17	2	0	3	0	2	.00	8	.231	.261	.398
06	LAD	NL	21	57	21	4	0	0	(0	0)	25	2	8	7	2	2	5	0	0	1	0	0	-	2	.368	.383	.439
	9 ML YEARS		686	2350	616	123	1	46	(22	24)	879	211	269	240	104	14	216	25	7	28	2	8	.20	80	.262	.297	.374

Roy Halladay

Pitches: R **Bats:** R **Pos:** SP-32 **Ht:** 6'6" **Wt:** 230 **Born:** 5/14/1977 **Age:** 33

Year	Team	Lg	G	GS	CG	GF	IP	BFP	H	R	ER	HR	SH	SF	HB	TBB	IBB	SO	WP	Bk	W	L	Pct	Sh	Sv-Op	Hld	ERC	ERA
1998	Tor	AL	2	2	1	0	14.0	53	9	4	3	2	0	0	0	2	0	13	0	0	1	0	1.000	0	0-0	0	1.61	1.93
1999	Tor	AL	36	18	1	2	149.1	668	156	76	65	19	3	4	4	79	1	82	6	0	8	7	.533	1	1-1	2	5.19	3.92
2000	Tor	AL	19	13	0	4	67.2	349	107	87	80	14	2	3	2	42	0	44	6	1	4	7	.364	0	0-0	0	9.70	10.64
2001	Tor	AL	17	16	1	0	105.1	432	97	41	37	3	3	1	1	25	0	96	4	1	5	3	.625	1	0-0	0	2.61	3.16
2002	Tor	AL	34	34	2	0	**239.1**	993	223	93	78	10	9	2	7	62	6	168	4	1	19	7	.731	1	0-0	0	2.85	2.93
2003	Tor	AL	36	36	9	0	**266.0**	1071	253	111	96	26	3	2	9	32	1	204	6	1	**22**	7	.759	2	0-0	0	2.86	3.25
2004	Tor	AL	21	21	1	0	133.0	561	140	66	62	13	4	3	1	39	1	95	2	2	8	8	.500	1	0-0	0	4.00	4.20
2005	Tor	AL	19	19	5	0	141.2	553	118	39	38	11	2	1	7	18	2	108	2	1	12	4	.750	2	0-0	0	2.26	2.41
2006	Tor	AL	32	32	4	0	220.0	876	208	82	78	19	3	5	5	34	5	132	3	0	16	5	.762	0	0-0	0	2.87	3.19
2007	Tor	AL	31	31	7	0	225.1	927	232	101	93	15	2	7	3	48	3	139	4	0	16	7	.696	1	0-0	0	3.37	3.71
2008	Tor	AL	34	33	9	0	**246.0**	987	220	88	76	18	5	4	12	39	3	206	4	0	20	11	.645	2	0-0	1	**2.62**	2.78
2009	Tor	AL	32	32	9	0	239.0	963	234	82	74	22	1	9	5	35	0	208	2	0	17	10	.630	4	0-0	0	3.06	2.79
12 ML YEARS			313	287	49	6	2046.2	8433	1997	870	780	172	37	41	56	455	22	1495	43	7	148	76	.661	15	1-1	3	3.26	3.43

Cole Hamels

Pitches: L **Bats:** L **Pos:** SP-32 **Ht:** 6'3" **Wt:** 190 **Born:** 12/27/1983 **Age:** 26

Year	Team	Lg	G	GS	CG	GF	IP	BFP	H	R	ER	HR	SH	SF	HB	TBB	IBB	SO	WP	Bk	W	L	Pct	Sh	Sv-Op	Hld	ERC	ERA
2006	Phi	NL	23	23	0	0	132.1	558	117	66	60	19	6	8	3	48	4	145	5	0	9	8	.529	0	0-0	0	3.61	4.08
2007	Phi	NL	28	28	2	0	183.1	743	163	72	69	25	5	5	3	43	4	177	5	0	15	5	.750	0	0-0	0	3.12	3.39
2008	Phi	NL	33	33	2	0	227.1	914	193	89	78	28	6	2	1	53	7	196	0	0	14	10	.583	2	0-0	0	2.76	3.09
2009	Phi	NL	32	32	2	0	193.2	814	206	95	93	24	7	5	5	43	4	168	1	0	10	11	.476	2	0-0	0	3.98	4.32
Postseason			6	6	0	0	41.2	158	26	10	10	2	1	1	0	13	0	37	0	0	4	1	.800	0	0-0	0	1.65	2.16
4 ML YEARS			116	116	6	0	736.2	3029	679	322	300	96	24	20	12	187	19	686	11	0	48	34	.585	4	0-0	0	3.31	3.67

Josh Hamilton

Bats: L **Throws:** L **Pos:** CF-56; RF-24; DH-6; PH-4 **Ht:** 6'4" **Wt:** 235 **Born:** 5/21/1981 **Age:** 29

					BATTING														BASERUNNING				AVERAGES		
Year	Team	Lg	G	AB	H	2B	3B	HR	(Hm | Rd)	TB	R	RBI	RC	TBB	IBB	SO	HBP	SH	SF	SB	CS	SB%	GDP	Avg	OBP	Slg
2009	Okla*	AAA	7	28	5	2	1	0	(- | -)	9	3	0	2	4	1	7	0	0	0	1	0	1.00	0	.179	.281	.321
2009	Frisco*	AA	1	4	1	0	0	0	(- | -)	1	1	1	0	1	0	1	0	0	0	1	0	1.00	0	.250	.400	.250
2007	Cin	NL	90	298	87	17	2	19	(11 | 8)	165	52	47	58	33	4	65	4	0	2	3	3	.50	6	.292	.368	.554
2008	Tex	AL	156	624	190	35	5	32	(19 | 13)	**331**	98	**130**	119	64	9	126	7	0	9	9	1	.90	8	.304	.371	.530
2009	Tex	AL	89	336	90	19	2	10	(6 | 4)	143	43	54	51	24	2	79	1	0	4	8	3	.73	5	.268	.315	.426
3 ML YEARS			335	1258	367	71	9	61	(36 | 25)	639	193	231	228	121	15	270	12	0	15	20	7	.74	19	.292	.356	.508

Jason Hammel

Pitches: R **Bats:** R **Pos:** SP-30; RP-4 **Ht:** 6'6" **Wt:** 220 **Born:** 9/2/1982 **Age:** 27

Year	Team	Lg	G	GS	CG	GF	IP	BFP	H	R	ER	HR	SH	SF	HB	TBB	IBB	SO	WP	Bk	W	L	Pct	Sh	Sv-Op	Hld	ERC	ERA
2006	TB	AL	9	9	0	0	44.0	208	61	38	38	7	0	3	1	21	0	32	3	2	0	6	.000	0	0-0	0	7.40	7.77
2007	TB	AL	24	14	0	2	85.0	384	100	58	58	12	2	0	2	40	1	64	3	0	3	5	.375	0	0-0	0	5.86	6.14
2008	TB	AL	40	5	0	21	78.1	346	83	45	40	11	2	2	2	35	4	44	7	0	4	4	.500	0	2-2	1	4.94	4.60
2009	Col	NL	34	30	1	0	176.2	771	203	94	85	17	10	9	9	42	6	133	4	0	10	8	.556	0	0-0	0	4.37	4.33
4 ML YEARS			107	58	1	23	384.0	1709	447	235	221	47	14	14	14	138	11	273	17	2	17	23	.425	0	2-2	1	5.13	5.18

Mike Hampton

Pitches: L **Bats:** R **Pos:** SP-21 **Ht:** 5'10" **Wt:** 195 **Born:** 9/9/1972 **Age:** 37

Year	Team	Lg	G	GS	CG	GF	IP	BFP	H	R	ER	HR	SH	SF	HB	TBB	IBB	SO	WP	Bk	W	L	Pct	Sh	Sv-Op	Hld	ERC	ERA
1993	Sea	AL	13	3	0	2	17.0	95	28	20	18	3	1	1	0	17	3	8	1	1	1	3	.250	0	1-1	2	11.09	9.53
1994	Hou	NL	44	0	0	7	41.1	181	46	19	17	4	0	0	2	16	1	24	5	1	2	1	.667	0	0-1	10	4.88	3.70
1995	Hou	NL	24	24	0	0	150.2	641	141	73	56	13	11	5	4	49	3	115	3	1	9	8	.529	0	0-0	0	3.37	3.35
1996	Hou	NL	27	27	2	0	160.1	691	175	79	64	12	10	3	3	49	1	101	7	2	10	10	.500	1	0-0	0	4.11	3.59
1997	Hou	NL	34	34	7	0	223.0	941	217	105	95	16	11	7	2	77	2	139	6	1	15	10	.600	2	0-0	0	3.56	3.83
1998	Hou	NL	32	32	1	0	211.2	917	227	92	79	18	7	7	5	81	1	137	4	2	11	7	.611	1	0-0	0	4.45	3.36
1999	Hou	NL	34	34	3	0	239.0	979	206	86	77	12	10	9	5	101	2	177	9	0	**22**	4	**.846**	2	0-0	0	3.25	2.90
2000	NYM	NL	33	33	3	0	217.2	929	194	89	76	10	11	5	8	99	5	151	10	0	15	10	.600	1	0-0	0	3.44	3.14
2001	Col	NL	32	32	2	0	203.0	904	236	138	122	31	8	6	8	85	7	122	6	0	14	13	.519	1	0-0	0	5.69	5.41
2002	Col	NL	30	30	0	0	178.2	838	228	**135**	122	24	2	9	7	91	4	74	9	2	7	15	.318	0	0-0	0	6.61	6.15
2003	Atl	NL	31	31	1	0	190.0	823	186	91	81	14	10	5	1	78	4	110	10	1	14	8	.636	0	0-0	0	3.77	3.84
2004	Atl	NL	29	29	1	0	172.1	760	198	86	82	15	8	3	1	65	3	87	3	2	13	9	.591	0	0-0	0	4.76	4.28
2005	Atl	NL	12	12	1	0	69.1	284	74	28	27	5	2	1	0	18	0	27	1	0	5	3	.625	1	0-0	0	3.85	3.50
2008	Atl	NL	13	13	0	0	78.0	331	83	45	42	10	5	2	1	28	6	38	0	0	3	4	.429	0	0-0	0	4.52	4.85
2009	Hou	NL	21	21	0	0	112.0	494	128	71	66	13	11	5	2	46	6	74	1	0	7	10	.412	0	0-0	0	5.12	5.30
Postseason			11	10	1	0	65.0	271	48	27	27	8	2	0	1	32	2	53	4	0	2	4	.333	1	0-0	0	3.19	3.74
15 ML YEARS			409	355	21	9	2264.0	9808	2367	1157	1024	200	107	68	49	900	48	1384	75	13	148	115	.563	9	1-2	12	4.33	4.07

Ryan Hanigan

Bats: R Throws: R Pos: C-88; PH-6   Ht: 6'0" Wt: 201 Born: 8/16/1980 Age: 29

							BATTING												BASERUNNING				AVERAGES		
Year	Team	Lg	G	AB	H	2D	3B	HR	(Hm | Rd)	TB	R	RBI	RC	TBB	IBB	SO	HBP	SH	SF	SB	CS	SB%	GDP	Avg	OBP	Slg
2009	Lsvlle*	AAA	5	18	7	2	0	0	(- | -)	9	4	2	3	1	0	0	0	0	0	0	0	-	0	.389	.421	.500
2007	Cin	NL	5	10	3	1	0	0	(0 | 0)	4	3	2	2	1	1	2	0	0	0	0	0	-	0	.300	.364	.400
2008	Cin	NL	31	85	23	2	0	2	(1 | 1)	31	9	9	12	10	1	9	3	0	0	0	0	-	2	.271	.367	.365
2009	Cin	NL	90	251	66	6	1	3	(3 | 0)	83	22	11	25	37	7	31	2	2	1	0	0	-	9	.263	.361	.331
	3 ML YEARS		126	346	92	9	1	5	(4 | 1)	118	34	22	39	48	9	42	5	2	1	0	0	-	11	.266	.363	.341

Jack Hannahan

Bats: L Throws: R Pos: 3B-84; 1B-18; SS-2; PH-2; 2B-1; PR-1   Ht: 6'2" Wt: 210 Born: 3/4/1980 Age: 30

							BATTING												BASERUNNING				AVERAGES		
Year	Team	Lg	G	AB	H	2B	3B	HR	(Hm | Rd)	TB	R	RBI	RC	TBB	IBB	SO	HBP	SH	SF	SB	CS	SB%	GDP	Avg	OBP	Slg
2009	Scrmto*	AAA	21	81	18	7	0	2	(- | -)	31	8	11	8	7	0	27	0	0	0	0	1	.00	0	.222	.284	.383
2006	Det	AL	3	9	0	0	0	0	(0 | 0)	0	0	0	0	1	0	1	0	0	0	0	0	-	0	.000	.100	.000
2007	Oak	AL	41	144	40	12	0	3	(1 | 2)	61	16	24	23	21	0	39	1	1	2	1	0	1.00	6	.278	.369	.424
2008	Oak	AL	143	436	95	27	0	9	(4 | 5)	149	48	47	38	55	4	131	2	3	5	2	0	1.00	5	.218	.305	.342
2009	2 Tms	AL	103	267	57	14	2	4	(2 | 2)	87	27	19	20	30	0	71	2	1	1	1	1	.50	4	.213	.297	.326
09	Oak	AL	52	119	23	6	2	1	(1 | 0)	36	12	8	7	13	0	36	1	1	0	0	0	-	2	.193	.278	.303
09	Sea	AL	51	148	34	8	0	3	(1 | 2)	51	15	11	13	17	0	35	1	0	1	1	1	.50	2	.230	.311	.345
	4 ML YEARS		290	856	192	53	2	16	(7 | 9)	297	91	90	81	107	4	242	5	5	8	4	1	.80	15	.224	.311	.347

Joel Hanrahan

Pitches: R Bats: R Pos: RP-67   Ht: 6'4" Wt: 251 Born: 10/6/1981 Age: 28

			HOW MUCH HE PITCHED						WHAT HE GAVE UP										THE RESULTS						
Year	Team	Lg	G	GS	CG	GF	IP	BFP	H	R	ER	HR	SH	SF	HB	TBB	IBB	SO	WP	Bk	W	L	Pct	Sh	Sv-Op	Hld	ERC	ERA
2007	Was	NL	12	11	0	0	51.0	247	59	35	34	9	2	1	0	38	0	43	3	0	5	3	.625	0	0-0	0	7.01	6.00
2008	Was	NL	69	0	0	34	84.1	364	73	40	37	9	2	6	1	42	7	93	6	0	6	3	.667	0	9-13	3	3.65	3.95
2009	2 Tms	NL	67	0	0	30	64.0	297	73	40	34	3	0	1	3	34	1	72	11	1	1	4	.200	0	5-10	9	5.12	4.78
09	Was	NL	34	0	0	23	32.2	163	50	28	28	3	0	1	2	14	0	35	6	1	1	3	.250	0	5-10	2	7.49	7.71
09	Pit	NL	33	0	0	7	31.1	134	23	12	6	0	0	0	1	20	1	37	5	0	0	1	.000	0	0-0	7	2.92	1.72
	3 ML YEARS		148	11	0	64	199.1	908	205	115	105	21	4	8	4	114	8	208	20	1	12	10	.545	0	14-23	12	4.93	4.74

Craig Hansen

Pitches: R Bats: R Pos: RP-5   Ht: 6'6" Wt: 226 Born: 11/15/1983 Age: 26

			HOW MUCH HE PITCHED						WHAT HE GAVE UP										THE RESULTS						
Year	Team	Lg	G	GS	CG	GF	IP	BFP	H	R	ER	HR	SH	SF	HB	TBB	IBB	SO	WP	Bk	W	L	Pct	Sh	Sv-Op	Hld	ERC	ERA
2005	Bos	AL	4	0	0	1	3.0	16	6	2	2	1	0	1	0	1	0	3	0	0	0	0	-	0	0-1	0	12.18	6.00
2006	Bos	AL	38	0	0	11	38.0	176	46	32	28	5	3	3	4	15	0	30	1	0	2	2	.500	0	0-2	8	5.93	6.63
2008	2 Tms		48	0	0	15	46.1	224	40	37	32	3	2	1	2	43	2	32	6	0	2	7	.222	0	3-7	7	5.05	6.22
2009	Pit	NL	5	0	0	1	6.1	30	6	4	4	1	0	0	1	4	0	5	0	0	0	0	-	0	0-0	0	5.66	5.68
08	Bos	AL	32	0	0	6	30.2	146	29	23	19	2	0	1	1	23	1	25	3	0	1	3	.250	0	2-4	7	4.78	5.58
08	Pit	NL	16	0	0	9	15.2	78	11	14	13	1	2	0	1	20	1	7	3	0	1	4	.200	0	1-3	0	5.55	7.47
	4 ML YEARS		95	0	0	28	93.2	446	98	75	66	10	5	5	7	63	2	70	7	0	4	9	.308	0	3-10	15	5.66	6.34

Tommy Hanson

Pitches: R Bats: R Pos: SP-21   Ht: 6'6" Wt: 220 Born: 8/28/1986 Age: 23

			HOW MUCH HE PITCHED						WHAT HE GAVE UP										THE RESULTS						
Year	Team	Lg	G	GS	CG	GF	IP	BFP	H	R	ER	HR	SH	SF	HB	TBB	IBB	SO	WP	Bk	W	L	Pct	Sh	Sv-Op	Hld	ERC	ERA
2006	Danvle	R+	13	8	0	0	51.2	208	42	15	12	2	3	2	1	9	0	56	3	0	4	1	.800	0	0--	-	1.94	2.09
2007	Rome	A	15	14	0	0	73.0	296	51	28	21	6	1	0	6	26	0	90	5	0	2	6	.250	0	0--	-	2.54	2.59
2007	MrtlBh	A+	11	11	0	0	60.0	260	53	33	28	10	2	3	4	32	0	64	0	1	3	3	.500	0	0--	-	4.77	4.20
2008	MrtlBh	A+	7	7	0	0	40.0	148	15	6	4	0	1	2	5	11	0	49	5	0	3	1	.750	0	0--	-	0.91	0.90
2008	Missi	AA	18	18	1	0	98.0	410	70	39	33	9	4	0	9	41	0	114	5	0	8	4	.667	1	0--	-	2.89	3.03
2009	Gwnntt	AAA	11	11	0	0	66.1	257	40	16	11	5	0	0	4	17	0	90	4	0	3	3	.500	0	0--	-	1.66	1.49
2009	Atl	NL	21	21	0	0	127.2	522	105	42	41	10	4	1	5	46	1	116	2	0	11	4	.733	0	0-0	0	3.02	2.89

J.A. Happ

Pitches: L Bats: L Pos: SP-23; RP-12   Ht: 6'6" Wt: 200 Born: 10/19/1982 Age: 27

			HOW MUCH HE PITCHED						WHAT HE GAVE UP										THE RESULTS						
Year	Team	Lg	G	GS	CG	GF	IP	BFP	H	R	ER	HR	SH	SF	HB	TBB	IBB	SO	WP	Bk	W	L	Pct	Sh	Sv-Op	Hld	ERC	ERA
2007	Phi	NL	1	1	0	0	4.0	21	7	5	5	3	0	0	0	2	0	5	0	0	0	1	.000	0	0-0	0	15.13	11.25
2008	Phi	NL	8	4	0	1	31.2	138	28	13	13	3	2	1	1	14	1	26	1	0	1	0	1.000	0	0-0	1	3.55	3.69
2009	Phi	NL	35	23	3	4	166.0	685	149	55	54	20	7	6	5	56	2	119	2	0	12	4	.750	2	0-0	0	3.57	2.93
	Postseason		1	0	0	0	3.0	13	4	1	1	0	0	0	0	2	0	2	0	0	0	0	-	0	0-0	0	7.18	3.00
	3 ML YEARS		44	28	3	5	201.2	844	184	73	72	26	9	7	6	72	3	150	3	0	13	5	.722	2	0-0	1	3.75	3.21

Aaron Harang

Pitches: R **Bats:** R **Pos:** SP-26   **Ht:** 6'7" **Wt:** 261 **Born:** 5/9/1978 **Age:** 32

Year	Team	Lg	G	GS	CG	GF	IP	BFP	H	R	ER	HR	SH	SF	HB	TBB	IBB	SO	WP	Bk	W	L	Pct	Sh	Sv-Op	Hld	ERC	ERA
2002	Oak	AL	16	15	0	0	78.1	354	78	44	42	7	3	4	3	45	2	64	1	0	5	4	.556	0	0-0	0	4.76	4.83
2003	2 Tms		16	15	0	1	76.1	327	89	47	45	11	5	1	1	19	0	42	3	1	5	6	.455	0	0-0	0	4.84	5.31
2004	Cin	NL	28	28	1	0	161.0	711	177	90	87	26	13	6	5	53	5	125	7	0	10	9	.526	1	0-0	0	4.81	4.86
2005	Cin	NL	32	32	1	0	211.2	887	217	93	90	22	11	5	8	51	3	163	6	0	11	13	.458	1	0-0	0	3.77	3.83
2006	Cin	NL	36	**35**	6	0	234.1	**993**	242	109	98	28	**21**	8	8	56	8	**216**	6	1	**16**	11	.593	2	0-0	0	3.82	3.76
2007	Cin	NL	34	34	2	0	231.2	948	213	100	96	28	4	5	8	52	3	218	**12**	1	16	6	.727	1	0-0	0	3.22	3.73
2008	Cin	NL	30	29	1	0	184.1	793	205	104	98	35	11	7	2	50	5	153	2	0	6	**17**	.261	1	0-0	0	4.83	4.78
2009	Cin	NL	26	26	2	0	162.1	703	186	82	76	24	6	2	4	43	6	142	6	0	6	14	.300	1	0-0	0	4.76	4.21
03	Oak	AL	7	6	0	1	30.1	136	41	19	18	5	2	1	0	9	0	16	0	1	1	3	.250	0	0-0	0	6.32	5.34
03	Cin	NL	9	9	0	0	46.0	191	48	28	27	6	3	0	1	10	0	26	3	0	4	3	.571	0	0-0	0	3.94	5.28
8 ML YEARS			218	214	13	1	1340.0	5716	1407	669	632	181	74	38	39	369	32	1123	43	3	75	80	.484	6	0-0	0	4.18	4.24

Rich Harden

Pitches: R **Bats:** L **Pos:** SP-26   **Ht:** 6'1" **Wt:** 195 **Born:** 11/30/1981 **Age:** 28

Year	Team	Lg	G	GS	CG	GF	IP	BFP	H	R	ER	HR	SH	SF	HB	TBB	IBB	SO	WP	Bk	W	L	Pct	Sh	Sv-Op	Hld	ERC	ERA
2009	Iowa*	AAA	1	1	0	0	4.2	20	3	2	1	0	1	0	0	2	0	6	0	0	0	0	-	0	0- -	-	1.62	1.93
2003	Oak	AL	15	13	0	0	74.2	324	72	38	37	5	2	3	1	40	1	67	6	0	5	4	.556	0	0-0	0	4.28	4.46
2004	Oak	AL	31	31	0	0	189.2	803	171	90	84	16	5	6	3	81	6	167	4	1	11	7	.611	0	0-0	0	3.57	3.99
2005	Oak	AL	22	19	2	0	128.0	514	93	42	36	7	4	2	2	43	0	121	6	0	10	5	.667	1	0-0	1	2.20	2.53
2006	Oak	AL	9	9	0	0	46.2	191	31	22	22	5	0	2	1	26	0	49	0	0	4	0	1.000	0	0-0	0	3.07	4.24
2007	Oak	AL	7	4	0	2	25.2	100	18	7	7	3	0	0	0	11	1	27	0	0	1	2	.333	0	0-0	0	2.80	2.45
2008	2 Tms		25	25	0	0	148.0	595	96	38	34	11	2	3	3	61	2	181	3	0	10	2	.833	0	0-0	0	2.20	2.07
2009	ChC	NL	26	26	0	0	141.0	609	122	74	64	23	12	3	6	67	5	171	7	0	9	9	.500	0	0-0	0	4.15	4.09
08	Oak	AL	13	13	0	0	77.0	311	57	21	20	5	0	2	1	31	1	92	1	0	5	1	.833	0	0-0	0	2.56	2.34
08	ChC	NL	12	12	0	0	71.0	284	39	17	14	6	2	1	2	30	1	89	2	0	5	1	.833	0	0-0	0	1.84	1.77
Postseason			4	2	0	2	11.1	55	12	8	8	2	0	0	0	10	3	9	1	0	1	3	.250	0	0-0	0	6.49	6.35
7 ML YEARS			135	127	2	2	753.2	3136	603	311	284	70	25	19	16	329	15	783	26	1	50	29	.633	1	0-0	1	3.16	3.39

J.J. Hardy

Bats: R **Throws:** R **Pos:** SS-112; PH-4   **Ht:** 6'2" **Wt:** 189 **Born:** 8/19/1982 **Age:** 27

Year	Team	Lg	G	AB	H	2B	3B	HR	(Hm	Rd)	TB	R	RBI	RC	TBB	IBB	SO	HBP	SH	SF	SB	CS	SB%	GDP	Avg	OBP	Slg
2009	Nashv*	AAA	18	71	18	2	0	4	(-	-)	32	7	12	9	3	0	9	0	0	0	0	0	-	1	.254	.284	.451
2005	Mil	NL	124	372	92	22	1	9	(6	3)	143	46	50	49	44	7	48	1	8	2	0	0	-	10	.247	.327	.384
2006	Mil	NL	35	128	31	5	0	5	(4	1)	51	13	14	13	10	0	23	0	0	1	1	1	.50	4	.242	.295	.398
2007	Mil	NL	151	592	164	30	1	26	(15	11)	274	89	80	84	40	1	73	1	4	1	2	3	.40	13	.277	.323	.463
2008	Mil	NL	146	569	161	31	4	24	(14	10)	272	78	74	78	52	3	98	1	5	2	2	1	.67	18	.283	.343	.478
2009	Mil	NL	115	414	95	16	2	11	(6	5)	148	53	47	32	43	0	85	0	1	5	0	1	.00	14	.229	.302	.357
Postseason			4	14	6	1	0	0	(0	0)	7	2	2	3	2	0	0	0	0	0	0	0	-	0	.429	.500	.500
5 ML YEARS			571	2075	543	104	8	75	(45	30)	888	279	265	256	189	11	327	5	18	11	5	6	.45	59	.262	.323	.428

Dan Haren

Pitches: R **Bats:** R **Pos:** SP-33   **Ht:** 6'5" **Wt:** 215 **Born:** 9/17/1980 **Age:** 29

Year	Team	Lg	G	GS	CG	GF	IP	BFP	H	R	ER	HR	SH	SF	HB	TBB	IBB	SO	WP	Bk	W	L	Pct	Sh	Sv-Op	Hld	ERC	ERA
2003	StL	NL	14	14	0	0	72.2	320	84	44	41	9	4	5	0	22	0	43	3	0	3	7	.300	0	0-0	0	5.07	5.08
2004	StL	NL	14	5	0	2	46.0	195	45	23	23	4	4	2	2	17	2	32	1	0	3	3	.500	0	0-0	0	3.91	4.50
2005	Oak	AL	34	34	3	0	217.0	897	212	101	90	26	3	5	6	53	5	163	6	0	14	12	.538	0	0-0	0	3.58	3.73
2006	Oak	AL	34	**34**	2	0	223.0	930	224	109	102	31	3	3	10	45	6	176	10	0	14	13	.519	0	0-0	0	3.72	4.12
2007	Oak	AL	34	**34**	0	0	222.2	935	214	91	76	24	2	8	3	55	1	192	1	0	15	9	.625	0	0-0	0	3.32	3.07
2008	Ari	NL	33	33	1	0	216.0	881	204	86	80	19	7	3	6	40	4	206	11	0	16	8	.667	1	0-0	0	2.96	3.33
2009	Ari	NL	33	33	3	0	229.1	909	192	83	80	27	8	3	4	38	2	223	13	0	14	10	.583	1	0-0	0	2.50	3.14
Postseason			7	2	0	0	19.1	86	24	7	7	3	1	0	0	7	0	16	2	0	2	0	1.000	0	0-0	0	5.83	3.26
7 ML YEARS			196	187	9	2	1226.2	5067	1175	537	492	140	31	26	36	270	20	1035	54	0	79	62	.560	2	0-0	0	3.33	3.61

Brendan Harris

Bats: R **Throws:** R **Pos:** SS-56; 3B-44; 2B-11; PH-11; DH-9; 1B-3; PR-2   **Ht:** 6'1" **Wt:** 210 **Born:** 8/26/1980 **Age:** 29

Year	Team	Lg	G	AB	H	2B	3B	HR	(Hm	Rd)	TB	R	RBI	RC	TBB	IBB	SO	HBP	SH	SF	SB	CS	SB%	GDP	Avg	OBP	Slg
2004	2 Tms	NL	23	59	10	3	0	1	(0	1)	16	4	3	2	3	0	12	1	0	0	0	0	-	0	.169	.222	.271
2005	Was	NL	4	9	3	1	0	1	(0	1)	7	1	3	3	0	0	0	1	0	0	0	0	-	0	.333	.400	.778
2006	2 Tms	NL	25	42	10	2	0	1	(1	0)	15	5	3	4	4	0	7	1	0	0	0	0	-	2	.238	.319	.357
2007	TB	AL	137	521	149	35	3	12	(5	7)	226	72	59	70	42	1	96	4	8	1	4	1	.80	19	.286	.343	.434
2008	Min	AL	130	434	115	29	3	7	(3	4)	171	57	49	52	39	0	98	4	7	6	1	1	.50	13	.265	.327	.394
2009	Min	AL	123	414	108	22	1	6	(5	1)	150	44	37	43	29	0	78	3	1	6	0	2	.00	16	.261	.310	.362
04	ChC	NL	3	9	2	1	0	0	(0	0)	3	0	1	1	1	0	1	0	0	0	0	0	-	0	.222	.300	.333
04	Mon	NL	20	50	8	2	0	1	(0	1)	13	4	2	1	2	0	11	1	0	0	0	0	-	0	.160	.208	.260
06	Was	NL	17	32	8	2	0	0	(0	0)	10	3	2	3	3	0	3	1	0	0	0	0	-	1	.250	.333	.313
06	Cin	NL	8	10	2	0	0	1	(1	0)	5	2	1	1	1	0	4	0	0	0	0	0	-	1	.200	.273	.500
6 ML YEARS			442	1479	395	92	7	28	(14	14)	585	183	154	174	117	1	291	14	16	13	5	4	.56	52	.267	.324	.396

Willie Harris

Bats: L Throws: R Pos: CF-63; LF-45; PH-27; 2B-19; 3B-4; PR-3; RF-1   Ht: 5'9" Wt: 191 Born: 6/22/1978 Age: 32

						BATTING														BASERUNNING				AVERAGES		
Year	Team	Lg	G	AB	H	2B	3B	HR	(Hm	Rd)	TB	R	RBI	RC	TBB	IBB	SO	HBP	SH	SF	SB	CS	SB%	GDP	Avg	OBP	Slg
2009	Syrcse*	AAA	5	18	4	1	0	0	(-	-)	5	2	1	1	2	0	3	1	0	0	0	1	.00	0	.222	.333	.278
2001	Bal	AL	9	24	3	1	0	0	(0	0)	4	3	0	0	0	0	7	0	1	0	0	0	-	0	.125	.125	.167
2002	CWS	AL	49	163	38	4	0	2	(2	0)	48	14	12	15	9	0	21	0	3	2	8	0	1.00	3	.233	.270	.294
2003	CWS	AL	79	137	28	3	1	0	(0	0)	33	19	5	11	10	0	28	0	3	0	12	2	.86	1	.204	.259	.241
2004	CWS	AL	129	409	107	15	2	2	(2	0)	132	68	27	53	51	0	79	1	7	3	19	7	.73	4	.262	.343	.323
2005	CWS	AL	56	121	31	2	1	1	(1	0)	38	17	8	15	13	0	25	1	4	0	10	3	.77	1	.256	.333	.314
2006	Bos	AL	47	45	7	2	0	0	(0	0)	9	17	1	1	4	0	11	2	0	1	6	3	.67	0	.156	.250	.200
2007	Atl	NL	117	344	93	20	8	2	(1	1)	135	56	32	47	40	0	71	3	1	3	17	11	.61	3	.270	.349	.392
2008	Was	NL	140	367	92	14	4	13	(4	9)	153	58	43	60	50	2	66	3	3	1	13	3	.81	8	.251	.344	.417
2009	Was	NL	137	323	76	18	6	7	(6	1)	127	47	27	47	57	1	62	9	3	1	11	4	.73	4	.235	.364	.393
	Postseason		3	2	2	0	0	0	(0	0)	2	1	1	2	0	0	0	0	0	0	1	0	1.00	0	1.000	1.000	1.000
	9 ML YEARS		763	1933	475	79	22	27	(16	11)	679	299	155	239	234	3	370	19	25	11	96	33	.74	24	.246	.331	.351

Matt Harrison

Pitches: L Bats: L Pos: SP-11   Ht: 6'4" Wt: 225 Born: 9/16/1985 Age: 24

				HOW MUCH HE PITCHED					WHAT HE GAVE UP										THE RESULTS						
Year	Team	Lg	G	GS	CG	GF	IP	BFP	H	R	ER	HR	SH	SF	HB	TBB	IBB	SO	WP	Bk	W	L	Pct	Sh	Sv-Op	Hld	ERC	ERA
2003	Braves	R	11	6	0	1	39.0	161	40	18	16	2	0	0	0	9	0	33	3	0	3	1	.750	0	1--	-	3.28	3.69
2004	Danvle	R+	13	12	1	0	66.0	278	72	36	30	3	4	4	1	10	1	49	3	1	4	4	.500	0	0--	-	3.24	4.09
2005	Rome	A	27	27	2	0	167.0	672	151	65	60	17	1	3	6	30	0	118	3	2	12	7	.632	1	0--	-	2.89	3.23
2006	MrtlBh	A+	13	13	2	0	81.1	327	77	30	28	6	1	1	4	16	0	60	0	1	8	4	.667	1	0--	-	3.11	3.10
2006	Missi	AA	13	12	1	0	77.1	330	83	36	31	6	4	3	1	17	0	54	5	5	3	4	.429	0	0--	-	3.62	3.61
2007	Missi	AA	20	20	0	0	116.2	487	118	51	44	6	2	3	1	34	0	78	2	3	5	7	.417	0	0--	-	3.46	3.39
2008	Frisco	AA	9	9	1	0	46.0	200	49	23	17	3	0	0	0	14	0	35	0	1	3	2	.600	1	0--	-	3.75	3.33
2008	Okla	AAA	6	6	0	0	39.0	159	40	16	16	1	0	2	0	14	0	18	1	0	3	1	.750	0	0--	-	4.25	3.55
2009	Frisco	AA	3	3	0	0	9.0	38	9	3	3	0	1	1	0	4	0	7	0	0	0	1	.000	0	0--	-	3.65	3.00
2008	Tex	AL	15	15	1	0	83.2	372	100	57	51	12	1	5	2	31	2	42	2	2	9	3	.750	1	0-0	0	5.53	5.49
2009	Tex	AL	11	11	2	0	63.1	283	81	43	43	9	1	1	2	23	0	34	0	0	4	5	.444	1	0-0	0	6.17	6.11
	2 ML YEARS		26	26	3	0	147.0	655	181	100	94	21	2	6	4	54	2	76	2	2	13	8	.619	2	0-0	0	5.80	5.76

Corey Hart

Bats: R Throws: R Pos: RF-112; PH-9   Ht: 6'6" Wt: 229 Born: 3/24/1982 Age: 28

						BATTING														BASERUNNING				AVERAGES		
Year	Team	Lg	G	AB	H	2B	3B	HR	(Hm	Rd)	TB	R	RBI	RC	TBB	IBB	SO	HBP	SH	SF	SB	CS	SB%	GDP	Avg	OBP	Slg
2009	Nashv*	AAA	4	10	5	1	0	1	(-	-)	9	5	3	4	2	0	2	2	0	0	0	0	-	0	.500	.643	.900
2004	Mil	NL	1	1	0	0	0	0	(0	0)	0	0	0	0	0	0	1	0	0	0	0	0	-	0	.000	.000	.000
2005	Mil	NL	21	57	11	2	1	2	(2	0)	21	9	7	4	6	0	11	0	0	0	2	0	1.00	6	.193	.270	.368
2006	Mil	NL	87	237	67	13	2	9	(6	3)	111	32	33	30	17	1	58	0	0	2	5	8	.38	7	.283	.328	.468
2007	Mil	NL	140	505	149	31	9	24	(15	9)	272	86	81	94	36	3	99	13	5	7	23	7	.77	6	.295	.353	.539
2008	Mil	NL	157	612	164	45	6	20	(7	13)	281	76	91	81	27	2	109	5	4	9	23	7	.77	14	.268	.300	.459
2009	Mil	NL	115	419	109	24	3	12	(9	3)	175	64	48	51	43	0	92	8	1	3	11	6	.65	9	.260	.335	.418
	Postseason		4	13	3	0	0	0	(0	0)	3	0	0	0	1	0	3	1	1	0	0	0	-	1	.231	.333	.231
	6 ML YEARS		521	1831	500	117	21	67	(39	28)	860	267	260	260	129	6	370	24	10	21	64	28	.70	45	.273	.326	.470

Kevin Hart

Pitches: R Bats: R Pos: SP-14; RP-4   Ht: 6'4" Wt: 220 Born: 11/29/1982 Age: 27

				HOW MUCH HE PITCHED					WHAT HE GAVE UP										THE RESULTS						
Year	Team	Lg	G	GS	CG	GF	IP	BFP	H	R	ER	HR	SH	SF	HB	TBB	IBB	SO	WP	Bk	W	L	Pct	Sh	Sv-Op	Hld	ERC	ERA
2009	Iowa*	AAA	22	6	0	12	52.1	217	39	20	18	5	2	1	5	20	0	57	3	0	3	3	.500	0	3--	-	2.98	3.10
2009	Peoria*	A	1	1	0	0	4.0	16	3	2	2	1	0	0	0	1	0	3	0	0	0	0	-	0	0--	-	3.01	4.50
2007	ChC	NL	8	0	0	2	11.0	42	7	1	1	0	1	0	0	4	0	13	0	0	0	0	-	0	0-0	0	1.62	0.82
2008	ChC	NL	21	0	0	4	27.2	142	39	24	20	2	1	0	3	18	3	23	1	0	2	2	.500	0	0-0	1	7.48	6.51
2009	2 Tms	NL	18	14	0	0	81.0	374	97	55	49	11	3	6	4	44	3	52	4	0	4	9	.308	0	0-0	0	6.35	5.44
	09 ChC	NL	8	4	0	3	27.2	120	23	8	8	3	2	3	2	18	1	13	0	0	3	1	.750	0	0-0	0	4.53	2.60
	09 Pit	NL	10	10	0	0	53.1	254	74	47	41	8	1	3	2	26	2	39	4	0	1	8	.111	0	0-0	0	7.35	6.92
	Postseason		1	0	0	0	1.0	5	0	2	2	0	0	0	0	2	0	2	1	0	0	0	-	0	0-0	0	3.47	18.00
	3 ML YEARS		47	14	0	9	119.2	558	143	80	70	13	5	6	7	66	6	88	5	0	6	11	.353	0	0-0	1	6.11	5.26

LaTroy Hawkins

Pitches: R Bats: R Pos: RP-65   Ht: 6'5" Wt: 215 Born: 12/21/1972 Age: 37

				HOW MUCH HE PITCHED					WHAT HE GAVE UP										THE RESULTS						
Year	Team	Lg	G	GS	CG	GF	IP	BFP	H	R	ER	HR	SH	SF	HB	TBB	IBB	SO	WP	Bk	W	L	Pct	Sh	Sv-Op	Hld	ERC	ERA
1995	Min	AL	6	6	1	0	27.0	131	39	29	26	3	0	3	1	12	0	9	1	1	2	3	.400	0	0-0	0	7.14	8.67
1996	Min	AL	7	6	0	1	26.1	124	42	24	24	8	1	1	0	9	0	24	1	1	1	1	.500	0	0-0	0	9.49	8.20
1997	Min	AL	20	20	0	0	103.1	478	134	71	67	19	2	2	4	47	0	58	6	3	6	12	.333	0	0-0	0	7.01	5.84
1998	Min	AL	33	33	0	0	190.1	840	227	126	111	27	4	10	5	61	1	105	10	2	7	14	.333	0	0-0	0	5.31	5.25
1999	Min	AL	33	33	1	0	174.1	803	238	136	129	29	1	5	1	60	2	103	9	0	10	14	.417	0	0-0	0	6.55	6.66
2000	Min	AL	66	0	0	38	87.2	370	85	34	33	7	4	1	1	32	1	59	6	0	2	5	.286	0	14-14	7	3.70	3.39
2001	Min	AL	62	0	0	51	51.1	248	59	34	34	3	4	1	4	39	3	36	7	0	1	5	.167	0	28-37	1	6.02	5.96
2002	Min	AL	65	0	0	15	80.1	310	63	23	19	5	2	3	0	15	1	63	5	0	6	0	1.000	0	0-3	13	1.99	2.13
2003	Min	AL	74	0	0	12	77.1	310	69	20	16	4	4	1	1	15	1	75	5	0	9	3	.750	0	2-8	28	2.48	1.86
2004	ChC	NL	77	0	0	50	82.0	333	72	27	24	10	6	2	2	14	5	69	2	0	5	4	.556	0	25-34	4	2.66	2.63
2005	2 Tms	NL	66	0	0	21	56.1	247	58	27	24	7	3	1	0	24	3	43	1	0	2	5	.200	0	6-15	15	4.41	3.83
2006	Bal	AL	60	0	0	12	60.1	261	73	30	30	4	1	2	0	15	3	27	2	0	3	2	.600	0	0-4	16	4.37	4.48

Year Team	Lg	HOW MUCH HE PITCHED						WHAT HE GAVE UP												THE RESULTS							
		G	GS	CG	GF	IP	BFP	H	R	ER	HR	SH	SF	HB	TBB	IBB	SO	WP	Bk	W	L	Pct	Sh	Sv-Op	Hld	ERC	ERA
2007 Col	NL	62	0	0	10	55.1	225	52	21	21	6	2	1	0	16	1	29	2	0	2	5	.286	0	0-5	18	3.43	3.42
2008 2 Tms		57	0	0	15	62.0	252	53	29	27	3	1	3	0	22	4	48	3	0	3	1	.750	0	1-2	13	2.75	3.92
2009 Hou		65	0	0	34	63.1	259	60	16	15	7	2	2	2	16	2	45	2	0	1	4	.200	0	11-15	19	3.42	2.13
05 ChC	NL	21	0	0	12	19.0	80	18	9	7	4	1	0	0	7	0	13	0	0	1	4	.200	0	4-8	0	4.44	3.32
05 SF	NL	45	0	0	9	37.1	167	40	18	17	3	2	1	0	17	3	30	1	0	1	4	.200	0	2-7	15	4.36	4.10
08 NYY	AL	33	0	0	11	41.0	173	42	26	26	3	1	2	0	17	3	23	2	0	1	1	.500	0	0-1	1	4.09	5.71
08 Hou		24	0	0	4	21.0	79	11	3	1	0	0	1	0	5	1	25	1	0	2	0	1.000	0	1-1	12	0.95	0.43
Postseason		15	0	0	4	11.2	48	11	7	6	0	2	1	0	2	0	14	0	0	1	0	1.000	0	0-0	4	2.24	4.63
15 ML YEARS		753	98	2	259	1197.1	5191	1324	647	600	142	34	41	18	397	27	793	62	7	60	81	.426	0	87-137	134	4.58	4.51

Blake Hawksworth

Pitches: R **Bats:** R **Pos:** RP-30 **Ht:** 6'3" **Wt:** 195 **Born:** 3/1/1983 **Age:** 27

Year Team	Lg	HOW MUCH HE PITCHED						WHAT HE GAVE UP												THE RESULTS							
		G	GS	CG	GF	IP	BFP	H	R	ER	HR	SH	SF	HB	TBB	IBB	SO	WP	Bk	W	L	Pct	Sh	Sv-Op	Hld	ERC	ERA
2002 JhsCty	R+	13	12	0	0	66.0	275	58	31	23	8	1	1	4	18	0	61	4	0	2	4	.333	0	0--	-	3.27	3.14
2002 NewJrs	A-	2	2	0	0	9.2	37	6	0	0	0	0	0	0	2	0	8	0	0	1	0	1.000	0	0--	-	1.18	0.00
2003 Peoria	A	10	10	0	0	54.2	213	37	16	14	0	1	1	1	12	0	57	1	1	5	1	.833	0	0--	-	1.41	2.30
2003 PlmBh	A+	6	6	0	0	32.0	132	28	14	14	2	0	1	1	11	0	32	2	0	1	3	.250	0	0--	-	3.09	3.94
2004 PlmBh	A+	2	2	0	0	10.2	45	10	7	7	2	1	1	0	3	0	11	3	1	1	0	1.000	0	0--	-	3.76	5.91
2005 NewJrs	A-	7	6	0	0	14.2	72	18	18	13	0	0	1	5	10	0	12	3	0	0	3	.000	0	0--	-	7.46	7.98
2006 PlmBh	A+	14	14	0	0	83.2	333	75	23	23	0	2	2	6	19	0	55	5	2	7	2	.778	0	0--	-	2.60	2.47
2006 Sprgfld	AA	13	13	0	0	79.2	329	72	34	30	8	3	3	2	31	1	66	2	0	4	2	.667	0	0--	-	3.69	3.39
2007 Memp	AAA	25	25	0	0	129.2	571	150	82	76	24	6	5	10	41	0	88	9	1	4	13	.235	0	0--	-	5.66	5.28
2008 Memp	AAA	18	16	0	0	88.2	413	111	71	60	12	3	3	8	38	1	83	7	1	5	7	.417	0	0--	-	6.33	6.09
2008 Cards	R	2	2	0	0	7.0	24	2	0	0	0	0	0	0	2	0	6	0	0	0	0	-	0	0--	-	0.54	0.00
2009 Memp	AAA	12	12	1	0	73.0	303	61	31	29	3	4	2	2	20	1	57	0	0	5	4	.556	0	0--	-	2.39	3.58
2009 StL	NL	30	0	0	10	40.0	160	29	10	9	2	4	1	1	15	3	20	0	0	4	0	1.000	0	0-0	2	2.26	2.03

Brad Hawpe

Bats: L **Throws:** L **Pos:** RF-141; PH-3; DH-1 **Ht:** 6'3" **Wt:** 205 **Born:** 6/22/1979 **Age:** 31

Year Team	Lg	BATTING																			BASERUNNING				AVERAGES		
		G	AB	H	2B	3B	HR	(Hm	Rd)	TB	R	RBI	RC	TBB	IBB	SO	HBP	SH	SF		SB	CS	SB%	GDP	Avg	OBP	Slg
2004 Col	NL	42	105	26	3	2	3	(1	2)	42	12	9	11	11	3	34	1	0	1		1	1	.50	4	.248	.322	.400
2005 Col	NL	101	305	80	10	3	9	(5	4)	123	38	47	44	43	3	70	0	0	3		2	2	.50	5	.262	.350	.403
2006 Col	NL	150	499	146	33	6	22	(6	16)	257	67	84	85	74	11	123	0	0	2		5	5	.50	8	.293	.383	.515
2007 Col	NL	152	516	150	33	4	29	(19	10)	278	80	116	103	81	11	137	3	1	5		2	2	.00	13	.291	.387	.539
2008 Col	NL	138	488	138	24	3	25	(14	11)	243	69	85	86	76	6	134	3	0	2		2	2	.50	7	.283	.381	.498
2009 Col	NL	145	501	143	42	3	23	(9	14)	260	82	86	91	79	7	145	4	0	4		1	3	.25	18	.285	.384	.519
Postseason		11	39	11	0	1	1	(1	0)	16	4	4	6	8	0	16	0	0	0		0	0	-	0	.282	.404	.410
6 ML YEARS		728	2414	683	145	21	111	(54	57)	1203	348	427	420	364	41	643	11	1	17		11	15	.42	55	.283	.377	.498

Brett Hayes

Bats: R **Throws:** R **Pos:** PH-10; PR-3; 1B-1 **Ht:** 6'1" **Wt:** 202 **Born:** 2/13/1984 **Age:** 26

Year Team	Lg	BATTING																			BASERUNNING				AVERAGES		
		G	AB	H	2B	3B	HR	(Hm	Rd)	TB	R	RBI	RC	TBB	IBB	SO	HBP	SH	SF		SB	CS	SB%	GDP	Avg	OBP	Slg
2005 Mrlns	R	3	12	5	1	0	0	(-	-)	6	2	2	1	0	0	2	0	0	0		0	1	.00	0	.417	.417	.500
2005 Jmstwn	A-	36	117	28	6	1	1	(-	-)	39	11	12	12	12	0	21	1	0	1		3	3	.50	3	.239	.313	.333
2006 Grnsbr	A	82	278	68	13	1	9	(-	-)	110	39	38	37	29	0	61	4	1	4		4	3	.57	5	.245	.321	.396
2007 Jupiter	A+	17	65	22	3	1	1	(-	-)	30	10	11	12	9	1	10	0	0	1		2	3	.40	2	.338	.413	.462
2007 Carlina	AA	74	273	64	16	0	3	(-	-)	89	22	31	26	18	0	51	0	2	2		2	0	1.00	7	.234	.280	.326
2008 Albq	AAA	37	116	34	3	1	5	(-	-)	54	21	17	17	4	0	23	3	2	1		1	1	.50	3	.293	.331	.466
2008 Carlina	AA	54	181	42	8	0	6	(-	-)	68	19	18	17	10	0	43	1	1	1		1	4	.20	1	.232	.275	.376
2009 NewOr	AAA	90	321	77	15	0	4	(-	-)	104	27	37	31	20	2	66	1	4	7		2	0	1.00	10	.240	.281	.324
2009 Fla	NL	14	11	3	1	0	1	(0	1)	7	5	2	1	0	0	4	1	0	0		0	0	-	1	.273	.333	.636

Dirk Hayhurst

Pitches: R **Bats:** L **Pos:** RP-15 **Ht:** 6'2" **Wt:** 215 **Born:** 3/24/1981 **Age:** 29

Year Team	Lg	HOW MUCH HE PITCHED						WHAT HE GAVE UP												THE RESULTS							
		G	GS	CG	GF	IP	BFP	H	R	ER	HR	SH	SF	HB	TBB	IBB	SO	WP	Bk	W	L	Pct	Sh	Sv-Op	Hld	ERC	ERA
2003 Eugene	A-	25	1	0	5	37.2	168	38	23	16	3	1	0	4	12	0	49	0	0	4	3	.571	0	0--	-	3.95	3.82
2004 FtWyn	A	26	17	0	1	118.1	475	114	41	35	6	5	5	4	19	0	106	4	1	9	4	.692	0	0--	-	2.84	2.66
2004 Lk Els	A+	5	5	0	0	22.2	109	25	18	14	2	0	1	1	16	0	18	1	1	1	2	.333	0	0--	-	5.92	5.56
2005 Lk Els	A+	38	7	0	7	93.2	414	106	66	56	9	1	7	4	27	0	69	3	1	5	5	.500	0	1--	-	4.46	5.38
2005 Mobile	AA	1	1	1	0	7.0	26	5	2	2	1	0	0	0	4	0	4	1	0	1	0	1.000	0	0--	-	4.01	2.57
2006 Lk Els	A+	12	11	0	0	59.0	259	61	34	26	3	2	2	5	20	0	51	4	0	2	7	.222	0	0--	-	3.97	3.97
2006 PortInd	AAA	4	4	0	0	20.0	95	29	15	15	4	0	2	0	9	0	12	0	0	1	2	.333	0	0--	-	7.94	6.75
2006 Mobile	AA	12	10	0	0	52.1	230	58	35	28	6	1	1	3	18	3	49	1	0	3	5	.375	0	0--	-	4.73	4.82
2007 Lk Els	A+	13	0	0	4	20.0	87	23	11	4	0	0	0	1	6	2	16	1	0	0	1	.000	0	0--	-	3.86	1.80
2007 SnAnt	AA	32	1	0	8	59.1	242	54	24	21	6	2	0	2	9	1	55	4	0	4	1	.800	0	2--	-	2.72	3.19
2007 PortInd	AAA	2	0	0	0	2.2	17	9	7	7	2	1	0	1	0	0	1	1	0	0	0	-	0	0--	-	30.21	23.63
2008 PortInd	AAA	46	2	0	7	84.0	362	84	36	35	7	4	3	3	28	4	98	3	1	2	3	.400	0	2--	-	3.73	3.75
2009 LsVgs	AAA	25	6	0	3	57.2	248	70	33	25	6	4	1	1	12	3	48	1	1	4	6	.400	0	0--	-	4.58	3.90
2008 SD	NL	10	3	0	3	16.2	84	27	18	18	2	0	0	0	10	1	14	4	0	0	2	.000	0	0-0	0	8.97	9.72
2009 Tor	AL	15	0	0	5	22.2	97	23	7	7	2	0	2	2	9	2	13	1	0	0	0	-	0	0-0	0	4.40	2.78
2 ML YEARS		25	3	0	8	39.1	181	50	25	25	4	0	2	2	19	3	27	5	0	0	2	.000	0	0-0	0	6.23	5.72

Chase Headley

Bats: B **Throws:** R **Pos:** LF-114; 3B-28; PH-16; DH-2; 1B-1   **Ht:** 6'2" **Wt:** 211 **Born:** 5/9/1984 **Age:** 26

Year	Team	Lg	G	AB	H	2B	3B	HR	(Hm	Rd)	TB	R	RBI	RC	TBB	IBB	SO	HBP	SH	SF	SB	CS	SB%	GDP	Avg	OBP	Slg
2007	SD	NL	8	18	4	1	0	0	(0	0)	5	1	0	1	2	0	4	1	0	0	0	0	-	2	.222	.333	.278
2008	SD	NL	91	331	89	19	2	9	(4	5)	139	34	38	42	30	1	104	5	0	2	4	1	.80	5	.269	.337	.420
2009	SD	NL	156	543	142	31	2	12	(7	5)	213	62	64	68	62	3	133	5	0	2	10	2	.83	19	.262	.342	.392
	3 ML YEARS		255	892	235	51	4	21	(11	10)	357	97	102	111	94	4	241	11	0	4	14	3	.82	26	.263	.340	.400

Aaron Heilman

Pitches: R **Bats:** R **Pos:** RP-70   **Ht:** 6'5" **Wt:** 227 **Born:** 11/12/1978 **Age:** 31

Year	Team	Lg	G	GS	CG	GF	IP	BFP	H	R	ER	HR	SH	SF	HB	TBB	IBB	SO	WP	Bk	W	L	Pct	Sh	Sv-Op	Hld	ERC	ERA
2003	NYM	NL	14	13	0	0	65.1	315	79	53	49	13	5	3	3	41	2	51	5	0	2	7	.222	0	0-0	0	7.16	6.75
2004	NYM	NL	5	5	0	0	28.0	119	27	17	17	4	1	0	0	13	0	22	0	0	1	3	.250	0	0-0	0	4.54	5.46
2005	NYM	NL	53	7	1	20	108.0	439	87	40	38	6	4	1	6	37	4	106	1	1	5	3	.625	1	5-6	5	2.74	3.17
2006	NYM	NL	74	0	0	14	87.0	356	73	37	35	7	2	3	2	28	2	73	5	0	4	5	.444	0	0-5	27	2.76	3.62
2007	NYM	NL	81	0	0	28	86.0	352	72	36	29	8	4	2	5	20	1	63	2	0	7	7	.500	0	1-6	22	2.71	3.03
2008	NYM	NL	78	0	0	23	76.0	356	75	48	44	10	8	2	9	46	8	80	2	0	3	8	.273	0	3-8	15	5.26	5.21
2009	ChC	NL	70	0	0	11	72.1	313	68	34	33	9	9	4	1	34	4	65	4	0	4	4	.500	0	1-7	10	4.16	4.11
	Postseason		6	0	0	1	7.1	30	7	3	3	2	0	0	0	1	1	6	1	0	0	1	.000	0	0-0	1	3.60	3.68
	7 ML YEARS		375	25	1	96	522.2	2250	481	265	245	55	38	14	27	219	21	460	19	1	26	37	.413	1	10-32	79	3.88	4.22

Wes Helms

Bats: R **Throws:** R **Pos:** 3B-70; PH-56; 1B-4; PR-2   **Ht:** 6'4" **Wt:** 227 **Born:** 5/12/1976 **Age:** 34

Year	Team	Lg	G	AB	H	2B	3B	HR	(Hm	Rd)	TB	R	RBI	RC	TBB	IBB	SO	HRP	SH	SF	SB	CS	SB%	GDP	Avg	OBP	Slg
1998	Mil	NL	7	13	4	1	0	1	(0	1)	8	2	2	2	0	0	4	0	0	0	0	0	-	0	.308	.308	.615
2000	Atl	NL	8	5	1	0	0	0	(0	0)	1	0	0	0	0	0	2	0	0	0	0	0	-	0	.200	.200	.200
2001	Atl	NL	100	216	48	10	3	10	(6	4)	94	28	36	27	21	2	56	1	0	1	1	1	.50	3	.222	.293	.435
2002	Atl	NL	85	210	51	16	0	6	(4	2)	85	20	22	15	11	2	57	3	1	6	1	1	.50	5	.243	.283	.405
2003	Mil	NL	134	476	124	21	0	23	(16	7)	214	56	67	66	43	3	131	10	0	7	0	1	.00	10	.261	.330	.450
2004	Mil	NL	92	274	72	13	1	4	(3	1)	99	34	28	28	24	1	66	8	1	2	0	1	.00	10	.263	.331	.361
2005	Mil	NL	95	168	50	13	1	4	(2	2)	77	18	24	26	14	0	30	3	0	3	0	1	.00	7	.298	.356	.458
2006	Fla	NL	140	240	79	19	5	10	(4	6)	138	30	47	45	21	1	55	6	6	5	0	4	.00	7	.329	.390	.575
2007	Phi	NL	112	280	69	19	0	5	(3	2)	103	21	39	24	19	2	62	3	2	4	0	0	-	10	.246	.297	.368
2008	Fla	NL	132	251	61	11	0	5	(1	4)	87	28	31	29	17	0	65	5	0	5	0	0	-	6	.243	.299	.347
2009	Fla	NL	113	214	58	11	0	3	(1	2)	78	18	33	26	13	1	54	3	1	3	1	1	.50	10	.271	.318	.364
	Postseason		3	2	0	0	0	0	(0	0)	0	1	0	0	1	0	0	0	0	0	0	0	-	0	.000	.333	.000
	11 ML YEARS		1016	2347	617	134	10	71	(40	31)	984	245	329	288	183	12	576	39	11	36	3	10	.23	68	.263	.322	.419

Todd Helton

Bats: L **Throws:** L **Pos:** 1B-149; PH-2   **Ht:** 6'2" **Wt:** 210 **Born:** 8/20/1973 **Age:** 36

Year	Team	Lg	G	AB	H	2B	3B	HR	(Hm	Rd)	TB	R	RBI	RC	TBB	IBB	SO	HBP	SH	SF	SB	CS	SB%	GDP	Avg	OBP	Slg
1997	Col	NL	35	93	26	2	1	5	(3	2)	45	13	11	15	8	0	11	0	0	0	0	1	.00	1	.280	.337	.484
1998	Col	NL	152	530	167	37	1	25	(13	12)	281	78	97	101	53	5	54	6	1	5	3	3	.50	15	.315	.380	.530
1999	Col	NL	159	578	185	39	5	35	(23	12)	339	114	113	124	68	6	77	6	0	4	7	6	.54	14	.320	.395	.587
2000	Col	NL	160	580	216	59	2	42	(27	15)	405	138	147	169	103	22	61	4	0	10	5	3	.63	12	.372	.463	.698
2001	Col	NL	159	587	197	54	2	49	(27	22)	402	132	146	157	98	16	104	5	1	5	7	5	.58	14	.336	.432	.685
2002	Col	NL	156	553	182	39	4	30	(18	12)	319	107	109	127	99	21	91	5	0	10	5	1	.83	10	.329	.429	.577
2003	Col	NL	160	583	209	49	5	33	(23	10)	367	135	117	160	111	21	72	2	0	7	0	4	.00	19	.358	.458	.630
2004	Col	NL	154	547	190	49	2	32	(21	11)	339	115	96	143	127	19	72	3	0	6	3	0	1.00	14	.347	.469	.620
2005	Col	NL	144	509	163	45	2	20	(13	7)	272	92	79	114	106	22	80	9	1	1	3	0	1.00	14	.320	.445	.534
2006	Col	NL	145	546	165	40	5	15	(8	7)	260	94	81	118	91	15	64	6	0	6	3	2	.60	10	.302	.404	.476
2007	Col	NL	154	557	178	42	2	17	(9	8)	275	86	91	115	116	16	74	2	0	7	0	1	.00	14	.320	.434	.494
2008	Col	NL	83	299	79	16	0	7	(5	2)	116	39	29	45	61	8	50	1	0	0	0	0	-	9	.264	.391	.388
2009	Col	NL	151	544	177	38	3	15	(10	5)	266	79	86	108	89	5	73	2	0	0	0	1	.00	15	.325	.416	.489
	Postseason		11	41	9	2	1	0	(0	0)	13	6	2	2	5	0	9	0	0	1	0	0	-	0	.220	.298	.317
	13 ML YEARS		1812	6506	2134	509	34	325	(200	125)	3686	1222	1202	1496	1130	175	883	51	3	71	36	27	.57	160	.328	.427	.567

Mark Hendrickson

Pitches: L **Bats:** L **Pos:** RP-42; SP-11   **Ht:** 6'9" **Wt:** 240 **Born:** 6/23/1974 **Age:** 36

Year	Team	Lg	G	GS	CG	GF	IP	BFP	H	R	ER	HR	SH	SF	HB	TBB	IBB	SO	WP	Bk	W	L	Pct	Sh	Sv-Op	Hld	ERC	ERA
2002	Tor	AL	16	4	0	0	36.2	142	25	11	10	1	2	2	2	12	3	21	0	0	3	0	1.000	0	0-1	1	1.90	2.45
2003	Tor	AL	30	30	1	0	158.1	703	207	111	97	24	1	8	0	40	3	76	4	0	9	9	.500	1	0-0	0	5.64	5.51
2004	TB	AL	32	30	2	1	183.1	803	211	113	98	21	4	5	7	46	5	87	4	5	10	15	.400	0	0-0	0	4.51	4.81
2005	TB	AL	31	31	1	0	178.1	796	227	126	117	24	8	7	2	49	1	89	4	1	11	8	.579	0	0-0	0	5.44	5.90
2006	2 Tms		31	25	1	0	164.2	719	173	87	77	17	5	4	4	62	0	99	6	1	6	15	.286	1	0-1	1	4.38	4.21
2007	LAD	NL	39	15	0	4	122.2	532	142	75	71	15	12	4	1	29	4	92	4	0	4	8	.333	0	0-0	0	4.42	5.21
2008	Fla	NL	36	19	0	4	133.2	590	148	87	81	17	9	5	5	48	7	81	4	0	7	8	.467	0	0-0	0	4.78	5.45
2009	Bal	AL	53	11	0	12	105.0	457	116	59	51	16	2	5	2	33	4	61	2	1	6	5	.545	0	1-3	2	4.71	4.37
06	BAL	AL	13	13	1	0	89.2	377	81	42	38	10	2	3	2	34	0	51	4	0	4	8	.333	1	0-0	0	3.65	3.81
06	LAD	NL	18	12	0	0	75.0	342	92	45	39	7	3	1	2	28	0	48	2	1	2	7	.222	0	0-0	1	5.29	4.68
	Postseason		3	0	0	0	2.2	10	1	0	0	0	0	0	1	1	0	1	0	0	0	0	-	0	0-0	0	1.70	0.00
	8 ML YEARS		268	165	5	21	1082.2	4742	1249	669	602	135	43	40	23	319	27	606	29	5	56	68	.452	2	1-5	4	4.74	5.00

Sean Henn

Pitches: L **Bats:** R **Pos:** RP-20   **Ht:** 6'4" **Wt:** 225 **Born:** 4/23/1981 **Age:** 29

Year	Team	Lg	G	GS	CG	GF	IP	BFP	H	R	ER	HR	SH	SF	HB	TBB	IBB	SO	WP	Bk	W	L	Pct	Sh	Sv-Op	Hld	ERC	ERA
2009	Roch*	AAA	28	0	0	11	38.2	172	37	18	10	3	2	0	2	16	1	45	1	0	1	1	.500	0	6--	-	3.53	2.33
2005	NYY	AL	3	3	0	0	11.1	61	18	16	14	3	0	0	0	11	0	3	0	0	0	3	.000	0	0-0	0	12.12	11.12
2006	NYY	AL	4	1	0	0	9.1	44	11	5	5	2	0	1	1	5	0	7	0	0	0	1	.000	0	0-0	0	7.09	4.82
2007	NYY	AL	29	1	0	8	36.2	181	44	32	29	6	1	0	3	27	1	28	1	0	2	2	.500	0	0-0	2	7.47	7.12
2008	SD	NL	4	0	0	2	9.1	47	11	8	8	1	1	0	0	9	1	9	1	0	0	0	-	0	0-0	0	7.32	7.71
2009	2 Tms	NL	20	0	0	3	14.1	69	15	12	12	2	0	1	1	12	1	15	1	0	0	3	.000	0	0-2	2	6.67	7.53
09	Min	AL	14	0	0	3	11.1	50	9	9	9	2	0	1	1	8	1	9	0	0	0	3	.000	0	0-1	2	4.99	7.15
09	Bal	AL	6	0	0	0	3.0	19	6	3	3	0	0	0	0	4	0	6	1	0	0	0	-	0	0-1	0	13.56	9.00
5 ML YEARS			60	5	0	13	81.0	402	99	73	68	14	2	2	5	64	3	62	3	0	2	9	.182	0	0-2	4	7.88	7.56

Matt Herges

Pitches: R **Bats:** L **Pos:** RP-30   **Ht:** 6'0" **Wt:** 210 **Born:** 4/1/1970 **Age:** 40

Year	Team	Lg	G	GS	CG	GF	IP	BFP	H	R	ER	HR	SH	SF	HB	TBB	IBB	SO	WP	Bk	W	L	Pct	Sh	Sv-Op	Hld	ERC	ERA
2009	Clmbs*	AAA	11	0	0	6	10.0	45	12	6	6	0	0	2	0	5	0	7	0	0	1	2	.333	0	4--	-	4.95	5.40
2009	ColSpr*	AAA	13	0	0	1	18.1	73	13	4	4	1	0	0	1	4	1	14	0	0	3	2	.600	0	0--	-	1.76	1.96
1999	LAD	NL	17	0	0	9	24.1	104	24	13	11	5	1	0	1	8	0	18	0	0	0	2	.000	0	0-2	1	4.61	4.07
2000	LAD	NL	59	4	0	17	110.2	461	100	43	39	7	9	4	6	40	5	75	4	0	11	3	.786	0	1-3	4	3.35	3.17
2001	LAD	NL	75	0	0	22	99.1	435	97	39	38	8	4	3	8	46	12	76	2	0	9	8	.529	0	1-8	15	4.20	3.44
2002	Mon	NL	62	0	0	25	64.2	298	80	33	29	10	6	2	2	26	8	50	3	0	2	5	.286	0	6-14	9	5.74	4.04
2003	2 Tms	NL	67	0	0	24	79.0	332	68	27	23	3	2	6	3	29	2	68	1	1	3	2	.600	0	3-6	9	2.87	2.62
2004	SF	NL	70	0	0	43	65.1	301	90	44	38	8	7	4	3	21	4	39	2	0	4	5	.444	0	23-31	5	6.29	5.23
2005	2 Tms	NL	28	0	0	7	29.0	132	35	23	23	6	2	2	1	12	1	9	0	0	1	1	.500	0	0-0	3	6.26	7.14
2006	Fla	NL	66	0	0	21	71.0	328	94	42	34	5	3	1	3	28	5	36	1	0	2	3	.400	0	0-4	9	5.81	4.31
2007	Col	NL	35	0	0	9	48.2	191	34	17	16	4	3	1	0	15	2	30	0	0	5	1	.833	0	0-2	3	2.05	2.96
2008	Col	NL	58	0	0	10	64.1	294	79	40	36	5	1	4	5	24	5	46	3	1	3	4	.429	0	0-5	4	5.29	5.04
2009	2 Tms	NL	30	0	0	11	34.2	147	34	14	13	5	1	0	0	8	0	26	0	0	3	1	.750	0	0-1	1	3.50	3.38
03	SD	NL	40	0	0	21	44.0	192	40	16	14	2	1	5	2	20	2	40	1	0	2	2	.500	0	3-5	4	3.45	2.86
03	SF	NL	27	0	0	3	35.0	140	28	11	9	1	1	1	1	9	0	28	0	1	1	0	1.000	0	0-1	5	2.18	2.31
05	SF	NL	21	0	0	5	21.0	90	23	11	11	2	2	1	0	7	1	6	0	0	1	1	.500	0	0-0	3	4.29	4.71
05	Ari	NL	7	0	0	2	8.0	42	12	12	12	4	0	1	1	5	0	3	0	0	0	0	-	0	0-0	0	12.23	13.50
09	Cle	AL	21	0	0	6	25.1	107	24	10	10	3	1	0	0	6	0	18	0	0	2	1	.667	0	0-1	1	3.17	3.55
09	Col	NL	9	0	0	5	9.1	40	10	4	3	2	0	0	0	2	0	8	0	0	1	0	1.000	0	0-0	0	4.41	2.89
Postseason			10	0	0	0	11.1	41	3	0	0	0	1	0	1	5	0	11	0	0	0	0	-	0	0-1	1	0.88	0.00
11 ML YEARS			567	4	0	198	691.0	3023	735	335	300	66	39	27	32	257	44	473	16	2	43	35	.551	0	34-76	63	4.38	3.91

Jeremy Hermida

Bats: L **Throws:** R **Pos:** RF-81; LF-51; PH-9; DH-2   **Ht:** 6'3" **Wt:** 222 **Born:** 1/30/1984 **Age:** 26

Year	Team	Lg	G	AB	H	2B	3B	HR	(Hm	Rd)	TB	R	RBI	RC	TBB	IBB	SO	HBP	SH	SF	SB	CS	SB%	GDP	Avg	OBP	Slg
2005	Fla	NL	23	41	12	2	0	4	(4	0)	26	9	11	10	6	1	12	0	0	0	2	0	1.00	1	.293	.383	.634
2006	Fla	NL	99	307	77	19	1	5	(3	2)	113	37	28	38	33	3	70	5	2	1	4	1	.80	6	.251	.332	.368
2007	Fla	NL	123	429	127	32	1	18	(8	10)	215	54	63	69	47	2	105	4	1	3	3	4	.43	10	.296	.369	.501
2008	Fla	NL	142	502	125	22	3	17	(4	13)	204	74	61	65	48	5	138	7	1	1	6	1	.86	12	.249	.323	.406
2009	Fla	NL	129	429	111	14	2	13	(4	9)	168	48	47	57	56	4	101	4	0	2	5	2	.71	6	.259	.348	.392
5 ML YEARS			516	1708	452	89	7	57	(23	34)	726	222	210	239	190	15	426	20	4	7	20	8	.71	35	.265	.344	.425

Anderson Hernandez

Bats: B **Throws:** R **Pos:** 2B-74; SS-38; PH-17; LF-1   **Ht:** 5'9" **Wt:** 186 **Born:** 10/30/1982 **Age:** 27

Year	Team	Lg	G	AB	H	2B	3B	HR	(Hm	Rd)	TB	R	RBI	RC	TBB	IBB	SO	HBP	SH	SF	SB	CS	SB%	GDP	Avg	OBP	Slg
2009	Syrcse*	AAA	1	4	0	0	0	0	(-	-)	0	0	0	0	0	0	0	0	0	0	0	0	-	0	.000	.000	.000
2005	NYM	NL	6	18	1	0	0	0	(0	0)	1	1	0	0	1	0	4	0	0	0	0	1	.00	0	.056	.105	.056
2006	NYM	NL	25	66	10	1	1	1	(1	0)	16	4	3	0	1	0	12	0	0	0	0	0	-	3	.152	.164	.242
2007	NYM	NL	4	3	1	0	0	0	(0	0)	1	1	0	0	0	0	1	0	0	0	0	0	-	0	.333	.333	.333
2008	Was	NL	28	81	27	4	0	0	(0	0)	31	11	17	18	10	0	8	0	0	0	0	0	-	1	.333	.407	.383
2009	2 Tms	NL	123	366	92	15	4	3	(0	3)	124	39	37	38	33	2	63	0	3	2	7	5	.58	10	.251	.312	.339
09	Was	NL	77	231	58	9	2	1	(0	1)	74	25	23	21	20	1	41	0	3	1	5	3	.63	6	.251	.310	.320
09	NYM	NL	46	135	34	6	2	2	(0	2)	50	14	14	17	13	1	22	0	0	1	2	2	.50	4	.252	.315	.370
Postseason			2	1	0	0	0	0	(0	0)	0	0	0	0	0	0	1	0	0	0	0	0	-	0	.000	.000	.000
5 ML YEARS			186	534	131	20	5	4	(1	3)	173	56	57	56	45	2	88	0	3	2	7	6	.54	14	.245	.303	.324

David Hernandez

Pitches: R **Bats:** R **Pos:** SP-19; RP-1   **Ht:** 6'3" **Wt:** 215 **Born:** 5/13/1985 **Age:** 25

Year	Team	Lg	G	GS	CG	GF	IP	BFP	H	R	ER	HR	SH	SF	HB	TBB	IBB	SO	WP	Bk	W	L	Pct	Sh	Sv-Op	Hld	ERC	ERA
2005	Abrdn	A-	12	8	0	0	41.2	188	41	21	18	2	1	2	1	17	0	47	3	1	1	2	.333	0	0--	-	4.23	3.89
2006	Dlmrva	A	28	28	0	0	145.1	639	134	83	67	13	4	3	10	71	0	154	22	0	7	8	.467	0	0--	-	4.17	4.15
2007	Frdrck	A+	28	27	0	0	145.1	622	139	86	80	16	1	4	11	47	0	168	12	1	7	11	.389	0	0--	-	3.89	4.95
2008	Bowie	AA	27	27	0	0	141.0	599	112	53	42	10	4	2	7	71	0	166	6	1	10	4	.714	0	0--	-	3.35	2.68
2009	Norfolk	AAA	11	11	0	0	57.1	232	42	26	21	5	1	0	2	18	1	79	3	0	3	2	.600	0	0--	-	2.37	3.30
2009	Bowie	AA	1	1	0	0	4.0	15	2	1	1	0	0	0	0	1	0	4	0	0	0	0	-	0	0--	-	0.94	2.25
2009	Bal	AL	20	19	0	0	101.1	462	118	62	61	27	2	3	1	46	0	68	3	0	4	10	.286	0	0-0	0	6.55	5.42

Diory Hernandez

Bats: R **Throws:** R **Pos:** SS-22; PH-6; 2B-4; 3B-3; PR-1　　　　**Ht:** 6'0" **Wt:** 185 **Born:** 4/8/1984 **Age:** 26

Year Team	Lg	G	AB	H	2B	3B	HR	(Hm	Rd)	TB	R	RBI	RC	TBB	IBB	SO	HBP	SH	SF	SB	CS	SB%	GDP	Avg	OBP	Slg
2003 Braves	R	54	190	42	9	2	1	(-	-)	58	26	12	16	14	0	24	4	1	1	2	4	.33	3	.221	.287	.305
2004 Rome	A	90	306	83	20	1	3	(-	-)	114	40	38	39	26	1	67	1	2	5	7	4	.64	8	.271	.325	.373
2005 Braves	R	7	28	10	1	0	1	(-	-)	14	5	4	4	0	0	2	0	0	0	2	0	.00	3	.357	.357	.500
2005 MrtlBh	A+	73	265	67	15	1	5	(-	-)	99	30	30	32	18	0	53	8	4	5	5	5	.50	5	.253	.314	.374
2006 MrtlBh	A+	76	286	68	10	0	6	(-	-)	96	37	47	31	19	2	51	5	0	2	11	1	.92	8	.238	.295	.336
2006 Braves	R	8	30	8	1	0	1	(-	-)	12	6	2	4	3	0	5	2	0	0	0	0	-	0	.267	.371	.400
2007 MrtlBh	A+	17	64	20	8	2	0	(-	-)	32	9	9	10	2	0	11	1	0	0	2	2	.50	1	.313	.343	.500
2007 Missi	AA	115	433	133	25	1	7	(-	-)	181	50	59	65	29	1	68	14	5	0	22	21	.51	13	.307	.370	.418
2008 Missi	AA	22	77	22	3	1	2	(-	-)	33	8	8	10	6	0	8	1	0	1	1	4	.20	3	.286	.341	.429
2008 Rchmd	AAA	120	459	132	23	3	5	(-	-)	176	46	53	57	20	0	73	2	4	5	7	5	.58	16	.288	.317	.383
2009 Gwnntt	AAA	54	204	65	16	1	1	(-	)	86	10	32	35	21	0	34	7	1	1	8	6	.57	5	.319	.399	.422
2009 Atl	NL	33	85	12	3	0	1	(1	0)	18	6	6	0	6	3	22	0	2	0	0	1	.00	4	.141	.198	.212

Felix Hernandez

Pitches: R **Bats:** R **Pos:** SP-34　　　　**Ht:** 6'3" **Wt:** 225 **Born:** 4/8/1986 **Age:** 24

Year Team	Lg	G	GS	CG	GF	IP	BFP	H	R	ER	HR	SH	SF	HB	TBB	IBB	SO	WP	Bk	W	L	Pct	Sh	Sv-Op	Hld	ERC	ERA
2005 Sea	AL	12	12	0	0	84.1	328	61	26	25	5	1	2	2	23	0	77	3	0	4	4	.500	1	0-0	0	2.08	2.67
2006 Sea	AL	31	31	0	0	191.0	816	195	105	96	23	2	3	6	60	2	176	11	0	12	14	.462	1	0-0	0	4.11	4.52
2007 Sea	AL	30	30	1	0	190.1	808	209	88	83	20	6	1	3	53	4	165	7	1	14	7	.667	1	0-0	0	4.27	3.92
2008 Sea	AL	31	31	2	0	200.2	857	198	85	77	17	4	8	8	80	7	175	8	1	9	11	.450	0	0-0	0	4.05	3.45
2009 Sea	AL	34	34	2	0	238.2	977	200	81	66	15	6	11	8	71	0	217	17	1	19	5	.792	1	0-0	0	2.72	2.49
5 ML YEARS		138	138	7	0	905.0	3786	863	385	347	80	19	23	27	287	13	810	46	3	58	41	.586	3	0-0	0	3.55	3.45

Livan Hernandez

Pitches: R **Bats:** R **Pos:** SP-31　　　　**Ht:** 6'2" **Wt:** 245 **Born:** 2/20/1975 **Age:** 35

Year Team	Lg	G	GS	CG	GF	IP	BFP	H	R	ER	HR	SH	SF	HB	TBB	IBB	SO	WP	Bk	W	L	Pct	Sh	Sv-Op	Hld	ERC	ERA
1996 Fla	NL	1	0	0	0	3.0	13	3	0	0	0	0	0	0	2	0	2	0	0	0	0	-	0	0-0	0	4.60	0.00
1997 Fla	NL	17	17	0	0	96.1	405	81	36	34	5	4	7	3	38	1	72	0	0	9	3	.750	0	0-0	0	2.96	3.18
1998 Fla	NL	33	33	9	0	234.1	1040	265	133	123	37	8	6	6	104	8	162	4	3	10	12	.455	0	0-0	0	5.58	4.72
1999 2 Tms	NL	30	30	2	0	199.2	886	227	110	103	23	7	6	2	76	5	144	2	2	8	12	.400	0	0-0	0	4.88	4.64
2000 SF	NL	33	33	5	0	240.0	1030	254	114	100	22	12	9	4	73	3	165	3	0	17	11	.607	2	0-0	0	4.01	3.75
2001 SF	NL	34	34	2	0	226.2	1008	266	143	132	24	12	12	3	85	7	138	7	0	13	15	.464	0	0-0	0	5.03	5.24
2002 SF	NL	33	33	5	0	216.0	921	233	113	105	19	14	8	4	71	5	134	1	1	12	16	.429	3	0-0	0	4.26	4.38
2003 Mon	NL	33	33	8	0	233.1	967	225	92	83	27	6	4	10	67	3	170	0	1	15	10	.600	0	0-0	0	3.55	3.20
2004 Mon	NL	35	35	9	0	255.0	1053	234	105	102	26	11	4	10	83	9	186	1	0	11	15	.423	2	0-0	0	3.52	3.60
2005 Was	NL	35	35	2	0	246.1	1065	268	116	109	25	15	9	13	84	14	147	3	2	15	10	.600	0	0-0	0	4.54	3.98
2006 2 Tms	NL	34	34	0	0	216.0	959	246	125	116	29	16	8	4	78	6	128	1	0	13	13	.500	0	0-0	0	4.97	4.83
2007 Ari	NL	33	33	1	0	204.1	913	247	116	112	34	17	8	6	79	1	90	3	2	11	11	.500	0	0-0	0	5.94	4.93
2008 2 Tms	NL	31	31	2	0	180.0	811	257	129	121	25	5	9	2	43	4	67	3	1	13	11	.542	0	0-0	0	6.35	6.05
2009 2 Tms	NL	31	31	2	0	183.2	806	220	112	111	19	13	10	1	67	5	102	1	0	9	12	.429	0	0-0	0	5.17	5.44
99 Fla	NL	20	20	2	0	136.0	612	161	78	72	17	3	4	2	55	3	97	2	1	5	9	.357	0	0-0	0	5.37	4.76
99 SF	NL	10	10	0	0	63.2	274	66	32	31	6	4	2	0	21	2	47	0	1	3	3	.500	0	0-0	0	3.88	4.38
06 Was	NL	24	24	0	0	146.2	661	176	94	87	22	10	7	2	52	4	89	0	0	9	8	.529	0	0-0	0	5.38	5.34
06 Ari	NL	10	10	0	0	69.1	298	70	31	29	7	6	1	2	26	2	39	1	0	4	5	.444	0	0-0	0	4.13	3.76
08 Min	AL	23	23	2	0	139.2	627	199	93	85	18	4	9	1	29	3	54	2	1	10	8	.556	0	0-0	0	6.06	5.48
08 Col	NL	8	8	0	0	40.1	184	58	36	36	7	1	0	1	14	1	13	1	0	3	3	.500	0	0-0	0	7.38	8.03
09 NYM	NL	23	23	1	0	135.0	593	164	83	82	16	8	8	1	51	3	75	1	0	7	8	.467	0	0-0	0	5.50	5.47
09 Was	NL	8	8	1	0	48.2	213	56	29	29	3	5	2	0	16	2	27	0	0	2	4	.333	0	0-0	0	4.30	5.36
Postseason		12	10	1	0	68.0	305	67	32	30	6	5	2	4	36	3	47	1	0	7	3	.700	0	0-0	0	4.56	3.97
14 ML YEARS		413	412	47	0	2734.2	11877	3026	1447	1351	315	140	99	68	940	71	1715	35	12	156	151	.508	7	0-0	0	4.66	4.45

Luis Hernandez

Bats: B **Throws:** R **Pos:** SS-23; 2B-8; PH-6; 3B-5; PR-3　　　　**Ht:** 5'10" **Wt:** 180 **Born:** 6/26/1984 **Age:** 26

Year Team	Lg	G	AB	H	2B	3B	HR	(Hm	Rd)	TB	R	RBI	RC	TBB	IBB	SO	HBP	SH	SF	SB	CS	SB%	GDP	Avg	OBP	Slg
2009 Omha*	AAA	55	198	60	10	0	1	(-	-)	73	24	26	27	16	0	17	1	7	1	1	3	.25	6	.303	.356	.369
2007 Bal	AL	30	69	20	2	0	1	(1	0)	25	5	7	6	1	0	10	0	1	0	2	2	.50	1	.290	.300	.362
2008 Bal	AL	36	79	19	1	0	0	(0	0)	20	9	3	6	7	0	11	0	3	2	2	0	1.00	2	.241	.295	.253
2009 KC	AL	37	73	15	1	0	0	(0	0)	16	4	4	4	4	0	18	1	3	0	1	0	1.00	2	.205	.256	.219
3 ML YEARS		103	221	54	4	0	1	(1	0)	61	18	14	16	12	0	39	1	7	2	5	2	.71	5	.244	.284	.276

Michel Hernandez

Bats: R **Throws:** R **Pos:** C-35　　　　**Ht:** 6'0" **Wt:** 215 **Born:** 8/12/1978 **Age:** 31

Year Team	Lg	G	AB	H	2B	3B	HR	(Hm	Rd)	TB	R	RBI	RC	TBB	IBB	SO	HBP	SH	SF	SB	CS	SB%	GDP	Avg	OBP	Slg
2009 Drham*	AAA	13	46	9	0	0	0	(-	-)	9	2	6	2	6	0	7	0	0	3	0	0	-	2	.196	.273	.196
2003 NYY	AL	5	4	1	0	0	0	(0	0)	1	0	0	1	1	0	1	0	0	0	0	0	-	0	.250	.400	.250
2008 TB	AL	5	15	3	0	0	0	(0	0)	3	2	0	0	0	0	3	0	0	0	0	0	-	0	.200	.200	.200
2009 TB	AL	35	99	24	3	1	1	(1	0)	32	12	12	7	7	0	12	0	1	0	2	1	.67	5	.242	.292	.323
3 ML YEARS		45	118	28	3	1	1	(1	0)	36	14	12	8	8	0	16	0	1	0	2	1	.67	5	.237	.286	.305

Ramon Hernandez

Bats: R **Throws:** R **Pos:** C-55; 1B-30; PH-2; 3B-1   **Ht:** 6'0" **Wt:** 225 **Born:** 5/20/1976 **Age:** 34

								BATTING													BASERUNNING				AVERAGES		
Year	Team	Lg	G	AB	H	2B	3B	HR	(Hm	Rd)	TB	R	RBI	RC	TBB	IBB	SO	HBP	SH	SF	SB	CS	SB%	GDP	Avg	OBP	Slg
1999	Oak	AL	40	136	38	7	0	3	(1	2)	54	13	21	20	18	0	11	1	1	2	1	0	1.00	5	.279	.363	.397
2000	Oak	AL	143	419	101	19	0	14	(7	7)	162	52	62	49	38	1	64	7	10	5	1	0	1.00	14	.241	.311	.387
2001	Oak	AL	136	453	115	25	0	15	(5	10)	185	55	60	58	37	3	68	6	9	4	1	1	.50	11	.254	.316	.408
2002	Oak	AL	136	403	94	20	0	7	(3	4)	135	51	42	41	43	1	64	5	3	3	0	0	-	11	.233	.313	.335
2003	Oak	AL	140	483	132	24	1	21	(9	12)	221	70	78	69	33	2	79	12	2	6	0	0	-	14	.273	.331	.458
2004	SD	NL	111	384	106	23	0	18	(10	8)	183	45	63	50	35	0	45	5	4	4	1	0	1.00	16	.276	.341	.477
2005	SD	NL	99	369	107	19	2	12	(5	7)	166	36	58	44	18	0	40	1	1	3	1	0	1.00	15	.290	.322	.450
2006	Bal	AL	144	501	138	29	2	23	(17	6)	240	66	91	82	43	2	79	11	0	5	1	0	1.00	13	.275	.343	.479
2007	Bal	AL	106	364	94	18	0	9	(4	5)	139	40	62	56	36	1	59	6	0	3	1	3	.25	9	.258	.333	.382
2008	Bal	AL	133	463	119	22	1	15	(10	5)	188	49	65	59	32	3	62	5	1	6	0	0	-	9	.257	.308	.406
2009	Cin	NL	81	287	74	13	1	5	(2	3)	104	25	37	42	33	2	34	3	4	4	1	0	1.00	7	.258	.336	.362
	Postseason		22	69	15	2	0	1	(1	0)	20	6	6	7	5	0	13	3	2	0	0	0	-	2	.217	.299	.290
11 ML YEARS			1269	4262	1118	219	7	142	(73	69)	1777	502	639	570	366	15	605	62	35	45	8	4	.67	122	.262	.327	.417

Daniel Ray Herrera

Pitches: L **Bats:** L **Pos:** RP-70   **Ht:** 5'6" **Wt:** 165 **Born:** 10/21/1984 **Age:** 25

			HOW MUCH HE PITCHED						WHAT HE GAVE UP											THE RESULTS						
Year	Team	Lg	G	GS	CG	GF	IP	BFP	H	R	ER	HR	SH	SF	HB	TBB	IBB	SO	WP	Bk	W	L	Pct	Sh	Sv-Op	Hld	ERC	ERA
2006	Rngrs	R	3	0	0	3	8.2	29	5	2	2	0	0	0	0	0	0	11	1	0	0	1	.000	0	2--	-	0.75	2.08
2006	Bkrsfld	A+	14	5	0	3	53.1	211	39	16	8	0	0	0	5	12	0	61	3	0	4	2	.667	0	1--	-	1.82	1.35
2007	Bkrsfld	A+	7	1	0	4	11.0	52	14	4	4	1	0	0	0	5	1	11	0	0	2	0	1.000	0	1--	-	5.51	3.27
2007	Frisco	AA	34	0	0	10	52.1	212	43	24	22	3	2	2	3	20	1	64	2	0	5	2	.714	0	0--	-	3.06	3.78
2008	Chatt	AA	10	0	0	1	17.2	69	12	6	5	0	1	3	1	7	0	10	0	0	3	0	1.000	0	0--	-	2.08	2.55
2008	Lsvlle	AAA	48	0	0	12	55.0	221	47	20	17	4	3	1	0	10	2	50	0	1	4	4	.500	0	6--	-	2.26	2.78
2008	Cin	NL	7	0	0	0	7.1	37	10	7	6	1	2	0	2	3	2	8	0	0	0	0	-	0	0-0	0	7.05	7.36
2009	Cin	NL	70	0	0	13	61.2	262	63	30	21	5	3	5	2	24	2	44	1	0	4	4	.500	0	0-0	9	4.20	3.06
2 ML YEARS			77	0	0	13	69.0	299	73	37	27	6	5	5	4	27	4	52	1	0	4	4	.500	0	0-0	9	4.49	3.52

John Hester

Bats: R **Throws:** R **Pos:** C-8; PH-7   **Ht:** 6'4" **Wt:** 210 **Born:** 9/14/1983 **Age:** 26

								BATTING													BASERUNNING				AVERAGES		
Year	Team	Lg	G	AB	H	2B	3B	HR	(Hm	Rd)	TB	R	RBI	RC	TBB	IBB	SO	HBP	SH	SF	SB	CS	SB%	GDP	Avg	OBP	Slg
2006	Msoula	R+	56	192	52	16	4	6	(-	-)	94	36	41	36	27	1	52	5	0	3	6	2	.75	5	.271	.370	.490
2007	Visalia	A+	79	297	78	16	1	10	(-	-)	126	38	43	40	22	0	64	1	0	0	4	2	.67	6	.263	.316	.424
2008	Mobile	AA	92	306	82	26	2	11	(-	-)	145	38	49	45	16	0	78	2	0	7	3	2	.60	10	.268	.302	.474
2009	Reno	AAA	92	329	108	31	5	9	(-	-)	176	61	66	65	22	1	65	3	0	1	13	3	.81	7	.328	.375	.535
2009	Ari	NL	15	28	7	2	0	1	(1	0)	12	4	4	5	2	0	7	0	0	0	0	0	-	0	.250	.300	.429

Aaron Hill

Bats: R **Throws:** R **Pos:** 2B-156; DH-2; PH-1   **Ht:** 5'11" **Wt:** 205 **Born:** 3/21/1982 **Age:** 28

								BATTING													BASERUNNING				AVERAGES		
Year	Team	Lg	G	AB	H	2B	3B	HR	(Hm	Rd)	TB	R	RBI	RC	TBB	IBB	SO	HBP	SH	SF	SB	CS	SB%	GDP	Avg	OBP	Slg
2005	Tor	AL	105	361	99	25	3	3	(3	0)	139	49	40	50	34	0	41	5	3	4	2	1	.67	5	.274	.342	.385
2006	Tor	AL	155	546	159	28	3	6	(4	2)	211	70	50	68	42	5	66	9	4	5	5	2	.71	15	.291	.349	.386
2007	Tor	AL	160	608	177	47	2	17	(8	9)	279	87	78	88	41	1	102	0	3	5	4	3	.57	21	.291	.333	.459
2008	Tor	AL	55	205	54	14	0	2	(1	1)	74	19	20	24	16	0	31	3	4	1	4	2	.67	4	.263	.324	.361
2009	Tor	AL	158	682	195	37	0	36	(21	15)	340	103	108	110	42	1	98	5	1	4	6	2	.75	17	.286	.330	.499
5 ML YEARS			633	2402	684	151	8	64	(37	27)	1043	328	296	340	175	7	338	22	15	19	21	10	.68	62	.285	.337	.434

Koyie Hill

Bats: B **Throws:** R **Pos:** C-79; PH-7; 3B-1   **Ht:** 6'0" **Wt:** 190 **Born:** 3/9/1979 **Age:** 31

								BATTING													BASERUNNING				AVERAGES		
Year	Team	Lg	G	AB	H	2B	3B	HR	(Hm	Rd)	TB	R	RBI	RC	TBB	IBB	SO	HBP	SH	SF	SB	CS	SB%	GDP	Avg	OBP	Slg
2003	LAD	NL	3	3	1	0	0	0	(0	0)	2	0	0	0	0	0	2	0	0	0	0	0	-	0	.333	.333	.667
2004	Ari	NL	13	36	9	1	0	1	(1	0)	13	3	6	5	2	1	6	0	0	0	1	0	1.00	1	.250	.289	.361
2005	Ari	NL	34	78	17	5	0	0	(0	0)	22	6	6	6	11	0	27	0	0	2	0	1	.00	0	.218	.308	.282
2007	ChC	NL	36	93	15	4	0	2	(1	1)	25	7	12	3	8	0	18	1	1	2	0	0	-	4	.161	.231	.269
2008	ChC	NL	10	21	2	1	0	0	(0	0)	3	0	1	0	0	0	12	0	1	0	0	0	-	0	.095	.095	.143
2009	ChC	NL	83	253	60	12	2	2	(1	1)	82	26	24	23	27	6	78	1	2	1	0	0	-	9	.237	.312	.324
6 ML YEARS			179	484	104	24	2	5	(3	2)	147	42	49	37	48	7	143	2	4	5	1	1	.50	14	.215	.286	.304

Rich Hill

Pitches: L **Bats:** L **Pos:** SP-13; RP-1   **Ht:** 6'5" **Wt:** 205 **Born:** 3/11/1980 **Age:** 30

			HOW MUCH HE PITCHED						WHAT HE GAVE UP											THE RESULTS						
Year	Team	Lg	G	GS	CG	GF	IP	BFP	H	R	ER	HR	SH	SF	HB	TBB	IBB	SO	WP	Bk	W	L	Pct	Sh	Sv-Op	Hld	ERC	ERA
2009	Frdrck*	A+	1	1	0	0	3.0	11	1	1	1	0	0	0	1	0	0	3	0	0	0	1	.000	0	0--	-	0.69	3.00
2009	Norfolk*	AAA	3	3	0	0	13.1	53	5	2	2	1	0	0	1	9	0	14	0	0	1	1	.500	0	0--	-	2.04	1.35
2005	ChC	NL	10	4	0	1	23.2	115	25	24	24	3	1	0	1	17	1	21	0	0	0	2	.000	0	0-0	0	5.81	9.13
2006	ChC	NL	17	16	2	1	99.1	417	83	51	46	16	8	3	2	39	1	90	3	0	6	7	.462	1	0-0	0	3.59	4.17
2007	ChC	NL	32	32	0	0	195.0	812	170	89	85	27	9	4	12	63	3	183	1	1	11	8	.579	0	0-0	0	3.56	3.92

Year	Team	Lg	G	GS	CG	GF	IP	BFP	H	R	ER	HR	SH	SF	HB	TBB	IBB	SO	WP	Bk	W	L	Pct	Sh	Sv-Op	Hld	ERC	ERA
2008	ChC	NL	5	5	0	0	19.2	89	13	9	9	2	0	2	1	18	0	15	1	0	1	0	1.000	0	0-0	0	4.38	4.12
2009	Bal	AL	14	13	0	0	57.2	275	68	53	50	7	2	2	1	40	2	46	1	1	3	3	.500	0	0-0	0	6.55	7.80
	Postseason		1	1	0	0	3.0	18	6	3	3	1	0	0	1	2	0	3	0	0	0	1	.000	0	0-0	0	15.68	9.00
	5 ML YEARS		78	70	2	2	395.1	1708	359	226	214	55	20	11	17	177	7	355	6	2	21	20	.512	1	0-0	0	4.16	4.87

Shawn Hill

Pitches: R Bats: R Pos: SP-3   Ht: 6'2" Wt: 225 Born: 4/28/1981 Age: 29

Year	Team	Lg	G	GS	CG	GF	IP	BFP	H	R	ER	HR	SH	SF	HB	TBB	IBB	SO	WP	Bk	W	L	Pct	Sh	Sv-Op	Hld	ERC	ERA
2004	Mon	NL	3	3	0	0	9.0	51	17	16	16	1	0	2	1	7	0	10	0	0	1	2	.333	0	0-0	0	12.14	16.00
2006	Was	NL	6	6	0	0	38.2	163	43	20	19	2	2	1	3	12	2	16	1	0	1	3	.250	0	0-0	0	4.70	4.66
2007	Was	NL	16	16	0	0	97.1	399	86	42	37	9	2	1	5	25	2	65	2	0	4	5	.444	0	0-0	0	3.03	3.42
2008	Was	NL	12	12	0	0	63.1	296	88	47	41	5	3	3	1	23	2	39	2	1	1	5	.167	0	0-0	0	6.04	5.83
2009	SD	NL	3	3	0	0	12.0	56	15	7	7	1	2	1	1	3	0	7	0	0	1	1	.500	0	0-0	0	4.90	5.25
	5 ML YEARS		40	40	0	0	218.1	965	249	132	120	18	9	8	11	70	6	137	5	1	8	16	.333	0	0-0	0	4.57	4.95

Mike Hinckley

Pitches: L Bats: R Pos: RP-14   Ht: 6'3" Wt: 203 Born: 10/5/1982 Age: 27

Year	Team	Lg	G	GS	CG	GF	IP	BFP	H	R	ER	HR	SH	SF	HB	TBB	IBB	SO	WP	Bk	W	L	Pct	Sh	Sv-Op	Hld	ERC	ERA
2001	Expos	R	8	5	0	0	34.1	158	46	23	20	1	1	2	3	12	0	28	6	1	2	2	.500	0	0--	-	5.74	5.24
2002	Vrmnt	A-	16	16	0	0	91.2	357	60	19	14	4	3	1	4	30	0	66	6	3	6	2	.750	0	0--	-	1.92	1.37
2003	Savann	A	23	23	2	0	121.0	515	124	54	49	4	2	6	9	41	1	111	8	2	9	5	.643	1	0--	-	3.86	3.64
2003	BrvdCt	A+	4	4	1	0	25.0	89	14	2	2	1	0	0	0	1	0	23	2	0	4	0	1.000	0	0--	-	0.85	0.72
2004	BrvdCt	A+	10	10	0	0	62.0	250	47	23	18	6	2	1	6	18	0	51	1	0	6	2	.750	0	0--	-	2.70	2.61
2004	Hrsbrg	AA	16	16	0	0	94.0	376	83	34	30	5	8	5	7	23	0	80	1	0	5	2	.711	0	0--	-	2.94	2.87
2005	Ptsma	AA	22	21	1	-	127.2	585	151	90	70	10	-	-	9	51	0	80	6	2	3	9	.250	0	0--	-	5.20	4.93
2006	Ptsma	A+	28	28	-	0	148.1	686	178	102	91	18	-	9	9	63	-	79	10	5	6	8	.429	-	0--	-	5.70	5.52
2007	Hrsbrg	AA	25	23	0	1	117.1	553	145	85	76	15	6	1	10	59	2	70	9	1	9	10	.474	-	0--	-	6.45	5.83
2008	Hrsbrg	AA	23	6	0	6	65.0	305	79	40	37	6	3	2	3	40	3	53	4	1	5	3	.625	0	0--	-	6.38	5.12
2008	Clmbs	AAA	20	1	0	0	25.2	114	27	11	9	0	1	1	0	15	0	20	1	0	2	0	.000	0	1--	-	4.42	3.16
2009	Okla	AAA	33	0	0	12	40.2	217	53	20	18	1	0	1	1	33	1	32	6	1	1	1	.500	0	0--	-	4.70	3.26
2008	Was	NL	14	0	0	2	13.2	49	8	1	0	0	0	0	1	3	0	9	0	1	0	0	-	0	0-0	4	1.35	0.00
2009	Was	NL	14	0	0	1	9.2	44	8	5	5	1	1	0	1	11	0	3	1	0	0	0	-	0	0-1	4	7.10	4.66
	2 ML YEARS		28	0	0	3	23.1	93	16	6	5	1	1	0	2	14	0	12	1	1	0	0	-	0	0-1	8	3.33	1.93

Alex Hinshaw

Pitches: L Bats: L Pos: RP-0   Ht: 6'3" Wt: 170 Born: 10/31/1982 Age: 27

Year	Team	Lg	G	GS	CG	GF	IP	BFP	H	R	ER	HR	SH	SF	HB	TBB	IBB	SO	WP	Bk	W	L	Pct	Sh	Sv-Op	Hld	ERC	ERA
2005	SlmKzr	A-	25	0	0	2	22.0	102	17	9	9	1	3	3	3	18	0	33	2	0	0	1	.000	0	0--	-	4.50	3.68
2006	SnJos	A+	30	10	0	8	69.2	330	58	48	33	6	1	4	10	60	0	78	6	0	6	3	.667	0	0--	-	5.38	4.26
2007	Conn	AA	17	5	0	0	41.1	165	22	13	9	2	1	1	2	19	0	50	2	0	3	1	.750	0	0--	-	1.78	1.96
2008	Fresno	AAA	13	0	0	9	15.2	55	5	1	1	0	0	0	0	4	0	21	0	0	0	0	-	0	7--	-	0.55	0.57
2009	Fresno	AAA	46	0	0	8	52.1	237	42	25	23	3	1	3	3	32	0	72	3	0	1	2	.333	0	1--	-	3.57	3.96
2008	SF	NL	48	0	0	12	39.2	179	31	16	15	5	4	2	3	29	4	47	5	0	2	1	.667	0	0-0	4	4.43	3.40
2009	SF	NL	9	0	0	3	6.0	33	10	8	8	2	0	0	0	7	0	2	1	0	0	0	-	0	0-0	0	14.88	12.00
	2 ML YEARS		57	0	0	15	45.2	212	41	24	23	7	4	2	3	36	4	49	6	0	2	1	.667	0	0-0	4	5.58	4.53

Eric Hinske

Bats: L Throws: R Pos: PH-38; RF-35; 3B-13; 1B-6; DH-5; LF-2; PR-1   Ht: 6'1" Wt: 235 Born: 8/5/1977 Age: 32

									BATTING														BASERUNNING				AVERAGES		
Year	Team	Lg	G	AB	H	2B	3B	HR	(Hm	Rd)	TB	R	RBI	RC	TBB	IBB	SO	HBP	SH	SF	SB	CS	SB%	GDP	Avg	OBP	Slg
2002	Tor	AL	151	566	158	38	2	24	(15	9)	272	99	84	103	77	5	138	2	0	5	13	1	.93	12	.279	.365	.481
2003	Tor	AL	124	449	109	45	3	12	(4	8)	196	74	63	66	59	1	104	1	0	5	12	2	.86	11	.243	.329	.437
2004	Tor	AL	155	570	140	23	3	15	(6	9)	214	66	69	60	54	2	109	4	0	6	12	8	.60	14	.246	.312	.375
2005	Tor	AL	147	477	125	31	2	15	(7	8)	205	79	68	71	46	4	121	8	0	4	8	4	.67	8	.262	.333	.430
2006	2 Tms	AL	109	277	75	17	2	13	(7	6)	135	43	34	39	35	2	79	0	0	0	2	2	.50	8	.271	.353	.487
2007	Bos	AL	84	186	38	12	3	6	(4	2)	74	25	21	22	28	2	54	3	0	1	3	0	1.00	7	.204	.317	.398
2008	TB	AL	133	381	94	21	1	20	(8	12)	177	59	60	53	47	4	88	3	0	1	10	3	.77	13	.247	.333	.465
2009	2 Tms	AL	93	190	46	12	0	8	(2	6)	82	31	25	27	27	1	52	5	0	2	1	0	1.00	2	.242	.348	.432
06	Pit	NL	78	197	52	9	2	12	(6	6)	101	35	29	29	27	2	49	0	0	0	1	1	.50	6	.264	.353	.513
06	Bos	AL	31	80	23	8	0	1	(1	0)	34	8	5	10	8	0	30	0	0	0	1	1	.50	2	.288	.352	.425
09	Pit	NL	54	106	27	9	0	1	(0	1)	39	18	11	16	17	0	27	3	0	0	0	0	-	0	.255	.373	.368
00	NYY	AL	39	84	19	3	0	7	(2	5)	43	13	14	11	10	1	25	2	0	2	1	0	1.00	2	.226	.316	.512
	Postseason		5	4	1	0	0	1	(0	1)	4	2	1	0	0	0	3	0	0	0	0	0	-	0	.250	.250	1.000
	8 ML YEARS		996	3096	785	199	16	113	(53	60)	1355	476	424	441	373	21	745	26	0	26	61	20	.75	75	.254	.336	.438

Luke Hochevar

Pitches: R Bats: R Pos: SP-25 Ht: 6'5" Wt: 210 Born: 9/15/1983 Age: 26

Year	Team	Lg	G	GS	CG	GF	IP	BFP	H	R	ER	HR	SH	SF	HB	TBB	IBB	SO	WP	Bk	W	L	Pct	Sh	Sv-Op	Hld	ERC	ERA
2009	Omha*	AAA	8	8	1	0	48.0	187	41	11	8	2	1	2	0	12	0	36	0	0	5	1	.833	1	0- -	-	2.49	1.50
2007	KC	AL	4	1	0	1	12.2	54	11	4	3	1	1	0	3	4	0	5	1	0	0	1	.000	0	0-0	0	3.86	2.13
2008	KC	AL	22	22	0	0	129.0	566	143	84	79	12	1	2	5	47	1	72	7	0	6	12	.333	0	0-0	0	4.67	5.51
2009	KC	AL	25	25	2	0	143.0	631	167	109	104	23	2	0	8	46	0	106	9	0	7	13	.350	0	0-0	0	5.46	6.55
3 ML YEARS			51	48	2	1	284.2	1251	321	197	186	36	4	2	16	97	1	183	17	0	13	26	.333	1	0-0	0	5.03	5.88

Trevor Hoffman

Pitches: R Bats: R Pos: RP-55 Ht: 6'0" Wt: 221 Born: 10/13/1967 Age: 42

Year	Team	Lg	G	GS	CG	GF	IP	BFP	H	R	ER	HR	SH	SF	HB	TBB	IBB	SO	WP	Bk	W	L	Pct	Sh	Sv-Op	Hld	ERC	ERA
2009	Nashv*	AAA	2	1	0	0	2.0	10	4	2	2	0	0	2	0	0	0	2	0	0	0	0	-	0	0- -	-	7.48	9.00
1993	2 Tms	NL	67	0	0	26	90.0	391	80	43	39	10	4	5	1	39	13	79	5	0	4	6	.400	0	5-8	15	3.40	3.90
1994	SD	NL	47	0	0	41	56.0	225	39	16	16	4	1	2	0	20	6	68	3	0	4	4	.500	0	20-23	1	2.02	2.57
1995	SD	NL	55	0	0	51	53.1	218	48	25	23	10	0	0	0	14	3	52	1	0	7	4	.636	0	31-38	0	3.48	3.88
1996	SD	NL	70	0	0	62	88.0	348	50	23	22	6	2	2	2	31	5	111	2	0	9	5	.643	0	42-49	0	1.58	2.25
1997	SD	NL	70	0	0	59	81.1	322	59	25	24	9	2	1	0	24	4	111	7	0	6	4	.600	0	37-44	0	2.27	2.66
1998	SD	NL	66	0	0	61	73.0	274	41	12	12	2	3	0	1	21	2	86	8	0	4	2	.667	0	53-54	0	1.32	1.48
1999	SD	NL	64	0	0	54	67.1	263	48	23	16	5	1	3	0	15	2	73	4	0	2	3	.400	0	40-43	0	1.78	2.14
2000	SD	NL	70	0	0	59	72.1	291	61	29	24	7	3	5	0	11	4	85	4	0	4	7	.364	0	43-50	0	2.18	2.99
2001	SD	NL	62	0	0	55	60.1	248	48	25	23	10	2	2	1	21	2	63	3	0	3	4	.429	0	43-46	0	3.20	3.43
2002	SD	NL	61	0	0	52	59.1	245	52	20	18	2	2	2	1	18	2	69	3	0	2	5	.286	0	38-41	0	2.63	2.73
2003	SD	NL	9	0	0	8	9.0	36	7	2	2	1	0	0	0	3	0	11	0	0	0	0	-	0	0-0	0	2.76	2.00
2004	SD	NL	55	0	0	51	54.2	209	42	14	14	5	2	0	0	8	1	53	2	0	3	3	.500	0	41-45	0	1.92	2.30
2005	SD	NL	60	0	0	54	57.2	240	52	23	19	3	2	3	1	12	1	54	1	0	1	6	.143	0	43-46	0	2.49	2.97
2006	SD	NL	65	0	0	50	63.0	248	48	16	15	6	0	0	1	13	1	50	2	0	0	2	.000	0	46-51	0	2.14	2.14
2007	SD	NL	61	0	0	50	57.1	235	49	21	19	2	3	2	0	15	5	44	0	0	4	5	.444	0	42-49	0	2.23	2.98
2008	SD	NL	48	0	0	42	45.1	180	38	19	19	8	1	0	0	9	2	46	0	0	3	6	.333	0	30-34	0	2.86	3.77
2009	Mil	NL	55	0	0	54	54.0	210	35	11	11	2	2	2	1	14	2	48	2	0	3	2	.600	0	37-41	0	1.53	1.83
93	Fla	NL	28	0	0	13	35.2	152	24	13	13	5	2	1	0	19	7	26	3	0	2	2	.500	0	2-3	8	2.71	3.28
93	SD	NL	39	0	0	13	54.1	239	56	30	26	5	2	4	1	20	6	53	2	0	2	4	.333	0	3-5	7	3.88	4.31
Postseason			12	0	0	11	13.0	55	11	6	5	2	0	1	0	5	1	14	0	0	1	2	.333	0	4-6	0	3.35	3.46
17 ML YEARS			985	0	0	820	1042.0	4183	797	347	316	92	30	29	9	288	55	1103	47	0	59	68	.465	0	591-662	16	2.26	2.73

Jaime Hoffmann

Bats: R Throws: R Pos: PH-9; RF-5 Ht: 6'3" Wt: 235 Born: 8/20/1984 Age: 25

Year	Team	Lg	G	AB	H	2B	3B	HR	(Hm	Rd)	TB	R	RBI	RC	TBB	IBB	SO	HBP	SH	SF	SB	CS	SB%	GDP	Avg	OBP	Slg
2005	Clmbs	A	79	321	99	13	9	1	(-	-)	133	53	24	54	39	1	73	1	5	2	10	4	.71	6	.308	.383	.414
2005	VeroB	A+	46	166	40	6	2	1	(-	-)	53	26	10	15	10	0	45	1	0	1	3	1	.75	5	.241	.287	.319
2006	VeroB	A+	121	433	109	16	0	5	(-	-)	140	50	29	44	35	0	94	2	7	2	15	11	.58	9	.252	.309	.323
2006	LsVgs	AAA	4	10	3	0	0	0	(-	-)	3	0	0	1	1	0	3	1	1	0	1	0	1.00	0	.300	.417	.300
2007	InldEm	A+	116	433	134	22	7	9	(-	-)	197	67	81	78	47	3	70	4	5	6	19	7	.73	5	.309	.378	.455
2008	Jaxnvl	AA	133	478	133	20	3	10	(-	-)	189	64	71	73	54	3	72	4	4	6	29	9	.76	9	.278	.350	.395
2009	Chatt	AA	29	101	31	9	2	2	(-	-)	50	25	16	24	22	0	18	6	0	0	5	3	.63	4	.307	.457	.495
2009	Albq	AAA	68	257	73	14	3	8	(-	-)	117	44	48	43	32	2	37	0	1	3	10	8	.56	6	.284	.360	.455
2009	LAD	NL	14	22	4	2	0	1	(1	0)	9	2	7	2	0	0	5	0	0	2	0	0	-	2	.182	.167	.409

Jarrett Hoffpauir

Bats: R Throws: R Pos: 2B-5; PH-5; 3B-1 Ht: 5'9" Wt: 190 Born: 6/18/1983 Age: 27

Year	Team	Lg	G	AB	H	2B	3B	HR	(Hm	Rd)	TB	R	RBI	RC	TBB	IBB	SO	HBP	SH	SF	SB	CS	SB%	GDP	Avg	OBP	Slg
2004	NewJrs	A-	9	36	13	3	0	3	(-	-)	25	8	6	9	3	0	2	0	0	0	1	0	1.00	1	.361	.410	.694
2004	Peoria	A	62	231	62	20	1	5	(-	-)	99	34	30	37	29	2	21	6	0	1	2	4	.33	4	.268	.363	.429
2005	QuadC	A	61	227	71	15	1	2	(-	-)	94	27	28	38	21	1	14	4	1	3	5	1	.83	3	.313	.376	.414
2005	PlmBch	A+	63	226	58	10	1	0	(-	-)	70	23	19	28	32	0	26	0	5	2	11	5	.69	2	.257	.346	.310
2006	Sprgfld	AA	120	393	98	20	1	7	(-	-)	141	55	46	53	54	4	41	5	5	3	9	6	.60	9	.249	.345	.359
2007	Sprgfld	AA	61	203	70	16	0	7	(-	-)	107	23	33	45	26	2	18	1	5	1	3	1	.75	9	.345	.420	.527
2007	Memp	AAA	55	190	57	10	0	4	(-	-)	79	27	24	33	29	0	21	1	4	1	2	3	.40	8	.300	.394	.416
2008	Memp	AAA	121	410	112	31	1	4	(-	-)	157	48	45	59	49	3	45	4	6	6	2	4	.33	12	.273	.352	.383
2009	Memp	AAA	108	358	104	22	3	14	(-	-)	174	53	53	64	35	1	28	3	4	2	4	1	.80	10	.291	.357	.486
2009	StL	NL	8	12	3	2	0	0	(0	0)	5	1	2	3	4	0	2	0	0	0	0	0	-	1	.250	.438	.417

Micah Hoffpauir

Bats: L Throws: L Pos: PH-47; 1B-27; RF-25; LF-11; DH-2 Ht: 6'3" Wt: 215 Born: 3/1/1980 Age: 30

Year	Team	Lg	G	AB	H	2B	3B	HR	(Hm	Rd)	TB	R	RBI	RC	TBB	IBB	SO	HBP	SH	SF	SB	CS	SB%	GDP	Avg	OBP	Slg
2002	Boise	A-	60	216	65	10	3	10	(-	-)	111	35	44	34	7	1	35	3	1	1	2	6	.25	1	.301	.330	.514
2003	Dytona	A+	124	477	121	33	2	8	(-	-)	182	59	58	62	44	7	96	7	0	5	2	1	.67	11	.254	.323	.382
2004	WTenn	AA	94	340	104	20	6	11	(-	-)	169	58	75	59	27	6	61	1	1	12	1	4	.20	4	.306	.347	.497
2004	Iowa	AAA	1	3	1	1	0	0	(-	-)	2	0	1	0	1	0	0	0	0	0	0	0	-	0	.333	.500	.667
2005	Iowa	AAA	119	392	105	14	3	3	(-	-)	134	48	47	49	38	4	59	3	1	4	3	0	1.00	11	.268	.334	.342
2005	WTenn	AA	7	25	4	0	0	1	(-	-)	7	1	2	0	0	0	6	0	0	0	0	0	-	1	.160	.160	.280
2006	WTenn	AA	40	138	37	11	2	10	(-	-)	82	28	31	30	20	2	29	2	0	3	0	0	-	2	.268	.362	.594
2006	Iowa	AAA	77	255	68	9	1	12	(-	-)	115	34	49	41	33	4	59	1	1	7	1	2	.33	6	.267	.345	.451

Year	Team	Lg	G	AB	H	2B	3B	HR	(Hm	Rd)	TB	R	RBI	RC	TBB	IBB	SO	HDP	SH	SF	SB	CS	SB%	GDP	Avg	OBP	Slg
2007	Iowa	AAA	82	310	99	24	0	16	(-	-)	171	56	73	62	24	3	34	2	0	8	2	1	.67	3	.319	.365	.552
2008	Iowa	AAA	71	290	105	34	2	25	(-	-)	218	63	100	79	17	1	46	1	0	5	2	0	1.00	0	.362	.393	.752
2009	Iowa	AAA	23	83	18	4	0	3	(-	-)	31	12	13	9	6	1	12	0	0	1	2	0	1.00	0	.217	.267	.373
2008	ChC	NL	33	73	25	8	0	2	(0	2)	39	14	8	14	6	0	24	1	0	0	1	0	1.00	1	.342	.400	.534
2009	ChC	NL	105	234	56	12	1	10	(4	6)	100	28	35	27	20	1	46	1	0	2	1	0	1.00	3	.239	.300	.427
2 ML YEARS			138	307	81	20	1	12	(4	8)	139	42	43	41	26	1	70	2	0	2	2	0	1.00	3	.264	.323	.453

Derek Holland

Pitches: L Bats: B Pos: SP-21; RP-12
Ht: 6'2" Wt: 185 Born: 10/9/1986 Age: 23

			HOW MUCH HE PITCHED						WHAT HE GAVE UP										THE RESULTS							
Year	Team	Lg	G	GS	CG	GF	IP	BFP	H	R	ER	HR	SH	SF	HB	TBB	IBB	SO	WP	Bk	W	L	Pct	Sh	Sv-Op	Hld	FRC	ERA
2007	Spkane	A-	16	14	0	0	67.0	284	57	33	24	7	1	1	6	21	0	83	7	0	4	5	.444	0	0--	-	3.25	3.22
2008	Clinton	A	17	17	0	0	93.2	376	77	30	25	2	4	3	2	29	0	91	3	0	7	0	1.000	0	0--	-	2.43	2.40
2008	Bkrsfld	A+	5	5	0	0	31.0	114	20	12	11	1	0	0	1	5	0	37	1	1	3	1	.750	0	0--	-	1.40	3.19
2008	Frisco	AA	4	4	0	0	26.0	94	14	4	2	0	2	0	0	6	0	29	0	0	3	0	1.000	0	0--	-	1.05	0.69
2009	Okla	AAA	1	1	0	0	4.0	17	5	4	4	1	0	0	0	3	0	5	0	0	0	1	.000	0	0--	-	9.72	9.00
2009	Tex	AL	33	21	1	0	138.1	611	160	98	94	26	2	3	4	47	0	107	3	3	8	13	.381	1	0-1	2	5.52	6.12

Matt Holliday

Bats: R Throws: R Pos: LF-155; PH-2
Ht: 6'4" Wt: 235 Born: 1/15/1980 Age: 30

Year	Team	Lg	G	AB	H	2B	3B	HR	(Hm	Rd)	TB	R	RBI	RC	TBB	IBB	SO	HRP	SH	SF	SB	CS	SB%	GDP	Avg	OBP	Slg
2004	Col	NL	121	400	116	31	3	14	(10	4)	195	65	57	61	31	0	86	6	1	1	3	3	.50	9	.290	.349	.488
2005	Col	NL	125	479	147	24	7	19	(12	7)	242	68	87	88	36	1	79	7	0	4	14	3	.82	11	.307	.361	.505
2006	Col	NL	155	602	196	45	5	34	(22	12)	353	119	114	112	47	3	110	15	0	3	10	5	.07	22	.326	.387	.586
2007	Col	NL	158	636	216	50	6	36	(25	11)	386	120	137	134	63	7	126	10	0	1	11	4	.75	13	.340	.405	.607
2008	Col	NL	139	539	173	38	2	25	(15	10)	290	107	88	104	74	6	104	8	0	2	28	2	.93	9	.321	.409	.538
2009 2 Tms		156	581	182	39	3	24	(16	8)	299	94	109	112	72	8	101	10	0	7	14	7	.67	13	.313	.394	.515
09	Oak	AL	93	346	99	23	1	11	(7	4)	157	52	54	62	46	3	58	6	0	2	12	3	.80	8	.286	.378	.454
09	StL	NL	63	235	83	16	2	13	(9	4)	142	42	55	50	26	5	43	4	0	5	2	4	.33	5	.353	.419	.604
Postseason		11	45	13	0	0	5	(3	2)	28	6	10	7	1	0	12	1	0	0	0	0	-	1	.289	.319	.622
6 ML YEARS		854	3237	1030	227	26	152	(100	52)	1765	573	592	611	323	25	606	56	1	21	80	24	.77	87	.318	.387	.545

Steve Holm

Bats: R Throws: R Pos: C-4; PR-1
Ht: 6'0" Wt: 210 Born: 10/21/1979 Age: 30

Year	Team	Lg	G	AB	H	2B	3B	HR	(Hm	Rd)	TB	R	RBI	RC	TBB	IBB	SO	HBP	SH	SF	SB	CS	SB%	GDP	Avg	OBP	Slg
2001	SlmKzr	A-	33	72	15	3	1	0	(-	-)	20	8	2	7	10	0	16	1	1	1	1	0	1.00	4	.208	.310	.278
2002	SlmKzr	A-	50	128	22	4	0	0	(-	-)	26	15	11	6	15	0	16	0	4	2	0	0	-	4	.172	.255	.203
2003	Hgrstn	A	55	173	38	10	1	1	(-	-)	53	12	17	14	8	0	32	3	2	1	3	1	.75	5	.220	.265	.306
2004	SnJos	A+	61	201	52	12	0	9	(-	-)	91	27	29	35	33	0	52	4	4	0	1	2	.33	5	.259	.374	.453
2005	Augsta	A	56	176	41	7	0	5	(-	-)	63	16	31	20	17	0	36	3	2	3	1	1	.50	2	.233	.307	.358
2005	Nrwich	AA	11	23	5	1	0	0	(-	-)	6	4	2	3	4	0	7	2	2	0	1	0	1.00	1	.217	.379	.261
2006	SnJos	A+	69	229	59	13	0	15	(-	-)	117	44	30	40	24	0	59	5	5	0	0	0	-	0	.258	.341	.511
2007	Conn	AA	84	254	69	14	0	9	(-	)	110	35	28	48	42	2	39	6	3	0	3	1	.75	7	.272	.387	.433
2008	Fresno	AAA	22	66	18	4	0	0	(-	-)	22	7	11	9	10	1	12	1	0	2	0	0	-	0	.273	.367	.333
2009	Fresno	AAA	63	198	48	12	0	6	(-	-)	78	23	16	24	15	1	40	2	3	4	0	0	-	0	.242	.297	.394
2008	SF	NL	49	84	22	9	0	1	(1	0)	34	10	6	8	10	1	16	3	0	1	0	1	.00	3	.262	.357	.405
2009	SF	NL	4	7	2	0	0	0	(0	0)	2	1	0	2	2	0	0	0	0	0	0	0	-	0	.286	.444	.286
2 ML YEARS		53	91	24	9	0	1	(1	0)	36	11	6	10	12	1	16	3	0	1	0	1	.00	3	.264	.364	.396

Paul Hoover

Bats: R Throws: R Pos: C-3
Ht: 6'1" Wt: 210 Born: 4/14/1976 Age: 34

Year	Team	Lg	G	AB	H	2B	3B	HR	(Hm	Rd)	TB	R	RBI	RC	TBB	IBB	SO	HBP	SH	SF	SB	CS	SB%	GDP	Avg	OBP	Slg
2009	LV*	AAA	73	245	62	16	1	1	(-	-)	83	26	28	29	29	0	66	1	1	5	1	2	.33	4	.253	.329	.339
2001	TB	AL	3	4	1	0	0	0	(0	0)	1	1	0	0	0	0	0	0	0	0	0	0	-	0	.250	.250	.250
2002	TB	AL	5	17	3	0	0	0	(0	0)	3	1	2	1	0	0	5	0	0	0	0	0	-	0	.176	.176	.176
2006	Fla	NL	4	5	2	0	0	0	(0	0)	2	0	1	1	0	0	0	0	0	0	0	0	-	0	.400	.400	.400
2007	Fla	NL	3	8	3	0	0	0	(0	0)	3	1	0	0	0	0	2	0	0	0	0	0	-	0	.375	.375	.375
2008	Fla	NL	13	40	8	1	0	0	(0	0)	9	1	2	0	2	1	17	0	0	0	0	0	-	2	.200	.238	.225
2009	Phi	NL	3	4	3	0	0	0	(0	0)	3	0	1	2	0	0	1	0	0	0	0	0	-	0	.750	.750	.750
6 ML YEARS		31	78	20	1	0	0	(0	0)	21	4	6	4	2	1	26	0	0	0	0	0	-	2	.256	.275	.269

Ryan Howard

Bats: L Throws: L Pos: 1B-156; DH-3; PH-2
Ht: 6'4" Wt: 259 Born: 11/19/1979 Age: 30

Year	Team	Lg	G	AB	H	2B	3B	HR	(Hm	Rd)	TB	R	RBI	RC	TBB	IBB	SO	HBP	SH	SF	SB	CS	SB%	GDP	Avg	OBP	Slg
2004	Phi	NL	19	39	11	5	0	2	(1	1)	22	5	5	7	2	0	13	1	0	0	0	0	-	2	.282	.333	.564
2005	Phi	NL	88	312	90	17	2	22	(11	11)	177	52	63	50	33	8	100	1	0	2	0	1	.00	6	.288	.356	.567
2006	Phi	NL	159	581	182	25	1	58	(29	29)	383	104	149	138	108	37	181	9	0	6	0	0	-	7	.313	.425	.659
2007	Phi	NL	144	529	142	26	0	47	(23	24)	309	94	136	119	107	35	199	5	0	1	1	0	1.00	13	.268	.392	.584

Year	Team	Lg	G	AB	H	2B	3B	HR	(Hm	Rd)	TB	R	RBI	RC	TBB	IBB	SO	HBP	SH	SF	SB	CS	SB%	GDP	Avg	OBP	Slg
2008	Phi	NL	**162**	610	153	26	4	48	(26	22)	331	105	146	117	81	17	199	3	0	6	1	1	.50	11	.251	.339	.543
2009	Phi	NL	160	616	172	37	4	45	(18	27)	352	105	141	117	75	8	186	6	0	6	8	1	.89	11	.279	.360	.571
	Postseason		17	64	17	3	0	4	(4	0)	32	9	10	9	11	4	23	1	0	0	0	0	-	1	.266	.382	.500
	6 ML YEARS		732	2687	750	136	11	222	(108	114)	1574	465	640	548	406	105	878	25	0	27	10	3	.77	50	.279	.376	.586

J.P. Howell

Pitches: L Bats: L Pos: RP-69

Ht: 6'0" Wt: 180 Born: 4/25/1983 Age: 27

			HOW MUCH HE PITCHED					WHAT HE GAVE UP											THE RESULTS						
Year	Team	Lg	G	GS	CG	GF	IP	BFP	H	R	ER	HR	SH	SF	HB	TBB	IBB	SO	WP	Bk	W	L	Pct	Sh	Sv-Op	Hld	ERC	ERA
2005	KC	AL	15	15	0	0	72.2	328	73	55	50	9	3	3	6	39	0	54	7	0	3	5	.375	0	0-0	0	5.18	6.19
2006	TB	AL	8	8	0	0	42.1	187	52	25	24	4	0	2	3	14	0	33	1	0	1	3	.250	0	0-0	0	5.51	5.10
2007	TB	AL	10	10	0	0	51.0	244	69	45	43	8	2	1	3	21	0	49	3	0	1	6	.143	0	0-0	0	6.84	7.59
2008	TB	AL	64	0	0	0	89.1	370	62	29	22	6	6	1	4	39	1	92	5	0	6	1	.857	0	3-5	14	2.51	2.22
2009	TB	AL	69	0	0	41	66.2	278	47	22	21	7	2	1	3	33	3	79	3	1	7	5	.583	0	17-25	4	2.99	2.84
	Postseason		12	0	0	1	12.0	50	9	4	4	0	0	1	2	4	1	17	1	0	0	3	.000	0	0-0	4	2.33	3.00
	5 ML YEARS		166	33	0	50	322.0	1407	303	176	160	34	13	8	19	146	4	307	19	1	18	20	.474	0	20-30	18	4.20	4.47

Bob Howry

Pitches: R Bats: L Pos: RP-63

Ht: 6'5" Wt: 220 Born: 8/4/1973 Age: 36

			HOW MUCH HE PITCHED					WHAT HE GAVE UP											THE RESULTS						
Year	Team	Lg	G	GS	CG	GF	IP	BFP	H	R	ER	HR	SH	SF	HB	TBB	IBB	SO	WP	Bk	W	L	Pct	Sh	Sv-Op	Hld	ERC	ERA
1998	CWS	AL	44	0	0	15	54.1	217	37	20	19	7	2	3	2	19	2	51	2	0	0	3	.000	0	9-11	19	2.50	3.15
1999	CWS	AL	69	0	0	54	67.2	298	58	34	27	8	3	1	3	38	3	80	3	1	5	3	.625	0	28-34	1	4.11	3.59
2000	CWS	AL	65	0	0	29	71.0	289	54	26	25	6	2	4	4	29	2	60	2	0	2	4	.333	0	7-12	14	2.96	3.17
2001	CWS	AL	69	0	0	23	78.2	346	85	41	41	11	4	3	4	30	9	64	6	0	4	5	.444	0	5-11	21	4.78	4.69
2002	2 Tms	AL	67	0	0	26	68.2	292	67	37	32	9	4	6	5	21	4	45	2	0	3	5	.375	0	0-1	15	4.00	4.19
2003	Bos	AL	4	0	0	3	4.1	27	11	6	6	1	0	1	0	3	1	4	0	0	0	0	-	0	0-1	0	16.51	12.46
2004	Cle	AL	37	0	0	6	42.2	178	37	14	13	5	1	1	2	12	0	39	0	0	4	2	.667	0	0-2	8	3.15	2.74
2005	Cle	AL	79	0	0	24	73.0	277	49	23	20	4	3	2	2	16	1	48	0	0	7	4	.636	0	3-5	29	1.58	2.47
2006	ChC	NL	84	0	0	26	76.2	314	70	28	27	8	5	3	3	17	4	71	1	0	4	5	.444	0	5-9	21	3.03	3.17
2007	ChC	NL	78	0	0	32	81.1	336	76	31	30	8	4	1	2	19	3	72	1	0	6	7	.462	0	8-12	22	3.10	3.32
2008	ChC	NL	72	0	0	27	70.2	311	90	44	42	13	1	4	2	13	5	59	0	0	7	5	.583	0	1-5	15	5.37	5.35
2009	SF	NL	63	0	0	20	63.2	268	50	26	24	5	3	6	2	23	6	46	4	0	2	6	.250	0	0-3	10	2.55	3.39
	02 CWS	AL	47	0	0	17	50.2	209	45	22	22	7	1	4	3	17	2	31	1	0	2	2	.500	0	0-0	10	3.72	3.91
	02 Bos	AL	20	0	0	9	18.0	83	22	15	10	2	3	2	2	4	2	14	1	0	1	3	.250	0	0-1	5	4.79	5.00
	Postseason		4	0	0	1	5.2	21	3	1	1	0	1	0	0	2	0	10	0	0	0	0	-	0	0-0	1	1.27	1.59
	12 ML YEARS		731	0	0	285	752.2	3153	684	330	306	85	32	35	29	240	40	639	21	1	44	49	.473	0	66-106	175	3.42	3.66

Chin-lung Hu

Bats: R Throws: R Pos: SS-3; PR-2; PH-1

Ht: 5'11" Wt: 195 Born: 2/2/1984 Age: 26

				BATTING																BASERUNNING			AVERAGES		
Year	Team	Lg	G	AB	H	2B	3B	HR	(Hm	Rd)	TB	R	RBI	RC	TBB	IBB	SO	HBP	SH	SF	SB	CS	SB%	GDP	Avg	OBP	Slg
2009	Albq*	AAA	130	496	146	21	5	6	(-	-)	195	66	53	68	25	0	54	5	14	4	14	5	.74	6	.294	.332	.393
2007	LAD	NL	12	29	7	0	1	2	(2	0)	15	5	5	5	0	0	8	0	2	0	0	0	-	0	.241	.241	.517
2008	LAD	NL	65	116	21	2	2	0	(0	0)	27	16	9	5	11	4	23	0	2	0	2	0	1.00	5	.181	.252	.233
2009	LAD	NL	5	5	2	1	0	0	(0	0)	3	2	2	1	0	0	2	0	0	1	0	0	-	1	.400	.333	.600
	3 ML YEARS		82	150	30	3	3	2	(2	0)	45	23	16	11	11	4	33	0	4	1	2	0	1.00	6	.200	.253	.300

Justin Huber

Bats: R Throws: R Pos: 1B-1

Ht: 6'2" Wt: 205 Born: 7/1/1982 Age: 27

				BATTING																BASERUNNING			AVERAGES		
Year	Team	Lg	G	AB	H	2B	3B	HR	(Hm	Rd)	TB	R	RBI	RC	TBB	IBB	SO	HBP	SH	SF	SB	CS	SB%	GDP	Avg	OBP	Slg
2009	Roch*	AAA	121	440	120	22	2	22	(-	-)	212	60	76	78	51	1	84	9	0	6	4	3	.57	16	.273	.356	.482
2005	KC	AL	25	78	17	3	0	0	(0	0)	20	6	6	4	5	0	20	1	0	1	0	0	-	1	.218	.271	.256
2006	KC	AL	5	10	2	1	0	0	(0	0)	3	1	1	1	1	0	4	0	0	0	1	0	1.00	0	.200	.273	.300
2007	KC	AL	8	10	1	0	0	0	(0	0)	1	2	0	0	0	0	2	0	0	0	0	0	-	0	.100	.100	.100
2008	SD	NL	33	61	15	3	0	2	(0	2)	24	5	8	9	3	0	19	2	1	0	0	0	-	0	.246	.303	.393
2009	Min	AL	1	2	1	0	0	0	(0	0)	1	0	0	0	0	0	0	0	0	0	0	0	-	1	.500	.500	.500
	5 ML YEARS		72	161	36	7	0	2	(0	2)	49	14	15	14	9	0	45	3	1	1	1	0	1.00	2	.224	.276	.304

Daniel Hudson

Pitches: R Bats: R Pos: RP-4; SP-2

Ht: 6'4" Wt: 220 Born: 3/9/1987 Age: 23

			HOW MUCH HE PITCHED					WHAT HE GAVE UP											THE RESULTS						
Year	Team	Lg	G	GS	CG	GF	IP	BFP	H	R	ER	HR	SH	SF	HB	TBB	IBB	SO	WP	Bk	W	L	Pct	Sh	Sv-Op	Hld	ERC	ERA
2008	Gr Falls	A-	14	14	0	0	69.2	283	52	30	26	6	1	0	3	22	0	90	3	0	5	4	.556	0	0--	-	2.49	3.36
2009	Knapol	A	4	4	0	0	22.0	85	15	5	3	0	1	0	3	2	0	30	0	0	1	2	.333	0	0--	-	1.41	1.23
2009	WinSa	A+	8	8	1	0	45.0	178	31	19	17	3	2	2	2	13	0	49	1	0	4	3	.571	0	0--	-	2.04	3.40
2009	Brham	AA	9	9	0	0	56.1	211	37	11	10	1	0	1	3	10	0	63	1	0	7	0	1.000	0	0--	-	1.45	1.60
2009	Charltt	AAA	5	5	0	0	24.0	103	22	10	8	1	0	3	2	9	0	24	1	0	2	0	1.000	0	0--	-	3.43	3.00
2009	CWS	AL	6	2	0	1	18.2	82	16	9	7	3	0	1	1	9	0	14	1	0	1	1	.500	0	0-0	0	4.15	3.38

Orlando Hudson

Bats: B Throws: R Pos: 2B-145; PH-4　　　　　　　Ht: 6'0" Wt: 191 Born: 12/12/1977 Age: 32

								BATTING														BASERUNNING				AVERAGES		
Year	Team	Lg	G	AB	H	2B	3B	HR	(Hm	Rd)	TB	R	RBI	RC	TBB	IBB	SO	HBP	SH	SF	SB	CS	SB%	GDP	Avg	OBP	Slg
2002	Tor	AL	54	192	53	10	5	4	(2	2)	85	20	23	30	11	0	27	2	0	2	0	1	.00	6	.276	.319	.443
2003	Tor	AL	142	474	127	21	6	9	(5	4)	187	54	57	64	39	1	87	5	0	3	5	4	.56	13	.268	.328	.395
2004	Tor	AL	135	489	132	32	7	12	(5	7)	214	73	58	71	51	0	98	4	3	4	7	3	.70	12	.270	.341	.438
2005	Tor	AL	131	461	125	25	5	10	(4	6)	190	62	63	59	30	1	65	3	0	7	7	1	.88	10	.271	.315	.412
2006	Ari	NL	157	579	166	34	9	15	(7	8)	263	87	67	89	61	5	78	2	4	4	9	6	.60	17	.287	.354	.454
2007	Ari	NL	139	517	152	28	9	10	(7	3)	228	69	63	82	70	1	87	2	5	7	10	2	.83	21	.294	.376	.441
2008	Ari	NL	107	407	124	29	3	8	(6	2)	183	54	41	66	40	2	62	2	3	3	4	1	.80	18	.305	.367	.450
2009	LAD	NL	149	551	156	35	6	9	(4	5)	230	74	62	78	62	4	99	4	9	5	8	1	.89	16	.283	.357	.417
	8 ML YEARS		1014	3670	1035	214	50	77	(40	37)	1580	493	434	539	364	14	603	24	24	35	50	19	.72	113	.282	.348	.431

Tim Hudson

Pitches: R Bats: R Pos: SP-7　　　　　　　Ht: 6'1" Wt: 170 Born: 7/14/1975 Age: 34

				HOW MUCH HE PITCHED						WHAT HE GAVE UP										THE RESULTS							
Year	Team	Lg	G	GS	CG	GF	IP	BFP	H	R	ER	HR	SH	SF	HB	TBB	IBB	SO	WP	Bk	W	L	Pct	Sh	Sv-Op	Hld	ERC	ERA
2009 Gwnntt*	AAA		4	4	0	0	18.2	78	24	7	7	0	0	1	0	2	0	11	0	0	1	0	1.000	0	0--	-	3.93	3.38
1999	Oak	AL	21	21	1	0	136.1	580	121	56	49	8	1	2	4	62	2	132	6	0	11	2	.846	0	0-0	0	3.50	3.23
2000	Oak	AL	32	32	2	0	202.1	847	169	100	93	24	5	7	7	82	5	169	7	0	20	6	.769	2	0-0	0	3.43	4.14
2001	Oak	AL	35	35	3	0	235.0	980	216	100	88	20	12	8	6	71	5	181	9	1	18	9	.667	0	0-0	0	3.22	3.37
2002	Oak	AL	34	34	4	0	238.1	983	237	87	79	19	6	5	8	62	9	152	7	1	15	9	.625	2	0-0	0	3.51	2.98
2003	Oak	AL	34	34	3	0	240.0	967	197	84	72	15	11	2	10	61	9	162	6	0	16	7	.696	2	0-0	0	2.47	2.70
2004	Oak	AL	27	27	3	0	188.2	793	194	82	74	8	7	4	12	44	3	103	4	1	12	6	.667	2	0-0	0	3.44	3.53
2005	Atl	NL	29	29	2	0	192.0	817	194	79	75	20	9	1	9	65	5	115	4	0	14	9	.609	0	0-0	0	4.12	3.52
2006	Atl	NL	35	35	2	0	218.1	959	235	129	118	25	8	3	9	79	10	141	7	0	13	12	.520	1	0-0	0	4.54	4.86
2007	Atl	NL	34	34	1	0	224.1	925	221	87	83	10	11	8	8	53	8	132	5	2	16	10	.615	1	0-0	0	3.12	3.33
2008	Atl	NL	23	22	1	0	142.0	573	125	53	50	11	5	4	2	40	5	86	0	1	11	7	.611	0	0-0	0	2.90	3.17
2009	Atl	NL	7	7	0	0	42.1	180	49	17	17	4	1	0	0	13	0	30	0	0	2	1	.667	0	0-0	0	4.70	3.61
	Postseason		9	8	1	0	47.2	207	50	27	21	5	4	2	2	16	1	32	1	0	1	3	.250	0	0-0	0	4.25	3.97
	11 ML YEARS		311	310	22	0	2059.2	8604	1958	874	798	164	76	42	75	632	61	1402	58	6	148	78	.655	11	0-0	0	3.43	3.49

Aubrey Huff

Bats: L Throws: R Pos: 1B-93; DH-47; PH-13　　　　　　　Ht: 6'4" Wt: 204 Born: 12/20/1976 Age: 33

								BATTING														BASERUNNING				AVERAGES		
Year	Team	Lg	G	AB	H	2B	3B	HR	(Hm	Rd)	TB	R	RBI	RC	TBB	IBB	SO	HBP	SH	SF	SB	CS	SB%	GDP	Avg	OBP	Slg
2000	TB	AL	39	122	35	7	0	4	(3	1)	54	12	14	15	5	1	18	1	0	1	0	0	--	6	.287	.318	.443
2001	TB	AL	111	411	102	25	1	8	(5	3)	153	42	45	37	23	2	72	0	0	0	1	3	.25	18	.248	.288	.372
2002	TB	AL	113	454	142	25	0	23	(17	6)	236	67	59	60	37	7	55	1	0	2	4	1	.80	17	.313	.364	.520
2003	TB	AL	162	636	198	47	3	34	(15	19)	353	91	107	112	53	17	80	8	0	9	2	3	.40	19	.311	.367	.555
2004	TB	AL	157	600	178	27	2	29	(16	13)	296	92	104	96	56	6	74	6	0	5	5	1	.83	9	.297	.360	.493
2005	TB	AL	154	575	150	26	2	22	(9	13)	246	70	92	77	49	13	88	5	0	7	8	7	.53	12	.261	.321	.428
2006	2 Tms		131	454	121	25	2	21	(9	12)	213	57	66	55	50	6	64	7	0	6	0	0	--	11	.267	.344	.469
2007	Bal	AL	151	550	154	34	6	15	(8	7)	245	68	72	79	48	2	87	1	0	4	1	1	.50	13	.280	.337	.442
2008	Bal	AL	154	598	182	48	2	32	(18	14)	330	96	108	111	53	7	89	3	0	7	4	0	1.00	9	.304	.360	.552
2009	2 Tms		150	536	129	30	1	15	(11	4)	206	59	85	67	51	7	87	5	0	5	0	6	.00	15	.241	.310	.384
06	TB	AL	63	230	65	15	1	8	(4	4)	106	26	28	28	24	3	25	0	0	2	0	0	--	4	.283	.348	.461
06	Hou	NL	68	224	56	10	1	13	(5	8)	107	31	38	27	26	3	39	7	0	4	0	0	--	7	.250	.341	.478
09	Bal	AL	110	430	100	24	1	13	(10	3)	174	51	72	58	41	7	74	4	0	5	0	6	.00	12	.233	.321	.405
09	Det	AL	40	106	29	6	0	2	(1	1)	32	8	13	9	10	0	13	1	0	0	0	0	--	3	.189	.265	.302
	10 ML YEARS		1322	4936	1391	294	18	203	(111	92)	2330	654	752	715	425	68	714	37	0	46	25	22	.53	129	.282	.340	.472

David Huff

Pitches: L Bats: L Pos: SP-23　　　　　　　Ht: 6'2" Wt: 190 Born: 8/22/1984 Age: 25

				HOW MUCH HE PITCHED						WHAT HE GAVE UP										THE RESULTS							
Year	Team	Lg	G	GS	CG	GF	IP	BFP	H	R	ER	HR	SH	SF	HB	TBB	IBB	SO	WP	Bk	W	L	Pct	Sh	Sv-Op	Hld	ERC	ERA
2006	MhVlly	A-	4	4	0	0	7.2	38	9	5	5	0	0	0	1	7	0	8	1	0	0	1	.000	0	0--	-	7.07	5.87
2007	Knstn	A+	11	11	0	0	59.2	249	57	23	18	4	4	2	1	15	0	46	2	0	4	2	.667	0	0--	-	3.08	2.72
2008	Akron	AA	11	10	1	0	65.2	253	44	17	14	5	4	1	1	14	0	62	1	0	5	1	.833	1	0--	-	1.67	1.92
2008	Buffalo	AAA	16	16	0	0	80.2	323	68	31	27	8	2	0	3	15	1	81	3	0	6	4	.600	0	0--	-	2.56	3.01
2009	Clmbs	AAA	7	7	0	0	39.1	163	35	19	19	5	1	1	0	16	0	32	1	0	5	1	.833	0	0--	-	3.75	4.35
2009	Cle	AL	23	23	0	0	128.1	574	159	82	80	16	2	2	1	41	1	65	1	0	11	8	.579	0	0-0	0	5.33	5.61

Dustin Hughes

Pitches: L Bats: L Pos: RP-7; SP-1　　　　　　　Ht: 5'10" Wt: 187 Born: 6/29/1982 Age: 28

				HOW MUCH HE PITCHED						WHAT HE GAVE UP										THE RESULTS							
Year	Team	Lg	G	GS	CG	GF	IP	BFP	H	R	ER	HR	SH	SF	HB	TBB	IBB	SO	WP	Bk	W	L	Pct	Sh	Sv-Op	Hld	ERC	ERA
2003	Royals	R	11	6	0	1	50.2	202	38	21	16	4	0	0	4	18	0	54	4	1	5	2	.714	0	0--	-	2.51	2.84
2004	Burlgtn	A	8	8	0	0	52.0	203	39	12	9	2	3	1	1	15	0	36	1	0	4	2	.667	0	0--	-	2.13	1.56
2004	Wilmg	A+	18	18	0	0	108.1	437	95	37	29	5	8	7	3	31	3	68	1	1	5	5	.500	0	0--	-	2.77	2.41
2005	Hi Dsrt	A+	19	19	0	0	92.0	432	119	74	58	13	5	4	5	45	0	87	9	1	5	7	.417	0	0--	-	6.81	5.67
2007	Wichta	AA	25	15	0	3	108.0	467	98	44	37	5	1	4	8	45	1	77	6	1	6	2	.750	0	1--	-	3.50	3.08
2008	NWArk	AA	20	4	0	7	52.2	209	47	17	17	3	2	1	0	16	1	43	1	1	5	2	.714	0	3--	-	2.95	2.91
2008	Omha	AAA	12	11	0	0	55.1	245	65	32	31	8	1	1	0	25	0	36	3	0	3	2	.600	0	0--	-	5.78	5.04
2009	Omha	AAA	34	11	0	12	87.1	371	79	35	34	6	4	5	2	41	0	76	8	0	3	3	.500	0	1--	-	3.74	3.50
2009	KC	AL	8	1	0	0	14.0	63	13	9	8	2	0	0	2	8	0	15	1	0	0	2	.000	0	0-0	2	5.31	5.14

Phil Hughes

Pitches: R **Bats:** R **Pos:** RP-44; SP-7 **Ht:** 6'5" **Wt:** 240 **Born:** 6/24/1986 **Age:** 24

Year	Team	Lg	G	GS	CG	GF	IP	BFP	H	R	ER	HR	SH	SF	HB	TBB	IBB	SO	WP	Bk	W	L	Pct	Sh	Sv-Op	Hld	ERC	ERA
2009	S-WB*	AAA	3	3	0	0	19.1	77	17	4	4	2	0	1	0	3	0	19	0	0	3	0	1.000	0	0- -	-	2.53	1.86
2007	NYY	AL	13	13	0	0	72.2	306	64	39	36	8	2	1	2	29	0	58	4	0	5	3	.625	0	0-0	0	3.61	4.46
2008	NYY	AL	8	8	0	0	34.0	157	43	26	25	3	1	3	1	15	0	23	2	0	0	4	.000	0	0-0	0	5.84	6.62
2009	NYY	AL	51	7	0	6	86.0	351	68	31	29	8	0	4	5	28	1	96	4	2	8	3	.727	0	3-6	18	2.86	3.03
	Postseason		2	0	0	1	5.2	21	3	1	1	1	0	0	0	0	0	6	1	0	1	0	1.000	0	0-0	0	0.99	1.59
3 ML YEARS			72	28	0	6	192.2	814	175	96	90	19	3	8	8	72	1	177	10	2	13	10	.565	0	3-6	18	3.63	4.20

Tug Hulett

Bats: L **Throws:** R **Pos:** PH-6; 2B-5; PR-4; RF-2; DH-2; 3B-1; SS-1; LF-1 **Ht:** 5'10" **Wt:** 192 **Born:** 2/28/1983 **Age:** 27

Year	Team	Lg	G	AB	H	2B	3B	HR	(Hm	Rd)	TB	R	RBI	RC	TBB	IBB	SO	HBP	SH	SF	SB	CS	SB%	GDP	Avg	OBP	Slg
2004	Spkane	A-	70	247	69	17	0	0	(-	-)	86	54	23	48	68	0	67	5	1	0	19	7	.73	1	.279	.444	.348
2005	Clinton	A	106	385	102	22	3	1	(-	-)	133	70	45	66	90	0	87	2	9	5	20	6	.77	7	.265	.402	.345
2006	Bkrsfld	A+	77	289	84	19	7	2	(-	-)	123	46	37	58	61	0	61	3	4	4	15	5	.75	2	.291	.415	.426
2006	Frisco	AA	48	185	57	8	4	0	(-	-)	73	36	15	34	31	0	36	1	3	3	9	2	.82	5	.308	.405	.395
2007	Okla	AAA	132	517	141	30	2	11	(-	-)	208	95	67	82	64	0	114	7	1	6	20	5	.80	11	.273	.357	.402
2008	Tacom	AAA	91	336	100	22	5	14	(-	-)	174	71	47	68	49	3	73	0	8	7	10	5	.67	4	.298	.380	.518
2009	Omha	AAA	99	374	109	27	4	11	(-	-)	177	62	53	72	58	2	79	1	5	4	9	2	.82	8	.291	.384	.473
2008	Sea	AL	30	49	11	1	0	1	(0	1)	15	2	2	2	5	0	17	1	1	0	0	0	-	3	.224	.309	.306
2009	KC	AL	15	18	2	0	0	0	(0	0)	2	4	1	0	1	0	6	0	0	0	0	0	-	0	.111	.158	.111
2 ML YEARS			45	67	13	1	0	1	(0	1)	17	6	3	2	6	0	23	1	1	0	0	0	-	3	.194	.270	.254

Philip Humber

Pitches: R **Bats:** R **Pos:** RP-8 **Ht:** 6'4" **Wt:** 210 **Born:** 12/21/1982 **Age:** 27

Year	Team	Lg	G	GS	CG	GF	IP	BFP	H	R	ER	HR	SH	SF	HB	TBB	IBB	SO	WP	Bk	W	L	Pct	Sh	Sv-Op	Hld	ERC	ERA
2009	Roch*	AAA	23	22	1	0	119.2	539	135	79	71	15	0	4	8	45	3	87	4	0	7	9	.438	0	0- -	-	5.09	5.34
2006	NYM	NL	2	0	0	1	2.0	7	0	0	0	0	0	0	0	1	0	2	0	0	0	0	-	0	0-0	0	0.27	0.00
2007	NYM	NL	3	1	0	2	7.0	32	9	6	6	1	0	0	0	2	0	2	0	0	0	0	-	0	0-0	0	5.46	7.71
2008	Min	AL	5	0	0	2	11.2	50	11	6	6	4	0	0	1	5	0	6	0	0	0	0	-	0	0-0	0	6.11	4.63
2009	Min	AL	8	0	0	3	9.0	50	17	8	8	1	0	0	0	9	2	9	1	0	0	0	-	0	0-0	0	12.62	8.00
4 ML YEARS			18	1	0	8	29.2	139	37	20	20	6	0	0	1	17	2	19	1	0	0	0	-	0	0-0	0	7.24	6.07

Nick Hundley

Bats: R **Throws:** R **Pos:** C-74; PH-4; LF-1; PR-1 **Ht:** 6'1" **Wt:** 205 **Born:** 9/8/1983 **Age:** 26

Year	Team	Lg	G	AB	H	2B	3B	HR	(Hm	Rd)	TB	R	RBI	RC	TBB	IBB	SO	HBP	SH	SF	SB	CS	SB%	GDP	Avg	OBP	Slg
2005	Eugene	A-	43	148	37	7	1	7	(-	-)	67	30	22	29	33	1	35	2	0	1	1	0	1.00	0	.250	.391	.453
2005	FtWyn	A	10	36	8	2	0	0	(-	-)	10	2	5	3	4	0	9	1	0	1	0	0	-	0	.222	.310	.278
2006	FtWyn	A	57	215	59	19	0	8	(-	-)	102	29	44	37	25	0	45	4	0	4	1	1	.50	3	.274	.355	.474
2006	Lk Els	A+	47	176	49	13	0	3	(-	-)	71	18	23	26	20	1	44	2	1	1	1	1	.50	2	.278	.357	.403
2007	SnAnt	AA	101	373	92	22	1	20	(-	-)	176	55	71	58	42	0	75	2	2	3	0	2	.00	7	.247	.324	.472
2008	PortInd	AAA	58	224	52	13	0	12	(-	-)	101	33	39	29	17	0	44	0	1	1	0	0	-	8	.232	.285	.451
2009	PortInd	AAA	5	16	4	1	0	1	(-	-)	8	2	2	2	2	0	4	0	0	0	0	0	-	0	.250	.333	.500
2008	SD	NL	60	198	47	7	1	5	(4	1)	71	21	24	17	11	0	52	2	0	5	0	0	-	1	.237	.278	.359
2009	SD	NL	78	256	61	15	2	8	(4	4)	104	23	30	33	28	1	76	1	1	3	5	1	.83	2	.238	.313	.406
2 ML YEARS			138	454	108	22	3	13	(8	5)	175	44	54	50	39	1	128	3	1	8	5	1	.83	3	.238	.298	.385

Tommy Hunter

Pitches: R **Bats:** R **Pos:** SP-19 **Ht:** 6'3" **Wt:** 255 **Born:** 7/3/1986 **Age:** 23

Year	Team	Lg	G	GS	CG	GF	IP	BFP	H	R	ER	HR	SH	SF	HB	TBB	IBB	SO	WP	Bk	W	L	Pct	Sh	Sv-Op	Hld	ERC	ERA
2007	Spkane	A-	10	0	0	5	17.2	69	15	7	5	0	0	0	0	1	0	13	0	0	2	3	.400	0	1- -	-	1.53	2.55
2008	Bkrsfld	A+	9	9	0	0	58.1	241	63	26	23	6	4	1	2	8	0	50	4	0	5	4	.556	0	0- -	-	3.68	3.55
2008	Okla	AA	8	8	0	0	52.1	218	52	24	22	5	2	1	3	17	1	28	2	0	4	2	.667	0	0- -	-	4.04	3.78
2008	Okla	AAA	8	8	0	0	53.0	219	55	18	17	6	0	2	0	9	0	28	1	0	4	2	.667	0	0- -	-	3.47	2.89
2009	Frisco	AA	5	3	0	1	21.2	102	30	15	12	1	1	1	0	4	0	16	1	0	1	0	1.000	0	0- -	-	4.73	4.98
2009	Okla	AAA	8	8	0	0	49.1	210	53	25	21	5	3	0	2	16	0	35	0	0	3	2	.600	0	0- -	-	3.47	3.83
2008	Tex	AL	3	3	0	0	11.0	63	23	20	20	4	0	0	0	3	0	9	0	0	0	2	.000	0	0-0	0	12.66	16.36
2009	Tex	AL	19	19	1	0	112.0	475	113	55	51	13	2	1	2	33	2	64	6	1	9	6	.600	0	0-0	0	3.86	4.10
2 ML YEARS			22	22	1	0	123.0	538	136	75	71	17	2	1	3	36	2	73	6	1	9	8	.529	0	0-0	0	4.54	5.20

Torii Hunter

Bats: R **Throws:** R **Pos:** CF-115; DH-4; PH-1 **Ht:** 6'2" **Wt:** 225 **Born:** 7/18/1975 **Age:** 34

Year	Team	Lg	G	AB	H	2B	3B	HR	(Hm	Rd)	TB	R	RBI	RC	TBB	IBB	SO	HBP	SH	SF	SB	CS	SB%	GDP	Avg	OBP	Slg
2009	RCuca*	A+	3	9	3	0	0	1	(-	-)	6	3	3	3	3	0	2	0	0	0	1	0	1.00	0	.333	.500	.667
1997	Min	AL	1	0	0	0	0	0	(0	0)	0	0	0	0	0	0	0	0	0	0	0	0	-	0			
1998	Min	AL	6	17	4	1	0	0	(0	0)	5	0	2	1	2	0	6	0	0	0	0	1	.00	1	.235	.316	.294
1999	Min	AL	135	384	98	17	2	9	(7	2)	146	52	35	44	26	1	72	6	1	5	10	6	.63	9	.255	.309	.380
2000	Min	AL	99	336	94	14	7	5	(4	1)	137	44	44	39	18	2	68	2	0	2	4	3	.57	13	.280	.318	.408
2001	Min	AL	148	564	147	32	5	27	(13	14)	270	82	92	79	29	0	125	8	1	1	9	6	.60	12	.261	.306	.479

Year	Team	Lg	G	AB	H	2B	3D	HR	(Hm	Rd)	TB	R	RBI	RC	TBB	IBB	SO	HBP	SH	SF	SB	CS	SB%	GDP	Avg	OBP	Slg
																									BATTING		
2002	Min	AL	148	561	162	37	4	29	(13	16)	294	89	94	85	35	3	118	5	0	3	23	8	.74	17	.289	.334	.524
2003	Min	AL	154	581	145	31	4	26	(12	14)	262	83	102	76	50	7	106	5	0	6	6	7	.46	15	.250	.312	.451
2004	Min	AL	138	520	141	37	0	23	(9	14)	247	79	81	69	40	4	101	7	0	2	21	7	.75	23	.271	.330	.475
2005	Min	AL	98	372	100	24	1	14	(6	8)	168	63	56	53	34	3	65	6	0	4	23	7	.77	8	.269	.337	.452
2006	Min	AL	147	557	155	21	2	31	(15	16)	273	86	98	81	45	2	108	5	0	4	12	6	.67	19	.278	.336	.490
2007	Min	AL	160	600	172	45	1	28	(11	17)	303	94	107	99	40	10	101	5	0	5	18	9	.67	17	.287	.334	.505
2008	LAA	AL	146	551	153	37	2	21	(10	11)	257	85	78	80	50	6	108	6	0	1	19	5	.79	15	.278	.344	.466
2009	LAA	AL	119	451	135	26	1	22	(15	7)	229	74	90	84	47	4	92	3	0	5	18	4	.82	9	.299	.366	.508
	Postseason		25	98	31	8	1	3	(0	3)	50	15	13	12	6	1	14	0	2	1	2	0	1.00	2	.316	.352	.510
	13 ML YEARS		1499	5494	1506	322	29	235	(110	125)	2591	831	879	790	416	42	1070	58	2	38	163	69	.70	158	.274	.330	.472

Eric Hurley

Pitches: R Bats: R Pos: P   Ht: 6'4" Wt: 195 Born: 9/17/1985 Age: 24

Year	Team	Lg	G	GS	CG	GF	IP	BFP	H	R	ER	HR	SH	SF	HB	TBB	IBB	SO	WP	Bk	W	L	Pct	Sh	Sv-Op	Hld	ERC	ERA
2004	Rngrs	R	6	2	0	1	15.1	69	20	8	4	1	0	1	1	4	0	15	1	0	0	1	.000	0	0--	-	5.31	2.35
2004	Spkane	A-	8	6	0	0	28.1	115	31	18	17	6	1	2	1	6	1	21	0	0	0	2	.000	0	0--	-	4.97	5.40
2005	Clinton	A	28	28	0	0	155.1	653	135	72	65	11	2	7	8	59	0	152	11	0	12	6	.667	0	0--	-	3.30	3.77
2006	Bkrsfld	A+	18	18	1	0	100.2	425	92	60	46	12	1	3	4	32	0	106	4	0	5	6	.455	0	0--	-	3.54	4.11
2006	Frisco	AA	6	6	0	0	37.0	140	21	9	8	4	1	0	3	11	0	31	0	0	3	1	.750	0	0--	-	1.94	1.95
2007	Frisco	AA	15	14	1	0	88.2	357	71	39	32	13	1	0	4	27	0	76	2	1	7	2	.778	1	0--	-	3.16	3.25
2007	Okla	AAA	13	13	0	0	73.1	313	65	45	40	13	4	2	3	28	0	59	4	0	4	7	.364	0	0--	-	4.02	4.91
2008	Okla	AAA	13	13	0	0	74.2	338	86	51	44	15	1	2	4	29	0	72	1	1	2	5	.286	0	0--	-	5.86	5.30
2008	Frisco	AA	1	1	0	0	7.1	24	4	0	0	0	0	0	0	1	0	2	0	0	1	0	1.000	0	0--	-	0.96	0.00
2008	Tex	AL	5	5	0	0	24.2	107	26	15	15	5	0	0	1	9	0	13	1	0	1	2	.333	0	0-0	0	5.19	5.47

Chris Iannetta

Bats: R Throws: R Pos: C-89; PH-5   Ht: 6'0" Wt: 225 Born: 4/8/1983 Age: 27

Year	Team	Lg	G	AB	H	2B	3B	HR	(Hm	Rd)	TB	R	RBI	RC	TBB	IBB	SO	HBP	SH	SF	SB	CS	SB%	GDP	Avg	OBP	Slg
																									BATTING		
2009	ColSpr*	AAA	4	15	5	2	0	1	(-	-)	10	3	3	3	2	0	6	0	0	0	0	0	-	0	.333	.412	.667
2006	Col	NL	21	77	20	4	0	2	(0	2)	30	12	10	9	13	2	17	1	1	1	0	1	.00	1	.260	.370	.390
2007	Col	NL	67	197	43	8	3	4	(1	3)	69	22	27	27	29	3	58	5	1	2	0	0	-	3	.218	.330	.350
2008	Col	NL	104	333	88	22	2	18	(11	7)	168	50	65	65	56	0	92	14	2	2	0	0	-	6	.264	.390	.505
2009	Col	NL	93	289	66	15	2	16	(8	8)	133	41	52	47	43	3	75	11	1	6	0	1	.00	4	.228	.344	.460
	4 ML YEARS		285	896	217	49	7	40	(20	20)	400	125	154	148	141	8	242	31	5	11	0	2	.00	14	.242	.361	.446

Raul Ibanez

Bats: L Throws: R Pos: LF-129; PH-5; DH-2   Ht: 6'2" Wt: 225 Born: 6/2/1972 Age: 38

Year	Team	Lg	G	AB	H	2B	3B	HR	(Hm	Rd)	TB	R	RBI	RC	TBB	IBB	SO	HBP	SH	SF	SB	CS	SB%	GDP	Avg	OBP	Slg
																									BATTING		
2009	Rdng*	AA	1	2	0	0	0	0	(-	-)	0	1	0	0	1	0	1	0	0	0	0	0	-	0	.000	.333	.000
2009	LV*	AAA	2	5	2	1	0	0	(-	-)	3	1	2	2	3	0	2	0	0	0	0	0	-	0	.400	.625	.600
1996	Sea	AL	4	5	0	0	0	0	(0	0)	0	0	0	0	0	0	1	1	0	0	0	0	-	0	.000	.167	.000
1997	Sea	AL	11	26	4	0	1	1	(1	0)	9	3	4	1	0	0	6	0	0	0	0	0	-	0	.154	.154	.346
1998	Sea	AL	37	98	25	7	1	2	(1	1)	40	12	12	10	5	0	22	0	0	0	0	0	-	4	.255	.291	.408
1999	Sea	AL	87	209	54	7	0	9	(3	6)	88	23	27	28	17	1	32	0	0	1	5	1	.83	4	.258	.313	.421
2000	Sea	AL	92	140	32	8	0	2	(2	0)	46	21	15	15	14	1	25	1	0	1	2	0	1.00	1	.229	.301	.329
2001	KC	AL	104	279	78	11	5	13	(5	8)	138	44	54	46	32	2	51	0	0	2	0	0	.00	6	.280	.353	.495
2002	KC	AL	137	497	146	37	6	24	(14	10)	267	70	103	89	40	5	76	2	1	4	5	3	.63	11	.294	.346	.537
2003	KC	AL	157	608	179	33	5	18	(8	10)	276	95	90	91	49	5	81	3	1	10	8	4	.67	10	.294	.345	.454
2004	Sea	AL	123	481	146	31	1	16	(9	7)	227	67	62	67	36	5	72	3	0	4	1	2	.33	10	.304	.353	.472
2005	Sea	AL	162	614	172	32	2	20	(9	11)	268	92	89	99	71	6	99	2	0	3	9	4	.69	12	.280	.355	.436
2006	Sea	AL	159	626	181	33	5	33	(17	16)	323	103	123	114	65	15	115	1	0	7	2	4	.33	13	.289	.353	.516
2007	Sea	AL	149	573	167	35	5	21	(7	14)	275	80	105	101	53	4	97	3	0	7	0	0	-	14	.291	.351	.480
2008	Sea	AL	162	635	186	43	3	23	(14	9)	304	85	110	107	64	11	110	3	0	5	2	4	.33	13	.293	.358	.479
2009	Phi	NL	134	500	136	32	3	34	(13	21)	276	93	93	80	56	8	119	4	0	5	4	0	1.00	16	.272	.347	.552
	Postseason		9	17	3	0	0	0	(0	0)	3	2	0	1	0	0	2	0	0	0	0	0	-	0	.176	.176	.176
	14 ML YEARS		1518	5291	1506	309	37	216	(103	113)	2537	788	887	848	502	63	906	23	2	48	38	24	.61	114	.285	.346	.479

Ryota Igarashi

Pitches: R Bats: R Pos: P   Ht: 5'11" Wt: 163 Born: 5/28/1979 Age: 31

Year	Team	Lg	G	GS	CG	GF	IP	BFP	H	R	ER	HR	SH	SF	HB	TBB	IBB	SO	WP	Bk	W	L	Pct	Sh	Sv-Op	Hld	ERC	ERA
1999	Yakult	Jap	36	0	0	14	47.2	207	34	27	26	4	-	-	1	29	-	55	3	1	6	4	.600	0	1--	-	3.21	4.91
2000	Yakult	Jap	56	0	0	19	75.1	301	42	28	26	11	-	-	1	33	-	90	6	0	11	4	.733	0	1--	-	2.24	3.11
2001	Yakult	Jap	41	0	0	13	41.2	180	25	13	12	2	4	1	2	28	2	51	1	0	2	3	.400	0	0--	-	2.64	2.59
2002	Yakult	Jap	64	0	0	21	78.0	300	49	19	18	8	-	-	3	18	-	97	8	0	8	2	.800	0	4--	-	1.76	2.08
2003	Yakult	Jap	66	0	0	21	74.0	310	60	33	32	9	-	-	1	33	-	83	7	1	5	5	.500	0	0--	-	3.42	3.89
2004	Yakult	Jap	66	0	0	56	74.1	313	57	24	22	9	5	0	1	36	5	86	4	0	5	3	.625	0	37--	-	3.21	2.66
2005	Yakult	Jap	49	0	0	18	56.2	246	52	24	22	6	6	2	1	27	2	60	6	0	3	2	.600	0	4--	-	3.95	3.49
2006	Yakult	Jap	29	0	0	18	25.0	119	33	20	17	3	4	0	2	11	1	18	4	0	1	2	.333	0	1--	-	6.52	6.12
2008	Yakult	Jap	44	0	0	-	43.2	171	35	13	12	3	2	0	2	6	0	42	3	0	3	2	.600	0	3--	-	2.08	2.47
2009	Yakult	Jap	56	0	0	10	53.2	221	42	19	19	3	-	-	3	20	1	44	1	0	3	2	.600	0	3--	-	2.72	3.19

Omar Infante

Bats: R **Throws:** R **Pos:** 2B-30; PH-15; 3B-10; SS-10; CF-8; LF-7; RF-3; PR-3   **Ht:** 6'0" **Wt:** 180 **Born:** 12/26/1981 **Age:** 28

Year	Team	Lg	G	AB	H	2B	3B	HR	(Hm	Rd)	TB	R	RBI	RC	TBB	IBB	SO	HBP	SH	SF	SB	CS	SB%	GDP	Avg	OBP	Slg
2009	Rome*	A	5	17	5	0	0	0	(-	-)	5	1	0	2	3	0	2	0	0	0	1	0	1.00	0	.294	.400	.294
2009	Gwnntt*	AAA	1	3	1	0	0	1	(-	-)	4	1	2	1	0	0	0	1	0	0	0	0	-	0	.333	.500	1.333
2002	Det	AL	18	72	24	3	0	1	(0	1)	30	4	6	12	3	0	10	0	0	0	0	1	.00	0	.333	.360	.417
2003	Det	AL	69	221	49	6	1	0	(0	0)	57	24	8	16	18	0	37	0	3	2	6	3	.67	1	.222	.278	.258
2004	Det	AL	142	503	133	27	9	16	(7	9)	226	69	55	69	40	3	112	1	7	5	13	7	.65	4	.264	.317	.449
2005	Det	AL	121	406	90	28	2	9	(3	6)	149	36	43	38	16	0	73	2	8	2	8	0	1.00	5	.222	.254	.367
2006	Det	AL	78	224	62	11	4	4	(0	4)	93	35	25	26	14	0	45	3	2	2	3	2	.60	5	.277	.325	.415
2007	Det	AL	66	166	45	6	1	2	(0	2)	59	24	17	23	9	0	29	0	2	1	4	1	.80	4	.271	.307	.355
2008	Atl	NL	96	317	93	24	3	3	(1	2)	132	45	40	45	22	2	44	2	2	5	0	1	.00	4	.293	.338	.416
2009	Atl	NL	70	203	62	9	1	2	(1	1)	79	24	27	29	19	0	28	1	2	4	2	0	1.00	5	.305	.361	.389
	Postseason		2	3	1	0	0	0	(0	0)	1	0	0	1	1	0	1	0	0	0	1	0	1.00	0	.333	.500	.333
	8 ML YEARS		660	2112	558	114	21	37	(12	25)	825	261	221	258	141	5	378	9	26	21	36	15	.71	28	.264	.310	.391

Brandon Inge

Bats: R **Throws:** R **Pos:** 3B-161   **Ht:** 5'11" **Wt:** 188 **Born:** 5/19/1977 **Age:** 33

Year	Team	Lg	G	AB	H	2B	3B	HR	(Hm	Rd)	TB	R	RBI	RC	TBB	IBB	SO	HBP	SH	SF	SB	CS	SB%	GDP	Avg	OBP	Slg
2001	Det	AL	79	189	34	11	0	0	(0	0)	45	13	15	6	9	0	41	0	2	2	1	4	.20	2	.180	.215	.238
2002	Det	AL	95	321	65	15	3	7	(3	4)	107	27	24	24	24	0	101	4	1	1	1	3	.25	7	.202	.266	.333
2003	Det	AL	104	330	67	15	3	8	(4	4)	112	32	30	23	24	0	79	5	4	3	4	4	.50	8	.203	.265	.339
2004	Det	AL	131	408	117	15	7	13	(9	4)	185	43	64	63	32	0	72	4	8	6	5	4	.56	4	.287	.340	.453
2005	Det	AL	160	616	161	31	9	16	(6	10)	258	75	72	82	63	1	140	3	6	6	7	6	.54	14	.261	.330	.419
2006	Det	AL	159	542	137	29	2	27	(12	15)	251	83	83	79	43	2	128	7	4	5	7	4	.64	12	.253	.313	.463
2007	Det	AL	151	508	120	25	2	14	(9	5)	191	64	71	65	47	5	150	11	7	4	9	2	.82	8	.236	.312	.376
2008	Det	AL	113	347	71	16	4	11	(8	3)	128	41	51	44	43	2	94	8	5	4	4	3	.57	4	.205	.303	.369
2009	Det	AL	161	562	129	16	1	27	(14	13)	228	71	84	70	54	1	170	17	1	3	2	5	.29	12	.230	.314	.406
	Postseason		13	44	12	3	0	1	(0	1)	18	4	4	5	4	2	15	0	1	1	0	0	-	1	.273	.327	.409
	9 ML YEARS		1153	3823	901	173	31	123	(69	54)	1505	449	494	456	339	11	975	59	38	34	40	35	.53	71	.236	.305	.394

Joe Inglett

Bats: L **Throws:** R **Pos:** LF-14; RF-11; PH-6; 2B-3; PR-3; CF-1; DH-1   **Ht:** 5'10" **Wt:** 185 **Born:** 6/29/1978 **Age:** 32

Year	Team	Lg	G	AB	H	2B	3B	HR	(Hm	Rd)	TB	R	RBI	RC	TBB	IBB	SO	HBP	SH	SF	SB	CS	SB%	GDP	Avg	OBP	Slg
2009	LsVgs*	AAA	40	161	58	14	1	3	(-	-)	83	29	25	34	16	0	18	2	6	1	4	2	.67	7	.360	.422	.516
2006	Cle	AL	64	201	57	8	3	2	(1	1)	77	26	21	28	14	0	39	1	5	1	5	1	.83	1	.284	.332	.383
2007	Tor	AL	2	5	3	0	1	0	(0	0)	5	0	2	3	0	0	0	0	0	0	1	0	1.00	0	.600	.600	1.000
2008	Tor	AL	109	344	102	15	7	3	(2	1)	140	45	39	52	28	0	43	4	8	1	9	2	.82	5	.297	.355	.407
2009	Tor	AL	36	89	25	4	1	0	(0	0)	31	11	6	14	8	0	21	1	1	0	3	1	.75	0	.281	.347	.348
	4 ML YEARS		211	639	187	27	12	5	(3	2)	253	82	68	97	50	0	103	6	14	2	18	4	.82	6	.293	.349	.396

Hernan Iribarren

Bats: L **Throws:** R **Pos:** PH-10; 2B-2; 3B-1; LF-1   **Ht:** 6'1" **Wt:** 195 **Born:** 6/29/1984 **Age:** 26

Year	Team	Lg	G	AB	H	2B	3B	HR	(Hm	Rd)	TB	R	RBI	RC	TBB	IBB	SO	HBP	SH	SF	SB	CS	SB%	GDP	Avg	OBP	Slg
2004	Brewrs	R	46	189	83	6	9	4	(-	-)	119	40	36	52	19	2	23	0	3	0	15	7	.68	2	.439	.490	.630
2004	Beloit	A	15	67	25	6	5	1	(-	-)	44	12	10	17	5	0	16	0	0	1	1	0	1.00	1	.373	.411	.657
2005	WV	A-	126	486	141	15	8	4	(-	-)	184	72	48	73	51	2	99	5	13	5	38	15	.72	9	.290	.360	.379
2006	BrvdCt	A+	108	398	127	12	4	2	(-	-)	153	50	50	60	39	0	57	1	11	6	19	15	.56	8	.319	.376	.384
2007	Hntsvl	AA	124	479	147	23	12	4	(-	-)	206	72	52	75	44	2	109	1	13	5	18	16	.53	3	.307	.363	.430
2008	Nashv	AAA	99	361	100	17	3	0	(-	-)	123	47	30	43	28	0	61	1	5	2	19	8	.70	6	.277	.329	.341
2009	Nashv	AAA	105	379	118	19	5	3	(-	-)	156	46	54	58	28	3	63	4	7	3	13	7	.65	3	.311	.362	.412
2008	Mil	NL	12	14	2	1	0	0	(0	0)	3	1	1	1	1	0	3	0	0	0	0	0	-	0	.143	.200	.214
2009	Mil	NL	12	13	3	2	0	0	(0	0)	5	1	1	2	1	0	5	0	0	0	0	0	-	0	.231	.286	.385
	2 ML YEARS		24	27	5	3	0	0	(0	0)	8	2	2	3	2	0	8	0	0	0	0	0	-	0	.185	.241	.296

Travis Ishikawa

Bats: L **Throws:** L **Pos:** 1B-113; PH-14   **Ht:** 6'3" **Wt:** 225 **Born:** 9/24/1983 **Age:** 26

Year	Team	Lg	G	AB	H	2B	3B	HR	(Hm	Rd)	TB	R	RBI	RC	TBB	IBB	SO	HBP	SH	SF	SB	CS	SB%	GDP	Avg	OBP	Slg
2006	SF	NL	12	24	7	3	1	0	(0	0)	12	1	4	4	1	0	6	0	0	0	0	0	-	1	.292	.320	.500
2008	SF	NL	33	95	26	6	0	3	(1	2)	41	12	15	17	9	1	27	0	0	0	1	0	1.00	1	.274	.337	.432
2009	SF	NL	120	326	85	10	2	9	(7	2)	126	49	39	44	30	3	89	4	1	2	2	2	.50	7	.261	.329	.387
	3 ML YEARS		165	445	118	19	3	12	(8	4)	179	62	58	65	40	4	122	4	1	2	3	2	.60	9	.265	.330	.402

Jason Isringhausen

Pitches: R **Bats:** R **Pos:** RP-9   **Ht:** 6'3" **Wt:** 230 **Born:** 9/7/1972 **Age:** 37

	HOW MUCH HE PITCHED						WHAT HE GAVE UP											THE RESULTS							
Year	Team	Lg	G	GS	CG	GF	IP	BFP	H	R	ER	HR	SH	SF	HB	TBB	IBB	SO	WP	Bk	W	L	Pct	Sh	Sv-Op	Hld	ERC	ERA
2009	Mont*	AA	4	0	0	0	4.0	17	2	1	1	0	0	1	0	4	0	3	0	0	0	0	-	0	0- -	-	2.99	2.25
2009	Drham*	AAA	6	0	0	1	7.0	30	7	4	4	0	0	1	0	2	0	0	0	0	0	0	-	0	0- -	-	2.89	5.14
1995	NYM	NL	14	14	1	0	93.0	385	88	29	29	6	3	3	2	31	2	55	4	1	9	2	.818	0	0-0	0	3.40	2.81
1996	NYM	NL	27	27	2	0	171.2	766	190	103	91	13	7	9	8	73	5	114	14	0	6	14	.300	1	0-0	0	4.75	4.77

HOW MUCH HE PITCHED / WHAT HE GAVE UP / THE RESULTS

Year	Team	Lg	G	GS	CG	GF	IP	BFP	H	R	ER	HR	SH	SF	HB	TBB	IBB	SO	WP	Bk	W	L	Pct	Sh	Sv-Op	Hld	ERC	ERA
1997	NYM	NL	6	6	0	0	29.2	145	40	27	25	3	1	2	1	22	0	25	3	0	2	2	.500	0	0-0	0	7.99	7.58
1999	2 Tms		33	5	0	20	64.2	286	64	35	34	9	0	1	3	34	4	51	4	0	1	4	.200	0	9-9	0	4.94	4.73
2000	Oak	AL	66	0	0	57	69.0	304	67	34	29	6	2	1	3	32	5	57	5	1	6	4	.600	0	33-40	0	4.09	3.78
2001	Oak	AL	65	0	0	54	71.1	293	54	24	21	5	3	1	0	23	5	74	2	0	4	3	.571	0	34-43	0	2.18	2.65
2002	StL	NL	60	0	0	51	65.1	257	46	22	18	0	4	3	1	18	1	68	0	0	3	2	.600	0	32-37	0	1.61	2.48
2003	StL	NL	40	0	0	31	42.0	174	31	14	11	2	1	0	0	18	1	41	6	0	0	1	.000	0	22-25	1	2.40	2.36
2004	StL	NL	74	0	0	66	75.1	308	55	27	24	5	6	1	2	23	4	71	1	0	4	2	.667	0	47-54	0	2.09	2.87
2005	StL	NL	63	0	0	52	59.0	245	43	14	14	4	3	1	1	27	5	51	2	0	1	2	.333	0	39-43	1	2.56	2.14
2006	StL	NL	59	0	0	51	58.1	257	47	25	23	10	1	3	3	38	3	52	3	0	4	8	.333	0	33-43	0	4.63	3.55
2007	StL	NL	63	0	0	54	65.1	267	42	21	18	4	1	1	2	28	3	54	3	0	4	0	1.000	0	32-34	0	2.11	2.48
2008	StL	NL	42	0	0	27	42.2	200	48	28	27	5	0	1	5	22	0	36	1	0	1	5	.167	0	12-19	2	5.84	5.70
2009	TB	AL	9	0	0	4	8.0	37	6	2	2	0	0	0	2	5	0	6	1	0	0	1	.000	0	0-1	0	3.64	2.25
99	NYM	NI	13	5	0	2	39.1	179	43	29	28	7	0	1	2	22	2	31	2	0	1	3	.250	0	1-1	0	6.07	6.41
99	Oak	AL	20	0	0	18	25.1	107	21	6	6	2	0	0	1	12	2	20	2	0	0	1	.000	0	8-8	0	3.33	2.13
	Postseason		23	0	0	22	26.2	110	17	8	7	2	2	1	1	12	4	23	0	0	1	1	.500	0	11-12	0	2.10	2.36
	14 ML YEARS		621	52	3	467	915.1	3924	821	405	366	72	32	27	33	394	38	755	49	2	45	50	.474	1	293-348	4	3.54	3.60

Akinori Iwamura

Bats: L Throws: R Pos: 2B-67; PH-3; 3B-1   Ht: 5'9" Wt: 200 Born: 2/9/1979 Age: 31

Year	Team	Lg	G	AB	H	2B	3B	HR	(Hm	Rd)	TB	R	RBI	RC	TBB	IBB	SO	HBP	SH	SF	SB	CS	SB%	GDP	Avg	OBP	Slg
2009	Drham*	AAA	11	33	10	3	0	0	(-	-)	13	9	2	6	9	0	7	0	0	0	0	0	-	3	.303	.452	.394
2007	TB	AL	123	491	140	21	10	7	(4	3)	202	82	34	68	58	0	114	1	4	5	12	8	.60	2	.285	.359	.411
2008	TB	AL	152	627	172	30	9	6	(3	3)	238	91	48	85	70	3	131	4	3	3	8	6	.57	2	.274	.349	.380
2009	TB	AL	69	231	67	16	2	1	(0	1)	90	28	22	29	24	0	44	1	1	3	9	1	.90	1	.290	.355	.390
	Postseason		16	66	18	4	1	1	(1	0)	27	8	5	12	7	1	12	0	0	0	2	0	1.00	0	.273	.342	.409
	3 ML YEARS		344	1349	379	67	21	14	(7	7)	530	201	104	182	152	3	289	6	8	11	29	15	.66	6	.281	.351	.393

Cesar Izturis

Bats: B Throws: R Pos: SS-112; PH-1; PR-1   Ht: 5'9" Wt: 155 Born: 2/10/1980 Age: 30

Year	Team	Lg	G	AB	H	2B	3B	HR	(Hm	Rd)	TB	R	RBI	RC	TBB	IBB	SO	HBP	SH	SF	SB	CS	SB%	GDP	Avg	OBP	Slg
2009	Bowie*	AA	2	6	2	0	0	0	(-	-)	2	2	0	1	0	0	0	1	0	0	1	0	1.00	0	.333	.429	.333
2001	Tor	AL	46	134	36	6	2	2	(1	1)	52	19	9	16	2	0	15	0	4	0	8	1	.89	0	.269	.279	.388
2002	LAD	NL	135	439	102	24	2	1	(0	1)	133	43	31	26	14	1	39	0	10	5	7	7	.50	12	.232	.253	.303
2003	LAD	NL	158	558	140	21	6	1	(0	1)	176	47	40	42	25	8	70	0	7	3	10	5	.67	8	.251	.282	.315
2004	LAD	NL	159	670	193	32	9	4	(1	3)	255	90	62	95	43	2	70	0	12	3	25	9	.74	6	.288	.330	.381
2005	LAD	NL	106	444	114	19	2	2	(1	1)	143	48	31	37	25	1	51	4	4	1	8	8	.50	11	.257	.302	.322
2006	2 Tms	NL	54	192	47	9	1	1	(1	0)	61	14	18	14	12	3	14	2	1	1	4	.20	4	.245	.295	.318
2007	2 Tms	NL	110	314	81	14	2	0	(0	0)	99	31	16	27	19	2	19	1	3	0	3	3	.50	7	.258	.302	.315
2008	StL	NL	135	414	109	10	3	1	(0	1)	128	50	24	39	29	1	26	6	3	2	24	6	.80	6	.263	.319	.309
2009	Bal	AL	114	387	99	14	4	2	(1	1)	127	34	30	37	18	0	38	3	4	0	12	4	.75	11	.256	.294	.328
06	LAD	NL	32	119	30	7	1	1	(1	0)	42	10	12	10	7	3	6	2	0	1	1	3	.25	1	.252	.302	.353
06	ChC	NL	22	73	17	2	0	0	(0	0)	19	4	6	4	5	0	8	0	1	0	3	0	1.00	3	.233	.282	.260
07	ChC	NL	65	191	47	11	0	0	(0	0)	58	15	8	13	13	2	16	1	2	0	3	0	1.00	6	.246	.298	.304
07	Pit	NL	45	123	34	3	2	0	(0	0)	41	16	8	14	6	0	3	0	1	0	0	3	.00	1	.276	.310	.333
	Postseason		4	17	3	1	0	0	(0	0)	4	1	0	0	1	0	2	0	0	0	0	0	-	0	.176	.222	.235
	9 ML YEARS		1017	3552	921	149	31	14	(5	9)	1174	376	261	333	187	18	342	16	48	15	98	47	.68	65	.259	.298	.331

Maicer Izturis

Bats: B Throws: R Pos: 2B-68; SS-28; PH-13; DH-7; 3B-5; LF-1   Ht: 5'8" Wt: 170 Born: 9/12/1980 Age: 29

Year	Team	Lg	G	AB	H	2B	3B	HR	(Hm	Rd)	TB	R	RBI	RC	TBB	IBB	SO	HBP	SH	SF	SB	CS	SB%	GDP	Avg	OBP	Slg
2004	Mon	NL	32	107	22	5	2	1	(1	0)	34	10	4	8	10	1	20	2	2	0	4	0	1.00	1	.206	.286	.318
2005	LAA	AL	77	191	47	8	4	1	(0	1)	66	18	15	25	17	2	21	0	1	1	9	3	.75	5	.246	.306	.346
2006	LAA	AL	104	352	103	21	3	5	(1	4)	145	64	44	56	38	1	35	3	5	1	14	6	.70	7	.293	.365	.412
2007	LAA	AL	102	336	97	17	2	6	(4	2)	136	47	51	65	33	2	39	0	1	4	7	1	.88	4	.289	.349	.405
2008	LAA	AL	79	290	78	14	2	3	(1	2)	105	44	37	39	26	0	27	1	2	2	11	2	.85	9	.269	.329	.362
2009	LAA	AL	114	387	116	22	3	8	(3	5)	168	74	65	66	35	2	41	5	3	7	13	5	.72	7	.300	.359	.434
	Postseason		4	12	4	2	0	0	(0	0)	6	1	0	1	0	0	2	0	0	0	2	0	1.00	0	.333	.333	.500
	6 ML YEARS		508	1663	463	87	16	24	(10	14)	654	257	216	259	159	8	183	11	14	15	58	17	.77	33	.278	.343	.393

Conor Jackson

Bats: R Throws: R Pos: LF-23; 1B-6; PH-5   Ht: 6'2" Wt: 215 Born: 5/7/1982 Age: 28

Year	Team	Lg	G	AB	H	2B	3B	HR	(Hm	Rd)	TB	R	RBI	RC	TBB	IBB	SO	HBP	SH	SF	SB	CS	SB%	GDP	Avg	OBP	Slg
2009	Visalia*	A+	3	10	0	0	0	0	(-	-)	0	1	1	0	1	0	1	0	0	0	0	0	-	1	.000	.091	.000
2005	Ari	NL	40	85	17	3	0	2	(2	0)	26	8	8	6	12	0	11	1	0	1	0	0	-	0	.200	.303	.306
2006	Ari	NL	140	485	141	26	1	15	(8	7)	214	75	79	77	54	2	73	9	1	7	1	0	1.00	18	.291	.368	.441
2007	Ari	NL	130	415	118	29	1	15	(8	7)	194	56	60	67	53	2	50	4	2	3	2	2	.50	8	.284	.368	.467
2008	Ari	NL	144	540	162	31	6	12	(6	6)	241	87	75	88	59	3	61	9	1	3	10	2	.83	14	.300	.376	.446
2009	Ari	NL	30	99	18	4	0	1	(1	0)	25	8	14	10	11	0	16	0	0	0	5	0	1.00	1	.182	.264	.253
	Postseason		6	17	4	1	0	0	(0	0)	5	1	2	1	0	0	3	0	0	1	0	0	-	1	.235	.222	.294
	5 ML YEARS		484	1624	456	93	8	45	(25	20)	700	234	236	248	189	7	211	23	4	14	18	4	.82	47	.281	.361	.431

Edwin Jackson

Pitches: R **Bats:** R **Pos:** SP-33 **Ht:** 6'3" **Wt:** 210 **Born:** 9/9/1983 **Age:** 26

				HOW MUCH HE PITCHED					WHAT HE GAVE UP									THE RESULTS						
Year	Team	Lg	G	GS	CG	GF	IP	BFP	H	R	ER	HR	SH	SF	HB	TBB	IBB	SO	WP	Bk	W	L	Pct	Sh	Sv-Op	Hld	ERC	ERA
2003	LAD	NL	4	3	0	0	22.0	91	17	6	6	2	1	1	1	11	1	19	3	0	2	1	.667	0	0-0	0	3.36	2.45
2004	LAD	NL	8	5	0	1	24.2	113	31	20	20	7	1	0	0	11	1	16	0	0	2	1	.667	0	0-0	0	7.21	7.30
2005	LAD	NL	7	6	0	0	28.2	134	31	22	20	2	0	2	1	17	0	13	2	1	2	2	.500	0	0-0	0	5.13	6.28
2006	TB	AL	23	1	0	7	36.1	174	42	27	22	2	2	2	1	25	0	27	3	1	0	0	-	0	0-0	0	5.86	5.45
2007	TB	AL	32	31	1	0	161.0	755	195	116	103	19	5	6	4	88	3	128	7	1	5	15	.250	1	0-0	0	6.11	5.76
2008	TB	AL	32	31	0	0	183.1	792	199	91	90	23	3	3	2	77	1	108	7	1	14	11	.560	0	0-1	0	4.99	4.42
2009	Det	AL	33	33	1	0	214.0	890	200	93	86	27	4	2	5	70	3	161	6	0	13	9	.591	0	0-0	0	3.72	3.62
	Postseason		3	0	0	2	4.1	17	2	1	1	1	0	0	0	3	1	5	0	0	0	0	-	0	0-0	0	2.98	2.08
	7 ML YEARS		139	110	2	8	670.0	2949	715	375	347	82	16	16	14	299	9	472	28	4	38	39	.494	1	0-1	0	4.91	4.66

Steven Jackson

Pitches: R **Bats:** R **Pos:** RP-40 **Ht:** 6'5" **Wt:** 215 **Born:** 3/15/1982 **Age:** 28

				HOW MUCH HE PITCHED					WHAT HE GAVE UP									THE RESULTS						
Year	Team	Lg	G	GS	CG	GF	IP	BFP	H	R	ER	HR	SH	SF	HB	TBB	IBB	SO	WP	Bk	W	L	Pct	Sh	Sv-Op	Hld	ERC	ERA
2004	Msoula	R+	7	0	0	0	10.0	50	16	9	4	1	0	0	2	2	0	8	1	0	0	1	.000	0	0- -	-	7.56	3.60
2004	Yakima	A-	9	2	0	1	23.2	102	24	12	12	4	1	1	0	6	0	18	3	0	1	0	1.000	0	0- -	-	3.91	4.56
2005	Sbend	A	28	28	0	0	158.2	708	205	109	94	14	1	10	2	57	0	89	12	0	10	5	.667	0	0- -	-	5.71	5.33
2006	Tenn	AA	24	24	1	0	149.2	605	131	52	44	6	3	8	1	45	2	125	3	0	8	11	.421	1	0- -	-	2.71	2.65
2007	S-WB	AAA	18	11	0	0	69.0	327	93	57	45	11	1	1	3	29	1	50	3	0	4	8	.333	0	0- -	-	6.82	5.87
2007	Trntn	AA	10	0	0	4	21.0	91	20	11	9	1	0	3	1	9	0	16	5	0	0	1	.000	0	1- -	-	3.73	3.86
2008	Trntn	AA	15	0	0	6	31.1	129	28	20	20	2	1	0	1	12	1	37	0	0	1	3	.250	0	2- -	-	3.35	5.74
2008	S-WB	AAA	34	1	0	11	48.1	208	44	18	17	2	1	4	3	19	0	54	4	0	3	0	1.000	0	4- -	-	3.36	3.17
2009	S-WB	AAA	7	1	0	3	14.1	61	16	3	3	1	0	0	0	3	0	8	0	0	0	0	-	0	1- -	-	3.74	1.88
2009	Indy	AAA	12	0	0	1	18.0	81	23	14	13	1	2	2	0	5	0	17	2	0	1	0	1.000	0	0- -	-	4.79	6.50
2009	Pit	NL	40	0	0	10	43.0	186	38	20	15	2	1	2	0	22	3	21	3	0	2	3	.400	0	0-1	4	3.35	3.14

Zach Jackson

Pitches: L **Bats:** L **Pos:** RP-2; SP-1 **Ht:** 6'5" **Wt:** 220 **Born:** 5/13/1983 **Age:** 27

				HOW MUCH HE PITCHED					WHAT HE GAVE UP									THE RESULTS						
Year	Team	Lg	G	GS	CG	GF	IP	BFP	H	R	ER	HR	SH	SF	HB	TBB	IBB	SO	WP	Bk	W	L	Pct	Sh	Sv-Op	Hld	ERC	ERA
2009	Clmbs*	AAA	30	14	0	5	99.2	454	128	76	67	13	0	4	8	33	1	67	2	0	4	8	.333	0	0- -	-	6.07	6.05
2006	Mil	NL	8	7	0	1	38.1	178	48	26	23	6	1	1	4	14	0	22	1	0	2	2	.500	0	0-0	0	6.26	5.40
2008	2 Tms		11	9	0	2	58.1	256	69	38	36	7	1	1	3	16	0	31	2	0	2	3	.400	0	0-0	0	5.00	5.55
2009	Cle	AL	3	1	0	0	8.2	47	14	10	9	2	0	1	2	4	0	10	0	0	0	0	-	0	0-0	1	9.99	9.35
08	Mil	NL	2	0	0	2	3.2	18	5	2	2	0	0	0	0	2	0	1	1	0	0	0	-	0	0-0	0	5.84	4.91
08	Cle	AL	9	9	0	0	54.2	238	64	36	34	7	1	1	3	14	0	30	1	0	2	3	.400	0	0-0	0	4.94	5.60
	3 ML YEARS		22	17	0	3	105.1	481	131	74	68	15	2	3	9	34	0	63	3	0	4	5	.444	0	0-0	1	5.84	5.81

Mike Jacobs

Bats: L **Throws:** R **Pos:** DH-105; 1B-15; PH-13 **Ht:** 6'3" **Wt:** 215 **Born:** 10/30/1980 **Age:** 29

									BATTING											BASERUNNING				AVERAGES		
Year	Team	Lg	G	AB	H	2B	3B	HR	(Hm	Rd)	TB	R	RBI	RC	TBB	IBB	SO	HBP	SH	SF	SB	CS	SB%	GDP	Avg	OBP	Slg
2005	NYM	NL	30	100	31	7	0	11	(6	5)	71	19	23	21	10	0	22	1	0	1	0	0	-	5	.310	.375	.710
2006	Fla	NL	136	469	123	37	1	20	(12	8)	222	54	77	66	45	2	105	1	0	5	0	1	1.00	16	.262	.325	.473
2007	Fla	NL	114	426	113	27	2	17	(10	7)	195	57	54	51	31	3	101	2	0	1	1	2	.33	12	.265	.317	.458
2008	Fla	NL	141	477	118	27	2	32	(14	18)	245	67	93	69	36	10	119	1	0	5	1	0	1.00	7	.247	.299	.514
2009	KC	AL	128	434	99	16	1	19	(8	11)	174	46	61	50	41	2	132	2	0	1	0	0	-	9	.228	.297	.401
	5 ML YEARS		549	1906	484	114	6	99	(50	49)	907	243	308	257	163	17	479	7	0	13	2	2	.71	49	.254	.313	.476

Chris Jakubauskas

Pitches: R **Bats:** L **Pos:** RP-27; SP-8 **Ht:** 6'2" **Wt:** 215 **Born:** 12/22/1978 **Age:** 31

				HOW MUCH HE PITCHED					WHAT HE GAVE UP									THE RESULTS						
Year	Team	Lg	G	GS	CG	GF	IP	BFP	H	R	ER	HR	SH	SF	HB	TBB	IBB	SO	WP	Bk	W	L	Pct	Sh	Sv-Op	Hld	ERC	ERA
2007	WTenn	AA	16	3	1	3	51.0	219	53	30	28	3	1	2	1	21	0	39	2	0	0	4	.000	0	0- -	-	4.21	4.94
2008	WTenn	AA	6	6	0	0	32.2	127	25	4	3	1	1	0	1	7	0	24	0	0	3	0	1.000	0	0- -	-	1.93	0.83
2008	Tacom	AAA	12	9	0	0	55.2	231	52	22	16	5	1	1	1	14	0	48	4	2	5	1	.833	0	0- -	-	3.13	2.59
2008	Everett	A-	1	1	0	0	2.2	9	1	0	0	0	0	0	0	0	0	7	0	0	0	0	-	0	0- -	-	0.31	0.00
2009	Tacom	AAA	1	0	0	0	1.0	3	0	0	0	0	0	0	0	1	0	1	0	0	0	0	-	0	0- -	-	1.26	0.00
2009	Sea	AL	35	8	1	6	93.0	390	91	60	55	15	0	3	2	27	3	47	8	1	6	7	.462	0	0-1	3	3.99	5.32

Chuck James

Pitches: L **Bats:** L **Pos:** P **Ht:** 6'0" **Wt:** 190 **Born:** 11/9/1981 **Age:** 28

				HOW MUCH HE PITCHED					WHAT HE GAVE UP									THE RESULTS						
Year	Team	Lg	G	GS	CG	GF	IP	BFP	H	R	ER	HR	SH	SF	HB	TBB	IBB	SO	WP	Bk	W	L	Pct	Sh	Sv-Op	Hld	ERC	ERA
2005	Atl	NL	2	0	0	0	5.2	23	4	1	1	0	0	0	0	3	0	5	1	0	0	0	-	0	0-0	0	2.41	1.59
2006	Atl	NL	25	18	0	0	119.0	504	101	54	50	20	8	7	6	47	2	91	2	0	11	4	**.733**	0	0-0	0	3.84	3.78
2007	Atl	NL	30	30	0	0	161.1	691	164	77	76	32	9	4	1	58	5	116	1	1	11	10	.524	0	0-0	0	4.69	4.24
2008	Atl	NL	7	7	0	0	29.2	146	36	30	30	10	4	3	3	20	2	22	1	1	2	5	.286	0	0-0	0	8.81	9.10
	4 ML YEARS		64	55	0	0	315.2	1364	305	162	157	62	21	14	10	128	9	234	5	2	24	19	.558	0	0-0	0	4.67	4.48

Paul Janish

Bats: R **Throws:** R **Pos:** SS-82; PH-7; 3B-2; PR-2   **Ht:** 6'2" **Wt:** 193 **Born:** 10/12/1982 **Age:** 27

								BATTING												BASERUNNING				AVERAGES		
Year	Team	Lg	G	AB	H	2B	3B	HR	(Hm | Rd)	TB	R	RBI	RC	TBB	IBB	SO	HBP	SH	SF	SB	CS	SB%	GDP	Avg	OBP	Slg
2004	Billings	R+	66	205	54	11	0	2	(- | -)	71	39	22	35	45	0	45	5	7	1	7	3	.70	2	.263	.406	.346
2005	Dayton	A	55	208	51	10	2	5	(- | -)	80	30	29	31	29	2	38	5	8	4	5	2	.71	1	.245	.346	.385
2006	Dayton	A	26	98	39	6	0	5	(- | -)	60	19	18	24	7	0	10	1	0	2	0	0	-	0	.398	.435	.612
2006	Srsota	A+	91	335	93	17	2	9	(- | -)	141	53	55	55	38	0	39	6	7	7	8	2	.80	8	.278	.355	.421
2006	Chatt	AA	4	15	4	1	0	0	(- | -)	5	1	2	1	1	0	5	0	0	0	0	0	-	1	.267	.313	.333
2007	Chatt	AA	88	324	79	21	2	1	(- | -)	107	46	20	45	50	1	54	9	5	3	10	3	.77	5	.244	.358	.330
2007	Lsvlle	AAA	55	199	44	8	1	3	(- | -)	63	20	19	18	14	1	31	2	11	1	2	0	1.00	7	.221	.278	.317
2008	Lsvlle	AAA	92	318	80	20	1	7	(- | -)	123	45	42	43	26	3	71	9	10	2	2	0	1.00	8	.252	.324	.387
2008	Cin	NL	38	80	15	2	0	1	(1 | 0)	20	5	6	5	7	0	18	2	0	0	0	0	-	2	.188	.270	.250
2009	Cin	NL	90	256	54	21	0	1	(1 | 0)	78	36	16	18	26	1	40	5	5	0	2	0	1.00	8	.211	.296	.305
	2 ML YEARS		128	336	69	23	0	2	(2 | 0)	98	41	22	23	33	1	58	7	5	0	2	0	1.00	10	.205	.290	.292

Casey Janssen

Pitches: R **Bats:** R **Pos:** RP-16; SP-5   **Ht:** 6'4" **Wt:** 210 **Born:** 9/17/1981 **Age:** 28

			HOW MUCH HE PITCHED						WHAT HE GAVE UP												THE RESULTS						
Year	Team	Lg	G	GS	CG	GF	IP	BFP	H	R	ER	HR	SH	SF	HB	TBB	IBB	SO	WP	Bk	W	L	Pct	Sh	Sv-Op	Hld	ERC	ERA
2009	B Jays*	R	1	0	0	0	1.0	5	2	1	1	0	0	0	0	0	0	0	0	0	0	0	-	0	0- -	-	7.48	9.00
2009	Dnedin*	A+	4	3	0	0	13.0	46	6	1	1	0	0	0	0	2	0	10	0	0	0	0	-	0	0- -	-	0.71	0.69
2009	NHam*	AA	6	1	0	0	15.0	61	12	6	4	0	1	0	0	5	0	12	1	1	1	0	1.000	0	0- -	-	2.15	2.40
2009	LsVgs*	AAA	7	0	0	2	6.2	25	4	4	4	0	0	0	0	1	0	7	0	0	0	0	-	0	0- -	-	1.02	5.40
2006	Tor	AL	19	17	0	1	94.0	407	103	58	53	12	2	2	7	21	3	44	3	2	6	10	.375	0	0-0	0	4.32	5.07
2007	Tor	AL	70	0	0	21	72.2	297	67	22	19	4	0	3	3	20	2	39	4	0	2	3	.400	0	6-11	24	3.06	2.35
2000	Tor	AL	21	5	0	5	40.0	192	59	29	26	5	1	2	2	14	1	24	1	0	2	4	.333	0	1-1	2	7.04	5.85
	3 ML YEARS		110	22	0	27	206.2	896	229	100	98	21	5	7	12	55	6	107	8	2	10	17	.370	0	7-12	26	4.35	4.27

Jason Jaramillo

Bats: B **Throws:** R **Pos:** C-62; PH-2   **Ht:** 6'0" **Wt:** 200 **Born:** 10/9/1982 **Age:** 27

								BATTING												BASERUNNING				AVERAGES		
Year	Team	Lg	G	AB	H	2B	3B	HR	(Hm	Rd)	TB	R	RBI	RC	TBB	IBB	SO	HBP	SH	SF	SB	CS	SB%	GDP	Avg	OBP	Slg
2004	Phillies	R	1	3	2	0	0	0	(-	-)	2	1	1	1	0	0	0	0	0	0	0	0	-	0	.667	.667	.667
2004	Batvia	A-	31	112	25	5	0	1	(-	-)	33	11	14	10	12	0	27	1	0	2	0	1	.00	3	.223	.299	.295
2005	Lakwd	A	119	448	136	28	4	8	(-	-)	196	46	63	73	44	3	72	2	1	1	2	3	.40	15	.304	.368	.438
2006	Rdng	AA	93	322	80	25	1	6	(-	-)	125	35	39	42	32	2	55	4	1	5	0	1	.00	13	.248	.320	.388
2006	S-WB	AAA	2	6	1	0	0	0	(-	-)	1	0	1	0	0	0	1	0	0	0	0	0	-	0	.167	.143	.167
2007	Ottawa	AAA	118	435	118	14	4	6	(-	-)	158	52	56	60	50	3	79	5	2	4	0	1	.00	18	.271	.350	.363
2008	LV	AAA	115	421	112	20	0	8	(-	-)	156	48	39	56	42	4	82	6	2	2	1	1	.50	12	.266	.340	.371
2009	Pit	NL	63	206	52	14	0	3	(3	0)	75	20	26	18	17	2	33	0	1	0	1	0	1.00	11	.252	.300	.364

Bobby Jenks

Pitches: R **Bats:** R **Pos:** RP-52   **Ht:** 6'3" **Wt:** 275 **Born:** 3/14/1981 **Age:** 29

			HOW MUCH HE PITCHED						WHAT HE GAVE UP												THE RESULTS						
Year	Team	Lg	G	GS	CG	GF	IP	BFP	H	R	ER	HR	SH	SF	HB	TBB	IBB	SO	WP	Bk	W	L	Pct	Sh	Sv-Op	Hld	ERC	ERA
2005	CWS	AL	32	0	0	18	39.1	168	34	15	12	3	1	0	1	15	3	50	4	0	1	1	.500	0	6-8	3	3.02	2.75
2006	CWS	AL	67	0	0	50	69.2	300	66	32	31	5	4	2	2	31	10	80	3	0	3	4	.429	0	41-45	0	3.65	4.00
2007	CWS	AL	66	0	0	62	65.0	249	45	20	20	2	5	3	1	13	4	56	4	0	3	5	.375	0	40-46	0	1.49	2.77
2008	CWS	AL	57	0	0	52	61.2	243	51	18	18	3	2	1	1	17	4	38	3	0	3	1	.750	0	30-34	0	2.43	2.63
2009	CWS	AL	52	0	0	46	53.1	228	52	24	22	9	0	2	2	16	1	49	0	0	3	4	.429	0	29-35	0	4.08	3.71
	Postseason		7	0	0	5	9.0	36	5	2	2	0	1	0	1	3	0	9	0	0	0	0	-	0	5-6	0	1.47	2.00
	5 ML YEARS		274	0	0	236	289.0	1188	248	109	103	22	12	8	7	92	22	273	14	0	13	15	.464	0	146-168	3	2.84	3.21

Jason Jennings

Pitches: R **Bats:** L **Pos:** RP-44   **Ht:** 6'2" **Wt:** 235 **Born:** 7/17/1978 **Age:** 31

			HOW MUCH HE PITCHED						WHAT HE GAVE UP												THE RESULTS						
Year	Team	Lg	G	GS	CG	GF	IP	BFP	H	R	ER	HR	SH	SF	HB	TBB	IBB	SO	WP	Bk	W	L	Pct	Sh	Sv-Op	Hld	ERC	ERA
2001	Col	NL	7	7	1	0	39.1	174	42	21	20	2	1	1	1	19	0	26	1	0	4	1	.800	1	0-0	0	4.58	4.58
2002	Col	NL	32	32	0	0	185.1	808	201	102	93	26	9	3	8	70	2	127	10	0	16	8	.667	0	0-0	0	4.98	4.52
2003	Col	NL	32	32	1	0	181.1	820	212	115	103	20	11	6	5	88	7	119	7	0	12	13	.480	0	0-0	0	5.60	5.11
2004	Col	NL	33	33	0	0	201.0	925	241	125	123	27	9	3	7	101	14	133	6	1	11	12	.478	0	0-0	0	5.99	5.51
2005	Col	NL	20	20	1	0	122.0	551	130	73	68	11	6	3	5	64	4	75	8	0	6	9	.400	0	0-0	0	4.91	5.02
2006	Col	NL	32	32	3	0	212.0	902	206	94	89	17	8	6	3	85	7	142	10	0	9	13	.409	2	0-0	0	3.83	3.78
2007	Hou	NL	19	18	0	0	99.0	445	119	73	71	19	6	7	2	34	2	71	5	0	2	9	.182	0	0-0	0	5.72	6.45
2008	Tex	AL	6	6	0	0	27.1	135	35	27	26	8	2	0	1	18	2	12	1	0	0	5	.000	0	0-0	0	8.42	8.56
2009	Tex	AL	44	0	0	8	61.0	272	67	31	28	7	3	5	2	28	3	44	3	0	2	4	.333	0	1-2	12	5.07	4.13
	9 ML YEARS		225	180	6	8	1128.1	5032	1253	661	621	137	55	34	34	505	41	749	51	1	62	74	.456	3	1-2	12	5.16	4.95

Kevin Jepsen

Pitches: R **Bats:** R **Pos:** RP-54   **Ht:** 6'3" **Wt:** 215 **Born:** 7/26/1984 **Age:** 25

Year	Team	Lg	G	GS	CG	GF	IP	BFP	H	R	ER	HR	SH	SF	HB	TBB	IBB	SO	WP	Bk	W	L	Pct	Sh	Sv-Op	Hld	ERC	ERA
2002	Angels	R	8	5	0	1	26.1	125	29	22	20	3	0	2	5	12	0	19	1	0	1	3	.250	0	0- -	-	5.63	6.84
2003	CRpds	A	10	10	0	0	51.0	211	32	24	15	2	1	2	2	28	0	42	0	0	6	3	.667	0	0- -	-	2.42	2.65
2004	CRpds	A	27	27	1	0	144.1	628	122	68	55	6	10	2	12	77	1	136	14	2	8	10	.444	1	0- -	-	3.63	3.43
2005	Angels	R	7	7	0	0	14.2	67	8	10	9	1	0	0	3	11	0	17	4	1	1	0	1.000	0	0- -	-	3.31	5.52
2005	RCuca	A+	4	4	0	0	12.2	68	19	18	15	2	0	0	1	10	0	11	0	0	0	1	.000	0	0- -	-	9.56	10.66
2006	RCuca	A+	47	0	0	41	50.1	237	51	26	20	2	7	3	4	34	0	46	6	0	4	4	.500	0	16- -	-	5.02	3.58
2007	RCuca	A+	44	0	0	16	53.2	252	61	29	25	2	1	1	3	38	2	50	4	0	1	5	.167	0	3- -	-	5.88	4.19
2008	Ark	AA	25	0	0	21	31.2	131	22	5	5	0	2	0	0	18	1	35	3	0	2	1	.667	0	11- -	-	2.40	1.42
2008	Salt Lk	AAA	15	0	0	9	23.0	95	17	9	6	3	3	0	0	12	1	21	2	0	1	3	.250	0	2- -	-	3.32	2.35
2009	Salt Lk	AAA	14	0	0	7	18.0	103	30	24	18	4	0	0	1	16	1	20	0	0	1	0	1.000	0	2- -	-	11.36	9.00
2008	LAA	AL	9	0	0	0	8.1	36	8	5	4	0	0	0	0	4	0	7	1	0	0	1	.000	0	0-0	3	3.46	4.32
2009	LAA	AL	54	0	0	13	54.2	237	63	33	30	2	0	2	0	19	2	48	6	0	6	4	.600	0	1-2	17	4.27	4.94
	2 ML YEARS		63	0	0	13	63.0	273	71	38	34	2	0	2	0	23	2	55	7	0	6	5	.545	0	1-2	20	4.16	4.86

Derek Jeter

Bats: R **Throws:** R **Pos:** SS-150; DH-5; PH-1   **Ht:** 6'3" **Wt:** 195 **Born:** 6/26/1974 **Age:** 36

Year	Team	Lg	G	AB	H	2B	3B	HR	(Hm	Rd)	TB	R	RBI	RC	TBB	IBB	SO	HBP	SH	SF	SB	CS	SB%	GDP	Avg	OBP	Slg
1995	NYY	AL	15	48	12	4	1	0	(0	0)	18	5	7	5	3	0	11	0	0	0	0	0	-	0	.250	.294	.375
1996	NYY	AL	157	582	183	25	6	10	(3	7)	250	104	78	92	48	1	102	9	6	9	14	7	.67	13	.314	.370	.430
1997	NYY	AL	159	654	190	31	7	10	(5	5)	265	116	70	99	74	0	125	10	8	2	23	12	.66	14	.291	.370	.405
1998	NYY	AL	149	626	203	25	8	19	(9	10)	301	127	84	115	57	1	119	5	3	3	30	6	.83	13	.324	.384	.481
1999	NYY	AL	158	627	**219**	37	9	24	(15	9)	346	134	102	146	91	5	116	12	3	6	19	8	.70	12	.349	.438	.552
2000	NYY	AL	148	593	201	31	4	15	(8	7)	285	119	73	118	68	4	99	12	3	3	22	4	.85	14	.339	.416	.481
2001	NYY	AL	150	614	191	35	3	21	(13	8)	295	110	74	112	56	3	99	10	5	1	27	3	.90	13	.311	.377	.480
2002	NYY	AL	157	644	191	26	0	18	(8	10)	271	124	75	108	73	2	114	7	3	3	32	3	.91	14	.297	.373	.421
2003	NYY	AL	119	482	156	25	3	10	(7	3)	217	87	52	86	43	2	88	13	3	1	11	5	.69	10	.324	.393	.450
2004	NYY	AL	154	643	188	44	1	23	(11	12)	303	111	78	100	46	1	99	14	16	2	23	4	.85	19	.292	.352	.471
2005	NYY	AL	159	654	202	25	5	19	(12	7)	294	122	70	105	77	3	117	11	7	3	14	5	.74	15	.309	.389	.450
2006	NYY	AL	154	623	214	39	3	14	(8	6)	301	118	97	**132**	69	4	102	12	7	4	34	5	.87	13	.343	.417	.483
2007	NYY	AL	156	639	206	39	4	12	(4	8)	289	102	73	112	56	3	100	14	3	2	15	8	.65	21	.322	.388	.452
2008	NYY	AL	150	596	179	25	3	11	(3	8)	243	88	69	88	52	0	85	9	7	4	11	5	.69	24	.300	.363	.408
2009	NYY	AL	153	634	212	27	1	18	(13	5)	295	107	66	109	72	4	90	5	4	1	30	5	.86	18	.334	.406	.465
	Postseason		123	495	153	22	3	17	(10	7)	232	85	49	77	51	1	96	5	8	4	16	4	.80	10	.309	.377	.469
	15 ML YEARS		2138	8659	2747	438	58	224	(119	105)	3973	1574	1068	1527	885	33	1466	143	78	44	305	80	.79	213	.317	.388	.459

Ubaldo Jimenez

Pitches: R **Bats:** R **Pos:** SP-33   **Ht:** 6'4" **Wt:** 200 **Born:** 1/22/1984 **Age:** 26

Year	Team	Lg	G	GS	CG	GF	IP	BFP	H	R	ER	HR	SH	SF	HB	TBB	IBB	SO	WP	Bk	W	L	Pct	Sh	Sv-Op	Hld	ERC	ERA
2006	Col	NL	2	1	0	0	7.2	30	5	4	3	1	0	0	0	3	0	3	0	0	0	0	-	0	0-0	0	2.48	3.52
2007	Col	NL	15	15	0	0	82.0	354	70	46	39	10	3	1	6	37	4	68	3	0	4	4	.500	0	0-0	0	3.80	4.28
2008	Col	NL	34	**34**	1	0	198.2	868	182	97	88	11	7	4	10	103	4	172	16	0	12	12	.500	0	0-0	0	3.92	3.99
2009	Col	NL	33	33	1	0	218.0	914	183	87	84	13	15	6	10	85	6	198	8	3	15	12	.556	0	0-0	0	3.03	3.47
	Postseason		3	3	0	0	16.0	71	11	4	4	1	0	1	1	13	1	13	1	0	0	1	.000	0	0-0	0	3.80	2.25
	4 ML YEARS		84	83	2	0	506.1	2166	440	234	214	35	25	11	26	228	14	441	27	3	31	28	.525	0	0-0	0	3.49	3.80

Waldis Joaquin

Pitches: R **Bats:** R **Pos:** RP-10   **Ht:** 6'2" **Wt:** 235 **Born:** 12/25/1986 **Age:** 23

Year	Team	Lg	G	GS	CG	GF	IP	BFP	H	R	ER	HR	SH	SF	HB	TBB	IBB	SO	WP	Bk	W	L	Pct	Sh	Sv-Op	Hld	ERC	ERA
2005	Giants	R	10	5	0	3	29.2	129	28	17	12	1	1	1	1	10	0	37	1	1	1	1	.500	0	1- -	-	3.10	3.64
2007	SlmKzr	A-	15	5	0	4	38.0	155	24	13	12	2	0	1	2	16	0	30	2	0	3	0	1.000	0	0- -	-	2.12	2.84
2008	Augsta	A	27	3	0	6	52.0	223	49	32	25	1	1	3	1	20	0	49	3	1	1	2	.333	0	2- -	-	3.19	4.33
2008	SnJos	A+	9	4	0	2	19.1	85	20	13	10	2	0	1	0	11	1	23	0	0	1	0	1.000	0	0- -	-	5.01	4.66
2009	Conn	AA	36	0	0	9	54.0	222	36	17	16	0	4	1	0	28	3	40	3	0	4	5	.444	0	1- -	-	2.04	2.67
2009	Fresno	AAA	8	0	0	1	10.0	37	5	0	0	0	0	0	0	2	0	16	0	0	1	0	1.000	0	1- -	-	0.86	0.00
2009	SF	NL	10	0	0	4	10.2	51	10	5	5	1	0	0	2	7	0	12	3	0	0	0	-	0	0-0	0	5.30	4.22

Kenji Johjima

Bats: R **Throws:** R **Pos:** C-70; PH-1   **Ht:** 6'0" **Wt:** 205 **Born:** 6/8/1976 **Age:** 34

Year	Team	Lg	G	AB	H	2B	3B	HR	(Hm	Rd)	TB	R	RBI	RC	TBB	IBB	SO	HBP	SH	SF	SB	CS	SB%	GDP	Avg	OBP	Slg
2009	Tacom*	AAA	4	14	4	0	0	0	(-	-)	4	2	0	1	0	0	3	0	0	0	0	0	-	0	.286	.286	.286
2006	Sea	AL	144	506	147	25	1	18	(6	12)	228	61	76	79	20	1	46	13	0	3	3	1	.75	15	.291	.332	.451
2007	Sea	AL	135	485	139	29	0	14	(8	6)	210	52	61	55	15	0	41	11	0	2	0	2	.00	22	.287	.322	.433
2008	Sea	AL	112	379	86	19	0	7	(3	4)	126	29	39	37	19	1	33	8	1	2	2	0	1.00	12	.227	.277	.332
2009	Sea	AL	71	239	59	11	0	9	(3	6)	97	24	22	23	12	0	28	5	1	1	2	2	.50	4	.247	.296	.406
	4 ML YEARS		462	1609	431	84	1	48	(20	28)	661	166	198	194	66	2	148	37	2	8	7	5	.58	53	.268	.310	.411

Chris Johnson

Bats: R **Throws**: R **Pos**: 3B-7; PH-5   **Ht**: 6'3" **Wt**: 220 **Born**: 10/1/1984 **Age**: 25

Year	Team	Lg	G	AB	H	2B	3B	HR	(Hm	Rd)	TB	R	RBI	RC	TBB	IBB	SO	HBP	SH	SF	SB	CS	SB%	GDP	Avg	OBP	Slg
2006	TriCity	A-	60	222	47	7	1	1	(-	-)	59	18	29	14	11	1	35	2	0	4	7	3	.70	13	.212	.251	.266
2007	Lxngtn	A	64	255	66	14	0	8	(-	-)	104	37	44	32	17	0	38	1	1	3	3	4	.43	8	.259	.304	.408
2007	Salem	A+	60	224	59	11	0	6	(-	-)	88	24	38	27	8	1	41	3	0	5	1	0	1.00	9	.263	.292	.393
2008	CpChr	AA	85	334	107	24	0	12	(-	-)	167	43	58	61	20	0	63	3	1	4	5	0	1.00	14	.320	.360	.500
2008	RdRck	AAA	30	101	22	2	1	1	(-	-)	29	10	9	7	5	0	25	0	0	1	0	0	-	1	.218	.252	.287
2009	RdRck	AAA	104	384	108	20	5	13	(-	-)	177	48	42	58	21	1	90	4	0	3	2	1	.67	16	.281	.323	.461
2009	Lancst	A+	4	16	7	5	0	0	(-	-)	12	5	6	4	1	0	3	0	0	-	1	0	-	1	.438	.471	.750
2009	Hou	NL	11	22	2	0	0	0	(0	0)	2	1	1	0	1	0	6	0	0	0	0	0	-	0	.091	.130	.091

Jim Johnson

Pitches: R **Bats**: R **Pos**: RP-64   **Ht**: 6'5" **Wt**: 224 **Born**: 6/27/1983 **Age**: 27

Year	Team	Lg	G	GS	CG	GF	IP	BFP	H	R	ER	HR	SH	SF	HB	TBB	IBB	SO	WP	Bk	W	L	Pct	Sh	Sv-Op	Hld	ERC	ERA
2006	Bal	AL	1	1	0	0	3.0	21	9	8	8	1	0	1	1	3	0	0	0	0	0	1	.000	0	0-0	0	26.81	24.00
2007	Bal	AL	1	0	0	1	2.0	11	3	2	2	0	0	1	0	2	0	1	0	0	0	0	-	0	0-0	0	8.58	9.00
2008	Bal	AL	54	0	0	18	68.2	281	54	18	17	0	2	1	3	28	3	38	1	1	2	4	.333	0	1-1	19	2.45	2.23
2009	Bal	AL	64	0	0	29	70.0	300	73	32	32	8	2	2	3	23	3	49	2	1	4	6	.400	0	10-16	14	4.28	4.11
	4 ML YEARS		120	1	0	48	143.2	613	139	60	59	9	4	5	7	56	6	88	3	2	6	11	.353	0	11-17	33	3.76	3.70

Josh Johnson

Pitches: R **Bats**: L **Pos**: SP-33   **Ht**: 6'7" **Wt**: 252 **Born**: 1/31/1984 **Age**: 26

Year	Team	Lg	G	GS	CG	GF	IP	BFP	H	R	ER	HR	SH	SF	HB	TBB	IBB	SO	WP	Bk	W	L	Pct	Sh	Sv-Op	Hld	ERC	ERA
2005	Fla	NL	1	1	0	0	12.1	55	11	5	5	0	1	0	1	10	0	10	0	0	0	0	-	0	0-0	0	4.82	3.65
2006	Fla	NL	31	24	0	1	157.0	659	136	63	54	14	11	0	4	68	6	133	3	1	12	7	.632	0	0-1	0	3.48	3.10
2007	Fla	NL	4	4	0	0	15.2	82	26	17	13	1	2	1	0	12	3	14	1	0	0	3	.000	0	0-0	0	9.16	7.47
2008	Fla	NL	14	14	1	0	87.1	365	91	36	35	7	5	1	4	27	1	77	4	0	7	1	.875	0	0-0	0	3.94	3.61
2009	Fla	NL	33	33	2	0	209.0	855	184	77	75	14	11	4	6	58	6	191	10	0	15	5	.750	0	0-0	0	2.84	3.23
	5 ML YEARS		86	76	3	1	481.1	2010	448	198	182	38	30	6	12	175	16	425	18	1	34	16	.680	0	0-1	0	3.47	3.40

Kelly Johnson

Bats: L **Throws**: R **Pos**: 2B-84; PH-26; PR-5   **Ht**: 6'1" **Wt**: 205 **Born**: 2/22/1982 **Age**: 28

Year	Team	Lg	G	AB	H	2B	3B	HR	(Hm	Rd)	TB	R	RBI	RC	TBB	IBB	SO	HBP	SH	SF	SB	CS	SB%	GDP	Avg	OBP	Slg
2009	Gwnnll*	AAA	13	52	16	2	2	3	(-	-)	31	9	16	11	4	0	8	0	0	3	1	0	1.00	1	.308	.339	.596
2005	Atl	NL	87	290	70	12	3	9	(2	7)	115	46	40	41	40	1	75	1	2	1	2	1	.67	11	.241	.334	.397
2007	Atl	NL	147	521	144	26	10	16	(5	11)	238	91	68	87	79	3	117	4	2	2	9	5	.64	8	.276	.375	.457
2008	Atl	NL	150	547	157	39	6	12	(5	7)	244	86	69	87	52	2	113	2	9	4	11	6	.65	3	.287	.349	.446
2009	Atl	NL	106	303	68	20	3	8	(4	4)	118	47	29	31	32	1	54	3	6	2	7	2	.78	4	.224	.303	.389
	Postseason		4	2	0	0	0	0	(0	0)	0	0	0	0	1	0	0	0	0	0	0	0	-	0	.000	.333	.000
	4 ML YEARS		490	1661	439	97	22	45	(16	29)	715	270	206	246	203	7	359	10	19	9	29	14	.67	26	.264	.346	.430

Nick Johnson

Bats: L **Throws**: L **Pos**: 1B-129; PH-4   **Ht**: 6'3" **Wt**: 236 **Born**: 9/19/1978 **Age**: 31

Year	Team	Lg	G	AB	H	2B	3B	HR	(Hm	Rd)	TB	R	RBI	RC	TBB	IBB	SO	HBP	SH	SF	SB	CS	SB%	GDP	Avg	OBP	Slg
2009	Jupiter*	A+	2	3	1	1	0	0	(-	-)	2	0	0	0	0	0	2	0	0	0	0	0	-	0	.333	.333	.667
2001	NYY	AL	23	67	13	2	0	2	(1	1)	21	6	8	6	7	0	15	4	0	0	0	0	-	3	.194	.308	.313
2002	NYY	AL	129	378	92	15	0	15	(7	8)	152	56	58	59	48	5	98	12	3	0	1	3	.25	11	.243	.347	.402
2003	NYY	AL	96	324	92	19	0	14	(8	6)	153	60	47	65	70	4	57	8	3	1	5	2	.71	9	.284	.422	.472
2004	Mon	NL	73	251	63	16	0	7	(4	3)	100	35	33	36	40	2	58	3	0	1	6	3	.67	5	.251	.359	.398
2005	Was	NL	131	453	131	35	3	15	(7	8)	217	66	74	83	80	8	87	12	0	2	3	8	.27	15	.289	.408	.479
2006	Was	NL	147	500	145	46	0	23	(10	13)	260	100	77	104	110	15	99	13	2	3	10	3	.77	12	.290	.428	.520
2008	Was	NL	38	109	24	8	0	5	(2	3)	47	15	20	21	33	4	25	4	0	1	0	0	-	2	.220	.415	.431
2009	2 Tms	NL	133	457	133	24	2	8	(2	6)	185	71	62	85	99	4	84	12	1	5	2	4	.33	15	.291	.426	.405
09	Was	NL	98	353	104	16	2	6	(2	4)	142	47	44	60	63	3	66	6	0	2	2	2	.50	11	.295	.408	.402
09	Fla	NL	35	104	29	8	0	2	(0	2)	43	24	18	25	36	1	18	6	1	3	0	2	.00	4	.279	.477	.413
	Postseason		20	67	14	3	0	1	(1	0)	20	10	6	6	8	1	14	1	0	0	0	0	-	2	.209	.303	.299
	8 ML YEARS		770	2539	693	165	5	89	(41	48)	1135	409	379	459	487	42	523	68	9	13	27	23	.54	72	.273	.402	.447

Randy Johnson

Pitches: L **Bats**: R **Pos**: SP-17; RP-5   **Ht**: 6'10" **Wt**: 225 **Born**: 9/10/1963 **Age**: 46

Year	Team	Lg	G	GS	CG	GF	IP	BFP	H	R	ER	HR	SH	SF	HB	TBB	IBB	SO	WP	Bk	W	L	Pct	Sh	Sv-Op	Hld	ERC	ERA
1988	Mon	NL	4	4	1	0	26.0	109	23	8	7	3	0	0	0	7	0	25	3	0	3	0	1.000	0	0-0	0	2.96	2.42
1989	2 Tms		29	28	2	1	160.2	715	147	100	86	13	10	13	3	96	2	130	7	7	7	13	.350	0	0-0	0	4.26	4.82
1990	Sea	AL	33	33	5	0	219.2	944	174	103	89	26	7	6	5	120	2	194	4	2	14	11	.560	2	0-0	0	3.68	3.65
1991	Sea	AL	33	33	2	0	201.1	889	151	96	89	15	9	8	12	152	0	228	12	2	13	10	.565	1	0-0	0	4.15	3.98
1992	Sea	AL	31	31	6	0	210.1	922	154	104	88	13	3	8	18	144	1	241	13	1	12	14	.462	2	0-0	0	3.75	3.77
1993	Sea	AL	35	34	10	1	255.1	1043	185	97	92	22	8	7	16	99	1	308	8	2	19	8	.704	3	1-1	0	2.73	3.24
1994	Sea	AL	23	23	9	0	172.0	694	132	65	61	14	3	1	6	72	2	204	5	0	13	6	.684	4	0-0	0	2.99	3.19
1995	Sea	AL	30	30	6	0	214.1	866	159	65	59	12	2	1	6	65	1	294	5	2	18	2	.900	3	0-0	0	2.18	2.48

(Pitcher statistics — name not shown)

Year	Team	Lg	G	GS	CG	GF	IP	BFP	H	R	ER	HR	SH	SF	HB	TBB	IBB	SO	WP	Bk	W	L	Pct	Sh	Sv-Op	Hld	ERC	ERA
1996	Sea	AL	14	8	0	2	61.1	256	48	27	25	8	1	0	2	25	0	85	3	1	5	0	1.000	0	1-2	0	3.24	3.67
1997	Sea	AL	30	29	5	0	213.0	850	147	60	54	20	4	1	10	77	2	291	4	0	20	4	.833	0	0-0	0	2.47	2.28
1998	2 Tms		34	34	10	0	244.1	1014	203	102	89	23	5	2	14	86	1	329	7	2	19	11	.633	6	0-0	0	3.16	3.28
1999	Ari	NL	35	35	12	0	271.2	1079	207	86	75	30	4	3	9	70	3	364	4	2	17	9	.654	2	0-0	0	2.49	2.48
2000	Ari	NL	35	35	8	0	248.2	1001	202	89	73	23	14	5	6	76	1	347	5	2	19	7	.731	3	0-0	0	2.80	2.64
2001	Ari	NL	35	34	3	1	249.2	994	181	74	69	19	10	5	18	71	2	372	8	1	21	6	.778	2	0-0	0	2.35	2.49
2002	Ari	NL	35	35	8	0	260.0	1035	197	78	67	26	4	2	13	71	1	334	3	2	24	5	.828	4	0-0	0	2.54	2.32
2003	Ari	NL	18	18	1	0	114.0	489	125	61	54	16	4	3	8	27	3	125	1	1	6	8	.429	1	0-0	0	4.52	4.26
2004	Ari	NL	35	35	4	0	245.2	964	177	88	71	18	7	5	10	44	1	290	3	1	16	14	.533	2	0-0	0	1.82	2.60
2005	NYY	AL	34	34	4	0	225.2	920	207	102	95	32	5	5	12	47	2	211	3	1	17	8	.680	0	0-0	0	3.38	3.79
2006	NYY	AL	33	33	2	0	205.0	860	194	125	114	28	6	7	10	60	1	172	3	2	17	11	.607	0	0-0	0	3.80	5.00
2007	Ari	NL	10	10	0	0	56.2	233	52	26	24	7	4	0	4	13	3	72	1	0	4	3	.571	0	0-0	0	3.34	3.81
2008	Ari	NL	30	30	2	0	184.0	778	184	92	80	24	13	6	6	44	6	173	2	1	11	10	.524	0	0-0	0	3.69	3.91
2009	SF	NL	22	17	0	2	96.0	412	97	55	52	19	8	1	2	31	2	86	5	1	8	6	.571	0	0-1	0	4.53	4.88
89	Mon	NL	7	6	0	1	29.2	143	29	25	22	2	3	4	0	26	1	26	2	2	0	4	.000	0	0-0	0	5.42	6.67
89	Sea	AL	22	22	2	0	131.0	572	118	75	64	11	7	9	3	70	1	104	5	5	7	9	.438	1	0-0	0	4.01	4.40
98	Sea	AL	23	23	6	0	160.0	685	146	90	77	19	5	1	11	60	0	213	7	2	9	10	.474	2	0-0	0	3.88	4.33
98	Hou	NL	11	11	4	0	84.1	329	57	12	12	4	0	1	3	26	1	116	0	0	10	1	.909	4	0-0	0	1.93	1.28
Postseason			19	16	3	2	121.0	493	106	51	47	15	5	5	0	32	2	132	0	0	9	4	.438	2	0-0	0	3.02	3.50
22 ML YEARS			618	603	100	7	4135.1	17067	3346	1703	1513	411	131	89	190	1497	37	4875	109	33	303	166	.646	37	2-4	0	3.08	3.29

Reed Johnson

Bats: R **Throws:** R **Pos:** CF-42; PH-18; LF-10; RF-7; PR-1　　**Ht:** 5'10" **Wt:** 180 **Born:** 12/8/1976 **Age:** 33

Year	Team	Lg	G	AB	H	2B	3B	HR	(Hm	Rd)	TB	R	RBI	RC	TBB	IBB	SO	HBP	SH	SF	SB	CS	SB%	GDP	Avg	OBP	Slg
2009	Peoria*	A	3	6	2	0	0	0	(-	-)	2	2	0	1	1	0	1	1	0	0	0	0	-	0	.333	.500	.333
2003	Tor	AL	114	412	121	21	2	10	(6	4)	176	79	52	64	20	1	67	20	1	4	5	3	.63	10	.294	.353	.427
2004	Tor	AL	141	537	145	25	2	10	(8	2)	204	68	61	65	28	2	98	12	3	2	6	3	.67	17	.270	.320	.380
2005	Tor	AL	142	398	107	21	6	8	(4	4)	164	55	58	57	22	1	82	16	2	1	5	6	.45	8	.269	.332	.412
2006	Tor	AL	134	461	147	34	2	12	(4	8)	221	86	49	76	33	4	81	21	1	1	8	2	.80	9	.319	.390	.479
2007	Tor	AL	79	275	65	13	2	2	(1	1)	88	31	14	24	16	0	56	11	5	0	4	2	.67	7	.236	.305	.320
2008	ChC	NL	109	333	101	21	0	6	(3	3)	140	52	50	57	19	1	68	12	5	5	5	6	.45	3	.303	.358	.420
2009	ChC	NL	65	165	42	10	2	4	(3	1)	68	23	22	19	13	0	27	6	1	1	2	1	.67	5	.255	.330	.412
7 ML YEARS			784	2581	728	145	16	52	(29	23)	1061	394	306	362	151	9	479	98	18	14	35	23	.60	59	.282	.344	.411

Rob Johnson

Bats: R **Throws:** R **Pos:** C-80; PR-1　　**Ht:** 6'1" **Wt:** 215 **Born:** 7/22/1982 **Age:** 27

Year	Team	Lg	G	AB	H	2B	3B	HR	(Hm	Rd)	TB	R	RBI	RC	TBB	IBB	SO	HBP	SH	SF	SB	CS	SB%	GDP	Avg	OBP	Slg
2007	Sea	AL	6	3	1	0	0	0	(0	0)	1	1	0	0	0	0	0	0	0	0	1	0	1.00	0	.333	.333	.333
2008	Sea	AL	14	31	4	0	0	0	(1	0)	7	2	2	0	0	0	6	0	1	0	0	0	-	1	.129	.129	.226
2009	Sea	AL	80	258	55	19	2	2	(2	0)	84	21	27	22	26	1	60	2	3	1	1	1	.50	11	.213	.289	.326
3 ML YEARS			100	292	60	19	2	3	(3	0)	92	24	29	22	26	1	66	2	4	1	2	1	.67	12	.205	.274	.315

Adam Jones

Bats: R **Throws:** R **Pos:** CF-119; PH-1　　**Ht:** 6'2" **Wt:** 210 **Born:** 8/1/1985 **Age:** 24

Year	Team	Lg	G	AB	H	2B	3B	HR	(Hm	Rd)	TB	R	RBI	RC	TBB	IBB	SO	HBP	SH	SF	SB	CS	SB%	GDP	Avg	OBP	Slg
2006	Sea	AL	32	74	16	4	0	1	(0	1)	23	6	8	4	2	0	22	0	0	0	3	1	.75	3	.216	.237	.311
2007	Sea	AL	41	65	16	2	1	2	(1	1)	26	16	4	5	4	0	21	1	1	0	2	1	.67	0	.246	.300	.400
2008	Bal	AL	132	477	129	21	7	9	(4	5)	191	61	57	56	23	0	108	7	2	5	10	3	.77	12	.270	.311	.400
2009	Bal	AL	119	473	131	22	3	19	(11	8)	216	83	70	71	36	3	93	7	0	3	10	4	.71	13	.277	.335	.457
4 ML YEARS			324	1089	292	49	11	31	(16	15)	456	166	139	136	65	3	244	15	3	8	25	9	.74	28	.268	.316	.419

Andruw Jones

Bats: R **Throws:** R **Pos:** DH-55; LF-12; 1B-8; PH-8; RF-5　　**Ht:** 6'1" **Wt:** 240 **Born:** 4/23/1977 **Age:** 33

Year	Team	Lg	G	AB	H	2B	3B	HR	(Hm	Rd)	TB	R	RBI	RC	TBB	IBB	SO	HBP	SH	SF	SB	CS	SB%	GDP	Avg	OBP	Slg
2009	Frisco*	AA	3	9	2	0	0	0	(-	-)	2	0	0	1	3	0	1	0	0	0	1	0	1.00	1	.222	.417	.222
1996	Atl	NL	31	106	23	7	1	5	(3	2)	47	11	13	13	7	0	29	0	0	0	3	0	1.00	1	.217	.265	.443
1997	Atl	NL	153	399	92	18	1	18	(5	13)	166	60	70	54	56	2	107	4	5	3	20	11	.65	11	.231	.329	.416
1998	Atl	NL	159	582	158	33	8	31	(16	15)	300	89	90	97	40	8	129	4	1	4	27	4	.87	10	.271	.321	.515
1999	Atl	NL	162	592	163	35	5	26	(10	16)	286	97	84	103	76	11	103	9	0	2	24	12	.67	12	.275	.365	.483
2000	Atl	NL	161	656	199	36	6	36	(15	21)	355	122	104	127	59	0	100	9	0	5	21	6	.78	12	.303	.366	.541
2001	Atl	NL	161	625	157	25	2	34	(16	18)	288	104	104	90	56	3	142	10	3	9	11	4	.73	10	.251	.312	.461
2002	Atl	NL	154	560	148	34	0	35	(18	17)	287	91	94	94	83	4	135	10	0	6	8	3	.73	14	.264	.366	.513
2003	Atl	NL	156	595	165	28	2	36	(16	20)	305	101	116	92	53	2	125	5	0	6	4	3	.57	18	.277	.338	.513
2004	Atl	NL	154	570	149	34	4	29	(13	16)	278	85	91	75	71	9	147	3	0	2	6	6	.50	24	.261	.345	.488
2005	Atl	NL	160	586	154	24	3	51	(21	30)	337	95	128	91	64	13	112	15	0	7	5	3	.63	19	.263	.347	.575
2006	Atl	NL	156	565	148	29	0	41	(19	22)	300	107	129	108	82	9	127	13	0	9	4	1	.80	13	.262	.363	.531
2007	Atl	NL	154	572	127	27	2	26	(16	10)	236	83	94	71	70	4	138	8	0	9	5	2	.71	16	.222	.311	.413
2008	LAD	NL	75	209	33	8	1	3	(0	3)	52	21	14	6	27	0	76	1	0	1	0	1	.00	5	.158	.256	.249
2009	Tex	AL	82	281	60	18	0	17	(9	8)	129	43	43	42	45	3	72	2	0	3	5	1	.83	7	.214	.323	.459
Postseason			75	238	65	8	0	10	(5	5)	103	43	33	34	34	2	50	2	1	3	5	5	.50	5	.273	.365	.433
14 ML YEARS			1918	6898	1776	356	35	388	(177	211)	3366	1109	1174	1063	789	68	1542	86	6	66	143	57	.72	172	.257	.338	.488

Brandon Jones

Bats: L Throws: R Pos: LF-4; PH-1 Ht: 6'1" Wt: 210 Born: 12/10/1983 Age: 26

Year	Team	Lg	G	AB	H	2B	3B	HR	(Hm	Rd)	TB	R	RBI	RC	TBB	IBB	SO	HBP	SH	SF	SB	CS	SB%	GDP	Avg	OBP	Slg
2009	Gwnntt*	AAA	107	384	108	29	2	7	(-	-)	162	50	57	62	50	3	76	1	1	7	6	3	.67	10	.281	.360	.422
2007	Atl	NL	5	19	3	1	0	0	(0	0)	4	0	4	1	0	0	8	1	0	1	0	0	-	0	.158	.190	.211
2008	Atl	NL	41	116	31	10	1	1	(0	1)	46	16	17	15	7	2	28	1	3	1	1	0	1.00	3	.267	.312	.397
2009	Atl	NL	5	13	4	0	0	0	(0	0)	4	2	1	2	4	0	3	0	0	0	0	0	-	0	.308	.471	.308
	3 ML YEARS		51	148	38	11	1	1	(0	1)	54	18	22	18	11	2	39	2	3	2	1	0	1.00	3	.257	.313	.365

Chipper Jones

Bats: B Throws: R Pos: 3B-133; PH-9; DH-3 Ht: 6'4" Wt: 210 Born: 4/24/1972 Age: 38

Year	Team	Lg	G	AB	H	2B	3B	HR	(Hm	Rd)	TB	R	RBI	RC	TBB	IBB	SO	HBP	SH	SF	SB	CS	SB%	GDP	Avg	OBP	Slg
1993	Atl	NL	8	3	2	1	0	0	(0	0)	3	2	0	2	1	0	1	0	0	0	0	0	-	0	.667	.750	1.000
1995	Atl	NL	140	524	139	22	3	23	(15	8)	236	87	86	84	73	1	99	0	1	4	8	4	.67	10	.265	.353	.450
1996	Atl	NL	157	598	185	32	5	30	(18	12)	317	114	110	123	87	0	88	0	1	7	14	1	.93	14	.309	.393	.530
1997	Atl	NL	157	597	176	41	3	21	(7	14)	286	100	111	104	76	8	88	0	0	6	20	5	.80	19	.295	.371	.479
1998	Atl	NL	160	601	188	29	5	34	(17	17)	329	123	107	129	96	1	93	1	1	8	16	6	.73	17	.313	.404	.547
1999	Atl	NL	157	567	181	41	1	45	(25	20)	359	116	110	150	126	18	94	2	0	6	25	3	.89	20	.319	.441	.633
2000	Atl	NL	156	579	180	38	1	36	(18	18)	328	118	111	128	95	10	64	2	0	10	14	7	.67	14	.311	.404	.566
2001	Atl	NL	159	572	189	33	5	38	(19	19)	346	113	102	136	98	20	82	2	0	5	9	10	.47	13	.330	.427	.605
2002	Atl	NL	158	548	179	35	1	26	(17	9)	294	90	100	119	107	23	89	2	0	5	8	2	.80	18	.327	.435	.536
2003	Atl	NL	153	555	169	33	2	27	(16	11)	287	103	106	110	94	13	83	1	0	6	2	2	.50	10	.305	.402	.517
2004	Atl	NL	137	472	117	20	1	30	(19	11)	229	69	96	82	84	8	96	4	0	7	2	0	1.00	14	.248	.362	.485
2005	Atl	NL	109	358	106	30	0	21	(9	12)	199	66	72	78	72	5	56	0	0	2	5	1	.83	9	.296	.412	.556
2006	Atl	NL	110	411	133	28	3	26	(12	14)	245	87	86	94	61	4	73	1	0	4	6	1	.86	12	.324	.409	.596
2007	Atl	NL	134	513	173	42	4	29	(14	15)	310	108	102	110	82	10	75	0	0	5	5	1	.83	21	.337	.425	.604
2008	Atl	NL	128	439	160	24	1	22	(12	10)	252	82	75	98	90	16	61	1	0	4	4	0	1.00	13	.364	.470	.574
2009	Atl	NL	143	488	129	23	2	18	(10	8)	210	80	71	85	101	18	89	1	0	6	4	1	.80	14	.264	.388	.430
	Postseason		92	333	96	18	0	13	(7	6)	153	58	47	60	72	11	60	1	1	5	8	3	.73	10	.288	.411	.459
	16 ML YEARS		2166	7825	2406	472	37	426	(228	198)	4230	1458	1445	1632	1343	155	1231	17	3	85	142	44	.76	218	.307	.406	.541

Garrett Jones

Bats: L Throws: L Pos: RF-39; 1B-30; LF-15 Ht: 6'4" Wt: 245 Born: 6/21/1981 Age: 29

Year	Team	Lg	G	AB	H	2B	3B	HR	(Hm	Rd)	TB	R	RBI	RC	TBB	IBB	SO	HBP	SH	SF	SB	CS	SB%	GDP	Avg	OBP	Slg
1999	Braves	R	46	170	41	3	0	3	(-	-)	53	17	18	16	16	0	47	1	0	1	2	3	.33	1	.241	.309	.312
2000	Danvle	R	40	138	24	7	2	0	(-	-)	35	12	16	6	13	0	55	0	0	2	0	3	.00	1	.174	.242	.254
2001	Danvle	R	40	149	43	11	0	3	(-	-)	63	13	23	20	9	0	58	1	0	0	0	1	.00	0	.289	.333	.423
2002	QuadC	A	63	223	45	8	0	10	(-	-)	83	21	32	19	11	1	82	0	3	1	3	1	.75	5	.202	.238	.372
2003	FtMyrs	A+	117	404	89	12	5	18	(-	-)	165	52	67	47	32	1	98	2	3	2	5	4	.56	8	.220	.280	.408
2004	FtMyrs	A+	19	66	16	5	0	1	(-	-)	24	6	6	7	4	2	19	0	0	0	2	0	1.00	0	.242	.286	.364
2004	NwBrit	AA	122	450	140	33	2	30	(-	-)	267	68	92	93	28	0	98	7	1	7	10	4	.71	5	.311	.356	.593
2005	Roch	AAA	134	488	119	22	2	24	(-	-)	217	71	72	66	36	4	109	1	1	1	5	1	.83	5	.244	.297	.445
2006	Roch	AAA	140	525	125	32	3	21	(-	-)	226	72	92	70	49	3	121	2	0	6	3	4	.43	8	.238	.302	.430
2007	Roch	AAA	107	400	112	32	3	13	(-	-)	189	57	70	65	32	4	83	5	0	9	2	2	.50	4	.280	.334	.473
2008	Roch	AAA	139	530	148	33	3	24	(-	-)	259	83	93	91	51	5	99	1	0	9	9	2	.82	11	.279	.338	.489
2009	Indy	AAA	72	277	85	18	0	12	(-	-)	139	44	49	49	18	7	47	1	0	3	14	4	.78	4	.307	.348	.502
2007	Min	AL	31	77	16	2	1	2	(1	1)	26	7	5	0	0	0	20	0	0	1	1	1	.50	2	.208	.262	.338
2009	Pit	NL	82	314	92	21	1	21	(13	8)	178	45	44	47	40	8	76	1	0	3	10	2	.83	6	.293	.372	.567
	2 ML YEARS		113	391	108	23	2	23	(14	9)	204	52	49	50	46	8	96	1	0	4	11	3	.79	8	.276	.351	.522

Hunter Jones

Pitches: L Bats: L Pos: RP-11 Ht: 6'4" Wt: 235 Born: 1/10/1984 Age: 26

Year	Team	Lg	G	GS	CG	GF	IP	BFP	H	R	ER	HR	SH	SF	HB	TBB	IBB	SO	WP	Bk	W	L	Pct	Sh	Sv-Op	Hld	ERC	ERA
2005	Lowell	A-	12	1	0	1	28.0	118	29	12	10	2	0	0	0	5	0	30	2	0	1	1	.500	0	1- -	-	3.15	3.21
2006	Grnville	A	35	5	0	18	94.1	385	87	41	35	8	1	5	5	20	0	100	7	0	4	5	.444	0	5- -	-	3.07	3.34
2007	Lancst	A+	24	0	0	4	47.0	192	35	16	11	2	2	1	3	21	0	40	1	0	4	1	.800	0	0- -	-	2.82	2.11
2007	Portlnd	AA	23	0	0	8	42.1	175	35	17	15	3	2	1	1	16	1	43	3	0	2	1	.667	0	2- -	-	2.94	3.19
2008	Portlnd	AA	13	0	0	6	22.2	94	21	3	3	0	1	1	1	4	1	26	3	0	0	1	.000	0	4- -	-	2.26	1.19
2008	Pwtckt	AAA	35	0	0	15	50.2	217	55	19	17	3	1	1	0	14	1	50	1	0	7	2	.778	0	8- -	-	3.73	3.02
2009	Pwtckt	AAA	36	0	0	15	53.0	228	45	27	25	7	5	4	1	24	6	39	1	1	4	3	.571	0	2- -	-	3.51	4.25
2009	Bos	AL	11	0	0	1	12.2	63	16	13	13	3	1	1	1	7	1	9	2	0	0	0	-	0	0-0	1	7.32	9.24

Mitch Jones

Bats: R Throws: R Pos: PH-5; DH-2; RF-1 Ht: 6'0" Wt: 215 Born: 10/15/1977 Age: 32

Year	Team	Lg	G	AB	H	2B	3B	HR	(Hm	Rd)	TB	R	RBI	RC	TBB	IBB	SO	HBP	SH	SF	SB	CS	SB%	GDP	Avg	OBP	Slg
2000	StlsInd	A-	74	284	76	28	3	11	(-	-)	143	46	54	52	35	0	66	3	0	2	8	2	.80	1	.268	.352	.504
2001	Tampa	A+	137	487	109	36	3	21	(-	-)	214	85	71	79	81	3	135	7	1	5	9	2	.82	12	.224	.340	.439
2002	Nrwich	AA	61	216	47	16	0	10	(-	-)	93	31	27	26	18	1	59	4	2	0	1	4	.20	4	.218	.290	.431
2002	Tampa	A+	61	229	61	19	0	13	(-	-)	119	36	49	40	20	1	71	3	0	3	0	0	-	8	.266	.329	.520
2003	Trnton	AA	136	463	112	18	0	23	(-	-)	199	76	91	72	58	1	131	14	1	10	5	4	.56	6	.242	.338	.430
2004	Trnton	AA	137	496	122	25	4	39	(-	-)	272	92	97	94	64	4	152	4	0	5	8	1	.89	6	.246	.334	.548
2005	Clmbs	AAA	128	489	131	29	3	27	(-	-)	247	82	79	85	52	3	174	6	0	5	2	5	.29	10	.268	.347	.505
2006	Clmbs	AAA	121	441	103	27	2	21	(-	-)	197	56	78	65	51	1	145	6	0	5	4	3	.57	11	.234	.318	.447

Year	Team	Lg	G	AB	H	2B	3B	HR	(Hm	Rd)	TB	R	RBI	RC	TBB	IBB	SO	HBP	SH	SF	SB	CS	SB%	GDP	Avg	OBP	Slg
2007	LsVgs	AAA	52	185	56	14	1	19	(-	-)	129	42	60	50	29	0	60	3	0	2	2	0	1.00	2	.303	.402	.697
2008	LsVgs	AAA	54	200	55	14	1	16	(-	-)	119	38	45	42	20	0	55	3	0	2	4	0	1.00	3	.275	.347	.595
2009	Albq	AAA	108	387	115	26	3	35	(-	-)	252	72	103	90	40	3	102	3	0	4	9	3	.75	7	.297	.364	.651
2009	LAD	NL	8	13	4	1	0	0	(0	0)	5	1	0	2	0	0	6	2	0	0	0	0	-	0	.308	.400	.385

Matt Joyce

Bats: L **Throws:** R **Pos:** RF-5; CF-4; PH-2; DH-1   **Ht:** 6'2" **Wt:** 185 **Born:** 8/3/1984 **Age:** 25

Year	Team	Lg	G	AB	H	2B	3B	HR	(Hm	Rd)	TB	R	RBI	RC	TBB	IBB	SO	HBP	SH	SF	SB	CS	SB%	GDP	Avg	OBP	Slg
2005	Oneont	A-	65	247	82	10	4	4	(-	-)	112	51	46	46	28	0	29	1	1	6	9	5	.64	4	.332	.394	.453
2006	WMich	A	122	465	120	30	5	11	(-	-)	193	75	86	69	56	2	70	3	1	5	5	4	.56	7	.258	.338	.415
2007	Erie	AA	130	456	117	33	3	17	(-	-)	207	61	70	70	51	1	127	3	1	3	4	6	.40	7	.257	.333	.454
2008	Toledo	AAA	56	200	54	13	2	13	(-	-)	110	36	41	38	24	1	62	2	0	1	2	3	.40	1	.270	.352	.550
2009	Drham	AAA	111	417	114	35	2	16	(-	-)	201	73	66	79	67	3	98	3	0	6	14	5	.74	5	.273	.373	.482
2008	Det	AL	92	242	61	16	3	12	(6	6)	119	40	33	36	31	0	65	2	0	2	0	2	.00	3	.252	.339	.492
2009	TB	AL	11	32	6	1	0	3	(2	1)	16	3	7	5	3	0	7	1	0	1	1	0	1.00	0	.188	.270	.500
2 ML YEARS			103	274	67	17	3	15	(8	7)	135	43	40	41	34	0	72	3	0	3	1	2	.33	3	.245	.331	.493

Jorge Julio

Pitches: R **Bats:** R **Pos:** RP-15   **Ht:** 6'1" **Wt:** 225 **Born:** 3/3/1979 **Age:** 31

Year	Team	Lg	G	GS	CG	GF	IP	BFP	H	R	ER	HR	SH	SF	HB	TBB	IBB	SO	WP	Bk	W	L	Pct	Sh	Sv-Op	Hld	ERC	ERA
2009	Drham*	AAA	19	0	0	5	22.2	105	22	16	15	2	1	1	2	15	1	24	6	0	1	1	.000	0	0- -	-	5.11	5.96
2009	Indy*	AAA	4	0	0	1	5.1	28	8	7	4	0	2	0	0	2	0	7	4	0	0	2	.000	0	0- -	-	5.50	6.75
2001	Bal	AL	18	0	0	8	21.1	99	25	13	9	2	2	0	1	9	0	22	1	0	1	1	.500	0	0-1	3	5.17	3.80
2002	Bal	AL	67	0	0	61	68.0	289	55	22	15	5	1	1	2	27	3	55	8	0	5	6	.455	0	25-31	1	2.83	1.99
2003	Bal	AL	64	0	0	51	61.2	273	60	36	30	10	2	1	2	34	4	52	0	0	0	7	.000	0	36-44	2	5.05	4.38
2004	Bal	AL	65	0	0	50	69.0	306	59	35	35	11	2	3	3	39	4	70	7	0	2	5	.286	0	22-26	2	4.35	4.57
2005	Bal	AL	67	0	0	19	71.2	313	76	50	47	14	1	3	2	24	4	58	10	0	3	5	.375	0	0-2	12	4.82	5.90
2006	2 Tms	NL	62	0	0	44	66.0	285	52	35	31	10	1	0	1	35	2	88	9	0	2	4	.333	0	16-20	1	3.72	4.23
2007	2 Tms	NL	68	0	0	14	62.0	280	68	39	36	8	2	4	3	31	2	56	6	1	0	5	.000	0	0-7	17	5.44	5.23
2008	2 Tms		27	0	0	11	30.0	132	27	12	12	3	0	2	1	19	2	34	6	0	3	0	1.000	0	0-1	0	4.52	3.60
2009	Mil	NL	15	0	0	7	17.1	88	15	17	15	2	0	0	4	15	0	13	5	0	1	1	.500	0	0-1	0	5.92	7.79
06	NYM	NL	18	0	0	12	21.1	96	21	15	12	4	0	0	1	10	1	33	2	0	1	2	.333	0	1-1	0	4.90	5.06
06	Ari	NL	44	0	0	32	44.2	189	31	20	19	6	1	0	0	25	1	55	7	0	1	2	.333	0	15-19	1	3.18	3.83
07	Fla	NL	10	0	0	5	9.1	59	18	14	13	2	1	0	2	11	1	6	1	1	0	2	.000	0	0-2	1	15.51	12.54
07	Col	NL	58	0	0	9	52.2	221	50	25	23	6	1	4	1	20	1	50	5	0	0	3	.000	0	0-5	16	3.93	3.93
08	Cle	AL	15	0	0	6	17.2	78	18	11	11	3	0	2	0	11	1	15	3	0	0	0	-	0	0-0	0	5.70	5.60
08	Atl	NL	12	0	0	5	12.1	54	9	1	1	0	0	0	1	8	1	19	3	0	3	0	1.000	0	0-1	0	2.97	0.73
9 ML YEARS			453	0	0	265	467.0	2065	437	259	230	65	11	14	19	233	21	448	52	1	17	34	.333	0	99-133	38	4.43	4.43

Jair Jurrjens

Pitches: R **Bats:** R **Pos:** SP-34   **Ht:** 6'1" **Wt:** 200 **Born:** 1/29/1986 **Age:** 24

Year	Team	Lg	G	GS	CG	GF	IP	BFP	H	R	ER	HR	SH	SF	HB	TBB	IBB	SO	WP	Bk	W	L	Pct	Sh	Sv-Op	Hld	ERC	ERA
2007	Det	AL	7	7	0	0	30.2	122	24	16	16	4	0	1	1	11	0	13	2	0	3	1	.750	0	0-0	0	3.19	4.70
2008	Atl	NL	31	31	0	0	188.1	813	188	87	77	11	12	5	4	70	9	139	3	0	13	10	.565	0	0-0	0	3.65	3.68
2009	Atl	NL	34	34	0	0	215.0	884	186	71	62	15	16	4	3	75	1	152	3	2	14	10	.583	0	0-0	0	3.03	2.60
3 ML YEARS			72	72	0	0	434.0	1819	398	174	155	30	28	10	8	156	10	304	8	2	30	21	.588	0	0-0	0	3.31	3.21

Gabe Kapler

Bats: R **Throws:** R **Pos:** RF-66; PH-17; LF-14; CF-12; PR-8; DH-2   **Ht:** 6'2" **Wt:** 205 **Born:** 7/31/1975 **Age:** 34

Year	Team	Lg	G	AB	H	2B	3B	HR	(Hm	Rd)	TB	R	RBI	RC	TBB	IBB	SO	HBP	SH	SF	SB	CS	SB%	GDP	Avg	OBP	Slg
1998	Det	AL	7	25	5	0	1	0	(0	0)	7	3	0	2	1	0	4	0	0	0	2	0	1.00	0	.200	.231	.280
1999	Det	AL	130	416	102	22	4	18	(12	6)	186	60	49	59	42	0	74	2	4	4	11	5	.69	7	.245	.315	.447
2000	Tex	AL	116	444	134	32	1	14	(11	3)	210	59	66	72	42	2	57	0	2	3	8	4	.67	12	.302	.360	.473
2001	Tex	AL	134	483	129	29	1	17	(11	6)	211	77	72	77	61	2	70	3	2	7	23	6	.79	10	.267	.348	.437
2002	2 Tms		112	315	88	16	4	2	(1	1)	118	37	34	44	16	0	53	1	7	3	11	4	.73	5	.279	.313	.375
2003	2 Tms		107	225	61	13	1	4	(2	1)	88	39	27	28	22	1	41	0	0	0	6	2	.75	4	.271	.336	.391
2004	Bos	AL	136	290	79	14	1	6	(3	3)	113	51	33	32	15	0	49	2	1	2	5	4	.56	5	.272	.311	.390
2005	Bos	AL	36	97	24	7	0	1	(0	1)	34	15	9	7	3	0	15	2	1	1	1	0	1.00	1	.247	.282	.351
2006	Bos	AL	72	130	33	7	0	2	(1	1)	46	21	12	14	14	0	15	3	0	0	1	1	.50	5	.254	.340	.354
2008	Mil	NL	96	229	69	17	2	8	(4	4)	114	36	38	35	13	0	39	1	1	1	3	1	.75	3	.301	.340	.498
2009	TB	AL	99	205	49	15	1	8	(3	5)	90	26	32	26	29	1	39	0	1	3	5	2	.71	9	.239	.329	.439
02	Tex	AL	72	196	51	12	1	0	(0	0)	65	25	17	20	8	0	30	0	7	3	5	2	.71	3	.260	.285	.332
02	Col	NL	40	119	37	4	3	2	(1	1)	53	12	17	24	8	0	23	1	0	0	6	2	.75	2	.311	.359	.445
03	Col	NL	39	67	15	2	0	0	(0	0)	17	10	4	5	8	1	18	0	0	0	2	0	1.00	0	.224	.307	.254
03	Bos	AL	68	158	46	11	1	4	(2	2)	71	29	23	23	14	0	23	0	0	0	4	2	.67	5	.291	.349	.449
Postseason			15	27	3	0	0	0	(0	0)	3	2	0	1	0	0	7	0	0	0	0	1	.00	2	.111	.111	.111
11 ML YEARS			1045	2859	773	172	16	80	(48	32)	1217	424	372	396	258	6	456	14	19	24	76	29	.72	65	.270	.331	.426

Jeff Karstens

Pitches: R **Bats:** R **Pos:** RP-26; SP-13   **Ht:** 6'3" **Wt:** 185 **Born:** 9/24/1982 **Age:** 27

			HOW MUCH HE PITCHED					WHAT HE GAVE UP										THE RESULTS							
Year	Team	Lg	G	GS	CG	GF	IP	BFP	H	R	ER	HR	SH	SF	HB	TBB	IBB	SO	WP	Bk	W	L	Pct	Sh	Sv-Op Hld	FRC	ERA
2009	Indy*	AAA	3	0	0	1	6.0	22	4	0	0	0	0	0	0	0	0	7	0	0	0	0	-	0	0-- -	0.91	0.00
2006	NYY	AL	8	6	0	2	42.2	179	40	20	18	6	0	2	1	11	2	16	3	1	2	1	.667	0	0-0 0	3.42	3.80
2007	NYY	AL	7	3	0	2	14.2	80	27	21	18	4	2	1	0	9	0	5	2	0	1	4	.200	0	0-0 0	11.86	11.05
2008	Pit	NL	9	9	1	0	51.1	220	56	32	23	7	2	4	0	13	0	23	1	0	2	6	.250	1	0-0 0	4.22	4.03
2009	Pit	NL	39	13	0	8	108.0	471	115	66	65	12	6	6	2	45	5	52	1	0	4	6	.400	0	0-0 1	4.64	5.42
4 ML YEARS			63	31	1	12	216.2	950	238	139	124	29	10	13	3	78	7	96	7	1	9	17	.346	1	0-0 1	4.71	5.15

Matt Kata

Bats: B **Throws:** R **Pos:** PH-29; 2B-7; LF-4; PR-3; 1B-1   **Ht:** 6'1" **Wt:** 185 **Born:** 3/14/1978 **Age:** 32

									BATTING												BASERUNNING				AVERAGES		
Year	Team	Lg	G	AB	H	2B	3B	HR	(Hm	Rd)	TB	R	RBI	RC	TBB	IBB	SO	HBP	SH	SF	SB	CS	SB%	GDP	Avg	OBP	Slg
2009	RdRck*	AAA	66	227	61	10	1	2	(-	-)	79	22	22	27	12	1	25	3	1	1	8	0	1.00	4	.269	.313	.348
2003	Ari	NL	78	288	74	16	5	7	(3	4)	121	42	29	40	25	0	53	1	5	3	3	2	.60	4	.257	.315	.420
2004	Ari	NL	42	162	40	9	2	2	(1	1)	59	17	13	19	13	2	29	0	1	0	4	1	.80	1	.247	.301	.364
2005	2 Tms	NL	40	37	7	2	1	0	(0	0)	11	7	0	2	5	0	6	0	2	0	0	1	.00	0	.189	.286	.297
2007	2 Tms	NL	78	158	35	9	1	3	(2	1)	55	21	16	14	5	0	33	2	2	0	1	0	1.00	3	.222	.255	.348
2009	Hou	NL	40	50	10	1	0	0	(0	0)	11	2	5	2	0	0	5	1	0	1	1	0	1.00	3	.200	.212	.220
05	Ari	NL	30	31	6	2	1	0	(0	0)	10	6	0	2	5	0	4	0	2	0	0	1	.00	0	.194	.306	.323
05	Phi	NL	10	6	1	0	0	0	(0	0)	1	1	0	0	0	0	2	0	0	0	0	0	-	0	.167	.167	.167
07	Tex	AL	31	70	13	2	0	2	(1	1)	21	12	6	5	5	0	18	1	1	0	1	0	1.00	0	.186	.250	.300
07	Pit	NL	47	88	22	7	1	1	(1	0)	34	9	10	9	0	0	15	1	1	0	0	0	-	3	.250	.258	.386
5 ML YEARS			278	695	166	37	9	12	(6	6)	257	89	63	77	48	2	126	4	10	5	9	4	.69	11	.239	.290	.370

Kenshin Kawakami

Pitches: R **Bats:** R **Pos:** SP-25; RP-7   **Ht:** 5'11" **Wt:** 200 **Born:** 6/22/1975 **Age:** 35

					HOW MUCH HE PITCHED						WHAT HE GAVE UP								THE RESULTS						
Year	Team	Lg	G	GS	CG	GF	IP	BFP	H	R	ER	HR	SH	SF	HB	TBB	IBB	SO	WP	Bk	W	L	Pct	Sh	Sv-Op Hld	ERC	ERA
1998	Chnchi	Jap	24	21	4	1	161.1	649	123	48	46	14	-	2	2	51	-	124	4	6	14	6	.700	3	0-- -	2.48	2.57
1999	Chnchi	Jap	29	22	3	1	162.0	695	173	84	80	20	-	3	13	-	108	3	0	8	9	.471	1	1-- -	4.10	4.44
2000	Chnchi	Jap	14	10	0	2	60.1	280	65	32	32	10	-	8	20	-	24	1	0	2	3	.400	0	0	4.81	4.77
2001	Chnchi	Jap	26	22	3	1	145.0	608	153	61	60	12	-	4	36	-	127	4	0	6	10	.375	1	0-- -	3.83	3.72
2002	Chnchi	Jap	27	24	3	0	187.2	760	170	54	49	13	-	8	34	-	149	0	0	12	6	.667	3	0-- -	2.72	2.35
2003	Chnchi	Jap	8	7	1	0	53.2	234	60	22	18	2	-	1	14	0	37	3	0	4	3	.571	0	0-- -	3.76	3.02
2004	Chnchi	Jap	27	22	5	0	192.1	774	173	72	71	27	11	1	4	38	2	176	2	0	17	7	.708	2	0-- -	3.10	3.32
2005	Chnchi	Jap	25	22	3	0	180.1	738	186	75	75	20	9	3	4	28	4	138	1	0	11	8	.579	2	0-- -	3.45	3.74
2006	Chnchi	Jap	29	22	6	0	215.0	841	166	74	60	22	11	2	5	39	1	194	3	0	17	7	.708	5	0-- -	2.19	2.51
2007	Chnchi	Jap	26	26	0	0	167.1	696	175	72	66	18	-	6	23	2	145	1	0	12	8	.600	0	0-- -	3.45	3.55
2008	Chnchi	Jap	20	16	1	1	117.1	466	99	33	30	11	-	5	25	-	112	1	0	9	5	.643	0	0-- -	2.72	2.30
2009	Atl	NL	32	25	0	3	156.1	669	153	73	67	15	10	7	6	57	6	105	8	1	7	12	.368	0	1-1 0	3.89	3.86

Scott Kazmir

Pitches: L **Bats:** L **Pos:** SP-26   **Ht:** 6'0" **Wt:** 190 **Born:** 1/24/1984 **Age:** 26

					HOW MUCH HE PITCHED						WHAT HE GAVE UP								THE RESULTS						
Year	Team	Lg	G	GS	CG	GF	IP	BFP	H	R	ER	HR	SH	SF	HB	TBB	IBB	SO	WP	Bk	W	L	Pct	Sh	Sv-Op Hld	ERC	ERA
2009	Charltt*	A+	1	1	0	0	4.2	19	3	0	0	0	0	0	0	1	0	5	0	0	0	0	-	0	0-- -	1.19	0.00
2009	Drhm*	AAA	1	1	0	0	6.0	21	5	1	1	0	0	0	0	0	0	5	0	0	1	0	1.000	0	0-- -	1.50	1.50
2004	TB	AL	8	7	0	0	33.1	152	33	22	21	4	0	0	2	21	0	41	3	0	2	3	.400	0	0-0 0	5.36	5.67
2005	TB	AL	32	32	0	0	186.0	818	172	90	78	12	6	9	10	100	3	174	7	1	10	9	.526	0	0-0 0	4.13	3.77
2006	TB	AL	24	24	1	0	144.2	610	132	59	52	15	0	5	2	52	3	163	6	0	10	8	.556	1	0-0 0	3.47	3.24
2007	TB	AL	34	34	0	0	206.2	887	196	91	80	18	6	3	7	89	1	239	10	0	13	9	.591	0	0-0 0	3.97	3.48
2008	TB	AL	27	27	0	0	152.1	641	123	61	59	23	4	5	4	70	2	166	5	0	12	8	.600	0	0-0 0	3.69	3.49
2009	2 Tms	AL	26	26	0	0	147.1	647	149	85	80	16	1	4	5	60	0	117	13	0	10	9	.526	0	0-0 0	4.36	4.89
09	TB	AL	20	20	0	0	111.0	504	121	77	73	15	1	4	5	50	0	91	10	0	8	7	.533	0	0-0 0	5.18	5.92
09	LAA	AL	6	6	0	0	36.1	143	28	8	7	1	0	0	1	10	0	26	3	0	2	2	.500	0	0-0 0	2.13	1.73
Postseason			5	5	0	0	25.2	124	26	12	12	4	1	1	3	18	0	22	1	0	1	1	.500	0	0-0 0	6.16	4.21
6 ML YEARS			151	150	1	0	870.1	3755	805	408	370	88	17	26	31	392	9	900	44	1	57	46	.553	1	0-0 0	3.99	3.83

Austin Kearns

Bats: R **Throws:** R **Pos:** RF-54; PH-29; CF-3; PR-1   **Ht:** 6'3" **Wt:** 243 **Born:** 5/20/1980 **Age:** 30

									BATTING												BASERUNNING				AVERAGES		
Year	Team	Lg	G	AB	H	2B	3B	HR	(Hm	Rd)	TB	R	RBI	RC	TBB	IBB	SO	HBP	SH	SF	SB	CS	SB%	GDP	Avg	OBP	Slg
2002	Cin	NL	107	372	117	24	3	13	(7	6)	186	66	56	70	54	3	81	6	0	3	6	3	.67	11	.315	.407	.500
2003	Cin	NL	82	292	77	11	0	15	(8	7)	133	39	58	52	41	1	68	5	0	0	5	2	.71	7	.264	.364	.455
2004	Cin	NL	64	217	50	10	2	9	(3	6)	91	28	32	26	28	0	71	1	0	0	2	1	.67	8	.230	.321	.419
2005	Cin	NL	112	387	93	26	1	18	(9	9)	175	62	67	55	48	2	107	8	0	5	0	0	-	8	.240	.333	.452
2006	2 Tms	NL	150	537	142	33	2	24	(12	12)	251	86	86	81	76	4	135	10	1	5	9	4	.69	18	.264	.363	.467
2007	Was	NL	161	587	156	35	1	16	(8	8)	241	84	74	87	71	5	106	12	0	4	2	2	.50	13	.266	.355	.411
2008	Was	NL	86	313	68	10	0	7	(1	6)	99	40	32	28	35	0	63	8	0	1	2	2	.50	11	.217	.311	.316
2009	Was	NL	80	174	34	6	2	3	(1	2)	53	20	17	17	32	1	51	5	0	0	1	1	.50	12	.195	.336	.305
06	Cin	NL	87	325	89	21	1	16	(8	8)	160	53	50	46	35	2	85	5	0	3	7	1	.88	14	.274	.351	.492
06	Was	NL	63	212	53	12	1	8	(4	4)	91	33	36	35	41	2	50	5	1	2	2	3	.40	4	.250	.381	.429
8 ML YEARS			842	2879	737	155	11	105	(49	56)	1229	425	422	416	385	16	682	55	1	18	27	15	.64	88	.256	.353	.427

Shawn Kelley

Pitches: R **Bats:** R **Pos:** RP-41   **Ht:** 6'2" **Wt:** 215 **Born:** 4/26/1984 **Age:** 26

		HOW MUCH HE PITCHED						WHAT HE GAVE UP												THE RESULTS							
Year	Team	Lg	G	GS	CG	GF	IP	BFP	H	R	ER	HR	SH	SF	HB	TBB	IBB	SO	WP	Bk	W	L	Pct	Sh	Sv-Op	Hld	ERC	ERA
2007	Everett	A-	3	0	0	0	3.0	10	2	1	1	0	0	0	0	0	0	4	0	0	1	0	1.000	0	0--	-	2.25	3.00
2007	Wisc	A	9	0	0	4	12.0	57	16	4	3	1	1	0	0	4	1	14	2	0	1	1	.500	0	0--	-	5.23	2.25
2008	Wisc	A	8	0	0	8	7.2	33	10	3	3	0	0	0	0	2	0	12	0	0	0	0	-	0	3--	-	4.69	3.52
2008	Hi Dsrt	A+	12	0	0	10	12.0	47	8	1	0	0	0	0	1	3	1	12	1	0	0	0	-	0	3--	-	1.52	0.00
2008	WTenn	AA	29	0	0	24	42.2	172	31	12	10	2	3	0	1	17	4	44	2	1	3	1	.750	0	9--	-	2.29	2.11
2009	Ms	R	2	2	0	0	2.0	6	0	0	0	0	0	0	0	0	0	3	0	0	0	0	-	0	0--	-	0.00	0.00
2009	Tacom	AAA	1	0	0	0	1.0	3	0	0	0	0	0	0	0	0	0	0	0	0	0	0	-	0	0--	-	0.00	0.00
2009	Sea	AL	41	0	0	12	46.0	191	45	23	23	9	2	2	3	9	1	41	2	1	5	4	.556	0	0-4	9	4.02	4.50

Don Kelly

Bats: L **Throws:** R **Pos:** LF-18; PH-5; 3B-4; DH-3; PR-3; 1B-2; RF-2; 2B-1   **Ht:** 6'4" **Wt:** 190 **Born:** 2/15/1980 **Age:** 30

					BATTING															BASERUNNING				AVERAGES		
Year	Team	Lg	G	AB	H	2B	3B	HR	(Hm	Rd)	TB	R	RBI	RC	TBB	IBB	SO	HBP	SH	SF	SB	CS	SB%	GDP	Avg	OBP	Slg
2001	Oneont	A-	67	262	75	8	3	0	(-	-)	89	41	25	33	25	1	16	0	2	3	8	5	.62	6	.286	.345	.340
2002	WMich	A	128	455	130	21	5	1	(-	-)	164	72	59	66	59	1	40	3	2	5	9	6	.60	11	.286	.368	.360
2003	Erie	AA	87	303	96	17	4	1	(-	-)	124	48	38	56	45	1	25	1	1	5	15	2	.88	8	.317	.401	.409
2003	Erie	AA	22	83	22	5	1	1	(-	-)	32	14	13	13	15	0	9	0	3	0	0	0	-	2	.265	.378	.386
2004	Erie	AA	28	101	23	6	2	0	(-	-)	33	17	9	12	15	0	13	1	1	1	3	1	.75	4	.228	.331	.327
2004	Tigers	R	3	10	4	0	0	0	(-	-)	4	2	0	1	0	0	2	0	0	0	1	0	1.00	0	.400	.400	.400
2005	Erie	AA	82	328	112	22	3	9	(-	-)	167	54	54	69	36	5	43	1	0	6	10	2	.83	6	.341	.402	.509
2005	Toledo	AAA	43	160	40	8	0	1	(-	-)	51	22	13	17	13	0	15	0	3	0	8	2	.80	2	.250	.306	.319
2006	Toledo	AAA	66	237	54	14	3	0	(-	-)	74	23	19	25	24	0	32	2	4	0	18	7	.72	3	.228	.304	.312
2006	Erie	AA	58	207	57	11	1	0	(-	-)	70	30	24	28	27	0	23	1	0	5	5	3	.63	5	.275	.354	.338
2007	Indy	AAA	52	150	37	5	2	0	(-	-)	46	20	11	17	18	0	17	2	4	0	6	4	.60	4	.247	.335	.307
2008	Tucsn	AAA	124	436	120	24	5	8	(-	-)	178	61	55	60	32	1	44	2	4	5	2	1	.67	3	.275	.324	.408
2009	Toledo	AAA	105	372	123	20	6	6	(-	-)	173	57	40	75	43	1	51	3	2	0	27	4	.87	6	.331	.404	.465
2007	Pit	NL	25	27	4	0	0	0	(0	0)	4	2	0	1	3	0	3	2	0	0	0	0	-	1	.148	.281	.148
2009	Det	AL	31	56	14	3	1	0	(0	0)	19	8	3	7	4	0	10	1	1	0	1	0	1.00	0	.250	.311	.339
	2 ML YEARS		56	83	18	3	1	0	(0	0)	23	10	3	8	7	0	13	3	1	0	1	0	1.00	1	.217	.301	.277

Matt Kemp

Bats: R **Throws:** R **Pos:** CF-158; RF-7; PH-3   **Ht:** 6'3" **Wt:** 226 **Born:** 9/23/1984 **Age:** 25

					BATTING															BASERUNNING				AVERAGES		
Year	Team	Lg	G	AB	H	2B	3B	HR	(Hm	Rd)	TB	R	RBI	RC	TBB	IBB	SO	HBP	SH	SF	SB	CS	SB%	GDP	Avg	OBP	Slg
2006	LAD	NL	52	154	39	7	1	7	(4	3)	69	30	23	20	9	1	53	0	0	1	8	0	1.00	1	.253	.289	.448
2007	LAD	NL	98	292	100	12	5	10	(9	1)	152	47	42	49	16	0	66	0	0	3	10	5	.67	6	.342	.373	.521
2008	LAD	NL	155	606	176	38	5	18	(14	4)	278	93	76	86	46	6	153	1	1	3	35	11	.76	11	.290	.340	.459
2009	LAD	NL	159	606	180	25	7	26	(13	13)	297	97	101	100	52	6	139	3	0	6	34	8	.81	14	.297	.352	.490
	Postseason		8	28	7	3	0	0	(0	0)	10	1	1	0	4	0	9	0	0	0	0	1	.00	2	.250	.344	.357
	4 ML YEARS		464	1658	495	82	18	61	(40	21)	796	267	242	255	123	13	411	4	1	15	85	24	.78	32	.299	.346	.480

Jason Kendall

Bats: R **Throws:** R **Pos:** C-133; PH-1; PR-1   **Ht:** 6'0" **Wt:** 192 **Born:** 6/26/1974 **Age:** 36

					BATTING															BASERUNNING				AVERAGES		
Year	Team	Lg	G	AB	H	2B	3B	HR	(Hm	Rd)	TB	R	RBI	RC	TBB	IBB	SO	HBP	SH	SF	SB	CS	SB%	GDP	Avg	OBP	Slg
1996	Pit	NL	130	414	124	23	5	3	(2	1)	166	54	42	63	35	11	30	15	3	4	5	2	.71	7	.300	.372	.401
1997	Pit	NL	144	486	143	36	4	8	(5	3)	211	71	49	86	49	2	53	31	1	5	18	6	.75	11	.294	.391	.434
1998	Pit	NL	149	535	175	36	3	12	(6	6)	253	95	75	110	51	3	51	31	2	8	26	5	.84	6	.327	.411	.473
1999	Pit	NL	78	280	93	20	3	8	(5	3)	143	61	41	63	38	3	32	12	0	4	22	3	.88	8	.332	.428	.511
2000	Pit	NL	152	579	185	33	6	14	(7	7)	272	112	58	112	79	3	79	15	1	4	22	12	.65	13	.320	.412	.470
2001	Pit	NL	157	606	161	22	2	10	(3	7)	217	84	53	68	44	4	48	20	0	2	13	14	.48	18	.266	.335	.358
2002	Pit	NL	145	545	154	25	3	3	(1	2)	194	59	44	66	49	1	29	9	0	2	15	8	.65	11	.283	.350	.356
2003	Pit	NL	150	587	191	29	3	6	(3	3)	244	84	58	97	49	3	40	25	1	3	8	7	.53	9	.325	.399	.416
2004	Pit	NL	147	574	183	32	0	3	(2	1)	224	86	51	95	60	2	41	19	1	4	11	8	.58	12	.319	.399	.390
2005	Oak	AL	150	601	163	28	1	0	(0	0)	193	70	53	79	50	0	39	20	0	5	8	3	.73	27	.271	.345	.321
2006	Oak	AL	143	552	163	23	0	1	(1	0)	189	76	50	80	53	2	54	12	4	5	11	5	.69	19	.295	.367	.342
2007	2 Tms		137	466	113	20	1	3	(1	2)	144	45	41	43	31	2	42	9	5	3	3	4	.43	8	.242	.301	.309
2008	Mil	NL	151	516	127	30	2	2	(1	1)	167	46	49	59	50	7	45	13	6	2	8	3	.73	5	.246	.327	.324
2009	Mil	NL	134	452	109	19	2	2	(0	2)	138	48	43	48	46	6	58	17	6	5	7	2	.78	11	.241	.331	.305
07	Oak	AL	80	292	66	10	0	2	(0	2)	82	24	22	18	12	0	27	3	2	3	3	1	.75	7	.226	.261	.281
07	ChC	NL	57	174	47	10	1	1	(1	0)	62	21	19	25	19	2	15	6	3	0	0	3	.00	1	.270	.362	.356
	Postseason		12	49	11	1	0	0	(0	0)	12	1	3	3	2	0	9	0	0	0	0	0	-	0	.224	.255	.245
	14 ML YEARS		1967	7193	2084	376	35	75	(37	38)	2755	991	707	1069	684	49	641	248	30	56	177	82	.68	165	.290	.369	.383

Howie Kendrick

Bats: R **Throws:** R **Pos:** 2B-95; PH-7; DH-5; PR-1   **Ht:** 5'10" **Wt:** 200 **Born:** 7/12/1983 **Age:** 26

					BATTING															BASERUNNING				AVERAGES		
Year	Team	Lg	G	AB	H	2B	3B	HR	(Hm	Rd)	TB	R	RBI	RC	TBB	IBB	SO	HBP	SH	SF	SB	CS	SB%	GDP	Avg	OBP	Slg
2009	Salt Lk*	AAA	20	78	27	6	1	2	(-	-)	41	11	11	16	7	0	12	2	0	0	4	2	.67	3	.346	.414	.526
2006	LAA	AL	72	267	76	21	1	4	(2	2)	111	25	30	32	9	2	44	4	0	3	6	0	1.00	5	.285	.314	.416
2007	LAA	AL	88	338	109	24	2	5	(3	2)	152	55	39	41	9	2	61	4	1	1	5	4	.56	15	.322	.347	.450

Year Team	Lg	G	AB	H	2B	3B	HR	(Hm	Rd)	TB	R	RBI	RC	TBB	IBB	SO	HBP	SH	SF	SB	CS	SB%	GDP	Avg	OBP	Slg
							BATTING													**BASERUNNING**				**AVERAGES**		
2008 LAA	AL	92	340	104	26	2	3	(1	2)	143	43	37	50	12	3	58	4	1	4	11	4	.73	8	.306	.333	.421
2009 LAA	AL	105	374	109	21	3	10	(5	5)	166	61	61	58	20	1	71	4	2	0	11	4	.73	8	.291	.334	.444
Postseason		7	27	4	0	0	0	(0	0)	4	0	1	0	0	0	8	0	2	1	2	0	1.00	1	.148	.143	.148
4 ML YEARS		357	1319	398	92	8	22	(11	11)	572	184	167	181	50	8	234	16	4	8	33	12	.73	36	.302	.333	.434

Kyle Kendrick

Pitches: R **Bats:** R **Pos:** RP-7; SP-2   Ht: 6'3" **Wt:** 205 **Born:** 8/26/1984 **Age:** 25

Year Team	Lg	G	GS	CG	GF	IP	BFP	H	R	ER	HR	SH	SF	HB	TBB	IBB	SO	WP	Bk	W	L	Pct	Sh	Sv-Op	Hld	ERC	ERA
				HOW MUCH HE PITCHED						**WHAT HE GAVE UP**												**THE RESULTS**					
2009 LV*	AAA	24	24	1	0	143.0	584	133	59	53	9	7	5	6	35	1	02	2	2	9	7	.563	0	0- -	-	3.03	3.34
2007 Phi	NL	20	20	0	0	121.0	499	129	53	52	16	4	2	7	25	3	49	0	0	10	4	.714	0	0-0	0	4.23	3.87
2008 Phi	NL	31	30	0	1	155.2	722	194	103	95	23	8	4	14	57	2	68	4	1	11	9	.550	0	0-0	0	6.05	5.49
2009 Phi	NL	9	2	0	2	26.1	112	27	11	10	1	1	2	1	9	0	15	0	1	3	1	.750	0	0-0	0	3.75	3.42
Postseason		1	1	0	0	3.2	18	5	5	5	2	0	0	1	2	1	2	0	0	0	1	.000	0	0-0	0	9.97	12.27
3 ML YEARS		60	52	0	3	303.0	1333	350	167	157	40	13	8	22	91	5	132	4	2	24	14	.632	0	0-0	0	5.11	4.66

Adam Kennedy

Bats: L **Throws:** R **Pos:** 3B-82; 2B-50; PH-2; 1B-1; RF-1   Ht: 6'1" **Wt:** 195 **Born:** 1/10/1976 **Age:** 34

Year Team	Lg	G	AB	H	2B	3B	HR	(Hm	Rd)	TB	R	RBI	RC	TBB	IBB	SO	HBP	SH	SF	SB	CS	SB%	GDP	Avg	OBP	Slg
								BATTING												**BASERUNNING**				**AVERAGES**		
2009 Drhm*	AAA	23	82	23	4	0	3	(-	-)	36	11	9	13	10	1	12	1	0	0	2	1	.67	0	.280	.366	.439
1999 StL	NL	33	102	26	10	1	1	(1	0)	41	12	16	12	3	0	8	2	1	2	0	1	.00	1	.255	.284	.402
2000 LAA	AL	156	598	159	33	11	9	(7	2)	241	82	72	72	28	5	73	3	8	4	22	8	.73	10	.266	.300	.403
2001 LAA	AL	137	478	129	25	3	6	(4	2)	178	40	40	57	27	3	71	11	7	9	12	7	.63	7	.270	.318	.372
2002 LAA	AL	144	474	148	32	6	7	(6	1)	213	65	52	70	19	1	80	7	5	4	17	4	.81	5	.312	.345	.449
2003 LAA	AL	143	449	121	17	1	13	(8	5)	179	71	49	61	48	4	73	9	2	5	22	9	.71	7	.269	.344	.399
2004 LAA	AL	144	468	130	20	5	10	(5	5)	190	70	48	60	41	7	92	13	9	2	15	5	.75	10	.278	.351	.406
2005 LAA	AL	129	416	125	23	0	2	(1	1)	154	49	37	62	29	1	64	7	5	3	19	4	.83	5	.300	.354	.370
2006 LAA	AL	139	451	123	26	6	4	(3	1)	173	50	55	62	39	5	72	5	3	6	16	10	.62	15	.273	.334	.384
2007 StL	NL	87	279	61	9	1	3	(0	3)	81	27	18	19	22	6	33	3	1	1	6	2	.75	9	.219	.282	.290
2008 StL	NL	115	339	95	17	4	2	(1	1)	126	42	36	39	21	4	43	1	0	4	7	1	.88	13	.280	.321	.372
2009 Oak	AL	130	650	155	29	1	11	(4	7)	217	66	63	60	46	2	86	4	5	3	20	6	.77	8	.289	.348	.410
Postseason		25	78	24	3	1	4	(4	0)	41	13	13	11	1	0	15	1	3	2	1	2	.33	1	.308	.317	.526
11 ML YEARS		1356	4583	1270	241	39	68	(40	28)	1793	581	486	602	319	38	695	65	46	42	156	57	.73	90	.277	.330	.391

Ian Kennedy

Pitches: R **Bats:** R **Pos:** RP-1   Ht: 6'0" **Wt:** 195 **Born:** 12/19/1984 **Age:** 25

Year Team	Lg	G	GS	CG	GF	IP	BFP	H	R	ER	HR	SH	SF	HB	TBB	IBB	SO	WP	Bk	W	L	Pct	Sh	Sv-Op	Hld	ERC	ERA
				HOW MUCH HE PITCHED						**WHAT HE GAVE UP**												**THE RESULTS**					
2009 S-WB*	AAA	4	4	0	0	22.2	91	18	5	4	0	2	0	0	7	0	25	1	0	1	0	1.000	0	0- -	-	2.06	1.59
2007 NYY	AL	3	3	0	0	19.0	77	13	6	4	1	0	0	0	9	0	15	0	0	1	0	1.000	0	0-0	0	2.42	1.89
2008 NYY	AL	10	9	0	0	39.2	194	50	37	36	5	1	4	1	26	0	27	3	0	0	4	.000	0	0-0	0	6.93	8.17
2009 NYY	AL	1	0	0	0	1.0	6	0	0	0	0	0	0	1	2	0	1	0	0	0	0		0	0-0	1	7.00	0.00
3 ML YEARS		14	12	0	1	59.2	277	63	43	40	6	1	4	2	37	0	43	3	0	1	4	.200	0	0-0	1	5.38	6.03

Logan Kensing

Pitches: R **Bats:** R **Pos:** RP-32   Ht: 6'1" **Wt:** 190 **Born:** 7/3/1982 **Age:** 27

Year Team	Lg	G	GS	CG	GF	IP	BFP	H	R	ER	HR	SH	SF	HB	TBB	IBB	SO	WP	Bk	W	L	Pct	Sh	Sv-Op	Hld	ERC	ERA
				HOW MUCH HE PITCHED						**WHAT HE GAVE UP**												**THE RESULTS**					
2009 Syrcse*	AAA	31	0	0	27	33.1	132	28	11	11	2	0	1	0	6	2	35	2	0	2	1	.667	0	17- -	-	2.11	2.97
2004 Fla	NL	5	3	0	2	13.2	66	19	15	15	5	0	1	1	9	0	7	2	0	0	3	.000	0	0-0	0	10.74	9.88
2005 Fla	NL	3	0	0	0	5.2	31	11	7	7	2	0	1	0	3	0	4	0	0	0	0	-	0	0-0	1	12.96	11.12
2006 Fla	NL	37	0	0	10	37.2	161	30	19	19	6	3	0	3	19	2	45	0	0	1	3	.250	0	1-7	14	4.02	4.54
2007 Fla	NL	9	0	0	0	13.1	59	11	2	2	0	1	0	0	7	2	13	0	0	3	0	1.000	0	0-0	0	3.15	1.35
2008 Fla	NL	48	0	0	7	55.1	254	50	26	26	7	1	2	4	33	5	55	7	0	3	1	.750	0	0-3	5	4.50	4.23
2009 2 Tms	NL	32	0	0	12	35.1	172	54	35	35	8	3	1	0	17	1	19	4	1	1	2	.333	0	1-3	1	8.78	8.92
09 Fla	NL	6	0	0	2	7.1	40	14	8	8	1	1	0	0	5	0	7	2	1	0	1	.000	0	0-0	0	11.61	9.82
09 Was	NL	26	0	0	10	28.0	132	40	27	27	7	2	1	0	12	1	12	2	0	1	1	.500	0	1-3	1	8.04	8.68
6 ML YEARS		134	3	0	31	161.0	743	175	104	104	28	8	5	10	88	10	143	13	1	8	9	.471	0	2-13	21	5.87	5.81

Bobby Keppel

Pitches: R **Bats:** R **Pos:** RP-37   Ht: 6'5" **Wt:** 215 **Born:** 6/11/1982 **Age:** 28

Year Team	Lg	G	GS	CG	GF	IP	BFP	H	R	ER	HR	SH	SF	HB	TBB	IBB	SO	WP	Bk	W	L	Pct	Sh	Sv-Op	Hld	ERC	ERA
				HOW MUCH HE PITCHED						**WHAT HE GAVE UP**												**THE RESULTS**					
2009 Roch*	AAA	23	3	1	6	55.2	227	51	18	15	1	2	1	3	13	1	28	3	0	3	3	.500	0	1- -	-	2.68	2.43
2006 KC	AL	8	6	0	0	34.1	157	45	21	21	6	2	1	1	15	2	20	0	0	0	4	.000	0	0-0	0	6.85	5.50
2007 Col	NL	4	0	0	1	4.0	20	6	5	5	1	0	0	0	3	0	1	0	0	0	0	-	0	0-0	0	10.40	11.25
2009 Min	AL	37	0	0	8	54.0	242	63	30	29	4	1	3	5	21	2	32	2	0	1	1	.500	0	0-1	4	5.18	4.83
3 ML YEARS		49	6	0	9	92.1	419	114	56	55	11	2	5	6	39	4	53	2	0	1	5	.167	0	0-1	4	5.99	5.36

Jeff Keppinger

Bats: R **Throws:** R **Pos:** 3B-67; 2B-22; PH-17; SS-11; LF-2; PR-2   **Ht:** 6'0" **Wt:** 184 **Born:** 4/21/1980 **Age:** 30

Year	Team	Lg	G	AB	H	2B	3B	HR	(Hm	Rd)	TB	R	RBI	RC	TBB	IBB	SO	HBP	SH	SF	SB	CS	SB%	GDP	Avg	OBP	Slg
2004	NYM	NL	33	116	33	2	0	3	(3	0)	44	9	9	12	6	0	7	0	0	1	2	1	.67	6	.284	.317	.379
2006	KC	AL	22	60	16	2	0	2	(0	2)	24	11	8	8	5	1	6	0	2	0	0	0	-	2	.267	.323	.400
2007	Cin	NL	67	241	80	16	2	5	(2	3)	115	39	32	42	24	0	12	4	6	1	2	1	.67	11	.332	.400	.477
2008	Cin	NL	121	459	122	24	2	3	(3	0)	159	45	43	52	30	3	24	2	6	5	3	1	.75	14	.266	.310	.346
2009	Hou	NL	107	305	78	13	3	7	(1	6)	118	35	29	28	27	3	33	3	7	2	0	2	.00	13	.256	.320	.387
	5 ML YEARS		350	1181	329	57	7	20	(9	11)	460	139	121	142	92	7	82	9	21	9	7	5	.58	46	.279	.333	.390

Clayton Kershaw

Pitches: L **Bats:** L **Pos:** SP-30; RP-1   **Ht:** 6'3" **Wt:** 223 **Born:** 3/19/1988 **Age:** 22

Year	Team	Lg	G	GS	CG	GF	IP	BFP	H	R	ER	HR	SH	SF	HB	TBB	IBB	SO	WP	Bk	W	L	Pct	Sh	Sv-Op	Hld	ERC	ERA
2006	Ddgrs	R	10	8	0	1	37.0	144	28	10	8	0	0	0	0	5	0	54	8	0	2	0	1.000	0	1--	-	1.42	1.95
2007	Gt Lks	A	20	20	0	0	97.1	413	72	39	30	5	5	1	2	50	0	134	8	0	7	5	.583	0	0--	-	2.82	2.77
2007	Jaxnvl	AA	5	5	0	0	24.2	107	17	13	10	4	2	0	0	17	0	29	1	1	1	2	.333	0	0--	-	3.88	3.65
2008	Jaxnvl	AA	13	11	0	0	61.1	241	39	19	13	0	2	2	0	19	0	59	7	2	2	3	.400	0	0--	-	1.44	1.91
2008	LAD	NL	22	21	0	0	107.2	470	109	51	51	11	3	3	1	52	3	100	7	0	5	5	.500	0	0-0	1	4.53	4.26
2009	LAD	NL	31	30	0	1	171.0	701	119	55	53	7	11	2	1	91	4	185	11	2	8	8	.500	0	0-0	0	2.60	2.79
	Postseason		2	0	0	0	2.0	9	1	1	1	0	1	0	0	2	0	1	0	0	0	0	-	0	0-0	1	2.80	4.50
	2 ML YEARS		53	51	0	1	278.2	1171	228	106	104	18	14	5	2	143	7	285	18	2	13	13	.500	0	0-0	1	3.31	3.36

Brad Kilby

Pitches: L **Bats:** L **Pos:** RP-10; SP-1   **Ht:** 6'2" **Wt:** 230 **Born:** 2/19/1983 **Age:** 27

Year	Team	Lg	G	GS	CG	GF	IP	BFP	H	R	ER	HR	SH	SF	HB	TBB	IBB	SO	WP	Bk	W	L	Pct	Sh	Sv-Op	Hld	ERC	ERA
2006	Kane	A	49	0	0	26	60.2	243	38	13	11	0	3	1	4	23	0	73	2	0	5	1	.833	0	9--	-	1.72	1.63
2007	Stcktn	A+	7	0	0	5	8.1	41	6	5	3	0	1	0	0	6	1	16	2	0	0	0	-	0	3--	-	2.44	3.24
2007	Mdland	AA	47	0	0	11	65.2	272	63	24	21	6	3	1	2	22	1	69	1	1	3	3	.500	0	0--	-	3.73	2.88
2008	Scrmto	AA	51	0	0	14	70.0	287	51	33	27	9	4	1	3	26	1	66	3	0	7	2	.778	0	2--	-	2.83	3.47
2009	Scrmto	AAA	45	0	0	6	63.1	252	40	15	15	5	0	1	2	24	1	77	5	0	4	2	.667	0	2--	-	2.08	2.13
2009	Oak	AL	11	1	0	1	17.0	65	10	2	1	1	0	0	0	4	0	20	0	0	1	0	1.000	0	0-0	1	1.36	0.53

Josh Kinney

Pitches: R **Bats:** R **Pos:** RP-17   **Ht:** 6'1" **Wt:** 214 **Born:** 3/31/1979 **Age:** 31

Year	Team	Lg	G	GS	CG	GF	IP	BFP	H	R	ER	HR	SH	SF	HB	TBB	IBB	SO	WP	Bk	W	L	Pct	Sh	Sv-Op	Hld	ERC	ERA
2009	Memp*	AAA	38	0	0	16	44.1	197	43	21	19	6	1	1	6	20	2	52	7	0	3	3	.500	0	1--	-	4.85	3.86
2006	StL	NL	21	0	0	4	25.0	99	17	9	9	3	0	0	1	8	0	22	0	0	0	0	-	0	0-0	2	2.40	3.24
2008	StL	NL	7	0	0	1	7.0	25	3	0	0	0	0	0	0	1	0	8	0	0	0	0	-	0	0-0	0	0.60	0.00
2009	StL	NL	17	0	0	3	15.1	81	23	15	15	2	1	0	2	11	1	8	0	0	1	0	1.000	0	0-1	2	9.17	8.80
	Postseason		7	0	0	1	6.1	25	3	0	0	0	0	1	0	4	0	6	0	0	1	0	1.000	0	0-0	3	2.24	0.00
	3 ML YEARS		45	0	0	8	47.1	205	43	24	24	5	1	0	3	20	1	38	0	0	1	0	1.000	0	0-1	4	3.88	4.56

Ian Kinsler

Bats: R **Throws:** R **Pos:** 2B-144   **Ht:** 6'0" **Wt:** 200 **Born:** 6/22/1982 **Age:** 28

Year	Team	Lg	G	AB	H	2B	3B	HR	(Hm	Rd)	TB	R	RBI	RC	TBB	IBB	SO	HBP	SH	SF	SB	CS	SB%	GDP	Avg	OBP	Slg
2009	Frisco*	AA	2	7	0	0	0	0	(-	-)	0	1	0	0	1	0	1	1	0	0	0	0	-	0	.000	.222	.000
2006	Tex	AL	120	423	121	27	1	14	(10	4)	192	65	55	65	40	1	64	3	1	7	11	4	.73	12	.286	.347	.454
2007	Tex	AL	130	483	127	22	2	20	(12	8)	213	96	61	79	62	2	83	9	8	4	23	2	.92	14	.263	.355	.441
2008	Tex	AL	121	518	165	41	4	18	(4	14)	268	102	71	106	45	1	67	6	7	7	26	3	.90	12	.319	.375	.517
2009	Tex	AL	144	566	143	32	4	31	(20	11)	276	101	86	99	59	0	77	6	3	6	31	5	.86	9	.253	.327	.488
	4 ML YEARS		515	1990	556	122	11	83	(46	37)	949	364	273	349	206	4	291	24	19	24	91	13	.88	47	.279	.350	.477

Masa Kobayashi

Pitches: R **Bats:** R **Pos:** RP-10   **Ht:** 6'0" **Wt:** 195 **Born:** 5/24/1974 **Age:** 36

Year	Team	Lg	G	GS	CG	GF	IP	BFP	H	R	ER	HR	SH	SF	HB	TBB	IBB	SO	WP	Bk	W	L	Pct	Sh	Sv-Op	Hld	ERC	ERA
1999	Chiba	Jap	46	7	3	9	124.1	507	93	42	37	8	-	-	4	55	-	107	6	4	5	5	.500	0	0--	-	2.84	2.68
2000	Chiba	Jap	65	3	0	33	109.2	441	87	34	26	4	-	-	1	37	-	72	4	0	11	6	.647	0	14--	-	2.42	2.13
2001	Chiba	Jap	48	0	0	41	52.0	218	54	25	25	7	-	-	1	13	-	47	1	0	0	4	.000	0	33--	-	4.04	4.33
2002	Chiba	Jap	43	0	0	43	43.1	158	26	4	4	1	-	0	0	6	-	41	1	0	2	1	.667	0	37--	-	1.10	0.83
2003	Chiba	Jap	44	0	0	40	47.0	192	45	18	15	2	-	-	1	11	-	30	1	0	2	2	.000	0	33--	-	2.96	2.87
2004	Chiba	Jap	51	0	0	46	57.2	235	51	25	25	4	2	2	2	19	6	50	3	0	8	5	.615	0	20--	-	3.03	3.90
2005	Chiba	Jap	46	0	0	43	45.1	186	49	14	13	6	2	0	1	9	1	33	0	0	2	2	.500	0	29--	-	4.13	2.58
2006	Chiba	Jap	53	0	0	48	53.2	214	49	16	16	4	4	1	2	8	0	48	0	0	6	2	.750	0	34--	-	2.68	2.68
2007	Chiba	Jap	49	0	0	-	47.1	207	53	24	19	4	-	-	2	12	4	35	0	0	2	7	.222	0	27--	-	4.03	3.61
2009	Clmbs	AAA	18	0	0	14	19.1	88	28	10	10	4	0	0	1	7	2	11	0	1	2	2	.500	0	1--	-	7.90	4.66
2008	Cle	AL	57	0	0	31	55.2	244	65	30	28	8	1	1	1	14	2	35	4	0	4	5	.444	0	6-9	2	4.71	4.53
2009	Cle	AL	10	0	0	5	9.2	45	12	9	9	2	0	0	1	4	0	4	1	0	0	0	-	0	0-0	0	6.86	8.38
	2 ML YEARS		67	0	0	36	65.1	289	77	39	37	10	1	1	2	18	2	39	5	0	4	5	.444	0	6-9	2	5.01	5.10

Paul Konerko

Bats: R **Throws:** R **Pos:** 1B-134; DH-18; PH-2 **Ht:** 6'2" **Wt:** 215 **Born:** 3/5/1976 **Age:** 34

Year	Team	Lg	G	AB	H	2B	3B	HR	(Hm	Rd)	TB	R	RBI	RC	TBB	IBB	SO	HBP	SH	SF	SB	CS	SB%	GDP	Avg	OBP	Slg
1997	LAD	NL	6	7	1	0	0	0	(0	0)	1	0	0	0	1	0	2	0	0	0	0	0	-	1	.143	.250	.143
1998	2 Tms	NL	75	217	47	4	0	7	(2	5)	72	21	29	17	16	0	40	3	0	3	0	1	.00	10	.217	.276	.332
1999	CWS	AL	142	513	151	31	4	24	(16	8)	262	71	81	86	45	0	68	2	1	3	1	0	1.00	19	.294	.352	.511
2000	CWS	AL	143	524	156	31	1	21	(10	11)	252	84	97	86	47	0	72	10	0	5	1	0	1.00	22	.298	.363	.481
2001	CWS	AL	156	582	164	35	0	32	(19	13)	295	92	99	99	54	6	89	9	0	5	1	0	1.00	17	.282	.349	.507
2002	CWS	AL	151	570	173	30	0	27	(13	14)	284	81	104	96	44	2	72	9	0	7	0	0	-	17	.304	.359	.498
2003	CWS	AL	137	444	104	19	0	18	(9	9)	177	49	65	42	43	7	50	4	0	4	0	0	-	28	.234	.305	.399
2004	CWS	AL	155	563	156	22	0	41	(29	12)	301	84	117	106	69	5	107	6	0	5	1	0	1.00	23	.277	.359	.535
2005	CWS	AL	158	575	163	24	0	40	(23	17)	307	98	100	106	81	10	109	5	0	3	0	0	-	9	.283	.375	.534
2006	CWS	AL	152	566	177	30	0	35	(21	14)	312	97	113	110	60	3	104	8	0	9	1	0	1.00	25	.313	.381	.551
2007	CWS	AL	151	549	142	34	0	31	(17	14)	269	71	90	88	78	9	102	3	0	6	0	1	.00	21	.259	.351	.490
2008	CWS	AL	122	438	105	19	1	22	(15	7)	192	59	62	60	65	4	80	7	0	4	2	0	1.00	17	.240	.344	.438
2009	CWS	AL	152	546	151	30	1	28	(18	10)	267	75	88	91	58	4	89	10	0	7	1	0	1.00	16	.277	.353	.489
98	LAD	NL	49	144	31	1	0	4	(2	2)	44	14	16	10	10	0	30	2	0	2	0	1	.00	5	.215	.272	.306
98	Cin	NL	26	73	16	3	0	3	(0	3)	28	7	13	7	6	0	10	1	0	1	0	0	-	5	.219	.284	.384
	Postseason		19	74	18	2	0	7	(3	4)	41	10	17	12	5	2	10	1	0	0	0	0	-	4	.243	.300	.554
	13 ML YEARS		1700	6094	1690	309	7	326	(192	134)	2991	882	1045	987	661	50	984	76	1	61	8	2	.80	224	.277	.352	.491

Bobby Korecky

Pitches: R **Bats:** R **Pos:** RP-5 **Ht:** 5'11" **Wt:** 185 **Born:** 9/16/1979 **Age:** 30

			HOW MUCH HE PITCHED						WHAT HE GAVE UP										THE RESULTS						
Year	Team	Lg	G	GS	CG	GF	IP	BFP	H	R	ER	HR	SH	SF	HB	TBB	IBB	SO	WP	Bk	W	L	Pct	Sh	Sv-Op	Hld	ERC	ERA
2002	Batvia	A-	7	5	0	0	35.0	132	30	12	9	2	1	1	0	6	0	25	2	0	2	2	.500	0	0--	-	2.37	2.31
2002	Lakwd	A	8	4	2	3	27.0	106	25	10	9	1	0	0	1	3	0	16	1	0	2	2	.500	0	1--	-	2.03	3.00
2003	Clrwtr	A+	49	0	0	44	59.2	234	52	19	15	3	3	0	2	0	1	46	3	0	6	1	.550	0	23--	-	1.52	2.26
2004	NwBrit	AA	55	0	0	48	67.0	275	52	29	25	5	1	0	3	20	2	58	3	0	3	4	.429	0	31--	-	2.45	3.36
2005	NwBrit	AA	2	0	0	1	1.1	7	2	1	1	0	0	0	0	1	0	1	0	0	0	0	-	0	0--	-	7.52	6.75
2006	NwBrit	AA	16	0	0	13	25.0	118	30	15	9	1	1	2	1	13	5	14	1	0	1	2	.333	0	5--	-	4.94	3.24
2006	Roch	AAA	34	0	0	22	51.1	219	52	25	19	4	1	2	0	16	7	28	5	0	5	3	.625	0	8		3.41	3.33
2007	Roch	AAA	66	0	0	59	85.0	358	80	42	35	5	3	4	0	34	9	71	3	0	5	6	.455	0	35--	-	3.34	3.71
2008	Roch	AAA	50	0	0	44	74.1	300	66	26	24	3	4	3	1	22	3	71	3	0	6	5	.545	0	26--	-	2.67	2.91
2009	Reno	AAA	27	0	0	24	30.0	116	26	9	7	1	1	0	0	3	0	25	2	0	2	1	.667	0	13--	-	1.93	2.10
2008	Min	AL	16	0	0	9	17.2	74	19	9	9	2	0	0	0	8	0	6	0	0	2	0	1.000	0	0-0	-	5.13	4.58
2009	Ari	NL	5	0	0	0	6.0	32	11	9	9	0	1	1	0	4	0	3	3	0	0	0	-	0	0-0	1	9.65	13.50
	2 ML YEARS		21	0	0	9	23.2	106	30	18	18	2	1	1	0	12	0	9	3	0	2	0	1.000	0	0-0	1	6.24	6.85

John Koronka

Pitches: L **Bats:** L **Pos:** SP-2 **Ht:** 6'0" **Wt:** 200 **Born:** 7/3/1980 **Age:** 29

			HOW MUCH HE PITCHED						WHAT HE GAVE UP										THE RESULTS						
Year	Team	Lg	G	GS	CG	GF	IP	BFP	H	R	ER	HR	SH	SF	HB	TBB	IBB	SO	WP	Bk	W	L	Pct	Sh	Sv-Op	Hld	ERC	ERA
2009	NewOr*	AAA	30	23	0	3	128.2	583	159	79	69	17	5	6	4	43	3	77	10	0	4	10	.286	0	0--	-	5.46	4.83
2005	ChC	NL	4	3	0	1	15.2	76	19	13	13	2	1	0	0	8	0	10	1	2	1	2	.333	0	0-0	0	5.68	7.47
2006	Tex	AL	23	23	0	0	125.0	554	145	80	79	17	1	7	5	47	2	61	4	1	7	7	.500	0	0-0	0	5.37	5.69
2007	Tex	AL	2	2	0	0	10.1	52	16	9	9	0	2	1	1	5	0	2	0	0	0	2	.000	0	0-0	0	7.26	7.84
2009	Fla	NL	2	2	0	0	7.1	41	11	11	9	4	2	0	0	7	0	4	0	0	0	2	.000	0	0-0	0	13.44	11.05
	4 ML YEARS		31	30	0	1	158.1	723	191	113	110	23	6	8	6	67	2	77	5	3	8	13	.381	0	0-0	0	5.86	6.25

Casey Kotchman

Bats: L **Throws:** L **Pos:** 1B-114; PH-13; PR-1 **Ht:** 6'3" **Wt:** 215 **Born:** 2/22/1983 **Age:** 27

Year	Team	Lg	G	AB	H	2B	3B	HR	(Hm	Rd)	TB	R	RBI	RC	TBB	IBB	SO	HBP	SH	SF	SB	CS	SB%	GDP	Avg	OBP	Slg
2009	Gwnntt*	AAA	2	3	0	0	0	0	(-	-)	0	2	3	0	1	0	1	0	0	1	0	0	-	0	.000	.200	.000
2004	LAA	AL	38	116	26	6	0	0	(0	0)	32	7	15	14	7	3	11	4	0	1	3	0	1.00	3	.224	.289	.276
2005	LAA	AL	47	126	35	5	0	7	(5	2)	61	16	22	21	15	0	18	0	1	1	1	1	.50	3	.278	.352	.484
2006	LAA	AL	29	79	12	2	0	1	(0	1)	17	6	6	1	7	0	13	0	2	0	0	1	.00	2	.152	.221	.215
2007	LAA	AL	137	443	131	37	3	11	(5	6)	207	64	68	74	53	1	43	4	3	5	2	4	.33	17	.296	.372	.467
2008	2 Tms		143	525	143	28	1	14	(3	11)	215	65	74	70	36	5	39	9	0	3	2	1	.67	18	.272	.328	.410
2009	2 Tms		126	385	103	23	0	7	(1	6)	147	37	48	49	39	6	42	4	0	3	1	0	1.00	11	.268	.339	.382
08	LAA	AL	100	373	107	24	0	12	(2	10)	167	47	54	53	18	3	23	5	0	2	2	1	.67	14	.287	.327	.448
08	Atl	NL	43	152	36	4	1	2	(1	1)	48	18	20	17	18	2	16	4	0	1	0	0	-	4	.237	.331	.316
09	Atl	NL	87	298	84	20	0	6	(1	5)	122	28	41	43	32	6	28	3	0	3	0	0	-	7	.282	.354	.409
09	Bos	AL	39	87	19	3	0	1	(0	1)	25	9	7	6	7	0	14	1	0	0	1	0	1.00	4	.218	.284	.287
	Postseason		8	15	2	1	0	0	(0	0)	3	1	1	1	3	0	2	0	0	0	0	0	-	0	.133	.278	.200
	6 ML YEARS		520	1674	450	101	4	40	(14	26)	679	195	233	229	157	15	166	21	6	13	9	7	.56	54	.269	.337	.406

Mark Kotsay

Bats: L **Throws:** L **Pos:** 1B-41; PH-15; RF-12; CF-5; LF-4; DH-3; PR-3 **Ht:** 6'0" **Wt:** 204 **Born:** 12/2/1975 **Age:** 34

Year	Team	Lg	G	AB	H	2B	3B	HR	(Hm	Rd)	TB	R	RBI	RC	TBB	IBB	SO	HBP	SH	SF	SB	CS	SB%	GDP	Avg	OBP	Slg
2009	Pwtckt*	AAA	10	33	10	1	0	0	(-	-)	11	2	5	3	0	0	1	0	0	1	1	0	1.00	2	.303	.294	.333
1997	Fla	NL	14	52	10	1	1	0	(0	0)	13	5	4	3	4	0	7	0	1	0	3	0	1.00	1	.192	.250	.250
1998	Fla	NL	154	578	161	25	7	11	(5	6)	233	72	68	70	34	2	61	1	7	3	10	5	.67	17	.279	.318	.403
1999	Fla	NL	148	495	134	23	9	8	(5	3)	199	57	50	58	29	5	50	0	2	9	7	6	.54	11	.271	.306	.402
2000	Fla	NL	152	530	158	31	5	12	(5	7)	235	87	57	78	42	2	46	0	2	4	19	9	.68	17	.298	.347	.443

159

Year	Team	Lg	BATTING G	AB	H	2B	3B	HR	(Hm	Rd)	TB	R	RBI	RC	TBB	IBB	SO	HBP	SH	SF	BASERUNNING SB	CS	SB%	GDP	AVERAGES Avg	OBP	Slg
2001	SD	NL	119	406	118	29	1	10	(3	7)	179	67	58	65	48	1	58	2	1	3	13	5	.72	11	.291	.366	.441
2002	SD	NL	153	578	169	27	7	17	(11	6)	261	82	61	92	59	0	89	3	2	4	11	9	.55	10	.292	.359	.452
2003	SD	NL	128	482	128	28	4	7	(1	6)	185	64	38	59	56	3	82	1	1	1	6	3	.67	8	.266	.343	.384
2004	Oak	AL	148	606	190	37	3	15	(9	6)	273	78	63	94	55	5	70	2	5	5	8	5	.62	6	.314	.370	.459
2005	Oak	AL	139	582	163	35	1	15	(4	11)	245	75	82	86	40	3	51	1	2	4	5	5	.50	13	.280	.325	.421
2006	Oak	AL	129	502	138	29	3	7	(1	6)	194	57	59	63	44	1	55	2	4	6	6	3	.67	18	.275	.332	.386
2007	Oak	AL	56	206	44	14	0	1	(0	1)	61	20	20	19	19	3	20	0	0	1	1	1	.50	4	.214	.279	.296
2008	2 Tms	AL	110	402	111	25	4	6	(4	2)	162	45	49	49	32	3	45	0	1	1	2	4	.33	14	.276	.329	.403
2009	2 Tms	AL	67	187	52	9	0	4	(4	0)	73	16	23	22	15	3	21	0	1	3	3	2	.60	6	.278	.327	.390
08	Atl	NL	88	318	92	17	3	6	(4	2)	133	39	37	37	25	2	34	0	1	1	2	3	.40	13	.289	.340	.418
08	Bos	AL	22	84	19	8	1	0	(0	0)	29	6	12	12	7	1	11	0	0	0	0	1	.00	1	.226	.286	.345
09	Bos	AL	27	74	19	2	0	1	(1	0)	24	4	5	6	4	1	12	0	0	1	2	1	.67	1	.257	.291	.324
09	CWS	AL	40	113	33	7	0	3	(3	0)	49	12	18	16	11	2	9	0	1	2	1	1	.50	5	.292	.349	.434
Postseason			17	70	16	5	0	1	(0	1)	24	7	2	3	2	0	10	0	0	0	0	0	-	4	.229	.250	.343
13 ML YEARS			1517	5606	1576	313	45	113	(52	61)	2318	725	632	758	477	31	655	12	29	44	94	57	.62	136	.281	.336	.413

George Kottaras

Bats: L **Throws:** R **Pos:** C-39; PR-7; DH-2; PH-2; 3B-1   **Ht:** 6'0" **Wt:** 185 **Born:** 5/10/1983 **Age:** 27

Year	Team	Lg	BATTING G	AB	H	2B	3B	HR	(Hm	Rd)	TB	R	RBI	RC	TBB	IBB	SO	HBP	SH	SF	BASERUNNING SB	CS	SB%	GDP	AVERAGES Avg	OBP	Slg
2003	Idaho	R+	42	143	37	8	1	7	(-	-)	68	27	24	24	19	1	36	1	0	1	1	1	.50	2	.259	.348	.476
2004	FtWyn	A	78	271	84	18	1	7	(-	-)	125	40	46	55	51	2	41	0	1	3	0	0	-	7	.310	.415	.461
2005	Lk Els	A+	91	337	102	29	0	9	(-	-)	158	54	50	64	50	2	60	1	2	4	2	1	.67	6	.303	.390	.469
2005	Mobile	AA	29	101	29	7	0	2	(-	-)	42	16	15	18	19	1	23	0	0	1	0	0	-	1	.287	.397	.416
2006	Mobile	AA	78	257	71	19	1	8	(-	-)	116	40	34	48	50	4	68	1	0	2	0	1	.00	9	.276	.394	.451
2006	Portlnd	AAA	33	119	25	10	1	2	(-	-)	43	14	17	13	12	0	30	1	0	1	0	0	-	6	.210	.286	.361
2007	Pwtckt	AAA	87	294	71	22	0	9	(-	-)	120	32	39	40	32	1	71	2	2	4	1	1	.50	12	.241	.316	.408
2008	Pwtckt	AAA	107	395	96	18	0	22	(-	-)	180	63	65	66	64	3	110	1	0	2	0	0	-	6	.243	.348	.456
2009	Pwtckt	AAA	10	24	7	3	0	0	(-	-)	10	1	0	4	6	0	6	0	0	0	0	0	-	0	.292	.433	.417
2008	Bos	AL	3	5	1	1	0	0	(0	0)	2	1	0	0	0	0	2	0	0	0	0	0	-	0	.200	.200	.400
2009	Bos	AL	45	93	22	11	0	1	(1	0)	36	15	10	10	11	0	25	0	0	3	0	0	-	1	.237	.308	.387
2 ML YEARS			48	98	23	12	0	1	(1	0)	38	16	10	10	11	0	27	0	0	3	0	0	-	1	.235	.304	.388

Kevin Kouzmanoff

Bats: R **Throws:** R **Pos:** 3B-139; PH-2   **Ht:** 6'1" **Wt:** 210 **Born:** 7/25/1981 **Age:** 28

Year	Team	Lg	BATTING G	AB	H	2B	3B	HR	(Hm	Rd)	TB	R	RBI	RC	TBB	IBB	SO	HBP	SH	SF	BASERUNNING SB	CS	SB%	GDP	AVERAGES Avg	OBP	Slg
2006	Cle	AL	16	56	12	2	0	3	(0	3)	23	4	11	7	5	0	12	0	0	0	0	0	-	3	.214	.279	.411
2007	SD	NL	145	484	133	30	2	18	(5	13)	221	57	74	69	32	2	94	10	2	6	1	0	1.00	9	.275	.329	.457
2008	SD	NL	154	624	162	31	4	23	(11	12)	270	71	84	70	23	3	139	15	0	6	0	0	-	14	.260	.299	.433
2009	SD	NL	141	529	135	31	1	18	(9	9)	222	50	88	64	27	3	106	11	0	6	1	0	1.00	25	.255	.302	.420
4 ML YEARS			456	1693	442	94	7	62	(25	37)	736	182	257	210	87	8	351	36	2	18	2	0	1.00	51	.261	.308	.435

Jason Kubel

Bats: L **Throws:** R **Pos:** DH-80; RF-30; LF-29; PH-13   **Ht:** 6'0" **Wt:** 218 **Born:** 5/25/1982 **Age:** 28

Year	Team	Lg	BATTING G	AB	H	2B	3B	HR	(Hm	Rd)	TB	R	RBI	RC	TBB	IBB	SO	HBP	SH	SF	BASERUNNING SB	CS	SB%	GDP	AVERAGES Avg	OBP	Slg
2004	Min	AL	23	60	18	2	0	2	(0	2)	26	10	7	13	6	0	9	0	0	1	1	1	.50	0	.300	.358	.433
2006	Min	AL	73	220	53	8	0	8	(3	5)	85	23	26	20	12	0	45	0	2	1	2	0	1.00	13	.241	.279	.386
2007	Min	AL	128	418	114	31	2	13	(6	7)	188	49	65	64	41	2	79	1	1	5	5	0	1.00	9	.273	.335	.450
2008	Min	AL	141	463	126	22	5	20	(9	11)	218	74	78	66	47	2	91	0	0	7	0	1	.00	12	.272	.335	.471
2009	Min	AL	146	514	154	35	2	28	(15	13)	277	73	103	95	56	9	106	3	0	5	1	1	.50	13	.300	.369	.539
Postseason			2	7	1	1	0	0	(0	0)	2	0	0	0	0	0	2	0	0	0	0	0	-	0	.143	.143	.286
5 ML YEARS			511	1675	465	98	9	71	(33	38)	794	229	279	258	162	13	330	4	3	19	9	3	.75	47	.278	.339	.474

Hong-Chih Kuo

Pitches: L **Bats:** L **Pos:** RP-35   **Ht:** 6'1" **Wt:** 242 **Born:** 7/23/1981 **Age:** 28

Year	Team	Lg	HOW MUCH HE PITCHED G	GS	CG	GF	IP	BFP	WHAT HE GAVE UP H	R	ER	HR	SH	SF	HB	TBB	IBB	SO	WP	Bk	THE RESULTS W	L	Pct	Sh	Sv-Op	Hld	ERC	ERA
2009	Ddgrs*	R	3	1	0	0	3.0	12	2	0	0	0	0	0	0	1	0	5	0	0	0	0	-	0	0--	-	3	1.57	0.00
2009	Albq*	AAA	2	0	0	1	2.0	8	2	1	1	0	0	0	0	1	0	1	0	0	0	0	-	0	0--	-	4.15	4.50
2009	InldEm*	A+	4	0	0	0	4.0	15	3	0	0	0	0	0	1	0	0	6	0	0	0	0	-	0	0--	-	1.79	0.00
2005	LAD	NL	9	0	0	0	5.1	26	5	4	4	1	0	0	0	5	1	10	0	1	0	1	.000	0	0-1	3	6.10	6.75
2006	LAD	NL	28	5	0	6	59.2	258	54	30	28	3	2	1	1	33	5	71	2	0	1	5	.167	0	0-0	2	3.76	4.22
2007	LAD	NL	8	6	0	1	30.1	140	35	26	25	3	1	1	1	14	0	27	1	0	1	4	.200	0	0-0	0	5.25	7.42
2008	LAD	NL	42	3	0	10	80.0	323	60	21	19	4	4	1	3	21	2	96	1	1	5	3	.625	0	1-3	12	2.05	2.14
2009	LAD	NL	35	0	0	2	30.0	124	21	10	10	2	3	0	2	13	2	32	5	0	2	0	1.000	0	0-1	14	2.54	3.00
Postseason			4	1	0	2	7.1	29	6	3	3	0	1	0	0	2	1	7	1	0	0	1	.000	0	0-0	1	1.90	3.68
5 ML YEARS			122	14	0	19	205.1	871	175	91	86	13	10	3	7	86	10	236	9	2	9	13	.409	0	1-5	31	3.13	3.77

Hiroki Kuroda

Pitches: R **Bats:** R **Pos:** SP-20; RP-1 **Ht:** 6'1" **Wt:** 220 **Born:** 2/10/1975 **Age:** 35

			HOW MUCH HE PITCHED						WHAT HE GAVE UP										THE RESULTS							
Year	Team	Lg	G	GS	CG	GF	IP	BFP	H	R	ER	HR	SH	SF	HB	TBB	IBB	SO	WP	Bk	W	L	Pct	Sh	Sv-Op	Hld	ERC	ERA
1997	Hrshm	Jap	23	23	4	0	135.0	601	147	72	66	17	-	-	4	63	-	64	8	1	6	9	.400	1	0- -	-	5.21	4.40
1998	Hrshm	Jap	18	6	0	3	45.0	199	53	34	33	5	-	-	1	24	-	25	1	0	1	4	.200	0	0- -	-	6.14	6.60
1999	Hrshm	Jap	21	16	2	1	87.2	406	106	70	66	20	-	-	3	39	-	55	4	0	5	8	.385	1	0- -	-	6.58	6.78
2000	Hrshm	Jap	29	21	7	3	144.0	623	147	73	69	21	-	-	1	61	-	116	3	0	9	6	.600	1	0- -	-	4.69	4.31
2001	Hrshm	Jap	27	27	13	0	190.0	786	175	72	64	19	-	-	8	45	-	146	7	0	12	8	.600	0	0- -	-	3.17	3.03
2002	Hrshm	Jap	23	23	8	0	164.1	671	166	69	67	16	-	-	1	34	-	144	1	0	10	10	.500	2	0- -	-	3.44	3.67
2003	Hrshm	Jap	28	28	8	0	205.2	827	197	77	71	18	-	-	3	45	2	137	5	1	13	9	.591	4	0- -	-	3.20	3.11
2004	Hrshm	Jap	21	21	7	0	147.0	639	187	81	76	17	6	6	2	29	1	138	1	0	7	9	.438	1	0- -	-	5.02	4.65
2005	Hrshm	Jap	29	29	11	0	212.2	863	183	76	75	17	16	3	7	42	2	165	7	0	15	12	.556	1	0- -	-	2.54	3.17
2006	Hrshm	Jap	26	26	7	0	189.1	757	169	49	39	12	16	4	7	21	4	144	5	0	13	6	.684	2	1- -	-	2.30	1.85
2007	Hrshm	Jap	26	26	7	0	179.2	738	176	78	71	20	-	-	4	42	3	123	1	0	12	8	.600	1	0- -	-	3.53	3.56
2009	InldEm	A+	3	3	0	0	13.2	58	15	9	5	0	0	1	1	1	0	10	0	0	0	0	-	0	0- -	-	2.89	3.29
2008	LAD	NL	31	31	2	0	183.1	776	181	85	76	13	7	5	7	42	8	116	5	0	9	10	.474	2	0-0	0	3.18	3.73
2009	LAD	NL	21	20	0	0	117.1	485	110	59	49	12	7	1	1	24	1	87	5	0	8	7	.533	0	0-0	0	2.98	3.76
	Postseason		2	2	0	0	12.1	50	11	2	2	0	0	0	0	3	1	7	0	0	2	0	1.000	0	0-0	0	2.18	1.46
	2 ML YEARS		52	51	2	0	300.2	1261	291	144	125	25	14	6	8	66	9	203	10	0	17	17	.500	2	0-0	0	3.10	3.74

John Lackey

Pitches: R **Bats:** R **Pos:** SP-27 **Ht:** 6'6" **Wt:** 245 **Born:** 10/23/1978 **Age:** 31

			HOW MUCH HE PITCHED						WHAT HE GAVE UP										THE RESULTS							
Year	Team	Lg	G	GS	CG	GF	IP	BFP	H	R	ER	HR	SH	SF	HB	TBB	IBB	SO	WP	Bk	W	L	Pct	Sh	Sv-Op	Hld	ERC	ERA
2009	Salt Lk*	AAA	2	2	0	0	9.2	36	6	3	3	1	0	0	1	1	0	8	0	0	1	0	1.000	0	0- -	-	1.59	2.79
2002	LAA	AL	18	18	1	0	108.1	465	113	52	44	10	0	4	4	33	0	69	7	2	9	4	.692	0	0-0	0	4.03	3.66
2003	LAA	AL	33	33	2	0	204.0	885	223	117	105	31	2	0	10	60	4	151	11	1	10	16	.385	2	0-0	0	4.00	4.63
2004	LAA	AL	33	33	1	0	198.1	866	215	108	103	22	9	4	6	60	4	144	11	1	14	13	.519	1	0-0	0	4.39	4.67
2005	LAA	AL	33	33	1	0	209.0	892	208	85	80	13	1	2	11	71	3	199	18	0	14	5	.737	0	0-0	0	3.76	3.44
2006	LAA	AL	33	33	3	0	217.2	922	203	98	86	14	8	6	9	72	4	190	16	0	13	11	.542	2	0-0	0	3.31	3.56
2007	LAA	AL	33	33	2	0	224.0	929	219	87	75	18	1	1	12	52	2	179	9	1	19	9	.679	2	0-0	0	3.40	3.01
2008	LAA	AL	24	24	3	0	163.1	675	161	71	68	26	5	1	10	40	1	130	5	0	12	5	.706	0	0-0	0	4.10	3.75
2009	LAA	AL	27	27	1	0	176.1	748	177	84	75	17	9	10	9	47	1	139	6	0	11	8	.579	1	0-0	0	3.73	3.83
	Postseason		11	9	0	0	50.1	244	50	22	22	4	2	2	1	22	4	39	3	0	2	3	.400	0	0-0	0	3.58	3.39
	8 ML YEARS		234	233	14	0	1501.0	6371	1519	702	636	151	35	34	73	441	19	1201	83	5	102	71	.590	8	0-0	0	3.92	3.81

Aaron Laffey

Pitches: L **Bats:** L **Pos:** SP-19; RP-6 **Ht:** 6'0" **Wt:** 185 **Born:** 4/15/1985 **Age:** 25

			HOW MUCH HE PITCHED						WHAT HE GAVE UP										THE RESULTS							
Year	Team	Lg	G	GS	CG	GF	IP	BFP	H	R	ER	HR	SH	SF	HB	TBB	IBB	SO	WP	Bk	W	L	Pct	Sh	Sv-Op	Hld	ERC	ERA
2009	Akron*	AA	2	2	0	0	7.1	35	6	3	3	0	1	0	1	7	0	6	0	0	0	0	-	0	0- -	-	4.93	3.68
2009	Clmbs*	AAA	3	3	0	0	10.1	52	21	13	13	2	0	1	0	5	0	4	0	0	0	2	.000	0	0- -	-	13.00	11.32
2007	Cle	AL	9	9	0	0	49.1	207	54	26	25	2	1	2	4	12	0	25	2	1	4	2	.667	0	0-0	0	4.02	4.56
2008	Cle	AL	16	16	0	0	93.2	409	103	52	44	10	2	0	9	31	1	43	5	1	5	7	.417	0	0-0	0	4.86	4.23
2009	Cle	AL	25	19	0	3	121.2	539	140	69	60	9	0	4	2	57	1	59	1	1	7	9	.438	0	1-1	0	5.20	4.44
	Postseason		1	0	0	0	4.2	16	1	0	0	0	0	0	0	1	0	3	0	0	0	0	-	0	0-0	0	0.30	0.00
	3 ML YEARS		50	44	0	3	264.2	1155	297	147	129	21	3	6	15	100	2	127	8	3	16	18	.471	0	1-1	0	4.85	4.39

Gerald Laird

Bats: R **Throws:** R **Pos:** C-135; PH-5; 1B-1 **Ht:** 6'1" **Wt:** 225 **Born:** 11/13/1979 **Age:** 30

			BATTING																			BASERUNNING				AVERAGES		
Year	Team	Lg	G	AB	H	2B	3B	HR	(Hm	Rd)	TB	R	RBI	RC	TBB	IBB	SO	HBP	SH	SF	SB	CS	SB%	GDP	Avg	OBP	Slg
2003	Tex	AL	19	44	12	2	1	1	(0	1)	19	9	4	5	5	0	11	1	0	0	0	0	-	2	.273	.360	.432
2004	Tex	AL	49	147	33	6	0	1	(1	0)	42	20	16	11	12	0	35	2	4	3	0	1	.00	5	.224	.287	.286
2005	Tex	AL	13	40	9	2	0	1	(0	1)	14	7	4	4	2	0	7	0	0	0	0	0	-	1	.225	.262	.350
2006	Tex	AL	78	243	72	20	1	7	(3	4)	115	46	22	24	12	0	54	2	1	2	3	1	.75	7	.296	.332	.473
2007	Tex	AL	120	407	91	18	3	9	(6	3)	142	48	47	45	30	1	103	2	5	4	6	2	.75	3	.224	.278	.349
2008	Tex	AL	95	344	95	24	0	6	(3	3)	137	54	41	46	23	2	63	6	4	4	2	4	.33	5	.276	.329	.398
2009	Det	AL	135	413	93	23	2	4	(1	3)	132	49	33	41	40	0	68	10	10	4	5	0	1.00	11	.225	.306	.320
	7 ML YEARS		509	1638	405	95	7	29	(14	15)	601	233	167	176	124	3	341	23	24	17	16	8	.67	34	.247	.306	.367

Chris Lambert

Pitches: R **Bats:** R **Pos:** RP-6 **Ht:** 6'1" **Wt:** 205 **Born:** 3/8/1983 **Age:** 27

			HOW MUCH HE PITCHED						WHAT HE GAVE UP										THE RESULTS							
Year	Team	Lg	G	GS	CG	GF	IP	BFP	H	R	ER	HR	SH	SF	HB	TBB	IBB	SO	WP	Bk	W	L	Pct	Sh	Sv-Op	Hld	ERC	ERA
2004	Peoria	A	9	9	0	0	38.1	169	31	15	11	2	0	2	1	24	1	46	2	0	1	1	.500	0	0- -	-	3.56	2.58
2005	PlmBh	A+	10	10	0	0	54.2	231	53	20	16	4	2	1	5	15	0	46	6	1	7	1	.875	0	0- -	-	3.61	2.63
2005	Sprgfld	AA	18	18	0	0	85.0	403	97	69	60	10	2	10	10	48	0	69	8	3	3	8	.273	0	0- -	-	6.17	6.35
2006	Sprgfld	AA	23	23	0	0	120.2	548	126	84	71	20	3	6	5	63	1	113	13	1	10	9	.526	0	0- -	-	5.44	5.30
2006	Memp	AAA	1	1	0	0	4.0	17	5	3	3	0	1	1	1	0	0	2	1	0	0	1	.000	0	0- -	-	4.32	6.75
2007	Sprgfld	AA	5	5	0	0	26.1	108	24	11	10	5	0	0	2	8	0	17	2	0	0	2	.000	0	0- -	-	4.24	3.42
2007	Memp	AAA	28	4	0	6	57.2	271	74	49	48	10	5	2	3	29	1	50	4	0	1	4	.200	0	0- -	-	7.04	7.49
2007	Toledo	AAA	1	1	0	0	6.0	22	1	0	0	0	0	0	0	2	0	10	0	0	0	0	-	0	0- -	-	0.57	0.00
2008	Toledo	AAA	26	26	3	0	149.1	631	143	69	58	7	6	9	2	48	0	124	3	1	12	8	.600	1	0- -	-	3.22	3.50
2009	Toledo	AAA	21	21	1	0	126.2	530	121	54	50	8	5	5	8	31	1	106	3	0	6	7	.462	0	0- -	-	3.11	3.55
2009	Norfolk	AAA	3	3	0	0	11.2	53	18	9	9	3	0	0	2	3	0	9	0	0	1	2	.333	0	0- -	-	8.34	6.94
2008	Det	AL	8	3	0	0	20.2	102	31	18	13	3	0	1	2	7	1	15	0	0	1	2	.333	0	0-0	0	7.37	5.66

Year	Team	Lg	G	GS	CG	GF	IP	BFP	H	R	ER	HR	SH	SF	HB	TBB	IBB	SO	WP	Bk	W	L	Pct	Sh	Sv-Op	Hld	ERC	ERA
2009	2 Tms	AL	6	0	0	2	12.1	62	20	14	14	5	0	0	0	7	0	11	1	0	0	1	.000	0	0-0	0	11.67	10.22
09	Det	AL	2	0	0	0	6.2	36	12	11	11	3	0	0	0	6	0	4	0	0	0	1	.000	0	0-0	0	15.70	14.85
09	Bal	AL	4	0	0	2	5.2	26	8	3	3	2	0	0	0	1	0	7	1	0	0	0	-	0	0-0	0	7.35	4.76
2 ML YEARS			14	3	0	3	33.0	164	51	32	27	8	0	1	2	14	1	26	1	0	1	3	.250	0	0-0	0	8.90	7.36

Ryan Langerhans

Bats: L **Throws:** L **Pos:** LF-30; RF-5; CF-4; PR-3; DH-1   **Ht:** 6'3" **Wt:** 221 **Born:** 2/20/1980 **Age:** 30

Year	Team	Lg	G	AB	H	2B	3B	HR	(Hm	Rd)	TB	R	RBI	RC	TBB	IBB	SO	HBP	SH	SF	SB	CS	SB%	GDP	Avg	OBP	Slg
2009	Syrcse*	AAA	64	205	57	16	0	9	(-	-)	100	34	40	37	30	2	50	2	2	3	7	6	.54	3	.278	.371	.488
2002	Atl	NL	1	1	0	0	0	0	(0	0)	0	0	0	0	0	0	0	0	0	0	0	0	-	0	.000	.000	.000
2003	Atl	NL	16	15	4	0	0	0	(0	0)	4	2	0	1	0	0	6	0	0	0	0	0	-	1	.267	.267	.267
2005	Atl	NL	128	326	87	22	3	8	(3	5)	139	48	42	53	37	3	75	5	2	3	0	2	.00	2	.267	.348	.426
2006	Atl	NL	131	315	76	16	3	7	(3	4)	119	46	28	45	50	8	91	3	0	1	1	2	.33	9	.241	.350	.378
2007	3 Tms		125	210	35	7	2	6	(1	5)	64	27	23	22	29	2	81	2	1	2	3	1	.75	4	.167	.272	.305
2008	Was	NL	73	111	26	5	2	3	(1	2)	44	17	12	18	25	1	31	1	2	0	2	0	1.00	1	.234	.380	.396
2009	Sea	NL	38	101	22	6	1	3	(2	1)	39	12	10	11	14	1	28	1	3	3	0	1	.00	0	.218	.311	.386
07	Atl	NL	20	44	3	1	0	0	(0	0)	4	3	1	0	6	1	16	1	0	1	0	1	.00	3	.068	.192	.091
07	Oak	AL	2	4	0	0	0	0	(0	0)	0	0	0	0	1	0	2	0	0	0	0	0	-	0	.000	.200	.000
07	Was	NL	103	162	32	6	2	6	(1	5)	60	24	22	22	22	1	63	1	1	1	3	0	1.00	1	.198	.296	.370
Postseason			4	12	4	1	0	0	(0	0)	5	1	0	2	3	1	3	1	0	0	1	0	1.00	1	.333	.500	.417
7 ML YEARS			512	1079	250	56	11	27	(10	17)	409	152	115	150	155	15	312	12	8	9	6	6	.50	17	.232	.332	.379

John Lannan

Pitches: L **Bats:** L **Pos:** SP-33   **Ht:** 6'4" **Wt:** 215 **Born:** 9/27/1984 **Age:** 25

Year	Team	Lg	G	GS	CG	GF	IP	BFP	H	R	ER	HR	SH	SF	HB	TBB	IBB	SO	WP	Bk	W	L	Pct	Sh	Sv-Op	Hld	ERC	ERA
2007	Was	NL	6	6	0	0	34.2	153	36	17	16	3	2	0	2	17	1	10	1	0	2	2	.500	0	0-0	0	4.82	4.15
2008	Was	NL	31	31	0	0	182.0	779	172	89	79	23	13	5	7	72	1	117	6	2	9	15	.375	0	0-0	0	4.09	3.91
2009	Was	NL	33	33	2	0	206.1	875	210	100	89	22	12	1	6	68	5	89	3	0	9	13	.409	1	0-0	0	4.07	3.88
3 ML YEARS			70	70	2	0	423.0	1807	418	206	184	48	27	6	15	157	7	216	10	2	20	30	.400	1	0-0	0	4.14	3.91

Matt LaPorta

Bats: R **Throws:** R **Pos:** LF-29; 1B-10; RF-10; DH-1; PH-1; PR-1   **Ht:** 6'2" **Wt:** 210 **Born:** 1/8/1985 **Age:** 25

Year	Team	Lg	G	AB	H	2B	3B	HR	(Hm	Rd)	TB	R	RBI	RC	TBB	IBB	SO	HBP	SH	SF	SB	CS	SB%	GDP	Avg	OBP	Slg
2007	Helena	R+	7	27	7	1	0	2	(-	-)	14	4	4	4	1	0	8	0	0	0	0	0	-	2	.259	.286	.519
2007	WV	A-	23	88	28	8	0	10	(-	-)	66	18	27	24	7	1	22	5	0	2	0	1	.00	2	.318	.392	.750
2008	Hntsvl	AA	84	302	87	23	2	20	(-	-)	174	56	66	71	45	3	63	15	0	4	2	1	.67	9	.288	.402	.576
2008	Akron	AA	17	60	14	1	0	2	(-	-)	21	6	8	6	4	1	12	2	0	1	0	0	-	1	.233	.299	.350
2009	Clmbs	AAA	93	338	101	23	2	17	(-	-)	179	63	60	69	42	1	57	9	1	3	1	3	.25	11	.299	.388	.530
2009	Cle	AL	52	181	46	13	0	7	(2	5)	80	29	21	22	12	0	37	3	0	2	2	0	1.00	6	.254	.308	.442

Jeff Larish

Bats: L **Throws:** R **Pos:** DH-15; 1B-11; PH-8; 3B-1   **Ht:** 6'2" **Wt:** 200 **Born:** 10/11/1982 **Age:** 27

Year	Team	Lg	G	AB	H	2B	3B	HR	(Hm	Rd)	TB	R	RBI	RC	TBB	IBB	SO	HBP	SH	SF	SB	CS	SB%	GDP	Avg	OBP	Slg
2005	Tigers	R	6	18	4	1	0	0	(-	-)	5	1	4	2	4	0	5	1	0	1	0	1	.00	0	.222	.375	.278
2005	Oneont	A-	18	64	19	3	0	6	(-	-)	40	16	13	17	13	0	6	2	0	0	0	0	-	0	.297	.430	.625
2006	Lkland	A+	135	457	118	34	2	18	(-	-)	210	76	65	84	81	8	101	10	0	4	9	7	.56	10	.258	.379	.460
2007	Erie	AA	132	454	121	25	2	28	(-	-)	234	71	101	96	87	9	108	9	0	6	5	2	.71	2	.267	.390	.515
2008	Toledo	AAA	103	384	96	20	2	21	(-	-)	183	49	64	64	50	4	109	4	0	2	0	1	.00	13	.250	.341	.477
2009	Toledo	AAA	61	211	56	13	0	6	(-	-)	87	38	26	37	42	6	56	4	0	0	2	2	.50	6	.265	.397	.412
2008	Det	AL	42	104	27	6	0	2	(1	1)	39	12	16	14	7	0	34	0	0	0	2	2	.50	2	.260	.306	.375
2009	Det	AL	32	74	16	3	1	4	(1	3)	33	13	7	5	15	0	25	0	0	1	0	1	.00	4	.216	.344	.446
2 ML YEARS			74	178	43	9	1	6	(2	4)	72	25	23	19	22	0	59	0	0	1	2	3	.40	6	.242	.323	.404

Adam LaRoche

Bats: L **Throws:** L **Pos:** 1B-148; PH-3; DH-1   **Ht:** 6'3" **Wt:** 203 **Born:** 11/6/1979 **Age:** 30

Year	Team	Lg	G	AB	H	2B	3B	HR	(Hm	Rd)	TB	R	RBI	RC	TBB	IBB	SO	HBP	SH	SF	SB	CS	SB%	GDP	Avg	OBP	Slg
2004	Atl	NL	110	324	90	27	1	13	(7	6)	158	45	45	43	27	1	78	1	2	2	0	0	-	10	.278	.333	.488
2005	Atl	NL	141	451	117	28	0	20	(11	9)	205	53	78	63	39	7	87	4	2	6	0	2	.00	15	.259	.320	.455
2006	Atl	NL	149	492	140	38	1	32	(11	21)	276	89	90	83	55	5	128	2	1	7	0	2	.00	9	.285	.354	.561
2007	Pit	NL	152	563	153	42	0	21	(10	11)	258	71	88	84	62	5	131	3	0	4	1	1	.50	18	.272	.345	.458
2008	Pit	NL	136	492	133	32	3	25	(14	11)	246	66	85	76	54	7	122	2	0	6	1	1	.50	9	.270	.341	.500
2009	3 Tms		150	555	154	38	2	25	(15	10)	271	78	83	84	69	12	142	0	0	5	2	2	.50	11	.277	.355	.488
09	Pit	NL	87	324	80	25	1	12	(7	5)	143	46	40	38	41	6	81	0	0	3	2	2	.50	9	.247	.329	.441
09	Bos	AL	6	19	5	2	0	1	(1	0)	10	2	3	3	0	0	2	0	0	0	0	0	-	1	.263	.263	.526
09	Atl	NL	57	212	69	11	1	12	(7	5)	118	30	40	43	28	6	59	0	0	2	0	0	-	1	.325	.401	.557
Postseason			8	25	8	2	0	2	(0	2)	16	3	10	6	5	1	6	0	1	0	0	0	-	1	.320	.433	.640
6 ML YEARS			838	2877	787	205	7	136	(68	68)	1414	402	469	433	306	37	688	12	5	30	4	8	.33	72	.274	.343	.491

Andy LaRoche

Bats: R Throws: R Pos: 3B-146; PH-5

Ht: 6'1" Wt: 210 Born: 9/13/1983 Age: 26

Year	Team	Lg	G	AB	H	2B	3B	HR	(Hm	Rd)	TB	R	RBI	RC	TBB	IBB	SO	HBP	SH	SF	SB	CS	SB%	GDP	Avg	OBP	Slg
2007	LAD	NL	35	93	21	5	0	1	(0	1)	29	16	10	12	20	5	24	1	0	1	2	1	.67	1	.226	.365	.312
2008	2 Tms	NL	76	223	37	5	0	5	(1	4)	57	17	18	10	24	1	37	2	2	1	2	0	1.00	8	.166	.252	.256
2009	Pit	NL	150	524	135	29	5	12	(7	5)	210	64	64	64	50	1	84	8	6	2	3	1	.75	16	.258	.330	.401
08	LAD	NL	27	59	12	1	0	2	(0	2)	19	6	6	3	10	0	7	0	0	0	0	0	-	5	.203	.319	.322
08	Pit	NL	49	164	25	4	0	3	(1	2)	38	11	12	7	14	1	30	2	2	1	2	0	1.00	3	.152	.227	.232
3 ML YEARS			261	840	193	39	5	18	(8	10)	296	97	92	86	94	7	145	11	8	4	7	2	.78	25	.230	.314	.352

Jason LaRue

Bats: R Throws: R Pos: C-43; PH-11; 1B-2

Ht: 5'11" Wt: 205 Born: 3/19/1974 Age: 36

Year	Team	Lg	G	AB	H	2B	3B	HR	(Hm	Rd)	TB	R	RBI	RC	TBB	IBB	SO	HBP	SH	SF	SB	CS	SB%	GDP	Avg	OBP	Slg
1999	Cin	NL	36	90	19	7	0	3	(1	2)	35	12	10	10	11	1	32	2	0	0	4	1	.80	4	.211	.311	.389
2000	Cin	NL	31	98	23	3	0	5	(1	4)	41	12	12	12	5	2	19	4	0	0	0	0	-	1	.235	.299	.418
2001	Cin	NL	121	364	86	21	2	12	(3	9)	147	39	43	42	27	4	106	9	1	2	3	3	.50	11	.236	.303	.404
2002	Cin	NL	113	353	88	17	1	12	(5	7)	143	42	52	44	27	6	117	13	2	2	1	2	.33	13	.249	.324	.405
2003	Cin	NL	118	379	87	23	1	16	(12	4)	160	52	50	47	33	4	111	20	1	4	3	3	.50	9	.230	.321	.422
2004	Cin	NL	114	390	98	24	2	14	(3	11)	168	46	55	53	26	5	108	24	2	3	0	2	.00	7	.251	.334	.431
2005	Cin	NL	110	361	94	27	0	14	(6	8)	163	38	60	63	41	7	101	13	5	2	0	0	-	8	.260	.355	.452
2006	Cin	NL	72	191	37	5	0	8	(5	3)	66	22	21	17	27	9	51	8	3	1	1	0	1.00	3	.194	.317	.346
2007	KC	AL	66	169	25	9	0	4	(2	2)	46	14	13	7	17	0	66	4	3	2	1	0	1.00	6	.148	.240	.272
2008	StL	NL	61	164	35	8	1	4	(1	3)	57	17	21	16	15	1	20	5	3	2	0	0	-	6	.213	.296	.348
2009	StL	NL	51	104	25	3	0	2	(1	1)	34	10	6	7	3	0	22	4	1	0	1	0	1.00	3	.240	.288	.327
11 ML YEARS			893	2663	617	147	7	94	(40	54)	1060	304	343	318	232	39	753	106	21	18	14	11	.56	71	.232	.316	.398

Mat Latos

Pitches: R Bats: R Pos: SP-10

Ht: 6'6" Wt: 225 Born: 12/9/1987 Age: 22

Year	Team	Lg	G	GS	CG	GF	IP	BFP	H	R	ER	HR	SH	SF	HB	TBB	IBB	SO	WP	Bk	W	L	Pct	Sh	Sv-Op	Hld	ERC	ERA
2007	Eugene	A-	16	13	0	0	56.1	246	58	30	24	1	1	1	4	22	0	74	8	4	1	4	.200	0	0--	-	3.90	3.83
2008	FtWyn	A	7	5	0	0	24.2	106	24	12	9	3	1	0	1	8	0	23	0	0	0	3	.000	0	0--	-	3.89	3.28
2008	Padres	R	5	3	0	0	14.0	56	12	5	5	0	0	0	2	2	0	23	2	0	1	0	1.000	0	0--	-	2.31	3.21
2008	Eugene	A-	3	3	0	0	17.1	70	13	3	2	1	0	0	1	3	0	23	2	1	2	0	1.000	0	0--	-	1.86	1.04
2009	FtWyn	A	4	2	0	1	25.1	86	10	1	1	1	0	0	0	3	0	27	0	0	3	0	1.000	0	0--	-	0.62	0.36
2009	SnAnt	AA	9	9	0	0	47.0	181	32	11	10	0	0	4	1	9	0	46	1	0	5	1	.833	0	0--	-	1.38	1.91
2009	SD	NL	10	10	0	0	50.2	212	43	29	26	7	3	1	0	23	1	39	0	2	4	5	.444	0	0-0	0	3.72	4.62

Brent Leach

Pitches: L Bats: L Pos: RP-38

Ht: 6'4" Wt: 219 Born: 11/18/1982 Age: 27

Year	Team	Lg	G	GS	CG	GF	IP	BFP	H	R	ER	HR	SH	SF	HB	TBB	IBB	SO	WP	Bk	W	L	Pct	Sh	Sv-Op	Hld	ERC	ERA
2005	Ogden	R+	14	13	1	0	66.2	269	53	21	18	4	2	0	5	29	0	77	4	0	5	3	.625	0	0--	-	3.28	2.43
2006	Clmbs	A	10	10	0	0	52.1	215	41	22	19	2	1	2	3	31	0	67	9	2	4	2	.667	0	0--	-	3.62	3.27
2006	VeroB	A+	30	0	0	8	49.1	225	48	34	25	1	1	3	8	32	0	57	13	2	3	4	.429	0	1--	-	5.04	4.56
2007	InldEm	A+	14	0	0	12	20.0	80	14	2	1	1	0	0	0	11	0	23	1	0	0	0	-	0	4--	-	2.85	0.45
2008	InldEm	A+	9	0	0	8	13.1	51	11	2	2	0	1	0	0	4	1	13	1	0	0	1	.000	0	3--	-	2.21	1.35
2008	Jaxnvl	AA	40	0	0	19	59.1	245	44	23	19	2	4	0	2	34	2	49	7	0	2	2	.500	0	12--	-	3.06	2.88
2009	Chatt	AA	9	0	0	3	13.0	61	12	3	1	1	0	0	0	8	1	17	0	0	0	1	.000	0	1--	-	3.93	0.69
2009	Albq	AAA	18	0	0	6	18.2	89	17	17	14	2	1	2	2	16	2	20	3	0	2	0	1.000	0	1--	-	5.67	6.75
2009	LAD	NL	38	0	0	6	20.1	88	16	13	13	3	0	0	1	12	3	19	5	0	2	0	1.000	0	0-0	4	3.93	5.75

Brandon League

Pitches: R Bats: R Pos: RP-67

Ht: 6'2" Wt: 205 Born: 3/16/1983 Age: 27

Year	Team	Lg	G	GS	CG	GF	IP	BFP	H	R	ER	HR	SH	SF	HB	TBB	IBB	SO	WP	Bk	W	L	Pct	Sh	Sv-Op	Hld	ERC	ERA
2004	Tor	AL	3	0	0	0	4.2	18	3	0	0	0	0	0	0	1	0	2	0	0	1	0	1.000	0	0-0	1	1.26	0.00
2005	Tor	AL	20	0	0	4	35.2	162	42	27	26	8	0	1	2	20	1	17	5	0	1	0	1.000	0	0-0	1	7.24	6.56
2006	Tor	AL	33	0	0	8	42.2	173	34	17	12	3	2	0	3	9	2	29	0	0	1	2	.333	0	1-4	12	2.30	2.53
2007	Tor	AL	14	0	0	2	11.2	58	19	8	8	1	0	1	0	7	0	7	3	0	0	0	-	0	0-1	0	8.98	6.17
2008	Tor	AL	31	0	0	8	33.0	141	28	9	8	2	1	0	3	15	2	23	2	0	1	2	.333	0	1-1	5	3.45	2.18
2009	Tor	AL	67	0	0	18	74.2	313	72	40	38	8	5	0	7	21	2	76	9	0	3	6	.333	0	0-3	9	3.85	4.58
6 ML YEARS			168	0	0	40	202.1	865	198	101	92	22	8	2	15	73	7	154	19	0	7	10	.412	0	2-9	28	4.15	4.09

Wade LeBlanc

Pitches: L Bats: L Pos: SP-9

Ht: 6'3" Wt: 202 Born: 8/7/1984 Age: 25

Year	Team	Lg	G	GS	CG	GF	IP	BFP	H	R	ER	HR	SH	SF	HB	TBB	IBB	SO	WP	Bk	W	L	Pct	Sh	Sv-Op	Hld	ERC	ERA
2006	Eugene	A-	7	3	0	0	21.0	85	19	10	10	1	0	2	1	6	0	20	1	0	1	0	1.000	0	0--	-	2.54	4.29
2006	FtWyn	A	7	7	0	0	32.2	136	31	8	8	1	1	0	1	10	0	27	0	0	4	1	.800	0	0--	-	3.12	2.20
2007	Lk Els	A+	16	16	0	0	92.0	363	72	32	27	5	2	4	1	17	0	90	7	0	6	5	.545	0	0--	-	1.93	2.64
2007	SnAnt	AA	12	11	0	0	57.1	233	48	22	22	8	1	0	0	19	0	55	1	0	7	3	.700	0	0--	-	3.22	3.45
2008	Portlnd	AAA	26	25	0	0	138.2	587	136	85	82	21	8	5	7	42	0	139	2	0	11	9	.550	0	0--	-	4.16	5.32

		HOW MUCH HE PITCHED						WHAT HE GAVE UP												THE RESULTS							
Year	Team	Lg	G	GS	CG	GF	IP	BFP	H	R	ER	HR	SH	SF	HB	TBB	IBB	SO	WP	Bk	W	L	Pct	Sh	Sv-Op	Hld	ERC	ERA
2009	Portlnd	AAA	24	20	0	1	121.0	498	109	54	52	15	4	7	2	31	0	95	9	0	4	9	.308	0	0- -	-	3.19	3.87
2008	SD	NL	5	4	0	0	21.1	104	29	19	19	7	1	0	0	15	2	14	0	0	1	3	.250	0	0-0	0	9.57	8.02
2009	SD	NL	9	9	0	0	46.1	194	35	19	19	6	3	1	4	19	1	30	0	0	3	1	.750	0	0-0	0	3.28	3.69
	2 ML YEARS		14	13	0	0	67.2	298	64	38	38	13	4	1	4	34	3	44	0	0	4	4	.500	0	0-0	0	5.03	5.05

Wil Ledezma

Pitches: L **Bats:** L **Pos:** RP-5   **Ht:** 6'4" **Wt:** 227 **Born:** 1/21/1981 **Age:** 29

		HOW MUCH HE PITCHED						WHAT HE GAVE UP												THE RESULTS							
Year	Team	Lg	G	GS	CG	GF	IP	BFP	H	R	ER	HR	SH	SF	HB	TBB	IBB	SO	WP	Bk	W	L	Pct	Sh	Sv-Op	Hld	ERC	ERA
2009	Syrcse*	AAA	18	0	0	4	19.1	95	29	12	9	0	1	0	1	12	0	17	2	0	0	2	.000	0	1- -	-	7.60	4.19
2009	Dnedin*	A+	3	0	0	1	3.0	10	1	0	0	0	0	0	0	0	0	2	0	0	0	0	-	0	0- -	-	0.25	0.00
2009	NHam*	AA	8	0	0	3	16.1	74	19	7	6	1	1	2	1	6	1	21	1	0	1	1	.500	0	0- -	-	4.67	3.31
2003	Det	AL	34	8	0	13	84.0	376	99	55	54	12	1	4	3	35	3	49	2	0	3	7	.300	0	0-1	1	5.67	5.79
2004	Det	AL	15	8	0	1	53.1	225	55	28	26	3	0	3	2	18	0	29	3	1	4	3	.571	0	0-1	0	3.94	4.39
2005	Det	AL	10	10	0	0	49.2	234	61	46	39	10	3	4	2	24	0	30	2	2	2	4	.333	0	0-0	0	6.66	7.07
2006	Det	AL	24	7	0	2	60.1	264	60	28	24	5	2	1	2	23	0	39	2	0	3	3	.500	0	0-1	2	3.92	3.58
2007	3 Tms		44	1	0	13	59.1	280	70	42	37	7	2	3	0	38	4	47	3	2	3	3	.500	0	0-2	4	6.13	5.61
2008	2 Tms	NL	28	6	0	8	58.1	266	51	29	27	4	4	4	3	41	2	53	4	0	0	2	.000	0	0-0	0	4.41	4.17
2009	Was		5	0	0	2	5.2	30	8	7	6	1	0	2	0	4	0	8	1	0	0	0	-	0	0-0	0	8.09	9.53
07	Det	AL	23	0	0	5	35.2	166	38	21	19	4	2	1	0	26	2	24	3	2	3	1	.750	0	0-2	2	5.83	4.79
07	Atl	NL	12	0	0	4	9.1	45	12	10	8	1	0	1	0	4	0	7	0	0	0	2	.000	0	0-0	2	5.64	7.71
07	SD	NL	9	1	0	4	14.1	69	20	11	10	2	0	1	0	8	2	16	0	0	0	0	-	0	0-0	0	7.23	6.28
08	SD	NL	25	6	0	6	54.1	249	49	29	27	4	4	4	3	38	2	49	4	0	0	2	.000	0	0-0	0	4.61	4.47
08	Ari	NL	3	0	0	2	4.0	17	2	0	0	0	0	0	0	3	0	4	0	0	0	0	-	0	0-0	0	2.03	0.00
	Postseason		4	0	0	1	4.0	17	4	1	1	1	0	0	0	1	0	2	0	0	1	0	1.000	0	0-0	1	4.38	2.25
	7 ML YEARS		160	40	0	39	370.2	1675	404	235	213	42	12	21	12	183	9	255	17	5	15	22	.405	0	0-5	7	5.15	5.17

Carlos Lee

Bats: R **Throws:** R **Pos:** LF-154; DH-6; 1B-1   **Ht:** 6'2" **Wt:** 240 **Born:** 6/20/1976 **Age:** 34

			BATTING																	BASERUNNING				AVERAGES		
Year	Team	Lg	G	AB	H	2B	3B	HR	(Hm	Rd)	TB	R	RBI	RC	TBB	IBB	SO	HBP	SH	SF	SB	CS	SB%	GDP	Avg	OBP	Slg
1999	CWS	AL	127	492	144	32	2	16	(10	6)	228	66	84	68	13	0	72	4	1	7	4	2	.67	11	.293	.312	.463
2000	CWS	AL	152	572	172	29	2	24	(12	12)	277	107	92	91	38	1	94	3	1	5	13	4	.76	17	.301	.345	.484
2001	CWS	AL	150	558	150	33	3	24	(12	12)	261	75	84	81	38	2	85	6	1	2	17	7	.71	15	.269	.321	.468
2002	CWS	AL	140	492	130	26	2	26	(14	12)	238	82	80	86	75	4	73	2	0	7	1	4	.20	5	.264	.359	.484
2003	CWS	AL	158	623	181	35	1	31	(18	13)	311	100	113	105	37	2	91	4	0	7	18	4	.82	20	.291	.331	.499
2004	CWS	AL	153	591	180	37	0	31	(17	14)	310	103	99	112	54	3	86	7	0	6	11	5	.69	10	.305	.366	.525
2005	Mil	NL	162	618	164	41	0	32	(15	17)	301	85	114	98	57	7	87	2	0	11	13	4	.76	8	.265	.324	.487
2006	2 Tms		161	624	187	37	1	37	(15	22)	337	102	116	113	58	6	65	2	0	11	19	2	.90	22	.300	.355	.540
2007	Hou	NL	162	627	190	43	1	32	(17	15)	331	93	119	104	53	10	63	4	0	13	10	5	.67	27	.303	.354	.528
2008	Hou	NL	115	436	137	27	0	28	(11	17)	248	61	100	85	37	7	49	3	0	5	4	1	.80	8	.314	.368	.569
2009	Hou	NL	160	610	183	35	1	26	(16	10)	298	65	102	85	41	5	51	3	0	8	5	3	.63	21	.300	.343	.489
06	Mil	NL	102	388	111	18	0	28	(10	18)	213	60	81	75	38	4	39	2	0	7	12	2	.86	13	.286	.347	.549
06	Tex	AL	59	236	76	19	1	9	(5	4)	124	42	35	38	20	2	26	0	0	4	7	0	1.00	9	.322	.369	.525
	Postseason		3	11	1	1	0	0	(0	0)	2	0	1	0	0	0	2	0	0	1	0	0	-	0	.091	.083	.182
	11 ML YEARS		1640	6243	1818	375	13	307	(157	150)	3140	939	1103	1028	501	47	816	40	3	82	115	41	.74	164	.291	.344	.503

Cliff Lee

Pitches: L **Bats:** L **Pos:** SP-34   **Ht:** 6'3" **Wt:** 190 **Born:** 8/30/1978 **Age:** 31

			HOW MUCH HE PITCHED					WHAT HE GAVE UP												THE RESULTS							
Year	Team	Lg	G	GS	CG	GF	IP	BFP	H	R	ER	HR	SH	SF	HB	TBB	IBB	SO	WP	Bk	W	L	Pct	Sh	Sv-Op	Hld	ERC	ERA
2002	Cle	AL	2	2	0	0	10.1	44	6	2	2	0	1	0	0	8	1	6	0	1	0	1	.000	0	0-0	0	2.38	1.74
2003	Cle	AL	9	9	0	0	52.1	210	41	28	21	7	1	1	2	20	1	44	3	0	3	3	.500	0	0-0	0	3.29	3.61
2004	Cle	AL	33	33	0	0	179.0	802	188	113	108	30	2	6	11	81	1	161	6	0	14	8	.636	0	0-0	0	5.31	5.43
2005	Cle	AL	32	32	1	0	202.0	838	194	91	85	22	5	7	0	52	1	143	4	0	18	5	.783	0	0-0	0	3.35	3.79
2006	Cle	AL	33	33	1	0	200.2	882	224	114	98	29	3	6	8	58	3	129	3	0	14	11	.560	0	0-0	0	4.69	4.40
2007	Cle	AL	20	16	1	1	97.1	443	112	73	68	17	3	2	7	36	1	66	5	0	5	8	.385	0	0-0	0	5.59	6.29
2008	Cle	AL	31	31	4	0	223.1	891	214	68	63	12	2	3	5	34	1	170	4	0	22	3	.880	2	0-0	0	2.75	2.54
2009	2 Tms		34	34	6	0	231.2	969	245	88	83	17	11	9	5	43	1	181	7	0	14	13	.519	2	0-0	0	3.45	3.22
09	Cle	AL	22	22	3	0	152.0	641	165	53	53	10	6	5	3	33	1	107	6	0	7	9	.438	1	0-0	0	3.68	3.14
09	Phi	NL	12	12	3	0	79.2	328	80	35	30	7	5	4	2	10	0	74	1	0	7	4	.636	1	0-0	0	3.03	3.39
	8 ML YEARS		194	190	13	1	1196.2	5079	1224	577	528	134	28	34	38	332	10	900	32	1	90	52	.634	4	0-0	0	3.92	3.97

Derrek Lee

Bats: R **Throws:** R **Pos:** 1B-140; DH-1   **Ht:** 6'5" **Wt:** 245 **Born:** 9/6/1975 **Age:** 34

			BATTING																	BASERUNNING				AVERAGES		
Year	Team	Lg	G	AB	H	2B	3B	HR	(Hm	Rd)	TB	R	RBI	RC	TBB	IBB	SO	HBP	SH	SF	SB	CS	SB%	GDP	Avg	OBP	Slg
1997	Fla	NL	22	54	14	3	0	1	(0	1)	20	9	4	8	9	0	24	0	0	0	0	0	-	1	.259	.365	.370
1998	Fla	NL	141	454	106	29	1	17	(4	13)	188	62	74	59	47	1	120	10	0	2	5	2	.71	12	.233	.318	.414
1999	Fla	NL	70	218	45	9	1	5	(0	5)	71	21	20	18	17	1	70	0	0	1	2	1	.67	3	.206	.263	.326
2000	Fla	NL	158	477	134	18	3	28	(9	19)	242	70	70	84	63	6	123	4	0	2	3	0	.00	14	.281	.368	.507
2001	Fla	NL	158	561	158	37	4	21	(8	13)	266	83	75	88	50	1	126	8	0	6	4	2	.67	18	.282	.346	.474
2002	Fla	NL	162	581	157	35	7	27	(9	18)	287	95	86	96	98	8	164	5	0	4	19	9	.68	14	.270	.378	.494
2003	Fla	NL	155	539	146	31	2	31	(11	20)	274	91	92	99	88	7	131	10	0	6	21	8	.72	9	.271	.379	.508
2004	ChC	NL	161	605	168	39	1	32	(18	14)	305	90	98	101	68	4	128	8	2	5	12	5	.71	14	.278	.356	.504
2005	ChC	NL	158	594	199	50	3	46	(24	22)	393	120	107	135	85	23	109	5	0	7	15	3	.83	12	.335	.418	.662
2006	ChC	NL	50	175	50	9	0	8	(5	3)	83	30	30	27	25	1	41	0	0	4	8	4	.67	11	.286	.368	.474

Year	Team	Lg	G	AB	H	2B	3B	HR	(Hm	Rd)	TB	R	RBI	RC	TBB	IBB	SO	HBP	SH	SF	SB	CS	SB%	GDP	Avg	OBP	Slg
2007	ChC	NL	150	567	180	43	1	22	(16	6)	291	91	82	108	71	0	114	9	0	3	6	5	.55	15	.317	.400	.513
2008	ChC	NL	155	623	181	41	3	20	(15	5)	288	93	90	93	71	3	119	0	0	4	8	2	.80	27	.291	.361	.462
2009	ChC	NL	141	532	163	36	2	35	(20	15)	308	91	111	112	76	6	109	3	0	4	1	0	1.00	12	.306	.393	.579
	Postseason		23	95	25	6	0	1	(0	1)	34	9	8	6	5	0	23	3	0	0	2	1	1.00	5	.263	.320	.358
	13 ML YEARS		1681	5980	1701	380	28	293	(139	154)	3016	946	939	1028	768	69	1378	62	2	48	101	44	.70	162	.284	.369	.504

Justin Lehr

Pitches: R Bats: R Pos: SP-11   Ht: 6'2" Wt: 215 Born: 8/3/1977 Age: 32

			HOW MUCH HE PITCHED					WHAT HE GAVE UP										THE RESULTS								
Year	Team	Lg	G	GS	CG	GF	IP	BFP	H	R	ER	HR	SH	SF	HB	TBB	IBB	SO	WP	Bk	W	L	Pct	Sh	Sv-Op	Hld	ERC	ERA
2009	LV*	AAA	8	7	1	1	41.2	177	43	23	22	5	2	1	0	16	0	20	4	0	5	2	.714	1	0- -	-	4.42	4.75
2000	Lovlle*	AAA	12	11	1	1	75.1	284	57	22	21	3	0	1	2	10	0	40	0	0	8	1	.889	0	0- -	-	1.70	2.51
2004	Oak	AL	27	0	0	11	32.2	144	35	19	19	3	1	2	2	14	2	16	2	0	1	1	.500	0	0-1	5	4.73	5.23
2005	Mil	NL	23	0	0	4	34.2	154	32	19	15	4	2	1	1	18	2	23	1	1	1	1	.500	0	0-1	3	4.17	3.89
2006	Mil	NL	16	0	0	4	15.2	75	24	16	15	2	1	1	1	7	1	12	1	0	2	1	.667	0	0-0	0	8.17	8.62
2009	Cin	NL	11	11	1	0	65.1	286	72	39	39	14	1	2	3	28	1	33	3	0	5	3	.625	1	0-0	0	5.96	5.37
	4 ML YEARS		77	11	1	24	148.1	659	163	93	88	23	5	6	7	67	6	84	7	1	9	6	.600	1	0-2	8	5.47	5.34

Anthony Lerew

Pitches: R Bats: L Pos: SP-2; RP-1   Ht: 6'3" Wt: 220 Born: 10/28/1982 Age: 27

			HOW MUCH HE PITCHED					WHAT HE GAVE UP										THE RESULTS								
Year	Team	Lg	G	GS	CG	GF	IP	BFP	H	R	ER	HR	SH	SF	HB	TBB	IBB	SO	WP	Bk	W	L	Pct	Sh	Sv-Op	Hld	ERC	ERA
2009	NWArk*	AA	27	27	1	0	152.0	667	164	79	69	14	6	4	6	55	3	101	9	1	10	6	.625	1	0- -	-	4.43	4.09
2005	Atl	NL	7	0	0	4	8.0	37	9	5	5	1	1	0	0	5	2	5	0	0	0	0	-	0	0-1	0	5.47	5.63
2006	Atl	NL	1	0	0	0	2.0	15	5	5	5	0	0	0	1	3	0	1	0	0	0	0	-	0	0-0	0	20.57	22.50
2007	Atl	NL	3	3	0	0	11.2	57	14	10	10	4	3	0	0	7	1	9	1	0	0	2	.000	0	0-0	0	7.02	7.71
2009	KC	AL	3	2	0	0	13.1	62	14	8	6	4	0	1	0	8	0	7	0	0	0	1	.000	0	0-0	0	6.60	4.05
	4 ML YEARS		14	5	0	4	35.0	171	42	28	26	9	4	1	1	23	3	22	1	0	0	3	.000	0	0-1	0	7.45	6.69

Chris Leroux

Pitches: R Bats: L Pos: RP-5   Ht: 6'6" Wt: 210 Born: 4/14/1984 Age: 26

			HOW MUCH HE PITCHED					WHAT HE GAVE UP										THE RESULTS								
Year	Team	Lg	G	GS	CG	GF	IP	BFP	H	R	ER	HR	SH	SF	HB	TBB	IBB	SO	WP	Bk	W	L	Pct	Sh	Sv-Op	Hld	ERC	ERA
2006	Grnsbr	A	3	3	0	0	10.1	50	13	7	7	2	2	0	2	6	0	9	0	0	0	3	.000	0	0- -	-	8.18	6.10
2006	Mrlns	R	4	4	0	0	11.0	45	10	9	5	0	2	0	2	1	0	9	2	0	0	0	-	0	0- -	-	2.48	4.09
2006	Jmstwn	A-	4	4	0	0	11.1	61	13	13	10	0	0	1	2	12	0	4	2	0	0	1	.000	0	0- -	-	7.30	7.94
2007	Grnsbr	A	46	0	0	8	71.2	316	72	38	33	6	3	3	5	29	3	76	4	1	2	3	.400	0	0- -	-	4.18	4.14
2008	Jupiter	A+	57	0	0	19	74.0	305	60	37	30	6	4	2	6	26	2	78	6	0	6	7	.462	0	1- -	-	3.05	3.65
2009	Jaxnvl	AA	46	0	0	11	60.0	250	59	19	18	0	2	1	1	17	1	55	2	0	5	3	.625	0	2- -	-	2.92	2.70
2009	Fla	NL	5	0	0	3	6.2	35	11	8	8	0	0	0	0	4	0	2	0	0	0	0	-	0	0-0	0	7.84	10.80

Jon Lester

Pitches: L Bats: L Pos: SP-32   Ht: 6'2" Wt: 190 Born: 1/7/1984 Age: 26

			HOW MUCH HE PITCHED					WHAT HE GAVE UP										THE RESULTS								
Year	Team	Lg	G	GS	CG	GF	IP	BFP	H	R	ER	HR	SH	SF	HB	TBB	IBB	SO	WP	Bk	W	L	Pct	Sh	Sv-Op	Hld	ERC	ERA
2006	Bos	AL	15	15	0	0	81.1	367	91	43	43	7	2	8	5	43	1	60	5	0	7	2	.778	0	0-0	0	5.52	4.76
2007	Bos	AL	12	11	0	0	63.0	275	61	33	32	10	1	5	1	31	0	50	1	0	4	0	1.000	0	0-0	0	4.78	4.57
2008	Bos	AL	33	33	2	0	210.1	874	202	78	75	14	6	3	10	66	1	152	3	1	16	6	.727	2	0-0	0	3.55	3.21
2009	Bos	AL	32	32	2	0	203.1	843	186	80	77	20	2	6	3	64	0	225	6	0	15	8	.652	0	0-0	0	3.35	3.41
	Postseason		7	5	0	2	36.0	147	30	11	9	4	0	0	0	9	0	34	0	0	2	2	.500	0	0-0	0	2.64	2.25
	4 ML YEARS		92	91	4	0	558.0	2359	540	234	227	51	11	22	19	204	2	487	15	1	42	16	.724	2	0-0	0	3.88	3.66

Colby Lewis

Pitches: R Bats: R Pos: P   Ht: 6'4" Wt: 230 Born: 8/2/1979 Age: 30

			HOW MUCH HE PITCHED					WHAT HE GAVE UP										THE RESULTS								
Year	Team	Lg	G	GS	CG	GF	IP	BFP	H	R	ER	HR	SH	SF	HB	TBB	IBB	SO	WP	Bk	W	L	Pct	Sh	Sv-Op	Hld	ERC	ERA
2009	Hrshm*	Jap	29	28	3	0	176.1	715	156	68	58	13	-	-	14	19	0	186	3	0	11	9	550	1	0- -	-	2.47	2.96
2002	Tex	AL	15	4	0	4	34.1	168	42	26	24	4	2	0	2	26	2	28	3	1	1	3	.250	0	0-2	1	7.22	6.29
2003	Tex	AL	26	26	0	0	127.0	594	163	104	103	23	2	2	5	70	1	88	5	0	10	9	.526	0	0-0	0	7.38	7.30
2004	Tex	AL	3	3	0	0	15.1	71	13	7	7	1	0	0	0	13	0	11	0	0	1	1	.500	0	0-0	0	4.98	4.11
2006	Det	AL	2	0	0	1	3.0	18	8	1	1	1	0	0	0	1	0	5	0	0	0	0	-	0	0-0	0	17.35	3.00
2007	Oak	AL	26	1	0	8	37.2	170	44	28	27	7	1	2	3	14	3	23	1	1	0	2	.000	0	0-1	3	5.79	6.45
	5 ML YEARS		72	34	0	13	217.1	1021	270	166	162	36	5	4	11	124	6	155	9	2	12	15	.444	0	0-3	4	7.03	6.71

Fred Lewis

Bats: L Throws: R Pos: LF-83; PH-43; PR-4; DH-1   Ht: 6'2" Wt: 198 Born: 12/9/1980 Age: 29

			BATTING																	BASERUNNING				AVERAGES		
Year	Team	Lg	G	AB	H	2B	3B	HR	(Hm	Rd)	TB	R	RBI	RC	TBB	IBB	SO	HBP	SH	SF	SB	CS	SB%	GDP	Avg	OBP	Slg
2006	SF	NL	13	11	5	1	0	0	(0	0)	6	5	2	4	0	0	3	0	0	0	0	0		0	.455	.455	.545
2007	SF	NL	58	157	45	6	2	3	(0	3)	64	34	19	27	19	0	32	3	1	0	5	1	.83	4	.287	.374	.408
2008	SF	NL	133	468	132	25	11	9	(4	5)	206	81	40	67	51	3	124	0	0	2	21	7	.75	5	.282	.351	.440
2009	SF	NL	122	295	76	21	3	4	(2	2)	115	49	20	37	36	3	84	5	0	0	8	4	.67	4	.258	.348	.390
	4 ML YEARS		326	931	258	53	16	16	(6	10)	391	169	81	135	106	6	243	8	1	2	34	12	.74	13	.277	.355	.420

Jensen Lewis

Pitches: R Bats: R Pos: RP-47 Ht: 6'3" Wt: 210 Born: 5/16/1984 Age: 26

Year	Team	Lg	G	GS	CG	GF	IP	BFP	H	R	ER	HR	SH	SF	HB	TBB	IBB	SO	WP	Bk	W	L	Pct	Sh	Sv-Op	Hld	ERC	ERA
2009	Clmbs*	AAA	12	0	0	4	18.2	73	13	0	0	0	0	0	1	7	0	28	0	0	1	0	1.000	0	0- -	-	2.08	0.00
2007	Cle	AL	26	0	0	5	29.1	125	26	8	7	1	2	1	1	10	1	34	1	0	1	1	.500	0	0-0	5	2.81	2.15
2008	Cle	AL	51	0	0	28	66.0	292	68	29	28	8	2	2	5	27	3	52	0	0	4	4	.000	0	13-14	4	4.66	3.82
2009	Cle	AL	47	0	0	15	66.1	285	62	37	34	13	3	2	2	29	3	62	2	1	2	4	.333	0	1-5	4	4.61	4.61
	Postseason		7	0	0	1	7.2	27	6	4	4	2	0	0	0	0	0	7	0	0	0	0	-	0	0-0	1	2.46	4.70
	3 ML YEARS		124	0	0	48	161.2	702	156	74	69	22	7	5	8	66	7	148	3	1	3	9	.250	0	14-19	13	4.28	3.84

Scott Lewis

Pitches: L Bats: B Pos: SP-1 Ht: 6'0" Wt: 185 Born: 9/26/1983 Age: 26

Year	Team	Lg	G	GS	CG	GF	IP	BFP	H	R	ER	HR	SH	SF	HB	TBB	IBB	SO	WP	Bk	W	L	Pct	Sh	Sv-Op	Hld	ERC	ERA
2004	MhVlly	A-	3	3	0	0	5.1	21	5	3	3	0	0	0	0	1	0	13	2	0	0	2	.000	0	0- -	-	2.40	5.06
2005	MhVlly	A-	7	6	0	0	15.2	66	13	8	8	2	0	0	2	6	0	24	3	0	0	1	.000	0	0- -	-	3.81	4.60
2006	Knstn	A+	27	26	0	0	115.2	445	84	24	19	3	3	0	0	28	0	123	4	0	3	3	.500	0	0- -	-	1.73	1.48
2007	Akron	AA	27	25	0	0	134.2	556	135	63	55	13	2	2	3	34	0	121	4	0	7	9	.438	0	0- -	-	3.64	3.68
2008	Akron	AA	13	13	0	0	73.1	288	62	22	19	2	1	0	1	9	0	61	2	0	6	2	.750	0	0- -	-	1.89	2.33
2008	Buffalo	AAA	4	4	1	0	24.0	93	19	8	7	2	0	3	0	4	0	21	0	0	2	2	.500	0	0- -	-	2.07	2.63
2009	Lk Cty	A	1	1	0	0	3.0	9	0	0	0	0	0	0	0	0	0	3	0	0	0	0	-	0	0- -	-	0.00	0.00
2009	Akron	AA	2	2	0	0	7.2	30	3	1	1	0	0	0	0	3	0	6	0	0	0	0	-	0	0- -	-	0.89	1.17
2009	Indns	R	2	2	0	0	7.0	26	4	3	1	1	0	0	0	0	0	11	0	0	0	0	-	0	0- -	-	1.03	1.29
2009	Knstn	A+	1	1	0	0	3.2	14	2	1	1	0	0	0	0	1	0	0	0	0	0	0	-	0	0- -	-	1.10	2.45
2009	Clmbs	AAA	1	1	0	0	2.0	11	5	4	4	1	0	0	0	1	0	2	0	1	0	0	.000	0	0- -	-	20.52	18.00
2008	Cle	AL	4	4	0	0	24.0	97	20	9	7	4	1	0	0	6	0	15	1	0	4	0	1.000	0	0-0	0	3.01	2.63
2009	Cle	AL	1	1	0	0	4.1	20	7	4	4	2	0	0	0	1	0	3	0	0	0	0	-	0	0-0	0	10.46	8.31
	2 ML YEARS		5	5	0	0	28.1	117	27	13	11	6	1	0	0	7	0	18	1	0	4	0	1.000	0	0-0	0	3.94	3.49

Brad Lidge

Pitches: R Bats: R Pos: RP-67 Ht: 6'5" Wt: 215 Born: 12/23/1976 Age: 33

Year	Team	Lg	G	GS	CG	GF	IP	BFP	H	R	ER	HR	SH	SF	HB	TBB	IBB	SO	WP	Bk	W	L	Pct	Sh	Sv-Op	Hld	ERC	ERA
2009	Rdng*	AA	1	1	0	0	1.0	4	1	0	0	0	0	0	0	0	0	2	0	0	0	0	-	0	0- -	-	1.95	0.00
2002	Hou	NL	6	1	0	2	8.2	48	12	6	6	0	1	0	2	9	1	12	0	0	1	0	1.000	0	0-0	0	8.90	6.23
2003	Hou	NL	78	0	0	9	85.0	349	60	36	34	6	2	3	5	42	7	97	4	1	6	3	.667	0	1-6	28	2.82	3.60
2004	Hou	NL	80	0	0	44	94.2	369	57	21	20	8	3	2	6	30	5	157	3	1	6	5	.545	0	29-33	17	1.85	1.90
2005	Hou	NL	70	0	0	65	70.2	291	58	21	18	5	4	1	3	23	1	103	8	0	4	4	.500	0	42-46	6	2.79	2.29
2006	Hou	NL	78	0	0	52	75.0	340	69	44	47	10	6	2	6	36	4	104	11	0	1	5	.167	0	32-38	6	4.25	5.28
2007	Hou	NL	66	0	0	34	67.0	287	54	29	25	9	5	1	4	30	4	88	6	0	5	3	.625	0	19-27	7	3.52	3.36
2008	Phi	NL	72	0	0	61	69.1	292	50	17	15	2	2	1	1	35	4	92	5	0	2	0	1.000	0	41-41	6	2.45	1.95
2009	Phi	NL	67	0	0	55	58.2	283	72	51	47	11	4	1	5	34	3	61	4	0	0	8	.000	0	31-42	1	7.11	7.21
	Postseason		26	0	0	21	34.1	137	23	8	8	2	2	0	1	12	0	51	2	0	1	3	.250	0	13-15	0	2.05	2.10
	8 ML YEARS		517	1	0	322	529.0	2259	432	228	209	51	27	11	32	239	29	714	41	2	25	28	.472	0	195-233	59	3.37	3.56

Brent Lillibridge

Bats: R Throws: R Pos: 2B-23; CF-12; SS-7; PR-6; PH-5; 3B-1; DH-1 Ht: 5'11" Wt: 190 Born: 9/18/1983 Age: 26

Year	Team	Lg	G	AB	H	2B	3B	HR	(Hm	Rd)	TB	R	RBI	RC	TBB	IBB	SO	HBP	SH	SF	SB	CS	SB%	GDP	Avg	OBP	Slg
2005	Wmspt	A-	42	169	41	12	4	4	(-	-)	73	19	18	24	14	0	35	2	4	2	10	3	.77	4	.243	.305	.432
2006	Hkry	A	74	274	82	18	5	11	(-	-)	143	59	43	63	51	0	61	4	2	2	29	8	.78	4	.299	.414	.522
2006	Lynbrg	A+	54	201	63	10	3	2	(-	-)	85	47	28	42	36	0	43	5	8	2	24	5	.83	4	.313	.426	.423
2007	Missi	AA	52	204	56	8	3	3	(-	-)	79	31	17	30	20	0	60	6	6	1	14	7	.67	1	.275	.355	.387
2007	Rchmd	AAA	87	321	92	14	2	10	(-	-)	140	47	41	51	20	0	59	3	8	3	28	5	.85	2	.287	.331	.436
2008	Rchmd	AAA	90	355	78	18	7	4	(-	-)	122	46	39	40	33	0	90	6	5	4	24	7	.77	6	.220	.294	.344
2009	Charltt	AAA	67	246	62	9	4	3	(-	-)	88	34	24	35	29	0	57	4	3	1	17	1	.94	5	.252	.339	.358
2008	Atl	NL	29	80	16	6	1	1	(0	1)	27	9	8	6	3	0	23	1	1	0	2	0	1.00	0	.200	.238	.338
2009	CWS	AL	46	95	15	2	0	0	(0	0)	17	9	3	5	14	0	26	1	2	0	6	3	.67	2	.158	.273	.179
	2 ML YEARS		75	175	31	8	1	1	(0	1)	44	18	11	11	17	0	49	2	3	0	8	3	.73	2	.177	.258	.251

Ted Lilly

Pitches: L Bats: L Pos: SP-27 Ht: 6'1" Wt: 190 Born: 1/4/1976 Age: 34

Year	Team	Lg	G	GS	CG	GF	IP	BFP	H	R	ER	HR	SH	SF	HB	TBB	IBB	SO	WP	Bk	W	L	Pct	Sh	Sv-Op	Hld	ERC	ERA
2009	Peoria*	A	1	1	0	0	5.0	17	2	0	0	0	0	0	0	1	0	2	0	0	1	0	1.000	0	0- -	-	0.67	0.00
1999	Mon	NL	9	3	0	1	23.2	110	30	20	20	7	0	1	3	9	0	28	1	0	0	1	.000	0	0-0	0	7.76	7.61
2000	NYY	AL	7	0	0	1	8.0	39	8	6	5	1	0	0	1	5	0	11	1	1	0	0	-	0	0-0	0	4.76	5.63
2001	NYY	AL	26	21	0	2	120.2	537	126	81	72	20	2	5	7	51	1	112	9	2	5	6	.455	0	0-0	0	5.10	5.37
2002	2 Tms	AL	22	16	2	1	100.0	413	80	43	41	15	0	3	6	31	3	77	6	1	5	7	.417	1	0-0	0	3.14	3.69
2003	Oak	AL	32	31	0	0	178.1	773	179	92	86	24	3	4	5	58	3	147	5	4	12	10	.545	0	0-0	0	4.06	4.34
2004	Tor	AL	32	32	2	0	197.1	845	171	92	89	26	3	3	6	89	2	168	6	4	12	10	.545	1	0-0	0	3.84	4.06
2005	Tor	AL	25	25	0	0	126.1	566	135	79	78	23	3	5	3	58	1	96	2	2	10	11	.476	0	0-0	0	5.38	5.56
2006	Tor	AL	32	32	0	0	181.2	797	179	98	87	28	4	2	4	81	6	160	7	4	15	13	.536	0	0-0	0	4.57	4.31
2007	ChC	NL	34	34	0	0	207.0	847	181	91	88	28	11	9	3	55	2	174	7	0	15	8	.652	0	0-0	0	3.14	3.83
2008	ChC	NL	34	**34**	0	0	204.2	861	187	96	93	32	5	3	7	64	2	184	4	4	17	9	.654	0	0-0	0	3.73	4.09
2009	ChC	NL	27	27	0	0	177.0	706	151	66	61	22	9	3	2	36	2	151	3	3	12	9	.571	0	0-0	0	2.74	3.10

Year Team	Lg	G	GS	CG	GF	IP	BFP	H	R	ER	HR	SH	SF	HB	TBB	IBB	SO	WP	Bk	W	L	Pct	Sh	Sv-Op	Hld	ERC	ERA
02 NYY	AL	16	11	2	1	76.2	314	57	31	29	10	0	3	5	24	3	59	6	0	3	6	.333	1	0-0	0	2.74	3.40
02 Oak	AL	6	5	0	0	23.1	99	23	12	12	5	0	0	1	7	0	18	0	1	2	1	.667	0	0-0	0	4.56	4.63
Postseason		5	2	0	0	16.1	76	19	13	12	2	1	0	1	7	0	14	1	0	0	2	.000	0	0-1	0	5.43	6.61
11 ML YEARS		280	255	4	5	1524.2	6494	1427	764	720	226	40	38	46	537	22	1308	51	25	103	84	.551	2	0-0	0	3.93	4.25

Tim Lincecum

Pitches: R **Bats:** L **Pos:** SP-32

Ht: 5'11" **Wt:** 170 **Born:** 6/15/1984 **Age:** 26

Year Team	Lg	G	GS	CG	GF	IP	BFP	H	R	ER	HR	SH	SF	HB	TBB	IBB	SO	WP	Bk	W	L	Pct	Sh	Sv-Op	Hld	ERC	ERA
2007 SF	NL	24	24	0	0	146.1	618	122	70	65	12	5	7	2	65	5	150	10	0	7	5	.583	1	0-0	0	3.21	4.00
2008 SF	NL	34	33	2	0	227.0	928	182	72	66	11	11	3	6	84	1	265	17	2	18	5	.783	1	0-0	0	2.60	2.62
2009 SF	NL	32	32	4	0	225.1	905	168	69	62	10	12	5	6	68	2	261	11	0	15	7	.682	2	0-0	0	2.14	2.48
3 ML YEARS		90	89	6	0	598.2	2451	472	211	193	33	28	15	14	217	8	676	38	2	40	17	.702	3	0-0	0	2.60	2.90

Mike Lincoln

Pitches: R **Bats:** R **Pos:** RP-19

Ht: 6'2" **Wt:** 218 **Born:** 4/10/1975 **Age:** 35

Year Team	Lg	G	GS	CG	GF	IP	BFP	H	R	ER	HR	SH	SF	HB	TBB	IBB	SO	WP	Bk	W	L	Pct	Sh	Sv-Op	Hld	ERC	ERA
1999 Min	AL	18	15	0	0	76.1	353	102	59	58	11	2	6	1	26	0	27	4	0	3	10	.231	0	0-0	1	6.16	6.84
2000 Min	AL	8	4	0	1	20.2	109	36	25	25	10	0	0	2	13	0	15	1	0	0	3	.000	0	0-0	0	14.32	10.89
2001 Pit	NL	31	0	0	5	40.1	168	34	16	12	3	1	1	4	11	0	24	2	0	2	1	.667	0	0-2	7	2.94	2.68
2002 Pit	NL	55	0	0	9	72.1	309	80	28	25	7	2	4	0	27	8	50	2	0	2	4	.333	0	0-3	11	4.49	3.11
2003 Pit	NL	36	0	0	14	36.1	153	38	22	21	5	1	1	1	13	0	28	1	0	3	4	.429	0	5-8	5	4.70	5.20
2004 StL	NL	13	0	0	1	17.1	71	10	12	10	1	1	2	1	6	0	14	0	0	3	2	.600	0	0-2	1	1.63	5.19
2008 Cin	NL	64	0	0	12	70.1	297	66	37	35	10	3	3	3	24	1	57	3	0	2	5	.286	0	0-1	10	3.98	4.48
2009 Cin	NL	19	0	0	8	23.0	115	29	21	21	7	2	0	4	19	2	9	1	0	1	1	.500	0	0-0	1	10.28	8.22
8 ML YEARS		244	19	0	50	356.2	1575	395	220	207	54	13	17	16	139	11	224	14	0	16	30	.348	0	5-16	36	5.20	5.22

Adam Lind

Bats: L **Throws:** L **Pos:** DH-95; LF-55; PH-4

Ht: 6'1" **Wt:** 215 **Born:** 7/17/1983 **Age:** 26

							BATTING												BASERUNNING				AVERAGES		
Year Team	Lg	G	AB	H	2B	3B	HR	(Hm Rd)	TB	R	RBI	RC	TBB	IBB	SO	HBP	SH	SF	SB	CS	SB%	GDP	Avg	OBP	Slg
2006 Tor	AL	18	60	22	8	0	2	(0 2)	36	8	8	13	5	0	12	0	0	0	0	0	-	0	.367	.415	.600
2007 Tor	AL	89	290	69	14	0	11	(10 1)	116	34	46	38	16	0	65	1	2	2	1	2	.33	7	.238	.278	.400
2008 Tor	AL	88	326	92	16	4	9	(2 7)	143	48	40	39	16	3	59	2	1	4	2	0	1.00	6	.282	.316	.439
2009 Tor	Al	151	587	179	46	0	35	(14 21)	330	93	114	114	58	7	110	5	0	4	1	1	.50	15	.305	.370	.562
4 ML YEARS		346	1263	362	84	4	57	(26 31)	625	183	208	204	95	10	246	8	3	10	4	3	.57	30	.287	.338	.495

Matt Lindstrom

Pitches: R **Bats:** R **Pos:** RP-54

Ht: 6'3" **Wt:** 218 **Born:** 2/11/1980 **Age:** 30

Year Team	Lg	G	GS	CG	GF	IP	BFP	H	R	ER	HR	SH	SF	HB	TBB	IBB	SO	WP	Bk	W	L	Pct	Sh	Sv-Op	Hld	ERC	ERA
2009 Jupiter*	A+	2	2	0	0	2.0	6	1	0	0	0	0	0	0	0	0	1	0	0	0	0	-	0	0--	-	0.63	0.00
2009 Jaxnvl*	AA	2	2	0	0	2.0	8	2	2	2	1	0	0	0	0	0	3	0	0	0	1	.000	0	0--	-	4.70	9.00
2007 Fla	NL	71	0	0	11	67.0	284	66	27	23	2	3	1	3	21	4	62	5	0	3	4	.429	0	0-2	19	3.26	3.09
2008 Fla	NL	66	0	0	27	57.1	245	57	21	20	1	6	1	1	26	4	43	4	0	3	3	.500	0	5-6	14	3.69	3.14
2009 Fla	NL	54	0	0	32	47.1	219	54	35	31	5	1	0	2	24	2	39	0	1	2	1	.667	0	15-17	8	5.41	5.89
3 ML YEARS		191	0	0	70	171.2	748	177	83	74	8	10	2	6	71	10	144	9	1	8	8	.500	0	20-25	41	3.98	3.88

Scott Linebrink

Pitches: R **Bats:** R **Pos:** RP-57

Ht: 6'2" **Wt:** 210 **Born:** 8/4/1976 **Age:** 33

Year Team	Lg	G	GS	CG	GF	IP	BFP	H	R	ER	HR	SH	SF	HB	TBB	IBB	SO	WP	Bk	W	L	Pct	Sh	Sv-Op	Hld	ERC	ERA
2000 2 Tms	NL	11	0	0	4	12.0	63	18	8	8	4	0	0	3	8	0	6	0	0	0	0	-	0	0-0	0	11.88	6.00
2001 Hou	NL	9	0	0	2	10.1	44	6	4	3	0	1	1	2	6	0	9	1	0	0	0	-	0	0-0	1	2.54	2.61
2002 Hou	NL	22	0	0	4	24.1	120	31	21	19	2	0	2	1	13	4	24	0	0	0	0	-	0	0-0	1	5.70	7.03
2003 2 Tms	NL	52	6	0	8	92.1	397	93	37	34	9	4	6	6	36	4	68	11	0	3	2	.600	0	0-0	6	4.32	3.31
2004 SD	NL	73	0	0	7	84.0	326	61	22	20	8	2	3	3	26	2	83	3	0	7	3	.700	0	0-5	28	2.48	2.14
2005 SD	NL	73	0	0	17	73.2	288	55	17	15	4	2	0	0	23	4	70	3	0	8	1	.889	0	1-6	26	2.15	1.83
2006 SD	NL	73	0	0	11	75.2	314	70	31	30	9	1	2	2	22	3	68	2	0	7	4	.636	0	2-11	36	3.36	3.57
2007 2 Tms	NL	71	0	0	11	70.1	295	68	33	29	12	0	0	1	25	3	50	6	0	5	6	.455	0	1-8	21	4.26	3.71
2008 CWS	AL	50	0	0	13	46.1	186	41	20	19	8	2	0	0	9	1	40	3	0	2	2	.500	0	1-4	19	3.09	3.69
2009 CWS	AL	57	0	0	24	56.0	259	70	34	29	9	0	3	3	23	6	55	5	0	3	7	.300	0	2-4	7	6.07	4.66
00 SF	NL	3	0	0	1	2.1	16	7	3	3	1	0	0	0	2	0	0	0	0	0	0	-	0	0-0	0	24.13	11.57
00 SD	NL	8	0	0	3	9.2	47	11	5	5	3	0	0	3	6	0	6	0	0	0	0	-	0	0-0	0	9.21	4.66
03 Hou	NL	9	6	0	2	31.2	140	38	15	15	4	2	1	3	14	1	17	5	0	1	1	.500	0	0-0	0	6.27	4.26
03 SD	NL	43	0	0	6	60.2	257	55	22	19	5	2	5	3	22	3	51	6	0	2	1	.667	0	0-0	6	3.41	2.82
07 Hou	NL	44	0	0	7	45.0	186	41	19	19	9	0	0	1	14	1	25	4	0	3	3	.500	0	1-7	15	3.99	3.80
07 Mil	NL	27	0	0	4	25.1	109	27	14	10	3	0	0	0	11	2	25	2	0	2	3	.400	0	0-1	6	4.71	3.55
Postseason		4	0	0	3	3.1	15	4	1	1	1	0	0	0	2	1	2	0	0	0	0	-	0	0-0	1	7.51	2.70
10 ML YEARS		491	6	0	101	545.0	2292	513	227	206	65	12	17	20	191	27	473	34	0	35	25	.583	0	7-38	144	3.79	3.40

Francisco Liriano

Pitches: L **Bats:** L **Pos:** SP-24; RP-5   **Ht:** 6'2" **Wt:** 225 **Born:** 10/26/1983 **Age:** 26

Year	Team	Lg	HOW MUCH HE PITCHED						WHAT HE GAVE UP													THE RESULTS							
			G	GS	CG	GF	IP	BFP	H	R	ER	HR	SH	SF	HB	TBB	IBB	SO	WP	Bk	W	L	Pct	Sh	Sv-Op	Hld	ERC	ERA
2005	Min	AL	6	4	0	2	23.2	93	19	15	15	4	0	0	0	7	0	33	0	0	1	2	.333	0	0-0	0	3.15	5.70
2006	Min	AL	28	16	0	2	121.0	473	89	31	29	9	4	2	1	32	0	144	9	1	12	3	.800	0	1-1	1	2.12	2.16
2008	Min	AL	14	14	0	0	76.0	329	74	40	33	7	2	3	1	32	1	67	3	0	6	4	.600	0	0-0	0	3.97	3.91
2009	Min	AL	29	24	0	2	136.2	609	147	93	88	21	5	6	6	65	0	122	5	1	5	13	.278	0	0-0	0	5.46	5.80
4 ML YEARS			77	58	0	6	357.1	1504	329	179	165	41	11	11	8	136	1	366	17	2	24	22	.522	0	1-1	1	3.78	4.16

Jesse Litsch

Pitches: R **Bats:** R **Pos:** SP-2   **Ht:** 6'1" **Wt:** 215 **Born:** 3/9/1985 **Age:** 25

Year	Team	Lg	HOW MUCH HE PITCHED						WHAT HE GAVE UP													THE RESULTS							
			G	GS	CG	GF	IP	BFP	H	R	ER	HR	SH	SF	HB	TBB	IBB	SO	WP	Bk	W	L	Pct	Sh	Sv-Op	Hld	ERC	ERA
2007	Tor	AL	20	20	0	0	111.0	478	116	56	47	14	3	3	7	36	2	50	2	0	7	9	.438	0	0-0	0	4.48	3.81
2008	Tor	AL	29	28	2	0	176.0	735	178	79	70	20	1	4	8	39	2	99	4	0	13	9	.591	2	0-0	0	3.71	3.58
2009	Tor	AL	2	2	0	0	9.0	42	14	9	9	4	0	0	1	1	0	8	0	0	0	1	.000	0	0-0	0	9.55	9.00
3 ML YEARS			51	50	2	0	296.0	1255	308	144	126	38	4	7	16	76	4	157	6	0	20	19	.513	2	0-0	0	4.15	3.83

Radhames Liz

Pitches: R **Bats:** R **Pos:** RP-2   **Ht:** 6'2" **Wt:** 185 **Born:** 10/6/1983 **Age:** 26

Year	Team	Lg	HOW MUCH HE PITCHED						WHAT HE GAVE UP													THE RESULTS							
			G	GS	CG	GF	IP	BFP	H	R	ER	HR	SH	SF	HB	TBB	IBB	SO	WP	Bk	W	L	Pct	Sh	Sv-Op	Hld	ERC	ERA
2009	Norfolk*	AAA	17	6	0	3	44.1	201	56	31	28	2	2	4	5	12	0	37	1	0	0	3	.000	0	0--	-	5.11	5.68
2009	Bowie*	AA	8	8	0	0	48.0	200	46	18	14	1	1	3	2	14	0	39	3	0	4	1	.800	0	0--	-	3.09	2.63
2007	Bal	AL	9	4	0	5	24.2	122	25	21	19	3	1	1	1	23	1	24	3	0	0	2	.000	0	0-0	0	6.49	6.93
2008	Bal	AL	17	17	0	0	84.1	393	99	67	63	16	1	3	3	51	3	57	6	0	6	6	.500	0	0-0	0	6.84	6.72
2009	Bal	AL	2	0	0	0	1.1	16	8	10	10	1	0	0	2	2	0	1	0	0	0	0	-	0	0-0	0	68.38	67.50
3 ML YEARS			28	21	0	5	110.1	531	132	98	92	20	2	4	6	76	4	82	9	0	6	8	.429	0	0-0	0	7.33	7.50

Jose Lobaton

Bats: B **Throws:** R **Pos:** C-6; 2B-1   **Ht:** 6'0" **Wt:** 193 **Born:** 10/21/1984 **Age:** 25

Year	Team	Lg	BATTING																			BASERUNNING				AVERAGES		
			G	AB	H	2B	3B	HR	(Hm	Rd)	TB	R	RBI	RC	TBB	IBB	SO	HBP	SH	SF	SB	CS	SB%	GDP	Avg	OBP	Slg
2003	Idaho	R+	56	191	52	15	0	1	(-	-)	70	22	32	26	22	2	50	2	1	1	0	1	.00	4	.272	.352	.366
2004	Eugene	A-	44	151	33	12	0	7	(-	-)	66	13	23	20	17	0	35	0	1	0	0	0	-	3	.219	.298	.437
2005	Padres	R	5	14	5	2	0	0	(-	-)	7	2	2	4	6	0	4	0	0	0	1	0	1.00	0	.357	.550	.500
2005	FtWyn	A	9	34	6	1	0	0	(-	-)	7	2	1	1	2	0	5	0	1	0	0	0	-	2	.176	.222	.206
2005	Eugene	A-	11	32	9	2	0	0	(-	-)	11	4	3	5	6	0	8	1	3	0	0	0	-	2	.281	.410	.344
2006	Lk Els	A+	42	122	26	7	0	4	(-	-)	45	12	15	15	20	0	42	1	1	1	0	2	.00	3	.213	.326	.369
2006	FtWyn	A	20	61	17	3	1	1	(-	-)	25	15	11	11	12	0	12	2	1	1	0	0	-	2	.279	.408	.410
2007	Lk Els	A+	90	304	79	15	3	10	(-	-)	130	50	47	48	41	1	79	3	2	7	0	0	-	4	.260	.346	.428
2008	SnAnt	AA	92	294	76	21	0	9	(-	-)	124	35	45	45	39	1	75	0	2	7	1	1	.50	8	.259	.338	.422
2009	Portlnd	AAA	39	133	32	6	0	3	(-	-)	47	14	8	14	10	0	35	0	4	1	0	0	-	0	.241	.292	.353
2009	Mont	AA	26	84	22	7	0	3	(-	-)	38	13	11	15	15	1	19	1	1	1	0	0	-	2	.262	.376	.452
2009	SD	NL	7	17	3	0	0	0	(0	0)	3	0	0	0	0	0	5	0	0	0	0	0	-	1	.176	.176	.176

Kameron Loe

Pitches: R **Bats:** R **Pos:** P   **Ht:** 6'8" **Wt:** 240 **Born:** 9/10/1981 **Age:** 28

Year	Team	Lg	HOW MUCH HE PITCHED						WHAT HE GAVE UP													THE RESULTS							
			G	GS	CG	GF	IP	BFP	H	R	ER	HR	SH	SF	HB	TBB	IBB	SO	WP	Bk	W	L	Pct	Sh	Sv-Op	Hld	ERC	ERA
2009	Fk Dai*	Jap	5	5	0	0	27.0	133	36	26	19	2	-	-	2	12	1	18	0	1	0	4	.000	0	0--	-	6.00	6.33
2004	Tex	AL	2	1	0	0	6.2	29	6	5	4	0	0	0	1	6	0	3	0	0	0	0	-	0	0-0	0	5.87	5.40
2005	Tex	AL	48	8	0	13	92.0	392	89	43	35	7	5	1	2	31	6	45	2	0	9	6	.600	0	1-4	4	3.45	3.42
2006	Tex	AL	15	15	1	0	78.1	358	105	54	51	10	1	3	1	22	0	34	3	0	3	6	.333	1	0-0	0	5.79	5.86
2007	Tex	AL	28	23	0	0	136.0	615	162	96	81	13	1	5	4	56	6	78	6	0	6	11	.353	0	0-0	0	5.24	5.36
2008	Tex	AL	14	0	0	4	30.2	134	36	18	11	3	0	1	0	8	1	20	0	0	1	0	1.000	0	0-1	2	4.40	3.23
5 ML YEARS			107	47	1	17	343.2	1528	398	216	182	33	7	10	8	123	13	180	11	0	19	23	.452	1	1-5	6	4.80	4.77

Boone Logan

Pitches: L **Bats:** R **Pos:** RP-20   **Ht:** 6'5" **Wt:** 215 **Born:** 8/13/1984 **Age:** 25

Year	Team	Lg	HOW MUCH HE PITCHED						WHAT HE GAVE UP													THE RESULTS							
			G	GS	CG	GF	IP	BFP	H	R	ER	HR	SH	SF	HB	TBB	IBB	SO	WP	Bk	W	L	Pct	Sh	Sv-Op	Hld	ERC	ERA
2009	Gwnntt*	AAA	29	0	0	10	35.2	152	26	15	13	2	1	1	6	17	2	39	4	0	4	2	.667	0	2--	-	3.16	3.28
2006	CWS	AL	21	0	0	4	17.1	93	21	18	16	2	1	1	3	15	2	15	1	0	0	0	-	0	1-2	2	7.56	8.31
2007	CWS	AL	68	0	0	13	50.2	226	59	30	28	7	2	6	0	20	3	35	2	0	2	1	.667	0	0-2	11	5.18	4.97
2008	CWS	AL	55	0	0	12	42.1	197	57	31	28	7	2	0	1	14	3	42	1	0	2	3	.400	0	0-1	3	6.24	5.95
2009	Atl	NL	20	0	0	7	17.1	82	21	12	10	1	0	0	1	9	3	10	0	0	1	1	.500	0	0-0	1	5.29	5.19
4 ML YEARS			164	0	0	36	127.2	598	158	91	82	17	5	7	5	58	11	102	4	0	5	5	.500	0	1-5	17	5.88	5.78

Kyle Lohse

Pitches: R **Bats:** R **Pos:** SP-22; RP-1   **Ht:** 6'2" **Wt:** 210 **Born:** 10/4/1978 **Age:** 31

Year	Team	Lg					**HOW MUCH HE PITCHED**							**WHAT HE GAVE UP**								**THE RESULTS**						
			G	GS	CG	GF	IP	BFP	H	R	ER	HR	SH	SF	HB	TBB	IBB	SO	WP	Bk	W	L	Pct	Sh	Sv-Op	Hld	ERC	ERA
2009	Sprgfld*	AA	1	1	0	0	4.2	21	3	2	2	1	0	0	0	4	0	3	0	0	0	0	-	0	0- -	-	4.60	3.86
2009	Memp*	AAA	1	1	0	0	6.0	23	2	0	0	0	0	0	1	2	0	6	0	0	1	0	1.000	0	0- -	-	0.96	0.00
2001	Min	AL	19	16	0	2	90.1	402	102	60	57	16	1	5	8	29	0	64	5	0	4	7	.364	0	0-0	0	5.43	5.68
2002	Min	AL	32	31	1	0	180.2	783	181	92	85	26	3	3	9	70	2	124	8	0	13	8	.619	1	0-1	0	4.55	4.23
2003	Min	AL	33	33	2	0	201.0	850	211	107	103	28	8	5	5	45	1	130	10	1	14	11	.560	1	0-0	0	4.00	4.61
2004	Min	AL	35	34	1	1	194.0	883	240	128	115	28	5	7	7	76	5	111	6	0	9	13	.409	1	0-0	0	5.89	5.34
2005	Min	AL	31	30	0	1	178.2	769	211	85	83	22	3	7	9	44	5	86	4	1	9	13	.409	0	0-0	0	4.91	4.18
2006	2 Tms		34	19	0	6	126.2	567	150	83	82	15	8	5	6	44	4	97	3	1	5	10	.333	0	0-0	0	5.20	5.83
2007	2 Tms	NL	34	32	2	0	192.2	829	207	109	99	22	14	4	12	57	3	122	3	0	9	12	.429	1	0-0	0	4.45	4.02
2008	StL	NL	33	33	0	0	200.0	839	211	88	84	18	6	4	3	49	3	119	5	0	15	6	.714	0	0-0	0	3.77	3.78
2009	StL	NL	23	22	1	0	117.2	512	126	69	62	10	3	5	3	36	2	77	3	1	6	10	.375	1	0-0	0	4.33	4.74
06	Min	AL	22	8	0	5	63.2	295	80	50	50	8	1	3	6	25	2	46	1	1	2	5	.286	0	0-0	0	6.10	7.07
06	Cin	NL	12	11	0	1	63.0	272	70	33	32	7	7	2	0	19	2	51	2	0	3	5	.375	0	0-0	0	4.34	4.57
07	Cin	NL	21	21	2	0	131.2	561	143	76	67	16	8	4	6	33	1	80	3	0	6	12	.333	1	0-0	0	4.32	4.58
07	Phi	NL	13	11	0	0	61.0	268	64	33	32	6	6	0	6	24	2	42	0	0	3	0	1.000	0	0-0	0	4.71	4.72
	Postseason		6	1	0	3	13.1	52	10	5	5	2	0	0	0	2	0	15	1	0	0	2	.000	0	0-0	0	2.12	3.38
	9 ML YEARS		274	250	7	10	1481.2	6434	1638	821	770	191	51	45	62	450	25	930	47	4	84	90	.483	5	0-1	0	4.65	4.68

James Loney

Bats: L **Throws:** L **Pos:** 1B-155; PH-6   **Ht:** 6'3" **Wt:** 220 **Born:** 5/7/1984 **Age:** 26

Year	Team	Lg							**BATTING**												**BASERUNNING**				**AVERAGES**		
			G	AB	H	2B	3B	HR	(Hm	Rd)	TB	R	RBI	RC	TBB	IBB	SO	HBP	SH	SF	SB	CS	SB%	GDP	Avg	OBP	Slg
2006	LAD	NL	48	102	29	6	5	4	(1	3)	57	20	18	17	8	1	10	1	0	1	1	0	1.00	8	.284	.342	.559
2007	LAD	NL	96	344	114	18	4	15	(5	10)	185	41	67	71	28	5	40	1	0	2	0	1	.00	6	.331	.381	.538
2008	LAD	NL	161	595	172	35	6	13	(5	8)	258	66	90	79	45	6	85	3	1	7	7	4	.64	16	.289	.338	.434
2009	LAD	NL	158	576	162	25	2	13	(1	12)	230	73	90	84	70	10	68	0	1	4	7	3	.70	16	.281	.357	.399
	Postseason		9	34	13	3	0	1	(0	1)	19	2	11	8	4	1	7	0	0	0	0	0	-	1	.382	.447	.559
	4 ML YEARS		463	1617	477	84	17	45	(12	33)	730	200	265	251	151	22	211	5	2	13	15	8	.65	55	.295	.354	.451

Evan Longoria

Bats: R **Throws:** R **Pos:** 3B-151; DH-3; PH-3   **Ht:** 6'2" **Wt:** 210 **Born:** 10/7/1985 **Age:** 24

Year	Team	Lg							**BATTING**												**BASERUNNING**				**AVERAGES**		
			G	AB	H	2B	3B	HR	(Hm	Rd)	TB	R	RBI	RC	TBB	IBB	SO	HBP	SH	SF	SB	CS	SB%	GDP	Avg	OBP	Slg
2006	HudVal	A-	8	33	14	1	1	4	(-	-)	29	5	11	12	5	0	5	0	0	1	1	0	1.00	0	.424	.487	.879
2006	Visalia	A+	28	110	36	8	0	8	(-	-)	68	22	28	26	13	4	19	2	1	2	1	1	.50	2	.327	.402	.618
2006	Mont	AA	26	105	28	5	0	6	(-	-)	51	14	19	14	1	0	20	0	0	3	2	1	.67	1	.267	.266	.486
2007	Mont	AA	105	381	117	21	0	21	(-	-)	201	78	76	83	51	5	81	12	0	3	4	0	1.00	7	.307	.403	.528
2007	Drham	AAA	31	104	28	8	0	5	(-	-)	51	19	10	21	22	0	29	1	0	1	0	0	-	1	.269	.398	.490
2008	Drham	AAA	7	25	5	0	0	0	(-	-)	5	2	1	2	4	1	5	1	0	0	0	0	-	1	.200	.333	.200
2008	TB	AL	122	440	122	31	2	27	(18	9)	238	67	85	72	46	4	122	6	0	8	7	0	1.00	8	.272	.343	.531
2009	TB	AL	157	584	164	44	0	33	(16	17)	307	100	113	102	72	11	140	6	0	7	9	0	1.00	27	.281	.364	.526
	Postseason		16	62	12	3	0	6	(3	3)	33	10	13	6	5	0	20	0	0	0	1	0	1.00	3	.194	.254	.532
	2 ML YEARS		279	1032	286	75	2	60	(34	26)	545	167	198	174	118	15	262	14	0	15	16	0	1.00	35	.277	.355	.528

Braden Looper

Pitches: R **Bats:** R **Pos:** SP-34   **Ht:** 6'3" **Wt:** 235 **Born:** 10/28/1974 **Age:** 35

Year	Team	Lg					**HOW MUCH HE PITCHED**							**WHAT HE GAVE UP**								**THE RESULTS**						
			G	GS	CG	GF	IP	BFP	H	R	ER	HR	SH	SF	HB	TBB	IBB	SO	WP	Bk	W	L	Pct	Sh	Sv-Op	Hld	ERC	ERA
1998	StL	NL	4	0	0	3	3.1	16	5	4	2	1	0	1	0	1	0	4	1	0	0	1	.000	0	0-2	0	8.14	5.40
1999	Fla	NL	72	0	0	22	83.0	370	96	43	35	7	5	5	1	31	6	50	2	2	3	3	.500	0	0-4	8	4.65	3.80
2000	Fla	NL	73	0	0	23	67.1	311	71	41	33	3	3	2	5	36	6	29	5	0	5	1	.833	0	2-5	18	4.55	4.41
2001	Fla	NL	71	0	0	21	71.0	295	63	28	28	8	0	3	2	30	3	52	0	0	3	3	.500	0	3-6	16	3.77	3.55
2002	Fla	NL	78	0	0	40	86.0	349	73	31	30	8	3	0	1	28	3	55	1	0	2	5	.286	0	13-16	16	2.98	3.14
2003	Fla	NL	74	0	0	64	80.2	347	82	34	33	4	3	3	1	29	1	56	2	0	6	4	.600	0	28-34	0	3.67	3.68
2004	NYM	NL	71	0	0	60	83.1	346	86	28	25	5	2	2	3	16	3	60	1	0	2	5	.286	0	29-34	0	3.28	2.70
2005	NYM	NL	60	0	0	54	59.1	271	65	31	26	7	4	0	5	22	3	27	1	0	4	7	.364	0	28-36	0	4.75	3.94
2006	StL	NL	69	0	0	28	73.1	308	76	30	29	3	7	5	2	20	5	41	0	0	9	3	.750	0	0-2	15	3.41	3.56
2007	StL	NL	31	0	0	10	175.0	746	183	100	96	22	4	6	4	51	2	87	0	3	12	12	.500	0	0-0	0	4.16	4.94
2008	StL	NL	33	33	1	0	199.0	842	216	101	92	25	7	5	11	45	1	108	3	1	12	14	.462	1	0-0	0	4.31	4.16
2009	Mil	NL	34	34	0	0	194.2	866	226	123	113	39	9	7	5	64	6	100	5	0	14	7	.667	0	0-0	0	5.47	5.22
	Postseason		15	0	0	10	15.2	69	17	9	8	3	2	0	1	3	2	7	0	0	2	0	1.000	0	1-1	2	4.24	4.60
	12 ML YEARS		670	97	1	315	1176.0	5067	1242	594	542	132	47	39	40	373	39	669	21	6	72	65	.526	1	103-139	73	4.24	4.15

Arturo Lopez

Pitches: L **Bats:** L **Pos:** RP-4   **Ht:** 5'10" **Wt:** 165 **Born:** 2/22/1983 **Age:** 27

Year	Team	Lg					**HOW MUCH HE PITCHED**							**WHAT HE GAVE UP**								**THE RESULTS**						
			G	GS	CG	GF	IP	BFP	H	R	ER	HR	SH	SF	HB	TBB	IBB	SO	WP	Bk	W	L	Pct	Sh	Sv-Op	Hld	ERC	ERA
2001	Ddgrs	R	14	7	0	3	61.2	230	46	20	14	2	0	2	0	12	0	45	2	0	5	1	.833	0	1- -	-	1.76	2.04
2002	VeroB	A+	1	0	0	0	0.1	7	2	4	2	0	0	0	0	3	0	0	0	0	0	0	-	0	0- -	-	74.92	54.00
2002	Gr Falls	R+	15	15	0	0	76.1	325	79	44	31	5	1	2	4	21	0	72	2	0	7	3	.700	0	0- -	-	3.76	3.66
2003	VeroB	A+	11	0	0	5	16.2	61	11	8	8	0	0	0	0	3	0	16	1	0	1	1	.500	0	0- -	-	1.30	4.32
2003	SoGA	A	20	4	0	8	37.1	177	48	40	36	5	0	1	4	15	0	27	1	1	1	4	.200	0	0- -	-	6.42	8.68
2004	Clmbs	A	29	7	0	10	86.2	380	88	51	46	11	1	0	4	29	0	83	5	0	4	5	.556	0	0- -	-	4.19	4.78
2005	Lk Els	A+	27	27	0	0	140.0	641	174	108	91	18	4	3	8	49	0	94	7	1	5	11	.313	0	0- -	-	5.42	5.85

Year	Team	Lg	G	GS	CG	GF	IP	BFP	H	R	ER	HR	SH	SF	HB	TBB	IBB	SO	WP	Bk	W	L	Pct	Sh	Sv-Op Hld	ERC	ERA
2006	Mobile	AA	14	0	0	6	17.2	80	20	12	10	0	2	0	0	5	3	15	1	0	0	1	.000	0	0- -	3.17	5.09
2007	SnAnt	AA	30	1	0	10	35.2	154	34	19	18	3	4	1	1	18	1	28	1	0	2	2	.500	0	0- -	4.25	4.54
2008	PortInd	AAA	3	3	0	0	12.1	64	18	18	18	4	0	1	0	11	0	7	0	0	0	3	.000	0	0- -	11.36	13.14
2009	PortInd	AAA	20	0	0	1	31.0	134	27	14	13	0	2	1	1	13	1	23	1	0	0	0		0	0- -	2.77	3.77
2009	Buffalo	AAA	15	1	0	6	30.1	137	36	17	13	1	1	1	0	13	0	19	1	1	0	2	.000	0	0- -	4.74	3.86
2009	SD	NL	4	0	0	2	2.1	17	7	5	5	2	0	0	1	3	0	0	0	0	0	0	-	0	0-0 0	36.74	19.29

Felipe Lopez

Bats: B **Throws:** R **Pos:** 2B-144; PH-8; DH-1   **Ht:** 6'0" **Wt:** 203 **Born:** 5/12/1980 **Age:** 30

						BATTING																BASERUNNING				AVERAGES		
Year	Team	Lg	G	AB	H	2B	3B	HR	(Hm	Rd)	TB	R	RBI	RC	TBB	IBB	SO	HBP	SH	SF	SB	CS	SB%	GDP	Avg	OBP	Slg
2001	Tor	AL	49	177	46	5	4	5	(3	2)	74	21	23	22	12	1	39	0	1	2	4	3	.57	2	.260	.304	.418
2002	Tor	AL	85	282	64	15	3	8	(5	3)	109	35	34	32	23	1	90	1	2	1	5	4	.56	4	.227	.287	.387
2003	Cin	NL	59	197	42	7	2	2	(0	2)	59	28	13	21	28	1	59	1	2	1	8	5	.62	2	.213	.313	.299
2004	Cin	NL	79	264	64	18	2	7	(3	4)	107	35	31	34	25	0	81	3	2	1	1	1	.50	1	.242	.314	.405
2005	Cin	NL	148	580	169	34	5	23	(16	7)	282	97	85	95	57	2	111	1	3	7	15	7	.68	8	.291	.352	.486
2006	2 Tms	NL	156	617	169	27	3	11	(5	6)	235	98	52	84	81	1	126	2	11	3	44	12	.79	9	.274	.358	.381
2007	Was	NL	154	603	148	25	6	9	(2	7)	212	70	50	63	53	1	109	4	5	6	24	9	.73	11	.245	.308	.352
2008	2 Tms	NL	143	481	136	28	2	6	(2	4)	186	64	46	56	43	2	82	3	2	3	8	8	.50	13	.283	.343	.387
2009	2 Tms	NL	151	604	187	38	3	9	(8	1)	258	88	57	98	71	4	100	2	1	2	6	6	.50	5	.310	.383	.427
06	Cin	NL	85	343	92	14	1	9	(5	4)	135	55	30	48	47	1	66	0	3	1	23	6	.79	6	.268	.355	.394
06	Was	NL	71	274	77	13	2	2	(0	2)	100	43	22	36	34	0	60	2	8	2	21	6	.78	3	.281	.362	.365
08	Was	NL	100	325	76	20	0	2	(1	1)	102	34	25	25	32	1	54	2	2	2	4	5	.44	13	.234	.305	.314
08	StL	NL	43	156	60	8	2	4	(1	3)	84	30	21	31	11	1	28	1	0	1	4	3	.57	0	.385	.426	.538
09	Ari	NL	85	345	104	18	1	6	(5	1)	142	44	25	49	34	3	59	1	1	2	6	3	.67	2	.301	.364	.412
09	Mil	NL	66	259	83	20	2	3	(3	0)	116	44	32	49	37	1	41	1	0	0	0	3	.00	3	.320	.407	.448
	9 ML YEARS		1024	3805	1025	197	30	80	(44	36)	1522	536	391	505	393	13	797	17	29	26	115	55	.68	55	.269	.338	.400

Javier Lopez

Pitches: L **Bats:** L **Pos:** RP-14   **Ht:** 6'4" **Wt:** 220 **Born:** 7/11/1977 **Age:** 32

				HOW MUCH HE PITCHED						WHAT HE GAVE UP										THE RESULTS							
Year	Team	Lg	G	GS	CG	GF	IP	BFP	H	R	ER	HR	SH	SF	HB	TBB	IBB	SO	WP	Bk	W	L	Pct	Sh	Sv-Op Hld	ERC	ERA
2009	Pwtckt*	AAA	38	0	0	15	39.2	159	35	15	14	2	1	1	1	13	1	23	0	0	1	1	.500	0	0- -	3.02	3.18
2003	Col	NL	75	0	0	11	58.1	242	58	25	24	5	1	0	4	12	2	40	1	3	4	1	.800	0	1-2 15	3.44	3.70
2004	Col	NL	64	0	0	10	40.2	187	45	34	34	1	1	0	3	26	4	20	3	0	1	2	.333	0	0-1 12	5.28	7.52
2005	2 Tms	NL	32	0	0	6	16.1	87	26	20	20	2	1	1	1	11	3	12	0	1	1	1	.500	0	2-4 6	8.82	11.02
2006	Bos	AL	27	0	0	8	16.2	69	13	10	5	1	0	1	2	10	1	11	0	0	1	0	1.000	0	1-1 6	3.96	2.70
2007	Bos	AL	61	0	0	11	40.2	174	36	16	14	2	1	1	4	18	2	26	1	0	2	1	.667	0	0-2 13	3.59	3.10
2008	Bos	AL	70	0	0	10	59.1	247	53	18	16	4	1	1	2	27	0	38	1	0	2	0	1.000	0	0-1 10	3.73	2.43
2009	Bos	AL	14	0	0	5	11.2	64	20	13	12	1	1	1	2	9	0	5	1	0	0	2	.000	0	0-0 0	11.00	9.26
05	Col	NL	3	0	0	1	2.0	13	7	5	5	0	0	0	0	0	0	1	0	0	0	0	-	0	0-1 0	18.39	22.50
05	Ari	NL	29	0	0	5	14.1	74	19	15	15	2	1	0	1	11	3	11	0	1	1	1	.500	0	2-3 6	7.63	9.42
	Postseason		8	0	0	1	5.0	28	11	5	5	0	1	1	0	2	1	1	1	0	0	1	.000	0	0-0 0	10.18	9.00
	7 ML YEARS		343	0	0	61	243.2	1070	251	136	125	16	6	4	18	113	12	152	7	3	11	7	.611	0	4-11 62	4.53	4.62

Jose Lopez

Bats: R **Throws:** R **Pos:** 2B-141; 1B-16; PH-1   **Ht:** 6'0" **Wt:** 205 **Born:** 11/24/1983 **Age:** 26

						BATTING																BASERUNNING				AVERAGES		
Year	Team	Lg	G	AB	H	2B	3B	HR	(Hm	Rd)	TB	R	RBI	RC	TBB	IBB	SO	HBP	SH	SF	SB	CS	SB%	GDP	Avg	OBP	Slg
2004	Sea	AL	57	207	48	13	0	5	(4	1)	76	28	22	20	8	0	31	1	1	1	0	1	.00	1	.232	.263	.367
2005	Sea	AL	54	190	47	19	0	2	(1	1)	72	18	25	24	6	0	25	4	1	2	4	2	.67	5	.247	.282	.379
2006	Sea	AL	151	603	170	28	8	10	(4	6)	244	78	79	84	26	1	80	9	12	5	5	2	.71	17	.282	.319	.405
2007	Sea	AL	149	524	132	17	2	11	(5	6)	186	58	62	52	20	0	64	5	9	3	2	3	.40	16	.252	.284	.355
2008	Sea	AL	159	644	191	41	1	17	(13	4)	285	80	89	83	27	5	67	1	6	9	6	3	.67	14	.297	.322	.443
2009	Sea	AL	153	613	167	42	0	25	(8	17)	284	69	96	71	24	5	69	6	3	7	3	3	.50	25	.272	.303	.463
	6 ML YEARS		723	2781	755	160	11	70	(35	35)	1147	331	373	334	111	11	336	26	32	27	20	14	.59	78	.271	.303	.412

Rodrigo Lopez

Pitches: R **Bats:** R **Pos:** SP-5; RP-2   **Ht:** 6'1" **Wt:** 185 **Born:** 12/14/1975 **Age:** 34

				HOW MUCH HE PITCHED						WHAT HE GAVE UP										THE RESULTS							
Year	Team	Lg	G	GS	CG	GF	IP	BFP	H	R	ER	HR	SH	SF	HB	TBB	IBB	SO	WP	Bk	W	L	Pct	Sh	Sv-Op Hld	ERC	ERA
2009	LV*	AAA	18	18	1	0	100.1	427	122	57	48	9	2	5	2	14	0	71	2	1	7	5	.583	0	0- -	4.29	4.31
2000	SD	NL	6	6	0	0	24.2	120	40	24	24	5	0	1	0	13	0	17	0	0	0	3	.000	0	0-0 0	9.78	8.76
2002	Bal	AL	33	28	1	0	196.2	809	172	83	78	23	2	4	5	62	4	136	2	1	15	9	.625	0	0-0 0	3.27	3.57
2003	Bal	AL	26	26	3	0	147.0	663	188	101	95	24	3	7	10	43	6	103	2	1	7	10	.412	1	0-0 0	6.00	5.82
2004	Bal	AL	37	23	1	3	170.2	714	164	71	68	21	5	2	2	54	2	121	4	1	14	9	.609	1	0-1 4	3.74	3.59
2005	Bal	AL	35	35	0	0	209.1	918	232	126	114	28	3	5	7	63	1	118	5	1	15	12	.556	0	0-0 0	4.62	4.90
2006	Bal	AL	36	29	0	2	189.0	847	234	129	124	32	5	5	4	59	2	136	6	1	9	18	.333	0	0-0 0	5.68	5.90
2007	Col	NL	14	14	0	0	79.1	333	83	43	39	11	3	5	0	21	6	43	0	0	5	4	.556	0	0-0 0	3.97	4.42
2009	Phi	NL	7	5	0	0	30.0	137	42	24	19	3	0	2	0	11	1	19	0	0	3	1	.750	0	0-0 0	6.39	5.70
	8 ML YEARS		194	166	5	5	1046.2	4541	1155	601	561	147	21	31	28	326	22	693	19	5	68	66	.507	2	0-1 4	4.68	4.82

Wilton Lopez

Pitches: R **Bats:** R **Pos:** RP-6; SP-2   **Ht:** 6'0" **Wt:** 199 **Born:** 7/19/1983 **Age:** 26

		HOW MUCH HE PITCHED						WHAT HE GAVE UP												THE RESULTS							
Year	Team	Lg	G	GS	CG	GF	IP	BFP	H	R	ER	HR	SH	SF	HB	TBB	IBB	SO	WP	Bk	W	L	Pct	Sh	Sv-Op	Hld	ERC	ERA
2004	Tampa	A+	1	0	0	0	2.0	9	2	1	1	0	0	0	0	1	0	2	0	0	0	0	-	0	0- -	-	3.63	4.50
2004	Btl Crk	A	2	0	0	1	1.2	10	4	5	0	0	0	0	0	1	0	2	0	0	0	1	.000	0	0- -	-	13.02	0.00
2004	StlsInd	A-	2	0	0	1	3.0	16	5	5	4	2	0	0	1	1	0	2	0	0	0	0	-	0	0- -	-	14.65	12.00
2004	Yanks	R	4	0	0	3	5.2	22	2	0	0	0	0	0	1	0	0	6	2	0	1	0	1.000	0	1- -	-	0.45	0.00
2007	FtWyn	A	22	0	0	7	30.0	121	34	11	11	2	0	1	1	2	0	17	1	0	1	0	1.000	0	0- -	-	3.53	3.30
2007	Lk Els	A+	22	0	0	15	20.2	95	35	16	14	3	0	0	0	1	0	19	3	0	2	1	.667	0	3- -	-	7.19	6.10
2008	SnAnt	AA	27	0	0	4	38.1	162	41	21	21	2	1	0	1	9	2	24	0	0	0	2	.000	0	0- -	-	3.52	4.93
2008	Portlnd	AAA	1	0	0	0	1.0	6	1	1	1	0	0	0	0	2	0	1	1	0	0	0	-	0	0- -	-	9.51	9.00
2008	Lk Els	A+	30	0	0	29	30.2	126	34	10	9	0	0	1	1	4	1	26	2	0	2	1	.667	0	12- -	-	3.09	2.64
2009	CpChr	AA	20	15	1	4	110.1	469	133	62	58	8	2	4	1	13	1	69	2	0	4	5	.444	1	0- -	-	3.92	4.73
2009	Hou	NL	8	2	0	0	19.1	97	32	21	18	4	3	2	1	8	0	9	1	0	0	2	.000	0	0-1	0	9.39	8.38

Mark Loretta

Bats: R **Throws:** R **Pos:** PH-66; 3B-23; 1B-17; DH-5; 2B-3   **Ht:** 6'0" **Wt:** 200 **Born:** 8/14/1971 **Age:** 38

			BATTING																		BASERUNNING				AVERAGES		
Year	Team	Lg	G	AB	H	2B	3B	HR	(Hm	Rd)	TB	R	RBI	RC	TBB	IBB	SO	HBP	SH	SF	SB	CS	SB%	GDP	Avg	OBP	Slg
1995	Mil	AL	19	50	13	3	0	1	(0	1)	19	13	3	6	4	0	7	1	1	0	1	1	.50	1	.260	.327	.380
1996	Mil	AL	73	154	43	3	0	1	(0	1)	49	20	13	16	14	0	15	0	2	0	2	1	.67	7	.279	.339	.318
1997	Mil	AL	132	418	120	17	5	5	(2	3)	162	56	47	56	47	2	60	2	5	10	5	5	.50	15	.287	.354	.388
1998	Mil	NL	140	434	137	29	0	6	(3	3)	184	55	54	68	42	1	47	7	4	4	9	6	.60	14	.316	.382	.424
1999	Mil	NL	153	587	170	34	5	5	(2	3)	229	93	67	82	52	1	59	10	9	6	4	1	.80	14	.290	.354	.390
2000	Mil	NL	91	352	99	21	1	7	(3	4)	143	49	40	48	37	2	38	1	8	1	0	3	.00	9	.281	.350	.406
2001	Mil	NL	102	384	111	14	2	2	(0	2)	135	40	29	48	28	0	46	7	7	3	1	2	.33	8	.289	.346	.352
2002	2 Tms	NL	107	283	86	18	0	4	(2	2)	116	33	27	50	32	1	37	6	6	3	1	1	.50	7	.304	.381	.410
2003	SD	NL	154	509	105	28	4	13	(10	3)	200	74	72	93	54	2	62	3	3	4	5	4	.56	17	.314	.379	.411
2004	SD	NL	154	620	108	47	2	16	(11	5)	307	108	76	112	58	3	45	9	4	16	5	3	.63	10	.335	.391	.495
2005	SD	NL	106	404	113	16	1	3	(1	2)	140	54	38	53	45	4	34	8	2	4	8	4	.67	11	.280	.360	.347
2006	Bos	NL	155	635	181	33	0	5	(4	1)	229	75	59	80	49	1	63	12	2	5	4	1	.80	16	.285	.345	.361
2007	Hou	NL	133	460	132	23	2	4	(4	0)	171	52	41	60	44	0	41	3	3	1	1	2	.33	15	.287	.352	.372
2008	Hou	NL	101	261	73	15	0	4	(3	1)	100	27	38	37	29	1	30	2	0	5	0	0	-	9	.280	.350	.383
2009	LAD	NL	107	181	42	0	0	0	(0	0)	50	19	25	20	20	2	21	1	0	2	1	1	.50	6	.232	.309	.270
02	Mil	NL	86	217	58	14	0	2	(1	1)	78	23	19	33	23	1	32	5	6	1	0	0	-	6	.267	.350	.359
02	Hou	NL	21	66	28	4	0	2	(1	1)	38	10	0	17	9	0	5	0	0	2	1	1	.50	1	.424	.481	.576
	Postseason		3	15	4	0	0	0	(0	0)	4	0	2	1	0	0	0	0	0	0	0	0	-	1	.267	.267	.267
	15 ML YEARS		1726	5812	1713	309	22	76	(45	31)	2294	768	629	829	555	20	605	71	56	64	47	35	.57	157	.295	.360	.395

Shane Loux

Pitches: R **Bats:** R **Pos:** RP-12; SP-6   **Ht:** 6'2" **Wt:** 235 **Born:** 8/31/1979 **Age:** 30

			HOW MUCH HE PITCHED						WHAT HE GAVE UP												THE RESULTS							
Year	Team	Lg	G	GS	CG	GF	IP	BFP	H	R	ER	HR	SH	SF	HB	TBB	IBB	SO	WP	Bk	W	L	Pct	Sh	Sv-Op	Hld	ERC	ERA
2009	RCuca*	A+	1	1	0	0	1.0	6	1	0	0	0	0	0	0	2	0	0	1	0	0	0	-	0	0- -	-	0.51	0.00
2009	Salt Lk*	AAA	8	5	0	0	25.0	106	24	12	11	2	0	0	0	14	0	13	1	0	1	2	.333	0	0- -	-	4.54	3.96
2002	Det	AL	3	3	0	0	14.0	64	19	16	14	4	0	0	1	3	0	7	1	0	0	1	.000	0	0-0	0	7.12	9.00
2003	Det	AL	11	4	0	1	30.1	140	37	24	24	4	1	1	4	12	1	8	1	0	1	1	.500	0	0-0	0	6.12	7.12
2008	LAA	AL	7	0	0	5	16.0	66	16	6	5	1	1	0	2	2	0	4	0	0	0	0	-	0	0-0	0	3.28	2.81
2009	LAA	AL	18	6	0	0	58.1	271	84	42	38	4	0	3	4	19	0	19	3	0	2	3	.400	0	0-0	0	6.54	5.86
	4 ML YEARS		39	13	0	13	118.2	541	156	88	81	13	2	4	11	36	1	38	5	0	3	7	.300	0	0-0	0	6.04	6.14

Derek Lowe

Pitches: R **Bats:** R **Pos:** SP-34   **Ht:** 6'6" **Wt:** 230 **Born:** 6/1/1973 **Age:** 37

			HOW MUCH HE PITCHED						WHAT HE GAVE UP												THE RESULTS							
Year	Team	Lg	G	GS	CG	GF	IP	BFP	H	R	ER	HR	SH	SF	HB	TBB	IBB	SO	WP	Bk	W	L	Pct	Sh	Sv-Op	Hld	ERC	ERA
1997	2 Tms	AL	20	9	0	1	69.0	298	74	49	47	11	4	2	4	23	3	52	2	0	2	6	.250	0	0-2	1	4.88	6.13
1998	Bos	AL	63	10	0	8	123.0	527	126	65	55	5	4	5	4	42	5	77	8	0	3	9	.250	0	4-9	12	3.64	4.02
1999	Bos	AL	74	0	0	32	109.1	436	84	35	32	7	1	2	4	25	1	80	1	0	6	3	.667	0	15-20	22	2.14	2.63
2000	Bos	AL	74	0	0	64	91.1	379	90	27	26	6	4	1	2	22	5	79	2	1	4	4	.500	0	42-47	0	3.17	2.56
2001	Bos	AL	67	3	0	50	91.2	404	103	39	36	7	5	1	5	29	9	82	4	0	5	10	.333	0	24-30	4	4.31	3.53
2002	Bos	AL	32	32	1	0	219.2	854	166	65	63	12	5	2	12	48	0	127	9	0	21	8	.724	1	0-0	0	2.13	2.58
2003	Bos	AL	33	33	1	0	203.1	886	216	113	101	17	3	5	11	72	4	110	3	0	17	7	.708	0	0-0	0	4.32	4.47
2004	Bos	AL	33	33	0	0	182.2	839	224	138	110	15	8	4	8	71	2	105	3	0	14	12	.538	0	0-0	0	5.31	5.42
2005	LAD	NL	35	35	2	0	222.0	934	223	113	89	28	12	5	5	55	1	146	3	2	12	15	.444	2	0-0	0	3.75	3.61
2006	LAD	NL	35	34	1	1	218.0	913	221	97	88	14	7	2	5	55	2	123	3	2	16	8	.667	0	0-0	0	3.42	3.63
2007	LAD	NL	33	32	3	0	199.1	831	194	100	86	20	6	2	1	59	2	147	3	1	12	14	.462	0	0 0	1	3.55	3.88
2008	LAD	NL	34	34	1	0	211.0	851	194	84	76	14	8	7	1	45	7	147	2	0	14	11	.560	0	0-0	0	2.72	3.24
2009	Atl	NL	34	34	0	0	194.2	855	232	109	101	16	11	6	4	63	7	111	4	2	15	10	.600	0	0-0	0	4.80	4.67
97	Sea	AL	12	9	0	1	53.0	234	59	43	41	11	2	1	2	20	2	39	2	0	2	4	.333	0	0-0	1	5.55	6.96
97	Sea	AL	8	0	0	0	16.0	64	15	6	6	0	2	1	2	3	1	13	0	0	0	2	.000	0	0-2	1	2.78	3.38
	Postseason		21	10	0	3	83.2	352	72	38	31	9	5	0	4	26	5	55	1	0	5	5	.500	0	1-2	1	3.07	3.33
	13 ML YEARS		567	289	9	156	2135.0	9007	2147	1034	910	172	78	44	66	609	48	1386	43	8	141	117	.547	3	85-108	40	3.63	3.84

Mark Lowe

Pitches: R **Bats:** L **Pos:** RP-75　　　　**Ht:** 6'3" **Wt:** 210 **Born:** 6/7/1983 **Age:** 27

Year	Team	Lg	G	GS	CG	GF	IP	BFP	H	R	ER	HR	SH	SF	HB	TBB	IBB	SO	WP	Bk	W	L	Pct	Sh	Sv-Op	Hld	ERC	ERA
2006	Sea	AL	15	0	0	3	18.2	75	12	4	4	1	1	0	2	9	1	20	1	0	1	0	1.000	0	0-0	6	2.61	1.93
2007	Sea	AL	4	0	0	1	2.2	13	2	2	2	1	0	0	0	3	0	3	0	0	0	0	-	0	0-0	2	7.69	6.75
2008	Sea	AL	57	0	0	19	63.2	303	78	44	38	6	3	3	4	34	0	55	2	0	1	5	.167	0	1-5	6	6.10	5.37
2009	Sea	AL	75	0	0	18	80.0	339	71	39	29	7	0	4	0	29	1	69	4	0	2	7	.222	0	3-13	26	3.16	3.26
	4 ML YEARS		151	0	0	41	165.0	730	163	89	73	15	4	7	6	75	2	147	7	0	4	12	.250	0	4-18	35	4.23	3.98

Mike Lowell

Bats: R **Throws:** R **Pos:** 3B-107; DH-8; PH-4; PR-1　　　　**Ht:** 6'3" **Wt:** 210 **Born:** 2/24/1974 **Age:** 36

Year	Team	Lg	G	AB	H	2B	3B	HR	(Hm	Rd)	TB	R	RBI	RC	TBB	IBB	SO	HBP	SH	SF	SB	CS	SB%	GDP	Avg	OBP	Slg
1998	NYY	AL	8	15	4	0	0	0	(0	0)	4	1	0	1	0	0	1	0	0	0	0	0	-	0	.267	.267	.267
1999	Fla	NL	97	308	78	15	0	12	(7	5)	129	32	47	40	26	1	69	5	0	5	0	0	-	8	.253	.317	.419
2000	Fla	NL	140	508	137	38	4	22	(11	11)	241	73	91	86	54	4	75	9	0	11	4	0	1.00	4	.270	.344	.474
2001	Fla	NL	146	551	156	37	0	18	(12	6)	247	65	100	84	43	3	79	10	0	10	1	2	.33	9	.283	.340	.448
2002	Fla	NL	160	597	165	44	0	24	(13	11)	281	88	92	84	65	5	92	4	0	11	4	3	.57	16	.276	.346	.471
2003	Fla	NL	130	492	136	27	1	32	(14	18)	261	76	105	88	56	6	78	3	0	6	3	1	.75	14	.276	.350	.530
2004	Fla	NL	158	598	175	44	1	27	(14	13)	302	87	85	96	64	8	77	6	0	3	5	1	.83	17	.293	.365	.505
2005	Fla	NL	150	500	118	36	1	8	(5	3)	180	56	58	46	46	1	58	2	1	9	4	0	1.00	14	.236	.298	.360
2006	Bos	AL	153	573	163	47	1	20	(9	11)	272	79	80	77	47	5	61	4	0	7	2	2	.50	22	.284	.339	.475
2007	Bos	AL	154	589	191	37	2	21	(14	7)	295	79	120	106	53	4	71	3	0	8	3	2	.60	19	.324	.378	.501
2008	Bos	AL	113	419	115	27	0	17	(6	11)	193	58	73	59	38	2	61	5	0	6	2	2	.50	14	.274	.338	.461
2009	Bos	AL	119	445	129	29	1	17	(12	5)	211	54	75	66	33	5	61	1	0	5	2	1	.67	24	.290	.337	.474
	Postseason		31	105	27	8	0	4	(2	2)	47	16	20	16	12	2	15	1	0	3	1	0	1.00	2	.257	.331	.448
	12 ML YEARS		1528	5595	1567	381	7	218	(117	101)	2616	748	926	833	525	44	783	52	1	81	30	14	.68	161	.280	.343	.468

Jed Lowrie

Bats: B **Throws:** R **Pos:** SS-26; 3B-4; PR-3; 2B-2; PH-1　　　　**Ht:** 6'0" **Wt:** 180 **Born:** 4/17/1984 **Age:** 26

Year	Team	Lg	G	AB	H	2B	3B	HR	(Hm	Rd)	TB	R	RBI	RC	TBB	IBB	SO	HBP	SH	SF	SB	CS	SB%	GDP	Avg	OBP	Slg
2005	Lowell	A-	53	201	66	12	0	4	(-	-)	90	36	32	40	34	0	30	2	2	1	7	5	.58	3	.328	.429	.448
2006	Wilmg	A+	97	374	98	21	6	3	(-	-)	140	43	50	54	54	1	65	2	0	8	2	2	.50	11	.262	.352	.374
2007	Portlnd	AA	93	337	100	31	7	8	(-	-)	169	61	49	72	65	2	58	1	3	2	5	3	.63	11	.297	.410	.501
2007	Pwtckt	AAA	40	160	48	16	1	5	(-	-)	81	21	21	28	12	0	33	3	0	2	0	1	.00	1	.300	.356	.506
2008	Pwtckt	AAA	53	198	53	14	2	5	(-	-)	86	35	32	33	31	2	43	0	0	5	1	0	1.00	5	.268	.359	.434
2009	Pwtckt	AAA	22	68	12	3	0	3	(-	-)	24	9	8	8	13	0	13	1	0	1	0	0	-	1	.176	.313	.353
2009	Portlnd	AA	1	5	3	1	0	0	(-	-)	4	1	2	1	0	0	0	0	0	0	0	0	-	0	.600	.600	.800
2009	Lowell	A-	3	11	2	2	0	0	(-	-)	4	2	1	1	2	0	1	0	0	0	0	0	-	0	.182	.308	.364
2008	Bos	AL	81	260	67	25	3	2	(0	2)	104	34	46	35	35	0	68	1	2	8	1	0	1.00	8	.258	.339	.400
2009	Bos	AL	32	68	10	2	0	2	(1	1)	18	5	11	5	6	0	20	0	0	2	0	0	-	0	.147	.211	.265
	Postseason		9	29	6	1	0	0	(0	0)	7	4	2	2	5	0	7	1	0	1	0	0	-	0	.207	.333	.241
	2 ML YEARS		113	328	77	27	3	4	(1	3)	122	39	57	40	41	0	88	1	2	10	1	0	1.00	8	.235	.313	.372

Ryan Ludwick

Bats: R **Throws:** L **Pos:** RF-133; PH-15; LF-1; CF-1　　　　**Ht:** 6'3" **Wt:** 218 **Born:** 7/13/1978 **Age:** 31

Year	Team	Lg	G	AB	H	2B	3B	HR	(Hm	Rd)	TB	R	RBI	RC	TBB	IBB	SO	HBP	SH	SF	SB	CS	SB%	GDP	Avg	OBP	Slg
2002	Tex	AL	23	81	19	6	0	1	(1	0)	28	10	9	6	7	0	24	0	0	0	2	1	.67	4	.235	.295	.346
2003	2 Tms	AL	47	162	40	8	1	7	(2	5)	71	17	26	28	12	1	48	0	1	0	2	0	1.00	1	.247	.299	.438
2004	Cle	AL	15	50	11	2	0	2	(0	2)	19	3	4	4	2	0	14	2	0	0	0	0	-	0	.220	.278	.380
2005	Cle	AL	19	41	9	0	0	4	(3	1)	21	8	5	3	7	0	13	0	0	0	0	1	.00	1	.220	.333	.512
2007	StL	NL	120	303	81	22	0	14	(7	7)	145	42	52	45	26	1	72	7	3	0	4	4	.50	1	.267	.339	.479
2008	StL	NL	152	538	161	40	3	37	(19	18)	318	104	113	100	62	3	146	8	1	8	4	4	.50	9	.299	.375	.591
2009	StL	NL	139	486	129	20	1	22	(4	18)	217	63	97	82	41	3	106	7	1	4	4	2	.67	6	.265	.329	.447
03	Tex	AL	8	26	4	1	0	0	(0	0)	5	3	0	1	4	0	9	0	0	0	0	0	-	0	.154	.267	.192
03	Cle	AL	39	136	36	7	1	7	(2	5)	66	14	26	27	8	1	39	0	1	0	2	0	1.00	1	.265	.306	.485
	7 ML YEARS		515	1661	450	98	5	87	(35	52)	819	247	306	268	157	8	423	24	6	12	16	12	.57	22	.271	.340	.493

Julio Lugo

Bats: R **Throws:** R **Pos:** SS-56; 2B-30; PH-13; PR-3; DH-1　　　　**Ht:** 6'1" **Wt:** 175 **Born:** 11/16/1975 **Age:** 34

Year	Team	Lg	G	AB	H	2B	3B	HR	(Hm	Rd)	TB	R	RBI	RC	TBB	IBB	SO	HBP	SH	SF	SB	CS	SB%	GDP	Avg	OBP	Slg
2009	Pwtckt*	AAA	4	17	4	1	0	0	(-	-)	5	1	0	1	2	0	5	0	0	0	0	0	-	0	.235	.316	.294
2000	Hou	NL	116	420	119	22	5	10	(6	4)	181	78	40	62	37	0	93	4	3	1	22	9	.71	9	.283	.346	.431
2001	Hou	NL	140	513	135	20	3	10	(6	4)	191	93	37	63	46	0	116	5	15	7	12	11	.52	7	.263	.326	.372
2002	Hou	NL	88	322	84	15	1	8	(6	2)	125	45	35	43	28	3	74	2	4	2	9	3	.75	6	.261	.322	.388
2003	2 Tms	AL	139	498	135	16	4	15	(5	10)	204	64	53	68	44	1	100	4	7	3	12	4	.75	7	.271	.333	.410
2004	TB	AL	157	581	160	41	4	7	(3	4)	230	83	75	86	54	0	106	5	7	8	21	5	.81	8	.275	.338	.396
2005	TB	AL	158	616	182	36	6	6	(0	6)	248	89	57	94	61	0	72	6	4	3	39	11	.78	5	.295	.362	.403
2006	2 Tms	AL	122	435	121	22	2	12	(7	5)	183	69	37	61	39	0	76	4	5	3	24	9	.73	9	.278	.341	.421
2007	Bos	AL	147	570	135	36	2	8	(2	6)	199	71	73	65	48	0	82	6	8	4	33	6	.85	9	.237	.294	.349
2008	Bos	AL	82	261	70	13	0	1	(1	0)	86	27	22	20	34	0	51	4	9	1	12	4	.75	13	.268	.355	.330
2009	2 Tms	AL	88	257	72	13	5	3	(2	1)	104	40	21	37	29	0	45	1	3	3	9	0	1.00	3	.280	.352	.405
03	Hou	NL	22	65	16	3	0	0	(0	0)	19	6	2	7	9	1	12	0	0	0	2	1	.67	2	.246	.338	.292
03	TB	AL	117	433	119	13	4	15	(5	10)	185	58	51	61	35	0	88	4	7	3	10	3	.77	5	.275	.333	.427

Year	Team	Lg	G	AB	H	2B	3B	HR	(Hm	Rd)	TB	R	RBI	RC	TBB	IBB	SO	HBP	SH	SF	SB	CS	SB%	GDP	Avg	OBP	Slg
																					BASERUNNING				**AVERAGES**		
06	TB	AL	73	289	89	17	1	12	(7	5)	144	53	27	52	27	0	47	3	3	0	10	4	.82	7	.308	.373	.498
06	LAD	NL	49	146	32	5	1	0	(0	0)	39	16	10	9	12	0	29	1	2	3	6	5	.55	2	.219	.278	.267
09	Bos	AL	37	109	31	4	1	1	(1	0)	40	16	8	15	12	0	18	0	1	1	3	0	1.00	0	.284	.352	.367
09	StL	NL	51	148	41	9	4	2	(1	1)	64	24	13	22	17	0	27	1	2	2	6	0	1.00	3	.277	.351	.432
	Postseason		19	60	14	4	0	0	(0	0)	18	8	3	3	6	0	12	0	2	0	1	1	.50	6	.233	.303	.300
	10 ML YEARS		1237	4473	1213	234	32	80	(38	42)	1751	659	452	599	420	4	815	35	58	40	193	62	.76	76	.271	.336	.391

Brandon Lyon

Pitches: R Bats: R Pos: RP-65   Ht: 6'1" Wt: 195 Born: 8/10/1979 Age: 30

Year	Team	Lg	G	GS	CG	GF	IP	BFP	H	R	ER	HR	SH	SF	HB	TBB	IBB	SO	WP	Bk	W	L	Pct	Sh	Sv-Op	Hld	ERC	ERA
2001	Tor	AL	11	11	0	0	63.0	201	63	31	30	6	2	6	1	15	0	35	0	1	5	4	.556	0	0-0	0	3.50	4.29
2002	Tor	AL	15	10	0	0	62.0	279	78	47	45	14	3	2	2	19	2	30	2	0	1	4	.200	0	0-0	0	6.24	6.53
2003	Bos	AL	49	0	0	31	59.0	273	73	33	27	6	1	4	2	19	5	50	0	0	4	6	.400	0	9-12	2	4.96	4.12
2005	Ari	NL	32	0	0	22	29.1	144	44	25	21	6	2	1	2	10	2	17	1	1	0	2	.000	0	14-15	1	7.72	6.44
2006	Ari	NL	68	0	0	22	69.1	293	68	32	30	7	3	4	0	22	7	46	1	0	2	4	.333	0	0-7	23	3.49	3.89
2007	Ari	NL	73	0	0	20	74.0	307	70	25	22	2	3	2	1	22	2	40	3	1	6	4	.600	0	2-5	35	2.93	2.68
2008	Ari	NL	61	0	0	50	59.1	265	75	34	31	7	2	1	0	13	1	44	1	0	3	5	.375	0	26-31	3	4.86	4.70
2009	Det	AL	65	0	0	27	78.2	314	56	25	25	7	5	3	2	31	9	57	3	0	6	5	.545	0	3-6	15	2.46	2.86
	Postseason		5	0	0	1	6.0	20	1	0	0	0	0	0	1	1	0	5	0	0	0	0	-	0	0-0	2	0.19	0.00
	8 ML YEARS		374	21	0	172	494.2	2136	527	252	231	55	21	23	10	151	28	319	11	3	27	34	.443	0	54-77	79	4.11	4.20

Mike MacDougal

Pitches: R Bats: R Pos: RP-57   Ht: 6'4" Wt: 180 Born: 3/5/1977 Age: 33

Year	Team	Lg	G	GS	CG	GF	IP	BFP	H	R	ER	HR	SH	SF	HB	TBB	IBB	SO	WP	Bk	W	L	Pct	Sh	Sv-Op	Hld	ERC	ERA
2009	Syrcse*	AAA	8	0	0	5	8.1	37	7	3	3	1	1	0	0	5	0	6	1	0	0	0	-	0	2--		4.02	3.24
2001	KC	AL	3	3	0	0	15.1	67	18	10	8	2	0	0	1	4	0	7	3	0	1	1	.500	0	0-0	0	5.04	4.70
2002	KC	AL	6	0	0	1	9.0	38	5	5	5	0	0	0	0	7	1	10	1	0	0	1	.000	0	0-0	0	2.26	5.00
2003	KC	AL	68	0	0	61	64.0	285	64	36	29	4	3	2	8	32	0	57	6	0	3	5	.375	0	27-35	1	4.76	4.08
2004	KC	AL	13	0	0	8	11.1	61	16	8	7	2	0	0	1	9	0	14	2	0	1	1	.500	0	1-3	0	9.04	5.56
2005	KC	AL	68	0	0	53	70.1	298	69	32	26	6	1	1	3	24	2	72	6	1	5	6	.455	0	21-25	0	3.80	3.33
2006	2 Tms	AL	29	0	0	7	29.0	110	21	5	5	1	1	0	1	6	0	21	1	0	1	1	.500	0	1-2	11	1.80	1.55
2007	CWS	AL	54	0	0	8	42.1	208	50	37	32	3	0	1	2	33	3	39	8	0	2	5	.286	0	0-3	19	6.49	6.80
2008	CWS	AL	16	0	0	8	17.0	78	16	4	4	0	0	0	2	12	2	12	4	1	0	0	-	0	0-0	0	4.45	2.12
2009	2 Tms		57	0	0	41	54.1	246	52	31	26	3	2	3	3	38	3	34	10	0	1	1	.500	0	20-21	0	4.87	4.31
06	KC	AL	4	0	0	3	4.0	13	2	0	0	0	0	0	0	0	0	2	0	0	0	0	-	0	1-1	0	0.58	0.00
06	CWS	AL	25	0	0	4	25.0	97	19	5	5	1	1	0	1	6	0	19	1	0	1	1	.500	0	0-1	11	2.10	1.80
09	CWS	AL	5	0	0	1	4.1	25	7	6	6	0	0	0	0	7	0	3	3	0	0	0	-	0	0-0	0	13.09	12.46
09	Was	NL	52	0	0	40	50.0	221	45	25	20	3	2	3	3	31	3	31	7	0	1	1	.500	0	20-21	0	4.26	3.60
	9 ML YEARS		314	3	0	187	312.2	1391	311	168	142	21	7	7	21	165	11	266	41	2	14	21	.400	0	70-80	31	4.55	4.09

Drew Macias

Bats: L Throws: L Pos: PH-22; LF-17; RF-7; CF-6   Ht: 6'3" Wt: 200 Born: 3/7/1983 Age: 27

Year	Team	Lg	G	AB	H	2B	3B	HR	(Hm	Rd)	TB	R	RBI	RC	TBB	IBB	SO	HBP	SH	SF	SB	CS	SB%	GDP	Avg	OBP	Slg
2000	Portlnd*	AAA	86	297	69	18	0	5	(-	-)	102	43	27	37	39	2	56	5	1	2	5	3	.63	2	232	.329	.343
2007	SD	NL	1	0	0	0	0	0	(0	0)	0	1	0	0	0	0	0	0	0	0	0	0	-	0	-	-	-
2008	SD	NL	17	20	4	0	0	2	(1	1)	10	2	5	1	2	0	6	1	0	1	0	0	-	1	.200	.250	.500
2009	SD	NL	51	76	15	6	0	1	(0	1)	24	8	7	7	13	1	15	1	0	0	0	1	.00	2	.197	.322	.316
	3 ML YEARS		69	96	19	6	0	3	(1	2)	34	11	12	8	15	1	21	1	1	2	0	1	.00	3	.198	.307	.354

Warner Madrigal

Pitches: R Bats: R Pos: RP-13   Ht: 6'0" Wt: 200 Born: 3/21/1984 Age: 26

Year	Team	Lg	G	GS	CG	GF	IP	BFP	H	R	ER	HR	SH	SF	HB	TBB	IBB	SO	WP	Bk	W	L	Pct	Sh	Sv-Op	Hld	ERC	ERA
2006	Angels	R	12	0	0	11	12.0	50	11	5	5	0	2	0	1	3	0	13	0	1	2	1	.667	0	5--	-	2.71	3.75
2007	CRpds	A	54	0	0	40	61.0	247	44	18	14	3	4	1	1	23	1	75	3	1	5	4	.556	0	20--	-	2.26	2.07
2008	Frisco	AA	14	0	0	13	15.2	61	11	4	3	1	0	1	0	8	1	18	1	0	1	0	1.000	0	10--	-	2.62	1.72
2008	Okla	AAA	17	0	0	11	20.1	91	20	10	9	2	0	2	0	8	2	25	3	0	0	0	-	0	4--	-	3.61	3.98
2009	Okla	AAA	42	0	0	35	49.0	198	42	15	14	5	3	2	0	11	0	48	1	0	2	2	.500	0	17--	-	2.65	2.57
2008	Tex	AL	31	1	0	10	36.0	154	36	22	19	4	1	2	0	14	0	22	2	0	0	2	.000	0	1-3	3	4.13	4.75
2009	Tex	AL	13	0	0	6	12.2	67	18	14	14	2	0	0	1	12	1	5	2	0	0	0	-	0	0-0	0	9.87	9.95
	2 ML YEARS		44	1	0	16	48.2	221	54	36	33	6	1	2	1	26	1	27	4	0	0	2	.000	0	1-3	3	5.51	6.10

Ryan Madson

Pitches: R Bats: L Pos: RP-79   Ht: 6'6" Wt: 200 Born: 8/28/1980 Age: 29

Year	Team	Lg	G	GS	CG	GF	IP	BFP	H	R	ER	HR	SH	SF	HB	TBB	IBB	SO	WP	Bk	W	L	Pct	Sh	Sv-Op	Hld	ERC	ERA
2003	Phi	NL	1	0	0	0	2.0	6	0	0	0	0	0	0	0	0	0	0	0	0	0	0	-	0	0-0	0	0.00	0.00
2004	Phi	NL	52	1	0	14	77.0	312	68	23	20	6	1	1	5	19	4	55	7	0	9	3	.750	0	1-2	7	2.95	2.34
2005	Phi	NL	78	0	0	10	87.0	365	84	44	40	11	5	5	6	25	6	79	6	1	6	5	.545	0	0-7	32	3.83	4.14
2006	Phi	NL	50	17	0	8	134.1	620	176	92	85	20	9	3	10	50	4	99	12	0	11	9	.550	0	2-4	6	6.50	5.69
2007	Phi	NL	38	0	0	9	56.0	237	48	19	19	5	2	2	2	23	4	43	2	2	2	2	.500	0	1-2	7	3.28	3.05

		HOW MUCH HE PITCHED			WHAT HE GAVE UP					THE RESULTS			
Year Team	Lg	G GS CG GF	IP	BFP	H R ER	HR SH SF HB	TBB IBB	SO	WP Bk	W L	Pct	Sh	Sv-Op Hld	ERC	ERA
2008 Phi	NL	76 0 0 14	82.2	340	79 29 28	6 3 2 1	23 4	67	2 1	4 2	.667	0	1-3 17	3.20	3.05
2009 Phi	NL	79 0 0 28	77.1	320	73 29 28	7 3 1 3	22 3	78	1 0	5 5	.500	0	10-16 26	3.39	3.26
Postseason		11 0 0 1	12.2	49	10 3 3	1 2 0 0	1 0	12	0 0	1 0	1.000	0	0-2 5	1.70	2.13
7 ML YEARS		374 18 0 83	516.1	2200	528 236 220	55 23 14 27	162 25	421	30 4	37 26	.587	0	15-34 95	4.08	3.83

Ron Mahay

Pitches: L **Bats:** L **Pos:** RP-57   **Ht:** 6'2" **Wt:** 193 **Born:** 6/28/1971 **Age:** 39

		HOW MUCH HE PITCHED			WHAT HE GAVE UP					THE RESULTS			
Year Team	Lg	G GS CG GF	IP	BFP	H R ER	HR SH SF HB	TBB IBB	SO	WP Bk	W L	Pct	Sh	Sv-Op Hld	ERC	ERA
1997 Bos	AL	28 0 0 7	25.0	105	19 7 7	3 1 0 0	11 0	22	3 0	3 0	1.000	0	0-1 5	3.01	2.52
1998 Bos	AL	29 0 0 6	26.0	120	26 16 10	2 0 4 2	15 1	14	3 0	1 1	.500	0	1-2 7	4.76	3.46
1999 Oak	AL	6 1 0 2	19.1	68	8 4 4	2 0 0 0	3 0	15	0 0	2 0	1.000	0	1-1 0	0.88	1.86
2000 2 Tms		23 2 0 7	41.1	199	57 35 33	10 1 2 0	25 1	32	4 0	1 1	.500	0	0-0 2	8.55	7.19
2001 ChC	NL	17 0 0 4	20.2	86	14 6 6	4 0 0 0	15 1	24	1 0	0 0	-	0	0-0 2	4.32	2.61
2002 ChC	NL	11 0 0 1	14.2	65	13 14 14	6 0 0 0	8 0	14	0 0	2 0	1.000	0	0-0 0	6.11	8.59
2003 Tex	AL	35 0 0 5	45.1	189	33 19 16	3 0 0 0	20 7	38	4 0	3 3	.500	0	0-3 9	2.31	3.18
2004 Tex	AL	60 0 0 12	67.0	290	60 23 19	5 4 0 2	29 5	54	2 0	3 0	1.000	0	0-2 14	3.39	2.55
2005 Tex	AL	30 0 0 9	35.2	167	47 28 27	8 0 1 0	16 1	30	2 0	0 2	.000	0	1-1 6	7.10	6.81
2006 Tex	AL	62 0 0 14	57.0	246	54 30 25	7 1 1 0	28 2	56	1 0	1 3	.250	0	0-1 9	4.28	3.95
2007 2 Tms		58 0 0 8	67.0	281	52 20 19	4 3 2 1	37 2	55	1 1	3 0	1.000	0	1-2 7	3.23	2.55
2008 KC	AL	57 0 0 3	64.2	278	61 27 25	6 0 6 1	29 0	49	1 0	5 0	1.000	0	0-1 21	3.98	3.48
2009 2 Tms		57 0 0 11	50.1	239	62 29 24	10 1 2 4	22 2	42	5 0	2 1	.667	0	0-0 6	6.49	4.29
00 Oak	AL	5 2 0 1	16.0	82	26 18 16	4 1 1 0	9 0	5	2 0	0 1	.000	0	0-0 0	9.97	9.00
00 Fla	NL	18 0 0 6	25.1	117	31 17 17	6 0 1 0	16 1	27	2 0	1 0	1.000	0	0-0 2	7.67	6.04
07 Tex	AL	28 0 0 8	39.0	164	33 12 12	3 1 1 1	21 0	32	0 1	2 0	1.000	0	1-1 1	3.81	2.77
07 Atl	NL	30 0 0 0	28.0	117	19 8 7	1 2 1 0	16 2	23	1 0	1 0	1.000	0	0-1 6	2.47	2.25
09 KC	AL	41 0 0 11	41.1	200	55 26 22	9 1 2 2	19 1	34	4 0	1 1	.500	0	0-0 4	7.27	4.79
09 Min	AL	16 0 0 0	9.0	39	7 3 2	1 0 0 2	3 1	8	1 0	1 0	1.000	0	0-0 2	3.29	2.00
13 ML YEARS		473 3 0 89	534.0	2333	506 258 229	70 11 18 10	258 22	445	27 1	26 11	.703	0	4-14 88	4.33	3.86

Paul Maholm

Pitches: L **Bats:** L **Pos:** SP-31   **Ht:** 6'2" **Wt:** 224 **Born:** 6/25/1982 **Age:** 28

		HOW MUCH HE PITCHED			WHAT HE GAVE UP					THE RESULTS			
Year Team	Lg	G GS CG GF	IP	BFP	H R ER	HR SH SF HB	TBB IBB	SO	WP Bk	W L	Pct	Sh	Sv-Op Hld	ERC	ERA
2005 Pit	NL	6 6 0 0	41.1	168	31 10 10	2 0 0 3	17 0	26	0 0	3 1	.750	0	0-0 0	2.79	2.18
2006 Pit	NL	30 30 0 0	176.0	788	202 98 93	19 7 4 12	81 6	117	3 1	8 10	.444	0	0-0 0	5.58	4.76
2007 Pit	NL	29 29 2 0	177.2	765	204 110 99	22 13 6 6	49 3	105	5 0	10 15	.400	1	0-0 0	4.77	5.02
2008 Pit	NL	31 31 1 0	206.1	853	201 89 85	21 8 8 9	63 2	139	2 1	9 9	.500	0	0-0 0	3.84	3.71
2009 Pit	NL	31 31 0 0	194.2	836	221 102 96	14 7 1 6	60 4	119	11 1	8 9	.471	0	0-0 0	4.45	4.44
5 ML YEARS		127 127 3 0	796.0	3410	859 409 383	78 35 19 36	270 15	506	21 3	38 44	.463	1	0-0 0	4.51	4.33

Mitch Maier

Bats: L **Throws:** R **Pos:** CF-85; RF-36; LF-17; PR-10; PH-6   **Ht:** 6'2" **Wt:** 211 **Born:** 6/30/1982 **Age:** 28

						BATTING											BASERUNNING		AVERAGES		
Year Team	Lg	G	AB	H	2B	3B HR	(Hm Rd)	TB	R	RBI	RC	TBB IBB	SO	HBP SH SF			SB CS SB% GDP		Avg	OBP	Slg
2009 Omha*	AAA	12	51	16	3	0 2	(- -)	25	8	10	10	8 2	8	0 0 1			1 1 .50 1		.314	.400	.490
2006 KC	AL	5	13	2	0	0 0	(0 0)	2	3	0	0	2 0	4	0 0 0			0 0 -		.154	.267	.154
2008 KC	AL	34	91	26	1	1 0	(0 0)	29	9	9	7	2 0	18	2 2 0			0 2 .00 3		.286	.316	.319
2009 KC	AL	127	341	83	15	3 3	(1 2)	113	42	31	42	43 2	76	4 7 2			9 2 .82 6		.243	.333	.331
3 ML YEARS		166	445	111	16	4 3	(1 2)	144	54	40	49	47 2	98	6 9 2			9 4 .69 10		.249	.328	.324

John Maine

Pitches: R **Bats:** R **Pos:** SP-15   **Ht:** 6'4" **Wt:** 200 **Born:** 5/8/1981 **Age:** 29

		HOW MUCH HE PITCHED			WHAT HE GAVE UP					THE RESULTS			
Year Team	Lg	G GS CG GF	IP	BFP	H R ER	HR SH SF HB	TBB IBB	SO	WP Bk	W L	Pct	Sh	Sv-Op Hld	ERC	ERA
2004 Bal	AL	1 1 0 0	3.2	19	7 4 4	1 0 0 0	3 0	1	1 0	0 1	.000	0	0-0 0	14.87	9.82
2005 Bal	AL	10 8 0 1	40.0	184	39 30 28	8 0 2 1	24 0	24	0 1	2 3	.400	0	0-0 0	5.47	6.30
2006 NYM	NL	16 15 1 1	90.0	365	69 40 36	15 3 1 2	33 1	71	3 0	6 5	.545	1	0-0 0	3.22	3.60
2007 NYM	NL	32 32 1 0	191.0	810	168 90 83	23 11 4 5	75 3	180	2 0	15 10	.600	1	0-0 0	3.58	3.91
2008 NYM	NL	25 25 0 0	140.0	608	122 70 65	16 10 5 4	67 2	122	10 0	10 8	.556	0	0-0 0	3.81	4.18
2009 NYM	NL	15 15 0 0	81.1	349	67 42 40	8 6 2 4	38 2	55	5 0	7 6	.538	0	0-0 0	3.48	4.43
Postseason		3 3 0 0	13.2	62	10 5 4	1 1 0 1	11 2	13	0 0	1 0	1.000	0	0-0 0	3.93	2.63
6 ML YEARS		99 96 2 2	546.0	2335	472 276 256	71 30 14 16	240 8	453	21 1	40 33	.548	2	0-0 0	3.75	4.22

Matt Maloney

Pitches: L **Bats:** L **Pos:** SP-7   **Ht:** 6'4" **Wt:** 220 **Born:** 1/16/1984 **Age:** 26

		HOW MUCH HE PITCHED			WHAT HE GAVE UP					THE RESULTS			
Year Team	Lg	G GS CG GF	IP	BFP	H R ER	HR SH SF HB	TBB IBB	SO	WP Bk	W L	Pct	Sh	Sv-Op Hld	ERC	ERA
2005 Batvia	A-	8 8 0 0	37.0	156	38 20 16	2 1 2 1	15 0	36	3 0	2 1	.667	0	0- -	4.18	3.89
2006 Lakwd	A	27 27 2 0	168.2	709	120 54 38	5 7 1 8	73 0	180	10 1	16 9	.640	1	0- -	2.34	2.03
2007 Rdng	AA	21 21 1 0	125.2	541	117 70 55	13 9 8 4	45 0	115	5 1	9 7	.563	0	0- -	3.61	3.94
2007 Chatt	AA	4 4 0 0	28.0	104	17 9 8	4 2 1 1	3 0	39	2 0	2 2	.500	0	0- -	1.51	2.57
2007 Lsvlle	AAA	3 3 0 0	17.0	66	10 6 6	2 1 0 0	6 1	23	2 0	2 1	.667	0	0- -	1.86	3.18
2008 Lsvlle	AAA	25 25 2 0	140.1	601	143 75 73	18 10 3 7	39 2	132	4 0	11 5	.688	1	0- -	4.05	4.68

Year	Team	Lg	G	GS	CG	GF	IP	BFP	H	R	ER	HR	SH	SF	HB	TBB	IBB	SO	WP	Bk	W	L	Pct	Sh	Sv-Op	Hld	ERC	FRA
2008	Rodo	R	1	0	0	0	5.2	18	1	0	0	0	0	0	0	0	0	9	0	0	1	0	1.000	0	0--	-	0.07	0.00
2009	Lsvlle	AAA	22	22	3	0	143.0	591	143	56	49	11	10	5	7	24	0	125	4	0	9	9	.500	1	0--	-	3.22	3.08
2009	Carlina	AA	1	1	0	0	7.0	24	3	1	1	1	0	0	0	2	0	5	1	0	0	0	-	0	0--	-	1.39	1.29
2009	Cin	NL	7	7	0	0	40.2	170	43	22	22	9	2	4	3	8	1	28	0	0	2	4	.333	0	0-0	0	4.76	4.87

Jeff Manship

Pitches: R **Bats:** R **Pos:** RP-6; SP-5   **Ht:** 6'2" **Wt:** 202 **Born:** 1/16/1985 **Age:** 25

			HOW MUCH HE PITCHED						WHAT HE GAVE UP												THE RESULTS							
Year	Team	Lg	G	GS	CG	GF	IP	BFP	H	R	ER	HR	SH	SF	HB	TBB	IBB	SO	WP	Bk	W	L	Pct	Sh	Sv-Op	Hld	ERC	ERA
2006	Twins	R	2	0	0	0	5.2	21	3	0	0	0	0	0	0	1	0	10	0	1	0	0	-	0	0--	-	0.89	0.00
2006	FtMyrs	A+	4	3	0	0	8.2	36	7	3	2	0	1	0	0	2	0	12	0	0	0	0	-	0	0--	-	1.78	2.08
2007	Beloit	A	13	13	0	0	77.2	288	51	15	13	4	1	1	1	9	0	77	7	0	7	1	.875	0	0--	-	1.33	1.51
2007	FtMyrs	A+	13	13	0	0	71.1	314	77	38	25	5	1	1	2	25	0	59	1	0	8	5	.615	0	0--	-	4.18	3.15
2008	FtMyrs	A+	13	13	1	0	78.2	320	68	31	25	0	0	2	4	20	0	63	4	0	7	3	.700	1	0--	-	2.38	2.86
2008	NwBrit	AA	14	14	0	0	76.2	340	90	47	38	8	2	3	3	24	0	62	6	1	3	6	.333	0	0--	-	4.90	4.46
2009	NwBrit	AA	13	13	0	0	75.2	314	72	37	36	2	1	2	2	20	0	45	1	0	6	4	.600	0	0--	-	2.92	4.28
2009	Roch	AAA	8	8	0	0	50.1	212	53	23	18	1	2	1	1	17	0	30	1	1	4	2	.667	0	0--	-	3.73	3.22
2009	Min	AL	11	5	0	0	31.2	146	39	21	20	4	1	3	1	15	0	21	2	0	1	1	.500	0	0-0	0	6.11	5.68

Robert Manuel

Pitches: R **Bats:** R **Pos:** RP-3   **Ht:** 6'3" **Wt:** 205 **Born:** 7/9/1983 **Age:** 26

			HOW MUCH HE PITCHED						WHAT HE GAVE UP												THE RESULTS							
Year	Team	Lg	G	GS	CG	GF	IP	BFP	H	R	ER	HR	SH	SF	HB	TBB	IBB	SO	WP	Bk	W	L	Pct	Sh	Sv-Op	Hld	ERC	ERA
2005	Mets	R	12	5	0	4	58.2	228	55	19	13	2	2	1	1	4	0	49	1	0	8	1	.889	0	0--	-	2.33	2.06
2005	Bklyn	A-	2	0	0	0	5.0	20	5	1	1	1	0	0	0	0	0	5	0	0	0	0	-	0	0--	-	3.05	1.80
2006	Dayton	A	12	7	0	1	10.0	200	58	27	23	3	2	2	2	4	1	36	1	0	0	3	.000	0	1--	-	4.04	4.31
2006	Srsota	A+	6	0	0	1	8.0	36	10	7	4	3	1	1	0	2	0	4	0	0	0	0	-	0	0--	-	6.80	4.50
2007	Srsota	A+	33	11	0	3	98.1	411	100	47	44	3	4	4	3	22	0	93	1	0	6	5	.545	0	1--	-	3.14	4.03
2008	Srsota	A+	4	0	0	0	7.2	32	5	1	0	0	0	0	0	3	0	11	0	0	1	0	1.000	0	0--	-	1.60	0.00
2008	Chatt	AA	47	0	0	13	77.0	300	47	16	12	2	6	2	3	15	6	92	0	0	5	3	.625	0	3--	-	1.22	1.40
2008	Lsvlle	AAA	1	0	0	0	2.0	8	2	0	0	0	0	0	0	0	0	0	0	0	0	0	-	0	0--	-	1.95	0.00
2009	Lsvlle	AAA	36	0	0	17	46.2	198	37	17	14	2	4	0	2	10	0	38	0	0	3	4	.429	0	10--	-	2.10	2.70
2009	Tacom	AAA	15	0	0	11	19.0	75	13	8	7	1	0	0	0	6	0	11	1	0	1	1	.500	0	4--	-	2.76	3.32
2009	Cin	NL	3	0	0	1	4.1	18	5	0	0	0	0	0	0	1	0	2	0	0	0	0	-	0	0-0	0	3.69	0.00

Tommy Manzella

Bats: R **Throws:** R **Pos:** PR-4; SS-2; PH-2   **Ht:** 6'2" **Wt:** 190 **Born:** 4/16/1983 **Age:** 27

			BATTING																		BASERUNNING				AVERAGES		
Year	Team	Lg	G	AB	H	2B	3B	HR	(Hm	Rd)	TB	R	RBI	RC	TBB	IBB	SO	HBP	SH	SF	SB	CS	SB%	GDP	Avg	OBP	Slg
2005	TriCity	A-	53	220	51	6	4	0	(-	-)	65	24	18	16	9	0	39	0	2	2	5	3	.63	7	.232	.260	.295
2006	Lxngtn	A	99	338	93	22	1	7	(-	-)	138	50	43	50	33	1	80	3	8	5	16	8	.67	12	.275	.340	.408
2007	Salem	A+	57	223	53	13	0	0	(-	-)	66	28	24	22	19	0	30	3	5	1	5	2	.71	3	.238	.305	.296
2007	CpChr	AA	64	228	66	12	3	1	(-	-)	87	35	15	32	19	0	40	0	6	1	10	2	.83	4	.289	.343	.382
2008	CpChr	AA	54	224	67	11	5	4	(-	-)	100	27	34	35	17	0	35	1	3	4	4	4	.60	7	.299	.346	.446
2008	RdRck	AAA	61	228	50	15	1	0	(-	-)	67	19	15	17	17	0	39	0	2	0	4	4	.00	7	.219	.273	.294
2009	RdRck	AAA	133	530	153	31	5	9	(-	-)	221	68	56	78	40	2	99	1	7	2	12	3	.80	18	.289	.339	.417
2009	Hou	NL	7	5	1	0	0	0	(0	0)	1	0	0	0	0	0	4	0	0	0	0	0	-	0	.200	.200	.200

Shaun Marcum

Pitches: R **Bats:** R **Pos:** P   **Ht:** 6'0" **Wt:** 180 **Born:** 12/14/1981 **Age:** 28

			HOW MUCH HE PITCHED						WHAT HE GAVE UP												THE RESULTS							
Year	Team	Lg	G	GS	CG	GF	IP	BFP	H	R	ER	HR	SH	SF	HB	TBB	IBB	SO	WP	Bk	W	L	Pct	Sh	Sv-Op	Hld	ERC	ERA
2009	NHam*	AA	2	2	0	0	7.2	35	8	5	1	1	0	0	0	2	0	8	0	0	0	1	.000	0	0--	-	3.63	1.17
2009	LsVgs*	AAA	1	1	0	0	2.0	9	2	1	1	0	0	0	0	1	0	1	0	0	0	0	-	0	0--	-	3.63	4.50
2005	Tor	AL	5	0	0	3	8.0	32	6	0	0	0	0	0	0	4	0	4	0	0	0	0	-	0	0-0	0	2.58	0.00
2006	Tor	AL	21	14	0	3	78.1	357	87	44	44	14	1	2	4	38	3	65	1	0	3	4	.429	0	0-0	0	5.80	5.06
2007	Tor	AL	38	25	0	6	159.0	660	149	76	73	27	3	3	5	49	1	122	1	0	12	6	.667	0	1-2	1	4.00	4.13
2008	Tor	AL	25	25	0	0	151.1	630	126	60	57	21	1	3	8	50	2	123	3	0	9	7	.563	0	0-0	0	3.32	3.39
	4 ML YEARS		89	64	0	12	396.2	1079	368	180	174	62	5	8	17	141	6	314	5	0	24	17	.585	0	1-2	1	4.04	3.95

Nick Markakis

Bats: L **Throws:** L **Pos:** RF-161   **Ht:** 6'2" **Wt:** 195 **Born:** 11/17/1983 **Age:** 26

			BATTING																		BASERUNNING				AVERAGES		
Year	Team	Lg	G	AB	H	2B	3B	HR	(Hm	Rd)	TB	R	RBI	RC	TBB	IBB	SO	HBP	SH	SF	SB	CS	SB%	GDP	Avg	OBP	Slg
2006	Bal	AL	147	491	143	25	2	16	(9	7)	220	72	62	67	43	3	72	3	3	2	2	0	1.00	15	.291	.351	.448
2007	Bal	AL	161	637	191	43	3	23	(15	8)	309	97	112	103	61	5	112	5	1	6	18	6	.75	22	.300	.362	.485
2008	Bal	AL	157	595	182	48	1	20	(11	9)	292	106	87	113	99	7	113	2	0	1	10	7	.59	10	.306	.406	.491
2009	Bal	AL	161	642	188	45	2	18	(8	10)	291	94	101	97	56	0	98	3	0	10	6	2	.75	12	.293	.347	.453
	4 ML YEARS		626	2365	704	161	8	77	(43	34)	1112	369	362	380	259	15	395	13	4	19	36	15	.71	59	.298	.367	.470

Carlos Marmol

Pitches: R **Bats:** R **Pos:** RP-79   **Ht:** 6'2" **Wt:** 180 **Born:** 10/14/1982 **Age:** 27

		HOW MUCH HE PITCHED						WHAT HE GAVE UP												THE RESULTS							
Year Team	Lg	G	GS	CG	GF	IP	BFP	H	R	ER	HR	SH	SF	HB	TBB	IBB	SO	WP	Bk	W	L	Pct	Sh	Sv-Op	Hld	ERC	ERA
2006 ChC	NL	19	13	0	1	77.0	356	71	54	52	14	6	2	5	59	2	59	3	1	5	7	.417	0	0-0	0	6.01	6.08
2007 ChC	NL	59	0	0	6	69.1	285	41	11	11	3	1	2	4	35	3	96	5	1	5	1	.833	0	1-2	16	2.11	1.43
2008 ChC	NL	82	0	0	22	87.1	348	40	30	26	10	2	3	6	41	3	114	6	1	2	4	.333	0	7-9	30	1.86	2.68
2009 ChC	NL	79	0	0	29	74.0	335	43	29	28	2	4	1	12	65	3	93	6	1	2	4	.333	0	15-19	27	3.55	3.41
Postseason		4	0	0	0	5.2	26	6	5	5	2	1	1	0	3	0	9	0	0	0	1	.000	0	0-0	0	6.73	7.94
4 ML YEARS		239	13	0	58	307.2	1324	195	124	117	29	13	8	27	200	11	362	20	4	14	16	.467	0	23-30	73	3.26	3.42

Jason Marquis

Pitches: R **Bats:** L **Pos:** SP-33   **Ht:** 6'1" **Wt:** 210 **Born:** 8/21/1978 **Age:** 31

		HOW MUCH HE PITCHED						WHAT HE GAVE UP												THE RESULTS							
Year Team	Lg	G	GS	CG	GF	IP	BFP	H	R	ER	HR	SH	SF	HB	TBB	IBB	SO	WP	Bk	W	L	Pct	Sh	Sv-Op	Hld	ERC	ERA
2000 Atl	NL	15	0	0	7	23.1	103	23	16	13	4	1	1	1	12	1	17	1	0	1	0	1.000	0	0-1	1	5.13	5.01
2001 Atl	NL	38	16	0	9	129.1	556	113	62	50	14	6	5	4	59	4	98	1	2	5	6	.455	0	0-2	2	3.70	3.48
2002 Atl	NL	22	22	0	0	114.1	507	127	66	64	19	4	3	3	49	3	84	4	0	8	9	.471	0	0-0	0	5.43	5.04
2003 Atl	NL	21	2	0	10	40.2	182	43	27	25	3	0	3	2	18	2	19	2	0	0	0	-	0	1-1	0	4.45	5.53
2004 StL	NL	32	32	0	0	201.1	874	215	90	83	26	5	6	10	70	1	138	6	0	15	7	.682	0	0-0	0	4.69	3.71
2005 StL	NL	33	32	3	0	207.0	868	206	110	95	29	4	3	5	69	2	100	10	3	13	14	.481	1	0-0	0	4.23	4.13
2006 StL	NL	33	33	0	0	194.1	870	221	136	130	35	12	3	16	75	2	96	2	1	14	16	.467	0	0-0	0	5.79	6.02
2007 ChC	NL	34	33	1	0	191.2	846	190	111	98	22	13	1	13	76	6	109	3	0	12	9	.571	1	0-0	0	4.28	4.60
2008 ChC	NL	29	28	0	0	167.0	738	172	87	84	15	10	7	8	70	6	91	8	1	11	9	.550	0	0-0	1	4.35	4.53
2009 Col	NL	33	33	2	0	216.0	921	218	104	97	15	10	10	4	80	6	115	6	1	15	13	.536	1	0-0	0	3.86	4.04
Postseason		10	3	0	5	22.2	111	24	17	12	6	4	1	0	18	1	14	0	0	0	2	.000	0	0-0	0	7.10	4.76
10 ML YEARS		290	231	6	26	1485.0	6465	1528	809	739	182	65	42	66	578	33	867	43	8	94	83	.531	3	1-4	4	4.52	4.48

Jay Marshall

Pitches: L **Bats:** L **Pos:** RP-10   **Ht:** 6'5" **Wt:** 205 **Born:** 2/25/1983 **Age:** 27

		HOW MUCH HE PITCHED						WHAT HE GAVE UP												THE RESULTS							
Year Team	Lg	G	GS	CG	GF	IP	BFP	H	R	ER	HR	SH	SF	HB	TBB	IBB	SO	WP	Bk	W	L	Pct	Sh	Sv-Op	Hld	ERC	ERA
2003 Bristol	R+	10	10	0	0	41.1	173	38	15	12	3	0	0	4	13	0	42	2	0	2	0	1.000	0	0--	-	3.54	2.61
2004 Bristol	R+	11	11	0	0	57.2	241	63	31	23	8	4	2	2	8	1	52	4	1	1	6	.143	0	0--	-	3.93	3.59
2004 Gr Falls	R+	4	2	0	1	15.2	69	19	9	6	2	0	0	0	6	0	17	0	0	2	0	1.000	0	0--	-	5.57	3.45
2005 Gr Falls	R+	29	0	0	16	43.1	174	35	20	13	3	0	1	3	7	0	43	1	0	2	0	1.000	0	6--	-	2.23	2.70
2006 WinSa	A+	58	0	0	16	62.0	234	46	11	7	2	5	0	2	8	0	44	2	1	5	1	.833	0	4--	-	1.61	1.02
2008 Mdland	AA	20	0	0	4	32.1	120	23	4	3	1	0	0	1	7	1	21	1	0	1	1	.500	0	1--	-	1.74	0.84
2008 Scrmto	AAA	37	0	0	19	38.0	184	55	26	26	3	4	1	0	20	4	21	0	0	3	5	.375	0	2--	-	6.94	6.16
2009 Scrmto	AAA	50	0	0	20	50.2	212	53	23	18	2	5	2	1	15	4	30	5	0	5	3	.625	0	7--	-	3.53	3.20
2007 Oak	AL	51	0	0	15	42.0	198	50	33	30	3	3	1	4	22	6	18	2	0	1	2	.333	0	0-2	9	5.56	6.43
2009 Oak	AL	10	0	0	2	7.1	35	13	12	12	1	2	0	1	0	0	1	0	0	0	2	.000	0	0-0	1	8.04	14.73
2 ML YEARS		61	0	0	17	49.1	233	63	45	42	4	5	1	5	22	6	19	2	0	1	4	.200	0	0-2	10	5.92	7.66

Sean Marshall

Pitches: L **Bats:** L **Pos:** RP-46; SP-9   **Ht:** 6'7" **Wt:** 220 **Born:** 8/30/1982 **Age:** 27

		HOW MUCH HE PITCHED						WHAT HE GAVE UP												THE RESULTS							
Year Team	Lg	G	GS	CG	GF	IP	BFP	H	R	ER	HR	SH	SF	HB	TBB	IBB	SO	WP	Bk	W	L	Pct	Sh	Sv-Op	Hld	ERC	ERA
2006 ChC	NL	24	24	0	0	125.2	563	132	85	78	20	7	1	7	59	3	77	6	0	6	9	.400	0	0-0	0	5.27	5.59
2007 ChC	NL	21	19	0	0	103.1	446	107	52	45	13	7	2	1	35	3	67	4	0	7	8	.467	0	0-0	0	4.18	3.92
2008 ChC	NL	34	7	0	6	65.1	279	60	28	28	9	4	3	4	23	4	58	3	0	3	5	.375	0	1-2	3	3.82	3.86
2009 ChC	NL	55	9	1	10	85.1	373	91	43	41	10	7	1	4	32	4	68	2	0	3	7	.300	0	0-0	7	4.43	4.32
Postseason		2	0	0	0	3.1	13	2	1	1	1	0	0	0	1	0	5	0	0	0	0	-	0	0-0	0	2.70	2.70
4 ML YEARS		134	59	1	16	379.2	1661	390	208	192	52	25	7	13	149	14	270	15	0	19	29	.396	0	1-2	10	4.53	4.55

Lou Marson

Bats: R **Throws:** R **Pos:** C-21   **Ht:** 6'1" **Wt:** 198 **Born:** 6/26/1986 **Age:** 24

		BATTING																		BASERUNNING				AVERAGES		
Year Team	Lg	G	AB	H	2B	3B	HR	(Hm	Rd)	TB	R	RBI	RC	TBB	IBB	SO	HBP	SH	SF	SB	CS	SB%	GDP	Avg	OBP	Slg
2004 Phillies	R	38	113	29	3	0	4	(-	-)	44	18	8	16	13	0	18	0	0	0	4	0	1.00	4	.257	.333	.389
2005 Batvia	A-	60	220	54	11	3	5	(-	-)	86	25	25	29	27	0	52	1	3	1	0	1	.00	12	.245	.329	.391
2006 Lakwd	A	104	350	85	16	5	4	(-	-)	123	44	39	47	49	1	82	5	5	1	4	0	1.00	13	.243	.343	.351
2007 Clrwtr	A+	111	393	113	24	1	7	(-	-)	160	68	63	64	52	2	80	5	1	6	3	1	.75	10	.288	.373	.407
2008 Rdng	AA	94	322	101	18	0	5	(-	-)	134	55	46	64	68	2	70	2	0	3	3	3	.50	10	.314	.433	.416
2009 LV	AAA	63	211	62	13	0	1	(-	-)	78	32	24	32	30	1	40	0	0	0	3	1	.75	9	.294	.382	.370
2009 Clmbs	AAA	28	103	25	5	1	1	(-	-)	35	10	9	12	10	0	19	2	0	1	1	0	1.00		.243	.319	.340
2008 Phi	NL	1	4	2	0	0	1	(1	0)	5	2	2	2	0	0	2	0	0	0	0	0	-	0	.500	.500	1.250
2009 2 Tms		21	61	15	7	0	0	(0	0)	22	9	4	7	10	0	21	0	0	1	0	0	-	3	.246	.347	.361
09 Phi	NL	7	17	4	1	0	0	(0	0)	5	3	0	1	3	0	7	0	0	0	0	0	-		.235	.350	.294
09 Cle	AL	14	44	11	6	0	0	(0	0)	17	6	4	6	7	0	14	0	0	1	0	0	-	2	.250	.346	.386
2 ML YEARS		22	65	17	7	0	1	(1	0)	27	11	6	9	10	0	23	0	0	1	0	0	-	3	.262	.355	.415

Andy Marte

Bats: R Throws: R Pos: 1B-45; PH-3; DH-1   Ht: 6'1" Wt: 205 Born: 10/21/1983 Age: 26

Year	Team	Lg	G	AB	H	2B	3B	HR	(Hm	Rd)	TB	R	RBI	RC	TBB	IBB	SO	HBP	SH	SF	SB	CS	SB%	GDP	Avg	OBP	Slg
2009	Clmbs*	AAA	82	300	98	24	1	18	(-	-)	178	48	66	64	22	1	50	0	1	3	3	0	1.00	2	.327	.369	.593
2005	Atl	NL	24	57	8	2	1	0	(0	0)	12	3	4	1	7	0	13	0	0	2	0	1	.00	2	.140	.227	.211
2006	Cle	AL	50	164	37	15	1	5	(3	2)	69	20	23	21	13	0	38	1	0	0	0	0	-	3	.226	.287	.421
2007	Cle	AL	20	57	11	4	0	1	(0	1)	18	3	8	4	2	0	9	1	0	0	0	0	-	0	.193	.233	.316
2008	Cle	AL	80	235	52	11	1	3	(2	1)	74	21	17	17	14	0	52	1	7	0	1	2	.33	5	.221	.268	.315
2009	Cle	AL	47	155	36	6	1	6	(2	4)	62	20	25	20	14	1	30	1	1	4	0	0	-	5	.232	.293	.400
5 ML YEARS			221	668	144	38	4	15	(7	8)	235	67	77	63	50	1	142	4	8	6	1	3	.25	15	.216	.272	.352

Damaso Marte

Pitches: L Bats: L Pos: RP-21   Ht: 6'2" Wt: 213 Born: 2/14/1975 Age: 35

Year	Team	Lg	G	GS	CG	GF	IP	BFP	H	R	ER	HR	SH	SF	HB	TBB	IBB	SO	WP	Bk	W	L	Pct	Sh	Sv-Op	Hld	ERC	ERA
2009	Yanks*	R	2	2	0	0	2.0	8	2	1	1	0	0	0	0	0	0	2	0	0	0	0	-	0	0--	-	1.95	4.50
2009	S-WB*	AAA	11	0	0	1	11.0	46	10	3	3	2	1	0	0	4	0	9	0	1	0	1	.000	0	0--	-	4.00	2.45
1999	Sea	AL	5	0	0	2	8.2	47	16	9	9	3	0	0	0	6	0	3	0	0	0	1	.000	0	0-0	0	13.32	9.35
2001	Pit	NL	23	0	0	4	36.1	154	34	21	19	5	1	2	3	12	3	39	1	0	0	1	.000	0	0-0	0	3.93	4.71
2002	CWS	AL	68	0	0	22	60.1	240	44	19	19	5	1	1	4	18	2	72	3	1	1	1	.500	0	10-12	14	2.42	2.83
2003	CWS	AL	71	0	0	25	79.2	314	50	16	14	3	3	3	3	34	6	87	1	0	4	2	.667	0	11-18	14	1.96	1.58
2004	CWS	AL	74	0	0	24	73.2	303	56	28	28	10	2	6	3	34	4	68	3	0	6	5	.545	0	6-12	21	3.39	3.42
2005	CWS	AL	66	0	0	15	45.1	213	45	21	19	5	1	0	3	33	4	54	1	1	3	4	.429	0	4-8	22	5.51	3.77
2006	Pit	NL	75	0	0	15	58.1	255	51	30	24	5	8	3	4	31	6	63	3	1	1	7	.125	0	0-4	13	3.88	3.70
2007	Pit	NL	65	0	0	11	45.1	182	32	14	12	2	0	2	2	18	1	51	0	1	2	0	1.000	0	0-0	15	2.35	2.38
2008	2 Tms		72	0	0	10	65.0	272	52	29	29	5	1	0	2	26	2	71	1	0	5	3	.625	0	5-7	25	2.90	4.02
2000	NYY	AL	21	0	0	0	13.1	62	15	14	14	3	1	0	1	9	1	13	0	0	1	3	.250	0	0-1	5	8.01	9.45
08	Pit	NL	47	0	0	8	46.2	192	38	18	18	4	1	0	1	16	1	47	1	0	4	0	1.000	0	5-7	15	2.82	3.47
08	NYY	AL	25	0	0	2	18.1	80	14	11	11	1	1	0	1	10	1	24	0	0	1	3	.250	0	0-0	10	3.07	5.40
Postseason			2	0	0	0	1.2	11	1	0	0	0	0	0	0	4	0	3	0	0	1	0	1.000	0	0-0	0	7.68	0.00
10 ML YEARS			540	0	0	134	486.0	2042	395	201	187	46	18	17	25	218	29	521	13	4	23	27	.460	0	36-62	129	3.34	3.46

Victor Marte

Pitches: R Bats: R Pos: RP-8   Ht: 6'2" Wt: 207 Born: 11/8/1980 Age: 29

Year	Team	Lg	G	GS	CG	GF	IP	BFP	H	R	ER	HR	SH	SF	HB	TBB	IBB	SO	WP	Bk	W	L	Pct	Sh	Sv-Op	Hld	ERC	ERA
2006	Hshma	Jap	12	0	0	-	11.1	45	5	7	2	1	-	-	1	6	-	5	3	0	0	1	.000	0	0--	-	1.97	1.59
2007	Hshma	Jap	17	0	0	-	17.1	90	28	16	16	2	-	-	2	10	-	13	1	0	0	1	.000	0	0--	-	9.34	8.31
2008	Hshma	Jap	1	0	0	-	2.0	11	4	3	3	0	-	-	0	1	0	2	1	0	0	0	-	0	0--	-	9.72	13.50
2009	NWArk	AA	13	0	0	6	16.0	67	5	7	6	1	0	1	1	5	0	17	1	0	2	1	.667	0	4--	-	1.69	2.45
2000	Omha	AAA	20	0	0	17	42.1	182	35	14	10	0	3	2	1	20	2	36	4	0	1	4	.200	0	4--	-	2.69	2.13
2009	KC	AL	8	0	0	4	12.0	58	13	12	11	2	0	0	0	12	1	7	1	0	0	0	-	0	0-0	0	7.71	8.25

J.D. Martin

Pitches: R Bats: R Pos: SP-15   Ht: 6'4" Wt: 200 Born: 1/2/1983 Age: 27

Year	Team	Lg	G	GS	CG	GF	IP	BFP	H	R	ER	HR	SH	SF	HB	TBB	IBB	SO	WP	Bk	W	L	Pct	Sh	Sv-Op	Hld	ERC	ERA
2001	Burlgtn	A	10	10	0	0	45.2	174	26	9	7	3	0	0	4	11	0	72	3	1	5	1	.833	0	0--	-	1.56	1.38
2002	Clmbs	AAA	27	26	0	0	138.1	594	141	76	60	12	2	3	13	46	0	131	2	1	14	5	.737	0	0--	-	4.26	3.90
2003	Knstn	A+	16	16	0	0	86.1	375	95	50	41	7	3	1	3	30	0	57	3	0	5	3	.625	0	0--	-	4.48	4.27
2004	Knstn	A+	25	25	2	0	147.2	605	139	75	72	15	6	8	12	41	0	98	6	0	11	10	.524	0	0--	-	3.73	4.39
2004	Buffalo	AA	1	1	0	0	5.0	26	9	6	6	1	0	0	0	2	0	2	0	1	0	0	-	0	0--	-	9.81	10.80
2005	Akron	AA	10	10	0	0	56.2	223	43	17	15	3	1	1	3	8	0	63	1	0	3	1	.750	0	0--	-	1.81	2.38
2006	MhVlly	A-	6	6	0	0	18.0	67	11	3	3	1	0	0	1	1	0	13	1	0	1	0	1.000	0	0--	-	1.15	1.50
2006	Lk Cty	A	5	5	0	0	15.0	60	13	7	7	2	0	2	1	3	0	16	0	0	0	1	.000	0	0--	-	3.12	4.20
2006	Knstn	A+	3	2	0	0	11.1	40	6	0	0	0	0	0	0	1	0	11	0	0	1	0	1.000	0	0--	-	0.76	0.00
2007	Akron	AA	9	9	0	0	42.1	185	42	22	20	4	4	0	3	16	0	23	1	0	2	3	.400	0	0--	-	4.16	4.25
2008	Akron	AA	31	8	0	8	79.2	323	73	25	22	5	3	4	4	19	0	71	2	2	11	3	.786	0	0--	-	3.02	2.49
2008	Buffalo	AAA	4	1	0	0	10.0	37	6	2	2	2	0	0	0	2	0	8	0	0	1	0	1.000	0	0--	-	1.91	1.80
2009	Syrcse	AAA	16	15	0	0	88.0	338	75	33	26	4	2	7	2	10	1	63	2	1	8	3	.727	0	0--	-	2.06	2.66
2009	Was	NL	15	15	0	0	77.0	341	85	40	38	14	4	2	6	24	4	37	0	0	5	4	.556	0	0-0	0	5.10	4.44

Russell Martin

Bats: R Throws: R Pos: C-137; PH-5; DH-3; 3B-1; PR-1   Ht: 5'10" Wt: 210 Born: 2/15/1983 Age: 27

Year	Team	Lg	G	AB	H	2B	3B	HR	(Hm	Rd)	TB	R	RBI	RC	TBB	IBB	SO	HBP	SH	SF	SB	CS	SB%	GDP	Avg	OBP	Slg
2006	LAD	NL	121	415	117	26	4	10	(8	2)	181	65	65	58	45	8	57	4	1	3	10	5	.67	17	.282	.355	.436
2007	LAD	NL	151	540	158	32	3	19	(8	11)	253	87	87	84	67	1	89	7	0	6	21	9	.70	16	.293	.374	.469
2008	LAD	NL	155	553	155	25	0	13	(6	7)	219	87	69	89	90	8	83	5	0	2	18	6	.75	16	.280	.385	.396
2009	LAD	NL	143	505	126	19	0	7	(3	4)	166	63	53	62	69	9	80	11	2	1	11	6	.65	18	.250	.352	.329
Postseason			11	42	10	3	0	1	(0	1)	16	7	6	3	5	0	12	2	0	1	1	0	1.00	1	.238	.347	.381
4 ML YEARS			570	2013	556	102	7	49	(25	24)	819	302	274	293	271	26	309	27	3	12	60	26	.70	67	.276	.368	.407

Carlos Martinez

Pitches: R **Bats:** R **Pos:** RP-2 **Ht:** 6'2" **Wt:** 220 **Born:** 5/26/1982 **Age:** 28

Year	Team	Lg	G	GS	CG	GF	IP	BFP	H	R	ER	HR	SH	SF	HB	TBB	IBB	SO	WP	Bk	W	L	Pct	Sh	Sv-Op	Hld	ERC	ERA
2009	NewOr*	AAA	17	0	0	4	17.1	79	23	14	13	4	0	1	0	8	2	14	0	0	0	0	.000	0	0--	-	7.35	6.75
2006	Fla	NL	12	0	0	4	10.1	44	9	2	2	0	0	2	0	6	0	11	0	0	0	1	.000	0	0-0	5	3.42	1.74
2007	Fla	NL	2	0	0	1	2.2	13	4	4	4	3	0	0	0	1	0	2	0	0	0	0	-	0	0-0	0	15.48	13.50
2009	Fla	NL	2	0	0	0	2.1	13	3	1	1	1	0	0	1	2	0	2	0	0	0	0	-	0	0-0	1	12.75	3.86
3 ML YEARS			16	0	0	5	15.1	70	16	7	7	4	0	2	1	9	0	15	0	0	0	1	.000	0	0-0	6	6.69	4.11

Cristhian Martinez

Pitches: R **Bats:** R **Pos:** RP-15 **Ht:** 6'1" **Wt:** 160 **Born:** 3/6/1982 **Age:** 28

Year	Team	Lg	G	GS	CG	GF	IP	BFP	H	R	ER	HR	SH	SF	HB	TBB	IBB	SO	WP	Bk	W	L	Pct	Sh	Sv-Op	Hld	ERC	ERA
2003	Tigers	R	9	5	0	2	35.1	155	34	25	23	9	0	1	3	11	0	39	1	0	3	2	.600	0	0--	-	4.79	5.86
2004	Oneont	A-	2	2	0	0	13.0	47	9	3	3	1	0	0	1	1	0	12	0	0	1	0	1.000	0	0--	-	1.65	2.08
2004	WMich	A	12	12	1	0	73.2	296	59	27	20	6	4	1	7	20	0	45	3	0	5	2	.714	1	0--	-	2.84	2.44
2005	Lkland	A+	3	2	0	0	11.0	49	11	6	6	0	0	0	2	4	0	9	0	0	2	0	1.000	0	0--	-	3.88	4.91
2006	Lkland	A+	5	5	0	0	21.2	93	27	14	12	3	0	1	1	5	0	15	1	0	1	1	.500	0	0--	-	5.46	4.98
2006	Tigers	R	7	6	0	0	35.0	135	30	11	6	1	1	0	1	4	0	27	2	1	3	2	.600	0	0--	-	2.02	1.54
2006	Oneont	A-	7	7	0	0	41.2	167	38	15	10	4	0	1	3	5	0	30	1	0	1	2	.333	0	0--	-	2.81	2.16
2007	Grnsbr	A	18	18	0	0	97.0	404	97	55	44	16	3	3	6	18	0	74	4	0	9	5	.643	0	0--	-	3.91	4.08
2008	Grnsbr	A	8	8	0	0	44.1	187	44	24	23	2	1	2	3	9	0	14	2	0	4	1	.800	0	0--	-	3.13	4.67
2008	Jupiter	A+	20	19	1	1	109.1	462	117	56	46	7	8	4	4	16	0	78	0	0	2	7	.222	0	0--	-	3.32	3.79
2009	Jaxnvl	AA	17	16	0	0	104.0	417	96	39	34	7	3	3	4	22	0	62	1	0	9	3	.750	0	0--	-	2.96	2.94
2009	Fla	NL	15	0	0	4	26.1	112	27	16	15	2	1	0	0	8	1	18	1	0	1	1	.500	0	0-1	0	3.60	5.13

Fernando Martinez

Bats: L **Throws:** R **Pos:** LF-11; CF-8; RF-6; PH-5 **Ht:** 6'1" **Wt:** 200 **Born:** 10/10/1988 **Age:** 21

Year	Team	Lg	G	AB	H	2B	3B	HR	(Hm	Rd)	TB	R	RBI	RC	TBB	IBB	SO	HBP	SH	SF	SB	CS	SB%	GDP	Avg	OBP	Slg
2006	Hgrstn	A	45	192	64	14	2	5	(-	-)	97	24	28	37	15	0	36	3	0	1	7	4	.64	5	.333	.389	.505
2006	Mets	R	1	4	1	0	0	0	(-	-)	1	1	0	0	0	0	1	0	0	0	0	0	-	0	.250	.250	.250
2006	StLuci	A+	30	119	23	4	2	5	(-	-)	46	18	11	12	6	0	24	4	0	1	1	1	.50	1	.193	.254	.387
2007	Mets	R	3	9	1	0	1	0	(-	-)	3	1	1	0	1	0	6	0	0	0	0	0	-	0	.111	.200	.333
2007	Bnghtn	AA	60	236	64	11	1	4	(-	-)	89	32	21	30	20	2	51	3	0	0	3	4	.43	5	.271	.336	.377
2008	Bnghtn	AA	86	352	101	19	4	8	(-	-)	152	48	43	53	27	2	73	3	0	3	6	2	.75	9	.287	.340	.432
2008	Mets	R	4	14	6	1	1	0	(-	-)	9	2	0	3	0	0	2	1	0	0	0	0	-	0	.429	.467	.643
2009	Buffalo	AAA	45	176	51	16	2	8	(-	-)	95	24	28	32	11	0	33	2	0	1	2	1	.67	4	.290	.337	.540
2009	NYM	NL	29	91	16	6	0	1	(0	1)	25	11	8	5	5	0	14	3	1	0	2	0	1.00	0	.176	.242	.275

Joe Martinez

Pitches: R **Bats:** L **Pos:** SP-5; RP-4 **Ht:** 6'2" **Wt:** 193 **Born:** 2/26/1983 **Age:** 27

Year	Team	Lg	G	GS	CG	GF	IP	BFP	H	R	ER	HR	SH	SF	HB	TBB	IBB	SO	WP	Bk	W	L	Pct	Sh	Sv-Op	Hld	ERC	ERA
2005	SlmKzr	A-	15	13	0	1	69.0	285	69	33	33	9	4	0	5	15	0	59	4	1	4	3	.571	0	0--	-	3.93	4.30
2006	Augsta	A	27	27	1	0	167.2	682	156	66	56	9	6	5	11	26	0	135	7	3	15	5	.750	1	0--	-	2.74	3.01
2007	SnJos	A+	28	28	0	0	162.2	678	172	85	77	11	4	8	5	36	0	151	7	2	10	10	.500	0	0--	-	3.65	4.26
2008	Conn	AA	27	27	0	0	148.0	611	131	58	41	6	7	8	4	37	0	112	3	0	10	10	.500	0	0--	-	2.59	2.49
2009	Giants	R	1	1	0	0	2.2	13	4	3	3	0	0	1	1	0	0	1	0	0	0	0	-	0	0--	-	5.97	10.13
2009	SnJos	A+	2	2	0	0	7.1	26	3	2	2	1	0	0	2	0	0	7	0	0	0	0	-	0	0--	-	1.22	2.45
2009	Fresno	AAA	7	5	0	0	35.0	150	39	21	19	1	1	1	1	8	0	22	1	1	0	2	.000	0	0--	-	3.64	4.89
2009	SF	NL	9	5	0	1	30.0	148	46	27	25	4	2	2	1	12	2	19	0	0	3	2	.600	0	0-0	0	7.49	7.50

Pedro Martinez

Pitches: R **Bats:** R **Pos:** SP-9 **Ht:** 5'11" **Wt:** 195 **Born:** 10/25/1971 **Age:** 38

Year	Team	Lg	G	GS	CG	GF	IP	BFP	H	R	ER	HR	SH	SF	HB	TBB	IBB	SO	WP	Bk	W	L	Pct	Sh	Sv-Op	Hld	ERC	ERA
2009	LV*	AAA	1	1	0	0	5.0	21	3	5	4	1	0	1	0	3	0	4	0	0	0	1	.000	0	0--	-	3.28	7.20
2009	Rdng*	AA	1	1	0	0	6.0	23	5	4	3	1	0	0	0	3	0	11	0	0	0	1	1.000	0	0--	-	2.06	4.50
1992	LAD	NL	2	1	0	1	8.0	31	6	2	2	0	0	0	0	1	0	8	0	0	0	1	.000	0	0-0	0	1.38	2.25
1993	LAD	NL	65	2	0	20	107.0	444	76	34	31	5	0	5	4	57	4	119	3	1	10	5	.667	0	2-3	14	2.79	2.61
1994	Mon	NL	24	23	1	1	144.2	584	115	58	55	11	2	3	11	45	3	142	6	0	11	5	.688	1	1-1	0	2.81	3.42
1995	Mon	NL	30	30	2	0	194.2	784	158	79	76	21	7	3	11	66	1	174	5	2	14	10	.583	2	0-0	0	3.19	3.51
1996	Mon	NL	33	33	4	0	216.2	901	189	100	89	19	9	6	3	70	3	222	6	0	13	10	.565	1	0-0	0	3.02	3.70
1997	Mon	NL	31	31	13	0	241.1	947	158	65	51	16	9	1	9	67	3	305	3	1	17	8	.680	4	0-0	0	1.79	1.90
1998	Bos	AL	33	33	3	0	233.2	951	188	82	75	26	4	7	8	67	3	251	9	0	19	7	.731	2	0-0	0	2.78	2.89
1999	Bos	AL	31	29	5	1	213.1	835	160	56	49	9	3	6	9	37	1	313	6	0	23	4	.852	1	0-0	0	1.79	2.07
2000	Bos	AL	29	29	7	0	217.0	817	128	44	42	17	2	1	14	32	0	284	1	0	18	6	.750	4	0-0	0	1.39	1.74
2001	Bos	AL	18	18	1	0	116.2	456	84	33	31	5	2	0	6	25	0	163	4	0	7	3	.700	0	0-0	0	1.84	2.39
2002	Bos	AL	30	30	2	0	199.1	787	144	62	50	13	2	4	15	40	1	239	3	0	20	4	.833	0	0-0	0	1.98	2.26
2003	Bos	AL	29	29	3	0	186.2	749	147	52	46	7	4	4	9	47	0	206	5	0	14	4	.778	0	0-0	0	2.22	2.22
2004	Bos	AL	33	33	1	0	217.0	903	193	99	94	26	5	9	16	61	2	227	2	0	16	9	.640	1	0-0	0	3.44	3.90
2005	NYM	NL	31	31	4	0	217.0	843	159	69	68	19	9	2	4	47	3	208	4	0	15	8	.652	1	0-0	0	2.03	2.82
2006	NYM	NL	23	23	0	0	132.2	550	108	72	66	19	6	5	10	39	2	137	2	1	9	8	.529	0	0-0	0	3.18	4.48
2007	NYM	NL	5	5	0	0	28.0	128	33	11	8	0	1	2	2	7	1	32	1	0	3	1	.750	0	0-0	0	3.80	2.57

Year	Team	Lg	HOW MUCH HE PITCHED							WHAT HE GAVE UP												THE RESULTS							
			G	GS	CG	GF	IP	BFP	H	R	ER	HR	SH	SF	HB	TBB	IBB	SO	WP	Bk	W	L	Pct	Sh	Sv-Op	Hld	ERC	ERA
2008	NYM	NL	20	20	0	0	109.0	493	127	70	68	19	7	4	6	44	3	87	2	1	5	6	.455	0	0-0	0	5.80	5.61
2009	Phi	NL	9	9	0	0	44.2	191	48	18	18	7	2	1	4	8	0	37	0	0	5	1	.833	0	0-0	0	4.34	3.63
	Postseason		13	11	0	1	79.1	324	63	30	30	7	0	0	6	26	0	80	1	0	6	2	.750	0	0-0	0	2.95	3.40
	18 ML YEARS		476	409	46	23	2827.1	11394	2221	1006	919	239	74	63	141	760	30	3154	62	6	219	100	.687	17	3-4	14	2.54	2.93

Ramon Martinez

Bats: R Throws: R Pos: SS-10; 2B-2   Ht: 6'0" Wt: 190 Born: 10/10/1972 Age: 37

Year	Team	Lg	BATTING																		BASERUNNING				AVERAGES		
			G	AB	H	2B	3B	HR	(Hm	Rd)	TB	R	RBI	RC	TBB	IBB	SO	HBP	SH	SF	SB	CS	SB%	GDP	Avg	OBP	Slg
2009	Buffalo*	AAA	9	31	9	1	0	0	(	-)	10	5	1	3	4	0	5	0	0	0	0	1	.00	0	.290	.371	.323
1998	SF	NL	19	19	6	1	0	0	(0	0)	7	4	0	4	4	0	2	0	1	0	0	0	-	0	.316	.435	.368
1999	SF	NL	61	144	38	6	0	5	(3	2)	59	21	19	19	14	0	17	0	6	1	1	2	.33	2	.264	.327	.410
2000	SF	NL	88	189	57	13	2	6	(4	2)	92	30	25	31	15	1	22	1	4	1	3	2	.60	6	.302	.354	.487
2001	SF	NL	128	391	99	18	3	5	(1	4)	138	48	37	44	38	6	52	5	6	6	1	2	.33	11	.253	.323	.353
2002	SF	NL	72	181	49	10	2	4	(4	0)	75	26	25	33	14	2	26	4	0	1	2	0	1.00	1	.271	.335	.414
2003	ChC	NL	108	293	83	16	1	3	(3	0)	110	30	34	34	24	1	50	2	6	8	0	1	.00	8	.283	.333	.375
2004	ChC	NL	102	260	64	15	1	3	(1	2)	90	22	30	28	26	3	40	1	7	4	1	0	1.00	5	.246	.313	.346
2005	2 Tms		52	112	31	3	0	1	(1	0)	37	11	14	14	6	0	11	1	4	4	0	0	-	2	.277	.309	.330
2006	LAD	NL	82	176	49	7	1	2	(1	1)	64	20	24	24	15	1	20	1	2	0	0	0	-	9	.278	.339	.364
2007	LAD	NL	67	129	25	4	0	0	(0	0)	29	10	27	11	11	0	15	0	2	5	1	0	1.00	1	.194	.248	.225
2008	NYM	NL	7	16	4	3	0	0	(0	0)	7	0	3	2	2	0	3	0	0	0	0	0	-	1	.250	.333	.438
2009	NYM	NL	12	42	7	2	0	0	(0	0)	9	1	4	1	1	0	9	0	0	1	1	0	1.00	1	.167	.182	.214
05	Det	AL	19	56	15	1	0	0	(0	0)	16	4	5	7	3	0	4	0	2	1	0	0	-	1	.268	.300	.286
05	Phi	NL	33	56	16	2	0	1	(1	0)	21	7	9	7	3	0	7	1	2	3	0	0	-	1	.286	.317	.375
	Postseason		16	20	3	1	0	0	(0	0)	4	0	2	1	1	0	8	0	1	0	0	0	-	0	.150	.190	.200
	12 ML YEARS		798	1952	512	98	10	29	(18	11)	717	223	242	243	170	14	267	15	38	31	10	7	.59	46	.262	.321	.367

Victor Martinez

Bats: B Throws: R Pos: C-85; 1B-70; PH-4; DH-3   Ht: 6'2" Wt: 210 Born: 12/23/1978 Age: 31

Year	Team	Lg	BATTING																		BASERUNNING				AVERAGES		
			G	AB	H	2B	3B	HR	(Hm	Rd)	TB	R	RBI	RC	TBB	IBB	SO	HBP	SH	SF	SB	CS	SB%	GDP	Avg	OBP	Slg
2002	Cle	AL	12	32	9	1	0	1	(1	0)	13	2	5	5	3	0	2	0	0	1	0	0	-	1	.281	.333	.406
2003	Cle	AL	49	159	46	4	0	1	(0	1)	53	15	16	17	13	0	21	1	0	1	1	1	.50	8	.289	.345	.333
2004	Cle	AL	141	520	147	38	1	23	(8	15)	256	77	108	90	60	11	69	5	0	6	0	1	.00	16	.283	.359	.492
2005	Cle	AL	147	547	167	33	0	20	(10	10)	260	73	80	90	63	9	78	5	0	7	0	1	.00	16	.305	.378	.475
2006	Cle	AL	153	572	181	37	0	16	(4	12)	266	82	93	96	71	8	78	3	0	6	0	0	-	27	.316	.391	.465
2007	Cle	AL	147	562	169	40	0	25	(12	13)	284	78	114	108	62	12	76	10	0	11	0	0	-	19	.301	.374	.505
2008	Cle	AL	73	266	74	17	0	2	(2	0)	97	30	35	30	24	4	32	1	0	3	0	0	-	12	.278	.337	.365
2009	2 Tms	AL	155	588	178	33	1	23	(7	16)	282	88	108	101	75	3	74	3	0	6	1	0	1.00	17	.303	.381	.480
09	Cle	AL	99	377	107	21	1	15	(6	9)	175	56	67	64	51	3	51	2	0	5	0	0	-	11	.284	.368	.464
09	Bos	AL	56	211	71	12	0	8	(1	7)	107	32	41	37	24	0	23	1	0	1	1	0	1.00	6	.336	.405	.507
	Postseason		11	44	14	2	0	2	(1	1)	22	6	7	8	4	3	8	1	0	0	0	0	-	0	.318	.388	.500
	8 ML YEARS		877	3246	971	203	2	111	(44	67)	1511	445	559	543	371	47	430	28	0	41	2	3	.40	116	.299	.372	.465

Shairon Martis

Pitches: R Bats: R Pos: SP-15   Ht: 6'1" Wt: 226 Born: 3/30/1987 Age: 23

Year	Team	Lg	HOW MUCH HE PITCHED							WHAT HE GAVE UP												THE RESULTS							
			G	GS	CG	GF	IP	BFP	H	R	ER	HR	SH	SF	HB	TBB	IBB	SO	WP	Bk	W	L	Pct	Sh	Sv-Op	Hld	ERC	ERA
2005	Giants	R	11	5	0	4	34.0	137	28	10	7	1	3	0	1	9	0	50	3	0	2	1	.667	0	1--	-	2.33	1.85
2006	Augsta	A	15	15	0	0	76.2	325	76	39	31	3	2	2	4	21	0	66	3	0	6	4	.600	0	0--	-	3.31	3.64
2006	Savann	A	4	4	0	0	21.1	86	23	9	9	2	0	1	0	4	0	14	0	1	1	1	.500	0	0--	-	3.79	3.80
2006	Ptomc	A+	2	2	0	0	12.0	47	9	5	4	0	0	0	1	3	0	7	1	0	0	2	.000	0	0--	-	1.99	3.00
2006	Hrsbrg	A	1	1	0	0	5.0	26	8	7	7	4	0	0	0	3	0	1	0	0	0	1	.000	0	0--	-	14.97	12.60
2007	Ptomc	A+	27	26	1	0	151.0	645	150	83	71	9	3	4	5	52	0	108	11	2	14	8	.636	0	0--	-	3.68	4.23
2008	Hrsbrg	AA	14	14	0	0	74.2	317	73	35	33	5	4	2	0	28	1	57	3	0	4	4	.500	0	0--	-	3.62	3.98
2008	Clmbs	AAA	7	7	0	0	41.2	182	42	17	14	2	0	3	1	17	0	42	3	1	1	2	.333	0	0--	-	3.85	3.02
2009	Syrcse	AAA	13	13	0	0	74.1	323	90	42	41	7	2	5	1	18	1	40	2	1	4	4	.500	0	0--	-	4.86	4.96
2008	Was	NL	5	4	0	0	20.2	92	18	14	13	5	0	1	0	12	0	23	1	0	1	3	.250	0	0-0	0	4.98	5.66
2009	Was	NL	15	15	1	0	85.2	377	83	52	50	11	5	3	4	39	3	34	3	0	5	3	.625	0	0-0	0	4.43	5.25
	2 ML YEARS		20	19	1	0	106.1	469	101	66	63	16	5	4	4	51	3	57	4	0	6	6	.500	0	0-0	0	4.54	5.33

Nick Masset

Pitches: R Bats: R Pos: RP-74   Ht: 6'4" Wt: 235 Born: 5/17/1982 Age: 28

Year	Team	Lg	HOW MUCH HE PITCHED							WHAT HE GAVE UP												THE RESULTS							
			G	GS	CG	GF	IP	BFP	H	R	ER	HR	SH	SF	HB	TBB	IBB	SO	WP	Bk	W	L	Pct	Sh	Sv-Op	Hld	ERC	ERA
2006	Tex	AL	8	0	0	7	8.2	36	9	4	4	0	2	0	2	2	0	4	0	0	0	0	-	0	0-0	0	4.05	4.15
2007	CWS	AL	27	1	0	4	39.1	193	52	33	31	2	1	3	2	26	5	21	4	0	2	3	.400	0	0-1	2	6.63	7.09
2008	2 Tms		42	1	0	12	62.0	271	71	32	27	7	3	1	2	26	4	43	3	1	2	0	1.000	0	1-3	2	5.27	3.92
2009	Cin	NL	74	0	0	15	76.0	292	54	22	20	6	1	4	1	24	0	70	6	0	5	1	.833	0	2-2	20	2.24	2.37
08	CWS	AL	32	1	0	11	44.2	203	55	26	23	4	3	1	2	21	4	32	2	1	1	0	1.000	0	1-1	1	5.78	4.63
08	Cin	NL	10	0	0	1	17.1	68	16	6	4	3	0	0	0	5	0	11	1	0	1	0	1.000	0	0-2	1	3.93	2.08
	4 ML YEARS		151	2	0	38	186.0	792	186	91	82	15	5	7	6	78	9	138	13	1	9	4	.692	0	1-6	24	4.16	3.97

Justin Masterson

Pitches: R **Bats:** R **Pos:** RP-26; SP-16   **Ht:** 6'6" **Wt:** 250 **Born:** 3/22/1985 **Age:** 25

Year	Team	Lg	G	GS	CG	GF	IP	BFP	H	R	ER	HR	SH	SF	HB	TBB	IBB	SO	WP	Bk	W	L	Pct	Sh	Sv-Op	Hld	ERC	ERA
2006	Lowell	A-	14	0	0	1	31.2	120	20	4	3	0	0	0	3	2	0	33	1	0	3	1	.750	0	0- -	-	1.12	0.85
2007	Lancst	A+	17	17	0	0	95.2	410	103	56	46	4	2	5	6	22	0	56	1	0	8	5	.615	0	0- -	-	3.66	4.33
2007	Portlnd	AA	10	10	0	0	58.0	239	49	29	28	4	1	0	2	18	0	59	3	0	4	3	.571	0	0- -	-	2.83	4.34
2008	Portlnd	AA	8	8	0	0	38.1	169	37	22	18	0	1	1	3	16	0	37	2	0	1	3	.250	0	0- -	-	3.48	4.23
2008	Pwtckt	AAA	4	1	0	0	9.1	35	6	4	3	1	2	0	1	1	0	8	1	0	1	0	1.000	0	0- -	-	1.70	2.89
2008	Bos	AL	36	9	0	6	88.1	365	68	31	31	10	1	1	8	40	3	68	1	0	6	5	.545	0	0-1	3	3.51	3.16
2009	2 Tms	AL	42	16	1	4	129.1	568	128	73	65	12	10	7	8	60	3	119	5	0	4	10	.286	0	0-1	6	4.45	4.52
09	Bos	AL	31	6	0	4	72.0	312	72	38	36	7	9	6	6	25	2	67	3	0	3	3	.500	0	0-1	6	4.13	4.50
09	Cle	AL	11	10	1	0	57.1	256	56	35	29	5	1	1	2	35	1	52	2	0	1	7	.125	0	0-0	0	4.85	4.55
	Postseason		9	0	0	1	9.2	40	10	3	2	0	1	0	1	5	0	9	0	0	1	0	1.000	0	0-1	4	4.85	1.86
	2 ML YEARS		78	25	1	10	217.2	933	196	104	96	22	11	8	16	100	6	187	6	0	10	15	.400	0	0-2	9	4.06	3.97

Tom Mastny

Pitches: R **Bats:** R **Pos:** P   **Ht:** 6'6" **Wt:** 225 **Born:** 2/4/1981 **Age:** 29

Year	Team	Lg	G	GS	CG	GF	IP	BFP	H	R	ER	HR	SH	SF	HB	TBB	IBB	SO	WP	Bk	W	L	Pct	Sh	Sv-Op	Hld	ERC	ERA
2009	Yokha*	Jap	15	12	0	1	61.2	296	79	45	39	8	-	-	11	25	0	43	6	0	1	5	.167	0	0- -	-	6.69	5.69
2006	Cle	AL	15	0	0	12	16.1	73	17	10	10	1	1	2	1	8	1	14	0	0	0	1	.000	0	5-7	0	4.53	5.51
2007	Cle	AL	51	0	0	18	57.2	262	63	30	30	6	3	2	2	32	9	52	5	0	7	2	.778	0	0-0	7	5.16	4.68
2008	Cle	AL	14	1	0	4	20.0	100	28	24	24	6	0	1	0	11	2	19	0	0	2	2	.500	0	0-1	0	8.39	10.80
	Postseason		3	0	0	1	4.2	18	2	0	0	0	0	2	0	2	0	3	0	0	1	0	1.000	0	0-0	0	1.08	0.00
	3 ML YEARS		80	1	0	34	94.0	435	108	64	64	13	4	5	3	51	12	85	5	0	9	5	.643	0	5-8	7	5.71	6.13

Doug Mathis

Pitches: R **Bats:** R **Pos:** RP-22; SP-2   **Ht:** 6'3" **Wt:** 220 **Born:** 6/7/1983 **Age:** 27

Year	Team	Lg	G	GS	CG	GF	IP	BFP	H	R	ER	HR	SH	SF	HB	TBB	IBB	SO	WP	Bk	W	L	Pct	Sh	Sv-Op	Hld	ERC	ERA
2005	Spkane	A-	17	16	0	0	84.0	346	78	33	25	2	2	0	6	17	0	78	7	0	4	7	.364	0	0- -	-	2.72	2.68
2006	Bkrsfld	A+	26	25	2	1	150.2	641	160	76	70	14	2	2	8	47	0	109	8	1	10	7	.588	1	0- -	-	4.32	4.18
2006	Frisco	AA	2	2	0	0	10.0	49	14	5	4	0	0	1	0	5	1	10	0	0	0	0	-	0	0- -	-	6.21	3.60
2007	Okla	AAA	3	2	0	0	12.2	63	21	16	15	2	0	1	0	6	0	8	1	0	0	3	.000	0	0- -	-	9.09	10.66
2007	Frisco	AA	22	22	1	0	131.2	559	140	59	55	7	3	4	5	40	0	92	3	0	11	7	.611	1	0- -	-	3.93	3.76
2007	Rngrs	R	1	1	0	0	2.2	15	7	5	5	0	0	0	0	1	0	2	0	0	0	0	-	0	0- -	-	14.52	16.88
2008	Okla	AAA	10	10	0	0	53.2	222	51	28	20	7	2	4	1	14	0	36	0	0	5	1	.833	0	0- -	-	3.55	3.35
2008	Rngrs	R	1	1	0	0	2.0	7	1	1	1	0	0	0	0	0	0	3	0	0	0	0	-	0	0- -	-	1.73	4.50
2009	Okla	AAA	11	10	2	0	57.0	244	64	23	18	3	2	1	2	15	0	38	4	0	4	2	.667	1	0- -	-	4.07	2.84
2008	Tex	AL	8	4	0	3	22.1	112	37	20	17	3	1	0	0	14	2	9	1	0	2	1	.667	0	0-0	0	9.60	6.85
2009	Tex	AL	24	2	0	13	42.2	172	39	17	15	4	0	2	2	10	0	25	0	0	0	1	.000	0	1-1	1	3.20	3.16
	2 ML YEARS		32	6	0	16	65.0	284	76	37	32	7	1	0	2	24	2	34	1	0	2	2	.500	0	1-1	1	5.18	4.43

Jeff Mathis

Bats: R **Throws:** R **Pos:** C-79; PH-5; DH-4   **Ht:** 6'0" **Wt:** 200 **Born:** 3/31/1983 **Age:** 27

Year	Team	Lg	G	AB	H	2B	3B	HR	(Hm	Rd)	TB	R	RBI	RC	TBB	IBB	SO	HBP	SH	SF	SB	CS	SB%	GDP	Avg	OBP	Slg
2005	LAA	AL	5	3	1	0	0	0	(0	0)	1	1	0	0	0	0	1	0	0	0	0	0	-	0	.333	.333	.333
2006	LAA	AL	23	55	8	2	0	2	(1	1)	16	9	6	4	7	1	14	0	0	1	0	0	-	0	.145	.238	.291
2007	LAA	AL	59	171	36	12	0	4	(3	1)	60	24	23	13	15	0	49	2	3	4	0	1	.00	3	.211	.276	.351
2008	LAA	AL	94	283	55	8	0	9	(4	5)	90	35	42	33	30	4	90	3	8	4	2	2	.50	1	.194	.275	.318
2009	LAA	AL	84	237	50	8	0	5	(3	2)	73	26	28	24	22	0	73	4	8	1	2	3	.40	2	.211	.288	.308
	Postseason		3	5	1	0	0	0	(0	0)	1	0	1	0	0	0	1	0	0	0	0	0	-	0	.200	.200	.200
	5 ML YEARS		265	749	150	30	0	20	(11	9)	240	95	99	74	74	5	227	9	19	10	4	6	.40	6	.200	.277	.320

Osiris Matos

Pitches: R **Bats:** R **Pos:** RP-5   **Ht:** 6'1" **Wt:** 202 **Born:** 8/6/1984 **Age:** 25

Year	Team	Lg	G	GS	CG	GF	IP	BFP	H	R	ER	HR	SH	SF	HB	TBB	IBB	SO	WP	Bk	W	L	Pct	Sh	Sv-Op	Hld	ERC	ERA
2002	Giants	R	13	13	0	0	62.0	268	63	35	32	3	1	5	3	22	0	51	1	1	4	2	.667	0	0- -	-	3.81	4.65
2003	Giants	R	9	6	0	0	34.2	151	35	21	18	1	1	4	2	0	0	28	3	0	2	2	.500	0	0- -	-	2.15	4.67
2004	Giants	R	11	8	0	0	48.0	212	43	23	13	1	1	1	3	20	0	47	2	1	2	0	1.000	0	1- -	-	3.14	2.44
2005	Augsta	A	29	22	0	3	135.1	594	162	83	75	12	4	6	8	31	0	79	1	1	8	8	.500	0	0- -	-	4.66	4.99
2006	Augsta	A	44	0	0	30	61.1	237	42	13	12	3	3	4	0	12	0	81	3	0	7	3	.700	0	13- -	-	1.53	1.76
2006	Conn	AA	6	0	0	3	9.2	41	11	4	4	0	0	0	0	2	1	5	0	0	0	0	-	0	2- -	-	3.23	3.72
2007	Conn	AA	35	0	0	12	56.0	239	50	20	18	3	5	2	1	21	2	43	1	0	5	0	1.000	0	4- -	-	3.04	2.89
2007	Augsta	A	7	0	0	6	9.0	29	1	0	0	0	0	0	0	1	0	9	0	0	5	0	1.000	0	4- -	-	0.09	0.00
2008	Conn	AA	27	0	0	14	36.2	144	25	5	5	0	1	0	1	11	0	37	1	0	0	0	-	0	8- -	-	1.64	1.23
2008	Fresno	AAA	5	0	0	1	9.2	36	5	0	0	0	0	0	0	2	0	13	0	0	1	0	1.000	0	1- -	-	0.91	0.00
2009	Fresno	AAA	45	0	0	11	54.1	231	56	23	21	7	6	2	2	13	0	48	3	0	3	3	.500	0	2- -	-	3.92	3.48
2008	SF	NL	20	0	0	5	20.2	98	26	17	11	3	1	3	1	9	1	16	0	0	1	2	.333	0	0-1	0	6.06	4.79
2009	SF	NL	5	0	0	2	6.0	31	11	7	6	2	0	0	0	1	0	5	0	0	0	0	-	0	0-0	0	9.74	9.00
	2 ML YEARS		25	0	0	7	26.2	129	37	24	17	5	1	3	1	10	1	21	0	0	1	2	.333	0	0-1	0	6.87	5.74

Hideki Matsui

Bats: L Throws: R Pos: DH-118; PH-26   Ht: 6'2" Wt: 210 Born: 6/12/1974 Age: 36

Year	Team	Lg	G	AB	H	2B	3B	HR	(Hm	Rd)	TB	R	RBI	RC	TBB	IBB	SO	HBP	SH	SF	SB	CS	SB%	GDP	Avg	OBP	Slg
2003	NYY	AL	163	623	179	42	1	16	(9	7)	271	82	106	96	63	5	86	3	0	6	2	2	.50	25	.287	.353	.435
2004	NYY	AL	162	584	174	34	2	31	(18	13)	305	109	108	117	88	2	103	3	0	5	3	0	1.00	11	.298	.390	.522
2005	NYY	AL	162	629	192	45	3	23	(15	8)	312	108	116	109	63	7	78	3	0	8	2	2	.50	16	.305	.367	.496
2006	NYY	AL	51	172	52	9	0	8	(1	7)	85	32	29	30	27	2	23	0	0	2	1	0	1.00	6	.302	.393	.494
2007	NYY	AL	143	547	156	28	4	25	(16	9)	267	100	103	91	73	2	73	3	0	10	4	2	.67	9	.285	.367	.488
2008	NYY	AL	93	337	99	17	0	9	(3	6)	143	43	45	56	38	6	47	3	0	0	0	0	-	10	.294	.370	.424
2009	NYY	AL	142	456	125	21	1	28	(13	15)	232	62	90	88	64	1	75	4	0	2	0	1	.00	4	.274	.367	.509
	Postseason		41	162	49	13	1	6	(2	4)	82	27	26	25	18	2	23	1	0	2	0	0	-	4	.302	.372	.506
	7 ML YEARS		916	3348	977	196	11	140	(75	65)	1615	536	597	587	416	25	485	19	0	33	12	7	.63	81	.292	.370	.482

Kaz Matsui

Bats: B Throws: R Pos: 2B-130; PH-2; PR-2   Ht: 5'10" Wt: 185 Born: 10/23/1975 Age: 34

Year	Team	Lg	G	AB	H	2B	3B	HR	(Hm	Rd)	TB	R	RBI	RC	TBB	IBB	SO	HBP	SH	SF	SB	CS	SB%	GDP	Avg	OBP	Slg
2009	CpChr*	AA	4	14	3	0	0	0	(-	-)	3	3	2	1	2	0	4	0	0	0	0	0	-	0	.214	.313	.214
2004	NYM	NL	114	460	125	32	2	7	(4	3)	182	65	44	63	40	4	97	2	5	2	14	3	.82	3	.272	.331	.396
2005	NYM	NL	87	267	68	9	4	3	(1	2)	94	31	24	27	14	1	43	5	5	4	6	1	.86	2	.255	.300	.352
2006	2 Tms	NL	70	243	65	12	3	3	(0	3)	92	32	26	28	16	1	46	0	4	2	10	1	.91	1	.267	.310	.379
2007	Col	NL	104	410	118	24	6	4	(0	4)	166	84	37	61	34	1	69	0	8	1	32	4	.89	1	.288	.342	.405
2008	Hou	NL	96	375	110	26	3	6	(4	2)	160	58	33	53	37	0	53	0	7	3	20	5	.80	3	.293	.354	.427
2009	Hou	NL	132	476	119	20	2	9	(5	4)	170	56	46	59	34	2	85	3	16	4	19	3	.86	4	.250	.302	.357
06	NYM	NL	38	130	26	6	0	1	(0	1)	35	10	7	5	6	1	19	0	3	0	2	0	1.00	1	.200	.235	.260
06	Col	NL	32	113	39	6	3	2	(0	2)	57	22	19	23	10	0	27	0	1	2	8	1	.89	0	.345	.392	.504
	Postseason		11	46	14	2	2	1	(0	1)	23	5	8	9	3	1	12	0	1	0	2	0	1.00	0	.304	.347	.500
	6 ML YEARS		603	2231	605	123	20	32	(18	14)	864	326	210	291	175	9	393	10	45	16	101	17	.86	14	.271	.325	.387

Daisuke Matsuzaka

Pitches: R Bats: R Pos: SP-12   Ht: 6'0" Wt: 185 Born: 9/13/1980 Age: 29

			HOW MUCH HE PITCHED						WHAT HE GAVE UP										THE RESULTS						
Year	Team	Lg	G	GS	CG	GF	IP	BFP	H	R	ER	HR	SH	SF	HB	TBB	IBB	SO	WP	Bk	W	L	Pct	Sh	Sv-Op	Hld	ERC	ERA
2009	RedSx*	R	1	1	0	0	3.0	11	1	0	0	0	0	0	1	0	0	4	1	0	0	0	-	0	0--	-	0.69	0.00
2009	Portlnd*	AA	1	1	0	0	2.0	13	4	5	5	1	0	1	0	3	0	2	0	0	0	1	.000	0	0--	-	20.26	22.50
2009	Pwtckt*	AAA	4	4	0	0	16.0	67	13	4	4	2	0	0	1	6	0	17	0	0	0	1	.000	0	0--	-	3.36	2.25
2007	Bos	AL	32	32	1	0	204.2	874	191	100	100	25	3	2	13	80	1	201	5	0	15	12	.556	0	0-0	0	4.10	4.40
2008	Bos	AL	29	29	0	0	167.2	716	128	58	54	12	3	4	7	94	1	154	5	0	18	3	.857	0	0-0	0	3.36	2.90
2009	Bos	AL	12	12	0	0	59.1	283	81	38	38	10	1	1	2	30	1	54	8	0	4	6	.400	0	0-0	0	7.45	5.76
	Postseason		7	7	0	0	35.2	163	39	19	19	4	0	1	1	17	0	33	4	0	3	1	.750	0	0-0	0	5.04	4.79
	3 ML YEARS		73	73	1	0	431.2	1873	400	196	192	47	7	7	22	204	3	409	18	0	37	21	.638	0	0-0	0	4.22	4.00

Gary Matthews Jr.

Bats: B Throws: R Pos: CF-56; RF-28; PH-14; LF-12; DH-3; PR-2   Ht: 6'3" Wt: 225 Born: 8/25/1974 Age: 35

Year	Team	Lg	G	AB	H	2B	3B	HR	(Hm	Rd)	TB	R	RBI	RC	TBB	IBB	SO	HBP	SH	SF	SB	CS	SB%	GDP	Avg	OBP	Slg
1999	SD	NL	23	36	8	0	0	0	(0	0)	8	4	7	4	9	0	9	0	0	0	2	0	1.00	1	.222	.378	.222
2000	ChC	NL	80	158	30	1	2	4	(2	2)	47	24	14	13	15	1	28	1	1	0	3	0	1.00	2	.190	.264	.297
2001	2 Tms	NL	152	405	92	15	2	14	(4	10)	153	63	44	51	60	2	100	1	5	1	8	5	.62	8	.227	.328	.378
2002	2 Tms		111	345	95	25	3	7	(6	1)	147	54	38	55	43	1	69	1	5	4	15	5	.75	4	.275	.354	.426
2003	2 Tms		144	468	116	31	2	6	(3	3)	169	71	42	51	43	0	95	2	0	0	12	8	.60	8	.248	.314	.361
2004	Tex	AL	87	280	77	17	1	11	(7	4)	129	37	36	48	33	5	64	1	0	3	5	1	.83	1	.275	.350	.461
2005	Tex	AL	131	475	121	25	5	17	(8	9)	207	72	55	63	47	1	90	0	1	3	9	2	.82	11	.255	.320	.436
2006	Tex	AL	147	620	194	44	6	19	(11	8)	307	102	79	109	58	5	99	4	0	8	10	7	.59	8	.313	.371	.495
2007	LAA	AL	140	516	130	26	3	18	(7	11)	216	79	72	66	55	6	102	2	0	6	18	4	.82	12	.252	.323	.419
2008	LAA	AL	127	426	103	19	3	8	(2	6)	152	53	46	47	45	2	95	4	0	2	8	3	.73	12	.242	.319	.357
2009	LAA	AL	103	316	79	19	2	4	(2	2)	114	44	50	50	40	2	74	2	0	2	4	1	.80	4	.250	.336	.361
01	ChC	NL	106	258	56	9	1	9	(2	7)	94	41	30	31	38	2	55	1	5	0	5	3	.63	4	.217	.320	.364
01	Pit	NL	46	147	36	6	1	5	(2	3)	59	22	14	20	22	0	45	0	0	1	3	2	.60	4	.245	.341	.401
02	NYM	NL	2	1	0	0	0	0	(0	0)	0	0	0	0	0	0	0	0	0	0	0	0	-	0	.000	.000	.000
02	Bal	AL	109	344	95	25	3	7	(6	1)	147	54	38	55	43	1	69	1	5	4	15	5	.75	4	.276	.355	.427
03	Bal	AL	41	162	33	12	1	0	(0	0)	53	21	20	15	9	0	29	1	0	0	0	3	.00	4	.204	.240	.327
03	SD	NL	103	306	83	19	1	4	(1	3)	116	50	22	36	34	0	66	1	0	0	12	5	.71	4	.271	.346	.379
	Postseason		3	5	0	0	0	0	(0	0)	0	0	0	0	0	0	2	0	0	0	0	0	-	0	.000	.000	.000
	11 ML YEARS		1245	4045	1045	222	29	108	(52	56)	1649	603	483	557	448	25	825	18	12	29	94	36	.72	71	.258	.333	.408

Brian Matusz

Pitches: L Bats: L Pos: SP-8   Ht: 6'5" Wt: 200 Born: 2/11/1987 Age: 23

			HOW MUCH HE PITCHED						WHAT HE GAVE UP										THE RESULTS						
Year	Team	Lg	G	GS	CG	GF	IP	BFP	H	R	ER	HR	SH	SF	HB	TBB	IBB	SO	WP	Bk	W	L	Pct	Sh	Sv-Op	Hld	ERC	ERA
2009	Frdrck	A+	11	11	0	0	66.2	276	56	22	16	5	4	1	2	21	0	75	5	0	4	2	.667	0	0--	-	2.76	2.16
2009	Bowie	AA	8	8	1	0	46.1	176	31	9	8	2	0	0	1	11	0	46	0	0	7	0	1.000	1	0--	-	1.65	1.55
2009	Bal	AL	8	8	0	0	44.2	196	52	24	23	6	2	2	0	14	0	38	0	0	5	2	.714	0	0-0	0	4.91	4.63

Joe Mauer

Bats: L **Throws:** R **Pos:** C-109; DH-28; PH-5   **Ht:** 6'5" **Wt:** 225 **Born:** 4/19/1983 **Age:** 27

Year	Team	Lg	G	AB	H	2B	3B	HR	(Hm	Rd)	TB	R	RBI	RC	TBB	IBB	SO	HBP	SH	SF	SB	CS	SB%	GDP	Avg	OBP	Slg
2009	FtMyrs*	A+	5	15	6	2	0	0	(-	-)	8	2	4	3	2	0	1	0	0	1	0	0	-	0	.400	.444	.533
2004	Min	AL	35	107	33	8	1	6	(4	2)	61	18	17	21	11	0	14	1	0	3	1	0	1.00	1	.308	.369	.570
2005	Min	AL	131	489	144	26	2	9	(4	5)	201	61	55	78	61	12	64	1	0	3	13	1	.93	9	.294	.372	.411
2006	Min	AL	140	521	181	36	4	13	(3	10)	264	86	84	103	79	21	54	1	0	7	8	3	.73	24	.347	.429	.507
2007	Min	AL	109	406	119	27	3	7	(2	5)	173	62	60	69	57	10	51	3	2	3	7	1	.88	11	.293	.382	.426
2008	Min	AL	146	536	176	31	4	9	(7	2)	242	98	85	103	84	8	50	1	1	11	1	1	.50	21	.328	.413	.451
2009	Min	AL	138	523	191	30	1	28	(16	12)	307	94	96	123	76	14	63	2	0	5	4	1	.80	13	.365	.444	.587
Postseason			3	11	2	0	0	0	(0	0)	2	0	0	0	1	0	0	0	0	0	0	0	-	0	.182	.250	.182
6 ML YEARS			699	2582	844	158	15	72	(36	36)	1248	419	397	497	368	65	296	9	3	32	34	7	.83	79	.327	.408	.483

Justin Maxwell

Bats: R **Throws:** R **Pos:** CF-32; PH-5; PR-5; LF-2; RF-2   **Ht:** 6'5" **Wt:** 235 **Born:** 11/6/1983 **Age:** 26

Year	Team	Lg	G	AB	H	2B	3B	HR	(Hm	Rd)	TB	R	RBI	RC	TBB	IBB	SO	HBP	SH	SF	SB	CS	SB%	GDP	Avg	OBP	Slg
2006	Savann	A	17	58	10	2	2	1	(-	-)	19	8	7	6	8	0	23	2	0	0	1	0	1.00	1	.172	.294	.328
2006	Vrmnt	A-	74	271	73	11	3	4	(-	-)	102	36	33	39	27	0	61	6	0	2	20	5	.80	3	.269	.346	.376
2007	Hgrstn	A-	56	209	63	12	2	14	(-	-)	121	51	40	47	26	0	57	6	0	3	14	3	.82	0	.301	.389	.579
2007	Ptomc	A+	58	228	60	13	0	13	(-	-)	112	35	43	41	24	0	65	4	0	4	21	5	.81	7	.263	.338	.491
2008	Hrsbrg	AA	43	146	34	6	3	7	(-	-)	67	35	28	27	31	2	28	1	0	2	13	4	.76	3	.233	.367	.459
2009	Syrcse	AAA	111	384	93	10	5	13	(-	-)	152	68	42	59	54	2	136	6	3	1	35	8	.81	10	.242	.344	.396
2007	Was	NL	15	26	7	0	0	2	(0	2)	13	5	5	4	1	0	8	0	0	0	0	0	-	0	.269	.296	.500
2009	Was	NL	40	89	22	4	1	4	(1	3)	40	13	9	15	12	0	32	1	0	0	6	1	.86	1	.247	.343	.449
2 ML YEARS			55	115	29	4	1	6	(1	5)	53	18	14	19	13	0	40	1	0	0	6	1	.86	1	.252	.333	.461

John Mayberry

Bats: R **Throws:** R **Pos:** LF-26; PH-12; PR-5; RF-4   **Ht:** 6'6" **Wt:** 230 **Born:** 12/21/1983 **Age:** 26

Year	Team	Lg	G	AB	H	2B	3B	HR	(Hm	Rd)	TB	R	RBI	RC	TBB	IBB	SO	HBP	SH	SF	SB	CS	SB%	GDP	Avg	OBP	Slg
2005	Spkane	A-	71	265	67	16	0	11	(-	-)	116	51	26	41	26	1	71	10	0	1	7	3	.70	1	.253	.341	.438
2006	Clinton	A	126	459	123	26	4	21	(-	-)	220	77	77	83	59	2	117	9	0	6	9	3	.75	7	.268	.358	.479
2007	Bkrsfld	A+	63	244	56	15	1	16	(-	-)	121	47	45	41	28	2	64	3	0	2	9	1	.90	7	.230	.314	.496
2007	Frisco	AA	69	245	59	10	0	14	(-	-)	111	35	38	36	20	0	62	4	1	1	7	1	.88	6	.241	.307	.453
2008	Frisco	AA	21	82	22	8	0	4	(-	-)	42	16	13	14	4	0	21	3	0	1	4	1	.80	3	.268	.322	.512
2008	Okla	AAA	114	437	115	30	7	16	(-	-)	207	49	58	67	30	2	85	5	1	2	6	2	.75	9	.263	.316	.474
2009	LV	AAA	89	316	81	20	2	13	(-	-)	144	44	43	50	34	0	94	4	0	4	6	2	.75	6	.256	.332	.456
2009	Phi	NL	39	57	12	3	0	4	(1	3)	27	8	8	5	2	0	23	1	0	0	0	0	-	2	.211	.250	.474

Cameron Maybin

Bats: R **Throws:** R **Pos:** CF-52; PR-3; PH-1   **Ht:** 6'3" **Wt:** 206 **Born:** 4/4/1987 **Age:** 23

Year	Team	Lg	G	AB	H	2B	3B	HR	(Hm	Rd)	TB	R	RBI	RC	TBB	IBB	SO	HBP	SH	SF	SB	CS	SB%	GDP	Avg	OBP	Slg
2009	NewOr*	AAA	82	298	95	18	8	3	(-	-)	138	44	39	57	38	0	58	3	2	2	8	2	.80	2	.319	.399	.463
2007	Det	AL	24	49	7	3	0	1	(0	1)	13	8	2	2	3	0	21	1	0	0	5	0	1.00	0	.143	.208	.265
2008	Fla	NL	8	32	16	2	0	0	(0	0)	18	9	2	8	3	0	8	0	1	0	4	0	1.00	0	.500	.543	.563
2009	Fla	NL	54	176	44	12	2	4	(1	3)	72	30	13	15	17	1	51	1	4	1	1	3	.25	2	.250	.318	.409
3 ML YEARS			86	257	67	17	2	5	(1	4)	103	47	17	25	23	1	80	2	5	1	10	3	.77	2	.261	.325	.401

Edwin Maysonet

Bats: R **Throws:** R **Pos:** 2B-15; PH-12; 3B-7; PR-4; SS-3   **Ht:** 6'1" **Wt:** 180 **Born:** 10/17/1981 **Age:** 28

Year	Team	Lg	G	AB	H	2B	3B	HR	(Hm	Rd)	TB	R	RBI	RC	TBB	IBB	SO	HBP	SH	SF	SB	CS	SB%	GDP	Avg	OBP	Slg
2003	TriCity	A-	45	138	38	7	1	1	(-	-)	50	30	13	26	29	0	28	5	3	3	9	1	.90	0	.275	.411	.362
2004	Lxngtn	A	109	391	102	22	10	11	(-	-)	177	79	63	72	64	1	91	9	14	7	18	7	.72	4	.261	.372	.453
2005	Salem	A+	66	236	46	9	2	1	(-	-)	62	29	16	19	26	0	69	3	12	4	4	2	.67	4	.195	.279	.263
2005	Lxngtn	A	45	173	45	11	1	4	(-	-)	70	29	17	27	15	0	29	10	2	1	11	4	.73	0	.260	.352	.405
2006	Salem	A+	113	378	96	32	0	8	(-	-)	152	58	38	51	20	1	58	8	11	4	21	3	.88	3	.254	.302	.402
2007	CpChr	AA	107	341	92	14	2	5	(-	-)	125	35	39	40	17	0	65	2	10	2	5	2	.71	9	.270	.307	.367
2008	RdRck	AAA	117	406	110	24	1	6	(-	-)	154	59	34	57	44	0	70	4	6	6	4	3	.57	5	.271	.343	.379
2009	RdRck	AAA	59	187	44	11	0	1	(-	-)	58	21	14	22	26	0	39	1	2	1	3	0	1.00	6	.235	.330	.310
2008	Hou	NL	7	7	1	0	0	0	(0	0)	1	0	0	0	0	0	2	0	0	0	0	0	-	0	.143	.143	.143
2009	Hou	NL	39	69	20	2	0	1	(0	1)	25	9	7	9	5	0	19	0	4	1	0	0	-	1	.290	.333	.362
2 ML YEARS			46	76	21	2	0	1	(0	1)	26	9	7	9	5	0	21	0	4	1	0	0	-	1	.276	.317	.342

Vin Mazzaro

Pitches: R **Bats:** R **Pos:** SP-17   **Ht:** 6'1" **Wt:** 215 **Born:** 9/27/1986 **Age:** 23

	HOW MUCH HE PITCHED							WHAT HE GAVE UP											THE RESULTS						
Year	Team	Lg	G	GS	CG	GF	IP	BFP	H	R	ER	HR	SH	SF	HB	TBB	IBB	SO	WP	Bk	W	L	Pct	Sh	Sv-Op Hld	ERC	ERA
2006	Kane	A	24	24	0	0	119.1	530	146	81	67	7	2	4	11	42	0	81	10	3	9	9	.500	0	0- - -	5.38	5.05
2007	Stcktn	A+	28	28	0	0	153.2	678	159	97	91	13	2	6	13	71	0	115	13	1	9	12	.429	0	0- - -	4.82	5.33

Year	Team	Lg	G	GS	CG	GF	IP	BFP	H	R	ER	HR	SH	SF	HB	TBB	IBB	SO	WP	Bk	W	L	Pct	Sh	Sv-Op	Hld	ERC	ERA
2008	Mdland	AA	23	23	0	0	145.1	585	119	40	29	3	6	2	11	36	0	114	6	0	13	3	.813	0	0- -	-	2.37	1.80
2008	Scrmto	AAA	6	5	0	0	33.2	161	49	26	23	3	1	2	5	9	0	27	2	0	3	3	.500	0	0- -	-	6.75	6.15
2009	Scrmto	AAA	10	9	0	1	56.2	230	42	17	15	2	1	1	6	17	1	44	5	0	2	2	.500	0	0- -	-	2.32	2.38
2009	Oak	AL	17	17	0	0	91.1	423	120	61	54	12	1	3	4	39	3	59	5	0	4	9	.308	0	0-0	0	6.49	5.32

Brian McCann

Bats: L Throws: R Pos: C-127; PH-13; DH-1 **Ht: 6'3" Wt: 230 Born: 2/20/1984 Age: 26**

Year	Team	Lg	G	AB	H	2B	3B	HR	(Hm	Rd)	TB	R	RBI	RC	TBB	IBB	SO	HBP	SH	SF	SB	CS	SB%	GDP	Avg	OBP	Slg
2009	MrtlBh*	A+	2	6	2	0	0	0	(-	-)	4	1	1	1	1	0	2	0	0	0	0	0	-	0	.333	.429	.667
2009	Gwnntt*	AAA	1	3	1	1	0	0	(-	-)	2	0	1	0	1	1	0	0	0	0	0	0	-	0	.333	.500	.667
2005	Atl	NL	59	180	50	7	0	5	(2	3)	72	20	23	25	18	5	26	1	4	1	1	1	.50	5	.278	.345	.400
2006	Atl	NL	130	442	147	34	0	24	(10	14)	253	61	93	94	41	8	54	3	0	6	2	0	1.00	16	.333	.388	.572
2007	Atl	NL	139	504	136	38	0	18	(6	12)	228	51	92	68	35	7	74	5	2	6	0	1	.00	19	.270	.320	.452
2008	Atl	NL	145	509	153	42	1	23	(10	13)	266	68	87	84	57	4	64	4	0	3	5	0	1.00	17	.301	.373	.523
2009	Atl	NL	138	488	137	35	1	21	(12	9)	237	63	94	83	49	3	83	5	3	6	4	1	.80	17	.281	.349	.486
	Postseason		3	16	3	0	0	2	(1	1)	9	2	5	2	0	0	6	0	0	0	0	0	-	0	.188	.188	.563
	5 ML YEARS		611	2123	623	156	2	91	(40	51)	1056	263	389	354	200	27	301	18	9	22	12	3	.80	70	.293	.356	.497

Brandon McCarthy

Pitches: R Bats: R Pos: SP-17 **Ht: 6'7" Wt: 200 Born: 7/7/1983 Age: 26**

Year	Team	Lg	G	GS	CG	GF	IP	BFP	H	R	ER	HR	SH	SF	HB	TBB	IBB	SO	WP	Bk	W	L	Pct	Sh	Sv-Op	Hld	ERC	ERA
2009	Okla*	AAA	5	5	0	0	21.2	93	20	10	10	1	2	0	1	9	0	22	0	0	0	1	.000	0	0- -	-	3.51	4.15
2005	CWS	AL	12	10	0	0	67.0	277	62	30	30	13	1	1	2	17	0	48	1	1	3	2	.600	0	0-0	0	3.83	4.03
2006	CWS	AL	63	2	0	13	84.2	354	77	44	44	17	3	1	0	33	9	69	5	0	4	7	.001	0	0-1	11	4.10	4.68
2007	Tex	AL	22	22	0	0	101.2	459	111	62	55	9	3	5	3	48	0	59	4	1	5	10	.333	0	0-0	0	4.89	4.87
2008	Tex	AL	5	5	0	0	22.0	93	20	11	10	3	0	2	1	8	0	10	0	0	1	1	.500	0	0-0	0	3.87	4.09
2009	Tex	AL	17	17	1	0	97.1	420	96	55	50	13	0	5	3	36	0	65	0	0	7	4	.636	1	0-0	0	4.22	4.62
	5 ML YEARS		110	56	1	13	372.2	1603	366	202	189	55	7	14	9	142	9	251	10	2	20	24	.455	1	0-1	11	4.29	4.56

Kyle McClellan

Pitches: R Bats: R Pos: RP-66 **Ht: 6'2" Wt: 215 Born: 6/12/1984 Age: 26**

Year	Team	Lg	G	GS	CG	GF	IP	BFP	H	R	ER	HR	SH	SF	HB	TBB	IBB	SO	WP	Bk	W	L	Pct	Sh	Sv-Op	Hld	ERC	ERA
2002	JhsCty	R+	7	3	0	1	12.0	60	17	17	15	3	0	0	1	7	0	8	3	0	0	2	.000	0	0- -	-	9.06	11.25
2003	JhsCty	R+	12	12	0	0	67.2	298	74	34	30	4	1	1	5	16	1	44	5	0	3	6	.333	0	0- -	-	3.83	3.99
2004	Peoria	A	24	24	1	0	128.0	562	143	85	76	12	4	5	14	34	1	84	18	0	4	12	.250	0	0- -	-	4.59	5.34
2005	QuadC	A	17	8	0	4	54.0	243	59	33	29	4	1	4	6	26	0	36	7	0	1	4	.200	0	1- -	-	5.28	4.83
2006	JhsCty	R+	3	3	0	0	6.2	32	7	7	7	0	1	0	1	3	0	4	0	0	0	1	.000	0	0- -	-	4.11	9.45
2007	PlmBh	A+	16	1	0	4	29.0	112	22	4	4	0	1	0	2	4	0	24	2	0	4	1	.800	0	0- -	-	1.63	1.24
2007	Sprgfld	AA	24	0	0	8	30.2	118	24	9	8	2	0	0	0	6	1	30	2	0	2	0	1.000	0	0- -	-	2.01	2.35
2008	StL	NL	68	0	0	7	75.2	327	79	37	34	7	2	1	4	26	2	59	6	0	2	7	.222	0	1-6	30	4.24	4.04
2009	StL	NL	66	0	0	14	66.2	288	56	27	25	4	5	2	2	34	2	51	4	0	4	4	.500	0	3-6	15	3.38	3.38
	2 ML YEARS		134	0	0	21	142.1	615	135	64	59	11	7	3	6	60	4	110	10	0	6	11	.353	0	4-12	45	3.83	3.73

Seth McClung

Pitches: R Bats: L Pos: RP-39; SP-2 **Ht: 6'6" Wt: 262 Born: 2/7/1981 Age: 29**

Year	Team	Lg	G	GS	CG	GF	IP	BFP	H	R	ER	HR	SH	SF	HB	TBB	IBB	SO	WP	Bk	W	L	Pct	Sh	Sv-Op	Hld	ERC	ERA
2003	TB	AL	12	5	0	2	38.2	167	33	23	23	6	1	1	3	25	1	25	2	0	4	1	.800	0	0-0	1	5.11	5.35
2005	TB	AL	34	17	0	3	109.1	500	106	85	80	20	0	5	7	62	1	92	6	0	7	11	.389	0	0-1	2	5.36	6.59
2006	TB	AL	39	15	0	20	103.0	489	120	77	72	14	1	9	3	68	5	59	7	0	6	12	.333	0	6-7	0	6.44	6.29
2007	Mil	NL	14	0	0	1	12.0	51	11	9	5	0	1	1	1	5	0	11	0	0	0	1	.000	0	0-0	0	3.35	3.75
2008	Mil	NL	37	12	0	10	105.1	456	93	47	47	10	5	6	7	55	3	87	5	0	6	6	.500	0	0-0	1	4.13	4.02
2009	Mil	NL	41	2	0	8	62.0	278	62	34	34	11	3	3	1	39	1	40	3	0	3	3	.500	0	0-1	5	5.72	4.94
	Postseason		1	0	0	0	2.0	11	2	0	0	0	0	0	0	3	1	1	0	0	0	0	-	0	0-0	0	6.30	0.00
	6 ML YEARS		177	51	0	44	430.1	1941	425	275	261	61	10	25	22	254	11	314	23	0	26	34	.433	0	6-9	9	5.27	5.46

Mike McCoy

Bats: R Throws: R Pos: PH-5; PR-5; 2B-2; RF-1 **Ht: 5'9" Wt: 175 Born: 4/2/1981 Age: 29**

Year	Team	Lg	G	AB	H	2B	3B	HR	(Hm	Rd)	TB	R	RBI	RC	TBB	IBB	SO	HBP	SH	SF	SB	CS	SB%	GDP	Avg	OBP	Slg
2002	JhsCty	R+	50	154	48	9	1	4	(-	-)	71	46	22	37	42	0	23	3	2	1	18	7	.72	0	.312	.465	.461
2003	Peoria	A	131	464	117	16	5	5	(-	-)	158	67	46	61	51	0	77	16	10	3	24	10	.71	2	.252	.345	.341
2004	Peoria	A	55	194	42	8	3	2	(-	-)	62	26	17	22	24	1	35	3	2	0	9	3	.75	4	.216	.309	.320
2004	PlmBh	A+	61	176	53	12	1	2	(-	-)	73	34	23	33	31	2	32	5	2	1	7	4	.64	1	.301	.418	.415
2004	Tenn	AA	3	6	0	0	0	0	(-	-)	0	0	0	0	0	0	3	0	0	0	0	0	-	0	.000	.000	.000
2005	PlmBh	A+	86	282	76	13	2	1	(-	-)	96	47	27	40	36	1	56	3	8	3	18	3	.86	2	.270	.355	.340
2005	Sprgfld	AA	5	14	2	0	0	0	(-	-)	2	1	1	0	0	0	5	1	0	1	0	0	-	0	.143	.188	.143
2006	Sprgfld	AA	130	474	118	14	2	3	(-	-)	145	64	37	59	62	0	98	7	16	0	30	9	.77	7	.249	.344	.306
2007	Sprgfld	AA	24	68	15	3	1	0	(-	-)	20	5	10	7	14	1	14	0	2	1	1	3	.25	0	.221	.349	.294
2007	Memp	AAA	89	238	59	8	0	3	(-	-)	76	31	16	34	45	0	42	1	11	0	12	4	.75	3	.248	.370	.319
2008	Norfolk	AAA	53	152	42	6	1	2	(-	-)	56	25	16	21	19	0	27	0	4	1	6	3	.67	3	.276	.355	.368

Year	Team	Lg	G	AB	H	2B	3B	HR	(Hm	Rd)	TB	R	RBI	RC	TBB	IBB	SO	HBP	SH	SF	SB	CS	SB%	GDP	Avg	OBP	Slg
2008	Frdrck	A+	1	5	3	0	0	0	(-	-)	3	1	1	1	0	0	1	0	0	0	0	1	.00	0	.600	.600	.600
2008	ColSpr	AAA	39	140	48	7	2	4	(-	-)	71	32	27	29	15	0	20	0	1	6	7	1	.88	3	.343	.391	.507
2009	ColSpr	AAA	132	462	142	27	5	2	(-	-)	185	102	52	90	80	1	70	3	16	11	40	6	.87	7	.307	.405	.400
2009	Col	NL	12	5	0	0	0	0	(0	0)	0	1	0	0	0	0	2	0	1	0	2	0	1.00	0	.000	.000	.000

Bob McCrory

Pitches: R Bats: R Pos: RP-7   Ht: 6'1" Wt: 205 Born: 5/3/1982 Age: 28

			HOW MUCH HE PITCHED						WHAT HE GAVE UP										THE RESULTS								
Year	Team	Lg	G	GS	CG	GF	IP	BFP	H	R	ER	HR	SH	SF	HB	TBB	IBB	SO	WP	Bk	W	L	Pct	Sh	Sv-Op	Hld	ERC	ERA
2004	Dlmrva	A	8	0	0	1	10.2	59	13	16	9	3	0	0	0	15	0	11	5	0	0	0	.000	0	0- -	-	11.55	7.59
2004	Bluefld	R+	11	11	0	0	51.2	222	42	21	11	3	1	2	1	32	0	51	8	1	4	3	.571	0	0- -	-	3.72	1.92
2004	Abrdn	A-	1	1	0	0	1.0	8	3	3	3	1	0	0	0	2	0	1	0	0	0	1	.000	0	0- -	-	38.33	27.00
2005	Abrdn	A-	5	5	0	0	24.2	101	21	9	9	2	0	0	3	8	0	21	3	0	2	1	.667	0	0- -	-	3.43	3.28
2006	Abrdn	A-	20	1	0	4	38.2	161	32	12	10	2	3	1	2	16	0	57	3	0	2	2	.500	0	2- -	-	3.11	2.33
2007	Frdrck	A+	22	0	0	18	22.0	93	16	4	3	1	0	1	2	12	1	22	5	0	0	0	-	0	14- -	-	3.08	1.23
2007	Bowie	AA	22	0	0	19	23.0	113	23	17	10	0	1	0	3	16	0	22	3	0	1	2	.333	0	13- -	-	4.72	3.91
2008	Norfolk	AAA	35	1	0	18	45.0	199	41	22	19	1	4	5	2	24	1	35	2	0	2	3	.400	0	5- -	-	3.63	3.80
2008	Abrdn	A-	1	0	0	0	1.0	6	1	2	2	0	0	0	0	2	0	2	0	0	0	0	-	0	0- -	-	9.51	18.00
2009	Norfolk	AAA	50	0	0	19	62.2	273	66	28	27	6	1	1	1	24	0	43	4	0	0	3	.000	0	5- -	-	4.34	3.88
2008	Bal	AL	8	0	0	2	6.1	37	10	12	11	0	1	1	0	8	0	5	1	0	0	0	-	0	0-0	0	10.26	15.63
2009	Bal	AL	7	0	0	2	7.1	49	17	19	14	3	0	1	0	10	0	4	1	0	0	0	-	0	0-0	0	21.02	17.18
	2 ML YEARS		15	0	0	4	13.2	86	27	31	25	3	1	2	0	18	0	9	2	0	0	0	-	0	0-0	0	15.83	16.46

Andrew McCutchen

Bats: R Throws: R Pos: CF-108   Ht: 5'11" Wt: 175 Born: 10/10/1986 Age: 23

			BATTING																	BASERUNNING				AVERAGES		
Year	Team	Lg	G	AB	H	2B	3B	HR	(Hm	Rd)	TB	R	RBI	RC	TBB	IBB	SO	HBP	SH	SF	SB	CS	SB%	GDP	Avg	OBP	Slg
2005	Pirates	R	45	158	47	9	3	2	(-	-)	68	36	30	32	29	0	24	3	0	2	13	1	.93	3	.297	.411	.430
2005	Wmspt	A-	13	52	18	3	1	0	(-	-)	23	12	5	11	8	0	6	1	1	0	4	1	.80	0	.346	.443	.442
2006	Hkry	A	114	453	132	20	4	14	(-	-)	202	77	62	75	42	3	91	5	0	3	22	7	.76	8	.291	.356	.446
2006	Altna	AA	20	78	24	4	0	3	(-	-)	37	12	12	14	8	0	20	1	0	0	1	1	.50	2	.308	.379	.474
2007	Altna	AA	118	446	115	20	3	10	(-	-)	171	70	48	62	44	1	83	3	2	3	17	1	.94	9	.258	.327	.383
2007	Indy	AAA	17	67	21	4	0	1	(-	-)	28	7	5	9	4	0	11	0	0	1	4	3	.57	1	.313	.347	.418
2008	Indy	AAA	135	512	145	26	3	9	(-	-)	204	75	50	81	68	1	87	6	1	3	34	19	.64	8	.283	.372	.398
2009	Indy	AAA	49	201	61	10	8	4	(-	-)	99	41	20	37	17	0	24	1	0	0	10	2	.83	0	.303	.361	.493
2009	Pit	NL	108	433	124	26	9	12	(8	4)	204	74	54	78	54	2	83	2	0	4	22	5	.81	3	.286	.365	.471

Daniel McCutchen

Pitches: R Bats: R Pos: SP-6   Ht: 6'2" Wt: 214 Born: 9/26/1982 Age: 27

			HOW MUCH HE PITCHED						WHAT HE GAVE UP										THE RESULTS								
Year	Team	Lg	G	GS	CG	GF	IP	BFP	H	R	ER	HR	SH	SF	HB	TBB	IBB	SO	WP	Bk	W	L	Pct	Sh	Sv-Op	Hld	ERC	ERA
2006	StIsInd	A-	2	2	0	0	8.0	28	4	1	1	1	0	0	0	1	0	11	0	0	1	0	1.000	0	0- -	-	1.13	1.13
2006	CtnSC	A	7	0	0	4	21.0	76	13	5	5	2	1	0	0	5	0	18	0	0	1	0	1.000	0	1- -	-	1.69	2.14
2007	Tampa	A+	17	16	0	1	101.0	391	86	29	28	7	2	0	4	21	1	67	1	0	11	2	.846	0	0- -	-	2.64	2.50
2007	Trntn	AA	7	7	0	0	41.0	162	30	11	11	2	2	1	1	12	0	36	2	0	3	2	.600	0	0- -	-	2.10	2.41
2008	Trntn	AA	9	9	0	0	53.0	215	43	16	15	4	0	0	1	18	0	52	3	0	4	3	.571	0	0- -	-	2.79	2.55
2008	S-WB	AAA	11	11	2	0	70.1	288	73	32	28	10	0	1	1	11	0	58	0	0	4	6	.400	2	0- -	-	3.70	3.58
2008	Indy	AAA	8	8	0	0	48.0	198	49	25	25	12	1	0	2	7	0	41	0	0	3	3	.500	0	0- -	-	4.33	4.69
2009	Indy	AAA	24	24	0	0	142.2	594	145	63	55	10	7	5	3	29	1	110	5	0	13	6	.684	0	0- -	-	3.27	3.47
2009	Pit	NL	6	6	0	0	36.1	155	38	17	17	6	3	0	1	11	2	19	0	0	1	2	.333	0	0-0	0	4.45	4.21

Darnell McDonald

Bats: R Throws: R Pos: LF-20; PH-15; RF-10; CF-8   Ht: 5'11" Wt: 208 Born: 11/17/1978 Age: 31

			BATTING																	BASERUNNING				AVERAGES		
Year	Team	Lg	G	AB	H	2B	3B	HR	(Hm	Rd)	TB	R	RBI	RC	TBB	IBB	SO	HBP	SH	SF	SB	CS	SB%	GDP	Avg	OBP	Slg
2009	Lsvlle*	AAA	73	280	88	22	7	9	(-	-)	151	42	40	52	16	1	56	1	3	4	8	3	.73	8	.314	.349	.539
2004	Bal	AL	17	32	5	1	0	0	(0	0)	6	3	1	2	2	0	6	0	0	0	1	0	1.00	0	.156	.206	.188
2007	Min	AL	4	10	1	0	0	0	(0	0)	1	0	0	0	1	0	3	0	0	0	0	0	-	0	.100	.182	.100
2009	Cin	NL	47	105	28	6	1	2	(2	0)	42	12	10	10	5	0	31	1	0	0	1	0	1.00	4	.267	.306	.400
	3 ML YEARS		68	147	34	7	1	2	(2	0)	49	15	11	12	8	0	40	1	0	0	2	0	1.00	4	.231	.276	.333

James McDonald

Pitches: R Bats: L Pos: RP-41; SP-4   Ht: 6'5" Wt: 195 Born: 10/19/1984 Age: 25

			HOW MUCH HE PITCHED						WHAT HE GAVE UP										THE RESULTS								
Year	Team	Lg	G	GS	CG	GF	IP	BFP	H	R	ER	HR	SH	SF	HB	TBB	IBB	SO	WP	Bk	W	L	Pct	Sh	Sv-Op	Hld	ERC	ERA
2003	Ddgrs	R	12	9	0	0	48.2	199	39	20	18	3	1	0	6	15	0	47	3	0	2	4	.333	0	0- -	-	2.93	3.33
2005	Ogden	R+	4	0	0	0	6.0	26	4	3	1	0	0	0	1	2	0	9	0	0	0	0	-	0	0- -	-	1.92	1.50
2006	Clmbia	A	30	22	2	4	142.1	600	119	72	63	15	2	2	11	65	0	146	12	0	5	10	.333	1	0- -	-	3.80	3.98
2007	InldEm	A+	16	15	0	0	82.0	341	79	37	36	8	0	3	5	21	0	104	3	0	6	7	.462	0	0- -	-	3.57	3.95
2007	Jaxnvl	AA	10	10	0	0	52.2	215	41	14	9	5	3	1	2	16	0	64	1	1	7	2	.778	0	0- -	-	2.63	1.54
2008	Jaxnvl	AA	22	22	0	0	118.2	491	98	47	42	12	6	2	6	46	2	113	4	2	8	3	.625	0	0- -	-	3.30	3.19
2008	LsVgs	AAA	5	4	0	0	22.1	95	17	9	9	3	0	0	3	7	0	28	0	0	2	1	.667	0	0- -	-	3.10	3.63
2009	Albq	AAA	6	6	0	0	30.1	122	21	11	11	2	0	1	0	14	0	40	0	0	1	0	1.000	0	0- -	-	2.52	3.26

Year	Team	Lg	G	GS	CG	GF	IP	BFP	H	R	ER	HR	SH	SF	HB	TBB	IBB	SO	WP	Bk	W	L	Pct	Sh	Sv-Op	Hld	ERC	ERA
2008	LAD	NL	4	0	0	1	6.0	24	5	0	0	1	0	0	0	1	0	2	0	0	0	0	-	0	0-0	0	1.74	0.00
2009	LAD	NL	45	4	0	10	63.0	280	60	34	28	6	2	3	5	34	5	54	4	0	5	5	.500	0	0-0	5	4.53	4.00
	Postseason		2	0	0	0	5.1	21	3	0	0	0	0	0	0	2	0	7	0	0	0	0	-	0	0-0	1	1.35	0.00
	2 ML YEARS		49	4	0	11	69.0	304	65	34	28	6	3	3	5	35	5	56	4	0	5	5	.500	0	0-0	5	4.25	3.65

John McDonald

Bats: R **Throws:** R **Pos:** SS-31; PR-21; 3B-10; 2B-8; LF-4; DH-2; PH-2   **Ht:** 5'10" **Wt:** 177 **Born:** 9/24/1974 **Age:** 35

								BATTING													BASERUNNING				AVERAGES		
Year	Team	Lg	G	AB	H	2B	3B	HR	(Hm	Rd)	TB	R	RBI	RC	TBB	IBB	SO	HBP	SH	SF	SB	CS	SB%	GDP	Avg	OBP	Slg
1999	Cle	AL	18	21	7	0	0	0	(0	0)	7	2	0	1	0	0	3	0	0	0	0	1	.00	2	.333	.333	.333
2000	Cle	AL	9	9	4	0	0	0	(0	0)	4	0	0	2	0	0	1	0	0	0	0	0	-	0	.444	.444	.444
2001	Cle	AL	17	22	2	1	0	0	(0	0)	3	1	0	0	1	0	7	1	1	0	0	0	-	0	.091	.167	.136
2002	Cle	AL	93	264	66	11	3	1	(0	1)	86	35	12	24	10	0	50	5	7	2	3	0	1.00	6	.250	.288	.326
2003	Cle	AL	82	214	46	9	1	1	(0	1)	60	21	14	18	11	0	31	2	4	2	3	3	.50	4	.215	.258	.280
2004	Cle	AL	66	93	19	5	1	2	(0	2)	32	17	7	7	4	0	11	0	3	0	0	0	-	2	.204	.237	.344
2005	2 Tms	AL	68	166	46	6	1	0	(0	0)	54	18	16	19	11	0	24	2	3	2	6	1	.86	6	.277	.326	.325
2006	Tor	AL	104	260	58	7	3	3	(1	2)	80	35	23	20	16	0	41	2	6	2	7	2	.78	5	.223	.271	.308
2007	Tor	AL	123	327	82	20	2	1	(1	0)	109	32	31	35	11	0	48	2	12	1	7	2	.78	4	.251	.279	.333
2008	Tor	AL	84	186	39	8	0	1	(1	0)	50	21	18	11	10	0	25	2	7	2	3	1	.75	3	.210	.255	.269
2009	Tor	AL	73	151	39	7	0	4	(2	2)	58	18	13	16	1	0	18	2	1	1	0	2	.00	1	.258	.271	.384
05	Tor	AL	37	93	27	3	0	0	(0	0)	30	8	12	13	6	0	12	2	3	2	5	0	1.00	3	.290	.340	.323
05	Det	AL	31	73	19	3	1	0	(0	0)	24	10	4	6	5	0	12	0	0	0	1	1	.50	3	.260	.308	.329
	11 ML YEARS		737	1713	408	74	11	13	(5	8)	543	200	134	152	75	0	259	18	44	12	29	12	.71	34	.238	.276	.317

Casey McGehee

Bats: R **Throws:** R **Pos:** 3B-71; DH-27, 2B-22, 1B-3; DH-3; RF-1   **Ht:** 6'1" **Wt:** 195 **Born:** 10/12/1982 **Age:** 27

								BATTING													BASERUNNING				AVERAGES		
Year	Team	Lg	G	AB	H	2B	3B	HR	(Hm	Rd)	TB	R	RBI	RC	TBB	IBB	SO	HBP	SH	SF	SB	CS	SB%	GDP	Avg	OBP	Slg
2003	Lansng	A	64	243	66	18	1	3	(-	-)	95	24	23	28	10	0	46	2	0	3	2	3	.40	8	.272	.302	.391
2004	Dytona	A+	119	449	117	30	0	10	(-	-)	177	56	66	57	33	3	69	1	4	4	2	1	.67	9	.261	.310	.394
2005	WTenn	AA	124	455	135	31	1	8	(-	-)	192	67	72	71	43	5	64	1	0	6	2	2	.50	21	.297	.354	.422
2006	Iowa	AAA	135	497	139	28	1	11	(-	-)	202	55	60	69	41	0	70	3	1	4	0	3	.00	17	.280	.336	.406
2007	Iowa	AAA	18	52	9	2	0	1	(-	-)	14	3	5	2	3	0	10	1	0	1	0	1	.00	2	.173	.228	.269
2007	Tenn	AA	105	384	105	26	2	9	(-	-)	162	53	54	57	40	5	73	0	0	5	1	2	.33	15	.273	.338	.422
2008	Iowa	AAA	133	497	147	30	0	12	(-	-)	213	68	92	76	40	0	89	3	0	10	0	3	.00	14	.296	.345	.429
2008	ChC	NL	9	24	4	1	0	0	(0	0)	5	1	5	0	0	0	8	0	0	1	0	0	-	1	.167	.160	.208
2009	Mil	NL	116	355	107	20	1	16	(6	10)	177	58	66	65	34	2	67	1	0	4	0	2	.00	13	.301	.360	.499
	2 ML YEARS		125	379	111	21	1	16	(6	10)	182	59	71	65	34	2	75	1	0	5	0	2	.00	14	.293	.348	.480

Dustin McGowan

Pitches: R **Bats:** R **Pos:** P   **Ht:** 6'3" **Wt:** 220 **Born:** 3/24/1982 **Age:** 28

									HOW MUCH HE PITCHED	WHAT HE GAVE UP											THE RESULTS							
Year	Team	Lg	G	GS	CG	GF	IP	BFP	H	R	ER	HR	SH	SF	HB	TBB	IBB	SO	WP	Bk	W	L	Pct	Sh	Sv-Op	Hld	ERC	ERA
2005	Tor	AL	13	7	0	2	45.1	205	49	34	32	7	0	4	7	17	0	34	7	0	1	3	.250	0	0-0	1	5.47	6.35
2006	Tor	AL	16	3	0	3	27.1	143	35	27	22	2	0	1	2	25	2	22	3	1	1	2	.333	0	0-1	1	7.72	7.24
2007	Tor	AL	27	27	2	0	169.2	705	146	80	77	14	0	6	2	61	3	144	13	0	12	10	.545	1	0-0	0	3.07	4.08
2008	Tor	AL	19	19	1	0	111.1	474	115	60	54	9	2	8	5	38	1	85	5	0	6	7	.462	0	0-0	0	4.13	4.37
	4 ML YEARS		75	56	3	5	353.2	1527	345	201	185	32	2	19	16	141	6	285	28	1	20	22	.476	1	0-1	2	4.03	4.71

Nate McLouth

Bats: L **Throws:** R **Pos:** CF-129; PH-1   **Ht:** 5'11" **Wt:** 180 **Born:** 10/28/1981 **Age:** 28

								BATTING													BASERUNNING				AVERAGES		
Year	Team	Lg	G	AB	H	2B	3B	HR	(Hm	Rd)	TB	R	RBI	RC	TBB	IBB	SO	HBP	SH	SF	SB	CS	SB%	GDP	Avg	OBP	Slg
2009	Missi*	AA	2	3	0	0	0	0	(-	-)	0	1	0	0	2	0	1	0	0	0	0	0	-	0	.000	.400	.000
2009	Rome*	A	1	2	0	0	0	0	(-	-)	0	0	0	0	0	0	1	1	0	0	0	0	-	0	.000	.333	.000
2005	Pit	NL	41	109	28	6	0	5	(2	3)	49	20	12	9	3	0	20	5	2	1	2	0	1.00	3	.257	.305	.450
2006	Pit	NL	106	270	63	16	2	7	(3	4)	104	50	16	25	18	0	59	5	3	1	10	1	.91	7	.233	.293	.385
2007	Pit	NL	137	329	85	21	3	13	(5	8)	151	62	38	52	39	2	77	9	3	2	22	1	.96	2	.258	.351	.459
2008	Pit	NL	152	597	165	46	4	26	(15	11)	297	113	94	105	65	11	93	12	5	6	23	3	.88	5	.276	.356	.497
2009	2 Tms	NL	129	507	130	27	2	20	(9	11)	221	86	70	85	68	1	99	9	3	4	19	6	.76	8	.256	.352	.436
09	Pit	NL	45	168	43	7	1	9	(5	4)	79	27	34	33	21	0	29	4	0	2	7	0	1.00	2	.256	.349	.470
09	Atl	NL	84	339	87	20	1	11	(4	7)	142	59	36	52	47	1	70	5	3	2	12	6	.67	6	.257	.354	.419
	5 ML YEARS		565	1812	471	116	11	71	(34	37)	822	331	230	276	193	14	348	40	16	14	76	11	.87	25	.260	.342	.454

Gil Meche

Pitches: R **Bats:** R **Pos:** SP-23   **Ht:** 6'3" **Wt:** 214 **Born:** 9/8/1978 **Age:** 31

									HOW MUCH HE PITCHED	WHAT HE GAVE UP											THE RESULTS							
Year	Team	Lg	G	GS	CG	GF	IP	BFP	H	R	ER	HR	SH	SF	HB	TBB	IBB	SO	WP	Bk	W	L	Pct	Sh	Sv-Op	Hld	ERC	ERA
2009	Omha*	AAA	2	2	0	0	8.2	33	3	3	3	0	0	1	0	7	0	4	1	1	1	1	.500	0	0- -	-	1.73	3.12
1999	Sea	AL	16	15	0	0	85.2	375	73	48	45	9	5	3	2	57	1	47	1	0	8	4	.667	0	0-0	0	4.47	4.73
2000	Sea	AL	15	15	1	0	85.2	363	75	37	36	7	5	4	1	40	0	60	2	0	4	4	.500	1	0-0	0	3.60	3.78
2003	Sea	AL	32	32	1	0	186.1	785	187	97	95	30	3	5	3	63	2	130	7	0	15	13	.536	0	0-0	0	4.39	4.59
2004	Sea	AL	23	23	1	0	127.2	565	139	73	71	21	1	3	5	47	0	99	4	0	7	7	.500	1	0-0	0	5.06	5.01
2005	Sea	AL	29	26	0	0	143.1	638	153	92	81	18	1	5	2	72	1	83	4	0	10	8	.556	0	0-0	0	5.15	5.09
2006	Sea	AL	32	32	1	0	186.2	811	183	106	93	24	3	2	8	84	2	156	4	2	11	8	.579	0	0-0	0	4.56	4.48

Year	Team	Lg	HOW MUCH HE PITCHED						WHAT HE GAVE UP												THE RESULTS							
			G	GS	CG	GF	IP	BFP	H	R	ER	HR	SH	SF	HB	TBB	IBB	SO	WP	Bk	W	L	Pct	Sh	Sv-Op	Hld	ERC	ERA
2007	KC	AL	34	34	1	0	216.0	906	218	98	88	22	5	7	3	62	2	156	3	0	9	13	.409	0	0-0	0	3.77	3.67
2008	KC	AL	34	34	0	0	210.1	886	204	98	93	19	4	10	3	73	2	183	5	0	14	11	.560	0	0-0	0	3.64	3.98
2009	KC	AL	23	23	1	0	129.0	581	144	81	73	17	1	6	3	58	0	95	7	0	6	10	.375	1	0-0	0	5.26	5.09
	9 ML YEARS		238	234	6	2	1370.2	5910	1376	730	675	167	28	45	27	556	10	1009	37	2	84	78	.519	3	0-0	0	4.37	4.43

Brandon Medders

Pitches: R **Bats:** R **Pos:** RP-61   **Ht:** 6'1" **Wt:** 191 **Born:** 1/26/1980 **Age:** 30

Year	Team	Lg	HOW MUCH HE PITCHED						WHAT HE GAVE UP												THE RESULTS							
			G	GS	CG	GF	IP	BFP	H	R	ER	HR	SH	SF	HB	TBB	IBB	SO	WP	Bk	W	L	Pct	Sh	Sv-Op	Hld	ERC	ERA
2005	Ari	NL	27	0	0	10	30.1	122	21	6	6	2	0	2	1	11	0	31	1	0	4	1	.800	0	0-0	2	2.25	1.78
2006	Ari	NL	60	0	0	13	71.2	316	76	37	29	5	3	2	2	28	3	47	2	0	5	3	.625	0	0-1	10	4.17	3.64
2007	Ari	NL	30	0	0	7	29.1	128	30	16	14	9	1	0	1	16	0	23	1	0	1	2	.333	0	0-1	1	6.76	4.30
2008	Ari	NL	18	0	0	3	19.2	88	17	11	10	2	1	2	2	11	2	8	1	0	1	0	1.000	0	0-1	0	4.13	4.58
2009	SF	NL	61	0	0	11	68.2	300	63	26	23	6	5	6	3	32	5	58	2	0	5	1	.833	0	1-4	8	3.80	3.01
	5 ML YEARS		196	0	0	44	219.2	954	207	96	82	24	10	12	9	98	10	167	7	0	16	7	.696	0	1-7	21	4.08	3.36

Kris Medlen

Pitches: R **Bats:** B **Pos:** RP-33; SP-4   **Ht:** 5'10" **Wt:** 190 **Born:** 10/7/1985 **Age:** 24

Year	Team	Lg	HOW MUCH HE PITCHED						WHAT HE GAVE UP												THE RESULTS							
			G	GS	CG	GF	IP	BFP	H	R	ER	HR	SH	SF	HB	TBB	IBB	SO	WP	Bk	W	L	Pct	Sh	Sv-Op	Hld	ERC	ERA
2006	Danvle	R+	20	0	0	19	22.0	83	14	2	1	0	0	0	1	2	0	36	2	0	1	0	1.000	0	10--	-	1.09	0.41
2007	Rome	A	17	0	0	15	20.2	80	13	4	2	1	0	0	0	3	0	33	0	0	0	1	.000	0	8--	-	1.22	0.87
2007	Missi	AA	3	0	0	1	2.1	11	4	3	3	0	0	0	0	2	0	2	0	0	0	0	-	0	1--	-	11.20	11.57
2007	MrtlBh	A+	18	0	0	8	24.0	101	22	7	3	1	1	1	0	7	2	28	0	0	2	0	1.000	0	2--	-	2.65	1.13
2008	Missi	AA	36	17	0	8	120.1	491	121	47	47	8	4	4	5	27	2	120	3	0	7	8	.467	0	1--	-	3.44	3.52
2009	Gwnntt	AAA	8	6	0	1	37.2	138	20	5	5	0	1	0	0	10	0	44	0	1	5	0	1.000	0	0--	-	1.09	1.19
2009	Atl	NL	37	4	0	10	67.2	294	65	34	32	5	6	2	2	30	2	72	3	1	3	5	.375	0	0-2	1	3.90	4.26

Evan Meek

Pitches: R **Bats:** R **Pos:** RP-41   **Ht:** 6'0" **Wt:** 220 **Born:** 5/12/1983 **Age:** 27

Year	Team	Lg	HOW MUCH HE PITCHED						WHAT HE GAVE UP												THE RESULTS							
			G	GS	CG	GF	IP	BFP	H	R	ER	HR	SH	SF	HB	TBB	IBB	SO	WP	Bk	W	L	Pct	Sh	Sv-Op	Hld	ERC	ERA
2003	Elizab	R+	14	8	0	3	51.0	209	33	15	14	2	0	0	0	24	0	47	6	0	7	1	.875	0	1--	-	2.10	2.47
2004	QuadC	A	3	3	0	0	5.2	39	7	7	7	0	1	0	2	15	0	3	4	0	0	0	-	0	0--	-	16.39	11.12
2004	Elizab	R+	12	3	0	3	22.1	117	18	26	20	1	2	3	8	25	0	23	11	0	1	2	.333	0	0--	-	6.65	8.06
2005	Beloit	A	13	0	0	2	18.0	107	15	26	20	0	1	3	2	36	0	11	8	1	0	1	.000	0	0--	-	8.86	10.00
2006	Lk Els	A+	26	25	0	0	119.1	546	136	80	66	5	1	3	8	62	0	113	9	1	6	6	.500	0	0--	-	5.23	4.98
2006	Visalia	A+	2	0	0	0	5.0	26	6	5	5	0	0	0	2	4	0	7	1	0	1	0	1.000	0	0--	-	7.80	9.00
2007	Mont	AA	44	0	0	9	67.0	297	74	36	32	2	2	2	1	34	5	69	11	0	2	1	.667	0	1--	-	4.58	4.30
2008	Altna	AA	9	0	0	7	16.0	65	14	5	5	0	2	0	1	3	0	17	3	1	1	1	.500	0	2--	-	2.22	2.81
2008	Indy	AAA	23	0	0	2	41.1	167	30	12	11	2	0	0	0	14	4	34	4	0	0	0	-	0	2--	-	1.96	2.40
2009	Indy	AAA	6	0	0	2	8.2	35	3	1	1	0	0	0	0	7	0	7	1	0	0	0	-	0	0--	-	1.62	1.04
2008	Pit	NL	9	0	0	7	13.0	61	11	11	10	3	1	1	1	12	2	7	3	0	0	1	.000	0	0-0	0	6.46	6.92
2009	Pit	NL	41	0	0	14	47.0	195	34	18	18	2	2	1	0	29	2	42	5	0	1	1	.500	0	0-1	4	3.03	3.45
	2 ML YEARS		50	0	0	21	60.0	256	45	29	28	5	3	2	1	41	4	49	8	0	1	2	.333	0	0-1	4	3.71	4.20

Mark Melancon

Pitches: R **Bats:** R **Pos:** RP-13   **Ht:** 6'2" **Wt:** 215 **Born:** 3/28/1985 **Age:** 25

Year	Team	Lg	HOW MUCH HE PITCHED						WHAT HE GAVE UP												THE RESULTS							
			G	GS	CG	GF	IP	BFP	H	R	ER	HR	SH	SF	HB	TBB	IBB	SO	WP	Bk	W	L	Pct	Sh	Sv-Op	Hld	ERC	ERA
2006	StIslnd	A-	7	0	0	3	7.2	36	9	7	3	0	2	0	0	2	0	8	1	0	0	1	.000	0	2--	-	3.45	3.52
2008	Tampa	A+	13	0	0	2	25.1	107	26	9	8	2	1	1	1	6	1	20	0	0	1	0	1.000	0	0--	-	3.53	2.84
2008	Trntn	AA	19	0	0	13	49.2	190	32	14	10	3	3	0	0	12	0	47	1	0	6	0	1.000	0	2--	-	1.57	1.81
2008	S-WB	AAA	12	0	0	0	20.0	75	11	7	6	1	1	1	1	4	0	22	1	0	1	1	.500	0	1--	-	1.26	2.70
2009	S-WB	AAA	32	0	0	20	53.0	208	37	22	17	3	0	2	6	11	0	54	5	0	4	0	1.000	0	3--	-	2.00	2.89
2009	NYY	AL	13	0	0	4	16.1	74	13	8	7	0	0	0	4	10	0	10	3	0	0	1	.000	0	0-1	0	3.94	3.86

John Meloan

Pitches: R **Bats:** R **Pos:** RP-6   **Ht:** 6'3" **Wt:** 225 **Born:** 7/11/1984 **Age:** 25

Year	Team	Lg	HOW MUCH HE PITCHED						WHAT HE GAVE UP												THE RESULTS							
			G	GS	CG	GF	IP	BFP	H	R	ER	HR	SH	SF	HB	TBB	IBB	SO	WP	Bk	W	L	Pct	Sh	Sv-Op	Hld	ERC	ERA
2009	Clmbs*	AAA	25	2	0	8	44.0	201	52	27	27	6	2	1	1	17	0	37	1	0	0	0	-	0	0--	-	5.34	5.52
2009	Drham*	AAA	10	0	0	1	13.1	64	13	5	5	2	1	0	1	10	1	15	1	0	0	0	-	0	0--	-	5.77	3.38
2009	Indy*	AAA	6	0	0	1	7.2	27	3	1	1	1	0	1	0	1	0	8	0	0	0	0	-	0	0--	-	0.83	1.17
2009	Scrmto*	AAA	3	0	0	1	3.0	10	0	0	0	0	0	0	0	2	0	1	0	0	0	0	-	0	0--	-	0.50	0.00
2007	LAD	NL	5	0	0	3	7.1	38	8	9	9	1	1	0	1	8	0	7	0	0	0	0	-	0	0-0	0	8.45	11.05
2008	Cle	AL	2	0	0	1	2.0	6	0	0	0	0	0	0	0	1	0	2	0	0	0	0	-	0	0-0	0	0.32	0.00
2009	Oak	AL	6	0	0	2	8.1	29	3	1	0	0	0	0	0	2	0	11	0	0	0	0	-	0	0-0	0	0.62	0.00
	3 ML YEARS		13	0	0	6	17.2	73	11	10	9	1	1	0	1	11	0	20	0	0	0	0	-	0	0-0	0	2.88	4.58

Luis Mendoza

Pitches: R Bats: R Pos: RP-1   Ht: 6'3" Wt: 210 Born: 10/31/1983 Age: 26

			HOW MUCH HE PITCHED						WHAT HE GAVE UP									THE RESULTS							
Year	Team	Lg	G	GS	CG	GF	IP	BFP	H	R	ER	HR	SH	SF	HB	TBB	IBB	SO	WP	Bk	W	L	Pct	Sh	Sv-Op Hld	ERC	ERA
2009	Okla*	AAA	25	10	2	2	111.1	509	130	62	56	4	1	5	11	50	1	78	3	2	6	7	.462	1	0- - -	5.16	4.53
2007	Tex	AL	6	3	0	2	16.0	64	13	4	4	1	0	2	2	4	0	7	0	0	1	0	1.000	0	0-0 0	2.83	2.25
2008	Tex	AL	25	11	0	6	63.1	316	97	74	61	7	0	2	6	25	4	35	5	0	3	8	.273	0	1-2 0	7.53	8.67
2009	Tex	AL	1	0	0	0	1.0	7	2	4	4	1	0	0	1	1	0	0	0	0	0	0	-	0	0-0 0	29.25	36.00
	3 ML YEARS		32	14	0	8	80.1	387	112	82	69	9	0	4	9	30	4	42	5	0	4	8	.333	0	1-2 0	6.73	7.73

Cla Meredith

Pitches: R Bats: R Pos: RP-64   Ht: 6'0" Wt: 189 Born: 6/4/1983 Age: 27

			HOW MUCH HE PITCHED						WHAT HE GAVE UP									THE RESULTS							
Year	Team	Lg	G	GS	CG	GF	IP	BFP	H	R	ER	HR	SH	SF	HB	TBB	IBB	SO	WP	Bk	W	L	Pct	Sh	Sv-Op Hld	ERC	ERA
2005	Bos	AL	3	0	0	0	2.1	18	6	7	7	1	0	0	1	4	0	0	1	0	0	0	-	0	0-0 0	27.60	27.00
2006	SD	NL	45	0	0	11	50.2	185	30	6	6	3	1	0	2	6	3	37	0	2	5	1	.833	0	0-2 16	1.19	1.07
2007	SD	NL	80	0	0	18	79.2	342	94	38	31	6	1	3	3	17	4	59	3	1	5	6	.455	0	0-5 10	4.28	3.50
2008	SD	NL	73	0	0	19	70.1	302	79	34	32	6	2	3	1	24	3	49	2	0	0	3	.000	0	0-6 11	4.52	4.09
2009	2 Tms		64	0	0	25	65.1	283	73	31	29	4	3	3	4	25	8	37	3	0	4	2	.667	0	0-3 4	4.56	3.99
09	SD	NL	35	0	0	13	36.2	165	47	19	17	1	2	3	2	13	4	20	3	0	4	2	.667	0	0-3 1	5.08	4.17
09	Bal	AL	29	0	0	12	28.2	118	26	12	12	3	1	0	2	12	4	17	0	0	0	0	-	0	0-0 3	3.91	3.77
	Postseason		2	0	0	0	3.2	15	3	2	0	0	1	0	1	0	0	3	0	0	0	0	-	0	0-0 0	2.00	0.00
	5 ML YEARS		265	0	0	73	268.1	1130	282	116	105	20	7	9	11	76	18	182	9	3	14	12	.538	0	0-16 41	3.85	3.52

Randy Messenger

Pitches: R Bats: R Pos: RP-12   Ht: 6'6" Wt: 265 Born: 8/13/1981 Age: 28

			HOW MUCH HE PITCHED						WHAT HE GAVE UP									THE RESULTS							
Year	Team	Lg	G	GS	CG	GF	IP	BFP	H	R	ER	HR	SH	SF	HB	TBB	IBB	SO	WP	Bk	W	L	Pct	Sh	Sv-Op Hld	ERC	ERA
2009	Tacom*	AAA	52	0	0	48	56.2	240	68	24	18	4	1	4	2	14	0	40	1	0	0	2	.000	0	25- - -	4.16	2.86
2005	Fla	NL	29	0	0	8	37.0	178	39	22	22	5	2	3	0	30	7	29	1	0	0	0	-	0	0-0 2	5.91	5.35
2006	Fla	NL	59	0	0	10	60.1	275	72	42	38	8	5	2	1	24	2	45	3	0	2	7	.222	0	0-1 9	5.38	5.67
2007	2 Tms	NL	60	0	0	21	64.1	291	85	30	30	4	6	5	1	21	5	34	1	0	2	4	.333	0	1-5 11	5.32	4.20
2008	Sea	AL	13	0	0	3	12.2	57	16	5	5	1	0	0	1	5	1	7	0	0	0	0	-	0	1-1 2	5.78	3.55
2009	Sea	AL	12	0	0	7	10.1	43	13	6	5	3	0	0	0	0	0	5	1	0	0	1	.000	0	0-0 1	5.19	4.35
07	Fla	NL	23	0	0	8	23.2	103	27	7	7	0	4	1	0	9	2	12	0	0	1	1	.500	0	0-0 6	3.97	2.66
07	SF	NL	37	0	0	13	40.2	188	58	23	23	4	2	4	1	12	3	22	1	0	1	3	.250	0	1-5 5	6.14	5.09
	5 ML YEARS		173	0	0	49	184.2	844	225	104	100	21	13	10	3	80	15	120	6	0	4	12	.250	0	2-7 25	5.50	4.87

Dan Meyer

Pitches: L Bats: R Pos: RP-71   Ht: 6'2" Wt: 222 Born: 7/3/1981 Age: 28

			HOW MUCH HE PITCHED						WHAT HE GAVE UP									THE RESULTS							
Year	Team	Lg	G	GS	CG	GF	IP	BFP	H	R	ER	HR	SH	SF	HB	TBB	IBB	SO	WP	Bk	W	L	Pct	Sh	Sv-Op Hld	ERC	ERA
2004	Atl	NL	2	0	0	1	2.0	8	2	0	0	0	0	0	0	1	1	1	0	0	0	0	-	0	0-0 0	3.21	0.00
2007	Oak	AL	6	3	0	2	16.1	79	20	19	16	2	1	1	0	9	0	11	3	0	0	2	.000	0	0-0 0	5.97	8.82
2008	Oak	AL	11	4	0	5	27.2	132	35	28	23	6	0	2	1	14	0	20	0	0	0	4	.000	0	0-0 0	7.10	7.48
2009	Fla	NL	71	0	0	8	58.1	242	47	24	20	7	3	2	1	21	2	56	2	0	3	2	.600	0	2-2 20	2.99	3.09
	4 ML YEARS		90	7	0	16	104.1	461	104	71	59	15	4	5	2	45	3	88	5	0	3	8	.273	0	2-2 20	4.45	5.09

Jason Michaels

Bats: R Throws: R Pos: PH-65; LF-31; CF-14; RF-3; PR-3   Ht: 6'0" Wt: 206 Born: 5/4/1976 Age: 34

			BATTING																	BASERUNNING				AVERAGES		
Year	Team	Lg	G	AB	H	2B	3B	HR	(Hm Rd)	TB	R	RBI	RC	TBB	IBB	SO	HBP	SH	SF	SB	CS	SB%	GDP	Avg	OBP	Slg
2001	Phi	NL	6	6	1	0	0	0	(0 0)	1	0	1	0	0	0	2	0	0	0	0	0	-	0	.167	.167	.167
2002	Phi	NL	81	105	28	10	3	2	(0 2)	50	16	11	14	13	1	33	1	0	2	1	1	.50	1	.267	.347	.476
2003	Phi	NL	76	109	36	11	0	5	(1 4)	62	20	17	19	15	1	22	1	0	0	0	0	-	3	.330	.416	.569
2004	Phi	NL	115	299	82	12	0	10	(5 5)	124	44	40	47	42	1	80	2	0	3	2	2	.50	3	.274	.364	.415
2005	Phi	NL	105	289	88	16	2	4	(1 3)	120	54	31	47	44	1	45	4	2	4	3	3	.50	3	.304	.399	.415
2006	Cle	AL	123	494	132	32	1	9	(4 5)	193	77	55	62	43	0	101	3	2	6	9	5	.64	6	.267	.326	.391
2007	Cle	AL	105	267	72	11	1	7	(5 2)	106	43	39	37	20	1	50	3	2	3	3	4	.43	3	.270	.324	.397
2008	2 Tms		123	286	64	13	1	8	(4 4)	103	28	53	37	27	0	65	2	2	4	2	1	.67	9	.224	.292	.360
2009	Hou	NL	102	135	32	12	1	4	(3 1)	68	17	10	15	16	0	38	1	0	0	1	2	.33	2	.237	.322	.430
08	Cle	AL	21	58	12	4	0	0	(0 0)	16	3	9	5	4	0	13	1	1	3	1	1	.50	0	.207	.258	.276
08	Pit	NL	102	228	52	9	1	8	(4 4)	87	25	44	32	23	0	52	1	1	1	1	0	1.00	9	.228	.300	.382
	Postseason		2	1	1	1	0	0	(0 0)	2	1	0	1	0	0	0	0	1	0	0	0	-	0	1.000	1.000	2.000
	9 ML YEARS		836	1990	535	117	9	49	(23 26)	817	299	263	278	220	5	436	17	8	22	21	18	.54	30	.269	.343	.411

Kam Mickolio

Pitches: R Bats: R Pos: RP-11   Ht: 6'9" Wt: 256 Born: 5/10/1984 Age: 26

			HOW MUCH HE PITCHED						WHAT HE GAVE UP									THE RESULTS							
Year	Team	Lg	G	GS	CG	GF	IP	BFP	H	R	ER	HR	SH	SF	HB	TBB	IBB	SO	WP	Bk	W	L	Pct	Sh	Sv-Op Hld	ERC	ERA
2006	Everett	A-	21	0	0	11	32.1	140	34	14	10	1	1	0	3	7	0	26	3	1	1	0	1.000	0	4- - -	3.47	2.78
2007	WTenn	AA	18	0	0	8	29.2	123	24	9	6	0	1	0	2	12	1	27	2	0	3	1	.750	0	2- - -	2.63	1.82
2007	Tacom	AAA	14	0	0	7	24.0	102	19	12	10	3	1	0	2	10	0	28	3	1	3	3	.500	0	1- - -	3.46	3.75
2008	Bowie	AA	28	0	0	6	38.1	178	39	21	20	2	2	2	3	22	0	40	3	0	2	1	.667	0	1- - -	4.71	4.70
2008	Norfolk	AAA	17	0	0	3	20.0	87	13	7	4	0	1	0	2	9	0	23	0	0	1	0	1.000	0	2- - -	2.01	1.80

		HOW MUCH HE PITCHED				WHAT HE GAVE UP							THE RESULTS						
Year Team	Lg	G GS CG GF	IP	BFP	H	R	ER	HR SH SF HB	TBB IBB	SO WP Bk	W	L	Pct	Sh	Sv-Op Hld	ERC	ERA
2009 Norfolk AAA	35 0 0 8	43.2	177	32	21	17	4 1 2 0	16 0	52 3 0	3	3	.500	0	0-- -	2.48	3.50
2008 Bal AL	9 0 0 5	7.2	36	8	5	5	0 1 1 0	4 0	8 2 0	0	1	.000	0	0-1 0	3.81	5.87
2009 Bal AL	11 0 0 7	13.2	59	11	4	4	0 0 2 0	7 1	14 0 0	0	2	.000	0	0-0 2	2.58	2.63
2 ML YEARS	20 0 0 12	21.1	95	19	9	9	0 1 3 0	11 1	22 2 0	0	3	.000	0	0-1 2	3.01	3.80

Doug Mientkiewicz

Bats: L **Throws:** R **Pos:** PH-17; 1B-4   **Ht:** 6'0" **Wt:** 211 **Born:** 6/19/1974 **Age:** 36

		BATTING														BASERUNNING				AVERAGES		
Year Team	Lg	G	AB	H	2B	3B	HR	(Hm Rd)	TB	R	RBI	RC	TBB IBB	SO	HBP SH SF	SB	CS	SB%	GDP	Avg	OBP	Slg
2009 Albq* AAA	11	49	15	6	1	1	(- -)	26	9	10	8	1 0	6	0 0 2	0	0	-	1	.306	.308	.531
2009 InldEm* A+	3	9	2	0	0	1	(- -)	5	2	2	2	2 0	3	1 0 0	0	0	-	0	.222	.417	.556
1998 Min AL	8	25	5	1	0	0	(0 0)	6	1	2	2	4 0	3	0 0 0	1	1	.50	0	.200	.310	.240
1999 Min AL	118	327	75	21	3	2	(0 2)	108	34	32	34	43 3	51	4 3 2	1	1	.50	13	.229	.324	.330
2000 Min AL	3	14	6	0	0	0	(0 0)	6	0	4	2	0 0	0	0 0 1	0	0	-	1	.429	.400	.429
2001 Min AL	151	543	166	39	1	15	(11 4)	252	77	74	96	67 6	92	9 0 7	2	6	.25	10	.306	.387	.464
2002 Min AL	143	467	122	29	1	10	(6 4)	183	60	64	76	74 8	69	6 0 7	1	2	.33	7	.261	.365	.392
2003 Min AL	142	487	146	38	1	11	(6 5)	219	67	65	89	74 4	55	5 2 6	4	1	.80	9	.300	.393	.450
2004 2 Tms AL	127	391	93	24	1	6	(1 5)	137	47	35	46	48 2	56	4 2 2	2	3	.40	12	.238	.326	.350
2005 NYM NL	87	275	66	13	0	11	(3 8)	112	36	29	28	32 7	39	2 2 2	0	1	.00	11	.240	.322	.407
2006 KC AL	91	314	89	24	2	4	(1 3)	129	37	43	48	35 1	50	5 1 5	3	0	1.00	6	.283	.359	.411
2007 NYY AL	72	166	46	12	0	5	(4 1)	73	26	24	25	16 0	23	3 6 1	0	0	-	3	.277	.349	.440
2008 Pit NL	125	285	79	19	2	2	(0 2)	108	37	30	47	44 3	28	2 0 3	0	0	-	6	.277	.374	.379
2009 LAD NL	20	18	6	1	0	0	(0 0)	7	0	3	4	1 0	6	1 0 0	0	0	-	0	.333	.400	.389
04 Min AL	78	284	70	18	0	5	(1 4)	103	34	25	34	38 2	38	3 2 1	2	2	.50	9	.246	.340	.363
04 Bos AL	49	107	23	6	1	1	(0 1)	34	13	10	12	10 0	18	1 0 1	0	1	.00	3	.215	.286	.318
Postseason	29	68	16	2	0	2	(1 1)	24	4	7	8	4 0	6	0 2 0	0	0	-	5	.235	.278	.353
12 ML YEARS	1087	3312	899	221	11	66	(32 34)	1340	422	405	497	438 34	472	41 16 36	14	15	.48	78	.271	.360	.405

Jose Mijares

Pitches: L **Bats:** L **Pos:** RP-71   **Ht:** 6'0" **Wt:** 231 **Born:** 10/29/1984 **Age:** 25

		HOW MUCH HE PITCHED				WHAT HE GAVE UP							THE RESULTS						
Year Team	Lg	G GS CG GF	IP	BFP	H	R	ER	HR SH SF HB	TBB IBB	SO WP Bk	W	L	Pct	Sh	Sv-Op Hld	ERC	ERA
2004 Twins R	19 0 0 13	29.2	126	22	9	8	1 2 1 2	15 0	25 3 1	4	0	1.000	0	5-- -	2.87	2.43
2005 Beloit A	20 6 0 5	54.1	240	43	28	26	6 1 1 2	40 0	78 3 1	6	3	.667	0	2-- -	4.50	4.31
2005 FtMyrs A+	5 1 0 1	12.0	49	5	4	2	1 0 0 0	5 0	17 0 0	0	0	-	0	0-- -	1.24	1.50
2006 FtMyrs A+	27 5 0 6	63.0	267	52	30	25	10 4 2 4	27 0	77 5 0	3	5	.375	0	0-- -	3.88	3.57
2007 NwBrit AA	46 0 0 31	61.0	275	40	26	24	7 5 2 2	48 1	75 3 0	5	3	.625	0	9-- -	3.75	3.54
2007 Roch AAA	5 0 0 0	8.2	41	9	7	6	3 0 1 1	5 1	6 0 0	0	1	.000	0	0-- -	7.11	6.23
2008 Twins R	7 0 0 1	11.0	44	10	3	1	0 0 0 0	1 0	16 0 0	2	1	.667	0	0-- -	1.84	0.82
2008 FtMyrs A+	5 0 0 1	10.1	40	7	3	3	0 0 1 0	3 0	8 2 0	0	0	-	0	2-- -	1.55	2.61
2008 NwBrit AA	11 0 0 3	15.1	69	16	5	5	2 0 0 0	7 0	17 0 0	1	1	.500	0	2-- -	4.66	2.93
2009 Roch AAA	5 0 0 4	6.1	21	2	0	0	0 0 0 0	1 0	4 0 0	1	0	1.000	0	1-- -	0.43	0.00
2008 Min AL	10 0 0 3	10.1	34	3	1	1	0 0 0 0	0 0	5 1 0	0	1	.000	0	0-0 2	0.19	0.87
2009 Min AL	71 0 0 12	61.2	253	50	17	16	7 2 3 2	23 1	55 0 0	2	2	.500	0	0-1 27	3.18	2.34
2 ML YEARS	81 0 0 15	72.0	287	53	18	17	7 2 3 2	23 1	60 1 0	2	3	.400	0	0-1 29	2.49	2.13

Aaron Miles

Bats: B **Throws:** R **Pos:** 2B-35; PH-34; SS-8; 3B-4   **Ht:** 5'8" **Wt:** 180 **Born:** 12/15/1976 **Age:** 33

		BATTING														BASERUNNING				AVERAGES		
Year Team	Lg	G	AB	H	2B	3B	HR	(Hm Rd)	TB	R	RBI	RC	TBB IBB	SO	HBP SH SF	SB	CS	SB%	GDP	Avg	OBP	Slg
2009 Iowa* AAA	21	87	22	4	0	0	(- -)	26	8	8	6	2 0	14	0 1 1	1	2	.33	1	.253	.267	.299
2003 CWS AL	8	12	4	3	0	0	(0 0)	7	3	2	3	0 0	0	0 0 0	0	0	-	0	.333	.333	.583
2004 Col NL	134	522	153	15	3	6	(4 2)	192	75	47	70	29 0	53	2 7 6	12	7	.63	12	.293	.329	.368
2005 Col NL	99	324	91	12	3	2	(2 0)	115	37	28	42	8 1	38	4 10 1	4	2	.67	6	.281	.306	.355
2006 StL NL	135	426	112	20	5	2	(1 1)	148	48	30	49	38 9	42	2 2 3	2	1	.67	5	.263	.324	.347
2007 StL NL	133	414	120	16	1	2	(0 2)	144	55	32	49	25 1	40	1 4 5	2	1	.67	11	.290	.328	.348
2008 StL NL	134	379	120	15	2	4	(1 3)	151	49	31	44	23 2	37	0 5 1	3	3	.50	13	.317	.355	.398
2009 ChC NL	74	157	29	7	1	0	(0 0)	38	17	5	3	8 1	21	0 5 0	3	0	1.00	4	.185	.224	.242
Postseason	7	11	4	0	1	0	(0 0)	6	2	0	2	1 1	2	0 0 0	1	0	1.00	0	.364	.417	.545
7 ML YEARS	717	2234	629	88	15	16	(6 10)	795	284	175	260	131 14	231	9 33 16	26	14	.65	54	.282	.322	.356

Kevin Millar

Bats: R **Throws:** R **Pos:** 1B-46; DH-22; PH-9; 3B-4; PR-1   **Ht:** 6'0" **Wt:** 217 **Born:** 9/24/1971 **Age:** 38

		BATTING														BASERUNNING				AVERAGES		
Year Team	Lg	G	AB	H	2B	3B	HR	(Hm Rd)	TB	R	RBI	RC	TBB IBB	SO	HBP SH SF	SB	CS	SB%	GDP	Avg	OBP	Slg
1998 Fla NL	2	2	1	0	0	0	(0 0)	1	1	0	1	1 0	0	0 0 0	0	0	-	0	.500	.667	.500
1999 Fla NL	105	351	100	17	4	9	(3 6)	152	48	67	57	40 2	64	7 1 8	1	0	1.00	7	.285	.362	.433
2000 Fla NL	123	259	67	14	3	14	(6 8)	129	36	42	47	36 0	47	8 0 2	0	0	-	5	.259	.364	.498
2001 Fla NL	144	449	141	39	5	20	(13 7)	250	62	85	89	39 2	70	5 0 2	0	0	-	8	.314	.374	.557
2002 Fla NL	126	438	134	41	0	16	(11 5)	223	58	57	63	40 0	74	5 0 6	0	2	.00	15	.306	.366	.509
2003 Bos AL	148	544	150	30	1	25	(10 15)	257	83	96	87	60 5	108	5 0 9	3	2	.60	14	.276	.348	.472
2004 Bos AL	150	508	151	36	4	18	(12 6)	249	74	74	90	57 0	91	17 0 6	1	1	.50	16	.297	.383	.474
2005 Bos AL	134	449	122	26	1	9	(8 1)	179	57	50	58	54 0	74	8 0 8	0	1	.00	12	.272	.355	.399
2006 Bal AL	132	430	117	26	0	15	(7 8)	188	64	64	67	59 3	74	12 0 2	1	1	.50	14	.272	.374	.437
2007 Bal AL	140	476	121	26	1	17	(12 5)	200	63	63	71	76 2	94	8 0 2	1	1	.50	8	.254	.365	.420

Year Team	Lg	G	AB	H	2B	3B	HR	Hm	Rd	TB	R	RBI	RC	TBB	IBB	SO	HBP	SH	SF	SB	CS	SB%	GDP	Avg	OBP	Slg
2008 Bal	AL	145	531	124	25	0	20	11	0	200	73	72	07	71	3	93	2	0	6	0	1	.00	8	.234	.323	.394
2009 Tor	AL	78	251	56	14	0	7	4	3	91	29	29	25	31	0	49	1	0	0	0	0	-	10	.223	.311	.363
Postseason		20	95	23	5	0	2	0	2	34	11	10	9	11	0	21	1	0	0	0	0	-	2	.242	.327	.358
12 ML YEARS		1427	4688	1284	296	15	170	97	73	2120	648	699	722	564	17	838	78	1	51	7	9	.44	117	.274	.358	.452

Lastings Milledge

Bats: R Throws: R Pos: LF-56; CF-5; PH-4 **Ht: 6'0" Wt: 203 Born: 4/5/1985 Age: 25**

Year Team	Lg	G	AB	H	2B	3B	HR	Hm	Rd	TB	R	RBI	RC	TBB	IBB	SO	HBP	SH	SF	SB	CS	SB%	GDP	Avg	OBP	Slg
2009 Syrcse*	AAA	22	79	20	5	0	0	-	-	25	11	4	7	3	0	16	0	0	1	6	1	.86	2	.253	.277	.316
2009 Nats*	R	3	5	1	0	0	1	-	-	4	1	3	2	3	0	0	0	0	0	1	0	1.00	0	.200	.500	.800
2009 Pirates*	R	7	17	5	2	0	1	-	-	10	2	3	5	5	0	2	0	0	0	2	0	1.00	0	.294	.455	.588
2009 Lynbrg*	A+	3	12	3	1	0	2	-	-	10	3	4	3	1	0	3	0	0	0	0	0	-	0	.250	.308	.833
2009 Indy*	AAA	17	60	20	6	0	0	-	-	26	7	7	12	8	0	10	3	1	2	3	2	.60	2	.333	.425	.433
2006 NYM	NL	56	166	40	7	2	4	2	2	63	14	22	21	12	4	39	5	1	1	1	2	.33	4	.241	.310	.380
2007 NYM	NL	59	184	50	9	1	7	6	1	82	27	29	27	13	2	42	7	1	1	3	2	.60	5	.272	.341	.446
2008 Was	NL	138	523	140	24	2	14	7	7	210	65	61	60	38	1	96	14	5	7	24	9	.73	19	.268	.330	.402
2009 2 Tms	NL	65	244	68	11	0	4	3	1	91	21	21	24	13	0	47	4	2	2	7	4	.64	5	.279	.323	.373
09 Was	NL	7	24	4	0	0	0	0	0	4	1	1	1	1	0	10	1	0	0	1	0	1.00	1	.167	.231	.167
09 Pit	NL	58	220	64	11	0	4	3	1	87	20	20	23	12	0	37	3	2	2	6	4	.60	4	.291	.333	.395
4 ML YEARS		318	1117	298	51	5	29	18	11	446	127	133	132	76	7	224	30	9	11	35	17	.67	33	.267	.325	.399

Andrew Miller

Pitches: L Bats: L Pos: SP-14; RP-6 **Ht: 6'7" Wt: 207 Born: 5/21/1985 Age: 25**

Year Team	Lg	G	GS	CG	GF	IP	BFP	H	R	ER	HR	SH	SF	HB	TBB	IBB	SO	WP	Bk	W	L	Pct	Sh	Sv-Op	Hld	ERC	ERA
2009 Jupiter*	A+	1	1	0	0	4.0	16	3	1	1	0	0	0	0	1	0	5	0	0	0	0	-	0	0--	-	1.65	2.25
2009 Jaxnvl*	AA	1	1	0	0	6.0	24	5	1	1	0	1	0	0	2	0	5	0	0	0	0	-	0	0--	-	2.37	1.50
2009 NewOr*	AAA	3	3	0	0	11.2	58	9	10	10	0	0	1	0	13	0	16	1	0	1	2	.333	0	0--	-	4.91	7.71
2009 Mrlns*	R	2	2	0	0	7.0	32	8	2	2	0	0	0	0	4	0	10	2	1	0	0	-	0	0--	-	4.83	2.57
2006 Det	AL	8	0	0	3	10.1	51	8	9	7	0	0	0	2	10	0	6	1	0	0	0	.000	0	0-0	1	4.70	6.10
2007 Det	AL	13	13	0	0	64.0	309	73	43	40	8	3	1	7	39	0	50	4	1	5	5	.500	0	0-0	0	6.31	5.63
2008 Fla	NL	29	20	0	1	107.1	492	120	78	70	7	10	7	4	56	4	89	4	0	6	10	.375	0	0-0	2	5.04	5.87
2009 Fla	NL	20	14	0	1	80.0	366	85	52	43	7	6	4	2	43	1	59	10	0	3	5	.375	0	0-0	1	4.90	4.84
4 ML YEARS		70	47	0	5	261.2	1218	286	182	160	22	19	12	15	148	5	210	19	1	14	21	.400	0	0-0	4	6.20	5.50

Corky Miller

Bats: R Throws: R Pos: C-32; PH-4; DH-1 **Ht: 6'1" Wt: 245 Born: 3/18/1976 Age: 34**

Year Team	Lg	G	AB	H	2B	3B	HR	Hm	Rd	TB	R	RBI	RC	TBB	IBB	SO	HBP	SH	SF	SB	CS	SB%	GDP	Avg	OBP	Slg
2009 Charltt*	AAA	4	7	1	0	0	0	-	-	1	0	0	0	2	0	2	1	0	0	0	0	-	0	.143	.400	.143
2009 Lsvlle*	AAA	23	77	22	5	0	0	-	-	27	13	8	11	8	2	7	3	2	0	0	0	-	5	.286	.375	.351
2001 Cin	NL	17	49	9	2	0	3	1	2	20	5	7	6	4	0	16	2	0	2	1	0	1.00	1	.184	.263	.408
2002 Cin	NL	39	114	29	10	0	3	2	1	48	9	15	15	9	2	20	4	1	1	0	0	-	7	.254	.328	.421
2003 Cin	NL	14	30	8	0	0	0	0	0	8	4	1	5	5	0	7	2	0	1	0	0	-	1	.267	.395	.267
2004 Cin	NL	13	39	1	0	0	0	0	0	1	2	3	0	6	0	12	3	0	1	0	0	-	3	.026	.204	.026
2005 Mln	AL	5	12	0	0	0	0	0	0	0	0	0	0	0	0	2	0	0	0	0	0	-	0	.000	.000	.000
2006 Bos	AL	1	4	0	0	0	0	0	0	0	0	0	0	0	0	1	0	0	0	0	0	-	0	.000	.000	.000
2007 Atl	NL	12	27	7	2	0	1	0	1	12	3	4	4	1	0	5	1	0	0	0	0	-	1	.259	.310	.444
2008 Atl	NL	31	60	5	0	0	1	0	1	8	4	5	5	5	0	15	0	1	0	0	0	-	2	.083	.152	.133
2009 2 Tms	NL	35	95	18	4	0	1	1	0	25	9	15	11	12	0	23	1	2	1	0	0	-	2	.189	.284	.263
09 CWS	AL	14	39	8	3	0	0	0	0	11	5	5	3	3	0	9	0	0	0	0	0	-	1	.205	.262	.282
09 Cin	NL	21	56	10	1	0	1	1	0	14	4	10	8	9	0	14	1	2	1	0	0	-	1	.179	.299	.250
9 ML YEARS		167	430	77	18	0	9	4	5	122	36	50	41	42	2	101	13	4	7	1	0	1.00	17	.179	.268	.284

Justin Miller

Pitches: R Bats: R Pos: RP-44 **Ht: 6'2" Wt: 200 Born: 8/27/1977 Age: 32**

Year Team	Lg	G	GS	CG	GF	IP	BFP	H	R	ER	HR	SH	SF	HB	TBB	IBB	SO	WP	Bk	W	L	Pct	Sh	Sv-Op	Hld	ERC	ERA
2002 Tor	AL	25	18	0	0	102.1	469	103	70	63	12	1	6	11	66	2	68	6	0	9	5	.643	0	0-0	0	5.73	5.54
2004 Tor	AL	19	15	0	0	81.2	375	101	58	55	14	2	6	5	42	3	47	3	1	3	4	.429	0	0-0	0	6.91	6.06
2005 Tor	AL	1	0	0	0	2.1	12	5	4	4	3	0	0	0	0	2	0	0	0	0	0	-	0	0-0	0	20.19	15.43
2007 Fla	NL	62	0	0	10	61.2	259	53	27	25	5	3	0	6	24	6	74	4	1	5	0	1.000	0	0-3	17	2.98	3.65
2008 Fla	NL	46	0	0	8	46.2	202	46	26	22	4	0	1	3	20	3	43	1	1	4	2	.667	0	0-1	7	4.21	4.24
2009 SF	NL	44	0	0	6	56.2	236	47	20	20	7	4	5	1	27	2	36	3	0	3	3	.500	0	0-0	1	3.69	3.18
6 ML YEARS		197	33	0	26	351.1	1553	355	205	189	45	10	18	20	179	16	270	17	3	24	14	.632	0	0-4	26	5.00	4.84

Trever Miller

Pitches: L Bats: R Pos: RP-70 **Ht: 6'3" Wt: 185 Born: 5/29/1973 Age: 37**

Year Team	Lg	G	GS	CG	GF	IP	BFP	H	R	ER	HR	SH	SF	HB	TBB	IBB	SO	WP	Bk	W	L	Pct	Sh	Sv-Op	Hld	ERC	ERA
1996 Det	AL	5	4	0	0	16.2	88	28	17	17	3	2	2	2	9	0	8	1	0	0	4	.000	0	0-0	0	10.15	9.18
1998 Hou	NL	37	1	0	15	53.1	235	57	21	18	4	0	0	1	20	1	30	1	0	2	0	1.000	0	1-2	1	4.18	3.04
1999 Hou	NL	47	0	0	11	49.2	232	58	29	28	6	2	2	5	29	1	37	4	0	3	2	.600	0	1-1	4	6.48	5.07
2000 2 Tms	NL	16	0	0	2	16.1	90	27	22	19	3	1	1	2	12	1	11	1	0	0	0	-	0	0-0	2	10.68	10.47

Year	Team	Lg	G	GS	CG	GF	IP	BFP	H	R	ER	HR	SH	SF	HB	TBB	IBB	SO	WP	Bk	W	L	Pct	Sh	Sv-Op	Hld	ERC	ERA
2003	Tor	AL	79	0	0	18	52.2	233	46	30	27	7	1	0	5	28	3	44	2	0	2	2	.500	0	3-4	16	4.38	4.61
2004	TB	AL	60	0	0	15	49.0	208	48	21	17	3	0	3	15	4	43	1	0	1	1	.500	0	1-3	9	3.45	3.12	
2005	TB	AL	61	0	0	13	44.1	206	45	23	20	4	3	5	7	29	6	35	2	0	2	2	.500	0	0-3	11	5.57	4.06
2006	Hou	NL	70	0	0	14	50.2	207	42	17	17	7	1	2	4	13	2	56	1	0	2	3	.400	0	1-3	12	3.11	3.02
2007	Hou	NL	76	0	0	12	46.1	211	45	26	25	6	3	0	4	23	6	46	1	0	0	0	-	0	1-3	12	4.52	4.86
2008	TB	AL	68	0	0	16	43.1	187	39	21	20	2	1	1	4	20	1	44	1	0	2	0	1.000	0	2-3	11	3.73	4.15
2009	StL	NL	70	0	0	9	43.2	173	31	11	10	5	2	1	2	11	1	46	1	0	4	1	.800	0	0-1	13	2.25	2.06
00	Phi	NL	14	0	0	2	14.0	72	19	16	13	3	1	1	1	9	1	10	1	0	0	0	-	0	0-0	0	8.14	8.36
00	LAD	NL	2	0	0	0	2.1	18	8	6	6	0	0	0	1	3	0	1	0	0	0	0	-	0	0-0	0	28.18	23.14
Postseason			9	0	0	2	3.0	16	3	2	2	1	0	0	0	4	0	4	1	0	0	0	-	0	0-0	1	9.98	6.00
11 ML YEARS			589	5	0	125	466.0	2070	466	238	218	50	19	14	39	209	26	400	16	0	18	15	.545	0	10-23	89	4.55	4.21

Brad Mills

Pitches: L **Bats:** R **Pos:** SP-2   **Ht:** 5'11" **Wt:** 185 **Born:** 3/5/1985 **Age:** 25

Year	Team	Lg	G	GS	CG	GF	IP	BFP	H	R	ER	HR	SH	SF	HB	TBB	IBB	SO	WP	Bk	W	L	Pct	Sh	Sv-Op	Hld	ERC	ERA
2007	Auburn	A-	6	2	0	0	18.0	70	9	4	4	0	0	0	1	6	0	21	0	0	2	0	1.000	0	0--	-	1.20	2.00
2008	Lansng	A	15	15	0	0	81.1	341	71	30	23	3	2	1	5	28	1	92	2	0	6	3	.667	0	0--	-	2.97	2.55
2008	Dnedin	A+	6	6	0	0	33.1	133	25	9	5	2	1	1	0	12	0	35	1	0	4	0	1.000	0	0--	-	2.41	1.35
2008	NHam	AA	6	6	0	0	32.2	131	24	11	4	2	0	1	1	12	0	32	2	0	3	2	.600	0	0--	-	2.47	1.10
2009	LsVgs	AAA	14	14	1	0	84.1	362	83	43	38	6	4	2	4	35	0	72	4	1	2	8	.200	0	0--	-	4.09	4.06
2009	Tor	AL	2	2	0	0	7.2	42	14	12	12	4	0	1	0	6	0	9	0	0	0	1	.000	0	0-0	0	15.52	14.09

Kevin Millwood

Pitches: R **Bats:** R **Pos:** SP-31   **Ht:** 6'4" **Wt:** 230 **Born:** 12/24/1974 **Age:** 35

Year	Team	Lg	G	GS	CG	GF	IP	BFP	H	R	ER	HR	SH	SF	HB	TBB	IBB	SO	WP	Bk	W	L	Pct	Sh	Sv-Op	Hld	ERC	ERA
1997	Atl	NL	12	8	0	2	51.1	227	55	26	23	1	3	5	2	21	1	42	1	0	5	3	.625	0	0-0	0	4.03	4.03
1998	Atl	NL	31	29	3	1	174.1	748	175	86	79	18	8	3	3	56	3	163	6	1	17	8	.680	1	0-0	1	3.81	4.08
1999	Atl	NL	33	33	2	0	228.0	906	168	80	68	24	9	3	4	59	2	205	5	0	18	7	.720	0	0-0	0	2.26	2.68
2000	Atl	NL	36	35	0	0	212.2	903	213	115	110	26	8	5	3	62	2	168	4	0	10	13	.435	0	0-0	0	3.83	4.66
2001	Atl	NL	21	21	0	0	121.0	515	121	66	58	20	7	2	1	40	6	84	5	1	7	7	.500	0	0-0	0	4.20	4.31
2002	Atl	NL	35	34	1	0	217.0	895	186	83	78	16	9	4	8	65	7	178	4	1	18	8	.692	1	0-0	0	2.85	3.24
2003	Phi	NL	35	35	5	0	222.0	930	210	103	99	19	12	5	4	68	6	169	2	0	14	12	.538	3	0-0	0	3.35	4.01
2004	Phi	NL	25	25	0	0	141.0	628	155	81	76	14	11	2	7	51	5	125	4	0	9	6	.600	0	0-0	0	4.57	4.85
2005	Cle	AL	30	30	1	0	192.0	799	182	72	61	20	6	4	4	52	0	146	2	0	9	11	.450	0	0-0	0	3.40	2.86
2006	Tex	AL	34	34	2	0	215.0	907	228	114	108	23	8	3	4	53	4	157	6	0	16	12	.571	0	0-0	0	3.92	4.52
2007	Tex	AL	31	31	0	0	172.2	788	213	111	99	19	1	4	8	67	2	123	4	0	10	14	.417	0	0-0	0	5.64	5.16
2008	Tex	AL	29	29	3	0	168.2	767	220	104	95	18	5	2	6	49	3	125	2	1	9	10	.474	0	0-0	0	5.54	5.07
2009	Tex	AL	31	31	0	0	198.2	850	195	88	81	26	4	5	11	71	0	123	8	0	13	10	.565	0	0-0	0	4.27	3.67
Postseason			9	7	1	1	41.1	164	33	20	18	7	1	1	0	6	0	38	1	1	3	3	.500	0	1-1	0	2.41	3.92
13 ML YEARS			383	375	20	3	2314.1	9863	2321	1129	1035	244	91	47	65	714	41	1808	53	3	155	121	.562	5	0-0	1	3.84	4.02

Eric Milton

Pitches: L **Bats:** L **Pos:** SP-5   **Ht:** 6'1" **Wt:** 220 **Born:** 8/4/1975 **Age:** 34

Year	Team	Lg	G	GS	CG	GF	IP	BFP	H	R	ER	HR	SH	SF	HB	TBB	IBB	SO	WP	Bk	W	L	Pct	Sh	Sv-Op	Hld	ERC	ERA
2009	Albq*	AAA	7	7	0	0	35.0	138	29	12	11	3	2	1	0	6	0	27	1	0	3	2	.600	0	0--	-	2.25	2.83
2009	InldEm*	A+	1	1	0	0	5.1	18	4	0	0	0	0	0	0	1	0	3	0	0	1	0	1.000	0	0--	-	1.80	0.00
1998	Min	AL	32	32	1	0	172.1	772	195	113	108	25	2	6	2	70	0	107	1	0	8	14	.364	0	0-0	0	5.21	5.64
1999	Min	AL	34	34	4	0	206.1	858	190	111	103	28	3	6	3	63	2	163	2	0	7	11	.389	2	0-0	0	3.56	4.49
2000	Min	AL	33	33	0	0	200.0	849	205	123	108	35	4	6	7	44	0	160	5	0	13	10	.565	0	0-0	0	4.09	4.86
2001	Min	AL	35	34	2	0	220.2	944	222	106	106	35	8	6	5	61	0	157	2	0	15	7	.682	1	0-0	0	4.05	4.32
2002	Min	AL	29	29	2	0	171.0	707	173	96	92	24	0	4	3	30	0	121	4	0	13	9	.591	1	0-0	0	3.59	4.84
2003	Min	AL	3	3	0	0	17.0	66	15	5	5	2	0	1	0	1	0	7	0	0	1	0	1.000	0	0-0	0	2.29	2.65
2004	Min	AL	34	34	0	0	201.0	862	196	110	106	43	11	6	1	75	6	161	3	0	14	6	.700	0	0-0	0	4.57	4.75
2005	Cin	NL	34	34	0	0	186.1	855	237	141	134	40	6	6	7	52	2	123	8	0	8	15	.348	0	0-0	0	6.03	6.47
2006	Cin	NL	26	26	0	0	152.2	662	163	94	88	29	6	3	6	42	4	90	2	0	8	8	.500	0	0-0	0	4.62	5.19
2007	Cin	NL	6	6	0	0	31.1	143	39	21	18	4	3	0	0	9	0	18	2	0	0	4	.000	0	0-0	0	5.07	5.17
2009	LAD	NL	5	5	0	0	23.2	108	30	12	10	2	1	0	2	6	0	20	0	0	2	1	.667	0	0-0	0	5.18	3.80
Postseason			3	2	0	0	16.1	65	13	3	3	2	0	0	0	3	0	9	0	0	1	0	1.000	0	0-0	0	2.30	1.65
11 ML YEARS			271	270	9	0	1582.1	6826	1665	935	878	267	44	44	35	453	14	1127	29	0	89	85	.511	4	0-0	0	4.42	4.99

Zach Miner

Pitches: R **Bats:** R **Pos:** RP-46; SP-5   **Ht:** 6'3" **Wt:** 200 **Born:** 3/12/1982 **Age:** 28

Year	Team	Lg	G	GS	CG	GF	IP	BFP	H	R	ER	HR	SH	SF	HB	TBB	IBB	SO	WP	Bk	W	L	Pct	Sh	Sv-Op	Hld	ERC	ERA
2006	Det	AL	27	16	1	4	93.0	398	100	53	50	11	2	2	0	32	1	59	1	0	7	6	.538	0	0-0	1	4.44	4.84
2007	Det	AL	34	1	0	8	53.2	232	56	22	18	3	4	1	0	22	4	34	1	0	3	4	.429	0	0-2	9	3.95	3.02
2008	Det	AL	45	13	0	3	118.0	509	118	60	56	10	4	3	6	46	3	62	4	0	8	5	.615	0	0-3	8	4.12	4.27
2009	Det	AL	51	5	0	9	92.1	409	101	49	44	11	2	1	2	45	1	62	2	0	7	5	.583	0	1-5	8	5.28	4.29
Postseason			1	0	0	1	0.2	2	0	0	0	0	0	0	0	0	0	0	1	0	0	0	-	0	0-0	0	3.22	0.00
4 ML YEARS			157	35	1	24	357.0	1548	375	184	168	35	12	7	8	145	9	217	8	0	25	20	.556	0	1-10	24	4.47	4.24

Juan Miranda

Bats: L Throws: L Pos: 1B-8; PH-1; PR-1   Ht: 6'0" Wt: 220 Born: 4/25/1983 Age: 27

								BATTING												BASERUNNING				AVERAGES		
Year Team	Lg	G	AB	H	2B	3B	HR	(Hm Rd)	TB	R	RBI	RC	TBB	IBB	SO	HBP	SH	SF	SB	CS	SB%	GDP	Avg	OBP	Slg
2007 Tampa	A+	67	250	66	17	3	9	(- -)	116	35	50	43	29	3	60	7	0	7	1	0	1.00	1	.264	.348	.464
2007 Trntn	AA	55	196	52	17	2	7	(- -)	94	29	46	34	23	2	46	5	0	3	0	1	.00	4	.265	.352	.480
2008 S-WB	AAA	99	356	102	22	0	12	(- -)	160	40	52	65	55	3	79	3	0	3	2	1	.67	6	.287	.384	.449
2009 S-WB	AAA	122	438	127	30	2	19	(- -)	218	74	82	82	55	3	101	3	0	6	1	0	1.00	9	.290	.369	.498
2008 NYY	AL	5	10	4	1	0	0	(0 0)	5	2	1	3	2	0	4	1	0	1	0	0	-	0	.400	.500	.500
2009 NYY	AL	8	9	3	0	0	1	(0 1)	6	2	3	2	0	0	4	0	0	0	0	0	-	0	.333	.333	.667
2 ML YEARS		13	19	7	1	0	1	(0 1)	11	4	4	5	2	0	8	1	0	1	0	0	-	0	.368	.435	.579

Pat Misch

Pitches: L Bats: R Pos: RP-19; SP-7   Ht: 6'2" Wt: 196 Born: 8/18/1981 Age: 28

		HOW MUCH HE PITCHED						WHAT HE GAVE UP												THE RESULTS							
Year Team	Lg	G	GS	CG	GF	IP	BFP	H	R	ER	HR	SH	SF	HB	TBB	IBB	SO	WP	Bk	W	L	Pct	Sh	Sv-Op	Hld	ERC	ERA
2009 Fresno*	AAA	12	1	0	2	27.0	105	24	7	6	1	1	0	2	4	0	12	0	1	3	0	1.000	0	1--	-	2.55	2.00
2009 Buffalo*	AAA	6	4	1	0	25.1	107	27	14	12	1	0	1	1	4	0	21	0	1	1	2	.333	0	0--	-	3.20	4.26
2006 SF	NL	1	0	0	0	1.0	5	2	0	0	0	0	0	0	0	0	1	0	0	0	0	-	0	0-0	0	7.48	0.00
2007 SF	NL	18	4	0	2	40.1	176	47	21	19	3	1	2	2	12	2	26	0	0	0	4	.000	0	0-0	2	4.59	4.24
2008 SF	NL	15	7	0	6	52.1	230	56	34	33	11	3	4	3	15	2	38	1	1	0	3	.000	0	0-0	0	4.88	5.68
2009 2 Tms	NL	26	7	1	2	62.1	270	68	31	31	9	6	1	2	22	2	23	1	0	3	4	.429	1	0-1	0	4.86	4.12
09 SF	NL	4	0	0	2	3.1	19	6	4	4	0	0	0	0	3	0	0	1	0	0	0	-	0	0-0	0	10.16	10.80
09 NYM	NL	22	7	1	0	59.0	251	62	27	27	9	6	1	2	19	2	23	1	0	3	4	.429	1	0-1	0	4.58	4.12
4 ML YEARS		60	18	1	10	156.0	681	173	86	83	23	10	7	7	49	6	88	2	1	3	11	.214	1	0-1	2	4.82	4.79

Sergio Mitre

Pitches: R Bats: R Pos: SP-9; RP-3   Ht: 6'3" Wt: 225 Born: 2/16/1981 Age: 29

		HOW MUCH HE PITCHED						WHAT HE GAVE UP												THE RESULTS							
Year Team	Lg	G	GS	CG	GF	IP	BFP	H	R	ER	HR	SH	SF	HB	TBB	IBB	SO	WP	Bk	W	L	Pct	Sh	Sv-Op	Hld	ERC	ERA
2009 Tampa*	A+	2	2	0	0	9.1	44	10	6	2	0	0	0	1	2	0	8	1	0	1	0	1.000	0	0--	-	3.10	1.93
2009 S-WB*	AAA	7	7	0	0	45.0	175	40	13	12	3	1	0	3	5	0	35	1	0	3	1	.750	0	0--	-	2.54	2.40
2003 ChC	NL	7	2	0	1	8.2	43	15	8	8	1	0	1	0	4	1	3	0	0	0	1	.000	0	0-0	0	8.02	8.31
2004 ChC	NL	12	9	0	2	51.2	244	71	38	38	6	3	0	4	20	1	37	5	1	2	4	.333	0	0-0	0	6.69	6.62
2005 ChC	NL	21	7	1	7	60.1	268	62	37	36	11	1	3	3	23	2	37	5	0	2	5	.286	1	0-0	0	4.81	5.37
2006 Fla	NL	15	7	0	3	41.0	189	44	28	26	7	2	1	6	20	3	31	1	0	1	5	.167	0	0-1	2	5.87	5.71
2007 Fla	NL	27	27	0	0	149.0	602	180	88	77	9	8	10	10	41	3	80	6	0	5	8	.385	0	0-0	0	4.71	4.66
2009 NYY	AL	12	9	0	2	51.2	241	71	45	39	10	0	4	3	13	0	32	3	0	3	3	.500	0	0-0	0	6.53	6.79
6 ML YEARS		90	61	1	15	362.1	1647	443	244	224	44	12	19	26	121	10	220	20	1	13	26	.333	1	0-1	2	5.48	5.56

Garrett Mock

Pitches: R Bats: R Pos: SP-15; RP-13   Ht: 6'3" Wt: 228 Born: 4/25/1983 Age: 27

		HOW MUCH HE PITCHED						WHAT HE GAVE UP												THE RESULTS							
Year Team	Lg	G	GS	CG	GF	IP	BFP	H	R	ER	HR	SH	SF	HB	TBB	IBB	SO	WP	Bk	W	L	Pct	Sh	Sv-Op	Hld	ERC	ERA
2004 Yakima	A-	5	5	0	0	23.1	86	18	8	4	1	1	2	0	4	0	14	0	0	2	0	1.000	0	0--	-	1.89	1.54
2004 Sbend	A	8	8	1	0	54.0	215	49	21	18	2	5	1	2	12	0	37	2	2	3	2	.600	0	0--	-	2.73	3.00
2005 Lancst	A+	28	28	0	0	174.1	757	202	95	81	19	2	2	9	33	0	160	7	0	14	7	.667	0	0--	-	4.36	4.18
2006 Tenn	AA	23	23	0	0	131.0	683	144	81	72	14	7	4	7	50	0	117	5	0	4	8	.333	0	0--	-	4.82	4.95
2006 Hrsbrg	AA	4	4	0	0	16.2	84	29	21	19	2	0	2	2	5	0	9	2	0	0	4	.000	0	0--	-	8.97	10.26
2007 Ptomc	A+	1	1	0	0	6.0	23	3	0	0	0	0	0	1	1	0	5	0	0	1	0	1.000	0	0--	-	1.09	0.00
2007 Nats	R	3	2	0	0	7.2	34	11	7	4	3	0	0	1	1	0	8	0	0	0	2	.000	0	0--	-	7.80	4.70
2007 Hrsbrg	AA	11	11	0	0	51.1	254	66	41	33	5	6	5	3	28	0	41	8	0	1	5	.167	0	0--	-	6.36	5.79
2008 Clmbs	AAA	19	17	0	0	104.2	436	98	41	35	9	7	5	6	25	0	96	5	1	6	3	.667	0	0--	-	3.23	3.01
2009 Syrcse	AAA	13	8	1	4	51.0	198	36	15	15	2	0	1	3	13	2	48	3	0	5	1	.833	1	2--	-	1.89	2.65
2008 Was	NL	26	3	0	5	41.0	180	37	20	19	4	1	1	0	23	3	46	3	1	1	3	.250	0	0-0	0	4.00	4.17
2009 Was	NL	28	15	0	1	91.1	422	114	65	57	9	4	3	1	44	3	72	10	0	3	10	.231	0	0-2	4	5.86	5.62
2 ML YEARS		54	18	0	6	132.1	602	151	85	76	13	5	4	1	67	6	118	13	1	4	13	.235	0	0-2	4	5.26	5.17

Brian Moehler

Pitches: R Bats: R Pos: SP-29   Ht: 6'3" Wt: 235 Born: 12/31/1971 Age: 38

		HOW MUCH HE PITCHED						WHAT HE GAVE UP												THE RESULTS							
Year Team	Lg	G	GS	CG	GF	IP	BFP	H	R	ER	HR	SH	SF	HB	TBB	IBB	SO	WP	Bk	W	L	Pct	Sh	Sv-Op	Hld	ERC	ERA
2009 RdRck*	AAA	1	1	0	0	4.0	19	3	2	1	0	0	0	0	3	0	0	0	0	0	0	-	0	0--	-	3.01	2.25
2009 CpChr*	AA	1	1	0	0	5.0	26	11	8	8	0	0	0	0	0	0	2	0	0	0	0	-	0	0--	-	8.80	14.40
1996 Det	AL	2	2	0	0	10.1	51	11	10	5	1	1	0	0	8	1	2	1	0	0	1	.000	0	0-0	0	5.49	4.35
1997 Det	AL	31	31	2	0	175.1	770	198	97	91	22	1	8	5	61	1	97	3	0	11	12	.478	1	0-0	0	4.92	4.67
1998 Det	AL	33	33	4	0	221.1	912	220	103	96	30	3	3	2	56	1	123	4	0	14	13	.519	3	0-0	0	3.79	3.90
1999 Det	AL	32	32	2	0	196.1	859	229	116	110	22	8	5	7	59	5	106	4	0	10	16	.385	2	0-0	0	4.85	5.04
2000 Det	AL	29	29	2	0	178.0	776	222	99	89	20	3	4	2	40	0	103	2	1	12	9	.571	0	0-0	0	4.95	4.50
2001 Det	AL	1	1	0	0	8.0	30	6	3	3	0	0	0	0	1	0	2	0	0	0	0	-	0	0-0	0	1.43	3.38
2002 2 Tms	AL	13	12	0	0	63.0	278	78	39	34	11	4	2	1	13	0	31	0	0	3	5	.375	0	0-0	0	5.20	4.86
2003 Hou	NL	3	3	0	0	13.2	66	22	12	12	4	1	1	0	6	0	5	0	0	0	0	-	0	0-0	0	9.97	7.90
2005 Fla	NL	37	25	0	4	158.1	696	198	82	80	16	13	4	5	42	9	95	1	0	6	12	.333	0	0-0	1	5.07	4.55
2006 Fla	NL	29	21	0	2	122.0	556	164	95	89	19	7	2	5	38	3	58	2	1	7	11	.389	0	0-1	0	6.36	6.57
2007 Hou	NL	42	0	0	29	59.2	257	67	29	27	8	1	0	6	17	3	36	1	0	1	4	.200	0	1-1	1	4.48	4.07
2008 Hou	NL	31	26	0	0	150.0	650	166	79	76	20	7	8	4	36	1	82	3	0	11	8	.579	0	0-0	0	4.31	4.56

Year	Team	Lg		HOW MUCH HE PITCHED							WHAT HE GAVE UP												THE RESULTS						
			G	GS	CG	GF	IP	BFP	H	R	ER	HR	SH	SF	HB	TBB	IBB	SO	WP	Bk	W	L	Pct	Sh	Sv-Op	Hld	ERC	ERA
2009	Hou	NL	29	29	1	0	154.2	694	187	101	94	21	9	3	4	51	12	91	4	0	8	12	.400	0	0-0	0	5.21	5.47
02	Det	AL	3	3	0	0	19.2	77	17	5	5	3	1	1	0	2	0	13	0	0	1	1	.500	0	0-0	0	2.54	2.29
02	Cin	NL	10	9	0	0	43.1	201	61	34	29	8	3	1	1	11	0	18	0	0	2	4	.333	0	0-0	0	6.56	6.02
13 ML YEARS			312	244	11	35	1510.2	6595	1768	865	806	194	58	41	35	428	36	831	25	2	83	103	.446	6	1-2	2	4.86	4.80

Chad Moeller

Bats: R **Throws:** R **Pos:** C-30   **Ht:** 6'3" **Wt:** 210 **Born:** 2/18/1975 **Age:** 35

Year	Team	Lg	G	AB	H	2B	3B	HR	(Hm	Rd)	TB	R	RBI	RC	TBB	IBB	SO	HBP	SH	SF	SB	CS	SB%	GDP	Avg	OBP	Slg
2009	Norfolk*	AAA	35	118	24	6	0	0	(-	-)	30	7	10	6	5	0	22	1	1	0	0	1	.00	5	.203	.242	.254
2000	Min	AL	48	128	27	3	1	1	(1	0)	35	13	9	8	9	0	33	0	1	1	1	0	1.00	3	.211	.261	.273
2001	Ari	NL	25	56	13	0	1	1	(1	0)	18	8	2	5	6	1	12	0	1	0	0	0	-	2	.232	.306	.321
2002	Ari	NL	37	105	30	11	1	2	(2	0)	49	10	16	17	17	3	23	0	1	0	0	1	.00	6	.286	.385	.467
2003	Ari	NL	78	239	64	17	1	7	(2	5)	104	29	29	28	23	11	59	2	3	2	1	2	.33	7	.268	.335	.435
2004	Mil	NL	101	317	66	13	1	5	(3	2)	96	25	27	14	21	1	74	4	6	1	0	1	.00	12	.208	.265	.303
2005	Mil	NL	66	199	41	9	1	7	(5	2)	73	23	23	14	13	1	48	1	2	1	0	0	-	9	.206	.257	.367
2006	Mil	NL	29	98	18	3	0	2	(2	0)	27	9	5	3	4	0	26	2	0	0	0	0	-	3	.184	.231	.276
2007	2 Tms	NL	37	56	9	1	0	1	(1	0)	13	8	2	5	0	0	18	1	1	0	0	0	-	3	.161	.175	.232
2008	NYY	AL	41	91	21	6	0	1	(0	1)	30	13	9	9	7	1	18	4	0	1	0	0	-	2	.231	.311	.330
2009	Bal	AL	30	89	23	8	1	2	(1	1)	39	6	10	8	7	0	16	1	1	2	0	0	-	3	.258	.313	.438
07	Cin	NL	30	48	8	1	0	1	(1	0)	12	6	2	0	0	0	17	0	1	0	0	0	-	2	.167	.167	.250
07	LAD	NL	7	8	1	0	0	0	(0	0)	1	2	0	0	0	0	1	1	0	0	0	0	-	1	.125	.222	.125
	Postseason		3	5	2	0	0	0	(0	0)	2	0	0	1	0	0	1	0	0	0	0	0	-	0	.400	.400	.400
10 ML YEARS			492	1378	312	71	7	29	(18	11)	484	144	132	106	107	18	327	15	16	8	2	4	.33	50	.226	.288	.351

Bengie Molina

Bats: R **Throws:** R **Pos:** C-123; PH-11; DH-1   **Ht:** 5'11" **Wt:** 225 **Born:** 7/20/1974 **Age:** 35

Year	Team	Lg	G	AB	H	2B	3B	HR	(Hm	Rd)	TB	R	RBI	RC	TBB	IBB	SO	HBP	SH	SF	SB	CS	SB%	GDP	Avg	OBP	Slg
1998	LAA	AL	2	1	0	0	0	0	(0	0)	0	0	0	0	0	0	0	0	0	0	0	0	-	0	.000	.000	.000
1999	LAA	AL	31	101	26	5	0	1	(1	0)	34	8	10	9	6	0	6	2	0	0	0	1	.00	5	.257	.312	.337
2000	LAA	AL	130	473	133	20	2	14	(11	3)	199	59	71	60	23	0	33	6	4	7	1	0	1.00	17	.281	.318	.421
2001	LAA	AL	96	325	85	11	0	6	(6	0)	114	31	40	34	16	3	51	8	2	4	1	0	1.00	8	.262	.309	.351
2002	LAA	AL	122	428	105	18	0	5	(2	3)	138	34	47	33	15	3	34	4	6	6	0	0	-	15	.245	.274	.322
2003	LAA	AL	119	409	115	24	0	14	(7	7)	181	37	71	57	13	2	31	2	2	4	1	1	.50	17	.281	.304	.443
2004	LAA	AL	97	337	93	13	0	10	(5	5)	136	36	54	44	18	1	35	2	2	4	0	1	.00	18	.276	.313	.404
2005	LAA	AL	119	410	121	17	0	15	(8	7)	183	45	69	53	27	2	41	1	5	6	0	2	.00	14	.295	.336	.446
2006	Tor	AL	117	433	123	20	1	19	(12	7)	202	44	57	58	19	1	47	4	0	2	1	1	.50	15	.284	.319	.467
2007	SF	NL	134	497	137	19	1	19	(9	10)	215	38	81	64	15	2	53	2	1	2	0	0	-	13	.276	.298	.433
2008	SF	NL	145	530	155	33	0	16	(9	7)	236	46	95	70	19	5	38	9	0	11	0	0	-	23	.292	.322	.445
2009	SF	NL	132	491	130	25	1	20	(12	8)	217	52	80	56	13	3	68	5	0	11	0	0	-	14	.265	.285	.442
	Postseason		29	91	24	4	1	3	(2	1)	39	7	12	14	4	2	8	3	2	0	0	0	-	3	.264	.316	.429
12 ML YEARS			1244	4435	1223	205	5	139	(81	58)	1855	430	675	538	184	22	437	45	22	57	3	7	.30	159	.276	.308	.418

Jose Molina

Bats: R **Throws:** R **Pos:** C-49; 1B-3; 3B-1; DH-1; PH-1   **Ht:** 6'2" **Wt:** 235 **Born:** 6/3/1975 **Age:** 35

Year	Team	Lg	G	AB	H	2B	3B	HR	(Hm	Rd)	TB	R	RBI	RC	TBB	IBB	SO	HBP	SH	SF	SB	CS	SB%	GDP	Avg	OBP	Slg
2009	S-WB*	AAA	2	4	1	1	0	0	(-	-)	2	0	1	0	1	0	0	0	0	0	0	0	-	0	.250	.400	.500
2009	Trntn*	AA	3	7	0	0	0	0	(-	-)	0	0	0	0	2	0	4	1	0	0	0	0	-	0	.000	.300	.000
1999	ChC	NL	10	19	5	1	0	0	(0	0)	6	3	1	2	2	1	4	0	0	0	0	0	-	0	.263	.333	.316
2001	LAA	AL	15	37	10	3	0	2	(0	2)	19	8	4	6	3	0	8	0	2	0	0	0	-	2	.270	.325	.514
2002	LAA	AL	29	70	19	3	0	0	(0	0)	22	5	5	4	5	0	15	0	4	2	0	2	.00	2	.271	.312	.314
2003	LAA	AL	53	114	21	4	0	0	(0	0)	25	12	6	5	1	0	26	3	4	1	0	0	-	1	.184	.210	.219
2004	LAA	AL	73	203	53	10	2	3	(1	2)	76	26	25	19	10	0	52	0	5	0	4	1	.80	6	.261	.296	.374
2005	LAA	AL	75	184	42	4	0	6	(2	4)	64	14	25	19	13	0	41	2	4	0	2	0	1.00	5	.228	.286	.348
2006	LAA	AL	78	225	54	17	0	4	(0	4)	83	18	22	21	9	0	49	2	7	2	1	0	1.00	6	.240	.273	.369
2007	2 Tms	AL	69	191	49	13	0	1	(1	0)	65	18	19	20	5	0	43	0	5	1	2	1	.67	4	.257	.274	.340
2008	NYY	AL	100	268	58	17	0	3	(2	1)	84	32	18	15	12	0	52	6	8	3	0	0	-	9	.216	.263	.313
2009	NYY	AL	52	138	30	4	0	1	(0	1)	37	15	11	12	14	0	28	1	1	1	0	0	-	6	.217	.292	.268
07	LAA	AL	40	125	28	8	0	0	(0	0)	36	9	10	9	3	0	30	0	3	0	2	1	.67	3	.224	.242	.288
07	NYY	AL	29	66	21	5	0	1	(1	0)	29	9	9	11	2	0	13	0	2	1	0	0	-	1	.318	.333	.439
	Postseason		10	8	3	0	0	0	(0	0)	3	1	3	1	2	0	0	1	0	0	0	0	-	0	.375	.500	.375
10 ML YEARS			554	1449	341	76	2	20	(6	14)	481	151	136	123	74	1	318	14	40	10	9	4	.69	41	.235	.277	.332

Yadier Molina

Bats: R **Throws:** R **Pos:** C-138; 1B-6; PH-3   **Ht:** 5'11" **Wt:** 230 **Born:** 7/13/1982 **Age:** 27

Year	Team	Lg	G	AB	H	2B	3B	HR	(Hm	Rd)	TB	R	RBI	RC	TBB	IBB	SO	HBP	SH	SF	SB	CS	SB%	GDP	Avg	OBP	Slg
2004	StL	NL	51	135	36	6	0	2	(1	1)	48	12	15	15	13	3	20	0	2	1	0	1	.00	4	.267	.329	.356
2005	StL	NL	114	385	97	15	1	8	(6	2)	138	36	49	46	23	3	30	2	8	3	2	3	.40	10	.252	.295	.358
2006	StL	NL	129	417	90	26	0	6	(2	4)	134	29	49	35	26	2	41	8	8	2	1	2	.33	15	.216	.274	.321
2007	StL	NL	111	353	97	15	0	6	(4	2)	130	30	40	38	34	5	43	3	2	4	1	1	.50	18	.275	.340	.368
2008	StL	NL	124	444	135	18	0	7	(2	5)	174	37	56	57	32	4	29	1	3	5	0	2	.00	21	.304	.349	.392
2009	StL	NL	140	481	141	23	1	6	(5	1)	184	45	54	64	50	2	39	6	6	1	9	3	.75	27	.293	.366	.383
	Postseason		29	95	30	7	0	2	(1	1)	43	7	11	12	6	1	9	0	0	0	0	1	.00	3	.316	.356	.453
6 ML YEARS			669	2215	596	103	2	35	(20	15)	808	189	263	255	178	19	202	20	29	16	13	12	.52	95	.269	.327	.365

Craig Monroe

Bats: R Throws: R Pos: PH-16; RF-9; LF-8; DH-3   Ht: 6'1" Wt: 215 Born: 2/27/1977 Age: 33

									BATTING												BASERUNNING				AVERAGES		
Year	Team	Lg	G	AB	H	2B	3B	HR	(Hm	Rd)	TB	R	RBI	RC	TBB	IBB	SO	HBP	SH	SF	SB	CS	SB%	GDP	Avg	OBP	Slg
2001	Tex	AL	27	52	11	1	0	2	(1	1)	18	8	5	6	6	0	18	0	0	0	2	0	1.00	1	.212	.293	.346
2002	Det	AL	13	25	3	1	0	1	(0	1)	7	3	1	0	0	0	5	1	0	0	0	2	.00	1	.120	.154	.280
2003	Det	AL	128	425	102	18	1	23	(10	13)	191	51	70	61	27	2	89	2	1	3	4	2	.67	10	.240	.287	.449
2004	Det	AL	128	447	131	27	3	18	(9	9)	218	65	72	66	29	1	79	2	0	3	3	4	.43	8	.293	.337	.488
2005	Det	AL	157	567	157	30	3	20	(9	11)	253	69	89	77	40	4	95	3	1	12	8	3	.73	16	.277	.322	.446
2006	Det	AL	147	541	138	35	2	28	(12	16)	261	89	92	76	37	3	126	1	0	6	2	2	.50	14	.255	.301	.482
2007	2 Tms		122	392	86	23	0	12	(5	7)	145	53	59	36	26	0	107	2	1	6	0	4	.00	13	.219	.268	.370
2008	Min	AL	58	163	33	9	0	8	(5	3)	66	22	29	22	16	1	48	0	0	0	0	1	.00	3	.202	.274	.405
2009	Pit	NL	34	79	17	2	0	3	(2	1)	28	8	16	11	7	1	21	1	0	0	0	0	-	4	.215	.287	.354
07	Det	AL	99	343	76	19	0	11	(5	6)	128	47	55	32	20	0	94	2	1	6	0	3	.00	10	.222	.264	.373
07	ChC	NL	23	49	10	4	0	1	(0	1)	17	6	4	4	6	0	13	0	0	0	0	1	.00	3	.204	.291	.347
	Postseason		13	50	12	4	0	5	(4	1)	31	11	9	6	4	0	12	0	0	1	0	0	-	0	.240	.291	.620
	9 ML YEARS		814	2691	678	146	9	115	(53	62)	1187	368	433	355	188	12	588	12	3	30	19	18	.51	70	.252	.301	.441

Lou Montanez

Bats: R Throws: R Pos: LF-19; PH-7; DH-3; CF-2; RF-2; PR-1   Ht: 6'1" Wt: 200 Born: 12/15/1981 Age: 28

									BATTING												BASERUNNING				AVERAGES		
Year	Team	Lg	G	AB	H	2B	3B	HR	(Hm	Rd)	TB	R	RBI	RC	TBB	IBB	SO	HBP	SH	SF	SB	CS	SB%	GDP	Avg	OBP	Slg
2000	Cubs	R	50	192	66	16	7	2	(-	-)	102	50	37	44	25	1	42	8	3	1	11	6	.65	5	.344	.438	.531
2000	Lansng	A	8	29	4	1	0	0	(-	-)	5	2	0	0	3	0	6	0	0	0	0	1	.00	0	.138	.219	.172
2001	Lansng	A	124	499	127	33	6	5	(-	-)	187	70	54	63	34	0	121	12	3	3	20	7	.74	12	.255	.316	.375
2002	Dytona	A+	124	487	129	21	5	4	(-	-)	172	69	59	61	44	0	89	9	0	7	14	8	.64	16	.265	.333	.353
2003	Dytona	A+	126	486	123	18	3	5	(-	-)	162	51	38	53	33	0	89	6	6	6	11	4	.73	11	.253	.305	.333
2004	Dytona	A+	21	79	17	4	2	1	(-	-)	28	8	7	8	7	0	18	2	1	1	2	3	.40	0	.215	.292	.354
2004	Boise	A-	72	188	75	13	7	6	(-	-)	132	47	48	50	35	2	53	3	2	3	5	5	.50	5	.297	.381	.496
2005	Peoria	A	82	315	96	28	2	12	(-	-)	164	54	48	64	32	1	48	10	2	2	10	4	.71	6	.305	.384	.521
2005	WTenn	AA	45	153	41	9	1	2	(-	-)	58	20	14	19	12	1	21	2	2	2	0	2	.00	1	.268	.325	.379
2006	WTenn	AA	38	141	52	11	0	2	(-	-)	69	24	25	30	15	1	26	3	2	1	5	3	.63	2	.369	.438	.489
2006	Iowa	AAA	82	245	55	12	0	8	(-	-)	91	23	31	26	17	0	44	3	2	2	0	1	.00	8	.224	.281	.371
2007	Norfolk	AAA	69	212	55	11	0	7	(-	-)	87	27	26	29	22	0	35	2	3	2	1	3	.25	9	.259	.332	.410
2007	Bowie	AA	31	121	41	2	0	3	(-	-)	52	24	11	21	10	0	16	2	2	0	3	2	.60	1	.339	.398	.430
2008	Bowie	AA	116	451	151	32	5	26	(-	-)	271	90	97	101	36	2	63	6	0	8	4	4	.50	9	.335	.395	.601
2009	Norfolk	AAA	10	42	18	3	0	0	(-	-)	21	8	3	10	5	0	9	1	0	0	3	0	1.00	0	.429	.500	.500
2009	Orioles	R	2	6	2	0	0	0	(-	-)	2	0	1	1	0	0	0	1	0	0	0	0	-	0	.333	.429	.333
2009	Frdrck	A+	2	9	3	0	0	0	(-	-)	3	0	2	1	0	0	0	0	0	1	0	0	-	0	.333	.300	.333
2009	Bowie	AA	2	8	3	0	0	0	(-	-)	3	2	2	1	0	0	0	0	0	0	0	0	-	0	.375	.375	.375
2008	Bal	AL	38	112	33	6	1	3	(2	1)	50	18	14	17	4	0	20	0	0	1	0	0	-	0	.295	.316	.446
2009	Bal	AL	29	82	15	5	0	1	(1	0)	23	5	6	8	5	0	16	2	1	1	0	1	.00	0	.183	.244	.280
	2 ML YEARS		67	194	48	11	1	4	(3	1)	73	23	20	25	9	0	36	2	1	2	0	1	.00	0	.247	.285	.376

Miguel Montero

Bats: L Throws: R Pos: C-111; PH-20; DH-2   Ht: 5'11" Wt: 190 Born: 7/9/1983 Age: 26

									BATTING												BASERUNNING				AVERAGES		
Year	Team	Lg	G	AB	H	2B	3B	HR	(Hm	Rd)	TB	R	RBI	RC	TBB	IBB	SO	HBP	SH	SF	SB	CS	SB%	GDP	Avg	OBP	Slg
2006	Ari	NL	6	16	4	1	0	0	(0	0)	5	0	3	2	1	0	3	0	0	0	0	0	-	0	.260	.294	.313
2007	Ari	NL	84	214	48	7	0	10	(7	3)	85	30	37	19	20	2	35	3	1	6	0	0	-	7	.224	.292	.397
2008	Ari	NL	70	184	47	16	1	5	(1	4)	80	24	18	21	19	3	49	2	1	1	0	0	-	1	.255	.330	.435
2009	Ari	NL	128	425	125	30	0	16	(5	11)	203	61	59	65	38	5	78	3	2	2	1	2	.33	6	.294	.355	.478
	Postseason		4	7	2	0	0	0	(0	0)	2	1	0	0	1	0	0	0	0	0	0	0	-	0	.286	.375	.286
	4 ML YEARS		288	839	224	54	1	31	(13	18)	373	115	117	107	78	10	165	8	4	9	1	2	.33	14	.267	.332	.445

Adam Moore

Bats: R Throws: R Pos: C-6; PH-1   Ht: 6'3" Wt: 220 Born: 5/8/1984 Age: 26

									BATTING												BASERUNNING				AVERAGES		
Year	Team	Lg	G	AB	H	2B	3B	HR	(Hm	Rd)	TB	R	RBI	RC	TBB	IBB	SO	HBP	SH	SF	SB	CS	SB%	GDP	Avg	OBP	Slg
2006	Everett	A-	16	63	20	9	0	0	(-	-)	29	8	9	10	2	0	10	1	0	0	0	0	-	3	.317	.348	.460
2006	Wisc	A	44	165	44	6	0	7	(-	-)	71	21	24	25	14	1	38	6	0	2	0	0	-	0	.267	.342	.430
2007	Hi Dsrt	A+	115	433	133	30	3	22	(-	-)	235	74	102	88	41	1	84	8	0	9	1	0	1.00	18	.307	.371	.543
2008	WTenn	AA	119	428	137	35	2	14	(-	-)	218	60	71	87	41	0	77	16	3	2	0	1	.00	16	.320	.398	.509
2009	WTenn	AA	27	95	25	5	0	3	(-	-)	39	14	13	16	16	2	21	2	0	3	0	0	-	2	.263	.371	.411
2009	Tacom	AAA	91	340	100	19	0	9	(-	-)	146	41	43	51	26	0	51	1	1	0	1	1	.50	6	.294	.346	.429
2009	Sea	AL	6	23	5	1	0	1	(1	0)	9	4	2	2	0	0	7	1	0	0	1	0	1.00	1	.217	.250	.391

Melvin Mora

Bats: R Throws: R Pos: 3B-124; PH-1   Ht: 5'11" Wt: 200 Born: 2/7/1972 Age: 38

									BATTING												BASERUNNING				AVERAGES		
Year	Team	Lg	G	AB	H	2B	3B	HR	(Hm	Rd)	TB	R	RBI	RC	TBB	IBB	SO	HBP	SH	SF	SB	CS	SB%	GDP	Avg	OBP	Slg
1999	NYM	NL	66	31	5	0	0	0	(0	0)	5	6	1	2	4	0	7	1	3	0	2	1	.67	0	.161	.278	.161
2000	2 Tms		132	414	114	22	5	8	(5	3)	170	60	47	56	35	3	80	6	4	5	12	11	.52	5	.275	.337	.411
2001	Bal	AL	128	436	109	28	0	7	(6	1)	158	49	48	55	41	2	91	14	5	7	16	10	.73	6	.250	.329	.362
2002	Bal	AL	149	557	130	30	4	19	(8	11)	225	86	64	78	70	2	108	20	1	4	16	10	.62	7	.233	.338	.404
2003	Bal	AL	96	344	109	17	1	15	(8	7)	173	68	48	67	49	0	71	12	6	2	6	3	.67	3	.317	.418	.503
2004	Bal	AL	140	550	187	41	0	27	(15	12)	309	111	104	115	66	0	95	11	6	3	11	6	.65	10	.340	.419	.562
2005	Bal	AL	149	593	168	30	1	27	(13	14)	281	86	88	88	50	0	112	10	8	3	7	4	.64	9	.283	.348	.474

Year	Team	Lg	G	AB	H	2B	3B	HR	(Hm	Rd)	TB	R	RBI	RC	TBB	IBB	SO	HBP	SH	SF	SB	CS	SB%	GDP	Avg	OBP	Slg
2006	Bal	AL	155	624	171	25	0	16	(8	8)	244	96	83	93	54	1	99	14	6	7	11	1	.92	9	.274	.342	.391
2007	Bal	AL	126	467	128	23	1	14	(7	7)	195	67	58	61	47	3	83	3	5	5	9	3	.75	22	.274	.341	.418
2008	Bal	AL	135	513	146	29	2	23	(15	8)	248	77	104	88	37	3	70	11	3	6	3	7	.30	14	.285	.342	.483
2009	Bal	AL	125	450	117	20	0	8	(8	0)	161	44	48	48	34	1	60	8	1	3	3	3	.50	13	.260	.321	.358
00	NYM	NL	79	215	56	13	2	6	(4	2)	91	35	30	29	18	3	48	2	2	5	3	3	.70	3	.260	.317	.423
00	Bal	AL	53	199	58	9	3	2	(1	1)	79	25	17	27	17	0	32	4	2	0	5	8	.38	2	.291	.359	.397
Postseason			9	15	6	0	0	1	(0	1)	9	4	2	4	3	0	2	0	1	0	2	0	1.00	0	.400	.500	.600
11 ML YEARS			1401	4979	1384	265	14	164	(93	71)	2169	750	693	751	487	15	876	110	48	45	91	53	.63	98	.278	.352	.436

Franklin Morales

Pitches: L **Bats:** L **Pos:** RP-38; SP-2   **Ht:** 6'0" **Wt:** 170 **Born:** 1/24/1986 **Age:** 24

			HOW MUCH HE PITCHED					WHAT HE GAVE UP												THE RESULTS							
Year	Team	Lg	G	GS	CG	GF	IP	BFP	H	R	ER	HR	SH	SF	HB	TBB	IBB	SO	WP	Bk	W	L	Pct	Sh	Sv-Op	Hld	ERC	ERA
2009	ColSpr*	AAA	8	8	0	0	41.1	178	39	17	16	4	2	0	3	19	0	37	0	0	2	2	.500	0	0--	-	4.34	3.48
2007	Col	NL	8	8	0	0	39.1	163	34	15	15	2	4	2	2	14	1	26	0	0	3	2	.600	0	0-0	0	3.04	3.43
2008	Col	NL	5	5	0	0	25.1	120	28	18	18	2	2	2	1	17	2	9	1	3	1	2	.333	0	0-0	0	5.58	6.39
2009	Col	NL	40	2	0	14	40.0	179	38	22	20	4	3	0	1	23	4	41	2	0	3	2	.600	0	7-8	7	4.38	4.50
Postseason			4	2	0	0	10.0	49	15	11	11	1	0	0	2	4	0	6	0	0	0	0	-	0	0-0	0	8.14	9.90
3 ML YEARS			53	15	0	14	104.2	462	100	55	53	8	9	4	4	54	7	76	3	3	7	6	.538	0	7-8	7	4.14	4.56

Jose Morales

Bats: B **Throws:** R **Pos:** C-29; PH-17; DH-10; PR-2   **Ht:** 5'11" **Wt:** 197 **Born:** 2/20/1983 **Age:** 27

Year	Team	Lg	G	AB	H	2B	3B	HR	(Hm	Rd)	TB	R	RBI	RC	TBB	IBB	SO	HBP	SH	SF	SB	CS	SB%	GDP	Avg	OBP	Slg
2001	Twins	R	35	117	29	6	2	0	(-	-)	39	13	18	12	6	0	26	2	2	0	4	1	.80	1	.248	.296	.333
2002	Twins	R	53	175	54	7	2	0	(-	-)	65	25	28	24	7	0	28	5	2	3	3	1	.75	5	.309	.347	.371
2003	FtMyrs	A+	12	42	15	3	1	0	(-	-)	20	6	2	6	1	1	5	0	0	0	0	2	.00	1	.357	.372	.476
2003	QuadC	A	48	170	46	10	1	2	(-	-)	64	14	25	19	5	0	32	3	3	1	1	0	1.00	6	.271	.302	.376
2004	FtMyrs	A+	91	331	95	13	4	4	(-	-)	128	30	46	45	29	3	77	0	0	5	0	1	.00	5	.287	.340	.387
2005	NwBrit	AA	7	20	5	1	0	0	(-	-)	6	1	0	1	1	0	3	0	0	0	0	0	-	3	.250	.286	.300
2006	NwBrit	AA	80	251	53	14	1	3	(-	-)	78	23	26	22	19	0	56	5	3	4	2	1	.67	11	.211	.276	.311
2006	Roch	AAA	2	7	1	0	0	0	(-	-)	1	0	0	0	0	0	0	0	0	0	0	0	-	0	.143	.143	.143
2007	Roch	AAA	108	376	117	25	1	2	(-	-)	150	42	37	56	30	5	44	3	1	1	1	4	.20	13	.311	.366	.399
2008	Roch	AAA	54	197	61	7	1	4	(-	-)	82	18	15	28	8	1	28	2	1	0	0	1	.00	7	.310	.343	.416
2009	Roch	AAA	58	211	71	13	1	2	(-	-)	92	30	26	39	28	1	27	1	0	2	1	3	.25	12	.336	.413	.436
2007	Min	AL	1	3	3	1	0	0	(0	0)	4	1	0	2	0	0	0	0	0	0	0	0	-	0	1.000	1.000	1.333
2009	Min	AL	54	119	37	6	0	0	(0	0)	43	14	7	19	14	1	22	0	0	1	0	0	-	4	.311	.381	.361
2 ML YEARS			55	122	40	7	0	0	(0	0)	47	15	7	21	14	1	22	0	0	1	0	0	-	4	.328	.394	.385

Kendry Morales

Bats: B **Throws:** R **Pos:** 1B-152; PH-8   **Ht:** 6'1" **Wt:** 225 **Born:** 6/20/1983 **Age:** 27

Year	Team	Lg	G	AB	H	2B	3B	HR	(Hm	Rd)	TB	R	RBI	RC	TBB	IBB	SO	HBP	SH	SF	SB	CS	SB%	GDP	Avg	OBP	Slg
2006	LAA	AL	57	197	46	10	1	5	(1	4)	73	21	22	19	17	1	28	0	0	1	1	1	.50	11	.234	.293	.371
2007	LAA	AL	43	119	35	10	0	4	(2	2)	57	12	15	15	6	2	21	1	0	0	0	1	.00	5	.294	.333	.479
2008	LAA	AL	27	61	13	2	0	3	(0	3)	24	7	8	3	4	0	7	1	0	0	0	1	.00	3	.213	.273	.393
2009	LAA	AL	152	566	173	43	2	34	(21	13)	322	86	108	105	46	10	117	2	0	8	3	7	.30	15	.306	.355	.569
Postseason			7	13	3	1	0	0	(0	0)	4	1	0	0	0	0	2	0	0	0	0	0	-	0	.231	.231	.308
4 ML YEARS			279	943	267	65	3	46	(24	22)	476	126	153	142	73	13	173	4	0	9	4	10	.29	34	.283	.334	.505

Edwin Moreno

Pitches: R **Bats:** R **Pos:** RP-19   **Ht:** 6'1" **Wt:** 218 **Born:** 7/30/1980 **Age:** 29

			HOW MUCH HE PITCHED					WHAT HE GAVE UP												THE RESULTS							
Year	Team	Lg	G	GS	CG	GF	IP	BFP	H	R	ER	HR	SH	SF	HB	TBB	IBB	SO	WP	Bk	W	L	Pct	Sh	Sv-Op	Hld	ERC	ERA
2000	Savann	A	23	22	1	0	133.0	562	127	58	48	9	1	2	7	46	0	89	6	0	9	8	.529	1	0--	-	3.63	3.25
2001	Charltt	A+	28	28	1	0	152.0	645	142	83	68	10	2	5	11	51	0	92	4	0	8	9	.471	1	0--	-	3.52	4.03
2002	Rngrs	R	9	7	0	1	37.1	152	30	14	14	2	0	0	1	10	0	23	1	0	2	2	.500	0	0--	-	2.34	3.38
2002	Charltt	A+	6	6	0	0	30.2	116	20	2	2	0	0	0	2	3	0	23	0	0	3	0	1.000	0	0--	-	1.19	0.59
2003	Frisco	AA	29	15	0	9	112.0	465	105	50	41	7	2	4	3	33	0	74	4	2	6	5	.545	0	0--	-	3.21	3.29
2004	Frisco	AA	18	13	0	1	70.1	313	90	54	47	8	4	3	4	18	0	37	6	0	5	6	.455	0	0--	-	5.50	6.01
2005	Rdng	AA	4	4	0	0	20.2	86	20	10	10	4	0	0	2	2	0	17	0	0	1	3	.250	0	0--	-	3.61	4.35
2007	SnAnt	AA	17	0	0	17	16.2	68	10	3	3	2	2	1	0	8	0	18	0	0	0	0	-	0	9--	-	2.38	1.62
2008	SnAnt	AA	15	0	0	11	21.1	82	16	8	7	1	1	2	0	6	1	19	0	0	2	0	.000	0	8--	-	2.06	2.95
2008	Portlnd	AAA	45	0	0	37	49.2	215	37	29	24	8	2	0	3	26	2	47	2	0	5	6	.455	0	18--	-	3.67	4.35
2009	Portlnd	AAA	39	0	0	29	45.1	198	46	24	21	7	4	1	3	20	2	40	1	0	3	3	.500	0	10--	-	4.99	4.17
2009	SD	NL	19	0	0	5	22.1	108	28	13	12	3	1	0	2	15	3	15	0	0	1	3	.250	0	0-1	4	7.24	4.84

Nyjer Morgan

Bats: L **Throws:** L **Pos:** LF-63; CF-57; PR-2; PH-1   **Ht:** 6'0" **Wt:** 175 **Born:** 7/2/1980 **Age:** 29

Year	Team	Lg	G	AB	H	2B	3B	HR	(Hm	Rd)	TB	R	RBI	RC	TBB	IBB	SO	HBP	SH	SF	SB	CS	SB%	GDP	Avg	OBP	Slg
2007	Pit	NL	28	107	32	3	4	1	(1	0)	46	15	7	18	9	0	19	1	1	0	7	3	.70	0	.299	.359	.430
2008	Pit	NL	58	160	47	13	0	0	(0	0)	60	26	7	18	10	0	32	3	1	1	9	5	.64	0	.294	.345	.375

Year Team	Lg	G	AB	H	2B	3B	HR	(Hm	Rd)	TB	R	RBI	RC	TBB	IBB	SO	HBP	SH	SF	SB	CS	SB%	GDP	Avg	OBP	Slg
2009 2 Tms	NL	120	469	144	15	7	3	(1	2)	182	74	39	69	40	2	74	9	10	5	42	17	.71	9	.307	.369	.388
09 Pit	NL	71	278	77	6	5	2	(1	1)	99	39	27	37	29	2	49	5	5	4	18	10	.64	6	.277	.351	.356
09 Was	NL	49	191	67	9	2	1	(0	1)	83	35	12	32	11	0	25	4	5	1	24	7	.77	3	.351	.396	.435
3 ML YEARS		206	736	223	31	11	4	(2	2)	288	115	53	105	59	2	125	13	12	6	58	25	.70	9	.303	.362	.391

Juan Morillo

Pitches: R **Bats:** R **Pos:** RP-3   **Ht:** 6'3" **Wt:** 190 **Born:** 11/5/1983 **Age:** 26

Year Team	Lg	G	GS	CG	GF	IP	BFP	H	R	ER	HR	SH	SF	HB	TBB	IBB	SO	WP	Bk	W	L	Pct	Sh	Sv-Op	Hld	ERC	ERA
2009 Roch*	AAA	46	0	0	19	67.0	305	56	30	29	1	1	3	2	51	0	87	9	1	6	6	.500	0	5--	-	3.98	3.90
2006 Col	NL	1	1	0	0	4.0	24	8	7	7	3	1	0	1	3	0	4	0	0	0	0	-	0	0-0	0	20.26	15.75
2007 Col	NL	4	0	0	1	3.2	16	3	4	4	1	0	0	1	1	0	3	0	0	0	0	-	0	0-0	0	4.74	9.82
2008 Col	NL	1	0	0	1	1.0	4	1	0	0	0	0	0	0	0	0	0	0	0	0	0	-	0	0-0	0	1.95	0.00
2009 Min	AL	3	0	0	2	2.0	12	3	5	5	1	0	0	0	3	0	1	0	0	0	0	-	0	0-0	0	16.26	22.50
4 ML YEARS		9	1	0	4	10.2	56	15	16	16	5	1	0	2	7	0	8	0	0	0	0	-	0	0-0	0	11.74	13.50

Justin Morneau

Bats: L **Throws:** R **Pos:** 1B-123; DH-12   **Ht:** 6'4" **Wt:** 235 **Born:** 5/15/1981 **Age:** 29

Year Team	Lg	G	AB	H	2B	3B	HR	(Hm	Rd)	TB	R	RBI	RC	TBB	IBB	SO	HBP	SH	SF	SB	CS	SB%	GDP	Avg	OBP	Slg
2003 Min	AL	40	106	24	4	0	4	(1	3)	40	14	16	11	9	1	30	0	0	0	0	0	-	4	.226	.287	.377
2004 Min	AL	74	280	76	17	0	19	(9	10)	150	39	58	48	28	8	54	2	0	2	0	0	-	4	.271	.340	.536
2005 Min	AL	141	490	117	23	4	22	(9	13)	214	62	79	58	44	8	94	4	0	5	0	2	.00	12	.239	.304	.437
2006 Min	AL	157	592	190	37	1	34	(17	17)	331	97	130	110	53	9	93	5	0	11	3	3	.50	10	.321	.375	.559
2007 Min	AL	157	590	160	31	3	31	(15	16)	290	84	111	95	64	11	91	5	0	9	1	1	.50	17	.271	.343	.492
2008 Min	AL	163	623	187	47	4	23	(12	11)	311	97	129	123	76	16	85	8	0	8	0	1	.00	20	.300	.374	.499
2009 Min	AL	135	508	139	31	1	30	(14	16)	262	85	100	91	72	12	86	3	0	7	0	0	-	12	.274	.363	.516
Postseason		7	29	9	3	0	2	(1	1)	18	4	4	3	0	0	3	0	0	0	0	0	-	0	.310	.310	.621
7 ML YEARS		867	3189	893	190	13	163	(77	86)	1598	478	623	543	346	65	533	22	0	44	4	7	.36	79	.280	.350	.501

Brandon Morrow

Pitches: R **Bats:** R **Pos:** RP-16; SP-10   **Ht:** 6'3" **Wt:** 195 **Born:** 7/26/1984 **Age:** 25

Year Team	Lg	G	GS	CG	GF	IP	BFP	H	R	ER	HR	SH	SF	HB	TBB	IBB	SO	WP	Bk	W	L	Pct	Sh	Sv-Op	Hld	ERC	ERA
2009 Tacom*	AAA	10	10	1	0	55.0	235	50	24	22	2	4	2	1	23	0	46	6	0	5	3	.625	1	0--	-	3.26	3.60
2007 Sea	AL	60	0	0	18	63.1	209	56	29	29	3	4	4	1	50	5	66	4	0	3	4	.429	0	0-2	18	4.47	4.12
2008 Sea	AL	45	5	0	24	64.2	265	40	26	24	10	1	0	0	34	1	75	5	0	3	4	.429	0	10-12	3	2.84	3.34
2009 Sea	AL	26	10	0	9	69.2	313	66	38	34	10	1	2	0	44	1	63	3	0	2	4	.333	0	6-8	1	4.99	4.39
3 ML YEARS		131	15	0	51	197.2	867	162	93	87	23	6	6	1	128	7	204	12	0	8	12	.400	0	16-22	22	4.11	3.96

Mike Morse

Bats: R **Throws:** R **Pos:** PH-19; 1B-11; RF-3; LF-2; 3B-1   **Ht:** 6'5" **Wt:** 230 **Born:** 3/22/1982 **Age:** 28

Year Team	Lg	G	AB	H	2B	3B	HR	(Hm	Rd)	TB	R	RBI	RC	TBB	IBB	SO	HBP	SH	SF	SB	CS	SB%	GDP	Avg	OBP	Slg
2009 Tacom*	AAA	66	260	81	14	0	10	(-	)	125	38	52	47	20	3	50	6	0	3	0	0	-	8	.312	.370	.481
2009 Syrcse*	AAA	44	165	56	12	3	6	(-	-)	92	21	34	36	15	0	27	3	0	0	2	1	.67	5	.339	.404	.558
2005 Sea	AL	72	230	64	10	1	3	(3	0)	85	27	23	28	18	0	50	8	0	2	3	1	.75	9	.278	.349	.370
2006 Sea	AL	21	43	16	5	0	0	(0	0)	21	5	11	9	3	0	7	0	0	2	1	0	1.00	0	.372	.396	.488
2007 Sea	AL	9	18	8	2	0	0	(0	0)	10	1	3	6	1	0	4	1	0	0	0	0	-	0	.444	.500	.556
2008 Sea	AL	5	9	2	1	0	0	(0	0)	3	0	1	1	1	0	4	1	0	0	0	0	-	0	.222	.364	.333
2009 Was	NL	32	52	13	3	0	3	(3	0)	25	4	10	8	3	0	16	0	0	0	0	0	-	1	.250	.291	.481
5 ML YEARS		139	352	103	21	1	6	(6	0)	144	37	47	52	26	0	81	10	0	4	4	1	.80	12	.293	.355	.409

Clayton Mortensen

Pitches: R **Bats:** R **Pos:** SP-6; RP-1   **Ht:** 6'4" **Wt:** 180 **Born:** 4/10/1985 **Age:** 25

Year Team	Lg	G	GS	CG	GF	IP	BFP	H	R	ER	HR	SH	SF	HB	TBB	IBB	SO	WP	Bk	W	L	Pct	Sh	Sv-Op	Hld	ERC	ERA
2007 Batvia	A-	6	4	0	0	20.1	83	13	4	4	0	1	0	2	11	0	23	1	0	1	1	.500	0	0--	-	2.46	1.77
2007 QuadC	A	10	10	0	0	40.1	172	44	17	14	2	0	0	4	8	0	45	2	0	0	2	.000	0	0--	-	3.85	3.12
2008 Sprgfld	AA	11	11	0	0	59.2	258	59	31	28	6	0	1	4	22	0	48	4	0	3	4	.429	0	0--	-	4.17	4.22
2008 Memp	AAA	15	14	0	0	80.0	361	87	50	49	12	1	2	6	42	1	57	14	1	5	6	.455	0	0--	-	5.87	5.51
2009 Memp	AAA	17	17	1	0	105.0	443	103	58	51	11	4	2	4	34	0	82	3	0	7	6	.538	0	0--	-	3.89	4.37
2009 Scrmto	AAA	6	6	0	0	32.1	145	40	20	16	2	0	2	0	14	0	18	2	0	2	2	.500	0	0--	-	5.39	4.45
2009 2 Tms		7	6	0	1	30.2	149	42	34	26	6	1	4	3	13	0	13	1	0	2	4	.333	0	0-0	0	7.50	7.63
09 StL	NL	1	0	0	1	3.0	16	5	6	2	1	1	1	1	1	0	2	0	0	0	0	-	0	0-0	0	11.45	6.00
09 Oak	AL	6	6	0	0	27.2	133	37	28	24	5	0	3	2	12	0	11	1	0	2	4	.333	0	0-0	0	7.10	7.81

Charlie Morton

Pitches: R **Bats:** R **Pos:** SP-18   Ht: 6'4" Wt: 190 Born: 11/12/1983 Age: 26

Year	Team	Lg	G	GS	CG	GF	IP	BFP	H	R	ER	HR	SH	SF	HB	TBB	IBB	SO	WP	Bk	W	L	Pct	Sh	Sv-Op	Hld	ERC	ERA
2002	Braves	R	11	5	0	1	39.2	186	37	34	20	1	1	1	2	30	0	32	5	0	1	7	.125	0	0--	-	4.63	4.54
2003	Danvle	R+	14	13	0	0	54.0	246	65	32	28	3	2	3	1	25	0	46	9	5	2	5	.286	0	0--	-	5.27	4.67
2004	Rome	A	27	18	0	3	117.2	558	140	76	63	7	4	8	7	68	2	102	10	0	7	9	.438	0	2--	-	5.76	4.82
2005	Rome	A	26	22	0	4	124.2	561	124	84	72	7	2	7	14	62	0	86	12	2	5	9	.357	0	1--	-	4.54	5.20
2006	MrtlBh	A+	30	14	0	6	100.0	466	116	70	60	14	7	3	4	54	0	75	9	0	6	7	.462	0	2--	-	6.03	5.40
2007	Missi	AA	41	6	0	9	79.2	350	80	41	38	3	6	4	6	37	2	67	11	0	4	6	.400	0	0--	-	4.19	4.29
2008	Rchmd	AAA	13	12	0	1	79.0	312	51	20	18	0	2	0	2	27	0	72	2	0	5	2	.714	0	0--	-	1.60	2.05
2009	Gwnntt	AAA	10	10	1	0	64.2	254	52	18	18	3	1	1	2	16	0	55	2	0	7	2	.778	1	0--	-	2.34	2.51
2009	Indy	AAA	1	1	0	0	7.0	25	4	0	0	0	0	0	1	1	0	7	0	0	-	0	-	0	0--	-	1.29	0.00
2008	Atl	NL	16	15	0	0	74.2	345	80	56	51	9	5	4	2	41	2	48	2	0	4	8	.333	0	0-0	0	5.21	6.15
2009	Pit	NL	18	18	1	0	97.0	416	102	49	49	7	1	1	5	40	0	62	4	0	5	9	.357	1	0-0	0	4.56	4.55
	2 ML YEARS		34	33	1	0	171.2	761	182	105	100	16	6	5	7	81	2	110	6	0	9	17	.346	1	0-0	0	4.84	5.24

Guillermo Moscoso

Pitches: R **Bats:** R **Pos:** RP-10   Ht: 6'1" Wt: 165 Born: 11/14/1983 Age: 26

Year	Team	Lg	G	GS	CG	GF	IP	BFP	H	R	ER	HR	SH	SF	HB	TBB	IBB	SO	WP	Bk	W	L	Pct	Sh	Sv-Op	Hld	ERC	ERA
2005	Oneont	A-	11	10	0	0	47.1	202	49	27	23	4	0	2	1	11	0	44	4	0	2	2	.500	0	0--	-	3.53	4.37
2006	Tigers	R	13	3	0	2	36.0	151	37	14	10	3	0	2	0	8	0	33	2	1	3	2	.600	0	0--	-	3.40	2.50
2007	Lkland	A+	1	1	0	0	3.0	12	2	0	0	0	0	0	0	1	0	4	0	0	-	0	-	0	0--	-	1.57	0.00
2007	Oneont	A-	14	14	2	0	79.2	320	75	25	21	3	2	0	1	15	0	68	1	1	8	2	.800	1	0--	-	2.65	2.37
2007	WMich	A	1	1	0	0	8.0	28	5	1	1	1	1	0	0	0	0	7	0	0	-	0	-	0	0--	-	1.21	1.13
2008	Lkland	A+	15	6	0	3	52.0	205	36	16	14	4	2	4	2	13	0	72	2	0	2	3	.400	0	1--	-	1.95	2.42
2008	Erie	AA	6	6	0	0	34.2	135	24	17	12	4	0	1	0	8	0	50	1	0	3	1	.750	0	0--	-	1.97	3.12
2009	Frisco	AA	9	7	0	0	42.1	182	41	23	21	1	0	1	0	14	0	36	3	0	3	1	.750	0	0--	-	3.04	4.46
2009	Okla	AAA	12	11	0	0	70.0	277	56	20	18	2	0	2	3	15	0	60	1	0	5	4	.556	0	0--	-	2.10	2.31
2009	Tex	AL	10	0	0	6	14.0	64	15	7	5	1	0	1	1	6	0	12	4	0	0	0	-	0	0-0	0	4.55	3.21

Bobby Mosebach

Pitches: R **Bats:** R **Pos:** RP-3   Ht: 6'4" Wt: 195 Born: 9/14/1984 Age: 25

Year	Team	Lg	G	GS	CG	GF	IP	BFP	H	R	ER	HR	SH	SF	HB	TBB	IBB	SO	WP	Bk	W	L	Pct	Sh	Sv-Op	Hld	ERC	ERA
2005	Orem	R+	15	13	0	1	65.0	278	69	36	33	6	4	2	8	18	0	52	7	3	3	3	.500	0	0--	-	4.47	4.57
2006	CRpds	A	24	24	3	0	159.2	655	166	61	54	5	2	7	9	29	0	97	10	2	10	6	.625	0	0--	-	3.28	3.04
2006	RCuca	A+	4	4	0	0	22.2	101	23	17	16	1	0	0	4	8	0	15	1	0	1	1	.500	0	0--	-	4.24	6.35
2007	RCuca	A+	25	23	1	0	155.2	677	171	88	74	16	4	8	15	49	0	93	9	0	11	7	.611	0	0--	-	4.78	4.28
2007	Ark	AA	2	2	0	0	14.0	63	16	9	8	1	0	1	1	8	0	3	1	0	1	1	.500	0	0--	-	5.91	5.14
2008	Ark	AA	29	29	2	0	177.1	782	209	106	91	6	6	7	14	69	2	88	10	0	9	12	.429	0	0--	-	5.00	4.62
2009	Ark	AA	19	0	0	15	26.1	101	12	1	1	0	3	0	3	9	0	16	0	0	2	0	1.000	0	6--	-	1.23	0.34
2009	Salt Lk	AAA	33	0	0	21	40.1	165	33	11	10	1	1	2	2	18	1	31	0	0	2	2	.500	0	7--	-	3.02	2.23
2009	LAA	AL	3	0	0	1	2.1	15	4	3	2	0	0	0	1	3	0	2	1	0	0	0	-	0	0-0	0	13.24	7.71

Dustin Moseley

Pitches: R **Bats:** R **Pos:** SP-3   Ht: 6'4" Wt: 215 Born: 12/26/1981 Age: 28

Year	Team	Lg	G	GS	CG	GF	IP	BFP	H	R	ER	HR	SH	SF	HB	TBB	IBB	SO	WP	Bk	W	L	Pct	Sh	Sv-Op	Hld	ERC	ERA
2006	LAA	AL	3	2	0	1	11.0	54	22	11	11	3	0	1	0	2	0	3	0	0	1	0	1.000	0	0-0	0	11.45	9.00
2007	LAA	AL	46	8	0	13	92.0	383	97	45	45	7	1	2	3	27	3	50	6	1	4	3	.571	0	0-0	4	4.00	4.40
2008	LAA	AL	12	10	0	1	50.1	237	70	38	38	6	1	3	2	20	0	37	3	1	2	4	.333	0	0-0	0	6.74	6.79
2009	LAA	AL	3	3	0	0	14.2	65	20	8	7	3	0	0	0	3	1	8	0	0	1	0	1.000	0	0-0	0	6.13	4.30
	Postseason		1	0	0	1	1.0	3	1	0	0	0	0	0	0	0	0	1	0	0	0	0	-	0	0-0	0	2.79	0.00
	4 ML YEARS		64	23	0	15	168.0	739	209	102	101	19	2	6	5	52	4	98	9	2	8	7	.533	0	0-0	4	5.41	5.41

Brandon Moss

Bats: L **Throws:** R **Pos:** RF-79; PH-37; LF-21   Ht: 6'0" Wt: 205 Born: 9/16/1983 Age: 26

Year	Team	Lg	G	AB	H	2B	3B	HR	(Hm	Rd)	TB	R	RBI	RC	TBB	IBB	SO	HBP	SH	SF	SB	CS	SB%	GDP	Avg	OBP	Slg
2007	Bos	AL	15	25	7	2	1	0	(0	0)	11	6	1	3	4	0	6	0	0	0	0	0	-	1	.280	.379	.440
2008	2 Tms		79	236	58	15	3	8	(4	4)	103	19	34	30	21	1	70	1	0	5	1	2	.33	2	.246	.304	.436
2009	Pit	NL	133	385	91	20	4	7	(4	3)	140	47	41	37	34	3	84	4	0	1	1	5	.17	7	.236	.304	.364
08	Bos	AL	34	78	23	5	1	2	(1	1)	36	7	11	11	6	0	25	0	0	2	1	1	.50	0	.295	.337	.462
08	Pit	NL	45	158	35	10	2	6	(3	3)	67	12	23	19	15	1	45	1	0	3	0	1	.00	2	.222	.288	.424
	3 ML YEARS		227	646	156	37	8	15	(8	7)	254	72	76	70	59	4	160	5	0	6	2	7	.22	10	.241	.307	.393

Guillermo Mota

Pitches: R **Bats:** R **Pos:** RP-61   Ht: 6'5" Wt: 233 Born: 7/25/1973 Age: 36

Year	Team	Lg	G	GS	CG	GF	IP	BFP	H	R	ER	HR	SH	SF	HB	TBB	IBB	SO	WP	Bk	W	L	Pct	Sh	Sv-Op	Hld	ERC	ERA
1999	Mon	NL	51	0	0	18	55.1	243	54	24	18	5	3	3	2	25	3	27	1	1	2	4	.333	0	0-1	3	4.10	2.93
2000	Mon	NL	29	0	0	7	30.0	126	27	21	20	3	1	1	2	12	0	24	1	1	1	1	.500	0	0-0	5	3.86	6.00
2001	Mon	NL	53	0	0	12	49.2	212	51	30	29	4	3	1	2	18	1	31	1	0	3	1	.250	0	0-3	12	4.77	5.26
2002	LAD	NL	43	0	0	11	60.2	256	45	30	28	4	3	1	2	27	6	49	3	0	1	3	.250	0	0-1	4	2.57	4.15

196

		HOW MUCH HE PITCHED						WHAT HE GAVE UP												THE RESULTS							
Year	Team	Lg	G	GS	CG	GF	IP	BFP	H	R	ER	HR	SH	SF	HB	TBB	IBB	SO	WP	Bk	W	L	Pct	Sh	Sv-Op	Hld	ERC	ERA
2003	LAD	NL	76	0	0	18	105.0	410	78	23	23	7	3	1	1	26	4	99	0	0	6	3	.667	0	1-3	13	2.01	1.97
2004	2 Tms		78	0	0	18	96.2	393	75	33	33	8	5	3	4	37	6	85	5	0	9	8	.529	0	4-8	30	2.82	3.07
2005	Fla	NL	56	0	0	24	67.0	293	65	38	35	5	1	3	1	32	7	60	4	0	2	2	.500	0	2-4	14	3.90	4.70
2006	2 Tms		52	0	0	17	55.2	241	55	29	28	11	0	3	0	24	4	46	2	0	4	3	.571	0	0-0	9	4.71	4.53
2007	NYM	NL	52	0	0	10	59.1	261	63	39	38	8	2	0	2	18	2	47	2	0	2	2	.500	0	0-3	6	4.26	5.76
2008	Mil	NL	58	0	0	18	57.0	244	52	28	26	7	1	3	0	28	0	50	4	1	5	6	.455	0	1-4	11	4.14	4.11
2009	LAD	NL	61	0	0	27	65.1	273	53	25	25	6	3	4	5	24	8	39	3	0	3	4	.429	0	0-2	2	2.98	3.44
04	LAD	NL	52	0	0	11	63.0	259	51	15	15	4	4	2	2	27	5	52	5	0	8	4	.667	0	1-1	17	2.98	2.14
04	Fla	NL	26	0	0	7	33.2	134	24	18	18	4	1	1	2	10	1	33	0	0	1	4	.200	0	3-7	13	2.51	4.81
06	Cle	AL	34	0	0	13	37.2	173	45	27	26	9	0	3	0	19	3	27	2	0	1	3	.250	0	0-0	5	6.62	6.21
06	NYM	NL	18	0	0	4	18.0	68	10	2	2	2	0	0	0	5	1	19	0	0	3	0	1.000	0	0-0	4	1.51	1.00
	Postseason		9	0	0	4	10.0	42	12	6	6	1	0	0	0	2	0	7	0	0	1	0	1.000	0	0-2	3	4.53	5.40
11 ML YEARS			609	0	0	180	701.2	2952	618	320	303	73	25	24	20	271	41	557	26	3	36	39	.480	0	8-29	109	3.42	3.80

Jason Motte

Pitches: R Bats: R Pos: RP-69 **Ht: 6'0" Wt: 200 Born: 6/22/1982 Age: 28**

		HOW MUCH HE PITCHED						WHAT HE GAVE UP												THE RESULTS							
Year	Team	Lg	G	GS	CG	GF	IP	BFP	H	R	ER	HR	SH	SF	HB	TBB	IBB	SO	WP	Bk	W	L	Pct	Sh	Sv-Op	Hld	ERC	ERA
2006	StCol	A-	21	0	0	16	26.1	114	30	12	9	1	1	2	0	4	0	25	0	0	1	2	.333	0	8- -	-	3.33	3.08
2006	QuadC	A	8	0	0	0	12.2	58	16	8	7	1	0	0	1	3	0	13	0	0	1	1	.500	0	0- -	-	4.97	4.97
2007	PlmBh	A+	9	0	0	8	10.0	40	7	2	1	0	0	1	0	1	0	6	0	0	1	0	1.000	0	3- -	-	1.13	0.90
2007	Sprgfld	AA	45	0	0	23	49.0	200	36	13	11	3	1	1	3	22	2	63	2	0	3	3	.500	0	8- -	-	2.82	2.02
2008	Memp	AAA	63	0	0	28	66.2	290	64	25	24	6	2	0	1	26	3	110	7	0	4	3	.571	0	9- -	-	3.66	3.24
2008	StL	NL	12	0	0	4	11.0	40	5	2	1	0	1	0	0	3	0	16	0	0	0	0	-	0	1-1	4	0.89	0.82
2009	StL	NL	69	0	0	14	56.2	244	57	32	30	10	0	3	2	23	1	54	2	1	4	4	.500	0	0-3	15	4.86	4.76
2 ML YEARS			81	0	0	10	67.2	284	62	34	31	10	1	3	2	26	1	70	2	1	4	4	.500	0	1-4	19	4.03	4.12

Jamie Moyer

Pitches: L Bats: L Pos: SP-25; RP-5 **Ht: 6'0" Wt: 185 Born: 11/18/1962 Age: 47**

		HOW MUCH HE PITCHED						WHAT HE GAVE UP												THE RESULTS							
Year	Team	Lg	G	GS	CG	GF	IP	BFP	H	R	ER	HR	SH	SF	HB	TBB	IBB	SO	WP	Bk	W	L	Pct	Sh	Sv-Op	Hld	ERC	ERA
1986	ChC	NL	16	16	1	0	87.1	385	107	52	49	10	3	3	3	42	1	45	3	3	7	4	.636	1	0-0	0	6.13	5.05
1987	ChC	NL	35	33	1	1	201.0	899	210	127	114	28	14	7	5	97	9	147	11	2	12	15	.444	1	0-0	0	4.96	5.10
1988	ChC	NL	34	30	3	1	202.0	855	212	84	78	20	14	4	4	55	7	121	4	0	9	15	.375	1	0-2	0	3.89	3.48
1989	Tex	AL	15	15	1	0	76.0	337	84	51	41	10	1	4	2	33	0	44	1	0	4	9	.308	0	0-0	0	5.20	4.86
1990	Tex	AL	33	10	1	6	102.1	447	115	59	53	6	1	7	4	39	4	58	1	0	2	6	.250	0	0-0	1	4.57	4.66
1991	StL	NL	8	7	0	1	31.1	142	38	21	20	5	4	2	1	16	0	20	2	1	0	5	.000	0	0-0	0	6.58	5.74
1993	Bal	AL	25	25	3	0	152.0	630	154	63	58	11	3	1	6	38	2	90	1	1	12	9	.571	1	0-0	0	3.58	3.43
1994	Bal	AL	23	23	0	0	149.0	631	158	81	79	23	5	2	2	38	3	87	1	0	5	7	.417	0	0-0	0	4.24	4.77
1995	Bal	AL	27	18	0	3	115.2	483	117	70	67	18	5	3	3	30	0	65	0	0	8	6	.571	0	0-0	0	4.11	5.21
1996	2 Tms	AL	34	21	0	1	160.2	703	177	86	71	23	7	6	2	46	5	79	3	1	13	3	.813	0	0-1	0	4.42	3.98
1997	Sea	AL	30	30	2	0	188.2	787	187	82	81	21	6	1	7	43	2	113	3	0	17	5	.773	0	0-0	0	3.56	3.86
1998	Sea	AL	34	34	4	0	234.1	974	234	99	92	23	4	3	10	42	2	158	3	1	15	9	.625	3	0-0	0	3.34	3.53
1999	Sea	AL	32	32	4	0	228.0	945	235	108	98	23	6	2	9	48	1	137	3	0	14	8	.636	0	0-0	0	3.71	3.87
2000	Sea	AL	26	26	0	0	154.0	678	173	103	94	22	3	3	3	53	2	98	4	1	13	10	.565	0	0-0	0	4.91	5.49
2001	Sea	AL	33	33	1	0	209.2	851	187	84	80	24	5	11	10	44	4	119	1	0	20	6	.769	0	0-0	0	3.03	3.43
2002	Sea	AL	34	34	4	0	230.2	931	198	89	85	28	5	7	9	50	4	147	3	0	13	8	.619	2	0-0	0	2.89	3.32
2003	Sea	AL	33	33	1	0	215.0	897	199	83	78	19	7	6	8	66	3	129	0	0	21	7	.750	0	0-0	0	3.37	3.27
2004	Sea	AL	34	34	4	0	202.0	888	217	127	117	44	9	6	11	63	3	125	1	0	7	13	.350	0	0-0	0	5.13	5.21
2005	Sea	AL	32	32	1	0	200.0	868	225	99	95	23	6	6	8	52	2	102	3	0	13	7	.650	0	0-0	0	4.46	4.28
2006	2 Tms	AL	33	33	2	0	211.1	894	228	110	101	33	5	9	5	51	5	108	3	1	11	14	.440	1	0-0	0	4.36	4.30
2007	Phi	NL	33	33	1	0	199.1	867	222	118	111	30	11	5	5	66	3	133	2	0	14	12	.538	0	0-0	0	4.92	5.01
2008	Phi	NL	33	33	0	0	196.1	841	199	85	81	20	7	2	11	62	4	123	3	0	16	7	.696	0	0-0	0	4.03	3.71
2009	Phi	NL	30	25	0	1	162.0	699	177	91	89	27	8	4	10	43	1	94	1	1	12	10	.545	0	0-0	1	4.79	4.94
96	Bos	AL	23	10	0	1	90.0	405	111	50	45	14	4	3	1	27	2	50	2	1	7	1	.875	0	0-0	1	5.37	4.50
96	Sea	AL	11	11	0	0	70.2	298	66	36	26	9	3	3	1	19	3	29	1	0	6	2	.750	0	0-0	0	3.31	3.31
06	Sea	AL	25	25	2	0	160.0	685	179	85	78	25	3	7	3	44	3	82	3	1	6	12	.333	1	0-0	0	4.74	4.39
06	Phi	NL	8	8	0	0	51.1	209	49	25	23	8	2	2	2	7	2	26	0	0	5	2	.714	0	0-0	0	3.24	4.03
	Postseason		8	8	0	0	41.1	168	37	19	19	3	2	2	2	10	0	29	1	0	3	3	.500	0	0-0	0	2.96	4.14
23 ML YEARS			667	609	31	15	3908.2	16642	4053	1972	1832	491	139	104	138	1117	67	2342	57	12	258	195	.570	9	0-2	3	4.13	4.22

Peter Moylan

Pitches: R Bats: R Pos: RP-87 **Ht: 6'2" Wt: 200 Born: 12/2/1978 Age: 31**

		HOW MUCH HE PITCHED						WHAT HE GAVE UP												THE RESULTS							
Year	Team	Lg	G	GS	CG	GF	IP	BFP	H	R	ER	HR	SH	SF	HB	TBB	IBB	SO	WP	Bk	W	L	Pct	Sh	Sv-Op	Hld	ERC	ERA
2006	Atl	NL	15	0	0	5	15.0	68	18	8	8	1	1	0	0	5	1	14	0	0	0	0	-	0	0-0	0	4.47	4.80
2007	Atl	NL	80	0	0	16	90.0	359	65	27	18	6	4	4	7	31	12	63	2	0	5	3	.625	0	1-2	8	2.36	1.80
2008	Atl	NL	7	0	0	2	5.2	22	5	1	1	1	0	0	1	1	0	5	0	0	1	0	1.000	0	1-2	4	3.51	1.59
2009	Atl	NL	87	0	0	6	73.0	309	65	29	23	0	4	3	2	35	8	61	1	0	6	2	.750	0	0-5	25	3.06	2.84
4 ML YEARS			189	0	0	29	183.2	761	153	65	50	8	9	7	10	72	21	143	3	0	11	6	.647	0	2-9	37	2.84	2.45

Edward Mujica

Pitches: R Bats: R Pos: RP-63; SP-4 Ht: 6'2" Wt: 215 Born: 5/10/1984 Age: 26

Year	Team	Lg	G	GS	CG	GF	IP	BFP	H	R	ER	HR	SH	SF	HB	TBB	IBB	SO	WP	Bk	W	L	Pct	Sh	Sv-Op	Hld	ERC	ERA
2006	Cle	AL	10	0	0	2	18.1	78	25	6	6	1	0	2	1	0	0	12	0	0	0	1	.000	0	0-0	0	4.50	2.95
2007	Cle	AL	10	0	0	5	13.0	60	19	12	12	3	0	1	0	2	0	7	0	0	0	0	-	0	0-0	0	6.63	8.31
2008	Cle	AL	33	0	0	13	38.2	168	46	29	29	5	0	4	1	10	3	27	1	0	3	2	.600	0	0-2	1	4.82	6.75
2009	SD	NL	67	4	0	15	93.2	393	101	47	41	14	1	3	0	19	4	76	3	1	3	5	.375	0	2-3	11	4.00	3.94
	4 ML YEARS		120	4	0	35	163.2	699	191	94	88	23	1	10	2	31	7	122	4	1	6	8	.429	0	2-5	12	4.45	4.84

Kevin Mulvey

Pitches: R Bats: R Pos: SP-4; RP-4 Ht: 6'2" Wt: 194 Born: 5/26/1985 Age: 25

Year	Team	Lg	G	GS	CG	GF	IP	BFP	H	R	ER	HR	SH	SF	HB	TBB	IBB	SO	WP	Bk	W	L	Pct	Sh	Sv-Op	Hld	ERC	ERA
2006	Mets	R	1	1	0	0	2.0	7	1	0	0	0	0	0	0	0	0	1	0	0	0	0	-	0	0--	-	0.54	0.00
2006	Bnghtn	AA	3	3	1	0	13.1	51	10	4	2	1	0	0	0	5	0	10	1	0	0	1	.000	0	0--	-	2.70	1.35
2007	Bnghtn	AA	26	26	0	0	151.2	639	145	74	56	4	7	6	7	43	0	110	12	1	11	10	.524	0	0--	-	3.06	3.32
2007	NewOr	AAA	1	1	0	0	6.0	21	2	0	0	0	0	0	0	0	0	3	0	0	1	0	1.000	0	0--	-	0.24	0.00
2008	Roch	AAA	27	27	1	0	148.0	640	152	80	62	16	7	6	6	48	0	121	7	2	7	9	.438	0	0--	-	4.12	3.77
2009	Roch	AAA	24	24	2	0	149.0	644	153	84	65	12	4	8	7	54	1	113	8	0	5	8	.385	1	0--	-	4.13	3.93
2009	2 Tms		8	4	0	1	24.1	114	29	22	22	5	1	2	2	12	0	18	1	0	0	3	.000	0	0-0	0	6.76	8.14
09	Min	AL	2	0	0	1	1.1	10	6	4	4	0	0	0	0	0	0	0	1	0	0	0	-	0	0-0	0	26.58	27.00
09	Ari	NL	6	4	0	0	23.0	104	23	18	18	5	1	2	2	12	0	18	0	0	0	3	.000	0	0-0	0	5.81	7.04

Eric Munson

Bats: L Throws: R Pos: PH-1 Ht: 6'3" Wt: 220 Born: 10/3/1977 Age: 32

Year	Team	Lg	G	AB	H	2B	3B	HR	(Hm	Rd)	TB	R	RBI	RC	TBB	IBB	SO	HBP	SH	SF	SB	CS	SB%	GDP	Avg	OBP	Slg
2009	Scrmto*	AAA	99	351	93	22	2	13			158	50	68	61	54	2	71	3	1	6	0	1	.00	10	.265	.362	.450
2000	Det	AL	3	5	0	0	0	0	(0	0)	0	0	1	0	0	0	1	0	0	0	0	0	-	0	.000	.000	.000
2001	Det	AL	17	66	10	3	1	1	(1	0)	18	4	6	2	3	0	21	0	0	0	0	1	.00	2	.152	.188	.273
2002	Det	AL	18	59	11	0	0	2	(0	2)	17	3	5	3	6	0	11	1	0	1	0	0	-	1	.186	.269	.288
2003	Det	AL	99	313	75	9	0	18	(7	11)	138	28	50	45	35	1	61	1	1	7	3	0	1.00	4	.240	.312	.441
2004	Det	AL	109	321	68	14	2	19	(13	6)	143	36	49	44	29	3	90	6	1	0	1	1	.50	1	.212	.289	.445
2005	TB	AL	11	18	3	1	0	0	(0	0)	4	2	2	2	4	0	3	1	0	1	0	0	-	2	.167	.333	.222
2006	Hou	NL	53	141	28	6	0	5	(2	3)	49	10	19	12	11	1	32	3	0	1	0	0	-	2	.199	.269	.348
2007	Hou	NL	50	132	31	4	0	4	(3	1)	47	14	15	15	16	1	15	0	0	2	0	0	-	8	.235	.313	.356
2009	Oak	AL	1	1	0	0	0	0	(0	0)	0	0	0	0	0	0	0	0	0	0	0	0	-	0	.000	.000	.000
	9 ML YEARS		361	1056	226	37	3	49	(26	23)	416	97	147	122	104	6	234	12	2	12	4	2	.67	20	.214	.289	.394

Bill Murphy

Pitches: L Bats: L Pos: RP-8 Ht: 5'11" Wt: 207 Born: 5/9/1981 Age: 29

Year	Team	Lg	G	GS	CG	GF	IP	BFP	H	R	ER	HR	SH	SF	HB	TBB	IBB	SO	WP	Bk	W	L	Pct	Sh	Sv-Op	Hld	ERC	ERA
2002	Vancvr	A-	13	9	0	0	41.1	187	28	23	21	2	1	3	2	35	0	46	4	0	1	4	.200	0	0--	-	3.75	4.57
2003	Kane	A	14	14	1	0	92.0	363	61	27	23	5	1	4	2	32	0	87	1	3	7	4	.636	1	0--	-	1.98	2.25
2003	Mdland	AA	11	11	0	0	55.0	233	44	25	25	4	1	3	3	26	1	34	1	3	3	3	.500	0	0--	-	3.26	4.09
2004	Carlina	AA	20	20	0	0	103.2	438	80	48	47	17	6	8	3	59	1	113	4	2	6	4	.600	0	0--	-	4.09	4.08
2004	ElPaso	AA	6	6	0	0	31.0	141	41	28	23	6	0	2	1	17	0	24	2	1	3	3	.500	0	0--	-	8.01	6.68
2005	Tucsn	AAA	23	21	0	0	121.0	570	135	81	76	14	6	4	7	78	0	87	7	1	6	8	.429	0	0--	-	6.12	5.65
2006	Tucsn	AAA	37	9	0	5	80.2	358	86	53	50	5	6	5	1	38	0	72	3	2	5	4	.556	0	0--	-	4.51	5.58
2006	Tenn	AA	5	4	0	0	21.0	93	22	13	13	2	2	0	1	9	0	26	0	0	0	1	.000	0	0--	-	4.61	5.57
2007	Tucsn	AAA	54	9	0	13	100.1	435	93	53	41	10	3	2	9	43	0	102	9	1	3	3	.500	0	1--	-	4.15	3.68
2008	Syrcse	AAA	32	24	0	4	142.0	652	155	91	84	14	4	4	7	84	0	152	10	1	8	10	.444	0	2--	-	5.62	5.32
2009	LsVgs	AAA	45	0	0	13	53.1	270	70	48	45	5	5	3	4	35	1	51	8	0	0	6	.000	0	0--	-	7.05	7.59
2007	Ari	NL	10	0	0	2	6.1	34	9	4	4	0	0	0	1	7	2	2	0	0	0	0	-	0	0-0	1	8.97	5.68
2009	Tor	AL	8	0	0	2	11.1	45	4	4	4	1	0	1	0	8	0	6	2	0	0	0	-	0	0-0	0	1.85	3.18
	2 ML YEARS		18	0	0	4	17.2	79	13	8	8	1	0	1	1	15	2	8	2	0	0	0	-	0	0-0	1	4.08	4.08

Daniel Murphy

Bats: L Throws: R Pos: 1B-101; PH-29; LF-27 Ht: 6'2" Wt: 215 Born: 4/1/1985 Age: 25

Year	Team	Lg	G	AB	H	2B	3B	HR	(Hm	Rd)	TB	R	RBI	RC	TBB	IBB	SO	HBP	SH	SF	SB	CS	SB%	GDP	Avg	OBP	Slg
2006	Mets	R	8	18	1	0	0	0	(-	-)	1	2	0	0	4	0	3	0	0	0	0	0	-	0	.056	.227	.056
2006	Kngspt	R+	9	33	9	0	0	2	(-	-)	15	2	7	5	4	0	1	0	0	0	0	0	-	4	.273	.351	.455
2006	Bklyn	A-	8	29	7	1	0	0	(-	-)	8	2	3	3	4	1	3	0	0	1	0	0	-	0	.241	.324	.276
2007	StLuci	A+	135	502	143	34	3	11	(-	-)	216	68	78	77	42	5	61	4	0	11	6	3	.67	8	.285	.338	.430
2008	Bnghtn	AA	95	357	110	26	1	13	(-	-)	177	56	67	69	39	7	46	3	1	7	14	5	.74	10	.308	.374	.496
2008	Bklyn	A-	3	14	7	0	0	0	(-	-)	7	1	2	3	0	0	2	0	0	0	0	0	-	0	.500	.500	.500
2008	NewOr	AAA	1	4	1	0	0	0	(-	-)	1	2	0	0	1	0	0	0	0	0	0	0	-	1	.250	.400	.250
2008	NYM	NL	49	131	41	9	3	2	(1	1)	62	24	17	26	18	1	28	1	0	1	0	2	.00	4	.313	.397	.473
2009	NYM	NL	155	508	135	38	4	12	(7	5)	217	60	63	60	38	4	69	0	4	6	4	2	.67	13	.266	.313	.427
	2 ML YEARS		204	639	176	47	7	14	(8	6)	279	84	80	86	56	5	97	1	4	7	4	4	.50	17	.275	.331	.437

David Murphy

Bats: L **Throws:** L **Pos:** LF-104; DH-11; RF-10; PH-4; PR-2; CF-1   **Ht:** 6'4" **Wt:** 205 **Born:** 10/18/1981 **Age:** 28

Year	Team	Lg	G	AB	H	2B	3B	HR	(Hm	Rd)	TB	R	RBI	RC	TBB	IBB	SO	HBP	SH	SF	SB	CS	SB%	GDP	Avg	OBP	Slg
2006	Bos	AL	20	22	5	1	0	1	(0	1)	9	4	2	2	4	0	4	0	0	0	0	0	-	1	.227	.346	.409
2007	2 Tms	AL	46	105	36	12	2	2	(1	1)	58	17	14	23	7	0	20	0	0	0	0	0	-	1	.343	.384	.552
2008	Tex	AL	108	415	114	28	3	15	(8	7)	193	64	74	62	31	3	70	0	2	6	7	2	.78	7	.275	.321	.465
2009	Tex	AL	128	432	116	24	1	17	(8	9)	193	61	57	60	49	3	106	1	2	9	9	4	.69	5	.269	.338	.447
07	Bos	AL	3	2	1	0	1	0	(0	0)	3	1	0	1	0	0	1	0	0	0	0	0	-	0	.500	.500	1.500
07	Tex	AL	43	103	35	12	1	2	(1	1)	55	16	14	22	7	0	19	0	0	0	0	0	-	1	.340	.382	.534
	4 ML YEARS		302	974	271	65	6	35	(17	18)	453	146	147	147	91	6	200	1	4	15	16	6	.73	14	.278	.336	.465

Matt Murton

Bats: R **Throws:** R **Pos:** PH-17; LF-12; RF-5; PR-1   **Ht:** 6'1" **Wt:** 220 **Born:** 10/3/1981 **Age:** 28

Year	Team	Lg	G	AB	H	2B	3B	HR	(Hm	Rd)	TB	R	RBI	RC	TBB	IBB	SO	HBP	SH	SF	SB	CS	SB%	GDP	Avg	OBP	Slg
2009	ColSpr*	AAA	97	373	121	27	1	12	(-	-)	186	72	79	75	39	3	52	5	0	7	2	2	.86	6	.324	.389	.499
2005	ChC	NL	51	140	45	3	2	7	(2	5)	73	19	14	19	16	4	22	0	2	2	2	1	.67	4	.321	.386	.521
2006	ChC	NL	144	455	135	22	3	13	(7	6)	202	70	62	68	45	1	62	5	1	2	5	2	.71	16	.297	.365	.444
2007	ChC	NL	94	235	66	13	0	8	(2	6)	103	35	22	28	26	0	39	0	0	1	1	0	1.00	4	.281	.352	.438
2008	2 Tms		28	70	13	3	0	0	(0	0)	16	3	8	2	2	0	12	1	0	0	0	0	-	3	.186	.219	.229
2009	Col	NL	29	52	13	5	0	1	(1	0)	21	7	6	7	4	0	14	0	0	0	2	0	1.00	0	.250	.304	.404
08	ChC	NL	19	40	10	2	0	0	(0	0)	12	2	6	2	1	0	5	1	0	0	0	0	-	2	.250	.286	.300
08	Oak	AL	9	30	3	1	0	0	(0	0)	4	1	2	0	1	0	7	0	0	0	0	0	-	1	.100	.129	.133
	Postseason		1	4	1	0	0	0	(0	0)	1	1	0	0	0	0	0	0	0	0	0	0	-	0	.250	.250	.250
	5 ML YEARS		346	952	272	46	5	29	(12	17)	415	134	112	124	93	5	149	6	3	4	10	3	.77	27	.286	.352	.436

Brett Myers

Pitches: R **Bats:** R **Pos:** SP-10; RP-8   **Ht:** 6'4" **Wt:** 238 **Born:** 8/17/1980 **Age:** 29

Year	Team	Lg	G	GS	CG	GF	IP	BFP	H	R	ER	HR	SH	SF	HB	TBB	IBB	SO	WP	Bk	W	L	Pct	Sh	Sv-Op	Hld	ERC	ERA
2009	Clrwtr*	A+	1	0	0	0	1.0	5	2	0	0	0	0	0	0	0	0	3	0	0	0	0	-	0	0--	-	7.48	0.00
2009	Lakwd*	A	1	1	0	0	1.0	4	0	0	0	0	0	0	0	1	0	1	0	0	0	0	-	0	0--	-	0.95	0.00
2009	Rdng*	AA	2	1	0	0	4.0	14	2	1	1	1	0	0	0	1	0	7	0	0	0	1	.000	0	0--	-	1.96	2.25
2009	LV*	AAA	2	0	0	1	2.0	6	0	0	0	0	0	0	0	0	0	3	0	0	0	0	-	0	1---	-	0.00	0.00
2002	Phi	NL	12	12	1	0	72.0	307	73	38	34	11	6	2	6	29	1	34	2	1	4	5	.444	0	0-0	0	5.04	4.25
2003	Phi	NL	32	32	1	0	193.0	848	205	99	95	20	6	3	9	76	8	143	9	0	14	9	.609	1	0-0	0	4.56	4.43
2004	Phi	NL	32	31	1	1	176.0	778	196	113	108	31	9	3	6	62	4	116	5	0	11	11	.500	1	0-0	0	5.17	5.52
2005	Phi	NL	34	34	2	0	215.1	905	193	94	89	31	9	3	11	68	2	208	4	4	13	8	.619	0	0-0	0	3.64	3.72
2006	Phi	NL	31	31	1	0	198.0	833	194	93	86	29	7	4	3	63	3	189	3	0	12	7	.632	0	0-0	0	4.02	3.91
2007	Phi	NL	51	3	0	37	68.2	293	61	33	33	9	3	1	1	27	1	83	5	0	5	7	.417	0	21-24	3	3.63	4.33
2008	Phi	NL	30	30	2	0	190.0	817	197	103	96	29	4	3	6	65	0	103	2	0	10	13	.435	0	0-0	0	4.53	4.55
2009	Phi	NL	18	10	0	1	70.2	304	74	38	38	18	3	2	4	23	1	50	1	0	4	3	.571	0	0-0	3	5.41	4.84
	Postseason		5	3	0	2	20.1	87	17	11	10	1	1	0	1	10	2	15	1	0	2	1	.667	0	0-0	0	3.21	4.43
	8 ML YEARS		240	183	8	39	1183.2	5085	1193	611	579	178	47	21	46	413	26	906	31	5	73	63	.537	3	21-24	6	4.40	4.40

Xavier Nady

Bats: R **Throws:** R **Pos:** RF-6; DH-1   **Ht:** 6'1" **Wt:** 185 **Born:** 11/14/1978 **Age:** 31

Year	Team	Lg	G	AB	H	2B	3B	HR	(Hm	Rd)	TB	R	RBI	RC	TBB	IBB	SO	HBP	SH	SF	SB	CS	SB%	GDP	Avg	OBP	Slg
2009	S-WB*	AAA	2	5	1	1	0	0	(-	-)	2	0	0	0	1	0	1	0	0	0	0	0	-	0	.200	.333	.400
2000	SD	NL	1	1	1	0	0	0	(0	0)	1	1	0	1	0	0	0	0	0	0	0	0	-	0	1.000	1.000	1.000
2003	SD	NL	110	371	99	17	1	9	(5	4)	145	50	39	39	24	0	74	6	2	1	6	2	.75	14	.267	.321	.391
2004	SD	NL	34	77	19	4	0	3	(1	2)	32	7	9	8	5	0	13	1	1	0	0	1	-	5	.247	.301	.416
2005	SD	NL	124	326	85	15	2	13	(5	8)	143	40	43	37	22	1	67	7	1	0	2	1	.67	5	.261	.321	.439
2006	2 Tms		130	468	131	28	1	17	(10	7)	212	57	63	62	30	7	85	11	2	1	3	3	.50	12	.280	.337	.453
2007	Pit	NL	125	431	120	23	1	20	(7	13)	205	55	72	60	23	2	101	12	0	4	1	1	.75	16	.278	.330	.476
2008	2 Tms		148	555	169	37	1	25	(11	14)	283	76	97	93	39	2	103	9	0	4	2	1	.67	14	.305	.357	.510
2009	NYY	AL	7	28	8	4	0	0	(0	0)	12	4	2	2	1	0	6	0	0	0	0	0	-	2	.286	.310	.429
06	NYM	NL	75	265	70	15	1	14	(10	4)	129	37	40	35	19	4	51	6	1	1	2	1	.67	7	.264	.326	.487
06	Pit		55	203	61	13	0	3	(0	3)	83	20	23	27	11	3	34	5	1	0	1	2	.33	5	.300	.352	.409
08	Pit	NL	89	327	108	26	1	13	(6	7)	175	50	57	59	25	1	55	5	0	3	1	0	1.00	9	.330	.383	.535
08	NYY	AL	59	228	61	11	0	12	(5	7)	108	26	40	34	14	1	48	4	0	1	1	1	.50	5	.268	.320	.474
	Postseason		2	3	1	0	0	0	(0	0)	1	0	2	1	0	0	1	2	0	0	0	0	-	0	.333	.600	.333
	8 ML YEARS		679	2257	632	128	6	87	(39	48)	1033	290	325	302	144	12	449	46	6	10	16	8	.67	67	.280	.335	.458

Mike Napoli

Bats: R **Throws:** R **Pos:** C-96; DH-18; PH-7   **Ht:** 6'0" **Wt:** 215 **Born:** 10/31/1981 **Age:** 28

Year	Team	Lg	G	AB	H	2B	3B	HR	(Hm	Rd)	TB	R	RBI	RC	TBB	IBB	SO	HBP	SH	SF	SB	CS	SB%	GDP	Avg	OBP	Slg
2006	LAA	AL	99	268	61	13	0	16	(10	6)	122	47	42	40	51	0	90	5	0	1	2	3	.40	2	.228	.360	.455
2007	LAA	AL	75	219	54	11	1	10	(5	5)	97	40	34	35	33	2	63	5	1	5	5	2	.71	5	.247	.351	.443
2008	LAA	AL	78	227	62	9	1	20	(10	10)	133	39	49	46	35	5	70	5	1	6	7	3	.70	3	.273	.374	.586
2009	LAA	AL	114	382	104	22	1	20	(10	10)	188	60	56	52	40	1	103	7	0	3	3	3	.50	6	.272	.350	.492
	Postseason		7	18	4	0	0	2	(0	2)	10	3	4	3	2	0	6	1	0	0	0	0	-	0	.222	.333	.556
	4 ML YEARS		366	1096	281	55	3	66	(35	31)	540	186	181	173	159	8	326	22	2	15	17	11	.61	16	.256	.358	.493

Chris Narveson

Pitches: L **Bats:** L **Pos:** RP-17; SP-4   **Ht:** 6'3" **Wt:** 205 **Born:** 12/20/1981 **Age:** 28

Year	Team	Lg	G	GS	CG	GF	IP	BFP	H	R	ER	HR	SH	SF	HB	TBB	IBB	SO	WP	Bk	W	L	Pct	Sh	Sv-Op	Hld	ERC	ERA
2000	JhsCty	R+	12	12	0	0	55.0	247	57	33	20	7	1	1	3	25	0	63	3	0	2	4	.333	0	0--	-	4.87	3.27
2001	Peoria	A	8	8	0	0	50.0	190	32	14	11	3	2	1	1	11	0	53	0	0	3	3	.500	0	0--	-	1.66	1.98
2001	Ptomc	A+	11	11	1	0	66.2	263	52	22	19	4	2	3	0	13	1	53	3	0	4	3	.571	0	0--	-	1.93	2.57
2002	JhsCty	R+	6	6	0	0	18.1	83	23	12	10	2	0	1	1	6	0	16	0	0	0	2	.000	0	0--	-	5.56	4.91
2002	Peoria	A	9	9	0	0	42.1	184	49	24	21	5	0	3	0	8	0	36	3	0	2	1	.667	0	0--	-	4.14	4.46
2003	PlmBh	A+	15	14	1	0	91.1	369	83	34	29	4	3	2	2	19	0	65	4	0	7	7	.500	0	0--	-	2.61	2.86
2003	Tenn	AA	10	10	0	0	57.0	247	56	21	19	6	4	3	0	26	2	34	4	1	4	3	.571	0	0--	-	4.19	3.00
2004	Tenn	AA	23	23	0	0	127.2	538	114	64	59	11	11	4	5	51	0	121	7	0	5	10	.333	0	0--	-	3.57	4.16
2004	Tulsa	AA	4	4	0	0	20.0	87	16	14	7	1	1	3	2	13	0	14	2	0	0	3	.000	0	0--	-	4.04	3.15
2005	Pwtckt	AAA	21	20	0	1	111.1	477	109	62	59	15	4	1	10	46	0	66	4	1	4	5	.444	0	0--	-	4.75	4.77
2005	Memp	AAA	2	2	0	0	6.2	37	11	9	9	2	0	1	1	7	0	8	0	0	0	1	.000	0	0--	-	14.45	12.15
2006	PlmBh	A+	3	3	0	0	17.0	62	9	4	4	2	1	0	0	1	0	13	0	0	0	0	-	0	0--	-	0.99	2.12
2006	Memp	AAA	15	15	0	0	80.0	332	70	26	25	9	1	2	2	33	2	58	3	0	8	5	.615	0	0--	-	3.66	2.81
2007	Memp	AAA	9	9	1	0	45.2	192	41	29	29	6	1	1	1	21	0	35	3	0	3	2	.600	0	0--	-	4.15	5.72
2007	PlmBh	A+	3	3	0	0	10.0	42	10	4	3	1	1	1	0	3	0	6	1	0	0	0	-	0	0--	-	3.70	2.70
2008	Nashv	AAA	28	22	0	0	136.0	600	140	90	82	23	7	3	4	57	0	125	9	0	6	13	.316	0	0--	-	4.91	5.43
2009	Nashv	AAA	26	6	0	8	75.1	313	59	36	31	3	4	0	1	26	0	76	4	0	4	4	.500	0	5--	0	2.34	3.70
2006	StL	NL	5	1	0	1	9.1	40	6	5	5	1	0	0	1	5	0	12	1	1	0	0	-	0	0-0	0	3.06	4.82
2009	Mil	NL	21	4	0	5	47.0	205	45	22	20	7	2	3	2	16	1	46	4	0	2	0	1.000	0	0-0	0	3.96	3.83
2 ML YEARS			26	5	0	6	56.1	245	51	27	25	8	2	3	3	21	1	58	5	1	2	0	1.000	0	0-0	0	3.81	3.99

Joe Nathan

Pitches: R **Bats:** R **Pos:** RP-70   **Ht:** 6'4" **Wt:** 225 **Born:** 11/22/1974 **Age:** 35

Year	Team	Lg	G	GS	CG	GF	IP	BFP	H	R	ER	HR	SH	SF	HB	TBB	IBB	SO	WP	Bk	W	L	Pct	Sh	Sv-Op	Hld	ERC	ERA
1999	SF	NL	19	14	0	2	90.1	395	84	45	42	17	2	0	1	46	0	54	2	0	7	4	.636	0	1-1	0	4.78	4.18
2000	SF	NL	20	15	0	0	93.1	426	89	63	54	12	5	5	4	63	4	61	5	0	5	2	.714	0	0-1	0	5.23	5.21
2002	SF	NL	4	0	0	3	3.2	12	1	0	0	0	0	0	0	0	0	2	0	0	0	0	-	0	0-0	0	0.17	0.00
2003	SF	NL	78	0	0	9	79.0	316	51	26	26	7	2	4	3	33	3	83	4	1	12	4	.750	0	0-3	20	2.34	2.96
2004	Min	AL	73	0	0	63	72.1	284	48	14	13	3	2	0	2	23	3	89	5	0	1	2	.333	0	44-47	0	1.78	1.62
2005	Min	AL	69	0	0	58	70.0	276	46	22	21	5	1	2	0	22	1	94	2	0	7	4	.636	0	43-48	0	1.83	2.70
2006	Min	AL	64	0	0	61	68.1	262	38	12	12	3	3	2	1	16	4	95	3	0	7	0	1.000	0	36-38	0	1.18	1.58
2007	Min	AL	68	0	0	60	71.2	282	54	15	15	4	2	2	1	19	2	77	3	0	4	2	.667	0	37-41	0	2.08	1.88
2008	Min	AL	68	0	0	57	67.2	261	43	13	10	5	1	0	2	18	4	74	2	0	1	2	.333	0	39-45	0	1.67	1.33
2009	Min	AL	70	0	0	62	68.2	271	42	16	16	7	1	0	2	22	1	89	4	0	2	2	.500	0	47-52	0	1.89	2.10
Postseason			6	0	0	2	6.0	31	7	5	5	1	0	0	0	6	2	8	1	0	0	2	.000	0	1-2	0	7.30	7.50
10 ML YEARS			533	29	0	375	685.0	2785	496	226	209	63	19	15	16	262	22	718	30	1	46	22	.676	0	247-276	20	2.55	2.75

Dioner Navarro

Bats: B **Throws:** R **Pos:** C-113; PH-4; PR-1   **Ht:** 5'9" **Wt:** 205 **Born:** 2/9/1984 **Age:** 26

Year	Team	Lg	G	AB	H	2B	3B	HR	(Hm	Rd)	TB	R	RBI	RC	TBB	IBB	SO	HBP	SH	SF	SB	CS	SB%	GDP	Avg	OBP	Slg
2004	NYY	AL	5	7	3	0	0	0	(0	0)	3	2	1	1	0	0	0	0	0	0	0	0	-	1	.429	.429	.429
2005	LAD	NL	50	176	48	9	0	3	(3	0)	66	21	14	18	20	1	21	2	1	0	0	0	-	3	.273	.354	.375
2006	2 Tms		81	268	68	9	0	6	(4	2)	95	28	28	27	31	6	51	1	1	1	2	1	.67	7	.254	.332	.354
2007	TB	AL	119	388	88	19	2	9	(5	4)	138	46	44	35	33	3	67	1	7	5	3	1	.75	11	.227	.286	.356
2008	TB	AL	120	427	126	27	0	7	(4	3)	174	43	54	59	34	1	49	3	3	3	0	4	.00	16	.295	.349	.407
2009	TB	AL	115	376	82	15	0	8	(4	4)	121	38	32	22	18	1	51	5	8	3	5	2	.71	14	.218	.261	.322
06	LAD	NL	25	75	21	2	0	2	(1	1)	29	5	8	8	11	4	18	0	0	0	1	0	1.00	1	.280	.372	.387
06	TB	AL	56	193	47	7	0	4	(3	1)	66	23	20	19	20	2	33	1	1	1	1	1	.50	6	.244	.316	.342
Postseason			16	58	17	4	0	0	(0	0)	21	4	5	6	4	0	11	0	0	0	0	1	.00	2	.293	.339	.362
6 ML YEARS			490	1642	415	79	2	33	(20	13)	597	178	173	162	136	12	239	12	20	12	10	8	.56	52	.253	.312	.364

Brad Nelson

Bats: L **Throws:** R **Pos:** PH-17; LF-1; RF-1   **Ht:** 6'2" **Wt:** 266 **Born:** 12/23/1982 **Age:** 27

Year	Team	Lg	G	AB	H	2B	3B	HR	(Hm	Rd)	TB	R	RBI	RC	TBB	IBB	SO	HBP	SH	SF	SB	CS	SB%	GDP	Avg	OBP	Slg
2001	Brewrs	R	17	63	19	6	1	0	(-	-)	27	10	13	11	8	0	18	2	1	1	0	0	-	1	.302	.392	.429
2001	Ogden	R+	13	42	11	4	0	0	(-	-)	15	5	10	4	3	0	9	0	0	2	0	0	-	1	.262	.298	.357
2002	Beloit	A	106	417	124	38	2	17	(-	-)	217	70	99	77	34	4	86	4	0	4	4	1	.80	9	.297	.353	.520
2002	Hi Dsrt	A+	26	102	26	11	0	3	(-	-)	46	24	17	15	12	1	28	0	0	0	0	0	-	4	.255	.333	.451
2003	Hi Dsrt	A+	41	167	52	9	1	1	(-	-)	66	23	18	24	12	0	22	2	0	1	2	2	.50	4	.311	.363	.395
2003	Hntsvl	AA	39	143	30	12	0	1	(-	-)	45	15	14	12	11	2	34	2	0	1	2	2	.50	4	.210	.274	.315
2004	Hntsvl	AA	137	500	127	31	1	19	(-	-)	217	61	77	71	47	3	146	5	0	6	11	10	.52	9	.254	.321	.434
2005	Nashv	AAA	81	281	71	16	2	7	(-	-)	112	50	39	42	45	4	74	2	2	1	5	4	.55	5	.253	.359	.399
2005	Hntsvl	AA	55	208	61	8	1	6	(-	-)	89	27	38	34	26	5	42	1	0	3	1	2	.33	5	.293	.370	.428
2006	Nashv	AAA	40	130	28	10	0	3	(-	-)	47	22	17	16	18	0	36	2	0	2	4	3	.57	5	.215	.316	.362
2006	Hntsvl	AA	80	265	70	14	1	6	(-	-)	104	47	39	48	63	4	62	0	0	4	6	3	.67	6	.264	.401	.392
2007	Nashv	AAA	116	411	108	23	1	20	(-	-)	193	54	65	61	31	1	98	2	0	1	9	6	.60	5	.263	.317	.470
2008	Nashv	AAA	132	475	136	36	1	18	(-	-)	228	78	78	89	73	3	77	1	0	4	13	8	.62	13	.286	.380	.480
2009	Tacom	AAA	78	275	68	9	1	15	(-	-)	124	35	45	41	30	5	56	1	0	1	0	0	-	6	.247	.322	.451
2008	Mil	NL	9	7	2	2	0	0	(0	0)	4	0	0	1	1	0	0	0	0	0	0	0	-	0	.286	.375	.571
2009	Mil	NL	19	21	0	0	0	0	(0	0)	0	0	0	0	2	0	9	0	0	0	0	0	-	1	.000	.087	.000
Postseason			2	2	0	0	0	0	(0	0)	0	0	0	0	0	0	2	0	0	0	0	0	-	0	.000	.000	.000
2 ML YEARS			28	28	2	2	0	0	(0	0)	4	0	0	1	3	0	9	0	0	0	0	0	-	1	.071	.161	.143

Joe Nelson

Pitches: R Bats: R Pos: RP-42 **Ht: 6'1" Wt: 205 Born: 10/25/1974 Age: 35**

		HOW MUCH HE PITCHED						WHAT HE GAVE UP											THE RESULTS							
Year Team	Lg	G	GS	CG	GF	IP	BFP	H	R	ER	HR	SH	SF	HB	TRR	IBB	SO	WP	Bk	W	L	Pct	Sh	Sv-Op	Hld	ERC	ERA
2009 Drham*	AAA	13	0	0	4	17.1	85	22	14	12	4	2	0	2	11	1	14	0	0	2	2	.500	0	0- -	0	8.22	6.23
2001 Atl	NL	2	0	0	0	2.0	16	7	9	8	1	0	1	1	2	0	0	0	0	0	0	-	0	0-0	0	33.03	36.00
2004 Bos	AL	3	0	0	1	2.2	17	4	5	5	0	1	0	2	3	0	5	0	0	0	0	-	0	0-0	0	12.43	16.88
2006 KC	AL	43	0	0	20	44.2	193	37	22	22	5	3	1	1	24	4	44	1	0	1	1	.500	0	9-10	5	3.67	4.43
2008 Fla	NL	59	0	0	20	54.0	230	42	16	12	5	2	0	2	22	4	60	3	0	3	1	.750	0	1-5	11	2.80	2.00
2009 TB	AL	42	0	0	13	40.1	182	32	22	18	7	2	2	1	27	1	36	3	1	3	0	1.000	0	3-4	7	4.44	4.02
5 ML YEARS		149	0	0	54	143.2	638	122	74	65	18	8	4	7	78	9	145	7	1	7	2	.778	0	13-19	23	3.97	4.07

Pat Neshek

Pitches: R Bats: B Pos: P **Ht: 6'3" Wt: 210 Born: 9/4/1980 Age: 29**

		HOW MUCH HE PITCHED						WHAT HE GAVE UP											THE RESULTS							
Year Team	Lg	G	GS	CG	GF	IP	BFP	H	R	ER	HR	SH	SF	HB	TBB	IBB	SO	WP	Bk	W	L	Pct	Sh	Sv-Op	Hld	ERC	ERA
2006 Min	AL	32	0	0	3	37.0	138	23	9	9	6	0	1	0	6	0	53	0	0	4	2	.667	0	0-2	10	1.68	2.19
2007 Min	AL	74	0	0	20	70.1	278	44	25	23	7	4	5	2	27	5	74	2	0	7	2	.778	0	0-3	15	2.12	2.94
2008 Min	AL	15	0	0	3	13.1	56	12	7	7	2	1	1	0	4	1	15	0	0	0	1	.000	0	0-2	6	3.29	4.73
Postseason		2	0	0	1	1.0	4	1	1	1	0	0	0	0	1	0	1	0	0	0	1	.000	0	0-0	1	1.95	9.00
3 ML YEARS		121	0	0	26	120.2	472	79	41	39	15	5	7	2	37	6	142	2	0	11	5	.688	0	0-7	31	2.11	2.91

Fu-Te Ni

Pitches: L Bats: L Pos: RP-36 **Ht: 6'0" Wt: 172 Born: 11/14/1982 Age: 27**

		HOW MUCH HE PITCHED						WHAT HE GAVE UP											THE RESULTS							
Year Team	Lg	G	GS	CG	GF	IP	BFP	H	R	ER	HR	SH	SF	HB	TBB	IBB	SO	WP	Bk	W	L	Pct	Sh	Sv-Op	Hld	ERC	ERA
2009 Toledo	AAA	24	0	0	10	31.2	130	31	10	10	4	0	1	0	9	0	32	2	0	3	0	1.000	0	0- -		3.13	2.60
2009 Det	AL	26	0	0	0	31.0	121	28	9	9	3	1	1	1	11	2	21	2	0	0	0	-	0	0-2	3	2.15	2.61

Jeff Niemann

Pitches: R Bats: R Pos: SP-30; RP-1 **Ht: 6'9" Wt: 260 Born: 2/28/1983 Age: 27**

		HOW MUCH HE PITCHED						WHAT HE GAVE UP											THE RESULTS							
Year Team	Lg	G	GS	CG	GF	IP	BFP	H	R	ER	HR	SH	SF	HB	TBB	IBB	SO	WP	Bk	W	L	Pct	Sh	Sv-Op	Hld	ERC	ERA
2005 Visalia	A+	5	5	0	0	20.1	83	12	10	9	3	-	-	2	10	0	28	1	0	0	1	.000	0	0- -		2.95	3.90
2005 Mont	AA	6	3	0	1	10.1	43	7	7	5	0	0	0	0	5	0	14	0	0	0	1	.000	0	0- -		2.02	4.35
2006 Mont	AA	14	14	0	0	77.1	320	56	24	23	6	4	3	7	29	0	84	3	0	5	5	.600	0	0- -		2.70	2.08
2007 Drham	AAA	25	25	0	0	131.0	580	144	69	58	13	3	3	9	46	1	123	8	0	12	6	.667	0	0- -		4.69	3.98
2008 Drham	AAA	24	24	3	0	133.0	647	101	60	53	15	2	1	5	50	0	128	2	0	9	5	.643	1	0- -		2.92	3.59
2008 TB	AL	5	2	0	0	16.0	76	18	12	9	3	2	0	1	8	0	14	0	0	2	2	.500	0	0-0	0	5.93	5.06
2009 TB	AL	31	30	2	1	180.2	769	185	84	79	17	2	4	9	59	1	125	6	0	13	6	.684	2	0-0	0	4.12	3.94
2 ML YEARS		36	32	2	3	196.2	845	203	96	88	20	4	4	10	67	1	139	6	0	15	8	.652	2	0-0	0	4.26	4.03

Jonathon Niese

Pitches: L Bats: L Pos: SP-5 **Ht: 6'4" Wt: 215 Born: 10/27/1986 Age: 23**

		HOW MUCH HE PITCHED						WHAT HE GAVE UP											THE RESULTS							
Year Team	Lg	G	GS	CG	GF	IP	BFP	H	R	ER	HR	SH	SF	HB	TBB	IBB	SO	WP	Bk	W	L	Pct	Sh	Sv-Op	Hld	ERC	ERA
2005 Mets	R	7	5	0	0	24.2	105	23	10	10	1	0	0	1	10	0	24	2	0	1	0	1.000	0	0- -		3.49	3.65
2006 Hgrstn	A	25	25	1	0	123.2	549	121	67	54	7	3	3	9	62	0	132	15	1	11	9	.550	1	0- -		4.33	3.93
2006 StLuci	A+	2	2	0	0	10.0	45	8	8	5	0	2	1	0	5	0	10	1	0	0	2	.000	0	0- -		2.49	4.50
2007 StLuci	A+	27	27	2	0	134.1	575	151	78	64	9	4	4	7	31	0	110	7	0	11	7	.611	1	0- -		4.11	4.29
2008 Bnghtn	AA	22	22	2	0	124.1	521	118	53	42	5	5	3	2	44	0	112	7	0	6	7	.462	1	0- -		3.31	3.04
2008 NewOr	AAA	7	7	0	0	39.2	167	34	15	15	4	2	2	2	14	0	32	1	0	5	1	.833	0	0- -		3.29	3.40
2009 Buffalo	AAA	16	16	2	0	94.1	400	95	47	40	7	1	1	5	25	0	82	4	0	5	6	.455	2	0- -		3.61	3.82
2008 NYM	NL	3	3	0	0	14.0	69	20	11	11	2	1	0	0	8	0	11	0	0	1	1	.500	0	0-0	0	7.71	7.07
2009 NYM	NL	5	5	0	0	25.2	110	27	12	12	1	2	1	0	9	0	18	1	0	1	1	.500	0	0-0	0	3.76	4.21
2 ML YEARS		8	8	0	0	39.2	179	47	23	23	3	3	1	0	17	0	29	1	0	2	2	.500	0	0-0	0	5.07	5.22

Fernando Nieve

Pitches: R Bats: R Pos: SP-7; RP-1 **Ht: 6'0" Wt: 195 Born: 7/15/1982 Age: 27**

		HOW MUCH HE PITCHED						WHAT HE GAVE UP											THE RESULTS							
Year Team	Lg	G	GS	CG	GF	IP	BFP	H	R	ER	HR	SH	SF	HB	TBB	IBB	SO	WP	Bk	W	L	Pct	Sh	Sv-Op	Hld	ERC	ERA
2009 Bnghtn*	AA	5	4	0	0	18.1	75	16	10	10	1	1	0	1	6	0	19	2	0	0	1	.000	0	0- -		3.09	4.91
2009 Buffalo*	AAA	4	4	0	0	24.1	98	18	10	10	2	0	0	0	10	0	23	2	0	0	1	1.000	0	0- -		2.67	3.70
2006 Hou	NL	40	11	0	11	96.1	411	87	46	45	18	5	3	2	41	5	70	1	0	3	3	.500	0	0-0	0	4.24	4.20
2008 Hou	NL	11	0	0	1	10.2	49	17	10	10	2	0	0	0	2	0	12	0	0	1	0	1.000	0	0-1	0	7.62	8.44
2009 NYM	NL	8	7	0	1	36.2	161	36	13	12	4	3	1	1	19	1	23	2	0	3	3	.500	0	0-0	0	4.62	2.95
3 ML YEARS		59	18	0	13	143.2	621	140	69	67	24	8	4	3	62	6	105	3	0	6	7	.462	0	0-1	0	4.57	4.20

Wil Nieves

Bats: R **Throws:** R **Pos:** C-71; PH-2; PR-2   **Ht:** 5'10" **Wt:** 182 **Born:** 9/25/1977 **Age:** 32

Year	Team	Lg	G	AB	H	2B	3B	HR	(Hm	Rd)	TB	R	RBI	RC	TBB	IBB	SO	HBP	SH	SF	SB	CS	SB%	GDP	Avg	OBP	Slg
2002	SD	NL	28	72	13	3	1	0	(0	0)	18	2	3	4	4	4	15	0	0	0	1	0	1.00	1	.181	.224	.250
2005	NYY	AL	3	4	0	0	0	0	(0	0)	0	0	0	0	0	0	1	0	0	0	0	0	-	0	.000	.000	.000
2006	NYY	AL	6	6	0	0	0	0	(0	0)	0	0	0	0	0	0	1	0	0	0	0	0	-	0	.000	.000	.000
2007	NYY	AL	26	61	10	4	0	0	(0	0)	14	6	8	4	2	0	9	0	3	0	0	0	-	3	.164	.190	.230
2008	Was	NL	68	176	46	9	1	1	(1	0)	60	15	20	20	13	1	29	0	5	2	0	1	.00	7	.261	.309	.341
2009	Was	NL	72	224	58	6	0	1	(0	1)	67	20	26	21	17	1	45	3	0	5	1	0	1.00	7	.259	.313	.299
	6 ML YEARS		203	543	127	22	2	2	(1	1)	159	43	57	49	36	6	100	3	8	7	2	1	.67	18	.234	.282	.293

Dustin Nippert

Pitches: R **Bats:** R **Pos:** SP-10; RP-10   **Ht:** 6'8" **Wt:** 225 **Born:** 5/6/1981 **Age:** 29

Year	Team	Lg	G	GS	CG	GF	IP	BFP	H	R	ER	HR	SH	SF	HB	TBB	IBB	SO	WP	Bk	W	L	Pct	Sh	Sv-Op	Hld	ERC	ERA
2009	Frisco*	AA	4	3	0	0	12.2	50	8	4	4	1	0	0	0	6	0	8	0	0	0	1	.000	0	0--	-	2.37	2.84
2009	Okla*	AAA	1	1	0	0	5.0	19	2	1	1	1	0	0	0	2	0	6	0	0	1	0	1.000	0	0--	-	1.65	1.80
2005	Ari	NL	3	3	0	0	14.2	68	10	9	9	1	0	0	1	13	0	11	1	0	1	0	1.000	0	0-0	0	4.09	5.52
2006	Ari	NL	2	2	0	0	10.0	51	15	13	13	5	1	0	0	7	0	9	0	0	0	2	.000	0	0-0	0	12.21	11.70
2007	Ari	NL	36	0	0	8	45.1	196	48	30	28	5	0	0	0	16	1	38	4	0	1	1	.500	0	0-0	2	4.25	5.56
2008	Tex	AL	20	6	0	6	71.2	341	92	52	51	10	3	1	1	37	3	55	1	1	3	5	.375	0	0-0	0	6.47	6.40
2009	Tex	AL	20	10	0	3	69.2	300	64	31	30	7	1	5	4	29	0	54	2	0	5	3	.625	0	0-0	1	3.91	3.88
	Postseason		2	0	0	1	2.1	8	1	0	0	0	0	0	0	0	0	2	0	0	0	0	-	0	0-0	0	0.40	0.00
	5 ML YEARS		81	21	0	17	211.1	956	229	135	131	28	5	6	6	102	4	167	8	1	10	11	.476	0	0-0	3	5.18	5.58

Jayson Nix

Bats: R **Throws:** R **Pos:** 2B-52; SS-15; PH-15; 3B-12; RF-4; DH-4; PR-4; LF-3   **Ht:** 5'11" **Wt:** 185 **Born:** 8/26/1982 **Age:** 27

Year	Team	Lg	G	AB	H	2B	3B	HR	(Hm	Rd)	TB	R	RBI	RC	TBB	IBB	SO	HBP	SH	SF	SB	CS	SB%	GDP	Avg	OBP	Slg
2001	Casper	R+	42	153	45	10	1	5	(-	-)	72	28	24	27	21	1	43	3	0	2	1	5	.17	1	.294	.385	.471
2002	Ashvll	A	132	487	120	29	2	14	(-	-)	195	73	79	72	62	2	105	9	3	4	14	5	.74	10	.246	.340	.400
2003	Visalia	A+	137	562	158	46	0	21	(-	-)	267	107	86	98	54	2	131	10	3	6	24	8	.75	3	.281	.351	.475
2004	Tulsa	AA	123	456	97	17	1	14	(-	-)	158	58	58	50	40	1	101	12	1	2	14	3	.82	9	.213	.292	.346
2005	Tulsa	AA	131	501	118	27	0	11	(-	-)	178	68	47	53	29	1	92	11	4	6	10	6	.63	8	.236	.289	.355
2006	ColSpr	AAA	103	358	90	14	1	2	(-	-)	112	39	26	40	32	0	61	3	3	1	15	3	.83	4	.251	.317	.313
2007	ColSpr	AAA	124	439	128	33	2	11	(-	-)	198	80	58	70	31	1	79	4	7	2	24	8	.75	5	.292	.342	.451
2008	ColSpr	AAA	67	264	80	21	2	17	(-	-)	156	63	51	58	27	1	64	5	3	4	11	5	.69	6	.303	.373	.591
2009	Brham	AA	3	10	3	0	0	0	(-	-)	3	1	3	1	2	0	0	0	0	0	0	0	-	0	.300	.417	.300
2009	Charltt	AAA	5	20	9	1	0	0	(-	-)	10	4	5	5	4	0	0	0	0	0	1	0	1.00	0	.450	.542	.500
2008	Col	NL	22	56	7	2	0	0	(0	0)	9	2	2	0	7	2	17	1	1	0	1	0	1.00	1	.125	.234	.161
2009	CWS	AL	94	255	57	11	0	12	(4	8)	104	36	32	31	28	1	64	4	1	2	10	2	.83	5	.224	.308	.408
	2 ML YEARS		116	311	64	13	0	12	(4	8)	113	38	34	31	35	3	81	5	2	2	11	2	.85	6	.206	.295	.363

Laynce Nix

Bats: L **Throws:** L **Pos:** LF-72; PH-40; RF-10; CF-5   **Ht:** 6'1" **Wt:** 220 **Born:** 10/30/1980 **Age:** 29

Year	Team	Lg	G	AB	H	2B	3B	HR	(Hm	Rd)	TB	R	RBI	RC	TBB	IBB	SO	HBP	SH	SF	SB	CS	SB%	GDP	Avg	OBP	Slg
2003	Tex	AL	53	184	47	10	0	8	(7	1)	81	25	30	25	9	0	53	0	1	1	3	0	1.00	1	.255	.289	.440
2004	Tex	AL	115	371	92	20	4	14	(9	5)	162	58	46	44	23	4	113	2	1	3	1	1	.50	6	.248	.293	.437
2005	Tex	AL	63	229	55	12	3	6	(3	3)	91	28	32	26	9	3	45	0	0	2	2	0	1.00	3	.240	.267	.397
2006	2 Tms		19	67	11	2	0	1	(1	0)	16	3	10	3	0	0	28	2	0	1	0	0	-	1	.164	.186	.239
2007	Mil	NL	10	12	0	0	0	0	(0	0)	0	0	0	0	0	0	4	0	0	0	0	0	-	0	.000	.000	.000
2008	Mil	NL	10	12	1	0	0	0	(0	0)	1	1	0	0	1	0	3	0	0	0	0	0	-	0	.083	.154	.083
2009	Cin	NL	116	309	74	26	1	15	(5	10)	147	42	46	35	22	3	81	2	0	4	0	1	.00	5	.239	.291	.476
06	Tex	AL	9	32	3	1	0	0	(0	0)	4	1	4	0	0	0	17	1	0	1	0	0	-	0	.094	.118	.125
06	Mil	NL	10	35	8	1	0	1	(1	0)	12	2	6	3	0	0	11	1	0	0	0	0	-	1	.229	.250	.343
	7 ML YEARS		386	1184	280	70	8	44	(25	19)	498	157	164	133	64	10	327	6	2	11	6	2	.75	16	.236	.277	.421

Ricky Nolasco

Pitches: R **Bats:** R **Pos:** SP-31   **Ht:** 6'2" **Wt:** 230 **Born:** 12/13/1982 **Age:** 27

Year	Team	Lg	G	GS	CG	GF	IP	BFP	H	R	ER	HR	SH	SF	HB	TBB	IBB	SO	WP	Bk	W	L	Pct	Sh	Sv-Op	Hld	ERC	ERA
2009	NewOr*	AAA	2	2	1	0	15.0	58	12	4	4	0	1	0	0	3	1	12	1	0	1	1	.500	0	0--	-	1.69	2.40
2006	Fla	NL	35	22	0	0	140.0	613	157	86	75	20	8	6	10	41	5	99	7	0	11	11	.500	0	0-0	2	4.89	4.82
2007	Fla	NL	5	4	0	0	21.1	99	26	16	13	3	3	5	1	9	2	11	1	0	1	2	.333	0	0-0	0	5.71	5.48
2008	Fla	NL	34	32	1	0	212.1	868	192	88	83	28	6	9	6	42	6	186	1	3	15	8	.652	1	0-0	0	3.03	3.52
2009	Fla	NL	31	31	2	0	185.0	785	188	111	104	23	8	5	2	44	7	195	2	0	13	9	.591	0	0-0	0	3.62	5.06
	4 ML YEARS		105	89	3	0	558.2	2365	563	301	275	74	25	25	19	136	20	491	11	3	40	30	.571	1	0-0	2	3.77	4.43

Bud Norris

Pitches: R Bats: R Pos: SP-10; RP-1   Ht: 6'0" Wt: 195 Born: 3/2/1985 Age: 25

Year Team	Lg	G	GS	CG	GF	IP	BFP	H	R	ER	HR	SH	SF	HB	TBB	IBB	SO	WP	Bk	W	L	Pct	Sh	Sv-Op	Hld	ERC	ERA
2006 TriCity A-		15	3	0	6	38.0	161	28	20	16	1	3	1	4	13	0	46	1	0	2	0	1.000	0	2--	-	2.30	3.79
2007 Lxngtn A		22	22	0	0	96.2	416	85	58	51	8	2	2	6	41	0	117	6	0	2	8	.200	0	0--	-	3.60	4.75
2007 Salem A+		1	1	0	0	6.0	22	4	1	1	0	0	0	0	1	0	2	0	0	1	0	1.000	0	0--	-	1.29	1.50
2008 CpChr AA		19	19	0	0	80.0	352	89	42	36	8	2	1	7	31	0	84	1	3	3	8	.273	0	0--	-	5.13	4.05
2009 RdRck AAA		19	19	0	0	120.0	509	104	42	35	6	11	3	4	53	4	112	4	0	4	9	.308	0	0--	-	3.25	2.63
2009 Hou	NL	11	10	0	0	55.2	249	59	29	28	9	1	3	3	25	1	54	3	0	6	3	.667	0	0-0	0	5.26	4.53

Greg Norton

Bats: B Throws: R Pos: PH-91; 1B-3; PR-1   Ht: 6'1" Wt: 205 Born: 7/6/1972 Age: 37

Year Team	Lg	G	AB	H	2B	3B	HR	(Hm	Rd)	TB	R	RBI	RC	TBB	IBB	SO	HBP	SH	SF	SB	CS	SB%	GDP	Avg	OBP	Slg
2009 Gwnntt* AAA		12	37	12	0	1	1	(-	-)	17	3	10	6	3	1	7	0	0	1	1	0	1.00	0	.324	.366	.459
1996 CWS	AL	11	23	5	0	0	2	(0	2)	11	4	3	3	4	0	6	0	0	0	0	1	.00	0	.217	.333	.478
1997 CWS	AL	18	34	9	2	2	0	(0	0)	15	5	1	5	2	0	8	0	1	0	0	0	-	0	.265	.306	.441
1998 CWS	AL	105	299	71	17	2	9	(6	3)	119	38	36	33	26	1	77	2	1	2	3	3	.50	11	.237	.301	.398
1999 CWS	AL	132	436	111	26	0	16	(5	11)	185	62	50	66	69	3	93	2	1	2	4	4	.50	11	.255	.358	.424
2000 CWS	AL	71	201	49	6	1	6	(4	2)	75	25	28	27	26	0	47	2	0	2	1	0	1.00	5	.244	.333	.373
2001 Col	NL	117	225	60	13	2	13	(7	6)	116	30	40	36	19	2	65	0	0	0	1	0	1.00	6	.267	.321	.516
2002 Col	NL	113	168	37	8	1	7	(3	4)	68	19	37	22	24	0	52	0	1	2	2	3	.40	4	.220	.314	.405
2003 Col	NL	114	179	47	15	0	6	(2	4)	80	19	31	26	16	0	47	1	0	1	2	1	.67	4	.263	.325	.447
2004 Det	AL	41	86	15	1	0	2	(1	1)	22	9	2	1	12	1	21	0	1	0	0	0	-	3	.174	.276	.256
2006 TB	AL	98	294	87	15	0	17	(9	8)	153	47	45	53	35	2	69	3	1	2	1	5	.17	2	.296	.374	.520
2007 TB	Al	75	202	49	9	0	4	(2	2)	70	25	23	28	37	3	55	0	0	1	1	1	.50	1	.243	.358	.347
2008 2 Tms		117	187	49	12	0	7	(2	5)	82	29	35	32	33	4	44	0	0	0	0	0	-	7	.262	.373	.439
2009 All	NL	95	76	11	2	0	2	(0	0)	19	3	7	7	20	0	20	1	0	0	0	0	-	0	.145	.000	.171
08 3rd	AL	6	16	7	2	0	0	(0	0)	9	2	4	6	2	0	4	0	0	0	0	0	-	0	.438	.500	.563
08 All	NL	111	171	42	10	0	7	(2	5)	73	27	31	26	31	4	40	0	0	0	0	0	-	7	.246	.361	.427
13 ML YEARS		1107	2410	600	126	8	89	(41	48)	1009	315	338	339	323	16	604	11	6	14	15	18	45	52	.249	.339	.419

Jhonny Nunez

Pitches: R Bats: R Pos: RP-7   Ht: 6'3" Wt: 185 Born: 11/26/1985 Age: 24

Year Team	Lg	G	GS	CG	GF	IP	BFP	H	R	ER	HR	SH	SF	HB	TBB	IBB	SO	WP	Bk	W	L	Pct	Sh	Sv-Op	Hld	ERC	ERA
2006 Ddgrs R		10	7	0	1	57.0	223	35	12	10	0	1	2	3	19	0	56	3	1	6	0	1.000	0	0--	-	1.58	1.58
2007 Hgrstn A		23	22	0	0	106.2	474	97	59	48	10	5	4	11	48	1	86	7	1	4	6	.400	0	0--	-	4.03	4.05
2008 Ptomc A+		21	17	0	1	81.0	346	88	51	47	11	1	1	4	21	0	82	6	1	2	8	.200	0	0--	-	4.49	5.22
2008 Hrsbrg AA		5	0	0	0	8.0	37	9	1	1	0	1	0	0	6	0	8	0	0	0	0	-	0	0--	-	5.56	1.13
2008 Trntn AA		8	0	0	2	19.1	81	16	5	4	2	2	2	1	6	0	26	0	0	1	0	1.000	0	0--	-	2.97	1.86
2009 Brham AA		26	0	0	11	46.1	191	38	12	11	3	1	3	0	21	2	57	2	1	3	0	1.000	0	3--	-	3.06	2.14
2009 Charltt AAA		16	0	0	5	24.1	94	19	9	9	3	0	2	1	5	0	22	2	1	2	0	1.000	0	1--	-	2.58	3.33
2009 CWS	AL	7	0	0	4	5.2	29	10	6	6	1	0	0	2	2	0	3	2	0	0	0	-	0	0-0	0	9.12	9.53

Leo Nunez

Pitches: R Bats: R Pos: RP-75   Ht: 6'2" Wt: 182 Born: 8/14/1983 Age: 26

Year Team	Lg	G	GS	CG	GF	IP	BFP	H	R	ER	HR	SH	SF	HB	TBB	IBB	SO	WP	Bk	W	L	Pct	Sh	Sv-Op	Hld	ERC	ERA
2005 KC	AL	41	0	0	10	53.2	246	73	45	45	9	1	2	3	18	2	32	1	0	3	2	.600	0	0-1	2	6.76	7.55
2006 KC	AL	7	0	0	5	13.1	58	15	7	7	2	0	1	2	5	0	7	0	0	0	0	-	0	0-0	0	5.98	4.73
2007 KC	AL	13	6	0	2	43.2	182	44	21	19	8	0	2	0	10	0	37	1	0	2	4	.333	0	0-0	1	3.98	3.92
2008 KC	AL	45	0	0	12	48.1	205	45	19	16	2	3	2	4	15	2	26	3	0	4	1	.800	0	0-3	7	3.20	2.98
2009 Fla	NL	75	0	0	41	68.2	293	59	33	31	13	4	2	4	27	5	60	1	1	4	6	.400	0	26-33	14	3.96	4.06
5 ML YEARS		181	6	0	70	227.2	984	236	125	118	34	8	9	13	75	9	162	6	1	13	13	.500	0	26-37	24	4.53	4.66

Vladimir Nunez

Pitches: R Bats: R Pos: RP-1   Ht: 6'4" Wt: 240 Born: 3/15/1975 Age: 35

Year Team	Lg	G	GS	CG	GF	IP	BFP	H	R	ER	HR	SH	SF	HB	TBB	IBB	SO	WP	Bk	W	L	Pct	Sh	Sv-Op	Hld	ERC	ERA
2009 Gwnntt* AAA		45	2	0	13	83.1	354	69	23	20	7	7	3	3	37	0	79	0	0	3	2	.600	0	5--	-	3.32	2.16
1998 Ari	NL	4	0	0	2	5.1	25	7	6	6	0	0	1	0	2	0	2	0	0	0	0	-	0	0-0	0	4.87	10.13
1999 2 Tms	NL	44	12	0	12	108.2	463	95	63	49	11	7	6	4	54	6	86	8	1	7	10	.412	0	1-3	4	3.88	4.06
2000 Fla	NL	17	12	0	0	68.1	322	88	63	60	12	5	5	2	34	2	45	5	0	0	6	.000	0	0-0	1	6.88	7.90
2001 Fla	NL	52	3	0	13	92.0	380	79	33	28	9	2	5	5	30	5	64	1	1	4	5	.444	0	0-1	4	3.17	2.74
2002 Fla	NL	77	0	0	43	97.2	404	80	38	37	8	6	4	0	37	1	73	2	0	6	5	.545	0	20-28	11	2.88	3.41
2003 Fla	NL	14	0	0	4	10.2	63	21	21	19	7	1	2	0	7	0	10	0	0	0	3	.000	0	0-3	2	16.12	16.03
2004 Col	NL	22	0	0	6	25.2	114	26	22	20	6	1	5	1	14	0	22	4	0	3	3	.500	0	0-3	3	6.01	7.01
2008 Atl	NL	23	0	0	7	32.2	146	32	14	14	0	0	3	1	19	5	24	2	0	1	2	.333	0	0-0	0	3.77	3.86
2009 Atl	NL	1	0	0	1	1.0	7	2	4	4	2	0	0	0	2	0	1	0	0	0	0	-	0	0-0	0	41.82	36.00
99 Ari	NL	27	0	0	11	34.0	146	29	15	11	2	2	3	1	20	5	28	3	0	3	2	.600	0	1-2	3	3.63	2.91
99 Fla	NL	17	12	0	1	74.2	317	66	48	38	9	5	3	3	34	1	58	5	1	4	8	.333	0	0-1	1	3.98	4.58
9 ML YEARS		254	27	0	91	442.0	1924	430	264	237	55	22	31	13	199	19	327	22	3	21	34	.382	0	21-38	25	4.35	4.83

Darren O'Day

Pitches: R Bats: R Pos: RP-68   Ht: 6'4" Wt: 220 Born: 10/22/1982 Age: 27

Year	Team	Lg	G	GS	CG	GF	IP	BFP	H	R	ER	HR	SH	SF	HB	TBB	IBB	SO	WP	Bk	W	L	Pct	Sh	Sv-Op Hld	ERC	ERA
2006	Orem	R+	14	0	0	13	14.1	60	11	5	4	1	1	0	1	5	0	15	3	0	0	1	.000	0	7- - -	2.66	2.51
2006	CRpds	A	17	0	0	6	23.1	90	20	8	7	1	1	1	1	2	0	14	2	0	3	1	.750	0	1- - -	2.05	2.70
2007	RCuca	A+	24	0	0	22	24.0	90	10	3	2	1	0	0	1	6	2	26	1	1	4	0	1.000	0	11- - -	0.87	0.75
2007	Ark	AA	29	0	0	26	29.1	126	27	13	13	3	2	1	2	14	0	22	1	0	3	4	.429	0	10- - -	4.30	3.99
2008	Salt Lk	AAA	21	0	0	16	33.0	130	29	13	12	3	1	2	1	7	0	30	0	0	2	2	.500	0	7- - -	2.87	3.27
2008	LAA	AL	30	0	0	17	43.1	194	49	24	22	2	2	1	4	14	6	29	1	0	0	1	.000	0	0-0 -	4.20	4.57
2009	2 Tms		68	0	0	15	58.2	233	41	14	12	3	1	3	5	18	1	56	1	0	2	1	.667	0	2-2 20	2.20	1.84
09	NYM	NL	4	0	0	1	3.0	17	5	2	0	0	0	1	1	1	0	2	0	0	0	0	-	0	0-0 0	7.72	0.00
09	Tex	AL	64	0	0	14	55.2	216	36	12	12	3	1	2	4	17	1	54	1	0	2	1	.667	0	2-2 20	1.95	1.94
	2 ML YEARS		98	0	0	32	102.0	427	90	38	34	5	3	4	9	32	7	85	2	0	2	2	.500	0	2-2 21	3.01	3.00

Trent Oeltjen

Bats: L Throws: L Pos: LF-11; CF-5; PR-4; RF-3; PH-2   Ht: 6'1" Wt: 190 Born: 2/28/1983 Age: 27

Year	Team	Lg	G	AB	H	2B	3B	HR	(Hm	Rd)	TB	R	RBI	RC	TBB	IBB	SO	HBP	SH	SF	SB	CS	SB%	GDP	Avg	OBP	Slg
2001	Twins	R	45	134	43	7	3	0	(-	-)	56	21	18	24	14	0	16	3	2	2	10	3	.77	2	.321	.387	.418
2001	Elizab	R+	9	30	7	1	0	0	(-	-)	8	4	4	2	0	0	6	0	1	1	2	0	1.00	0	.233	.226	.267
2002	Elizab	R+	54	215	64	7	2	3	(-	-)	84	36	18	32	16	0	34	7	3	2	7	5	.58	0	.298	.363	.391
2002	QuadC	A	10	25	6	1	0	0	(-	-)	7	4	1	2	3	0	2	0	1	0	1	0	1.00	1	.240	.321	.280
2003	QuadC	A	123	466	139	12	8	4	(-	-)	179	73	44	72	37	1	57	20	4	5	29	14	.67	3	.298	.371	.384
2004	FtMyrs	A+	90	324	90	8	5	2	(-	-)	114	45	28	42	18	2	61	12	4	2	25	8	.76	6	.278	.337	.352
2005	FtMyrs	A+	98	341	98	17	4	4	(-	-)	135	44	43	54	26	0	77	20	5	3	21	9	.70	3	.287	.369	.396
2006	NwBrit	AA	113	401	120	16	10	3	(-	-)	165	61	44	67	36	1	58	16	9	2	24	11	.69	3	.299	.378	.411
2007	Roch	AAA	97	244	58	9	5	2	(-	-)	83	33	23	26	10	1	44	13	4	0	14	7	.67	4	.238	.303	.340
2008	Tucsn	AAA	127	442	140	28	10	6	(-	-)	206	75	60	76	24	1	68	10	4	11	15	7	.68	6	.317	.357	.466
2009	Reno	AAA	114	442	134	29	14	10	(-	-)	221	78	64	81	31	3	101	10	4	1	22	8	.73	6	.303	.362	.500
2009	Ari	NL	24	70	17	4	1	3	(1	2)	32	11	4	4	1	0	13	0	1	1	3	1	.75	0	.243	.250	.457

Eric O'Flaherty

Pitches: L Bats: L Pos: RP-78   Ht: 6'2" Wt: 220 Born: 2/5/1985 Age: 25

Year	Team	Lg	G	GS	CG	GF	IP	BFP	H	R	ER	HR	SH	SF	HB	TBB	IBB	SO	WP	Bk	W	L	Pct	Sh	Sv-Op Hld	ERC	ERA
2006	Sea	AL	15	0	0	5	11.0	57	18	9	5	2	1	0	0	6	3	6	2	0	0	0	-	0	0-0 1	8.63	4.09
2007	Sea	AL	56	0	0	9	52.1	221	45	26	26	1	0	2	5	20	1	36	4	1	7	1	.875	0	0-1 4	3.04	4.47
2008	Sea	AL	7	0	0	1	6.2	42	16	15	15	2	0	1	2	4	2	4	0	0	0	1	.000	0	0-0 2	17.12	20.25
2009	Atl	NL	78	0	0	8	56.1	236	52	23	19	2	1	1	6	18	4	39	2	0	2	1	.667	0	0-2 15	3.26	3.04
	4 ML YEARS		156	0	0	23	126.1	556	131	73	65	7	2	4	13	48	10	85	8	1	9	3	.750	0	0-3 22	4.16	4.63

Tomo Ohka

Pitches: R Bats: R Pos: RP-12; SP-6   Ht: 6'1" Wt: 200 Born: 3/18/1976 Age: 34

Year	Team	Lg	G	GS	CG	GF	IP	BFP	H	R	ER	HR	SH	SF	HB	TBB	IBB	SO	WP	Bk	W	L	Pct	Sh	Sv-Op Hld	ERC	ERA
2009	Clmbs*	AAA	9	9	0	0	52.2	208	53	26	20	6	2	1	1	9	0	26	2	0	3	3	.500	0	0- - -	3.55	3.42
1999	Bos	AL	8	2	0	3	13.0	65	21	12	9	2	0	1	0	6	0	8	0	0	1	2	.333	0	0-0 0	8.56	6.23
2000	Bos	AL	13	12	0	1	69.1	297	70	25	24	7	1	2	2	26	0	40	3	0	3	6	.333	0	0-0 0	4.19	3.12
2001	2 Tms		22	21	0	1	107.0	469	134	70	65	15	2	2	3	29	0	68	2	1	3	9	.250	0	0-0 0	5.52	5.47
2002	Mon	NL	32	31	2	1	192.2	806	194	83	68	19	13	6	7	45	7	118	2	1	13	8	.619	0	0-0 0	3.55	3.18
2003	Mon	NL	34	34	2	0	199.0	864	233	106	92	24	8	3	9	45	11	118	8	0	10	12	.455	0	0-0 0	4.59	4.16
2004	Mon	NL	15	15	0	0	84.2	367	98	40	32	11	4	2	1	20	1	38	3	0	3	7	.300	0	0-0 0	4.53	3.40
2005	2 Tms	NL	32	29	1	0	180.1	774	189	88	81	22	7	4	3	55	5	98	8	0	11	9	.550	1	0-0 1	4.13	4.04
2006	Mil	NL	18	18	0	0	97.0	421	98	58	52	12	8	4	5	35	1	50	4	0	4	5	.444	0	0-0 0	4.32	4.82
2007	Tor	AL	10	10	0	0	56.0	251	68	39	36	10	1	1	0	22	1	21	2	0	2	5	.286	0	0-0 0	5.90	5.79
2009	Cle	AL	18	6	0	5	71.0	306	77	47	47	18	3	3	4	19	1	31	3	0	1	5	.167	0	0-0 0	5.33	5.96
01	Bos	AL	12	11	0	1	52.1	241	69	40	36	7	1	1	2	19	0	37	1	1	2	5	.286	0	0-0 0	6.24	6.19
01	Mon	NL	10	10	0	0	54.2	228	65	30	29	8	1	1	1	10	0	31	1	0	1	4	.200	0	0-0 0	4.83	4.77
05	Was	NL	10	9	0	0	54.0	231	44	23	20	6	6	1	1	27	1	17	3	0	4	3	.571	0	0-0 0	3.54	3.33
05	Mil	NL	22	20	1	0	126.1	543	145	65	61	16	1	3	2	28	4	81	5	0	7	6	.538	1	0-0 1	4.39	4.35
	10 ML YEARS		202	178	5	11	1070.0	4620	1182	568	506	140	47	28	34	302	27	590	35	2	51	68	.429	1	0-0 1	4.51	4.26

Ross Ohlendorf

Pitches: R Bats: R Pos: SP-29   Ht: 6'4" Wt: 235 Born: 8/8/1982 Age: 27

Year	Team	Lg	G	GS	CG	GF	IP	BFP	H	R	ER	HR	SH	SF	HB	TBB	IBB	SO	WP	Bk	W	L	Pct	Sh	Sv-Op Hld	ERC	ERA
2007	NYY	AL	6	0	0	3	6.1	26	5	2	2	1	0	0	0	2	0	9	0	0	0	0	-	0	0-0 1	2.94	2.84
2008	2 Tms		30	5	0	3	62.2	300	86	49	45	10	1	1	1	31	3	49	10	1	1	4	.200	0	0-0 4	7.16	6.46
2009	Pit	NL	29	29	0	0	176.2	725	165	80	77	25	11	8	7	53	1	109	2	1	11	10	.524	0	0-0 0	3.84	3.92
08	NYY	AL	25	0	0	3	40.0	187	50	31	29	7	0	0	1	19	3	36	6	0	1	1	.500	0	0-0 4	6.39	6.53
08	Pit	NL	5	5	0	0	22.2	113	36	18	16	3	1	1	0	12	0	13	4	1	0	3	.000	0	0-0 0	8.59	6.35
	Postseason		1	0	0	0	1.0	9	4	3	3	1	0	0	1	1	0	0	0	0	0	0	-	0	0-0 0	47.63	27.00
	3 ML YEARS		65	34	0	6	245.2	1051	256	131	124	36	12	9	8	86	4	167	12	2	12	14	.462	0	0-0 5	4.62	4.54

Will Ohman

Pitches: L **Bats:** L **Pos:** RP-21   **Ht:** 6'2" **Wt:** 210 **Born:** 8/13/1977 **Age:** 32

		HOW MUCH HE PITCHED						WHAT HE GAVE UP											THE RESULTS						
Year Team	Lg	G	GS	CG	GF	IP	BFP	H	R	ER	HR	SH	SF	HB	TBB	IBB	SO	WP	Bk	W	L	Pct	Sh	Sv-Op Hld	ERC	ERA
2009 InldEm*	A+	3	1	0	0	2.2	14	5	4	4	0	1	0	0	1	0	2	0	0	0	0	-	0	0- - -	8.33	13.50
2009 Albq*	AAA	8	1	0	1	7.2	28	3	1	1	1	0	0	0	3	0	9	0	0	0	0	-	0	0- - -	1.41	1.17
2000 ChC	NL	6	0	0	2	3.1	17	4	3	3	0	0	0	0	4	1	2	1	0	1	0	1.000	0	0-0 1	7.25	8.10
2001 ChC	NL	11	0	0	0	11.2	54	14	10	10	2	0	0	0	6	0	12	2	0	0	1	.000	0	0-0 1	6.26	7.71
2005 ChC	NL	69	0	0	13	43.1	187	32	14	14	6	1	0	3	24	3	45	6	1	2	2	.500	0	0-3 13	3.62	2.91
2006 ChC	NL	78	0	0	14	65.1	286	51	30	30	6	0	2	5	34	2	74	4	0	1	1	.500	0	0-0 9	3.44	4.13
2007 ChC	NL	56	0	0	11	36.1	168	42	20	20	3	2	0	1	16	4	33	2	0	2	4	.333	0	1-1 12	4.79	4.95
2008 Atl	NL	83	0	0	16	58.2	248	51	27	24	3	3	0	1	22	4	53	2	0	4	1	.800	0	1-4 23	2.87	3.68
2009 LAD	NL	21	0	0	5	12.1	54	12	8	8	4	0	0	0	8	1	7	0	0	1	0	1.000	0	1-2 4	6.76	5.84
7 ML YEARS		324	0	0	61	231.0	1014	206	112	109	24	6	2	10	114	15	226	17	1	11	9	.550	0	3-10 63	3.87	4.25

Saburo Ohmura

Bats: R **Throws:** R **Pos:** OF   **Ht:** 5'11" **Wt:** 187 **Born:** 6/1/1974 **Age:** 36

		BATTING																	BASERUNNING				AVERAGES		
Year Team	Lg	G	AB	H	2B	3B	HR	(Hm | Rd)	TB	R	RBI	RC	TBB	IBB	SO	HBP	SH	SF	SB	CS	SB%	GDP	Avg	OBP	Slg
1995 Chiba	Jap	28	48	9	2	0	0	(- | -)	11	4	2	3	11	-	17	0	1	1	3	4	.43	0	.188	.333	.229
1996 Chiba	Jap	9	1	1	0	0	0	(- | -)	1	1	0	0	0	-	0	0	0	0	0	0	-	0	1.000	1.000	1.000
1997 Chiba	Jap	33	32	5	2	0	0	(- | -)	7	2	1	1	2	-	8	0	2	0	1	0	1.00	0	.156	.206	.219
1998 Chiba	Jap	2	1	0	0	0	0	(- | -)	0	0	0	0	0	-	1	0	0	0	0	0	-	0	.000	.000	.000
1999 Chiba	Jap	108	130	30	9	0	0	(- | -)	39	26	8	11	12	-	27	2	12	0	1	5	.17	0	.231	.306	.300
2000 Chiba	Jap	95	263	71	13	1	5	(- | -)	101	42	23	40	35	-	41	0	15	1	8	2	.80	4	.270	.355	.384
2001 Chiba	Jap	108	240	55	12	1	1	(- | -)	72	37	25	22	23	-	45	1	17	3	9	7	.56	8	.229	.296	.300
2002 Chiba	Jap	131	441	126	33	2	9	(- | -)	190	87	43	71	36	0	93	9	6	13	13	1	.93	4	.286	.343	.431
2003 Chiba	Jap	80	286	78	23	1	10	(- | -)	133	44	46	45	24	1	66	6	13	4	4	7	.36	2	.273	.338	.466
2004 Chiba	Jap	89	258	66	16	3	5	(- | -)	103	31	33	36	26	0	64	1	5	2	12	10	.50	12	.256	.331	.399
2005 Chiba	Jap	107	351	110	19	6	14	(| -)	183	68	50	60	30	0	77	1	2	2	0	3	.07	6	.313	.380	.521
2006 Chiba	Jap	115	298	65	13	1	9	(- | -)	107	38	38	34	34	0	84	2	2	8	6	2	.75	6	.218	.295	.359
2007 Chiba	Jap	133	472	127	28	4	7	(- | -)	184	67	68	65	43	1	105	4	3	6	13	5	.72	5	.269	.331	.390
2008 Chiba	Jap	105	346	100	22	2	6	(- | -)	144	43	56	55	36	1	70	4	0	4	5	0	1.00	5	.289	.359	.416
2009 Chiba	Jap	119	427	134	24	2	22	(- | -)	228	71	68	84	48	2	121	1	7	9	4	7	.36	7	.314	.377	.534

Augie Ojeda

Bats: B **Throws:** R **Pos:** 2B-35; SS-34; 3B-28; PH-16; PR-2   **Ht:** 5'9" **Wt:** 174 **Born:** 12/20/1974 **Age:** 35

		BATTING																	BASERUNNING				AVERAGES		
Year Team	Lg	G	AB	H	2B	3B	HR	(Hm | Rd)	TB	R	RBI	RC	TBB	IBB	SO	HBP	SH	SF	SB	CS	SB%	GDP	Avg	OBP	Slg
2000 ChC	NL	28	77	17	3	1	2	(1 | 1)	20	10	8	9	10	1	9	0	1	1	0	1	.00	1	.221	.307	.364
2001 ChC	NL	78	144	29	5	1	1	(1 | 0)	39	16	12	10	12	1	20	2	2	2	1	0	1.00	2	.201	.269	.271
2002 ChC	NL	30	70	13	4	0	0	(0 | 0)	17	4	4	4	5	0	5	1	4	1	1	0	1.00	2	.186	.247	.243
2003 ChC	NL	12	25	3	0	0	0	(0 | 0)	3	2	0	0	1	1	5	1	0	0	0	0	-	1	.120	.185	.120
2004 Min	AL	30	59	20	1	0	2	(0 | 2)	27	16	7	11	10	0	3	0	2	1	1	1	.50	0	.339	.429	.458
2007 Ari	NL	57	113	31	2	2	1	(0 | 1)	40	16	12	16	16	3	13	0	2	2	1	0	1.00	1	.274	.354	.354
2008 Ari	NL	105	231	56	9	2	0	(0 | 0)	69	27	17	27	26	2	24	10	4	1	0	0	-	6	.242	.343	.299
2009 Ari	NL	103	264	65	17	3	1	(1 | 0)	91	38	16	29	32	3	28	6	6	1	3	1	.75	4	.246	.340	.345
Postseason		7	21	8	1	0	0	(0 | 0)	7	1	1	2	1	0	3	1	0	0	0	0	-	3	.286	.348	.333
8 ML YEARS		443	983	234	41	9	7	(3 | 4)	314	129	76	106	111	11	107	20	21	9	7	3	.70	17	.238	.325	.319

Hideki Okajima

Pitches: L **Bats:** L **Pos:** RP-68   **Ht:** 6'1" **Wt:** 194 **Born:** 12/25/1975 **Age:** 34

		HOW MUCH HE PITCHED						WHAT HE GAVE UP											THE RESULTS						
Year Team	Lg	G	GS	CG	GF	IP	BFP	H	R	ER	HR	SH	SF	HB	TBB	IBB	SO	WP	Bk	W	L	Pct	Sh	Sv-Op Hld	ERC	ERA
2007 Bos	AL	66	0	0	13	69.0	272	50	17	17	6	5	1	1	17	2	63	0	0	3	2	.600	0	5-7 27	2.03	2.22
2008 Bos	AL	64	0	0	11	62.0	258	49	18	18	6	0	3	1	23	1	60	2	0	3	2	.600	0	1-9 23	2.82	2.61
2009 Bos	AL	68	0	0	6	61.0	258	56	23	23	8	3	1	2	21	3	53	0	0	6	0	1.000	0	0-2 23	3.65	3.39
Postseason		16	0	0	1	21.0	81	13	5	5	2	0	0	0	5	1	16	0	0	0	0	-	0	0-0 8	1.55	2.14
3 ML YEARS		198	0	0	30	192.0	788	155	58	58	20	8	5	4	61	6	176	2	0	12	4	.750	0	6-18 73	2.78	2.72

Darren Oliver

Pitches: L **Bats:** R **Pos:** RP-62; SP-1   **Ht:** 6'2" **Wt:** 200 **Born:** 10/6/1970 **Age:** 39

		HOW MUCH HE PITCHED						WHAT HE GAVE UP											THE RESULTS						
Year Team	Lg	G	GS	CG	GF	IP	BFP	H	R	ER	HR	SH	SF	HB	TBB	IBB	SO	WP	Bk	W	L	Pct	Sh	Sv-Op Hld	ERC	ERA
1993 Tex	AL	2	0	0	0	3.1	14	2	1	1	1	0	0	0	1	1	4	0	0	0	0	-	0	0-0 0	2.15	2.70
1994 Tex	AL	43	0	0	10	50.0	226	40	24	19	4	6	0	6	35	4	50	2	2	4	0	1.000	0	2-3 9	4.29	3.42
1995 Tex	AL	17	7	0	2	49.0	222	47	25	23	3	5	1	1	32	1	39	4	0	4	2	.667	0	0-0 0	4.59	4.22
1996 Tex	AL	30	30	1	0	173.2	777	190	97	90	20	2	7	10	76	3	112	5	1	14	6	.700	1	0-0 0	5.10	4.66
1997 Tex	AL	32	32	3	0	201.1	887	213	111	94	29	2	5	11	82	3	104	7	0	13	12	.520	1	0-0 0	4.98	4.20
1998 2 Tms		29	29	2	0	160.1	749	204	115	102	18	8	8	10	66	2	87	7	4	10	11	.476	1	0-0 0	6.01	5.73
1999 StL	NL	30	30	2	0	196.1	842	197	96	93	16	11	4	11	74	4	119	6	2	9	9	.500	1	0-0 0	4.11	4.26
2000 Tex	AL	21	21	0	0	108.0	501	151	95	89	16	5	4	4	42	3	49	4	1	2	9	.182	0	0-0 0	7.04	7.42
2001 Tex	AL	28	28	1	0	154.0	696	189	109	103	23	1	5	6	65	0	104	8	2	11	11	.500	0	0-0 0	6.14	6.02
2002 Bos	AL	14	9	1	0	58.0	258	70	30	30	7	1	3	6	27	0	32	1	0	4	5	.444	1	0-0 0	6.49	4.66
2003 Col	NL	33	32	1	0	180.1	786	201	108	101	21	4	5	8	61	3	88	0	0	13	11	.542	0	0-0 0	4.80	5.04
2004 2 Tms	NL	27	10	0	5	72.2	314	87	50	48	14	4	3	1	21	1	46	1	0	3	3	.500	0	0-0 0	5.59	5.94
2006 NYM	NL	45	0	0	10	81.0	333	70	33	31	13	2	4	3	21	2	60	1	0	4	1	.800	0	0-0 3	3.27	3.44
2007 LAA	AL	61	0	0	20	64.1	273	58	31	27	5	2	4	1	23	2	51	1	1	3	1	.750	0	0-0 8	3.19	3.78

Year	Team	Lg	G	GS	CG	GF	IP	BFP	H	R	ER	HR	SH	SF	HB	TBB	IBB	SO	WP	Bk	W	L	Pct	Sh	Sv-Op	Hld	ERC	ERA
							HOW MUCH HE PITCHED				WHAT HE GAVE UP													THE RESULTS				
2008	LAA	AL	54	0	0	9	72.0	291	67	24	23	5	4	3	4	16	2	48	3	0	7	1	.875	0	0-2	12	3.07	2.88
2009	LAA	AL	63	1	0	9	73.0	293	61	22	22	5	4	5	5	22	8	65	7	0	5	1	.833	0	0-1	20	2.81	2.71
98	Tex	AL	19	19	2	0	103.1	493	140	84	75	11	3	6	10	43	1	58	6	1	6	7	.462	0	0-0	0	6.68	6.53
98	StL	NL	10	10	0	0	57.0	256	64	31	27	7	5	2	0	23	1	29	1	3	4	4	.500	0	0-0	0	4.85	4.26
04	Fla	NL	18	8	0	3	58.2	260	75	44	42	13	4	3	1	17	1	33	1	0	2	3	.400	0	0-0	0	6.30	6.44
04	Hou	NL	9	2	0	2	14.0	54	12	6	6	1	0	0	0	4	0	13	0	0	1	0	1.000	0	0-0	0	2.89	3.86
Postseason			6	1	0	0	17.1	66	14	8	8	2	2	0	1	4	0	7	1	0	0	1	.000	0	0-0	0	2.93	4.15
16 ML YEARS			529	229	11	65	1697.1	7462	1847	971	896	200	61	61	87	664	39	1058	57	13	106	83	.561	4	2-6	52	4.89	4.75

Miguel Olivo

Bats: R Throws: R Pos: C-103; DH-10; PH-4   Ht: 6'0" Wt: 229 Born: 7/15/1978 Age: 31

Year	Team	Lg	G	AB	H	2B	3B	HR	(Hm	Rd)	TB	R	RBI	RC	TBB	IBB	SO	HBP	SH	SF	SB	CS	SB%	GDP	Avg	OBP	Slg
2002	CWS	AL	6	19	4	1	0	1	(0	1)	8	2	5	4	2	0	5	0	0	0	0	0	-	1	.211	.286	.421
2003	CWS	AL	114	317	75	19	1	6	(4	2)	114	37	27	32	19	0	80	4	4	2	6	4	.60	3	.237	.287	.360
2004	2 Tms	AL	96	301	70	15	4	13	(8	5)	132	46	40	33	20	2	84	3	4	1	7	6	.54	4	.233	.286	.439
2005	2 Tms		91	267	58	11	1	9	(5	4)	98	30	34	23	8	2	80	3	1	2	7	2	.78	7	.217	.246	.367
2006	Fla	NL	127	430	113	22	3	16	(7	9)	189	52	58	49	9	4	103	7	3	3	2	3	.40	9	.263	.287	.440
2007	Fla	NL	122	452	107	20	4	16	(11	5)	183	43	60	43	14	2	123	2	0	1	3	2	.60	13	.237	.262	.405
2008	KC	AL	84	306	78	22	0	12	(3	9)	136	29	41	35	7	2	82	3	0	1	7	0	1.00	6	.255	.278	.444
2009	KC	AL	114	390	97	15	5	23	(10	13)	191	51	65	47	19	0	126	5	1	1	5	2	.71	10	.249	.292	.490
04	Fla	AL	46	141	38	7	2	7	(4	3)	70	21	26	21	10	1	29	0	4	1	5	4	.56	2	.270	.316	.496
04	Sea	AL	50	160	32	8	2	6	(4	2)	62	25	14	12	10	1	55	3	0	0	2	2	.50	2	.200	.260	.388
05	Sea	AL	54	152	23	4	0	5	(4	1)	42	14	18	6	4	0	49	0	0	1	1	1	.50	3	.151	.172	.276
05	SD	NL	37	115	35	7	1	4	(1	3)	56	16	16	17	4	2	31	3	1	1	6	1	.86	4	.304	.341	.487
Postseason			1	1	0	0	0	0	(0	0)	0	0	0	0	0	0	0	0	0	0	0	0	-	0	1.000	1.000	1.000
8 ML YEARS			754	2482	602	125	18	96	(48	48)	1051	290	330	266	98	12	683	27	13	11	37	19	.66	53	.243	.278	.423

Scott Olsen

Pitches: L Bats: L Pos: SP-11   Ht: 6'4" Wt: 211 Born: 1/12/1984 Age: 26

Year	Team	Lg	G	GS	CG	GF	IP	BFP	H	R	ER	HR	SH	SF	HB	TBB	IBB	SO	WP	Bk	W	L	Pct	Sh	Sv-Op	Hld	ERC	ERA
2009	Ptomc*	A+	1	1	0	0	3.0	11	3	0	0	0	0	0	0	0	0	4	0	0	0	0	-	0	0--	-	2.18	0.00
2009	Syrcse*	AAA	3	3	0	0	12.2	62	19	9	8	2	0	1	0	6	1	9	1	0	1	0	1.000	0	0--	-	7.72	5.68
2005	Fla	NL	5	4	0	0	20.1	91	21	13	9	5	0	0	0	10	0	21	1	0	1	1	.500	0	0-0	0	5.66	3.98
2006	Fla	NL	31	31	0	0	180.2	761	160	94	81	23	7	2	7	75	1	166	8	0	12	10	.545	0	0-0	0	3.88	4.04
2007	Fla	NL	33	33	0	0	176.2	826	226	134	114	29	14	8	1	85	4	133	8	0	10	15	.400	0	0-0	0	6.54	5.81
2008	Fla	NL	33	33	0	0	201.2	855	195	106	94	30	7	4	3	69	13	113	5	0	8	11	.421	0	0-0	0	3.96	4.20
2009	Was	NL	11	11	0	0	62.2	289	83	45	42	11	4	1	0	25	2	42	2	0	2	4	.333	0	0-0	0	6.55	6.03
5 ML YEARS			113	112	0	0	642.0	2822	685	392	340	98	32	15	11	264	20	475	24	0	33	41	.446	0	0-0	0	4.91	4.77

Garrett Olson

Pitches: L Bats: R Pos: RP-20; SP-11   Ht: 6'1" Wt: 205 Born: 10/18/1983 Age: 26

Year	Team	Lg	G	GS	CG	GF	IP	BFP	H	R	ER	HR	SH	SF	HB	TBB	IBB	SO	WP	Bk	W	L	Pct	Sh	Sv-Op	Hld	ERC	ERA
2009	Tacom*	AAA	9	9	0	0	47.1	200	38	26	26	2	1	1	4	23	0	38	2	0	2	3	.400	0	0--	-	3.30	4.94
2007	Bal	AL	7	7	0	0	32.1	162	42	28	28	4	0	3	2	28	1	28	1	1	1	3	.250	0	0-0	0	8.46	7.79
2008	Bal	AL	26	26	0	0	132.2	621	168	100	98	17	4	4	8	62	1	83	6	0	9	10	.474	0	0-0	0	6.40	6.65
2009	Sea	AL	31	11	0	5	80.1	347	79	52	50	19	1	2	4	34	0	47	2	0	3	5	.375	0	0-0	5	5.33	5.60
3 ML YEARS			64	44	0	5	245.1	1130	289	180	176	40	5	9	14	124	2	158	9	1	13	18	.419	0	0-0	5	6.33	6.46

Magglio Ordonez

Bats: R Throws: R Pos: RF-104; DH-24; PH-8   Ht: 6'0" Wt: 215 Born: 1/28/1974 Age: 36

Year	Team	Lg	G	AB	H	2B	3B	HR	(Hm	Rd)	TB	R	RBI	RC	TBB	IBB	SO	HBP	SH	SF	SB	CS	SB%	GDP	Avg	OBP	Slg
1997	CWS	AL	21	69	22	6	0	4	(2	2)	40	12	11	12	2	0	8	0	1	0	1	2	.33	1	.319	.338	.580
1998	CWS	AL	145	535	151	25	2	14	(8	6)	222	70	65	67	28	1	53	9	2	4	9	7	.56	19	.282	.326	.415
1999	CWS	AL	157	624	188	34	3	30	(16	14)	318	100	117	102	47	4	64	1	0	5	13	6	.68	24	.301	.349	.510
2000	CWS	AL	153	588	185	34	3	32	(21	11)	321	102	126	112	60	3	64	2	0	15	18	4	.82	28	.315	.371	.546
2001	CWS	AL	160	593	181	40	1	31	(17	14)	316	97	113	117	70	7	70	5	0	3	25	7	.78	14	.305	.382	.533
2002	CWS	AL	153	590	189	47	1	38	(24	14)	352	116	135	119	53	2	77	7	0	3	7	5	.58	21	.320	.381	.597
2003	CWS	AL	160	606	192	46	3	29	(17	12)	331	95	99	109	57	1	73	7	0	4	9	5	.64	20	.317	.380	.546
2004	CWS	AL	52	202	59	8	2	9	(4	5)	98	32	37	39	16	2	22	3	0	1	0	2	.00	4	.292	.351	.485
2005	Det	AL	82	305	92	17	0	8	(2	6)	133	38	46	51	30	1	35	1	0	7	0	0	-	8	.302	.359	.436
2006	Det	AL	155	593	177	32	1	24	(8	16)	283	82	104	97	45	3	87	4	0	4	1	4	.20	13	.298	.350	.477
2007	Det	AL	157	595	216	54	0	28	(17	11)	354	117	139	146	76	8	79	2	0	5	4	1	.80	20	.363	.434	.595
2008	Det	AL	146	561	178	32	2	21	(13	8)	277	72	103	92	53	2	76	3	0	6	1	5	.17	27	.317	.376	.494
2009	Det	AL	131	465	144	24	2	9	(3	6)	199	54	50	69	51	2	65	0	0	2	3	1	.75	19	.310	.376	.428
Postseason			16	62	12	1	1	3	(3	0)	24	8	9	4	6	0	10	0	0	0	1	1	.50	3	.194	.265	.387
13 ML YEARS			1672	6326	1974	399	20	277	(155	122)	3244	987	1145	1132	588	36	773	44	3	59	91	49	.65	218	.312	.371	.513

Pete Orr

Bats: L Throws: R Pos: 2B-18; PH-8; 3B-4; RF-1   Ht: 6'1" Wt: 194 Born: 6/8/1979 Age: 31

								BATTING											BASERUNNING				AVERAGES		
Year	Team	Lg	G	AB	H	2B	3B	HR	(Hm | Rd)	TB	R	RBI	RC	TBB	IBB	SO	HBP	SH	SF	SB	CS	SB%	GDP	Avg	OBP	Slg
2009	Syrcse*	AAA	120	412	101	13	5	9	(- | -)	151	50	50	49	27	3	77	11	8	6	18	8	.69	3	.245	.305	.367
2005	Atl	NL	112	150	45	8	1	1	(0 | 1)	58	32	8	18	6	0	23	1	5	0	7	1	.88	2	.300	.331	.387
2006	Atl	NL	102	154	39	3	4	1	(1 | 0)	53	22	8	16	5	1	30	0	5	0	2	4	.33	1	.253	.277	.344
2007	Atl	NL	57	65	13	1	0	0	(0 | 0)	14	11	2	3	3	0	14	0	1	0	1	0	1.00	1	.200	.235	.215
2008	Was	NL	49	75	19	2	1	0	(0 | 0)	23	10	7	6	2	0	16	1	1	0	1	0	1.00	0	.253	.282	.307
2009	Was	NL	27	75	19	2	1	1	(0 | 1)	26	5	10	8	3	0	15	0	0	3	2	1	.67	0	.253	.272	.347
	Postseason		3	2	0	0	0	0	(0 | 0)	0	0	0	0	0	0	0	0	0	0	0	0	-	0	.000	.000	.000
	5 ML YEARS		347	519	135	16	7	3	(1 | 2)	174	80	35	51	19	1	98	2	12	3	13	6	.68	4	.260	.287	.335

Anthony Ortega

Pitches: R Bats: R Pos: SP-3   Ht: 6'0" Wt: 210 Born: 8/24/1985 Age: 24

			HOW MUCH HE PITCHED						WHAT HE GAVE UP												THE RESULTS					
Year	Team	Lg	G	GS	CG	GF	IP	BFP	H	R	ER	HR	SH	SF	HB	TBB	IBB	SO	WP	Bk	W	L	Pct	Sh	Sv-Op	Hld	ERC	ERA
2006	RCuca	A+	5	1	0	3	8.2	37	9	6	2	0	0	0	0	5	0	5	0	0	0	1	.000	0	1--	-	4.49	2.08
2006	Orem	R+	2	2	0	0	11.1	41	6	3	1	0	1	0	1	2	0	11	1	0	1	1	.500	0	0--	-	1.10	0.79
2006	CRpds	A	12	12	0	0	66.1	287	71	36	31	5	2	2	2	27	0	55	11	0	1	6	.143	0	0--	-	4.53	4.21
2007	RCuca	A+	28	28	1	0	163.1	703	157	84	73	17	7	5	5	68	2	127	8	2	7	11	.389	1	0--	-	4.07	4.02
2008	Ark	AA	22	22	1	0	135.0	569	124	65	56	11	8	3	7	49	0	83	9	1	9	7	.563	1	0--	-	3.59	3.73
2008	Salt Lk	AAA	6	6	0	0	39.1	173	45	14	11	2	1	0	3	6	0	22	2	1	5	0	1.000	0	0--	-	3.74	2.52
2009	Salt Lk	AAA	4	4	0	0	18.2	89	30	21	20	5	0	0	1	6	0	5	0	0	2	1	.667	0	0--	-	9.39	9.64
2009	LAA	AL	3	3	0	0	12.2	62	19	15	13	4	1	0	0	6	0	7	0	0	0	2	.000	0	0-0	0	9.28	9.24

David Ortiz

Bats: L Throws: L Pos: DH-139; 1B-6; PH-6   Ht: 6'4" Wt: 230 Born: 11/18/1975 Age: 34

								BATTING											BASERUNNING				AVERAGES		
Year	Team	Lg	G	AB	H	2B	3B	HR	(Hm	Rd)	TB	R	RBI	RC	TBB	IBB	SO	HBP	SH	SF	SB	CS	SB%	GDP	Avg	OBP	Slg
1997	Min	AL	15	49	16	3	0	1	(0	1)	22	10	6	7	2	0	19	0	0	0	0	0	-	1	.327	.353	.449
1998	Min	AL	86	278	77	20	0	9	(2	7)	124	47	46	46	39	3	72	5	0	4	1	0	1.00	6	.277	.371	.446
1999	Min	Al	10	20	0	0	0	0	(0	0)	0	1	0	0	5	0	12	0	0	0	0	0	-	2	.000	.200	.000
2000	Min	AL	130	415	117	36	1	10	(7	3)	185	59	63	66	57	2	81	0	0	6	1	0	1.00	13	.282	.364	.446
2001	Min	AL	89	303	71	17	1	18	(6	12)	144	46	48	46	40	8	68	1	1	2	1	0	1.00	6	.234	.324	.475
2002	Min	Al	125	412	112	32	1	20	(5	15)	206	52	75	62	43	0	87	3	0	8	1	2	.33	5	.272	.339	.500
2003	Bos	AL	128	448	129	39	2	31	(17	14)	265	79	101	80	58	8	83	1	0	2	0	0	-	9	.288	.369	.592
2004	Bos	AL	150	582	175	47	3	41	(17	24)	351	94	139	127	75	8	133	4	0	8	0	0	-	12	.301	.380	.603
2005	Bos	AL	159	601	180	40	1	47	(20	27)	363	119	148	137	102	9	124	1	0	9	1	0	1.00	13	.300	.397	.604
2006	Bos	AL	151	558	160	29	2	54	(22	32)	355	115	137	129	119	23	117	4	0	5	1	0	1.00	12	.287	.413	.636
2007	Bos	AL	149	549	182	52	1	35	(16	19)	341	116	117	138	111	12	103	4	0	3	3	1	.75	16	.332	.445	.621
2008	Bos	AL	109	416	110	30	1	23	(12	11)	211	74	89	82	70	12	74	1	1	3	1	0	1.00	11	.264	.369	.507
2009	Bos	AL	150	541	129	35	1	28	(18	10)	250	77	99	79	74	5	134	5	0	7	0	2	.00	9	.238	.332	.462
	Postseason		63	232	68	18	2	12	(7	5)	126	39	47	51	41	7	60	2	0	2	0	1	.00	3	.293	.401	.543
	13 ML YEARS		1451	5172	1458	380	14	317	(142	175)	2817	889	1068	999	795	90	1107	29	2	57	10	5	.67	117	.282	.377	.545

Russ Ortiz

Pitches: R Bats: R Pos: SP-13; RP-10   Ht: 6'1" Wt: 219 Born: 6/5/1974 Age: 36

			HOW MUCH HE PITCHED						WHAT HE GAVE UP												THE RESULTS					
Year	Team	Lg	G	GS	CG	GF	IP	BFP	H	R	ER	HR	SH	SF	HB	TBB	IBB	SO	WP	Bk	W	L	Pct	Sh	Sv-Op	Hld	ERC	ERA
2009	S-WB*	AAA	3	3	0	0	17.0	74	14	4	3	1	0	0	0	8	0	12	2	1	2	1	.667	0	0--	-	2.99	1.59
2009	ColSpr*	AAA	3	2	0	0	14.0	68	18	12	11	2	1	0	0	10	0	9	1	0	0	1	.000	0	0--	-	7.54	7.07
1998	SF	NL	22	13	0	3	88.1	394	90	51	49	11	5	4	4	46	1	75	3	0	4	4	.500	0	0-0	1	5.05	4.99
1999	SF	NL	33	33	3	0	207.2	922	189	100	88	24	11	6	6	125	5	164	13	0	18	9	.667	0	0-0	0	4.56	3.81
2000	SF	NL	33	32	0	0	195.2	871	192	117	109	28	11	6	7	112	1	167	8	0	14	12	.538	0	0-0	0	5.17	5.01
2001	SF	NL	33	33	1	0	218.2	911	187	90	80	13	10	4	0	91	3	169	8	1	17	9	.654	1	0-0	0	3.08	3.29
2002	SF	NL	33	33	2	0	214.1	911	191	89	86	15	15	6	6	94	5	137	5	0	14	10	.583	0	0-0	0	3.46	3.61
2003	Atl	NL	34	34	1	0	212.1	912	177	101	90	17	6	7	4	102	7	149	5	0	21	7	.750	1	0-0	0	3.32	3.81
2004	Atl	NL	34	34	2	0	204.2	896	197	98	94	23	10	7	3	112	7	143	4	1	15	9	.625	1	0-0	0	4.60	4.13
2005	Ari	NL	22	22	0	0	115.0	551	147	92	88	18	5	8	4	65	3	46	5	0	5	11	.313	0	0-0	0	6.96	6.89
2006	2 Tms		26	11	0	5	63.0	303	86	60	57	18	1	1	3	40	1	44	2	0	0	8	.000	0	0-0	0	9.39	8.14
2007	3F	NL	12	8	0	1	49.0	223	57	32	30	4	3	1	6	20	1	27	0	0	2	3	.400	0	0-0	0	5.42	5.51
2009	Hou	NL	23	13	0	3	85.2	387	95	56	53	8	2	4	4	48	2	65	3	0	3	6	.333	0	0-1	5	5.57	5.57
	06 Ari	NL	6	6	0	0	22.2	113	27	21	19	3	1	0	1	22	1	21	0	0	0	5	.000	0	0-0	0	8.19	7.54
	06 Bal	AL	20	5	0	5	40.1	190	59	39	38	15	0	1	2	18	0	23	2	0	0	3	.000	0	0-0	0	9.99	8.48
	Postseason		9	9	0	0	44.0	204	51	28	28	5	0	2	0	25	3	27	3	0	3	1	.750	0	0-0	0	5.65	5.73
	11 ML YEARS		305	266	9	12	1654.1	7281	1608	895	824	179	78	54	45	855	36	1186	56	2	113	88	.562	3	0-0	2	4.53	4.48

Sean O'Sullivan

Pitches: R Bats: R Pos: SP-10; RP-2   Ht: 6'2" Wt: 230 Born: 9/1/1987 Age: 22

			HOW MUCH HE PITCHED						WHAT HE GAVE UP												THE RESULTS					
Year	Team	Lg	G	GS	CG	GF	IP	BFP	H	R	ER	HR	SH	SF	HB	TBB	IBB	SO	WP	Bk	W	L	Pct	Sh	Sv-Op	Hld	ERC	ERA
2006	Orem	R+	14	14	0	0	71.1	291	65	23	17	2	2	5	5	7	0	55	2	0	4	0	1.000	0	0--	-	2.25	2.14
2007	CRpds	A	25	25	0	0	158.1	656	136	58	39	6	2	5	9	40	0	125	9	0	10	7	.588	0	0--	-	2.55	2.22
2008	RCuca	A+	28	25	0	1	158.0	692	167	94	83	8	2	6	11	50	0	111	12	0	16	8	.667	0	0--	-	3.95	4.73
2009	Ark	AA	3	3	0	0	18.2	76	21	11	11	1	2	1	0	0	0	14	0	0	1	2	.333	0	0--	-	2.89	5.30
2009	Salt Lk	AAA	14	13	1	0	69.0	301	74	42	42	9	1	3	3	20	0	48	3	0	6	4	.600	1	0--	-	4.38	5.48
2009	LAA	AL	12	10	0	1	51.2	227	60	34	34	12	2	4	1	16	1	29	1	0	4	2	.667	0	0-0	0	5.66	5.92

Roy Oswalt

Pitches: R Bats: R Pos: SP-30 **Ht: 6'0" Wt: 185 Born: 8/29/1977 Age: 32**

			HOW MUCH HE PITCHED						WHAT HE GAVE UP											THE RESULTS							
Year	Team	Lg	G	GS	CG	GF	IP	BFP	H	R	ER	HR	SH	SF	HB	TBB	IBB	SO	WP	Bk	W	L	Pct	Sh	Sv-Op	Hld	ERC	ERA
2001	Hou	NL	28	20	3	4	141.2	575	126	48	43	13	4	4	6	24	2	144	0	0	14	3	.824	1	0-0	0	2.68	2.73
2002	Hou	NL	35	34	0	0	233.0	956	215	86	78	17	12	7	5	62	4	208	3	0	19	9	.679	0	0-0	0	3.05	3.01
2003	Hou	NL	21	21	0	0	127.1	514	116	48	42	15	7	1	5	29	0	108	1	0	10	5	.667	0	0-0	0	3.26	2.97
2004	Hou	NL	36	35	2	0	237.0	983	233	100	92	17	11	4	11	62	5	206	5	1	20	10	.667	2	0-0	0	3.46	3.49
2005	Hou	NL	35	35	4	0	241.2	1002	243	85	79	18	12	7	8	48	3	184	5	1	20	12	.625	1	0-0	0	3.27	2.94
2006	Hou	NL	33	32	2	1	220.2	896	220	76	73	18	12	4	6	38	4	166	1	1	15	8	.652	0	0-0	0	3.19	**2.98**
2007	Hou	NL	33	32	1	0	212.0	910	221	80	75	14	6	4	7	60	6	154	1	1	14	7	.667	0	0-0	1	3.68	3.18
2008	Hou	NL	32	32	3	0	208.2	862	199	89	82	23	8	9	10	47	2	165	1	0	17	10	.630	2	0-0	0	3.40	3.54
2009	Hou	NL	30	30	3	0	181.1	757	183	83	83	19	12	5	8	42	4	138	4	0	8	6	.571	0	0-0	0	3.67	4.12
	Postseason		8	7	0	1	46.2	206	48	19	19	5	2	2	4	19	0	32	0	0	4	0	1.000	0	0-0	0	4.67	3.66
	9 ML YEARS		283	271	18	5	1803.1	7455	1756	695	647	154	84	45	66	412	30	1473	21	4	137	70	.662	6	0-0	1	3.31	3.23

Josh Outman

Pitches: L Bats: L Pos: SP-12; RP-2 **Ht: 6'1" Wt: 186 Born: 9/14/1984 Age: 25**

			HOW MUCH HE PITCHED						WHAT HE GAVE UP											THE RESULTS							
Year	Team	Lg	G	GS	CG	GF	IP	BFP	H	R	ER	HR	SH	SF	HB	TBB	IBB	SO	WP	Bk	W	L	Pct	Sh	Sv-Op	Hld	ERC	ERA
2005	Batvia	A-	11	4	0	0	29.1	128	23	14	9	1	1	0	2	14	0	31	3	0	2	1	.667	0	0--	-	2.91	2.76
2006	Lakwd	A	27	27	1	0	155.1	652	119	61	51	5	5	5	8	75	0	161	12	1	14	6	.700	1	0--	-	2.88	2.95
2007	Clrwtr	A+	20	18	0	0	117.1	504	104	35	32	7	2	2	5	54	0	117	4	0	10	4	.714	0	0--	-	3.57	2.45
2007	Rdng	AA	7	7	1	0	42.0	184	38	25	21	5	1	2	1	23	1	34	2	0	2	3	.400	1	0--	-	4.32	4.50
2008	Rdng	AA	33	5	0	7	70.1	310	68	27	25	3	3	3	2	37	0	66	3	0	5	4	.556	0	1--	-	4.08	3.20
2008	Mdland	AA	4	4	0	0	12.2	54	13	7	6	1	1	0	0	3	0	5	1	0	1	0	1.000	0	0--	-	3.36	4.26
2008	Scrmto	AAA	5	2	0	1	15.1	59	9	3	3	1	0	0	0	5	1	15	2	0	1	0	1.000	0	0--	-	1.54	1.76
2008	Oak	AL	6	4	0	0	25.2	116	34	14	13	1	0	2	2	8	1	19	1	0	1	2	.333	0	0-0	0	5.49	4.56
2009	Oak	AL	14	12	0	1	67.1	276	53	30	26	9	1	0	0	25	0	53	1	0	4	1	.800	0	0-0	0	3.04	3.48
	2 ML YEARS		20	16	0	1	93.0	392	87	44	39	10	1	2	2	33	1	72	2	0	5	3	.625	0	0-0	0	3.68	3.77

Lyle Overbay

Bats: L Throws: L Pos: 1B-130; PH-5; PR-2 **Ht: 6'2" Wt: 235 Born: 1/28/1977 Age: 33**

			BATTING																			BASERUNNING				AVERAGES		
Year	Team	Lg	G	AB	H	2B	3B	HR	(Hm	Rd)	TB	R	RBI	RC	TBB	IBB	SO	HBP	SH	SF	SB	CS	SB%	GDP	Avg	OBP	Slg
2001	Ari	NL	2	2	1	0	0	0	(0	0)	1	0	0	0	0	0	1	0	0	0	0	0	-	0	.500	.500	.500
2002	Ari	NL	10	10	1	0	0	0	(0	0)	1	0	1	0	0	0	5	0	0	0	0	0	-	0	.100	.100	.100
2003	Ari	NL	86	254	70	20	0	4	(2	2)	102	23	28	34	35	7	67	2	0	2	1	0	1.00	8	.276	.365	.402
2004	Mil	NL	159	579	174	53	1	16	(6	10)	277	83	87	94	81	9	128	2	0	6	2	1	.67	11	.301	.385	.478
2005	Mil	NL	158	537	148	34	1	19	(10	9)	241	80	72	84	78	8	98	2	1	4	1	0	1.00	17	.276	.367	.449
2006	Tor	AL	157	581	181	46	1	22	(17	5)	295	82	92	89	55	7	96	2	0	2	5	3	.63	19	.312	.372	.508
2007	Tor	AL	122	425	102	30	2	10	(6	4)	166	49	44	45	47	4	78	1	0	3	2	0	1.00	12	.240	.315	.391
2008	Tor	AL	158	544	147	32	2	15	(7	8)	228	74	69	73	74	3	116	3	1	5	1	2	.33	24	.270	.358	.419
2009	Tor	AL	132	423	112	35	1	16	(6	10)	197	57	64	64	74	6	95	0	0	3	0	0	-	8	.265	.372	.466
	9 ML YEARS		984	3355	936	250	8	102	(54	48)	1508	448	457	483	444	44	684	12	2	25	12	6	.67	99	.279	.363	.449

Jerry Owens

Bats: L Throws: L Pos: CF-4; PH-4; LF-3; PR-3; DH-2 **Ht: 6'3" Wt: 195 Born: 2/16/1981 Age: 29**

			BATTING																			BASERUNNING				AVERAGES		
Year	Team	Lg	G	AB	H	2B	3B	HR	(Hm	Rd)	TB	R	RBI	RC	TBB	IBB	SO	HBP	SH	SF	SB	CS	SB%	GDP	Avg	OBP	Slg
2009	Charltt*	AAA	2	7	1	0	0	0	(-	-)	1	1	2	0	1	0	3	0	0	0	0	0	-	0	.143	.250	.143
2009	Tacom*	AAA	100	390	126	10	9	3	(-	-)	163	74	37	68	44	2	48	1	6	4	23	8	.74	6	.323	.390	.418
2006	CWS	AL	12	9	3	1	0	0	(0	0)	4	4	0	1	0	0	2	0	0	0	1	0	1.00	0	.333	.333	.444
2007	CWS	AL	93	356	95	9	2	1	(1	0)	111	44	17	41	27	0	63	3	3	0	32	8	.80	5	.267	.324	.312
2008	CWS	AL	12	16	4	0	0	0	(0	0)	4	1	1	0	0	0	4	0	1	0	2	1	.67	0	.250	.250	.250
2009	CWS	AL	12	12	1	0	0	0	(0	0)	1	0	0	0	3	0	3	0	0	0	1	0	1.00	1	.083	.267	.083
	4 ML YEARS		129	393	103	10	2	1	(1	0)	120	49	18	42	30	0	72	3	4	0	36	9	.80	6	.262	.319	.305

Micah Owings

Pitches: R Bats: R Pos: SP-19; RP-7 **Ht: 6'5" Wt: 220 Born: 9/28/1982 Age: 27**

			HOW MUCH HE PITCHED						WHAT HE GAVE UP											THE RESULTS							
Year	Team	Lg	G	GS	CG	GF	IP	BFP	H	R	ER	HR	SH	SF	HB	TBB	IBB	SO	WP	Bk	W	L	Pct	Sh	Sv-Op	Hld	ERC	ERA
2009	Lsville*	AAA	2	2	0	0	10.1	44	8	1	1	1	0	0	1	7	0	5	0	0	1	0	1.000	0	0--	-	4.46	0.87
2007	Ari	NL	29	27	2	0	152.2	651	146	81	73	20	7	3	14	50	2	106	5	0	8	8	.500	1	0-0	0	4.13	4.30
2008	2 Tms	NL	22	18	0	2	104.2	466	104	73	69	14	2	4	12	41	0	87	4	0	6	9	.400	0	0-0	1	4.66	5.93
2009	Cin	NL	26	19	0	4	119.2	542	126	75	71	18	3	5	6	64	3	68	1	0	7	12	.368	0	1-1	0	5.48	5.34
	Postseason		1	1	0	0	3.2	21	6	6	2	1	0	0	1	2	0	2	0	0	0	1	.000	0	0-0	0	10.83	4.91
	3 ML YEARS		77	64	2	6	377.0	1659	376	229	213	52	12	12	32	155	5	261	10	0	21	29	.420	1	1-1	1	4.70	5.08

Jorge Padilla

Bats: R Throws: R Pos: PH-14; LF-7; RF-5; PR-4; CF-1   Ht: 6'1" Wt: 213 Born: 8/11/1979 Age: 30

Year	Team	Lg	G	AB	H	2B	3B	HR	(Hm	Rd)	TB	R	RBI	RC	TBB	IBB	SO	HBP	SH	SF	SB	CS	SB%	GDP	Avg	OBP	Slg
1998	Mrtnsvl	R+	23	90	32	3	0	5	(-	-)	50	10	25	18	4	0	24	1	0	3	2	0	1.00	3	.356	.378	.556
1999	Pmont	A	44	168	35	10	1	3	(-	-)	56	13	17	13	5	0	44	4	0	5	0	0	-	5	.208	.247	.333
1999	Batvia	A-	65	238	60	10	1	3	(-	-)	81	28	30	29	22	1	79	7	1	2	2	1	.67	3	.252	.331	.340
2000	Pmont	A	108	413	126	24	8	11	(-	-)	199	62	67	69	26	0	89	2	0	4	8	4	.67	10	.305	.346	.482
2001	Clrwtr	A+	100	358	93	13	2	16	(-	-)	158	62	66	59	40	4	73	7	0	3	23	6	.79	11	.260	.343	.441
2002	Rdng	AA	127	484	124	30	2	7	(-	-)	179	71	65	64	40	1	77	11	2	8	32	11	.74	5	.256	.322	.370
2003	Rdng	AA	46	173	51	13	1	2	(-	-)	72	21	23	26	18	1	29	1	0	1	11	8	.58	7	.295	.363	.416
2004	S-WB	AAA	117	364	92	12	0	7	(-	-)	125	51	45	48	48	2	75	7	7	3	11	7	.61	12	.253	.348	.343
2005	Clrwtr	A+	14	59	18	4	0	0	(-	-)	22	9	6	8	3	0	7	2	0	0	1	0	1.00	1	.305	.359	.373
2005	S-WB	AAA	59	204	56	6	1	1	(-	-)	67	25	17	22	15	1	41	2	5	1	4	5	.44	9	.275	.329	.328
2006	Bnghtn	AA	129	482	142	26	1	10	(-	-)	200	66	54	74	42	1	87	6	3	1	8	5	.62	15	.295	.358	.415
2007	Wichta	AA	69	247	83	13	1	10	(-	-)	128	51	49	56	32	2	40	8	2	3	11	3	.79	10	.336	.424	.518
2007	Omha	AAA	56	196	57	9	1	6	(-	-)	86	27	20	30	14	1	26	1	4	3	8	3	.73	6	.291	.336	.439
2008	Hrsbrg	AA	33	106	35	4	0	1	(-	-)	42	25	14	20	17	0	12	3	1	0	2	2	.50	4	.330	.437	.396
2008	Clmbs	AAA	81	282	88	11	1	4	(-	-)	113	38	25	45	26	0	39	8	5	1	13	9	.59	7	.312	.385	.401
2009	Syrcse	AAA	95	311	114	18	3	4	(-	-)	150	58	21	62	24	1	32	8	6	1	14	11	.56	4	.367	.424	.482
2009	Was	NL	29	25	3	0	0	0	(0	0)	3	3	0	0	1	0	8	0	0	0	0	0	-	1	.120	.154	.120

Vicente Padilla

Pitches: R Bats: R Pos: SP-25; RP-1   Ht: 6'2" Wt: 220 Born: 9/27/1977 Age: 32

Year	Team	Lg	G	GS	CG	GF	IP	BFP	H	R	ER	HR	SH	SF	HB	TBB	IBB	SO	WP	Bk	W	L	Pct	Sh	Sv-Op	Hld	ERC	ERA
2009	Albq*	AAA	1	1	0	0	5.0	21	3	2	2	1	0	0	0	3	0	5	0	0	1	0	1.000	0	0- -	-	3.28	3.60
1999	Ari	NL	5	0	0	2	2.2	19	7	5	5	1	0	0	0	3	0	0	0	0	0	1	.000	0	0-1	1	20.05	10.00
2000	2 Tms	NL	55	0	0	16	65.1	291	72	33	27	2	6	3	1	29	7	51	4	0	1	7	.001	0	2-11	10	4.22	3.71
2001	Phi	NL	23	0	0	5	34.0	144	36	18	16	1	0	0	0	12	0	29	1	0	3	1	.750	0	0-3	1	3.80	4.24
2002	Phi	NL	32	32	1	0	206.0	862	198	83	75	16	10	3	15	53	5	128	6	2	14	11	.560	1	0-0	0	3.42	3.28
2003	Phi	NL	32	32	1	0	208.2	876	196	94	84	22	11	7	16	62	4	133	3	2	14	12	.538	1	0-0	0	3.68	3.62
2004	Phi	NL	20	20	0	0	115.1	503	119	63	58	16	7	5	10	36	6	82	2	0	7	7	.500	0	0-0	0	4.42	4.53
2005	Phi	NL	27	27	0	0	147.0	654	146	79	77	22	7	3	8	74	9	103	1	0	9	12	.429	0	0-0	0	4.94	4.71
2006	Tex	AL	33	33	0	0	200.0	872	206	108	100	21	6	6	17	70	2	156	4	2	15	10	.600	0	0-0	0	4.41	4.50
2007	Tex	AL	23	23	0	0	120.1	553	146	88	77	16	3	2	9	50	1	71	2	0	6	10	.375	0	0-0	0	5.95	5.76
2008	Tex	AL	29	29	1	0	171.0	757	185	100	90	26	1	3	15	65	4	127	12	3	14	8	.636	1	0-0	0	5.20	4.74
2009	2 Tms	NL	26	25	0	0	147.1	634	156	76	73	16	6	3	8	54	0	97	5	2	12	6	.667	0	0-0	0	4.65	4.46
00	Ari	NL	27	0	0	12	35.0	143	32	10	9	0	0	1	0	10	2	30	0	0	2	1	.667	0	0-1	7	2.48	2.31
00	Phi	NL	28	0	0	4	30.1	148	40	23	18	3	5	2	1	18	5	21	1	0	2	6	.250	0	2-6	8	6.52	5.34
09	Tex	AL	18	18	0	0	108.0	475	120	61	59	12	3	2	8	42	0	59	4	2	8	6	.571	0	0-0	0	5.15	4.92
09	LAD	NL	8	7	0	0	39.1	159	36	15	14	4	3	1	0	12	0	38	1	0	4	0	1.000	0	0-0	0	3.36	3.20
11 ML YEARS			305	221	3	23	1417.2	6165	1467	747	682	160	57	35	99	507	38	977	37	11	98	85	.536	3	2-11	17	4.45	4.33

Angel Pagan

Bats: B Throws: R Pos: CF-61; LF-20; PH-7; RF-6   Ht: 6'2" Wt: 195 Born: 7/2/1981 Age: 28

Year	Team	Lg	G	AB	H	2B	3B	HR	(Hm	Rd)	TB	R	RBI	RC	TBB	IBB	SO	HBP	SH	SF	SB	CS	SB%	GDP	Avg	OBP	Slg
2009	Buffalo*	AAA	3	14	4	0	2	0	(-	-)	8	2	2	2	0	0	3	0	0	0	0	0	-	1	.286	.286	.571
2009	StLuci*	A+	4	12	5	2	0	0	(-	-)	7	4	3	4	4	0	2	0	0	0	2	0	1.00	0	.417	.563	.583
2006	ChC	NL	77	170	42	6	2	5	(4	1)	67	28	18	21	15	0	28	0	1	1	4	2	.67	3	.247	.306	.394
2007	ChC	NL	71	148	39	10	2	4	(3	1)	65	21	21	23	10	0	32	1	0	2	4	1	.80	0	.264	.306	.439
2008	NYM	NL	31	91	25	7	1	0	(0	0)	34	12	13	15	11	0	18	0	1	2	4	0	1.00	0	.275	.346	.374
2009	NYM	NL	88	343	105	22	11	6	(5	1)	167	54	32	53	25	2	56	0	5	3	14	7	.67	3	.306	.350	.487
4 ML YEARS			267	752	211	45	16	15	(12	3)	333	115	84	112	61	2	134	0	8	8	26	10	.72	6	.281	.331	.443

Matt Pagnozzi

Bats: R Throws: R Pos: C-5; 1B-1; PH-1   Ht: 6'2" Wt: 195 Born: 11/10/1982 Age: 27

Year	Team	Lg	G	AB	H	2B	3B	HR	(Hm	Rd)	TB	R	RBI	RC	TBB	IBB	SO	HBP	SH	SF	SB	CS	SB%	GDP	Avg	OBP	Slg
2003	NewJrs	A-	59	152	27	4	1	1	(-	-)	36	13	19	12	23	0	42	5	3	2	3	2	.60	1	.178	.302	.237
2004	Peoria	A	74	215	45	10	1	0	(-	-)	57	29	14	16	15	1	54	5	4	0	4	1	.80	4	.209	.277	.265
2005	PlmBh	A+	61	187	36	11	0	1	(-	-)	50	14	18	14	20	1	49	2	2	0	3	2	.60	6	.193	.278	.267
2005	Sprgfld	AA	15	37	6	2	0	0	(-	-)	8	3	1	1	3	0	8	1	0	0	0	0	-	2	.162	.244	.216
2006	PlmBh	A+	77	268	58	15	3	3	(-	-)	88	25	27	25	20	0	67	5	2	0	1	0	1.00	4	.216	.283	.328
2007	Sprgfld	AA	13	43	9	3	0	0	(-	-)	12	5	3	3	2	0	11	1	1	0	0	0	-	2	.209	.261	.279
2007	Memp	AAA	47	139	31	6	0	2	(-	-)	43	10	0	12	6	0	36	4	2	1	1	0	1.00	4	.223	.273	.309
2008	Memp	AAA	3	5	1	1	0	0	(-	-)	2	0	1	1	2	1	1	0	0	0	0	0	-	1	.200	.429	.400
2008	Sprgfld	AA	68	216	51	10	0	3	(-	-)	70	24	19	22	16	1	47	3	6	3	2	1	.67	10	.236	.294	.324
2009	Memp	AAA	86	253	56	7	0	5	(-	-)	78	21	32	24	26	0	78	3	7	2	0	1	.00	11	.221	.299	.308
2009	StL	NL	6	3	0	0	0	0	(0	0)	0	1	0	0	1	0	0	0	1	0	0	0	-	0	.000	.250	.000

Matt Palmer

Pitches: R **Bats:** R **Pos:** RP-27; SP-13   **Ht:** 6'2" **Wt:** 225 **Born:** 3/21/1979 **Age:** 31

Year	Team	Lg	G	GS	CG	GF	IP	BFP	H	R	ER	HR	SH	SF	HB	TBB	IBB	SO	WP	Bk	W	L	Pct	Sh	Sv-Op	Hld	ERC	ERA
2002	Salem	A-	16	9	0	3	53.2	217	44	15	11	0	0	1	3	23	0	49	5	0	3	2	.600	0	0- -	-	2.89	1.84
2003	Hgrstn	A	44	0	0	41	52.1	195	21	7	7	3	2	0	4	15	0	56	3	1	5	0	1.000	0	25- -	-	1.10	1.20
2003	Nrwich	AA	5	0	0	1	6.2	41	12	11	10	0	0	1	2	5	0	5	3	0	0	0	-	0	0- -	-	10.28	13.50
2004	Nrwich	AA	42	5	0	17	79.1	358	66	35	27	4	4	4	7	51	4	81	7	0	4	7	.364	0	8- -	-	3.91	3.06
2005	Nrwich	AA	11	2	0	4	26.0	115	22	14	8	2	0	2	3	9	1	20	2	0	0	1	.000	0	1- -	-	3.09	2.77
2006	Conn	AA	15	9	0	2	62.1	253	50	20	9	1	4	0	7	10	0	51	1	0	5	3	.625	0	0- -	-	2.03	1.30
2006	Fresno	AAA	15	15	0	0	91.0	387	91	45	41	10	5	0	9	30	0	64	3	1	6	4	.600	0	0- -	-	4.35	4.05
2007	Fresno	AAA	29	25	1	1	150.0	644	155	80	72	17	7	1	12	51	0	98	6	0	11	8	.579	0	0- -	-	4.52	4.32
2007	Conn	AA	1	1	0	0	5.0	26	8	6	6	2	2	0	1	2	0	3	1	0	0	0	-	0	0- -	-	11.25	10.80
2008	Fresno	AAA	26	25	1	0	142.0	629	138	71	66	11	7	6	10	72	0	143	11	0	6	10	.375	0	0- -	-	4.47	4.18
2009	Salt Lk	AAA	2	2	0	0	7.2	38	13	10	10	2	0	0	1	3	0	5	0	0	1	1	.500	0	0- -	-	10.81	11.74
2008	SF	NL	3	3	0	0	12.2	67	17	13	12	1	1	0	2	13	1	3	0	0	0	2	.000	0	0-0	0	9.37	8.53
2009	LAA	AL	40	13	1	10	121.1	505	105	55	53	12	6	3	4	55	2	69	5	0	11	2	.846	0	0-0	0	3.74	3.93
	2 ML YEARS		43	16	1	10	134.0	572	122	68	65	13	7	3	6	68	3	72	5	0	11	4	.733	0	0-0	0	4.22	4.37

Jonathan Papelbon

Pitches: R **Bats:** R **Pos:** RP-66   **Ht:** 6'4" **Wt:** 225 **Born:** 11/23/1980 **Age:** 29

Year	Team	Lg	G	GS	CG	GF	IP	BFP	H	R	ER	HR	SH	SF	HB	TBB	IBB	SO	WP	Bk	W	L	Pct	Sh	Sv-Op	Hld	ERC	ERA
2005	Bos	AL	17	3	0	4	34.0	148	33	11	10	4	1	0	3	17	2	34	1	0	3	1	.750	0	0-1	4	4.82	2.65
2006	Bos	AL	59	0	0	49	68.1	257	40	8	7	3	1	2	1	13	2	75	2	0	4	2	.667	0	35-41	1	1.22	0.92
2007	Bos	AL	59	0	0	53	58.1	224	30	12	12	5	0	0	4	15	0	84	0	0	1	3	.250	0	37-40	2	1.43	1.85
2008	Bos	AL	67	0	0	62	69.1	273	58	24	18	4	4	1	0	8	0	77	2	0	5	4	.556	0	41-46	0	1.92	2.34
2009	Bos	AL	66	0	0	59	68.0	285	54	15	14	5	1	2	4	24	1	76	0	0	1	1	.500	0	38-41	0	2.78	1.85
	Postseason		16	0	0	11	25.0	90	10	0	0	0	0	1	0	6	2	22	0	0	2	0	1.000	0	7-8	0	0.64	0.00
	5 ML YEARS		268	3	0	227	298.0	1187	215	70	61	21	7	5	12	77	5	346	5	0	14	11	.560	0	151-169	7	2.06	1.84

Mike Parisi

Pitches: R **Bats:** R **Pos:** P   **Ht:** 6'3" **Wt:** 215 **Born:** 4/18/1983 **Age:** 27

Year	Team	Lg	G	GS	CG	GF	IP	BFP	H	R	ER	HR	SH	SF	HB	TBB	IBB	SO	WP	Bk	W	L	Pct	Sh	Sv-Op	Hld	ERC	ERA
2004	NewJrs	A-	7	7	0	0	36.1	147	40	18	18	3	0	2	1	6	0	26	1	0	4	2	.667	0	0- -	-	3.87	4.46
2004	Peoria	A	6	6	0	0	35.2	151	30	16	13	1	2	4	4	15	1	36	2	0	1	1	.500	0	0- -	-	3.21	3.28
2005	QuadC	A	14	14	0	0	86.0	379	98	42	39	5	3	4	4	25	0	66	2	2	5	5	.500	0	0- -	-	4.28	4.08
2005	PlmBh	A+	13	13	1	0	78.0	329	79	31	28	6	3	1	4	22	0	63	3	0	5	6	.455	0	0- -	-	3.77	3.23
2006	Sprgfld	AA	27	27	0	0	150.2	672	168	92	77	13	4	2	5	63	1	107	7	0	9	8	.529	0	0- -	-	4.83	4.60
2007	Memp	AAA	28	28	0	0	165.0	733	192	100	90	21	10	4	10	65	0	111	5	1	8	13	.381	0	0- -	-	5.55	4.91
2008	Memp	AAA	15	15	1	0	84.0	355	80	38	36	7	2	0	3	33	0	58	0	0	8	2	.800	0	0- -	-	3.87	3.86
2009	Cards	R	3	3	0	0	7.2	28	2	1	1	0	0	0	0	4	0	9	0	0	0	1	.000	0	0- -	-	0.84	1.17
2009	PlmBh	A+	2	2	0	0	7.2	38	15	7	7	0	0	0	1	3	0	4	0	1	0	1	.000	0	0- -	-	10.59	8.22
2008	StL	NL	12	2	0	6	23.0	121	37	24	21	2	3	1	0	15	2	13	3	0	0	4	.000	0	0-0	0	8.44	8.22

Chan Ho Park

Pitches: R **Bats:** R **Pos:** RP-38; SP-7   **Ht:** 6'2" **Wt:** 212 **Born:** 6/30/1973 **Age:** 37

Year	Team	Lg	G	GS	CG	GF	IP	BFP	H	R	ER	HR	SH	SF	HB	TBB	IBB	SO	WP	Bk	W	L	Pct	Sh	Sv-Op	Hld	ERC	ERA
1994	LAD	NL	2	0	0	0	4.0	23	5	5	5	1	0	0	1	5	0	6	0	0	0	0	-	0	0-0	0	11.69	11.25
1995	LAD	NL	2	1	0	0	4.0	16	2	2	2	1	0	0	0	2	0	7	0	1	0	0	-	0	0-0	0	2.70	4.50
1996	LAD	NL	48	10	0	7	108.2	477	82	48	44	7	8	1	4	71	3	119	4	3	5	5	.500	0	0-0	4	3.50	3.64
1997	LAD	NL	32	29	2	1	192.0	792	149	80	72	24	9	5	8	70	1	166	4	1	14	8	.636	0	0-0	0	3.04	3.38
1998	LAD	NL	34	34	2	0	220.2	946	199	101	91	16	11	10	11	97	1	191	6	2	15	9	.625	0	0-0	0	3.69	3.71
1999	LAD	NL	33	33	0	0	194.1	883	208	120	113	31	10	5	14	100	4	174	11	1	13	11	.542	0	0-0	0	5.68	5.23
2000	LAD	NL	34	34	3	0	226.0	963	173	92	82	21	12	5	12	124	4	217	13	0	18	10	.643	1	0-0	0	3.51	3.27
2001	LAD	NL	36	35	2	0	234.0	981	183	98	91	23	16	7	20	91	1	218	3	3	15	11	.577	1	0-0	0	3.15	3.50
2002	Tex	AL	25	25	0	0	145.2	666	154	95	93	20	4	3	17	78	2	121	9	0	9	8	.529	0	0-0	0	5.75	5.75
2003	Tex	AL	7	7	0	0	29.2	146	34	26	25	5	1	3	6	25	0	16	1	1	1	3	.250	0	0-0	0	8.56	7.58
2004	Tex	AL	16	16	0	0	95.2	428	105	63	58	22	4	4	13	33	0	63	1	1	4	7	.364	0	0-0	0	5.97	5.46
2005	2 Tms		30	29	0	0	155.1	715	180	103	99	11	7	3	10	80	1	113	6	0	12	8	.600	0	0-0	0	5.52	5.74
2006	SD	NL	24	21	1	0	136.2	606	146	81	73	20	10	4	10	44	7	96	5	0	7	7	.500	1	0-0	0	4.62	4.81
2007	NYM	NL	1	1	0	0	4.0	20	6	7	7	2	0	0	0	2	0	4	1	0	0	1	.000	0	0-0	0	10.88	15.75
2008	LAD	NL	54	5	0	11	95.1	412	97	43	36	12	4	0	4	36	7	79	2	1	4	4	.500	0	2-5	5	4.34	3.40
2009	Phi	NL	45	7	0	6	83.1	362	84	43	41	5	1	5	5	33	3	73	2	0	3	3	.500	0	0-1	13	4.01	4.43
05	Tex	AL	20	20	0	0	109.2	502	130	70	69	8	5	2	6	54	1	80	3	0	8	5	.615	0	0-0	0	5.58	5.66
05	SD	NL	10	9	0	0	45.2	213	50	33	30	3	2	1	4	26	0	33	3	0	4	3	.571	0	0-0	0	5.36	5.91
	Postseason		5	0	0	1	3.2	13	2	0	0	0	0	0	1	1	0	1	1	0	0	0	-	0	0-1	0	1.97	0.00
	16 ML YEARS		423	287	10	26	1929.1	8436	1807	1007	932	221	97	55	135	891	34	1663	68	14	120	95	.558	3	2-6	22	4.32	4.35

Bobby Parnell

Pitches: R Bats: R Pos: RP-60; SP-8   Ht: 6'4" Wt: 200 Born: 9/8/1984 Age: 25

		HOW MUCH HE PITCHED						WHAT HE GAVE UP												THE RESULTS							
Year Team	Lg	G	GS	CG	GF	IP	BFP	H	R	ER	HR	SH	SF	HB	TBB	IBB	SO	WP	Bk	W	L	Pct	Sh	Sv-Op	Hld	ERC	ERA
2005 Bklyn	A-	15	14	0	1	73.0	294	48	20	14	1	0	2	4	29	0	67	3	0	2	3	.400	0	0--	-	1.97	1.73
2006 Hgrstn	A	18	18	1	0	93.2	401	84	50	42	7	1	2	6	40	0	84	12	0	5	10	.333	0	0--	-	3.70	4.04
2006 StLuci	A+	3	3	0	0	11.2	58	16	13	12	3	0	1	0	9	0	13	2	0	0	1	.000	0	0--	-	9.50	9.26
2007 StLuci	A+	12	12	0	0	55.1	242	56	22	20	0	0	0	4	22	0	62	3	1	3	3	.500	0	0--	-	3.69	3.25
2007 Bnghtn	AA	17	17	0	0	88.2	401	98	54	47	9	1	2	4	38	1	74	3	0	5	5	.500	0	0--	-	4.91	4.77
2008 Bnghtn	AA	24	24	0	0	127.2	556	126	66	61	14	2	3	6	57	1	91	9	0	10	6	.625	0	0--	-	4.46	4.30
2008 NewOr	AAA	5	4	0	0	20.1	94	25	16	15	0	1	0	0	9	0	23	1	0	2	2	.500	0	0--	-	4.72	6.64
2008 NYM	NL	6	0	0	3	5.0	19	3	3	3	0	0	0	0	2	0	3	1	0	0	0	-	0	0-0	0	1.59	5.40
2009 NYM	NL	68	8	0	14	88.1	413	101	56	52	8	3	1	4	46	2	74	6	1	4	8	.333	0	1-5	16	5.37	5.30
2 ML YEARS		74	8	0	17	93.1	432	104	59	55	8	3	1	4	48	2	77	7	1	4	8	.333	0	1-5	16	5.14	5.30

Chad Paronto

Pitches: R Bats: R Pos: RP-6   Ht: 6'5" Wt: 250 Born: 7/28/1975 Age: 34

		HOW MUCH HE PITCHED						WHAT HE GAVE UP												THE RESULTS							
Year Team	Lg	G	GS	CG	GF	IP	BFP	H	R	ER	HR	SH	SF	HB	TBB	IBB	SO	WP	Bk	W	L	Pct	Sh	Sv-Op	Hld	ERC	ERA
2009 RdRck*	AAA	44	0	0	39	51.2	197	34	8	8	1	3	4	1	14	1	39	0	0	2	1	.667	0	24--	-	1.57	1.39
2001 Bal	AL	24	0	0	9	27.0	128	33	24	15	5	1	1	1	11	0	16	1	0	1	3	.250	0	0-1	5	5.98	5.00
2002 Cle	AL	29	0	0	11	35.2	154	34	19	16	3	0	4	2	11	1	23	2	0	0	2	.000	0	0-0	0	3.45	4.04
2003 Cle	AL	6	0	0	5	6.2	29	7	8	7	1	1	1	0	3	0	6	0	0	0	2	.000	0	0-0	0	5.00	9.45
2006 Atl	NL	65	0	0	11	56.2	237	53	23	20	5	4	1	3	19	3	41	3	0	2	3	.400	0	0-2	8	3.56	3.18
2007 Atl	NL	41	0	0	12	40.1	180	47	20	16	1	2	3	3	19	5	14	2	0	3	1	.750	0	1-2	2	4.95	3.57
2008 Hou	NL	6	0	0	3	10.1	41	11	5	5	2	1	0	0	2	0	4	0	0	1	0	1.000	0	0-0	4	4.49	4.35
2009 Hou	NL	6	0	0	1	6.2	36	15	9	9	4	1	1	0	1	0	3	0	0	0	0	-	0	0-0	0	15.69	12.15
7 ML YEARS		177	0	0	52	183.1	805	200	108	88	21	10	11	9	66	9	107	8	0	6	12	.333	0	1-5	15	4.67	4.32

James Parr

Pitches: R Bats: R Pos: RP-8   Ht: 6'1" Wt: 185 Born: 2/27/1986 Age: 24

		HOW MUCH HE PITCHED						WHAT HE GAVE UP												THE RESULTS							
Year Team	Lg	G	GS	CG	GF	IP	BFP	H	R	ER	HR	SH	SF	HB	TBB	IBB	SO	WP	Bk	W	L	Pct	Sh	Sv-Op	Hld	ERC	ERA
2004 Braves	R	10	10	0	0	40.1	187	39	19	19	2	0	0	0	12	0	40	2	1	3	2	.600	0	0--	-	3.20	4.24
2005 Rome	A	26	18	0	7	126.2	537	134	54	48	13	3	7	4	24	0	98	1	0	13	4	.765	0	3--	-	3.67	3.41
2006 MrtlBh	A+	24	22	2	1	134.2	566	138	76	72	14	6	9	1	37	0	90	2	1	7	8	.467	0	1--	-	3.80	4.81
2007 MrtlBh	A+	8	8	1	0	39.2	163	36	14	14	1	1	2	1	6	0	37	1	2	3	4	.429	1	0--	-	2.41	3.18
2007 Missi	AA	18	16	0	0	98.0	416	111	51	50	8	10	3	2	25	0	75	0	1	4	5	.444	0	0--	-	4.27	4.59
2008 Missi	AA	18	17	0	0	95.0	397	87	40	39	9	2	3	2	37	0	81	3	1	8	4	.667	0	0--	-	3.68	3.69
2008 Rchmd	AAA	10	9	0	0	55.2	226	49	20	20	4	0	1	1	14	0	44	0	1	5	3	.625	0	0--	-	2.78	3.23
2009 Braves	R	3	3	0	0	6.0	21	0	1	0	0	1	0	1	1	0	9	0	1	0	0	-	0	0--	-	0.03	0.00
2009 Gwnntt	AAA	7	6	0	0	30.0	126	34	18	18	5	2	0	0	5	1	20	1	0	1	1	.500	0	0--	-	4.31	5.40
2008 Atl	NL	5	5	0	0	22.1	102	29	13	12	4	1	0	0	9	0	14	1	0	1	0	1.000	0	0-0	0	6.53	4.84
2009 Atl	NL	8	0	0	4	14.0	66	17	9	9	1	1	1	1	5	0	12	0	0	0	0	-	0	0-0	0	4.99	5.79
2 ML YEARS		13	5	0	4	36.1	168	46	22	21	5	2	1	1	14	0	26	1	0	1	0	1.000	0	0-0	0	5.92	5.20

Gerardo Parra

Bats: L Throws: L Pos: LF-75; CF-43; PH-10; RF-9   Ht: 5'11" Wt: 197 Born: 5/6/1987 Age: 23

		BATTING																BASERUNNING				AVERAGES		
Year Team	Lg	G	AB	H	2B	3B	HR	(Hm	Rd)	TB	R	RBI	RC	TBB	IBB	SO	HBP	SH	SF	SB	CS	SB%	GDP	Avg	OBP	Slg
2006 Msoula	R+	69	271	89	18	4	4	(-	-)	127	46	43	52	25	3	30	3	0	4	23	7	.77	4	.328	.386	.469
2007 Sbend	A	110	444	142	25	4	6	(-	-)	193	64	57	75	30	2	51	8	1	5	24	8	.75	12	.320	.370	.435
2007 Visalia	A+	24	102	29	2	1	2	(-	-)	39	11	14	11	4	1	17	0	0	3	2	3	.40	1	.284	.303	.382
2008 Visalia	A+	50	196	59	8	4	2	(-	-)	81	26	19	33	23	1	31	3	1	1	12	4	.75	7	.301	.381	.413
2008 Mobile	AA	73	265	73	14	6	4	(-	-)	111	35	33	40	23	2	34	6	3	5	17	9	.65	11	.275	.341	.419
2009 Mobile	AA	29	108	39	3	1	3	(-	-)	53	23	12	25	22	4	13	0	0	0	7	4	.64	3	.361	.469	.491
2009 Ari	NL	120	455	132	21	8	5	(4	1)	184	59	60	58	25	1	89	1	4	6	5	7	.42	18	.290	.324	.404

Manny Parra

Pitches: L Bats: L Pos: SP-27   Ht: 6'3" Wt: 216 Born: 10/30/1982 Age: 27

		HOW MUCH HE PITCHED						WHAT HE GAVE UP												THE RESULTS							
Year Team	Lg	G	GS	CG	GF	IP	BFP	H	R	ER	HR	SH	SF	HB	TBB	IBB	SO	WP	Bk	W	L	Pct	Sh	Sv-Op	Hld	ERC	ERA
2009 Nashv*	AAA	4	4	0	0	24.2	103	16	10	8	0	0	0	0	13	0	19	1	0	1	2	.333	0	0--	-	2.02	2.92
2007 Mil	NL	9	2	0	3	26.1	116	25	13	11	1	1	3	2	12	0	26	1	0	0	1	.000	0	0-0	1	3.83	3.76
2008 Mil	NL	32	29	0	0	166.0	741	181	91	81	18	10	2	2	75	1	147	17	2	10	8	.556	0	0-0	0	4.89	4.39
2009 Mil	NL	27	27	0	0	140.0	671	179	108	99	19	5	3	1	77	5	116	4	1	11	11	.500	0	0-0	0	6.51	6.36
Postseason		2	0	0	0	2.1	9	2	0	0	0	0	0	0	1	0	3	0	0	0	0	-	0	0-0	0	3.03	0.00
3 ML YEARS		68	58	0	3	332.1	1528	385	212	191	38	16	8	5	164	6	289	22	3	21	20	.512	0	0-0	1	5.47	5.17

Corey Patterson

Bats: L **Throws:** R **Pos:** PH-9; CF-6; RF-2   **Ht:** 5'10" **Wt:** 173 **Born:** 8/13/1979 **Age:** 30

Year	Team	Lg	G	AB	H	2B	3B	HR	(Hm	Rd)	TB	R	RBI	RC	TBB	IBB	SO	HBP	SH	SF	SB	CS	SB%	GDP	Avg	OBP	Slg
2009	Syrcse*	AAA	84	263	72	16	1	7	(-	-)	111	30	40	36	13	0	65	4	3	0	14	5	.74	1	.274	.318	.422
2009	Nashv*	AAA	29	124	41	12	3	5	(-	-)	74	24	22	26	8	2	25	0	1	2	8	3	.73	1	.331	.366	.597
2000	ChC	NL	11	42	7	1	0	2	(1	1)	14	9	2	3	3	0	14	1	1	0	1	1	.50	1	.167	.239	.333
2001	ChC	NL	59	131	29	3	0	4	(1	3)	44	26	14	13	6	0	33	3	2	3	4	0	1.00	1	.221	.266	.336
2002	ChC	NL	153	592	150	30	5	14	(7	7)	232	71	54	61	19	1	142	8	4	5	18	3	.86	8	.253	.284	.392
2003	ChC	NL	83	329	98	17	7	13	(7	6)	168	49	55	55	15	2	77	1	0	2	16	5	.76	5	.298	.329	.511
2004	ChC	NL	157	631	168	33	6	24	(14	10)	285	91	72	87	45	7	168	5	5	1	32	9	.78	7	.266	.320	.452
2005	ChC	NL	126	451	97	15	3	13	(9	4)	157	47	34	32	23	3	118	1	5	1	15	5	.75	5	.215	.254	.348
2006	Bal	AL	135	463	128	19	5	16	(9	7)	205	75	53	66	21	5	94	5	8	1	45	9	.83	0	.276	.314	.443
2007	Bal	AL	132	461	124	26	2	8	(5	3)	178	65	45	51	21	1	65	4	13	4	37	9	.80	3	.269	.304	.386
2008	Cin	NL	135	366	75	17	2	10	(2	8)	126	46	34	23	16	0	57	1	5	4	14	9	.61	5	.205	.238	.344
2009	2 Tms	NL	16	29	3	0	0	0	(0	0)	3	0	0	0	0	0	13	0	1	0	2	1	.67	1	.103	.103	.103
09	Was	NL	5	15	2	0	0	0	(0	0)	2	0	0	0	0	0	6	0	0	0	2	0	1.00	1	.133	.133	.133
09	Mil	NL	11	14	1	0	0	0	(0	0)	1	0	0	0	0	0	7	0	1	0	1	1	.00	1	.071	.071	.071
	10 ML YEARS		1007	3495	879	161	30	104	(55	49)	1412	479	363	391	169	19	781	29	44	21	184	51	.78	33	.252	.290	.404

Eric Patterson

Bats: L **Throws:** R **Pos:** LF-26; PR-6; 2B-5; CF-4; DH-4; RF-2   **Ht:** 5'11" **Wt:** 170 **Born:** 4/8/1983 **Age:** 27

Year	Team	Lg	G	AB	H	2B	3B	HR	(Hm	Rd)	TB	R	RBI	RC	TBB	IBB	SO	HBP	SH	SF	SB	CS	SB%	GDP	Avg	OBP	Slg
2009	Scrmto*	AAA	110	466	143	29	11	12	(-	-)	230	91	56	94	52	3	81	2	6	4	43	6	.88	2	.307	.376	.494
2007	Oak	NL	7	8	2	1	0	0	(0	0)	3	0	0	0	0	0	3	0	1	0	0	0	-	0	.250	.250	.375
2008	2 Tms		43	130	25	4	0	1	(1	0)	32	16	15	11	17	0	36	0	0	1	10	1	.91	1	.192	.284	.246
2009	Oak	AL	39	94	27	5	1	1	(1	0)	37	15	11	14	14	0	25	0	0	2	6	1	.86	0	.287	.373	.394
08	ChC	NL	13	38	9	1	0	1	(1	0)	13	5	7	5	5	0	12	0	0	1	2	1	.67	1	.237	.318	.342
08	Oak	AL	30	92	16	3	0	0	(0	0)	19	11	8	6	12	0	24	0	0	0	8	0	1.00	0	.174	.269	.207
	3 ML YEARS		89	232	54	10	1	2	(2	0)	72	31	26	25	31	0	64	0	1	3	16	2	.89	1	.233	.320	.310

David Patton

Pitches: R **Bats:** R **Pos:** RP-20   **Ht:** 6'3" **Wt:** 205 **Born:** 5/18/1984 **Age:** 26

Year	Team	Lg	G	GS	CG	GF	IP	BFP	H	R	ER	HR	SH	SF	HB	TBB	IBB	SO	WP	Bk	W	L	Pct	Sh	Sv-Op	Hld	ERC	ERA
2004	Casper	R+	17	7	0	0	50.0	245	60	48	35	2	4	4	3	30	0	43	5	0	2	3	.400	0	0--	-	5.62	6.30
2005	Ashvll	A	4	4	0	0	14.0	78	26	23	17	4	0	0	1	8	0	9	1	0	0	3	.000	0	0--	-	12.09	10.93
2005	TriCity	A-	8	7	0	0	42.0	185	49	29	28	7	1	3	1	13	0	39	1	0	3	5	.375	0	0--	-	5.25	6.00
2006	Ashvll	A	52	0	0	21	73.2	304	51	18	16	1	4	1	6	26	0	79	4	0	7	4	.636	0	3--	-	2.02	1.95
2007	Mdest	A+	49	0	0	14	67.2	300	73	37	34	6	5	3	0	34	1	59	6	0	5	5	.500	0	1--	-	4.88	4.52
2008	Mdest	A+	50	0	0	28	73.2	317	74	31	29	8	1	2	1	28	3	87	5	0	4	5	.444	0	4--	-	4.07	3.54
2009	Tenn	AA	3	3	0	0	7.2	33	7	6	3	1	0	0	0	1	0	6	0	0	0	1	.000	0	0--	-	2.52	3.52
2009	Iowa	AAA	5	1	0	0	7.0	31	5	4	4	1	1	1	0	7	0	4	1	0	1	1	.500	0	0--	-	5.39	5.14
2009	ChC	NL	20	0	0	5	27.2	134	31	22	21	4	3	1	0	19	2	23	3	0	3	1	.750	0	0-0	0	5.98	6.83

Xavier Paul

Bats: L **Throws:** R **Pos:** PH-7; RF-3; CF-1; PR-1   **Ht:** 5'9" **Wt:** 203 **Born:** 2/25/1985 **Age:** 25

Year	Team	Lg	G	AB	H	2B	3B	HR	(Hm	Rd)	TB	R	RBI	RC	TBB	IBB	SO	HBP	SH	SF	SB	CS	SB%	GDP	Avg	OBP	Slg
2003	Ogden	R+	69	264	81	15	6	7	(-	-)	129	60	47	51	34	2	58	2	3	5	11	4	.73	2	.307	.384	.489
2004	Clmbs	A	128	465	122	26	6	9	(-	-)	187	69	72	67	56	4	127	3	5	7	10	7	.59	4	.262	.341	.402
2005	VeroB	A+	85	288	71	15	3	7	(-	-)	113	42	41	37	32	2	81	4	4	2	1	5	.17	3	.247	.328	.392
2006	VeroB	A+	120	470	134	23	3	13	(-	-)	202	62	49	69	38	4	114	4	7	1	22	15	.59	10	.285	.343	.430
2007	Jaxnvl	AA	118	422	123	21	2	11	(-	-)	181	64	50	69	48	2	112	3	7	2	18	9	.67	6	.291	.366	.429
2008	LsVgs	AAA	115	443	140	28	5	9	(-	-)	205	82	68	80	43	2	96	5	9	6	17	7	.71	9	.316	.378	.463
2009	Albq	AAA	31	116	38	10	2	2	(-	-)	58	13	16	22	10	1	22	0	2	1	8	2	.80	2	.328	.378	.500
2009	LAD	NL	11	14	3	1	0	1	(0	1)	7	3	1	0	2	0	4	0	0	0	1	0	1.00	1	.214	.313	.500

Felipe Paulino

Pitches: R **Bats:** R **Pos:** SP-17; RP-6   **Ht:** 6'2" **Wt:** 180 **Born:** 10/5/1983 **Age:** 26

Year	Team	Lg	G	GS	CG	GF	IP	BFP	H	R	ER	HR	SH	SF	HB	TBB	IBB	SO	WP	Bk	W	L	Pct	Sh	Sv-Op	Hld	ERC	ERA
2003	Mrtnsvl	R+	16	0	0	6	25.2	126	23	20	16	0	0	1	8	19	0	27	8	0	2	2	.500	0	1--	-	5.12	5.61
2004	Grnsvle	R	10	10	0	0	32.0	149	30	30	27	4	0	1	4	22	0	37	6	0	1	3	.250	0	0--	-	5.55	7.59
2005	TriCity	A-	13	2	0	10	30.2	126	21	15	13	2	1	0	3	11	0	34	8	0	2	2	.500	0	1--	-	2.39	3.82
2005	Lxngtn	A	7	5	0	0	24.1	100	21	8	5	2	3	1	0	6	0	30	2	0	1	1	.500	0	0--	-	2.61	1.85
2006	Salem	A+	27	26	0	0	126.1	546	119	67	61	13	2	2	7	59	0	91	9	0	9	7	.563	0	0--	-	4.31	4.35
2007	CpChr	AA	22	21	0	0	112.0	488	103	55	45	6	0	4	3	49	0	110	7	1	4	5	.444	0	0--	-	3.49	3.62
2008	RdRck	AAA	1	0	0	0	0.2	4	1	0	0	0	0	0	0	1	0	1	0	0	0	0	-	0	0--	-	10.76	0.00
2009	RdRck	AAA	7	7	0	0	34.2	158	30	13	12	1	2	2	2	23	1	29	0	0	2	1	.667	0	0--	-	3.90	3.12
2007	Hou	NL	5	3	0	0	19.0	85	22	15	15	5	2	0	0	7	1	11	1	0	2	1	.667	0	0-0	1	5.93	7.11
2009	Hou	NL	23	17	0	0	97.2	448	126	73	68	20	8	1	4	37	2	93	5	0	3	11	.214	0	0-1	0	6.70	6.27
	2 ML YEARS		28	20	0	0	116.2	533	148	88	83	25	10	1	4	44	3	104	6	0	5	12	.294	0	0-1	1	6.58	6.40

Ronny Paulino

Bats: R Throws: R Pos: C-77; PH-10   Ht: 6'3" Wt: 210 Born: 4/21/1981 Age: 29

Year Team	Lg	G	AB	H	2B	3B	HR	(Hm	Rd)	TB	R	RBI	RC	TBB	IBB	SO	HBP	SH	SF	SB	CS	SB%	GDP	Avg	OBP	Slg
2005 Pit	NL	2	4	2	0	0	0	(0	0)	2	1	0	1	1	0	0	0	0	0	0	0	-	0	.500	.600	.500
2006 Pit	NL	129	442	137	19	0	6	(2	4)	174	37	55	60	34	5	79	2	1	2	0	0	-	17	.310	.360	.394
2007 Pit	NL	133	457	120	25	0	11	(7	4)	178	56	55	49	33	0	79	2	0	2	2	2	.50	14	.263	.314	.389
2008 Pit	NL	40	118	25	5	0	2	(0	2)	36	8	18	14	11	1	24	0	0	1	0	0	-	4	.212	.277	.305
2009 Fla	NL	80	239	65	10	1	8	(4	4)	101	24	27	31	25	2	48	0	1	1	1	0	1.00	8	.272	.340	.423
5 ML YEARS		384	1260	349	59	1	27	(13	14)	491	126	155	155	104	8	230	4	2	6	3	2	.60	43	.277	.333	.390

Carl Pavano

Pitches: R Bats: R Pos: SP-33   Ht: 6'5" Wt: 240 Born: 1/8/1976 Age: 34

Year Team	Lg	G	GS	CG	GF	IP	BFP	H	R	ER	HR	SH	SF	HB	TBB	IBB	SO	WP	Bk	W	L	Pct	Sh	Sv-Op	Hld	ERC	ERA
1998 Mon	NL	24	23	0	0	134.2	580	130	70	63	18	5	6	8	43	1	83	1	0	6	9	.400	0	0-0	0	3.97	4.21
1999 Mon	NL	19	18	1	0	104.0	457	117	66	65	8	5	2	4	35	1	70	1	3	6	8	.429	1	0-0	0	4.51	5.63
2000 Mon	NL	15	15	0	0	97.0	408	89	40	33	8	4	3	8	34	1	64	1	1	8	4	.667	0	0-0	0	3.67	3.06
2001 Mon	NL	8	8	0	0	42.2	199	59	33	30	7	2	1	2	16	1	36	0	1	1	6	.143	0	0-0	0	6.99	6.33
2002 2 Tms	NL	37	22	0	2	136.0	619	174	88	78	19	4	4	10	45	8	92	3	2	6	10	.375	0	0-0	3	5.98	5.16
2003 Fla	NL	33	32	2	1	201.0	846	204	99	96	19	9	10	7	49	10	133	3	2	12	13	.480	0	0-0	0	3.57	4.30
2004 Fla	NL	31	31	2	0	222.1	909	212	80	74	16	7	4	11	49	13	139	2	3	18	8	.692	2	0-0	0	3.10	3.00
2005 NYY	AL	17	17	1	0	100.0	442	129	66	53	17	4	3	8	18	1	56	2	1	4	6	.400	1	0-0	0	5.74	4.77
2007 NYY	AL	2	2	0	0	11.1	40	12	7	6	1	0	0	0	2	0	4	0	0	1	0	1.000	0	0-0	0	3.54	4.76
2008 NYY	AL	7	7	0	0	34.1	154	41	23	22	5	3	3	4	10	0	15	0	1	4	2	.667	0	0-0	0	5.60	5.77
2009 2 Tms	AL	33	33	1	0	199.1	854	235	119	113	26	2	7	6	39	1	147	5	0	14	12	.538	1	0-0	0	4.63	5.10
02 Mon	NL	15	14	0	0	74.1	350	98	55	52	14	2	2	7	31	5	51	2	1	3	8	.273	0	0-0	0	7.07	6.30
02 Fla	NL	22	8	0	2	61.2	269	76	33	26	5	2	2	3	14	3	41	1	1	3	2	.600	0	0-0	3	4.74	3.79
09 Clv	AL	21	21	1	0	125.2	534	150	80	75	19	1	6	3	23	0	88	4	0	9	8	.529	1	0-0	0	4.88	5.37
09 Min	AL	12	12	0	0	73.2	320	85	39	38	7	1	1	3	16	1	59	1	0	5	4	.556	0	0-0	0	4.29	4.64
Postseason		8	2	0	1	19.1	75	17	3	3	0	1	1	1	3	1	15	0	0	2	0	1.000	0	0-0	0	2.13	1.40
11 ML YEARS		226	208	7	3	1282.2	5514	1402	691	633	144	45	43	68	340	37	839	18	14	80	78	.506	5	0-0	3	4.34	4.44

Steve Pearce

Bats: R Throws: R Pos: 1B-42; PH-18; RF-1   Ht: 5'11" Wt: 214 Born: 4/13/1983 Age: 27

Year Team	Lg	G	AB	H	2B	3B	HR	(Hm	Rd)	TB	R	RBI	RC	TBB	IBB	SO	HBP	SH	SF	SB	CS	SB%	GDP	Avg	OBP	Slg
2009 Indy*	AAA	77	273	78	18	1	13	(-	-)	137	37	54	50	34	1	46	6	1	3	3	7	.30	7	.286	.373	.502
2007 Pit	NL	23	68	20	5	1	0	(0	0)	27	13	6	9	5	0	12	0	0	0	2	1	.67	0	.294	.342	.397
2008 Pit	NL	37	109	27	7	0	4	(0	4)	46	6	15	13	5	0	22	3	0	2	2	0	1.00	1	.248	.294	.422
2009 Pit	NL	60	165	34	13	1	4	(3	1)	61	19	16	17	21	0	43	0	0	0	1	0	1.00	2	.206	.296	.370
3 ML YEARS		120	342	81	25	2	8	(3	5)	134	38	37	39	31	0	77	3	0	2	5	1	.83	5	.237	.304	.392

Jake Peavy

Pitches: R Bats: R Pos: SP-16   Ht: 6'1" Wt: 193 Born: 5/31/1981 Age: 29

Year Team	Lg	G	GS	CG	GF	IP	BFP	H	R	ER	HR	SH	SF	HB	TBB	IBB	SO	WP	Bk	W	L	Pct	Sh	Sv-Op	Hld	ERC	ERA
2009 Charltt*	AAA	4	4	0	0	15.1	64	14	6	5	1	0	0	1	4	0	17	0	0	1	1	.500	0	0--	-	3.08	2.93
2002 SD	NL	17	17	0	0	97.2	430	106	54	49	11	5	2	3	33	4	90	4	1	6	7	.462	0	0-0	0	4.41	4.52
2003 SD	NL	32	32	0	0	194.2	827	173	94	89	33	7	5	6	82	3	156	2	0	12	11	.522	0	0-0	0	4.13	4.11
2004 SD	NL	27	27	0	0	166.1	694	146	49	42	13	5	6	11	53	4	173	1	1	15	6	.714	0	0-0	0	3.18	2.27
2005 SD	NL	30	30	3	0	203.0	812	162	70	65	18	4	5	7	50	3	216	3	1	13	7	.650	3	0-0	0	2.49	2.88
2006 SD	NL	32	32	2	0	202.1	846	187	93	92	23	5	1	6	62	11	215	4	0	11	14	.440	0	0-0	0	3.42	4.09
2007 SD	NL	34	34	0	0	223.1	898	169	67	63	13	5	7	6	68	5	240	4	0	19	6	.760	0	0-0	0	2.27	2.54
2008 SD	NL	27	27	1	0	173.2	709	146	57	55	17	7	1	5	59	1	166	6	0	10	11	.476	1	0-0	0	3.12	2.85
2009 2 Tms	AL	16	16	1	0	101.2	410	80	41	39	8	3	2	1	34	0	110	2	2	9	6	.600	0	0-0	0	2.63	3.45
09 SD	NL	13	13	1	0	81.2	335	69	38	36	7	2	2	1	28	0	92	2	1	6	6	.500	0	0-0	0	3.00	3.97
09 CWS	AL	3	3	0	0	20.0	75	11	3	3	1	1	0	0	6	0	18	0	1	3	0	1.000	0	0-0	0	1.38	1.35
Postseason		2	2	0	0	9.2	49	19	13	13	3	1	1	0	4	3	5	1	0	0	2	.000	0	0-0	0	12.16	12.10
8 ML YEARS		215	215	7	0	1362.2	5626	1169	525	494	136	41	29	45	441	31	1366	26	5	95	68	.583	5	0-0	0	3.12	3.26

Dustin Pedroia

Bats: R Throws: R Pos: 2B-154   Ht: 5'9" Wt: 180 Born: 8/17/1983 Age: 26

Year Team	Lg	G	AB	H	2B	3B	HR	(Hm	Rd)	TB	R	RBI	RC	TBB	IBB	SO	HBP	SH	SF	SB	CS	SB%	GDP	Avg	OBP	Slg
2006 Bos	AL	31	89	17	4	0	2	(1	1)	27	5	7	3	7	0	7	1	1	0	0	1	.00	1	.191	.258	.303
2007 Bos	AL	139	520	165	39	1	8	(5	3)	230	86	50	79	47	1	42	7	5	2	7	1	.88	8	.317	.380	.442
2008 Bos	AL	157	653	213	54	2	17	(7	10)	322	118	83	107	50	1	52	7	1	9	20	1	.95	11	.326	.376	.493
2009 Bos	AL	154	626	185	48	1	15	(10	5)	280	115	72	104	74	3	45	5	3	6	20	8	.71	19	.296	.371	.447
Postseason		25	103	27	8	0	5	(2	3)	50	21	16	17	13	0	12	2	1	0	2	1	.67	3	.262	.356	.485
4 ML YEARS		481	1888	580	145	4	42	(23	19)	859	324	212	293	178	5	146	20	16	17	47	11	.81	45	.307	.370	.455

Mike Pelfrey

Pitches: R **Bats:** R **Pos:** SP-31   **Ht:** 6'7" **Wt:** 230 **Born:** 1/14/1984 **Age:** 26

Year	Team	Lg	G	GS	CG	GF	IP	BFP	H	R	ER	HR	SH	SF	HB	TBB	IBB	SO	WP	Bk	W	L	Pct	Sh	Sv-Op	Hld	ERC	ERA
2006	NYM	NL	4	4	0	0	21.1	99	25	14	13	1	1	1	3	12	0	13	2	0	2	1	.667	0	0-0	0	6.05	5.48
2007	NYM	NL	15	13	0	0	72.2	342	85	47	45	6	6	3	9	39	1	45	3	0	3	8	.273	0	0-0	0	5.99	5.57
2008	NYM	NL	32	32	2	0	200.2	851	209	86	83	12	11	5	13	64	1	110	2	0	13	11	.542	0	0-0	0	4.04	3.72
2009	NYM	NL	31	31	0	0	184.1	824	213	112	103	18	8	5	7	66	8	107	1	6	10	12	.455	0	0-0	0	4.83	5.03
	4 ML YEARS		82	80	2	0	479.0	2116	532	259	244	37	26	14	32	181	10	275	8	6	28	32	.467	0	0-0	0	4.72	4.58

Brayan Pena

Bats: B **Throws:** R **Pos:** C-30; DH-20; PH-20   **Ht:** 5'11" **Wt:** 247 **Born:** 1/7/1982 **Age:** 28

Year	Team	Lg	G	AB	H	2B	3B	HR	(Hm	Rd)	TB	R	RBI	RC	TBB	IBB	SO	HBP	SH	SF	SB	CS	SB%	GDP	Avg	OBP	Slg
2009	Omha*	AAA	22	88	27	6	1	4	(-	-)	47	11	18	16	4	2	9	3	2	1	2	1	.67	5	.307	.354	.534
2005	Atl	NL	18	39	7	2	0	0	(0	0)	9	2	4	0	1	1	7	0	0	0	0	0	-	1	.179	.200	.231
2006	Atl	NL	23	41	11	2	0	1	(0	1)	16	9	5	4	2	0	5	0	0	0	0	0	-	2	.268	.302	.390
2007	Atl	NL	16	33	7	0	0	1	(1	0)	10	2	3	0	0	0	3	0	0	0	0	1	.00	2	.212	.212	.303
2008	Atl	NL	14	14	4	1	0	0	(0	0)	5	3	0	0	1	0	2	0	0	0	0	0	-	0	.286	.333	.357
2009	KC	AL	64	165	45	10	0	6	(3	3)	73	17	18	18	12	2	18	0	4	2	0	0	-	5	.273	.318	.442
	5 ML YEARS		135	292	74	15	0	8	(4	4)	113	33	30	22	16	3	35	0	4	2	0	1	.00	10	.253	.290	.387

Carlos Pena

Bats: L **Throws:** L **Pos:** 1B-134; PH-3   **Ht:** 6'2" **Wt:** 225 **Born:** 5/17/1978 **Age:** 32

Year	Team	Lg	G	AB	H	2B	3B	HR	(Hm	Rd)	TB	R	RBI	RC	TBB	IBB	SO	HBP	SH	SF	SB	CS	SB%	GDP	Avg	OBP	Slg
2001	Tex	AL	22	62	16	4	1	3	(2	1)	31	6	12	11	10	0	17	0	0	0	0	0	-	1	.258	.361	.500
2002	2 Tms	AL	115	397	96	17	4	19	(10	9)	178	43	52	56	41	0	111	3	0	2	2	2	.50	7	.242	.316	.448
2003	Det	AL	131	452	112	21	6	18	(8	10)	199	51	50	61	53	1	123	6	1	4	4	5	.44	6	.248	.332	.440
2004	Det	AL	142	481	116	22	4	27	(10	17)	227	89	82	73	70	2	146	3	2	5	7	1	.88	11	.241	.338	.472
2005	Det	AL	79	260	61	9	0	18	(14	4)	124	37	44	40	31	2	95	4	0	0	0	1	.00	3	.235	.325	.477
2006	Bos	AL	18	33	9	2	0	1	(1	0)	14	3	3	3	4	0	10	0	0	0	0	0	-	1	.273	.351	.424
2007	TB	AL	148	490	138	29	1	46	(23	23)	307	99	121	114	103	10	142	10	1	8	1	0	1.00	6	.282	.411	.627
2008	TB	AL	139	490	121	24	2	31	(14	17)	242	76	102	92	96	7	166	12	0	9	1	1	.50	6	.247	.377	.494
2009	TB	AL	135	471	107	25	2	39	(19	20)	253	91	100	88	87	11	163	9	0	3	3	3	.50	5	.227	.356	.537
02	Oak	AL	40	124	27	4	0	7	(5	2)	52	12	16	17	15	0	38	1	0	1	0	0	-	2	.218	.305	.419
02	Det	AL	75	273	69	13	4	12	(5	7)	126	31	36	39	26	0	73	2	0	1	2	2	.50	5	.253	.321	.462
	Postseason		15	53	14	2	0	3	(0	3)	25	9	10	11	10	2	17	0	0	0	3	2	.60	1	.264	.381	.472
	9 ML YEARS		929	3136	776	153	20	202	(101	101)	1575	495	566	538	495	33	973	47	4	31	18	13	.58	47	.247	.355	.502

Ramiro Pena

Bats: B **Throws:** R **Pos:** SS-34; 3B-27; PR-14; 2B-8; PH-3; DH-2   **Ht:** 5'11" **Wt:** 165 **Born:** 7/18/1985 **Age:** 24

Year	Team	Lg	G	AB	H	2B	3B	HR	(Hm	Rd)	TB	R	RBI	RC	TBB	IBB	SO	HBP	SH	SF	SB	CS	SB%	GDP	Avg	OBP	Slg
2005	Tampa	A+	23	73	18	4	1	1	(-	-)	27	11	6	9	9	0	12	0	2	2	1	0	1.00	4	.247	.321	.370
2005	Trntn	AA	68	236	59	5	2	0	(-	-)	68	28	11	19	10	0	48	0	8	1	4	1	.80	5	.250	.279	.288
2006	Trntn	AA	26	86	17	2	0	0	(-	-)	19	6	6	4	5	0	19	1	5	1	0	1	.00	0	.198	.247	.221
2006	Tampa	A+	54	218	61	4	2	0	(-	-)	69	31	23	25	16	0	26	4	4	4	8	4	.67	2	.280	.335	.317
2007	Trntn	AA	52	203	51	7	1	0	(-	-)	60	23	10	22	22	1	33	2	6	0	7	3	.70	7	.251	.330	.296
2008	Trntn	AA	110	439	115	20	7	2	(-	-)	155	56	45	54	40	1	85	4	12	6	8	5	.62	7	.262	.325	.353
2009	S-WB	AAA	43	156	36	9	0	2	(-	-)	51	18	9	17	18	0	28	0	6	0	5	1	.83	6	.231	.310	.327
2009	NYY	AL	69	115	33	6	1	1	(1	0)	44	17	10	15	5	0	20	0	1	0	4	1	.80	2	.287	.317	.383

Tony Pena

Pitches: R **Bats:** R **Pos:** RP-72   **Ht:** 6'2" **Wt:** 219 **Born:** 1/9/1982 **Age:** 28

Year	Team	Lg	G	GS	CG	GF	IP	BFP	H	R	ER	HR	SH	SF	HB	TBB	IBB	SO	WP	Bk	W	L	Pct	Sh	Sv-Op	Hld	ERC	ERA
2006	Ari	NL	25	0	0	6	30.2	135	36	21	19	6	2	1	0	8	0	21	1	0	3	4	.429	0	1-1	2	5.12	5.58
2007	Ari	NL	75	0	0	13	85.1	344	63	36	31	8	1	3	5	31	4	63	3	1	5	4	.556	0	2-5	30	2.71	3.27
2008	Ari	NL	72	0	0	20	72.2	313	80	38	35	5	4	4	3	17	5	52	4	0	3	2	.600	0	3-8	23	3.79	4.33
2009	2 Tms		72	0	0	28	70.0	312	81	37	31	7	2	2	2	20	3	55	3	0	6	5	.545	0	2-4	13	4.46	3.99
09	Ari	NL	37	0	0	13	34.0	153	41	20	16	3	1	1	1	11	0	26	2	0	5	3	.625	0	1-2	8	4.93	4.24
09	CWS	AL	35	0	0	15	36.0	159	40	17	15	4	1	1	1	9	3	29	1	0	1	2	.333	0	1-2	5	4.03	3.75
	Postseason		5	0	0	1	5.1	17	3	0	0	0	0	0	0	0	0	7	0	0	0	0	-	0	0-0	1	0.75	0.00
	4 ML YEARS		244	0	0	67	258.2	1104	260	132	116	26	9	10	10	76	12	191	11	1	17	15	.531	0	8-18	68	3.75	4.04

Tony Pena

Bats: R **Throws:** R **Pos:** SS-40; PR-2; PH-1   **Ht:** 6'2" **Wt:** 180 **Born:** 3/23/1981 **Age:** 29

Year	Team	Lg	G	AB	H	2B	3B	HR	(Hm	Rd)	TB	R	RBI	RC	TBB	IBB	SO	HBP	SH	SF	SB	CS	SB%	GDP	Avg	OBP	Slg
2009	Omha*	AAA	1	0	0	0	0	0	(-	-)	0	0	0	0	0	0	0	0	0	0	0	0	-	0	-	-	-
2006	Atl	NL	40	44	10	2	0	1	(1	0)	15	12	3	3	2	1	10	0	0	0	0	0	-	1	.227	.261	.341
2007	KC	AL	152	509	136	25	7	2	(1	1)	181	58	47	48	10	0	78	4	8	5	5	6	.45	13	.267	.284	.356
2008	KC	AL	95	225	38	4	1	1	(0	1)	47	22	14	7	6	2	49	0	2	2	3	1	.75	4	.169	.189	.209
2009	KC	AL	40	51	5	1	0	0	(0	0)	6	3	2	0	2	0	13	0	0	0	0	0	-	1	.098	.132	.118
	4 ML YEARS		327	829	189	32	8	4	(2	2)	249	95	66	58	20	3	150	4	10	7	8	7	.53	19	.228	.248	.300

Year	Team	Lg	G	GS	CG	GF	IP	BFP	H	R	ER	HR	SH	SF	HB	TBB	IBB	SO	WP	Bk	W	l	Pct	Sh	Sv-Op	Hld	ERC	ERA
			HOW MUCH HE PITCHED						WHAT HE GAVE UP												THE RESULTS							
2009	Royals	R	2	2	0	0	2.0	10	2	2	0	0	0	0	0	1	0	1	1	0	0	0	-	0	0--	-	3.21	0.00
2009	Burlgtn	A	7	1	0	0	14.1	56	8	6	5	1	0	0	1	5	0	14	1	0	1	2	.333	0	0--	-	1.75	3.14
2009	Omha	AAA	1	0	0	0	3.0	11	2	0	0	0	1	0	0	0	0	3	0	0	0	0	-	0	0--	-	0.91	0.00
2008	KC	AL	1	0	0	1	1.0	3	0	0	0	0	0	0	0	0	0	1	0	0	0	0	-	0	0-0		0.00	0.00

Hunter Pence

Bats: R **Throws:** R **Pos:** RF-157; PH-2   **Ht:** 6'4" **Wt:** 210 **Born:** 4/13/1983 **Age:** 27

Year	Team	Lg	G	AB	H	2B	3B	HR	(Hm	Rd)	TB	R	RBI	RC	TBB	IBB	SO	HBP	SH	SF	SB	CS	SB%	GDP	Avg	OBP	Slg
			BATTING																		BASERUNNING				AVERAGES		
2007	Hou	NL	108	456	147	30	9	17	(7	10)	246	57	69	77	26	0	95	1	0	1	11	5	.69	10	.322	.360	.539
2008	Hou	NL	157	595	160	34	4	25	(14	11)	277	78	83	82	40	2	124	4	0	3	11	10	.52	14	.269	.318	.466
2009	Hou	NL	159	585	165	26	5	25	(14	11)	276	76	72	80	58	1	109	1	0	3	14	11	.56	25	.282	.346	.472
	3 ML YEARS		424	1636	472	90	18	67	(35	32)	799	211	224	239	124	3	328	6	0	7	36	26	.58	49	.289	.340	.488

Hayden Penn

Pitches: R **Bats:** R **Pos:** RP-15; SP-1   **Ht:** 6'3" **Wt:** 200 **Born:** 10/13/1984 **Age:** 25

Year	Team	Lg	G	GS	CG	GF	IP	BFP	H	R	ER	HR	SH	SF	HB	TBB	IBB	SO	WP	Bk	W	L	Pct	Sh	Sv-Op	Hld	ERC	ERA
			HOW MUCH HE PITCHED						WHAT HE GAVE UP												THE RESULTS							
2009	NewOr	AAA	14	13	2	0	70.0	304	71	35	32	9	0	3	0	26	1	62	4	0	2	4	.333	1	0--	-	4.17	4.11
2005	Bal	AL	8	8	0	0	38.1	178	46	30	27	6	1	0	0	21	3	18	3	1	3	2	.600	0	0-0	0	6.17	6.34
2006	Bal	AL	6	6	0	0	19.2	112	38	33	33	8	0	0	2	13	0	8	0	0	0	4	.000	0	0-0	0	14.68	15.10
2009	Fla	NL	16	1	0	5	22.0	120	30	27	19	3	4	0	2	20	2	27	1	0	1	0	1.000	0	0-0	1	8.66	7.77
	3 ML YEARS		30	15	0	5	80.0	410	114	90	79	17	5	0	4	54	5	53	4	1	4	6	.400	0	0-0	1	8.81	8.89

Cliff Pennington

Bats: B **Throws:** R **Pos:** SS-60   **Ht:** 5'11" **Wt:** 188 **Born:** 6/15/1984 **Age:** 26

Year	Team	Lg	G	AB	H	2B	3B	HR	(Hm	Rd)	TB	R	RBI	RC	TBB	IBB	SO	HBP	SH	SF	SB	CS	SB%	GDP	Avg	OBP	Slg
			BATTING																		BASERUNNING				AVERAGES		
2005	Kane	A	89	290	80	15	0	3	(-	-)	104	49	29	44	39	0	47	2	2	1	25	6	.81	4	.276	.364	.359
2006	Stcktn	A+	46	177	36	7	0	2	(-	-)	49	36	21	17	24	0	35	1	0	0	7	1	.88	5	.203	.302	.277
2006	As	R	9	28	13	3	1	0	(-	-)	18	3	6	8	4	0	2	0	0	0	0	0	-	0	.464	.531	.643
2007	Stcktn	A+	68	286	73	17	3	6	(-	-)	114	50	36	44	43	2	54	1	0	0	9	2	.82	2	.255	.348	.399
2007	Mdland	AA	70	271	68	13	2	2	(-	-)	91	41	21	35	38	0	35	1	2	2	8	2	.80	5	.251	.343	.336
2008	Mdland	AA	50	204	53	7	2	0	(-	-)	64	42	18	32	39	0	36	0	1	0	20	1	.95	7	.260	.379	.314
2008	Scrmto	AAA	65	236	70	9	3	2	(-	-)	91	47	16	45	54	2	34	0	3	1	11	5	.69	2	.297	.426	.386
2009	Scrmto	AAA	99	360	95	22	3	3	(-	-)	132	48	40	53	45	1	54	2	6	4	27	4	.87	2	.264	.345	.367
2008	Oak	AL	36	99	24	5	0	0	(0	0)	29	14	9	12	13	0	18	2	2	1	4	1	.80	1	.242	.339	.293
2009	Oak	AL	60	208	58	11	3	4	(3	1)	87	27	21	29	19	0	46	1	1	0	7	5	.58	5	.279	.342	.418
	2 ML YEARS		96	307	82	16	3	4	(3	1)	116	41	30	41	32	0	64	3	3	1	11	6	.65	6	.267	.341	.378

Brad Penny

Pitches: R **Bats:** R **Pos:** SP-30   **Ht:** 6'4" **Wt:** 240 **Born:** 5/24/1978 **Age:** 32

Year	Team	Lg	G	GS	CG	GF	IP	BFP	H	R	ER	HR	SH	SF	HB	TBB	IBB	SO	WP	Bk	W	L	Pct	Sh	Sv-Op	Hld	ERC	ERA
			HOW MUCH HE PITCHED						WHAT HE GAVE UP												THE RESULTS							
2000	Fla	NL	23	22	0	0	119.2	529	120	70	64	13	6	2	5	60	4	80	4	1	8	7	.533	0	0-0	0	4.70	4.81
2001	Fla	NL	31	31	1	0	205.0	833	183	92	84	15	8	2	7	54	3	154	2	0	10	10	.500	1	0-0	0	2.96	3.69
2002	Fla	NL	24	24	1	0	129.1	574	148	76	67	18	6	4	1	50	7	93	4	0	8	7	.533	1	0-0	0	5.08	4.66
2003	Fla	NL	32	32	0	0	196.1	811	195	96	90	21	7	5	3	56	6	138	3	4	14	10	.583	0	0-0	0	3.73	4.13
2004	2 Tms	NL	24	24	0	0	143.0	590	130	55	50	12	3	3	3	45	6	111	5	0	9	10	.474	0	0-0	0	3.20	3.15
2005	LAD	NL	29	29	1	0	175.1	738	185	78	76	17	7	1	3	41	2	122	3	0	7	9	.438	0	0-0	0	3.77	3.90
2006	LAD	NL	34	33	0	0	189.0	813	206	94	91	19	8	3	9	54	4	148	6	0	16	9	.640	0	0-0	1	4.32	4.33
2007	LAD	NL	33	33	0	0	208.0	865	199	75	70	13	9	5	5	73	2	135	6	0	16	4	.800	0	0-0	0	3.41	3.03
2008	LAD	NL	19	17	0	1	94.2	426	112	68	66	13	10	2	3	42	0	51	1	1	6	9	.400	0	0-0	0	5.82	6.27
2009	2 Tms	NL	30	30	1	0	173.1	751	191	102	94	22	0	7	5	51	0	109	6	0	11	9	.550	0	0-0	0	4.54	4.88
04	Fla	NL	21	21	0	0	131.1	545	124	50	46	10	3	3	3	39	6	105	5	0	8	8	.500	0	0-0	0	3.26	3.15
04	LAD	NL	3	3	0	0	11.2	45	6	5	4	2	0	0	0	6	0	6	0	0	1	2	.333	0	0-0	0	2.51	3.09
09	Bos	AL	24	24	0	0	131.2	590	160	89	82	17	0	7	5	42	0	89	4	0	7	8	.467	0	0-0	0	5.35	5.61
09	SF	NL	6	6	1	0	41.2	161	31	13	12	5	0	0	0	9	0	20	2	0	4	1	.800	0	0-0	0	2.22	2.59
	Postseason		8	4	0	0	23.0	106	31	17	16	3	2	1	0	11	1	14	0	0	3	2	.600	0	0-1	0	6.81	6.26
	10 ML YEARS		279	275	4	1	1633.2	6930	1669	806	752	159	68	38	44	526	34	1141	40	6	105	84	.556	2	0-0	1	3.98	4.14

Jhonny Peralta

Bats: R **Throws:** R **Pos:** 3B-105; SS-41; DH-8; PH-3   **Ht:** 6'1" **Wt:** 210 **Born:** 5/28/1982 **Age:** 28

Year	Team	Lg	G	AB	H	2B	3B	HR	(Hm	Rd)	TB	R	RBI	RC	TBB	IBB	SO	HBP	SH	SF	SB	CS	SB%	GDP	Avg	OBP	Slg
			BATTING																		BASERUNNING				AVERAGES		
2003	Cle	AL	77	242	55	10	1	4	(3	1)	79	24	21	24	20	0	65	4	2	2	1	3	.25	5	.227	.295	.326
2004	Cle	AL	8	25	6	1	0	0	(0	0)	7	2	2	2	3	0	6	0	0	0	0	1	.00	0	.240	.321	.280
2005	Cle	AL	141	504	147	35	4	24	(14	10)	262	82	78	87	58	3	128	3	1	4	0	2	.00	12	.292	.366	.520
2006	Cle	AL	149	569	146	28	3	13	(7	6)	219	84	68	66	56	0	152	1	3	3	0	1	.00	19	.257	.323	.385
2007	Cle	AL	152	574	155	27	1	21	(16	5)	247	87	72	85	61	2	146	4	1	7	4	4	.50	12	.270	.341	.430

Year	Team	Lg	G	AB	H	2B	3B	HR	(Hm	Rd)	TB	R	RBI	RC	TBB	IBB	SO	HBP	SH	SF	SB	CS	SB%	GDP	Avg	OBP	Slg
																									BATTING	BASERUNNING	AVERAGES
2008	Cle	AL	154	605	167	42	4	23	(11	12)	286	104	89	84	48	2	126	4	2	5	3	1	.75	26	.276	.331	.473
2009	Cle	AL	151	582	148	35	1	11	(2	9)	218	57	83	63	51	0	134	4	2	6	0	2	.00	20	.254	.316	.375
	Postseason		11	42	14	5	0	2	(1	1)	25	6	10	9	5	0	11	0	0	1	1	0	1.00	2	.333	.396	.595
	7 ML YEARS		832	3101	824	178	14	96	(53	43)	1318	440	413	411	297	7	757	20	11	27	8	14	.36	94	.266	.331	.425

Joel Peralta

Pitches: R **Bats:** R **Pos:** RP-27   **Ht:** 5'11" **Wt:** 193 **Born:** 3/23/1976 **Age:** 34

Year	Team	Lg	G	GS	CG	GF	IP	BFP	H	R	ER	HR	SH	SF	HB	TBB	IBB	SO	WP	Bk	W	L	Pct	Sh	Sv-Op	Hld	ERC	ERA
			HOW MUCH HE PITCHED						WHAT HE GAVE UP												THE RESULTS							
2009	ColSpr*	AAA	31	0	0	12	36.2	152	31	11	10	3	1	2	0	11	1	32	3	0	6	0	1.000	0	4- -	-	2.67	2.45
2005	LAA	AL	28	0	0	10	34.2	145	28	15	15	6	2	1	0	14	2	30	2	0	1	0	1.000	0	0-0	0	3.40	3.89
2006	KC	AL	64	0	0	21	73.2	304	74	37	36	10	1	3	2	17	2	57	5	0	1	3	.250	0	1-3	17	3.80	4.40
2007	KC	AL	62	0	0	18	87.2	366	93	39	37	9	2	4	2	19	5	66	2	0	1	3	.250	0	1-5	7	3.75	3.80
2008	KC	AL	40	0	0	12	52.2	224	56	37	35	15	1	3	2	14	0	38	1	0	1	2	.333	0	0-1	1	5.38	5.98
2009	Col	NL	27	0	0	6	24.2	113	27	17	17	3	0	1	3	12	2	22	0	0	0	3	.000	0	0-1	6	5.51	6.20
	5 ML YEARS		221	0	0	67	273.1	1152	278	145	140	43	6	12	9	76	11	213	10	0	4	11	.267	0	2-10	31	4.18	4.61

Troy Percival

Pitches: R **Bats:** R **Pos:** RP-14   **Ht:** 6'3" **Wt:** 255 **Born:** 8/9/1969 **Age:** 40

Year	Team	Lg	G	GS	CG	GF	IP	BFP	H	R	ER	HR	SH	SF	HB	TBB	IBB	SO	WP	Bk	W	L	Pct	Sh	Sv-Op	Hld	ERC	ERA
			HOW MUCH HE PITCHED						WHAT HE GAVE UP												THE RESULTS							
1995	LAA	AL	62	0	0	16	74.0	284	37	16	16	6	4	1	1	26	2	94	2	2	3	2	.600	0	3-6	29	1.44	1.95
1996	LAA	AL	62	0	0	52	74.0	291	38	20	19	8	2	1	2	31	4	100	2	0	0	2	.000	0	36-39	2	1.76	2.31
1997	LAA	AL	55	0	0	46	52.0	224	40	20	20	6	1	2	4	22	2	72	5	0	5	5	.500	0	27-31	0	3.15	3.46
1998	LAA	AL	67	0	0	60	66.2	287	45	31	27	5	3	2	3	37	4	87	3	0	2	7	.222	0	42-48	0	2.74	3.65
1999	LAA	AL	60	0	0	50	57.0	230	38	24	24	9	0	1	3	22	0	58	3	0	4	6	.400	0	31-39	0	2.83	3.79
2000	LAA	AL	54	0	0	45	50.0	221	42	27	25	7	3	2	2	30	4	49	1	0	5	5	.500	0	32-42	0	4.24	4.50
2001	LAA	AL	57	0	0	50	57.2	230	39	19	17	3	1	0	2	18	1	71	2	0	4	2	.667	0	39-42	0	1.90	2.65
2002	LAA	AL	58	0	0	50	56.1	228	38	12	12	5	0	1	0	25	1	68	5	0	4	1	.800	0	40-44	0	2.45	1.92
2003	LAA	AL	52	0	0	49	49.1	206	33	22	19	7	0	1	3	23	1	48	1	0	0	5	.000	0	33-37	0	2.99	3.47
2004	LAA	AL	52	0	0	48	49.2	211	43	19	16	7	0	2	3	19	3	33	2	0	2	3	.400	0	33-38	0	3.67	2.90
2005	Det	AL	26	0	0	23	25.0	107	19	16	16	7	1	1	2	11	3	20	0	0	1	3	.250	0	8-11	0	4.17	5.76
2007	StL	NL	34	1	0	9	40.0	150	24	8	8	3	0	0	0	10	0	36	2	0	3	0	1.000	0	0-0	3	1.52	1.80
2008	TB	AL	50	0	0	38	45.2	194	29	26	23	9	1	2	1	27	0	38	2	0	2	1	.667	0	28-32	4	3.50	4.53
2009	TB	AL	14	0	0	10	11.1	52	14	8	8	3	0	0	1	5	0	7	2	0	0	1	.000	0	6-6	0	7.48	6.35
	Postseason		9	0	0	9	9.2	39	8	3	3	1	0	0	1	1	0	10	0	0	0	0	-	0	7-7	0	2.42	2.79
	14 ML YEARS		703	1	0	546	708.2	2915	479	271	250	85	16	16	27	306	25	781	32	2	35	43	.449	0	358-415	38	2.68	3.17

Luis Perdomo

Pitches: R **Bats:** B **Pos:** RP-35   **Ht:** 6'0" **Wt:** 170 **Born:** 4/27/1984 **Age:** 26

Year	Team	Lg	G	GS	CG	GF	IP	BFP	H	R	ER	HR	SH	SF	HB	TBB	IBB	SO	WP	Bk	W	L	Pct	Sh	Sv-Op	Hld	ERC	ERA
			HOW MUCH HE PITCHED						WHAT HE GAVE UP												THE RESULTS							
2006	Indns	R	19	0	0	17	20.0	79	11	9	8	1	0	1	2	5	0	29	3	0	0	2	.000	0	9- -	-	1.43	3.60
2007	Lk Cty	A	56	0	0	40	66.0	270	43	28	24	6	1	1	4	26	1	81	3	1	4	6	.400	0	10- -	-	2.35	3.27
2008	Knstn	A+	31	0	0	25	39.0	153	19	6	4	0	2	2	2	17	0	43	5	0	3	1	.750	0	18- -	-	1.37	0.92
2008	Akron	AA	9	0	0	5	15.1	63	12	6	6	1	0	1	0	7	0	17	0	0	2	0	1.000	0	1- -	-	2.94	3.52
2008	Sprgfld	AA	15	0	0	5	18.0	80	18	12	9	2	0	0	1	6	0	22	2	0	2	2	.500	0	1- -	-	3.96	4.50
2009	Portlnd	AAA	1	0	0	0	1.0	7	3	2	2	0	0	0	1	1	0	1	0	0	0	0	-	0	0- -	-	19.55	18.00
2009	SD	NL	35	0	0	10	60.0	268	57	36	32	11	1	1	0	34	3	55	8	0	1	0	1.000	0	0-1	0	4.94	4.80

Chris Perez

Pitches: R **Bats:** R **Pos:** RP-61   **Ht:** 6'4" **Wt:** 230 **Born:** 7/1/1985 **Age:** 24

Year	Team	Lg	G	GS	CG	GF	IP	BFP	H	R	ER	HR	SH	SF	HB	TBB	IBB	SO	WP	Bk	W	L	Pct	Sh	Sv-Op	Hld	ERC	ERA
			HOW MUCH HE PITCHED						WHAT HE GAVE UP												THE RESULTS							
2006	QuadC	A	25	0	0	21	29.1	126	20	9	6	0	1	1	4	19	0	32	9	0	2	0	1.000	0	12- -	-	3.13	1.84
2007	Sprgfld	AA	39	0	0	37	40.2	172	17	11	11	3	1	0	8	28	0	62	2	0	2	0	1.000	0	27- -	-	2.61	2.43
2007	Memp	AAA	15	0	0	15	14.0	58	6	7	7	2	2	0	1	13	0	15	2	0	0	1	.000	0	9- -	-	3.75	4.50
2008	Memp	AAA	26	0	0	21	25.1	105	18	9	9	3	1	0	1	12	0	38	4	0	1	1	.500	0	11- -	-	3.08	3.20
2009	Memp	AAA	3	0	0	3	4.0	14	0	0	0	0	0	0	0	3	0	4	1	0	1	0	1.000	0	2- -	-	0.61	0.00
2008	StL	NL	41	0	0	23	41.2	177	34	18	16	5	1	3	1	22	0	42	2	0	3	3	.500	0	7-11	6	3.83	3.46
2009	2 Tms		61	0	0	16	57.0	239	41	28	27	8	1	1	6	27	0	68	8	0	1	2	.333	0	2-5	7	3.54	4.26
09	StL	NL	29	0	0	8	23.2	106	17	12	11	3	0	1	3	15	0	30	4	0	1	1	.500	0	1-2	3	4.01	4.18
09	Cle	AL	32	0	0	8	33.1	133	24	16	16	5	0	1	3	12	0	38	4	0	0	1	.000	0	1-3	4	3.19	4.32
	2 ML YEARS		102	0	0	39	98.2	416	75	46	43	13	1	5	7	49	0	110	10	0	4	5	.444	0	9-16	13	3.66	3.92

Fernando Perez

Bats: B **Throws:** R **Pos:** CF-8; LF-5; PR-4; DH-2; RF-1   **Ht:** 6'1" **Wt:** 195 **Born:** 4/23/1983 **Age:** 27

Year	Team	Lg	G	AB	H	2B	3B	HR	(Hm	Rd)	TB	R	RBI	RC	TBB	IBB	SO	HBP	SH	SF	SB	CS	SB%	GDP	Avg	OBP	Slg
																					BATTING				BASERUNNING	AVERAGES	
2004	HudVal	A-	69	267	62	8	5	2	(-	-)	86	46	20	32	30	0	70	3	1	3	24	4	.86	0	.232	.314	.322
2005	SWMch	A	134	522	151	17	13	6	(-	-)	212	93	48	85	58	0	86	3	6	5	57	17	.77	14	.289	.361	.406
2006	Visalia	A+	133	547	168	19	9	4	(-	-)	217	123	56	94	78	0	134	6	8	2	33	16	.67	5	.307	.398	.397
2007	Mont	AA	102	393	121	24	10	8	(-	-)	189	84	33	82	76	0	104	2	5	0	32	18	.64	2	.308	.423	.481
2008	Drham	AAA	129	511	147	17	11	5	(-	-)	201	86	36	80	58	2	156	2	4	0	43	12	.78	3	.288	.361	.393
2009	Rays	R	1	3	0	0	0	0	(-	-)	0	0	0	0	0	0	3	0	0	0	0	0	.	0	.000	.000	.000

Year	Team	Lg	G	AB	H	2B	3B	HR	(Hm	Rd)	TB	R	RBI	RC	TBB	IBB	SO	HDP	SH	SF	SB	CS	SB%	GDP	Avg	OBP	Slg
2009	Charltt	A+	3	10	2	0	0	0	(-	-)	2	1	0	0	1	0	1	0	0	0	2	0	1.00	0	.200	.273	.200
2009	Drham	AAA	13	36	10	3	0	0	(-	-)	13	10	2	6	7	0	17	0	0	0	8	1	.89	0	.278	.395	.361
2008	TB	AL	23	60	15	2	0	3	(2	1)	26	18	8	10	8	1	16	1	3	0	5	0	1.00	3	.250	.348	.433
2009	TB	AL	18	34	7	0	0	0	(0	0)	7	4	2	0	0	0	11	0	1	0	2	0	.206	0	.206	.206	.206
	Postseason		5	9	1	0	0	0	(0	0)	1	2	0	0	0	0	2	0	0	0	1	0	1.00	0	.111	.111	.111
	2 ML YEARS		41	94	22	2	0	3	(2	1)	33	22	10	10	8	1	27	1	4	0	5	2	.71	3	.234	.301	.351

Oliver Perez

Pitches: L **Bats:** L **Pos:** SP-14   **Ht:** 6'3" **Wt:** 205 **Born:** 8/15/1981 **Age:** 28

			HOW MUCH HE PITCHED					WHAT HE GAVE UP										THE RESULTS								
Year	Team	Lg	G	GS	CG	GF	IP	BFP	H	R	ER	HR	SH	SF	HB	TBB	IBB	SO	WP	Bk	W	L	Pct	Sh	Sv-Op Hld	ERC	ERA
2009	StLuci*	A+	1	1	0	0	3.0	18	7	6	2	1	0	1	0	1	0	3	1	0	0	1	.000	0	0- -	13.87	6.00
2009	Bklyn*	A-	1	1	0	0	5.0	17	2	0	0	0	0	0	0	1	0	6	0	0	1	0	1.000	0	0- -	0.67	0.00
2009	Buffalo*	AAA	2	2	0	0	9.1	44	8	4	4	1	0	0	0	9	0	9	0	0	0	2	.000	0	0- -	5.56	3.86
2002	SD	NL	16	15	0	0	90.0	387	71	37	35	13	5	3	5	48	1	94	3	0	4	5	.444	0	0-0	3.93	3.50
2003	2 Tms	NL	24	24	0	0	126.2	579	129	80	77	22	5	2	4	77	3	141	7	1	4	10	.286	0	0-0	5.66	5.47
2004	Pit	NL	30	30	2	0	196.0	805	145	71	65	22	9	6	0	81	2	239	2	1	12	10	.545	1	0-0	2.99	2.98
2005	Pit	NL	20	20	0	0	103.0	471	102	68	67	23	5	4	6	70	1	97	3	0	7	5	.583	0	0-0	6.44	5.85
2006	2 Tms	NL	22	22	1	0	112.2	529	129	90	82	20	5	10	4	68	0	102	5	1	3	13	.188	1	0-0	6.62	6.55
2007	NYM	NL	29	29	0	0	177.0	765	153	90	70	22	4	7	7	79	1	174	6	0	15	10	.600	0	0-0	3.76	3.56
2008	NYM	NL	34	34	0	0	194.0	847	167	100	91	24	9	7	11	105	4	180	9	1	10	7	.588	0	0-0	4.21	4.22
2009	NYM	NL	14	14	0	0	66.0	324	69	51	50	12	5	4	4	58	2	62	2	0	3	4	.429	0	0-0	7.16	6.82
03	SD	NL	19	19	0	0	103.2	473	103	65	62	20	4	2	3	65	2	117	6	1	4	7	.364	0	0-0	5.74	5.38
03	Pit	NL	5	5	0	0	23.0	106	26	15	15	2	1	0	1	12	1	24	1	0	0	3	.000	0	0-0	5.29	5.87
06	Pit	NL	15	15	0	0	76.0	364	88	64	56	13	5	8	3	51	0	61	4	1	2	10	.167	0	0-0	6.85	6.63
06	NYM	NL	7	7	1	0	36.2	165	41	26	26	7	0	2	3	17	0	41	1	0	1	3	.250	1	0-0	6.16	6.38
	Postseason		2	2	0	0	11.2	50	13	6	6	3	2	0	1	3	1	7	0	0	1	0	1.000	0	0-0	5.61	4.63
	8 ML YEARS		189	188	3	0	1065.1	4707	865	587	537	158	47	42	32	580	14	1089	37	4	58	64	.475	2	0-0	4.66	4.54

Rafael Perez

Pitches: L **Bats:** L **Pos:** RP 54   **Ht:** 6'3" **Wt:** 195 **Born:** 5/15/1982 **Age:** 28

			HOW MUCH HE PITCHED					WHAT HE GAVE UP										THE RESULTS								
Year	Team	Lg	G	GS	CG	GF	IP	BFP	H	R	ER	HR	SH	SF	HB	TBB	IBB	SO	WP	Bk	W	L	Pct	Sh	Sv-Op Hld	ERC	ERA
2009	Clmbs*	AAA	16	0	0	9	21.2	91	23	3	2	0	0	0	1	5	0	23	1	0	1	0	1.000	0	3- -	3.29	0.83
2006	Cle	AL	18	0	0	5	16.2	56	10	6	6	2	1	0	0	6	1	15	4	1	0	0	-	0	0-1	1.37	4.38
2007	Cle	AL	44	0	0	11	60.2	236	41	15	12	5	1	1	0	15	2	62	4	0	1	2	.333	0	1-2 12	1.74	1.78
2008	Cle	AL	73	0	0	14	76.1	313	67	32	30	8	2	0	2	23	3	86	3	0	4	4	.500	0	2-7 25	3.14	3.54
2009	Cle	AL	54	0	0	12	48.0	230	66	41	39	5	4	2	2	25	6	32	1	2	3	4	.571	0	0-1 6	6.85	7.31
	Postseason		6	0	0	1	7.0	34	10	9	6	3	0	0	0	3	0	6	0	0	1	0	1.000	0	0-0	9.36	7.71
	4 ML YEARS		189	0	0	42	197.1	835	184	94	87	20	8	3	4	69	12	195	12	3	9	9	.500	0	3-11 44	3.49	3.97

Glen Perkins

Pitches: L **Bats:** L **Pos:** SP-17; RP-1   **Ht:** 6'0" **Wt:** 200 **Born:** 3/2/1983 **Age:** 27

			HOW MUCH HE PITCHED					WHAT HE GAVE UP										THE RESULTS								
Year	Team	Lg	G	GS	CG	GF	IP	BFP	H	R	ER	HR	SH	SF	HB	TBB	IBB	SO	WP	Bk	W	L	Pct	Sh	Sv-Op Hld	ERC	ERA
2009	FtMyrs*	A+	2	2	1	0	11.0	42	8	5	3	2	0	0	0	1	0	9	0	0	1	0	1.000	1	0- -	1.96	2.45
2009	Twins*	R	1	1	0	0	1.0	3	0	0	0	0	0	0	0	0	0	0	0	0	0	0	-	0	0- -	0.00	0.00
2006	Min	AL	4	0	0	1	5.2	20	3	1	1	0	0	0	0	0	0	6	0	0	0	0	-	0	0-0 1	0.60	1.59
2007	Min	AL	19	0	0	3	28.2	115	23	10	10	2	1	1	2	12	0	20	2	0	0	0	-	0	0-0 3	3.32	3.14
2008	Min	AL	26	26	0	0	151.0	661	183	81	74	25	7	4	3	39	0	74	2	1	12	4	.750	0	0-0 0	5.30	4.41
2009	Min	AL	18	17	0	0	96.1	423	120	64	63	13	1	3	1	23	0	45	2	1	6	7	.462	0	0-0 0	5.14	5.89
	Postseason		1	0	0	0	0.1	3	2	0	0	0	0	0	0	0	0	0	0	0	0	0	-	0	0-0 0	39.65	0.00
	4 ML YEARS		67	43	0	5	281.2	1219	329	156	148	40	9	8	6	74	0	145	6	2	18	11	.621	0	0-0 4	4.91	4.73

Ryan Perry

Pitches: R **Bats:** R **Pos:** RP-53   **Ht:** 6'4" **Wt:** 200 **Born:** 2/13/1987 **Age:** 23

			HOW MUCH HE PITCHED					WHAT HE GAVE UP										THE RESULTS								
Year	Team	Lg	G	GS	CG	GF	IP	BFP	H	R	ER	HR	SH	SF	HB	TBB	IBB	SO	WP	Bk	W	L	Pct	Sh	Sv-Op Hld	ERC	ERA
2008	Tigers	R	2	0	0	0	2.0	6	0	0	0	0	0	0	0	0	4	0	0	0	0	0	-	0	0- -	0.00	0.00
2008	Lkland	A+	12	0	0	9	11.2	59	15	6	5	0	0	1	1	7	0	12	2	0	1	2	.333	0	4- -	5.83	3.86
2009	Toledo	AAA	8	0	0	5	13.2	58	13	4	4	1	1	0	0	4	0	12	1	0	1	0	1.000	0	3- -	3.15	2.63
2009	Det	AL	53	0	0	12	61.2	273	56	30	26	7	3	3	1	38	5	60	6	1	0	1	.000	0	0-3 6	4.45	3.79

Gregorio Petit

Bats: R **Throws:** R **Pos:** 2B-8; 3B-3; PH-1   **Ht:** 5'10" **Wt:** 200 **Born:** 12/10/1984 **Age:** 25

			BATTING																	BASERUNNING				AVERAGES		
Year	Team	Lg	G	AB	H	2B	3B	HR	(Hm	Rd)	TB	R	RBI	RC	TBB	IBB	SO	HBP	SH	SF	SB	CS	SB%	GDP	Avg	OBP	Slg
2003	As	R	32	117	31	6	0	0	(-	-)	37	13	12	11	10	0	22	0	2	1	3	5	.38	5	.265	.323	.316
2004	Vancvr	A-	68	254	65	9	2	4	(-	-)	90	34	35	29	20	0	67	3	4	2	3	3	.50	9	.256	.315	.354
2005	Kane	A	87	287	83	10	4	9	(-	-)	128	55	33	46	26	0	44	1	3	1	8	2	.80	9	.289	.349	.446
2006	Stcktn	A+	137	519	133	25	7	8	(-	-)	196	71	63	63	38	0	96	5	9	5	22	13	.63	15	.256	.310	.378
2007	Mdland	AA	66	268	82	14	0	4	(-	-)	108	33	31	42	25	0	44	1	4	1	9	3	.75	5	.306	.366	.403
2007	Scrmto	AAA	67	235	65	12	0	2	(-	-)	83	20	28	28	16	0	48	3	3	3	1	2	.33	15	.277	.327	.353
2008	Scrmto	AAA	79	308	83	14	3	1	(-	-)	106	39	35	34	23	0	60	1	7	0	3	5	.38	11	.269	.322	.344

Year	Team	Lg	G	AB	H	2B	3B	HR	(Hm	Rd)	TB	R	RBI	RC	TBB	IBB	SO	HBP	SH	SF	SB	CS	SB%	GDP	Avg	OBP	Slg
2009	Scrmto	AAA	98	357	87	18	0	5	(-	-)	120	45	32	36	26	2	83	1	7	7	0	2	.00	15	.244	.292	.336
2008	Oak	AL	14	23	8	2	0	0	(0	0)	10	4	0	2	2	0	9	0	0	0	0	0	-	0	.348	.400	.435
2009	Oak	AL	11	31	7	1	0	0	(0	0)	8	2	1	1	0	0	6	0	0	0	0	0	-	2	.226	.226	.258
2 ML YEARS			25	54	15	3	0	0	(0	0)	18	6	1	3	2	0	15	0	0	0	0	0	-	2	.278	.304	.333

Yusmeiro Petit

Pitches: R **Bats:** R **Pos:** SP-17; RP-6   **Ht:** 6'1" **Wt:** 253 **Born:** 11/22/1984 **Age:** 25

	HOW MUCH HE PITCHED						WHAT HE GAVE UP												THE RESULTS							
Year	Team	Lg	G	GS	CG	GF	IP	BFP	H	R	ER	HR	SH	SF	HB	TBB	IBB	SO	WP	Bk	W	L	Pct	Sh	Sv-Op	Hld	ERC	ERA
2009	Reno*	AAA	5	5	0	0	15.2	73	21	13	12	4	1	1	0	5	0	13	0	0	0	1	.000	0	0- -	-	6.81	6.89
2006	Fla	NL	15	1	0	5	26.1	129	46	28	28	7	1	1	0	9	1	20	0	0	1	1	.500	0	0-0	0	10.07	9.57
2007	Ari	NL	14	10	0	2	57.0	243	58	30	29	12	1	1	0	18	1	40	0	1	3	4	.429	0	0-0	0	4.56	4.58
2008	Ari	NL	19	8	0	6	56.1	229	45	29	27	12	4	2	1	14	2	42	3	1	3	5	.375	0	0-0	0	3.08	4.31
2009	Ari	NL	23	17	0	2	89.2	407	102	62	58	19	3	0	0	34	1	74	3	0	3	10	.231	0	0-0	0	5.44	5.82
4 ML YEARS			71	36	0	15	229.1	1008	251	149	142	50	9	4	1	75	5	176	6	2	10	20	.333	0	0-0	0	5.07	5.57

Chris Pettit

Bats: R **Throws:** R **Pos:** RF-4; PR-4; DH-3; LF-2; PH-1   **Ht:** 6'0" **Wt:** 194 **Born:** 8/15/1984 **Age:** 25

										BATTING										BASERUNNING				AVERAGES		
Year	Team	Lg	G	AB	H	2B	3B	HR	(Hm | Rd)	TB	R	RBI	RC	TBB	IBB	SO	HBP	SH	SF	SB	CS	SB%	GDP	Avg	OBP	Slg
2006	Orem	R+	68	226	76	25	3	7	(- | -)	128	41	54	57	31	1	48	14	0	1	5	1	.83	5	.336	.445	.566
2007	CRpds	A	64	228	79	24	1	9	(- | -)	132	47	41	57	23	3	41	12	0	3	17	4	.81	4	.346	.429	.579
2007	RCuca	A+	69	265	82	20	2	9	(- | -)	133	54	54	55	36	1	48	3	1	2	13	3	.81	5	.309	.395	.502
2008	Ark	AA	61	222	55	12	2	6	(- | -)	89	27	26	30	16	0	39	8	4	1	5	2	.71	4	.248	.320	.401
2008	Angels	R	3	13	3	1	0	0	(- | -)	4	3	2	1	2	0	2	0	0	0	0	0	-	0	.231	.333	.308
2009	Angels	R	4	14	5	1	0	0	(- | -)	6	2	1	3	3	0	6	0	0	0	1	0	1.00	0	.357	.471	.429
2009	Salt Lk	AAA	96	371	120	30	3	8	(- | -)	180	70	59	72	31	0	62	8	1	3	18	2	.90	9	.323	.385	.485
2009	LAA	AL	10	7	2	0	0	0	(0 | 0)	2	2	0	0	0	0	1	0	0	0	0	0	-	1	.286	.286	.286

Andy Pettitte

Pitches: L **Bats:** L **Pos:** SP-32   **Ht:** 6'5" **Wt:** 225 **Born:** 6/15/1972 **Age:** 38

	HOW MUCH HE PITCHED						WHAT HE GAVE UP												THE RESULTS							
Year	Team	Lg	G	GS	CG	GF	IP	BFP	H	R	ER	HR	SH	SF	HB	TBB	IBB	SO	WP	Bk	W	L	Pct	Sh	Sv-Op	Hld	ERC	ERA
1995	NYY	AL	31	26	3	1	175.0	745	183	86	81	15	4	5	1	63	3	114	8	1	12	9	.571	0	0-0	0	4.13	4.17
1996	NYY	AL	35	34	2	1	221.0	929	229	105	95	23	7	3	3	72	2	162	6	1	21	8	.724	0	0-0	0	4.14	3.87
1997	NYY	AL	35	35	4	0	240.1	986	233	86	77	7	6	2	3	65	0	166	7	0	18	7	.720	1	0-0	0	3.05	2.88
1998	NYY	AL	33	32	5	0	216.1	932	226	110	102	20	6	7	6	87	1	146	5	0	16	11	.593	0	0-0	0	4.46	4.24
1999	NYY	AL	31	31	0	0	191.2	851	216	105	100	20	6	6	3	89	3	121	3	1	14	11	.560	0	0-0	0	5.22	4.70
2000	NYY	AL	32	32	3	0	204.2	903	219	111	99	17	7	4	4	80	4	125	2	3	19	9	.679	1	0-0	0	4.32	4.35
2001	NYY	AL	31	31	2	0	200.2	858	224	103	89	14	8	7	4	41	3	164	2	2	15	10	.600	0	0-0	0	3.82	3.99
2002	NYY	AL	22	22	3	0	134.2	570	144	58	49	6	3	2	4	32	2	97	2	1	13	5	.722	1	0-0	0	3.55	3.27
2003	NYY	AL	33	33	1	0	208.1	896	227	109	93	21	5	5	1	50	3	180	5	0	21	8	.724	0	0-0	0	3.89	4.02
2004	Hou	NL	15	15	0	0	83.0	346	71	37	36	8	1	0	0	31	2	79	4	0	6	4	.600	0	0-0	0	3.12	3.90
2005	Hou	NL	33	33	0	0	222.1	875	188	66	59	17	10	4	3	41	0	171	2	0	17	9	.654	0	0-0	0	2.40	2.39
2006	Hou	NL	36	35	2	1	214.1	929	238	114	100	27	14	5	2	70	9	178	2	1	14	13	.519	1	0-0	0	4.58	4.20
2007	NYY	AL	36	34	0	0	215.1	916	238	106	97	16	5	9	1	69	1	141	3	0	15	9	.625	0	0-0	1	4.27	4.05
2008	NYY	AL	33	33	0	0	204.0	881	233	112	103	19	8	7	7	55	4	158	6	1	14	14	.500	0	0-0	0	4.45	4.54
2009	NYY	AL	32	32	0	0	194.2	834	193	101	90	20	4	4	4	76	1	148	3	0	14	8	.636	0	0-0	0	4.11	4.16
Postseason			35	35	0	0	218.1	923	235	100	96	24	11	6	3	60	3	139	3	1	14	9	.609	0	0-0	0	4.16	3.96
15 ML YEARS			468	458	25	3	2926.1	12451	3062	1409	1270	250	94	70	48	921	38	2150	60	11	229	135	.629	4	0-0	1	3.97	3.91

Brandon Phillips

Bats: R **Throws:** R **Pos:** 2B-151; PH-3   **Ht:** 6'0" **Wt:** 195 **Born:** 6/28/1981 **Age:** 29

										BATTING										BASERUNNING				AVERAGES		
Year	Team	Lg	G	AB	H	2B	3B	HR	(Hm | Rd)	TB	R	RBI	RC	TBB	IBB	SO	HBP	SH	SF	SB	CS	SB%	GDP	Avg	OBP	Slg
2002	Cle	AL	11	31	8	3	1	0	(0 | 0)	13	5	4	5	3	0	6	1	1	0	0	0	-	0	.258	.343	.419
2003	Cle	AL	112	370	77	18	1	6	(3 | 3)	115	36	33	22	14	0	77	3	5	1	4	5	.44	12	.208	.242	.311
2004	Cle	AL	6	22	4	2	0	0	(0 | 0)	6	1	1	0	2	0	5	0	0	0	0	2	.00	1	.182	.250	.273
2005	Cle	AL	6	9	0	0	0	0	(0 | 0)	0	1	0	0	0	0	4	0	0	0	0	0	-	0	.000	.000	.000
2006	Cin	NL	149	536	148	28	1	17	(9 | 8)	229	65	75	74	35	3	88	6	4	6	25	2	.93	19	.276	.324	.427
2007	Cin	NL	158	650	187	26	6	30	(17 | 13)	315	107	94	88	33	4	109	12	2	5	32	8	.80	26	.288	.331	.485
2008	Cin	NL	141	559	146	24	7	21	(13 | 8)	247	80	78	74	39	6	93	5	0	6	23	10	.70	13	.261	.312	.442
2009	Cin	NL	153	584	161	30	5	20	(10 | 10)	261	78	98	80	44	3	75	6	2	8	25	9	.74	21	.276	.329	.447
8 ML YEARS			736	2761	731	131	21	94	(52 | 42)	1186	373	383	343	170	16	457	33	14	26	109	36	.75	92	.265	.312	.430

Kyle Phillips

Bats: L **Throws:** R **Pos:** C-5; PH-1   **Ht:** 6'2" **Wt:** 210 **Born:** 4/3/1984 **Age:** 26

										BATTING										BASERUNNING				AVERAGES		
Year	Team	Lg	G	AB	H	2B	3B	HR	(Hm | Rd)	TB	R	RBI	RC	TBB	IBB	SO	HBP	SH	SF	SB	CS	SB%	GDP	Avg	OBP	Slg
2002	Twins	R	35	101	20	4	1	1	(- | -)	29	10	12	9	14	0	18	0	0	1	0	0	-	0	.198	.293	.287
2003	Elizab	R+	63	246	71	12	0	8	(- | -)	107	36	49	40	26	2	34	3	0	4	1	0	1.00	4	.289	.358	.435
2003	FtMyrs	A+	1	2	1	0	0	0	(- | -)	1	0	0	0	0	0	0	0	0	0	0	0	-	0	.500	.500	.500
2004	QuadC	A	97	347	79	16	0	11	(- | -)	128	49	44	42	38	4	69	3	0	7	1	0	1.00	11	.228	.304	.369
2005	FtMyrs	A+	83	278	64	12	1	2	(- | -)	84	20	32	29	31	2	47	2	1	3	2	0	1.00	8	.230	.309	.302
2005	NwBrit	AA	22	67	14	1	0	2	(- | -)	21	6	8	6	6	2	17	0	1	3	0	0	-	0	.209	.263	.313

Year	Team	Lg	BATTING																				BASERUNNING				AVERAGES		
			G	AB	H	2B	3B	HR	(Hm	Rd)	TB	R	RBI	RC	TBB	IBB	SO	HBP	SH	SF			SB	CS	SB%	GDP	Avg	OBP	Slg
2006	BrvdCt	A+	58	216	51	4	0	3	(-	-)	64	13	35	20	21	2	40	1	2	2			1	1	.50	9	.236	.304	.296
2007	Dnedin	A+	104	389	119	19	0	10	(-	-)	168	44	62	62	35	1	51	0	0	4			0	0	-	4	.306	.360	.432
2008	NHam	AA	78	268	82	16	0	8	(-	-)	122	33	34	45	27	2	41	1	4	1			0	2	.00	3	.306	.370	.455
2009	NHam	AA	12	40	7	0	0	1	(-	-)	10	1	1	2	3	0	8	0	0	0			0	0	-	0	.175	.233	.250
2009	LsVgs	AAA	76	277	83	13	0	8	(-	-)	120	37	29	46	29	2	53	4	4	2			0	0	-	7	.300	.372	.433
2009	Tor	AL	5	18	5	3	0	0	(0	0)	8	1	2	1	0	0	4	0	0	0			0	0	-	1	.278	.278	.444

Paul Phillips

Bats: R **Throws:** R **Pos:** C-15; PH-2   **Ht:** 5'11" **Wt:** 205 **Born:** 4/15/1977 **Age:** 33

Year	Team	Lg	BATTING																				BASERUNNING				AVERAGES		
			G	AB	H	2B	3B	HR	(Hm	Rd)	TB	R	RBI	RC	TBB	IBB	SO	HBP	SH	SF			SB	CS	SB%	GDP	Avg	OBP	Slg
2009	ColSpr*	AAA	38	123	34	6	2	1	(-	-)	47	11	14	14	4	0	18	0	1	2			0	0	-	3	.276	.295	.382
2004	KC	AL	4	5	1	0	0	0	(0	0)	1	2	0	0	0	0	1	1	0	0			0	0	-	0	.200	.333	.200
2005	KC	AL	23	67	18	4	1	1	(0	1)	27	6	9	8	0	0	5	0	0	0			0	0	-	4	.269	.269	.403
2006	KC	AL	23	65	18	3	0	1	(0	1)	24	8	5	8	1	0	8	0	2	1			0	0	-	0	.277	.284	.369
2007	KC	AL	8	14	2	1	0	0	(0	0)	3	2	2	1	1	0	1	0	0	0			0	0	-	1	.143	.200	.214
2008	CWS	AL	4	2	0	0	0	0	(0	0)	0	0	0	0	0	0	1	0	0	0			0	0	-	0	.000	.000	.000
2009	Col	NL	17	45	14	2	0	1	(0	1)	19	5	9	11	7	1	3	0	1	1			0	0	-	0	.311	.396	.422
	6 ML YEARS		79	198	53	10	1	3	(0	3)	74	23	25	28	9	1	19	1	3	2			0	0	-	5	.268	.300	.374

Felix Pie

Bats: L **Throws:** L **Pos:** LF-44; CF-41; PR-14; PH-8; DH-3   **Ht:** 6'2" **Wt:** 170 **Born:** 2/8/1985 **Age:** 25

Year	Team	Lg	BATTING																				BASERUNNING				AVERAGES		
			G	AB	H	2B	3B	HR	(Hm	Rd)	TB	R	RBI	RC	TBB	IBB	SO	HBP	SH	SF			SB	CS	SB%	GDP	Avg	OBP	Slg
2007	ChC	NL	87	177	38	9	3	2	(0	2)	59	26	20	21	14	0	43	0	2	1			8	1	.80	0	.215	.271	.333
2008	ChC	NL	43	83	20	2	1	1	(1	0)	27	9	10	9	7	0	29	2	0	1			3	0	1.00	8	.241	.312	.325
2009	Bal	AL	101	252	67	10	3	9	(6	3)	110	38	29	30	24	1	58	0	0	3			1	3	.26	6	.266	.326	.437
	Postseason		2	1	0	0	0	0	(0	0)	0	0	0	0	1	0	1	0	0	0			0	0	-	0	.000	.500	.000
	3 ML YEARS		231	512	125	21	7	12	(7	5)	196	73	59	60	45	1	130	2	4	5			12	4	.75	9	.244	.305	.383

Juan Pierre

Bats: L **Throws:** L **Pos:** LF-94; PH-51; CF-15; PR-5   **Ht:** 5'10" **Wt:** 187 **Born:** 8/14/1977 **Age:** 32

Year	Team	Lg	BATTING																				BASERUNNING				AVERAGES		
			G	AB	H	2B	3B	HR	(Hm	Rd)	TB	R	RBI	RC	TBB	IBB	SO	HBP	SH	SF			SB	CS	SB%	GDP	Avg	OBP	Slg
2000	Col	NL	51	200	62	2	0	0	(0	0)	64	26	20	23	13	0	15	1	4	1			7	6	.54	2	.310	.353	.320
2001	Col	NL	156	617	202	26	11	2	(0	2)	256	108	55	101	41	1	29	10	14	1			46	17	.73	6	.327	.378	.415
2002	Col	NL	152	592	170	20	5	1	(0	1)	203	90	35	70	31	0	52	9	8	0			47	12	.80	7	.287	.332	.343
2003	Fla	NL	162	668	204	28	7	1	(1	0)	249	100	41	92	55	1	35	5	15	3			65	20	.76	9	.305	.361	.373
2004	Fla	NL	162	678	221	22	12	3	(1	2)	276	100	49	101	45	1	35	8	13	2			45	24	.65	9	.326	.374	.407
2005	Fla	NL	162	656	181	19	13	2	(1	1)	232	96	47	76	41	1	45	9	10	2			57	17	.77	10	.276	.326	.354
2006	ChC	NL	162	699	204	32	13	3	(1	2)	271	87	40	84	32	0	38	8	10	1			58	20	.74	6	.292	.330	.388
2007	LAD	NL	162	668	196	24	8	0	(0	0)	236	96	41	75	33	0	37	6	20	2			64	15	.81	10	.293	.331	.353
2008	LAD	NL	119	375	106	10	2	1	(0	1)	123	44	28	48	22	1	24	3	5	1			40	12	.77	3	.283	.327	.328
2009	LAD	NL	145	380	117	16	8	0	(0	0)	149	57	31	58	27	3	27	8	9	1			30	12	.71	7	.308	.365	.392
	Postseason		19	77	24	5	2	0	(0	0)	33	14	7	14	8	2	4	1	1	0			3	5	.38	0	.312	.384	.429
	10 ML YEARS		1433	5533	1663	199	79	13	(4	9)	2059	804	387	737	340	8	337	67	110	14			459	155	.75	69	.301	.348	.372

A.J. Pierzynski

Bats: L **Throws:** R **Pos:** C-131; PH-11; DH-1   **Ht:** 6'3" **Wt:** 230 **Born:** 12/30/1976 **Age:** 33

Year	Team	Lg	BATTING																				BASERUNNING				AVERAGES		
			G	AB	H	2B	3B	HR	(Hm	Rd)	TB	R	RBI	RC	TBB	IBB	SO	HBP	SH	SF			SB	CS	SB%	GDP	Avg	OBP	Slg
1998	Min	AL	7	10	3	0	0	0	(0	0)	3	1	1	2	1	0	2	1	0	1			0	0	-	0	.300	.385	.300
1999	Min	AL	9	22	6	2	0	0	(0	0)	8	3	3	3	1	0	4	1	0	0			0	0	-	0	.273	.333	.364
2000	Min	AL	33	88	27	5	1	2	(1	1)	40	12	11	14	5	0	14	2	0	1			1	0	1.00	1	.307	.354	.455
2001	Min	AL	114	381	110	33	2	7	(3	4)	168	51	55	50	16	4	57	4	1	3			1	7	.13	7	.289	.322	.441
2002	Min	AL	130	440	132	31	6	6	(2	4)	193	54	49	60	13	1	61	11	2	3			1	2	.33	14	.300	.334	.439
2003	Min	AL	137	487	152	35	4	11	(6	5)	226	63	74	80	24	12	55	15	2	5			3	1	.75	13	.312	.360	.464
2004	SF	NL	131	471	128	28	2	11	(3	8)	193	45	77	58	19	4	27	15	2	3			0	1	.00	27	.272	.319	.410
2005	CWS	AL	128	460	118	21	0	18	(12	6)	193	61	56	55	23	5	68	12	1	1			0	2	.00	13	.257	.308	.420
2006	CWS	AL	140	509	150	24	0	16	(9	7)	222	65	64	68	22	6	72	8	1	1			1	0	1.00	10	.295	.333	.436
2007	CWS	AL	136	472	124	31	1	14	(8	6)	190	54	50	49	25	5	66	8	1	3			1	1	.50	21	.263	.309	.403
2008	CWS	AL	134	534	150	31	1	13	(7	6)	222	66	60	64	19	5	71	8	3	6			1	0	1.00	14	.281	.312	.416
2009	CWS	AL	138	504	151	22	1	13	(8	5)	214	57	49	59	24	6	52	1	3	3			1	1	.50	18	.300	.331	.425
	Postseason		30	100	30	5	1	5	(3	2)	52	16	17	19	10	1	13	2	1	1			2	3	.40	2	.300	.372	.520
	12 ML YEARS		1237	4378	1251	256	16	111	(59	52)	1872	532	549	562	192	48	549	86	18	30			10	15	.40	138	.286	.326	.428

Joel Pineiro

Pitches: R **Bats:** R **Pos:** SP-32   **Ht:** 6'1" **Wt:** 200 **Born:** 9/25/1978 **Age:** 31

Year	Team	Lg	HOW MUCH HE PITCHED						WHAT HE GAVE UP											THE RESULTS							
			G	GS	CG	GF	IP	BFP	H	R	ER	HR	SH	SF	HB	TBB	IBB	SO	WP	Bk	W	L	Pct	Sh	Sv-Op	Hld	ERC	ERA
2000	Sea	AL	8	1	0	5	19.1	94	25	13	12	3	0	2	0	13	0	10	0	0	1	0	1.000	0	0-0	0	7.44	5.59
2001	Sea	AL	17	11	0	1	75.1	289	50	24	17	2	1	2	3	21	0	56	2	0	6	2	.750	0	0-0	1	1.71	2.03
2002	Sea	AL	37	28	2	4	194.1	812	189	75	70	24	5	7	7	54	1	136	8	0	14	7	.667	1	0-0	3	3.77	3.24
2003	Sea	AL	32	32	3	0	211.2	890	192	94	89	19	3	9	6	76	3	151	5	0	16	11	.593	2	0-0	0	3.43	3.78
2004	Sea	AL	21	21	1	0	140.2	596	144	77	73	21	1	4	3	43	1	111	4	0	6	11	.353	0	0-0	0	4.32	4.67

Year	Team	Lg	G	GS	CG	GF	IP	BFP	H	R	ER	HR	SH	SF	HB	TBB	IBB	SO	WP	Bk	W	L	Pct	Sh	Sv-Op Hld	ERC	ERA
							HOW MUCH HE PITCHED					**WHAT HE GAVE UP**											**THE RESULTS**				
2005	Sea	AL	30	30	2	0	189.0	822	224	118	118	23	5	7	6	56	4	107	7	1	7	11	.389	0	0-0 0	5.05	5.62
2006	Sea	AL	40	25	1	6	165.2	753	209	123	117	23	1	6	10	64	13	87	4	1	8	13	.381	0	1-2 4	6.05	6.36
2007	2 Tms		42	11	0	15	97.2	419	110	49	47	14	3	1	2	26	0	60	3	0	7	5	.583	0	0-0 1	4.68	4.33
2008	StL	NL	26	25	0	1	148.2	645	180	89	85	22	7	3	2	35	0	81	1	0	7	7	.500	0	1-1 0	5.05	5.15
2009	StL	NL	32	32	3	0	214.0	865	218	94	83	11	12	6	8	27	1	105	4	0	15	12	.556	2	0-0 0	3.00	3.49
07	Bos	AL	31	0	0	15	34.0	157	41	20	19	3	1	1	1	14	0	20	3	0	1	1	.500	0	0-0 1	5.25	5.03
07	StL	NL	11	11	0	0	63.2	262	69	29	28	11	2	0	1	12	0	40	0	0	6	4	.600	0	0-0 0	4.36	3.96
	Postseason		1	0	0	0	2.0	12	4	1	1	0	0	0	0	2	0	5	1	0	0	0	-	0	0-0 0	12.01	4.50
	10 ML YEARS		285	216	12	32	1456.1	6185	1541	756	711	162	38	48	48	415	23	904	38	2	87	79	.524	5	2-3 10	4.17	4.39

Renyel Pinto

Pitches: L Bats: L Pos: RP-73   Ht: 6'4" Wt: 265 Born: 7/8/1982 Age: 27

Year	Team	Lg	G	GS	CG	GF	IP	BFP	H	R	ER	HR	SH	SF	HB	TBB	IBB	SO	WP	Bk	W	L	Pct	Sh	Sv-Op Hld	ERC	ERA
2009	Jupiter*	A+	2	0	0	1	2.0	7	0	0	0	0	0	0	1	1	0	1	1	0	0	0	-	0	0-- -	0.27	0.00
2009	NewOr*	AAA	2	0	0	0	2.0	6	1	0	0	0	0	0	0	0	0	1	0	0	0	0	-	0	0-- -	0.63	0.00
2006	Fla	NL	27	0	0	7	29.2	135	20	12	10	3	0	1	1	27	0	36	4	0	0	0	-	0	1-1 3	4.33	3.03
2007	Fla	NL	57	0	0	4	58.2	242	45	25	24	7	1	3	3	32	2	56	2	0	2	4	.333	0	1-6 16	3.79	3.68
2008	Fla	NL	67	0	0	11	64.2	284	52	33	32	9	6	5	4	39	2	56	8	0	2	5	.286	0	0-2 17	4.24	4.45
2009	Fla	NL	73	0	0	11	61.1	275	53	25	22	4	1	3	2	45	2	58	4	0	4	1	.800	0	0-4 13	4.46	3.23
	4 ML YEARS		224	0	0	33	214.1	936	170	95	88	23	8	12	10	143	6	206	18	0	8	10	.444	0	2-13 49	4.20	3.70

Scott Podsednik

Bats: L Throws: L Pos: LF-78; CF-50; DH-13; RF-3; PH-2; PR-2   Ht: 6'2" Wt: 190 Born: 3/18/1976 Age: 34

Year	Team	Lg	G	AB	H	2B	3B	HR	(Hm	Rd)	TB	R	RBI	RC	TBB	IBB	SO	HBP	SH	SF	SB	CS	SB%	GDP	Avg	OBP	Slg
										BATTING													**BASERUNNING**			**AVERAGES**	
2009	Charltt*	AAA	10	42	11	4	0	0	(-	-)	15	6	2	6	5	0	5	2	0	0	1	0	1.00	6	.262	.367	.357
2001	Sea	AL	5	6	1	0	1	0	(0	0)	3	1	3	0	0	0	1	0	0	0	0	0	-	1	.167	.167	.500
2002	Sea	AL	14	20	4	0	0	1	(0	1)	7	2	5	3	4	0	6	0	0	1	0	0	-	1	.200	.320	.350
2003	Mil	NL	154	558	175	29	8	9	(7	2)	247	100	58	101	56	2	91	4	8	2	43	10	.81	11	.314	.379	.443
2004	Mil	NL	154	640	156	27	7	12	(3	9)	233	85	39	76	58	2	105	7	6	1	70	13	.84	7	.244	.313	.364
2005	CWS	AL	129	507	147	28	1	0	(0	0)	177	80	25	64	47	0	75	3	6	5	59	23	.72	7	.290	.351	.349
2006	CWS	AL	139	524	137	27	6	3	(2	1)	185	86	45	65	54	1	96	2	8	4	40	19	.68	7	.261	.330	.353
2007	Col	NL	62	214	52	13	4	2	(1	1)	79	30	11	17	13	0	36	4	4	0	12	5	.71	9	.243	.299	.369
2008	Col	AL	93	162	41	8	1	0	(0	1)	51	19	15	19	16	0	28	1	1	1	12	4	.75	3	.253	.322	.333
2009	CWS	AL	132	537	163	25	6	7	(3	4)	221	75	48	78	39	1	74	3	6	2	30	13	.70	8	.304	.353	.412
	Postseason		12	49	14	1	3	2	(2	0)	27	9	6	10	7	0	10	2	1	0	6	3	.67	1	.286	.397	.551
	9 ML YEARS		882	3168	876	157	34	35	(16	19)	1206	481	249	423	287	6	512	24	39	16	266	87	.75	54	.277	.340	.381

Placido Polanco

Bats: R Throws: R Pos: 2B-151; PH-5   Ht: 5'10" Wt: 194 Born: 10/10/1975 Age: 34

Year	Team	Lg	G	AB	H	2B	3B	HR	(Hm	Rd)	TB	R	RBI	RC	TBB	IBB	SO	HBP	SH	SF	SB	CS	SB%	GDP	Avg	OBP	Slg
										BATTING													**BASERUNNING**			**AVERAGES**	
1998	StL	NL	45	114	29	3	2	1	(1	0)	39	10	11	12	5	0	9	1	2	0	2	0	1.00	1	.254	.292	.342
1999	StL	NL	88	220	61	9	3	1	(0	1)	79	24	19	23	15	1	24	0	3	2	1	3	.25	7	.277	.321	.359
2000	StL	NL	118	323	102	12	3	5	(2	3)	135	50	39	44	16	0	26	1	7	3	4	4	.50	8	.316	.347	.418
2001	StL	NL	144	564	173	26	4	3	(1	2)	216	87	38	70	25	0	43	6	14	1	12	3	.80	22	.307	.342	.383
2002	2 Tms	NL	147	548	158	32	2	9	(8	1)	221	75	49	64	26	1	41	8	13	0	5	3	.63	15	.288	.330	.403
2003	Phi	NL	122	492	142	30	3	14	(7	7)	220	87	63	74	42	1	38	8	8	4	14	2	.88	16	.289	.352	.447
2004	Phi	NL	126	503	150	21	0	17	(10	7)	222	74	55	71	27	0	39	12	7	6	7	4	.64	13	.298	.345	.441
2005	2 Tms	AL	129	501	166	27	2	9	(6	3)	224	84	56	86	33	0	25	11	2	4	4	3	.57	12	.331	.383	.447
2006	Det	AL	110	461	136	18	1	4	(2	2)	168	58	52	65	17	0	27	7	8	2	1	2	.33	18	.295	.329	.364
2007	Det	AL	142	587	200	36	3	9	(7	2)	269	105	67	100	37	3	30	11	2	4	7	3	.70	9	.341	.388	.458
2008	Det	AL	141	580	178	34	3	8	(2	6)	242	90	58	81	35	2	43	6	4	4	7	1	.88	14	.307	.350	.417
2009	Det	AL	153	618	176	31	4	10	(5	5)	245	82	72	84	36	2	46	9	7	5	7	2	.78	15	.285	.331	.396
02	StL	NL	94	342	97	19	1	5	(5	0)	133	47	27	38	12	1	27	4	9	0	3	1	.75	12	.284	.316	.389
02	Phi	NL	53	206	61	13	1	4	(3	1)	88	28	22	26	14	0	14	4	4	0	2	2	.50	3	.296	.353	.427
05	Phi	NL	43	158	50	7	0	3	(2	1)	66	26	20	26	12	0	9	3	0	0	0	0	-	3	.316	.376	.418
05	Det	AL	86	343	116	20	2	6	(4	2)	158	58	36	60	21	0	16	8	2	4	4	3	.57	9	.338	.386	.461
	Postseason		25	81	24	2	0	0	(0	0)	26	7	8	8	8	2	5	1	3	1	2	1	.67	3	.296	.363	.321
	12 ML YEARS		1465	5511	1671	279	30	90	(51	39)	2280	826	579	774	314	10	391	80	77	35	71	30	.70	150	.303	.348	.414

Sidney Ponson

Pitches: R Bats: R Pos: SP-9; RP-5   Ht: 6'1" Wt: 260 Born: 11/2/1976 Age: 33

Year	Team	Lg	G	GS	CG	GF	IP	BFP	H	R	ER	HR	SH	SF	HB	TBB	IBB	SO	WP	Bk	W	L	Pct	Sh	Sv-Op Hld	ERC	ERA
2009	Omha*	AAA	6	6	0	0	33.0	127	34	8	8	2	1	1	0	5	0	19	1	0	2	1	.667	0	0-- -	3.26	2.18
1998	Bal	AL	31	20	0	5	135.0	588	157	82	79	19	3	4	3	42	2	85	4	1	8	9	.471	0	1-2 0	5.07	5.27
1999	Bal	AL	32	32	6	0	210.0	897	227	118	110	35	4	7	1	80	2	112	4	0	12	12	.500	0	0-0 0	5.08	4.71
2000	Bal	AL	32	32	6	0	222.0	953	223	125	119	30	3	3	1	83	0	152	5	0	9	13	.409	1	0-0 0	4.26	4.82
2001	Bal	AL	23	23	3	0	138.1	605	161	83	76	21	3	2	6	37	0	84	2	0	5	10	.333	1	0-0 0	5.04	4.94
2002	Bal	AL	28	28	3	0	176.0	736	172	84	80	26	2	3	2	63	1	120	3	0	7	9	.438	0	0-0 0	4.24	4.09
2003	2 Tms		31	31	4	0	216.0	898	211	94	90	16	6	5	5	61	5	134	9	0	17	12	.586	0	0-0 0	3.41	3.75
2004	Bal	AL	33	33	5	0	215.2	954	265	136	127	23	6	3	8	69	3	115	8	2	11	15	.423	2	0-0 0	5.33	5.30
2005	Bal	AL	23	23	1	0	130.1	595	177	97	90	16	2	8	3	48	1	68	10	0	7	11	.389	0	0-0 0	6.45	6.21
2006	2 Tms		19	16	0	1	85.0	384	108	62	59	10	4	0	4	36	1	48	2	0	4	5	.444	0	0-0 0	6.25	6.25
2007	Min	AL	7	7	0	0	37.2	181	54	31	29	7	0	0	3	17	1	23	0	0	2	5	.286	0	0-0 0	8.04	6.93

Year	Team	Lg	G	GS	CG	GF	IP	BFP	H	R	ER	HR	SH	SF	HB	TBB	IBB	SO	WP	Bk	W	L	Pct	Sh	Sv-Op	Hld	ERC	ERA
2008	2 Tms	AL	26	24	1	1	135.2	612	170	89	78	14	2	8	7	48	2	58	4	0	8	5	.615	0	0-0	1	5.63	5.04
2009	KC	AL	14	9	0	0	58.2	273	79	50	48	6	4	4	2	25	1	32	2	0	1	7	.125	0	0-1	0	6.44	7.36
03	Bal	AL	21	21	4	0	148.0	622	147	65	62	10	2	3	4	43	2	100	6	0	14	6	.700	0	0-0	0	3.50	3.77
03	SF	NL	10	10	0	0	68.0	276	64	29	28	6	4	2	1	18	3	34	3	0	3	6	.333	0	0-0	0	3.23	3.71
06	StL	NL	14	13	0	0	68.2	303	82	42	40	7	4	0	4	29	1	33	2	0	4	4	.500	0	0-0	0	5.74	5.24
06	NYY	AL	5	3	0	1	16.1	81	26	20	19	3	0	0	0	7	0	15	0	0	0	1	.000	0	0-0	0	8.48	10.47
08	Tex	AL	9	9	1	0	55.2	252	71	36	24	3	0	3	2	16	0	25	2	0	4	1	.800	0	0-0	0	4.96	3.88
08	NYY	AL	16	15	0	1	80.0	360	99	53	52	11	2	5	5	32	2	33	2	0	4	4	.500	0	0-0	0	6.11	5.85
	Postseason		1	1	0	0	5.0	22	7	4	4	0	0	0	0	0	0	3	1	0	0	0	-	0	0-0	0	3.92	7.20
	12 ML YEARS		298	278	29	7	1760.1	7676	2004	1051	983	223	39	47	45	609	19	1031	53	3	91	113	.446	4	1-3	0	5.00	5.03

Rick Porcello

Pitches: R **Bats:** R **Pos:** SP-31   **Ht:** 6'5" **Wt:** 200 **Born:** 12/27/1988 **Age:** 21

			HOW MUCH HE PITCHED						WHAT HE GAVE UP											THE RESULTS							
Year	Team	Lg	G	GS	CG	GF	IP	BFP	H	R	ER	HR	SH	SF	HB	TBB	IBB	SO	WP	Bk	W	L	Pct	Sh	Sv-Op	Hld	ERC	ERA
2008	Lkland	A+	24	24	0	0	125.0	527	116	51	37	7	4	3	11	33	0	72	3	0	8	6	.571	0	0--	-	3.18	2.66
2009	Det	AL	31	31	0	0	170.2	720	176	81	75	23	4	2	3	52	0	89	6	1	14	9	.609	0	0-0	0	4.24	3.96

Aaron Poreda

Pitches: L **Bats:** L **Pos:** RP-14   **Ht:** 6'6" **Wt:** 240 **Born:** 10/1/1986 **Age:** 23

Year	Team	Lg	G	GS	CG	GF	IP	BFP	H	R	ER	HR	SH	SF	HB	TBB	IBB	SO	WP	Bk	W	L	Pct	Sh	Sv-Op	Hld	ERC	ERA
2007	Gr Falls	R+	12	8	0	1	46.1	172	29	7	6	1	1	1	0	10	0	48	1	0	4	0	1.000	0	0--	-	1.34	1.17
2008	WinSa	A+	12	12	1	0	73.1	304	67	31	27	1	2	0	2	18	0	46	2	1	5	5	.500	0	0--	-	2.55	3.31
2008	Brham	AA	15	15	1	0	87.2	355	81	34	29	6	4	1	3	22	0	72	1	0	3	4	.429	0	0--	-	3.02	2.98
2009	Brham	AA	11	11	1	0	64.1	273	47	20	17	1	3	1	6	36	0	60	4	0	5	4	.556	1	0--	-	2.95	2.38
2009	Charltt	AAA	2	2	0	0	10.0	44	8	4	4	0	2	0	2	3	0	9	1	0	0	0	-	0	0--	-	2.56	3.60
2009	Portlnd	AAA	7	6	0	0	32.2	162	28	27	26	3	2	3	3	37	1	30	5	0	0	3	.000	0	0--	-	6.43	7.16
2009	2 Tms		14	0	0	6	13.1	61	10	4	4	0	1	0	1	13	1	12	2	0	1	0	1.000	0	0-0	0	4.34	2.70
09	CWS	AL	10	0	0	5	11.0	49	9	3	3	0	1	0	1	8	1	12	2	0	1	0	1.000	0	0-0	0	3.81	2.45
09	SD	NL	4	0	0	1	2.1	12	1	1	1	0	0	0	0	5	0	0	0	0	0	0	-	0	0-0	0	6.99	3.86

Jorge Posada

Bats: B **Throws:** R **Pos:** C-100; PH-14; DH-9; 1B-2   **Ht:** 6'2" **Wt:** 215 **Born:** 8/17/1971 **Age:** 38

			BATTING																		BASERUNNING				AVERAGES		
Year	Team	Lg	G	AB	H	2B	3B	HR	(Hm	Rd)	TB	R	RBI	RC	TBB	IBB	SO	HBP	SH	SF	SB	CS	SB%	GDP	Avg	OBP	Slg
1995	NYY	AL	1	0	0	0	0	0	(0	0)	0	0	0	0	0	0	0	0	0	0	0	0	-	0	-	-	-
1996	NYY	AL	8	14	1	0	0	0	(0	0)	1	1	0	0	1	0	6	0	0	0	0	0	-	1	.071	.133	.071
1997	NYY	AL	60	188	47	12	0	6	(2	4)	77	29	25	29	30	2	33	3	1	2	1	2	.33	2	.250	.359	.410
1998	NYY	AL	111	358	96	23	0	17	(6	11)	170	56	63	56	47	7	92	0	0	4	0	1	.00	14	.268	.350	.475
1999	NYY	AL	112	379	93	19	2	12	(4	8)	152	50	57	52	53	2	91	3	0	2	1	0	1.00	9	.245	.341	.401
2000	NYY	AL	151	505	145	35	1	28	(18	10)	266	92	86	110	107	10	151	8	0	4	2	2	.50	11	.287	.417	.527
2001	NYY	AL	138	484	134	28	1	22	(14	8)	230	59	95	80	62	10	132	6	0	5	2	6	.25	10	.277	.363	.475
2002	NYY	AL	143	511	137	40	1	20	(12	8)	239	79	99	92	81	9	143	3	0	3	1	0	1.00	23	.268	.370	.468
2003	NYY	AL	142	481	135	24	0	30	(15	15)	249	83	101	98	93	6	110	10	0	4	2	4	.33	13	.281	.405	.518
2004	NYY	AL	137	449	122	31	0	21	(11	10)	216	72	81	78	88	5	92	9	0	1	1	3	.25	24	.272	.400	.481
2005	NYY	AL	142	474	124	23	0	19	(11	8)	204	67	71	71	66	5	94	2	0	4	1	0	1.00	8	.262	.352	.430
2006	NYY	AL	143	465	129	27	2	23	(11	12)	229	65	93	89	64	1	97	11	0	5	3	0	1.00	10	.277	.374	.492
2007	NYY	AL	144	506	171	42	1	20	(11	9)	275	91	90	99	74	7	98	6	0	3	2	1	1.00	18	.338	.426	.543
2008	NYY	AL	51	168	45	13	1	3	(1	2)	69	18	22	23	24	3	38	2	0	1	0	0	-	7	.268	.364	.411
2009	NYY	AL	111	383	109	25	0	22	(14	8)	200	55	81	73	48	4	101	2	0	5	1	0	1.00	13	.285	.363	.522
	Postseason		96	322	76	19	0	9	(4	5)	122	41	31	36	57	8	77	2	0	2	2	3	.40	13	.236	.352	.379
	15 ML YEARS		1594	5365	1488	342	9	243	(130	113)	2577	817	964	950	838	71	1278	65	1	43	17	18	.49	163	.277	.379	.480

Buster Posey

Bats: R **Throws:** R **Pos:** C-7; PH-1   **Ht:** 6'1" **Wt:** 205 **Born:** 3/27/1987 **Age:** 23

			BATTING																		BASERUNNING				AVERAGES		
Year	Team	Lg	G	AB	H	2B	3B	HR	(Hm	Rd)	TB	R	RBI	RC	TBB	IBB	SO	HBP	SH	SF	SB	CS	SB%	GDP	Avg	OBP	Slg
2008	Giants	R	7	26	10	3	1	1	(-	-)	18	8	4	8	5	1	4	0	0	0	0	0	-	0	.385	.484	.692
2008	SlmKzr	A-	3	11	3	2	0	0	(-	-)	5	2	2	2	3	0	0	0	0	0	0	0	-	0	.273	.429	.455
2009	SnJos	A+	80	291	95	23	0	13	(-	-)	157	63	58	69	45	0	45	8	0	2	6	0	1.00	6	.326	.428	.540
2009	Fresno	AAA	35	131	42	8	1	5	(-	-)	67	21	22	26	17	0	23	0	0	3	0	1	.00	5	.321	.391	.511
2009	SF	NL	7	17	2	0	0	0	(0	0)	2	1	0	0	0	0	4	0	0	0	0	0	-	0	.118	.118	.118

Landon Powell

Bats: B **Throws:** R **Pos:** C-36; 1B-6; DH-4; PH-2   **Ht:** 6'3" **Wt:** 260 **Born:** 3/19/1982 **Age:** 28

			BATTING																		BASERUNNING				AVERAGES		
Year	Team	Lg	G	AB	H	2B	3B	HR	(Hm	Rd)	TB	R	RBI	RC	TBB	IBB	SO	HBP	SH	SF	SB	CS	SB%	GDP	Avg	OBP	Slg
2004	Vancvr	A-	38	135	32	6	1	3	(-	-)	49	24	19	20	26	1	22	1	0	1	0	0	-	4	.237	.362	.363
2006	Stcktn	A+	90	326	86	12	0	15	(-	-)	143	44	47	53	43	0	77	2	1	3	0	0	-	6	.264	.350	.439
2006	Mdland	AA	12	41	11	0	0	1	(-	-)	14	4	4	4	3	0	12	1	0	0	0	0	-	1	.268	.333	.341
2007	Mdland	AA	60	219	64	9	2	11	(-	-)	110	46	39	44	36	2	40	0	0	1	1	0	1.00	7	.292	.391	.502
2007	Scrmto	AAA	4	17	5	0	0	3	(-	-)	14	3	3	4	0	0	4	0	0	0	0	0	-	0	.294	.294	.824
2008	Scrmto	AAA	88	300	68	11	0	15	(-	-)	124	42	52	49	63	1	85	0	0	4	0	1	.00	5	.227	.357	.413
2009	Oak	AL	46	140	32	7	0	7	(4	3)	60	19	30	22	14	0	36	0	0	1	0	0	-	3	.229	.297	.429

Martin Prado

Bats: R **Throws:** R **Pos:** 2B-63; 3B-41; 1B-29; PH-13; RF-1; DH-1; PR-1   **Ht:** 6'1" **Wt:** 190 **Born:** 10/27/1983 **Age:** 26

Year	Team	Lg	G	AB	H	2B	3B	HR	(Hm	Rd)	TB	R	RBI	RC	TBB	IBB	SO	HBP	SH	SF	SB	CS	SB%	GDP	Avg	OBP	Slg
2006	Atl	NL	24	42	11	1	1	1	(1	0)	17	3	9	9	5	0	7	0	2	0	0	0	-	2	.262	.340	.405
2007	Atl	NL	28	59	17	3	0	0	(0	0)	20	5	2	6	3	0	6	0	0	0	0	0	-	0	.288	.323	.339
2008	Atl	NL	78	228	73	18	4	2	(1	1)	105	36	33	39	21	0	29	1	2	2	3	1	.75	3	.320	.377	.461
2009	Atl	NL	128	450	138	38	0	11	(4	7)	209	64	49	57	36	1	59	2	11	4	1	3	.25	17	.307	.358	.464
	4 ML YEARS		258	779	239	60	5	14	(6	8)	351	108	93	111	65	1	101	3	15	6	4	4	.50	22	.307	.360	.451

David Price

Pitches: L **Bats:** L **Pos:** SP-23   **Ht:** 6'6" **Wt:** 225 **Born:** 8/26/1985 **Age:** 24

Year	Team	Lg	G	GS	CG	GF	IP	BFP	H	R	ER	HR	SH	SF	HB	TBB	IBB	SO	WP	Bk	W	L	Pct	Sh	Sv-Op	Hld	ERC	ERA
2008	VeroB	A+	6	6	0	0	34.2	134	28	7	7	0	0	0	0	7	0	37	1	0	4	0	1.000	0	0- -	-	1.83	1.82
2008	Mont	AA	9	9	1	0	57.0	224	42	13	12	7	0	0	4	16	1	55	1	0	7	0	1.000	0	0- -	-	2.70	1.89
2008	Drham	AAA	4	4	0	0	18.0	82	22	10	9	0	0	0	0	9	0	17	1	0	1	1	.500	0	0- -	-	5.04	4.50
2009	Drham	AAA	8	8	0	0	34.1	147	28	20	15	5	3	4	1	18	0	35	0	1	1	4	.200	0	0- -	-	3.98	3.93
2008	TB	AL	5	1	0	0	14.0	57	9	4	3	1	0	1	1	4	0	12	0	0	0	0	-	0	0-0	1	1.86	1.93
2009	TB	AL	23	23	0	0	128.1	557	119	72	63	17	3	2	4	54	0	102	2	0	10	7	.588	0	0-0	0	4.05	4.42
	Postseason		5	0	0	5	5.2	24	2	2	1	1	0	0	0	4	0	8	0	0	1	0	1.000	0	1-1	0	2.19	1.59
	2 ML YEARS		28	24	0	0	142.1	614	128	76	66	18	3	3	5	58	0	114	2	0	10	7	.588	0	0-0	1	3.81	4.17

Jason Pridie

Bats: L **Throws:** R **Pos:** PR-1   **Ht:** 6'1" **Wt:** 205 **Born:** 10/9/1983 **Age:** 26

Year	Team	Lg	G	AB	H	2B	3B	HR	(Hm	Rd)	TB	R	RBI	RC	TBB	IBB	SO	HBP	SH	SF	SB	CS	SB%	GDP	Avg	OBP	Slg
2002	Princtn	R+	67	285	105	12	9	7	(-	-)	156	60	33	60	19	1	35	2	1	1	13	9	.59	2	.368	.410	.547
2002	HudVal	A-	8	32	11	1	1	1	(-	-)	17	4	1	6	3	1	6	0	0	0	0	0	-	0	.344	.400	.531
2003	CtnSC	A	128	530	138	28	10	7	(-	-)	207	75	48	63	30	1	113	4	3	5	26	17	.60	2	.260	.302	.391
2004	CtnSC	A	128	515	142	27	11	17	(-	-)	242	103	86	82	37	3	114	6	9	8	17	6	.74	1	.276	.327	.470
2005	Visalia	A+	1	2	1	0	0	0	(-	-)	1	0	0	0	0	0	0	0	0	0	0	0	-	0	.500	.500	.500
2005	Mont	AA	28	95	20	4	2	3	(-	-)	37	14	8	10	8	0	30	0	2	0	5	1	.83	3	.211	.272	.389
2006	Mont	AA	132	461	106	11	4	5	(-	-)	140	39	34	41	31	5	93	3	4	5	16	5	.76	6	.230	.280	.304
2007	Mont	AA	71	280	81	16	7	4	(-	-)	123	42	27	41	14	1	45	4	1	2	14	7	.67	8	.289	.330	.439
2007	Drham	AAA	63	245	78	16	4	10	(-	-)	132	47	39	50	22	2	47	2	2	3	12	3	.80	1	.318	.375	.539
2008	Roch	AAA	138	559	151	21	16	13	(-	-)	243	84	61	77	30	2	152	1	7	6	25	9	.74	8	.270	.305	.435
2009	Roch	AAA	121	513	136	23	5	9	(-	-)	196	69	53	61	19	0	85	5	3	6	25	7	.78	6	.265	.295	.382
2008	Min	AL	10	4	0	0	0	0	(0	0)	0	3	0	0	1	0	1	0	1	0	0	0	-	0	.000	.200	.000
2009	Min	AL	1	0	0	0	0	0	(0	0)	0	0	0	0	0	0	0	0	0	0	0	0	-	0	-	-	-
	2 ML YEARS		11	4	0	0	0	0	(0	0)	0	3	0	0	1	0	1	0	1	0	0	0	-	0	.000	.200	.000

Scott Proctor

Pitches: R **Bats:** R **Pos:** P   **Ht:** 6'1" **Wt:** 195 **Born:** 1/2/1977 **Age:** 33

Year	Team	Lg	G	GS	CG	GF	IP	BFP	H	R	ER	HR	SH	SF	HB	TBB	IBB	SO	WP	Bk	W	L	Pct	Sh	Sv-Op	Hld	ERC	ERA
2004	NYY	AL	26	0	0	12	25.0	118	29	18	15	5	0	2	0	14	0	21	1	1	2	1	.667	0	0-0	2	6.32	5.40
2005	NYY	AL	29	1	0	11	44.2	199	46	32	30	10	0	1	2	17	4	36	4	1	1	0	1.000	0	0-0	0	4.98	6.04
2006	NYY	AL	83	0	0	12	102.1	426	89	41	40	12	2	6	2	33	6	89	2	0	6	4	.600	0	1-8	26	3.15	3.52
2007	2 Tms		83	0	0	14	86.1	382	78	41	35	12	3	7	6	44	4	64	5	1	5	5	.500	0	0-6	18	4.41	3.65
2008	LAD	NL	41	0	0	11	38.2	184	41	30	26	7	1	2	0	24	1	46	6	0	2	0	1.000	0	0-1	2	5.67	6.05
07	NYY	AL	52	0	0	10	54.1	245	53	27	23	8	1	6	3	29	3	37	3	0	2	5	.286	0	0-4	11	4.90	3.81
07	LAD	NL	31	0	0	4	32.0	137	25	14	12	4	2	1	3	15	1	27	2	1	3	0	1.000	0	0-2	7	3.61	3.38
	Postseason		5	0	0	2	6.0	26	8	1	1	0	0	0	0	1	0	2	1	0	0	0	-	0	0-0	1	4.37	1.50
	5 ML YEARS		262	1	0	60	297.0	1309	283	162	146	46	6	18	10	132	15	256	18	3	16	10	.615	0	1-15	48	4.36	4.42

Albert Pujols

Bats: R **Throws:** R **Pos:** 1B-159; PH-2; DH-1   **Ht:** 6'3" **Wt:** 230 **Born:** 1/16/1980 **Age:** 30

Year	Team	Lg	G	AB	H	2B	3B	HR	(Hm	Rd)	TB	R	RBI	RC	TBB	IBB	SO	HBP	SH	SF	SB	CS	SB%	GDP	Avg	OBP	Slg
2001	StL	NL	161	590	194	47	4	37	(18	19)	360	112	130	132	69	6	93	9	1	7	1	3	.25	21	.329	.403	.610
2002	StL	NL	157	590	185	40	2	34	(14	20)	331	118	127	121	72	13	69	9	0	4	2	4	.33	20	.314	.394	.561
2003	StL	NL	157	591	212	51	1	43	(21	22)	394	137	124	160	79	12	65	10	0	5	5	1	.83	13	.359	.439	.667
2004	StL	NL	154	592	196	51	2	46	(18	28)	389	133	123	143	84	12	52	7	0	9	5	5	.50	21	.331	.415	.657
2005	StL	NL	161	591	195	38	2	41	(23	18)	360	129	117	139	97	27	65	9	0	3	16	2	.89	19	.330	.430	.609
2006	StL	NL	143	535	177	33	1	49	(24	25)	359	119	137	146	92	28	50	4	0	3	7	2	.78	20	.331	.431	.671
2007	StL	NL	158	565	185	38	1	32	(12	20)	321	99	103	118	99	22	58	7	0	8	2	6	.25	27	.327	.429	.568
2008	StL	NL	148	524	187	44	0	37	(19	18)	342	100	116	130	104	34	54	5	0	8	7	3	.70	16	.357	.462	.653
2009	StL	NL	160	568	186	45	1	47	(22	25)	374	124	135	145	115	44	64	9	0	8	16	4	.80	23	.327	.443	.658
	Postseason		53	189	61	10	1	13	(7	6)	112	39	35	43	33	9	27	3	0	1	0	1	.00	5	.323	.429	.593
	9 ML YEARS		1399	5146	1717	387	14	366	(171	195)	3230	1071	1112	1234	811	198	570	69	1	55	61	30	.67	180	.334	.427	.628

Nick Punto

Bats: B **Throws:** R **Pos:** 2B-63; SS-58; 3B-5; PR-4   **Ht:** 5'9" **Wt:** 190 **Born:** 11/8/1977 **Age:** 32

								BATTING													BASERUNNING				AVERAGES		
Year	Team	Lg	G	AB	H	2B	3B	HR	(I lm	Rd)	TB	R	RBI	RC	TBB	IBB	SO	HBP	SH	SF	SB	CS	SB%	GDP	Avg	OBP	Slg
2001	Phi	NL	4	5	2	0	0	0	(0	0)	2	0	0	1	0	0	0	0	0	0	0	0	-	0	.400	.400	.400
2002	Phi	NL	9	6	1	0	0	0	(0	0)	1	0	0	0	0	0	3	0	1	0	0	0	-	0	.167	.167	.167
2003	Phi	NL	64	92	20	2	0	1	(0	1)	25	14	4	7	7	1	22	0	0	0	2	1	.67	0	.217	.273	.272
2004	Min	AL	38	91	23	0	0	2	(2	0)	29	17	12	15	12	0	19	0	0	0	6	0	1.00	2	.253	.340	.319
2005	Min	AL	112	394	94	18	4	4	(3	1)	132	45	26	35	36	0	86	0	7	2	13	8	.62	9	.239	.301	.335
2006	Min	AL	135	459	133	21	7	1	(0	1)	171	73	45	59	47	0	68	1	10	7	17	5	.77	8	.290	.352	.373
2007	Min	AL	150	472	99	18	4	1	(0	1)	128	53	25	37	55	1	90	0	6	3	16	6	.73	7	.210	.291	.271
2008	Min	AL	99	338	96	19	4	2	(1	1)	129	43	28	42	32	1	57	0	5	2	15	6	.71	10	.284	.344	.382
2009	Min	AL	125	359	82	15	1	1	(0	1)	102	56	38	46	61	1	70	1	13	6	16	3	.04	7	.228	.337	.284
	Postseason		3	12	2	0	0	0	(0	0)	2	0	0	0	0	0	1	0	1	0	0	0	-	0	.167	.167	.167
9 ML YEARS			736	2216	550	93	20	12	(6	6)	719	301	178	242	250	4	415	2	42	20	85	29	.75	43	.248	.322	.324

David Purcey

Pitches: L **Bats:** L **Pos:** SP-9   **Ht:** 6'5" **Wt:** 235 **Born:** 4/22/1982 **Age:** 28

			HOW MUCH HE PITCHED						WHAT HE GAVE UP										THE RESULTS							
Year	Team	Lg	G	GS	CG	GF	IP	BFP	H	R	ER	HR	SH	SF	HB	TBB	IBB	SO	WP	Bk	W	L	Pct	Sh	Sv-Op	Hld	ERC	ERA
2004	Auburn	A-	3	2	0	0	12.0	43	6	2	2	0	1	2	1	1	0	13	0	0	1	0	1.000	0	0- -	-	0.82	1.50
2005	Dnedin	A+	21	21	0	0	94.1	422	80	51	38	8	2	4	10	56	0	116	8	0	5	4	.556	0	0- -	-	4.25	3.63
2005	NHam	AA	8	8	1	0	43.0	184	32	17	14	2	0	2	1	25	0	45	4	0	4	3	.571	0	0- -	-	3.08	2.93
2006	Syrcse	AAA	12	12	1	0	51.2	242	49	41	31	7	1	4	2	38	0	45	2	0	2	7	.222	0	0- -	-	5.48	5.40
2006	NHam	AA	16	16	0	0	88.1	414	101	59	55	9	4	1	12	44	0	81	6	0	4	5	.444	0	0- -	-	5.86	5.60
2007	NHam	AA	11	11	1	0	62.0	266	67	41	37	4	1	3	4	16	0	55	4	1	5	3	.375	1	0- -	-	3.99	5.37
2008	Syrcse	AAA	19	19	0	0	117.0	471	97	41	35	8	1	5	4	34	0	120	11	1	8	6	.571	0	0- -	-	2.73	2.69
2009	LsVgs	AAA	24	24	1	0	139.1	617	132	83	69	7	4	7	0	78	0	109	9	0	9	6	.000	1	0- -	-	4.33	4.46
2008	Tor	AL	12	12	1	0	65.0	290	67	41	40	9	0	0	4	28	0	58	3	0	5	3	.555	0	0-0	0	4.90	5.54
2009	Tor	AL	9	9	0	0	40.0	223	54	35	33	6	3	1	1	30	1	39	3	0	1	3	.250	0	0-0	0	6.00	6.19
2 ML YEARS			21	21	1	0	113.0	512	121	76	73	15	5	4	5	59	1	97	6	0	4	9	.308	0	0-0	0	5.40	5.81

J.J. Putz

Pitches: R **Bats:** R **Pos:** RP-29   **Ht:** 6'5" **Wt:** 250 **Born:** 2/22/1977 **Age:** 33

			HOW MUCH HE PITCHED						WHAT HE GAVE UP										THE RESULTS							
Year	Team	Lg	G	GS	CG	GF	IP	BFP	H	R	ER	HR	SH	SF	HB	TBB	IBB	SO	WP	Bk	W	L	Pct	Sh	Sv-Op	Hld	ERC	ERA
2003	Sea	AL	3	0	0	0	3.2	18	4	2	2	0	0	0	0	3	0	3	0	0	0	0	-	0	0-0	0	5.31	4.91
2004	Sea	AL	54	0	0	0	63.0	275	66	35	33	10	3	2	5	24	4	47	1	0	0	3	.000	0	9-13	3	4.97	4.71
2005	Sea	AL	64	0	0	20	60.0	259	58	27	24	8	3	3	2	23	2	45	2	0	6	5	.545	0	1-4	21	4.11	3.60
2006	Sea	AL	72	0	0	57	78.1	303	59	20	20	4	1	2	2	13	1	104	1	0	4	1	.800	0	36-43	5	1.78	2.30
2007	Sea	AL	68	0	0	65	71.2	260	37	11	11	6	2	1	2	13	0	82	3	0	6	1	.857	0	40-42	0	1.21	1.38
2008	Sea	AL	47	0	0	35	46.1	211	46	20	20	4	0	1	2	28	2	56	2	0	6	5	.545	0	15-23	0	4.82	3.88
2009	NYM	NL	29	0	0	6	29.1	135	29	18	17	1	1	2	0	19	4	19	1	0	1	4	.200	0	2-4	10	4.16	5.22
7 ML YEARS			337	0	0	213	352.1	1461	299	133	127	33	10	11	13	123	13	356	10	0	23	19	.548	0	103-129	39	3.12	3.24

Chad Qualls

Pitches: R **Bats:** R **Pos:** RP-51   **Ht:** 6'5" **Wt:** 220 **Born:** 8/17/1978 **Age:** 31

			HOW MUCH HE PITCHED						WHAT HE GAVE UP										THE RESULTS							
Year	Team	Lg	G	GS	CG	GF	IP	BFP	H	R	ER	HR	SH	SF	HB	TBB	IBB	SO	WP	Bk	W	L	Pct	Sh	Sv-Op	Hld	ERC	ERA
2004	Hou	NL	25	0	0	4	33.0	141	34	13	13	3	0	1	4	8	1	24	0	0	4	0	1.000	0	1-2	9	4.02	3.55
2005	Hou	NL	77	0	0	19	79.2	329	73	33	29	7	4	3	6	23	2	60	1	0	6	4	.600	0	0-0	22	3.42	3.28
2006	Hou	NL	81	0	0	13	88.2	356	76	38	37	10	4	4	6	28	6	56	0	0	7	3	.700	0	0-6	23	3.36	3.76
2007	Hou	NL	79	0	0	16	82.2	345	84	29	28	10	6	2	3	25	5	78	2	0	6	5	.545	0	5-10	21	4.07	3.05
2008	Ari	NL	77	0	0	21	73.2	300	61	29	23	4	4	3	3	18	2	71	6	0	4	8	.333	0	9-17	22	2.40	2.81
2009	Ari	NL	51	0	0	44	52.0	217	53	23	21	5	1	0	2	7	2	45	2	0	2	2	.500	0	24-29	0	3.17	3.63
	Postseason		15	0	0	0	21.0	85	20	11	11	2	1	0	0	7	3	17	0	0	1	1	.500	0	0-2	2	3.45	4.71
6 ML YEARS			390	0	0	117	409.2	1688	381	165	151	39	19	13	24	109	18	334	11	0	29	22	.569	0	39-64	97	3.36	3.32

Carlos Quentin

Bats: R **Throws:** R **Pos:** LF-89; DH-9; PH-3   **Ht:** 6'1" **Wt:** 230 **Born:** 8/28/1982 **Age:** 27

								BATTING													BASERUNNING				AVERAGES		
Year	Team	Lg	G	AB	H	2B	3B	HR	(Hm	Rd)	TB	R	RBI	RC	TBB	IBB	SO	HBP	SH	SF	SB	CS	SB%	GDP	Avg	OBP	Slg
2009	Charltt*	AAA	12	37	14	3	0	1	(-	-)	20	10	9	9	5	0	2	2	0	1	0	0	-	1	.378	.467	.541
2009	Knapol*	A	2	3	1	1	0	0	(-	-)	2	0	1	1	2	0	0	0	0	0	0	0	-	0	.333	.600	.667
2006	Ari	NL	57	166	42	13	3	9	(3	6)	88	23	32	29	15	2	34	8	1	1	1	0	1.00	6	.253	.342	.530
2007	Ari	NL	81	229	49	16	0	5	(5	0)	80	29	31	27	18	1	54	11	1	4	2	2	.50	5	.214	.298	.349
2008	CWS	AL	130	480	138	26	1	36	(21	15)	274	96	100	104	66	0	80	20	0	3	7	3	.70	16	.288	.394	.571
2009	CWS	AL	99	351	83	14	0	21	(12	9)	160	47	56	47	31	2	52	15	0	2	3	0	1.00	11	.236	.323	.456
4 ML YEARS			367	1226	312	69	4	71	(41	30)	602	195	219	207	130	5	220	54	2	10	13	5	.72	38	.254	.349	.491

Robb Quinlan

Bats: R Throws: R Pos: 1B-17; LF-17; 3B-9; RF-6; PH-5; DH-4; PR-2   Ht: 6'1" Wt: 215 Born: 3/17/1977 Age: 33

Year Team	Lg	G	AB	H	2B	3B	HR	(Hm	Rd)	TB	R	RBI	RC	TBB	IBB	SO	HBP	SH	SF	SB	CS	SB%	GDP	Avg	OBP	Slg
2003 LAA	AL	38	94	27	4	2	0	(0	0)	35	13	4	8	6	0	16	0	1	0	1	2	.33	3	.287	.330	.372
2004 LAA	AL	56	160	55	14	0	5	(3	2)	84	23	23	33	14	0	26	2	0	1	3	1	.75	1	.344	.401	.525
2005 LAA	AL	54	134	31	8	0	5	(3	2)	54	17	14	11	7	0	26	1	0	1	0	1	.00	4	.231	.273	.403
2006 LAA	AL	86	234	75	11	1	9	(3	6)	115	28	32	36	7	1	28	2	0	1	2	1	.67	6	.321	.344	.491
2007 LAA	AL	79	178	44	9	0	3	(1	2)	62	21	21	15	14	1	27	1	0	1	3	2	.60	6	.247	.304	.348
2008 LAA	AL	68	164	43	1	2	1	(1	0)	51	15	11	17	14	0	28	2	0	1	4	2	.67	5	.262	.326	.311
2009 LAA	AL	54	115	28	5	0	2	(1	1)	39	13	14	12	5	0	30	0	0	0	1	1	.50	3	.243	.275	.339
Postseason		4	6	2	0	0	1	(0	1)	5	1	1	2	0	0	2	0	0	0	0	0	-	0	.333	.333	.833
7 ML YEARS		435	1079	303	52	5	25	(12	13)	440	130	119	132	67	2	181	8	1	5	14	10	.58	28	.281	.326	.408

Omar Quintanilla

Bats: L Throws: R Pos: 2B-25; PH-22; SS-13; 3B-10; PR-7   Ht: 5'9" Wt: 190 Born: 10/24/1981 Age: 28

Year Team	Lg	G	AB	H	2B	3B	HR	(Hm	Rd)	TB	R	RBI	RC	TBB	IBB	SO	HBP	SH	SF	SB	CS	SB%	GDP	Avg	OBP	Slg
2005 Col	NL	39	128	28	1	1	0	(0	0)	31	16	7	9	9	0	15	0	6	0	2	1	.67	3	.219	.270	.242
2006 Col	NL	11	34	6	1	1	0	(0	0)	9	3	3	2	3	1	9	0	1	0	1	1	.50	1	.176	.243	.265
2007 Col	NL	27	70	16	4	0	0	(0	0)	20	6	5	6	5	0	15	0	0	0	0	0	-	3	.229	.280	.286
2008 Col	NL	81	210	50	17	0	2	(1	1)	73	28	15	18	15	3	46	0	8	1	0	0	-	3	.238	.288	.348
2009 Col	NL	58	58	10	2	0	0	(0	0)	12	7	2	4	8	0	27	0	3	0	0	0	-	0	.172	.273	.207
5 ML YEARS		216	500	110	25	2	2	(1	1)	145	60	32	39	40	4	112	0	18	1	3	2	.60	10	.220	.277	.290

Humberto Quintero

Bats: R Throws: R Pos: C-59; PH-2   Ht: 5'9" Wt: 215 Born: 8/2/1979 Age: 30

Year Team	Lg	G	AB	H	2B	3B	HR	(Hm	Rd)	TB	R	RBI	RC	TBB	IBB	SO	HBP	SH	SF	SB	CS	SB%	GDP	Avg	OBP	Slg
2009 RdRck*	AAA	4	10	1	1	0	0	(-	-)	2	0	1	0	2	0	4	2	0	0	0	0	-	0	.100	.250	.200
2003 SD	NL	12	23	5	0	0	0	(0	0)	5	1	2	2	1	1	6	0	0	0	0	0	-	0	.217	.250	.217
2004 SD	NL	23	72	18	3	0	2	(1	1)	27	7	10	6	5	0	16	0	0	1	0	2	.00	5	.250	.295	.375
2005 Hou	NL	18	54	10	1	0	1	(1	0)	14	6	8	2	1	1	10	0	2	0	0	0	-	3	.185	.200	.259
2006 Hou	NL	11	21	7	2	0	0	(0	0)	9	2	2	1	1	0	3	0	0	0	0	0	-	2	.333	.364	.429
2007 Hou	NL	29	53	12	2	0	0	(0	0)	14	2	1	3	2	1	13	2	0	0	0	0	-	2	.226	.281	.264
2008 Hou	NL	59	168	38	6	0	2	(1	1)	50	16	12	10	6	0	34	4	5	0	0	0	-	5	.226	.270	.298
2009 Hou	NL	60	157	37	8	1	4	(3	1)	59	11	14	13	7	1	41	4	0	0	0	0	-	8	.236	.286	.376
7 ML YEARS		212	548	127	22	1	9	(6	3)	178	45	49	37	23	4	123	10	7	1	0	2	.00	25	.232	.275	.325

Guillermo Quiroz

Bats: R Throws: R Pos: C-4   Ht: 6'1" Wt: 215 Born: 11/29/1981 Age: 28

Year Team	Lg	G	AB	H	2B	3B	HR	(Hm	Rd)	TB	R	RBI	RC	TBB	IBB	SO	HBP	SH	SF	SB	CS	SB%	GDP	Avg	OBP	Slg
2009 Tacom*	AAA	13	48	12	2	0	1	(-	-)	17	2	6	4	0	0	9	0	2	0	0	0	-	1	.250	.250	.354
2009 WTenn*	AA	47	157	38	9	1	5	(-	-)	64	18	25	19	11	0	26	1	0	2	0	0	-	3	.242	.292	.408
2004 Tor	AL	17	52	11	2	0	0	(0	0)	13	2	6	4	2	0	8	2	0	1	1	0	1.00	0	.212	.263	.250
2005 Tor	AL	12	36	7	2	0	0	(0	0)	9	3	4	3	2	0	13	1	0	0	0	0	-	0	.194	.256	.250
2006 Sea	AL	1	2	0	0	0	0	(0	0)	0	0	0	0	0	0	2	0	0	0	0	0	-	0	.000	.000	.000
2007 Tex	AL	9	10	4	1	0	0	(0	0)	5	1	2	3	1	0	2	0	0	0	0	0	-	0	.400	.455	.500
2008 Bal	AL	56	134	25	5	0	2	(1	1)	36	12	14	10	12	0	34	1	1	0	0	0	-	3	.187	.259	.269
2009 Sea	AL	4	14	4	0	0	0	(0	0)	4	0	2	1	0	0	3	0	1	0	0	0	-	0	.286	.286	.286
6 ML YEARS		99	248	51	10	0	2	(1	1)	67	18	28	21	17	0	62	4	2	1	1	0	1.00	4	.206	.267	.270

Ryan Raburn

Bats: R Throws: R Pos: LF-70; PH-25; RF-14; 1B-10; CF-7; PR-7; 3B-6; DH-5   Ht: 6'0" Wt: 185 Born: 4/17/1981 Age: 29

Year Team	Lg	G	AB	H	2B	3B	HR	(Hm	Rd)	TB	R	RBI	RC	TBB	IBB	SO	HBP	SH	SF	SB	CS	SB%	GDP	Avg	OBP	Slg
2009 Toledo*	AAA	12	47	12	3	0	5	(-	-)	30	11	9	10	7	0	13	1	0	1	2	1	.67	0	.255	.357	.638
2004 Det	AL	12	29	4	1	0	0	(0	0)	5	4	1	1	2	0	15	0	0	0	1	0	1.00	0	.138	.194	.172
2007 Det	AL	49	138	42	12	2	4	(2	2)	70	28	27	21	8	1	33	0	1	1	3	0	1.00	7	.304	.340	.507
2008 Det	AL	92	182	43	10	1	4	(2	2)	67	26	20	20	16	1	49	0	1	0	3	1	.75	2	.236	.298	.368
2009 Det	AL	113	261	76	11	2	16	(9	7)	139	44	45	42	26	2	60	2	1	1	5	4	.56	6	.291	.359	.533
4 ML YEARS		266	610	165	34	5	24	(13	11)	281	102	93	84	52	4	157	2	3	2	12	5	.71	15	.270	.329	.461

Alexei Ramirez

Bats: R Throws: R Pos: SS-148   Ht: 6'2" Wt: 170 Born: 9/22/1981 Age: 28

Year Team	Lg	G	AB	H	2B	3B	HR	(Hm	Rd)	TB	R	RBI	RC	TBB	IBB	SO	HBP	SH	SF	SB	CS	SB%	GDP	Avg	OBP	Slg
2008 CWS	AL	136	480	139	22	2	21	(13	8)	228	65	77	78	18	3	61	4	3	4	13	9	.59	14	.290	.317	.475
2009 CWS	AL	148	542	150	14	1	15	(9	6)	211	71	68	74	49	3	66	1	6	8	14	5	.74	15	.277	.333	.389
Postseason		4	12	3	0	0	0	(0	0)	3	1	2	1	1	0	1	0	0	2	0	0	-	0	.250	.267	.250
2 ML YEARS		284	1022	289	36	3	36	(22	14)	439	136	145	152	67	6	127	4	10	12	27	14	.66	29	.283	.326	.430

Aramis Ramirez

Bats: R **Throws:** R **Pos:** 3B-79; PH-3　　　　　**Ht:** 6'1" **Wt:** 215 **Born:** 6/25/1978 **Age:** 32

							BATTING													BASERUNNING				AVERAGES		
Year	Team	Lg	G	AB	H	2B	3B	HR	(Hm | Rd)	TB	R	RBI	RC	TBB	IBB	SO	HBP	SH	SF	SB	CS	SB%	GDP	Avg	OBP	Slg
2009 Peoria*	A		3	6	3	1	0	0	(- | -)	4	2	1	2	3	0	0	0	0	0	0	0	-	1	.500	.667	.667
1998 Pit	NL		72	251	59	9	1	6	(3 | 3)	88	23	24	26	18	0	72	4	1	1	0	1	.00	3	.235	.296	.351
1999 Pit	NL		18	56	10	2	1	0	(0 | 0)	14	2	7	4	6	0	9	0	1	1	0	0	-	0	.179	.254	.250
2000 Pit	NL		73	254	65	15	2	6	(4 | 2)	102	19	35	28	10	0	36	5	1	4	0	0	-	9	.256	.293	.402
2001 Pit	NL		158	603	181	40	0	34	(16 | 18)	323	83	112	108	40	4	100	8	0	4	5	4	.56	9	.300	.350	.536
2002 Pit	NL		142	522	122	26	0	18	(7 | 11)	202	51	71	49	29	3	95	8	0	11	2	0	1.00	17	.234	.279	.387
2003 2 Tms	NL		159	607	165	32	2	27	(10 | 17)	282	75	106	88	42	3	99	10	0	11	2	2	.50	21	.272	.324	.465
2004 ChC	NL		145	547	174	32	1	36	(22 | 14)	316	99	103	100	49	6	62	3	0	7	0	2	.00	25	.318	.373	.578
2005 ChC	NL		123	463	140	30	1	31	(20 | 11)	263	72	92	79	35	4	60	6	0	2	0	1	.00	15	.302	.358	.568
2006 ChC	NL		157	594	173	38	4	38	(14 | 24)	333	93	119	109	50	4	63	9	0	7	2	1	.67	15	.291	.352	.561
2007 ChC	NL		132	506	157	35	4	26	(17 | 9)	278	72	101	95	43	8	66	4	0	5	0	0	-	13	.310	.366	.549
2008 ChC	NL		149	554	160	44	1	27	(17 | 10)	287	97	111	108	74	7	94	11	0	6	2	2	.50	13	.289	.380	.518
2009 ChC	NL		82	306	97	14	1	15	(7 | 8)	158	46	65	66	28	3	43	8	0	0	2	1	.67	8	.317	.389	.516
03 Pit	NL		96	375	105	25	1	12	(6 | 6)	168	44	67	49	25	3	68	7	0	8	1	1	.50	17	.280	.330	.448
03 ChC	NL		63	232	60	7	1	15	(4 | 11)	114	31	39	39	17	0	31	3	0	3	1	1	.50	4	.259	.314	.491
Postseason			18	67	13	2	1	4	(1 | 3)	29	7	10	8	9	0	15	1	0	0	0	0	-	5	.194	.299	.433
12 ML YEARS			1410	5263	1503	317	17	264	(128 | 136)	2646	732	946	860	424	42	799	76	3	59	15	14	.52	148	.286	.344	.503

Edwar Ramirez

Pitches: R **Bats:** R **Pos:** RP-20　　　　　**Ht:** 6'3" **Wt:** 165 **Born:** 3/28/1981 **Age:** 29

			HOW MUCH HE PITCHED						WHAT HE GAVE UP										THE RESULTS					
Year	Team	Lg	G	GS	CG	GF	IP	BFP	H	R	ER	HR	SH	SF	HB	TBB	IBB	SO	WP	Bk	W	L	Pct	Sh	Sv-Op	Hld	ERC	ERA
2009 S-WB*	AAA		29	0	0	19	51.0	206	39	19	18	3	0	0	6	16	0	62	8	0	1	5	.167	0	4--		2.28	3.18
2007 NYY	AL		21	0	0	5	21.0	103	24	19	19	6	1	1	3	14	2	31	4	0	1	1	.500	0	1-3	3	7.95	8.14
2008 NYY	AL		55	0	0	16	55.1	233	44	25	24	7	0	1	3	24	2	63	3	0	5	1	.833	0	1-4	5	3.42	3.90
2009 NYY	AL		20	0	0	2	22.0	110	25	15	14	6	0	2	0	18	0	22	1	0	0	0		0	0 0	1	7.06	5.73
3 ML YEARS			96	0	0	23	98.1	446	93	59	57	19	1	4	6	56	4	116	8	0	6	2	.750	0	2-7	9	5.25	5.22

Hanley Ramirez

Bats: R **Throws:** R **Pos:** SS-147; PH-5　　　　　**Ht:** 6'3" **Wt:** 225 **Born:** 12/23/1983 **Age:** 26

							BATTING													BASERUNNING				AVERAGES		
Year	Team	Lg	G	AB	H	2B	3B	HR	(Hm	Rd)	TB	R	RBI	RC	TBB	IBB	SO	IDP	SH	SF	SB	CS	SB%	GDP	Avg	OBP	Slg
2005 Bos	AL		2	2	0	0	0	0	(0	0)	0	0	0	0	0	0	2	0	0	0	0	0	-	0	.000	.000	.000
2006 Fla	NL		158	633	185	46	11	17	(9	8)	304	119	59	101	56	0	128	4	5	2	51	15	.77	7	.292	.353	.480
2007 Fla	NL		154	639	212	48	6	29	(15	14)	359	125	81	115	52	3	95	7	4	4	51	14	.78	10	.332	.386	.562
2008 Fla	NL		153	589	177	34	4	33	(17	16)	318	125	67	116	92	9	122	8	0	4	35	12	.74	5	.301	.400	.540
2009 Fla	NL		151	576	197	42	1	24	(17	7)	313	101	106	122	61	14	101	9	1	5	27	8	.77	9	.342	.410	.543
5 ML YEARS			618	2439	771	170	22	103	(58	45)	1294	470	313	454	261	26	448	28	10	15	164	49	.77	31	.316	.386	.531

Horacio Ramirez

Pitches: L **Bats:** L **Pos:** RP-18; SP-1　　　　　**Ht:** 6'1" **Wt:** 221 **Born:** 11/24/1979 **Age:** 30

			HOW MUCH HE PITCHED						WHAT HE GAVE UP										THE RESULTS					
Year	Team	Lg	G	GS	CG	GF	IP	BFP	H	R	ER	HR	SH	SF	HB	TBB	IBB	SO	WP	Bk	W	L	Pct	Sh	Sv-Op	Hld	ERC	ERA
2009 Syrcse*	AAA		16	16	1	0	85.0	376	111	53	51	10	4	3	2	24	1	35	3	1	3	7	.300	0	0--		5.71	5.40
2003 Atl	NL		29	29	1	0	182.1	781	181	91	81	21	12	3	6	72	10	100	5	1	12	4	.750	0	0-0	0	4.21	4.00
2004 Atl	NL		10	9	1	0	60.1	259	51	24	16	7	2	1	0	30	5	31	0	2	4	4	.333	0	0-0	0	3.55	2.39
2005 Atl	NL		33	32	1	0	202.1	847	214	108	104	31	13	5	2	67	4	80	4	1	11	9	.550	1	0-0	0	4.66	4.63
2006 Atl	NL		14	14	0	0	76.1	337	85	42	38	6	3	3	4	31	2	37	0	1	5	5	.500	0	0-0	0	4.82	4.48
2007 Sea	AL		20	20	0	0	98.0	459	139	86	78	13	1	1	2	42	1	40	1	0	8	7	.533	0	0-0	0	7.17	7.16
2008 2 Tms	AL		32	0	0	7	37.1	168	45	20	18	1	3	1	2	9	1	13	2	0	1	4	.200	0	0-0	2	4.13	4.34
2009 KC	AL		19	1	0	1	22.2	104	27	16	15	3	1	0	0	11	3	13	1	0	0	2	.000	0	0-1	2	5.53	5.96
08 CWS	AL		17	0	0	3	13.0	72	24	11	11	0	3	0	0	8	1	2	1	0	0	3	.000	0	0-0	1	8.89	7.62
08 KC	AL		15	0	0	4	24.1	96	21	9	7	1	0	1	2	1	0	11	1	0	1	1	.500	0	0-0	1	1.99	2.59
7 ML YEARS			157	105	3	8	679.1	2955	742	387	350	82	35	14	16	262	26	314	13	5	39	35	.527	1	0-1	4	4.79	4.64

Manny Ramirez

Bats: R **Throws:** R **Pos:** LF-101; PH-5　　　　　**Ht:** 6'0" **Wt:** 200 **Born:** 5/30/1972 **Age:** 38

							BATTING													BASERUNNING				AVERAGES		
Year	Team	Lg	G	AB	H	2B	3B	HR	(Hm	Rd)	TB	R	RBI	RC	TBB	IBB	SO	HBP	SH	SF	SB	CS	SB%	GDP	Avg	OBP	Slg
2009 Albq*	AAA		2	3	0	0	0	0	(-	-)	0	0	0	0	1	0	1	0	0	0	0	0	-	0	.000	.250	.000
2009 InldEm*	A+		3	7	3	0	0	1	(-	-)	6	2	1	2	2	0	4	0	0	0	0	0	-	0	.429	.556	.857
1993 Cle	AL		22	53	9	1	0	2	(0	2)	16	5	5	2	2	0	8	0	0	0	0	0	-	3	.170	.200	.302
1994 Cle	AL		91	290	78	22	0	17	(9	8)	151	51	60	53	42	4	72	4	0	4	4	2	.67	6	.269	.357	.521
1995 Cle	AL		137	484	149	26	1	31	(12	19)	270	85	107	103	75	6	112	5	2	5	6	6	.50	13	.308	.402	.558
1996 Cle	AL		152	550	170	45	3	33	(19	14)	320	94	112	120	85	8	104	3	0	9	8	5	.62	18	.309	.399	.582
1997 Cle	AL		150	561	184	40	0	26	(14	12)	302	99	88	117	79	5	115	7	0	4	2	3	.40	19	.328	.415	.538
1998 Cle	AL		150	571	168	35	2	45	(25	20)	342	108	145	121	76	6	121	6	0	10	5	3	.63	18	.294	.377	.599
1999 Cle	AL		147	522	174	34	3	44	(21	23)	346	131	165	141	96	9	131	13	0	9	2	1	.67	12	.333	.442	.663
2000 Cle	AL		118	439	154	34	2	38	(22	16)	306	92	122	122	86	9	117	3	0	4	1	1	.50	9	.351	.457	.697
2001 Bos	AL		142	529	162	33	2	41	(21	20)	322	93	125	122	81	25	147	8	0	2	0	0	-	16	.306	.405	.609
2002 Bos	AL		120	436	152	31	0	33	(18	15)	282	84	107	125	73	14	85	8	0	6	0	0	-	13	.349	.450	.647
2003 Bos	AL		154	569	185	36	1	37	(18	19)	334	117	104	128	97	28	94	8	0	5	3	1	.75	22	.325	.427	.587
2004 Bos	AL		152	568	175	44	0	43	(23	20)	348	108	130	124	82	15	124	6	0	7	2	4	.33	17	.308	.397	.613
2005 Bos	AL		152	554	162	30	1	45	(22	23)	329	112	144	134	80	9	119	10	0	6	1	0	1.00	20	.292	.388	.594

Year	Team	Lg	G	AB	H	2B	3B	HR	(Hm	Rd)	TB	R	RBI	RC	TBB	IBB	SO	HBP	SH	SF	SB	CS	SB%	GDP	Avg	OBP	Slg
2006	Bos	AL	130	449	144	27	1	35	(16	19)	278	79	102	114	100	16	102	1	0	8	0	1	.00	13	.321	**.439**	.619
2007	Bos	AL	133	483	143	33	1	20	(10	10)	238	84	88	78	71	13	92	7	0	8	0	-	-	21	.296	.388	.493
2008	2 Tms		153	552	183	36	1	37	(17	20)	332	102	121	133	87	24	124	11	0	4	3	0	1.00	17	.332	.430	.601
2009	LAD	NL	104	352	102	24	2	19	(10	9)	187	62	63	73	71	21	81	7	0	1	0	1	.00	7	.290	.418	.531
08	Bos	AL	100	365	109	22	1	20	(8	12)	193	66	68	69	52	8	86	8	0	0	1	0	1.00	12	.299	.398	.529
08	LAD	NL	53	187	74	14	0	17	(9	8)	139	36	53	64	35	16	38	3	0	4	2	0	1.00	5	.396	.489	.743
Postseason			103	378	108	16	0	28	(11	17)	208	64	74	81	70	12	85	5	0	6	1	1	.50	16	.286	.399	.550
17 ML YEARS			2207	7962	2494	531	20	546	(277	269)	4703	1506	1788	1815	1283	212	1748	103	2	87	37	32	.54	237	.313	.411	.591

Ramon Ramirez

Pitches: R **Bats:** R **Pos:** RP-11 **Ht:** 6'0" **Wt:** 188 **Born:** 9/16/1982 **Age:** 27

			HOW MUCH HE PITCHED						WHAT HE GAVE UP									THE RESULTS							
Year	Team	Lg	G	GS	CG	GF	IP	BFP	H	R	ER	HR	SH	SF	HB	TBB	IBB	SO	WP	Bk	W	L	Pct	Sh	Sv-Op	Hld	ERC	ERA
2004	Billings	R+	17	12	0	2	74.1	310	63	36	28	7	10	3	9	36	0	60	5	2	3	6	.333	0	1--	-	4.19	3.39
2005	Dayton	A	30	19	0	2	114.0	502	114	69	57	8	0	7	15	50	0	90	9	1	5	7	.417	0	0--	-	4.60	4.50
2006	Srsota	A+	15	11	1	2	65.0	279	66	33	31	11	1	1	3	21	0	53	5	2	4	5	.444	0	0--	-	4.53	4.29
2007	Srsota	A+	15	12	0	1	73.1	303	64	37	33	5	1	0	1	25	0	86	4	0	5	2	.714	0	1--	-	3.02	4.05
2007	Chatt	AA	16	0	0	3	31.1	132	30	16	16	3	2	0	0	12	1	34	3	1	5	1	.833	0	1--	-	3.74	4.60
2007	Lsvlle	AAA	5	2	0	1	14.2	54	7	0	0	1	0	1	0	6	0	16	1	0	1	0	1.000	0	0--	-	1.24	0.00
2008	Chatt	AA	11	9	0	2	46.0	193	41	29	24	6	1	2	2	15	0	52	4	0	2	3	.400	0	1--	-	3.55	4.70
2008	Lsvlle	AAA	19	15	0	2	99.1	400	76	37	34	8	3	0	1	42	1	93	4	1	4	5	.444	0	1--	-	2.89	3.08
2009	Lsvlle	AAA	31	20	0	4	127.1	546	122	68	57	13	4	9	6	50	0	78	7	3	6	7	.462	0	0--	-	4.03	4.03
2008	Cin	NL	5	4	0	0	27.0	105	17	8	8	3	0	0	1	11	0	21	0	1	1	1	.500	0	0-0	0	2.48	2.67
2009	Cin	NL	11	0	0	3	12.1	48	8	5	5	2	0	0	1	4	0	8	0	0	0	0	-	0	0-0	3	2.73	3.65
2 ML YEARS			16	4	0	3	39.1	153	25	13	13	5	0	0	2	15	0	29	0	1	1	1	.500	0	0-0	3	2.56	2.97

Ramon Ramirez

Pitches: R **Bats:** R **Pos:** RP-70 **Ht:** 5'11" **Wt:** 190 **Born:** 8/31/1981 **Age:** 28

			HOW MUCH HE PITCHED						WHAT HE GAVE UP									THE RESULTS							
Year	Team	Lg	G	GS	CG	GF	IP	BFP	H	R	ER	HR	SH	SF	HB	TBB	IBB	SO	WP	Bk	W	L	Pct	Sh	Sv-Op	Hld	ERC	ERA
2006	Col	NL	61	0	0	14	67.2	285	58	28	26	5	2	3	1	27	3	61	2	0	4	3	.571	0	0-2	10	3.09	3.46
2007	Col	NL	22	0	0	5	17.1	78	21	16	16	2	2	2	1	6	2	15	2	0	2	2	.500	0	0-0	3	5.24	8.31
2008	KC	AL	71	0	0	15	71.2	295	57	23	21	2	4	3	0	31	6	70	6	1	3	2	.600	0	1-5	21	2.53	2.64
2009	Bos	AL	70	0	0	16	69.2	301	61	26	22	7	3	0	4	32	4	52	2	2	7	4	.636	0	0-4	12	3.73	2.84
4 ML YEARS			224	0	0	50	226.1	959	197	93	85	16	11	8	6	96	15	198	12	3	16	11	.593	0	1-11	46	3.26	3.38

Wilkin Ramirez

Bats: R **Throws:** R **Pos:** PR-9; DH-5; LF-3; RF-2 **Ht:** 6'2" **Wt:** 190 **Born:** 10/25/1985 **Age:** 24

									BATTING											BASERUNNING				AVERAGES		
Year	Team	Lg	G	AB	H	2B	3B	HR	(Hm	Rd)	TB	R	RBI	RC	TBB	IBB	SO	HBP	SH	SF	SB	CS	SB%	GDP	Avg	OBP	Slg
2003	Tigers	R	54	200	55	6	7	5	(-	-)	90	34	35	30	13	2	51	1	1	1	6	1	.86	4	.275	.321	.450
2005	WMich	A	131	493	129	21	2	16	(-	-)	202	69	65	67	35	1	143	7	1	5	21	8	.72	9	.262	.317	.410
2006	Lkland	A+	66	249	56	10	4	8	(-	-)	98	31	33	26	10	0	69	2	0	2	8	2	.80	8	.225	.259	.394
2007	Lkland	A+	88	319	87	7	4	10	(-	-)	132	48	41	45	20	0	86	1	0	3	28	6	.82	4	.273	.315	.414
2007	Erie	AA	34	121	26	3	1	2	(-	-)	37	15	14	10	8	0	38	2	1	1	6	2	.75	1	.215	.273	.306
2008	Erie	AA	110	433	131	24	7	19	(-	-)	226	74	73	83	43	1	138	5	0	1	26	12	.68	3	.303	.371	.522
2008	Toledo	AAA	11	36	3	1	0	0	(-	-)	4	2	0	0	1	0	11	1	0	0	1	0	1.00	1	.083	.132	.111
2009	Toledo	AAA	113	434	112	18	6	17	(-	-)	193	69	51	67	41	0	143	4	0	2	34	10	.77	6	.258	.326	.445
2009	Det	AL	15	11	4	0	1	1	(1	0)	9	6	3	3	1	0	3	0	0	1	0	0	-	1	.364	.385	.818

Cesar Ramos

Pitches: L **Bats:** L **Pos:** RP-3; SP-2 **Ht:** 6'2" **Wt:** 203 **Born:** 6/22/1984 **Age:** 26

			HOW MUCH HE PITCHED						WHAT HE GAVE UP									THE RESULTS							
Year	Team	Lg	G	GS	CG	GF	IP	BFP	H	R	ER	HR	SH	SF	HB	TBB	IBB	SO	WP	Bk	W	L	Pct	Sh	Sv-Op	Hld	ERC	ERA
2005	Eugene	A-	6	4	0	0	20.2	101	27	21	15	3	0	2	3	7	0	13	2	0	0	1	.000	0	0--	-	6.31	6.53
2005	FtWyn	A	7	7	1	0	38.2	160	42	19	18	0	0	3	1	7	0	32	2	0	3	2	.600	0	0--	-	3.18	4.19
2006	Lk Els	A+	26	24	0	1	141.0	608	161	72	58	9	3	1	8	44	0	70	4	0	7	8	.467	0	0--	-	4.60	3.70
2007	SnAnt	AA	27	27	2	0	163.2	670	153	69	62	15	3	2	6	43	0	90	5	0	13	9	.591	2	0--	-	3.34	3.41
2008	Portlnd	AAA	28	27	0	1	149.2	671	183	108	88	17	4	7	5	57	0	105	2	0	9	11	.450	0	0--	-	5.60	5.29
2009	Portlnd	AAA	15	15	1	0	76.2	344	84	42	34	7	5	1	0	31	2	45	5	0	5	6	.455	0	0--	-	4.43	3.99
2009	Padres	R	4	2	0	0	8.0	32	8	3	2	0	0	0	0	0	0	8	0	0	0	1	.000	0	0--	-	1.95	2.25
2009	Lk Els	A+	2	1	0	0	9.0	41	9	1	1	0	0	0	0	5	0	6	0	0	1	0	1.000	0	0--	-	3.83	1.00
2009	SD	NL	5	2	0	0	14.2	62	19	5	5	0	0	0	0	4	0	10	0	0	0	1	.000	0	0-0	0	4.78	3.07

Cody Ransom

Bats: R **Throws:** R **Pos:** 3B-23; PR-6; SS-3; DH-2; 1B-1; 2B-1 **Ht:** 6'2" **Wt:** 190 **Born:** 2/17/1976 **Age:** 34

									BATTING											BASERUNNING				AVERAGES		
Year	Team	Lg	G	AB	H	2B	3B	HR	(Hm	Rd)	TB	R	RBI	RC	TBB	IBB	SO	HBP	SH	SF	SB	CS	SB%	GDP	Avg	OBP	Slg
2009	S-WB*	AAA	31	96	23	7	1	3	(-	-)	41	24	16	17	19	2	22	2	0	3	0	0	-	1	.240	.367	.427
2001	SF	NL	9	7	0	0	0	0	(0	0)	0	1	0	0	0	0	5	0	0	0	0	0	-	0	.000	.000	.000
2002	SF	NL	7	3	2	0	0	0	(0	0)	2	2	1	1	1	1	1	0	0	0	0	0	-	0	.667	.750	.667
2003	SF	NL	20	27	6	1	0	1	(1	0)	10	7	1	1	1	0	11	0	0	0	0	0	-	0	.222	.250	.370
2004	SF	NL	78	68	17	6	0	1	(0	1)	26	13	11	9	6	0	20	1	3	0	2	2	.50	2	.250	.320	.382

		BATTING																				BASERUNNING				AVERAGES		
Year	Team	Lg	G	AB	H	2B	3B	HR	(Hm	Rd)	TB	R	RBI	RC	TBB	IBB	SO	HBP	SH	SF	SB	CS	SB%	GDP	Avg	OBP	Slg
2007	Hou	NL	19	35	8	2	0	1	(1	0)	13	9	3	6	9	1	9	2	0	0	0	0	-	1	.229	.413	.371
2008	NYY	AL	33	43	13	3	0	4	(1	3)	28	9	8	10	6	0	12	1	1	0	0	0	-	-	.302	.400	.651
2009	NYY	AL	31	79	15	9	1	0	(0	0)	26	11	10	5	7	0	25	0	0	0	2	0	1.00	3	.190	.256	.329
7 ML YEARS			197	262	61	21	1	7	(3	4)	105	52	34	32	30	2	83	4	4	0	4	2	.67	6	.233	.321	.401

Clay Rapada

Pitches: L **Bats:** R **Pos:** RP-3   **Ht:** 6'5" **Wt:** 200 **Born:** 3/9/1981 **Age:** 29

			HOW MUCH HE PITCHED				WHAT HE GAVE UP										THE RESULTS						
Year	Team	Lg	G	GS	CG	GF	IP	BFP	H	R	ER	HR	SH	SF	HB	TBB	IBB	SO	WP	Bk	W	L	Pct	Sh	Sv-Op	Hld	ERC	ERA
2009	Toledo*	AAA	42	0	0	18	45.2	197	50	15	14	1	2	1	0	17	3	47	1	0	4	2	.667	0	5--	-	3.87	2.76
2007	2 Tms		5	0	0	2	2.2	13	3	3	3	2	0	0	0	2	0	4	2	0	0	0	-	0	0-0	0	11.59	10.13
2008	Det	AL	25	0	0	3	21.1	94	19	11	10	0	1	0	1	14	1	15	1	0	3	0	1.000	0	0-0	2	3.87	4.22
2009	Det	AL	3	0	0	1	3.1	16	4	2	2	1	0	0	0	2	1	2	0	0	0	0	-	0	0-0	0	7.00	5.40
07	ChC	NL	1	0	0	0	0.1	1	0	0	0	0	0	0	0	0	0	0	0	0	0	0	-	0	0-0	0	0.00	0.00
07	Det	AL	4	0	0	2	2.1	12	3	3	3	2	0	0	0	2	0	4	2	0	0	0	-	0	0-0	0	14.48	11.57
3 ML YEARS			33	0	0	6	27.1	123	26	16	15	3	1	0	1	18	2	21	3	0	3	0	1.000	0	0-0	2	4.97	4.94

Colby Rasmus

Bats: L **Throws:** L **Pos:** CF-124; PH-20; LF-9; RF-6; PR-1   **Ht:** 6'2" **Wt:** 200 **Born:** 8/11/1986 **Age:** 23

			BATTING																		BASERUNNING				AVERAGES		
Year	Team	Lg	G	AB	H	2B	3B	HR	(Hm	Rd)	TB	R	RBI	RC	TBB	IBB	SO	HBP	SH	SF	SB	CS	SB%	GDP	Avg	OBP	Slg
2005	JhsCty	R+	62	216	64	16	5	7	(-	-)	111	47	27	41	21	2	73	3	1	3	13	3	.81	0	.296	.362	.514
2006	QuadC	A	78	303	94	22	3	11	(-	-)	155	49	50	59	29	2	55	3	3	3	17	5	.77	2	.310	.373	.512
2006	PlmBh	A+	53	193	49	4	5	5	(-	-)	78	22	35	30	27	3	35	3	0	2	11	3	.79	3	.254	.351	.404
2007	Sprgfld	AA	128	472	130	37	3	29	(-	-)	260	93	72	103	70	0	108	12	0	2	18	3	.86	2	.275	.381	.551
2008	Memp	AAA	90	331	83	15	0	11	(	)	131	50	30	51	49	3	72	1	3	3	15	2	.88	7	.251	.010	.000
2008	Sarus	R	3	9	5	1	0	1	(-	-)	9	1	2	4	3	0	2	0	0	0	0	0	-	0	.556	.667	1.000
2008	PlmBh	A+	3	9	0	0	0	0	(-	-)	0	1	0	0	1	0	3	1	0	0	0	0	-	0	.000	.182	.000
2009	StL	NL	147	474	119	22	2	16	(7	9)	193	72	52	60	36	3	95	3	5	2	3	1	.75	5	.251	.307	.407

Jon Rauch

Pitches: R **Bats:** R **Pos:** RP-75   **Ht:** 6'11" **Wt:** 291 **Born:** 9/27/1978 **Age:** 31

			HOW MUCH HE PITCHED				WHAT HE GAVE UP										THE RESULTS						
Year	Team	Lg	G	GS	CG	GF	IP	BFP	H	R	ER	HR	SH	SF	HB	TBB	IBB	SO	WP	Bk	W	L	Pct	Sh	Sv-Op	Hld	ERC	ERA
2002	CWS	AL	8	6	0	1	28.2	130	28	26	21	7	0	1	2	14	2	19	1	1	2	1	.667	0	0-0	0	5.41	6.59
2004	2 Tms		11	4	0	1	32.0	131	30	10	10	1	2	1	0	11	2	22	2	0	4	1	.800	0	0-0	0	3.05	2.81
2005	Was	NL	15	1	0	4	30.0	124	24	12	12	3	1	1	1	11	2	23	2	0	2	4	.333	0	0-0	0	2.90	3.60
2006	Was	NL	85	0	0	19	91.1	383	78	37	34	13	1	6	2	36	6	86	4	1	4	5	.444	0	2-5	18	3.52	3.35
2007	Was	NL	88	0	0	26	87.1	354	75	37	35	7	2	5	0	21	4	71	2	0	8	4	.667	0	4-10	33	2.53	3.61
2008	2 Tms	NL	74	0	0	51	71.2	295	69	36	33	11	6	3	0	16	2	66	1	0	4	8	.333	0	18-24	6	3.48	4.14
2009	2 Tms	NL	75	0	0	15	70.0	299	70	30	28	6	3	4	2	23	1	49	6	0	7	3	.700	0	2-5	17	3.78	3.60
04	CWS	AL	2	2	0	0	8.2	43	16	6	6	0	1	1	0	4	0	4	1	0	1	1	.500	0	0-0	0	9.15	6.23
04	Mon	NL	9	2	0	1	23.1	88	14	4	4	1	1	0	0	7	2	18	1	0	3	0	1.000	0	0-0	0	1.44	1.54
08	Was	NL	48	0	0	41	48.1	192	42	18	16	5	3	1	0	7	1	44	0	0	4	2	.667	0	17-22	0	2.41	2.98
08	Ari	NL	26	0	0	10	23.1	103	27	18	17	6	3	2	0	9	1	22	1	0	0	6	.000	0	1-2	6	6.09	6.56
09	Ari	NL	58	0	0	13	54.1	235	57	27	25	5	1	2	1	17	0	35	6	0	2	2	.500	0	2-3	12	3.98	4.14
09	Min	AI	17	0	0	2	15.2	64	13	3	3	1	2	2	1	6	1	14	0	0	5	1	.833	0	0-2	5	3.09	1.72
7 ML YEARS			356	11	0	117	411.0	1716	374	188	173	48	15	21	7	132	19	336	18	2	31	26	.544	0	26-44	74	3.38	3.79

Chris Ray

Pitches: R **Bats:** R **Pos:** RP-46   **Ht:** 6'3" **Wt:** 223 **Born:** 1/12/1982 **Age:** 28

			HOW MUCH HE PITCHED				WHAT HE GAVE UP										THE RESULTS						
Year	Team	Lg	G	GS	CG	GF	IP	BFP	H	R	ER	HR	SH	SF	HB	TBB	IBB	SO	WP	Bk	W	L	Pct	Sh	Sv-Op	Hld	ERC	ERA
2009	Norfolk*	AAA	8	0	0	5	12.0	44	5	3	3	0	0	0	0	4	0	13	0	0	0	1	.000	0	1--	-	0.90	2.25
2009	Bowie*	AA	3	0	0	0	3.0	11	0	0	0	0	0	0	0	2	0	2	0	0	0	0	-	0	0--	-	0.46	0.00
2005	Bal	AL	41	0	0	8	40.2	174	34	15	12	5	1	1	1	18	3	43	0	1	1	3	.250	0	0-4	8	3.43	2.66
2006	Bal	AL	61	0	0	56	66.0	267	45	22	20	10	2	4	1	27	2	51	2	0	4	4	.500	0	33-38	0	2.77	2.73
2007	Bal	AL	43	0	0	37	42.2	179	35	22	21	5	0	1	2	18	2	44	1	0	5	6	.455	0	16-20	0	3.42	4.43
2009	Bal	AL	46	0	0	12	43.1	214	64	36	35	8	4	4	1	23	7	39	0	0	0	4	.000	0	0-3	6	6.03	7.27
4 ML YEARS			191	0	0	113	192.2	834	178	95	88	28	7	10	5	86	14	177	3	1	10	17	.370	0	49-65	14	4.12	4.11

Robert Ray

Pitches: R **Bats:** R **Pos:** SP-4   **Ht:** 6'5" **Wt:** 190 **Born:** 1/21/1984 **Age:** 26

			HOW MUCH HE PITCHED				WHAT HE GAVE UP										THE RESULTS						
Year	Team	Lg	G	GS	CG	GF	IP	BFP	H	R	ER	HR	SH	SF	HB	TBB	IBB	SO	WP	Bk	W	L	Pct	Sh	Sv-Op	Hld	ERC	ERA
2005	Auburn	A-	15	13	0	0	61.2	253	46	22	19	2	0	3	4	20	0	58	3	1	4	3	.571	0	0--	-	2.25	2.77
2006	Dnedin	A+	14	9	0	1	48.2	216	59	34	27	2	2	2	6	13	0	37	2	0	2	4	.333	0	0--	-	4.88	4.99
2007	Dnedin	A+	18	15	1	2	66.2	304	83	40	36	3	1	0	6	24	0	57	4	0	3	3	.500	0	1--	-	5.30	4.86
2008	Dnedin	A+	13	13	1	0	70.2	299	71	37	33	6	0	0	5	18	0	60	5	0	5	3	.625	0	0--	-	3.72	4.20
2008	NHam	AA	16	16	2	0	96.1	421	108	43	34	6	3	1	7	27	2	72	7	0	8	6	.571	1	0--	-	4.27	3.18
2009	Dnedin	A+	2	2	0	0	6.2	28	8	3	2	0	0	0	0	4	0	4	0	0	1	0	1.000	0	0--	-	2.89	2.70
2009	LsVgs	AAA	1	1	0	0	4.1	18	2	0	0	0	0	0	0	3	0	3	0	0	0	0	-	0	0--	-	1.70	0.00
2009	B Jays	R	2	2	0	0	2.0	10	4	1	1	0	0	0	0	0	0	2	1	0	0	1	.000	0	0--	-	7.48	4.50
2009	Tor	AL	4	4	0	0	24.1	101	23	15	12	4	1	1	2	6	0	13	0	0	1	2	.333	0	0-0	0	3.97	4.44

Josh Reddick

Bats: L **Throws:** R **Pos:** LF-12; RF-10; PH-8; CF-2; PR-2   **Ht:** 6'2" **Wt:** 180 **Born:** 2/19/1987 **Age:** 23

Year	Team	Lg	G	AB	H	2B	3B	HR	(Hm	Rd)	TB	R	RBI	RC	TBB	IBB	SO	HBP	SH	SF	SB	CS	SB%	GDP	Avg	OBP	Slg
2007	Grnville	A	94	369	113	17	6	18	(-	-)	196	60	72	68	26	2	51	3	0	5	8	5	.62	7	.306	.352	.531
2007	Portlnd	AA	1	1	0	0	0	0	(-	-)	0	0	0	0	0	0	0	0	0	0	0	0	-	0	.000	.000	.000
2008	Grnville	A	14	53	18	4	2	0	(-	-)	26	7	9	10	5	0	8	0	0	0	2	1	.67	0	.340	.397	.491
2008	Lancst	A+	76	312	107	11	8	17	(-	-)	185	60	57	67	17	0	49	0	0	2	9	1	.90	4	.343	.375	.593
2008	Portlnd	AA	34	117	25	4	2	6	(-	-)	51	22	25	15	12	1	25	1	1	1	3	1	.75	1	.214	.290	.436
2009	Portlnd	AA	63	256	71	17	3	13	(-	-)	133	47	29	46	30	3	62	0	0	1	5	5	.50	2	.277	.352	.520
2009	Pwtckt	AAA	18	71	9	0	2	0	(-	-)	13	1	6	1	6	0	13	0	0	2	0	1	.00	1	.127	.190	.183
2009	Bos	AL	27	59	10	4	0	2	(0	2)	20	5	4	4	2	0	17	1	0	0	0	0	-	0	.169	.210	.339

Tim Redding

Pitches: R **Bats:** R **Pos:** SP-17; RP-13   **Ht:** 5'11" **Wt:** 230 **Born:** 2/12/1978 **Age:** 32

Year	Team	Lg	G	GS	CG	GF	IP	BFP	H	R	ER	HR	SH	SF	HB	TBB	IBB	SO	WP	Bk	W	L	Pct	Sh	Sv-Op	Hld	ERC	ERA
2009	Buffalo*	AAA	2	2	0	0	13.0	53	13	4	4	1	2	0	0	2	0	9	0	0	0	0	-	0	0--	-	2.98	2.77
2001	Hou	NL	13	9	0	1	55.2	249	62	38	34	11	2	3	3	24	0	55	2	0	3	1	.750	0	0-0	0	5.87	5.50
2002	Hou	NL	18	14	0	1	73.1	325	78	49	44	10	4	3	0	35	3	63	5	1	3	6	.333	0	0-0	0	4.96	5.40
2003	Hou	NL	33	32	0	0	176.0	769	179	85	72	16	7	3	7	65	4	116	3	0	10	14	.417	0	0-0	0	4.07	3.68
2004	Hou	NL	27	17	0	2	100.2	465	125	73	64	15	10	3	5	43	3	56	2	0	5	7	.417	0	0-0	0	6.14	5.72
2005	2 Tms		10	7	0	0	30.2	154	44	41	36	7	3	3	2	17	1	19	1	0	0	6	.000	0	0-0	0	8.60	10.57
2007	Was	NL	15	15	0	0	84.0	366	84	35	34	10	6	1	4	38	4	47	1	1	3	6	.333	0	0-0	0	4.59	3.64
2008	Was	NL	33	33	1	0	182.0	791	195	110	100	27	5	5	7	65	5	120	10	0	10	11	.476	0	0-0	0	4.80	4.95
2009	NYM	NL	30	17	0	2	120.0	525	122	72	68	18	3	6	2	50	5	76	4	0	3	6	.333	0	0-0	0	4.57	5.10
05	SD	NL	9	6	0	0	29.2	143	40	35	30	7	3	3	2	13	1	17	1	0	0	5	.000	0	0-0	0	7.56	9.10
05	NYY	AL	1	1	0	0	1.0	11	4	6	6	0	0	0	0	4	0	2	0	0	0	1	.000	0	0-0	0	43.35	54.00
	8 ML YEARS		179	144	1	6	822.1	3644	889	503	452	114	40	27	30	337	25	552	28	2	37	57	.394	0	0-0	0	4.96	4.95

Mike Redmond

Bats: R **Throws:** R **Pos:** C-44; PH-2   **Ht:** 5'11" **Wt:** 200 **Born:** 5/5/1971 **Age:** 39

Year	Team	Lg	G	AB	H	2B	3B	HR	(Hm	Rd)	TB	R	RBI	RC	TBB	IBB	SO	HBP	SH	SF	SB	CS	SB%	GDP	Avg	OBP	Slg
1998	Fla	NL	37	118	39	9	0	2	(1	1)	54	10	12	18	5	2	16	2	4	0	0	0	-	6	.331	.368	.458
1999	Fla	NL	84	242	73	9	0	1	(0	1)	85	22	27	33	26	2	34	5	5	0	0	0	-	6	.302	.381	.351
2000	Fla	NL	87	210	53	8	1	0	(0	0)	63	17	15	20	13	3	19	8	1	3	0	0	-	5	.252	.316	.300
2001	Fla	NL	48	141	44	4	0	4	(3	1)	60	19	14	21	13	4	13	2	1	1	0	0	-	6	.312	.376	.426
2002	Fla	NL	89	256	78	15	0	2	(1	1)	99	19	28	37	21	8	34	8	2	3	0	2	.00	4	.305	.372	.387
2003	Fla	NL	59	125	30	7	1	0	(0	0)	39	12	11	10	7	0	16	5	2	2	0	0	-	2	.240	.302	.312
2004	Fla	NL	81	246	63	15	0	2	(0	2)	84	19	25	27	14	0	28	8	3	2	1	0	1.00	10	.256	.315	.341
2005	Min	AL	45	148	46	9	0	1	(0	1)	58	17	26	23	6	0	14	3	2	0	0	0	-	9	.311	.350	.392
2006	Min	AL	47	179	61	13	0	0	(0	0)	74	20	23	22	4	0	18	4	1	2	0	0	-	9	.341	.365	.413
2007	Min	AL	82	272	80	13	0	1	(1	0)	96	23	38	38	18	3	23	5	0	3	0	0	-	9	.294	.346	.353
2008	Min	AL	38	129	37	6	0	0	(0	0)	43	14	12	12	5	0	11	2	0	1	0	0	-	8	.287	.321	.333
2009	Min	AL	45	135	32	5	1	0	(0	0)	39	9	7	8	11	0	19	1	0	0	0	0	-	8	.237	.299	.289
	Postseason		2	1	0	0	0	0	(0	0)	0	1	0	0	1	0	0	0	0	0	0	0	-	0	.000	.500	.000
	12 ML YEARS		742	2201	636	113	3	13	(6	7)	794	201	238	269	143	22	245	53	21	17	1	2	.33	82	.289	.345	.361

Jeremy Reed

Bats: L **Throws:** L **Pos:** PH-60; LF-50; CF-12; RF-8; 1B-4; PR-1   **Ht:** 6'0" **Wt:** 212 **Born:** 6/15/1981 **Age:** 29

Year	Team	Lg	G	AB	H	2B	3B	HR	(Hm	Rd)	TB	R	RBI	RC	TBB	IBB	SO	HBP	SH	SF	SB	CS	SB%	GDP	Avg	OBP	Slg
2004	Sea	AL	18	58	23	4	0	0	(0	0)	27	11	5	11	7	1	4	1	0	0	3	1	.75	2	.397	.470	.466
2005	Sea	AL	141	488	124	33	3	3	(0	3)	172	61	45	49	48	1	74	2	4	2	12	11	.52	10	.254	.322	.352
2006	Sea	AL	67	212	46	6	5	6	(1	5)	80	27	17	13	11	1	31	2	2	2	2	3	.40	5	.217	.260	.377
2007	Sea	AL	13	17	3	0	1	0	(0	0)	5	2	0	0	0	0	3	0	0	0	0	0	-	0	.176	.176	.294
2008	Sea	AL	97	286	77	18	1	2	(1	1)	103	30	31	31	18	0	38	1	3	3	2	3	.40	5	.269	.314	.360
2009	NYM	NL	126	161	39	6	2	0	(0	0)	49	9	9	12	14	1	36	0	1	1	0	3	.00	4	.242	.301	.304
	6 ML YEARS		462	1222	312	67	12	11	(2	9)	436	140	107	116	98	4	186	7	10	8	19	21	.48	26	.255	.312	.357

Steven Register

Pitches: R **Bats:** R **Pos:** RP-1   **Ht:** 6'1" **Wt:** 180 **Born:** 5/16/1983 **Age:** 27

Year	Team	Lg	G	GS	CG	GF	IP	BFP	H	R	ER	HR	SH	SF	HB	TBB	IBB	SO	WP	Bk	W	L	Pct	Sh	Sv-Op	Hld	ERC	ERA
2004	TriCity	A-	15	15	0	0	79.1	326	68	41	32	5	6	2	7	20	0	63	2	0	6	7	.462	0	0--	-	2.85	3.63
2005	Mdest	A+	27	27	1	0	156.0	676	184	98	77	16	3	4	1	35	0	108	6	0	9	11	.450	0	0--	-	4.41	4.44
2006	Tulsa	AA	27	27	2	0	155.0	694	189	114	96	25	10	7	10	53	1	77	5	1	4	10	.286	0	0--	-	5.91	5.57
2007	Tulsa	AA	61	0	0	55	58.0	250	63	27	26	3	3	4	1	16	1	48	3	0	1	3	.250	0	37--	-	3.74	4.03
2008	ColSpr	AAA	56	0	0	45	59.0	251	57	25	22	4	3	1	3	19	0	52	3	0	5	3	.625	0	16--	-	3.56	3.36
2009	ColSpr	AAA	16	0	0	13	16.0	77	22	11	8	3	2	0	0	9	4	13	0	0	0	2	.000	0	6--	-	7.30	4.50
2009	LV	AAA	34	0	0	19	41.1	176	44	18	17	4	1	1	0	12	2	28	3	0	2	3	.400	0	7--	-	3.91	3.70
2008	Col	NL	10	0	0	5	10.0	49	13	10	10	4	0	1	0	6	1	8	0	0	0	0	-	0	0-0	0	8.89	9.00
2009	Phi	NL	1	0	0	1	2.0	11	3	1	1	0	0	0	1	1	0	1	0	0	0	0	-	0	0-0	0	8.58	4.50
	2 ML YEARS		11	0	0	6	12.0	60	16	11	11	4	0	1	1	7	1	9	0	0	0	0	-	0	0-0	0	8.91	8.25

Nolan Reimold

Bats: R **Throws:** R **Pos:** LF-88; DH-10; PH-8; RF-2 **Ht:** 6'4" **Wt:** 205 **Born:** 10/12/1983 **Age:** 26

Year	Team	Lg	G	AB	H	2B	3B	HR	(Hm	Rd)	TB	R	RBI	RC	TBB	IBB	SO	HBP	SH	SF	SB	CS	SB%	GDP	Avg	OBP	Slg
2005	Abrdn	A-	50	180	53	15	2	9	(-	-)	99	33	30	39	29	1	44	1	0	2	2	0	1.00	2	.294	.392	.550
2005	Frdrck	A+	23	83	22	6	0	6	(-	-)	46	17	11	17	12	0	27	2	0	0	3	0	1.00	0	.265	.371	.554
2006	Frdrck	A+	119	415	106	26	0	19	(-	-)	189	73	75	77	76	4	107	9	0	4	14	8	.64	4	.255	.379	.455
2007	Bowie	AA	50	186	57	15	0	11	(-	-)	105	30	34	36	17	1	47	0	0	0	2	3	.40	5	.306	.365	.565
2007	Orioles	R	9	30	7	4	1	0	(-	-)	13	4	8	6	6	0	4	3	0	0	0	0	-	0	.233	.410	.433
2008	Bowie	AA	139	507	144	30	3	25	(-	-)	255	87	84	97	63	1	82	8	0	8	7	3	.70	9	.284	.367	.503
2009	Norfolk	AAA	31	109	43	11	0	9	(-	-)	81	21	27	36	18	2	25	2	0	1	6	1	.86	2	.394	.485	.743
2009	Bal	AL	104	358	100	18	2	15	(8	7)	167	49	45	57	47	1	77	3	0	3	8	2	.80	8	.279	.365	.466

Chad Reineke

Pitches: R **Bats:** R **Pos:** SP-1 **Ht:** 6'6" **Wt:** 228 **Born:** 4/9/1982 **Age:** 28

Year	Team	Lg	G	GS	CG	GF	IP	BFP	H	R	ER	HR	SH	SF	HB	TBB	IBB	SO	WP	Bk	W	L	Pct	Sh	Sv-Op	Hld	ERC	ERA
2004	TriCity	A-	23	0	0	16	36.2	160	27	13	10	0	0	0	0	23	0	52	3	0	1	2	.333	0	3--	-	2.74	2.45
2005	Lxngtn	A	42	11	0	16	102.1	425	84	46	40	5	5	1	4	49	0	108	6	0	10	8	.556	0	4--	-	3.29	3.52
2006	Salem	A+	17	17	1	0	99.2	414	82	42	33	5	4	4	5	29	0	87	7	0	6	5	.545	0	0--	-	2.55	2.98
2006	CpChr	AA	15	4	0	2	44.1	187	33	17	15	3	2	0	1	26	1	45	1	0	1	3	.250	0	0--	-	3.27	3.05
2007	RdRck	AAA	16	16	0	4	100.0	439	99	61	52	7	4	4	0	52	7	95	7	0	5	5	.500	0	0--	-	4.17	4.68
2008	RdRck	AAA	20	19	1	0	112.1	480	112	62	55	15	3	1	1	35	0	100	2	0	5	9	.357	0	0--	-	3.93	4.41
2008	Portlnd	AAA	3	3	0	0	17.1	72	17	8	8	5	0	0	1	6	0	13	0	0	0	1	.000	0	0--	-	5.17	4.15
2009	Scrmto	AAA	30	22	0	2	125.0	557	134	73	66	17	2	6	5	52	2	91	9	0	9	4	.692	0	2--	-	4.92	4.75
2008	SD	NL	4	3	0	1	18.0	78	14	10	10	1	1	1	0	12	1	13	0	0	2	1	.667	0	0-0	0	3.48	5.00
2009	Oak	AL	1	1	0	0	5.0	22	7	4	4	2	0	0	1	0	0	1	0	0	0	0	-	0	0-0	0	8.12	7.20
	2 ML YEARS		5	4	0	1	23.0	100	21	14	14	3	1	1	1	12	1	14	0	0	2	1	.667	0	0-0	0	4.43	5.48

Edgar Renteria

Bats: R **Throws:** R **Pos:** SS-123; PH-3 **Ht:** 6'1" **Wt:** 200 **Born:** 8/7/1975 **Age:** 34

Year	Team	Lg	G	AB	H	2B	3B	HR	(Hm	Rd)	TB	R	RBI	RC	TBB	IBB	SO	HBP	SH	SF	SB	CS	SB%	GDP	Avg	OBP	Slg
1996	Fla	NL	106	431	133	18	3	5	(2	3)	172	68	31	62	33	0	68	2	2	3	16	2	.89	12	.309	.358	.399
1997	Fla	NL	154	617	171	21	3	4	(3	1)	210	90	52	68	45	1	100	4	19	8	32	15	.68	17	.277	.327	.340
1998	Fla	NL	133	517	146	18	2	3	(2	1)	177	79	31	61	48	1	78	4	9	2	41	22	.65	13	.282	.347	.342
1999	StL	NL	154	585	161	36	2	11	(6	5)	234	92	63	81	53	0	82	2	6	7	37	8	.82	16	.275	.334	.400
2000	StL	NL	160	562	156	32	1	16	(4	12)	238	94	76	80	63	3	77	1	8	9	21	13	.62	19	.278	.346	.423
2001	StL	NL	141	493	128	19	3	10	(3	7)	183	54	57	57	39	4	73	3	8	6	17	4	.81	15	.260	.314	.371
2002	StL	NL	152	544	166	36	2	11	(4	7)	239	77	83	94	49	7	57	4	7	5	22	7	.76	17	.305	.364	.439
2003	StL	NL	157	587	194	47	1	13	(4	9)	282	96	100	103	65	12	54	1	3	7	34	7	.83	21	.330	.394	.480
2004	StL	NL	149	586	168	37	0	10	(7	3)	235	84	72	74	39	5	78	1	6	10	17	11	.61	14	.287	.327	.401
2005	Bos	AL	153	623	172	36	4	8	(3	5)	240	100	70	82	55	0	100	3	6	5	9	4	.69	15	.276	.335	.385
2006	Atl	NL	149	598	175	40	2	14	(4	10)	261	100	70	89	62	0	89	3	8	2	17	6	.74	17	.293	.361	.436
2007	Atl	NL	124	494	164	30	1	12	(5	7)	232	87	57	82	46	0	77	1	2	0	11	2	.85	14	.332	.390	.470
2008	Det	NL	138	503	136	22	2	10	(5	5)	192	69	55	61	37	1	64	0	2	5	6	3	.67	19	.270	.317	.382
2009	SF	NL	124	460	115	19	1	5	(3	2)	151	50	48	50	39	5	69	1	5	5	7	2	.78	17	.250	.307	.328
	Postseason		55	207	51	12	0	1	(1	0)	66	30	17	23	23	1	34	3	6	2	9	1	.90	8	.246	.328	.319
	14 ML YEARS		1984	7600	2185	411	27	132	(55	77)	3046	1140	865	1044	673	39	1074	30	91	72	287	106	.73	226	.288	.345	.401

Jason Repko

Bats: R **Throws:** R **Pos:** CF-3; RF-3; PR-3; LF-2; PH-1 **Ht:** 5'10" **Wt:** 192 **Born:** 12/27/1980 **Age:** 29

Year	Team	Lg	G	AB	H	2B	3B	HR	(Hm	Rd)	TB	R	RBI	RC	TBB	IBB	SO	HBP	SH	SF	SB	CS	SB%	GDP	Avg	OBP	Slg
2009	Albq*	AAA	110	393	109	20	4	16	(-	-)	185	70	47	64	28	0	81	5	2	5	24	7	.77	4	.277	.329	.471
2005	LAD	NL	129	276	61	15	3	8	(4	4)	106	43	30	28	16	1	80	7	2	0	5	0	1.00	7	.221	.281	.384
2006	LAD	NL	69	130	33	5	1	3	(1	2)	49	21	16	21	15	1	24	3	2	0	10	4	.71	2	.254	.345	.377
2008	LAD	NL	22	18	3	1	0	0	(0	0)	4	0	0	0	2	0	9	0	0	0	1	0	1.00	0	.167	.250	.222
2009	Cle	NL	10	5	0	0	0	0	(0	0)	0	1	1	0	0	0	2	1	0	1	1	0	1.00	0	.000	.143	.000
	Postseason		1	0	0	0	0	0	(0	0)	0	0	0	0	0	0	0	0	0	0	0	0	-	0			
	4 ML YEARS		230	429	97	21	4	11	(5	6)	159	65	47	49	33	2	115	11	4	1	17	4	.81	9	.226	.297	.371

Anthony Reyes

Pitches: R **Bats:** R **Pos:** SP-8 **Ht:** 6'2" **Wt:** 230 **Born:** 10/16/1981 **Age:** 28

Year	Team	Lg	G	GS	CG	GF	IP	BFP	H	R	ER	HR	SH	SF	TB	TBB	IBB	SO	WP	Bk	W	L	Pct	Sh	Sv-Op	Hld	ERC	ERA
2005	StL	NL	4	1	0	0	13.1	51	6	4	4	2	1	1	0	4	1	12	2	0	1	1	.500	0	0-0	0	1.32	2.70
2006	StL	NL	17	17	1	0	85.1	370	84	48	48	17	5	3	7	34	0	72	2	0	5	8	.385	0	0-0	0	5.08	5.06
2007	StL	NL	22	20	1	1	107.1	474	108	77	72	16	1	7	9	43	0	74	1	2	2	14	.125	0	0-0	0	4.78	6.04
2008	2 Tms		16	6	0	6	49.0	203	47	15	15	4	1	0	1	15	0	25	0	0	4	2	.667	0	1-1	2	3.50	2.76
2009	Cle	AL	8	8	0	0	38.1	176	40	30	28	5	2	3	2	23	0	22	2	0	1	1	.500	0	0-0	0	5.59	6.57
08	StL	NL	10	0	0	6	14.2	61	16	8	8	2	0	0	0	3	0	10	0	0	2	1	.667	0	1-1	2	4.11	4.91
08	Cle	AL	6	6	0	0	34.1	142	31	7	7	2	1	0	1	12	0	15	0	0	2	1	.667	0	0-0	0	3.24	1.83
	Postseason		2	2	0	0	12.0	48	7	4	4	3	0	0	0	5	0	8	0	0	1	0	1.000	0	0-0	0	2.81	3.00
	5 ML YEARS		67	52	2	7	293.1	1274	285	174	167	44	10	14	19	119	1	205	7	2	13	26	.333	0	1-1	2	4.56	5.12

Argenis Reyes

Bats: B **Throws:** R **Pos:** PH-5; 2B-3; SS-1   **Ht:** 5'10" **Wt:** 180 **Born:** 9/25/1982 **Age:** 27

Year	Team	Lg	G	AB	H	2B	3B	HR	(Hm	Rd)	TB	R	RBI	RC	TBB	IBB	SO	HBP	SH	SF	SB	CS	SB%	GDP	Avg	OBP	Slg
2003	Burlgtn	R+	39	151	42	2	0	0	(-	-)	44	26	9	17	7	1	23	1	4	1	14	1	.93	3	.278	.321	.291
2004	MhVlly	A-	73	324	101	11	0	0	(-	-)	112	53	20	43	15	2	36	5	0	3	27	9	.75	4	.312	.349	.346
2005	Lk Cty	A	71	317	102	14	5	2	(-	-)	132	51	36	48	16	1	36	1	3	2	16	6	.73	4	.322	.354	.416
2005	Knstn	A+	52	202	52	4	1	1	(-	-)	61	23	13	18	8	0	38	1	5	1	8	3	.73	7	.257	.288	.302
2006	Knstn	A+	130	516	137	16	6	2	(-	-)	171	71	58	64	48	2	73	4	10	8	24	6	.80	14	.266	.328	.331
2007	Akron	AA	126	467	130	21	4	3	(-	-)	168	66	32	56	23	0	56	1	11	1	27	8	.77	14	.278	.313	.360
2008	NewOr	AAA	81	311	88	11	1	0	(-	-)	101	41	22	39	31	1	47	1	7	3	13	6	.68	2	.283	.347	.325
2009	Buffalo	AAA	101	379	107	19	4	3	(-	-)	143	43	31	51	29	3	46	2	5	1	10	3	.77	9	.282	.336	.377
2008	NYM	NL	49	110	24	0	0	1	(1	0)	27	13	3	4	4	0	20	2	5	0	2	0	1.00	2	.218	.259	.245
2009	NYM	NL	9	17	2	0	0	0	(0	0)	2	0	0	0	1	0	4	0	0	0	1	0	1.00	0	.118	.167	.118
2 ML YEARS			58	127	26	0	0	1	(1	0)	29	13	3	4	5	0	24	2	5	0	3	0	1.00	2	.205	.246	.228

Dennys Reyes

Pitches: L **Bats:** R **Pos:** RP-75   **Ht:** 6'3" **Wt:** 250 **Born:** 4/19/1977 **Age:** 33

Year	Team	Lg	G	GS	CG	GF	IP	BFP	H	R	ER	HR	SH	SF	HB	TBB	IBB	SO	WP	Bk	W	L	Pct	Sh	Sv-Op	Hld	ERC	ERA
1997	LAD	NL	14	5	0	0	47.0	207	51	21	20	4	5	1	1	18	3	36	2	1	2	3	.400	0	0-0	0	4.34	3.83
1998	2 Tms	NL	19	10	0	4	67.1	300	62	36	34	3	7	2	1	47	5	77	6	1	3	5	.375	0	0-0	0	4.37	4.54
1999	Cin	NL	65	1	0	12	61.2	277	53	30	26	5	4	3	3	39	1	72	5	1	2	2	.500	0	2-3	14	4.16	3.79
2000	Cin	NL	62	0	0	15	43.2	200	43	31	22	5	3	3	1	29	0	36	5	0	2	1	.667	0	0-1	10	5.24	4.53
2001	Cin	NL	35	6	0	2	53.0	246	51	35	29	5	2	2	1	35	1	52	5	0	2	6	.250	0	0-0	6	4.77	4.92
2002	2 Tms	NL	58	5	0	15	82.2	378	98	52	49	10	3	2	0	45	4	59	10	1	4	4	.500	0	0-0	4	5.90	5.33
2003	2 Tms	NL	15	0	0	4	12.2	63	15	16	15	2	1	2	0	10	1	16	5	0	0	0	-	0	0-0	2	6.96	10.66
2004	KC	AL	40	12	0	5	108.0	483	114	64	57	12	7	5	4	50	3	91	6	2	4	8	.333	0	0-1	5	4.81	4.75
2005	SD	NL	36	1	0	9	43.2	215	57	30	25	3	1	0	1	32	2	35	3	1	3	2	.600	0	0-1	0	7.06	5.15
2006	Min	AL	66	0	0	8	50.2	194	35	8	5	3	1	0	0	15	2	49	4	0	5	0	1.000	0	0-1	16	1.90	0.89
2007	Min	AL	50	0	0	7	29.1	139	34	14	13	1	3	3	2	21	1	21	4	0	2	1	.667	0	0-0	8	6.08	3.99
2008	Min	AL	75	0	0	16	46.1	188	40	12	12	4	1	0	2	15	2	39	5	0	3	0	1.000	0	0-3	17	3.14	2.33
2009	StL	NL	75	0	0	10	41.0	180	35	17	15	2	5	1	3	21	1	33	5	1	0	2	.000	0	1-1	18	3.53	3.29
98	LAD	NL	11	3	0	4	28.2	130	27	17	15	1	3	1	0	20	4	33	1	1	0	4	.000	0	0-0	0	4.16	4.71
98	Cin	NL	8	7	0	0	38.2	170	35	19	19	2	4	1	1	27	1	44	5	0	3	1	.750	0	0-0	0	4.54	4.42
02	Col	NL	43	0	0	13	40.1	182	43	19	19	1	2	2	0	24	3	30	4	0	0	1	.000	0	0-0	4	4.55	4.24
02	Tex	AL	15	5	0	2	42.1	196	55	33	30	9	1	0	0	21	1	29	6	1	4	3	.571	0	0-0	0	7.24	6.38
03	Pit	NL	12	0	0	4	10.1	50	10	13	12	1	1	2	0	9	1	11	5	0	0	0	-	0	0-0	2	5.43	10.45
03	Ari	NL	3	0	0	0	2.1	13	5	3	3	1	0	0	0	1	0	5	0	0	0	0	-	0	0-0	0	14.73	11.57
Postseason			2	0	0	0	1.0	6	1	3	1	1	0	0	0	2	1	0	0	0	0	0	-	0	0-0	0	17.98	9.00
13 ML YEARS			610	40	0	107	687.0	3070	688	366	322	59	43	24	19	377	26	616	65	8	32	34	.485	0	3-11	100	4.62	4.22

Jo-Jo Reyes

Pitches: L **Bats:** L **Pos:** SP-5; RP-1   **Ht:** 6'2" **Wt:** 230 **Born:** 11/20/1984 **Age:** 25

Year	Team	Lg	G	GS	CG	GF	IP	BFP	H	R	ER	HR	SH	SF	HB	TBB	IBB	SO	WP	Bk	W	L	Pct	Sh	Sv-Op	Hld	ERC	ERA
2009	Gwnntt*	AAA	15	14	0	0	66.0	281	68	23	21	6	3	3	1	24	0	32	3	1	4	2	.667	0	0--	-	4.16	2.86
2007	Atl	NL	11	10	0	0	50.2	230	55	39	35	9	5	2	1	30	2	27	1	0	2	2	.500	0	0-0	0	6.06	6.22
2008	Atl	NL	23	22	0	0	113.0	512	134	77	73	18	9	3	3	52	4	78	2	0	3	11	.214	0	0-0	0	5.97	5.81
2009	Atl	NL	6	5	0	0	27.0	119	27	25	21	4	1	1	1	13	3	21	0	0	0	2	.000	0	0-0	0	4.73	7.00
3 ML YEARS			40	37	0	0	190.2	861	216	141	129	31	15	6	5	95	9	126	3	0	5	15	.250	0	0-0	0	5.81	6.09

Jose Reyes

Bats: B **Throws:** R **Pos:** SS-35; PH-1   **Ht:** 6'1" **Wt:** 200 **Born:** 6/11/1983 **Age:** 27

Year	Team	Lg	G	AB	H	2B	3B	HR	(Hm	Rd)	TB	R	RBI	RC	TBB	IBB	SO	HBP	SH	SF	SB	CS	SB%	GDP	Avg	OBP	Slg
2003	NYM	NL	69	274	84	12	4	5	(1	4)	119	47	32	46	13	0	36	0	2	3	13	3	.81	1	.307	.334	.434
2004	NYM	NL	53	220	56	16	2	2	(1	1)	82	33	14	25	5	0	31	0	4	0	19	2	.90	1	.255	.271	.373
2005	NYM	NL	161	696	190	24	17	7	(2	5)	269	99	58	84	27	0	78	2	4	4	60	15	.80	7	.273	.300	.386
2006	NYM	NL	153	647	194	30	17	19	(9	10)	315	122	81	121	53	6	81	1	2	0	64	17	.79	6	.300	.354	.487
2007	NYM	NL	160	681	191	36	12	12	(7	5)	287	119	57	99	77	13	78	1	5	1	78	21	.79	6	.280	.354	.421
2008	NYM	NL	159	688	204	37	19	16	(9	7)	327	113	68	117	66	8	82	1	5	3	56	15	.79	9	.297	.358	.475
2009	NYM	NL	36	147	41	7	2	2	(1	1)	58	18	15	20	18	1	19	0	0	1	11	2	.85	2	.279	.355	.395
Postseason			10	44	11	1	1	1	(1	0)	17	7	5	6	3	1	5	0	0	0	3	1	.75	0	.250	.298	.386
7 ML YEARS			791	3353	960	162	73	63	(30	33)	1457	551	325	512	259	28	405	5	22	12	301	75	.80	32	.286	.337	.435

Greg Reynolds

Pitches: R **Bats:** R **Pos:** P   **Ht:** 6'7" **Wt:** 225 **Born:** 7/3/1985 **Age:** 24

Year	Team	Lg	G	GS	CG	GF	IP	BFP	H	R	ER	HR	SH	SF	HB	TBB	IBB	SO	WP	Bk	W	L	Pct	Sh	Sv-Op	Hld	ERC	ERA
2006	Mdest	A+	11	11	0	0	48.2	205	51	22	18	7	0	0	3	14	0	29	3	0	2	1	.667	0	0--	-	3.67	3.33
2007	Tulsa	AA	8	8	0	0	50.2	190	32	10	8	2	1	0	2	9	0	35	0	0	4	1	.800	0	0--	-	1.41	1.42
2008	ColSpr	AAA	13	13	0	0	63.1	286	84	38	30	4	2	3	3	22	0	37	0	0	1	3	.250	0	0--	-	5.81	4.26
2009	ColSpr	AAA	1	1	0	0	4.1	24	6	5	5	0	0	2	0	3	0	3	0	0	0	0	-	0	0--	-	5.97	10.38
2008	Col	NL	14	13	0	0	62.0	294	83	58	56	14	4	2	4	26	3	22	2	0	2	8	.200	0	0-0	0	7.36	8.13

Mark Reynolds

Bats: R **Throws:** R **Pos:** 3B-130, 1B-28; PH-3 **Ht:** 6'2" **Wt:** 220 **Born:** 8/3/1983 **Age:** 26

					BATTING																	BASERUNNING				AVERAGES		
Year	Team	Lg	G	AB	H	2B	3B	HR	(Hm	Rd)	TB	R	RBI	RC	TBB	IBB	SO	HBP	SH	SF		SB	CS	SB%	GDP	Avg	OBP	Slg
2007	Ari	NL	111	366	102	20	4	17	(7	10)	181	62	62	62	37	4	129	5	1	5		0	1	.00	5	.279	.349	.405
2008	Ari	NL	152	539	129	28	3	28	(13	15)	247	87	97	82	64	0	204	3	1	6		11	2	.85	10	.239	.320	.458
2009	Ari	NL	155	578	150	30	1	44	(19	25)	314	98	102	94	76	3	223	7	0	3		24	9	.73	8	.260	.349	.543
	Postseason		7	26	4	0	0	2	(1	1)	10	3	2	1	2	0	9	1	0	0		0	0	-	0	.154	.241	.385
	3 ML YEARS		418	1483	381	78	8	89	(39	50)	742	247	261	238	177	7	556	13	2	14		35	12	.74	23	.257	.338	.500

Arthur Rhodes

Pitches: L **Bats:** L **Pos:** RP-66 **Ht:** 6'2" **Wt:** 212 **Born:** 10/24/1969 **Age:** 40

			HOW MUCH HE PITCHED						WHAT HE GAVE UP										THE RESULTS							
Year	Team	Lg	G	GS	CG	GF	IP	BFP	H	R	ER	HR	SH	SF	HB	TBB	IBB	SO	WP	Bk	W	L	Pct	Sh	Sv-Op	Hld	ERC	ERA
1991	Bal	AL	8	8	0	0	36.0	174	47	35	32	4	1	3	0	23	0	23	2	0	0	3	.000	0	0-0	0	7.00	8.00
1992	Bal	AL	15	15	2	0	94.1	394	87	39	38	6	5	1	1	38	2	77	2	1	7	5	.583	1	0-0	0	3.48	3.63
1993	Bal	AL	17	17	0	0	85.2	387	91	62	62	16	2	3	1	49	1	49	2	0	5	6	.455	0	0-0	0	5.88	6.51
1994	Bal	AL	10	10	3	0	52.2	238	51	34	34	8	2	3	2	30	1	47	3	0	3	5	.375	2	0-0	0	5.03	5.81
1995	Bal	AL	19	9	0	3	75.1	336	68	53	52	13	4	0	0	48	1	77	3	1	2	5	.286	0	0-1	0	4.97	6.21
1996	Bal	AL	28	2	0	5	53.0	224	48	28	24	6	1	1	0	23	3	62	0	0	9	1	.900	0	1-1	2	3.72	4.08
1997	Bal	AL	53	0	0	6	95.1	378	75	32	32	9	0	4	4	26	5	102	2	0	10	3	.769	0	1-2	9	2.58	3.02
1998	Bal	AL	45	0	0	10	77.0	321	65	30	30	8	2	5	1	34	2	83	1	1	4	4	.500	0	4-8	10	3.47	3.51
1999	Bal	AL	43	0	0	11	53.0	244	43	37	32	9	2	2	0	45	6	59	4	0	3	4	.429	0	3-5	5	5.07	5.43
2000	Sea	AL	72	0	0	9	69.1	281	51	34	33	6	1	2	0	29	3	77	4	0	5	8	.385	0	0-7	24	2.62	4.28
2001	Sea	AL	71	0	0	16	68.0	258	46	14	13	5	1	0	1	12	0	83	3	0	8	0	1.000	0	3-7	32	1.61	1.72
2002	Sea	AL	66	0	0	9	69.2	257	45	18	18	4	2	1	0	13	1	81	2	0	10	4	.714	0	2-7	27	1.46	2.33
2003	Sea	AL	67	0	0	14	54.0	228	53	25	25	4	2	0	1	18	2	48	2	0	3	3	.500	0	3-6	18	3.57	4.17
2004	Oak	AL	37	0	0	25	38.2	182	46	23	22	9	3	1	0	21	4	34	2	0	3	3	.500	0	9-14	3	6.54	5.12
2005	Cle	AL	47	0	0	8	43.1	176	33	13	10	2	0	2	1	12	2	43	0	0	3	1	.750	0	0-3	10	2.08	2.08
2006	Phi	NL	55	0	0	10	16.0	211	47	27	27	2	1	0	2	30	7	48	7	0	0	5	.000	0	4-7	23	4.63	5.32
2008	2 Tms		61	0	0	8	35.1	146	28	9	8	0	4	1	0	16	4	40	1	0	4	1	.800	0	2-3	24	2.36	2.04
2009	Cin	NL	66	0	0	10	53.1	215	37	16	15	3	5	2	1	20	3	48	1	0	1	1	.500	0	0-2	25	2.11	2.53
08	Sea	AL	36	0	0	4	22.0	92	17	8	7	0	3	1	0	13	2	26	1	0	2	1	.667	0	1-2	13	2.79	2.86
08	Fla	AL	25	0	0	2	13.1	54	11	1	1	0	1	0	0	3	2	14	0	0	2	0	1.000	0	1-1	11	1.69	0.68
	Postseason		20	0	0	0	17.0	75	16	9	9	2	2	1	0	10	2	19	4	0	0	1	.000	0	0-0	4	4.44	4.70
	18 ML YEARS		780	61	5	142	1099.2	4652	961	529	507	114	38	31	15	487	47	1081	41	3	80	62	.563	3	32-73	218	3.58	4.15

Danny Richar

Bats: L **Throws:** R **Pos:** 3B-4; PH-2; 2B-1; PR-1 **Ht:** 6'1" **Wt:** 195 **Born:** 6/9/1983 **Age:** 27

					BATTING																	BASERUNNING				AVERAGES		
Year	Team	Lg	G	AB	H	2B	3B	HR	(Hm	Rd)	TB	R	RBI	RC	TBB	IBB	SO	HBP	SH	SF		SB	CS	SB%	GDP	Avg	OBP	Slg
2009	Lsvlle*	AAA	47	169	49	11	1	4	(-	-)	74	20	16	24	10	0	17	0	2	0		2	3	.40	1	.290	.330	.438
2007	CWS		56	187	43	9	3	6	(3	3)	76	30	15	21	16	0	33	0	2	1		1	3	.25	5	.230	.289	.406
2008	Cin	NL	16	36	8	2	0	0	(0	0)	10	4	3	1	0	0	9	0	1	0		1	0	1.00	0	.222	.222	.278
2009	Cin	NL	7	8	2	0	0	0	(0	0)	2	1	0	1	1	0	1	0	0	0		0	0	-	0	.250	.333	.250
	3 ML YEARS		79	231	53	11	3	6	(3	3)	88	35	18	23	17	0	43	0	3	1		2	3	.40	6	.229	.281	.381

Chris Richard

Bats: L **Throws:** L **Pos:** 1B-13 **Ht:** 6'2" **Wt:** 210 **Born:** 6/7/1974 **Age:** 36

					BATTING																	BASERUNNING				AVERAGES		
Year	Team	Lg	G	AB	H	2B	3B	HR	(Hm	Rd)	TB	R	RBI	RC	TBB	IBB	SO	HBP	SH	SF		SB	CS	SB%	GDP	Avg	OBP	Slg
2009	Drhm*	AAA	100	365	96	22	0	24	(-	-)	190	56	75	70	52	2	83	6	0	0		2	1	.67	3	.263	.364	.521
2000	2 Tms		62	215	57	14	2	14	(4	10)	117	39	37	36	17	3	40	4	0	3		7	5	.58	5	.265	.326	.544
2001	Bal	AL	136	483	128	31	3	15	(6	9)	210	74	61	66	45	4	100	8	2	4		11	9	.55	15	.265	.335	.435
2002	Bal	AL	50	155	36	11	0	4	(2	2)	59	15	21	15	12	0	30	2	0	2		0	3	.00	2	.232	.292	.381
2003	Col	NL	19	27	6	1	1	1	(0	1)	12	3	3	2	3	0	6	0	0	0		0	1	.00	1	.222	.300	.444
2009	TB	AL	13	19	2	0	0	0	(0	0)	2	1	0	0	4	0	7	0	0	0		0	0	-	0	.105	.261	.105
00	StL	NL	6	16	2	0	0	1	(0	1)	5	1	1	1	2	0	2	0	0	0		0	0	-	0	.125	.222	.313
00	Bal	AL	56	199	55	14	2	13	(4	9)	112	38	36	35	15	3	38	4	0	3		7	5	.58	5	.276	.335	.563
	5 ML YEARS		280	899	229	57	6	34	(12	22)	400	132	122	119	81	7	183	14	2	9		18	18	.50	23	.255	.323	.445

Clayton Richard

Pitches: L **Bats:** L **Pos:** SP-26; RP-12 **Ht:** 6'5" **Wt:** 240 **Born:** 9/12/1983 **Age:** 26

			HOW MUCH HE PITCHED						WHAT HE GAVE UP										THE RESULTS							
Year	Team	Lg	G	GS	CG	GF	IP	BFP	H	R	ER	HR	SH	SF	HB	TBB	IBB	SO	WP	Bk	W	L	Pct	Sh	Sv-Op	Hld	ERC	ERA
2005	Gr Falls	R+	10	9	0	0	41.0	168	37	19	13	2	0	1	1	12	0	39	0	1	2	1	.667	0	0- -	-	2.93	2.85
2005	Knapol	A-	3	2	0	1	10.1	44	14	7	6	1	0	0	0	1	0	8	1	2	0	1	.000	0	0- -	-	4.97	5.23
2006	Knapol	A-	18	17	0	0	95.2	423	117	47	39	0	4	6	7	28	0	54	8	0	6	6	.500	0	0- -	-	4.52	3.67
2006	WinSa	A+	4	4	1	0	23.2	104	29	18	12	2	2	3	1	6	0	12	1	0	1	3	.250	0	0- -	-	4.86	4.56
2007	WinSa	A+	28	27	1	1	161.1	684	159	86	65	11	5	8	5	59	0	99	4	2	8	12	.400	1	0- -	-	3.81	3.63
2008	Brham	AA	13	13	1	0	83.2	327	66	29	23	2	2	1	4	16	0	53	3	0	6	6	.500	1	0- -	-	1.98	2.47
2008	Charltt	AAA	7	7	1	0	44.0	167	33	12	12	3	0	0	1	4	0	33	0	2	6	0	1.000	0	0- -	-	1.64	2.45
2008	CWS	AL	13	8	0	3	47.2	215	61	37	32	5	0	1	0	13	2	29	1	1	2	5	.286	0	0-0	0	5.06	6.04
2009	2 Tms		38	26	1	3	153.0	663	154	81	75	17	8	5	3	71	0	114	7	3	9	5	.643	0	0-0	0	4.60	4.41
09	CWS	AL	26	14	1	3	89.0	387	94	50	46	10	3	4	3	37	0	66	5	2	4	3	.571	0	0-0	0	4.76	4.65
09	SD	NL	12	12	0	0	64.0	276	60	31	29	7	5	1	0	34	0	48	2	1	5	2	.714	0	0-0	0	4.38	4.08
	Postseason		2	0	0	0	6.1	25	5	1	1	0	0	0	0	3	0	6	0	0	0	0	-	0	0-0	0	2.74	1.42
	2 ML YEARS		51	34	1	6	200.2	878	215	118	107	22	8	6	3	84	2	143	8	4	11	10	.524	0	0-0	0	4.71	4.80

Dustin Richardson

Pitches: L Bats: L Pos: RP-3   Ht: 6'6" Wt: 220 Born: 1/9/1984 Age: 26

			HOW MUCH HE PITCHED						WHAT HE GAVE UP												THE RESULTS						
Year	Team	Lg	G	GS	CG	GF	IP	BFP	H	R	ER	HR	SH	SF	HB	TBB	IBB	SO	WP	Bk	W	L	Pct	Sh	Sv-Op	Hld	ERC	ERA
2006	Lowell	A-	16	1	0	4	39.2	162	28	16	14	2	1	4	3	13	0	44	2	0	4	1	.800	0	2--	-	2.22	3.18
2007	Grnville	A	21	21	0	0	99.2	423	86	46	37	4	1	3	6	47	0	98	4	1	5	7	.417	0	0--	-	3.46	3.34
2007	Lancst	A+	4	4	0	0	23.0	89	14	8	7	1	1	1	1	5	0	25	0	0	4	0	1.000	0	0--	-	1.41	2.74
2008	Portlnd	AA	22	22	0	0	106.2	469	108	76	75	17	3	5	5	51	0	114	0	0	7	10	.412	0	0--	-	5.15	6.33
2008	Lowell	A-	2	2	0	0	5.0	27	8	5	5	2	0	0	1	2	0	4	2	0	0	1	.000	0	0--	-	10.81	9.00
2009	Portlnd	AA	38	0	0	11	63.1	271	42	22	19	2	1	1	3	40	2	80	3	0	2	2	.500	0	4--	-	2.77	2.70
2009	Pwtckt	AAA	7	0	0	2	10.2	40	8	2	2	1	0	0	0	2	0	16	0	0	0	0	-	0	0--	-	2.08	1.69
2009	Bos	AL	3	0	0	1	3.1	14	3	0	0	0	0	1	0	1	0	0	1	1	0	0	-	0	0-0	0	2.46	0.00

Kevin Richardson

Bats: R Throws: R Pos: C-4   Ht: 6'3" Wt: 230 Born: 9/12/1980 Age: 29

									BATTING													BASERUNNING				AVERAGES		
Year	Team	Lg	G	AB	H	2B	3B	HR	(Hm	Rd)	TB	R	RBI	RC	TBB	IBB	SO	HBP	SH	SF	SB	CS	SB%	GDP	Avg	OBP	Slg
2002	Pulaski	R+	24	83	13	4	0	1	(-	-)	20	8	7	5	12	1	32	2	0	0	1	1	.50	3	.157	.278	.241
2003	Clinton	A	22	67	11	0	0	0	(-	-)	11	4	4	3	10	1	22	3	0	1	0	1	.00	1	.164	.296	.164
2003	Spkane	A	32	112	34	10	0	6	(-	-)	62	19	26	24	18	0	34	1	0	0	0	0	-	4	.304	.405	.554
2004	Clinton	A	100	345	77	19	0	13	(-	-)	135	50	55	43	33	0	121	10	0	4	1	1	.50	8	.223	.306	.391
2005	Clinton	A	56	202	54	8	1	6	(-	-)	82	28	37	32	23	0	56	10	0	1	3	2	.60	2	.267	.369	.406
2005	Frisco	AA	18	59	18	4	0	2	(-	-)	28	12	11	11	6	0	23	4	0	0	0	1	.00	2	.305	.406	.475
2006	Frisco	AA	93	303	82	12	3	17	(-	-)	151	54	47	55	33	1	95	9	2	1	4	1	.80	6	.271	.358	.498
2007	Frisco	AA	91	320	71	8	0	14	(-	-)	121	42	45	36	25	0	85	8	3	1	0	2	.00	10	.222	.294	.378
2008	Okla	AAA	55	187	47	10	1	6	(-	-)	77	25	22	26	18	0	53	4	2	2	0	0	-	5	.251	.327	.412
2009	Okla	AAA	74	255	55	10	1	13	(-	-)	106	33	36	30	19	0	105	4	3	0	0	0	-	4	.216	.281	.416
2009	Tex	AL	4	6	3	0	0	0	(0	0)	3	2	0	1	0	0	2	0	0	0	0	0	-	0	.500	.500	.500

Scott Richmond

Pitches: R Bats: R Pos: SP-24; RP-3   Ht: 6'5" Wt: 215 Born: 8/30/1979 Age: 30

									WHAT HE GAVE UP														THE RESULTS					
Year	Team	Lg	G	GS	CG	GF	IP	BFP	H	R	ER	HR	SH	SF	HB	TBB	IBB	SO	WP	Bk	W	L	Pct	Sh	Sv-Op	Hld	ERC	ERA
2008	NHam	AA	16	16	0	0	89.2	390	89	55	49	14	1	1	3	30	0	84	4	3	5	8	.385	0	0--	-	4.22	4.92
2008	Syrcse	AAA	8	8	1	0	48.0	197	44	20	19	6	2	1	1	13	0	40	2	0	1	3	.250	0	0--	-	3.39	3.56
2009	B Jays	R	1	1	0	0	3.1	19	9	3	3	1	0	0	0	1	0	5	1	0	0	0	-	0	0--	-	17.99	8.10
2009	LsVgs	AAA	1	1	0	0	5.1	20	3	2	1	1	0	1	0	1	0	5	0	0	1	0	1.000	0	0--	-	1.61	1.69
2008	Tor	AL	5	5	1	0	27.0	113	32	12	12	2	0	1	2	2	0	20	0	0	1	3	.250	1	0-0	0	3.99	4.00
2009	Tor	AL	27	24	1	1	138.2	610	147	90	85	27	1	2	0	59	1	117	5	1	8	11	.421	0	0-0	0	5.20	5.52
	2 ML YEARS		32	29	2	1	165.2	723	179	102	97	29	1	3	2	61	1	137	5	1	9	14	.391	1	0-0	0	5.00	5.27

Shawn Riggans

Bats: R Throws: R Pos: C-7   Ht: 6'2" Wt: 200 Born: 7/25/1980 Age: 29

									BATTING													BASERUNNING				AVERAGES		
Year	Team	Lg	G	AB	H	2B	3B	HR	(Hm	Rd)	TB	R	RBI	RC	TBB	IBB	SO	HBP	SH	SF	SB	CS	SB%	GDP	Avg	OBP	Slg
2009	Mont*	AA	3	7	2	0	0	0	(-	-)	2	2	0	0	0	0	2	0	0	0	0	0	-	0	.286	.286	.286
2009	Charltt*	A+	12	39	10	2	0	0	(-	-)	12	5	2	5	4	0	6	2	0	0	1	0	1.00	1	.256	.356	.308
2009	Drham*	AAA	11	40	8	2	0	1	(-	-)	13	4	5	3	1	0	7	1	0	0	0	0	-	1	.200	.238	.325
2006	TB	AL	10	29	5	1	0	0	(0	0)	6	3	1	0	4	0	7	0	0	0	0	0	-	1	.172	.273	.207
2007	TB	AL	3	10	1	0	0	0	(0	0)	1	1	2	0	0	0	1	0	0	0	0	0	-	0	.100	.100	.100
2008	TB	AL	44	135	30	7	0	6	(3	3)	55	21	24	17	12	0	30	1	2	2	0	0	-	4	.222	.287	.407
2009	TB	AL	7	14	2	0	0	1	(0	1)	5	2	1	0	0	0	3	0	0	0	0	0	-	1	.143	.143	.357
	4 ML YEARS		64	188	38	8	0	7	(3	4)	67	27	28	17	16	0	41	1	2	2	0	0	-	7	.202	.266	.356

Juan Rincon

Pitches: R Bats: R Pos: RP-33   Ht: 5'11" Wt: 210 Born: 1/23/1979 Age: 31

									WHAT HE GAVE UP														THE RESULTS					
Year	Team	Lg	G	GS	CG	GF	IP	BFP	H	R	ER	HR	SH	SF	HB	TBB	IBB	SO	WP	Bk	W	L	Pct	Sh	Sv-Op	Hld	ERC	ERA
2009	ColSpr*	AAA	14	0	0	9	17.1	67	8	3	3	1	0	0	2	7	0	22	1	0	1	0	1.000	0	3--	-	1.62	1.56
2001	Min	AL	4	0	0	1	5.2	28	7	5	4	1	1	0	0	5	0	4	0	0	0	0	-	0	0-0	0	8.33	6.35
2002	Min	AL	10	3	0	0	28.2	135	44	23	20	5	0	1	0	9	0	21	2	0	0	2	.000	0	0-1	0	7.62	6.28
2003	Min	AL	58	0	0	20	85.2	370	74	38	35	5	2	5	4	38	7	63	7	0	5	6	.455	0	0-1	5	3.21	3.68
2004	Min	AL	77	0	0	18	82.0	327	52	27	24	5	3	3	2	32	1	106	2	0	11	6	.647	0	2-6	16	2.00	2.63
2005	Min	AL	75	0	0	18	77.0	319	63	26	21	2	4	1	4	30	3	84	5	1	6	6	.500	0	0-5	25	2.68	2.45
2006	Min	AL	75	0	0	22	74.1	315	76	30	24	2	5	1	3	24	3	65	2	0	3	1	.750	0	1-3	26	3.53	2.91
2007	Min	AL	63	0	0	16	59.2	272	65	38	34	9	2	1	3	28	3	49	4	0	3	3	.500	0	0-2	14	5.31	5.13
2008	2 Tms	AL	47	0	0	15	55.1	254	67	39	36	8	2	0	3	24	2	39	5	0	3	3	.500	0	0-0	3	5.96	5.86
2009	2 Tms	AL	33	0	0	7	36.2	165	30	29	28	4	2	1	1	26	4	35	2	0	4	2	.667	0	0-0	1	4.20	6.87
	08 Min	AL	24	0	0	6	28.0	133	33	21	19	5	2	0	2	16	2	20	3	0	2	2	.500	0	0-0	1	6.59	6.11
	08 Cle	AL	23	0	0	9	27.1	121	34	18	17	3	0	0	1	8	0	19	2	0	1	1	.500	0	0-0	2	5.33	5.60
	09 Det	AL	7	0	0	6	10.1	49	12	6	6	2	1	1	0	6	0	10	1	0	1	0	1.000	0	0-0	0	6.37	5.23
	09 Col	NL	26	0	0	1	26.1	116	18	23	22	2	1	0	1	20	4	25	1	0	3	2	.600	0	0-0	1	3.41	7.52
	Postseason		8	0	0	2	8.2	36	6	5	5	1	0	0	0	6	0	9	1	0	0	0	-	0	0-0	1	3.77	5.19
	9 ML YEARS		442	3	0	117	505.0	2185	478	255	226	41	21	13	19	216	23	466	29	1	35	29	.547	0	3-18	90	3.82	4.03

Alex Rios

Bats: R Throws: R Pos: RF-110; CF-42   Ht: 6'5" Wt: 215 Born: 2/18/1981 Age: 29

										BATTING											BASERUNNING				AVERAGES		
Year	Team	Lg	G	AB	H	2B	3B	HR	(Hm	Rd)	TB	R	RBI	RC	TBB	IBB	SO	HBP	SH	SF	SB	CS	SB%	GDP	Avg	OBP	Slg
2004	Tor	AL	111	426	122	24	7	1	(0	1)	163	55	28	49	31	0	84	2	1	0	15	3	.83	14	.286	.338	.383
2005	Tor	AL	146	481	126	23	6	10	(5	5)	191	71	59	56	28	1	101	5	0	5	14	9	.61	14	.262	.306	.397
2006	Tor	AL	128	450	136	33	6	17	(12	5)	232	68	82	83	35	1	89	3	0	10	15	6	.71	10	.302	.349	.516
2007	Tor	AL	161	643	191	43	7	24	(13	11)	320	114	85	105	55	3	103	6	0	7	17	4	.81	9	.297	.354	.498
2008	Tor	AL	155	635	185	47	8	15	(9	6)	293	91	79	92	44	2	112	2	0	5	32	8	.80	20	.291	.337	.461
2009	2 Tms	AL	149	582	144	31	2	17	(15	2)	230	63	71	64	37	1	107	6	1	7	24	5	.83	21	.247	.296	.395
09	Tor	AL	108	436	115	25	2	14	(12	2)	186	52	62	60	31	1	78	6	0	6	19	3	.86	14	.264	.317	.427
09	CWS	AL	41	146	29	6	0	3	(3	0)	44	11	9	4	6	0	29	0	1	1	5	2	.71	7	.199	.229	.301
6 ML YEARS			850	3217	904	201	36	84	(54	30)	1429	462	404	449	230	8	596	24	2	34	117	35	.77	88	.281	.330	.444

David Riske

Pitches: R Bats: R Pos: RP-1   Ht: 6'2" Wt: 189 Born: 10/23/1976 Age: 33

				HOW MUCH HE PITCHED						WHAT HE GAVE UP										THE RESULTS						
Year	Team	Lg	G	GS	CG	GF	IP	BFP	H	R	ER	HR	SH	SF	HB	TBB	IBB	SO	WP	Bk	W	L	Pct	Sh	Sv-Op	Hld	ERC	ERA
1999	Cle	AL	12	0	0	3	14.0	68	20	15	13	2	1	1	0	6	0	16	0	0	0	1	.000	0	0-1	0	6.96	8.36
2001	Cle	AL	26	0	0	6	27.1	118	20	7	6	3	0	1	2	18	3	29	1	0	2	0	1.000	0	1-1	3	3.81	1.98
2002	Cle	AL	51	0	0	17	51.1	237	49	32	30	8	4	3	4	35	4	65	1	0	2	2	.500	0	1-1	5	5.55	5.26
2003	Cle	AL	68	0	0	24	74.2	293	52	21	19	9	4	1	3	20	3	82	1	0	2	2	.500	0	8-13	17	2.26	2.29
2004	Cle	AL	72	0	0	27	77.1	336	69	32	32	11	3	2	2	41	4	78	3	0	7	3	.700	0	5-12	9	4.32	3.72
2005	Cle	AL	58	0	0	33	72.2	288	55	28	25	11	3	1	4	15	0	48	0	0	3	4	.429	0	1-1	0	2.59	3.10
2006	2 Tms	AL	41	0	0	12	44.0	189	40	20	19	6	1	2	3	17	1	28	0	0	1	2	.333	0	0-1	2	3.98	3.89
2007	KC	AL	65	0	0	27	69.2	289	61	19	19	8	4	3	1	27	4	52	0	0	1	4	.200	0	4-8	16	3.46	2.45
2008	Mil	NL	45	0	0	6	42.1	193	47	25	25	6	0	4	0	25	0	27	1	0	1	2	.333	0	2-7	11	5.88	5.31
2009	Mil	NL	1	0	0	0	1.0	6	4	2	2	2	0	0	1	0	0	0	0	0	0	-	0	0-0	0	26.25	18.00
06	Bos	AL	8	0	0	2	9.2	42	9	4	4	2	1	0	2	3	0	5	0	0	0	1	.000	0	0-0	0	4.23	3.72
06	CWS	AL	33	0	0	10	34.1	147	31	16	15	4	0	2	1	14	1	23	0	0	1	1	.500	0	0-1	2	3.91	3.93
Postseason			3	0	0	0	3.2	14	2	0	0	0	0	0	0	1	0	5	0	0	0	0	-	0	0-0	0	1.10	0.00
10 ML YEARS			439	0	0	155	474.1	2017	417	201	190	64	20	19	19	204	19	425	7	0	20	20	.500	0	22-45	63	3.87	3.61

Juan Rivera

Bats: R Throws: R Pos: LF-124; DH-10; RF-7   Ht: 6'2" Wt: 230 Born: 7/3/1978 Age: 31

										BATTING											BASERUNNING				AVERAGES		
Year	Team	Lg	G	AB	H	2B	3B	HR	(Hm	Rd)	TB	R	RBI	RC	TBB	IBB	SO	HBP	SH	SF	SB	CS	SB%	GDP	Avg	OBP	Slg
2001	NYY	AL	3	4	0	0	0	0	(0	0)	0	0	0	0	0	0	0	0	0	0	0	0	-	0	.000	.000	.000
2002	NYY	AL	28	83	22	5	0	1	(0	1)	30	9	6	8	6	0	10	0	1	1	1	1	.50	4	.265	.311	.361
2003	NYY	AL	57	173	46	14	0	7	(4	3)	81	22	26	23	10	1	27	0	1	1	0	0	-	8	.266	.304	.468
2004	Mon	NL	134	391	120	24	1	12	(6	6)	182	48	49	60	34	7	45	1	0	0	6	2	.75	11	.307	.364	.465
2005	LAA	AL	106	350	95	17	1	15	(8	7)	159	46	59	49	23	0	44	0	2	1	1	9	.10	15	.271	.316	.454
2006	LAA	AL	124	448	139	27	0	23	(12	11)	235	65	85	80	33	0	59	7	0	6	0	4	.00	14	.310	.362	.525
2007	LAA	AL	14	43	12	1	0	2	(1	1)	19	3	8	5	1	0	4	0	0	0	0	0	-	5	.279	.295	.442
2008	LAA	AL	89	256	63	13	0	12	(5	7)	112	31	45	28	16	0	33	0	0	8	1	1	.50	10	.246	.282	.438
2009	LAA	AL	138	529	152	24	1	25	(11	14)	253	72	88	82	36	1	57	2	0	5	0	1	.00	19	.287	.332	.478
Postseason			27	69	17	3	0	1	(1	0)	23	9	6	5	8	2	11	0	1	0	0	0	-	6	.246	.325	.333
9 ML YEARS			693	2277	649	125	3	97	(47	50)	1071	296	366	335	159	9	279	10	4	22	9	18	.33	86	.285	.331	.470

Mariano Rivera

Pitches: R Bats: R Pos: RP-66   Ht: 6'2" Wt: 185 Born: 11/29/1969 Age: 40

				HOW MUCH HE PITCHED						WHAT HE GAVE UP										THE RESULTS						
Year	Team	Lg	G	GS	CG	GF	IP	BFP	H	R	ER	HR	SH	SF	HB	TBB	IBB	SO	WP	Bk	W	L	Pct	Sh	Sv-Op	Hld	ERC	ERA
1995	NYY	AL	19	10	0	2	67.0	301	71	43	41	11	0	2	2	30	0	51	0	1	5	3	.625	0	0-1	0	5.14	5.51
1996	NYY	AL	61	0	0	14	107.2	425	73	25	25	1	2	1	2	34	3	130	1	0	8	3	.727	0	5-8	27	1.65	2.09
1997	NYY	AL	66	0	0	56	71.2	301	65	17	15	5	3	4	0	20	6	68	2	0	6	4	.600	0	43-52	0	2.73	1.88
1998	NYY	AL	54	0	0	49	61.1	246	48	13	13	3	2	3	1	17	1	36	0	0	3	0	1.000	0	36-41	0	2.21	1.91
1999	NYY	AL	66	0	0	63	69.0	268	43	15	14	2	0	2	3	18	3	52	2	1	4	3	.571	0	45-49	0	1.47	1.83
2000	NYY	AL	66	0	0	61	75.2	311	58	26	24	4	5	2	0	25	3	58	2	0	7	4	.636	0	36-41	0	2.20	2.85
2001	NYY	AL	71	0	0	66	80.2	310	61	24	21	5	4	1	1	12	2	83	1	0	4	6	.400	0	50-57	0	1.74	2.34
2002	NYY	AL	45	0	0	36	46.0	187	35	16	14	3	2	0	2	11	2	41	1	1	1	4	.200	0	28-32	2	2.08	2.74
2003	NYY	AL	64	0	0	57	70.2	277	61	15	13	3	1	2	4	10	1	63	0	0	5	2	.714	0	40-46	0	2.29	1.66
2004	NYY	AL	74	0	0	09	78.2	316	65	17	17	3	2	0	5	20	3	66	0	0	4	2	.667	0	53-57	0	2.45	1.94
2005	NYY	AL	71	0	0	67	78.1	306	50	18	12	2	0	1	4	18	6	80	0	0	7	4	.636	0	43-47	0	1.48	1.38
2006	NYY	AL	63	0	0	59	75.0	293	61	16	15	3	1	2	5	11	4	55	0	0	5	5	.500	0	34-37	0	2.03	1.80
2007	NYY	AL	67	0	0	59	71.1	295	68	25	25	4	1	1	6	12	2	74	1	0	3	4	.429	0	30-34	0	2.92	3.15
2008	NYY	AL	64	0	0	60	70.2	259	41	11	11	4	1	1	2	6	5	77	1	0	6	5	.545	0	39-40	0	1.09	1.40
2009	NYY	AL	66	0	0	55	66.1	257	48	14	13	7	0	0	1	12	1	72	1	0	3	3	.500	0	44-46	0	1.93	1.76
Postseason			76	0	0	61	117.1	438	72	12	10	2	5	3	3	16	3	93	3	0	8	1	.889	0	34-39	4	1.13	0.77
15 ML YEARS			917	10	0	773	1090.0	4352	848	295	273	60	24	22	38	256	31	1006	12	3	71	52	.577	0	526-588	29	2.13	2.25

Mike Rivera

Bats: R **Throws:** R **Pos:** C-34; PH-9   **Ht:** 6'1" **Wt:** 236 **Born:** 9/8/1976 **Age:** 33

Year Team	Lg	G	AB	H	2B	3B	HR	(Hm Rd)	TB	R	RBI	RC	TBB	IBB	SO	HBP	SH	SF	SB	CS	SB%	GDP	Avg	OBP	Slg
2009 Nashv*	AAA	3	13	3	1	0	0	(- -)	4	1	3	0	0	0	5	0	0	0	0	0	-	0	.231	.231	.308
2001 Det	AL	4	12	4	2	0	0	(0 0)	6	2	1	2	0	0	2	0	0	0	0	0	-	0	.333	.333	.500
2002 Det	AL	39	132	30	8	1	1	(0 1)	43	11	11	8	4	0	35	1	0	1	0	0	-	5	.227	.254	.326
2003 SD	NL	19	53	9	1	0	1	(0 1)	13	2	2	0	5	0	11	0	0	0	0	0	-	4	.170	.241	.245
2006 Mil	NL	46	142	38	9	0	6	(3 3)	65	16	24	19	10	5	21	3	1	2	0	0	-	3	.268	.325	.458
2007 Mil	NL	11	13	3	0	0	2	(1 1)	9	2	3	2	1	0	3	0	1	0	0	0	-	0	.231	.286	.692
2008 Mil	NL	21	62	19	5	0	1	(0 1)	27	8	14	13	6	0	10	1	0	0	2	0	1.00	2	.306	.377	.435
2009 Mil	NL	41	114	26	7	0	2	(2 0)	39	10	14	15	15	3	32	2	0	1	1	0	1.00	6	.228	.326	.342
7 ML YEARS		181	528	129	32	1	13	(6 7)	202	51	69	59	41	8	114	7	2	4	3	0	1.00	20	.244	.305	.383

Saul Rivera

Pitches: R **Bats:** B **Pos:** RP-30   **Ht:** 5'10" **Wt:** 175 **Born:** 12/7/1977 **Age:** 32

Year Team	Lg	G	GS	CG	GF	IP	BFP	H	R	ER	HR	SH	SF	HB	TBB	IBB	SO	WP	Bk	W	L	Pct	Sh	Sv-Op	Hld	ERC	ERA
2009 Syrcse*	AAA	30	0	0	8	45.2	214	57	26	18	1	3	3	2	25	7	32	4	1	2	5	.286	0	2--	-	5.42	3.55
2006 Was	NL	54	0	0	16	60.1	277	59	28	23	4	4	1	4	32	6	41	3	0	3	0	1.000	0	1-3	9	4.17	3.43
2007 Was	NL	85	0	0	17	93.0	398	88	39	38	1	5	4	2	42	4	64	4	0	4	6	.400	0	3-5	19	3.39	3.68
2008 Was	NL	76	0	0	14	84.0	371	90	41	37	3	3	6	2	35	2	65	4	1	5	6	.455	0	0-6	17	4.11	3.96
2009 Was	NL	30	0	0	9	38.1	176	48	28	26	7	3	1	3	14	4	21	1	0	1	3	.250	0	0-1	2	6.20	6.10
4 ML YEARS		245	0	0	56	275.2	1222	285	136	124	15	15	12	11	123	16	191	12	1	13	15	.464	0	4-15	47	4.15	4.05

Brian Roberts

Bats: B **Throws:** R **Pos:** 2B-158; PH-4   **Ht:** 5'9" **Wt:** 175 **Born:** 10/9/1977 **Age:** 32

Year Team	Lg	G	AB	H	2B	3B	HR	(Hm Rd)	TB	R	RBI	RC	TBB	IBB	SO	HBP	SH	SF	SB	CS	SB%	GDP	Avg	OBP	Slg
2001 Bal	AL	75	273	69	12	3	2	(0 2)	93	42	17	27	13	0	36	0	3	3	12	3	.80	3	.253	.284	.341
2002 Bal	AL	38	128	29	6	0	1	(1 0)	38	18	11	12	15	0	21	1	3	2	9	2	.82	3	.227	.308	.297
2003 Bal	AL	112	460	124	22	4	5	(3 2)	169	65	41	62	46	1	58	1	4	1	23	6	.79	9	.270	.337	.367
2004 Bal	AL	159	641	175	50	2	4	(0 4)	241	107	53	91	71	1	95	1	15	6	29	12	.71	3	.273	.344	.376
2005 Bal	AL	143	561	176	45	7	18	(9 9)	289	92	73	106	67	5	83	3	5	4	27	10	.73	6	.314	.387	.515
2006 Bal	AL	138	563	161	34	3	10	(6 4)	231	85	55	74	55	4	66	0	6	5	36	7	.84	16	.286	.347	.410
2007 Bal	AL	156	621	180	42	5	12	(6 6)	268	103	57	105	89	6	99	0	2	4	50	7	.88	8	.290	.377	.432
2008 Bal	AL	155	611	181	51	8	9	(6 3)	275	107	57	101	82	3	104	2	3	6	40	10	.80	8	.296	.378	.450
2009 Bal	AL	159	632	179	56	1	16	(4 12)	285	110	79	106	74	3	112	2	1	8	30	7	.81	7	.283	.356	.451
9 ML YEARS		1135	4490	1274	318	33	77	(35 42)	1889	729	443	684	512	23	674	10	42	39	256	64	.80	63	.284	.356	.421

Ryan Roberts

Bats: R **Throws:** R **Pos:** 2B-57; PH-31; 3B-19; LF-16; PR-4   **Ht:** 5'11" **Wt:** 195 **Born:** 9/19/1980 **Age:** 29

Year Team	Lg	G	AB	H	2B	3B	HR	(Hm Rd)	TB	R	RBI	RC	TBB	IBB	SO	HBP	SH	SF	SB	CS	SB%	GDP	Avg	OBP	Slg
2009 Reno*	AAA	10	42	13	1	1	1	(- -)	19	10	10	9	6	0	6	0	0	0	7	0	1.00	1	.310	.396	.452
2006 Tor	AL	9	13	1	0	0	1	(0 1)	4	1	1	0	1	0	4	0	0	0	0	0	-	1	.077	.143	.308
2007 Tor	AL	8	13	1	0	0	0	(0 0)	1	2	0	0	2	0	7	1	0	0	0	0	-	0	.077	.250	.077
2008 Tex	AL	1	1	0	0	0	0	(0 0)	0	0	0	0	0	0	1	0	0	0	0	0	-	0	.000	.000	.000
2009 Ari	NL	110	305	85	17	2	7	(3 4)	127	41	25	41	40	1	55	3	2	1	7	3	.70	2	.279	.367	.416
4 ML YEARS		128	332	87	17	2	8	(3 5)	132	44	26	41	43	1	67	4	2	1	7	3	.70	3	.262	.353	.398

David Robertson

Pitches: R **Bats:** R **Pos:** RP-45   **Ht:** 5'11" **Wt:** 190 **Born:** 4/9/1985 **Age:** 25

Year Team	Lg	G	GS	CG	GF	IP	BFP	H	R	ER	HR	SH	SF	HB	TBB	IBB	SO	WP	Bk	W	L	Pct	Sh	Sv-Op	Hld	ERC	ERA
2007 CtnSC	A	24	0	0	9	47.0	183	25	5	4	0	1	1	0	15	0	67	5	0	5	2	.714	0	3--	-	1.14	0.77
2007 Tampa	A+	18	0	0	7	33.1	129	18	6	4	0	1	0	0	15	0	37	2	0	3	1	.750	0	1--	-	1.48	1.08
2007 Trntn	AA	2	0	0	0	4.0	16	2	1	1	0	0	0	0	2	0	9	1	0	0	0	-	0	0--	-	1.41	2.25
2008 Trntn	AA	9	0	0	5	18.2	68	8	2	2	0	1	0	1	6	0	26	1	0	0	0	-	0	2--	-	1.03	0.96
2008 S-WB	AAA	21	0	0	4	35.0	146	20	11	8	1	0	2	1	17	1	51	1	0	4	0	1.000	0	1--	-	1.74	2.06
2009 S-WB	AAA	8	0	0	4	14.2	59	10	7	3	0	1	1	0	6	1	25	0	0	0	3	.000	0	2--	-	1.76	1.84
2008 NYY	AL	25	0	0	8	30.1	131	29	18	18	3	0	3	0	15	2	36	6	0	4	0	1.000	0	0-0	0	4.12	5.34
2009 NYY	AL	45	0	0	20	43.2	191	36	19	16	4	0	0	1	23	1	63	6	0	2	1	.667	0	1-1	5	3.51	3.30
2 ML YEARS		70	0	0	28	74.0	322	65	37	34	7	0	3	1	38	3	99	12	0	6	1	.857	0	1-1	5	3.76	4.14

Nate Robertson

Pitches: L **Bats:** R **Pos:** RP-22; SP-6   **Ht:** 6'2" **Wt:** 225 **Born:** 9/3/1977 **Age:** 32

Year Team	Lg	G	GS	CG	GF	IP	BFP	H	R	ER	HR	SH	SF	HB	TBB	IBB	SO	WP	Bk	W	L	Pct	Sh	Sv-Op	Hld	ERC	ERA
2009 Toledo*	AAA	5	5	0	0	19.0	76	19	7	4	1	1	0	1	4	0	21	0	0	1	1	.500	0	0--	-	3.40	1.89
2002 Fla	NL	6	1	0	0	8.1	46	15	11	11	3	0	0	2	4	1	3	0	0	0	1	.000	0	0-0	0	12.69	11.88
2003 Det	AL	8	8	0	0	44.2	203	55	27	27	6	0	0	0	23	2	33	3	0	1	2	.333	0	0-0	0	6.24	5.44
2004 Det	AL	34	32	1	1	196.2	852	210	116	107	30	12	4	4	66	1	155	5	1	12	10	.545	0	1-1	0	4.65	4.90
2005 Det	AL	32	32	0	0	196.2	846	202	113	98	28	3	11	7	65	2	122	6	1	7	16	.304	0	0-0	0	4.38	4.48
2006 Det	AL	32	32	1	0	208.2	881	206	98	89	29	4	7	8	67	4	137	6	0	13	13	.500	0	0-0	0	4.14	3.84
2007 Det	AL	30	30	0	0	177.2	781	199	98	94	22	5	6	3	63	2	119	5	1	9	13	.409	0	0-0	0	4.80	4.76

Year	Team	Lg	G	GS	CG	GF	IP	BFP	H	R	ER	HR	SH	SF	HB	TBB	IBB	SO	WP	Bk	W	L	Pct	Sh	Sv-Op	Hld	ERC	ERA
			HOW MUCH HE PITCHED						**WHAT HE GAVE UP**												**THE RESULTS**							
2008	Det	AL	32	28	0	1	168.2	761	218	124	119	26	4	0	2	62	7	108	5	0	7	11	.389	0	0-0	0	6.14	6.35
2009	Det	AL	28	6	0	3	49.2	234	59	33	30	4	2	2	2	28	3	35	2	0	2	3	.400	0	0-0	0	5.70	5.44
Postseason			3	3	0	0	15.2	74	23	9	9	1	0	0	2	6	1	8	0	0	1	2	.333	0	0-0	0	7.15	5.17
8 ML YEARS			202	169	4	6	1051.0	4604	1164	620	575	148	30	30	28	378	20	712	32	3	51	69	.425	0	1-1	0	4.92	4.92

Shane Robinson

Bats: R **Throws:** R **Pos:** RF-6; PH-5; CF-2; LF-1   **Ht:** 5'9" **Wt:** 160 **Born:** 10/30/1984 **Age:** 25

Year	Team	Lg	G	AB	H	2B	3B	HR	(Hm	Rd)	TB	R	RBI	RC	TBB	IBB	SO	HBP	SH	SF	SB	CS	SB%	GDP	Avg	OBP	Slg
			BATTING																		**BASERUNNING**				**AVERAGES**		
2006	QuadC	A	63	252	71	9	2	0	(-	-)	84	41	21	33	20	1	20	6	1	2	13	3	.81	9	.282	.346	.333
2007	PlmBh	A+	43	166	42	6	1	3	(-	-)	59	22	13	21	16	0	16	2	3	3	14	4	.78	4	.253	.321	.355
2007	Cards	R	4	11	2	0	0	0	(	)	2	1	1	0	2	0	1	0	0	1	0	0	-	0	.182	.286	.182
2008	Sprgfld	AA	63	244	86	17	3	4	(-	-)	121	46	32	48	17	0	34	3	3	4	13	5	.72	4	.352	.396	.496
2008	Memp	AAA	42	141	31	4	1	1	(-	-)	40	10	10	9	5	0	24	1	2	2	2	3	.40	3	.220	.248	.284
2009	Memp	AAA	100	345	82	18	3	5	(-	-)	121	46	40	42	28	0	42	8	8	4	16	3	.84	14	.238	.306	.351
2009	StL	NL	11	25	6	1	0	0	(0	0)	7	1	1	1	0	0	2	0	0	1	1	0	1.00	1	.240	.231	.280

Fernando Rodney

Pitches: R **Bats:** R **Pos:** RP-73   **Ht:** 5'11" **Wt:** 218 **Born:** 3/18/1977 **Age:** 33

Year	Team	Lg	G	GS	CG	GF	IP	BFP	H	R	ER	HR	SH	SF	HB	TBB	IBB	SO	WP	Bk	W	L	Pct	Sh	Sv-Op	Hld	ERC	ERA
			HOW MUCH HE PITCHED						**WHAT HE GAVE UP**												**THE RESULTS**							
2002	Det	AL	20	0	0	10	18.0	89	25	15	12	2	2	1	0	10	2	10	0	1	1	3	.250	0	0-4	0	6.77	6.00
2003	Det	AL	27	0	0	11	29.2	143	35	20	20	2	3	3	1	17	1	33	0	0	1	3	.250	0	3-6	3	5.46	6.07
2005	Det	AL	39	0	0	26	44.0	185	39	14	14	5	2	0	2	17	3	42	2	0	2	3	.400	0	9-15	3	3.59	2.86
2006	Det	AL	63	0	0	30	71.2	304	51	36	28	6	2	0	8	34	4	65	3	0	7	4	.636	0	7-11	18	3.01	3.52
2007	Det	AL	48	0	0	12	50.2	223	48	27	24	5	4	2	3	21	0	54	4	0	2	6	.250	0	1-3	12	3.74	4.26
2008	Det	AL	38	0	0	25	40.1	188	34	22	22	3	1	2	3	30	5	49	3	0	0	6	.000	0	13-19	5	4.29	4.91
2009	Det	AL	73	0	0	65	75.2	330	70	38	37	8	4	2	2	41	4	61	5	0	2	5	.286	0	37-38	0	4.31	4.40
Postseason			7	0	0	0	7.2	33	6	4	2	0	0	0	0	5	1	9	0	0	0	0	-	0	0-1	2	2.94	2.35
7 ML YEARS			308	0	0	179	330.0	1462	300	172	157	31	18	10	19	170	19	314	17	1	15	30	.333	0	70-96	41	4.06	4.28

Alex Rodriguez

Bats: R **Throws:** R **Pos:** 3B-116; DH-9; PH-2   **Ht:** 6'3" **Wt:** 228 **Born:** 7/27/1975 **Age:** 34

Year	Team	Lg	G	AB	H	2B	3B	HR	(Hm	Rd)	TB	R	RBI	RC	TBB	IBB	SO	HBP	SH	SF	SB	CS	SB%	GDP	Avg	OBP	Slg
			BATTING																		**BASERUNNING**				**AVERAGES**		
1994	Sea	AL	17	54	11	0	0	0	(0	0)	11	4	2	3	3	0	20	0	1	1	3	0	1.00	0	.204	.241	.204
1995	Sea	AL	48	142	33	6	2	5	(1	4)	58	15	19	15	6	0	42	0	1	0	4	2	.67	0	.232	.264	.408
1996	Sea	AL	146	601	215	54	1	36	(18	18)	379	141	123	144	59	1	104	4	6	7	15	4	.79	15	.358	.414	.631
1997	Sea	AL	141	587	176	40	3	23	(16	7)	291	100	84	100	41	1	99	5	4	1	29	6	.83	14	.300	.350	.496
1998	Sea	AL	161	686	213	35	5	42	(18	24)	384	123	124	135	45	0	121	10	3	4	46	13	.78	12	.310	.360	.560
1999	Sea	AL	129	502	143	25	0	42	(20	22)	294	110	111	102	56	2	109	5	1	8	21	7	.75	12	.285	.357	.586
2000	Sea	AL	148	554	175	34	2	41	(13	28)	336	134	132	138	100	5	121	7	0	11	15	4	.79	10	.316	.420	.606
2001	Tex	AL	162	632	201	34	1	52	(26	26)	393	133	135	148	75	6	131	16	0	9	18	3	.86	17	.318	.399	.622
2002	Tex	AL	162	624	187	27	2	57	(34	23)	389	125	142	152	87	12	122	10	0	4	9	4	.69	14	.300	.392	.623
2003	Tex	AL	161	607	181	30	6	47	(26	21)	364	124	118	131	87	10	126	15	0	8	17	3	.85	16	.298	.396	.600
2004	NYY	AL	155	601	172	24	2	36	(17	19)	308	112	106	112	80	4	131	10	0	7	28	4	.88	18	.286	.375	.512
2005	NYY	AL	162	605	194	29	1	48	(26	22)	369	124	130	137	91	8	139	16	0	3	21	6	.78	8	.321	.421	.610
2006	NYY	AL	154	572	166	26	1	35	(20	15)	299	113	121	112	90	8	139	8	0	4	15	4	.79	22	.290	.392	.523
2007	NYY	AL	158	583	183	31	0	54	(26	28)	376	143	156	159	95	11	120	21	0	9	24	4	.86	15	.314	.422	.645
2008	NYY	AL	138	510	154	33	0	35	(21	14)	292	104	103	97	65	9	117	14	0	5	18	3	.86	14	.302	.392	.573
2009	NYY	AL	124	444	127	17	1	30	(18	12)	236	78	100	89	80	7	97	8	0	3	14	2	.88	13	.286	.402	.532
Postseason			39	147	41	9	0	7	(3	4)	71	21	17	21	17	1	38	5	1	0	4	3	.57	4	.279	.373	.483
16 ML YEARS			2166	8304	2531	445	27	583	(300	283)	4779	1683	1706	1774	1060	86	1738	149	16	82	297	69	.81	202	.305	.390	.576

Fernando Rodriguez

Pitches: R **Bats:** R **Pos:** RP-1   **Ht:** 6'3" **Wt:** 215 **Born:** 6/18/1984 **Age:** 26

Year	Team	Lg	G	GS	CG	GF	IP	BFP	H	R	ER	HR	SH	SF	HB	TBB	IBB	SO	WP	Bk	W	L	Pct	Sh	Sv-Op	Hld	ERC	ERA
			HOW MUCH HE PITCHED						**WHAT HE GAVE UP**												**THE RESULTS**							
2003	Angels	R	15	0	0	5	25.0	121	29	24	18	2	2	1	2	14	1	27	1	1	0	2	.000	0	0--	-	5.66	6.48
2003	Provo	R+	4	0	0	3	6.0	28	9	4	1	1	0	0	0	1	0	9	1	0	0	0	-	0	1--	-	6.43	1.50
2004	Provo	R+	14	12	0	1	58.2	238	64	35	27	7	1	4	2	18	0	54	5	0	4	3	.571	0	0--	-	4.84	4.14
2005	CRpds	A	28	28	4	0	157.1	675	161	87	73	8	2	3	13	49	0	128	2	1	8	10	.444	0	0--	-	3.86	4.18
2006	RCuca	A+	28	27	1	1	163.1	706	188	92	83	15	3	5	7	49	0	112	10	0	11	8	.579	0	0--	-	4.73	4.57
2007	Ark	AA	22	22	1	0	125.1	547	137	71	63	14	5	7	5	46	2	61	3	0	8	4	.667	0	0--	-	4.74	4.52
2008	Ark	AA	33	22	1	2	136.2	617	153	96	84	10	7	8	10	62	1	86	6	0	7	11	.389	1	0--	-	5.09	5.53
2009	Salt Lk	AAA	23	0	0	5	37.0	172	44	33	31	5	2	4	2	23	0	25	3	0	1	1	.500	0	0--	-	6.79	7.54
2009	Ark	AA	26	0	0	12	42.1	173	20	7	6	0	3	1	1	22	2	52	3	0	3	1	.750	0	4--	-	1.35	1.28
2009	LAA	AL	1	0	0	0	0.2	6	1	3	2	1	0	0	0	2	0	1	1	0	0	0	-	0	0-0	0	31.03	27.00

Francisco Rodriguez

Pitches: R **Bats:** R **Pos:** RP-70   **Ht:** 6'0" **Wt:** 195 **Born:** 1/7/1982 **Age:** 28

Year	Team	Lg	G	GS	CG	GF	IP	BFP	H	R	ER	HR	SH	SF	HB	TBB	IBB	SO	WP	Bk	W	L	Pct	Sh	Sv-Op	Hld	ERC	ERA
2002	LAA	AL	5	0	0	4	5.2	21	3	0	0	0	0	0	1	2	1	13	0	0	0	0	.---	0	0-0	0	1.52	0.00
2003	LAA	AL	59	0	0	23	86.0	334	50	30	29	12	2	4	2	35	5	95	7	0	8	3	.727	0	2-6	7	2.25	3.03
2004	LAA	AL	69	0	0	29	84.0	335	51	21	17	2	2	1	1	33	1	123	5	0	4	1	.800	0	12-19	27	1.64	1.82
2005	LAA	AL	66	0	0	58	67.1	279	45	20	20	7	1	1	0	32	3	91	8	0	2	5	.286	0	45-50	0	2.52	2.67
2006	LAA	AL	69	0	0	58	73.0	296	52	16	14	6	3	0	1	28	5	98	10	0	2	3	.400	0	47-51	0	2.35	1.73
2007	LAA	AL	64	0	0	56	67.1	285	50	22	21	3	1	1	4	34	0	90	7	1	5	2	.714	0	40-46	0	2.74	2.81
2008	LAA	AL	76	0	0	69	68.1	288	54	21	17	4	1	1	2	34	4	77	6	0	2	3	.400	0	62-69	0	3.06	2.24
2009	NYM	NL	70	0	0	66	68.0	295	51	34	28	7	4	1	0	38	6	73	1	0	3	6	.333	0	35-42	0	3.18	3.71
	Postseason		21	0	0	8	31.2	134	27	14	11	5	0	3	1	14	2	41	5	0	5	4	.556	0	3-5	3	3.86	3.13
	8 ML YEARS		478	0	0	363	519.2	2133	356	164	146	41	14	12	9	236	25	660	44	1	26	23	.531	0	243-283	34	2.47	2.53

Guillermo Rodriguez

Bats: R **Throws:** R **Pos:** C-6; DH-1; PH-1   **Ht:** 5'11" **Wt:** 221 **Born:** 5/15/1978 **Age:** 32

Year	Team	Lg	G	AB	H	2B	3B	HR	(Hm	Rd)	TB	R	RBI	RC	TBB	IBB	SO	HBP	SH	SF	SB	CS	SB%	GDP	Avg	OBP	Slg
1996	Bllghm	A-	3	4	0	0	0	0	(-	-)	0	1	0	0	0	0	1	0	0	0	0	0	-	0	.000	.000	.000
1997	SlmKzr	A-	11	39	9	3	0	0	(-	-)	12	3	3	3	5	0	12	0	0	0	0	1	.00	1	.231	.318	.308
1997	SnJos	A+	13	27	4	3	1	0	(-	-)	9	2	2	1	0	0	9	0	2	0	0	0	-	1	.148	.148	.333
1998	SlmKzr	A+	1	4	1	0	0	0	(-	-)	1	0	0	0	0	0	0	1	0	0	0	1	.00	0	.250	.250	.250
1998	SnJos	A+	1	1	0	0	0	0	(-	-)	0	0	0	0	0	0	0	0	0	0	0	0	-	0	.000	.000	.000
1999	Bkrsfld	A+	41	93	27	5	0	1	(-	-)	35	10	11	13	3	0	18	4	3	2	4	0	1.00	2	.290	.333	.376
1999	SlmKzr	A+	33	114	29	5	0	6	(-	-)	52	16	34	16	9	1	28	3	0	0	1	3	.25	2	.254	.325	.456
2000	Bkrsfld	A+	118	437	105	27	1	10	(-	-)	164	63	58	53	30	2	101	13	4	3	20	8	.71	11	.240	.306	.375
2001	Shreve	AA	65	216	44	7	0	5	(-	-)	66	21	25	17	8	0	40	6	5	3	3	0	1.00	5	.204	.249	.306
2001	SnJos	A+	35	126	34	10	0	2	(-	-)	50	18	21	18	9	0	26	8	4	1	2	2	.50	4	.270	.354	.397
2002	SnJos	A+	42	152	55	15	1	1	(-	-)	75	24	20	29	10	0	26	1	1	0	2	1	.67	4	.362	.405	.493
2002	Fresno	AAA	32	115	27	5	0	2	(-	-)	38	9	8	11	6	0	23	5	1	1	0	1	.00	4	.235	.299	.330
2002	Shreve	AA	13	41	11	1	1	1	(-	-)	17	4	6	5	4	0	10	1	0	0	1	2	.33	0	.268	.348	.415
2003	Fresno	AAA	78	239	66	8	4	5	(-	-)	97	31	36	33	14	0	25	5	1	1	1	0	1.00	9	.276	.328	.406
2004	Toledo	AAA	73	219	41	8	2	7	(-	-)	74	17	21	18	14	0	45	3	3	2	2	2	.50	6	.187	.244	.338
2005	SnJos	A+	67	209	57	14	3	9	(-	-)	104	36	43	36	12	0	50	10	3	7	5	1	.83	5	.273	.332	.498
2005	Nrwich	AA	6	15	4	1	0	0	(-	-)	5	1	1	2	3	0	4	1	0	1	0	0	-	0	.267	.400	.333
2006	SnJos	A+	26	77	28	6	1	5	(-	-)	51	20	21	22	10	0	12	3	0	1	2	0	1.00	6	.364	.451	.662
2006	Fresno	AAA	40	127	28	8	1	8	(-	-)	62	20	16	19	12	0	25	4	0	2	1	0	.00	3	.220	.303	.488
2007	Fresno	AAA	33	103	25	6	0	1	(-	-)	34	15	16	12	11	1	8	1	3	1	1	0	1.00	1	.243	.319	.330
2008	Fresno	AAA	33	94	25	2	0	2	(-	-)	38	9	7	12	12	1	14	0	0	0	0	0	-	5	.266	.349	.351
2009	Bowie	AA	71	226	57	14	1	5	(-	-)	88	24	21	28	13	0	42	2	5	4	6	0	1.00	11	.252	.294	.389
2009	Norfolk	AAA	18	72	16	6	0	0	(-	-)	22	4	9	4	1	0	11	0	1	0	0	0	-	2	.222	.233	.306
2007	SF	NL	39	87	22	6	0	1	(1	0)	31	10	14	13	10	0	17	0	0	1	0	1	.00	3	.253	.327	.356
2009	Bal	AL	7	5	0	0	0	0	(0	0)	0	1	1	0	2	0	1	0	0	0	0	0	-	1	.000	.286	.000
	2 ML YEARS		46	92	22	6	0	1	(1	0)	31	11	15	13	12	0	18	0	0	1	0	1	.00	4	.239	.324	.337

Henry Rodriguez

Pitches: R **Bats:** R **Pos:** RP-3   **Ht:** 6'1" **Wt:** 175 **Born:** 2/25/1987 **Age:** 23

Year	Team	Lg	G	GS	CG	GF	IP	BFP	H	R	ER	HR	SH	SF	HB	TBB	IBB	SO	WP	Bk	W	L	Pct	Sh	Sv-Op	Hld	ERC	ERA
2006	As	R	15	4	0	3	43.2	222	46	39	36	1	2	2	6	50	0	59	10	1	5	2	.714	0	1--	-	7.51	7.42
2007	Kane	A	20	18	1	1	99.2	419	75	38	34	2	3	3	4	58	0	106	13	0	6	8	.429	0	0--	-	3.08	3.07
2008	Stcktn	A+	20	13	0	6	75.0	319	57	38	33	5	2	1	2	40	0	104	9	0	2	3	.400	0	2--	-	3.14	3.96
2008	Mdland	AA	14	9	0	2	41.0	215	51	39	34	1	1	0	1	44	0	43	16	0	2	7	.222	0	0--	-	7.73	7.46
2009	Stcktn	A+	3	0	0	0	5.0	20	3	0	0	0	0	0	1	1	0	11	1	0	0	0	.---	0	0--	-	1.51	0.00
2009	Scrmto	AAA	37	0	0	18	43.2	207	38	28	28	4	1	1	0	38	2	71	8	0	2	1	.667	0	4--	-	4.92	5.77
2009	Oak	AL	3	0	0	1	4.0	20	4	2	1	0	0	0	1	2	0	4	3	0	0	0	.---	0	0-0	0	4.28	2.25

Ivan Rodriguez

Bats: R **Throws:** R **Pos:** C-115; PH-7; DH-3   **Ht:** 5'9" **Wt:** 190 **Born:** 11/30/1971 **Age:** 38

Year	Team	Lg	G	AB	H	2B	3B	HR	(Hm	Rd)	TB	R	RBI	RC	TBB	IBB	SO	HBP	SH	SF	SB	CS	SB%	GDP	Avg	OBP	Slg
1991	Tex	AL	88	280	74	16	0	3	(3	0)	99	24	27	23	5	0	42	0	2	1	0	1	.00	10	.264	.276	.354
1992	Tex	AL	123	420	109	16	1	8	(4	4)	151	39	37	41	24	2	73	1	7	2	0	0	-	15	.260	.300	.360
1993	Tex	AL	137	473	129	28	4	10	(7	3)	195	56	66	57	29	3	70	4	5	8	8	7	.53	16	.273	.315	.412
1994	Tex	AL	99	363	108	19	1	16	(7	9)	177	56	57	61	31	5	42	7	0	4	6	3	.67	10	.298	.360	.488
1995	Tex	AL	130	492	149	32	2	12	(5	7)	221	56	67	68	16	2	48	4	0	5	0	2	.00	11	.303	.327	.449
1996	Tex	AL	153	639	192	47	3	19	(10	9)	302	116	86	99	38	7	55	4	0	4	5	1	.83	18	.300	.342	.473
1997	Tex	AL	150	597	187	34	4	20	(12	8)	289	98	77	98	38	7	89	8	1	4	7	3	.70	18	.313	.360	.484
1998	Tex	AL	145	579	186	40	4	21	(12	9)	297	88	91	100	32	4	88	3	0	3	9	0	1.00	18	.321	.358	.513
1999	Tex	AL	144	600	199	29	1	35	(12	23)	335	116	113	104	24	2	64	1	0	5	25	12	.68	31	.332	.356	.558
2000	Tex	AL	91	363	126	27	4	27	(16	11)	242	66	83	78	19	5	48	1	0	6	5	5	.50	17	.347	.375	.667
2001	Tex	AL	111	442	136	24	2	25	(16	9)	239	70	65	77	23	3	73	4	0	1	10	3	.77	13	.308	.347	.541
2002	Tex	AL	108	408	128	32	2	19	(15	4)	221	67	60	63	25	2	71	2	1	4	5	4	.56	13	.314	.353	.542
2003	Fla	NL	144	511	152	36	3	16	(8	8)	242	90	85	91	55	6	92	6	1	5	10	4	.63	18	.297	.369	.474
2004	Det	AL	135	527	176	32	2	19	(7	12)	269	72	86	98	41	6	91	3	0	4	7	4	.64	15	.334	.383	.510
2005	Det	AL	129	504	139	33	5	14	(8	6)	224	71	50	44	11	2	93	2	1	7	7	3	.70	19	.276	.290	.444
2006	Det	AL	136	547	164	28	4	13	(5	8)	239	74	69	82	26	4	86	1	4	2	8	3	.73	16	.300	.332	.437
2007	Det	AL	129	502	141	31	3	11	(4	7)	211	50	63	55	9	1	96	1	1	2	2	2	.50	16	.281	.294	.420
2008	2 Tms	AL	115	398	110	20	3	7	(5	2)	157	44	35	40	23	2	67	3	3	2	10	1	.91	15	.276	.319	.394

Year Team	Lg	G	AB	H	2B	3B	HR	(Hm Rd)	TB	R	RBI	RC	TBB	IBB	SO	HBP	SH	SF	SB	CS	SB%	GDP	Avg	OBP	Slg
2009 2 Tms		121	425	106	23	2	10	(3 7)	163	55	47	30	18	0	92	1	1	3	1	2	.33	20	.249	.280	.384
08 Det	AL	82	302	89	16	3	5	(3 2)	126	33	32	36	19	1	52	2	3	2	6	1	.86	9	.295	.338	.417
08 NYY	AL	33	96	21	4	0	2	(2 0)	31	11	3	4	4	1	15	1	0	0	4	0	1.00	6	.219	.257	.323
09 Hou	NL	93	327	82	15	2	8	(3 5)	125	41	34	21	13	0	74	1	1	2	1	2	.00	13	.251	.280	.382
09 Tex	AL	28	98	24	8	0	2	(0 2)	38	14	13	9	5	0	18	0	0	1	1	0	1.00	7	.245	.279	.388
Postseason		40	153	39	9	0	4	(2 2)	60	17	25	22	14	3	32	0	1	2	1	0	1.00	3	.255	.314	.392
19 ML YEARS		2388	9070	2711	547	50	305	(159 146)	4273	1308	1264	1309	487	63	1380	56	27	72	125	61	.67	306	.299	.336	.471

Luis Rodriguez

Bats: B **Throws:** R **Pos:** SS-34; 2B-30; PH-30; 3B-1; PR-1   **Ht:** 5'9" **Wt:** 188 **Born:** 6/27/1980 **Age:** 30

Year Team	Lg	G	AB	H	2B	3B	HR	(Hm Rd)	TB	R	RBI	RC	TBB	IBB	SO	HBP	SH	SF	SB	CS	SB%	GDP	Avg	OBP	Slg
2009 Lk Els*	A+	4	14	4	0	0	1	(- -)	7	1	1	2	0	0	2	0	0	0	0	0	-	2	.286	.286	.500
2005 Min	AL	79	175	47	10	2	1	(1 1)	67	21	20	27	18	0	23	1	6	3	2	2	.50	4	.269	.335	.383
2006 Min	AL	59	115	27	4	0	2	(1 1)	37	11	6	8	14	1	16	0	2	1	0	0	-	3	.235	.315	.322
2007 Min	AL	68	155	34	5	1	2	(1 1)	47	18	12	11	12	0	14	2	2	2	1	0	1.00	8	.219	.281	.303
2008 SD	NL	64	202	58	11	1	0	(0 0)	71	22	12	19	13	0	13	0	7	3	1	1	.50	9	.287	.326	.351
2009 SD	NL	93	208	42	6	0	2	(0 2)	54	18	16	19	37	4	23	0	3	3	1	0	1.00	5	.202	.319	.260
5 ML YEARS		363	855	208	36	4	8	(3 5)	276	90	66	84	94	5	89	3	20	12	5	3	.63	29	.243	.316	.323

Rafael Rodriguez

Pitches: R **Bats:** R **Pos:** RP-18   **Ht:** 6'1" **Wt:** 175 **Born:** 9/24/1984 **Age:** 25

Year Team	Lg	G	GS	CG	GF	IP	BFP	H	R	ER	HR	SH	SF	HB	TBB	IBB	SO	WP	Bk	W	L	Pct	Sh	Sv-Op	Hld	ERC	ERA
2002 Angels	R	8	8	0	0	38.1	172	37	19	17	4	2	0	5	20	0	50	3	0	2	1	.667	0	0--	-	4.95	3.99
2002 Provo	R+	8	8	0	0	25.2	118	26	17	17	3	0	2	3	14	0	25	3	0	1	1	.500	0	0--	-	5.40	5.96
2003 CRpds	A	26	26	1	0	144.0	623	129	85	69	7	4	6	7	59	2	100	19	1	10	11	.476	1	0		3.20	4.31
2004 CRpds	A	7	7	0	0	33.1	158	36	27	24	5	2	0	5	19	0	35	4	0	1	5	.167	0	0--	-	6.19	6.48
2004 Angels	A	4	4	0	0	15.1	68	18	12	11	1	0	0	2	5	0	13	2	0	0	2	.000	0	0--	-	5.15	6.46
2005 CRpds	A	13	13	0	0	74.1	311	61	24	23	5	1	1	4	27	0	74	2	1	5	2	.714	0	0--	-	2.94	2.78
2005 RCuca	AA	14	14	0	0	72.0	328	84	58	54	11	2	4	1	33	0	44	11	0	4	4	.500	0	0--	-	5.72	6.75
2006 RCuca	A+	3	3	0	0	17.0	67	15	1	1	0	0	0	1	2	0	20	0	0	3	0	1.000	0	0--	-	2.06	0.53
2006 Ark	AA	24	24	0	0	133.0	615	174	111	98	28	3	5	7	56	0	83	12	1	5	10	.333	0	0--	-	7.21	6.63
2007 Ark	AA	16	1	0	10	71.1	315	79	36	33	6	1	8	3	30	3	42	8	0	0	6	.000	0	0--	-	4.81	4.16
2008 Salt Lk	AAA	9	0	0	2	14.1	65	20	12	10	2	2	0	0	6	0	8	1	0	2	0	1.000	0	0--	-	7.12	6.28
2008 Ark	AA	42	0	0	28	53.1	212	46	11	11	3	3	1	2	11	0	48	4	0	2	4	.333	0	11--	-	2.54	1.86
2009 Salt Lk	AAA	22	0	0	9	34.0	131	27	7	7	3	0	0	1	10	1	23	1	0	1	0	1.000	0	3--	-	2.75	1.85
2009 LAA	AL	18	0	0	6	30.2	145	47	22	19	4	1	2	1	9	1	10	1	0	0	1	.000	0	0-2	2	7.21	5.58

Sean Rodriguez

Bats: R **Throws:** R **Pos:** 2B-5; LF-3; CF-2; RF-2; PH-1   **Ht:** 6'0" **Wt:** 190 **Born:** 4/26/1985 **Age:** 25

Year Team	Lg	G	AB	H	2B	3B	HR	(Hm Rd)	TB	R	RBI	RC	TBB	IBB	SO	HBP	SH	SF	SB	CS	SB%	GDP	Avg	OBP	Slg
2003 Angels	R	54	216	58	8	5	2	(- -)	82	30	25	29	14	0	37	7	1	1	11	4	.73	6	.269	.332	.380
2004 CRpds	A	57	196	49	8	1	4	(- -)	77	35	17	20	10	0	54	7	2	1	14	4	.78	2	.250	.333	.393
2004 Provo	R+	64	225	76	14	4	10	(- -)	128	64	55	64	51	0	62	15	0	1	9	3	.75	2	.338	.486	.569
2005 CRpds	A	124	440	112	29	3	14	(- -)	189	88	48	78	78	0	85	9	9	2	27	11	.71	8	.250	.371	.422
2006 RCuca	A+	116	455	137	29	5	24	(- -)	248	78	77	95	47	3	124	12	3	6	15	3	.83	9	.301	.377	.545
2006 Ark	AA	18	65	23	5	0	5	(- -)	43	16	9	17	11	0	18	2	1	0	0	3	.00	1	.354	.462	.662
2006 Salt Lk	AAA	1	2	0	0	0	0	(- -)	0	0	0	0	0	0	2	0	0	0	0	0	-	0	.000	.000	.000
2007 Ark	AA	136	508	129	31	2	17	(- -)	215	84	73	79	54	0	132	19	2	4	15	8	.65	5	.254	.345	.423
2008 Salt Lk	AAA	66	248	76	19	1	21	(- -)	160	68	52	62	29	0	45	9	2	1	4	1	.80	5	.306	.397	.645
2009 Salt Lk	AAA	103	365	109	17	6	29	(- -)	225	81	93	89	51	0	119	13	3	3	9	2	.82	5	.299	.400	.616
2009 Drham	AAA	5	20	4	2	0	1	(- -)	9	6	5	3	4	0	3	0	0	0	2	0	-	1	.200	.333	.450
2008 LAA	AL	59	167	34	8	1	3	(2 1)	53	18	10	12	14	0	55	3	2	1	3	1	.75	3	.204	.276	.317
2009 LAA	AL	12	25	5	0	0	2	(0 2)	11	4	4	2	3	0	7	0	0	1	0	0	-	2	.200	.276	.440
2 ML YEARS		71	192	39	8	1	5	(2 3)	64	22	14	14	17	0	62	3	2	2	3	1	.75	5	.203	.276	.333

Wandy Rodriguez

Pitches: L **Bats:** B **Pos:** SP-33   **Ht:** 5'11" **Wt:** 160 **Born:** 1/18/1979 **Age:** 31

Year Team	Lg	G	GS	CG	GF	IP	BFP	H	R	ER	HR	SH	SF	HB	TBB	IBB	SO	WP	Bk	W	L	Pct	Sh	Sv-Op	Hld	ERC	ERA
2005 Hou	NL	25	22	0	0	128.2	560	135	82	79	19	3	3	8	53	2	80	3	3	10	10	.500	0	0-0	0	5.08	5.53
2006 Hou	NL	30	24	0	1	135.2	611	154	96	85	17	7	4	6	63	7	98	6	0	9	10	.474	0	0-0	0	5.45	5.64
2007 Hou	NL	31	31	1	0	182.2	782	179	102	93	22	6	4	5	62	2	158	3	0	9	13	.409	1	0-0	0	3.94	4.58
2008 Hou	NL	25	25	0	0	137.1	587	136	65	54	14	2	5	4	44	3	131	2	3	9	7	.563	1	0-0	0	3.82	3.54
2009 Hou	NL	33	33	1	0	205.2	849	192	77	69	21	8	4	5	63	5	193	2	1	14	12	.538	1	0-0	0	3.47	3.02
Postseason		3	0	0	1	4.2	22	5	2	2	1	0	0		5	1	4	0	0	0	1	.000	0	0-0	0	10.58	3.86
5 ML YEARS		144	135	2	1	790.0	3389	796	422	380	93	26	20	29	285	19	660	16	7	51	52	.495	2	0-0	0	4.22	4.33

Josh Roenicke

Pitches: R Bats: R Pos: RP-24   Ht: 6'3" Wt: 194 Born: 8/4/1982 Age: 27

Year	Team	Lg	G	GS	CG	GF	IP	BFP	H	R	ER	HR	SH	SF	HB	TBB	IBB	SO	WP	Bk	W	L	Pct	Sh	Sv-Op	Hld	ERC	ERA
2006	Reds	R	7	0	0	4	7.2	36	8	2	1	0	1	0	1	3	0	9	1	0	1	0	1.000	0	0--	-	3.81	1.17
2006	Billings	R+	14	0	0	12	15.2	68	10	11	11	1	0	0	0	12	0	24	1	0	1	0	1.000	0	6--	-	3.22	6.32
2007	Srsota	A+	27	0	0	25	27.2	119	23	10	10	1	1	0	1	15	2	41	1	0	2	1	.667	0	16--	-	3.28	3.25
2007	Chatt	AA	19	0	0	15	19.0	72	12	3	2	0	1	0	0	6	0	15	0	0	1	1	.500	0	8--	-	1.49	0.95
2008	Chatt	AA	22	0	0	19	22.0	100	21	10	8	2	2	3	0	12	1	28	1	0	4	2	.667	0	10--	-	4.10	3.27
2008	Lsvlle	AAA	35	0	0	12	39.0	161	34	11	11	2	1	1	0	14	3	43	8	0	2	0	1.000	0	12--	-	2.81	2.54
2009	Lsvlle	AAA	27	0	0	21	28.0	122	30	9	8	0	2	0	2	6	1	32	1	0	1	0	1.000	0	12--	-	3.19	2.57
2008	Cin	NL	5	0	0	0	3.0	18	6	3	3	0	0	0	1	2	0	6	0	0	0	0	-	0	0-0	0	12.01	9.00
2009	2 Tms		24	0	0	5	31.0	138	32	19	18	2	0	1	1	16	1	33	2	0	0	0	-	0	0-0	1	4.55	5.23
09	Cin	NL	11	0	0	2	13.1	54	13	4	4	0	0	0	0	4	0	14	1	0	0	0	-	0	0-0	0	3.00	2.70
09	Tor	AL	13	0	0	3	17.2	84	19	15	14	2	0	1	1	12	1	19	1	0	0	0	-	0	0-0	1	5.81	7.13
	2 ML YEARS		29	0	0	5	34.0	156	38	22	21	2	0	1	2	18	1	39	2	0	0	0	-	0	0-0	1	5.15	5.56

Esmil Rogers

Pitches: R Bats: R Pos: SP-1   Ht: 6'1" Wt: 146 Born: 8/14/1985 Age: 24

Year	Team	Lg	G	GS	CG	GF	IP	BFP	H	R	ER	HR	SH	SF	HB	TBB	IBB	SO	WP	Bk	W	L	Pct	Sh	Sv-Op	Hld	ERC	ERA
2006	Casper	R+	15	15	1	0	63.1	297	78	53	49	8	2	3	13	24	0	40	8	1	3	6	.333	0	0--	-	6.45	6.96
2007	Ashvll	A	19	18	1	0	117.2	517	125	60	49	6	3	4	7	42	0	90	10	4	7	4	.636	0	0--	-	4.12	3.75
2008	Mdest	A+	25	25	0	0	143.2	609	146	73	63	9	2	6	4	45	0	116	6	3	9	7	.563	0	0--	-	3.70	3.95
2009	Tulsa	AA	15	15	0	0	94.1	384	87	30	27	2	0	1	6	19	0	83	3	1	8	2	.800	0	0--	-	2.67	2.58
2009	ColSpr	AAA	12	11	0	0	60.2	287	77	50	50	4	2	4	3	35	2	46	7	3	3	5	.375	0	0--	-	7.06	7.42
2009	Col	NL	1	1	0	0	4.0	16	3	2	2	0	0	1	0	2	0	3	0	0	0	0	-	0	0-0	0	2.58	4.50

Ryan Rohlinger

Bats: R Throws: R Pos: 3B-8; SS-3; PH-2; 2B-1   Ht: 6'1" Wt: 195 Born: 10/7/1983 Age: 26

Year	Team	Lg	G	AB	H	2B	3B	HR	(Hm	Rd)	TB	R	RBI	RC	TBB	IBB	SO	HBP	SH	SF	SB	CS	SB%	GDP	Avg	OBP	Slg
2006	SlmKzr	A-	65	234	59	13	1	3	(-	-)	83	34	28	30	27	1	27	5	2	5	0	2	.00	13	.252	.336	.355
2007	Augsta	A	135	506	119	31	3	18	(-	-)	210	86	78	74	62	3	83	13	1	4	3	3	.50	7	.235	.332	.415
2008	SnJos	A+	73	277	79	16	0	7	(-	-)	116	45	46	46	34	0	50	5	1	5	1	1	.83	6	.285	.368	.419
2008	Conn	AA	44	159	47	12	1	6	(-	-)	79	27	19	28	13	0	20	3	3	1	1	1	.50	8	.296	.358	.497
2009	Fresno	AAA	126	474	133	37	2	16	(-	-)	222	74	78	80	42	1	90	12	2	5	4	2	.67	9	.281	.351	.468
2008	SF	NL	21	32	3	1	1	0	(0	0)	6	2	2	0	1	0	8	0	0	0	0	1	.00	2	.094	.121	.188
2009	SF	NL	12	19	3	1	0	0	(0	0)	4	0	4	1	1	0	6	0	0	0	0	0	-	1	.158	.200	.211
	2 ML YEARS		33	51	6	2	1	0	(0	0)	10	2	6	1	2	0	14	0	0	0	0	1	.00	3	.118	.151	.196

Scott Rolen

Bats: R Throws: R Pos: 3B-127; PH-1   Ht: 6'4" Wt: 250 Born: 4/4/1975 Age: 35

Year	Team	Lg	G	AB	H	2B	3B	HR	(Hm	Rd)	TB	R	RBI	RC	TBB	IBB	SO	HBP	SH	SF	SB	CS	SB%	GDP	Avg	OBP	Slg
2009	Lsvlle*	AAA	2	6	2	0	0	0	(-	-)	2	1	1	0	0	0	1	0	0	0	0	0	-	0	.333	.333	.333
1996	Phi	NL	37	130	33	7	0	4	(2	2)	52	10	18	16	13	0	27	1	0	2	4	2	.00	4	.254	.322	.400
1997	Phi	NL	156	561	159	35	3	21	(11	10)	263	93	92	103	76	4	138	13	0	7	16	6	.73	6	.283	.377	.469
1998	Phi	NL	160	601	174	45	4	31	(19	12)	320	120	110	124	93	6	141	11	0	6	14	7	.67	10	.290	.391	.532
1999	Phi	NL	112	421	113	28	1	26	(9	17)	221	74	77	83	67	2	114	3	0	6	12	2	.86	8	.268	.368	.525
2000	Phi	NL	128	483	144	32	4	26	(12	14)	266	88	89	97	51	9	99	5	0	2	8	1	.89	8	.298	.370	.551
2001	Phi	NL	151	554	160	39	1	25	(12	13)	276	96	107	108	74	6	127	13	0	12	16	5	.76	6	.289	.378	.498
2002	2 Tms	NL	155	580	154	29	8	31	(14	17)	292	89	110	98	72	4	102	12	0	3	8	4	.67	22	.266	.357	.503
2003	StL	NL	154	559	160	49	1	28	(12	16)	295	98	104	104	82	5	104	9	0	7	13	3	.81	19	.286	.382	.528
2004	StL	NL	142	500	157	32	4	34	(10	24)	299	109	124	124	72	5	92	13	1	7	4	3	.57	8	.314	.409	.598
2005	StL	NL	56	196	46	12	1	5	(2	3)	75	28	28	22	25	1	28	1	0	1	1	2	.33	3	.235	.323	.383
2006	StL	NL	142	521	154	48	1	22	(12	10)	270	94	95	89	56	7	69	9	0	8	7	4	.64	10	.296	.369	.518
2007	StL	NL	112	392	104	24	2	8	(4	4)	156	55	58	47	37	2	56	5	0	7	5	3	.63	13	.265	.331	.398
2008	Tor	AL	115	408	107	30	3	11	(6	5)	176	58	50	57	46	2	71	10	0	3	5	0	1.00	14	.262	.349	.431
2009	2 Tms	NL	128	475	145	36	1	11	(8	3)	216	76	67	82	45	1	62	7	0	8	5	4	.56	4	.305	.368	.455
02	Phi	NL	100	375	97	21	4	17	(8	9)	177	52	66	60	52	2	68	8	0	3	5	2	.71	12	.259	.358	.472
02	StL	NL	55	205	57	8	4	14	(6	8)	115	37	44	38	20	2	34	4	0	0	3	2	.60	10	.278	.354	.561
09	Tor	AL	88	338	108	29	0	8	(6	2)	161	52	43	60	26	1	42	4	0	5	4	2	.67	2	.320	.370	.476
09	Cin	NL	40	137	37	7	1	3	(2	1)	55	24	24	22	19	0	20	3	0	3	1	2	.33	2	.270	.364	.401
	Postseason		32	114	26	7	0	5	(3	2)	48	17	11	14	14	0	22	2	0	1	0	1	.00	5	.228	.321	.421
	14 ML YEARS		1748	6381	1810	446	36	283	(133	150)	3177	1088	1129	1154	809	54	1230	112	1	79	114	46	.71	129	.284	.370	.498

Jimmy Rollins

Bats: B Throws: R Pos: SS-155; PH-3   Ht: 5'8" Wt: 170 Born: 11/27/1978 Age: 31

Year	Team	Lg	G	AB	H	2B	3B	HR	(Hm	Rd)	TB	R	RBI	RC	TBB	IBB	SO	HBP	SH	SF	SB	CS	SB%	GDP	Avg	OBP	Slg
2000	Phi	NL	14	53	17	1	1	0	(0	0)	20	5	5	8	2	0	7	0	0	0	3	0	1.00	0	.321	.345	.377
2001	Phi	NL	158	656	180	29	12	14	(8	6)	275	97	54	96	48	2	108	2	9	5	46	8	.85	5	.274	.323	.419
2002	Phi	NL	154	637	156	33	10	11	(5	6)	242	82	60	72	54	3	103	4	6	4	31	13	.70	14	.245	.306	.380
2003	Phi	NL	156	628	165	42	6	8	(5	3)	243	85	62	76	54	4	113	0	5	2	20	12	.63	9	.263	.320	.387
2004	Phi	NL	154	657	190	43	12	14	(8	6)	299	119	73	108	57	3	73	3	6	2	30	9	.77	4	.289	.348	.455
2005	Phi	NL	158	677	196	38	11	12	(5	7)	292	115	54	100	47	8	71	4	2	2	41	6	.87	9	.290	.338	.431
2006	Phi	NL	158	689	191	45	9	25	(15	10)	329	127	83	114	57	2	80	5	0	7	36	4	.90	12	.277	.334	.478

Year	Team	Lg	G	AB	H	2B	3B	HR	(Hm	Rd)	TB	R	RBI	RC	TBB	IBB	SO	HBP	SH	SF	SB	CS	SB%	GDP	Avg	OBP	Slg
2007	Phi	NL	162	716	212	38	20	30	(18	12)	380	139	94	124	49	5	85	7	0	6	41	6	.87	11	.296	.344	.531
2008	Phi	NL	137	556	154	38	9	11	(5	6)	243	76	59	95	58	7	55	5	3	3	47	3	.94	11	.277	.349	.437
2009	Phi	NL	155	672	168	43	5	21	(10	11)	284	100	77	88	44	1	70	2	2	5	31	8	.79	7	.250	.296	.423
	Postseason		17	70	16	4	1	3	(1	2)	31	11	6	4	6	0	16	0	1	0	4	2	.67	2	.229	.289	.443
	10 ML YEARS		1406	5941	1629	350	95	146	(77	69)	2607	945	621	881	470	35	765	32	33	36	326	69	.83	82	.274	.329	.439

Alex Romero

Bats: L **Throws:** R **Pos:** PH-26; LF-21; RF-21; CF-4; PR-1   **Ht:** 6'0" **Wt:** 198 **Born:** 9/9/1983 **Age:** 26

Year	Team	Lg	G	AB	H	2B	3B	HR	(Hm	Rd)	TB	R	RBI	RC	TBB	IBB	SO	HBP	SH	SF	SB	CS	SB%	GDP	Avg	OBP	Slg
2002	Twins	R	56	186	62	13	2	2	(-	-)	85	31	42	40	29	3	14	5	3	7	16	6	.73	5	.333	.423	.457
2003	QuadC	A	120	423	125	16	3	4	(-	-)	159	50	40	60	43	3	43	1	5	4	11	8	.58	10	.296	.359	.376
2004	FtMyrs	A+	105	380	111	21	2	6	(-	-)	154	59	42	64	54	3	47	6	5	2	6	4	.60	4	.292	.387	.405
2005	NwBrit	AA	139	510	153	31	2	15	(-	-)	233	65	77	83	36	5	69	8	4	2	14	10	.58	11	.300	.354	.457
2006	Roch	AAA	71	236	59	8	2	0	(-	-)	71	20	26	23	15	2	22	3	5	3	6	2	.75	11	.250	.300	.301
2006	NwBrit	AA	48	167	47	11	2	5	(-	-)	77	29	16	31	26	2	19	3	2	2	15	7	.68	2	.281	.384	.461
2007	Tucsn	AAA	131	533	166	32	6	5	(-	-)	225	82	66	81	37	2	52	1	8	3	13	10	.57	20	.311	.355	.422
2008	Tucsn	AAA	41	173	56	9	2	3	(-	-)	78	28	19	28	11	0	19	1	1	0	4	3	.57	4	.324	.368	.451
2009	Reno	AAA	70	279	97	20	3	2	(-	-)	129	40	47	55	32	4	26	3	0	3	7	4	.64	8	.348	.416	.462
2008	Ari	NL	78	135	31	8	2	1	(1	0)	46	13	12	11	3	0	20	1	2	1	4	0	1.00	3	.230	.250	.341
2009	Ari	NL	66	145	36	6	2	1	(1	0)	49	14	18	15	11	1	23	1	0	0	2	0	1.00	7	.248	.306	.338
	2 ML YEARS		144	280	67	14	4	2	(2	0)	95	27	30	26	14	1	43	2	2	1	6	0	1.00	10	.239	.279	.339

J.C. Romero

Pitches: L **Bats:** B **Pos:** RP-21   **Ht:** 5'11" **Wt:** 203 **Born:** 6/4/1976 **Age:** 34

			HOW MUCH HE PITCHED						WHAT HE GAVE UP											THE RESULTS						
Year	Team	Lg	G	GS	CG	GF	IP	BFP	H	R	ER	HR	SH	SF	HB	TBB	IBB	SO	WP	Bk	W	L	Pct	Sh	Sv-Op	Hld	ERC	ERA
2009	LV*	AAA	5	1	0	0	4.2	20	5	2	2	0	0	0	0	2	0	5	0	0	0	1	.000	0	0--	-	3.97	3.86
2009	Rdng*	AA	1	0	0	0	1.0	3	0	0	0	0	0	0	1	0	0	0	0	0	0	0	-	0	0--	-	1.26	0.00
2009	Lakwd*	A	1	0	0	0	2.0	6	0	0	0	0	0	0	0	0	0	2	0	0	0	0	-	0	0--	-	0.00	0.00
2009	Clrwtr*	A+	1	0	0	0	0.1	2	0	0	0	0	0	0	0	1	0	1	0	0	0	0	-	0	0--	-	7.00	0.00
1999	Min	AL	5	0	0	3	9.2	39	13	4	4	0	0	0	0	9	0	1	0	0	0	0	-	0	0-0	0	3.95	3.72
2000	Min	AL	12	11	0	0	57.2	260	72	51	45	8	4	2	1	30	0	50	2	1	2	7	.222	0	0-0	0	6.48	7.02
2001	Min	AL	14	11	0	1	65.0	286	71	48	45	10	3	2	1	24	1	39	1	0	1	4	.200	0	0-0	0	4.89	6.23
2002	Min	AL	81	0	0	15	81.0	332	62	17	17	3	1	6	4	36	4	76	9	0	9	2	.818	0	1-5	33	2.74	1.89
2003	Min	AL	73	0	0	17	63.0	295	66	37	35	7	4	0	6	42	7	50	9	2	2	0	1.000	0	0-4	22	5.72	5.00
2004	Min	AL	74	0	0	12	74.1	319	61	32	29	4	3	1	5	38	6	69	5	0	7	4	.636	0	1-8	16	3.33	3.51
2005	Min	AL	68	0	0	11	57.0	264	50	26	22	6	5	1	6	39	8	48	1	1	4	3	.571	0	0-1	11	4.62	3.47
2006	LAA	AL	65	0	0	16	48.1	226	57	40	36	3	1	5	1	28	2	31	1	0	1	2	.333	0	0-1	7	5.54	6.70
2007	2 Tms		74	0	0	10	56.1	237	39	12	12	3	1	1	2	40	5	42	4	0	2	2	.500	0	1-2	24	3.35	1.92
2008	Phi	NL	81	0	0	14	59.0	255	41	18	18	5	4	0	5	38	5	52	2	1	4	4	.500	0	1-5	24	3.42	2.70
2009	Phi	NL	21	0	0	5	16.2	73	13	6	5	2	0	0	2	13	0	12	0	0	0	0	-	0	0-1	6	5.20	2.70
07	Bos	AL	23	0	0	5	20.0	94	24	7	7	2	0	1	0	15	3	11	0	0	1	0	1.000	0	1-1	2	6.61	3.15
07	Phi	NL	51	0	0	5	36.1	143	15	5	5	1	1	0	2	25	2	31	4	0	1	2	.333	0	0-1	22	1.86	1.24
	Postseason		23	0	0	7	19.0	79	15	7	7	1	2	1	0	9	1	15	1	0	2	2	.500	0	0-0	5	2.85	3.32
	11 ML YEARS		568	22	0	104	588.0	2594	545	291	268	51	26	12	33	328	38	473	34	5	32	28	.533	0	4-27	143	4.33	4.10

Niuman Romero

Bats: B **Throws:** R **Pos:** SS-4; PR-3; DH-2; PH-2; 1B-1; 3B-1   **Ht:** 6'0" **Wt:** 160 **Born:** 1/24/1985 **Age:** 25

Year	Team	Lg	G	AB	H	2B	3B	HR	(Hm	Rd)	TB	R	RBI	RC	TBB	IBB	SO	HBP	SH	SF	SB	CS	SB%	GDP	Avg	OBP	Slg
2005	Burlgtn	A	63	218	60	12	2	2	(-	-)	82	33	29	32	31	1	45	4	3	1	6	6	.50	5	.275	.374	.376
2006	Lk Cty	A	114	412	94	11	1	2	(-	-)	113	45	36	40	55	0	83	1	9	3	10	8	.56	13	.228	.318	.274
2007	Knstn	A+	12	40	14	2	0	0	(-	-)	16	5	6	7	4	0	9	0	0	1	1	0	1.00	6	.350	.400	.400
2007	Lk Cty	A	69	215	45	10	2	1	(-	-)	62	31	24	27	44	0	45	5	2	3	3	1	.75	6	.209	.352	.288
2008	Knstn	A+	108	395	117	22	1	6	(-	-)	159	64	53	59	34	1	55	2	4	5	10	4	.71	8	.296	.351	.403
2009	Akron	AA	38	115	24	4	0	0	(-	-)	28	13	8	9	12	0	19	2	4	1	3	1	.75	7	.209	.292	.243
2009	Clmbs	AAA	81	252	64	10	1	1	(-	-)	79	34	27	27	21	0	27	2	6	3	10	4	.71	6	.254	.313	.313
2009	Cle	AL	10	14	2	0	0	0	(0	0)	2	2	0	0	1	0	5	0	0	0	0	0	-	0	.143	.200	.143

Ricky Romero

Pitches: L **Bats:** R **Pos:** SP-29   **Ht:** 6'0" **Wt:** 210 **Born:** 11/6/1984 **Age:** 25

			HOW MUCH HE PITCHED						WHAT HE GAVE UP											THE RESULTS						
Year	Team	Lg	G	GS	CG	GF	IP	BFP	H	R	ER	HR	SH	SF	HB	TBB	IBB	SO	WP	Bk	W	L	Pct	Sh	Sv-Op	Hld	ERC	ERA
2006	Dnedin	A+	8	8	0	0	30.2	134	36	13	13	2	0	0	0	7	0	22	5	1	1	0	1.000	0	0--	-	4.06	3.82
2005	Auburn	A-	1	1	0	0	2.0	9	2	0	0	0	0	0	0	1	0	1	0	0	0	0	-	0	0--	-	3.63	0.00
2006	Dnedin	A+	10	10	1	0	58.1	234	48	17	16	5	2	3	1	14	0	61	0	0	2	1	.667	1	0--	-	2.52	2.47
2006	NHam	AA	12	12	0	0	67.1	288	65	43	38	7	5	2	1	26	0	41	6	0	2	7	.222	0	0--	-	3.92	5.08
2007	NHam	AA	18	18	1	0	88.1	409	98	57	48	9	1	2	4	51	0	80	9	0	3	6	.333	0	0--	-	5.62	4.89
2007	Dnedin	A+	1	1	0	0	4.2	17	4	2	2	0	0	0	0	1	0	2	0	0	0	0	-	0	0--	-	2.29	3.86
2008	NHam	AA	21	21	0	0	121.2	540	139	70	67	9	2	4	6	55	0	78	11	1	5	5	.500	0	0--	-	5.23	4.96
2008	Syrcse	AAA	7	7	1	0	42.2	184	42	17	16	3	1	1	2	20	0	38	2	0	3	3	.500	0	0--	-	4.32	3.38
2009	Dnedin	A+	1	1	0	0	4.0	19	6	6	6	2	0	0	0	1	0	5	1	0	1	0	1.000	0	0--	-	9.51	13.50
2009	NHam	AA	1	1	0	0	5.1	22	3	2	1	0	0	0	0	2	0	6	0	0	0	0	-	0	0--	-	3.21	1.69
2009	LsVgs	AAA	1	1	0	0	5.0	24	8	4	4	0	0	0	1	2	0	3	0	0	0	0	-	0	0--	-	8.20	7.20
2009	Tor	AL	29	29	0	0	178.0	771	192	88	85	18	3	3	10	79	0	141	6	1	13	9	.591	0	0-0	0	5.12	4.30

Sergio Romo

Pitches: R **Bats:** R **Pos:** RP-45   **Ht:** 5'11" **Wt:** 191 **Born:** 3/4/1983 **Age:** 27

Year	Team	Lg	G	GS	CG	GF	IP	BFP	H	R	ER	HR	SH	SF	HB	TBB	IBB	SO	WP	Bk	W	L	Pct	Sh	Sv-Op	Hld	ERC	ERA
2005	SlmKzr	A-	15	14	0	0	68.2	283	70	24	21	7	3	0	3	9	0	65	1	1	7	1	.875	0	0- -	-	3.31	2.75
2006	Augsta	A	31	10	0	10	103.1	405	78	33	29	9	0	6	5	19	0	95	2	0	10	2	.833	0	4- -	-	2.13	2.53
2007	SnJos	A+	41	0	0	27	66.1	247	35	12	10	4	2	3	1	15	1	106	2	0	6	2	.750	0	9- -	-	1.20	1.36
2008	Conn	AA	24	0	0	21	27.0	108	22	15	12	1	2	1	2	7	2	30	0	0	1	3	.250	0	11- -	-	2.40	4.00
2008	Fresno	AAA	3	0	0	2	6.0	22	3	0	0	0	0	0	0	2	1	7	0	0	0	0	-	0	0- -	-	1.00	0.00
2009	SnJos	A+	3	1	0	0	4.2	17	2	0	0	0	0	0	0	2	0	6	0	0	0	0	-	0	0- -	-	1.14	0.00
2009	Fresno	AAA	3	0	0	0	3.0	12	2	1	0	0	0	0	0	0	0	3	1	0	0	0	-	0	0- -	-	0.84	0.00
2008	SF	NL	29	0	0	8	34.0	130	16	13	8	3	2	1	3	8	1	33	0	0	3	1	.750	0	0-0	5	1.27	2.12
2009	SF	NL	45	0	0	9	34.0	143	30	15	15	1	2	0	1	11	0	41	2	0	5	2	.714	0	2-2	10	2.76	3.97
	2 ML YEARS		74	0	0	17	68.0	273	46	28	23	4	4	1	4	19	1	74	2	0	8	3	.727	0	2-2	15	1.90	3.04

Carlos Rosa

Pitches: R **Bats:** R **Pos:** RP-7   **Ht:** 6'1" **Wt:** 208 **Born:** 9/21/1984 **Age:** 25

Year	Team	Lg	G	GS	CG	GF	IP	BFP	H	R	ER	HR	SH	SF	HB	TBB	IBB	SO	WP	Bk	W	L	Pct	Sh	Sv-Op	Hld	ERC	ERA
2002	Royals	R	10	9	0	0	32.0	161	52	32	22	3	1	2	2	12	0	11	3	1	0	4	.000	0	0- -	-	7.89	6.19
2003	Royals	R	15	11	0	0	69.1	297	79	36	28	4	1	0	4	18	1	54	9	1	5	3	.625	0	0- -	-	4.29	3.63
2004	Burlgtn	A	8	8	0	0	34.2	159	41	24	18	1	2	0	2	17	0	23	0	0	0	5	.000	0	0- -	-	5.21	4.67
2004	Royals	R	4	4	0	0	11.0	53	14	6	6	1	0	0	0	9	0	8	2	2	0	0	-	0	0- -	-	8.21	4.91
2006	Burlgtn	A	24	24	1	0	138.2	575	121	50	39	6	5	2	7	54	0	102	4	3	8	6	.571	1	0- -	-	3.22	2.53
2006	Hi Dsrt	A+	3	3	0	0	11.1	59	20	12	9	1	1	2	1	4	0	13	0	0	1	0	1.000	0	0- -	-	8.72	7.15
2007	Wilmg	A+	4	4	0	0	23.0	89	18	2	1	0	0	0	0	3	0	15	0	0	2	1	.667	0	0- -	-	1.51	0.39
2007	Wichta	AA	21	17	0	2	97.0	419	101	50	47	8	3	1	1	43	1	70	4	0	6	6	.500	0	1- -	-	4.46	4.36
2008	NWArk	AA	8	8	0	0	45.0	166	30	8	6	2	0	0	0	7	0	42	3	0	4	2	.667	0	0- -	-	1.41	1.20
2008	Omha	AAA	11	11	0	0	50.2	204	51	24	23	3	0	1	0	12	0	44	3	1	4	3	.571	0	0- -	-	3.34	4.09
2009	Omha	AAA	43	0	0	24	71.0	306	69	40	36	6	5	1	1	32	2	80	6	0	2	8	.200	0	7- -	-	4.05	4.56
2008	KC	AL	2	0	0	1	3.1	12	3	1	1	0	0	0	0	0	0	3	0	0	0	0	-	0	0-0	0	1.70	2.70
2009	KC	AL	7	0	0	5	10.2	43	10	4	4	1	0	1	0	3	0	4	0	0	0	0	-	0	1-1	0	3.34	3.38
	2 ML YEARS		9	0	0	6	14.0	55	13	5	5	1	0	1	0	3	0	7	0	0	0	0	-	0	1-1	0	2.93	3.21

Adam Rosales

Bats: R **Throws:** R **Pos:** 3B-57; PH-15; 1B-11; SS-6; 2B-4; PR-2   **Ht:** 6'2" **Wt:** 195 **Born:** 5/20/1983 **Age:** 27

Year	Team	Lg	G	AB	H	2B	3B	HR	(Hm	Rd)	TB	R	RBI	RC	TBB	IBB	SO	HBP	SH	SF	SB	CS	SB%	GDP	Avg	OBP	Slg
2005	Billings	R+	34	140	45	14	0	5	(-	-)	74	29	25	28	13	0	37	5	0	1	2	2	.50	0	.321	.396	.529
2005	Dayton	A	32	134	44	8	0	9	(-	-)	79	24	21	29	10	0	24	2	0	2	3	1	.75	3	.328	.378	.590
2006	Srsota	A+	34	122	26	8	2	2	(-	-)	44	15	14	15	20	0	27	2	1	2	3	3	.50	1	.213	.329	.361
2006	Dayton	A	55	222	60	9	3	6	(-	-)	93	36	29	32	15	1	40	5	0	2	5	1	.83	1	.270	.328	.419
2007	Srsota	A+	69	248	73	23	5	5	(-	-)	121	47	48	51	31	1	46	13	2	6	9	2	.82	8	.294	.393	.488
2007	Chatt	AA	67	255	71	18	6	13	(-	-)	140	51	31	53	37	3	66	5	2	3	4	4	.50	1	.278	.377	.549
2008	Lsvlle	AAA	117	432	124	29	7	11	(-	-)	200	70	58	70	22	0	82	14	1	4	7	1	.88	0	.287	.339	.463
2009	Lsvlle	AAA	30	109	38	8	2	5	(-	-)	65	27	20	26	12	2	15	1	0	3	4	0	1.00	3	.349	.408	.596
2008	Cin	NL	18	29	6	1	0	0	(0	0)	7	0	2	2	1	0	4	0	0	0	1	0	1.00	0	.207	.233	.241
2009	Cin	NL	87	230	49	10	1	4	(2	2)	73	23	19	22	26	0	46	5	2	3	1	2	.33	2	.213	.303	.317
	2 ML YEARS		105	259	55	11	1	4	(2	2)	80	23	21	24	27	0	50	5	2	3	2	2	.50	2	.212	.296	.309

Leo Rosales

Pitches: R **Bats:** R **Pos:** RP-33   **Ht:** 6'1" **Wt:** 205 **Born:** 5/28/1981 **Age:** 29

Year	Team	Lg	G	GS	CG	GF	IP	BFP	H	R	ER	HR	SH	SF	HB	TBB	IBB	SO	WP	Bk	W	L	Pct	Sh	Sv-Op	Hld	ERC	ERA
2003	Eugene	A-	36	0	0	11	43.0	178	32	13	10	4	0	2	1	16	0	58	1	0	3	1	.750	0	3- -	-	2.61	2.09
2004	FtWyn	A	53	1	0	40	57.2	230	38	11	9	4	0	0	0	15	1	66	1	0	6	1	.857	0	26- -	-	1.62	1.40
2005	Lk Els	A+	61	0	0	56	65.0	275	53	26	23	5	5	3	1	24	0	77	1	0	8	7	.533	0	27- -	-	2.79	3.18
2006	Mobile	AA	53	0	0	21	61.2	264	53	35	22	6	2	4	2	18	6	54	5	0	5	6	.455	0	0- -	-	2.74	3.21
2006	Lk Els	A+	5	0	0	4	6.1	23	1	0	0	1	0	0	2	0	7	0	0	1	0	1.000	0	0- -	-	0.31	0.00
2007	Portlnd	AAA	24	0	0	22	24.2	104	23	9	9	3	0	0	0	10	1	27	0	0	1	1	.500	0	14- -	-	3.85	3.28
2008	Tucsn	AAA	29	0	0	25	36.1	159	39	22	18	5	1	2	0	14	1	28	4	0	2	2	.500	0	9- -	-	4.65	4.46
2009	Reno	AAA	17	0	0	8	19.1	77	12	3	3	1	2	0	1	8	0	12	3	0	2	1	.667	0	3- -	-	2.09	1.40
2008	Ari	NL	27	0	0	6	30.0	136	32	15	14	2	1	1	1	15	3	18	2	0	1	1	.500	0	0-1	1	4.51	4.20
2009	Ari	NL	33	0	0	8	45.1	186	40	24	24	5	1	4	0	12	2	31	3	0	2	1	.667	0	0-0	2	2.91	4.76
	2 ML YEARS		60	0	0	14	75.1	322	72	39	38	7	2	5	1	27	5	49	5	0	3	2	.600	0	0-1	3	3.54	4.54

Cody Ross

Bats: R **Throws:** L **Pos:** CF-103; RF-58; PH-1   **Ht:** 5'10" **Wt:** 194 **Born:** 12/20/1980 **Age:** 29

Year	Team	Lg	G	AB	H	2B	3B	HR	(Hm	Rd)	TB	R	RBI	RC	TBB	IBB	SO	HBP	SH	SF	SB	CS	SB%	GDP	Avg	OBP	Slg
2003	Det	AL	6	19	4	1	0	1	(1	0)	8	1	5	4	1	0	3	1	1	0	0	0	-	0	.211	.286	.421
2005	LAD	NL	14	25	4	1	0	0	(0	0)	5	1	1	0	1	0	10	0	0	0	0	0	-	0	.160	.192	.200
2006	3 Tms	NL	101	269	61	12	2	13	(6	7)	116	34	46	36	22	0	65	4	1	2	1	1	.50	8	.227	.293	.431
2007	Fla	NL	66	173	58	19	0	12	(8	4)	113	35	39	42	20	3	38	3	0	1	2	0	1.00	2	.335	.411	.653
2008	Fla	NL	145	461	120	29	5	22	(7	15)	225	59	73	68	33	2	116	7	0	5	6	1	.86	5	.260	.316	.488
2009	Fla	NL	151	559	151	37	1	24	(13	11)	262	73	90	75	34	1	122	9	0	2	5	2	.71	18	.270	.321	.469

							BATTING										BASERUNNING				AVERAGES		
Year	Team	Lg	G	AB	H	2B	3B	HR	(Hm | Rd)	TB	R	RBI	RC	TBB	IBB	SO	HBP	SH	SF	SB	CS	SB%	GDP	Avg	OBP	Slg
06	LAD	NL	8	14	7	1	1	2	(0 | 2)	16	4	9	6	0	0	2	0	0	0	1	0	1.00	0	.500	.500	1.143
06	Cin	NL	2	5	1	0	0	0	(0 | 0)	1	0	0	1	0	0	2	0	0	0	0	0	-	0	.200	.200	.200
06	Fla	NL	91	250	53	11	1	11	(6 | 5)	99	30	37	29	22	0	61	4	1	2	0	1	.00	8	.212	.284	.396
	6 ML YEARS		483	1506	398	99	8	72	(35 | 37)	729	203	254	225	111	6	354	24	2	10	14	4	.78	34	.264	.323	.484

David Ross

Bats: R Throws: R Pos: C-52; PH-3; PR-2   Ht: 6'2" Wt: 238 Born: 3/19/1977 Age: 33

							BATTING										BASERUNNING				AVERAGES		
Year	Team	Lg	G	AB	H	2B	3B	HR	(Hm | Rd)	TB	R	RBI	RC	TBB	IBB	SO	HBP	SH	SF	SB	CS	SB%	GDP	Avg	OBP	Slg
2009	Rome*	A	2	6	3	0	0	1	(- | -)	6	1	4	2	1	0	1	0	0	0	0	0	-	0	.500	.571	1.000
2002	LAD	NL	8	10	2	1	0	1	(0 | 1)	6	2	2	2	2	0	4	1	0	0	0	0	-	0	.200	.385	.600
2003	LAD	NL	40	124	32	7	0	10	(5 | 5)	69	19	18	18	13	0	42	2	0	1	0	0	-	4	.258	.336	.556
2004	LAD	NL	70	165	28	3	1	5	(2 | 3)	48	13	15	11	15	1	62	5	0	5	0	0	-	3	.170	.253	.291
2005	2 Tms	NL	51	125	30	8	1	3	(2 | 1)	49	11	15	13	6	0	28	2	2	3	0	0	-	3	.240	.279	.392
2006	Cin	NL	90	247	63	15	1	21	(13 | 8)	143	37	52	43	37	7	75	3	4	5	0	0	-	4	.255	.353	.579
2007	Cin	NL	112	311	63	10	0	17	(12 | 5)	124	32	39	27	30	4	92	0	5	2	0	0	-	9	.203	.271	.399
2008	2 Tms	NL	60	142	32	9	0	3	(1 | 2)	50	18	13	19	32	4	39	1	6	1	0	1	.00	3	.225	.369	.352
2009	Atl	NL	54	128	35	9	0	7	(2 | 5)	65	18	20	20	21	0	39	1	1	0	0	0	-	1	.273	.380	.508
05	Pit	NL	40	108	24	8	0	3	(2 | 1)	41	9	15	9	6	0	24	1	1	3	0	0	-	3	.222	.263	.380
05	SD	NL	11	17	6	0	1	0	(0 | 0)	8	2	0	4	0	0	4	1	1	0	0	0	-	0	.353	.389	.471
08	Cin	NL	52	134	31	9	0	3	(1 | 2)	49	17	13	19	32	4	36	1	5	1	0	1	.00	3	.231	.381	.366
08	Bos	AL	8	8	1	0	0	0	(0 | 0)	1	1	0	0	0	0	3	0	1	0	0	0	-	0	.125	.125	.125
	Postseason		3	3	0	0	0	0	(0 | 0)	0	0	0	0	1	0	0	0	0	0	0	0	-	0	.000	.250	.000
	8 ML YEARS		485	1252	285	62	3	67	(37 | 30)	554	150	174	153	156	16	381	15	18	17	0	1	.00	27	.228	.317	.442

Aaron Rowand

Bats: R Throws: R Pos: CF-137; PH-9   Ht: 6'0" Wt: 219 Born: 8/29/1977 Age: 32

							BATTING										BASERUNNING				AVERAGES		
Year	Team	Lg	G	AB	H	2B	3B	HR	(Hm | Rd)	TB	R	RBI	RC	TBB	IBB	SO	HBP	SH	SF	SB	CS	SB%	GDP	Avg	OBP	Slg
2001	CWS	AL	63	123	36	5	0	4	(3 | 1)	53	21	20	22	15	0	28	4	5	1	5	1	.83	2	.293	.385	.431
2002	CWS	AL	126	302	78	16	2	7	(5 | 2)	119	41	29	37	12	1	54	6	8	2	0	1	.00	8	.258	.291	.394
2003	CWS	AL	90	157	45	8	0	6	(5 | 1)	71	22	24	20	7	0	21	3	2	1	0	0	-	1	.287	.327	.452
2004	CWS	AL	140	487	151	38	2	24	(12 | 12)	265	94	69	92	30	1	91	10	5	2	17	5	.77	5	.310	.361	.544
2005	CWS	AL	157	578	156	30	5	13	(8 | 5)	235	77	69	78	32	3	116	21	5	4	16	5	.76	17	.270	.329	.407
2006	Phi	NL	109	405	106	24	3	12	(6 | 6)	172	59	47	47	18	2	76	18	2	2	10	4	.71	13	.262	.321	.425
2007	Phi	NL	161	612	189	45	0	27	(17 | 10)	315	105	89	100	47	3	119	19	2	4	6	3	.67	18	.309	.374	.515
2008	SF	NL	152	549	149	37	0	13	(6 | 7)	225	57	70	67	44	7	126	14	0	4	2	4	.33	21	.271	.339	.410
2009	SF	NL	144	499	130	30	2	15	(5 | 10)	209	61	64	63	30	2	125	14	0	3	4	1	.80	12	.261	.319	.419
	Postseason		15	57	13	6	0	1	(1 | 0)	22	9	4	3	4	1	13	1	0	1	1	0	1.00	3	.228	.286	.386
	9 ML YEARS		1145	3712	1040	233	14	121	(67 | 54)	1664	537	481	534	235	19	756	109	30	23	60	24	.71	97	.280	.339	.448

Ryan Rowland-Smith

Pitches: L Bats: L Pos: SP-15   Ht: 6'3" Wt: 240 Born: 1/26/1983 Age: 27

			HOW MUCH HE PITCHED						WHAT HE GAVE UP									THE RESULTS						
Year	Team	Lg	G	GS	CG	GF	IP	BFP	H	R	ER	HR	SH	SF	HB	TBB	IBB	SO	WP	Bk	W	L	Pct	Sh	Sv-Op	Hld	ERC	ERA
2009	Tacom*	AAA	10	10	0	0	56.1	238	61	28	27	5	2	3	3	10	0	38	1	1	5	3	.625	0	0-0	3	3.79	4.31
2007	Sea	AL	26	0	0	6	38.2	168	39	19	17	4	1	4	2	15	1	42	0	0	1	0	1.000	0	0-0	3	4.27	3.96
2008	Sea	AL	47	12	0	9	118.1	506	114	49	45	13	2	3	2	48	0	77	2	1	5	3	.625	0	2-3	1	4.05	3.42
2009	Sea	AL	15	15	0	0	96.1	401	87	43	40	9	1	5	4	27	0	52	2	1	5	4	.556	0	0-0	0	3.19	3.74
	3 ML YEARS		88	27	0	15	253.1	1075	240	111	102	26	4	12	8	90	1	171	4	2	11	7	.611	0	2-3	4	3.75	3.62

Carlos Ruiz

Bats: R Throws: R Pos: C-107; PH-3; PR-1   Ht: 5'10" Wt: 204 Born: 1/22/1979 Age: 31

							BATTING										BASERUNNING				AVERAGES		
Year	Team	Lg	G	AB	H	2B	3B	HR	(Hm | Rd)	TB	R	RBI	RC	TBB	IBB	SO	HBP	SH	SF	SB	CS	SB%	GDP	Avg	OBP	Slg
2009	LV*	AAA	4	13	3	1	0	0	(- | -)	4	1	2	1	3	0	2	0	0	0	0	0	-	0	.231	.375	.308
2006	Phi	NL	27	69	18	1	1	3	(2 | 1)	30	5	10	10	5	2	8	1	2	1	0	0	-	3	.261	.316	.435
2007	Phi	NL	115	374	97	29	2	6	(4 | 2)	148	42	54	49	42	10	49	5	5	3	6	1	.86	17	.259	.340	.396
2008	Phi	NL	117	320	70	14	0	4	(2 | 2)	96	47	31	20	44	6	38	4	4	1	1	2	.33	14	.219	.320	.300
2009	Phi	NL	107	322	82	26	1	9	(5 | 4)	137	32	43	49	47	8	39	4	4	2	3	2	.60	8	.255	.355	.425
	Postseason		17	55	15	4	0	1	(1 | 0)	22	7	4	7	7	0	2	0	0	0	2	0	1.00	1	.273	.355	.400
	4 ML YEARS		366	1085	267	70	4	22	(13 | 9)	411	126	138	136	138	26	134	14	15	7	10	5	.67	42	.246	.337	.379

Randy Ruiz

Bats: R Throws: R Pos: DH-30; 1B-3; PR-1   Ht: 6'3" Wt: 250 Born: 10/19/1977 Age: 32

							BATTING										BASERUNNING				AVERAGES		
Year	Team	Lg	G	AB	H	2B	3B	HR	(Hm | Rd)	TB	R	RBI	RC	TBB	IBB	SO	HBP	SH	SF	SB	CS	SB%	GDP	Avg	OBP	Slg
1999	Reds	R	33	102	29	8	0	3	(- | -)	46	12	9	18	12	0	33	4	0	1	5	2	.71	5	.284	.378	.451
1999	Clinton	A	2	8	5	2	0	0	(- | -)	7	3	2	3	1	0	0	0	0	1	0	0	-	1	.625	.667	.875
2000	Billings	R+	61	231	88	15	1	10	(- | -)	135	55	55	60	29	0	56	10	1	2	1	2	.33	6	.381	.467	.584
2001	Dayton	A	123	466	125	34	3	20	(- | -)	225	82	92	82	48	4	116	14	0	3	21	9	.70	10	.268	.352	.483
2002	Stcktn	A+	28	100	26	9	0	3	(- | -)	44	16	17	15	13	0	29	2	0	0	3	3	.50	4	.260	.357	.440
2002	Dayton	A	78	285	86	17	4	8	(- | -)	135	47	49	55	36	1	88	8	0	4	9	3	.75	8	.302	.390	.474
2003	Frdrck	A+	17	68	17	4	1	1	(- | -)	26	7	8	7	4	0	24	1	0	0	0	1	-	1	.250	.301	.382
2003	Dlmrva	A	67	239	74	18	2	11	(- | -)	129	33	51	50	29	1	70	5	0	3	3	3	.50	4	.310	.391	.540

				BATTING																		BASERUNNING				AVERAGES		
Year	Team	Lg	G	AB	H	2B	3B	HR	(Hm	Rd)	TB	R	RBI	RC	TBB	IBB	SO	HBP	SH	SF	SB	CS	SB%	GDP	Avg	OBP	Slg
2004	Lakwd	A	110	417	120	31	2	17	(-	-)	206	85	91	77	42	0	140	13	0	5	1	1	.50	10	.288	.367	.494
2005	Rdng	AA	89	345	122	29	0	27	(-	-)	232	59	89	88	30	11	85	6	0	5	0	2	.00	6	.354	.409	.672
2006	Wichta	AA	6	23	5	1	0	2	(-	-)	12	3	3	4	6	0	8	0	0	0	0	0	-	0	.217	.379	.522
2006	Trntn	AA	119	468	134	35	1	26	(-	-)	249	72	87	90	41	6	132	15	0	2	2	0	1.00	12	.286	.361	.532
2007	Altna	AA	47	162	47	9	1	7	(-	-)	79	20	30	29	18	1	32	2	0	3	0	1	.00	2	.290	.362	.488
2007	Rdng	AA	22	82	31	10	0	3	(-	-)	50	16	12	19	6	0	21	1	0	0	1	0	1.00	1	.378	.427	.610
2007	Ottawa	AAA	22	79	17	4	0	4	(-	-)	33	11	11	10	9	0	23	0	0	0	0	0	-	3	.215	.295	.418
2007	Conn	AA	39	151	44	6	3	8	(-	-)	80	25	27	27	11	1	40	3	0	0	0	0	-	2	.291	.352	.530
2008	Roch	AAA	111	416	133	33	3	17	(-	-)	223	58	68	80	23	1	115	11	0	6	1	2	.33	10	.320	.366	.536
2009	LsVgs	AAA	114	462	148	43	2	25	(-	-)	270	81	106	103	47	5	99	9	0	3	0	0	-	14	.320	.392	.584
2008	Min	AL	22	62	17	2	0	1	(0	1)	22	13	7	11	6	1	21	0	0	0	0	0	-	1	.274	.338	.355
2009	Tor	AL	33	115	36	7	0	10	(3	7)	73	25	17	18	10	0	35	4	0	1	1	1	.50	6	.313	.385	.635
	2 ML YEARS		55	177	53	9	0	11	(3	8)	95	38	24	29	16	1	56	4	0	1	1	1	.50	7	.299	.369	.537

Rich Rundles

Pitches: L **Bats:** L **Pos:** RP-1   **Ht:** 6'5" **Wt:** 210 **Born:** 6/3/1981 **Age:** 29

				HOW MUCH HE PITCHED					WHAT HE GAVE UP												THE RESULTS						
Year	Team	Lg	G	GS	CG	GF	IP	BFP	H	R	ER	HR	SH	SF	HB	TBB	IBB	SO	WP	Bk	W	L	Pct	Sh	Sv-Op	Hld	ERC	ERA
1999	RedSx	R	5	1	0	0	12.2	53	13	3	3	1	0	1	0	1	0	11	2	0	1	0	1.000	0	0- -		2.73	2.13
2000	RedSx	R	9	6	0	0	40.1	158	31	15	11	3	2	0	4	10	0	32	0	1	3	1	.750	0	0- -		2.60	2.45
2001	Augsta	A	19	19	0	0	115.0	468	109	46	31	5	5	5	7	10	0	94	4	0	7	6	.538	0	0- -		2.46	2.43
2001	Clinton	A	4	4	0	0	27.0	112	26	10	7	0	0	1	3	3	1	20	1	0	1	1	.500	0	0- -		2.47	2.33
2002	BrvdCt	A+	12	11	0	0	57.1	243	66	34	26	5	1	1	2	16	1	31	2	0	2	7	.222	0	0- -		4.62	4.08
2003	BrvdCt	A+	19	19	2	0	106.2	446	111	44	35	2	4	2	2	24	0	76	4	1	5	6	.455	1	0- -		3.16	2.95
2004	Hrsbrg	AA	20	20	0	0	102.2	441	107	50	39	7	3	5	8	35	2	65	8	0	3	6	.333	0	0- -		4.20	3.42
2004	BrvdCt	A+	1	1	0	0	3.0	13	4	2	2	0	0	0	0	2	0	0	0	0	1	0	1.000	0	0- -		7.18	6.00
2005	Hrsbrg	AA	27	26	2	0	159.1	695	177	95	73	14	6	2	6	49	1	91	5	0	6	13	.316	0	0- -		4.38	4.12
2006	Sprgfld	AA	15	14	1	0	86.0	379	100	52	44	9	1	4	4	28	0	47	3	0	5	6	.455	0	0- -		4.97	4.60
2006	Bnghtn	AA	12	7	0	2	43.1	206	53	32	22	4	4	1	4	23	1	23	1	0	1	3	.250	0	0- -		6.18	4.57
2006	StLuci	A+	3	3	0	0	19.2	86	27	8	4	2	0	0	1	6	0	9	0	0	2	2	.333	0	0- -		6.25	1.83
2007	Akron	AA	23	2	0	6	34.1	140	27	10	7	0	1	0	4	10	0	29	0	0	3	0	1.000	0	2- -		2.36	1.83
2007	Buffalo	AAA	17	0	0	8	26.2	131	28	15	8	1	1	1	5	16	3	19	2	0	2	4	.333	0	0- -		4.97	2.70
2008	Buffalo	AAA	55	0	0	22	52.2	221	40	18	17	3	1	0	1	24	1	60	1	0	5	4	.556	0	4- -		2.73	2.91
2009	Clmbs	AAA	45	0	0	14	41.2	194	54	29	22	3	1	1	2	17	0	36	0	0	2	2	.500	0	1- -		5.80	4.75
2008	Cle	AL	8	0	0	0	5.0	22	5	1	1	0	0	0	0	3	0	6	0	0	0	0	-	0	0-0	1	4.20	1.80
2009	Cle	AL	1	0	0	0	1.0	6	1	1	1	0	0	0	1	1	0	1	0	0	0	0	-	0	0-0	0	9.51	0.00
	2 ML YEARS		9	0	0	0	6.0	28	6	1	1	0	0	0	1	4	0	7	0	0	0	0	-	0	0-0	1	5.04	1.50

Dan Runzler

Pitches: L **Bats:** L **Pos:** RP-11   **Ht:** 6'4" **Wt:** 230 **Born:** 3/30/1985 **Age:** 25

				HOW MUCH HE PITCHED					WHAT HE GAVE UP												THE RESULTS						
Year	Team	Lg	G	GS	CG	GF	IP	BFP	H	R	ER	HR	SH	SF	HB	TBB	IBB	SO	WP	Bk	W	L	Pct	Sh	Sv-Op	Hld	ERC	ERA
2007	Giants	R	15	0	0	9	18.1	77	15	8	7	1	4	1	4	6	0	24	4	0	1	2	.333	0	4- -		3.39	3.44
2007	SlmKzr	A-	1	0	0	0	1.0	7	2	1	1	0	0	0	0	2	0	1	0	0	0	0	-	0	0- -		16.69	9.00
2008	Augsta	A	20	0	0	10	24.2	117	25	18	15	2	2	1	2	19	1	26	3	2	0	1	.000	0	0- -		5.75	5.47
2008	SlmKzr	A-	27	0	0	2	30.0	127	19	8	7	1	2	0	1	21	0	43	4	0	0	1	.000	0	0- -		2.93	2.10
2009	Augsta	A	19	0	0	17	26.1	103	8	2	2	0	0	0	4	13	0	45	5	0	1	1	.500	0	11- -		1.15	0.68
2009	SnJos	A+	19	0	0	12	21.1	81	8	3	2	1	0	0	0	4	0	26	0	0	1	0	1.000	0	5- -		0.64	0.84
2009	Conn	AA	7	0	0	3	9.1	40	5	1	1	1	2	1	1	7	1	11	0	0	3	0	1.000	0	1- -		3.18	0.96
2009	Fresno	AAA	2	0	0	0	2.0	7	2	0	0	0	0	0	0	0	0	1	0	0	0	0	-	0	0- -		2.31	0.00
2009	SF	NL	11	0	0	0	8.2	38	6	1	1	1	0	0	1	5	0	11	0	0	0	0	-	0	0-0	2	3.54	1.04

Josh Rupe

Pitches: R **Bats:** R **Pos:** RP-4   **Ht:** 6'2" **Wt:** 210 **Born:** 8/18/1982 **Age:** 27

				HOW MUCH HE PITCHED					WHAT HE GAVE UP												THE RESULTS						
Year	Team	Lg	G	GS	CG	GF	IP	BFP	H	R	ER	HR	SH	SF	HB	TBB	IBB	SO	WP	Bk	W	L	Pct	Sh	Sv-Op	Hld	ERC	ERA
2009	Okla*	AAA	24	14	0	6	89.0	415	115	75	66	5	5	6	6	41	1	62	8	0	5	7	.417	0	1- -		6.01	6.67
2005	Tex	AL	4	1	0	1	9.2	39	7	4	3	0	1	0	2	4	0	6	1	0	1	0	1.000	0	0-0	0	2.91	2.79
2006	Tex	AL	16	0	0	3	29.0	126	33	11	11	2	1	0	1	9	0	14	2	0	0	1	.000	0	0-1	1	4.45	3.41
2008	Tex	AL	46	0	0	10	89.1	392	93	52	51	8	2	7	10	46	3	53	3	0	3	1	.750	0	0-2	2	5.30	5.14
2009	Tex	AL	4	0	0	2	4.2	31	12	8	8	2	0	0	0	5	0	2	0	0	0	0	-	0	0-0	0	21.74	15.43
	4 ML YEARS		70	1	0	16	132.2	588	145	75	73	12	4	7	13	64	3	75	6	0	4	2	.667	0	0-3	3	5.40	4.95

Glendon Rusch

Pitches: L **Bats:** L **Pos:** RP-11   **Ht:** 6'1" **Wt:** 225 **Born:** 11/7/1974 **Age:** 35

				HOW MUCH HE PITCHED					WHAT HE GAVE UP												THE RESULTS						
Year	Team	Lg	G	GS	CG	GF	IP	BFP	H	R	ER	HR	SH	SF	HB	TBB	IBB	SO	WP	Bk	W	L	Pct	Sh	Sv-Op	Hld	ERC	ERA
1997	KC	AL	30	27	1	0	170.1	758	206	111	104	28	8	7	7	52	0	116	0	1	6	9	.400	0	0-0	0	5.56	5.50
1998	KC	AL	29	24	1	2	154.2	686	191	104	101	22	1	2	4	50	0	94	1	0	6	15	.286	1	1-1	0	5.62	5.88
1999	2 Tms		4	0	0	2	5.0	26	8	7	7	1	0	0	1	3	0	4	0	0	1	0	.000	0	0-0	0	10.75	12.60
2000	NYM	NL	31	30	2	0	190.2	802	196	91	85	18	10	7	6	44	2	157	2	0	11	11	.500	0	0-0	0	3.64	4.01
2001	NYM	NL	33	33	1	0	179.0	785	216	101	92	23	11	5	7	43	2	156	3	2	8	12	.400	0	0-0	0	4.97	4.63
2002	Mil	NL	34	34	4	0	210.2	913	227	118	110	30	14	5	5	76	1	140	6	0	10	16	.385	1	0-0	0	4.80	4.70
2003	Mil	NL	32	19	1	1	123.1	573	171	93	88	11	5	2	4	45	3	93	3	0	1	12	.077	0	1-1	7	6.27	6.42
2004	ChC	NL	32	16	0	5	129.2	545	127	54	50	10	8	2	4	33	1	90	1	1	6	2	.750	0	2-2	3	3.33	3.47
2005	ChC	NL	46	19	0	5	145.1	655	175	79	73	14	13	9	1	53	8	111	1	1	9	8	.529	1	0-1	3	4.97	4.52
2006	ChC	NL	25	9	0	5	66.1	311	86	57	55	21	7	1	1	33	2	59	0	0	3	8	.273	0	0-0	0	8.09	7.46

HOW MUCH HE PITCHED								WHAT HE GAVE UP												THE RESULTS							
Year	Team	Lg	G	GS	CG	GF	IP	BFP	H	R	ER	HR	SH	SF	HB	TBB	IBB	SO	WP	Bk	W	L	Pct	Sh	Sv-Op	Hld	ERC	ERA
2008	2 Tms	NL	35	9	0	9	83.2	367	94	50	48	10	5	5	0	25	7	55	2	0	5	5	.500	0	0-1	1	4.31	5.16
2009	Col	NL	11	0	0	1	18.2	92	35	15	14	3	1	0	0	3	1	13	0	0	2	0	1.000	0	0-0	1	8.91	6.75
99	KC	AL	3	0	0	1	4.0	23	7	7	7	1	0	0	1	3	0	4	0	0	0	1	.000	0	0-0	0	12.89	15.75
99	NYM	NL	1	0	0	1	1.0	3	1	0	0	0	0	0	0	0	0	0	0	0	0	0	-	0	0-0	0	2.79	0.00
08	SD	NL	12	0	0	6	19.2	92	22	15	14	2	1	1	0	11	4	12	1	0	1	2	.333	0	0-0	0	4.92	6.41
08	Col	NL	23	9	0	3	64.0	275	72	35	34	8	4	4	0	14	3	43	1	0	4	3	.571	0	0-1	1	4.11	4.78
	Postseason		6	0	0	1	8.1	35	9	1	1	0	0	1	1	2	1	7	2	0	1	0	1.000	0	0-0	0	3.58	1.08
	12 ML YEARS		342	220	11	31	1477.1	6513	1732	880	827	191	83	45	40	460	27	1088	19	5	67	99	.404	3	4-6	15	5.01	5.04

Adam Russell

Pitches: R Bats: R Pos: RP-15   Ht: 6'8" Wt: 255 Born: 4/14/1983 Age: 27

HOW MUCH HE PITCHED								WHAT HE GAVE UP												THE RESULTS							
Year	Team	Lg	G	GS	CG	GF	IP	BFP	H	R	ER	HR	SH	SF	HB	TBB	IBB	SO	WP	Bk	W	L	Pct	Sh	Sv-Op	Hld	ERC	ERA
2004	Gr Falls	R+	15	4	0	2	38.0	158	31	11	10	2	3	1	0	18	0	33	0	0	4	0	1.000	0	0--	-	3.08	2.37
2004	Knapol	A-	2	2	0	0	10.0	52	18	11	10	3	0	0	1	7	0	3	1	0	0	2	.000	0	0--	-	13.80	9.00
2005	Knapol	A-	24	24	0	0	126.1	542	116	61	53	10	4	5	6	55	0	82	5	0	9	7	.563	0	0--	-	3.82	3.78
2006	WinSa	A+	17	17	0	0	94.2	393	80	35	28	5	4	2	7	39	0	61	4	0	7	3	.700	0	0--	-	3.32	2.66
2006	Brham	AA	10	10	0	0	55.0	242	59	33	29	5	0	1	3	19	0	47	3	1	3	3	.500	0	0--	-	4.39	4.75
2007	Brham	AA	38	20	0	1	138.2	622	158	81	73	8	7	2	6	58	0	95	4	0	9	11	.450	0	1--	-	4.81	4.74
2008	Charltt	AAA	25	0	0	0	37.1	160	28	13	12	3	1	1	1	19	0	28	2	0	3	2	.600	0	0--	-	3.04	2.89
2009	Charltt	AAA	34	0	0	16	56.1	221	39	20	20	5	3	2	3	18	1	51	2	0	2	2	.500	0	5--	-	2.35	3.20
2009	Portlnd	AAA	9	0	0	7	12.0	52	12	7	7	1	0	0	0	6	0	7	1	0	0	0	-	0	4--	-	4.43	5.25
2008	CWS	AL	22	0	0	16	26.0	118	30	15	15	1	2	1	2	10	1	22	3	0	4	0	1.000	0	0-0	4	4.63	5.19
2009	SD	NL	15	0	0	1	12.1	61	13	6	5	0	0	0	0	11	0	14	0	0	3	1	.750	0	0-0	4	5.38	3.65
	2 ML YEARS		37	0	0	17	38.1	179	43	21	20	1	2	1	2	21	1	36	3	0	7	1	.875	0	0-0	4	4.88	4.70

Rusty Ryal

Bats: R Throws: R Pos: PH-14; 2B-13; 1B-10; PR-1   Ht: 6'2" Wt: 200 Born: 3/16/1983 Age: 27

BATTING																					BASERUNNING				AVERAGES		
Year	Team	Lg	G	AB	H	2B	3B	HR	(Hm	Rd)	TB	R	RBI	RC	TBB	IBB	SO	HBP	SH	SF	SB	CS	SB%	GDP	Avg	OBP	Slg
2005	Msoula	R+	72	294	98	22	4	6	(-	-)	146	59	46	58	14	1	47	15	1	2	11	3	.79	7	.333	.391	.497
2006	Lancst	A+	97	350	97	17	6	11	(-	-)	159	53	42	64	23	1	70	12	1	1	8	8	.50	15	.277	.342	.454
2007	Visalia	A+	70	276	83	15	3	11	(-	-)	137	46	46	47	16	0	47	8	0	2	2	4	.33	8	.301	.354	.496
2007	Mobile	AA	47	168	40	6	2	6	(-	-)	68	18	21	22	8	1	42	5	5	1	4	3	.57	4	.238	.291	.405
2008	Mobile	AA	128	460	126	22	4	16	(-	-)	204	65	66	70	35	2	96	9	0	5	4	4	.50	8	.274	.334	.443
2009	Reno	AAA	103	404	117	33	6	17	(-	-)	213	65	70	74	33	0	94	4	2	3	5	3	.63	13	.290	.347	.527
2009	Ari	NL	30	59	16	6	2	3	(2	1)	35	11	9	10	6	1	21	2	0	1	0	0	-	0	.271	.353	.593

B.J. Ryan

Pitches: L Bats: L Pos: RP-25   Ht: 6'6" Wt: 255 Born: 12/28/1975 Age: 34

HOW MUCH HE PITCHED								WHAT HE GAVE UP												THE RESULTS							
Year	Team	Lg	G	GS	CG	GF	IP	BFP	H	R	ER	HR	SH	SF	HB	TBB	IBB	SO	WP	Bk	W	L	Pct	Sh	Sv-Op	Hld	ERC	ERA
2009	Dnedin*	A+	3	0	0	0	3.0	11	1	1	1	0	0	1	0	1	0	2	0	0	0	1	.000	0	0--	-	0.69	3.00
2009	Iowa*	AAA	5	0	0	0	5.2	21	0	0	0	0	1	0	1	5	0	4	0	0	0	0	-	0	0--	-	1.14	0.00
1999	2 Tms		14	0	0	3	20.1	82	13	7	7	0	0	1	0	13	1	29	1	0	1	0	1.000	0	0-0	0	2.42	3.10
2000	Bal	AL	42	0	0	9	42.2	193	36	29	28	7	1	1	0	31	1	41	2	1	2	3	.400	0	0-3	7	4.87	5.91
2001	Bal	AL	61	0	0	9	53.0	237	47	31	25	6	1	2	2	30	4	54	0	0	2	4	.333	0	2-4	14	4.13	4.25
2002	Bal	AL	67	0	0	13	57.2	252	51	31	30	7	3	0	4	33	4	56	4	0	2	1	.667	0	1-2	12	4.48	4.68
2003	Bal	AL	76	0	0	17	50.1	219	42	19	19	1	1	3	3	27	0	63	2	0	4	1	.800	0	0-2	19	3.33	3.40
2004	Bal	AL	76	0	0	19	87.0	361	64	24	22	4	3	2	1	35	9	122	0	0	4	6	.400	0	3-7	21	2.20	2.28
2005	Bal	AL	69	0	0	61	70.1	290	54	20	19	4	1	1	2	26	2	100	5	0	1	4	.200	0	36-41	0	2.50	2.43
2006	Tor	AL	65	0	0	57	72.1	270	42	12	11	3	1	1	0	20	1	86	4	0	2	2	.500	0	38-42	1	1.39	1.37
2007	Tor	AL	5	0	0	4	4.1	25	7	7	6	1	0	0	0	4	0	3	0	0	0	2	.000	0	3-5	0	10.86	12.46
2008	Tor	AL	60	0	0	48	58.0	249	46	21	19	4	2	1	4	28	3	58	2	1	2	4	.333	0	32-36	1	3.20	2.95
2009	Tor	AL	25	0	0	9	20.2	95	22	15	15	5	1	1	1	17	2	13	1	0	1	1	.500	0	2-4	2	7.83	6.53
99	Cin	NL	1	0	0	0	2.0	9	4	1	1	0	0	0	0	1	0	1	0	0	0	0	-	0	0-0	0	12.01	4.50
99	Bal	AL	13	0	0	3	18.1	73	9	6	6	0	0	1	0	12	1	28	1	0	1	0	1.000	0	0-0	0	1.73	2.95
	11 ML YEARS		560	0	0	249	536.2	2273	424	216	201	42	14	13	17	264	27	625	21	2	21	28	.429	0	117-146	77	3.18	3.37

Brendan Ryan

Bats: R Throws: R Pos: SS-105; 2B-19; PH-12; PR-2   Ht: 6'2" Wt: 195 Born: 3/26/1982 Age: 28

BATTING																					BASERUNNING				AVERAGES		
Year	Team	Lg	G	AB	H	2B	3B	HR	(Hm	Rd)	TB	R	RBI	RC	TBB	IBB	SO	HBP	SH	SF	SB	CS	SB%	GDP	Avg	OBP	Slg
2009	Memp*	AAA	3	11	0	0	0	0	(-	-)	0	0	0	0	0	0	5	0	0	0	0	0	-	0	.000	.000	.000
2007	StL	NL	67	180	52	9	0	4	(2	2)	73	30	12	21	15	0	19	1	3	0	7	0	1.00	3	.289	.347	.406
2008	StL	NL	80	197	48	9	0	0	(0	0)	57	30	10	12	16	0	31	2	0	3	7	2	.78	4	.244	.307	.289
2009	StL	NL	129	390	114	19	7	3	(1	2)	156	55	37	48	24	3	56	6	6	3	14	7	.67	9	.292	.340	.400
	3 ML YEARS		276	767	214	37	7	7	(3	4)	286	115	59	81	55	3	106	9	12	3	28	9	.76	16	.279	.333	.373

243

Dusty Ryan

Bats: R **Throws:** R **Pos:** C-12; PH-1 **Ht:** 6'4" **Wt:** 220 **Born:** 9/2/1984 **Age:** 25

									BATTING													BASERUNNING					AVERAGES		
Year	Team	Lg	G	AB	H	2B	3B	HR	(Hm	Rd)	TB	R	RBI	RC	TBB	IBB	SO	HBP	SH	SF		SB	CS	SB%	GDP		Avg	OBP	Slg
2004	Oneont	A-	54	157	43	11	1	4	(-	-)	68	20	26	26	24	0	52	2	2	4		6	4	.60	1		.274	.369	.433
2005	WMich	A	75	241	44	11	0	4	(-	-)	67	21	21	16	22	0	70	2	4	2		3	3	.50	6		.183	.255	.278
2006	WMich	A	98	322	79	13	2	6	(-	-)	114	49	35	42	44	2	102	5	3	1		3	4	.43	6		.245	.344	.354
2007	Lkland	A+	46	145	31	0	0	7	(-	-)	52	17	22	17	18	0	52	3	0	2		0	1	.00	5		.214	.310	.359
2007	Tigers	R	6	16	1	0	0	0	(-	-)	1	1	1	0	4	0	5	0	0	0		0	0	-	2		.063	.250	.063
2008	Erie	AA	82	296	75	17	2	15	(-	-)	141	46	50	49	38	1	95	2	0	2		2	1	.67	6		.253	.340	.476
2008	Toledo	AAA	20	73	23	7	2	2	(-	-)	40	12	13	14	6	0	27	1	0	1		0	0	-	2		.315	.370	.548
2009	Toledo	AAA	63	202	52	8	1	10	(-	-)	92	25	35	34	29	0	64	3	1	0		2	0	1.00	4		.257	.359	.455
2008	Det	AL	15	44	14	2	0	2	(1	1)	22	6	7	9	5	0	13	0	0	1		0	0	-	0		.318	.380	.500
2009	Det	AL	12	26	4	1	0	0	(0	0)	5	1	4	2	4	0	12	0	0	0		0	1	.00	2		.154	.267	.192
	2 ML YEARS		27	70	18	3	0	2	(1	1)	27	7	11	11	9	0	25	0	0	1		0	1	.00	2		.257	.338	.386

Marc Rzepczynski

Pitches: L **Bats:** L **Pos:** SP-11 **Ht:** 6'3" **Wt:** 205 **Born:** 8/29/1985 **Age:** 24

			HOW MUCH HE PITCHED						WHAT HE GAVE UP										THE RESULTS						
Year	Team	Lg	G	GS	CG	GF	IP	BFP	H	R	ER	HR	SH	SF	HB	TBB	IBB	SO	WP	Bk	W	L	Pct	Sh	Sv-Op	Hld	ERC	ERA
2007	Auburn	A-	11	7	0	0	45.2	183	33	21	14	2	1	0	1	17	0	49	0	0	5	0	1.000	0	0- -	-	2.29	2.76
2008	Lansng	A	22	22	0	0	121.0	491	100	41	38	2	6	1	8	42	1	124	11	0	7	6	.538	0	0- -	-	2.71	2.83
2009	NHam	AA	14	14	0	0	76.2	344	80	38	25	1	2	1	4	36	1	88	1	0	7	5	.583	0	0- -	-	4.09	2.93
2009	LsVgs	AAA	2	2	0	0	11.1	45	7	1	1	0	0	0	0	4	0	16	1	0	2	0	1.000	0	0- -	-	1.46	0.79
2009	Tor	AL	11	11	0	0	61.1	261	51	27	25	7	2	1	1	30	0	60	4	1	2	4	.333	0	0-0	0	3.65	3.67

CC Sabathia

Pitches: L **Bats:** L **Pos:** SP-34 **Ht:** 6'7" **Wt:** 290 **Born:** 7/21/1980 **Age:** 29

			HOW MUCH HE PITCHED						WHAT HE GAVE UP										THE RESULTS						
Year	Team	Lg	G	GS	CG	GF	IP	BFP	H	R	ER	HR	SH	SF	HB	TBB	IBB	SO	WP	Bk	W	L	Pct	Sh	Sv-Op	Hld	ERC	ERA
2001	Cle	AL	33	33	0	0	180.1	763	149	93	88	19	3	5	7	95	1	171	7	3	17	5	.773	0	0-0	0	3.86	4.39
2002	Cle	AL	33	33	2	0	210.0	891	198	109	102	17	5	10	1	88	2	149	6	3	13	11	.542	0	0-0	0	3.74	4.37
2003	Cle	AL	30	30	2	0	197.2	832	190	85	79	19	10	4	6	66	3	141	4	2	13	9	.591	1	0-0	0	3.70	3.60
2004	Cle	AL	30	30	1	0	188.0	787	176	90	86	20	3	6	7	72	3	139	1	1	11	10	.524	1	0-0	0	3.91	4.12
2005	Cle	AL	31	31	1	0	196.2	823	185	92	88	19	6	3	7	62	1	161	7	0	15	10	.600	0	0-0	0	3.55	4.03
2006	Cle	AL	28	28	6	0	192.2	802	182	83	69	17	8	5	7	44	3	172	3	0	12	11	.522	2	0-0	0	3.13	3.22
2007	Cle	AL	34	34	4	0	241.0	975	238	94	86	20	6	6	8	37	1	209	1	0	19	7	.731	1	0-0	0	3.12	3.21
2008	2 Tms		35	35	10	0	253.0	1023	223	85	76	19	9	6	7	59	1	251	2	2	17	10	.630	5	0-0	0	2.78	2.70
2009	NYY	AL	34	34	2	0	230.0	938	197	96	86	18	4	9	9	67	7	197	5	0	19	8	.704	1	0-0	0	2.89	3.37
	08 Cle	AL	18	18	3	0	122.1	507	117	54	52	13	3	3	3	34	1	123	1	2	6	8	.429	2	0-0	0	3.52	3.83
	08 Mil	NL	17	17	7	0	130.2	516	106	31	24	6	6	3	4	25	0	128	1	0	11	2	.846	3	0-0	0	2.13	1.65
	Postseason		5	5	0	0	25.0	126	33	22	22	4	1	0	3	22	4	24	1	0	2	3	.400	0	0-0	0	9.12	7.92
	9 ML YEARS		288	288	28	0	1889.1	7834	1738	827	760	168	54	54	59	590	22	1590	36	11	136	81	.627	11	0-0	0	3.36	3.62

Billy Sadler

Pitches: R **Bats:** R **Pos:** RP-1 **Ht:** 6'0" **Wt:** 194 **Born:** 9/21/1981 **Age:** 28

			HOW MUCH HE PITCHED						WHAT HE GAVE UP										THE RESULTS						
Year	Team	Lg	G	GS	CG	GF	IP	BFP	H	R	ER	HR	SH	SF	HB	TBB	IBB	SO	WP	Bk	W	L	Pct	Sh	Sv-Op	Hld	ERC	ERA
2009	Fresno	AAA	13	13	0	0	55.2	253	64	34	33	4	4	0	1	29	0	51	2	0	5	3	.625	0	0- -	-	5.33	5.34
2009	Astros*	R	3	1	0	0	5.1	21	2	2	2	0	0	0	1	1	0	12	0	0	0	1	.000	0	0- -	-	0.81	3.38
2009	RdRck*	AAA	3	3	0	0	7.2	32	9	4	3	0	0	0	1	2	0	6	0	0	0	0	-	0	0- -	-	4.60	3.52
2006	SF	NL	5	0	0	2	4.0	20	5	3	3	2	0	0	1	2	0	6	0	0	0	0	-	0	0-0	0	10.38	6.75
2008	SF	NL	33	0	0	8	44.1	197	34	21	20	6	2	2	8	27	4	42	8	0	0	1	.000	0	0-0	1	4.42	4.06
2009	Hou	NL	1	0	0	0	1.1	7	2	2	2	0	0	0	0	1	0	2	0	0	0	0	-	0	0-0	0	7.52	13.50
	3 ML YEARS		39	0	0	10	49.2	224	41	26	25	8	2	2	9	30	4	50	8	0	0	1	.000	0	0-0	1	4.94	4.53

Ryan Sadowski

Pitches: R **Bats:** R **Pos:** SP-6 **Ht:** 6'4" **Wt:** 195 **Born:** 10/4/1982 **Age:** 27

			HOW MUCH HE PITCHED						WHAT HE GAVE UP										THE RESULTS						
Year	Team	Lg	G	GS	CG	GF	IP	BFP	H	R	ER	HR	SH	SF	HB	TBB	IBB	SO	WP	Bk	W	L	Pct	Sh	Sv-Op	Hld	ERC	ERA
2003	SlmKzr	A-	15	3	0	4	31.1	133	22	11	11	2	0	1	2	22	0	26	3	0	1	2	.333	0	0- -	-	3.70	3.16
2004	Hgrstn	A	26	16	0	4	91.0	423	106	84	70	12	7	7	7	45	0	90	13	0	3	9	.250	0	0- -	-	5.97	6.92
2005	SnJos	A+	24	23	0	0	126.0	542	120	70	65	12	0	5	9	42	0	118	15	0	9	6	.600	0	0- -	-	3.76	4.64
2007	Conn	AA	35	3	0	6	68.0	287	56	29	23	3	4	5	2	27	1	50	9	0	4	3	.571	0	1- -	-	2.79	3.04
2008	Conn	AA	9	0	0	0	11.0	55	13	5	4	0	0	3	2	9	2	9	3	0	1	0	1.000	0	0- -	-	6.42	3.27
2008	Fresno	AAA	31	11	0	4	80.2	364	93	47	43	7	1	3	7	33	2	72	10	0	8	4	.667	0	0- -	-	5.24	4.80
2009	Fresno	AAA	18	17	0	0	89.1	394	84	54	50	14	8	5	2	43	1	73	7	0	6	3	.667	0	0- -	-	4.48	5.04
2009	SnJos	A+	1	1	0	0	6.0	24	5	1	0	0	0	0	0	1	0	8	0	0	1	0	1.000	0	0- -	-	1.74	0.00
2009	SF	NL	6	6	0	0	28.1	128	28	15	14	2	1	3	1	17	1	17	2	0	2	4	.333	0	0-0	0	4.65	4.45

Takashi Saito

Pitches: R Bats: R Pos: RP-56   Ht: 6'2" Wt: 214 Born: 2/14/1970 Age: 40

			HOW MUCH HE PITCHED						WHAT HE GAVE UP											THE RESULTS						
Year	Team	Lg	G	GS	CG	GF	IP	RFP	H	R	ER	HR	SH	SF	HB	TBB	IBB	SO	WP	Bk	W	L	Pct	Sh	Sv-Op	Hld	ERC	ERA
2006	LAD	NL	72	0	0	48	78.1	303	48	19	18	3	3	4	2	23	3	107	2	0	6	2	.750	0	24-26	7	1.52	2.07
2007	LAD	NL	63	0	0	55	64.1	234	33	10	10	5	0	3	2	13	0	78	0	0	2	1	.667	0	39-43	1	1.28	1.40
2008	LAD	NL	45	0	0	35	47.0	197	40	14	13	1	0	2	2	16	3	60	1	0	4	4	.500	0	18-22	0	2.57	2.49
2009	Bos	AL	56	0	0	30	55.2	240	50	16	15	6	1	4	5	25	2	52	1	0	3	3	.500	0	2-4	3	4.08	2.43
	Postseason		3	0	0	2	2.2	12	3	2	2	0	0	0	0	0	0	4	0	0	0	0	-	0	0-0	0	2.27	6.75
	4 ML YEARS		236	0	0	168	245.1	974	171	59	56	15	4	10	12	77	8	297	4	0	15	10	.600	0	83-95	11	2.11	2.05

Jeff Salazar

Bats: L Throws: L Pos: PH-19; CF-2; LF-1; RF-1   Ht: 6'0" Wt: 195 Born: 11/24/1980 Age: 29

						BATTING														BASERUNNING				AVERAGES		
Year	Team	Lg	G	AB	H	2B	3B	HR	(Hm	Rd)	TB	R	RBI	RC	TBB	IBB	SO	HBP	SH	SF	SB	CS	SB%	GDP	Avg	OBP	Slg
2009	Indy*	AAA	84	315	85	7	3	10	(-	-)	128	43	39	48	30	0	57	2	1	3	16	0	1.00	4	.270	.334	.406
2006	Col	NL	19	53	15	4	0	1	(1	0)	22	13	8	11	11	2	16	1	1	1	2	0	1.00	1	.283	.409	.415
2007	Ari	NL	38	94	26	6	1	1	(0	1)	37	13	10	16	9	0	19	0	0	0	2	0	1.00	1	.277	.340	.394
2008	Ari	NL	90	128	27	5	3	2	(0	2)	44	17	12	17	21	1	41	2	1	0	0	2	.00	2	.211	.331	.344
2009	Pit	NL	21	23	1	0	0	0	(0	0)	1	1	1	0	3	0	7	0	0	0	1	0	1.00	1	.043	.154	.043
	Postseason		6	10	1	0	0	0	(0	0)	1	0	0	0	1	0	3	0	0	0	0	0	-	0	.100	.182	.100
	4 ML YEARS		168	298	69	15	4	4	(1	3)	104	44	31	44	44	3	83	3	2	1	5	2	.71	4	.232	.335	.349

Oscar Salazar

Bats: R Throws: R Pos: PH-42; LF-16; 1B-8; 3B-5; RF-4; 2B-3; SS-2; DH-1   Ht: 6'0" Wt: 195 Born: 6/27/1978 Age: 32

						BATTING														BASERUNNING				AVERAGES		
Year	Team	Lg	G	AB	H	2B	3B	HR	(Hm	Rd)	TB	R	RBI	RC	TBB	IBB	SO	HBP	SH	SF	SB	CS	SB%	GDP	Avg	OBP	Slg
2009	Norfolk	AAA	90	199	74	17	1	10	(-	-)	123	31	43	45	13	0	27	0	0	1	0	3	.00	5	.372	.408	.618
2002	Det	AL	8	21	4	1	0	1	(0	1)	8	2	3	3	1	0	2	0	1	0	0	0	-	0	.190	.227	.381
2008	Bal	AL	34	81	23	3	0	5	(4	1)	41	13	15	14	12	0	13	0	0	1	0	1	.00	1	.284	.372	.506
2009	2 Tms		72	139	42	8	2	5	(3	2)	69	16	25	26	14	1	20	0	0	1	0	0	-	8	.302	.364	.496
09	Bal	AL	17	31	13	0	0	2	(2	0)	19	4	6	9	2	0	4	0	0	0	0	0	-	2	.419	.455	.613
09	SD	NL	55	108	29	8	2	3	(1	2)	50	12	19	17	12	1	16	0	0	1	0	0	-	6	.269	.339	.463
	3 ML YEARS		114	241	69	12	2	11	(7	4)	118	31	43	43	27	1	35	0	1	2	0	1	.00	9	.286	.356	.490

Jarrod Saltalamacchia

Bats: B Throws: R Pos: C-83; DH-1   Ht: 6'4" Wt: 235 Born: 5/2/1985 Age: 25

						BATTING														BASERUNNING				AVERAGES		
Year	Team	Lg	G	AB	H	2B	3B	HR	(Hm	Rd)	TB	R	RBI	RC	TBB	IBB	SO	HBP	SH	SF	SB	CS	SB%	GDP	Avg	OBP	Slg
2009	Frisco*	AA	2	4	0	0	0	0	(-	-)	0	1	0	0	1	0	1	1	0	0	0	0	-	0	.000	.333	.000
2007	2 Tms		93	308	82	13	1	11	(6	5)	130	39	33	32	19	1	75	1	0	1	0	0	-	8	.266	.310	.422
2008	Tex	AL	61	198	50	13	0	3	(2	1)	72	27	26	29	31	1	74	0	0	1	0	2	.00	1	.253	.352	.364
2009	Tex	AL	84	283	66	12	0	9	(6	3)	105	34	34	30	22	1	97	1	3	1	0	2	.00	3	.233	.290	.371
07	Atl	NL	47	144	40	6	0	4	(2	2)	58	11	12	13	10	1	28	1	0	1	0	0	-	4	.278	.333	.411
07	Tex	AL	46	164	42	7	1	7	(4	3)	72	28	21	19	9	0	47	0	0	0	0	0	-	4	.256	.290	.439
	3 ML YEARS		238	789	198	38	1	23	(14	9)	307	100	93	91	72	3	246	2	3	3	0	4	.00	12	.251	.314	.389

Jeff Samardzija

Pitches: R Bats: R Pos: RP-18; SP-2   Ht: 6'5" Wt: 218 Born: 1/23/1985 Age: 25

			HOW MUCH HE PITCHED						WHAT HE GAVE UP											THE RESULTS						
Year	Team	Lg	G	GS	CG	GF	IP	BFP	H	R	ER	HR	SH	SF	HB	TBB	IBB	SO	WP	Bk	W	L	Pct	Sh	Sv-Op	Hld	ERC	ERA
2006	Boise	A-	5	5	0	0	19.0	84	18	5	5	1	0	0	5	6	0	13	2	0	1	1	.500	0	0- -	-	4.13	2.37
2006	Peoria	A	2	2	0	0	11.0	43	6	5	4	1	0	1	0	6	0	4	0	0	0	1	.000	0	0- -	-	2.30	3.27
2007	Dytona	A+	24	20	1	0	107.1	479	142	69	59	8	2	1	1	35	1	45	3	0	3	8	.273	0	0- -	-	5.60	4.95
2007	Tenn	AA	6	6	0	0	34.1	145	33	15	13	8	2	1	1	9	0	20	0	0	3	3	.500	0	0- -	-	4.26	3.41
2008	Tenn	AA	16	15	0	0	76.0	332	71	43	41	6	4	2	2	42	0	44	4	0	3	5	.375	0	0- -	-	4.30	4.86
2008	Iowa	AAA	6	6	1	0	37.1	152	32	13	13	5	1	1	1	16	0	40	3	0	4	1	.800	0	0- -	-	3.91	3.13
2009	Iowa	AAA	18	17	1	0	89.0	384	98	46	43	12	5	3	3	27	1	71	3	0	6	6	.500	0	0- -	-	4.67	4.35
2008	ChC	NL	26	0	0	6	27.2	124	24	12	7	0	1	1	1	15	2	25	2	0	1	0	1.000	0	1-4	3	3.08	2.28
2009	ChC	NL	20	2	0	7	34.2	161	46	29	29	7	4	1	1	15	1	21	2	0	1	3	.250	0	0-0	0	7.13	7.53
	Postseason		1	0	0	0	1.0	4	2	1	1	0	0	0	0	0	0	0	0	0	0	0	-	0	0-0	0	9.49	9.00
	2 ML YEARS		46	2	0	13	62.1	285	70	41	36	7	5	2	2	30	3	46	4	0	2	3	.400	0	1-4	3	5.20	5.20

Clint Sammons

Bats: R Throws: R Pos: C-6   Ht: 6'0" Wt: 200 Born: 5/15/1983 Age: 27

						BATTING														BASERUNNING				AVERAGES		
Year	Team	Lg	G	AB	H	2B	3B	HR	(Hm	Rd)	TB	R	RBI	RC	TBB	IBB	SO	HBP	SH	SF	SB	CS	SB%	GDP	Avg	OBP	Slg
2009	Gwnntt*	AAA	80	299	64	12	0	9	(-	-)	103	34	37	29	20	0	61	3	1	5	7	0	1.00	5	.214	.266	.344
2007	Atl	NL	2	3	2	1	0	0	(0	0)	3	0	0	1	0	0	0	0	0	0	0	0	-	1	.667	.667	1.000
2008	Atl	NL	23	54	8	0	0	1	(1	0)	11	2	4	2	5	0	12	0	0	0	0	0	-	2	.148	.220	.204
2009	Atl	NL	6	11	2	0	0	0	(0	0)	2	1	0	0	1	0	3	0	0	0	0	0	-	0	.182	.250	.182
	3 ML YEARS		31	68	12	1	0	1	(1	0)	16	3	4	3	6	0	15	0	0	0	0	0	-	3	.176	.243	.235

Chris Sampson

Pitches: R **Bats:** R **Pos:** RP-49   **Ht:** 6'1" **Wt:** 190 **Born:** 5/23/1978 **Age:** 32

Year	Team	Lg	G	GS	CG	GF	IP	BFP	H	R	ER	HR	SH	SF	HB	TBB	IBB	SO	WP	Bk	W	L	Pct	Sh	Sv-Op	Hld	ERC	ERA
2009	RdRck*	AAA	6	0	0	1	6.0	26	7	5	5	0	0	0	0	2	0	5	1	0	0	0	-	0	0--	-	4.08	7.50
2006	Hou	NL	12	3	0	0	34.0	130	25	10	8	3	1	1	1	5	1	15	0	0	2	1	.667	0	0-0	0	1.84	2.12
2007	Hou	NL	24	19	0	2	121.2	522	138	64	62	20	6	6	7	30	2	51	3	0	7	8	.467	0	0-0	0	4.96	4.59
2008	Hou	NL	54	11	0	6	117.1	478	118	60	55	8	3	5	3	23	5	61	0	0	6	4	.600	0	0-2	11	3.21	4.22
2009	Hou	NL	49	0	0	9	55.1	248	66	34	31	2	1	1	0	21	6	33	2	1	4	2	.667	0	3-6	15	4.40	5.04
	4 ML YEARS		139	33	0	17	328.1	1378	347	168	156	33	11	13	11	79	14	160	5	1	19	15	.559	0	3-8	26	3.88	4.28

Brian Sanches

Pitches: R **Bats:** R **Pos:** RP-47   **Ht:** 6'0" **Wt:** 189 **Born:** 8/8/1978 **Age:** 31

Year	Team	Lg	G	GS	CG	GF	IP	BFP	H	R	ER	HR	SH	SF	HB	TBB	IBB	SO	WP	Bk	W	L	Pct	Sh	Sv-Op	Hld	ERC	ERA
2009	NewOr*	AAA	16	0	0	16	17.2	70	13	6	4	1	2	1	0	4	0	22	1	0	1	1	.500	0	4--	-	1.82	2.04
2006	Phi	NL	18	0	0	5	21.1	98	23	14	14	5	0	0	1	13	3	22	0	1	0	0	-	0	0-0	0	6.18	5.91
2007	Phi	NL	12	0	0	4	14.2	68	13	11	9	6	1	0	1	12	2	9	1	0	1	1	.500	0	0-0	1	7.73	5.52
2008	Was	NL	12	0	0	2	11.0	54	16	10	9	2	0	1	1	5	0	10	0	0	2	0	1.000	0	0-1	0	8.15	7.36
2009	Fla	NL	47	0	0	7	56.1	248	50	18	16	5	3	0	6	26	8	51	5	0	4	2	.667	0	0-3	9	3.75	2.56
	4 ML YEARS		89	0	0	18	103.1	468	102	53	48	18	4	1	8	56	13	92	6	1	7	3	.700	0	0-4	10	5.20	4.18

Anibal Sanchez

Pitches: R **Bats:** R **Pos:** SP-16   **Ht:** 6'0" **Wt:** 219 **Born:** 2/27/1984 **Age:** 26

Year	Team	Lg	G	GS	CG	GF	IP	BFP	H	R	ER	HR	SH	SF	HB	TBB	IBB	SO	WP	Bk	W	L	Pct	Sh	Sv-Op	Hld	ERC	ERA
2009	Jupiter*	A+	3	3	0	0	13.1	49	7	2	1	0	0	0	0	3	0	12	1	0	1	0	1.000	0	0--	-	0.98	0.68
2009	Mrlns*	R	1	1	0	0	2.2	13	3	1	1	0	0	0	0	2	0	0	1	0	0	0	-	0	0--	-	5.24	3.38
2009	Jaxnvl*	AA	2	2	0	0	10.1	39	5	3	3	1	0	0	0	3	0	8	0	0	1	0	1.000	0	0--	-	1.30	2.61
2006	Fla	NL	18	17	2	0	114.1	469	90	39	36	9	3	1	4	46	1	72	4	1	10	3	.769	1	0-0	0	2.96	2.83
2007	Fla	NL	6	6	0	0	30.0	151	43	17	16	3	2	2	2	19	1	14	3	0	2	1	.667	0	0-0	0	7.90	4.80
2008	Fla	NL	10	10	0	0	51.2	241	54	35	32	7	4	2	6	27	2	50	1	0	2	5	.286	0	0-0	0	5.40	5.57
2009	Fla	NL	16	16	0	0	86.0	383	84	39	37	10	2	2	1	46	5	71	0	1	4	8	.333	0	0-0	0	4.51	3.87
	4 ML YEARS		50	49	2	0	282.0	1244	271	130	121	29	11	7	13	138	9	207	8	2	18	17	.514	1	0-0	0	4.35	3.86

Duaner Sanchez

Pitches: R **Bats:** R **Pos:** RP-12   **Ht:** 6'2" **Wt:** 210 **Born:** 10/14/1979 **Age:** 30

Year	Team	Lg	G	GS	CG	GF	IP	BFP	H	R	ER	HR	SH	SF	HB	TBB	IBB	SO	WP	Bk	W	L	Pct	Sh	Sv-Op	Hld	ERC	ERA
2002	2 Tms	NL	9	0	0	5	6.0	31	6	6	6	2	0	0	0	7	0	6	0	0	0	0	-	0	0-1	1	9.19	9.00
2003	Pit	NL	6	0	0	2	6.0	34	15	11	11	2	0	1	2	1	0	3	0	0	1	0	1.000	0	0-0	0	17.96	16.50
2004	LAD	NL	67	0	0	27	80.0	342	81	34	30	9	2	3	6	27	2	44	6	0	3	1	.750	0	0-1	4	4.31	3.38
2005	LAD	NL	79	0	0	31	82.0	353	75	36	34	8	10	1	3	36	6	71	7	1	4	7	.364	0	8-12	13	3.76	3.73
2006	NYM	NL	49	0	0	15	55.1	229	43	19	16	3	4	4	4	24	6	44	1	0	5	1	.833	0	0-1	14	2.85	2.60
2008	NYM	NL	66	0	0	14	58.1	254	54	28	28	6	1	0	3	23	3	44	2	0	5	1	.833	0	0-1	21	3.71	4.32
2009	SD	NL	12	0	0	1	11.0	57	18	11	11	3	1	0	1	8	1	2	1	0	1	1	.500	0	0-1	5	11.81	9.00
	02 Ari	NL	6	0	0	3	3.2	19	3	2	2	1	0	0	0	5	0	4	0	0	0	0	-	0	0-1	1	8.32	4.91
	02 Pit	NL	3	0	0	2	2.1	12	3	4	4	1	0	0	0	2	0	2	0	0	0	0	-	0	0-0	0	10.55	15.43
	Postseason		2	0	0	2	2.0	8	1	0	0	0	0	0	0	1	0	3	0	0	0	0	-	0	0-0	0	1.41	0.00
	7 ML YEARS		288	0	0	95	298.2	1300	292	145	136	33	17	10	19	126	18	214	17	1	19	11	.633	0	8-17	58	4.28	4.10

Freddy Sanchez

Bats: R **Throws:** R **Pos:** 2B-110; PH-2   **Ht:** 5'10" **Wt:** 189 **Born:** 12/21/1977 **Age:** 32

Year	Team	Lg	G	AB	H	2B	3B	HR	(Hm	Rd)	TB	R	RBI	RC	TBB	IBB	SO	HBP	SH	SF	SB	CS	SB%	GDP	Avg	OBP	Slg
2009	Fresno*	AAA	3	9	3	1	0	0	(-	-)	4	1	0	1	1	0	1	0	0	0	0	0	-	0	.333	.400	.444
2002	Bos	AL	12	16	3	0	0	0	(0	0)	3	2	1	2	2	0	3	0	0	0	0	0	-	0	.188	.278	.188
2003	Bos	AL	20	34	8	2	0	0	(0	0)	10	6	2	1	0	0	8	0	0	0	0	0	-	0	.235	.235	.294
2004	Pit	NL	9	19	3	0	0	0	(0	0)	3	2	2	2	0	0	3	0	1	0	0	0	-	0	.158	.158	.158
2005	Pit	NL	132	453	132	26	4	5	(3	2)	181	54	35	57	27	1	36	5	4	3	2	2	.50	6	.291	.336	.400
2006	Pit	NL	157	582	200	53	2	6	(2	4)	275	85	85	101	31	6	52	7	3	9	3	2	.60	12	**.344**	.378	.473
2007	Pit	NL	147	602	183	42	4	11	(5	6)	266	77	81	94	32	2	76	8	2	9	0	1	.00	13	.304	.343	.442
2008	Pit	NL	145	569	154	26	2	9	(1	8)	211	75	52	61	21	1	63	4	8	6	0	1	.00	13	.271	.298	.371
2009	2 Tms	NL	111	457	134	29	3	7	(3	4)	190	56	41	59	22	4	76	2	4	4	5	1	.83	12	.293	.326	.416
	09 Pit	NL	86	355	105	28	3	6	(3	3)	157	45	34	49	20	4	60	2	2	3	5	1	.83	9	.296	.334	.442
	09 SF	NL	25	102	29	1	0	1	(0	1)	33	11	7	10	2	0	16	0	2	1	0	0	-	3	.284	.295	.324
	8 ML YEARS		733	2732	817	178	15	38	(14	24)	1139	358	300	376	135	14	317	26	22	31	10	7	.59	56	.299	.334	.417

Gaby Sanchez

Bats: R **Throws:** R **Pos:** PH-20; 1B-1   **Ht:** 6'1" **Wt:** 234 **Born:** 9/2/1983 **Age:** 26

Year	Team	Lg	G	AB	H	2B	3B	HR	(Hm	Rd)	TB	R	RBI	RC	TBB	IBB	SO	HBP	SH	SF	SB	CS	SB%	GDP	Avg	OBP	Slg
2005	Jmstwn	A-	62	234	83	16	0	5	(-	-)	114	34	42	46	16	0	24	4	0	3	11	5	.69	6	.355	.401	.487
2006	Grnsbr	A	55	189	60	12	0	14	(-	-)	114	43	40	51	39	2	20	7	0	2	6	2	.75	4	.317	.447	.603
2006	Mrlns	R	3	6	2	1	0	0	(-	-)	3	1	3	2	5	0	0	0	0	0	0	0	-	0	.333	.636	.500
2006	Jupiter	A+	16	55	10	3	1	1	(-	-)	18	13	7	7	12	0	12	0	0	1	1	0	1.00	0	.182	.324	.327

Year	Team	Lg	G	AB	H	2B	3B	HR	(Hm	Rd)	TB	R	RBI	RC	TBB	IBB	SO	HBP	SH	SF	SB	CS	SB%	GDP	Avg	OBP	Slg
2007	Jupiter	A+	133	473	132	40	3	9	(-	-)	205	89	70	79	64	0	74	6	0	4	6	6	.50	15	.279	.369	.433
2008	Carlina	AA	133	478	150	42	1	17	(-	-)	245	70	92	101	69	4	70	6	0	4	17	8	.68	13	.314	.404	.513
2009	NewOr	AAA	85	318	92	11	0	16	(-	-)	151	55	56	60	41	2	44	5	1	5	5	0	1.00	10	.289	.374	.475
2008	Fla	NL	5	8	3	2	0	0	(0	0)	5	0	1	2	0	0	2	0	0	0	0	0	-	0	.375	.375	.625
2009	Fla	NL	21	21	5	0	0	2	(2	0)	11	2	3	3	2	0	3	0	0	0	0	0	-	0	.238	.304	.524
2 ML YEARS			26	29	8	2	0	2	(2	0)	16	2	4	5	2	0	5	0	0	0	0	0	-	1	.276	.323	.552

Jonathan Sanchez

Pitches: L Bats: L Pos: SP-29; RP-3 **Ht: 6'2" Wt: 189 Born: 11/19/1982 Age: 27**

Year	Team	Lg	G	GS	CG	GF	IP	BFP	H	R	ER	HR	SH	SF	HB	TBB	IBB	SO	WP	Bk	W	L	Pct	Sh	Sv-Op	Hld	ERC	ERA
2006	SF	NL	27	4	0	4	40.0	185	39	26	22	2	0	2	4	23	0	33	2	0	3	1	.750	0	0-0	5	4.54	4.95
2007	SF	NL	33	4	0	8	52.0	238	57	34	34	8	2	2	5	28	1	62	4	0	1	5	.167	0	0-0	2	6.06	5.88
2008	SF	NL	29	29	0	0	158.0	695	154	90	88	14	9	5	7	75	1	157	7	0	9	12	.429	0	0-0	4	4.31	5.01
2009	SF	NL	32	29	1	2	163.1	710	135	82	77	19	3	1	6	88	5	177	11	0	8	12	.400	1	0-0	1	3.83	4.24
4 ML YEARS			121	66	1	14	413.1	1828	385	232	221	43	14	10	22	214	7	429	24	0	21	30	.412	1	0-0	8	4.35	4.81

Freddy Sandoval

Bats: B Throws: R Pos: 2B-3; 3B-2 **Ht: 6'1" Wt: 200 Born: 8/16/1982 Age: 27**

Year	Team	Lg	G	AB	H	2B	3B	HR	(Hm	Rd)	TB	R	RBI	RC	TBB	IBB	SO	HBP	SH	SF	SB	CS	SB%	GDP	Avg	OBP	Slg
2005	CRpds	A	117	427	120	34	4	4	(-	-)	174	54	63	66	53	3	58	4	6	7	17	12	.59	11	.281	.360	.407
2006	RCuca	A+	113	434	112	28	2	5	(-	-)	159	60	54	63	59	0	98	1	7	8	30	8	.79	14	.258	.343	.366
2007	Ark	AA	127	472	144	32	6	11	(-	-)	221	84	72	91	67	3	78	6	12	7	21	11	.00	12	.305	.392	.468
2008	Salt Lk	AAA	131	525	176	45	2	15	(-	-)	270	92	88	105	47	3	74	4	4	7	6	3	.67	20	.335	.389	.514
2009	Salt Lk	AAA	67	277	83	16	5	6	(-	-)	127	46	46	47	26	2	39	0	0	0	12	2	.90	9	.300	.360	.458
2008	Angels	R	6	19	5	1	0	0	(-	-)	6	5	1	3	4	0	2	1	0	0	1	0	1.00	0	.263	.417	.316
2008	LAA	AL	6	6	1	0	0	0	(0	0)	1	0	0	0	1	0	0	0	0	0	0	0	-	0	.167	.286	.167
2009	LAA	AL	5	11	2	1	0	0	(0	0)	3	1	0	0	0	0	3	0	0	0	0	0	-	0	.182	.182	.273
2 ML YEARS			11	17	3	1	0	0	(0	0)	4	1	0	0	1	0	3	0	0	0	0	0	-	0	.176	.222	.235

Pablo Sandoval

Bats: B Throws: R Pos: 3B-120; 1B-26; PH-4; C-3; DH-2 **Ht: 5'11" Wt: 246 Born: 8/11/1986 Age: 23**

Year	Team	Lg	G	AB	H	2B	3B	HR	(Hm	Rd)	TB	R	RBI	RC	TBB	IBB	SO	HBP	SH	SF	SB	CS	SB%	GDP	Avg	OBP	Slg
2004	Giants	R	46	177	47	9	5	0	(-	-)	66	21	26	20	5	1	17	2	3	4	4	1	.80	2	.266	.287	.373
2005	SlmKzr	A	76	294	97	15	2	3	(-	-)	125	40	50	49	21	3	33	0	3	3	2	3	.40	9	.330	.383	.425
2006	Augsta	A	117	438	116	27	2	6	(-	-)	141	43	49	45	22	4	74	8	1	4	3	4	.43	18	.265	.309	.322
2007	SnJos	A+	102	401	115	33	5	11	(-	-)	191	66	62	60	10	0	52	0	3	3	3	1	.75	10	.287	.312	.476
2008	SnJos	A+	68	273	98	25	2	12	(-	-)	163	61	59	64	23	2	39	3	0	2	2	1	.67	1	.359	.412	.597
2008	Conn	AA	44	175	59	13	0	8	(-	-)	96	29	37	33	8	2	20	0	0	1	0	1	1.00	4	.337	.364	.549
2008	SF	NL	41	145	50	10	1	3	(1	2)	71	24	24	24	4	1	14	1	0	4	0	0	-	6	.345	.357	.490
2009	SF	NL	153	572	189	44	5	25	(13	12)	318	79	90	113	52	13	83	4	0	5	5	5	.50	10	.330	.387	.556
2 ML YEARS			194	717	239	54	6	28	(14	14)	389	103	114	137	56	14	97	5	0	9	5	5	.50	16	.333	.381	.543

Ervin Santana

Pitches: R Bats: R Pos: SP-23; RP-1 **Ht: 6'2" Wt: 185 Born: 12/12/1982 Age: 27**

Year	Team	Lg	G	GS	CG	GF	IP	BFP	H	R	ER	HR	SH	SF	HB	TBB	IBB	SO	WP	Bk	W	L	Pct	Sh	Sv-Op	Hld	ERC	ERA
2009	RCuca*	A+	1	1	0	0	4.2	18	4	3	3	2	0	0	0	3	0	3	0	0	0	0	-	0	0--	-	3.45	5.79
2009	Salt Lk*	AAA	1	1	0	0	5.0	21	3	2	2	0	0	0	0	1	0	4	1	0	1	0	1.000	0	0--	-	1.44	3.60
2009	Angels*	R	1	1	0	0	3.1	13	3	0	0	0	0	0	0	0	0	7	0	0	0	0	-	0	0--	-	1.57	0.00
2005	LAA	AL	23	23	1	0	133.2	583	139	73	69	17	1	4	8	47	2	99	4	0	12	8	.600	1	0-0	0	4.51	4.65
2006	LAA	AL	33	33	0	0	204.0	846	181	106	97	21	4	10	11	70	2	141	10	2	16	8	.667	0	0-0	0	3.51	4.28
2007	LAA	AL	28	26	0	1	150.0	675	174	103	96	26	3	2	8	58	3	126	7	0	7	14	.333	0	0-0	0	5.69	5.76
2008	LAA	AL	32	32	2	0	219.0	897	198	89	85	23	3	5	8	47	2	214	5	1	16	7	.696	1	0-0	0	3.00	3.49
2009	LAA	AL	24	23	2	0	139.2	614	159	83	78	24	2	1	10	47	4	107	4	0	8	8	.500	2	0-0	1	5.47	5.03
Postseason			4	2	0	1	17.0	75	16	14	13	4	0	1	2	5	0	9	0	0	1	1	.500	0	0-0	0	4.56	6.88
5 ML YEARS			140	137	5	1	846.1	3615	851	454	425	111	13	22	45	269	13	687	30	3	59	45	.567	4	0-0	1	4.20	4.52

Johan Santana

Pitches: L Bats: L Pos: SP-25 **Ht: 6'0" Wt: 208 Born: 3/13/1979 Age: 31**

Year	Team	Lg	G	GS	CG	GF	IP	BFP	H	R	ER	HR	SH	SF	HB	TBB	IBB	SO	WP	Bk	W	L	Pct	Sh	Sv-Op	Hld	ERC	ERA
2000	Min	AL	30	5	0	9	86.0	398	102	64	62	11	1	3	2	54	0	64	5	2	2	3	.400	0	0-0	0	6.59	6.49
2001	Min	AL	15	4	0	5	43.2	195	50	25	23	6	2	3	3	16	0	28	3	0	1	0	1.000	0	0-0	0	5.36	4.74
2002	Min	AL	27	14	0	2	108.1	452	84	41	36	7	3	3	1	49	0	137	15	2	8	6	.571	0	1-1	3	2.86	2.99
2003	Min	AL	45	18	0	7	158.1	644	127	56	54	17	2	4	3	47	1	169	6	2	12	3	.800	0	0-0	5	2.73	3.07
2004	Min	AL	34	34	1	0	228.0	881	156	70	66	24	3	3	9	54	0	265	7	0	20	6	.769	1	0-0	0	2.07	2.61
2005	Min	AL	33	33	3	0	231.2	910	180	77	74	22	6	2	1	45	0	238	8	0	16	7	.696	2	0-0	0	2.14	2.87
2006	Min	AL	34	34	1	0	233.2	923	186	79	72	24	6	4	4	47	0	245	4	1	19	6	.760	0	0-0	0	2.36	2.77
2007	Min	AL	33	33	1	0	219.0	878	183	88	81	33	4	4	4	52	0	235	7	1	15	13	.536	1	0-0	0	2.98	3.33

Year	Team	Lg	G	GS	CG	GF	IP	BFP	H	R	ER	HR	SH	SF	HB	TBB	IBB	SO	WP	Bk	W	L	Pct	Sh	Sv-Op	Hld	ERC	ERA
2008	NYM	NL	34	34	3	0	234.1	964	206	74	66	23	9	1	4	63	5	206	9	2	16	7	.696	2	0-0	0	2.93	2.53
2009	NYM	NL	25	25	0	0	166.2	701	156	67	58	20	8	3	3	46	3	146	1	0	13	9	.591	0	0-0	0	3.37	3.13
Postseason			11	5	0	0	34.0	143	35	15	15	2	0	0	1	10	1	32	2	0	1	3	.250	0	0-0	1	3.66	3.97
10 ML YEARS			310	234	9	23	1709.2	6946	1430	641	592	187	44	30	34	473	10	1733	65	10	122	60	.670	6	1-1	8	2.86	3.12

Ramon Santiago

Bats: B Throws: R Pos: SS-69; 2B-29; PH-8; PR-4; 3B-2 — Ht: 5'11" Wt: 175 Born: 8/31/1979 Age: 30

Year	Team	Lg	G	AB	H	2B	3B	HR	(Hm	Rd)	TB	R	RBI	RC	TBB	IBB	SO	HBP	SH	SF	SB	CS	SB%	GDP	Avg	OBP	Slg
2002	Det	AL	65	222	54	5	5	4	(3	1)	81	33	20	23	13	0	48	8	4	2	8	5	.62	2	.243	.306	.365
2003	Det	AL	141	444	100	18	1	2	(1	1)	126	41	29	38	33	0	66	10	18	2	10	4	.71	9	.225	.292	.284
2004	Sea	AL	19	39	7	1	0	0	(0	0)	8	8	2	1	3	0	3	1	2	0	0	0	-	1	.179	.256	.205
2005	Sea	AL	8	8	1	0	0	0	(0	0)	1	2	0	1	1	0	2	3	1	0	0	0	-	0	.125	.417	.125
2006	Det	AL	43	80	18	1	1	0	(0	0)	21	9	3	3	1	0	14	1	4	0	2	0	1.00	1	.225	.244	.263
2007	Det	AL	32	67	19	5	1	0	(0	0)	26	10	7	11	1	0	10	3	3	0	3	0	1.00	0	.284	.324	.388
2008	Det	AL	58	124	35	6	2	4	(4	0)	57	30	18	26	22	0	17	5	5	0	1	0	1.00	1	.282	.411	.460
2009	Det	AL	93	262	70	6	2	7	(4	3)	101	29	35	33	17	1	57	4	10	3	1	2	.33	3	.267	.318	.385
Postseason			6	12	1	0	0	0	(0	0)	1	0	0	0	1	0	2	0	1	0	0	0	-	0	.083	.154	.083
8 ML YEARS			459	1246	304	42	12	17	(12	5)	421	162	114	136	91	1	217	35	47	7	25	11	.69	17	.244	.312	.338

Omir Santos

Bats: R Throws: R Pos: C-91; PH-11; PR-3 — Ht: 6'0" Wt: 213 Born: 4/29/1981 Age: 29

Year	Team	Lg	G	AB	H	2B	3B	HR	(Hm	Rd)	TB	R	RBI	RC	TBB	IBB	SO	HBP	SH	SF	SB	CS	SB%	GDP	Avg	OBP	Slg
2001	StIsInd	A-	44	117	32	5	1	0	(-	-)	39	11	8	12	6	0	25	1	1	2	0	1	.00	2	.274	.310	.333
2002	Grnsbr	A	23	73	17	2	1	1	(-	-)	24	7	8	6	2	0	15	3	0	2	0	0	-	2	.233	.275	.329
2002	StIsInd	A-	61	232	67	10	0	7	(-	-)	98	22	44	33	12	0	32	4	0	3	2	1	.67	6	.289	.331	.422
2003	Btl Crk	A	82	277	65	11	0	2	(-	-)	82	35	30	27	25	0	36	3	6	8	0	0	-	8	.235	.297	.296
2003	Yanks	R	1	0	0	0	0	0	(-	-)	0	0	0	0	0	0	0	0	0	0	0	0	-	0	-	-	-
2004	Btl Crk	A	56	171	41	7	0	2	(-	-)	54	21	16	16	7	0	27	3	0	3	4	0	1.00	2	.240	.277	.316
2004	Tampa	A+	37	119	34	6	1	2	(-	-)	48	18	13	17	4	0	17	4	1	0	1	0	1.00	5	.286	.341	.403
2005	Trntn	AA	111	401	102	17	0	10	(-	-)	149	44	48	43	11	1	75	9	1	3	1	0	.00	12	.254	.288	.372
2006	Trntn	AA	101	324	87	18	0	4	(-	-)	117	31	38	39	19	0	65	6	3	4	1	0	1.00	6	.269	.317	.361
2007	S-WB	AAA	51	167	39	8	0	3	(-	-)	56	13	19	15	10	1	35	1	2	2	1	1	.50	7	.234	.278	.335
2007	Trntn	AA	10	38	8	2	0	0	(-	-)	10	4	0	2	1	0	8	0	0	0	0	0	-	0	.211	.231	.263
2008	Norfolk	AAA	84	297	80	13	0	1	(-	-)	96	31	36	33	20	0	57	8	3	4	1	2	.33	5	.269	.328	.323
2009	Buffalo	AAA	3	13	3	0	0	0	(-	-)	3	1	0	1	1	0	2	1	0	0	0	0	-	0	.231	.333	.231
2008	Bal	AL	11	10	1	0	0	0	(0	0)	1	0	0	0	0	0	2	0	0	0	0	0	-	0	.100	.100	.100
2009	NYM	NL	96	281	73	14	1	7	(2	5)	110	28	40	29	15	1	44	2	2	6	0	0	-	9	.260	.296	.391
2 ML YEARS			107	291	74	14	1	7	(2	5)	111	28	40	29	15	1	46	2	2	6	0	0	-	9	.254	.290	.381

Dane Sardinha

Bats: R Throws: R Pos: C-12 — Ht: 6'0" Wt: 215 Born: 4/8/1979 Age: 31

Year	Team	Lg	G	AB	H	2B	3B	HR	(Hm	Rd)	TB	R	RBI	RC	TBB	IBB	SO	HBP	SH	SF	SB	CS	SB%	GDP	Avg	OBP	Slg
2009	Toledo*	AAA	39	118	21	7	0	3	(-	-)	37	10	16	9	11	0	34	1	3	2	0	0	-	3	.178	.250	.314
2003	Cin	NL	1	2	0	0	0	0	(0	0)	0	0	0	0	0	0	1	0	0	0	0	0	-	0	.000	.000	.000
2005	Cin	NL	1	3	0	0	0	0	(0	0)	0	0	0	0	0	0	1	0	0	0	0	0	-	0	.000	.000	.000
2008	Det	AL	17	44	7	0	1	0	(0	0)	9	2	3	3	4	0	11	0	1	0	0	0	-	1	.159	.229	.205
2009	Det	AL	12	31	3	1	0	0	(0	0)	4	1	3	0	0	0	16	0	1	2	0	0	-	1	.097	.091	.129
4 ML YEARS			31	80	10	1	1	0	(0	0)	13	3	6	3	4	0	29	0	2	2	0	0	-	2	.125	.163	.163

Dennis Sarfate

Pitches: R Bats: R Pos: RP-20 — Ht: 6'4" Wt: 225 Born: 4/9/1981 Age: 29

Year	Team	Lg	G	GS	CG	GF	IP	BFP	H	R	ER	HR	SH	SF	HB	TBB	IBB	SO	WP	Bk	W	L	Pct	Sh	Sv-Op	Hld	ERC	ERA
2009	Bowie	AA	1	0	0	0	1.0	3	0	0	0	0	0	0	0	0	0	2	0	0	0	0	-	0	0--	-	0.00	0.00
2009	Frdrck*	A+	1	0	0	0	2.0	9	2	2	2	0	0	0	0	1	0	2	0	0	1	0	1.000	0	0--	-	3.63	9.00
2009	Norfolk*	AAA	12	0	0	0	12.2	53	13	10	9	4	0	0	1	2	0	13	1	0	1	1	.500	0	0--	-	5.01	6.39
2006	Mil	NL	8	0	0	5	8.1	38	9	4	4	0	0	0	0	4	1	11	2	0	0	0	-	0	0-0	0	3.77	4.32
2007	Hou	NL	7	0	0	1	8.1	31	5	1	1	0	0	1	0	1	0	14	0	0	1	0	1.000	0	0-0	3	0.96	1.08
2008	Bal	AL	57	4	0	15	79.2	359	62	47	42	8	2	3	7	62	2	86	6	1	4	3	.571	0	0-2	3	4.65	4.74
2009	Bal	AL	20	0	0	5	23.0	101	21	15	13	3	2	0	1	14	0	20	0	0	0	1	.000	0	0-0	1	4.91	5.09
4 ML YEARS			92	4	0	26	119.1	529	97	67	60	11	4	4	8	81	3	131	8	1	5	4	.556	0	0-2	7	4.30	4.53

Joe Saunders

Pitches: L Bats: L Pos: SP-31 — Ht: 6'3" Wt: 210 Born: 6/16/1981 Age: 29

Year	Team	Lg	G	GS	CG	GF	IP	BFP	H	R	ER	HR	SH	SF	HB	TBB	IBB	SO	WP	Bk	W	L	Pct	Sh	Sv-Op	Hld	ERC	ERA
2005	LAA	AL	2	2	0	0	9.1	41	10	8	8	3	0	0	0	4	0	4	1	0	0	0	-	0	0-0	0	6.27	7.71
2006	LAA	AL	13	13	0	0	70.2	302	71	42	37	6	1	2	1	29	1	51	2	1	7	3	.700	0	0-0	0	4.13	4.71
2007	LAA	AL	18	18	0	0	107.1	473	129	56	53	11	0	5	1	34	1	69	3	0	8	5	.615	0	0-0	0	4.96	4.44

Year	Team	Lg		HOW MUCH HE PITCHED							WHAT HE GAVE UP										THE RESULTS						
			G	GS	CG	GF	IP	BFP	H	R	ER	HR	SH	SF	HB	TBB	IBB	SO	WP	Bk	W	L	Pct	Sh	Sv-Op Hld	ERC	ERA
2008	LAA	AL	31	31	1	0	198.0	807	187	82	75	21	5	2	6	53	2	103	3	0	17	7	.708	0	0-0 0	3.49	3.41
2009	LAA	AL	31	31	1	0	186.0	805	202	102	95	29	6	4	6	64	2	101	5	1	16	7	.696	1	0-0 0	4.91	4.60
	Postseason		1	1	0	0	4.2	23	5	4	4	0	0	0	1	4	0	2	0	0	0	0		0	0-0 0	6.47	7.71
	5 ML YEARS		95	95	2	0	571.1	2428	599	290	268	70	12	13	14	184	6	328	14	2	48	22	.686	1	0-0 0	4.34	4.22

Michael Saunders

Bats: L **Throws:** R **Pos:** LF-39; PR-6; DH-4; PH-1   **Ht:** 6'4" **Wt:** 212 **Born:** 11/19/1986 **Age:** 23

Year	Team	Lg						BATTING														BASERUNNING				AVERAGES		
			G	AB	H	2B	3B	HR	(Hm	Rd)	TB	R	RBI	RC	TBB	IBB	SO	HBP	SH	SF		SB	CS	SB%	GDP	Avg	OBP	Slg
2005	Everett	A-	56	196	53	13	3	7	(-	-)	93	24	39	32	27	1	74	2	1	1		2	7	.22	1	.270	.361	.474
2006	Wisc	A	104	359	86	10	8	4	(-	-)	124	48	39	46	48	2	103	2	2	5		22	7	.76	2	.240	.329	.345
2007	Hi Dsrt	A+	108	431	129	25	4	14	(-	-)	204	91	77	84	60	2	116	8	5	3		27	10	.73	7	.299	.392	.473
2007	WTenn	AA	15	52	15	1	2	1	(-	-)	23	8	7	8	7	0	20	0	1	0		2	1	.67	0	.288	.373	.442
2008	WTenn	AA	67	248	72	18	3	8	(-	-)	120	46	30	46	30	2	66	4	6	1		12	6	.67	3	.290	.375	.484
2008	Tacom	AAA	24	95	23	4	1	3	(-	-)	38	12	16	11	9	0	30	0	1	0		1	2	.33	0	.242	.308	.400
2009	Tacorn	AAA	64	248	77	15	2	13	(-	-)	135	58	32	50	25	0	48	3	4	2		6	3	.67	2	.310	.378	.544
2009	Sea	AL	46	122	27	1	3	0	(0	0)	34	13	4	8	6	0	40	0	1	0		4	1	.80	1	.221	.258	.279

Bobby Scales

Bats: D **Throws:** D **Pos:** LF-17; DH-15; 2B-11; 3B-9; RF-4; PR-2   **Ht:** 6'0" **Wt:** 185 **Born:** 10/4/1977 **Age:** 32

Year	Team	Lg						BATTING														BASERUNNING				AVERAGES		
			G	AB	H	2B	3B	HR	(Hm	Rd)	TB	R	RBI	RC	TBB	IBB	SO	HBP	SH	SF		SB	CS	SB%	GDP	Avg	OBP	Slg
1999	Idaho	R+	44	169	49	14	6	1	(-	-)	78	47	30	33	29	0	31	2	2	1		7	2	.78	6	.290	.398	.462
2000	FtWyn	A	81	269	76	14	3	1	(-	-)	99	42	27	41	39	5	52	3	3	0		14	7	.67	9	.283	.379	.368
2001	Lk Els	A+	90	362	98	24	4	5	(-	-)	145	46	42	68	44	1	78	10	1	0		20	7	.74	7	.271	.365	.401
2002	Mobile	AA	97	250	69	13	3	4	(-	-)	100	40	27	37	27	1	56	4	1	0		6	3	.67	3	.276	.356	.400
2003	Mobile	AA	100	301	85	22	3	3	(-	-)	122	41	37	47	36	2	63	2	1	2		8	2	.80	4	.282	.361	.405
2003	Portlnd	AAA	11	43	16	7	0	0	(-	-)	23	8	2	11	7	0	6	0	0	0		3	0	1.00	0	.372	.460	.535
2004	Portlnd	AAA	73	213	50	13	2	1	(-	-)	70	26	24	26	27	2	56	5	0	0		3	1	.75	8	.235	.335	.329
2004	Mobile	AA	20	68	18	6	0	0	(-	-)	24	12	5	11	13	2	15	3	0	0		2	0	1.00	0	.265	.405	.353
2005	Portlnd	AAA	120	376	104	19	2	14	(-	-)	169	50	61	66	53	0	98	6	0	1		9	4	.69	9	.277	.374	.449
2006	S-WB	AAA	105	356	104	22	7	7	(-	-)	161	46	44	62	44	3	99	3	6	5		3	3	.50	3	.292	.370	.452
2007	Pwtckt	AAA	122	432	127	28	8	11	(-	-)	204	64	57	80	50	4	94	8	3	6		14	3	.82	5	.294	.373	.472
2008	Iowa	AAA	121	387	124	20	2	15	(-	-)	193	94	59	81	59	1	90	5	4	2		7	5	.58	8	.320	.415	.499
2009	Iowa	AAA	91	306	85	15	1	5	(-	-)	117	41	39	47	46	0	61	5	1	2		8	8	.50	6	.278	.379	.382
2009	ChC	NL	51	124	30	8	2	3	(2	1)	51	15	15	14	11	1	32	2	0	1		0	0	-	5	.242	.312	.411

Jordan Schafer

Bats: L **Throws:** L **Pos:** CF-50   **Ht:** 6'1" **Wt:** 200 **Born:** 9/4/1986 **Age:** 23

Year	Team	Lg						BATTING														BASERUNNING				AVERAGES		
			G	AB	H	2B	3B	HR	(Hm	Rd)	TB	R	RBI	RC	TBB	IBB	SO	HBP	SH	SF		SB	CS	SB%	GDP	Avg	OBP	Slg
2005	Braves	R	49	182	37	12	3	3	(-	-)	64	18	19	17	13	0	49	1	1	3		13	6	.68	4	.203	.256	.352
2006	Rome	A	114	388	93	15	7	8	(-	-)	146	49	60	43	28	0	95	1	5	0		15	9	.63	4	.240	.293	.376
2007	Rome	A	30	129	48	13	2	5	(-	-)	82	16	20	32	16	0	31	0	0	0		4	4	.50	1	.372	.441	.636
2007	MrtlBh	A+	106	436	128	34	8	10	(-	-)	208	70	43	73	40	4	95	1	3	1		10	11	.63	7	.294	.351	.477
2008	Missi	AA	84	297	80	18	6	10	(-	-)	140	46	51	55	49	2	88	3	0	0		12	5	.71	6	.269	.378	.471
2009	Gwnntt	AAA	9	35	8	0	0	2	(-	-)	14	6	3	4	2	0	10	0	0	1		3	1	.75	0	.229	.263	.400
2009	Atl	NL	50	167	34	8	0	2	(0	2)	48	18	8	11	27	3	63	0	0	1		2	1	.67	2	.204	.313	.287

Max Scherzer

Pitches: R **Bats:** R **Pos:** SP-30   **Ht:** 6'3" **Wt:** 213 **Born:** 7/27/1984 **Age:** 25

Year	Team	Lg		HOW MUCH HE PITCHED							WHAT HE GAVE UP										THE RESULTS						
			G	GS	CG	GF	IP	BFP	H	R	ER	HR	SH	SF	HB	TBB	IBB	SO	WP	Bk	W	L	Pct	Sh	Sv-Op Hld	ERC	ERA
2007	FtWth	IND	3	3	0	0	16.0	60	9	2	1	0	0	0	1	4	0	25	2	1	1	0	1.000	0	0-- -	1.27	0.56
2007	Visalia	A+	3	3	0	0	17.0	59	5	1	1	0	0	0	1	2	0	30	0	0	2	0	1.000	0	0-- -	0.39	0.53
2007	Mobile	AA	14	14	0	0	73.2	320	64	38	32	3	3	1	4	40	0	76	3	0	4	4	.500	0	0-- -	3.71	3.91
2008	Tucsn	AAA	13	10	0	0	53.0	219	35	19	16	2	1	2	2	22	0	79	1	0	1	1	.500	0	0-- -	2.07	2.72
2009	Visalia	A+	1	1	0	0	4.2	20	1	2	1	0	0	0	0	4	0	5	0	0	0	0		0	0-- -	1.71	1.93
2008	Ari	NL	16	7	0	2	56.0	237	48	24	19	5	4	2	5	21	1	66	2	0	0	4	.000	0	0-0 0	3.45	3.05
2009	Ari	NL	30	30	0	0	170.1	741	166	94	78	20	5	6	10	63	1	174	5	1	9	11	.450	0	0-0 0	4.12	4.12
	2 ML YEARS		46	37	0	2	226.1	978	214	118	97	25	9	8	15	84	2	240	7	1	9	15	.375	0	0-0 0	3.95	3.86

Nate Schierholtz

Bats: L **Throws:** R **Pos:** RF-86; PH-37   **Ht:** 6'2" **Wt:** 217 **Born:** 2/15/1984 **Age:** 26

Year	Team	Lg						BATTING														BASERUNNING				AVERAGES		
			G	AB	H	2B	3B	HR	(Hm	Rd)	TB	R	RBI	RC	TBB	IBB	SO	HBP	SH	SF		SB	CS	SB%	GDP	Avg	OBP	Slg
2009	Fresno*	AAA	5	18	4	1	0	0	(-	-)	5	2	1	1	1	0	1	0	0	0		1	0	1.00	1	.222	.263	.278
2007	SF	NL	39	112	34	5	3	0	(0	0)	45	9	10	14	2	0	19	1	0	2		3	1	.75	0	.304	.316	.402
2008	SF	NL	19	75	24	8	1	1	(1	0)	37	12	5	12	3	0	8	3	0	0		0	1	.00	1	.320	.370	.493
2009	SF	NL	116	285	76	19	2	5	(1	4)	114	33	29	35	16	3	58	1	0	6		3	1	.75	5	.267	.302	.400
	3 ML YEARS		174	472	134	32	6	6	(2	4)	196	54	44	61	21	3	85	5	0	8		6	3	.67	6	.284	.316	.415

Daniel Schlereth

Pitches: L Bats: L Pos: RP-21   Ht: 6'0" Wt: 210 Born: 5/9/1986 Age: 24

Year Team	Lg	G	GS	CG	GF	IP	BFP	H	R	ER	HR	SH	SF	HB	TBB	IBB	SO	WP	Bk	W	L	Pct	Sh	Sv-Op	Hld	ERC	ERA
2009 Mobile	AA	21	0	0	11	26.2	109	14	3	3	1	3	2	1	16	0	39	3	0	0	0	-	0	4--	-	2.09	1.01
2009 Reno	AAA	1	0	0	0	1.0	6	1	0	0	0	0	0	1	1	0	1	0	0	0	0	-	0	0--	-	9.51	0.00
2009 Ari	NL	21	0	0	4	18.1	86	15	13	12	1	2	0	1	15	1	22	4	0	1	4	.200	0	0-3	0	4.32	5.89

Travis Schlichting

Pitches: R Bats: R Pos: RP-2   Ht: 6'4" Wt: 214 Born: 10/19/1984 Age: 25

Year Team	Lg	G	GS	CG	GF	IP	BFP	H	R	ER	HR	SH	SF	HB	TBB	IBB	SO	WP	Bk	W	L	Pct	Sh	Sv-Op	Hld	ERC	ERA
2006 Angels	R	5	0	0	3	7.2	30	4	0	0	0	0	1	2	0	13	0	0	0	0	0	-	0	0--	-	1.26	0.00
2007 KC	IND	41	0	0	9	51.0	256	72	33	30	4	4	4	6	29	1	47	11	0	1	2	.333	0	0--	-	7.50	5.29
2008 Jaxnvl	AA	33	0	0	11	59.2	254	58	31	25	4	6	1	6	18	3	49	1	0	6	4	.600	0	0--	-	3.64	3.77
2009 Chatt	AA	9	0	0	1	13.2	56	7	5	1	1	0	1	0	7	0	12	1	0	1	0	1.000	0	1--	-	1.77	0.66
2009 Albq	AAA	13	0	0	3	12.2	54	8	3	2	0	2	0	1	8	0	7	1	0	1	0	1.000	0	0--	-	2.57	1.42
2009 Ddgrs	R	3	3	0	0	3.0	11	2	0	0	0	0	0	0	0	0	4	0	0	0	0	-	0	0--	-	0.91	0.00
2009 LAD	NL	2	0	0	1	2.2	15	1	2	1	1	0	1	0	5	0	2	1	0	0	0	-	0	0-0	0	8.03	3.38

Jason Schmidt

Pitches: R Bats: R Pos: SP-4   Ht: 6'5" Wt: 220 Born: 1/29/1973 Age: 37

Year Team	Lg	G	GS	CG	GF	IP	BFP	H	R	ER	HR	SH	SF	HB	TBB	IBB	SO	WP	Bk	W	L	Pct	Sh	Sv-Op	Hld	ERC	ERA
2009 InldEm*	A+	2	2	0	0	12.0	52	8	4	3	0	0	0	1	7	0	12	1	0	1	1	.500	0	0--	-	2.54	2.25
2009 Albq*	AAA	6	5	0	0	32.1	136	35	16	15	3	5	1	2	7	0	25	0	0	2	0	1.000	0	0--	-	4.07	4.18
1995 Atl	NL	9	2	0	1	25.0	119	27	17	16	2	2	4	1	18	3	19	1	0	2	2	.500	0	0-1	0	5.56	5.76
1996 2 Tms	NL	19	17	1	0	96.1	445	108	67	61	10	4	9	2	53	0	74	8	1	5	6	.455	0	0-0	0	5.46	5.70
1997 Pit	NL	32	32	2	0	187.2	825	193	106	96	16	10	3	9	76	2	136	8	0	10	9	.526	0	0-0	0	4.31	4.60
1998 Pit	NL	33	33	0	0	214.1	916	228	106	97	24	10	3	4	71	3	158	15	1	11	14	.440	0	0-0	0	4.35	4.07
1999 Pit	NL	33	33	2	0	212.2	937	219	110	99	24	7	7	3	85	4	148	6	4	13	11	.542	0	0-0	0	4.30	4.19
2000 Pit	NL	11	11	0	0	63.1	295	71	43	38	6	1	2	1	41	2	51	1	0	2	5	.286	0	0-0	0	5.77	5.40
2001 2 Tms	NL	25	25	1	0	150.1	641	138	75	68	13	5	3	7	61	3	142	8	1	13	7	.650	0	0-0	0	3.72	4.07
2002 SF	NL	29	29	2	0	185.1	769	148	78	71	15	11	5	2	73	1	196	12	0	13	8	.619	2	0-0	0	2.87	3.45
2003 SF	NL	29	29	5	0	207.2	819	152	56	54	14	6	3	5	46	1	208	7	1	17	5	.773	3	0-0	0	1.93	2.34
2004 SF	NL	32	32	4	0	225.0	907	165	84	80	18	7	3	3	77	3	251	7	1	18	7	.720	3	0-0	0	2.37	3.20
2005 SF	NL	29	29	0	0	172.0	757	160	90	84	16	8	3	5	85	4	165	7	1	12	7	.632	0	0-0	0	4.04	4.40
2006 SF	NL	32	32	3	0	213.1	894	189	94	85	21	7	7	6	80	6	180	11	1	11	9	.550	1	0-0	0	3.43	3.59
2007 LAD	NL	6	6	0	0	25.2	125	32	20	18	4	2	0	1	14	2	22	2	0	1	4	.200	0	0-0	0	6.40	6.31
2009 LAD	NL	4	4	0	0	17.2	83	16	12	11	1	1	0	3	12	1	8	0	0	2	2	.500	0	0-0	0	4.80	5.60
96 Atl	NL	13	11	0	0	58.2	274	69	48	44	8	3	6	0	32	0	48	5	1	3	4	.429	0	0-0	0	5.92	6.75
96 Pit	NL	6	6	1	0	37.2	171	39	19	17	2	1	3	2	21	0	26	3	0	2	2	.500	0	0-0	0	4.75	4.06
01 Pit	NL	14	14	1	0	84.0	357	81	46	43	11	3	2	7	28	2	77	3	1	6	6	.500	0	0-0	0	4.17	4.61
01 SF	NL	11	11	0	0	66.1	284	57	29	25	2	2	1	0	33	1	65	5	0	7	1	.875	0	0-0	0	3.16	3.39
Postseason		5	5	1	0	32.1	132	26	11	11	3	2	1	0	9	1	32	1	0	3	1	.750	1	0-0	0	2.45	3.06
14 ML YEARS		323	314	20	1	1996.1	8532	1846	958	878	184	81	57	52	792	35	1758	93	11	130	96	.575	9	0-1	0	3.65	3.96

Brian Schneider

Bats: L Throws: R Pos: C-57; PH-2   Ht: 6'1" Wt: 210 Born: 11/26/1976 Age: 33

Year Team	Lg	G	AB	H	2B	3B	HR	(Hm	Rd)	TB	R	RBI	RC	TBB	IBB	SO	HBP	SH	SF	SB	CS	SB%	GDP	Avg	OBP	Slg
2000 Mon	NL	45	115	27	6	0	0	(0	0)	33	6	11	8	7	2	24	0	0	1	0	1	.00	1	.235	.276	.287
2001 Mon	NL	27	41	13	3	0	1	(1	0)	19	4	6	8	6	1	3	0	0	1	0	0	-	0	.317	.396	.463
2002 Mon	NL	73	207	57	19	2	5	(3	2)	95	21	29	29	21	8	41	0	2	2	1	2	.33	7	.275	.339	.459
2003 Mon	NL	108	335	77	26	1	9	(9	0)	132	34	46	36	37	8	75	2	1	2	0	2	.00	12	.230	.309	.394
2004 Mon	NL	135	436	112	20	3	12	(5	7)	174	40	49	52	42	10	63	3	5	2	0	1	.00	8	.257	.325	.399
2005 Was	NL	116	369	99	20	1	10	(5	5)	151	38	44	48	29	7	48	6	2	2	1	0	1.00	10	.268	.330	.409
2006 Was	NL	124	410	105	18	0	4	(3	1)	135	30	55	45	38	10	67	2	2	3	2	2	.50	14	.256	.320	.329
2007 Was	NL	129	408	96	21	1	6	(2	4)	137	33	54	41	56	7	56	2	4	7	0	0	-	15	.235	.326	.336
2008 NYM	NL	110	335	86	10	0	9	(4	5)	123	30	38	36	42	9	53	1	4	2	0	0	-	11	.257	.339	.367
2009 NYM	NL	59	170	37	11	0	3	(3	0)	57	11	24	16	18	1	21	1	2	3	0	0	-	5	.218	.292	.335
10 ML YEARS		926	2826	709	154	8	59	(35	24)	1056	247	356	319	296	63	451	17	22	25	4	8	.33	83	.251	.323	.374

Scott Schoeneweis

Pitches: L Bats: L Pos: RP-45   Ht: 6'0" Wt: 190 Born: 10/2/1973 Age: 36

Year Team	Lg	G	GS	CG	GF	IP	BFP	H	R	ER	HR	SH	SF	HB	TBB	IBB	SO	WP	Bk	W	L	Pct	Sh	Sv-Op	Hld	ERC	ERA
1999 LAA	AL	31	0	0	6	39.1	175	47	27	24	4	0	1	0	14	1	22	1	0	1	1	.500	0	0-0	3	4.99	5.49
2000 LAA	AL	27	27	1	0	170.0	742	183	112	103	21	2	5	6	67	2	78	4	3	7	10	.412	1	0-0	0	4.84	5.45
2001 LAA	AL	32	32	1	0	205.1	910	227	122	116	21	3	8	14	77	2	104	4	1	10	11	.476	0	0-0	0	4.87	5.08
2002 LAA	AL	54	15	0	4	118.0	510	119	68	64	17	1	5	5	49	4	65	1	1	9	8	.529	0	1-4	11	4.68	4.88
2003 2 Tms	AL	59	0	0	19	64.2	276	63	35	30	3	2	1	4	19	5	56	3	0	3	2	.600	0	0-2	4	3.25	4.18
2004 CWS	AL	20	19	0	0	112.2	500	129	74	70	17	3	2	3	49	0	69	3	0	6	9	.400	0	0-0	0	5.65	5.59
2005 Tor	AL	80	0	0	15	57.0	250	54	23	21	2	1	0	4	25	5	43	2	0	3	4	.429	0	1-4	21	3.56	3.32
2006 2 Tms	AL	71	0	0	16	51.2	221	48	28	28	4	1	0	2	24	6	29	3	0	4	2	.667	0	4-6	19	3.79	4.88
2007 NYM	NL	70	0	0	17	59.0	265	62	36	33	8	4	1	3	28	5	41	3	1	0	2	.000	0	2-3	11	4.97	5.03
2008 NYM	NL	73	0	0	12	56.2	243	55	23	21	7	2	2	4	23	6	34	3	0	2	6	.250	0	1-5	15	4.28	3.34
2009 Ari	NL	45	0	0	9	24.0	117	29	20	19	6	1	0	2	13	1	14	0	0	1	2	.333	0	0-3	6	7.18	7.13

Year	Team	Lg	G	GS	CG	GF	IP	BFP	H	R	ER	HR	SH	SF	HB	TBB	IBB	SO	WP	Bk	W	L	Pct	Sh	Sv-Op	Hld	ERC	ERA
03	LAA	AL	39	0	0	12	38.2	163	37	19	17	2	1	1	3	10	3	29	1	0	1	1	.500	0	0-1	4	3.14	3.96
03	CWS	AL	20	0	0	7	26.0	113	26	16	13	1	1	0	1	9	2	27	2	0	2	1	.667	0	0-1	0	3.41	4.50
06	Tor	AL	55	0	0	8	37.1	161	39	27	27	3	1	0	1	16	5	18	2	0	2	2	.500	0	1-3	18	4.27	6.51
06	Cin	NL	16	0	0	8	14.1	60	9	1	1	1	0	0	1	8	1	11	1	0	2	0	1.000	0	3-3	1	2.64	0.63
Postseason			6	0	0	1	3.0	12	3	1	1	0	0	0	0	1	0	2	0	0	0	0	-	0	0-1	0	3.35	3.00
11 ML YEARS			562	93	2	98	958.1	4209	1016	568	529	110	20	25	47	388	37	555	27	6	46	57	.447	1	9-27	90	4.71	4.97

Skip Schumaker

Bats: L **Throws:** R **Pos:** 2B-133; LF-39; PH-19; RF-11; CF-6 **Ht:** 5'10" **Wt:** 195 **Born:** 2/3/1980 **Age:** 30

Year	Team	Lg	G	AB	H	2B	3B	HR	(Hm	Rd)	TB	R	RBI	RC	TBB	IBB	SO	HBP	SH	SF	SB	CS	SB%	GDP	Avg	OBP	Slg
2005	StL	NL	27	24	6	1	0	0	(0	0)	7	9	1	2	2	0	2	0	0	0	1	0	1.00	0	.250	.308	.292
2006	StL	NL	28	54	10	1	0	1	(0	1)	14	3	2	2	5	1	6	0	1	0	2	1	.67	1	.185	.254	.259
2007	StL	NL	88	177	59	12	2	2	(1	1)	81	19	19	30	8	0	20	0	1	2	1	1	.50	5	.333	.358	.458
2008	StL	NL	153	540	163	22	5	8	(4	4)	219	87	46	74	47	2	60	2	4	1	8	2	.80	19	.302	.359	.406
2009	StL	NL	153	532	161	34	1	4	(2	2)	209	85	35	74	52	2	69	0	1	1	2	2	.50	4	.303	.364	.393
5 ML YEARS			449	1327	399	70	8	15	(7	8)	530	203	103	182	114	5	157	2	7	4	14	6	.70	29	.301	.356	.399

Luke Scott

Bats: L **Throws:** R **Pos:** DH-89; LF-26; 1B-10; PH-7 **Ht:** 6'0" **Wt:** 210 **Born:** 6/25/1978 **Age:** 32

Year	Team	Lg	G	AB	H	2B	3B	HR	(Hm	Rd)	TB	R	RBI	RC	TBB	IBB	SO	HBP	SH	SF	SB	CS	SB%	GDP	Avg	OBP	Slg
2009 Dlmrva*	A		2	4	3	0	0	1	(-	-)	6	1	1	3	2	0	0	0	0	0	0	0	-	0	.750	.833	1.500
2005	Hou	NL	34	80	15	4	2	0	(0	0)	23	6	4	6	9	1	23	0	0	0	1	1	.50	0	.188	.270	.288
2006	Hou	NL	65	214	72	19	6	10	(8	2)	133	31	37	48	30	4	43	4	0	1	2	1	.67	2	.336	.426	.621
2007	Hou	NL	132	369	94	28	5	18	(8	10)	186	49	64	55	53	4	55	0	0	1	2	1	.75	8	.255	.351	.504
2008	Bal	AL	148	475	122	29	2	23	(11	12)	224	67	65	68	53	10	102	5	0	3	2	2	.50	7	.257	.336	.472
2009	Bal	AL	128	449	116	26	1	25	(18	7)	219	61	77	69	55	5	104	1	0	1	0	0	-	4	.258	.340	.488
Postseason			2	2	0	0	0	0	(0	0)	0	1	0	0	1	0	1	0	0	0	0	0	-	0	.000	.333	.000
5 ML YEARS			507	1587	419	106	16	76	(45	31)	785	214	247	246	200	24	367	12	0	6	8	5	.62	21	.264	.350	.495

Marco Scutaro

Bats: R **Throws:** R **Pos:** SS-143; 2B-2; DH-1 **Ht:** 5'10" **Wt:** 185 **Born:** 10/30/1975 **Age:** 34

Year	Team	Lg	G	AB	H	2B	3B	HR	(Hm	Rd)	TB	R	RBI	RC	TBB	IBB	SO	HBP	SH	SF	SB	CS	SB%	GDP	Avg	OBP	Slg
2002	NYM	NL	27	36	8	0	1	1	(1	0)	13	2	6	2	0	0	11	0	1	1	0	1	.00	1	.222	.216	.361
2003	NYM	NL	48	75	16	4	0	2	(0	2)	26	10	6	10	13	2	14	1	1	1	2	0	1.00	1	.213	.333	.347
2004	Oak	AL	137	455	124	32	1	7	(6	1)	179	50	43	48	16	1	58	0	5	1	0	0	-	9	.273	.297	.393
2005	Oak	AL	118	381	94	22	3	9	(5	4)	149	48	37	45	36	1	48	0	4	2	5	2	.71	6	.247	.310	.391
2006	Oak	AL	117	365	97	21	6	5	(1	4)	145	52	41	47	50	0	66	0	3	5	5	1	.83	16	.266	.350	.397
2007	Oak	AL	104	338	88	13	0	7	(2	5)	122	49	41	42	35	1	40	2	2	2	2	1	.67	13	.260	.332	.361
2008	Tor	AL	145	517	138	23	1	7	(5	2)	184	76	60	72	57	0	65	5	6	7	7	2	.78	8	.267	.341	.356
2009	Tor	AL	144	574	162	35	1	12	(7	5)	235	100	60	97	90	0	75	4	5	7	14	5	.74	12	.282	.379	.409
Postseason			7	27	5	4	0	0	(0	0)	9	1	6	3	0	0	4	0	0	0	0	0	-	1	.185	.185	.333
8 ML YEARS			840	2741	727	150	13	50	(27	23)	1053	387	294	363	297	5	377	12	27	26	35	12	.74	66	.265	.337	.384

Bobby Seay

Pitches: L **Bats:** L **Pos:** RP-67 **Ht:** 6'2" **Wt:** 235 **Born:** 6/20/1978 **Age:** 32

Year	Team	Lg	G	GS	CG	GF	IP	BFP	H	R	ER	HR	SH	SF	HB	TBB	IBB	SO	WP	Bk	W	L	Pct	Sh	Sv-Op	Hld	ERC	ERA
2001	TB	AL	12	0	0	4	13.0	58	13	11	9	3	2	0	1	5	1	12	1	0	1	1	.500	0	0-0	0	5.03	6.23
2003	TB	AL	12	0	0	2	9.0	39	7	3	3	0	0	2	0	6	0	5	0	0	0	0	-	0	0-1	0	3.17	3.00
2004	TB	AL	21	0	0	6	22.2	95	21	6	6	2	0	0	2	5	1	17	1	0	0	0	-	0	0-0	3	3.15	2.38
2005	Col	NL	17	0	0	5	11.2	58	18	11	11	3	1	0	0	8	1	11	0	1	0	0	-	0	0-1	1	10.28	8.49
2006	Det	AL	14	0	0	6	15.1	71	14	11	11	1	1	1	3	9	1	12	0	0	0	0	-	0	0-0	0	4.65	6.46
2007	Det	AL	58	0	0	19	46.1	189	38	12	12	1	2	2	2	15	4	38	1	1	3	0	1.000	0	1-2	10	2.39	2.33
2008	Det	AL	60	0	0	14	56.1	246	59	28	28	4	3	4	2	25	7	58	3	0	1	2	.333	0	0-1	13	4.29	4.47
2009	Det	AL	67	0	0	7	48.2	208	46	23	23	3	3	3	3	17	3	37	3	0	6	3	.667	0	0-4	28	3.44	4.25
8 ML YEARS			261	0	0	63	223.0	964	216	105	103	17	12	12	13	90	18	190	9	2	11	6	.647	0	1-9	52	3.85	4.16

Zack Segovia

Pitches: R **Bats:** R **Pos:** RP-8 **Ht:** 6'2" **Wt:** 245 **Born:** 4/11/1983 **Age:** 27

Year	Team	Lg	G	GS	CG	GF	IP	BFP	H	R	ER	HR	SH	SF	HB	TBB	IBB	SO	WP	Bk	W	L	Pct	Sh	Sv-Op	Hld	ERC	ERA
2002	Phillies	R	8	8	0	0	34.1	128	21	11	8	0	0	1	3	3	0	30	1	0	3	2	.600	0	0- -	-	1.11	2.10
2003	Lakwd	A	11	10	0	0	49.2	225	63	25	22	2	2	2	2	14	1	27	2	0	1	5	.167	0	0- -	-	4.76	3.99
2003	Phillies	R	5	4	0	0	9.0	35	8	5	4	0	0	0	1	0	0	6	0	0	0	1	.000	0	0- -	-	1.88	4.00
2005	Clrwtr	A+	27	27	0	0	144.2	654	168	84	89	18	5	6	17	48	0	83	9	1	4	14	.222	0	0- -	-	5.38	5.54
2006	Clrwtr	A+	7	7	0	0	49.1	193	39	14	12	2	0	0	5	12	0	41	1	0	5	1	.833	0	0- -	-	2.51	2.19
2006	Rdng	AA	17	16	3	0	107.0	437	90	45	37	8	4	2	8	24	2	75	5	0	11	5	.688	1	0- -	-	2.65	3.11
2007	Ottawa	AAA	13	13	1	0	77.1	348	99	55	52	8	2	2	2	28	0	22	4	0	1	9	.100	0	0- -	-	5.78	6.05
2007	Rdng	AA	10	10	0	0	57.2	258	65	34	31	4	4	3	5	22	0	30	1	0	5	3	.625	0	0- -	-	4.87	4.84
2008	Rdng	AA	4	1	0	1	5.0	28	7	9	8	1	1	0	0	6	0	1	1	0	0	1	.000	0	0- -	-	10.82	14.40
2008	Clrwtr	A+	7	7	0	0	38.2	171	50	26	23	6	0	1	0	12	2	32	0	0	1	3	.250	0	0- -	-	5.86	5.35
2008	Nats	R	2	1	0	0	6.0	25	5	3	3	0	0	0	1	1	0	6	1	0	1	0	1.000	0	0- -	-	2.26	4.50

Year	Team	Lg	G	GS	CG	GF	IP	BFP	H	R	ER	HR	SH	SF	HB	TBB	IBB	SO	WP	Bk	W	L	Pct	Sh	Sv-Op	Hld	ERC	ERA
2008	Hgrstn	A	1	1	0	0	5.0	23	8	4	4	0	0	0	1	0	0	3	0	0	0	1	.000	0	0--	-	6.13	7.20
2008	Ptomc	A+	3	3	0	0	16.2	68	17	8	5	2	1	1	2	3	0	13	0	0	2	1	.667	0	0--	-	4.10	2.70
2008	Hrsbrg	AA	8	6	0	0	37.2	174	50	29	27	5	1	3	2	13	0	24	1	0	4	1	.800	0	0--	-	6.26	6.45
2009	Hrsbrg	AA	24	3	0	11	44.0	205	57	19	18	2	5	4	3	19	7	39	1	0	1	3	.250	0	1--	-	5.51	3.68
2009	Syrcse	AAA	27	4	0	11	28.1	112	18	8	8	1	0	2	4	8	1	27	0	0	2	2	.500	0	5--	-	1.88	2.54
2007	Phi	NL	1	1	0	0	5.0	23	8	5	5	1	1	1	0	1	1	2	0	0	0	1	.000	0	0-0	0	7.45	9.00
2009	Was	NL	8	0	0	2	10.1	47	11	10	9	1	0	2	0	6	1	4	1	0	1	0	1.000	0	0-1	0	4.96	7.84
	2 ML YEARS		9	1	0	2	15.1	70	19	15	14	2	1	3	0	7	2	6	1	0	1	1	.500	0	0-1	0	5.74	8.22

Ben Sheets

Pitches: R **Bats:** R **Pos:** P **Ht:** 6'1" **Wt:** 226 **Born:** 7/18/1978 **Age:** 31

Year	Team	Lg	G	GS	CG	GF	IP	BFP	H	R	ER	HR	SH	SF	HB	TBB	IBB	SO	WP	Bk	W	L	Pct	Sh	Sv-Op	Hld	ERC	ERA
2001	Mil	NL	25	25	1	0	151.1	653	166	89	80	23	8	5	5	48	6	94	3	0	11	10	.524	1	0-0	0	4.78	4.76
2002	Mil	NL	34	34	1	0	216.2	934	237	105	100	21	10	0	10	70	10	170	9	0	11	**16**	.407	0	0-0	0	4.45	4.15
2003	Mil	NL	34	34	1	0	220.2	931	232	122	109	29	11	6	6	43	2	157	7	0	11	13	.458	0	0-0	0	3.83	4.45
2004	Mil	NL	34	34	5	0	237.0	937	201	85	71	25	6	4	4	32	1	264	8	1	12	14	.462	0	0-0	0	2.37	2.70
2005	Mil	NL	22	22	3	0	156.2	633	142	66	58	19	6	2	2	25	1	141	7	0	10	9	.526	0	0-0	0	2.81	3.33
2006	Mil	NL	17	17	0	0	106.0	430	105	47	45	9	6	5	2	11	1	116	3	0	6	7	.462	0	0-0	0	2.84	3.82
2007	Mil	NL	24	24	2	0	141.1	592	138	62	60	17	4	5	1	37	2	106	4	0	12	5	.706	0	0-0	0	3.53	3.82
2008	Mil	NL	31	31	5	0	198.1	812	181	74	68	17	6	7	1	47	2	158	8	0	13	9	.591	**3**	0-0	0	2.89	3.09
	8 ML YEARS		221	221	18	0	1428.0	5922	1402	650	591	160	57	34	31	313	25	1206	49	1	86	83	.509	4	0-0	0	3.41	3.72

Gary Sheffield

Bats: R **Throws:** R **Pos:** LF-46; PH-32; RF-18; DH-6 **Ht:** 6'0" **Wt:** 215 **Born:** 11/18/1968 **Age:** 41

Year	Team	Lg	G	AB	H	2B	3B	HR	(Hm	Rd)	TB	R	RBI	RC	TBB	IBB	SO	HBP	SH	SF	SB	CS	SB%	GDP	Avg	OBP	Slg
1988	Mil	AL	24	80	19	1	0	4	(1	3)	32	12	12	8	7	0	7	0	1	1	3	1	.75	5	.238	.295	.400
1989	Mil	AL	95	368	91	18	0	5	(2	3)	124	34	32	38	27	0	33	4	3	3	10	6	.63	4	.247	.303	.337
1990	Mil	AL	125	487	143	30	1	10	(3	7)	205	67	67	73	44	1	41	3	4	9	25	10	.71	11	.294	.350	.421
1991	Mil	AL	50	175	34	12	2	2	(2	0)	56	25	22	15	19	1	15	3	1	5	5	5	.50	3	.194	.277	.320
1992	SD	NL	146	557	184	34	3	33	(23	10)	323	87	100	113	48	5	40	6	0	7	5	6	.45	19	**.330**	.385	.580
1993	2 Tms	NL	140	494	145	20	5	20	(10	10)	235	67	73	84	47	6	64	9	0	7	17	5	.77	11	.294	.361	.476
1994	Fla	NL	87	322	89	16	1	27	(15	12)	188	61	78	68	51	11	50	6	0	5	12	6	.67	10	.276	.380	.584
1995	Fla	NL	63	213	69	8	0	16	(4	12)	125	46	46	60	55	8	45	4	0	2	19	4	.83	3	.324	.467	.587
1996	Fla	NL	161	519	163	33	1	42	(19	**23**)	324	118	120	144	142	19	66	10	0	6	16	9	.64	16	.314	**.465**	.624
1997	Fla	NL	135	444	111	22	1	21	(13	8)	198	86	71	92	121	11	79	15	0	2	11	7	.61	7	.250	.424	.446
1998	2 Tms	NL	130	437	132	27	2	22	(11	11)	229	73	85	102	95	12	46	8	0	9	22	7	.76	7	.302	.428	.524
1999	LAD	NL	152	549	165	20	0	34	(15	19)	287	103	101	118	101	4	64	4	0	9	11	5	.69	10	.301	.407	.523
2000	LAD	NL	141	501	163	24	3	43	(23	20)	322	105	109	131	101	7	71	4	0	6	4	6	.40	13	.325	.438	.643
2001	LAD	NL	143	515	160	28	2	36	(16	20)	300	98	100	120	94	13	67	4	0	5	10	4	.71	12	.311	.417	.583
2002	Atl	NL	135	492	151	26	0	25	(10	15)	252	82	84	102	72	2	53	11	0	4	12	2	.86	16	.307	.404	.512
2003	Atl	NL	155	576	190	37	2	39	(20	19)	348	126	132	134	86	6	55	8	0	8	18	4	.82	16	.330	.419	.604
2004	NYY	AL	154	573	166	30	1	36	(19	17)	306	117	121	123	92	7	83	11	0	8	5	6	.45	16	.290	.393	.534
2005	NYY	AL	154	584	170	27	0	34	(19	15)	299	104	123	130	78	7	76	8	0	5	10	2	.83	11	.291	.379	.512
2006	NYY	AL	39	151	45	5	0	6	(5	1)	68	22	25	21	13	2	16	1	0	1	5	1	.83	6	.298	.355	.450
2007	Det	AL	133	494	131	20	1	25	(14	11)	228	107	75	90	84	2	71	9	0	6	22	5	.81	10	.265	.378	.462
2008	Det	AL	114	418	94	16	0	19	(13	6)	167	52	57	51	58	3	83	5	0	1	9	2	.82	19	.225	.326	.400
2009	NYM	NL	100	268	74	13	2	10	(5	5)	121	44	43	39	40	3	46	2	0	2	2	1	.67	10	.276	.372	.451
93	SD	NL	68	258	76	12	2	10	(6	4)	122	34	36	40	18	0	30	3	0	3	5	1	.83	9	.295	.344	.473
93	Fla	NL	72	236	69	8	3	10	(4	6)	113	33	37	44	29	6	34	6	0	4	12	4	.75	2	.292	.378	.479
98	Fla	NL	40	136	37	11	1	6	(6	0)	68	21	28	27	26	1	16	2	0	2	4	2	.67	3	.272	.392	.500
98	LAD	NL	90	301	95	16	1	16	(5	11)	161	52	57	75	69	11	30	6	0	7	18	5	.78	4	.316	.444	.535
	Postseason		44	161	40	6	0	6	(4	2)	64	27	19	27	39	2	26	2	0	0	1	1	.50	6	.248	.401	.398
	22 ML YEARS		2576	9217	2689	467	27	509	(262	247)	4737	1636	1676	1856	1475	130	1171	135	9	111	253	104	.71	235	.292	.393	.514

Steven Shell

Pitches: R **Bats:** R **Pos:** RP-4 **Ht:** 6'4" **Wt:** 225 **Born:** 3/10/1983 **Age:** 27

Year	Team	Lg	G	GS	CG	GF	IP	BFP	H	R	ER	HR	SH	SF	HB	TBB	IBB	SO	WP	Bk	W	L	Pct	Sh	Sv-Op	Hld	ERC	ERA
2001	Angels	R	3	0	0	1	4.0	15	1	0	0	0	0	0	0	2	0	3	0	0	1	0	1.000	0	0--	-	0.75	0.00
2001	Provo	R+	14	4	0	3	37.2	182	52	31	30	3	0	1	9	15	0	33	3	0	0	3	.000	0	1--	-	7.31	7.17
2002	CRpds	A	22	21	1	0	121.0	506	119	59	50	12	1	3	9	26	0	86	3	2	11	4	.733	0	0--	-	3.56	3.72
2003	RCuca	A+	22	21	1	0	127.1	540	123	66	60	13	4	3	12	26	0	100	3	1	6	8	.429	1	0--	-	3.45	4.24
2004	RCuca	A+	28	28	2	0	165.1	672	151	76	66	19	6	2	16	40	0	190	4	1	12	7	.632	1	0--	-	3.57	3.59
2005	Ark	AA	27	27	1	0	159.2	712	175	90	81	18	-	-	9	58	0	126	10	0	10	8	.556	1	0--	-	4.75	4.57
2006	Ark	AA	3	3	0	0	18.0	75	20	12	8	1	0	0	1	4	0	10	0	0	1	2	.333	0	0--	-	4.04	4.00
2006	Salt Lk	AAA	24	22	0	1	122.2	542	156	91	84	16	3	5	12	32	0	82	2	1	5	9	.357	0	0--	-	5.88	6.16
2007	Ark	AA	5	0	0	0	13.1	54	10	1	1	1	0	0	3	1	0	19	0	0	0	0	-	0	0--	-	2.21	0.68
2007	Salt Lk	AAA	31	7	0	10	70.1	297	83	43	37	15	1	4	2	19	0	52	1	0	7	3	.700	0	0--	-	5.76	4.73
2008	Clmbs	AAA	22	4	0	3	58.1	232	49	19	17	5	2	1	3	14	1	54	2	1	3	2	.600	0	1--	-	2.77	2.62
2009	Tacom	AAA	17	5	0	6	40.0	191	56	35	31	10	0	2	0	15	0	27	3	0	3	3	.500	0	1--	-	7.42	6.98
2009	WTenn	AA	5	3	0	1	21.0	80	9	2	1	0	0	0	1	6	1	16	0	0	3	0	1.000	0	0--	-	0.86	0.43
2008	Was	NL	39	0	0	7	50.0	199	34	14	12	5	1	1	2	20	1	41	1	0	2	2	.500	0	2-3	7	2.58	2.16
2009	Was	NL	4	0	0	0	5.0	22	5	3	3	1	0	0	0	2	0	5	0	0	0	0	-	0	0-0	1	4.68	5.40
	2 ML YEARS		43	0	0	7	55.0	221	39	17	15	6	1	1	2	22	1	46	1	0	2	2	.500	0	2-3	8	2.76	2.45

Chris Shelton

Bats: R Throws: R Pos: 1B-4; PH-3; DH-2 **Ht: 6'0" Wt: 215 Born: 6/26/1980 Age: 30**

Year	Team	Lg	G	AB	H	2B	3B	HR	(Hm	Rd)	TB	R	RBI	RC	TBB	IBB	SO	HBP	SH	SF	SB	CS	SB%	GDP	Avg	OBP	Slg
2009	Tacom*	AAA	105	405	127	30	2	15	(-	-)	206	71	85	83	58	1	86	2	0	7	0	2	.00	5	.314	.396	.509
2004	Det	AL	27	46	9	1	0	1	(1	0)	13	6	3	4	9	0	14	0	0	1	0	0	-	2	.196	.321	.283
2005	Det	AL	107	388	116	22	3	18	(10	8)	198	61	59	65	34	0	87	5	0	4	0	0	-	11	.299	.360	.510
2006	Det	AL	115	373	102	16	4	16	(5	11)	174	50	47	50	34	1	107	4	0	1	1	2	.33	10	.273	.340	.466
2008	Tex	AL	41	97	21	5	0	2	(1	1)	32	14	11	11	17	0	33	0	3	0	1	0	1.00	3	.216	.333	.330
2009	Sea	AL	9	26	6	2	0	0	(0	0)	8	1	4	3	2	0	11	0	0	0	0	0	-	0	.231	.286	.308
5 ML YEARS			299	930	254	46	7	37	(17	20)	425	132	124	133	96	1	252	9	3	6	2	2	.50	26	.273	.345	.457

George Sherrill

Pitches: L Bats: L Pos: RP-72 **Ht: 6'0" Wt: 230 Born: 4/19/1977 Age: 33**

Year	Team	Lg	G	GS	CG	GF	IP	BFP	H	R	ER	HR	SH	SF	HB	TBB	IBB	SO	WP	Bk	W	L	Pct	Sh	Sv-Op	Hld	ERC	ERA
2004	Sea	AL	21	0	0	4	23.2	104	24	12	10	3	0	1	1	9	1	16	4	1	2	1	.667	0	0-0	3	4.31	3.80
2005	Sea	AL	29	0	0	2	19.0	77	13	12	11	3	1	1	1	7	2	24	0	0	4	3	.571	0	0-0	9	2.70	5.21
2006	Sea	AL	72	0	0	6	40.0	174	30	19	19	0	4	2	0	27	4	42	0	0	2	4	.333	0	1-1	17	2.86	4.28
2007	Sea	AL	73	0	0	16	45.2	182	28	12	12	4	4	4	1	17	1	56	1	1	2	0	1.000	0	3-7	22	1.96	2.36
2008	Bal	AL	57	0	0	49	53.1	239	47	28	28	6	1	3	1	33	6	58	1	0	3	5	.375	0	31-37	0	4.18	4.73
2009	2 Tms		72	0	0	39	69.0	282	53	13	13	4	1	1	2	24	4	61	1	0	1	1	.500	0	21-26	11	2.41	1.70
09	Bal	AL	42	0	0	38	41.1	171	34	11	11	3	0	1	2	13	2	39	0	0	0	1	.000	0	20-23	0	2.72	2.40
09	LAD	NL	30	0	0	1	27.2	111	19	2	2	1	1	0	0	11	2	22	1	0	1	0	1.000	0	1-3	11	1.96	0.65
6 ML YEARS			324	0	0	116	250.2	1058	195	96	93	20	11	12	6	117	18	257	7	2	14	14	.500	0	56-71	62	2.95	3.34

James Shields

Pitches: R Bats: R Pos: SP-33 **Ht: 6'4" Wt: 220 Born: 12/20/1981 Age: 28**

Year	Team	Lg	G	GS	CG	GF	IP	BFP	H	R	ER	HR	SH	SF	HB	TBB	IBB	SO	WP	Bk	W	L	Pct	Sh	Sv-Op	Hld	ERC	ERA
2006	TB	AL	21	21	1	0	124.2	540	141	69	67	18	4	3	5	38	5	104	9	0	6	8	.429	0	0-0	0	4.92	4.04
2007	TB	AL	31	31	1	0	215.0	874	202	98	92	28	4	5	10	36	0	184	9	0	12	8	.600	0	0-0	0	3.24	3.85
2008	TB	AL	33	33	3	0	215.0	877	208	94	85	24	8	0	12	40	1	160	6	0	14	8	.636	2	0-0	0	3.41	3.56
2009	TB	AL	33	33	0	0	219.2	900	230	117	101	29	6	3	1	52	1	167	3	1	11	12	.478	0	0-0	0	4.16	4.14
Postseason			4	4	0	0	25.0	108	28	9	8	3	1	1	1	8	0	17	1	0	2	2	.500	0	0-0	0	4.82	2.88
4 ML YEARS			118	118	5	0	774.1	3221	790	374	345	99	20	11	28	166	6	615	27	1	43	36	.544	2	0-0	0	3.81	4.01

Scot Shields

Pitches: R Bats: R Pos: RP-20 **Ht: 6'1" Wt: 180 Born: 7/22/1975 Age: 34**

Year	Team	Lg	G	GS	CG	GF	IP	BFP	H	R	ER	HR	SH	SF	HB	TBB	IBB	SO	WP	Bk	W	L	Pct	Sh	Sv-Op	Hld	ERC	ERA
2001	LAA	AL	8	0	0	6	11.0	48	8	1	0	0	0	0	0	7	0	7	2	0	0	0	-	0	0-0	0	3.10	0.00
2002	LAA	AL	29	1	0	13	49.0	188	31	13	12	4	1	0	1	21	1	30	3	0	5	3	.625	0	0-0	3	2.35	2.20
2003	LAA	AL	44	13	0	5	148.1	609	138	56	47	12	3	4	5	38	6	111	4	0	5	6	.455	0	1-1	3	3.12	2.85
2004	LAA	AL	60	0	0	12	105.1	454	97	42	39	6	2	2	3	40	5	109	4	0	8	2	.800	0	4-7	17	3.24	3.33
2005	LAA	AL	78	0	0	21	91.2	375	66	33	28	5	4	3	2	37	2	98	12	0	10	11	.476	0	7-13	33	2.37	2.75
2006	LAA	AL	74	0	0	13	87.2	351	70	30	28	8	3	1	1	24	4	84	8	0	7	7	.500	0	2-8	31	2.48	2.87
2007	LAA	AL	71	0	0	13	77.0	320	62	36	33	7	0	1	4	33	0	77	6	0	4	5	.444	0	2 8	31	3.31	3.86
2008	LAA	AL	64	0	0	12	63.1	270	56	29	19	6	1	1	2	29	2	64	2	0	6	4	.600	0	4-9	31	3.72	2.70
2009	LAA	AL	20	0	0	2	17.2	83	16	14	13	1	1	0	0	15	0	12	1	0	1	3	.250	0	1-4	6	4.90	6.62
Postseason			17	0	0	3	25.1	109	24	13	9	3	1	1	0	11	2	25	0	0	1	2	.333	0	0-1	1	3.91	3.20
9 ML YEARS			448	14	0	97	651.0	2698	544	254	219	49	15	12	19	244	20	592	42	0	46	41	.529	0	21-50	155	3.01	3.03

Kelly Shoppach

Bats: R Throws: R Pos: C-81; DH-7; PH-4 **Ht: 6'0" Wt: 220 Born: 4/29/1980 Age: 30**

Year	Team	Lg	G	AB	H	2B	3B	HR	(Hm	Rd)	TB	R	RBI	RC	TBB	IBB	SO	HBP	SH	SF	SB	CS	SB%	GDP	Avg	OBP	Slg
2005	Bos	AL	9	15	0	0	0	0	(0	0)	0	1	0	0	0	0	7	1	0	0	0	0	-	0	.000	.063	.000
2006	Cle	AL	41	110	27	6	0	3	(2	1)	42	7	16	13	8	0	45	0	2	0	0	0	-	2	.245	.297	.382
2007	Cle	AL	59	161	42	13	0	7	(4	3)	76	26	30	24	11	0	56	1	3	1	0	0	-	2	.261	.310	.472
2008	Cle	AL	112	352	92	27	0	21	(9	12)	182	67	55	58	36	3	133	11	3	1	0	0	-	7	.261	.348	.517
2009	Cle	AL	89	271	58	14	0	12	(5	7)	108	33	40	32	33	0	98	18	2	3	0	0	-	8	.214	.335	.399
Postseason			2	6	3	2	0	0	(0	0)	5	1	0	2	0	0	2	2	0	0	0	0	-	0	.500	.625	.833
5 ML YEARS			310	909	219	60	0	43	(20	23)	408	134	141	127	88	3	339	31	10	5	0	0	-	19	.241	.327	.449

Brian Shouse

Pitches: L Bats: L Pos: RP-45 **Ht: 5'10" Wt: 190 Born: 9/26/1968 Age: 41**

Year	Team	Lg	G	GS	CG	GF	IP	BFP	H	R	ER	HR	SH	SF	HB	TBB	IBB	SO	WP	Bk	W	L	Pct	Sh	Sv-Op	Hld	ERC	ERA
2009	Charltt*	A+	4	0	0	2	4.0	17	5	1	1	0	0	0	1	0	0	2	0	0	0	0	-	0	1- -	-	4.32	2.25
1993	Pit	NL	6	0	0	1	4.0	22	7	4	4	1	0	1	0	2	0	3	1	0	0	0	-	0	0-0	0	9.92	9.00
1998	Bos	AL	7	0	0	4	8.0	36	9	5	5	2	0	0	0	4	0	5	0	0	0	1	.000	0	0-0	1	6.42	5.63
2002	KC	AL	23	0	0	7	14.2	71	15	10	10	3	1	1	2	9	1	11	2	0	0	0	-	0	0-0	2	6.11	6.14
2003	Tex	AL	62	0	0	14	61.0	253	62	24	21	3	3	0	4	14	6	40	0	0	1	1	.000	0	1-1	10	3.10	3.10
2004	Tex	AL	53	0	0	14	44.1	184	36	12	11	3	2	2	1	18	3	34	0	0	2	0	1.000	0	0-0	12	2.87	2.23
2005	Tex	AL	64	0	0	12	53.1	233	55	37	31	7	2	3	3	18	4	35	2	0	3	2	.600	0	0-2	11	4.29	5.23

Year	Team	Lg	G	GS	CG	GF	IP	BFP	H	R	ER	HR	SH	SF	HB	TBB	IBB	SO	WP	Bk	W	L	Pct	Sh	Sv-Op	Hld	ERC	ERA
2006	2 Tms		65	0	0	10	38.1	174	40	18	17	4	1	1	6	18	5	23	0	0	1	3	.250	0	2-5	15	5.06	3.99
2007	Mil	NL	73	0	0	13	47.2	201	46	19	16	4	2	2		14	5	32	0	1	1	1	.500	0	1-4	21	2.79	3.02
2008	Mil	NL	69	0	0	17	51.1	212	46	19	16	5	4	1	0	14	4	33	1	0	5	1	.833	0	2-5	15	2.87	2.81
2009	TB	AL	45	0	0	9	28.0	122	31	15	14	5	1	0	2	7	3	17	1	1	1	1	.500	0	0-1	10	4.73	4.50
06	Tex	AL	6	0	0	2	4.1	20	6	2	2	1	0	0	0	1	1	3	0	0	0	0	-	0	0-1	1	6.09	4.15
06	Mil	NL	59	0	0	8	34.0	154	34	16	15	3	1	1	6	17	4	20	0	0	1	3	.250	0	2-4	14	4.92	3.97
10 ML YEARS			467	0	0	101	350.2	1508	347	163	145	31	18	11	20	118	31	233	7	2	13	10	.565	0	6-18	97	3.76	3.72

Carlos Silva

Pitches: R **Bats:** R **Pos:** SP-6; RP-2   **Ht:** 6'4" **Wt:** 250 **Born:** 4/23/1979 **Age:** 31

Year	Team	Lg	G	GS	CG	GF	IP	BFP	H	R	ER	HR	SH	SF	HB	TBB	IBB	SO	WP	Bk	W	L	Pct	Sh	Sv-Op	Hld	ERC	ERA
2009	Everett*	A-	1	1	0	0	1.0	7	3	2	1	0	0	0	0	0	0	3	1	0	0	0	-	0	0--	-	12.36	9.00
2009	Tacom*	AAA	2	1	0	0	3.0	12	3	1	1	0	0	0	0	0	0	2	0	0	0	0	-	0	0--	-	1.95	3.00
2002	Phi	NL	68	0	0	21	84.0	350	88	34	30	4	9	3	4	22	6	41	3	0	5	0	1.000	0	1-5	8	3.60	3.21
2003	Phi	NL	62	1	0	15	87.1	381	92	43	43	7	6	1	8	37	5	48	12	1	3	1	.750	0	1-3	4	4.71	4.43
2004	Min	AL	33	33	1	0	203.0	869	255	100	95	23	6	0	5	35	2	76	5	1	14	8	.636	1	0-0	0	4.89	4.21
2005	Min	AL	27	27	2	0	188.1	749	212	83	72	25	2	5	3	9	2	71	0	0	9	8	.529	0	0-0	0	3.78	3.44
2006	Min	AL	36	31	0	2	180.1	811	246	130	119	38	6	7	7	32	4	70	1	0	11	15	.423	0	0-0	2	6.23	5.94
2007	Min	AL	33	33	2	0	202.0	848	229	99	94	20	4	5	4	36	2	89	4	1	13	14	.481	1	0-0	0	4.05	4.19
2008	Sea	AL	28	28	1	0	153.1	689	213	114	110	20	3	7	4	32	2	69	1	0	4	15	.211	0	0-0	0	5.93	6.46
2009	Sea	AL	8	6	0	1	30.1	142	41	29	29	5	1	0	3	11	0	10	2	1	1	3	.250	0	0-0	0	7.01	8.60
Postseason			1	1	0	0	5.0	24	10	6	6	1	0	0	0	0	0	1	0	0	0	1	.000	0	0-0	0	9.65	10.80
8 ML YEARS			295	159	6	39	1128.2	4839	1376	632	592	142	39	28	38	214	23	474	28	4	60	64	.484	2	2-8	14	4.84	4.72

Walter Silva

Pitches: R **Bats:** R **Pos:** SP-6   **Ht:** 6'1" **Wt:** 190 **Born:** 1/4/1977 **Age:** 33

Year	Team	Lg	G	GS	CG	GF	IP	BFP	H	R	ER	HR	SH	SF	HB	TBB	IBB	SO	WP	Bk	W	L	Pct	Sh	Sv-Op	Hld	ERC	ERA
2009	Portlnd	AAA	23	13	0	2	81.1	358	98	57	55	10	4	3	2	27	1	56	5	1	7	5	.583	0	0--	-	5.31	6.09
2009	SD	NL	6	6	0	0	24.2	121	34	28	24	4	0	3	0	15	0	11	0	0	0	2	.000	0	0-0	0	7.74	8.76

Alfredo Simon

Pitches: R **Bats:** R **Pos:** SP-2   **Ht:** 6'4" **Wt:** 230 **Born:** 5/8/1981 **Age:** 29

Year	Team	Lg	G	GS	CG	GF	IP	BFP	H	R	ER	HR	SH	SF	HB	TBB	IBB	SO	WP	Bk	W	L	Pct	Sh	Sv-Op	Hld	ERC	ERA
2001	Phillies	R	10	8	0	0	43.1	194	35	23	14	2	2	3	7	23	0	40	6	3	2	2	.500	0	0--	-	3.67	2.91
2002	Batvia	A-	15	14	0	1	90.1	388	79	44	36	5	2	2	5	46	0	77	3	1	9	2	.818	0	0--	-	3.75	3.59
2003	Lakwd	A	14	7	0	4	71.1	298	59	32	30	4	4	3	3	25	0	66	5	1	5	0	1.000	0	2--	-	2.80	3.79
2004	Clrwtr	A+	22	21	4	0	134.2	552	121	58	49	13	8	2	5	38	2	107	10	4	7	9	.438	3	0--	-	3.21	3.27
2004	SnJos	A+	6	6	0	0	31.2	142	44	24	20	7	3	2	0	12	0	21	5	0	1	2	.333	0	0--	-	7.62	5.68
2005	Nrwich	AA	43	9	0	28	91.1	395	104	54	51	6	7	5	3	24	2	60	5	0	3	8	.273	0	19--	-	4.17	5.03
2006	Fresno	AAA	10	10	0	0	52.0	245	76	41	39	8	3	2	3	19	0	35	7	0	0	6	.000	0	0--	-	7.52	6.75
2006	SnJos	A+	18	7	-	-	36.1	166	43	28	26	7	-	-	1	14	-	35	1	1	2	4	.333	-	0--	-	5.80	6.44
2007	Okla	AAA	22	22	1	0	119.0	539	152	92	85	19	3	1	6	46	0	73	4	0	5	10	.333	0	0--	-	6.46	6.43
2008	Norfolk	AAA	1	1	0	0	4.2	25	9	7	4	1	0	1	1	2	0	5	0	0	0	1	.000	0	0--	-	12.56	7.71
2008	Bal	AL	4	1	0	0	13.0	59	16	10	9	4	0	1	2	2	0	8	2	0	0	0	-	0	0-0	0	6.45	6.23
2009	Bal	AL	2	2	0	0	6.1	28	8	7	7	5	0	0	0	2	0	3	0	0	0	1	.000	0	0-0	0	10.74	9.95
2 ML YEARS			6	3	0	0	19.1	87	24	17	16	9	0	1	2	4	0	11	2	0	0	1	.000	0	0-0	0	7.81	7.45

Tony Sipp

Pitches: L **Bats:** L **Pos:** RP-46   **Ht:** 6'0" **Wt:** 190 **Born:** 7/12/1983 **Age:** 26

Year	Team	Lg	G	GS	CG	GF	IP	BFP	H	R	ER	HR	SH	SF	HB	TBB	IBB	SO	WP	Bk	W	L	Pct	Sh	Sv-Op	Hld	ERC	ERA
2004	MhVlly	A-	10	10	0	0	42.2	174	33	23	15	5	3	1	1	13	0	74	3	3	3	1	.750	0	0--	-	2.68	3.16
2005	Lk Cty	A	13	12	0	1	69.0	263	47	19	17	5	3	1	0	19	0	71	5	0	4	1	.800	0	0--	-	1.91	2.22
2005	Knstn	A+	22	5	0	8	47.1	196	34	19	14	4	4	1	2	23	0	59	3	0	2	2	.500	0	2--	-	2.97	2.66
2006	Akron	AA	29	4	0	13	60.1	245	44	23	21	2	3	3	0	21	0	80	3	0	4	2	.667	0	3--	-	2.04	3.13
2008	Indns	R	3	1	0	0	4.0	12	0	0	0	0	0	0	0	1	0	4	0	0	0	0	-	0	0--	-	0.08	0.00
2008	Knstn	A+	5	0	0	1	8.0	31	4	2	1	0	0	1	0	3	0	10	0	0	0	0	-	0	0--	-	1.17	1.13
2008	Akron	AA	16	0	0	2	21.2	90	19	12	9	4	2	0	0	7	1	32	5	0	0	3	.000	0	1--	-	3.56	3.74
2009	Clmbs	AAA	12	0	0	3	17.0	74	17	8	7	1	0	1	0	6	0	22	5	0	1	0	1.000	0	1--	-	3.52	3.71
2009	Cle	AL	46	0	0	8	40.0	168	27	16	13	5	3	1	0	25	2	48	3	0	2	0	1.000	0	0-0	9	3.29	2.93

Grady Sizemore

Bats: L **Throws:** L **Pos:** CF-92; DH-14   **Ht:** 6'2" **Wt:** 200 **Born:** 8/2/1982 **Age:** 27

Year	Team	Lg	G	AB	H	2B	3B	HR	(Hm	Rd)	TB	R	RBI	RC	TBB	IBB	SO	HBP	SH	SF	SB	CS	SB%	GDP	Avg	OBP	Slg
2004	Cle	AL	43	138	34	6	2	4	(2	2)	56	15	24	21	14	0	34	5	0	2	2	0	1.00	0	.246	.333	.406
2005	Cle	AL	158	640	185	37	11	22	(10	12)	310	111	81	101	52	1	132	7	5	2	22	10	.69	17	.289	.348	.484
2006	Cle	AL	162	655	190	53	11	28	(14	14)	349	134	76	121	78	8	153	13	1	4	22	6	.79	2	.290	.375	.533
2007	Cle	AL	162	628	174	34	5	24	(11	13)	290	118	78	123	101	9	155	17	0	2	33	10	.77	3	.277	.390	.462

								BATTING													BASERUNNING				AVERAGES		
Year	Team	Lg	G	AB	H	2B	3B	HR	(Hm	Rd)	TB	R	RBI	RC	TBB	IBB	SO	HBP	SH	SF	SB	CS	SB%	GDP	Avg	OBP	Slg
2008	Cle	AL	157	634	170	39	5	33	(21	12)	318	101	90	121	98	14	130	11	0	2	38	6	.88	5	.268	.374	.502
2009	Cle	AL	106	436	108	20	6	18	(6	13)	194	73	64	68	60	1	92	4	2	1	13	8	.62	4	.248	.343	.445
	Postseason		11	43	12	2	1	2	(0	2)	22	9	3	5	8	3	9	1	0	1	2	1	.67	2	.270	.396	.512
6 ML YEARS			788	3131	861	189	40	129	(63	66)	1517	552	413	555	403	33	696	57	8	13	130	39	.77	31	.275	.367	.485

Doug Slaten

Pitches: L Bats: L Pos: RP-11 Ht: 6'5" Wt: 210 Born: 2/4/1980 Age: 30

			HOW MUCH HE PITCHED						WHAT HE GAVE UP											THE RESULTS						
Year	Team	Lg	G	GS	CG	GF	IP	BFP	H	R	ER	HR	SH	SF	HB	TBB	IBB	SO	WP	Bk	W	L	Pct	Sh	Sv-Op	Hld	ERC	ERA
2009	Reno*	AAA	39	0	0	16	43.2	181	41	17	15	3	0	0	0	15	2	40	5	0	3	2	.600	0	9--	-	3.29	3.09
2006	Ari	NL	9	0	0	0	5.2	21	3	0	0	0	1	0	0	2	1	3	0	0	0	0	-	0	0-0	2	1.11	0.00
2007	Ari	NL	61	0	0	13	36.1	163	41	15	11	4	0	0	0	14	0	28	3	0	3	2	.600	0	0-1	7	4.74	2.72
2008	Ari	NL	45	0	0	13	32.1	147	33	20	17	4	1	1	4	14	1	20	0	0	0	3	.000	0	0-0	4	4.86	4.73
2009	Ari	NL	11	0	0	1	6.1	30	10	5	5	1	0	0	0	1	0	4	0	0	0	0	-	0	0-0	0	6.82	7.11
	Postseason		3	0	0	1	1.1	7	1	0	0	0	0	0	0	2	1	1	1	0	0	0	-	0	0-0	0	4.29	0.00
4 ML YEARS			126	0	0	27	80.2	361	87	40	33	9	2	1	4	31	2	55	3	0	3	5	.375	0	0-1	13	4.63	3.68

Kevin Slowey

Pitches: R Bats: R Pos: SP-16 Ht: 6'3" Wt: 195 Born: 5/4/1984 Age: 26

			HOW MUCH HE PITCHED						WHAT HE GAVE UP											THE RESULTS						
Year	Team	Lg	G	GS	CG	GF	IP	BFP	H	R	ER	HR	SH	SF	HB	TBB	IBB	SO	WP	Bk	W	L	Pct	Sh	Sv-Op	Hld	ERC	ERA
2007	Min	AL	13	11	0	0	66.2	297	82	36	35	11	0	1	0	11	0	47	3	0	4	1	.800	0	0-0	0	5.22	4.73
2008	Min	AL	27	27	3	0	160.1	653	161	74	71	22	1	5	4	24	1	123	1	0	12	11	.522	2	0-0	0	3.48	3.99
2009	Min	AL	16	16	0	0	90.2	394	113	50	49	15	3	5	5	15	1	75	3	0	10	3	.769	0	0-0	0	5.25	4.86
0 ML YEARS			56	54	3	0	317.2	1344	356	163	155	53	4	11	9	50	2	245	7	0	26	15	.634	2	0-0	0	4.33	4.39

Chris Smith

Pitches: R Bats: R Pos: RP-35 Ht: 6'0" Wt: 190 Born: 4/9/1981 Age: 29

			HOW MUCH HE PITCHED						WHAT HE GAVE UP											THE RESULTS						
Year	Team	Lg	G	GS	CG	GF	IP	BFP	H	R	ER	HR	SH	SF	HB	TBB	IBB	SO	WP	Bk	W	L	Pct	Sh	Sv-Op	Hld	ERC	ERA
2002	Lowell	A-	14	14	0	0	56.2	237	54	29	26	3	1	0	2	14	0	50	5	0	3	3	.500	0	0--	-	3.03	4.13
2003	RedSx	R	3	2	0	0	8.1	39	11	8	6	0	0	0	0	4	0	3	1	0	0	2	.000	0	0--	-	5.47	6.48
2003	Augsta	A	8	8	0	0	46.1	188	48	22	22	4	1	3	3	5	0	25	3	1	3	3	.500	0	0--	-	3.37	4.27
2003	Srsota	A+	2	2	0	0	12.0	47	8	2	0	0	0	0	1	2	0	9	0	0	2	0	1.000	0	0--	-	1.40	0.00
2004	PortInd	AA	14	14	0	0	74.1	317	77	34	31	10	4	1	2	21	0	85	1	3	5	2	.714	0	0--	-	4.15	3.75
2005	PortInd	AA	15	15	0	0	75.2	331	95	46	44	13	6	4	4	15	1	49	3	0	4	4	.500	0	0--	-	5.50	5.23
2005	RedSx	AA	1	1	0	0	3.0	9	0	0	0	0	-	0	0	0	0	4	0	0	0	0	-	0	0--	-	0.00	0.00
2006	PortInd	AA	20	20	1	0	115.2	492	114	57	52	9	6	4	10	29	3	78	4	3	9	6	.600	1	0--	-	3.54	4.05
2006	Pwtckt	AAA	7	6	0	0	33.2	144	33	16	12	2	2	0	1	9	0	23	1	0	1	1	.500	0	0--	-	3.22	3.21
2007	PortInd	AA	30	14	0	4	104.0	466	126	57	51	10	5	3	8	42	2	80	7	1	6	9	.400	0	1--	-	5.72	4.41
2007	Pwtckt	AAA	2	0	0	0	5.0	29	12	5	1	1	0	1	0	3	0	2	0	0	0	0	-	0	0--	-	12.68	1.80
2008	Pwtckt	AAA	37	4	0	27	59.1	239	54	23	21	6	1	2	2	11	2	52	2	0	1	5	.167	0	15--	-	2.89	3.19
2009	Nashv	AAA	28	0	0	23	42.2	162	31	7	6	3	2	0	2	6	1	49	1	0	2	0	1.000	0	17--	-	1.77	1.27
2008	Bos	AL	12	0	0	3	10.1	78	18	16	16	6	1	1	0	7	0	13	0	0	1	0	1.000	0	0-0	0	5.53	7.85
2009	Mil	NL	35	0	0	12	46.0	200	41	21	21	11	1	0	3	19	0	35	1	0	0	0	-	0	0-1	0	4.68	4.11
2 ML YEARS			47	0	0	15	64.1	278	59	37	37	17	2	1	3	26	0	48	1	0	1	0	1.000	0	0-1	0	4.92	5.18

Jason Smith

Bats: L Throws: R Pos: PH-14; 2B-5; PR-4; 3B-1; SS-1 Ht: 6'3" Wt: 190 Born: 7/24/1977 Age: 32

								BATTING													BASERUNNING				AVERAGES		
Year	Team	Lg	G	AB	H	2B	3B	HR	(Hm	Rd)	TB	R	RBI	RC	TBB	IBB	SO	HBP	SH	SF	SB	CS	SB%	GDP	Avg	OBP	Slg
2009	RdRck*	AAA	83	262	52	6	2	6	(-	-)	80	32	28	20	13	1	83	3	4	3	11	2	.85	0	.198	.242	.305
2001	ChC	NL	2	1	0	0	0	0	(0	0)	0	0	0	0	0	0	1	0	0	0	0	0	-	0	.000	.000	.000
2002	TB	AL	26	65	13	1	2	1	(0	1)	21	9	6	5	2	0	24	0	2	0	3	0	1.00	0	.200	.224	.323
2003	TB	AL	1	4	1	0	0	0	(0	0)	1	0	0	0	0	0	0	0	0	0	0	0	-	0	.250	.250	.250
2004	Det	AL	61	155	37	7	4	5	(0	5)	67	20	19	13	8	0	37	1	5	0	1	2	.33	0	.239	.280	.432
2005	Det	AL	27	58	11	1	2	0	(0	0)	16	4	2	4	0	0	16	1	4	0	2	1	.67	0	.190	.203	.276
2006	Col	NL	49	99	26	1	0	5	(1	4)	42	9	13	15	7	1	29	2	0	1	3	0	1.00	1	.263	.324	.424
2007	3 Tms		69	141	28	3	2	6	(0	6)	53	16	18	11	6	0	53	1	0	1	0	0	-	2	.199	.235	.376
2008	KC	AL	22	28	6	2	0	0	(0	0)	8	6	1	1	0	0	12	0	0	0	0	1	.00	0	.214	.214	.286
2009	Hou	NL	21	25	0	0	0	0	(0	0)	0	0	0	0	0	0	9	0	1	1	0	0	-	1	.000	.000	.000
07	Tor	AL	27	52	11	1	0	0	(0	0)	14	7	4	3	3	0	22	1	0	0	0	0	-	0	.212	.268	.269
07	Ari	NL	2	4	1	0	0	0	(0	0)	1	0	0	0	0	0	2	0	0	0	0	0	-	0	.250	.250	.250
07	KC	AL	40	85	16	2	1	6	(0	6)	38	9	14	8	3	0	29	0	0	1	0	0	-	2	.188	.213	.447
9 ML YEARS			278	576	122	15	10	17	(1	16)	208	65	60	49	23	1	181	5	12	2	9	4	.69	4	.212	.248	.361

Joe Smith

Pitches: R Bats: R Pos: RP-37 Ht: 6'2" Wt: 205 Born: 3/22/1984 Age: 26

			HOW MUCH HE PITCHED						WHAT HE GAVE UP											THE RESULTS						
Year	Team	Lg	G	GS	CG	GF	IP	BFP	H	R	ER	HR	SH	SF	HB	TBB	IBB	SO	WP	Bk	W	L	Pct	Sh	Sv-Op	Hld	ERC	ERA
2009	Clmbs*	AAA	5	0	0	1	5.0	20	4	0	0	0	0	0	0	1	0	6	0	0	0	0	-	0	0--	-	1.70	0.00
2007	NYM	NL	54	0	0	14	44.1	205	48	18	17	3	2	0	7	21	4	45	2	0	3	2	.600	0	0-0	10	5.04	3.45
2008	NYM	NL	82	0	0	12	63.1	271	51	28	25	4	4	0	4	31	4	52	1	0	6	3	.667	0	0-3	18	3.23	3.55
2009	Cle	AL	37	0	0	5	34.0	142	30	16	13	4	1	1	0	13	0	30	2	0	0	0	-	0	0-1	10	3.49	3.44
3 ML YEARS			173	0	0	31	141.2	618	129	62	55	11	7	1	11	65	8	127	5	0	9	5	.643	0	0-4	38	3.85	3.49

Seth Smith

Bats: L Throws: L Pos: LF-86; PH-48; DH-3   Ht: 6'3" Wt: 215 Born: 9/30/1982 Age: 27

									BATTING													BASERUNNING				AVERAGES		
Year	Team	Lg	G	AB	H	2B	3B	HR	(Hm	Rd)	TB	R	RBI	RC	TBB	IBB	SO	HBP	SH	SF		SB	CS	SB%	GDP	Avg	OBP	Slg
2007	Col	NL	7	8	5	0	1	0	(0	0)	7	4	0	3	0	0	1	0	0	0		0	0	-	0	.625	.625	.875
2008	Col	NL	67	108	28	7	0	4	(2	2)	47	13	15	18	15	0	23	0	0	0		1	0	1.00	0	.259	.350	.435
2009	Col	NL	133	335	98	20	4	15	(8	7)	171	61	55	63	46	3	67	2	1	3		4	1	.80	5	.293	.378	.510
	Postseason		6	6	3	1	0	0	(0	0)	4	2	2	2	0	0	1	0	0	0		0	0	-	0	.500	.500	.667
	3 ML YEARS		207	451	131	27	5	19	(10	9)	225	78	70	84	61	3	91	2	1	3		5	1	.83	5	.290	.375	.499

John Smoltz

Pitches: R Bats: R Pos: SP-15   Ht: 6'3" Wt: 220 Born: 5/15/1967 Age: 43

			HOW MUCH HE PITCHED						WHAT HE GAVE UP												THE RESULTS							
Year	Team	Lg	G	GS	CG	GF	IP	BFP	H	R	ER	HR	SH	SF	HB	TBB	IBB	SO	WP	Bk	W	L	Pct	Sh	Sv-Op	Hld	ERC	ERA
2009	Portlnd*	AA	1	1	0	0	3.1	13	3	1	1	0	0	0	0	0	0	2	0	0	0	0	-	0	0-	-	1.57	2.70
2009	Grnvlle*	A	2	2	0	0	8.0	29	5	1	1	0	0	0	0	0	0	8	1	0	0	0	-	0	0-	-	0.81	1.13
2009	Pwtckt*	AAA	3	3	1	0	16.0	63	10	6	6	2	0	2	1	4	0	11	2	0	1	1	.500	0	0-	-	1.97	3.38
1988	Atl	NL	12	12	0	0	64.0	297	74	40	39	10	2	0	2	33	4	37	2	1	2	7	.222	0	0-0	0	5.86	5.48
1989	Atl	NL	29	29	5	0	208.0	847	160	79	68	15	10	7	2	72	2	168	8	3	12	11	.522	0	0-0	0	2.50	2.94
1990	Atl	NL	34	34	6	0	231.1	966	206	109	99	20	9	8	1	90	3	170	14	3	14	11	.560	2	0-0	0	3.37	3.85
1991	Atl	NL	36	36	5	0	229.2	947	206	101	97	16	9	9	3	77	1	148	20	2	14	13	.519	0	0-0	0	3.15	3.80
1992	Atl	NL	35	35	9	0	246.2	1021	206	90	78	17	7	8	5	80	5	215	17	1	15	12	.556	3	0-0	0	2.73	2.85
1993	Atl	NL	35	35	3	0	243.2	1028	208	104	98	23	13	4	6	100	12	208	13	1	15	11	.577	1	0-0	0	3.29	3.62
1994	Atl	NL	21	21	1	0	134.2	568	120	69	62	15	7	6	4	48	4	113	7	0	6	10	.375	0	0-0	0	3.44	4.14
1995	Atl	NL	29	29	2	0	192.2	808	166	76	68	15	13	5	4	72	8	193	13	0	12	7	.632	1	0-0	0	3.08	3.18
1996	Atl	NL	35	35	6	0	253.2	995	199	93	83	19	12	4	2	55	3	276	10	1	24	8	.750	2	0-0	0	2.17	2.94
1997	Atl	NL	35	35	7	0	256.0	1043	234	97	86	21	10	3	1	63	9	241	10	1	15	12	.556	2	0-0	0	2.89	3.02
1998	Atl	NL	26	26	2	0	167.2	681	145	58	54	10	4	2	4	44	2	173	3	1	17	3	.850	2	0-0	0	2.67	2.90
1999	Atl	NL	29	29	1	0	186.1	746	168	70	66	14	10	5	4	40	2	156	2	0	11	8	.579	1	0-0	0	2.81	3.19
2001	Atl	NL	36	5	0	20	59.0	238	53	24	22	7	1	2	2	10	2	57	0	0	3	3	.500	0	10-11	5	2.85	3.36
2002	Atl	NL	75	0	0	68	80.1	314	59	30	29	4	2	1	0	24	1	85	1	1	3	2	.600	0	55-59	0	2.06	3.25
2003	Atl	NL	62	0	0	55	64.1	244	48	9	8	2	0	1	0	8	1	73	2	0	0	2	.000	0	45-49	0	1.50	1.12
2004	Atl	NL	73	0	0	61	81.2	323	75	25	25	8	4	0	0	13	2	85	6	0	0	1	.000	0	44-49	0	2.73	2.76
2005	Atl	NL	33	33	3	0	229.2	931	210	83	78	18	10	3	5	53	7	169	2	1	14	7	.667	1	0-0	0	2.83	3.06
2006	Atl	NL	35	35	3	0	232.0	960	221	93	90	23	4	10	9	55	4	211	5	0	16	9	.640	1	0-0	0	3.32	3.49
2007	Atl	NL	32	32	0	0	205.2	853	196	78	71	18	10	5	4	47	9	197	8	0	14	8	.636	0	0-0	0	3.07	3.11
2008	Atl	NL	6	5	0	0	28.0	117	25	8	8	2	0	0	0	8	1	36	2	0	3	2	.600	0	0-1	0	2.77	2.57
2009	2 Tms		15	15	0	0	78.0	344	95	55	55	11	2	4	3	18	2	73	0	0	3	8	.273	0	0-0	0	5.03	6.35
09	Bos	AL	8	8	0	0	40.0	186	59	37	37	8	1	1	3	9	1	33	0	0	2	5	.286	0	0-0	0	7.31	8.33
09	StL	NL	7	7	0	0	38.0	158	36	18	18	3	1	3	0	9	1	40	0	0	1	3	.250	0	0-0	0	2.95	4.26
	Postseason		40	27	2	11	207.0	846	168	66	61	17	4	3	3	67	6	194	6	0	15	4	.789	1	4-5	0	2.68	2.65
	21 ML YEARS		723	481	53	204	3473.0	14271	3074	1391	1284	288	139	87	57	1010	84	3084	145	16	213	155	.579	16	154-169	5	2.96	3.33

Ian Snell

Pitches: R Bats: R Pos: SP-27   Ht: 5'11" Wt: 198 Born: 10/30/1981 Age: 28

			HOW MUCH HE PITCHED						WHAT HE GAVE UP												THE RESULTS							
Year	Team	Lg	G	GS	CG	GF	IP	BFP	H	R	ER	HR	SH	SF	HB	TBB	IBB	SO	WP	Bk	W	L	Pct	Sh	Sv-Op	Hld	ERC	ERA
2009	Indy*	AAA	6	6	1	0	37.1	150	28	7	4	0	1	1	1	13	0	47	0	1	2	2	.500	1	0-	-	2.08	0.96
2004	Pit	NL	3	1	0	1	12.0	56	14	10	10	2	0	0	0	9	0	9	0	0	0	1	.000	0	0-0	0	7.31	7.50
2005	Pit	NL	15	5	0	2	42.0	189	43	25	24	5	2	1	1	24	3	34	4	0	1	2	.333	0	0-0	1	5.03	5.14
2006	Pit	NL	32	32	0	0	186.0	813	198	104	98	29	16	6	2	74	4	169	8	0	14	11	.560	0	0-0	0	4.86	4.74
2007	Pit	NL	32	32	1	0	208.0	882	209	94	87	22	6	7	8	68	4	177	12	0	9	12	.429	0	0-0	0	4.02	3.76
2008	Pit	NL	31	31	0	0	164.1	766	201	107	99	18	7	6	8	89	0	135	8	1	7	12	.368	0	0-0	0	6.11	5.42
2009	2 Tms		27	27	1	0	145.0	649	148	82	78	14	7	1	2	83	3	89	6	0	7	10	.412	0	0-0	0	4.91	4.84
09	Pit	NL	15	15	1	0	80.2	360	87	50	48	7	5	1	1	44	3	52	3	0	2	8	.200	0	0-0	0	5.08	5.36
09	Sea	AL	12	12	0	0	64.1	289	61	32	30	7	2	0	1	39	0	37	3	0	5	2	.714	0	0-0	0	4.70	4.20
	6 ML YEARS		140	128	2	3	757.1	3355	813	422	396	90	38	21	15	347	14	613	38	1	38	48	.442	0	0-0	1	4.95	4.71

Travis Snider

Bats: L Throws: L Pos: LF-56; RF-21; PH-3; DH-2; PR-2   Ht: 6'0" Wt: 235 Born: 2/2/1988 Age: 22

									BATTING													BASERUNNING				AVERAGES		
Year	Team	Lg	G	AB	H	2B	3B	HR	(Hm	Rd)	TB	R	RBI	RC	TBB	IBB	SO	HBP	SH	SF		SB	CS	SB%	GDP	Avg	OBP	Slg
2006	Pulaski	R+	54	194	63	12	1	11	(-	-)	110	36	41	44	30	4	47	0	0	2		6	3	.67	2	.325	.412	.567
2007	Lansng	A	118	457	143	35	7	16	(-	-)	240	72	93	87	49	5	129	3	0	8		3	10	.23	8	.313	.377	.525
2008	Dnedin	A+	17	61	17	5	0	4	(-	-)	34	15	7	11	5	0	22	0	0	0		1	0	1.00	1	.279	.333	.557
2008	NHam	AA	98	362	95	21	0	17	(-	-)	167	65	67	62	52	0	116	4	0	5		1	1	.50	10	.262	.357	.461
2008	Syrcse	AAA	18	64	22	5	0	2	(-	-)	33	9	17	12	4	0	16	1	0	1		1	0	1.00	0	.344	.386	.516
2009	LsVgs	AAA	48	175	59	13	1	14	(-	-)	116	32	40	46	28	0	47	1	0	0		2	3	.40	2	.337	.431	.663
2008	Tor	AL	24	73	22	6	0	2	(1	1)	34	9	13	13	5	0	23	0	0	2		0	0	-	0	.301	.338	.466
2009	Tor	AL	77	241	58	14	1	9	(5	4)	101	34	29	30	29	1	78	3	2	1		1	1	.50	5	.241	.328	.419
	2 ML YEARS		101	314	80	20	1	11	(6	5)	135	43	42	43	34	1	101	3	2	3		1	1	.50	5	.255	.331	.430

Chris Snyder

Bats: R **Throws:** R **Pos:** C-56; PH-4; 1B-1; DH-1   **Ht:** 6'4" **Wt:** 245 **Born:** 2/12/1981 **Age:** 29

Year	Team	Lg	G	AB	H	2B	3B	HR	(Hm	Rd)	TB	R	RBI	RC	TBB	IBB	SO	HBP	SH	SF	SB	CS	SB%	GDP	Avg	OBP	Slg
2009	Visalia*	A+	3	7	1	0	0	0	(-	-)	1	1	0	1	3	0	3	1	0	0	0	0	-	0	.143	.455	.143
2009	Reno*	AAA	3	13	4	1	0	1	(-	-)	8	2	4	2	0	0	3	0	0	0	0	0	-	0	.308	.308	.615
2004	Ari	NL	29	96	23	6	0	5	(1	4)	44	10	15	11	13	1	25	0	0	1	0	0	-	0	.240	.327	.458
2005	Ari	NL	115	326	66	14	0	6	(2	4)	98	24	28	25	40	5	87	4	3	0	0	1	.00	4	.202	.297	.301
2006	Ari	NL	61	184	51	9	0	6	(4	2)	78	19	32	27	22	4	39	1	1	5	0	0	-	5	.277	.349	.424
2007	Ari	NL	110	326	82	20	0	13	(4	9)	141	37	47	48	40	3	67	7	3	4	0	1	.00	9	.252	.342	.433
2008	Ari	NL	115	334	79	22	1	16	(6	10)	151	47	64	53	56	5	101	4	5	5	0	0	-	7	.237	.348	.452
2009	Ari	NL	61	165	33	7	0	6	(3	3)	68	20	22	17	32	4	47	2	1	2	0	0	-	5	.200	.333	.352
	Postseason		6	19	5	2	0	1	(0	1)	10	3	3	2	2	0	6	0	0	0	0	0	-	3	.263	.333	.526
	6 ML YEARS		491	1431	334	78	1	52	(20	32)	570	157	208	181	203	22	366	18	13	17	0	2	.00	32	.233	.333	.398

Andy Sonnanstine

Pitches: R **Bats:** L **Pos:** SP-18; RP-4   **Ht:** 6'3" **Wt:** 190 **Born:** 3/18/1983 **Age:** 27

Year	Team	Lg	G	GS	CG	GF	IP	BFP	H	R	ER	HR	SH	SF	HB	TBB	IBB	SO	WP	Bk	W	L	Pct	Sh	Sv-Op	Hld	ERC	ERA
2009	Drhm*	AAA	9	9	0	0	57.1	244	68	29	28	4	3	4	1	9	0	36	0	0	5	3	.625	0	0- -	-	4.02	4.40
2007	TB	AL	22	22	0	0	130.2	554	151	87	85	18	3	5	5	26	2	97	2	0	6	10	.375	0	0-0	0	4.62	5.85
2008	TB	AL	32	32	1	0	193.1	819	212	105	94	21	4	9	5	37	2	124	6	0	13	9	.591	1	0-0	0	3.92	4.38
2009	TB	AL	22	18	0	2	99.2	459	131	85	75	19	0	2	2	34	3	60	3	0	6	9	.400	0	0-0	0	6.38	6.77
	Postseason		3	3	0	0	17.0	74	15	11	8	4	0	0	0	5	0	8	0	0	2	1	.667	0	0-0	0	3.64	4.24
	3 ML YEARS		76	72	1	2	423.2	1832	494	277	254	58	7	16	12	97	7	281	11	0	25	28	.472	1	0-0	0	4.69	5.40

Joakim Soria

Pitches: R **Bats:** R **Pos:** RP-47   **Ht:** 6'3" **Wt:** 204 **Born:** 5/18/1984 **Age:** 26

Year	Team	Lg	G	GS	CG	GF	IP	BFP	H	R	ER	HR	SH	SF	HB	TBB	IBB	SO	WP	Bk	W	L	Pct	Sh	Sv-Op	Hld	ERC	ERA
2007	KC	AL	62	0	0	38	69.0	270	46	20	19	3	1	3	1	19	3	75	2	0	2	3	.400	0	17-21	9	1.63	2.48
2008	KC	AL	63	0	0	57	67.1	260	39	13	12	5	2	2	8	19	1	66	1	1	2	3	.400	0	42-45	0	1.72	1.60
2009	KC	AL	47	0	0	41	53.0	222	44	14	13	5	1	2	1	16	1	69	3	0	3	2	.600	0	30-33	0	2.80	2.21
	3 ML YEARS		172	0	0	136	189.1	752	129	47	44	13	4	7	0	54	5	210	6	1	7	8	.467	0	89-99	9	1.97	2.09

Alfonso Soriano

Bats: R **Throws:** R **Pos:** LF-116; 2B-2; 3B-1; PH-1   **Ht:** 6'1" **Wt:** 180 **Born:** 1/7/1976 **Age:** 34

Year	Team	Lg	G	AB	H	2B	3B	HR	(Hm	Rd)	TB	R	RBI	RC	TBB	IBB	SO	HBP	SH	SF	SB	CS	SB%	GDP	Avg	OBP	Slg
1999	NYY	AL	9	8	1	0	0	1	(1	0)	4	2	1	0	0	0	3	0	0	0	0	1	.00	0	.125	.125	.500
2000	NYY	AL	22	50	9	3	0	2	(0	2)	18	5	3	4	1	0	15	0	2	0	2	0	1.00	0	.180	.196	.360
2001	NYY	AL	158	574	154	34	3	18	(8	10)	248	77	73	77	29	0	125	3	3	5	43	14	.75	7	.268	.304	.432
2002	NYY	AL	156	696	209	51	2	39	(17	22)	381	128	102	121	23	1	157	14	1	7	41	13	.76	8	.300	.332	.547
2003	NYY	AL	156	682	198	36	5	38	(15	23)	358	114	91	110	38	7	130	12	0	2	35	8	.81	8	.290	.338	.525
2004	Tex	AL	145	608	170	32	4	28	(12	16)	294	77	91	90	33	4	121	10	0	7	18	5	.78	7	.280	.324	.484
2005	Tex	AL	156	637	171	43	2	36	(25	11)	326	102	104	93	33	3	125	7	0	5	30	2	.94	6	.268	.309	.512
2006	Was	NL	159	647	179	41	2	46	(24	22)	362	119	95	114	67	16	160	9	2	3	41	17	.71	3	.277	.351	.560
2007	ChC	NL	135	579	173	42	5	33	(13	20)	324	97	70	91	31	4	130	4	0	3	19	6	.76	9	.299	.337	.560
2008	ChC	NL	109	453	127	27	0	29	(17	12)	241	76	75	77	43	11	103	3	0	4	19	3	.86	9	.280	.344	.532
2009	ChC	NL	117	477	115	25	1	20	(7	13)	202	64	55	61	40	6	118	3	0	2	9	2	.82	7	.241	.303	.423
	Postseason		44	174	37	3	0	4	(3	1)	52	14	18	14	9	0	53	3	0	0	10	3	.77	3	.213	.263	.299
	11 ML YEARS		1322	5411	1506	334	24	290	(139	151)	2758	861	760	838	338	52	1187	65	8	38	257	71	.78	64	.278	.326	.510

Rafael Soriano

Pitches: R **Bats:** R **Pos:** RP-77   **Ht:** 6'1" **Wt:** 220 **Born:** 12/19/1979 **Age:** 30

Year	Team	Lg	G	GS	CG	GF	IP	BFP	H	R	ER	HR	SH	SF	HB	TBB	IBB	SO	WP	Bk	W	L	Pct	Sh	Sv-Op	Hld	ERC	ERA
2002	Sea	AL	10	8	0	1	47.1	202	45	25	24	8	1	0	6	16	1	32	2	0	0	3	.000	0	1-1	0	3.93	4.56
2003	Sea	AL	40	0	0	12	53.0	201	30	9	9	2	0	1	3	12	1	68	0	0	3	0	1.000	0	1-2	5	1.32	1.53
2004	Sea	AL	6	0	0	0	3.1	23	9	6	5	0	0	0	0	3	0	3	0	0	0	3	.000	0	0-1	0	15.97	13.50
2005	Sea	AL	7	0	0	4	7.1	30	6	2	2	0	0	1	1	1	0	9	0	0	0	0	-	0	0-0	1	2.00	2.45
2006	Sea	AL	53	0	0	14	60.0	241	44	15	15	6	1	1	2	21	0	65	2	0	1	2	.333	0	2-6	18	2.64	2.25
2007	Atl	NL	71	0	0	28	72.0	276	47	26	24	12	0	0	2	15	2	70	0	0	3	3	.500	0	9-12	19	2.05	3.00
2008	Atl	NL	14	0	0	5	14.0	57	7	5	4	1	0	0	1	9	2	16	1	0	0	1	.000	0	3-4	6	2.27	2.57
2009	Atl	NL	77	0	0	52	75.2	307	53	25	25	6	4	2	1	27	4	102	0	0	1	6	.143	0	27-31	6	2.18	2.97
	8 ML YEARS		278	8	0	116	332.2	1337	241	113	108	35	6	5	10	104	10	365	5	0	8	18	.308	0	43-57	49	2.41	2.92

Jorge Sosa

Pitches: R **Bats:** R **Pos:** RP-18   **Ht:** 6'2" **Wt:** 220 **Born:** 4/28/1977 **Age:** 33

Year	Team	Lg	G	GS	CG	GF	IP	BFP	H	R	ER	HR	SH	SF	HB	TBB	IBB	SO	WP	Bk	W	L	Pct	Sh	Sv-Op	Hld	ERC	ERA
2009	Syrcse*	AAA	20	4	0	7	48.1	193	40	16	15	3	1	1	1	13	0	53	0	0	1	2	.333	0	3- -	-	2.56	2.79
2002	TB	AL	31	14	0	10	99.1	434	88	63	61	16	0	5	2	54	0	48	5	0	2	7	.222	0	0-0	1	4.51	5.53
2003	TB	AL	29	19	1	4	128.2	566	137	71	66	14	4	5	4	60	4	72	8	1	5	12	.294	1	0-0	0	4.93	4.62
2004	TB	AL	43	8	0	6	99.1	447	100	67	61	17	2	4	1	54	3	94	2	0	4	7	.364	0	1-1	6	5.17	5.53
2005	Atl	NL	44	20	0	5	134.0	577	122	42	38	12	5	2	0	64	8	85	3	0	13	3	.813	0	0-0	4	3.70	2.55

Year	Team	Lg	G	GS	CG	GF	IP	BFP	H	R	ER	HR	SH	SF	HB	TBB	IBB	SO	WP	Bk	W	L	Pct	Sh	Sv-Op	Hld	ERC	ERA
			HOW MUCH HE PITCHED						**WHAT HE GAVE UP**												**THE RESULTS**							
2006	2 Tms	NL	45	13	0	12	118.0	524	138	79	71	30	7	4	1	40	6	75	2	0	3	11	.214	0	4-7	0	5.88	5.42
2007	NYM	NL	42	14	0	2	112.2	481	109	58	56	10	10	3	0	41	2	69	0	0	9	8	.529	0	0-2	9	3.63	4.47
2008	NYM	NL	20	0	0	8	21.2	107	30	23	17	4	3	0	0	11	4	12	2	0	4	1	.800	0	0-0	1	6.95	7.06
2009	Was	NL	18	0	0	4	22.1	103	28	16	16	5	0	1	0	12	2	17	2	0	2	1	.667	0	2-2	3	7.12	6.45
06	Atl	NL	26	13	0	8	87.1	394	105	61	53	20	5	4	1	32	5	58	2	0	3	10	.231	0	3-6	0	6.00	5.46
06	StL	NL	19	0	0	4	30.2	130	33	18	18	10	2	0	0	8	1	17	0	0	0	1	1.000	0	1-1	0	5.48	5.28
	Postseason		1	1	0	0	6.0	27	7	3	3	1	0	1	1	2	2	3	0	0	0	1	.000	0	0-0	0	5.45	4.50
8 ML YEARS			272	88	1	51	736.0	3239	752	419	386	108	31	24	8	336	29	472	24	1	42	50	.457	1	7-12	24	4.74	4.72

Geovany Soto

Bats: R Throws: R Pos: C-96; PH-8　　　　　　　　　　　**Ht: 6'1" Wt: 225 Born: 1/20/1983 Age: 27**

Year	Team	Lg	G	AB	H	2B	3B	HR	(Hm	Rd)	TB	R	RBI	RC	TBB	IBB	SO	HBP	SH	SF	SB	CS	SB%	GDP	Avg	OBP	Slg
						BATTING															**BASERUNNING**				**AVERAGES**		
2009	Cubs*	R	1	3	1	1	0	0	(-	-)	2	0	2	0	0	0	1	0	0	0	0	0	-	0	.333	.333	.667
2009	Tenn*	AA	3	9	3	0	0	2	(-	-)	9	2	4	3	2	0	4	0	0	0	0	0	-	0	.333	.455	1.000
2005	ChC	NL	1	1	0	0	0	0	(0	0)	0	0	0	0	0	0	0	0	0	0	0	0	-	0	.000	.000	.000
2006	ChC	NL	11	25	5	1	0	0	(0	0)	6	1	2	0	0	0	5	1	0	0	0	0	-	0	.200	.231	.240
2007	ChC	NL	18	54	21	6	0	3	(2	1)	36	12	8	13	5	0	14	0	0	1	0	0	-	1	.389	.433	.667
2008	ChC	NL	141	494	141	35	2	23	(11	12)	249	66	86	81	62	6	121	2	0	5	0	1	.00	11	.285	.364	.504
2009	ChC	NL	102	331	72	19	1	11	(6	5)	126	27	47	34	50	3	77	3	0	5	1	0	1.00	19	.218	.321	.381
	Postseason		5	17	3	1	0	1	(0	1)	7	1	2	1	3	0	4	0	0	0	0	0	-	0	.176	.300	.412
5 ML YEARS			273	905	239	61	3	37	(19	18)	417	106	143	128	117	9	217	6	0	11	1	1	.50	31	.264	.348	.461

Jeremy Sowers

Pitches: L Bats: L Pos: SP-22; RP-1　　　　　　　　　　　**Ht: 6'1" Wt: 180 Born: 5/17/1983 Age: 27**

Year	Team	Lg	G	GS	CG	GF	IP	BFP	H	R	ER	HR	SH	SF	HB	TBB	IBB	SO	WP	Bk	W	L	Pct	Sh	Sv-Op	Hld	ERC	ERA
			HOW MUCH HE PITCHED						**WHAT HE GAVE UP**												**THE RESULTS**							
2009	Clmbs*	AAA	6	6	0	0	37.1	159	36	12	12	2	2	0	1	9	1	27	1	0	2	2	.500	0	0- -		2.94	2.89
2006	Cle	AL	14	14	2	0	88.1	360	85	36	35	10	1	0	2	20	1	35	1	0	7	4	.636	2	0-0	0	3.41	3.57
2007	Cle	AL	13	13	0	0	67.1	303	84	49	48	10	0	5	4	21	2	24	3	0	1	6	.143	0	0-0	0	5.75	6.42
2008	Cle	AL	22	22	0	0	121.0	533	141	84	75	18	3	4	3	39	1	64	3	1	4	9	.308	0	0-0	0	5.17	5.58
2009	Cle	AL	23	22	0	1	123.1	545	134	73	72	11	5	8	3	52	3	51	2	0	6	11	.353	0	0-0	0	4.64	5.25
4 ML YEARS			72	71	2	1	400.0	1741	444	242	230	49	9	17	12	132	7	174	9	1	18	30	.375	2	0-0	0	4.70	5.18

Denard Span

Bats: L Throws: L Pos: CF-84; LF-74; RF-39; PH-2　　　　　**Ht: 6'0" Wt: 205 Born: 2/27/1984 Age: 26**

Year	Team	Lg	G	AB	H	2B	3B	HR	(Hm	Rd)	TB	R	RBI	RC	TBB	IBB	SO	HBP	SH	SF	SB	CS	SB%	GDP	Avg	OBP	Slg
						BATTING															**BASERUNNING**				**AVERAGES**		
2003	Elizab	R+	50	207	56	5	1	1	(-	-)	66	34	18	26	23	0	34	4	0	0	14	5	.74	2	.271	.355	.319
2004	QuadC	A	64	240	64	4	3	0	(-	-)	74	29	14	31	34	0	49	3	4	1	15	8	.65	2	.267	.363	.308
2005	FtMyrs	A+	49	186	63	3	3	1	(-	-)	75	38	19	33	22	0	25	1	2	1	13	4	.76	3	.339	.410	.403
2005	NwBrit	AA	68	267	76	6	5	0	(-	-)	92	47	26	34	22	1	41	8	5	2	10	8	.56	2	.285	.355	.345
2006	NwBrit	AA	134	536	153	16	6	2	(-	-)	187	80	45	68	40	0	78	5	15	1	25	11	.69	11	.285	.340	.349
2007	Roch	AAA	139	487	130	20	7	3	(-	-)	173	59	55	66	40	1	90	0	21	0	25	14	.64	10	.267	.323	.355
2008	Roch	AAA	40	156	53	11	1	3	(-	-)	75	32	14	33	26	1	36	0	2	0	15	8	.65	1	.340	.434	.481
2009	Roch	AAA	2	6	2	1	0	0	(-	-)	3	1	0	1	1	0	1	1	0	0	1	1	.50	0	.333	.500	.500
2008	Min	AL	93	347	102	16	7	6	(2	4)	150	70	47	68	50	3	60	4	8	2	18	7	.72	3	.294	.387	.432
2009	Min	AL	145	578	180	16	**10**	8	(5	3)	240	97	68	100	70	3	89	10	12	6	23	10	.70	7	.311	.392	.415
2 ML YEARS			238	925	282	32	17	14	(7	7)	390	167	115	168	120	6	149	14	20	8	41	17	.71	10	.305	.390	.422

Justin Speier

Pitches: R Bats: R Pos: RP-41　　　　　　　　　　　　　　**Ht: 6'3" Wt: 205 Born: 11/6/1973 Age: 36**

Year	Team	Lg	G	GS	CG	GF	IP	BFP	H	R	ER	HR	SH	SF	HB	TBB	IBB	SO	WP	Bk	W	L	Pct	Sh	Sv-Op	Hld	ERC	ERA
			HOW MUCH HE PITCHED						**WHAT HE GAVE UP**												**THE RESULTS**							
1998	2 Tms	NL	19	0	0	10	20.2	99	27	20	20	7	2	1	0	13	1	17	3	0	0	3	.000	0	0-1	1	8.94	8.71
1999	Atl	NL	19	0	0	8	28.2	127	28	18	18	8	0	1	0	13	1	22	0	0	0	0	-	0	0-0	0	5.27	5.65
2000	Cle	AL	47	0	0	12	68.1	290	57	27	25	9	2	4	4	28	3	69	7	1	5	2	.714	0	0-1	6	3.56	3.29
2001	2 Tms	NL	54	0	0	10	76.2	324	71	40	39	13	2	7	8	20	3	62	6	1	6	3	.667	0	0-1	4	3.93	4.58
2002	Col	NL	63	0	0	7	62.1	259	51	31	30	9	0	1	3	19	4	47	1	2	5	1	.833	0	1-4	18	3.06	4.33
2003	Col	NL	72	0	0	31	73.1	319	73	37	33	11	1	4	7	23	6	66	0	0	3	1	.750	0	9-12	12	4.27	4.05
2004	Tor	AL	62	0	0	32	69.0	294	61	32	30	8	6	3	5	25	6	52	4	0	3	8	.273	0	7-11	7	3.52	3.91
2005	Tor	AL	65	0	0	36	66.2	264	48	20	19	10	4	0	3	15	2	56	1	1	3	2	.600	0	0-4	11	2.38	2.57
2006	Tor	AL	58	0	0	8	51.1	222	47	18	17	5	0	0	1	21	3	55	4	0	2	0	1.000	0	0-3	25	3.55	2.98
2007	LAA	AL	51	0	0	9	50.0	198	36	17	16	6	2	2	4	12	1	47	2	0	2	3	.400	0	0-1	24	2.43	2.88
2008	LAA	AL	62	0	0	19	68.0	305	69	41	38	15	4	4	6	25	1	56	8	0	2	8	.200	0	0-2	10	5.17	5.03
2009	LAA	AL	41	0	0	8	40.0	182	44	23	23	7	3	1	4	15	2	39	2	0	4	2	.667	0	0-1	8	5.34	5.18
98	ChC	NL	1	0	0	0	1.1	7	2	2	2	0	0	0	0	1	0	2	1	0	0	0	-	0	0-0	0	7.52	13.50
98	Fla	NL	18	0	0	10	19.1	92	25	18	18	7	2	1	0	12	1	15	2	0	0	3	.000	0	0-1	1	9.02	8.38
01	Cle	AL	12	0	0	2	20.2	96	24	16	16	5	0	3	3	8	0	15	2	0	2	0	1.000	0	0-0	0	6.61	6.97
01	Col	NL	42	0	0	8	56.0	228	47	24	23	8	2	4	5	12	3	47	4	1	4	3	.571	0	0-1	4	3.04	3.70
	Postseason		2	0	0	0	1.2	10	4	5	5	0	0	1	0	1	0	0	0	0	0	1	.000	0	0-0	0	13.02	27.00
12 ML YEARS			613	0	0	190	675.0	2883	612	324	308	108	26	28	45	231	37	588	38	5	35	33	.515	0	17-41	126	3.88	4.11

258

Ryan Speier

Pitches: R **Bats:** R **Pos:** RP-5   **Ht:** 6'7" **Wt:** 210 **Born:** 7/24/1979 **Age:** 30

			HOW MUCH HE PITCHED						WHAT HE GAVE UP												THE RESULTS							
Year	Team	Lg	G	GS	CG	GF	IP	BFP	H	R	ER	HR	SH	SF	HB	TBB	IBB	SO	WP	Bk	W	L	Pct	Sh	Sv-Op	Hld	ERC	ERA
2009	Mdest*	A+	3	0	0	1	3.0	15	5	1	1	0	1	0	0	3	1	2	0	0	0	0	-	0	0--	-	10.17	3.00
2009	Tulsa*	AA	3	0	0	0	3.0	12	3	1	1	0	0	0	0	2	0	2	1	0	0	0	-	0	0--	-	5.03	3.00
2009	ColSpr*	AAA	30	0	0	6	30.2	146	42	19	16	3	1	0	1	14	2	24	2	0	2	2	.500	0	0--	-	6.49	4.70
2005	Col	NL	22	0	0	10	24.2	111	26	12	10	0	2	1	1	13	0	10	2	0	2	1	.667	0	0-1	2	4.29	3.65
2007	Col	NL	20	0	0	5	18.0	77	20	8	8	1	1	0	1	8	1	13	2	1	3	1	.750	0	0-1	2	4.95	4.00
2008	Col	NL	43	0	0	8	51.0	217	52	23	23	3	1	3	4	18	2	33	2	0	2	1	.667	0	0-1	3	4.05	4.06
2009	Col	NL	5	0	0	3	5.2	25	6	3	3	0	1	1	1	3	0	2	0	0	0	0	-	0	0-0	0	5.12	4.76
	Postseason		3	0	0	1	2.1	11	1	1	0	0	0	0	0	3	0	1	0	0	0	0	-	0	1-1	0	3.36	0.00
	4 ML YEARS		90	0	0	26	99.1	430	104	46	44	4	5	5	7	42	3	58	6	1	7	3	.700	0	0-3	7	4.33	3.99

Ryan Spilborghs

Bats: R **Throws:** R **Pos:** LF-65; PH-38; RF-37; CF-16; PR-2   **Ht:** 6'1" **Wt:** 190 **Born:** 9/5/1979 **Age:** 30

			BATTING																		BASERUNNING				AVERAGES		
Year	Team	Lg	G	AB	H	2B	3B	HR	(Hm	Rd)	TB	R	RBI	RC	TBB	IBB	SO	HBP	SH	SF	SB	CS	SB%	GDP	Avg	OBP	Slg
2005	Col	NL	1	4	2	0	0	0	(0	0)	2	0	1	1	0	0	1	0	0	0	0	0	-	0	.500	.500	.500
2006	Col	NL	67	167	48	6	3	4	(3	1)	72	26	21	22	14	0	30	0	2	3	5	2	.71	7	.287	.337	.431
2007	Col	NL	97	264	79	14	1	11	(5	6)	128	40	51	48	28	1	45	2	0	6	4	1	.80	5	.299	.363	.485
2008	Col	NL	89	233	73	14	2	6	(3	3)	109	38	36	42	38	0	41	1	0	3	7	4	.64	8	.313	.407	.468
2009	Col	NL	133	352	85	24	3	8	(4	4)	139	55	48	44	34	0	79	2	3	2	9	5	.64	9	.241	.310	.395
	Postseason		9	20	3	0	0	0	(0	0)	3	3	0	1	5	0	7	0	0	0	0	0	-	0	.150	.320	.150
	5 ML YEARS		387	1020	287	58	9	29	(15	14)	450	159	157	157	114	1	196	5	5	14	25	12	.68	29	.281	.352	.441

Russ Springer

Pitches: R **Bats:** R **Pos:** RP-74   **Ht:** 6'4" **Wt:** 225 **Born:** 11/7/1968 **Age:** 41

			HOW MUCH HE PITCHED						WHAT HE GAVE UP												THE RESULTS							
Year	Team	Lg	G	GS	CG	GF	IP	BFP	H	R	ER	HR	SH	SF	HB	TBB	IBB	SO	WP	Bk	W	L	Pct	Sh	Sv-Op	Hld	ERC	ERA
1992	NYY	AL	14	0	0	5	16.0	75	18	11	11	0	0	0	1	10	0	12	0	0	0	0	-	0	0-0	2	5.15	6.19
1993	LAA	AL	14	9	1	3	60.0	270	73	48	48	11	1	1	3	32	1	31	6	0	1	6	.143	0	0-0	0	6.87	7.20
1994	LAA	AL	18	5	0	6	45.2	198	53	28	28	9	1	1	0	14	0	20	2	0	2	2	.500	0	2-0	1	6.38	5.52
1995	2 Tms		33	6	0	6	78.1	350	82	40	40	16	2	2	7	35	4	70	2	0	1	2	.333	0	1-2	0	5.63	5.29
1996	Phi	NL	51	7	0	12	96.2	437	106	60	50	12	5	3	1	38	6	94	5	0	3	10	.231	0	0-3	6	4.57	4.66
1997	Hou	NL	54	0	0	13	55.1	241	48	28	26	4	1	2	4	27	2	74	4	0	3	3	.500	0	3-7	9	3.69	4.23
1998	2 Tms	NL	48	0	0	14	52.2	232	51	26	24	4	2	1	1	30	4	56	5	0	5	4	.556	0	0-4	7	4.38	4.10
1999	Atl	NL	49	0	0	8	47.1	194	31	20	18	5	0	2	2	22	2	49	0	0	2	1	.667	0	1-1	8	2.63	3.42
2000	Ari	NL	52	0	0	10	62.0	282	63	36	35	11	2	3	2	34	6	59	3	0	2	4	.333	0	0-2	3	5.25	5.08
2001	Ari	NL	18	0	0	9	17.2	79	20	16	14	5	1	1	0	4	0	12	2	0	0	0	-	0	1-1	2	5.13	7.13
2003	StL	NL	17	0	0	4	17.1	77	19	16	16	8	0	0	1	6	0	11	1	0	1	1	.500	0	0-1	5	7.27	8.31
2004	Hou	NL	16	0	0	3	13.2	62	15	4	4	1	0	1	1	6	0	9	2	0	0	1	.000	0	0-0	4	4.84	2.63
2005	Hou	NL	62	0	0	11	59.0	246	49	34	31	9	1	0	3	21	3	54	2	0	4	4	.500	0	0-3	10	3.45	4.73
2006	Hou	NL	72	0	0	17	59.2	240	46	23	23	10	2	0	4	16	1	46	2	0	1	1	.500	0	0-0	9	3.03	3.47
2007	StL	NL	76	0	0	18	66.0	257	41	18	16	3	3	6	3	19	1	66	1	0	8	1	.889	0	0-2	11	1.63	2.18
2008	StL	NL	70	0	0	9	50.1	205	39	14	13	4	2	0	1	18	0	45	2	0	2	1	.667	0	0-2	15	2.68	2.32
2009	2 Tms		74	0	0	20	57.0	256	68	27	28	9	0	6	1	17	3	58	0	0	1	4	.200	0	1-3	14	5.08	4.11
95	LAA	AL	19	6	0	3	51.2	238	60	37	35	11	1	0	5	25	1	38	1	0	1	2	.333	0	1-2	0	6.69	6.10
95	Phi	NL	14	0	0	3	26.2	112	22	11	11	5	1	2	2	10	3	32	1	0	0	0	-	0	0-0	0	3.73	3.71
98	Ari	NL	26	0	0	13	32.2	140	29	16	15	4	0	0	1	14	1	37	3	0	4	3	.571	0	0-3	1	4.13	4.13
98	Atl	NL	22	0	0	1	20.0	92	22	10	9	0	2	1	0	16	3	19	2	0	1	1	.500	0	0-1	6	5.36	4.05
09	Oak	AL	48	0	0	11	41.2	191	52	20	19	5	0	3	0	14	2	47	0	0	0	1	.000	0	0-1	7	5.19	4.10
09	TB	AL	26	0	0	9	15.1	65	16	7	7	4	0	3	1	3	1	11	0	0	1	3	.250	0	1-2	7	4.74	4.11
	Postseason		14	0	0	4	14.1	63	15	7	7	1	1	0	1	6	0	14	0	0	1	1	.500	0	0-0	3	4.51	4.40
	17 ML YEARS		738	27	1	168	854.2	3709	822	457	429	121	23	29	35	349	33	774	39	0	36	45	.444	0	9-34	107	4.27	4.52

Matt Stairs

Bats: L **Throws:** R **Pos:** PH-85; RF-9; LF-6; DH-2   **Ht:** 5'9" **Wt:** 215 **Born:** 2/27/1968 **Age:** 42

			BATTING																		BASERUNNING				AVERAGES		
Year	Team	Lg	G	AB	H	2B	3B	HR	(Hm	Rd)	TB	R	RBI	RC	TBB	IBB	SO	HBP	SH	SF	SB	CS	SB%	GDP	Avg	OBP	Slg
1992	Mon	NL	13	30	5	2	0	0	(0	0)	7	2	5	3	7	0	7	0	0	1	0	0	-	0	.167	.316	.233
1993	Mon	NL	6	8	3	1	0	0	(0	0)	4	1	2	1	0	0	1	0	0	0	0	0	-	1	.375	.375	.500
1995	Bos	AL	39	88	23	7	1	1	(0	1)	35	8	17	9	4	0	14	1	1	1	0	1	.00	4	.261	.298	.398
1996	Oak	AL	61	137	38	5	1	10	(5	5)	75	21	23	27	19	2	23	1	0	1	1	1	.50	2	.277	.367	.547
1997	Oak	AL	133	352	105	19	0	27	(20	7)	205	62	73	77	50	1	60	3	1	4	3	2	.60	6	.298	.386	.582
1998	Oak	AL	149	523	154	33	1	26	(16	10)	267	88	106	96	59	6	93	6	1	4	8	3	.73	13	.294	.370	.511
1999	Oak	AL	146	531	137	26	3	38	(15	23)	283	94	102	101	89	6	124	2	0	1	2	7	.22	8	.258	.366	.533
2000	Oak	AL	143	476	108	26	0	21	(9	12)	197	74	81	69	78	4	122	1	1	6	5	2	.71	7	.227	.333	.414
2001	ChC	NL	128	340	85	21	0	17	(5	12)	157	48	61	57	52	7	76	7	1	3	2	3	.40	7	.250	.358	.462
2002	Mil	NL	107	270	66	15	0	16	(6	10)	129	41	41	48	36	4	50	8	0	1	2	0	1.00	7	.244	.349	.478
2003	Pit	NL	121	305	89	20	1	20	(13	7)	171	49	57	58	45	3	64	5	0	2	1	0	1.00	7	.292	.389	.561
2004	KC	AL	126	439	117	21	3	18	(6	12)	198	48	66	66	49	2	92	6	0	3	1	0	1.00	15	.267	.345	.451
2005	KC	AL	127	396	109	26	1	13	(5	8)	176	55	66	70	60	4	69	4	0	5	1	2	.33	9	.275	.373	.444
2006	3 Tms	AL	117	348	86	21	0	13	(7	6)	146	42	51	51	40	3	86	3	0	2	0	0	-	7	.247	.328	.420
2007	Tor	AL	125	357	103	28	1	21	(7	14)	196	58	64	65	44	5	66	2	0	2	2	1	.67	7	.289	.368	.549
2008	2 Tms		121	337	85	12	1	13	(7	6)	138	46	49	44	42	9	90	5	0	3	1	1	.50	10	.252	.341	.409
2009	Phi	NL	99	103	20	4	0	5	(3	2)	39	15	17	15	23	2	30	3	0	0	0	0	-	2	.194	.357	.379
06	KC	AL	77	226	59	14	0	8	(3	5)	97	31	32	35	31	2	52	2	0	2	0	0	-	5	.261	.352	.429
06	Tex	AL	26	81	17	4	0	3	(2	1)	30	6	11	10	6	1	22	1	0	0	0	0	-	1	.210	.273	.370
06	Det	AL	14	41	10	3	0	2	(1	0)	19	5	8	6	3	0	12	0	0	0	0	0	-	1	.244	.295	.463

259

							BATTING															BASERUNNING				AVERAGES		
Year	Team	Lg	G	AB	H	2B	3B	HR	(Hm	Rd)	TB	R	RBI	RC	TBB	IBB	SO	HBP	SH	SF	SB	CS	SB%	GDP	Avg	OBP	Slg
08	Tor	AL	105	320	80	11	1	11	(6	5)	126	42	44	41	41	9	87	5	0	2	1	1	.50	10	.250	.342	.394
08	Phi	NL	16	17	5	1	0	2	(1	1)	12	4	5	3	1	0	3	0	0	1	0	0	-	0	.294	.316	.706
	Postseason		8	14	2	1	0	1	(0	1)	6	1	2	2	0	0	3	0	0	0	0	0	-	1	.143	.143	.429
	17 ML YEARS		1761	5040	1333	287	13	259	(123	136)	2423	752	881	846	697	57	1067	57	5	39	28	24	.54	107	.264	.358	.481

Craig Stammen

Pitches: R **Bats:** R **Pos:** SP-19   **Ht:** 6'3" **Wt:** 200 **Born:** 3/9/1984 **Age:** 26

			HOW MUCH HE PITCHED						WHAT HE GAVE UP											THE RESULTS						
Year	Team	Lg	G	GS	CG	GF	IP	BFP	H	R	ER	HR	SH	SF	HB	TBB	IBB	SO	WP	Bk	W	L	Pct	Sh	Sv-Op Hld	ERC	ERA
2005	Vrmnt	A-	13	7	0	3	51.0	225	62	36	23	2	0	2	2	12	0	32	3	1	4	5	.444	0	0-- -	4.33	4.06
2006	Savann	A	21	21	0	0	113.0	479	110	55	45	10	3	6	2	29	0	93	8	0	6	9	.400	0	0-- -	3.30	3.58
2006	Ptomc	A+	7	6	0	0	29.2	128	34	20	19	5	2	0	1	7	0	16	4	0	2	2	.000	0	0-- -	4.88	5.76
2007	Ptomc	A+	28	22	0	0	125.0	566	156	79	58	9	1	6	4	54	0	96	16	0	8	6	.571	0	0-- -	5.67	4.18
2007	Clmbs	AAA	1	1	0	0	3.2	18	4	5	5	1	0	0	0	3	0	2	0	0	0	1	.000	0	0-- -	7.64	12.27
2008	Ptomc	A+	15	9	0	1	69.1	279	59	24	17	6	1	0	1	17	0	62	2	0	4	2	.667	0	1-- -	2.69	2.21
2008	Clmbs	AAA	9	8	0	0	43.0	198	62	35	35	3	2	3	2	16	3	35	4	0	1	4	.200	0	0-- -	6.63	7.33
2008	Hrsbrg	AA	6	6	0	0	38.1	144	22	8	7	1	2	2	0	11	1	31	0	0	3	1	.750	0	0-- -	1.32	1.64
2009	Syrcse	AAA	7	7	0	0	40.0	162	33	10	8	4	5	1	0	8	0	14	0	0	4	2	.667	0	0-- -	2.35	1.80
2009	Was	NL	19	19	1	0	105.2	448	112	67	60	14	4	3	3	24	1	48	7	0	4	7	.364	0	0-0 0	4.03	5.11

Craig Stansberry

Bats: R **Throws:** R **Pos:** PH-1   **Ht:** 6'0" **Wt:** 185 **Born:** 3/8/1982 **Age:** 28

							BATTING															BASERUNNING				AVERAGES		
Year	Team	Lg	G	AB	H	2B	3B	HR	(Hm	Rd)	TB	R	RBI	RC	TBB	IBB	SO	HBP	SH	SF	SB	CS	SB%	GDP	Avg	OBP	Slg
2009	Portlnd*	AAA	118	427	115	25	4	7	(-	-)	169	52	41	61	45	1	72	3	3	2	9	4	.69	12	.269	.342	.396
2007	SD	NL	11	7	2	0	0	0	(0	0)	2	1	1	1	0	0	3	1	2	0	0	0	-	0	.286	.375	.286
2008	SD	NL	12	16	6	1	0	0	(0	0)	7	4	2	4	2	0	3	0	0	0	0	0	-	0	.375	.444	.438
2009	SD	NL	1	1	0	0	0	0	(0	0)	0	0	0	0	0	0	0	0	0	0	0	0	-	0	.000	.000	.000
	3 ML YEARS		24	24	8	1	0	0	(0	0)	9	5	3	5	2	0	6	1	2	0	0	0	-	0	.333	.407	.375

Denny Stark

Pitches: R **Bats:** R **Pos:** RP-9   **Ht:** 6'2" **Wt:** 210 **Born:** 10/27/1974 **Age:** 35

			HOW MUCH HE PITCHED						WHAT HE GAVE UP											THE RESULTS						
Year	Team	Lg	G	GS	CG	GF	IP	BFP	H	R	ER	HR	SH	SF	HB	TBB	IBB	SO	WP	Bk	W	L	Pct	Sh	Sv-Op Hld	ERC	ERA
2009	Tacom*	AAA	38	0	0	10	51.1	243	55	33	33	6	2	5	5	35	2	43	4	0	2	2	.500	0	1-- -	6.11	5.79
1999	Sea	AL	5	0	0	2	6.1	31	10	8	7	0	0	0	0	4	0	4	0	0	0	0	-	0	0-0 0	8.05	9.95
2001	Sea	AL	4	3	0	0	14.2	68	21	15	15	5	0	1	0	4	0	12	0	0	1	1	.500	0	0-0 0	7.99	9.20
2002	Col	NL	32	20	0	1	128.1	554	108	69	57	25	2	4	5	64	4	64	2	0	11	4	.733	0	0-1 1	4.33	4.00
2003	Col	NL	17	13	0	0	78.2	366	98	57	51	12	2	7	3	33	2	30	2	1	3	3	.500	0	0-0 0	6.05	5.83
2004	Col	NL	6	6	0	0	26.0	150	53	43	33	9	4	4	0	18	3	10	1	0	0	5	.000	0	0-0 0	14.12	11.42
2009	Sea	AL	9	0	0	6	11.0	54	13	9	8	2	0	1	0	10	0	7	1	0	0	1	.000	0	0-0 0	8.15	6.55
	6 ML YEARS		73	42	0	9	265.0	1223	303	201	171	53	8	17	8	133	9	127	6	1	15	14	.517	0	0-1 1	6.12	5.81

Tim Stauffer

Pitches: R **Bats:** R **Pos:** SP-14   **Ht:** 6'1" **Wt:** 205 **Born:** 6/2/1982 **Age:** 28

			HOW MUCH HE PITCHED						WHAT HE GAVE UP											THE RESULTS						
Year	Team	Lg	G	GS	CG	GF	IP	BFP	H	R	ER	HR	SH	SF	HB	TBB	IBB	SO	WP	Bk	W	L	Pct	Sh	Sv-Op Hld	ERC	ERA
2009	SnAnt*	AA	12	0	0	5	19.0	75	13	5	4	1	0	0	0	4	0	12	0	0	1	0	1.000	0	1-- -	1.55	1.89
2009	Portlnd*	AAA	4	4	0	0	23.0	89	16	7	6	1	2	2	0	4	0	16	1	0	2	1	.667	0	0-- -	1.49	2.35
2005	SD	NL	15	14	0	0	81.0	355	92	50	48	10	2	0	2	29	0	49	0	0	3	6	.333	0	0-0 0	5.00	5.33
2006	SD	NL	1	1	0	0	6.0	21	3	2	1	0	0	0	0	1	0	2	0	0	1	0	1.000	0	0-0 0	0.84	1.50
2007	SD	NL	2	2	0	0	7.2	45	15	18	18	5	0	0	1	6	0	6	0	0	0	1	.000	0	0-0 0	18.32	21.13
2009	SD	NL	14	14	0	0	73.0	316	71	31	29	8	2	1	5	34	1	53	1	0	4	7	.364	0	0-0 0	4.60	3.58
	4 ML YEARS		32	31	0	0	167.2	737	181	101	96	23	4	1	8	70	1	110	1	0	8	14	.364	0	0-0 0	5.13	5.15

Nick Stavinoha

Bats: R **Throws:** R **Pos:** PH-16; LF-13; RF-10; DH-1   **Ht:** 6'2" **Wt:** 240 **Born:** 5/3/1982 **Age:** 28

							BATTING															BASERUNNING				AVERAGES		
Year	Team	Lg	G	AB	H	2B	3B	HR	(Hm	Rd)	TB	R	RBI	RC	TBB	IBB	SO	HBP	SH	SF	SB	CS	SB%	GDP	Avg	OBP	Slg
2005	QuadC	A	65	250	86	9	2	14	(-	-)	141	54	53	55	23	1	25	2	0	4	4	0	1.00	7	.344	.398	.564
2006	Sprgfld	AA	111	417	124	26	3	12	(-	-)	192	55	73	66	28	0	81	2	0	6	2	1	.67	10	.297	.340	.460
2007	Memp	AAA	139	501	131	17	0	13	(-	-)	187	50	49	60	31	0	81	4	1	2	7	1	.88	7	.261	.309	.373
2008	Memp	AAA	112	427	144	23	4	16	(-	-)	221	67	74	79	20	0	50	2	0	4	2	1	.67	12	.337	.366	.518
2009	Memp	AAA	72	259	73	17	2	11	(-	-)	127	39	56	46	25	2	48	6	0	5	2	0	1.00	4	.282	.353	.490
2008	StL	NL	29	57	11	1	0	0	(0	0)	12	4	4	0	2	1	11	0	1	1	0	0	-	2	.193	.217	.211
2009	StL	NL	39	87	20	7	0	2	(1	1)	33	6	17	9	2	0	15	0	0	2	1	0	1.00	2	.230	.242	.379
	2 ML YEARS		68	144	31	8	0	2	(1	1)	45	10	21	9	4	1	26	0	1	3	1	0	1.00	4	.215	.232	.313

Mitch Stetter

Pitches: L Bats: L Pos: RP-71   Ht: 6'4" Wt: 212 Born: 1/16/1981 Age: 29

Year	Team	Lg	G	GS	CG	GF	IP	BFP	H	R	ER	HR	SH	SF	HB	TBB	IBB	SO	WP	Bk	W	L	Pct	Sh	Sv-Op	Hld	ERC	FRA
2007	Mil	NL	6	0	0	2	5.0	20	2	2	2	0	0	1	2	2	0	4	3	0	1	0	1.000	0	0-0	0	1.86	3.60
2008	Mil	NL	30	0	0	7	25.1	109	14	9	9	2	1	0	4	19	1	31	1	0	3	1	.750	0	0-1	4	3.40	3.20
2009	Mil	NL	71	0	0	13	45.0	203	37	19	18	4	0	0	5	27	6	44	2	0	4	1	.800	0	1-2	20	3.90	3.60
	Postseason		3	0	0	0	1.1	4	0	0	0	0	0	0	0	0	0	2	0	0	0	0	-	0	0-0	1	0.00	0.00
	3 ML YEARS		107	0	0	22	75.1	332	53	30	29	6	1	1	11	48	7	79	6	0	8	2	.800	0	1-3	24	3.59	3.46

Jeff Stevens

Pitches: R Bats: R Pos: RP-11   Ht: 6'2" Wt: 205 Born: 9/5/1983 Age: 26

Year	Team	Lg	G	GS	CG	GF	IP	BFP	H	R	ER	HR	SH	SF	HB	TBB	IBB	SO	WP	Bk	W	L	Pct	Sh	Sv-Op	Hld	ERC	ERA
2005	Billings	R+	13	8	0	1	54.1	222	44	20	18	4	0	2	5	15	0	58	1	0	4	4	.500	0	0--	-	2.79	2.98
2006	Dayton	A	14	6	0	1	42.2	179	42	22	21	6	1	0	1	16	0	43	3	0	2	4	.333	0	0--	-	4.38	4.43
2006	Lk Cty	A	16	15	0	0	73.1	319	65	40	36	4	2	2	12	23	0	60	5	0	7	3	.700	0	0--	-	3.36	4.42
2007	Knstn	A+	15	0	0	2	35.0	134	18	13	9	2	1	1	3	9	0	37	2	0	3	2	.600	0	0--	-	1.37	2.31
2007	Akron	AA	34	0	0	6	48.1	202	40	17	17	4	2	3	2	16	1	65	4	0	3	1	.750	0	2--	-	2.86	3.17
2008	Akron	AA	17	0	0	3	28.2	114	19	8	8	2	1	0	1	11	0	37	1	0	5	1	.833	0	1--	-	2.24	2.51
2008	Buffalo	AAA	19	0	0	11	29.2	123	19	14	13	3	0	1	1	16	0	44	0	0	0	3	.000	0	5--	-	2.82	3.94
2009	Iowa	AAA	42	0	0	10	57.2	232	35	15	13	1	3	2	2	25	4	61	5	0	1	3	.250	0	1--	-	1.71	2.03
2009	ChC	NL	11	0	0	2	12.2	59	14	10	10	2	1	0	1	8	1	9	0	0	1	0	1.000	0	0-0	0	6.37	7.11

Ian Stewart

Bats: L Throws: R Pos: 3B 121; 2B-21; PH 21; LF-6, RF-3   Ht: 6'3" Wt: 205 Born: 4/5/1985 Age: 25

Year	Team	Lg	G	AB	H	2B	3B	HR	(Hm	Rd)	TB	R	RBI	RC	TBB	IBB	SO	HBP	SH	SF	SB	CS	SB%	GDP	Avg	OBP	Slg
2007	Col	NL	35	43	9	4	0	1	(1	0)	16	3	9	5	1	0	17	2	0	0	0	0	.--	0	.209	.261	.372
2008	Col	NL	81	266	69	18	2	10	(5	5)	121	33	41	44	30	4	94	7	0	1	1	1	.50	3	.259	.349	.455
2009	Col	NL	147	425	97	19	3	25	(13	12)	197	74	70	59	56	3	138	5	0	5	7	4	.64	7	.228	.322	.404
	3 ML YEARS		263	734	175	41	5	36	(19	17)	334	110	120	108	87	7	249	14	0	6	8	5	.62	10	.238	.328	.455

Brian Stokes

Pitches: R Bats: R Pos: RP-69   Ht: 6'1" Wt: 210 Born: 9/7/1979 Age: 30

Year	Team	Lg	G	GS	CG	GF	IP	BFP	H	R	ER	HR	SH	SF	HB	TBB	IBB	SO	WP	Bk	W	L	Pct	Sh	Sv-Op	Hld	ERC	ERA
2006	TB	AL	5	4	0	0	24.0	110	31	13	13	2	0	3	1	9	0	15	0	0	1	0	1.000	0	0-0	0	5.75	4.88
2007	TB	AL	59	0	0	22	62.1	294	90	49	49	11	1	3	3	25	1	35	1	0	2	7	.222	0	0-2	8	7.70	7.07
2008	NYM	NL	24	1	0	5	33.1	138	35	13	13	5	2	3	0	8	3	26	1	0	1	0	1.000	0	1-3	4	3.99	3.51
2009	NYM	NL	69	0	0	19	70.1	316	72	33	31	6	2	3	2	38	7	45	1	0	2	4	.333	0	0-2	10	4.59	3.97
	4 ML YEARS		157	5	0	46	190.0	858	228	108	106	24	5	12	6	80	11	121	3	0	6	11	.353	0	1-7	22	5.60	5.02

Tobi Stoner

Pitches: R Bats: B Pos: RP-4   Ht: 6'2" Wt: 215 Born: 12/3/1984 Age: 25

Year	Team	Lg	G	GS	CG	GF	IP	BFP	H	R	ER	HR	SH	SF	HB	TBB	IBB	SO	WP	Bk	W	L	Pct	Sh	Sv-Op	Hld	ERC	ERA
2006	Bklyn	A-	14	14	0	0	83.2	329	66	25	20	1	4	3	4	17	0	62	2	1	6	2	.750	0	0--	-	1.94	2.15
2007	Savann	A	11	11	0	0	57.1	247	59	32	23	1	0	1	1	17	0	50	3	0	3	5	.375	0	0--	-	3.28	3.61
2007	StLuci	A+	16	16	0	0	82.2	356	90	57	45	9	2	5	2	25	0	57	3	1	4	5	.444	0	0--	-	4.36	4.90
2008	StLuci	A+	9	9	0	0	52.0	208	46	17	15	3	4	0	2	9	1	48	1	0	1	5	.167	0	0--	-	2.49	2.60
2008	Bnghtn	AA	15	15	0	0	79.0	338	79	39	38	7	1	5	3	29	1	59	4	0	4	6	.400	0	0--	-	4.03	4.33
2009	Bnghtn	AA	7	7	1	0	47.0	182	28	15	14	5	2	1	1	13	0	28	0	0	2	2	.500	1	0--	-	1.71	2.68
2009	Buffalo	AAA	16	16	0	0	97.2	414	92	45	43	9	3	5	2	34	0	64	3	0	7	7	.500	0	0--	-	3.57	3.96
2009	NYM	NL	4	0	0	1	9.0	36	9	4	4	2	1	0	0	3	0	5	0	0	0	0	-	0	0-0	0	4.98	4.00

Huston Street

Pitches: R Bats: R Pos: RP-64   Ht: 6'0" Wt: 200 Born: 8/2/1983 Age: 26

Year	Team	Lg	G	GS	CG	GF	IP	BFP	H	R	ER	HR	SH	SF	HB	TBB	IBB	SO	WP	Bk	W	L	Pct	Sh	Sv-Op	Hld	ERC	ERA
2005	Oak	AL	67	0	0	47	78.1	306	53	17	15	3	3	2	2	26	4	72	1	0	5	1	.833	0	23-27	0	1.87	1.72
2006	Oak	AL	69	0	0	55	70.2	290	64	28	26	4	3	3	2	13	3	67	4	0	4	4	.500	0	37-48	1	2.49	3.31
2007	Oak	AL	48	0	0	35	50.0	199	35	20	16	5	2	1	0	12	3	63	0	0	5	2	.714	0	16-21	5	1.84	2.88
2008	Oak	AL	63	0	0	37	70.0	287	58	29	29	6	3	3	1	27	6	69	2	0	7	5	.583	0	18-25	6	2.98	3.73
2009	Col	NL	64	0	0	52	61.2	240	43	22	21	7	3	2	0	13	4	70	0	0	4	1	.800	0	35-37	2	1.83	3.06
	Postseason		5	0	0	5	6.1	26	8	5	5	2	0	0	0	1	0	4	0	0	0	1	.000	0	2-2	0	6.51	7.11
	5 ML YEARS		311	0	0	226	330.2	1322	253	116	107	25	14	11	5	91	20	341	7	0	25	13	.658	0	129-158	14	2.22	2.91

Pedro Strop

Pitches: R **Bats:** R **Pos:** RP-7   **Ht:** 6'0" **Wt:** 160 **Born:** 6/13/1985 **Age:** 25

			HOW MUCH HE PITCHED					WHAT HE GAVE UP											THE RESULTS						
Year	Team	Lg	G	GS	CG	GF	IP	BFP	H	R	ER	HR	SH	SF	HB	TBB	IBB	SO	WP	Bk	W	L	Pct	Sh	Sv-Op Hld	ERC	ERA
2006	Casper	R+	11	0	0	10	13.0	51	9	3	3	1	0	0	1	2	0	22	3	1	1	0	1.000	0	0-- -	1.75	2.08
2006	Ashvll	A	11	0	0	2	13.1	53	10	7	7	3	1	0	0	5	0	13	0	0	2	1	.667	0	0-- -	3.51	4.73
2007	Mdest	A+	48	0	0	25	54.2	237	43	28	26	4	2	3	3	29	1	75	11	0	5	2	.714	0	7-- -	3.36	4.28
2008	Tulsa	AA	7	0	0	5	7.0	31	6	2	2	0	0	0	1	4	0	7	0	0	0	0	-	0	3-- -	3.77	2.57
2009	Okla	AAA	11	0	0	6	12.2	54	13	11	11	2	0	1	1	4	0	13	2	0	1	1	.500	0	1-- -	4.70	7.82
2009	Frisco	AA	36	0	0	11	51.1	229	48	28	25	1	0	2	2	29	1	48	7	2	5	5	.500	0	4-- -	3.85	4.38
2009	Tex	AL	7	0	0	3	7.0	30	6	6	6	0	0	0	0	4	0	9	0	0	0	0	-	0	0-0 0	3.27	7.71

Drew Stubbs

Bats: R **Throws:** R **Pos:** CF-42   **Ht:** 6'4" **Wt:** 205 **Born:** 10/4/1984 **Age:** 25

			BATTING																		BASERUNNING				AVERAGES		
Year	Team	Lg	G	AB	H	2B	3B	HR	(Hm	Rd)	TB	R	RBI	RC	TBB	IBB	SO	HBP	SH	SF	SB	CS	SB%	GDP	Avg	OBP	Slg
2006	Billings	R+	56	210	53	7	3	6	(-	-)	84	39	24	36	32	0	64	7	2	1	19	4	.83	0	.252	.368	.400
2007	Dayton	A	129	497	134	29	5	12	(-	-)	209	93	43	79	69	1	142	6	1	2	23	15	.61	7	.270	.364	.421
2008	Srsota	A+	86	303	79	21	4	5	(-	-)	123	49	38	51	50	1	82	2	0	3	27	8	.77	3	.261	.366	.406
2008	Chatt	AA	26	92	29	8	0	0	(-	-)	37	12	9	16	11	0	21	2	1	0	3	1	.75	1	.315	.400	.402
2008	Lsvlle	AAA	19	75	22	4	2	2	(-	-)	36	14	10	13	6	0	20	1	2	0	3	0	1.00	0	.293	.354	.480
2009	Lsvlle	AAA	107	411	110	25	2	3	(-	-)	148	57	39	62	51	0	104	4	4	2	46	8	.85	4	.268	.353	.360
2009	Cin	NL	42	180	48	5	1	8	(7	1)	79	27	17	22	15	0	49	0	1	0	10	4	.71	1	.267	.323	.439

Eric Stults

Pitches: L **Bats:** L **Pos:** SP-10   **Ht:** 6'1" **Wt:** 222 **Born:** 12/9/1979 **Age:** 30

			HOW MUCH HE PITCHED					WHAT HE GAVE UP											THE RESULTS						
Year	Team	Lg	G	GS	CG	GF	IP	BFP	H	R	ER	HR	SH	SF	HB	TBB	IBB	SO	WP	Bk	W	L	Pct	Sh	Sv-Op Hld	ERC	ERA
2009	InldEm*	A+	2	2	0	0	7.1	27	5	2	1	0	0	0	0	0	0	5	0	0	0	0	-	0	0-- -	0.95	1.23
2009	Albq*	AAA	12	11	0	0	64.0	292	86	43	37	5	4	3	0	24	2	40	1	0	5	4	.556	0	0-- -	5.83	5.20
2006	LAD	NL	6	2	0	2	17.2	73	17	12	11	4	2	0	0	7	0	5	0	0	1	0	1.000	0	0-0 0	4.91	5.60
2007	LAD	NL	12	5	0	0	38.2	179	50	26	25	5	1	1	1	17	2	30	2	0	1	4	.200	0	0-0 1	6.25	5.82
2008	LAD	NL	7	7	1	0	38.2	167	38	18	15	6	2	0	1	13	2	30	0	0	2	3	.400	1	0-0 0	4.07	3.49
2009	LAD	NL	10	10	1	0	50.0	223	51	27	27	3	3	0	4	26	2	33	2	0	4	3	.571	1	0-0 0	4.67	4.86
	4 ML YEARS		35	24	2	2	145.0	642	156	83	78	18	8	1	6	63	6	98	4	0	8	10	.444	2	0-0 1	4.95	4.84

Cory Sullivan

Bats: L **Throws:** L **Pos:** LF-38; PH-23; CF-6; RF-2; PR-1   **Ht:** 6'0" **Wt:** 198 **Born:** 8/20/1979 **Age:** 30

			BATTING																		BASERUNNING				AVERAGES		
Year	Team	Lg	G	AB	H	2B	3B	HR	(Hm	Rd)	TB	R	RBI	RC	TBB	IBB	SO	HBP	SH	SF	SB	CS	SB%	GDP	Avg	OBP	Slg
2009	Buffalo*	AAA	85	286	83	16	0	2	(-	-)	105	37	24	39	29	0	30	0	2	3	2	2	.50	9	.290	.352	.367
2005	Col	NL	139	378	111	15	4	4	(1	3)	146	64	30	54	28	0	83	3	10	5	12	3	.80	6	.294	.343	.386
2006	Col	NL	126	386	103	26	10	2	(0	2)	155	47	30	47	32	3	100	1	19	5	10	6	.63	5	.267	.321	.402
2007	Col	NL	72	140	40	6	1	2	(0	2)	54	19	14	20	9	1	25	2	1	1	2	0	1.00	5	.286	.336	.386
2008	Col	NL	18	23	5	0	1	0	(0	0)	7	3	4	3	0	0	5	1	0	0	1	0	1.00	5	.217	.250	.304
2009	NYM	NL	64	136	34	2	5	2	(2	0)	52	17	15	18	19	1	22	0	0	2	7	1	.88	5	.250	.338	.382
	Postseason		6	6	2	0	0	0	(0	0)	2	0	0	0	0	0	1	0	0	0	0	0	-	0	.333	.333	.333
	5 ML YEARS		419	1063	293	49	21	10	(3	7)	414	150	93	142	88	5	235	7	30	13	32	10	.76	21	.276	.331	.389

Jeff Suppan

Pitches: R **Bats:** R **Pos:** SP-30   **Ht:** 6'2" **Wt:** 230 **Born:** 1/2/1975 **Age:** 35

			HOW MUCH HE PITCHED					WHAT HE GAVE UP											THE RESULTS						
Year	Team	Lg	G	GS	CG	GF	IP	BFP	H	R	ER	HR	SH	SF	HB	TBB	IBB	SO	WP	Bk	W	L	Pct	Sh	Sv-Op Hld	ERC	ERA
2009	Wisc*	AAA	1	1	0	0	3.1	15	5	4	4	0	0	0	0	0	0	1	0	0	0	1	.000	0	0-- -	4.47	10.80
2009	Nashv*	AAA	1	1	0	0	3.2	19	8	5	5	0	0	1	0	0	0	3	0	0	0	1	.000	0	0-- -	8.67	12.27
1995	Bos	AL	8	3	0	1	22.2	100	29	15	15	4	1	1	0	5	1	19	0	0	1	2	.333	0	0-0 1	5.43	5.96
1996	Bos	AL	8	4	0	2	22.2	107	29	19	19	3	1	4	1	13	0	13	3	0	1	1	.500	0	0-0 0	7.03	7.54
1997	Bos	AL	23	22	0	1	112.1	503	140	75	71	12	0	4	4	36	1	67	5	0	7	3	.700	0	0-0 0	5.39	5.69
1998	2 Tms		17	14	1	2	78.2	345	91	56	50	13	3	2	1	22	1	51	2	0	1	7	.125	0	0-0 0	4.95	5.72
1999	KC	AL	32	32	4	0	208.2	887	222	113	105	28	7	5	3	62	4	103	5	1	10	12	.455	1	0-0 0	4.33	4.53
2000	KC	AL	35	33	3	0	217.0	948	240	121	119	36	5	6	7	84	3	128	7	1	10	9	.526	1	0-0 0	5.31	4.94
2001	KC	AL	34	34	1	0	218.1	946	227	120	106	26	5	6	12	74	3	120	6	0	10	14	.417	0	0-0 0	4.40	4.37
2002	KC	AL	33	33	3	0	208.0	912	229	134	123	32	4	11	7	68	3	109	10	1	9	16	.360	1	0-0 0	4.84	5.32
2003	2 Tms		32	31	3	0	204.0	873	217	98	91	23	11	6	8	51	5	110	7	0	13	11	.542	2	0-0 0	4.03	4.19
2004	StL	NL	31	31	0	0	188.0	811	192	98	87	25	8	5	8	65	1	110	4	1	16	9	.640	0	0-0 0	4.38	4.16
2005	StL	NL	32	32	0	0	194.1	834	206	93	77	24	11	5	7	63	1	114	6	1	16	10	.615	0	0-0 0	4.46	3.57
2006	StL	NL	32	32	0	0	190.0	837	207	100	87	21	9	3	8	69	6	104	8	0	12	7	.632	0	0-0 0	4.62	4.12
2007	Mil	NL	34	34	1	0	206.2	919	243	116	106	18	14	11	11	68	10	114	7	0	12	12	.500	0	0-0 0	4.84	4.62
2008	Mil	NL	31	31	0	0	177.2	780	207	110	98	30	10	4	4	67	7	90	3	0	10	10	.500	0	0-0 0	5.58	4.96
2009	Mil	NL	30	30	0	0	161.2	748	200	106	95	25	11	4	11	74	8	80	12	0	7	12	.368	0	0-0 0	6.39	5.29
	98 Ari	NL	13	13	1	0	66.0	299	82	55	49	12	3	2	1	21	1	39	2	0	1	7	.125	0	0-0 0	5.73	6.68
	98 KC	AL	4	1	0	2	12.2	46	9	1	1	1	0	0	0	1	0	12	0	0	0	0	-	0	0-0 0	1.51	0.71
	03 Pit	NL	21	21	3	0	141.0	597	147	57	56	11	10	2	6	31	5	78	3	0	10	7	.588	2	0-0 0	3.55	3.57
	03 Bos	AL	11	10	0	0	63.0	276	70	41	39	12	1	4	2	20	0	32	4	0	3	4	.429	0	0-0 0	5.15	5.57
	Postseason		10	10	0	0	57.0	241	46	24	23	9	1	2	3	24	4	36	1	0	3	4	.429	0	0-0 0	3.56	3.63
	15 ML YEARS		412	396	16	6	2410.2	10550	2679	1371	1253	320	100	77	92	821	54	1332	85	6	135	135	.500	5	0-0 1	4.85	4.68

Drew Sutton

Bats: B Throws: R Pos: PH-27; 2B-8; SS-7; LF-5; 3B-2; PR-2; RF-1 Ht: 6'3" Wt: 185 Born: 6/30/1983 Age: 27

Year	Team	Lg	G	AB	H	2B	3B	HR	Hm	Rd	TB	R	RBI	RC	TBB	IBB	SO	HBP	SH	SF	SB	CS	SB%	GDP	Avg	OBP	Slg
2004	TriCity	A-	63	250	70	10	0	1	-	-	83	43	16	35	39	2	50	2	2	2	2	4	.33	5	.280	.379	.332
2005	Salem	A+	43	148	38	5	1	3	-	-	54	22	12	23	29	1	34	1	0	0	4	3	.57	3	.257	.382	.365
2005	Lxngtn	A	62	231	66	19	2	13	-	-	128	46	42	51	36	1	51	6	1	1	4	2	.67	5	.286	.394	.554
2006	Salem	A+	125	456	120	27	2	15	-	-	196	65	48	74	69	6	84	3	17	6	20	15	.57	7	.263	.360	.430
2007	CpChr	AA	128	480	129	28	1	9	-	-	186	81	53	73	57	3	86	7	8	6	24	5	.83	11	.269	.351	.388
2008	CpChr	AA	134	524	166	39	4	20	-	-	273	102	69	113	76	3	99	6	1	3	20	7	.74	8	.317	.407	.521
2009	RdRck	AAA	5	15	4	0	0	0	-	-	4	1	0	1	2	0	2	1	0	0	0	0	-	0	.267	.389	.267
2009	Lsvlle	AAA	44	157	40	13	2	5	-		72	32	22	28	26	1	39	5	1	1	1	2	.33	2	.255	.376	.459
2009	Cin	NL	42	66	14	4	1	1	1	0	23	10	9	12	7	0	20	1	2	0	0	2	.00	1	.212	.297	.348

Ichiro Suzuki

Bats: L Throws: R Pos: RF-145; DH-1 Ht: 5'11" Wt: 172 Born: 10/22/1973 Age: 36

Year	Team	Lg	G	AB	H	2B	3B	HR	Hm	Rd	TB	R	RBI	RC	TBB	IBB	SO	HBP	SH	SF	SB	CS	SB%	GDP	Avg	OBP	Slg
2001	Sea	AL	157	692	242	34	8	8	5	3	316	127	69	124	30	10	53	8	4	4	56	14	.80	3	.350	.381	.457
2002	Sea	AL	157	647	208	27	8	8	4	4	275	111	51	110	68	27	62	5	3	5	31	15	.67	8	.321	.388	.425
2003	Sea	AL	159	679	212	29	8	13	8	5	296	111	62	107	36	7	69	6	3	1	34	8	.81	3	.312	.352	.436
2004	Sea	AL	161	704	262	24	5	8	4	4	320	101	60	125	49	19	63	4	2	3	36	11	.77	6	.372	.414	.455
2005	Sea	AL	162	679	206	21	12	15	8	7	296	111	68	109	48	23	66	4	2	6	33	8	.80	5	.303	.350	.436
2006	Sea	AL	161	695	224	20	9	9	6	3	289	110	49	107	49	16	71	5	1	2	45	2	.96	2	.322	.370	.416
2007	Sea	AL	161	678	238	22	7	6	3	3	292	111	68	128	49	13	77	3	4	2	37	8	.82	7	.351	.396	.431
2008	Sea	AL	162	686	213	20	7	6	3	3	265	103	42	100	51	12	65	5	3	4	43	4	.91	8	.310	.361	.386
2009	Sea	AL	146	639	225	31	4	11	6	6	297	88	46	111	32	15	71	4	2	1	26	9	.74	1	.352	.386	.465
Postseason			10	38	16	2	0	0	0	0	19	7	3	8	5	2	4	0	0	0	3	2	.60	0	.421	.400	.474
9 ML YEARS			1426	6099	2030	228	68	84	47	37	2040	973	515	1021	412	142	597	44	24	28	341	70	.91	43	.333	.378	.434

Kurt Suzuki

Bats: R Throws: R Pos: C-135; DH-8; PH-7 Ht: 5'11" Wt: 199 Born: 10/4/1983 Age: 26

Year	Team	Lg	G	AB	H	2B	3B	HR	Hm	Rd	TB	R	RBI	RC	TBB	IBB	SO	HBP	SH	SF	SB	CS	SB%	GDP	Avg	OBP	Slg
2007	Oak	AL	68	213	53	13	0	7	4	3	87	27	39	33	24	0	39	3	3	5	0	0	-	5	.249	.327	.408
2008	Oak	AL	148	530	148	25	1	7	5	2	196	54	42	66	44	2	69	11	2	1	2	3	.40	20	.279	.346	.370
2009	Oak	AL	147	570	156	37	1	15	8	7	240	74	88	77	28	0	59	8	1	7	8	2	.80	14	.274	.313	.421
3 ML YEARS			363	1313	357	75	2	29	17	12	523	155	169	176	96	2	167	22	6	13	10	5	.67	38	.272	.329	.398

Anthony Swarzak

Pitches: R Bats: R Pos: SP-12 Ht: 6'4" Wt: 225 Born: 9/10/1985 Age: 24

Year	Team	Lg	G	GS	CG	GF	IP	BFP	H	R	ER	HR	SH	SF	HB	TBB	IBB	SO	WP	Bk	W	L	Pct	Sh	Sv-Op	Hld	ERC	ERA
2004	Twins	R	11	9	0	2	48.0	193	46	20	14	1	3	0	1	6	0	42	2	1	5	3	.625	0	1--	-	2.41	2.63
2005	Beloit	A	18	18	0	0	91.1	386	81	48	41	7	4	2	7	32	0	101	3	1	9	5	.643	0	0--	-	3.40	4.04
2006	FtMyrs	A+	10	10	0	0	59.0	257	72	25	24	3	3	2	1	11	0	55	1	1	3	4	.429	0	0--	-	4.15	3.66
2006	FtMyrs	A+	27	27	2	0	145.2	613	131	56	50	0	6	5	1	60	0	131	4	3	11	7	.611	1	0--	-	3.31	3.27
2007	NwBrlt	AA	15	14	1	0	86.1	354	78	34	31	6	0	3	5	23	0	76	2	0	5	4	.556	0	0--	-	3.11	3.23
2007	FtMyrs	A+	3	3	0	0	15.2	66	14	6	4	0	1	1	1	5	0	18	0	0	0	0	-	0	0--	-	2.75	2.30
2008	NwBrlt	AA	20	20	0	0	101.2	462	126	71	64	12	2	6	3	37	0	76	1	0	3	8	.273	0	0--	-	5.56	5.67
2008	Roch	AAA	7	7	0	0	45.0	189	41	14	9	4	1	1	4	14	0	26	1	0	5	0	1.000	0	0--	-	3.54	1.80
2009	Roch	AAA	13	13	0	0	79.2	330	79	31	29	4	1	2	3	21	1	45	2	0	4	5	.444	0	0--	-	3.35	3.28
2009	Min	AL	12	12	0	0	59.0	268	76	43	41	12	1	1	2	20	0	34	0	0	3	7	.300	0	0-0	0	6.50	6.25

Mike Sweeney

Bats: R Throws: R Pos: DH-57; PH-12; 1B-5 Ht: 6'3" Wt: 225 Born: 7/22/1973 Age: 36

Year	Team	Lg	G	AB	H	2B	3B	HR	Hm	Rd	TB	R	RBI	RC	TBB	IBB	SO	HBP	SH	SF	SB	CS	SB%	GDP	Avg	OBP	Slg
1995	KC	AL	4	4	1	0	0	0	0	0	1	1	0	0	0	0	0	0	0	0	0	0	-	0	.250	.250	.250
1996	KC	AL	50	165	46	10	0	4	1	3	68	23	24	23	18	0	21	4	0	3	1	2	.33	7	.279	.358	.412
1997	KC	AL	84	240	58	8	0	7	5	2	87	30	31	25	17	0	33	6	1	2	3	2	.60	8	.242	.306	.363
1998	KC	AL	92	282	73	18	0	8	6	2	115	32	35	35	24	1	38	2	2	1	2	3	.40	7	.259	.320	.408
1999	KC	AL	150	575	185	44	2	22	10	12	299	101	102	109	54	0	48	10	0	4	6	1	.86	21	.322	.387	.520
2000	KC	AL	159	610	206	30	0	29	17	12	323	105	144	128	71	5	67	15	0	13	8	3	.73	15	.333	.407	.523
2001	KC	AL	147	559	170	46	0	29	14	15	303	97	99	109	64	13	84	2	1	6	10	3	.77	13	.304	.374	.542
2002	KC	AL	126	471	160	31	1	24	14	10	265	81	86	112	61	10	46	6	0	7	9	7	.56	9	.340	.417	.563
2003	KC	AL	108	392	115	18	1	16	7	9	183	62	83	83	64	5	56	2	0	5	3	2	.60	13	.293	.391	.467
2004	KC	AL	106	411	118	23	0	22	8	14	207	56	79	75	33	9	44	6	0	2	3	2	.60	7	.287	.347	.504
2005	KC	AL	122	470	141	39	0	21	7	14	243	63	83	80	33	7	61	4	1	6	3	0	1.00	16	.300	.347	.517
2006	KC	AL	60	217	56	15	0	8	4	4	95	29	33	34	28	5	48	4	0	2	2	0	1.00	5	.258	.349	.438
2007	KC	AL	74	265	69	15	1	7	6	1	107	26	38	39	17	4	29	5	0	2	0	0	-	9	.260	.315	.404
2008	Oak	AL	42	126	36	8	0	2	1	1	50	13	12	16	7	0	6	2	0	1	0	0	-	5	.286	.331	.397
2009	Sea	AL	74	242	68	15	0	8	2	6	107	25	34	34	17	2	31	4	0	3	0	0	-	4	.281	.335	.442
15 ML YEARS			1398	5037	1502	320	5	207	102	105	2453	738	883	901	508	61	592	72	5	58	50	25	.67	137	.298	.367	.487

Ryan Sweeney

Bats: L Throws: L Pos: RF-85; CF-57; LF-7; PH-4   Ht: 6'4" Wt: 221 Born: 2/20/1985 Age: 25

Year	Team	Lg	G	AB	H	2B	3B	HR	(Hm	Rd)	TB	R	RBI	RC	TBB	IBB	SO	HBP	SH	SF	SB	CS	SB%	GDP	Avg	OBP	Slg
2006	CWS	AL	18	35	8	0	0	0	(0	0)	8	1	5	1	0	0	7	0	0	0	0	0	-	1	.229	.229	.229
2007	CWS	AL	15	45	9	3	0	1	(1	0)	15	5	5	2	4	0	5	0	0	0	0	1	.00	2	.200	.265	.333
2008	Oak	AL	115	384	110	18	2	5	(1	4)	147	53	45	56	38	3	67	3	2	6	9	1	.90	9	.286	.350	.383
2009	Oak	AL	134	484	142	31	3	6	(2	4)	197	68	53	63	40	1	67	3	2	5	6	5	.55	14	.293	.348	.407
4 ML YEARS			282	948	269	52	5	12	(4	8)	367	127	108	122	82	4	146	6	4	11	15	7	.68	26	.284	.341	.387

R.J. Swindle

Pitches: L Bats: L Pos: RP-6   Ht: 6'3" Wt: 190 Born: 7/7/1983 Age: 26

Year	Team	Lg	G	GS	CG	GF	IP	BFP	H	R	ER	HR	SH	SF	HB	TBB	IBB	SO	WP	Bk	W	L	Pct	Sh	Sv-Op	Hld	ERC	ERA
2004	Lowell	A-	12	1	0	4	51.0	199	42	18	11	0	3	3	2	4	0	56	1	0	5	1	.833	0	0--	-	1.60	1.94
2005	Schbrg	IND	18	16	2	0	118.1	491	117	46	43	5	8	4	3	27	0	102	1	0	6	4	.600	0	0--	-	3.08	3.27
2006	Schbrg	IND	5	5	0	0	31.2	131	32	15	12	1	1	0	1	8	0	22	0	0	2	2	.500	0	0--	-	3.28	3.41
2006	CtnSC	A	21	0	0	6	44.1	174	35	5	3	0	1	0	1	5	0	46	1	0	4	2	.667	0	2--	-	1.52	0.61
2006	Clmbs	AAA	1	0	0	1	2.0	7	1	0	0	0	0	0	0	0	0	0	0	0	0	0	-	0	1--	-	1.62	0.00
2007	Newark	IND	9	0	0	1	9.1	40	8	3	2	0	0	0	1	3	0	9	0	0	1	0	1.000	0	1--	-	2.67	1.93
2007	Lakwd	A	20	0	0	16	29.0	107	16	3	3	0	2	4	1	5	2	37	1	0	2	1	.667	0	10--	-	0.96	0.93
2007	Clrwtr	A+	12	0	0	8	15.0	62	15	8	8	3	0	0	0	3	0	20	0	0	0	1	.000	0	3--	-	3.93	4.80
2008	Rdng	AA	11	0	0	4	16.2	60	8	1	1	0	2	0	1	1	1	16	0	1	1	0	1.000	0	1--	-	0.64	0.54
2008	LV	AAA	27	0	0	11	36.1	147	33	9	8	1	1	1	1	7	1	51	0	0	2	1	.667	0	1--	-	2.43	1.98
2009	Nashv	AAA	31	0	0	6	43.2	174	30	6	5	1	2	2	2	13	1	41	1	0	3	1	.750	0	2--	-	1.77	1.03
2009	Clmbs	AAA	6	0	0	3	6.2	31	9	4	3	2	0	0	1	3	0	5	0	0	1	0	1.000	0	0--	-	9.17	4.05
2008	Phi	NL	3	0	0	0	4.2	24	9	4	4	2	0	0	0	2	0	4	0	0	0	0	-	0	0-0	0	13.63	7.71
2009	Mil	NL	6	0	0	2	6.2	37	12	12	12	3	0	0	1	4	1	8	1	0	0	0	-	0	0-0	0	13.69	16.20
2 ML YEARS			9	0	0	2	11.1	61	21	16	16	5	0	0	1	6	1	12	1	0	0	0	-	0	0-0	0	13.67	12.71

Nick Swisher

Bats: B Throws: L Pos: RF-130; 1B-20; LF-8; PH-6; DH-3   Ht: 5'11" Wt: 210 Born: 11/25/1980 Age: 29

Year	Team	Lg	G	AB	H	2B	3B	HR	(Hm	Rd)	TB	R	RBI	RC	TBB	IBB	SO	HBP	SH	SF	SB	CS	SB%	GDP	Avg	OBP	Slg
2004	Oak	AL	20	60	15	4	0	2	(1	1)	25	11	8	8	8	0	11	2	0	1	0	0	-	2	.250	.352	.417
2005	Oak	AL	131	462	109	32	1	21	(11	10)	206	66	74	62	55	3	110	4	0	1	0	1	.00	9	.236	.322	.446
2006	Oak	AL	157	556	141	24	2	35	(17	18)	274	106	95	95	97	7	152	11	2	6	1	2	.33	13	.254	.372	.493
2007	Oak	AL	150	539	141	36	1	22	(8	14)	245	84	78	89	100	12	131	10	1	9	3	2	.60	13	.262	.381	.455
2008	CWS	AL	153	497	109	21	1	24	(19	5)	204	86	69	69	82	6	135	4	1	4	3	3	.50	14	.219	.332	.410
2009	NYY	AL	150	498	124	35	1	29	(8	21)	248	84	82	84	97	2	126	3	3	6	0	0	-	13	.249	.371	.498
Postseason			10	24	5	2	0	0	(0	0)	7	4	1	4	9	0	8	0	0	0	0	0	-	0	.208	.424	.292
6 ML YEARS			761	2612	639	152	6	133	(64	69)	1202	437	406	407	439	30	665	34	7	27	7	8	.47	64	.245	.357	.460

Jon Switzer

Pitches: L Bats: L Pos: RP-4   Ht: 6'3" Wt: 210 Born: 8/13/1979 Age: 30

Year	Team	Lg	G	GS	CG	GF	IP	BFP	H	R	ER	HR	SH	SF	HB	TBB	IBB	SO	WP	Bk	W	L	Pct	Sh	Sv-Op	Hld	ERC	ERA
2009	Buffalo*	AAA	41	0	0	16	52.0	225	46	23	19	4	4	1	2	23	0	49	0	0	1	3	.250	0	4--	-	3.54	3.29
2003	TB	AL	5	0	0	1	9.2	46	13	8	8	2	0	1	2	3	0	7	1	0	0	0	-	0	0-0	0	8.88	7.45
2005	TB	AL	2	0	0	0	4.0	25	5	4	3	0	0	0	0	7	0	5	0	0	0	0	-	0	0-0	0	9.71	6.75
2006	TB	AL	40	0	0	6	33.2	157	38	19	17	5	2	1	1	19	3	18	3	0	2	2	.500	0	0-3	5	5.78	4.54
2007	TB	AL	21	0	0	2	19.0	88	27	17	17	2	0	1	0	7	1	13	1	0	0	2	.000	0	0-0	3	6.47	8.05
2009	NYM	NL	4	0	0	1	3.1	17	4	3	3	1	0	0	1	2	0	3	0	0	0	0	-	0	0-1	1	8.99	8.10
5 ML YEARS			72	0	0	10	69.2	333	87	51	48	10	2	3	6	38	4	46	5	0	2	4	.333	0	0-4	9	6.76	6.20

So Taguchi

Bats: R Throws: R Pos: LF-3; PH-3; RF-1; PR-1   Ht: 5'10" Wt: 169 Born: 7/2/1969 Age: 40

Year	Team	Lg	G	AB	H	2B	3B	HR	(Hm	Rd)	TB	R	RBI	RC	TBB	IBB	SO	HBP	SH	SF	SB	CS	SB%	GDP	Avg	OBP	Slg
2009	Iowa*	AAA	85	258	64	8	1	4	(-	-)	86	37	29	33	32	0	32	9	1	4	4	4	.50	11	.248	.347	.333
2002	StL	NL	19	15	6	0	0	0	(0	0)	6	4	2	4	2	0	1	0	2	0	1	0	1.00	0	.400	.471	.400
2003	StL	NL	43	54	14	3	1	3	(1	2)	28	9	13	11	4	1	11	0	1	0	0	0	-	2	.259	.310	.519
2004	StL	NL	109	179	52	10	2	3	(1	2)	75	26	25	27	12	1	23	2	10	3	6	3	.67	6	.291	.337	.419
2005	StL	NL	143	396	114	21	2	8	(5	3)	163	45	53	59	20	2	62	2	2	4	11	2	.85	11	.288	.322	.412
2006	StL	NL	134	316	84	19	1	2	(0	2)	111	46	31	35	32	1	48	2	9	2	11	3	.79	9	.266	.335	.351
2007	StL	NL	130	307	89	15	0	3	(0	3)	113	48	30	41	23	0	32	6	3	1	7	4	.64	10	.290	.330	.368
2008	Phi	NL	88	91	20	5	1	0	(0	0)	27	18	9	8	8	0	14	0	4	0	3	0	1.00	2	.220	.283	.297
2009	ChC	NL	6	11	3	1	0	0	(0	0)	4	1	0	1	1	0	4	0	0	0	0	0	-	0	.273	.333	.364
Postseason			30	32	7	1	0	2	(1	1)	14	6	5	4	1	0	8	0	3	0	0	0	-	0	.219	.242	.438
8 ML YEARS			672	1369	382	74	7	19	(7	12)	527	197	163	186	102	5	195	12	31	10	39	12	.76	40	.279	.332	.385

Hisanori Takahashi

Pitches: L Bats: L Pos: P   Ht: 5'10" Wt: 172 Born: 4/2/1975 Age: 35

			HOW MUCH HE PITCHED						WHAT HE GAVE UP											THE RESULTS							
Year	Team	Lg	G	GS	CG	GF	IP	BFP	H	R	ER	HR	SH	SF	HB	TBB	IBB	SO	WP	Bk	W	L	Pct	Sh	Sv-Op	Hld	ERC	ERA
2000	Yomiuri	Jap	24	23	3	0	135.2	563	133	59	48	10	-	-	2	36	-	102	1	0	9	6	.600	2	0--	-	3.35	3.18
2001	Yomiuri	Jap	30	23	3	1	134.2	584	126	65	59	20	17	4	3	52	2	99	4	0	9	9	.500	1	0--	-	3.98	3.94
2002	Yomiuri	Jap	24	23	2	0	163.1	669	143	58	56	16	-	-	6	39	-	145	4	1	10	4	.714	0	0--	-	2.91	3.09
2003	Yomiuri	Jap	13	13	3	0	86.2	364	79	42	37	14	-	-	4	27	1	78	1	1	4	4	.500	0	0--	-	3.81	3.84
2004	Yomiuri	Jap	16	16	3	0	91.0	402	107	59	55	18	6	2	3	26	0	61	3	0	5	10	.333	1	0--	-	5.45	5.44
2005	Yomiuri	Jap	27	26	4	0	163.0	695	171	88	81	18	14	7	4	48	1	135	1	0	8	12	.400	2	0--	-	4.11	4.47
2006	Yomiuri	Jap	35	4	0	0	62.0	266	70	36	34	10	5	0	1	15	2	51	1	0	2	6	.250	0	15--	-	4.62	4.94
2007	Yomiuri	Jap	28	27	2	0	186.2	704	168	63	57	21	-	-	2	50	4	141	1	0	14	4	.778	2	0--	-	3.13	2.75
2008	Yomiuri	Jap	23	22	0	0	122.0	518	127	63	56	16	7	5	5	30	0	94	2	0	8	5	.615	0	0--	-	4.07	4.13
2009	Yomiuri	Jap	25	25	1	0	144.0	610	147	58	47	16	-	-	8	36	1	126	0	2	10	6	.625	0	0--	-	3.82	2.94

Ken Takahashi

Pitches: L Bats: L Pos: RP-28   Ht: 6'0" Wt: 198 Born: 4/16/1969 Age: 41

			HOW MUCH HE PITCHED						WHAT HE GAVE UP											THE RESULTS							
Year	Team	Lg	G	GS	CG	GF	IP	BFP	H	R	ER	HR	SH	SF	HB	TBB	IBB	SO	WP	Bk	W	L	Pct	Sh	Sv-Op	Hld	ERC	ERA
1995	Hshma	Jap	39	6	0	-	90.0	393	55	44	39	12	-	-	0	45	0	54	1	1	4	4	.500	0	0--	-	2.39	4.90
1996	Hshma	Jap	24	4	0	-	52.2	233	57	33	29	4	-	-	1	20	0	40	4	0	2	1	.667	0	1--	-	4.31	4.96
1997	Hshma	Jap	34	4	0	-	62.0	282	69	37	33	8	-	-	0	34	0	35	3	0	3	4	.429	0	0--	-	5.57	4.79
1998	Hshma	Jap	41	9	0	-	101.0	431	92	45	43	10	-	2	2	46	0	76	5	1	3	8	.273	0	0--	-	3.90	3.83
1999	Hshma	Jap	36	11	2	-	102.0	448	102	64	53	21	-	-	2	40	0	90	9	0	3	7	.300	1	0--	-	4.79	4.68
2000	Hshma	Jap	50	8	2	-	112.1	482	89	56	49	13	-	-	3	57	0	88	6	0	5	9	.357	1	4--	-	3.52	3.93
2001	Hshma	Jap	30	20	5	-	173.0	736	165	89	82	23	-	-	8	60	0	132	6	0	10	8	.556	1	0--	-	4.03	4.27
2002	Hshma	Jap	26	19	6	-	173.1	750	107	92	74	22	-	-	3	38	0	142	2	0	9	14	.391	3	0--	-	4.28	3.84
2003	Hshma	Jap	24	18	6	-	167.0	700	171	79	68	26	-	-	8	36	2	127	2	0	9	8	.529	1	0--	-	4.12	3.66
2004	Hshma	Jap	18	17	0	-	98.0	428	122	66	59	24	4	2	2	24	0	66	0	1	3	10	.231	0	0--	-	6.23	5.53
2005	Hshma	Jap	14	4	0	-	26.2	133	43	28	28	7	3	4	1	9	1	14	1	0	0	2	.000	0	0--	-	8.88	9.45
2006	Hshma	Jap	54	0	0	-	46.0	201	46	27	24	9	4	1	1	16	2	40	0	0	2	3	.400	0	0--	-	4.45	4.70
2007	Hshma	Jap	22	20	0	-	112.0	481	116	54	46	18	-	-	5	36	1	74	3	0	5	4	.556	0	0--	-	4.58	3.70
2008	Hshma	Jap	21	20	1	-	115.0	503	124	50	45	11	12	2	5	42	2	71	1	0	8	5	.615	1	0--	-	4.51	3.52
2009	Buffalo	AAA	18	7	1	1	56.2	245	55	21	15	2	3	0	2	23	0	38	3	0	1	3	.250	1	0--	-	3.61	2.38
2009	NYM	NL	20	0	0	5	27.1	116	23	9	9	2	0	2	2	14	1	23	2	1	0	1	.000	0	0-0	0	3.75	2.96

Brian Tallet

Pitches: L Bats: L Pos: SP-25; RP-12   Ht: 6'6" Wt: 220 Born: 9/21/1977 Age: 32

			HOW MUCH HE PITCHED						WHAT HE GAVE UP											THE RESULTS							
Year	Team	Lg	G	GS	CG	GF	IP	BFP	H	R	ER	HR	SH	SF	HB	TBB	IBB	SO	WP	Bk	W	L	Pct	Sh	Sv-Op	Hld	ERC	ERA
2002	Cle	AL	2	2	0	0	12.0	47	9	3	2	0	0	0	1	4	0	5	0	0	1	0	1.000	0	0-0	0	2.31	1.50
2003	Cle	AL	5	3	0	1	19.0	87	23	14	10	2	2	0	1	8	0	9	0	0	0	2	.000	0	0-0	0	6.66	4.74
2005	Cle	AL	2	0	0	0	4.2	24	6	4	4	2	0	0	1	3	0	2	0	0	0	0	-	0	0-0	0	10.55	7.71
2006	Tor	AL	44	1	0	8	54.1	229	45	24	23	5	1	5	3	31	4	57	0	0	3	0	1.000	0	0-0	5	3.97	3.81
2007	Tor	AL	48	0	0	11	62.1	267	49	26	24	1	2	3	6	28	7	54	1	0	2	4	.333	0	0-3	1	2.68	3.47
2008	Tor	AL	51	0	0	15	56.1	240	52	19	18	4	1	2	1	22	3	47	0	0	1	2	.333	0	0-0	4	3.39	2.88
2009	Tor	AL	37	25	0	3	160.2	717	169	99	95	20	1	7	6	72	2	120	2	0	7	9	.438	0	0-0	0	4.85	5.32
7 ML YEARS			189	31	0	38	369.1	1611	353	189	176	34	7	17	19	168	16	274	5	1	14	17	.452	0	0-3	10	4.12	4.20

Taylor Tankersley

Pitches: L Bats: L Pos: P   Ht: 6'1" Wt: 220 Born: 3/7/1983 Age: 27

			HOW MUCH HE PITCHED						WHAT HE GAVE UP											THE RESULTS							
Year	Team	Lg	G	GS	CG	GF	IP	BFP	H	R	ER	HR	SH	SF	HB	TBB	IBB	SO	WP	Bk	W	L	Pct	Sh	Sv-Op	Hld	ERC	ERA
2006	Fla	NL	49	0	0	10	41.0	178	33	14	13	4	3	3	1	26	5	46	3	0	2	1	.667	0	3-7	22	3.80	2.85
2007	Fla	NL	67	0	0	12	47.1	205	42	22	21	4	0	2	3	29	3	49	2	0	6	1	.857	0	1-3	16	4.45	3.99
2008	Fla	NL	25	0	0	3	17.2	84	22	16	16	6	1	0	1	8	0	13	3	0	0	1	.000	0	0-2	4	7.76	8.15
3 ML YEARS			141	0	0	25	106.0	467	97	52	50	14	4	5	5	63	8	108	8	0	8	3	.727	0	4-12	42	4.72	4.25

Jack Taschner

Pitches: L Bats: L Pos: RP-24   Ht: 6'3" Wt: 207 Born: 4/21/1978 Age: 32

			HOW MUCH HE PITCHED						WHAT HE GAVE UP											THE RESULTS							
Year	Team	Lg	G	GS	CG	GF	IP	BFP	H	R	ER	HR	SH	SF	HB	TBB	IBB	SO	WP	Bk	W	L	Pct	Sh	Sv-Op	Hld	ERC	ERA
2009	LV*	AAA	20	0	0	7	21.2	89	16	6	5	1	2	2	0	10	1	15	3	0	0	2	.000	0	2--	-	2.52	2.08
2005	SF	NL	24	0	0	7	22.2	95	15	5	4	0	0	1	0	13	0	19	0	0	2	0	1.000	0	0-1	3	2.25	1.59
2006	SF	NL	24	0	0	6	19.1	101	31	23	18	4	0	2	2	7	0	15	3	0	0	1	.000	0	0-1	3	8.55	8.38
2007	SF	NL	63	0	0	16	50.0	222	44	31	30	4	2	3	1	29	2	51	2	0	3	1	.750	0	0-2	13	3.92	5.40
2008	SF	NL	67	0	0	7	48.0	227	57	27	26	5	3	3	2	24	2	39	5	0	3	2	.600	0	0-4	14	5.56	4.88
2009	Phi	NL	24	0	0	8	29.1	143	38	18	16	3	1	0	2	20	2	19	1	0	1	1	.500	0	0-1	0	7.29	4.91
5 ML YEARS			202	0	0	44	169.1	788	185	104	94	16	6	9	7	93	6	143	11	0	9	5	.643	0	0-9	33	5.18	5.00

Fernando Tatis

Bats: R **Throws:** R **Pos:** 1B-41; PH-40; 3B-27; LF-26; 2B-7; SS-2; RF-2; PR-1
Ht: 5'11" **Wt:** 187 **Born:** 1/1/1975 **Age:** 35

Year	Team	Lg	G	AB	H	2B	3B	HR	(Hm	Rd)	TB	R	RBI	RC	TBB	IBB	SO	HBP	SH	SF	SB	CS	SB%	GDP	Avg	OBP	Slg
1997	Tex	AL	60	223	57	9	0	8	(6	2)	90	29	29	26	14	0	42	0	2	2	3	0	1.00	6	.256	.297	.404
1998	2 Tms		150	532	147	33	4	11	(6	5)	221	69	58	69	36	3	123	6	4	1	13	5	.72	16	.276	.329	.415
1999	StL	NL	149	537	160	31	2	34	(16	18)	297	104	107	117	82	4	128	16	0	4	21	9	.70	11	.298	.404	.553
2000	StL	NL	96	324	82	21	1	18	(11	7)	159	59	64	58	57	1	94	10	1	2	2	3	.40	13	.253	.379	.491
2001	Mon	NL	41	145	37	9	0	2	(0	2)	52	20	11	18	16	0	43	4	0	3	0	0	-	5	.255	.339	.359
2002	Mon	NL	114	381	87	18	1	15	(5	10)	152	43	55	39	35	1	90	8	1	5	2	2	.50	15	.228	.303	.399
2003	Mon	NL	53	175	34	6	0	2	(1	1)	46	15	15	15	18	0	40	3	0	0	2	1	.67	7	.194	.281	.263
2006	Bal	AL	28	56	14	6	1	2	(1	1)	28	7	8	9	6	1	17	0	0	2	0	0	-	2	.250	.313	.500
2008	NYM	NL	92	273	81	16	1	11	(6	5)	132	33	47	55	29	3	59	3	0	1	3	0	1.00	7	.297	.369	.484
2009	NYM	NL	125	340	96	21	4	8	(5	3)	149	42	48	42	22	3	54	9	4	4	4	1	.80	13	.282	.339	.438
98	Tex	AL	95	330	89	17	2	3	(1	2)	119	41	32	33	12	2	66	4	4	0	6	2	.75	10	.270	.303	.361
98	StL	NL	55	202	58	16	2	8	(5	3)	102	28	26	36	24	1	57	2	0	1	7	3	.70	6	.287	.367	.505
Postseason			5	13	3	2	0	0	(0	0)	5	1	2	1	1	0	5	0	0	1	0	0	-	0	.231	.267	.385
10 ML YEARS			908	2986	795	170	14	111	(57	54)	1326	421	442	448	315	16	690	59	12	24	50	21	.70	95	.266	.345	.444

Craig Tatum

Bats: R **Throws:** R **Pos:** C-26; PH-3
Ht: 6'1" **Wt:** 224 **Born:** 3/18/1983 **Age:** 27

Year	Team	Lg	G	AB	H	2B	3B	HR	(Hm	Rd)	TB	R	RBI	RC	TBB	IBB	SO	HBP	SH	SF	SB	CS	SB%	GDP	Avg	OBP	Slg
2004	Billings	R+	42	149	33	8	3	2	(-	-)	53	19	21	19	21	0	36	2	0	2	2	0	1.00	9	.221	.322	.356
2005	Dayton	A	37	128	24	7	1	1	(-	-)	36	16	12	12	21	0	30	2	0	0	0	2	.00	2	.188	.311	.281
2006	Dayton	A	98	343	95	21	0	8	(-	-)	140	41	37	50	32	2	70	4	0	2	3	1	.75	7	.277	.344	.408
2007	Srsota	A+	58	219	70	15	0	10	(-	-)	115	29	39	38	9	0	41	1	1	1	1	1	.00	5	.320	.348	.525
2007	Chatt	AA	46	173	40	10	1	2	(-	-)	58	21	22	18	17	0	49	1	0	3	0	1	.00	3	.231	.299	.335
2008	Chatt	AA	86	293	74	18	1	8	(-	-)	118	31	57	39	26	2	58	2	1	6	1	1	.50	7	.253	.312	.403
2008	Lsvlle	AAA	10	39	7	0	0	0	(-	-)	7	1	4	0	0	0	16	0	0	1	0	0	-	4	.179	.175	.179
2009	Lsvlle	AAA	64	213	51	12	0	3	(-	-)	72	22	21	22	17	0	55	2	0	1	0	0	-	4	.239	.300	.338
2009	Cin	NL	26	68	11	1	0	1	(1	0)	15	3	6	4	7	1	10	1	1	0	0	0	-	0	.162	.250	.221

Julian Tavarez

Pitches: R **Bats:** L **Pos:** RP-42
Ht: 6'2" **Wt:** 195 **Born:** 5/22/1973 **Age:** 37

Year	Team	Lg	G	GS	CG	GF	IP	BFP	H	R	ER	HR	SH	SF	HB	TBB	IBB	SO	WP	Bk	W	L	Pct	Sh	Sv-Op	Hld	ERC	ERA
1993	Cle	AL	8	7	0	0	37.0	172	53	29	27	7	0	1	2	13	2	19	3	1	2	2	.500	0	0-0	0	7.48	6.57
1994	Cle	AL	1	1	0	0	1.2	14	6	8	4	1	0	1	0	1	1	0	0	0	0	1	.000	0	0-0	0	24.13	21.60
1995	Cle	AL	57	0	0	15	85.0	350	76	36	23	7	0	2	3	21	0	68	3	2	10	2	.833	0	0-4	19	2.93	2.44
1996	Cle	AL	51	4	0	13	80.2	353	101	49	48	9	5	4	1	22	5	46	1	0	4	7	.364	0	0-0	13	5.12	5.36
1997	SF	NL	89	0	0	13	88.1	378	91	43	38	6	3	8	4	34	5	38	4	0	6	4	.600	0	0-3	26	4.13	3.87
1998	SF	NL	60	0	0	12	85.1	374	96	41	36	5	5	3	8	36	11	52	1	1	5	3	.625	0	1-6	10	4.89	3.80
1999	SF	NL	47	0	0	12	54.2	258	65	38	36	7	3	2	8	25	3	33	4	1	2	0	1.000	0	0-2	5	6.10	5.93
2000	Col	NL	51	12	1	8	120.0	530	124	68	59	11	3	4	7	53	9	62	2	1	11	5	.688	0	1-1	6	4.49	4.43
2001	ChC	NL	34	28	0	1	161.1	712	172	98	81	13	8	4	11	69	4	107	2	1	10	9	.526	0	0-0	2	4.70	4.43
2002	Fla	NL	29	27	0	1	153.2	714	188	100	92	9	13	2	15	74	7	67	7	2	10	12	.455	0	0-0	1	5.75	5.39
2003	Pit	NL	64	0	0	29	83.2	350	75	37	34	1	9	1	5	27	8	39	3	0	3	3	.500	0	11-14	9	2.72	3.66
2004	StL	NL	77	0	0	27	64.1	268	57	21	17	1	3	1	6	19	0	48	2	1	7	4	.636	0	4-6	19	2.87	2.38
2005	StL	NL	74	0	0	16	65.2	278	68	28	25	6	3	3	8	19	4	47	1	0	2	3	.400	0	4-6	32	4.29	3.43
2006	Bos	AL	58	6	1	11	98.2	431	110	54	49	10	3	3	6	44	3	56	2	0	5	4	.556	0	1-3	2	5.32	4.47
2007	Bos	AL	34	23	0	2	134.2	604	151	89	77	14	3	5	7	51	4	77	4	0	7	11	.389	0	0-0	1	4.83	5.15
2008	3 Tms	NL	52	0	0	15	54.2	267	73	42	31	5	5	2	3	28	4	51	2	1	1	5	.167	0	0-0	6	6.42	5.10
2009	Was	NL	42	0	0	9	35.0	169	34	27	19	1	1	3	2	27	2	32	2	0	3	7	.300	0	1-2	5	4.76	4.89
08	Bos	AL	9	0	0	2	12.2	64	18	12	9	0	1	1	1	9	0	6	1	0	0	1	.000	0	0-0	0	7.43	6.39
08	Mil	NL	7	0	0	1	7.1	41	13	10	7	0	0	0	0	5	0	10	0	0	0	1	.000	0	0-0	0	8.77	8.59
08	Atl	NL	36	0	0	12	34.2	162	42	20	15	5	3	1	2	14	4	35	1	1	1	3	.250	0	0-0	6	5.56	3.89
Postseason			31	0	0	7	30.2	135	31	13	12	6	2	0	4	10	3	16	3	0	2	4	.333	0	0-1	4	4.86	3.52
17 ML YEARS			828	108	2	184	1404.1	6222	1540	808	696	113	67	49	96	563	72	842	43	11	88	82	.518	0	23-48	155	4.71	4.46

Willy Taveras

Bats: R **Throws:** R **Pos:** CF-98; PH-5; PR-1
Ht: 6'0" **Wt:** 160 **Born:** 12/25/1981 **Age:** 28

Year	Team	Lg	G	AB	H	2B	3B	HR	(Hm	Rd)	TB	R	RBI	RC	TBB	IBB	SO	HBP	SH	SF	SB	CS	SB%	GDP	Avg	OBP	Slg
2004	Hou	NL	10	1	0	0	0	0	(0	0)	0	2	0	0	0	0	1	0	1	0	1	0	1.00	0	.000	.000	.000
2005	Hou	NL	152	592	172	13	4	3	(2	1)	202	82	29	61	25	1	103	7	7	4	34	11	.76	4	.291	.325	.341
2006	Hou	NL	149	529	147	19	5	1	(0	1)	179	83	30	64	34	0	88	11	11	2	33	9	.79	6	.278	.333	.338
2007	Col	NL	97	372	119	13	2	2	(2	0)	142	64	24	56	21	0	55	7	7	1	33	9	.79	1	.320	.367	.382
2008	Col	NL	133	479	120	15	2	1	(0	1)	142	64	26	49	36	0	79	5	15	3	68	7	.91	4	.251	.308	.296
2009	Cin	NL	102	404	97	11	2	1	(1	0)	115	56	15	33	18	2	58	2	11	2	25	6	.81	2	.240	.275	.285
Postseason			21	69	18	4	1	0	(0	0)	24	9	1	8	4	0	13	3	4	0	2	1	.67	0	.261	.329	.348
6 ML YEARS			643	2377	655	71	15	8	(5	3)	780	351	124	263	134	1	384	32	52	12	194	42	.82	17	.276	.321	.328

Graham Taylor

Pitches: L **Bats:** L **Pos:** SP-3   **Ht:** 6'3" **Wt:** 225 **Born:** 5/25/1984 **Age:** 26

		HOW MUCH HE PITCHED						WHAT HE GAVE UP										THE RESULTS						
Year	Team	Lg	G	GS	CG	GF	IP	BFP	H	R	ER	HR	SH	SF	HB	TBB	IBB	SO	WP	Bk	W	L	Pct	Sh	Sv-Op	Hld	ERC	ERA
2006	Jmstwn	A-	13	13	0	0	65.2	257	59	26	18	2	3	4	3	4	0	48	4	0	3	5	.375	0	0- -	-	2.07	2.47
2007	Grnsbr	A	25	25	3	0	164.1	639	135	59	49	16	6	0	8	18	0	135	7	0	11	3	.786	1	0- -	-	2.26	2.68
2007	Jupiter	A+	2	2	0	0	10.0	51	16	9	9	0	0	1	0	5	0	3	0	0	1	1	.500	0	0- -	-	7.10	8.10
2008	Jupiter	A+	23	22	1	0	140.1	583	147	59	54	7	2	4	3	25	0	95	2	0	11	6	.647	1	0- -	-	3.23	3.46
2008	Carlina	AA	5	5	0	0	23.2	102	29	11	8	4	1	0	0	8	0	15	1	0	2	1	.667	0	0- -	-	5.87	3.04
2009	Jaxnvl	AA	23	23	0	0	126.2	543	115	62	52	9	9	3	9	54	2	71	7	0	8	7	.533	0	0- -	-	3.74	3.69
2009	Fla	NL	3	3	0	0	11.0	63	16	14	10	0	1	2	1	12	0	5	2	0	0	2	.000	0	0-0	0	8.91	8.18

Junichi Tazawa

Pitches: R **Bats:** R **Pos:** SP-4; RP-2   **Ht:** 5'11" **Wt:** 180 **Born:** 6/6/1986 **Age:** 24

		HOW MUCH HE PITCHED						WHAT HE GAVE UP										THE RESULTS						
Year	Team	Lg	G	GS	CG	GF	IP	BFP	H	R	ER	HR	SH	SF	HB	TBB	IBB	SO	WP	Bk	W	L	Pct	Sh	Sv-Op	Hld	ERC	ERA
2009	Portlnd	AA	18	18	0	0	98.0	394	80	31	28	8	2	3	3	26	0	88	4	2	9	5	.643	0	0- -	-	2.62	2.57
2009	Pwtckt	AAA	2	2	0	0	11.1	41	7	4	3	0	1	0	1	1	0	6	0	0	0	2	.000	0	0- -	-	1.17	2.38
2009	Bos	AL	6	4	0	1	25.1	130	43	23	21	4	0	3	3	9	0	13	0	0	2	3	.400	0	0-0	0	9.14	7.46

Taylor Teagarden

Bats: R **Throws:** R **Pos:** C-60; PH-2   **Ht:** 6'1" **Wt:** 200 **Born:** 12/21/1983 **Age:** 26

						BATTING										BASERUNNING				AVERAGES		
Year	Team	Lg	G	AB	H	2B	3B	HR	(Hm Rd)	TB	R	RBI	RC	TBB	IBB	SO	HBP	SH	SF	SB	CS	SB%	GDP	Avg	OBP	Slg
2005	Spokane	A-	31	96	27	5	4	7	(- -)	61	23	16	25	23	0	32	2	0	1	1	1	.50	1	.281	.426	.635
2006	Rngrs	R	7	20	1	0	0	0	(-)	1	4	1	1	9	0	7	0	0	0	1	0	1.00	0	.050	.345	.050
2007	Bkrsfld	A+	81	292	92	25	0	20	(- -)	177	75	67	78	65	0	80	6	0	1	2	1	.67	4	.315	.440	.606
2007	Frisco	AA	29	102	30	3	0	7	(- -)	54	19	16	19	10	0	39	1	0	2	0	0	-	1	.294	.357	.520
2008	Frisco	AA	16	59	10	2	0	2	(- -)	18	6	6	8	8	0	23	1	0	0	1	0	1.00	0	.169	.279	.305
2008	Okla	AAA	57	187	42	6	3	7	(- -)	74	26	16	26	28	0	59	2	1	0	0	1	.00	6	.225	.332	.396
2008	Tex	AL	16	47	15	5	0	6	(3 3)	38	10	17	15	5	0	19	1	0	0	0	0	-	0	.319	.396	.809
2009	Tex	AL	60	198	43	13	0	6	(2 4)	74	26	24	16	14	0	76	1	3	2	0	0	-	6	.217	.270	.374
	2 ML YEARS		76	245	58	18	0	12	(5 7)	112	36	41	31	19	0	95	2	3	2	0	0	-	6	.237	.295	.457

Mark Teahen

Bats: L **Throws:** R **Pos:** 3B-107; RF-32; 1B-11; 2B-3; PH-2; PR-2   **Ht:** 6'3" **Wt:** 210 **Born:** 9/6/1981 **Age:** 28

						BATTING										BASERUNNING				AVERAGES		
Year	Team	Lg	G	AB	H	2B	3B	HR	(Hm Rd)	TB	R	RBI	RC	TBB	IBB	SO	HBP	SH	SF	SB	CS	SB%	GDP	Avg	OBP	Slg
2005	KC	AL	130	447	110	29	4	7	(3 4)	168	60	55	52	40	2	107	1	2	1	7	2	.78	13	.246	.309	.376
2006	KC	AL	109	393	114	21	7	18	(9 9)	203	70	69	79	40	2	85	2	2	2	10	0	1.00	5	.290	.357	.517
2007	KC	AL	144	544	155	31	8	7	(6 1)	223	78	60	82	55	8	127	3	4	2	13	5	.72	23	.285	.353	.410
2008	KC	AL	149	572	146	31	4	15	(4 11)	230	66	59	66	46	4	131	3	0	2	4	3	.57	6	.255	.313	.402
2009	KC	AL	144	524	142	34	1	12	(6 6)	214	69	50	60	37	4	123	6	2	2	8	1	.89	12	.271	.325	.408
	5 ML YEARS		676	2480	687	146	24	59	(28 31)	1038	343	293	339	218	20	573	15	10	9	42	11	.79	59	.269	.331	.419

Mark Teixeira

Bats: B **Throws:** R **Pos:** 1B-152; DH-5; PH-1   **Ht:** 6'3" **Wt:** 220 **Born:** 4/11/1980 **Age:** 30

						BATTING										BASERUNNING				AVERAGES		
Year	Team	Lg	G	AB	H	2B	3B	HR	(Hm Rd)	TB	R	RBI	RC	TBB	IBB	SO	HBP	SH	SF	SB	CS	SB%	GDP	Avg	OBP	Slg
2003	Tex	AL	146	529	137	29	5	26	(19 7)	254	66	84	78	44	5	120	14	0	2	1	2	.33	14	.259	.331	.480
2004	Tex	AL	145	545	153	34	2	38	(18 20)	305	101	112	120	68	12	117	10	0	2	4	1	.80	6	.281	.370	.560
2005	Tex	AL	162	644	194	41	3	43	(30 13)	370	112	144	148	72	5	124	11	0	3	4	0	1.00	18	.301	.379	.575
2006	Tex	AL	162	628	177	45	1	33	(12 21)	323	99	110	114	89	12	128	4	0	6	2	0	1.00	17	.282	.371	.514
2007	2 Tms		132	494	151	33	2	30	(14 16)	278	86	105	116	72	13	112	7	0	2	0	0	-	16	.306	.400	.563
2008	2 Tms		157	574	177	41	0	33	(19 14)	317	102	121	119	97	13	93	7	0	7	2	0	1.00	17	.308	.410	.552
2009	NYY	AL	156	609	178	43	3	39	(24 15)	344	103	122	112	81	9	114	12	0	5	2	0	1.00	13	.292	.383	.565
07	Tex	AL	78	286	85	24	1	13	(5 8)	150	48	49	58	45	10	66	3	0	1	0	0	-	6	.297	.397	.524
07	Atl	NL	54	208	66	9	1	17	(9 8)	128	38	56	58	27	3	46	4	0	1	0	0	-	2	.317	.404	.615
08	Atl	NL	103	381	108	27	0	20	(11 9)	195	63	78	69	65	9	70	3	0	2	0	0	-	13	.283	.390	.512
08	LAA	AL	54	193	69	14	0	13	(8 5)	122	39	43	50	32	4	23	4	0	5	2	0	1.00	4	.358	.449	.632
	Postseason		4	15	7	0	0	0	(0 0)	7	4	1	2	4	0	3	0	0	1	0	0	-	0	.467	.550	.467
	7 ML YEARS		1060	4023	1167	266	16	242	(136 106)	2191	669	798	807	523	69	808	65	0	27	15	3	.83	92	.290	.378	.545

Miguel Tejada

Bats: R **Throws:** R **Pos:** SS-158   **Ht:** 5'9" **Wt:** 213 **Born:** 5/25/1974 **Age:** 36

						BATTING										BASERUNNING				AVERAGES		
Year	Team	Lg	G	AB	H	2B	3B	HR	(Hm Rd)	TB	R	RBI	RC	TBB	IBB	SO	HBP	SH	SF	SB	CS	SB%	GDP	Avg	OBP	Slg
1997	Oak	AL	26	99	20	3	2	2	(1 1)	33	10	7	7	2	0	22	3	0	0	2	0	1.00	3	.202	.240	.333
1998	Oak	AL	105	365	85	20	1	11	(5 6)	140	53	45	40	28	0	86	7	4	3	5	6	.45	8	.233	.298	.384
1999	Oak	AL	159	593	149	33	4	21	(12 9)	253	93	84	82	57	3	94	10	9	5	8	7	.53	11	.251	.325	.427
2000	Oak	AL	160	607	167	32	1	30	(16 14)	291	105	115	99	66	6	102	4	2	2	6	0	1.00	15	.275	.349	.479
2001	Oak	AL	162	622	166	31	3	31	(17 14)	296	107	113	94	43	5	89	13	1	4	11	5	.69	14	.267	.326	.476
2002	Oak	AL	162	662	204	30	0	34	(17 17)	336	108	131	123	38	3	84	11	0	4	7	2	.78	21	.308	.354	.508
2003	Oak	AL	162	636	177	42	0	27	(15 12)	300	98	106	103	53	7	65	6	0	8	10	0	1.00	12	.278	.336	.472
2004	Bal	AL	162	653	203	40	2	34	(17 17)	349	107	150	124	48	6	73	10	0	14	4	1	.80	24	.311	.360	.534
2005	Bal	AL	162	654	199	50	5	26	(16 10)	337	89	98	102	40	9	83	7	0	3	5	1	.83	26	.304	.349	.515

Year	Team	Lg	G	AB	H	2B	3B	HR	(Hm	Rd)	TB	R	RBI	RC	TBB	IBB	SO	HBP	SH	SF	SB	CS	SB%	GDP	Avg	OBP	Slg
												BATTING										**BASERUNNING**				**AVERAGES**	
2006	Bal	AL	162	648	214	37	0	24	(17	7)	323	99	100	99	46	10	79	9	0	6	6	2	.75	28	.330	.379	.498
2007	Bal	AL	133	514	152	19	1	18	(12	6)	227	72	81	76	41	9	55	10	0	3	2	1	.67	22	.296	.357	.442
2008	Hou	NL	158	632	179	38	3	13	(8	5)	262	92	66	61	24	4	72	6	1	3	7	7	.50	32	.283	.314	.415
2009	Hou	NL	158	635	199	46	1	14	(10	4)	289	83	86	84	19	2	48	11	0	8	5	2	.71	29	.313	.340	.455
Postseason			20	85	18	7	0	1	(0	1)	28	9	8	6	3	0	16	1	0	2	1	0	1.00	0	.212	.242	.329
13 ML YEARS			1871	7320	2114	421	23	285	(163	122)	3436	1116	1185	1094	505	64	952	107	17	63	78	34	.70	245	.289	.341	.469

Robinson Tejeda

Pitches: R **Bats:** R **Pos:** RP-29; SP-6　　　　　**Ht:** 6'3" **Wt:** 248 **Born:** 3/24/1982 **Age:** 28

Year	Team	Lg	G	GS	CG	GF	IP	BFP	H	R	ER	HR	SH	SF	HB	TBB	IBB	SO	WP	Bk	W	L	Pct	Sh	Sv-Op Hld	ERC	ERA
							HOW MUCH HE PITCHED					**WHAT HE GAVE UP**											**THE RESULTS**				
2009	NWArk*	AA	2	2	0	0	3.2	14	3	2	2	1	0	0	0	2	0	5	0	0	0	1	.000	0	0-- -	5.50	4.91
2009	Omha*	AAA	1	1	0	0	2.0	10	1	2	0	0	0	0	0	3	0	1	0	0	0	1	.000	0	0-- -	4.47	0.00
2005	Phi	NL	26	13	0	5	85.2	371	67	36	34	5	3	2	8	51	4	72	3	1	4	3	.571	0	0-0 1	3.64	3.57
2006	Tex	AL	14	14	0	0	73.2	329	83	40	35	10	1	5	3	32	1	40	1	1	5	5	.500	0	0-0 0	5.41	4.28
2007	Tex	AL	19	19	0	0	95.1	454	110	78	70	17	3	6	6	60	2	69	10	0	5	9	.357	0	0-0 0	6.77	6.61
2008	2 Tms	AL	29	1	0	15	45.1	186	27	23	20	4	0	3	1	24	0	45	5	0	2	2	.500	0	0-1 1	2.43	3.97
2009	KC	AL	35	6	0	5	73.2	313	43	30	29	4	2	1	3	50	2	87	6	1	4	2	.667	0	0-0 0	2.68	3.54
08	Tex	AL	4	0	0	1	6.0	29	5	6	6	1	0	1	0	5	0	4	0	0	0	0	-	0	0-1 0	5.04	9.00
08	KC	AL	25	1	0	14	39.1	157	22	17	14	3	0	2	1	19	0	41	5	0	2	2	.500	0	0-0 1	2.08	3.20
5 ML YEARS			123	53	0	25	373.2	1653	330	207	188	40	9	17	21	217	9	313	25	3	20	21	.488	0	0-1 4	4.36	4.53

Marcus Thames

Bats: R **Throws:** R **Pos:** DH-54; LF-20; PH-18; 1B-2　　　　　**Ht:** 6'2" **Wt:** 220 **Born:** 3/6/1977 **Age:** 33

Year	Team	Lg	G	AB	H	2B	3B	HR	(Hm	Rd)	TB	R	RBI	RC	TBB	IBB	SO	HBP	SH	SF	SB	CS	SB%	GDP	Avg	OBP	Slg
												BATTING										**BASERUNNING**				**AVERAGES**	
2009	Toledo*	AAA	12	49	12	0	0	2	(-	-)	18	6	6	5	5	0	14	0	0	0	0	0	-	2	.245	.315	.367
2002	NYY	AL	7	13	3	1	0	1	(1	0)	7	2	2	2	0	0	4	0	0	0	0	0	-	0	.231	.231	.538
2003	Tex	AL	30	73	15	2	0	1	(0	1)	20	12	4	5	8	0	18	2	0	1	0	1	.00	2	.205	.298	.274
2004	Det	AL	61	165	42	12	0	10	(5	5)	84	24	33	30	16	0	42	2	0	1	0	1	.00	3	.255	.326	.509
2005	Det	AL	38	107	21	2	0	7	(3	4)	44	11	16	10	9	1	38	1	0	1	0	0	-	1	.196	.263	.411
2006	Det	AL	110	348	89	20	2	26	(11	15)	191	61	60	60	37	0	92	4	0	1	1	1	.50	0	.256	.333	.549
2007	Det	AL	86	269	65	15	0	18	(14	4)	134	37	54	39	13	1	72	1	0	1	2	1	.67	6	.242	.278	.498
2008	Det	AL	103	316	76	12	0	25	(10	15)	163	50	56	44	24	0	95	0	0	2	0	3	.00	6	.241	.292	.516
2009	Det	AL	87	258	65	11	1	13	(6	7)	117	33	36	31	29	2	72	1	0	6	0	2	.00	5	.252	.323	.453
Postseason			8	21	5	2	0	0	(0	0)	7	3	1	3	1	0	6	0	0	0	0	0	-	0	.238	.273	.333
8 ML YEARS			522	1549	376	75	3	101	(50	51)	760	230	261	221	136	4	433	11	0	13	3	9	.25	23	.243	.306	.491

Joe Thatcher

Pitches: L **Bats:** L **Pos:** RP-52　　　　　**Ht:** 6'2" **Wt:** 229 **Born:** 10/4/1981 **Age:** 28

Year	Team	Lg	G	GS	CG	GF	IP	BFP	H	R	ER	HR	SH	SF	HB	TBB	IBB	SO	WP	Bk	W	L	Pct	Sh	Sv-Op Hld	ERC	ERA
							HOW MUCH HE PITCHED					**WHAT HE GAVE UP**											**THE RESULTS**				
2009	Portlnd	AAA	19	0	0	5	19.0	81	18	7	4	1	0	0	1	5	1	22	1	0	1	2	.333	0	1-- -	3.00	1.89
2007	SD	NL	22	0	0	5	21.0	85	13	6	3	1	0	0	1	6	2	16	0	0	2	2	.500	0	0-0 2	1.49	1.29
2008	SD	NL	25	0	0	7	25.2	128	42	25	24	4	2	3	0	13	2	17	0	0	0	4	.000	0	0-3 5	8.91	8.42
2009	SD	NL	52	0	0	7	45.0	188	37	14	14	2	1	2	4	18	7	55	2	1	1	0	1.000	0	0-1 9	2.87	2.80
3 ML YEARS			99	0	0	19	91.2	401	92	45	41	7	3	5	5	37	11	88	2	1	3	6	.333	0	0-4 16	3.94	4.03

Dale Thayer

Pitches: R **Bats:** R **Pos:** RP-11　　　　　**Ht:** 6'0" **Wt:** 195 **Born:** 12/17/1980 **Age:** 29

Year	Team	Lg	G	GS	CG	GF	IP	BFP	H	R	ER	HR	SH	SF	HB	TBB	IBB	SO	WP	Bk	W	L	Pct	Sh	Sv-Op Hld	ERC	ERA
							HOW MUCH HE PITCHED					**WHAT HE GAVE UP**											**THE RESULTS**				
2003	FtWyn	A	45	0	0	35	48.0	194	31	15	11	2	5	2	2	15	1	72	1	0	1	3	.250	0	25-- -	1.69	2.06
2004	Lk Els	A+	50	0	0	42	55.1	214	36	12	10	1	0	2	0	11	0	54	0	0	2	1	.667	0	23-- -	1.31	1.63
2004	Mobile	AA	8	0	0	4	7.1	31	8	3	3	1	0	0	0	1	0	7	0	0	1	1	.500	0	0-- -	3.69	3.68
2005	Mobile	AA	56	0	0	50	57.2	249	60	16	15	5	5	2	1	26	2	59	1	0	3	5	.375	0	28-- -	4.52	2.34
2006	Mobile	AA	57	0	0	51	65.1	274	59	18	18	3	6	0	3	22	5	57	0	0	7	4	.636	0	27-- -	3.01	2.48
2006	Portlnd	AAA	2	0	0	2	3.0	11	2	1	1	1	0	0	0	1	0	4	1	0	0	0	-	0	0-- -	3.72	3.00
2007	Mont	AA	47	0	0	43	59.2	239	40	16	15	4	2	3	2	19	2	54	1	0	9	0	1.000	0	21-- -	1.95	2.26
2007	Drham	AAA	8	0	0	4	9.1	35	5	3	3	0	1	0	0	4	0	9	2	0	0	1	.000	0	0-- -	1.46	2.89
2008	Drham	AAA	52	0	0	24	68.1	301	73	26	21	2	2	2	0	24	1	76	4	0	3	1	.750	0	9-- -	3.65	2.77
2009	Drham	AAA	51	0	0	40	63.1	264	59	24	16	3	4	1	3	15	1	44	2	0	2	5	.286	0	17-- -	2.87	2.27
2009	TB	AL	11	0	0	3	13.2	59	18	9	7	3	0	0	0	1	0	8	1	0	0	0	-	0	1-1 0	5.38	4.61

Ryan Theriot

Bats: R **Throws:** R **Pos:** SS-151; PH-5　　　　　**Ht:** 5'11" **Wt:** 175 **Born:** 12/7/1979 **Age:** 30

Year	Team	Lg	G	AB	H	2B	3B	HR	(Hm	Rd)	TB	R	RBI	RC	TBB	IBB	SO	HBP	SH	SF	SB	CS	SB%	GDP	Avg	OBP	Slg
												BATTING										**BASERUNNING**				**AVERAGES**	
2005	ChC	NL	9	13	2	1	0	0	(0	0)	3	3	0	0	1	0	2	0	0	0	1	0	1.00	0	.154	.214	.231
2006	ChC	NL	53	134	44	11	3	3	(3	0)	70	34	16	31	17	0	18	2	6	0	13	2	.87	5	.328	.412	.522
2007	ChC	NL	148	537	143	30	2	3	(3	0)	186	80	45	64	49	1	50	0	8	3	28	4	.88	12	.266	.326	.346
2008	ChC	NL	149	580	178	19	4	1	(1	0)	208	85	38	78	73	1	58	3	4	1	22	13	.63	13	.307	.387	.359
2009	ChC	NL	154	602	171	20	5	7	(5	2)	222	81	54	69	51	1	93	6	13	5	21	10	.68	13	.284	.343	.369
Postseason			6	23	6	0	0	0	(0	0)	6	0	1	2	2	1	4	0	0	0	1	0	1.00	1	.261	.320	.261
5 ML YEARS			513	1866	538	81	14	14	(12	2)	689	283	153	252	191	3	221	11	31	9	84	29	.74	49	.288	.356	.369

Josh Thole

Bats: L Throws: R Pos: C-16; PH-1 Ht: 6'1" Wt: 205 Born: 10/28/1986 Age: 23

Year	Team	Lg	G	AB	H	2B	3B	HR	(Hm	Rd)	TB	R	RBI	RC	TBB	IBB	SO	HBP	SH	SF	SB	CS	SB%	GDP	Avg	OBP	Slg
2005	Mets	R	35	104	28	2	1	1	(-	-)	35	14	12	17	20	0	11	4	2	0	1	1	.50	2	.269	.406	.337
2006	Kngspt	R+	36	98	23	4	0	1	(-	-)	30	13	12	9	7	1	25	3	0	2	1	1	.50	1	.235	.300	.306
2007	Savann	A	117	389	104	17	0	0	(-	-)	121	46	36	51	61	1	57	4	4	0	4	4	.50	10	.267	.372	.311
2008	StLuci	A+	111	347	104	25	2	5	(-	-)	148	49	56	60	45	2	38	4	1	5	2	1	.67	8	.300	.382	.427
2009	Bnghtn	AA	103	384	126	29	2	1	(-	-)	162	48	46	68	43	4	34	5	1	9	8	4	.67	14	.328	.395	.422
2009	NYM	NL	17	53	17	2	1	0	(0	0)	21	2	9	9	4	0	5	0	0	2	1	0	1.00	1	.321	.356	.396

Clete Thomas

Bats: L Throws: R Pos: RF-87; LF-23; PR-10; CF-7; PH-5 Ht: 5'11" Wt: 195 Born: 11/14/1983 Age: 26

Year	Team	Lg	G	AB	H	2B	3B	HR	(Hm	Rd)	TB	R	RBI	RC	TBB	IBB	SO	HBP	SH	SF	SB	CS	SB%	GDP	Avg	OBP	Slg
2005	Oneont	A-	18	70	27	5	1	1	(-	-)	37	19	14	19	12	1	11	2	0	0	9	0	1.00	0	.386	.488	.529
2005	WMich	A	51	194	55	8	5	0	(-	-)	73	39	11	29	21	3	37	2	2	2	11	3	.79	3	.284	.356	.376
2006	Lkland	A+	132	529	136	30	5	6	(-	-)	194	67	40	70	56	3	127	6	1	3	34	13	.72	3	.257	.333	.367
2007	Erie	AA	137	528	148	30	6	8	(-	-)	214	97	53	80	59	0	110	7	3	2	18	11	.62	3	.280	.359	.405
2008	Toledo	AAA	76	291	72	18	2	9	(-	-)	121	44	45	43	37	2	88	1	3	1	29	11	.73	3	.247	.333	.416
2009	Toledo	AAA	45	175	51	17	1	1	(-	-)	73	27	17	32	26	1	49	3	0	1	18	3	.86	4	.291	.390	.417
2008	Det	AL	40	116	33	9	1	1	(1	0)	47	7	9	17	14	1	26	1	2	0	2	0	1.00	1	.284	.366	.405
2009	Det	AL	102	275	66	13	3	7	(4	3)	106	46	39	36	33	0	77	1	1	0	3	0	1.00	3	.240	.324	.385
	2 ML YEARS		142	391	99	22	4	8	(5	3)	153	53	48	53	47	1	103	2	3	0	5	0	1.00	4	.253	.336	.391

Jim Thome

Bats: L Throws: R Pos: DH-99; PH-20 Ht: 6'3" Wt: 260 Born: 8/27/1970 Age: 39

Year	Team	Lg	G	AB	H	2B	3B	HR	(Hm	Rd)	TB	R	RBI	RC	TBB	IBB	SO	HBP	SH	SF	SB	CS	SB%	GDP	Avg	OBP	Slg
1991	Cle	AL	27	98	25	4	2	1	(0	1)	36	7	9	9	5	1	16	1	0	0	1	1	.50	4	.255	.298	.367
1992	Cle	AL	40	117	24	3	1	2	(1	1)	35	8	12	9	10	2	34	2	0	2	2	0	1.00	3	.205	.275	.299
1993	Cle	AL	47	154	41	11	0	7	(5	2)	73	28	22	30	29	1	36	4	0	5	2	1	.67	3	.266	.385	.474
1994	Cle	AL	98	321	86	20	1	20	(10	10)	168	58	52	56	46	6	84	0	1	1	3	3	.50	11	.268	.359	.523
1995	Cle	AL	137	452	142	29	3	25	(13	12)	252	92	73	109	97	3	113	5	0	3	4	3	.57	8	.314	.438	.558
1996	Cle	AL	151	505	157	28	5	38	(18	20)	309	122	116	132	123	8	141	6	0	2	2	2	.60	12	.311	.450	.612
1997	Cle	AL	147	496	142	25	0	40	(17	23)	287	104	102	120	120	9	146	3	0	8	1	1	.50	9	.286	.423	.579
1998	Cle	AL	123	440	129	34	2	30	(18	12)	257	89	85	104	89	8	141	4	0	4	1	0	1.00	7	.293	.413	.584
1999	Cle	AL	146	494	137	27	2	33	(19	14)	267	101	108	116	127	13	171	4	0	4	0	0	-	6	.277	.426	.540
2000	Cle	AL	158	557	150	33	1	37	(21	16)	296	106	106	119	118	4	171	4	0	5	1	0	1.00	8	.269	.398	.531
2001	Cle	AL	156	526	153	26	1	49	(30	19)	328	101	124	130	111	14	185	4	0	9	0	1	.00	9	.291	.416	.624
2002	Cle	AL	147	480	146	19	2	52	(30	22)	325	101	118	139	122	18	139	5	0	6	1	2	.33	5	.304	.445	.677
2003	Phi	NL	159	578	154	30	3	47	(28	19)	331	111	131	125	111	11	182	4	0	5	0	3	.00	6	.266	.385	.573
2004	Phi	NL	143	508	139	28	1	42	(19	23)	295	97	105	97	104	26	144	2	0	4	0	2	.00	10	.274	.396	.581
2005	Phi	NL	59	193	40	7	0	7	(6	1)	68	26	30	25	45	4	59	2	0	2	0	0	-	5	.207	.360	.352
2006	CWS	AL	143	490	141	26	0	42	(25	17)	293	108	109	120	107	12	147	0	0	7	0	0	-	4	.288	.416	.598
2007	CWS	AL	130	432	119	19	0	35	(21	14)	243	79	96	104	95	11	134	6	0	3	0	1	.00	10	.275	.410	.563
2008	CWS	AL	149	503	123	28	0	34	(19	15)	253	93	90	96	91	9	147	4	0	4	1	0	1.00	18	.245	.362	.503
2009	2 Tms		124	362	90	15	0	23	(14	9)	174	55	77	65	69	3	123	0	0	3	0	0	-	0	.249	.366	.481
09	CWS	AL	107	345	86	15	0	23	(14	9)	170	55	74	65	69	3	116	0	0	3	0	0	-	8	.249	.372	.493
09	LAD	NL	17	17	4	0	0	0	(0	0)	4	0	3	0	0	0	7	0	0	0	0	0	-	0	.235	.235	.235
	Postseason		59	204	45	2	1	17	(13	4)	100	33	37	30	26	1	64	2	1	0	0	0	-	3	.221	.315	.490
	19 ML YEARS		2284	7706	2138	412	24	564	(314	250)	4290	1486	1565	1705	1619	162	2313	66	1	71	19	20	.49	146	.277	.404	.557

Brad Thompson

Pitches: R Bats: R Pos: RP-24; SP-8 Ht: 6'1" Wt: 190 Born: 1/31/1982 Age: 28

Year	Team	Lg	G	GS	CG	GF	IP	BFP	H	R	ER	HR	SH	SF	HB	TBB	IBB	SO	WP	Bk	W	L	Pct	Sh	Sv-Op	Hld	ERC	ERA
2009	Memp*	AAA	3	3	0	0	15.2	59	13	6	6	1	1	0	0	1	0	9	0	0	2	0	1.000	0	0--	-	1.83	3.45
2005	StL	NL	40	0	0	8	55.0	225	46	22	18	5	3	0	4	15	2	29	0	0	4	0	1.000	0	1-1	7	2.90	2.95
2006	StL	NL	43	1	0	16	56.2	245	58	23	21	4	3	0	5	20	3	32	1	0	1	2	.333	0	0-0	3	4.11	3.34
2007	StL	NL	44	17	0	10	129.1	580	157	76	68	23	4	2	13	40	2	53	4	0	8	6	.571	0	0-0	0	5.99	4.73
2008	StL	NL	26	6	0	10	64.2	273	72	38	37	5	2	3	3	19	1	32	2	0	3	6	.667	0	0-1	1	4.44	5.15
2009	StL	NL	32	8	0	17	80.0	345	85	45	43	8	2	2	7	23	2	34	5	1	2	6	.250	0	0-0	0	4.32	4.84
	Postseason		8	0	0	1	4.1	23	8	5	4	2	0	1	0	1	0	4	0	0	0	1	.000	0	0-0	0	11.13	8.31
	5 ML YEARS		185	32	0	61	385.2	1668	418	204	187	45	14	7	32	117	10	180	12	1	21	17	.553	0	1-2	11	4.63	4.36

Rich Thompson

Pitches: R Bats: R Pos: RP-13 Ht: 6'1" Wt: 180 Born: 7/1/1984 Age: 25

Year	Team	Lg	G	GS	CG	GF	IP	BFP	H	R	ER	HR	SH	SF	HB	TBB	IBB	SO	WP	Bk	W	L	Pct	Sh	Sv-Op	Hld	ERC	ERA
2009	Salt Lk*	AAA	29	0	0	10	43.1	185	41	19	15	7	3	2	2	11	0	51	2	0	3	1	.750	0	0--	-	3.69	3.12
2007	LAA	AL	7	0	0	0	6.2	32	10	8	8	4	0	0	0	3	0	9	2	0	0	0	-	0	0-0	0	11.85	10.80
2008	LAA	AL	2	0	0	1	2.0	12	4	5	5	0	0	0	0	2	0	1	1	0	0	0	-	0	0-0	0	12.01	22.50
2009	LAA	AL	13	0	0	2	19.1	92	27	11	11	6	1	1	1	7	0	21	5	0	0	0	-	0	0-0	0	8.17	5.12
	3 ML YEARS		22	0	0	5	28.0	136	41	24	24	10	1	1	1	12	0	31	8	0	0	0	-	0	0-0	0	9.33	7.71

Matt Thornton

Pitches: L Bats: L Pos: RP-70

Ht: 6'6" Wt: 235 Born: 9/15/1976 Age: 33

Year	Team	Lg	G	GS	CG	GF	IP	BFP	H	R	ER	HR	SH	SF	HB	TBB	IBB	SO	WP	Bk	W	L	Pct	Sh	Sv-Op	Hld	ERC	ERA
2004	Sea	AL	19	1	0	8	32.2	148	30	15	15	2	2	1	0	25	1	30	2	0	1	2	.333	0	0-0	0	4.75	4.13
2005	Sea	AL	55	0	0	15	57.0	262	54	33	33	13	1	1	0	42	2	57	7	0	0	4	.000	0	0-1	5	6.06	5.21
2006	CWS	AL	63	0	0	20	54.0	227	46	20	20	5	1	3	1	21	4	49	1	0	5	3	.625	0	2-5	18	3.12	3.33
2007	CWS	AL	68	0	0	13	56.1	249	59	31	30	4	0	2	2	26	6	55	3	0	4	4	.500	0	2-7	17	4.35	4.79
2008	CWS	AL	74	0	0	12	67.1	268	48	20	20	5	1	1	2	19	2	77	3	0	5	3	.625	0	1-6	20	2.07	2.67
2009	CWS	AL	70	0	0	17	72.1	291	58	22	22	5	2	1	1	20	2	87	4	0	6	3	.667	0	4-9	24	2.40	2.74
	Postseason		3	0	0	1	3.1	14	2	0	0	0	0	0	0	2	1	2	0	0	0	0	-	0	0-0	1	1.62	0.00
	6 ML YEARS		349	1	0	85	339.2	1445	295	141	140	34	7	9	6	153	17	355	20	0	21	19	.525	0	9-28	84	3.54	3.71

Joe Thurston

Bats: L Throws: R Pos: 3B-68; 2B-47; PH-43; LF-5; PR-4

Ht: 5'11" Wt: 210 Born: 9/29/1979 Age: 30

Year	Team	Lg	G	AB	H	2B	3B	HR	(Hm	Rd)	TB	R	RBI	RC	TBB	IBB	SO	HBP	SH	SF	SB	CS	SB%	GDP	Avg	OBP	Slg
2002	LAD	NL	8	13	6	1	0	0	(0	0)	7	1	1	3	0	0	1	0	1	1	0	0	-	0	.462	.429	.538
2003	LAD	NL	12	10	2	0	0	0	(0	0)	2	2	0	0	1	0	1	0	0	0	0	0	-	0	.200	.273	.200
2004	LAD	NL	17	17	3	1	1	0	(0	0)	6	1	1	1	0	0	5	0	0	1	0	0	-	0	.176	.167	.353
2006	Phi	NL	18	18	4	1	0	0	(0	0)	5	3	0	1	1	0	2	1	0	0	0	0	-	0	.222	.300	.278
2008	Bos	AL	4	8	0	0	0	0	(0	0)	0	0	0	0	0	0	1	1	0	0	0	0	-	0	.000	.111	.000
2009	StL	NL	124	267	60	17	4	1	(0	1)	88	27	25	29	33	5	56	3	3	1	4	2	.67	9	.225	.316	.330
	6 ML YEARS		183	333	75	20	5	1	(0	1)	108	34	27	34	35	5	66	5	4	3	4	2	.67	9	.225	.306	.324

Chris Tillman

Pitches: R Bats: R Pos: SP-12

Ht: 6'5" Wt: 195 Born: 4/15/1988 Age: 22

Year	Team	Lg	G	GS	CG	GF	IP	BFP	H	R	ER	HR	SH	SF	HB	TBB	IBB	SO	WP	Bk	W	L	Pct	Sh	Sv-Op	Hld	ERC	ERA
2006	Ms	R	5	0	0	2	11.0	48	9	4	1	0	0	0	1	5	0	16	1	0	2	0	1.000	0	1--	-	2.87	0.82
2006	Everett	A-	5	5	0	0	19.2	97	25	17	17	4	2	0	3	15	0	29	3	0	1	3	.250	0	0--	-	9.13	7.78
2007	Wisc	A	8	8	0	0	33.0	145	31	21	13	1	1	0	1	13	0	34	3	1	1	4	.200	0	0--	-	3.24	3.55
2007	Hi Dsrt	A+	20	20	0	0	102.2	472	107	79	60	12	4	5	12	48	0	105	13	0	6	7	.462	0	0--	-	5.10	5.26
2008	Bowie	AA	28	28	0	0	135.2	580	115	53	48	10	3	1	4	65	1	154	10	0	11	4	.733	0	0--	-	3.46	3.18
2009	Norfolk	AAA	18	18	0	0	96.2	399	85	36	29	5	2	1	4	26	1	99	6	2	8	6	.571	0	0--	-	2.75	2.70
2009	Bal	AL	12	12	0	0	65.0	285	77	40	39	15	0	0	2	24	1	39	4	0	2	5	.286	0	0-0	0	6.28	5.40

Jesse Todd

Pitches: R Bats: R Pos: RP-20

Ht: 5'11" Wt: 210 Born: 4/20/1986 Age: 24

Year	Team	Lg	G	GS	CG	GF	IP	BFP	H	R	ER	HR	SH	SF	HB	TBB	IBB	SO	WP	Bk	W	L	Pct	Sh	Sv-Op	Hld	ERC	ERA
2007	Batvia	A-	16	7	0	2	58.1	231	48	23	18	2	0	0	1	14	1	69	2	0	4	1	.800	0	0--	-	2.23	2.78
2008	PlmBh	A+	7	4	0	1	27.1	108	18	7	5	0	2	0	1	7	0	35	0	1	3	0	1.000	0	1--	-	1.46	1.65
2008	Sprgfld	AA	17	16	0	1	103.0	405	79	37	34	12	3	0	13	24	1	81	1	0	4	5	.444	0	0--	-	2.89	2.97
2008	Memp	AAA	4	4	0	0	22.2	96	19	10	10	4	0	2	1	11	0	20	2	0	1	1	.500	0	0--	-	4.28	3.97
2009	Memp	AAA	41	0	0	34	49.0	199	39	13	12	3	3	1	0	13	1	59	7	0	4	2	.667	0	24--	-	2.21	2.21
2009	Clmbs	AAA	3	0	0	2	4.0	13	1	0	0	0	0	0	0	0	0	7	0	0	0	0	-	0	1--	-	0.14	0.00
2009	2 Tms		20	0	0	6	22.1	109	34	19	19	4	1	4	0	9	1	20	1	0	0	1	.000	0	0-0	1	7.74	7.66
09	StL	NL	1	0	0	0	1.2	10	3	2	2	1	0	0	0	2	0	2	0	0	0	0	-	0	0-0	0	18.11	10.80
09	Cle	AL	19	0	0	6	20.2	99	31	17	17	3	1	4	0	7	1	18	1	0	0	1	.000	0	0-0	1	7.01	7.40

Matt Tolbert

Bats: B Throws: R Pos: 2B-36; 3B-27; PR-9; SS-3; 1B-1; DH-1; PH-1

Ht: 6'0" Wt: 185 Born: 5/4/1982 Age: 28

Year	Team	Lg	G	AB	H	2B	3B	HR	(Hm	Rd)	TB	R	RBI	RC	TBB	IBB	SO	HBP	SH	SF	SB	CS	SB%	GDP	Avg	OBP	Slg
2004	Elizab	R+	33	104	32	7	2	3	(-	-)	52	23	18	19	12	0	13	0	1	1	3	2	.60	4	.308	.376	.500
2005	FtMyrs	A+	111	417	111	20	6	3	(-	-)	152	55	46	53	35	1	80	3	15	2	11	4	.73	3	.266	.326	.365
2006	FtMyrs	A+	40	155	47	6	3	4	(-	-)	71	20	24	27	14	1	17	1	1	2	7	2	.78	4	.303	.360	.458
2006	NwBrit	AA	72	248	64	15	1	3	(-	-)	90	33	35	34	30	1	43	4	5	5	5	1	.83	3	.258	.341	.363
2007	Roch	AAA	121	417	122	24	7	6	(-	-)	178	65	53	67	37	0	56	5	12	6	11	3	.79	4	.293	.353	.427
2008	NwBrit	AA	14	56	14	3	0	0	(-	-)	17	6	6	3	1	0	6	0	0	0	4	3	.57	0	.250	.263	.304
2009	Roch	AAA	56	236	68	11	6	3	(-	-)	100	35	22	33	14	0	32	1	0	0	7	4	.64	1	.288	.331	.424
2008	Min	AL	41	113	32	6	3	0	(0	0)	44	18	6	13	7	0	19	0	2	1	7	1	.88	5	.283	.322	.389
2009	Min	AL	71	198	46	7	1	2	(0	2)	61	28	19	22	21	1	37	0	10	2	6	2	.75	1	.232	.303	.308
	2 ML YEARS		112	311	78	13	4	2	(0	2)	105	46	25	35	28	1	56	0	12	3	13	3	.81	6	.251	.310	.338

Brett Tomko

Pitches: R Bats: R Pos: RP-15; SP-6

Ht: 6'4" Wt: 220 Born: 4/7/1973 Age: 37

Year	Team	Lg	G	GS	CG	GF	IP	BFP	H	R	ER	HR	SH	SF	HB	TBB	IBB	SO	WP	Bk	W	L	Pct	Sh	Sv-Op	Hld	ERC	ERA
2009	S-WB*	AAA	10	0	0	8	14.0	53	8	1	1	0	0	0	0	4	0	17	0	0	1	0	1.000	0	4--	-	1.49	0.64
2009	Scrmto*	AAA	3	2	0	0	5.2	29	9	6	5	0	0	0	1	2	0	8	1	0	0	0	-	0	0--	-	7.15	7.94
1997	Cin	NL	22	19	0	1	126.0	519	106	50	48	14	5	9	4	47	4	95	5	0	11	7	.611	0	0-0	0	3.31	3.43
1998	Cin	NL	34	34	1	0	210.2	887	198	111	104	22	12	2	7	64	3	162	9	1	13	12	.520	0	0-0	0	3.50	4.44
1999	Cin	NL	33	26	1	1	172.0	744	175	103	94	31	9	5	4	60	10	132	8	0	5	7	.417	0	0-0	1	4.51	4.92
2000	Sea	AL	32	8	0	10	92.1	401	92	53	48	12	5	5	3	40	4	59	1	1	7	5	.583	0	1-2	3	4.49	4.68

Year	Team	Lg	G	GS	CG	GF	IP	BFP	H	R	ER	HR	SH	SF	IIB	TBB	IBB	SO	WP	Bk	W	L	Pct	Sh	Sv-Op	Hld	ERC	ERA
							HOW MUCH HE PITCHED					WHAT HE GAVE UP												THE RESULTS					
2001	Sea	AL	11	4	0	1	34.2	164	42	24	20	9	1	2	0	15	2	22	1	0	3	1	.750	0	0-1	0	6.31	5.19
2002	SD	NL	32	32	3	0	204.1	871	212	107	102	31	6	8	2	60	9	126	3	0	10	10	.500	0	0-0	0	4.18	4.49
2003	StL	NL	33	32	2	0	202.2	903	252	126	119	35	12	3	5	57	2	114	6	0	13	9	.591	0	0-0	0	5.63	5.28
2004	SF	NL	32	31	2	1	194.0	825	196	98	87	19	7	1	0	64	3	108	10	0	11	7	.611	1	0-0	0	3.82	4.04
2005	SF	NL	33	30	3	1	190.2	823	205	99	95	20	6	5	7	57	11	114	5	0	8	15	.348	0	1-1	1	4.18	4.48
2006	LAD	NL	44	15	0	2	112.1	491	123	67	59	17	7	7	2	29	0	76	3	1	8	7	.533	0	0-3	5	4.37	4.73
2007	2 Tms	NL	40	19	0	9	131.1	588	149	89	81	18	8	6	2	48	1	105	5	0	4	12	.250	0	0-0	0	4.96	5.55
2008	2 Tms		22	10	0	3	70.0	307	83	51	49	11	1	2	0	18	2	49	4	0	2	7	.222	0	0-2	0	4.88	6.30
2009	2 Tms	AL	21	6	1	7	57.1	227	50	24	24	12	1	0	1	13	0	33	2	0	5	3	.625	1	0-0	0	3.56	3.77
07	LAD	NL	33	15	0	8	104.0	475	124	75	67	13	5	6	2	42	1	79	3	0	2	11	.154	0	0-0	0	5.39	5.80
07	SD	NL	7	4	0	1	27.1	113	25	14	14	5	3	0	0	6	0	26	2	0	2	1	.667	0	0-0	0	3.37	4.61
08	KC	AL	16	10	0	1	60.2	271	80	49	47	11	1	2	0	13	0	40	4	0	2	7	.222	0	0-2	0	5.73	6.97
08	SD	NL	6	0	0	2	9.1	36	3	2	2	0	0	0	0	5	2	9	0	0	0	0	-	0	0-0	0	0.81	1.93
09	NYY	AL	15	0	0	7	20.2	85	19	12	12	5	1	0	0	7	0	11	1	0	1	2	.333	0	0-0	0	4.42	5.23
09	Oak	AL	6	6	1	0	36.2	142	31	12	12	7	0	0	1	6	0	22	1	0	4	1	.800	1	0-0	0	3.10	2.95
	Postseason		5	0	0	0	8.2	40	8	8	5	0	1	1	0	7	1	4	2	1	0	0	-	0	0-0	0	4.23	5.19
13 ML YEARS			389	266	13	36	1798.1	7750	1883	1002	930	251	80	55	37	572	51	1195	62	3	100	102	.495	2	2-9	10	4.31	4.65

Wyatt Toregas

Bats: R Throws: R Pos: C-19   Ht: 5'11" Wt: 200 Born: 12/2/1982 Age: 27

Year	Team	Lg	G	AB	H	2B	3B	HR	(Hm	Rd)	TB	R	RBI	RC	TBB	IBB	SO	HBP	SH	SF	SB	CS	SB%	GDP	Avg	OBP	Slg
												BATTING									BASERUNNING				AVERAGES		
2004	MhVlly	A-	59	214	63	18	1	7	(-	-)	104	38	48	36	11	1	26	5	1	4	1	0	1.00	6	.294	.338	.486
2005	Lk Cty	A	104	411	95	22	0	5	(-	-)	132	57	42	42	37	0	76	6	2	3	0	1	.00	15	.231	.302	.321
2006	Knbh	A+	44	146	49	14	0	4	(-	-)	75	25	23	31	20	0	28	2	1	2	0	0	-	4	.336	.418	.514
2006	Akron	AA	10	162	42	10	0	4	(-	-)	84	21	20	20	14	0	33	2	2	3	1	3	.25	10	.258	.319	.393
2007	Akron	AA	86	284	71	16	0	6	(-	-)	105	36	39	30	27	1	46	4	2	7	3	1	.75	6	.250	.317	.370
2008	Buffalo	AAA	50	155	34	8	0	2	(-	-)	48	15	25	16	15	0	32	3	5	0	2	0	1.00	1	.219	.301	.310
2008	Akron	AA	47	162	48	9	0	12	(-	-)	93	22	35	34	17	2	20	4	0	3	0	1	.00	2	.296	.371	.574
2009	Clmbs	AAA	60	208	59	10	0	9	(-	-)	90	22	29	31	16	0	43	2	0	3	1	0	.00	5	.284	.336	.433
2009	Cle	AL	19	51	9	1	0	0	(0	0)	10	1	6	4	6	0	12	1	0	2	0	0	-	1	.176	.267	.196

Yorvit Torrealba

Bats: R Throws: R Pos: C-64; PR-1   Ht: 5'11" Wt: 200 Born: 7/19/1978 Age: 31

Year	Team	Lg	G	AB	H	2B	3B	HR	(Hm	Rd)	TB	R	RBI	RC	TBB	IBB	SO	HBP	SH	SF	SB	CS	SB%	GDP	Avg	OBP	Slg
												BATTING									BASERUNNING				AVERAGES		
2009	ColSpr*	AAA	4	15	4	0	0	0	(-	-)	4	1	1	1	1	0	0	0	0	0	0	0	-	2	.267	.313	.267
2001	SF	NL	3	4	2	0	1	0	(0	0)	5	0	2	2	0	0	0	0	0	0	0	0	-	0	.500	.500	1.000
2002	SF	NL	53	136	38	10	0	2	(0	2)	54	17	14	16	14	2	20	2	3	0	0	0	-	11	.279	.355	.397
2003	SF	NL	66	200	52	10	2	4	(3	1)	78	22	29	25	14	1	39	2	3	2	1	0	1.00	3	.260	.312	.390
2004	SF	NL	64	172	39	7	3	6	(3	3)	70	19	23	18	17	3	31	2	4	1	2	0	1.00	7	.227	.302	.407
2005	2 Tms		76	201	47	12	0	3	(2	1)	68	32	15	14	16	1	50	2	5	0	1	0	1.00	8	.234	.297	.338
2006	Col	NL	65	223	55	16	3	7	(3	4)	98	23	43	30	11	1	49	4	2	1	4	3	.57	7	.247	.293	.439
2007	Col	NL	113	396	101	22	1	8	(6	2)	149	47	47	34	34	1	73	6	6	1	2	1	.67	19	.255	.323	.376
2008	Col	NL	70	236	58	17	0	6	(5	1)	93	19	31	23	12	0	44	5	5	3	1	1	.50	10	.246	.293	.394
2009	Col	NL	64	213	62	11	1	2	(1	1)	81	27	31	37	21	5	42	1	3	4	1	1	.50	7	.291	.351	.380
05	SF	NL	34	93	21	8	0	1	(1	0)	32	18	7	7	9	1	25	1	2	0	1	0	1.00	3	.226	.301	.344
05	Sea	AL	42	108	26	4	0	2	(1	1)	36	14	8	7	7	0	25	1	3	0	0	0	-	5	.241	.293	.333
	Postseason		13	42	10	2	0	1	(1	0)	15	5	9	6	4	1	6	0	2	1	0	0	-	2	.238	.298	.357
9 ML YEARS			574	1781	454	105	11	38	(23	15)	695	206	235	199	139	14	348	24	31	12	11	9	.55	69	.255	.315	.390

Andres Torres

Bats: B Throws: R Pos: CF-37; LF-33; PH-12; RF-5; PR-4   Ht: 5'10" Wt: 190 Born: 1/26/1978 Age: 32

Year	Team	Lg	G	AB	H	2B	3B	HR	(Hm	Rd)	TB	R	RBI	RC	TBB	IBB	SO	HBP	SH	SF	SB	CS	SB%	GDP	Avg	OBP	Slg
												BATTING									BASERUNNING				AVERAGES		
2009	Giants*	R	3	6	2	1	0	0	(-	-)	3	1	1	2	4	0	3	0	0	0	1	1	.50	0	.333	.600	.500
2009	SnJos*	A+	3	10	1	1	0	0	(-	-)	2	0	0	0	0	0	5	0	0	0	0	0	-	0	.100	.100	.200
2009	Fresno*	AAA	11	43	13	1	1	1	(-	-)	19	7	2	6	1	0	18	0	1	0	1	0	1.00	0	.302	.318	.442
2002	Det	AL	19	70	14	1	1	0	(0	0)	17	7	3	2	6	0	16	1	0	2	2	2	.50	2	.200	.266	.243
2003	Det	AL	59	168	37	4	3	1	(1	0)	50	23	9	9	10	0	35	0	6	1	5	5	.50	5	.220	.263	.298
2004	Det	AL	3	0	0	0	0	0	(0	0)	0	1	0	0	0	0	0	0	0	0	1	0	1.00	0	-	-	-
2005	Tex	AL	8	19	3	1	0	0	(0	0)	4	2	1	1	1	0	6	0	0	1	1	0	1.00	0	.158	.190	.211
2009	SF	NL	75	152	41	6	8	6	(4	2)	81	30	23	31	16	0	45	1	1	0	6	1	.86	0	.270	.343	.533
5 ML YEARS			104	400	95	12	12	7	(5	2)	152	63	36	43	33	0	102	2	7	4	15	8	.65	7	.232	.290	.372

Carlos Torres

Pitches: R Bats: R Pos: SP-5; RP-3   Ht: 6'1" Wt: 185 Born: 10/22/1982 Age: 27

Year	Team	Lg	G	GS	CG	GF	IP	BFP	H	R	ER	HR	SH	SF	HB	TBB	IBB	SO	WP	Bk	W	L	Pct	Sh	Sv-Op	Hld	ERC	ERA
							HOW MUCH HE PITCHED					WHAT HE GAVE UP												THE RESULTS					
2004	Bristol	R+	19	0	0	9	38.0	166	43	30	20	2	1	0	0	12	2	28	6	0	2	2	.500	0	1--	-	4.03	4.74
2005	Gr Falls	R+	5	5	0	0	25.0	97	18	8	8	1	1	0	0	8	0	26	0	0	1	1	.500	0	0--	-	2.05	2.88
2005	Knapol	A	8	8	0	0	43.1	182	28	20	17	4	0	2	1	23	0	54	3	0	1	3	.250	0	0--	-	2.67	3.53
2006	WinSa	A+	25	20	0	3	94.0	446	116	66	49	7	3	5	1	55	0	76	7	0	3	8	.273	0	1--	-	6.01	4.69
2007	WinSa	A+	19	0	0	7	36.1	147	33	16	15	0	2	0	2	10	0	41	4	0	0	2	.000	0	3--	-	2.74	3.72
2007	Brham	AA	36	0	0	8	56.0	240	57	26	23	3	4	1	1	22	1	59	5	0	2	2	.500	0	1--	-	3.90	3.70

HOW MUCH HE PITCHED								WHAT HE GAVE UP												THE RESULTS							
Year	Team	Lg	G	GS	CG	GF	IP	BFP	H	R	ER	HR	SH	SF	HB	TBB	IBB	SO	WP	Bk	W	L	Pct	Sh	Sv-Op	Hld	ERC	ERA
2008	Brham	AA	21	17	0	0	101.1	407	86	40	36	4	3	2	5	29	0	93	4	0	9	5	.643	0	0--	-	2.71	3.20
2008	Charltt	AAA	8	1	0	4	19.2	91	23	10	10	2	2	0	0	11	1	19	0	0	0	0	-	0	0--	-	5.63	4.58
2009	Charltt	AAA	23	20	2	2	128.0	528	96	38	34	4	1	3	4	56	0	130	2	0	10	4	.714	1	1--	-	2.57	2.39
2009	CWS	AL	8	5	0	2	28.1	130	30	20	19	5	3	3	2	17	2	22	0	0	1	2	.333	0	0-0	0	6.05	6.04

Josh Towers

Pitches: R Bats: R Pos: RP-2　　　　　　　　　　**Ht: 6'1" Wt: 183 Born: 2/26/1977 Age: 33**

HOW MUCH HE PITCHED								WHAT HE GAVE UP												THE RESULTS							
Year	Team	Lg	G	GS	CG	GF	IP	BFP	H	R	ER	HR	SH	SF	HB	TBB	IBB	SO	WP	Bk	W	L	Pct	Sh	Sv-Op	Hld	ERC	ERA
2009	Syrcse*	AAA	1	0	0	0	1.2	11	6	4	4	0	0	0	0	0	0	0	0	0	0	0	-	0	0--	-	19.18	21.60
2009	S-WB*	AAA	19	18	0	0	101.2	404	89	32	31	13	2	1	4	24	0	55	1	0	7	6	.538	0	0--	-	3.20	2.74
2001	Bal	AL	24	20	1	2	140.1	586	165	74	70	21	3	4	6	16	0	58	1	0	8	10	.444	1	0-0	0	4.51	4.49
2002	Bal	AL	5	3	0	1	27.1	124	42	24	24	11	1	2	0	5	0	13	1	0	0	3	.000	0	0-0	0	9.00	7.90
2003	Tor	AL	14	8	1	2	64.1	265	67	34	32	15	0	2	4	7	1	42	1	0	8	1	.889	0	1-1	0	4.26	4.48
2004	Tor	AL	21	21	0	0	116.1	518	148	70	66	16	2	4	9	26	4	51	0	1	9	9	.500	0	0-0	0	5.50	5.11
2005	Tor	AL	33	33	2	0	208.2	876	237	101	86	24	3	7	6	29	2	112	1	1	13	12	.520	1	0-0	0	4.02	3.71
2006	Tor	AL	15	12	0	1	62.0	295	93	62	58	17	1	3	3	17	3	35	1	1	2	10	.167	0	0-0	0	8.05	8.42
2007	Tor	AL	25	15	0	6	107.0	469	129	73	64	18	3	4	6	22	2	76	1	0	5	10	.333	0	0-0	0	5.15	5.38
2009	NYY	AL	2	0	0	2	5.1	25	6	3	2	0	0	1	1	1	1	2	0	0	0	0	-	0	0-0	0	3.36	3.38
8 ML YEARS			139	112	4	14	731.1	3158	887	441	402	122	13	27	35	123	13	389	6	3	45	55	.450	2	1-1	0	5.02	4.95

J.R. Towles

Bats: R Throws: R Pos: C-15; PR-1　　　　　　　　　　**Ht: 6'2" Wt: 190 Born: 2/11/1984 Age: 26**

						BATTING														BASERUNNING				AVERAGES		
Year	Team	Lg	G	AB	H	2B	3B	HR	(Hm	Rd)	TB	R	RBI	RC	TBB	IBB	SO	HBP	SH	SF	SB	CS	SB%	GDP	Avg	OBP	Slg
2009	RdRck*	AAA	56	145	40	12	1	4	(-	-)	66	23	22	28	22	0	27	6	2	3	3	0	1.00	2	.276	.386	.455
2007	Hou	NL	14	40	15	5	0	1	(0	1)	23	9	12	11	3	1	1	0	0	0	0	0	1.00	1	.375	.432	.575
2008	Hou	NL	54	146	20	5	0	4	(3	1)	37	10	16	10	16	1	40	6	3	0	0	0	-	3	.137	.250	.253
2009	Hou	NL	16	48	9	2	0	2	(0	2)	17	7	3	2	3	1	16	1	1	0	0	0	-	1	.188	.250	.354
3 ML YEARS			84	234	44	12	0	7	(3	4)	77	26	31	23	22	3	57	8	4	0	0	1	.00	5	.188	.280	.329

Billy Traber

Pitches: L Bats: L Pos: RP-1　　　　　　　　　　**Ht: 6'5" Wt: 205 Born: 9/18/1979 Age: 30**

HOW MUCH HE PITCHED								WHAT HE GAVE UP												THE RESULTS							
Year	Team	Lg	G	GS	CG	GF	IP	BFP	H	R	ER	HR	SH	SF	HB	TBB	IBB	SO	WP	Bk	W	L	Pct	Sh	Sv-Op	Hld	ERC	ERA
2009	Pwtckt*	AAA	38	7	0	12	84.1	356	88	36	33	8	2	1	4	25	3	53	2	1	7	8	.467	0	0--	-	4.08	3.52
2003	Cle	AL	33	18	1	0	111.2	503	132	67	65	15	4	3	5	40	4	88	6	0	6	9	.400	1	0-0	1	5.31	5.24
2006	Was	NL	15	8	0	0	43.1	202	53	33	31	5	3	1	8	14	2	25	0	0	4	3	.571	0	0-0	2	5.81	6.44
2007	Was	NL	28	2	0	5	39.2	182	50	22	21	4	3	5	2	13	3	27	0	0	2	2	.500	0	0-1	2	5.30	4.76
2008	NYY	AL	19	0	0	3	16.2	80	23	13	13	3	0	0	2	7	1	11	2	0	0	0	-	0	0-0	1	7.54	7.02
2009	Bos	AL	1	0	0	0	3.2	20	9	5	5	2	0	0	0	1	0	1	0	0	0	0	-	0	0-0	0	18.46	12.27
5 ML YEARS			96	28	1	8	215.0	987	267	140	135	29	10	9	17	75	10	152	8	0	12	14	.462	1	0-1	6	5.76	5.65

Andy Tracy

Bats: L Throws: R Pos: PH-8; 1B-1　　　　　　　　　　**Ht: 6'3" Wt: 239 Born: 12/11/1973 Age: 36**

						BATTING														BASERUNNING				AVERAGES		
Year	Team	Lg	G	AB	H	2B	3B	HR	(Hm	Rd)	TB	R	RBI	RC	TBB	IBB	SO	HBP	SH	SF	SB	CS	SB%	GDP	Avg	OBP	Slg
2009	LV*	AAA	129	453	115	23	1	26	(-	-)	218	76	96	84	74	5	110	6	0	7	1	1	.88	9	.254	.361	.481
2000	Mon	NL	83	192	50	8	1	11	(	)	93	29	32	31	22	1	61	2	0	2	1	0	1.00	3	.260	.339	.484
2001	Mon	NL	38	55	6	1	0	2	(	)	13	4	8	1	6	0	26	0	0	2	0	0	-	1	.109	.190	.236
2004	Col	NL	15	16	3	1	0	0	(0	0)	4	1	1	1	1	0	8	0	0	0	0	0	-	0	.188	.235	.250
2008	Phi	NL	4	2	0	0	0	0	(0	0)	0	0	1	0	1	0	1	0	0	1	0	0	-	0	.000	.250	.000
2009	Phi	NL	9	12	5	0	1	0	(0	0)	7	1	1	3	0	0	3	0	0	0	0	0	-	0	.417	.417	.583
5 ML YEARS			149	277	64	10	2	13	(0	0)	117	35	43	36	30	1	99	2	0	5	1	0	1.00	4	.231	.306	.422

Chad Tracy

Bats: L Throws: R Pos: 1B-66; PH-33; 3B-8　　　　　　　　　　**Ht: 6'2" Wt: 215 Born: 5/22/1980 Age: 30**

						BATTING														BASERUNNING				AVERAGES		
Year	Team	Lg	G	AB	H	2B	3B	HR	(Hm	Rd)	TB	R	RBI	RC	TBB	IBB	SO	HBP	SH	SF	SB	CS	SB%	GDP	Avg	OBP	Slg
2009	Reno*	AAA	10	35	10	1	1	0	(-	-)	13	4	4	4	3	0	8	1	0	1	0	1	.00	2	.286	.350	.371
2004	Ari	NL	143	481	137	29	3	8	(6	2)	196	45	53	63	45	3	60	0	1	5	2	3	.40	11	.285	.343	.407
2005	Ari	NL	145	503	155	34	4	27	(9	18)	278	73	72	82	35	4	78	8	1	6	3	1	.75	10	.308	.359	.553
2006	Ari	NL	154	597	168	41	0	20	(14	6)	269	91	80	85	54	5	129	5	1	5	5	1	.83	11	.281	.343	.451
2007	Ari	NL	76	227	60	18	2	7	(3	4)	103	30	35	33	29	4	43	1	0	3	0	0	-	8	.264	.346	.454
2008	Ari	NL	88	273	73	16	0	8	(3	5)	113	25	39	32	16	2	49	1	0	2	0	0	-	5	.267	.308	.414
2009	Ari	NL	98	257	61	15	0	8	(7	1)	100	29	39	28	26	7	38	1	0	4	1	0	1.00	3	.237	.306	.389
6 ML YEARS			704	2338	654	153	9	78	(42	36)	1059	293	318	323	205	25	397	16	3	25	11	5	.69	48	.280	.339	.453

Matt Treanor

Bats: R **Throws:** R **Pos:** C-4   **Ht:** 6'0" **Wt:** 210 **Born:** 3/3/1976 **Age:** 34

Year	Team	Lg	G	AB	H	2B	3B	HR	(Hm	Rd)	TB	R	RBI	RC	TBB	IBB	SO	HBP	SH	SF	SB	CS	SB%	GDP	Avg	OBP	Slg
2004	Fla	NL	29	55	13	2	0	0	(0	0)	15	7	1	4	4	0	13	2	0	0	0	0	-	3	.236	.311	.273
2005	Fla	NL	58	134	27	8	0	0	(0	0)	35	10	13	13	16	1	28	3	1	0	0	0	-	5	.201	.301	.261
2006	Fla	NL	67	157	36	6	1	2	(0	2)	50	12	14	16	19	4	34	5	2	2	0	1	.00	4	.229	.328	.318
2007	Fla	NL	55	171	46	7	1	4	(2	2)	67	16	19	26	19	1	29	5	2	1	0	0	-	2	.269	.357	.392
2008	Fla	NL	65	206	49	7	0	2	(1	1)	62	18	23	25	18	1	53	3	5	2	1	0	1.00	2	.238	.306	.301
2009	Det	AL	4	13	0	0	0	0	(0	0)	0	0	0	0	1	0	4	0	0	0	0	0	-	3	.000	.071	.000
	6 ML YEARS		278	736	171	30	2	8	(3	5)	229	63	70	84	77	7	161	18	10	5	1	1	.50	19	.232	.318	.311

Ramon Troncoso

Pitches: R **Bats:** R **Pos:** RP-73   **Ht:** 6'1" **Wt:** 220 **Born:** 2/16/1983 **Age:** 27

Year	Team	Lg	G	GS	CG	GF	IP	BFP	H	R	ER	HR	SH	SF	HB	TBB	IBB	SO	WP	Bk	W	L	Pct	Sh	Sv-Op Hld	ERC	ERA
2005	Clmbs	A	13	6	0	3	37.2	183	58	33	28	2	0	5	4	13	0	27	2	0	2	3	.400	0	1- - -	7.19	6.69
2005	Ogden	R+	29	0	0	27	36.2	167	40	19	15	0	1	2	8	12	0	30	4	0	6	2	.750	0	13- - -	4.37	3.68
2006	VeroB	A+	18	0	0	9	29.1	146	43	27	22	1	4	1	3	14	3	31	1	0	1	3	.250	0	0- - -	6.79	6.75
2006	Clmbs	A	23	0	0	23	33.2	129	28	11	9	1	1	1	4	7	0	22	1	0	4	0	1.000	0	15- - -	2.66	2.41
2007	InldEm	A+	16	0	0	12	26.0	100	18	6	3	0	2	1	1	3	0	30	2	0	3	1	.750	0	7- - -	1.28	1.04
2007	Jaxnvl	AA	35	0	0	22	52.0	219	52	19	18	3	1	1	1	18	1	39	1	0	7	3	.700	0	7- - -	3.68	3.12
2008	LsVgs	AAA	22	0	0	6	30.2	149	43	24	17	1	2	0	3	16	0	18	1	0	4	0	1.000	0	0- - -	6.90	4.99
2008	LAD	NL	32	0	0	12	38.0	160	37	19	18	2	4	3	3	12	1	38	2	0	1	1	.500	0	0-0 2	3.60	4.26
2009	LAD	NL	73	0	0	20	82.2	357	83	30	25	3	7	3	3	34	9	55	4	0	5	4	.556	0	6-7 14	3.67	2.72
	2 ML YEARS		105	0	0	32	120.2	517	120	49	43	5	11	6	6	46	10	93	6	0	6	5	.545	0	6-7 16	3.65	3.21

Matt Tuiasosopo

Bats: R **Throws:** R **Pos:** 2B-6; PH-1   **Ht:** 6'2" **Wt:** 225 **Born:** 5/10/1986 **Age:** 24

Year	Team	Lg	G	AB	H	2B	3B	HR	(Hm	Rd)	TB	R	RBI	RC	TBB	IBB	SO	HBP	SH	SF	SB	CS	SB%	GDP	Avg	OBP	Slg
2004	Ms	R	20	68	28	5	2	4	(-	-)	49	18	12	23	13	1	14	6	0	2	1	2	.33	2	.412	.528	.721
2004	Everett	A-	29	101	25	6	1	2	(-	-)	39	18	14	13	10	0	36	4	0	1	4	3	.57	3	.248	.336	.386
2005	Wisc	A	107	409	113	21	3	6	(-	-)	158	72	45	60	44	2	96	9	1	1	8	5	.62	7	.276	.359	.386
2006	InldEm	A+	59	232	71	14	0	1	(-	-)	88	31	34	31	14	1	58	5	2	0	5	6	.45	8	.306	.359	.379
2006	SnAnt	AA	62	216	40	4	0	1	(-	-)	47	16	10	11	20	0	64	2	2	1	2	1	.67	4	.185	.259	.218
2007	WTenn	AA	129	446	116	27	5	9	(-	-)	180	74	57	73	76	2	113	11	1	14	4	8	.33	14	.260	.371	.404
2008	Tacom	AAA	111	437	123	32	2	13	(-	-)	198	87	73	76	47	0	104	12	0	4	4	0	1.00	9	.281	.364	.453
2009	Ms	R	9	27	11	0	0	1	(-	-)	14	9	3	6	4	0	6	1	0	0	0	0	-	0	.407	.500	.519
2009	Tacom	AAA	59	226	59	15	0	11	(- | -)	107	43	35	41	36	0	83	3	3	.75	5	3	1	.75	5	.261	.368	.473
2008	Sea	AL	14	44	7	2	1	0	(0	0)	11	1	2	1	2	0	16	1	0	0	0	0	-	0	.159	.213	.250
2009	Sea	AL	7	22	5	1	0	1	(-	-)	9	2	2	2	2	0	5	0	0	1	0	0	-	0	.227	.280	.409
	2 ML YEARS		21	66	12	3	1	1	(0	1)	20	3	4	3	4	0	21	1	0	1	0	0	-	0	.182	.236	.303

Troy Tulowitzki

Bats: R **Throws:** R **Pos:** SS-151   **Ht:** 6'3" **Wt:** 205 **Born:** 10/10/1984 **Age:** 25

Year	Team	Lg	G	AB	H	2B	3B	HR	(Hm	Rd)	TB	R	RBI	RC	TBB	IBB	SO	HBP	SH	SF	SB	CS	SB%	GDP	Avg	OBP	Slg
2006	Col	NL	25	96	23	2	0	1	(0	1)	28	15	6	10	10	3	25	1	1	0	3	0	1.00	1	.240	.318	.292
2007	Col	NL	155	609	177	33	5	24	(15	9)	292	104	99	95	57	3	130	9	5	2	7	6	.54	14	.291	.359	.479
2008	Col	NL	101	377	99	24	2	8	(4	4)	151	48	46	42	38	5	56	2	2	1	1	6	.14	16	.263	.332	.401
2009	Col	NL	151	543	161	25	9	32	(17	15)	300	101	92	96	73	4	112	3	0	9	20	11	.65	20	.297	.377	.552
	Postseason		11	41	8	3	0	1	(0	1)	14	3	3	2	4	0	15	0	0	0	0	1	.00	1	.195	.267	.341
	4 ML YEARS		432	1625	460	84	16	65	(36	29)	771	268	243	243	178	15	323	15	8	13	31	23	.57	51	.283	.357	.474

Justin Turner

Bats: R **Throws:** R **Pos:** 3B-7; PH-5; 2B-3; DH-1; PR-1   **Ht:** 5'11" **Wt:** 180 **Born:** 11/23/1984 **Age:** 25

Year	Team	Lg	G	AB	H	2B	3B	HR	(Hm	Rd)	TB	R	RBI	RC	TBB	IBB	SO	HBP	SH	SF	SB	CS	SB%	GDP	Avg	OBP	Slg
2006	Billings	R+	60	231	78	16	3	6	(-	-)	118	53	41	50	23	1	38	7	0	2	12	2	.86	7	.338	.411	.511
2007	Dayton	A	117	466	145	25	4	10	(-	-)	208	70	59	79	39	0	72	9	0	4	12	8	.60	7	.311	.374	.446
2007	Srsota	A+	6	20	4	0	0	0	(-	-)	4	2	0	0	1	0	2	0	0	0	0	0	-	0	.200	.238	.200
2008	Srsota	A+	33	136	43	8	1	0	(-	-)	53	23	11	21	12	0	19	3	0	0	3	1	.75	3	.316	.384	.390
2008	Chatt	AA	78	280	81	14	1	8	(-	-)	121	45	42	46	33	0	54	1	3	6	2	1	.67	4	.289	.359	.432
2009	Norfolk	AAA	108	387	116	28	0	2	(-	-)	150	54	43	59	34	0	37	8	4	8	9	4	.69	12	.300	.362	.388
2009	Bal	AL	12	18	3	0	0	0	(0	0)	3	2	3	1	4	0	3	0	0	0	0	0	-	1	.167	.318	.167

Koji Uehara

Pitches: R **Bats:** R **Pos:** SP-12   **Ht:** 6'1" **Wt:** 190 **Born:** 4/3/1975 **Age:** 35

Year	Team	Lg	G	GS	CG	GF	IP	BFP	H	R	ER	HR	SH	SF	HB	TBB	IBB	SO	WP	Bk	W	L	Pct	Sh	Sv-Op Hld	ERC	ERA
1999	Yomiuri	Jap	25	25	12	0	197.2	769	153	49	46	12	-	-	4	24	-	179	3	0	20	4	.833	1	0- - -	1.75	2.09
2000	Yomiuri	Jap	20	20	6	0	131.0	519	112	53	52	20	-	-	1	22	-	126	1	0	9	7	.563	1	0- - -	2.78	3.57
2001	Yomiuri	Jap	24	22	4	0	138.2	573	133	66	62	18	15	3	5	28	3	108	2	0	10	7	.588	1	0- - -	3.38	4.02
2002	Yomiuri	Jap	26	26	8	0	204.0	808	173	65	59	18	-	-	6	23	-	182	2	0	17	5	.773	3	0- - -	2.24	2.60
2003	Yomiuri	Jap	27	27	11	0	207.1	821	190	76	73	28	-	-	5	23	3	194	0	0	16	5	.762	1	0- - -	2.84	3.17

Year	Team	Lg	G	GS	CG	GF	IP	BFP	H	R	ER	HR	SH	SF	HB	TBB	IBB	SO	WP	Bk	W	L	Pct	Sh	Sv-Op	Hld	ERC	ERA
2004	Yomiuri	Jap	22	22	2	0	163.0	637	135	54	47	24	6	3	5	23	0	153	1	0	13	5	.722	0	0--	-	2.62	2.60
2005	Yomiuri	Jap	27	27	6	0	187.1	747	164	73	69	24	19	3	0	22	0	145	0	1	9	12	.429	2	0--	-	2.48	3.31
2006	Yomiuri	Jap	24	24	5	0	168.1	673	157	67	60	24	15	5	1	21	3	151	0	1	8	9	.471	0	0--	-	2.92	3.21
2007	Yomiuri	Jap	55	0	0	-	62.0	237	47	12	12	4	-	-	-	4	1	66	1	0	4	3	.571	0	32--	-	1.54	1.74
2008	Yomiuri	Jap	26	14	2	3	89.2	345	90	43	38	11	-	-	0	16	-	72	0	0	6	5	.545	0	1--	-	3.65	3.81
2009	Bal	AL	12	12	0	0	66.2	279	71	33	30	7	1	3	0	12	1	48	0	0	2	4	.333	0	0-0	0	3.56	4.05

Dan Uggla

Bats: R **Throws:** R **Pos:** 2B-158; PH-1   **Ht:** 5'11" **Wt:** 213 **Born:** 3/11/1980 **Age:** 30

Year	Team	Lg	G	AB	H	2B	3B	HR	(Hm	Rd)	TB	R	RBI	RC	TBB	IBB	SO	HBP	SH	SF	SB	CS	SB%	GDP	Avg	OBP	Slg
2006	Fla	NL	154	611	172	26	7	27	(10	17)	293	105	90	97	48	1	123	9	7	8	6	6	.50	5	.282	.339	.480
2007	Fla	NL	159	632	155	49	3	31	(18	13)	303	113	88	81	68	0	167	13	4	11	2	1	.67	10	.245	.326	.479
2008	Fla	NL	146	531	138	37	1	32	(15	17)	273	97	92	93	77	6	171	8	0	3	5	5	.50	10	.260	.360	.514
2009	Fla	NL	158	564	137	27	1	31	(21	10)	259	84	90	81	92	4	150	7	1	4	2	1	.67	10	.243	.354	.459
4 ML YEARS			617	2338	602	139	12	121	(64	57)	1128	399	360	352	285	11	611	37	12	26	15	13	.54	35	.257	.344	.482

B.J. Upton

Bats: R **Throws:** R **Pos:** CF-144; PH-2   **Ht:** 6'3" **Wt:** 185 **Born:** 8/21/1984 **Age:** 25

Year	Team	Lg	G	AB	H	2B	3B	HR	(Hm	Rd)	TB	R	RBI	RC	TBB	IBB	SO	HBP	SH	SF	SB	CS	SB%	GDP	Avg	OBP	Slg
2009	Charltt*	A+	3	9	4	0	0	0	(-	-)	4	1	2	2	4	0	2	1	0	0	4	3	.57	0	.444	.643	.444
2004	TB	AL	45	159	41	8	2	4	(2	2)	65	19	12	22	15	0	46	1	1	1	4	1	.80	1	.258	.324	.409
2006	TB	AL	50	175	43	5	0	1	(1	0)	51	20	10	17	13	0	40	1	0	0	11	3	.79	1	.246	.302	.291
2007	TB	AL	129	474	142	25	1	24	(13	11)	241	86	82	93	65	4	154	4	1	4	22	8	.73	14	.300	.386	.508
2008	TB	AL	145	531	145	37	2	9	(4	5)	213	85	67	87	97	4	134	2	3	7	44	16	.73	13	.273	.383	.401
2009	TB	AL	144	560	135	33	4	11	(7	4)	209	79	55	68	57	0	152	3	3	3	42	14	.75	7	.241	.313	.373
Postseason			16	66	19	1	1	7	(2	5)	43	16	16	13	5	1	16	0	0	1	6	0	1.00	4	.288	.333	.652
5 ML YEARS			513	1899	506	108	9	49	(27	22)	779	289	226	287	247	8	526	11	8	15	123	42	.75	36	.266	.352	.410

Justin Upton

Bats: R **Throws:** R **Pos:** RF-136; DH-1; PH-1; PR-1   **Ht:** 6'2" **Wt:** 205 **Born:** 8/25/1987 **Age:** 22

Year	Team	Lg	G	AB	H	2B	3B	HR	(Hm	Rd)	TB	R	RBI	RC	TBB	IBB	SO	HBP	SH	SF	SB	CS	SB%	GDP	Avg	OBP	Slg
2007	Ari	NL	43	140	31	8	3	2	(2	0)	51	17	11	13	11	4	37	1	0	0	2	0	1.00	3	.221	.283	.364
2008	Ari	NL	108	356	89	19	6	15	(12	3)	165	52	42	47	54	6	121	4	0	3	1	4	.20	3	.250	.353	.463
2009	Ari	NL	138	526	158	30	7	26	(14	12)	280	84	86	94	55	3	137	2	1	4	20	5	.80	10	.300	.366	.532
Postseason			6	14	5	1	1	0	(0	0)	8	2	1	4	3	0	3	2	0	0	1	0	1.00	0	.357	.526	.571
3 ML YEARS			289	1022	278	57	16	43	(28	15)	496	153	139	154	120	13	295	7	1	7	23	9	.72	16	.272	.350	.485

Juan Uribe

Bats: R **Throws:** R **Pos:** 3B-44; SS-41; 2B-38; PH-10   **Ht:** 6'0" **Wt:** 230 **Born:** 3/22/1979 **Age:** 31

Year	Team	Lg	G	AB	H	2B	3B	HR	(Hm	Rd)	TB	R	RBI	RC	TBB	IBB	SO	HBP	SH	SF	SB	CS	SB%	GDP	Avg	OBP	Slg
2001	Col	NL	72	273	82	15	11	8	(3	5)	143	32	53	44	8	1	55	2	0	0	3	0	1.00	6	.300	.325	.524
2002	Col	NL	155	566	136	25	7	6	(4	2)	193	69	49	53	34	1	120	5	7	6	9	2	.82	17	.240	.286	.341
2003	Col	NL	87	316	80	19	3	10	(6	4)	135	45	33	45	17	0	60	3	6	1	7	2	.78	3	.253	.297	.427
2004	CWS	AL	134	502	142	31	6	23	(16	7)	254	82	74	81	34	1	96	1	4	1	9	11	.45	10	.283	.327	.506
2005	CWS	AL	146	481	121	23	3	16	(10	6)	198	58	71	59	34	0	77	4	11	10	4	6	.40	7	.252	.301	.412
2006	CWS	AL	132	463	109	28	2	21	(13	8)	204	53	71	52	13	1	82	3	9	7	1	1	.50	10	.235	.257	.441
2007	CWS	AL	150	513	120	18	2	20	(15	5)	202	55	68	52	34	2	112	4	7	5	1	9	.10	6	.234	.284	.394
2008	CWS	AL	110	324	80	22	1	7	(5	2)	125	38	40	43	22	0	64	1	5	1	1	3	.25	5	.247	.296	.386
2009	SF	NL	122	398	115	26	4	16	(9	7)	197	50	55	55	25	2	82	1	3	5	3	1	.75	7	.289	.329	.495
Postseason			16	54	14	5	0	1	(1	0)	22	7	7	7	5	0	13	0	2	0	2	0	1.00	1	.259	.322	.407
9 ML YEARS			1108	3836	985	207	39	127	(81	46)	1651	482	514	484	219	8	748	26	59	40	38	35	.52	71	.257	.298	.430

Chase Utley

Bats: L **Throws:** R **Pos:** 2B-155; PH-2   **Ht:** 6'1" **Wt:** 190 **Born:** 12/17/1978 **Age:** 31

Year	Team	Lg	G	AB	H	2B	3B	HR	(Hm	Rd)	TB	R	RBI	RC	TBB	IBB	SO	HBP	SH	SF	SB	CS	SB%	GDP	Avg	OBP	Slg
2003	Phi	NL	43	134	32	10	1	2	(1	1)	50	13	21	19	11	0	22	6	0	1	2	0	1.00	3	.239	.322	.373
2004	Phi	NL	94	267	71	11	2	13	(8	5)	125	36	57	37	15	1	40	2	1	2	4	1	.80	6	.266	.308	.468
2005	Phi	NL	147	543	158	39	6	28	(12	16)	293	93	105	102	69	5	109	9	0	7	16	3	.84	10	.291	.376	.540
2006	Phi	NL	160	658	203	40	4	32	(16	16)	347	131	102	122	63	1	132	14	0	4	15	4	.79	9	.309	.379	.527
2007	Phi	NL	132	530	176	48	5	22	(14	8)	300	104	103	111	50	1	89	25	1	7	9	1	.90	7	.332	.410	.566
2008	Phi	NL	159	607	177	41	4	33	(20	13)	325	113	104	113	64	14	104	27	1	8	14	2	.88	9	.292	.380	.535
2009	Phi	NL	156	571	161	28	4	31	(16	15)	290	112	93	115	88	3	110	24	0	4	23	0	1.00	5	.282	.397	.508
Postseason			17	61	13	3	0	3	(2	1)	25	10	9	11	15	1	19	1	0	0	3	1	.75	1	.213	.377	.410
7 ML YEARS			891	3310	978	217	26	161	(87	74)	1730	602	585	619	360	25	606	107	3	33	83	11	.88	49	.295	.379	.523

Luis Valbuena

Bats: L **Throws:** R **Pos:** 2B-77; SS-28; PH-3; PR-2; 3B-1   **Ht:** 5'10" **Wt:** 195 **Born:** 11/30/1985 **Age:** 24

						BATTING														BASERUNNING				AVERAGES		
Year	Team	Lg	G	AB	H	2B	3B	HR	(Hm	Rd)	TB	R	RBI	RC	TBB	IBB	SO	HBP	SH	SF	SB	CS	SB%	GDP	Avg	OBP	Slg
2005	Tacom	AAA	3	4	0	0	0	0	(-	-)	0	0	0	0	1	0	2	0	0	0	0	0	-	0	.000	.200	.000
2005	Everett	A-	74	287	75	10	3	12	(-	-)	127	47	51	45	31	0	37	0	2	1	14	6	.70	3	.261	.333	.443
2006	Wisc	A	89	325	93	16	6	3	(-	-)	130	45	38	53	44	0	44	1	1	2	21	7	.75	8	.286	.371	.400
2006	InldEm	A+	43	163	41	10	1	2	(-	-)	59	18	10	18	14	2	26	1	3	0	1	3	.25	5	.252	.315	.362
2007	WTenn	AA	122	444	106	23	3	11	(-	-)	168	55	44	55	48	2	83	1	6	6	10	6	.63	9	.239	.311	.378
2008	WTenn	AA	70	240	73	12	2	9	(-	-)	116	43	40	45	31	0	37	0	4	2	8	4	.67	4	.304	.381	.483
2008	Tacom	AAA	58	212	64	9	0	2	(-	-)	79	41	20	33	28	0	32	0	6	0	10	4	.71	1	.302	.383	.373
2009	Clmbs	AAA	22	78	25	4	2	3	(-	-)	42	15	13	18	16	0	13	0	1	0	3	3	.50	1	.321	.436	.538
2008	Sea	AL	18	49	12	5	0	0	(0	0)	17	6	1	5	4	0	11	1	0	0	0	0	-	0	.245	.315	.347
2009	Cle	AL	103	368	92	25	3	10	(2	8)	153	52	31	35	26	0	83	0	2	2	2	3	.40	8	.250	.298	.416
	2 ML YEARS		121	417	104	30	3	10	(2	8)	170	58	32	40	30	0	94	1	2	2	2	3	.40	8	.249	.300	.408

Luis Valdez

Pitches: R **Bats:** R **Pos:** RP-3   **Ht:** 6'2" **Wt:** 205 **Born:** 5/5/1984 **Age:** 26

			HOW MUCH HE PITCHED					WHAT HE GAVE UP										THE RESULTS						
Year	Team	Lg	G	GS	CG	GF	IP	BFP	H	R	ER	HR	SH	SF	HB	TBB	IBB	SO	WP	Bk	W	L	Pct	Sh	Sv-Op	Hld	ERC	ERA
2004	Pirates	R	11	11	2	0	61.1	250	58	22	19	1	2	1	4	10	0	41	3	2	7	2	.778	1	0- -	-	2.61	2.79
2005	Hkry	A	7	2	0	1	18.0	87	24	19	15	1	1	1	1	9	0	9	2	0	0	2	.000	0	0- -	-	6.25	7.50
2005	Wmspt	A-	16	7	0	2	59.2	259	67	39	30	4	0	2	4	17	0	30	3	1	4	5	.444	0	0- -	-	4.38	4.53
2006	Hkry	A	22	22	2	0	122.0	521	131	73	58	20	5	3	7	26	0	71	8	0	7	8	.467	1	0- -	-	4.40	4.28
2006	Lynbrg	A+	1	1	0	0	3.2	22	7	6	6	0	0	0	0	5	0	1	0	0	0	0	-	0	0- -	-	13.66	14.73
2007	Lynbrg	A+	36	1	0	15	73.1	331	87	44	39	4	2	0	4	20	1	78	6	0	3	4	.429	0	5- -	-	4.78	4.79
2008	Missi	AA	66	0	0	45	65.1	282	48	30	20	3	8	2	4	36	3	77	4	0	4	3	.571	0	28- -	-	2.95	2.76
2009	Gwnnll	AAA	58	0	0	51	71.1	000	66	27	26	4	0	5	0	19	0	75	2	0	5	4	.556	0	27-	-	2.78	3.28
2009	Atl	NL	3	0	0	2	2.2	13	3	1	1	0	0	0	0	2	0	0	0	0	0	1	.000	0	0-0	0	6.04	3.38

Merkin Valdez

Pitches: R **Bats:** R **Pos:** RP-48   **Ht:** 6'5" **Wt:** 232 **Born:** 11/10/1981 **Age:** 28

			HOW MUCH HE PITCHED					WHAT HE GAVE UP										THE RESULTS						
Year	Team	Lg	G	GS	CG	GF	IP	BFP	H	R	ER	HR	SH	SF	HB	TBB	IBB	SO	WP	Bk	W	L	Pct	Sh	Sv-Op	Hld	ERC	ERA
2004	SF	NL	2	0	0	1	1.2	12	4	5	5	1	0	0	0	3	0	2	0	0	0	0	-	0	0-0	0	26.50	27.00
2008	SF	NL	17	1	0	3	16.0	69	14	5	3	1	1	0	2	7	2	13	2	1	1	0	1.000	0	0-0	2	3.57	1.69
2009	SF	NL	48	0	0	20	49.1	225	57	33	31	5	1	1	0	28	2	38	5	0	2	1	.667	0	0-3	4	5.67	5.66
	3 ML YEARS		67	1	0	23	67.0	306	75	43	39	7	2	1	2	38	4	53	7	1	3	1	.750	0	0-3	6	5.55	5.24

Wilson Valdez

Bats: R **Throws:** R **Pos:** SS-32; PH-5; PR-3; LF-2; 2B-1; 3B-1   **Ht:** 5'11" **Wt:** 170 **Born:** 5/20/1978 **Age:** 32

						BATTING														BASERUNNING				AVERAGES		
Year	Team	Lg	G	AB	H	2B	3B	HR	(Hm	Rd)	TB	R	RBI	RC	TBB	IBB	SO	HBP	SH	SF	SB	CS	SB%	GDP	Avg	OBP	Slg
2009	Clmbs*	AAA	41	121	24	1	0	0	(-	-)	25	17	6	7	10	0	19	1	4	1	5	1	.83	5	.198	.263	.207
2009	Buffalo*	AAA	36	114	34	4	0	0	(-	-)	38	13	6	13	7	0	10	1	3	1	1	1	.50	4	.298	.341	.333
2004	CWS	AL	19	43	10	1	0	1	(1	0)	14	8	4	2	2	0	5	0	1	0	1	2	.33	1	.233	.267	.326
2005	2 Tms		51	139	28	7	1	0	(0	0)	37	9	9	8	8	0	26	0	1	0	2	2	.50	2	.201	.245	.266
2007	LAD	NL	41	74	16	2	1	0	(0	0)	20	12	7	7	4	0	12	1	0	1	1	0	1.00	0	.216	.263	.270
2009	NYM	NL	41	86	22	3	2	0	(0	0)	29	11	7	6	8	0	10	1	0	0	0	1	.00	6	.256	.326	.337
05	Sea	AL	42	126	25	5	1	0	(0	0)	32	9	8	6	6	0	25	0	1	0	2	2	.50	1	.198	.235	.254
05	SD	NL	9	13	3	2	0	0	(0	0)	5	0	1	2	2	0	1	0	0	0	0	0	-	1	.231	.333	.385
	4 ML YEARS		152	342	76	13	4	1	(1	0)	100	40	27	23	22	0	53	2	2	1	4	5	.44	9	.222	.272	.292

Jose Valverde

Pitches: R **Bats:** R **Pos:** RP-52   **Ht:** 6'4" **Wt:** 254 **Born:** 3/24/1978 **Age:** 32

			HOW MUCH HE PITCHED					WHAT HE GAVE UP										THE RESULTS						
Year	Team	Lg	G	GS	CG	GF	IP	BFP	H	R	ER	HR	SH	SF	HB	TBB	IBB	SO	WP	Bk	W	L	Pct	Sh	Sv-Op	Hld	ERC	ERA
2009	CpChr*	AA	2	0	0	0	2.0	8	0	0	0	0	0	0	0	2	0	2	1	0	0	0	-	0	0- -	-	0.95	0.00
2003	Ari	NL	54	0	0	33	50.1	204	24	16	12	4	0	1	2	26	2	71	2	0	2	1	.667	0	10-11	8	1.77	2.15
2004	Ari	NL	29	0	0	20	29.2	131	23	17	14	7	3	2	1	17	4	38	4	0	1	2	.333	0	8-10	5	4.25	4.25
2005	Ari	NL	61	0	0	34	66.1	268	51	19	18	5	3	1	2	20	1	75	3	0	3	4	.429	0	15-17	7	2.43	2.44
2006	Ari	NL	44	0	0	35	49.1	223	50	32	32	6	1	3	2	22	3	69	2	0	2	3	.400	0	18-22	1	4.42	5.84
2007	Ari	NL	65	0	0	59	64.1	265	46	21	19	7	0	1	3	26	1	78	1	0	1	4	.200	0	47-54	1	2.77	2.66
2008	Hou	NL	74	0	0	71	72.0	303	62	28	27	10	0	2	2	23	6	83	3	2	6	3	.667	0	44-51	0	3.18	3.38
2009	Hou	NL	52	0	0	45	54.0	219	40	15	14	5	1	2	2	21	1	56	1	0	4	2	.667	0	25-29	1	2.76	2.33
	Postseason		4	0	0	3	4.2	21	2	1	1	0	0	0	0	4	0	2	0	0	0	1	.000	0	1-1	0	1.91	1.93
	7 ML YEARS		379	0	0	297	386.0	1613	296	148	136	44	8	12	14	155	18	470	16	2	19	19	.500	0	167-194	22	2.95	3.17

Jonathan Van Every

Bats: L **Throws:** L **Pos:** RF-4; CF-2; PR-1   **Ht:** 6'1" **Wt:** 190 **Born:** 11/27/1979 **Age:** 30

						BATTING														BASERUNNING				AVERAGES		
Year	Team	Lg	G	AB	H	2B	3B	HR	(Hm	Rd)	TB	R	RBI	RC	TBB	IBB	SO	HBP	SH	SF	SB	CS	SB%	GDP	Avg	OBP	Slg
2001	MhVlly	A-	41	135	34	4	2	6	(-	-)	60	30	17	26	28	1	50	7	0	0	1	2	.33	1	.252	.406	.444
2002	MhVlly	A-	42	140	36	7	6	6	(-	-)	73	31	26	27	20	0	45	1	1	2	6	0	1.00	3	.257	.350	.521
2002	Clmbs	A	15	43	6	0	1	3	(-	-)	17	10	4	7	13	1	25	2	0	0	1	0	1.00	0	.140	.362	.395
2003	Lk Cty	A	59	197	38	9	2	5	(-	-)	66	22	24	18	12	0	89	7	3	2	15	5	.75	0	.193	.261	.335

BATTING																					BASERUNNING				AVERAGES		
Year	Team	Lg	G	AB	H	2B	3B	HR	(Hm	Rd)	TB	R	RBI	RC	TBB	IBB	SO	HBP	SH	SF	SB	CS	SB%	GDP	Avg	OBP	Slg
2003	MhVlly	A-	22	65	17	6	1	1	(-	-)	28	13	9	11	9	0	23	3	0	2	7	4	.64	1	.262	.367	.431
2004	Knstn	A+	113	392	108	22	2	21	(-	-)	197	67	71	76	53	0	129	8	0	6	11	3	.79	3	.276	.368	.503
2005	Akron	AA	118	389	95	14	2	27	(-	-)	194	71	64	75	66	5	155	8	3	1	16	6	.73	3	.244	.364	.499
2006	Akron	AA	66	236	61	16	5	10	(-	-)	117	35	40	41	26	4	80	5	0	5	5	1	.83	1	.258	.338	.496
2006	Buffalo	AAA	47	151	39	9	2	5	(-	-)	67	23	16	23	16	0	51	3	0	1	5	2	.71	2	.258	.339	.444
2007	Akron	AA	44	151	52	14	5	4	(-	-)	88	27	34	34	19	2	48	1	3	2	4	5	.44	1	.344	.416	.583
2007	Buffalo	AAA	51	158	43	5	1	8	(-	-)	74	17	23	27	23	1	57	2	2	1	2	3	.40	1	.272	.370	.468
2008	Pwtckt	AAA	119	380	100	15	3	26	(-	-)	199	84	70	73	54	1	157	4	3	1	6	1	.86	4	.263	.360	.524
2009	Pwtckt	AAA	20	65	14	4	0	4	(-	-)	30	7	10	12	16	1	25	1	0	0	0	0	-	1	.215	.378	.462
2008	Bos	AL	11	17	4	0	1	0	(0	0)	6	0	5	3	1	0	6	0	0	0	0	0	-	0	.235	.278	.353
2009	Bos	AL	7	11	4	0	0	1	(0	1)	7	1	3	4	2	0	5	0	0	0	0	0	-	0	.364	.462	.636
2 ML YEARS			18	28	8	0	1	1	(0	1)	13	1	8	7	3	0	11	0	0	0	0	0	-	0	.286	.355	.464

Rick VandenHurk

Pitches: R Bats: R Pos: SP-11　　　　Ht: 6'5" Wt: 219 Born: 5/22/1985 Age: 25

HOW MUCH HE PITCHED							WHAT HE GAVE UP												THE RESULTS							
Year	Team	Lg	G	GS	CG	GF	IP	BFP	H	R	ER	HR	SH	SF	HB	TBB	IBB	SO	WP	Bk	W	L	Pct	Sh	Sv-Op	Hld	ERC	ERA
2009	Jupiter*	A+	1	1	0	0	3.0	14	3	1	1	0	0	0	0	2	0	3	0	0	0	0	-	0	0--	-	4.23	3.00
2009	NewOr*	AAA	11	11	0	0	59.2	241	43	20	19	3	2	1	2	16	2	51	3	0	5	2	.714	0	0--	-	1.90	2.87
2007	Fla	NL	18	17	0	0	81.2	379	94	63	62	15	5	3	3	48	5	82	4	4	6	9	.400	0	0-0	0	6.50	6.83
2008	Fla	NL	4	4	0	0	14.0	74	20	12	12	1	2	0	2	10	0	20	0	0	1	1	.500	0	0-0	0	8.20	7.71
2009	Fla	NL	11	11	0	0	58.2	256	57	29	28	11	3	2	4	21	3	49	2	0	3	2	.600	0	0-0	0	4.49	4.30
3 ML YEARS			33	32	0	0	154.1	709	171	104	102	27	10	5	9	79	8	151	6	4	8	9	.471	0	0-0	0	5.87	5.95

Claudio Vargas

Pitches: R Bats: R Pos: RP-36　　　　Ht: 6'4" Wt: 234 Born: 6/19/1978 Age: 32

HOW MUCH HE PITCHED							WHAT HE GAVE UP												THE RESULTS							
Year	Team	Lg	G	GS	CG	GF	IP	BFP	H	R	ER	HR	SH	SF	HB	TBB	IBB	SO	WP	Bk	W	L	Pct	Sh	Sv-Op	Hld	ERC	ERA
2009	InldEm*	A+	3	3	0	0	5.0	20	3	3	3	1	0	0	0	1	0	3	0	0	0	1	.000	0	0--	-	1.73	5.40
2009	Albq*	AAA	7	0	0	4	13.0	53	15	5	5	3	0	0	0	1	0	12	0	0	0	0	-	0	1--	-	4.59	3.46
2003	Mon	NL	23	20	0	0	114.0	492	111	59	55	16	5	4	7	41	5	62	2	0	6	8	.429	0	0-0	0	4.21	4.34
2004	Mon	NL	45	14	0	6	118.1	530	120	75	69	26	4	4	7	64	7	89	8	0	5	5	.500	0	0-0	3	5.84	5.25
2005	2 Tms	NL	25	23	0	0	132.1	586	146	81	77	25	6	1	7	47	5	95	6	0	9	9	.500	0	0-0	0	5.28	5.24
2006	Ari	NL	31	30	0	1	167.2	747	185	101	90	27	8	3	8	52	2	123	9	1	12	10	.545	0	0-0	0	4.81	4.83
2007	Mil	NL	29	23	0	1	134.1	605	153	86	76	23	5	7	2	54	3	107	4	0	11	6	.647	0	1-2	0	5.38	5.09
2008	NYM	NL	11	4	0	2	37.0	150	33	20	19	4	1	1	2	11	0	20	1	0	3	2	.600	0	0-1	1	3.46	4.62
2009	2 Tms	NL	36	0	0	6	41.1	159	25	8	8	3	0	1	2	15	1	30	0	0	1	0	1.000	0	0-2	11	1.98	1.74
05	Was	NL	4	4	0	0	12.2	66	22	15	13	4	0	0	0	7	2	5	0	0	0	3	.000	0	0-0	0	11.04	9.24
05	Ari	NL	21	19	0	0	119.2	520	124	66	64	21	6	1	7	40	3	90	6	0	9	6	.600	0	0-0	0	4.74	4.81
09	LAD	NL	8	0	0	4	11.0	43	7	2	2	1	0	0	0	4	0	10	0	0	0	0	-	0	0-0	0	2.42	1.64
09	Mil	NL	28	0	0	2	30.1	116	18	6	6	2	0	1	1	11	1	20	0	0	1	0	1.000	0	0-2	11	1.83	1.78
7 ML YEARS			200	114	0	16	745.0	3269	773	424	394	124	29	21	35	284	23	526	30	1	47	40	.540	0	1-5	15	4.82	4.76

Jason Vargas

Pitches: L Bats: L Pos: SP-14; RP-9　　　　Ht: 6'0" Wt: 215 Born: 2/2/1983 Age: 27

HOW MUCH HE PITCHED							WHAT HE GAVE UP												THE RESULTS							
Year	Team	Lg	G	GS	CG	GF	IP	BFP	H	R	ER	HR	SH	SF	HB	TBB	IBB	SO	WP	Bk	W	L	Pct	Sh	Sv-Op	Hld	ERC	ERA
2009	Tacom*	AAA	9	9	0	0	51.2	205	48	19	18	3	1	1	0	15	0	46	1	0	4	3	.571	0	0--	-	3.15	3.14
2005	Fla	NL	17	13	1	0	73.2	325	71	34	33	4	4	1	4	31	4	59	0	0	5	5	.500	0	0-0	0	3.68	4.03
2006	Fla	NL	12	5	0	3	43.0	213	50	39	35	9	4	4	4	30	3	25	2	0	1	2	.333	0	0-0	0	7.30	7.33
2007	NYM	NL	2	2	0	0	10.1	51	17	14	14	4	0	0	0	2	1	4	1	1	1	0	1.000	0	0-0	0	8.95	12.19
2009	Sea	AL	23	14	0	4	91.2	385	98	53	50	16	3	6	3	24	1	54	1	0	3	6	.333	0	0-0	0	4.64	4.91
4 ML YEARS			54	34	1	7	218.2	974	236	140	132	33	11	11	11	87	9	142	4	1	9	14	.391	0	0-0	0	5.00	5.43

Jason Varitek

Bats: B Throws: R Pos: C-108; PH-1　　　　Ht: 6'2" Wt: 230 Born: 4/11/1972 Age: 38

BATTING																					BASERUNNING				AVERAGES		
Year	Team	Lg	G	AB	H	2B	3B	HR	(Hm	Rd)	TB	R	RBI	RC	TBB	IBB	SO	HBP	SH	SF	SB	CS	SB%	GDP	Avg	OBP	Slg
1997	Bos	AL	1	1	1	0	0	0	(0	0)	1	0	0	1	0	0	0	0	0	0	0	0	-	0	1.000	1.000	1.000
1998	Bos	AL	86	221	56	13	0	7	(1	6)	90	31	33	26	17	1	45	2	4	3	2	2	.50	8	.253	.309	.407
1999	Bos	AL	144	483	130	39	2	20	(12	8)	233	70	76	75	46	2	85	2	5	8	1	2	.33	13	.269	.330	.482
2000	Bos	AL	139	448	111	31	1	10	(2	8)	174	55	65	59	60	3	84	6	1	4	1	1	.50	16	.248	.342	.388
2001	Bos	AL	51	174	51	11	1	7	(2	5)	85	19	25	30	21	3	35	1	1	1	0	0	-	6	.293	.371	.489
2002	Bos	AL	132	467	124	27	1	10	(6	4)	183	58	61	52	41	3	95	7	1	3	4	3	.57	13	.266	.332	.392
2003	Bos	AL	142	451	123	31	1	25	(13	12)	231	63	85	79	51	8	106	7	5	7	3	2	.60	10	.273	.351	.512
2004	Bos	AL	137	463	137	30	1	18	(8	10)	223	67	73	79	62	9	126	10	0	1	10	3	.77	11	.296	.390	.482
2005	Bos	AL	133	470	132	30	1	22	(7	15)	230	70	70	78	62	3	117	3	1	3	2	0	1.00	10	.281	.366	.489
2006	Bos	AL	103	365	87	19	2	12	(2	10)	146	46	55	45	46	7	87	2	1	2	1	2	.33	10	.238	.325	.400
2007	Bos	AL	131	435	111	15	3	17	(9	8)	183	57	68	61	71	9	122	8	0	4	1	2	.33	9	.255	.367	.421
2008	Bos	AL	131	423	93	20	0	13	(4	9)	152	37	43	36	52	3	122	6	0	2	0	1	.00	13	.220	.313	.359
2009	Bos	AL	109	364	76	24	0	14	(10	4)	142	41	51	43	56	6	90	3	0	4	0	0	-	6	.209	.313	.390
Postseason			63	228	54	12	2	11	(3	8)	103	37	33	27	14	4	56	5	2	3	0	0	-	6	.237	.292	.452
13 ML YEARS			1439	4765	1232	290	13	175	(76	99)	2073	614	705	664	583	57	1114	57	19	42	25	18	.58	125	.259	.344	.435

Esmerling Vasquez

Pitches: R Bats: R Pos: RP-53
Ht: 6'1" Wt: 173 Born: 11/7/1983 Age: 26

Year	Team	Lg	G	GS	CG	GF	IP	BFP	H	R	ER	HR	SH	SF	HB	TBB	IBB	SO	WP	Bk	W	L	Pct	Sh	Sv-Op	Hld	ERC	ERA
2004	Msoula	R+	19	0	0	12	30.2	141	22	15	12	1	0	0	6	21	2	33	11	0	3	2	.600	0	5--	-	3.62	3.52
2004	Yakima	A-	5	0	0	4	5.2	27	10	6	4	1	0	0	6	0	0	7	1	0	0	0	-	0	1--	-	7.45	6.35
2005	Sbend	A	53	0	0	17	71.2	327	63	33	29	2	4	6	5	47	0	79	13	1	6	4	.600	0	3--	-	4.05	3.64
2006	Lancst	A+	34	18	0	6	117.2	547	129	89	77	9	6	2	12	51	0	115	6	1	4	9	.308	0	0--	-	4.85	5.89
2007	Mobile	AA	29	29	0	0	165.1	663	125	61	55	11	7	6	13	60	0	151	6	0	10	6	.625	0	0--	-	2.81	2.99
2008	Tucsn	AAA	24	15	0	2	83.0	398	79	68	62	11	8	4	12	73	2	57	2	0	3	6	.333	0	0--	-	6.66	6.72
2009	Reno	AAA	6	0	0	1	9.2	38	7	2	1	0	0	0	0	3	0	9	0	0	0	0	-	0	1--	-	1.77	0.93
2009	Arl	NL	53	0	0	10	53.0	238	52	27	26	4	1	1	3	29	2	45	4	0	3	3	.500	0	0-4	4	4.51	4.42

Virgil Vasquez

Pitches: R Bats: R Pos: SP-7; RP-7
Ht: 6'3" Wt: 205 Born: 6/7/1982 Age: 28

Year	Team	Lg	G	GS	CG	GF	IP	BFP	H	R	ER	HR	SH	SF	HB	TBB	IBB	SO	WP	Bk	W	L	Pct	Sh	Sv-Op	Hld	ERC	ERA
2003	Oneont	A-	11	11	0	0	53.1	245	76	43	41	5	0	1	2	10	0	35	1	0	3	4	.429	0	0--	-	5.73	6.92
2004	WMich	A	27	27	0	0	168.1	681	156	73	68	14	8	5	15	34	1	120	6	1	14	6	.700	0	0--	-	3.23	3.64
2005	Lkland	A+	8	8	1	0	47.0	191	52	23	22	6	1	0	3	7	0	31	2	0	4	1	.800	1	0--	-	4.31	4.21
2005	Erie	AA	15	15	0	0	83.2	361	93	57	47	10	5	5	7	13	0	53	1	0	2	8	.200	0	0--	-	4.14	5.06
2006	Erie	AA	27	27	3	0	173.2	734	174	79	72	21	4	3	20	50	2	129	2	0	7	12	.368	0	0--	-	4.33	3.73
2007	Toledo	AAA	25	25	2	0	155.0	626	139	64	60	18	3	5	8	33	1	127	1	1	12	5	.706	2	0--	-	3.14	3.48
2008	Toledo	AAA	27	27	2	0	159.0	690	179	91	85	27	3	6	11	37	2	115	4	0	12	12	.500	2	0--	-	4.87	4.81
2009	Indy	AAA	19	19	1	0	107.2	447	116	50	47	14	5	3	3	16	1	72	3	0	7	4	.636	0	0--	-	3.83	3.93
2007	Det	AL	5	3	0	0	16.2	81	27	16	16	7	0	1	0	5	0	7	0	0	0	1	.000	0	0-0	0	10.58	8.64
2009	Pit	NL	14	7	0	4	44.2	208	58	30	29	6	2	2	3	18	1	29	0	0	2	5	.286	0	0-0	0	6.44	5.84
	2 ML YEARS		19	10	0	4	61.1	287	85	46	45	13	2	2	4	23	1	36	0	0	2	6	.250	0	0-0	0	7.53	6.60

Javier Vazquez

Pitches: R Bats: R Pos: SP-32
Ht: 6'2" Wt: 210 Born: 7/25/1976 Age: 33

Year	Team	Lg	G	GS	CG	GF	IP	BFP	H	R	ER	HR	SH	SF	HB	TBB	IBB	SO	WP	Bk	W	L	Pct	Sh	Sv-Op	Hld	ERC	ERA
1998	Mon	NL	33	32	0	1	172.1	704	190	121	116	21	9	4	11	68	2	139	2	0	5	15	.250	0	0-0	0	5.79	6.06
1999	Mon	NL	26	26	3	0	154.2	667	154	98	86	20	3	3	4	52	4	113	2	0	9	8	.529	1	0-0	0	4.02	5.00
2000	Mon	NL	33	33	2	0	217.2	945	247	104	98	24	11	3	5	61	10	196	3	0	11	9	.550	1	0-0	0	4.45	4.05
2001	Mon	NL	32	32	5	0	223.2	898	197	92	85	24	9	2	3	44	4	208	3	1	16	11	.593	3	0-0	0	2.75	3.42
2002	Mon	NL	34	34	2	0	230.1	971	243	111	100	28	15	7	4	49	6	179	3	0	10	13	.435	0	0-0	0	3.80	3.91
2003	Mon	NL	34	34	4	0	230.2	938	198	93	83	28	6	6	4	57	5	241	11	1	13	12	.520	1	0-0	0	2.90	3.24
2004	NYY	AL	32	32	0	0	198.0	849	195	114	108	33	4	8	11	60	3	150	12	2	14	10	.583	0	0-0	0	4.23	4.91
2005	Ari	AL	33	33	3	0	215.2	904	223	112	106	35	13	3	5	46	4	192	7	0	11	15	.423	1	0-0	0	4.00	4.42
2006	CWS	AL	33	32	1	0	202.2	872	206	116	109	23	2	4	15	56	2	184	7	0	11	12	.478	0	0-0	0	4.02	4.84
2007	CWS	AL	32	32	2	0	216.2	882	197	95	90	29	5	7	7	50	2	213	5	0	15	8	.652	0	0-0	0	3.29	3.74
2008	CWS	AL	33	33	1	0	208.1	890	214	113	108	25	4	4	6	61	2	200	2	0	12	16	.429	0	0-0	0	4.03	4.67
2009	Atl	NL	32	32	3	0	219.1	874	181	75	70	20	12	2	4	44	2	238	6	0	15	10	.600	0	0-0	0	2.42	2.87
	Postseason		4	2	0	0	15.2	80	24	18	18	6	0	3	2	10	0	18	0	0	1	1	.500	0	0-0	0	11.90	10.34
	12 ML YEARS		387	385	26	1	2490.0	10454	2451	1244	1159	320	93	53	70	648	46	2253	63	4	142	139	.505	7	0-0	0	3.73	4.19

Ramon Vazquez

Bats: L Throws: R Pos: PH-45; SS-28; 2B-22; 3B-14
Ht: 5'11" Wt: 170 Born: 8/21/1976 Age: 33

Year	Team	Lg	G	AB	H	2B	3B	HR	(Hm	Rd)	TB	R	RBI	RC	TBB	IBB	SO	HBP	SH	SF	SB	CS	SB%	GDP	Avg	OBP	Slg
2001	Sea	AL	17	35	8	0	0	0	(0	0)	8	5	4	2	0	0	3	0	1	1	0	0	-	0	.229	.222	.229
2002	SD	NL	128	423	116	21	5	2	(0	2)	153	50	32	55	45	3	79	1	3	2	7	2	.78	6	.274	.344	.362
2003	SD	NL	116	422	110	17	4	3	(1	2)	144	56	30	49	52	2	88	2	5	3	10	3	.77	4	.261	.342	.341
2004	SD	NL	52	115	27	3	2	1	(1	0)	37	12	13	9	11	2	24	0	4	2	1	1	.50	2	.235	.297	.322
2005	2 Tms	AL	39	85	18	5	0	0	(0	0)	23	7	5	5	5	0	17	0	2	0	0	0	-	0	.212	.256	.271
2006	Cle	AL	34	67	14	2	0	1	(1	0)	19	11	8	7	6	0	18	1	4	2	0	0	-	3	.209	.267	.284
2007	Tex	AL	104	300	69	13	3	8	(2	6)	112	42	28	36	29	0	72	2	12	2	1	0	1.00	4	.230	.300	.373
2008	Tex	AL	105	300	87	18	3	6	(4	2)	129	44	40	46	38	3	66	0	5	4	0	1	.00	4	.290	.365	.430
2009	Pit	NL	101	204	47	7	0	1	(0	1)	57	17	16	20	31	4	47	2	0	2	1	0	1.00	2	.230	.335	.279
05	Bos	AL	27	61	12	2	0	0	(0	0)	14	6	4	3	3	0	14	0	2	0	0	0	-	0	.197	.234	.230
05	Cle	AL	12	24	6	3	0	0	(0	0)	9	1	1	2	2	0	3	0	0	0	0	0	-	0	.250	.308	.375
	Postseason		1	0	0	0	0	0	(0	0)	0	0	0	0	0	0	0	0	0	0	0	0	-	0	-	-	-
	9 ML YEARS		696	1951	496	86	17	22	(9	13)	682	244	176	229	217	14	414	7	34	18	20	7	.74	25	.254	.328	.350

Donnie Veal

Pitches: L Bats: L Pos: RP-19
Ht: 6'4" Wt: 230 Born: 9/18/1984 Age: 25

Year	Team	Lg	G	GS	CG	GF	IP	BFP	H	R	ER	HR	SH	SF	HB	TBB	IBB	SO	WP	Bk	W	L	Pct	Sh	Sv-Op	Hld	ERC	ERA
2005	Cubs	R	4	3	0	0	10.2	45	8	6	6	2	0	1	5	0	14	2	0	0	1	.000	0	0--	-	3.95	5.06
2005	Boise	A-	7	6	0	0	29.0	117	18	11	8	2	1	1	0	15	0	34	4	3	1	2	.333	0	0--	-	2.36	2.48
2006	Peoria	A	14	14	0	0	73.2	296	45	26	22	4	1	2	2	40	0	86	9	0	5	3	.625	0	0--	-	2.44	2.69
2006	Dytona	A+	14	14	0	0	80.2	317	46	18	15	3	2	1	2	42	0	88	8	1	6	2	.750	0	0--	-	2.08	1.67
2007	Tenn	AA	28	27	0	0	130.1	585	126	80	72	11	9	5	6	73	0	131	6	3	8	10	.444	0	0--	-	4.57	4.97

Year	Team	Lg	G	GS	CG	GF	IP	BFP	H	R	ER	HR	SH	SF	HB	TBB	IBB	SO	WP	Bk	W	L	Pct	Sh	Sv-Op	Hld	ERC	ERA
2008	Tenn	AA	29	29	0	0	145.1	643	150	89	74	19	8	5	5	81	0	123	17	2	5	10	.333	0	0--	-	5.40	4.58
2009	Indy	AAA	9	1	0	2	14.0	62	6	10	10	0	1	1	0	16	0	13	1	0	0	1	.000	0	0--	-	3.01	6.43
2009	Altna	AA	7	5	0	0	13.1	55	5	2	2	0	0	1	1	10	0	18	1	0	0	0	-	0	0--	-	1.75	1.35
2009	Pit	NL	19	0	0	10	16.1	87	18	13	13	2	0	1	2	20	0	16	2	0	1	0	1.000	0	0-0	1	8.89	7.16

Gil Velazquez

Bats: R **Throws:** R **Pos:** SS-4; 3B-2; PR-1 **Ht:** 6'2" **Wt:** 170 **Born:** 10/17/1979 **Age:** 30

Year	Team	Lg	G	AB	H	2B	3B	HR	(Hm	Rd)	TB	R	RBI	RC	TBB	IBB	SO	HBP	SH	SF	SB	CS	SB%	GDP	Avg	OBP	Slg
1998	Kngspt	R+	12	29	3	1	0	0	(-	-)	4	2	4	0	2	0	7	0	3	1	2	0	1.00	0	.103	.156	.138
1998	Mets	R	33	97	18	3	0	0	(-	-)	21	7	7	5	8	0	10	2	3	1	2	1	.67	1	.186	.259	.216
1999	Clmbia	A	21	75	17	4	1	0	(-	-)	23	9	6	5	3	0	14	1	2	3	0	1	.00	2	.227	.256	.307
1999	Kngspt	R+	62	225	59	8	0	1	(-	-)	70	24	19	25	19	0	43	3	2	4	4	1	.80	5	.262	.323	.311
2000	StLuci	A+	125	440	101	16	1	1	(-	-)	122	37	43	33	25	0	69	9	4	3	3	9	.25	15	.230	.283	.277
2001	Bnghtn	AA	106	358	74	11	2	3	(-	-)	98	33	19	25	26	1	84	3	4	0	1	1	.50	12	.207	.266	.274
2002	Bnghtn	AA	27	72	14	2	0	0	(-	-)	16	6	5	3	7	0	15	1	1	0	0	3	.00	3	.194	.275	.222
2002	StLuci	A+	33	118	25	6	0	0	(-	-)	31	13	16	7	6	0	30	0	1	0	2	0	1.00	1	.212	.250	.263
2002	Norfolk	AAA	12	33	7	1	0	0	(-	-)	8	2	1	2	4	0	9	0	0	0	0	0	-	0	.212	.297	.242
2003	Bnghtn	AA	59	141	32	6	0	3	(-	-)	47	17	19	14	15	0	30	0	5	1	1	3	.25	4	.227	.299	.333
2003	Norfolk	AAA	5	16	4	0	0	0	(-	-)	4	0	2	0	0	0	5	0	0	0	0	1	.00	0	.250	.250	.250
2003	StLuci	A+	19	57	12	3	0	1	(-	-)	18	6	6	5	6	0	5	0	1	0	0	0	-	2	.211	.286	.316
2004	Norfolk	AAA	17	33	3	1	0	0	(-	-)	4	0	0	0	5	0	12	0	2	0	1	0	1.00	1	.091	.211	.121
2004	Bnghtn	AA	105	359	86	16	3	5	(-	-)	123	42	37	39	32	1	94	2	6	2	4	3	.57	3	.240	.304	.343
2005	NwBrit	AA	81	286	66	13	0	1	(-	-)	82	36	28	26	22	0	52	6	6	3	3	2	.60	2	.231	.297	.287
2005	Roch	AA	17	34	9	1	1	0	(-	-)	12	3	3	3	0	0	8	0	0	0	0	0	-	1	.265	.265	.353
2006	NwBrit	AA	6	16	6	2	0	0	(-	-)	8	1	3	3	3	0	2	0	0	0	0	0	-	0	.375	.474	.500
2006	Roch	AAA	56	164	41	4	1	1	(-	-)	50	26	17	15	11	0	33	2	3	2	2	2	.50	5	.250	.302	.305
2007	NwBrit	AA	17	45	12	2	3	1	(-	-)	23	6	13	10	10	0	13	0	3	3	1	0	1.00	0	.267	.379	.511
2007	Roch	AAA	69	183	44	9	1	1	(-	-)	58	26	16	19	13	0	35	3	5	2	3	0	1.00	6	.240	.299	.317
2008	Pwtckt	AAA	101	350	90	17	4	10	(-	-)	145	54	46	46	22	0	73	5	5	4	3	3	.50	13	.257	.307	.414
2009	Pwtckt	AAA	94	290	56	13	0	3	(-	-)	78	26	18	18	19	0	49	0	4	3	3	1	.75	9	.193	.240	.269
2008	Bos	AL	3	8	1	0	0	0	(0	0)	1	0	1	1	0	0	0	0	0	0	0	0	-	0	.125	.125	.125
2009	Bos	AL	6	2	0	0	0	0	(0	0)	0	0	0	0	0	0	0	1	0	0	0	0	-	0	.000	.333	.000
	2 ML YEARS		9	10	1	0	0	0	(0	0)	1	0	1	1	0	0	0	1	0	0	0	0	-	0	.100	.182	.100

Eugenio Velez

Bats: B **Throws:** R **Pos:** LF-42; 2B-31; PH-14; CF-12; RF-5; PR-3 **Ht:** 6'1" **Wt:** 162 **Born:** 5/16/1982 **Age:** 28

Year	Team	Lg	G	AB	H	2B	3B	HR	(Hm	Rd)	TB	R	RBI	RC	TBB	IBB	SO	HBP	SH	SF	SB	CS	SB%	GDP	Avg	OBP	Slg
2009	Fresno*	AAA	45	182	54	13	3	3	(-	-)	82	30	26	28	13	2	26	0	0	2	16	9	.64	4	.297	.340	.451
2007	SF	NL	14	11	3	0	2	0	(0	0)	7	5	2	4	2	0	3	0	0	0	4	0	1.00	0	.273	.385	.636
2008	SF	NL	98	275	72	16	7	1	(0	1)	105	32	30	29	14	2	40	1	1	1	15	6	.71	11	.262	.299	.382
2009	SF	NL	84	285	76	13	5	5	(3	2)	114	40	31	33	16	1	55	2	2	2	11	5	.69	6	.267	.308	.400
	3 ML YEARS		196	571	151	29	14	6	(3	3)	226	77	63	66	32	3	98	3	3	3	30	11	.73	17	.264	.305	.396

Will Venable

Bats: L **Throws:** L **Pos:** RF-68; CF-16; PH-16; LF-6 **Ht:** 6'2" **Wt:** 210 **Born:** 10/29/1982 **Age:** 27

Year	Team	Lg	G	AB	H	2B	3B	HR	(Hm	Rd)	TB	R	RBI	RC	TBB	IBB	SO	HBP	SH	SF	SB	CS	SB%	GDP	Avg	OBP	Slg
2005	Padres	R	15	59	19	4	2	1	(-	-)	30	13	12	12	2	0	9	4	0	0	4	0	1.00	1	.322	.385	.508
2005	Eugene	A-	42	139	30	5	2	2	(-	-)	45	17	14	14	14	0	38	2	0	1	2	1	.67	1	.216	.295	.324
2006	FtWyn	A	124	472	148	34	5	11	(-	-)	225	86	91	92	55	4	81	7	1	6	18	5	.78	8	.314	.389	.477
2007	SnAnt	AA	134	515	143	19	3	8	(-	-)	192	66	68	72	38	3	84	10	5	4	21	2	.91	8	.278	.337	.373
2008	Portlnd	AAA	120	442	129	26	4	14	(-	-)	205	70	58	76	44	0	104	5	3	2	7	3	.70	7	.292	.361	.464
2009	Portlnd	AAA	53	200	52	10	3	12	(-	-)	104	33	30	35	20	0	46	2	1	3	1	0	1.00	3	.260	.329	.520
2008	SD	NL	28	110	29	4	2	2	(0	2)	43	16	10	15	13	1	21	0	0	1	1	1	.50	1	.264	.339	.391
2009	SD	NL	95	293	75	14	2	12	(5	7)	129	38	38	34	25	2	89	4	2	0	6	1	.86	6	.256	.323	.440
	2 ML YEARS		123	403	104	18	4	14	(5	9)	172	54	48	49	38	3	110	4	2	1	7	2	.78	7	.258	.327	.427

Jose Veras

Pitches: R **Bats:** R **Pos:** RP-47 **Ht:** 6'5" **Wt:** 235 **Born:** 10/20/1980 **Age:** 29

Year	Team	Lg	G	GS	CG	GF	IP	BFP	H	R	ER	HR	SH	SF	HB	TBB	IBB	SO	WP	Bk	W	L	Pct	Sh	Sv-Op	Hld	ERC	ERA
2009	Clmbs*	AAA	7	0	0	1	7.0	24	3	1	1	1	0	0	0	2	0	9	0	0	0	1	.000	0	0--	-	1.39	1.29
2006	NYY	AL	12	0	0	4	11.0	43	8	5	5	2	0	0	0	5	0	6	1	1	0	0	-	0	1-1	1	3.55	4.09
2007	NYY	AL	9	0	0	3	9.1	41	6	6	6	0	0	0	0	7	1	7	1	0	0	0	-	0	2-2	1	2.52	5.79
2008	NYY	AL	60	0	0	15	57.2	253	52	23	23	7	2	1	3	29	6	63	4	0	5	3	.625	0	0-2	10	4.09	3.59
2009	2 Tms	AL	47	0	0	19	50.1	225	42	33	29	8	4	0	6	28	0	40	0	1	4	3	.571	0	0-0	6	4.60	5.19
09	NYY	AL	25	0	0	10	25.2	118	23	17	17	5	2	0	4	14	0	18	0	0	3	1	.750	0	0-0	3	5.29	5.96
09	Cle	AL	22	0	0	9	24.2	107	19	16	12	3	2	0	2	14	0	22	0	1	1	2	.333	0	0-0	3	3.92	4.38
	Postseason		2	0	0	0	0.2	4	1	0	0	0	0	0	0	1	1	1	0	0	0	0	-	0	0-0	0	6.98	0.00
	4 ML YEARS		128	0	0	41	128.1	562	108	67	63	16	6	1	9	69	7	116	6	2	9	6	.600	0	3-5	18	4.13	4.42

Justin Verlander

Pitches: R Bats: R Pos: SP-35 Ht: 6'5" Wt: 225 Born: 2/20/1983 Age: 27

			HOW MUCH HE PITCHED						WHAT HE GAVE UP										THE RESULTS							
Year	Team	Lg	G	GS	CG	GF	IP	BFP	H	R	ER	HR	SH	SF	HB	TBB	IBB	SO	WP	Bk	W	L	Pct	Sh	Sv-Op	Hld	ERC	ERA
2005	Det	AL	2	2	0	0	11.1	54	15	9	9	1	0	0	1	5	0	7	1	0	0	2	.000	0	0-0	0	6.41	7.15
2006	Det	AL	30	30	1	0	186.0	776	187	78	75	21	2	4	6	60	1	124	5	1	17	9	.654	1	0-0	0	4.12	3.63
2007	Det	AL	32	32	1	0	201.2	866	181	88	82	20	3	1	19	67	3	183	17	2	18	6	.750	1	0-0	0	3.53	3.66
2008	Det	AL	33	33	1	0	201.0	880	195	119	108	18	4	6	14	87	8	163	6	3	11	17	.393	0	0-0	0	4.17	4.84
2009	Det	AL	35	35	3	0	240.0	982	219	99	92	20	6	4	6	63	5	269	8	4	19	9	.679	1	0-0	0	3.06	3.45
	Postseason		4	4	0	0	21.2	100	26	17	14	5	1	0	0	10	0	23	3	1	1	2	.333	0	0-0	0	6.45	5.82
	5 ML YEARS		132	132	6	0	840.0	3558	797	393	366	80	15	15	46	282	17	746	37	10	65	43	.602	3	0-0	0	3.71	3.92

Shane Victorino

Bats: B Throws: R Pos: CF-150; PH 5; PR-1 Ht: 5'9" Wt: 187 Born: 11/30/1980 Age: 29

						BATTING														BASERUNNING				AVERAGES		
Year	Team	Lg	G	AB	H	2B	3B	HR	(Hm	Rd)	TB	R	RBI	RC	TBB	IBB	SO	HBP	SH	SF	SB	CS	SB%	GDP	Avg	OBP	Slg
2003	SD	NL	36	73	11	2	0	0	(0	0)	13	8	4	1	7	0	17	1	1	1	7	2	.78	5	.151	.232	.178
2005	Phi	NL	21	17	5	0	0	2	(1	1)	11	5	8	4	0	0	3	0	0	2	0	0	-	0	.294	.263	.647
2006	Phi	NL	153	415	119	19	8	6	(3	3)	172	70	46	58	24	0	54	14	8	1	4	3	.57	5	.287	.346	.414
2007	Phi	NL	131	456	128	23	3	12	(6	6)	193	78	46	65	37	1	62	10	5	2	37	4	.90	10	.281	.347	.423
2008	Phi	NL	146	570	167	30	8	14	(6	8)	255	102	58	86	45	2	69	7	5	0	36	11	.77	6	.293	.352	.447
2009	Phi	NL	156	620	181	39	13	10	(4	6)	276	102	62	99	60	1	71	6	4	4	25	8	.76	5	.292	.358	.445
	Postseason		17	61	16	3	1	3	(1	2)	30	7	14	10	6	4	5	0	1	0	4	0	1.00	2	.262	.328	.492
	6 ML YEARS		643	2151	611	113	32	44	(20	24)	920	365	224	313	173	4	276	38	23	10	109	28	.80	33	.284	.347	.428

Carlos Villanueva

Pitches: R Bats: R Pos: RP 58; SP 6 Ht: 6'2" Wt: 220 Born: 11/28/1983 Age: 26

						HOW MUCH HE PITCHED						WHAT HE GAVE UP										THE RESULTS							
Year	Team	Lg	G	GS	CG	GF	IP	BFP	H	R	ER	HR	SH	SF	HB	TBB	IBB	SO	WP	Bk	W	L	Pct	Sh	Sv-Op	Hld	ERC	ERA
2006	Mil	NL	10	6	0	2	53.2	215	43	22	22	8	1	0	4	11	1	39	0	0	2	2	.500	0	0-0	0	2.85	3.69
2007	Mil	NL	59	6	0	8	114.1	409	101	52	50	16	4	1	3	53	3	99	3	0	8	5	.615	0	1-3	16	4.03	3.94
2008	Mil	NL	17	9	0	0	108.1	464	112	53	49	18	9	1	3	30	1	93	4	0	4	7	.364	0	1-1	11	4.29	4.07
2009	Mil	NL	64	6	0	23	96.0	422	102	58	57	13	4	0	2	35	8	83	4	0	4	10	.000	0	3-9	9	4.44	5.34
	Postseason		2	0	0	0	7.2	11	0	0	0	0	0	0	0	0	0	3	0	0	0	0	-	0	0-0	1	0.00	0.00
	4 ML YEARS		180	27	0	42	372.1	1590	358	185	178	55	18	2	12	129	13	314	11	0	18	24	.429	0	5-12	36	4.04	4.30

Ron Villone

Pitches: L Bats: L Pos: RP-63 Ht: 6'3" Wt: 245 Born: 1/16/1970 Age: 40

						HOW MUCH HE PITCHED						WHAT HE GAVE UP										THE RESULTS							
Year	Team	Lg	G	GS	CG	GF	IP	BFP	H	R	ER	HR	SH	SF	HB	TBB	IBB	SO	WP	Bk	W	L	Pct	Sh	Sv-Op	Hld	ERC	ERA
2009	Syrcse*	AAA	8	0	0	0	7.2	29	4	2	2	1	1	0	1	2	0	5	0	0	0	0	0--	-	0--	-	1.87	2.35
1995	2 Tms		38	0	0	15	45.0	212	44	31	29	11	3	1	1	34	0	63	3	0	2	3	.400	0	1-5	6	6.57	5.80
1996	2 Tms		44	0	0	19	43.0	182	31	15	15	6	0	2	5	25	0	38	2	0	1	1	.500	0	2-3	9	4.08	3.14
1997	Mil	AL	50	0	0	15	52.2	238	54	23	20	4	2	0	1	36	2	40	3	0	1	0	1.000	0	0-2	8	5.30	3.42
1998	Cle	AL	25	0	0	6	27.0	129	30	18	18	3	2	2	2	22	0	15	0	0	0	0	-	0	0-0	1	7.01	6.00
1999	Cin	NL	29	2	0	2	142.2	610	114	70	67	8	9	3	5	73	2	97	8	0	9	7	.563	0	2-2	0	3.20	4.23
2000	Cin	NL	35	23	2	5	141.0	643	154	95	85	22	10	8	9	78	3	77	7	0	10	10	.500	0	0-0	1	5.97	5.43
2001	2 Tms		53	12	0	12	114.2	523	133	81	75	18	1	1	5	53	5	113	4	1	6	10	.375	0	0-0	6	5.81	5.89
2002	Pit	NL	45	7	0	6	93.0	399	95	63	60	8	5	3	5	34	3	55	1	0	4	6	.400	0	0-1	0	4.18	5.81
2003	Hou	NL	19	19	0	0	106.2	449	91	51	49	16	3	3	5	48	1	91	1	0	6	6	.500	0	0-0	0	4.04	4.13
2004	Sea	AL	56	10	0	14	117.0	523	102	64	53	12	4	4	12	64	3	86	6	0	8	6	.571	0	0-1	7	4.26	4.08
2005	2 Tms		79	0	0	24	64.0	287	57	34	29	4	3	5	7	35	2	70	3	1	5	5	.500	0	1-9	21	4.09	4.08
2006	NYY	AL	70	0	0	19	80.1	365	75	48	45	9	6	4	4	51	9	72	5	0	3	3	.500	0	0-1	6	4.69	5.04
2007	NYY	AL	37	0	0	13	42.1	176	36	20	20	5	0	1	3	18	3	25	4	0	0	0	-	0	0-1	4	3.74	4.25
2008	StL	NL	74	0	0	11	50.0	229	45	27	26	4	2	3	2	37	2	50	2	0	1	2	.333	0	1-2	16	4.77	4.68
2009	Was	NL	63	0	0	7	48.2	228	54	25	23	6	4	2	2	29	4	33	1	0	5	6	.455	0	1-4	7	5.65	4.25
95	Sea	AL	19	0	0	7	19.1	101	20	19	17	6	3	0	1	23	0	26	1	0	0	2	.000	0	0-3	3	9.67	7.91
95	SD	NL	19	0	0	8	25.2	111	24	12	12	5	0	1	0	11	0	37	2	0	2	1	.667	0	1-2	3	4.44	4.21
96	SD	NL	21	0	0	9	18.1	78	17	6	6	2	0	0	1	7	0	19	0	0	1	1	.500	0	0-1	4	3.90	2.95
96	Mil	AL	23	0	0	10	24.2	104	14	9	9	4	0	2	4	18	0	19	2	0	0	0	-	0	2-2	5	4.21	3.28
01	Col	NL	22	6	0	6	46.2	222	56	35	33	6	1	1	1	29	4	48	2	0	1	3	.250	0	0-0	2	6.30	6.36
01	Hou	NL	31	6	0	6	68.0	301	77	46	42	12	0	0	4	24	1	65	2	1	5	7	.417	0	0-0	4	5.46	5.56
05	Sea	AL	52	0	0	14	40.1	178	33	14	11	2	1	3	5	23	1	41	2	1	2	3	.400	0	1-6	17	3.79	2.45
05	Fla	NL	27	0	0	10	23.2	109	24	20	18	2	2	2	2	12	1	29	1	0	3	2	.600	0	0-3	4	4.61	6.85
	Postseason		3	0	0	2	2.0	8	1	0	0	0	0	0	0	1	0	1	0	0	0	0	-	0	0-0	0	1.41	0.00
	15 ML YEARS		717	93	2	168	1168.0	5193	1115	665	614	136	54	42	68	637	39	925	48	2	61	65	.484	0	8-31	92	4.71	4.73

Pedro Viola

Pitches: L Bats: R Pos: RP-9 Ht: 6'1" Wt: 185 Born: 6/29/1983 Age: 27

						HOW MUCH HE PITCHED						WHAT HE GAVE UP										THE RESULTS							
Year	Team	Lg	G	GS	CG	GF	IP	BFP	H	R	ER	HR	SH	SF	HB	TBB	IBB	SO	WP	Bk	W	L	Pct	Sh	Sv-Op	Hld	ERC	ERA
2007	Dayton	A	22	0	0	8	43.1	174	29	14	9	3	1	2	1	17	1	49	2	0	3	1	.750	0	2--	-	2.20	1.87
2007	Srsota	A+	10	0	0	5	20.0	82	14	2	2	0	0	0	0	7	2	28	1	0	0	1	.000	0	2--	-	1.59	0.90
2007	Chatt	AA	14	0	0	4	19.0	76	12	3	2	2	2	0	0	6	0	17	0	0	0	0	-	0	2--	-	1.87	0.95
2008	Chatt	AA	52	7	0	17	82.1	369	88	50	41	6	8	3	4	36	4	84	6	0	4	7	.364	0	2--	-	4.49	4.48
2009	Lsvlle	AAA	54	0	0	16	49.1	230	48	30	30	7	5	1	0	33	1	57	4	0	2	2	.500	0	8--	-	5.13	5.47
2009	Cin	NL	9	0	0	1	7.0	30	7	4	4	2	1	0	0	3	0	5	0	0	0	0	-	0	0-0	-	5.60	5.14

Luis Vizcaino

Pitches: R **Bats:** R **Pos:** RP-15   **Ht:** 5'11" **Wt:** 210 **Born:** 8/6/1974 **Age:** 35

Year	Team	Lg	G	GS	CG	GF	IP	BFP	H	R	ER	HR	SH	SF	HB	TBB	IBB	SO	WP	Bk	W	L	Pct	Sh	Sv-Op	Hld	ERC	ERA
1999	Oak	AL	1	0	0	1	3.1	16	3	2	2	1	0	0	0	3	0	2	1	0	0	0	-	0	0-0	0	7.01	5.40
2000	Oak	AL	12	0	0	1	19.1	96	25	17	16	2	0	1	2	11	0	18	1	0	0	1	.000	0	0-0	0	6.83	7.45
2001	Oak	AL	36	0	0	15	36.2	156	38	19	19	8	0	1	0	12	1	31	3	0	2	1	.667	0	1-1	3	4.80	4.66
2002	Mil	NL	76	0	0	30	81.1	326	55	27	27	6	3	3	3	30	4	79	3	2	5	3	.625	0	5-6	19	2.20	2.99
2003	Mil	NL	75	0	0	21	62.0	272	64	45	44	16	2	1	1	25	3	61	3	0	4	3	.571	0	0-6	9	5.37	6.39
2004	Mil	NL	73	0	0	21	72.0	298	61	35	30	12	1	5	1	24	3	63	9	0	4	4	.500	0	1-5	21	3.40	3.75
2005	CWS	AL	65	0	0	20	70.0	305	74	30	29	8	4	1	2	29	6	43	3	0	6	5	.545	0	0-3	15	4.58	3.73
2006	Ari	NL	70	0	0	15	65.1	272	51	26	26	8	2	0	4	29	6	72	1	0	4	6	.400	0	0-2	25	3.34	3.58
2007	NYY	AL	77	0	0	13	75.1	334	66	37	36	6	2	6	2	43	11	62	1	0	8	2	.800	0	0-3	14	3.70	4.30
2008	Col	NL	43	0	0	13	46.0	203	48	28	27	10	1	2	1	19	1	49	0	0	1	2	.333	0	0-1	1	5.25	5.28
2009	2 Tms		15	0	0	6	15.1	69	10	7	7	2	1	1	0	12	2	12	1	0	1	3	.250	0	1-1	2	3.49	4.11
09	ChC	NL	4	0	0	2	3.2	13	2	0	0	0	0	0	0	0	0	3	0	0	0	0	-	0	0-0	1	0.63	0.00
09	Cle	AL	11	0	0	4	11.2	56	8	7	7	2	1	1	0	12	2	9	1	0	1	3	.250	0	1-1	1	4.79	5.40
	Postseason		2	0	0	1	1.2	10	2	1	1	0	1	0	0	3	1	0	0	0	0	1	.000	0	0-0	0	8.50	5.40
	11 ML YEARS		543	0	0	156	546.2	2347	495	273	263	79	16	21	16	237	37	492	26	2	35	30	.538	0	8-28	103	3.99	4.33

Omar Vizquel

Bats: B **Throws:** R **Pos:** SS-27; 3B-20; 2B-16; PH-4; PR-2   **Ht:** 5'9" **Wt:** 175 **Born:** 4/24/1967 **Age:** 43

							BATTING														BASERUNNING				AVERAGES		
Year	Team	Lg	G	AB	H	2B	3B	HR	(Hm	Rd)	TB	R	RBI	RC	TBB	IBB	SO	HBP	SH	SF	SB	CS	SB%	GDP	Avg	OBP	Slg
1989	Sea	AL	143	387	85	7	3	1	(1	0)	101	45	20	25	28	0	40	1	13	2	1	4	.20	6	.220	.273	.261
1990	Sea	AL	81	255	63	3	2	2	(0	2)	76	19	18	22	18	0	22	0	10	2	4	1	.80	7	.247	.295	.298
1991	Sea	AL	142	426	98	16	4	1	(1	0)	125	42	41	39	45	0	37	0	8	3	7	2	.78	8	.230	.302	.293
1992	Sea	AL	136	483	142	20	4	0	(0	0)	170	49	21	54	32	0	38	2	9	1	15	13	.54	14	.294	.340	.352
1993	Sea	AL	158	560	143	14	2	2	(1	1)	167	68	31	53	50	2	71	4	13	3	12	14	.46	7	.255	.319	.298
1994	Cle	AL	69	286	78	10	1	1	(0	1)	93	39	33	32	23	0	23	0	11	2	13	4	.76	4	.273	.325	.325
1995	Cle	AL	136	542	144	28	0	6	(3	3)	190	87	56	70	59	0	59	1	10	10	29	11	.73	4	.266	.333	.351
1996	Cle	AL	151	542	161	36	1	9	(2	7)	226	98	64	87	56	0	42	4	12	9	35	9	.80	10	.297	.362	.417
1997	Cle	AL	153	565	158	23	6	5	(3	2)	208	89	49	75	57	1	58	2	16	2	43	12	.78	16	.280	.347	.368
1998	Cle	AL	151	576	166	30	6	2	(0	2)	214	86	50	82	62	1	64	4	12	6	37	12	.76	10	.288	.358	.372
1999	Cle	AL	144	574	191	36	4	5	(3	2)	250	112	66	106	65	0	50	1	17	7	42	9	.82	8	.333	.397	.436
2000	Cle	AL	156	613	176	27	3	7	(1	6)	230	101	66	92	87	0	72	5	7	5	22	10	.69	13	.287	.377	.375
2001	Cle	AL	155	611	156	26	8	2	(2	0)	204	84	50	66	61	0	72	2	15	4	13	9	.59	14	.255	.323	.334
2002	Cle	AL	151	582	160	31	5	14	(9	5)	243	85	72	91	56	3	64	8	7	10	18	10	.64	7	.275	.341	.418
2003	Cle	AL	64	250	61	13	2	2	(2	0)	84	43	19	25	29	0	20	0	5	1	8	3	.73	11	.244	.321	.336
2004	Cle	AL	148	567	165	28	3	7	(2	5)	220	82	59	86	57	0	62	1	20	6	19	6	.76	12	.291	.353	.388
2005	SF	NL	152	568	154	28	4	3	(0	3)	199	66	45	76	56	0	58	5	20	2	24	10	.71	10	.271	.341	.350
2006	SF	NL	153	579	171	22	10	4	(2	2)	225	88	58	90	56	3	51	6	13	5	24	7	.77	13	.295	.361	.389
2007	SF	NL	145	513	126	18	3	4	(2	2)	162	54	51	53	44	6	48	1	14	3	14	6	.70	14	.246	.305	.316
2008	SF	NL	92	266	59	10	1	0	(0	0)	71	24	23	24	24	9	29	0	7	3	5	4	.56	4	.222	.283	.267
2009	Tex	AL	62	177	47	7	2	1	(0	1)	61	17	14	24	13	0	27	0	5	0	4	0	1.00	0	.266	.316	.345
	Postseason		57	228	57	7	4	0	(0	0)	72	28	20	27	25	0	36	2	7	2	23	3	.88	5	.250	.327	.316
	21 ML YEARS		2742	9922	2704	433	74	78	(34	44)	3519	1378	906	1272	978	25	1007	47	244	86	389	156	.71	192	.273	.338	.355

Edinson Volquez

Pitches: R **Bats:** R **Pos:** SP-9   **Ht:** 6'0" **Wt:** 210 **Born:** 7/3/1983 **Age:** 26

Year	Team	Lg	G	GS	CG	GF	IP	BFP	H	R	ER	HR	SH	SF	HB	TBB	IBB	SO	WP	Bk	W	L	Pct	Sh	Sv-Op	Hld	ERC	ERA
2005	Tex	AL	6	3	0	0	12.2	75	25	20	20	3	0	1	2	10	0	11	0	0	0	4	.000	0	0-0	0	14.15	14.21
2006	Tex	AL	8	8	0	0	33.1	164	52	28	27	7	0	1	1	17	0	15	0	0	1	6	.143	0	0-0	0	9.27	7.29
2007	Tex	AL	6	6	0	0	34.0	149	34	18	17	4	0	2	2	15	0	29	0	0	1	2	.667	0	0-0	0	4.63	4.50
2008	Cin	NL	33	32	0	1	196.0	838	167	82	70	14	6	5	14	93	5	206	10	1	17	6	.739	0	0-0	0	3.61	3.21
2009	Cin	NL	9	9	0	0	49.2	218	34	25	24	6	2	1	5	32	0	47	2	1	4	2	.667	0	0-0	0	3.77	4.35
	5 ML YEARS		62	58	0	1	325.2	1444	312	175	158	34	8	10	24	167	5	308	12	2	24	19	.558	0	0-0	0	4.60	4.37

Chris Volstad

Pitches: R **Bats:** R **Pos:** SP-29   **Ht:** 6'8" **Wt:** 227 **Born:** 9/23/1986 **Age:** 23

Year	Team	Lg	G	GS	CG	GF	IP	BFP	H	R	ER	HR	SH	SF	HB	TBB	IBB	SO	WP	Bk	W	L	Pct	Sh	Sv-Op	Hld	ERC	ERA
2005	Mrlns	R	6	6	0	0	27.0	111	25	14	7	1	1	1	2	4	0	26	1	0	1	1	.500	0	0- -	-	2.58	2.33
2005	Jmstwn	A-	7	7	0	0	38.0	170	43	19	9	0	1	1	3	11	0	29	2	1	3	2	.600	0	0- -	-	3.88	2.13
2006	Grnsbr	A	26	26	0	0	152.0	636	161	73	52	12	6	2	6	36	0	99	6	0	11	8	.579	0	0- -	-	3.84	3.08
2007	Jupiter	A+	21	20	2	0	126.0	567	152	76	63	8	2	4	6	37	1	93	9	0	8	9	.471	1	0- -	-	4.67	4.50
2007	Carlina	AA	7	7	0	0	42.2	177	41	19	15	4	3	0	1	10	0	25	3	0	4	2	.667	0	0- -	-	3.27	3.16
2008	Carlina	AA	15	15	1	0	91.0	383	86	37	34	0	7	2	2	30	3	55	3	0	4	4	.500	0	0- -	-	2.86	3.36
2009	NewOr	AAA	1	1	0	0	4.0	18	5	3	3	2	1	0	2	0	0	7	0	0	1	0	1.000	0	0- -	-	9.58	6.75
2008	Fla	NL	15	14	0	0	84.1	365	76	30	27	3	6	1	5	36	4	52	0	0	6	4	.600	0	0-0	0	3.30	2.88
2009	Fla	NL	29	29	1	0	159.0	682	169	100	92	29	8	3	3	59	3	107	8	0	9	13	.409	1	0-0	0	5.05	5.21
	2 ML YEARS		44	43	1	0	243.1	1047	245	130	119	32	14	4	8	95	7	159	8	0	15	17	.469	1	0-0	0	4.43	4.40

Joey Votto

Bats: L Throws: R Pos: 1B-130; PH-2   Ht: 6'3" Wt: 233 Born: 9/10/1983 Age: 26

									BATTING													BASERUNNING				AVERAGES		
Year	Team	Lg	G	AB	H	2B	3B	HR	(Hm	Rd)	TB	R	RBI	RC	TBB	IBB	SO	HBP	SH	SF		SB	CS	SB%	GDP	Avg	OBP	Slg
2009	Srsota*	A+	1	2	0	0	0	0	(-	-)	0	0	0	0	1	0	1	0	0	0		1	0	1.00	0	.000	.333	.000
2009	Dayton	A	2	7	3	0	0	1	(-	-)	6	3	3	3	2	0	3	0	0	0		1	0	1.00	0	.429	.556	.857
2007	Cin	NL	24	84	27	7	0	4	(4	0)	46	11	17	17	5	1	15	0	0	0		1	0	1.00	0	.321	.360	.548
2008	Cin	NL	151	526	156	32	3	24	(14	10)	266	69	84	91	59	9	102	2	0	2		7	5	.58	7	.297	.368	.506
2009	Cin	NL	131	469	151	38	1	25	(14	11)	266	82	84	99	70	10	106	4	0	1		4	1	.80	8	.322	.414	.567
	3 ML YEARS		306	1079	334	77	4	53	(32	21)	578	162	185	207	134	20	223	6	0	3		12	6	.67	15	.310	.388	.536

Jason Waddell

Pitches: L Bats: R Pos: RP-3   Ht: 6'2" Wt: 199 Born: 6/11/1981 Age: 29

			HOW MUCH HE PITCHED						WHAT HE GAVE UP												THE RESULTS						
Year	Team	Lg	G	GS	CG	GF	IP	BFP	H	R	ER	HR	SH	SF	HB	TBB	IBB	SO	WP	Bk		W	L	Pct	Sh	Sv-Op	Hld	ERC	ERA
2001	SlmKzr	R	15	1	0	1	28.0	125	30	19	17	2	1	1	1	11	1	30	3	0		1	1	.500	0	0--	-	4.25	5.46
2001	Giants	R	1	1	0	0	6.0	26	8	3	2	2	0	0	1	0	0	3	0	0		0	1	.000	0	0--	-	4.37	3.00
2002	SlmKzr	A-	11	2	0	4	20.0	82	19	12	12	2	0	0	2	10	1	13	2	0		0	2	.000	0	0--	-	5.02	5.40
2002	Hgrstn	A	4	0	0	2	6.2	30	6	5	5	1	0	0	1	1	0	4	0	0		0	0	-	0	0--	-	3.14	6.75
2003	Hgrstn	A	36	2	0	13	61.1	256	52	32	24	7	3	3	4	21	1	54	2	0		4	2	.667	0	0--	-	3.35	3.52
2004	SnJos	A+	47	2	0	18	70.2	309	76	39	32	4	0	0	1	24	1	60	6	1		6	4	.600	0	0--	-	3.94	4.08
2005	SnJos	A+	26	2	0	5	47.2	196	42	20	18	4	2	3	1	15	0	44	4	0		5	1	.833	0	0--	-	3.11	3.40
2006	Conn	AA	38	3	0	13	48.2	222	64	27	20	4	5	2	2	15	3	49	2	0		1	3	.250	0	1--	-	5.45	3.70
2007	SnJos	A+	30	0	0	9	44.0	187	48	14	9	0	3	1	1	12	1	50	1	0		1	1	.500	0	1--	-	3.47	1.84
2008	Conn	AA	44	0	0	21	64.0	268	47	27	24	6	1	4	2	36	2	70	2	0		0	3	.000	0	2--	-	3.33	3.38
2009	Iowa	AAA	26	0	0	8	27.2	116	26	12	10	1	2	0	1	8	0	20	1	0		1	0	1.000	0	2--	-	3.02	3.25
2009	Erie	AA	11	0	0	5	14.1	57	11	5	5	0	0	0	1	4	1	14	0	0		1	2	.333	0	2--	-	2.00	3.14
2009	Cin	NL	2	0	0	0	1.2	8	3	1	1	0	0	0	0	0	0	2	0	0		0	0	-	0	0-0	1	6.23	5.40

Cory Wade

Pitches: R Bats: R Pos: RP-27   Ht: 6'1" Wt: 190 Born: 5/28/1983 Age: 27

			HOW MUCH HE PITCHED						WHAT HE GAVE UP												THE RESULTS						
Year	Team	Lg	G	GS	CG	GF	IP	BFP	H	R	ER	HR	SH	SF	HB	TBB	IBB	SO	WP	Bk		W	L	Pct	Sh	Sv-Op	Hld	ERC	ERA
2004	Ddgrs	R	11	2	0	8	32.2	129	28	12	11	2	1	0	4	1	0	26	0	0		2	1	.667	0	1--	-	2.19	3.03
2004	Ogden	R+	8	0	0	8	14.0	70	24	9	8	0	0	0	4	4	1	19	1	0		1	2	.333	0	0--	-	6.77	5.14
2005	Clmbs	A	12	0	0	8	20.0	102	29	19	9	2	3	3	1	10	0	14	1	0		0	2	.000	0	2--	-	7.11	4.05
2005	Ogden	R+	16	11	1	0	72.1	306	81	42	35	12	3	1	5	19	0	60	3	0		2	3	.400	0	0--	-	5.13	4.35
2006	Clmbs	A	23	14	1	5	94.1	401	101	56	52	9	1	3	10	11	0	94	5	0		6	5	.545	1	2--	-	3.69	4.96
2006	VeroB	A+	7	7	0	0	39.1	184	52	40	36	9	1	2	4	13	0	32	0	0		2	4	.333	0	0--	-	7.13	8.24
2007	InldEm	A+	25	2	0	7	66.0	265	50	19	18	6	0	1	6	17	1	67	4	0		7	0	1.000	0	6--	-	2.55	2.45
2007	Jaxnvl	AA	14	0	0	3	33.0	136	22	5	5	2	3	1	0	11	2	33	0	0		0	1	.000	0	0--	-	1.72	1.36
2008	Jaxnvl	AA	6	0	0	2	14.2	58	14	7	7	3	0	0	2	1	0	13	1	0		0	0	-	0	1--	-	3.87	4.30
2008	Gt Lks	A	1	1	0	0	1.0	4	1	0	0	0	0	0	0	0	0	0	0	0		0	0	-	0	0--	-	1.95	0.00
2009	InldEm	A+	1	1	0	0	1.0	5	0	0	0	0	0	0	0	2	0	1	0	0		0	0	-	0	0--	-	3.47	0.00
2009	Albq	AAA	18	0	0	5	22.2	94	20	17	17	5	0	1	1	7	1	19	0	0		1	1	.500	0	1--	-	3.99	6.75
2008	LAD	NL	55	0	0	21	71.1	275	51	22	18	7	2	1	4	15	3	51	2	0		2	1	.667	0	0-1	9	2.11	2.27
2009	LAD	NL	27	0	0	6	27.2	121	28	17	17	3	0	1	1	10	3	18	4	0		2	3	.400	0	0-6	7	3.96	5.53
	Postseason		7	0	0	1	7.1	28	6	3	3	1	0	0	0	0	0	4	1	0		0	1	.000	0	0-1	2	1.84	3.68
	2 ML YEARS		82	0	0	23	99.0	396	79	39	35	10	2	2	5	25	6	69	6	0		4	4	.500	0	0-7	16	2.60	3.18

Doug Waechter

Pitches: R Bats: R Pos: RP-5   Ht: 6'4" Wt: 227 Born: 1/28/1981 Age: 29

			HOW MUCH HE PITCHED						WHAT HE GAVE UP												THE RESULTS						
Year	Team	Lg	G	GS	CG	GF	IP	BFP	H	R	ER	HR	SH	SF	HB	TBB	IBB	SO	WP	Bk		W	L	Pct	Sh	Sv-Op	Hld	ERC	ERA
2009	Omha*	AAA	13	0	0	3	18.2	77	22	11	10	0	1	2	0	1	0	10	1	0		1	1	.500	0	1--	-	3.06	4.82
2003	TB	AL	6	5	1	0	35.1	145	29	13	13	4	0	0	1	15	0	29	0	0		3	2	.600	1	0-0	0	3.48	3.31
2004	TB	AL	14	14	0	0	70.1	309	68	54	47	20	0	2	4	33	1	36	1	1		5	7	.417	0	0-0	0	5.74	6.01
2005	TB	AL	29	25	0	3	157.0	692	191	109	98	29	4	4	3	38	5	87	4	2		5	12	.294	0	0-0	0	5.29	5.62
2006	TB	AL	11	10	0	0	53.0	249	67	40	39	6	3	6	5	19	1	25	0	0		1	4	.200	0	0-0	0	5.79	6.62
2008	Fla	NL	48	0	0	10	63.1	275	63	29	26	7	2	2	2	21	3	46	2	0		4	2	.667	0	0-1	9	3.82	3.69
2009	KC	AL	6	0	0	3	5.1	28	9	5	5	2	0	1	0	3	0	3	1	0		0	0	-	0	0-0	0	11.46	8.44
	6 ML YEARS		113	54	1	16	384.1	1698	427	250	228	68	9	15	15	129	10	226	8	3		18	27	.400	1	0-1	9	5.09	5.34

Billy Wagner

Pitches: L Bats: L Pos: RP-17   Ht: 5'11" Wt: 203 Born: 7/25/1971 Age: 38

			HOW MUCH HE PITCHED						WHAT HE GAVE UP												THE RESULTS						
Year	Team	Lg	G	GS	CG	GF	IP	BFP	H	R	ER	HR	SH	SF	HB	TBB	IBB	SO	WP	Bk		W	L	Pct	Sh	Sv-Op	Hld	ERC	ERA
2009	Mets*	R	2	0	0	0	2.0	?	0	0	0	0	0	0	0	0	0	2	0	0		0	0	-	0	0--	-	0.00	0.00
2009	StLuci*	A+	5	0	0	0	5.0	16	3	0	0	0	0	0	0	0	0	8	0	0		0	0	-	0	0--	-	0.85	0.00
1995	Hou	NL	1	0	0	0	0.1	1	0	0	0	0	0	0	0	0	0	0	0	0		0	0	-	0	0-0	0	0.00	0.00
1996	Hou	NL	37	0	0	20	51.2	212	28	16	14	6	7	2	3	30	2	67	1	0		2	2	.500	0	9-13	3	2.61	2.44
1997	Hou	NL	62	0	0	49	66.1	277	49	23	21	5	3	1	3	30	1	106	3	0		7	8	.467	0	23-29	1	2.85	2.85
1998	Hou	NL	58	0	0	50	60.0	247	46	19	18	6	4	0	0	25	1	97	2	0		4	3	.571	0	30-35	1	2.87	2.70
1999	Hou	NL	66	0	0	55	74.2	286	35	14	13	5	2	1	1	23	1	124	2	0		4	1	.800	0	39-42	1	1.20	1.57
2000	Hou	NL	28	0	0	19	27.2	129	28	19	19	6	0	0	1	18	0	28	7	0		2	4	.333	0	6-15	0	6.15	6.18
2001	Hou	NL	64	0	0	58	62.2	251	44	19	19	5	3	1	5	20	0	79	3	0		2	5	.286	0	39-41	0	2.42	2.73
2002	Hou	NL	70	0	0	61	75.0	289	51	21	21	7	2	3	2	22	5	88	6	0		4	2	.667	0	35-41	0	2.08	2.52
2003	Hou	NL	78	0	0	67	86.0	335	52	18	17	8	1	0	3	23	5	105	4	0		1	4	.200	0	44-47	0	1.63	1.78

281

Year	Team	Lg	G	GS	CG	GF	IP	BFP	H	R	ER	HR	SH	SF	HB	TBB	IBB	SO	WP	Bk	W	L	Pct	Sh	Sv-Op	Hld	ERC	ERA
2004	Phi	NL	45	0	0	38	48.1	182	31	16	13	5	3	0	2	6	1	59	1	0	4	0	1.000	0	21-25	1	1.52	2.42
2005	Phi	NL	75	0	0	70	77.2	297	45	17	13	6	0	2	3	20	2	87	3	1	4	3	.571	0	38-41	1	1.53	1.51
2006	NYM	NL	70	0	0	59	72.1	297	59	22	18	7	2	0	4	21	1	94	2	0	3	2	.600	0	40-45	0	2.83	2.24
2007	NYM	NL	66	0	0	57	68.1	282	55	22	20	6	1	2	2	22	4	80	4	0	2	2	.500	0	34-39	0	2.66	2.63
2008	NYM	NL	45	0	0	34	47.0	184	32	17	12	4	0	1	0	10	0	52	2	0	0	1	.000	0	27-34	0	1.68	2.30
2009	2 Tms		17	0	0	2	15.2	63	8	5	3	1	2	0	1	8	0	26	1	0	1	1	.500	0	0-0	6	1.99	1.72
09	NYM	NL	2	0	0	0	2.0	7	0	0	0	0	0	0	0	1	0	4	0	0	0	0	-	0	0-0	0	0.27	0.00
09	Bos	AL	15	0	0	2	13.2	56	8	5	3	1	2	0	1	7	0	22	1	0	1	1	.500	0	0-0	6	2.42	1.98
Postseason			11	0	0	9	10.1	51	18	11	11	3	0	0	1	1	0	11	1	0	1	1	.500	0	3-4	0	9.19	9.58
15 ML YEARS			782	0	0	639	833.2	3332	563	248	221	77	30	13	30	278	23	1092	41	1	40	38	.513	0	385-447	13	2.20	2.39

Adam Wainwright

Pitches: R Bats: R Pos: SP-34   Ht: 6'7" Wt: 228 Born: 8/30/1981 Age: 28

Year	Team	Lg	G	GS	CG	GF	IP	BFP	H	R	ER	HR	SH	SF	HB	TBB	IBB	SO	WP	Bk	W	L	Pct	Sh	Sv-Op	Hld	ERC	ERA
2005	StL	NL	2	0	0	1	2.0	9	2	3	3	1	0	0	0	1	0	0	0	0	0	0	-	0	0-0	0	7.30	13.50
2006	StL	NL	61	0	0	10	75.0	309	64	26	26	6	4	1	4	22	2	72	3	0	2	1	.667	0	3-5	17	2.92	3.12
2007	StL	NL	32	32	1	0	202.0	882	212	93	83	13	9	5	9	70	4	136	6	0	14	12	.538	0	0-0	0	4.01	3.70
2008	StL	NL	20	20	1	0	132.0	544	122	51	47	12	6	4	3	34	1	91	3	0	11	3	.786	0	0-0	0	3.14	3.20
2009	StL	NL	34	34	1	0	233.0	970	216	75	68	17	10	5	3	66	1	212	7	0	19	8	.704	0	0-0	0	3.08	2.63
Postseason			9	0	0	9	9.2	38	7	0	0	0	0	0	0	2	0	15	1	0	1	0	1.000	0	4-5	0	1.48	0.00
5 ML YEARS			149	86	3	11	644.0	2714	616	248	227	49	29	15	19	193	8	511	19	0	46	24	.657	0	3-5	17	3.37	3.17

Tim Wakefield

Pitches: R Bats: R Pos: SP-21   Ht: 6'2" Wt: 210 Born: 8/2/1966 Age: 43

Year	Team	Lg	G	GS	CG	GF	IP	BFP	H	R	ER	HR	SH	SF	HB	TBB	IBB	SO	WP	Bk	W	L	Pct	Sh	Sv-Op	Hld	ERC	ERA
2009	Pwtckt*	AAA	2	2	0	0	9.1	37	5	3	3	1	0	0	2	2	0	7	0	1	1	1	.500	0	0--	-	1.85	2.89
1992	Pit	NL	13	13	4	0	92.0	373	76	26	22	3	6	4	1	35	1	51	3	1	8	1	.889	1	0-0	0	2.72	2.15
1993	Pit	NL	24	20	3	1	128.1	595	145	83	80	14	7	5	9	75	2	59	6	0	6	11	.353	2	0-0	0	5.97	5.61
1995	Bos	AL	27	27	6	0	195.1	804	163	76	64	22	3	7	9	68	0	119	11	0	16	8	.667	1	0-0	0	3.28	2.95
1996	Bos	AL	32	32	6	0	211.2	963	238	151	121	38	1	9	12	90	0	140	4	1	14	13	.519	0	0-0	0	5.68	5.14
1997	Bos	AL	35	29	4	2	201.1	866	193	109	95	24	3	7	16	87	5	151	6	0	12	15	.444	2	0-0	1	4.47	4.25
1998	Bos	AL	36	33	2	1	216.0	939	211	123	110	30	1	8	14	79	1	146	6	1	17	8	.680	0	0-0	0	4.30	4.58
1999	Bos	AL	49	17	0	28	140.0	635	146	93	79	19	1	8	5	72	2	104	1	0	6	11	.353	0	15-18	5	5.12	5.08
2000	Bos	AL	51	17	0	13	159.1	706	170	107	97	31	4	8	4	65	3	102	4	0	6	10	.375	0	0-1	3	5.23	5.48
2001	Bos	AL	45	17	0	5	168.2	732	156	84	73	13	3	9	18	73	5	148	5	1	9	12	.429	0	3-5	3	4.02	3.90
2002	Bos	AL	45	15	0	10	163.1	657	121	57	51	15	1	4	9	51	2	134	5	2	11	5	.688	0	3-5	5	2.54	2.81
2003	Bos	AL	35	33	0	2	202.1	872	193	106	92	23	2	4	12	71	0	169	8	0	11	7	.611	0	1-1	0	3.92	4.09
2004	Bos	AL	32	30	0	0	188.1	831	197	121	102	29	2	4	16	63	3	116	9	0	12	10	.545	0	0-0	1	4.73	4.87
2005	Bos	AL	33	33	3	0	225.1	943	210	113	104	35	1	6	11	68	4	151	8	0	16	12	.571	0	0-0	0	3.87	4.15
2006	Bos	AL	23	23	1	0	140.0	610	135	80	72	19	1	3	10	51	0	90	6	0	7	11	.389	0	0-0	0	4.22	4.63
2007	Bos	AL	31	31	0	0	189.0	800	191	104	100	22	2	6	4	64	1	110	10	0	17	12	.586	0	0-0	0	4.14	4.76
2008	Bos	AL	30	30	1	0	181.0	754	154	89	83	25	2	4	13	60	0	117	12	0	10	11	.476	0	0-0	0	3.54	4.13
2009	Bos	AL	21	21	2	0	129.2	572	137	67	66	12	4	1	10	50	0	72	4	0	11	5	.688	0	0-0	0	4.60	4.58
Postseason			18	11	2	2	72.0	329	68	56	54	13	1	3	9	38	2	54	1	0	5	7	.417	0	0-0	0	5.25	6.75
17 ML YEARS			562	421	32	62	2931.2	12652	2836	1589	1411	374	44	97	173	1122	29	1979	108	6	189	162	.538	6	22-30	13	4.24	4.33

Jamie Walker

Pitches: L Bats: L Pos: RP-22   Ht: 6'2" Wt: 194 Born: 7/1/1971 Age: 38

Year	Team	Lg	G	GS	CG	GF	IP	BFP	H	R	ER	HR	SH	SF	HB	TBB	IBB	SO	WP	Bk	W	L	Pct	Sh	Sv-Op	Hld	ERC	ERA
1997	KC	AL	50	0	0	15	43.0	197	46	28	26	6	2	2	3	20	3	24	2	0	3	3	.500	0	0-1	3	5.10	5.44
1998	KC	AL	6	2	0	0	17.1	86	30	20	19	5	1	1	4	3	0	15	0	0	0	1	.000	0	0-0	1	9.69	9.87
2002	Det	AL	57	0	0	16	43.2	175	32	19	18	9	0	1	4	9	1	40	1	1	1	1	.500	0	1-4	5	2.86	3.71
2003	Det	AL	78	0	0	19	65.0	273	61	30	24	9	5	2	2	17	1	45	1	0	4	3	.571	0	3-7	12	3.51	3.32
2004	Det	AL	70	0	0	18	64.2	277	69	28	23	8	1	1	1	12	3	53	4	0	3	4	.429	0	1-7	18	3.65	3.20
2005	Det	AL	66	0	0	11	48.2	208	49	22	20	5	1	1	2	13	3	30	0	0	4	3	.571	0	0-2	14	3.63	3.70
2006	Det	AL	56	0	0	14	48.0	196	47	15	15	8	1	0	0	8	3	37	1	0	0	1	.000	0	0-0	11	3.38	2.81
2007	Bal	AL	81	0	0	19	61.1	258	57	25	22	6	0	5	2	17	4	41	3	0	3	2	.600	0	7-13	21	3.19	3.23
2008	Bal	AL	59	0	0	11	38.0	178	53	31	29	12	1	2	1	11	3	24	2	0	1	3	.250	0	0-4	9	7.53	6.87
2009	Bal	AL	22	0	0	2	12.1	55	19	8	7	5	1	2	1	0	0	9	1	1	0	0	-	0	0-1	2	8.46	5.11
Postseason			5	0	0	3	4.1	16	3	2	2	2	0	0	0	1	0	3	1	0	1	0	1.000	0	0-0	0	4.01	4.15
10 ML YEARS			545	2	0	127	442.0	1903	463	226	203	73	13	17	18	110	21	318	15	2	19	21	.475	0	12-39	96	4.22	4.13

Neil Walker

Bats: B Throws: R Pos: 3B-9; PH-8   Ht: 6'3" Wt: 215 Born: 9/10/1985 Age: 24

Year	Team	Lg	G	AB	H	2B	3B	HR	(Hm	Rd)	TB	R	RBI	RC	TBB	IBB	SO	HBP	SH	SF	SB	CS	SB%	GDP	Avg	OBP	Slg
2004	Pirates	R	52	192	52	12	3	4	(-	-)	82	28	20	26	10	2	33	3	0	3	3	1	.75	2	.271	.313	.427
2004	Wmspt	A-	8	32	10	3	0	0	(-	-)	13	2	7	4	2	0	1	0	0	1	1	2	.33	0	.313	.343	.406
2005	Hkry	A	120	485	146	33	2	12	(-	-)	219	78	68	74	20	2	71	6	0	7	7	4	.64	10	.301	.332	.452
2005	Lynbrg	A+	9	42	11	2	1	0	(-	-)	15	4	12	3	0	0	12	0	0	0	0	0	-	0	.262	.244	.357
2006	Lynbrg	A+	72	264	75	22	1	3	(-	-)	108	32	35	37	19	1	41	6	4	1	3	5	.38	6	.284	.345	.409
2006	Altna	AA	10	31	5	0	0	2	(-	-)	11	5	3	1	1	0	4	0	0	0	0	0	-	1	.161	.188	.355
2007	Altna	AA	117	431	124	30	3	13	(-	-)	199	77	66	75	53	3	73	0	1	5	9	4	.69	6	.288	.362	.462
2007	Indy	AAA	19	64	13	3	0	0	(-	-)	16	7	0	3	2	0	13	3	0	0	1	1	.50	2	.203	.261	.250

BATTING																					BASERUNNING				AVERAGES		
Year	Team	Lg	G	AB	H	2B	3B	HR	(Hm Rd)	TB	R	RDI	RC	TBB	IBB	SO	HBP	SH	SF	SB	CS	SB%	GDP	Avg	OBP	Slg
2008	Indy	AAA	133	505	122	25	7	16	(- -)	209	69	80	61	29	0	102	2	4	10	10	6	.63	11	.242	.280	.414
2009	Pirates	R	8	30	5	2	0	1	(- -)	10	2	1	1	1	0	5	1	0	0	0	1	.00	0	.167	.219	.333
2009	Indy	AAA	95	356	94	31	2	14	(- -)	171	38	69	55	26	1	60	1	1	6	5	2	.71	13	.264	.311	.480
2009	Pit	NL	17	36	7	1	0	0	(0 0)	8	5	0	2	4	0	11	0	0	0	1	0	1.00	1	.194	.275	.222

Tyler Walker

Pitches: R Bats: R Pos: RP-32   Ht: 6'3" Wt: 262 Born: 5/15/1976 Age: 34

			HOW MUCH HE PITCHED					WHAT HE GAVE UP										THE RESULTS						
Year	Team	Lg	G	GS	CG	GF	IP	BFP	H	R	ER	HR	SH	SF	HB	TBB	IBB	SO	WP	Bk	W	L	Pct	Sh	Sv-Op Hld	ERC	ERA
2009	LV*	AAA	15	0	0	7	19.1	70	8	4	3	1	0	2	1	3	0	20	1	0	2	1	.667	0	3- -	0.82	1.40
2002	NYM	NL	5	1	0	3	10.2	49	11	7	7	3	0	0	0	5	1	7	0	0	1	0	1.000	0	0-0	0	5.46	5.91
2004	SF	NL	52	0	0	13	63.2	275	69	31	30	8	3	7	1	24	1	48	1	0	5	1	.833	0	1-1	5	4.76	4.24
2005	SF	NL	67	0	0	39	61.2	279	68	31	29	9	5	1	3	27	6	54	4	0	6	4	.600	0	23-28	2	5.15	4.23
2006	2 Tms		26	0	0	17	25.1	111	27	20	20	1	1	0	0	12	0	19	1	0	1	4	.200	0	10-14	1	4.35	7.11
2007	SF	NL	15	0	0	1	14.1	53	12	2	2	0	0	1	0	4	1	9	0	0	2	0	1.000	0	0-1	7	2.30	1.26
2008	SF	NL	65	0	0	19	53.1	226	47	29	27	7	2	1	1	21	3	49	5	0	5	8	.385	0	0-4	19	3.57	4.56
2009	Phi	NL	32	0	0	10	35.1	150	31	12	12	4	1	2	3	9	1	27	2	0	2	1	.667	0	0-0	1	3.13	3.06
06	SF	NL	6	0	0	1	5.1	28	9	9	9	1	0	0	0	5	0	3	1	0	0	1	.000	0	0-2	1	12.35	15.19
06	TB	AL	20	0	0	16	20.0	83	18	11	11	0	1	0	0	7	0	16	0	0	1	3	.250	0	10-12	0	2.70	4.95
7 ML YEARS			262	1	0	102	264.1	1143	265	132	127	32	12	12	8	102	13	213	13	0	22	18	.550	0	34-48	35	4.23	4.32

P.J. Walters

Pitches: R Bats: R Pos: RP-7, SP-1   Ht: 6'4" Wt: 200 Born: 3/12/1985 Age: 25

			HOW MUCH HE PITCHED					WHAT HE GAVE UP										THE RESULTS						
Year	Team	Lg	G	GS	CG	GF	IP	BFP	H	R	ER	HR	SH	SF	HB	TBB	IBB	SO	WP	Bk	W	L	Pct	Sh	Sv-Op Hld	ERC	ERA
2006	StCol	A-	26	0	0	19	30.1	131	29	15	12	1	0	0	2	9	0	31	2	0	2	1	.667	0	8	2.15	2.66
2007	QuadC	A	17	10	0	4	68.2	282	59	25	20	2	1	2	9	12	0	73	4	0	6	1	.857	0	1- -	2.51	2.62
2007	PlmBh	A+	5	5	0	0	33.2	138	29	10	10	2	2	0	1	6	0	37	1	0	3	1	.750	0	0- -	2.31	2.67
2007	Sprgfld	AA	8	8	1	0	49.1	200	42	13	13	4	3	0	4	15	0	37	3	0	3	4	.429	0	0- -	3.08	2.37
2008	Sprgfld	AA	6	6	0	0	36.0	150	35	17	13	5	0	0	3	8	0	34	2	0	1	2	.333	0	0- -	3.85	3.25
2008	Memp	AAA	23	23	0	0	122.0	547	123	71	66	17	7	7	8	62	2	122	11	1	9	4	.692	0	0	5.09	4.87
2009	Memp	AAA	21	20	2	0	121.0	539	128	73	61	6	9	2	10	44	1	113	10	0	8	10	.444	0	0- -	4.14	4.54
2009	StL	NL	8	1	0	4	16.0	80	21	19	17	6	1	1	0	9	1	14	0	0	0	0	-	0	0-0	8.42	9.56

Chien-Ming Wang

Pitches: R Bats: R Pos: SP-9; RP-3   Ht: 6'3" Wt: 230 Born: 3/31/1980 Age: 30

			HOW MUCH HE PITCHED					WHAT HE GAVE UP										THE RESULTS						
Year	Team	Lg	G	GS	CG	GF	IP	BFP	H	R	ER	HR	SH	SF	HB	TBB	IBB	SO	WP	Bk	W	L	Pct	Sh	Sv-Op Hld	ERC	ERA
2009	S-WB*	AAA	2	2	1	0	13.0	47	7	0	0	0	0	0	0	3	0	7	0	0	1	0	1.000	1	0- -	1.05	0.00
2005	NYY	AL	18	17	0	0	116.1	486	113	58	52	9	3	4	6	32	3	47	3	0	8	5	.615	0	0-0	0	3.47	4.02
2006	NYY	AL	34	33	2	1	218.0	900	233	92	88	12	3	2	2	52	4	76	6	1	19	6	.760	1	1-1	0	3.62	3.63
2007	NYY	AL	30	30	1	0	199.1	823	199	84	82	9	2	3	8	59	1	104	9	1	19	7	.731	0	0-0	0	3.54	3.70
2008	NYY	AL	15	15	1	0	95.0	402	90	44	43	4	0	3	3	35	1	54	0	0	8	2	.800	0	0-0	0	3.39	4.07
2009	NYY	AL	12	9	0	2	42.0	206	66	46	45	7	3	1	2	19	1	29	3	0	1	6	.143	0	0-0	0	8.67	9.64
	Postseason		4	4	0	0	10.0	90	28	19	16	5	2	0	3	5	0	7	0	0	1	3	.250	0	0-0	0	8.53	7.58
5 ML YEARS			109	104	4	3	670.2	2817	701	324	310	41	11	13	21	197	10	310	21	2	55	26	.679	1	1-1	0	3.82	4.16

Jarrod Washburn

Pitches: L Bats: L Pos: SP-28   Ht: 6'1" Wt: 195 Born: 8/13/1974 Age: 35

			HOW MUCH HE PITCHED					WHAT HE GAVE UP										THE RESULTS						
Year	Team	Lg	G	GS	CG	GF	IP	BFP	H	R	ER	HR	SH	SF	HB	TBB	IBB	SO	WP	Bk	W	L	Pct	Sh	Sv-Op Hld	ERC	ERA
1998	LAA	AL	15	11	0	0	74.0	317	70	40	38	11	2	3	3	27	1	48	0	0	6	3	.667	0	0-0	1	4.09	4.62
1999	LAA	AL	16	10	0	3	61.2	264	61	36	36	6	1	2	1	26	0	39	2	0	4	5	.444	0	0-0	1	4.20	5.25
2000	LAA	AL	14	14	0	0	84.1	340	64	38	35	16	1	3	1	37	0	49	1	0	7	2	.778	0	0-0	0	3.66	3.74
2001	LAA	AL	30	30	1	0	193.1	813	196	89	81	25	4	4	7	54	4	126	3	0	11	10	.524	0	0-0	0	4.03	3.77
2002	LAA	AL	32	32	1	0	206.0	852	183	75	72	19	4	7	3	59	1	139	5	1	18	6	.750	0	0-0	0	3.02	3.15
2003	LAA	AL	32	32	2	0	207.1	876	205	106	102	34	5	6	11	54	4	118	4	1	10	15	.400	0	0-0	0	4.07	4.43
2004	LAA	AL	25	25	1	0	149.1	640	159	81	77	20	2	4	4	40	1	86	5	0	11	8	.579	1	0-0	0	4.23	4.64
2005	LAA	AL	29	29	1	0	177.1	740	184	66	63	19	4	6	8	51	0	94	2	0	8	8	.500	1	0-0	0	4.19	3.20
2006	Sea	AL	31	31	0	0	187.0	809	198	103	97	25	3	6	7	55	2	103	3	0	8	14	.364	0	0-0	0	4.33	4.67
2007	Sea	AL	32	32	1	0	193.2	839	201	102	93	23	9	6	8	67	5	114	2	1	10	15	.400	1	0-0	0	4.33	4.32
2008	Sea	AL	28	26	1	1	153.2	675	174	87	80	19	6	4	5	50	2	87	2	0	5	14	.263	0	1-1	0	4.88	4.69
2009	2 Tms	AL	28	28	1	0	176.0	724	160	77	74	23	8	4	5	49	1	100	1	0	9	9	.500	1	0-0	0	3.44	3.78
09	Sea	AL	20	20	1	0	133.0	531	109	42	39	11	5	2	3	33	1	79	1	0	8	6	.571	1	0-0	0	2.55	2.64
09	Det	AL	8	8	0	0	43.0	193	51	35	35	12	3	2	2	16	0	21	0	0	1	3	.250	0	0-0	0	6.65	7.33
	Postseason		8	7	0	1	36.2	164	40	26	20	8	3	3	2	14	2	21	0	0	1	3	.250	0	0-0	0	5.48	4.91
12 ML YEARS			312	300	9	4	1863.2	7889	1855	900	848	240	49	56	65	569	21	1103	30	3	107	109	.495	4	1-1	2	4.01	4.10

Chris Waters

Pitches: L **Bats:** L **Pos:** RP-4; SP-1   **Ht:** 6'0" **Wt:** 170 **Born:** 8/17/1980 **Age:** 29

Year	Team	Lg	G	GS	CG	GF	IP	BFP	H	R	ER	HR	SH	SF	HB	TBB	IBB	SO	WP	Bk	W	L	Pct	Sh	Sv-Op	Hld	ERC	ERA
2000	Danvle	R+	13	13	1	0	69.0	286	64	33	30	4	2	2	2	29	0	73	6	0	5	3	.625	0	0- -	-	3.71	3.91
2001	Macon	A	25	24	3	0	147.2	616	131	71	55	14	4	4	7	52	0	78	8	2	8	6	.571	1	0- -	-	3.45	3.35
2002	MrtlBh	A+	28	28	2	0	182.2	752	154	63	56	12	7	7	24	43	0	103	12	0	13	7	.650	1	0- -	-	2.90	2.76
2003	MrtlBh	A+	2	2	0	0	9.1	43	7	7	3	0	1	3	1	6	0	6	3	0	1	1	.500	0	0- -	-	3.13	2.89
2003	Grnville	AA	17	17	0	0	85.2	381	104	53	42	11	7	6	1	26	1	54	2	1	3	8	.273	0	0- -	-	5.13	4.41
2004	MrtlBh	A+	4	1	0	0	7.1	39	14	10	10	0	0	0	0	4	0	5	1	0	0	1	.000	0	0- -	-	9.57	12.27
2005	MrtlBh	A+	17	17	1	0	103.1	434	106	54	49	10	1	5	4	31	0	67	0	0	4	5	.444	0	0- -	-	4.04	4.27
2006	Missi	AA	27	27	0	0	155.0	673	152	90	83	24	9	6	2	79	1	117	5	2	8	14	.364	0	0- -	-	4.93	4.82
2007	Bowie	AA	27	27	0	0	152.1	673	144	83	76	17	4	2	6	86	3	117	12	2	8	9	.471	0	0- -	-	4.67	4.49
2007	Norfolk	AAA	1	1	0	0	6.0	28	9	2	2	0	0	0	0	3	0	3	0	0	0	0	-	0	0- -	-	6.98	3.00
2008	Bowie	AA	6	6	0	0	32.0	120	20	6	6	2	0	0	0	8	0	22	2	0	5	0	1.000	0	0- -	-	1.56	1.69
2008	Norfolk	AAA	18	16	1	1	90.0	406	97	62	57	10	4	4	7	43	1	72	4	1	3	6	.333	0	0- -	-	5.24	5.70
2009	Norfolk	AAA	29	20	0	2	114.1	504	114	66	57	12	3	4	9	47	1	71	7	1	9	7	.563	0	0- -	-	4.42	4.49
2008	Bal	AL	11	11	1	0	64.2	291	70	38	36	9	0	3	3	29	0	33	1	1	3	5	.375	1	0-0	0	5.20	5.01
2009	Bal	AL	5	1	0	0	11.2	49	9	7	7	3	0	0	0	5	0	5	0	0	1	0	1.000	0	0-0	0	3.89	5.40
2 ML YEARS			16	12	1	0	76.1	340	79	45	43	12	0	3	3	34	0	38	1	1	4	5	.444	1	0-0	0	5.00	5.07

David Weathers

Pitches: R **Bats:** R **Pos:** RP-68   **Ht:** 6'3" **Wt:** 238 **Born:** 9/25/1969 **Age:** 40

Year	Team	Lg	G	GS	CG	GF	IP	BFP	H	R	ER	HR	SH	SF	HB	TBB	IBB	SO	WP	Bk	W	L	Pct	Sh	Sv-Op	Hld	ERC	ERA
1991	Tor	AL	15	0	0	4	14.2	79	15	9	8	1	2	1	2	17	3	13	0	0	1	0	1.000	0	0-0	1	6.88	4.91
1992	Tor	AL	2	0	0	0	3.1	15	5	3	3	1	0	0	0	2	0	3	0	0	0	0	-	0	0-0	0	10.97	8.10
1993	Fla	NL	14	6	0	2	45.2	202	57	26	26	3	2	0	1	13	1	34	6	0	2	3	.400	0	0-0	0	4.86	5.12
1994	Fla	NL	24	24	0	0	135.0	621	166	87	79	13	12	4	4	59	9	72	7	1	8	12	.400	0	0-0	0	5.52	5.27
1995	Fla	NL	28	15	0	0	90.1	419	104	68	60	8	7	3	5	52	3	60	3	0	4	5	.444	0	0-0	1	5.79	5.98
1996	2 Tms		42	12	0	9	88.2	409	108	60	54	8	5	2	6	42	5	53	3	0	2	4	.333	0	0-0	3	5.80	5.48
1997	2 Tms	AL	19	1	0	5	25.2	126	38	24	24	3	2	1	1	15	0	18	3	0	1	3	.250	0	0-1	0	8.27	8.42
1998	2 Tms	NL	44	9	0	9	110.0	492	130	69	60	6	6	2	3	41	3	94	7	2	6	5	.545	0	0-1	3	4.73	4.91
1999	Mil	NL	63	0	0	14	93.0	414	102	49	48	14	4	4	2	38	3	74	1	1	7	4	.636	0	2-6	9	5.04	4.65
2000	Mil	NL	69	0	0	23	76.1	320	73	29	26	7	4	1	2	32	8	50	0	0	3	5	.375	0	1-7	14	3.90	3.07
2001	2 Tms	NL	80	0	0	25	86.0	351	65	24	23	6	10	3	3	34	8	66	0	0	4	5	.444	0	4-10	16	2.59	2.41
2002	NYM	NL	71	0	0	12	77.1	331	69	30	25	6	6	4	3	36	7	61	2	0	6	3	.667	0	0-5	18	3.60	2.91
2003	NYM	NL	77	0	0	20	87.2	384	87	33	30	6	8	0	6	40	6	75	1	0	1	6	.143	0	7-9	26	4.21	3.08
2004	3 Tms	NL	66	2	0	20	82.1	357	85	44	38	12	5	2	5	35	2	61	1	1	7	7	.500	0	0-4	12	5.01	4.15
2005	Cin	NL	73	0	0	41	77.2	331	71	36	34	7	4	2	2	29	2	61	4	0	7	4	.636	0	15-19	8	3.46	3.94
2006	Cin	NL	67	0	0	32	73.2	314	61	31	29	12	5	3	2	34	4	50	0	0	4	4	.500	0	12-19	9	3.79	3.54
2007	Cin	NL	70	0	0	60	77.2	328	67	33	31	4	5	4	5	27	4	48	1	0	2	6	.250	0	33-39	0	2.95	3.59
2008	Cin	NL	72	0	0	17	69.1	311	76	27	25	6	2	1	3	30	8	46	1	1	4	6	.400	0	0-4	19	4.61	3.25
2009	2 Tms	NL	68	0	0	11	62.0	267	53	29	27	10	6	3	2	28	2	37	1	0	4	6	.400	0	1-5	21	3.92	3.92
96	Fla	NL	31	8	0	8	71.1	319	85	41	36	7	5	1	4	28	4	40	2	0	2	2	.500	0	0-0	3	5.35	4.54
96	NYY	AL	11	4	0	1	17.1	90	23	19	18	1	0	1	2	14	1	13	1	0	0	2	.000	0	0-0	0	7.66	9.35
97	NYY	AL	10	0	0	3	9.0	47	15	10	10	1	0	0	0	7	0	4	2	0	0	1	.000	0	0-1	0	10.26	10.00
97	Cle	AL	9	1	0	2	16.2	79	23	14	14	2	2	1	1	8	0	14	1	0	1	2	.333	0	0-0	0	7.23	7.56
98	Cin	NL	16	9	0	0	62.1	294	86	47	43	3	4	1	1	27	2	51	5	1	2	4	.333	0	0-0	0	6.04	6.21
98	Mil	NL	28	0	0	9	47.2	198	44	22	17	3	2	1	2	14	1	43	2	1	4	1	.800	0	0-1	3	3.15	3.21
01	Mil	NL	52	0	0	21	57.2	233	37	14	13	3	8	1	2	25	7	46	0	0	3	4	.429	0	4-7	10	2.01	2.03
01	ChC	NL	28	0	0	4	28.1	118	28	10	10	3	2	2	1	9	1	20	0	0	1	1	.500	0	0-3	6	3.90	3.18
04	NYM	NL	32	0	0	10	33.2	156	41	19	16	5	2	2	2	15	0	25	1	1	5	3	.625	0	0-1	6	6.15	4.28
04	Hou	NL	26	0	0	9	32.0	137	31	20	17	5	2	0	3	13	1	26	0	0	1	4	.200	0	0-3	5	4.77	4.78
04	Fla	NL	8	2	0	1	16.2	64	13	5	5	2	1	0	0	7	1	10	0	0	1	0	1.000	0	0-0	1	3.28	2.70
09	Cin	NL	43	0	0	7	38.0	160	27	14	14	7	5	2	0	17	1	27	1	0	3	3	.500	0	1-4	13	3.10	3.32
09	Mil	NL	25	0	0	4	24.0	107	26	15	13	3	1	1	2	11	1	10	0	0	1	3	.250	0	0-1	8	5.33	4.88
Postseason			7	0	0	2	11.0	41	6	1	1	0	1	1	0	3	1	8	0	1	2	0	1.000	0	0-0	1	1.05	0.82
19 ML YEARS			964	69	0	304	1376.1	6071	1432	711	650	133	95	40	57	604	78	976	41	6	73	88	.453	0	75-129	160	4.51	4.25

Jeff Weaver

Pitches: R **Bats:** R **Pos:** RP-21; SP-7   **Ht:** 6'5" **Wt:** 200 **Born:** 8/22/1976 **Age:** 33

Year	Team	Lg	G	GS	CG	GF	IP	BFP	H	R	ER	HR	SH	SF	HB	TBB	IBB	SO	WP	Bk	W	L	Pct	Sh	Sv-Op	Hld	ERC	ERA
2009	Albq*	AAA	5	1	0	1	12.2	51	11	6	5	1	0	0	0	2	0	12	0	0	1	0	1.000	0	1- -	-	2.31	3.55
1999	Det	AL	30	29	0	1	163.2	717	176	104	101	27	5	5	17	56	2	114	0	0	9	12	.429	0	0-0	0	5.21	5.55
2000	Det	AL	31	30	2	0	200.0	849	205	102	96	26	3	9	15	52	2	136	3	2	11	15	.423	0	0-0	0	4.18	4.32
2001	Det	AL	33	33	5	0	229.1	985	235	116	104	19	12	7	14	68	4	152	3	0	13	16	.448	0	0-0	0	3.89	4.08
2002	2 Tms	AL	32	25	3	3	199.2	840	193	88	78	16	4	3	11	48	4	132	6	0	11	11	.500	3	2-2	0	3.30	3.52
2003	NYY	AL	32	24	0	3	159.1	735	211	113	106	16	9	9	11	47	2	93	2	0	7	9	.438	0	0-0	1	5.77	5.99
2004	LAD	NL	34	34	0	0	220.0	935	219	103	98	19	5	7	14	60	9	153	9	0	13	13	.500	0	0-0	0	3.79	4.01
2005	LAD	NL	34	34	3	0	224.0	930	220	111	105	35	8	3	18	43	1	157	2	0	14	11	.560	2	0-0	0	3.87	4.22
2006	2 Tms		31	31	0	0	172.0	770	213	117	110	34	7	4	10	47	1	107	5	0	8	14	.364	0	0-0	0	5.90	5.76
2007	Sea	AL	27	27	3	0	146.2	657	190	105	101	23	4	7	8	35	5	80	3	1	7	13	.350	2	0-0	0	5.74	6.20
2009	LAD	NL	28	7	0	5	79.0	355	87	34	32	7	5	2	5	33	9	64	4	0	6	4	.600	0	0-0	0	4.68	3.65
02	Det	AL	17	17	3	0	121.2	509	112	50	43	4	5	2	8	33	1	75	4	0	6	8	.429	3	0-0	0	2.94	3.18
02	NYY	AL	15	8	0	3	78.0	331	81	38	35	12	1	1	3	15	3	57	2	0	5	3	.625	0	2-2	0	3.86	4.04
06	LAA	AL	16	16	0	0	88.2	397	114	68	62	18	2	1	4	21	0	62	4	0	3	10	.231	0	0-0	0	6.03	6.29
06	StL	NL	15	15	0	0	83.1	373	99	49	48	16	5	3	6	26	1	45	1	0	5	4	.556	0	0-0	0	5.78	5.18
Postseason			9	6	0	2	38.0	169	38	18	17	4	3	1	4	14	2	24	1	0	4	3	.429	0	0-0	0	4.24	4.03
10 ML YEARS			312	274	16	12	1793.2	7773	1949	993	931	222	64	56	123	496	39	1188	37	3	99	118	.456	7	2-2	1	4.49	4.67

Jered Weaver

Pitches: R Bats: R Pos: SP-33 Ht: 6'7" Wt: 205 Born: 10/4/1982 Age: 27

				HOW MUCH HE PITCHED				WHAT HE GAVE UP										THE RESULTS						
Year Team	Lg	G	GS	CG	GF	IP	BFP	H	R	ER	HR	SH	SF	HB	TBB	IBB	SO	WP	Bk	W	L	Pct	Sh	Sv-Op	Hld	ERC	ERA
2006 LAA	AL	19	19	0	0	123.0	490	94	36	35	15	2	2	3	33	1	105	2	0	11	2	.846	0	0-0	0	2.57	2.56
2007 LAA	AL	28	28	0	0	161.0	695	178	77	70	17	5	5	2	45	3	115	4	0	13	7	.650	0	0-0	0	4.24	3.91
2008 LAA	AL	30	30	0	0	176.2	745	173	88	85	20	1	4	6	54	4	152	3	0	11	10	.524	0	0-0	0	3.80	4.33
2009 LAA	AL	33	33	4	0	211.0	882	196	91	88	26	6	8	4	66	3	174	3	0	16	8	.667	2	0-0	0	3.56	3.75
Postseason		2	1	0	1	7.0	29	5	2	2	2	0	0	0	4	0	8	0	0	1	1	.500	0	0-0	0	4.51	2.57
4 ML YEARS		110	110	4	0	671.2	2812	641	292	278	78	14	19	15	198	11	546	12	0	51	27	.654	2	0-0	0	3.59	3.73

Brandon Webb

Pitches: R Bats: R Pos: SP-1 Ht: 6'3" Wt: 228 Born: 5/9/1979 Age: 31

				HOW MUCH HE PITCHED				WHAT HE GAVE UP										THE RESULTS						
Year Team	Lg	G	GS	CG	GF	IP	BFP	H	R	ER	HR	SH	SF	HB	TBB	IBB	SO	WP	Bk	W	L	Pct	Sh	Sv-Op	Hld	ERC	ERA
2003 Ari	NL	29	28	1	1	180.2	750	140	65	57	12	9	1	13	68	4	172	9	1	10	9	.526	1	0-0	0	2.80	2.84
2004 Ari	NL	35	35	1	0	208.0	933	194	111	83	17	14	6	11	119	11	164	17	1	7	16	.304	0	0-0	0	4.32	3.59
2005 Ari	NL	33	33	1	0	229.0	943	229	98	90	21	10	7	2	59	4	172	14	1	14	12	.538	0	0-0	0	3.54	3.54
2006 Ari	NL	33	33	5	0	235.0	950	216	91	81	15	10	6	6	50	4	178	5	2	16	8	.667	3	0-0	0	2.81	3.10
2007 Ari	NL	34	34	4	0	236.1	975	209	91	79	12	9	6	5	72	6	194	3	0	18	10	.643	3	0-0	0	2.82	3.01
2008 Ari	NL	34	34	3	0	226.2	944	206	95	83	13	8	9	12	65	5	183	8	1	22	7	.759	1	0-0	0	3.04	3.30
2009 Ari	NL	1	1	0	0	4.0	20	6	6	6	2	0	0	1	2	0	2	0	0	0	0	-	0	0-0	0	12.87	13.50
Postseason		2	2	0	0	13.0	55	11	5	5	0	0	0	1	5	0	13	2	0	1	1	.500	0	0-0	0	2.79	3.46
7 ML YEARS		199	198	15	1	1319.2	5515	1200	557	479	92	60	35	50	435	34	1065	56	6	87	62	.584	8	0-0	0	3.23	3.27

Ryan Webb

Pitches: R Bats: R Pos: RP-28 Ht: 6'6" Wt: 214 Born: 2/5/1986 Age: 24

				HOW MUCH HE PITCHED				WHAT HE GAVE UP										THE RESULTS						
Year Team	Lg	G	GS	CG	GF	IP	BFP	H	R	ER	HR	SH	SF	HB	TBB	IDD	SO	WP	Bk	W	L	Pct	Sh	Sv-Op	Hld	ERC	ERA
2004 As	R	8	7	0	0	20.1	83	18	11	11	2	0	0	3	1	0	23	1	0	1	1	.500	0	0--	-	2.63	4.87
2005 Kane	A	24	23	0	0	128.2	561	139	82	68	16	5	10	9	41	0	84	7	1	5	11	.313	0	0--	-	4.68	4.76
2006 Stcktn	A+	23	23	0	0	117.2	529	160	75	68	9	1	6	4	37	0	96	6	1	8	9	.471	0	0--	-	5.94	5.28
2007 Stcktn	A+	15	15	0	0	83.0	356	83	59	53	13	1	3	5	22	0	71	6	1	4	7	.364	0	0--	-	4.12	6.76
2007 Mdland	AA	5	5	0	0	25.2	118	34	27	26	10	1	2	0	10	0	16	1	0	0	4	.000	0	0--	-	8.33	9.12
2008 Mdland	AA	25	22	0	0	130.0	590	165	86	75	12	3	8	2	44	0	94	3	1	9	8	.529	0	0--	-	5.37	5.19
2009 Scrmto	AAA	32	2	0	8	46.2	206	57	22	22	3	4	0	2	15	2	41	0	1	7	1	.875	0	2--	-	4.94	4.24
2009 Portlnd	AAA	3	0	0	1	3.0	12	3	1	1	0	1	0	0	1	0	0	0	0	0	0	-	0	0--	-	3.35	3.00
2009 SD	NL	28	0	0	9	25.2	117	27	14	11	3	2	1	1	11	1	19	4	0	2	1	.667	0	0-0	6	4.54	3.86

Rickie Weeks

Bats: R Throws: R Pos: 2B-36; PH-1 Ht: 5'10" Wt: 213 Born: 9/13/1982 Age: 27

							BATTING												BASERUNNING				AVERAGES		
Year Team	Lg	G	AB	H	2B	3B	HR	(Hm	Rd)	TB	R	RBI	RC	TBB	IBB	SO	HBP	SH	SF	SB	CS	SB%	GDP	Avg	OBP	Slg
2003 Mil	NL	7	12	2	1	0	0	(0	0)	3	1	0	0	1	0	6	1	0	0	0	0	-	0	.167	.286	.250
2005 Mil	NL	96	360	86	13	2	13	(8	5)	142	56	42	49	40	2	96	11	2	1	15	2	.88	11	.239	.333	.394
2006 Mil	NL	95	359	100	15	3	8	(6	2)	145	73	34	53	30	1	92	19	2	3	19	5	.79	6	.279	.363	.404
2007 Mil	NL	118	409	96	21	6	16	(5	11)	177	87	36	65	78	5	116	14	3	2	25	2	.93	3	.235	.374	.433
2008 Mil	NL	129	475	111	22	7	14	(3	11)	189	89	46	67	66	0	115	14	1	4	19	5	.79	5	.234	.342	.398
2009 Mil	NL	37	147	40	5	2	9	(7	2)	76	28	24	27	12	0	39	3	0	0	2	2	.50	1	.272	.340	.517
Postseason		3	4	0	0	0	0	(0	0)	0	0	0	0	0	0	2	0	0	0	0	0	-	0	.000	.000	.000
6 ML YEARS		482	1762	435	77	20	60	(29	31)	732	334	182	261	227	8	464	62	8	10	80	16	.83	26	.247	.351	.415

Todd Wellemeyer

Pitches: R Bats: R Pos: SP-21; RP-7 Ht: 6'3" Wt: 225 Born: 8/30/1978 Age: 31

				HOW MUCH HE PITCHED				WHAT HE GAVE UP										THE RESULTS						
Year Team	Lg	G	GS	CG	GF	IP	BFP	H	R	ER	HR	SH	SF	HB	TBB	IBB	SO	WP	Bk	W	L	Pct	Sh	Sv-Op	Hld	ERC	ERA
2009 Memp*	AAA	2	2	0	0	2.0	13	4	4	4	1	0	0	0	3	0	4	0	0	0	0	-	0	0--	-	20.26	18.00
2003 ChC	NL	15	0	0	8	27.2	122	25	22	20	5	1	0	0	19	1	30	0	0	1	1	.500	0	1-1	0	5.33	6.51
2004 ChC	NL	20	0	0	7	24.1	119	27	16	16	1	3	2	0	20	2	30	0	1	2	1	.667	0	0-0	0	5.67	5.92
2005 ChC	NL	22	0	0	6	32.1	146	32	23	22	7	2	1	0	22	1	32	3	0	2	1	.667	0	1-1	3	6.29	6.12
2006 2 Tms		46	0	0	10	78.1	345	68	38	36	6	3	6	4	50	3	54	9	0	1	4	.200	0	1-1	3	4.28	4.14
2007 2 Tms		32	11	0	7	79.1	353	77	50	40	11	3	4	3	40	2	60	4	0	3	3	.500	0	0-0	2	4.68	4.54
2008 StL	NL	32	32	0	0	191.2	807	178	84	79	25	6	6	7	62	1	134	7	1	13	9	.591	0	0-0	0	3.72	3.71
2009 StL	NL	28	21	0	4	122.1	561	160	88	80	19	9	4	3	57	2	78	2	0	7	10	.412	0	0-0	0	6.87	5.89
06 Fla	NL	18	0	0	6	21.1	97	20	13	13	1	1	3	2	13	1	17	2	0	0	2	.000	0	0-0	0	4.41	5.48
06 KC	AL	28	0	0	4	57.0	248	48	25	23	5	2	3	2	37	2	37	7	0	1	2	.333	0	1-1	3	4.23	3.63
07 KC	AL	12	0	0	5	15.2	84	25	19	18	4	1	0	1	11	2	9	2	0	0	1	.000	0	0-0	1	10.40	10.34
07 StL	NL	20	11	0	2	63.2	269	52	31	22	7	2	4	2	29	0	51	2	0	3	2	.600	0	0-0	1	3.48	3.11
7 ML YEARS		195	64	0	42	556.0	2453	567	321	293	74	27	23	17	270	12	418	25	2	29	29	.500	0	3-3	9	4.90	4.74

Kip Wells

Pitches: R Bats: R Pos: RP-26; SP-7 — Ht: 6'3" Wt: 205 Born: 4/21/1977 Age: 33

Year	Team	Lg	G	GS	CG	GF	IP	BFP	H	R	ER	HR	SH	SF	HB	TBB	IBB	SO	WP	Bk	W	L	Pct	Sh	Sv-Op	Hld	ERC	ERA
2009	Syrcse*	AAA	2	2	0	0	11.0	42	9	3	3	1	0	0	0	2	0	11	0	0	1	0	1.000	0	0--	-	2.36	2.45
2009	Ptomc*	A+	4	1	0	1	5.0	17	3	1	1	0	0	0	0	1	0	1	0	0	0	0	-	0	0--	-	1.24	1.80
2009	Lsvlle*	AAA	5	1	0	0	14.2	59	12	5	5	2	1	0	0	5	0	16	0	0	1	0	1.000	0	0--	-	3.17	3.07
1999	CWS	AL	7	7	0	0	35.2	153	33	17	16	2	0	2	3	15	0	29	1	2	4	1	.800	0	0-0	0	3.80	4.04
2000	CWS	AL	20	20	0	0	98.2	468	126	76	66	15	1	3	3	58	4	71	7	0	6	9	.400	0	0-0	0	7.07	6.02
2001	CWS	AL	40	20	0	3	133.1	603	145	80	71	14	8	6	12	61	5	99	14	0	10	11	.476	0	0-2	6	5.16	4.79
2002	Pit	NL	33	33	1	0	198.1	845	197	92	79	21	7	5	7	71	11	134	7	0	12	14	.462	1	0-0	0	4.00	3.58
2003	Pit	NL	31	31	1	0	197.1	835	171	77	72	24	15	2	7	76	7	147	7	0	10	9	.526	0	0-0	0	3.49	3.28
2004	Pit	NL	24	24	0	0	138.1	621	145	71	70	14	5	6	6	66	4	116	3	0	5	7	.417	0	0-0	0	4.77	4.55
2005	Pit	NL	33	33	1	0	182.0	828	186	116	103	23	9	10	12	99	8	132	8	0	8	18	.308	1	0-0	0	5.14	5.09
2006	2 Tms		9	9	0	0	44.1	208	61	33	32	3	1	1	4	21	1	20	5	0	2	5	.286	0	0-0	0	6.90	6.50
2007	StL	NL	34	26	0	4	162.2	750	186	116	103	19	8	7	9	78	9	122	8	1	7	17	.292	0	0-0	0	5.44	5.70
2008	2 Tms		25	2	0	8	37.2	176	39	29	26	4	3	0	2	30	2	31	3	0	1	3	.250	0	0-0	1	6.20	6.21
2009	2 Tms	NL	33	7	0	0	72.2	314	60	43	43	6	4	1	5	40	1	43	0	0	2	5	.286	0	2-2	5	3.84	5.33
06	Pit	NL	7	7	0	0	36.1	168	46	27	27	3	1	1	4	18	1	16	5	0	1	5	.167	0	0-0	0	6.51	6.69
06	Tex	AL	2	2	0	0	8.0	40	15	6	5	0	0	0	0	3	0	4	0	0	1	0	1.000	0	0-0	0	8.77	5.63
08	Col	NL	15	2	0	6	27.1	126	29	19	16	3	3	0	1	19	2	22	2	0	1	2	.333	0	0-0	0	5.82	5.27
08	KC	AL	10	0	0	2	10.1	50	10	10	10	1	0	0	1	11	0	9	1	0	0	1	.000	0	0-0	1	7.23	8.71
09	Was	NL	23	0	0	8	26.1	117	23	19	19	1	1	1	0	18	1	18	0	0	0	2	.000	0	2-2	5	3.95	6.49
09	Cin	NL	10	7	0	1	46.1	197	37	24	24	5	3	0	5	22	0	25	0	0	2	3	.400	0	0-0	0	3.77	4.66
11 ML YEARS			289	212	3	24	1301.0	5801	1349	750	681	145	61	43	70	615	52	944	63	3	67	99	.404	2	2-4	12	4.81	4.71

Randy Wells

Pitches: R Bats: R Pos: SP-27 — Ht: 6'3" Wt: 230 Born: 8/28/1982 Age: 27

Year	Team	Lg	G	GS	CG	GF	IP	BFP	H	R	ER	HR	SH	SF	HB	TBB	IBB	SO	WP	Bk	W	L	Pct	Sh	Sv-Op	Hld	ERC	ERA
2003	Lansng	A	1	0	0	1	1.0	3	1	0	0	0	0	0	0	0	0	0	0	0	0	0	-	0	0--	-	2.79	0.00
2003	Cubs	R	3	0	0	0	5.0	25	5	2	2	0	1	0	0	4	0	4	0	0	0	0	-	0	0--	-	4.51	3.60
2004	Lansng	A	36	15	0	4	107.2	466	112	64	53	9	0	4	5	40	1	121	4	1	6	6	.500	0	1--	-	4.28	4.43
2005	Dytona	A+	41	10	0	12	98.2	407	93	33	30	5	3	0	3	22	0	106	5	0	10	2	.833	0	2--	-	2.88	2.74
2005	WTenn	AA	6	0	0	2	8.1	41	12	4	4	0	2	1	0	6	1	4	0	0	0	1	.000	0	1--	-	7.12	4.32
2006	WTenn	AA	12	12	0	0	62.1	247	45	13	11	2	3	2	3	13	1	54	1	0	4	2	.667	0	0--	-	1.71	1.59
2006	Iowa	AAA	13	12	0	0	69.0	314	87	42	38	7	5	3	1	23	1	59	2	0	5	5	.500	0	0--	-	5.30	4.96
2007	Iowa	AAA	40	9	0	6	95.2	425	100	54	48	11	4	2	5	41	0	101	2	1	5	6	.455	0	2--	-	4.75	4.52
2008	Iowa	AAA	27	19	0	1	118.2	513	127	64	53	15	2	3	1	34	1	102	3	0	10	4	.714	0	0--	-	4.17	4.02
2009	Iowa	AAA	5	5	0	0	26.0	101	19	8	8	1	1	0	0	7	0	21	0	0	3	0	1.000	0	0--	-	1.90	2.77
2008	2 Tms		4	0	0	2	5.1	18	0	0	0	0	0	0	0	3	0	1	0	0	0	0	-	0	0-0	0	0.35	0.00
2009	ChC	NL	27	27	0	0	165.1	694	165	67	56	14	7	4	6	46	4	104	3	1	12	10	.545	0	0-0	0	3.62	3.05
08	Tor	AL	1	0	0	1	1.0	4	0	0	0	0	0	0	0	1	0	0	0	0	0	0	-	0	0-0	0	0.95	0.00
08	ChC	NL	3	0	0	1	4.1	14	0	0	0	0	0	0	0	2	0	1	0	0	0	0	-	0	0-0	0	0.25	0.00
2 ML YEARS			31	27	0	2	170.2	712	165	67	56	14	7	4	6	49	4	105	3	1	12	10	.545	0	0-0	0	3.47	2.95

Vernon Wells

Bats: R Throws: R Pos: CF-155; DH-1; PH-1; PR-1 — Ht: 6'1" Wt: 230 Born: 12/8/1978 Age: 31

Year	Team	Lg	G	AB	H	2B	3B	HR	(Hm	Rd)	TB	R	RBI	RC	TBB	IBB	SO	HBP	SH	SF	SB	CS	SB%	GDP	Avg	OBP	Slg
1999	Tor	AL	24	88	23	5	0	1	(1	0)	31	8	8	7	4	0	18	0	0	0	1	1	.50	6	.261	.293	.352
2000	Tor	AL	3	2	0	0	0	0	(0	0)	0	0	0	0	0	0	0	0	0	0	0	0	-	0	.000	.000	.000
2001	Tor	AL	30	96	30	8	0	1	(1	0)	41	14	6	16	5	0	15	1	0	1	5	0	1.00	0	.313	.350	.427
2002	Tor	AL	159	608	167	34	4	23	(10	13)	278	87	100	88	27	0	85	3	2	8	9	4	.69	15	.275	.305	.457
2003	Tor	AL	161	678	215	49	5	33	(13	20)	373	118	117	124	42	2	80	7	0	8	4	1	.80	21	.317	.359	.550
2004	Tor	AL	134	536	146	34	2	23	(14	9)	253	82	67	72	51	2	83	2	0	1	9	2	.82	17	.272	.337	.472
2005	Tor	AL	156	620	167	30	3	28	(14	14)	287	78	97	96	47	3	86	3	0	8	8	3	.73	13	.269	.320	.463
2006	Tor	AL	154	611	185	40	5	32	(24	8)	331	91	106	107	54	0	90	3	0	9	17	4	.81	13	.303	.357	.542
2007	Tor	AL	149	584	143	36	4	16	(8	8)	235	85	80	74	49	4	89	3	0	6	10	4	.71	9	.245	.304	.402
2008	Tor	AL	108	427	128	22	1	20	(11	9)	212	63	78	68	29	5	46	3	0	7	4	2	.67	16	.300	.343	.496
2009	Tor	AL	158	630	164	37	3	15	(8	7)	252	84	66	65	48	2	86	1	0	5	17	4	.81	18	.260	.311	.400
11 ML YEARS			1236	4880	1368	295	27	192	(104	88)	2293	710	725	717	356	18	678	26	2	53	84	25	.77	128	.280	.329	.470

Jayson Werth

Bats: R Throws: R Pos: RF-146; CF-12; PH-4; LF-3 — Ht: 6'5" Wt: 212 Born: 5/20/1979 Age: 31

Year	Team	Lg	G	AB	H	2B	3B	HR	(Hm	Rd)	TB	R	RBI	RC	TBB	IBB	SO	HBP	SH	SF	SB	CS	SB%	GDP	Avg	OBP	Slg
2002	Tor	AL	15	46	12	2	1	0	(0	0)	16	4	6	5	6	0	11	0	0	1	1	0	1.00	4	.261	.340	.348
2003	Tor	AL	26	48	10	4	0	2	(0	2)	20	7	10	6	3	0	22	0	0	0	1	0	1.00	6	.208	.255	.417
2004	LAD	NL	89	290	76	11	3	16	(11	5)	141	56	47	47	30	0	85	4	1	1	4	1	.80	1	.262	.338	.486
2005	LAD	NL	102	337	79	22	2	7	(1	6)	126	46	43	44	48	2	114	6	1	3	11	2	.85	10	.234	.338	.374
2007	Phi	NL	94	255	76	11	3	8	(1	7)	117	43	49	57	44	1	73	2	2	1	7	1	.88	0	.298	.404	.459
2008	Phi	NL	134	418	114	16	3	24	(11	13)	208	73	67	74	57	1	119	4	0	3	20	1	.95	2	.273	.363	.498
2009	Phi	NL	159	571	153	26	1	36	(21	15)	289	98	99	107	91	8	156	8	0	6	20	3	.87	11	.268	.373	.506
Postseason			20	72	21	8	1	4	(2	2)	43	12	7	12	11	0	22	0	0	0	4	0	1.00	1	.292	.386	.597
7 ML YEARS			619	1965	520	92	13	93	(45	48)	917	327	321	340	279	12	580	24	4	15	64	8	.89	28	.265	.360	.467

Sean West

Pitches: L Bats: R Pos: SP-20   Ht: 6'8" Wt: 240 Born: 6/15/1986 Age: 24

Year	Team	Lg	G	GS	CG	GF	IP	BFP	H	R	ER	HR	SH	SF	HB	TBB	IBB	SO	WP	Bk	W	L	Pct	Sh	Sv-Op	Hld	ERC	ERA
2005	Mrlns	R	9	8	0	1	38.1	157	33	12	10	2	0	3	3	7	0	40	2	1	2	3	.400	0	0- -	-	2.48	2.35
2005	Jmstwn	A-	3	3	0	0	11.0	52	17	7	7	1	0	0	3	5	0	14	1	0	0	2	.000	0	0- -	-	7.83	5.73
2006	Grnsbr	A	21	21	0	0	120.1	509	115	55	50	13	4	2	12	40	0	102	0	0	8	5	.615	0	0- -	-	4.09	3.74
2008	Jupiter	A+	21	20	0	1	100.2	426	79	33	27	3	5	3	6	60	1	92	13	0	6	5	.545	0	0- -	-	3.46	2.41
2009	Jaxnvl	AA	12	11	0	0	64.0	287	68	37	34	12	0	2	2	28	2	65	1	0	7	3	.700	0	0- -	-	5.25	4.78
2009	Fla	NL	20	20	0	0	103.1	467	115	62	55	11	5	4	3	44	0	70	3	0	8	6	.571	0	0-0	0	4.93	4.79

Jake Westbrook

Pitches: R Bats: R Pos: P   Ht: 6'3" Wt: 215 Born: 9/29/1977 Age: 32

Year	Team	Lg	G	GS	CG	GF	IP	BFP	H	R	ER	HR	SH	SF	HB	TBB	IBB	SO	WP	Bk	W	L	Pct	Sh	Sv-Op	Hld	ERC	ERA
2009	Akron*	AA	3	3	0	0	9.0	34	8	2	2	1	0	0	0	1	0	6	2	0	0	1	.000	0	0- -	-	2.60	2.00
2000	NYY	AL	3	2	0	1	6.2	38	15	10	10	1	0	2	0	4	1	1	0	0	0	2	.000	0	0-0	0	13.53	13.50
2001	Cle	AL	23	6	0	3	64.2	290	79	43	42	6	1	5	4	22	4	48	4	0	4	4	.500	0	0-0	5	5.25	5.85
2002	Cle	AL	11	4	0	1	41.2	185	50	30	27	6	2	1	1	12	1	20	1	0	1	3	.250	0	0-2	1	5.12	5.83
2003	Cle	AL	34	22	1	4	133.0	580	142	70	64	9	4	3	12	56	1	58	3	0	7	10	.412	0	0-0	1	4.78	4.33
2004	Cle	AL	33	30	5	2	215.2	895	208	95	81	19	6	6	5	61	3	116	4	1	14	9	.609	1	0-0	0	3.45	3.38
2005	Cle	AL	34	34	2	0	210.2	895	218	121	105	19	5	4	7	56	3	119	3	0	15	15	.500	0	0-0	0	3.78	4.49
2006	Cle	AL	32	32	3	0	211.1	904	247	106	98	15	5	4	4	55	4	109	5	0	15	10	.600	2	0-0	0	4.39	4.17
2007	Cle	AL	25	25	0	0	152.0	648	159	78	73	13	6	4	6	55	5	93	3	0	6	9	.400	0	0-0	0	4.28	4.32
2008	Clo	AL	5	5	1	0	34.2	139	33	13	12	5	0	2	1	7	0	19	1	0	1	2	.333	0	0-0	0	3.54	3.12
	Postseason		3	3	0	0	17.2	74	25	11	11	2	0	1	0	4	1	8	0	0	1	2	.333	0	0-0	0	6.33	5.60
9 ML YEARS			200	160	12	11	1070.1	4574	1161	566	512	93	29	31	40	328	22	583	24	1	63	64	.496	3	0-2	7	4.21	4.31

Dan Wheeler

Pitches: R Bats: R Pos: RP-69   Ht: 6'3" Wt: 220 Born: 12/10/1977 Age: 32

Year	Team	Lg	G	GS	CG	GF	IP	BFP	H	R	ER	HR	SH	SF	HB	TBB	IBB	SO	WP	Bk	W	L	Pct	Sh	Sv-Op	Hld	ERC	ERA
1999	TB	AL	6	6	0	0	30.2	136	35	20	20	7	1	0	0	13	1	32	1	0	0	4	.000	0	0-0	0	5.96	5.87
2000	TB	AL	11	2	0	6	23.0	111	29	14	14	2	1	1	2	11	2	17	2	0	1	1	.500	0	0-1	1	5.87	5.48
2001	TB	AL	13	0	0	3	17.2	87	30	17	17	3	0	2	0	5	0	12	1	1	1	0	1.000	0	0-0	0	8.38	8.66
2003	NYM	NL	35	0	0	10	51.0	215	49	23	21	6	0	3	1	17	4	35	1	0	1	3	.250	0	2-3	0	3.69	3.71
2004	2 Tms	NL	46	1	0	11	65.0	287	76	33	31	10	2	1	1	20	2	55	4	1	3	1	.750	0	0-0	5	5.05	4.29
2005	Hou	NL	71	0	0	20	73.1	288	53	18	18	7	5	1	3	19	3	69	0	0	2	3	.400	0	3-5	17	2.22	2.21
2006	Hou	NL	75	0	0	25	71.1	295	58	22	20	5	3	3	2	24	8	68	0	0	3	5	.375	0	9-12	24	2.57	2.52
2007	2 Tms	NL	70	0	0	29	74.2	321	74	48	44	11	3	3	3	23	3	82	2	0	1	9	.100	0	11-18	18	4.04	5.30
2008	TB	AL	70	0	0	26	66.1	264	44	25	23	10	0	2	0	22	4	53	1	0	5	6	.455	0	13-18	26	2.28	3.12
2009	TB	AL	69	0	0	20	57.2	219	41	22	21	11	3	1	0	9	2	45	3	0	4	5	.444	0	2-6	16	2.17	3.28
04	NYM	NL	32	1	0	7	50.2	232	65	29	27	9	2	1	0	17	2	46	4	1	3	1	.750	0	0-0	3	5.91	4.80
04	NYM	NL	14	0	0	4	14.1	55	11	4	4	1	0	0	1	3	0	9	0	0	0	0	-	0	0-0	2	2.35	2.51
07	Hou	NL	45	0	0	25	49.2	205	46	28	28	8	1	1	2	13	1	56	1	0	1	4	.200	0	11-15	6	3.69	5.07
07	TB	AL	25	0	0	4	25.0	116	28	20	16	3	2	2	1	10	2	26	1	0	0	5	.000	0	0-3	12	4.72	5.76
	Postseason		20	0	0	5	25.2	108	21	10	10	3	1	0	3	8	1	26	1	0	1	0	1.000	0	1-3	5	3.22	3.51
10 ML YEARS			466	9	0	150	530.2	2223	489	242	229	72	18	17	12	163	29	468	15	2	21	37	.362	0	40-63	107	3.51	3.88

Wes Whisler

Pitches: L Bats: L Pos: RP-3   Ht: 6'5" Wt: 240 Born: 4/7/1983 Age: 27

Year	Team	Lg	G	GS	CG	GF	IP	BFP	H	R	ER	HR	SH	SF	HB	TBB	IBB	SO	WP	Bk	W	L	Pct	Sh	Sv-Op	Hld	ERC	ERA
2004	Knapol	A	10	7	0	0	45.1	199	52	29	17	2	1	7	2	11	0	28	4	0	4	1	.800	0	0- -	-	4.00	3.38
2004	WinSa	A+	5	5	0	0	26.2	102	17	10	10	3	2	0	0	7	0	13	0	0	2	1	.667	0	0- -	-	1.84	3.38
2005	WinSa	A+	26	21	1	2	112.1	523	153	93	84	10	2	2	6	42	0	79	6	0	4	9	.308	0	1- -	-	6.28	6.73
2006	WinSa	A+	20	20	1	0	118.1	507	112	52	39	0	3	3	9	44	0	57	4	0	10	7	.588	1	0- -	-	3.27	2.97
2006	Brham	AA	7	7	0	0	44.2	195	50	28	22	5	1	1	2	15	0	28	1	0	2	3	.400	0	0- -	-	4.81	4.43
2007	Brham	AA	28	27	0	0	156.2	700	195	107	87	10	6	6	6	42	0	74	6	1	6	13	.316	0	0- -	-	4.81	5.00
2008	Charltt	AAA	27	27	1	0	156.0	682	175	86	66	12	7	1	6	45	0	71	2	0	12	10	.545	0	0- -	-	4.28	3.81
2009	Charltt	AAA	26	26	1	0	152.2	664	166	83	69	10	3	5	3	56	4	77	4	0	10	12	.455	1	0- -	-	4.25	4.07
2009	CWS	AL	3	0	0	2	1.1	7	0	2	2	0	0	0	0	3	0	2	1	0	0	0	-	0	0-0	0	4.30	13.50

Sean White

Pitches: R Bats: R Pos: RP-52   Ht: 6'4" Wt: 210 Born: 4/25/1981 Age: 29

Year	Team	Lg	G	GS	CG	GF	IP	BFP	H	R	ER	HR	SH	SF	HB	TBB	IBB	SO	WP	Bk	W	L	Pct	Sh	Sv-Op	Hld	ERC	ERA
2003	Danvle	R	14	10	0	2	51.1	219	53	22	17	1	1	0	5	16	0	32	4	0	3	3	.500	0	1- -	-	3.79	2.98
2004	Rome	A	13	1	0	4	36.1	160	42	30	26	4	1	2	0	12	0	20	1	0	3	2	.600	0	1- -	-	4.74	6.44
2004	MrtlBh	A+	18	10	0	0	70.0	291	62	34	28	2	3	4	0	24	0	41	4	0	6	6	.500	0	0- -	-	2.77	3.60
2005	MrtlBh	A+	18	18	0	0	97.0	417	112	46	40	5	3	1	5	29	0	65	11	0	9	3	.750	0	0- -	-	4.52	3.71
2005	Missi	AA	8	8	0	0	50.1	211	43	25	23	2	2	0	4	18	2	33	6	0	2	5	.286	0	0- -	-	2.97	4.11
2006	Missi	AA	21	16	0	2	102.1	469	124	58	50	3	5	5	3	43	3	73	6	0	5	6	.455	0	1- -	-	4.86	4.40
2006	Braves	R	3	0	0	0	7.0	24	3	0	0	0	0	0	0	0	0	6	1	0	0	0	-	0	0- -	-	0.40	0.00
2007	Ms	R	3	3	0	0	10.1	54	19	10	9	0	0	0	1	4	0	11	4	0	0	2	.000	0	0- -	-	8.74	7.84
2007	Wisc	A-	1	1	0	0	5.0	18	2	0	0	0	0	0	0	1	0	4	0	0	1	0	1.000	0	0- -	-	0.63	0.00
2007	Tacom	AAA	2	2	0	0	10.2	45	11	4	3	0	0	0	0	2	0	7	0	0	1	1	.500	0	0- -	-	3.11	2.53
2008	Tacom	AAA	22	22	0	0	125.0	569	176	85	76	12	3	0	4	43	0	52	2	0	6	11	.353	0	0- -	-	6.56	5.47

			HOW MUCH HE PITCHED						WHAT HE GAVE UP												THE RESULTS						
Year	Team	Lg	G	GS	CG	GF	IP	BFP	H	R	ER	HR	SH	SF	HB	TBB	IBB	SO	WP	Bk	W	L	Pct	Sh	Sv-Op	Hld	ERC	ERA
2008	Everett	A-	1	1	0	0	2.0	8	3	2	2	1	0	0	0	0	0	1	0	0	0	0	-	0	0--	-	9.22	9.00
2009	Tacom	AAA	2	0	0	1	4.1	17	4	2	2	0	0	0	1	0	0	1	1	0	0	0	-	0	0--	-	2.51	4.15
2007	Sea	AL	15	0	0	4	35.1	165	35	24	22	2	0	3	8	20	0	16	5	1	1	1	.500	0	0-0	0	5.24	5.60
2009	Sea	AL	52	0	0	15	64.1	261	50	23	20	3	2	4	2	20	1	28	3	0	3	2	.600	0	1-3	15	2.33	2.80
	2 ML YEARS		67	0	0	19	99.2	426	85	47	42	5	2	7	10	40	1	44	8	1	4	3	.571	0	1-3	15	3.29	3.79

Josh Whitesell

Bats: L **Throws:** L **Pos:** 1B-30; PH-16   **Ht:** 6'1" **Wt:** 225 **Born:** 4/14/1982 **Age:** 28

						BATTING														BASERUNNING				AVERAGES		
Year	Team	Lg	G	AB	H	2B	3B	HR	(Hm	Rd)	TB	R	RBI	RC	TBB	IBB	SO	HBP	SH	SF	SB	CS	SB%	GDP	Avg	OBP	Slg
2003	Vrmnt	A-	49	167	41	10	1	5	(-	-)	68	13	19	27	28	2	53	4	0	1	0	0	-	2	.246	.365	.407
2004	Savann	A	113	380	95	29	0	16	(-	-)	172	56	54	63	58	2	91	2	1	2	0	1	.00	5	.250	.351	.453
2005	Ptomc	A+	113	389	114	32	2	18	(-	-)	204	59	66	87	74	3	125	9	1	1	1	1	.50	3	.293	.416	.524
2006	Hrsbrg	AA	127	402	106	11	0	19	(-	-)	174	47	56	63	53	3	125	4	6	2	6	2	.25	17	.264	.354	.433
2007	Hrsbrg	AA	119	387	110	23	1	21	(-	-)	198	78	74	89	87	5	107	10	0	3	6	2	.75	6	.284	.425	.512
2008	Tucsn	AAA	127	475	156	36	0	26	(-	-)	270	86	110	112	74	4	136	8	0	3	1	2	.33	9	.328	.425	.568
2009	Reno	AAA	63	225	66	14	1	8	(-	-)	106	35	58	45	40	3	48	3	0	6	1	1	.50	7	.293	.398	.471
2008	Ari	NL	7	7	2	0	0	1	(0	1)	5	1	1	2	1	0	2	1	0	0	0	0	-	0	.286	.444	.714
2009	Ari	NL	46	108	21	7	0	1	(0	1)	31	7	14	15	24	4	29	1	0	0	0	0	-	2	.194	.346	.287
	2 ML YEARS		53	115	23	7	0	2	(0	2)	36	8	15	17	25	4	31	2	0	0	0	0	-	2	.200	.352	.313

Eli Whiteside

Bats: R **Throws:** R **Pos:** C-47; PR-3; PH-1   **Ht:** 6'2" **Wt:** 215 **Born:** 10/22/1979 **Age:** 30

						BATTING														BASERUNNING				AVERAGES		
Year	Team	Lg	G	AB	H	2B	3B	HR	(Hm	Rd)	TB	R	RBI	RC	TBB	IBB	SO	HBP	SH	SF	SB	CS	SB%	GDP	Avg	OBP	Slg
2001	Dlmrva	A	61	212	53	11	0	7	(-	-)	85	30	28	26	9	1	45	7	0	2	1	1	.50	11	.250	.300	.401
2002	Frdrck	A+	80	313	81	19	0	8	(-	-)	124	34	42	38	14	0	57	4	0	4	0	0	-	8	.259	.296	.396
2002	Bowie	AA	27	99	26	5	0	2	(-	-)	37	11	11	11	4	0	18	3	1	0	0	1	.00	4	.263	.311	.374
2003	Bowie	AA	81	265	54	13	1	1	(-	-)	72	21	23	14	5	0	44	4	1	0	0	0	-	7	.204	.230	.272
2003	Orioles	R	1	3	1	1	0	0	(-	-)	2	0	0	0	1	0	1	0	0	0	0	0	-	0	.333	.500	.667
2003	Abrdn	A-	2	10	7	3	0	0	(-	-)	10	0	4	4	0	0	1	0	0	0	1	0	1.00	0	.700	.700	1.000
2004	Bowie	AA	90	297	75	18	0	18	(-	-)	147	41	60	46	25	0	65	1	0	3	2	2	.50	3	.253	.310	.495
2005	Ottawa	AAA	95	317	74	22	1	4	(-	-)	110	28	27	31	21	1	65	2	1	3	1	3	.25	7	.233	.283	.347
2006	Ottawa	AAA	92	315	77	18	1	11	(-	-)	130	37	47	36	10	0	73	7	2	6	1	3	.25	4	.244	.278	.413
2007	Norfolk	AAA	18	61	11	1	0	2	(-	-)	18	5	6	3	1	1	12	2	2	1	1	1	.50	2	.180	.215	.295
2007	Bowie	AA	42	141	41	7	4	4	(-	-)	68	18	30	22	8	0	32	2	3	2	0	3	.00	2	.291	.333	.482
2008	Roch	AAA	8	24	4	0	0	1	(-	-)	7	2	1	1	1	0	6	0	0	0	0	0	-	1	.167	.200	.292
2008	Fresno	AAA	49	151	36	7	0	2	(-	-)	49	13	22	15	12	0	27	1	1	4	2	0	1.00	8	.238	.292	.325
2009	Fresno	AAA	34	116	28	7	1	6	(-	-)	55	16	24	16	8	1	40	0	2	0	0	0	-	2	.241	.290	.474
2005	Bal	AL	9	12	3	0	0	0	(0	0)	3	1	1	0	0	0	2	0	0	0	0	0	-	1	.250	.250	.250
2009	SF	NL	49	127	29	6	1	2	(1	1)	43	15	13	11	4	1	30	3	0	0	0	0	-	4	.228	.269	.339
	2 ML YEARS		58	139	32	6	1	2	(1	1)	46	16	14	11	4	1	32	3	0	0	0	0	-	5	.230	.267	.331

Matt Wieters

Bats: B **Throws:** R **Pos:** C-86; DH-10; PH-1   **Ht:** 6'5" **Wt:** 230 **Born:** 5/21/1986 **Age:** 24

						BATTING														BASERUNNING				AVERAGES		
Year	Team	Lg	G	AB	H	2B	3B	HR	(Hm	Rd)	TB	R	RBI	RC	TBB	IBB	SO	HBP	SH	SF	SB	CS	SB%	GDP	Avg	OBP	Slg
2008	Frdrck	A+	69	229	79	8	0	15	(-	-)	132	48	40	58	44	5	47	2	1	4	1	2	.33	6	.345	.448	.576
2008	Bowie	AA	61	208	76	14	2	12	(-	-)	130	41	51	58	38	3	29	1	0	3	1	0	1.00	9	.365	.460	.625
2009	Norfolk	AAA	39	141	43	9	2	5	(-	-)	71	25	30	28	20	1	30	0	0	2	0	0	-	6	.305	.387	.504
2009	Bal	AL	96	354	102	15	1	9	(5	4)	146	35	43	43	28	2	86	1	0	2	0	0	-	11	.288	.340	.412

Ty Wigginton

Bats: R **Throws:** R **Pos:** 1B-40; 3B-39; DH-24; PH-20; SS-9; 2B-8; LF-2   **Ht:** 6'0" **Wt:** 190 **Born:** 10/11/1977 **Age:** 32

						BATTING														BASERUNNING				AVERAGES		
Year	Team	Lg	G	AB	H	2B	3B	HR	(Hm	Rd)	TB	R	RBI	RC	TBB	IBB	SO	HBP	SH	SF	SB	CS	SB%	GDP	Avg	OBP	Slg
2002	NYM	NL	46	116	35	8	0	6	(4	2)	61	18	18	15	8	0	19	2	0	1	2	1	.67	4	.302	.354	.526
2003	NYM	NL	156	573	146	36	6	11	(4	7)	227	73	71	76	46	2	124	9	1	4	12	2	.86	15	.255	.318	.396
2004	2 Tms	NL	144	494	129	30	2	17	(6	11)	214	63	66	59	45	6	82	2	1	3	7	1	.88	15	.261	.324	.433
2005	Pit	NL	57	155	40	9	1	7	(1	6)	72	20	25	22	14	0	30	1	1	0	1	0	1.00	3	.258	.324	.465
2006	TB	AL	122	444	122	25	1	24	(18	6)	221	55	79	69	32	3	97	6	1	3	4	3	.57	11	.275	.330	.498
2007	2 Tms	NL	148	547	152	33	0	22	(15	7)	251	71	67	64	41	0	113	8	0	8	3	4	.43	16	.278	.333	.459
2008	Hou	NL	111	386	110	22	1	23	(15	8)	203	50	58	57	32	1	69	8	0	3	4	6	.40	9	.285	.350	.526
2009	Bal	AL	122	410	112	19	0	11	(9	2)	164	44	41	41	23	1	57	2	0	1	1	2	.33	16	.273	.314	.400
04	NYM	NL	86	312	89	23	2	12	(5	7)	152	46	42	38	23	4	48	1	1	2	6	1	.86	11	.285	.334	.487
04	Pit	NL	58	182	40	7	0	5	(1	4)	62	17	24	21	22	2	34	1	0	1	1	0	1.00	4	.220	.306	.341
07	TB	AL	98	378	104	21	0	16	(9	7)	173	47	49	42	28	0	73	5	0	6	1	4	.20	8	.275	.329	.458
07	Hou	NL	50	169	48	12	0	6	(6	0)	78	24	18	22	13	0	40	3	0	2	2	0	1.00	8	.284	.342	.462
	8 ML YEARS		906	3125	846	182	11	121	(72	49)	1413	394	425	403	241	13	591	38	4	23	33	20	.62	89	.271	.328	.452

Randy Williams

Pitches: L Bats: L Pos: RP-25

Ht: 6'3" Wt: 190 Born: 9/18/1975 Age: 34

Year	Team	Lg	G	GS	CG	GF	IP	BFP	H	R	ER	HR	SH	SF	HB	TBB	IBB	SO	WP	Bk	W	L	Pct	Sh	Sv-Op	Hld	ERC	ERA
2009	Charltt*	AAA	33	0	0	19	36.2	156	31	17	14	3	1	2	1	11	2	40	2	0	3	0	1.000	0	1- -	-	2.66	3.44
2004	Sea	AL	6	0	0	1	4.2	22	3	3	3	0	0	0	0	6	0	4	0	0	0	0	-	0	0-0	1	4.73	5.79
2005	2 Tms	NL	32	0	0	6	26.1	125	33	21	20	5	0	1	1	13	3	21	0	0	3	1	.750	0	0-2	4	6.54	6.84
2009	CWS	NL	25	0	0	6	17.2	80	13	9	9	2	1	1	3	12	4	22	0	0	0	1	.000	0	0-0	3	4.00	4.58
05	SD	NL	2	0	0	0	4.1	25	7	6	6	1	0	0	1	4	0	2	0	0	1	0	1.000	0	0-0	0	12.46	12.46
05	Col	NL	30	0	0	6	22.0	100	26	15	14	4	0	1	0	9	3	19	0	0	2	1	.667	0	0-2	4	5.48	5.73
3 ML YEARS			63	0	0	13	48.2	227	49	33	32	7	1	2	4	31	7	47	0	0	3	2	.600	0	0-2	8	5.43	5.92

Josh Willingham

Bats: R Throws: R Pos: LF-87; RF-35; PH-17; 1B-1

Ht: 6'2" Wt: 215 Born: 2/17/1979 Age: 31

Year	Team	Lg	G	AB	H	2B	3B	HR	(Hm	Rd)	TB	R	RBI	RC	TBB	IBB	SO	HBP	SH	SF	SB	CS	SB%	GDP	Avg	OBP	Slg
2004	Fla	NL	12	25	5	0	0	1	(0	1)	8	2	1	1	4	0	8	0	0	0	0	0	-	1	.200	.310	.320
2005	Fla	NL	16	23	7	1	0	0	(0	0)	8	3	4	3	2	0	5	2	1	0	0	0	-	1	.304	.407	.348
2006	Fla	NL	142	502	139	28	2	26	(11	15)	249	62	74	74	54	2	109	11	0	6	2	0	1.00	13	.277	.356	.496
2007	Fla	NL	144	521	138	32	4	21	(10	11)	241	75	89	94	66	1	122	16	0	1	8	1	.89	11	.265	.364	.463
2008	Fla	NL	102	351	89	21	5	15	(6	9)	165	54	51	56	48	2	82	14	1	2	3	2	.60	7	.254	.364	.470
2009	Was	NL	133	427	111	29	0	24	(7	17)	212	70	61	61	61	2	104	12	0	2	4	3	.57	11	.260	.367	.496
6 ML YEARS			549	1849	489	111	11	87	(34	53)	883	266	280	289	235	7	430	55	2	11	17	6	.74	44	.264	.362	.478

Dontrelle Willis

Pitches: L Bats: L Pos: SP-7

Ht: 6'4" Wt: 225 Born: 1/12/1982 Age: 28

Year	Team	Lg	G	GS	CG	GF	IP	BFP	H	R	ER	HR	SH	SF	HB	TBB	IBB	SO	WP	Bk	W	L	Pct	Sh	Sv-Op	Hld	ERC	ERA
2009	Lkland*	A+	1	1	0	0	7.0	27	8	4	4	1	1	0	0	0	0	2	0	0	0	1	.000	0	0- -	-	3.77	5.14
2009	Erie*	AA	1	1	0	0	6.0	23	3	2	2	1	0	0	0	3	0	6	0	0	1	0	1.000	0	0- -	-	2.36	3.00
2009	Toledo*	AAA	5	5	0	0	24.1	108	22	13	13	1	0	0	1	17	0	15	2	0	1	2	.333	0	0- -	-	4.52	4.81
2003	Fla	NL	27	27	2	0	160.2	668	148	61	59	10	3	1	3	58	0	142	7	1	14	6	.700	2	0-0	0	3.49	3.30
2004	Fla	NL	32	32	3	0	197.0	848	210	99	88	20	8	2	8	61	8	139	2	0	10	11	.476	0	0-0	0	4.21	4.02
2005	Fla	NL	34	34	7	0	236.1	960	213	79	69	11	14	5	8	55	3	170	2	1	22	10	.688	5	0-0	0	2.71	2.63
2006	Fla	NL	34	34	4	0	223.1	975	234	106	96	21	11	6	19	83	6	160	6	1	12	12	.500	1	0-0	0	4.53	3.87
2007	Fla	NL	35	35	0	0	205.1	942	241	131	118	29	15	7	14	87	4	146	9	1	10	15	.400	0	0-0	0	5.72	5.17
2008	Det	AL	8	7	0	0	24.0	122	18	25	25	4	0	0	1	35	1	18	5	1	0	2	.000	0	0-0	0	7.65	9.38
2009	Det	AL	7	7	0	0	33.2	160	37	28	28	4	2	3	1	28	0	17	1	0	1	4	.200	0	0-0	0	6.87	7.49
Postseason			7	2	0	0	12.2	63	15	12	12	1	1	2	0	10	0	10	1	0	0	1	.000	0	0-0	1	6.43	8.53
7 ML YEARS			177	176	15	0	1080.1	4675	1101	529	483	102	53	24	54	407	22	792	32	5	69	60	.535	8	0-0	0	4.24	4.02

Reggie Willits

Bats: B Throws: R Pos: LF-27; PR-12; RF-10; PH-7; CF-6

Ht: 5'11" Wt: 185 Born: 5/30/1981 Age: 29

Year	Team	Lg	G	AB	H	2B	3B	HR	(Hm	Rd)	TB	R	RBI	RC	TBB	IBB	SO	HBP	SH	SF	SB	CS	SB%	GDP	Avg	OBP	Slg
2009	Salt Lk*	AAA	62	234	61	10	1	1	(-	-)	76	40	27	31	34	0	44	2	4	6	11	4	.73	5	.261	.361	.325
2006	LAA	AL	28	45	12	1	0	0	(0	0)	13	12	2	6	11	0	10	0	2	0	4	3	.57	0	.267	.411	.289
2007	LAA	AL	136	430	126	20	1	0	(0	0)	148	74	34	68	69	2	83	3	11	5	27	8	.77	7	.293	.391	.344
2008	LAA	AL	82	108	21	4	0	0	(0	0)	25	21	7	10	21	0	26	0	5	2	2	1	.67	1	.194	.321	.231
2009	LAA	AL	49	80	17	2	0	0	(0	0)	19	16	6	3	5	0	17	0	6	1	5	1	.83	0	.213	.256	.238
Postseason			6	4	0	0	0	0	(0	0)	0	0	0	0	1	0	2	0	0	0	1	1	.50	0	.000	.200	.000
4 ML YEARS			295	663	176	27	1	0	(0	0)	205	123	49	87	106	2	136	3	24	8	38	13	.75	8	.265	.365	.309

Bobby Wilson

Bats: R Throws: R Pos: C-11; 1B-1

Ht: 6'0" Wt: 220 Born: 4/8/1983 Age: 27

Year	Team	Lg	G	AB	H	2B	3B	HR	(Hm	Rd)	TB	R	RBI	RC	TBB	IBB	SO	HBP	SH	SF	SB	CS	SB%	GDP	Avg	OBP	Slg
2003	Provo	R+	57	236	67	12	0	6	(-	-)	97	36	62	33	18	0	31	0	0	4	0	0	-	11	.284	.329	.411
2004	CRpds	A	105	396	106	23	0	8	(-	-)	153	45	64	52	30	3	55	5	1	9	5	2	.71	3	.268	.320	.386
2005	RCuca	A+	115	466	135	32	1	14	(-	-)	211	66	77	71	30	0	61	2	0	3	2	1	.67	5	.290	.333	.453
2006	Ark	AA	103	374	107	26	0	9	(-	-)	160	46	53	56	33	2	47	5	4	2	1	6	.14	7	.286	.350	.428
2007	Ark	AA	50	181	49	9	0	6	(-	-)	76	24	27	27	22	1	26	0	0	1	5	3	.63	5	.271	.348	.420
2007	Salt Lk	AAA	40	132	39	13	1	3	(-	-)	63	15	22	21	8	1	18	0	1	0	1	0	1.00	6	.295	.336	.477
2008	Salt Lk	AAA	72	260	81	20	0	4	(-	-)	113	33	45	45	29	1	45	4	3	2	0	0	-	5	.312	.386	.435
2009	Salt Lk	AAA	97	354	96	19	1	8	(-	-)	141	38	55	45	22	0	56	1	4	0	0	0	-	10	.271	.316	.398
2008	LAA	AL	7	6	1	0	0	0	(0	0)	1	0	1	0	1	0	3	0	0	0	0	0	-	0	.167	.286	.167
2009	LAA	AL	12	5	1	1	0	0	(0	0)	2	0	0	0	0	0	1	0	1	0	0	0	-	1	.200	.200	.400
2 ML YEARS			19	11	2	1	0	0	(0	0)	3	0	1	0	1	0	4	0	1	0	0	0	-	1	.182	.250	.273

Brian Wilson

Pitches: R Bats: R Pos: RP-68   Ht: 6'1" Wt: 196 Born: 3/16/1982 Age: 28

			HOW MUCH HE PITCHED						WHAT HE GAVE UP										THE RESULTS						
Year	Team	Lg	G	GS	CG	GF	IP	BFP	H	R	ER	HR	SH	SF	HB	TBB	IBB	SO	WP	Bk	W	L	Pct	Sh	Sv-Op	Hld	ERC	ERA
2006	SF	NL	31	0	0	9	30.0	141	32	19	18	1	1	4	1	21	2	23	0	0	2	3	.400	0	1-2	4	5.11	5.40
2007	SF	NL	24	0	0	9	23.2	93	16	6	6	1	0	0	1	7	0	18	0	0	1	2	.333	0	6-7	9	1.87	2.28
2008	SF	NL	63	0	0	54	62.1	274	62	32	32	7	2	5	3	28	4	67	2	0	3	2	.600	0	41-47	0	4.41	4.62
2009	SF	NL	68	0	0	60	72.1	303	60	27	22	3	4	2	1	27	4	83	4	0	5	6	.455	0	38-45	1	2.61	2.74
4 ML YEARS			186	0	0	132	188.1	811	170	84	78	12	7	11	6	83	10	191	6	0	11	13	.458	0	86-101	14	3.46	3.73

C.J. Wilson

Pitches: L Bats: L Pos: RP-74   Ht: 6'1" Wt: 215 Born: 11/18/1980 Age: 29

			HOW MUCH HE PITCHED						WHAT HE GAVE UP										THE RESULTS						
Year	Team	Lg	G	GS	CG	GF	IP	BFP	H	R	ER	HR	SH	SF	HB	TBB	IBB	SO	WP	Bk	W	L	Pct	Sh	Sv-Op	Hld	ERC	ERA
2005	Tex	AL	24	6	0	5	48.0	220	63	39	37	5	1	2	2	18	1	30	4	1	1	7	.125	0	1-1	4	6.03	6.94
2006	Tex	AL	44	0	0	12	44.1	191	39	23	20	7	1	0	5	18	1	43	0	0	2	4	.333	0	1-2	7	4.25	4.06
2007	Tex	AL	66	0	0	22	68.1	285	50	25	23	4	2	4	6	33	1	63	5	0	2	1	.667	0	12-14	15	3.01	3.03
2008	Tex	AL	50	0	0	41	46.1	214	49	35	31	8	1	1	2	27	2	41	3	0	2	2	.500	0	24-28	1	5.77	6.02
2009	Tex	AL	74	0	0	30	73.2	323	66	29	23	3	3	0	6	32	3	84	3	0	5	6	.455	0	14-18	19	3.40	2.81
5 ML YEARS			258	6	0	110	280.2	1233	267	151	134	27	8	7	21	128	8	261	15	1	12	20	.375	0	52-63	46	4.23	4.30

Jack Wilson

Bats: R Throws: R Pos: SS-105; PH-1   Ht: 6'0" Wt: 200 Born: 12/29/1977 Age: 32

			BATTING																	BASERUNNING				AVERAGES		
Year	Team	Lg	G	AB	H	2B	3B	HR	(Hm	Rd)	TB	R	RBI	RC	TBB	IBB	SO	HBP	SH	SF	SB	CS	SB%	GDP	Avg	OBP	Slg
2009	Indy*	AAA	2	6	2	2	0	0	(-	-)	4	0	3	1	0	0	2	0	0	1	0	0	-	0	.333	.286	.667
2001	Pit	NL	108	390	87	17	1	3	(0	3)	115	44	25	27	16	2	70	1	17	1	1	3	.25	4	.223	.255	.295
2002	Pit	NL	147	527	133	22	4	4	(2	2)	175	77	47	60	37	2	74	4	17	1	2	.71	7	.252	.306	.332
2003	Pit	NL	150	558	143	21	3	9	(2	7)	197	58	62	62	36	3	74	4	11	6	5	5	.50	11	.256	.303	.353
2004	Pit	NL	157	652	201	41	12	11	(7	4)	299	82	59	84	26	0	71	3	7	5	8	4	.67	15	.308	.335	.459
2005	Pit	NL	158	587	151	24	7	8	(3 | 5)	213	60	52	60	31	6	58	4	6	11	4	7	3	.70	11	.257	.299	.363
2006	Pit	NL	142	543	148	27	1	8	(5	3)	201	70	35	58	33	0	65	4	9	5	4	3	.57	15	.273	.316	.370
2007	Pit	NL	135	477	141	29	2	12	(3	9)	210	67	56	70	38	9	46	6	7	7	2	5	.29	8	.296	.350	.440
2008	Pit	NL	87	305	83	18	1	1	(1	0)	106	24	22	32	13	0	27	5	6	1	2	2	.50	6	.272	.312	.348
2009	2 Tms		106	373	95	23	1	5	(2	3)	135	37	39	40	21	2	48	0	5	3	3	1	.75	6	.255	.292	.362
09	Pit	NL	75	266	71	18	1	4	(1	3)	103	26	31	31	15	2	31	0	3	2	2	1	.67	4	.267	.304	.387
09	Sea	AL	31	107	24	5	0	1	(1	0)	32	11	8	9	6	0	17	0	2	1	1	0	1.00	2	.224	.263	.299
9 ML YEARS			1190	4412	1182	222	32	61	(25	36)	1651	519	397	493	251	24	533	33	90	33	37	28	.57	83	.268	.310	.374

Josh Wilson

Bats: R Throws: R Pos: SS-55; 3B-6; PR-6; 2B-4; PH-3; DH-2   Ht: 6'0" Wt: 175 Born: 3/26/1981 Age: 29

			BATTING																	BASERUNNING				AVERAGES		
Year	Team	Lg	G	AB	H	2B	3B	HR	(Hm	Rd)	TB	R	RBI	RC	TBB	IBB	SO	HBP	SH	SF	SB	CS	SB%	GDP	Avg	OBP	Slg
2009	Reno*	AAA	15	50	13	3	1	1	(-	-)	21	5	10	8	7	0	8	1	1	2	1	1	.50	2	.260	.350	.420
2009	Tacom*	AAA	16	53	13	2	0	1	(-	-)	18	10	3	5	2	0	6	1	3	1	1	0	1.00	1	.245	.281	.340
2005	Fla	NL	11	10	1	1	0	0	(0	0)	2	2	0	0	0	0	4	1	0	0	0	0	-	0	.100	.182	.200
2007	2 Tms		105	282	67	15	3	2	(0	2)	94	28	24	24	17	0	57	5	3	3	6	2	.75	5	.238	.290	.333
2009	3 Tms		72	192	42	11	1	3	(1	2)	64	19	13	14	12	1	44	4	3	0	1	2	.33	4	.219	.279	.333
07	Was	NL	15	19	1	0	0	0	(0	0)	1	3	0	0	5	0	6	1	0	0	0	0	-	0	.053	.280	.053
07	TB	AL	90	263	66	15	3	2	(0	2)	93	25	24	24	12	0	51	4	3	3	6	2	.75	5	.251	.291	.354
09	Ari	NL	11	26	6	1	0	0	(0	0)	7	1	2	4	3	0	3	1	0	0	0	0	-	2	.231	.333	.269
09	SD	NL	16	38	4	2	0	0	(0	0)	6	2	1	1	3	1	9	1	1	0	0	0	-	0	.105	.190	.158
09	Sea	AL	45	128	32	8	1	3	(1	2)	51	16	10	9	6	0	32	2	2	0	1	2	.33	2	.250	.294	.398
3 ML YEARS			188	484	110	27	4	5	(1	4)	160	49	37	38	29	1	105	10	6	3	7	4	.64	9	.227	.283	.331

Randy Winn

Bats: B Throws: R Pos: RF-104; LF-54; CF-22; PH-7; DH-1   Ht: 6'2" Wt: 193 Born: 6/9/1974 Age: 36

			BATTING																	BASERUNNING				AVERAGES		
Year	Team	Lg	G	AB	H	2B	3B	HR	(Hm	Rd)	TB	R	RBI	RC	TBB	IBB	SO	HBP	SH	SF	SB	CS	SB%	GDP	Avg	OBP	Slg
1998	TB	AL	109	338	94	9	9	1	(0	1)	124	51	17	44	29	0	69	1	11	0	26	12	.68	2	.278	.337	.367
1999	TB	AL	79	303	81	16	4	2	(2	0)	111	44	24	32	17	0	63	1	1	2	9	9	.50	3	.267	.307	.366
2000	TB	AL	51	159	40	5	0	1	(1	0)	48	28	16	18	26	0	25	2	2	1	6	7	.46	2	.252	.362	.302
2001	TB	AL	128	429	117	25	6	6	(3	3)	172	54	50	56	38	0	81	6	5	2	12	10	.55	10	.273	.339	.401
2002	TB	AL	152	607	181	39	9	14	(9	5)	280	87	75	104	55	3	109	6	1	5	27	8	.77	9	.298	.360	.461
2003	Sea	AL	157	600	177	37	4	11	(6	5)	255	103	75	96	41	0	108	8	6	5	23	5	.82	9	.295	.346	.425
2004	Sea	AL	157	626	179	34	6	14	(8	6)	267	84	81	91	53	1	98	8	9	7	21	7	.75	16	.286	.346	.427
2005	2 Tms		160	617	189	47	6	20	(9	11)	308	85	63	95	48	4	91	5	10	3	19	11	.63	11	.306	.360	.499
2006	SF	NL	149	573	150	34	5	11	(5	6)	227	82	56	69	48	3	63	7	3	4	10	8	.56	7	.262	.324	.396
2007	SF	NL	155	593	178	42	1	14	(4	10)	264	73	65	86	44	3	85	7	4	5	15	3	.83	12	.300	.353	.445
2008	SF	NL	155	598	183	38	2	10	(6	4)	255	84	64	90	59	6	88	0	1	9	25	2	.93	6	.306	.363	.426
2009	SF	NL	149	538	141	33	5	2	(1	1)	190	65	51	73	47	2	93	1	3	8	16	2	.89	6	.262	.318	.353
05	Sea	AL	102	386	106	25	1	6	(2	4)	151	46	37	52	37	3	53	4	6	3	12	6	.67	7	.275	.342	.391
05	SF	NL	58	231	83	22	5	14	(7	7)	157	39	26	43	11	1	38	1	4	0	7	5	.58	4	.359	.391	.680
12 ML YEARS			1601	5981	1710	359	57	106	(50	56)	2501	840	637	854	505	22	973	52	56	51	209	84	.71	93	.286	.344	.418

DeWayne Wise

Bats: L **Throws:** L **Pos:** CF-35; RF-34; PR-19; PH-9; LF-5; DH-2   **Ht:** 6'1" **Wt:** 190 **Born:** 2/24/1978 **Age:** 32

Year	Team	Lg	G	AB	H	2B	3B	HR	(Hm	Rd)	TB	R	RBI	RC	TBB	IBB	SO	HBP	SH	SF	SB	CS	SB%	GDP	Avg	OBP	Slg
2009	Charltt*	AAA	7	27	9	3	1	0	(-	-)	14	2	3	4	1	0	4	0	0	0	0	0	-	0	.333	.357	.519
2000	Tor	AL	28	22	3	0	0	0	(0	0)	3	3	0	0	1	0	5	1	0	0	1	0	1.00	0	.136	.208	.136
2002	Tor	AL	42	112	20	4	1	3	(2	1)	35	14	13	8	4	0	15	0	0	0	5	0	1.00	0	.179	.207	.313
2004	Atl	NL	77	162	37	9	4	6	(3	3)	72	24	17	20	9	1	28	1	2	1	6	1	.86	1	.228	.272	.444
2006	Cin	NL	31	38	7	2	0	0	(0	0)	9	3	1	0	0	0	6	0	2	0	0	0	-	2	.184	.184	.237
2007	Cin	NL	5	5	1	0	1	0	(0	0)	3	1	1	1	1	1	1	0	0	0	0	0	-	0	.200	.333	.600
2008	CWS	AL	57	129	32	4	2	6	(2	4)	58	20	18	14	8	0	32	1	3	2	9	0	1.00	0	.248	.293	.450
2009	CWS	AL	84	142	32	8	3	2	(2	0)	52	17	11	10	3	0	27	4	4	0	4	5	.44	1	.225	.262	.366
	Postseason		8	12	3	2	0	1	(0	1)	8	3	5	3	1	0	4	0	0	0	1	0	1.00	0	.250	.308	.667
	7 ML YEARS		324	610	132	27	11	17	(9	8)	232	82	61	53	26	2	114	7	11	3	25	6	.81	9	.216	.255	.380

Randy Wolf

Pitches: L **Bats:** L **Pos:** SP-34   **Ht:** 5'10" **Wt:** 202 **Born:** 8/22/1976 **Age:** 33

Year	Team	Lg	G	GS	CG	GF	IP	BFP	H	R	ER	HR	SH	SF	HB	TBB	IBB	SO	WP	Bk	W	L	Pct	Sh	Sv-Op	Hld	ERC	ERA
1999	Phi	NL	22	21	0	0	121.2	552	126	78	75	20	5	1	5	67	0	116	4	0	6	9	.400	0	0-0	0	5.54	5.55
2000	Phi	NL	32	32	1	0	206.1	889	210	107	100	25	10	8	6	83	2	160	1	0	11	9	.550	0	0-0	0	4.54	4.36
2001	Phi	NL	28	25	4	1	163.0	684	150	74	67	15	11	7	10	51	4	152	1	0	10	11	.476	2	0-0	0	3.46	3.70
2002	Phi	NL	31	31	3	0	210.2	855	172	77	75	23	7	6	7	63	5	172	4	0	11	9	.550	2	0-0	0	2.88	3.20
2003	Phi	NL	33	33	2	0	200.0	850	176	101	94	27	8	4	6	78	4	177	6	0	16	10	.615	2	0-0	0	3.67	4.23
2004	Phi	NL	23	23	1	0	136.2	585	145	73	65	20	6	3	5	36	4	89	2	0	5	8	.385	1	0-0	0	4.29	4.28
2005	Phi	NL	13	13	0	0	80.0	346	87	40	39	14	4	1	6	26	2	61	1	0	6	4	.600	0	0-0	0	5.17	4.39
2006	Phi	NL	12	12	0	0	56.2	261	83	37	35	13	2	3	2	33	2	44	2	0	4	0	1.000	0	0-0	0	6.63	5.56
2007	LAD	NL	18	18	0	0	102.2	458	110	55	54	10	5	5	8	39	2	94	1	0	9	6	.600	0	0-0	0	4.52	4.73
2008	2 Tms	NL	33	33	1	0	190.1	823	191	100	91	21	10	4	12	71	4	162	3	0	12	12	.500	1	0-0	0	4.30	4.30
2009	LAD	NL	34	34	0	0	214.1	862	178	81	77	24	12	2	6	58	1	160	4	0	11	7	.611	0	0-0	0	2.89	3.23
08	SD	NL	21	21	0	0	119.2	522	123	69	63	14	6	2	8	47	0	105	2	0	6	10	.375	0	0-0	0	4.63	4.74
08	Hou	NL	12	12	1	0	70.2	301	68	31	28	7	4	2	4	24	4	57	1	0	6	2	.750	1	0-0	0	3.77	3.57
	11 ML YEARS		279	275	12	1	1682.1	7165	1608	823	772	212	80	44	73	605	30	1387	32	0	101	85	.543	8	0-0	0	4.01	4.13

Brian Wolfe

Pitches: R **Bats:** R **Pos:** RP-14   **Ht:** 6'3" **Wt:** 225 **Born:** 11/29/1980 **Age:** 29

Year	Team	Lg	G	GS	CG	GF	IP	BFP	H	R	ER	HR	SH	SF	HB	TBB	IBB	SO	WP	Bk	W	L	Pct	Sh	Sv-Op	Hld	ERC	ERA
2009	LsVgs*	AAA	34	0	0	15	46.1	208	59	29	28	3	0	4	2	12	0	27	4	0	2	3	.400	0	3--	-	4.97	5.05
2007	Tor	AL	38	0	0	12	45.1	174	36	17	15	5	0	2	2	9	2	22	0	0	3	1	.750	0	0-2	8	2.52	2.98
2008	Tor	AL	20	0	0	4	22.0	86	18	6	6	2	2	1	0	6	1	14	1	0	0	2	.000	0	0-0	3	2.61	2.45
2009	Tor	AL	14	0	0	8	15.1	77	25	15	14	5	1	2	1	7	1	11	1	0	2	2	.500	0	0-1	0	10.52	8.22
	3 ML YEARS		72	0	0	24	82.2	337	79	38	35	12	3	5	3	22	4	47	2	0	5	5	.500	0	0-3	9	3.78	3.81

Brandon Wood

Bats: R **Throws:** R **Pos:** 3B-9; SS-5; 1B-4; PH-3   **Ht:** 6'3" **Wt:** 210 **Born:** 3/2/1985 **Age:** 25

Year	Team	Lg	G	AB	H	2B	3B	HR	(Hm	Rd)	TB	R	RBI	RC	TBB	IBB	SO	HBP	SH	SF	SB	CS	SB%	GDP	Avg	OBP	Slg
2009	Salt Lk*	AAA	99	386	113	28	4	22	(-	-)	215	65	72	75	36	3	80	2	0	4	1	1	.50	11	.293	.353	.557
2007	LAA	AL	13	33	5	1	0	1	(0	1)	9	2	3	1	0	0	12	0	0	0	0	0	-	0	.152	.152	.273
2008	LAA	AL	55	150	30	4	0	5	(2	3)	49	12	13	7	4	0	43	1	1	1	4	0	1.00	3	.200	.224	.327
2009	LAA	AL	18	41	8	1	0	1	(1	0)	12	5	3	0	3	0	19	1	1	0	0	0	-	3	.195	.267	.293
	3 ML YEARS		86	224	43	6	0	7	(3	4)	70	19	19	8	7	0	74	2	2	1	4	0	1.00	6	.192	.222	.313

Kerry Wood

Pitches: R **Bats:** R **Pos:** RP-58   **Ht:** 6'5" **Wt:** 211 **Born:** 6/16/1977 **Age:** 33

Year	Team	Lg	G	GS	CG	GF	IP	BFP	H	R	ER	HR	SH	SF	HB	TBB	IBB	SO	WP	Bk	W	L	Pct	Sh	Sv-Op	Hld	ERC	ERA
1998	ChC	NL	26	26	1	0	166.2	699	117	69	63	14	2	4	11	85	1	233	6	3	13	6	.684	1	0-0	0	3.03	3.40
2000	ChC	NL	23	23	1	0	137.0	603	112	77	73	17	7	5	9	87	0	132	5	1	8	7	.533	0	0-0	0	4.43	4.80
2001	ChC	NL	28	28	1	0	174.1	740	127	70	65	16	4	5	10	92	3	217	9	0	12	6	.667	1	0-0	0	3.22	3.36
2002	ChC	NL	33	33	4	0	213.2	895	169	92	87	22	13	5	16	97	5	217	8	1	12	11	.522	1	0-0	0	3.46	3.66
2003	ChC	NL	32	32	4	0	211.0	887	152	77	75	24	11	6	21	100	2	266	10	0	14	11	.560	2	0-0	0	3.31	3.20
2004	ChC	NL	22	22	0	0	140.1	595	127	62	58	16	6	6	11	51	0	144	7	0	8	9	.471	0	0-0	0	3.83	3.72
2005	ChC	NL	21	10	0	4	66.0	273	52	32	31	14	2	1	2	26	0	77	0	0	3	4	.429	0	0-0	4	3.75	4.23
2006	ChC	NL	4	4	0	0	19.2	86	19	13	9	5	0	2	1	8	0	13	1	0	1	2	.333	0	0-0	0	5.17	4.12
2007	ChC	NL	22	0	0	2	24.1	101	18	9	9	0	1	0	0	13	1	24	1	0	1	1	.500	0	0-0	0	2.49	3.33
2008	ChC	NL	65	0	0	56	66.1	276	54	24	24	3	2	2	7	18	4	84	1	0	5	4	.556	0	34-40	0	2.52	3.26
2009	Cle	AL	58	0	0	50	55.0	241	48	26	26	7	1	3	3	28	0	63	5	0	3	3	.500	0	20-26	0	4.16	4.25
	Postseason		8	5	0	2	36.2	157	29	16	15	3	1	0	0	18	1	38	1	0	2	2	.500	0	0-0	0	3.06	3.68
	11 ML YEARS		334	178	11	112	1274.1	5396	995	551	520	138	49	39	91	605	16	1470	53	5	80	64	.556	5	54-66	4	3.49	3.67

Tim Wood

Pitches: R **Bats:** R **Pos:** RP-18   **Ht:** 6'0" **Wt:** 175 **Born:** 11/16/1982 **Age:** 27

			HOW MUCH HE PITCHED						WHAT HE GAVE UP										THE RESULTS						
Year	Team	Lg	G	GS	CG	GF	IP	BFP	H	R	ER	HR	SH	SF	HB	TBB	IBB	SO	WP	Bk	W	L	Pct	Sh	Sv-Op	Hld	ERC	ERA
2003	Jmstwn	A-	16	4	0	5	38.2	185	44	33	23	2	1	3	1	28	0	32	6	0	0	2	.000	0	2--	-	5.89	5.35
2004	Grnsbr	A	24	8	0	7	70.1	305	73	47	33	12	2	2	1	22	0	70	6	0	2	3	.400	0	1--	-	4.42	4.22
2005	Grnsbr	A	5	5	0	0	21.1	109	29	23	22	2	0	1	0	15	0	10	5	0	1	2	.333	0	0--	-	7.22	9.28
2006	Jupiter	A+	16	16	0	0	63.1	275	65	43	41	4	3	4	5	25	0	52	4	0	2	7	.222	0	0--	-	4.31	5.83
2007	Jupiter	A+	17	0	0	5	26.0	109	24	14	11	1	3	0	0	8	1	26	0	0	0	2	.000	0	0--	-	2.81	3.81
2008	Jupiter	A+	27	1	0	9	40.0	158	25	10	8	1	1	1	4	15	1	22	2	0	5	2	.714	0	1--	-	1.97	1.80
2008	Carlina	AA	12	0	0	5	20.1	88	20	14	13	2	0	0	2	6	0	15	1	0	2	1	.667	0	0--	-	3.91	5.75
2009	NewOr	AAA	31	0	0	9	39.2	176	42	16	14	1	2	1	0	17	2	37	3	0	1	2	.333	0	0--	-	3.83	3.18
2009	Fla	NL	18	0	0	8	22.1	97	22	8	7	2	2	3	1	10	1	16	2	0	1	0	1.000	0	0-0	1	4.25	2.82

Chris Woodward

Bats: R **Throws:** R **Pos:** 3B-18; 2B-11; SS-5; PR-4   **Ht:** 6'0" **Wt:** 190 **Born:** 6/27/1976 **Age:** 34

			BATTING																			BASERUNNING				AVERAGES		
Year	Team	Lg	G	AB	H	2B	3B	HR	(Hm	Rd)	TB	R	RBI	RC	TBB	IBB	SO	HBP	SH	SF		SB	CS	SB%	GDP	Avg	OBP	Slg
2009	Tacom*	AAA	51	174	52	12	1	1	(-	-)	69	24	15	27	19	2	30	1	2	1		4	0	1.00	3	.299	.369	.397
2009	Pwtckt*	AAA	12	31	4	0	0	0	(-	-)	4	1	0	0	5	0	7	0	1	0		0	1	.00	0	.129	.250	.129
1999	Tor	AL	14	26	6	1	0	0	(0	0)	7	1	2	2	2	0	6	0	0	1		0	0	-	1	.231	.276	.269
2000	Tor	AL	37	104	19	7	0	3	(1	2)	35	16	14	9	10	3	28	0	1	0		1	0	1.00	1	.183	.254	.337
2001	Tor	AL	37	63	12	3	2	2	(2	0)	25	9	5	4	1	0	14	0	2	0		1	0	1.00	1	.190	.203	.397
2002	Tor	AL	90	312	86	13	4	13	(9	4)	146	48	45	45	26	0	72	3	1	8		3	0	1.00	8	.276	.330	.468
2003	Tor	AL	104	349	91	22	2	7	(4	3)	138	49	45	42	28	0	72	3	0	6		1	2	.33	6	.261	.316	.395
2004	Tor	AL	69	213	50	13	4	1	(0	1)	74	21	24	24	14	0	46	1	2	2		1	2	.33	3	.235	.283	.347
2005	NYM	NL	81	173	49	10	0	3	(2	1)	68	16	18	20	13	0	46	2	2	2		2	2	.50	2	.283	.337	.393
2006	NYM	NL	83	222	48	10	1	3	(2	1)	69	25	25	18	23	2	55	1	4	3		1	1	.50	2	.216	.289	.311
2007	Atl	NL	92	136	27	6	1	1	(1	0)	38	16	8	9	10	1	29	0	4	1		1	0	1.00	3	.199	.252	.279
2009	2 Tms	AL	33	79	17	1	0	0	(0	0)	18	7	5	5	7	0	19	2	1	1		1	0	1.00	1	.215	.292	.228
09	Sea	AL	20	67	16	1	0	0	(0	0)	17	7	5	5	5	0	15	0	1	1		1	0	1.00	1	.239	.288	.254
09	Bos	AL	13	12	1	0	0	0	(0	0)	1	0	0	0	2	0	4	2	0	0		0	0	-	0	.083	.313	.083
	Postseason		1	1	1	1	0	0	(0	0)	2	1	0	1	0	0	0	0	0	0		0	0	-	0	1.000	1.000	2.000
	10 ML YEARS		640	1677	405	86	14	33	(21	12)	618	208	191	178	134	6	387	12	17	24		9	6	.60	28	.242	.298	.369

David Wright

Bats: R **Throws:** R **Pos:** 3B-142; PH-2   **Ht:** 6'0" **Wt:** 208 **Born:** 12/20/1982 **Age:** 27

			BATTING																			BASERUNNING				AVERAGES		
Year	Team	Lg	G	AB	H	2B	3B	HR	(Hm	Rd)	TB	R	RBI	RC	TBB	IBB	SO	HBP	SH	SF		SB	CS	SB%	GDP	Avg	OBP	Slg
2004	NYM	NL	69	263	77	17	1	14	(8	6)	138	41	40	42	14	0	40	3	0	3		6	0	1.00	7	.293	.332	.525
2005	NYM	NL	160	575	176	42	1	27	(12	15)	301	99	102	105	72	2	113	7	0	3		17	7	.71	16	.306	.388	.523
2006	NYM	NL	154	582	181	40	5	26	(13	13)	309	96	116	119	66	13	113	5	0	8		20	5	.80	15	.311	.381	.531
2007	NYM	NL	160	604	196	42	1	30	(16	14)	330	113	107	127	94	6	115	6	0	7		34	5	.87	14	.325	.416	.546
2008	NYM	NL	160	626	189	42	2	33	(21	12)	334	115	124	116	94	5	118	4	0	11		15	5	.75	15	.302	.390	.534
2009	NYM	NL	144	535	164	39	3	10	(5	5)	239	88	72	86	74	8	140	3	0	6		27	9	.75	16	.307	.390	.447
	Postseason		10	37	8	3	0	1	(0	1)	14	3	6	5	5	1	8	0	0	0		0	0	-	0	.216	.310	.378
	6 ML YEARS		847	3185	983	222	13	140	(75	65)	1651	552	561	595	414	34	639	28	0	38		119	31	.79	83	.309	.389	.518

Jamey Wright

Pitches: R **Bats:** R **Pos:** RP-65   **Ht:** 6'5" **Wt:** 225 **Born:** 12/24/1974 **Age:** 35

			HOW MUCH HE PITCHED						WHAT HE GAVE UP												THE RESULTS						
Year	Team	Lg	G	GS	CG	GF	IP	BFP	H	R	ER	HR	SH	SF	HB	TBB	IBB	SO	WP	Bk	W	L	Pct	Sh	Sv-Op	Hld	ERC	ERA
1996	Col	NL	16	15	0	0	91.1	406	105	60	50	8	4	2	7	41	1	45	1	2	4	4	.500	0	0-0	1	5.50	4.93
1997	Col	NL	26	26	1	0	149.2	698	198	113	104	19	8	3	11	71	3	59	6	2	8	12	.400	0	0-0	0	6.96	6.25
1998	Col	NL	34	34	1	0	206.1	919	235	143	130	24	8	6	11	95	3	86	6	3	9	14	.391	0	0-0	0	5.57	5.67
1999	Col	NL	16	16	0	0	94.1	423	110	52	51	10	3	4	4	54	3	49	3	0	4	3	.571	0	0-0	0	6.19	4.87
2000	Mil	NL	26	25	0	1	164.2	718	157	81	75	12	4	6	18	88	5	96	9	2	7	9	.438	0	0-0	0	4.67	4.10
2001	Mil	NL	33	33	1	0	194.2	868	201	115	106	26	7	5	20	98	10	129	6	1	11	12	.478	1	0-0	0	5.36	4.90
2002	2 Tms	NL	23	22	1	0	129.1	585	130	80	76	17	9	6	11	75	9	77	9	0	7	13	.350	1	0-0	0	5.35	5.29
2003	KC	AL	4	4	2	0	25.1	106	23	14	12	1	0	0	1	11	0	19	0	0	1	2	.333	1	0-0	0	3.53	4.26
2004	Col	NL	14	14	0	0	78.2	361	82	39	36	8	1	1	6	45	3	41	3	0	2	3	.400	0	0-0	0	5.26	4.12
2005	Col	NL	34	27	0	1	171.1	782	201	110	104	22	4	3	15	81	4	101	2	2	8	16	.333	0	0-0	1	6.02	5.46
2006	SF	NL	34	21	0	2	156.0	676	167	95	90	16	5	4	10	64	4	79	6	0	6	10	.375	0	0-0	0	4.89	5.19
2007	Tex	AL	20	9	0	3	77.0	330	72	35	31	6	3	2	5	41	2	39	4	0	4	5	.444	0	0-0	0	4.44	3.62
2008	Tex	AL	75	0	0	17	84.1	379	93	54	48	5	3	4	8	35	3	60	5	0	8	7	.533	0	0-6	17	4.74	5.12
2009	KC	AL	65	0	0	14	79.0	350	73	51	38	8	4	0	7	44	5	60	7	0	3	5	.375	0	0-3	12	4.56	4.33
02	Mil	NL	19	19	1	0	114.1	515	115	72	68	15	9	6	11	63	8	69	8	0	5	13	.278	1	0-0	0	5.28	5.35
02	StL	NL	4	3	0	0	15.0	70	15	8	8	2	0	0	0	12	1	8	1	0	2	0	1.000	0	0-0	0	5.87	4.80
	14 ML YEARS		420	246	6	38	1702.0	7601	1847	1054	951	182	63	46	134	843	55	940	67	12	82	115	.416	3	0-9	32	5.38	5.03

Wesley Wright

Pitches: L **Bats:** R **Pos:** RP-49   **Ht:** 5'11" **Wt:** 160 **Born:** 1/28/1985 **Age:** 25

			HOW MUCH HE PITCHED						WHAT HE GAVE UP												THE RESULTS						
Year	Team	Lg	G	GS	CG	GF	IP	BFP	H	R	ER	HR	SH	SF	HB	TBB	IBB	SO	WP	Bk	W	L	Pct	Sh	Sv-Op	Hld	ERC	ERA
2003	Ddgrs	R	14	5	0	1	37.2	157	37	15	15	1	0	0	1	19	0	26	4	0	3	1	.750	0	0--	-	4.21	3.58
2005	Clmbs	A	30	0	0	9	60.2	254	38	21	13	2	0	1	7	33	0	68	5	0	1	5	.167	0	1--	-	2.62	1.93
2005	VeroB	A+	6	0	0	1	6.2	37	8	7	7	0	0	0	0	10	0	8	0	0	0	0	-	0	0--	-	8.99	9.45
2006	VeroB	A+	26	0	0	15	42.1	174	29	11	7	0	3	0	1	23	1	51	6	0	3	3	.500	0	0--	-	2.37	1.49

			HOW MUCH HE PITCHED						WHAT HE GAVE UP												THE RESULTS							
Year	Team	Lg	G	GS	CG	GF	IP	BFP	H	R	FR	HR	SH	SF	HB	TBB	IBB	SO	WP	Bk	W	L	Pct	Sh	Sv-Op	Hld	ERC	ERA
2006	Jaxnvl	AA	15	0	0	11	21.1	90	14	13	11	2	1	2	2	11	0	28	4	1	1	1	.500	0	1--	1	2.96	4.64
2007	Jaxnvl	AA	30	1	0	9	61.1	258	45	19	17	4	2	4	0	31	0	67	6	1	6	2	.750	0	2--	-	2.79	2.49
2007	LsVgs	AAA	14	1	0	6	16.2	92	28	23	17	4	2	2	1	18	1	18	2	0	1	2	.333	0	0--	-	13.54	9.18
2009	RdRck	AAA	13	1	0	1	19.0	80	13	7	7	0	6	0	1	10	2	18	2	0	2	1	.667	0	0--	-	2.22	3.32
2008	Hou	NL	71	0	0	15	55.2	250	45	34	31	8	1	1	4	34	4	57	2	1	4	3	.571	0	1-1	13	4.21	5.01
2009	Hou	NL	49	0	0	5	44.2	204	53	27	27	9	0	2	0	25	3	47	2	0	3	4	.429	0	0-2	6	6.64	5.44
	2 ML YEARS		120	0	0	20	100.1	454	98	61	58	17	1	3	4	59	7	104	4	1	7	7	.500	0	1-3	19	5.24	5.20

Mike Wuertz

Pitches: R **Bats:** R **Pos:** RP-74   **Ht:** 6'3" **Wt:** 205 **Born:** 12/15/1978 **Age:** 31

			HOW MUCH HE PITCHED						WHAT HE GAVE UP												THE RESULTS							
Year	Team	Lg	G	GS	CG	GF	IP	BFP	H	R	ER	HR	SH	SF	HB	TBB	IBB	SO	WP	Bk	W	L	Pct	Sh	Sv-Op	Hld	ERC	ERA
2004	ChC	NL	31	0	0	11	29.0	124	22	14	14	4	4	2	0	17	1	30	2	1	1	0	1.000	0	1-1	1	3.67	4.34
2005	ChC	NL	75	0	0	12	75.2	319	60	36	32	6	3	2	0	40	7	75	7	0	6	2	.750	0	0-3	18	3.17	3.81
2006	ChC	NL	41	0	0	4	40.2	175	35	14	12	5	3	0	1	16	2	42	1	0	3	1	.750	0	0-1	6	3.37	2.66
2007	ChC	NL	73	0	0	19	72.1	312	64	30	28	8	3	1	0	35	6	79	6	0	2	3	.400	0	0-0	8	3.68	3.48
2008	ChC	NL	45	0	0	13	44.2	189	44	23	18	4	1	3	0	20	2	30	2	0	1	1	.500	0	0-3	3	4.15	3.63
2009	Oak	AL	74	0	0	9	78.2	304	52	25	23	6	2	3	0	23	1	102	6	0	6	1	.857	0	4-6	23	1.84	2.63
	Postseason		2	0	0	0	1.2	7	0	0	0	0	1	0	0	1	0	2	1	0	0	0	-	0	0-0	0	0.32	0.00
	6 ML YEARS		339	0	0	68	341.0	1423	277	142	127	33	16	11	1	151	19	372	24	1	19	8	.704	0	5-14	59	3.14	3.35

Yasuhiko Yabuta

Pitches: R **Bats:** R **Pos:** RP-12   **Ht:** 6'2" **Wt:** 189 **Born:** 6/19/1973 **Age:** 37

			HOW MUCH HE PITCHED						WHAT HE GAVE UP												THE RESULTS							
Year	Team	Lg	G	GS	CG	GF	IP	BFP	H	R	ER	HR	SH	SF	HB	TBB	IBB	SO	WP	Bk	W	L	Pct	Sh	Sv-Op	Hld	ERC	ERA
1996	Chiba	Jap	18	10	1	3	92.0	376	79	39	37	8	-	-	3	20	-	98	5	0	1	6	.100	1	0--	-	3.07	3.02
1997	Chiba	Jap	25	20	4	0	146.1	621	144	69	64	16	-	-	2	48	-	74	7	2	5	9	.357	0	0--	-	3.82	3.94
1998	Chiba	Jap	17	14	2	0	100.1	448	123	61	54	15	-	-	1	40	-	45	8	6	2	9	.182	0	0--	-	5.91	4.84
1999	Chiba	Jap	12	10	0	1	57.0	260	68	33	31	9	-	-	2	30	-	33	3	1	5	4	.556	0	0--	-	6.48	4.89
2000	Chiba	Jap	2	2	0	0	6.2	31	9	10	10	3	-	-	0	2	-	3	0	0	0	1	.000	0	0--	-	8.30	13.50
2001	Chiba	Jap	27	13	0	8	87.1	414	94	44	42	16	-	-	3	40	-	70	1	0	4	6	.400	0	0--	-	4.51	3.88
2002	Chiba	Jap	3	3	0	0	11.1	52	16	11	11	4	-	-	0	4	-	8	0	0	1	2	.333	0	0--	-	6.57	8.74
2003	Chiba	Jap	17	13	0	1	68.2	304	74	45	45	12	-	-	2	27	-	44	3	0	5	6	.455	0	0--	-	5.13	5.90
2004	Chiba	Jap	66	1	0	24	77.1	328	62	26	24	4	5	2	3	34	4	71	2	1	3	4	.429	0	2--	-	2.86	2.79
2005	Chiba	Jap	51	0	0	15	55.2	220	42	20	19	7	4	0	2	13	1	54	1	0	7	4	.636	0	2--	-	2.45	3.07
2006	Chiba	Jap	47	0	0	16	55.0	232	43	19	16	3	6	3	0	26	4	48	0	0	4	2	.667	0	1--	-	2.73	2.62
2007	Chiba	Jap	58	0	0	-	62.2	264	64	21	19	5	-	-	2	10	2	45	1	0	4	6	.400	0	4--	-	3.13	2.73
2008	Omha	AAA	20	0	0	15	40.1	178	46	24	24	3	3	1	0	16	0	33	1	0	4	3	.571	0	3--	-	4.70	5.36
2009	Omha	AAA	26	0	0	5	45.2	191	39	19	18	5	3	0	0	17	0	53	1	0	2	1	.667	0	0--	-	3.21	3.55
2008	KC	AL	31	0	0	12	37.2	168	41	21	20	6	1	1	0	17	0	25	1	0	1	3	.250	0	0-1	0	5.21	4.78
2009	KC	AL	12	0	0	3	14.0	77	29	21	21	3	0	1	0	7	0	9	4	0	2	1	.667	0	0-1	0	12.56	13.50
	2 ML YEARS		43	0	0	15	51.2	245	70	42	41	9	1	2	0	24	0	34	5	0	3	4	.429	0	0-2	0	7.03	7.14

Tyler Yates

Pitches: R **Bats:** R **Pos:** RP-15   **Ht:** 6'4" **Wt:** 250 **Born:** 8/7/1977 **Age:** 32

			HOW MUCH HE PITCHED						WHAT HE GAVE UP												THE RESULTS							
Year	Team	Lg	G	GS	CG	GF	IP	BFP	H	R	ER	HR	SH	SF	HB	TBB	IBB	SO	WP	Bk	W	L	Pct	Sh	Sv-Op	Hld	ERC	ERA
2004	NYM	NL	21	7	0	2	46.2	228	61	36	33	6	2	2	3	25	3	35	1	1	2	4	.333	0	0-0	2	6.73	6.36
2006	Atl	NL	56	0	0	11	50.0	217	42	23	22	6	2	0	0	31	8	46	1	0	2	5	.286	0	1-6	12	3.95	3.96
2007	Atl	NL	75	0	0	14	66.0	294	64	44	38	6	4	1	3	31	8	69	2	0	2	3	.400	0	2-3	13	4.02	5.18
2008	Pit	NL	72	0	0	16	73.1	331	72	39	38	6	4	1	2	41	4	63	5	0	6	3	.667	0	1-5	14	4.43	4.66
2009	Pit	NL	15	0	0	2	12.0	56	14	12	10	2	2	1	1	7	1	9	0	0	0	2	.000	0	0-0	3	6.64	7.50
	5 ML YEARS		239	7	0	45	248.0	1126	253	154	141	26	14	5	9	135	24	222	9	1	12	17	.414	0	4-14	44	4.73	5.12

Kevin Youkilis

Bats: R **Throws:** R **Pos:** 1B-78; 3B-63; LF-2; PH-1   **Ht:** 6'1" **Wt:** 220 **Born:** 3/15/1979 **Age:** 31

			BATTING																		BASERUNNING				AVERAGES		
Year	Team	Lg	G	AB	H	2B	3B	HR	(Hm	Rd)	TB	R	RBI	RC	TBB	IBB	SO	HBP	SH	SF	SB	CS	SB%	GDP	Avg	OBP	Slg
2009	Pwtckt*	AAA	2	6	0	0	0	0	(-	-)	0	0	0	0	1	0	2	0	0	0	0	0	.000	0	.000	.143	.000
2004	Bos	AL	72	208	54	11	0	7	(2	5)	86	38	35	36	33	0	45	4	0	3	0	1	.00	1	.260	.367	.413
2005	Bos	AL	44	79	22	7	0	1	(0	1)	32	11	9	13	14	0	19	2	0	0	0	1	.00	0	.278	.400	.405
2006	Bos	AL	147	569	159	42	2	13	(6	7)	244	100	72	104	91	0	120	9	0	11	5	2	.71	12	.279	.381	.429
2007	Bos	AL	145	528	152	35	2	16	(8	8)	239	85	83	101	77	0	105	15	0	5	4	2	.67	9	.288	.390	.453
2008	Bos	AL	145	538	168	43	4	29	(17	12)	306	91	115	120	62	7	108	12	0	9	3	5	.38	11	.312	.390	.569
2009	Bos	AL	136	491	150	36	1	27	(14	13)	269	99	94	114	77	6	125	16	0	4	7	2	.78	9	.305	.413	.548
	Postseason		26	99	33	8	1	6	(2	4)	61	22	17	20	13	0	16	0	0	1	0	0	-	4	.333	.407	.616
	6 ML YEARS		689	2413	705	174	9	93	(47	46)	1176	424	408	488	354	13	522	58	0	32	19	13	.59	42	.292	.391	.407

Chris Young

Pitches: R Bats: R Pos: SP-14   Ht: 6'10" Wt: 278 Born: 5/25/1979 Age: 31

			HOW MUCH HE PITCHED						WHAT HE GAVE UP											THE RESULTS						
Year	Team	Lg	G	GS	CG	GF	IP	BFP	H	R	ER	HR	SH	SF	HB	TBB	IBB	SO	WP	Bk	W	L	Pct	Sh	Sv-Op	Hld	ERC	ERA
2004	Tex	AL	7	7	0	0	36.1	158	36	21	19	7	1	0	2	10	0	27	1	0	3	2	.600	0	0-0	0	4.26	4.71
2005	Tex	AL	31	31	0	0	164.2	700	162	84	78	19	2	4	7	45	2	137	3	0	12	7	.632	0	0-0	0	3.71	4.26
2006	SD	NL	31	31	0	0	179.1	735	134	72	69	28	8	3	6	69	4	164	6	1	11	5	.688	0	0-0	0	3.12	3.46
2007	SD	NL	30	30	0	0	173.0	705	118	66	60	10	3	6	7	72	0	167	7	4	9	8	.529	0	0-0	0	2.35	3.12
2008	SD	NL	18	18	1	0	102.1	434	84	46	45	13	4	1	1	48	4	93	3	1	7	6	.538	0	0-0	0	3.50	3.96
2009	SD	NL	14	14	0	0	76.0	336	70	47	44	12	4	5	2	40	3	50	1	0	4	6	.400	0	0-0	0	4.55	5.21
Postseason			1	1	0	0	6.2	25	4	0	0	0	0	0	0	2	1	9	0	0	1	0	1.000	0	0-0	0	1.22	0.00
6 ML YEARS			131	131	1	0	731.2	3068	604	336	315	89	22	19	25	284	13	638	21	6	46	34	.575	0	0-0	0	3.31	3.87

Chris Young

Bats: R Throws: R Pos: CF-124; PH-13   Ht: 6'2" Wt: 200 Born: 9/5/1983 Age: 26

						BATTING															BASERUNNING				AVERAGES		
Year	Team	Lg	G	AB	H	2B	3B	HR	(Hm	Rd)	TB	R	RBI	RC	TBB	IBB	SO	HBP	SH	SF	SB	CS	SB%	GDP	Avg	OBP	Slg
2009	Reno*	AAA	13	54	20	5	1	3	(-	-)	36	17	9	14	9	0	13	0	0	0	2	2	.50	1	.370	.460	.667
2006	Ari	NL	30	70	17	4	0	2	(1	1)	27	10	10	11	6	0	12	1	0	1	2	1	.67	0	.243	.308	.386
2007	Ari	NL	148	569	135	29	3	32	(14	18)	266	85	68	68	43	1	141	6	1	5	27	6	.82	5	.237	.295	.467
2008	Ari	NL	160	625	155	42	7	22	(9	13)	277	85	85	84	62	2	165	1	6	5	14	5	.74	10	.248	.315	.443
2009	Ari	NL	134	433	92	28	4	15	(7	8)	173	54	42	47	59	2	133	4	3	2	11	4	.73	3	.212	.311	.400
Postseason			7	25	7	1	0	2	(1	1)	14	4	5	7	7	0	13	1	0	0	1	2	.33	0	.280	.455	.560
4 ML YEARS			472	1697	399	103	14	71	(31	40)	743	234	205	210	170	5	451	12	10	13	54	16	.77	18	.235	.307	.438

Delmon Young

Bats: R Throws: R Pos: LF-98; DH-8; PR-2; PH-1   Ht: 6'3" Wt: 200 Born: 9/14/1985 Age: 24

						BATTING															BASERUNNING				AVERAGES		
Year	Team	Lg	G	AB	H	2B	3B	HR	(Hm	Rd)	TB	R	RBI	RC	TBB	IBB	SO	HBP	SH	SF	SB	CS	SB%	GDP	Avg	OBP	Slg
2006	TB	AL	30	126	40	9	1	3	(1	2)	60	16	10	15	1	0	24	3	0	1	2	2	.50	0	.317	.336	.476
2007	TB	AL	162	645	186	38	0	13	(9	4)	263	65	93	90	26	2	127	3	0	7	10	3	.77	23	.288	.316	.408
2008	Min	AL	152	575	167	28	4	10	(7	3)	233	80	69	74	35	7	105	7	1	5	14	5	.74	19	.290	.336	.405
2009	Min	AL	108	395	112	16	2	12	(7	5)	168	50	60	46	12	1	92	4	0	5	2	5	.29	17	.284	.308	.425
4 ML YEARS			452	1741	505	91	7	38	(24	14)	724	211	232	225	74	10	348	17	1	18	28	15	.65	59	.290	.322	.416

Delwyn Young

Bats: B Throws: R Pos: 2B-53; PH-42; RF-26; LF-4   Ht: 5'10" Wt: 191 Born: 6/30/1982 Age: 28

						BATTING															BASERUNNING				AVERAGES		
Year	Team	Lg	G	AB	H	2B	3B	HR	(Hm	Rd)	TB	R	RBI	RC	TBB	IBB	SO	HBP	SH	SF	SB	CS	SB%	GDP	Avg	OBP	Slg
2009	Albq*	AAA	3	9	1	0	0	0	(-	-)	1	0	0	0	1	0	2	0	0	0	0	0	-	1	.111	.200	.111
2006	LAD	NL	8	5	0	0	0	0	(0	0)	0	0	0	0	0	0	1	0	0	0	0	0	-	0	.000	.000	.000
2007	LAD	NL	19	34	13	1	1	2	(2	0)	22	4	3	8	2	0	5	0	0	0	1	0	1.00	0	.382	.417	.647
2008	LAD	NL	83	126	31	9	0	1	(1	0)	43	10	7	11	14	0	34	0	3	0	0	0	-	2	.246	.321	.341
2009	Pit	NL	124	354	94	16	2	7	(4	3)	135	40	43	43	29	0	90	3	1	1	2	0	1.00	13	.266	.326	.381
4 ML YEARS			234	519	138	26	3	10	(7	3)	200	54	53	62	45	0	130	3	4	1	3	0	1.00	15	.266	.327	.385

Dmitri Young

Bats: B Throws: R Pos: 1B   Ht: 6'2" Wt: 298 Born: 10/11/1973 Age: 36

						BATTING															BASERUNNING				AVERAGES		
Year	Team	Lg	G	AB	H	2B	3B	HR	(Hm	Rd)	TB	R	RBI	RC	TBB	IBB	SO	HBP	SH	SF	SB	CS	SB%	GDP	Avg	OBP	Slg
2009	Nats*	R	3	6	1	0	0	0	(-	-)	1	2	0	0	1	0	0	1	0	0	0	0	-	1	.167	.375	.167
2009	Hrsbrg*	AA	10	29	7	2	0	0	(-	-)	9	4	2	3	3	1	4	1	0	1	0	0	-	0	.241	.324	.310
2009	Ptomc*	A+	1	3	1	0	0	1	(-	-)	4	1	1	1	1	0	1	0	0	0	0	0	-	0	.333	.500	1.333
1996	StL	NL	16	29	7	0	0	0	(0	0)	7	3	2	2	4	0	5	1	0	0	0	1	.00	1	.241	.353	.241
1997	StL	NL	110	333	86	14	3	5	(2	3)	121	38	34	40	38	3	63	2	1	3	6	5	.55	8	.258	.335	.363
1998	Cin	NL	144	536	166	48	1	14	(3	11)	258	81	83	88	47	4	94	2	0	5	2	4	.33	16	.310	.364	.481
1999	Cin	NL	127	373	112	30	2	14	(9	5)	188	63	56	63	30	1	71	2	0	4	3	1	.75	11	.300	.352	.504
2000	Cin	NL	152	548	166	37	6	18	(6	12)	269	68	88	86	36	6	80	3	1	5	0	3	.00	16	.303	.346	.491
2001	Cin	NL	142	540	163	28	3	21	(8	13)	260	68	69	83	37	10	77	5	1	3	8	5	.62	22	.302	.350	.481
2002	Det	AL	54	201	57	14	0	7	(5	2)	92	25	27	27	12	5	39	2	0	1	2	0	1.00	12	.284	.329	.458
2003	Det	AL	155	562	167	34	7	29	(10	19)	302	78	85	101	58	16	130	11	0	4	2	1	.67	16	.297	.372	.537
2004	Det	AL	104	389	106	23	2	18	(8	10)	187	72	60	57	33	4	71	6	0	4	0	1	.00	8	.272	.336	.481
2005	Det	AL	126	469	127	25	3	21	(10	11)	221	61	72	60	29	7	100	9	0	1	1	0	1.00	16	.271	.325	.471
2006	Det	AL	48	172	43	4	1	7	(2	5)	70	19	23	20	11	0	39	0	0	1	1	1	.50	3	.250	.293	.407
2007	Was	NL	136	460	147	38	1	13	(7	6)	226	57	74	74	44	6	74	1	0	3	0	0	-	13	.320	.378	.491
2008	Was	NL	50	150	42	6	0	4	(1	3)	60	15	10	16	28	4	28	1	0	1	0	0	-	4	.280	.394	.400
Postseason			4	7	2	0	1	0	(0	0)	4	1	2	1	0	0	2	0	0	0	0	0	-	0	.286	.286	.571
13 ML YEARS			1364	4762	1389	301	29	171	(71	100)	2261	648	683	717	407	66	871	45	3	35	25	22	.53	150	.292	.351	.475

Michael Young

Bats: R **Throws:** R **Pos:** 3B-134; DH-1   **Ht:** 6'1" **Wt:** 200 **Born:** 10/19/1976 **Age:** 33

								BATTING												BASERUNNING				AVERAGES		
Year Team	Lg	G	AB	H	2B	3B	HR	(Hm Rd)	TB	R	RBI	RC	TBB	IBB	SO	HBP	SH	SF	SB	CS	SB%	GDP	Avg	OBP	Slg
2000 Tex	AL	2	2	0	0	0	0	(0 0)	0	0	0	0	0	0	1	0	0	0	0	0	-	0	.000	.000	.000
2001 Tex	AL	106	386	96	18	4	11	(7 4)	155	57	49	45	26	0	91	3	9	5	3	1	.75	9	.249	.298	.402
2002 Tex	AL	156	573	150	26	8	9	(3 6)	219	77	62	64	41	1	112	0	13	6	6	7	.46	14	.262	.308	.382
2003 Tex	AL	160	666	204	33	9	14	(9 5)	297	106	72	106	36	1	103	1	3	7	13	2	.87	14	.306	.339	.446
2004 Tex	AL	160	690	216	33	9	22	(9 13)	333	114	99	124	44	1	89	1	0	4	12	3	.80	11	.313	.353	.483
2005 Tex	AL	159	668	221	40	5	24	(12 12)	343	114	91	131	58	0	91	3	0	3	5	2	.71	20	.331	.385	.513
2006 Tex	AL	162	691	217	52	3	14	(8 6)	317	93	103	120	48	0	96	1	0	8	7	3	.70	27	.314	.356	.459
2007 Tex	AL	156	639	201	37	1	9	(8 1)	267	80	94	107	47	5	107	5	0	1	13	3	.81	21	.315	.366	.418
2008 Tex	AL	155	645	183	36	2	12	(8 4)	259	102	82	86	55	0	109	2	0	6	10	0	1.00	19	.284	.339	.402
2009 Tex	AL	135	541	174	36	2	22	(10 12)	280	76	68	87	47	2	90	1	0	4	8	3	.73	16	.322	.374	.518
10 ML YEARS		1351	5501	1662	311	43	137	(74 63)	2470	819	720	870	402	10	889	17	25	44	77	24	.76	151	.302	.349	.449

Eric Young Jr.

Bats: B **Throws:** R **Pos:** PH-17; 2B-6; CF-5; PR-2   **Ht:** 5'10" **Wt:** 180 **Born:** 5/25/1985 **Age:** 25

								BATTING												BASERUNNING				AVERAGES		
Year Team	Lg	G	AB	H	2B	3B	HR	(Hm Rd)	TB	R	RBI	RC	TBB	IBB	SO	HBP	SH	SF	SB	CS	SB%	GDP	Avg	OBP	Slg
2004 Casper	R+	23	87	23	5	1	0	(- -)	30	20	7	17	20	0	13	1	2	0	14	1	.93	0	.264	.407	.345
2005 Casper	R+	63	219	66	7	7	3	(- -)	96	48	25	42	35	0	52	4	4	2	25	10	.71	4	.301	.404	.438
2006 Ashvll	A	128	482	142	28	6	5	(- -)	197	92	49	88	67	0	75	10	9	1	87	31	.74	2	.295	.391	.409
2007 Mdest	A+	130	540	157	29	11	8	(- -)	232	113	63	94	46	1	105	13	12	2	73	18	.80	5	.291	.359	.430
2008 Tulsa	AA	105	403	117	23	4	3	(- -)	157	74	33	70	61	1	77	6	6	0	46	16	.74	6	.290	.391	.390
2009 ColSpr	AAA	119	472	141	21	10	7	(- -)	203	118	43	88	56	1	79	12	12	0	57	14	.80	2	.299	.387	.430
2009 Col	NL	30	57	14	1	0	1	(1 0)	18	7	1	2	4	0	12	0	0	0	4	4	.50	1	.246	.295	.316

Carlos Zambrano

Pitches: R **Bats:** B **Pos:** SP-28   **Ht:** 6'5" **Wt:** 255 **Born:** 6/1/1981 **Age:** 29

					HOW MUCH HE PITCHED			WHAT HE GAVE UP												THE RESULTS						
Year Team	Lg	G	GS	CG	GF	IP	BFP	H	R	ER	HR	SH	SF	HB	TBB	IBB	SO	WP	Bk	W	L	Pct	Sh	Sv-Op	Hld	ERC	ERA
2000 Dytona*	A+	1	1	0	0	3.2	19	5	4	4	0	0	0	0	3	0	1	0	0	0	1	.000	0	0--	-	6.95	9.82
2009 Peoria*	A	1	1	0	0	5.0	19	4	0	0	0	0	0	0	0	0	5	1	0	0	0	-	0	0--	-	1.27	0.00
2001 ChC	NL	6	1	0	1	7.2	42	11	13	13	2	1	1	1	8	0	4	1	0	1	2	.333	0	0-1	0	11.88	15.26
2002 ChC	NL	32	16	0	3	108.1	477	94	53	44	9	9	1	4	63	2	93	6	0	4	8	.333	0	0-0	0	4.02	3.66
2003 ChC	NL	32	32	3	0	214.0	907	188	88	74	9	11	6	10	94	12	168	6	1	13	11	.542	1	0-0	0	3.28	3.11
2004 ChC	NL	31	31	1	0	209.2	887	174	73	64	14	10	3	20	81	4	188	6	2	16	8	.667	1	0-0	0	3.20	2.75
2005 ChC	NL	33	33	2	0	223.1	909	170	88	81	21	9	5	8	86	3	202	7	0	14	6	.700	0	0-0	0	2.86	3.26
2006 ChC	NL	33	33	0	0	214.0	917	162	91	81	20	11	4	9	115	4	210	9	1	16	7	.696	0	0-0	0	3.34	3.41
2007 ChC	NL	34	34	1	0	216.1	925	187	100	95	23	6	3	14	101	4	177	3	0	18	13	.581	0	0-0	0	3.88	3.95
2008 ChC	NL	30	30	1	0	188.2	796	172	85	82	18	5	0	6	72	1	130	4	0	14	6	.700	1	0-0	0	3.62	3.91
2009 ChC	NL	28	28	1	0	169.1	733	155	78	71	10	10	5	9	78	6	152	7	0	9	7	.563	1	0-0	0	3.70	3.77
Postseason		5	5	0	0	29.0	132	35	19	14	6	1	1	2	8	0	27	1	0	0	2	.000	0	0-0	0	5.72	4.34
9 ML YEARS		259	238	9	4	1551.1	6593	1313	669	605	126	72	28	81	698	36	1324	49	4	105	68	.607	4	0-1	0	3.47	3.51

Gregg Zaun

Bats: B **Throws:** R **Pos:** C-83; PH-12   **Ht:** 5'10" **Wt:** 170 **Born:** 4/14/1971 **Age:** 39

								BATTING												BASERUNNING				AVERAGES		
Year Team	Lg	G	AB	H	2B	3B	HR	(Hm Rd)	TB	R	RBI	RC	TBB	IBB	SO	HBP	SH	SF	SB	CS	SB%	GDP	Avg	OBP	Slg
1995 Bal	AL	40	104	27	5	0	3	(1 1)	41	18	14	15	16	0	14	0	2	0	1	1	.50	2	.260	.358	.394
1996 2 Tms	AL	60	139	34	9	1	2	(1 1)	51	20	15	16	14	3	20	2	1	2	1	0	1.00	5	.245	.318	.367
1997 Fla	NL	58	143	43	10	2	2	(0 2)	63	21	20	27	26	4	18	2	1	0	1	0	1.00	3	.301	.415	.441
1998 Fla	NL	106	298	56	12	2	5	(2 3)	87	19	29	23	35	2	52	1	2	2	5	2	.71	7	.188	.274	.292
1999 Tex	AL	43	93	23	2	1	1	(0 1)	30	12	12	10	10	0	7	0	1	2	1	0	1.00	2	.247	.314	.323
2000 KC	AL	83	234	64	11	0	7	(2 5)	96	36	33	40	43	3	34	3	0	2	7	3	.70	4	.274	.390	.410
2001 KC	AL	39	125	40	9	0	6	(1 5)	67	15	18	24	12	0	16	0	0	1	1	2	.33	2	.320	.377	.536
2002 Hou	NL	76	185	41	7	1	3	(3 0)	59	18	24	17	12	1	36	2	2	1	1	0	1.00	4	.222	.275	.319
2003 2 Tms	NL	74	166	38	8	0	4	(1 3)	58	15	21	20	19	0	21	1	1	2	1	1	.50	5	.229	.309	.349
2004 Tor	AL	107	338	91	24	0	6	(2 4)	133	46	36	50	47	3	61	6	0	1	0	2	.00	7	.269	.367	.393
2005 Tor	AL	133	434	109	18	1	11	(7 4)	162	61	61	65	73	2	70	4	0	5	2	3	.40	11	.251	.355	.373
2006 Tor	AL	99	290	79	19	0	12	(7 5)	134	39	40	41	43	3	42	3	0	5	0	2	.00	10	.272	.363	.462
2007 Tor	AL	110	331	80	24	1	10	(6 4)	136	43	52	48	51	8	55	2	1	6	0	-		9	.242	.341	.411
2008 Tor	AL	86	245	58	12	0	6	(5 1)	88	29	30	32	38	1	38	1	3	1	2	1	.67	6	.237	.340	.359
2009 2 Tms	AL	90	262	68	17	0	8	(3 5)	109	34	27	35	31	0	48	3	0	0	0	2	.00	4	.260	.345	.416
96 Bal	AL	50	108	25	8	1	1	(1 0)	38	16	13	12	11	2	15	2	0	2	0	0	-	3	.231	.309	.352
96 Fla	NL	10	31	9	1	0	1	(0 1)	13	4	2	4	3	1	5	0	1	0	1	0	1.00	2	.290	.353	.419
03 Hou	NL	50	120	26	7	0	1	(1 0)	36	9	13	12	14	0	14	1	1	2	1	0	1.00	5	.217	.299	.300
03 Col	NL	15	46	12	1	0	3	(0 3)	22	6	8	8	5	0	7	0	0	0	0	1	.00	0	.261	.333	.478
09 Bal	AL	56	168	41	10	0	4	(1 3)	63	23	13	23	27	0	30	2	0	0	0	0	-	2	.244	.355	.375
09 TB	AL	34	94	27	7	0	4	(2 2)	46	11	14	12	4	0	18	1	0	0	0	2	.00	2	.287	.323	.489
Postseason		3	2	0	0	0	0	(0 0)	0	0	0	0	0	0	0	0	0	0	0	0	-	0	.000	.000	.000
15 ML YEARS		1204	3387	851	187	9	86	(41 45)	1314	426	432	463	468	30	532	26	14	30	23	19	.55	81	.251	.344	.388

Clay Zavada

Pitches: L **Bats:** L **Pos:** RP-49
Ht: 6'1" **Wt:** 195 **Born:** 6/28/1984 **Age:** 26

Year	Team	Lg	G	GS	CG	GF	IP	BFP	H	R	ER	HR	SH	SF	HB	TBB	IBB	SO	WP	Bk	W	L	Pct	Sh	Sv-Op	Hld	ERC	ERA
2006	Msoula	R+	22	0	0	5	49.1	208	41	29	17	3	6	2	2	15	0	51	2	2	2	3	.400	0	2- -	-	2.63	3.10
2008	So Ill	IND	12	0	0	7	15.2	58	7	3	3	0	1	1	1	4	0	22	1	0	2	1	.667	0	4- -	-	0.95	1.72
2008	Sbend	A	24	0	0	15	35.1	115	6	2	2	1	1	0	1	5	0	54	0	0	3	1	.750	0	8- -	-	0.25	0.51
2009	Mobile	AA	11	0	0	2	17.1	69	10	5	5	2	1	1	0	7	0	18	0	0	1	0	1.000	0	0- -	-	2.00	2.60
2009	Ari	NL	49	0	0	9	51.0	221	45	22	19	5	2	1	3	24	2	52	1	0	3	3	.500	0	0-0	4	3.84	3.35

Brad Ziegler

Pitches: R **Bats:** R **Pos:** RP-69
Ht: 6'4" **Wt:** 205 **Born:** 10/10/1979 **Age:** 30

Year	Team	Lg	G	GS	CG	GF	IP	BFP	H	R	ER	HR	SH	SF	HB	TBB	IBB	SO	WP	Bk	W	L	Pct	Sh	Sv-Op	Hld	ERC	ERA
2003	Batvia	A-	3	0	0	1	6.0	23	5	1	1	0	0	0	0	1	0	6	0	0	1	0	1.000	0	0- -	-	1.84	1.50
2004	Schbrg	IND	4	4	1	0	24.0	84	12	5	4	0	1	0	2	1	0	26	0	0	3	0	1.000	0	0- -	-	0.76	1.50
2004	Mdest	A+	16	15	0	1	92.1	389	94	51	40	11	4	2	2	22	0	77	0	1	9	2	.818	0	0- -	-	3.74	3.90
2005	Mdland	AA	4	4	0	0	21.0	96	27	16	16	1	1	4	3	4	0	20	1	0	2	1	.667	0	0- -	-	4.98	6.86
2005	Stcktn	A+	24	24	0	0	141.0	605	166	84	73	13	1	2	6	20	0	144	4	0	9	7	.563	0	0- -	-	4.13	4.66
2006	Mdland	AA	23	22	1	0	141.2	596	151	60	53	17	5	5	7	37	0	88	3	1	9	6	.600	0	0- -	-	4.32	3.37
2006	Scrmto	AAA	4	4	0	0	21.0	97	32	17	14	3	1	1	1	5	0	11	1	0	0	1	.000	0	0- -	-	7.24	6.00
2007	Mdland	AA	15	0	0	4	23.2	94	19	6	3	0	1	2	0	4	0	18	0	0	4	0	1.000	0	1- -	-	1.64	1.14
2007	Scrmto	AAA	35	0	0	5	54.2	218	46	20	18	0	2	1	2	14	0	44	0	1	8	3	.727	0	1- -	-	2.27	2.96
2008	Scrmto	AAA	19	0	0	14	24.1	91	15	2	1	0	1	0	0	4	1	20	0	0	2	0	1.000	0	8- -	-	1.07	0.37
2008	Oak	AL	47	0	0	21	59.2	229	47	8	7	2	4	3	1	22	3	30	0	0	3	0	1.000	0	11-13	9	2.60	1.06
2009	Oak	AL	69	0	0	23	73.1	313	82	27	25	2	1	3	1	28	4	54	0	0	2	4	.333	0	7-10	14	4.25	3.07
	2 ML YEARS		116	0	0	44	133.0	542	129	35	32	4	5	6	2	50	7	84	0	0	5	4	.556	0	18-23	23	3.49	2.17

Ryan Zimmerman

Bats: R **Throws:** R **Pos:** 3B-154; PH-3; DH-1
Ht: 6'3" **Wt:** 228 **Born:** 9/28/1984 **Age:** 25

Year	Team	Lg	G	AB	H	2B	3B	HR	(Hm	Rd)	TB	R	RBI	RC	TBB	IBB	SO	HBP	SH	SF	SB	CS	SB%	GDP	Avg	OBP	Slg
2005	Was	NL	20	58	23	10	0	0	(0	0)	33	6	6	9	3	0	12	0	0	-	1	0	-	1	.397	.419	.569
2006	Was	NL	157	614	176	47	3	20	(10	10)	289	84	110	101	61	7	120	2	1	4	11	8	.58	15	.287	.351	.471
2007	Was	NL	162	653	174	43	5	24	(11	13)	299	99	91	83	61	3	125	3	0	5	4	1	.80	26	.266	.330	.458
2008	Was	NL	106	428	121	24	1	14	(7	7)	189	51	51	48	31	1	71	3	0	4	1	1	.50	12	.283	.333	.442
2009	Was	NL	157	610	178	37	3	33	(17	16)	320	110	106	96	72	9	119	2	0	9	2	0	1.00	22	.292	.364	.525
	5 ML YEARS		602	2363	672	161	12	91	(45	46)	1130	350	364	337	228	20	447	10	1	23	18	10	.64	76	.284	.347	.478

Jordan Zimmermann

Pitches: R **Bats:** R **Pos:** SP-16
Ht: 6'2" **Wt:** 218 **Born:** 5/23/1986 **Age:** 24

Year	Team	Lg	G	GS	CG	GF	IP	BFP	H	R	ER	HR	SH	SF	HB	TBB	IBB	SO	WP	Bk	W	L	Pct	Sh	Sv-Op	Hld	ERC	ERA
2007	Vrmnt	A-	13	11	0	0	53.0	216	45	14	14	2	0	1	0	18	0	71	2	2	5	2	.714	0	0- -	-	2.67	2.38
2008	Ptomc	A+	5	4	0	1	27.1	99	15	6	5	1	1	0	0	8	0	31	0	0	3	1	.750	0	1- -	-	1.36	1.65
2008	Hrsbrg	AA	20	20	0	0	106.2	439	89	42	38	9	2	1	3	39	2	103	2	1	7	2	.778	0	0- -	-	3.06	3.21
2009	Syrcse	AAA	1	1	0	0	5.1	21	4	3	3	2	0	0	0	1	0	4	0	0	0	0	-	0	0- -	-	3.42	5.06
2009	Ptomc	A+	1	1	0	0	3.1	14	2	2	1	1	1	0	0	1	0	6	0	0	0	0	-	0	0- -	-	2.47	2.70
2009	Was	NL	16	16	0	0	91.1	391	95	51	47	10	5	3	4	29	0	92	0	0	3	5	.375	0	0-0	0	4.25	4.63

Barry Zito

Pitches: L **Bats:** L **Pos:** SP-33
Ht: 6'4" **Wt:** 215 **Born:** 5/13/1978 **Age:** 32

Year	Team	Lg	G	GS	CG	GF	IP	BFP	H	R	ER	HR	SH	SF	HB	TBB	IBB	SO	WP	Bk	W	L	Pct	Sh	Sv-Op	Hld	ERC	ERA
2000	Oak	AL	14	14	1	0	92.2	376	64	30	28	6	1	0	2	45	2	78	2	0	7	4	.636	1	0-0	0	2.63	2.72
2001	Oak	AL	35	**35**	3	0	214.1	902	184	92	83	18	5	4	13	80	0	205	6	1	17	8	.680	2	0-0	0	3.33	3.49
2002	Oak	AL	35	**35**	1	0	229.1	939	182	79	70	24	9	7	9	78	2	182	2	1	23	5	.821	0	0-0	0	2.92	2.75
2003	Oak	AL	35	35	4	0	231.2	957	186	98	85	19	7	7	6	88	3	146	4	0	14	12	.538	1	0-0	0	2.91	3.30
2004	Oak	AL	34	34	0	0	213.0	926	216	106	106	28	7	9	9	81	2	163	4	1	11	11	.500	0	0-0	0	4.45	4.48
2005	Oak	AL	35	**35**	0	0	228.1	953	185	106	98	26	8	7	13	89	0	171	4	0	14	13	.519	0	0-0	0	3.32	3.86
2006	Oak	AL	34	34	0	0	221.0	**945**	211	99	94	27	7	6	13	99	5	151	4	2	16	10	.615	0	0-0	0	4.47	3.83
2007	SF	NL	34	33	0	0	196.2	850	182	105	99	24	12	4	4	83	4	131	5	0	11	13	.458	0	0-0	0	3.91	4.53
2008	SF	NL	32	32	0	0	180.0	818	186	115	103	16	8	**14**	4	102	10	120	3	0	10	**17**	.370	0	0-0	0	4.81	5.15
2009	SF	NL	33	33	1	0	192.0	818	179	89	86	21	11	1	8	81	8	154	2	2	10	13	.435	0	0-0	0	4.00	4.03
	Postseason		7	7	0	0	44.1	184	34	16	16	6	1	0	3	17	0	33	1	0	4	3	.571	0	0-0	0	3.24	3.25
	10 ML YEARS		321	320	10	0	1999.0	8484	1775	929	852	209	75	59	81	826	36	1501	36	7	133	106	.556	4	0-0	0	3.68	3.84

Ben Zobrist

Bats: B **Throws:** R **Pos:** 2B-91; RF-59; PH-14; SS-13; LF-9; CF-7; 1B-3; 3B-1; DH-1; PR-1
Ht: 6'3" **Wt:** 200 **Born:** 5/26/1981 **Age:** 29

Year	Team	Lg	G	AB	H	2B	3B	HR	(Hm	Rd)	TB	R	RBI	RC	TBB	IBB	SO	HBP	SH	SF	SB	CS	SB%	GDP	Avg	OBP	Slg
2006	TB	AL	52	183	41	6	2	2	(2	0)	57	10	18	13	10	1	26	0	2	3	2	3	.40	2	.224	.260	.311
2007	TB	AL	31	97	15	2	0	1	(0	1)	20	8	9	0	3	0	21	1	2	2	2	0	1.00	1	.155	.184	.206

			BATTING																					BASERUNNING				AVERAGES		
Year	Team	Lg	G	AB	H	2B	3B	HR	(1Im	Rd)	TB	R	RBI	RC	TBB	IBB	SO	HBP	SH	SF	SB	CS	SB%	GDP	Avg	OBP	Slg
2008	TB	AL	62	198	50	10	2	12	(4	8)	100	32	30	31	25	1	37	2	0	2	3	0	1.00	4	.253	.339	.505
2009	TB	AL	152	501	149	28	7	27	(18	9)	272	91	91	109	91	4	104	2	1	4	17	6	.74	7	.297	.405	.543
Postseason			7	11	1	0	0	0	(0	0)	1	0	0	0	2	0	0	0	0	0	0	0	-	0	.091	.231	.091
4 ML YEARS			297	979	255	46	11	42	(24	18)	449	141	148	153	129	6	188	5	5	11	24	9	.73	14	.260	.346	.459

Joel Zumaya

Pitches: R **Bats:** R **Pos:** RP-29

Ht: 6'3" **Wt:** 210 **Born:** 11/9/1984 **Age:** 25

			HOW MUCH HE PITCHED						WHAT HE GAVE UP												THE RESULTS							
Year	Team	Lg	G	GS	CG	GF	IP	BFP	H	R	ER	HR	SH	SF	HB	TBB	IBB	SO	WP	Bk	W	L	Pct	Sh	Sv-Op	Hld	ERC	ERA
2009	Lkland*	A+	2	2	0	0	2.1	16	3	5	3	1	0	1	0	5	0	4	1	0	0	1	.000	0	0--	-	16.01	11.57
2009	Toledo*	AAA	3	0	0	0	4.0	15	3	0	0	0	0	0	0	0	0	5	0	0	0	0	-	0	0--	-	1.13	0.00
2006	Det	AL	62	0	0	12	83.1	350	56	20	18	6	2	4	2	42	2	97	4	0	6	3	.667	0	1-6	30	2.55	1.94
2007	Det	AL	28	0	0	7	33.2	142	23	16	16	3	1	1	1	17	2	27	3	0	2	3	.400	0	1-5	8	2.68	4.28
2008	Det	AL	21	0	0	5	23.1	114	24	13	9	3	0	1	0	22	4	22	6	0	0	2	.000	0	1-5	5	6.32	3.47
2009	Det	AL	29	0	0	5	31.0	149	34	18	17	5	1	1	1	22	3	30	1	0	3	3	.500	0	1-7	7	6.26	4.94
Postseason			6	0	0	2	6.0	24	2	4	2	0	0	0	0	3	0	6	1	0	0	1	.000	0	0-0	1	0.92	3.00
4 ML YEARS			140	0	0	29	171.1	755	137	67	60	17	4	7	4	103	11	176	14	0	11	11	.500	0	4-23	50	3.66	3.15

2009 Fielding Statistics

Fielding statistics have come a long ways in the past few years. At the beginning of the book, we list the Runs Saved and Plus/Minus leaders and the Fielding Bible Award winners. If you need our best estimate at how Ryan Zimmerman stacks up defensively, that's the place to check.

However, the newfangled defensive metrics don't mean the traditional ones are useless. There's still many a bar bet to be won with the knowledge that Jose Bautista had eight times as many assists as Juan Pierre in half as many innings in left field, or that Barbaro Canizares managed to start five games for the Braves at first base, or that Toronto second-sacker Aaron Hill turned 52 more double plays than former Blue Jay second baseman Orlando Hudson in only 100 more innings. (If you actually know a bar where these facts win drinks, let me know!)

It's possible that our fielding stats won't entirely match up with the official, Major League Baseball-sanctioned results when they arrive later this year. It's possible we differ by an assist or a double play somewhere. We had a choice: publish the book in November or wait for the official totals. Well, we hope you'll agree it's worth putting the book out early. Our totals may not be official, but they're no less accurate. In fact, we've been known to review dozens of games just to find a missing assist, only to find that our totals were correct all along.

Each position is broken down into "The Regulars" and "The Rest." This way, we get a clearer sense of how the starters at each position compare to one another, and we don't have to sift through the handful of games played by players away from their regular positions. September call-ups and players playing out of position have their own lists, so if you want to know which Nix brother was more defensively versatile, or how the Cincinnati Reds' Drew Stubbs handled his late season audition in center field, we have that as well.

The last column for the non-catchers is Range Factor, labeled "Rng." Range Factor is the number of successful chances (putouts plus assists) times nine, divided by the number of defensive innings played.

Don't miss our "Catchers Special" section where we offer catcher statistics like catcher ERA and caught stealing percentages. The Texas Rangers used four different catchers in 2009—which one managed to keep his Catcher ERA below 4.50?

Two clarifications before you start reading: PCS is the number of Total Caught Stealing attributed to the pitcher, not to the catcher in question. So CS% is the percentage of runners caught stealing not including PCS. And lastly, if you are looking for a pitcher's fielding statistics, you will find them in the "Pitchers Hitting, Fielding & Holding Runners" section.

First Basemen - Regulars

Player	Tm	G	GS	Inn	PO	A	E	DP	Pct.	Rng
Kotchman,Casey	TOT	114	100	893.1	859	80	0	63	1.000	-
LaRoche,Adam	TOT	148	147	1308.1	1325	108	2	148	.999	-
Youkilis,Kevin	Bos	78	77	647.0	565	52	1	56	.998	-
Overbay,Lyle	Tor	130	117	1055.1	1028	102	2	113	.998	-
Helton,Todd	Col	149	147	1275.0	1349	96	3	115	.998	-
Morneau,Justin	Min	123	123	1071.2	952	90	3	88	.997	-
Teixeira,Mark	NYY	152	150	1303.2	1222	49	4	110	.997	-
Konerko,Paul	CWS	134	133	1141.0	1159	79	4	112	.997	-
Davis,Chris	Tex	100	92	825.1	845	47	3	82	.997	-
Ishikawa,Travis	SF	113	88	817.1	745	55	3	83	.996	-
Huff,Aubrey	TOT	93	93	826.0	822	59	4	82	.995	-
Fielder,Prince	Mil	162	162	1431.0	1387	66	7	142	.995	-
Berkman,Lance	Hou	131	131	1141.1	1107	116	6	122	.995	-
Lee,Derrek	ChC	139	139	1231.1	1088	94	6	110	.995	-
Gonzalez,Adrian	SD	156	153	1359.2	1224	136	7	116	.995	-
Loney,James	LAD	155	147	1341.0	1269	85	7	110	.995	-
Cabrera,Miguel	Det	153	153	1315.0	1215	105	7	128	.995	-
Garko,Ryan	TOT	84	77	637.2	637	50	4	70	.994	-
Morales,Kendry	LAA	152	142	1279.0	1274	86	8	145	.994	-
Cantu,Jorge	Fla	111	93	850.0	829	38	6	72	.993	-
Pujols,Albert	StL	159	157	1376.2	1473	185	13	150	.992	-
Butler,Billy	KC	145	143	1248.0	1141	92	10	123	.992	-
Pena,Carlos	TB	133	129	1155.0	1055	71	10	102	.991	-
Votto,Joey	Cin	130	128	1097.0	960	101	10	108	.991	-
Branyan,Russell	Sea	116	116	1034.1	947	74	10	94	.990	-
Howard,Ryan	Phi	156	155	1388.1	1300	95	14	109	.990	-
Johnson,Nick	TOT	129	124	1067.0	1025	91	12	95	.989	-
Murphy,Daniel	NYM	101	97	849.1	790	74	10	81	.989	-

First Basemen - The Rest

Player	Tm	G	GS	Inn	PO	A	E	DP	Pct.	Rng
Allen,Brandon	Ari	32	29	254.2	260	11	2	23	.993	-
Atkins,Garrett	Col	28	11	126.1	124	5	1	8	.992	-
Aubrey,Michael	Bal	25	21	191.0	189	17	0	23	1.000	-
Aurilia,Rich	SF	22	16	158.1	125	14	0	13	1.000	-
Aybar,Willy	TB	31	26	204.1	168	18	1	16	.995	-
Bailey,Jeff	Bos	23	19	180.0	158	11	2	12	.988	-
Baker,Jeff	Col	1	0	3.0	3	0	0	2	1.000	-
Baker,Jeff	ChC	2	0	7.0	8	0	0	2	1.000	-
Barker,Kevin	Cin	6	1	25.0	32	1	0	5	1.000	-
Barton,Daric	Oak	51	46	416.2	418	25	1	38	.998	-
Bates,Aaron	Bos	5	3	30.0	35	0	1	3	.972	-
Belliard,Ronnie	Was	15	1	31.0	31	3	1	3	.971	-
Betemit,Wilson	CWS	7	4	46.0	41	7	1	6	.980	-
Blake,Casey	LAD	2	0	1.1	2	0	0	1	1.000	-
Blalock,Hank	Tex	66	66	567.2	535	26	6	64	.989	-
Blanks,Kyle	SD	8	4	45.0	36	3	0	8	1.000	-
Bloomquist,Willie	KC	3	0	6.0	3	0	0	1	1.000	-
Blum,Geoff	Hou	10	7	59.1	58	3	0	2	1.000	-
Boone,Aaron	Hou	2	1	10.0	9	1	0	1	1.000	-
Bowker,John	SF	4	2	18.2	15	0	0	0	1.000	-
Bruntlett,Eric	Phi	2	1	7.1	6	0	0	0	1.000	-
Burke,Jamie	Sea	1	1	9.0	7	1	1	2	.889	-
Buscher,Brian	Min	13	6	72.1	69	6	0	13	1.000	-
Canizares,Barbaro	Atl	5	5	43.0	33	2	0	3	1.000	-
Carp,Mike	Sea	16	15	127.1	115	15	0	13	1.000	-
Clark,Tony	Ari	21	14	131.0	128	13	3	11	.979	-
Cora,Alex	NYM	1	0	1.0	0	0	0	0	-	-
Coste,Chris	Phi	1	1	9.0	3	0	0	1	1.000	-
Coste,Chris	Hou	15	13	115.2	118	7	1	16	.992	-
Crosby,Bobby	Oak	54	24	268.0	235	13	0	26	1.000	-
Cuddyer,Michael	Min	34	34	296.0	278	14	4	27	.986	-
Delgado,Carlos	NYM	25	25	217.2	192	9	2	16	.990	-
DeRosa,Mark	Cle	7	4	41.0	41	1	1	3	.977	-
DeRosa,Mark	StL	3	1	8.0	6	0	0	2	1.000	-
Dobbs,Greg	Phi	6	4	41.0	24	1	1	3	.962	-
Duncan,Chris	StL	6	3	27.0	26	3	2	1	.935	-
Dunn,Adam	Was	67	66	540.0	531	37	8	63	.986	-
Erstad,Darin	Hou	15	10	98.2	94	7	0	13	1.000	-
Evans,Nick	NYM	5	5	38.0	36	2	1	1	.974	-
Everidge,Tommy	Oak	21	19	166.0	138	11	1	11	.993	-

Player	Tm	G	GS	Inn	PO	A	E	DP	Pct.	Rng
Fields,Josh	CWS	17	10	94.0	100	4	0	9	1.000	-
Fox,Jake	ChC	7	5	40.0	40	1	2	3	.953	-
Freese,David	StL	3	0	4.0	7	0	0	1	1.000	-
Garciaparra,Nomar	Oak	16	11	101.1	95	5	0	13	1.000	-
Garko,Ryan	Cle	51	47	407.0	418	36	3	53	.993	-
Garko,Ryan	SF	33	30	230.2	219	14	1	17	.996	-
German,Esteban	Tex	1	0	2.0	0	0	0	0	-	-
Giambi,Jason	Oak	58	58	450.0	441	17	3	45	.993	-
Giambi,Jason	Col	5	4	34.0	29	2	0	3	1.000	-
Gimenez,Chris	Cle	18	13	123.0	133	4	1	6	.993	-
Glaus,Troy	StL	2	1	10.0	15	0	0	0	1.000	-
Gload,Ross	Fla	41	32	294.2	266	20	1	23	.997	-
Gonzalez,Edgar	SD	2	1	9.0	6	0	0	2	1.000	-
Greene,Tyler	StL	1	0	1.0	1	0	0	1	1.000	-
Guillen,Carlos	Det	2	2	18.0	19	0	0	2	1.000	-
Guzman,Jesus	SF	3	2	14.0	10	0	0	1	1.000	-
Hannahan,Jack	Oak	1	0	2.0	1	0	0	0	1.000	-
Hannahan,Jack	Sea	17	9	90.0	92	8	0	8	1.000	-
Harris,Brendan	Min	3	0	9.0	11	0	0	1	1.000	-
Hayes,Brett	Fla	1	0	2.0	1	0	0	1	1.000	-
Headley,Chase	SD	1	0	1.0	1	0	0	0	1.000	-
Helms,Wes	Fla	4	4	31.0	33	5	1	2	.974	-
Hernandez,Ramon	Cin	30	26	251.2	238	12	4	30	.984	-
Hinske,Eric	Pit	6	5	44.0	39	3	0	4	1.000	-
Hoffpauir,Micah	ChC	27	17	167.0	136	10	1	11	.993	-
Huber,Justin	Min	1	0	3.0	0	0	0	0	-	-
Jackson,Conor	Ari	6	6	43.0	42	1	1	5	.977	-
Jacobs,Mike	KC	15	13	112.0	94	14	2	13	.982	-
Johnson,Nick	Was	96	92	806.1	833	67	7	73	.992	-
Johnson,Nick	Fla	33	32	260.2	192	24	5	22	.977	-
Jones,Andruw	Tex	8	4	39.2	12	3	1	6	1.000	-
Jones,Garrett	Pit	30	29	255.2	246	37	1	26	.996	-
Kata,Matt	Hou	1	0	4.0	5	0	0	1	1.000	-
Kelly,Don	Det	2	0	7.0	7	0	0	1	1.000	-
Kennedy,Adam	Oak	1	0	3.0	1	0	0	0	1.000	-
Kotchman,Casey	Atl	85	81	703.1	674	61	0	51	1.000	-
Kotchman,Casey	Bos	29	19	190.0	185	19	0	12	1.000	-
Kotsay,Mark	Bos	19	12	125.1	103	11	0	9	1.000	-
Kotsay,Mark	CWS	22	15	158.2	155	12	0	13	1.000	-
Laird,Gerald	Det	1	0	1.0	1	0	0	1	1.000	-
LaPorta,Matt	Cle	10	10	78.0	78	4	2	8	.976	-
Larish,Jeff	Det	11	6	67.0	68	5	0	4	1.000	-
LaRoche,Adam	Pit	87	86	756.2	776	59	1	86	.999	-
LaRoche,Adam	Bos	4	4	36.0	29	6	0	1	1.000	-
LaRoche,Adam	Atl	57	57	515.2	520	43	1	61	.998	-
LaRue,Jason	StL	2	0	3.0	7	0	0	0	1.000	-
Lee,Carlos	Hou	1	0	1.0	2	0	0	0	1.000	-
Lopez,Jose	Sea	16	12	122.0	115	8	1	12	.992	-
Loretta,Mark	LAD	17	14	119.0	122	9	0	12	1.000	-
Marte,Andy	Cle	45	43	390.1	380	23	5	47	.988	-
Martinez,Victor	Cle	47	44	385.2	348	17	3	41	.992	-
Martinez,Victor	Bos	23	22	189.1	160	3	0	14	1.000	-
McGehee,Casey	Mil	3	0	4.0	3	0	0	0	1.000	-
Mientkiewicz,Doug	LAD	4	1	12.0	9	0	0	0	1.000	-
Millar,Kevin	Tor	46	44	386.2	376	27	4	40	.990	-
Miranda,Juan	NYY	8	1	23.0	19	1	0	2	1.000	-
Molina,Jose	NYY	3	0	6.1	4	2	0	1	1.000	-
Molina,Yadier	StL	6	0	10.0	10	1	0	2	1.000	-
Morse,Mike	Was	11	3	46.0	46	6	0	6	1.000	-
Norton,Greg	Atl	3	2	18.0	21	2	0	1	1.000	-
Ortiz,David	Bos	6	6	39.0	42	6	1	2	.980	-
Pagnozzi,Matt	StL	1	0	1.0	1	0	0	0	1.000	-
Pearce,Steve	Pit	42	41	362.0	360	30	2	31	.995	-
Posada,Jorge	NYY	2	0	5.0	3	2	0	0	1.000	-
Powell,Landon	Oak	6	4	40.1	39	4	1	5	.977	-
Prado,Martin	Atl	28	17	182.2	160	14	1	25	.994	-
Quinlan,Robb	LAA	17	16	126.0	119	16	0	11	1.000	-
Raburn,Ryan	Det	10	2	36.0	35	2	0	6	1.000	-
Ransom,Cody	NYY	1	1	8.0	5	2	0	1	1.000	-
Reed,Jeremy	NYM	4	3	23.1	26	1	1	4	.964	-
Reynolds,Mark	Ari	28	24	218.0	186	11	5	28	.975	-
Richard,Chris	TB	13	5	55.0	59	2	1	2	.984	-
Romero,Niuman	Cle	1	1	9.0	7	0	0	1	1.000	-
Rosales,Adam	Cin	11	7	84.2	68	11	0	5	1.000	-

Player	Tm	G	GS	Inn	PO	A	E	DP	Pct.	Rng
Ruiz,Randy	Tor	3	1	9.0	7	1	0	1	1.000	-
Ryal,Rusty	Ari	10	5	45.2	39	5	1	2	.978	-
Salazar,Oscar	Bal	2	2	16.0	20	1	0	0	1.000	-
Salazar,Oscar	SD	6	4	36.0	30	4	0	2	1.000	-
Sanchez,Gaby	Fla	1	1	8.0	12	0	0	1	1.000	-
Sandoval,Pablo	SF	26	24	207.0	181	10	3	10	.985	-
Scott,Luke	Bal	10	8	63.0	54	3	1	4	.983	-
Shelton,Chris	Sea	4	4	35.0	31	2	0	3	1.000	-
Snyder,Chris	Ari	1	0	4.0	1	0	0	0	1.000	-
Sweeney,Mike	Sea	5	5	35.0	29	0	2	3	.935	-
Swisher,Nick	NYY	20	10	104.0	89	5	1	7	.989	-
Tatis,Fernando	NYM	41	32	296.2	274	28	1	20	.997	-
Teahen,Mark	KC	11	6	60.0	60	3	0	4	1.000	-
Thames,Marcus	Det	2	0	3.0	3	0	0	1	1.000	-
Tolbert,Matt	Min	1	0	1.0	1	0	0	1	1.000	-
Tracy,Andy	Phl	1	1	10.0	8	1	0	2	1.000	-
Tracy,Chad	Ari	66	56	501.0	471	37	2	39	.996	-
Whitesell,Josh	Ari	30	28	250.1	246	12	1	16	.996	-
Wigginton,Ty	Bal	40	38	333.0	315	30	4	30	.989	-
Willingham,Josh	Was	1	0	1.0	0	0	0	0	-	-
Wilson,Bobby	LAA	1	0	6.0	5	0	0	0	1.000	-
Wood,Brandon	LAA	4	4	34.0	35	5	0	4	1.000	-
Zobrist,Ben	TB	3	2	13.0	6	1	1	2	.875	-

Second Basemen - Regulars

Player	Tm	G	GS	Inn	PO	A	E	DP	Pct.	Rng
Valbuena,Luis	Cle	77	75	652.0	162	228	6	64	.985	5.38
Matsui,Kaz	Hou	130	127	1101.1	279	373	6	99	.991	5.33
Hill,Aaron	Tor	156	155	1372.0	307	484	7	129	.991	5.19
Barmes,Clint	Col	139	130	1147.1	241	413	12	91	.982	5.13
Polanco,Placido	Det	151	146	1289.1	290	439	2	112	.997	5.09
Utley,Chase	Phi	155	154	1357.0	264	108	12	97	.984	5.05
Kinsler,Ian	Tex	144	143	1258.0	249	451	11	100	.985	5.01
Getz,Chris	CWS	106	100	896.1	196	298	7	75	.986	4.96
Johnson,Kelly	Atl	84	69	655.2	135	222	10	56	.973	4.90
Sanchez,Freddy	TOT	110	109	949.2	228	289	5	75	.990	4.90
Schumaker,Skip	StL	133	124	989.1	188	347	9	80	.983	4.87
Hudson,Orlando	LAD	145	143	1272.1	326	360	8	77	.988	4.84
Phillips,Brandon	Cin	151	150	1332.1	307	409	9	100	.988	4.84
Castillo,Luis	NYM	137	135	1146.2	266	344	11	71	.982	4.79
Ellis,Mark	Oak	105	102	906.2	197	285	5	68	.990	4.78
Kendrick,Howie	LAA	95	90	805.2	156	271	4	70	.991	4.77
López,Felipe	TOT	144	142	1257.2	243	419	17	102	.975	4.74
Cano,Robinson	NYY	161	158	1399.2	308	424	12	96	.984	4.71
Zobrist,Ben	TB	91	81	714.2	143	225	4	44	.989	4.63
Roberts,Brian	Bal	158	155	1340.2	249	432	11	106	.984	4.57
Eckstein,David	SD	131	124	1093.1	228	326	2	79	.996	4.56
Callaspo,Alberto	KC	146	142	1240.0	233	379	17	96	.973	4.44
Uggla,Dan	Fla	158	157	1401.1	264	426	16	95	.977	4.43
Pedroia,Dustin	Bos	154	154	1346.2	253	404	6	93	.991	4.39
Lopez,Jose	Sea	141	139	1234.0	235	351	15	89	.975	4.27

Second Basemen - The Rest

Player	Tm	G	GS	Inn	PO	A	E	DP	Pct.	Rng
Abreu,Tony	LAD	1	1	9.0	4	3	0	1	1.000	7.00
Andino,Robert	Bal	8	3	39.0	12	8	0	4	1.000	4.62
Arias,Joaquin	Tex	2	2	16.2	4	4	0	2	1.000	4.32
Aybar,Willy	TB	28	16	139.1	35	46	5	13	.942	5.23
Baker,Jeff	Col	3	2	17.0	4	5	1	1	.900	4.76
Baker,Jeff	ChC	49	43	368.2	103	116	1	33	.995	5.35
Barden,Brian	StL	1	1	7.0	4	0	0	0	1.000	5.14
Barfield,Josh	Cle	8	3	36.0	12	12	0	4	1.000	6.00
Belliard,Ronnie	Was	50	36	316.2	73	116	3	28	.984	5.37
Belliard,Ronnie	LAD	10	10	87.0	11	19	1	6	.968	3.10
Bixler,Brian	Pit	5	3	30.0	4	12	1	1	.941	4.80
Blanco,Andres	ChC	40	21	224.1	52	71	0	20	1.000	4.93
Bloomquist,Willie	KC	14	12	107.0	24	35	2	10	.967	4.96
Bonifacio,Emilio	Fla	7	4	38.0	6	13	0	4	1.000	4.50
Brignac,Reid	TB	3	1	8.0	0	4	0	0	1.000	4.50
Bruntlett,Eric	Phi	13	5	65.1	20	20	2	6	.952	5.51
Burke,Chris	SD	1	0	4.0	0	0	0	0	-	.00
Burriss,Emmanuel	SF	61	57	494.0	115	131	7	33	.972	4.48

Player	Tm	G	GS	Inn	PO	A	E	DP	Pct.	Rng
Cabrera,Asdrubal	Cle	28	28	244.0	59	82	1	30	.993	5.20
Cairo,Miguel	Phi	5	3	33.1	10	9	0	3	1.000	5.13
Carroll,Jamey	Cle	56	52	467.0	89	137	1	26	.996	4.36
Casilla,Alexi	Min	72	64	571.1	141	170	5	35	.984	4.90
Castro,Juan	LAD	20	8	94.2	29	24	2	7	.964	5.04
Catalanotto,Frank	Mil	3	0	7.0	1	0	0	0	1.000	1.29
Cedeno,Ronny	Sea	13	8	82.2	22	21	1	9	.977	4.68
Cintron,Alex	Was	2	0	3.0	1	0	0	0	1.000	3.00
Coghlan,Chris	Fla	1	1	7.0	2	0	0	0	1.000	2.57
Conrad,Brooks	Atl	11	9	84.0	22	31	0	10	1.000	5.68
Cora,Alex	NYM	19	13	131.1	38	40	2	7	.975	5.35
Counsell,Craig	Mil	50	45	396.1	92	131	0	37	1.000	5.06
Crosby,Bobby	Oak	5	4	37.0	12	8	1	3	.952	4.86
Cruz,Luis	Pit	5	4	39.1	6	11	0	1	1.000	3.89
Cuddyer,Michael	Min	1	0	1.0	1	1	0	1	1.000	18.00
DeRosa,Mark	StL	2	0	2.0	0	0	0	0	-	.00
Desmond,Ian	Was	5	5	39.2	12	12	2	2	.923	5.45
DeWitt,Blake	LAD	2	0	4.0	2	1	0	0	1.000	6.75
Dillon,Joe	TB	2	1	10.0	1	1	0	0	1.000	1.80
Downs,Matt	SF	17	16	143.0	31	42	0	13	1.000	4.59
Figgins,Chone	LAA	2	2	14.0	2	2	0	0	1.000	2.57
Fontenot,Mike	ChC	70	63	529.1	112	149	3	36	.989	4.44
Frandsen,Kevin	SF	14	7	73.2	21	22	1	9	.977	5.25
Freel,Ryan	Bal	2	0	4.0	0	1	0	0	1.000	2.25
Freel,Ryan	KC	1	0	2.0	0	0	0	0	-	.00
German,Esteban	Tex	6	3	34.0	4	13	1	3	.944	4.50
Gonzalez,Alberto	Was	55	40	363.0	86	121	1	34	.995	5.13
Gonzalez,Edgar	SD	15	11	110.0	20	20	3	4	.930	3.27
Graffanino,Tony	Cle	4	4	35.0	10	10	1	3	.952	5.14
Green,Andy	NYM	1	0	3.0	0	1	0	0	1.000	3.00
Green,Nick	Bos	7	6	58.0	12	17	0	2	1.000	4.50
Greene,Tyler	StL	7	1	18.1	4	6	0	2	1.000	4.91
Hairston,Jerry	Cin	9	8	75.0	16	22	1	5	.974	4.56
Hairston,Jerry	NYY	3	0	9.0	3	2	0	0	1.000	5.00
Hall,Bill	Sea	3	2	19.0	3	3	0	0	1.000	2.84
Hannahan,Jack	Oak	1	0	2.0	0	0	0	0	-	.00
Harris,Brendan	Min	11	10	85.1	19	24	0	2	1.000	4.54
Harris,Willie	Was	19	9	82.0	21	26	2	7	.959	5.16
Hernandez,And	Was	66	57	497.0	132	174	6	33	.981	5.54
Hernandez,And	NYM	8	5	53.2	11	14	0	4	1.000	4.10
Hernandez,Diory	Atl	4	1	10.2	4	5	0	1	1.000	7.59
Hernandez,Luis	KC	8	3	36.0	3	7	0	0	1.000	2.50
Hoffpauir,Jarrett	StL	5	2	22.0	1	10	0	2	1.000	4.50
Hulett,Tug	KC	5	2	18.0	2	7	0	1	1.000	4.50
Infante,Omar	Atl	30	22	199.0	42	62	2	12	.981	4.70
Inglett,Joe	Tor	3	2	20.0	5	6	0	1	1.000	4.95
Iribarren,Hernan	Mil	2	0	6.0	3	4	0	2	1.000	10.50
Iwamura,Akinori	TB	67	63	555.1	114	163	6	37	.979	4.49
Izturis,Maicer	LAA	68	64	567.1	114	180	2	49	.993	4.66
Kata,Matt	Hou	7	5	47.0	9	24	0	4	1.000	6.32
Kelly,Don	Det	1	0	1.0	0	0	0	0	-	.00
Kennedy,Adam	Oak	50	49	421.0	87	121	7	30	.967	4.45
Keppinger,Jeff	Hou	22	14	138.2	33	48	1	12	.988	5.26
Lillibridge,Brent	CWS	23	14	137.1	29	43	2	6	.973	4.72
Lobaton,Jose	SD	1	0	1.0	0	0	0	0	-	.00
Lopez,Felipe	Ari	82	80	715.1	138	243	9	56	.977	4.79
Lopez,Felipe	Mil	62	62	542.1	105	176	8	46	.972	4.66
Loretta,Mark	LAD	3	0	6.1	2	2	0	1	1.000	5.68
Lowrie,Jed	Bos	2	0	5.0	0	0	0	0	-	.00
Lugo,Julio	StL	30	17	168.1	33	59	2	12	.979	4.92
Martinez,Ramon	NYM	2	2	17.0	3	6	0	3	1.000	4.76
Maysonet,Edwin	Hou	15	13	112.0	22	46	2	9	.971	5.46
McCoy,Mike	Col	2	0	2.0	0	0	0	0	-	.00
McDonald,John	Tor	8	5	55.0	8	30	0	7	1.000	6.22
McGehee,Casey	Mil	22	20	179.2	37	61	2	13	.980	4.91
Miles,Aaron	ChC	35	26	253.2	71	69	2	21	.986	4.97
Nix,Jayson	CWS	52	48	406.0	81	137	6	34	.973	4.83
Ojeda,Augie	Ari	35	27	247.2	44	93	0	19	1.000	4.98
Orr,Pete	Was	18	15	123.0	31	51	2	15	.976	6.00
Patterson,Eric	Oak	5	3	30.2	9	9	2	1	.900	5.28
Pena,Ramiro	NYY	8	3	32.1	7	10	0	2	1.000	4.73
Petit,Gregorio	Oak	8	4	50.0	14	15	1	5	.967	5.22
Prado,Martin	Atl	63	61	513.1	116	162	4	37	.986	4.87
Punto,Nick	Min	63	58	510.1	119	150	0	36	1.000	4.74

Player	Tm	G	GS	Inn	PO	A	E	DP	Pct.	Rng
Quintanilla,Omar	Col	25	4	75.2	23	28	1	11	.981	6.07
Ransom,Cody	NYY	1	1	9.0	4	2	0	1	1.000	6.00
Reyes,Argenis	NYM	3	2	20.0	4	3	0	0	1.000	3.15
Richar,Danny	Cin	1	0	1.0	0	0	0	0	-	.00
Roberts,Ryan	Ari	57	45	407.1	99	117	2	18	.991	4.77
Rodriguez,Luis	SD	30	25	226.0	51	69	3	15	.976	4.78
Rodriguez,Sean	LAA	5	4	36.0	5	6	0	4	1.000	2.75
Rohlinger,Ryan	SF	1	1	10.0	5	3	0	1	1.000	7.20
Rosales,Adam	Cin	4	1	11.0	2	3	0	1	1.000	4.09
Ryal,Rusty	Ari	13	10	77.1	9	27	0	7	1.000	4.19
Ryan,Brendan	StL	19	10	95.2	21	31	1	9	.981	4.89
Salazar,Oscar	SD	3	2	16.1	4	6	2	1	.833	5.51
Sanchez,Freddy	Pit	85	84	739.2	184	224	2	63	.995	4.96
Sanchez,Freddy	SF	25	25	210.0	44	65	3	12	.973	4.67
Sandoval,Freddy	LAA	3	2	22.0	4	8	0	1	1.000	4.91
Santiago,Ramon	Det	29	17	156.2	33	52	0	15	1.000	4.88
Scales,Bobby	ChC	11	8	67.2	14	19	1	4	.971	4.39
Scutaro,Marco	Tor	2	0	4.0	0	2	0	0	1.000	4.50
Smith,Jason	Hou	5	3	31.0	4	8	0	5	1.000	3.48
Soriano,Alfonso	ChC	2	0	1.2	0	0	0	0	-	.00
Stewart,Ian	Col	21	20	152.1	36	43	3	9	.963	4.67
Sutton,Drew	Cin	8	3	39.0	9	11	0	2	1.000	4.62
Tatis,Fernando	NYM	7	5	51.1	8	13	0	1	1.000	3.68
Teahen,Mark	KC	3	3	23.0	5	6	0	1	1.000	4.30
Thurston,Joe	StL	47	7	138.0	32	48	2	13	.976	5.22
Tolbert,Matt	Min	36	31	285.0	74	110	2	29	.989	5.81
Tuiasosopo,Matt	Sea	6	6	56.0	12	20	0	4	1.000	5.14
Turner,Justin	Bal	3	0	6.0	3	3	0	1	1.000	9.00
Uribe,Juan	SF	38	34	299.2	59	82	1	20	.993	4.23
Valdez,Wilson	NYM	1	0	3.0	0	0	0	0	-	.00
Vazquez,Ramon	Pit	22	18	161.0	33	50	0	13	1.000	4.64
Velez,Eugenio	SF	31	22	215.2	55	68	6	8	.953	5.13
Vizquel,Omar	Tex	16	14	126.0	23	49	0	12	1.000	5.14
Weeks,Rickie	Mil	35	35	303.2	66	95	6	21	.964	4.77
Wigginton,Ty	Bal	8	4	39.1	8	11	0	2	1.000	4.35
Wilson,Josh	Sea	4	3	26.0	6	13	0	4	1.000	6.58
Woodward,Chris	Sea	5	4	35.0	8	3	0	1	1.000	2.83
Woodward,Chris	Bos	6	2	27.0	5	6	0	0	1.000	3.67
Young,Delwyn	Pit	53	52	448.1	102	131	4	37	.983	4.68
Young Jr.,Eric	Col	6	6	44.0	8	10	0	1	1.000	3.68

Third Basemen - Regulars

Player	Tm	G	GS	Inn	PO	A	E	DP	Pct.	Rng
Mora,Melvin	Bal	124	122	1050.1	113	254	11	20	.971	3.14
LaRoche,Andy	Pit	146	142	1246.0	97	321	14	34	.968	3.02
Beltre,Adrian	Sea	111	110	988.1	103	224	14	19	.959	2.98
Zimmerman,Ryan	Was	154	153	1337.2	117	325	17	28	.963	2.97
Hannahan,Jack	TOT	84	66	613.0	53	149	7	21	.967	2.97
Peralta,Jhonny	Cle	104	102	902.0	78	211	15	19	.951	2.88
Longoria,Evan	TB	151	150	1302.2	112	302	13	43	.970	2.86
Crede,Joe	Min	84	84	728.0	60	171	4	18	.983	2.86
Figgins,Chone	LAA	154	154	1339.0	109	314	14	38	.968	2.84
Feliz,Pedro	Phi	155	150	1342.1	110	312	15	35	.966	2.83
Beckham,Gordon	CWS	102	102	885.0	73	205	14	21	.952	2.83
Blake,Casey	LAD	134	131	1161.0	99	263	10	32	.973	2.81
Inge,Brandon	Det	161	157	1387.0	143	281	20	41	.955	2.75
Kennedy,Adam	Oak	82	78	691.2	50	156	13	8	.941	2.68
Reynolds,Mark	Ari	130	128	1125.2	88	240	19	30	.945	2.62
Rolen,Scott	TOT	127	125	1118.1	91	232	5	19	.985	2.60
Lowell,Mike	Bos	107	105	895.0	82	174	9	14	.966	2.57
Wright,David	NYM	142	142	1232.0	119	224	18	19	.950	2.51
Bonifacio,Emilio	Fla	86	82	717.2	48	151	14	13	.934	2.50
DeRosa,Mark	TOT	105	99	874.0	66	173	8	21	.968	2.46
Rodriguez,Alex	NYY	116	113	974.1	66	200	9	17	.967	2.46
Teahen,Mark	KC	107	99	869.0	66	171	11	14	.956	2.45
Encarnacion,Edwin	TOT	85	84	726.1	52	146	11	14	.947	2.45
Ramirez,Aramis	ChC	79	79	683.2	45	137	10	14	.948	2.40
Stewart,Ian	Col	121	85	831.0	43	176	7	11	.969	2.37
Kouzmanoff,Kevin	SD	139	134	1186.2	94	214	3	24	.990	2.34
Sandoval,Pablo	SF	120	120	1028.0	70	195	11	13	.960	2.32
Jones,Chipper	Atl	133	131	1136.2	85	208	22	30	.930	2.32
Blum,Geoff	Hou	102	94	830.1	45	164	3	15	.986	2.27
Young,Michael	Tex	134	134	1165.2	72	208	9	29	.969	2.16

Third Basemen - The Rest

Player	Tm	G	GS	Inn	PO	A	E	DP	Pct.	Rng
Abreu,Tony	LAD	1	1	10.0	1	3	0	0	1.000	3.60
Andino,Robert	Bal	2	0	7.0	0	1	0	0	1.000	1.29
Arias,Joaquin	Tex	1	0	2.0	0	0	0	0	-	.00
Atkins,Garrett	Col	78	75	577.0	37	137	8	13	.956	2.71
Aurilia,Rich	SF	13	6	65.2	3	11	0	2	1.000	1.92
Aviles,Mike	KC	2	1	10.0	0	0	0	0	-	.00
Aybar,Willy	TB	18	11	114.0	8	26	2	2	.944	2.68
Baker,Jeff	Col	3	2	14.1	0	2	0	0	1.000	1.26
Baker,Jeff	ChC	17	8	84.0	6	18	1	0	.960	2.57
Baldelli,Rocco	Bos	1	0	3.0	0	0	0	0	-	.00
Barden,Brian	StL	46	20	216.2	9	50	4	4	.937	2.45
Bautista,Jose	Tor	26	22	209.0	18	48	3	4	.957	2.84
Belliard,Ronnie	Was	2	2	16.0	0	5	1	1	.833	2.81
Belliard,Ronnie	LAD	10	9	79.2	8	13	0	1	1.000	2.37
Berroa,Angel	NYY	16	6	63.0	6	16	3	3	.880	3.14
Betemit,Wilson	CWS	6	5	43.0	0	4	4	0	.500	.84
Blalock,Hank	Tex	1	1	9.0	0	3	0	1	1.000	3.00
Blanco,Henry	SD	1	0	1.0	0	0	0	0	-	.00
Bloomquist,Willie	KC	3	2	21.0	2	5	0	0	1.000	3.00
Boone,Aaron	Hou	1	1	8.0	0	2	0	0	1.000	2.25
Bruntlett,Eric	Phi	7	0	15.2	0	1	0	0	1.000	.57
Burke,Chris	SD	2	0	7.0	1	0	0	0	1.000	1.29
Buscher,Brian	Min	25	22	195.2	19	31	1	4	.980	2.30
Cairo,Miguel	Phi	1	1	9.0	1	1	0	0	1.000	2.00
Callaspo,Alberto	KC	14	11	99.0	11	13	0	3	1.000	2.18
Cantu,Jorge	Fla	45	44	355.0	26	45	7	9	.910	1.80
Carroll,Jamey	Cle	23	17	156.0	11	37	2	8	.960	2.77
Castro,Juan	LAD	8	2	22.2	2	5	0	0	1.000	2.78
Cedeno,Ronny	Sea	2	2	17.0	0	3	0	0	1.000	1.59
Chavez,Eric	Oak	8	8	67.0	5	15	0	2	1.000	2.69
Conrad,Brooks	Atl	1	0	2.0	0	0	0	0	-	.00
Counsell,Craig	Mil	43	26	255.2	27	58	4	5	.955	2.99
Crosby,Bobby	Oak	42	33	297.1	23	72	7	6	.931	2.88
Davis,Chris	Tex	11	10	85.0	9	8	2	1	.895	1.80
DeRosa,Mark	Cle	42	41	355.0	25	74	8	12	.925	2.51
DeRosa,Mark	StL	63	58	519.0	41	99	0	9	1.000	2.43
DeWitt,Blake	LAD	14	5	68.0	5	13	1	1	.947	2.38
Dillon,Joe	TB	3	0	4.0	0	1	0	0	1.000	2.25
Dlugach,Brent	Det	2	0	5.0	1	3	0	0	1.000	7.20
Dobbs,Greg	Phi	16	11	88.2	3	25	0	1	1.000	2.84
Encarnacion,Edwin	Cin	43	42	362.1	25	69	4	8	.959	2.33
Encarnacion,Edwin	Tor	42	42	364.0	27	77	7	6	.937	2.57
Fields,Josh	CWS	49	47	421.2	27	101	8	9	.941	2.73
Fontenot,Mike	ChC	50	37	360.0	26	77	4	7	.963	2.58
Fox,Jake	ChC	27	23	195.1	8	38	2	2	.958	2.12
Francisco,Juan	Cin	4	3	30.0	1	8	1	2	.900	2.70
Freel,Ryan	Bal	2	1	3.0	0	0	0	0	-	.00
Freel,Ryan	ChC	7	7	50.2	2	10	1	1	.923	2.13
Freese,David	StL	7	5	41.1	6	5	0	1	1.000	2.40
Gamel,Mat	Mil	27	24	191.0	19	35	7	5	.885	2.54
Garciaparra,Nomar	Oak	6	6	32.0	1	8	0	0	1.000	2.53
German,Esteban	Tex	10	8	72.0	5	12	4	1	.810	2.13
Glaus,Troy	StL	8	4	40.2	1	6	1	0	.875	1.55
Gonzalez,Alberto	Was	3	0	4.2	0	0	0	0	-	.00
Gonzalez,Andy	Fla	2	1	8.0	0	1	0	0	1.000	1.13
Gonzalez,Edgar	SD	5	3	28.0	2	6	1	0	.889	2.57
Gordon,Alex	KC	49	48	406.0	21	94	10	8	.920	2.55
Graffanino,Tony	Cle	3	2	18.0	0	8	0	0	1.000	4.00
Green,Andy	NYM	1	0	1.0	0	0	1	0	.000	.00
Green,Nick	Bos	9	0	19.1	4	4	1	0	.889	3.72
Greene,Khalil	StL	16	13	96.0	5	27	1	5	.970	3.00
Greene,Tyler	StL	11	7	61.0	3	8	1	1	.917	1.62
Hairston,Jerry	Cin	33	31	275.1	33	40	7	7	.913	2.39
Hairston,Jerry	NYY	16	9	76.0	3	20	2	3	.920	2.72
Hall,Bill	Mil	66	50	457.0	33	123	4	13	.975	3.07
Hall,Bill	Sea	3	1	17.2	1	4	0	1	1.000	2.55
Hannahan,Jack	Oak	51	34	335.1	35	89	4	10	.969	3.33
Hannahan,Jack	Sea	33	32	277.2	18	60	3	11	.963	2.53
Harris,Brendan	Min	44	34	312.0	20	57	6	1	.928	2.22
Harris,Willie	Was	4	4	32.0	4	8	1	2	.923	3.38
Headley,Chase	SD	28	25	225.2	10	39	5	2	.907	1.95
Helms,Wes	Fla	70	35	365.2	31	70	7	11	.935	2.49

Player	Tm	G	GS	Inn	PO	A	E	DP	Pct.	Rng
Hernandez,Diory	Atl	3	1	13.0	1	5	0	2	1.000	4.15
Hernandez,Luis	KC	5	1	19.0	4	2	0	0	1.000	2.84
Hernandez,Ramon	Cin	1	0	1.0	1	0	0	0	1.000	9.00
Hill,Koyie	ChC	1	0	1.0	0	0	0	0	-	.00
Hinske,Eric	Pit	3	2	19.0	0	3	0	0	1.000	1.42
Hinske,Eric	NYY	10	2	35.1	3	3	0	0	1.000	1.53
Hoffpauir,Jarrett	StL	1	0	3.0	0	1	0	0	1.000	3.00
Hulett,Tug	KC	1	0	2.0	0	0	1	0	.000	.00
Infante,Omar	Atl	10	4	45.0	1	14	1	0	.938	3.00
Iribarren,Hernan	Mil	1	0	1.0	0	0	0	0	-	.00
Iwamura,Akinori	TB	1	0	1.0	1	0	0	0	1.000	9.00
Izturis,Maicer	LAA	5	2	25.0	3	4	0	1	1.000	2.52
Janish,Paul	Cin	2	1	6.0	1	3	0	1	1.000	6.00
Johnson,Chris	Hou	7	5	48.0	2	5	0	0	1.000	1.31
Kelly,Don	Det	4	1	14.0	2	5	0	1	1.000	4.50
Keppinger,Jeff	Hou	67	59	507.2	38	110	7	16	.955	2.62
Kottaras,George	Bos	1	0	4.0	0	2	0	0	1.000	4.50
Larish,Jeff	Det	1	1	6.0	1	1	0	0	1.000	3.00
Lillibridge,Brent	CWS	1	0	1.0	0	0	0	0	-	.00
Loretta,Mark	LAD	23	14	131.2	11	31	2	3	.955	2.87
Lowrie,Jed	Bos	4	1	10.0	1	4	0	0	1.000	4.50
Martin,Russell	LAD	1	0	0.1	0	0	0	0	-	.00
Maysonet,Edwin	Hou	7	3	35.0	1	8	0	0	1.000	2.31
McDonald,John	Tor	10	9	78.0	3	17	2	2	.909	2.31
McGehee,Casey	Mil	71	62	530.1	31	111	13	11	.916	2.41
Miles,Aaron	ChC	4	0	12.0	1	1	0	0	1.000	1.50
Millar,Kevin	Tor	4	2	21.0	4	4	0	2	1.000	3.43
Molina,Jose	NYY	1	0	2.0	0	0	0	0	-	.00
Morse,Mike	Was	1	0	4.0	1	2	0	0	1.000	6.75
Nix,Jayson	CWS	12	8	89.0	2	20	1	2	.957	2.22
Ojeda,Augie	Ari	28	14	143.0	14	25	5	5	.886	2.45
Orr,Pete	Was	3	3	30.0	2	6	2	0	.800	2.40
Pena,Ramiro	NYY	27	14	135.1	10	30	2	5	.952	2.66
Petit,Gregorio	Oak	3	3	24.0	1	4	0	0	1.000	1.88
Prado,Martin	Atl	41	26	266.0	14	65	2	8	.975	2.67
Punto,Nick	Min	5	3	27.0	3	6	0	1	1.000	3.00
Quinlan,Robb	LAA	9	2	31.0	2	4	1	0	.857	1.74
Quintanilla,Omar	Col	10	0	16.0	1	6	0	0	1.000	3.94
Raburn,Ryan	Det	6	4	33.0	2	4	4	0	.600	1.64
Ransom,Cody	NYY	23	18	164.0	10	31	4	2	.911	2.25
Richar,Danny	Cin	4	2	19.2	1	2	1	0	.750	1.37
Roberts,Ryan	Ari	19	15	132.0	14	24	3	3	.927	2.59
Rodriguez,Luis	SD	1	0	1.0	0	0	0	0	-	.00
Rohlinger,Ryan	SF	8	2	29.0	2	7	0	0	1.000	2.79
Rolen,Scott	Tor	88	87	779.0	62	168	5	16	.979	2.66
Rolen,Scott	Cin	39	38	339.1	29	64	0	3	1.000	2.47
Romero,Niuman	Cle	1	0	1.0	0	0	0	0	-	.00
Rosales,Adam	Cin	57	44	419.1	37	81	7	8	.944	2.53
Salazar,Oscar	Bal	5	1	17.0	4	0	0	0	1.000	2.12
Sandoval,Freddy	LAA	2	0	9.0	0	3	0	0	1.000	3.00
Santiago,Ramon	Det	2	0	2.0	0	0	0	0	-	.00
Scales,Bobby	ChC	8	7	58.1	6	11	1	1	.944	2.62
Smith,Jason	Hou	1	0	1.0	0	1	0	0	1.000	9.00
Soriano,Alfonso	ChC	1	0	0.1	0	0	0	0	-	.00
Sutton,Drew	Cin	2	1	5.1	1	1	0	0	1.000	3.38
Tatis,Fernando	NYM	27	20	192.0	22	45	2	3	.971	3.14
Thurston,Joe	StL	68	55	463.0	38	109	10	11	.936	2.86
Tolbert,Matt	Min	27	20	190.1	11	43	2	5	.964	2.55
Tracy,Chad	Ari	8	5	47.0	5	9	0	0	1.000	2.68
Turner,Justin	Bal	7	3	34.0	3	7	0	1	1.000	2.65
Uribe,Juan	SF	44	34	323.1	28	67	4	8	.960	2.64
Valbuena,Luis	Cle	1	0	2.0	0	1	0	0	1.000	4.50
Valdez,Wilson	NYM	1	0	1.0	0	0	0	0	-	.00
Vazquez,Ramon	Pit	14	9	83.2	7	20	1	3	.964	2.90
Velazquez,Gil	Bos	2	0	4.0	0	3	1	0	.750	6.75
Vizquel,Omar	Tex	20	9	101.0	5	22	0	2	1.000	2.41
Walker,Neil	Pit	9	8	69.2	6	15	1	1	.955	2.71
Wigginton,Ty	Bal	39	35	317.2	24	54	4	4	.951	2.21
Wilson,Josh	SD	1	0	1.1	0	0	0	0	-	.00
Wilson,Josh	Sea	5	3	29.0	2	6	0	1	1.000	2.48
Wood,Brandon	LAA	9	4	41.0	6	1	0	0	1.000	1.54
Woodward,Chris	Sea	15	14	123.0	9	38	4	6	.922	3.44
Woodward,Chris	Bos	3	0	7.0	1	1	0	0	1.000	2.57
Youkilis,Kevin	Bos	63	56	494.1	52	99	4	5	.974	2.75

Player	Tm	G	GS	Inn	PO	A	E	DP	Pct.	Rng
Zobrist,Ben	TB	1	1	5.2	0	0	0	0	-	.00

Shortstops - Regulars

Player	Tm	G	GS	Inn	PO	A	E	DP	Pct.	Rng
Ryan,Brendan	StL	105	95	830.2	145	354	8	71	.984	5.41
Izturis,Cesar	Bal	112	107	934.2	171	337	8	70	.984	4.89
Andrus,Elvis	Tex	145	140	1238.0	261	407	22	98	.968	4.86
Aybar,Erick	LAA	136	135	1189.1	240	378	11	102	.983	4.68
Wilson,Jack	TOT	105	105	917.1	152	317	12	81	.975	4.60
Guzman,Cristian	Was	117	115	993.2	154	353	20	74	.962	4.59
Tejada,Miguel	Hou	158	157	1371.1	214	475	21	105	.970	4.52
Cedeno,Ronny	TOT	82	81	711.2	110	247	9	45	.975	4.51
Tulowitzki,Troy	Col	151	148	1294.0	215	433	9	89	.986	4.51
Escobar,Yunel	Atl	139	138	1208.2	191	409	13	83	.979	4.47
Cabrera,Asdrubal	Cle	100	99	870.0	143	288	9	75	.980	4.46
Cabrera,Everth	SD	102	101	896.2	140	304	23	66	.951	4.46
Cabrera,Orlando	TOT	158	157	1388.2	258	428	25	98	.965	4.45
Hardy,J.J.	Mil	112	110	949.1	146	318	6	61	.983	4.40
Scutaro,Marco	Tor	143	143	1252.2	190	421	10	99	.984	4.39
Ramirez,Alexei	CWS	148	147	1293.2	220	410	20	94	.969	4.38
Betancourt,Yuniesky	TOT	133	131	1159.0	212	340	18	78	.968	4.29
Furcal,Rafael	LAD	149	141	1282.1	187	419	20	76	.968	4.25
Theriot,Ryan	ChC	151	147	1311.0	206	411	15	90	.976	4.24
Everett,Adam	Det	116	107	942.2	161	282	14	70	.969	4.23
Green,Nick	Bos	81	74	644.1	104	198	14	40	.956	4.22
Drew,Stephen	Ari	132	128	1142.0	173	362	11	70	.980	4.22
Ramirez,Hanley	Fla	146	144	1259.0	221	349	10	77	.983	4.07
Bartlett,Jason	TB	134	133	1153.2	170	339	20	57	.962	3.97
Gonzalez,Alex	TOT	112	110	948.1	148	270	7	59	.984	3.97
Rollins,Jimmy	Phi	155	152	1364.2	212	389	6	72	.990	3.96
Jeter,Derek	NYY	150	147	1260.2	206	340	8	75	.986	3.90
Renteria,Edgar	SF	123	121	1071.2	161	290	14	63	.970	3.86

Shortstops - The Rest

Player	Tm	G	GS	Inn	PO	A	E	DP	Pct.	Rng
Amezaga,Alfredo	Fla	5	5	42.0	5	15	0	1	1.000	4.29
Andino,Robert	Bal	62	55	478.1	76	163	8	37	.968	4.50
Aviles,Mike	KC	34	33	269.1	61	92	4	29	.973	4.78
Barden,Brian	StL	4	3	27.0	4	11	0	2	1.000	5.00
Barmes,Clint	Col	16	12	103.1	13	49	1	8	.984	5.40
Berroa,Angel	NYM	8	6	57.2	7	22	2	4	.935	4.53
Betancourt,Yuniesky	Sea	62	61	548.0	101	159	9	38	.967	4.27
Betancourt,Yuniesky	KC	71	70	611.0	111	181	9	40	.970	4.30
Bixler,Brian	Pit	10	10	77.0	15	24	2	3	.951	4.56
Blanco,Andres	ChC	15	9	90.1	15	31	3	7	.939	4.58
Bloomquist,Willie	KC	38	29	237.2	51	80	6	22	.956	4.96
Blum,Geoff	Hou	1	0	1.0	0	0	0	0	-	.00
Bonifacio,Emilio	Fla	20	12	135.1	11	32	3	5	.935	2.86
Brignac,Reid	TB	28	23	211.2	26	62	2	9	.978	3.74
Bruntlett,Eric	Phi	9	9	75.0	13	18	1	2	.969	3.72
Burke,Chris	SD	25	21	184.1	27	52	6	9	.929	3.86
Cabrera,Orlando	Oak	101	100	887.2	156	273	14	63	.968	4.35
Cabrera,Orlando	Min	57	57	501.0	102	155	11	35	.959	4.62
Cairo,Miguel	Phi	3	1	13.0	1	4	0	0	1.000	3.46
Callaspo,Alberto	KC	1	0	2.0	1	0	0	0	1.000	4.50
Casilla,Alexi	Min	2	0	2.0	0	1	0	1	1.000	4.50
Castro,Juan	LAD	28	19	170.0	20	39	1	6	.983	3.12
Cedeno,Ronny	Sea	40	39	344.2	44	114	5	18	.969	4.13
Cedeno,Ronny	Pit	42	42	367.0	66	133	4	27	.980	4.88
Cintron,Alex	Was	2	2	15.0	4	2	1	0	.857	3.60
Cora,Alex	NYM	56	54	466.1	106	140	6	36	.976	4.75
Counsell,Craig	Mil	27	19	185.2	35	70	1	20	.991	5.09
Crosby,Bobby	Oak	6	2	26.0	3	8	0	2	1.000	3.12
Cruz,Luis	Pit	17	14	134.0	37	48	2	9	.977	5.71
Desmond,Ian	Was	17	14	136.1	37	43	4	14	.952	5.28
DeWitt,Blake	LAD	2	1	8.0	1	2	0	0	1.000	3.38
Dlugach,Brent	Det	2	0	2.0	0	0	0	0	-	.00
Escobar,Alcides	Mil	37	33	300.0	59	94	6	20	.962	4.59
Feliz,Pedro	Phi	2	0	3.0	0	0	0	0	-	.00
Frandsen,Kevin	SF	7	5	42.2	4	12	1	2	.941	3.38
Gonzalez,Alberto	Was	41	31	279.1	39	84	9	13	.932	3.96
Gonzalez,Alex	Cin	68	67	587.1	97	163	6	42	.977	3.98

303

Player	Tm	G	GS	Inn	PO	A	E	DP	Pct.	Rng
Gonzalez,Alex	Bos	44	43	361.0	51	107	1	17	.994	3.94
Gonzalez,Andy	Fla	4	1	10.0	0	2	0	0	1.000	1.80
Greene,Khalil	StL	30	26	240.1	43	80	7	17	.946	4.61
Greene,Tyler	StL	30	20	184.2	28	65	3	12	.969	4.53
Hairston,Jerry	Cin	31	25	217.1	47	56	2	8	.981	4.27
Hairston,Jerry	NYY	11	2	28.1	6	10	0	2	1.000	5.08
Hannahan,Jack	Sea	2	0	11.0	0	4	0	0	1.000	3.27
Harris,Brendan	Min	56	50	451.0	64	150	6	25	.973	4.27
Hernandez,And	NYM	38	34	289.2	40	88	6	16	.955	3.98
Hernandez,Diory	Atl	22	18	181.0	26	61	1	18	.989	4.33
Hernandez,Luis	KC	23	15	139.0	20	52	1	13	.986	4.66
Hu,Chin-lung	LAD	3	1	13.0	1	1	0	0	1.000	1.38
Hulett,Tug	KC	1	0	1.0	0	0	0	0	-	.00
Infante,Omar	Atl	10	6	73.0	11	21	0	3	1.000	3.95
Izturis,Maicer	LAA	28	25	224.2	33	52	2	15	.977	3.41
Janish,Paul	Cin	82	63	592.1	110	212	3	54	.991	4.89
Keppinger,Jeff	Hou	11	3	38.2	5	13	0	2	1.000	4.19
Lillibridge,Brent	CWS	7	3	35.0	8	7	1	2	.938	3.86
Lowrie,Jed	Bos	26	18	163.2	22	52	1	16	.987	4.07
Lugo,Julio	Bos	32	27	243.1	39	51	7	8	.928	3.33
Lugo,Julio	StL	24	18	158.0	35	55	2	16	.978	5.13
Manzella,Tommy	Hou	2	1	8.0	1	3	0	1	1.000	4.50
Martinez,Ramon	NYM	10	9	81.1	12	26	4	6	.905	4.20
Maysonet,Edwin	Hou	3	1	9.0	1	1	0	1	1.000	2.00
McDonald,John	Tor	31	19	198.1	38	66	1	22	.990	4.72
Miles,Aaron	ChC	8	5	44.0	7	13	0	2	1.000	4.09
Nix,Jayson	CWS	15	12	111.0	19	39	6	10	.906	4.70
Ojeda,Augie	Ari	34	27	241.2	31	74	3	15	.972	3.91
Pena,Ramiro	NYY	34	11	145.0	21	40	3	9	.953	3.79
Pena,Tony F	KC	40	15	166.0	29	44	5	9	.936	3.96
Pennington,Cliff	Oak	60	60	533.2	90	181	8	41	.971	4.57
Peralta,Jhonny	Cle	34	38	334.0	62	123	4	36	.979	4.99
Punto,Nick	Min	58	56	491.0	100	153	7	29	.973	4.64
Quintanilla,Omar	Col	13	2	41.0	13	15	1	5	.966	6.15
Ransom,Cody	NYY	3	2	16.0	2	5	0	0	1.000	3.94
Reyes,Argenis	NYM	1	1	8.0	2	3	0	2	1.000	5.63
Reyes,Jose	NYM	35	35	305.1	50	90	5	12	.966	4.13
Rodriguez,Luis	SD	34	30	263.2	45	74	3	23	.975	4.06
Rohlinger,Ryan	SF	3	1	13.0	4	5	0	2	1.000	6.23
Romero,Niuman	Cle	4	3	25.0	1	6	0	1	1.000	2.52
Rosales,Adam	Cin	6	4	33.0	4	12	0	2	1.000	4.36
Salazar,Oscar	Bal	2	0	3.0	0	2	1	0	.667	6.00
Santiago,Ramon	Det	69	56	502.1	78	159	6	35	.975	4.25
Smith,Jason	Hou	1	0	2.0	0	0	0	0	-	.00
Sutton,Drew	Cin	7	3	28.1	7	16	0	4	1.000	7.31
Tatis,Fernando	NYM	2	0	7.0	4	2	0	1	1.000	7.71
Tolbert,Matt	Min	3	0	8.0	2	4	0	2	1.000	6.75
Uribe,Juan	SF	41	35	318.2	61	94	4	20	.975	4.38
Valbuena,Luis	Cle	28	22	205.0	37	73	5	6	.957	4.83
Valdez,Wilson	NYM	32	23	210.2	41	69	1	16	.991	4.70
Vazquez,Ramon	Pit	28	21	189.2	37	54	1	13	.989	4.32
Velazquez,Gil	Bos	4	0	11.2	3	3	0	1	1.000	4.63
Vizquel,Omar	Tex	27	22	196.2	32	76	0	22	1.000	4.94
Wigginton,Ty	Bal	9	0	13.0	3	8	0	1	1.000	7.62
Wilson,Jack	Pit	74	74	650.0	105	242	7	64	.980	4.80
Wilson,Jack	Sea	31	31	266.2	47	75	5	17	.961	4.12
Wilson,Josh	Ari	8	7	64.0	12	27	2	6	.951	5.48
Wilson,Josh	SD	15	10	106.0	13	20	2	3	.943	2.80
Wilson,Josh	Sea	32	30	273.1	42	74	2	16	.983	3.82
Wood,Brandon	LAA	5	2	31.0	6	8	3	3	.824	4.06
Woodward,Chris	Sea	1	1	9.0	2	0	0	0	1.000	2.00
Woodward,Chris	Bos	4	0	12.2	0	2	1	0	.667	1.42
Zobrist,Ben	TB	13	6	62.0	9	16	2	5	.926	3.63

Left Fielders - Regulars

Player	Tm	G	GS	Inn	PO	A	E	DP	Pct.	Rng
Crawford,Carl	TB	154	149	1282.2	327	6	4	1	.988	2.34
DeJesus,David	KC	139	138	1204.1	294	13	0	3	1.000	2.29
Bay,Jason	Bos	150	150	1279.1	310	15	0	2	1.000	2.29
Reimold,Nolan	Bal	88	83	732.1	172	7	5	1	.973	2.20
Willingham,Josh	Was	87	82	691.2	165	2	5	2	.971	2.17
Rivera,Juan	LAA	124	120	1032.1	231	10	2	3	.992	2.10
Murphy,David	Tex	104	96	858.1	195	4	1	1	.995	2.09

Player	Tm	G	GS	Inn	PO	A	E	DP	Pct.	Rng
Podsednik,Scott	CWS	78	67	615.2	139	3	0	1	1.000	2.08
Braun,Ryan	Mil	158	156	1364.0	304	8	2	2	.994	2.06
Headley,Chase	SD	114	111	982.1	215	5	3	2	.987	2.02
Young,Delmon	Min	98	93	806.2	175	4	5	1	.973	2.00
Smith,Seth	Col	86	76	627.1	135	4	1	1	.993	1.99
Quentin,Carlos	CWS	88	87	753.0	157	6	2	2	.988	1.95
Holliday,Matt	TOT	155	154	1353.1	275	7	5	1	.983	1.88
Soriano,Alfonso	ChC	116	116	1004.1	201	7	11	2	.950	1.86
Coghlan,Chris	Fla	123	120	1039.1	209	3	5	1	.977	1.84
Damon,Johnny	NYY	132	128	1117.2	220	6	5	2	.978	1.82
Ibanez,Raul	Phi	129	127	1123.2	213	9	2	0	.991	1.78
Pierre,Juan	LAD	94	63	653.1	128	1	0	0	1.000	1.78
Anderson,Garret	Atl	124	123	1026.1	193	4	4	0	.980	1.73
Ramirez,Manny	LAD	101	99	812.0	139	3	4	0	.973	1.57
Lee,Carlos	Hou	154	154	1272.1	211	9	2	0	.991	1.56

Left Fielders - The Rest

Player	Tm	G	GS	Inn	PO	A	E	DP	Pct.	Rng
Abreu,Bobby	LAA	10	10	85.0	20	0	0	0	1.000	2.12
Adams,Russ	Tor	5	3	31.0	1	0	0	0	1.000	.29
Amezaga,Alfredo	Fla	2	0	3.0	1	0	0	0	1.000	3.00
Anderson,Brian	Bos	4	1	11.0	0	0	0	0	-	.00
Anderson,Josh	Det	48	31	305.1	66	3	2	0	.972	2.03
Anderson,Josh	KC	1	0	1.0	0	0	0	0	-	.00
Andino,Robert	Bal	1	0	1.0	0	0	0	0	-	.00
Ankiel,Rick	StL	25	17	153.1	41	2	0	1	1.000	2.52
Bailey,Jeff	Bos	2	1	13.0	2	0	0	0	1.000	1.38
Baldelli,Rocco	Bos	2	1	11.0	3	0	0	0	1.000	2.45
Balentien,Wladimir	Sea	42	34	338.2	83	5	1	0	.989	2.34
Balentien,Wladimir	Cin	19	17	155.2	39	1	1	0	.976	2.31
Barfield,Josh	Cle	1	0	4.0	0	0	0	0	-	.00
Bautista,Jose	Tor	42	35	322.1	54	8	1	2	.984	1.73
Bernadina,Roger	Was	1	0	2.0	1	0	0	0	1.000	4.50
Blake,Casey	LAD	2	0	2.0	0	0	0	0	-	.00
Blanco,Gregor	Atl	3	0	8.0	0	1	1	0	.500	1.13
Blanks,Kyle	SD	18	13	110.0	26	1	0	0	1.000	2.21
Bloomquist,Willie	KC	9	9	69.0	24	0	0	0	1.000	3.13
Boggs,Brandon	Tex	3	3	26.0	8	0	1	0	.889	2.77
Bonifacio,Emilio	Fla	6	2	21.1	3	0	0	0	1.000	1.27
Borbon,Julio	Tex	16	14	128.0	31	0	3	0	.912	2.18
Bourgeois,Jason	Mil	1	0	3.0	0	0	0	0	-	.00
Bowker,John	SF	13	11	84.2	20	1	0	0	1.000	2.23
Brantley,Michael	Cle	8	7	63.1	13	0	0	0	1.000	1.85
Bruntlett,Eric	Phi	4	1	10.0	5	0	1	0	.833	4.50
Buck,Travis	Oak	5	3	29.0	0	0	0	0	-	.00
Burrell,Pat	TB	1	0	1.0	0	0	0	0	-	.00
Byrd,Marlon	Tex	36	35	305.2	73	0	0	0	1.000	2.15
Byrnes,Eric	Ari	49	46	385.2	92	3	3	0	.969	2.22
Cabrera,Melky	NYY	40	20	204.1	38	0	1	0	.974	1.67
Carroll,Brett	Fla	15	0	32.0	11	0	0	0	1.000	3.09
Carroll,Jamey	Cle	4	4	35.0	7	0	1	0	.875	1.80
Carson,Matt	Oak	1	0	2.0	0	0	0	0	-	.00
Castro,Juan	LAD	2	0	4.0	0	0	0	0	-	.00
Catalanotto,Frank	Mil	7	3	35.0	4	0	0	0	1.000	1.03
Cedeno,Ronny	Sea	7	4	41.0	11	0	0	0	1.000	2.41
Chavez,Endy	Sea	40	35	303.2	81	1	1	1	.988	2.52
Choo,Shin-Soo	Cle	20	20	164.0	37	0	0	0	1.000	2.03
Crowe,Trevor	Cle	32	28	251.0	50	4	2	0	.964	1.94
Cruz,Nelson	Tex	2	2	17.0	7	0	1	0	.875	3.71
Cunningham,Aaron	Oak	9	0	17.0	1	0	0	0	1.000	.53
De Aza,Alejandro	Fla	6	0	10.0	2	0	0	0	1.000	1.80
Dellucci,David	Cle	1	1	8.0	1	0	0	0	1.000	1.13
Dellucci,David	Tor	6	6	49.2	8	0	0	0	1.000	1.45
Denorfia,Chris	Oak	1	0	2.0	0	0	0	0	-	.00
DeRosa,Mark	Cle	16	15	130.0	22	1	0	0	1.000	1.59
DeRosa,Mark	StL	2	1	10.0	5	0	0	0	1.000	4.50
Diaz,Matt	Atl	50	30	301.0	67	0	1	0	.985	2.00
Dickerson,Chris	Cin	37	27	251.2	58	1	3	0	.952	2.11
Dobbs,Greg	Phi	13	11	83.0	17	0	0	0	1.000	1.84
Duffy,Chris	Mil	3	1	18.0	4	0	0	0	1.000	2.00
Dukes,Elijah	Was	5	1	11.2	1	0	0	0	1.000	.77
Duncan,Chris	StL	68	64	507.1	79	3	3	1	.965	1.45
Dunn,Adam	Was	62	61	505.0	99	2	5	0	.953	1.80

Player	Tm	G	GS	Inn	PO	A	E	DP	Pct.	Rng
Durango,Luis	3D	1	1	10.0	2	0	0	0	1.000	1.80
Erstad,Darin	Hou	24	4	61.1	7	0	0	0	1.000	1.03
Evans,Nick	NYM	10	9	74.1	16	1	0	0	1.000	2.06
Evans,Terry	LAA	2	0	10.0	2	0	0	0	1.000	1.80
Figgins,Chone	LAA	1	0	0.0	0	0	0	0	-	-
Fiorentino,Jeff	Bal	7	5	51.0	9	1	0	0	1.000	1.76
Fox,Jake	ChC	23	15	140.2	34	1	3	0	.921	2.24
Francisco,Ben	Cle	51	43	393.0	97	0	1	0	.990	2.22
Francisco,Ben	Phi	10	8	71.1	19	0	0	0	1.000	2.40
Freel,Ryan	Bal	5	3	31.0	8	0	0	0	1.000	2.32
Freel,Ryan	ChC	1	0	3.0	0	0	0	0	-	.00
Freel,Ryan	KC	1	1	9.0	2	1	0	0	1.000	3.00
Fuld,Sam	ChC	29	4	79.1	24	1	1	0	.962	2.84
Garko,Ryan	Cle	7	6	48.0	10	1	1	0	.917	2.06
Gathright,Joey	Bos	7	0	12.0	4	0	0	0	1.000	3.00
German,Esteban	Tex	1	0	1.0	0	0	0	0	-	.00
Gerut,Jody	Mil	3	0	7.0	1	0	0	0	1.000	1.29
Gimenez,Chris	Cle	14	9	81.0	20	0	0	0	1.000	2.22
Gload,Ross	Fla	1	0	0.2	1	0	0	0	1.000	13.50
Gomes,Jonny	Cin	37	33	253.0	46	3	1	1	.980	1.74
Gonzalez,Carlos	Col	47	30	294.1	67	2	0	0	1.000	2.11
Gonzalez,Edgar	SD	1	0	0.2	0	0	0	0	-	.00
Gorecki,Reid	Atl	22	1	56.0	15	0	1	0	.938	2.41
Green,Nick	Bos	3	0	7.0	3	0	1	0	.750	3.86
Griffey Jr,Ken	Sea	8	8	60.0	9	0	0	0	1.000	1.35
Guillen,Carlos	Det	12	10	90.2	20	0	2	0	.975	2.20
Guillen,Jose	KC	4	4	33.0	2	0	0	0	1.000	.55
Guzman,Freddy	NYY	5	0	10.0	3	0	0	0	1.000	2.70
Hairston,Jerry	Cin	9	9	80.0	24	0	0	0	1.000	2.70
Hairston,Jerry	NYY	10	8	65.0	17	1	0	0	1.000	2.49
Hairston,Scott	SD	16	14	131.0	36	1	0	0	1.000	2.54
Hairston,Scott	Oak	44	42	361.1	90	1	0	1	1.000	2.27
Hall,Bill	Mil	1	1	1.0	2	0	0	0	1.000	18.00
Hall,Bill	Sea	21	21	176.2	43	1	1	0	.978	2.24
Harris,Willie	Was	45	15	175.2	34	0	0	0	1.000	1.74
Hermida,Jeremy	Fla	51	40	340.0	61	0	1	0	.984	1.61
Hernandez,And	Was	1	0	2.0	0	0	0	0	-	.00
Hinske,Eric	NYY	2	2	17.0	7	0	0	0	1.000	3.71
Hoffpauir,Micah	ChC	11	9	64.1	12	0	0	0	1.000	1.68
Holliday,Matt	Oak	93	92	812.2	189	6	4	1	.980	2.16
Holliday,Matt	StL	62	62	540.2	86	1	1	0	.989	1.45
Hulett,Tug	KC	1	0	1.0	0	0	0	0	-	.00
Hundley,Nick	SD	1	0	1.0	1	0	0	0	1.000	9.00
Infante,Omar	Atl	7	4	36.1	11	0	0	0	1.000	2.72
Inglett,Joe	Tor	14	12	115.0	25	0	0	0	1.000	1.96
Iribarren,Hernan	Mil	1	0	1.0	0	0	0	0	-	.00
Izturis,Maicer	LAA	1	0	0.1	0	0	0	0	-	.00
Jackson,Conor	Ari	23	19	179.1	35	0	1	0	.972	1.76
Johnson,Reed	ChC	10	1	25.0	5	0	0	0	1.000	1.80
Jones,Andruw	Tex	12	12	98.2	24	0	0	0	1.000	2.19
Jones,Brandon	Atl	4	4	35.0	5	0	0	0	1.000	1.29
Jones,Garrett	Pit	15	15	127.0	24	0	0	0	1.000	1.70
Kapler,Gabe	TB	14	7	73.2	8	0	0	0	1.000	.98
Kata,Matt	Hou	4	0	2.2	0	0	0	0	-	.00
Kelly,Don	Det	18	10	97.1	23	0	0	0	1.000	2.13
Keppinger,Jeff	Hou	2	0	3.1	0	1	0	0	1.000	2.70
Kotsay,Mark	Bos	2	1	8.0	2	0	0	0	1.000	2.25
Kotsay,Mark	CWS	2	2	18.0	3	0	0	0	1.000	1.50
Kubel,Jason	Min	29	25	208.1	51	1	0	0	1.000	2.25
Langerhans,Ryan	Sea	30	26	230.2	68	1	0	0	1.000	2.69
LaPorta,Matt	Cle	29	29	256.2	53	2	1	0	.982	1.93
Lewis,Fred	SF	83	69	589.2	127	3	3	1	.977	1.98
Lind,Adam	Tor	55	55	475.2	80	1	1	0	.988	1.53
Ludwick,Ryan	StL	1	1	8.0	1	0	0	0	1.000	1.13
Macias,Drew	SD	17	8	80.2	14	0	0	0	1.000	1.56
Maier,Mitch	KC	17	10	108.2	23	0	0	0	1.000	1.90
Marshall,Sean	ChC	1	0	0.1	0	0	0	0	-	.00
Martinez,Fernando	NYM	11	10	82.0	17	1	0	0	1.000	1.98
Matthews Jr.,Gary	LAA	12	10	84.0	25	0	1	0	.962	2.68
Maxwell,Justin	Was	2	0	2.0	0	0	0	0	-	.00
Mayberry,John	Phi	26	7	96.1	25	0	0	0	1.000	2.34
McDonald,Darnell	Cin	20	12	124.0	27	1	1	1	.966	2.03
McDonald,John	Tor	4	2	22.0	3	0	0	0	1.000	1.23
Michaels,Jason	Hou	31	4	90.1	18	0	0	0	1.000	1.79

Player	Tm	G	GS	Inn	PO	A	E	DP	Pct.	Rng
Milledge,Lastings	Pit	56	56	500.0	111	6	0	0	1.000	2.11
Monroe,Craig	Pit	8	7	62.0	17	0	0	0	1.000	2.47
Montanez,Lou	Bal	19	14	135.2	34	0	0	0	1.000	2.26
Morgan,Nyjer	Pit	63	61	530.2	141	5	1	1	.993	2.48
Morse,Mike	Was	2	1	9.2	4	0	0	0	1.000	3.72
Moss,Brandon	Pit	21	19	170.2	46	1	1	0	.979	2.48
Murphy,Daniel	NYM	27	27	213.2	56	1	3	1	.950	2.40
Murton,Matt	Col	12	8	74.2	12	0	0	0	1.000	1.45
Nelson,Brad	Mil	1	1	6.0	3	0	0	0	1.000	4.50
Nix,Jayson	CWS	3	3	22.0	4	0	0	0	1.000	1.64
Nix,Laynce	Cin	72	60	558.0	118	2	1	2	.992	1.94
Oeltjen,Trent	Ari	11	8	80.0	20	1	1	0	.955	2.36
Owens,Jerry	CWS	3	1	13.0	4	0	0	0	1.000	2.77
Padilla,Jorge	Was	7	2	24.2	7	1	0	0	1.000	2.92
Pagan,Angel	NYM	20	17	146.2	40	0	0	0	1.000	2.45
Parra,Gerardo	Ari	75	66	577.0	129	4	3	0	.978	2.07
Patterson,Eric	Oak	26	20	179.1	33	1	0	0	1.000	1.71
Perez,Fernando	TB	5	4	31.0	10	0	0	0	1.000	2.90
Pettit,Chris	LAA	2	0	3.0	1	0	0	0	1.000	3.00
Pie,Felix	Bal	44	33	272.0	85	3	1	0	.989	2.91
Quinlan,Robb	LAA	17	9	79.0	16	1	0	0	1.000	1.94
Raburn,Ryan	Det	70	43	437.2	112	9	5	2	.960	2.49
Ramirez,Wilkin	Det	3	3	17.0	3	1	0	0	1.000	2.12
Rasmus,Colby	StL	4	4	43.0	9	0	0	0	1.000	1.88
Reddick,Josh	Bos	12	6	81.1	20	0	0	0	1.000	2.21
Reed,Jeremy	NYM	50	7	141.1	39	1	0	0	1.000	2.55
Repko,Jason	LAD	2	0	2.0	1	0	0	0	1.000	4.50
Roberts,Ryan	Ari	16	12	114.0	22	0	1	0	.957	1.74
Robinson,Shane	StL	1	0	2.0	0	0	0	0	-	.00
Rodriguez,Sean	LAA	3	2	19.0	2	0	0	0	1.000	.95
Romero,Alex	Ari	21	11	111.2	29	0	0	0	1.000	2.34
Salazar,Jeff	Pit	1	0	2.0	0	0	0	0	-	.00
Salazar,Oscar	Bal	1	0	1.0	0	0	0	0	-	.00
Salazar,Oscar	SD	15	12	102.2	19	0	0	0	1.000	1.67
Saunders,Michael	Sea	39	34	312.1	89	0	1	0	.989	2.56
Scales,Bobby	ChC	14	14	113.1	32	0	0	0	1.000	2.54
Schumaker,Skip	StL	39	1	82.1	16	0	1	0	.941	1.75
Scott,Luke	Bal	26	24	199.0	53	0	0	0	1.000	2.40
Sheffield,Gary	NYM	46	44	358.1	78	3	2	0	.976	2.03
Snider,Travis	Tor	56	49	435.1	87	3	1	0	.989	1.86
Span,Denard	Min	74	45	438.0	115	3	2	0	.983	2.42
Spilborghs,Ryan	Col	65	45	415.0	83	5	1	1	.989	1.91
Stairs,Matt	Phi	6	5	43.0	14	1	0	1	1.000	3.14
Stavinoha,Nick	StL	13	10	77.0	6	0	0	0	1.000	.70
Stewart,Ian	Col	6	3	27.0	4	1	0	0	1.000	1.67
Sullivan,Cory	NYM	38	26	227.0	50	2	0	0	1.000	2.06
Sutton,Drew	Cin	5	4	36.0	11	0	0	0	1.000	2.75
Sweeney,Ryan	Oak	7	5	44.0	8	2	0	0	1.000	2.05
Swisher,Nick	NYY	8	4	36.0	10	0	0	0	1.000	2.50
Taguchi,So	ChC	3	2	15.0	1	1	0	0	1.000	1.20
Tatis,Fernando	NYM	26	22	178.2	56	0	0	0	1.000	2.82
Thames,Marcus	Det	20	17	125.0	19	0	0	0	1.000	1.37
Thomas,Clete	Det	23	17	142.0	38	0	2	0	.950	2.41
Thurston,Joe	StL	5	2	17.0	3	0	0	0	1.000	1.59
Torres,Andres	SF	33	16	163.1	33	1	0	1	1.000	1.87
Valdez,Wilson	NYM	2	0	4.0	2	0	0	0	1.000	4.50
Velez,Eugenio	SF	42	32	288.2	49	2	2	0	.962	1.59
Venable,Will	SD	6	3	32.1	5	0	1	0	.833	1.39
Werth,Jayson	Phi	3	3	28.1	3	1	0	0	1.000	1.27
Wigginton,Ty	Bal	2	0	6.0	1	0	0	0	1.000	1.50
Willits,Reggie	LAA	27	11	132.1	19	0	0	0	1.000	1.29
Winn,Randy	SF	54	34	319.2	72	1	0	0	1.000	2.06
Wise,DeWayne	CWS	5	2	18.0	0	0	0	0	-	.00
Youkilis,Kevin	Bos	2	2	14.0	3	1	1	0	.800	2.57
Young,Delwyn	Pit	4	3	26.0	6	1	1	0	.875	2.42
Zobrist,Ben	TB	9	2	38.0	8	0	0	0	1.000	1.89

Center Fielders - Regulars

Player	Tm	G	GS	Inn	PO	A	E	DP	Pct.	Rng
Jones,Adam	Bal	118	116	1005.0	349	9	5	1	.986	3.21
Gomez,Carlos	Min	132	86	848.2	297	3	1	0	.997	3.18
Gwynn,Tony	SD	102	87	812.0	269	4	7	0	.975	3.03
Gutierrez,Franklin	Sea	153	152	1353.1	445	6	7	2	.985	3.00

Player	Tm	G	GS	Inn	PO	A	E	DP	Pct.	Rng
Taveras,Willy	Cin	98	95	839.0	266	7	4	2	.986	2.93
Sizemore,Grady	Cle	92	92	806.1	259	1	0	0	1.000	2.90
Cameron,Mike	Mil	147	146	1267.2	404	4	4	1	.990	2.90
Hunter,Torii	LAA	115	114	977.1	308	2	1	0	.997	2.85
Beltran,Carlos	NYM	77	77	676.0	208	3	2	1	.991	2.81
Davis,Rajai	Oak	113	93	856.1	259	8	4	1	.985	2.81
Upton,B.J.	TB	144	141	1228.2	375	6	4	1	.990	2.79
Gardner,Brett	NYY	99	63	628.2	186	3	2	2	.990	2.71
Granderson,Curtis	Det	160	155	1384.0	400	4	3	2	.993	2.63
Bourn,Michael	Hou	154	150	1326.0	371	11	3	0	.992	2.59
McLouth,Nate	TOT	129	126	1120.1	313	9	1	4	.997	2.59
McCutchen,Andrew	Pit	108	108	952.2	263	10	2	1	.993	2.58
Young,Chris	Ari	124	117	1020.1	287	3	2	1	.993	2.56
Cabrera,Melky	NYY	103	97	806.1	226	2	0	1	1.000	2.54
Kemp,Matt	LAD	158	148	1355.1	367	14	2	4	.995	2.53
Ellsbury,Jacoby	Bos	153	150	1302.2	357	5	2	1	.995	2.50
Byrd,Marlon	Tex	104	100	889.0	242	5	3	4	.988	2.50
Ross,Cody	Fla	103	100	858.1	233	4	2	2	.992	2.49
Rasmus,Colby	StL	124	104	945.2	258	3	5	1	.981	2.48
Rowand,Aaron	SF	137	133	1127.0	299	5	3	2	.990	2.43
Wells,Vernon	Tor	155	153	1356.2	352	6	1	1	.997	2.37
Victorino,Shane	Phi	149	149	1330.1	336	8	1	1	.997	2.33
Fowler,Dexter	Col	127	105	977.2	247	5	4	2	.984	2.32
Fukudome,Kosuke	ChC	113	105	903.0	226	4	2	1	.991	2.29

Center Fielders - The Rest

Player	Tm	G	GS	Inn	PO	A	E	DP	Pct.	Rng
Amezaga,Alfredo	Fla	14	7	81.1	27	0	0	0	1.000	2.99
Anderson,Brian	CWS	61	49	438.0	108	2	2	1	.982	2.26
Anderson,Brian	Bos	6	0	12.0	2	0	0	0	1.000	1.50
Anderson,Josh	Det	1	1	5.0	0	0	0	0	-	.00
Anderson,Josh	KC	31	21	199.2	55	2	0	0	1.000	2.57
Andino,Robert	Bal	1	0	2.0	1	0	0	0	1.000	4.50
Ankiel,Rick	StL	66	52	458.2	134	1	4	0	.971	2.65
Baldelli,Rocco	Bos	8	5	51.0	14	1	0	1	1.000	2.65
Bautista,Jose	Tor	6	3	32.1	9	0	0	0	1.000	2.51
Bernadina,Roger	Was	1	1	7.2	3	0	0	0	1.000	3.52
Bixler,Brian	Pit	1	0	1.0	0	0	0	0	-	.00
Blanco,Gregor	Atl	9	7	72.0	20	0	0	0	1.000	2.50
Bloomquist,Willie	KC	22	20	164.1	34	0	0	0	1.000	1.86
Boggs,Brandon	Tex	3	1	11.0	1	0	0	0	1.000	.82
Bonifacio,Emilio	Fla	11	6	58.2	20	0	0	0	1.000	3.07
Borbon,Julio	Tex	4	3	26.0	7	0	0	0	1.000	2.42
Bradley,Milton	ChC	1	0	1.0	0	0	0	0	-	.00
Brantley,Michael	Cle	20	19	166.0	46	0	1	0	.979	2.49
Bruntlett,Eric	Phi	1	0	1.0	0	0	0	0	-	.00
Byrnes,Eric	Ari	6	4	38.1	14	0	0	0	1.000	3.29
Carroll,Brett	Fla	2	0	2.0	1	1	0	1	1.000	9.00
Chavez,Endy	Sea	8	7	67.0	17	1	0	0	1.000	2.42
Choo,Shin-Soo	Cle	1	1	8.0	1	0	0	0	1.000	1.13
Church,Ryan	NYM	6	6	49.0	15	0	0	0	1.000	2.76
Church,Ryan	Atl	17	15	127.0	31	0	0	0	1.000	2.20
Colvin,Tyler	ChC	6	5	45.0	16	0	0	0	1.000	3.20
Crisp,Coco	KC	49	49	412.0	120	0	3	0	.976	2.62
Crowe,Trevor	Cle	30	19	193.0	68	0	1	0	.986	3.17
Cuddyer,Michael	Min	3	2	17.0	10	0	0	0	1.000	5.29
De Aza,Alejandro	Fla	5	2	30.0	17	0	1	0	.944	5.10
DeJesus,David	KC	3	3	25.0	10	0	0	0	1.000	3.60
Denorfia,Chris	Oak	1	0	2.1	0	0	0	0	-	.00
Diaz,Matt	Atl	2	1	6.0	1	0	0	0	1.000	1.50
Dickerson,Chris	Cin	27	19	170.2	57	4	0	3	1.000	3.22
Duffy,Chris	Mil	5	3	32.0	11	0	0	0	1.000	3.09
Dukes,Elijah	Was	35	32	272.2	79	6	1	0	.988	2.81
Durango,Luis	SD	1	1	7.0	1	1	0	0	1.000	2.57
Erstad,Darin	Hou	1	0	2.0	0	0	0	0	-	.00
Evans,Terry	LAA	1	0	4.0	1	0	0	0	1.000	2.25
Fiorentino,Jeff	Bal	14	11	101.1	26	1	0	0	1.000	2.40
Francisco,Ben	Cle	33	31	260.2	71	5	0	3	1.000	2.62
Francisco,Ben	Phi	7	7	62.0	21	1	0	0	1.000	3.19
Freel,Ryan	ChC	1	1	7.0	1	0	0	0	1.000	1.29
Freel,Ryan	KC	4	4	32.0	5	0	0	0	1.000	1.41
Fuld,Sam	ChC	26	18	161.2	39	0	0	0	1.000	2.17
Gathright,Joey	ChC	11	1	22.1	6	0	0	0	1.000	2.42
Gathright,Joey	Bos	4	2	20.0	5	0	0	0	1.000	2.25
Gentry,Craig	Tex	7	3	33.0	8	1	0	1	1.000	2.45
Gerut,Jody	SD	23	21	191.2	56	2	0	0	1.000	2.72
Gerut,Jody	Mil	19	11	113.1	25	1	1	0	.963	2.06
Golson,Greg	Tex	1	0	1.0	1	0	0	0	1.000	9.00
Gonzalez,Carlos	Col	43	38	309.2	82	3	2	0	.977	2.47
Gorecki,Reid	Atl	5	4	36.0	9	1	0	0	1.000	2.50
Greene,Tyler	StL	1	1	3.0	1	0	0	0	1.000	3.00
Hairston,Jerry	Cin	3	3	17.0	5	0	0	0	1.000	2.65
Hairston,Jerry	NYY	2	2	15.0	3	0	0	0	1.000	1.80
Hairston,Scott	SD	38	34	290.2	70	1	1	0	.986	2.20
Hairston,Scott	Oak	13	12	106.0	30	0	1	0	.968	2.55
Hall,Bill	Mil	1	0	1.0	1	0	0	0	1.000	9.00
Hamilton,Josh	Tex	56	55	472.2	132	2	0	0	1.000	2.55
Harris,Willie	Was	63	54	467.1	143	1	1	0	.993	2.77
Infante,Omar	Atl	8	4	49.1	7	0	0	0	1.000	1.28
Inglett,Joe	Tor	1	0	1.0	0	0	0	0	-	.00
Johnson,Reed	ChC	42	31	305.1	74	3	1	1	.987	2.27
Joyce,Matt	TB	4	4	32.0	9	0	0	0	1.000	2.53
Kapler,Gabe	TB	12	6	68.0	27	1	0	0	1.000	3.71
Kearns,Austin	Was	3	2	19.0	3	0	0	0	1.000	1.42
Kotsay,Mark	Bos	4	3	28.0	5	0	0	0	1.000	1.61
Kotsay,Mark	CWS	1	1	9.0	2	0	0	0	1.000	2.00
Langerhans,Ryan	Sea	4	3	32.1	16	0	0	0	1.000	4.45
Lillibridge,Brent	CWS	12	9	79.0	15	1	1	1	.941	1.82
Ludwick,Ryan	StL	1	1	7.0	2	0	0	0	1.000	2.57
Macias,Drew	SD	6	3	32.1	5	0	0	0	1.000	1.39
Maier,Mitch	KC	85	65	593.0	181	10	0	4	1.000	2.90
Martinez,Fernando	NYM	8	7	64.0	21	0	0	0	1.000	2.95
Matthews Jr.,Gary	LAA	56	46	435.2	125	1	1	0	.992	2.60
Maxwell,Justin	Was	32	20	203.1	58	1	0	1	1.000	2.61
Maybin,Cameron	Fla	52	47	416.0	124	1	1	0	.992	2.70
McDonald,Darnell	Cin	8	2	29.0	10	0	1	0	.909	3.10
McLouth,Nate	Pit	45	44	380.0	117	5	0	2	1.000	2.89
McLouth,Nate	Atl	84	82	740.1	196	4	1	2	.995	2.43
Michaels,Jason	Hou	14	12	102.0	30	0	0	0	1.000	2.65
Milledge,Lastings	Was	5	5	42.1	11	0	0	0	1.000	2.34
Montanez,Lou	Bal	2	1	9.0	2	0	0	0	1.000	2.00
Morgan,Nyjer	Pit	9	8	71.2	22	1	0	0	1.000	2.89
Morgan,Nyjer	Was	47	46	391.0	135	7	3	1	.979	3.27
Murphy,David	Tex	1	0	2.0	0	0	0	0	-	.00
Nix,Laynce	Cin	5	3	34.0	9	0	1	0	.900	2.38
Oeltjen,Trent	Ari	5	4	34.1	6	0	0	0	1.000	1.57
Owens,Jerry	CWS	4	1	16.0	7	0	0	0	1.000	3.94
Padilla,Jorge	Was	1	0	3.0	0	0	0	0	-	.00
Pagan,Angel	NYM	61	59	506.1	132	4	2	0	.986	2.42
Parra,Gerardo	Ari	43	34	328.0	89	3	3	0	.968	2.52
Patterson,Corey	Was	2	2	18.0	3	0	0	0	1.000	1.50
Patterson,Corey	Mil	4	2	21.0	6	0	0	0	1.000	2.57
Patterson,Eric	Oak	4	4	30.0	6	0	0	0	1.000	1.80
Paul,Xavier	LAD	1	1	7.0	1	0	0	0	1.000	1.29
Perez,Fernando	TB	8	6	52.0	19	0	0	0	1.000	3.29
Pie,Felix	Bal	41	34	311.2	112	2	1	0	.991	3.29
Pierre,Juan	LAD	15	13	102.0	28	0	1	0	.966	2.47
Podsednik,Scott	CWS	49	47	397.0	115	3	1	1	.992	2.68
Raburn,Ryan	Det	7	5	33.0	14	0	0	0	1.000	3.82
Reddick,Josh	Bos	2	1	8.0	1	0	0	0	1.000	1.13
Reed,Jeremy	NYM	12	9	86.2	29	0	0	0	1.000	3.01
Repko,Jason	LAD	3	0	9.0	1	0	0	0	1.000	1.00
Rios,Alex	Tor	8	6	61.0	19	0	0	0	1.000	2.80
Rios,Alex	CWS	34	31	285.0	82	0	2	0	.976	2.59
Robinson,Shane	StL	2	1	2.2	0	0	0	0	-	.00
Rodriguez,Sean	LAA	2	0	2.0	1	0	0	0	1.000	4.50
Romero,Alex	Ari	4	3	26.2	11	1	0	0	1.000	4.05
Salazar,Jeff	Pit	2	1	13.0	7	1	0	0	1.000	5.54
Schafer,Jordan	Atl	50	49	432.0	127	4	0	1	1.000	2.73
Schumaker,Skip	StL	6	3	23.2	8	0	0	0	1.000	3.04
Span,Denard	Min	84	75	587.1	179	11	1	1	.994	2.76
Spilborghs,Ryan	Col	16	15	113.0	30	2	2	0	.941	2.55
Stubbs,Drew	Cin	42	40	368.2	111	4	0	0	1.000	2.81
Sullivan,Cory	NYM	6	4	44.0	14	1	0	0	1.000	3.07
Sweeney,Ryan	Oak	57	53	452.2	146	4	1	0	.993	2.98
Thomas,Clete	Det	7	2	25.0	8	0	0	0	1.000	2.88
Torres,Andres	SF	37	12	152.1	53	1	0	0	1.000	3.19

Player	Tm	G	GS	Inn	PO	A	E	DP	Pct.	Rng
Van Every,Jonathan	Bos	2	1	15.0	2	0	0	0	1.000	1.20
Velez,Eugenio	SF	12	6	65.1	13	0	1	0	.929	1.79
Venable,Will	SD	16	16	117.0	30	1	0	0	1.000	2.38
Werth,Jayson	Phi	12	6	62.1	23	0	2	0	.920	3.32
Willits,Reggie	LAA	6	2	26.0	8	0	0	0	1.000	2.77
Winn,Randy	SF	22	11	101.1	23	0	0	1	1.000	2.13
Wise,DeWayne	CWS	35	24	215.2	72	2	1	1	.987	3.09
Young Jr.,Eric	Col	5	4	38.0	4	0	0	0	1.000	.95
Zobrist,Ben	TB	7	5	46.2	15	0	0	0	1.000	2.89

Right Fielders - Regulars

Player	Tm	G	GS	Inn	PO	A	E	DP	Pct.	Rng
Cruz,Nelson	Tex	120	117	1035.2	294	11	3	2	.990	2.65
Sweeney,Ryan	Oak	85	63	600.0	165	5	2	2	.988	2.55
Moss,Brandon	Pit	79	76	665.0	171	8	1	4	.994	2.42
Choo,Shin-Soo	Cle	124	121	1084.2	279	11	7	2	.976	2.41
Werth,Jayson	Phi	146	143	1288.2	327	10	4	4	.988	2.35
Bruce,Jay	Cin	98	89	810.1	200	11	2	2	.991	2.34
Upton,Justin	Ari	136	134	1180.0	294	4	12	1	.961	2.27
Suzuki,Ichiro	Sea	145	145	1291.0	317	5	4	2	.988	2.24
Winn,Randy	SF	104	90	770.0	187	3	0	1	1.000	2.22
Gross,Gabe	TB	100	67	638.2	149	6	3	1	.981	2.18
Pence,Hunter	Hou	157	156	1375.2	316	16	5	2	.985	2.17
Abreu,Bobby	LAA	126	126	1081.0	249	10	8	4	.970	2.16
Rios,Alex	TOT	110	109	982.0	228	4	3	0	.987	2.13
Hermida,Jeremy	Fla	81	73	620.1	140	3	0	1	1.000	2.07
Church,Ryan	TOT	86	71	642.0	141	6	2	5	.987	2.06
Swisher,Nick	NYY	130	126	1052.2	239	2	5	1	.980	2.06
Drew,J.D.	Bos	131	124	1083.1	242	5	2	2	.992	2.05
Francoeur,Jeff	TOT	154	152	1338.1	294	11	1	0	.997	2.05
Markakis,Nick	Bal	161	160	1402.0	298	13	6	1	.981	2.00
Bradley,Milton	ChC	108	107	914.0	197	5	3	4	.985	1.99
Dye,Jermaine	CWS	133	133	1120.2	238	9	5	3	.980	1.90
Ethier,Andre	LAD	158	150	1365.1	279	6	7	0	.976	1.88
Cuddyer,Michael	Min	117	112	991.2	199	5	2	0	.990	1.85
Ludwick,Ryan	StL	133	120	1068.1	210	9	1	4	.995	1.84
Hart,Corey	Mil	112	105	930.1	187	3	5	0	.974	1.84
Ordonez,Magglio	Det	104	102	796.1	149	6	2	1	.987	1.75
Hawpe,Brad	Col	141	141	1195.2	213	4	5	1	.977	1.63

Right Fielders - The Rest

Player	Tm	G	GS	Inn	PO	A	E	DP	Pct.	Rng
Amezaga,Alfredo	Fla	3	1	10.0	5	0	0	0	1.000	4.50
Anderson,Brian	CWS	6	2	28.0	10	1	0	0	1.000	3.54
Anderson,Brian	Bos	11	3	41.0	4	0	0	0	1.000	.88
Anderson,Josh	Det	18	8	87.2	13	1	0	1	1.000	1.44
Anderson,Josh	KC	11	9	87.0	38	0	1	0	.974	3.93
Ankiel,Rick	StL	27	21	183.2	28	2	1	1	.968	1.47
Bailey,Jeff	Bos	1	1	8.0	2	0	0	0	1.000	2.25
Baldelli,Rocco	Bos	35	28	228.2	49	2	3	0	.944	2.01
Balentien,Wladimir	Sea	5	3	25.2	5	0	0	0	1.000	1.75
Balentien,Wladimir	Cin	17	11	110.0	28	0	0	0	1.000	2.29
Barton,Brian	Atl	1	0	2.0	1	0	0	0	1.000	4.50
Bautista,Jose	Tor	36	32	286.1	69	3	0	0	1.000	2.26
Bernadina,Roger	Was	1	0	3.0	0	0	0	0	-	.00
Blanco,Gregor	Atl	2	1	10.0	1	0	0	0	1.000	.90
Blanks,Kyle	SD	22	21	174.0	29	0	0	0	1.000	1.50
Bloomquist,Willie	KC	61	33	329.0	76	3	2	1	.975	2.16
Bourgeois,Jason	Mil	6	6	45.0	14	0	0	0	1.000	2.80
Bowker,John	SF	5	4	29.0	6	0	0	0	1.000	1.86
Brown,Emil	NYM	1	1	8.0	1	0	0	0	1.000	1.13
Bruntlett,Eric	Phi	5	2	22.1	4	1	0	0	1.000	2.01
Buck,Travis	Oak	28	24	217.2	61	0	0	0	1.000	2.52
Burrell,Pat	TB	1	1	7.0	2	0	0	0	1.000	2.57
Byrd,Marlon	Tex	6	6	52.0	17	1	0	0	1.000	3.12
Byrnes,Eric	Ari	5	4	40.0	12	0	0	0	1.000	2.70
Cabrera,Melky	NYY	48	13	177.0	36	1	2	0	.949	1.88
Carroll,Brett	Fla	60	32	319.1	85	4	0	0	1.000	2.51
Carroll,Jamey	Cle	6	4	35.0	10	0	0	0	1.000	2.57
Carson,Matt	Oak	8	6	54.0	12	0	0	0	1.000	2.00
Carter,Chris	Bos	1	0	6.0	2	0	0	0	1.000	3.00
Catalanotto,Frank	Mil	31	29	230.2	60	2	1	0	.984	2.42

Player	Tm	G	GS	Inn	PO	A	E	DP	Pct.	Rng
Chavez,Endy	Sea	4	2	23.0	6	0	0	0	1.000	2.35
Church,Ryan	NYM	60	52	469.0	105	3	1	3	.991	2.07
Church,Ryan	Atl	26	19	173.0	36	3	1	2	.975	2.03
Crosby,Bobby	Oak	1	0	1.0	0	0	0	0	-	.00
Crowe,Trevor	Cle	5	3	28.0	12	0	1	0	.923	3.86
Cunningham,Aaron	Oak	16	14	119.0	21	0	2	0	.913	1.59
Cust,Jack	Oak	51	50	401.2	69	1	2	1	.972	1.57
Davis,Rajai	Oak	5	4	35.0	6	0	0	0	1.000	1.54
DeJesus,David	KC	2	1	10.0	6	0	0	0	1.000	5.40
Denorfia,Chris	Oak	1	0	2.0	0	0	0	0	-	.00
DeRosa,Mark	Cle	9	8	68.0	16	0	0	0	1.000	2.12
DeRosa,Mark	StL	1	1	8.0	2	0	0	0	1.000	2.25
Desmond,Ian	Was	1	1	7.0	3	0	0	0	1.000	3.86
Diaz,Matt	Atl	66	61	540.2	89	2	2	0	.978	1.51
Dickerson,Chris	Cin	20	13	122.0	31	0	0	0	1.000	2.29
Dobbs,Greg	Phi	2	2	15.0	6	0	0	0	1.000	3.60
Doumit,Ryan	Pit	1	1	9.0	2	0	0	0	1.000	2.00
Duffy,Chris	Mil	2	1	11.1	6	1	0	0	1.000	5.56
Dukes,Elijah	Was	65	61	548.1	129	6	7	1	.951	2.22
Duncan,Shelley	NYY	8	2	24.1	5	0	0	0	1.000	1.85
Dunn,Adam	Was	22	22	180.0	43	0	3	0	.935	2.15
Erstad,Darin	Hou	4	4	34.0	8	0	0	0	1.000	2.12
Evans,Terry	LAA	7	1	12.0	3	0	0	0	1.000	2.25
Florentino,Jeff	Bal	2	0	3.0	1	0	0	0	1.000	3.00
Fox,Jake	ChC	3	2	17.0	2	0	0	0	1.000	1.06
Francisco,Ben	Cle	19	9	74.0	15	0	0	0	1.000	1.82
Francisco,Ben	Phi	6	5	48.0	11	1	0	0	1.000	2.25
Francoeur,Jeff	Atl	80	78	701.0	157	6	0	0	1.000	2.09
Francoeur,Jeff	NYM	74	74	637.1	137	5	1	0	.993	2.01
Freel,Ryan	Bal	1	1	3.0	0	0	0	0	-	.00
Freel,Ryan	ChC	1	0	4.0	0	0	0	0	-	.00
Freel,Ryan	KC	12	6	64.0	9	0	0	0	1.000	1.27
Fukudome,Kosuke	ChC	44	24	263.1	79	1	0	1	1.000	2.73
Fuld,Sam	ChC	2	0	2.0	2	0	0	0	1.000	9.00
Garko,Ryan	Cle	5	4	28.0	6	0	0	0	1.000	1.93
Gathright,Joey	Bos	2	1	11.0	4	0	0	0	1.000	3.27
Gentry,Craig	Tex	2	2	13.0	3	0	0	0	1.000	2.08
Gerut,Jody	SD	5	3	29.0	7	0	0	0	1.000	2.17
Gerut,Jody	Mil	32	16	172.2	43	0	0	0	1.000	2.24
Giles,Brian	SD	58	56	502.2	113	6	0	3	1.000	2.13
Gimenez,Chris	Cle	7	4	34.0	8	0	0	0	1.000	2.12
Gload,Ross	Fla	10	5	46.2	10	0	1	0	.909	1.93
Gomes,Jonny	Cin	34	33	269.1	57	2	0	0	1.000	1.97
Gonzalez,Carlos	Col	8	2	28.2	3	1	0	0	1.000	1.26
Gonzalez,Edgar	SD	14	13	98.1	24	0	0	0	1.000	2.20
Gorecki,Reid	Atl	1	0	1.0	1	0	0	0	1.000	9.00
Griffey Jr.,Ken	Sea	3	3	23.0	4	0	0	0	1.000	1.57
Guerrero,Vladimir	LAA	2	2	16.0	4	0	0	0	1.000	2.25
Guillen,Jose	KC	65	64	504.0	96	4	4	0	.962	1.79
Guzman,Freddy	NYY	3	0	6.0	1	0	0	0	1.000	1.50
Gwynn,Tony	SD	11	9	81.1	28	1	1	1	.967	3.21
Hairston,Jerry	Cin	5	1	14.0	6	0	0	0	1.000	3.86
Hairston,Jerry	NYY	9	0	15.0	2	0	0	0	1.000	1.20
Hall,Bill	Mil	5	4	36.0	13	0	0	0	1.000	3.25
Hall,Bill	Sea	10	8	72.0	22	2	0	0	1.000	3.00
Hamilton,Josh	Tex	24	24	210.0	53	2	1	0	.982	2.36
Harris,Willie	Was	1	0	1.0	0	0	0	0	-	.00
Hinske,Eric	Pit	13	13	111.2	30	3	0	0	1.000	2.66
Hinske,Eric	NYY	22	15	129.0	25	0	0	0	1.000	1.74
Hoffmann,Jaime	LAD	5	3	32.0	10	1	0	1	1.000	3.09
Hoffpauir,Micah	ChC	25	23	187.0	43	1	1	0	.978	2.12
Hulett,Tug	KC	2	0	3.0	2	0	0	0	1.000	6.00
Infante,Omar	Atl	3	3	33.0	6	0	0	0	1.000	1.64
Inglett,Joe	Tor	11	9	76.2	10	2	2	0	.857	1.41
Johnson,Reed	ChC	7	4	37.0	4	0	0	0	1.000	.97
Jones,Andruw	Tex	5	5	50.0	6	0	0	0	1.000	1.08
Jones,Garrett	Pit	39	38	343.1	76	4	0	0	1.000	2.10
Jones,Mitch	LAD	1	1	7.0	2	0	0	0	1.000	2.57
Joyce,Matt	TB	5	4	36.0	6	0	0	0	1.000	1.50
Kapler,Gabe	TB	66	53	414.1	108	4	2	0	.982	2.43
Kearns,Austin	Was	54	39	363.0	81	5	0	0	1.000	2.13
Kelly,Don	Det	2	2	14.0	6	1	0	0	1.000	4.50
Kemp,Matt	LAD	7	7	50.0	10	0	0	0	1.000	1.80
Kennedy,Adam	Oak	1	0	5.0	1	0	0	0	1.000	1.80

Player	Tm	G	GS	Inn	PO	A	E	DP	Pct.	Rng
Kotsay,Mark	Bos	4	1	8.2	1	0	0	0	1.000	1.04
Kotsay,Mark	CWS	8	7	54.0	13	1	0	0	1.000	2.33
Kubel,Jason	Min	30	28	219.1	52	0	0	0	1.000	2.13
Langerhans,Ryan	Sea	5	1	18.0	1	0	0	0	1.000	.50
LaPorta,Matt	Cle	10	10	82.1	24	1	1	0	.962	2.73
Lopez,Javier	Bos	1	0	0.2	0	0	0	0	-	.00
Macias,Drew	SD	7	4	43.2	5	0	1	0	.833	1.03
Maier,Mitch	KC	36	18	178.0	46	1	0	1	1.000	2.38
Martinez,Fernando	NYM	6	6	56.0	11	0	0	0	1.000	1.77
Matthews Jr.,Gary	LAA	28	24	218.0	43	1	1	0	.978	1.82
Maxwell,Justin	Was	2	1	9.0	2	0	0	0	1.000	2.00
Mayberry,John	Phi	4	3	30.2	6	1	0	1	1.000	2.05
McCoy,Mike	Col	1	0	1.1	1	0	0	0	1.000	6.75
McDonald,Darnell	Cin	10	8	66.2	24	1	0	0	1.000	3.38
McGehee,Casey	Mil	1	0	1.0	0	0	0	0	-	.00
Michaels,Jason	Hou	3	2	20.1	4	0	0	0	1.000	1.77
Monroe,Craig	Pit	9	6	59.0	14	0	0	0	1.000	2.14
Montanez,Lou	Bal	2	1	12.0	1	0	0	0	1.000	.75
Morse,Mike	Was	3	3	23.0	7	0	0	0	1.000	2.74
Murphy,David	Tex	10	8	74.0	19	3	1	1	.957	2.68
Murton,Matt	Col	5	0	10.1	1	0	0	0	1.000	.87
Nady,Xavier	NYY	6	6	46.0	10	0	0	0	1.000	1.96
Nelson,Brad	Mil	1	1	8.0	1	0	0	0	1.000	1.13
Nix,Jayson	CWS	4	1	14.0	7	0	0	0	1.000	4.50
Nix,Laynce	Cin	10	7	63.0	14	0	0	0	1.000	2.00
Oeltjen,Trent	Ari	3	3	25.0	10	1	0	0	1.000	3.96
Orr,Pete	Was	1	0	1.0	0	0	0	0	-	.00
Padilla,Jorge	Was	5	1	13.0	3	0	0	0	1.000	2.08
Pagan,Angel	NYM	6	4	44.0	11	1	0	0	1.000	2.45
Parra,Gerardo	Ari	9	6	60.2	11	1	0	0	1.000	1.78
Patterson,Corey	Was	2	1	11.2	3	0	0	0	1.000	2.31
Patterson,Eric	Oak	2	1	12.0	2	0	0	0	1.000	1.50
Paul,Xavier	LAD	3	1	12.0	1	0	0	0	1.000	.75
Pearce,Steve	Pit	1	1	9.0	1	0	0	0	1.000	1.00
Perez,Fernando	TB	1	0	2.0	0	0	0	0	-	.00
Pettit,Chris	LAA	4	0	18.0	3	0	0	0	1.000	1.50
Podsednik,Scott	CWS	3	2	18.0	4	0	1	0	.800	2.00
Prado,Martin	Atl	1	0	2.0	0	0	0	0	-	.00
Quinlan,Robb	LAA	6	1	15.0	4	0	0	0	1.000	2.40
Raburn,Ryan	Det	14	4	43.2	10	0	0	0	1.000	2.06
Ramirez,Wilkin	Det	2	0	3.0	1	0	0	0	1.000	3.00
Rasmus,Colby	StL	6	6	46.2	9	0	1	0	.900	1.74
Reddick,Josh	Bos	10	3	35.0	9	0	1	0	.900	2.31
Reed,Jeremy	NYM	8	5	49.0	11	0	0	0	1.000	2.02
Reimold,Nolan	Bal	2	1	9.0	1	0	0	0	1.000	1.00
Repko,Jason	LAD	3	0	7.0	1	0	0	0	1.000	1.29
Rios,Alex	Tor	103	102	914.2	217	4	3	0	.987	2.17
Rios,Alex	CWS	7	7	67.1	11	0	0	0	1.000	1.47
Rivera,Juan	LAA	7	5	42.0	6	1	0	0	1.000	1.50
Robinson,Shane	StL	6	4	41.1	6	0	0	0	1.000	1.31
Rodriguez,Sean	LAA	2	0	4.0	0	0	0	0	-	.00
Romero,Alex	Ari	21	15	142.0	24	1	1	0	.962	1.58
Ross,Cody	Fla	57	49	450.0	104	2	1	1	.991	2.12
Salazar,Jeff	Pit	1	0	3.1	0	0	0	0	-	.00
Salazar,Oscar	SD	4	4	28.0	6	0	0	0	1.000	1.93
Scales,Bobby	ChC	4	1	18.0	3	0	0	0	1.000	1.50
Schierholtz,Nate	SF	86	61	597.2	135	10	2	2	.986	2.18
Schumaker,Skip	StL	11	0	25.1	5	0	0	0	1.000	1.78
Sheffield,Gary	NYM	18	18	143.2	18	1	0	0	1.000	1.19
Snider,Travis	Tor	21	19	173.1	36	0	3	0	.923	1.87
Span,Denard	Min	39	23	242.0	56	2	2	1	.967	2.16
Spilborghs,Ryan	Col	37	18	192.1	37	1	1	0	.974	1.78
Stairs,Matt	Phi	9	7	51.0	9	1	0	1	1.000	1.76
Stavinoha,Nick	StL	10	10	67.1	6	0	0	0	1.000	.80
Stewart,Ian	Col	3	1	10.0	1	0	0	0	1.000	.90
Sullivan,Cory	NYM	2	2	17.0	4	0	0	0	1.000	2.12
Sutton,Drew	Cin	1	0	3.0	0	0	0	0	-	.00
Taguchi,So	ChC	1	0	3.0	1	0	0	0	1.000	3.00
Tatis,Fernando	NYM	2	0	2.0	0	0	0	0	-	.00
Teahen,Mark	KC	32	31	251.0	39	0	1	0	.975	1.40
Thomas,Clete	Det	87	47	502.1	127	5	2	3	.985	2.36
Torres,Andres	SF	5	5	35.1	7	0	0	0	1.000	1.78
Van Every,Jonathan	Bos	4	1	14.1	4	0	0	0	1.000	2.51
Velez,Eugenio	SF	5	2	14.0	3	0	0	0	1.000	1.93

Player	Tm	G	GS	Inn	PO	A	E	DP	Pct.	Rng
Venable,Will	SD	68	52	493.2	123	2	1	0	.992	2.28
Willingham,Josh	Was	35	33	264.1	68	0	2	0	.971	2.32
Willits,Reggie	LAA	10	3	39.0	9	0	0	0	1.000	2.08
Wise,DeWayne	CWS	34	10	137.2	24	4	0	2	1.000	1.83
Young,Delwyn	Pit	26	26	218.0	60	0	1	0	.984	2.48
Zobrist,Ben	TB	59	37	329.1	89	5	0	4	1.000	2.57

Catchers - Regulars

Player	Tm	G	GS	Inn	PO	A	E	DP	PB	Pct.
Hanigan,Ryan	Cin	88	72	670.1	494	44	1	6	3	.998
Laird,Gerald	Det	135	123	1090.1	844	78	3	7	9	.997
Varitek,Jason	Bos	108	106	924.0	856	37	3	3	1	.997
Ruiz,Carlos	Phi	107	100	882.1	707	49	3	7	1	.996
Mauer,Joe	Min	109	105	939.0	724	31	3	3	9	.996
Hill,Koyie	ChC	79	69	627.1	573	46	3	8	2	.995
Molina,Bengie	SF	123	120	1042.0	942	77	5	8	4	.995
Suzuki,Kurt	Oak	135	132	1173.1	923	68	5	7	3	.995
Molina,Yadier	StL	138	136	1176.2	884	82	5	6	4	.995
Pierzynski,A.J.	CWS	131	124	1104.0	879	50	5	8	7	.995
Santos,Omir	NYM	91	74	680.1	502	26	3	4	3	.994
Martin,Russell	LAD	137	133	1201.0	1039	87	7	9	3	.994
Navarro,Dioner	TB	113	105	921.1	732	47	5	7	6	.994
Soto,Geovany	ChC	96	92	811.0	720	50	5	9	3	.994
Johnson,Rob	Sea	80	75	684.1	511	42	4	5	9	.993
Baker,John	Fla	105	99	864.0	748	42	6	2	5	.992
Martinez,Victor	TOT	85	82	687.0	500	22	4	3	4	.992
Shoppach,Kelly	Cle	81	74	672.0	476	31	4	3	6	.992
Iannetta,Chris	Col	89	87	763.2	542	59	5	10	2	.992
Rodriguez,Ivan	TOT	115	108	962.0	786	52	7	5	7	.992
Kendall,Jason	Mil	133	131	1162.0	882	61	8	2	4	.992
Barajas,Rod	Tor	120	110	974.1	806	58	8	7	6	.991
Wieters,Matt	Bal	86	84	738.1	489	35	5	12	3	.991
Posada,Jorge	NYY	100	88	785.0	648	48	7	6	8	.990
Olivo,Miguel	KC	103	97	845.2	718	47	8	6	10	.990
Hundley,Nick	SD	74	71	643.1	515	35	6	5	7	.989
Montero,Miguel	Ari	111	101	924.2	733	60	9	4	4	.989
Bard,Josh	Was	79	71	630.2	397	27	5	3	3	.988
McCann,Brian	Atl	127	124	1078.2	924	58	12	7	7	.988
Zaun,Gregg	TOT	83	74	643.0	462	23	6	2	2	.988
Mathis,Jeff	LAA	79	78	657.0	507	58	7	5	6	.988
Doumit,Ryan	Pit	71	70	615.1	418	53	6	3	3	.987
Saltalamacchia,J	Tex	83	82	714.0	502	28	7	4	2	.987
Napoli,Mike	LAA	96	84	758.0	526	48	8	7	5	.986

Catchers - The Rest

Player	Tm	G	GS	Inn	PO	A	E	DP	PB	Pct.
Alfonzo,Eliezer	SD	30	28	255.1	203	23	1	5	3	.996
Ausmus,Brad	LAD	30	27	244.2	203	11	0	1	2	1.000
Avila,Alex	Det	25	17	153.1	101	7	0	0	1	1.000
Bako,Paul	Phi	42	33	299.1	254	9	5	1	6	.981
Barrett,Michael	Tor	7	4	39.1	34	1	0	0	1	1.000
Bellorin,Edwin	Col	2	2	18.0	11	0	0	0	0	1.000
Blanco,Henry	SD	60	58	508.0	444	28	0	4	2	1.000
Brown,Dusty	Bos	6	0	12.0	6	2	0	0	0	1.000
Buck,John	KC	46	41	366.2	309	14	8	4	2	.976
Budde,Ryan	LAA	2	0	6.0	7	1	0	0	1	1.000
Burke,Jamie	Sea	12	11	96.2	68	6	2	1	1	.974
Burke,Jamie	Was	6	3	34.1	27	1	0	0	0	1.000
Carlin,Luke	Ari	4	4	34.0	24	1	0	0	1	1.000
Cash,Kevin	NYY	10	7	67.0	57	10	0	1	0	1.000
Castro,Ramon	NYM	23	21	181.0	159	9	2	3	0	.988
Castro,Ramon	CWS	29	25	220.2	163	7	3	2	0	.983
Cervelli,Francisco	NYY	40	25	241.1	207	14	1	1	0	.995
Chavez,Raul	Tor	51	44	399.0	327	40	2	2	5	.995
Corporan,Carlos	Mil	1	0	2.0	2	1	0	0	0	1.000
Coste,Chris	Phi	29	22	211.0	164	6	0	1	3	1.000
Coste,Chris	Hou	26	14	141.0	116	5	0	0	0	1.000
Diaz,Robinzon	Pit	33	33	283.0	188	23	2	1	7	.991
Ellis,A.J.	LAD	7	2	27.2	36	2	0	0	0	1.000
Flores,Jesus	Was	24	23	205.2	139	10	1	0	2	.993
Flowers,Tyler	CWS	6	3	27.0	20	1	0	0	1	1.000
Fox,Jake	ChC	3	0	7.0	6	1	0	0	0	1.000

Player	Tm	G	GS	Inn	PO	A	E	DP	PB	Pct.
Freese,David	StL	1	0	1.0	1	0	0	0	0	1.000
Gimenez,Chris	Cle	8	6	56.0	36	4	0	0	0	1.000
Hernandez,Michel	TB	35	29	264.1	217	11	2	2	1	.991
Hernandez,Ramon	Cin	55	53	451.0	353	26	1	2	0	.997
Hester,John	Ari	8	6	53.0	45	3	0	0	0	1.000
Holm,Steve	SF	4	2	23.0	14	1	0	0	0	1.000
Hoover,Paul	Phi	3	1	11.0	9	1	0	0	0	1.000
Jaramillo,Jason	Pit	62	58	520.0	322	28	4	5	4	.989
Johjima,Kenji	Sea	70	67	580.0	413	35	1	2	4	.998
Kottaras,George	Bos	39	25	243.2	196	8	1	1	8	.995
LaRue,Jason	StL	43	26	254.0	174	13	1	0	1	.995
Lobaton,Jose	SD	6	5	44.0	52	2	1	0	0	.982
Marson,Lou	Phi	7	6	52.0	48	6	0	0	0	1.000
Marson,Lou	Cle	14	14	123.0	95	8	1	1	0	.990
Martinez,Victor	Cle	52	51	430.0	285	14	0	2	3	1.000
Martinez,Victor	Bos	33	31	257.0	215	8	4	1	1	.982
Miller,Corky	CWS	11	10	88.0	68	3	0	1	1	1.000
Miller,Corky	Cin	21	18	164.0	125	12	0	3	1	1.000
Moeller,Chad	Bal	30	28	239.1	194	6	0	0	3	1.000
Molina,Jose	NYY	49	42	356.2	366	21	1	1	3	.997
Moore,Adam	Sea	6	5	57.0	40	2	0	0	1	1.000
Morales,Jose	Min	29	19	183.1	135	9	3	0	5	.980
Nieves,Wil	Was	71	65	553.2	380	41	6	4	4	.986
Pagnozzi,Matt	StL	5	0	9.0	9	1	0	1	0	1.000
Paulino,Ronny	Fla	77	63	582.1	511	16	2	1	3	.996
Pena,Brayan	KC	30	24	213.2	100	7	0	0	0	1.000
Phillips,Kyle	Tor	5	4	38.1	28	2	1	0	1	.968
Phillips,Paul	Col	15	12	111.1	95	8	1	0	2	.990
Posey,Buster	SF	7	4	40.0	32	4	0	0	0	1.000
Powell,Landon	Oak	36	30	274.0	214	13	3	3	2	.987
Quintero,Humberto	Hou	59	51	427.0	358	36	5	6	5	.987
Quiroz,Guillermo	Sea	4	4	34.2	25	2	0	0	1	1.000
Redmond,Mike	Min	44	39	330.2	228	8	0	2	2	1.000
Richardson,Kevin	Tex	4	1	15.0	13	0	0	0	0	1.000
Riggans,Shawn	TB	7	3	34.0	29	1	1	0	0	.968
Rivera,Mike	Mil	34	31	271.0	234	14	0	1	2	1.000
Rodriguez,Guillermo	Bal	6	1	16.0	10	0	0	0	0	1.000
Rodriguez,Ivan	Hou	90	83	748.0	618	41	4	4	5	.994
Rodriguez,Ivan	Tex	25	25	214.0	168	11	3	1	2	.984
Ross,David	Atl	52	36	354.0	314	37	1	6	5	.997
Ryan,Dusty	Det	12	8	78.2	60	6	0	0	1	1.000
Sammons,Clint	Atl	6	2	30.0	23	2	0	0	0	1.000
Sandoval,Pablo	SF	3	3	27.0	21	2	0	0	0	1.000
Sardinha,Dane	Det	12	11	92.2	90	7	0	2	1	1.000
Schneider,Brian	NYM	57	52	437.1	329	25	1	3	1	.997
Snyder,Chris	Ari	56	51	436.0	363	21	0	1	3	1.000
Tatum,Craig	Cin	26	19	173.0	137	10	1	0	0	.993
Teagarden,Taylor	Tex	60	54	491.2	360	31	6	4	5	.985
Thole,Josh	NYM	16	15	127.1	72	3	1	0	3	.987
Toregas,Wyatt	Cle	19	17	153.0	119	9	0	0	1	1.000
Torrealba,Yorvit	Col	64	61	545.1	505	27	0	2	2	1.000
Towles,J.R.	Hou	15	14	114.0	83	8	0	0	1	1.000
Treanor,Matt	Det	4	4	32.0	28	0	0	0	0	1.000
Whiteside,Eli	SF	47	33	314.0	286	25	5	2	5	.984
Wilson,Bobby	LAA	11	0	24.0	19	1	0	0	0	1.000
Zaun,Gregg	Bal	54	49	435.1	294	17	5	1	2	.984
Zaun,Gregg	TB	29	25	207.2	168	6	1	1	0	.994

Catchers Special - Regulars

Player	Tm	G	GS	Inn	SBA	CS	PCS	CS%	ER	CERA
Hanigan,Ryan	Cin	88	72	670.1	49	21	2	.40	318	4.27
Laird,Gerald	Det	135	123	1090.1	101	42	2	.40	513	4.23
Hill,Koyie	ChC	79	69	627.1	50	20	0	.40	257	3.69
Molina,Yadier	StL	138	136	1176.2	54	22	6	.33	455	3.48
Rodriguez,Ivan	TOT	115	108	962.0	63	22	3	.32	488	4.57
Barajas,Rod	Tor	120	110	974.1	80	27	5	.29	461	4.26
Johnson,Rob	Sea	80	75	684.1	59	18	1	.29	245	3.22
Soto,Geovany	ChC	96	92	811.0	82	23	0	.28	360	4.00
Martin,Russell	LAD	137	133	1201.0	107	33	8	.25	450	3.37
Mathis,Jeff	LAA	79	78	657.0	70	18	1	.25	291	3.99
Olivo,Miguel	KC	103	97	845.2	78	22	4	.24	422	4.49
Mauer,Joe	Min	109	105	939.0	73	19	2	.24	448	4.29
Navarro,Dioner	TB	113	105	921.1	83	22	3	.24	433	4.23

Player	Tm	G	GS	Inn	SBA	CS	PCS	CS%	ER	CERA
Iannetta,Chris	Col	89	87	763.2	68	18	3	.23	357	4.21
Posada,Jorge	NYY	100	88	785.0	111	31	8	.22	440	5.04
Saltalamacchia,J	Tex	83	82	714.0	80	19	2	.22	324	4.03
Wieters,Matt	Bal	86	84	738.1	86	21	3	.22	413	5.03
McCann,Brian	Atl	127	124	1078.2	100	24	3	.22	438	3.65
Molina,Bengie	SF	123	120	1042.0	110	25	2	.21	434	3.75
Montero,Miguel	Ari	111	101	924.2	90	23	5	.21	422	4.01
Shoppach,Kelly	Cle	81	74	672.0	64	15	2	.21	349	4.67
Santos,Omir	NYM	91	74	680.1	50	15	6	.20	337	4.46
Doumit,Ryan	Pit	71	70	615.1	64	20	9	.20	306	4.48
Ruiz,Carlos	Phi	107	100	802.1	84	23	8	.20	392	4.00
Zaun,Gregg	TOT	83	74	643.0	54	11	5	.19	362	5.07
Baker,John	Fla	105	99	864.0	99	20	2	.19	425	4.43
Suzuki,Kurt	Oak	135	132	1173.1	108	27	10	.17	553	4.24
Kendall,Jason	Mil	133	131	1162.0	80	16	3	.17	640	4.96
Pierzynski,A.J.	CWS	131	124	1104.0	129	30	10	.17	503	4.10
Hundley,Nick	SD	74	71	643.1	70	14	4	.15	286	4.00
Napoli,Mike	LAA	96	84	758.0	95	21	8	.15	409	4.86
Bard,Josh	Was	79	71	630.2	59	16	9	.14	347	4.95
Martinez,Victor	TOT	85	82	687.0	65	9	1	.13	425	5.57
Varitek,Jason	Bos	108	106	924.0	124	16	1	.08	397	3.87

Catchers Special - The Rest

Player	Tm	G	GS	Inn	SBA	CS	PCS	CS%	ER	CERA
Alfonzo,Eliezer	SD	30	28	255.1	24	9	0	.38	128	4.51
Ausmus,Brad	LAD	30	27	244.2	20	6	2	.22	99	3.64
Avila,Alex	Det	25	17	153.1	15	4	0	.27	94	5.52
Bako,Paul	Phi	42	33	299.1	22	7	4	.17	130	3.91
Barrett,Michael	Tor	7	4	39.1	2	0	0	.00	19	4.35
Bellorin,Edwin	Col	2	2	18.0	0	0	0	-	4	2.00
Blanco,Henry	SD	60	58	508.0	45	18	4	.34	265	4.69
Brown,Dusty	Bos	6	0	12.0	0	0	0	-	4	0.00
Buck,John	KC	46	41	366.2	49	8	0	.16	211	5.18
Budde,Ryan	LAA	2	0	6.0	1	0	0	.00	7	10.50
Burke,Jamie	Sea	12	11	96.2	9	4	1	.38	32	2.98
Burke,Jamie	Was	6	3	34.1	2	1	0	.50	18	4.72
Carlin,Luke	Ari	4	4	34.0	6	0	0	.00	35	9.26
Cash,Kevin	NYY	10	7	67.0	11	2	0	.18	26	3.49
Castro,Ramon	NYM	23	21	181.0	15	7	1	.43	85	4.23
Castro,Ramon	CWS	29	25	220.2	33	10	7	.12	112	4.57
Cervelli,Francisco	NYY	40	25	241.1	23	10	2	.38	92	3.43
Chavez,Raul	Tor	51	44	399.0	47	18	2	.36	215	4.85
Corporan,Carlos	Mil	1	0	2.0	0	0	0	-	0	0.00
Coste,Chris	Phi	29	22	211.0	20	5	3	.12	110	4.69
Coste,Chris	Hou	26	14	141.0	7	0	0	.00	73	4.66
Diaz,Robinson	Pit	33	33	283.0	36	9	3	.18	127	4.04
Ellis,A.J.	LAD	7	2	27.2	1	0	0	.00	10	3.25
Flores,Jesus	Was	24	23	205.2	19	8	4	.27	118	5.16
Flowers,Tyler	CWS	6	3	27.0	2	0	0	.00	17	5.67
Fox,Jake	ChC	3	0	7.0	0	0	0	-	0	0.00
Freese,David	StL	1	0	1.0	1	0	0	.00	2	18.00
Gimenez,Chris	Cle	8	6	56.0	5	1	0	.20	26	4.18
Hernandez,Michel	TB	35	29	264.1	18	5	1	.24	130	4.43
Hernandez,Ramon	Cin	55	53	451.0	51	18	7	.25	221	4.41
Hester,John	Ari	8	6	53.0	8	2	1	.14	33	5.60
Holm,Steve	SF	4	2	23.0	2	2	1	1.00	11	4.30
Hoover,Paul	Phi	3	1	11.0	2	0	0	.00	8	6.55
Jaramillo,Jason	Pit	62	58	520.0	50	14	3	.23	291	5.04
Johjima,Kenji	Sea	70	67	580.0	41	22	3	.50	312	4.84
Kottaras,George	Bos	39	25	243.2	31	5	1	.13	145	5.36
LaRue,Jason	StL	43	26	254.0	15	5	2	.23	126	4.46
Lobaton,Jose	SD	6	5	44.0	3	1	0	.33	26	5.32
Marson,Lou	Phi	7	6	52.0	4	2	0	.50	33	5.71
Marson,Lou	Cle	14	14	123.0	17	8	2	.40	72	5.27
Martinez,Victor	Cle	52	51	430.0	46	7	1	.13	276	5.78
Martinez,Victor	Bos	33	31	257.0	19	2	0	.11	149	5.22
Miller,Corky	CWS	11	10	88.0	10	2	1	.11	33	3.38
Miller,Corky	Cin	21	18	164.0	15	4	0	.27	55	5.02
Moeller,Chad	Bal	30	28	239.1	27	2	1	.04	151	5.68
Molina,Jose	NYY	49	42	356.2	32	9	4	.18	131	3.31
Moore,Adam	Sea	6	5	57.0	1	0	0	.00	16	2.53
Morales,Jose	Min	29	19	183.1	26	8	7	.05	83	4.07
Nieves,Wil	Was	71	65	553.2	47	13	0	.28	311	5.06

309

Player	Tm	G	GS	Inn	SBA	CS	PCS	CS%	ER	CERA
Pagnozzi,Matt	StL	5	0	9.0	2	1	0	.50	3	3.00
Paulino,Ronny	Fla	77	63	582.1	72	22	3	.28	269	4.16
Pena,Brayan	KC	30	24	213.2	26	9	5	.19	132	5.56
Phillips,Kyle	Tor	5	4	38.1	6	1	0	.17	25	5.87
Phillips,Paul	Col	15	12	111.1	17	1	0	.06	51	4.12
Posey,Buster	SF	7	4	40.0	2	1	0	.50	16	3.60
Powell,Landon	Oak	36	30	274.0	22	11	2	.45	137	4.50
Quintero,Humberto	Hou	59	51	427.0	26	12	3	.39	206	4.34
Quiroz,Guillermo	Sea	4	4	34.2	1	0	0	.00	20	5.19
Redmond,Mike	Min	44	39	330.2	40	5	3	.05	195	5.31
Richardson,Kevin	Tex	4	1	15.0	2	0	0	.00	10	6.00
Riggans,Shawn	TB	7	3	34.0	2	0	0	.00	14	3.71
Rivera,Mike	Mil	34	31	271.0	23	5	0	.22	132	4.38
Rodriguez,Guillermo	Bal	6	1	16.0	0	0	0	-	8	4.50
Rodriguez,Ivan	Hou	90	83	748.0	50	16	2	.29	372	4.48
Rodriguez,Ivan	Tex	25	25	214.0	13	6	1	.42	116	4.88
Ross,David	Atl	52	36	354.0	40	19	3	.43	135	3.43
Ryan,Dusty	Det	12	8	78.2	6	2	0	.33	34	3.89
Sammons,Clint	Atl	6	2	30.0	3	3	1	1.00	8	2.40
Sandoval,Pablo	SF	3	3	27.0	2	1	0	.50	5	1.67
Sardinha,Dane	Det	12	11	92.2	12	2	0	.17	36	3.50
Schneider,Brian	NYM	57	52	437.1	29	10	1	.32	225	4.63
Snyder,Chris	Ari	56	51	436.0	34	8	3	.16	224	4.62
Tatum,Craig	Cin	26	19	173.0	11	4	1	.30	83	4.32
Teagarden,Taylor	Tex	60	54	491.2	47	18	3	.34	249	4.56
Thole,Josh	NYM	16	15	127.1	6	2	1	.20	60	4.24
Toregas,Wyatt	Cle	19	17	153.0	12	2	0	.17	85	5.00
Torrealba,Yorvit	Col	64	61	545.1	57	8	4	.08	265	4.37
Towles,J.R.	Hou	15	14	114.0	11	1	0	.09	71	5.61
Treanor,Matt	Det	4	4	32.0	4	0	0	.00	21	5.91
Whiteside,Eli	SF	47	33	314.0	33	13	5	.29	105	3.01
Wilson,Bobby	LAA	11	0	24.0	1	0	0	.00	8	3.00
Zaun,Gregg	Bal	54	49	435.1	39	10	1	.24	248	5.13
Zaun,Gregg	TB	29	25	207.2	15	1	0	.07	114	4.94

2009 Baserunning

Bill James

Chone Gone Figgins was on first base when a single was hit 43 times in 2009, and he made it to third 23 times. Prince Fielder was on first base when a single was hit 45 times, and he made it to third only once—1 for 45. Not that that's a bad thing.

Chone Figgins was on second base when a single was hit last year 31 times. He scored 26 times. David Ortiz was on second base when a single was hit 16 times. He scored only twice. In part this was because it is very difficult to score from second base on a single to left in Fenway Park, since the left fielder is just behind the shortstop. In part it is because David Ortiz is not nearly as fast as Chone Figgins, who led the majors in both of these categories.

Emilio Bonafacio was on first base when a double was hit 10 times in 2009. He scored all 10 times. Mike Lowell was also on first base when a double was hit 10 times. He didn't score any of those times.

Denard Span in 2009 moved up a base 31 times on a Wild Pitch, a Passed Ball, a Balk, a Sacrifice Fly, or Defensive Indifference. Geoff Blum of the Astros—appearing in 120 games, and going to the plate more than 400 times— never advanced a base on any of those plays.

Juan Rivera and Carlos Lee in 2009 were thrown out 8 times each attempting to go first-to-third on a single, or attempting to stretch a hit. Many major league players, including dozens of major league regulars, went through the season without ever being thrown out trying to take a base too far.

Rookie Elvis Andrus was doubled off base on a line drive caught by an infielder or a fly ball caught by an outfielder 7 times in 2009. Almost one-half of major league regulars or near-regulars were not doubled off base at all during the season.

We are attempting to measure base running here—not just base stealing, but base *running*. We measure it by looking at all of these things. And then, because these events are also obviously a part of the "baserunning" equation, we also consider stolen bases, caught stealing, and grounding into double plays.

All of our baserunning system is zero-centered except the stolen bases. In the major leagues last year there were 9,297 runners on first base when a single was hit, of whom 2,490 went to third base, or 26.8%.   Chone Figgins at 23-for-43 was 11.5 bases better than average.   Prince Fielder at 1 for 45 was 11.1 bases worse than average, in that regard.

We sum up all of the positives and negatives from players being above or below average, and then we add 1.0 for a stolen base, take away 2.0 for a caught stealing.   The major league stolen base percentage is higher than 66.7%, so that pushes the chart off of its zero center a little bit.

The biggest element in our baserunning analysis, actually, is running into outs.   When a player makes an out on the bases (beyond the normal frequency for such occurrences), we charge a negative 3 for each additional out—or a positive 3 for each out not made, compared to the average.   Those events (baserunning outs) have a huge "drag" effect on an offense. . .and actually, the 3.0 weighting given to them may not be enough.   Suppose that one runner goes from first to third on a single three times but is thrown out once, while his teammate goes first-to-second each time but is not thrown out.   Which is more valuable?   I'm not sure, but I suspect it's the guy who isn't thrown out.

Of course, that's one situation; the math is very different if you're talking about scoring three runs as opposed to being left on third base three times.   Anyway, we've studied it and concluded that a 3-to-1 weighting is approximate but appropriate, so that's what we use.   This is an all-star team of the best and worst baserunners of 2009:

	BEST				**WORST**	
C	Kurt Suzuki	+15		C	Yadier Molina	-26
1B	Carlos Pena	+9		1B	Adrian Gonzalez	-29
2B	Chase Utley	+50		2B	Robinson Cano	-23
3B	Chone Figgins	+35		3B	Mike Lowell	-27
SS	Jason Bartlett	+30		SS	Yuniesky Betancourt	-28
LF	Ryan Braun	+35		LF	Juan Rivera	-40
CF	Michael Bourn	+55		CF	Kosuke Fukudome	-11
RF	Ichiro Suzuki	+32		RF	Gabe Kapler	-19

From which we learn that all players named "Suzuki" are outstanding baserunners, except possibly Mac Suzuki.   It is a surprise to see Gabe Kapler—traditionally a good baserunner—ranking at the bottom of the right field list.   In 2009 he was just 1-for-10 going first-to-third on a single, was 3-for-9 scoring from second on a single (below average), was 0-for-2 scoring from first on a double, made four outs on the bases in limited playing time and grounded into 9 double plays in just 47 double play situations.   The major league norm is just over 10%.

Most people will tell you that we should have Carl Crawford in left field ahead of Ryan Braun, and people will tell you that Yadier Molina actually runs well for a catcher, or at least for a Molina. We don't base this on reputation. Carl Crawford was 8-for-27 going first-to-third on a single. Ryan Braun was 15-for-41, which is better. Crawford was 4-for-9 scoring from first on a double. Braun was 7-for-9. Crawford moved up 24 bases on Wild Pitches, Passed Balls, Balks, Sacrifice Flies and Defensive Indifference. Braun moved up 26 times. Crawford grounded into 7 double plays in 136 DP situations; Braun grounded into 7 in 172 situations. Braun was thrown out 5 times on the bases. Crawford was thrown out 10. Crawford *is* a very good baserunner—the second-best baserunner among major league left fielders in 2009, including his base stealing—but Braun was better. And Yadi Molina grounded into 27 frigging double plays, which is a record even for a Molina brother.

And if you want to know why Juan Rivera is cited as the worst baserunner in the major leagues, here's why.

On May 14 against the Red Sox in Anaheim, Rivera singled leading off the fourth inning, tried to stretch it into a double and was thrown out.

On May 24 at Dodger Stadium, Rivera singled leading off the second inning, tried to stretch it into a double and was thrown out.

On May 27 against the White Sox, Rivera singled leading off the bottom of the fifth. The next hitter lined to the shortstop, and Rivera was doubled off.

On June 13 against San Diego, Rivera hit an RBI single in the bottom of the first, attempted to take second on the throw home and was thrown out by the cutoff man.

On July 1 at Texas, Rivera batted in the second inning with Vladimir Guerrero on second base. He grounded back to the mound, and Guerrero was trapped off second. Guerrero tried to stay in a rundown long enough to allow Rivera to get to second, but Guerrero was out at third and then Rivera was out at second (1-6-5-4 DP).

In the sixth inning of the same game, Rivera was on first with Guerrero on third, one out. Maicer Izturis hit a fly ball, scoring Guerrero—but Rivera was doubled off of first base.

On July 6 against Texas in Anaheim, Rivera hit an RBI single but was thrown out at second by the cutoff man.

On August 14, in the first inning of a game at Baltimore, Rivera hit an RBI double, but was thrown out at third base, ending the inning.

On September 9 against the Mariners, bottom of the 6th, Rivera walked and was on second with one out. Jeff Mathis lined to Adrian Beltre at third base, and Beltre picked Rivera off of second, ending the inning.

On September 28 against Texas, bottom of the first inning, Rivera reached on an error by the second baseman, but was thrown out attempting to take second on the play.

Of course, the Angels as a team are really, really good baserunners. Chone Figgins was +35 on the season, Maicer Izturis was +28, Torii Hunter was +23, Bobby Abreu was +21, and many of the other Angels were positive baserunners. Even Mike Napoli was +7.

Almost a hundred years ago, Ping Bodie was caught stealing and Bugs Baer wrote that "he had larceny in his heart, but his feet were honest." Rivera tried to play the game the way his teammates played it, stealing a run here and there, but he has honest feet.

We have made a couple of changes to the way we tally baserunning, which I should explain here. This ties into a philosophical dispute that I have with. . .well, almost everybody else, so let me explain my position on the issue. The general issue is one that comes up constantly in the process of creating and studying new records.

When counting something like how often a runner goes from first to third on a single, it is my very strong opinion that every event should be included, and by "every event" what I mean is every event. Infield hit? I don't care. Slow runner on base ahead of you? I don't care. It counts anyway.

A runner will move from first to third on a single more often if the single is hit to center field than if it is hit to left, and more often if it is hit to right than if it is hit to center. A runner will move from first to third on a single hit 190 feet much more often than he will move from first to third on a single hit 130 feet. These situations are not the same.

The way that A. E. Else thinks about this problem, the thing to do is to focus on the "meaningful" situations that distinguish the good baserunners from the poor baserunners. This is dead wrong. It is completely wrong. What A. E. Else always wants to do is to ignore the outliers. Everybody goes first-to-third on a single hit 185 feet to right field, so we'll ignore those. Nobody goes to first-to-third on a ground ball single to left in Fenway Park, so we'll ignore those. A runner doesn't have a fair chance to go first-to-third on a single if there's a slow runner on in front of him, so we'll ignore those.

The problem is. . .well, there are several problems. The first problem is, the cases you are ignoring are often the MOST telling examples. If almost nobody goes first to third on a single hit 115 feet to left field, it becomes a telling event when somebody does. If almost everybody goes first to third on a single hit 190 feet to right field, it is very instructive when somebody doesn't.

But the second problem is, you wind up discarding most of the data. If you can't "penalize" a runner for not going first-to-third when there is a slow runner on base in front of him, of course, then you also can't "reward" him for going first to third when the slow runner does happen to vacate the base, because obviously, those are no longer "typical" events. You wind up discarding all first-to-third events which start with a runner on second base.

Or what A. E. Else always wants to do is to "balance" the data by situations. If a single is hit to left field, we'll have a .15 expectation of going to third base, if center field, a .27 expectation, if right field, a .40 expectation, or whatever the data is. We'll "correct" the data for those differences. . .but wait, we can do better than that. If it's hit to left field and less than 130 feet, we'll make it .11; left field and 130-180 feet, .15, left field and 180+ feet, .19. That way we can *really* get at the truth.

But wait a minute—what about the fielder? They go first-to-third more often against Mark Teahen than they do against Ichiro, so. . .let's adjust the data for that, too.

The problem is that if you *don't* do any of that nonsense, you have perfectly sensible data. Chone Figgins was 23-for-43 going first-to-third on a single; Prince Fielder was 1-for-45. Whaddaya think, it's a coincidence? Chase Utley was 10-for-13 scoring from first on a double; Dioner Navarro was 2-for-10. What's wrong with that data?

Absolutely nothing. Yes, *of course* there are outside influences on the data. There are outside influences on ALL data. It is the nature of data. Some players have more RBI opportunities than others. You can adjust for that—but we still count RBI. It is easier to hit home runs in some parks than it is in others, easier to pitch in the Oakland Coliseum than it is in Coors Field. We all know that, and it is not inappropriate to adjust for those things—AFTER you have the data. When you have enough data that you can study it, sift through it, see the biases in it, then you can build in all kinds of sophisticated adjustments.

But when we publish a book that says that a player was 10-for-22 going first to third on a single, what that should mean is that he was 10-for-22 going first to third on a single. Period.

Unfortunately, that *isn't* the way we have been doing it in years past. Because of the influence of A. E. Else, we've been screening out situations in which there was a runner on second, in front of the "focus" runner, at the start of the play. . .in other words, if there were runners on first *and* second and a single was hit, we would ignore the play because of the "interference" of the other runner.

Because of that policy, we were ignoring almost one-third of the first-to-third situations, and also the same percentage of scoring-from-first-on-a-double situations. In doing this book, I made once again the argument that I have just made here, and A. E. Else made the opposite argument, and we studied the data.

In 2009 when there was NOT a runner on second, runners went from first to third 26.6% of the time. When there WAS a runner on second, runners went from first to third 27.3% of the time. The percentage goes up because, while there are some plays in which the lead runners stops at third and impedes the runner on first, there are slightly MORE plays on which the runner from second draws a throw, creating an opportunity for the runner from first to go to third. On balance it makes little difference.

When there was NOT a runner on second, runners scored from first on a double 42.6% of the time. When there WAS a runner on second, they scored from first on a double 45.3% of the time. The whole theory of those being plays on which the runner from first had no opportunity to advance turns out, on investigation, to be bogus.

Our data last year showed runners going first-to-third on a single, for the major leagues as a whole, complete season, 1,786 times in 6,600 chances. The data this year shows 2,490 advances in 9,297 chances. The 2700-chance increase is not a difference between 2009 and 2008 baseball; it is the chances that we *would* have screened out, under the old policy. The old policy was in place because A. E. Else thought it would be more fair and more accurate. It was in fact neither more fair nor more accurate, and we have made the data better by including everything.

Baserunning in baseball is a significant element of a team's performance. The difference between the best baserunner in the majors (Michael Bourn) and the worst (Juan Rivera) was 95 bases, or about 24 runs. That's nowhere near as large as the difference between Ryan Howard's bat and Willie Bloomquist's. It is not as large as the difference between Tim Lincecum's arm and R. A. Dickey's, or the difference between Zach Greinke and Luke Hochever. It is not as large the difference between having Franklin Gutierrez in center fielder or Vernon Wells, nor even as large as the difference between Franklin Gutierrez and an average defensive center fielder.

It is not *that* large, but it is not meaningless or insignificant, either. It counts. We count everything because everything counts; that's our motto, or ought to be. On a team level the difference between best and worst baserunners is about 170 bases, or 40+ runs.

2009 Baserunning

Player	1st to 3rd Moved	Chances	2nd to Home Moved	Chances	1st to Home Moved	Chances	Bases Taken	Out Adv	Doubled Off	BR Outs	GDP	GDP Opps	BR Gain	SB Gain	Net Gain
Abreu,Bobby	11	39	16	24	6	9	18	3	1	4	15	144	+7	+14	+21
Anderson,Brian	3	14	7	9	3	6	3	0	0	0	6	46	+2	-9	-7
Anderson,Garret	7	26	9	14	0	5	9	0	1	1	11	102	+2	+1	+3
Anderson,Josh	4	14	8	11	4	6	13	3	0	3	7	58	+4	+15	+19
Andino,Robert	3	12	3	7	1	8	8	0	0	0	6	45	+2	-3	-1
Andrus,Elvis	7	24	12	18	5	10	14	1	7	8	4	76	-6	+21	+15
Ankiel,Rick	3	12	10	13	2	4	9	1	1	2	5	88	+8	-2	+6
Atkins,Garrett	3	12	3	5	3	7	7	2	0	2	8	82	-1	0	-1
Aybar,Erick	17	34	12	14	3	4	20	3	3	6	9	107	+14	0	+14
Aybar,Willy	4	15	1	2	0	7	14	2	0	2	4	66	+6	+1	+7
Baker,Jeff	0	10	4	8	4	5	6	0	1	1	8	46	-3	+1	-2
Baker,John	3	29	6	14	1	6	14	2	0	2	10	91	-3	0	-3
Baldelli,Rocco	3	10	6	7	1	4	0	1	0	1	6	50	-3	+1	-2
Balentien,Wladimir	6	16	6	7	0	0	10	3	0	3	3	52	+6	0	+6
Barajas,Rod	1	16	7	12	2	5	6	1	0	1	4	74	+2	+1	+3
Bard,Josh	2	15	4	11	1	2	1	2	0	2	5	46	-11	-2	-13
Barmes,Clint	7	15	11	14	5	6	16	3	3	6	6	104	+8	-8	+0
Bartlett,Jason	10	27	10	23	7	16	21	0	2	2	6	77	+14	+16	+30
Barton,Daric	3	12	4	7	0	3	9	1	0	2	1	50	+5	-4	+1
Bautista,Jose	9	24	10	14	4	7	13	3	1	4	9	61	+2	+4	+6
Bay,Jason	12	37	11	12	6	19	17	4	1	5	9	129	+7	+7	+14
Beckham,Gordon	6	12	15	21	3	4	17	4	1	5	10	71	+4	-1	+3
Belliard,Ronnie	5	14	5	7	1	3	10	0	0	0	10	67	+7	+3	+10
Beltran,Carlos	6	19	10	16	4	11	13	5	2	7	9	65	-12	+9	-3
Beltre,Adrian	10	20	6	10	4	10	14	3	0	3	19	105	1	+9	+8
Berkman,Lance	11	40	11	22	2	5	15	5	1	6	13	117	-9	-1	-10
Betancourt,Yuniesky	9	27	8	20	2	3	9	7	1	8	17	100	-25	-3	-28
Blake,Casey	13	44	16	22	4	12	17	2	0	2	12	118	+11	-5	+6
Blalock,Hank	1	16	8	17	1	8	11	0	2	2	6	83	-2	+2	+0
Blanco,Henry	2	14	2	7	1	1	4	1	1	2	5	34	-8	0	-8
Blanks,Kyle	2	10	1	6	2	3	5	1	0	1	4	32	-2	-1	-3
Bloomquist,Willie	2	15	9	14	4	8	9	1	2	3	7	94	0	+13	+13
Blum,Geoff	3	18	6	10	3	4	0	1	1	2	9	100	-7	-2	-9
Bonifacio,Emilio	11	27	17	19	10	10	16	2	2	4	5	87	+21	+3	+24
Borbon,Julio	5	12	3	10	1	3	7	0	2	2	3	31	-1	+11	+10
Bourn,Michael	13	37	19	29	6	7	25	3	3	6	1	80	+18	+37	+55
Bradley,Milton	6	33	8	14	3	17	10	2	1	3	10	99	-9	-4	-13
Branyan,Russell	6	29	8	14	2	8	13	5	0	5	6	109	-2	+2	0
Braun,Ryan	15	41	12	17	7	9	26	4	1	5	7	172	+27	+8	+35
Bruce,Jay	6	13	4	7	0	1	13	0	1	1	5	80	+14	-3	+11
Buck,John	2	8	0	3	0	0	3	0	0	0	2	32	+2	-1	+1
Burrell,Pat	4	21	3	9	1	9	6	3	1	5	6	87	-15	+2	-13
Burriss,Emmanuel	3	10	4	5	2	2	5	0	0	0	3	34	+7	+3	+10
Buscher,Brian	2	9	4	5	0	0	4	0	1	1	3	33	+1	0	+1
Butler,Billy	4	38	13	24	4	12	8	2	1	3	20	131	-19	+1	-18
Byrd,Marlon	5	25	9	20	5	11	16	3	1	4	11	122	-2	0	-2
Byrnes,Eric	4	6	3	3	3	5	6	2	0	2	4	46	+4	+3	+7
Cabrera,Asdrubal	11	30	11	20	6	11	20	4	2	6	13	119	+2	+9	+11
Cabrera,Everth	4	19	11	17	3	3	15	1	3	4	3	56	+5	+9	+14
Cabrera,Melky	10	26	12	16	2	6	12	4	0	5	15	107	-5	+6	+1
Cabrera,Miguel	7	47	13	27	0	4	16	2	1	3	22	146	-14	+2	-12
Cabrera,Orlando	20	45	10	18	7	11	22	2	0	2	22	134	+14	+5	+19
Callaspo,Alberto	6	38	9	17	3	7	12	5	1	6	15	118	-17	0	-17
Cameron,Mike	13	31	8	20	6	8	14	2	0	2	12	138	+11	+1	+12
Cano,Robinson	9	31	12	20	3	9	16	5	1	6	22	130	-14	-9	-23
Cantu,Jorge	5	38	5	19	4	8	18	2	2	4	15	133	-9	+1	-8
Carroll,Brett	0	3	2	6	2	2	8	0	0	0	2	32	+7	0	+7
Carroll,Jamey	10	24	8	11	2	11	13	1	1	2	8	65	+6	0	+6
Casilla,Alexi	3	13	5	8	0	2	4	1	1	2	6	64	-4	+11	+7
Castillo,Luis	12	36	19	27	5	14	16	1	3	4	15	93	-1	+8	+7
Catalanotto,Frank	1	8	5	6	1	2	3	0	0	0	2	28	+4	+2	+6
Cedeno,Ronny	5	15	2	3	4	7	3	2	1	3	9	58	-8	+1	-7

317

2009 Baserunning

Player	1st to 3rd Moved	Chances	2nd to Home Moved	Chances	1st to Home Moved	Chances	Bases Taken	Out Adv	Doubled Off	BR Outs	GDP	GDP Opps	BR Gain	SB Gain	Net Gain
Chavez,Endy	2	4	3	3	1	4	5	1	1	2	4	29	-2	+7	+5
Chavez,Raul	3	10	1	3	0	2	5	0	0	0	4	31	+2	-1	+1
Choo,Shin-Soo	10	37	13	19	6	14	22	1	5	6	9	130	+6	+17	+23
Church,Ryan	3	20	8	21	3	4	12	1	0	1	11	85	-1	+2	+1
Coghlan,Chris	11	33	14	21	3	8	21	3	4	7	3	78	+5	-2	+3
Cora,Alex	7	16	6	13	2	2	7	1	1	2	2	36	+3	+2	+5
Coste,Chris	0	9	1	7	2	2	3	1	1	2	5	52	-8	0	-8
Counsell,Craig	5	23	4	14	2	10	16	3	0	3	12	75	-7	-5	-12
Crawford,Carl	8	27	20	24	4	9	24	4	4	10	7	136	+4	+28	+32
Crede,Joe	1	11	7	8	3	8	7	1	1	2	6	67	+0	0	+0
Crisp,Coco	3	8	4	6	1	2	4	0	1	1	4	24	0	+9	+9
Crosby,Bobby	3	22	8	9	4	6	11	0	0	0	7	56	+10	0	+10
Crowe,Trevor	1	10	5	8	3	4	4	1	0	1	7	43	-3	+6	+3
Cruz,Nelson	4	20	6	13	3	9	15	2	0	2	9	80	+2	+12	+14
Cuddyer,Michael	12	26	9	19	3	5	22	1	3	6	22	138	-3	+4	+1
Cust,Jack	5	34	11	17	6	16	10	3	3	6	7	108	-11	+2	-9
Damon,Johnny	13	32	14	21	9	16	20	6	3	9	9	160	+6	+12	+18
Davis,Chris	2	24	5	6	3	5	4	0	1	1	6	70	-1	0	-1
Davis,Rajai	10	20	10	16	6	6	19	0	1	1	12	83	+19	+17	+36
DeJesus,David	12	42	11	17	5	10	10	4	2	6	10	104	-8	-14	-22
DeRosa,Mark	9	28	16	21	4	8	21	3	2	5	11	121	+11	-1	+10
Diaz,Matt	4	24	10	19	2	4	9	2	1	3	14	87	-11	+2	-9
Diaz,Robinzon	2	9	2	2	0	2	1	2	0	2	5	22	-9	-2	-11
Dickerson,Chris	4	16	8	13	1	2	8	2	2	4	3	44	-4	+5	+1
Doumit,Ryan	3	12	4	10	1	2	7	3	0	3	12	59	-11	+4	-7
Drew,J.D.	6	24	13	19	4	14	16	0	0	0	6	85	+15	-10	+5
Drew,Stephen	10	25	9	20	6	12	16	3	0	4	5	110	+9	+3	+12
Dukes,Elijah	6	19	5	9	3	3	13	2	0	2	8	89	+8	-17	-9
Duncan,Chris	6	19	3	6	2	3	5	1	2	3	6	60	-4	-2	-6
Dunn,Adam	6	28	3	9	3	10	9	0	1	1	8	139	+4	-2	+2
Dye,Jermaine	8	28	7	13	3	7	16	3	0	3	15	130	+3	-4	-1
Eckstein,David	11	34	12	22	5	10	16	3	1	4	8	105	+6	+1	+7
Ellis,Mark	10	22	12	17	3	9	11	2	2	4	10	86	+1	+4	+5
Ellsbury,Jacoby	8	30	12	26	2	9	26	4	1	6	13	110	-3	+46	+43
Encarnacion,Edwin	4	16	4	6	2	4	8	2	2	4	5	54	-5	0	-5
Escobar,Yunel	13	39	19	25	8	14	13	5	1	6	21	101	-10	-3	-13
Ethier,Andre	6	37	15	18	6	12	17	2	1	4	19	137	-2	-2	-4
Everett,Adam	10	24	9	14	2	5	9	0	0	0	9	82	+11	+1	+12
Feliz,Pedro	6	34	7	18	3	13	11	1	1	2	12	120	-7	-2	-9
Fielder,Prince	1	45	7	20	6	13	16	2	1	3	14	137	-12	-4	-16
Fields,Josh	4	17	3	6	0	3	5	1	0	1	5	49	-2	-4	-6
Figgins,Chone	23	43	26	31	9	14	29	7	1	8	8	117	+27	+8	+35
Fontenot,Mike	3	22	4	13	4	8	14	1	1	2	7	87	+2	+2	+4
Fowler,Dexter	14	22	10	17	6	6	28	5	5	10	4	70	+10	+7	+17
Fox,Jake	1	11	2	6	0	2	6	1	0	1	5	62	-1	0	-1
Francisco,Ben	9	19	10	17	4	5	8	2	1	3	12	95	+0	0	+0
Francoeur,Jeff	12	30	15	28	1	5	15	4	4	8	13	136	-9	-2	-11
Fukudome,Kosuke	8	26	16	24	6	11	14	3	0	3	15	114	+3	-14	-11
Fuld,Sam	3	7	3	6	2	4	3	0	1	1	1	16	+1	0	+1
Furcal,Rafael	13	47	13	22	5	11	22	1	0	1	11	100	+16	0	+16
Garciaparra,Nomar	2	8	3	6	1	6	9	0	0	0	4	47	+7	+2	+9
Gardner,Brett	11	21	4	14	1	1	14	2	0	2	3	48	+10	+16	+26
Garko,Ryan	2	21	3	4	0	5	7	2	1	3	8	82	-9	0	-9
Gerut,Jody	2	22	3	7	4	6	10	1	0	2	8	52	-3	+2	-1
Getz,Chris	7	22	15	24	5	8	12	4	0	4	4	76	+5	+21	+26
Giambi,Jason	1	17	1	6	2	7	7	1	1	2	6	86	-5	0	-5
Giles,Brian	5	11	2	4	0	1	3	2	0	2	6	41	-5	+1	-4
Gload,Ross	6	21	8	10	0	1	6	1	0	1	3	60	+7	0	+7
Gomes,Jonny	2	10	6	9	0	0	4	0	0	0	8	71	+2	+1	+3
Gomez,Carlos	7	18	11	14	1	3	11	0	3	3	1	56	+9	0	+9
Gonzalez,Adrian	7	45	12	24	5	10	7	3	3	6	23	154	-28	-1	-29
Gonzalez,Alberto	2	17	5	11	2	4	7	2	1	3	8	70	-8	-1	-9
Gonzalez,Alex	2	18	9	15	0	1	4	0	0	0	7	69	-1	0	-1
Gonzalez,Carlos	4	9	4	6	2	5	18	2	1	3	3	48	+11	+8	+19

2009 Baserunning

Player	1st to 3rd Moved	Chances	2nd to Home Moved	Chances	1st to Home Moved	Chances	Bases Taken	Out Adv	Doubled Off	BR Outs	GDP	GDP Opps	BR Gain	SB Gain	Net Gain
Gordon,Alex	3	8	9	11	1	2	1	0	0	0	5	39	+3	+5	+8
Granderson,Curtis	13	31	5	12	8	11	10	4	5	9	1	106	-4	+8	+4
Green,Nick	4	15	10	15	5	7	10	3	1	4	10	65	-4	-7	-11
Griffey Jr.,Ken	3	28	4	10	2	8	3	0	0	0	6	83	-4	0	-4
Gross,Gabe	5	14	1	11	2	3	8	5	0	5	2	64	-7	0	-7
Guerrero,Vladimir	5	26	9	12	1	5	15	1	1	2	16	81	-2	0	-2
Guillen,Carlos	3	13	7	9	1	5	8	2	2	4	7	79	-4	-5	-9
Guillen,Jose	4	15	4	7	0	6	4	1	0	1	13	58	-10	+1	-9
Gutierrez,Franklin	10	42	12	19	4	8	12	2	0	2	14	125	+2	+6	+8
Guzman,Cristian	8	30	12	17	7	11	21	0	2	2	9	96	+17	-6	+11
Gwynn,Tony	7	30	16	17	2	5	19	3	1	4	2	56	+13	-3	+10
Hafner,Travis	2	19	4	11	3	7	14	1	0	1	7	80	+5	0	+5
Hairston,Jerry	5	18	10	13	4	9	8	4	3	7	3	75	-8	-1	-9
Hairston,Scott	4	13	2	8	4	5	8	1	1	2	9	98	+1	+5	+6
Hall,Bill	3	8	5	6	0	2	8	0	1	1	11	73	+2	-2	0
Hamilton,Josh	3	14	6	11	1	3	8	0	2	2	5	78	+2	+2	+4
Hanigan,Ryan	1	13	3	6	0	4	4	1	0	1	9	56	-9	0	-9
Hannahan,Jack	2	20	7	10	0	2	4	1	2	3	4	54	-8	-1	-9
Hardy,J.J.	5	30	5	11	3	8	12	0	0	0	14	104	+3	-2	+1
Harris,Brendan	7	25	6	12	2	8	22	0	1	1	16	85	+9	-4	+5
Harris,Willie	3	13	10	15	1	2	13	3	0	3	4	81	+5	+3	+8
Hart,Corey	5	23	18	21	2	5	13	3	0	3	9	102	+8	-1	+7
Hawpe,Brad	5	26	11	14	5	8	26	0	0	0	18	115	+19	-5	+14
Headley,Chase	8	29	11	18	3	8	17	3	0	3	19	119	-2	+6	+4
Helms,Wes	2	15	6	10	0	0	10	1	0	1	10	60	+0	-1	-1
Helton,Todd	5	41	9	18	4	18	19	4	1	5	15	111	-15	-2	-17
Hermida,Jeremy	7	27	7	15	4	8	8	5	1	6	6	95	-10	+1	-9
Hernandez,Anderson	7	16	10	13	1	3	5	0	1	1	10	69	+2	-3	-1
Hernandez,Ramon	3	14	1	6	2	5	6	5	0	5	7	60	-15	+1	-14
Hill,Aaron	10	37	12	20	5	8	20	1	0	1	17	174	+16	+2	+18
Hill,Koyie	6	11	3	7	1	1	7	0	0	0	9	56	+5	0	+5
Hinske,Eric	2	14	5	8	2	3	3	1	1	2	2	52	-1	+1	0
Hoffpauir,Micah	2	12	5	10	1	2	3	0	0	0	3	70	+4	+1	+5
Holliday,Matt	9	37	15	27	4	5	20	4	2	6	13	128	-2	0	-2
Howard,Ryan	1	25	11	25	4	12	11	0	1	1	11	149	-1	+6	+5
Hudson,Orlando	13	29	15	25	8	11	17	5	1	6	16	134	+2	+6	+8
Huff,Aubrey	7	35	11	24	1	8	12	2	1	3	15	126	-10	-12	-22
Hundley,Nick	2	10	4	9	2	4	7	0	0	0	2	46	+7	+3	+10
Hunter,Torii	11	24	10	15	3	7	17	2	1	3	9	106	+13	+10	+23
Iannetta,Chris	4	11	5	7	3	4	8	4	0	4	4	63	+0	-2	-2
Ibanez,Raul	11	29	9	23	0	4	16	0	0	1	16	101	+2	+4	+6
Infante,Omar	2	9	3	5	1	3	10	0	2	2	5	35	+1	+2	+3
Inge,Brandon	8	37	3	13	3	7	13	0	1	1	12	150	+4	-8	-4
Ishikawa,Travis	5	19	8	8	4	8	13	0	1	1	7	75	+13	-2	+11
Iwamura,Akinori	3	17	8	17	2	3	11	1	0	1	1	44	+7	+7	+14
Izturis,Cesar	4	22	6	10	2	5	6	1	1	2	11	78	-7	+4	-3
Izturis,Maicer	13	34	20	27	3	4	28	2	2	4	7	84	+25	+3	+28
Jacobs,Mike	2	27	5	10	5	12	1	2	1	3	9	97	-15	0	-15
Janish,Paul	8	14	3	11	2	4	6	1	0	1	8	58	+1	+2	+3
Jaramillo,Jason	4	18	3	10	0	1	4	2	1	3	11	51	-16	+1	-15
Jeter,Derek	16	47	15	22	2	13	17	2	1	3	18	106	-2	+20	+18
Johjima,Kenji	2	11	4	6	0	3	2	1	0	1	4	52	-2	-2	-4
Johnson,Kelly	4	16	10	13	3	5	8	1	0	1	4	47	+7	+3	+10
Johnson,Nick	14	40	9	23	1	9	22	3	0	3	15	114	+2	-6	-4
Johnson,Reed	2	9	4	5	1	3	11	2	0	2	5	31	+2	0	+2
Johnson,Rob	2	9	2	10	2	5	6	1	0	1	11	57	-8	-1	-9
Jones,Adam	6	25	11	19	8	12	14	2	2	5	13	101	-4	+2	-2
Jones,Andruw	1	13	5	11	1	5	5	1	0	1	7	65	-5	+3	-2
Jones,Chipper	10	39	17	21	2	9	11	1	3	4	14	122	-3	+2	-1
Jones,Garrett	9	17	6	8	3	4	5	2	1	3	6	66	+2	+6	+8
Kapler,Gabe	1	10	3	9	0	2	2	4	0	4	9	47	-20	+1	-19
Kearns,Austin	1	4	3	4	2	3	3	0	0	1	12	52	-6	-1	-7
Kemp,Matt	12	34	14	18	6	9	20	2	3	5	14	143	+11	+18	+29
Kendall,Jason	5	23	4	18	3	5	14	0	0	0	11	102	+4	+3	+7

319

2009 Baserunning

Player	1st to 3rd		2nd to Home		1st to Home		Bases Taken	Out Adv	Doubled Off	BR Outs	GDP	GDP Opps	BR Gain	SB Gain	Net Gain
	Moved	Chances	Moved	Chances	Moved	Chances									
Kendrick,Howie	7	22	11	21	4	5	17	4	3	7	8	79	-4	+3	-1
Kennedy,Adam	9	33	8	16	5	13	17	4	5	9	8	81	-15	+8	-7
Keppinger,Jeff	5	14	6	6	3	4	4	0	0	0	13	66	+1	-4	-3
Kinsler,Ian	9	27	7	14	6	12	19	0	1	1	9	105	+16	+21	+37
Konerko,Paul	6	40	8	16	1	7	11	2	1	3	15	124	-11	+1	-10
Kotchman,Casey	5	19	6	11	1	7	8	1	0	1	11	98	-1	+1	+0
Kotsay,Mark	4	14	0	4	1	5	3	3	0	3	6	48	-11	-1	-12
Kouzmanoff,Kevin	4	24	8	14	4	8	9	1	1	2	25	119	-14	+1	-13
Kubel,Jason	2	23	8	16	1	8	11	3	0	3	13	113	-10	-1	-11
Laird,Gerald	11	26	11	16	1	4	16	2	2	4	11	98	+6	+5	+11
LaPorta,Matt	4	10	3	7	0	2	6	4	0	4	6	42	-9	+2	-7
LaRoche,Adam	5	20	10	19	2	5	11	3	3	6	11	124	-10	-2	-12
LaRoche,Andy	8	35	12	18	5	7	14	5	1	6	16	125	-8	+1	-7
Lee,Carlos	5	38	4	16	3	8	10	8	0	8	21	138	-35	-1	-36
Lee,Derrek	13	46	10	24	5	12	12	3	1	4	12	149	-3	+1	-2
Lewis,Fred	5	15	6	12	5	7	13	0	0	0	4	52	+14	0	+14
Lind,Adam	13	35	11	21	5	17	13	2	0	2	15	124	+2	-1	+1
Loney,James	9	37	11	17	5	13	15	4	3	8	16	133	+1	-15	-14
Longoria,Evan	11	34	10	15	3	14	16	0	4	4	27	136	-12	+9	-3
Lopez,Felipe	12	44	11	21	5	10	27	2	2	4	5	74	+13	-6	+7
Lopez,Jose	4	28	9	18	3	14	21	3	0	3	25	132	-10	-3	-13
Loretta,Mark	3	13	3	5	0	0	7	0	0	0	6	38	+4	-1	+3
Lowell,Mike	4	14	7	13	0	10	2	2	1	3	24	104	-27	0	-27
Ludwick,Ryan	10	26	11	16	2	3	10	0	0	0	6	101	+17	0	+17
Lugo,Julio	5	18	8	12	4	5	5	0	1	1	3	58	+6	+9	+15
Maier,Mitch	11	19	7	14	4	5	9	4	0	4	6	72	+3	+5	+8
Markakis,Nick	12	47	21	25	5	7	13	1	1	2	12	143	+14	+2	+16
Martin,Russell	8	30	15	21	4	8	17	3	3	6	18	102	-8	-1	-9
Martinez,Victor	4	33	13	20	2	5	18	2	1	3	17	152	+1	+1	+2
Mathis,Jeff	3	12	4	5	0	3	5	0	0	0	2	55	+7	-4	+3
Matsui,Hideki	6	22	8	15	4	7	9	2	0	2	4	96	+7	-2	+5
Matsui,Kaz	3	14	9	17	1	3	8	0	1	1	4	71	+4	+13	+17
Matthews Jr.,Gary	4	19	12	16	4	8	16	2	1	3	4	58	+9	+2	+11
Mauer,Joe	7	34	13	17	3	9	16	4	1	5	13	125	-3	+2	-1
Maybin,Cameron	1	6	5	7	3	3	5	0	0	0	2	45	+9	-5	+4
McCann,Brian	11	36	5	15	1	11	6	2	1	3	17	119	-16	+2	-14
McCutchen,Andrew	4	24	11	16	7	10	16	1	3	4	3	58	+6	+12	+18
McDonald,John	0	3	3	7	1	2	9	0	1	1	1	24	+5	-4	+1
McGehee,Casey	2	14	6	9	4	7	9	2	0	2	13	88	-3	-4	-7
McLouth,Nate	8	28	13	20	2	7	18	0	1	1	8	88	+14	+7	+21
Michaels,Jason	1	4	4	5	0	1	3	2	1	3	2	26	-5	-3	-8
Millar,Kevin	1	12	6	7	1	7	8	2	0	2	10	59	-6	0	-6
Milledge,Lastings	1	12	5	9	3	6	2	1	1	2	5	59	-6	-1	-7
Molina,Bengie	2	24	3	15	1	11	9	1	1	2	14	95	-17	0	-17
Molina,Yadier	7	33	5	9	1	5	12	4	2	6	27	100	-29	+3	-26
Montero,Miguel	5	26	11	13	5	9	10	2	2	4	6	81	+1	-3	-2
Mora,Melvin	6	23	6	13	3	13	8	5	1	6	13	94	-20	-3	-23
Morales,Jose	2	9	4	7	1	2	1	0	0	0	4	28	-1	0	-1
Morales,Kendry	9	43	12	17	2	9	19	3	1	5	15	111	-5	-11	-16
Morgan,Nyjer	8	37	18	24	3	5	20	2	3	5	9	68	+3	+8	+11
Morneau,Justin	7	28	8	13	3	6	15	4	1	5	12	137	0	0	0
Moss,Brandon	5	22	8	15	3	5	8	3	0	3	7	83	-2	-9	-11
Murphy,Daniel	13	27	10	13	3	5	20	4	2	6	13	114	+7	0	+7
Murphy,David	4	21	10	21	4	10	17	2	1	3	5	90	+6	+1	+7
Napoli,Mike	10	24	13	16	2	7	6	1	0	1	6	84	+10	-3	+7
Navarro,Dioner	6	19	7	9	2	10	10	1	0	1	14	79	0	+1	+1
Nieves,Wil	3	13	5	11	2	7	4	2	0	2	7	45	-9	+1	-8
Nix,Jayson	4	18	4	7	4	4	7	2	2	4	5	46	-5	+6	+1
Nix,Laynce	3	12	5	7	2	3	7	0	1	1	5	75	+7	-2	+5
Ojeda,Augie	3	17	6	7	3	5	11	1	0	1	4	56	+9	+1	+10
Olivo,Miguel	3	17	1	4	3	6	11	1	2	3	10	97	-2	+1	-1
Ordonez,Magglio	2	27	3	15	4	13	11	1	1	2	19	114	-18	+1	-17
Ortiz,David	2	27	2	16	0	6	13	3	0	3	9	145	-8	-4	-12
Overbay,Lyle	5	24	4	16	2	3	12	2	0	2	8	98	-1	0	-1

2009 Baserunning

Player	1st to 3rd Moved	Chances	2nd to Home Moved	Chances	1st to Home Moved	Chances	Bases Taken	Out Adv	Doubled Off	BR Outs	GDP	GDP Opps	BR Gain	SB Gain	Net Gain
Pagan,Angel	8	18	8	16	1	2	15	0	1	1	3	35	+12	0	+12
Parra,Gerardo	9	26	14	18	1	6	25	5	0	5	18	104	+4	-9	-5
Paulino,Ronny	1	10	4	7	0	1	7	3	0	3	8	49	-8	+1	-7
Pearce,Steve	1	5	2	4	1	2	3	0	0	0	2	30	+3	+1	+4
Pedroia,Dustin	9	36	17	23	4	16	25	4	0	5	19	133	+1	+4	+5
Pena,Brayan	2	10	2	3	0	1	2	2	0	2	5	33	-7	0	-7
Pena,Carlos	10	23	9	15	2	8	15	1	2	3	5	106	+12	-3	+9
Pena,Ramiro	1	7	4	7	1	3	1	0	1	1	2	23	-4	+2	-2
Pence,Hunter	15	37	13	19	5	5	12	4	0	4	25	107	-8	-8	-16
Pennington,Cliff	5	7	5	10	1	2	8	2	0	2	5	39	+2	-3	-1
Peralta,Jhonny	7	21	10	15	1	12	15	2	1	3	20	112	-7	-4	-11
Phillips,Brandon	10	27	13	18	2	5	22	4	2	7	21	124	-5	+7	+2
Pie,Felix	5	11	3	6	4	6	4	3	1	4	6	53	-7	-5	-12
Pierre,Juan	9	21	7	10	5	9	16	3	4	7	7	70	-2	+6	+4
Pierzynski,A.J.	10	30	6	14	2	10	18	4	0	4	18	114	-5	-1	-6
Podsednik,Scott	10	26	12	16	1	5	17	1	2	3	8	65	+8	+4	+12
Polanco,Placido	6	37	20	30	2	8	17	0	1	1	15	120	+5	+3	+8
Posada,Jorge	4	20	4	15	1	7	8	4	0	4	13	91	-18	+1	-17
Prado,Martin	4	20	10	20	4	5	19	3	0	3	17	105	+0	-5	-5
Pujols,Albert	14	17	26	33	3	9	16	5	4	9	23	170	-15	+8	-7
Punto,Nick	12	33	14	21	1	3	16	1	0	1	7	88	+17	+10	+27
Quentin,Carlos	5	16	1	6	4	7	9	4	0	4	11	98	-6	+3	-3
Raburn,Ryan	6	12	3	4	0	2	12	3	1	4	6	48	0	-3	-3
Ramirez,Alexei	9	29	12	22	6	8	13	3	3	6	15	125	-7	+4	-3
Ramirez,Aramis	1	22	3	11	2	7	5	4	0	4	8	73	-19	0	-19
Ramirez,Hanley	8	31	17	26	4	10	15	3	3	6	9	146	+0	+11	+11
Ramirez,Manny	6	26	14	21	0	3	11	2	1	3	7	93	+2	-2	0
Rasmus,Colby	9	18	12	13	7	8	17	1	1	2	5	102	+26	+1	+27
Redmond,Mike	0	7	0	2	0	1	1	1	0	2	8	35	-14	0	-14
Reed,Jeremy	4	16	3	7	0	2	1	1	0	1	4	34	-6	-6	-12
Reimold,Nolan	9	18	7	13	0	6	5	1	1	2	8	76	-2	+4	+2
Renteria,Edgar	9	29	1	9	2	4	14	3	2	5	17	77	-15	+3	-12
Reyes,Jose	3	12	1	5	1	1	6	3	1	4	2	20	-8	+7	-1
Reynolds,Mark	3	22	7	10	3	10	13	2	1	3	8	114	+2	+6	+8
Rios,Alex	3	18	11	17	4	7	16	2	2	4	21	162	-3	+14	+11
Rivera,Juan	8	29	6	14	1	8	10	8	1	10	19	107	-35	-2	-37
Roberts,Brian	9	37	11	23	6	16	24	3	2	5	7	110	+5	+16	+21
Roberts,Ryan	8	19	8	12	2	3	10	1	3	4	2	59	+5	+1	+6
Rodriguez,Alex	9	22	9	13	2	10	13	5	4	9	13	102	-17	+10	-7
Rodriguez,Ivan	6	23	11	17	7	10	5	0	0	0	20	90	-4	-3	-7
Rodriguez,Luis	4	16	5	5	0	2	6	1	1	2	5	41	-1	+1	0
Rolen,Scott	13	26	14	19	5	9	18	3	0	3	4	87	+21	-3	+18
Rollins,Jimmy	9	34	12	26	4	10	15	2	1	3	7	74	0	+15	+15
Romero,Alex	3	9	4	4	0	1	3	2	0	2	7	32	-6	+2	-4
Rosales,Adam	2	7	5	10	1	1	6	0	0	0	2	46	+7	-3	+4
Ross,Cody	9	27	9	17	1	3	16	1	1	3	18	133	+1	+1	+2
Ross,David	0	5	3	6	0	0	0	0	0	0	1	28	-1	0	-1
Rowand,Aaron	8	32	11	21	1	7	18	1	0	1	12	93	+6	+2	+8
Ruiz,Carlos	2	6	5	9	2	2	6	3	2	5	8	66	-11	-1	-12
Ryan,Brendan	9	19	11	18	4	5	11	1	0	1	9	75	+11	0	+11
Salazar,Oscar	3	5	2	4	2	3	3	2	1	3	8	35	-9	0	-9
Saltalamacchia,J.	5	14	3	7	0	4	7	0	0	0	3	36	+5	-4	+1
Sanchez,Freddy	10	27	9	16	3	5	13	2	2	4	12	95	0	+3	+3
Sandoval,Pablo	12	34	9	18	4	6	21	5	2	7	10	133	+3	-5	-2
Santiago,Ramon	7	17	9	10	0	5	7	1	1	2	3	53	+6	-3	+3
Santos,Omir	3	12	3	11	2	5	5	2	0	2	9	67	-8	0	-8
Schafer,Jordan	1	5	5	8	1	2	3	3	0	3	2	34	-5	0	-5
Schierholtz,Nate	5	14	5	9	3	4	8	0	1	1	5	56	+7	+1	+8
Schneider,Brian	2	9	0	3	1	1	6	0	0	0	5	39	+3	0	+3
Schumaker,Skip	4	45	14	22	4	11	20	1	0	1	4	66	+9	-2	+7
Scott,Luke	7	30	8	18	1	4	9	2	1	3	4	106	+0	0	+0
Scutaro,Marco	4	38	12	19	7	17	24	1	1	2	12	101	+7	+4	+11
Sheffield,Gary	6	23	5	10	2	6	13	1	2	3	10	71	-2	0	-2
Shoppach,Kelly	2	19	3	10	1	3	7	1	0	1	8	68	-5	0	-5

321

2009 Baserunning

Player	1st to 3rd		2nd to Home		1st to Home		Bases Taken	Out Adv	Doubled Off	BR Outs	GDP	GDP Opps	BR Gain	SB Gain	Net Gain
	Moved	Chances	Moved	Chances	Moved	Chances									
Sizemore,Grady	9	32	5	10	6	8	13	4	1	5	4	104	+4	-3	+1
Smith,Seth	7	20	10	13	6	7	12	1	1	3	5	55	+9	+2	+11
Snider,Travis	5	20	6	11	0	3	8	2	0	2	5	50	-1	-1	-2
Snyder,Chris	2	12	3	9	1	5	0	2	0	2	5	37	-13	0	-13
Soriano,Alfonso	4	13	9	12	4	7	6	2	3	5	7	84	-6	+5	-1
Soto,Geovany	1	14	3	5	2	5	2	1	0	1	19	87	-16	+1	-15
Span,Denard	15	40	17	28	9	14	31	3	3	6	7	109	+21	+3	+24
Spilborghs,Ryan	10	17	9	15	4	6	14	0	1	1	9	88	+16	-1	+15
Stewart,Ian	9	22	14	22	1	3	10	1	0	1	7	96	+12	-1	+11
Stubbs,Drew	1	8	5	6	3	4	3	1	0	1	1	23	+2	+2	+4
Sullivan,Cory	3	9	3	6	1	3	4	1	2	3	5	33	-8	+5	-3
Suzuki,Ichiro	7	39	13	20	7	11	23	1	0	1	1	93	+24	+8	+32
Suzuki,Kurt	6	29	19	28	1	5	16	0	0	0	14	119	+11	+4	+15
Sweeney,Mike	3	8	2	6	1	3	4	2	0	2	4	43	-4	0	-4
Sweeney,Ryan	8	32	6	13	7	9	13	1	2	3	14	102	-1	-4	-5
Swisher,Nick	9	37	9	17	7	13	9	4	3	7	13	119	-16	0	-16
Tatis,Fernando	6	22	10	14	1	6	14	3	1	4	13	83	-4	+2	-2
Taveras,Willy	6	23	12	15	4	7	16	2	1	3	2	50	+12	+13	+25
Teagarden,Taylor	1	8	4	8	2	2	2	0	0	0	6	39	-1	0	-1
Teahen,Mark	9	30	15	21	4	9	7	6	2	8	12	111	-17	+6	-11
Teixeira,Mark	8	39	17	26	5	11	13	6	0	6	13	176	-4	+2	-2
Tejada,Miguel	5	30	10	22	7	12	20	6	0	6	29	125	-22	+1	-21
Thames,Marcus	3	20	6	7	0	4	5	0	0	0	5	57	+2	-4	-2
Theriot,Ryan	13	40	10	16	4	10	20	1	0	1	13	104	+14	+1	+15
Thomas,Clete	3	18	9	10	3	5	8	0	1	1	3	71	+10	+3	+13
Thome,Jim	3	19	4	14	0	7	7	2	2	4	8	88	-15	0	-15
Thurston,Joe	6	18	5	7	2	4	9	4	1	5	9	55	-9	0	-9
Tolbert,Matt	2	9	9	13	0	0	15	1	1	2	1	46	+13	+2	+15
Torrealba,Yorvit	3	16	3	5	3	5	8	1	2	3	4	42	-2	-1	-3
Torres,Andres	4	9	4	5	3	3	9	1	0	1	0	27	+12	+4	+16
Tracy,Chad	2	13	2	4	0	2	3	2	0	2	3	49	-5	+1	-4
Tulowitzki,Troy	10	22	13	19	3	9	27	6	2	8	20	153	+1	-2	-1
Uggla,Dan	8	35	9	16	5	9	18	4	1	5	10	136	+3	0	+3
Upton,B.J.	10	37	12	20	3	6	20	3	1	4	7	88	+8	+14	+22
Upton,Justin	9	26	11	14	2	4	14	4	2	6	10	136	+2	+10	+12
Uribe,Juan	4	21	5	10	1	2	19	1	2	3	7	91	+8	+1	+9
Utley,Chase	19	33	13	15	10	13	24	2	5	7	5	134	+27	+23	+50
Valbuena,Luis	4	14	6	12	3	8	16	4	1	5	8	88	-1	-4	-5
Varitek,Jason	2	20	4	13	0	2	8	1	0	1	6	76	-3	0	-3
Vazquez,Ramon	1	7	2	4	2	3	9	0	0	0	2	46	+10	+1	+11
Velez,Eugenio	6	17	5	9	4	5	12	0	0	0	6	45	+12	+1	+13
Venable,Will	0	11	2	8	1	2	6	0	1	1	6	64	-3	+4	+1
Victorino,Shane	14	31	11	19	3	6	21	0	2	3	5	92	+18	+9	+27
Vizquel,Omar	0	8	3	4	1	6	8	3	1	4	0	27	-5	+4	-1
Votto,Joey	16	35	13	19	2	9	15	4	2	6	8	84	+1	+2	+3
Weeks,Rickie	2	6	3	7	1	3	9	1	0	1	1	22	+5	-2	+3
Wells,Vernon	10	30	14	16	7	11	14	1	0	1	18	141	+13	+9	+22
Werth,Jayson	9	39	11	15	2	8	13	0	0	0	11	124	+11	+14	+25
Wieters,Matt	2	21	4	16	0	2	3	2	0	2	11	77	-18	0	-18
Wigginton,Ty	6	21	6	15	3	5	5	5	0	5	16	87	-21	-3	-24
Willingham,Josh	9	31	13	22	2	5	10	0	0	0	11	116	+9	-2	+7
Wilson,Jack	4	17	11	16	2	2	12	3	1	4	6	70	+2	+1	+3
Wilson,Josh	3	10	1	6	2	3	4	1	0	1	4	40	-1	-3	-4
Winn,Randy	6	32	17	27	4	7	23	3	0	3	6	93	+14	+12	+26
Wise,DeWayne	2	5	2	3	1	4	8	1	0	1	1	27	+6	-6	+0
Wright,David	13	41	12	20	4	9	31	4	1	5	16	148	+14	+9	+23
Youkilis,Kevin	12	32	11	21	7	13	15	3	2	5	9	127	+4	+3	+7
Young,Chris	5	17	7	11	6	8	10	1	3	4	3	90	+6	+3	+9
Young,Delmon	4	21	8	16	2	3	14	0	2	2	17	79	-5	-8	-13
Young,Delwyn	2	17	5	9	2	6	7	2	1	3	13	69	-13	+2	-11
Young,Michael	4	21	9	24	4	11	12	5	1	6	16	106	-22	+2	-20
Zaun,Gregg	8	18	2	13	0	2	6	1	1	2	4	52	-3	-4	-7
Zimmerman,Ryan	6	29	20	27	6	12	18	0	0	0	22	182	+15	+2	+17
Zobrist,Ben	8	22	11	18	4	9	22	1	2	3	7	122	+18	+5	+23

2009 Team Baserunning

Team	1st to 3rd Moved	1st to 3rd Chances	2nd to Home Moved	2nd to Home Chances	1st to Home Moved	1st to Home Chances	Bases Taken	Out Adv	Doubled Off	BR Outs	GDP	GDP Opps	BR Gain	SB Gain	Net Gain
Philadelphia Phillies	82	280	94	175	32	82	142	11	16	29	90	1122	+46	+63	+109
Los Angeles Angels	128	367	161	223	41	88	212	36	16	54	128	1201	+77	+22	+99
Toronto Blue Jays	78	309	115	185	46	102	175	21	6	27	130	1215	+62	+27	+89
Tampa Bay Rays	87	292	101	183	32	100	177	27	17	47	104	1135	+10	+72	+82
Oakland Athletics	83	320	109	196	50	106	182	19	17	37	130	1213	+32	+37	+69
Arizona D-Backs	80	282	95	149	42	85	157	27	13	41	94	1142	+45	+22	+67
San Francisco Giants	80	299	93	174	38	79	176	19	12	31	115	1070	+45	+22	+67
Colorado Rockies	86	262	111	171	49	92	204	30	18	49	111	1149	+70	-4	+66
Texas Rangers	59	262	99	194	39	103	147	18	19	37	97	1041	-13	+77	+64
Minnesota Twins	94	328	130	208	33	72	197	20	18	41	146	1265	+42	+21	+63
Los Angeles Dodgers	102	349	131	200	46	94	172	27	17	46	140	1278	+21	+20	+41
St Louis Cardinals	91	313	129	194	35	65	145	23	13	36	128	1148	+27	+13	+40
Florida Marlins	80	336	114	201	41	76	178	30	14	45	110	1270	+27	+5	+32
Milwaukee Brewers	67	328	97	190	43	83	179	24	3	28	129	1252	+36	-6	+30
Boston Red Sox	78	313	113	206	37	115	160	28	8	38	137	1269	-19	+48	+29
Washington Nationals	76	303	119	195	33	79	146	18	9	28	132	1269	+29	-7	+22
Cincinnati Reds	86	276	97	170	25	59	142	33	13	47	103	1101	-8	+16	+8
Detroit Tigers	84	334	111	187	28	82	146	17	17	34	131	1258	+1	+6	+7
Cleveland Indians	84	315	105	180	40	106	180	34	15	49	140	1258	-15	+22	+7
New York Mets	102	337	118	213	34	83	181	32	20	52	144	1167	-27	+34	+7
Seattle Mariners	66	299	91	165	35	92	137	30	5	35	124	1134	-28	+23	-5
New York Yankees	108	344	125	208	39	102	142	43	16	59	143	1295	-64	+55	-9
San Diego Padres	71	296	101	178	35	70	135	25	13	39	131	1107	-34	+24	-10
Chicago Cubs	73	304	95	180	43	101	135	20	9	29	134	1252	-7	-12	-19
Chicago White Sox	87	309	105	189	31	82	156	36	11	46	139	1174	-35	+15	-20
Pittsburgh Pirates	66	292	101	178	38	70	142	31	18	49	124	1092	-53	+26	-27
Atlanta Braves	79	320	128	215	32	89	132	22	13	35	142	1209	-33	+6	-27
Houston Astros	67	283	98	187	39	65	122	33	7	40	153	1063	-79	+25	-54
Baltimore Orioles	92	338	102	206	36	97	126	29	11	41	131	1102	59	+2	-57
Kansas City Royals	74	307	105	177	40	88	100	35	13	48	136	1128	-97	+30	-67
MLB Totals	2490	9297	3293	5677	1132	2607	4725	797	397	1217	3796	35469			

323

2009 Relief Pitchers
Bill James

Does Mariano Rivera have the same job assignment as Joe Thatcher? Does Bob Howry have the same duties as Randy Choate? Does C. J. Wilson do the same job for the Rangers as Jason Jennings? Does either of them have the same job as Frank Francisco?

Of course they do not; the answer to all of those questions is "no". Being a "reliever", in modern baseball, is not one job; it is six different jobs. Which are:

Closer (CL, in the chart below)
Setup Man (SU)
Lefty Relief Specialist (LT)
Long Man (LM)
Utility Reliever (UR)
Emergency Reliever (ER)

In our structure the other job descriptions, other than "Utility Reliever", are all carefully spelled out and formally defined, and then "Utility Reliever" is a catch-all term for a pitcher who doesn't fit the usage pattern assigned to any other bullpen role. There are many, many utility relievers in the lists below, but they're almost all relievers who pitched in 15 games or fewer, and consequently failed to earn their stripes in any specific bullpen position.

There are 22 categories of the reliever's records detailed below, which I shall endeavor here to make clear.

Games Pitched The major league leaders in Game Pitched in 2009 were Pedro Feliciano of the Mets (88 games), Peter Moylan of the Braves (87 games), and Mike Gonzalez of the Braves (80 games). Those are all setup men. Setup men, in modern baseball, pitch more often than any other kind of reliever.

Early Entries An "Early Entry" is any time a relief pitcher enters the game in the sixth inning or before. Baltimore's Brian Bass led the majors in early entries, with 29, followed by D. J. Carrasco with 27, then Brandon Medders, Zach Miner and Justin Miller with 26 each. Lance Cormier, who led the majors in early entries in 2008 with 28, was among several pitchers last year with 25.

19% of major league relief appearances in 2009 were early entries. Given the number of relievers who appear in games now, that's still 91 early entries per team, which strikes me as an enormous number.

Pitching on Consecutive Days   Pedro Feliciano pitched more times on consecutive days in 2009 than any other pitcher, 34 times—exactly the same as he had in 2008.   The major league leader in 2008 was the same pitcher, and with the same number. Eleven other pitchers pitched 25 times or more on consecutive days—Ryan Madson and Rafael Soriano (29), Mike Gonzalez (28), Eric O'Flaherty and Peter Moylan (27), Carlos Marmol and Jonathan Broxton (26), and Craig Breslow, Nick Masset, Sean Green and David Aardsma (25).

By our definition there were 28 Closers in the majors last year who pitched in 50 or more games.   Those pitchers pitched an average of 65 relief games, and made an average of 18 appearances on consecutive days.

Long Outings   Anything more than 25 pitches is considered a long outing for a reliever.   Brian Bass, who led in Early Entries, also led in Long Outings, with 30. D. J. Carrasco and Alfredo Aceves had 25 each, no one else more than 22.

Leverage Index   We use the Leverage Index calculated by Tom Tango. An average Leverage Index is 1.000.   If a pitcher pitches in critical situations, his Leverage Index will be high; if he pitches in non-essential situations, it will be low. A Leverage Index of 2.00 would indicate that the pitcher pitched at moments when a run allowed would be twice as damaging as at a nominal moment.

In 2008, when he had all the save opportunities, K-Rod had a Leverage Index of 2.5.   In 2009 the highest leverage index for any pitcher pitching more than 2 games was 2.3, by Brian Wilson.

Inherited Runners   Mitch Stetter of Milwaukee and Grant Balfour of Tampa Bay each entered the game in 2009 with 67 runners on base.   No other major league pitcher was over 58.

Closers, in modern baseball, do not inherit a lot of runners.   The 28 closers who pitched in 50 or more games (average 65 games) inherited an average of only 14 runners for the season, or slightly more than one for each five games. Setup men and Lefty specialists inherit far more baserunners.

Inherited Runners Who Scored   Remarkably enough, the three worst pitchers in the majors at allowing inherited runners to score in 2009 were all Kansas City Royals—Jamey Wright (22), Ron Mahay (22) and John Bale (21).

Inherited Runners Allowed Percentage Detroit's Fu-Te Ni entered games with 35 runners on base, of whom only 3 scored, or 9%. This was the lowest percentage in the majors. John Bale allowed the highest percentage to score, 21 of 36, or 58%.

Overall, 32% of inherited runners eventually scored. The average for closers was 24%.

Easy Save Opportunity (etc.) We sort Save Opportunities into Easy, Tough, and Regular Opportunities. An Easy Save Opportunity is one in which the reliever enters the game with the tying run not on base or at the plate, and with three outs or less to go. A Tough Save is one in which the reliever enters with the tying run on base. A regular save opportunity is neither of those—that is, a save opportunity in which the reliever either must face the potential tying run or must pitch more than one inning.

In the majors in 2009 relievers converted 89% of easy save chances, 61% of regular save chances, and 24% of tough save chances. The latter figure could be misleading, however, in that many of those became "holds". The 24% figure is calculated by contrasting the Saves with the Blown Saves, but there are three possible outcomes from a save situation—Save, Blown Save, or Hold.

Joe Nathan led the majors in easy save chances in 2009, with 35, and Brian Wilson led in tough save chances, with 8. Nathan converted 32 of his 35, and Wilson 6 of his 8. Those figures (32 and 6) also led the majors.

Clean Outing A clean outing is any game appearance in which a reliever does not allow a run to score or allow an inherited runner to score. The major league leaders in the percentage of clean outings were Mike Adams of San Diego (32 of 37, 86%), David Aardsma of Seattle (63 of 73, 86%), Joe Nathan (60 of 70, 86%) and Trevor Hoffman (47 of 55, 85%). The lowest percentage by a pitcher appearing in 50 or more games was 48%, by Jamey Wright of the Royals (31 Clean Outings in 65 games.) For the major leagues as a whole, 64% of appearances by relievers were Clean Outings.

Blown Save Win (or Vultured Win, or BS Win) is a "win" credited to a reliever after he has blown a save. No major league reliever in 2009 had more than two BS Wins. If you went back to the 1950s and 1960s, however, you might find pitchers with double-digit totals of BS Wins.

Saves and Save Opportunities Self explanatory.

Holds A reliever is credited with a "Hold" if he enters the game in a potential save situation, records at least one out, does not surrender the lead, and passes off the save opportunity to another pitcher.

Save/Hold Percentage We used to figure the "Save Percentage" for each pitcher, but this was a very misleading figure because middle relievers had theoretical "save opportunities" in which they had absolutely no chance to be credited with a save.   If a lefty reliever is called into the 7th inning of a 4-3 game to face Ryan Howard, in theory that's a Save Situation. In reality, however, that reliever has a better chance to marry the Queen than he does of being credited with a save, since his job is not to finish the game, but merely to get out of that situation and pass it on to the next reliever.

The Save/Hold Percentage is Saves PLUS Holds, divided by Saves Plus Holds Plus Blown Saves. This is a much more accurate way to measure whether the reliever has been successful in his assigned role.

The most successful major league reliever of 2009, by this measure, was Jeremy Affeldt of San Francisco, who had 33 holds in 33 Save Opportunities, or 100%. Other relievers who did well were Darren O'Day (22 of 22, 100%), Dan Meyer (22 of 22, 100%), Fernando Rodney (37 of 38, 97%) and Mariano Rivera (44 of 46, 96%).

The lowest percentages, for pitchers with 20 or more Save or Hold Opportunities, were by J. P. Howell (21 of 29, 72%), Mark Lowe of Seattle (29 of 39, 74%), and Brad Lidge (32 of 43, 74%).

Opposition OPS Self-explanatory, but to complete the record, the lowest opposition OPS by any reliever pitching 50 or more games in 2009 was .476, by the hitters facing Andrew Bailey of Oakland. Jonathan Broxton and Trevor Hoffman had almost the same figures (.479 and .481), while Mike Adams and Phil Hughes had even lower numbers, but in less than 50 relief games.

The highest Opposition OPS vs any reliever in 50 or more games was .912, vs. Brad Lidge, followed closely by Matt Capps of Pittsburgh at .907. More than 100 relievers had figures worse than Lidge, but in less than 50 game appearances.

Relief Pitching

			Usage					Inherited Runners			Saves			Relief Results							
Pitcher	Pos	T	Rel G	Early Entry	Cons Days	Long	Lev Ind	#	Scrd	Pct	Easy	Reg	Tough	Clean	BS Win	Saves	Opps	Holds	Sv/Hld Pct	Opp OPS	Rel ERA
Arizona Diamondbacks																					
Qualls, Chad, Ari	CL	R	51	0	10	4	1.8	15	5	.33	15 - 17	6 - 7	3 - 5	33	0	24	29	0	.83	.683	3.63
Zavada, Clay, Ari	LT	L	49	10	9	8	0.9	21	9	.43	0 - 0	0 - 0	0 - 0	33	0	0	0	4	1.00	.685	3.35
Schoeneweis, Scott, Ari	LT	L	45	1	10	1	1.0	34	10	.29	0 - 0	0 - 1	0 - 2	29	0	0	3	6	.67	.864	7.13
Schlereth, Daniel, Ari	LT	L	21	6	1	1	1.0	12	7	.58	0 - 0	0 - 1	0 - 2	15	0	0	3	0	.00	.648	5.89
Slaten, Doug, Ari	LT	L	11	5	2	0	0.8	8	3	.38	0 - 0	0 - 0	0 - 0	4	0	0	0	0		.953	7.11
Rosales, Leo, Ari	LM	R	33	16	2	12	0.5	17	5	.29	0 - 0	0 - 0	0 - 0	15	0	0	0	2	1.00	.678	4.76
Gutierrez, Juan, Ari	UR	R	65	5	11	11	1.2	44	18	.41	7 - 7	2 - 2	0 - 1	41	0	9	10	7	.94	.660	4.06
Vasquez, Esmerling, Ari	UR	R	53	8	6	10	0.9	29	10	.34	0 - 2	0 - 1	0 - 1	32	1	0	4	4	.50	.737	4.42
Boyer, Blaine, Atl-StL-Ari	UR	R	48	10	11	9	0.6	21	11	.52	0 - 0	0 - 0	0 - 0	27	0	0	0	4	1.00	.669	4.12
Petit, Yusmeiro, Ari	UR	R	6	4	0	2	0.7	0	0		0 - 0	0 - 0	0 - 0	3	0	0	0	0		.906	7.11
Cabrera, Daniel, Was-Ari	UR	R	6	0	0	1	0.1	0	0		0 - 0	0 - 0	0 - 0	5	0	0	0	0		.787	6.75
Augenstein, Bryan, Ari	UR	R	5	2	0	1	0.3	4	2	.50	0 - 0	0 - 0	0 - 0	2	0	0	0	0		.929	7.94
Korecky, Bobby, Ari	UR	R	5	3	1	2	0.4	0	0		0 - 0	0 - 0	0 - 0	2	0	0	0	1	1.00	1.138	13.50
Mulvey, Kevin, Min-Ari	UR	R	4	2	0	2	0.2	1	0	.00	0 - 0	0 - 0	0 - 0	2	0	0	0	0		.935	10.38
Gordon, Tom, Ari	UR	R	3	1	0	0	1.7	0	0		0 - 0	0 - 1	0 - 0	2	0	0	1	0	.00	1.314	21.60
Buckner, Billy, Ari	UR	R	3	3	0	2	0.7	1	0	.00	0 - 0	0 - 0	0 - 0	1	0	0	0	0		1.483	15.75
Atlanta Braves																					
Soriano, Rafael, Atl	CL	R	77	0	29	8	1.6	5	0	.00	17 - 18	9 - 12	1 - 1	61	0	27	31	6	.89	.586	2.97
Moylan, Peter, Atl	SU	R	87	9	27	7	1.4	56	16	.29	0 - 1	0 - 2	0 - 2	65	0	0	5	25	.83	.651	2.84
Gonzalez, Mike, Atl	SU	L	80	0	28	7	1.7	9	2	.22	5 - 5	5 - 11	0 - 1	60	2	10	17	17	.79	.658	2.42
O'Flaherty, Eric, Atl	LT	L	78	12	27	2	0.8	45	8	.18	0 - 1	0 - 0	0 - 1	59	0	0	2	15	.88	.619	3.04
Logan, Boone, Atl	LT	L	20	5	3	4	0.7	13	2	.15	0 - 0	0 - 0	0 - 0	12	0	0	0	1	1.00	.767	5.19
Medlen, Kris, Atl	LM	R	35	15	6	11	0.8	12	6	.50	0 - 1	0 - 0	0 - 1	22	0	0	2	1	.33	.711	3.47
Carlyle, Buddy, Atl	LM	R	16	7	2	7	0.7	12	4	.33	0 - 0	0 - 0	0 - 0	5	0	0	0	2	1.00	1.078	8.86
Acosta, Manny, Atl	UR	R	38	1	8	9	0.6	20	4	.20	0 - 0	0 - 0	0 - 0	23	0	0	0	2	1.00	.846	4.34
Parr, James, Atl	UR	R	8	3	1	4	0.4	3	3	1.00	0 - 0	0 - 0	0 - 0	3	0	0	0	0		.940	5.79
Kawakami, Kenshin, Atl	UR	R	7	3	0	4	1.6	0	0		0 - 0	1 - 1	0 - 0	4	0	1	1	0	1.00	.769	2.63
Campillo, Jorge, Atl	UR	R	5	0	1	0	1.3	5	5	1.00	0 - 0	0 - 0	0 - 1	2	0	0	1	0	.00	1.087	4.15
Valdez, Luis, Atl	UR	R	3	0	0	0	0.8	0	0		0 - 0	0 - 0	0 - 0	2	0	0	0	0		.839	3.38
Reyes, Jo-Jo, Atl	UR	L	1	0	0	0	0.0	0	0		0 - 0	0 - 0	0 - 0	0	0	0	0	0		1.100	18.00
Nunez, Vladimir, Atl	UR	R	1	0	0	1	0.2	0	0		0 - 0	0 - 0	0 - 0	0	0	0	0	0		2.171	36.00
Baltimore Orioles																					
Johnson, Jim, Bal	SU	R	64	0	14	9	1.6	9	3	.33	5 - 5	4 - 10	1 - 1	42	1	10	16	14	.80	.747	4.11
Walker, Jamie, Bal	LT	L	22	1	4	0	0.8	23	9	.39	0 - 0	0 - 0	0 - 1	14	0	0	1	2	.67	1.135	5.11
Castillo, Alberto, Bal	LT	L	20	5	6	0	1.1	17	1	.06	0 - 0	0 - 0	0 - 0	16	0	0	0	5	1.00	.703	2.25
Henn, Sean, Min-Bal	LT	L	20	4	2	3	0.8	14	3	.21	0 - 1	0 - 0	0 - 1	12	0	0	2	2	.50	.897	7.53
Waters, Chris, Bal	LT	L	4	2	0	3	0.4	3	0	.00	0 - 0	0 - 0	0 - 0	2	0	0	0	0		.792	8.10
Albers, Matt, Bal	LM	R	56	24	5	19	0.8	48	18	.38	0 - 1	0 - 1	0 - 2	32	0	0	4	10	.71	.797	5.51
Bass, Brian, Bal	LM	R	48	29	2	30	0.8	24	5	.21	0 - 0	0 - 0	0 - 0	24	0	0	0	1	1.00	.844	4.90
Hendrickson, Mark, Bal	LM	L	42	16	7	11	0.5	36	8	.22	0 - 0	1 - 1	0 - 2	24	0	1	3	2	.60	.708	3.44
Meredith, Cla, SD-Bal	UR	R	64	15	12	4	0.7	41	13	.32	0 - 0	0 - 0	0 - 3	40	0	0	3	4	.57	.747	3.99
Baez, Danys, Bal	UR	R	59	10	5	13	1.3	28	12	.43	0 - 0	0 - 1	0 - 1	36	0	0	2	15	.88	.634	4.02
Ray, Chris, Bal	UR	R	46	11	7	6	0.8	29	11	.38	0 - 0	0 - 2	0 - 1	25	0	0	3	6	.67	.985	7.27
Sarfate, Dennis, Bal	UR	R	20	6	2	7	0.6	10	4	.40	0 - 0	0 - 0	0 - 0	12	0	0	0	1	1.00	.804	5.09
Mickolio, Kam, Bal	UR	R	11	3	0	4	0.7	6	1	.17	0 - 0	0 - 0	0 - 0	7	0	0	0	2	1.00	.565	2.63
McCrory, Bob, Bal	UR	R	7	0	0	4	0.4	6	3	.50	0 - 0	0 - 0	0 - 0	0	0	0	0	0		1.340	17.18
Lambert, Chris, Det-Bal	UR	R	6	3	0	3	0.4	5	4	.80	0 - 0	0 - 0	0 - 0	1	0	0	0	0		1.108	10.22
Liz, Radhames, Bal	UR	R	2	1	0	1	0.1	3	3	1.00	0 - 0	0 - 0	0 - 0	0	0	0	0	0		2.000	67.50
Hill, Rich, Bal	UR	L	1	0	0	0	0.1	0	0		0 - 0	0 - 0	0 - 0	0	0	0	0	0		1.750	54.00
Hernandez, David, Bal	ER	R	1	1	0	1	1.0	1	1	1.00	0 - 0	0 - 0	0 - 0	0	0	0	0	0		.750	.00
Boston Red Sox																					
Papelbon, Jonathan, Bos	CL	R	66	0	11	10	2.2	16	4	.25	20 - 21	15 - 16	3 - 4	54	0	38	41	0	.93	.600	1.85
Okajima, Hideki, Bos	SU	L	68	5	14	6	1.3	37	6	.16	0 - 0	0 - 1	0 - 1	51	1	0	2	23	.92	.704	3.39
Bard, Daniel, Bos	SU	R	49	8	4	8	1.0	29	7	.24	1 - 1	0 - 1	0 - 2	33	0	1	4	13	.82	.690	3.65
Wagner, Billy, NYM-Bos	LT	L	17	0	1	1	0.9	1	0	.00	0 - 0	0 - 0	0 - 0	13	0	0	0	6	1.00	.548	1.72
Lopez, Javier, Bos	LT	L	14	1	5	1	0.7	1	0	.00	0 - 0	0 - 0	0 - 0	6	0	0	0	0		1.080	9.26
Jones, Hunter, Bos	LT	L	11	7	0	6	0.5	16	3	.19	0 - 0	0 - 0	0 - 0	4	0	0	0	1	1.00	.934	9.24
Richardson, Dustin, Bos	LT	L	3	2	0	0	0.1	4	2	.50	0 - 0	0 - 0	0 - 0	2	0	0	0	0		.636	.00
Traber, Billy, Bos	LT	L	1	1	0	1	0.2	3	3	1.00	0 - 0	0 - 0	0 - 0	0	0	0	0	0		1.342	12.27
Ramirez, Ramon, Bos	UR	R	70	9	17	12	1.2	41	9	.22	0 - 0	0 - 3	0 - 1	49	0	0	4	12	.75	.711	2.84
Delcarmen, Manny, Bos	UR	R	64	23	8	13	1.1	33	8	.24	0 - 1	0 - 2	0 - 0	38	0	0	3	6	.67	.796	4.53
Saito, Takashi, Bos	UR	R	56	4	5	8	0.7	18	11	.61	2 - 2	0 - 1	0 - 1	38	0	2	4	3	.71	.701	2.43
Bowden, Michael, Bos	UR	R	7	3	1	5	0.3	4	3	.75	0 - 0	0 - 0	0 - 0	4	0	0	0	1	1.00	.834	6.92
Cabrera, Fernando, Bos	UR	R	6	2	0	2	0.3	1	0	.00	0 - 0	0 - 0	0 - 0	4	0	0	0	1	1.00	.863	8.44

Relief Pitching

Pitcher	Pos	T	Rel G	Early Entry	Cons Days	Long	Lev Ind	#	Scrd	Pct	Easy	Reg	Tough	Clean	Win	Saves	Opps	Holds	Sv/Hld Pct	Opp OPS	Rel ERA
Tazawa, Junichi, Bos	UR	R	2	1	0	2	1.0	1	0	.00	0-0	0-0	0-0	0	0	0	0	0		.969	11.81
Gonzalez, Enrique, Bos	UR	R	2	0	0	2	0.3	2	1	.50	0-0	0-0	0-0	1	0	0	0	0		.889	4.91
Byrd, Paul, Bos	UR	R	1	1	0	1	0.4	0	0		0-0	0-0	0-0	0	0	0	0	0		.818	6.00
Van Every, Jonathan, Bos	ER	L	1	0	0	0	0.0	1	1	1.00	0-0	0-0	0-0	0	0	0	0	0		1.167	.00
Green, Nick, Bos	ER	R	1	0	0	1	0.0	0	0		0-0	0-0	0-0	1	0	0	0	0		.333	.00
Brown, Dusty, Bos	ER	R	1	0	0	0	0.0	0	0		0-0	0-0	0-0	0	0	0	0	0		1.000	9.00
Chicago Cubs																					
Gregg, Kevin, ChC	CL	R	72	0	20	13	1.6	22	4	.18	15-17	7-10	1-3	48	1	23	30	1	.77	.740	4.72
Marmol, Carlos, ChC	SU	R	79	0	26	12	1.8	20	4	.20	11-11	3-5	1-3	57	0	15	19	27	.91	.612	3.41
Grabow, John, Pit-ChC	SU	L	75	2	22	8	1.1	28	10	.36	0-1	0-1	0-0	57	0	0	2	23	.92	.670	3.36
Marshall, Sean, ChC	LT	L	46	11	16	5	0.9	42	9	.21	0-0	0-0	0-0	34	0	0	0	7	1.00	.709	3.23
Cotts, Neal, ChC	LT	L	19	1	6	0	1.1	14	1	.07	0-0	0-1	0-0	12	0	0	1	2	.67	1.014	7.36
Gorzelanny, Tom, Pit-ChC	LT	L	15	5	3	2	1.0	12	1	.08	0-0	0-1	0-0	9	0	0	1	2	.67	.553	5.87
Waddell, Jason, ChC	LT	L	3	1	0	2	0.8	1	0	.00	0-0	0-0	0-0	2	0	0	0	1	1.00	.750	5.40
Patton, David, ChC	LM	R	20	9	2	9	0.5	11	3	.27	0-0	0-0	0-0	9	0	0	0	0		.796	6.83
Heilman, Aaron, ChC	UR	R	70	12	20	16	1.2	37	18	.49	0-0	0-1	0-3	43	0	1	7	10	.65	.754	4.11
Guzman, Angel, ChC	UR	R	55	9	15	9	1.2	25	4	.16	1-1	0-0	0-0	39	0	1	1	15	1.00	.617	2.95
Samardzija, Jeff, ChC	UR	R	18	6	2	7	0.6	8	5	.63	0-0	0-0	0-0	6	0	0	0	0		.928	6.49
Caridad, Esmailin, ChC	UR	R	14	2	1	2	0.5	6	4	.67	0-0	0-0	0-0	11	0	0	0	2	1.00	.622	1.40
Berg, Justin, ChC	UR	R	11	3	2	1	0.2	7	3	.43	0-0	0-0	0-0	8	0	0	0	0		.494	.75
Stevens, Jeff, ChC	UR	R	11	5	2	3	0.6	3	1	.33	0-0	0-0	0-0	7	0	0	0	0		.927	7.11
Fox, Chad, ChC	UR	R	2	0	0	0	0.2	0	0		0-0	0-0	0-0	0	0	0	0	0		2.833	135.00
Atkins, Mitch, ChC	UR	R	2	0	1	0	0.0	0	0		0-0	0-0	0-0	2	0	0	0	0		.286	.00
Chicago White Sox																					
Jenks, Bobby, CWS	CL	R	52	0	9	4	1.9	9	1	.11	21-23	8-10	0-2	35	2	29	35	0	.83	.725	3.71
Thornton, Matt, CWS	SU	L	70	4	15	9	1.5	47	15	.32	1-1	3-4	0-4	47	1	4	9	24	.85	.599	2.74
Dotel, Octavio, CWS	SU	R	62	10	12	15	1.0	25	13	.52	0-0	0-1	0-2	37	0	0	3	16	.84	.764	3.32
Williams, Randy, CWS	LT	L	25	7	6	2	0.8	20	6	.30	0-0	0-0	0-0	17	0	0	0	3	1.00	.688	4.58
Gobble, Jimmy, CWS	LT	L	12	4	1	4	0.2	6	4	.67	0-0	0-0	0-0	9	0	0	0	0		.910	7.50
Whisler, Wes, CWS	LT	L	3	1	0	0	0.2	1	0	.00	0-0	0-0	0-0	2	0	0	0	0		.429	13.50
Carrasco, D.J., CWS	LM	R	48	27	7	25	0.6	31	14	.45	0-0	0-0	0-1	23	0	0	1	0	.00	.689	3.43
Pena, Tony, Ari-CWS	UR	R	72	4	17	9	1.3	39	16	.41	1-2	0-1	1-1	40	0	2	4	13	.88	.748	3.99
Linebrink, Scott, CWS	UR	R	57	1	9	11	0.9	12	4	.33	1-2	1-2	0-0	37	1	2	4	7	.82	.875	4.66
Nunez, Jhonny, CWS	UR	R	7	0	0	1	0.0	3	0	.00	0-0	0-0	0-0	4	0	0	0	0		1.043	9.53
Hudson, Daniel, CWS	UR	R	4	2	0	2	0.1	0	0		0-0	0-0	0-0	1	0	0	0	0		.803	4.70
Torres, Carlos, CWS	UR	R	3	1	0	1	0.7	1	1	1.00	0-0	0-0	0-0	2	0	0	0	0		.817	3.38
Egbert, Jack, CWS	UR	R	2	1	0	1	0.1	2	1	.50	0-0	0-0	0-0	0	0	0	0	0		1.422	27.00
Cincinnati Reds																					
Cordero, Francisco, Cin	CL	R	68	0	22	9	1.9	4	3	.75	27-29	12-13	0-1	55	0	39	43	0	.91	.628	2.16
Masset, Nick, Cin	SU	R	74	15	25	6	1.1	50	16	.32	0-0	0-0	0-2	51	0	0	2	20	.91	.584	2.37
Rhodes, Arthur, Cin	SU	L	66	0	20	3	1.5	19	4	.21	0-1	0-1	0-0	53	0	0	2	25	.93	.576	2.53
Herrera, Daniel Ray, Cin	LT	L	70	22	17	9	0.8	52	11	.21	0-0	0-0	0-0	46	0	0	0	9	1.00	.747	3.06
Viola, Pedro, Cin	LT	L	9	4	2	1	0.4	3	0	.00	0-0	0-0	0-0	6	0	0	0	0		.845	5.14
Lincoln, Mike, Cin	LM	R	19	7	0	7	0.7	9	1	.11	0-0	0-0	0-0	9	0	0	0	1	1.00	1.127	8.22
Burton, Jared, Cin	UR	R	53	16	7	13	0.9	38	14	.37	0-0	0-0	0-0	30	0	0	0	7	1.00	.759	4.40
Fisher, Carlos, Cin	UR	R	39	12	7	15	0.5	12	6	.50	0-0	0-1	0-0	20	0	0	1	2	.67	.743	4.47
Wells, Kip, Was-Cin	UR	R	26	4	9	9	1.3	16	1	.06	0-0	2-2	0-0	12	0	2	2	5	1.00	.686	5.91
Ramirez, Ramon, Cin	UR	R	11	5	1	1	0.6	4	1	.25	0-0	0-0	0-0	7	0	0	0	3	1.00	.643	3.65
Owings, Micah, Cin	UR	R	7	2	0	5	1.2	2	0	.00	0-0	1-1	0-0	4	0	1	1	0		.531	3.06
Manuel, Robert, Cin	UR	R	3	2	0	2	0.2	0	0		0-0	0-0	0-0	3	0	0	0	0		.686	.00
Janish, Paul, Cin	ER	R	2	0	0	2	0.0	0	0		0-0	0-0	0-0	0	0	0	0	0		1.780	49.50
Cleveland Indians																					
Wood, Kerry, Cle	CL	R	58	0	13	10	1.8	5	1	.20	11-14	9-11	0-1	43	1	20	26	0	.77	.703	4.25
Smith, Joe, Cle	SU	R	37	5	7	3	1.0	25	7	.28	0-0	0-0	0-1	24	0	0	1	10	.91	.707	3.44
Perez, Rafael, Cle	LT	L	54	9	11	6	0.8	32	9	.28	0-0	0-0	0-1	30	0	0	1	6	.86	.899	7.31
Sipp, Tony, Cle	LT	L	46	8	10	7	1.0	37	7	.19	0-0	0-0	0-0	33	0	0	0	9	1.00	.682	2.93
Gosling, Mike, Cle	LT	L	15	7	1	7	0.1	2	0	.00	0-0	0-0	0-0	7	0	0	0	0		.865	5.04
Jackson, Zach, Cle	LT	L	2	2	0	1	0.4	2	2	1.00	0-0	0-0	0-0	0	0	0	0	1	1.00	.837	5.79
Rundles, Rich, Cle	LT	L	1	1	0	1	0.1	2	2	1.00	0-0	0-0	0-0	0	0	0	0	0		1.000	.00
Lewis, Jensen, Cle	LM	R	47	21	3	19	0.8	35	16	.46	0-0	0-0	1-5	22	1	1	5	4	.56	.804	4.61
Masterson, Justin, Bos-Cle	LM	R	26	12	2	11	0.8	14	6	.43	0-0	0-0	0-1	15	0	0	1	6	.86	.694	4.08
Perez, Chris, StL-Cle	UR	R	61	6	9	10	0.9	38	14	.37	1-1	0-2	1-2	43	0	2	5	7	.75	.667	4.26
Veras, Jose, NYY-Cle	UR	R	47	9	8	14	0.7	17	5	.29	0-0	0-0	0-0	24	0	0	0	6	1.00	.756	5.19
Todd, Jesse, StL-Cle	UR	R	20	4	2	4	0.5	8	6	.75	0-0	0-0	0-0	9	0	0	0	1	1.00	.914	7.66
Vizcaino, Luis, ChC-Cle	UR	R	15	2	2	4	1.1	5	3	.60	0-0	1-1	0-0	8	0	1	1	2	1.00	.651	4.70
Ohka, Tomo, Cle	UR	R	12	8	0	8	0.5	6	3	.50	0-0	0-0	0-0	4	0	0	0	0		.773	4.70
Aquino, Greg, Cle	UR	R	10	7	2	7	1.3	6	1	.17	0-0	0-0	0-0	5	0	0	0	1	1.00	.729	4.50

Relief Pitching

Pitcher	Pos	T	Rel G	Early Entry	Cons Days	Long	Lev Ind	#	Scrd	Pct	Easy	Reg	Tough	Clean	BS Win	Saves	Opps	Holds	Sv/Hld Pct	Opp OPS	Rel ERA
			Usage					**Inherited Runners**			**Saves**			**Relief Results**							
Kobayashi, Masa, Cle	UR	R	10	3	1	1	0.2	6	6	1.00	0 - 0	0 - 0	0 - 0	6	0	0	0	0		.878	8.38
Chulk, Vinnie, Cle	UR	R	8	3	1	5	0.9	8	6	.75	0 - 0	0 - 1	0 - 0	2	0	0	1	0	.00	.726	3.75
Laffey, Aaron, Cle	UR	L	6	1	0	4	0.9	3	0	.00	0 - 0	1 - 1	0 - 0	2	0	1	1	0	1.00	.604	3.65
Abreu, Winston, TB-Cle	UR	R	5	2	0	2	0.0	1	0	.00	0 - 0	0 - 0	0 - 0	1	0	0	0	0		1.098	10.50
Sowers, Jeremy, Cle	ER	L	1	1	0	1	0.0	0	0		0 - 0	0 - 0	0 - 0	1	0	0	0	0		.458	.00
Colorado Rockies																					
Street, Huston, Col	CL	R	64	0	22	1	1.7	8	4	.50	25 - 26	10 - 11	0 - 0	48	0	35	37	2	.95	.561	3.00
Betancourt, Rafael, Cle-Col	SU	R	61	3	18	8	1.5	38	11	.29	1 - 1	1 - 1	0 - 4	44	0	2	6	20	.85	.604	2.73
Morales, Franklin, Col	SU	L	38	4	10	5	1.6	27	8	.30	5 - 5	2 - 2	0 - 1	27	0	7	8	7	.93	.681	4.78
Beimel, Joe, Was-Col	LT	L	71	0	24	5	1.3	48	12	.25	0 - 0	1 - 4	0 - 2	46	0	1	6	13	.74	.760	3.58
Embree, Alan, Col	LT	L	36	2	9	0	1.1	26	6	.23	0 - 0	0 - 1	0 - 2	25	0	3	6		.67	.824	5.84
Flores, Randy, Col	LT	L	27	4	5	0	0.9	18	5	.28	0 - 0	0 - 0	0 - 0	20	0	0	0	10	1.00	.808	5.25
Belisle, Matt, Col	LM	R	24	10	3	5	0.6	15	8	.53	0 - 0	0 - 0	0 - 0	12	0	0	0	1	1.00	.780	5.52
Fogg, Josh, Col	LM	R	23	12	2	12	0.3	20	8	.40	0 - 0	0 - 0	0 - 0	11	0	0	0	1	1.00	.594	2.74
Rusch, Glendon, Col	LM	L	11	10	1	6	0.6	11	5	.45	0 - 0	0 - 0	0 - 0	4	0	0	0	1	1.00	1.008	6.75
Daley, Matt, Col	UR	R	57	4	12	10	0.9	28	9	.32	0 - 0	0 - 0	0 - 3	38	0	0	3	12	.80	.742	4.24
Corpas, Manny, Col	UR	R	35	1	11	3	0.8	11	3	.27	1 - 3	0 - 0	0 - 0	22	1	1	3	7	.80	.813	5.88
Rincon, Juan, Det-Col	UR	R	33	8	3	9	0.7	20	1	.05	0 - 0	0 - 0	0 - 0	19	0	0	0	1	1.00	.735	6.87
Herges, Matt, Cle-Col	UR	R	30	5	3	10	0.8	21	11	.52	0 - 0	0 - 0	0 - 1	18	0	0	1	1	.50	.693	3.38
Peralta, Joel, Col	UR	R	27	2	6	4	1.0	18	6	.33	0 - 0	0 - 1	0 - 0	18	0	0	1	6	.86	.877	6.20
Chacin, Jhoulys, Col	UR	R	8	2	0	0	0.4	2	1	.50	0 - 0	0 - 0	0 - 0	5	0	0	0	0		.001	0.10
Contreras, Jose, CWS-Col	UR	R	5	3	2	1	1.7	0	0		0 - 0	0 - 1	0 - 0	4	0	0	1	1	.50	.760	1.23
Speier, Ryan, Col	UR	R	5	2	0	1	0.4	4	4	1.00	0 - 0	0 - 0	0 - 0	1	0	0	0	0		.838	4.76
Eaton, Adam, Bal-Col	UR	R	4	1	1	3	1.2	0	0		0 - 0	0 - 0	0 - 0	2	0	0	0	0		.956	5.63
Hammel, Jason, Col	ER	R	4	4	0	3	0.0	0	0		0 - 0	0 - 0	0 - 0	3	0	0	0	0		.739	2.08
de la Rosa, Jorge, Col	ER	L	1	1	0	0	0.8	0	0		0 - 0	0 - 0	0 - 0	0	0	0	0	0		1.500	18.00
Detroit Tigers																					
Rodney, Fernando, Det	CL	R	73	0	23	12	1.8	8	1	.13	26 - 26	10 - 11	1 - 1	51	0	37	38	0	.97	.731	4.40
Seay, Bobby, Det	SU	L	67	5	20	2	1.2	38	11	.29	0 - 0	0 - 1	0 - 3	47	0	0	4	28	.88	.696	4.25
Lyon, Brandon, Det	SU	R	65	4	16	15	1.3	44	16	.36	2 - 2	1 - 3	0 - 1	45	1	3	6	15	.86	.629	2.86
Zumaya, Joel, Det	SU	R	29	1	6	7	1.8	15	2	.13	1 - 1	0 - 5	0 - 1	16	1	1	7	7	.57	.829	4.94
Ni, Fu-Te, Det	LT	L	36	13	2	6	0.6	35	3	.09	0 - 1	0 - 0	0 - 0	27	0	0	2	3	.60	.603	2.61
Rapada, Clay, Det	LT	L	3	1	0	1	0.4	4	4	1.00	0 - 0	0 - 0	0 - 0	1	0	0	0	0		.946	5.40
Miner, Zach, Det	LM	R	46	26	6	18	1.0	29	10	.34	1 - 1	0 - 1	0 - 3	27	1	1	5	8	.69	.733	3.80
Robertson, Nate, Det	LM	L	22	9	3	4	0.5	17	8	.47	0 - 0	0 - 0	0 - 0	12	0	0	0	0		.794	7.48
Perry, Ryan, Det	UR	R	53	13	6	17	0.7	33	13	.39	0 - 0	0 - 0	0 - 3	30	0	0	3	6	.67	.738	3.79
Fien, Casey, Det	UR	R	9	3	1	4	0.2	8	3	.38	0 - 0	0 - 0	0 - 0	2	0	0	0	0		.914	7.94
Bonderman, Jeremy, Det	UR	R	7	1	1	0	0.3	5	1	.20	0 - 0	0 - 0	0 - 0	4	0	0	0	0		.972	5.68
Bonine, Eddie, Det	UR	R	6	4	0	3	0.4	9	4	.44	0 - 0	0 - 0	0 - 0	1	0	0	0	0		1.069	6.94
Dolsi, Freddy, Det	UR	R	6	1	1	5	1.0	6	4	.67	0 - 0	0 - 1	0 - 0	1	1	0	1	0	.00	.766	1.60
Figaro, Alfredo, Det	UR	R	2	2	0	2	0.2	3	0	.00	0 - 0	0 - 0	0 - 0	1	0	0	0	0		.449	1.93
Galarraga, Armando, Det	ER	R	4	3	0	2	0.8	5	0	.00	0 - 0	0 - 0	0 - 0	1	0	0	0	0		1.038	12.00
Florida Marlins																					
Nunez, Leo, Fla	CL	R	75	0	23	6	1.7	24	7	.29	18 - 20	6 - 10	2 - 3	49	1	26	33	14	.85	.745	4.06
Lindstrom, Matt, Fla	CL	R	54	1	12	5	1.6	5	0	.00	9 - 10	5 - 6	1 - 1	38	1	15	17	8	.92	.804	5.89
Meyer, Dan, Fla	SU	L	71	8	20	5	1.1	34	9	.26	2 - 2	0 - 0	0 - 0	51	0	2	2	20	1.00	.638	3.09
Donnelly, Brendan, Fla	SU	R	30	2	7	1	1.0	15	3	.20	1 - 1	0 - 0	1 - 1	22	0	2	2	9	1.00	.662	1.78
Pinto, Renyel, Fla	LT	L	73	7	22	8	1.2	37	11	.30	0 - 0	0 - 2	0 - 2	52	0	0	4	13	.76	.713	3.23
Davidson, Dave, Fla	LT	L	1	1	0	1	0.1	0	0		0 - 0	0 - 0	0 - 0	0	0	0	0	0		1.442	45.00
Sanches, Brian, Fla	LM	R	47	20	9	14	1.2	28	10	.36	0 - 1	0 - 1	0 - 1	30	0	0	3	9	.75	.687	2.56
Badenhop, Burke, Fla	LM	R	33	25	1	22	0.9	22	7	.32	0 - 0	0 - 1	0 - 0	20	0	0	1	2	.67	.638	3.31
Penn, Hayden, Fla	LM	R	15	8	3	8	0.5	14	8	.57	0 - 0	0 - 0	0 - 0	5	0	0	0	1	1.00	.888	7.45
Martinez, Cristhian, Fla	LM	R	15	8	1	9	0.6	12	2	.17	0 - 0	0 - 1	0 - 0	6	0	0	1	0	.00	.723	5.13
Calero, Kiko, Fla	UR	R	67	5	13	5	0.9	40	12	.30	0 - 0	0 - 2	0 - 3	51	0	0	5	12	.71	.520	1.95
Ayala, Luis, Min-Fla	UR	R	38	6	8	6	0.8	24	8	.33	0 - 0	0 - 1	0 - 3	19	0	0	4	3	.43	.894	5.63
Wood, Tim, Fla	UR	R	18	8	1	4	0.5	20	11	.55	0 - 0	0 - 0	0 - 0	11	0	0	0	1	1.00	.742	2.82
Miller, Andrew, Fla	UR	L	6	3	0	1	0.4	2	2	1.00	0 - 0	0 - 0	0 - 0	2	0	0	0	1	1.00	1.141	4.76
Leroux, Chris, Fla	UR	R	5	1	0	2	0.1	1	0	.00	0 - 0	0 - 0	0 - 0	1	0	0	0	0		1.009	10.80
Martinez, Carlos, Fla	UR	R	2	1	0	1	0.8	0	0		0 - 0	0 - 0	0 - 0	1	0	0	0	1	1.00	1.062	3.86
Ross, Cody, Fla	ER	R	1	0	0	0	0.0	0	0		0 - 0	0 - 0	0 - 0	1	0	0	0	0		.500	.00
Gload, Ross, Fla	ER	L	1	0	0	0	0.0	0	0		0 - 0	0 - 0	0 - 0	1	0	0	0	0		.500	.00
Houston Astros																					
Valverde, Jose, Hou	CL	R	52	0	16	5	1.6	11	0	.00	12 - 12	12 - 16	1 - 1	41	0	25	29	1	.87	.626	2.33
Hawkins, LaTroy, Hou	SU	R	65	0	21	4	1.5	5	3	.60	7 - 7	3 - 6	1 - 2	50	1	11	15	19	.88	.679	2.13
Sampson, Chris, Hou	SU	R	49	12	15	12	1.2	28	16	.57	1 - 2	2 - 4	0 - 0	29	0	3	6	15	.86	.779	5.04
Byrdak, Tim, Hou	LT	L	76	17	18	9	0.7	58	19	.33	0 - 0	0 - 0	0 - 2	51	0	0	2	9	.82	.669	3.23
Wright, Wesley, Hou	LT	L	49	20	13	10	0.7	22	6	.27	0 - 0	0 - 0	0 - 2	28	0	0	2	6	.75	.880	5.44

Relief Pitching

Pitcher	Pos	T	Rel G	Early Entry	Cons Days	Long	Lev Ind	#	Scrd	Pct	Easy	Reg	Tough	Clean	BS Win	Saves	Opps	Holds	Sv/Hld Pct	Opp OPS	Rel ERA
Fulchino, Jeff, Hou	UR	R	61	14	12	19	0.9	33	9	.27	0-0	0-1	0-2	35	1	0	3	12	.80	.680	3.40
Arias, Alberto, Hou	UR	R	42	7	9	9	0.9	19	2	.11	0-0	0-2	0-0	28	0	0	2	9	.82	.715	3.35
Gervacio, Sammy, Hou	UR	R	29	9	16	2	0.7	25	6	.24	0-0	0-0	0-1	23	0	0	1	6	.86	.620	2.14
Brocail, Doug, Hou	UR	R	20	4	3	3	0.6	4	3	.75	0-0	0-0	0-1	13	0	0	1	3	.75	.968	4.58
Geary, Geoff, Hou	UR	R	16	3	1	7	1.2	6	2	.33	0-0	0-1	0-1	3	0	0	2	2	.50	1.027	8.10
Ortiz, Russ, Hou	UR	R	10	7	0	5	0.7	3	2	.67	0-0	0-0	0-0	7	0	0	0	1	1.00	.728	2.49
Paulino, Felipe, Hou	UR	R	6	5	0	4	0.8	8	4	.50	0-0	0-0	0-1	0	0	0	1	0	.00	1.194	10.97
Lopez, Wilton, Hou	UR	R	6	4	1	3	0.3	1	1	1.00	0-0	0-1	0-0	1	0	0	1	0	.00	1.075	8.44
Paronto, Chad, Hou	UR	R	6	3	1	1	0.1	0	0		0-0	0-0	0-0	2	0	0	0	0		1.366	12.15
Backe, Brandon, Hou	UR	R	4	2	0	3	0.2	0	0		0-0	0-0	0-0	0	0	0	0	0		1.170	12.00
Bazardo, Yorman, Hou	UR	R	4	2	0	1	0.2	1	0	.00	0-0	0-0	0-0	3	0	0	0	0		.497	4.26
Sadler, Billy, Hou	UR	R	1	1	0	0	0.6	0	0		0-0	0-0	0-0	0	0	0	0	0		.762	13.50
Norris, Bud, Hou	UR	R	1	1	0	1	0.0	0	0		0-0	0-0	0-0	0	0	0	0	0		.671	3.00
Kansas City Royals																					
Soria, Joakim, KC	CL	R	47	0	13	8	2.1	18	8	.44	16-16	11-13	3-4	32	1	30	33	0	.91	.614	2.21
Bale, John, KC	SU	L	43	3	14	1	1.2	36	21	.58	0-0	1-2	0-3	19	0	1	5	10	.73	.859	5.72
Ramirez, Horacio, KC	LT	L	18	8	3	2	0.6	11	2	.18	0-0	0-1	0-0	12	0	0	1	2	.67	.762	4.42
Hughes, Dustin, KC	LT	L	7	4	1	2	0.7	5	1	.20	0-0	0-0	0-0	3	0	0	0	2	1.00	.684	4.66
Tejeda, Robinson, KC	LM	R	29	21	2	18	0.7	25	9	.36	0-0	0-0	0-0	14	0	0	0	2	1.00	.572	4.07
Wright, Jamey, KC	UR	R	65	13	12	17	1.1	46	22	.48	0-0	0-2	0-1	31	0	0	3	12	.80	.724	4.33
Cruz, Juan, KC	UR	R	46	4	7	10	1.0	22	8	.36	1-1	1-3	0-2	28	1	2	6	7	.69	.760	5.72
Colon, Roman, KC	UR	R	43	6	6	9	0.9	35	13	.37	0-0	0-2	0-1	19	1	0	3	6	.67	.758	4.83
Farnsworth, Kyle, KC	UR	R	41	3	5	5	0.9	21	9	.43	0-0	0-2	0-0	25	0	0	2	5	.71	.727	4.58
Yabuta, Yasuhiko, KC	UR	R	12	6	0	6	0.7	5	2	.40	0-0	0-1	0-0	3	0	0	1	0	.00	1.134	13.50
Chen, Bruce, KC	UR	L	8	3	0	4	0.1	2	0	.00	0-0	0-0	0-0	1	0	0	0	0		.800	5.65
Marte, Victor, KC	UR	R	8	4	1	4	0.2	5	4	.80	0-0	0-0	0-0	4	0	0	0	0		.888	8.25
Rosa, Carlos, KC	UR	R	7	1	0	3	0.1	5	4	.80	1-1	0-0	0-0	4	0	1	1	0	1.00	.661	3.38
Waechter, Doug, KC	UR	R	5	0	0	1	0.0	0	0		0-0	0-0	0-0	3	0	0	0	0		1.137	8.44
Ponson, Sidney, KC	UR	R	5	3	0	2	0.6	7	2	.29	0-0	0-0	0-1	0	0	0	1	0	.00	.914	12.96
Lerew, Anthony, KC	UR	R	1	1	0	1	0.2	0	0		0-0	0-0	0-0	0	0	0	0	0		.985	6.75
Los Angeles Angels																					
Fuentes, Brian, LAA	CL	L	65	0	18	2	2.1	17	3	.18	28-30	19-24	1-1	48	0	48	55	0	.87	.720	3.93
Oliver, Darren, LAA	SU	L	62	16	11	11	1.3	44	13	.30	0-0	0-0	0-1	41	0	1	1	20	.95	.650	2.74
Jepsen, Kevin, LAA	SU	R	54	8	12	8	1.4	26	8	.31	1-1	0-1	0-0	31	0	1	2	17	.95	.693	4.94
Arredondo, Jose, LAA	SU	R	43	4	10	6	1.1	18	7	.39	0-0	0-0	0-1	25	0	0	1	16	.94	.769	6.00
Shields, Scot, LAA	SU	R	20	1	0	2	2.0	11	5	.45	0-0	1-3	0-1	12	0	1	4	6	.70	.721	6.62
Davidson, Daniel, LAA	LT	L	4	1	2	0	0.5	6	2	.33	0-0	0-0	0-0	1	0	0	0	0		1.045	5.40
Palmer, Matt, LAA	LM	R	27	8	3	16	0.6	16	4	.25	0-0	0-0	0-0	17	0	0	0	0		.681	2.74
Rodriguez, Rafael, LAA	LM	R	18	8	3	8	0.5	13	7	.54	0-0	0-1	0-1	6	0	0	2	2	.50	.934	5.58
Thompson, Rich, LAA	LM	R	13	8	2	7	0.3	9	5	.56	0-0	0-0	0-0	5	0	0	0	0		.994	5.12
Bulger, Jason, LAA	UR	R	64	17	16	6	1.0	45	12	.27	0-0	0-1	1-3	45	0	1	4	9	.77	.682	3.56
Speier, Justin, LAA	UR	R	41	11	10	5	0.9	14	2	.14	0-0	0-0	0-1	28	1	0	1	8	.89	.792	5.18
Loux, Shane, LAA	UR	R	12	4	3	9	0.3	4	1	.25	0-0	0-0	0-0	5	0	0	0	0		.983	7.46
Bell, Trevor, LAA	UR	R	4	1	0	2	0.7	2	0	.00	0-0	0-0	0-0	2	0	0	0	0		.862	6.75
Mosebach, Bobby, LAA	UR	R	3	1	1	1	0.1	0	0		0-0	0-0	0-0	1	0	0	0	0		1.079	7.71
O'Sullivan, Sean, LAA	UR	R	2	1	0	0	0.4	0	0		0-0	0-0	0-0	2	0	0	0	0		.473	.00
Rodriguez, Fernando, LAA	UR	R	1	0	0	1	0.0	0	0		0-0	0-0	0-0	0	0	0	0	0		1.500	27.00
Santana, Ervin, LAA	ER	R	1	1	0	1	1.2	0	0		0-0	0-0	0-0	1	0	0	0	1	1.00	.750	.00
Los Angeles Dodgers																					
Broxton, Jonathan, LAD	CL	R	73	0	26	10	1.8	19	5	.26	19-22	15-17	2-3	57	2	36	42	1	.86	.479	2.61
Sherrill, George, Bal-LAD	CL	R	72	0	21	10	1.6	17	4	.24	13-14	8-10	0-2	59	1	21	26	11	.86	.588	1.70
Kuo, Hong-Chih, LAD	SU	L	35	3	3	1	1.5	10	2	.20	0-1	0-0	0-0	28	1	0	1	14	.93	.599	3.00
Wade, Cory, LAD	SU	R	27	7	3	3	1.7	12	3	.25	0-0	0-4	0-2	16	1	0	6	7	.54	.735	5.53
Leach, Brent, LAD	LT	L	38	3	14	0	0.9	29	7	.24	0-0	0-0	0-0	26	0	0	0	4	1.00	.783	5.75
Ohman, Will, LAD	LT	L	21	3	5	0	0.9	17	4	.24	1-1	0-0	0-1	12	0	1	2	4	.83	.979	5.84
Elbert, Scott, LAD	LT	L	19	8	5	7	0.4	16	6	.38	0-0	0-0	0-0	11	0	0	0	3	1.00	.784	5.03
Weaver, Jeff, LAD	LM	R	21	14	1	15	1.1	13	4	.31	0-0	0-0	0-0	12	0	0	0	0		.803	3.99
Troncoso, Ramon, LAD	UR	R	73	14	16	13	1.4	32	5	.16	3-4	2-2	1-1	55	0	6	7	14	.95	.675	2.72
Belisario, Ronald, LAD	UR	R	69	16	19	10	1.2	36	10	.28	0-1	0-4	0-2	50	1	0	7	12	.63	.580	2.04
Mota, Guillermo, LAD	UR	R	61	11	14	14	0.7	38	17	.45	0-0	0-1	0-1	38	0	0	2	2	.50	.671	3.44
McDonald, James, LAD	UR	R	41	11	7	13	0.9	10	5	.50	0-0	0-0	0-0	25	0	0	0	5	1.00	.695	2.72
Haeger, Charlie, LAD	UR	R	3	1	0	0	0.1	0	0		0-0	0-0	0-0	3	0	0	0	0		.384	.00
Schlichting, Travis, LAD	UR	R	2	0	0	2	0.0	0	0		0-0	0-0	0-0	0	0	0	0	0		.844	3.38
Kuroda, Hiroki, LAD	ER	R	1	0	0	0	0.4	1	1	1.00	0-0	0-0	0-0	0	0	0	0	0		1.042	20.25
Loretta, Mark, LAD	ER	R	1	0	0	0	0.0	1	0	.00	0-0	0-0	0-0	1	0	0	0	0		.500	.00
Kershaw, Clayton, LAD	ER	L	1	0	0	1	0.0	0	0		0-0	0-0	0-0	1	0	0	0	0		.143	.00
Billingsley, Chad, LAD	ER	R	1	0	0	1	0.2	0	0		0-0	0-0	0-0	0	0	0	0	0		1.323	10.80

Relief Pitching

Pitcher	Pos	T	Rel G	Early Entry	Cons Days	Long	Lev Ind	#	Scrd	Pct	Easy	Reg	Tough	Clean	BS Win	Saves	Opps	Holds	Sv/Hld Pct	Opp OPS	Rel ERA
Padilla, Vicente, Tex-LAD	ER	R	1	1	0	1	0.1	0	0		0 - 0	0 - 0	0 - 0	1	0	0	0	0		.167	.00
Milwaukee Brewers																					
Hoffman, Trevor, Mil	CL	R	55	0	16	3	1.9	8	4	.50	25 - 26	12 - 15	0 - 0	47	1	37	41	0	.90	.481	1.83
Coffey, Todd, Mil	SU	R	78	13	21	11	1.3	51	18	.35	1 - 2	0 - 0	1 - 4	54	0	2	6	27	.88	.670	2.90
Stetter, Mitch, Mil	SU	L	71	12	22	2	1.1	67	14	.21	0 - 0	0 - 1	1 - 1	51	0	1	2	20	.95	.685	3.60
Weathers, David, Cin-Mil	SU	R	68	3	15	5	1.4	21	9	.43	1 - 1	0 - 3	0 - 1	47	0	1	5	21	.85	.748	3.92
Vargas, Claudio, LAD-Mil	SU	R	36	6	9	8	1.1	26	3	.12	0 - 0	0 - 1	0 - 1	27	0	0	2	11	.85	.534	1.74
Swindle, R.J., Mil	LT	L	6	2	1	3	0.1	3	1	1.00	0 - 0	0 - 0	0 - 0	0	0	0	0	0		1.209	16.20
McClung, Seth, Mil	LM	R	39	18	7	17	0.8	22	4	.18	0 - 0	0 - 1	0 - 0	22	0	0	1	5	.83	.758	3.95
Narveson, Chris, Mil	LM	L	17	11	2	7	0.5	6	5	.83	0 - 0	0 - 0	0 - 0	7	0	0	0	0		.754	4.13
DiFelice, Mark, Mil	UR	R	59	21	12	5	0.9	46	17	.37	0 - 0	0 - 0	0 - 1	41	0	0	1	9	.90	.706	3.66
Villanueva, Carlos, Mil	UR	R	58	10	13	12	0.9	8	2	.25	2 - 3	1 - 5	0 - 0	40	0	3	8	9	.71	.722	4.84
Smith, Chris, Mil	UR	R	35	10	6	10	0.4	15	4	.27	0 - 1	0 - 0	0 - 0	20	0	0	1	0	.00	.780	4.11
Colome, Jesus, Was-Mil	UR	R	21	6	6	4	0.6	15	10	.67	0 - 0	0 - 0	0 - 1	10	0	0	1	0	.00	.955	7.59
Julio, Jorge, Mil	UR	R	15	5	3	4	0.4	6	3	.50	0 - 1	0 - 0	0 - 0	7	0	0	1	0	.00	.749	7.79
Burns, Mike, Mil	UR	R	7	2	1	3	0.3	0	0		0 - 0	0 - 0	0 - 0	5	0	0	0	0		.646	1.64
Axford, John, Mil	UR	R	7	1	2	2	0.2	0	0		1 - 1	0 - 0	0 - 0	5	0	1	1	0	1.00	.538	3.52
Butler, Josh, Mil	UR	R	3	1	0	2	0.2	1	1	1.00	0 - 0	0 - 0	0 - 0	0	0	0	0	0		.992	9.00
Dillard, Tim, Mil	UR	R	2	2	0	1	0.7	0	0		0 - 0	0 - 1	0 - 0	0	0	0	1	0	.00	1.169	12.46
Riske, David, Mil	UR	R	1	0	0	0	0.1	0	0		0 - 0	0 - 0	0 - 0	0	0	0	0	0		1.667	18.00
Bush, David, Mil	ER	R	1	0	0	0	0.2	0	0		0 - 0	0 - 0	0 - 0	0	0	0	0	0		1.022	19.00
Minnesota Twins																					
Nathan, Joe, Min	CL	R	70	0	22	7	1.9	13	0	.00	32 - 35	14 - 16	1 - 1	60	2	47	52	0	.90	.549	2.10
Guerrier, Matt, Min	SU	R	79	5	23	5	1.3	54	13	.24	0 - 0	0 - 2	1 - 2	66	0	1	4	33	.92	.598	2.36
Mijares, Jose, Min	SU	L	71	5	18	4	1.2	55	15	.27	0 - 1	0 - 0	0 - 0	48	0	0	1	27	.96	.649	2.34
Mahay, Ron, KC-Min	LT	L	57	20	13	8	0.6	45	22	.49	0 - 0	0 - 0	0 - 0	30	0	0	0	6	1.00	.879	4.29
Keppel, Bobby, Min	LM	R	37	21	7	14	0.8	25	9	.36	0 - 0	0 - 0	0 - 1	10	0	0	1	4	.80	.813	4.83
Dickey, R.A., Min	LM	R	34	15	7	18	0.5	27	17	.63	0 - 0	0 - 0	0 - 0	16	0	0	0	1	1.00	.834	4.55
Duensing, Brian, Min	LM	L	15	9	2	11	0.4	15	11	.73	0 - 0	0 - 0	0 - 0	4	0	0	0	1	1.00	.728	5.17
Rauch, Jon, Ari-Min	UR	R	75	11	16	5	1.2	32	14	.44	1 - 1	1 - 1	0 - 3	52	1	2	5	17	.86	.722	3.60
Crain, Jesse, Min	UR	R	56	13	11	9	1.0	33	13	.39	0 - 0	0 - 0	0 - 0	35	0	0	0	4	1.00	.722	4.70
Humber, Philip, Min	UR	R	8	4	2	4	0.7	3	1	.33	0 - 0	0 - 0	0 - 0	4	0	0	0	0		1.008	8.00
Manship, Jeff, Min	UR	R	6	4	1	5	0.3	4	1	.25	0 - 0	0 - 0	0 - 0	2	0	0	0	0		.733	4.22
Liriano, Francisco, Min	UR	L	5	2	0	3	0.6	3	0	.00	0 - 0	0 - 0	0 - 0	3	0	0	0	0		.808	3.52
Morillo, Juan, Min	UR	R	3	0	0	0	0.0	0	0		0 - 0	0 - 0	0 - 0	1	0	0	0	0		1.278	22.50
Gabino, Armando, Min	UR	R	1	1	0	1	0.0	0	0		0 - 0	0 - 0	0 - 0	0	0	0	0	0		1.810	27.00
Perkins, Glen, Min	ER	L	1	0	0	0	0.0	0	0		0 - 0	0 - 0	0 - 0	1	0	0	0	0		.650	.00
New York Mets																					
Rodriguez, Fr., NYM	CL	R	70	0	17	11	1.0	17	3	.18	24 - 26	11 - 15	0 - 1	50	1	35	42	0	.83	.644	3.71
Feliciano, Pedro, NYM	SU	L	88	4	34	1	1.3	54	10	.19	0 - 0	0 - 1	0 - 1	65	1	0	2	24	.92	.681	3.03
Parnell, Bobby, NYM	SU	R	60	8	13	5	1.3	18	6	.33	0 - 2	1 - 3	0 - 0	41	1	1	5	16	.81	.698	3.46
Putz, J.J., NYM	SU	R	29	0	5	4	1.5	4	1	.25	1 - 1	1 - 3	0 - 0	18	0	2	4	10	.86	.739	5.22
Takahashi, Ken, NYM	LT	L	28	10	3	5	0.6	23	5	.22	0 - 0	0 - 0	0 - 0	17	0	0	0	0		.724	2.96
Switzer, Jon, NYM	LT	L	4	2	1	1	0.5	2	2	1.00	0 - 0	0 - 0	0 - 1	2	0	0	1	1	.50	.983	8.10
Fossum, Casey, NYM	LT	L	3	3	1	1	0.5	8	3	.38	0 - 0	0 - 0	0 - 0	1	0	0	0	0		.688	2.25
Dessens, Elmer, NYM	LM	R	28	13	8	4	0.3	19	3	.16	0 - 0	0 - 0	0 - 0	19	0	0	0	0		.676	3.31
Misch, Pat, SF-NYM	LM	L	19	9	5	6	0.6	15	4	.27	0 - 0	0 - 1	0 - 0	10	0	0	1	0	.00	.780	4.09
Broadway, L., CWS-NYM	LM	R	16	9	2	11	0.3	5	1	.20	0 - 0	0 - 0	0 - 0	6	0	0	0	0		.744	4.87
Green, Sean, NYM	UR	R	79	13	25	5	1.1	34	14	.41	0 - 0	1 - 2	0 - 1	50	0	1	3	14	.88	.716	4.52
Stokes, Brian, NYM	UR	R	69	14	19	13	0.9	35	9	.26	0 - 0	0 - 2	0 - 0	49	1	0	2	10	.83	.769	3.97
Redding, Tim, NYM	UR	R	13	7	2	7	0.4	6	2	.33	0 - 0	0 - 0	0 - 0	5	0	0	0	0		.935	5.63
Figueroa, Nelson, NYM	UR	R	6	4	1	4	0.6	5	1	.20	0 - 0	0 - 0	0 - 0	2	0	0	0	0		.834	3.65
Stoner, Tobi, NYM	UR	R	4	4	0	2	0.3	0	0		0 - 0	0 - 0	0 - 0	2	0	0	0	0		.843	4.00
Nieve, Fernando, NYM	UR	R	1	0	0	0	0.0	0	0		0 - 0	0 - 0	0 - 0	1	0	0	0	0		.286	.00
New York Yankees																					
Rivera, Mariano, NYY	CL	R	66	0	20	5	1.7	20	5	.25	28 - 28	12 - 14	4 - 4	56	0	44	46	0	.96	.549	1.76
Coke, Phil, NYY	SU	L	72	10	23	7	1.3	54	12	.22	0 - 0	2 - 3	0 - 4	48	2	2	7	21	.82	.668	4.50
Bruney, Brian, NYY	SU	R	44	3	7	5	1.0	13	4	.31	0 - 1	0 - 0	0 - 0	31	1	0	1	14	.93	.759	3.92
Hughes, Phil, NYY	SU	R	44	4	8	10	1.4	16	1	.06	0 - 0	2 - 4	1 - 2	37	2	3	6	18	.88	.456	1.40
Marte, Damaso, NYY	LT	L	21	4	2	1	1.1	21	4	.19	0 - 0	0 - 1	0 - 0	13	0	0	1	5	.83	.861	9.45
Dunn, Mike, NYY	LT	L	4	0	0	0	0.1	2	1	.50	0 - 0	0 - 0	0 - 0	2	0	0	0	0		.800	6.75
Aceves, Alfredo, NYY	LM	R	42	25	7	25	1.1	29	8	.28	0 - 0	0 - 1	0 - 1	23	0	1	2	5	.86	.616	3.35
Robertson, David, NYY	UR	R	45	9	7	10	0.7	25	9	.36	0 - 0	1 - 1	0 - 0	28	0	1	1	5	1.00	.685	3.30
Albaladejo, Jonathan, NYY	UR	R	32	12	4	4	0.6	22	5	.23	0 - 0	0 - 1	0 - 0	21	0	0	1	0	.50	.905	5.24
Ramirez, Edwar, NYY	UR	R	20	6	3	6	0.5	21	7	.33	0 - 0	0 - 0	0 - 0	11	0	0	0	1	1.00	.911	5.73
Melancon, Mark, NYY	UR	R	13	5	1	2	0.4	15	8	.53	0 - 0	0 - 0	0 - 1	6	0	0	1	0	.00	.665	3.86
Gaudin, Chad, SD-NYY	UR	R	6	1	0	5	0.8	4	3	.75	0 - 0	0 - 0	0 - 0	4	0	0	0	0		.848	3.46

Relief Pitching

Pitcher	Pos	T	Rel G	Early Entry	Cons Days	Long	Lev Ind	#	Scrd	Pct	Easy	Reg	Tough	Clean	BS Win	Saves	Opps	Holds	Sv/Hld Pct	Opp OPS	Rel ERA
Wang, Chien-Ming, NYY	UR	R	3	1	0	3	0.5	0	0		0 - 0	0 - 0	0 - 0	2	0	0	0	0		.744	2.25
Mitre, Sergio, NYY	UR	R	3	1	0	2	0.2	1	1	1.00	0 - 0	0 - 0	0 - 0	1	0	0	0	0		.802	4.70
Towers, Josh, NYY	UR	R	2	1	0	2	0.1	3	1	.33	0 - 0	0 - 0	0 - 0	0	0	0	0	0		.729	3.38
Kennedy, Ian, NYY	UR	R	1	0	0	1	4.2	0	0		0 - 0	0 - 0	0 - 0	1	0	0	0	1	1.00	.500	.00
Chamberlain, Joba, NYY	ER	R	1	0	0	0	0.1	0	0		0 - 0	0 - 0	0 - 0	1	0	0	0	0		.000	.00
Swisher, Nick, NYY	ER	L	1	0	0	0	0.0	0	0		0 - 0	0 - 0	0 - 0	1	0	0	0	0		.650	.00
Oakland Athletics																					
Bailey, Andrew, Oak	CL	R	68	6	17	11	1.4	22	8	.36	15 - 15	10 - 12	1 - 3	53	1	26	30	2	.88	.476	1.84
Wuertz, Mike, Oak	SU	R	74	13	16	10	1.3	40	8	.20	1 - 1	3 - 5	0 - 0	54	0	4	6	23	.93	.567	2.63
Ziegler, Brad, Oak	SU	R	69	12	17	9	1.1	31	12	.39	4 - 4	3 - 4	0 - 2	47	0	7	10	14	.88	.734	3.07
Breslow, Craig, Min-Oak	LT	L	77	20	25	6	1.0	50	12	.24	0 - 0	0 - 1	0 - 1	52	1	0	2	15	.88	.613	3.36
Blevins, Jerry, Oak	LT	L	20	5	3	5	0.4	9	2	.22	0 - 0	0 - 0	0 - 0	13	0	0	0	0		.651	4.84
Kilby, Brad, Oak	LT	L	10	8	1	3	0.5	7	2	.29	0 - 0	0 - 0	0 - 0	8	0	0	0	1	1.00	.533	.60
Marshall, Jay, Oak	LT	L	10	3	2	1	0.7	7	0	.00	0 - 0	0 - 0	0 - 0	6	0	0	0	1	1.00	1.018	14.73
Gonzalez, Edgar, Oak	LM	R	20	8	2	10	0.5	11	2	.18	0 - 0	0 - 0	0 - 0	9	0	0	0	0		.778	5.21
Casilla, Santiago, Oak	UR	R	46	11	7	8	0.8	19	15	.79	0 - 0	0 - 0	0 - 0	27	0	0	0	5	1.00	.866	5.96
Gray, Jeff, Oak	UR	R	24	9	5	4	0.5	9	3	.33	0 - 0	0 - 0	0 - 0	14	0	0	0	1	1.00	.723	3.76
Tomko, Brett, NYY-Oak	UR	R	15	5	1	8	0.7	6	0	.00	0 - 0	0 - 0	0 - 0	8	0	0	0	0		.790	5.23
Cameron, Kevin, Oak	UR	R	11	3	1	6	0.4	2	1	.50	0 - 0	1 - 1	0 - 0	7	0	1	1	1	1.00	.578	3.44
Meloan, John, Oak	UR	R	6	3	1	2	0.2	1	0	.00	0 - 0	0 - 0	0 - 0	5	0	0	0	0		.284	.00
Giese, Dan, Oak	UR	R	6	3	0	5	0.9	2	1	.50	0 - 0	0 - 0	0 - 0	1	0	0	0	0		.776	5.51
Eveland, Dana, Oak	UR	L	4	1	0	1	0.5	0	0		0 - 0	0 - 0	0 - 0	2	0	0	0	0		.894	2.25
Rodriguez, Henry, Oak	UR	R	3	0	0	1	0.1	1	1	1.00	0 - 0	0 - 0	0 - 0	1	0	0	0	0		.585	2.25
Outman, Josh, Oak	UR	L	2	0	1	0	0.9	0	0		0 - 0	0 - 0	0 - 0	2	0	0	0	0		.286	.00
Mortensen, C., StL-Oak	UR	R	1	0	0	1	0.1	0	0		0 - 0	0 - 0	0 - 0	0	0	0	0	0		1.300	6.00
Gonzalez, Gio, Oak	ER	L	3	1	0	2	1.4	3	3	1.00	0 - 0	0 - 0	0 - 0	0	0	0	0	0		.848	7.45
Philadelphia Phillies																					
Lidge, Brad, Phi	CL	R	67	0	21	6	2.0	6	1	.17	22 - 24	9 - 18	0 - 0	36	0	31	42	1	.74	.912	7.21
Madson, Ryan, Phi	SU	R	79	0	29	6	1.6	13	0	.00	4 - 6	4 - 8	2 - 2	61	1	10	16	26	.86	.673	3.26
Eyre, Scott, Phi	SU	L	42	3	7	2	1.1	30	7	.23	0 - 0	0 - 0	0 - 0	34	0	0	0	13	1.00	.655	1.50
Park, Chan Ho, Phi	SU	R	38	11	5	13	1.1	25	8	.32	0 - 0	0 - 1	0 - 0	24	0	0	1	13	.93	.576	2.52
Romero, J.C., Phi	SU	L	21	0	5	1	1.6	18	2	.11	0 - 0	0 - 0	0 - 1	15	0	0	1	6	.86	.711	2.70
Taschner, Jack, Phi	LT	L	24	6	1	9	0.6	8	1	.13	0 - 0	0 - 1	0 - 0	14	0	0	1	0	.00	.881	4.91
Escalona, Sergio, Phi	LT	L	14	4	3	1	0.4	4	1	.25	0 - 0	0 - 0	0 - 0	10	0	0	0	2	1.00	.613	4.61
Durbin, Chad, Phi	UR	R	59	13	10	20	0.8	22	5	.23	0 - 0	2 - 2	0 - 1	34	0	2	3	8	.91	.724	4.39
Condrey, Clay, Phi	UR	R	45	10	14	3	1.1	28	8	.29	0 - 0	1 - 1	0 - 1	30	0	1	2	7	.89	.645	3.00
Walker, Tyler, Phi	UR	R	32	8	6	8	0.4	20	11	.55	0 - 0	0 - 0	0 - 0	22	0	0	0	1	1.00	.652	3.06
Happ, J.A., Phi	UR	L	12	6	1	7	0.5	10	2	.20	0 - 0	0 - 0	0 - 0	8	0	0	0	0		.536	2.49
Myers, Brett, Phi	UR	R	8	2	3	0	1.2	0	0		0 - 0	0 - 0	0 - 0	5	0	0	0	3	1.00	.879	6.43
Kendrick, Kyle, Phi	UR	R	7	4	1	4	1.1	1	1	1.00	0 - 0	0 - 0	0 - 0	4	0	0	0	0		.577	3.60
Moyer, Jamie, Phi	UR	L	5	5	0	4	0.9	1	0	.00	0 - 0	0 - 0	0 - 0	2	0	0	0	1	1.00	.442	1.93
Lopez, Rodrigo, Phi	UR	R	2	1	0	2	0.6	2	2	1.00	0 - 0	0 - 0	0 - 0	0	0	0	0	0		1.411	27.00
Carpenter, Drew, Phi	UR	R	2	0	1	0	0.1	0	0		0 - 0	0 - 0	0 - 0	0	0	0	0	0		1.500	13.50
Register, Steven, Phi	UR	R	1	0	0	1	0.0	0	0		0 - 0	0 - 0	0 - 0	0	0	0	0	0		1.121	4.50
Bastardo, Antonio, Phi	UR	L	1	0	0	0	0.5	0	0		0 - 0	0 - 0	0 - 0	1	0	0	0	0		.250	.00
Pittsburgh Pirates																					
Capps, Matt, Pit	CL	R	57	0	9	7	1.6	7	4	.57	22 - 22	5 - 9	0 - 1	36	1	27	32	1	.85	.907	5.80
Veal, Donnie, Pit	LT	L	19	4	0	6	0.3	3	0	.00	0 - 0	0 - 0	0 - 0	12	0	0	0	1	1.00	.913	7.16
Dumatrait, Phil, Pit	LT	L	15	4	3	1	0.8	10	6	.60	0 - 0	0 - 0	0 - 1	7	0	0	1	1	.50	.933	6.92
Karstens, Jeff, Pit	LM	R	26	12	4	11	0.8	9	3	.33	0 - 0	0 - 0	0 - 0	13	0	0	0	1	1.00	.835	5.83
Chavez, Jesse, Pit	UR	R	73	11	18	6	0.9	44	17	.39	0 - 0	0 - 0	0 - 4	45	0	0	4	15	.79	.783	4.01
Hanrahan, Joel, Was-Pit	UR	R	67	4	14	16	1.2	22	9	.41	1 - 2	3 - 5	1 - 3	42	0	5	10	9	.74	.780	4.78
Meek, Evan, Pit	UR	R	41	5	7	7	0.6	10	6	.60	0 - 0	0 - 0	0 - 1	29	0	0	1	4	.80	.670	3.45
Jackson, Steven, Pit	UR	R	40	8	13	8	0.9	22	6	.27	0 - 0	0 - 0	0 - 1	29	0	0	1	4	.80	.660	3.14
Ascanio, Jose, ChC-Pit	UR	R	16	3	1	5	1.4	3	3	1.00	0 - 0	0 - 0	0 - 0	7	0	0	0	1	1.00	.819	4.00
Yates, Tyler, Pit	UR	R	15	0	3	0	1.1	3	0	.00	0 - 0	0 - 0	0 - 0	9	0	0	0	3	1.00	.941	7.50
Bautista, Denny, Pit	UR	R	14	3	1	2	0.7	10	6	.60	0 - 0	0 - 0	0 - 1	7	0	0	1	1	.50	.791	5.27
Bootcheck, Chris, Pit	UR	R	13	6	1	3	0.5	7	3	.43	0 - 0	0 - 0	0 - 0	6	0	0	0	1	1.00	.834	11.05
Vasquez, Virgil, Pit	UR	R	7	1	1	4	0.1	2	0	.00	0 - 0	0 - 0	0 - 0	3	0	0	0	0		.806	5.06
Hansen, Craig, Pit	UR	R	5	1	1	1	0.3	0	0		0 - 0	0 - 0	0 - 0	4	0	0	0	0		.807	5.68
Hart, Kevin, ChC-Pit	UR	R	4	0	0	1	0.2	0	0		0 - 0	0 - 0	0 - 0	3	0	0	0	0		.681	1.59
Hacker, Eric, Pit	UR	R	3	0	0	1	0.0	0	0		0 - 0	0 - 0	0 - 0	2	0	0	0	0		1.012	6.00
Claggett, Anthony, NYY-Pit	UR	R	3	1	0	2	0.1	1	1	1.00	0 - 0	0 - 0	0 - 0	0	0	0	0	0		1.649	27.00
San Diego Padres																					
Bell, Heath, SD	CL	R	68	0	22	9	2.0	12	1	.08	26 - 26	13 - 19	3 - 3	55	0	42	48	0	.88	.568	2.71
Gregerson, Luke, SD	SU	R	72	7	20	6	1.5	27	5	.19	0 - 1	0 - 4	1 - 2	54	0	1	7	27	.82	.615	3.24
Adams, Mike, SD	SU	R	37	0	11	2	1.1	5	2	.40	0 - 0	0 - 0	0 - 1	32	0	0	1	15	.94	.315	.73

Relief Pitching

Pitcher	Pos	T	Rel G	Early Entry	Cons Days	Long	Lev Ind	#	Scrd	Pct	Easy	Reg	Tough	Clean	BS Win	Saves	Opps	Holds	Sv/Hld Pct	Opp OPS	Rel ERA
Sanchez, Duaner, SD	SU	R	12	2	3	2	1.5	1	1	1.00	0 - 0	0 - 1	0 - 0	6	0	0	1	5	.83	1.142	9.00
Thatcher, Joe, SD	LT	L	52	14	15	8	0.6	43	7	.16	0 - 0	0 - 0	0 - 1	38	0	0	1	9	.90	.628	2.80
Poreda, Aaron, CWS-SD	LT	L	14	4	0	5	0.5	11	4	.36	0 - 0	0 - 0	0 - 0	8	0	0	0	0		.639	2.70
Lopez, Arturo, SD	LT	L	4	2	1	0	0.1	3	3	1.00	0 - 0	0 - 0	0 - 0	1	0	0	0	0		1.878	19.29
Ramos, Cesar, SD	LT	L	3	2	0	1	0.8	2	0	.00	0 - 0	0 - 0	0 - 0	2	0	0	0	0		.571	1.69
Perdomo, Luis, SD	LM	R	35	19	3	21	0.3	25	10	.40	0 - 0	0 - 1	0 - 0	14	0	0	1	0	.00	.806	4.00
Moreno, Edwin, SD	LM	R	19	7	2	8	1.2	4	3	.75	0 - 0	0 - 1	0 - 0	11	0	0	1	4	.80	.898	4.84
Mujica, Edward, SD	UR	R	63	17	10	12	0.8	27	6	.22	1 - 2	1 - 1	0 - 0	41	0	2	3	11	.93	.708	3.51
Burke, Greg, SD	UR	R	48	9	11	6	0.9	14	2	.14	0 - 0	0 - 2	0 - 0	30	1	0	2	10	.83	.765	4.14
Webb, Ryan, SD	UR	R	28	6	5	5	0.6	14	4	.29	0 - 0	0 - 0	0 - 0	16	0	0	0	6	1.00	.771	3.86
Russell, Adam, SD	UR	R	15	6	4	5	1.2	6	1	.17	0 - 0	0 - 0	0 - 0	11	0	0	0	4	1.00	.673	3.65
Richard, Clayton, CWS-SD	UR	L	12	8	0	3	0.4	12	5	.42	0 - 0	0 - 0	0 - 0	6	0	0	0	0		.902	4.32
Ekstrom, Mike, SD	UR	R	12	6	1	6	0.3	7	2	.29	0 - 0	0 - 0	0 - 0	5	0	0	0	0		.806	6.38
Gallagher, Sean, Oak-SD	UR	R	12	3	3	2	0.9	6	1	.17	0 - 0	0 - 0	0 - 0	10	0	0	0	0		.703	2.19
Banks, Josh, SD	UR	R	3	3	0	2	0.9	6	4	.67	0 - 0	0 - 0	0 - 0	0	0	0	0	0		.772	2.45
de la Cruz, Eulogio, SD	UR	R	3	0	0	1	0.0	1	0	.00	0 - 0	0 - 0	0 - 0	2	0	0	0	0		.671	5.40
Frieri, Ernesto, SD	UR	R	2	0	0	0	0.1	0	0		0 - 0	0 - 0	0 - 0	2	0	0	0	0		.143	.00
Geer, Josh, SD	ER	R	2	2	0	2	0.3	0	0		0 - 0	0 - 0	0 - 0	0	0	0	0	0		1.105	12.60
San Francisco Giants																					
Wilson, Brian, SF	CL	R	68	0	19	16	2.3	34	6	.18	19 - 21	13 - 16	6 - 8	53	2	38	45	1	.86	.595	2.74
Affeldt, Jeremy, SF	SU	L	74	2	18	2	1.5	54	15	.28	0 - 0	0 - 0	0 - 0	53	0	0	0	33	1.00	.500	1.70
Runzler, Dan, SF	LT	L	11	3	2	2	0.9	9	3	.33	0 - 0	0 - 0	0 - 0	9	0	0	0	2	1.00	.597	1.04
Hinshaw, Alex, SF	LT	L	9	0	2	0	0.2	2	1	.50	0 - 0	0 - 0	0 - 0	3	0	0	0	0		1.169	12.00
Bumgarner, Madison, SF	LT	L	3	2	0	2	0.4	3	1	.33	0 - 0	0 - 0	0 - 0	2	0	0	0	0		.611	.00
Medders, Brandon, SF	LM	R	61	26	9	15	1.0	43	18	.42	0 - 0	1 - 3	0 - 1	34	0	1	4	8	.75	.698	3.01
Miller, Justin, SF	LM	R	44	26	9	13	0.6	46	14	.30	0 - 0	0 - 0	0 - 0	23	0	0	0	1	1.00	.730	3.18
Howry, Bob, SF	UR	R	63	7	9	12	1.0	23	7	.30	0 - 0	0 - 2	0 - 1	44	0	0	3	10	.77	.633	3.39
Valdez, Merkin, SF	UR	R	48	11	8	10	0.5	22	13	.59	0 - 0	0 - 1	0 - 2	29	1	0	3	4	.57	.800	5.66
Romo, Sergio, SF	UR	R	45	1	7	0	1.4	26	2	.08	1 - 1	0 - 0	1 - 1	34	0	2	2	10	1.00	.631	3.97
Joaquin, Waldis, SF	UR	R	10	3	1	2	0.3	2	1	.50	0 - 0	0 - 0	0 - 0	6	0	0	0	0		.754	4.22
Matos, Osiris, SF	UR	R	5	1	0	2	0.1	2	1	.50	0 - 0	0 - 0	0 - 0	2	0	0	0	0		.987	9.00
Johnson, Randy, SF	UR	L	5	1	0	0	1.2	0	0		0 - 0	0 - 1	0 - 0	1	0	0	1	0	.00	1.084	8.23
Martinez, Joe, SF	UR	R	4	2	0	3	0.6	1	0	.00	0 - 0	0 - 0	0 - 0	1	0	0	0	0		.919	7.11
Sanchez, Jonathan, SF	ER	L	3	1	0	0	0.4	0	0		0 - 0	0 - 0	0 - 0	3	0	0	0	1	1.00	.414	.00
Seattle Mariners																					
Aardsma, David, Sea	CL	R	73	0	25	6	2.1	3	0	.00	20 - 22	17 - 19	1 - 1	63	0	38	42	6	.92	.555	2.52
Morrow, Brandon, Sea	CL	R	16	4	1	7	1.5	2	1	.50	5 - 6	1 - 2	0 - 0	8	0	6	8	1	.78	.789	6.38
Lowe, Mark, Sea	SU	R	75	3	20	11	1.6	29	9	.31	2 - 4	1 - 5	0 - 4	52	0	3	13	26	.74	.664	3.26
Batista, Miguel, Sea	SU	R	56	17	12	19	1.1	12	8	.67	0 - 0	1 - 3	0 - 2	35	1	1	5	14	.79	.783	4.04
White, Sean, Sea	SU	R	52	10	7	9	1.1	40	11	.28	1 - 1	0 - 1	0 - 1	32	1	1	3	15	.89	.581	2.80
Kelley, Shawn, Sea	SU	R	41	10	3	11	1.3	25	10	.40	0 - 0	0 - 1	0 - 3	28	0	0	4	9	.69	.742	4.50
Olson, Garrett, Sea	LT	L	20	4	3	5	0.5	17	5	.29	0 - 0	0 - 0	0 - 0	12	0	0	0	5	1.00	.721	3.90
Jakubauskas, Chris, Sea	LM	R	27	18	2	16	0.9	21	7	.33	0 - 0	0 - 0	0 - 1	12	0	0	1	3	.75	.739	4.30
Corcoran, Roy, Sea	UR	R	16	7	0	3	0.9	12	8	.67	0 - 0	0 - 0	0 - 1	8	0	0	1	2	.67	.935	6.16
Messenger, Randy, Sea	UR	R	12	0	1	1	0.3	6	2	.33	0 - 0	0 - 0	0 - 0	7	0	0	0	1	1.00	.860	4.35
Stark, Denny, Sea	UR	R	9	2	2	4	0.5	5	0	.00	0 - 0	0 - 0	0 - 0	6	0	0	0	0		.891	6.55
Vargas, Jason, Sea	UR	L	9	6	0	3	0.8	16	0	.00	0 - 0	0 - 0	0 - 0	6	0	0	0	0		.585	2.87
French, Luke, Det-Sea	UR	L	3	1	0	1	0.5	2	0	.00	0 - 0	0 - 0	0 - 0	2	0	0	0	0		.835	4.15
Silva, Carlos, Sea	UR	R	2	0	0	1	0.0	0	0		0 - 0	0 - 0	0 - 0	0	0	0	0	0		1.125	10.80
Fister, Doug, Sea	UR	R	1	0	0	0	0.0	0	0		0 - 0	0 - 0	0 - 0	1	0	0	0	0		.650	.00
Wilson, Josh, Ari-SD-Sea	ER	R	2	0	0	1	1.8	0	0		0 - 0	0 - 0	0 - 0	1	0	0	0	0		1.556	13.50
St Louis Cardinals																					
Franklin, Ryan, StL	CL	R	62	0	13	9	1.9	19	2	.11	20 - 20	14 - 19	4 - 4	52	2	38	43	1	.89	.592	1.92
McClellan, Kyle, StL	SU	R	66	8	12	17	1.4	30	5	.17	0 - 0	2 - 5	1 - 1	48	0	3	6	15	.86	.639	3.38
Reyes, Dennys, StL	LT	L	75	12	24	0	1.0	50	13	.26	0 - 0	1 - 1	0 - 0	57	0	1	1	18	1.00	.657	3.29
Miller, Trever, StL	LT	L	70	16	19	0	0.8	54	9	.17	0 - 0	0 - 0	0 - 1	58	0	0	1	13	.93	.589	2.06
Motte, Jason, StL	UR	R	69	11	17	6	1.0	36	8	.22	0 - 1	0 - 1	0 - 1	49	1	0	3	15	.83	.804	4.76
Hawksworth, Blake, StL	UR	R	30	8	1	6	0.8	11	4	.36	0 - 0	0 - 0	0 - 0	23	0	0	0	2	1.00	.612	2.03
Thompson, Brad, StL	UR	R	24	4	4	10	0.5	9	3	.33	0 - 0	0 - 0	0 - 0	11	0	0	0	0		.748	3.89
Kinney, Josh, StL	UR	R	17	7	2	1	0.7	13	3	.23	0 - 0	0 - 1	0 - 0	10	0	0	1	2	.67	.957	8.80
Walters, P.J., StL	UR	R	7	3	0	4	0.2	3	3	1.00	0 - 0	0 - 0	0 - 0	1	0	0	0	0		1.046	10.50
Boggs, Mitchell, StL	UR	R	7	3	0	3	1.1	2	2	1.00	0 - 0	0 - 0	0 - 0	3	0	0	0	1	1.00	.749	4.66
Wellemeyer, Todd, StL	UR	R	7	0	0	2	1.1	3	2	.67	0 - 0	0 - 0	0 - 0	4	0	0	0	0		.836	3.24
Lohse, Kyle, StL	ER	R	1	1	0	0	0.4	0	0		0 - 0	0 - 0	0 - 0	1	0	0	0	0		.000	.00
Tampa Bay Rays																					
Howell, J.P., TB	CL	L	69	5	23	7	1.8	44	16	.36	11 - 12	6 - 8	0 - 5	44	2	17	25	4	.72	.627	2.84
Percival, Troy, TB	CL	R	14	0	2	0	1.8	2	0	.00	4 - 4	2 - 2	0 - 0	10	0	6	6	0	1.00	.972	6.35

335

Relief Pitching

Pitcher	Pos	T	Rel G	Early Entry	Cons Days	Long	Lev Ind	#	Scrd	Pct	Easy	Reg	Tough	Clean	BS Win	Saves	Opps	Holds	Sv/Hld Pct	Opp OPS	Rel ERA
Balfour, Grant, TB	SU	R	73	16	21	11	1.1	67	18	.27	1 - 2	2 - 3	1 - 4	45	0	4	9	18	.81	.681	4.81
Wheeler, Dan, TB	SU	R	69	0	19	0	1.2	38	13	.34	1 - 2	1 - 1	0 - 3	50	0	2	6	16	.82	.659	3.28
Choate, Randy, TB	LT	L	61	4	24	4	0.9	57	9	.16	2 - 2	3 - 3	0 - 0	44	0	5	5	9	1.00	.588	3.47
Shouse, Brian, TB	LT	L	45	3	10	1	0.9	29	7	.24	0 - 0	0 - 0	0 - 1	31	0	0	1	10	.91	.804	4.50
Cormier, Lance, TB	LM	R	53	25	9	17	0.7	33	14	.42	0 - 0	2 - 2	0 - 0	30	0	2	2	6	1.00	.679	3.26
Springer, Russ, Oak-TB	UR	R	74	12	24	5	1.0	40	19	.48	1 - 1	0 - 1	0 - 1	46	0	1	3	14	.88	.806	4.11
Bennett, Jeff, Atl-TB	UR	R	44	13	12	10	0.7	23	10	.43	0 - 0	0 - 0	0 - 1	24	0	0	0	2	1.00	.927	5.01
Nelson, Joe, TB	UR	R	42	12	9	9	1.0	24	8	.33	2 - 2	1 - 1	0 - 1	29	1	3	4	7	.91	.753	4.02
Bradford, Chad, TB	UR	R	20	6	6	0	1.0	21	10	.48	0 - 0	0 - 0	0 - 1	10	0	0	1	2	.67	.946	4.35
Thayer, Dale, TB	UR	R	11	3	1	4	0.1	6	1	.17	0 - 0	1 - 1	0 - 0	6	0	1	1	0	1.00	.822	4.61
Isringhausen, Jason, TB	UR	R	9	1	0	1	0.8	2	1	.50	0 - 0	0 - 1	0 - 0	8	0	0	1	0	.00	.585	2.25
Sonnanstine, Andy, TB	ER	R	4	3	0	3	0.9	2	2	1.00	0 - 0	0 - 0	0 - 0	1	0	0	0	0		.991	4.76
Niemann, Jeff, TB	ER	R	1	1	0	1	0.0	0	0		0 - 0	0 - 0	0 - 0	0	0	0	0	0		.904	9.00
Texas Rangers																					
Francisco, Frank, Tex	CL	R	51	0	13	4	1.7	13	6	.46	15 - 18	9 - 9	1 - 2	41	1	25	29	4	.88	.639	3.83
Wilson, C.J., Tex	SU	L	74	0	21	14	1.6	23	6	.26	9 - 10	4 - 6	1 - 2	55	0	14	18	19	.89	.651	2.81
O'Day, Darren, NYM-Tex	SU	R	68	5	21	5	1.0	45	15	.33	0 - 0	0 - 0	2 - 2	49	0	2	2	20	1.00	.543	1.84
Feliz, Neftali, Tex	SU	R	20	14	0	12	1.0	18	4	.22	0 - 0	2 - 2	0 - 1	15	1	2	3	9	.92	.416	1.74
Guardado, Eddie, Tex	LT	L	48	4	9	4	0.7	15	7	.47	0 - 0	0 - 2	0 - 0	31	0	0	2	5	.71	.823	4.46
Jennings, Jason, Tex	LM	R	44	17	3	21	0.9	29	17	.59	1 - 1	0 - 1	0 - 0	17	0	1	2	12	.93	.814	4.13
Mathis, Doug, Tex	LM	R	22	7	1	11	0.4	8	2	.25	0 - 0	1 - 1	0 - 0	15	0	1	1	1	1.00	.595	2.14
Grilli, Jason, Col-Tex	UR	R	52	10	10	6	0.8	34	9	.26	0 - 0	1 - 1	0 - 0	32	0	1	1	7	1.00	.813	5.32
Eyre, Willie, Tex	UR	R	17	2	2	1	0.3	6	2	.33	0 - 0	0 - 0	0 - 0	14	0	0	0	0		.749	4.50
Madrigal, Warner, Tex	UR	R	13	4	0	4	0.3	9	3	.33	0 - 0	0 - 0	0 - 0	5	0	0	0	0		.981	9.95
Holland, Derek, Tex	UR	L	12	6	0	6	0.9	17	8	.47	0 - 0	0 - 0	0 - 1	3	0	0	1	2	.67	.857	5.48
Moscoso, Guillermo, Tex	UR	R	10	3	1	5	0.3	5	1	.20	0 - 0	0 - 0	0 - 0	6	0	0	0	0		.772	3.21
Nippert, Dustin, Tex	UR	R	10	7	2	6	0.8	10	2	.20	0 - 0	0 - 0	0 - 0	6	0	0	0	1	1.00	.534	1.86
Strop, Pedro, Tex	UR	R	7	2	1	1	0.2	1	1	1.00	0 - 0	0 - 0	0 - 0	4	0	0	0	0		.679	7.71
Benson, Kris, Tex	UR	R	6	3	0	3	0.1	3	2	.67	0 - 0	0 - 0	0 - 0	2	0	0	0	0		1.033	7.94
Rupe, Josh, Tex	UR	R	4	0	1	2	0.1	5	4	.80	0 - 0	0 - 0	0 - 0	1	0	0	0	0		1.395	15.43
Mendoza, Luis, Tex	UR	R	1	1	0	0	0.1	0	0		0 - 0	0 - 0	0 - 0	0	0	0	0	0		1.571	36.00
Feldman, Scott, Tex	ER	R	3	3	0	3	0.4	2	0	.00	0 - 0	0 - 0	0 - 0	1	0	0	0	0		1.138	12.15
Toronto Blue Jays																					
Downs, Scott, Tor	SU	L	48	0	15	3	1.7	16	5	.31	4 - 6	4 - 5	1 - 2	34	0	9	13	10	.83	.688	3.09
Carlson, Jesse, Tor	LT	L	73	17	18	8	1.0	31	6	.19	0 - 1	0 - 1	0 - 1	49	1	0	3	12	.80	.730	4.66
Ryan, B.J., Tor	LT	L	25	2	5	3	1.0	2	0	.00	1 - 2	1 - 2	0 - 0	17	1	2	4	2	.67	.986	6.53
Murphy, Bill, Tor	LT	L	8	3	1	3	0.2	4	0	.00	0 - 0	0 - 0	0 - 0	5	0	0	0	0		.544	3.18
Roenicke, Josh, Cin-Tor	LM	R	24	10	2	9	0.4	17	6	.35	0 - 0	0 - 0	0 - 0	11	0	0	0	1	1.00	.705	5.23
League, Brandon, Tor	UR	R	67	5	14	11	1.0	28	9	.32	0 - 0	0 - 1	0 - 2	42	1	0	3	9	.75	.735	4.58
Frasor, Jason, Tor	UR	R	61	2	13	8	1.4	23	9	.39	4 - 5	5 - 5	2 - 4	47	1	11	14	4	.83	.556	2.50
Camp, Shawn, Tor	UR	R	59	20	6	19	1.1	36	11	.31	0 - 0	1 - 1	0 - 0	38	0	1	1	6	1.00	.705	3.50
Accardo, Jeremy, Tor	UR	R	26	1	6	4	1.3	7	1	.14	0 - 0	0 - 0	1 - 1	20	0	1	1	4	1.00	.765	2.55
Janssen, Casey, Tor	UR	R	16	7	1	3	1.1	10	3	.30	1 - 1	0 - 0	0 - 0	9	0	1	1	2	1.00	.816	5.14
Hayhurst, Dirk, Tor	UR	R	15	6	2	5	0.3	6	4	.67	0 - 0	0 - 0	0 - 0	7	0	0	0	0		.767	2.78
Wolfe, Brian, Tor	UR	R	14	3	1	5	0.6	10	5	.50	0 - 0	0 - 1	0 - 0	6	0	0	1	0	.00	1.101	8.22
Tallet, Brian, Tor	UR	L	12	5	0	5	0.9	8	6	.75	0 - 0	0 - 0	0 - 0	4	0	0	0	0		.753	4.71
Bullington, Bryan, Tor	UR	R	4	1	1	1	0.2	2	2	1.00	0 - 0	0 - 0	0 - 0	3	0	0	0	0		.868	3.00
Richmond, Scott, Tor	ER	R	3	2	0	2	1.1	2	1	.50	0 - 0	0 - 0	0 - 0	0	0	0	0	0		.646	4.05
Cecil, Brett, Tor	ER	L	1	0	0	0	0.2	1	0	.00	0 - 0	0 - 0	0 - 0	1	0	0	0	0		.667	.00
Washington Nationals																					
Burnett, Sean, Pit-Was	LT	L	71	18	22	12	1.1	51	8	.16	0 - 0	1 - 3	0 - 0	53	0	1	3	11	.86	.607	3.12
Villone, Ron, Was	LT	L	63	21	23	9	1.1	54	18	.33	0 - 0	0 - 1	1 - 3	36	0	1	4	7	.73	.840	4.25
Hinckley, Mike, Was	LT	L	14	5	4	2	1.6	11	3	.27	0 - 0	0 - 1	0 - 0	9	0	0	1	4	.80	.852	4.66
Ledezma, Wil, Was	LT	L	5	2	1	2	0.5	2	2	1.00	0 - 0	0 - 0	0 - 0	0	0	0	0	0		1.025	9.53
Garate, Victor, Was	LT	L	4	1	0	0	0.1	5	4	.80	0 - 0	0 - 0	0 - 0	0	0	0	0	0		1.800	22.50
Clippard, Tyler, Was	LM	R	41	15	6	19	0.9	19	7	.37	0 - 0	0 - 0	0 - 1	21	0	0	1	3	.75	.633	2.69
Rivera, Saul, Was	LM	R	30	11	5	10	0.9	21	8	.38	0 - 0	0 - 1	0 - 0	9	0	0	1	2	.67	.898	6.10
MacDougal, M., CWS-Was	UR	R	57	3	21	7	1.6	24	4	.17	10 - 10	6 - 7	4 - 4	37	0	20	21	0	.95	.731	4.31
Bergmann, Jason, Was	UR	R	56	24	18	5	1.0	50	7	.14	0 - 0	0 - 1	0 - 0	37	0	0	1	10	.91	.825	4.50
Tavarez, Julian, Was	UR	R	42	7	11	7	1.1	22	4	.18	1 - 1	0 - 0	0 - 1	26	0	1	2	5	.86	.743	4.89
Kensing, Logan, Fla-Was	UR	R	32	9	8	9	0.6	19	9	.47	1 - 1	0 - 1	0 - 1	13	0	1	3	1	.50	1.023	8.92
Sosa, Jorge, Was	UR	R	18	1	5	8	0.8	9	3	.33	1 - 1	1 - 1	0 - 0	8	0	2	2	3	1.00	.966	6.45
Mock, Garrett, Was	UR	R	13	6	5	1	1.5	10	3	.30	0 - 1	0 - 0	0 - 1	7	0	0	2	4	.67	.769	6.92
Segovia, Zack, Was	UR	R	8	1	0	4	0.8	3	2	.67	0 - 1	0 - 0	0 - 0	2	1	0	1	0	.00	.798	7.84
Shell, Steven, Was	UR	R	4	4	0	2	1.3	5	4	.80	0 - 0	0 - 0	0 - 0	1	0	0	0	1	1.00	.818	5.00
Estrada, Marco, Was	UR	R	3	2	0	2	0.7	2	2	1.00	0 - 0	0 - 0	0 - 0	1	0	0	0	0		.488	.00
Detwiler, Ross, Was	UR	L	1	1	0	1	0.4	0	0		0 - 0	0 - 0	0 - 0	0	0	0	0	0		.250	.00

Pitchers Hitting, Fielding & Holding Runners, and Hitters Pitching

One of the perils of interleague play is that American League pitchers, when playing in a National League park, have to get up there and take their cuts with the other eight defensive positions: They can't hide behind a designated hitter. Usually these at-bats work out more or less as you'd imagine. The pitcher goes to the plate, watches three fastballs cruise past, then goes back to the dugout and sits down again.

But sometimes there are consequences. Just ask Toronto Blue Jays reliever Scott Downs. He was the team's closer midway through June, racking up eight saves, until he sprained his big toe in a 10th-inning at-bat. After two stints on the disabled list, he eventually lost the closer's job. It was his only at-bat in 2009, and it dropped his career batting average from .068 to .067 (3-for-45).

In this section, you can see how pitchers fared when it was time to take their turn at the plate. The Houston Astros' Mike Hampton got healthy enough to log over 100 innings in 2009. But who besides Mike Hampton knows he's a lifetime .246 hitter with 16 homers and 79 RBI? His .324 batting average in 2009 paced all pitchers with more than 25 at-bats.

We also have 2009 fielding statistics for pitchers and data on how well they held runners last season. It can be quite interesting to compare pitchers in their ability to control the running game. Mark Buehrle only allowed four steals, but also caught four attempting to steal (all on his own throws to first) and directly picked off four more. In less than half of Buehrle's innings, San Diego's Chris Young allowed 20 steals, caught none (either by his catcher or his own throw to first) and picked off just one.

And you can see how hitters pitch. Not too well is the answer. Nine hitters pitched a collective 11.0 innings with a 12.27 ERA.

All active position players who have pitched have their career pitching statistics listed, as well as any 2009 pitching statistics that they may have accrued. The Royals' Tony Pena is not included because he converted to pitching during the season. His entire pitching record is in the Register.

Pitchers Hitting, Fielding and Holding Runners

Pitcher	T	2009 Hitting						Career Hitting										2009 Fielding and Holding Runners											
		Avg	AB	H	HR	RBI	SH	Avg	AB	H	2B	3B	HR	RBI	BB	SO	SH	G	Inn	PO	A	E	DP	Pct	SBA	CS	PCS	PPO	CS%
Aardsma,David, Sea	R	-	0	0	0	0	0	.000	3	0	0	0	0	0	0	1	1	73	71.1	2	5	0	1	1.000	4	2	0	0	.50
Abreu,Winston, TB-Cle	R	-	0	0	0	0	0	.000	2	0	0	0	0	0	0	1	0	5	6.0	0	1	0	0	1.000	1	0	0	0	.00
Accardo,Jeremy, Tor	R	-	0	0	0	0	0	.143	7	1	0	0	0	0	0	1	0	26	24.2	0	3	0	0	1.000	5	3	0	0	.60
Aceves,Alfredo, NYY	R	.000	2	0	0	0	0	.000	2	0	0	0	0	0	0	1	0	43	84.0	2	9	2	1	.846	12	2	1	0	.17
Acosta,Manny, Atl	R	.000	1	0	0	0	0	.000	6	0	0	0	0	0	1	4	0	36	37.1	2	9	1	1	.917	5	1	0	0	.20
Adams,Mike, SD	R	-	0	0	0	0	0	.000	2	0	0	0	0	0	0	0	0	37	37.0	4	2	0	0	1.000	3	1	0	0	.33
Adenhart,Nick, LAA	R	-	0	0	0	0	0	-	0	0	0	0	0	0	0	0	0	1	6.0	0	0	0	0	-	0	0	0	0	-
Affeldt,Jeremy, SF	L	.500	2	1	0	0	0	.250	12	3	0	0	0	2	1	2	0	74	62.1	4	12	1	2	.941	5	1	1	0	.20
Albaladejo,J, NYY	R	-	0	0	0	0	0	-	0	0	0	0	0	0	0	0	0	32	34.1	1	7	0	0	1.000	5	2	1	0	.40
Albers,Matt, Bal	R	.000	1	0	0	0	0	.059	34	2	0	0	0	0	0	21	3	56	67.0	4	6	0	0	1.000	12	3	0	0	.25
Anderson,Brett, Oak	L	.000	3	0	0	0	0	.000	3	0	0	0	0	0	0	2	0	30	175.1	0	29	0	5	1.000	18	4	4	0	.22
Aquino,Greg, Cle	R	-	0	0	0	0	0	.000	2	0	0	0	0	0	0	0	0	10	16.0	2	4	0	0	1.000	1	0	0	1	.00
Arias,Alberto, Hou	R	.000	1	0	0	0	0	.000	6	0	0	0	0	0	1	5	0	42	45.2	5	9	3	2	.824	3	0	0	0	.00
Arredondo,Jose, LAA	R	-	0	0	0	0	0	-	0	0	0	0	0	0	0	0	0	43	45.0	5	3	0	0	1.000	3	1	0	0	.33
Arroyo,Bronson, Cin	R	.113	62	7	0	0	14	.128	329	42	13	0	4	16	10	142	42	33	220.1	18	31	2	3	.961	18	6	1	0	.33
Ascanio,Jose, ChC-Pit	R	.000	2	0	0	0	0	.000	2	0	0	0	0	0	0	1	0	16	18.0	1	1	0	0	1.000	4	1	0	0	.25
Atkins,Mitch, ChC	R	-	0	0	0	0	0	-	0	0	0	0	0	0	0	0	0	2	2.0	0	0	0	0	-	0	0	0	0	-
Augenstein,Bryan, Ari	R	.000	3	0	0	0	0	.000	3	0	0	0	0	0	1	1	0	7	17.0	0	5	1	0	.833	1	0	0	0	.00
Axford,John, Mil	R	-	0	0	0	0	0	-	0	0	0	0	0	0	0	0	0	7	7.2	1	0	0	0	1.000	1	0	0	0	.00
Ayala,Luis, Min-Fla	R	-	0	0	0	0	1	.286	14	4	1	0	0	0	3	3	0	38	40.0	2	7	0	0	1.000	7	2	1	0	.29
Backe,Brandon, Hou	R	.000	1	0	0	0	0	.256	133	34	5	2	4	16	10	48	13	5	13.0	0	2	0	0	1.000	1	0	0	0	.00
Badenhop,Burke, Fla	R	.000	10	0	0	1	3	.045	22	1	0	0	0	1	0	12	5	35	72.0	4	11	0	1	1.000	4	0	0	0	.00
Baez,Danys, Bal	R	1.000	1	1	0	0	0	.250	4	1	0	0	0	0	0	0	0	59	71.2	9	11	0	1	1.000	4	0	0	0	.00
Bailey,Andrew, Oak	R	-	0	0	0	0	0	-	0	0	0	0	0	0	0	0	0	68	83.1	7	9	1	0	.941	1	0	0	0	.00
Bailey,Homer, Cin	R	.079	38	3	0	2	5	.119	59	7	2	0	0	4	0	27	8	20	113.1	13	11	2	0	.923	15	5	0	1	.33
Baker,Scott, Min	R	.000	6	0	0	0	0	.059	17	1	0	0	0	0	0	6	3	33	200.0	9	17	0	1	1.000	13	3	0	1	.23
Bale,John, KC	L	-	0	0	0	0	0	.118	17	2	0	0	0	0	0	8	0	43	28.1	3	5	1	1	.889	4	0	0	0	.00
Balester,Collin, Was	R	.125	8	1	0	0	2	.174	23	4	0	0	0	1	2	10	10	7	30.1	1	0	1	0	.500	2	2	0	0	1.00
Balfour,Grant, TB	R	-	0	0	0	0	0	.000	1	0	0	0	0	0	0	1	0	73	67.1	1	3	0	1	1.000	7	1	0	0	.14
Banks,Josh, SD	R	.000	4	0	0	0	0	.111	27	3	0	0	0	0	4	6	2	6	22.2	0	6	0	1	1.000	6	2	0	0	.33
Bannister,Brian, KC	R	.200	5	1	0	1	0	.292	24	7	3	0	0	3	0	6	2	26	154.0	10	24	0	1	1.000	16	1	0	0	.06
Bard,Daniel, Bos	R	-	0	0	0	0	0	-	0	0	0	0	0	0	0	0	0	49	49.1	4	2	2	1	.750	4	0	0	0	.00
Bass,Brian, Bal	R	.000	1	0	0	0	0	.000	1	0	0	0	0	0	0	1	0	48	86.1	6	18	3	0	.889	10	5	2	1	.50
Bastardo,Antonio, Phi	L	.000	6	0	0	0	1	.000	6	0	0	0	0	0	0	3	1	6	23.2	0	2	0	0	1.000	3	1	1	0	.33
Batista,Miguel, Sea	R	.000	1	0	0	0	0	.093	291	27	5	0	2	9	11	162	24	56	71.1	4	8	0	0	1.000	9	2	0	0	.22
Bautista,Denny, Pit	R	-	0	0	0	0	0	.143	7	1	0	0	0	1	0	4	0	14	13.2	1	2	0	0	1.000	1	1	0	0	1.00
Bazardo,Yorman, Hou	R	.000	10	0	0	0	0	.000	11	0	0	0	0	0	0	4	0	10	32.0	7	6	2	0	.867	2	0	0	0	.00
Beckett,Josh, Bos	R	.200	5	1	1	1	0	.148	216	32	9	0	3	16	10	80	26	32	212.1	11	14	2	2	.926	18	3	0	0	.17
Bedard,Erik, Sea	L	-	0	0	0	0	0	.267	15	4	0	0	0	1	1	6	1	15	83.0	4	6	0	0	1.000	8	3	1	0	.38
Beimel,Joe, Was-Col	L	-	0	0	0	0	0	.233	43	10	1	0	0	1	2	17	6	71	55.1	3	8	3	0	.786	3	1	0	0	.33
Belisario,Ronald, LAD	R	.000	4	0	0	0	0	.000	4	0	0	0	0	0	0	3	0	69	70.2	3	8	1	0	.917	7	1	0	0	.14
Belisle,Matt, Col	R	.000	3	0	0	0	1	.068	74	5	1	0	0	1	3	43	15	24	31.0	4	4	0	2	1.000	4	0	0	0	.00
Bell,Heath, SD	R	-	0	0	0	0	1	.000	5	0	0	0	0	0	0	2	1	68	69.2	7	9	0	1	1.000	6	1	0	1	.17
Bell,Trevor, LAA	R	-	0	0	0	0	0	-	0	0	0	0	0	0	0	0	0	8	20.1	1	1	0	0	1.000	2	1	0	0	.50
Bennett,Jeff, Atl-TB	R	.000	2	0	0	0	0	.118	17	2	1	0	0	1	2	7	1	44	46.2	1	5	1	1	.857	4	1	1	0	.25
Benson,Kris, Tex	R	-	0	0	0	0	0	.130	316	41	7	0	1	22	15	126	46	8	22.1	2	1	0	0	1.000	0	0	0	0	-
Berg,Justin, ChC	R	-	0	0	0	0	0	-	0	0	0	0	0	0	0	0	0	11	12.0	0	3	0	0	1.000	1	0	0	0	.00
Bergesen,Brad, Bal	R	.200	5	1	0	0	2	.200	5	1	0	0	0	0	0	0	2	19	123.1	13	26	2	1	1.000	4	3	0	0	.75
Bergmann,Jason, Was	R	.000	2	0	0	0	1	.067	90	6	0	0	0	3	39	11	56	44.0	0	3	2	0	.600	5	1	0	0	.20
Berken,Jason, Bal	R	.000	1	0	0	0	0	.000	1	0	0	0	0	0	0	1	0	24	119.2	4	16	2	3	.909	15	3	0	0	.20
Betancourt,R., Cle-Col	R	-	0	0	0	0	0	.000	1	0	0	0	0	0	0	1	0	61	56.0	3	2	0	0	1.000	9	1	0	0	.11
Billingsley,Chad, LAD	R	.179	56	10	1	4	7	.123	179	22	3	0	1	11	11	94	17	33	196.1	11	22	4	1	.892	16	9	1	0	.56
Blackburn,Nick, Min	R	.000	4	0	0	0	0	.143	7	1	0	0	0	0	2	0	0	33	205.2	25	23	1	2	.980	14	2	1	2	.14
Blanton,Joe, Phi	R	.127	55	7	0	1	9	.111	81	9	0	0	0	2	4	36	18	31	195.1	12	23	0	2	1.000	12	4	0	0	.33
Blevins,Jerry, Oak	L	-	0	0	0	0	0	-	0	0	0	0	0	0	0	0	0	20	22.1	0	1	0	0	1.000	0	0	0	0	-
Boggs,Mitchell, StL	R	.071	14	1	0	0	3	.045	22	1	1	0	0	0	0	11	3	16	58.0	6	10	0	1	1.000	5	2	1	0	.40
Bonderman,Jeremy, Det	R	-	0	0	0	0	0	.038	26	1	0	0	0	0	0	15	1	8	10.1	0	0	0	0	-	2	1	0	0	.50
Bonine,Eddie, Det	R	-	0	0	0	0	0	.000	2	0	0	0	0	0	0	0	0	10	34.1	3	3	0	1	1.000	4	4	0	0	1.00
Bootcheck,Chris, Pit	R	.000	2	0	0	0	0	.000	2	0	0	0	0	0	0	2	0	13	14.2	1	2	1	0	.750	2	0	0	0	.00
Bowden,Michael, Bos	R	-	0	0	0	0	0	-	0	0	0	0	0	0	0	0	0	4	8.1	1	1	0	0	1.000	1	0	0	0	.00
Boyer,Blaine, Atl-StL-Ari	R	.000	4	0	0	0	0	.000	6	0	0	0	0	0	5	1	48	54.2	4	5	3	0	.750	7	1	0	0	.14
Braden,Dallas, Oak	L	.000	3	0	0	0	1	.000	3	0	0	0	0	0	0	2	1	22	136.2	6	15	3	1	.875	2	2	1	1	1.00
Bradford,Chad, TB	R	-	0	0	0	0	0	-	0	0	0	0	0	0	0	0	0	20	10.1	1	1	0	0	1.000	3	0	0	0	.00
Breslow,Craig, Min-Oak	L	-	0	0	0	0	0	.000	1	0	0	0	0	0	0	1	0	77	69.2	5	7	0	0	1.000	13	5	3	0	.38
Broadway,L., CWS-NYM	R	-	0	0	0	0	0	-	0	0	0	0	0	0	0	0	0	16	30.2	2	7	1	0	.900	2	1	0	0	.50
Brocail,Doug, Hou	R	-	0	0	0	0	0	.174	69	12	0	1	0	1	0	19	16	20	17.2	3	4	0	1	1.000	3	1	0	0	.33
Broxton,Jonathan, LAD	R	.000	1	0	0	0	0	.000	5	0	0	0	0	0	2	2	1	73	76.0	2	7	0	0	1.000	8	1	0	0	.13
Bruney,Brian, NYY	R	-	0	0	0	0	0	.000	1	0	0	0	0	0	0	0	0	44	39.0	0	3	0	0	1.000	2	0	0	0	.00

Pitchers Hitting, Fielding and Holding Runners

Pitcher	T	2009 Hitting						Career Hitting										2009 Fielding and Holding Runners											
		Avg	AB	H	HR	RBI	SH	Avg	AB	H	2B	3B	HR	RBI	BB	SO	SH	G	Inn	PO	A	E	DP	Pct	SBA	CS	PCS	PPO	CS%
Buchholz,Clay, Bos	R	-	0	0	0	0	0	-	0	0	0	0	0	0	0	0	0	16	92.0	8	8	1	0	.941	6	0	0	0	.00
Buckner,Billy, Ari	R	.238	21	5	0	6	2	.227	22	5	2	0	0	6	0	8	2	16	77.1	5	7	1	0	.923	6	2	1	1	.33
Buehrle,Mark, CWS	L	.250	4	1	1	1	1	.100	40	4	0	0	1	2	1	21	7	33	213.1	13	41	1	5	.982	8	4	4	4	.50
Bulger,Jason, LAA	R	-	0	0	0	0	0	-	0	0	0	0	0	0	0	0	0	64	65.2	5	8	1	2	.929	3	0	0	0	.00
Bullington,Bryan, Tor	R	-	0	0	0	0	0	.333	3	1	0	0	0	0	0	1	1	4	6.0	0	0	0	0	-	0	0	0	0	
Bumgarner,Madison, SF	L	.000	2	0	0	0	0	.000	2	0	0	0	0	0	0	1	0	4	10.0	0	3	0	0	1.000	0	0	0	0	
Burke,Greg, SD	R	-	0	0	0	0	0	-	0	0	0	0	0	0	0	0	0	48	45.2	4	5	0	0	1.000	3	2	0	0	.67
Burnett,A.J., NYY	R	.200	5	1	0	0	0	.132	266	35	6	3	3	9	12	126	34	33	207.0	5	20	3	0	.893	35	12	2	2	.34
Burnett,Sean, Pit-Was	L	.000	2	0	0	0	0	.036	28	1	1	0	0	0	2	9	2	71	57.2	12	12	1	0	.960	8	1	1	0	.13
Burns,Mike, Mil	R	.077	13	1	0	2	3	.077	13	1	0	0	0	2	2	7	3	15	51.2	2	2	0	0	1.000	0	0	0	0	
Burres,Brian, Tor	L	-	0	0	0	0	0	.500	2	1	0	0	0	1	0	1	1	2	6.1	0	4	0	0	1.000	1	0	0	0	
Burton,Jared, Cin	R	.000	1	0	0	0	0	.000	2	0	0	0	0	0	0	2	0	53	59.1	2	7	2	0	.818	4	0	0	1	.00
Bush,David, Mil	R	.118	34	4	0	0	2	.129	210	27	6	0	0	11	5	73	22	22	114.1	5	8	0	2	1.000	16	4	0	0	.25
Butler,Josh, Mil	R	-	0	0	0	0	0	-	0	0	0	0	0	0	0	0	0	3	4.0	0	0	0	0	-	0	0	0	0	
Byrd,Paul, Bos	R	-	0	0	0	0	0	.154	156	24	0	0	0	10	12	39	27	7	34.0	2	5	0	1	1.000	3	1	0	0	.33
Byrdak,Tim, Hou	L	.000	3	0	0	0	0	.182	11	2	1	0	0	0	0	3	0	76	61.1	6	10	0	0	1.000	6	4	2	0	.67
Cabrera,Daniel, Was-Ari	R	.000	12	0	0	0	2	.000	26	0	0	0	0	0	2	24	3	15	51.0	1	2	0	0	1.000	4	1	0	0	.25
Cabrera,Fernando, Bos	R	-	0	0	0	0	0	-	0	0	0	0	0	0	0	0	0	6	5.1	0	0	0	0	-	2	0	0	0	.00
Cahill,Trevor, Oak	R	.500	2	1	0	0	0	.500	2	1	0	0	0	0	0	0	0	32	178.2	6	29	1	1	.972	27	10	2	0	.37
Cain,Matt, SF	R	.150	60	9	0	3	9	.116	251	29	6	1	4	11	11	131	31	33	217.2	17	22	0	1	1.000	20	9	0	0	.45
Calero,Kiko, Fla	R	-	0	0	0	0	0	.167	6	1	0	0	0	1	0	2	0	67	60.0	4	10	0	0	1.000	10	3	3	1	.30
Cameron,Kevin, Oak	R	-	0	0	0	0	0	.000	5	0	0	0	0	0	0	4	0	11	18.1	1	1	1	0	.667	2	1	0	0	.50
Camp,Shawn, Tor	R	-	0	0	0	0	0	-	0	0	0	0	0	0	0	0	1	59	79.2	8	10	2	2	.900	1	1	0	0	1.00
Campillo,Jorge, Atl	R	-	0	0	0	0	0	.178	45	8	1	0	0	1	1	16	5	5	4.1	1	1	0	0	1.000	2	2	1	0	1.00
Capps,Matt, Pit	R	-	0	0	0	0	0	.250	4	1	0	0	0	0	1	2	0	57	54.1	4	5	1	1	.900	6	0	0	0	.00
Caridad,Esmailin, ChC	R	.000	2	0	0	0	0	.000	2	0	0	0	0	0	0	0	0	14	19.1	0	2	1	0	.667	1	1	0	1	1.00
Carlson,Jesse, Tor	L	-	0	0	0	0	0	-	0	0	0	0	0	0	0	0	0	73	67.2	10	9	0	1	1.000	4	1	0	0	.25
Carlyle,Buddy, Atl	R	.000	2	0	0	0	0	.161	56	9	0	0	0	4	3	17	7	16	21.1	1	3	0	0	1.000	0	0	0	0	-
Carmona,Fausto, Cle	R	-	0	0	0	0	0	.000	7	0	0	0	0	0	0	1	1	24	125.1	10	19	0	2	1.000	12	4	0	0	.33
Carpenter,Chris, StL	R	.175	63	11	1	7	3	.110	290	32	5	0	1	12	9	92	28	28	192.2	21	19	0	2	1.000	6	4	1	0	.67
Carpenter,Drew, Phi	R	.000	3	0	0	0	0	.000	3	0	0	0	0	0	0	1	0	3	5.2	1	1	0	0	1.000	1	0	0	0	.00
Carrasco,Carlos, Cle	R	-	0	0	0	0	0	-	0	0	0	0	0	0	0	0	0	5	22.1	1	7	1	0	.889	6	3	2	1	.50
Carrasco,D.J., CWS	R	-	0	0	0	0	0	.000	9	0	0	0	0	0	0	2	1	49	93.1	2	23	1	2	.962	4	3	1	1	.75
Carrillo,Cesar, SD	R	.000	3	0	0	0	0	.000	3	0	0	0	0	0	0	1	0	3	10.1	1	2	0	1	1.000	0	0	0	0	-
Casilla,Santiago, Oak	R	-	0	0	0	0	0	-	0	0	0	0	0	0	0	0	0	46	48.1	2	5	1	1	.875	5	2	1	0	.40
Castillo,Alberto, Bal	L	-	0	0	0	0	0	-	0	0	0	0	0	0	0	0	0	20	12.0	2	3	0	0	1.000	1	1	1	1	1.00
Cecil,Brett, Tor	L	.000	2	0	0	0	0	.000	2	0	0	0	0	0	0	2	0	18	93.1	1	9	1	0	.909	8	4	0	0	.50
Chacin,Jhoulys, Col	R	-	0	0	0	0	0	-	0	0	0	0	0	0	0	0	0	9	11.0	0	2	0	0	1.000	4	1	0	0	.25
Chamberlain,Joba, NYY	R	.000	2	0	0	0	1	.000	5	0	0	0	0	0	1	1	2	32	157.1	8	28	2	4	.947	34	8	1	0	.24
Chavez,Jesse, Pit	R	.000	1	0	0	0	0	.000	1	0	0	0	0	0	0	1	0	73	67.1	6	5	0	1	1.000	3	0	0	0	.00
Chen,Bruce, KC	L	1.000	1	1	0	0	0	.138	116	16	1	0	0	3	3	53	17	17	62.1	3	9	1	0	.923	8	4	4	0	.50
Choate,Randy, TB	L	-	0	0	0	0	0	.000	5	0	0	0	0	0	0	3	0	61	36.1	1	9	0	1	1.000	3	1	0	0	.33
Chulk,Vinnie, Cle	R	-	0	0	0	0	0	.250	4	1	0	0	0	0	0	0	0	8	12.0	1	2	1	0	.750	0	0	0	0	-
Claggett,Anthony, NYY-Pit	R	-	0	0	0	0	0	-	0	0	0	0	0	0	0	0	0	3	3.2	0	0	0	0	-	0	0	0	0	-
Clippard,Tyler, Was	R	.000	7	0	0	0	0	.200	10	2	1	0	0	0	0	5	1	41	60.1	5	4	0	1	1.000	2	1	0	0	.50
Coffey,Todd, Mil	R	.000	3	0	0	0	3	.000	6	0	0	0	0	0	0	5	3	78	83.2	3	4	0	1	1.000	4	1	0	0	.25
Coke,Phil, NYY	L	.000	1	0	0	0	0	.000	1	0	0	0	0	0	0	1	0	72	60.0	3	9	2	0	.857	4	2	0	0	.50
Colome,Jesus, Was-Mil	R	-	0	0	0	0	0	.000	2	0	0	0	0	0	0	2	0	21	21.1	0	1	1	0	.500	5	0	0	0	.00
Colon,Bartolo, CWS	R	-	0	0	0	0	0	.118	85	10	0	0	0	5	0	49	5	12	62.1	1	12	1	0	.929	0	0	0	1	-
Colon,Roman, KC	R	-	0	0	0	0	0	.000	7	0	0	0	0	0	0	5	1	43	50.1	8	4	1	0	.923	8	1	0	0	.13
Condrey,Clay, Phi	R	-	0	0	0	0	0	.120	25	3	1	0	0	0	0	15	0	45	42.0	5	3	0	1	1.000	2	0	0	0	.00
Contreras,Jose, CWS-Col	R	.000	9	0	0	0	1	.000	29	0	0	0	0	0	3	18	1	28	131.2	4	17	4	1	.840	26	3	0	0	.10
Cook,Aaron, Col	R	.114	44	5	0	6	5	.153	308	47	5	1	0	16	21	102	61	27	158.0	19	35	4	4	.931	8	4	0	3	.50
Corcoran,Roy, Sea	R	-	0	0	0	0	0	.000	3	0	0	0	0	0	1	3	0	16	19.0	0	2	0	1	1.000	2	1	0	0	.50
Cordero,Francisco, Cin	R	-	0	0	0	0	0	.000	2	0	0	0	0	0	0	1	0	68	66.2	5	8	0	1	1.000	7	4	1	0	.57
Cormier,Lance, TB	R	-	0	0	0	0	0	.109	46	5	1	0	0	2	2	17	4	53	77.1	9	16	1	1	.962	7	1	0	0	.14
Corpas,Manny, Col	R	-	0	0	0	0	0	.000	1	0	0	0	0	0	0	0	0	35	33.2	2	2	0	0	1.000	2	1	0	0	.50
Correia,Kevin, SD	R	.145	55	8	0	0	11	.122	139	17	2	0	0	4	8	56	19	33	198.0	22	22	2	1	.957	14	7	1	0	.50
Cotts,Neal, ChC	L	-	0	0	0	0	0	.500	2	1	1	0	0	0	0	1	0	19	11.0	0	2	0	1	1.000	1	0	0	0	.00
Crain,Jesse, Min	R	-	0	0	0	0	0	-	0	0	0	0	0	0	0	0	0	56	51.2	6	8	0	1	1.000	5	1	0	1	.20
Cruz,Juan, KC	R	-	0	0	0	0	0	.114	70	8	1	1	0	2	4	28	7	46	50.1	1	5	0	0	1.000	5	3	0	0	.60
Cueto,Johnny, Cin	R	.130	46	6	0	1	10	.088	91	8	0	0	0	2	5	32	18	30	171.1	7	12	2	2	.905	7	5	2	0	.71
Daley,Matt, Col	R	-	0	0	0	0	0	-	0	0	0	0	0	0	0	0	0	57	51.0	2	4	0	0	1.000	2	0	0	0	.00
Danks,John, CWS	L	.000	2	0	0	0	1	.100	10	1	0	0	0	0	1	5	1	32	200.1	7	33	2	1	.952	25	7	4	2	.28
Davidson,Daniel, LAA	L	-	0	0	0	0	0	-	0	0	0	0	0	0	0	0	0	4	1.2	0	0	0	0	-	1	0	0	0	.00
Davidson,Dave, Fla	L	1.000	1	1	0	0	0	1.000	1	1	0	0	0	0	0	0	0	1	1.0	0	0	0	0	-	0	0	0	0	-
Davies,Kyle, KC	R	.000	1	0	0	0	1	.134	67	9	1	0	2	9	4	24	15	22	123.0	10	10	2	1	.909	21	4	0	0	.19
Davis,Doug, Ari	L	.159	63	10	0	3	6	.087	389	34	4	2	0	12	4	166	44	34	203.1	4	23	5	0	.844	17	6	4	3	.35
Davis,Wade, TB	R	-	0	0	0	0	0	-	0	0	0	0	0	0	0	0	0	6	36.1	1	9	0	0	1.000	5	1	0	0	.20
de la Cruz,Eulogio, SD	R	-	0	0	0	0	0	.000	2	0	0	0	0	0	0	2	0	3	3.1	1	1	0	1	1.000	1	0	0	0	.00

Pitchers Hitting, Fielding and Holding Runners

Pitcher	T	2009 Hitting Avg	AB	H	HR	RBI	SH	Career Hitting Avg	AB	H	2B	3B	HR	RBI	BB	SO	SH	2009 Fielding and Holding Runners G	Inn	PO	A	E	DP	Pct	SBA	CS	PCS	PPO	CS%
de la Rosa,Jorge, Col	L	.123	57	7	0	3	5	.115	113	13	2	0	0	9	1	55	10	33	185.0	11	22	5	3	.868	19	3	2	0	.16
Delcarmen,Manny, Bos	R	-	0	0	0	0	0	-	0	0	0	0	0	0	0	0	0	64	59.2	2	4	1	0	.857	10	1	0	0	.10
Dempster,Ryan, ChC	R	.125	64	8	0	5	7	.096	439	42	8	1	0	14	12	174	58	31	200.0	17	33	3	5	.943	27	11	0	0	.41
Dessens,Elmer, NYM	R	-	0	0	0	0	0	.163	240	39	4	1	0	16	22	65	38	28	32.2	4	6	0	0	1.000	0	0	0	0	-
Detwiler,Ross, Was	L	.053	19	1	0	1	0	.053	19	1	0	0	0	1	0	12	0	15	75.2	5	13	0	1	1.000	9	3	3	0	.33
Dickey,R.A., Min	R	-	0	0	0	0	0	.400	5	2	0	0	0	0	0	0	0	35	64.1	6	8	1	0	.933	6	1	0	1	.17
DiFelice,Mark, Mil	R	.000	1	0	0	0	0	.000	1	0	0	0	0	0	0	1	2	59	51.2	1	6	1	0	.875	2	0	0	0	.00
Dillard,Tim, Mil	R	.000	1	0	0	0	0	.500	2	1	0	0	0	0	0	1	0	2	4.1	1	0	0	0	1.000	0	0	0	0	-
DiNardo,Lenny, KC	L	-	0	0	0	0	0	.200	5	1	0	0	0	0	0	3	0	5	21.1	0	1	0	0	1.000	1	0	0	0	.00
Dolsi,Freddy, Det	R	-	0	0	0	0	0	.000	1	0	0	0	0	0	0	1	0	6	10.2	0	0	1	0	.000	2	1	0	0	.50
Donnelly,Brendan, Fla	R	-	0	0	0	0	0	.000	1	0	0	0	0	0	0	0	0	30	25.1	0	2	0	0	1.000	2	0	0	0	.00
Dotel,Octavio, CWS	R	-	0	0	0	0	0	.068	74	5	0	0	0	1	5	42	9	62	62.1	2	3	1	0	.833	19	5	1	0	.26
Downs,Scott, Tor	L	.000	1	0	0	0	0	.067	45	3	0	0	0	1	3	17	10	48	46.2	4	9	0	1	1.000	2	1	0	0	.50
Duensing,Brian, Min	L	-	0	0	0	0	0	-	0	0	0	0	0	0	0	0	0	24	84.0	6	17	0	2	1.000	4	3	2	0	.75
Duke,Zach, Pit	L	.200	60	12	0	5	14	.188	245	46	5	0	0	17	9	92	32	32	213.0	16	35	2	5	.962	15	8	4	0	.53
Dumatrait,Phil, Pit	L	-	0	0	0	0	0	.037	27	1	0	0	0	1	0	11	5	15	13.0	2	0	0	0	1.000	1	1	0	0	1.00
Dunn,Mike, NYY	L	-	0	0	0	0	0	-	0	0	0	0	0	0	0	0	0	4	4.0	0	0	0	0	-	0	0	0	0	-
Durbin,Chad, Phi	R	.143	7	1	0	0	0	.091	22	2	0	0	0	1	0	6	1	59	69.2	6	4	0	0	1.000	6	1	0	0	.17
Eaton,Adam, Bal-Col	R	-	0	0	0	1	0	.194	341	66	16	1	3	26	33	113	26	12	49.0	1	3	0	0	1.000	9	0	0	0	.00
Egbert,Jack, CWS	R	-	0	0	0	0	0	-	0	0	0	0	0	0	0	0	0	2	2.2	0	4	0	0	1.000	0	0	0	0	-
Ekstrom,Mike, SD	R	.000	1	0	0	0	1	.000	2	0	0	0	0	0	0	1	1	12	18.1	1	1	0	0	1.000	4	0	0	0	.00
Elbert,Scott, LAD	L	.200	5	1	0	1	0	.167	6	1	1	0	0	1	0	2	0	19	19.2	0	2	0	0	1.000	2	1	0	0	.50
Embree,Alan, Col	L	-	0	0	0	0	0	.000	3	0	0	0	0	0	1	2	0	36	24.2	3	4	0	0	1.000	6	3	2	0	.50
Escalona,Sergio, Phi	L	-	0	0	0	0	0	-	0	0	0	0	0	0	0	0	0	14	13.2	0	0	0	0	-	1	0	0	0	.00
Escobar,Kelvim, LAA	R	-	0	0	0	0	0	.111	27	3	0	0	0	1	0	13	2	1	5.0	2	0	0	0	1.000	3	1	0	0	.33
Estrada,Marco, Was	R	-	0	0	0	0	2	-	0	0	0	0	0	0	1	0	3	4	7.1	0	0	0	0	-	0	0	0	0	-
Eveland,Dana, Oak	L	-	0	0	0	0	0	.083	12	1	0	0	0	1	6	4	0	13	44.0	0	6	1	0	.857	5	0	0	0	.00
Eyre,Scott, Phi	L	-	0	0	0	0	0	.154	13	2	0	0	0	1	6	0	42	30.0	1	2	0	0	1.000	1	0	0	0	.00
Eyre,Willie, Tex	R	-	0	0	0	0	0	.000	1	0	0	0	0	0	0	1	0	17	18.0	0	2	0	0	1.000	1	1	0	0	1.00
Farnsworth,Kyle, KC	R	-	0	0	0	0	0	.074	54	4	1	0	0	3	2	18	8	41	37.1	0	3	1	0	.750	4	2	0	0	.50
Feldman,Scott, Tex	R	.000	5	0	0	0	3	.125	8	1	0	0	0	0	0	2	3	34	189.2	15	27	4	4	.913	22	7	0	0	.32
Feliciano,Pedro, NYM	L	-	0	0	0	0	0	.000	6	0	0	0	0	0	2	2	1	88	59.1	4	17	0	3	1.000	0	0	0	0	-
Feliz,Neftali, Tex	R	-	0	0	0	0	0	-	0	0	0	0	0	0	0	0	0	20	31.0	1	3	1	0	.800	1	0	0	0	.00
Fien,Casey, Det	R	-	0	0	0	0	0	-	0	0	0	0	0	0	0	0	0	9	11.1	0	0	0	0	-	0	0	0	0	-
Figaro,Alfredo, Det	R	.000	2	0	0	0	0	.000	2	0	0	0	0	0	0	2	0	5	17.0	0	2	0	0	1.000	6	0	0	0	.00
Figueroa,Nelson, NYM	R	.136	22	3	0	3	2	.156	90	14	1	1	0	8	5	38	9	16	70.1	4	9	0	0	1.000	6	2	0	0	.33
Fisher,Carlos, Cin	R	.000	1	0	0	0	0	.000	1	0	0	0	0	0	0	1	0	39	52.1	2	7	1	0	.900	6	5	1	1	.83
Fister,Doug, Sea	R	-	0	0	0	0	0	-	0	0	0	0	0	0	0	0	0	11	61.0	6	6	1	1	.923	1	1	0	0	1.00
Flores,Randy, Col	L	-	0	0	0	0	0	.000	8	0	0	0	0	0	0	5	0	27	12.0	1	3	0	0	1.000	1	0	0	0	.00
Floyd,Gavin, CWS	R	.000	1	0	0	0	2	.043	46	2	0	0	0	0	0	26	0	30	193.0	10	21	1	1	.969	18	4	0	0	.22
Fogg,Josh, Col	R	.111	9	1	0	0	2	.119	335	40	4	0	0	11	13	113	55	24	45.2	3	4	1	0	.875	3	0	0	1	.00
Fossum,Casey, NYM	L	-	0	0	0	0	0	.087	46	4	0	0	0	0	1	16	4	3	4.0	0	0	0	0	-	2	0	0	0	.00
Fox,Chad, ChC	R	-	0	0	0	0	0	.000	7	0	0	0	0	0	0	3	1	2	0.1	0	0	0	0	-	0	0	0	0	-
Francisco,Frank, Tex	R	-	0	0	0	0	0	-	0	0	0	0	0	0	0	0	0	51	49.1	1	0	1	0	.500	4	0	0	0	.00
Franklin,Ryan, StL	R	-	0	0	0	0	0	.118	17	2	0	0	0	1	2	8	2	62	61.0	8	5	0	1	1.000	2	1	0	1	.50
Frasor,Jason, Tor	R	-	0	0	0	0	0	-	0	0	0	0	0	0	0	0	0	61	57.2	3	5	0	0	1.000	8	2	0	0	.25
French,Luke, Det-Sea	L	-	0	0	0	0	0	-	0	0	0	0	0	0	0	0	0	15	67.1	2	5	0	0	1.000	3	1	0	1	.33
Frieri,Ernesto, SD	R	-	0	0	0	0	0	-	0	0	0	0	0	0	0	0	0	2	2.0	0	0	0	0	-	0	0	0	0	-
Fuentes,Brian, LAA	L	-	0	0	0	0	0	.000	1	0	0	0	0	0	0	0	0	65	55.0	1	6	0	0	1.000	2	1	1	0	.50
Fulchino,Jeff, Hou	R	.333	3	1	0	0	0	.333	3	1	0	0	0	0	0	0	0	61	82.0	6	7	0	1	1.000	6	2	0	1	.33
Gabino,Armando, Min	R	-	0	0	0	0	0	-	0	0	0	0	0	0	0	0	0	2	3.2	0	1	0	0	.000	0	0	0	0	-
Galarraga,Armando, Det	R	.000	1	0	0	0	0	.000	3	0	0	0	0	0	3	2	1	29	143.2	7	11	2	2	.900	8	5	0	0	.63
Gallagher,Sean, Oak-SD	R	-	0	0	0	0	0	.000	11	0	0	0	0	0	0	6	0	14	19.2	0	3	0	0	1.000	3	1	0	0	.33
Gallardo,Yovani, Mil	R	.172	58	10	2	8	5	.196	107	21	6	0	4	14	3	34	6	30	185.2	7	20	0	1	1.000	21	6	0	0	.10
Garate,Victor, Was	L	-	0	0	0	0	0	-	0	0	0	0	0	0	0	0	0	4	2.0	0	0	0	0	-	0	0	0	0	-
Garcia,Freddy, CWS	R	-	0	0	0	0	0	.207	58	12	2	0	0	4	2	19	13	9	56.0	4	6	0	1	1.000	11	1	0	0	.09
Garland,Jon, Ari-LAD	R	.086	70	6	0	1	3	.101	89	9	0	0	1	5	3	39	10	33	204.0	21	33	4	4	.931	10	2	0	0	.20
Garza,Matt, TB	R	.000	2	0	0	0	0	.000	8	0	0	0	0	0	1	6	2	32	203.0	10	11	1	1	.955	7	4	0	0	.57
Gaudin,Chad, SD-NYY	R	.036	28	1	0	0	1	.031	32	1	0	0	0	0	2	16	3	31	147.1	12	21	2	2	.943	9	5	0	1	.56
Geary,Geoff, Hou	R	-	0	0	0	0	0	.118	17	2	1	0	0	1	1	10	0	16	20.0	0	1	1	0	.500	0	0	0	0	-
Geer,Josh, SD	R	.167	24	4	0	1	5	.152	33	5	1	0	0	2	3	14	5	19	102.2	4	22	1	2	.963	3	1	1	2	.33
Gervacio,Sammy, Hou	R	-	0	0	0	0	0	-	0	0	0	0	0	0	0	0	0	29	21.0	2	0	0	0	1.000	4	1	0	0	.25
Giese,Dan, Oak	R	-	0	0	0	0	0	-	0	0	0	0	0	0	0	0	0	7	22.0	3	2	0	0	1.000	2	0	0	0	.00
Gobble,Jimmy, CWS	L	-	0	0	0	0	0	.000	2	0	0	0	0	0	0	1	1	12	12.0	0	0	0	0	-	0	0	0	0	-
Gonzalez,Edgar, Oak	R	1.000	2	2	0	0	0	.175	63	11	1	0	0	2	0	13	7	26	65.1	2	10	1	1	.923	5	2	0	0	.40
Gonzalez,Enrique, Bos	R	-	0	0	0	0	0	.281	32	9	1	0	3	0	8	3	2	3.2	2	0	0	0	1.000	0	0	0	0	-
Gonzalez,Gio, Oak	L	-	0	0	0	0	0	-	0	0	0	0	0	0	0	0	0	20	98.2	1	14	1	1	.938	6	2	2	0	.33
Gonzalez,Mike, Atl	L	-	0	0	0	0	0	.333	3	1	1	0	0	2	0	0	0	80	74.1	4	11	0	1	1.000	9	2	2	0	.22
Gordon,Tom, Ari	R	-	0	0	0	0	0	.000	2	0	0	0	0	0	0	0	0	3	1.2	1	0	0	0	1.000	0	0	0	0	-
Gorzelanny,Tom, Pit-ChC	L	.143	14	2	0	2	1	.072	125	9	0	0	0	9	6	60	15	22	47.0	1	7	2	1	.800	1	0	0	0	.00

Pitchers Hitting, Fielding and Holding Runners

Pitcher	T	2009 Hitting						Career Hitting										2009 Fielding and Holding Runners											
		Avg	AB	H	HR	RBI	SH	Avg	AB	H	2B	3B	HR	RBI	BB	SO	SH	G	Inn	PO	A	E	DP	Pct	SBA	CS	PCS	PPO	CS%
Gosling,Mike, Cle	L	-	0	0	0	0	0	.000	17	0	0	0	0	0	1	11	2	15	25.0	1	1	1	0	.667	0	0	0	0	-
Grabow,John, Pit-ChC	L	.000	1	0	0	0	1	.000	5	0	0	0	0	0	1	1	1	75	72.1	0	9	1	0	.900	6	1	1	0	.17
Gray,Jeff, Oak	R	-	0	0	0	0	0	-	0	0	0	0	0	0	0	0	0	24	26.1	2	2	0	1	1.000	0	0	0	0	-
Green,Sean, NYM	R	.000	1	0	0	0	0	.000	2	0	0	0	0	0	0	2	0	79	69.2	8	14	2	2	.917	3	1	0	0	.33
Gregerson,Luke, SD	R	.000	1	0	0	0	1	.000	1	0	0	0	0	0	0	1	1	72	75.0	9	9	0	0	1.000	2	1	0	0	.50
Gregg,Kevin, ChC	R	-	0	0	0	0	0	.000	6	0	0	0	0	0	0	5	0	72	68.2	3	0	0	1	1.000	1	0	0	0	.00
Greinke,Zack, KC	R	.167	6	1	0	0	0	.222	18	4	2	0	1	1	0	5	1	33	229.1	11	35	1	4	.979	14	9	1	1	.64
Grilli,Jason, Col-Tex	R	.000	2	0	0	0	0	.214	14	3	0	0	1	3	0	2	3	52	45.2	4	10	1	0	.933	6	1	1	0	.17
Guardado,Eddie, Tex	L	-	0	0	0	0	0	.000	1	0	0	0	0	0	0	0	0	48	38.1	0	4	0	0	1.000	6	2	0	0	.33
Guerrier,Matt, Min	R	-	0	0	0	0	0	.000	2	0	0	0	0	0	0	1	0	79	76.1	8	12	0	1	1.000	6	2	0	0	.33
Guthrie,Jeremy, Bal	R	.000	2	0	0	0	1	.071	14	1	1	0	0	0	0	9	1	33	200.0	10	25	1	3	.972	11	2	0	4	.18
Gutierrez,Juan, Ari	R	-	0	0	0	0	0	.000	6	0	0	0	0	0	0	4	1	65	71.0	1	6	0	0	1.000	12	1	0	1	.08
Guzman,Angel, ChC	R	.000	3	0	0	0	0	.091	22	2	1	0	0	2	0	7	4	55	61.0	4	11	1	0	.938	6	4	0	0	.67
Hacker,Eric, Pit	R	-	0	0	0	0	0	-	0	0	0	0	0	0	0	0	0	3	3.0	1	2	0	0	1.000	0	0	0	0	-
Haeger,Charlie, LAD	R	.000	4	0	0	0	1	.200	5	1	0	0	0	0	0	4	1	6	19.0	0	3	0	0	1.000	3	0	0	0	.00
Halladay,Roy, Tor	R	.000	1	0	0	0	1	.079	38	3	0	0	0	1	0	17	3	32	239.0	26	24	1	2	.980	24	6	0	0	.25
Hamels,Cole, Phi	L	.148	61	9	0	5	7	.163	245	40	7	0	0	13	9	108	22	32	193.2	7	27	0	0	1.000	29	11	5	0	.38
Hammel,Jason, Col	R	.109	55	6	0	0	3	.125	56	7	2	0	0	1	2	25	3	34	176.2	11	20	0	1	1.000	20	2	0	1	.10
Hampton,Mike, Hou	L	.324	37	12	1	7	1	.246	725	178	22	5	16	79	47	195	63	21	112.0	9	17	2	1	.929	7	2	0	0	.29
Hanrahan,Joel, Was-Pit	R	.000	1	0	0	0	0	.235	17	4	2	1	0	3	0	5	4	67	64.0	6	4	1	1	.909	9	3	0	0	.33
Hansen,Craig, Pit	R	-	0	0	0	0	0	-	0	0	0	0	0	0	0	0	0	5	6.1	0	0	0	0	-	1	0	0	0	.00
Hanson,Tommy, Atl	R	.054	37	2	0	0	8	.054	37	2	0	0	0	1	1	20	8	21	127.2	12	16	2	1	.933	26	8	1	0	.31
Happ,J.A., Phi	L	.093	43	4	0	1	7	.078	51	4	1	0	0	1	1	20	9	35	166.0	6	20	0	0	1.000	8	1	1	0	.50
Harang,Aaron, Cin	R	.149	47	7	1	6	6	.090	401	36	4	0	1	15	3	182	35	26	162.1	3	15	2	0	.900	18	5	2	0	.28
Harden,Rich, ChC	R	.186	43	8	0	0	4	.147	75	11	1	0	0	1	1	31	8	26	141.0	7	9	2	2	.889	12	4	0	0	.33
Haren,Dan, Ari	R	.247	73	18	1	10	9	.188	202	38	15	0	1	19	7	56	17	33	229.1	19	24	0	2	1.000	24	6	0	0	.25
Harrison,Matt, Tex	L	.000	1	0	0	0	0	.000	1	0	0	0	0	0	0	0	0	11	63.1	3	13	0	2	1.000	6	3	1	0	.50
Hart,Kevin, ChC-Pit	R	.160	25	4	0	2	1	.133	30	4	0	0	0	2	3	9	1	18	81.0	12	12	1	2	.960	19	3	0	1	.16
Hawkins,LaTroy, Hou	R	-	0	0	0	0	0	.000	6	0	0	0	0	0	0	5	1	65	63.1	8	11	0	0	1.000	8	3	1	0	.38
Hawksworth,Blake, StL	R	-	0	0	0	0	0	-	0	0	0	0	0	0	0	0	0	30	40.0	4	8	0	0	1.000	1	1	0	1	1.00
Hayhurst,Dirk, Tor	R	-	0	0	0	0	0	.000	3	0	0	0	0	0	1	3	0	15	22.2	0	1	0	0	1.000	0	0	0	0	-
Heilman,Aaron, ChC	R	.000	1	0	0	0	0	.022	45	1	0	0	0	1	2	23	5	70	72.1	3	16	0	1	1.000	5	2	0	0	.40
Hendrickson,Mark, Bal	L	-	0	0	0	0	0	.134	97	13	3	1	1	3	6	53	4	53	105.0	6	13	0	1	1.000	15	0	0	0	.00
Henn,Sean, Min-Bal	L	-	0	0	0	0	0	.000	1	0	0	0	0	0	0	0	0	20	14.1	1	1	0	1	1.000	2	1	0	0	.50
Herges,Matt, Cle-Col	R	-	0	0	0	0	0	.167	36	6	0	0	0	1	1	22	2	30	34.2	2	5	1	0	.875	3	1	0	0	.33
Hernandez,David, Bal	R	-	0	0	0	0	0	-	0	0	0	0	0	0	0	0	0	20	101.1	7	7	0	0	1.000	10	2	0	0	.20
Hernandez,Felix, Sea	R	.000	6	0	0	0	0	.133	15	2	0	0	1	5	1	9	2	34	238.2	29	24	1	3	.981	28	8	1	0	.29
Hernandez,L., NYM-Was	R	.148	54	8	0	0	11	.227	862	196	36	2	9	75	8	114	99	31	183.2	11	36	0	3	1.000	17	6	1	2	.35
Herrera,Daniel Ray, Cin	L	.000	2	0	0	0	1	.000	2	0	0	0	0	0	1	1	1	70	61.2	9	9	0	0	1.000	3	2	0	0	.67
Hill,Rich, Bal	L	.125	8	1	0	1	0	.123	114	14	3	0	0	6	2	51	6	14	57.2	1	9	1	0	.909	13	2	2	0	.15
Hill,Shawn, SD	R	.000	4	0	0	0	0	.067	45	3	0	0	0	0	6	19	15	3	12.0	0	1	0	0	1.000	1	0	0	0	.00
Hinckley,Mike, Was	L	.000	1	0	0	0	0	.000	1	0	0	0	0	0	0	1	0	11	9.2	0	3	0	0	1.000	0	0	0	0	-
Hinshaw,Alex, SF	L	-	0	0	0	0	0	-	0	0	0	0	0	0	0	0	0	9	6.0	1	1	0	0	1.000	1	1	1	0	1.00
Hochevar,Luke, KC	R	.000	5	0	0	0	0	.000	8	0	0	0	0	0	0	7	1	25	143.0	10	20	0	1	1.000	23	4	2	2	.17
Hoffman,Trevor, Mil	R	-	0	0	0	0	0	.121	33	4	2	0	0	5	0	10	2	55	54.0	2	3	1	0	.833	1	0	0	0	.00
Holland,Derek, Tex	L	.000	5	0	0	0	1	.000	5	0	0	0	0	0	0	2	1	33	138.1	5	13	5	2	.783	11	3	2	1	.27
Howell,J.P., TB	L	-	0	0	0	0	0	.200	10	2	0	0	0	1	0	4	0	69	66.2	3	8	0	0	1.000	5	2	1	0	.40
Howry,Bob, SF	R	.000	2	0	0	0	1	.200	5	1	0	0	0	0	0	2	1	63	63.2	4	2	0	1	1.000	4	0	0	0	.00
Hudson,Daniel, CWS	R	-	0	0	0	0	0	-	0	0	0	0	0	0	0	0	0	6	18.2	0	3	1	0	.750	4	0	0	0	.00
Hudson,Tim, Atl	R	.333	12	4	1	2	1	.170	283	48	8	1	1	23	13	86	30	7	42.1	3	4	0	1	1.000	5	4	0	0	.80
Huff,David, Cle	L	.000	2	0	0	0	2	.000	2	0	0	0	0	0	0	1	2	23	128.1	7	10	0	0	1.000	8	1	0	0	.13
Hughes,Dustin, KC	L	-	0	0	0	0	0	-	0	0	0	0	0	0	0	0	0	8	14.0	1	0	0	0	1.000	1	1	1	0	.50
Hughes,Phil, NYY	R	-	0	0	0	0	0	-	0	0	0	0	0	0	0	0	0	51	86.0	4	5	0	0	1.000	7	2	0	0	.29
Humber,Phillip, Min	R	-	0	0	0	0	0	.000	1	0	0	0	0	0	0	0	1	8	9.0	0	1	1	0	.500	1	0	0	0	.00
Hunter,Tommy, Tex	R	-	0	0	0	0	0	-	0	0	0	0	0	0	0	0	0	19	112.0	3	14	1	1	.944	12	3	1	0	.25
Isringhausen,Jason, TB	R	-	0	0	0	0	0	.202	104	21	4	1	2	16	5	36	8	9	8.0	0	0	0	0	-	2	0	0	0	.00
Jackson,Edwin, Det	R	.000	4	0	0	0	0	.133	30	4	0	0	0	2	3	10	3	33	214.0	16	11	4	3	.871	32	9	0	0	.28
Jackson,Steven, Pit	R	.000	1	0	0	0	0	.000	1	0	0	0	0	0	0	0	0	40	43.0	3	4	0	1	1.000	5	0	0	0	.00
Jackson,Zach, Cle	L	-	0	0	0	0	0	.111	9	1	0	0	0	0	0	2	4	3	8.2	0	2	0	0	1.000	1	0	0	0	.00
Jakubauskas,Chris, Sea	R	.000	2	0	0	0	0	.000	2	0	0	0	0	0	0	1	0	35	93.0	10	10	2	1	.909	4	2	1	1	.50
Janssen,Casey, Tor	R	.000	1	0	0	0	1	.000	2	0	0	0	0	0	0	1	1	21	40.0	2	6	1	0	.889	1	1	0	1	1.00
Jenks,Bobby, CWS	R	-	0	0	0	0	0	-	0	0	0	0	0	0	0	0	0	52	53.1	1	2	0	0	1.000	9	0	0	0	.00
Jennings,Jason, Tex	R	.000	1	0	0	0	0	.207	329	68	14	0	2	26	19	80	28	44	61.0	1	6	1	0	.875	10	3	0	0	.30
Jepsen,Kevin, LAA	R	-	0	0	0	0	0	-	0	0	0	0	0	0	0	0	0	54	54.2	6	5	0	1	1.000	3	0	0	0	.00
Jimenez,Ubaldo, Col	R	.220	59	13	0	2	12	.124	153	19	0	0	0	2	12	50	23	33	218.0	12	47	2	2	.967	21	6	2	0	.29
Joaquin,Waldis, SF	R	-	0	0	0	0	0	-	0	0	0	0	0	0	0	0	0	10	10.2	0	1	0	0	1.000	3	0	0	0	.00
Johnson,Jim, Bal	R	-	0	0	0	0	0	-	0	0	0	0	0	0	0	0	0	64	70.0	4	10	1	0	.933	5	1	0	0	.20
Johnson,Josh, Fla	R	.194	62	12	3	10	9	.150	140	21	5	0	3	15	8	77	19	33	209.0	17	33	0	1	1.000	26	8	0	0	.31
Johnson,Randy, SF	L	.077	26	2	0	0	1	.125	625	78	14	0	1	40	19	296	44	22	96.0	0	13	1	0	.929	10	3	2	0	.30
Jones,Hunter, Bos	L	-	0	0	0	0	0	-	0	0	0	0	0	0	0	0	0	11	12.2	0	1	0	0	1.000	1	0	0	0	.00

Pitchers Hitting, Fielding and Holding Runners

Pitcher	T	2009 Hitting						Career Hitting										2009 Fielding and Holding Runners											
		Avg	AB	H	HR	RBI	SH	Avg	AB	H	2B	3B	HR	RBI	BB	SO	SH	G	Inn	PO	A	E	DP	Pct	SBA	CS	PCS	PPO	CS%
Julio,Jorge, Mil	R	.000	1	0	0	0	0	.000	2	0	0	0	0	0	2	2	0	15	17.1	1	0	0	0	1.000	3	0	0	0	.00
Jurrjens,Jair, Atl	R	.123	65	8	0	4	7	.114	123	14	2	1	0	4	14	42	14	34	215.0	15	32	4	2	.922	21	7	0	1	.33
Karstens,Jeff, Pit	R	.045	22	1	0	0	1	.083	36	3	0	0	0	0	4	20	3	39	108.0	4	12	0	0	1.000	11	2	0	1	.18
Kawakami,Kenshin, Atl	R	.098	41	4	0	0	5	.098	41	4	0	0	0	0	3	13	5	32	156.1	13	28	1	3	.976	11	5	0	0	.45
Kazmir,Scott, TB-LAA	L	-	0	0	0	0	0	.125	8	1	0	0	0	1	0	3	0	26	147.1	6	12	0	0	1.000	7	3	2	0	.43
Kelley,Shawn, Sea	R	-	0	0	0	0	0	-	0	0	0	0	0	0	0	0	0	41	46.0	1	3	0	0	1.000	2	0	0	0	.00
Kendrick,Kyle, Phi	R	.250	8	2	0	0	1	.134	97	13	1	0	0	4	6	46	12	9	26.1	1	3	1	1	.800	0	0	0	0	-
Kennedy,Ian, NYY	R	-	0	0	0	0	0	-	0	0	0	0	0	0	0	0	0	1	1.0	0	0	0	-		0	0	0	0	-
Kensing,Logan, Fla-Was	R	.000	2	0	0	0	0	.000	8	0	0	0	0	0	0	2	1	32	35.1	0	8	0	0	1.000	4	0	0	0	.00
Keppel,Bobby, Min	R	-	0	0	0	0	0	.000	2	0	0	0	0	0	1	1	0	37	54.0	4	7	0	0	1.000	3	1	0	1	.33
Kershaw,Clayton, LAD	L	.104	48	5	0	2	8	.091	77	7	0	0	0	2	3	29	17	31	171.0	8	19	0	2	1.000	13	7	4	3	.54
Kilby,Brad, Oak	L	-	0	0	0	0	0	-	0	0	0	0	0	0	0	0	0	11	17.0	0	1	0	0	1.000	0	0	0	0	.00
Kinney,Josh, StL	R	.000	1	0	0	0	0	.000	1	0	0	0	0	0	0	1	0	17	15.1	1	0	0	0	1.000	3	0	0	0	.00
Kobayashi,Masa, Cle	R	-	0	0	0	0	0	-	0	0	0	0	0	0	0	0	0	10	9.2	1	2	0	1	1.000	0	0	0	0	-
Korecky,Bobby, Ari	R	-	0	0	0	0	0	1.000	1	1	0	0	0	0	0	0	0	5	6.0	0	1	0	0	1.000	1	0	0	0	.00
Koronka,John, Fla	L	.000	1	0	0	0	1	.000	13	0	0	0	0	0	1	8	1	2	7.1	0	3	2	0	.600	0	0	0	0	-
Kuo,Hong-Chih, LAD	L	-	0	0	0	0	0	.192	26	5	2	0	1	1	0	13	7	35	30.0	0	5	0	0	1.000	2	0	0	0	.00
Kuroda,Hiroki, LAD	R	.143	28	4	0	0	9	.146	82	12	1	0	0	2	7	27	15	21	117.1	8	12	1	0	.952	10	0	1	0	.00
Lackey,John, LAA	R	.125	8	1	0	1	1	.033	30	1	0	0	0	1	0	9	1	27	176.1	13	22	2	3	.946	16	3	0	0	.19
Laffey,Aaron, Cle	L	-	0	0	0	0	0	.500	2	1	0	0	0	0	0	0	0	25	121.2	6	13	1	2	.950	5	4	0	0	.80
Lambert,Chris, Det-Bal	R	-	0	0	0	0	0	-	0	0	0	0	0	0	0	0	0	6	12.1	1	3	0	0	1.000	2	1	0	0	.50
Lannan,John, Was	L	.155	58	9	0	0	5	.103	116	12	2	0	0	1	6	50	11	33	206.1	8	28	0	1	1.000	17	7	3	1	.41
Latos,Mat, SD	R	.053	19	1	0	0	2	.053	19	1	0	0	0	0	0	9	2	10	50.2	3	3	0	0	1.000	7	3	0	0	.43
Leach,Brent, LAD	L	-	0	0	0	0	0	-	0	0	0	0	0	0	0	0	0	38	20.1	2	2	0	0	1.000	1	1	1	0	1.00
League,Brandon, Tor	R	-	0	0	0	0	0	-	0	0	0	0	0	0	0	0	0	67	74.2	10	4	2	2	.875	10	1	0	0	.10
LeBlanc,Wade, SD	L	.077	13	1	0	0	3	.190	21	4	0	0	0	1	6	4	3	9	46.1	1	6	1	0	.875	2	1	1	0	.50
Ledezma,Wil, Was	L	-	0	0	0	0	0	.000	12	0	0	0	0	0	1	6	2	5	5.2	1	0	0	0	1.000	1	0	0	0	.00
Lee,Cliff, Cle-Phi	L	.184	38	7	0	1	2	.138	65	9	2	0	0	1	1	25	2	34	231.2	11	29	2	2	.952	10	3	2	0	.30
Lehr,Justin, Cin	R	.091	22	2	0	1	5	.080	25	2	1	0	0	1	1	10	5	11	65.1	4	12	0	1	1.000	7	1	0	2	.14
Lerew,Anthony, KC	R	-	0	0	0	0	0	.000	3	0	0	0	0	0	0	0	0	3	13.1	2	2	0	1	1.000	1	0	0	0	.00
Leroux,Chris, Fla	R	-	0	0	0	0	0	-	0	0	0	0	0	0	0	0	0	5	6.2	0	1	0	0	1.000	0	0	0	0	-
Lester,Jon, Bos	L	.000	3	0	0	0	2	.000	12	0	0	0	0	0	0	7	2	32	203.1	7	24	2	1	.939	25	6	6	0	.24
Lewis,Jensen, Cle	R	.000	1	0	0	0	0	.000	1	0	0	0	0	0	0	1	0	47	66.1	5	7	0	1	1.000	2	0	0	0	.00
Lewis,Scott, Cle	L	-	0	0	0	0	0	-	0	0	0	0	0	0	0	0	0	1	4.1	0	0	0	0	-	0	0	0	0	-
Lidge,Brad, Phi	R	-	0	0	0	0	0	.286	7	2	1	0	0	2	0	4	0	67	58.2	4	8	2	1	.857	12	1	1	0	.08
Lilly,Ted, ChC	L	.088	57	5	0	2	5	.126	215	27	4	1	0	12	4	98	24	27	177.0	4	16	5	1	.800	16	4	0	1	.25
Lincecum,Tim, SF	R	.152	66	10	0	3	13	.140	179	25	3	1	0	8	13	89	25	32	225.1	13	25	2	3	.950	25	5	0	0	.20
Lincoln,Mike, Cin	R	.000	2	0	0	0	0	.071	14	1	0	0	0	0	0	7	1	19	23.0	2	6	0	1	1.000	2	2	1	0	1.00
Lindstrom,Matt, Fla	R	-	0	0	0	0	0	.000	1	0	0	0	0	0	0	1	0	54	47.1	2	4	2	0	.750	7	2	0	0	.29
Linebrink,Scott, CWS	R	-	0	0	0	0	0	.222	18	4	1	0	0	0	0	10	2	57	56.0	2	5	0	0	1.000	12	1	0	0	.08
Liriano,Francisco, Min	L	.000	5	0	0	0	1	.100	10	1	0	0	0	1	1	6	2	29	136.2	1	15	0	1	1.000	24	9	6	0	.38
Litsch,Jesse, Tor	R	-	0	0	0	0	0	.000	4	0	0	0	0	0	0	0	0	2	9.0	1	1	0	0	1.000	2	1	0	0	.50
Liz,Radhames, Bal	R	-	0	0	0	0	0	.000	6	0	0	0	0	0	0	3	0	2	1.1	0	0	0	-		0	0	0	0	-
Logan,Boone, Atl	L	-	0	0	0	0	0	-	0	0	0	0	0	0	0	0	0	20	17.1	3	2	0	0	1.000	4	0	0	0	.00
Lohse,Kyle, StL	R	.216	37	8	0	2	5	.161	192	31	3	0	0	13	3	57	31	23	117.2	20	13	1	0	.971	5	1	0	0	.20
Looper,Braden, Mil	R	.200	60	12	0	8	11	.215	186	40	6	1	0	18	10	63	30	34	194.2	13	31	2	1	.957	8	3	1	2	.38
Lopez,Arturo, SD	L	-	0	0	0	0	0	-	0	0	0	0	0	0	0	0	0	4	2.1	1	0	0	0	1.000	0	0	0	0	-
Lopez,Javier, Bos	L	-	0	0	0	0	0	.125	8	1	0	0	0	1	0	4	1	14	11.2	2	2	1	0	.800	1	0	0	0	.00
Lopez,Rodrigo, Phi	R	.000	9	0	0	0	0	.039	51	2	0	0	0	0	1	29	2	7	30.0	3	0	0	0	1.000	4	1	0	0	.25
Lopez,Wilton, Hou	R	.000	5	0	0	0	0	.000	5	0	0	0	0	0	0	2	0	8	19.1	1	4	0	0	1.000	1	0	0	0	.00
Loux,Shane, LAA	R	-	0	0	0	0	0	-	0	0	0	0	0	0	0	0	0	18	58.1	6	11	0	0	1.000	10	3	0	0	.30
Lowe,Derek, Atl	R	.222	54	12	0	1	12	.141	327	46	5	0	0	15	20	97	47	34	194.2	17	24	2	1	.953	17	4	0	2	.24
Lowe,Mark, Sea	R	-	0	0	0	0	0	.000	1	0	0	0	0	0	0	1	0	75	80.0	3	5	2	0	.800	4	2	0	0	.50
Lyon,Brandon, Det	R	-	0	0	0	0	0	-	0	0	0	0	0	0	1	0	0	65	78.2	10	16	0	2	1.000	5	2	0	0	.40
MacDougal,M., CWS-Was	R	-	0	0	0	0	0	-	0	0	0	0	0	0	0	0	0	57	54.1	4	6	1	2	.909	6	1	0	0	.17
Madrigal,Warner, Tex	R	-	0	0	0	0	0	-	0	0	0	0	0	0	0	0	0	13	12.2	0	1	0	0	1.000	0	0	0	0	-
Madson,Ryan, Phi	R	-	0	0	0	0	0	.128	47	6	1	0	0	2	2	19	7	79	77.1	5	9	1	0	.933	6	1	1	0	.17
Mahay,Ron, KC-Min	L	-	0	0	0	0	0	.214	28	6	3	0	1	3	1	8	1	57	50.1	5	4	0	0	1.000	1	1	0	0	1.00
Maholm,Paul, Pit	L	.069	58	4	1	2	6	.123	252	31	2	0	1	12	14	130	12	31	194.0	9	39	2	3	.960	21	6	3	1	.29
Maine,John, NYM	R	.148	27	4	0	2	2	.103	156	16	1	0	1	8	11	78	24	15	81.1	8	6	0	0	1.000	9	4	0	0	.44
Maloney,Matt, Cin	L	.250	12	3	0	0	2	.250	12	3	0	0	0	0	1	5	2	7	40.2	0	4	0	0	1.000	5	3	1	0	.60
Manship,Jeff, Min	R	-	0	0	0	0	0	-	0	0	0	0	0	0	0	0	0	11	31.2	3	2	0	0	1.000	6	0	0	0	.00
Manuel,Robert, Cin	R	-	0	0	0	0	0	-	0	0	0	0	0	0	0	0	0	3	4.1	0	0	0	0	-	1	1	0	0	1.00
Marmol,Carlos, ChC	R	-	0	0	0	0	0	.200	30	6	1	0	1	1	0	11	3	79	74.0	1	7	2	1	.800	2	0	0	1	.00
Marquis,Jason, Col	R	.172	64	11	0	8	9	.202	505	102	28	2	5	48	13	123	32	33	216.0	15	39	2	3	.964	22	4	0	0	.18
Marshall,Jay, Oak	L	-	0	0	0	0	0	-	0	0	0	0	0	0	0	0	0	10	7.1	1	1	0	0	1.000	0	0	0	0	-
Marshall,Sean, ChC	L	.231	13	3	0	2	1	.165	97	16	1	0	1	5	2	44	8	55	85.1	7	16	0	0	1.000	4	1	0	0	.25
Marte,Damaso, NYY	L	-	0	0	0	0	0	.000	8	0	0	0	0	0	0	2	0	21	13.1	0	1	0	0	1.000	1	0	0	0	.00
Marte,Victor, KC	R	-	0	0	0	0	0	-	0	0	0	0	0	0	0	0	0	8	12.0	3	0	0	0	1.000	2	2	0	0	1.00
Martin,J.D., Was	R	.160	25	4	0	0	2	.160	25	4	0	0	0	0	1	13	2	15	77.0	8	17	3	0	.893	1	1	0	0	1.00

Pitchers Hitting, Fielding and Holding Runners

Pitcher	T	2009 Hitting Avg	AB	H	HR	RBI	SH	Career Avg	AB	H	2B	3B	HR	RBI	BB	SO	SH	G	Inn	PO	A	E	DP	Pct	SBA	CS	PCS	PPO	CS%
Martinez,Carlos, Fla	R	-	0	0	0	0	0	.000	1	0	0	0	0	0	0	1	0	2	2.1	0	0	0	0	-	1	0	0	0	.00
Martinez,Cristhian, Fla	R	.000	2	0	0	0	0	.000	2	0	0	0	0	0	0	0	0	15	26.1	2	3	1	0	.833	0	0	0	0	-
Martinez,Joe, SF	R	.250	8	2	0	0	1	.250	8	2	1	0	0	0	0	1	1	9	30.0	0	7	0	0	1.000	5	0	0	0	.00
Martinez,Pedro, Phi	R	.071	14	1	0	1	1	.099	434	43	6	2	0	18	15	190	63	9	44.2	1	6	0	1	1.000	4	0	0	0	.00
Martis,Shairon, Was	R	.208	24	5	0	2	3	.161	31	5	1	0	0	2	1	8	3	15	85.2	8	18	0	1	1.000	3	0	0	0	.00
Masset,Nick, Cin	R	.000	1	0	0	0	0	.000	5	0	0	0	0	0	0	5	1	74	76.0	5	11	0	1	1.000	4	2	0	0	.50
Masterson,J., Bos-Cle	R	-	0	0	0	0	0	.000	5	0	0	0	0	0	0	4	0	42	129.1	4	22	2	1	.929	21	6	1	0	.29
Mathis,Doug, Tex	R	-	0	0	0	0	0	-	0	0	0	0	0	0	0	0	0	24	42.2	3	8	0	1	1.000	0	0	0	0	-
Matos,Osiris, SF	R	1.000	1	1	0	1	0	.333	3	1	0	0	0	1	0	2	0	5	6.0	0	0	0	0	-	1	0	0	0	.00
Matsuzaka,Daisuke, Bos	R	.000	2	0	0	0	0	.000	8	0	0	0	0	0	0	4	0	12	59.1	2	5	0	2	1.000	7	0	0	0	.00
Matusz,Brian, Bal	L	-	0	0	0	0	0	-	0	0	0	0	0	0	0	0	0	8	44.2	0	5	0	0	1.000	11	2	0	0	.18
Mazzaro,Vin, Oak	R	-	0	0	0	0	4	-	0	0	0	0	0	0	0	0	4	17	91.1	1	5	1	0	.857	11	3	0	1	.27
McCarthy,Brandon, Tex	R	.000	4	0	0	0	0	.000	9	0	0	0	0	0	0	4	1	17	97.1	8	9	1	1	.944	7	2	0	0	.29
McClellan,Kyle, StL	R	.000	3	0	0	0	0	.000	8	0	0	0	0	0	0	5	1	66	66.2	7	8	0	2	1.000	0	0	0	0	-
McClung,Seth, Mil	R	.000	7	0	0	0	0	.185	27	5	1	0	0	0	0	14	3	41	62.0	2	4	0	0	1.000	7	1	0	0	.14
McCrory,Bob, Bal	R	-	0	0	0	0	0	-	0	0	0	0	0	0	0	0	0	7	7.1	0	1	0	0	1.000	0	0	0	0	-
McCutchen,Daniel, Pit	R	.091	11	1	0	1	0	.091	11	1	0	0	0	1	1	3	0	6	36.1	3	4	0	0	1.000	3	0	0	1	.00
McDonald,James, LAD	R	.000	9	0	0	0	1	.000	9	0	0	0	0	0	0	6	1	45	63.0	3	3	0	1	1.000	6	2	0	0	.33
Meche,Gil, KC	R	.000	2	0	0	0	0	.130	23	3	0	0	0	2	0	9	0	23	129.0	8	21	0	2	1.000	16	1	0	0	.06
Medders,Brandon, SF	R	.000	2	0	0	0	0	.000	5	0	0	0	0	0	0	2	0	61	68.2	2	9	0	1	1.000	3	1	0	0	.33
Medlen,Kris, Atl	R	.000	13	0	0	0	0	.000	13	0	0	0	0	0	0	7	0	37	67.2	5	8	0	0	1.000	2	1	0	1	.50
Meek,Evan, Pit	R	-	0	0	0	0	0	-	0	0	0	0	0	0	0	0	0	41	47.0	6	5	0	1	1.000	6	2	0	0	.33
Melancon,Mark, NYY	R	-	0	0	0	0	0	0	0	0	0	0	0	0	0	0	0	13	16.1	1	4	0	0	1.000	2	0	0	0	.00
Meloan,John, Oak	R	-	0	0	0	0	0	-	0	0	0	0	0	0	0	0	0	6	8.1	0	0	0	0	-	1	1	0	0	1.00
Mendoza,Luis, Tex	R	-	0	0	0	0	0	.000	1	0	0	0	0	0	0	1	1	1	1.0	0	0	0	0	-	0	0	0	0	-
Meredith,Cla, SD-Bal	R	-	0	0	0	0	0	.000	2	0	0	0	0	0	0	1	1	64	65.1	6	10	0	1	1.000	11	1	0	0	.09
Messenger,Randy, Sea	R	-	0	0	0	0	0	.167	6	1	0	0	0	0	1	3	1	12	10.1	0	1	0	0	1.000	0	0	0	0	-
Meyer,Dan, Fla	L	.000	2	0	0	0	0	.000	2	0	0	0	0	0	0	2	0	71	58.1	2	2	2	0	.667	3	0	0	0	.00
Mickolio,Kam, Bal	R	-	0	0	0	0	0	-	0	0	0	0	0	0	0	0	0	11	13.2	0	2	0	0	1.000	0	0	0	0	-
Mijares,Jose, Min	L	-	0	0	0	0	0	-	0	0	0	0	0	0	0	0	0	71	61.2	2	6	0	0	1.000	5	0	0	1	.00
Miller,Andrew, Fla	L	.083	24	2	0	0	2	.068	59	4	0	0	0	3	0	29	4	20	80.0	6	8	1	1	.933	16	3	0	0	.19
Miller,Justin, SF	R	.000	3	0	0	0	0	.000	8	0	0	0	0	0	0	4	0	44	56.2	3	8	0	1	1.000	3	1	0	0	.33
Miller,Trever, StL	L	-	0	0	0	0	0	.167	6	1	1	0	0	0	0	1	2	70	43.2	4	6	1	0	.900	2	1	1	0	.50
Mills,Brad, Tor	L	.000	1	0	0	0	0	.000	1	0	0	0	0	0	0	0	0	2	7.2	0	0	0	0	-	1	1	0	0	1.00
Millwood,Kevin, Tex	R	.000	2	0	0	0	0	.122	443	54	15	0	2	24	20	203	52	31	198.2	9	26	0	4	1.000	21	8	0	0	.38
Milton,Eric, LAD	L	.000	8	0	0	0	2	.176	205	36	5	1	2	16	10	90	20	5	23.2	0	4	0	0	1.000	1	1	1	0	1.00
Milner,Zach, Det	R	.000	1	0	0	0	0	.143	7	1	1	0	0	0	0	4	0	51	92.1	3	12	0	0	1.000	6	2	0	0	.33
Misch,Pat, SF-NYM	L	.000	13	0	0	0	2	.065	31	2	0	0	0	1	3	10	7	26	62.1	1	15	0	2	1.000	3	2	2	0	.67
Mitre,Sergio, NYY	R	-	0	0	0	0	0	.141	78	11	4	0	0	2	3	33	13	12	51.2	3	12	3	1	.833	4	1	0	0	.25
Mock,Garrett, Was	R	.087	23	2	0	0	3	.074	27	2	0	0	0	0	0	16	4	28	91.1	7	10	2	0	.895	6	3	0	1	.50
Moehler,Brian, Hou	R	.024	42	1	0	0	3	.042	192	8	2	0	0	5	9	90	18	29	154.2	13	20	1	4	.971	15	3	0	0	.20
Morales,Franklin, Col	L	.400	5	2	0	1	0	.250	28	7	0	0	0	2	1	9	2	40	40.0	2	4	0	0	1.000	2	1	0	1	.50
Moreno,Edwin, SD	R	-	0	0	0	0	0	-	0	0	0	0	0	0	0	0	0	19	22.1	4	1	0	1	1.000	5	2	0	0	.40
Morillo,Juan, Min	R	-	0	0	0	0	0	.000	1	0	0	0	0	0	0	0	0	3	2.0	0	0	0	0	-	0	0	0	0	-
Morrow,Brandon, Sea	R	.000	2	0	0	0	0	.000	3	0	0	0	0	0	0	1	0	26	69.2	5	7	0	1	1.000	6	1	0	0	.17
Mortensen,C., StL-Oak	R	.000	1	0	0	0	0	.000	1	0	0	0	0	0	0	0	0	7	30.2	2	3	1	0	.833	7	2	0	0	.29
Morton,Charlie, Pit	R	.129	31	4	0	1	2	.104	48	5	1	0	0	1	0	24	5	18	97.0	7	11	0	2	1.000	13	4	1	0	.31
Moscoso,Guillermo, Tex	R	-	0	0	0	0	0	-	0	0	0	0	0	0	0	0	0	10	14.0	0	1	0	0	1.000	1	0	0	0	.00
Mosebach,Bobby, LAA	R	-	0	0	0	0	0	-	0	0	0	0	0	0	0	0	0	3	2.1	0	1	1	0	.500	0	0	0	0	-
Moseley,Dustin, LAA	R	-	0	0	0	0	0	-	0	0	0	0	0	0	0	0	0	3	14.2	2	3	0	0	1.000	3	1	0	0	.33
Mota,Guillermo, LAD	R	.333	3	1	0	1	1	.216	37	8	1	0	2	7	0	18	1	61	65.1	1	10	0	0	1.000	7	1	0	0	.14
Motte,Jason, StL	R	.000	1	0	0	0	0	.000	1	0	0	0	0	0	0	1	0	69	56.2	4	6	0	1	1.000	1	1	1	0	1.00
Moyer,Jamie, Phi	L	.119	42	5	0	2	9	.130	361	47	5	0	0	12	31	129	55	30	162.0	7	19	1	0	.963	19	5	4	0	.26
Moylan,Peter, Atl	R	.000	3	0	0	0	0	.000	7	0	0	0	0	0	1	6	0	87	73.0	7	15	3	1	.880	14	3	1	0	.21
Mujica,Edward, SD	R	.250	8	2	0	0	2	.250	8	2	0	0	0	0	0	2	2	67	93.2	6	8	0	0	1.000	6	3	0	0	.50
Mulvey,Kevin, Min-Ari	R	.143	7	1	0	0	0	.143	7	1	0	0	0	0	0	3	0	8	24.1	3	4	0	0	1.000	2	1	0	0	.50
Murphy,Bill, Tor	L	-	0	0	0	0	0	-	0	0	0	0	0	0	0	0	0	8	11.1	2	2	0	1	1.000	0	0	0	0	-
Myers,Brett, Phi	R	.222	18	4	0	0	1	.121	346	42	9	0	0	10	19	114	45	18	70.2	6	10	0	0	1.000	6	3	1	1	.50
Narveson,Chris, Mil	L	.125	8	1	0	0	1	.111	9	1	0	0	0	0	0	6	1	21	47.0	2	7	0	0	1.000	6	1	0	0	.17
Nathan,Joe, Min	R	-	0	0	0	0	0	.159	63	10	3	0	2	4	3	17	10	70	68.2	5	6	1	1	.917	5	0	0	0	.00
Nelson,Joe, TB	R	-	0	0	0	0	0	.000	1	0	0	0	0	0	0	0	0	42	40.1	1	3	1	0	.800	6	0	0	0	.00
Ni,Fu-Te, Det	L	-	0	0	0	0	0	-	0	0	0	0	0	0	0	0	0	36	31.0	3	2	0	0	1.000	2	1	1	0	.50
Niemann,Jeff, TB	R	.000	5	0	0	0	1	.000	5	0	0	0	0	0	0	4	1	31	180.2	9	12	0	4	1.000	30	6	0	1	.20
Niese,Jonathon, NYM	L	.125	8	1	0	0	0	.143	14	2	0	0	0	0	0	7	1	5	25.2	1	3	0	0	1.000	3	2	1	0	.67
Nieve,Fernando, NYM	R	.333	9	3	0	1	0	.192	26	5	0	0	0	2	2	11	5	8	36.2	2	6	0	0	1.000	3	1	0	0	.33
Nippert,Dustin, Tex	R	-	0	0	0	0	0	.125	8	1	0	0	0	0	1	6	0	20	69.2	3	5	1	0	.889	13	1	1	1	.08
Nolasco,Ricky, Fla	R	.140	50	7	0	0	3	.144	160	23	2	0	1	13	6	82	27	31	185.0	12	19	0	1	1.000	17	4	1	0	.24
Norris,Bud, Hou	R	.188	16	3	0	0	1	.188	16	3	0	0	0	0	0	4	1	11	55.2	1	3	0	0	1.000	1	0	0	1	.00
Nunez,Jhonny, CWS	R	-	0	0	0	0	0	-	0	0	0	0	0	0	0	0	0	7	5.2	0	0	0	0	-	0	0	0	0	-
Nunez,Leo, Fla	R	-	0	0	0	0	0	-	0	0	0	0	0	0	0	0	0	75	68.2	2	6	1	0	.889	9	1	0	0	.11

Pitchers Hitting, Fielding and Holding Runners

Pitcher	T	2009 Hitting						Career Hitting										2009 Fielding and Holding Runners											
		Avg	AB	H	HR	RBI	SH	Avg	AB	H	2B	3B	HR	RBI	BB	SO	SH	G	Inn	PO	A	E	DP	Pct	SBA	CS	PCS	PPO	CS%
Nunez,Vladimir, Atl	R	-	0	0	0	0	0	.133	60	8	0	0	1	5	1	20	8	1	1.0	0	0	0	0	1.000	0	0	0	0	-
O'Day,Darren, NYM-Tex	R	-	0	0	0	0	0	-	0	0	0	0	0	0	0	0	0	68	58.2	1	6	0	0	1.000	11	4	0	0	.36
O'Flaherty,Eric, Atl	L	.000	1	0	0	0	0	.000	2	0	0	0	0	0	0	2	0	78	56.1	0	5	0	0	1.000	7	3	1	0	.43
Ohka,Tomo, Cle	R	.000	2	0	0	0	0	.138	240	33	2	0	0	15	10	95	24	18	71.0	7	9	0	1	1.000	3	0	0	0	.00
Ohlendorf,Ross, Pit	R	.068	59	4	0	0	4	.061	66	4	0	0	0	0	1	25	4	29	176.2	14	27	1	3	.976	20	8	4	4	.40
Ohman,Will, LAD	L	.500	2	1	0	1	1	.400	5	2	0	0	0	1	1	2	1	21	12.1	0	0	0	-	-	3	0	0	0	.00
Okajima,Hideki, Bos	L	.000	1	0	0	0	0	.000	1	0	0	0	0	0	0	0	0	68	61.0	3	6	1	0	.900	0	0	0	1	-
Oliver,Darren, LAA	L	-	0	0	0	0	0	.221	217	48	11	0	1	20	8	74	15	63	73.0	2	7	0	1	1.000	12	3	1	1	.25
Olsen,Scott, Was	L	.133	15	2	0	1	4	.159	189	30	5	0	0	15	7	77	28	11	62.2	0	7	1	0	.875	9	4	3	0	.44
Olson,Garrett, Sea	L	.000	3	0	0	0	1	.167	6	1	0	0	0	1	0	2	2	31	80.1	2	7	0	0	1.000	8	3	0	0	.38
Ortega,Anthony, LAA	R	-	0	0	0	0	0	-	0	0	0	0	0	0	0	0	0	3	12.2	0	2	0	0	1.000	1	0	0	0	.00
Ortiz,Russ, Hou	R	.179	28	5	1	2	2	.205	507	104	23	0	7	49	35	135	60	23	85.2	8	10	1	1	.947	9	3	0	0	.33
O'Sullivan,Sean, LAA	R	.333	3	1	0	0	0	.333	3	1	0	0	0	0	0	1	0	12	51.2	4	3	0	0	1.000	5	0	0	0	.00
Oswalt,Roy, Hou	R	.122	49	6	0	2	14	.158	556	88	7	0	1	33	21	150	87	30	181.1	11	29	0	1	1.000	3	1	0	0	.33
Outman,Josh, Oak	L	.000	2	0	0	0	0	.000	2	0	0	0	0	0	0	0	0	14	67.1	2	3	1	0	.833	1	0	0	0	.00
Owings,Micah, Cin	R	.259	54	14	3	10	1	.300	170	51	14	2	8	31	8	56	3	26	119.2	17	11	2	0	.933	9	2	0	0	.22
Padilla,Vicente, Tex-LAD	R	.200	15	3	0	2	2	.103	224	23	3	1	0	15	14	118	24	26	147.1	6	20	2	1	.929	11	7	1	1	.64
Palmer,Matt, LAA	R	.167	6	1	0	0	1	.200	10	2	0	0	0	1	5	1	1	40	121.1	7	10	0	1	1.000	16	4	0	0	.25
Papelbon,Jonathan, Bos	R	-	0	0	0	0	0	-	0	0	0	0	0	0	0	0	0	66	68.0	1	4	1	0	.833	11	1	0	0	.09
Park,Chan Ho, Phi	R	.143	14	2	1	1	1	.179	429	77	15	1	3	31	20	155	54	45	83.1	5	9	1	1	.933	4	2	0	0	.50
Parnell,Bobby, NYM	R	.125	8	1	0	0	4	.125	8	1	0	0	0	0	0	3	4	68	88.1	6	15	0	1	1.000	3	2	0	0	.67
Paronto,Chad, Hou	R	-	0	0	0	0	0	.000	3	0	0	0	0	0	0	3	0	6	6.2	0	0	0	-	-	0	0	0	0	-
Parr,James, Atl	R	.000	1	0	0	0	0	.222	9	2	1	0	0	0	2	5	0	8	14.0	0	1	0	0	1.000	5	0	0	0	.00
Parra,Manny, Mil	L	.133	45	6	0	4	6	.187	107	20	9	1	0	12	3	43	10	27	140.0	0	13	3	0	.769	10	2	0	0	.20
Patton,David, ChC	R	-	0	0	0	0	0	-	0	0	0	0	0	0	0	0	0	20	27.2	0	2	1	0	.667	6	0	0	0	.00
Paulino,Felipe, Hou	R	.040	25	1	0	0	3	.032	31	1	0	0	0	0	0	20	3	23	97.2	3	13	0	1	1.000	4	2	1	2	.50
Pavano,Carl, Cle-Min	R	.000	2	0	0	0	0	.138	297	41	8	2	2	14	4	116	34	33	199.1	11	22	0	2	1.000	39	6	0	0	.15
Peavy,Jake, SD-CWS	R	.087	23	2	0	0	4	.180	405	73	14	1	2	26	18	116	45	16	101.2	5	13	1	1	.947	11	2	0	0	.18
Pelfrey,Mike, NYM	R	.096	52	5	0	4	5	.085	141	12	0	0	0	6	7	43	13	31	184.1	12	25	2	2	.949	22	6	2	0	.27
Pena,Tony, Ari-CWS	R	.000	1	0	0	0	0	.143	7	1	0	0	0	1	0	2	0	72	70.0	6	4	0	0	1.000	9	2	0	0	.22
Penn,Hayden, Fla	R	-	0	0	0	0	1	.000	1	0	0	0	0	0	2	0	1	16	22.0	0	2	0	0	1.000	5	1	0	0	.20
Penny,Brad, Bos-SF	R	.105	19	2	0	0	2	.156	499	78	16	2	2	30	3	161	40	30	173.1	13	15	1	1	.966	31	3	1	0	.10
Peralta,Joel, Col	R	-	0	0	0	0	0	1.000	1	1	1	0	0	2	0	0	0	27	24.2	1	4	1	0	.833	2	0	0	1	.00
Percival,Troy, TB	R	-	0	0	0	0	0	-	5	0	0	0	0	0	0	5	0	14	11.1	1	0	0	0	1.000	5	1	0	0	.20
Perdomo,Luis, SD	R	.000	6	0	0	0	0	.000	6	0	0	0	0	0	0	5	0	35	60.0	8	7	1	0	.938	6	1	0	0	.17
Perez,Chris, StL-Cle	R	-	0	0	0	0	0	.000	1	0	0	0	0	0	0	1	0	61	57.0	2	6	0	0	1.000	11	4	0	0	.36
Perez,Oliver, NYM	L	.273	22	6	0	0	1	.160	332	53	1	0	0	14	13	112	38	14	66.0	3	12	0	1	1.000	8	3	2	0	.38
Perez,Rafael, Cle	L	.000	1	0	0	0	0	.000	1	0	0	0	0	0	0	1	0	54	48.0	1	9	1	0	.909	6	2	0	0	.33
Perkins,Glen, Min	L	.000	1	0	0	0	2	.000	4	0	0	0	0	0	0	4	3	18	96.1	3	8	1	1	.917	7	0	0	0	.00
Perry,Ryan, Det	R	-	0	0	0	0	0	-	0	0	0	0	0	0	0	0	0	53	61.2	3	3	1	0	.857	13	3	0	0	.23
Petit,Yusmeiro, Ari	R	.037	27	1	0	0	0	.049	61	3	0	0	0	1	1	25	4	23	89.2	5	8	1	0	.929	10	1	0	0	.10
Pettitte,Andy, NYY	L	.200	5	1	0	1	1	.134	186	25	6	0	1	13	6	60	32	32	194.2	3	27	2	1	.938	22	8	4	2	.36
Pineiro,Joel, StL	R	.136	66	9	0	4	9	.107	159	17	6	0	0	10	9	91	20	32	214.0	27	31	1	3	.983	5	4	0	0	.80
Pinto,Renyel, Fla	L	.000	1	0	0	0	0	.000	6	0	0	0	0	0	1	4	2	73	61.1	3	6	1	0	.900	8	4	0	0	.67
Ponson,Sidney, KC	R	-	0	0	0	0	0	.138	65	9	3	0	0	1	3	22	12	14	58.2	4	16	1	1	.952	1	0	0	0	.00
Porcello,Rick, Det	R	.400	5	2	0	2	0	.400	5	2	0	0	0	2	0	1	0	31	170.2	11	25	2	1	.947	10	2	0	1	.20
Poreda,Aaron, CWS-SD	L	-	0	0	0	0	0	-	0	0	0	0	0	0	0	0	0	14	13.1	0	3	0	0	1.000	2	1	0	1	.50
Price,David, TB	L	.333	3	1	0	0	0	.333	3	1	0	0	0	0	0	0	0	23	128.1	5	17	1	0	.957	14	6	3	0	.43
Purcey,David, Tor	L	-	0	0	0	0	0	.000	1	0	0	0	0	0	0	1	0	9	48.0	2	5	1	0	.875	8	2	0	0	.25
Putz,J.J., NYM	R	-	0	0	0	0	0	-	0	0	0	0	0	0	0	0	0	29	29.1	4	5	0	1	1.000	5	1	0	0	.20
Qualls,Chad, Ari	R	.000	2	0	0	0	0	.000	6	0	0	0	0	0	0	5	0	51	52.0	3	8	0	1	1.000	3	0	0	0	.00
Ramirez,Edwar, NYY	R	-	0	0	0	0	0	-	0	0	0	0	0	0	0	0	0	20	22.0	1	2	0	0	1.000	4	1	0	0	.25
Ramirez,Horacio, KC	L	-	0	0	0	0	0	.151	179	27	3	1	0	5	2	36	13	19	22.2	4	2	0	0	1.000	1	0	0	0	.00
Ramirez,Ramon, Cin	R	-	0	0	0	0	1	.100	10	1	0	0	0	0	3	3	1	11	12.1	0	0	0	-	-	1	0	0	0	.00
Ramirez,Ramon, Bos	R	.000	1	0	0	0	0	.400	5	2	0	0	0	0	3	1	0	70	69.2	7	4	1	1	.917	6	0	0	0	.00
Ramos,Cesar, SD	L	.000	4	0	0	0	0	.000	4	0	0	0	0	0	0	2	0	5	14.2	2	2	0	0	1.000	4	1	1	0	.25
Rapada,Clay, Det	L	-	0	0	0	0	0	-	0	0	0	0	0	0	0	0	0	3	3.1	0	1	0	0	1.000	0	0	0	0	-
Rauch,Jon, Ari-Min	R	-	0	0	0	0	0	.095	21	2	0	0	1	3	0	15	1	75	70.0	4	8	0	0	1.000	5	0	0	0	.00
Ray,Chris, Bal	R	-	0	0	0	0	0	-	0	0	0	0	0	0	0	0	0	46	43.1	2	5	2	2	.778	7	1	0	0	.14
Ray,Robert, Tor	R	-	0	0	0	0	0	-	0	0	0	0	0	0	0	0	0	4	24.1	3	3	0	0	1.000	6	1	0	0	.17
Redding,Tim, NYM	R	.069	29	2	0	0	3	.138	225	31	5	0	0	10	7	94	30	30	120.0	7	13	0	2	1.000	4	1	0	0	.25
Register,Steven, Phi	R	-	0	0	0	0	0	-	0	0	0	0	0	0	0	0	0	1	2.0	0	0	0	0	-	2	0	0	0	.00
Reineke,Chad, Oak	R	-	0	0	0	0	0	.167	6	1	0	0	0	1	0	4	0	1	5.0	0	0	0	0	-	0	0	0	0	-
Reyes,Anthony, Cle	R	.000	1	0	0	0	0	.088	57	5	0	0	0	1	1	22	8	8	38.1	1	8	0	1	1.000	9	2	0	0	.22
Reyes,Dennys, StL	L	-	0	0	0	0	0	.074	54	4	1	0	0	2	2	25	2	75	41.0	2	7	2	0	.818	7	3	2	1	.43
Reyes,Jo-Jo, Atl	L	.111	9	1	0	0	0	.138	58	8	2	0	0	2	3	22	7	6	27.0	0	3	1	0	.750	1	0	0	0	.00
Richard,Arthur, Cin	L	.000	1	0	0	0	0	.200	5	1	0	0	0	0	0	4	0	66	53.1	3	6	1	0	.900	4	2	1	0	.50
Richard,C., CWS-SD	L	.087	23	2	0	2	3	.087	23	2	1	0	0	2	0	10	3	38	153.0	9	26	3	1	.921	23	10	8	1	.43
Richardson,Dustin, Bos	L	-	0	0	0	0	0	-	0	0	0	0	0	0	0	0	0	3	3.1	1	0	0	0	1.000	0	0	0	0	-
Richmond,Scott, Tor	R	.000	6	0	0	0	0	.000	6	0	0	0	0	0	0	5	0	27	138.2	14	17	0	1	1.000	9	3	0	1	.33

Pitchers Hitting, Fielding and Holding Runners

Pitcher	T	Avg	AB	H	HR	RBI	SH	Avg	AB	H	2B	3B	HR	RBI	BB	SO	SH	G	Inn	PO	A	E	DP	Pct	SBA	CS	PCS	PPO	CS%
					2009 Hitting							**Career Hitting**										**2009 Fielding and Holding Runners**							
Rincon,Juan, Det-Col	R	.000	1	0	0	0	0	.333	3	1	0	0	0	0	0	1	0	33	36.2	5	7	0	0	1.000	4	0	0	0	.00
Riske,David, Mil	R	-	0	0	0	0	0	.000	1	0	0	0	0	0	0	0	0	1	1.0	0	0	0	0	-	0	0	0	0	-
Rivera,Mariano, NYY	R	.000	1	0	0	1	0	.000	2	0	0	0	0	1	1	1	0	66	66.1	2	16	0	1	1.000	3	1	0	0	.33
Rivera,Saul, Was	R	.333	3	1	0	0	1	.111	9	1	0	0	0	0	2	2	1	30	38.1	7	7	0	1	1.000	2	1	1	0	.50
Robertson,David, NYY	R	-	0	0	0	0	0	-	0	0	0	0	0	0	0	0	0	45	43.2	0	3	0	0	1.000	4	2	1	0	.50
Robertson,Nate, Det	L	-	0	0	0	0	0	.056	18	1	0	0	0	1	0	9	1	28	49.2	3	7	1	0	.909	6	1	0	0	.17
Rodney,Fernando, Det	R	-	0	0	0	0	0	.000	1	0	0	0	0	0	0	0	0	73	75.2	6	10	0	0	1.000	2	0	0	0	.00
Rodriguez,Fernando, LAA	R	-	0	0	0	0	0	-	0	0	0	0	0	0	0	0	0	1	0.2	0	0	0	0	-	0	0	0	0	-
Rodriguez,Fr., NYM	R	-	0	0	0	0	0	-	0	0	0	0	0	0	0	0	0	70	68.0	4	4	0	0	1.000	9	2	0	0	.22
Rodriguez,Henry, Oak	R	-	0	0	0	0	0	-	0	0	0	0	0	0	0	0	0	3	4.0	1	0	0	0	1.000	1	0	0	0	.00
Rodriguez,Rafael, LAA	R	-	0	0	0	0	0	-	0	0	0	0	0	0	0	0	0	18	30.2	3	9	1	0	.923	3	1	0	0	.33
Rodriguez,Wandy, Hou	L	.127	63	8	0	4	6	.122	230	28	5	0	0	9	6	71	28	33	205.2	8	24	0	0	1.000	7	4	1	0	.57
Roenicke,Josh, Cin-Tor	R	-	0	0	0	0	0	-	0	0	0	0	0	0	0	0	0	24	31.0	2	3	0	1	1.000	7	0	0	0	.00
Rogers,Esmil, Col	R	.000	1	0	0	0	0	.000	1	0	0	0	0	0	0	0	0	1	4.0	0	0	0	0	-	0	0	0	0	-
Romero,J.C., Phi	L	-	0	0	0	0	0	.250	4	1	1	0	0	0	0	1	0	21	16.2	1	3	0	0	1.000	2	0	0	1	.00
Romero,Ricky, Tor	L	.000	6	0	0	0	0	.000	6	0	0	0	0	0	0	4	0	29	178.0	15	25	2	2	.952	16	7	2	2	.44
Romo,Sergio, SF	R	.000	1	0	0	0	0	.000	2	0	0	0	0	0	0	1	0	45	34.0	0	5	0	0	1.000	2	0	0	0	.00
Rosa,Carlos, KC	R	-	0	0	0	0	0	-	0	0	0	0	0	0	0	0	0	7	10.2	0	0	0	0	-	0	0	0	0	-
Rosales,Leo, Ari	R	.000	3	0	0	0	0	.000	3	0	0	0	0	0	0	2	0	33	45.1	4	5	1	0	.900	1	0	0	0	.00
Rowland-Smith,R., Sea	L	-	0	0	0	0	0	-	0	0	0	0	0	0	0	0	0	15	96.1	1	2	1	1	.750	1	1	0	0	1.00
Rundles,Rich, Cle	L	-	0	0	0	0	0	-	0	0	0	0	0	0	0	0	0	1	1.0	0	0	0	0	-	0	0	0	0	-
Runzler,Dan, SF	L	-	0	0	0	0	0	-	0	0	0	0	0	0	0	0	0	11	8.2	0	3	0	1	1.000	1	0	0	0	.00
Rupe,Josh, Tex	R	-	0	0	0	0	0	-	0	0	0	0	0	0	0	0	0	4	4.2	1	0	0	0	1.000	1	0	0	0	.00
Rusch,Glendon, Col	L	.333	6	2	0	0	0	.151	331	50	5	0	3	19	9	104	41	11	18.2	1	2	0	0	1.000	0	0	0	0	-
Russell,Adam, SD	R	.000	1	0	0	0	0	.000	1	0	0	0	0	0	0	0	0	15	12.1	0	2	0	0	1.000	3	1	0	0	.33
Ryan,B.J., Tor	L	-	0	0	0	0	0	.000	2	0	0	0	0	0	0	0	0	25	20.2	0	3	0	0	1.000	4	3	1	0	.75
Rzepczynski,Marc, Tor	L	-	0	0	0	0	0	-	0	0	0	0	0	0	0	0	0	11	61.1	2	10	0	2	1.000	10	3	2	0	.30
Sabathia,CC, NYY	L	.250	4	1	0	1	0	.261	92	24	3	0	3	14	1	23	3	34	230.0	3	28	0	0	1.000	20	7	3	0	.35
Sadler,Dilly, Hou	R	.000	1	0	0	0	0	.000	2	0	0	0	0	0	0	1	0	1	1.1	1	0	0	0	1.000	0	0	0	0	-
Sadowski,Ryan, SF	R	.100	10	1	0	0	2	.100	10	1	0	0	0	0	0	6	2	6	28.1	2	4	0	0	1.000	1	0	0	0	.00
Salto,Takashi, Bos	R	-	0	0	0	0	0	.000	1	0	0	0	0	0	0	1	0	56	55.2	3	7	1	1	.909	9	2	0	0	.22
Samardzija,Jeff, ChC	R	.200	5	1	1	1	1	.167	6	1	0	0	1	1	0	2	1	20	34.2	4	4	1	0	.889	4	1	0	0	.25
Sampson,Chris, Hou	R	.000	2	0	0	0	0	.127	55	7	0	0	0	1	22	13	49	55.1	7	3	0	1	1.000	1	0	0	0	.00
Sanches,Brian, Fla	R	.000	4	0	0	1	1	.000	4	0	0	0	0	0	1	0	1	47	56.1	4	4	1	2	.889	9	3	0	0	.33
Sanchez,Anibal, Fla	R	.000	23	0	0	0	5	.058	86	5	0	0	0	2	6	36	10	16	86.0	6	10	2	2	.889	12	1	0	0	.08
Sanchez,Duaner, SD	R	-	0	0	0	0	0	.111	9	1	1	0	0	2	0	2	2	12	11.0	1	2	1	0	.750	0	0	0	0	-
Sanchez,Jonathan, SF	L	.073	41	3	0	0	8	.087	103	9	2	0	0	5	6	56	14	32	163.1	3	15	0	1	1.000	29	5	2	0	.17
Santana,Ervin, LAA	R	-	0	0	0	0	0	.133	15	2	1	0	0	2	0	8	0	24	139.2	6	9	1	0	.938	20	5	0	0	.25
Santana,Johan, NYM	L	.167	42	7	0	4	10	.172	151	26	9	1	0	8	9	42	12	25	166.2	7	24	2	3	.939	3	2	2	0	.67
Sarfate,Dennis, Bal	R	-	0	0	0	0	0	-	0	0	0	0	0	0	0	0	0	20	23.0	2	2	0	0	1.000	4	1	0	0	.25
Saunders,Joe, LAA	L	-	0	0	0	0	0	.000	3	0	0	0	0	0	0	2	0	31	186.0	7	24	1	3	.909	25	7	4	0	.28
Scherzer,Max, Ari	R	.226	53	12	0	3	6	.182	66	12	2	0	0	3	4	21	6	30	170.1	15	18	2	3	.943	16	6	1	0	.38
Schlereth,Daniel, Ari	L	-	0	0	0	0	0	-	0	0	0	0	0	0	0	0	0	21	18.1	1	1	0	0	1.000	0	0	0	0	-
Schlichting,Travis, LAD	R	-	0	0	0	0	0	-	0	0	0	0	0	0	0	0	0	2	2.2	0	1	0	0	1.000	0	0	0	0	-
Schmidt,Jason, LAD	R	.167	6	1	0	0	1	.106	597	63	9	0	7	21	22	282	90	4	17.2	0	2	0	0	1.000	6	0	0	0	.00
Schoeneweis,Scott, Ari	L	-	0	0	0	0	0	.250	8	2	1	0	0	1	2	2	0	45	24.0	1	1	0	0	1.000	7	0	0	0	.00
Seay,Bobby, Det	L	-	0	0	0	0	0	.000	1	0	0	0	0	0	0	1	0	67	48.2	3	4	0	0	1.000	1	1	0	0	1.00
Segovia,Zack, Was	R	-	0	0	0	0	0	.000	2	0	0	0	0	0	0	0	0	8	10.1	1	2	0	0	1.000	1	0	0	0	.00
Shell,Steven, Was	R	-	0	0	0	0	0	.000	4	0	0	0	0	0	0	2	0	4	5.0	1	0	0	0	1.000	1	0	0	0	.00
Sherrill,George, Bal-LAD	L	-	0	0	0	0	0	-	0	0	0	0	0	0	0	0	0	72	69.0	1	4	0	0	1.000	5	0	0	0	.00
Shields,James, TB	R	.000	4	0	0	0	0	.227	22	5	0	0	0	1	2	5	1	33	219.2	16	25	2	5	.953	7	2	0	1	.29
Shields,Scot, LAA	R	-	0	0	0	0	0	.000	3	0	0	0	0	0	0	2	0	20	17.2	3	2	2	2	.714	2	0	0	0	.00
Shouse,Brian, TB	L	-	0	0	0	0	0	-	0	0	0	0	0	0	0	0	0	45	28.0	2	7	0	1	1.000	2	0	0	0	.00
Silva,Carlos, Sea	R	-	0	0	0	0	0	.111	27	3	1	0	0	1	1	10	3	8	30.1	1	3	0	1	1.000	2	1	0	0	.50
Silva,Walter, SD	R	.375	8	3	0	0	0	.375	8	3	0	0	0	0	0	3	0	6	24.2	1	1	0	0	1.000	0	0	0	0	-
Simon,Alfredo, Bal	R	-	0	0	0	0	0	-	0	0	0	0	0	0	0	0	0	2	6.1	1	1	0	0	1.000	2	1	0	0	.50
Sipp,Tony, Cle	L	-	0	0	0	0	0	-	0	0	0	0	0	0	0	0	0	46	40.0	1	5	0	0	1.000	3	0	0	0	.00
Slaten,Doug, Ari	L	-	0	0	0	0	0	-	0	0	0	0	0	0	0	0	0	11	6.1	0	1	0	0	1.000	1	0	0	0	.00
Slowey,Kevin, Min	R	.000	3	0	0	0	1	.182	11	2	1	0	0	2	0	2	1	16	90.2	4	6	0	0	1.000	13	3	0	0	.23
Smith,Chris, Mil	R	.000	2	0	0	0	0	.000	2	0	0	0	0	0	1	1	0	35	46.0	2	3	0	0	1.000	1	0	0	0	.00
Smith,Joe, Cle	R	-	0	0	0	0	0	.000	2	0	0	0	0	0	0	2	0	37	34.0	3	9	0	0	1.000	1	0	0	0	.00
Smoltz,John, Bos-StL	R	.067	15	1	0	0	0	.159	948	151	26	2	5	61	79	365	136	15	78.0	6	12	0	1	1.000	4	1	0	0	.25
Snell,Ian, Pit-Sea	R	.174	23	4	0	1	4	.094	192	18	2	0	6	7	8	84	33	27	145.0	13	22	1	1	.972	15	5	1	0	.33
Sonnanstine,Andy, TB	R	.273	11	3	0	1	0	.333	21	7	1	0	0	2	3	11	2	22	99.2	7	12	3	0	.864	3	2	0	0	.67
Soria,Joakim, KC	R	-	0	0	0	0	0	-	0	0	0	0	0	0	0	0	0	47	53.0	2	5	1	0	.875	1	1	0	0	1.00
Soriano,Rafael, Atl	R	-	0	0	0	0	0	.000	4	0	0	0	0	0	0	1	0	77	75.2	3	8	0	0	1.000	0	0	0	0	.00
Sosa,Jorge, Was	R	-	0	0	0	0	1	.136	81	11	2	0	3	4	7	36	12	18	22.1	2	2	0	0	1.000	0	0	0	0	-
Sowers,Jeremy, Cle	L	.000	2	0	0	0	0	.250	4	1	0	0	0	0	2	1	1	23	123.1	1	20	0	0	1.000	8	3	2	0	.38
Speier,Justin, LAA	R	-	0	0	0	0	0	.176	17	3	0	0	0	0	0	8	0	41	40.0	0	1	0	0	1.000	3	0	0	0	.00
Speier,Ryan, Col	R	-	0	0	0	0	0	.000	5	0	0	0	0	0	0	3	0	5	5.2	0	2	0	0	1.000	0	0	0	0	-

Pitchers Hitting, Fielding and Holding Runners

Pitcher	T	2009 Hitting						Career Hitting										2009 Fielding and Holding Runners											
		Avg	AB	H	HR	RBI	SH	Avg	AB	H	2B	3B	HR	RBI	BB	SO	SH	G	Inn	PO	A	E	DP	Pct	SBA	CS	PCS	PPO	CS%
Springer,Russ, Oak-TB	R	-	0	0	0	0	0	.074	27	2	0	0	0	0	0	17	4	74	57.0	1	0	0	0	1.000	6	0	0	0	.00
Stammen,Craig, Was	R	.194	31	6	0	4	4	.194	31	6	3	0	0	4	2	10	4	19	105.2	6	12	0	1	1.000	19	2	0	0	.11
Stark,Denny, Sea	R	-	0	0	0	0	0	.099	71	7	3	0	1	8	5	28	4	9	11.0	0	1	0	0	1.000	5	3	0	0	.60
Stauffer,Tim, SD	R	.174	23	4	0	0	2	.170	53	9	1	0	0	3	1	26	6	14	73.0	8	5	0	2	1.000	3	2	0	0	.67
Stetter,Mitch, Mil	L	-	0	0	0	0	0	.000	1	0	0	0	0	0	0	1	0	71	45.0	2	3	1	0	.833	2	1	1	0	.50
Stevens,Jeff, ChC	R	-	0	0	0	0	0	-	0	0	0	0	0	0	0	0	0	11	12.2	0	4	0	0	1.000	2	1	0	0	.50
Stokes,Brian, NYM	R	-	0	0	0	0	1	.667	3	2	0	0	0	0	0	1	1	69	70.1	3	8	0	1	1.000	2	0	0	0	.00
Stoner,Tobi, NYM	R	-	0	0	0	0	0	-	0	0	0	0	0	0	0	0	0	4	9.0	2	2	0	1	1.000	1	0	0	0	.00
Street,Huston, Col	R	-	0	0	0	0	0	-	0	0	0	0	0	0	0	0	0	64	61.2	7	10	1	0	.944	9	0	0	0	.00
Strop,Pedro, Tex	R	-	0	0	0	0	0	-	0	0	0	0	0	0	0	0	0	7	7.0	1	0	0	0	1.000	0	0	0	0	-
Stults,Eric, LAD	L	.067	15	1	0	2	2	.213	47	10	2	0	0	4	5	20	3	10	50.0	4	8	0	1	1.000	6	3	1	0	.50
Suppan,Jeff, Mil	R	.143	42	6	0	5	10	.174	403	70	6	0	1	23	22	94	67	30	161.2	6	25	1	2	.969	9	3	0	2	.33
Swarzak,Anthony, Min	R	.000	2	0	0	0	0	.000	2	0	0	0	0	0	0	2	0	12	59.0	2	5	0	0	1.000	3	2	0	0	.67
Swindle,R.J., Mil	L	-	0	0	0	0	0	.000	2	0	0	0	0	1	0	0	0	6	6.2	0	0	0	0	-	0	0	0	0	-
Switzer,Jon, NYM	L	-	0	0	0	0	0	-	0	0	0	0	0	0	0	0	0	4	3.1	1	1	0	0	1.000	0	0	0	0	-
Takahashi,Ken, NYM	L	.000	2	0	0	0	0	.000	2	0	0	0	0	0	0	2	0	28	27.1	1	6	0	2	1.000	0	0	0	0	-
Tallet,Brian, Tor	L	.000	2	0	0	0	0	.000	4	0	0	0	0	0	0	2	0	37	160.2	11	10	2	0	.913	12	5	2	0	.42
Taschner,Jack, Phi	L	.000	1	0	0	0	1	.000	2	0	0	0	0	0	0	0	2	24	29.1	1	2	0	0	1.000	6	2	0	0	.33
Tavarez,Julian, Was	R	.000	1	0	0	0	0	.114	140	16	0	0	0	8	7	60	21	42	35.0	2	2	0	0	1.000	6	1	0	0	.17
Taylor,Graham, Fla	L	.000	3	0	0	0	2	.000	3	0	0	0	0	0	0	2	2	3	11.0	1	0	0	0	1.000	0	0	0	0	-
Tazawa,Junichi, Bos	R	-	0	0	0	0	0	-	0	0	0	0	0	0	0	0	0	6	25.1	0	1	0	0	1.000	1	0	0	0	.00
Tejeda,Robinson, KC	R	-	0	0	0	0	0	.080	25	2	0	1	0	0	0	13	0	35	73.2	3	5	0	1	1.000	14	3	1	0	.21
Thatcher,Joe, SD	L	-	0	0	0	0	0	.000	1	0	0	0	0	0	0	1	0	52	45.0	1	4	0	0	1.000	6	1	1	0	.17
Thayer,Dale, TB	R	.000	1	0	0	0	0	.000	1	0	0	0	0	0	0	0	0	11	13.2	1	0	0	0	1.000	1	0	0	0	.00
Thompson,Brad, StL	R	.083	12	1	0	0	2	.179	56	10	0	0	0	2	2	27	13	32	80.0	8	10	1	2	.947	3	1	0	0	.33
Thompson,Rich, LAA	R	-	0	0	0	0	0	-	0	0	0	0	0	0	0	0	0	13	19.1	0	1	1	0	.500	6	0	0	0	.00
Thornton,Matt, CWS	L	-	0	0	0	0	0	.000	1	0	0	0	0	0	0	1	0	70	72.1	2	9	1	2	.917	9	5	1	0	.56
Tillman,Chris, Bal	R	-	0	0	0	0	0	-	0	0	0	0	0	0	0	0	0	12	65.0	3	3	0	0	1.000	6	5	0	0	.83
Todd,Jesse, StL-Cle	R	-	0	0	0	0	0	-	0	0	0	0	0	0	0	0	0	20	22.1	2	0	0	1	1.000	0	0	0	0	-
Tomko,Brett, NYY-Oak	R	.000	1	0	0	0	0	.156	455	71	9	0	0	29	19	180	71	21	57.1	2	3	0	1	1.000	5	1	0	0	.20
Torres,Carlos, CWS	R	.000	3	0	0	0	0	.000	3	0	0	0	0	0	0	3	0	8	28.1	1	4	0	0	1.000	5	1	0	0	.20
Towers,Josh, NYY	R	-	0	0	0	0	0	.063	16	1	0	0	0	0	0	3	2	2	5.1	0	0	0	0	-	0	0	0	0	-
Traber,Billy, Bos	L	-	0	0	0	0	0	.048	21	1	0	0	0	1	1	13	2	1	3.2	0	1	0	0	1.000	0	0	0	0	-
Troncoso,Ramon, LAD	R	.000	5	0	0	0	1	.000	5	0	0	0	0	0	0	5	1	73	82.2	0	12	1	0	.923	7	2	0	0	.29
Uehara,Koji, Bal	R	.000	2	0	0	0	0	.000	2	0	0	0	0	0	1	1	0	12	66.2	0	5	0	1	1.000	4	0	0	1	.00
Valdez,Luis, Atl	R	-	0	0	0	0	0	-	0	0	0	0	0	0	0	0	0	3	2.2	0	0	0	0	-	0	0	0	0	-
Valdez,Merkin, SF	R	-	0	0	0	0	0	-	0	0	0	0	0	0	0	0	1	48	49.1	1	5	0	0	1.000	8	4	0	0	.50
Valverde,Jose, Hou	R	-	0	0	0	0	0	.500	2	1	1	0	0	0	0	1	1	52	54.0	1	1	1	0	.667	8	3	0	0	.38
VandenHurk,Rick, Fla	R	.000	21	0	0	0	1	.021	47	1	0	0	0	0	1	31	6	11	58.2	2	5	0	0	1.000	5	1	0	0	.20
Vargas,Claudio, LAD-Mil	R	-	0	0	0	0	0	.081	185	15	4	0	0	7	3	57	33	36	41.1	1	9	1	0	.909	5	2	1	1	.40
Vargas,Jason, Sea	L	.250	4	1	0	0	0	.292	48	14	3	0	0	3	2	11	1	23	91.2	3	13	0	3	1.000	8	6	1	1	.75
Vasquez,Esmerling, Ari	R	-	0	0	0	0	0	-	0	0	0	0	0	0	0	0	0	53	53.0	2	6	1	0	.889	7	1	1	0	.14
Vasquez,Virgil, Pit	R	.000	10	0	0	0	1	.000	10	0	0	0	0	0	0	4	1	14	44.2	0	7	1	0	.875	0	0	0	0	-
Vazquez,Javier, Atl	R	.176	68	12	0	3	20	.207	503	104	13	2	1	27	20	85	94	32	219.1	11	29	0	0	1.000	12	5	0	0	.42
Veal,Donnie, Pit	L	-	0	0	0	0	1	-	0	0	0	0	0	0	0	0	1	19	16.1	2	1	0	1	1.000	2	1	1	0	.50
Veras,Jose, NYY-Cle	R	-	0	0	0	0	0	-	0	0	0	0	0	0	0	0	0	47	50.1	5	4	1	0	.900	5	1	0	0	.20
Verlander,Justin, Det	R	.000	2	0	0	0	2	.000	12	0	0	0	0	0	0	7	4	35	240.0	14	20	2	4	.944	25	16	1	2	.64
Villanueva,Carlos, Mil	R	.091	11	1	0	0	1	.089	56	5	0	0	0	3	2	27	10	64	96.0	2	18	0	1	1.000	6	1	0	0	.17
Villone,Ron, Was	L	-	0	0	0	0	0	.129	170	22	3	1	1	7	1	51	12	63	48.2	1	7	1	0	.889	1	1	1	0	1.00
Viola,Pedro, Cin	L	-	0	0	0	0	0	-	0	0	0	0	0	0	0	0	0	9	7.0	0	0	0	0	-	0	0	0	0	-
Vizcaino,Luis, ChC-Cle	R	-	0	0	0	0	0	.000	6	0	0	0	0	0	0	5	0	15	15.1	0	3	0	0	1.000	5	0	0	0	.00
Volquez,Edinson, Cin	R	.063	16	1	0	0	3	.091	77	7	0	0	0	1	0	39	11	9	49.2	2	9	2	0	.846	2	0	0	0	.00
Volstad,Chris, Fla	R	.128	47	6	0	3	6	.123	73	9	3	0	0	3	1	37	8	29	159.0	7	30	1	2	.974	31	10	1	0	.32
Waddell,Jason, ChC	L	-	0	0	0	0	0	-	0	0	0	0	0	0	0	0	0	3	1.2	0	1	0	0	1.000	0	0	0	0	-
Wade,Cory, LAD	R	.000	2	0	0	0	0	.000	2	0	0	0	0	1	1	0	0	27	27.2	2	2	0	0	1.000	1	0	0	0	.00
Waechter,Doug, KC	R	-	0	0	0	0	0	.125	8	1	0	0	0	0	0	1	2	5	5.1	0	0	0	0	-	0	0	0	0	-
Wagner,Billy, NYM-Bos	L	-	0	0	0	0	0	.100	20	2	0	0	0	1	1	12	0	17	15.2	0	2	0	0	1.000	2	0	0	0	.00
Wainwright,Adam, StL	R	.180	89	16	2	4	6	.244	217	53	11	1	5	17	6	64	17	34	233.0	27	29	0	0	1.000	17	5	1	0	.29
Wakefield,Tim, Bos	R	.500	2	1	0	0	0	.126	103	13	2	0	1	4	2	41	13	21	129.2	10	11	0	1	1.000	26	3	0	0	.12
Walker,Jamie, Bal	L	-	0	0	0	0	0	-	0	0	0	0	0	0	0	0	0	22	12.1	0	3	0	0	1.000	2	1	0	0	.50
Walker,Tyler, Phi	R	-	0	0	0	0	1	.000	10	0	0	0	0	0	1	6	1	32	35.1	0	5	0	0	1.000	3	0	0	0	.00
Walters,P.J., StL	R	.000	3	0	0	0	2	.000	3	0	0	0	0	0	0	1	2	8	16.0	3	7	0	1	1.000	1	0	0	0	.00
Wang,Chien-Ming, NYY	R	.000	3	0	0	0	1	.000	14	0	0	0	0	0	0	8	1	12	42.0	3	7	0	1	1.000	13	3	1	0	.23
Washburn,J., Sea-Det	L	.000	3	0	0	0	0	.220	41	9	0	0	0	4	5	13	7	28	176.0	8	18	2	0	.929	9	4	0	0	.44
Waters,Chris, Bal	L	-	0	0	0	0	0	-	0	0	0	0	0	0	0	0	0	5	11.2	1	0	0	0	1.000	1	0	0	0	.00
Weathers,David, Cin-Mil	R	-	0	0	0	0	1	.101	139	14	0	0	2	4	7	85	17	68	62.0	5	7	1	0	.923	2	0	0	0	.00
Weaver,Jeff, LAD	R	.231	13	3	0	0	2	.207	203	42	6	1	0	13	6	70	24	20	76.0	6	10	1	0	.941	11	2	0	0	.18
Weaver,Jered, LAA	R	.000	4	0	0	1	0	.083	12	1	0	0	0	1	1	4	0	33	211.0	9	20	1	0	.967	25	6	1	2	.24
Webb,Brandon, Ari	R	.000	2	0	0	0	0	.113	391	44	9	0	0	29	10	182	55	1	4.0	0	1	0	0	1.000	2	1	0	0	.50
Webb,Ryan, SD	R	-	0	0	0	0	0	-	0	0	0	0	0	0	0	0	0	28	25.2	1	5	1	0	.857	0	0	0	0	-

Pitchers Hitting, Fielding and Holding Runners

Pitcher	T	2009 Hitting						Career Hitting										2009 Fielding and Holding Runners											
		Avg	AB	H	HR	RBI	SH	Avg	AB	H	2B	3B	HR	RBI	BB	SO	SH	G	Inn	PO	A	E	DP	Pct	SBA	CS	PCS	PPO	CS%
Wellemeyer,Todd, StL	R	.128	39	5	0	0	6	.142	120	17	0	0	0	6	2	57	22	28	122.1	8	12	1	1	.952	6	1	0	0	.17
Wells,Kip, Was-Cin	R	.091	11	1	0	0	6	.194	319	62	10	1	4	17	4	138	33	33	72.2	2	8	0	0	1.000	14	3	0	0	.21
Wells,Randy, ChC	R	.191	47	9	0	2	12	.191	47	9	3	0	0	2	2	7	12	27	165.1	15	18	1	1	.971	18	4	0	0	.22
West,Sean, Fla	L	.065	31	2	0	0	4	.065	31	2	1	0	0	0	0	19	4	20	103.1	3	7	2	0	.833	3	0	0	0	.00
Wheeler,Dan, TB	R	-	0	0	0	0	0	.143	7	1	0	0	0	0	0	1	1	69	57.2	0	8	0	1	1.000	5	0	0	0	.00
Whisler,Wes, CWS	L	-	0	0	0	0	0	-	0	0	0	0	0	0	0	0	0	3	1.1	0	0	0	0	-	1	0	0	0	.00
White,Sean, Sea	R	-	0	0	0	0	0	-	0	0	0	0	0	0	0	0	0	52	64.1	9	8	1	1	.944	8	3	1	2	.38
Williams,Randy, CWS	L	-	0	0	0	0	0	.000	1	0	0	0	0	0	0	0	0	25	17.2	4	5	0	0	1.000	7	2	2	0	.29
Willis,Dontrelle, Det	L	.000	1	0	0	0	0	.233	352	82	10	5	8	35	21	64	29	7	33.2	2	9	0	1	1.000	4	0	0	0	.00
Wilson,Brian, SF	R	.000	2	0	0	0	0	.000	4	0	0	0	0	0	0	1	0	68	72.1	1	9	1	2	.909	6	1	0	0	.17
Wilson,C.J., Tex	L	-	0	0	0	0	0	-	0	0	0	0	0	0	0	0	0	74	73.2	1	15	2	2	.889	6	2	0	0	.33
Wolf,Randy, LAD	L	.162	68	11	1	11	9	.181	509	92	26	0	5	49	31	170	66	34	214.1	9	32	1	1	.976	12	5	2	0	.42
Wolfe,Brian, Tor	R	-	0	0	0	0	0	-	0	0	0	0	0	0	0	0	0	14	15.1	1	0	0	0	1.000	0	0	0	0	-
Wood,Kerry, Cle	R	-	0	0	0	0	0	.171	345	59	6	0	7	32	11	113	46	58	55.0	1	7	0	0	1.000	10	0	0	0	.00
Wood,Tim, Fla	R	.500	2	1	0	0	0	.500	2	1	0	0	0	0	0	0	0	18	22.1	1	1	0	0	1.000	1	0	0	0	.00
Wright,Jamey, KC	R	-	0	0	0	0	0	.147	436	64	15	1	1	17	12	175	51	65	79.0	1	16	2	2	.895	10	3	0	2	.30
Wright,Wesley, Hou	L	.250	4	1	0	0	0	.250	4	1	0	0	0	0	0	1	0	49	44.2	3	3	1	0	.857	5	0	0	0	.00
Wuertz,Mike, Oak	R	-	0	0	0	0	0	.000	6	0	0	0	0	0	0	5	1	74	78.2	4	7	0	0	1.000	12	3	1	0	.25
Yabuta,Yasuhiko, KC	R	-	0	0	0	0	0	-	0	0	0	0	0	0	0	0	0	12	14.0	0	1	0	0	1.000	2	0	0	0	.00
Yates,Tyler, Pit	R	-	0	0	0	0	0	.083	12	1	0	0	0	0	0	6	1	15	12.0	0	2	0	0	1.000	1	1	0	0	1.00
Young,Chris, SD	R	.261	23	6	0	2	1	.141	156	22	4	1	1	10	8	62	21	14	76.0	9	9	0	0	1.000	20	0	0	1	.00
Zambrano,Carlos, ChC	R	.217	69	15	4	11	1	.238	593	133	24	3	20	58	6	203	31	28	169.1	10	23	3	2	.933	13	8	0	2	.62
Zavada,Clay, Ari	L	-	0	0	0	0	1	-	0	0	0	0	0	0	0	0	0	49	51.0	3	5	0	0	1.000	1	2	0	0	.50
Ziegler,Brad, Oak	R	-	0	0	0	0	0	-	0	0	0	0	0	0	0	0	0	69	73.1	10	13	0	3	1.000	4	1	0	1	.25
Zimmermann,J., Was	R	.148	27	4	0	2	6	.148	27	4	0	0	0	2	1	11	6	16	91.1	7	16	1	1	.958	13	5	1	1	.38
Zito,Barry, SF	L	.118	51	6	0	0	12	.104	193	20	0	0	0	5	10	57	23	33	192.0	3	26	2	1	.935	20	9	0	0	.45
Zumaya,Joel, Det	R	-	0	0	0	0	0	-	0	0	0	0	0	0	0	0	0	29	31.0	2	2	1	0	.800	2	0	0	0	.00

Hitters Pitching

Player	2009 Pitching											Career Pitching										
	G	W	L	Sv	IP	H	R	ER	BB	SO	ERA	G	W	L	Sv	IP	H	R	ER	BB	SO	ERA
Ankiel,Rick, StL	0	0	0	0	0.0	0	0	0	0	0	-	51	13	10	1	242.0	198	119	105	130	269	3.90
Brown,Dusty, Bos	1	0	0	0	1.0	2	1	1	0	1	9.00	1	0	0	0	1.0	2	1	1	0	1	9.00
Burke,Jamie, Sea-Was	0	0	0	0	0.0	0	0	0	0	0	-	1	0	1	0	1.0	1	1	1	0	0	9.00
Gload,Ross, Fla	1	0	0	0	1.0	0	0	0	2	0	0.00	1	0	0	0	1.0	0	0	0	2	0	0.00
Green,Nick, Bos	1	0	0	0	2.0	0	0	0	3	0	0.00	1	0	0	0	2.0	0	0	0	3	0	0.00
Janish,Paul, Cin	2	0	0	0	2.0	9	11	11	2	3	49.50	2	0	0	0	2.0	9	11	11	2	3	49.50
Loretta,Mark, LAD	1	0	0	0	0.1	0	0	0	0	0	0.00	2	0	0	0	1.1	1	0	0	1	2	0.00
Miles,Aaron, ChC	0	0	0	0	0.0	0	0	0	0	0	-	3	0	0	0	3.0	3	2	2	0	0	6.00
Ojeda,Augie, Ari	0	0	0	0	0.0	0	0	0	0	0	-	1	0	0	0	1.0	0	0	0	0	0	0.00
Ross,Cody, Fla	1	0	0	0	1.0	1	0	0	0	0	0.00	1	0	0	0	1.0	1	0	0	0	0	0.00
Swisher,Nick, NYY	1	0	0	0	1.0	1	0	0	1	1	0.00	1	0	0	0	1.0	1	0	0	1	1	0.00
Van Every,Jonathan, Bos	1	0	0	0	0.2	1	0	0	1	0	0.00	1	0	0	0	0.2	1	0	0	1	0	0.00
Wilson,Josh, Ari-SD-Sea	2	0	1	0	2.0	3	3	3	2	0	13.50	3	0	1	0	3.0	4	3	3	3	0	9.00

2009 Pinch Hitting

Pinch hitting might be the most thankless job in the big leagues. Usually called upon with the game on the line, pinch hitters step to the plate more or less cold. They need to be versatile. They are asked to get a hit or a walk, but once in a while they are called upon to bunt, work the count, or make contact to advance the runner. They also need to have short memories. Being employed as a pinch hitter is just a series of isolated incidents—without a past and with no certain future. Except, of course, if you collect all the data for every pinch hit at-bat and offer it in an easy-to-read table. Then, pinch hitting becomes not a series of isolated incidents, but a measurable skill.

Which is why we're excited to offer this brand new section, Pinch Hitting Analysis. This sort of thing was a staple of the old Sporting News *Baseball Guide,* one of our favorite publications. Unfortunately, the *Guide* is no longer being published, so we decided to take up the torch—at least as far as pinch hitting is concerned.

In this section, we see every player who made a pinch-hit appearance in 2009. This allows us to see how a player performed as a pinch hitter last season in comparison to his entire career.

It also allows us to see who the best pinch hitter in baseball really is. Maybe it's Cleveland's Jamey Carroll, who has hit .351 with an on-base percentage of .431 and a slugging percentage of .394 in almost 100 career at-bats as a pinch hitter (well above his .273/.351/.350 overall career numbers). Maybe it's Mark Kotsay. Most recently with the White Sox, he's displayed his pinch-hitting talents on a half-dozen teams in his career with his .342 average and a slugging percentage of .526. But I'm going with Colorado's Seth Smith. In 78 career pinch-hit at bats (nearly 100 plate appearances) he has hit .397 with a .500 on-base percentage and .718 slugging. Smith had a .472 batting average in 2009 in 36 pinch-hit at bats.

Pinch Hitting

Batter	B	AB	H	2B	3B	HR	RBI	TBB	IBB	SO	GDP	Avg	OBP	Slg	AB	H	2B	3B	HR	RBI	TBB	IBB	SO	GDP	Avg	OBP	Slg
		\	\	\	2009 Pinch Hitting										\	\	\	Career Pinch Hitting									
Bobby Abreu	L	2	0	0	0	0	0	0	0	0	0	.000	.000	.000	44	9	0	1	0	6	9	3	14	0	.205	.340	.250
Tony Abreu	B	3	0	0	0	0	0	1	0	0	0	.000	.250	.000	13	3	0	0	1	1	1	0	3	0	.231	.286	.462
Russ Adams	L	2	1	0	0	0	0	0	0	0	0	.500	.500	.500	33	10	3	0	1	5	0	0	6	3	.303	.303	.485
Eliezer Alfonzo	R	7	1	0	0	0	0	0	0	3	0	.143	.143	.143	23	4	1	0	0	4	0	0	12	0	.174	.174	.217
Brandon Allen	L	1	0	0	0	0	0	0	0	1	0	.000	.000	.000	1	0	0	0	0	0	0	0	1	0	.000	.000	.000
Alfredo Amezaga	B	8	2	1	0	0	0	1	0	0	0	.250	.333	.375	83	20	3	2	0	2	7	0	20	1	.241	.300	.325
Brian Anderson	R	9	2	0	0	0	0	1	0	3	1	.222	.300	.222	29	7	2	0	1	3	5	0	9	2	.241	.343	.414
Garret Anderson	L	11	3	0	0	1	4	0	0	1	0	.273	.273	.545	37	11	1	0	1	8	2	1	5	0	.297	.341	.405
Josh Anderson	L	12	2	0	0	0	0	0	0	3	0	.167	.167	.167	18	3	0	0	0	0	2	0	4	0	.167	.250	.167
Marlon Anderson	L	4	0	0	0	0	0	1	0	1	0	.000	.000	.000	309	84	15	0	9	46	30	1	63	5	.272	.336	.408
Robert Andino	R	5	0	0	0	0	0	0	0	3	0	.000	.000	.000	31	4	1	0	0	2	3	0	17	0	.129	.206	.161
Elvis Andrus	R	0	0	0	0	0	0	1	0	0	0	-	1.000	-	0	0	0	0	0	0	1	0	0	0	-	1.000	-
Rick Ankiel	L	22	6	1	0	2	3	4	1	6	0	.273	.385	.591	44	10	1	0	3	6	7	1	17	0	.227	.346	.455
Garrett Atkins	R	24	4	1	0	0	4	4	0	9	0	.167	.286	.208	42	8	2	0	1	8	6	0	13	0	.190	.286	.310
Michael Aubrey	L	4	2	0	0	0	0	1	0	1	0	.500	.600	.500	6	3	0	0	0	0	1	0	1	0	.500	.571	.500
Rich Aurilia	R	27	6	1	0	0	2	3	0	5	3	.222	.300	.259	117	31	3	0	4	25	14	2	24	5	.265	.338	.393
Brad Ausmus	R	5	0	0	0	0	0	0	0	2	0	.000	.167	.000	28	4	0	0	0	1	4	0	5	1	.143	.273	.143
Alex Avila	L	4	2	0	0	0	3	2	0	1	0	.500	.571	.500	4	2	0	0	0	3	2	0	1	0	.500	.571	.500
Mike Aviles	R	1	1	0	0	0	1	0	0	0	0	1.000	1.000	1.000	1	1	0	0	0	1	0	0	0	0	1.000	1.000	1.000
Erick Aybar	B	1	0	0	0	0	0	0	0	0	0	.000	.000	.000	28	5	1	2	0	5	4	0	8	1	.179	.294	.357
Willy Aybar	B	24	5	1	0	1	5	1	0	6	0	.208	.231	.375	47	11	1	0	1	6	4	0	10	1	.234	.288	.319
Brandon Backe	R	0	0	0	0	0	0	1	0	0	0	-	1.000	-	4	0	0	0	0	0	1	0	1	0	.000	.200	.000
Homer Bailey	R	1	0	0	0	0	0	0	0	1	0	.000	.000	.000	1	0	0	0	0	0	0	0	1	0	.000	.000	.000
Jeff Bailey	R	1	0	0	0	0	0	0	0	0	0	.000	.000	.000	11	2	0	1	0	1	0	0	6	0	.182	.182	.364
Jeff Baker	R	15	3	0	0	1	1	1	0	7	0	.200	.250	.400	91	16	3	0	2	5	9	1	37	2	.176	.255	.275
John Baker	L	9	0	0	0	0	0	1	0	4	0	.000	.100	.000	12	1	0	0	1	3	2	0	5	0	.083	.214	.333
Paul Bako	L	3	0	0	0	0	1	0	0	1	0	.000	.000	.000	35	4	0	0	0	1	4	0	10	1	.114	.205	.114
Rocco Baldelli	R	14	5	2	0	0	3	2	0	3	0	.357	.438	.500	29	8	2	0	1	6	5	1	9	1	.276	.382	.448
W. Balentien	R	13	0	0	0	0	0	0	0	1	0	.000	.000	.000	19	1	1	0	0	2	0	0	2	1	.053	.053	.105
Rod Barajas	R	5	3	0	0	2	2	1	0	0	0	.600	.667	1.800	24	10	1	0	2	4	3	1	6	0	.417	.481	.708
Josh Bard	B	14	5	2	0	0	2	1	0	3	0	.357	.400	.500	58	16	3	0	0	7	15	1	10	4	.276	.421	.328
Brian Barden	R	11	2	0	0	0	0	0	0	1	0	.182	.167	.182	27	5	1	0	0	3	1	0	4	1	.185	.207	.222
Josh Barfield	R	2	0	0	0	0	0	0	0	1	0	.000	.000	.000	9	2	1	0	1	4	0	0	3	0	.222	.222	.667
Kevin Barker	L	24	7	3	0	0	1	3	1	9	2	.292	.370	.417	44	10	3	0	0	2	5	1	17	2	.227	.306	.295
Clint Barmes	R	3	1	0	0	1	3	0	0	0	0	.333	.500	1.333	28	8	2	0	1	6	0	0	6	0	.286	.310	.464
Daric Barton	L	2	0	0	0	0	0	0	0	1	0	.000	.000	.000	10	1	0	0	0	2	0	0	6	0	.100	.100	.100
Jose Bautista	R	6	2	0	0	0	0	2	0	2	0	.333	.500	.333	49	7	1	0	0	1	11	2	20	0	.143	.300	.163
Ronnie Belliard	R	35	9	1	0	1	7	2	0	11	2	.257	.289	.371	115	29	6	0	3	23	13	0	26	3	.252	.323	.383
Carlos Beltran	B	1	0	0	0	0	0	0	0	0	0	.000	.000	.000	19	3	0	0	1	1	2	0	6	0	.158	.238	.316
Lance Berkman	B	4	2	0	0	0	0	1	0	1	0	.500	.600	.500	45	5	1	0	1	4	6	2	19	1	.111	.216	.200
Angel Berroa	R	5	1	0	0	0	0	1	0	2	0	.200	.333	.200	12	2	0	0	0	0	1	0	5	0	.167	.286	.167
Y. Betancourt	R	0	0	0	0	0	0	1	0	0	0	-	1.000	-	5	1	0	0	0	1	1	0	1	0	.200	.333	.200
Wilson Betemit	B	7	1	0	0	0	0	1	0	2	0	.143	.250	.143	131	31	7	0	4	15	23	0	46	2	.237	.351	.382
Brian Bixler	R	1	1	1	0	0	0	1	0	0	0	1.000	1.000	2.000	6	2	1	0	0	0	1	0	2	0	.333	.429	.500
Casey Blake	R	5	0	0	0	0	0	1	0	4	0	.000	.167	.000	20	4	2	0	0	3	3	0	8	0	.200	.296	.300
Hank Blalock	L	6	0	0	0	0	0	1	0	1	0	.000	.143	.000	26	6	2	0	2	12	2	1	6	1	.231	.286	.538
Andres Blanco	B	6	2	1	0	0	0	0	0	0	0	.333	.333	.500	6	2	1	0	0	0	0	0	0	0	.333	.333	.500
Gregor Blanco	L	6	1	0	0	0	0	0	0	3	0	.167	.167	.167	14	2	1	0	0	0	1	0	6	0	.143	.200	.214
Henry Blanco	R	4	0	0	0	0	0	2	0	2	0	.000	.333	.000	44	10	1	0	0	6	5	0	12	2	.227	.306	.250
Kyle Blanks	R	7	1	1	0	0	0	1	0	3	0	.143	.250	.286	7	1	1	0	0	0	1	0	3	0	.143	.250	.286
Willie Bloomquist	R	9	4	0	0	0	1	1	0	2	0	.444	.500	.444	46	13	1	0	0	3	3	0	10	1	.283	.320	.304
Geoff Blum	B	10	1	0	0	0	1	4	1	2	1	.100	.357	.100	194	45	10	0	1	21	29	6	42	5	.232	.333	.299
Brandon Boggs	B	2	0	0	0	0	0	1	0	2	0	.000	.333	.000	15	4	1	0	0	2	3	0	7	0	.267	.421	.333
Emilio Bonifacio	B	6	2	0	0	0	0	0	0	2	0	.333	.333	.333	16	4	1	0	0	2	1	0	5	0	.250	.294	.313
Aaron Boone	R	7	0	0	0	0	0	0	0	1	0	.000	.125	.000	74	16	3	1	1	11	9	0	17	1	.216	.302	.324
Julio Borbon	L	3	2	0	0	0	1	1	0	0	0	.667	.750	.667	3	2	0	0	0	1	1	0	0	0	.667	.750	.667
Jason Bourgeois	R	14	2	0	0	0	0	2	0	5	0	.143	.250	.143	15	2	0	0	0	0	2	0	5	0	.133	.235	.133
Michael Bourn	L	2	0	0	0	0	0	0	0	1	0	.000	.000	.000	25	2	0	0	0	0	1	0	6	0	.080	.115	.080
John Bowker	L	10	2	0	1	0	1	1	0	3	0	.200	.273	.400	33	11	1	2	0	4	4	0	8	0	.333	.405	.485
Milton Bradley	B	13	3	0	0	1	1	2	0	4	0	.231	.333	.462	31	5	0	0	1	1	8	1	10	1	.161	.333	.258
Michael Brantley	L	1	1	0	0	0	1	1	0	0	0	1.000	1.000	1.000	1	1	0	0	0	1	1	0	0	0	1.000	1.000	1.000
Ryan Braun	R	1	1	1	0	0	2	0	0	0	0	1.000	1.000	2.000	4	2	2	0	0	2	0	0	1	0	.500	.600	1.000
Reid Brignac	L	4	0	0	0	0	0	1	0	0	0	.000	.200	.000	5	0	0	0	0	0	1	0	0	0	.000	.000	.000
Emil Brown	R	1	0	0	0	0	0	1	0	0	0	.000	.500	.000	77	12	4	0	0	8	12	0	31	1	.156	.278	.208
Jay Bruce	L	4	2	1	0	0	2	0	0	0	0	.500	.500	.750	8	5	2	0	0	2	0	0	0	0	.625	.625	.875
Eric Bruntlett	R	28	4	4	0	0	3	1	0	12	0	.143	.194	.286	100	25	10	0	0	9	12	0	24	2	.250	.330	.350
John Buck	R	5	0	0	0	0	0	1	0	3	0	.000	.167	.000	15	2	0	0	0	0	1	0	7	2	.133	.188	.133
Travis Buck	L	6	0	0	0	0	0	0	0	2	0	.000	.000	.000	9	1	0	0	0	1	0	0	3	0	.111	.111	.111

Pinch Hitting

Batter	B	2009 Pinch Hitting													Career Pinch Hitting												
		AB	H	2B	3B	HR	RBI	TBB	IBB	SO	GDP	Avg	OBP	Slg	AB	H	2B	3B	HR	RBI	TBB	IBB	SO	GDP	Avg	OBP	Slg
Chris Burke	R	7	1	1	0	0	0	1	0	4	0	.143	.250	.286	79	14	4	0	1	6	12	0	21	1	.177	.313	.266
Pat Burrell	R	8	2	0	0	0	0	1	0	4	0	.250	.333	.250	44	10	1	0	2	6	13	1	16	1	.227	.404	.386
Brian Buscher	L	15	3	0	0	0	0	6	0	6	0	.200	.455	.200	25	6	1	0	0	3	9	0	8	1	.240	.457	.280
Billy Butler	R	3	0	0	0	0	0	1	0	3	0	.000	.250	.000	17	5	1	0	0	0	3	0	4	0	.294	.400	.353
Marlon Byrd	R	2	0	0	0	0	0	0	0	0	0	.000	.000	.000	45	13	6	0	1	5	5	0	10	1	.289	.377	.489
Eric Byrnes	R	24	4	1	0	1	3	1	0	2	0	.167	.200	.333	59	10	4	0	1	5	4	0	12	0	.169	.222	.288
Asdrubal Cabrera	B	2	0	0	0	0	0	1	0	0	0	.000	.333	.000	6	2	1	0	0	0	3	0	1	0	.333	.556	.500
Everth Cabrera	B	1	0	0	0	0	0	0	0	0	0	.000	.000	.000	1	0	0	0	0	0	0	0	0	0	.000	.000	.000
Melky Cabrera	B	6	0	0	0	0	0	1	0	2	0	.000	.143	.000	17	1	0	0	0	1	4	0	8	0	.059	.227	.059
Miguel Cabrera	R	0	0	0	0	0	0	1	0	0	0	-	1.000	-	5	2	0	0	0	2	1	0	1	0	.400	.500	.400
Orlando Cabrera	R	1	0	0	0	0	0	0	0	0	0	.000	.000	.000	9	1	0	0	0	2	1	0	2	0	.111	.182	.111
Miguel Cairo	R	18	2	0	0	0	0	0	0	2	0	.111	.158	.111	187	50	11	2	1	27	17	3	26	3	.267	.330	.364
Alberto Callaspo	B	2	1	0	0	0	0	0	0	0	0	.500	.500	.500	50	10	2	0	0	3	3	0	8	2	.200	.241	.240
Mike Cameron	R	2	0	0	0	0	0	1	0	0	0	.000	.333	.000	18	3	2	0	1	6	4	0	6	0	.167	.348	.444
Robinson Cancel	R	1	0	0	0	0	0	0	0	0	0	.000	.000	.000	12	4	1	0	0	2	2	0	0	0	.333	.429	.417
Robinson Cano	L	2	1	0	0	0	0	0	0	0	0	.500	.500	.500	12	6	0	0	2	4	0	0	2	0	.500	.500	1.000
Jorge Cantu	R	5	3	1	0	0	2	0	0	1	0	.600	.600	.800	31	10	4	0	0	4	3	0	7	0	.323	.400	.452
Luke Carlin	B	3	0	0	0	0	0	3	0	1	0	.000	.500	.000	4	0	0	0	0	0	3	0	1	0	.000	.429	.000
Mike Carp	L	4	0	0	0	0	1	1	0	3	0	.000	.167	.000	4	0	0	0	0	1	1	0	3	0	.000	.167	.000
Brett Carroll	R	21	5	2	0	1	7	2	0	7	1	.238	.304	.476	30	5	2	0	1	7	4	0	10	2	.167	.265	.333
Jamey Carroll	R	10	2	0	0	0	3	1	0	3	1	.200	.273	.200	93	32	1	0	1	12	14	0	21	4	.344	.426	.387
Matt Burson	R	1	1	0	0	0	1	0	0	0	0	1.000	1.000	1.000	1	1	0	0	0	1	0	0	0	0	1.000	1.000	1.000
Chris Carter	L	3	0	0	0	0	0	0	0	2	0	.000	.000	.000	7	1	0	0	0	0	0	0	2	0	.143	.143	.143
Alexi Casilla	B	1	0	0	0	0	0	0	0	0	0	.000	.000	.000	3	0	0	0	0	0	2	0	0	0	.000	.400	.000
Luis Castillo	B	6	1	0	0	0	2	0	0	2	0	.167	.143	.167	26	6	1	0	0	3	1	0	5	0	.231	.241	.269
Wilkin Castillo	B	3	2	0	0	0	1	0	0	0	0	.667	.667	.667	11	3	0	0	0	1	1	0	2	0	.273	.273	.273
Juan Castro	R	5	3	0	0	0	0	1	0	1	0	.600	.667	.600	102	20	1	1	3	10	5	0	26	2	.196	.234	.314
Ramon Castro	R	4	0	0	0	0	0	1	0	1	0	.000	.200	.000	73	19	3	0	3	10	5	0	18	0	.260	.308	.425
Frank Catalanotto	L	33	6	2	0	0	0	3	1	8	0	.182	.250	.242	227	62	14	4	2	35	29	3	38	7	.273	.358	.396
Ronny Cedeno	R	6	3	2	0	0	0	0	0	0	0	.500	.500	.833	53	14	4	0	1	4	6	0	11	0	.264	.361	.396
Francisco Cervelli	R	1	0	0	0	0	0	0	0	0	0	.000	.000	.000	1	0	0	0	0	0	0	0	0	0	.000	.000	.000
Endy Chavez	L	1	1	0	0	0	0	0	0	0	0	1.000	1.000	1.000	101	27	4	3	1	11	7	1	10	3	.267	.315	.396
Shin-Soo Choo	L	1	0	0	0	0	1	0	0	1	0	.000	.333	.000	21	6	1	1	0	9	3	0	7	1	.286	.393	.429
Ryan Church	L	10	4	1	0	1	2	0	0	6	0	.400	.400	.800	72	17	3	0	3	13	13	2	24	2	.236	.366	.403
Alex Cintron	B	18	2	0	0	0	0	0	0	6	0	.111	.111	.111	131	29	5	1	4	17	9	1	25	4	.221	.270	.366
Tony Clark	B	17	4	2	0	1	5	3	0	7	0	.235	.350	.529	266	60	12	0	12	62	33	1	89	8	.226	.316	.406
Chris Coghlan	L	5	1	0	0	1	1	0	0	1	0	.200	.200	.800	5	1	0	0	1	1	0	0	1	0	.200	.200	.800
Brooks Conrad	B	18	1	0	0	1	3	1	0	4	1	.056	.105	.222	18	1	0	0	1	3	1	0	4	1	.056	.105	.222
Aaron Cook	R	1	0	0	0	0	0	0	0	0	0	.000	.000	.000	5	2	0	0	0	0	1	0	0	0	.400	.400	.400
Alex Cora	L	8	4	0	1	0	1	0	0	0	0	.500	.500	.750	88	25	4	1	1	9	4	1	8	1	.284	.323	.386
Kevin Correia	R	1	0	0	0	0	0	0	0	1	0	.000	.000	.000	1	0	0	0	0	0	0	0	1	0	.000	.000	.000
Chris Coste	R	15	1	0	0	0	1	3	0	7	0	.067	.222	.133	61	13	3	0	1	7	3	0	19	1	.213	.262	.311
Craig Counsell	L	16	5	1	0	0	0	6	0	1	0	.313	.542	.375	184	39	6	1	1	7	31	1	23	4	.212	.336	.272
Carl Crawford	L	3	0	0	0	0	0	2	1	1	0	.000	.400	.000	15	1	0	0	0	1	4	1	3	0	.067	.263	.067
Joe Crede	R	3	0	0	0	0	0	0	0	1	0	.000	.000	.000	11	2	0	0	0	3	1	0	3	0	.182	.250	.182
Bobby Crosby	R	4	0	0	0	0	0	0	0	2	0	.000	.000	.000	7	0	0	0	0	0	0	0	4	0	.000	.000	.000
Trevor Crowe	B	2	0	0	0	0	0	0	0	0	0	.000	.000	.000	2	0	0	0	0	0	0	0	0	0	.000	.000	.000
Luis Cruz	R	5	1	0	0	0	0	0	0	0	0	.200	.200	.200	5	1	0	0	0	0	0	0	0	0	.200	.200	.200
Nelson Cruz	R	4	0	0	0	0	0	0	0	2	0	.000	.000	.000	12	0	0	0	0	1	0	0	5	0	.000	.000	.000
Michael Cuddyer	R	1	1	1	0	0	2	1	0	0	0	1.000	1.000	2.000	35	14	4	1	2	12	4	1	4	1	.400	.462	.743
A. Cunningham	R	1	0	0	0	0	0	0	0	0	0	.000	.000	.000	3	1	1	0	0	2	0	0	1	0	.333	.333	.667
Jack Cust	L	3	1	0	0	0	1	0	0	1	0	.333	.333	.333	36	6	0	0	0	3	13	0	17	1	.167	.388	.167
Johnny Damon	L	4	0	0	0	0	0	3	0	2	0	.000	.500	.000	53	9	1	0	1	4	8	1	14	1	.170	.281	.245
Chris Davis	L	2	1	0	0	0	0	1	0	1	0	.500	.500	.500	3	2	0	0	0	1	1	0	1	0	.667	.667	.667
Rajai Davis	R	8	2	0	1	0	2	0	0	4	0	.250	.250	.500	39	8	2	1	0	2	4	0	10	0	.205	.279	.308
Alejandro De Aza	L	8	1	0	0	0	0	3	0	2	0	.125	.333	.125	18	3	0	0	0	2	3	0	5	0	.167	.273	.167
David DeJesus	L	1	0	0	0	0	0	0	0	0	0	.000	.000	.000	5	0	0	0	0	0	1	0	2	0	.000	.167	.000
Carlos Delgado	L	0	0	0	0	0	0	1	0	0	0	-	1.000	-	49	9	1	0	2	9	5	0	16	2	.184	.268	.327
David Dellucci	L	3	2	0	0	0	0	0	0	1	0	.667	.667	.667	281	76	12	2	10	58	33	3	95	3	.270	.357	.434
Mark DeRosa	R	5	1	0	0	0	0	0	0	1	0	.200	.200	.200	103	27	5	2	0	15	10	0	17	0	.262	.336	.359
Ian Desmond	R	1	0	0	0	0	0	0	0	0	0	.000	.000	.000	1	0	0	0	0	0	0	0	0	0	.000	.000	.000
Blake DeWitt	L	18	5	1	0	2	2	2	0	3	1	.278	.350	.667	25	8	2	0	2	5	2	0	4	1	.320	.370	.640
Matt Diaz	R	15	4	1	0	0	1	2	0	2	0	.267	.389	.333	127	35	5	2	0	11	3	0	25	5	.276	.301	.346
Robinzon Diaz	R	7	2	1	0	0	1	1	0	0	0	.286	.375	.429	8	3	1	0	0	1	1	0	0	0	.375	.444	.500
Chris Dickerson	L	19	4	0	0	0	0	8	1	8	1	.211	.444	.211	23	5	1	0	0	2	9	1	11	1	.217	.438	.261
Joe Dillon	R	5	0	0	0	0	0	0	0	2	0	.000	.167	.000	82	18	5	1	1	5	6	0	19	3	.220	.289	.341
Greg Dobbs	L	54	9	1	0	1	4	6	0	11	0	.167	.250	.241	210	58	15	2	6	48	18	2	47	4	.276	.332	.452
Ryan Doumit	B	3	3	0	0	0	0	0	0	0	0	1.000	1.000	1.000	61	16	3	0	2	14	5	1	16	3	.262	.329	.410
J.D. Drew	L	6	2	0	0	0	1	3	0	1	0	.333	.556	.333	89	22	3	1	4	16	16	1	28	2	.247	.358	.438
Stephen Drew	L	3	1	0	0	0	0	2	0	0	0	.333	.600	.333	13	5	0	0	1	1	3	0	2	0	.385	.500	.615

Pinch Hitting

Batter	B	2009 Pinch Hitting													Career Pinch Hitting												
		AB	H	2B	3B	HR	RBI	TBB	IBB	SO	GDP	Avg	OBP	Slg	AB	H	2B	3B	HR	RBI	TBB	IBB	SO	GDP	Avg	OBP	Slg
Chris Duffy	L	7	1	0	0	0	1	2	0	2	0	.143	.333	.143	25	4	1	0	0	3	2	0	9	0	.160	.222	.200
Elijah Dukes	R	5	0	0	0	0	0	2	0	3	0	.000	.286	.000	11	0	0	0	0	0	3	0	5	1	.000	.214	.000
Chris Duncan	L	12	4	1	0	0	0	2	0	2	1	.333	.429	.417	79	19	4	0	6	16	11	1	27	3	.241	.333	.519
Shelley Duncan	R	3	0	0	0	0	0	0	0	1	0	.000	.000	.000	12	0	0	0	0	0	0	0	5	0	.000	.000	.000
Adam Dunn	L	3	1	0	0	0	1	1	0	1	0	.333	.500	.333	29	8	1	0	3	9	5	0	10	0	.276	.382	.621
Luis Durango	B	4	2	0	0	0	0	2	0	1	0	.500	.667	.500	4	2	0	0	0	0	2	0	1	0	.500	.667	.500
Jermaine Dye	R	1	0	0	0	0	0	0	0	0	0	.000	.000	.000	25	8	0	0	0	3	0	0	6	1	.320	.346	.320
David Eckstein	R	8	4	1	0	1	3	0	0	0	0	.500	.500	1.000	22	6	1	0	1	4	3	0	2	0	.273	.360	.455
A.J. Ellis	R	1	0	0	0	0	0	0	0	0	0	.000	.000	.000	1	0	0	0	0	0	0	0	0	0	.000	.000	.000
Jacoby Ellsbury	L	2	0	0	0	0	0	0	0	1	0	.000	.000	.000	3	1	0	0	0	0	1	0	1	0	.333	.500	.333
Darin Erstad	L	62	12	2	2	1	6	8	1	16	0	.194	.282	.339	136	33	9	2	2	20	12	2	36	0	.243	.302	.382
Yunel Escobar	R	2	1	0	0	0	0	0	0	0	0	.500	.500	.500	14	4	0	0	0	1	5	0	1	0	.286	.474	.286
Andre Ethier	L	4	1	1	0	0	1	2	0	1	0	.250	.500	.500	40	11	2	0	2	9	8	0	13	1	.275	.396	.475
Nick Evans	R	15	1	0	1	0	0	0	0	7	2	.067	.067	.200	31	5	1	1	0	2	1	0	14	2	.161	.188	.258
Adam Everett	R	3	0	0	0	0	0	0	0	3	0	.000	.000	.000	13	2	1	0	0	1	2	0	5	0	.154	.353	.231
Tommy Everidge	R	1	0	0	0	0	0	0	0	1	0	.000	.000	.000	1	0	0	0	0	0	0	0	1	0	.000	.000	.000
Pedro Feliz	R	6	1	1	0	0	2	0	0	2	0	.167	.167	.333	124	34	10	2	2	20	6	0	35	0	.274	.308	.435
Josh Fields	R	6	0	0	0	0	0	3	0	2	1	.000	.333	.000	11	1	0	0	1	2	4	0	4	1	.091	.333	.364
Jeff Fiorentino	L	4	1	0	0	0	0	1	0	2	0	.250	.400	.250	5	1	0	0	0	0	2	0	3	0	.200	.429	.200
Jesus Flores	R	4	0	0	0	0	1	2	0	1	0	.000	.333	.000	35	8	1	0	1	8	7	0	9	0	.229	.349	.343
Tyler Flowers	R	2	0	0	0	0	0	0	0	1	0	.000	.000	.000	2	0	0	0	0	0	0	0	1	0	.000	.000	.000
Cliff Floyd	L	8	1	0	0	0	0	0	0	3	0	.125	.125	.125	148	25	4	1	5	23	25	1	51	2	.169	.291	.311
Mike Fontenot	L	23	5	4	0	0	3	1	0	5	1	.217	.240	.391	77	16	8	0	1	10	11	0	18	1	.208	.308	.351
Dexter Fowler	B	10	4	1	0	0	1	2	0	3	0	.400	.500	.500	13	4	1	0	0	1	2	0	3	0	.308	.400	.385
Jake Fox	R	24	5	2	0	0	3	2	0	9	0	.208	.300	.292	27	5	2	0	0	3	2	0	10	1	.185	.273	.259
Ben Francisco	R	15	3	2	0	0	2	2	0	6	0	.200	.294	.333	30	6	3	0	1	5	4	0	11	1	.200	.294	.400
Juan Francisco	L	8	4	1	0	1	4	3	0	2	0	.500	.636	1.000	8	4	1	0	1	4	3	0	2	0	.500	.636	1.000
Jeff Francoeur	R	3	1	0	0	0	0	0	0	1	0	.333	.333	.333	8	2	0	0	0	0	1	0	2	0	.250	.333	.250
Kevin Frandsen	R	4	1	0	0	0	0	0	0	0	0	.250	.250	.250	40	10	0	0	0	6	2	0	8	1	.250	.286	.250
Ryan Freel	R	6	1	0	0	0	0	0	0	1	0	.167	.167	.167	48	9	2	0	1	2	5	0	11	2	.188	.278	.292
David Freese	R	7	2	1	0	0	1	1	0	1	0	.286	.375	.429	7	2	1	0	0	1	1	0	1	0	.286	.375	.429
K. Fukudome	L	8	1	0	0	0	1	2	0	2	0	.125	.300	.125	22	7	1	0	1	4	3	0	3	0	.318	.400	.500
Sam Fuld	L	14	3	0	0	0	0	2	0	1	0	.214	.313	.214	16	3	0	0	0	0	2	0	2	0	.188	.278	.188
Rafael Furcal	B	7	4	0	0	1	2	2	1	1	0	.571	.667	1.000	25	8	0	0	1	2	3	1	4	1	.320	.393	.440
Yovani Gallardo	R	1	0	0	0	0	0	0	0	0	0	.000	.000	.000	1	0	0	0	0	0	0	0	0	0	.000	.000	.000
Mat Gamel	L	20	3	1	0	0	2	7	1	13	0	.150	.370	.200	22	4	2	0	0	2	7	1	14	0	.182	.379	.273
N. Garciaparra	R	28	4	1	0	0	3	0	0	6	2	.143	.143	.179	56	11	1	0	0	7	6	2	11	2	.196	.281	.214
Brett Gardner	L	6	2	1	0	0	0	0	0	1	0	.333	.333	.500	7	2	1	0	0	0	0	0	1	0	.286	.286	.429
Ryan Garko	R	17	1	0	0	0	1	1	0	2	0	.059	.105	.059	38	8	1	0	2	7	2	0	11	0	.211	.244	.395
Jon Garland	R	1	0	0	0	0	0	0	0	1	0	.000	.000	.000	1	0	0	0	0	0	0	0	1	0	.000	.000	.000
Joey Gathright	L	9	1	0	0	0	0	1	0	5	0	.111	.200	.111	23	5	0	0	0	3	5	0	7	0	.217	.357	.217
Esteban German	R	3	0	0	0	0	0	0	0	1	0	.000	.000	.000	58	12	4	1	0	3	9	0	23	0	.207	.324	.310
Jody Gerut	L	48	10	2	0	0	10	8	0	7	2	.208	.328	.250	91	20	2	0	0	14	9	0	14	2	.220	.294	.242
Chris Getz	L	2	0	0	0	0	0	0	0	0	0	.000	.000	.000	3	1	0	0	0	0	1	0	0	0	.333	.333	.333
Jason Giambi	L	13	5	1	0	1	7	4	0	3	0	.385	.529	.692	63	19	3	0	4	16	9	2	21	1	.302	.397	.540
Brian Giles	L	4	2	1	0	0	0	0	0	0	0	.500	.500	.750	44	15	3	0	3	15	10	2	7	0	.341	.456	.614
Chris Gimenez	R	1	0	0	0	0	0	0	0	0	0	.000	.000	.000	1	0	0	0	0	0	0	0	0	0	.000	.000	.000
Troy Glaus	R	6	0	0	0	0	0	2	0	4	0	.000	.250	.000	18	2	0	0	1	4	7	2	9	0	.111	.360	.278
Ross Gload	L	66	21	1	1	2	15	11	3	10	0	.318	.418	.455	160	48	3	1	5	29	14	3	26	3	.300	.358	.425
Jonny Gomes	R	19	3	2	0	0	2	3	0	11	0	.158	.273	.263	59	10	4	0	2	10	6	0	22	1	.169	.269	.339
Carlos Gomez	R	2	0	0	0	0	0	0	0	1	0	.000	.000	.000	8	0	0	0	0	0	0	0	4	0	.000	.000	.000
Adrian Gonzalez	L	3	2	0	0	1	2	0	0	0	0	.667	.667	1.667	12	2	0	0	1	2	1	1	3	0	.167	.231	.417
Alberto Gonzalez	R	12	5	1	0	0	4	1	0	1	1	.417	.462	.500	20	7	1	0	0	6	1	0	3	1	.350	.381	.400
Andy Gonzalez	R	8	1	0	1	0	0	0	0	2	0	.125	.125	.375	16	4	1	1	0	0	0	0	4	0	.250	.250	.438
Carlos Gonzalez	L	9	0	0	0	0	0	1	0	7	0	.000	.100	.000	15	2	0	0	0	2	1	0	9	0	.133	.188	.133
Edgar Gonzalez	R	42	9	1	0	2	6	5	0	12	1	.214	.298	.381	72	17	1	0	3	10	9	0	21	1	.236	.321	.375
Curtis Granderson	L	1	1	0	0	0	0	0	0	0	0	1.000	1.000	1.000	18	5	0	0	0	1	1	0	8	0	.278	.300	.278
Andy Green	R	3	0	0	0	0	0	1	0	1	0	.000	.250	.000	67	14	3	0	2	5	11	0	23	0	.209	.321	.343
Nick Green	R	1	0	0	0	0	1	1	0	0	1	.000	.500	.000	18	3	1	0	0	1	2	0	6	1	.167	.286	.222
Khalil Greene	R	32	5	1	0	1	6	3	1	13	2	.156	.216	.281	34	5	1	0	1	6	3	1	13	2	.147	.205	.265
Tyler Greene	R	6	3	0	0	1	1	0	0	2	0	.500	.571	1.000	6	3	0	0	1	1	0	0	2	0	.500	.571	1.000
Ken Griffey Jr.	L	14	4	0	0	1	3	1	0	4	0	.286	.333	.500	86	22	3	0	6	20	19	6	29	2	.256	.389	.500
Gabe Gross	L	27	2	1	0	0	1	5	0	15	0	.074	.219	.111	129	21	4	0	3	19	24	0	49	1	.163	.299	.264
Vladimir Guerrero	R	5	3	0	0	0	0	0	0	0	0	.600	.600	.600	15	4	1	0	2	1	1	0	0	0	.267	.294	.400
Carlos Guillen	B	3	0	0	0	0	0	1	0	1	0	.000	.250	.000	25	5	1	0	0	2	7	1	10	0	.200	.364	.240
Jose Guillen	R	3	0	0	0	0	2	0	0	0	0	.000	.000	.000	83	21	0	1	2	11	3	1	23	5	.253	.303	.349
Cristian Guzman	B	16	3	1	0	0	2	1	0	3	0	.188	.235	.250	36	5	1	0	0	2	3	1	9	2	.139	.205	.167
Jesus Guzman	R	9	3	0	0	0	0	0	0	2	2	.333	.333	.333	9	3	0	0	0	0	0	0	2	2	.333	.333	.333
Tony Gwynn	L	11	4	1	0	0	0	3	0	0	0	.364	.500	.455	66	19	3	1	0	5	10	0	11	1	.288	.382	.364
Travis Hafner	L	5	3	0	0	0	1	1	0	1	0	.600	.667	.600	34	9	1	0	2	10	11	2	7	2	.265	.447	.471

Pinch Hitting

Batter	B	2009 AB	H	2B	3B	HR	RBI	TBB	IBB	SO	GDP	Avg	OBP	Slg	Career AB	H	2B	3B	HR	RBI	TBB	IBB	SO	GDP	Avg	OBP	Slg
Jerry Hairston	R	8	1	1	0	0	1	2	0	2	0	.125	.273	.250	52	8	3	1	0	2	3	0	9	2	.154	.196	.231
Scott Hairston	R	7	3	1	0	1	2	1	0	3	0	.429	.500	1.000	81	14	3	0	2	8	12	0	30	2	.173	.280	.284
Bill Hall	R	7	0	0	0	0	0	0	0	5	0	.000	.000	.000	100	18	3	0	4	17	6	0	42	0	.180	.224	.330
Josh Hamilton	L	4	1	0	0	0	1	0	0	1	0	.250	.250	.250	14	3	0	0	2	5	1	0	3	0	.214	.267	.643
Ryan Hanigan	R	6	2	0	0	0	0	0	0	1	0	.333	.333	.333	9	3	1	0	0	2	2	0	1	0	.333	.455	.444
Jack Hannahan	L	1	0	0	0	0	1	0	0	0	0	.000	.000	.000	10	2	0	0	0	1	1	0	5	0	.200	.250	.200
J.J. Hardy	R	3	1	1	0	0	0	0	0	1	0	.333	.333	.667	15	3	1	0	0	1	1	0	4	0	.200	.250	.267
Dan Haren	R	1	0	0	0	0	1	0	0	1	0	.000	.000	.000	1	0	0	0	0	1	1	0	1	0	.000	.333	.000
Brendan Harris	R	7	2	1	0	0	0	2	0	0	1	.286	.500	.429	37	8	2	0	2	5	5	0	11	1	.216	.328	.432
Willie Harris	L	26	6	0	0	1	1	1	0	5	0	.231	.259	.346	99	22	2	0	3	7	12	0	17	1	.222	.313	.333
Corey Hart	R	7	1	0	0	0	1	1	0	1	0	.143	.222	.143	54	19	2	1	3	12	5	1	12	4	.352	.410	.593
Brad Hawpe	L	3	1	0	0	0	0	0	0	0	0	.333	.333	.333	51	11	2	0	2	9	6	0	24	1	.216	.293	.373
Brett Hayes	R	9	2	1	0	1	2	0	0	3	1	.222	.300	.667	9	2	1	0	1	2	0	0	3	1	.222	.300	.667
Chase Headley	L	12	4	1	0	2	2	4	0	5	0	.333	.500	.917	17	6	1	0	2	2	4	0	6	0	.353	.500	.765
Wes Helms	R	49	17	3	0	0	12	4	0	12	3	.347	.429	.408	266	77	19	3	7	49	25	0	76	11	.289	.362	.462
Todd Helton	L	2	1	0	0	0	0	0	0	0	0	.500	.500	.500	41	7	1	0	1	7	6	2	14	1	.171	.277	.268
Jeremy Hermida	L	9	2	0	0	0	2	0	0	5	0	.222	.222	.222	41	10	1	0	2	8	6	0	11	1	.244	.354	.415
A. Hernandez	B	17	4	1	1	0	0	0	0	5	0	.235	.235	.412	32	6	1	1	0	1	1	0	10	0	.188	.212	.281
Diory Hernandez	R	5	0	0	0	0	0	0	0	3	0	.000	.000	.000	5	0	0	0	0	0	0	0	3	0	.000	.000	.000
Livan Hernandez	R	1	0	0	0	0	0	0	0	0	1	.000	.000	.000	12	1	0	0	0	1	0	0	5	1	.083	.083	.083
Luis Hernandez	R	8	0	0	0	0	0	0	0	4	0	.000	.000	.000	10	0	0	0	0	0	0	0	5	0	.000	.000	.000
R. Hernandez	R	2	1	0	0	0	0	0	0	1	0	.500	.500	.500	54	8	0	0	2	0	3	0	16	2	.148	.193	.259
John Hester	R	6	2	0	0	1	3	0	0	3	0	.333	.333	.833	6	2	0	0	1	3	0	0	3	0	.333	.333	.833
Aaron Hill	R	1	1	0	0	0	1	0	0	0	0	1.000	1.000	1.000	6	3	1	0	0	1	0	0	0	1	.500	.500	.667
Koyie Hill	B	5	1	1	0	0	0	1	0	1	0	.200	.333	.400	20	4	2	0	0	0	2	0	7	1	.200	.273	.300
Rich Hill	L	1	0	0	0	0	0	0	0	0	0	.000	.000	.000	1	0	0	0	0	0	0	0	0	0	.000	.000	.000
Eric Hinske	L	30	9	3	0	0	4	7	0	8	0	.300	.421	.400	102	26	6	0	2	14	19	0	28	2	.255	.371	.373
Jaime Hoffmann	R	9	1	0	0	0	0	0	0	0	2	.111	.111	.111	9	1	0	0	0	0	0	0	0	2	.111	.111	.111
Jarrett Hoffpauir	R	2	1	1	0	0	0	3	0	1	0	.500	.800	1.000	2	1	1	0	0	0	3	0	1	0	.500	.800	1.000
Micah Hoffpauir	L	41	9	4	0	1	10	5	1	10	0	.220	.304	.390	54	12	4	0	1	11	6	1	17	0	.222	.300	.352
Matt Holliday	L	2	1	0	0	0	0	1	0	1	0	.500	.500	.500	14	3	1	0	0	1	4	0	4	0	.214	.267	.286
Ryan Howard	L	1	1	0	0	0	3	1	0	0	0	1.000	1.000	4.000	28	11	3	0	5	12	3	0	12	1	.393	.452	1.036
Chin-lung Hu	R	1	0	0	0	0	0	0	0	1	0	.000	.000	.000	3	1	0	0	1	1	0	0	1	0	.333	.333	1.333
Orlando Hudson	B	4	0	0	0	0	0	0	0	2	1	.000	.000	.000	24	8	1	0	2	5	4	0	8	1	.333	.429	.625
Aubrey Huff	L	12	4	1	1	1	6	0	0	3	0	.333	.385	.833	39	8	1	1	1	11	3	1	10	0	.205	.273	.359
Tug Hulett	L	6	1	0	0	0	1	0	0	2	0	.167	.167	.167	17	3	1	0	0	1	2	0	4	0	.176	.263	.235
Nick Hundley	R	3	1	0	0	0	2	1	0	0	0	.333	.500	.333	4	1	0	0	0	2	1	0	0	0	.250	.400	.250
Torii Hunter	R	1	1	0	0	0	0	0	0	0	0	1.000	1.000	1.000	20	3	0	1	0	0	0	0	5	2	.150	.150	.250
Chris Iannetta	R	4	2	0	0	1	2	0	0	0	0	.500	.600	1.250	16	7	0	0	2	5	2	0	4	0	.438	.526	.813
Raul Ibanez	L	4	0	0	0	0	0	1	1	1	0	.000	.200	.000	89	13	2	0	1	11	11	1	17	2	.146	.238	.202
Omar Infante	R	14	6	0	0	0	4	0	0	1	0	.429	.429	.429	46	11	2	2	0	11	3	0	13	2	.239	.275	.370
Joe Inglett	L	6	1	0	0	0	0	0	0	2	0	.167	.167	.167	24	5	1	0	0	2	1	0	3	0	.208	.240	.250
Hernan Iribarren	L	9	2	2	0	0	0	1	0	3	0	.222	.300	.444	18	4	3	0	0	1	2	0	6	0	.222	.300	.389
Travis Ishikawa	L	13	3	0	0	0	0	1	0	6	0	.231	.286	.231	22	5	1	0	0	0	1	0	10	1	.227	.261	.273
Akinori Iwamura	L	2	0	0	0	0	0	1	0	1	0	.000	.333	.000	3	0	0	0	0	0	1	0	2	0	.000	.250	.000
Cesar Izturis	B	1	0	0	0	0	0	0	0	1	0	.000	.000	.000	34	10	2	0	0	0	3	0	4	0	.294	.368	.353
Maicer Izturis	B	7	3	1	0	0	1	6	2	2	0	.429	.692	.571	20	5	1	0	0	2	8	2	4	1	.250	.464	.300
Conor Jackson	R	4	1	0	0	1	4	1	0	0	0	.250	.400	1.000	43	6	0	0	3	12	12	0	5	0	.140	.321	.349
Mike Jacobs	L	12	4	0	0	1	4	1	0	4	1	.333	.385	.583	47	11	1	0	3	13	3	2	15	1	.234	.275	.447
Paul Janish	R	5	1	0	0	0	0	2	0	0	0	.286	.429	.200	7	2	0	0	0	2	2	0	3	0	.286	.444	.286
Jason Jaramillo	B	2	0	0	0	0	0	0	0	0	0	.000	.000	.000	2	0	0	0	0	0	0	0	0	0	.000	.000	.000
Derek Jeter	R	1	0	0	0	0	0	0	0	0	0	.000	.000	.000	4	0	0	0	0	0	1	0	2	0	.000	.200	.000
Chris Johnson	R	5	0	0	0	0	0	2	0	0	0	.000	.000	.000	5	0	0	0	0	0	2	0	0	0	.000	.000	.000
Josh Johnson	L	0	0	0	0	0	0	1	0	0	0	-	1.000	-	0	0	0	0	0	0	1	0	0	0	-	1.000	-
Kelly Johnson	L	19	7	2	1	0	2	6	0	1	0	.368	.520	.579	44	14	2	1	1	8	14	1	8	0	.318	.483	.477
Nick Johnson	L	2	1	0	0	0	0	1	0	0	0	.500	.750	.500	23	5	0	0	0	3	5	0	3	1	.217	.379	.217
Reed Johnson	R	15	4	0	0	0	2	1	0	4	0	.267	.353	.267	80	19	5	0	2	12	6	1	18	2	.238	.303	.375
Adam Jones	R	1	0	0	0	0	0	0	0	0	0	.000	.000	.000	7	2	0	0	1	3	1	0	2	0	.286	.375	.714
Andruw Jones	R	8	1	1	0	0	0	0	0	3	1	.125	.125	.250	49	9	3	0	2	8	10	0	15	1	.184	.322	.367
Brandon Jones	L	0	0	0	0	0	0	1	0	0	0	-	1.000	-	6	0	0	0	0	0	3	0	2	0	.000	.333	.000
Chipper Jones	B	8	4	2	0	0	5	1	1	2	0	.500	.556	.750	50	12	2	0	2	15	11	3	16	0	.240	.371	.400
Mitch Jones	R	5	2	0	0	0	0	0	0	2	0	.400	.400	.400	5	2	0	0	0	0	0	0	2	0	.400	.400	.400
Matt Joyce	L	2	0	0	0	0	0	0	0	0	0	.000	.000	.000	11	1	0	1	0	1	0	0	3	0	.091	.167	.273
Gabe Kapler	R	11	3	1	0	2	3	4	0	1	0	.273	.467	.909	102	31	5	1	4	14	12	0	19	1	.304	.377	.490
Matt Kata	B	28	7	0	0	0	4	0	0	3	2	.250	.241	.250	85	21	4	1	1	13	3	0	14	3	.247	.267	.353
K. Kawakami	R	2	0	0	0	0	0	0	0	2	0	.000	.000	.000	2	0	0	0	0	0	0	0	2	0	.000	.000	.000
Austin Kearns	R	22	4	1	0	0	2	6	0	8	1	.182	.379	.227	52	14	2	1	2	13	10	0	17	1	.269	.397	.462
Don Kelly	L	4	1	0	0	0	0	0	0	1	0	.250	.250	.250	20	3	0	0	0	0	2	0	3	1	.150	.261	.150
Matt Kemp	R	3	1	0	0	0	1	0	0	1	0	.333	.333	.333	26	5	0	0	1	1	2	0	13	0	.192	.250	.308
Jason Kendall	R	1	0	0	0	0	0	0	0	0	0	.000	.000	.000	34	8	1	0	0	5	5	2	3	0	.235	.366	.265

Pinch Hitting

Batter	B	AB	H	2B	3B	HR	RBI	TBB	IBB	SO	GDP	Avg	OBP	Slg	AB	H	2B	3B	HR	RBI	TBB	IBB	SO	GDP	Avg	OBP	Slg
						2009 Pinch Hitting														**Career Pinch Hitting**							
Howie Kendrick	R	7	2	0	0	0	1	0	0	1	0	.286	.286	.286	8	2	0	0	0	1	0	0	1	0	.250	.250	.250
Adam Kennedy	L	1	0	0	0	0	1	0	0	0	1	.000	.000	.000	79	16	4	0	1	9	5	1	17	4	.203	.253	.291
Jeff Keppinger	R	15	5	0	0	0	1	0	0	1	1	.333	.313	.333	31	9	1	0	0	4	1	0	3	1	.290	.303	.323
Paul Konerko	R	2	0	0	0	0	0	0	0	0	0	.000	.000	.000	52	14	0	0	2	12	7	3	7	2	.269	.350	.385
Casey Kotchman	L	11	0	0	0	0	1	2	0	3	0	.000	.154	.000	41	10	6	0	0	9	11	0	15	0	.244	.404	.390
Mark Kotsay	L	15	2	1	0	0	0	0	0	6	0	.133	.133	.200	76	26	5	0	3	12	5	2	17	0	.342	.383	.526
George Kottaras	L	2	0	0	0	0	0	0	0	2	0	.000	.000	.000	2	0	0	0	0	0	0	0	2	0	.000	.000	.000
Kevin Kouzmanoff	R	1	0	0	0	0	1	0	0	0	0	.000	.000	.000	11	3	1	0	0	6	2	0	2	0	.273	.333	.364
Jason Kubel	L	10	3	0	0	3	5	3	0	4	0	.300	.462	1.200	55	13	3	0	4	8	10	1	17	0	.236	.354	.509
Gerald Laird	R	4	0	0	0	0	1	0	0	1	0	.000	.000	.000	10	2	0	0	0	1	2	0	1	0	.200	.333	.200
Matt LaPorta	R	1	0	0	0	0	0	0	0	1	0	.000	.000	.000	1	0	0	0	0	0	0	0	1	0	.000	.000	.000
Jeff Larish	L	5	0	0	0	0	0	2	0	3	0	.000	.286	.000	16	5	2	0	0	2	3	0	6	0	.313	.421	.438
Adam LaRoche	L	3	0	0	0	0	0	0	0	1	0	.000	.000	.000	56	12	2	0	1	8	2	1	14	2	.214	.237	.304
Andy LaRoche	R	4	1	0	0	0	0	0	0	2	0	.250	.250	.250	21	4	0	0	0	1	2	0	5	0	.190	.261	.190
Jason LaRue	R	8	0	0	0	0	0	2	0	1	0	.000	.273	.000	40	10	3	0	4	12	2	0	10	2	.250	.318	.625
Fred Lewis	L	38	10	7	0	0	7	5	0	13	0	.263	.349	.447	62	17	7	1	0	11	10	1	21	0	.274	.384	.419
Brent Lillibridge	R	5	0	0	0	0	0	0	0	1	0	.000	.000	.000	6	0	0	0	0	0	0	0	2	0	.000	.000	.000
Adam Lind	L	4	2	0	0	0	1	0	0	1	0	.500	.500	.500	19	7	0	0	1	6	0	0	8	0	.368	.350	.526
James Loney	L	5	0	0	0	0	0	1	0	1	1	.000	.167	.000	26	2	0	1	0	2	1	0	5	1	.077	.111	.154
Evan Longoria	R	2	0	0	0	0	0	1	1	0	0	.000	.333	.000	3	1	0	0	0	1	1	1	0	0	.333	.500	.333
Felipe Lopez	B	7	0	0	0	0	0	1	0	2	0	.000	.125	.000	38	6	1	0	0	3	3	0	12	1	.158	.238	.184
Jose Lopez	R	1	0	0	0	0	0	0	0	0	0	.000	.000	.000	6	0	0	0	0	0	0	0	1	0	.000	.000	.000
Mark Loretta	R	60	14	2	0	0	7	6	1	8	1	.233	.303	.267	180	47	9	0	4	36	23	2	33	8	.261	.348	.378
Mike Lowell	R	3	0	0	0	0	0	1	1	0	0	.000	.250	.000	41	10	2	0	1	8	2	1	6	1	.244	.267	.366
Jed Lowrie	B	1	1	0	0	0	0	0	0	0	0	1.000	1.000	1.000	3	1	0	0	0	0	0	0	1	0	.333	.333	.333
Ryan Ludwick	R	13	4	1	0	1	4	2	0	3	1	.308	.400	.615	65	18	4	0	4	11	9	1	14	1	.277	.373	.523
Julio Lugo	R	10	2	0	0	0	0	2	0	2	1	.200	.333	.200	41	9	1	0	0	2	6	0	9	1	.220	.340	.244
Drew Macias	L	17	2	1	0	0	2	5	0	5	0	.118	.318	.176	25	2	1	0	0	3	7	0	9	0	.080	.273	.120
Mitch Maier	L	5	1	1	0	0	0	1	0	2	0	.200	.333	.400	6	1	1	0	0	0	1	0	2	0	.167	.286	.333
Matt Maloney	L	1	0	0	0	0	0	0	0	1	0	.000	.000	.000	1	0	0	0	0	0	0	0	1	0	.000	.000	.000
Tommy Manzella	R	2	1	0	0	0	0	0	0	0	0	.500	.500	.500	2	1	0	0	0	0	0	0	0	0	.500	.500	.500
Andy Marte	R	3	0	0	0	0	0	0	0	1	0	.000	.000	.000	15	1	0	0	0	0	2	0	7	1	.067	.176	.067
Russell Martin	R	3	0	0	0	0	0	0	0	0	0	.000	.250	.000	17	2	0	0	1	2	0	0	2	1	.118	.167	.294
F. Martinez	L	4	1	0	0	0	0	0	0	0	0	.250	.250	.250	4	1	0	0	0	0	0	0	0	0	.250	.250	.250
Victor Martinez	B	4	2	1	0	4	4	0	0	0	0	.500	.500	.750	28	11	2	0	1	9	10	1	1	1	.393	.538	.571
Jeff Mathis	R	5	1	0	0	0	1	0	0	1	0	.200	.200	.200	10	1	0	0	0	1	0	0	3	0	.100	.100	.100
Hideki Matsui	L	21	8	2	0	1	4	5	1	5	0	.381	.500	.619	30	10	2	0	1	5	5	1	9	1	.333	.417	.500
Kaz Matsui	B	2	1	0	0	0	0	0	0	0	0	.500	.500	.500	41	10	0	1	0	1	0	0	9	0	.244	.244	.293
Gary Matthews Jr.	B	11	5	0	0	1	6	3	0	4	0	.455	.571	.727	101	24	3	1	4	21	14	1	27	3	.238	.330	.406
Joe Mauer	L	5	3	0	0	1	3	0	0	0	0	.600	.600	1.200	25	6	0	0	1	6	4	1	5	1	.240	.333	.360
Justin Maxwell	R	3	1	1	0	0	0	1	0	2	0	.333	.600	.667	9	3	1	0	1	4	1	0	3	0	.333	.455	.778
John Mayberry	R	11	3	1	0	1	1	1	0	4	1	.273	.333	.636	11	3	1	0	1	1	1	0	4	1	.273	.333	.636
Cameron Maybin	R	1	0	0	0	0	0	0	0	1	0	.000	.000	.000	5	1	0	0	0	0	0	0	3	0	.200	.200	.200
Edwin Maysonet	R	9	3	0	0	0	0	0	0	3	0	.333	.333	.333	11	4	0	0	0	0	0	0	3	0	.364	.364	.364
Brian McCann	L	12	4	3	0	2	1	0	0	3	0	.333	.385	.583	38	10	5	0	2	7	4	6	6	1	.263	.378	.395
Mike McCoy	R	4	0	0	0	0	0	0	0	1	0	.000	.000	.000	4	0	0	0	0	0	0	0	1	0	.000	.000	.000
Darnell McDonald	R	14	3	1	1	0	1	1	0	3	2	.214	.267	.429	17	4	1	1	0	1	1	0	4	2	.235	.278	.412
John McDonald	R	2	0	0	0	0	0	0	0	2	0	.000	.000	.000	37	8	0	0	0	2	2	0	8	0	.216	.256	.216
Casey McGehee	R	23	6	1	0	1	5	3	1	4	1	.261	.370	.435	26	6	1	0	1	5	3	1	6	2	.231	.333	.385
Nate McLouth	L	0	0	0	0	0	0	1	0	0	0	-	1.000	-	89	18	3	1	1	10	5	0	23	2	.202	.250	.292
Kris Medlen	B	1	0	0	0	0	0	0	0	1	0	.000	.000	.000	1	0	0	0	0	0	0	0	1	0	.000	.000	.000
Jason Michaels	R	53	12	5	1	0	4	11	0	17	0	.226	.369	.358	273	64	14	2	5	34	42	1	82	4	.234	.334	.355
D. Mientkiewicz	L	13	3	1	0	0	2	1	0	5	0	.231	.333	.308	90	25	6	1	0	12	13	1	17	2	.278	.377	.367
Aaron Miles	B	30	5	0	0	0	0	1	0	6	1	.167	.194	.167	134	30	5	1	0	13	4	0	18	4	.224	.248	.276
Kevin Millar	R	9	0	0	0	0	0	0	0	5	0	.000	.000	.000	126	25	6	0	2	25	18	1	35	4	.198	.309	.294
Lastings Milledge	R	4	2	0	0	0	0	0	0	1	0	.500	.500	.500	21	6	1	1	0	4	1	0	6	0	.286	.375	.429
Corky Miller	R	4	0	0	0	0	0	0	0	3	0	.000	.000	.000	14	2	0	0	1	2	1	0	5	0	.143	.200	.357
Eric Milton	L	1	0	0	0	0	0	0	0	1	0	.000	.000	.000	2	1	0	0	0	0	0	0	0	0	.500	.500	.500
Juan Miranda	L	1	1	0	0	0	0	0	0	0	0	1.000	1.000	1.000	1	1	0	0	0	0	0	0	0	0	1.000	1.000	1.000
Bengie Molina	R	9	2	1	0	1	6	0	0	2	1	.222	.273	.667	54	11	2	0	3	18	4	2	13	3	.204	.266	.407
Jose Molina	R	1	0	0	0	0	0	0	0	1	0	.000	.000	.000	14	4	0	0	0	2	0	0	3	0	.286	.286	.286
Yadier Molina	R	2	0	0	0	0	0	0	0	0	0	.000	.000	.000	13	3	0	0	0	1	2	2	1	1	.231	.333	.231
Craig Monroe	R	14	0	0	0	0	0	1	0	7	0	.000	.125	.000	56	9	0	0	3	9	10	2	22	1	.161	.299	.321
Lou Montanez	R	7	0	0	0	0	0	0	0	4	0	.000	.000	.000	12	1	0	0	0	0	0	0	4	0	.083	.083	.083
Miguel Montero	L	16	3	1	0	0	3	2	0	2	1	.188	.350	.250	55	13	2	0	3	12	9	1	16	2	.236	.368	.436
Adam Moore	R	1	0	0	0	0	0	0	0	1	0	.000	.000	.000	1	0	0	0	0	0	0	0	1	0	.000	.000	.000
Melvin Mora	R	1	0	0	0	0	0	0	0	1	0	.000	.000	.000	34	6	2	0	1	3	4	0	9	1	.176	.293	.324
Jose Morales	B	15	6	1	0	0	3	2	1	4	0	.400	.471	.467	15	6	1	0	0	3	2	1	4	0	.400	.471	.467
Kendry Morales	B	8	1	0	0	1	1	0	0	2	0	.125	.125	.500	28	4	1	0	1	2	0	0	7	0	.143	.143	.286
Nyjer Morgan	L	1	0	0	0	0	0	0	0	0	0	.000	.000	.000	16	3	1	0	0	0	2	0	5	0	.188	.316	.250

354

Pinch Hitting

Batter	B	AB	H	2B	3B	HR	RBI	TBB	IBB	SO	GDP	Avg	OBP	Slg	AB	H	2B	3B	HR	RBI	TBB	IBB	SO	GDP	Avg	OBP	Slg
		2009 Pinch Hitting													**Career Pinch Hitting**												
Mike Morse	R	17	6	1	0	1	8	1	0	5	0	.353	.389	.588	28	11	2	0	1	8	3	0	10	0	.393	.452	.571
Brandon Moss	L	34	9	3	0	1	5	1	0	12	1	.265	.306	.441	45	11	3	1	1	7	1	0	17	1	.244	.277	.422
Eric Munson	L	1	0	0	0	0	0	0	0	0	0	.000	.000	.000	41	5	0	0	1	5	9	0	12	3	.122	.302	.195
Daniel Murphy	L	28	7	0	1	1	7	0	0	5	0	.250	.241	.429	41	13	1	1	2	12	6	1	7	1	.317	.396	.537
David Murphy	L	2	0	0	0	0	0	2	0	0	0	.000	.500	.000	7	0	0	0	0	0	2	0	1	0	.000	.222	.000
Matt Murton	R	14	3	1	0	0	1	3	0	5	0	.214	.353	.286	78	15	2	0	2	11	11	0	21	3	.192	.292	.295
Mike Napoli	R	7	1	0	0	0	2	0	0	4	1	.143	.143	.143	17	2	0	0	0	3	4	0	11	1	.118	.318	.118
Dioner Navarro	B	4	0	0	0	0	0	0	0	0	1	.000	.000	.000	22	4	0	0	0	4	1	0	6	2	.182	.250	.182
Brad Nelson	L	14	0	0	0	0	0	2	0	7	1	.000	.125	.000	20	2	2	0	0	0	3	0	7	1	.100	.217	.200
Wil Nieves	R	2	0	0	0	0	0	0	0	1	0	.000	.000	.000	13	0	0	0	0	0	0	0	6	0	.000	.000	.000
Jayson Nix	R	11	0	0	0	0	0	4	0	3	0	.000	.267	.000	13	1	0	0	0	0	4	0	4	0	.077	.294	.077
Laynce Nix	L	34	8	4	0	1	5	6	1	13	1	.235	.350	.441	60	9	4	0	1	5	9	1	22	1	.150	.261	.267
Greg Norton	B	68	11	2	0	0	7	20	0	18	1	.162	.360	.191	413	96	21	2	13	73	72	4	122	10	.232	.348	.387
Trent Oeltjen	L	2	0	0	0	0	0	0	0	1	0	.000	.000	.000	2	0	0	0	0	0	0	0	1	0	.000	.000	.000
Augie Ojeda	B	16	2	2	0	0	0	2	0	2	0	.125	.125	.250	66	13	4	1	0	8	5	0	14	1	.197	.250	.288
Miguel Olivo	R	4	0	0	0	0	0	0	0	1	0	.000	.000	.000	33	6	1	0	2	7	0	0	10	0	.182	.200	.394
Magglio Ordonez	R	8	1	1	0	0	0	0	0	3	0	.125	.125	.250	26	5	2	0	2	4	5	2	7	1	.192	.303	.500
Pete Orr	L	6	3	0	0	0	2	0	0	0	0	.500	.375	.500	166	43	4	2	2	13	6	0	36	1	.259	.282	.343
David Ortiz	L	4	1	1	0	0	2	2	0	1	0	.250	.500	.500	71	14	3	1	3	16	16	1	18	1	.197	.341	.394
Russ Ortiz	R	2	0	0	0	0	0	0	0	1	0	.000	.000	.000	4	0	0	0	0	0	0	0	1	0	.000	.000	.000
Lyle Overbay	L	5	1	0	0	0	0	0	0	4	0	.200	.200	.200	43	11	3	0	2	13	5	0	16	2	.256	.320	.465
Jerry Owens	L	1	0	0	0	0	0	0	0	1	0	.000	.000	.000	14	2	0	0	0	0	0	0	2	0	.143	.143	.143
Micah Owings	R	16	4	2	0	1	3	0	0	7	0	.250	.250	.563	37	10	3	0	1	6	0	0	11	1	.270	.325	.514
Jorge Padilla	R	14	2	0	0	0	0	4	0	4	0	.143	.143	.143	14	2	0	0	0	0	0	0	4	0	.143	.143	.143
Angel Pagan	B	7	1	0	0	0	0	0	0	3	1	.143	.143	.143	52	9	0	1	0	0	1	0	17	1	.173	.189	.212
Matt Pagnozzi	R	1	0	0	0	0	0	0	0	0	0	.000	.000	.000	1	0	0	0	0	0	0	0	0	0	.000	.000	.000
Gerardo Parra	L	3	0	0	0	0	1	0	0	3	1	.000	.000	.000	9	0	0	0	0	1	0	0	3	1	.000	.000	.000
Corey Patterson	L	7	1	0	0	0	0	0	0	3	0	.143	.143	.143	89	14	3	0	1	4	1	0	24	1	.160	.211	.202
Xavier Paul	L	7	3	1	0	1	1	0	0	1	1	.429	.429	1.000	7	3	1	0	1	1	0	0	1	1	.429	.429	1.000
Ronny Paulino	R	9	2	0	0	1	2	1	0	3	0	.222	.300	.556	30	5	1	0	1	4	2	0	7	2	.167	.219	.300
Steve Pearce	R	14	3	2	1	0	1	3	0	4	0	.214	.353	.500	27	4	3	1	0	1	3	0	8	0	.148	.233	.333
Brayan Pena	B	19	5	1	0	1	1	1	0	4	1	.263	.300	.474	55	15	3	0	1	7	3	0	12	1	.273	.310	.382
Carlos Pena	L	2	0	0	0	0	0	1	0	2	0	.000	.333	.000	25	5	2	0	0	3	3	0	17	0	.200	.286	.280
Ramiro Pena	B	3	0	0	0	0	0	0	0	1	0	.000	.000	.000	3	0	0	0	0	0	0	0	1	0	.000	.000	.000
Tony Pena	R	1	0	0	0	0	0	0	0	0	0	.000	.000	.000	16	3	1	0	1	1	1	0	3	0	.188	.235	.438
Hunter Pence	R	2	0	0	0	0	0	0	0	0	0	.000	.000	.000	4	1	0	0	0	0	0	0	1	0	.250	.250	.250
Jhonny Peralta	R	2	0	0	0	0	1	1	0	0	0	.000	.333	.000	10	3	0	0	0	2	2	0	3	0	.300	.417	.300
Gregorio Petit	R	1	0	0	0	0	0	0	0	0	0	.000	.000	.000	1	0	0	0	0	0	0	0	0	0	.000	.000	.000
Chris Pettit	R	1	0	0	0	0	0	0	0	0	0	.000	.000	.000	1	0	0	0	0	0	0	0	0	0	.000	.000	.000
Brandon Phillips	R	3	0	0	0	0	0	0	0	0	0	.000	.000	.000	12	4	2	0	1	1	3	1	1	0	.333	.467	.750
Kyle Phillips	L	1	1	1	0	0	1	0	0	0	0	1.000	1.000	2.000	1	1	1	0	0	1	0	0	0	0	1.000	1.000	2.000
Paul Phillips	R	2	2	0	0	0	1	0	0	0	0	1.000	1.000	1.000	8	3	1	0	0	1	0	0	1	0	.375	.375	.500
Felix Pie	L	7	2	1	0	0	0	0	0	4	0	.286	.286	.429	18	4	1	0	0	0	0	0	9	0	.222	.222	.278
Juan Pierre	L	43	14	0	2	0	0	5	1	2	0	.326	.396	.419	89	27	1	2	0	4	9	1	6	0	.303	.374	.360
A.J. Pierzynski	L	10	1	0	0	0	0	1	0	1	2	.100	.182	.100	80	18	4	0	2	15	9	4	14	5	.225	.304	.350
Scott Podsednik	L	2	1	0	0	1	1	0	0	0	0	.500	.500	2.000	88	19	1	2	1	10	11	0	18	2	.216	.317	.307
Placido Polanco	R	5	1	0	0	0	0	0	0	0	0	.200	.200	.200	73	19	3	0	1	6	5	0	7	2	.260	.304	.342
Jorge Posada	B	11	4	0	0	2	7	2	0	6	1	.364	.429	.909	113	27	3	1	4	25	20	3	39	5	.239	.350	.389
Buster Posey	R	1	0	0	0	0	0	0	0	0	0	.000	.000	.000	1	0	0	0	0	0	0	0	0	0	.000	.000	.000
Landon Powell	B	2	0	0	0	0	0	0	0	0	0	.000	.000	.000	2	0	0	0	0	0	0	0	0	0	.000	.000	.000
Martin Prado	R	10	4	2	0	0	3	3	0	1	0	.400	.538	.600	43	13	5	0	1	12	8	0	7	0	.302	.412	.488
Albert Pujols	R	2	1	0	0	1	1	0	0	0	0	.500	.500	2.000	21	8	0	0	2	9	6	2	6	0	.381	.500	.667
Carlos Quentin	R	3	0	0	0	0	0	0	0	0	0	.000	.000	.000	20	6	4	0	1	9	0	0	5	0	.300	.364	.650
Robb Quinlan	R	4	1	0	0	0	0	0	0	0	0	.250	.250	.250	42	10	2	0	2	5	3	0	5	0	.238	.298	.429
Omar Quintanilla	L	17	3	1	0	0	0	3	0	10	0	.176	.300	.235	27	4	1	0	0	0	3	0	14	0	.148	.233	.185
H. Quintero	R	2	0	0	0	0	0	0	0	2	0	.000	.000	.000	14	3	0	0	0	0	0	0	4	3	.214	.214	.214
Ryan Raburn	R	18	3	0	0	1	3	4	1	8	0	.167	.348	.333	36	7	1	0	2	6	6	1	14	1	.194	.326	.389
Aramis Ramirez	R	3	1	0	0	0	0	0	0	0	0	.333	.333	.333	30	9	1	0	1	11	1	0	6	1	.300	.333	.433
Hanley Ramirez	R	5	2	0	0	0	1	0	0	1	0	.400	.400	.400	10	4	0	0	0	4	2	0	2	0	.400	.500	.700
Manny Ramirez	R	4	1	0	0	1	4	1	1	0	0	.250	.400	1.000	30	4	0	0	1	7	8	3	10	0	.133	.308	.233
Colby Rasmus	L	19	3	1	0	0	1	1	0	6	1	.158	.200	.211	19	3	1	0	0	1	1	0	6	1	.158	.200	.211
Josh Reddick	L	8	1	0	0	0	0	0	0	2	0	.125	.125	.125	8	1	0	0	0	0	0	0	2	0	.125	.125	.125
Mike Redmond	R	2	0	0	0	0	0	0	0	0	0	.000	.000	.000	52	10	3	1	0	6	1	0	10	1	.192	.232	.288
Jeremy Reed	L	54	15	2	1	0	4	4	0	13	0	.278	.322	.352	94	24	4	1	0	9	5	0	23	0	.255	.290	.319
Nolan Reimold	R	6	0	0	0	0	0	2	0	3	0	.000	.250	.000	6	0	0	0	0	0	2	0	3	0	.000	.250	.000
Edgar Renteria	R	3	0	0	0	0	0	0	0	1	0	.000	.000	.000	29	7	1	0	0	6	1	0	12	1	.241	.273	.276
Argenis Reyes	B	4	0	0	0	0	0	1	0	2	0	.000	.200	.000	25	5	0	0	0	0	2	0	10	1	.200	.259	.200
Jose Reyes	B	1	0	0	0	0	0	0	0	0	0	.000	.000	.000	7	1	0	0	0	0	1	0	1	0	.143	.333	.286
Mark Reynolds	R	3	1	0	0	1	2	0	0	1	1	.333	.333	1.333	13	2	0	0	2	5	0	0	7	2	.154	.143	.615
Danny Richar	L	2	0	0	0	0	0	0	0	0	0	.000	.000	.000	11	3	0	0	0	1	0	0	1	0	.273	.273	.273

Pinch Hitting

Batter	B	2009 Pinch Hitting													Career Pinch Hitting												
		AB	H	2B	3B	HR	RBI	TBB	IBB	SO	GDP	Avg	OBP	Slg	AB	H	2B	3B	HR	RBI	TBB	IBB	SO	GDP	Avg	OBP	Slg
Mike Rivera	R	7	1	0	0	0	0	1	0	2	0	.143	.333	.143	15	2	0	0	0	0	1	0	5	1	.133	.235	.133
Brian Roberts	B	4	0	0	0	0	0	0	0	2	0	.000	.000	.000	33	7	2	0	0	1	3	0	9	0	.212	.278	.273
Ryan Roberts	R	26	6	1	0	0	1	4	0	10	1	.231	.355	.269	29	6	1	0	0	1	5	0	11	1	.207	.361	.241
Shane Robinson	R	5	1	1	0	0	0	0	0	1	0	.200	.200	.400	5	1	1	0	0	0	0	0	1	0	.200	.200	.400
Alex Rodriguez	R	1	0	0	0	0	0	1	0	0	0	.000	.500	.000	9	0	0	0	0	0	1	0	3	0	.000	.100	.000
G. Rodriguez	R	1	0	0	0	0	0	0	0	0	0	.000	.000	.000	8	3	0	0	0	2	1	0	0	1	.375	.444	.375
Ivan Rodriguez	R	6	0	0	0	0	0	1	0	4	0	.000	.143	.000	72	19	1	0	2	15	6	3	20	3	.264	.325	.361
Luis Rodriguez	B	21	5	0	0	0	3	7	0	2	1	.238	.429	.238	64	10	0	0	1	7	9	0	5	5	.156	.257	.203
Sean Rodriguez	R	1	1	0	0	0	0	0	0	0	0	1.000	1.000	1.000	2	1	0	0	0	0	0	0	0	0	.500	.500	.500
Ryan Rohlinger	R	2	1	0	0	0	2	0	0	0	0	.500	.500	.500	5	1	0	0	0	2	0	0	1	1	.200	.200	.200
Scott Rolen	R	1	0	0	0	0	0	0	0	0	0	.000	.000	.000	7	2	0	0	1	1	0	0	3	0	.286	.286	.714
Jimmy Rollins	B	3	1	0	0	1	1	0	0	0	0	.333	.333	1.333	16	2	0	0	1	1	1	0	2	0	.125	.176	.313
Alex Romero	L	24	5	0	0	0	3	1	0	6	2	.208	.240	.208	50	10	0	0	0	6	1	0	11	3	.200	.212	.200
Niuman Romero	B	2	1	0	0	0	0	0	0	1	0	.500	.500	.500	2	1	0	0	0	0	0	0	1	0	.500	.500	.500
Adam Rosales	R	14	2	1	0	1	4	1	0	5	0	.143	.200	.429	27	4	1	0	1	5	1	0	9	0	.148	.179	.296
Cody Ross	R	1	1	1	0	0	1	0	0	0	0	1.000	1.000	2.000	49	13	4	0	4	10	5	0	16	0	.265	.357	.592
David Ross	R	2	0	0	0	0	0	1	0	1	0	.000	.333	.000	40	9	1	1	3	7	10	0	11	1	.225	.380	.525
Aaron Rowand	R	9	1	1	0	0	0	0	0	2	1	.111	.111	.222	45	9	4	0	0	3	3	0	18	1	.200	.250	.289
Carlos Ruiz	R	3	1	0	0	0	1	0	0	1	0	.333	.333	.333	20	6	2	0	0	4	1	0	2	1	.300	.333	.400
Rusty Ryal	R	13	3	1	0	1	1	1	0	4	0	.231	.286	.308	13	3	1	0	1	1	1	0	4	0	.231	.286	.308
Brendan Ryan	R	9	3	1	0	1	1	1	0	2	0	.333	.455	.444	32	8	3	0	1	1	6	0	6	0	.250	.400	.344
Dusty Ryan	R	1	0	0	0	0	0	0	0	1	0	.000	.000	.000	1	0	0	0	0	0	0	0	1	0	.000	.000	.000
Jeff Salazar	L	16	1	0	0	0	1	3	0	5	1	.063	.211	.063	71	17	3	1	3	10	13	0	24	1	.239	.357	.437
Oscar Salazar	R	35	11	2	0	3	9	5	1	8	1	.314	.390	.629	47	17	3	0	4	14	6	1	8	1	.362	.426	.681
Freddy Sanchez	R	1	1	0	0	0	0	1	0	0	0	1.000	1.000	1.000	55	16	3	2	0	6	7	0	6	1	.291	.371	.418
Gaby Sanchez	R	18	5	0	0	2	3	2	0	3	0	.278	.350	.611	21	5	0	0	2	3	2	0	4	0	.238	.304	.524
Pablo Sandoval	B	1	0	0	0	0	1	2	1	0	1	.000	.500	.000	8	4	2	0	0	6	2	1	1	1	.500	.545	.750
Ramon Santiago	B	8	3	0	0	0	0	0	0	3	0	.375	.375	.375	19	6	1	0	0	1	0	0	5	0	.316	.409	.368
Omir Santos	R	10	3	0	0	1	2	0	0	1	0	.300	.300	.600	11	3	0	0	1	2	0	0	1	0	.273	.273	.545
Michael Saunders	L	1	0	0	0	0	0	0	0	1	0	.000	.000	.000	1	0	0	0	0	0	0	0	1	0	.000	.000	.000
Bobby Scales	B	14	7	2	1	2	5	1	0	1	0	.500	.533	1.214	14	7	2	1	2	5	1	0	1	0	.500	.533	1.214
Max Scherzer	R	1	0	0	0	0	0	0	0	0	0	.000	.000	.000	1	0	0	0	0	0	0	0	0	0	.000	.000	.000
Nate Schierholtz	L	35	13	3	0	0	5	1	0	9	0	.371	.378	.457	46	16	4	0	0	6	1	0	12	0	.348	.347	.435
Jason Schmidt	R	1	1	0	0	0	0	0	0	0	0	1.000	1.000	1.000	1	1	0	0	0	0	0	0	0	0	1.000	1.000	1.000
Brian Schneider	R	2	0	0	0	0	0	0	0	0	0	.000	.000	.000	52	12	2	0	1	10	6	2	8	4	.231	.322	.327
Skip Schumaker	L	18	4	1	0	1	2	0	0	5	0	.222	.222	.444	86	20	4	0	1	7	2	0	14	2	.233	.247	.314
Luke Scott	L	6	1	0	0	0	1	0	0	2	0	.167	.167	.167	64	15	8	0	0	5	7	0	21	0	.234	.310	.359
Gary Sheffield	R	24	1	0	0	1	1	8	2	6	0	.042	.281	.167	49	10	0	0	2	11	16	3	8	2	.204	.394	.327
Chris Shelton	R	3	1	0	0	0	1	0	0	0	0	.333	.333	.333	30	7	0	0	0	4	3	0	9	1	.233	.314	.233
Kelly Shoppach	R	2	0	0	0	0	1	1	0	2	0	.000	.250	.000	12	3	0	0	1	5	3	0	5	0	.250	.375	.500
Jason Smith	L	13	0	0	0	0	1	0	0	5	0	.000	.000	.000	76	8	0	1	1	7	4	1	31	0	.105	.148	.171
Seth Smith	L	36	17	5	3	1	12	10	2	8	1	.472	.574	.861	78	31	8	4	3	20	17	2	16	1	.397	.500	.718
Travis Snider	L	3	1	1	0	0	0	0	0	2	0	.333	.333	.667	4	1	1	0	0	0	0	0	2	0	.250	.250	.500
Chris Snyder	R	4	0	0	0	0	0	0	0	2	0	.000	.000	.000	15	1	0	0	1	3	1	1	2	0	.067	.118	.267
Andy Sonnanstine	L	2	0	0	0	0	0	0	0	2	0	.000	.000	.000	2	0	0	0	0	0	0	0	2	0	.000	.000	.000
Alfonso Soriano	R	0	0	0	0	0	0	1	0	0	0	-	1.000	-	6	2	1	0	0	0	2	1	0	0	.333	.500	.500
Geovany Soto	R	6	1	1	0	0	0	2	1	2	0	.167	.375	.333	17	5	1	0	0	2	4	2	6	0	.294	.429	.353
Denard Span	L	2	1	0	0	0	2	0	0	0	0	.500	.500	.500	2	1	0	0	0	2	0	0	1	0	.500	.500	.500
Ryan Spilborghs	R	30	8	6	1	0	8	8	0	5	0	.267	.421	.533	106	33	9	1	1	25	20	0	25	4	.311	.414	.443
Matt Stairs	L	62	13	2	0	5	15	16	3	19	0	.210	.380	.484	325	87	17	2	19	77	53	9	78	4	.268	.377	.508
Craig Stansberry	R	1	0	0	0	0	0	0	0	0	0	.000	.000	.000	11	4	0	0	0	2	1	0	4	0	.364	.462	.364
Nick Stavinoha	R	15	5	3	0	1	3	1	0	2	0	.333	.375	.733	28	7	3	0	1	5	1	0	5	0	.250	.267	.464
Ian Stewart	L	20	6	3	0	1	2	1	0	6	1	.300	.333	.600	54	14	7	0	2	8	2	0	20	1	.259	.310	.500
Eric Stults	L	1	0	0	0	0	0	0	0	1	0	.000	.000	.000	4	0	0	0	0	0	0	0	3	0	.000	.000	.000
Cory Sullivan	L	21	5	0	1	0	2	2	0	8	0	.238	.304	.333	103	24	1	1	1	13	7	1	34	1	.233	.295	.291
Drew Sutton	B	22	4	1	0	0	3	1	0	8	0	.182	.250	.227	22	4	1	0	0	3	1	0	8	0	.182	.250	.227
Kurt Suzuki	R	4	1	0	0	0	2	2	0	0	0	.250	.571	.250	14	7	1	0	2	6	2	0	0	0	.500	.588	1.000
Mike Sweeney	R	11	5	1	0	0	3	0	0	3	0	.455	.500	.545	52	14	3	0	0	4	4	0	8	3	.269	.333	.327
Ryan Sweeney	L	4	0	0	0	0	0	0	0	3	1	.000	.000	.000	14	0	0	0	0	0	1	0	7	1	.000	.067	.000
Nick Swisher	B	5	1	1	0	0	0	1	0	1	0	.200	.333	.400	15	2	2	0	0	3	2	0	4	2	.133	.235	.267
So Taguchi	R	3	1	0	0	0	0	0	0	1	0	.333	.333	.333	138	33	7	1	1	22	13	0	30	4	.239	.305	.326
Fernando Tatis	R	35	9	1	0	2	8	3	1	7	4	.257	.325	.457	79	17	2	0	2	12	7	1	17	5	.215	.281	.316
Craig Tatum	R	2	0	0	0	0	0	0	0	0	0	.000	.333	.000	2	0	0	0	0	0	0	0	0	0	.000	.333	.000
Willy Taveras	R	5	1	0	1	0	0	0	0	1	0	.200	.200	.600	41	12	2	1	0	4	0	0	7	0	.293	.310	.390
Taylor Teagarden	R	2	0	0	0	0	0	0	0	1	0	.000	.000	.000	3	0	0	0	0	0	1	0	1	0	.000	.250	.000
Mark Teahen	L	1	0	0	0	0	0	0	0	0	0	.000	.500	.000	11	2	0	0	0	0	2	0	3	0	.182	.308	.182
Mark Teixeira	B	1	0	0	0	0	0	0	0	0	0	.000	.000	.000	4	0	0	0	0	0	1	0	0	0	.000	.200	.000
Marcus Thames	R	14	6	0	0	1	3	4	2	3	0	.429	.556	.643	55	18	2	0	5	14	10	2	20	1	.327	.431	.636
Ryan Theriot	R	5	0	0	0	0	0	0	0	0	0	.000	.000	.000	32	7	2	0	1	6	5	0	6	0	.219	.342	.375
Josh Thole	L	1	0	0	0	0	0	0	0	0	0	.000	.000	.000	1	0	0	0	0	0	0	0	0	0	.000	.000	.000

Pinch Hitting

Batter	B	2009 Pinch Hitting													Career Pinch Hitting												
		AB	H	2B	3B	HR	RBI	TBB	IBB	SO	GDP	Avg	OBP	Slg	AB	H	2B	3B	HR	RBI	TBB	IBB	SO	GDP	Avg	OBP	Slg
Clete Thomas	L	5	0	0	0	0	0	0	0	3	0	.000	.000	.000	7	1	1	0	0	0	0	0	4	0	.143	.143	.286
Jim Thome	L	25	4	0	0	0	3	1	0	10	0	.160	.192	.160	82	18	4	0	3	11	15	0	33	2	.220	.343	.378
Joe Thurston	L	35	8	3	0	0	3	4	0	10	1	.229	.308	.314	68	15	5	1	0	3	5	0	14	1	.221	.284	.324
Matt Tolbert	B	0	0	0	0	0	0	1	0	0	0	-	1.000	-	5	2	0	0	0	0	2	0	1	0	.400	.571	.400
Andres Torres	B	10	3	0	0	1	4	2	0	5	0	.300	.417	.600	20	5	0	0	1	5	2	0	9	0	.250	.318	.400
Andy Tracy	L	8	4	0	0	0	1	0	0	1	0	.500	.500	.500	69	13	1	1	2	9	8	0	28	1	.188	.266	.319
Chad Tracy	L	29	8	1	0	3	9	4	0	6	0	.276	.364	.621	86	26	9	0	5	24	11	0	17	2	.302	.384	.581
Matt Tulasosopo	R	1	0	0	0	0	0	0	0	0	0	.000	.000	.000	1	0	0	0	0	0	0	0	0	0	.000	.000	.000
Justin Turner	R	5	1	0	0	0	2	0	0	1	0	.200	.200	.200	5	1	0	0	0	2	0	0	1	0	.200	.200	.200
Dan Uggla	R	1	0	0	0	0	0	0	0	0	0	.000	.000	.000	4	0	0	0	0	0	2	0	0	0	.000	.333	.000
B.J. Upton	R	2	1	0	0	0	0	0	0	0	0	.500	.500	.500	9	4	0	0	1	2	0	0	2	1	.444	.444	.778
Justin Upton	R	1	1	1	0	0	0	0	0	0	0	1.000	1.000	2.000	11	4	2	0	0	0	0	0	6	0	.364	.364	.545
Juan Uribe	R	9	2	0	0	0	0	1	0	3	1	.222	.300	.222	31	10	4	0	1	7	2	0	8	1	.323	.364	.548
Chase Utley	L	2	0	0	0	0	0	0	0	1	0	.000	.000	.000	43	13	2	0	4	15	5	1	15	0	.302	.380	.628
Luis Valbuena	L	3	2	0	1	0	0	0	0	0	0	.667	.667	1.333	4	2	0	1	0	0	0	0	2	0	.500	.500	1.000
Wilson Valdez	R	3	1	0	0	0	0	1	0	0	0	.333	.600	.333	13	2	0	0	0	0	1	0	2	0	.154	.267	.154
Jason Varitek	B	1	0	0	0	0	0	0	0	0	0	.000	.000	.000	100	29	6	0	3	15	12	3	23	2	.290	.372	.440
Javier Vazquez	R	2	0	0	0	0	0	1	0	1	0	.000	.333	.000	2	0	0	0	0	0	1	0	1	0	.000	.333	.000
Ramon Vazquez	L	42	10	3	0	0	2	2	0	11	0	.238	.273	.310	96	21	5	0	0	9	9	0	25	1	.219	.280	.271
Eugenio Velez	R	12	2	1	0	0	0	0	0	4	0	.167	.167	.250	45	12	2	2	0	5	1	0	9	2	.267	.283	.400
Will Venable	L	15	3	1	0	0	2	1	0	6	0	.200	.250	.267	15	3	1	0	0	2	2	0	6	0	.200	.294	.267
Shane Victorino	B	5	1	0	0	0	1	0	0	1	0	.200	.200	.200	80	22	1	1	3	22	6	0	14	1	.275	.326	.425
Omar Vizquel	B	4	0	0	0	0	0	0	0	1	0	.000	.000	.000	54	6	3	0	0	0	0	0	11	1	.111	.158	.167
Joey Votto	L	0	0	0	0	0	0	2	1	0	0	-	1.000	-	12	3	0	0	1	4	2	1	4	0	.250	.357	.500
Adam Wainwright	R	5	0	0	0	0	0	0	0	4	0	.000	.000	.000	13	3	0	0	0	1	0	0	7	0	.231	.214	.231
Neil Walker	B	8	2	1	0	0	0	0	0	0	1	.250	.250	.375	8	2	1	0	0	0	0	0	0	1	.250	.250	.375
Rickie Weeks	R	1	0	0	0	0	0	0	0	0	0	.000	.000	.000	15	4	0	1	1	1	4	0	6	1	.267	.421	.600
Todd Wellemeyer	R	2	0	0	0	0	0	0	0	2	0	.000	.000	.000	2	0	0	0	0	0	0	0	2	0	.000	.000	.000
Vernon Wells	R	1	0	0	0	0	0	0	0	0	0	.000	.000	.000	8	2	0	0	0	4	0	0	0	0	.250	.250	.250
Jayson Werth	R	4	0	0	0	0	0	0	0	4	0	.000	.000	.000	50	12	1	0	3	11	7	0	21	0	.240	.333	.440
Josh Whitesell	L	15	1	1	0	0	1	1	0	6	0	.067	.125	.133	19	2	1	0	1	2	2	0	8	0	.105	.227	.316
Eli Whiteside	R	1	0	0	0	0	0	0	0	1	0	.000	.000	.000	1	0	0	0	0	0	0	0	1	0	.000	.000	.000
Matt Wieters	B	1	1	0	0	0	1	0	0	0	0	1.000	1.000	1.000	1	1	0	0	0	1	0	0	0	0	1.000	1.000	1.000
Ty Wigginton	R	17	6	1	0	1	9	1	0	1	1	.353	.400	.588	55	16	2	0	3	21	6	0	9	2	.291	.375	.491
Josh Willingham	R	16	3	0	0	1	2	1	0	0	0	.188	.235	.375	41	9	1	0	2	8	4	0	15	0	.220	.289	.390
Reggie Willits	B	3	1	0	0	0	0	0	0	1	0	.333	.333	.333	25	5	0	0	0	4	6	0	7	0	.200	.310	.200
Jack Wilson	R	1	1	0	0	0	0	0	0	0	0	1.000	1.000	1.000	31	14	2	0	1	2	1	0	7	0	.452	.469	.613
Josh Wilson	R	3	0	0	0	0	0	0	0	2	0	.000	.000	.000	18	4	0	0	0	3	1	0	6	1	.222	.263	.222
Randy Winn	B	6	3	1	0	0	2	0	0	1	0	.500	.429	.667	60	20	2	0	3	17	7	0	7	1	.333	.406	.517
DeWayne Wise	L	9	4	0	0	1	1	0	0	1	0	.444	.444	.778	61	20	2	1	3	12	0	0	14	1	.328	.323	.541
Randy Wolf	L	1	0	0	0	0	0	0	0	0	0	.000	.000	.000	6	1	0	0	0	0	0	0	2	0	.167	.167	.167
Brandon Wood	R	2	0	0	0	0	0	0	0	0	0	.000	.000	.000	4	2	1	0	1	3	0	0	0	0	.500	.500	1.500
David Wright	R	2	0	0	0	0	0	0	0	1	0	.000	.000	.000	3	1	0	0	0	1	0	0	1	0	.333	.333	.333
Kevin Youkilis	R	1	0	0	0	0	0	0	0	0	0	.000	.000	.000	19	2	0	0	0	2	3	0	8	0	.105	.227	.105
Chris Young	R	9	2	1	0	0	4	4	1	3	0	.222	.462	.333	14	3	2	0	0	5	4	1	4	0	.214	.389	.357
Delmon Young	R	1	1	0	0	0	0	0	0	0	0	1.000	1.000	1.000	2	2	1	0	0	0	0	0	0	0	1.000	1.000	1.500
Delwyn Young	R	38	12	4	0	0	4	3	0	10	1	.316	.381	.421	101	30	6	0	1	10	11	0	25	3	.297	.372	.386
Eric Young Jr.	B	15	3	0	0	0	0	2	0	2	0	.200	.294	.200	15	3	0	0	0	0	2	0	2	0	.200	.294	.200
Carlos Zambrano	B	7	1	0	0	0	0	0	0	4	0	.143	.143	.143	21	2	0	0	0	0	0	0	11	1	.095	.095	.095
Gregg Zaun	B	12	3	1	0	1	6	0	0	5	0	.250	.250	.583	178	41	7	0	6	34	24	2	31	6	.230	.317	.371
Ryan Zimmerman	R	3	2	1	0	0	1	0	0	0	0	.667	.667	1.000	9	3	2	0	0	3	0	0	1	0	.333	.300	.556
Ben Zobrist	B	13	4	0	0	3	9	1	1	0	0	.308	.357	1.000	25	4	0	0	3	9	2	1	6	0	.160	.222	.520

Manufactured Runs

Bill James

We are in the fourth year of our effort to track Manufactured Runs.   The term "Manufactured Run", which is used by all broadcasters and in almost every game, is used to describe a run that is put together out of small elements and by pro-active measures.   A batter reaches on a walk, steals second, scores on a single, the broadcaster will describe that as a Manufactured Run.

In 2007 we posed the question, "What, exactly, is a Manufactured Run?", which enabled us to begin edging toward the subsequent questions. . .how many Manufactured Runs are there? How important are they? What teams are good at Manufacturing Runs? What benefits do teams that are good at Manufacturing Runs derive from that?"

Beginning with the question, "What, exactly, is a Manufactured Run?" . . .we defined a Manufactured Run loosely as any run on which *two* of the four bases result from doing something other than playing station-to-station baseball. In other words, if a team combines two singles into a run, that's a Manufactured Run, since two singles will not make a run unless you add something else to the mix.   If a walk and a single are added together to make a run, that's a Manufactured Run.

If it's three singles, that's not a Manufactured Run.   If it's two singles and a walk, it's not a Manufactured Run.   If there's an extra-base hit involved, generally speaking, that's not a Manufactured Run.

Single, stolen base, single, run scores. . .that's a Manufactured Run.

Single, sac bunt, single, run scores. . .that's a Manufactured Run.

Single, single (runner to third), sacrifice fly. . .that's a Manufactured Run.

Infield single, wild pitch, single (run scores). . .that's a Manufactured Run.

Single, move up on ground ball, steal third, sac fly. . .that's a Manufactured Run.

Double, ground ball, fly ball, run scores. . .that's a Manufactured Run.

Double, single, run. . .that's *not* a Manufactured Run.

Single, double, run. . .that's not a Manufactured Run.

Single, stolen base, home run. . .those are not Manufactured Runs.

Walk, sac bunt, walk, double. . .those are not Manufactured Runs.

I'll give a more complete definition in just a moment.

The best teams in baseball at Manufacturing Runs, pretty much every year, are the Los Angeles Angels of Anaheim and the Minnesota Twins of

Bloomington.   Those two teams were 1-3 in 2006, 1-2 in 2007, 1-4 in 2008, and 1-2 in 2009.   They're good at that.   The Angels led the majors in 2009 with 221 Manufactured Runs.

On average, about one run per team per game is classified as a Manufactured Run. . .just a hair less than one per game.   There is no real difference between the leagues in regard to Manufactured Runs.   However, the two best teams at manufacturing runs are both American League teams, and, in 2009, four of the five worst teams at manufacturing runs were National League teams (the Pirates, Padres, Cubs and D-Backs.)

The most critical element to manufacturing runs, in modern baseball, is speed. . .the bunt, yes, but modern teams don't bunt that much, and it doesn't lead to a lot of runs even when they do.   The players who contribute to the most Manufactured Runs are the fastest players—Michael Bourn, Jacoby Ellsbury, Chone Figgins and Emilio Bonifacio.

OK, here's the technical definition of a Manufactured Run. Six rules:

1) A run that scores without a hit, or a run on which the only hit(s) is/are infield hits, is always scored as a Manufactured Run.

2) A run which is driven in by a home run is never scored a Manufactured Run, under any circumstance.

3) A run which is driven in by a double or a triple is scored as a Manufactured Run only if *two* of the four bases result from advancing on one of these four acts: a sacrifice bunt, a stolen base, a hit and run, or a bunt single.

4) Otherwise, a run is considered to be a Manufactured Run if two of the four bases do not result from the runner being forced along by a walk, a hit batsman, or a safe hit reaching the outfield.

5) A forceout or fielder's choice which does not improve the position of the base runners should not be counted as contributing toward a Manufactured Run. Advancing on a forceout or a fielder's choice DOES count toward a manufactured run, if the play is one which improves the position of the baserunners.

6) A base "gained" on a double play does not count as a contribution to a Manufactured Run. A run scored on a double play is a Manufactured Run only if two of the OTHER bases are not attributable to forced advancement.

2009 Manufactured Runs

American League

Team	MR
Los Angeles Angels	221
Minnesota Twins	189
Boston Red Sox	166
Oakland Athletics	165
Texas Rangers	162
Tampa Bay Rays	162
New York Yankees	158
Detroit Tigers	147
Toronto Blue Jays	141
Seattle Mariners	141
Baltimore Orioles	138
Cleveland Indians	137
Chicago White Sox	137
Kansas City Royals	130

American League Opponents

Team	MR
Kansas City Royals	193
Cleveland Indians	186
Los Angeles Angels	171
Oakland Athletics	166
Minnesota Twins	156
Chicago White Sox	155
New York Yankees	152
Boston Red Sox	151
Toronto Blue Jays	148
Tampa Bay Rays	142
Baltimore Orioles	137
Detroit Tigers	136
Seattle Mariners	133
Texas Rangers	132

National League

Team	MR
New York Mets	181
Cincinnati Reds	173
Los Angeles Dodgers	172
Colorado Rockies	172
Florida Marlins	169
San Francisco Giants	163
Atlanta Braves	162
St Louis Cardinals	153
Houston Astros	148
Washington Nationals	146
Philadelphia Phillies	144
Milwaukee Brewers	137
Arizona Diamondbacks	133
San Diego Padres	130
Chicago Cubs	123
Pittsburgh Pirates	121

National League Opponents

Team	MR
Washington Nationals	186
Arizona Diamondbacks	184
San Diego Padres	181
Pittsburgh Pirates	168
Colorado Rockies	168
Los Angeles Dodgers	164
Chicago Cubs	163
Florida Marlins	163
New York Mets	151
Houston Astros	145
Milwaukee Brewers	144
Cincinnati Reds	139
Atlanta Braves	138
San Francisco Giants	129
St Louis Cardinals	122
Philadelphia Phillies	118

2009 Manufactured Runs

American League Leaders

Player	Tm	MRC
Figgins, Chone	LAA	46
Ellsbury, Jacoby	Bos	40
Roberts, Brian	Bal	29
Span, Denard	Min	27
Upton, B.J.	TB	27
Crawford, Carl	TB	27
Kinsler, Ian	Tex	26
Podsednik, Scott	CWS	25
Bartlett, Jason	TB	25
Izturis, Maicer	LAA	25

National League Leaders

Player	Tm	MRC
Bourn, Michael	Hou	47
Bonifacio, Emilio	Fla	32
Wright, David	NYM	31
Fowler, Dexter	Col	29
Tulowitzki, Troy	Col	27
Kemp, Matt	LAD	27
Ramirez, Hanley	Fla	27
Castillo, Luis	NYM	26
Cabrera, Everth	SD	26
Furcal, Rafael	LAD	24
Victorino, Shane	Phi	24

MRC = Manufactured Runs Contribution

Top Three From Each Team

Arizona Diamondbacks

Player	MRC
Parra, Gerardo	19
Roberts, Ryan	13
Lopez, Felipe	13
Drew, Stephen	13

Atlanta Braves

Player	MRC
Escobar, Yunel	17
Jones, Chipper	15
Prado, Martin	15

Baltimore Orioles

Player	MRC
Roberts, Brian	29
Markakis, Nick	18
Jones, Adam	13

Boston Red Sox

Player	MRC
Ellsbury, Jacoby	40
Pedroia, Dustin	21
Bay, Jason	18

Chicago Cubs

Player	MRC
Theriot, Ryan	20
Fukudome, Kosuke	19
Soriano, Alfonso	12

Chicago White Sox

Player	MRC
Podsednik, Scott	25
Getz, Chris	20
Beckham, Gordon	13

Cincinnati Reds

Player	MRC
Taveras, Willy	23
Votto, Joey	21
Phillips, Brandon	18

Cleveland Indians

Player	MRC
Choo, Shin-Soo	20
Sizemore, Grady	16
Valbuena, Luis	15

Colorado Rockies

Player	MRC
Fowler, Dexter	29
Tulowitzki, Troy	27
Smith, Seth	15
Stewart, Ian	15

Detroit Tigers

Player	MRC
Granderson, Curtis	20
Laird, Gerald	19
Inge, Brandon	16
Polanco, Placido	16

Florida Marlins

Player	MRC
Bonifacio, Emilio	32
Ramirez, Hanley	27
Coghlan, Chris	21

Houston Astros

Player	MRC
Bourn, Michael	47
Matsui, Kaz	23
Pence, Hunter	15

Kansas City Royals

Player	MRC
Bloomquist, Willie	18
Teahen, Mark	16
Callaspo, Alberto	16

Los Angeles Angels

Player	MRC
Figgins, Chone	46
Izturis, Maicer	25
Kendrick, Howie	23

Los Angeles Dodgers

Player	MRC
Kemp, Matt	27
Furcal, Rafael	24
Pierre, Juan	21

Milwaukee Brewers

Player	MRC
Braun, Ryan	20
Counsell, Craig	15
Kendall, Jason	13

Minnesota Twins

Player	MRC
Span, Denard	27
Punto, Nick	24
Cuddyer, Michael	20

New York Mets

Player	MRC
Wright, David	31
Castillo, Luis	26
Murphy, Daniel	14
Pagan, Angel	14

New York Yankees

Player	MRC
Jeter, Derek	24
Cano, Robinson	18
Gardner, Brett	18

Oakland Athletics

Player	MRC
Davis, Rajai	24
Kennedy, Adam	22
Sweeney, Ryan	18

Philadelphia Phillies

Player	MRC
Victorino, Shane	24
Rollins, Jimmy	21
Werth, Jayson	21

Pittsburgh Pirates

Player	MRC
McCutchen, Andrew	23
Morgan, Nyjer	14
LaRoche, Adam	9
LaRoche, Andy	9

San Diego Padres

Player	MRC
Cabrera, Everth	26
Gwynn, Tony	19
Headley, Chase	15

San Francisco Giants

Player	MRC
Winn, Randy	20
Uribe, Juan	19
Rowand, Aaron	17

Seattle Mariners

Player	MRC
Gutierrez, Franklin	23
Suzuki, Ichiro	22
Lopez, Jose	15

St Louis Cardinals

Player	MRC
Pujols, Albert	18
Ludwick, Ryan	18
Schumaker, Skip	18

Tampa Bay Rays

Player	MRC
Upton, B.J.	27
Crawford, Carl	27
Bartlett, Jason	25

Texas Rangers

Player	MRC
Kinsler, Ian	26
Andrus, Elvis	22
Murphy, David	14

Toronto Blue Jays

Player	MRC
Scutaro, Marco	18
Wells, Vernon	18
Hill, Aaron	18

Washington Nationals

Player	MRC
Morgan, Nyjer	18
Guzman, Cristian	16
Harris, Willie	14

The Manager's Record

Bill James

There are many things that a manager does that are beyond the scope of our analysis. A good manager helps to calm down a rookie who is nervous, and helps to keep a veteran focused. A good manager knows when an older player needs a day off, and when a young player is ready for an opportunity to play. A good manager knows when a superstar needs to have his ego stroked, and when he needs to have his toes stomped on. These things are beyond our ability to study.

There are, however, certain things that one manager does differently than another manager that we can study. This section of the book is devoted to documenting those things. Among the things you can find by studying this data are the following:

1) Whether the manager likes to use a fixed lineup, or whether he likes to experiment. Felipe Alou with the Expos in 1999 used 143 different lineups in 162 games, the most in the National League. With the Giants in 2003 and 2004 he used 138 and 139 different lineups, again the most in the National League (ignoring the pitcher's spot, of course.) Charlie Manuel used only 68 different lineups last year, and in the five years he has managed the Phillies he has never used more than 87 lineups in a season.

2) Whether the manager likes to platoon. For the Yankees last year, a whopping 73% of hitters in the starting lineup had the platoon advantage at the start of the game. For Dusty Baker's Reds, on the other hand, only 45% had the platoon advantage.

But I should explain something here. This doesn't exactly work the way it was intended to. Up until the mid-1980s, many managers platooned players. With the Blue Jays in the early 1980s, Bobby Cox was at times platooning at five or maybe six positions, using Garth Iorg and Rance Mulliniks at third base, Ernie Whitt and Buck Martinez behind the plate, Hosken Powell and Jesse Barfield in right field, Barry Bonnell and Al Woods in left field.

But teams at that time carried 10 or 11 pitchers; now they carry 12 or 13. The expansion of the bullpens has cut down the benches to where platooning is no longer as common or as practical as it once was. Thus, the "platoon percentage", which was intended to measure whether a manager liked to platoon, in fact mostly measures how many switch hitters he has on the roster. The Yankees have a very high platoon percentage because they have Posada and Teixeira and Melky in the lineup, who always have the platoon advantage.

3) How many pinch hitters the manager uses. Jim Riggleman with the Cubs used to use 300 pinch hitters a year.   There aren't as many pinch hitting opportunities in the American League, but with the Mariners in 2008, Riggleman still used 75 pinch hitters in 90 games. With the same team in 2009, Don Wakamatsu used only 58 pinch hitters in 162 games. Joe Maddon of the Rays uses more than twice that many every year—133 in 2008, 140 in 2009.

4) How many pinch runners the manager uses. Bruce Bochy in his last season managing the Padres (2006) used 64 pinch runners. Bud Black, in his three years managing the same team, has used only 51 pinch runners total—17 per season.

5) How many defensive substitutions the manager makes. Manny Acta in 2007 used 78 defensive substitutes.   In his three-year career he has averaged 54 per season.   Sam Perlozzo with Baltimore averaged 57 per 162 games.   Buddy Bell, on the other hand, averaged only 18 defensive substitutes per season, and Eric Wedge only 19.

6) How often the manager pulls his pitcher out of the game early.   These are called "Quick Hooks" and "Slow Hooks", or, in the chart below, just "Quick" or "Slow". The definitions are in the glossary. Joe Torre in 2009 had 62 quick hooks, 23 slow hooks.   Dusty Baker had 30 quick hooks, 62 slow hooks, and Charlie Manuel was at 32-55.

7) How often the manager allows his pitcher to throw more than 110 pitches in a game, which we call a "Long Outing".   Jim Leyland's starting pitcher in 2009 through 110+ pitches 38 times.   Bob Geren, managing a young Oakland A's staff, left his starting pitcher in that long only 5 times.

8) Relievers Used on Consecutive Days. Manny Acta and Jim Riggleman combined in 2009 to use a reliever who had pitched the previous day 154 times, which was nothing compared to 2007, when Acta on his own did this 183 times, but was still enough to lead the majors.   Eric Wedge, Terry Francona and Don Wakamatsu in 2009 did this less than 80 times.

9) The number of relievers a manager uses.   Some managers now use about 530 relievers a season.   Joe Torre and Fredi Gonzalez in 2009 were all near that number.   Ozzie Guillen and Don Wakamatsu were just over 400.

10) The number of stolen base attempts the manager orders or allows.   Mike Scioscia's teams have averaged 187 stolen base attempts per season, and Joe Maddon's teams have averaged 194.   Ken Macha's teams averaged 74 stolen base attempts per season, and Bud Black over his three-year career has averaged only 81.

11) The number of sacrifice bunts that the manager attempts. Dusty Baker has ordered an average of 102 sacrifice bunt attempts per season. Dave Trembley has averaged 35 a year. Of course the data varies by league, but Bruce Bochy, a National League manager, averages only 73 per season—30 less than Baker.

12) The number of runners who are moving with the pitch (not including stolen base attempts, and not including runners moving on a 3-2 count with 2 out.) Mike Scioscia averages 143 runners per season moving with the pitch, which is still less than one per game. Jim Leyland averages 124. Ron Washington has averaged 74, Charlie Manuel 78, and Ken Macha averaged only 61.

There was a notable change in this regard last year for Joe Girardi. In 2008 Girardi had 173 runners moving with the pitch—an enormous number. Last year he had 83.

13) How often the manager orders a pitchout. Dusty Baker orders an average of 55 pitchouts a season. His predecessor with the Reds, Jerry Narron, averaged only 9, Cecil Cooper averages only 8, and Don Wakamatsu, in his first season with Seattle, ordered only 4.

14) How often the manager orders an intentional walk, and how that works out. If the manager gets a double play on the next hitter, or if he gets out of the inning without a run being scored, we count that as a "good" result from the intentional walk. If he doesn't get a double play and a run scores in the inning, we count that as a "not good" result, and if multiple runs are scored in the inning after the intentional walk, we count that as a "bomb", or "the intentional walk blew up in his face."

Ron Washington in 2008 ordered 44 intentional walks, of which 20 blew up on him—the most in the major leagues. Learning from experience, he ordered only 14 intentional walks in 2009, of which only 3 blew up on him.

Tony LaRussa, who has lots of experience, has had only two intentional walks blow up on him in the last two seasons—one in 2008, one in 2009. He issues between 20 and 30 a year, but his success ratio is very good, and apparently he is able to pick his moments pretty well.

Fredi Gonzalez, on the other hand, has had some real trouble with this. He orders 62 intentional walks per season, and, over the last three years, has had 45 intentional walks that blew up on him. That's a very high number, but Bobby Cox still orders almost as many intentional walks, and 50 have exploded on him over the last three years as well. Dusty Baker had those kind of numbers early in his career, but last year he had an exceptional year with the IBB. He ordered 36 intentional walks and got a good result 29 times—one of the highest percentages that we have yet seen.

Manny Acta, on the other hand, ordered 26 intentional walks and got a 13-13 split on it, which is not what you're looking for; you want to get out of the inning, if you can, 60% of the time after the IBB.   Manny had a tough year and was replaced mid-season.   But at ACTA Publications, we still believe in him.

Categories of this record are Games Managed (G), Number of Different Lineups Used (LUp), the percentage of players who had the platoon advantage at the start of the game (PL%), Pinch Hitters Used (PH), Pinch Runners Used (PR), Defensive Substitutes Used (DS), Quick Hooks (Quick), Slow Hooks (Slow), Long Outings by Starting Pitchers (LO), Relievers Used on Consecutive Days (RCD), Long Saves (LS), Relievers Used (Rel), Stolen Base Attempts (SBA), Sacrifice Bunts Attempts (SacA), Runners Moving with the Pitch (RM), Pitchouts ordered (PO), Intentional Walks issued (#), Intentional Walks resulting in a Good Outcome (Good), Intentional Walks resulting Not in a Good Outcome (NG), Intentional Walks Blowing up on the Manager (Bomb), Wins (W), Losses (L) and Winning Percentage (Pct.).

Manny Acta

Year	Team	Lg	G	LINEUPS		SUBSTITUTION			PITCHER USAGE						TACTICS				INTENTIONAL BB				RESULTS		
				LUp	PL%	PH	PR	DS	Quick	Slow	LO	RCD	LS	Rel	SBA	SacA	RM	PO	#	Good	NG	Bomb	W	L	Pct
2007	Nationals	NL	162	101	.65	295	32	78	53	28	5	183	1	588	92	86	70	28	44	28	16	8	73	89	.451
2008	Nationals	NL	161	133	.62	293	31	39	38	46	6	119	4	517	124	95	63	24	44	27	17	8	59	102	.366
2009	Nationals	NL	87	66	.62	145	11	20	14	25	1	91	1	282	54	43	62	5	26	13	13	6	26	61	.299
	162-Game Average			119	.63	290	29	54	41	39	5	155	2	548	107	89	77	23	45	27	18	9	62	100	.383

Felipe Alou

Year	Team	Lg	G	LINEUPS		SUBSTITUTION			PITCHER USAGE						TACTICS				INTENTIONAL BB				RESULTS		
				LUp	PL%	PH	PR	DS	Quick	Slow	LO	RCD	LS	Rel	SBA	SacA	RM	PO	#	Good	NG	Bomb	W	L	Pct
1994	Expos	NL	114	72	.48	143	33	7	51	18	0	60	26	259	173	72		20	28	21	7	3	74	40	.649
1995	Expos	NL	144	116	.49	200	36	10	48	28	7	80	18	396	169	74		22	26	13	13	6	66	78	.458
1996	Expos	NL	162	113	.49	240	31	30	60	27	13	85	18	433	142	97		25	33	24	9	2	88	74	.543
1997	Expos	NL	162	138	.58	205	22	40	52	41	15	78	13	390	121	91		30	45	28	17	9	78	84	.481
1998	Expos	NL	162	133	.50	235	27	37	56	26	2	109	15	443	137	111		18	39	30	9	7	65	97	.401
1999	Expos	NL	162	143	.49	247	33	55	45	36	5	101	10	432	121	84		26	39	27	12	5	68	94	.420
2000	Expos	NL	162	120	.61	211	24	32	51	36	5	113	15	452	106	103		18	40	30	10	5	67	95	.414
2001	Expos	NL	53	40	.58	84	4	5	18	12	1	37	1	171	39	28		7	13	9	4	0	21	32	.396
2003	Giants	NL	161	127	.50	202	32	42	46	27	26	113	5	461	90	93	33	9	34	19	15	7	100	61	.621
2004	Giants	NL	162	138	.67	239	47	60	25	50	45	154	8	521	66	105	109	2	35	21	14	8	91	71	.562
2005	Giants	NL	162	139	.62	242	33	49	29	46	37	145	6	511	106	109	120	12	42	26	16	7	75	87	.463
2006	Giants	NL	161	123	.64	215	57	57	23	50	44	98	5	438	83	100	84	14	37	24	13	6	76	85	.472
	162-Game Average			129	.56	226	35	39	46	36	18	108	13	450	124	98	87	19	38	25	13	6	80	82	.494

Dusty Baker

Year	Team	Lg	G	LINEUPS		SUBSTITUTION			PITCHER USAGE						TACTICS				INTENTIONAL BB				RESULTS		
				LUp	PL%	PH	PR	DS	Quick	Slow	LO	RCD	LS	Rel	SBA	SacA	RM	PO	#	Good	NG	Bomb	W	L	Pct
1994	Giants	NL	115	76	.53	177	16	9	29	25	2	86	12	288	154	88		78	40	24	16	8	55	60	.478
1995	Giants	NL	144	90	.41	230	26	13	32	50	8	90	8	381	184	101		77	51	32	19	14	67	77	.465
1996	Giants	NL	162	129	.51	250	17	15	24	58	15	94	8	425	166	103		96	60	37	23	9	68	94	.420
1997	Giants	NL	162	114	.71	212	17	22	46	25	17	132	4	481	170	85		93	57	36	21	12	90	72	.556
1998	Giants	NL	163	130	.62	224	20	12	43	38	8	113	5	433	153	111		41	68	42	26	9	89	74	.546
1999	Giants	NL	162	120	.62	233	16	16	30	51	27	111		450	165	113		40	41	25	16	10	86	76	.531
2000	Giants	NL	162	82	.56	233	26	22	38	50	25	91	3	384	118	86		37	20	17	0	2	97	65	.599
2001	Giants	NL	162	122	.48	261	22	19	40	48	10	114	4	439	99	95		45	49	33	16	6	90	72	.556
2002	Giants	NL	162	118	.43	223	32	38	29	56	53	106	8	417	95	89	42	41	44	28	16	10	95	66	.590
2003	Cubs	NL	162	114	.49	272	25	43	24	58	65	111	3	420	104	93	31	24	36	23	13	4	88	74	.543
2004	Cubs	NL	162	113	.44	254	16	19	37	41	42	129	8	460	94	108	71	62	33	22	11	7	89	73	.549
2005	Cubs	NL	162	121	.59	240	21	29	40	46	36	103	2	457	104	88	107	70	48	27	21	7	79	83	.488
2006	Cubs	NL	162	133	.56	271	9	26	45	39	22	165	2	542	170	108	139	46	44	28	16	11	66	96	.407
2008	Reds	NL	162	119	.58	285	28	27	26	63	39	124	2	507	132	100	101	37	40	28	12	4	74	88	.457
2009	Reds	NL	162	130	.45	252	15	35	30	62	36	116	1	478	136	120	118	23	36	29	7	4	78	84	.481
	162-Game Average			118	.53	248	22	24	35	49	28	115	5	449	140	102	87	55	46	30	17	8	83	79	.512

Buddy Bell

Year	Team	Lg	G	LINEUPS		SUBSTITUTION			PITCHER USAGE						TACTICS				INTENTIONAL BB				RESULTS		
				LUp	PL%	PH	PR	DS	Quick	Slow	LO	RCD	LS	Rel	SBA	SacA	RM	PO	#	Good	NG	Bomb	W	L	Pct
1996	Tigers	AL	162	128	.50	123	29	17	17	27	26	82	8	426	137	63		13	63	29	34	19	53	109	.327
1997	Tigers	AL	162	116	.61	163	19	22	24	7	12	113	11	417	233	44		32	33	17	16	10	79	83	.488
1998	Tigers	AL	137	88	.58	102	25	7	15	15	10	89	4	362	143	24		38	45	24	21	15	52	85	.380
2000	Rockies	NL	162	106	.64	285	21	8	12	18	10	106	8	480	192	100		40	72	39	33	16	82	80	.506
2001	Rockies	NL	162	116	.61	314	27	14	18	30	8	117	6	476	186	108		43	71	40	31	13	73	89	.451
2002	Rockies	NL	22	15	.55	42	1	5	5	11	3	21	0	69	17	10	8	5	11	5	6	4	6	16	.273
2005	Royals	AL	112	93	.61	97	18	8	32	23	3	50	4	310	48	38	80	25	17	9	8	6	43	69	.384
2006	Royals	AL	152	113	.62	87	27	25	40	37	13	86	4	439	95	63	84	13	40	20	20	10	58	94	.382
2007	Royals	AL	162	141	.55	119	30	28	49	28	16	74	10	448	122	59	125	25	54	33	21	9	69	93	.426
	162-Game Average			123	.58	175	26	18	28	26	13	97	7	450	154	67	107	31	53	28	25	13	68	94	.420

Bud Black

Year	Team	Lg	G	LINEUPS		SUBSTITUTION			PITCHER USAGE						TACTICS				INTENTIONAL BB				RESULTS		
				LUp	PL%	PH	PR	DS	Quick	Slow	LO	RCD	LS	Rel	SBA	SacA	RM	PO	#	Good	NG	Bomb	W	L	Pct
2007	Padres	NL	163	115	.62	279	18	13	63	28	13	122	0	485	79	85	73	56	48	28	20	11	89	74	.546
2008	Padres	NL	162	113	.63	286	25	20	55	36	17	109	0	491	53	75	78	31	61	30	31	17	63	99	.389
2009	Padres	NL	162	137	.64	264	8	34	50	37	8	118	5	527	111	99	84	55	58	42	16	6	75	87	.463
	162-Game Average			121	.63	276	17	22	56	34	13	116	2	500	81	86	78	47	56	33	22	11	76	86	.469

Bruce Bochy

Year	Team	Lg	G	LINEUPS LUp	PL%	SUBSTITUTION PH	PR	DS	PITCHER USAGE Quick	Slow	LO	RCD	LS	Rel	TACTICS SBA	SacA	RM	PO	INTENTIONAL BB #	Good	NG	Bomb	RESULTS W	L	Pct
1995	Padres	NL	144	96	.59	262	30	23	44	41	17	38	3	337	170	68		38	37	19	18	11	70	74	.486
1996	Padres	NL	162	114	.52	289	29	15	51	33	10	67	12	411	164	73		65	47	29	18	12	91	71	.562
1997	Padres	NL	162	111	.60	291	26	9	45	45	3	81	11	426	200	84		58	37	20	17	11	76	86	.469
1998	Padres	NL	162	110	**.65**	280	**62**	44	44	45	9	81	12	369	116	84		27	45	31	14	10	98	64	.605
1999	Padres	NL	162	137	.60	298	**51**	21	44	36	4	68	5	403	**241**	60		29	48	29	19	13	74	88	.457
2000	Padres	NL	162	134	.52	**285**	44	14	41	47	14	105	5	443	184	52		27	50	21	29	11	76	86	.469
2001	Padres	NL	162	116	.60	255	**54**	27	32	47	6	85	10	422	173	43		23	54	31	23	13	79	83	.488
2002	Padres	NL	162	123	**.66**	259	44	56	39	43	17	106	4	459	115	63	74	14	61	38	23	14	66	96	.407
2003	Padres	NL	162	134	.58	339	20	29	34	43	16	100	3	473	115	63	41	6	52	33	19	12	64	98	.395
2004	Padres	NL	162	96	.54	261	28	47	47	32	15	76	3	437	77	75	96	14	39	24	15	10	87	75	.537
2005	Padres	NL	162	128	.58	285	31	49	46	36	23	87	1	456	143	89	111	16	45	33	12	8	82	80	.506
2006	Padres	NL	162	111	.60	264	**64**	48	43	42	24	111	2	475	154	77	110	21	63	43	20	10	88	74	.543
2007	Giants	NL	162	128	**.72**	264	50	45	26	50	**36**	132	2	496	152	86	119	10	41	29	12	3	71	91	.438
2008	Giants	NL	162	134	**.68**	276	32	39	24	59	**42**	97	6	478	154	77	**155**	5	59	40	19	8	72	90	.444
2009	Giants	NL	162	134	.65	231	21	52	42	40	32	84	**8**	457	106	93	118	5	49	32	17	10	88	74	.543
162-Game Average				121	.61	278	39	35	40	43	18	89	6	439	152	73	103	24	49	30	18	10	79	83	.488

Dave Clark

Year	Team	Lg	G	LINEUPS LUp	PL%	SUBSTITUTION PH	PR	DS	PITCHER USAGE Quick	Slow	LO	RCD	LS	Rel	TACTICS SBA	SacA	RM	PO	INTENTIONAL BB #	Good	NG	Bomb	RESULTS W	L	Pct
2009	Astros	NL	13	9	.63	28	1	4	3	5	0	15	0	48	7	5	8	0	3	1	2	1	4	9	.308
162-Game Average				112	.63	349	12	50	37	62	0	187	0	598	87	62	100	0	37	12	25	12	50	112	.309

Cecil Cooper

Year	Team	Lg	G	LINEUPS LUp	PL%	SUBSTITUTION PH	PR	DS	PITCHER USAGE Quick	Slow	LO	RCD	LS	Rel	TACTICS SBA	SacA	RM	PO	INTENTIONAL BB #	Good	NG	Bomb	RESULTS W	L	Pct
2007	Astros	NL	31	26	.42	63	8	23	10	5	2	11	0	88	19	16	20	4	14	8	6	4	15	16	.484
2008	Astros	NL	161	115	.58	252	16	47	60	35	14	108	2	488	166	81	112	5	53	35	18	11	86	75	.534
2009	Astros	NL	149	94	.54	238	26	36	48	34	14	116	6	449	150	86	77	8	53	30	23	12	70	79	.470
162-Game Average				112	.55	263	24	50	56	35	14	112	4	487	159	87	99	8	57	35	22	13	81	81	.500

Bobby Cox

Year	Team	Lg	G	LINEUPS LUp	PL%	SUBSTITUTION PH	PR	DS	PITCHER USAGE Quick	Slow	LO	RCD	LS	Rel	TACTICS SBA	SacA	RM	PO	INTENTIONAL BB #	Good	NG	Bomb	RESULTS W	L	Pct
1994	Braves	NL	114	64	.60	163	30	25	22	31	5	60	5	244	79	83		44	52	33	19	9	68	46	.596
1995	Braves	NL	144	59	.56	224	48	40	41	34	13	80	6	339	116	77		41	46	31	15	4	90	54	.625
1996	Braves	NL	162	89	**.62**	254	32	27	48	43	19	110	9	408	126	90		34	64	38	26	14	**96**	66	.593
1997	Braves	NL	162	87	.64	276	**58**	29	40	37	**23**	90	4	374	166	**112**		13	56	42	14	10	**101**	61	.623
1998	Braves	NL	162	80	.64	245	28	25	44	33	14	70	1	354	141	97		40	37	22	15	8	**106**	56	.654
1999	Braves	NL	162	76	.58	272	**51**	34	44	39	13	99	6	394	214	89		54	55	35	20	11	**103**	59	.636
2000	Braves	NL	162	103	.59	252	**72**	11	**52**	41	6	81	13	376	**204**	109		59	52	35	17	5	95	67	.586
2001	Braves	NL	162	113	.57	278	50	23	49	40	4	93	8	412	131	84		**90**	**77**	49	28	13	88	74	.543
2002	Braves	NL	161	105	.48	282	33	44	60	30	20	113	9	469	115	89	47	51	63	41	22	12	**101**	59	.631
2003	Braves	NL	162	69	.52	262	49	45	40	45	23	113	10	489	90	85	23	49	69	**51**	18	11	**101**	61	.623
2004	Braves	NL	162	105	.57	243	**57**	28	50	34	25	128	**16**	483	118	105	87	25	50	30	20	14	96	66	.593
2005	Braves	NL	162	110	**.69**	247	**54**	35	46	27	20	125	7	484	124	104	93	11	52	34	18	14	90	72	.556
2006	Braves	NL	162	85	.58	299	24	35	44	38	24	144	3	522	87	99	58	24	69	48	21	12	79	83	.488
2007	Braves	NL	162	86	.68	290	33	21	60	24	10	143	1	528	94	77	68	28	**89**	**58**	**31**	**16**	84	78	.519
2008	Braves	NL	162	117	.67	**294**	31	17	59	34	6	**134**	6	**545**	85	90	77	23	80	45	**35**	**20**	72	90	.444
2009	Braves	NL	162	112	.62	252	37	32	48	34	19	**142**	1	488	84	**125**	47	21	59	35	24	14	86	76	.531
162-Game Average				94	.61	265	44	30	48	36	16	111	7	443	127	97	63	39	62	40	22	12	93	69	.574

Billy Doran

Year	Team	Lg	G	LINEUPS LUp	PL%	SUBSTITUTION PH	PR	DS	PITCHER USAGE Quick	Slow	LO	RCD	LS	Rel	TACTICS SBA	SacA	RM	PO	INTENTIONAL BB #	Good	NG	Bomb	RESULTS W	L	Pct
2006	Royals	AL	10	10	.50	5	2	0	4	1	0	4	0	34	4	7	4	0	5	4	1	0	4	6	.400
162-Game Average				162	.50	81	32	0	65	16	0	65	0	551	65	113	65	0	81	65	16	0	65	97	.401

Terry Francona

Year	Team	Lg	G	LINEUPS LUp	PL%	SUBSTITUTION PH	PR	DS	PITCHER USAGE Quick	Slow	LO	RCD	LS	Rel	TACTICS SBA	SacA	RM	PO	INTENTIONAL BB #	Good	NG	Bomb	RESULTS W	L	Pct
1997	Phillies	NL	162	98	.66	288	19	28	28	**54**	22	102	9	409	148	91		30	42	23	19	9	68	**94**	.420
1998	Phillies	NL	162	84	.53	256	20	19	34	**57**	20	88	7	385	142	85		16	27	10	17	8	75	87	.463
1999	Phillies	NL	162	85	.51	239	13	31	29	41	16	111	7	441	160	81		27	24	14	10	6	77	85	.475
2000	Phillies	NL	162	108	.53	278	17	14	38	43	**25**	102	5	414	132	89		16	32	22	10	7	65	**97**	.401

				LINEUPS		SUBSTITUTION			PITCHER USAGE						TACTICS				INTENTIONAL BB				RESULTS		
Year	Team	Lg	G	LUp	PL%	PH	PR	DS	Quick	Slow	LO	RCD	LS	Rel	SBA	SacA	RM	PO	#	Good	NG	Bomb	W	L	Pct
2004	Red Sox	AL	162	141	.65	116	65	58	41	48	32	105	8	437	98	18	91	28	28	22	6	4	98	64	.605
2005	Red Sox	AL	162	104	.67	110	46	37	25	55	30	99	3	442	57	21	79	11	28	18	10	5	95	67	.586
2006	Red Sox	AL	162	116	.59	93	54	49	36	44	13	94	9	454	74	33	98	16	25	11	14	7	86	76	.531
2007	Red Sox	AL	162	109	.60	84	34	23	41	35	32	89	4	451	120	45	90	14	20	14	6	4	96	66	.593
2008	Red Sox	AL	162	131	.59	62	40	40	50	30	20	90	11	466	155	40	87	8	17	10	7	4	95	67	.586
2009	Red Sox	AL	162	113	.58	85	47	28	36	50	30	68	6	463	165	29	68	9	24	15	9	6	95	67	.586
	162-Game Average			109	.59	161	36	33	36	46	24	95	7	436	125	53	86	18	27	16	11	6	85	77	.525

Ron Gardenhire

				LINEUPS		SUBSTITUTION			PITCHER USAGE						TACTICS				INTENTIONAL BB				RESULTS		
Year	Team	Lg	G	LUp	PL%	PH	PR	DS	Quick	Slow	LO	RCD	LS	Rel	SBA	SacA	RM	PO	#	Good	NG	Bomb	W	L	Pct
2002	Twins	AL	161	111	.69	141	36	42	54	25	10	84	1	435	141	48	44	11	24	16	8	4	94	67	.584
2003	Twins	AL	162	126	.63	144	50	26	49	33	13	85	2	399	138	59	37	14	35	16	19	6	90	72	.556
2004	Twins	AL	162	131	.59	129	45	29	56	21	20	106	4	435	162	66	121	18	27	15	12	7	92	70	.568
2005	Twins	AL	162	135	.58	104	45	26	50	21	5	87	1	396	146	59	138	16	38	28	10	3	83	79	.512
2006	Twins	AL	162	97	.62	93	36	21	60	31	3	82	5	421	143	48	130	11	25	14	11	4	96	66	.593
2007	Twins	AL	162	139	.63	104	42	25	45	30	8	99	4	438	142	45	148	11	33	14	19	9	79	83	.488
2008	Twins	AL	163	103	.64	109	26	12	47	29	5	115	3	485	144	73	143	17	38	25	13	8	88	75	.540
2009	Twins	AL	163	129	.63	83	54	34	43	25	12	115	3	480	117	62	100	21	20	9	11	6	87	76	.534
	162-Game Average			121	.63	113	42	27	50	27	9	97	3	436	142	57	108	15	30	17	13	6	89	73	.549

Phil Garner

				LINEUPS		SUBSTITUTION			PITCHER USAGE						TACTICS				INTENTIONAL BB				RESULTS		
Year	Team	Lg	G	LUp	PL%	PH	PR	DS	Quick	Slow	LO	RCD	LS	Rel	SBA	SacA	RM	PO	#	Good	NG	Bomb	W	L	Pct
1994	Brewers	AL	115	94	.53	53	33	24	31	35	0	44	5	252	96	46		23	28	18	10	9	53	62	.461
1995	Brewers	AL	144	120	.58	83	67	52	42	42	10	52	4	321	145	64		52	39	18	21	12	65	79	.451
1996	Brewers	AL	162	114	.58	115	48	46	50	30	13	61	12	386	119	72		82	30	14	19	11	80	83	.494
1997	Brewers	AL	161	128	.59	190	42	36	51	34	6	93	6	367	158	65		55	25	15	10	6	78	83	.484
1998	Brewers	NL	162	125	.59	265	54	46	52	43	6	90	9	416	140	85		59	29	20	9	4	74	88	.457
1999	Brewers	NL	112	69	.57	182	15	5	28	26	4	45	5	294	75	85		57	22	13	9	8	52	60	.464
2000	Tigers	AL	162	128	.53	126	30	25	35	38	8	109	3	429	121	58		26	22	14	8	6	79	83	.488
2001	Tigers	AL	162	116	.64	93	40	14	25	51	9	81	3	391	194	58		36	56	37	19	11	66	96	.407
2002	Tigers	AL	6	3	.63	1	1	0	1	3	3	2	0	15	4	2	3	0	2	0	2	2	0	6	.000
2004	Astros	NL	74	31	.54	142	20	35	27	15	14	71	4	241	78	40	40	7	24	20	4	1	48	26	.649
2005	Astros	NL	163	101	.48	251	40	63	55	34	21	118	3	434	159	99	140	10	20	17	12	7	89	73	.549
2006	Astros	NL	162	111	.47	287	17	47	55	36	18	157	2	497	115	123	114	26	65	31	34	17	82	80	.506
2007	Astros	NL	121	99	.52	230	14	36	31	44	17	120	0	388	79	88	84	23	48	27	21	11	58	73	.443
	162-Game Average			117	.55	191	40	41	46	41	12	99	5	418	143	84	118	43	40	25	17	10	73	84	.481

Cito Gaston

				LINEUPS		SUBSTITUTION			PITCHER USAGE						TACTICS				INTENTIONAL BB				RESULTS		
Year	Team	Lg	G	LUp	PL%	PH	PR	DS	Quick	Slow	LO	RCD	LS	Rel	SBA	SacA	RM	PO	#	Good	NG	Bomb	W	L	Pct
1994	Blue Jays	AL	115	59	.55	41	16	21	7	14	2	23	5	221	105	44		48	23	15	8	6	55	60	.478
1995	Blue Jays	AL	144	82	.65	85	24	7	15	27	40	29	10	265	91	47		57	42	24	18	10	56	88	.389
1996	Blue Jays	AL	162	87	.70	126	23	11	12	27	23	41	4	303	154	63		34	37	23	14	9	74	88	.457
1997	Blue Jays	AL	157	90	.59	71	19	6	13	22	36	74	6	322	177	50		30	29	20	9	2	72	85	.459
2008	Blue Jays	AL	88	65	.59	36	18	30	18	19	25	40	0	216	37	41	37	11	16	8	8	6	51	37	.580
2009	Blue Jays	AL	162	105	.49	48	36	18	36	47	25	83	3	445	96	32	64	25	26	15	11	6	75	87	.463
	162-Game Average			95	.60	80	27	18	20	31	30	57	5	347	129	54	65	40	34	21	13	8	75	87	.463

Bob Geren

				LINEUPS		SUBSTITUTION			PITCHER USAGE						TACTICS				INTENTIONAL BB				RESULTS		
Year	Team	Lg	G	LUp	PL%	PH	PR	DS	Quick	Slow	LO	RCD	LS	Rel	SBA	SacA	RM	PO	#	Good	NG	Bomb	W	L	Pct
2007	Athletics	AL	162	140	.57	64	31	24	39	43	14	112	9	446	72	31	91	22	60	38	22	10	76	86	.469
2008	Athletics	AL	161	133	.59	91	57	37	49	32	5	87	8	441	109	44	62	18	45	25	20	10	75	86	.466
2009	Athletics	AL	162	129	.59	77	27	40	54	40	5	108	11	488	181	37	71	5	30	15	16	7	75	87	.463
	162-Game Average			134	.59	77	38	34	47	38	8	103	9	459	121	37	75	15	45	26	19	9	75	87	.463

John Gibbons

				LINEUPS		SUBSTITUTION			PITCHER USAGE						TACTICS				INTENTIONAL BB				RESULTS		
Year	Team	Lg	G	LUp	PL%	PH	PR	DS	Quick	Slow	LO	RCD	LS	Rel	SBA	SacA	RM	PO	#	Good	NG	Bomb	W	L	Pct
2004	Blue Jays	AL	50	36	.68	42	3	2	16	8	7	22	1	130	34	2	47	21	11	5	6	3	20	30	.400
2005	Blue Jays	AL	162	124	.66	148	11	37	55	18	9	77	12	432	107	28	128	45	29	13	16	9	80	82	.494
2006	Blue Jays	AL	162	120	.53	112	32	40	59	33	17	94	16	482	98	20	127	40	56	32	24	12	87	75	.537

Year	Team	Lg	G	LUp	PL%	PH	PR	DS	Quick	Slow	LO	RCD	LS	Rel	SBA	SacA	RM	PO	#	Good	NG	Bomb	W	L	Pct
				LINEUPS		SUBSTITUTION			PITCHER USAGE						TACTICS				INTENTIONAL BB				RESULTS		
2007	Blue Jays	AL	162	131	.46	139	48	33	45	37	31	75	9	420	79	35	99	37	34	17	17	6	83	79	.512
2008	Blue Jays	AL	74	60	.48	53	15	18	12	20	12	43	0	205	70	23	39	10	26	16	10	6	35	39	.473
	162-Game Average			125	.56	131	29	35	50	31	20	83	10	443	103	29	117	41	41	22	19	10	81	81	.500

Joe Girardi

Year	Team	Lg	G	LUp	PL%	PH	PR	DS	Quick	Slow	LO	RCD	LS	Rel	SBA	SacA	RM	PO	#	Good	NG	Bomb	W	L	Pct
				LINEUPS		SUBSTITUTION			PITCHER USAGE						TACTICS				INTENTIONAL BB				RESULTS		
2006	Marlins	NL	162	117	.50	250	44	66	46	40	28	76	3	438	168	97	108	42	58	37	21	7	78	84	.481
2008	Yankees	AL	162	114	.63	97	37	42	60	37	12	88	10	475	157	38	173	36	37	22	15	8	89	73	.549
2009	Yankees	AL	162	106	.73	97	61	42	36	45	27	88	13	461	139	44	83	33	28	14	14	9	103	59	.636
	162-Game Average			112	.62	148	47	50	47	41	22	84	9	458	155	60	121	37	41	24	17	8	90	72	.556

Fredi Gonzalez

Year	Team	Lg	G	LUp	PL%	PH	PR	DS	Quick	Slow	LO	RCD	LS	Rel	SBA	SacA	RM	PO	#	Good	NG	Bomb	W	L	Pct
				LINEUPS		SUBSTITUTION			PITCHER USAGE						TACTICS				INTENTIONAL BB				RESULTS		
2007	Marlins	NL	162	96	.50	284	29	34	33	56	20	138	5	560	139	91	79	22	60	36	24	16	71	91	.438
2008	Marlins	NL	161	106	.51	255	38	49	38	39	8	120	3	511	104	61	75	17	66	42	24	14	84	77	.522
2009	Marlins	NL	162	97	.58	281	28	49	48	26	12	116	0	530	110	86	88	20	60	38	22	15	87	75	.537
	162-Game Average			100	.53	274	32	44	40	40	13	125	3	535	118	79	81	20	62	39	23	15	81	81	.500

Ozzie Guillen

Year	Team	Lg	G	LUp	PL%	PH	PR	DS	Quick	Slow	LO	RCD	LS	Rel	SBA	SacA	RM	PO	#	Good	NG	Bomb	W	L	Pct
				LINEUPS		SUBSTITUTION			PITCHER USAGE						TACTICS				INTENTIONAL BB				RESULTS		
2004	White Sox	AL	162	134	.58	132	35	15	28	65	48	86	8	399	129	84	97	17	36	15	21	8	83	79	.512
2005	White Sox	AL	162	112	.51	100	32	21	31	56	35	114	5	412	204	68	148	15	42	27	15	6	99	63	.611
2006	White Sox	AL	162	87	.60	135	42	38	28	68	35	83	7	398	141	61	85	27	59	39	20	9	90	72	.556
2007	White Sox	AL	162	124	.56	100	26	23	26	53	33	131	2	463	123	54	92	13	50	24	26	15	72	90	.444
2008	White Sox	AL	163	100	.52	75	49	37	42	48	14	100	3	463	101	44	98	8	42	29	13	6	89	74	.546
2009	White Sox	AL	162	124	.52	105	48	19	50	37	16	70	4	415	162	45	114	15	41	23	18	10	79	83	.488
	162-Game Average			113	.55	108	39	25	34	54	30	97	5	425	143	59	106	16	45	26	19	9	85	77	.525

Mike Hargrove

Year	Team	Lg	G	LUp	PL%	PH	PR	DS	Quick	Slow	LO	RCD	LS	Rel	SBA	SacA	RM	PO	#	Good	NG	Bomb	W	L	Pct
				LINEUPS		SUBSTITUTION			PITCHER USAGE						TACTICS				INTENTIONAL BB				RESULTS		
1994	Indians	AL	113	53	.67	79	18	31	23	31	3	41	4	222	179	43		40	28	14	14	7	66	47	.584
1995	Indians	AL	144	64	.66	101	34	21	36	23	12	61	3	335	185	40		22	16	9	7	3	100	44	.694
1996	Indians	AL	161	96	.56	115	20	25	39	31	14	70	5	382	210	58		41	42	22	20	11	99	62	.615
1997	Indians	AL	161	109	.58	86	17	14	34	46	14	101	9	429	177	60		37	53	30	23	10	86	75	.534
1998	Indians	AL	162	108	.62	88	21	32	29	39	19	104	9	423	203	53		47	48	26	22	13	89	73	.549
1999	Indians	AL	162	123	.66	99	25	22	41	44	15	99	3	466	197	82		28	55	33	22	13	97	65	.599
2000	Orioles	AL	162	107	.54	77	42	19	25	55	24	84	2	396	191	36		31	32	21	11	2	74	88	.457
2001	Orioles	AL	162	139	.53	82	27	20	39	42	3	74	10	392	186	57		71	28	18	10	7	63	98	.391
2002	Orioles	AL	162	125	.52	127	22	22	36	46	32	74	6	407	158	54	26	42	34	22	12	6	67	95	.414
2003	Orioles	AL	163	120	.52	78	37	22	29	52	48	89	5	425	125	67	45	16	43	20	23	11	71	91	.438
2005	Mariners	AL	162	97	.52	125	24	18	30	45	31	73	1	433	149	61	120	36	32	21	11	7	69	93	.426
2006	Mariners	AL	162	84	.51	121	21	20	24	52	24	81	14	429	143	40	124	17	50	26	24	16	78	84	.481
2007	Mariners	AL	78	48	.47	41	18	21	20	26	9	44	7	209	55	22	58	13	20	12	8	4	45	33	.577
	162-Game Average			106	.57	101	27	24	34	44	21	83	6	411	179	56	83	37	40	23	17	9	83	79	.512

Trey Hillman

Year	Team	Lg	G	LUp	PL%	PH	PR	DS	Quick	Slow	LO	RCD	LS	Rel	SBA	SacA	RM	PO	#	Good	NG	Bomb	W	L	Pct
				LINEUPS		SUBSTITUTION			PITCHER USAGE						TACTICS				INTENTIONAL BB				RESULTS		
2008	Royals	AL	162	134	.55	71	44	34	35	48	19	78	2	439	117	50	96	15	15	9	6	3	75	87	.463
2009	Royals	AL	162	141	.63	90	34	38	41	54	34	72	7	426	117	51	110	27	28	13	15	10	65	97	.401
	162-Game Average			138	.59	81	39	36	38	51	27	75	5	433	117	51	103	21	22	11	11	7	70	92	.432

A.J. Hinch

Year	Team	Lg	G	LUp	PL%	PH	PR	DS	Quick	Slow	LO	RCD	LS	Rel	SBA	SacA	RM	PO	#	Good	NG	Bomb	W	L	Pct
				LINEUPS		SUBSTITUTION			PITCHER USAGE						TACTICS				INTENTIONAL BB				RESULTS		
2009	Diamondbacks	NL	133	115	.63	222	10	13	24	50	24	61	5	392	113	64	41	5	24	12	12	6	58	75	.436
	162-Game Average			140	.63	270	12	16	29	61	29	74	6	477	138	78	50	6	29	15	15	7	71	91	.438

Clint Hurdle

Year	Team	Lg	G	LINEUPS		SUBSTITUTION			PITCHER USAGE						TACTICS				INTENTIONAL BB				RESULTS		
				LUp	PL%	PH	PR	DS	Quick	Slow	LO	RCD	LS	Rel	SBA	SacA	RM	PO	#	Good	NG	Bomb	W	L	Pct
2002	Rockies	NL	140	100	.52	274	28	41	33	45	17	104	3	437	139	46	50	13	38	22	16	11	67	73	.479
2003	Rockies	NL	162	108	.47	317	17	32	35	40	5	87	4	500	100	82	26	16	51	31	20	13	74	88	.457
2004	Rockies	NL	162	131	.57	289	18	35	36	63	20	74	1	473	77	128	67	12	84	54	30	12	68	94	.420
2005	Rockies	NL	162	135	.60	273	21	40	42	60	17	89	2	459	97	114	119	22	54	28	26	15	67	95	.414
2006	Rockies	NL	162	111	.49	259	17	22	34	52	17	107	2	499	135	156	114	28	81	45	36	23	76	86	.469
2007	Rockies	NL	163	96	.51	283	32	29	45	37	13	112	1	529	131	112	109	26	61	30	31	14	90	73	.552
2008	Rockies	NL	162	131	.49	253	20	31	40	43	16	85	2	485	178	111	116	43	49	31	18	6	74	88	.457
2009	Rockies	NL	46	42	.60	73	8	10	11	14	3	31	0	135	45	26	34	3	11	8	3	1	18	28	.391
	162-Game Average			119	.52	282	23	34	39	49	15	96	2	492	126	108	89	23	60	35	25	13	75	87	.463

Tony LaRussa

Year	Team	Lg	G	LINEUPS		SUBSTITUTION			PITCHER USAGE						TACTICS				INTENTIONAL BB				RESULTS		
				LUp	PL%	PH	PR	DS	Quick	Slow	LO	RCD	LS	Rel	SBA	SacA	RM	PO	#	Good	NG	Bomb	W	L	Pct
1994	Athletics	AL	114	97	.62	89	28	14	43	21	5	60	4	308	130	31		32	30	20	10	4	51	63	.447
1995	Athletics	AL	144	120	.54	113	38	24	33	38	19	46	7	358	158	42		42	26	18	8	4	67	77	.465
1996	Cardinals	NL	162	120	.52	246	25	13	32	48	24	90	8	413	207	117		41	43	28	15	7	88	74	.543
1997	Cardinals	NL	162	146	.54	307	17	18	34	42	16	81	2	399	224	77		79	34	26	8	2	73	89	.451
1998	Cardinals	NL	162	146	.52	259	7	18	62	31	13	82	14	429	174	85		34	38	25	13	8	83	79	.512
1999	Cardinals	NL	161	138	.47	264	32	28	50	41	13	96	14	454	182	103		30	38	20	18	11	75	86	.466
2000	Cardinals	NL	162	137	.53	240	35	25	40	31	11	63	18	386	138	107		34	28	21	7	6	95	67	.586
2001	Cardinals	NL	162	117	.47	256	26	13	46	36	7	140	7	485	126	102		25	36	21	15	4	93	69	.574
2002	Cardinals	NL	162	117	.52	340	27	41	58	33	23	110	8	472	128	100	75	13	39	25	14	8	97	65	.599
2003	Cardinals	NL	162	126	.50	352	28	51	38	49	36	113	9	460	114	108	56	9	36	28	8	2	85	77	.525
2004	Cardinals	NL	162	119	.53	275	25	69	30	48	31	120	16	469	158	88	158	9	24	17	7	4	105	57	.648
2005	Cardinals	NL	162	138	.55	270	25	48	40	38	22	88	4	436	119	92	153	9	27	16	11	7	100	62	.617
2006	Cardinals	NL	161	131	.56	272	11	53	50	34	21	95	6	469	91	86	123	13	35	21	14	3	83	78	.516
2007	Cardinals	NL	162	150	.60	317	19	37	46	44	8	102	5	516	89	86	120	23	25	10	15	11	78	84	.481
2008	Cardinals	NL	162	153	.64	275	26	57	52	40	18	101	11	506	105	87	114	18	21	13	8	1	86	76	.531
2009	Cardinals	NL	162	131	.52	289	12	51	55	38	17	102	8	481	106	93	91	17	23	15	8	1	91	71	.562
	162-Game Average			134	.54	267	24	36	46	39	18	96	9	452	144	90	111	27	32	21	11	5	87	75	.537

Jim Leyland

Year	Team	Lg	G	LINEUPS		SUBSTITUTION			PITCHER USAGE						TACTICS				INTENTIONAL BB				RESULTS		
				LUp	PL%	PH	PR	DS	Quick	Slow	LO	RCD	LS	Rel	SBA	SacA	RM	PO	#	Good	NG	Bomb	W	L	Pct
1994	Pirates	NL	114	94	.56	170	16	13	12	9	1	48	4	285	78	48		38	52	29	23	15	53	61	.465
1995	Pirates	NL	144	124	.56	282	8	4	13	12	11	71	4	391	139	69		51	50	30	20	10	58	86	.403
1996	Pirates	NL	162	117	.53	299	18	14	27	8	11	60	11	422	175	101		46	50	23	27	13	73	89	.451
1997	Marlins	NL	162	105	.59	258	36	31	21	12	18	65	2	404	173	91		38	41	25	16	9	92	70	.568
1998	Marlins	NL	162	98	.59	277	13	15	18	24	31	73	8	420	172	91		31	61	36	25	11	54	108	.333
1999	Rockies	NL	162	124	.56	294	11	12	11	29	21	72	5	421	113	88		11	46	24	22	14	72	90	.444
2006	Tigers	AL	162	120	.53	81	34	38	52	32	16	52	3	390	100	57	128	9	35	23	12	9	95	67	.586
2007	Tigers	AL	162	108	.53	77	31	49	46	43	14	70	5	443	133	35	123	20	41	24	17	13	88	74	.543
2008	Tigers	AL	162	131	.51	66	25	50	29	47	20	72	7	440	94	40	114	10	63	37	26	13	74	88	.457
2009	Tigers	AL	163	126	.55	125	52	50	47	47	38	86	3	439	105	60	132	19	42	26	16	6	86	77	.528
	162-Game Average			119	.55	201	25	29	29	27	19	70	5	422	134	71	124	28	50	29	21	12	78	84	.481

Grady Little

Year	Team	Lg	G	LINEUPS		SUBSTITUTION			PITCHER USAGE						TACTICS				INTENTIONAL BB				RESULTS		
				LUp	PL%	PH	PR	DS	Quick	Slow	LO	RCD	LS	Rel	SBA	SacA	RM	PO	#	Good	NG	Bomb	W	L	Pct
2002	Red Sox	AL	162	120	.59	127	51	23	63	28	18	53	11	338	108	35	38	50	29	18	11	3	93	69	.574
2003	Red Sox	AL	162	118	.64	130	80	32	43	36	19	78	8	437	123	32	42	28	41	22	19	13	95	67	.586
2006	Dodgers	NL	162	118	.67	291	34	37	56	27	11	106	9	454	177	82	144	63	40	22	18	7	88	74	.543
2007	Dodgers	NL	162	112	.61	273	35	61	44	31	11	125	4	483	187	77	133	45	34	21	13	7	82	80	.506
	162-Game Average			117	.63	205	50	38	52	31	15	91	8	428	149	57	89	47	36	21	15	8	90	72	.556

Ken Macha

Year	Team	Lg	G	LINEUPS		SUBSTITUTION			PITCHER USAGE						TACTICS				INTENTIONAL BB				RESULTS		
				LUp	PL%	PH	PR	DS	Quick	Slow	LO	RCD	LS	Rel	SBA	SacA	RM	PO	#	Good	NG	Bomb	W	L	Pct
2003	Athletics	AL	162	111	.57	140	29	23	44	38	30	72	12	364	62	31	28	9	42	25	17	10	96	66	.593
2004	Athletics	AL	162	119	.60	123	13	14	37	47	39	94	5	410	69	30	63	2	49	31	18	9	91	71	.562
2005	Athletics	AL	162	127	.62	83	17	11	43	36	30	79	13	410	53	29	53	13	42	27	15	6	88	74	.543
2006	Athletics	AL	162	121	.58	62	33	23	39	47	28	104	8	444	81	29	70	22	47	26	21	11	93	69	.574
2009	Brewers	NL	162	111	.48	267	7	32	35	51	19	120	1	512	105	70	90	12	60	35	25	17	80	82	.494
	162-Game Average			118	.57	135	20	21	40	44	29	94	8	429	74	38	61	12	48	29	19	11	90	72	.556

Pete Mackanin

Year	Team	Lg	G	LINEUPS LUp	PL%	SUBSTITUTION PH	PR	DS	PITCHER USAGE Quick	Slow	LO	RCD	LS	Rel	TACTICS SBA	SacA	RM	PO	INTENTIONAL BB #	Good	NG	Bomb	RESULTS W	L	Pct
2005	Pirates	NL	26	24	.52	54	1	5	11	4	1	22	0	94	19	19	20	2	5	2	3	1	12	14	.462
2007	Reds	NL	80	57	.59	130	10	26	20	22	9	58	3	266	62	44	36	12	18	10	8	3	41	39	.513
	162-Game Average			124	.57	281	17	47	47	40	15	122	5	550	124	96	86	21	35	18	17	6	81	81	.500

Joe Maddon

Year	Team	Lg	G	LINEUPS LUp	PL%	SUBSTITUTION PH	PR	DS	PITCHER USAGE Quick	Slow	LO	RCD	LS	Rel	TACTICS SBA	SacA	RM	PO	INTENTIONAL BB #	Good	NG	Bomb	RESULTS W	L	Pct
1996	Angels	AL	22	19	.64	21	5	0	7	6	6	10	3	48	11	20		6	4	3	1	1	8	14	.364
1998	Angels	AL	8	4	.57	2	4	0	1	5	3	5	3	12	2	7		0	1	0	1	0	6	2	.750
1999	Angels	AL	29	19	.58	29	4	1	6	0	4	20	0	85	23	12		7	3	1	2	1	19	10	.655
2006	Devil Rays	AL	162	145	.54	81	26	51	41	39	16	79	10	444	186	51	132	48	39	19	20	13	61	101	.377
2007	Devil Rays	AL	162	122	.53	80	19	16	31	56	19	113	1	483	179	40	118	50	31	18	13	4	66	96	.407
2008	Rays	AL	162	115	.69	133	16	39	48	37	14	112	7	448	192	31	113	26	29	15	14	8	97	65	.599
2009	Rays	AL	162	123	.66	140	21	18	28	51	23	139	3	510	255	29	99	15	22	10	12	7	84	78	.519
	162-Game Average			125	.60	111	22	29	37	44	19	110	6	465	194	44	116	35	30	15	14	8	78	84	.481

Charlie Manuel

Year	Team	Lg	G	LINEUPS LUp	PL%	SUBSTITUTION PH	PR	DS	PITCHER USAGE Quick	Slow	LO	RCD	LS	Rel	TACTICS SBA	SacA	RM	PO	INTENTIONAL BB #	Good	NG	Bomb	RESULTS W	L	Pct
2000	Indians	AL	162	102	.64	73	40	26	21	12	20	104	7	462	147	59		30	45	28	17	9	90	72	.556
2001	Indians	AL	162	114	.61	105	30	49	28	17	10	120	3	484	120	67		43	44	30	14	11	91	71	.562
2002	Indians	AL	86	67	.61	57	10	19	14	17	25	47	0	222	57	21	34	3	21	12	9	4	39	47	.453
2005	Phillies	NL	162	80	.64	265	36	19	42	28	13	119	6	442	143	86	76	11	51	35	16	9	88	74	.543
2006	Phillies	NL	162	81	.65	301	42	49	28	43	22	126	2	500	117	79	74	16	63	35	28	12	85	77	.525
2007	Phillies	NL	162	87	.64	264	56	75	40	40	19	128	6	498	157	84	90	30	62	41	21	16	89	73	.549
2008	Phillies	NL	162	77	.65	291	62	60	33	42	24	124	1	468	161	88	92	34	64	46	18	11	92	70	.568
2009	Phillies	NL	162	68	.67	283	20	16	32	55	32	107	3	459	147	74	65	3	31	19	12	3	93	69	.574
	162-Game Average			90	.64	218	39	42	32	34	22	116	4	469	139	74	78	23	51	33	18	10	89	73	.549

Jerry Manuel

Year	Team	Lg	G	LINEUPS LUp	PL%	SUBSTITUTION PH	PR	DS	PITCHER USAGE Quick	Slow	LO	RCD	LS	Rel	TACTICS SBA	SacA	RM	PO	INTENTIONAL BB #	Good	NG	Bomb	RESULTS W	L	Pct
1998	White Sox	AL	162	110	.56	65	19	31	43	35	6	72	14	405	173	54		26	20	14	6	4	80	82	.494
1999	White Sox	AL	161	109	.58	79	35	39	35	42	9	78	8	409	160	69		22	31	20	11	7	75	86	.466
2000	White Sox	AL	162	84	.53	84	35	20	41	31	8	91	18	466	161	75		32	27	16	11	10	95	67	.586
2001	White Sox	AL	162	115	.53	104	34	50	45	39	5	93	16	466	182	95		41	38	24	14	9	83	79	.512
2002	White Sox	AL	162	104	.55	86	10	39	50	44	17	86	10	423	106	73	38	18	31	17	14	11	81	81	.500
2003	White Sox	AL	162	105	.55	146	40	71	39	36	27	74	10	361	106	66	39	20	30	18	12	7	86	76	.531
2008	Mets	NL	93	58	.76	167	7	31	12	30	23	95	2	324	89	54	81	6	37	18	19	6	55	38	.591
2009	Mets	NL	162	117	.72	289	11	37	34	51	22	137	2	511	166	112	104	3	60	38	22	14	70	92	.432
	162-Game Average			106	.59	135	25	42	40	41	15	96	11	437	151	79	73	22	36	22	14	9	83	79	.512

John McLaren

Year	Team	Lg	G	LINEUPS LUp	PL%	SUBSTITUTION PH	PR	DS	PITCHER USAGE Quick	Slow	LO	RCD	LS	Rel	TACTICS SBA	SacA	RM	PO	INTENTIONAL BB #	Good	NG	Bomb	RESULTS W	L	Pct
2007	Mariners	AL	84	52	.48	55	40	18	17	23	19	49	6	247	56	20	76	18	19	10	9	5	43	41	.512
2008	Mariners	AL	72	48	.50	31	16	4	17	24	9	45	1	197	65	17	63	11	12	6	6	5	25	47	.347
	162-Game Average			104	.49	89	58	23	35	49	29	98	7	461	126	38	144	30	32	17	16	10	71	91	.438

Bob Melvin

Year	Team	Lg	G	LINEUPS LUp	PL%	SUBSTITUTION PH	PR	DS	PITCHER USAGE Quick	Slow	LO	RCD	LS	Rel	TACTICS SBA	SacA	RM	PO	INTENTIONAL BB #	Good	NG	Bomb	RESULTS W	L	Pct
2003	Mariners	AL	162	111	.62	81	62	33	27	46	43	56	6	366	145	44	37	5	24	14	10	4	93	69	.574
2004	Mariners	AL	162	151	.59	109	66	26	26	63	43	82	5	414	152	56	123	24	32	18	14	8	63	99	.389
2005	Diamondbacks	NL	162	120	.68	310	26	38	26	56	36	123	11	458	93	93	101	30	43	27	16	9	77	85	.475
2006	Diamondbacks	NL	162	114	.72	278	11	35	37	42	15	86	0	461	106	83	61	30	44	28	16	8	76	86	.469
2007	Diamondbacks	NL	162	146	.57	243	11	61	35	42	31	96	2	469	133	74	70	25	38	30	8	4	90	72	.556
2008	Diamondbacks	NL	162	134	.57	263	27	30	41	39	16	102	0	444	81	87	79	28	41	27	14	9	82	80	.506
2009	Diamondbacks	NL	29	29	.62	47	6	8	7	4	3	17	0	91	29	17	13	3	3	1	2	2	12	17	.414
	162-Game Average			130	.62	215	34	37	32	47	30	91	4	437	120	73	78	23	36	23	13	7	80	82	.494

Jerry Narron

Year	Team	Lg	G	LUp	PL%	PH	PR	DS	Quick	Slow	LO	RCD	LS	Rel	SBA	SacA	RM	PO	#	Good	NG	Bomb	W	L	Pct
2001	Rangers	AL	134	94	.66	92	14	19	9	18	6	60	5	340	106	29		5	24	10	14	8	62	72	.463
2002	Rangers	AL	162	128	.52	154	59	30	33	54	26	121	5	487	96	58	58	6	32	19	13	3	72	90	.444
2005	Reds	NL	93	73	.61	156	9	14	13	22	12	71	5	287	50	45	53	7	25	21	4	2	46	46	.500
2006	Reds	NL	162	140	.56	273	23	46	33	47	41	121	2	476	157	86	91	11	55	38	17	9	80	82	.494
2007	Reds	NL	82	63	.58	135	6	26	11	33	21	74	8	256	66	56	45	8	29	16	13	7	31	51	.378
	162-Game Average			128	.58	208	28	35	25	45	27	115	6	473	122	70	80	9	42	27	16	7	75	87	.463

Sam Perlozzo

Year	Team	Lg	G	LUp	PL%	PH	PR	DS	Quick	Slow	LO	RCD	LS	Rel	SBA	SacA	RM	PO	#	Good	NG	Bomb	W	L	Pct
2005	Orioles	AL	55	47	.61	28	23	26	15	11	5	46	2	180	41	24	25	8	3	1	2	1	23	32	.418
2006	Orioles	AL	162	124	.56	72	46	49	29	47	14	102	10	472	153	58	79	30	26	15	11	7	70	92	.432
2007	Orioles	AL	69	48	.60	29	26	25	16	15	13	64	1	211	62	30	29	13	8	3	5	5	29	40	.420
	162-Game Average			124	.58	73	54	57	34	41	18	120	7	489	145	63	75	29	21	11	10	7	69	93	.426

Lou Piniella

Year	Team	Lg	G	LUp	PL%	PH	PR	DS	Quick	Slow	LO	RCD	LS	Rel	SBA	SacA	RM	PO	#	Good	NG	Bomb	W	L	Pct
1994	Mariners	AL	112	98	.49	113	24	6	30	35	4	54	9	252	69	54		37	21	18	9		49	63	.438
1995	Mariners	AL	145	98	.58	137	41	22	37	39	30	58	20	324	151	66		40	37	18	19	12	79	66	.545
1996	Mariners	AL	161	99	.55	190	28	14	56	21	19	91	14	408	120	66		40	52	31	21	13	85	76	.528
1997	Mariners	AL	162	84	.57	147	35	27	38	47	25	79	11	392	129	61		32	36	18	18	10	90	72	.556
1998	Mariners	AL	161	111	.53	99	38	43	38	54	32	81	4	368	154	68		20	23	8	15	7	76	85	.472
1999	Mariners	AL	162	130	.46	122	38	30	31	40	21	51	10	346	175	49		31	39	15	24	8	79	83	.488
2000	Mariners	AL	162	130	.50	109	43	52	51	37	1	64	11	383	178	73		22	37	20	17	8	91	71	.562
2001	Mariners	AL	162	115	.64	121	44	64	55	33	5	62	9	392	216	62		33	28	19	9	3	116	46	.716
2002	Mariners	AL	162	129	.64	95	129	50	49	39	34	52	7	343	195	61	43	25	34	15	19	11	93	69	.574
2003	Devil Rays	AL	162	124	.60	188	43	26	38	41	29	59	5	372	184	53	52	23	37	21	16	10	63	99	.389
2004	Devil Rays	AL	161	137	.63	97	25	36	51	34	23	57	15	401	174	45	104	16	35	16	19	8	70	91	.435
2005	Devil Rays	AL	162	135	.54	127	18	52	38	54	32	67	10	401	200	53	128	16	41	19	22	13	67	95	.414
2007	Cubs	NL	161	125	.51	263	52	51	35	38	33	98	3	478	119	60	89	17	46	28	18	4	85	77	.525
2008	Cubs	NL	161	112	.47	286	22	31	42	37	27	111	3	478	121	93	98	15	45	28	17	9	97	64	.602
2009	Cubs	NL	161	131	.57	277	14	55	47	40	20	127	3	480	90	81	92	23	46	21	25	13	83	78	.516
	162-Game Average			121	.55	163	41	38	44	40	23	76	9	399	157	64	87	27	40	20	19	10	84	78	.519

Willie Randolph

Year	Team	Lg	G	LUp	PL%	PH	PR	DS	Quick	Slow	LO	RCD	LS	Rel	SBA	SacA	RM	PO	#	Good	NG	Bomb	W	L	Pct
2005	Mets	NL	162	105	.64	222	10	51	47	34	20	74	5	392	193	89	118	18	43	28	15	9	83	79	.512
2006	Mets	NL	162	101	.68	247	9	24	40	40	15	119	4	474	181	102	106	16	39	25	14	9	97	65	.599
2007	Mets	NL	162	102	.68	269	21	28	26	44	27	122	3	499	246	97	100	10	40	26	14	7	88	74	.543
2008	Mets	NL	69	46	.77	104	3	11	12	20	11	73	1	233	85	44	48	4	16	10	6	2	34	35	.493
	162-Game Average			103	.68	246	13	33	36	40	21	113	4	466	206	97	109	14	40	26	14	8	88	74	.543

Jim Riggleman

Year	Team	Lg	G	LUp	PL%	PH	PR	DS	Quick	Slow	LO	RCD	LS	Rel	SBA	SacA	RM	PO	#	Good	NG	Bomb	W	L	Pct
1994	Padres	NL	117	93	.63	184	28	19	11	5	3	53	10	273	116	80		52	62	34	28	11	47	70	.402
1995	Cubs	NL	144	92	.56	196	9	30	15	8	13	119	12	414	142	90		53	68	45	23	12	73	71	.507
1996	Cubs	NL	162	87	.54	326	34	21	17	11	7	114	11	439	158	79		65	55	33	22	10	76	86	.469
1997	Cubs	NL	162	127	.50	280	40	44	13	5	2	113	9	441	176	103		74	51	38	13	6	68	94	.420
1998	Cubs	NL	163	104	.60	273	26	35	16	14	20	133	6	449	109	89		26	48	22	26	15	90	73	.552
1999	Cubs	NL	162	122	.61	312	25	30	16	19	8	105	4	441	104	94		20	48	21	27	15	67	95	.414
2008	Mariners	AL	90	70	.60	76	30	22	21	25	19	50	4	272	57	27	88	10	25	17	8	3	36	54	.400
2009	Nationals	NL	75	60	.51	115	15	33	24	16	4	63	6	250	59	44	36	8	33	17	16	8	33	42	.440
	162-Game Average			114	.57	265	31	35	20	16	11	113	9	449	139	91	122	46	59	34	25	12	74	88	.457

Frank Robinson

Year	Team	Lg	G	LUp	PL%	PH	PR	DS	Quick	Slow	LO	RCD	LS	Rel	SBA	SacA	RM	PO	#	Good	NG	Bomb	W	L	Pct
2002	Expos	NL	162	121	.60	254	47	40	48	40	34	109	11	437	182	126	58	24	80	57	23	11	83	79	.512
2003	Expos	NL	162	134	.63	248	55	31	50	44	44	98	4	437	139	85	50	8	51	27	24	13	83	79	.512
2004	Expos	NL	162	131	.67	254	17	26	48	39	36	109	4	462	147	121	112	1	78	54	24	10	67	95	.414

Year	Team	Lg	G	LUp	PL%	PH	PR	DS	Quick	Slow	LO	RCD	LS	Rel	SBA	SacA	RM	PO	#	Good	NG	Bomb	W	L	Pct
2005	Nationals	NL	162	121	.63	266	48	35	45	47	42	140	3	470	90	115	109	4	77	50	27	9	81	81	.500
2006	Nationals	NL	162	110	.58	314	37	26	46	33	19	137	3	517	185	95	150	14	93	57	36	23	71	91	.438
	162-Game Average			123	.62	267	41	32	47	41	35	119	5	465	149	108	96	10	76	49	27	13	77	85	.475

John Russell

Year	Team	Lg	G	LUp	PL%	PH	PR	DS	Quick	Slow	LO	RCD	LS	Rel	SBA	SacA	RM	PO	#	Good	NG	Bomb	W	L	Pct
2008	Pirates	NL	162	128	.51	290	17	13	29	47	15	111	0	497	76	92	54	19	31	21	10	4	67	95	.414
2009	Pirates	NL	161	121	.60	251	3	5	44	45	12	89	0	456	122	78	97	15	37	20	17	10	62	99	.385
	162-Game Average			125	.56	271	10	9	37	46	14	100	0	478	99	85	76	17	34	21	14	7	65	97	.401

Mike Scioscia

Year	Team	Lg	G	LUp	PL%	PH	PR	DS	Quick	Slow	LO	RCD	LS	Rel	SBA	SacA	RM	PO	#	Good	NG	Bomb	W	L	Pct
2000	Angels	AL	162	75	.62	110	41	4	56	42	6	95	9	441	145	63		40	44	28	16	7	82	80	.506
2001	Angels	AL	162	130	.62	118	30	8	29	41	5	81	9	384	168	66		50	47	22	25	12	75	87	.463
2002	Angels	AL	162	102	.64	162	57	26	36	33	34	88	8	400	168	62	52	30	24	15	9	5	99	63	.611
2003	Angels	AL	162	130	.64	134	54	40	50	48	11	60	4	375	190	64	79	25	38	26	12	3	77	85	.475
2004	Angels	AL	162	126	.57	94	32	44	37	40	22	61	11	343	189	70	229	33	27	18	9	3	92	70	.568
2005	Angels	AL	162	124	.65	92	37	37	47	37	24	88	9	379	218	58	160	43	24	15	9	4	95	67	.586
2006	Angels	AL	162	114	.63	103	45	38	38	49	21	99	9	380	205	37	166	22	27	18	9	6	89	73	.549
2007	Angels	AL	162	127	.66	103	26	19	39	40	14	94	4	396	194	41	166	44	22	12	10	5	94	68	.580
2008	Angels	AL	162	125	.63	74	30	36	37	48	21	87	1	383	177	39	151	31	32	22	10	6	100	62	.617
2009	Angels	AL	162	123	.69	80	26	37	47	47	33	91	1	434	211	55	137	40	35	22	13	6	97	65	.599
	162-Game Average			118	.63	107	38	29	42	43	19	84	7	392	187	56	143	36	32	20	12	6	90	72	.556

Buck Showalter

Year	Team	Lg	G	LUp	PL%	PH	PR	DS	Quick	Slow	LO	RCD	LS	Rel	SBA	SacA	RM	PO	#	Good	NG	Bomb	W	L	Pct
1994	Yankees	AL	113	79	.59	95	31	3	24	30	0	38	7	241	95	34		22	24	13	11	4	70	43	.619
1995	Yankees	AL	145	107	.68	124	30	20	29	42	37	57	6	302	80	27		29	21	14	7	1	79	65	.549
1998	Diamondbacks	NL	162	124	.62	252	17	15	34	40	7	43	6	368	111	68		13	32	16	16	9	65	97	.401
1999	Diamondbacks	NL	162	97	.63	220	20	17	37	48	25	74	3	382	176	75		15	48	29	19	8	100	62	.617
2000	Diamondbacks	NL	162	99	.60	250	32	11	46	26	18	74	12	390	141	89		10	53	28	25	16	85	77	.525
2003	Rangers	AL	162	133	.61	88	51	41	35	33	12	93	7	494	90	35	80	12	45	24	21	14	71	91	.438
2004	Rangers	AL	162	120	.64	86	15	24	53	30	12	82	10	468	105	30	88	5	29	19	10	3	89	73	.549
2005	Rangers	AL	162	98	.59	57	22	11	42	39	17	79	8	454	82	11	103	5	31	10	21	16	79	83	.488
2006	Rangers	AL	162	95	.57	39	34	22	41	27	10	85	4	489	77	30	72	8	18	11	7	5	80	82	.494
	162-Game Average			111	.62	141	29	19	40	37	16	73	7	418	111	46	86	14	35	19	16	9	84	78	.519

Dale Sveum

Year	Team	Lg	G	LUp	PL%	PH	PR	DS	Quick	Slow	LO	RCD	LS	Rel	SBA	SacA	RM	PO	#	Good	NG	Bomb	W	L	Pct
2008	Brewers	NL	12	3	.48	32	2	1	7	2	1	12	0	46	5	13	6	1	2	1	1	0	7	5	.583
	162-Game Average			41	.48	432	27	14	95	27	14	162	0	621	68	176	81	14	27	14	14	0	94	68	.580

Joe Torre

Year	Team	Lg	G	LUp	PL%	PH	PR	DS	Quick	Slow	LO	RCD	LS	Rel	SBA	SacA	RM	PO	#	Good	NG	Bomb	W	L	Pct
1994	Cardinals	NL	115	79	.68	192	9	0	36	29	6	106	4	330	122	57		33	28	18	10	6	53	61	.465
1995	Cardinals	NL	47	36	.51	99	6	4	17	11	1	41	2	146	42	26		14	16	10	6	2	20	27	.426
1996	Yankees	AL	162	131	.59	92	62	55	59	23	22	97	10	411	142	53		19	35	17	18	14	92	70	.568
1997	Yankees	AL	162	118	.61	75	70	23	35	41	19	84	14	368	157	54		14	41	23	18	10	96	66	.593
1998	Yankees	AL	162	96	.62	94	36	28	43	38	27	71	17	334	216	44		9	25	17	8	4	114	48	.704
1999	Yankees	AL	162	76	.63	103	57	10	29	51	26	80	12	276	129	31		12	27	17	10	8	98	64	.605
2000	Yankees	AL	161	112	.63	86	49	27	43	53	27	92	16	382	147	22		8	23	9	14	7	87	74	.540
2001	Yankees	AL	161	94	.56	76	33	14	37	45	10	77	17	362	214	41		21	29	20	9	6	95	65	.594
2002	Yankees	AL	161	108	.58	89	53	31	39	49	44	86	13	334	138	35	46	18	44	33	11	4	103	58	.640
2003	Yankees	AL	163	104	.65	118	48	18	26	51	52	75	10	367	131	39	69	33	36	21	15	8	101	61	.623
2004	Yankees	AL	162	116	.65	86	35	46	48	35	29	129	10	436	117	50	126	36	32	16	16	9	101	61	.623
2005	Yankees	AL	162	117	.64	94	65	47	44	45	28	92	7	418	111	40	123	50	25	11	14	9	95	67	.586
2006	Yankees	AL	162	120	.66	108	50	59	50	30	9	109	7	489	174	48	118	50	41	22	19	4	97	65	.599
2007	Yankees	AL	162	102	.68	99	34	22	51	29	10	113	13	522	163	51	152	41	33	17	16	7	94	68	.580
2008	Dodgers	NL	162	124	.53	277	43	66	61	30	17	94	8	461	169	75	133	38	58	46	12	5	84	78	.519
2009	Dodgers	NL	162	113	.59	263	22	22	62	23	18	125	8	526	164	107	163	17	68	45	23	12	95	67	.586
	162-Game Average			110	.61	130	45	32	45	39	23	98	11	412	156	52	116	28	37	23	15	8	95	67	.586

Jim Tracy

Year	Team	Lg	G	LINEUPS		SUBSTITUTION			PITCHER USAGE						TACTICS				INTENTIONAL BB				RESULTS		
				LUp	PL%	PH	PR	DS	Quick	Slow	LO	RCD	LS	Rel	SBA	SacA	RM	PO	#	Good	NG	Bomb	W	L	Pct
2001	Dodgers	NL	162	111	.50	264	34	20	46	42	8	84	4	409	131	81		10	37	19	18	9	86	76	.531
2002	Dodgers	NL	162	102	.52	317	39	37	49	36	21	118	9	423	133	81	46	18	45	31	14	5	92	70	.568
2003	Dodgers	NL	162	103	.64	269	22	64	52	29	22	148	11	438	116	97	32	10	35	23	12	8	85	77	.525
2004	Dodgers	NL	162	94	.70	295	25	19	49	34	16	128	16	459	143	81	93	7	47	32	15	8	93	69	.574
2005	Dodgers	NL	162	129	.64	303	31	37	44	40	20	126	2	459	93	76	97	17	34	21	13	6	71	91	.438
2006	Pirates	NL	162	121	.43	264	22	22	37	43	12	156	3	505	91	80	75	12	62	39	23	15	67	95	.414
2007	Pirates	NL	162	124	.49	240	12	26	33	40	13	113	0	495	98	80	90	12	55	30	25	11	68	94	.420
2009	Rockies	NL	116	87	.63	186	25	28	28	27	27	83	3	349	116	73	82	9	40	28	12	7	74	42	.638
	162-Game Average			113	.57	277	27	33	44	38	18	124	6	458	119	84	77	12	46	29	17	9	82	80	.506

Dave Trembley

Year	Team	Lg	G	LINEUPS		SUBSTITUTION			PITCHER USAGE						TACTICS				INTENTIONAL BB				RESULTS		
				LUp	PL%	PH	PR	DS	Quick	Slow	LO	RCD	LS	Rel	SBA	SacA	RM	PO	#	Good	NG	Bomb	W	L	Pct
2007	Orioles	AL	93	71	.60	63	29	16	21	25	16	47	3	279	124	32	83	32	29	15	14	8	40	53	.430
2008	Orioles	AL	161	119	.58	117	36	25	41	44	11	87	4	492	118	38	143	11	44	18	26	12	68	93	.422
2009	Orioles	AL	162	132	.68	99	26	21	43	39	11	66	4	484	113	20	86	6	45	28	17	9	64	98	.395
	162-Game Average			125	.62	109	35	24	41	42	15	78	4	489	138	35	122	19	46	24	22	11	67	95	.414

Don Wakamatsu

Year	Team	Lg	G	LINEUPS		SUBSTITUTION			PITCHER USAGE						TACTICS				INTENTIONAL BB				RESULTS		
				LUp	PL%	PH	PR	DS	Quick	Slow	LO	RCD	LS	Rel	SBA	SacA	RM	PO	#	Good	NG	Bomb	W	L	Pct
2009	Mariners	AL	162	138	.51	58	31	19	50	27	18	76	1	410	122	61	91	4	13	3	10	6	85	77	.525
	162-Game Average			138	.51	58	31	19	50	27	18	76	1	410	122	61	91	4	13	3	10	6	85	77	.525

Ron Washington

Year	Team	Lg	G	LINEUPS		SUBSTITUTION			PITCHER USAGE						TACTICS				INTENTIONAL BB				RESULTS		
				LUp	PL%	PH	PR	DS	Quick	Slow	LO	RCD	LS	Rel	SBA	SacA	RM	PO	#	Good	NG	Bomb	W	L	Pct
2007	Rangers	AL	162	139	.60	89	30	53	47	46	4	78	9	467	113	76	67	13	38	19	19	11	75	87	.463
2008	Rangers	AL	162	129	.64	118	16	14	31	53	11	85	3	458	106	53	74	20	44	19	25	20	79	83	.488
2009	Rangers	AL	162	123	.55	48	11	11	39	47	28	80	9	436	185	44	80	5	14	9	5	3	87	75	.537
	162-Game Average			130	.60	85	19	26	39	49	14	81	7	454	135	58	74	13	32	16	16	11	80	82	.494

Eric Wedge

Year	Team	Lg	G	LINEUPS		SUBSTITUTION			PITCHER USAGE						TACTICS				INTENTIONAL BB				RESULTS		
				LUp	PL%	PH	PR	DS	Quick	Slow	LO	RCD	LS	Rel	SBA	SacA	RM	PO	#	Good	NG	Bomb	W	L	Pct
2003	Indians	AL	162	145	.67	117	43	27	47	34	18	89	5	428	147	67	54	12	37	22	15	8	68	94	.420
2004	Indians	AL	162	114	.72	91	34	20	44	38	22	121	0	479	149	57	129	28	47	26	21	18	80	82	.494
2005	Indians	AL	162	111	.66	88	18	16	45	45	15	90	3	409	98	53	79	9	20	11	9	7	93	69	.574
2006	Indians	AL	162	119	.59	98	13	13	31	52	27	48	1	377	78	40	83	15	35	21	14	11	78	84	.481
2007	Indians	AL	162	117	.60	116	41	25	34	38	20	79	2	395	113	40	108	16	42	24	18	9	96	66	.593
2008	Indians	AL	162	136	.54	112	31	18	40	35	17	78	4	399	106	56	98	5	28	6	22	11	81	81	.500
2009	Indians	AL	162	148	.59	63	28	11	32	41	21	67	3	445	115	52	74	8	31	14	17	9	65	97	.401
	162-Game Average			126	.63	98	30	19	39	40	20	82	3	419	115	52	89	13	34	18	17	10	80	82	.494

Ned Yost

Year	Team	Lg	G	LINEUPS		SUBSTITUTION			PITCHER USAGE						TACTICS				INTENTIONAL BB				RESULTS		
				LUp	PL%	PH	PR	DS	Quick	Slow	LO	RCD	LS	Rel	SBA	SacA	RM	PO	#	Good	NG	Bomb	W	L	Pct
2003	Brewers	NL	162	97	.44	304	22	39	23	59	18	90	6	460	138	85	40	23	43	28	15	9	68	94	.420
2004	Brewers	NL	161	131	.60	283	25	20	39	41	27	63	2	423	178	79	108	8	27	16	11	8	67	94	.416
2005	Brewers	NL	162	99	.46	259	18	35	26	41	42	71	2	395	113	89	97	50	52	23	29	10	81	81	.500
2006	Brewers	NL	162	106	.48	238	12	14	33	44	18	77	4	427	108	80	82	16	34	14	20	12	75	87	.463
2007	Brewers	NL	162	109	.60	259	11	41	37	42	18	117	7	492	128	74	94	19	37	28	9	9	83	79	.512
2008	Brewers	NL	150	93	.48	217	5	16	37	39	23	69	5	399	141	61	105	31	30	17	13	7	83	67	.553
	162-Game Average			107	.51	264	16	28	33	45	25	82	4	439	136	79	89	25	38	21	16	9	77	85	.475

2009 American League Managers

Manager	G	LINEUPS LUp	PL%	SUBSTITUTION PH	PR	DS	PITCHER USAGE Quick	Slow	LO	RCD	LS	Rel	TACTICS SBA	SacA	RM	PO	INTENTIONAL BB #	Good	NG	Bomb	RESULTS W	L	Pct
Terry Francona, Bos	162	113	.58	85	47	28	36	50	30	68	6	463	165	29	68	9	24	15	9	6	95	67	.586
Ron Gardenhire, Min	163	129	.63	83	54	34	43	25	12	115	3	480	117	62	100	21	20	9	11	6	87	76	.534
Cito Gaston, Tor	162	105	.49	48	36	18	36	47	25	83	3	445	96	32	64	25	26	15	11	6	75	87	.463
Bob Geren, Oak	162	129	.59	77	27	40	54	40	5	108	11	488	181	37	71	5	30	15	15	7	75	87	.463
Joe Girardi, NYY	162	106	.73	97	61	42	36	45	27	88	13	461	139	44	83	33	28	14	14	9	103	59	.636
Ozzie Guillen, CWS	162	124	.52	105	48	19	50	37	16	70	4	415	162	45	114	15	41	23	18	10	79	83	.488
Trey Hillman, KC	162	141	.63	90	34	38	41	54	34	72	7	426	117	51	110	27	28	13	15	10	65	97	.401
Jim Leyland, Det	163	126	.55	125	52	50	47	47	38	86	3	439	105	60	132	19	42	26	16	6	86	77	.528
Joe Maddon, TB	162	123	.66	140	21	18	28	51	23	139	3	510	255	29	99	15	22	10	12	7	84	78	.519
Mike Scioscia, LAA	162	123	.69	80	26	37	47	47	33	91	1	434	211	55	137	40	35	22	13	6	97	65	.599
Dave Trembley, Bal	162	132	.68	99	26	21	43	39	11	66	4	484	113	20	86	6	45	28	17	9	64	98	.395
Don Wakamatsu, Sea	162	138	.51	58	31	19	50	27	18	76	1	410	122	61	91	4	13	3	10	6	85	77	.525
Ron Washington, Tex	162	123	.55	48	11	11	39	47	28	80	9	436	185	44	80	5	14	9	5	3	87	75	.537
Eric Wedge, Cle	162	148	.59	63	28	11	32	41	21	67	3	445	115	52	74	8	31	14	17	9	65	97	.401
162-Game Average		126	.60	85	36	28	42	43	23	86	5	452	149	44	93	17	28	15	13	7	82	80	.506

2009 National League Managers

Manager	G	LINEUPS LUp	PL%	SUBSTITUTION PH	PR	DS	PITCHER USAGE Quick	Slow	LO	RCD	LS	Rel	TACTICS SBA	SacA	RM	PO	INTENTIONAL BB #	Good	NG	Bomb	RESULTS W	L	Pct
Dusty Baker, Cin	162	130	.45	252	15	35	30	62	35	115	1	478	136	120	118	23	36	29	7	4	78	84	.481
Bud Black, SD	162	137	.64	264	8	34	50	37	8	118	5	527	111	99	84	55	58	42	16	6	75	87	.463
Bruce Bochy, SF	162	134	.65	231	21	52	42	40	32	84	8	457	106	93	118	5	49	32	17	10	88	74	.543
Bobby Cox, Atl	162	112	.62	252	37	32	48	34	19	142	1	488	84	125	47	21	59	35	24	14	86	76	.531
Fredi Gonzalez, Fla	162	97	.58	281	28	49	48	26	12	116	0	530	110	86	88	20	60	38	22	15	87	75	.537
Tony LaRussa, StL	162	131	.52	289	12	51	55	38	17	102	8	481	106	93	91	17	23	15	8	1	91	71	.562
Ken Macha, Mil	162	111	.48	267	7	32	35	51	19	120	1	512	105	70	90	12	60	35	25	17	80	82	.494
Charlie Manuel, Phi	162	68	.67	283	20	16	32	55	32	107	3	459	147	74	65	3	31	19	12	3	93	69	.574
Jerry Manuel, NYM	162	117	.72	289	11	37	34	51	22	137	2	511	166	112	104	3	60	38	22	14	70	92	.432
Lou Piniella, ChC	161	131	.57	277	14	55	47	40	20	127	3	480	90	81	92	23	46	21	25	13	83	78	.516
John Russell, Pit	161	121	.60	251	3	5	44	45	12	89	0	456	122	78	97	15	37	20	17	10	62	99	.385
Joe Torre, LAD	162	113	.59	263	22	22	62	23	18	125	8	526	164	107	163	17	68	45	23	12	95	67	.586
162-Game Average		122	.59	269	20	38	42	43	18	120	4	501	127	92	95	15	47	28	19	10	77	85	.475

Manager	G	LINEUPS LUp	PL%	SUBSTITUTION PH	PR	DS	PITCHER USAGE Quick	Slow	LO	RCD	LS	Rel	TACTICS SBA	SacA	RM	PO	INTENTIONAL BB #	Good	NG	Bomb	RESULTS W	L	Pct
Manny Acta, Was	87	66	.62	145	11	20	14	25	1	91	1	282	54	43	62	5	26	13	13	6	26	61	.299
Dave Clark, Hou	13	9	.63	28	1	4	3	5	0	15	0	48	7	5	8	0	3	1	2	1	4	9	.308
Cecil Cooper, Hou	149	94	.54	238	26	36	48	34	14	116	6	449	150	86	77	8	53	30	23	12	70	79	.470
A.J. Hinch, Ari	133	115	.63	222	10	13	24	50	24	61	5	392	113	64	41	5	24	12	12	6	58	75	.436
Clint Hurdle, Col	46	42	.60	73	8	10	11	14	3	31	0	135	45	26	34	3	11	8	3	1	18	28	.391
Bob Melvin, Ari	29	29	.62	47	6	8	7	4	3	17	0	91	29	17	13	3	3	1	2	2	12	17	.414
Jim Riggleman, Was	75	60	.51	115	15	33	24	16	4	63	6	250	59	44	36	8	33	17	16	8	33	42	.440
Jim Tracy, Col	116	87	.63	186	25	28	28	27	27	83	3	349	116	73	82	9	40	28	12	7	74	42	.638

Categories of this record are Games Managed (G), Number of Different Lineups Used (LUp), the percentage of players who had the platoon advantage at the start of the game (PL%), Pinch Hitters Used (PH), Pinch Runners Used (PR), Defensive Substitutes Used (DS), Quick Hooks (Quick), Slow Hooks (Slow), Long Outings by Starting Pitchers (LO), Relievers Used on Consecutive Days (RCD), Long Saves (LS), Relievers Used (Rel), Stolen Base Attempts (SBA), Sacrifice Bunts Attempts (SacA), Runners Moving with the Pitch (RM), Pitchouts ordered (PO), Intentional Walks issued (#), Intentional Walks resulting in a Good Outcome (Good), Intentional Walks resulting Not in a Good Outcome (NG), Intentional Walks Blowing up on the Manager (Bomb), Wins (W), Losses (L) and Winning Percentage (Pct.).

2009 Park Indices

Major League Baseball opened two new ballparks in 2009, both in New York: Citi Field and the new Yankee Stadium. Early on, as home runs flew out of there at a record-breaking pace, Yankee Stadium played like The Launching Pad That Steinbrenner Built. There was some talk of wind studies. Others blamed the unusually warm spring. Still others blamed, well, Yankee pitching.

Meanwhile, over the bridge in Queens, Citi Field played like a pitchers' park just like its predecessor (Shea Stadium) had. Some blamed the ballpark's large dimensions for sapping the power of a few Mets superstars. But were they justified in blaming the architects for David Wright's meager home run total? And is Yankee Stadium really the new Coors Field, or was it all just early-season hoopla over a statistical quirk? In short, exactly what effects did these new parks have on performance? We tracked and measured it all with park indices.

Park indices are calculated in a way that neutralizes the effect of a team's makeup and isolates the effects of the park. The isolation is figured by comparing what both the team and its opponents accomplished at home, and comparing that to what the same team and its opponents accomplished on the road.

To calculate the park index for home runs in a given ballpark, we take the total home runs of both the home team and its opponents at the ballpark and compare it to the total home runs of the home team and its opponents in other games. We then divide each of those totals by the at-bats in the equivalent situations, so that if there are more at-bats in either situation the index is not skewed. The result is then multiplied by 100 to yield the familiar form.

The park indices for doubles, triples, walks, strikeouts and home runs by lefties and righties are determined like home runs above—relative to at-bats. Indices of at-bats, runs, hits, errors and infield fielding errors (E-Infield) are calculated relative to games. The three batting average indices are calculated as is, since these are already relative to at-bats.

A park with an index of exactly 100 is neutral and can be said to have had no effect on that particular stat. An index above 100 means the ballpark favors that statistic. For example, if a park has a home run index of 120, it was 20% easier to hit home runs in that park then the rest of the parks in that team's league.

Each year there are twists and turns in the data. 2009 is no different. The historical data for both the new Yankee Stadium and Citi Field show only one-year data instead of three—three years of the old Yankee Stadium and Shea Stadium, respectively, are shown for comparison.

Arizona Diamondbacks - Chase Field

| | 2009 Season | | | | | | | 2007-2009 | | | | | | |
| | Home Games | | | Away Games | | | | Home Games | | | Away Games | | | |
	D'Backs	Opp	Total	D'Backs	Opp	Total	Index	D'Backs	Opp	Total	D'Backs	Opp	Total	Index
G	81	81	162	81	81	162		243	243	486	243	243	486	
Avg	.270	.266	.268	.237	.260	.248	108	.266	.262	.264	.237	.259	.248	107
AB	2733	2877	5610	2832	2714	5546	101	8010	8518	16528	8362	8067	16429	101
R	386	431	817	334	351	685	119	1164	1171	2335	988	1049	2037	115
H	737	765	1502	671	705	1376	109	2131	2231	4362	1982	2088	4070	107
2B	177	158	335	130	127	257	129	500	464	964	411	390	801	120
3B	29	24	53	16	18	34	154	94	57	151	38	49	87	173
HR	87	87	174	86	81	167	103	255	256	511	248	228	476	107
BB	291	258	549	280	267	547	99	859	753	1612	831	769	1600	100
SO	597	601	1198	701	557	1258	94	1685	1772	3457	2011	1703	3714	93
E	62	46	108	62	57	119	91	170	130	300	173	148	321	93
E-Infield	27	15	42	15	21	36	117	75	44	119	60	55	115	103
LHB-Avg	.287	.264	.275	.245	.266	.255	108	.277	.262	.269	.250	.269	.260	103
LHB-HR	31	42	73	28	34	62	123	86	111	197	79	94	173	115
RHB-Avg	.255	.267	.262	.229	.255	.242	108	.259	.262	.260	.229	.251	.239	109
RHB-HR	56	45	101	58	47	105	91	169	145	314	169	134	303	102

Atlanta Braves - Turner Field

| | 2009 Season | | | | | | | 2007-2009 | | | | | | |
| | Home Games | | | Away Games | | | | Home Games | | | Away Games | | | |
	Braves	Opp	Total	Braves	Opp	Total	Index	Braves	Opp	Total	Braves	Opp	Total	Index
G	81	81	162	81	81	162		243	243	486	243	243	486	
Avg	.257	.245	.251	.269	.264	.266	94	.267	.254	.261	.272	.264	.268	97
AB	2700	2811	5511	2839	2696	5535	100	8207	8459	16666	8625	8085	16710	100
R	332	318	650	403	323	726	90	1093	1082	2175	1205	1070	2275	96
H	695	688	1383	764	711	1475	94	2193	2149	4342	2342	2131	4473	97
2B	137	136	273	163	159	322	85	419	439	858	525	453	978	88
3B	10	26	36	10	23	33	110	42	66	108	38	64	102	106
HR	69	55	124	80	64	144	86	213	225	438	242	222	464	95
BB	305	279	584	297	251	548	107	910	870	1780	844	783	1627	110
SO	529	657	1186	535	575	1110	107	1588	1800	3388	1648	1614	3262	104
E	53	45	98	43	47	90	109	172	143	315	138	142	280	113
E-Infield	33	24	57	17	21	38	150	84	66	150	59	64	123	122
LHB-Avg	.241	.253	.247	.271	.269	.271	91	.264	.257	.261	.273	.266	.270	97
LHB-HR	41	28	69	44	31	75	95	115	95	210	136	90	226	94
RHB-Avg	.275	.238	.255	.266	.259	.262	97	.270	.251	.260	.270	.262	.266	98
RHB-HR	28	27	55	36	33	69	78	98	130	228	106	132	238	96

Baltimore Orioles - Oriole Park at Camden Yards

| | 2009 Season | | | | | | | 2007-2009 | | | | | | |
| | Home Games | | | Away Games | | | | Home Games | | | Away Games | | | |
	Orioles	Opp	Total	Orioles	Opp	Total	Index	Orioles	Opp	Total	Orioles	Opp	Total	Index
G	81	81	162	81	81	162		242	242	484	243	243	486	
Avg	.288	.289	.288	.249	.286	.267	108	.281	.281	.281	.258	.275	.266	106
AB	2786	2948	5734	2832	2728	5560	103	8299	8683	16982	8509	8103	16612	103
R	411	412	823	330	464	794	104	1195	1323	2518	1084	1290	2374	107
H	802	852	1654	706	781	1487	111	2331	2437	4768	2192	2225	4417	108
2B	155	173	328	152	183	335	95	445	469	914	490	449	939	95
3B	12	12	24	7	16	23	101	38	32	70	41	36	77	89
HR	96	109	205	64	109	173	115	275	301	576	199	262	461	122
BB	258	253	511	259	293	552	90	763	934	1697	787	995	1782	93
SO	475	481	956	538	452	990	94	1371	1488	2859	1571	1454	3025	92
E	45	31	76	45	55	100	76	127	117	244	142	160	302	81
E-Infield	21	12	33	15	25	40	83	51	45	96	54	76	130	74
LHB-Avg	.289	.290	.290	.253	.289	.269	108	.286	.281	.284	.266	.281	.272	104
LHB-HR	53	55	108	41	48	89	112	136	134	270	111	111	222	115
RHB-Avg	.286	.288	.287	.245	.284	.266	108	.275	.281	.278	.250	.270	.260	107
RHB-HR	43	54	97	23	61	84	118	139	167	306	88	151	239	129

Boston Red Sox - Fenway Park

	2009 Season							2007-2009						
	Home Games			Away Games				Home Games			Away Games			
	Red Sox	Opp	Total	Red Sox	Opp	Total	Index	Red Sox	Opp	Total	Red Sox	Opp	Total	Index
G	81	81	162	81	81	162		243	243	486	243	243	486	
Avg	.284	.262	.273	.257	.272	.264	103	.291	.259	.275	.262	.250	.256	107
AB	2656	2804	5460	2887	2790	5677	96	8140	8413	16553	8588	8126	16714	99
R	481	351	832	391	385	776	107	1414	1040	2454	1170	1047	2217	111
H	764	736	1490	741	758	1499	99	2369	2178	4547	2252	2035	4287	106
2B	198	176	374	137	136	273	142	600	540	1140	440	356	796	145
3B	14	13	27	11	14	25	112	47	33	80	46	33	79	102
HR	114	72	186	98	95	193	100	272	209	481	279	256	535	91
BB	317	241	558	342	289	631	92	1010	743	1753	984	817	1801	98
SO	539	597	1136	581	633	1214	97	1521	1761	3282	1709	1803	3512	94
E	41	54	95	41	55	96	99	121	148	269	127	150	277	97
E-Infield	16	21	37	17	27	44	84	47	63	110	56	57	113	97
LHB-Avg	.271	.267	.268	.251	.278	.265	101	.282	.260	.271	.252	.250	.251	108
LHB-HR	42	30	72	38	41	79	93	104	93	197	115	115	230	85
RHB-Avg	.295	.259	.277	.261	.266	.263	105	.298	.258	.278	.270	.251	.261	107
RHB-HR	72	42	114	60	54	114	105	168	116	284	164	141	305	95

Chicago Cubs - Wrigley Field

	2009 Season							2007-2009						
	Home Games			Away Games				Home Games			Away Games			
	Cubs	Opp	Total	Cubs	Opp	Total	Index	Cubs	Opp	Total	Cubs	Opp	Total	Index
G	80	80	160	81	81	162		242	242	484	242	242	484	
Avg	.265	.245	.255	.245	.247	.246	103	.278	.246	.262	.259	.243	.251	104
AB	2654	2728	5382	2832	2674	5506	99	8161	8399	16560	8556	7950	16506	100
R	388	344	732	319	328	647	115	1230	1060	2290	1064	980	2044	113
H	703	668	1371	695	661	1356	102	2266	2066	4332	2214	1932	4146	104
2B	147	121	268	146	112	258	106	474	436	910	488	360	848	107
3B	13	17	30	16	17	33	93	35	46	81	43	56	99	82
HR	82	78	160	79	82	161	102	272	243	515	224	242	466	110
BB	303	294	597	289	292	581	105	889	850	1739	839	857	1696	102
SO	534	644	1178	651	628	1279	94	1813	1786	3599	1786	1787	3573	100
E	56	44	100	49	52	101	100	156	157	313	142	155	297	105
E-Infield	25	21	46	18	21	39	119	73	68	141	55	66	121	117
LHB-Avg	.237	.254	.245	.233	.254	.243	101	.247	.253	.250	.243	.248	.245	102
LHB-HR	25	35	60	24	23	47	139	66	99	165	61	75	136	126
RHB-Avg	.283	.239	.261	.255	.243	.249	105	.293	.242	.268	.267	.240	.255	105
RHB-HR	57	43	100	55	59	114	86	206	144	350	163	167	330	103

Chicago White Sox - U.S. Cellular Field

	2009 Season							2007-2009						
	Home Games			Away Games				Home Games			Away Games			
	White Sox	Opp	Total	White Sox	Opp	Total	Index	White Sox	Opp	Total	White Sox	Opp	Total	Index
G	81	81	162	81	81	162		244	244	488	243	243	486	
Avg	.252	.258	.255	.264	.264	.264	97	.257	.261	.259	.255	.272	.263	98
AB	2647	2819	5466	2816	2694	5510	99	8070	8614	16684	8387	8171	16558	100
R	367	383	750	357	349	706	106	1190	1176	2366	1038	1124	2162	109
H	666	727	1393	744	711	1455	96	2074	2246	4320	2135	2219	4354	99
2B	108	149	257	138	142	280	93	366	454	820	425	448	873	93
3B	8	11	19	12	12	24	80	18	35	53	35	55	90	58
HR	103	89	192	81	80	161	120	356	262	618	253	237	490	125
BB	273	280	553	261	227	488	114	826	758	1584	780	708	1488	106
SO	486	613	1099	536	506	1042	106	1509	1781	3290	1678	1500	3178	103
E	61	48	109	52	34	86	127	173	147	320	156	115	271	118
E-Infield	27	19	46	25	9	34	135	77	55	132	60	45	105	125
LHB-Avg	.274	.252	.262	.280	.264	.272	96	.261	.263	.262	.265	.272	.269	98
LHB-HR	31	39	70	20	35	55	122	117	110	227	79	101	180	122
RHB-Avg	.238	.262	.250	.255	.264	.259	96	.254	.259	.257	.249	.271	.259	99
RHB-HR	72	50	122	61	45	106	120	239	152	391	174	136	310	127

Cincinnati Reds - Great American Ballpark

	2009 Season							2007-2009						
	Home Games			Away Games				Home Games			Away Games			
	Reds	Opp	Total	Reds	Opp	Total	Index	Reds	Opp	Total	Reds	Opp	Total	Index
G	81	81	162	81	81	162		243	243	486	243	243	486	
Avg	.252	.254	.253	.242	.262	.252	100	.257	.266	.262	.251	.278	.264	99
AB	2670	2790	5460	2792	2718	5510	99	8105	8576	16681	8429	8227	16656	100
R	329	360	689	344	363	707	97	1122	1199	2321	1038	1177	2215	105
H	672	709	1381	677	711	1388	99	2080	2283	4363	2116	2284	4400	99
2B	133	146	279	147	127	274	103	420	484	904	422	456	878	103
3B	15	10	25	10	13	23	110	39	35	74	33	43	76	97
HR	94	93	187	64	95	159	119	314	318	632	235	269	504	125
BB	281	283	564	250	294	544	105	856	788	1644	771	828	1599	103
SO	561	578	1139	568	491	1059	109	1658	1769	3427	1709	1595	3304	104
E	38	45	83	51	51	102	81	140	139	279	158	144	302	92
E-Infield	17	17	34	23	21	44	77	50	60	110	61	65	126	87
LHB-Avg	.263	.263	.263	.276	.248	.259	102	.268	.267	.267	.260	.266	.263	102
LHB-HR	34	46	80	32	34	66	119	152	136	288	137	101	238	121
RHB-Avg	.247	.246	.247	.230	.273	.248	100	.250	.265	.258	.246	.287	.265	97
RHB-HR	60	47	107	32	61	93	118	162	182	344	98	168	266	129

Cleveland Indians - Progressive Field

	2009 Season							2007-2009						
	Home Games			Away Games				Home Games			Away Games			
	Indians	Opp	Total	Indians	Opp	Total	Index	Indians	Opp	Total	Indians	Opp	Total	Index
G	81	81	162	81	81	162		239	239	478	247	247	494	
Avg	.255	.277	.266	.272	.283	.277	96	.268	.273	.270	.262	.275	.268	101
AB	2711	2880	5591	2857	2732	5589	100	8018	8481	16499	8697	8393	17090	100
R	358	389	747	415	476	891	84	1197	1098	2295	1192	1232	2424	98
H	691	797	1488	777	773	1550	96	2146	2315	4461	2281	2304	4585	101
2B	148	166	314	166	145	311	101	445	463	908	513	444	957	98
3B	7	12	19	21	15	36	53	26	28	54	51	42	93	60
HR	66	72	138	95	111	206	67	250	205	455	260	294	554	85
BB	284	291	575	298	307	605	95	880	723	1603	852	729	1581	105
SO	580	522	1102	631	464	1095	101	1692	1618	3310	1934	1401	3335	103
E	43	53	96	54	49	103	93	136	157	293	147	142	289	105
E-Infield	21	23	44	25	16	41	107	73	64	137	68	51	119	119
LHB-Avg	.270	.267	.268	.286	.308	.296	91	.271	.272	.271	.265	.286	.275	99
LHB-HR	35	33	68	45	48	93	71	107	82	189	118	121	239	83
RHB-Avg	.241	.284	.264	.260	.266	.263	101	.265	.274	.270	.260	.267	.263	102
RHB-HR	31	39	70	50	63	113	64	143	123	266	142	173	315	87

Colorado Rockies - Coors Field

	2009 Season							2007-2009						
	Home Games			Away Games				Home Games			Away Games			
	Rockies	Opp	Total	Rockies	Opp	Total	Index	Rockies	Opp	Total	Rockies	Opp	Total	Index
G	81	81	162	81	81	162		244	244	488	243	243	486	
Avg	.287	.266	.276	.235	.256	.245	112	.288	.273	.280	.249	.262	.255	110
AB	2675	2836	5511	2723	2631	5354	103	8253	8658	16911	8393	8043	16436	102
R	464	379	843	340	336	676	125	1353	1195	2548	1058	1100	2158	118
H	767	754	1521	641	673	1314	116	2373	2364	4737	2088	2107	4195	112
2B	166	153	319	134	118	252	123	497	494	991	426	410	836	115
3B	32	30	62	18	17	35	172	75	79	154	39	59	98	153
HR	98	74	172	92	67	159	105	293	238	531	228	215	443	116
BB	338	276	614	322	252	574	104	946	760	1706	906	834	1740	95
SO	542	592	1134	735	562	1297	85	1616	1587	3203	2022	1575	3597	87
E	48	61	109	39	42	81	135	134	177	311	117	154	271	114
E-Infield	22	23	45	15	19	34	132	46	65	111	48	61	109	101
LHB-Avg	.289	.273	.282	.252	.260	.256	110	.279	.271	.275	.256	.267	.261	105
LHB-HR	48	27	75	47	27	74	102	110	92	202	91	93	184	109
RHB-Avg	.284	.260	.271	.219	.252	.236	115	.292	.274	.283	.244	.258	.251	113
RHB-HR	50	47	97	45	40	85	107	183	146	329	137	122	259	122

Detroit Tigers - Comerica Park

	2009 Season							2007-2009						
	Home Games			Away Games				Home Games			Away Games			
	Tigers	Opp	Total	Tigers	Opp	Total	Index	Tigers	Opp	Total	Tigers	Opp	Total	Index
G	81	81	162	82	82	164		243	243	486	244	244	488	
Avg	.270	.249	.259	.252	.277	.264	98	.282	.264	.273	.265	.272	.268	102
AB	2683	2749	5432	2857	2765	5622	98	8268	8505	16773	8670	8250	16920	100
R	401	348	749	342	397	739	103	1284	1198	2482	1167	1201	2368	105
H	724	684	1408	719	765	1484	96	2328	2248	4576	2296	2240	4536	101
2B	120	130	250	125	141	266	97	432	442	874	458	451	909	97
3B	19	15	34	16	16	32	110	74	58	132	52	52	104	128
HR	92	87	179	91	95	186	100	303	265	568	257	263	520	110
BB	282	289	571	258	305	563	105	795	878	1673	791	926	1717	98
SO	522	563	1085	592	539	1131	99	1495	1616	3111	1749	1524	3273	96
E	38	57	95	50	36	86	112	150	149	299	150	119	269	112
E-Infield	10	30	40	18	15	33	123	59	57	116	62	51	113	103
LHB-Avg	.246	.247	.246	.242	.287	.270	91	.271	.259	.264	.268	.277	.273	97
LHB-HR	29	35	64	35	44	79	85	78	104	182	77	116	193	96
RHB-Avg	.282	.251	.268	.256	.265	.260	103	.286	.268	.278	.264	.267	.265	105
RHB-HR	63	52	115	56	51	107	110	225	161	386	180	147	327	118

Florida Marlins - Land Shark Stadium

	2009 Season							2007-2009						
	Home Games			Away Games				Home Games			Away Games			
	Marlins	Opp	Total	Marlins	Opp	Total	Index	Marlins	Opp	Total	Marlins	Opp	Total	Index
G	81	81	162	81	81	162		243	243	486	242	242	484	
Avg	.273	.261	.267	.263	.253	.258	104	.264	.266	.265	.262	.268	.265	100
AB	2701	2807	5508	2811	2637	5448	104	8222	8657	16879	8476	8054	16530	102
R	393	425	818	379	341	720	114	1171	1270	2441	1161	1154	2315	105
H	755	757	1512	738	668	1406	108	2171	2306	4477	2223	2157	4380	102
2B	141	152	293	155	109	264	107	447	477	924	491	377	868	104
3B	14	14	28	11	33	44	61	57	42	99	34	58	92	105
HR	86	83	169	73	77	150	108	290	238	528	278	259	537	96
BB	298	325	623	270	276	546	110	840	990	1830	792	858	1650	109
SO	608	680	1288	618	568	1186	105	1988	1962	3950	1941	1555	3496	111
E	67	49	116	39	52	91	127	195	152	347	165	143	308	112
E-Infield	23	14	37	15	23	38	97	71	45	116	64	54	118	98
LHB-Avg	.272	.264	.268	.261	.250	.255	105	.251	.266	.259	.263	.259	.261	99
LHB-HR	18	43	61	25	29	54	106	69	105	174	84	90	174	94
RHB-Avg	.274	.259	.267	.264	.256	.260	103	.272	.267	.269	.262	.274	.267	101
RHB-HR	68	40	108	48	48	96	111	221	133	354	194	169	363	98

Houston Astros - Minute Maid Park

	2009 Season							2007-2009						
	Home Games			Away Games				Home Games			Away Games			
	Astros	Opp	Total	Astros	Opp	Total	Index	Astros	Opp	Total	Astros	Opp	Total	Index
G	81	81	162	81	81	162		240	240	480	245	245	490	
Avg	.269	.273	.271	.252	.278	.265	102	.271	.265	.268	.252	.277	.264	101
AB	2666	2850	5516	2770	2672	5442	101	8020	8520	16540	8472	8228	16700	101
R	334	347	681	309	423	732	93	1061	1072	2133	1017	1254	2271	96
H	717	777	1494	698	744	1442	104	2171	2259	4430	2133	2281	4414	102
2B	126	142	268	144	163	307	86	412	471	883	435	488	923	97
3B	19	16	35	13	22	35	99	54	44	98	30	64	94	105
HR	78	86	164	64	90	154	105	253	292	545	223	287	510	108
BB	241	240	489	207	298	505	96	728	747	1475	716	801	1517	98
SO	480	612	1092	510	532	1042	103	1449	1834	3283	1635	1514	3149	105
E	35	42	77	43	37	80	96	114	115	229	134	136	270	87
E-Infield	17	20	37	20	19	39	95	61	50	120	59	64	123	100
LHB-Avg	.263	.272	.268	.245	.280	.263	102	.263	.273	.269	.258	.273	.267	101
LHB-HR	20	31	51	19	35	54	92	73	112	185	80	107	187	100
RHB-Avg	.272	.273	.273	.256	.277	.266	103	.274	.260	.267	.249	.280	.263	102
RHB-HR	58	55	113	45	55	100	112	180	180	360	143	180	323	113

Kansas City Royals - Kauffman Stadium

| | 2009 Season | | | | | | | 2007-2009 | | | | | | |
| | Home Games | | | Away Games | | | | Home Games | | | Away Games | | | |
	Royals	Opp	Total	Royals	Opp	Total	Index	Royals	Opp	Total	Royals	Opp	Total	Index
G	81	81	162	81	81	162		243	243	486	243	243	486	
Avg	.276	.280	.278	.242	.256	.249	112	.273	.274	.273	.254	.265	.259	105
AB	2738	2881	5619	2794	2653	5447	103	8168	8589	16757	8506	8109	16615	101
R	367	438	805	319	404	723	111	1060	1208	2268	1023	1193	2216	102
H	756	808	1564	676	678	1354	116	2227	2356	4583	2159	2150	4309	106
2B	142	157	299	134	116	250	116	463	523	986	416	412	828	118
3B	30	23	53	21	15	36	143	70	55	125	55	54	109	114
HR	65	69	134	79	97	176	74	164	221	385	202	272	474	81
BB	258	288	546	199	312	511	104	666	806	1472	611	829	1440	101
SO	472	585	1057	619	568	1187	86	1422	1600	3022	1743	1631	3374	89
E	60	41	101	56	43	99	102	152	134	286	166	152	318	90
E-Infield	28	20	48	20	17	37	130	66	56	122	60	55	115	106
LHB-Avg	.275	.286	.280	.238	.242	.240	117	.276	.275	.276	.253	.259	.256	108
LHB-HR	29	17	46	40	45	85	53	70	87	157	88	127	215	73
RHB-Avg	.278	.276	.277	.246	.268	.257	108	.270	.273	.272	.254	.270	.262	104
RHB-HR	36	52	88	39	52	91	92	94	134	228	114	145	259	87

Los Angeles Angels - Angel Stadium of Anaheim

| | 2009 Season | | | | | | | 2007-2009 | | | | | | |
| | Home Games | | | Away Games | | | | Home Games | | | Away Games | | | |
	Angels	Opp	Total	Angels	Opp	Total	Index	Angels	Opp	Total	Angels	Opp	Total	Index
G	81	81	162	81	81	162		243	243	486	243	243	486	
Avg	.288	.273	.281	.283	.271	.277	101	.290	.264	.277	.269	.269	.269	103
AB	2716	2844	5560	2906	2718	5624	99	8194	8536	16730	8522	8160	16682	100
R	444	386	830	439	375	814	102	1287	1088	2375	1183	1101	2284	104
H	783	777	1560	821	736	1557	100	2378	2256	4634	2290	2192	4482	103
2B	141	143	284	152	155	307	94	454	443	897	437	416	853	105
3B	14	8	22	19	17	36	62	37	33	70	44	54	98	71
HR	90	104	194	83	76	159	123	223	254	477	232	237	469	101
BB	271	257	528	276	266	542	99	758	699	1457	777	758	1535	95
SO	473	548	1021	581	514	1095	94	1357	1669	3026	1567	1655	3222	94
E	44	59	103	41	59	100	103	140	178	318	137	177	314	101
E-Infield	18	20	38	18	25	43	88	54	70	124	54	72	126	98
LHB-Avg	.311	.278	.293	.283	.303	.293	100	.308	.263	.284	.267	.279	.273	104
LHB-HR	35	44	79	25	45	70	116	86	103	189	80	126	206	94
RHB-Avg	.272	.269	.271	.282	.241	.263	103	.277	.265	.271	.270	.260	.265	102
RHB-HR	55	60	115	58	31	89	129	137	151	288	152	111	263	107

Los Angeles Dodgers - Dodger Stadium

| | 2009 Season | | | | | | | 2007-2009 | | | | | | |
| | Home Games | | | Away Games | | | | Home Games | | | Away Games | | | |
	Dodgers	Opp	Total	Dodgers	Opp	Total	Index	Dodgers	Opp	Total	Dodgers	Opp	Total	Index
G	81	81	162	81	81	162		243	243	486	243	243	486	
Avg	.265	.229	.247	.275	.237	.257	96	.270	.240	.255	.270	.257	.264	97
AB	2712	2785	5497	2880	2643	5523	100	8142	8380	16522	8569	8068	16637	99
R	365	277	642	415	334	749	86	1092	916	2008	1123	1070	2193	92
H	720	639	1359	791	626	1417	96	2195	2014	4209	2315	2075	4390	96
2B	137	128	265	141	127	268	99	380	395	775	445	398	843	93
3B	18	8	26	21	22	43	61	40	24	64	63	56	119	54
HR	70	57	127	75	70	145	88	210	178	388	201	218	419	93
BB	261	261	522	346	323	669	78	806	729	1535	855	853	1708	90
SO	511	660	1171	557	612	1169	101	1449	1971	3420	1515	1690	3205	107
E	39	57	96	44	55	99	97	136	170	306	162	150	312	98
E-Infield	13	24	37	20	23	43	86	50	63	113	69	68	137	82
LHB-Avg	.272	.234	.255	.265	.223	.247	103	.276	.241	.259	.275	.257	.267	97
LHB-HR	30	25	55	28	20	48	112	81	80	161	83	63	146	111
RHB-Avg	.259	.226	.241	.283	.246	.264	91	.264	.240	.251	.266	.257	.262	96
RHB-HR	40	32	72	47	50	97	76	129	98	227	118	155	273	84

Milwaukee Brewers - Miller Park

| | 2009 Season | | | | | | | 2007-2009 | | | | | | |
| | Home Games | | | Away Games | | | | Home Games | | | Away Games | | |
	Brewers	Opp	Total	Brewers	Opp	Total	Index	Brewers	Opp	Total	Brewers	Opp	Total	Index
G	81	81	162	81	81	162		243	243	486	243	243	486	
Avg	.257	.258	.258	.268	.279	.273	94	.259	.254	.256	.259	.275	.267	96
AB	2677	2840	5517	2833	2744	5577	99	8056	8498	16554	8543	8236	16779	99
R	366	387	753	419	431	850	89	1168	1077	2245	1168	1206	2374	95
H	688	733	1421	759	765	1524	93	2084	2158	4242	2216	2268	4484	95
2B	130	178	317	142	154	296	108	460	450	910	455	464	919	100
3B	22	14	36	15	18	33	110	55	35	90	54	45	99	92
HR	100	101	201	82	106	188	108	321	263	584	290	280	570	104
BB	310	297	607	300	310	610	101	860	848	1708	801	794	1595	109
SO	607	621	1228	624	483	1107	112	1762	1836	3598	1809	1552	3361	109
E	43	39	82	55	41	96	85	154	141	295	154	150	304	97
E-Infield	20	12	32	24	23	47	68	64	54	118	67	69	136	87
LHB-Avg	.264	.268	.266	.279	.275	.276	96	.265	.259	.261	.256	.270	.264	99
LHB-HR	34	50	84	28	36	64	124	110	124	234	92	110	202	116
RHB-Avg	.253	.250	.252	.263	.262	.271	99	.266	.250	.253	.261	.279	.269	94
RHB-HR	66	51	117	54	70	124	99	211	139	350	198	170	368	91

Minnesota Twins - Hubert H. Humphrey Metrodome Surface: FieldTurf

| | 2009 Season | | | | | | | 2007-2009 | | | | | | |
| | Home Games | | | Away Games | | | | Home Games | | | Away Games | | |
	Twins	Opp	Total	Twins	Opp	Total	Index	Twins	Opp	Total	Twins	Opp	Total	Index
G	82	82	164	81	81	162		244	244	488	244	244	488	
Avg	.278	.273	.275	.271	.272	.271	101	.277	.261	.269	.269	.283	.276	97
AB	2766	2800	5566	2842	2697	5539	102	8194	8678	16872	8577	8288	16865	100
R	432	398	830	385	367	752	109	1190	1045	2235	1171	1190	2364	95
H	769	809	1578	770	733	1503	104	2267	2266	4533	2304	2349	4653	97
2B	135	148	283	136	142	278	98	417	435	852	425	447	872	98
3B	23	14	37	17	13	30	119	70	37	107	55	44	99	108
HR	96	93	189	76	92	168	109	200	257	457	201	296	497	92
BB	295	217	512	290	249	539	92	796	610	1406	830	682	1512	93
SO	493	560	1053	528	492	1020	100	1334	1671	3005	1505	1470	2975	101
E	29	43	72	47	55	102	70	122	148	270	157	179	336	80
E-Infield	13	16	29	16	19	35	82	44	53	97	57	69	126	77
LHB-Avg	.299	.260	.281	.280	.277	.278	101	.284	.264	.274	.282	.293	.287	96
LHB-HR	52	36	88	44	32	76	116	112	103	215	113	123	236	93
RHB-Avg	.255	.282	.270	.261	.268	.265	102	.269	.250	.261	.254	.278	.266	99
RHB-HR	44	57	101	32	60	92	103	88	154	242	88	173	261	91

New York Mets - Citi Field

| | 2009 Season | | | | | | | 2006-2008 | | | | | | |
| | Home Games | | | Away Games | | | | Home Games | | | Away Games | | |
	Mets	Opp	Total	Mets	Opp	Total	Index	Mets	Opp	Total	Mets	Opp	Total	Index
G	81	81	162	81	81	162		243	243	486	243	243	486	
Avg	.274	.248	.261	.266	.281	.273	95	.265	.242	.253	.272	.266	.269	94
AB	2664	2808	5472	2789	2683	5472	100	8139	8461	16600	8630	8193	16823	99
R	343	350	693	328	407	735	94	1150	1071	2221	1287	1125	2412	92
H	731	697	1428	741	755	1496	95	2153	2051	4204	2350	2181	4531	93
2B	144	152	296	151	159	310	95	427	413	840	464	421	885	96
3B	32	10	42	17	18	35	120	48	30	78	58	43	101	78
HR	49	81	130	46	77	123	106	274	240	514	275	268	543	96
BB	260	294	554	266	322	588	94	881	839	1720	834	848	1682	104
SO	458	564	1022	470	467	937	109	1477	1810	3287	1599	1666	3265	102
E	41	47	88	56	55	111	79	138	157	295	150	173	323	91
E-Infield	20	18	38	25	24	49	78	58	69	127	50	70	120	106
LHB-Avg	.272	.235	.254	.270	.284	.277	92	.259	.258	.259	.271	.268	.270	96
LHB-HR	18	35	53	17	38	55	100	139	99	238	156	104	260	93
RHB-Avg	.277	.260	.268	.261	.279	.270	99	.270	.232	.249	.274	.265	.269	93
RHB-HR	31	46	77	29	39	68	110	135	141	276	119	164	283	99

New York Yankees - Yankee Stadium

	2009 Season							2006-2008						
	Home Games			Away Games				Home Games			Away Games			
	Yankees	Opp	Total	Yankees	Opp	Total	Index	Yankees	Opp	Total	Yankees	Opp	Total	Index
G	81	81	162	81	81	162		243	243	486	243	243	486	
Avg	.284	.249	.266	.283	.253	.269	99	.288	.256	.272	.276	.275	.275	99
AB	2764	2837	5601	2896	2686	5582	100	8284	8457	16741	8656	8266	16922	99
R	460	359	819	455	394	849	96	1382	1097	2479	1305	1174	2479	100
H	785	706	1491	819	680	1499	99	2388	2166	4554	2388	2273	4661	98
2B	150	118	268	175	156	331	81	449	453	902	493	456	949	96
3B	5	10	15	16	14	30	50	29	30	59	44	44	88	68
HR	136	101	237	108	80	188	126	310	234	544	281	229	510	108
BB	348	301	649	315	273	588	110	906	761	1667	915	802	1717	98
SO	483	649	1132	531	611	1142	99	1428	1660	3088	1631	1509	3140	99
E	35	53	88	51	44	95	93	138	170	308	137	140	277	111
E-Infield	10	20	30	22	22	44	68	57	78	135	61	61	122	111
LHB-Avg	.290	.238	.268	.277	.259	.270	99	.288	.247	.271	.279	.279	.279	97
LHB-HR	90	42	132	74	34	108	120	182	111	293	164	82	246	120
RHB-Avg	.275	.257	.264	.292	.249	.267	99	.289	.263	.274	.272	.272	.272	101
RHB-HR	46	59	105	34	46	80	133	128	123	251	117	147	264	97

Oakland Athletics - McAfee Coliseum

	2009 Season							2007-2009						
	Home Games			Away Games				Home Games			Away Games			
	Athletics	Opp	Total	Athletics	Opp	Total	Index	Athletics	Opp	Total	Athletics	Opp	Total	Index
G	81	81	162	81	81	162		241	241	482	244	244	488	
Avg	.259	.260	.260	.265	.270	.267	97	.248	.250	.249	.259	.271	.265	94
AB	2690	2828	5518	2894	2776	5670	97	7998	8351	16349	8614	8223	16837	98
R	402	348	750	357	413	770	97	1049	1008	2057	1097	1201	2298	91
H	698	736	1434	766	750	1516	95	1980	2088	4068	2232	2230	4462	92
2B	147	143	290	160	162	322	93	412	396	808	460	475	935	89
3B	13	13	26	8	15	23	116	35	44	79	25	60	85	96
HR	71	69	140	64	87	151	95	207	194	401	224	235	459	90
BB	279	238	517	248	285	533	100	887	797	1684	878	832	1710	101
SO	507	580	1087	539	544	1083	103	1560	1625	3185	1831	1596	3427	96
E	49	56	105	56	46	102	103	145	150	295	148	126	274	109
E-Infield	22	16	38	20	21	41	93	53	55	108	44	53	97	113
LHB-Avg	.258	.272	.265	.259	.291	.273	97	.246	.250	.248	.250	.279	.263	94
LHB-HR	39	37	76	31	44	75	106	118	90	208	115	82	197	106
RHB-Avg	.261	.253	.256	.270	.257	.263	98	.249	.250	.249	.267	.266	.267	94
RHB-HR	32	32	64	33	43	76	85	89	104	193	109	153	262	77

Philadelphia Phillies - Citizens Bank Park

	2009 Season							2007-2009						
	Home Games			Away Games				Home Games			Away Games			
	Phillies	Opp	Total	Phillies	Opp	Total	Index	Phillies	Opp	Total	Phillies	Opp	Total	Index
G	81	81	162	81	81	162		243	243	486	243	243	486	
Avg	.263	.267	.265	.253	.262	.258	103	.268	.266	.267	.257	.267	.262	102
AB	2713	2848	5561	2865	2743	5608	99	8170	8568	16738	8605	8228	16833	99
R	408	367	775	412	342	754	103	1270	1126	2396	1241	1084	2325	103
H	713	759	1472	726	720	1446	102	2191	2279	4470	2213	2199	4412	101
2B	159	152	311	153	144	297	106	444	479	923	485	468	953	97
3B	19	9	28	16	15	31	91	58	27	85	54	48	102	84
HR	108	99	207	116	90	206	101	333	304	637	318	243	561	114
BB	298	246	544	291	243	534	103	901	774	1675	915	806	1721	98
SO	563	608	1171	592	545	1137	104	1670	1725	3395	1807	1559	3366	101
E	34	53	87	42	45	87	100	120	169	289	135	149	284	102
E-Infield	19	19	38	21	18	39	97	55	73	128	66	61	127	101
LHB-Avg	.261	.255	.259	.263	.259	.261	99	.273	.274	.274	.263	.266	.264	104
LHB-HR	63	34	97	82	26	108	90	181	117	298	189	82	271	111
RHB-Avg	.265	.273	.270	.241	.265	.255	106	.263	.261	.262	.251	.268	.260	101
RHB-HR	45	65	110	34	64	98	114	152	187	339	129	161	290	117

Pittsburgh Pirates - PNC Park

| | 2009 Season | | | | | | | 2007-2009 | | | | | | |
| | Home Games | | | Away Games | | | | Home Games | | | Away Games | | | |
	Pirates	Opp	Total	Pirates	Opp	Total	Index	Pirates	Opp	Total	Pirates	Opp	Total	Index
G	81	81	162	80	80	160		243	243	486	242	242	484	
Avg	.270	.265	.267	.234	.288	.260	103	.268	.276	.272	.247	.292	.269	101
AB	2713	2801	5514	2704	2606	5310	103	8209	8609	16818	8405	8144	16549	101
R	360	354	714	276	414	690	102	1094	1149	2243	1001	1349	2350	95
H	732	741	1473	632	750	1382	105	2202	2373	4575	2079	2376	4455	102
2B	143	168	311	146	181	327	92	472	529	1001	453	518	971	101
3B	20	14	34	14	33	47	70	46	33	79	40	68	108	72
HR	75	68	143	50	84	134	103	214	223	437	212	279	491	88
BB	251	275	526	248	288	536	95	698	845	1543	738	893	1631	93
SO	503	475	978	639	444	1083	87	1523	1446	2969	1793	1433	3226	91
E	40	41	81	33	40	73	110	117	145	262	146	135	281	93
E-Infield	16	21	37	14	17	31	118	58	62	120	66	49	115	104
LHB-Avg	.280	.267	.274	.222	.285	.250	109	.276	.275	.275	.240	.289	.263	105
LHB-HR	40	26	66	29	30	59	112	103	84	187	83	88	171	107
RHB-Avg	.261	.263	.262	.244	.289	.268	98	.263	.276	.270	.252	.293	.273	99
RHB-HR	35	42	77	21	54	75	96	111	139	250	129	191	320	77

San Diego Padres - PETCO Park

| | 2009 Season | | | | | | | 2007-2009 | | | | | | |
| | Home Games | | | Away Games | | | | Home Games | | | Away Games | | | |
	Padres	Opp	Total	Padres	Opp	Total	Index	Padres	Opp	Total	Padres	Opp	Total	Index
G	81	81	162	81	81	162		243	243	486	244	244	488	
Avg	.219	.233	.226	.264	.283	.273	83	.231	.230	.235	.263	.276	.269	87
AB	2594	2802	5396	2831	2718	5549	97	7967	8478	16445	8638	8249	16887	98
R	278	321	599	360	448	808	74	890	931	1821	1126	1268	2394	76
H	567	654	1221	748	768	1516	81	1841	2019	3860	2272	2275	4547	85
2B	106	108	214	159	142	301	73	349	339	688	502	442	944	75
3B	16	12	28	15	21	36	80	50	40	90	39	60	99	93
HR	61	68	129	80	99	179	74	199	183	382	267	268	535	73
BB	331	303	634	255	300	555	117	882	785	1667	779	853	1632	105
SO	597	647	1244	585	540	1125	114	1854	1835	3689	1816	1588	3404	111
E	44	43	87	50	47	97	90	130	104	234	141	131	272	86
E-Infield	17	17	34	20	19	39	87	47	40	87	53	60	113	77
LHB-Avg	.220	.247	.234	.271	.296	.283	83	.238	.249	.244	.272	.281	.276	88
LHB-HR	25	31	56	47	46	93	60	83	76	159	146	118	264	61
RHB-Avg	.217	.221	.219	.259	.271	.265	83	.225	.229	.227	.255	.272	.264	86
RHB-HR	36	37	73	33	53	86	90	116	107	223	121	150	271	86

San Francisco Giants - AT&T Park

| | 2009 Season | | | | | | | 2007-2009 | | | | | | |
| | Home Games | | | Away Games | | | | Home Games | | | Away Games | | | |
	Giants	Opp	Total	Giants	Opp	Total	Index	Giants	Opp	Total	Giants	Opp	Total	Index
G	81	81	162	81	81	162		243	243	486	243	243	486	
Avg	.268	.234	.251	.247	.239	.243	103	.264	.255	.259	.252	.248	.250	104
AB	2629	2746	5375	2864	2622	5486	98	8062	8483	16545	8512	7914	16426	101
R	358	292	650	299	319	618	105	1008	1054	2062	972	1036	2008	103
H	705	642	1347	706	626	1332	101	2127	2160	4287	2143	1966	4109	104
2B	129	132	261	146	111	257	104	424	464	888	429	400	829	106
3B	27	13	40	16	20	36	113	69	61	130	48	45	93	139
HR	65	64	129	57	76	133	99	164	203	367	183	217	400	91
BB	208	244	452	184	340	524	88	701	849	1550	675	980	1655	93
SO	539	663	1202	619	639	1258	98	1456	1824	3280	1653	1775	3428	95
E	48	44	92	40	48	88	105	152	153	305	120	137	257	119
E-Infield	22	14	36	16	21	37	97	79	56	135	53	54	107	126
LHB-Avg	.276	.227	.252	.249	.236	.243	104	.275	.249	.263	.253	.248	.251	105
LHB-HR	27	16	43	21	32	53	81	69	60	129	69	77	146	88
RHB-Avg	.262	.239	.249	.245	.241	.243	103	.254	.258	.256	.251	.249	.250	103
RHB-HR	38	48	86	36	44	80	112	95	143	238	114	140	254	93

Seattle Mariners - Safeco Field

	2009 Season							2007-2009						
	Home Games			Away Games				Home Games			Away Games			
	Mariners	Opp	Total	Mariners	Opp	Total	Index	Mariners	Opp	Total	Mariners	Opp	Total	Index
G	81	81	162	81	81	162		244	244	488	242	242	484	
Avg	.255	.243	.249	.260	.252	.256	97	.270	.262	.266	.270	.276	.273	97
AB	2728	2828	5556	2815	2668	5483	101	8262	8593	16855	8608	8096	16704	100
R	313	335	648	327	357	684	95	1036	1119	2155	1069	1197	2266	94
H	697	686	1383	733	673	1406	98	2229	2249	4478	2328	2232	4560	97
2B	132	125	257	148	134	282	90	406	457	863	443	484	927	92
3B	10	6	16	9	10	19	83	31	25	56	30	45	75	74
HR	76	80	156	84	92	176	87	212	231	443	225	249	474	93
BB	230	267	497	191	267	458	107	641	870	1511	586	836	1422	105
SO	555	551	1106	538	492	1030	106	1439	1669	3108	1405	1410	2815	109
E	46	47	93	59	36	95	98	134	169	303	160	153	313	96
E-Infield	25	20	45	27	18	45	100	58	68	126	69	73	142	88
LHB-Avg	.287	.247	.265	.261	.252	.256	103	.295	.259	.275	.281	.286	.283	97
LHB-HR	40	35	75	30	43	73	104	81	106	187	77	122	199	95
RHB-Avg	.238	.239	.239	.260	.252	.256	93	.255	.264	.260	.264	.268	.266	98
RHB-HR	36	45	81	54	49	103	77	131	125	256	148	127	275	91

St Louis Cardinals - Busch Stadium

	2009 Season							2007-2009						
	Home Games			Away Games				Home Games			Away Games			
	Cardinals	Opp	Total	Cardinals	Opp	Total	Index	Cardinals	Opp	Total	Cardinals	Opp	Total	Index
G	81	81	162	81	81	162		243	243	486	243	243	486	
Avg	.263	.254	.259	.263	.261	.262	99	.277	.261	.269	.268	.271	.270	100
AB	2654	2790	5444	2811	2670	5481	99	8089	8503	16592	8541	8175	16716	99
R	341	315	656	389	325	714	92	1080	1056	2136	1154	1138	2292	93
H	698	710	1408	738	697	1435	98	2241	2222	4463	2293	2216	4509	99
2B	145	132	277	149	142	291	96	403	463	866	453	482	935	93
3B	16	8	24	13	22	35	69	39	41	80	29	61	90	90
HR	66	54	120	94	69	163	74	207	203	410	268	251	519	80
BB	266	236	502	262	224	486	104	789	738	1527	822	727	1549	99
SO	495	550	1045	546	499	1045	101	1371	1489	2860	1564	1462	3026	95
E	49	51	100	47	46	93	108	158	140	298	144	135	279	107
E-Infield	22	24	46	22	21	43	107	66	60	126	60	57	117	108
LHB-Avg	.258	.270	.265	.251	.257	.254	104	.276	.263	.269	.260	.270	.265	101
LHB-HR	15	29	44	22	36	58	77	63	96	159	77	116	193	82
RHB-Avg	.265	.241	.254	.269	.265	.267	95	.278	.260	.269	.273	.272	.273	99
RHB-HR	51	25	76	72	33	105	73	144	107	251	191	135	326	78

Tampa Bay Rays - Tropicana Field Surface: FieldTurf

	2009 Season							2007-2009						
	Home Games			Away Games				Home Games			Away Games			
	Rays	Opp	Total	Rays	Opp	Total	Index	Rays	Opp	Total	Rays	Opp	Total	Index
G	81	81	162	81	81	162		237	237	474	249	249	498	
Avg	.273	.247	.260	.252	.268	.260	100	.267	.255	.261	.261	.274	.267	98
AB	2686	2814	5500	2776	2709	5485	100	7823	8249	16072	8773	8452	17225	98
R	433	344	777	370	410	780	100	1167	1064	2231	1192	1305	2497	94
H	734	696	1430	700	725	1425	100	2091	2101	4192	2286	2318	4604	96
2B	155	140	295	142	147	289	102	396	437	833	476	473	949	94
3B	21	15	36	15	9	24	150	58	48	106	51	46	97	117
HR	103	82	185	96	101	197	94	283	237	520	283	311	594	94
BB	313	252	565	329	263	592	95	873	774	1647	940	835	1775	99
SO	612	600	1212	617	525	1142	106	1753	1772	3525	2024	1690	3714	102
E	49	44	93	49	49	98	95	146	144	290	159	158	317	96
E-Infield	22	12	34	17	22	39	87	57	58	115	67	71	138	88
LHB-Avg	.270	.249	.260	.248	.257	.253	103	.275	.256	.265	.255	.275	.264	100
LHB-HR	52	32	84	44	46	90	94	141	96	237	143	134	277	91
RHB-Avg	.276	.246	.260	.256	.277	.266	98	.260	.254	.257	.266	.273	.270	95
RHB-HR	51	50	101	52	55	107	93	142	141	283	140	177	317	96

Texas Rangers - Rangers Ballpark In Arlington

| | 2009 Season | | | | | | | 2007-2009 | | | | | | |
| | Home Games | | | Away Games | | | | Home Games | | | Away Games | | | |
	Rangers	Opp	Total	Rangers	Opp	Total	Index	Rangers	Opp	Total	Rangers	Opp	Total	Index
G	81	81	162	81	81	162		243	243	486	243	243	486	
Avg	.273	.262	.267	.248	.258	.252	106	.282	.272	.277	.255	.277	.266	104
AB	2694	2829	5523	2832	2679	5511	100	8255	8629	16884	8554	8161	16715	101
R	426	367	793	358	373	731	108	1332	1278	2610	1169	1273	2442	107
H	735	742	1477	701	690	1391	106	2332	2343	4675	2183	2261	4444	105
2B	153	152	305	143	141	284	107	483	492	975	487	470	957	101
3B	18	14	32	9	13	22	145	67	52	119	31	36	67	176
HR	122	93	215	102	78	180	119	324	262	586	273	240	513	113
BB	255	264	519	217	267	484	107	829	878	1707	741	946	1687	100
SO	590	518	1108	663	490	1161	95	1783	1553	3336	1901	1402	3303	100
E	49	57	106	57	51	108	98	186	162	348	176	148	324	107
E-Infield	22	28	50	17	26	43	116	80	67	147	64	68	132	111
LHB-Avg	.245	.260	.253	.254	.260	.257	98	.277	.265	.270	.256	.283	.269	100
LHB-HR	44	47	91	39	37	76	120	148	129	277	121	114	235	117
RHB-Avg	.291	.264	.278	.243	.255	.249	112	.287	.277	.282	.255	.272	.263	107
RHB-HR	78	46	124	63	41	104	118	176	133	309	152	126	278	110

Toronto Blue Jays - Rogers Centre Surface: FieldTurf

| | 2009 Season | | | | | | | 2007-2009 | | | | | | |
| | Home Games | | | Away Games | | | | Home Games | | | Away Games | | | |
	Blue Jays	Opp	Total	Blue Jays	Opp	Total	Index	Blue Jays	Opp	Total	Blue Jays	Opp	Total	Index
G	81	81	162	81	81	162		243	243	486	243	243	486	
Avg	.259	.255	.257	.273	.284	.278	92	.261	.242	.251	.265	.268	.267	94
AB	2743	2826	5569	2960	2772	5725	97	8136	8388	16524	8599	8182	16701	98
R	389	370	759	409	401	810	94	1128	984	2112	1107	1006	2233	95
H	711	721	1432	805	788	1593	90	2124	2026	4150	2279	2196	4475	93
2B	170	160	330	169	163	332	102	492	448	940	494	408	902	106
3B	6	14	20	7	12	19	108	41	46	87	28	35	63	140
HR	104	90	194	105	91	196	102	263	229	492	237	243	480	104
BB	280	266	546	268	285	553	101	813	742	1555	789	755	1544	102
SO	517	613	1130	511	568	1079	108	1533	1842	3375	1477	1590	3067	112
E	38	54	92	38	40	78	118	114	150	264	148	126	274	96
E-Infield	9	21	30	14	18	32	94	45	63	108	57	58	115	94
LHB-Avg	.284	.248	.261	.263	.291	.281	93	.274	.249	.258	.253	.278	.268	96
LHB-HR	25	42	67	35	44	79	86	82	121	203	82	113	195	105
RHB-Avg	.251	.260	.255	.276	.279	.277	92	.256	.235	.247	.270	.260	.266	93
RHB-HR	79	48	127	70	47	117	112	181	108	289	155	130	285	104

Washington Nationals - Nationals Park

| | 2009 Season | | | | | | | 2008-2009 | | | | | | |
| | Home Games | | | Away Games | | | | Home Games | | | Away Games | | | |
	Nationals	Opp	Total	Nationals	Opp	Total	Index	Nationals	Opp	Total	Nationals	Opp	Total	Index
G	81	81	162	81	81	162		161	161	322	162	162	324	
Avg	.257	.263	.260	.258	.290	.274	95	.254	.266	.261	.254	.280	.267	98
AB	2701	2863	5564	2792	2686	5478	102	5354	5724	11078	5630	5370	11000	101
R	369	426	795	341	448	789	101	685	852	1537	666	847	1513	102
H	695	754	1449	721	779	1500	97	1362	1524	2886	1430	1505	2935	99
2B	127	189	316	144	172	316	98	253	350	603	287	316	603	99
3B	26	16	42	12	25	37	112	41	26	67	23	37	60	111
HR	76	86	162	80	87	167	96	127	183	310	146	180	326	94
BB	312	300	612	305	329	634	95	592	580	1172	559	637	1196	97
SO	575	456	1031	633	455	1088	93	1092	979	2071	1211	995	2206	93
E	75	53	128	68	32	100	128	134	99	233	132	95	227	103
E-Infield	29	21	50	26	15	41	122	55	45	100	50	38	88	114
LHB-Avg	.265	.278	.272	.260	.297	.278	98	.256	.279	.268	.249	.277	.263	102
LHB-HR	34	40	74	28	36	64	111	43	82	125	51	71	122	98
RHB-Avg	.251	.252	.251	.257	.285	.271	93	.253	.256	.255	.257	.282	.269	95
RHB-HR	42	46	88	52	51	103	86	84	101	185	95	109	204	92

2009 American League Ballpark Index Rankings - Runs

Home Park	TOTALS											LHB		RHB	
	Avg	AB	R	H	2B	3B	HR	BB	SO	E	E-Inf	Avg	HR	Avg	HR
Royals (Kauffman Stadium)	112	103	111	116	116	143	74	104	86	102	130	117	53	108	92
Twins (Hubert H. Humphrey Metrodome)	101	102	109	104	98	119	109	92	100	70	82	101	116	102	103
Rangers (Rangers Ballpark in Arlington)	106	100	108	106	107	145	119	107	95	98	116	98	120	112	118
Red Sox (Fenway Park)	103	96	107	99	142	112	100	92	97	99	84	101	93	105	105
White Sox (U.S. Cellular Field)	97	99	106	96	93	80	120	114	106	127	135	96	122	96	120
Orioles (Oriole Park at Camden Yards)	108	103	104	111	95	101	115	90	94	76	83	108	112	108	118
Tigers (Comerica Park)	98	98	103	96	97	110	100	105	99	112	123	91	85	103	110
Angels (Angel Stadium of Anaheim)	101	99	102	100	94	62	123	99	94	103	88	100	116	103	129
Rays (Tropicana Field)	100	100	100	100	102	150	94	95	106	95	87	103	94	98	93
Athletics (McAfee Coliseum)	97	97	97	95	93	116	95	100	103	103	93	97	106	98	85
Yankees (Yankee Stadium)	99	100	96	99	81	50	126	110	99	93	68	99	120	99	133
Mariners (Safeco Field)	97	101	95	98	90	83	87	107	106	98	100	103	104	93	77
Blue Jays (Rogers Centre)	92	97	94	90	102	108	102	101	108	118	94	93	86	92	112
Indians (Progressive Field)	96	100	84	96	101	53	67	95	101	93	107	91	71	101	64

2009 National League Ballpark Index Rankings - Runs

Home Park	TOTALS											LHB		RHB	
	Avg	AB	R	H	2B	3B	HR	BB	SO	E	E-Inf	Avg	HR	Avg	HR
Rockies (Coors Field)	112	103	125	116	123	172	105	104	85	135	132	110	102	115	107
Diamondbacks (Chase Field)	108	101	119	109	129	154	103	99	94	91	117	108	123	108	91
Cubs (Wrigley Field)	103	99	115	102	106	93	102	105	94	100	119	101	139	105	86
Marlins (Land Shark Stadium)	104	104	114	108	107	61	108	110	105	127	97	105	106	103	111
Giants (AT&T Park)	103	98	105	101	104	113	99	88	98	105	97	104	81	103	112
Phillies (Citizens Bank Park)	103	99	103	102	106	91	101	103	104	100	97	99	90	106	114
Pirates (PNC Park)	103	103	102	105	92	70	103	95	87	110	118	109	112	98	96
Nationals (Nationals Park)	95	102	101	97	98	112	96	95	93	128	122	98	111	93	86
Reds (Great American Ballpark)	100	99	97	99	103	110	119	105	109	81	77	102	119	100	118
Mets (Citi Field)	95	100	94	95	95	120	106	94	109	79	78	92	100	99	110
Astros (Minute Maid Park)	102	101	93	104	86	99	105	96	103	96	95	102	92	103	112
Cardinals (Busch Stadium)	99	99	92	98	96	69	74	104	101	108	107	104	77	95	73
Braves (Turner Field)	94	100	90	94	85	110	86	107	107	109	150	91	95	97	78
Brewers (Miller Park)	94	99	89	93	108	110	108	101	112	85	68	96	124	93	99
Dodgers (Dodger Stadium)	96	100	86	96	99	61	88	78	101	97	86	103	112	91	76
Padres (PETCO Park)	83	97	74	81	73	80	74	117	114	90	87	83	60	83	90

2009 AL Home Runs

Home Park	Index
Yankees	126
Angels	123
White Sox	120
Rangers	119
Orioles	115
Twins	109
Blue Jays	102
Red Sox	100
Tigers	100
Athletics	95
Rays	94
Mariners	87
Royals	74
Indians	67

2009 AL LHB Home Runs

Home Park	Index
White Sox	122
Rangers	120
Yankees	120
Twins	116
Angels	116
Orioles	112
Athletics	106
Mariners	104
Rays	94
Red Sox	93
Blue Jays	86
Tigers	85
Indians	71
Royals	53

2009 AL RHB Home Runs

Home Park	Index
Yankees	133
Angels	129
White Sox	120
Rangers	118
Orioles	118
Blue Jays	112
Tigers	110
Red Sox	105
Twins	103
Rays	93
Royals	92
Athletics	85
Mariners	77
Indians	64

2009 NL Home Runs

Home Park	Index
Reds	119
Marlins	108
Brewers	108
Mets	106
Rockies	105
Astros	105
Diamondbacks	103
Pirates	103
Cubs	102
Phillies	101
Giants	99
Nationals	96
Dodgers	88
Braves	86
Cardinals	74
Padres	74

2009 NL LHB Home Runs

Home Park	Index
Cubs	139
Brewers	124
Diamondbacks	123
Reds	119
Pirates	112
Dodgers	112
Nationals	111
Marlins	106
Rockies	102
Mets	100
Braves	95
Astros	92
Phillies	90
Giants	81
Cardinals	77
Padres	60

2009 NL RHB Home Runs

Home Park	Index
Reds	118
Phillies	114
Astros	112
Giants	112
Marlins	111
Mets	110
Rockies	107
Brewers	99
Pirates	96
Diamondbacks	91
Padres	90
Cubs	86
Nationals	86
Braves	78
Dodgers	76
Cardinals	73

2009 AL Avg	Index
Home Park	
Royals	112
Orioles	108
Rangers	106
Red Sox	103
Twins	101
Angels	101
Rays	100
Yankees	99
Tigers	98
Athletics	97
Mariners	97
White Sox	97
Indians	96
Blue Jays	92

2009 AL LHB Avg	Index
Home Park	
Royals	117
Orioles	108
Mariners	103
Rays	103
Red Sox	101
Twins	101
Angels	100
Yankees	99
Rangers	98
Athletics	97
White Sox	96
Blue Jays	93
Tigers	91
Indians	91

2009 AL RHB Avg	Index
Home Park	
Rangers	112
Orioles	108
Royals	108
Red Sox	105
Tigers	103
Angels	103
Twins	102
Indians	101
Yankees	99
Rays	98
Athletics	98
White Sox	96
Mariners	93
Blue Jays	92

2009 NL Avg	Index
Home Park	
Rockies	112
Diamondbacks	108
Marlins	104
Cubs	103
Giants	103
Phillies	103
Pirates	102
Astros	102
Reds	100
Cardinals	99
Dodgers	96
Mets	95
Nationals	95
Brewers	94
Braves	94
Padres	83

2009 NL LHB Avg	Index
Home Park	
Rockies	110
Pirates	109
Diamondbacks	108
Marlins	105
Cardinals	104
Giants	104
Dodgers	103
Astros	102
Reds	102
Cubs	101
Phillies	99
Nationals	98
Brewers	96
Mets	92
Braves	91
Padres	83

2009 NL RHB Avg	Index
Home Park	
Rockies	115
Diamondbacks	108
Phillies	106
Cubs	105
Giants	103
Marlins	103
Astros	103
Reds	100
Mets	99
Pirates	98
Braves	97
Cardinals	95
Nationals	93
Brewers	93
Dodgers	91
Padres	83

2009 AL Doubles	Index
Home Park	
Red Sox	142
Royals	116
Rangers	107
Blue Jays	102
Rays	102
Indians	101
Twins	98
Tigers	97
Orioles	95
Angels	94
Athletics	93
White Sox	93
Mariners	90
Yankees	81

2009 AL Triples	Index
Home Park	
Rays	150
Rangers	145
Royals	143
Twins	119
Athletics	116
Red Sox	112
Tigers	110
Blue Jays	108
Orioles	101
Mariners	83
White Sox	80
Angels	62
Indians	53
Yankees	50

2009 AL Errors	Index
Home Park	
White Sox	127
Blue Jays	118
Tigers	112
Angels	103
Athletics	103
Royals	102
Red Sox	99
Rangers	98
Mariners	98
Rays	95
Indians	93
Yankees	93
Orioles	76
Twins	70

2009 NL Doubles	Index
Home Park	
Diamondbacks	129
Rockies	123
Brewers	108
Marlins	107
Cubs	106
Phillies	106
Giants	104
Reds	103
Dodgers	99
Nationals	98
Cardinals	96
Mets	95
Pirates	92
Astros	86
Braves	85
Padres	73

2009 NL Triples	Index
Home Park	
Rockies	172
Diamondbacks	154
Mets	120
Giants	113
Nationals	112
Brewers	110
Reds	110
Braves	110
Astros	99
Cubs	93
Phillies	91
Padres	80
Pirates	70
Cardinals	69
Marlins	61
Dodgers	61

2009 NL Errors	Index
Home Park	
Rockies	135
Nationals	128
Marlins	127
Pirates	110
Braves	109
Cardinals	108
Giants	105
Cubs	100
Phillies	100
Dodgers	97
Astros	96
Diamondbacks	91
Padres	90
Brewers	85
Reds	81
Mets	79

2007-2009 American League Ballpark Index Rankings - Runs

Home Park	Avg	AB	R	H	2B	3B	HR	BB	SO	E	E-Inf	LHB Avg	LHB HR	RHB Avg	RHB HR
Red Sox (Fenway Park)	107	99	111	106	145	102	91	98	94	97	97	108	85	107	95
White Sox (U.S. Cellular Field)	98	100	109	99	93	58	125	106	103	118	125	98	122	99	127
Rangers (Rangers Ballpark in Arlington)	104	101	107	105	101	176	113	100	100	107	111	100	117	107	110
Orioles (Oriole Park at Camden Yards)	106	103	107	108	95	89	122	93	92	81	74	104	115	107	129
Tigers (Comerica Park)	102	100	105	101	97	128	110	98	96	112	103	97	96	105	118
Angels (Angel Stadium of Anaheim)	103	100	104	103	105	71	101	95	94	101	98	104	94	102	107
Royals (Kauffman Stadium)	105	101	102	106	118	114	81	101	89	90	106	108	73	104	87
Indians (Progressive Field)	101	100	98	101	98	60	85	105	103	105	119	99	83	102	87
Yankees (Yankee Stadium) *	99	100	96	99	81	50	126	110	99	93	68	99	120	99	133
Blue Jays (Rogers Centre)	94	98	95	93	106	140	104	102	112	96	94	96	105	93	104
Twins (Hubert H. Humphrey Metrodome)	97	100	95	97	98	108	92	93	101	80	77	96	93	99	91
Mariners (Safeco Field)	97	100	94	97	92	74	93	105	109	96	88	97	95	99	91
Rays (Tropicana Field)	98	98	94	96	94	117	94	99	102	96	88	100	91	95	96
Athletics (McAfee Coliseum)	94	98	91	92	89	96	90	101	96	109	113	94	106	94	77

2007-2009 National League Ballpark Index Rankings - Runs

Home Park	Avg	AB	R	H	2B	3B	HR	BB	SO	E	E-Inf	LHB Avg	LHB HR	RHB Avg	RHB HR
Rockies (Coors Field)	110	102	118	112	115	153	116	95	87	114	101	105	109	113	122
Diamondbacks (Chase Field)	107	101	115	107	120	173	107	100	93	93	103	103	115	109	102
Cubs (Wrigley Field)	104	100	113	104	107	82	110	102	100	105	117	102	126	105	103
Marlins (Land Shark Stadium)	100	102	105	102	104	105	96	109	111	112	98	99	94	101	98
Reds (Great American Ballpark)	99	100	105	99	103	97	125	103	104	92	87	102	121	97	129
Phillies (Citizens Bank Park)	102	99	103	101	97	84	114	98	101	102	101	104	111	101	117
Giants (AT&T Park)	104	101	103	104	106	139	91	93	95	119	126	105	88	103	93
Nationals (Nationals Park) **	98	101	102	99	99	111	94	97	93	103	114	102	98	95	92
Astros (Minute Maid Park)	101	101	96	102	97	105	108	98	105	87	100	101	100	102	113
Braves (Turner Field)	97	100	96	97	88	106	95	110	104	113	122	97	94	98	96
Pirates (PNC Park)	101	101	95	102	101	72	88	93	91	93	104	105	107	99	77
Brewers (Miller Park)	96	99	95	95	100	92	104	109	109	97	87	99	116	94	97
Mets (Citi Field) *	95	100	94	95	95	120	106	94	109	79	78	92	100	99	110
Cardinals (Busch Stadium)	100	99	93	99	93	90	80	99	95	107	108	101	82	99	78
Dodgers (Dodger Stadium)	97	99	92	96	93	54	93	90	107	98	82	97	111	96	84
Padres (PETCO Park)	87	98	76	85	75	93	73	105	111	86	77	88	61	86	86

2007-2009 AL Home Runs

Home Park	Index
Yankees *	126
White Sox	125
Orioles	122
Rangers	113
Tigers	110
Blue Jays	104
Angels	101
Rays	94
Mariners	93
Twins	92
Red Sox	91
Athletics	90
Indians	85
Royals	81

2007-2009 AL LHB Home Runs

Home Park	Index
White Sox	122
Yankees *	120
Rangers	117
Orioles	115
Athletics	106
Blue Jays	105
Tigers	96
Mariners	95
Angels	94
Twins	93
Rays	91
Red Sox	85
Indians	83
Royals	73

2007-2009 AL RHB Home Runs

Home Park	Index
Yankees *	133
Orioles	129
White Sox	127
Tigers	118
Rangers	110
Angels	107
Blue Jays	104
Rays	96
Red Sox	95
Twins	91
Mariners	91
Royals	87
Indians	87
Athletics	77

2007-2009 NL Home Runs

Home Park	Index
Reds	125
Rockies	116
Phillies	114
Cubs	110
Astros	108
Diamondbacks	107
Mets *	106
Brewers	104
Marlins	96
Braves	95
Nationals **	94
Dodgers	93
Giants	91
Pirates	88
Cardinals	80
Padres	73

2007-2009 NL LHB Home Runs

Home Park	Index
Cubs	126
Reds	121
Brewers	116
Diamondbacks	115
Dodgers	111
Phillies	111
Rockies	109
Pirates	107
Astros	100
Mets *	100
Nationals **	98
Marlins	94
Braves	94
Giants	88
Cardinals	82
Padres	61

2007-2009 NL RHB Home Runs

Home Park	Index
Reds	129
Rockies	122
Phillies	117
Astros	113
Mets *	110
Cubs	103
Diamondbacks	102
Marlins	98
Brewers	97
Braves	96
Giants	93
Nationals **	92
Padres	86
Dodgers	84
Cardinals	78
Pirates	77

* Data since 2009   ** Data since 2008

2007-2009 AL Avg	
Home Park	Index
Red Sox	107
Orioles	106
Royals	105
Rangers	104
Angels	103
Tigers	102
Indians	101
Yankees *	99
White Sox	98
Rays	98
Twins	97
Mariners	97
Blue Jays	94
Athletics	94

2007-2009 AL LHB Avg	
Home Park	Index
Red Sox	108
Royals	108
Angels	104
Orioles	104
Rays	100
Rangers	100
Yankees *	99
Indians	99
White Sox	98
Mariners	97
Tigers	97
Blue Jays	96
Twins	96
Athletics	94

2007-2009 AL RHB Avg	
Home Park	Index
Rangers	107
Orioles	107
Red Sox	107
Tigers	105
Royals	104
Indians	102
Angels	102
Twins	99
White Sox	99
Yankees *	99
Mariners	98
Rays	95
Athletics	94
Blue Jays	93

2007-2009 NL Avg	
Home Park	Index
Rockies	110
Diamondbacks	107
Cubs	104
Giants	104
Phillies	102
Astros	101
Pirates	101
Marlins	100
Cardinals	100
Reds	99
Nationals **	98
Braves	97
Dodgers	97
Brewers	96
Mets *	95
Padres	87

2007-2009 NL LHB Avg	
Home Park	Index
Rockies	105
Giants	105
Pirates	105
Phillies	104
Diamondbacks	103
Nationals **	102
Cubs	102
Reds	100
Cardinals	101
Astros	101
Marlins	99
Brewers	99
Dodgers	97
Braves	97
Mets *	92
Padres	88

2007-2009 NL RHB Avg	
Home Park	Index
Rockies	113
Diamondbacks	109
Cubs	105
Giants	103
Astros	102
Marlins	101
Phillies	101
Mets *	99
Pirates	99
Cardinals	99
Braves	98
Reds	97
Dodgers	96
Nationals **	95
Brewers	94
Padres	86

2007-2009 AL Doubles	
Home Park	Index
Red Sox	145
Royals	118
Blue Jays	106
Angels	105
Rangers	101
Indians	98
Twins	98
Tigers	97
Orioles	95
Rays	94
White Sox	93
Mariners	92
Athletics	89
Yankees *	81

2007-2009 AL Triples	
Home Park	Index
Rangers	176
Blue Jays	140
Tigers	128
Rays	117
Royals	114
Twins	108
Red Sox	102
Athletics	96
Orioles	89
Mariners	74
Angels	71
Indians	60
White Sox	58
Yankees *	50

2007-2009 AL Errors	
Home Park	Index
White Sox	118
Tigers	112
Athletics	109
Rangers	107
Indians	105
Angels	101
Red Sox	97
Blue Jays	96
Rays	90
Mariners	96
Yankees *	93
Royals	90
Orioles	81
Twins	80

2007-2009 NL Doubles	
Home Park	Index
Diamondbacks	120
Rockies	115
Cubs	107
Giants	106
Marlins	104
Reds	103
Pirates	101
Brewers	100
Nationals **	99
Phillies	97
Astros	97
Mets *	95
Cardinals	93
Dodgers	93
Braves	88
Padres	75

2007-2009 NL Triples	
Home Park	Index
Diamondbacks	173
Rockies	153
Giants	139
Mets *	120
Nationals **	111
Braves	106
Marlins	105
Astros	105
Reds	97
Padres	93
Brewers	92
Cardinals	90
Phillies	84
Cubs	82
Pirates	72
Dodgers	54

2007-2009 NL Errors	
Home Park	Index
Giants	119
Rockies	114
Braves	113
Marlins	112
Cardinals	107
Cubs	105
Nationals **	103
Phillies	102
Dodgers	98
Brewers	97
Diamondbacks	93
Pirates	93
Reds	92
Astros	87
Padres	86
Mets *	79

* Data since 2009   ** Data since 2008

2009 Lefty/Righty Statistics

Last year we had a little fun imagining dream tandems, players who maybe aren't perennial All-Stars on their own, but who, if somehow they could integrate with the exactly the right player, would be voted in every year. Here are our 2009 Dream Mash-Ups:

1. R.A. Dempster. A combination of Ryan Dempster and R.A. Dickey would be a top-of-the-rotation starter for almost any team. Dominating righties to the tune of .241/.286/.378 (Dempster), he would use a fluttering knuckleball to keep lefties in check at .246/.343/.404 (Dickey).

2. Jensen Ray Herrera. Imagine the entrance music for a hybrid of Daniel Ray Herrera and Jensen Lewis. He would stand 5'6'', never crease the bill of his cap, and hold right-handers to a .205/.284/.356 line (Lewis) while handcuffing left-handers with .183/.254/.266 (Herrera).

3. Felipe Castillo. A Vulcan Mind Meld of Luis Castillo and Felipe Lopez could hit .319/.411/.345 (Castillo) against righties and .320/.379/.456 against lefties (Lopez). Not a lot of power from the keystone sack, but not a lot of strikeouts either.

4. Esmerling Gutierrez. If the Arizona Diamondbacks' Chad Qualls has trouble returning from his knee injury, the D'backs may have the solution in-house. A one-two punch of Juan Gutierrez and Esmerling Vasquez would not only have a name that any broadcaster would love to pronounce, but would dominate righties to the tune of .207/.252/.307 (Gutierrez) and stymie lefties at .196/.312/.359 (Vasquez).

5. Yorvit Molina. Wait…there's a fourth Molina brother? Only in our dream world: A catching mash-up of Bengie Molina and Yorvit Torrealba would rake right-handed pitchers with a line of .318/.376/.403 (Torrealba) and punish left-handed pitchers with a line of .277/.315/.563 (Molina).

Special mention: Josh Barfield. Yes, the one and only Josh Barfield of the Cleveland Indians…the most symmetrical hitter in all of 2009. He only clocked twenty at-bats this season, but against righties he hit .400/.400/.467 while hitting .400/.400/.400 in five at-bats against lefties. Ah, the joys of small sample sizes…. Just don't call him "Mr. .400."

In the following section are lefty/righty splits for all batters and pitchers who appeared during the 2009 season. The batting side of each hitter is shown below his name; for pitchers, the hand that he throws with is indicated.

Batters vs. Left-Handed and Right-Handed Pitchers

Batter	vs	Avg	AB	H	2B	3B	HR	RBI	BB	SO	OBP	Slg
Abreu,Bobby	L	.267	176	47	8	2	3	26	22	40	.348	.386
Bats Left	R	.305	387	118	21	1	12	77	72	73	.408	.457
Abreu,Tony	L	-	0	0	0	0	0	0	2	0	1.000	-
Bats Both	R	.250	8	2	0	0	0	1	1	2	.333	.250
Adams,Russ	L	.000	1	0	0	0	0	0	0	0	.000	.000
Bats Left	R	.211	19	4	0	0	0	0	1	1	.250	.211
Alfonzo,Eliezer	L	.208	24	5	0	0	1	4	0	6	.208	.333
Bats Right	R	.167	90	15	3	0	1	4	3	28	.194	.233
Allen,Brandon	L	.091	22	2	1	0	0	0	4	11	.231	.136
Bats Left	R	.232	82	19	6	0	4	14	8	29	.300	.451
Amezaga,Alfredo	L	.133	15	2	0	0	0	1	2	6	.222	.133
Bats Both	R	.241	54	13	3	0	0	4	3	10	.281	.296
Anderson,Brian	L	.194	62	12	3	0	1	6	12	13	.324	.290
Bats Right	R	.264	140	37	6	0	3	12	11	41	.329	.371
Anderson,Garret	L	.283	145	41	6	0	4	19	4	30	.307	.407
Bats Left	R	.262	351	92	21	0	9	42	23	43	.302	.399
Anderson,Josh	L	.200	45	9	0	0	0	5	2	8	.250	.200
Bats Left	R	.248	238	59	7	4	1	19	11	35	.281	.324
Anderson,Marlon	L	-	0	0	0	0	0	0	0	0	-	-
Bats Left	R	.000	4	0	0	0	0	0	0	1	.000	.000
Andino,Robert	L	.226	62	14	3	0	1	4	3	16	.258	.323
Bats Right	R	.221	136	30	4	0	1	6	12	31	.282	.272
Andrus,Elvis	L	.279	129	36	5	3	1	10	18	21	.373	.388
Bats Right	R	.262	351	92	12	5	5	30	22	56	.311	.368
Ankiel,Rick	L	.234	94	22	6	0	0	8	2	29	.265	.298
Bats Left	R	.230	278	64	15	2	11	30	24	70	.291	.417
Arias,Joaquin	L	.000	6	0	0	0	0	0	0	3	.000	.000
Bats Right	R	.000	2	0	0	0	0	0	0	0	.000	.000
Atkins,Garrett	L	.268	138	37	5	1	5	22	20	27	.363	.428
Bats Right	R	.199	216	43	7	0	4	26	21	31	.272	.287
Aubrey,Michael	L	.150	20	3	2	0	0	0	1	3	.190	.250
Bats Left	R	.329	70	23	5	0	4	14	4	7	.365	.571
Aurilia,Rich	L	.250	52	13	1	0	0	3	3	11	.291	.269
Bats Right	R	.186	70	13	1	0	2	13	5	13	.231	.286
Ausmus,Brad	L	.286	28	8	1	0	0	3	2	7	.333	.321
Bats Right	R	.299	67	20	3	0	1	6	3	14	.347	.388
Avila,Alex	L	.400	10	4	1	0	1	3	1	1	.455	.800
Bats Left	R	.255	51	13	3	0	4	11	9	17	.361	.549
Aviles,Mike	L	.195	41	8	1	1	0	3	4	10	.267	.268
Bats Right	R	.177	79	14	2	0	1	5	0	16	.175	.241
Aybar,Erick	L	.325	163	53	6	1	4	15	6	14	.356	.448
Bats Both	R	.305	341	104	17	8	1	43	24	40	.351	.411
Aybar,Willy	L	.265	102	27	7	0	6	14	18	23	.372	.510
Bats Both	R	.247	194	48	5	0	6	27	16	31	.308	.366
Bailey,Jeff	L	.400	25	10	0	1	2	5	5	6	.500	.720
Bats Right	R	.115	52	6	3	1	1	4	5	15	.246	.269
Baker,Jeff	L	.279	61	17	3	1	2	9	3	12	.323	.459
Bats Right	R	.291	165	48	12	1	2	15	15	41	.350	.412
Baker,John	L	.171	35	6	2	0	1	3	4	10	.310	.314
Bats Left	R	.281	338	95	23	0	8	47	37	79	.354	.420
Bako,Paul	L	.000	10	0	0	0	0	0	1	3	.167	.000
Bats Left	R	.245	106	26	4	0	3	9	12	29	.322	.368
Baldelli,Rocco	L	.290	93	27	2	0	4	15	7	19	.343	.441
Bats Right	R	.193	57	11	2	1	3	8	4	18	.258	.421
Balentien,Wladimir	L	.165	79	13	7	0	1	8	8	28	.239	.291
Bats Right	R	.263	186	49	10	1	6	16	20	42	.333	.425
Barajas,Rod	L	.267	105	28	5	0	6	26	8	10	.308	.486
Bats Right	R	.213	324	69	14	0	13	45	12	66	.241	.377
Bard,Josh	L	.240	50	12	4	0	1	5	3	15	.283	.380
Bats Both	R	.228	224	51	14	0	5	26	21	35	.296	.357
Barden,Brian	L	.191	47	9	1	0	2	5	3	10	.240	.340
Bats Right	R	.268	56	15	2	0	2	5	3	11	.323	.411
Barfield,Josh	L	.400	5	2	0	0	0	0	0	2	.400	.400
Bats Right	R	.400	15	6	1	0	0	2	0	5	.400	.467
Barker,Kevin	L	.000	3	0	0	0	0	0	0	1	.000	.000
Bats Left	R	.310	29	9	3	0	0	3	3	8	.364	.414
Barmes,Clint	L	.245	139	34	6	1	9	23	13	28	.314	.496
Bats Right	R	.246	411	101	26	2	14	53	18	93	.287	.421
Barrett,Michael	L	.000	5	0	0	0	0	0	1	1	.167	.000
Bats Right	R	.231	13	3	0	1	0	2	0	4	.231	.462
Bartlett,Jason	L	.338	151	51	5	4	4	19	23	20	.427	.503
Bats Right	R	.312	349	109	24	3	10	47	31	69	.371	.484
Barton,Brian	L	-	0	0	0	0	0	0	0	0	-	-
Bats Right	R	-	0	0	0	0	0	0	0	0	-	-
Barton,Daric	L	.333	24	8	3	0	1	5	7	2	.500	.583
Bats Left	R	.257	136	35	9	1	2	19	19	23	.346	.382

Batter	vs	Avg	AB	H	2B	3B	HR	RBI	BB	SO	OBP	Slg
Bates,Aaron	L	.333	6	2	0	0	0	1	0	3	.333	.667
Bats Right	R	.400	5	2	0	0	0	1	1	1	.500	.400
Bautista,Jose	L	.293	123	36	8	2	6	18	19	21	.382	.537
Bats Right	R	.202	213	43	5	1	7	22	37	64	.331	.333
Bay,Jason	L	.292	154	45	11	0	11	34	28	36	.402	.578
Bats Right	R	.257	377	97	18	3	25	85	66	126	.377	.520
Beckham,Gordon	L	.318	110	35	13	0	3	17	10	13	.372	.518
Bats Right	R	.250	268	67	15	1	11	46	31	52	.338	.437
Belliard,Ronnie	L	.282	71	20	2	0	4	9	9	13	.363	.479
Bats Right	R	.275	193	53	12	1	6	30	11	43	.311	.440
Bellorin,Edwin	L	.000	2	0	0	0	0	0	1	1	.333	.000
Bats Right	R	.333	6	2	0	0	0	0	0	0	.333	.333
Beltran,Carlos	L	.326	86	28	9	1	5	20	8	12	.385	.628
Bats Both	R	.324	222	72	13	0	5	28	39	31	.425	.450
Beltre,Adrian	L	.298	121	36	9	0	4	14	14	26	.384	.471
Bats Right	R	.253	328	83	18	0	4	30	5	48	.271	.345
Berkman,Lance	L	.231	134	31	4	0	7	23	12	30	.293	.418
Bats Both	R	.291	326	95	21	1	18	57	85	68	.436	.546
Bernadina,Roger	L	-	0	0	0	0	0	0	1	0	1.000	-
Bats Left	R	.250	4	1	1	0	0	0	0	1	.250	.500
Berroa,Angel	L	.158	19	3	1	0	0	1	0	7	.200	.211
Bats Right	R	.133	30	4	1	0	0	2	3	5	.212	.167
Betancourt,Yuniesky	L	.283	120	34	5	1	4	20	9	6	.331	.442
Bats Right	R	.231	350	81	15	5	2	29	12	38	.253	.320
Betemit,Wilson	L	.200	15	3	3	0	0	1	1	7	.250	.400
Bats Both	R	.200	30	6	2	0	0	2	4	6	.294	.267
Bixler,Brian	L	.500	10	5	1	0	0	1	1	3	.545	.600
Bats Right	R	.147	34	5	4	0	0	2	1	23	.171	.265
Blake,Casey	L	.320	103	33	9	2	4	18	24	19	.442	.563
Bats Right	R	.270	382	103	16	4	14	61	39	97	.340	.442
Blalock,Hank	L	.221	131	29	5	2	6	17	1	39	.231	.427
Bats Left	R	.239	331	79	16	2	19	49	25	69	.294	.471
Blanco,Andres	L	.250	28	7	2	0	0	3	2	2	.300	.321
Bats Both	R	.253	95	24	6	0	1	9	6	12	.304	.347
Blanco,Gregor	L	.083	12	1	0	0	0	0	1	2	.154	.083
Bats Left	R	.226	31	7	0	1	0	1	3	7	.294	.290
Blanco,Henry	L	.322	59	19	5	0	4	6	11	15	.429	.610
Bats Right	R	.200	145	29	7	0	2	10	15	35	.273	.290
Blanks,Kyle	L	.220	41	9	3	0	1	6	5	11	.304	.366
Bats Right	R	.262	107	28	6	0	9	16	13	44	.373	.570
Bloomquist,Willie	L	.248	165	41	4	3	2	10	18	23	.321	.345
Bats Right	R	.275	269	74	7	5	2	19	9	50	.300	.361
Blum,Geoff	L	.345	29	10	4	0	0	5	4	7	.424	.483
Bats Both	R	.239	352	84	10	1	10	44	29	54	.305	.358
Boggs,Brandon	L	.100	10	1	1	0	0	0	0	4	.100	.200
Bats Both	R	.000	7	0	0	0	0	0	1	4	.125	.000
Bonifacio,Emilio	L	.315	143	45	1	3	0	7	6	31	.340	.364
Bats Both	R	.223	318	71	10	3	1	20	28	64	.288	.283
Boone,Aaron	L	.000	5	0	0	0	0	0	0	0	.000	.000
Bats Right	R	.000	8	0	0	0	0	0	0	2	.111	.000
Borbon,Julio	L	.125	16	2	0	0	0	0	0	5	.125	.125
Bats Left	R	.333	141	47	4	0	4	20	15	23	.401	.447
Bourgeois,Jason	L	.240	25	6	0	0	1	2	2	3	.296	.360
Bats Right	R	.083	12	1	0	0	0	0	1	4	.154	.083
Bourn,Michael	L	.287	143	41	6	2	2	12	7	35	.325	.399
Bats Left	R	.285	463	132	21	10	1	23	56	105	.362	.380
Bowker,John	L	.000	5	0	0	0	0	0	0	0	.000	.000
Bats Left	R	.210	62	13	2	2	2	6	4	16	.269	.403
Bradley,Milton	L	.333	99	33	6	1	1	9	7	13	.385	.444
Bats Right	R	.231	294	68	11	0	11	31	59	82	.376	.381
Brantley,Michael	L	.462	26	12	2	0	0	2	4	7	.533	.538
Bats Left	R	.267	86	23	2	0	0	9	4	12	.300	.291
Branyan,Russell	L	.222	158	35	9	1	10	26	20	64	.321	.481
Bats Left	R	.267	273	73	12	0	21	50	38	85	.363	.542
Braun,Ryan	L	.395	119	47	13	1	8	34	20	21	.475	.723
Bats Right	R	.302	516	156	26	5	24	80	37	100	.363	.512
Brignac,Reid	L	.050	20	1	0	0	0	0	1	7	.095	.050
Bats Left	R	.343	70	24	8	2	1	6	2	13	.361	.557
Brown,Dusty	L	.500	2	1	0	0	1	1	0	0	.500	2.000
Bats Right	R	.000	1	0	0	0	0	0	0	0	.500	.000
Brown,Emil	L	.200	5	1	0	0	0	0	1	0	.333	.200
Bats Right	R	-	0	0	0	0	0	0	0	0	-	-
Bruce,Jay	L	.210	100	21	6	0	2	14	15	28	.313	.330
Bats Left	R	.229	245	56	9	2	20	44	23	47	.299	.527
Bruntlett,Eric	L	.229	48	11	5	0	0	2	4	10	.315	.333
Bats Right	R	.123	57	7	2	0	0	5	1	16	.145	.158

Batters vs. Left-Handed and Right-Handed Pitchers

Batter	vs	Avg	AB	H	2B	3B	HR	RBI	BB	SO	OBP	Slg
Buck,John	L	.213	47	10	4	1	1	9	3	16	.260	.404
Bats Right	R	.259	139	36	8	3	7	27	10	39	.311	.511
Buck,Travis	L	.143	14	2	1	0	0	1	0	3	.143	.214
Bats Left	R	.231	91	21	2	0	3	9	10	17	.307	.352
Budde,Ryan	L	.000	1	0	0	0	0	0	0	1	.000	.000
Bats Right	R	.000	2	0	0	0	0	0	0	1	.000	.000
Burke,Chris	L	.091	22	2	1	0	0	1	2	7	.200	.136
Bats Right	R	.250	60	15	4	0	1	4	4	9	.297	.367
Burke,Jamie	L	.200	5	1	0	0	0	0	1	1	.333	.200
Bats Right	R	.109	46	5	0	0	1	2	2	17	.143	.174
Burrell,Pat	L	.202	119	24	6	0	0	12	23	35	.336	.252
Bats Right	R	.229	293	67	10	1	14	52	34	84	.306	.413
Burriss,Emmanuel	L	.333	48	16	2	0	0	3	1	5	.347	.375
Bats Both	R	.208	154	32	4	0	0	10	13	20	.276	.234
Buscher,Brian	L	.200	15	3	2	0	0	1	3	0	.333	.333
Bats Left	R	.240	121	29	1	1	2	11	21	35	.363	.314
Butler,Billy	L	.330	179	59	16	0	8	29	25	22	.413	.553
Bats Right	R	.289	429	124	35	1	13	64	33	81	.339	.466
Byrd,Marlon	L	.244	164	40	13	0	7	30	11	32	.293	.451
Bats Right	R	.300	383	115	30	2	13	59	21	66	.344	.491
Byrnes,Eric	L	.228	79	18	6	0	5	8	5	13	.274	.494
Bats Right	R	.225	160	36	8	1	3	23	7	17	.267	.344
Cabrera,Asdrubal	L	.306	147	45	12	1	0	16	12	26	.356	.401
Bats Both	R	.309	376	116	30	3	6	52	32	63	.363	.452
Cabrera,Everth	L	.238	105	20	0	0	0	5	13	25	.325	.303
Bats Both	R	.261	268	70	15	6	2	20	30	63	.349	.384
Cabrera,Melky	L	.268	157	42	9	0	5	20	15	16	.343	.420
Bats Both	R	.277	328	91	19	1	8	48	28	43	.332	.415
Cabrera,Miguel	L	.315	143	45	8	0	7	17	33	27	.441	.517
Bats Right	R	.327	468	153	26	0	27	86	35	80	.380	.556
Cabrera,Orlando	L	.271	199	54	12	0	2	16	18	18	.327	.302
Bats Right	R	.289	457	132	24	3	7	61	18	53	.311	.400
Cairo,Miguel	L	.000	3	0	0	0	0	0	0	1	.250	.000
Bats Right	R	.286	42	12	2	1	1	2	0	4	.286	.452
Callaspo,Alberto	L	.361	180	65	18	1	3	23	9	10	.391	.522
Bats Both	R	.273	396	108	23	7	8	50	43	41	.342	.427
Cameron,Mike	L	.271	118	32	8	1	7	19	30	32	.420	.594
Bats Right	R	.244	426	104	24	2	17	51	45	124	.318	.430
Cancel,Robinson	L	.000	1	0	0	0	0	0	0	0	.000	.000
Bats Right	R	-	0	0	0	0	0	0	0	0	-	
Canizares,Barbaro	L	.333	6	2	0	0	0	0	0	1	.333	.333
Bats Right	R	.133	15	2	1	0	0	0	0	5	.133	.200
Cano,Robinson	L	.309	220	68	19	1	10	32	9	33	.335	.541
Bats Left	R	.326	417	136	29	1	15	53	21	30	.360	.508
Cantu,Jorge	L	.322	143	46	11	0	5	24	15	21	.389	.503
Bats Right	R	.278	442	123	31	0	11	76	32	60	.331	.420
Carlin,Luke	L	.100	10	1	0	0	0	0	1	3	.182	.100
Bats Both	R	.250	4	1	0	0	0	1	2	0	.400	.250
Carp,Mike	L	.286	7	2	0	0	0	0	2	2	.444	.286
Bats Left	R	.319	47	15	3	1	1	5	6	8	.411	.489
Carroll,Brett	L	.258	66	17	4	2	3	10	3	17	.286	.515
Bats Right	R	.213	75	16	4	0	0	8	8	16	.322	.267
Carroll,Jamey	L	.271	85	23	4	0	0	7	14	15	.374	.318
Bats Right	R	.278	230	64	6	2	2	19	22	48	.348	.348
Carson,Matt	L	.308	13	4	0	0	1	5	0	4	.286	.538
Bats Right	R	.250	8	2	0	0	0	0	0	3	.250	.250
Carter,Chris	L	.000	1	0	0	0	0	0	0	1	.000	.000
Bats Left	R	.000	4	0	0	0	0	0	1	0	.000	.000
Cash,Kevin	L	.429	7	3	2	0	0	1	0	0	.375	.714
Bats Right	R	.158	57	9	3	0	0	2	0	5	.200	.158
Casilla,Alexi	L	.182	66	12	1	1	0	7	7	7	.260	.227
Bats Both	R	.210	162	34	6	2	0	10	15	29	.287	.272
Castillo,Luis	L	.264	144	38	7	1	1	14	16	13	.329	.347
Bats Both	R	.319	342	109	5	2	0	26	53	45	.411	.345
Castillo,Wilkin	L	1.000	1	1	0	0	0	1	0	0	1.000	1.000
Bats Both	R	.500	2	1	0	0	0	0	0	0	.500	.500
Castro,Juan	L	.240	25	6	1	0	1	3	1	7	.269	.400
Bats Right	R	.287	87	25	3	0	0	6	5	18	.323	.322
Castro,Ramon	L	.222	54	12	3	0	4	12	7	13	.311	.500
Bats Right	R	.218	101	22	5	0	3	13	9	26	.282	.356
Catalanotto,Frank	L	.091	11	1	0	0	0	1	0	3	.091	.091
Bats Left	R	.293	133	39	6	3	1	8	14	20	.364	.406
Cedeno,Ronny	L	.193	88	17	4	1	1	6	7	23	.253	.295
Bats Right	R	.213	253	54	4	2	9	32	12	56	.257	.352
Cervelli,Francisco	L	.345	29	10	1	0	0	4	0	2	.345	.379
Bats Right	R	.277	65	18	3	0	1	7	2	9	.294	.369

Batter	vs	Avg	AB	H	2B	3B	HR	RBI	BB	SO	OBP	Slg
Chavez,Endy	L	.258	31	8	0	0	0	3	1	5	.281	.258
Bats Left	R	.277	130	36	3	1	2	10	13	17	.338	.362
Chavez,Eric	L	.111	18	2	0	0	0	0	0	5	.111	.111
Bats Left	R	.083	12	1	1	0	0	1	1	2	.154	.167
Chavez,Raul	L	.244	41	10	2	0	0	2	4	3	.311	.293
Bats Right	R	.263	118	31	6	0	2	13	2	20	.275	.364
Choo,Shin-Soo	L	.275	182	50	11	2	6	25	20	56	.369	.456
Bats Left	R	.312	401	125	27	4	14	61	58	95	.406	.504
Church,Ryan	L	.213	80	17	5	0	1	9	10	12	.297	.313
Bats Left	R	.290	279	81	23	0	3	31	23	46	.350	.405
Cintron,Alex	L	.000	2	0	0	0	0	0	0	0	.000	.000
Bats Both	R	.083	24	2	0	0	0	2	0	7	.154	.083
Clark,Tony	L	.211	19	4	1	0	1	2	5	6	.375	.421
Bats Both	R	.170	47	8	3	0	3	9	6	18	.259	.426
Coghlan,Chris	L	.316	133	42	9	0	2	11	12	22	.385	.429
Bats Left	R	.323	371	120	22	6	7	36	41	55	.391	.472
Colvin,Tyler	L	.000	3	0	0	0	0	0	1	2	.250	.000
Bats Left	R	.214	14	3	0	0	0	2	1	3	.250	.214
Conrad,Brooks	L	.222	9	2	0	0	1	2	1	4	.300	.556
Bats Both	R	.200	45	9	1	2	1	6	2	10	.250	.378
Cora,Alex	L	.292	65	19	3	1	0	4	5	9	.352	.369
Bats Both	R	.238	206	49	8	0	1	14	20	19	.310	.291
Corporan,Carlos	L	-	0	0	0	0	0	0	0	0	-	
Bats Both	R	1.000	1	1	0	0	0	0	0	0	1.000	1.000
Coste,Chris	L	.222	54	12	3	0	2	7	0	12	.205	.389
Bats Right	R	.228	131	30	10	0	0	11	16	43	.304	.291
Counsell,Craig	L	.237	38	9	0	2	0	8	0	0	.366	.342
Bats Left	R	.290	366	106	22	6	4	33	36	46	.358	.415
Crawford,Carl	L	.269	193	52	13	1	2	18	11	32	.325	.378
Bats Left	R	.322	413	133	15	7	13	50	40	67	.382	.487
Crede,Joe	L	.202	99	20	8	0	0	7	7	18	.250	.283
Bats Right	R	.235	234	55	8	1	15	41	22	38	.305	.470
Crisp,Coco	L	.222	72	16	5	1	1	5	10	9	.317	.361
Bats Both	R	.231	108	25	3	4	2	9	19	14	.349	.389
Crosby,Bobby	L	.265	113	30	8	1	4	18	11	15	.333	.460
Bats Right	R	.184	125	23	2	1	2	11	13	29	.261	.264
Crowe,Trevor	L	.255	47	12	2	2	0	5	3	7	.300	.383
Bats Both	R	.228	136	31	7	1	1	12	8	32	.270	.316
Cruz,Luis	L	.172	29	5	1	0	0	1	4	3	.273	.207
Bats Right	R	.244	41	10	0	0	0	1	2	4	.289	.244
Cruz,Nelson	L	.235	132	31	5	0	7	17	16	28	.320	.432
Bats Right	R	.270	330	89	16	1	26	59	33	90	.337	.561
Cuddyer,Michael	L	.307	166	51	12	0	15	33	14	29	.363	.651
Bats Right	R	.263	422	111	22	7	17	61	40	89	.333	.469
Cunningham,Aaron	L	.176	17	3	1	0	0	2	2	3	.263	.235
Bats Right	R	.139	36	5	1	0	1	6	3	13	.184	.250
Cust,Jack	L	.221	140	31	2	0	3	9	20	47	.321	.300
Bats Left	R	.247	373	92	14	0	22	61	73	138	.369	.461
Damon,Johnny	L	.269	171	46	9	0	7	26	16	38	.332	.444
Bats Left	R	.288	379	109	27	3	17	56	55	60	.380	.509
Davis,Chris	L	.189	122	23	3	0	4	15	6	49	.235	.311
Bats Left	R	.260	269	70	12	1	17	44	18	101	.307	.502
Davis,Rajai	L	.316	136	43	7	2	0	12	12	19	.376	.397
Bats Right	R	.299	254	76	20	3	3	36	17	51	.352	.437
De Aza,Alejandro	L	.000	3	0	0	0	0	0	0	1	.000	.000
Bats Left	R	.294	17	5	1	0	0	3	5	4	.435	.353
DeJesus,David	L	.290	200	58	6	2	1	20	17	35	.335	.355
Bats Left	R	.277	358	99	22	7	12	51	40	60	.354	.478
Delgado,Carlos	L	.333	18	6	1	0	1	6	2	4	.409	.556
Bats Left	R	.289	76	22	6	1	3	17	10	16	.389	.513
Dellucci,David	L	.200	5	1	0	0	0	0	0	3	.200	.200
Bats Left	R	.183	60	11	4	0	0	3	5	16	.275	.250
Denorfia,Chris	L	-	0	0	0	0	0	0	0	0	-	
Bats Right	R	.000	2	0	0	0	0	0	0	1	.000	.000
DeRosa,Mark	L	.278	126	35	7	1	10	24	10	29	.341	.587
Bats Right	R	.242	389	94	16	0	13	54	37	92	.312	.383
Desmond,Ian	L	.300	10	3	0	0	0	1	1	2	.333	.300
Bats Right	R	.278	72	20	7	2	4	11	4	12	.316	.597
DeWitt,Blake	L	.200	5	1	1	0	0	0	0	1	.200	.400
Bats Left	R	.205	44	9	2	0	2	6	3	16	.250	.386
Diaz,Matt	L	.412	136	56	11	1	6	24	11	20	.464	.640
Bats Right	R	.255	235	60	7	3	7	34	24	70	.349	.400
Diaz,Robinson	L	.237	59	14	1	0	0	5	2	4	.254	.254
Bats Right	R	.314	70	22	6	0	1	14	1	5	.351	.443
Dickerson,Chris	L	.243	37	9	2	0	0	2	5	12	.326	.297
Bats Left	R	.280	218	61	11	3	2	13	34	54	.378	.385

Batter	vs	Avg	AB	H	2B	3B	HR	RBI	BB	SO	OBP	Slg
Dillon,Joe	L	.158	19	3	0	0	1	1	2	3	.304	.316
Bats Right	R	.545	11	6	0	0	0	1	1	1	.583	.545
Dlugach,Brent	L	.000	1	0	0	0	0	0	0	0	.000	.000
Bats Right	R	.000	2	0	0	0	0	0	0	2	.000	.000
Dobbs,Greg	L	.429	7	3	0	0	0	2	0	1	.429	.429
Bats Left	R	.238	147	35	6	0	5	18	11	28	.290	.381
Doumit,Ryan	L	.266	79	21	6	0	1	7	5	15	.306	.380
Bats Both	R	.244	201	49	10	0	9	31	15	34	.297	.428
Downs,Matt	L	.100	10	1	0	0	0	0	1	2	.182	.100
Bats Right	R	.186	43	8	2	0	1	2	5	11	.265	.302
Drew,J.D.	L	.272	114	31	6	0	6	15	19	36	.381	.482
Bats Left	R	.281	338	95	24	4	18	53	63	73	.396	.536
Drew,Stephen	L	.200	140	28	4	3	3	23	8	26	.237	.336
Bats Left	R	.282	393	111	25	9	9	42	41	61	.349	.461
Duffy,Chris	L	.000	3	0	0	0	0	0	0	1	.000	.000
Bats Left	R	.138	29	4	1	0	0	3	4	11	.242	.172
Dukes,Elijah	L	.243	74	18	4	0	2	8	12	14	.349	.378
Bats Right	R	.252	290	73	16	4	6	50	34	60	.333	.397
Duncan,Chris	L	.231	65	15	3	1	1	10	6	21	.296	.354
Bats Left	R	.226	195	44	12	1	4	22	35	46	.339	.359
Duncan,Shelley	L	.250	8	2	0	0	0	0	0	3	.250	.250
Bats Right	R	.143	7	1	0	0	0	1	0	2	.143	.143
Dunn,Adam	L	.268	149	40	4	0	7	28	17	48	.351	.436
Bats Left	R	.267	397	106	25	0	31	77	99	129	.414	.564
Durango,Luis	L	.571	7	4	0	0	0	0	0	1	.571	.571
Bats Both	R	.500	4	2	0	0	0	0	2	1	.667	.500
Dye,Jermaine	L	.292	130	38	7	0	7	24	20	23	.387	.508
Bats Right	R	.236	373	88	12	1	20	57	44	85	.323	.434
Eckstein,David	L	.244	164	40	12	0	1	13	15	17	.311	.335
Bats Right	R	.268	339	91	15	2	1	37	24	29	.328	.333
Ellis,A.J.	L	.000	2	0	0	0	0	0	0	0	.000	.000
Bats Right	R	.125	8	1	0	0	0	1	0	1	.125	.125
Ellis,Mark	L	.260	100	26	5	0	3	13	7	7	.306	.400
Bats Right	R	.264	277	73	18	0	7	48	16	47	.304	.404
Ellsbury,Jacoby	L	.318	192	61	6	3	2	16	17	29	.374	.411
Bats Left	R	.294	432	127	21	7	6	44	32	45	.346	.417
Encarnacion,Edwin	L	.250	60	15	2	1	3	7	9	15	.348	.467
Bats Right	R	.219	233	51	9	1	10	32	28	52	.312	.395
Erstad,Darin	L	.154	13	2	0	0	0	0	3	0	.154	.154
Bats Left	R	.198	121	24	8	2	2	11	14	28	.279	.347
Escobar,Alcides	L	.480	25	12	1	0	0	4	1	6	.500	.520
Bats Right	R	.260	100	26	2	1	1	7	3	12	.292	.330
Escobar,Yunel	L	.232	155	36	6	0	4	19	26	20	.343	.348
Bats Right	R	.327	373	122	20	2	10	57	31	42	.392	.472
Ethier,Andre	L	.194	165	32	7	0	6	25	13	39	.283	.345
Bats Left	R	.302	431	130	35	3	25	81	59	77	.390	.571
Evans,Nick	L	.321	28	9	1	1	0	2	3	6	.387	.429
Bats Right	R	.162	37	6	4	0	1	5	1	14	.184	.351
Evans,Terry	L	1.000	1	1	0	0	0	1	0	0	1.000	1.000
Bats Right	R	.167	6	1	0	0	0	0	0	2	.167	.167
Everett,Adam	L	.273	128	35	9	0	3	24	7	27	.312	.414
Bats Right	R	.217	217	47	12	0	0	20	15	34	.274	.272
Everidge,Tommy	L	.333	24	8	3	0	1	3	2	4	.393	.583
Bats Right	R	.180	61	11	3	0	1	4	6	13	.265	.279
Feliz,Pedro	L	.208	130	27	3	1	6	19	13	15	.278	.385
Bats Right	R	.282	450	127	27	1	6	63	22	53	.317	.387
Fielder,Prince	L	.292	178	52	11	1	13	47	14	46	.359	.584
Bats Left	R	.303	413	125	24	2	33	94	96	92	.432	.610
Fields,Josh	L	.243	70	17	1	0	4	9	9	18	.346	.429
Bats Right	R	.213	169	36	4	2	3	21	16	58	.281	.314
Figgins,Chone	L	.246	203	50	8	2	0	11	24	44	.325	.305
Bats Both	R	.323	412	133	22	5	5	43	77	70	.428	.437
Fiorentino,Jeff	L	.364	22	8	0	0	0	2	2	5	.400	.364
Bats Left	R	.238	42	10	1	0	0	6	6	11	.327	.262
Flores,Jesus	L	.276	29	8	1	0	1	3	3	6	.344	.414
Bats Right	R	.313	64	20	2	2	3	12	8	20	.384	.547
Flowers,Tyler	L	.250	8	2	1	0	0	0	2	3	.400	.375
Bats Right	R	.125	8	1	0	0	0	0	1	5	.300	.125
Floyd,Cliff	L	.000	1	0	0	0	0	0	0	0	.000	.000
Bats Left	R	.133	15	2	0	0	0	0	1	7	.188	.133
Fontenot,Mike	L	.212	52	11	3	1	0	5	2	12	.246	.308
Bats Left	R	.240	325	78	19	1	9	38	33	71	.309	.388
Fowler,Dexter	L	.321	137	44	14	1	2	11	13	29	.377	.482
Bats Both	R	.240	296	71	15	9	2	23	54	87	.357	.372
Fox,Jake	L	.250	56	14	4	0	1	11	3	11	.290	.375
Bats Right	R	.263	160	42	8	0	10	33	11	36	.318	.500

Batter	vs	Avg	AB	H	2B	3B	HR	RBI	BB	SO	OBP	Slg
Francisco,Ben	L	.247	97	24	8	0	2	10	15	21	.351	.392
Bats Right	R	.260	308	80	22	1	13	36	23	62	.326	.464
Francisco,Juan	L	.333	3	1	0	0	0	0	0	1	.500	.333
Bats Left	R	.444	18	8	1	0	1	7	3	6	.524	.667
Francoeur,Jeff	L	.344	163	56	13	2	4	22	5	20	.356	.521
Bats Right	R	.256	430	110	19	2	11	54	18	72	.291	.386
Frandsen,Kevin	L	.154	13	2	0	0	0	0	2	1	.267	.154
Bats Right	R	.135	37	5	2	0	0	1	1	3	.179	.189
Freel,Ryan	L	.143	35	5	1	0	1	4	4	8	.250	.171
Bats Right	R	.226	53	12	1	0	0	4	7	15	.317	.245
Freese,David	L	.176	17	3	0	0	0	3	1	5	.211	.176
Bats Right	R	.500	14	7	2	0	1	4	1	2	.533	.857
Fukudome,Kosuke	L	.164	55	9	2	0	1	8	9	20	.277	.255
Bats Left	R	.270	444	120	36	5	10	46	84	92	.387	.441
Fuld,Sam	L	.308	26	8	2	0	1	2	4	4	.400	.500
Bats Left	R	.296	71	21	4	1	0	0	13	6	.412	.380
Furcal,Rafael	L	.296	142	42	7	0	5	19	16	12	.365	.451
Bats Both	R	.261	471	123	21	5	4	28	45	77	.326	.352
Gamel,Mat	L	.304	23	7	2	0	1	3	1	8	.333	.522
Bats Left	R	.229	105	24	4	1	4	17	17	46	.339	.400
Garciaparra,Nomar	L	.297	74	22	4	0	2	6	2	14	.316	.432
Bats Right	R	.267	86	23	4	0	1	10	6	14	.312	.349
Gardner,Brett	L	.291	55	16	2	2	0	7	7	10	.381	.400
Bats Left	R	.264	193	51	4	4	3	16	19	30	.335	.373
Garko,Ryan	L	.308	117	36	5	0	5	17	13	21	.391	.479
Bats Right	R	.249	237	59	8	1	8	34	16	29	.321	.392
Gathright,Joey	L	.200	5	1	0	0	0	0	0	0	.200	.200
Bats Left	R	.280	25	7	0	0	0	0	2	6	.333	.280
Gentry,Craig	L	.250	4	1	1	0	0	0	0	2	.250	.500
Bats Right	R	.077	13	1	0	0	0	1	2	3	.200	.077
German,Esteban	L	.389	18	7	2	0	0	3	0	1	.389	.500
Bats Right	R	.250	28	7	2	0	0	1	4	6	.344	.321
Gerut,Jody	L	.194	31	6	0	0	2	5	1	9	.219	.387
Bats Left	R	.235	243	57	13	0	7	30	18	34	.286	.374
Getz,Chris	L	.246	65	16	3	2	0	9	4	10	.296	.354
Bats Left	R	.265	310	82	15	2	2	22	26	44	.329	.345
Giambi,Jason	L	.213	89	19	6	0	7	22	12	22	.333	.517
Bats Left	R	.196	204	40	8	0	6	29	45	58	.346	.324
Giles,Brian	L	.136	81	11	2	0	0	7	8	13	.213	.160
Bats Left	R	.222	144	32	8	1	2	16	18	18	.311	.333
Gimenez,Chris	L	.143	21	3	0	0	0	1	4	6	.280	.143
Bats Right	R	.144	90	13	2	0	3	6	13	30	.250	.267
Glaus,Troy	L	.000	3	0	0	0	0	0	1	0	.250	.000
Bats Right	R	.192	26	5	2	0	0	2	2	8	.250	.269
Gload,Ross	L	.194	31	6	0	0	0	4	1	6	.219	.194
Bats Left	R	.271	199	54	10	2	6	26	22	24	.345	.432
Golson,Greg	L	-	0	0	0	0	0	0	0	0	-	-
Bats Right	R	.000	1	0	0	0	0	0	0	1	.000	.000
Gomes,Jonny	L	.307	101	31	9	0	5	19	8	27	.369	.545
Bats Right	R	.244	180	44	8	0	15	32	18	58	.320	.539
Gomez,Carlos	L	.204	108	22	4	2	2	14	9	25	.275	.333
Bats Right	R	.242	207	50	11	3	1	14	13	47	.293	.338
Gonzalez,Adrian	L	.234	218	51	9	2	10	37	32	54	.339	.431
Bats Left	R	.305	334	102	18	0	30	62	87	55	.448	.629
Gonzalez,Alberto	L	.397	63	25	6	2	1	11	4	3	.429	.603
Bats Right	R	.228	228	52	10	1	0	22	10	24	.262	.281
Gonzalez,Alex	L	.212	99	21	3	0	1	11	3	20	.243	.273
Bats Right	R	.247	292	72	19	0	7	30	17	45	.291	.384
Gonzalez,Andy .	L	.143	7	1	0	1	0	0	0	3	.143	.429
Bats Right	R	.000	5	0	0	0	0	0	0	1	.000	.000
Gonzalez,Carlos	L	.276	58	16	5	0	2	6	5	19	.343	.466
Bats Left	R	.286	220	63	9	7	11	23	23	51	.355	.541
Gonzalez,Edgar	L	.204	54	11	4	0	1	6	4	12	.259	.333
Bats Right	R	.222	99	22	4	2	3	12	7	24	.288	.394
Gordon,Alex	L	.163	49	8	1	0	3	8	5	10	.268	.367
Bats Left	R	.261	115	30	5	0	3	14	16	33	.348	.383
Gorecki,Reid	L	.400	5	2	0	0	0	0	0	2	.400	.400
Bats Right	R	.150	20	3	0	0	0	3	1	10	.182	.150
Graffanino,Tony	L	.000	7	0	0	0	0	0	0	2	.000	.000
Bats Right	R	.188	16	3	1	0	0	0	1	3	.235	.250
Granderson,Curtis	L	.183	180	33	4	0	2	9	15	42	.245	.239
Bats Left	R	.275	451	124	19	8	28	62	57	99	.358	.539
Green,Andy	L	1.000	1	1	0	0	0	0	0	0	1.000	1.000
Bats Right	R	.000	3	0	0	0	0	0	1	1	.250	.000
Green,Nick	L	.235	68	16	4	0	1	3	5	18	.297	.338
Bats Right	R	.236	208	49	14	0	5	32	15	51	.305	.375

Batters vs. Left-Handed and Right-Handed Pitchers

Batter	vs	Avg	AB	H	2B	3B	HR	RBI	BB	SO	OBP	Slg
Greene,Khalil	L	.180	61	11	3	0	2	12	6	14	.257	.328
Bats Right	R	.211	109	23	4	0	4	12	9	21	.281	.358
Greene,Tyler	L	.188	32	6	0	0	1	2	3	11	.257	.281
Bats Right	R	.237	76	18	5	0	1	5	1	21	.275	.342
Griffey Jr.,Ken	L	.213	75	16	3	0	6	13	11	20	.310	.493
Bats Left	R	.215	312	67	16	0	13	44	52	60	.327	.391
Gross,Gabe	L	.172	29	5	2	1	1	8	7	10	.333	.414
Bats Left	R	.233	253	59	14	0	5	28	35	69	.325	.348
Guerrero,Vladimir	L	.250	100	25	4	0	4	12	4	16	.276	.410
Bats Right	R	.311	283	88	12	1	11	38	15	40	.354	.477
Guillen,Carlos	L	.244	45	11	4	0	1	8	6	6	.358	.400
Bats Both	R	.241	232	56	6	3	10	33	33	50	.335	.422
Guillen,Jose	L	.181	94	17	0	0	4	9	8	25	.245	.309
Bats Right	R	.273	187	51	8	0	5	31	14	25	.348	.396
Gutierrez,Franklin	L	.335	164	55	9	0	9	26	21	26	.409	.555
Bats Right	R	.262	401	105	15	1	9	44	25	96	.309	.372
Guzman,Cristian	L	.307	127	39	7	1	2	11	3	20	.323	.425
Bats Both	R	.277	404	112	17	6	4	41	13	55	.301	.379
Guzman,Freddy	L	1.000	1	1	0	0	0	1	0	0	.500	1.000
Bats Both	R	.000	5	0	0	0	0	0	0	1	.000	.000
Guzman,Jesus	L	.231	13	3	0	0	0	0	0	2	.231	.231
Bats Right	R	.286	7	2	0	0	0	0	0	1	.286	.286
Gwynn,Tony	L	.215	107	23	0	1	0	3	7	24	.267	.234
Bats Left	R	.290	286	83	11	5	2	18	41	41	.370	.385
Hafner,Travis	L	.210	81	17	1	0	4	12	8	19	.289	.407
Bats Left	R	.292	257	75	15	0	12	37	33	40	.376	.490
Hairston,Jerry	L	.242	128	31	5	0	6	11	14	12	.319	.422
Bats Right	R	.255	255	65	18	1	4	28	18	42	.313	.380
Hairston,Scott	L	.318	129	41	12	1	5	21	13	25	.378	.543
Bats Right	R	.240	321	77	16	1	12	43	12	58	.275	.419
Hall,Bill	L	.223	130	29	6	1	3	17	8	43	.252	.354
Bats Right	R	.186	204	38	14	0	5	10	21	77	.261	.328
Hamilton,Josh	L	.327	110	36	3	1	6	26	6	19	.361	.536
Bats Left	R	.239	226	54	16	1	4	28	18	60	.293	.372
Hanigan,Ryan	L	.291	55	16	1	0	1	2	8	5	.381	.364
Bats Right	R	.255	196	50	5	1	2	9	29	26	.355	.321
Hannahan,Jack	L	.191	89	17	2	1	1	2	8	26	.265	.270
Bats Left	R	.225	178	40	12	1	3	17	22	45	.312	.354
Hardy,J.J.	L	.169	83	14	2	0	1	2	17	22	.310	.229
Bats Right	R	.245	331	81	14	2	10	45	26	63	.299	.390
Harris,Brendan	L	.302	149	45	9	0	2	11	11	26	.348	.403
Bats Right	R	.238	265	63	13	1	4	26	18	52	.289	.340
Harris,Willie	L	.121	33	4	3	0	0	1	10	7	.356	.212
Bats Left	R	.248	290	72	15	6	7	26	47	55	.365	.414
Hart,Corey	L	.248	101	25	5	0	2	6	12	25	.333	.356
Bats Right	R	.264	318	84	19	3	10	42	31	67	.336	.437
Hawpe,Brad	L	.243	144	35	10	0	6	20	20	47	.337	.438
Bats Left	R	.303	357	108	32	3	17	66	59	98	.403	.552
Hayes,Brett	L	.333	3	1	0	0	1	1	0	0	.333	1.333
Bats Right	R	.250	8	2	1	0	0	1	0	4	.333	.375
Headley,Chase	L	.244	180	44	8	0	4	25	17	32	.315	.356
Bats Both	R	.270	363	98	23	2	8	39	45	101	.354	.410
Helms,Wes	L	.273	99	27	5	0	2	15	4	25	.295	.384
Bats Right	R	.270	115	31	6	0	1	18	9	29	.336	.348
Helton,Todd	L	.311	183	57	8	0	1	28	17	32	.369	.372
Bats Left	R	.332	361	120	30	3	14	58	72	41	.437	.548
Hermida,Jeremy	L	.189	106	20	4	0	3	10	13	30	.289	.311
Bats Left	R	.282	323	91	10	2	10	37	43	71	.368	.418
Hernandez,Anderson	L	.273	88	24	5	1	1	8	10	19	.347	.386
Bats Both	R	.245	278	68	10	3	2	29	23	44	.300	.324
Hernandez,Diory	L	.087	23	2	1	0	0	1	0	6	.087	.130
Bats Right	R	.161	62	10	2	0	1	5	6	16	.235	.242
Hernandez,Luis	L	.250	24	6	0	0	0	0	2	1	.333	.250
Bats Both	R	.184	49	9	1	0	0	4	2	17	.216	.204
Hernandez,Michel	L	.200	30	6	2	0	0	7	4	3	.294	.267
Bats Right	R	.261	69	18	1	1	1	5	3	9	.292	.348
Hernandez,Ramon	L	.288	80	23	4	1	1	8	6	9	.348	.400
Bats Right	R	.246	207	51	9	0	4	29	27	25	.332	.348
Hester,John	L	.167	18	3	2	0	0	1	0	6	.167	.278
Bats Right	R	.400	10	4	0	0	1	3	2	1	.500	.700
Hill,Aaron	L	.298	171	51	12	0	11	30	9	23	.335	.561
Bats Right	R	.282	511	144	25	0	25	78	33	75	.328	.477
Hill,Koyie	L	.256	43	11	4	1	0	4	4	7	.319	.395
Bats Both	R	.233	210	49	8	1	2	20	23	71	.311	.310
Hinske,Eric	L	.244	41	10	2	0	2	6	7	14	.347	.439
Bats Left	R	.242	149	36	10	0	6	19	20	38	.349	.430

Batter	vs	Avg	AB	H	2B	3B	HR	RBI	BB	SO	OBP	Slg
Hoffmann,Jaime	L	.167	6	1	1	0	0	3	0	1	.125	.333
Bats Right	R	.188	16	3	1	0	1	4	0	4	.188	.438
Hoffpauir,Jarrett	L	.143	7	1	0	0	0	2	2	2	.333	.143
Bats Right	R	.400	5	2	2	0	0	0	2	0	.571	.800
Hoffpauir,Micah	L	.172	29	5	2	0	1	2	2	7	.226	.345
Bats Left	R	.249	205	51	10	1	9	33	18	39	.310	.439
Holliday,Matt	L	.289	152	44	8	0	3	20	29	31	.405	.401
Bats Right	R	.322	429	138	31	3	21	89	43	70	.390	.555
Holm,Steve	L	-	0	0	0	0	0	0	0	0	-	-
Bats Right	R	.286	7	2	0	0	0	0	2	0	.444	.286
Hoover,Paul	L	.750	4	3	0	0	0	1	0	1	.750	.750
Bats Right	R	-	0	0	0	0	0	0	0	0	-	-
Howard,Ryan	L	.207	222	46	13	1	6	33	25	83	.298	.356
Bats Left	R	.320	394	126	24	3	39	108	50	103	.395	.693
Hu,Chin-lung	L	-	0	0	0	0	0	1	0	0	.000	-
Bats Right	R	.400	5	2	1	0	0	1	0	2	.400	.600
Huber,Justin	L	1.000	1	1	0	0	0	0	0	0	1.000	1.000
Bats Right	R	.000	1	0	0	0	0	0	0	0	.000	.000
Hudson,Orlando	L	.293	140	41	13	3	3	19	16	23	.361	.493
Bats Both	R	.280	411	115	22	3	6	43	46	76	.356	.392
Huff,Aubrey	L	.232	177	41	8	1	4	28	15	32	.294	.356
Bats Left	R	.245	359	88	22	0	11	57	36	55	.318	.398
Hulett,Tug	L	.500	2	1	0	0	0	0	0	0	.500	.500
Bats Left	R	.063	16	1	0	0	0	1	1	6	.118	.063
Hundley,Nick	L	.159	69	11	0	0	3	9	14	20	.298	.290
Bats Right	R	.267	187	50	18	2	5	24	14	60	.319	.449
Hunter,Torii	L	.336	116	39	7	0	7	32	13	23	.400	.578
Bats Right	R	.287	335	96	19	1	15	58	34	69	.354	.484
Iannetta,Chris	L	.296	81	24	9	1	4	11	11	24	.406	.580
Bats Right	R	.202	208	42	6	1	12	41	32	51	.320	.413
Ibanez,Raul	L	.285	144	41	10	1	13	40	16	41	.359	.639
Bats Left	R	.267	356	95	22	2	21	53	40	78	.342	.517
Infante,Omar	L	.323	62	20	2	0	0	0	7	3	.375	.355
Bats Right	R	.298	141	42	7	1	2	18	12	25	.355	.404
Inge,Brandon	L	.243	140	34	8	1	9	16	21	37	.381	.493
Bats Right	R	.225	422	95	10	0	18	68	33	133	.298	.377
Inglott,Joe	L	.000	3	0	0	0	0	0	1	1	.400	.000
Bats Left	R	.291	86	25	4	1	0	6	7	20	.344	.360
Iribarren,Hernan	L	.000	2	0	0	0	0	0	0	1	.000	.000
Bats Left	R	.273	11	3	2	0	0	1	1	4	.333	.455
Ishikawa,Travis	L	.278	36	10	0	0	0	1	2	8	.316	.278
Bats Left	R	.259	290	75	10	2	9	38	28	81	.330	.400
Iwamura,Akinori	L	.386	70	27	6	1	0	12	7	17	.442	.500
Bats Left	R	.248	161	40	10	1	1	10	17	27	.319	.342
Izturis,Cesar	L	.290	131	38	5	1	2	12	4	9	.316	.389
Bats Both	R	.238	256	61	9	3	0	18	14	29	.283	.297
Izturis,Maicer	L	.380	50	19	3	0	1	6	7	5	.475	.500
Bats Both	R	.288	337	97	19	3	7	59	28	36	.341	.424
Jackson,Conor	L	.172	29	5	1	0	0	2	2	3	.226	.207
Bats Right	R	.186	70	13	3	0	1	12	9	13	.278	.271
Jacobs,Mike	L	.178	101	18	4	0	1	6	9	36	.252	.248
Bats Left	R	.243	333	81	12	1	18	55	32	96	.311	.447
Janish,Paul	L	.230	74	17	4	0	0	2	7	14	.296	.284
Bats Right	R	.203	182	37	17	0	1	14	19	26	.296	.313
Jaramillo,Jason	L	.161	31	5	2	0	1	3	1	2	.188	.323
Bats Both	R	.269	175	47	12	0	2	23	16	31	.330	.371
Jeter,Derek	L	.395	177	70	8	0	6	23	23	27	.468	.542
Bats Right	R	.311	457	142	19	1	12	43	49	63	.381	.435
Johjima,Kenji	L	.244	78	19	0	0	3	5	4	11	.280	.359
Bats Right	R	.248	161	40	11	0	6	17	8	17	.303	.429
Johnson,Chris	L	.000	7	0	0	0	0	0	1	2	.125	.000
Bats Right	R	.133	15	2	0	0	0	1	0	4	.133	.133
Johnson,Kelly	L	.325	80	26	6	2	4	13	6	17	.368	.600
Bats Left	R	.188	223	42	14	1	4	16	26	37	.281	.314
Johnson,Nick	L	.316	133	42	9	1	2	21	28	29	.440	.444
Bats Left	R	.281	324	91	15	1	6	41	71	55	.420	.389
Johnson,Reed	L	.324	68	22	7	1	1	11	7	13	.403	.500
Bats Right	R	.206	97	20	3	1	3	11	6	14	.278	.351
Johnson,Rob	L	.171	82	14	5	0	0	7	10	16	.261	.232
Bats Right	R	.233	176	41	14	2	2	20	16	44	.303	.369
Jones,Adam	L	.246	171	42	5	1	4	18	13	39	.309	.357
Bats Right	R	.295	302	89	17	2	15	52	23	54	.350	.513
Jones,Andruw	L	.218	119	26	9	0	4	15	29	24	.367	.395
Bats Right	R	.210	162	34	9	0	13	28	16	48	.287	.506
Jones,Brandon	L	1.000	1	1	0	0	0	0	0	0	1.000	1.000
Bats Left	R	.250	12	3	0	0	0	1	4	3	.438	.250

Batters vs. Left-Handed and Right-Handed Pitchers

Batter	vs	Avg	AB	H	2B	3B	HR	RBI	BB	SO	OBP	Slg
Jones,Chipper	L	.289	159	46	11	1	9	33	22	28	.372	.541
Bats Both	R	.252	329	83	12	1	9	38	79	61	.395	.377
Jones,Garrett	L	.208	101	21	7	0	6	12	5	28	.243	.455
Bats Left	R	.333	213	71	14	1	15	32	35	48	.426	.620
Jones,Mitch	L	.286	7	2	1	0	0	0	0	3	.444	.429
Bats Right	R	.333	6	2	0	0	0	0	0	3	.333	.333
Joyce,Matt	L	.250	4	1	1	0	0	2	0	1	.250	.500
Bats Left	R	.179	28	5	0	0	3	5	3	6	.273	.500
Kapler,Gabe	L	.276	145	40	14	1	8	30	26	23	.379	.552
Bats Right	R	.150	60	9	1	0	0	2	3	16	.190	.167
Kata,Matt	L	.143	7	1	0	0	0	0	0	1	.143	.143
Bats Both	R	.209	43	9	1	0	0	5	0	4	.222	.233
Kearns,Austin	L	.122	49	6	1	0	1	1	14	15	.348	.204
Bats Right	R	.224	125	28	5	2	2	16	18	36	.331	.344
Kelly,Don	L	.125	8	1	1	0	0	0	0	2	.125	.250
Bats Left	R	.271	48	13	2	1	0	3	4	8	.340	.354
Kemp,Matt	L	.362	138	50	7	2	8	25	16	17	.429	.616
Bats Right	R	.278	468	130	18	5	18	76	36	122	.329	.453
Kendall,Jason	L	.218	78	17	2	2	0	4	14	9	.340	.295
Bats Right	R	.246	374	92	17	0	2	39	32	49	.329	.307
Kendrick,Howie	L	.313	144	45	9	0	6	21	4	26	.331	.500
Bats Right	R	.278	230	64	12	3	4	40	16	45	.336	.409
Kennedy,Adam	L	.241	141	34	8	1	1	17	12	23	.303	.333
Bats Left	R	.307	388	119	21	0	10	46	33	63	.364	.438
Keppinger,Jeff	L	.314	102	32	5	1	2	9	8	6	.360	.441
Bats Right	R	.227	203	46	8	2	5	20	19	27	.301	.360
Kinsler,Ian	L	.310	158	49	10	2	13	30	15	15	.366	.646
Bats Right	R	.230	408	94	22	2	18	56	44	62	.312	.426
Konerko,Paul	L	.338	151	51	8	0	10	27	20	24	.420	.589
Bats Right	R	.253	395	100	22	1	18	61	38	65	.327	.451
Kotchman,Casey	L	.250	112	28	4	0	1	16	9	20	.312	.313
Bats Left	R	.275	273	75	19	0	6	32	30	22	.350	.410
Kotsay,Mark	L	.219	32	7	1	0	0	0	0	4	.219	.250
Bats Left	R	.290	155	45	8	0	4	23	15	17	.347	.419
Kottaras,George	L	.111	18	2	1	0	0	1	3	5	.227	.167
Bats Left	R	.267	75	20	10	0	1	9	8	20	.329	.440
Kouzmanoff,Kevin	L	.291	148	43	10	1	6	20	11	27	.342	.493
Bats Right	R	.241	381	92	21	0	12	68	16	79	.286	.391
Kubel,Jason	L	.243	148	36	9	0	2	20	10	36	.299	.345
Bats Left	R	.322	366	118	26	2	26	83	46	70	.396	.617
Laird,Gerald	L	.248	101	25	6	0	2	9	16	13	.364	.366
Bats Right	R	.218	312	68	17	2	2	24	24	55	.286	.304
Langerhans,Ryan	L	.212	33	7	2	0	2	5	4	9	.229	.455
Bats Left	R	.221	68	15	4	1	1	5	14	19	.345	.353
LaPorta,Matt	L	.211	38	8	3	0	1	3	4	7	.311	.368
Bats Right	R	.266	143	38	10	0	6	18	8	30	.307	.462
LaRoche,Adam	L	.243	173	42	13	0	6	20	10	53	.284	.422
Bats Left	R	.293	382	112	25	2	19	63	59	89	.383	.518
LaRoche,Andy	L	.285	130	37	8	2	5	12	16	21	.363	.492
Bats Right	R	.249	394	98	21	3	7	52	34	63	.320	.371
LaRue,Jason	L	.259	27	7	1	0	0	2	1	4	.310	.296
Bats Right	R	.234	77	18	2	0	2	4	2	18	.280	.338
Lee,Carlos	L	.325	126	41	5	0	6	18	12	6	.384	.508
Bats Right	R	.293	484	142	30	1	20	84	29	45	.332	.483
Lee,Derrek	L	.300	90	27	5	0	3	18	14	18	.444	.456
Bats Right	R	.308	442	136	31	2	32	99	52	91	.382	.604
Lewis,Fred	L	.164	55	9	2	0	0	1	8	19	.292	.200
Bats Left	R	.279	240	67	19	3	4	19	28	65	.362	.433
Lillibridge,Brent	L	.214	28	6	0	0	0	1	2	5	.267	.214
Bats Right	R	.134	67	9	2	0	0	2	12	21	.275	.164
Lind,Adam	L	.275	167	46	10	0	7	26	11	46	.318	.461
Bats Left	R	.317	420	133	36	0	28	88	47	64	.389	.602
Lobaton,Jose	L	-	0	0	0	0	0	0	0	0	-	-
Bats Both	R	.176	17	3	0	0	0	0	0	5	.176	.176
Loney,James	L	.274	124	34	5	0	4	25	19	24	.368	.411
Bats Left	R	.283	452	128	20	2	9	65	51	44	.354	.396
Longoria,Evan	L	.289	173	50	17	0	9	29	22	37	.365	.543
Bats Right	R	.277	411	114	27	0	24	84	50	103	.363	.518
Lopez,Felipe	L	.320	147	47	11	0	3	19	13	22	.379	.456
Bats Both	R	.306	457	140	27	3	6	38	58	78	.384	.418
Lopez,Jose	L	.286	192	55	16	0	4	24	10	20	.327	.432
Bats Right	R	.266	421	112	26	0	21	72	14	49	.292	.477
Loretta,Mark	L	.273	55	15	4	0	0	11	9	5	.364	.345
Bats Right	R	.214	126	27	4	0	0	14	11	16	.283	.246
Lowell,Mike	L	.301	143	43	8	0	7	22	13	18	.363	.503
Bats Right	R	.285	302	86	21	1	10	53	20	43	.324	.460
Lowrie,Jed	L	.211	19	4	0	0	1	1	3	5	.318	.368
Bats Both	R	.122	49	6	2	0	1	10	3	15	.167	.224
Ludwick,Ryan	L	.269	130	35	9	1	2	16	14	30	.342	.400
Bats Right	R	.264	356	94	11	0	20	81	27	76	.324	.463
Lugo,Julio	L	.278	97	27	5	1	1	6	13	20	.366	.381
Bats Right	R	.281	160	45	8	4	2	15	16	25	.343	.419
Macias,Drew	L	.222	18	4	3	0	0	3	2	3	.333	.389
Bats Left	R	.190	58	11	3	0	1	4	11	12	.319	.293
Maier,Mitch	L	.299	87	26	6	1	1	13	13	16	.413	.425
Bats Left	R	.224	254	57	9	2	2	18	30	60	.304	.299
Manzella,Tommy	L	.500	2	1	0	0	0	0	0	1	.500	.500
Bats Right	R	.000	3	0	0	0	0	0	0	3	.000	.000
Markakis,Nick	L	.262	263	69	13	1	5	35	16	43	.305	.376
Bats Left	R	.314	379	119	32	1	13	66	40	55	.376	.507
Marson,Lou	L	.111	9	1	1	0	0	0	1	5	.200	.222
Bats Right	R	.269	52	14	0	0	0	4	9	16	.371	.385
Marte,Andy	L	.167	24	4	0	0	0	3	2	8	.259	.167
Bats Right	R	.244	131	32	6	1	6	23	11	22	.299	.443
Martin,Russell	L	.275	102	28	4	0	1	6	21	19	.413	.343
Bats Right	R	.243	403	98	15	0	6	47	48	61	.335	.325
Martinez,Fernando	L	.158	19	3	0	0	0	0	0	4	.200	.158
Bats Left	R	.181	72	13	6	0	1	8	5	10	.253	.306
Martinez,Ramon	L	.300	10	3	0	0	0	1	1	0	.364	.300
Bats Right	R	.125	32	4	2	0	0	3	0	9	.121	.188
Martinez,Victor	L	.273	176	48	5	1	10	34	25	24	.365	.483
Bats Both	R	.316	412	130	28	0	13	74	50	50	.388	.478
Mathis,Jeff	L	.228	79	18	2	0	2	10	8	21	.295	.329
Bats Right	R	.203	158	32	6	0	3	18	14	52	.284	.297
Matsui,Hideki	L	.282	131	37	5	0	13	46	15	24	.358	.618
Bats Left	R	.271	325	88	16	1	15	44	49	51	.370	.465
Matsui,Kaz	L	.271	107	29	6	0	3	9	12	14	.345	.411
Bats Both	R	.244	369	90	14	2	6	37	22	71	.289	.341
Matthews Jr.,Gary	L	.221	86	19	6	1	2	18	12	15	.323	.384
Bats Both	R	.261	230	60	13	1	2	32	28	59	.341	.352
Mauer,Joe	L	.345	197	68	9	0	7	31	22	21	.413	.497
Bats Left	R	.377	326	123	21	1	21	65	54	42	.462	.641
Maxwell,Justin	L	.242	33	8	1	0	0	1	5	12	.342	.273
Bats Right	R	.250	56	14	3	1	4	8	7	20	.344	.554
Mayberry,John	L	.243	37	9	3	0	3	7	1	12	.263	.568
Bats Right	R	.150	20	3	0	0	1	1	1	11	.227	.300
Maybin,Cameron	L	.254	59	15	4	1	0	0	3	18	.290	.356
Bats Right	R	.248	117	29	8	1	4	13	14	33	.331	.436
Maysonet,Edwin	L	.313	16	5	0	0	0	0	1	4	.353	.313
Bats Right	R	.283	53	15	2	0	1	7	4	15	.328	.377
McCann,Brian	L	.225	160	36	4	0	4	22	16	23	.309	.325
Bats Left	R	.308	328	101	31	1	17	72	33	60	.368	.564
McCoy,Mike	L	.000	2	0	0	0	0	0	0	1	.000	.000
Bats Right	R	.000	3	0	0	0	0	0	0	1	.000	.000
McCutchen,Andrew	L	.310	100	31	8	1	4	14	14	13	.391	.530
Bats Right	R	.279	333	93	18	8	8	40	40	70	.357	.453
McDonald,Darnell	L	.365	52	19	4	0	1	5	4	17	.421	.500
Bats Right	R	.170	53	9	2	1	1	5	1	14	.185	.302
McDonald,John	L	.260	50	13	2	0	1	4	0	2	.255	.360
Bats Right	R	.257	101	26	5	0	3	9	1	16	.279	.396
McGehee,Casey	L	.303	89	27	8	0	2	11	15	13	.404	.461
Bats Right	R	.301	266	80	12	1	14	55	19	54	.345	.511
McLouth,Nate	L	.230	161	37	4	1	6	22	15	27	.309	.379
Bats Left	R	.269	346	93	23	1	14	48	53	72	.371	.462
Michaels,Jason	L	.268	56	15	7	0	1	4	4	13	.317	.446
Bats Right	R	.215	79	17	5	1	3	12	12	25	.326	.418
Mientkiewicz,Doug	L	.333	3	1	0	0	0	0	0	1	.333	.333
Bats Left	R	.333	15	5	1	0	0	3	1	5	.412	.400
Miles,Aaron	L	.206	34	7	4	0	0	0	1	7	.229	.324
Bats Both	R	.179	123	22	3	1	0	5	7	14	.223	.220
Millar,Kevin	L	.250	136	34	10	0	3	17	16	28	.333	.390
Bats Right	R	.191	115	22	4	0	4	12	15	21	.285	.330
Milledge,Lastings	L	.327	55	18	3	0	1	5	4	8	.383	.436
Bats Right	R	.265	189	50	8	0	3	16	9	39	.305	.354
Miller,Corky	L	.226	31	7	3	0	1	6	4	4	.333	.419
Bats Right	R	.172	64	11	1	0	0	9	7	19	.260	.188
Miranda,Juan	L	.500	2	1	0	0	0	0	0	1	.500	.500
Bats Left	R	.286	7	2	0	0	0	1	0	3	.286	.714
Moeller,Chad	L	.160	25	4	1	0	0	4	1	7	.214	.240
Bats Right	R	.297	64	19	7	1	2	6	6	9	.352	.531

Batters vs. Left-Handed and Right-Handed Pitchers

Batter	vs	Avg	AB	H	2B	3B	HR	RBI	BB	SO	OBP	Slg
Molina,Bengie	L	.277	119	33	8	1	8	22	6	21	.315	.563
Bats Right	R	.261	372	97	17	0	12	58	7	47	.275	.403
Molina,Jose	L	.220	41	9	0	0	0	2	6	10	.319	.220
Bats Right	R	.216	97	21	4	0	1	9	8	18	.280	.289
Molina,Yadier	L	.248	113	28	6	0	2	14	20	6	.363	.354
Bats Right	R	.307	368	113	17	1	4	40	30	33	.367	.391
Monroe,Craig	L	.256	43	11	1	0	2	9	5	6	.347	.419
Bats Right	R	.167	36	6	1	0	1	7	2	15	.211	.278
Montanez,Lou	L	.114	35	4	1	0	0	2	1	6	.135	.143
Bats Right	R	.234	47	11	4	0	1	4	4	10	.321	.383
Montero,Miguel	L	.329	82	27	4	0	3	15	3	13	.356	.488
Bats Left	R	.286	343	98	26	0	13	44	35	65	.354	.475
Moore,Adam	L	.300	10	3	1	0	0	1	0	2	.300	.400
Bats Right	R	.154	13	2	0	0	1	1	0	5	.214	.385
Mora,Melvin	L	.242	165	40	5	0	5	14	16	23	.326	.364
Bats Right	R	.270	285	77	15	0	3	34	18	37	.318	.354
Morales,Jose	L	.412	17	7	3	0	0	0	2	3	.474	.588
Bats Both	R	.294	102	30	3	0	0	7	12	19	.365	.324
Morales,Kendry	L	.296	135	40	13	0	4	24	5	21	.319	.481
Bats Both	R	.309	431	133	30	2	30	84	41	96	.366	.596
Morgan,Nyjer	L	.175	103	18	2	0	1	12	14	30	.283	.223
Bats Left	R	.344	366	126	13	7	2	27	26	44	.395	.434
Morneau,Justin	L	.277	206	57	14	1	10	44	19	35	.336	.500
Bats Left	R	.272	302	82	17	0	20	56	63	61	.379	.526
Morse,Mike	L	.060	19	2	1	0	0	0	0	5	.250	.333
Bats Right	R	.250	40	10	2	0	3	10	3	11	.302	.525
Moss,Brandon	L	.232	56	13	3	0	1	7	5	10	.306	.339
Bats Left	R	.237	329	78	17	4	6	34	29	74	.304	.368
Munson,Eric	L	.000	1	0	0	0	0	0	0	0	.000	.000
Bats Left	R	-	0	0	0	0	0	0	0	0	-	-
Murphy,Daniel	L	.223	94	21	6	0	4	14	6	19	.207	.415
Bats Right	R	.275	414	114	32	4	8	40	32	50	.324	.430
Murphy,David	L	.235	102	24	3	0	3	14	7	33	.274	.353
Bats Left	R	.279	330	92	21	1	14	43	42	73	.357	.476
Murton,Matt	L	.233	30	7	3	0	1	3	1	9	.258	.433
Bats Right	R	.273	22	6	2	0	0	3	3	5	.360	.364
Nady,Xavier	L	.333	6	2	1	0	0	0	0	0	.333	.500
Bats Right	R	.273	22	6	3	0	0	2	1	6	.304	.409
Napoli,Mike	L	.330	94	31	8	0	6	15	12	25	.417	.606
Bats Right	R	.253	288	73	14	1	14	41	28	78	.327	.455
Navarro,Dioner	L	.279	140	39	7	0	5	19	4	13	.304	.436
Bats Both	R	.182	236	43	8	0	3	13	14	38	.236	.254
Nelson,Brad	L	.000	3	0	0	0	0	0	1	1	.250	.000
Bats Left	R	.000	18	0	0	0	0	0	1	8	.053	.000
Nieves,Wil	L	.186	43	8	2	0	0	4	4	9	.250	.233
Bats Right	R	.276	181	50	4	0	1	22	13	30	.320	.315
Nix,Jayson	L	.256	121	31	5	0	8	14	12	24	.326	.496
Bats Right	R	.194	134	26	6	0	4	18	16	40	.292	.328
Nix,Laynce	L	.156	32	5	3	0	0	3	2	12	.206	.250
Bats Left	R	.249	277	69	23	1	15	43	20	69	.300	.502
Norton,Greg	L	.286	14	4	1	0	0	3	4	4	.444	.357
Bats Both	R	.113	62	7	1	0	0	4	16	16	.304	.129
Oeltjen,Trent	L	.158	19	3	1	0	0	0	6	1	.158	.211
Bats Left	R	.275	51	14	3	1	3	4	1	7	.283	.549
Ojeda,Augie	L	.203	74	15	5	1	0	8	14	7	.337	.297
Bats Right	R	.263	190	50	12	2	1	8	18	21	.341	.363
Olivo,Miguel	L	.265	151	40	4	2	7	23	7	45	.297	.457
Bats Right	R	.238	239	57	11	3	16	42	12	81	.288	.510
Ordonez,Magglio	L	.352	145	51	10	0	5	20	15	21	.413	.524
Bats Right	R	.291	320	93	14	2	4	30	36	44	.360	.384
Orr,Pete	L	.143	7	1	0	0	0	0	0	3	.143	.143
Bats Left	R	.265	68	18	2	1	1	10	3	12	.284	.368
Ortiz,David	L	.212	165	35	16	0	6	29	19	44	.298	.418
Bats Left	R	.250	376	94	19	1	22	70	55	90	.346	.481
Overbay,Lyle	L	.190	79	15	4	0	1	8	7	20	.256	.278
Bats Left	R	.282	344	97	31	1	15	56	67	75	.396	.509
Owens,Jerry	L	.500	2	1	0	0	0	0	1	0	.667	.500
Bats Left	R	.000	10	0	0	0	0	0	2	3	.167	.000
Padilla,Jorge	L	.400	5	2	0	0	0	0	0	2	.400	.400
Bats Right	R	.050	20	1	0	0	0	0	1	6	.095	.050
Pagan,Angel	L	.280	93	26	7	0	4	9	6	8	.323	.484
Bats Both	R	.316	250	79	15	11	2	23	19	48	.360	.488
Pagnozzi,Matt	L	.000	2	0	0	0	0	0	0	0	.000	.000
Bats Right	R	.000	1	0	0	0	0	0	1	0	.500	.000
Parra,Gerardo	L	.220	100	22	0	0	0	8	3	22	.250	.220
Bats Left	R	.310	355	110	21	8	5	52	22	67	.345	.456
Patterson,Corey	L	.000	2	0	0	0	0	0	0	2	.000	.000
Bats Left	R	.111	27	3	0	0	0	0	0	6	.111	.111
Patterson,Eric	L	.375	16	6	0	0	0	1	3	4	.474	.375
Bats Left	R	.269	78	21	5	1	1	10	11	21	.352	.397
Paul,Xavier	L	.200	5	1	0	0	0	0	0	2	.200	.200
Bats Left	R	.222	9	2	1	0	1	1	2	2	.364	.667
Paulino,Ronny	L	.290	131	38	5	1	5	15	11	25	.343	.458
Bats Right	R	.250	108	27	5	0	3	12	14	23	.336	.380
Pearce,Steve	L	.268	56	15	8	0	2	9	7	15	.349	.518
Bats Right	R	.174	109	19	5	1	2	7	14	28	.268	.294
Pedroia,Dustin	L	.277	173	48	15	0	2	19	25	14	.366	.399
Bats Right	R	.302	453	137	33	1	13	53	49	31	.373	.466
Pena,Brayan	L	.258	62	16	3	0	1	6	5	9	.313	.355
Bats Both	R	.282	103	29	7	0	5	12	7	9	.321	.495
Pena,Carlos	L	.211	166	35	7	1	12	31	25	56	.332	.402
Bats Left	R	.236	305	72	18	1	27	69	62	107	.369	.567
Pena,Ramiro	L	.120	25	3	0	0	0	1	1	7	.154	.120
Bats Both	R	.333	90	30	6	1	1	9	4	13	.362	.456
Pence,Hunter	L	.294	119	35	8	2	6	16	10	17	.349	.546
Bats Right	R	.279	466	130	18	3	19	56	48	92	.346	.453
Pennington,Cliff	L	.200	55	11	2	0	1	3	3	14	.241	.291
Bats Both	R	.307	153	47	9	3	3	18	16	32	.376	.464
Peralta,Jhonny	L	.235	153	36	10	0	3	16	15	39	.302	.359
Bats Right	R	.261	429	112	25	1	8	67	38	95	.321	.380
Perez,Fernando	L	.154	13	2	0	0	0	1	0	4	.154	.154
Bats Right	R	.238	21	5	0	0	0	1	0	7	.238	.238
Petit,Gregorio	L	.308	13	4	0	0	0	0	0	2	.308	.308
Bats Right	R	.167	18	3	1	0	0	1	0	4	.167	.222
Pettit,Chris	L	.000	2	0	0	0	0	0	0	0	.000	.000
Bats Right	R	.400	5	2	0	0	0	0	0	1	.400	.400
Phillips,Brandon	L	.301	146	44	6	1	9	26	10	17	.342	.541
Bats Right	R	.267	438	117	24	4	11	72	34	58	.324	.416
Phillips,Kyle	L	.000	3	0	0	0	0	0	0	2	.000	.000
Bats Left	R	.333	15	5	3	0	0	2	0	2	.333	.533
Phillips,Paul	L	.125	8	1	0	0	0	0	2	1	.300	.125
Bats Right	R	.351	37	13	2	0	1	9	5	2	.419	.486
Pie,Felix	L	.250	40	10	1	0	1	4	2	12	.273	.350
Bats Left	R	.269	212	57	9	3	8	25	22	46	.336	.453
Pierre,Juan	L	.320	100	32	2	3	0	10	8	7	.414	.400
Bats Left	R	.304	280	85	14	5	0	21	19	20	.347	.389
Pierzynski,A.J.	L	.277	130	36	3	0	4	8	2	18	.288	.392
Bats Left	R	.307	374	115	19	1	9	41	22	34	.345	.436
Podsednik,Scott	L	.320	150	48	7	0	0	10	9	14	.356	.347
Bats Left	R	.297	387	115	18	6	7	38	30	60	.352	.429
Polanco,Placido	L	.266	173	46	15	1	4	17	10	10	.304	.434
Bats Right	R	.292	445	130	16	3	6	55	26	36	.341	.382
Posada,Jorge	L	.290	124	36	8	0	5	24	13	42	.360	.476
Bats Both	R	.282	259	73	17	0	17	57	35	59	.365	.544
Posey,Buster	L	.000	5	0	0	0	0	0	0	1	.000	.000
Bats Right	R	.167	12	2	0	0	0	0	0	3	.167	.167
Powell,Landon	L	.128	39	5	1	0	1	4	5	14	.227	.231
Bats Both	R	.267	101	27	6	0	6	26	9	22	.324	.505
Prado,Martin	L	.301	143	43	15	0	6	17	22	15	.392	.531
Bats Right	R	.309	307	95	23	0	5	32	14	44	.340	.433
Pridie,Jason	L	-	0	0	0	0	0	0	0	0	-	-
Bats Left	R	-	0	0	0	0	0	0	0	0	-	-
Pujols,Albert	L	.338	148	50	14	0	13	26	36	13	.465	.696
Bats Right	R	.324	420	136	31	1	34	109	79	51	.435	.645
Punto,Nick	L	.236	106	25	5	0	1	11	15	17	.331	.311
Bats Both	R	.225	253	57	10	1	0	27	46	53	.340	.273
Quentin,Carlos	L	.213	94	20	1	0	5	14	14	14	.333	.383
Bats Right	R	.245	257	63	13	0	16	42	17	38	.319	.482
Quinlan,Robb	L	.257	74	19	2	0	2	13	3	20	.286	.365
Bats Right	R	.220	41	9	3	0	0	1	2	16	.256	.293
Quintanilla,Omar	L	.083	12	1	0	0	0	0	2	7	.214	.083
Bats Left	R	.196	46	9	2	0	0	2	6	20	.288	.239
Quintero,Humberto	L	.273	33	9	3	0	2	4	0	10	.294	.545
Bats Right	R	.226	124	28	5	1	2	10	7	31	.284	.331
Quiroz,Guillermo	L	1.000	1	1	0	0	0	0	0	0	1.000	1.000
Bats Right	R	.231	13	3	0	0	0	2	0	3	.231	.231
Raburn,Ryan	L	.278	133	37	6	0	12	29	21	31	.382	.594
Bats Right	R	.305	128	39	5	2	4	16	5	29	.331	.469
Ramirez,Alexei	L	.370	127	47	4	0	5	14	16	10	.441	.520
Bats Right	R	.248	415	103	10	1	10	54	33	56	.300	.349
Ramirez,Aramis	L	.350	40	14	2	0	3	10	8	7	.458	.625
Bats Right	R	.312	266	83	12	1	12	55	20	36	.378	.500

Batters vs. Left-Handed and Right-Handed Pitchers

Batter	vs	Avg	AB	H	2B	3B	HR	RBI	BB	SO	OBP	Slg
Ramirez,Hanley	L	.316	158	50	13	0	1	22	13	25	.376	.418
Bats Right	R	.352	418	147	29	1	23	84	48	76	.423	.591
Ramirez,Manny	L	.270	74	20	6	0	4	9	12	14	.379	.514
Bats Right	R	.295	278	82	18	2	15	54	59	67	.427	.536
Ramirez,Wilkin	L	.333	9	3	0	1	1	2	1	3	.364	.889
Bats Right	R	.500	2	1	0	0	0	1	0	0	.500	.500
Ransom,Cody	L	.158	38	6	3	0	0	3	3	14	.220	.237
Bats Right	R	.220	41	9	6	1	0	7	4	11	.289	.415
Rasmus,Colby	L	.160	106	17	1	0	3	10	6	27	.219	.255
Bats Left	R	.277	368	102	21	2	13	42	30	68	.332	.451
Reddick,Josh	L	.200	5	1	1	0	0	0	1	2	.333	.400
Bats Left	R	.167	54	9	3	0	2	4	1	15	.196	.333
Redmond,Mike	L	.320	50	16	3	0	0	5	5	2	.382	.380
Bats Right	R	.188	85	16	2	1	0	2	6	17	.250	.235
Reed,Jeremy	L	.400	10	4	0	0	0	1	1	2	.455	.400
Bats Left	R	.232	151	35	6	2	0	8	13	34	.291	.298
Reimold,Nolan	L	.271	129	35	8	1	4	11	21	25	.373	.442
Bats Right	R	.284	229	65	10	1	11	34	26	52	.360	.480
Renteria,Edgar	L	.231	117	27	7	0	2	7	10	19	.287	.342
Bats Right	R	.257	343	88	12	1	3	41	29	50	.314	.324
Repko,Jason	L	.000	1	0	0	0	0	0	0	1	.000	.000
Bats Right	R	.000	4	0	0	0	0	1	0	1	.167	.000
Reyes,Argenis	L	.000	3	0	0	0	0	0	0	2	.000	.000
Bats Both	R	.143	14	2	0	0	0	0	1	2	.200	.143
Reyes,Jose	L	.400	30	12	3	0	1	6	5	4	.486	.600
Bats Both	R	.248	117	29	4	2	1	9	13	15	.321	.342
Reynolds,Mark	L	.235	119	28	6	0	8	18	34	46	.406	.487
Bats Right	R	.266	459	122	24	1	36	84	42	177	.331	.558
Richar,Danny	L	-	0	0	0	0	0	0	0	0	-	-
Bats Left	R	.250	8	2	0	0	0	0	1	1	.333	.250
Richard,Chris	L	.000	4	0	0	0	0	0	0	3	.000	.000
Bats Left	R	.133	15	2	0	0	0	0	4	4	.316	.133
Richardson,Kevin	L	.000	2	0	0	0	0	0	0	2	.000	.000
Bats Right	R	.750	4	3	0	0	0	0	0	0	.750	.750
Riggans,Shawn	L	.000	3	0	0	0	0	0	0	1	.000	.000
Bats Right	R	.182	11	2	0	0	1	1	0	2	.182	.455
Rios,Alex	L	.261	161	42	5	0	7	23	11	31	.301	.422
Bats Right	R	.242	421	102	26	2	10	48	26	76	.294	.385
Rivera,Juan	L	.333	141	47	8	0	12	26	13	7	.385	.645
Bats Right	R	.271	388	105	16	1	13	62	23	50	.313	.418
Rivera,Mike	L	.267	30	8	2	0	0	1	4	7	.371	.333
Bats Right	R	.214	84	18	5	0	2	13	11	25	.309	.345
Roberts,Brian	L	.294	211	62	19	1	1	20	29	29	.373	.408
Bats Both	R	.278	421	117	37	0	15	59	45	83	.347	.473
Roberts,Ryan	L	.325	117	38	9	1	5	12	16	17	.406	.547
Bats Right	R	.250	188	47	8	1	2	13	24	38	.343	.335
Robinson,Shane	L	.143	7	1	0	0	0	0	0	0	.143	.143
Bats Right	R	.278	18	5	1	0	0	1	0	2	.263	.333
Rodriguez,Alex	L	.277	119	33	7	0	8	21	25	30	.401	.538
Bats Right	R	.289	325	94	10	1	22	79	55	67	.402	.529
Rodriguez,Guillermo	L	.000	1	0	0	0	0	0	0	0	.000	.000
Bats Right	R	.000	4	0	0	0	0	1	2	1	.333	.000
Rodriguez,Ivan	L	.283	92	26	6	0	4	10	3	19	.305	.478
Bats Right	R	.240	333	80	17	2	6	37	15	73	.273	.357
Rodriguez,Luis	L	.294	51	15	1	0	1	4	7	1	.373	.373
Bats Both	R	.172	157	27	5	0	1	12	30	22	.302	.223
Rodriguez,Sean	L	.091	11	1	0	0	1	3	3	4	.267	.364
Bats Right	R	.286	14	4	0	0	1	1	0	3	.286	.500
Rohlinger,Ryan	L	.000	8	0	0	0	0	0	1	2	.111	.000
Bats Right	R	.273	11	3	1	0	0	4	0	4	.273	.364
Rolen,Scott	L	.374	115	43	14	1	3	11	17	16	.459	.591
Bats Right	R	.283	360	102	22	0	8	56	28	46	.338	.411
Rollins,Jimmy	L	.230	174	40	11	1	7	22	9	13	.266	.425
Bats Both	R	.257	498	128	32	4	14	55	35	57	.306	.422
Romero,Alex	L	.192	26	5	0	1	0	1	1	6	.222	.269
Bats Left	R	.261	119	31	6	1	1	17	10	17	.323	.353
Romero,Niuman	L	.000	4	0	0	0	0	0	0	3	.000	.000
Bats Both	R	.200	10	2	0	0	0	0	1	2	.273	.200
Rosales,Adam	L	.255	55	14	5	1	0	5	5	11	.311	.382
Bats Right	R	.200	175	35	5	0	4	14	21	35	.300	.297
Ross,Cody	L	.284	134	38	11	0	11	28	12	22	.347	.612
Bats Right	R	.266	425	113	26	1	13	62	22	100	.313	.424
Ross,David	L	.250	40	10	2	0	0	2	6	14	.348	.300
Bats Right	R	.284	88	25	7	0	7	18	15	25	.394	.602
Rowand,Aaron	L	.213	122	26	5	1	4	14	9	24	.267	.369
Bats Right	R	.276	377	104	25	1	11	50	21	101	.335	.435

Batter	vs	Avg	AB	H	2B	3B	HR	RBI	BB	SO	OBP	Slg
Ruiz,Carlos	L	.293	82	24	7	0	4	17	10	11	.370	.524
Bats Right	R	.242	240	58	19	1	5	26	37	28	.350	.392
Ruiz,Randy	L	.286	28	8	2	0	1	1	2	6	.333	.464
Bats Right	R	.322	87	28	5	0	9	16	8	29	.400	.690
Ryal,Rusty	L	.273	44	12	5	2	2	7	3	14	.347	.614
Bats Right	R	.267	15	4	1	0	1	2	3	7	.368	.533
Ryan,Brendan	L	.265	132	35	7	1	0	6	12	22	.331	.333
Bats Right	R	.306	258	79	12	6	3	31	12	34	.345	.434
Ryan,Dusty	L	.083	12	1	0	0	0	0	3	5	.267	.083
Bats Right	R	.214	14	3	1	0	0	4	1	7	.267	.286
Salazar,Jeff	L	.000	4	0	0	0	0	0	0	1	.000	.000
Bats Left	R	.053	19	1	0	0	0	1	3	6	.182	.053
Salazar,Oscar	L	.357	56	20	4	1	2	11	6	4	.419	.571
Bats Right	R	.265	83	22	4	1	3	14	8	16	.326	.446
Saltalamacchia,J.	L	.229	96	22	2	0	4	12	7	27	.282	.375
Bats Both	R	.235	187	44	10	0	5	22	15	70	.294	.369
Sammons,Clint	L	.250	4	1	0	0	0	0	0	0	.250	.250
Bats Right	R	.143	7	1	0	0	0	0	1	3	.250	.143
Sanchez,Freddy	L	.323	127	41	6	1	3	16	6	22	.351	.457
Bats Right	R	.282	330	93	23	2	4	25	16	54	.316	.400
Sanchez,Gaby	L	.333	6	2	0	0	1	1	0	0	.333	.833
Bats Right	R	.200	15	3	0	0	1	2	2	3	.294	.400
Sandoval,Freddy	L	.333	3	1	0	0	0	0	0	2	.333	.333
Bats Both	R	.125	8	1	1	0	0	0	0	1	.125	.250
Sandoval,Pablo	L	.379	145	55	14	0	6	25	12	15	.428	.600
Bats Both	R	.314	427	134	30	5	19	65	40	68	.373	.541
Santiago,Ramon	L	.270	37	10	0	0	1	5	0	8	.270	.351
Bats Both	R	.267	225	60	6	2	6	30	17	49	.325	.391
Santos,Omir	L	.218	101	22	3	0	4	14	5	17	.250	.366
Bats Right	R	.283	180	51	11	1	3	26	10	27	.321	.406
Sardinha,Dane	L	.077	13	1	1	0	0	1	0	6	.071	.154
Bats Right	R	.111	18	2	0	0	0	2	0	10	.105	.111
Saunders,Michael	L	.200	55	11	0	1	0	1	0	24	.200	.236
Bats Left	R	.239	67	16	1	2	0	3	6	16	.301	.313
Scales,Bobby	L	.208	24	5	0	0	2	3	1	2	.231	.458
Bats Both	R	.250	100	25	8	2	1	12	10	30	.330	.400
Schafer,Jordan	L	.212	52	11	2	0	1	4	8	19	.311	.308
Bats Left	R	.200	115	23	6	0	1	4	19	44	.313	.278
Schierholtz,Nate	L	.370	54	20	5	0	3	12	3	12	.397	.630
Bats Left	R	.242	231	56	14	2	2	17	13	46	.280	.346
Schneider,Brian	L	.000	9	0	0	0	0	0	0	1	.100	.000
Bats Left	R	.230	161	37	11	0	3	24	18	20	.302	.354
Schumaker,Skip	L	.220	100	22	2	0	0	2	8	19	.278	.240
Bats Left	R	.322	432	139	32	1	4	33	44	50	.384	.428
Scott,Luke	L	.260	146	38	8	0	10	27	12	41	.316	.521
Bats Left	R	.257	303	78	18	1	15	50	43	63	.351	.472
Scutaro,Marco	L	.269	145	39	10	0	4	15	28	15	.389	.421
Bats Right	R	.287	429	123	25	1	8	45	62	60	.376	.406
Sheffield,Gary	L	.294	85	25	3	1	3	10	11	11	.375	.459
Bats Right	R	.268	183	49	10	1	7	33	29	35	.370	.448
Shelton,Chris	L	.313	16	5	2	0	0	4	2	5	.389	.438
Bats Right	R	.100	10	1	0	0	0	0	0	6	.100	.100
Shoppach,Kelly	L	.304	56	17	3	0	5	18	8	23	.420	.625
Bats Right	R	.191	215	41	11	0	7	22	25	75	.313	.340
Sizemore,Grady	L	.216	134	29	5	1	6	19	18	24	.309	.403
Bats Left	R	.262	302	79	15	5	12	45	42	68	.358	.464
Smith,Jason	L	.000	2	0	0	0	0	0	0	0	.000	.000
Bats Left	R	.000	23	0	0	0	0	1	0	9	.000	.000
Smith,Seth	L	.259	58	15	3	1	3	10	10	16	.368	.500
Bats Left	R	.300	277	83	17	3	12	45	36	51	.381	.513
Snider,Travis	L	.225	40	9	2	0	0	4	5	20	.333	.275
Bats Left	R	.244	201	49	12	1	9	25	24	58	.327	.448
Snyder,Chris	L	.161	56	9	1	0	3	4	19	19	.373	.339
Bats Right	R	.220	109	24	6	0	3	18	13	28	.310	.358
Soriano,Alfonso	L	.184	98	18	4	0	2	8	14	30	.283	.286
Bats Right	R	.256	379	97	21	1	18	47	26	88	.308	.459
Soto,Geovany	L	.205	73	15	2	0	4	11	18	14	.370	.397
Bats Right	R	.221	258	57	17	1	7	36	32	63	.306	.376
Span,Denard	L	.330	182	60	5	6	3	22	21	34	.405	.473
Bats Left	R	.303	396	120	11	4	5	46	49	55	.385	.389
Spilborghs,Ryan	L	.230	148	34	12	2	5	22	18	24	.317	.439
Bats Right	R	.250	204	51	12	1	3	26	16	55	.305	.363
Stairs,Matt	L	.000	3	0	0	0	0	0	1	0	.250	.000
Bats Left	R	.200	100	20	4	0	5	17	22	30	.360	.390
Stansberry,Craig	L	.000	1	0	0	0	0	0	0	0	.000	.000
Bats Right	R	-	0	0	0	0	0	0	0	0	-	-

Batter	vs	Avg	AB	H	2B	3B	HR	RBI	BB	SO	OBP	Slg
Stavinoha,Nick	L	.262	42	11	4	0	1	9	2	8	.289	.429
Bats Right	R	.200	45	9	3	0	1	8	0	7	.196	.333
Stewart,Ian	L	.178	101	18	6	0	5	11	12	37	.278	.386
Bats Left	R	.244	324	79	13	3	20	59	44	101	.335	.488
Stubbs,Drew	L	.286	42	12	3	0	2	5	3	10	.333	.500
Bats Right	R	.261	138	36	2	1	6	12	12	39	.320	.420
Sullivan,Cory	L	.167	18	3	0	0	0	1	2	5	.250	.167
Bats Right	R	.263	118	31	2	5	2	14	17	17	.350	.415
Sutton,Drew	L	.167	6	1	1	0	0	1	1	0	.286	.333
Bats Both	R	.217	60	13	3	1	1	8	6	20	.299	.350
Suzuki,Ichiro	L	.339	224	76	15	1	3	17	11	26	.374	.455
Bats Left	R	.359	415	149	16	3	8	29	21	45	.393	.470
Suzuki,Kurt	L	.250	156	39	9	0	6	25	12	15	.304	.423
Bats Right	R	.283	414	117	28	1	9	63	16	44	.317	.420
Sweeney,Mike	L	.235	136	32	8	0	7	20	12	21	.303	.449
Bats Right	R	.340	106	36	7	0	1	14	5	10	.377	.434
Sweeney,Ryan	L	.268	112	30	9	0	1	7	12	21	.344	.375
Bats Left	R	.301	372	112	22	3	5	46	28	46	.349	.417
Swisher,Nick	L	.244	160	39	8	1	9	30	41	34	.393	.475
Bats Both	R	.251	338	85	27	0	20	52	56	92	.359	.509
Taguchi,So	L	.222	9	2	1	0	0	0	1	3	.300	.333
Bats Right	R	.500	2	1	0	0	0	0	0	1	.500	.500
Talis,Fernando	L	.278	133	37	9	3	3	19	15	25	.364	.459
Bats Right	R	.285	207	59	12	1	5	29	7	29	.321	.425
Tatum,Craig	L	.000	6	0	0	0	0	0	0	0	.167	.000
Bats Right	R	.175	63	11	1	0	1	6	7	10	.257	.238
Tavoras,Willy	L	.219	105	23	4	0	0	3	4	21	.245	.257
Bats Right	R	.247	299	74	7	2	1	12	14	37	.285	.294
Teagarden,Taylor	L	.288	52	15	4	0	3	5	2	16	.309	.538
Bats Right	R	.192	140	28	0	0	3	19	12	60	.256	.315
Teahen,Mark	L	.287	188	54	15	0	3	20	0	45	.328	.415
Bats Left	R	.262	336	88	19	1	9	30	29	78	.323	.405
Teixeira,Mark	L	.305	174	53	9	0	9	31	25	26	.400	.511
Bats Both	R	.287	435	125	34	3	30	91	66	88	.376	.586
Tejada,Miguel	L	.326	141	46	13	0	3	19	6	3	.349	.482
Bats Right	R	.310	494	153	33	1	11	67	13	45	.338	.447
Thames,Marcus	L	.257	105	27	7	1	4	14	10	26	.347	.467
Bats Right	R	.248	153	38	4	0	9	22	13	46	.306	.451
Theriot,Ryan	L	.306	121	37	8	1	2	13	9	11	.361	.438
Bats Right	R	.279	481	134	12	4	5	41	42	82	.339	.351
Thole,Josh	L	.200	10	2	2	0	0	0	0	2	.200	.400
Bats Left	R	.349	43	15	0	1	0	9	4	3	.388	.395
Thomas,Clete	L	.245	49	12	4	0	0	7	6	15	.327	.327
Bats Left	R	.239	226	54	9	3	7	32	27	62	.323	.398
Thome,Jim	L	.209	91	19	5	0	5	22	14	32	.314	.429
Bats Left	R	.262	271	71	10	0	18	55	55	91	.383	.498
Thurston,Joe	L	.196	46	9	5	1	0	4	10		.327	.348
Bats Left	R	.231	221	51	12	3	1	21	25	46	.313	.326
Tolbert,Matt	L	.321	53	17	3	1	2	8	4	7	.362	.528
Bats Both	R	.200	145	29	4	0	0	11	17	30	.282	.228
Toregas,Wyatt	L	.333	12	4	0	0	0	1	0	3	.333	.333
Bats Right	R	.128	39	5	1	0	0	5	6	9	.250	.154
Torrealba,Yorvit	L	.220	59	13	3	0	1	5	6	9	.288	.322
Bats Right	R	.318	154	49	8	1	1	26	15	33	.376	.403
Torres,Andres	L	.338	71	24	3	6	4	14	7	17	.397	.718
Bats Both	R	.210	81	17	3	2	2	9	9	28	.297	.370
Towles,J.R.	L	.286	14	4	2	0	0	0	2	2	.375	.429
Bats Right	R	.147	34	5	0	0	2	3	1	14	.194	.324
Tracy,Andy	L	.000	1	0	0	0	0	0	0	1	.000	.000
Bats Left	R	.455	11	5	0	1	0	1	0	2	.455	.636
Tracy,Chad	L	.146	48	7	1	0	2	7	5	6	.222	.292
Bats Left	R	.258	209	54	14	0	6	32	21	32	.325	.411
Treanor,Matt	L	.000	4	0	0	0	0	0	0	3	.000	.000
Bats Right	R	.000	9	0	0	0	0	0	1	1	.100	.000
Tuiasosopo,Matt	L	.278	18	5	1	0	1	2	1	3	.300	.500
Bats Right	R	.000	0	0	0	0	0	0	1	2	.200	.000
Tulowitzki,Troy	L	.269	156	42	7	1	10	28	28	33	.382	.519
Bats Right	R	.307	387	119	18	8	22	64	45	79	.376	.566
Turner,Justin	L	.429	7	3	0	0	0	3	1	1	.500	.429
Bats Right	R	.000	11	0	0	0	0	0	3	2	.214	.000
Uggla,Dan	L	.208	130	27	3	1	7	18	23	30	.344	.408
Bats Right	R	.253	434	110	24	0	24	72	69	120	.357	.475
Upton,B.J.	L	.190	163	31	8	1	1	11	25	46	.302	.270
Bats Right	R	.262	397	104	25	3	10	44	32	106	.318	.416
Upton,Justin	L	.377	122	46	7	2	12	30	15	24	.445	.762
Bats Right	R	.277	404	112	23	5	14	56	40	113	.342	.463

Batter	vs	Avg	AB	H	2B	3B	HR	RBI	BB	SO	OBP	Slg
Uribe,Juan	L	.255	94	24	3	1	4	9	9	21	.324	.436
Bats Right	R	.299	304	91	23	3	12	46	16	61	.330	.513
Utley,Chase	L	.288	191	55	14	1	11	33	35	37	.417	.545
Bats Left	R	.279	380	106	14	3	20	60	53	73	.387	.489
Valbuena,Luis	L	.205	39	8	3	0	2	7	1	11	.225	.436
Bats Left	R	.255	329	84	22	3	8	24	25	72	.306	.413
Valdez,Wilson	L	.115	26	3	0	1	0	3	2	1	.207	.192
Bats Right	R	.317	60	19	3	1	0	4	6	9	.379	.400
Van Every,Jonathan	L	.000	1	0	0	0	0	0	0	0	.000	.000
Bats Left	R	.400	10	4	0	0	1	3	2	5	.500	.700
Varitek,Jason	L	.231	104	24	7	0	6	18	16	20	.336	.471
Bats Both	R	.200	260	52	17	0	8	33	38	70	.304	.358
Vazquez,Ramon	L	.290	31	9	0	0	0	1	7	10	.436	.290
Bats Left	R	.220	173	38	7	0	1	15	24	37	.315	.277
Velazquez,Gil	L	-	0	0	0	0	0	0	0	0		
Bats Right	R	.000	2	0	0	0	0	0	0		.333	.000
Velez,Eugenio	L	.200	65	13	3	0	0	2	4	16	.257	.246
Bats Both	R	.286	220	63	10	5	5	29	12	39	.323	.445
Venable,Will	L	.225	71	16	1	0		6	5	22	.295	.239
Bats Left	R	.266	222	59	13	2	12	32	20	67	.332	.505
Victorino,Shane	L	.314	172	54	13	3	2	12	20	20	.385	.459
Bats Both	R	.283	448	127	26	10	8	50	40	51	.347	.440
Vizquel,Omar	L	.485	33	16	1	0	0	3	2	3	.514	.515
Bats Both	R	.215	144	31	6	2	1	11	11	24	.271	.306
Votto,Joey	L	.320	143	47	8	0	7	27	15	37	.400	.631
Bats Left	R	.315	528	181	28	1	19	57	55	89	.419	.583
Walker,Neil	L	.143	7	1	0	0	0	0	0	3	.143	.143
Bats Both	R	.207	29	6	1	0	0	0	4	8	.303	.241
Weeks,Rickie	L	.276	29	8	0	0	2	2	1	7	.300	.483
Bats Right	R	.271	118	32	5	2	7	22	11	32	.348	.525
Wells,Vernon	L	.206	155	32	5	2	3	9	10	21	.270	.323
Bats Right	R	.278	475	132	32	1	12	57	32	65	.322	.425
Werth,Jayson	L	.302	149	45	9	0	14	37	37	33	.436	.644
Bats Right	R	.256	422	108	17	1	22	62	54	123	.348	.457
Whitesell,Josh	L	.208	24	5	0	0	0	2	5	7	.345	.208
Bats Left	R	.190	84	16	7	0	1	12	19	22	.346	.310
Whiteside,Eli	L	.083	24	2	0	0	0	1	1	8	.120	.083
Bats Right	R	.262	103	27	6	1	2	12	3	22	.303	.398
Wieters,Matt	L	.248	137	34	6	0	3	17	13	40	.313	.358
Bats Both	R	.313	217	68	9	1	6	26	15	46	.357	.447
Wigginton,Ty	L	.252	147	37	6	0	2	7	14	19	.317	.333
Bats Right	R	.285	263	75	13	0	9	34	9	38	.313	.437
Willingham,Josh	L	.300	80	24	5	0	7	21	15	20	.424	.625
Bats Both	R	.251	347	87	24	0	17	40	46	84	.352	.467
Willits,Reggie	L	.222	18	4	0	0	0	3	0	3	.211	.222
Bats Both	R	.210	62	13	2	0	0	3	5	14	.269	.242
Wilson,Bobby	L	-	0	0	0	0	0	0	0	0		
Bats Right	R	.200	5	1	1	0	0	0	0	1	.200	.400
Wilson,Jack	L	.240	104	25	5	0	1	6	11	17	.310	.317
Bats Right	R	.260	269	70	18	1	4	33	10	31	.285	.379
Wilson,Josh	L	.188	64	12	3	1	2	5	7	12	.278	.359
Bats Right	R	.234	128	30	8	0	1	8	5	32	.279	.320
Winn,Randy	L	.158	120	19	1	2	0	8	4	14	.184	.200
Bats Both	R	.292	418	122	32	3	2	43	43	79	.354	.397
Wise,DeWayne	L	.400	15	6	1	0	0	2	0	1	.471	.467
Bats Left	R	.205	127	26	7	3	2	9	3	26	.235	.354
Wood,Brandon	L	.217	23	5	0	0	1	3	1	9	.250	.348
Bats Right	R	.167	18	3	1	0	0	0	2	10	.286	.222
Woodward,Chris	L	.107	28	3	0	0	0	2	2	9	.161	.107
Bats Right	R	.275	51	14	1	0	0	3	5	10	.362	.294
Wright,David	L	.416	113	47	12	1	4	16	19	12	.496	.646
Bats Right	R	.277	422	117	27	2	6	56	55	128	.361	.393
Youkilis,Kevin	L	.309	139	43	11	0	6	22	26	46	.435	.518
Bats Right	R	.304	352	107	25	1	21	72	51	79	.404	.560
Young,Chris	L	.262	107	28	8	2	5	13	26	30	.406	.514
Bats Right	R	.196	326	64	20	2	10	29	33	103	.277	.362
Young,Delmon	L	.310	129	40	3	1	7	19	3	31	.321	.512
Bats Right	R	.271	266	72	13	1	5	41	9	61	.301	.383
Young,Delwyn	L	.233	116	27	2	0	3	14	9	32	.294	.328
Bats Both	R	.282	238	67	14	2	4	29	20	58	.341	.408
Young,Michael	L	.297	148	44	12	0	5	20	20	27	.379	.480
Bats Right	R	.331	393	130	24	2	17	48	27	63	.373	.532
Young Jr.,Eric	L	.304	23	7	1	0	1	1	0	3	.304	.478
Bats Both	R	.206	34	7	0	0	0	0	4	9	.289	.206
Zaun,Gregg	L	.217	46	10	1	0	0	1	1	9	.333	.239
Bats Both	R	.269	216	58	16	0	8	26	23	41	.347	.454

Batters vs. Left-Handed and Right-Handed Pitchers

Batter	vs	Avg	AB	H	2B	3B	HR	RBI	BB	SO	OBP	Slg
Zimmerman,Ryan	L	.270	137	37	8	1	5	14	23	21	.373	.453
Bats Right	R	.298	473	141	29	2	28	92	49	98	.361	.545
Zobrist,Ben	L	.319	163	52	12	3	9	31	34	35	.440	.595
Bats Both	R	.287	338	97	16	4	18	60	57	69	.387	.518
AL	L	.267	-	-	-	-	-	-	-	-	.337	.426
	R	.266	-	-	-	-	-	-	-	-	.335	.429
NL	L	.256	-	-	-	-	-	-	-	-	.330	.407
	R	.260	-	-	-	-	-	-	-	-	.331	.409
MLB	L	.261	-	-	-	-	-	-	-	-	.334	.417
	R	.263	-	-	-	-	-	-	-	-	.333	.418

Pitchers vs. Left-Handed and Right-Handed Batters

Pitcher	vs	Avg	AB	H	2B	3B	HR	RBI	BB	SO	OBP	Slg
Aardsma,David	L	.197	132	26	4	0	1	4	21	41	.307	.250
Throws Right	R	.183	126	23	5	0	3	16	13	39	.257	.294
Abreu,Winston	L	.300	10	3	1	0	0	1	3	1	.500	.400
Throws Right	R	.412	17	7	0	0	2	5	1	5	.444	.765
Accardo,Jeremy	L	.143	42	6	2	0	0	1	7	11	.294	.190
Throws Right	R	.386	44	17	1	0	2	7	10	7	.482	.545
Aceves,Alfredo	L	.212	151	32	5	0	3	16	8	33	.255	.305
Throws Right	R	.228	162	37	9	0	7	16	8	36	.280	.414
Acosta,Manny	L	.297	64	19	5	1	1	8	11	17	.400	.453
Throws Right	R	.302	86	26	5	0	3	13	8	15	.375	.465
Adams,Mike	L	.130	69	9	0	0	1	8	3	27	.167	.174
Throws Right	R	.088	57	5	0	1	0	1	5	18	.161	.123
Adenhart,Nick	L	.250	12	3	0	0	0	0	3	4	.400	.250
Throws Right	R	.333	12	4	0	0	0	0	0	1	.333	.333
Affeldt,Jeremy	L	.211	90	19	4	0	2	11	18	26	.360	.322
Throws Left	R	.187	123	23	4	0	1	10	13	29	.263	.244
Albaladejo,Jonathan	L	.258	66	17	4	0	3	9	8	9	.329	.455
Throws Right	R	.353	68	24	7	0	3	15	8	12	.432	.588
Albers,Matt	L	.342	114	39	11	0	2	25	20	20	.438	.491
Throws Right	R	.273	150	41	8	0	1	24	16	29	.347	.347
Anderson,Brett	L	.313	182	57	5	0	6	23	9	36	.349	.440
Throws Left	R	.247	497	123	24	1	14	61	36	114	.299	.384
Aquino,Greg	L	.182	22	4	1	1	0	3	7	5	.367	.318
Throws Right	R	.257	35	9	1	0	1	3	8	6	.386	.371
Arias,Alberto	L	.276	76	21	5	2	0	8	10	17	.375	.395
Throws Right	R	.269	104	28	3	0	1	8	9	22	.347	.327
Arredondo,Jose	L	.238	80	19	2	0	2	11	13	23	.344	.338
Throws Right	R	.295	95	28	4	1	4	14	10	24	.358	.484
Arroyo,Bronson	L	.278	399	111	19	2	16	40	33	46	.334	.456
Throws Right	R	.236	436	103	22	0	15	52	32	81	.297	.390
Ascanio,Jose	L	.522	23	12	3	0	1	5	2	4	.571	.783
Throws Right	R	.213	47	10	1	0	0	2	7	16	.321	.234
Atkins,Mitch	L	.000	3	0	0	0	0	0	0	0	.000	.000
Throws Right	R	.250	4	1	0	0	0	0	0	0	.250	.250
Augenstein,Bryan	L	.250	24	6	0	0	1	6	2	3	.321	.375
Throws Right	R	.378	45	17	4	0	1	11	4	3	.431	.533
Axford,John	L	.067	15	1	0	0	0	1	1	6	.125	.067
Throws Right	R	.308	13	4	1	0	0	2	5	3	.500	.385
Ayala,Luis	L	.396	53	21	7	1	5	16	10	9	.484	.849
Throws Right	R	.279	104	29	4	1	0	13	4	19	.327	.337
Backe,Brandon	L	.370	27	10	2	0	2	5	3	3	.433	.667
Throws Right	R	.355	31	11	3	0	3	9	3	7	.400	.742
Badenhop,Burke	L	.250	128	32	4	1	3	13	20	23	.351	.367
Throws Right	R	.269	145	39	6	0	2	18	4	34	.289	.352
Baez,Danys	L	.248	129	32	7	0	4	20	11	21	.312	.395
Throws Right	R	.197	107	27	1	0	1	19	11	19	.273	.292
Bailey,Andrew	L	.146	137	20	2	0	4	14	14	40	.222	.248
Throws Right	R	.185	157	29	3	2	1	10	10	51	.234	.248
Bailey,Homer	L	.283	219	62	8	0	7	33	27	43	.360	.416
Throws Right	R	.248	214	53	8	2	5	15	25	43	.331	.374
Baker,Scott	L	.217	373	81	20	2	6	26	29	79	.278	.330
Throws Right	R	.275	396	109	20	1	22	62	19	83	.307	.497
Bale,John	L	.271	59	16	3	0	1	13	5	16	.338	.373
Throws Left	R	.321	56	18	6	1	2	14	13	8	.437	.571
Balester,Collin	L	.315	54	17	5	1	3	6	10	7	.422	.611
Throws Right	R	.254	67	17	2	0	7	15	4	13	.296	.597
Balfour,Grant	L	.240	100	24	3	1	3	12	11	27	.321	.380
Throws Right	R	.232	151	35	7	0	3	25	22	42	.330	.338
Banks,Josh	L	.357	42	15	2	2	3	9	1	3	.372	.714
Throws Right	R	.306	49	15	3	0	3	13	3	6	.345	.551
Bannister,Brian	L	.266	312	83	13	0	6	32	23	56	.315	.365
Throws Right	R	.270	289	78	15	0	9	46	27	42	.332	.415
Bard,Daniel	L	.263	80	21	4	1	4	13	13	28	.379	.488
Throws Right	R	.200	100	20	5	0	1	11	9	35	.265	.280
Bass,Brian	L	.298	161	48	6	0	7	22	25	26	.400	.466
Throws Right	R	.314	185	58	10	1	4	21	19	28	.382	.443
Bastardo,Antonio	L	.303	33	10	3	0	1	5	3	10	.361	.485
Throws Left	R	.258	62	16	5	0	3	10	6	9	.343	.484
Batista,Miguel	L	.331	127	42	8	0	3	24	26	22	.442	.465
Throws Right	R	.242	153	37	7	0	4	15	13	30	.310	.366
Bautista,Denny	L	.318	22	7	1	0	0	4	2	7	.360	.364
Throws Right	R	.296	27	8	1	0	1	6	5	8	.400	.444
Bazardo,Yorman	L	.293	58	17	6	1	0	8	12	9	.417	.431
Throws Right	R	.299	67	20	3	0	2	15	10	8	.385	.433
Beckett,Josh	L	.258	461	119	24	1	11	55	34	127	.310	.386
Throws Right	R	.226	350	79	17	2	14	37	21	72	.278	.406

Pitcher	vs	Avg	AB	H	2B	3B	HR	RBI	BB	SO	OBP	Slg
Bedard,Erik	L	.214	84	18	3	0	2	8	13	25	.327	.321
Throws Left	R	.211	223	47	7	1	6	15	21	65	.286	.332
Beimel,Joe	L	.258	93	24	5	2	4	17	5	22	.297	.484
Throws Left	R	.282	117	33	10	0	1	17	14	13	.348	.393
Belisario,Ronald	L	.270	100	27	4	0	1	13	18	23	.380	.340
Throws Right	R	.157	159	25	4	1	3	13	11	41	.234	.252
Belisle,Matt	L	.241	58	14	2	1	2	11	5	11	.308	.414
Throws Right	R	.313	67	21	2	0	4	14	0	11	.309	.522
Bell,Heath	L	.275	138	38	7	1	2	9	15	38	.346	.384
Throws Right	R	.138	116	16	1	0	1	13	9	41	.200	.172
Bell,Trevor	L	.409	49	20	4	0	2	10	7	6	.526	.673
Throws Right	R	.354	48	17	3	0	1	13	4	8	.396	.479
Bennett,Jeff	L	.393	89	35	7	1	3	20	16	12	.491	.596
Throws Right	R	.304	102	31	5	0	1	14	16	15	.407	.382
Benson,Kris	L	.255	55	14	3	0	3	9	5	10	.317	.473
Throws Right	R	.452	42	19	4	0	3	15	7	1	.549	.762
Berg,Justin	L	.263	19	5	1	0	0	0	1	1	.300	.316
Throws Right	R	.200	25	5	0	0	0	3	0	6	.200	.200
Bergesen,Brad	L	.263	228	60	13	0	5	24	22	26	.335	.386
Throws Right	R	.267	247	66	17	0	6	23	10	39	.297	.409
Bergmann,Jason	L	.339	62	21	1	2	3	10	13	9	.453	.565
Throws Right	R	.246	118	29	5	0	4	18	12	31	.331	.390
Berken,Jason	L	.335	263	88	17	2	8	41	27	31	.399	.506
Throws Right	R	.318	239	76	18	1	11	43	17	35	.367	.540
Betancourt,Rafael	L	.265	83	22	5	2	2	12	13	20	.357	.446
Throws Right	R	.169	118	20	3	0	2	14	7	41	.213	.246
Billingsley,Chad	L	.257	382	98	23	2	7	40	41	106	.329	.382
Throws Right	R	.229	328	75	14	1	10	47	45	74	.324	.369
Blackburn,Nick	L	.300	464	139	30	2	17	49	25	50	.335	.483
Throws Right	R	.277	364	101	17	1	8	41	16	48	.310	.396
Blanton,Joe	L	.252	349	88	10	3	12	32	33	75	.320	.401
Throws Right	R	.271	406	110	27	0	18	54	26	88	.321	.470
Blevins,Jerry	L	.250	28	7	2	0	1	6	2	10	.290	.429
Throws Left	R	.218	55	12	2	1	1	5	4	13	.271	.345
Boggs,Mitchell	L	.410	100	41	8	4	1	9	17	15	.496	.600
Throws Right	R	.234	128	30	5	1	2	16	16	31	.331	.336
Bonderman,Jeremy	L	.278	18	5	0	0	2	5	2	1	.350	.611
Throws Right	R	.423	26	11	1	1	2	4	8	4	.545	.769
Bonine,Eddie	L	.299	67	20	3	0	3	11	4	7	.342	.478
Throws Right	R	.317	63	20	4	0	4	10	8	12	.389	.571
Bootcheck,Chris	L	.250	16	4	1	0	0	4	7	3	.480	.313
Throws Right	R	.300	40	12	5	0	1	16	2	10	.333	.500
Bowden,Michael	L	.395	38	15	5	0	1	12	4	5	.452	.605
Throws Right	R	.258	31	8	3	0	2	8	2	7	.303	.548
Boyer,Blaine	L	.240	104	25	7	0	1	14	10	13	.319	.337
Throws Right	R	.290	107	31	3	0	0	19	10	16	.364	.318
Braden,Dallas	L	.203	133	27	5	0	2	17	10	31	.264	.286
Throws Left	R	.290	404	117	35	1	7	44	32	50	.340	.433
Bradford,Chad	L	.800	5	4	0	0	1	6	2	0	.750	1.400
Throws Right	R	.391	46	18	1	0	0	7	0	6	.383	.413
Breslow,Craig	L	.204	108	22	2	0	4	14	13	23	.298	.333
Throws Left	R	.191	136	26	5	0	4	10	16	32	.281	.316
Broadway,Lance	L	.350	60	21	6	0	0	10	9	6	.429	.450
Throws Right	R	.258	66	17	3	0	0	8	6	12	.315	.303
Brocail,Doug	L	.355	31	11	1	1	3	5	7	4	.462	.742
Throws Right	R	.270	37	10	2	0	1	7	6	5	.364	.405
Broxton,Jonathan	L	.138	130	18	0	0	2	11	15	62	.230	.185
Throws Right	R	.190	137	26	4	1	2	16	14	52	.263	.277
Bruney,Brian	L	.214	70	15	1	1	3	7	9	15	.309	.386
Throws Right	R	.269	78	21	4	0	3	10	14	21	.380	.436
Buchholz,Clay	L	.284	176	50	10	0	4	13	19	31	.354	.409
Throws Right	R	.228	180	41	4	0	9	30	17	37	.297	.400
Buckner,Billy	L	.347	144	50	8	2	5	23	18	22	.427	.535
Throws Right	R	.270	163	44	7	0	7	19	11	42	.318	.442
Buehrle,Mark	L	.298	215	64	14	2	8	27	13	25	.340	.493
Throws Left	R	.267	591	158	30	2	19	59	32	80	.304	.421
Bulger,Jason	L	.196	107	21	7	1	5	20	16	38	.304	.421
Throws Right	R	.217	115	25	7	1	2	11	14	30	.295	.348
Bullington,Bryan	L	.000	6	0	0	0	0	0	5	1	.455	.000
Throws Right	R	.412	17	7	1	1	0	4	1	4	.421	.588
Bumgarner,Madison	L	.083	12	1	0	0	0	1	0	4	.077	.083
Throws Left	R	.304	23	7	0	1	2	2	3	6	.385	.652
Burke,Greg	L	.346	81	28	6	1	3	13	12	14	.430	.556
Throws Right	R	.208	96	20	2	1	1	5	11	19	.296	.281
Burnett,A.J.	L	.217	419	91	16	2	11	39	53	123	.310	.344
Throws Right	R	.282	362	102	19	0	14	51	44	72	.366	.450

Pitchers vs. Left-Handed and Right-Handed Batters

Pitcher	vs	Avg	AB	H	2B	3B	HR	RBI	BB	SO	OBP	Slg
Burnett,Sean	L	.186	97	18	4	1	3	12	11	24	.273	.340
Throws Left	R	.176	102	18	3	0	3	9	17	19	.306	.294
Burns,Mike	L	.295	88	26	4	3	4	11	12	15	.386	.545
Throws Right	R	.293	116	34	10	0	6	23	5	24	.312	.534
Burres,Brian	L	.200	5	1	0	0	0	0	0	1	.200	.200
Throws Left	R	.407	27	11	2	2	0	7	5	3	.500	.630
Burton,Jared	L	.222	99	22	7	0	1	12	12	16	.313	.323
Throws Right	R	.289	135	39	14	1	4	28	11	29	.353	.496
Bush,David	L	.293	225	66	15	4	10	38	26	53	.370	.529
Throws Right	R	.295	220	65	19	1	9	30	11	36	.359	.514
Butler,Josh	L	.417	12	5	2	0	0	3	4	2	.529	.583
Throws Right	R	.286	7	2	0	0	0	2	2	1	.500	.286
Byrd,Paul	L	.405	74	30	7	0	3	15	9	4	.470	.622
Throws Right	R	.250	68	17	3	1	1	4	2	7	.268	.368
Byrdak,Tim	L	.184	103	19	3	0	6	25	17	31	.312	.388
Throws Left	R	.172	116	20	3	3	4	9	19	27	.287	.353
Cabrera,Daniel	L	.316	117	37	10	1	3	19	23	11	.427	.496
Throws Right	R	.244	90	22	5	1	1	14	19	12	.393	.356
Cabrera,Fernando	L	.500	6	3	1	0	0	2	2	1	.625	.667
Throws Right	R	.235	17	4	2	0	0	1	2	7	.350	.353
Cahill,Trevor	L	.286	360	103	23	6	21	57	40	46	.361	.558
Throws Right	R	.252	326	82	22	0	6	32	32	44	.315	.374
Cain,Matt	L	.233	412	96	16	4	10	34	31	79	.285	.364
Throws Right	R	.231	381	88	20	1	12	33	42	92	.310	.383
Calero,Kiko	L	.187	75	14	4	0	0	9	18	20	.347	.240
Throws Right	R	.176	125	22	0	2	1	11	12	49	.243	.232
Cameron,Kevin	L	.240	25	6	0	0	0	1	2	7	.296	.240
Throws Right	R	.209	43	9	2	0	1	7	4	8	.277	.326
Camp,Shawn	L	.260	146	38	12	0	4	19	16	28	.337	.425
Throws Right	R	.230	152	35	7	1	3	18	13	30	.302	.349
Campillo,Jorge	L	.500	8	4	0	1	0	6	3	3	.636	.750
Throws Right	R	.300	10	3	2	0	0	1	0	0	.300	.500
Capps,Matt	L	.342	117	40	9	1	8	25	7	22	.373	.641
Throws Right	R	.306	108	33	4	1	2	13	10	24	.374	.417
Caridad,Esmailin	L	.194	31	6	3	0	0	1	3	11	.265	.290
Throws Right	R	.243	37	9	3	1	0	6	0	6	.300	.378
Carlson,Jesse	L	.272	114	31	8	0	3	16	10	22	.333	.421
Throws Left	R	.247	146	36	10	1	4	15	11	29	.300	.411
Carlyle,Buddy	L	.316	38	12	2	0	2	8	9	10	.438	.526
Throws Right	R	.426	54	23	6	0	3	18	3	2	.456	.704
Carmona,Fausto	L	.331	296	98	19	3	12	61	47	41	.427	.537
Throws Right	R	.245	216	53	14	0	4	25	23	38	.331	.366
Carpenter,Chris	L	.239	326	78	16	2	3	20	20	66	.288	.328
Throws Right	R	.214	365	78	13	2	4	28	18	78	.257	.293
Carpenter,Drew	L	.400	15	6	2	0	0	4	1	3	.471	.533
Throws Right	R	.455	11	5	2	0	1	2	3	2	.571	.909
Carrasco,Carlos	L	.367	49	18	3	0	3	9	5	3	.426	.612
Throws Right	R	.431	51	22	6	0	3	14	6	8	.483	.725
Carrasco,D.J.	L	.317	164	52	12	0	4	27	22	23	.392	.463
Throws Right	R	.251	203	51	8	1	1	23	7	39	.282	.315
Carrillo,Cesar	L	.250	16	4	1	0	1	2	2	2	.368	.500
Throws Right	R	.400	30	12	2	0	3	12	10	2	.561	.767
Casilla,Santiago	L	.354	96	34	6	1	3	24	16	16	.439	.531
Throws Right	R	.257	105	27	10	0	3	14	9	19	.331	.438
Castillo,Alberto	L	.269	26	7	1	0	0	1	3	5	.345	.308
Throws Left	R	.294	17	5	2	0	0	1	1	3	.368	.412
Cecil,Brett	L	.295	132	39	6	0	9	27	8	29	.336	.545
Throws Left	R	.314	245	77	18	2	8	28	30	40	.397	.502
Chacin,Jhoulys	L	.263	19	5	1	0	1	2	3	4	.364	.474
Throws Right	R	.059	17	1	1	0	0	1	8	9	.360	.118
Chamberlain,Joba	L	.266	319	85	10	3	11	45	51	69	.376	.420
Throws Right	R	.282	291	82	20	1	10	45	25	64	.348	.460
Chavez,Jesse	L	.228	127	29	4	1	5	17	11	19	.288	.394
Throws Right	R	.299	134	40	10	1	6	28	11	28	.356	.522
Chen,Bruce	L	.292	72	21	3	0	0	6	6	16	.346	.333
Throws Left	R	.305	174	53	9	2	12	31	19	29	.382	.586
Choate,Randy	L	.141	78	11	1	0	1	9	5	22	.193	.192
Throws Left	R	.321	53	17	0	0	3	6	6	6	.390	.491
Chulk,Vinnie	L	.056	18	1	0	0	0	1	5	2	.261	.056
Throws Right	R	.360	25	9	0	1	1	7	5	2	.467	.560
Claggett,Anthony	L	.700	10	7	2	0	3	7	4	0	.786	1.800
Throws Right	R	.429	14	6	1	0	0	4	0	3	.429	.500
Clippard,Tyler	L	.122	115	14	3	0	3	7	13	38	.217	.226
Throws Right	R	.234	94	22	5	1	6	14	19	29	.360	.500
Coffey,Todd	L	.282	124	35	9	0	4	13	13	22	.355	.452
Throws Right	R	.223	184	41	5	0	4	27	8	43	.260	.315

Pitcher	vs	Avg	AB	H	2B	3B	HR	RBI	BB	SO	OBP	Slg
Coke,Phil	L	.195	123	24	3	0	6	24	5	32	.218	.366
Throws Left	R	.227	88	20	6	0	4	16	15	17	.346	.432
Colome,Jesus	L	.372	43	16	4	1	1	13	4	5	.438	.581
Throws Right	R	.353	51	18	4	1	1	9	2	10	.370	.529
Colon,Bartolo	L	.288	118	34	7	0	10	19	15	20	.365	.602
Throws Right	R	.273	128	35	12	0	3	16	6	18	.311	.438
Colon,Roman	L	.265	83	22	2	0	2	11	10	8	.351	.361
Throws Right	R	.250	112	28	3	3	5	22	12	21	.328	.464
Condrey,Clay	L	.172	58	10	3	0	1	8	7	8	.262	.276
Throws Right	R	.267	101	27	1	1	3	14	7	17	.321	.386
Contreras,Jose	L	.252	258	65	17	1	4	28	35	51	.341	.372
Throws Right	R	.292	260	76	16	1	9	41	18	55	.350	.465
Cook,Aaron	L	.282	319	90	11	3	10	33	40	31	.358	.429
Throws Right	R	.285	298	85	19	2	9	37	7	47	.304	.453
Corcoran,Roy	L	.345	29	10	0	0	2	8	11	4	.512	.552
Throws Right	R	.366	41	15	1	0	0	12	6	2	.449	.390
Cordero,Francisco	L	.228	114	26	4	0	0	6	20	33	.341	.263
Throws Right	R	.256	125	32	5	0	2	15	10	25	.304	.344
Cormier,Lance	L	.239	159	38	5	2	3	19	18	24	.318	.352
Throws Right	R	.261	142	37	8	1	3	13	7	12	.293	.394
Corpas,Manny	L	.400	60	24	2	0	2	12	5	10	.439	.533
Throws Right	R	.267	75	20	2	2	1	11	2	14	.295	.387
Correia,Kevin	L	.247	360	89	18	2	9	36	42	71	.330	.383
Throws Right	R	.269	390	105	21	0	8	41	22	71	.308	.385
Cotts,Neal	L	.318	22	7	1	0	3	5	6	4	.483	.773
Throws Left	R	.304	23	7	2	0	0	2	3	5	.385	.391
Crain,Jesse	L	.297	74	22	5	1	3	14	17	20	.441	.514
Throws Right	R	.220	118	26	5	1	0	13	10	23	.291	.280
Cruz,Juan	L	.244	90	22	5	1	2	15	14	16	.349	.389
Throws Right	R	.247	97	24	6	0	4	14	15	22	.348	.433
Cueto,Johnny	L	.250	336	84	18	4	15	44	40	71	.334	.461
Throws Right	R	.274	321	88	20	1	9	39	21	61	.338	.427
Daley,Matt	L	.266	79	21	9	2	0	9	13	18	.366	.430
Throws Right	R	.206	107	22	4	2	6	20	5	37	.250	.449
Danks,John	L	.244	197	48	10	2	8	19	20	39	.320	.437
Throws Left	R	.246	553	136	25	1	20	58	53	110	.312	.403
Davidson,Daniel	L	.429	7	3	1	0	0	3	1	0	.500	.571
Throws Left	R	.000	1	0	0	0	0	0	2	0	.667	.000
Davidson,Dave	L	.500	4	2	1	0	0	3	2	2	.667	.750
Throws Left	R	.667	3	2	0	0	0	2	2	1	.800	.667
Davies,Kyle	L	.239	197	47	6	2	5	23	37	43	.359	.365
Throws Right	R	.284	264	75	9	0	13	40	29	43	.359	.466
Davis,Doug	L	.264	163	43	10	1	7	24	22	44	.358	.466
Throws Left	R	.268	598	160	21	6	18	59	81	102	.354	.413
Davis,Wade	L	.238	84	20	5	0	1	5	7	21	.297	.333
Throws Right	R	.250	52	13	1	0	1	8	6	15	.328	.327
de la Cruz,Eulogio	L	.250	4	1	0	0	0	1	6	1	.700	.250
Throws Right	R	.167	6	1	0	0	0	1	0	1	.143	.167
de la Rosa,Jorge	L	.204	152	31	7	1	2	17	12	57	.265	.303
Throws Left	R	.262	538	141	28	7	18	69	71	136	.354	.441
Delcarmen,Manny	L	.221	122	27	8	1	1	10	20	24	.333	.328
Throws Right	R	.322	115	37	8	2	4	22	14	20	.409	.530
Dempster,Ryan	L	.281	359	101	26	3	9	45	42	88	.357	.446
Throws Right	R	.241	394	95	15	0	13	44	23	84	.286	.378
Dessens,Elmer	L	.193	57	11	3	0	3	8	5	9	.277	.404
Throws Right	R	.228	57	13	3	0	2	6	5	5	.286	.386
Detwiler,Ross	L	.288	73	21	5	0	0	8	7	13	.361	.356
Throws Left	R	.289	228	66	17	2	3	29	26	30	.362	.421
Dickey,R.A.	L	.246	114	28	4	1	4	22	18	19	.343	.404
Throws Right	R	.326	141	46	8	2	4	24	12	23	.395	.496
DiFelice,Mark	L	.278	54	15	5	0	3	10	7	14	.361	.537
Throws Right	R	.233	146	34	7	1	3	24	8	34	.277	.356
Dillard,Tim	L	.500	6	3	0	0	1	3	4	1	.700	1.000
Throws Right	R	.364	11	4	1	0	0	2	1	0	.385	.455
DiNardo,Lenny	L	.450	20	9	1	1	0	7	3	1	.542	.600
Throws Left	R	.405	79	32	3	1	2	16	12	7	.473	.544
Dolsi,Freddy	L	.368	19	7	2	0	0	2	4	3	.478	.474
Throws Right	R	.261	23	6	2	0	0	5	0	0	.250	.348
Donnelly,Brendan	L	.262	42	11	2	1	0	2	6	12	.354	.357
Throws Right	R	.220	50	11	1	1	1	4	3	13	.278	.340
Dotel,Octavio	L	.268	71	19	3	2	5	12	19	21	.422	.577
Throws Right	R	.226	155	35	12	1	2	24	17	54	.297	.355
Downs,Scott	L	.263	57	15	2	1	3	9	3	13	.295	.491
Throws Left	R	.246	126	31	8	0	1	12	10	30	.309	.333
Duensing,Brian	L	.244	82	20	2	0	0	11	6	19	.311	.268
Throws Left	R	.269	238	64	11	0	7	21	25	34	.338	.403

Pitchers vs. Left-Handed and Right-Handed Batters

Pitcher	vs	Avg	AB	H	2B	3B	HR	RBI	BB	SO	OBP	Slg
Duke,Zach	L	.284	183	52	12	1	4	28	12	30	.333	.426
Throws Left	R	.285	627	179	34	4	19	65	37	76	.322	.443
Dumatrait,Phil	L	.280	25	7	1	1	2	8	3	2	.357	.640
Throws Left	R	.222	27	6	1	0	2	5	8	5	.389	.481
Dunn,Mike	L	.000	4	0	0	0	0	0	4	3	.500	.000
Throws Left	R	.273	11	3	0	0	1	2	1	2	.333	.545
Durbin,Chad	L	.223	112	25	4	0	4	13	23	25	.358	.366
Throws Right	R	.218	142	31	8	1	4	19	24	37	.351	.373
Eaton,Adam	L	.342	111	30	11	2	5	22	19	19	.435	.613
Throws Right	R	.284	95	27	6	1	5	20	8	16	.340	.526
Egbert,Jack	L	.750	4	3	1	0	1	3	2	0	.833	1.750
Throws Right	R	.455	11	5	1	0	0	6	0	0	.417	.545
Ekstrom,Mike	L	.286	35	10	0	0	1	4	5	11	.381	.371
Throws Right	R	.297	37	11	2	0	2	10	3	8	.341	.514
Elbert,Scott	L	.222	36	8	1	0	2	4	3	14	.282	.417
Throws Left	R	.282	39	11	1	1	2	9	4	7	.349	.513
Embree,Alan	L	.326	43	14	2	0	2	10	3	4	.383	.512
Throws Left	R	.264	53	14	4	0	1	9	9	8	.371	.396
Escalona,Sergio	L	.200	15	3	0	0	0	3	2	2	.400	.200
Throws Left	R	.257	35	9	2	0	0	3	3	8	.300	.314
Escobar,Kelvim	L	.000	10	0	0	0	0	1	2	5	.154	.000
Throws Right	R	.571	7	4	0	0	0	1	2	0	.700	.571
Estrada,Marco	L	.300	10	3	2	0	0	3	4	3	.500	.500
Throws Right	R	.167	18	3	1	0	1	5	0	6	.167	.389
[illegible],Dana	L	.373	51	19	6	0	1	9	8	3	.450	.549
Throws Left	R	.362	141	51	6	0	3	28	18	19	.431	.468
Fyre,Scott	L	.210	62	13	3	0	2	6	5	12	.269	.355
Throws Left	R	.200	45	9	1	1	1	5	11	10	.356	.333
Eyre,Willie	L	.286	28	8	5	0	0	2	4	6	.375	.464
Throws Right	R	.278	36	10	3	0	0	8	2	2	.316	.361
Farnsworth,Kyle	L	.277	65	18	2	1	1	12	10	21	.368	.385
Throws Right	R	.294	85	25	1	0	2	12	4	21	.330	.376
Feldman,Scott	L	.226	385	87	11	0	13	35	39	66	.304	.356
Throws Right	R	.277	328	91	22	1	5	38	26	47	.337	.396
Feliciano,Pedro	L	.215	149	32	6	1	4	15	6	41	.245	.349
Throws Left	R	.264	72	19	5	1	3	8	12	18	.365	.486
Feliz,Neftali	L	.155	58	9	1	1	2	6	3	18	.222	.310
Throws Right	R	.085	47	4	0	0	0	2	5	21	.189	.085
Fien,Casey	L	.188	16	3	1	0	1	5	4	4	.333	.438
Throws Right	R	.345	29	10	3	1	1	6	2	5	.375	.621
Figaro,Alfredo	L	.480	25	12	1	1	1	6	6	1	.581	.720
Throws Right	R	.239	46	11	1	0	2	5	4	15	.314	.391
Figueroa,Nelson	L	.274	117	32	8	0	2	12	17	26	.374	.393
Throws Right	R	.294	163	48	8	1	6	22	7	33	.343	.466
Fisher,Carlos	L	.337	83	28	3	0	1	12	9	18	.402	.410
Throws Right	R	.204	108	22	5	1	3	16	23	30	.341	.352
Fister,Doug	L	.237	135	32	6	1	9	19	10	23	.290	.496
Throws Right	R	.298	104	31	6	1	2	6	5	13	.342	.433
Flores,Randy	L	.265	34	9	4	0	1	6	1	12	.286	.471
Throws Left	R	.313	16	5	1	0	1	1	1	2	.353	.563
Floyd,Gavin	L	.232	379	88	14	1	14	51	35	95	.295	.385
Throws Right	R	.256	352	90	20	0	7	28	24	68	.307	.372
Fogg,Josh	L	.221	77	17	5	2	4	13	13	15	.333	.494
Throws Right	R	.176	85	15	1	0	3	13	7	12	.240	.294
Fossum,Casey	L	.000	3	0	0	0	0	1	1	1	.250	.000
Throws Left	R	.333	12	4	0	0	0	2	3	2	.467	.333
Fox,Chad	L	1.000	1	1	0	1	0	0	1	0	1.000	3.000
Throws Right	R	.500	2	1	0	1	0	2	2	0	.750	1.500
Francisco,Frank	L	.238	101	24	6	0	2	14	6	26	.280	.356
Throws Right	R	.186	86	16	4	0	4	11	9	31	.271	.372
Franklin,Ryan	L	.196	97	19	4	0	0	5	17	17	.316	.237
Throws Right	R	.238	126	30	7	0	2	9	7	27	.279	.341
Frasor,Jason	L	.274	106	29	3	0	3	19	9	29	.325	.387
Throws Right	R	.140	100	14	1	0	1	5	7	27	.211	.180
French,Luke	L	.322	90	29	4	0	2	8	5	18	.371	.433
Throws Left	R	.310	187	58	16	2	9	34	23	24	.377	.561
Frieri,Ernesto	L	.000	4	0	0	0	0	0	1	2	.200	.000
Throws Right	R	.000	2	0	0	0	0	0	0	0	.000	.000
Fuentes,Brian	L	.239	71	17	3	0	0	2	7	13	.308	.282
Throws Left	R	.261	138	36	5	0	6	23	17	33	.358	.428
Fulchino,Jeff	L	.261	138	36	8	2	1	16	17	36	.342	.370
Throws Right	R	.209	163	34	9	1	6	23	10	35	.266	.387
Gabino,Armando	L	.400	15	6	3	0	0	4	3	1	.500	.600
Throws Right	R	.600	5	3	0	0	1	2	2	1	.714	1.200
Galarraga,Armando	L	.309	285	88	14	5	12	51	47	46	.405	.519
Throws Right	R	.257	272	70	13	2	12	36	20	49	.310	.452
Gallagher,Sean	L	.323	31	10	3	0	1	8	9	4	.476	.516
Throws Right	R	.327	49	16	1	0	0	4	3	10	.377	.347
Gallardo,Yovani	L	.213	352	75	20	2	6	25	53	114	.320	.332
Throws Right	R	.225	334	75	25	1	15	47	41	90	.312	.440
Garate,Victor	L	.000	2	0	0	0	0	0	1	0	.500	.000
Throws Left	R	.625	8	5	2	1	1	8	2	0	.636	1.500
Garcia,Freddy	L	.196	102	20	5	1	2	8	8	19	.252	.324
Throws Right	R	.316	114	36	10	0	2	13	4	18	.339	.456
Garland,Jon	L	.271	406	110	28	5	8	36	30	59	.326	.424
Throws Right	R	.293	392	115	17	0	15	60	31	50	.345	.452
Garza,Matt	L	.196	392	77	11	0	11	39	66	111	.300	.309
Throws Right	R	.271	369	100	21	4	14	47	23	78	.323	.463
Gaudin,Chad	L	.296	270	80	16	2	4	31	48	47	.408	.415
Throws Right	R	.224	295	66	14	1	10	42	28	92	.293	.380
Geary,Geoff	L	.355	31	11	3	0	3	7	5	3	.444	.742
Throws Right	R	.358	53	19	5	0	1	11	5	9	.424	.509
Geer,Josh	L	.290	200	58	12	1	10	30	9	30	.324	.510
Throws Right	R	.286	203	58	11	2	17	37	14	24	.333	.611
Gervacio,Sammy	L	.250	20	5	1	0	1	3	5	4	.400	.450
Throws Right	R	.208	53	11	3	0	0	6	3	21	.263	.264
Giese,Dan	L	.243	37	9	1	0	3	8	4	0	.310	.514
Throws Right	R	.277	47	13	2	0	2	6	5	3	.346	.447
Gobble,Jimmy	L	.227	22	5	1	0	1	4	2	9	.346	.409
Throws Left	R	.321	28	9	2	0	2	9	5	1	.424	.607
Gonzalez,Edgar	L	.351	134	47	13	2	3	22	19	15	.436	.545
Throws Right	R	.200	[illegible]	[illegible]	9	1	1	14	9	24	.298	.311
Gonzalez,Enrique	L	.091	11	1	0	0	0	1	2	1	.231	.091
Throws Right	R	.800	5	4	0	0	1	2	0	0	.800	1.400
Gonzalez,Gio	L	.340	94	32	9	1	6	23	18	30	.446	.649
Throws Left	R	.271	299	81	13	3	8	40	38	79	.352	.415
Gonzalez,Mike	L	.194	98	19	7	0	2	7	7	32	.256	.327
Throws Left	R	.218	170	37	9	0	5	18	26	58	.340	.359
Gordon,Tom	L	.000	2	0	0	0	0	0	1	0	.333	.000
Throws Right	R	.600	5	3	0	1	0	1	2	0	.714	1.000
Gorzelanny,Tom	L	.244	41	10	0	0	0	4	5	13	.319	.244
Throws Left	R	.252	139	35	4	2	6	19	12	34	.312	.439
Gosling,Mike	L	.289	38	11	3	0	0	2	4	4	.357	.368
Throws Left	R	.292	65	19	4	0	5	10	7	9	.361	.585
Grabow,John	L	.222	81	18	2	0	1	11	10	23	.323	.284
Throws Left	R	.238	185	44	10	0	4	27	30	34	.341	.357
Gray,Jeff	L	.300	50	15	2	1	1	9	2	6	.327	.440
Throws Right	R	.259	58	15	1	0	2	5	2	13	.306	.379
Green,Sean	L	.223	103	23	8	1	3	15	23	14	.380	.408
Throws Right	R	.250	164	41	7	1	2	23	13	40	.328	.341
Gregerson,Luke	L	.285	137	39	10	0	3	19	15	40	.365	.423
Throws Right	R	.161	143	23	6	0	0	9	16	53	.245	.203
Gregg,Kevin	L	.195	118	23	4	2	2	9	12	46	.278	.314
Throws Right	R	.257	144	37	5	0	11	27	18	25	.339	.521
Greinke,Zack	L	.250	408	102	26	3	4	25	25	129	.294	.358
Throws Right	R	.211	441	93	21	2	7	31	26	113	.259	.315
Grilli,Jason	L	.262	84	22	7	1	2	11	18	26	.392	.440
Throws Right	R	.289	97	28	5	2	2	19	9	23	.352	.443
Guardado,Eddie	L	.333	54	18	4	0	2	11	6	10	.400	.519
Throws Left	R	.228	92	21	3	0	6	13	9	10	.311	.457
Guerrier,Matt	L	.194	108	21	2	0	2	6	7	16	.256	.269
Throws Right	R	.215	172	37	3	1	8	24	9	31	.261	.384
Guthrie,Jeremy	L	.289	391	113	23	5	21	61	34	55	.351	.535
Throws Right	R	.274	405	111	28	1	14	53	26	55	.320	.452
Gutierrez,Juan	L	.297	128	38	4	2	0	21	22	28	.403	.359
Throws Right	R	.207	140	29	8	0	2	19	8	38	.252	.307
Guzman,Angel	L	.189	90	17	5	0	3	8	11	17	.275	.344
Throws Right	R	.194	124	24	4	0	5	14	12	30	.268	.347
Hacker,Eric	L	.375	8	3	2	0	0	1	0	1	.375	.625
Throws Right	R	.250	4	1	1	0	0	1	2	0	.500	.500
Haeger,Charlie	L	.125	24	3	1	0	1	2	4	6	.250	.292
Throws Right	R	.222	45	10	0	0	3	5	3	9	.300	.422
Halladay,Roy	L	.240	525	126	25	1	15	40	20	116	.270	.377
Throws Right	R	.278	388	108	22	0	7	39	15	92	.305	.389
Hamels,Cole	L	.242	161	39	7	0	7	20	12	34	.295	.416
Throws Left	R	.282	593	167	37	5	17	68	31	134	.320	.447
Hammel,Jason	L	.289	356	103	20	5	8	42	30	65	.344	.441
Throws Right	R	.290	345	100	21	2	9	40	12	68	.322	.441
Hampton,Mike	L	.238	101	24	4	1	4	12	5	29	.269	.416
Throws Left	R	.316	329	104	20	3	9	54	41	45	.392	.477
Hanrahan,Joel	L	.269	119	32	11	0	2	17	19	35	.383	.412
Throws Right	R	.293	140	41	13	0	1	18	15	37	.359	.407

Pitchers vs. Left-Handed and Right-Handed Batters

Pitcher	vs	Avg	AB	H	2B	3B	HR	RBI	BB	SO	OBP	Slg
Hansen,Craig	L	.000	8	0	0	0	0	0	3	4	.333	.000
Throws Right	R	.353	17	6	2	0	1	4	1	1	.389	.647
Hanson,Tommy	L	.256	242	62	11	2	6	19	33	63	.350	.393
Throws Right	R	.192	224	43	11	3	4	22	13	53	.245	.321
Happ,J.A.	L	.216	148	32	12	0	3	15	13	33	.285	.358
Throws Left	R	.253	462	117	19	2	17	39	43	86	.318	.413
Harang,Aaron	L	.285	326	93	13	1	11	28	25	66	.340	.433
Throws Right	R	.289	322	93	23	2	13	38	18	76	.328	.494
Harden,Rich	L	.251	235	59	6	0	12	32	23	80	.326	.430
Throws Right	R	.220	286	63	9	3	11	38	44	91	.327	.388
Haren,Dan	L	.229	445	102	21	5	15	44	29	120	.279	.400
Throws Right	R	.219	411	90	17	0	12	34	9	103	.238	.348
Harrison,Matt	L	.210	62	13	1	1	1	6	4	11	.258	.306
Throws Left	R	.351	194	68	17	0	8	33	19	23	.412	.562
Hart,Kevin	L	.335	155	52	12	1	4	18	19	21	.406	.503
Throws Right	R	.278	162	45	8	1	7	29	25	31	.378	.469
Hawkins,LaTroy	L	.203	118	24	3	1	1	7	9	28	.258	.271
Throws Right	R	.303	119	36	3	0	6	11	7	17	.349	.479
Hawksworth,Blake	L	.246	65	16	7	0	1	9	8	6	.324	.400
Throws Right	R	.176	74	13	1	1	1	5	7	14	.256	.257
Hayhurst,Dirk	L	.326	43	14	5	0	1	6	5	9	.408	.512
Throws Right	R	.220	41	9	1	0	1	5	4	4	.292	.317
Heilman,Aaron	L	.210	105	22	2	3	1	9	19	24	.328	.314
Throws Right	R	.288	160	46	5	1	8	39	15	41	.346	.481
Hendrickson,Mark	L	.275	131	36	12	0	2	19	9	27	.317	.412
Throws Left	R	.282	284	80	18	2	14	36	24	34	.339	.507
Henn,Sean	L	.323	31	10	4	0	2	9	5	11	.432	.645
Throws Left	R	.208	24	5	2	0	0	2	7	4	.375	.292
Herges,Matt	L	.277	65	18	5	0	3	11	2	7	.299	.492
Throws Right	R	.219	73	16	2	0	2	9	6	19	.278	.329
Hernandez,David	L	.280	225	63	14	1	15	35	30	33	.360	.551
Throws Right	R	.297	185	55	10	1	12	25	16	35	.356	.557
Hernandez,Felix	L	.228	469	107	20	2	8	35	46	114	.294	.330
Throws Right	R	.226	412	93	11	0	7	39	25	103	.279	.303
Hernandez,Livan	L	.287	376	108	31	4	9	52	41	50	.351	.463
Throws Right	R	.330	339	112	16	2	10	48	26	52	.377	.478
Herrera,Daniel Ray	L	.183	109	20	3	0	2	11	10	26	.254	.266
Throws Left	R	.361	119	43	7	2	3	18	14	18	.423	.529
Hill,Rich	L	.267	45	12	5	0	2	9	12	15	.414	.511
Throws Left	R	.303	185	56	18	0	5	39	28	31	.395	.481
Hill,Shawn	L	.286	28	8	2	0	1	3	3	4	.364	.464
Throws Right	R	.333	21	7	3	0	0	3	0	3	.333	.476
Hinckley,Mike	L	.077	13	1	0	0	0	1	2	0	.250	.077
Throws Left	R	.389	18	7	1	0	1	3	9	3	.593	.611
Hinshaw,Alex	L	.400	15	6	0	0	1	4	2	1	.471	.600
Throws Left	R	.364	11	4	1	0	1	3	5	1	.563	.727
Hochevar,Luke	L	.292	281	82	15	7	13	60	31	54	.368	.534
Throws Right	R	.289	294	85	23	0	10	39	15	52	.334	.469
Hoffman,Trevor	L	.222	90	20	3	0	0	5	9	24	.300	.256
Throws Right	R	.149	101	15	2	0	2	10	5	24	.185	.228
Holland,Derek	L	.287	129	37	9	1	3	22	17	25	.367	.442
Throws Left	R	.289	426	123	28	3	23	71	30	82	.340	.531
Howell,J.P.	L	.280	75	21	4	1	1	12	11	19	.372	.400
Throws Left	R	.159	164	26	4	0	6	19	22	60	.268	.293
Howry,Bob	L	.225	89	20	4	2	2	11	18	21	.348	.382
Throws Right	R	.207	145	30	7	1	3	14	5	25	.235	.331
Hudson,Daniel	L	.194	36	7	0	0	1	3	6	9	.318	.278
Throws Right	R	.257	35	9	1	1	2	4	3	5	.316	.514
Hudson,Tim	L	.329	70	23	5	0	2	9	2	8	.347	.486
Throws Right	R	.271	96	26	4	0	2	8	11	22	.346	.375
Huff,David	L	.317	186	59	14	1	6	25	20	29	.385	.500
Throws Left	R	.292	342	100	26	3	10	48	21	36	.332	.474
Hughes,Dustin	L	.267	15	4	0	0	0	2	0	5	.267	.267
Throws Left	R	.237	38	9	1	0	2	4	8	10	.396	.421
Hughes,Phil	L	.257	140	36	8	1	3	11	18	42	.348	.393
Throws Right	R	.184	174	32	7	0	5	12	10	54	.235	.310
Humber,Philip	L	.385	13	5	0	0	0	2	8	5	.619	.385
Throws Right	R	.429	28	12	0	0	1	5	1	4	.448	.536
Hunter,Tommy	L	.288	222	64	12	3	10	34	25	30	.364	.505
Throws Right	R	.228	215	49	15	0	3	15	8	34	.256	.340
Isringhausen,Jason	L	.167	12	2	0	0	0	3	3	2	.375	.167
Throws Right	R	.222	18	4	1	0	0	0	2	4	.333	.278
Jackson,Edwin	L	.247	454	112	24	4	9	35	41	94	.311	.377
Throws Right	R	.248	355	88	21	1	18	44	29	67	.309	.465
Jackson,Steven	L	.216	74	16	1	2	1	14	14	9	.337	.324
Throws Right	R	.253	87	22	5	0	1	7	8	12	.313	.345

Pitcher	vs	Avg	AB	H	2B	3B	HR	RBI	BB	SO	OBP	Slg
Jackson,Zach	L	.300	10	3	0	0	1	1	0	2	.417	.600
Throws Left	R	.367	30	11	1	0	1	10	4	8	.429	.500
Jakubauskas,Chris	L	.275	171	47	13	2	7	28	17	23	.340	.497
Throws Right	R	.235	187	44	10	1	8	29	10	24	.276	.428
Janssen,Casey	L	.313	83	26	11	0	3	12	7	10	.367	.554
Throws Right	R	.367	90	33	8	0	2	14	7	14	.416	.522
Jenks,Bobby	L	.309	94	29	6	0	4	15	8	22	.362	.500
Throws Right	R	.202	114	23	2	0	5	10	8	27	.260	.351
Jennings,Jason	L	.327	98	32	5	2	2	16	15	18	.414	.480
Throws Right	R	.257	136	35	9	0	5	23	13	26	.320	.434
Jepsen,Kevin	L	.373	110	41	3	0	2	20	11	16	.426	.455
Throws Right	R	.208	106	22	3	0	0	8	8	32	.261	.236
Jimenez,Ubaldo	L	.251	410	103	21	2	4	36	56	101	.340	.341
Throws Right	R	.206	388	80	11	1	9	38	29	97	.276	.309
Joaquin,Waldis	L	.188	16	3	0	0	0	1	3	7	.381	.188
Throws Right	R	.269	26	7	1	1	1	2	4	5	.367	.500
Johnson,Jim	L	.262	126	33	8	0	3	12	17	24	.350	.397
Throws Right	R	.278	144	40	3	2	5	20	6	25	.316	.431
Johnson,Josh	L	.242	413	100	13	3	3	26	33	98	.301	.310
Throws Right	R	.231	363	84	9	3	11	40	25	93	.286	.364
Johnson,Randy	L	.268	82	22	4	3	1	5	5	23	.318	.427
Throws Left	R	.260	288	75	18	2	18	42	26	63	.323	.524
Jones,Hunter	L	.200	20	4	2	0	0	3	2	4	.304	.300
Throws Left	R	.364	33	12	2	0	3	8	5	5	.436	.697
Julio,Jorge	L	.269	26	7	1	0	2	5	8	5	.441	.538
Throws Right	R	.186	43	8	1	1	0	7	7	8	.352	.256
Jurrjens,Jair	L	.264	371	98	15	3	8	34	46	66	.344	.385
Throws Right	R	.212	415	88	24	2	7	30	29	86	.267	.330
Karstens,Jeff	L	.263	194	51	16	4	5	25	31	22	.364	.464
Throws Right	R	.294	218	64	18	2	7	39	14	30	.333	.491
Kawakami,Kenshin	L	.252	305	77	16	2	6	28	32	48	.325	.377
Throws Right	R	.268	284	76	24	8	9	40	25	57	.331	.504
Kazmir,Scott	L	.261	134	35	7	1	5	17	14	27	.344	.440
Throws Left	R	.258	442	114	30	0	11	52	46	90	.329	.400
Kelley,Shawn	L	.209	86	18	2	0	2	5	4	25	.253	.302
Throws Right	R	.303	89	27	3	0	7	24	5	16	.347	.573
Kendrick,Kyle	L	.267	45	12	0	0	1	5	8	6	.370	.333
Throws Right	R	.278	54	15	0	0	0	7	1	9	.298	.278
Kennedy,Ian	L	.000	2	0	0	0	0	0	2	1	.500	.000
Throws Right	R	.000	1	0	0	0	0	0	0	0	.500	.000
Kensing,Logan	L	.292	65	19	3	0	4	17	11	11	.390	.523
Throws Right	R	.407	86	35	10	0	4	22	6	8	.446	.663
Keppel,Bobby	L	.317	104	33	8	2	1	10	10	11	.379	.462
Throws Right	R	.278	108	30	5	1	3	22	11	21	.360	.426
Kershaw,Clayton	L	.173	139	24	8	0	1	8	11	72	.237	.252
Throws Left	R	.208	457	95	20	0	6	35	80	113	.325	.291
Kilby,Brad	L	.217	23	5	1	1	1	3	0	5	.217	.478
Throws Left	R	.132	38	5	1	0	0	1	4	15	.214	.158
Kinney,Josh	L	.235	34	8	3	0	0	6	7	3	.366	.324
Throws Right	R	.455	33	15	2	0	2	8	4	5	.538	.697
Kobayashi,Masa	L	.294	17	5	1	0	1	7	0	2	.333	.529
Throws Right	R	.304	23	7	1	0	1	5	4	2	.407	.478
Korecky,Bobby	L	.455	11	5	2	1	0	2	1	1	.462	.818
Throws Right	R	.400	15	6	2	0	0	3	3	2	.500	.533
Koronka,John	L	.400	10	4	0	0	2	5	1	1	.455	1.000
Throws Left	R	.318	22	7	1	0	2	2	6	3	.464	.636
Kuo,Hong-Chih	L	.152	33	5	0	0	1	3	6	16	.282	.242
Throws Left	R	.219	73	16	3	1	1	4	7	16	.305	.329
Kuroda,Hiroki	L	.233	215	50	15	2	7	26	18	34	.294	.419
Throws Right	R	.253	237	60	11	1	5	26	6	53	.272	.371
Lackey,John	L	.276	384	106	24	2	11	39	22	67	.321	.435
Throws Right	R	.247	288	71	10	2	6	34	25	72	.309	.358
Laffey,Aaron	L	.255	137	35	2	1	2	16	10	27	.313	.328
Throws Left	R	.310	339	105	23	0	7	39	47	32	.391	.440
Lambert,Chris	L	.438	32	14	0	0	1	9	4	4	.500	.531
Throws Right	R	.261	23	6	0	1	4	9	3	7	.346	.870
Lannan,John	L	.290	193	56	12	2	9	28	17	38	.360	.513
Throws Left	R	.259	595	154	38	1	13	57	51	51	.319	.392
Latos,Mat	L	.271	85	23	1	0	4	10	15	15	.376	.424
Throws Right	R	.200	100	20	4	0	3	12	8	24	.259	.330
Leach,Brent	L	.256	43	11	2	1	2	8	6	7	.360	.488
Throws Left	R	.156	32	5	1	2	1	4	6	12	.289	.406
League,Brandon	L	.270	141	38	10	1	5	23	11	37	.327	.461
Throws Right	R	.245	139	34	7	0	3	18	10	39	.323	.360
LeBlanc,Wade	L	.235	34	8	1	1	2	4	6	6	.366	.500
Throws Left	R	.203	133	27	5	0	4	13	13	24	.287	.331

Pitchers vs. Left-Handed and Right-Handed Batters

Pitcher	vs	Avg	AB	H	2B	3B	HR	RBI	BB	SO	OBP	Slg
Ledezma,Wil	L	.273	11	3	0	0	1	5	1	4	.308	.545
Throws Left	R	.385	13	5	2	1	0	1	3	4	.471	.692
Lee,Cliff	L	.241	228	55	7	1	3	25	6	37	.263	.320
Throws Left	R	.283	672	190	44	1	14	59	37	144	.321	.414
Lehr,Justin	L	.234	107	25	6	0	5	12	16	14	.339	.430
Throws Right	R	.324	145	47	6	0	9	26	12	19	.379	.552
Lerew,Anthony	L	.294	34	10	1	0	3	3	5	3	.385	.588
Throws Right	R	.211	19	4	1	0	1	3	3	4	.304	.421
Leroux,Chris	L	.412	17	7	3	0	0	4	2	2	.474	.588
Throws Right	R	.286	14	4	4	0	0	4	2	0	.375	.571
Lester,Jon	L	.257	202	52	10	0	7	19	13	65	.306	.411
Throws Left	R	.237	566	134	21	2	13	53	51	160	.299	.350
Lewis,Jensen	L	.299	117	35	5	2	8	23	16	26	.381	.607
Throws Right	R	.205	132	27	6	1	4	20	14	37	.284	.356
Lewis,Scott	L	.500	2	1	0	0	1	2	0	0	.500	2.000
Throws Left	R	.353	17	6	2	0	1	2	1	3	.389	.647
Lidge,Brad	L	.319	116	37	10	1	3	21	21	29	.440	.500
Throws Right	R	.285	123	35	2	2	8	27	13	32	.355	.528
Lilly,Ted	L	.219	128	28	4	0	6	13	7	27	.265	.391
Throws Left	R	.233	528	123	35	1	16	49	29	124	.273	.394
Lincecum,Tim	L	.209	459	96	18	2	8	35	41	156	.274	.309
Throws Right	R	.203	355	72	14	1	2	24	27	105	.267	.265
Lincoln,Mike	L	.405	37	15	3	0	4	15	10	6	.551	.811
Throws Right	R	.269	52	14	6	0	3	5	9	3	.397	.550
Lindstrom,Matt	L	.278	97	27	4	1	4	20	16	15	.388	.404
Throws Right	R	.284	95	27	9	0	1	8	8	24	.340	.411
Linebrink,Scott	L	.297	101	30	8	3	2	13	15	22	.385	.495
Throws Right	R	.310	129	40	5	0	7	22	8	33	.359	.512
Liriano,Francisco	L	.255	137	35	4	0	1	13	14	31	.325	.307
Throws Left	R	.287	390	112	33	0	20	74	51	91	.373	.526
Litsch,Jesse	L	.261	23	6	0	1	1	4	1	7	.292	.478
Throws Right	R	.471	17	8	1	0	3	5	0	1	.500	1.059
Liz,Radhames	L	.250	4	1	0	0	0	1	1	1	.600	.250
Throws Right	R	.875	8	7	2	1	1	9	1	0	.900	1.750
Logan,Boone	L	.231	39	9	3	0	0	3	4	7	.318	.308
Throws Left	R	.364	33	12	1	0	1	7	5	3	.447	.485
Lohse,Kyle	L	.251	219	55	10	1	8	29	24	35	.324	.416
Throws Right	R	.285	246	70	18	3	8	35	12	42	.321	.480
Looper,Braden	L	.302	364	110	17	1	23	55	38	43	.365	.544
Throws Right	R	.278	417	116	21	5	16	56	26	57	.325	.468
Lopez,Arturo	L	.400	5	2	0	0	0	3	1	0	.571	.400
Throws Left	R	.625	8	5	1	1	2	5	2	0	.700	1.750
Lopez,Javier	L	.429	21	9	3	0	0	6	4	3	.538	.571
Throws Left	R	.367	30	11	4	0	1	4	5	2	.459	.600
Lopez,Rodrigo	L	.327	55	18	7	0	2	13	0	7	.327	.564
Throws Right	R	.348	69	24	7	0	1	10	5	12	.387	.493
Lopez,Wilton	L	.377	53	20	4	1	2	10	5	7	.424	.604
Throws Right	R	.400	30	12	0	0	2	10	3	2	.457	.600
Loux,Shane	L	.385	135	52	11	3	4	27	9	9	.426	.600
Throws Right	R	.291	110	32	6	1	0	12	10	10	.358	.364
Lowe,Derek	L	.300	377	113	21	4	6	35	30	49	.351	.424
Throws Right	R	.303	393	119	25	4	10	65	33	62	.358	.463
Lowe,Mark	L	.253	146	37	8	1	7	24	18	34	.335	.466
Throws Right	R	.213	160	34	11	0	0	19	11	35	.257	.281
Lyon,Brandon	L	.205	112	23	6	0	1	11	21	20	.331	.286
Throws Right	R	.205	161	33	8	1	6	28	10	37	.256	.379
MacDougal,Mike	L	.286	105	30	7	0	1	15	17	15	.379	.381
Throws Right	R	.232	95	22	2	0	2	11	21	19	.383	.316
Madrigal,Warner	L	.481	27	13	2	0	2	10	5	2	.563	.778
Throws Right	R	.185	27	5	2	0	0	4	7	3	.371	.259
Madson,Ryan	L	.257	136	35	4	0	4	14	16	29	.338	.375
Throws Right	R	.245	155	38	8	0	3	13	6	49	.282	.355
Mahay,Ron	L	.262	103	27	4	1	4	23	5	20	.306	.437
Throws Left	R	.327	107	35	7	1	6	17	17	22	.425	.579
Maholm,Paul	L	.182	148	27	7	1	1	9	9	37	.247	.264
Throws Left	R	.316	614	194	45	4	13	81	51	82	.370	.466
Maine,John	L	.159	164	26	7	1	3	17	26	30	.272	.268
Throws Right	R	.304	135	41	7	0	5	23	12	25	.375	.467
Maloney,Matt	L	.286	35	10	2	0	1	5	3	6	.341	.429
Throws Left	R	.280	118	33	9	0	8	15	5	22	.315	.559
Manship,Jeff	L	.318	66	21	6	0	0	7	8	11	.382	.409
Throws Right	R	.300	60	18	2	0	4	8	7	10	.377	.533
Manuel,Robert	L	.125	8	1	0	0	0	0	1	2	.222	.125
Throws Right	R	.444	9	4	1	0	0	0	0	0	.444	.556
Marmol,Carlos	L	.136	118	16	5	0	2	12	27	47	.320	.229
Throws Right	R	.200	135	27	7	1	0	14	38	46	.398	.267

Pitcher	vs	Avg	AB	H	2B	3B	HR	RBI	BB	SO	OBP	Slg
Marquis,Jason	L	.275	403	111	22	3	7	43	49	54	.350	.397
Throws Right	R	.258	414	107	20	5	8	48	31	61	.313	.389
Marshall,Jay	L	.333	12	4	1	0	0	1	0	0	.333	.417
Throws Left	R	.450	20	9	2	0	1	5	0	1	.476	.700
Marshall,Sean	L	.243	107	26	5	2	2	16	12	21	.325	.383
Throws Left	R	.289	225	65	11	2	8	29	20	47	.346	.462
Marte,Damaso	L	.120	25	3	1	0	1	7	2	5	.214	.280
Throws Left	R	.414	29	12	2	0	2	8	4	8	.485	.690
Marte,Victor	L	.167	18	3	1	0	1	2	6	2	.375	.389
Throws Right	R	.357	28	10	1	0	1	9	8	5	.471	.500
Martin,J.D.	L	.307	150	46	7	1	6	21	12	16	.360	.487
Throws Right	R	.252	155	39	13	0	8	17	12	21	.324	.490
Martinez,Carlos	L	.000	2	0	0	0	0	0	1	1	.333	.000
Throws Right	R	.375	8	3	0	0	1	1	1	1	.500	.750
Martinez,Cristhian	L	.163	49	8	4	0	1	6	5	9	.241	.306
Throws Right	R	.352	54	19	3	1	1	11	3	9	.386	.500
Martinez,Joe	L	.429	63	27	5	2	3	18	5	5	.457	.714
Throws Right	R	.279	68	19	5	0	1	8	7	14	.355	.397
Martinez,Pedro	L	.276	105	29	7	0	5	11	4	13	.315	.486
Throws Right	R	.268	71	19	5	1	2	7	4	24	.321	.451
Martis,Shairon	L	.315	178	56	15	1	7	29	25	13	.401	.528
Throws Right	R	.182	148	27	6	1	4	20	14	21	.261	.318
Masset,Nick	L	.219	96	21	4	1	1	10	12	21	.306	.313
Throws Right	R	.194	170	33	6	0	5	23	12	49	.246	.318
Masterson,Justin	L	.323	251	81	16	2	6	39	37	51	.407	.470
Throws Right	R	.203	232	47	3	1	6	29	23	68	.289	.302
Mathis,Doug	L	.250	68	17	4	0	2	8	4	10	.301	.397
Throws Right	R	.239	92	22	1	1	2	11	6	15	.293	.337
Matos,Osiris	L	.313	16	5	0	0	1	3	1	3	.353	.500
Throws Right	R	.429	14	6	1	0	1	5	0	2	.429	.714
Matsuzaka,Daisuke	L	.340	147	50	16	0	5	19	21	28	.424	.551
Throws Right	R	.304	102	31	4	1	5	16	9	26	.366	.510
Matusz,Brian	L	.200	35	7	0	2	2	5	1	11	.222	.486
Throws Left	R	.315	143	45	10	1	4	18	13	27	.367	.483
Mazzaro,Vin	L	.321	218	70	13	1	8	34	27	40	.390	.500
Throws Right	R	.316	158	50	12	0	4	21	12	19	.368	.468
McCarthy,Brandon	L	.264	193	51	11	1	8	27	23	33	.339	.456
Throws Right	R	.246	183	45	9	0	5	17	13	32	.302	.377
McClellan,Kyle	L	.198	106	21	2	0	1	8	16	28	.309	.245
Throws Right	R	.252	139	35	5	1	3	16	18	23	.338	.367
McClung,Seth	L	.291	117	34	6	0	4	13	19	18	.390	.444
Throws Right	R	.243	115	28	5	0	7	21	20	22	.353	.470
McCrory,Bob	L	.500	22	11	4	0	2	13	5	3	.571	.955
Throws Right	R	.375	16	6	0	0	1	6	5	1	.524	.563
McCutchen,Daniel	L	.262	65	17	2	0	2	7	6	8	.324	.385
Throws Right	R	.280	75	21	5	0	4	8	5	11	.333	.507
McDonald,James	L	.213	94	20	3	0	0	8	17	20	.345	.245
Throws Right	R	.282	142	40	6	0	6	18	17	28	.364	.451
Meche,Gil	L	.268	246	66	16	3	8	30	25	48	.330	.455
Throws Right	R	.292	267	78	16	2	9	38	33	47	.375	.468
Medders,Brandon	L	.258	97	25	3	2	2	15	20	24	.383	.392
Throws Right	R	.242	157	38	5	0	4	19	12	34	.297	.350
Medlen,Kris	L	.183	126	23	6	0	2	11	20	43	.291	.278
Throws Right	R	.328	128	42	14	0	3	21	10	29	.386	.508
Meek,Evan	L	.250	72	18	7	1	0	8	11	20	.349	.375
Throws Right	R	.176	91	16	5	1	2	12	18	22	.309	.319
Melancon,Mark	L	.276	29	8	1	2	0	6	5	3	.382	.448
Throws Right	R	.161	31	5	0	0	0	5	5	7	.350	.161
Meloan,John	L	.231	13	3	0	0	0	1	1	6	.286	.231
Throws Right	R	.000	14	0	0	0	0	0	1	5	.067	.000
Mendoza,Luis	L	1.000	2	2	0	0	1	4	0	0	1.000	2.500
Throws Right	R	.000	3	0	0	0	0	0	1	0	.400	.000
Meredith,Cla	L	.280	107	30	4	0	0	11	14	8	.373	.318
Throws Right	R	.305	141	43	4	1	4	30	11	29	.357	.433
Messenger,Randy	L	.320	25	8	1	0	3	4	0	3	.320	.720
Throws Right	R	.278	18	5	1	0	0	2	0	2	.278	.333
Moyer,Dan	L	.228	101	23	4	0	4	11	9	23	.288	.386
Throws Left	R	.211	114	24	3	0	3	12	12	33	.289	.316
Mickolio,Kam	L	.043	23	1	1	0	0	0	5	8	.214	.087
Throws Right	R	.370	27	10	1	0	0	5	2	6	.387	.407
Mijares,Jose	L	.155	103	16	1	0	3	13	10	31	.228	.252
Throws Left	R	.283	120	34	6	0	4	15	13	24	.358	.433
Miller,Andrew	L	.309	81	25	5	2	1	14	14	14	.408	.457
Throws Left	R	.261	230	60	15	2	6	34	29	45	.344	.422
Miller,Justin	L	.241	83	20	3	2	5	12	16	13	.364	.506
Throws Right	R	.233	116	27	4	1	2	15	11	23	.293	.336

Pitchers vs. Left-Handed and Right-Handed Batters

Pitcher	vs	Avg	AB	H	2B	3B	HR	RBI	BB	SO	OBP	Slg
Miller,Trever	L	.135	96	13	3	0	1	10	6	38	.200	.198
Throws Left	R	.295	61	18	3	0	4	9	5	8	.348	.541
Mills,Brad	L	.375	8	3	0	0	0	1	2	2	.500	.375
Throws Left	R	.407	27	11	2	0	4	9	4	7	.469	.926
Millwood,Kevin	L	.240	362	87	18	3	16	41	46	70	.337	.439
Throws Right	R	.272	397	108	20	2	10	38	25	53	.319	.408
Milton,Eric	L	.281	32	9	3	1	1	6	1	10	.303	.531
Throws Left	R	.313	67	21	4	0	1	6	5	10	.378	.418
Miner,Zach	L	.256	160	41	4	3	1	10	21	32	.343	.338
Throws Right	R	.302	199	60	8	1	10	35	24	30	.381	.503
Misch,Pat	L	.321	84	27	3	1	4	11	7	10	.380	.524
Throws Left	R	.265	155	41	8	0	5	22	15	13	.331	.413
Mitre,Sergio	L	.421	95	40	4	1	6	15	8	9	.466	.674
Throws Right	R	.246	126	31	4	1	4	24	5	23	.283	.389
Mock,Garrett	L	.344	189	65	15	1	4	30	24	27	.412	.497
Throws Right	R	.271	181	49	11	2	5	27	20	45	.347	.436
Moehler,Brian	L	.280	304	85	18	6	10	43	33	49	.351	.477
Throws Right	R	.316	323	102	25	1	11	47	18	42	.355	.502
Morales,Franklin	L	.205	39	8	0	0	1	5	5	12	.311	.282
Throws Left	R	.265	113	30	3	0	3	16	18	29	.366	.372
Moreno,Edwin	L	.352	54	19	5	0	2	8	7	7	.444	.556
Throws Right	R	.250	36	9	1	0	1	4	8	8	.386	.361
Morillo,Juan	L	.200	5	1	1	0	0	0	1	0	.333	.400
Throws Right	R	.500	4	2	0	0	1	2	2	1	.667	1.250
Morrow,Brandon	L	.277	148	41	7	0	7	24	28	32	.388	.466
Throws Right	R	.212	118	25	4	0	3	8	16	31	.306	.322
Mortensen,Clayton	L	.317	60	19	4	2	4	18	10	7	.397	.650
Throws Right	R	.338	68	23	5	0	2	13	3	6	.387	.500
Morton,Charlie	L	.316	187	59	11	5	7	31	20	35	.383	.540
Throws Right	R	.236	182	43	6	0	0	15	20	27	.325	.269
Moscoso,Guillermo	L	.412	17	7	1	0	0	3	5	2	.545	.471
Throws Right	R	.205	39	8	5	0	1	4	1	10	.238	.410
Mosebach,Bobby	L	.375	8	3	1	0	0	1	2	1	.545	.500
Throws Right	R	.333	3	1	1	0	0	2	1	1	.500	.667
Moseley,Dustin	L	.281	32	9	1	0	1	4	2	5	.324	.406
Throws Right	R	.367	30	11	2	0	2	3	1	3	.387	.633
Mota,Guillermo	L	.202	94	19	5	0	2	15	15	14	.313	.319
Throws Right	R	.238	143	34	11	0	4	25	9	25	.297	.399
Motte,Jason	L	.341	85	29	8	0	4	15	9	18	.411	.576
Throws Right	R	.214	131	28	6	0	6	17	14	36	.289	.397
Moyer,Jamie	L	.243	152	37	6	1	3	12	10	29	.326	.355
Throws Left	R	.290	482	140	25	1	24	71	33	65	.335	.496
Moylan,Peter	L	.309	94	29	6	2	0	17	22	11	.436	.415
Throws Right	R	.211	171	36	7	1	0	17	13	50	.271	.263
Mujica,Edward	L	.300	180	54	7	2	7	20	11	35	.337	.478
Throws Right	R	.247	190	47	9	0	7	24	8	41	.276	.405
Mulvey,Kevin	L	.228	57	13	2	0	1	4	11	12	.348	.316
Throws Right	R	.400	40	16	3	0	4	18	1	6	.432	.775
Murphy,Bill	L	.125	16	2	1	1	0	1	2	3	.222	.313
Throws Left	R	.100	20	2	0	0	1	3	6	3	.296	.250
Myers,Brett	L	.233	150	35	7	0	4	10	16	30	.314	.360
Throws Right	R	.320	122	39	11	0	14	25	7	20	.364	.754
Narveson,Chris	L	.313	48	15	5	0	1	6	4	12	.370	.479
Throws Left	R	.224	134	30	7	1	6	14	12	34	.289	.425
Nathan,Joe	L	.160	119	19	5	2	3	8	12	42	.237	.311
Throws Right	R	.181	127	23	3	0	4	6	10	47	.252	.299
Nelson,Joe	L	.212	99	21	6	0	5	20	13	23	.298	.424
Throws Right	R	.216	51	11	4	0	2	6	14	13	.394	.412
Ni,Fu-Te	L	.113	62	7	3	0	2	6	7	13	.211	.258
Throws Left	R	.289	45	13	4	0	1	3	4	8	.347	.444
Niemann,Jeff	L	.273	366	100	25	1	7	34	40	70	.346	.404
Throws Right	R	.258	329	85	12	1	10	37	19	55	.311	.392
Niese,Jonathon	L	.333	36	12	4	0	0	4	2	6	.368	.444
Throws Left	R	.242	62	15	5	0	1	7	7	12	.314	.371
Nieve,Fernando	L	.200	80	16	2	0	2	5	11	15	.297	.300
Throws Right	R	.351	57	20	4	0	2	5	8	8	.433	.526
Nippert,Dustin	L	.257	140	36	4	1	5	20	21	31	.352	.407
Throws Right	R	.231	121	28	6	0	2	11	8	23	.291	.331
Nolasco,Ricky	L	.251	398	100	28	2	12	44	30	102	.303	.422
Throws Right	R	.268	328	88	15	5	11	58	14	93	.299	.445
Norris,Bud	L	.200	90	18	3	0	1	9	19	27	.333	.267
Throws Right	R	.323	127	41	6	1	8	18	6	27	.365	.575
Nunez,Jhonny	L	.667	9	6	2	0	0	2	0	1	.667	.889
Throws Right	R	.222	18	4	2	0	1	4	2	2	.300	.500
Nunez,Leo	L	.234	145	34	2	5	5	13	18	39	.317	.421
Throws Right	R	.225	111	25	1	0	8	23	9	21	.304	.450

Pitcher	vs	Avg	AB	H	2B	3B	HR	RBI	BB	SO	OBP	Slg
Nunez,Vladimir	L	.333	3	1	0	0	1	3	2	0	.600	1.333
Throws Right	R	.500	2	1	0	0	1	1	0	1	.500	2.000
O'Day,Darren	L	.239	67	16	1	0	3	11	4	22	.278	.388
Throws Right	R	.180	139	25	4	0	0	13	14	34	.275	.209
O'Flaherty,Eric	L	.215	107	23	2	0	2	11	6	24	.270	.290
Throws Left	R	.282	103	29	2	0	0	10	12	15	.375	.301
Ohka,Tomo	L	.256	133	34	9	1	9	28	13	16	.322	.541
Throws Right	R	.299	144	43	6	0	9	20	6	15	.338	.528
Ohlendorf,Ross	L	.286	343	98	25	6	10	35	28	53	.337	.481
Throws Right	R	.221	303	67	11	0	15	35	25	56	.291	.406
Ohman,Will	L	.296	27	8	2	1	4	8	5	5	.406	.889
Throws Left	R	.211	19	4	0	0	0	1	3	2	.318	.211
Okajima,Hideki	L	.167	108	18	4	1	1	6	7	26	.217	.250
Throws Left	R	.309	123	38	5	0	7	15	14	27	.386	.520
Oliver,Darren	L	.263	114	30	8	0	3	19	4	37	.295	.412
Throws Left	R	.217	143	31	5	0	2	11	18	28	.311	.294
Olsen,Scott	L	.309	55	17	1	0	4	15	6	13	.377	.545
Throws Left	R	.324	204	66	17	6	7	29	19	29	.379	.569
Olson,Garrett	L	.275	91	25	2	1	4	16	11	15	.362	.451
Throws Left	R	.251	215	54	12	0	15	34	23	32	.328	.516
Ortega,Anthony	L	.273	33	9	2	0	2	5	4	5	.351	.515
Throws Right	R	.455	22	10	2	0	2	7	2	2	.500	.818
Ortiz,Russ	L	.272	162	44	8	2	5	27	28	34	.377	.438
Throws Right	R	.305	167	51	13	1	3	20	20	31	.387	.449
O'Sullivan,Sean	L	.263	95	25	9	0	7	15	5	14	.298	.579
Throws Right	R	.324	108	35	12	0	5	17	11	15	.383	.574
Oswalt,Roy	L	.279	341	95	21	2	8	28	20	73	.319	.422
Throws Right	R	.252	349	88	22	1	11	43	22	65	.307	.415
Outman,Josh	L	.123	57	7	1	0	1	2	4	23	.180	.193
Throws Left	R	.238	193	46	8	0	8	23	21	30	.313	.404
Owings,Micah	L	.272	206	56	8	1	6	30	39	27	.382	.408
Throws Right	R	.271	258	70	10	1	12	37	25	41	.348	.457
Padilla,Vicente	L	.303	307	93	10	3	10	36	37	57	.384	.453
Throws Right	R	.246	256	63	10	1	6	26	17	40	.301	.363
Palmer,Matt	L	.279	229	64	11	1	6	29	34	33	.371	.415
Throws Right	R	.197	208	41	9	0	6	22	21	36	.281	.327
Papelbon,Jonathan	L	.187	134	25	9	0	2	8	15	44	.272	.299
Throws Right	R	.242	120	29	1	0	3	10	9	32	.308	.325
Park,Chan Ho	L	.280	157	44	10	0	3	24	15	34	.350	.401
Throws Right	R	.248	161	40	9	1	2	22	18	39	.326	.354
Parnell,Bobby	L	.270	159	43	5	0	4	20	29	36	.384	.377
Throws Right	R	.290	200	58	14	0	4	34	17	38	.355	.420
Paronto,Chad	L	.467	15	7	2	0	0	1	1	1	.500	.600
Throws Right	R	.444	18	8	1	0	4	8	0	2	.421	1.167
Parr,James	L	.367	30	11	2	4	1	9	2	4	.424	.800
Throws Right	R	.214	28	6	2	1	0	3	3	8	.281	.357
Parra,Manny	L	.287	122	35	6	1	2	18	18	31	.376	.402
Throws Left	R	.311	463	144	34	1	17	78	59	85	.389	.499
Patton,David	L	.243	37	9	2	0	2	4	11	9	.417	.459
Throws Right	R	.297	74	22	1	0	2	13	8	14	.361	.392
Paulino,Felipe	L	.354	181	64	10	2	14	42	23	52	.427	.663
Throws Right	R	.286	217	62	10	0	6	25	14	41	.338	.415
Pavano,Carl	L	.271	409	111	23	6	10	47	26	92	.313	.430
Throws Right	R	.317	391	124	19	3	16	63	13	55	.345	.504
Peavy,Jake	L	.249	201	50	13	1	4	20	22	57	.324	.383
Throws Right	R	.178	169	30	2	1	4	17	12	53	.231	.272
Pelfrey,Mike	L	.284	422	120	23	3	12	61	40	60	.348	.438
Throws Right	R	.294	316	93	16	2	6	43	26	47	.353	.415
Pena,Tony	L	.288	118	34	8	1	5	24	17	19	.378	.500
Throws Right	R	.280	168	47	5	1	2	19	3	36	.297	.357
Pena,Tony F	L	-	0	0	0	0	0	0	0	0	-	-
Throws Right	R	-	0	0	0	0	0	0	0	0	-	-
Penn,Hayden	L	.400	45	18	4	0	0	10	10	13	.509	.489
Throws Right	R	.245	49	12	2	0	3	16	10	14	.393	.469
Penny,Brad	L	.259	359	93	21	4	11	39	29	66	.313	.432
Throws Right	R	.299	328	98	20	3	11	48	22	43	.347	.479
Peralta,Joel	L	.348	46	16	7	1	2	13	8	8	.455	.674
Throws Right	R	.216	51	11	4	0	1	8	4	14	.293	.353
Percival,Troy	L	.478	23	11	3	0	3	4	3	2	.538	1.000
Throws Right	R	.130	23	3	1	0	0	1	2	5	.231	.174
Perdomo,Luis	L	.293	116	34	6	1	8	24	17	25	.383	.569
Throws Right	R	.198	116	23	4	3	3	17	17	30	.299	.362
Perez,Chris	L	.188	69	13	3	0	3	13	12	30	.317	.362
Throws Right	R	.207	135	28	5	0	5	25	15	38	.306	.356
Perez,Oliver	L	.200	80	16	0	0	3	9	8	23	.278	.313
Throws Left	R	.306	173	53	14	2	9	36	50	39	.463	.566

Pitchers vs. Left-Handed and Right-Handed Batters

Pitcher	vs	Avg	AB	H	2B	3B	HR	RBI	BB	SO	OBP	Slg
Perez,Rafael	L	.412	85	35	4	1	3	16	12	12	.480	.588
Throws Left	R	.277	112	31	9	0	2	14	13	20	.359	.411
Perkins,Glen	L	.333	87	29	3	0	3	11	9	10	.402	.471
Throws Left	R	.295	308	91	16	2	10	49	14	35	.323	.458
Perry,Ryan	L	.294	102	30	4	0	4	20	18	20	.390	.451
Throws Right	R	.206	126	26	7	0	3	13	20	40	.320	.333
Petit,Yusmeiro	L	.282	195	55	6	2	12	30	15	34	.333	.518
Throws Right	R	.269	175	47	16	0	7	27	19	40	.340	.480
Pettitte,Andy	L	.282	220	62	10	0	6	25	12	55	.321	.409
Throws Left	R	.249	526	131	28	1	14	56	64	93	.332	.386
Pineiro,Joel	L	.272	394	107	25	1	7	42	17	47	.300	.393
Throws Right	R	.266	418	111	24	2	4	46	10	58	.294	.361
Pinto,Renyel	L	.277	94	26	3	1	2	16	22	32	.413	.394
Throws Left	R	.208	130	27	4	2	2	13	23	26	.327	.315
Ponson,Sidney	L	.372	129	48	6	2	4	25	16	17	.443	.543
Throws Right	R	.284	109	31	7	2	2	20	9	15	.333	.440
Porcello,Rick	L	.281	381	107	14	1	13	36	27	50	.328	.425
Throws Right	R	.248	278	69	13	0	10	33	25	39	.316	.403
Poreda,Aaron	L	.333	18	6	1	0	0	1	6	7	.500	.389
Throws Left	R	.143	28	4	0	0	0	4	7	5	.333	.143
Price,David	L	.236	110	26	7	0	1	11	13	28	.315	.327
Throws Left	R	.242	384	93	19	0	16	56	41	74	.321	.417
Purcey,David	L	.156	45	7	3	0	0	4	8	8	.291	.222
Throws Left	R	.329	143	47	7	2	6	25	22	31	.418	.531
Putz,J.J.	L	.296	54	16	3	1	1	8	15	8	.443	.444
Throws Right	R	.220	59	13	2	2	0	8	4	13	.266	.322
Qualls,Chad	L	.298	104	31	6	1	1	13	3	19	.324	.404
Throws Right	R	.214	103	22	6	0	4	12	4	26	.250	.388
Ramirez,Edwar	L	.302	53	16	0	0	3	8	12	16	.424	.472
Throws Right	R	.250	36	9	3	0	3	12	6	6	.349	.583
Ramirez,Horacio	L	.245	49	12	4	0	0	3	3	0	.288	.327
Throws Left	R	.349	43	15	4	1	3	9	8	4	.451	.698
Ramirez,Ramon A.	L	.273	11	3	0	0	1	1	1	2	.385	.545
Throws Right	R	.156	32	5	2	0	1	2	3	6	.229	.313
Ramirez,Ramon	L	.244	135	33	8	1	6	16	19	20	.342	.452
Throws Right	R	.220	127	28	7	1	1	14	13	32	.308	.315
Ramos,Cesar	L	.118	17	2	0	0	0	1	0	3	.118	.118
Throws Left	R	.415	41	17	1	1	0	2	4	7	.467	.488
Rapada,Clay	L	.333	6	2	1	0	0	3	0	2	.333	.500
Throws Left	R	.250	8	2	0	0	1	3	2	0	.400	.625
Rauch,Jon	L	.237	118	28	5	3	2	14	19	24	.343	.381
Throws Right	R	.282	149	42	6	1	4	22	4	25	.302	.416
Ray,Chris	L	.449	78	35	8	0	5	18	9	11	.506	.744
Throws Right	R	.279	104	29	7	0	3	24	14	28	.358	.433
Ray,Robert	L	.239	46	11	3	0	1	6	4	5	.308	.370
Throws Right	R	.267	45	12	3	0	3	8	2	8	.313	.533
Redding,Tim	L	.278	245	68	23	2	9	30	34	48	.362	.498
Throws Right	R	.247	219	54	10	0	9	36	16	28	.300	.416
Register,Steven	L	.500	4	2	1	0	0	0	0	1	.500	.750
Throws Right	R	.200	5	1	0	1	0	1	1	0	.429	.600
Reineke,Chad	L	.400	10	4	1	0	2	3	0	1	.400	1.100
Throws Right	R	.273	11	3	1	0	0	1	0	0	.333	.364
Reyes,Anthony	L	.292	72	21	4	0	4	16	10	10	.373	.514
Throws Right	R	.257	74	19	5	1	1	10	13	12	.374	.392
Reyes,Dennys	L	.207	92	19	2	0	0	10	8	17	.288	.228
Throws Left	R	.276	58	16	5	0	2	7	13	16	.408	.466
Reyes,Jo-Jo	L	.156	32	5	1	0	1	2	2	11	.229	.281
Throws Left	R	.310	71	22	9	2	3	16	11	10	.398	.620
Rhodes,Arthur	L	.141	85	12	1	0	0	5	9	22	.227	.153
Throws Left	R	.245	102	25	5	2	3	9	11	26	.319	.422
Richard,Clayton	L	.229	131	30	4	0	4	10	11	37	.294	.351
Throws Left	R	.279	445	124	20	3	13	66	60	77	.363	.425
Richardson,Dustin	L	.200	5	1	0	0	0	0	0	0	.200	.200
Throws Left	R	.286	7	2	0	0	0	2	1	0	.333	.286
Richmond,Scott	L	.292	329	96	26	4	17	54	46	68	.377	.550
Throws Right	R	.233	219	51	7	1	10	29	13	49	.276	.411
Rincon,Juan	L	.241	58	14	5	1	2	7	11	15	.362	.466
Throws Right	R	.208	77	16	3	0	2	11	15	20	.340	.325
Riske,David	L	1.000	3	3	1	0	0	0	0	0	1.000	1.333
Throws Right	R	.500	2	1	0	0	0	1	0	0	.333	.500
Rivera,Mariano	L	.182	121	22	0	1	3	6	9	35	.238	.273
Throws Right	R	.211	123	26	5	0	4	11	3	37	.236	.350
Rivera,Saul	L	.296	71	21	4	0	3	14	9	7	.390	.479
Throws Right	R	.321	84	27	8	0	4	16	5	14	.363	.560
Robertson,David	L	.189	74	14	2	1	2	6	9	30	.277	.324
Throws Right	R	.237	93	22	8	1	2	18	14	33	.343	.409

Pitcher	vs	Avg	AB	H	2B	3B	HR	RBI	BB	SO	OBP	Slg
Robertson,Nate	L	.295	78	23	4	0	1	16	7	18	.360	.385
Throws Left	R	.295	122	36	4	0	3	18	21	17	.399	.402
Rodney,Fernando	L	.269	160	43	6	1	3	14	20	40	.352	.375
Throws Right	R	.223	121	27	4	1	5	18	21	21	.340	.397
Rodriguez,Fernando	L	.500	2	1	0	0	1	2	2	0	.750	2.000
Throws Right	R	.000	2	0	0	0	0	0	0	1	.000	.000
Rodriguez,Francisco	L	.185	130	24	6	0	2	14	13	40	.264	.277
Throws Right	R	.223	121	27	6	0	5	19	25	33	.354	.397
Rodriguez,Henry	L	.429	7	3	0	0	0	2	2	0	.556	.429
Throws Right	R	.100	10	1	0	0	0	0	0	4	.182	.100
Rodriguez,Rafael	L	.371	62	23	4	2	3	9	4	3	.403	.645
Throws Right	R	.343	70	24	4	0	1	12	5	7	.390	.443
Rodriguez,Wandy	L	.192	151	29	5	0	2	6	9	39	.238	.265
Throws Left	R	.264	618	163	35	1	19	66	54	154	.326	.416
Roenicke,Josh	L	.351	57	20	4	0	1	14	11	13	.449	.474
Throws Right	R	.190	63	12	0	0	1	7	5	20	.261	.238
Rogers,Esmil	L	.250	8	2	0	0	0	2	0	2	.222	.250
Throws Right	R	.200	5	1	0	0	0	0	2	1	.429	.200
Romero,J.C.	L	.308	26	8	0	0	2	3	4	7	.438	.538
Throws Left	R	.156	32	5	0	0	0	2	9	5	.341	.156
Romero,Ricky	L	.297	209	62	19	0	10	30	16	55	.348	.531
Throws Left	R	.278	467	130	20	1	8	50	63	86	.373	.377
Romo,Sergio	L	.188	48	9	1	2	0	4	4	15	.250	.292
Throws Right	R	.259	81	21	3	1	1	5	7	26	.326	.358
Rosa,Carlos	L	.158	19	3	0	0	1	4	2	4	.227	.316
Throws Right	R	.350	20	7	1	0	0	4	1	0	.381	.400
Rosales,Leo	L	.235	85	20	4	2	1	9	6	10	.293	.365
Throws Right	R	.238	84	20	4	0	4	14	6	13	.280	.429
Rowland-Smith,Ryan	L	.195	87	17	4	0	2	8	5	15	.260	.310
Throws Left	R	.253	277	70	16	1	7	25	22	37	.306	.394
Rundles,Rich	L	.000	1	0	0	0	0	0	1	1	.500	.000
Throws Left	R	.333	3	1	1	0	0	2	0	0	.500	.667
Runzler,Dan	L	.059	17	1	0	0	0	1	2	6	.200	.059
Throws Left	R	.333	15	5	0	0	1	3	3	5	.444	.533
Rupe,Josh	L	.200	10	2	0	0	1	3	2	2	.333	.500
Throws Right	R	.625	16	10	2	1	1	9	3	0	.684	1.063
Rusch,Glendon	L	.368	19	7	1	0	0	4	0	3	.368	.421
Throws Left	R	.406	69	28	7	0	3	15	3	10	.431	.638
Russell,Adam	L	.286	21	6	1	0	0	5	4	5	.400	.333
Throws Right	R	.241	29	7	0	0	0	1	7	9	.389	.241
Ryan,B.J.	L	.250	36	9	2	0	1	3	7	9	.378	.389
Throws Left	R	.333	39	13	1	1	4	9	10	4	.469	.718
Rzepczynski,Marc	L	.220	50	11	2	1	1	9	4	15	.291	.360
Throws Left	R	.226	177	40	7	0	6	15	26	45	.324	.367
Sabathia,CC	L	.198	197	39	9	2	3	19	13	60	.250	.310
Throws Left	R	.242	652	158	34	4	15	70	54	137	.305	.376
Sadler,Billy	L	.500	4	2	0	0	0	1	1	1	.600	.500
Throws Right	R	.000	2	0	0	0	0	0	0	1	.000	.000
Sadowski,Ryan	L	.291	55	16	3	0	1	10	10	9	.388	.400
Throws Right	R	.235	51	12	1	0	1	4	7	8	.333	.314
Saito,Takashi	L	.195	113	22	1	0	2	13	12	32	.273	.257
Throws Right	R	.304	92	28	4	1	4	12	13	20	.405	.500
Samardzija,Jeff	L	.361	61	22	4	3	4	14	9	12	.443	.721
Throws Right	R	.304	79	24	5	0	3	18	6	9	.356	.481
Sampson,Chris	L	.315	111	35	7	2	0	18	7	13	.356	.414
Throws Right	R	.272	114	31	9	2	2	27	14	20	.349	.439
Sanches,Brian	L	.245	94	23	3	0	2	6	12	17	.349	.340
Throws Right	R	.227	119	27	7	0	3	17	14	34	.324	.361
Sanchez,Anibal	L	.231	169	39	11	1	3	18	29	32	.340	.361
Throws Right	R	.276	163	45	8	1	7	17	17	39	.348	.466
Sanchez,Duaner	L	.355	31	11	2	0	1	5	3	2	.412	.516
Throws Right	R	.438	16	7	2	0	2	6	5	0	.591	.938
Sanchez,Jonathan	L	.223	157	35	6	1	4	18	13	43	.299	.350
Throws Left	R	.220	455	100	33	1	15	52	75	134	.332	.396
Santana,Ervin	L	.323	291	94	17	3	12	43	27	54	.385	.526
Throws Right	R	.248	262	65	11	0	12	36	20	53	.318	.427
Santana,Johan	L	.267	180	48	13	0	10	19	10	40	.309	.506
Throws Left	R	.235	460	108	22	1	10	41	36	106	.291	.352
Sarfate,Dennis	L	.256	39	10	2	1	1	5	6	12	.356	.436
Throws Right	R	.244	45	11	3	0	2	11	8	8	.370	.444
Saunders,Joe	L	.257	191	49	3	2	5	16	16	35	.324	.372
Throws Left	R	.287	534	153	29	2	24	80	48	66	.346	.483
Scherzer,Max	L	.265	351	93	22	4	11	52	44	87	.348	.444
Throws Right	R	.239	306	73	20	2	9	31	19	87	.296	.405
Schlereth,Daniel	L	.222	27	6	1	0	1	8	8	6	.400	.370
Throws Left	R	.220	41	9	0	0	0	7	7	16	.347	.220

Pitchers vs. Left-Handed and Right-Handed Batters

Pitcher	vs	Avg	AB	H	2B	3B	HR	RBI	BB	SO	OBP	Slg
Schlichting,Travis	L	.143	7	1	0	0	1	1	2	1	.333	.571
Throws Right	R	.000	2	0	0	0	0	1	3	1	.500	.000
Schmidt,Jason	L	.226	31	7	0	0	0	2	7	0	.400	.226
Throws Right	R	.250	36	9	5	1	1	6	5	8	.357	.528
Schoeneweis,Scott	L	.276	58	16	0	0	4	10	5	11	.354	.483
Throws Left	R	.302	43	13	2	0	2	8	8	3	.412	.488
Seay,Bobby	L	.261	111	29	6	1	1	16	9	23	.328	.360
Throws Left	R	.239	71	17	3	1	2	9	8	14	.313	.394
Segovia,Zack	L	.318	22	7	1	1	1	6	4	1	.423	.591
Throws Right	R	.235	17	4	0	0	0	4	2	3	.286	.235
Shell,Steven	L	.000	7	0	0	0	0	0	1	1	.125	.000
Throws Right	R	.385	13	5	2	0	1	6	1	4	.429	.769
Sherrill,George	L	.128	78	10	2	0	0	2	6	29	.188	.154
Throws Left	R	.244	176	43	11	0	4	15	18	32	.321	.375
Shields,James	L	.272	448	122	29	3	17	58	27	95	.314	.464
Throws Right	R	.279	420	117	25	3	12	40	25	72	.318	.438
Shields,Scot	L	.250	32	8	3	0	0	5	6	5	.368	.344
Throws Right	R	.229	35	8	1	0	1	8	9	7	.386	.343
Shouse,Brian	L	.224	67	15	1	0	3	8	1	14	.246	.373
Throws Left	R	.356	45	16	6	0	2	8	6	3	.442	.622
Silva,Carlos	L	.380	71	27	12	0	4	16	7	4	.436	.718
Throws Right	R	.250	56	14	4	1	1	9	4	6	.333	.411
Silva,Walter	L	.323	62	20	3	0	1	11	8	7	.394	.419
Throws Right	R	.341	41	14	2	1	3	12	7	4	.420	.659
Simon,Alfredo	L	.333	15	5	0	0	3	4	1	0	.375	.933
Throws Right	R	.273	11	3	0	0	2	2	1	3	.333	.818
Sipp,Tony	L	.208	72	15	4	0	3	7	9	24	.296	.389
Throws Left	R	.179	67	12	5	0	2	11	16	24	.333	.343
Slaten,Doug	L	.389	18	7	2	0	1	5	0	4	.389	.667
Throws Left	R	.273	11	3	0	1	0	2	1	0	.333	.455
Slowey,Kevin	L	.354	175	62	14	1	6	20	13	38	.398	.549
Throws Right	R	.267	191	51	10	0	9	28	2	37	.285	.461
Smith,Chris	L	.232	82	19	2	0	6	10	13	16	.344	.476
Throws Right	R	.232	95	22	6	0	5	13	6	19	.291	.453
Smith,Joe	L	.355	31	11	4	0	1	5	3	9	.412	.581
Throws Right	R	.198	96	19	3	1	3	13	10	21	.271	.344
Smoltz,John	L	.342	161	55	14	1	8	31	11	33	.386	.590
Throws Right	R	.256	156	40	12	0	3	20	7	40	.289	.391
Snell,Ian	L	.265	283	75	27	1	6	32	50	39	.376	.431
Throws Right	R	.267	273	73	21	4	8	44	33	50	.349	.462
Sonnanstine,Andy	L	.275	255	70	16	0	7	33	19	33	.326	.420
Throws Right	R	.367	166	61	11	3	12	46	15	27	.421	.687
Soria,Joakim	L	.224	107	24	2	0	2	11	6	35	.261	.299
Throws Right	R	.213	94	20	4	1	3	10	10	34	.302	.372
Soriano,Rafael	L	.258	128	33	7	1	4	16	13	37	.324	.422
Throws Right	R	.138	145	20	5	1	2	9	14	65	.217	.228
Sosa,Jorge	L	.344	32	11	3	0	4	9	8	5	.463	.813
Throws Right	R	.293	58	17	6	0	1	9	4	12	.339	.448
Sowers,Jeremy	L	.291	134	39	9	0	3	17	10	24	.340	.425
Throws Left	R	.277	343	95	22	2	8	45	42	27	.354	.423
Speier,Justin	L	.328	67	22	3	0	4	11	10	19	.430	.552
Throws Right	R	.239	92	22	2	0	3	12	5	20	.290	.359
Speier,Ryan	L	.222	9	2	0	0	0	2	1	1	.300	.222
Throws Right	R	.400	10	4	0	1	0	5	2	1	.500	.600
Springer,Russ	L	.350	80	28	4	0	4	14	12	19	.430	.550
Throws Right	R	.263	152	40	8	1	5	26	5	39	.282	.428
Stammen,Craig	L	.290	224	65	18	1	6	26	11	13	.329	.460
Throws Right	R	.247	190	47	15	1	8	24	13	35	.294	.463
Stark,Denny	L	.333	21	7	1	0	2	5	7	3	.500	.667
Throws Right	R	.273	22	6	0	0	0	4	3	4	.346	.273
Stauffer,Tim	L	.239	138	33	4	2	2	12	17	26	.331	.341
Throws Right	R	.279	136	38	6	1	6	16	17	27	.369	.471
Stetter,Mitch	L	.178	90	16	5	0	2	14	12	31	.295	.300
Throws Left	R	.259	81	21	5	0	2	11	15	13	.388	.395
Stevens,Jeffrey	L	.318	22	7	3	0	0	2	3	4	.400	.455
Throws Right	R	.259	27	7	1	1	2	7	5	5	.394	.593
Stokes,Brian	L	.330	115	38	11	2	1	13	21	21	.435	.487
Throws Right	R	.219	155	34	4	1	5	25	17	24	.297	.355
Stoner,Tobi	L	.176	17	3	0	0	1	2	3	3	.300	.353
Throws Right	R	.400	15	6	1	0	1	2	0	2	.400	.667
Street,Huston	L	.167	102	17	4	0	2	8	8	23	.227	.265
Throws Right	R	.217	120	26	4	0	5	16	5	47	.244	.375
Strop,Pedro	L	.154	13	2	2	0	0	3	0	5	.154	.308
Throws Right	R	.308	13	4	1	0	0	4	4	4	.471	.385
Stults,Eric	L	.262	42	11	4	1	0	5	7	7	.392	.405
Throws Left	R	.270	148	40	12	1	3	17	19	26	.361	.426

Pitcher	vs	Avg	AB	H	2B	3B	HR	RBI	BB	SO	OBP	Slg
Suppan,Jeff	L	.311	302	94	15	6	10	45	43	40	.402	.500
Throws Right	R	.306	346	106	28	1	15	52	31	40	.373	.523
Swarzak,Anthony	L	.331	124	41	4	2	7	25	12	22	.391	.565
Throws Right	R	.292	120	35	5	0	5	13	8	12	.341	.458
Swindle,R.J.	L	.385	13	5	2	0	1	5	3	3	.529	.769
Throws Left	R	.368	19	7	1	0	2	6	1	5	.400	.737
Switzer,Jon	L	.333	6	2	1	0	1	3	2	2	.500	1.000
Throws Left	R	.250	8	2	0	0	0	1	0	1	.333	.250
Takahashi,Ken	L	.302	53	16	4	1	1	7	6	13	.387	.472
Throws Left	R	.156	45	7	3	0	1	5	8	10	.278	.289
Tallet,Brian	L	.290	176	51	15	2	7	30	22	31	.376	.517
Throws Left	R	.259	455	118	28	2	13	64	50	89	.333	.415
Tankersley,Taylor	L	-	0	0	0	0	0	0	0	0	-	-
Throws Left	R	-	0	0	0	0	0	0	0	0	-	-
Taschner,Jack	L	.324	37	12	1	1	0	7	9	8	.468	.405
Throws Left	R	.313	83	26	5	0	3	11	11	11	.400	.482
Tavarez,Julian	L	.315	54	17	5	1	1	7	13	12	.441	.500
Throws Right	R	.207	82	17	6	0	0	9	14	20	.330	.280
Taylor,Graham	L	.455	11	5	0	0	0	8	4	1	.588	.455
Throws Left	R	.306	36	11	2	0	0	2	8	4	.422	.361
Tazawa,Junichi	L	.323	65	21	5	0	0	9	5	6	.370	.400
Throws Right	R	.440	50	22	4	1	4	14	4	7	.491	.800
Tejeda,Robinson	L	.209	129	27	5	0	2	17	33	35	.376	.295
Throws Right	R	.125	128	16	2	0	2	10	17	52	.233	.188
Thatcher,Joe	L	.182	77	14	3	0	1	9	6	33	.253	.260
Throws Left	R	.267	86	23	5	0	1	10	12	22	.370	.360
Thayer,Dale	L	.208	24	5	0	0	1	3	1	6	.240	.333
Throws Right	R	.382	34	13	2	0	2	4	0	2	.382	.618
Thompson,Brad	L	.255	145	37	7	4	5	23	15	18	.325	.462
Throws Right	R	.289	166	48	13	0	3	20	8	16	.344	.422
Thompson,Rich	L	.351	37	13	3	0	3	6	4	8	.415	.676
Throws Right	R	.311	45	14	2	0	3	9	3	13	.360	.556
Thornton,Matt	L	.208	101	21	5	1	2	6	7	43	.259	.337
Throws Left	R	.223	166	37	5	1	3	22	13	44	.282	.319
Tillman,Chris	L	.254	130	33	5	2	6	14	17	27	.349	.462
Throws Right	R	.341	129	44	6	0	9	22	7	12	.375	.597
Todd,Jesse	L	.408	49	20	1	0	4	17	4	9	.444	.673
Throws Right	R	.304	46	14	2	0	0	7	5	11	.352	.348
Tomko,Brett	L	.218	101	22	5	0	3	6	7	14	.275	.356
Throws Right	R	.252	111	28	4	0	9	17	6	19	.291	.532
Torres,Carlos	L	.264	53	14	0	0	3	9	11	12	.385	.434
Throws Right	R	.308	52	16	5	0	2	9	6	10	.387	.519
Towers,Josh	L	.091	11	1	1	0	0	1	1	1	.154	.182
Throws Right	R	.455	11	5	2	0	0	2	0	1	.500	.636
Traber,Billy	L	.429	7	3	1	0	0	3	0	0	.429	.571
Throws Left	R	.500	12	6	0	0	2	5	1	1	.538	1.000
Troncoso,Ramon	L	.289	135	39	7	0	2	15	17	27	.365	.385
Throws Right	R	.251	175	44	4	0	1	9	17	28	.325	.291
Uehara,Koji	L	.273	139	38	7	3	4	10	4	25	.290	.453
Throws Right	R	.266	124	33	12	0	3	17	8	23	.308	.435
Valdez,Luis	L	.750	4	3	2	0	0	1	0	0	.750	1.250
Throws Right	R	.000	7	0	0	0	0	0	2	0	.222	.000
Valdez,Merkin	L	.250	84	21	1	0	2	6	14	20	.354	.333
Throws Right	R	.324	111	36	7	1	3	32	14	18	.400	.486
Valverde,Jose	L	.281	89	25	4	1	2	6	11	22	.356	.416
Throws Right	R	.144	104	15	4	0	3	9	10	34	.231	.269
VandenHurk,Rick	L	.273	128	35	10	2	7	22	12	30	.340	.547
Throws Right	R	.224	98	22	3	0	4	7	9	19	.303	.378
Vargas,Claudio	L	.203	59	12	3	0	1	5	7	10	.294	.305
Throws Right	R	.159	82	13	1	0	2	4	8	20	.242	.244
Vargas,Jason	L	.290	107	31	5	0	6	18	8	16	.336	.505
Throws Left	R	.277	242	67	13	1	10	29	16	38	.323	.463
Vasquez,Esmerling	L	.196	92	18	3	0	4	17	15	21	.312	.359
Throws Right	R	.304	112	34	9	1	0	14	14	24	.391	.402
Vasquez,Virgil	L	.342	76	26	9	1	1	11	12	13	.433	.526
Throws Right	R	.305	105	32	9	1	5	18	6	16	.351	.552
Vazquez,Javier	L	.235	405	95	14	4	14	36	26	112	.282	.393
Throws Right	R	.212	406	86	14	2	6	32	18	126	.249	.300
Veal,Donnie	L	.200	20	4	1	0	0	1	8	7	.448	.250
Throws Left	R	.318	44	14	2	1	2	10	12	9	.466	.545
Veras,Jose	L	.259	81	21	6	0	4	9	13	15	.368	.481
Throws Right	R	.198	106	21	5	0	4	21	15	25	.325	.358
Verlander,Justin	L	.248	505	125	26	1	14	58	37	157	.298	.386
Throws Right	R	.237	397	94	24	1	6	32	26	112	.292	.348
Villanueva,Carlos	L	.257	183	47	12	1	7	20	15	44	.317	.448
Throws Right	R	.278	198	55	10	2	6	30	20	39	.347	.439

Pitchers vs. Left-Handed and Right-Handed Batters

Pitcher	vs	Avg	AB	H	2B	3B	HR	RBI	BB	SO	OBP	Slg
Villone,Ron	L	.293	99	29	4	1	2	20	13	18	.386	.414
Throws Left	R	.272	92	25	8	1	4	14	16	15	.373	.511
Viola,Pedro	L	.077	13	1	0	0	0	0	2	2	.200	.077
Throws Left	R	.462	13	6	0	0	2	3	1	3	.500	.923
Vizcaino,Luis	L	.050	20	1	0	0	0	0	6	5	.269	.050
Throws Right	R	.257	35	9	2	0	2	7	6	7	.357	.486
Volquez,Edinson	L	.202	84	17	6	0	2	12	12	25	.299	.345
Throws Right	R	.181	94	17	5	0	4	10	20	22	.353	.362
Volstad,Chris	L	.255	318	81	13	3	18	45	33	50	.326	.484
Throws Right	R	.302	291	88	15	1	11	44	26	57	.362	.474
Waddell,Jason	L	.333	6	2	0	0	0	0	0	2	.333	.333
Throws Left	R	.500	2	1	0	0	0	0	0	0	.500	.500
Wade,Cory	L	.283	46	13	4	0	0	5	5	9	.346	.370
Throws Right	R	.238	63	15	2	1	3	12	5	9	.304	.444
Waechter,Doug	L	.214	14	3	1	0	1	3	2	1	.313	.500
Throws Right	R	.600	10	6	1	0	1	2	1	2	.583	1.000
Wagner,Billy	L	.111	18	2	1	0	0	2	3	9	.238	.167
Throws Right	R	.176	34	6	2	0	1	3	5	17	.300	.324
Wainwright,Adam	L	.275	403	111	27	2	9	33	42	101	.345	.419
Throws Right	R	.217	483	105	11	0	8	29	24	111	.255	.290
Wakefield,Tim	L	.280	207	58	11	0	5	29	20	23	.351	.406
Throws Right	R	.263	300	79	21	1	7	33	30	49	.344	.410
Walker,Jamie	L	.458	24	11	2	0	4	10	0	5	.462	1.042
Throws Left	R	.296	27	8	3	0	1	5	0	4	.286	.519
Walker,Tyler	L	.229	48	11	1	0	1	7	4	8	.283	.313
Throws Right	R	.230	87	20	3	1	3	14	3	15	.251	.391
Walters,P.J.	L	.355	31	11	2	0	4	11	8	3	.475	.806
Throws Right	R	.263	38	10	0	1	2	7	1	11	.282	.474
Wang,Chien-Ming	L	.394	99	39	11	1	5	30	12	10	.469	.677
Throws Right	R	.329	82	27	8	0	2	10	7	19	.378	.500
Washburn,Jarrod	L	.178	180	32	6	0	6	16	8	47	.224	.311
Throws Left	R	.268	478	128	22	2	17	55	41	53	.326	.429
Waters,Chris	L	.214	14	3	0	0	1	3	1	4	.267	.429
Throws Left	R	.200	30	6	1	0	2	2	4	1	.294	.433
Weathers,David	L	.218	87	19	9	0	3	12	16	12	.340	.425
Throws Right	R	.241	141	34	4	1	7	18	12	25	.303	.433
Weaver,Jeff	L	.286	133	38	12	3	4	16	17	24	.377	.511
Throws Right	R	.277	177	49	7	2	3	14	16	40	.342	.390
Weaver,Jered	L	.276	438	121	32	4	16	52	37	101	.335	.477
Throws Right	R	.208	360	75	21	0	10	28	29	73	.265	.350
Webb,Brandon	L	.222	9	2	1	0	0	4	1	2	.300	.333
Throws Right	R	.500	8	4	1	0	2	2	1	0	.600	1.375
Webb,Ryan	L	.250	48	12	2	1	3	11	8	10	.368	.521
Throws Right	R	.278	54	15	2	1	0	4	3	9	.310	.352
Wellemeyer,Todd	L	.351	245	86	14	4	16	56	36	34	.432	.637
Throws Right	R	.305	243	74	7	1	3	29	21	44	.363	.379
Wells,Kip	L	.248	113	28	7	1	3	18	22	16	.372	.407
Throws Right	R	.212	151	32	3	2	3	20	18	27	.312	.318
Wells,Randy	L	.310	287	89	13	0	8	29	26	47	.367	.439
Throws Right	R	.221	344	76	8	1	6	29	20	57	.273	.302
West,Sean	L	.338	74	25	7	0	2	14	5	15	.375	.514
Throws Left	R	.267	337	90	22	4	9	39	39	55	.346	.436
Wheeler,Dan	L	.305	59	18	6	0	5	10	5	6	.359	.661
Throws Right	R	.156	147	23	4	2	6	23	4	39	.178	.333
Whisler,Wes	L	.000	2	0	0	0	0	0	2	0	.500	.000
Throws Left	R	.000	2	0	0	0	0	0	1	2	.333	.000
White,Sean	L	.191	110	21	4	1	1	10	10	11	.258	.273
Throws Right	R	.238	122	29	5	0	2	18	10	17	.299	.328
Williams,Randy	L	.162	37	6	1	0	1	6	4	14	.279	.270
Throws Left	R	.269	26	7	1	0	1	6	8	8	.444	.423
Willis,Dontrelle	L	.306	36	11	1	0	3	13	8	8	.444	.583
Throws Left	R	.289	90	26	5	0	1	9	20	9	.407	.378
Wilson,Brian	L	.189	132	25	8	0	0	6	17	42	.282	.250
Throws Right	R	.255	137	35	4	0	3	23	10	41	.307	.350
Wilson,C.J.	L	.206	97	20	3	0	0	3	12	28	.319	.237
Throws Left	R	.249	185	46	12	1	3	25	20	56	.329	.373
Wolf,Randy	L	.159	170	27	2	1	1	9	13	60	.217	.200
Throws Left	R	.246	614	151	36	2	23	67	45	100	.303	.423
Wolfe,Brian	L	.444	27	12	2	0	1	9	5	4	.514	.630
Throws Right	R	.333	39	13	2	0	4	8	2	7	.366	.692
Wood,Kerry	L	.255	110	28	1	1	4	12	14	34	.336	.391
Throws Right	R	.208	96	20	3	1	3	14	14	29	.322	.354
Wood,Tim	L	.219	32	7	1	0	1	7	7	7	.359	.344
Throws Right	R	.306	49	15	1	1	1	10	3	9	.339	.429
Wright,Jamey	L	.200	130	26	4	1	2	21	28	31	.342	.292
Throws Right	R	.285	165	47	5	0	6	30	16	29	.372	.424

Pitcher	vs	Avg	AB	H	2B	3B	HR	RBI	BB	SO	OBP	Slg
Wright,Wesley	L	.359	64	23	5	0	1	5	10	21	.440	.484
Throws Left	R	.265	113	30	3	0	8	19	15	26	.349	.504
Wuertz,Mike	L	.183	115	21	5	2	3	10	9	42	.238	.339
Throws Right	R	.193	161	31	9	0	3	16	14	60	.256	.304
Yabuta,Yasuhiko	L	.467	30	14	5	0	1	9	4	5	.529	.733
Throws Right	R	.385	39	15	3	0	2	12	3	4	.419	.615
Yates,Tyler	L	.600	15	9	3	0	0	2	6	1	.714	.800
Throws Right	R	.167	30	5	1	0	2	4	1	8	.212	.400
Young,Chris	L	.210	167	35	8	1	5	16	24	31	.306	.359
Throws Right	R	.297	118	35	8	0	7	26	16	19	.381	.542
Zambrano,Carlos	L	.258	291	75	11	3	2	23	46	60	.366	.337
Throws Right	R	.235	340	80	13	3	8	44	32	92	.306	.362
Zavada,Clay	L	.284	74	21	2	0	1	12	13	19	.411	.351
Throws Left	R	.205	117	24	4	1	4	13	11	33	.271	.359
Ziegler,Brad	L	.336	110	37	9	2	1	13	18	14	.430	.482
Throws Right	R	.265	170	45	5	0	1	23	10	40	.304	.312
Zimmermann,Jordan	L	.279	183	51	10	2	4	22	19	45	.353	.421
Throws Right	R	.263	167	44	7	2	6	28	10	47	.307	.437
Zito,Barry	L	.230	174	40	8	0	4	24	11	41	.295	.345
Throws Left	R	.256	543	139	26	1	17	53	70	113	.344	.401
Zumaya,Joel	L	.344	61	21	4	0	4	11	14	17	.467	.607
Throws Right	R	.206	63	13	0	1	1	8	8	13	.301	.286
AL	L	.269	-	-	-	-	-	-	-	-	.342	.431
	R	.204	-	-	-	-	-	-	-	-	.328	.419
NL	L	.262	-	-	-	-	-	-	-	-	.341	.413
	R	.060	-	-	-	-	-	-	-	-	.304	.411
MLB	L	.265	-	-	-	-	-	-	-	-	.341	.422
	R	.260	-	-	-	-	-	-	-	-	.326	.415

413

2009 Leader Boards

Many of our leader boards are derived from the complex pitch data collected by Baseball Info Solutions. Our pitch charting data is the most complete and thorough in baseball, and the information found in these leader boards cannot be found anywhere else. We track which pitchers threw the highest percentage of changeups, for example, and Bill James offers his own leader boards for categories like Runs Created, Tough Losses, and Power/Speed Numbers.

Here's a little admission: We try to mention each of the 30 MLB teams at least once in all of these section introductions, because fans of every team deserve a shout-out. But we don't necessarily write them in sequential order, so the leader board section was one of the last to be written this year. As a result, we found ourselves in a bit of a lurch, faced with introducing the leader boards and still needing to mention... the Pittsburgh Pirates.

So Pirate fans, this is for you. You'll be hard-pressed to find a single Pirate in the next 34 pages. It feels a little bit like cheating to mention Nyjer Morgan who, although he ranked 10th in the National League with a .307 batting average, was traded from Pittsburgh to Washington mid-season. Our advice? Scan the leader boards for everywhere a guy named Andrew McCutchen is mentioned. Put a little Sister Sledge on the stereo. And remember that "rebuilding" is just a state of mind—there's always next year.

For the first time this year, our home run distance leader boards are fueled by Hit Tracker data. Please check out www.hittrackeronline.com and thank you Greg Rybarczyk.

Here are some definitions to help clarify parts of the leader boards that may not be familiar to all readers:

In the past we measured hitter performance against various pitch types by result only. The problem with that approach was that if a hitter regularly looked silly on non-result-pitch curveballs, but mashed just a few along the way, he could look like a great curveball hitter, even though nothing was further from the truth. Bill James designed a formula to rate hitters not only on the result pitches, but on every pitch the batter faced. The hitters you'll now see in these leader boards are a much better representation of the guys who mastered each pitch type this past year.

BPS stands for "Batting Average plus Slugging Percentage." We feel that BPS makes more sense than OPS for some leader boards because we wanted to know who was having success putting those balls in play, not just drawing walks.

OutZ is "Pitches Outside the Strike Zone."

Holds Adjusted Saves Percentage is calculated by dividing holds plus saves by holds plus save opportunities.

2009 American League Batting Leaders

Batting Average (minimum 502 PA)		On Base Percentage (minimum 502 PA)		Slugging Average (minimum 502 PA)		Home Runs	
Mauer,Joe, Min	.365	Mauer,Joe, Min	.444	Mauer,Joe, Min	.587	Pena,Carlos, TB	39
Suzuki,Ichiro, Sea	.352	Youkilis,Kevin, Bos	.413	Morales,Kendry, LAA	.569	Teixeira,Mark, NYY	39
Jeter,Derek, NYY	.334	Jeter,Derek, NYY	.406	Teixeira,Mark, NYY	.565	Bay,Jason, Bos	36
Cabrera,Miguel, Det	.324	Zobrist,Ben, TB	.405	Lind,Adam, Tor	.562	Hill,Aaron, Tor	36
Young,Michael, Tex	.322	Rodriguez,Alex, NYY	.402	Youkilis,Kevin, Bos	.548	Lind,Adam, Tor	35
Cano,Robinson, NYY	.320	Cabrera,Miguel, Det	.396	Cabrera,Miguel, Det	.547	Cabrera,Miguel, Det	34
Bartlett,Jason, TB	.320	Figgins,Chone, LAA	.395	Zobrist,Ben, TB	.543	Morales,Kendry, LAA	34
Aybar,Erick, LAA	.312	Choo,Shin-Soo, Cle	.394	Kubel,Jason, Min	.539	Cruz,Nelson, Tex	33
Span,Denard, Min	.311	Drew,J.D., Bos	.392	Pena,Carlos, TB	.537	Longoria,Evan, TB	33
Ordonez,Magglio, Det	.310	Span,Denard, Min	.392	Bay,Jason, Bos	.537	Cuddyer,Michael, Min	32

Games		Plate Appearances		At Bats		Hits	
Cano,Robinson, NYY	161	Hill,Aaron, Tor	734	Hill,Aaron, Tor	682	Suzuki,Ichiro, Sea	225
Inge,Brandon, Det	161	Figgins,Chone, LAA	729	Cabrera,Orlando, Oak-Min	656	Jeter,Derek, NYY	212
Markakis,Nick, Bal	161	Roberts,Brian, Bal	717	Markakis,Nick, Bal	642	Cano,Robinson, NYY	204
Cabrera,Miguel, Det	160	Jeter,Derek, NYY	716	Suzuki,Ichiro, Sea	639	Cabrera,Miguel, Det	198
Cabrera,Orlando, Oak-Min	160	Pedroia,Dustin, Bos	714	Cano,Robinson, NYY	637	Hill,Aaron, Tor	195
Granderson,Curtis, Det	160	Markakis,Nick, Bal	711	Jeter,Derek, NYY	634	Mauer,Joe, Min	191
Butler,Billy, KC	159	Granderson,Curtis, Det	710	Roberts,Brian, Bal	632	Ellsbury,Jacoby, Bos	188
Roberts,Brian, Bal	159	Cabrera,Orlando, Oak-Min	708	Granderson,Curtis, Det	631	Markakis,Nick, Bal	188
3 tied with	158	Teixeira,Mark, NYY	707	Wells,Vernon, Tor	630	Cabrera,Orlando, Oak-Min	186
		Ellsbury,Jacoby, Bos	693	Pedroia,Dustin, Bos	626	2 tied with	185

Singles		Doubles		Triples		Total Bases	
Suzuki,Ichiro, Sea	179	Roberts,Brian, Bal	56	Ellsbury,Jacoby, Bos	10	Teixeira,Mark, NYY	344
Jeter,Derek, NYY	166	Butler,Billy, KC	51	Span,Denard, Min	10	Hill,Aaron, Tor	340
Span,Denard, Min	146	Cano,Robinson, NYY	48	Aybar,Erick, LAA	9	Cabrera,Miguel, Det	334
Ellsbury,Jacoby, Bos	143	Pedroia,Dustin, Bos	48	DeJesus,David, KC	9	Cano,Robinson, NYY	331
Figgins,Chone, LAA	141	Lind,Adam, Tor	46	Andrus,Elvis, Tex	8	Lind,Adam, Tor	330
Cabrera,Orlando, Oak-Min	138	Markakis,Nick, Bal	45	Bloomquist,Willie, KC	8	Morales,Kendry, LAA	322
Crawford,Carl, TB	134	Longoria,Evan, TB	44	Callaspo,Alberto, KC	8	Longoria,Evan, TB	307
Mauer,Joe, Min	132	Byrd,Marlon, Tex	43	Crawford,Carl, TB	8	Mauer,Joe, Min	307
Polanco,Placido, Det	131	Morales,Kendry, LAA	43	Granderson,Curtis, Det	8	Cuddyer,Michael, Min	306
Cabrera,Miguel, Det	130	Teixeira,Mark, NYY	43	4 tied with	7	Butler,Billy, KC	299

Runs Scored		RBI		Walks		Strikeouts	
Pedroia,Dustin, Bos	115	Teixeira,Mark, NYY	122	Figgins,Chone, LAA	101	Cust,Jack, Oak	185
Figgins,Chone, LAA	114	Bay,Jason, Bos	119	Swisher,Nick, NYY	97	Inge,Brandon, Det	170
Roberts,Brian, Bal	110	Lind,Adam, Tor	114	Abreu,Bobby, LAA	94	Pena,Carlos, TB	163
Damon,Johnny, NYY	107	Longoria,Evan, TB	113	Bay,Jason, Bos	94	Bay,Jason, Bos	162
Jeter,Derek, NYY	107	Hill,Aaron, Tor	108	Cust,Jack, Oak	93	Upton,B.J., TB	152
Bay,Jason, Bos	103	Martinez,Victor, Cle-Bos	108	Zobrist,Ben, TB	91	Choo,Shin-Soo, Cle	151
Cano,Robinson, NYY	103	Morales,Kendry, LAA	108	Scutaro,Marco, Tor	90	Davis,Chris, Tex	150
Hill,Aaron, Tor	103	Abreu,Bobby, LAA	103	Pena,Carlos, TB	87	Branyan,Russell, Sea	149
Teixeira,Mark, NYY	103	Cabrera,Miguel, Det	103	Drew,J.D., Bos	82	Granderson,Curtis, Det	141
Kinsler,Ian, Tex	101	Kubel,Jason, Min	103	Teixeira,Mark, NYY	81	Longoria,Evan, TB	140

2009 American League Batting Leaders

Intentional Walks

Suzuki,Ichiro, Sea	15
Cabrera,Miguel, Det	14
Mauer,Joe, Min	14
Morneau,Justin, Min	12
Longoria,Evan, TB	11
Pena,Carlos, TB	11
Morales,Kendry, LAA	10
Kubel,Jason, Min	9
Teixeira,Mark, NYY	9
4 tied with	7

BA Bases Loaded
(minimum 10 PA)

Span,Denard, Min	.667
Hunter,Torii, LAA	.600
Davis,Rajai, Oak	.571
Matthews Jr.,Gary, LAA	.571
Zobrist,Ben, TB	.538
Bay,Jason, Bos	.533
Martinez,Victor, Cle-Bos	.533
4 tied with	.500

Sacrifice Hits

Everett,Adam, Det	15
Gutierrez,Franklin, Sea	13
Punto,Nick, Min	13
Andrus,Elvis, Tex	12
Aybar,Erick, LAA	12
Span,Denard, Min	12
Betancourt,Y., Sea-KC	11
4 tied with	10

Sacrifice Flies

Byrd,Marlon, Tex	10
Cabrera,Orlando, Oak-Min	10
Markakis,Nick, Bal	10
Abreu,Bobby, LAA	9
Murphy,David, Tex	9
Morales,Kendry, LAA	8
Ramirez,Alexei, CWS	8
Roberts,Brian, Bal	8
11 tied with	7

BA Close & Late
(minimum 50 PA)

DeRosa,Mark, Cle	463
Rolen,Scott, Tor	412
Choo,Shin-Soo, Cle	.405
Jeter,Derek, NYY	.366
Kendrick,Howie, LAA	.364
Davis,Rajai, Oak	.358
Valbuena,Luis, Cle	.358
Young,Michael, Tex	.357
Raburn,Ryan, Det	.354
Hunter,Torii, LAA	.353

Batting Average w/ RISP
(minimum 100 PA)

Bartlett,Jason, TB	.386
Kennedy,Adam, Oak	.368
Mauer,Joe, Min	.367
Youkilis,Kevin, Bos	.362
Bay,Jason, Bos	.360
Matthews Jr.,Gary, LAA	.358
Abreu,Bobby, LAA	.354
Rolen,Scott, Tor	.341
Ellis,Mark, Oak	.337
2 tied with	.333

SLG vs. LHP
(minimum 125 PA)

Cuddyer,Michael, Min	.651
Kinsler,Ian, Tex	.646
Rivera,Juan, LAA	.645
Matsui,Hideki, NYY	.618
Zobrist,Ben, TB	.595
Raburn,Ryan, Det	.594
Konerko,Paul, CWS	.589
Bay,Jason, Bos	.578
Hunter,Torii, LAA	.578
Hill,Aaron, Tor	.561

SLG vs. RHP
(minimum 377 PA)

Mauer,Joe, Min	.641
Kubel,Jason, Min	.617
Lind,Adam, Tor	.602
Morales,Kendry, LAA	.596
Teixeira,Mark, NYY	.586
Youkilis,Kevin, Bos	.560
Cabrera,Miguel, Det	.556
Granderson,Curtis, Det	.539
Drew,J.D., Bos	.536
Young,Michael, Tex	.532

Leadoff Hitters OBP
(minimum 150 PA)

Jeter,Derek, NYY	.409
Bartlett,Jason, TB	.398
Figgins,Chone, LAA	.395
Span,Denard, Min	.392
Suzuki,Ichiro, Sea	.386
Borbon,Julio, Tex	.385
Scutaro,Marco, Tor	.379
DeJesus,David, KC	.378
Podsednik,Scott, CWS	.355
Roberts,Brian, Bal	.355

Cleanup Hitters SLG
(minimum 150 PA)

Youkilis,Kevin, Bos	.573
Zobrist,Ben, TB	.660
Byrd,Marlon, Tex	.560
Cabrera,Miguel, Det	.538
Rodriguez,Alex, NYY	.533
Thome,Jim, CWS	.531
Kubel,Jason, Min	.529
Choo,Shin-Soo, Cle	.514
Sweeney,Mike, Sea	.507
Rolen,Scott, Tor	.504

BA vs. LHP
(minimum 125 PA)

Jeter,Derek, NYY	.395
Ramirez,Alexei, CWS	.370
Callaspo,Alberto, KC	.361
Ordonez,Magglio, Det	.352
Mauer,Joe, Min	.345
Suzuki,Ichiro, Sea	.339
Bartlett,Jason, TB	.338
Konerko,Paul, CWS	.338
Hunter,Torii, LAA	.336
Gutierrez,Franklin, Sea	.335

BA vs. RHP
(minimum 377 PA)

Mauer,Joe, Min	.377
Suzuki,Ichiro, Sea	.359
Young,Michael, Tex	.331
Cabrera,Miguel, Det	.327
Cano,Robinson, NYY	.326
Figgins,Chone, LAA	.323
Kubel,Jason, Min	.322
Crawford,Carl, TB	.322
Lind,Adam, Tor	.317
Martinez,Victor, Cle-Bos	.316

Home BA
(minimum 251 PA)

Mauer,Joe, Min	.388
Suzuki,Ichiro, Sea	.376
Butler,Billy, KC	.362
Cabrera,Miguel, Det	.348
Young,Michael, Tex	.347
Morales,Kendry, LAA	.341
Cano,Robinson, NYY	.338
Callaspo,Alberto, KC	.337
Jeter,Derek, NYY	.331
Span,Denard, Min	.325

Away BA
(minimum 251 PA)

Mauer,Joe, Min	.345
Aybar,Erick, LAA	.339
Jeter,Derek, NYY	.337
Bartlett,Jason, TB	.333
Suzuki,Ichiro, Sea	.329
Sweeney,Ryan, Oak	.326
Martinez,Victor, Cle-Bos	.323
Scutaro,Marco, Tor	.322
Cabrera,Asdrubal, Cle	.320
Choo,Shin-Soo, Cle	.317

OBP vs. LHP
(minimum 125 PA)

Jeter,Derek, NYY	.468
Cabrera,Miguel, Det	.441
Ramirez,Alexei, CWS	.441
Zobrist,Ben, TB	.440
Youkilis,Kevin, Bos	.435
Bartlett,Jason, TB	.427
Konerko,Paul, CWS	.420
Butler,Billy, KC	.413
Mauer,Joe, Min	.413
Ordonez,Magglio, Det	.413

OBP vs. RHP
(minimum 377 PA)

Mauer,Joe, Min	.462
Figgins,Chone, LAA	.428
Abreu,Bobby, LAA	.408
Choo,Shin-Soo, Cle	.406
Youkilis,Kevin, Bos	.404
Rodriguez,Alex, NYY	.402
Kubel,Jason, Min	.396
Overbay,Lyle, Tor	.396
Drew,J.D., Bos	.396
Suzuki,Ichiro, Sea	.393

2009 American League Batting Leaders

Stolen Bases

Ellsbury,Jacoby, Bos	70
Crawford,Carl, TB	60
Figgins,Chone, LAA	42
Upton,B.J., TB	42
Davis,Rajai, Oak	41
Andrus,Elvis, Tex	33
Kinsler,Ian, Tex	31
5 tied with	30

Caught Stealing

Figgins,Chone, LAA	17
Crawford,Carl, TB	16
Upton,B.J., TB	14
Podsednik,Scott, CWS	13
Davis,Rajai, Oak	12
Ellsbury,Jacoby, Bos	12
Span,Denard, Min	10
DeJesus,David, KC	9
Suzuki,Ichiro, Sea	9
3 tied with	8

Highest SB Success Pct
(minimum 20 SBA)

Getz,Chris, CWS	92.6
Choo,Shin-Soo, Cle	91.3
Kinsler,Ian, Tex	86.1
Jeter,Derek, NYY	85.7
Ellsbury,Jacoby, Bos	85.4
Andrus,Elvis, Tex	84.6
Gardner,Brett, NYY	83.9
Anderson,Josh, Det-KC	83.3
Cruz,Nelson, Tex	83.3
Rios,Alex, Tor-CWS	82.8

Lowest SB Success Pct
(minimum 20 SBA)

Sizemore,Grady, Cle	61.9
Aybar,Erick, LAA	66.7
Gomez,Carlos, Min	66.7
Span,Denard, Min	69.7
Podsednik,Scott, CWS	69.8
Figgins,Chone, LAA	71.2
Pedroia,Dustin, Bos	71.4
Zobrist,Ben, TB	73.9
Suzuki,Ichiro, Sea	74.3
Upton,B.J., TB	75.0

Steals of Third

Roberts,Brian, Bal	14
Ellsbury,Jacoby, Bos	13
Andrus,Elvis, Tex	11
Kinsler,Ian, Tex	11
Upton,B.J., TB	11
Suzuki,Ichiro, Sea	10
Davis,Rajai, Oak	9
Cruz,Nelson, Tex	7
4 tied with	6

Grounded Into DP

Longoria,Evan, TB	27
Lopez,Jose, Sea	25
Lowell,Mike, Bos	24
Cabrera,Miguel, Det	22
Cabrera,Orlando, Oak-Min	22
Cano,Robinson, NYY	22
Cuddyer,Michael, Min	22
Rios,Alex, Tor-CWS	21
Butler,Billy, KC	20
Peralta,Jhonny, Cle	20

Grounded Into DP Pct
(minimum 50 GIDP Ops)

Granderson,Curtis, Det	0.94
Suzuki,Ichiro, Sea	1.08
Gomez,Carlos, Min	1.79
Barton,Daric, Oak	2.00
Gross,Gabe, TB	3.13
Mathis,Jeff, LAA	3.64
Rolen,Scott, Tor	3.70
Scott,Luke, Bal	3.77
Sizemore,Grady, Cle	3.85
Matsui,Hideki, NYY	4.17

Hit By Pitch

Shoppach,Kelly, Cle	18
Choo,Shin-Soo, Cle	17
Inge,Brandon, Det	17
Youkilis,Kevin, Bos	16
Quentin,Carlos, CWS	15
Teixeira,Mark, NYY	12
5 tied with	10

Pitches Seen

Figgins,Chone, LAA	3084
Roberts,Brian, Bal	2901
Pedroia,Dustin, Bos	2829
Granderson,Curtis, Det	2818
Abreu,Bobby, LAA	2814
Choo,Shin-Soo, Cle	2775
Scutaro,Marco, Tor	2768
Markakis,Nick, Bal	2763
Jeter,Derek, NYY	2746
Martinez,Victor, Cle-Bos	2728

At Bats Per Home Run
(minimum 502 PA)

Pena,Carlos, TB	12.1
Branyan,Russell, Sea	13.9
Cruz,Nelson, Tex	14.0
Bay,Jason, Bos	14.8
Rodriguez,Alex, NYY	14.8
Teixeira,Mark, NYY	15.6
Matsui,Hideki, NYY	16.3
Morales,Kendry, LAA	16.6
Lind,Adam, Tor	16.8
Morneau,Justin, Min	16.9

Highest GB/FB Ratio
(minimum 502 PA)

Jeter,Derek, NYY	2.51
Andrus,Elvis, Tex	2.40
Suzuki,Ichiro, Sea	2.12
Jones,Adam, Bal	1.97
Span,Denard, Min	1.89
Crawford,Carl, TB	1.82
Ordonez,Magglio, Det	1.81
Podsednik,Scott, CWS	1.79
Teahen,Mark, KC	1.73
Cabrera,Melky, NYY	1.67

Lowest GB/FB Ratio
(minimum 502 PA)

Pena,Carlos, TB	0.54
Kinsler,Ian, Tex	0.56
Granderson,Curtis, Det	0.60
Ortiz,David, Bos	0.64
Branyan,Russell, Sea	0.65
Bay,Jason, Bos	0.68
Sizemore,Grady, Cle	0.76
Youkilis,Kevin, Bos	0.78
Konerko,Paul, CWS	0.78
Teixeira,Mark, NYY	0.83

Pitches Per Plate App
(minimum 502 PA)

Youkilis,Kevin, Bos	4.42
Swisher,Nick, NYY	4.27
Cust,Jack, Oak	4.25
Figgins,Chone, LAA	4.23
Abreu,Bobby, LAA	4.22
Dye,Jermaine, CWS	4.20
Mauer,Joe, Min	4.19
Ortiz,David, Bos	4.19
Drew,J.D., Bos	4.13
Branyan,Russell, Sea	4.11

Pct Pitches Taken
(minimum 1500 Pitches)

Abreu,Bobby, LAA	67.5
Carroll,Jamey, Cle	66.3
Scutaro,Marco, Tor	65.3
Swisher,Nick, NYY	64.4
Mauer,Joe, Min	63.9
Figgins,Chone, LAA	63.0
Drew,J.D., Bos	63.0
Zobrist,Ben, TB	62.5
Bautista,Jose, Tor	62.4
Overbay,Lyle, Tor	62.3

Best BPS on OutZ
(minimum 502 PA)

Zobrist,Ben, TB	.833
Mauer,Joe, Min	.671
Young,Michael, Tex	.659
Podsednik,Scott, CWS	.659
Suzuki,Ichiro, Sea	.644
Martinez,Victor, Cle-Bos	.634
Pierzynski,A.J., CWS	.618
Callaspo,Alberto, KC	.609
Scutaro,Marco, Tor	.591
Jones,Adam, Bal	.588

Worst BPS on OutZ
(minimum 502 PA)

Cust,Jack, Oak	.167
Swisher,Nick, NYY	.218
Sizemore,Grady, Cle	.220
Pena,Carlos, TB	.225
Branyan,Russell, Sea	.229
Drew,J.D., Bos	.237
Huff,Aubrey, Bal-Det	.255
Peralta,Jhonny, Cle	.280
Ordonez,Magglio, Det	.296
Cuddyer,Michael, Min	.305

2009 American League Batting Leaders

Best OPS vs Fastballs		Best OPS vs Curveballs		Best OPS vs Changeups		Best OPS vs Sliders	
(minimum 251 PA)		(minimum 50 PA)		(minimum 50 PA)		(minimum 32 PA)	
Mauer,Joe, Min	1.108	Morales,Kendry, LAA	1.166	Kinsler,Ian, Tex	1.144	Thome,Jim, CWS	1.156
Kubel,Jason, Min	1.080	Crawford,Carl, TB	1.130	Posada,Jorge, NYY	1.112	Guerrero,Vladimir, LAA	1.155
Martinez,Victor, Cle-Bos	1.036	Lind,Adam, Tor	1.085	Cabrera,Miguel, Det	1.050	Span,Denard, Min	1.151
Youkilis,Kevin, Bos	1.030	Matsui,Hideki, NYY	1.025	Cuddyer,Michael, Min	1.046	Buck,John, KC	1.089
Young,Michael, Tex	1.028	Suzuki,Ichiro, Sea	1.020	Markakis,Nick, Bal	1.036	Hairston,Scott, Oak	1.051
Teixeira,Mark, NYY	.984	Cabrera,Miguel, Det	.980	Overbay,Lyle, Tor	1.012	Varitek,Jason, Bos	1.044
Rodriguez,Alex, NYY	.978	Cruz,Nelson, Tex	.974	Mauer,Joe, Min	1.006	Sweeney,Ryan, Oak	1.024
Drew,J.D., Bos	.973	Cano,Robinson, NYY	.939	Ortiz,David, Bos	.995	Zobrist,Ben, TB	1.024
Zobrist,Ben, TB	.960	Kinsler,Ian, Tex	.933	Lind,Adam, Tor	.985	Bay,Jason, Bos	1.017
Choo,Shin-Soo, Cle	.958	Choo,Shin-Soo, Cle	.913	Jeter,Derek, NYY	.977	Suzuki,Kurt, Oak	1.015

OPS		OPS First Half		OPS Second Half		OPS by Catchers	
(minimum 502 PA)		(minimum 260 PA)		(minimum 201 PA)		(minimum 251 PA)	
Mauer,Joe, Min	1.031	Mauer,Joe, Min	1.089	Drew,J.D., Bos	.999	Mauer,Joe, Min	1.061
Youkilis,Kevin, Bos	.961	Zobrist,Ben, TB	1.012	Mauer,Joe, Min	.998	Posada,Jorge, NYY	.891
Teixeira,Mark, NYY	.948	Youkilis,Kevin, Bos	.985	Teixeira,Mark, NYY	.991	Napoli,Mike, LAA	.817
Zobrist,Ben, TB	.948	Scott,Luke, Bal	.976	Morales,Kendry, LAA	.989	Martinez,Victor, Cle-Bos	.783
Cabrera,Miguel, Det	.942	Morneau,Justin, Min	.965	Ordonez,Magglio, Det	.978	Pierzynski,A.J., CWS	.770
Rodriguez,Alex, NYY	.933	Branyan,Russell, Sea	.956	Young,Michael, Tex	.962	Wieters,Matt, Bal	.764
Lind,Adam, Tor	.932	Dye,Jermaine, CWS	.942	Cabrera,Miguel, Det	.960	Zaun,Gregg, Bal-TB	.757
Morales,Kendry, LAA	.924	Hunter,Torii, LAA	.938	Bay,Jason, Bos	.939	Olivo,Miguel, KC	.755
Bay,Jason, Bos	.921	Bartlett,Jason, TB	.930	Lind,Adam, Tor	.938	Shoppach,Kelly, Cle	.750
Drew,J.D., Bos	.914	Lind,Adam, Tor	.928	Youkilis,Kevin, Bos	.933	Suzuki,Kurt, Oak	.730

OPS by First Basemen		OPS by Second Basemen		OPS by Third Basemen		OPS by Shortstops	
(minimum 251 PA)		(minimum 251 PA)		(minimum 251 PA)		(minimum 251 PA)	
Youkilis,Kevin, Bos	.999	Cano,Robinson, NYY	.871	Rodriguez,Alex, NYY	.919	Bartlett,Jason, TB	.886
Cabrera,Miguel, Det	.958	Hill,Aaron, Tor	.838	Longoria,Evan, TB	.905	Jeter,Derek, NYY	.869
Teixeira,Mark, NYY	.947	Callaspo,Alberto, KC	.823	Young,Michael, Tex	.894	Cabrera,Asdrubal, Cle	.797
Martinez,Victor, Cle-Bos	.942	Zobrist,Ben, TB	.822	Rolen,Scott, Tor	.846	Scutaro,Marco, Tor	.790
Morales,Kendry, LAA	.928	Pedroia,Dustin, Bos	.819	Beckham,Gordon, CWS	.808	Aybar,Erick, LAA	.777
Pena,Carlos, TB	.896	Kinsler,Ian, Tex	.814	Lowell,Mike, Bos	.806	Ramirez,Alexei, CWS	.723
Branyan,Russell, Sea	.867	Roberts,Brian, Bal	.812	Figgins,Chone, LAA	.792	Cabrera,Orlando, Oak-Min	.706
Morneau,Justin, Min	.866	Izturis,Maicer, LAA	.785	Teahen,Mark, KC	.774	Andrus,Elvis, Tex	.701
Butler,Billy, KC	.857	Kendrick,Howie, LAA	.776	Crede,Joe, Min	.729	Green,Nick, Bos	.656
Overbay,Lyle, Tor	.843	Lopez,Jose, Sea	.760	Inge,Brandon, Det	.720	Izturis,Cesar, Bal	.624

OPS by Left Fielders		OPS by Center Fielders		OPS by Right Fielders		OPS by Designated Hitters	
(minimum 251 PA)		(minimum 251 PA)		(minimum 251 PA)		(minimum 125 PA)	
Bay,Jason, Bos	.925	Hunter,Torii, LAA	.848	Drew,J.D., Bos	.911	Ruiz,Randy, Tor	1.033
Damon,Johnny, NYY	.861	Byrd,Marlon, Tex	.808	Choo,Shin-Soo, Cle	.907	Lind,Adam, Tor	.897
Reimold,Nolan, Bal	.840	Sizemore,Grady, Cle	.807	Sweeney,Ryan, Oak	.873	Mauer,Joe, Min	.888
Holliday,Matt, Oak	.834	Span,Denard, Min	.795	Suzuki,Ichiro, Sea	.854	Thome,Jim, CWS	.882
Crawford,Carl, TB	.824	Jones,Adam, Bal	.794	Swisher,Nick, NYY	.851	Matsui,Hideki, NYY	.863
Quentin,Carlos, CWS	.788	Granderson,Curtis, Det	.778	Abreu,Bobby, LAA	.818	Kubel,Jason, Min	.846
Rivera,Juan, LAA	.787	Ellsbury,Jacoby, Bos	.772	Cruz,Nelson, Tex	.818	Scott,Luke, Bal	.845
DeJesus,David, KC	.776	Davis,Rajai, Oak	.766	Cuddyer,Michael, Min	.817	Hafner,Travis, Cle	.819
Murphy,David, Tex	.765	Gutierrez,Franklin, Sea	.764	Dye,Jermaine, CWS	.803	Jones,Andruw, Tex	.819
Podsednik,Scott, CWS	.738	Cabrera,Melky, NYY	.762	Markakis,Nick, Bal	.801	Blalock,Hank, Tex	.807

2009 American League Batting Leaders

OPS Batting Left vs. LHP (minimum 125 PA)	
Matsui,Hideki, NYY	.976
Mauer,Joe, Min	.910
Span,Denard, Min	.877
Cano,Robinson, NYY	.876
Drew,J.D., Bos	.863
Scott,Luke, Bal	.837
Morneau,Justin, Min	.836
Suzuki,Ichiro, Sea	.829
Choo,Shin-Soo, Cle	.825
Pena,Carlos, TB	.814

OPS Batting Left vs. RHP (minimum 377 PA)	
Mauer,Joe, Min	1.103
Kubel,Jason, Min	1.014
Lind,Adam, Tor	.992
Morales,Kendry, LAA	.962
Teixeira,Mark, NYY	.951
Drew,J.D., Bos	.932
Choo,Shin-Soo, Cle	.909
Overbay,Lyle, Tor	.905
Zobrist,Ben, TB	.905
Granderson,Curtis, Det	.897

OPS Batting Right vs. LHP (minimum 125 PA)	
Zobrist,Ben, TB	1.035
Rivera,Juan, LAA	1.030
Cuddyer,Michael, Min	1.013
Kinsler,Ian, Tex	1.011
Jeter,Derek, NYY	1.010
Konerko,Paul, CWS	1.006
Bay,Jason, Bos	.980
Hunter,Torii, LAA	.978
Raburn,Ryan, Det	.976
Butler,Billy, KC	.966

OPS Batting Right vs. RHP (minimum 377 PA)	
Youkilis,Kevin, Bos	.964
Cabrera,Miguel, Det	.935
Rodriguez,Alex, NYY	.931
Young,Michael, Tex	.906
Bay,Jason, Bos	.897
Longoria,Evan, TB	.881
Bartlett,Jason, TB	.856
Pedroia,Dustin, Bos	.839
Byrd,Marlon, Tex	.835
Jeter,Derek, NYY	.817

OPS vs. LHP (minimum 125 PA)	
Zobrist,Ben, TB	1.035
Rivera,Juan, LAA	1.030
Cuddyer,Michael, Min	1.013
Kinsler,Ian, Tex	1.011
Jeter,Derek, NYY	1.010
Konerko,Paul, CWS	1.009
Bay,Jason, Bos	.980
Hunter,Torii, LAA	.978
Matsui,Hideki, NYY	.976
Raburn,Ryan, Det	.976

OPS vs. RHP (minimum 377 PA)	
Mauer,Joe, Min	1.103
Kubel,Jason, Min	1.014
Lind,Adam, Tor	.992
Youkilis,Kevin, Bos	.964
Teixeira,Mark, NYY	.963
Morales,Kendry, LAA	.962
Cabrera,Miguel, Det	.935
Drew,J.D., Bos	.932
Rodriguez,Alex, NYY	.931
Choo,Shin-Soo, Cle	.909

RC Per 27 Outs vs. LHP (minimum 125 PA)	
Jeter,Derek, NYY	11.4
Hunter,Torii, LAA	11.0
Zobrist,Ben, TB	9.8
Konerko,Paul, CWS	9.5
Youkilis,Kevin, Bos	9.0
Bay,Jason, Bos	8.8
Bartlett,Jason, TB	8.8
Matsui,Hideki, NYY	8.6
Rivera,Juan, LAA	8.4
Kinsler,Ian, Tex	8.2

RC Per 27 Outs vs. RHP (minimum 377 PA)	
Mauer,Joe, Min	10.3
Kubel,Jason, Min	8.5
Youkilis,Kevin, Bos	8.4
Choo,Shin-Soo, Cle	7.9
Bay,Jason, Bos	7.7
Lind,Adam, Tor	7.6
Abreu,Bobby, LAA	7.2
Figgins,Chone, LAA	7.2
Suzuki,Ichiro, Sea	7.2
Morales,Kendry, LAA	7.0

Highest RBI % (minimum 502 PA)	
Bay,Jason, Bos	12.08
Pena,Carlos, TB	11.51
Rodriguez,Alex, NYY	11.49
Lind,Adam, Tor	11.23
Hunter,Torii, LAA	11.10
Morales,Kendry, LAA	11.04
Kubel,Jason, Min	10.95
Teixeira,Mark, NYY	10.86
Mauer,Joe, Min	10.86
Longoria,Evan, TB	10.78

Lowest RBI % (minimum 502 PA)	
Suzuki,Ichiro, Sea	4.85
Andrus,Elvis, Tex	5.12
Figgins,Chone, LAA	5.34
Teahen,Mark, KC	5.64
Ellsbury,Jacoby, Bos	5.81
Podsednik,Scott, CWS	5.85
Pierzynski,A.J., CWS	5.90
Betancourt,Y., Sea-KC	5.98
Wells,Vernon, Tor	6.07
Upton,B.J., TB	6.30

Highest Strikeout per PA (minimum 502 PA)	
Cust,Jack, Oak	.302
Branyan,Russell, Sea	.295
Pena,Carlos, TB	.286
Inge,Brandon, Det	.267
Bay,Jason, Bos	.254
Upton,B.J., TB	.243
Cruz,Nelson, Tex	.229
Choo,Shin-Soo, Cle	.220
Teahen,Mark, KC	.215
Ortiz,David, Bos	.214

Lowest Strikeout per PA (minimum 502 PA)	
Pedroia,Dustin, Bos	.063
Polanco,Placido, Det	.068
Callaspo,Alberto, KC	.080
Betancourt,Y., Sea-KC	.087
Cano,Robinson, NYY	.093
Suzuki,Kurt, Oak	.096
Aybar,Erick, LAA	.097
Pierzynski,A.J., CWS	.097
Cabrera,Orlando, Oak-Min	.100
Rivera,Juan, LAA	.100

Home Runs At Home	
Teixeira,Mark, NYY	24
Hill,Aaron, Tor	21
Morales,Kendry, LAA	21
Kinsler,Ian, Tex	20
Cabrera,Miguel, Det	19
Pena,Carlos, TB	19
7 tied with	18

Home Runs Away	
Bay,Jason, Bos	21
Lind,Adam, Tor	21
Swisher,Nick, NYY	21
Granderson,Curtis, Det	20
Pena,Carlos, TB	20
Longoria,Evan, TB	17
Lopez,Jose, Sea	17
Martinez,Victor, Cle-Bos	16
Morneau,Justin, Min	16
6 tied with	15

Longest Avg Home Run (min 10 over the wall)	
Kendrick,Howie, LAA	421
Hunter,Torii, LAA	417
Cuddyer,Michael, Min	416
Cruz,Nelson, Tex	416
Branyan,Russell, Sea	415
Cabrera,Miguel, Det	415
Jacobs,Mike, KC	415
Byrd,Marlon, Tex	414
Holliday,Matt, Oak	413
Hamilton,Josh, Tex	412

Shortest Avg Home Run (min 10 over the wall)	
Pedroia,Dustin, Bos	366
Kennedy,Adam, Oak	377
Ramirez,Alexei, CWS	378
Bautista,Jose, Tor	378
Lowell,Mike, Bos	378
Polanco,Placido, Det	378
Damon,Johnny, NYY	379
Scutaro,Marco, Tor	381
Suzuki,Ichiro, Sea	381
Aybar,Willy, TB	382

2009 American League Batting Leaders

Under Age 26: AB Per HR
(minimum 502 PA)

Longoria,Evan, TB	17.7
Lopez,Jose, Sea	24.5
Jones,Adam, Bal	24.9
Butler,Billy, KC	29.0
Markakis,Nick, Bal	35.7
Cabrera,Melky, NYY	37.3
Suzuki,Kurt, Oak	38.0
Upton,B.J., TB	50.9
Span,Denard, Min	72.3
Andrus,Elvis, Tex	80.0

Under Age 26: OPS
(minimum 502 PA)

Longoria,Evan, TB	.889
Butler,Billy, KC	.853
Span,Denard, Min	.807
Markakis,Nick, Bal	.801
Cabrera,Asdrubal, Cle	.799
Jones,Adam, Bal	.792
Aybar,Erick, LAA	.776
Lopez,Jose, Sea	.766
Sweeney,Ryan, Oak	.755
Cabrera,Melky, NYY	.752

Under Age 26: RC/27 Outs
(minimum 502 PA)

Span,Denard, Min	6.2
Longoria,Evan, TB	6.0
Butler,Billy, KC	5.9
Cabrera,Asdrubal, Cle	5.5
Markakis,Nick, Bal	5.4
Jones,Adam, Bal	5.2
Aybar,Erick, LAA	5.1
Cabrera,Melky, NYY	4.9
Suzuki,Kurt, Oak	4.7
Andrus,Elvis, Tex	4.6

Longest Home Run

Hamilton,Josh, Tex, 5/15	471
Cruz,Nelson, Tex, 7/27	467
Pena,Carlos, TB, 6/13	466
Konerko,Paul, CWS, 9/22	464
Dye,Jermaine, CWS, 7/5	461
Thames,Marcus, Det, 8/9	461
Inge,Brandon, Det, 4/7	460
Shoppach,Kelly, Cle, 4/9	460
Thome,Jim, CWS, 7/17	460
7 tied with	459

Swing and Miss %
(minimum 1500 Pitches Seen)

Davis,Chris, Tex	36.9
Olivo,Miguel, KC	35.5
Pena,Carlos, TB	34.7
Branyan,Russell, Sea	34.5
Cruz,Nelson, Tex	31.9
Cust,Jack, Oak	30.7
Thome,Jim, CWS	30.2
Bay,Jason, Bos	28.6
Napoli,Mike, LAA	28.1
Inge,Brandon, Det	27.8

Highest First Swing %
(minimum 502 PA)

Branyan,Russell, Sea	37.3
Pena,Carlos, TB	36.7
Ordonez,Magglio, Det	36.3
Pierzynski,A.J., CWS	36.1
Cruz,Nelson, Tex	36.0
Byrd,Marlon, Tex	35.8
Cabrera,Miguel, Det	34.5
Lopez,Jose, Sea	34.5
Hill,Aaron, Tor	34.3
Morneau,Justin, Min	33.8

Lowest First Swing %
(minimum 502 PA)

Mauer,Joe, Min	6.5
Pedroia,Dustin, Bos	6.6
Gutierrez,Franklin, Sea	7.7
Abreu,Bobby, LAA	9.5
Youkilis,Kevin, Bos	10.5
Damon,Johnny, NYY	10.8
Ellsbury,Jacoby, Bos	12.1
Morales,Kendry, LAA	13.7
Dye,Jermaine, CWS	13.8
Podsednik,Scott, CWS	13.8

Home RC Per 27 Outs
(minimum 251 PA)

Mauer,Joe, Min	10.4
Bay,Jason, Bos	10.0
Zobrist,Ben, TB	9.7
Youkilis,Kevin, Bos	9.7
Cabrera,Miguel, Det	9.0
Morales,Kendry, LAA	8.6
Butler,Billy, KC	8.5
Suzuki,Ichiro, Sea	8.3
Pena,Carlos, TB	7.8
Kubel,Jason, Min	7.7

Road RC Per 27 Outs
(minimum 251 PA)

Rodriguez,Alex, NYY	8.7
Mauer,Joe, Min	8.5
Choo,Shin-Soo, Cle	7.9
Youkilis,Kevin, Bos	7.5
Bartlett,Jason, TB	7.3
Martinez,Victor, Cle-Bos	7.1
Lind,Adam, Tor	6.9
Scutaro,Marco, Tor	6.9
Roberts,Brian, Bal	6.7
Abreu,Bobby, LAA	6.5

2009 National League Batting Leaders

Batting Average (minimum 502 PA)		On Base Percentage (minimum 502 PA)		Slugging Average (minimum 502 PA)		Home Runs	
Ramirez,Hanley, Fla	.342	Pujols,Albert, StL	.443	Pujols,Albert, StL	.658	Pujols,Albert, StL	47
Sandoval,Pablo, SF	.330	Johnson,Nick, Was-Fla	.426	Fielder,Prince, Mil	.602	Fielder,Prince, Mil	46
Pujols,Albert, StL	.327	Helton,Todd, Col	.416	Lee,Derrek, ChC	.579	Howard,Ryan, Phi	45
Helton,Todd, Col	.325	Votto,Joey, Cin	.414	Howard,Ryan, Phi	.571	Reynolds,Mark, Ari	44
Votto,Joey, Cin	.322	Fielder,Prince, Mil	.412	Votto,Joey, Cin	.567	Gonzalez,Adrian, SD	40
Coghlan,Chris, Fla	.321	Ramirez,Hanley, Fla	.410	Sandoval,Pablo, SF	.556	Dunn,Adam, Was	38
Braun,Ryan, Mil	.320	Gonzalez,Adrian, SD	.407	Tulowitzki,Troy, Col	.552	Werth,Jayson, Phi	36
Tejada,Miguel, Hou	.313	Berkman,Lance, Hou	.399	Ibanez,Raul, Phi	.552	Lee,Derrek, ChC	35
Lopez,Felipe, Ari-Mil	.310	Dunn,Adam, Was	.398	Braun,Ryan, Mil	.551	Ibanez,Raul, Phi	34
Morgan,Nyjer, Pit-Was	.307	Utley,Chase, Phi	.397	Gonzalez,Adrian, SD	.551	Zimmerman,Ryan, Was	33

Games		Plate Appearances		At Bats		Hits	
Fielder,Prince, Mil	162	Rollins,Jimmy, Phi	725	Rollins,Jimmy, Phi	672	Braun,Ryan, Mil	203
Ethier,Andre, LAD	160	Fielder,Prince, Mil	719	Braun,Ryan, Mil	635	Tejada,Miguel, Hou	199
Gonzalez,Adrian, SD	160	Braun,Ryan, Mil	708	Tejada,Miguel, Hou	635	Ramirez,Hanley, Fla	197
Howard,Ryan, Phi	160	Howard,Ryan, Phi	703	Victorino,Shane, Phi	620	Sandoval,Pablo, SF	189
Lee,Carlos, Hou	160	Pujols,Albert, StL	700	Howard,Ryan, Phi	616	Lopez,Felipe, Ari-Mil	187
Pujols,Albert, StL	160	Victorino,Shane, Phi	694	Furcal,Rafael, LAD	613	Pujols,Albert, StL	186
Dunn,Adam, Was	159	Zimmerman,Ryan, Was	694	Lee,Carlos, Hou	610	Lee,Carlos, Hou	183
Kemp,Matt, LAD	159	Utley,Chase, Phi	687	Zimmerman,Ryan, Was	610	Victorino,Shane, Phi	181
Pence,Hunter, Hou	159	Ethier,Andre, LAD	685	Bourn,Michael, Hou	606	Kemp,Matt, LAD	180
Werth,Jayson, Phi	159	Gonzalez,Adrian, SD	681	Kemp,Matt, LAD	606	Zimmerman,Ryan, Was	178

Singles		Doubles		Triples		Total Bases	
Theriot,Ryan, ChC	139	Tejada,Miguel, Hou	46	Victorino,Shane, Phi	13	Pujols,Albert, StL	374
Tejada,Miguel, Hou	138	Pujols,Albert, StL	45	Bourn,Michael, Hou	12	Fielder,Prince, Mil	356
Lopez,Felipe, Ari-Mil	137	Sandoval,Pablo, SF	44	Drew,Stephen, Ari	12	Howard,Ryan, Phi	352
Bourn,Michael, Hou	131	Rollins,Jimmy, Phi	43	Pagan,Angel, NYM	11	Braun,Ryan, Mil	350
Castillo,Luis, NYM	131	Cantu,Jorge, Fla	42	Fowler,Dexter, Col	10	Zimmerman,Ryan, Was	320
Ramirez,Hanley, Fla	130	Ethier,Andre, LAD	42	McCutchen,Andrew, Pit	9	Sandoval,Pablo, SF	318
Braun,Ryan, Mil	126	Hawpe,Brad, Col	42	Tulowitzki,Troy, Col	9	Reynolds,Mark, Ari	314
Furcal,Rafael, LAD	123	Ramirez,Hanley, Fla	42	5 tied with	8	Ramirez,Hanley, Fla	313
3 tied with	122	3 tied with	39			Lee,Derrek, ChC	308
						Gonzalez,Adrian, SD	304

Runs Scored		RBI		Walks		Strikeouts	
Pujols,Albert, StL	124	Fielder,Prince, Mil	141	Gonzalez,Adrian, SD	119	Reynolds,Mark, Ari	223
Braun,Ryan, Mil	113	Howard,Ryan, Phi	141	Dunn,Adam, Was	116	Howard,Ryan, Phi	186
Utley,Chase, Phi	112	Pujols,Albert, StL	135	Pujols,Albert, StL	115	Dunn,Adam, Was	177
Zimmerman,Ryan, Was	110	Braun,Ryan, Mil	114	Fielder,Prince, Mil	110	Cameron,Mike, Mil	156
Howard,Ryan, Phi	105	Lee,Derrek, ChC	111	Jones,Chipper, Atl	101	Werth,Jayson, Phi	156
Fielder,Prince, Mil	103	Ethier,Andre, LAD	106	Johnson,Nick, Was-Fla	99	Uggla,Dan, Fla	150
Victorino,Shane, Phi	102	Ramirez,Hanley, Fla	106	Berkman,Lance, Hou	97	Hawpe,Brad, Col	145
Ramirez,Hanley, Fla	101	Zimmerman,Ryan, Was	106	Fukudome,Kosuke, ChC	93	Bourn,Michael, Hou	140
Tulowitzki,Troy, Col	101	Dunn,Adam, Was	105	Uggla,Dan, Fla	92	LaRoche,Adam, Pit-Atl	140
Rollins,Jimmy, Phi	100	2 tied with	102	Werth,Jayson, Phi	91	Wright,David, NYM	140

2009 National League Batting Leaders

Intentional Walks		BA Bases Loaded (minimum 10 PA)		Sacrifice Hits		Sacrifice Flies	
Pujols,Albert, StL	44	Helton,Todd, Col	.625	Vazquez,Javier, Atl	20	Molina,Bengie, SF	11
Gonzalez,Adrian, SD	22	Matsui,Kaz, Hou	.625	Castillo,Luis, NYM	19	Blake,Casey, LAD	10
Fielder,Prince, Mil	21	Lee,Derrek, ChC	.600	Matsui,Kaz, Hou	16	Helton,Todd, Col	10
Ramirez,Manny, LAD	21	McCutchen,Andrew, Pit	.600	Arroyo,Bronson, Cin	14	Anderson,Garret, Atl	9
Jones,Chipper, Atl	18	Pujols,Albert, StL	.588	Duke,Zach, Pit	14	Fielder,Prince, Mil	9
Dunn,Adam, Was	16	Lee,Carlos, Hou	.571	Fowler,Dexter, Col	14	Francoeur,Jeff, Atl-NYM	9
Berkman,Lance, Hou	14	Renteria,Edgar, SF	.571	Oswalt,Roy, Hou	14	Tulowitzki,Troy, Col	9
Ramirez,Hanley, Fla	14	Fox,Jake, ChC	.500	Eckstein,David, SD	13	Zimmerman,Ryan, Was	9
Sandoval,Pablo, SF	13	McGehee,Casey, Mil	.500	Lincecum,Tim, SF	13	5 tied with	8
LaRoche,Adam, Pit-Atl	12	Fielder,Prince, Mil	.471	Theriot,Ryan, ChC	13		

BA Close & Late (minimum 50 PA)		Batting Average w/ RISP (minimum 100 PA)		SLG vs. LHP (minimum 125 PA)		SLG vs. RHP (minimum 377 PA)	
Gload,Ross, Fla	.387	Ramirez,Aramis, ChC	.425	Upton,Justin, Ari	.762	Howard,Ryan, Phi	.693
Beltran,Carlos, NYM	.002	Escobar,Yunel, Atl	.373	Braun,Ryan, Mil	.723	Pujols,Albert, StL	.646
Fielder,Prince, Mil	.380	Ramirez,Hanley, Fla	.373	Pujols,Albert, StL	.696	Gonzalez,Adrian, SD	.629
Winn,Randy, SF	.372	McGehee,Casey, Mil	.371	Wright,David, NYM	.646	Fielder,Prince, Mil	.610
Tejada,Miguel, Hou	.366	Pujols,Albert, StL	.361	Werth,Jayson, Phi	.644	Lee,Derrek, ChC	.604
Helms,Wes, Fla	.360	Bourn,Michael, Hou	.353	Diaz,Matt, Atl	.640	Ramirez,Hanley, Fla	.591
Rodriguez,Ivan, Hou	.359	Coghlan,Chris, Fla	.352	Ibanez,Raul, Phi	.639	Votto,Joey, Cin	.583
Smith,Seth, Col	.351	McLouth,Nate, Pit-Atl	.339	Kemp,Matt, LAD	.616	Ethier,Andre, LAD	.571
Upton,Justin, Ari	.341	Diaz,Matt, Atl	.337	Ross,Cody, Fla	.612	Tulowitzki,Troy, Col	.566
Blake,Casey, LAD	.340	Parra,Gerardo, Ari	.337	Sandoval,Pablo, SF	.600	Dunn,Adam, Was	.564

Leadoff Hitters OBP (minimum 150 PA)		Cleanup Hitters SLG (minimum 150 PA)		BA vs. LHP (minimum 125 PA)		BA vs. RHP (minimum 377 PA)	
Fukudome,Kosuke, ChC	.404	Lee,Derrek, ChC	.611	Wright,David, NYM	.416	Ramirez,Hanley, Fla	.352
Coghlan,Chris, Fla	.397	Tulowitzki,Troy, Col	.610	Diaz,Matt, Atl	.412	Morgan,Nyjer, Pit-Was	.344
Harris,Willie, Was	.392	Holliday,Matt, StL	.603	Braun,Ryan, Mil	.395	Helton,Todd, Col	.332
Lopez,Felipe, Ari-Mil	.388	Fielder,Prince, Mil	.602	Sandoval,Pablo, SF	.379	Escobar,Yunel, Atl	.327
Morgan,Nyjer, Pit-Was	.375	Howard,Ryan, Phi	.566	Upton,Justin, Ari	.377	Pujols,Albert, StL	.324
Pierre,Juan, LAD	.372	Reynolds,Mark, Ari	.551	Kemp,Matt, LAD	.362	Coghlan,Chris, Fla	.323
Schumaker,Skip, StL	.369	Gonzalez,Adrian, SD	.549	Francoeur,Jeff, Atl-NYM	.344	Schumaker,Skip, StL	.322
McCutchen,Andrew, Pit	.365	Ramirez,Aramis, ChC	.545	Pujols,Albert, StL	.338	Howard,Ryan, Phi	.320
Pagan,Angel, NYM	.358	Dunn,Adam, Was	.536	Votto,Joey, Cin	.329	Votto,Joey, Cin	.319
Reyes,Jose, NYM	.358	Ludwick,Ryan, StL	.509	Tejada,Miguel, Hou	.326	Castillo,Luis, NYM	.319

Home BA (minimum 251 PA)		Away BA (minimum 251 PA)		OBP vs. LHP (minimum 125 PA)		OBP vs. RHP (minimum 377 PA)	
Sandoval,Pablo, SF	.361	Ramirez,Hanley, Fla	.353	Wright,David, NYM	.496	Gonzalez,Adrian, SD	.448
Castillo,Luis, NYM	.350	Coghlan,Chris, Fla	.348	Braun,Ryan, Mil	.475	Helton,Todd, Col	.437
Helton,Todd, Col	.348	Braun,Ryan, Mil	.343	Pujols,Albert, StL	.465	Berkman,Lance, Hou	.436
Tejada,Miguel, Hou	.343	Votto,Joey, Cin	.336	Diaz,Matt, Atl	.464	Pujols,Albert, StL	.435
LaRoche,Adam, Pit-Atl	.333	Pujols,Albert, StL	.330	Upton,Justin, Ari	.445	Fielder,Prince, Mil	.432
Ramirez,Hanley, Fla	.332	Kemp,Matt, LAD	.314	Blake,Casey, LAD	.442	Ramirez,Hanley, Fla	.423
Lopez,Felipe, Ari-Mil	.331	Wright,David, NYM	.314	Johnson,Nick, Was-Fla	.440	Johnson,Nick, Was-Fla	.420
Tulowitzki,Troy, Col	.326	Fielder,Prince, Mil	.313	Werth,Jayson, Phi	.436	Votto,Joey, Cin	.419
Pujols,Albert, StL	.325	Loney,James, LAD	.309	Kemp,Matt, LAD	.429	Dunn,Adam, Was	.414
Lee,Derrek, ChC	.322	Gonzalez,Adrian, SD	.306	Sandoval,Pablo, SF	.428	Castillo,Luis, NYM	.411

2009 National League Batting Leaders

Stolen Bases

Bourn,Michael, Hou	61
Morgan,Nyjer, Pit-Was	42
Kemp,Matt, LAD	34
Rollins,Jimmy, Phi	31
Pierre,Juan, LAD	30
Fowler,Dexter, Col	27
Ramirez,Hanley, Fla	27
Wright,David, NYM	27
4 tied with	25

Caught Stealing

Morgan,Nyjer, Pit-Was	17
Bourn,Michael, Hou	12
Pierre,Juan, LAD	12
Pence,Hunter, Hou	11
Tulowitzki,Troy, Col	11
Barmes,Clint, Col	10
Dukes,Elijah, Was	10
Fowler,Dexter, Col	10
Fukudome,Kosuke, ChC	10
Theriot,Ryan, ChC	10

Highest SB Success Pct

(minimum 20 SBA)

Utley,Chase, Phi	100.0
Werth,Jayson, Phi	87.0
Matsui,Kaz, Hou	86.4
Bourn,Michael, Hou	83.6
McCutchen,Andrew, Pit	81.5
Kemp,Matt, LAD	81.0
Taveras,Willy, Cin	80.6
Gonzalez,Carlos, Col	80.0
Pujols,Albert, StL	80.0
Upton,Justin, Ari	80.0

Lowest SB Success Pct

(minimum 20 SBA)

Barmes,Clint, Col	54.5
Pence,Hunter, Hou	56.0
Tulowitzki,Troy, Col	64.5
Pagan,Angel, NYM	66.7
Ryan,Brendan, StL	66.7
Theriot,Ryan, ChC	67.7
Bonifacio,Emilio, Fla	70.0
Morgan,Nyjer, Pit-Was	71.2
Pierre,Juan, LAD	71.4
Reynolds,Mark, Ari	72.7

Steals of Third

Braun,Ryan, Mil	9
Werth,Jayson, Phi	8
Phillips,Brandon, Cin	7
Rollins,Jimmy, Phi	7
Bonifacio,Emilio, Fla	6
Cabrera,Everth, SD	6
Young,Chris, Ari	6
4 tied with	5

Grounded Into DP

Tejada,Miguel, Hou	29
Molina,Yadier, StL	27
Kouzmanoff,Kevin, SD	25
Pence,Hunter, Hou	25
Gonzalez,Adrian, SD	23
Pujols,Albert, StL	23
Zimmerman,Ryan, Was	22
Escobar,Yunel, Atl	21
Lee,Carlos, Hou	21
Phillips,Brandon, Cin	21

Grounded Into DP Pct

(minimum 50 GIDP Ops)

Bourn,Michael, Hou	1.25
Hairston,Jerry, Cin	3.33
Young,Chris, Ari	3.33
Roberts,Ryan, Ari	3.39
Gwynn,Tony, SD	3.57
Utley,Chase, Phi	3.73
Coghlan,Chris, Fla	3.85
Taveras,Willy, Cin	4.00
Braun,Ryan, Mil	4.07
Hoffpauir,Micah, ChC	4.29

Hit By Pitch

Utley,Chase, Phi	24
Kendall,Jason, Mil	17
Rowand,Aaron, SF	14
Braun,Ryan, Mil	13
Diaz,Matt, Atl	13
Ethier,Andre, LAD	13
Johnson,Nick, Was-Fla	12
Willingham,Josh, Was	12
5 tied with	11

Pitches Seen

Werth,Jayson, Phi	3046
Dunn,Adam, Was	2893
Howard,Ryan, Phi	2870
Utley,Chase, Phi	2845
Zimmerman,Ryan, Was	2827
Fielder,Prince, Mil	2805
Uggla,Dan, Fla	2777
Helton,Todd, Col	2768
Ethier,Andre, LAD	2758
Bourn,Michael, Hou	2742

At Bats Per Home Run

(minimum 502 PA)

Pujols,Albert, StL	12.1
Fielder,Prince, Mil	12.8
Reynolds,Mark, Ari	13.1
Howard,Ryan, Phi	13.7
Gonzalez,Adrian, SD	13.8
Dunn,Adam, Was	14.4
Ibanez,Raul, Phi	14.7
Lee,Derrek, ChC	15.2
Werth,Jayson, Phi	15.9
Tulowitzki,Troy, Col	17.0

Highest GB/FB Ratio

(minimum 502 PA)

Schumaker,Skip, StL	3.49
Castillo,Luis, NYM	3.14
Bourn,Michael, Hou	2.68
Hudson,Orlando, LAD	2.17
Morgan,Nyjer, Pit-Was	2.06
Lopez,Felipe, Ari-Mil	2.00
Bonifacio,Emilio, Fla	1.91
Furcal,Rafael, LAD	1.91
Guzman,Cristian, Was	1.89
Molina,Yadier, StL	1.73

Lowest GB/FB Ratio

(minimum 502 PA)

Molina,Bengie, SF	0.58
Barmes,Clint, Col	0.63
Dunn,Adam, Was	0.64
Ludwick,Ryan, StL	0.67
Soriano,Alfonso, ChC	0.68
Ross,Cody, Fla	0.69
Utley,Chase, Phi	0.71
Cameron,Mike, Mil	0.72
Reynolds,Mark, Ari	0.75
Rasmus,Colby, StL	0.76

Pitches Per Plate App

(minimum 502 PA)

Werth,Jayson, Phi	4.51
Johnson,Nick, Was-Fla	4.38
Dunn,Adam, Was	4.33
Blake,Casey, LAD	4.31
Helton,Todd, Col	4.29
Castillo,Luis, NYM	4.25
Hawpe,Brad, Col	4.24
Fowler,Dexter, Col	4.19
Fukudome,Kosuke, ChC	4.18
Uggla,Dan, Fla	4.16

Pct Pitches Taken

(minimum 1500 Pitches)

Castillo,Luis, NYM	68.1
Johnson,Nick, Was-Fla	65.9
Utley,Chase, Phi	63.7
Gwynn,Tony, SD	62.6
Fukudome,Kosuke, ChC	62.6
Harris,Willie, Was	62.3
Hardy,J.J., Mil	61.9
Atkins,Garrett, Col	61.8
Counsell,Craig, Mil	61.8
Werth,Jayson, Phi	61.4

Best BPS on OutZ

(minimum 502 PA)

Helton,Todd, Col	.661
Sandoval,Pablo, SF	.659
Schumaker,Skip, StL	.611
Coghlan,Chris, Fla	.602
Ramirez,Hanley, Fla	.600
Pujols,Albert, StL	.592
Murphy,Daniel, NYM	.585
Wright,David, NYM	.577
Ibanez,Raul, Phi	.570
Gonzalez,Adrian, SD	.540

Worst BPS on OutZ

(minimum 502 PA)

Willingham,Josh, Was	.212
Fukudome,Kosuke, ChC	.237
Uggla,Dan, Fla	.254
Ludwick,Ryan, StL	.278
Rowand,Aaron, SF	.286
Headley,Chase, SD	.307
Eckstein,David, SD	.307
Dunn,Adam, Was	.315
Johnson,Nick, Was-Fla	.348
Anderson,Garret, Atl	.350

2009 National League Batting Leaders

Best OPS vs Fastballs
(minimum 251 PA)

Pujols,Albert, StL	1.152
Lee,Derrek, ChC	1.060
Upton,Justin, Ari	1.044
Fielder,Prince, Mil	1.021
Gonzalez,Adrian, SD	.982
Dunn,Adam, Was	.975
Tulowitzki,Troy, Col	.973
Kemp,Matt, LAD	.967
Uggla,Dan, Fla	.959
Zimmerman,Ryan, Was	.951

Best OPS vs Curveballs
(minimum 50 PA)

Votto,Joey, Cin	1.089
Sandoval,Pablo, SF	.987
Barmes,Clint, Col	.955
Ethier,Andre, LAD	.946
Francoeur,Jeff, Atl-NYM	.881
Pence,Hunter, Hou	.863
Werth,Jayson, Phi	.862
Hawpe,Brad, Col	.860
Cameron,Mike, Mil	.858
McCann,Brian, Atl	.850

Best OPS vs Changeups
(minimum 50 PA)

Braun,Ryan, Mil	1.347
Hawpe,Brad, Col	1.141
McCutchen,Andrew, Pit	1.099
Ramirez,Hanley, Fla	1.074
Fukudome,Kosuke, ChC	1.048
McCann,Brian, Atl	1.027
Cantu,Jorge, Fla	1.018
Sandoval,Pablo, SF	1.016
Ibanez,Raul, Phi	1.011
Zimmerman,Ryan, Was	1.006

Best OPS vs Sliders
(minimum 32 PA)

Gerut,Jody, SD-Mil	1.330
Howard,Ryan, Phi	1.067
Berkman,Lance, Hou	1.063
Hundley,Nick, SD	.992
Braun,Ryan, Mil	.990
Wilson,Jack, Pit	.976
Holliday,Matt, StL	.972
Fielder,Prince, Mil	.961
Utley,Chase, Phi	.959
Hanigan,Ryan, Cin	.939

OPS
(minimum 502 PA)

Pujols,Albert, StL	1.101
Fielder,Prince, Mil	1.014
Votto,Joey, Cin	.981
Lee,Derrek, ChC	.972
Gonzalez,Adrian, SD	.958
Ramirez,Hanley, Fla	.954
Sandoval,Pablo, SF	.943
Braun,Ryan, Mil	.937
Howard,Ryan, Phi	.931
Tulowitzki,Troy, Col	.930

OPS First Half
(minimum 260 PA)

Pujols,Albert, StL	1.179
Fielder,Prince, Mil	1.055
Ibanez,Raul, Phi	1.015
Utley,Chase, Phi	1.004
Ramirez,Hanley, Fla	.979
Hawpe,Brad, Col	.973
Sandoval,Pablo, SF	.964
Beltran,Carlos, NYM	.952
Dunn,Adam, Was	.943
Berkman,Lance, Hou	.929

OPS Second Half
(minimum 201 PA)

Lee,Derrek, ChC	1.092
Tulowitzki,Troy, Col	1.042
Holliday,Matt, StL	1.023
Gonzalez,Adrian, SD	1.018
Pujols,Albert, StL	1.009
Howard,Ryan, Phi	1.003
Gonzalez,Carlos, Col	.992
Zimmerman,Ryan, Was	.969
Fielder,Prince, Mil	.967
Coghlan,Chris, Fla	.966

OPS by Catchers
(minimum 251 PA)

Montero,Miguel, Ari	.836
McCann,Brian, Atl	.830
Iannetta,Chris, Col	.785
Ruiz,Carlos, Phi	.781
Baker,John, Fla	.776
Paulino,Ronny, Fla	.759
Molina,Yadier, StL	.749
Molina,Bengie, SF	.729
Hundley,Nick, SD	.717
Doumit,Ryan, Pit	.710

OPS by First Basemen
(minimum 251 PA)

Pujols,Albert, StL	1.080
Fielder,Prince, Mil	1.014
Votto,Joey, Cin	.979
Lee,Derrek, ChC	.969
Gonzalez,Adrian, SD	.953
Howard,Ryan, Phi	.929
Berkman,Lance, Hou	.906
Helton,Todd, Col	.904
Dunn,Adam, Was	.896
LaRoche,Adam, Pit-Atl	.846

OPS by Second Basemen
(minimum 251 PA)

Prado,Martin, Atl	.913
Utley,Chase, Phi	.908
Lopez,Felipe, Ari-Mil	.820
Uggla,Dan, Fla	.814
Hudson,Orlando, LAD	.780
Phillips,Brandon, Cin	.779
Schumaker,Skip, StL	.771
Castillo,Luis, NYM	.738
Sanchez,Freddy, Pit-SF	.737
Barmes,Clint, Col	.723

OPS by Third Basemen
(minimum 251 PA)

Sandoval,Pablo, SF	.921
Ramirez,Aramis, ChC	.908
Zimmerman,Ryan, Was	.888
Reynolds,Mark, Ari	.867
Wright,David, NYM	.840
Blake,Casey, LAD	.836
Jones,Chipper, Atl	.820
McGehee,Casey, Mil	.799
Stewart,Ian, Col	.747
LaRoche,Andy, Pit	.733

OPS by Shortstops
(minimum 251 PA)

Ramirez,Hanley, Fla	.954
Tulowitzki,Troy, Col	.930
Escobar,Yunel, Atl	.812
Tejada,Miguel, Hou	.795
Ryan,Brendan, StL	.760
Drew,Stephen, Ari	.752
Theriot,Ryan, ChC	.718
Rollins,Jimmy, Phi	.714
Guzman,Cristian, Was	.706
Cabrera,Everth, SD	.704

OPS by Left Fielders
(minimum 251 PA)

Holliday,Matt, StL	1.019
Dunn,Adam, Was	1.016
Ramirez,Manny, LAD	.944
Braun,Ryan, Mil	.933
Ibanez,Raul, Phi	.901
Coghlan,Chris, Fla	.846
Lee,Carlos, Hou	.843
Willingham,Josh, Was	.831
Smith,Seth, Col	.802
Pierre,Juan, LAD	.778

OPS by Center Fielders
(minimum 251 PA)

Beltran,Carlos, NYM	.930
Kemp,Matt, LAD	.847
McCutchen,Andrew, Pit	.836
Pagan,Angel, NYM	.818
Ross,Cody, Fla	.818
Morgan,Nyjer, Pit-Was	.806
Victorino,Shane, Phi	.806
Fukudome,Kosuke, ChC	.800
Cameron,Mike, Mil	.796
McLouth,Nate, Pit-Atl	.787

OPS by Right Fielders
(minimum 251 PA)

Hawpe,Brad, Col	.908
Diaz,Matt, Atl	.905
Upton,Justin, Ari	.892
Werth,Jayson, Phi	.892
Ethier,Andre, LAD	.868
Pence,Hunter, Hou	.821
Ludwick,Ryan, StL	.777
Bradley,Milton, ChC	.774
Bruce,Jay, Cin	.767
Hermida,Jeremy, Fla	.761

OPS by Pitchers
(minimum 50 PA)

Zambrano,Carlos, ChC	.734
Haren,Dan, Ari	.637
Johnson,Josh, Fla	.609
Wainwright,Adam, StL	.545
Scherzer,Max, Ari	.542
Gallardo,Yovani, Mil	.516
Jimenez,Ubaldo, Col	.513
Billingsley,Chad, LAD	.501
Lowe,Derek, Atl	.498
Santana,Johan, NYM	.493

2009 National League Batting Leaders

OPS Batting Left vs. LHP
(minimum 125 PA)

Ibanez,Raul, Phi	.998
Utley,Chase, Phi	.962
Fielder,Prince, Mil	.943
Votto,Joey, Cin	.931
Johnson,Nick, Was-Fla	.883
Coghlan,Chris, Fla	.814
Dunn,Adam, Was	.787
Loney,James, LAD	.779
Hawpe,Brad, Col	.775
Gonzalez,Adrian, SD	.770

OPS Batting Left vs. RHP
(minimum 377 PA)

Howard,Ryan, Phi	1.088
Gonzalez,Adrian, SD	1.077
Fielder,Prince, Mil	1.042
Votto,Joey, Cin	1.002
Helton,Todd, Col	.986
Berkman,Lance, Hou	.982
Dunn,Adam, Was	.978
Ethier,Andre, LAD	.960
Hawpe,Brad, Col	.955
Sandoval,Pablo, SF	.914

OPS Batting Right vs. LHP
(minimum 125 PA)

Upton,Justin, Ari	1.208
Braun,Ryan, Mil	1.198
Pujols,Albert, StL	1.161
Wright,David, NYM	1.142
Diaz,Matt, Atl	1.103
Werth,Jayson, Phi	1.080
Kemp,Matt, LAD	1.045
Sandoval,Pablo, SF	1.028
Blake,Casey, LAD	1.005
Ross,Cody, Fla	.959

OPS Batting Right vs. RHP
(minimum 377 PA)

Pujols,Albert, StL	1.080
Ramirez,Hanley, Fla	1.014
Lee,Derrek, ChC	.986
Tulowitzki,Troy, Col	.941
Zimmerman,Ryan, Was	.906
Reynolds,Mark, Ari	.889
Braun,Ryan, Mil	.875
Escobar,Yunel, Atl	.864
Uggla,Dan, Fla	.832
Willingham,Josh, Was	.819

OPS vs. LHP
(minimum 125 PA)

Upton,Justin, Ari	1.208
Braun,Ryan, Mil	1.198
Pujols,Albert, StL	1.161
Wright,David, NYM	1.142
Diaz,Matt, Atl	1.103
Werth,Jayson, Phi	1.080
Kemp,Matt, LAD	1.045
Sandoval,Pablo, SF	1.028
Blake,Casey, LAD	1.005
Ibanez,Raul, Phi	.998

OPS vs. RHP
(minimum 377 PA)

Howard,Ryan, Phi	1.088
Pujols,Albert, StL	1.080
Gonzalez,Adrian, SD	1.077
Fielder,Prince, Mil	1.042
Ramirez,Hanley, Fla	1.014
Votto,Joey, Cin	1.002
Helton,Todd, Col	.986
Lee,Derrek, ChC	.986
Berkman,Lance, Hou	.982
Dunn,Adam, Was	.978

RC Per 27 Outs vs. LHP
(minimum 125 PA)

Braun,Ryan, Mil	12.3
Wright,David, NYM	11.4
Diaz,Matt, Atl	10.9
Pujols,Albert, StL	10.5
Werth,Jayson, Phi	10.1
Upton,Justin, Ari	10.0
Blake,Casey, LAD	9.6
Sandoval,Pablo, SF	9.5
Kemp,Matt, LAD	7.9
Fielder,Prince, Mil	7.6

RC Per 27 Outs vs. RHP
(minimum 377 PA)

Howard,Ryan, Phi	9.1
Ramirez,Hanley, Fla	9.0
Pujols,Albert, StL	8.9
Gonzalez,Adrian, SD	8.5
Fielder,Prince, Mil	8.4
Votto,Joey, Cin	8.3
Helton,Todd, Col	8.3
Lee,Derrek, ChC	7.9
Dunn,Adam, Was	7.8
Berkman,Lance, Hou	7.6

Highest RBI %
(minimum 502 PA)

Pujols,Albert, StL	12.83
Fielder,Prince, Mil	12.71
Howard,Ryan, Phi	12.54
Lee,Derrek, ChC	11.47
Ludwick,Ryan, StL	10.90
Votto,Joey, Cin	10.62
Ibanez,Raul, Phi	10.53
Ramirez,Hanley, Fla	10.50
McCann,Brian, Atl	10.49
Dunn,Adam, Was	10.25

Lowest RBI %
(minimum 502 PA)

Bonifacio,Emilio, Fla	3.65
Bourn,Michael, Hou	3.93
Schumaker,Skip, StL	4.41
Fowler,Dexter, Col	4.76
Castillo,Luis, NYM	4.82
Furcal,Rafael, LAD	5.01
Kendall,Jason, Mil	5.18
Morgan,Nyjer, Pit-Was	5.22
Theriot,Ryan, ChC	5.55
Eckstein,David, SD	5.84

Highest Strikeout per PA
(minimum 502 PA)

Reynolds,Mark, Ari	.337
Dunn,Adam, Was	.265
Howard,Ryan, Phi	.265
Cameron,Mike, Mil	.248
Hawpe,Brad, Col	.247
Upton,Justin, Ari	.233
Werth,Jayson, Phi	.231
LaRoche,Adam, Pit-Atl	.230
Rowand,Aaron, SF	.229
Wright,David, NYM	.227

Lowest Strikeout per PA
(minimum 502 PA)

Tejada,Miguel, Hou	.071
Molina,Yadier, StL	.072
Lee,Carlos, Hou	.077
Eckstein,David, SD	.081
Pujols,Albert, StL	.091
Rollins,Jimmy, Phi	.097
Castillo,Luis, NYM	.100
Victorino,Shane, Phi	.102
Escobar,Yunel, Atl	.103
Loney,James, LAD	.104

Home Runs At Home

Fielder,Prince, Mil	23
Ethier,Andre, LAD	22
Pujols,Albert, StL	22
Uggla,Dan, Fla	21
Werth,Jayson, Phi	21
Lee,Derrek, ChC	20
Dunn,Adam, Was	19
Reynolds,Mark, Ari	19
Howard,Ryan, Phi	18
3 tied with	17

Home Runs Away

Gonzalez,Adrian, SD	28
Howard,Ryan, Phi	27
Pujols,Albert, StL	25
Reynolds,Mark, Ari	25
Fielder,Prince, Mil	23
Ibanez,Raul, Phi	21
Dunn,Adam, Was	19
Ludwick,Ryan, StL	18
Braun,Ryan, Mil	17
Willingham,Josh, Was	17

Longest Avg Home Run
(min 10 over the wall)

Iannetta,Chris, Col	423
Reynolds,Mark, Ari	420
Stewart,Ian, Col	419
Tulowitzki,Troy, Col	416
Howard,Ryan, Phi	416
Pujols,Albert, StL	414
Hart,Corey, Mil	414
Beltran,Carlos, NYM	414
Smith,Seth, Col	414
Rasmus,Colby, StL	413

Shortest Avg Home Run
(min 10 over the wall)

Blum,Geoff, Hou	380
Rollins,Jimmy, Phi	383
Cantu,Jorge, Fla	385
Doumit,Ryan, Pit	385
Tejada,Miguel, Hou	386
Diaz,Matt, Atl	388
Lee,Carlos, Hou	388
LaRoche,Andy, Pit	389
Feliz,Pedro, Phi	389
Ramirez,Aramis, ChC	389

2009 National League Batting Leaders

Under Age 26: AB Per HR
(minimum 502 PA)

Fielder,Prince, Mil	12.8
Tulowitzki,Troy, Col	17.0
Zimmerman,Ryan, Was	18.5
Braun,Ryan, Mil	19.8
Upton,Justin, Ari	20.2
Sandoval,Pablo, SF	22.9
McCann,Brian, Atl	23.2
Kemp,Matt, LAD	23.3
Ramirez,Hanley, Fla	24.0
Rasmus,Colby, StL	29.6

Under Age 26: OPS
(minimum 502 PA)

Fielder,Prince, Mil	1.014
Ramirez,Hanley, Fla	.954
Sandoval,Pablo, SF	.943
Braun,Ryan, Mil	.937
Tulowitzki,Troy, Col	.930
Upton,Justin, Ari	.899
Zimmerman,Ryan, Was	.888
Coghlan,Chris, Fla	.850
Kemp,Matt, LAD	.842
McCann,Brian, Atl	.834

Under Age 26: RC/27 Outs
(minimum 502 PA)

Fielder,Prince, Mil	8.1
Ramirez,Hanley, Fla	8.1
Braun,Ryan, Mil	7.9
Sandoval,Pablo, SF	7.5
Coghlan,Chris, Fla	6.9
Upton,Justin, Ari	6.5
Tulowitzki,Troy, Col	6.1
Kemp,Matt, LAD	5.9
McCann,Brian, Atl	5.9
Zimmerman,Ryan, Was	5.5

Longest Home Run

Balentien,W., Cin, 10/2	495
Reynolds,Mark, Ari, 7/28	481
Ibanez,Raul, Phi, 5/22	477
Dunn,Adam, Was, 7/28	473
Howard,Ryan, Phi, 9/18	473
Votto,Joey, Cin, 7/16	473
Gonzalez,Adrian, SD, 4/26	471
Iannetta,Chris, Col, 4/6	471
Reynolds,Mark, Ari, 8/27	471
Dunn,Adam, Was, 5/10	469

Swing and Miss %
(minimum 1500 Pitches Seen)

Reynolds,Mark, Ari	38.1
Howard,Ryan, Phi	32.8
Hawpe,Brad, Col	28.5
Stewart,Ian, Col	28.2
Upton,Justin, Ari	27.5
Dunn,Adam, Was	27.0
Young,Chris, Ari	26.7
Dukes,Elijah, Was	26.2
Soriano,Alfonso, ChC	25.7
Rowand,Aaron, SF	25.3

Highest First Swing %
(minimum 502 PA)

Sandoval,Pablo, SF	47.2
Francoeur,Jeff, Atl-NYM	43.8
Molina,Bengie, SF	38.6
Phillips,Brandon, Cin	38.6
Ramirez,Hanley, Fla	37.9
Votto,Joey, Cin	37.9
Rasmus,Colby, StL	35.7
Hawpe,Brad, Col	35.0
Kouzmanoff,Kevin, SD	34.5
Molina,Yadier, StL	34.3

Lowest First Swing %
(minimum 502 PA)

Eckstein,David, SD	7.6
Johnson,Nick, Was-Fla	8.5
Utley,Chase, Phi	8.7
Castillo,Luis, NYM	9.7
Prado,Martin, Atl	11.6
Werth,Jayson, Phi	13.2
Blake,Casey, LAD	13.5
Pujols,Albert, StL	15.3
Ibanez,Raul, Phi	15.4
2 tied with	16.4

Home RC Per 27 Outs
(minimum 251 PA)

Sandoval,Pablo, SF	9.6
Lee,Derrek, ChC	9.4
Pujols,Albert, StL	9.1
Ramirez,Hanley, Fla	8.2
Helton,Todd, Col	7.9
McCutchen,Andrew, Pit	7.9
Fielder,Prince, Mil	7.7
Ethier,Andre, LAD	7.5
Tulowitzki,Troy, Col	7.4
Votto,Joey, Cin	7.2

Road RC Per 27 Outs
(minimum 251 PA)

Pujols,Albert, StL	9.5
Braun,Ryan, Mil	9.4
Votto,Joey, Cin	9.0
Fielder,Prince, Mil	8.5
Coghlan,Chris, Fla	8.1
Gonzalez,Adrian, SD	8.0
Ramirez,Hanley, Fla	8.0
Ludwick,Ryan, StL	7.9
Dunn,Adam, Was	7.7
Utley,Chase, Phi	7.7

2009 American League Pitching Leaders

Earned Run Average
(minimum 162 IP)

Greinke,Zack, KC	2.16
Hernandez,Felix, Sea	2.49
Halladay,Roy, Tor	2.79
Sabathia,CC, NYY	3.37
Lester,Jon, Bos	3.41
Verlander,Justin, Det	3.45
Jackson,Edwin, Det	3.62
Millwood,Kevin, Tex	3.67
Weaver,Jered, LAA	3.75
Danks,John, CWS	3.77

Winning Percentage
(minimum 15 Decisions)

Hernandez,Felix, Sea	.792
Beckett,Josh, Bos	.739
Sabathia,CC, NYY	.704
Saunders,Joe, LAA	.696
Wakefield,Tim, Bos	.688
Niemann,Jeff, TB	.684
Feldman,Scott, Tex	.680
Verlander,Justin, Det	.679
Greinke,Zack, KC	.667
Weaver,Jered, LAA	.667

Opponent Batting Average
(minimum 162 IP)

Hernandez,Felix, Sea	.227
Greinke,Zack, KC	.230
Sabathia,CC, NYY	.232
Garza,Matt, TB	.233
Lester,Jon, Bos	.242
Verlander,Justin, Det	.243
Washburn,Jarrod, Sea-Det	.243
Floyd,Gavin, CWS	.244
Beckett,Josh, Bos	.244
Danks,John, CWS	.245

Baserunners Per 9 IP
(minimum 162 IP)

Greinke,Zack, KC	9.81
Halladay,Roy, Tor	10.32
Hernandez,Felix, Sea	10.52
Sabathia,CC, NYY	10.68
Verlander,Justin, Det	10.80
Baker,Scott, Min	10.89
Washburn,Jarrod, Sea-Det	10.94
Beckett,Josh, Bos	11.02
Floyd,Gavin, CWS	11.15
Lester,Jon, Bos	11.20

Games

Guerrier,Matt, Min	79
Breslow,Craig, Min-Oak	77
Lowe,Mark, Sea	75
Springer,Russ, Oak-TB	74
Wilson,C.J., Tex	74
Wuertz,Mike, Oak	74
Aardsma,David, Sea	73
Balfour,Grant, TB	73
Carlson,Jesse, Tor	73
Rodney,Fernando, Det	73

Games Started

Verlander,Justin, Det	35
Hernandez,Felix, Sea	34
Sabathia,CC, NYY	34
10 tied with	33

Complete Games

Halladay,Roy, Tor	9
Greinke,Zack, KC	6
Beckett,Josh, Bos	4
Weaver,Jered, LAA	4
Blackburn,Nick, Min	3
Lee,Cliff, Cle	3
Millwood,Kevin, Tex	3
Verlander,Justin, Det	3
8 tied with	2

Shutouts

Halladay,Roy, Tor	4
Greinke,Zack, KC	3
Beckett,Josh, Bos	2
Niemann,Jeff, TB	2
Santana,Ervin, LAA	2
Weaver,Jered, LAA	2
18 tied with	1

Wins

Hernandez,Felix, Sea	19
Sabathia,CC, NYY	19
Verlander,Justin, Det	19
Beckett,Josh, Bos	17
Feldman,Scott, Tex	17
Halladay,Roy, Tor	17
Greinke,Zack, KC	16
Saunders,Joe, LAA	16
Weaver,Jered, LAA	16
2 tied with	15

Losses

Guthrie,Jeremy, Bal	17
Cahill,Trevor, Oak	13
Contreras,Jose, CWS	13
Hochevar,Luke, KC	13
Holland,Derek, Tex	13
Liriano,Francisco, Min	13
6 tied with	12

No Decisions

Chamberlain,Joba, NYY	16
Garza,Matt, TB	12
Blackburn,Nick, Min	11
Burnett,A.J., NYY	11
Jackson,Edwin, Det	11
Niemann,Jeff, TB	11
6 tied with	10

Wild Pitches

Burnett,A.J., NYY	17
Hernandez,Felix, Sea	17
Kazmir,Scott, TB-LAA	13
Bannister,Brian, KC	12
Davies,Kyle, KC	10
Hochevar,Luke, KC	9
League,Brandon, Tor	9
6 tied with	8

Strikeouts

Verlander,Justin, Det	269
Greinke,Zack, KC	242
Lester,Jon, Bos	225
Hernandez,Felix, Sea	217
Halladay,Roy, Tor	208
Beckett,Josh, Bos	199
Sabathia,CC, NYY	197
Burnett,A.J., NYY	195
Garza,Matt, TB	189
Weaver,Jered, LAA	174

Walks Allowed

Burnett,A.J., NYY	97
Garza,Matt, TB	79
Romero,Ricky, Tor	79
Chamberlain,Joba, NYY	76
Pettitte,Andy, NYY	76
Danks,John, CWS	73
Cahill,Trevor, Oak	72
Tallet,Brian, Tor	72
Hernandez,Felix, Sea	71
Millwood,Kevin, Tex	71

Intentional Walks Allowed

Lyon,Brandon, Det	9
Oliver,Darren, LAA	8
Ray,Chris, Bal	7
Sabathia,CC, NYY	7
Linebrink,Scott, CWS	6
Perez,Rafael, Cle	6
Bass,Brian, Bal	5
Perry,Ryan, Det	5
Verlander,Justin, Det	5
Wright,Jamey, KC	5

Hit Batters

Chamberlain,Joba, NYY	12
Garza,Matt, TB	11
Millwood,Kevin, Tex	11
Burnett,A.J., NYY	10
Romero,Ricky, Tor	10
Santana,Ervin, LAA	10
Wakefield,Tim, Bos	10
5 tied with	9

2009 American League Pitching Leaders

Runs Allowed		Hits Allowed		Doubles Allowed		Home Runs Allowed	
Guthrie,Jeremy, Bal	120	Blackburn,Nick, Min	240	Shields,James, TB	54	Guthrie,Jeremy, Bal	35
Pavano,Carl, Cle-Min	119	Shields,James, TB	239	Weaver,Jered, LAA	53	Saunders,Joe, LAA	29
Shields,James, TB	113	Pavano,Carl, Cle-Min	235	Guthrie,Jeremy, Bal	51	Shields,James, TB	29
Hochevar,Luke, KC	109	Halladay,Roy, Tor	234	Verlander,Justin, Det	50	Baker,Scott, Min	28
Blackburn,Nick, Min	103	Guthrie,Jeremy, Bal	224	Blackburn,Nick, Min	47	Danks,John, CWS	28
Saunders,Joe, LAA	102	Buehrle,Mark, CWS	222	Greinke,Zack, KC	47	Buehrle,Mark, CWS	27
Pettitte,Andy, NYY	101	Verlander,Justin, Det	219	Halladay,Roy, Tor	47	Cahill,Trevor, Oak	27
6 tied with	99	Saunders,Joe, LAA	202	Cahill,Trevor, Oak	45	Hernandez,David, Bal	27
		Hernandez,Felix, Sea	200	Jackson,Edwin, Det	45	Jackson,Edwin, Det	27
		Jackson,Edwin, Det	200	Buehrle,Mark, CWS	44	Richmond,Scott, Tor	27

Run Support Per Nine IP (minimum 162 IP)		% Pitches In Strike Zone (minimum 162 IP)		Pitches Per Start (minimum 30 GS)		Pitches Per Batter (minimum 162 IP)	
Saunders,Joe, LAA	6.02	Baker,Scott, Min	52.8	Verlander,Justin, Det	112.5	Blackburn,Nick, Min	3.52
Niemann,Jeff, TB	6.43	Danks,John, CWS	52.5	Garza,Matt, TB	106.0	Halladay,Roy, Tor	3.52
Beckett,Josh, Bos	6.36	Verlander,Justin, Det	52.4	Hernandez,Felix, Sea	106.8	Shields,James, TB	3.58
Millwood,Kevin, Tex	6.25	Halladay,Roy, Tor	51.5	Lester,Jon, Bos	106.4	Pavano,Carl, Cle-Min	3.64
Porcello,Rick, Det	6.06	Beckett,Josh, Bos	50.7	Halladay,Roy, Tor	106.1	Buehrle,Mark, CWS	3.68
Pavano,Carl, Cle-Min	5.96	Niemann,Jeff, TB	50.5	Millwood,Kevin, Tex	105.6	Lackey,John, LAA	3.68
Baker,Scott, Min	5.84	Blackburn,Nick, Min	50.5	Sabathia,CC, NYY	105.5	Hernandez,Felix, Sea	3.72
Cahill,Trevor, Oak	5.74	Shields,James, TB	50.2	Greinke,Zack, KC	105.4	Saunders,Joe, LAA	3.74
Burnett,A.J., NYY	5.74	Anderson,Brett, Oak	49.2	Beckett,Josh, Bos	105.2	Floyd,Gavin, CWS	3.74
Weaver,Jered, LAA	5.72	Guthrie,Jeremy, Bal	49.1	Jackson,Edwin, Det	105.0	Niemann,Jeff, TB	3.76

Quality Starts		Batters Faced		Innings Pitched		Most Pitches in a Game	
Hernandez,Felix, Sea	29	Verlander,Justin, Det	982	Verlander,Justin, Det	240.0	Halladay,Roy, Tor	133
Greinke,Zack, KC	26	Hernandez,Felix, Sea	977	Halladay,Roy, Tor	239.0	Jackson,Edwin, Det	132
Lester,Jon, Bos	23	Halladay,Roy, Tor	963	Hernandez,Felix, Sea	238.2	Meche,Gil, KC	132
Halladay,Roy, Tor	22	Sabathia,CC, NYY	938	Sabathia,CC, NYY	230.0	Lackey,John, LAA	131
Verlander,Justin, Det	22	Shields,James, TB	930	Greinke,Zack, KC	229.1	Verlander,Justin, Det	129
Blackburn,Nick, Min	21	Greinke,Zack, KC	915	Shields,James, TB	219.2	Verlander,Justin, Det	128
Burnett,A.J., NYY	21	Burnett,A.J., NYY	896	Jackson,Edwin, Det	214.0	Verlander,Justin, Det	127
Jackson,Edwin, Det	21	Jackson,Edwin, Det	890	Buehrle,Mark, CWS	213.1	4 tied with	126
Sabathia,CC, NYY	21	Beckett,Josh, Bos	883	Beckett,Josh, Bos	212.1		
3 tied with	20	2 tied with	882	Weaver,Jered, LAA	211.0		

Stolen Bases Allowed		Caught Stealing Off		Stolen Base Pct Allowed (minimum 162 IP)		Pickoffs	
Pavano,Carl, Cle-Min	33	Verlander,Justin, Det	16	Greinke,Zack, KC	35.7	Buehrle,Mark, CWS	8
Penny,Brad, Bos	27	Burnett,A.J., NYY	12	Verlander,Justin, Det	36.0	Danks,John, CWS	6
Chamberlain,Joba, NYY	26	Cahill,Trevor, Oak	10	Garza,Matt, TB	42.9	Lester,Jon, Bos	6
Niemann,Jeff, TB	24	Greinke,Zack, KC	9	Buehrle,Mark, CWS	50.0	Liriano,Francisco, Min	6
Burnett,A.J., NYY	23	Jackson,Edwin, Det	9	Washburn,Jarrod, Sea-Det	55.6	Pettitte,Andy, NYY	6
Jackson,Edwin, Det	23	Liriano,Francisco, Min	9	Romero,Ricky, Tor	56.3	Richard,Clayton, CWS	6
Wakefield,Tim, Bos	23	Chamberlain,Joba, NYY	8	Millwood,Kevin, Tex	61.9	7 tied with	4
Hernandez,Felix, Sea	20	Hernandez,Felix, Sea	8	Cahill,Trevor, Oak	63.0		
4 tied with	19	Millwood,Kevin, Tex	8	Pettitte,Andy, NYY	63.6		
		Pettitte,Andy, NYY	8	Sabathia,CC, NYY	65.0		

2009 American League Pitching Leaders

Strikeouts Per 9 IP
(minimum 162 IP)

Verlander,Justin, Det	10.09
Lester,Jon, Bos	9.96
Greinke,Zack, KC	9.50
Burnett,A.J., NYY	8.48
Beckett,Josh, Bos	8.43
Garza,Matt, TB	8.38
Hernandez,Felix, Sea	8.18
Halladay,Roy, Tor	7.83
Sabathia,CC, NYY	7.71
Anderson,Brett, Oak	7.70

Opp On-Base Percentage
(minimum 162 IP)

Greinke,Zack, KC	.276
Halladay,Roy, Tor	.285
Hernandez,Felix, Sea	.287
Sabathia,CC, NYY	.292
Baker,Scott, Min	.293
Verlander,Justin, Det	.295
Beckett,Josh, Bos	.296
Washburn,Jarrod, Sea-Det	.299
Floyd,Gavin, CWS	.301
Lester,Jon, Bos	.301

Opp Slugging Average
(minimum 162 IP)

Hernandez,Felix, Sea	.318
Greinke,Zack, KC	.336
Sabathia,CC, NYY	.360
Lester,Jon, Bos	.366
Verlander,Justin, Det	.369
Feldman,Scott, Tex	.374
Floyd,Gavin, CWS	.379
Halladay,Roy, Tor	.382
Garza,Matt, TB	.384
Pettitte,Andy, NYY	.393

Opponent OPS
(minimum 162 IP)

Hernandez,Felix, Sea	.605
Greinke,Zack, KC	.611
Sabathia,CC, NYY	.653
Verlander,Justin, Det	.665
Halladay,Roy, Tor	.667
Lester,Jon, Bos	.667
Floyd,Gavin, CWS	.680
Beckett,Josh, Bos	.691
Feldman,Scott, Tex	.693
Garza,Matt, TB	.695

Home Runs Per Nine IP
(minimum 162 IP)

Greinke,Zack, KC	0.43
Hernandez,Felix, Sea	0.57
Sabathia,CC, NYY	0.70
Verlander,Justin, Det	0.75
Halladay,Roy, Tor	0.83
Niemann,Jeff, TB	0.85
Feldman,Scott, Tex	0.85
Lackey,John, LAA	0.87
Lester,Jon, Bos	0.89
Romero,Ricky, Tor	0.91

Batting Average vs. LHB
(minimum 125 BF)

Bailey,Andrew, Oak	.146
Nathan,Joe, Min	.160
Washburn,Jarrod, Sea-Det	.178
Rivera,Mariano, NYY	.182
Wuertz,Mike, Oak	.183
Papelbon,Jonathan, Bos	.187
White,Sean, Sea	.191
Saito,Takashi, Bos	.195
Coke,Phil, NYY	.195
Bulger,Jason, LAA	.196

Batting Average vs. RHB
(minimum 225 BF)

Palmer,Matt, LAA	.197
Masterson,Justin, Bos-Cle	.203
Weaver,Jered, LAA	.208
Bedard,Erik, Sea	.211
Greinke,Zack, KC	.211
Beckett,Josh, Bos	.226
Hernandez,Felix, Sea	.226
Richmond,Scott, Tor	.233
Lester,Jon, Bos	.237
Verlander,Justin, Det	.237

Opp BA w/ RISP
(minimum 125 BF)

Greinke,Zack, KC	.199
Hernandez,Felix, Sea	.199
Weaver,Jered, LAA	.200
Washburn,Jarrod, Sea-Det	.203
Lester,Jon, Bos	.203
Danks,John, CWS	.205
Garza,Matt, TB	.214
Penny,Brad, Bos	.216
Cahill,Trevor, Oak	.218
Burnett,A.J., NYY	.226

OBP vs. Leadoff Hitter
(minimum 150 BF)

Niemann,Jeff, TB	.240
Beckett,Josh, Bos	.269
Sabathia,CC, NYY	.274
Halladay,Roy, Tor	.276
Lackey,John, LAA	.276
Verlander,Justin, Det	.282
Feldman,Scott, Tex	.284
Baker,Scott, Min	.286
Hernandez,Felix, Sea	.289
Weaver,Jered, LAA	.301

Strikeouts / Walks Ratio
(minimum 162 IP)

Halladay,Roy, Tor	5.94
Greinke,Zack, KC	4.75
Verlander,Justin, Det	4.27
Pavano,Carl, Cle-Min	3.77
Beckett,Josh, Bos	3.62
Lester,Jon, Bos	3.52
Baker,Scott, Min	3.38
Anderson,Brett, Oak	3.33
Shields,James, TB	3.21
Hernandez,Felix, Sea	3.06

Highest GB/FB Ratio
(minimum 162 IP)

Romero,Ricky, Tor	2.03
Porcello,Rick, Det	1.89
Hernandez,Felix, Sea	1.79
Halladay,Roy, Tor	1.71
Anderson,Brett, Oak	1.49
Beckett,Josh, Bos	1.49
Feldman,Scott, Tex	1.43
Cahill,Trevor, Oak	1.40
Lester,Jon, Bos	1.38
Floyd,Gavin, CWS	1.34

Lowest GB/FB Ratio
(minimum 162 IP)

Weaver,Jered, LAA	0.61
Baker,Scott, Min	0.71
Guthrie,Jeremy, Bal	0.75
Verlander,Justin, Det	0.84
Washburn,Jarrod, Sea-Det	0.88
Jackson,Edwin, Det	0.92
Garza,Matt, TB	0.93
Greinke,Zack, KC	0.99
Niemann,Jeff, TB	1.03
Danks,John, CWS	1.08

Sacrifice Flies Allowed

Galarraga,Armando, Det	11
Hernandez,Felix, Sea	11
Bannister,Brian, KC	10
Lackey,John, LAA	10
Halladay,Roy, Tor	9
Sabathia,CC, NYY	9
Garza,Matt, TB	8
Guthrie,Jeremy, Bal	8
Sowers,Jeremy, Cle	8
Weaver,Jered, LAA	8

Sacrifice Hits Allowed

Buehrle,Mark, CWS	11
Masterson,Justin, Bos-Cle	10
Lackey,John, LAA	9
Greinke,Zack, KC	8
Washburn,Jarrod, Sea-Det	8
Contreras,Jose, CWS	7
8 tied with	6

GIDP Induced

Romero,Ricky, Tor	30
Buehrle,Mark, CWS	28
Saunders,Joe, LAA	27
Laffey,Aaron, Cle	26
Anderson,Brett, Oak	24
Porcello,Rick, Det	24
Danks,John, CWS	22
Sabathia,CC, NYY	22
3 tied with	21

GIDP Per Nine IP
(minimum 162 IP)

Romero,Ricky, Tor	1.52
Saunders,Joe, LAA	1.31
Porcello,Rick, Det	1.27
Anderson,Brett, Oak	1.23
Buehrle,Mark, CWS	1.18
Feldman,Scott, Tex	1.00
Danks,John, CWS	0.99
Floyd,Gavin, CWS	0.98
Niemann,Jeff, TB	0.95
Cahill,Trevor, Oak	0.91

2009 American League Pitching Leaders

Saves

Fuentes,Brian, LAA	48
Nathan,Joe, Min	47
Rivera,Mariano, NYY	44
Aardsma,David, Sea	38
Papelbon,Jonathan, Bos	38
Rodney,Fernando, Det	37
Soria,Joakim, KC	30
Jenks,Bobby, CWS	29
Bailey,Andrew, Oak	26
Francisco,Frank, Tex	25

Blown Saves

Lowe,Mark, Sea	10
Howell,J.P., TB	8
Fuentes,Brian, LAA	7
Jenks,Bobby, CWS	6
Johnson,Jim, Bal	6
Wood,Kerry, Cle	6
Zumaya,Joel, Det	6
4 tied with	5

Save Pct
(minimum 20 Save Ops)

Rodney,Fernando, Det	97.4
Rivera,Mariano, NYY	95.7
Papelbon,Jonathan, Bos	92.7
Soria,Joakim, KC	90.9
Aardsma,David, Sea	90.5
Nathan,Joe, Min	90.4
Fuentes,Brian, LAA	87.3
Sherrill,George, Bal	87.0
Bailey,Andrew, Oak	86.7
Francisco,Frank, Tex	86.2

Save Opportunities

Fuentes,Brian, LAA	55
Nathan,Joe, Min	52
Rivera,Mariano, NYY	46
Aardsma,David, Sea	42
Papelbon,Jonathan, Bos	41
Rodney,Fernando, Det	38
Jenks,Bobby, CWS	35
Soria,Joakim, KC	33
Bailey,Andrew, Oak	30
Francisco,Frank, Tex	29

Easy Saves

Nathan,Joe, Min	32
Fuentes,Brian, LAA	28
Rivera,Mariano, NYY	28
Rodney,Fernando, Det	26
Jenks,Bobby, CWS	21
Aardsma,David, Sea	20
Papelbon,Jonathan, Bos	20
Soria,Joakim, KC	16
Bailey,Andrew, Oak	15
Francisco,Frank, Tex	15

Regular Saves

Fuentes,Brian, LAA	19
Aardsma,David, Sea	17
Papelbon,Jonathan, Bos	15
Nathan,Joe, Min	14
Rivera,Mariano, NYY	12
Soria,Joakim, KC	11
Bailey,Andrew, Oak	10
Rodney,Fernando, Det	10
Francisco,Frank, Tex	9
Wood,Kerry, Cle	9

Tough Saves

Rivera,Mariano, NYY	4
Papelbon,Jonathan, Bos	3
Soria,Joakim, KC	3
Frasor,Jason, Tor	2
O'Day,Darren, Tex	2
16 tied with	1

Holds Adjusted Saves %
(minimum 20 Save Ops)

Rodney,Fernando, Det	97.4
Rivera,Mariano, NYY	95.7
Papelbon,Jonathan, Bos	92.7
Aardsma,David, Sea	91.7
Soria,Joakim, KC	90.9
Nathan,Joe, Min	90.4
Francisco,Frank, Tex	87.9
Bailey,Andrew, Oak	87.5
Fuentes,Brian, LAA	87.3
Sherrill,George, Bal	87.0

Relief Wins

Aceves,Alfredo, NYY	10
Breslow,Craig, Min-Oak	8
Batista,Miguel, Sea	7
Crain,Jesse, Min	7
Frasor,Jason, Tor	7
Howell,J.P., TB	7
Ramirez,Ramon, Bos	7
8 tied with	6

Relief Losses

Breslow,Craig, Min-Oak	7
Linebrink,Scott, CWS	7
Lowe,Mark, Sea	7
8 tied with	6

Relief Games

Guerrier,Matt, Min	79
Breslow,Craig, Min-Oak	77
Lowe,Mark, Sea	75
Springer,Russ, Oak-TB	74
Wilson,C.J., Tex	74
Wuertz,Mike, Oak	74
Aardsma,David, Sea	73
Balfour,Grant, TB	73
Carlson,Jesse, Tor	73
Rodney,Fernando, Det	73

Holds

Guerrier,Matt, Min	33
Seay,Bobby, Det	28
Mijares,Jose, Min	27
Lowe,Mark, Sea	26
Thornton,Matt, CWS	24
Okajima,Hideki, Bos	23
Wuertz,Mike, Oak	23
Coke,Phil, NYY	21
O'Day,Darren, Tex	20
Oliver,Darren, LAA	20

Relief Innings

Carrasco,D.J., CWS	89.1
Bass,Brian, Bal	86.1
Bailey,Andrew, Oak	83.1
Aceves,Alfredo, NYY	80.2
Lowe,Mark, Sea	80.0
Camp,Shawn, Tor	79.2
Wright,Jamey, KC	79.0
Lyon,Brandon, Det	78.2
Wuertz,Mike, Oak	78.2
Cormier,Lance, TB	77.1

Inherited Runners Scrd %
(minimum 30 IR)

Ni,Fu-Te, Det	8.6
Choate,Randy, TB	15.8
Okajima,Hideki, Bos	16.2
Sipp,Tony, Cle	18.9
Carlson,Jesse, Tor	19.4
Wuertz,Mike, Oak	20.0
Ramirez,Ramon, Bos	22.0
Coke,Phil, NYY	22.2
Hendrickson,Mark, Bal	22.2
Breslow,Craig, Min-Oak	24.0

Relief Opp On Base Pct
(minimum 50 IP)

Hughes,Phil, NYY	.228
Bailey,Andrew, Oak	.228
Wheeler,Dan, TB	.231
Rivera,Mariano, NYY	.237
Nathan,Joe, Min	.244
Wuertz,Mike, Oak	.248
Guerrier,Matt, Min	.259
Aceves,Alfredo, NYY	.263
O'Day,Darren, Tex	.265
Frasor,Jason, Tor	.270

Relief Opp Slugging Avg
(minimum 50 IP)

Hughes,Phil, NYY	.228
Bailey,Andrew, Oak	.248
O'Day,Darren, Tex	.260
Aardsma,David, Sea	.271
Frasor,Jason, Tor	.286
White,Sean, Sea	.302
Nathan,Joe, Min	.305
Papelbon,Jonathan, Bos	.311
Rivera,Mariano, NYY	.311
Wuertz,Mike, Oak	.319

2009 American League Pitching Leaders

Relief Opp BA Vs LHB		Relief Opp BA Vs RHB		Relief Opp Batting Average		Relief Earned Run Average	
(minimum 50 AB)		(minimum 50 AB)		(minimum 50 IP)		(minimum 50 IP)	
Ni,Fu-Te, Det	.113	Frasor,Jason, Tor	.140	Bailey,Andrew, Oak	.167	Hughes,Phil, NYY	1.40
Choate,Randy, TB	.141	Tejeda,Robinson, KC	.150	Nathan,Joe, Min	.171	Rivera,Mariano, NYY	1.76
Bailey,Andrew, Oak	.146	Hughes,Phil, NYY	.152	Hughes,Phil, NYY	.172	Bailey,Andrew, Oak	1.84
Feliz,Neftali, Tex	.155	Wheeler,Dan, TB	.156	O'Day,Darren, Tex	.188	Papelbon,Jonathan, Bos	1.85
Mijares,Jose, Min	.155	Tallet,Brian, Tor	.158	Wuertz,Mike, Oak	.188	O'Day,Darren, Tex	1.94
Nathan,Joe, Min	.160	Howell,J.P., TB	.159	Aardsma,David, Sea	.190	Nathan,Joe, Min	2.10
Okajima,Hideki, Bos	.167	O'Day,Darren, Tex	.164	Howell,J.P., TB	.197	Soria,Joakim, KC	2.21
Rivera,Mariano, NYY	.182	Betancourt,Rafael, Cle	.179	Breslow,Craig, Min-Oak	.197	Mijares,Jose, Min	2.34
Wuertz,Mike, Oak	.183	Sipp,Tony, Cle	.179	Rivera,Mariano, NYY	.197	Guerrier,Matt, Min	2.36
Papelbon,Jonathan, Bos	.187	Nathan,Joe, Min	.181	Wheeler,Dan, TB	.199	Saito,Takashi, Bos	2.43

Rel OBP 1st Batter Faced		Rel Opp BA w/ Runners On		Relief Opp BA w/ RISP		Fastest Avg Fastball-Relief	
(minimum 40 BF)		(minimum 50 IP)		(minimum 50 IP)		(minimum 50 IP)	
Hendrickson,Mark, Bal	.095	Rivera,Mariano, NYY	.139	Hughes,Phil, NYY	.088	Lowe,Mark, Sea	96.3
Aceves,Alfredo, NYY	.119	Nathan,Joe, Min	.146	Nathan,Joe, Min	.103	Jepsen,Kevin, LAA	96.2
Nathan,Joe, Min	.171	Guerrier,Matt, Min	.155	Papelbon,Jonathan, Bos	.128	Rodney,Fernando, Det	95.8
Bailey,Andrew, Oak	.176	Bailey,Andrew, Oak	.157	Breslow,Craig, Min-Oak	.143	Thornton,Matt, CWS	95.7
Wheeler,Dan, TB	.194	Wuertz,Mike, Oak	.165	Bailey,Andrew, Oak	.152	Wood,Kerry, Cle	95.5
Wuertz,Mike, Oak	.203	Hughes,Phil, NYY	.167	Bulger,Jason, LAA	.153	League,Brandon, Tor	95.4
Hughes,Phil, NYY	.205	Breslow,Craig, Min-Oak	.171	Rivera,Mariano, NYY	.157	Perry,Ryan, Det	95.4
Okajima,Hideki, Bos	.209	Bulger,Jason, LAA	.175	Wuertz,Mike, Oak	.167	Jenks,Bobby, CWS	94.8
Jenks,Bobby, CWS	.212	Papelbon,Jonathan, Bos	.177	Cormier,Lance, TB	.172	Crain,Jesse, Min	94.8
2 tied with	.230	O'Day,Darren, Tex	.181	Guerrier,Matt, Min	.176	Hughes,Phil, NYY	94.7

Fastest Average Fastball		Slowest Average Fastball		Pitches 100+ Velocity		Pitches 95+ Velocity	
(minimum 162 IP)		(minimum 162 IP)					
Verlander,Justin, Det	95.6	Buehrle,Mark, CWS	85.7	Zumaya,Joel, Det	198	Verlander,Justin, Det	1901
Jackson,Edwin, Det	94.5	Washburn,Jarrod, Sea-Det	88.3	Bard,Daniel, Bos	39	Jackson,Edwin, Det	1157
Burnett,A.J., NYY	94.2	Weaver,Jered, LAA	88.9	Verlander,Justin, Det	39	Hernandez,Felix, Sea	977
Beckett,Josh, Bos	94.2	Pettitte,Andy, NYY	89.0	Feliz,Neftali, Tex	24	Burnett,A.J., NYY	947
Sabathia,CC, NYY	94.2	Cahill,Trevor, Oak	89.8	Rodriguez,Henry, Oak	22	Beckett,Josh, Bos	904
Hernandez,Felix, Sea	94.0	Millwood,Kevin, Tex	90.3	Farnsworth,Kyle, KC	15	Sabathia,CC, NYY	879
Greinke,Zack, KC	93.7	Danks,John, CWS	90.4	Rodney,Fernando, Det	9	Thornton,Matt, CWS	832
Lester,Jon, Bos	93.6	Shields,James, TB	90.5	Lowe,Mark, Sea	4	Penny,Brad, Bos	829
Garza,Matt, TB	92.9	Saunders,Joe, LAA	90.5	Jepsen,Kevin, LAA	3	Lowe,Mark, Sea	752
Halladay,Roy, Tor	92.6	Blackburn,Nick, Min	90.6	Morrow,Brandon, Sea	2	Greinke,Zack, KC	679

Pitches Less Than 80 MPH		Lowest % Fastballs		Highest % Fastballs		Highest % Curveballs	
		(minimum 162 IP)		(minimum 162 IP)		(minimum 162 IP)	
Wakefield,Tim, Bos	2005	Halladay,Roy, Tor	31.3	Niemann,Jeff, TB	71.4	Burnett,A.J., NYY	30.8
Beckett,Josh, Bos	806	Feldman,Scott, Tex	42.6	Garza,Matt, TB	70.7	Beckett,Josh, Bos	25.2
Weaver,Jered, LAA	806	Shields,James, TB	42.9	Cahill,Trevor, Oak	68.7	Lackey,John, LAA	24.3
Buehrle,Mark, CWS	776	Buehrle,Mark, CWS	43.0	Porcello,Rick, Det	68.5	Halladay,Roy, Tor	22.0
Washburn,Jarrod, Sea-Det	718	Floyd,Gavin, CWS	45.6	Verlander,Justin, Det	66.3	Verlander,Justin, Det	19.5
Braden,Dallas, Oak	704	Danks,John, CWS	51.7	Burnett,A.J., NYY	65.6	Lester,Jon, Bos	19.3
Dickey,R.A., Min	692	Anderson,Brett, Oak	52.2	Jackson,Edwin, Det	64.4	Floyd,Gavin, CWS	17.6
French,Luke, Det-Sea	660	Romero,Ricky, Tor	52.8	Millwood,Kevin, Tex	64.0	Saunders,Joe, LAA	15.2
Halladay,Roy, Tor	571	Pettitte,Andy, NYY	52.9	Saunders,Joe, LAA	62.5	Feldman,Scott, Tex	14.8
Kazmir,Scott, TB-LAA	532	Lester,Jon, Bos	54.4	Hernandez,Felix, Sea	61.4	Baker,Scott, Min	14.8

2009 American League Pitching Leaders

Highest % Changeups
(minimum 162 IP)

Shields,James, TB	23.3
Pavano,Carl, Cle-Min	22.9
Romero,Ricky, Tor	22.0
Buehrle,Mark, CWS	19.7
Cahill,Trevor, Oak	19.2
Sabathia,CC, NYY	18.3
Saunders,Joe, LAA	17.8
Danks,John, CWS	17.6
Weaver,Jered, LAA	16.3
Guthrie,Jeremy, Bal	13.8

Highest % Sliders
(minimum 162 IP)

Anderson,Brett, Oak	31.9
Jackson,Edwin, Det	27.0
Floyd,Gavin, CWS	25.8
Millwood,Kevin, Tex	21.7
Greinke,Zack, KC	19.9
Sabathia,CC, NYY	19.7
Pavano,Carl, Cle-Min	19.4
Guthrie,Jeremy, Bal	19.3
Weaver,Jered, LAA	15.8
Baker,Scott, Min	15.5

Balks

Verlander,Justin, Det	4
Holland,Derek, Tex	3
9 tied with	2

Strikeout/Hit Ratio
(minimum 50 IP)

Nathan,Joe, Min	2.12
Tejeda,Robinson, KC	2.02
Wuertz,Mike, Oak	1.96
Bailey,Andrew, Oak	1.86
Howell,J.P., TB	1.68
Aardsma,David, Sea	1.63
Soria,Joakim, KC	1.57
O'Day,Darren, Tex	1.50
Rivera,Mariano, NYY	1.50
Thornton,Matt, CWS	1.50

Opp OPS vs Fastballs
(minimum 251 BF)

Hernandez,Felix, Sea	.606
Greinke,Zack, KC	.607
Sabathia,CC, NYY	.639
Verlander,Justin, Det	.660
Baker,Scott, Min	.676
Porcello,Rick, Det	.692
Lee,Cliff, Cle	.698
Niemann,Jeff, TB	.702
Price,David, TB	.706
Halladay,Roy, Tor	.707

Opp OPS vs Curveballs
(minimum 100 BF)

Floyd,Gavin, CWS	.410
Bulger,Jason, LAA	.535
Hunter,Tommy, Tex	.538
Gonzalez,Gio, Oak	.571
Burnett,A.J., NYY	.603
Bedard,Erik, Sea	.605
Lester,Jon, Bos	.617
Feldman,Scott, Tex	.626
Greinke,Zack, KC	.626
Howell,J.P., TB	.627

Opp OPS vs Changeups
(minimum 100 BF)

Bannister,Brian, KC	.480
Braden,Dallas, Oak	.496
Sabathia,CC, NYY	.504
Hernandez,Felix, Sea	.508
Davies,Kyle, KC	.603
Tallet,Brian, Tor	.621
Romero,Ricky, Tor	.643
Buehrle,Mark, CWS	.651
Weaver,Jered, LAA	.662
Cahill,Trevor, Oak	.663

Opp OPS vs Sliders
(minimum 64 BF)

Lowe,Mark, Sea	.382
O'Day,Darren, Tex	.415
Wuertz,Mike, Oak	.478
Rzepczynski,Marc, Tor	.483
Nathan,Joe, Min	.557
Jackson,Edwin, Det	.574
Cruz,Juan, KC	.581
Oliver,Darren, LAA	.595
Greinke,Zack, KC	.596
Mazzaro,Vin, Oak	.598

Earned Runs

Pavano,Carl, Cle-Min	113
Guthrie,Jeremy, Bal	112
Hochevar,Luke, KC	104
Shields,James, TB	101
Baker,Scott, Min	97
Saunders,Joe, LAA	95
Tallet,Brian, Tor	95
Holland,Derek, Tex	94
Burnett,A.J., NYY	93
3 tied with	92

Hits Per Nine Innings
(minimum 162 IP)

Hernandez,Felix, Sea	7.54
Greinke,Zack, KC	7.65
Sabathia,CC, NYY	7.71
Garza,Matt, TB	7.85
Washburn,Jarrod, Sea-Det	8.18
Verlander,Justin, Det	8.21
Lester,Jon, Bos	8.23
Danks,John, CWS	8.27
Floyd,Gavin, CWS	8.30
Weaver,Jered, LAA	8.36

2009 National League Pitching Leaders

Earned Run Average (minimum 162 IP)		Winning Percentage (minimum 15 Decisions)		Opponent Batting Average (minimum 162 IP)		Baserunners Per 9 IP (minimum 162 IP)	
Carpenter,Chris, StL	2.24	Carpenter,Chris, StL	.810	Kershaw,Clayton, LAD	.200	Haren,Dan, Ari	9.18
Lincecum,Tim, SF	2.48	Happ,J.A., Phi	.750	Lincecum,Tim, SF	.206	Carpenter,Chris, StL	9.39
Jurrjens,Jair, Atl	2.60	Johnson,Josh, Fla	.750	Gallardo,Yovani, Mil	.219	Vazquez,Javier, Atl	9.40
Wainwright,Adam, StL	2.63	Hanson,Tommy, Atl	.733	Sanchez,Jonathan, SF	.221	Lilly,Ted, ChC	9.61
Kershaw,Clayton, LAD	2.79	Wainwright,Adam, StL	.704	Vazquez,Javier, Atl	.223	Lincecum,Tim, SF	9.67
Vazquez,Javier, Atl	2.87	Lincecum,Tim, SF	.682	Haren,Dan, Ari	.224	Wolf,Randy, LAD	10.16
Cain,Matt, SF	2.89	Looper,Braden, Mil	.667	Carpenter,Chris, StL	.226	Pineiro,Joel, StL	10.64
Happ,J.A., Phi	2.93	Cook,Aaron, Col	.647	Wolf,Randy, LAD	.227	Johnson,Josh, Fla	10.68
Rodriguez,Wandy, Hou	3.02	de la Rosa,Jorge, Col	.640	Jimenez,Ubaldo, Col	.229	Cain,Matt, SF	10.75
Wells,Randy, ChC	3.05	Cain,Matt, SF	.636	Lilly,Ted, ChC	.230	Wainwright,Adam, StL	11.01

Games		Games Started		Complete Games		Shutouts	
Feliciano,Pedro, NYM	88	Davis,Doug, Ari	34	Cain,Matt, SF	4	Arroyo,Bronson, Cin	2
Moylan,Peter, Atl	87	Jurrjens,Jair, Atl	34	Lincecum,Tim, SF	4	Hamels,Cole, Phi	2
Gonzalez,Mike, Atl	80	Looper,Braden, Mil	34	9 tied with	3	Happ,J.A., Phi	2
Green,Sean, NYM	79	Lowe,Derek, Atl	34			Lincecum,Tim, SF	2
Madson,Ryan, Phi	79	Wainwright,Adam, StL	34			Pineiro,Joel, StL	2
Marmol,Carlos, ChC	79	Wolf,Randy, LAD	34			20 tied with	1
Coffey,Todd, Mil	78	11 tied with	33				
O'Flaherty,Eric, Atl	78						
Soriano,Rafael, Atl	77						
Byrdak,Tim, Hou	76						

Wins		Losses		No Decisions		Wild Pitches	
Wainwright,Adam, StL	19	Duke,Zach, Pit	16	Oswalt,Roy, Hou	16	Billingsley,Chad, LAD	14
Carpenter,Chris, StL	17	Davis,Doug, Ari	14	Wolf,Randy, LAD	16	Haren,Dan, Ari	13
de la Rosa,Jorge, Col	16	Harang,Aaron, Cin	14	Kershaw,Clayton, LAD	14	Davis,Doug, Ari	12
8 tied with	15	Arroyo,Bronson, Cin	13	Maholm,Paul, Pit	14	de la Rosa,Jorge, Col	12
		Garland,Jon, Ari-LAD	13	Johnson,Josh, Fla	13	Suppan,Jeff, Mil	12
		Lannan,John, Was	13	Looper,Braden, Mil	13	7 tied with	11
		Marquis,Jason, Col	13	Hammel,Jason, Col	12		
		Volstad,Chris, Fla	13	Zambrano,Carlos, ChC	12		
		Zito,Barry, SF	13	7 tied with	11		
		11 tied with	12				

Strikeouts		Walks Allowed		Intentional Walks Allowed		Hit Batters	
Lincecum,Tim, SF	261	Davis,Doug, Ari	103	Moehler,Brian, Hou	12	Bush,David, Mil	15
Vazquez,Javier, Atl	238	Gallardo,Yovani, Mil	94	Gregerson,Luke, SD	9	Cueto,Johnny, Cin	14
Haren,Dan, Ari	223	Kershaw,Clayton, LAD	91	Troncoso,Ramon, LAD	9	Marmol,Carlos, ChC	12
Wainwright,Adam, StL	212	Sanchez,Jonathan, SF	88	Weaver,Jeff, LAD	9	Suppan,Jeff, Mil	11
Gallardo,Yovani, Mil	204	Billingsley,Chad, LAD	86	9 tied with	8	Jimenez,Ubaldo, Col	10
Jimenez,Ubaldo, Col	198	Jimenez,Ubaldo, Col	85			Moyer,Jamie, Phi	10
Nolasco,Ricky, Fla	195	de la Rosa,Jorge, Col	83			Scherzer,Max, Ari	10
de la Rosa,Jorge, Col	193	Zito,Barry, SF	81			6 tied with	9
Rodriguez,Wandy, Hou	193	Marquis,Jason, Col	80				
Johnson,Josh, Fla	191	Zambrano,Carlos, ChC	78				

2009 National League Pitching Leaders

Runs Allowed

Looper,Braden, Mil	123
Hernandez,L., NYM-Was	112
Pelfrey,Mike, NYM	112
Nolasco,Ricky, Fla	111
Lowe,Derek, Atl	109
Parra,Manny, Mil	108
Garland,Jon, Ari-LAD	106
Suppan,Jeff, Mil	106
Marquis,Jason, Col	104
Maholm,Paul, Pit	102

Hits Allowed

Lowe,Derek, Atl	232
Duke,Zach, Pit	231
Looper,Braden, Mil	226
Garland,Jon, Ari-LAD	225
Maholm,Paul, Pit	221
Hernandez,L., NYM-Was	220
Marquis,Jason, Col	218
Pineiro,Joel, StL	218
Wainwright,Adam, StL	216
Arroyo,Bronson, Cin	214

Doubles Allowed

Maholm,Paul, Pit	52
Lannan,John, Was	50
Pineiro,Joel, StL	49
Hernandez,L., NYM-Was	47
Duke,Zach, Pit	46
Lowe,Derek, Atl	46
Gallardo,Yovani, Mil	45
Garland,Jon, Ari-LAD	45
Hamels,Cole, Phi	44
4 tied with	43

Home Runs Allowed

Looper,Braden, Mil	39
Arroyo,Bronson, Cin	31
Blanton,Joe, Phi	30
Volstad,Chris, Fla	29
Geer,Josh, SD	27
Haren,Dan, Ari	27
Moyer,Jamie, Phi	27
Davis,Doug, Ari	25
Ohlendorf,Ross, Pit	25
Suppan,Jeff, Mil	25

Run Support Per Nine IP
(minimum 162 IP)

Looper,Braden, Mil	7.17
de la Rosa,Jorge, Col	6.47
Lowe,Derek, Atl	6.20
Wainwright,Adam, StL	5.95
Moyer,Jamie, Phi	5.78
Wells,Randy, ChC	5.66
Duke,Zach, Pit	5.62
Johnson,Josh, Fla	5.60
Vazquez,Javier, Atl	5.42
Happ,J.A., Phi	5.37

% Pitches In Strike Zone
(minimum 162 IP)

Lilly,Ted, ChC	56.2
Santana,Johan, NYM	53.8
Oswalt,Roy, Hou	52.7
Carpenter,Chris, StL	51.5
Hamels,Cole, Phi	51.4
Happ,J.A., Phi	51.3
Pineiro,Joel, StL	51.2
Wolf,Randy, LAD	50.9
Zito,Barry, SF	50.6
Cain,Matt, SF	50.6

Pitches Per Start
(minimum 30 GS)

Jimenez,Ubaldo, Col	108.2
Lincecum,Tim, SF	107.5
Gallardo,Yovani, Mil	106.7
Wainwright,Adam, StL	106.3
Blanton,Joe, Phi	104.9
Haren,Dan, Ari	104.8
Vazquez,Javier, Atl	103.6
Arroyo,Bronson, Cin	103.2
Scherzer,Max, Ari	102.4
Davis,Doug, Ari	102.1

Pitches Per Batter
(minimum 162 IP)

Pineiro,Joel, StL	3.42
Duke,Zach, Pit	3.45
Marquis,Jason, Col	3.53
Carpenter,Chris, StL	3.56
Lannan,John, Was	3.57
Hammel,Jason, Col	3.59
Maholm,Paul, Pit	3.65
Wells,Randy, ChC	3.66
Santana,Johan, NYM	3.67
Oswalt,Roy, Hou	3.68

Quality Starts

Lincecum,Tim, SF	26
Jurrjens,Jair, Atl	25
Wainwright,Adam, StL	25
Haren,Dan, Ari	24
Jimenez,Ubaldo, Col	24
Wolf,Randy, LAD	24
Arroyo,Bronson, Cin	23
Garland,Jon, Ari-LAD	23
Johnson,Josh, Fla	23
Rodriguez,Wandy, Hou	23

Batters Faced

Wainwright,Adam, StL	970
Arroyo,Bronson, Cin	923
Marquis,Jason, Col	921
Jimenez,Ubaldo, Col	914
Haren,Dan, Ari	909
Lincecum,Tim, SF	905
Duke,Zach, Pit	891
Davis,Doug, Ari	889
Cain,Matt, SF	886
Jurrjens,Jair, Atl	884

Innings Pitched

Wainwright,Adam, StL	233.0
Haren,Dan, Ari	229.1
Lincecum,Tim, SF	225.1
Arroyo,Bronson, Cin	220.1
Vazquez,Javier, Atl	219.1
Jimenez,Ubaldo, Col	218.0
Cain,Matt, SF	217.2
Marquis,Jason, Col	216.0
Jurrjens,Jair, Atl	215.0
Wolf,Randy, LAD	214.1

Most Pitches in a Game

Snell,Ian, Pit	131
Martinez,Pedro, Phi	130
Wainwright,Adam, StL	130
Happ,J.A., Phi	127
Hernandez,L., NYM-Was	127
Jimenez,Ubaldo, Col	127
Lincecum,Tim, SF	127
4 tied with	126

Stolen Bases Allowed

Sanchez,Jonathan, SF	24
Volstad,Chris, Fla	21
Lincecum,Tim, SF	20
Young,Chris, SD	20
Gallardo,Yovani, Mil	19
6 tied with	18

Caught Stealing Off

Dempster,Ryan, ChC	11
Hamels,Cole, Phi	11
Volstad,Chris, Fla	10
Billingsley,Chad, LAD	9
Cain,Matt, SF	9
Zito,Barry, SF	9
5 tied with	8

Stolen Base Pct Allowed
(minimum 162 IP)

Pineiro,Joel, StL	20.0
Cueto,Johnny, Cin	28.6
Carpenter,Chris, StL	33.3
Santana,Johan, NYM	33.3
Zambrano,Carlos, ChC	38.5
Rodriguez,Wandy, Hou	42.9
Billingsley,Chad, LAD	43.8
Kershaw,Clayton, LAD	46.2
Duke,Zach, Pit	46.7
2 tied with	50.0

Pickoffs

Ohlendorf,Ross, Pit	8
Davis,Doug, Ari	7
Kershaw,Clayton, LAD	7
Hamels,Cole, Phi	5
Calero,Kiko, Fla	4
Duke,Zach, Pit	4
Lannan,John, Was	4
Maholm,Paul, Pit	4
Moyer,Jamie, Phi	4
9 tied with	3

2009 National League Pitching Leaders

Strikeouts Per 9 IP
(minimum 162 IP)

Lincecum,Tim, SF	10.42
Gallardo,Yovani, Mil	9.89
Vazquez,Javier, Atl	9.77
Sanchez,Jonathan, SF	9.75
Kershaw,Clayton, LAD	9.74
Nolasco,Ricky, Fla	9.49
de la Rosa,Jorge, Col	9.39
Scherzer,Max, Ari	9.19
Haren,Dan, Ari	8.75
Rodriguez,Wandy, Hou	8.45

Opp On-Base Percentage
(minimum 162 IP)

Haren,Dan, Ari	.260
Vazquez,Javier, Atl	.266
Lincecum,Tim, SF	.271
Lilly,Ted, ChC	.271
Carpenter,Chris, StL	.272
Wolf,Randy, LAD	.285
Johnson,Josh, Fla	.294
Santana,Johan, NYM	.296
Pineiro,Joel, StL	.297
Wainwright,Adam, StL	.297

Opp Slugging Average
(minimum 162 IP)

Kershaw,Clayton, LAD	.282
Lincecum,Tim, SF	.290
Carpenter,Chris, StL	.310
Jimenez,Ubaldo, Col	.326
Johnson,Josh, Fla	.335
Vazquez,Javier, Atl	.346
Wainwright,Adam, StL	.349
Zambrano,Carlos, ChC	.350
Jurrjens,Jair, Atl	.356
Wells,Randy, ChC	.365

Opponent OPS
(minimum 162 IP)

Lincecum,Tim, SF	.561
Carpenter,Chris, StL	.581
Kershaw,Clayton, LAD	.588
Vazquez,Javier, Atl	.612
Johnson,Josh, Fla	.629
Haren,Dan, Ari	.635
Jimenez,Ubaldo, Col	.635
Wainwright,Adam, StL	.646
Jurrjens,Jair, Atl	.660
Wolf,Randy, LAD	.660

Home Runs Per Nine IP
(minimum 162 IP)

Carpenter,Chris, StL	0.33
Kershaw,Clayton, LAD	0.37
Lincecum,Tim, SF	0.40
Pineiro,Joel, StL	0.46
Zambrano,Carlos, ChC	0.53
Jimenez,Ubaldo, Col	0.54
Johnson,Josh, Fla	0.60
Marquis,Jason, Col	0.62
Jurrjens,Jair, Atl	0.63
Maholm,Paul, Pit	0.65

Batting Average vs. LHB
(minimum 125 BF)

Clippard,Tyler, Was	.122
Marmol,Carlos, ChC	.136
Broxton,Jonathan, LAD	.138
Maine,John, NYM	.159
Wolf,Randy, LAD	.159
Kershaw,Clayton, LAD	.173
Maholm,Paul, Pit	.182
Medlen,Kris, Atl	.183
Byrdak,Tim, Hou	.184
Rodriguez,Francisco, NYM	.185

Batting Average vs. RHB
(minimum 225 BF)

Hanson,Tommy, Atl	.192
Lincecum,Tim, SF	.203
Jimenez,Ubaldo, Col	.206
Kershaw,Clayton, LAD	.208
Vazquez,Javier, Atl	.212
Jurrjens,Jair, Atl	.212
Carpenter,Chris, StL	.214
Wainwright,Adam, StL	.217
Haren,Dan, Ari	.219
Sanchez,Jonathan, SF	.220

Opp BA w/ RISP
(minimum 125 BF)

Happ,J.A., Phi	.158
Cain,Matt, SF	.161
Gallardo,Yovani, Mil	.176
Kershaw,Clayton, LAD	.188
Jurrjens,Jair, Atl	.192
Ohlendorf,Ross, Pit	.198
Jimenez,Ubaldo, Col	.200
Wainwright,Adam, StL	.209
Johnson,Josh, Fla	.210
Haren,Dan, Ari	.213

OBP vs. Leadoff Hitter
(minimum 150 BF)

Wolf,Randy, LAD	.253
Rodriguez,Wandy, Hou	.254
Carpenter,Chris, StL	.258
Volstad,Chris, Fla	.261
Vazquez,Javier, Atl	.272
Haren,Dan, Ari	.273
Santana,Johan, NYM	.273
Blanton,Joe, Phi	.274
Scherzer,Max, Ari	.274
Lilly,Ted, ChC	.276

Strikeouts / Walks Ratio
(minimum 162 IP)

Haren,Dan, Ari	5.87
Vazquez,Javier, Atl	5.41
Nolasco,Ricky, Fla	4.43
Lilly,Ted, ChC	4.19
Hamels,Cole, Phi	3.91
Pineiro,Joel, StL	3.89
Lincecum,Tim, SF	3.84
Carpenter,Chris, StL	3.79
Harang,Aaron, Cin	3.30
Johnson,Josh, Fla	3.29

Highest GB/FB Ratio
(minimum 162 IP)

Pineiro,Joel, StL	2.54
Lowe,Derek, Atl	2.18
Marquis,Jason, Col	2.03
Carpenter,Chris, StL	1.96
Jimenez,Ubaldo, Col	1.88
Maholm,Paul, Pit	1.74
Lannan,John, Was	1.72
Pelfrey,Mike, NYM	1.71
Wainwright,Adam, StL	1.68
Johnson,Josh, Fla	1.58

Lowest GB/FB Ratio
(minimum 162 IP)

Lilly,Ted, ChC	0.63
Santana,Johan, NYM	0.75
Harang,Aaron, Cin	0.84
Happ,J.A., Phi	0.90
Cain,Matt, SF	0.92
Zito,Barry, SF	0.94
Wolf,Randy, LAD	0.94
Sanchez,Jonathan, SF	0.95
Kershaw,Clayton, LAD	0.95
Nolasco,Ricky, Fla	0.96

Sacrifice Flies Allowed

Billingsley,Chad, LAD	11
Duke,Zach, Pit	10
Hernandez,L., NYM-Was	10
Marquis,Jason, Col	10
Hammel,Jason, Col	9
Dempster,Ryan, ChC	8
Ohlendorf,Ross, Pit	8
Kawakami,Kenshin, Atl	7
Looper,Braden, Mil	7
17 tied with	6

Sacrifice Hits Allowed

Duke,Zach, Pit	18
Jurrjens,Jair, Atl	16
Davis,Doug, Ari	15
Jimenez,Ubaldo, Col	15
Hernandez,L., NYM-Was	13
7 tied with	12

GIDP Induced

Pineiro,Joel, StL	29
Lannan,John, Was	28
Lowe,Derek, Atl	28
Maholm,Paul, Pit	28
Marquis,Jason, Col	28
Arroyo,Bronson, Cin	25
Garland,Jon, Ari-LAD	25
Hernandez,L., NYM-Was	24
Rodriguez,Wandy, Hou	24
Carpenter,Chris, StL	23

GIDP Per Nine IP
(minimum 162 IP)

Lowe,Derek, Atl	1.29
Maholm,Paul, Pit	1.29
Lannan,John, Was	1.22
Pineiro,Joel, StL	1.22
Hernandez,L., NYM-Was	1.18
Marquis,Jason, Col	1.17
Garland,Jon, Ari-LAD	1.10
Wells,Randy, ChC	1.09
Carpenter,Chris, StL	1.07
Rodriguez,Wandy, Hou	1.05

2009 National League Pitching Leaders

Saves

Bell,Heath, SD	42
Cordero,Francisco, Cin	39
Franklin,Ryan, StL	38
Wilson,Brian, SF	38
Hoffman,Trevor, Mil	37
Broxton,Jonathan, LAD	36
Rodriguez,Francisco, NYM	35
Street,Huston, Col	35
Lidge,Brad, Phi	31
2 tied with	27

Blown Saves

Lidge,Brad, Phi	11
Belisario,Ronald, LAD	7
Gonzalez,Mike, Atl	7
Gregg,Kevin, ChC	7
Nunez,Leo, Fla	7
Rodriguez,Francisco, NYM	7
Wilson,Brian, SF	7
6 tied with	6

Save Pct
(minimum 20 Save Ops)

MacDougal,Mike, Was	95.2
Street,Huston, Col	94.6
Cordero,Francisco, Cin	90.7
Hoffman,Trevor, Mil	90.2
Franklin,Ryan, StL	88.4
Bell,Heath, SD	87.5
Soriano,Rafael, Atl	87.1
Valverde,Jose, Hou	86.2
Broxton,Jonathan, LAD	85.7
Wilson,Brian, SF	84.4

Save Opportunities

Bell,Heath, SD	48
Wilson,Brian, SF	45
Cordero,Francisco, Cin	43
Franklin,Ryan, StL	43
Broxton,Jonathan, LAD	42
Lidge,Brad, Phi	42
Rodriguez,Francisco, NYM	42
Hoffman,Trevor, Mil	41
Street,Huston, Col	37
Nunez,Leo, Fla	33

Easy Saves

Cordero,Francisco, Cin	27
Bell,Heath, SD	26
Hoffman,Trevor, Mil	25
Street,Huston, Col	25
Rodriguez,Francisco, NYM	24
Capps,Matt, Pit	22
Lidge,Brad, Phi	22
Franklin,Ryan, StL	20
Broxton,Jonathan, LAD	19
Wilson,Brian, SF	19

Regular Saves

Broxton,Jonathan, LAD	15
Franklin,Ryan, StL	14
Bell,Heath, SD	13
Wilson,Brian, SF	13
Cordero,Francisco, Cin	12
Hoffman,Trevor, Mil	12
Valverde,Jose, Hou	12
Rodriguez,Francisco, NYM	11
Street,Huston, Col	10
2 tied with	9

Tough Saves

Wilson,Brian, SF	6
Franklin,Ryan, StL	4
MacDougal,Mike, Was	4
Bell,Heath, SD	3
Qualls,Chad, Ari	3
Broxton,Jonathan, LAD	2
Madson,Ryan, Phi	2
Nunez,Leo, Fla	2
16 tied with	1

Holds Adjusted Saves %
(minimum 20 Save Ops)

MacDougal,Mike, Was	95.2
Street,Huston, Col	94.9
Cordero,Francisco, Cin	90.7
Hoffman,Trevor, Mil	90.2
Soriano,Rafael, Atl	89.2
Franklin,Ryan, StL	88.6
Bell,Heath, SD	87.5
Valverde,Jose, Hou	86.7
Broxton,Jonathan, LAD	86.0
Nunez,Leo, Fla	85.1

Relief Wins

Broxton,Jonathan, LAD	7
Badenhop,Burke, Fla	6
Bell,Heath, SD	6
Condrey,Clay, Phi	6
Feliciano,Pedro, NYM	6
Fulchino,Jeff, Hou	6
Moylan,Peter, Atl	6
10 tied with	5

Relief Losses

Capps,Matt, Pit	8
Lidge,Brad, Phi	8
Tavarez,Julian, Was	7
Villanueva,Carlos, Mil	7
10 tied with	6

Relief Games

Feliciano,Pedro, NYM	88
Moylan,Peter, Atl	87
Gonzalez,Mike, Atl	80
Green,Sean, NYM	79
Madson,Ryan, Phi	79
Marmol,Carlos, ChC	79
Coffey,Todd, Mil	78
O'Flaherty,Eric, Atl	78
Soriano,Rafael, Atl	77
Byrdak,Tim, Hou	76

Holds

Affeldt,Jeremy, SF	33
Coffey,Todd, Mil	27
Gregerson,Luke, SD	27
Marmol,Carlos, ChC	27
Madson,Ryan, Phi	26
Moylan,Peter, Atl	25
Rhodes,Arthur, Cin	25
Feliciano,Pedro, NYM	24
Grabow,John, Pit-ChC	23
Weathers,David, Cin-Mil	21

Relief Innings

Coffey,Todd, Mil	83.2
Troncoso,Ramon, LAD	82.2
Fulchino,Jeff, Hou	82.0
Madson,Ryan, Phi	77.1
Mujica,Edward, SD	77.0
Broxton,Jonathan, LAD	76.0
Masset,Nick, Cin	76.0
Soriano,Rafael, Atl	75.2
Gregerson,Luke, SD	75.0
Gonzalez,Mike, Atl	74.1

Inherited Runners Scrd %
(minimum 30 IR)

Bergmann,Jason, Was	14.0
Troncoso,Ramon, LAD	15.6
Burnett,Sean, Pit-Was	15.7
Thatcher,Joe, SD	16.3
McClellan,Kyle, StL	16.7
Miller,Trever, StL	16.7
Wilson,Brian, SF	17.6
O'Flaherty,Eric, Atl	17.8
Feliciano,Pedro, NYM	18.5
Stetter,Mitch, Mil	20.9

Relief Opp On Base Pct
(minimum 50 IP)

Street,Huston, Col	.236
Hoffman,Trevor, Mil	.240
Broxton,Jonathan, LAD	.247
Soriano,Rafael, Atl	.267
Masset,Nick, Cin	.268
Guzman,Angel, ChC	.271
Rhodes,Arthur, Cin	.276
Bell,Heath, SD	.281
Howry,Bob, SF	.283
Clippard,Tyler, Was	.284

Relief Opp Slugging Avg
(minimum 50 IP)

Broxton,Jonathan, LAD	.232
Calero,Kiko, Fla	.235
Hoffman,Trevor, Mil	.241
Marmol,Carlos, ChC	.249
Affeldt,Jeremy, SF	.277
Park,Chan Ho, Phi	.280
Belisario,Ronald, LAD	.286
Bell,Heath, SD	.287
O'Flaherty,Eric, Atl	.295
Franklin,Ryan, StL	.296

2009 National League Pitching Leaders

Relief Opp BA Vs LHB	
(minimum 50 AB)	
Clippard,Tyler, Was	.122
Adams,Mike, SD	.130
Miller,Trever, StL	.135
Marmol,Carlos, ChC	.136
Broxton,Jonathan, LAD	.138
Rhodes,Arthur, Cin	.141
Medlen,Kris, Atl	.161
Street,Huston, Col	.167
Condrey,Clay, Phi	.172
Stetter,Mitch, Mil	.178

Relief Opp BA Vs RHB	
(minimum 50 AB)	
Adams,Mike, SD	.088
Bell,Heath, SD	.138
Soriano,Rafael, Atl	.138
Valverde,Jose, Hou	.144
Happ,J.A., Phi	.145
Hoffman,Trevor, Mil	.149
Betancourt,Rafael, Col	.157
Belisario,Ronald, LAD	.157
Vargas,Claudio, LAD-Mil	.159
Gregerson,Luke, SD	.161

Relief Opp Batting Average	
(minimum 50 IP)	
Broxton,Jonathan, LAD	.165
Marmol,Carlos, ChC	.170
Clippard,Tyler, Was	.172
Byrdak,Tim, Hou	.178
Calero,Kiko, Fla	.180
Burnett,Sean, Pit-Was	.181
Hoffman,Trevor, Mil	.183
Guzman,Angel, ChC	.192
Street,Huston, Col	.194
Soriano,Rafael, Atl	.194

Relief Earned Run Average	
(minimum 50 IP)	
Affeldt,Jeremy, SF	1.73
Hoffman,Trevor, Mil	1.83
Franklin,Ryan, StL	1.92
Calero,Kiko, Fla	1.95
Belisario,Ronald, LAD	2.04
Hawkins,LaTroy, Hou	2.13
Cordero,Francisco, Cin	2.16
Valverde,Jose, Hou	2.33
Masset,Nick, Cin	2.37
Gonzalez,Mike, Atl	2.42

Rel OBP 1st Batter Faced	
(minimum 40 BF)	
Broxton,Jonathan, LAD	.205
Belisario,Ronald, LAD	.217
Hoffman,Trevor, Mil	.218
Gregerson,Luke, SD	.219
Masset,Nick, Cin	.219
Villanueva,Carlos, Mil	.224
Gregg,Kevin, ChC	.225
Medders,Brandon, SF	.230
Burnett,Sean, Pit-Was	.232
Street,Huston, Col	.234

Rel Opp BA w/ Runners On	
(minimum 50 IP)	
Marmol,Carlos, ChC	.131
Gonzalez,Mike, Atl	.142
Calero,Kiko, Fla	.147
Soriano,Rafael, Atl	.153
Burnett,Sean, Pit-Was	.161
Rodriguez,Francisco, NYM	.169
Bell,Heath, SD	.171
Byrdak,Tim, Hou	.172
Valverde,Jose, Hou	.174
Affeldt,Jeremy, SF	.179

Relief Opp BA w/ RISP	
(minimum 50 IP)	
Guzman,Angel, ChC	.102
Burnett,Sean, Pit-Was	.130
Valverde,Jose, Hou	.135
Miller,Justin, SF	.155
Bell,Heath, SD	.161
Feliciano,Pedro, NYM	.167
Franklin,Ryan, StL	.167
Rhodes,Arthur, Cin	.167
Gonzalez,Mike, Atl	.171
Gregg,Kevin, ChC	.173

Fastest Avg Fastball-Relief	
(minimum 50 IP)	
Broxton,Jonathan, LAD	97.7
Wilson,Brian, SF	96.6
MacDougal,Mike, Was	95.9
Motte,Jason, StL	95.9
Valverde,Jose, Hou	95.8
Parnell,Bobby, NYM	95.3
Madson,Ryan, Phi	95.0
Cordero,Francisco, Cin	95.0
Belisario,Ronald, LAD	94.9
Gutierrez,Juan, Ari	94.8

Fastest Average Fastball	
(minimum 162 IP)	
Jimenez,Ubaldo, Col	96.1
Johnson,Josh, Fla	95.0
Kershaw,Clayton, LAD	93.9
Scherzer,Max, Ari	93.6
de la Rosa,Jorge, Col	93.3
Oswalt,Roy, Hou	93.1
Carpenter,Chris, StL	93.0
Cueto,Johnny, Cin	92.7
Cain,Matt, SF	92.6
Pelfrey,Mike, NYM	92.6

Slowest Average Fastball	
(minimum 162 IP)	
Moyer,Jamie, Phi	81.4
Hernandez,L., NYM-Was	84.7
Davis,Doug, Ari	85.1
Zito,Barry, SF	86.5
Lilly,Ted, ChC	87.1
Lannan,John, Was	88.2
Arroyo,Bronson, Cin	88.5
Lowe,Derek, Atl	88.6
Duke,Zach, Pit	88.8
Wolf,Randy, LAD	89.0

Pitches 100+ Velocity	
Broxton,Jonathan, LAD	90
Jimenez,Ubaldo, Col	26
Wilson,Brian, SF	22
Parnell,Bobby, NYM	5
Lindstrom,Matt, Fla	3
Paulino,Felipe, Hou	2
Joaquin,Waldis, SF	1
Motte,Jason, StL	1
Valdez,Merkin, SF	1
Valverde,Jose, Hou	1

Pitches 95+ Velocity	
Jimenez,Ubaldo, Col	1705
Johnson,Josh, Fla	1519
Penny,Brad, SF	829
Broxton,Jonathan, LAD	813
Wilson,Brian, SF	790
Paulino,Felipe, Hou	751
Kershaw,Clayton, LAD	678
MacDougal,Mike, Was	678
Bailey,Homer, Cin	662
Scherzer,Max, Ari	657

Pitches Less Than 80 MPH	
Arroyo,Bronson, Cin	1327
Hernandez,L., NYM-Was	1322
Zito,Barry, SF	1294
Rodriguez,Wandy, Hou	1100
Moyer,Jamie, Phi	1042
Davis,Doug, Ari	941
Wolf,Randy, LAD	910
Wainwright,Adam, StL	872
Vazquez,Javier, Atl	741
Garland,Jon, Ari-LAD	688

Lowest % Fastballs	
(minimum 162 IP)	
Davis,Doug, Ari	25.1
Arroyo,Bronson, Cin	42.3
Haren,Dan, Ari	45.4
Carpenter,Chris, StL	46.0
Billingsley,Chad, LAD	47.4
Vazquez,Javier, Atl	47.8
Zito,Barry, SF	48.4
Looper,Braden, Mil	48.5
Wainwright,Adam, StL	49.4
Correia,Kevin, SD	49.7

Highest % Fastballs	
(minimum 162 IP)	
Pelfrey,Mike, NYM	77.4
Scherzer,Max, Ari	70.5
Pineiro,Joel, StL	70.2
Kershaw,Clayton, LAD	69.2
Happ,J.A., Phi	69.0
Johnson,Josh, Fla	67.0
Lowe,Derek, Atl	66.8
Harang,Aaron, Cin	66.8
Lannan,John, Was	65.9
Sanchez,Jonathan, SF	65.1

Highest % Curveballs	
(minimum 162 IP)	
Rodriguez,Wandy, Hou	36.1
Carpenter,Chris, StL	23.9
Wainwright,Adam, StL	23.8
Gallardo,Yovani, Mil	22.1
Billingsley,Chad, LAD	22.1
Duke,Zach, Pit	18.4
Zito,Barry, SF	17.9
Haren,Dan, Ari	17.9
Oswalt,Roy, Hou	17.5
Lincecum,Tim, SF	17.2

2009 National League Pitching Leaders

Highest % Changeups
(minimum 162 IP)

Santana,Johan, NYM	30.8
Hamels,Cole, Phi	29.9
Jurrjens,Jair, Atl	23.7
Lincecum,Tim, SF	21.2
Moyer,Jamie, Phi	18.4
Blanton,Joe, Phi	17.4
de la Rosa,Jorge, Col	16.9
Wells,Randy, ChC	16.9
Duke,Zach, Pit	16.9
Scherzer,Max, Ari	16.5

Highest % Sliders
(minimum 162 IP)

Dempster,Ryan, ChC	33.8
Cueto,Johnny, Cin	29.3
Correia,Kevin, SD	29.0
Carpenter,Chris, StL	27.2
Wells,Randy, ChC	27.0
Lowe,Derek, Atl	26.3
Lilly,Ted, ChC	25.6
Johnson,Josh, Fla	24.5
Nolasco,Ricky, Fla	24.3
Ohlendorf,Ross, Pit	24.2

Balks

Pelfrey,Mike, NYM	6
Jimenez,Ubaldo, Col	3
Lilly,Ted, ChC	3
Colome,Jesus, Was-Mil	2
Jurrjens,Jair, Atl	2
Kershaw,Clayton, LAD	2
Latos,Mat, SD	2
Lowe,Derek, Atl	2
Zito,Barry, SF	2
44 tied with	1

Strikeout/Hit Ratio
(minimum 50 IP)

Broxton,Jonathan, LAD	2.59
Marmol,Carlos, ChC	2.16
Calero,Kiko, Fla	1.92
Soriano,Rafael, Atl	1.92
Clippard,Tyler, Was	1.86
Street,Huston, Col	1.83
Gonzalez,Mike, Atl	1.61
Kershaw,Clayton, LAD	1.55
Lincecum,Tim, SF	1.55
Gregerson,Luke, SD	1.50

Opp OPS vs Fastballs
(minimum 251 BF)

Kershaw,Clayton, LAD	.556
Wolf,Randy, LAD	.600
Johnson,Josh, Fla	.602
Lilly,Ted, ChC	.610
Lincecum,Tim, SF	.617
Carpenter,Chris, StL	.627
Cain,Matt, SF	.631
Santana,Johan, NYM	.643
Zambrano,Carlos, ChC	.657
Pineiro,Joel, StL	.658

Opp OPS vs Curveballs
(minimum 100 BF)

Lincecum,Tim, SF	.448
Vazquez,Javier, Atl	.464
Arroyo,Bronson, Cin	.482
Zito,Barry, SF	.482
Wainwright,Adam, StL	.501
Wolf,Randy, LAD	.511
Carpenter,Chris, StL	.522
Duke,Zach, Pit	.549
Kawakami,Kenshin, Atl	.561
Rodriguez,Wandy, Hou	.590

Opp OPS vs Changeups
(minimum 100 BF)

Jimenez,Ubaldo, Col	.452
Lincecum,Tim, SF	.483
Vazquez,Javier, Atl	.488
de la Rosa,Jorge, Col	.550
Lannan,John, Was	.567
Blanton,Joe, Phi	.615
Duke,Zach, Pit	.618
Grabow,John, Pit-ChC	.621
Harden,Rich, ChC	.629
2 tied with	.671

Opp OPS vs Sliders
(minimum 64 BF)

Miller,Trever, StL	.386
Wainwright,Adam, StL	.406
Byrdak,Tim, Hou	.412
Street,Huston, Col	.412
Young,Chris, SD	.426
Gutierrez,Juan, Ari	.466
Gregerson,Luke, SD	.467
Broxton,Jonathan, LAD	.480
Jimenez,Ubaldo, Col	.515
2 tied with	.517

Earned Runs

Looper,Braden, Mil	113
Hernandez,L., NYM-Was	111
Nolasco,Ricky, Fla	104
Pelfrey,Mike, NYM	103
Lowe,Derek, Atl	101
Parra,Manny, Mil	99
Marquis,Jason, Col	97
Duke,Zach, Pit	96
Maholm,Paul, Pit	96
Suppan,Jeff, Mil	95

Hits Per Nine Innings
(minimum 162 IP)

Kershaw,Clayton, LAD	6.26
Lincecum,Tim, SF	6.71
Gallardo,Yovani, Mil	7.27
Carpenter,Chris, StL	7.29
Vazquez,Javier, Atl	7.43
Sanchez,Jonathan, SF	7.44
Wolf,Randy, LAD	7.47
Haren,Dan, Ari	7.53
Jimenez,Ubaldo, Col	7.56
Cain,Matt, SF	7.61

2009 American League Fielding Leaders

2B Pivot %	
(minimum 98 G)	
Pedroia,Dustin, Bos	0.789
Roberts,Brian, Bal	0.739
Kinsler,Ian, Tex	0.727
Lopez,Jose, Sea	0.688
Polanco,Placido, Det	0.667
Getz,Chris, CWS	0.652
Hill,Aaron, Tor	0.612
Ellis,Mark, Oak	0.604
Callaspo,Alberto, KC	0.596
Cano,Robinson, NYY	0.563

SS Pivot %	
(minimum 98 G)	
Betancourt,Y., Sea-KC	0.735
Andrus,Elvis, Tex	0.671
Cabrera,Asdrubal, Cle	0.646
Aybar,Erick, LAA	0.629
Scutaro,Marco, Tor	0.593
Ramirez,Alexei, CWS	0.578
Izturis,Cesar, Bal	0.576
Cabrera,Orlando, Oak-Min	0.557
Everett,Adam, Det	0.548
Jeter,Derek, NYY	0.541

Highest Pct CS by Catchers	
(minimum 600 INN or 50 SBA)	
Laird,Gerald, Det	40.4
Barajas,Rod, Tor	29.3
Johnson,Rob, Sea	29.3
Mathis,Jeff, LAA	24.6
Olivo,Miguel, KC	24.3
Mauer,Joe, Min	23.9
Navarro,Dioner, TB	23.8
Posada,Jorge, NYY	22.3
Saltalamacchia,J, Tex	21.8
Wieters,Matt, Bal	21.7

Lowest Pct CS by Catchers	
(minimum 600 INN or 50 SBA)	
Varitek,Jason, Bos	8.5
Martinez,Victor, Cle-Bos	12.5
Napoli,Mike, LAA	14.9
Pierzynski,A.J., CWS	16.8
Suzuki,Kurt, Oak	17.3
Zaun,Gregg, Bal-TB	18.9
Shoppach,Kelly, Cle	21.0
Wieters,Matt, Bal	21.7
Saltalamacchia,J, Tex	21.8
Posada,Jorge, NYY	22.3

2B Double Play %	
(minimum 98 G)	
Kinsler,Ian, Tex	0.605
Lopez,Jose, Sea	0.593
Polanco,Placido, Det	0.592
Roberts,Brian, Bal	0.572
Pedroia,Dustin, Bos	0.568
Hill,Aaron, Tor	0.557
Callaspo,Alberto, KC	0.555
Ellis,Mark, Oak	0.532
Cano,Robinson, NYY	0.518
Getz,Chris, CWS	0.489

3B Double Play %	
(minimum 98 G)	
Longoria,Evan, TB	0.636
Figgins,Chone, LAA	0.547
Young,Michael, Tex	0.545
Inge,Brandon, Det	0.507
Beckham,Gordon, CWS	0.447
Lowell,Mike, Bos	0.429
Beltre,Adrian, Sea	0.370
Peralta,Jhonny, Cle	0.349
Mora,Melvin, Bal	0.339
Rodriguez,Alex, NYY	0.333

SS Double Play %	
(minimum 98 G)	
Aybar,Erick, LAA	0.653
Andrus,Elvis, Tex	0.647
Cabrera,Asdrubal, Cle	0.634
Betancourt,Y., Sea-KC	0.622
Scutaro,Marco, Tor	0.591
Ramirez,Alexei, CWS	0.589
Everett,Adam, Det	0.569
Izturis,Cesar, Bal	0.560
Cabrera,Orlando, Oak-Min	0.527
Jeter,Derek, NYY	0.519

Errors	
Cabrera,Orlando, Oak-Min	25
Andrus,Elvis, Tex	22
Bartlett,Jason, TB	20
Inge,Brandon, Det	20
Kennedy,Adam, Oak	20
Ramirez,Alexei, CWS	20
Peralta,Jhonny, Cle	19
Betancourt,Y., Sea-KC	18
Callaspo,Alberto, KC	17
2 tied with	16

Fielding Errors	
Cabrera,Orlando, Oak-Min	15
Ramirez,Alexei, CWS	13
Callaspo,Alberto, KC	12
Lopez,Jose, Sea	12
Betancourt,Y., Sea-KC	10
Beckham,Gordon, CWS	9
Everett,Adam, Det	9
Kennedy,Adam, Oak	9
Kinsler,Ian, Tex	9
Peralta,Jhonny, Cle	9

Throwing Errors	
Andrus,Elvis, Tex	14
Bartlett,Jason, TB	13
Inge,Brandon, Det	13
Kennedy,Adam, Oak	11
Cabrera,Orlando, Oak-Min	10
Peralta,Jhonny, Cle	10
Green,Nick, Bos	9
Longoria,Evan, TB	9
4 tied with	8

Range Factor for 2B	
(minimum 98 games)	
Hill,Aaron, Tor	5.19
Polanco,Placido, Det	5.09
Kinsler,Ian, Tex	5.01
Getz,Chris, CWS	4.96
Ellis,Mark, Oak	4.78
Cano,Robinson, NYY	4.71
Roberts,Brian, Bal	4.57
Callaspo,Alberto, KC	4.44
Pedroia,Dustin, Bos	4.39
Lopez,Jose, Sea	4.27

Range Factor for 3B	
(minimum 98 games)	
Mora,Melvin, Bal	3.14
Beltre,Adrian, Sea	2.98
Peralta,Jhonny, Cle	2.88
Longoria,Evan, TB	2.86
Figgins,Chone, LAA	2.84
Beckham,Gordon, CWS	2.83
Inge,Brandon, Det	2.75
Lowell,Mike, Bos	2.57
Rodriguez,Alex, NYY	2.46
Teahen,Mark, KC	2.45

Range Factor for SS	
(minimum 98 games)	
Izturis,Cesar, Bal	4.89
Andrus,Elvis, Tex	4.86
Aybar,Erick, LAA	4.68
Cabrera,Asdrubal, Cle	4.46
Cabrera,Orlando, Oak-Min	4.45
Scutaro,Marco, Tor	4.39
Ramirez,Alexei, CWS	4.38
Betancourt,Y., Sea-KC	4.29
Everett,Adam, Det	4.23
Bartlett,Jason, TB	3.97

2009 National League Fielding Leaders

2B Pivot %
(minimum 98 G)

Schumaker,Skip, StL	0.722
Eckstein,David, SD	0.718
Matsui,Kaz, Hou	0.714
Utley,Chase, Phi	0.709
Lopez,Felipe, Ari-Mil	0.690
Barmes,Clint, Col	0.676
Sanchez,Freddy, Pit-SF	0.676
Uggla,Dan, Fla	0.659
Phillips,Brandon, Cin	0.644
Hudson,Orlando, LAD	0.635

SS Pivot %
(minimum 98 G)

Tulowitzki,Troy, Col	0.696
Guzman,Cristian, Was	0.660
Furcal,Rafael, LAD	0.651
Ryan,Brendan, StL	0.636
Drew,Stephen, Ari	0.619
Tejada,Miguel, Hou	0.596
Escobar,Yunel, Atl	0.575
Rollins,Jimmy, Phi	0.574
Ramirez,Hanley, Fla	0.566
Cabrera,Everth, SD	0.551

Highest Pct CS by Catchers
(minimum 600 INN or 50 SBA)

Hanigan,Ryan, Cin	40.4
Hill,Koyie, ChC	40.0
Molina,Yadier, StL	33.3
Rodriguez,Ivan, Hou	29.2
Soto,Geovany, ChC	28.0
Paulino,Ronny, Fla	27.5
Martin,Russell, LAD	25.3
Iannetta,Chris, Col	23.1
McCann,Brian, Atl	21.6
Molina,Bengie, SF	21.3

Lowest Pct CS by Catchers
(minimum 600 INN or 50 SBA)

Torrealba,Yorvit, Col	7.5
Bard,Josh, Was	14.0
Hundley,Nick, SD	15.2
Kendall,Jason, Mil	16.9
Baker,John, Fla	18.6
Ruiz,Carlos, Phi	19.7
Doumit,Ryan, Pit	20.0
Santos,Omir, NYM	20.5
Montero,Miguel, Ari	21.2
Molina,Bengie, SF	21.3

2B Double Play %
(minimum 98 G)

Schumaker,Skip, StL	0.571
Utley,Chase, Phi	0.537
Uggla,Dan, Fla	0.536
Phillips,Brandon, Cin	0.534
Barmes,Clint, Col	0.523
Matsui,Kaz, Hou	0.519
Lopez,Felipe, Ari-Mil	0.516
Sanchez,Freddy, Pit-SF	0.511
Eckstein,David, SD	0.476
Hudson,Orlando, LAD	0.463

3B Double Play %
(minimum 98 G)

Feliz,Pedro, Phi	0.457
LaRoche,Andy, Pit	0.448
Jones,Chipper, Atl	0.111
Blake,Casey, LAD	0.406
Blum,Geoff, Hou	0.406
Zimmerman,Ryan, Was	0.397
Reynolds,Mark, Ari	0.388
Kouzmanoff,Kevin, SD	0.368
Sandoval,Pablo, SF	0.278
Wright,David, NYM	0.262

SS Double Play %
(minimum 98 G)

Tulowitzki,Troy, Col	0.623
Guzman,Cristian, Was	0.621
Ryan,Brendan, StL	0.605
Furcal,Rafael, LAD	0.605
Cabrera,Everth, SD	0.598
Drew,Stephen, Ari	0.594
Escobar,Yunel, Atl	0.592
Tejada,Miguel, Hou	0.592
Rollins,Jimmy, Phi	0.579
Ramirez,Hanley, Fla	0.576

Errors

Reynolds,Mark, Ari	24
Cabrera,Everth, SD	23
Jones,Chipper, Atl	22
Tejada,Miguel, Hou	21
Furcal,Rafael, LAD	20
Guzman,Cristian, Was	20
Wright,David, NYM	18
Bonifacio,Emilio, Fla	17
Lopez,Felipe, Ari-Mil	17
Zimmerman,Ryan, Was	17

Fielding Errors

Guzman,Cristian, Was	15
Jones,Chipper, Atl	15
Reynolds,Mark, Ari	15
Cabrera,Everth, SD	14
Dunn,Adam, Was	14
Tejada,Miguel, Hou	14
Feliz,Pedro, Phi	11
Lopez,Felipe, Ari-Mil	11
McGehee,Casey, Mil	11
Pujols,Albert, StL	11

Throwing Errors

Zimmerman,Ryan, Was	13
Bonifacio,Emilio, Fla	10
Furcal,Rafael, LAD	10
Uggla,Dan, Fla	10
Cabrera,Everth, SD	9
Reynolds,Mark, Ari	9
Wright,David, NYM	9
Kendall,Jason, Mil	8
Montero,Miguel, Ari	8
Sandoval,Pablo, SF	8

Range Factor for 2B
(minimum 98 games)

Matsui,Kaz, Hou	5.33
Barmes,Clint, Col	5.13
Utley,Chase, Phi	5.05
Sanchez,Freddy, Pit-SF	4.90
Schumaker,Skip, StL	4.87
Hudson,Orlando, LAD	4.84
Phillips,Brandon, Cin	4.84
Castillo,Luis, NYM	4.79
Lopez,Felipe, Ari-Mil	4.74
Eckstein,David, SD	4.56

Range Factor for 3B
(minimum 98 games)

LaRoche,Andy, Pit	3.02
Zimmerman,Ryan, Was	2.97
Feliz,Pedro, Phi	2.83
Blake,Casey, LAD	2.81
Reynolds,Mark, Ari	2.62
Wright,David, NYM	2.51
Stewart,Ian, Col	2.37
Kouzmanoff,Kevin, SD	2.34
Jones,Chipper, Atl	2.32
Sandoval,Pablo, SF	2.32

Range Factor for SS
(minimum 98 games)

Ryan,Brendan, StL	5.41
Guzman,Cristian, Was	4.59
Tejada,Miguel, Hou	4.52
Tulowitzki,Troy, Col	4.51
Escobar,Yunel, Atl	4.47
Cabrera,Everth, SD	4.46
Hardy,J.J., Mil	4.40
Furcal,Rafael, LAD	4.25
Theriot,Ryan, ChC	4.24
Drew,Stephen, Ari	4.22

2009 Active Career Batting Leaders

Batting Average (minimum 1000 PA)		On Base Percentage (minimum 1000 PA)		Slugging Average (minimum 1000 PA)		Home Runs	
Pujols,Albert	.334	Helton,Todd	.427	Pujols,Albert	.628	Griffey Jr.,Ken	630
Suzuki,Ichiro	.333	Pujols,Albert	.427	Ramirez,Manny	.591	Rodriguez,Alex	583
Helton,Todd	.328	Berkman,Lance	.412	Howard,Ryan	.586	Thome,Jim	564
Mauer,Joe	.327	Ramirez,Manny	.411	Rodriguez,Alex	.576	Ramirez,Manny	546
Guerrero,Vladimir	.321	Mauer,Joe	.408	Braun,Ryan	.574	Sheffield,Gary	509
Holliday,Matt	.318	Jones,Chipper	.406	Guerrero,Vladimir	.568	Delgado,Carlos	473
Jeter,Derek	.317	Giambi,Jason	.405	Helton,Todd	.567	Jones,Chipper	426
Ramirez,Hanley	.316	Thome,Jim	.404	Thome,Jim	.557	Giambi,Jason	409
Ramirez,Manny	.313	Abreu,Bobby	.404	Berkman,Lance	.555	Guerrero,Vladimir	407
Garciaparra,Nomar	.313	Johnson,Nick	.402	Fielder,Prince	.550	Jones,Andruw	388

Games		At Bats		Hits		Total Bases	
Vizquel,Omar	2742	Vizquel,Omar	9922	Griffey Jr.,Ken	2763	Griffey Jr.,Ken	5251
Griffey Jr.,Ken	2638	Griffey Jr.,Ken	9703	Jeter,Derek	2747	Rodriguez,Alex	4779
Sheffield,Gary	2576	Sheffield,Gary	9217	Rodriguez,Ivan	2711	Sheffield,Gary	4737
Rodriguez,Ivan	2388	Rodriguez,Ivan	9070	Vizquel,Omar	2704	Ramirez,Manny	4703
Thome,Jim	2284	Jeter,Derek	8659	Sheffield,Gary	2689	Thome,Jim	4290
Ramirez,Manny	2207	Anderson,Garret	8485	Rodriguez,Alex	2531	Rodriguez,Ivan	4273
Jones,Chipper	2166	Damon,Johnny	8408	Anderson,Garret	2501	Jones,Chipper	4230
Rodriguez,Alex	2166	Rodriguez,Alex	8304	Ramirez,Manny	2494	Guerrero,Vladimir	3978
Anderson,Garret	2148	Ramirez,Manny	7962	Damon,Johnny	2425	Delgado,Carlos	3976
Jeter,Derek	2138	Jones,Chipper	7825	Jones,Chipper	2406	Jeter,Derek	3973

Doubles		Triples		Runs Scored		RBI	
Rodriguez,Ivan	547	Damon,Johnny	95	Rodriguez,Alex	1683	Griffey Jr.,Ken	1829
Ramirez,Manny	531	Rollins,Jimmy	95	Griffey Jr.,Ken	1656	Ramirez,Manny	1788
Griffey Jr.,Ken	522	Crawford,Carl	92	Sheffield,Gary	1636	Rodriguez,Alex	1706
Anderson,Garret	516	Guzman,Cristian	85	Jeter,Derek	1574	Sheffield,Gary	1676
Helton,Todd	509	Pierre,Juan	79	Ramirez,Manny	1506	Thome,Jim	1565
Abreu,Bobby	483	Vizquel,Omar	74	Thome,Jim	1486	Delgado,Carlos	1512
Delgado,Carlos	483	Reyes,Jose	73	Damon,Johnny	1483	Jones,Chipper	1445
Jones,Chipper	472	Suzuki,Ichiro	68	Jones,Chipper	1458	Anderson,Garret	1353
Sheffield,Gary	467	Beltran,Carlos	64	Vizquel,Omar	1378	Giambi,Jason	1330
Damon,Johnny	451	Cameron,Mike	59	Rodriguez,Ivan	1308	Guerrero,Vladimir	1318

Walks		Intentional Walks		Hit By Pitch		Strikeouts	
Thome,Jim	1619	Griffey Jr.,Ken	246	Kendall,Jason	248	Thome,Jim	2313
Sheffield,Gary	1475	Guerrero,Vladimir	242	Delgado,Carlos	172	Cameron,Mike	1798
Jones,Chipper	1343	Ramirez,Manny	212	Giambi,Jason	164	Griffey Jr.,Ken	1762
Griffey Jr.,Ken	1303	Pujols,Albert	198	Rodriguez,Alex	149	Ramirez,Manny	1748
Ramirez,Manny	1283	Delgado,Carlos	186	Jeter,Derek	143	Delgado,Carlos	1745
Giambi,Jason	1262	Helton,Todd	175	Sheffield,Gary	135	Rodriguez,Alex	1738
Abreu,Bobby	1254	Thome,Jim	162	Eckstein,David	134	Jones,Andruw	1542
Giles,Brian	1183	Jones,Chipper	155	Guillen,Jose	131	Abreu,Bobby	1518
Helton,Todd	1130	Suzuki,Ichiro	142	Rolen,Scott	112	Jeter,Derek	1466
Delgado,Carlos	1109	2 tied with	130	Mora,Melvin	110	Dunn,Adam	1433

2009 Active Career Batting Leaders

Sacrifice Hits		Sacrifice Flies		Stolen Bases		Seasons Played	
Vizquel,Omar	244	Sheffield,Gary	111	Pierre,Juan	459	Moyer,Jamie	23
Smoltz,John	136	Griffey Jr.,Ken	101	Vizquel,Omar	389	Johnson,Randy	22
Castillo,Luis	112	Delgado,Carlos	93	Damon,Johnny	374	Sheffield,Gary	22
Pierre,Juan	110	Ramirez,Manny	87	Castillo,Luis	362	Gordon,Tom	21
Hernandez,Livan	99	Vizquel,Omar	86	Crawford,Carl	362	Griffey Jr.,Ken	21
Eckstein,David	94	Anderson,Garret	85	Abreu,Bobby	348	Smoltz,John	21
Vazquez,Javier	94	Jones,Chipper	85	Suzuki,Ichiro	341	Vizquel,Omar	21
Renteria,Edgar	91	Giambi,Jason	82	Rollins,Jimmy	326	Rodriguez,Ivan	19
Schmidt,Jason	90	Lee,Carlos	82	Jeter,Derek	305	Thome,Jim	19
Wilson,Jack	90	Rodriguez,Alex	82	Reyes,Jose	301	Weathers,David	19

At Bats Per Home Run		Grounded Into DP		Highest SB Success Pct		Lowest SB Success Pct	
(minimum 1000 AB)				(minimum 100 SBA)		(minimum 100 SBA)	
Howard,Ryan	12.1	Rodriguez,Ivan	306	Beltran,Carlos	88.3	Guillen,Carlos	62.1
Thome,Jim	13.7	Tejada,Miguel	245	Kinsler,Ian	87.6	Kotsay,Mark	62.3
Dunn,Adam	14.0	Ramirez,Manny	237	Matsui,Kaz	85.6	Anderson,Garret	62.7
Pujols,Albert	14.1	Guerrero,Vladimir	235	Ellsbury,Jacoby	84.9	Mora,Melvin	63.2
Rodriguez,Alex	14.2	Sheffield,Gary	235	Byrnes,Eric	84.8	Guzman,Cristian	64.7
Ramirez,Manny	14.6	Renteria,Edgar	226	Bourn,Michael	82.9	Ordonez,Magglio	65.0
Branyan,Russell	14.8	Konerko,Paul	224	Rollins,Jimmy	82.5	Ausmus,Brad	65.8
Fielder,Prince	14.9	Jones,Chipper	218	Taveras,Willy	82.2	Berkman,Lance	66.4
Thames,Marcus	15.3	Ordonez,Magglio	218	Crawford,Carl	81.9	Bradley,Milton	66.7
Delgado,Carlos	15.4	Jeter,Derek	213	Bloomquist,Willie	81.4	Guerrero,Vladimir	66.8

Strikeouts / Walks Ratio		At Bats Per GIDP		OPS		Secondary Average	
(minimum 1000 AB)		(minimum 1000 AB)		(minimum 1000 PA)		(minimum 1000 PA)	
Pujols,Albert	.703	Iwamura,Akinori	269.8	Pujols,Albert	1.055	Thome,Jim	.492
Giles,Brian	.706	Bourn,Michael	240.0	Ramirez,Manny	1.002	Dunn,Adam	.490
Helton,Todd	.781	Matsui,Kaz	159.4	Helton,Todd	.994	Pujols,Albert	.463
Sheffield,Gary	.794	Granderson,Curtis	143.3	Berkman,Lance	.987	Howard,Ryan	.461
Mauer,Joe	.804	Suzuki,Ichiro	141.8	Rodriguez,Alex	.965	Berkman,Lance	.457
Pedroia,Dustin	.820	Taveras,Willy	139.8	Howard,Ryan	.961	Ramirez,Manny	.443
Keppinger,Jeff	.891	Gomez,Carlos	127.1	Thome,Jim	.961	Giambi,Jason	.438
Jones,Chipper	.917	Drew,Stephen	126.4	Guerrero,Vladimir	.954	Cust,Jack	.435
Kendall,Jason	.937	Patterson,Corey	105.9	Jones,Chipper	.947	Rodriguez,Alex	.434
Ruiz,Carlos	.971	Branyan,Russell	105.7	Braun,Ryan	.937	Jones,Chipper	.423

Highest Strikeout per PA		Lowest Strikeout per PA		Plate Appearances		At Bats Per RBI	
(minimum 1000 PA)		(minimum 1000 PA)				(minimum 1000 AB)	
Branyan,Russell	.335	Pierre,Juan	.056	Vizquel,Omar	11277	Howard,Ryan	4.2
Reynolds,Mark	.329	Keppinger,Jeff	.063	Griffey Jr.,Ken	11196	Ramirez,Manny	4.5
Shoppach,Kelly	.325	Polanco,Placido	.065	Sheffield,Gary	10947	Pujols,Albert	4.6
Cust,Jack	.321	Pedroia,Dustin	.069	Jeter,Derek	9809	Delgado,Carlos	4.8
Smoltz,John	.313	Eckstein,David	.073	Rodriguez,Ivan	9712	Ortiz,David	4.8
Gomes,Jonny	.279	Kendall,Jason	.078	Rodriguez,Alex	9611	Rodriguez,Alex	4.9
Howard,Ryan	.279	Callaspo,Alberto	.079	Thome,Jim	9463	Thome,Jim	4.9
Dunn,Adam	.265	Molina,Yadier	.082	Ramirez,Manny	9437	Giambi,Jason	5.0
Pena,Carlos	.262	3 tied with	.086	Damon,Johnny	9433	Teixeira,Mark	5.0
Ross,David	.261			Jones,Chipper	9273	Berkman,Lance	5.1

2009 Active Career Pitching Leaders

Earned Run Average
(minimum 750 IP)

Rivera,Mariano	2.25
Wagner,Billy	2.39
Hoffman,Trevor	2.73
Martinez,Pedro	2.93
Santana,Johan	3.12
Oswalt,Roy	3.23
Peavy,Jake	3.26
Webb,Brandon	3.27
Johnson,Randy	3.29
Smoltz,John	3.33

Winning Percentage
(minimum 100 Decisions)

Martinez,Pedro	.687
Santana,Johan	.670
Oswalt,Roy	.662
Halladay,Roy	.661
Hudson,Tim	.655
Johnson,Randy	.646
Lee,Cliff	.634
Pettitte,Andy	.629
Sabathia,CC	.627
Carpenter,Chris	.613

Opponent Batting Average
(minimum 750 IP)

Wagner,Billy	.189
Hoffman,Trevor	.208
Rivera,Mariano	.211
Martinez,Pedro	.214
Wood,Kerry	.216
Dotel,Octavio	.218
Harden,Rich	.220
Johnson,Randy	.221
Santana,Johan	.225
Zambrano,Carlos	.230

Baserunners Per 9 IP
(minimum 750 IP)

Wagner,Billy	9.40
Rivera,Mariano	9.43
Hoffman,Trevor	9.45
Martinez,Pedro	9.94
Santana,Johan	10.20
Smoltz,John	10.73
Haren,Dan	10.87
Peavy,Jake	10.93
Johnson,Randy	10.95
Sheets,Ben	11.00

Games

Hoffman,Trevor	985
Weathers,David	964
Rivera,Mariano	917
Guardado,Eddie	908
Gordon,Tom	890
Embree,Alan	882
Tavarez,Julian	828
Wagner,Billy	782
Rhodes,Arthur	780
Hawkins,LaTroy	753

Games Started

Moyer,Jamie	609
Johnson,Randy	603
Smoltz,John	481
Pettitte,Andy	458
Wakefield,Tim	421
Hernandez,Livan	412
Martinez,Pedro	409
Suppan,Jeff	396
Vazquez,Javier	385
Millwood,Kevin	375

Complete Games

Johnson,Randy	100
Smoltz,John	53
Halladay,Roy	49
Hernandez,Livan	47
Martinez,Pedro	46
Wakefield,Tim	32
Colon,Bartolo	31
Moyer,Jamie	31
Ponson,Sidney	29
2 tied with	28

Shutouts

Johnson,Randy	37
Martinez,Pedro	17
Smoltz,John	16
Halladay,Roy	15
Carpenter,Chris	13
Hudson,Tim	11
Sabathia,CC	11
4 tied with	9

Wins

Johnson,Randy	303
Moyer,Jamie	258
Pettitte,Andy	229
Martinez,Pedro	219
Smoltz,John	213
Wakefield,Tim	189
Hernandez,Livan	156
Millwood,Kevin	155
Colon,Bartolo	153
3 tied with	148

Losses

Moyer,Jamie	195
Johnson,Randy	166
Wakefield,Tim	162
Smoltz,John	155
Hernandez,Livan	151
Vazquez,Javier	139
Pettitte,Andy	135
Suppan,Jeff	135
Gordon,Tom	126
Millwood,Kevin	121

Innings Pitched

Johnson,Randy	4135.1
Moyer,Jamie	3908.2
Smoltz,John	3473.0
Wakefield,Tim	2931.2
Pettitte,Andy	2926.1
Martinez,Pedro	2827.1
Hernandez,Livan	2734.2
Vazquez,Javier	2490.0
Suppan,Jeff	2410.2
Millwood,Kevin	2314.1

Batters Faced

Johnson,Randy	17067
Moyer,Jamie	16642
Smoltz,John	14271
Wakefield,Tim	12652
Pettitte,Andy	12451
Hernandez,Livan	11877
Martinez,Pedro	11394
Suppan,Jeff	10550
Vazquez,Javier	10454
Millwood,Kevin	9863

Strikeouts

Johnson,Randy	4875
Martinez,Pedro	3154
Smoltz,John	3084
Moyer,Jamie	2342
Vazquez,Javier	2253
Pettitte,Andy	2150
Wakefield,Tim	1979
Gordon,Tom	1928
Millwood,Kevin	1808
Schmidt,Jason	1758

Walks Allowed

Johnson,Randy	1497
Wakefield,Tim	1122
Moyer,Jamie	1117
Smoltz,John	1010
Gordon,Tom	977
Hernandez,Livan	940
Pettitte,Andy	921
Hampton,Mike	900
Park,Chan Ho	891
Ortiz,Russ	855

Hit Batters

Johnson,Randy	190
Wakefield,Tim	173
Martinez,Pedro	141
Moyer,Jamie	138
Park,Chan Ho	135
Wright,Jamey	134
Weaver,Jeff	123
Padilla,Vicente	99
Tavarez,Julian	96
Suppan,Jeff	92

Wild Pitches

Smoltz,John	145
Gordon,Tom	112
Johnson,Randy	109
Wakefield,Tim	108
Batista,Miguel	94
Schmidt,Jason	93
Suppan,Jeff	85
Burnett,A.J.	83
Lackey,John	83
Garcia,Freddy	76

2009 Active Career Pitching Leaders

Saves		Save Pct (minimum 50 Save Ops)		Home Runs Allowed		Strikeouts Per 9 IP (minimum 750 IP)	
Hoffman,Trevor	591	Smoltz,John	91.1	Moyer,Jamie	491	Wagner,Billy	11.79
Rivera,Mariano	526	Soria,Joakim	89.9	Johnson,Randy	411	Dotel,Octavio	10.98
Wagner,Billy	385	Nathan,Joe	89.5	Wakefield,Tim	374	Johnson,Randy	10.61
Percival,Troy	358	Rivera,Mariano	89.5	Suppan,Jeff	320	Wood,Kerry	10.38
Isringhausen,Jason	293	Papelbon,Jonathan	89.3	Vazquez,Javier	320	Martinez,Pedro	10.04
Cordero,Francisco	250	Hoffman,Trevor	89.3	Hernandez,Livan	315	Hoffman,Trevor	9.53
Nathan,Joe	247	Saito,Takashi	87.4	Smoltz,John	288	Harden,Rich	9.35
Rodriguez,Francisco	243	Jenks,Bobby	86.9	Milton,Eric	267	Kazmir,Scott	9.31
Lidge,Brad	195	Percival,Troy	86.3	Colon,Bartolo	256	Perez,Oliver	9.20
Guardado,Eddie	187	Wagner,Billy	86.1	Tomko,Brett	251	Santana,Johan	9.12

Opp On-Base Percentage (minimum 750 IP)		Opp Slugging Average (minimum 750 IP)		Hits Per Nine Innings (minimum 750 IP)		Home Runs Per Nine IP (minimum 750 IP)	
Hoffman,Trevor	.263	Rivera,Mariano	.292	Wagner,Billy	6.00	Rivera,Mariano	0.50
Wagner,Billy	.264	Wagner,Billy	.299	Hoffman,Trevor	6.00	Webb,Brandon	0.63
Rivera,Mariano	.264	Hoffman,Trevor	.305	Rivera,Mariano	7.00	Isringhausen,Jason	0.71
Martinez,Pedro	.276	Martinez,Pedro	.337	Wood,Kerry	7.03	Hudson,Tim	0.72
Santana,Johan	.281	Harden,Rich	.342	Martinez,Pedro	7.07	Tavarez,Julian	0.72
Smoltz,John	.293	Isringhausen,Jason	.349	Harden,Rich	7.20	Lowe,Derek	0.73
Haren,Dan	.294	Zambrano,Carlos	.352	Dotel,Octavio	7.21	Zambrano,Carlos	0.73
Peavy,Jake	.296	Webb,Brandon	.352	Johnson,Randy	7.28	Smoltz,John	0.75
Johnson,Randy	.297	Johnson,Randy	.353	Santana,Johan	7.53	Gordon,Tom	0.75
Sheets,Ben	.298	Wood,Kerry	.360	Zambrano,Carlos	7.62	Cook,Aaron	0.75

Strikeouts / Walks Ratio (minimum 750 IP)		Stolen Base Pct Allowed (minimum 750 IP)		GIDP Induced		GIDP Per Nine IP (minimum 750 IP)	
Martinez,Pedro	4.15	Carpenter,Chris	38.0	Pettitte,Andy	322	Maholm,Paul	1.29
Rivera,Mariano	3.93	Buehrle,Mark	42.1	Moyer,Jamie	319	Cook,Aaron	1.28
Wagner,Billy	3.93	Verlander,Justin	42.6	Hampton,Mike	287	Westbrook,Jake	1.28
Sheets,Ben	3.85	Zambrano,Carlos	46.5	Hernandez,Livan	260	Wright,Jamey	1.23
Haren,Dan	3.83	Duke,Zach	48.5	Suppan,Jeff	257	Tavarez,Julian	1.23
Hoffman,Trevor	3.83	Santana,Johan	49.3	Johnson,Randy	252	Silva,Carlos	1.20
Shields,James	3.70	Colon,Bartolo	51.5	Lowe,Derek	247	Hampton,Mike	1.14
Santana,Johan	3.66	Greinke,Zack	52.2	Smoltz,John	245	Robertson,Nate	1.10
Oswalt,Roy	3.58	Rodriguez,Wandy	52.5	Buehrle,Mark	240	Schoeneweis,Scott	1.09
Vazquez,Javier	3.48	Ohka,Tomo	52.9	Wright,Jamey	233	Garland,Jon	1.06

Complete Game % (minimum 100 GS)		Quality Start Pct (minimum 100 GS)		Walks Per 9 IP (minimum 750 IP)		Games Finished	
Halladay,Roy	0.17	Oswalt,Roy	68.3	Silva,Carlos	1.71	Hoffman,Trevor	820
Johnson,Randy	0.17	Santana,Johan	67.1	Shields,James	1.93	Rivera,Mariano	773
Hernandez,Livan	0.11	Peavy,Jake	67.0	Sheets,Ben	1.97	Wagner,Billy	639
Martinez,Pedro	0.11	Johnson,Randy	66.8	Haren,Dan	1.98	Percival,Troy	546
Smoltz,John	0.11	Martinez,Pedro	66.7	Halladay,Roy	2.00	Isringhausen,Jason	467
Carpenter,Chris	0.11	Webb,Brandon	66.7	Buehrle,Mark	2.05	Cordero,Francisco	430
Ponson,Sidney	0.10	Haren,Dan	65.2	Oswalt,Roy	2.06	Guardado,Eddie	401
Sabathia,CC	0.10	Halladay,Roy	64.8	Rivera,Mariano	2.11	Nathan,Joe	375
Colon,Bartolo	0.10	Hudson,Tim	63.9	Byrd,Paul	2.13	Rodriguez,Francisco	363
Gordon,Tom	0.09	Buehrle,Mark	63.1	Bush,David	2.14	Gordon,Tom	347

2009 American League Bill James Leaders

Top Game Scores

Pitcher	Date	Opp	IP	H	R	ER	BB	SO	GS
Buehrle,Mark, CWS	7/23	TB	9.0	0	0	0	0	6	93
Verlander,Justin, Det	5/8	Cle	9.0	2	0	0	2	11	92
Halladay,Roy, Tor	9/4	NYY	9.0	1	0	0	3	9	91
Niemann,Jeff, TB	6/3	KC	9.0	2	0	0	1	9	91
Anderson,Brett, Oak	7/6	Bos	9.0	2	0	0	2	9	90
Greinke,Zack, KC	8/30	Sea	9.0	1	0	0	1	5	89
Baker,Scott, Min	8/14	Cle	9.0	2	0	0	0	5	88
Beckett,Josh, Bos	7/12	KC	9.0	3	0	0	0	7	88
Greinke,Zack, KC	4/24	Det	9.0	3	1	0	1	10	88
Holland,Derek, Tex	8/9	LAA	9.0	3	0	0	1	8	88
Lester,Jon, Bos	6/6	Tex	9.0	2	1	1	2	11	88
Washburn,Jarrod, Sea	7/6	Bal	9.0	1	0	0	0	3	88

Worst Game Scores

Pitcher	Date	Opp	IP	H	R	ER	BB	SO	GS
Gonzalez,Gio, Oak	7/20	Min	2.2	10	11	11	3	1	-8
Tallet,Brian, Tor	4/29	KC	4.0	11	10	10	3	2	-1
Holland,Derek, Tex	8/31	Tor	3.0	7	10	10	3	1	3
Pavano,Carl, Cle	4/9	Tex	1.0	6	9	9	3	1	3
Mitre,Sergio, NYY	9/6	Tor	4.1	11	11	9	2	5	4
Hughes,Phil, NYY	5/9	Bal	1.2	8	8	8	2	0	5
Meche,Gil, KC	6/21	StL	3.1	9	9	9	2	1	5
Perkins,Glen, Min	8/2	LAA	4.0	12	9	8	1	2	5
Pavano,Carl, Cle	6/10	KC	4.2	11	9	9	1	1	6
Perkins,Glen, Min	7/22	Oak	1.0	6	8	8	3	0	6

Runs Created

Mauer,Joe, Min	123
Bay,Jason, Bos	122
Cabrera,Miguel, Det	114
Lind,Adam, Tor	114
Youkilis,Kevin, Bos	114
Teixeira,Mark, NYY	112
Choo,Shin-Soo, Cle	111
Suzuki,Ichiro, Sea	111
Figgins,Chone, LAA	110
Hill,Aaron, Tor	110

Runs Created Per 27 Outs

Mauer,Joe, Min	9.3
Youkilis,Kevin, Bos	8.5
Bay,Jason, Bos	8.0
Zobrist,Ben, TB	7.8
Bartlett,Jason, TB	7.2
Lind,Adam, Tor	7.1
Rodriguez,Alex, NYY	7.1
Choo,Shin-Soo, Cle	6.9
Matsui,Hideki, NYY	6.9
Cabrera,Miguel, Det	6.9

Offensive Winning %

Mauer,Joe, Min	.782
Youkilis,Kevin, Bos	.736
Zobrist,Ben, TB	.725
Choo,Shin-Soo, Cle	.715
Bay,Jason, Bos	.711
Lind,Adam, Tor	.698
Rodriguez,Alex, NYY	.692
Suzuki,Ichiro, Sea	.690
Bartlett,Jason, TB	.688
Matsui,Hideki, NYY	.683

Secondary Average
(minimum 502 PA)

Pena,Carlos, TB	.501
Bay,Jason, Bos	.471
Zobrist,Ben, TB	.461
Rodriguez,Alex, NYY	.457
Swisher,Nick, NYY	.444
Drew,J.D., Bos	.429
Youkilis,Kevin, Bos	.413
Cruz,Nelson, Tex	.413
Teixeira,Mark, NYY	.409
Branyan,Russell, Sea	.408

Isolated Power
(minimum 502 PA)

Pena,Carlos, TB	.310
Teixeira,Mark, NYY	.273
Bay,Jason, Bos	.269
Branyan,Russell, Sea	.269
Cruz,Nelson, Tex	.264
Morales,Kendry, LAA	.263
Lind,Adam, Tor	.257
Swisher,Nick, NYY	.249
Zobrist,Ben, TB	.246
Rodriguez,Alex, NYY	.245

Power / Speed Number

Kinsler,Ian, Tex	31.0
Cruz,Nelson, Tex	24.9
Crawford,Carl, TB	24.0
Granderson,Curtis, Det	24.0
Jeter,Derek, NYY	22.5
Roberts,Brian, Bal	20.9
Zobrist,Ben, TB	20.9
Choo,Shin-Soo, Cle	20.5
Abreu,Bobby, LAA	20.0
Rios,Alex, Tor-CWS	19.9

Speed Scores (2008-2009)

Gomez,Carlos, Min	8.51
Ellsbury,Jacoby, Bos	8.13
Granderson,Curtis, Det	8.07
Span,Denard, Min	7.77
Crawford,Carl, TB	7.75
Sizemore,Grady, Cle	7.47
Suzuki,Ichiro, Sea	7.36
Kinsler,Ian, Tex	7.26
Roberts,Brian, Bal	7.11
Aybar,Erick, LAA	7.07

Cheap Wins

Romero,Ricky, Tor	6
Saunders,Joe, LAA	5
Shields,James, TB	5
Wakefield,Tim, Bos	5
Beckett,Josh, Bos	4
Berken,Jason, Bal	4
Davies,Kyle, KC	4
Huff,David, Cle	4
Palmer,Matt, LAA	4
Pettitte,Andy, NYY	4

Tough Losses

Garza,Matt, TB	5
Guthrie,Jeremy, Bal	5
Halladay,Roy, Tor	5
Shields,James, TB	5
Bannister,Brian, KC	4
Cahill,Trevor, Oak	4
Greinke,Zack, KC	4
Millwood,Kevin, Tex	4
7 tied with	3

2009 National League Bill James Leaders

Top Game Scores

Pitcher	Date	Opp	IP	H	R	ER	BB	SO	GS
Sanchez,Jonathan, SF	7/10	SD	9.0	0	0	0	0	11	98
Carpenter,Chris, StL	9/7	Mil	9.0	1	0	0	2	10	93
Lee,Cliff, Phi	8/19	Ari	9.0	2	1	0	0	11	92
Hamels,Cole, Phi	9/1	SF	9.0	2	0	0	1	9	91
Lincecum,Tim, SF	6/29	StL	9.0	2	0	0	0	8	91
Harang,Aaron, Cin	4/12	Pit	9.0	3	0	0	0	9	90
Zambrano,Carlos, ChC	9/25	SF	9.0	2	0	0	1	8	90
Carpenter,Chris, StL	5/25	Mil	8.0	2	0	0	0	10	88
Gallardo,Yovani, Mil	4/29	Pit	8.0	2	0	0	1	11	88
Haren,Dan, Ari	7/10	Fla	9.0	4	0	0	1	10	88

Worst Game Scores

Pitcher	Date	Opp	IP	H	R	ER	BB	SO	GS
Morton,Charlie, Pit	8/14	ChC	1.0	7	10	10	3	1	-3
Arroyo,Bronson, Cin	5/6	Mil	1.0	7	9	9	3	0	0
Rodriguez,Wandy, Hou	8/14	Mil	4.0	10	10	10	5	4	1
Marquis,Jason, Col	5/13	Hou	3.2	10	9	9	3	1	3
Nolasco,Ricky, Fla	8/12	Hou	3.1	8	10	10	2	1	3
Ortiz,Russ, Hou	7/30	ChC	2.1	9	9	9	3	3	3
Parra,Manny, Mil	6/2	Fla	4.0	11	10	10	2	5	3
Cueto,Johnny, Cin	7/6	Phi	0.2	5	9	9	3	1	4
Garland,Jon, Ari	5/29	Atl	2.2	9	9	8	3	1	4
Parnell,Bobby, NYM	8/19	Atl	3.0	9	9	9	2	1	4

Runs Created

Pujols,Albert, StL	145
Fielder,Prince, Mil	134
Braun,Ryan, Mil	133
Ramirez,Hanley, Fla	122
Howard,Ryan, Phi	117
Utley,Chase, Phi	115
Sandoval,Pablo, SF	113
Lee,Derrek, ChC	112
Dunn,Adam, Was	109
Gonzalez,Adrian, SD	109

Runs Created Per 27 Outs

Pujols,Albert, StL	9.3
Fielder,Prince, Mil	8.1
Ramirez,Hanley, Fla	8.1
Votto,Joey, Cin	8.1
Braun,Ryan, Mil	7.9
Lee,Derrek, ChC	7.8
Sandoval,Pablo, SF	7.5
Helton,Todd, Col	7.4
Utley,Chase, Phi	7.3
Dunn,Adam, Was	7.1

Offensive Winning %

Pujols,Albert, StL	.821
Fielder,Prince, Mil	.781
Braun,Ryan, Mil	.770
Votto,Joey, Cin	.767
Ramirez,Hanley, Fla	.753
Gonzalez,Adrian, SD	.747
Sandoval,Pablo, SF	.727
Utley,Chase, Phi	.725
Dunn,Adam, Was	.719
Lee,Derrek, ChC	.718

Secondary Average
(minimum 502 PA)

Pujols,Albert, StL	.562
Fielder,Prince, Mil	.492
Gonzalez,Adrian, SD	.491
Dunn,Adam, Was	.474
Berkman,Lance, Hou	.461
Reynolds,Mark, Ari	.457
Werth,Jayson, Phi	.433
Tulowitzki,Troy, Col	.427
Howard,Ryan, Phi	.427
Utley,Chase, Phi	.420

Isolated Power
(minimum 502 PA)

Pujols,Albert, StL	.331
Fielder,Prince, Mil	.303
Howard,Ryan, Phi	.292
Reynolds,Mark, Ari	.284
Ibanez,Raul, Phi	.280
Gonzalez,Adrian, SD	.274
Lee,Derrek, ChC	.273
Dunn,Adam, Was	.262
Tulowitzki,Troy, Col	.256
Votto,Joey, Cin	.245

Power / Speed Number

Reynolds,Mark, Ari	31.1
Kemp,Matt, LAD	29.5
Utley,Chase, Phi	26.4
Werth,Jayson, Phi	25.7
Ramirez,Hanley, Fla	25.4
Rollins,Jimmy, Phi	25.0
Braun,Ryan, Mil	24.6
Tulowitzki,Troy, Col	24.6
Pujols,Albert, StL	23.9
Upton,Justin, Ari	22.6

Speed Scores (2008-2009)

Taveras,Willy, Cin	8.84
Bourn,Michael, Hou	8.75
Reyes,Jose, NYM	8.04
Victorino,Shane, Phi	7.82
Rollins,Jimmy, Phi	7.55
McLouth,Nate, Pit-Atl	7.20
Winn,Randy, SF	7.07
Matsui,Kaz, Hou	7.05
Kemp,Matt, LAD	6.97
Drew,Stephen, Ari	6.93

Cheap Wins

Looper,Braden, Mil	5
Parra,Manny, Mil	5
Wainwright,Adam, Stl	5
Dempster,Ryan, ChC	4
Lehr,Justin, Cin	4
Lowe,Derek, Atl	4
Moyer,Jamie, Phi	4
Ohlendorf,Ross, Pit	4
Pelfrey,Mike, NYM	4
2 tied with	3

Tough Losses

Haren,Dan, Ari	7
Jimenez,Ubaldo, Col	7
Gallardo,Yovani, Mil	6
Jurrjens,Jair, Atl	6
Vazquez,Javier, Atl	6
Wainwright,Adam, StL	6
5 tied with	5

Additional Bill James Leaders

AL Batters Win Shares (2009)	
Mauer,Joe, Min	32
Bay,Jason, Bos	29
Jeter,Derek, NYY	28
Suzuki,Ichiro, Sea	28
Youkilis,Kevin, Bos	28
Zobrist,Ben, TB	27
Figgins,Chone, LAA	26
Teixeira,Mark, NYY	26
Cabrera,Miguel, Det	25
Hill,Aaron, Tor	25

NL Batters Win Shares (2009)	
Pujols,Albert, StL	39
Braun,Ryan, Mil	36
Fielder,Prince, Mil	36
Gonzalez,Adrian, SD	34
Ramirez,Hanley, Fla	34
Utley,Chase, Phi	32
Sandoval,Pablo, SF	27
Howard,Ryan, Phi	26
Kemp,Matt, LAD	26
Werth,Jayson, Phi	26

AL Pitchers Win Shares (2009)	
Greinke,Zack, KC	26
Hernandez,Felix, Sea	26
Halladay,Roy, Tor	21
Verlander,Justin, Det	21
Sabathia,CC, NYY	18
Bailey,Andrew, Oak	17
Jackson,Edwin, Det	17
Lester,Jon, Bos	17
Weaver,Jered, LAA	17
5 tied with	16

NL Pitchers Win Shares (2009)	
Lincecum,Tim, SF	22
Carpenter,Chris, StL	21
Wainwright,Adam, StL	21
Cain,Matt, SF	20
Haren,Dan, Ari	20
Jimenez,Ubaldo, Col	19
Johnson,Josh, Fla	19
Jurrjens,Jair, Atl	17
3 tied with	16

Batters Win Shares (Career)	
Sheffield,Gary	430
Rodriguez,Alex	422
Griffey Jr.,Ken	403
Ramirez,Manny	397
Jones,Chipper	369
Thome,Jim	352
Jeter,Derek	348
Rodriguez,Ivan	326
Pujols,Albert	315
Abreu,Bobby	312

Pitchers Win Shares (Career)	
Johnson,Randy	326
Smoltz,John	289
Martinez,Pedro	256
Rivera,Mariano	227
Moyer,Jamie	221
Pettitte,Andy	196
Hoffman,Trevor	187
Gordon,Tom	179
Wakefield,Tim	171
Halladay,Roy	169

AL Component ERA (minimum 162 IP)	
Greinke,Zack, KC	2.39
Hernandez,Felix, Sea	2.72
Sabathia,CC, NYY	2.89
Halladay,Roy, Tor	3.06
Verlander,Justin, Det	3.06
Lester,Jon, Bos	3.35
Floyd,Gavin, CWS	3.38
Beckett,Josh, Bos	3.39
Washburn,Jarrod, Sea-Det	3.44
Baker,Scott, Min	3.51

NL Component ERA (minimum 162 IP)	
Lincecum,Tim, SF	2.14
Carpenter,Chris, StL	2.14
Vazquez,Javier, Atl	2.42
Haren,Dan, Ari	2.50
Kershaw,Clayton, LAD	2.60
Lilly,Ted, ChC	2.74
Johnson,Josh, Fla	2.84
Wolf,Randy, LAD	2.89
Pineiro,Joel, StL	3.00
Jimenez,Ubaldo, Col	3.03

AL Highest Avg Game Score (AL - minimum 30 GS)	
Greinke,Zack, KC	63.42
Hernandez,Felix, Sea	60.76
Halladay,Roy, Tor	60.44
Verlander,Justin, Det	58.57
Lester,Jon, Bos	57.22
Sabathia,CC, NYY	57.18
Beckett,Josh, Bos	55.28
Garza,Matt, TB	54.41
Weaver,Jered, LAA	54.39
Jackson,Edwin, Det	54.09

AL Lowest Avg Game Score (AL - minimum 30 GS)	
Guthrie,Jeremy, Bal	46.12
Cahill,Trevor, Oak	47.00
Pavano,Carl, Cle-Min	47.09
Chamberlain,Joba, NYY	47.13
Saunders,Joe, LAA	47.26
Blackburn,Nick, Min	48.67
Porcello,Rick, Det	49.19
Pettitte,Andy, NYY	50.44
Shields,James, TB	50.79
Anderson,Brett, Oak	50.97

AL Lowest Offensive Win %	
Betancourt,Y., Sea-KC	.255
Wells,Vernon, Tor	.362
Rios,Alex, Tor-CWS	.366
Cabrera,Orlando, Oak-Min	.386
Teahen,Mark, KC	.403
Peralta,Jhonny, Cle	.405
Upton,B.J., TB	.407
Inge,Brandon, Det	.408
Pierzynski,A.J., CWS	.409
Lopez,Jose, Sea	.414

NL Highest Avg Game Score (NL - minimum 30 GS)	
Lincecum,Tim, SF	64.47
Vazquez,Javier, Atl	61.63
Haren,Dan, Ari	60.82
Wainwright,Adam, StL	59.32
Cain,Matt, SF	58.27
Kershaw,Clayton, LAD	58.00
Johnson,Josh, Fla	57.09
Jurrjens,Jair, Atl	57.06
Jimenez,Ubaldo, Col	56.94
Rodriguez,Wandy, Hou	56.58

NL Lowest Avg Game Score (NL - minimum 30 GS)	
Suppan,Jeff, Mil	42.30
Hernandez,L., NYM-Was	44.00
Looper,Braden, Mil	44.41
Pelfrey,Mike, NYM	45.23
Lowe,Derek, Atl	46.12
Maholm,Paul, Pit	48.03
Hammel,Jason, Col	48.33
Garland,Jon, Ari-LAD	48.79
Lannan,John, Was	49.64
Davis,Doug, Ari	49.79

NL Lowest Offensive Win %	
Bonifacio,Emilio, Fla	.287
Barmes,Clint, Col	.372
Renteria,Edgar, SF	.377
Francoeur,Jeff, Atl-NYM	.392
Kendall,Jason, Mil	.397
Anderson,Garret, Atl	.399
Molina,Bengie, SF	.416
Guzman,Cristian, Was	.432
Soriano,Alfonso, ChC	.446
Theriot,Ryan, ChC	.457

Win Shares

Bill James initially devised Win Shares as a way to relate a player's individual statistics to the number of wins he contributed to his team. As a single number, Win Shares allows us to easily compare the accomplishments of each player and to compare players across positions.

We credit a team with three Win Shares for each win. If a team wins 100 games, the players on the team will be credited with 300 Win Shares—or 300 thirds-of-a-win. If a team wins 70 games, the players on the team will be credited with 210 Win Shares, and so on.

The following pages contain the sum of a player's Win Shares prior to 2000, followed by his individual season totals from 2000 through 2009. Career totals are also included for each player.

The quality of the team does not affect an individual player's Win Shares. A great player on a bad team will rate just as well as a great player on a good team. In 2009, Adam Dunn's 24 Win Shares for the major-league worst 59-103 Washington Nationals were the equivalent of the 24 Win Shares contributed by Dustin Pedroia and Troy Tulowitzki to their respective teams—both of which made the playoffs.

Win Shares are also a great tool for evaluating award voting and Hall of Fame credentials. Generally, 30 Win Shares indicates an MVP-caliber season; 20 Win Shares indicates a season worthy of the Cy Young Award.

Based on Win Shares, the 2009 American League MVP should be Twins backstop Joe Mauer (32), just as it should have been in 2008 when Mauer led the league with 30. Below him, three players are tied at 28: the Yankees' Derek Jeter, the Mariners' Ichiro Suzuki, and the Red Sox' Kevin Youkilis. The AL Cy Young Award will come down to who voters like better between Kansas City's Zack Greinke and Seattle's Felix Hernandez, both of whom garnered 26 Win Shares, while the Rangers' Elvis Andrus and the Athletics' Andrew Bailey both had 17, and should compete for Rookie of the Year.

In the National League, Albert Pujols (39) was the best player in baseball, but two Brewers had outstanding seasons—Ryan Braun and Prince Fielder, both of whom had 36. The Marlins' Hanley Ramirez (34) and the Phillies' Chase Utley (32) also deserve recognition here. San Francisco Giant Tim Lincecum (22) should win his second-straight Cy Young Award, and as for Rookie of the Year, the Pirates' Andrew McCutchen (18) is the only rookie within three Win Shares of the Marlins' Chris Coghlan (21).

Win Shares can also be used to assess the value of trades. Does your favorite team have a net gain or loss from their transaction? A brand new book by Doug Decatur called *Traded* (ACTA Sports) does this exact thing as he analyzes the 400 most lopsided trades in history using Win Shares.

Win Shares also adjusts for offensive environment, so it is a great tool to use for looking at the greatest individual seasons in baseball history, as well as the greatest players of all time. For a complete description of how Win Shares are calculated as well as countless essays using Win Shares to analyze various facets of the game, check out Bill James' book, *Win Shares*.

WIN SHARES BY YEAR

Player	<00	00	01	02	03	04	05	06	07	08	09	Career
Aardsma,David						0		4	1	1	16	22
Abreu,Bobby	58	23	26	29	28	33	25	27	18	22	23	312
Abreu,Tony									4		1	5
Abreu,Winston									0	0	0	0
Accardo,Jeremy						2	4	14	0		2	22
Aceves,Alfredo										3	7	10
Acosta,Manny									2	4	1	7
Adams,Mike						5	1	0		6	5	17
Adams,Russ						2	10	3	1		0	16
Adenhart,Nick										0	1	1
Affeldt,Jeremy				5	12	4	1	3	5	6	10	46
Albaladejo,J									2	1	1	4
Albers,Matt							0	0		4	2	6
Alfonzo,Eliezer								9	1	0	1	11
Allen,Brandon											1	1
Amezaga,Alfredo				2	1	1	0	5	5	9	1	24
Anderson,Brett											8	8
Anderson,Brian							0	5	0	3	3	11
Anderson,Garret	67	15	17	23	25	14	16	14	13	19	7	230
Anderson,Josh									3	4	5	12
Anderson,Marlon	10	2	16	10	12	3	4	8	4	1	0	70
Andino,Robert							0	0	0	1	3	4
Andrus,Elvis											17	17
Ankiel,Rick	3	14	0			0			8	13	5	43
Aquino,Greg						6	0	3	0	0	1	10
Arias,Alberto									0	1	3	4
Arias,Joaquin							1		3	0		4
Arredondo,Jose										11	1	12
Arroyo,Bronson		0	3	2	2	11	11	20	11	10	13	83
Ascanio,Jose								0	0	1		1
Atkins,Garrett					0	2	13	23	18	13	7	76
Atkins,Mitch											0	0
Aubrey,Michael										0	2	2
Augenstein,Bryan											0	0
Aurilia,Rich	43	20	33	15	13	7	16	15	5	9	1	177
Ausmus,Brad	73	16	10	10	12	7	15	7	7	8	3	168
Avila,Alex											3	3
Aviles,Mike										17	2	19
Axford,John											1	1
Ayala,Luis				11	10	8			4	2	2	37
Aybar,Erick								1	2	15	20	38
Aybar,Willy							6	6		6	7	25
Backe,Brandon			0	1	5	7	3	3	2		0	21
Badenhop,Burke										0	5	5
Baez,Danys			6	11	9	10	10	6	1		5	58
Bailey,Andrew											17	17
Bailey,Homer									2	0	5	7
Bailey,Jeff									0	1	1	2
Baker,Jeff							1	3	1	7	7	19
Baker,John										9	13	22
Baker,Scott						4	0	8	13	12		37
Bako,Paul	10	5	3	3	6	2	1	2	2	7	2	43
Baldelli,Rocco					14	14		12	2	2	6	46
Bale,John	0	0	2		2				3	1	1	9
Balentien,Wladimir									0	1	5	6
Balester,Collin										1	0	1
Balfour,Grant			0		2	3			0	11	5	21
Banks,Josh									0	2	0	2
Bannister,Brian								3	11	2	6	22
Barajas,Rod	1	0	1	3	5	9	11	7	3	10	12	62
Bard,Daniel											4	4
Bard,Josh			1		7	2	2	10	16	2	4	44
Barden,Brian								0	0	1		1
Barfield,Josh								18	8	1	1	28
Barker,Kevin	4	2	0					0			1	7
Barmes,Clint					1	3	9	6	0	12	13	44
Barrett,Michael	12	1	2	12	7	14	18	13	3	1	0	83
Bartlett,Jason					0	6	13	16	14	23		72
Barton,Brian										3	0	3
Barton,Daric									3	9	6	18
Bass,Brian										3	4	7
Bastardo,Antonio											0	0
Bates,Aaron											1	1

WIN SHARES BY YEAR

Player	<00	00	01	02	03	04	05	06	07	08	09	Career
Batista,Miguel	12	0	11	9	14	11	8	10	12	0	5	92
Bautista,Denny						0	1	1	0	3	1	6
Bautista,Jose						0	0	9	12	8	6	35
Bay,Jason					5	15	30	21	12	24	29	136
Bazardo,Yorman							0		3	0	0	3
Beckett,Josh			3	5	11	9	12	11	18	11	16	96
Beckham,Gordon											12	12
Bedard,Erik			0		6	8	13	17	6	8		58
Beimel,Joe		4	3	2	0	1	7	6	7	4		34
Belisario,Ronald											7	7
Belisle,Matt					0		4	3	5	0	1	13
Bell,Heath						2	0	1	13	6	12	34
Bell,Trevor										0		0
Belliard,Ronnie	15	17	13	1	12	18	18	11	15	11	7	138
Bellorin,Edwin								0	0	1		1
Beltran,Carlos	20	5	27	20	28	29	21	34	25	29	14	252
Beltre,Adrian	19	22	12	16	13	33	13	17	16	13	10	184
Bennett,Jeff				2				1	7	2		12
Benoit,Joaquin			0	3	5	4	6	4	10	2		34
Benson,Kris	12	14		5	2	10	10	8			0	61
Berg,Justin											2	2
Bergesen,Brad											9	9
Bergmann,Jason							2	0	5	2	2	11
Berken,Jason											1	1
Berkman,Lance	1	10	32	29	25	30	20	31	24	36	22	260
Bernadina,Roger										1	0	1
Berroa,Angel			1	1	15	12	12	4	0	3	0	48
Betancourt,Rafael					4	5	7	5	16	3	8	48
Betancourt,Yuniesky							3	13	19	8	8	51
Betemit,Wilson			0			1	7	9	8	2	0	27
Billingsley,Chad								6	12	16	9	43
Bixler,Brian										1	0	1
Blackburn,Nick									0	10	12	22
Blake,Casey	1	0	1	0	11	17	9	11	11	18	19	98
Blalock,Hank			1	17	24	14	13	8	6	6		89
Blanco,Andres						3	1	2			2	11
Blanco,Gregor										11	0	11
Blanco,Henry	6	9	6	4	2	5	5	6	0	3	6	52
Blanks,Kyle											5	5
Blanton,Joe						0	13	10	13	7	11	54
Blevins,Jerry									0	3	1	4
Bloomquist,Willie				3	3	2	4	5	2	5	7	31
Blum,Geoff	3	10	8	15	5	3	7	6	9	9	6	81
Boggs,Brandon										5	0	5
Boggs,Mitchell										0	2	2
Bonderman,Jeremy					2	8	9	13	7	4	0	43
Bonifacio,Emilio									1	2	7	10
Bonine,Eddie										1	2	3
Bonser,Boof								6	4		0	10
Boone,Aaron	21	10	13	19	23		9	7	7	2	0	111
Bootcheck,Chris						0		1	0	4	0	5
Borbon,Julio										0	5	5
Bourgeois,Jason										0	0	0
Bourn,Michael								0	4	7	23	34
Bowden,Michael										1	0	1
Bowker,John										7	1	8
Boyer,Blaine							4	0	0	1	3	8
Braden,Dallas									0	4	8	12
Bradford,Chad	3	2	3	9	9	5	2	7	6	8	1	55
Bradley,Milton		3	3	6	18	16	10	13	11	19	11	110
Brantley,Michael											3	3
Branyan,Russell	1	5	10	8	5	5	9	6	5	5	14	73
Braun,Ryan									22	23	36	81
Bray,Bill								3	1	4		8
Breslow,Craig							1	1		6	6	14
Brignac,Reid										0	2	2
Broadway,Lance									2	0	0	2
Brocail,Doug	35	5				4	3	1	6	7	1	62
Brown,Dusty											0	0
Brown,Emil	1	1	2			18	13	8	7	0		50
Broxton,Jonathan							0	9	10	10	16	45
Bruce,Jay										7	9	16
Bruney,Brian						2	0	3	2	6	3	16

WIN SHARES BY YEAR

Player	<00	00	01	02	03	04	05	06	07	08	09	Career
Bruntlett,Eric				1	2	3	4	4	4	3	1	18
Buchholz,Clay									3	0	6	9
Buchholz,Taylor							1	5	9			15
Buck,John						4	10	8	7	8	6	43
Buck,Travis									10	5	1	16
Buckner,Billy									1	1	1	3
Budde,Ryan									0	0	0	0
Buehrle,Mark		4	18	17	13	17	22	9	17	16	16	149
Bulger,Jason							1	0	1	0	7	9
Bullington,Bryan					0			0	0	0	0	0
Bumgarner,Madison											1	1
Burke,Chris						0	6	10	5	2	0	23
Burke,Greg											2	2
Burke,Jamie			0		1	5	0		6	2	1	15
Burnett,A.J.	3	5	9	14	0	7	11	9	11	14	12	95
Burnett,Sean						2				2	5	9
Burns,Mike							1	0			0	1
Burrell,Pat		12	17	25	8	14	24	15	20	20	6	161
Burres,Brian								1	3	2	0	6
Burriss,Emmanuel										4	2	6
Burton,Jared									5	6	3	14
Buscher,Brian									1	8	4	13
Bush,David						7	6	12	6	8	0	39
Butler,Billy									7	8	18	33
Butler,Josh											0	0
Byrd,Marlon				0	10	3	0	2	13	12	20	74
Byrd,Paul	23	0	6	19		7	13	6	12	9	1	96
Byrdak,Tim	0	0					1	0	4	4	5	14
Byrnes,Eric		0	1	2	16	17	9	13	24	2	3	87
Cabrera,Asdrubal									7	12	18	37
Cabrera,Daniel						8	7	7	6	6	0	34
Cabrera,Everth											14	14
Cabrera,Fernando						0	4	2	1	1	0	8
Cabrera,Melky							0	13	12	5	14	44
Cabrera,Miguel					12	19	27	33	29	20	25	165
Cabrera,Orlando	14	9	26	14	19	11	15	18	25	19	14	184
Cahill,Trevor											7	7
Cain,Matt							5	11	12	14	20	62
Cairo,Miguel	20	10	4	3	3	14	5	5	4		4	72
Calero,Kiko				3	6	5	7	1	0	8		30
Callaspo,Alberto								1	1	6	17	25
Cameron,Kevin									4	0	1	5
Cameron,Mike	42	19	29	18	21	15	11	25	20	17	17	234
Camp,Shawn						4	0	5	0	3	5	17
Campillo,Jorge					0	0	0	0	0	0	0	0
Cancel,Robinson	0									0	0	0
Canizares,Barbaro											0	0
Cano,Robinson							12	17	21	12	18	80
Cantu,Jorge						4	18	5	1	19	17	64
Capps,Matt							0	7	14	7	2	30
Capuano,Chris					2	4	13	14	5			38
Caridad,Esmailin											3	3
Carlin,Luke										1	0	1
Carlson,Jesse										9	3	12
Carlyle,Buddy	0	0				0			3	4	0	7
Carmona,Fausto								1	22	3	0	26
Carp,Mike											2	2
Carpenter,Chris	22	5	13	3		12	20	19	0	1	21	116
Carpenter,Drew										0	0	0
Carrasco,Carlos										0	0	0
Carrasco,D.J.					6	1	4			3	7	21
Carrillo,Cesar										0		0
Carroll,Brett									0	0	5	5
Carroll,Jamey				3	3	6	9	13	5	10	8	57
Carson,Matt											1	1
Carter,Chris										0	0	0
Cash,Kevin				0	1	3	0		0	1	1	6
Casilla,Alexi								0	1	9	4	14
Casilla,Santiago						0	0	0	4	3	0	7
Castillo,Alberto										2	1	3
Castillo,Luis	23	18	14	20	23	22	18	18	16	8	16	196
Castillo,Wilkin										0	0	0
Castro,Juan	6	3	1	2	7	5	7	6	1	2	2	42

WIN SHARES BY YEAR

Player	<00	00	01	02	03	04	05	06	07	08	09	Career
Castro,Ramon	1	3	0	4	2	1	7	2	6	6	4	36
Catalanotto,Frank	10	8	17	7	15	5	16	14	9	4	4	109
Cecil,Brett											3	3
Cedeno,Ronny					2		5	1	5	7		20
Cervelli,Francisco										0	3	3
Chacin,Jhoulys											0	0
Chamberlain,Joba									5	11	6	22
Chavez,Endy		0	3	9	10	1	13	4	3	3		46
Chavez,Eric	11	16	26	24	23	18	20	16	6	3	0	163
Chavez,Jesse										0	4	4
Chavez,Raul	0	0		0	1	3	2	0		3	3	12
Chen,Bruce	2	11	4	1	0	4	13	0	0		1	36
Chico,Matt								5	0			5
Choate,Randy		1	4	0	0	3	0	1	0		5	14
Choo,Shin-Soo							0	4	1	16	23	44
Chulk,Vinnie				0	4	5	2	5	1	0		17
Church,Ryan						1	8	9	16	10	7	51
Cintron,Alex		0	1	14	8	7	6	4	2	0		42
Claggett,Anthony										0	0	0
Clark,Tony	68	6	16	1	4	7	18	0	4	3	1	128
Claussen,Brandon					1	0	7	1				9
Clement,Matt	7	5	4	11	11	12	11	1				62
Clippard,Tyler									1	1	5	7
Coffey,Todd							3	9	1	1	7	21
Coughlan,Chris											21	21
Coke,Phil										3	5	8
Colome,Jesus			4	0	4	5	2	0	5	3	0	23
Colon,Bartolo	34	15	14	22	17	10	18	1	1	2	3	137
Colon,Roman						2	1	2			3	8
Colvin,Tyler										0		0
Condrey,Clay				2	0		2	3	5	5		17
Conrad,Brooks										0	1	1
Contreras,Jose					7	6	17	13	5	7	4	59
Cook,Aaron				2	3	6	6	12	9	15	11	64
Cora,Alex	1	6	6	13	12	17	5	6	4	5	5	80
Corcoran,Roy						1	0	0		7	0	8
Cordero,Chad					2	12	15	12	10	0		51
Cordero,Francisco	2	3	0	8	12	17	11	12	12	11	13	101
Cormier,Lance						0	4	2	0	4	6	16
Corpas,Manny								3	15	6	1	25
Corporan,Carlos											0	0
Correia,Kevin					3	0	2	6	8	0	8	27
Coste,Chris								8	4	9	3	24
Cotts,Neal					0	2	9	2	1	2	0	16
Counsell,Craig	23	3	14	13	3	10	22	9	6	6	15	130
Crain,Jesse						4	10	7	0	5	4	30
Crawford,Carl				6	13	20	22	21	20	11	19	132
Crede,Joe		0	1	6	13	8	15	19	4	10	6	82
Crisp,Coco				3	8	14	20	9	16	11	4	85
Crosby,Bobby					0	14	12	8	4	10	2	50
Crowe,Trevor										2	2	2
Cruz,Juan				4	3	0	7	0	6	6	2	34
Cruz,Luis										1	1	2
Cruz,Nelson							0	3	4	7	16	30
Cuddyer,Michael			0	3	1	10	7	22	16	7	17	83
Cueto,Johnny										6	7	13
Cunningham,Aaron										3	0	3
Cust,Jack		0	0	4	0		0	19	17	14		54
Daley,Matt											4	4
Damon,Johnny	61	26	17	22	19	26	25	21	15	23	21	276
Danks,John									4	17	16	37
Davidson,Daniel											0	0
Davidson,Dave									0	0	0	0
Davies,Kyle							4	0	1	7	5	17
Davis,Chris										8	7	15
Davis,Doug	0	5	8	3	7	16	12	8	11	7	10	87
Davis,Rajai								0	5	5	13	23
Davis,Wade											2	2
De Aza,Alejandro									1		1	2
de la Cruz,Eulogio									0	0	0	0
de la Rosa,Jorge						0	2	2	3	5	12	24
DeJesus,David					0	9	16	14	15	22	16	92
Delcarmen,Manny							1	3	6	7	4	21

451

WIN SHARES BY YEAR

Player	<00	00	01	02	03	04	05	06	07	08	09	Career
Delgado,Carlos	78	36	23	26	32	16	29	22	13	23	5	303
Dellucci,David	16	1	7	4	4	10	15	8	2	5	0	72
Dempster,Ryan	6	17	7	4	0	2	14	6	8	18	12	94
Denorfia,Chris							0	2		2	0	4
DeRosa,Mark	0	1	6	7	5	2	4	14	16	23	13	91
Desmond,Ian											2	2
Dessens,Elmer	3	10	10	15	7	5	4	5	0	0	2	61
Detwiler,Ross										0	2	2
Devine,Joey								0	0	1	9	10
DeWitt,Blake										12	0	12
Diaz,Matt					0	0	2	7	11	1	15	36
Diaz,Robinzon										1	2	3
Dickerson,Chris										5	7	12
Dickey,R.A.			0		7	4	0	0		3	3	17
DiFelice,Mark										2	3	5
Dillard,Tim										0	0	0
Dillon,Joe						0			3	2	0	5
DiNardo,Lenny						1	1	0	6	0	0	8
Dlugach,Brent											0	0
Dobbs,Greg						1	2	1	7	8	2	21
Dolsi,Freddy										3	1	4
Donnelly,Brendan				6	11	5	6	5	2	0	4	39
Dotel,Octavio	3	7	12	17	12	14	2	0	3	6	6	82
Doumit,Ryan							6	2	6	20	4	38
Downs,Matt											1	1
Downs,Scott		3			0	0	5	6	8	11	6	39
Drew,J.D.	13	18	22	15	13	31	12	19	12	16	18	189
Drew,Stephen								6	16	21	16	59
Duchscherer,Justin			0		1	9	11	10	1	13		45
Duensing,Brian											6	6
Duffy,Chris							5	6	5			16
Duke,Zach							10	10	2	3	12	37
Dukes,Elijah									2	9	7	18
Dumatrait,Phil									0	1	0	1
Duncan,Chris							0	10	17	5	6	38
Duncan,Shelley									3	0	0	3
Dunn,Adam			10	20	13	29	25	18	18	21	24	178
Dunn,Mike											0	0
Durango,Luis											1	1
Durbin,Chad	0	0	8	0	0	1		1	6	8	3	27
Dye,Jermaine	25	21	18	13	2	12	17	25	11	17	14	175
Eaton,Adam		9	5	0	7	6	5	4	2	1	0	39
Eckstein,David			12	21	10	10	27	13	12	8	17	130
Egbert,Jack											0	0
Ekstrom,Mike										0	0	0
Elbert,Scott										0	1	1
Ellis,A.J.										0	0	0
Ellis,Mark				14	18		21	14	20	13	11	111
Ellsbury,Jacoby									6	16	21	43
Embree,Alan	16	3	2	7	5	4	0	5	8	2	1	53
Encarnacion,Edwin							4	14	16	14	6	54
Erstad,Darin	52	30	14	17	4	15	15	1	5	8	0	161
Escalona,Sergio											1	1
Escobar,Alcides										0	4	4
Escobar,Alex			1		1	3		4				9
Escobar,Kelvim	20	8	11	9	12	14	5	12	18		0	109
Escobar,Yunel									12	13	24	49
Estes,Shawn	29	10	7	4	0	9	5	0		1		65
Estrada,Johnny			5	0	0	18	9	13	7	0		52
Estrada,Marco										0	0	0
Ethier,Andre								11	13	23	21	68
Evans,Nick										1	1	2
Evans,Terry									0	0		0
Eveland,Dana							0	0	0	8	0	8
Everett,Adam			0	1	11	12	14	13	4	4	6	65
Everidge,Tommy											0	0
Eyre,Scott	4	0	2	4	5	4	9	5	3	3	5	44
Eyre,Willie									2	2	1	5
Falkenborg,B	0					0	0	0	0	0		0
Farnsworth,Kyle	5	0	9	0	7	3	14	5	3	3	2	51
Feierabend,Ryan								1	0	0		1
Feldman,Scott							1	3	1	4	14	23
Feliciano,Pedro				0	3	1		8	6	3	7	28

Player	<00	00	01	02	03	04	05	06	07	08	09	Career
Feliz,Neftali											6	6
Feliz,Pedro		0	0	2	7	9	9	13	12	8	18	78
Fielder,Prince							2	16	27	23	36	104
Fields,Josh								0	12	0	3	15
Fien,Casey											0	0
Figaro,Alfredo											0	0
Figgins,Chone				0	9	20	22	17	21	12	26	127
Figueroa,Nelson		0	6	1	3	0				2	4	16
Fiorentino,Jeff							0	1		0	1	2
Fisher,Carlos											2	2
Fister,Doug											4	4
Flores,Jesus									6	9	3	18
Flores,Randy			1			2	3	1	3	0	1	11
Flowers,Tyler											0	0
Floyd,Cliff	49	19	26	22	15	13	24	9	8	6	0	191
Floyd,Gavin						2	0	0	2	15	13	32
Fogg,Josh			2	10	4	7	3	6	6	0	3	41
Fontenot,Mike								0	5	12	7	24
Fossum,Casey			2	6	3	0	5	4	0	2	0	22
Fowler,Dexter										0	15	15
Fox,Chad	6	9	0	4	0	0				0	0	19
Fox,Jake										0	6	6
Francis,Jeff						2	6	13	14	5		40
Francisco,Ben									1	9	10	20
Francisco,Frank						6		0	3	6	9	24
Francisco,Juan											2	2
Francoeur,Jeff							12	15	20	5	9	61
Frandsen,Kevin								0	4	0	1	5
Franklin,Ryan	1		5	6	13	6	6	4	8	8	14	71
Frasor,Jason						9	6	4	3	2	10	34
Freel,Ryan			0		3	19	11	11	4	4	1	53
Freese,David											1	1
French,Luke											2	2
Frieri,Ernesto											0	0
Fuentes,Brian			1	2	10	2	14	12	10	12	9	72
Fukudome,Kosuke										15	17	32
Fulchino,Jeff									0	0	7	7
Fuld,Sam										0	4	4
Furcal,Rafael		17	9	20	26	20	26	27	15	8	17	185
Gabino,Armando										0	0	0
Galarraga,Armando									0	13	3	16
Gallagher,Sean									0	2	1	3
Gallardo,Yovani									9	2	10	21
Gamel,Mat										0	5	5
Garate,Victor										0	0	0
Garcia,Freddy	16	8	18	11	8	15	17	14	1	1	4	113
Garcia,Jaime										1		1
Garciaparra,Nomar	87	29	3	26	25	11	5	17	11	4	1	219
Gardner,Brett										3	9	12
Garko,Ryan							0	6	12	15	11	44
Garland,Jon		1	8	8	10	11	20	15	13	9	10	105
Garza,Matt								1	4	12	12	29
Gathright,Joey						0	4	7	6	6	0	23
Gaudin,Chad					3	1	0	7	9	5	3	28
Geary,Geoff					0	1	3	10	3	7	0	24
Geer,Josh										2	0	2
Gentry,Craig											0	0
German,Esteban				0	0	2	1	11	8	5	1	28
Gerut,Jody					14	10	3			13	2	42
Gervacio,Sammy											3	3
Getz,Chris										0	10	10
Giambi,Jason	91	38	38	34	27	8	24	22	6	14	7	309
Giese,Dan									0	2	0	2
Giles,Brian	61	27	29	31	25	23	32	21	17	20	1	287
Gimenez,Chris											1	1
Glaus,Troy	19	25	21	22	10	8	23	16	14	20	0	178
Gload,Ross		0			0	7	0	4	7	5	4	27
Gobble,Jimmy					3	5	1	4	5	0	0	18
Golson,Greg										0	0	0
Gomes,Jonny					0	0	14	6	8	2	10	40
Gomez,Carlos									2	13	6	21
Gonzalez,Adrian						1	1	16	25	24	34	101
Gonzalez,Alberto									0	3	5	8

Player	<00	00	01	02	03	04	05	06	07	08	09	Career
Gonzalez,Alex	12	3	10	3	20	15	14	10	10		8	105
Gonzalez,Andy								1	0	0		1
Gonzalez,Carlos										6	9	15
Gonzalez,Edgar				1	0	0	3	5	0	1		10
Gonzalez,Edgar V.									7	1		8
Gonzalez,Enrique							3	0	0	0		3
Gonzalez,Gio									0	2		2
Gonzalez,Mike				0	8	6	11	3	3	9		40
Gordon,Alex								12	15	2		29
Gordon,Tom	116		8	3	11	15	10	10	4	2	0	179
Gorecki,Reid											0	0
Gorzelanny,Tom					0	3	11	0	2			16
Gosling,Mike				1	1	0	1			1		4
Grabow,John			0	1	2	5	3	6	7			24
Graffanino,Tony	18	6	3	7	9	7	13	12	5		0	80
Granderson,Curtis					0	6	20	25	20	20		91
Gray,Jeff									0	1		1
Green,Andy				1	1	0			0	0		2
Green,Nick					8	6	2	0		6		22
Green,Sean							2	5	4	3		14
Greene,Khalil				1	20	16	13	19	4	4		77
Greene,Tyler										1		1
Gregerson,Luke										5		5
Gregg,Kevin				2	6	2	4	10	11	7		42
Greinke,Zack					9	3	1	9	15	26		63
Griffey Jr.,Ken	275	24	14	5	6	15	19	0	14	16	7	100
Grilli,Jason		0	1		0	1	4	4	7	2		19
Gross,Gabe					2	2	10	4	10	8		36
Guardado,Eddie	23	8	12	14	14	8	10	3	0	6	2	100
Guerrero,Vladimir	67	29	23	28	18	27	27	24	29	22	7	301
Guerrier,Matt					0	5	5	9	2	11		32
Guillen,Carlos	2	8	14	12	12	22	8	25	19	13	6	141
Guillen,Jose	21	6	2	2	20	20	15	3	18	10	4	121
Guthrie,Jeremy					1	0	0	12	13	7		33
Gutierrez,Franklin					0	1	6	5	21			33
Gutierrez,Juan							0			7		7
Guzman,Angel					0	2	0	7				9
Guzman,Cristian	5	12	18	14	14	16	6		7	20	9	121
Guzman,Freddy					1		0	0		0		1
Guzman,Jesus									0			0
Gwynn,Tony							1	3	0	13		17
Hacker,Eric									0			0
Haeger,Charlie							2	0	0	1		3
Hafner,Travis			1	7	21	26	24	16	2	8		105
Hairston,Jerry	5	4	10	12	7	8	9	1	2	12	8	78
Hairston,Scott					3	0	0	7	9	14		33
Hall,Bill				1	3	7	17	20	10	8	4	70
Hall,Toby		0	6	7	10	8	11	3	0	2		47
Halladay,Roy	12	0	9	21	23	9	15	20	16	23	21	169
Hamels,Cole							8	15	18	10		51
Hamilton,Josh								11	26	11		48
Hammel,Jason							0	2	3	10		15
Hampton,Mike	74	19	11	5	11	10	6			3	4	143
Hanigan,Ryan								1	4	8		13
Hannahan,Jack						0	5	5	4			14
Hanrahan,Joel							2	7	3			12
Hansen,Craig					0	0		1	0			1
Hanson,Tommy										10		10
Happ,J.A.								0	2	15		17
Harang,Aaron			4	3	5	11	18	17	6	7		71
Harden,Rich				4	14	12	4	2	16	7		59
Hardy,J.J.					11	3	19	20	6			59
Haren,Dan				1	2	13	14	17	19	20		86
Harris,Brendan					0	1	0	13	11	7		32
Harris,Willie			0	2	2	10	4	1	9	10	9	47
Harrison,Matt									3	1		4
Hart,Corey					0	0	5	21	16	9		51
Hart,Kevin							2	0	3			5
Hawkins,LaTroy	11	12	3	11	13	16	5	4	5	6	10	96
Hawksworth,Blake										5		5
Hawpe,Brad					1	8	15	20	16	19		79
Hayes,Brett									0			0
Hayhurst,Dirk									0	2		2

Player	<00	00	01	02	03	04	05	06	07	08	09	Career
Headley,Chase								0	8	16		24
Heilman,Aaron			0	0	10	8	8	2	5			33
Helms,Wes	1	0	5	1	14	4	5	10	2	5	5	52
Helton,Todd	38	29	26	27	35	30	25	21	22	8	23	284
Hendrickson,Mark			4	5	7	4	8	3	3	6		40
Henn,Sean					0	0	0	0				0
Herges,Matt	1	10	9	4	7	3	1	3	5	2	3	48
Hermida,Jeremy						3	6	13	13	11		46
Hernandez,And					0	1	0	4	7			12
Hernandez,David										3		3
Hernandez,Diory										1		1
Hernandez,Felix						8	8	14	13	26		69
Hernandez,Livan	24	14	5	7	22	19	13	10	10	3	3	130
Hernandez,Luis								1	1	1		3
Hernandez,Michel				0					0	1		2
Hernandez,Orlando	27	12	4	11		8	5	7	9			83
Hernandez,Ramon	6	10	13	12	18	13	10	21	11	11	11	136
Herrera,Daniel Ray									0	5		5
Hester,John										1	1	1
Hill,Aaron						9	14	20	5	25		73
Hill,Koyie				0	1	1		1	0	7		10
Hill,Rich				0	5	13	1	0				19
Hill,Shawn				0		1	6	0				7
Hinckley,Mike									2	0		2
Hinshaw,Alex								4	0			4
Hinske,Eric			22	12	6	11	7	3	10	5		76
Hochevar,Luke								1	3	1		5
Hoey,Jim							0	0				0
Hoffman,Trevor	92	13	9	8	1	11	10	14	11	7	11	187
Hoffmann,Jaime									0			0
Hoffpauir,Jarrett									1			1
Hoffpauir,Micah								3	4			7
Holland,Derek									2			2
Holliday,Matt					9	17	19	27	21	25		118
Holm,Stove								2	1			3
Hoover,Paul		0	0			0	0	0	1			1
Howard,Ryan				1	10	29	26	24	26			116
Howell,J.P.				1	2	0	11	11				25
Howry,Bob	17	9	5	3	0	4	11	9	11	3	5	77
Hu,Chin-lung								1	1	0		2
Huber,Justin						0	0	0	2	0		2
Hudson,Daniel										1		1
Hudson,Luke			0		4	1	5	0				10
Hudson,Orlando			7	17	16	15	20	21	17	20		133
Hudson,Tim	12	15	17	23	23	16	14	7	17	10	4	158
Huff,Aubrey		3	5	12	21	20	14	9	12	21	8	125
Huff,David										3		3
Hughes,Dustin										0		0
Hughes,Phil							4	0	10			14
Hulett,Tug									0	0		0
Humber,Philip							0	0	0	0		0
Hundley,Nick									3	10		13
Hunter,Tommy									0	8		8
Hunter,Torii	5	8	19	20	16	13	11	17	22	21	20	172
Hurley,Eric									1			1
Iannetta,Chris								1	5	17	10	33
Ibanez,Raul	5	1	9	12	15	12	17	25	23	21	17	157
Infante,Omar				3	3	12	7	5	4	9	7	50
Inge,Brandon			3	4	4	13	17	17	12	10	13	93
Inglett,Joe								6	1	12	2	21
Iribarren,Hernan									0	0		0
Ishikawa,Travis							1		4	9		14
Isringhausen,Jason	18	10	14	13		7	15	12	8	12	1	111
Iwamura,Akinori								13	21	6		40
Izturis,Cesar			4	4	10	25	6	3	5	9	8	74
Izturis,Maicer					1	6	13	16	11	17		64
Jackson,Conor						0	12	13	17	1		43
Jackson,Edwin			2	0	0	1	2	10	17			32
Jackson,Steven										3		3
Jackson,Zach							1		1	0		2
Jacobs,Mike							5	12	7	14	5	43
Jakubauskas,Chris										3		3
James,Chuck							1	8	8	0		17

453

Player	<00	00	01	02	03	04	05	06	07	08	09	Career
Janish,Paul										1	4	5
Janssen,Casey								4	10	0		14
Jaramillo,Jason											2	2
Jenks,Bobby							6	12	16	13	8	55
Jennings,Jason			3	14	8	9	5	14	0	0	4	57
Jepsen,Kevin										0	4	4
Jeter,Derek	100	23	28	24	19	26	26	32	24	18	28	348
Jimenez,Ubaldo								0	4	11	19	34
Joaquin,Waldis											1	1
Johjima,Kenji								20	17	8	7	52
Johnson,Chris											0	0
Johnson,Jim								0	0	8	7	15
Johnson,Josh							1	12	0	6	19	38
Johnson,Kelly								9	19	19	6	53
Johnson,Nick			0	11	14	6	20	25		4	18	98
Johnson,Randy	174	26	26	29	7	21	15	8	4	12	4	326
Johnson,Reed					11	9	10	16	3	13	3	65
Johnson,Rob									0	0	9	9
Jones,Adam								1	0	9	13	23
Jones,Andruw	70	30	22	27	23	17	21	22	15	2	6	255
Jones,Brandon									0	3	0	3
Jones,Chipper	130	27	29	31	26	18	18	22	25	23	20	369
Jones,Garrett										0	10	10
Jones,Hunter											0	0
Jones,Mitch											0	0
Joyce,Matt										6	1	7
Julio,Jorge			1	13	6	8	1	7	4	2	0	42
Jurrjens,Jair									2	11	17	30
Kapler,Gabe	8	10	13	7	4	5	1	2		8	5	63
Karstens,Jeff								3	0	1	2	6
Kata,Matt				8	3	0				1	0	12
Kawakami,Kenshin											7	7
Kazmir,Scott						1	10	13	13	12	6	55
Kearns,Austin				16	12	5	10	17	20	3	2	85
Kelley,Shawn											3	3
Kelly,Don								0			1	1
Kemp,Matt								3	10	19	26	58
Kendall,Jason	73	24	9	14	21	25	14	23	7	19	9	238
Kendrick,Howie								6	9	15	15	45
Kendrick,Kyle									9	3	2	14
Kennedy,Adam	2	11	8	17	13	13	17	15	2	8	18	124
Kennedy,Ian									2	0	0	2
Kensing,Logan						0	0	2	2	3	0	7
Keppel,Bobby									1	0	2	3
Keppinger,Jeff				2				1	9	10	5	27
Kershaw,Clayton										5	12	17
Kilby,Brad											2	2
Kinney,Josh								2		1	0	3
Kinsler,Ian								12	17	24	24	77
Kobayashi,Masa										4	0	4
Konerko,Paul	16	15	17	17	4	20	24	21	16	10	18	178
Korecky,Bobby										1	0	1
Koronka,John						0	4	0				4
Kotchman,Casey						2	4	0	15	14	10	45
Kotsay,Mark	20	12	16	22	13	21	19	11	3	9	4	150
Kottaras,George										0	1	1
Kouzmanoff,Kevin								1	15	14	16	46
Kubel,Jason						3		1	12	12	19	47
Kuo,Hong-Chih							0	3	0	10	3	16
Kuroda,Hiroki										10	5	15
Lackey,John				7	7	10	16	16	21	13	12	102
Laffey,Aaron									3	4	5	12
Laird,Gerald					1	3	1	5	10	9	14	43
Lambert,Chris									0	0	0	0
Langerhans,Ryan				0	0		12	8	5	4	2	31
Lannan,John									2	9	9	20
LaPorta,Matt											3	3
Larish,Jeff										2	0	2
LaRoche,Adam						7	11	16	16	16	17	83
LaRoche,Andy									2	2	12	16
LaRue,Jason	2	3	9	11	10	15	17	5	2	4	1	79
Latos,Mat											1	1
Leach,Brent											1	1

Player	<00	00	01	02	03	04	05	06	07	08	09	Career
League,Brandon			1	0	5	0	4	3				13
LeBlanc,Wade										0	2	2
Ledezma,Wil				2	3	0	4	2	2	0		13
Lee,Carlos	10	14	15	17	20	22	21	22	21	22	18	202
Lee,Cliff			1	3	6	13	10	1	24	17		75
Lee,Derek	13	16	16	22	25	19	34	4	21	17	24	211
Lehr,Justin				2	2	0					2	6
Lerew,Anthony								0	0	0	0	0
Leroux,Chris										0		0
Lester,Jon								5	4	18	17	44
Lewis,Colby				0	1	1				0	0	2
Lewis,Fred								1	5	13	7	26
Lewis,Jensen									4	6	3	13
Lewis,Scott										3	0	3
Lidge,Brad			1	8	22	15	7	10	15	0		78
Lillibridge,Brent										1	1	2
Lilly,Ted	0	0	3	6	10	15	4	11	15	12	14	90
Lincecum,Tim									8	25	22	55
Lincoln,Mike	1	0	4	6	2	1				4	0	18
Lind,Adam								3	7	7	21	38
Lindstrom,Matt									5	6	2	13
Linebrink,Scott		1	1	0	6	10	11	8	5	5	3	50
Liriano,Francisco								0	16	4	2	22
Litsch,Jesse									7	12	0	19
Liz,Radhames									0	0	0	0
Lobaton,Jose										0		0
Loe,Kameron							0	8	2	3	2	15
Logan,Boone								0	3	1	0	4
Lohse,Kyle			3	11	11	6	10	4	9	12	3	69
Loney,James								3	16	14	18	51
Longoria,Evan										19	24	43
Looper,Braden	5	5	7	11	11	13	6	8	6	11	5	88
Lopez,Arturo											0	0
Lopez,Felipe			5	6	3	9	21	16	11	10	23	104
Lopez,Javier						6	0	2	4	6	0	18
Lopez,Jose						3	5	16	10	18	12	64
Lopez,Rodrigo	0		15	2	14	8	4	4			0	47
Lopez,Wilton											0	0
Loretta,Mark	45	12	9	10	25	32	15	17	12	9	3	189
Loux,Shane				0	0					1	1	2
Lowe,Derek	27	19	11	22	12	6	11	15	11	16	7	157
Lowe,Mark								3	0	1	8	12
Lowell,Mike	8	20	20	19	22	22	8	16	23	12	13	183
Lowrie,Jed										7	1	8
Lowry,Noah						1	6	15	7	10		39
Ludwick,Ryan					0	6	0	0	10	24	19	59
Lugo,Julio		9	9	9	15	20	24	13	11	2	9	121
Lyon,Brandon				4	0	5	0	6	11	6	11	43
MacDougal,Mike			1	0	9	0	8	5	0	2	5	30
Macias,Drew									0	0	1	1
Madrigal,Warner										1	0	1
Madson,Ryan					0	9	6	4	5	8	10	42
Mahay,Ron	8	1	2	0	5	8	0	4	7	6	2	43
Maholm,Paul							4	7	5	9	8	33
Maier,Mitch									0	1	9	10
Maine,John						0	0	6	11	7	4	28
Maloney,Matt											1	1
Manship,Jeff											1	1
Manuel,Robert											1	1
Manzella,Tommy											0	0
Marcum,Shaun								1	3	10	12	26
Markakis,Nick								12	20	23	16	71
Marmol,Carlos								1	11	12	10	34
Marquis,Jason		1	8	3	1	14	12	2	8	8	15	72
Marshall,Jay									0	0		0
Marshall,Sean								2	6	4	5	17
Marson,Lou										1	1	2
Marte,Andy							0	4	0	2	3	9
Marte,Damaso	0		1	9	15	9	4	4	5	6	0	53
Marte,Victor											0	0
Martin,J.D.											3	3
Martin,Russell								14	22	20	16	72
Martinez,Carlos			1	0							0	1

454

Player	<00	00	01	02	03	04	05	06	07	08	09	Career
Martinez,Cristhian											1	1
Martinez,Fernando											0	0
Martinez,Joe											0	0
Martinez,Pedro	126	29	12	21	20	16	19	6	2	1	4	256
Martinez,Ramon	5	7	9	9	8	6	2	5	2	0		53
Martinez,Victor				1	3	20	22	18	29	7	21	121
Martis,Shairon										0	2	2
Masset,Nick								1	0	4	10	15
Masterson,Justin										7	5	12
Mastny,Tom								1	4	0		5
Mathieson,Scott							0					0
Mathis,Doug										0	4	4
Mathis,Jeff							0	0	2	7	4	13
Matos,Osiris										0	0	0
Matsui,Hideki					19	28	23	6	16	10	18	120
Matsui,Kaz						13	5	7	14	12	16	67
Matsuzaka,Daisuke									12	16	2	30
Matthews Jr.,Gary	1	1	10	10	9	11	11	21	14	8	10	106
Matusz,Brian											3	3
Mauer,Joe						6	22	30	21	30	32	141
Maxwell,Justin										1	3	4
Mayberry,John											1	1
Maybin,Cameron									0	3	2	5
Maysonet,Edwin										0	2	2
Mazzaro,Vin											2	2
McBride,Macay						0	4	1				6
McCann,Brian							8	22	15	18	20	81
McCarthy,Brandon							5	5	3	1	5	19
McClellan,Kyle										4	6	10
McClung,Seth				2			1	2	0	7	2	14
McCoy,Mike											0	0
McCrory,Bob										0	0	0
McCutchen,Andrew											18	18
McCutchen,Daniel											2	2
McDonald,Darnell				0				0			1	1
McDonald,James										1	3	4
McDonald,John	0	0	0	8	3	1	4	3	8	1	3	28
McGehee,Casey										0	17	17
McGowan,Dustin								0	0	11	5	16
McLouth,Nate							1	2	10	24	19	56
McPherson,Dallas							1	6	3		0	10
Meche,Gil	6	6			9	5	5	8	13	14	5	71
Medders,Brandon							5	6	2	1	7	21
Medlen,Kris											3	3
Meek,Evan										0	4	4
Melancon,Mark											1	1
Meloan,John									0	0	1	1
Mendoza,Luis									2	0	0	2
Meredith,Cla							0	9	5	3	4	21
Messenger,Randy							1	1	3	1	1	7
Meyer,Dan					0				0	0	6	6
Michaels,Jason			0	3	4	10	12	9	7	7	3	55
Mickolio,Kam										0	1	1
Mientkiewicz,Doug	3	0	18	17	20	6	4	8	4	10	1	91
Mijares,Jose										1	8	9
Miles,Aaron					1	12	8	10	10	9	2	52
Millar,Kevin	12	10	20	14	16	17	11	13	12	10	3	138
Milledge,Lastings								4	6	11	4	25
Miller,Andrew								0	2	0	2	4
Miller,Corky			2	5	1	0	0	0	1	1	3	13
Miller,Justin				3		2	0		5	3	5	18
Miller,Trever	6	0			4	4	2	6	2	3	6	33
Mills,Brad											0	0
Millwood,Kevin	35	10	5	19	12	5	14	13	5	6	15	139
Milton,Eric	18	11	15	9	2	9	0	7	1		1	73
Miner,Zach								4	5	8	6	23
Miranda,Juan										1	0	1
Misch,Pat								0	2	1	3	6
Mitre,Sergio						0	0	2	0	4	0	6
Mock,Garrett										2	0	2
Moehler,Brian	36	10	1	2	0		5	0	3	7	2	66
Moeller,Chad		2	0	6	6	5	3	1	0	3	1	27
Molina,Bengie	3	13	7	10	16	11	15	11	13	19	12	130

Player	<00	00	01	02	03	04	05	06	07	08	09	Career
Molina,Jose	0	1	2	2	6	7	5	4	9	4		40
Molina,Yadier						5	14	9	12	15	20	76
Monroe,Craig			1	0	9	11	13	13	3	3	2	55
Montanez,Lou										3	1	4
Montero,Miguel								0	3	4	13	20
Moore,Adam											1	1
Mora,Melvin	0	12	11	16	15	24	20	18	10	17	7	150
Morales,Franklin									4	0	4	8
Morales,Jose										1	4	5
Morales,Kendry								2	2	0	23	27
Moreno,Edwin										0		0
Morgan,Nyjer									4	3	15	22
Morillo,Juan								0	0	0		0
Morneau,Justin					1	9	7	26	18	28	18	107
Morrow,Brandon									5	7	4	16
Morse,Mike							5	2	2	0	2	11
Mortensen,Clayton											0	0
Morton,Charlie										0	4	4
Moscoso,Guillermo											1	1
Mosebach,Bobby											0	0
Moseley,Dustin								0	6	0	1	7
Moss,Brandon									1	5	5	11
Mota,Guillermo	5	1	2	2	14	12		3	3	1	4	51
Motte,Jason										2	2	4
Moyer,Jamie	110	5	15	16	18	8	12	10	8	13	8	221
Moylan,Peter								1	9	1	7	18
Mujica,Edward								1	0	0	4	5
Mulvey,Kevin											0	0
Munson,Eric			0	0	0	8	9	0	1	1	0	19
Murphy,Bill								0			1	1
Murphy,Daniel										6	10	16
Murphy,David								0	5	11	11	27
Murton,Matt							4	13	5	1	1	24
Myers,Brett				3	9	4	14	12	9	7	3	61
Nady,Xavier		0		7	1	8	12	10	20	0		58
Napoli,Mike								10	8	12	10	40
Narveson,Chris								0			2	2
Nathan,Joe	5	2		1	11	19	17	20	16	16	16	123
Navarro,Dioner						0	4	5	6	17	5	37
Nelson,Brad								0			0	0
Nelson,Joe		0				0			5	6	3	14
Neshek,Pat								6	8	1		15
Ni,Fu-Te											3	3
Niemann,Jeff										0	12	12
Niese,Jonathon										0	1	1
Nieve,Fernando								6		0	4	10
Nieves,Wil			1				0	0	1	4	4	10
Nippert,Dustin							1	0	1	1	5	8
Nix,Jayson										1	6	7
Nix,Laynce					4	7	4	0	0	0	6	21
Nolasco,Ricky								5	0	14	6	25
Norris,Bud											3	3
Norton,Greg	16	3	3	3	4	0		9	5	6	1	50
Nunez,Jhonny											0	0
Nunez,Leo							0	1	3	5	9	18
Nunez,Vladimir	5	0	8	14	0	1				2	0	30
O'Day,Darren										2	9	11
Oeltjen,Trent											0	0
O'Flaherty,Eric								0	4	0	4	8
Ohka,Tomo	0	6	2	14	12	5	10	4	1			55
Ohlendorf,Ross									1	0	11	12
Ohman,Will		0	0				4	5	2	5	0	16
Ojeda,Augie		2	2	1	0	3			4	6	5	23
Okajima,Hideki									11	8	7	26
Oliver,Darren	50	0	3	3	10	1		6	5	9	9	96
Olivo,Miguel				1	8	7	7	13	7	7	9	59
Olsen,Scott							1	10	1	8	1	21
Olson,Garrett									0	1	1	2
Ordonez,Magglio	36	22	25	25	23	8	10	19	34	16	13	231
Orr,Pete							3	2	0	1	1	7
Ortega,Anthony											0	0
Ortiz,David	11	8	7	11	14	24	30	27	27	15	11	185
Ortiz,Russ	15	7	15	13	16	12	0	1	1		1	81

Player	<00	00	01	02	03	04	05	06	07	08	09	Career
O'Sullivan,Sean											2	2
Oswalt,Roy			15	20	10	18	21	20	17	16	9	146
Outman,Josh										1	4	5
Overbay,Lyle			0	0	6	17	17	17	6	14	12	89
Owens,Henry									0	3		3
Owens,Jerry								0	6	0	0	6
Owings,Micah									13	2	4	19
Padilla,Jorge											0	0
Padilla,Vicente	0	6	3	14	13	5	6	12	2	8	8	77
Pagan,Angel								3	5	3	12	23
Pagnozzi,Matt											0	0
Palmer,Matt										0	10	10
Papelbon,Jonathan							4	19	15	15	15	68
Parisi,Mike										0		0
Park,Chan Ho	39	18	16	5	0	4	5	4	0	6	4	101
Parnell,Bobby										0	2	2
Paronto,Chad			0	2	0			4	3	0	0	9
Parr,James										1	0	1
Parra,Gerardo											9	9
Parra,Manny									2	8	0	10
Patterson,Corey		0	3	8	13	17	4	13	8	2	0	68
Patterson,Eric									0	2	3	5
Patton,David											0	0
Patton,Troy									1			1
Paul,Xavier											0	0
Paulino,Felipe										0	0	0
Paulino,Ronny							0	14	10	3	8	35
Pavano,Carl	9	8	0	3	9	19	3		1	1	7	60
Pearce,Steve									2	2	2	6
Peavy,Jake				3	7	15	16	12	21	13	6	93
Pedroia,Dustin								2	18	26	24	70
Pelfrey,Mike								0	1	12	4	17
Pena,Brayan							0	1	0	0	2	3
Pena,Carlos			3	11	9	11	7	0	28	22	17	108
Pena,Ramiro											4	4
Pena,Tony							1	11	6	6		24
Pena,Tony F							0	11	3	1		15
Pence,Hunter									18	19	17	54
Penn,Hayden							0	0				0
Pennington,Cliff										3	7	10
Penny,Brad		5	12	4	10	10	9	11	20	0	7	88
Peralta,Jhonny					5	0	25	15	21	19	10	95
Peralta,Joel						2	5	6	0	0		13
Percival,Troy	61	8	14	13	8	9	2		4	6	0	125
Perdomo,Luis											1	1
Perez,Chris										4	3	7
Perez,Fernando										3	0	3
Perez,Oliver				4	1	16	2	0	10	8	1	42
Perez,Rafael								1	9	8	0	18
Perkins,Glen								1	2	7	2	12
Perry,Ryan											4	4
Petit,Gregorio										1	0	1
Petit,Yusmeiro								0	3	3	1	7
Pettit,Chris											0	0
Pettitte,Andy	72	14	13	11	14	5	21	12	13	10	11	196
Phillips,Brandon				1	4	0	0	14	17	19	19	74
Phillips,Kyle											0	0
Phillips,Paul					0	2	2	0	0	3		7
Pie,Felix									5	2	5	12
Pierre,Juan		3	17	15	20	22	14	15	12	9	12	139
Pierzynski,A.J.	1	3	15	18	22	12	11	14	8	8	10	122
Pineiro,Joel		0	7	14	13	5	3	0	5	3	13	63
Pinto,Renyel								2	4	3	5	14
Podsednik,Scott				0	1	22	13	12	9	1	15	75
Polanco,Placido	5	11	14	16	18	17	22	14	24	15	21	177
Ponson,Sidney	15	11	4	10	16	8	0	3	0	5	0	72
Porcello,Rick											13	13
Poreda,Aaron										1	1	1
Posada,Jorge	31	29	23	22	28	21	19	24	24	5	19	245
Posey,Buster											0	0
Powell,Landon											5	5
Prado,Martin								2	1	9	12	24
Price,David										1	6	7

Player	<00	00	01	02	03	04	05	06	07	08	09	Career
Pridie,Jason										0	0	0
Prior,Mark				8	22	7	12	0				49
Proctor,Scott						1	0	9	6	0		16
Pujols,Albert			29	32	41	37	34	37	32	34	39	315
Punto,Nick			0	0	1	4	6	12	5	10	11	49
Purcey,David										1	0	1
Putz,J.J.					0	3	5	17	20	5	1	51
Qualls,Chad						4	7	9	9	11	8	48
Quentin,Carlos								5	5	23	8	41
Quinlan,Robb					1	8	2	8	1	3	2	25
Quintanilla,Omar							1	0	1	3	1	6
Quintero,Humberto					0	1	1	0	1	3	4	10
Quiroz,Guillermo						0	0	0	1	1	0	2
Raburn,Ryan						0			4	3	9	16
Ramirez,Alexei										18	15	33
Ramirez,Aramis	2	3	27	6	20	19	18	21	21	25	15	177
Ramirez,Edwar									0	5	0	5
Ramirez,Hanley							0	25	27	32	34	118
Ramirez,Horacio				9	5	8	3	0	2	0		27
Ramirez,Manny	140	27	25	29	28	25	33	27	14	31	18	397
Ramirez,Ramon A.										3	1	4
Ramirez,Ramon								7	0	9	8	24
Ramirez,Wilkin											1	1
Ramos,Cesar											1	1
Ransom,Cody			0	0	0	2			2	3	1	8
Rapada,Clay									0	2	0	2
Rasmus,Colby											13	13
Rauch,Jon				0		4	2	8	10	9	7	40
Ray,Chris							4	12	6		0	22
Ray,Robert										1		1
Reddick,Josh										0	0	0
Redding,Tim			2	1	10	1	0		5	6	2	27
Redmond,Mike	16	5	6	13	1	6	7	6	11	3	1	75
Reed,Jeremy					3	9	1	0	4	1		18
Register,Steven										0	0	0
Reimold,Nolan											10	10
Reineke,Chad										1	0	1
Renteria,Edgar	54	15	13	26	25	16	15	19	19	11	10	223
Repko,Jason							5	4	0	0		9
Reyes,Anthony							1	3	0	5	0	9
Reyes,Argenis										1	0	1
Reyes,Dennys	9	2	1	4	0	4	1	9	2	6	3	41
Reyes,Jo-Jo									0	0	0	0
Reyes,Jose				12		4	16	28	24	28	5	117
Reynolds,Greg										0		0
Reynolds,Mark									14	17	20	51
Rhodes,Arthur	35	6	12	11	4	2	6	3		6	7	92
Richar,Danny									3	0	0	3
Richard,Chris		6	12	1	0						0	19
Richard,Clayton										0	8	8
Richardson,Dustin											1	1
Richardson,Kevin										0	0	0
Richmond,Scott										1	3	4
Riggans,Shawn								1	0	4	0	5
Rincon,Juan			0	0	7	12	10	8	2	1	1	41
Rios,Alex						7	9	18	22	20	11	87
Riske,David	0		3	2	10	7	5	4	8	1	0	40
Rivera,Juan			0	1	4	12	9	18	1	4	16	65
Rivera,Mariano	66	16	19	9	17	18	19	16	12	20	15	227
Rivera,Mike			0	1	0			4	0	4	4	13
Rivera,Saul								5	7	6	0	18
Roberts,Brian			3	2	14	16	28	13	22	20	20	138
Roberts,Ryan								0	0	0	8	8
Robertson,David										2	3	5
Robertson,Nate				0	1	8	7	14	8	1	1	40
Robinson,Shane											0	0
Rodney,Fernando				0	1		6	8	3	4	10	32
Rodriguez,Alex	111	37	37	35	31	29	34	25	37	23	23	422
Rodriguez,Fernando											0	0
Rodriguez,Francisco				1	9	17	14	17	15	16	10	99
Rodriguez,Guillermo									3	0		3
Rodriguez,Henry										0	0	0
Rodriguez,Ivan	169	19	18	11	25	22	10	24	12	11	5	326

WIN SHARES BY YEAR

Player	<00	00	01	02	03	04	05	06	07	08	09	Career
Rodriguez,Luis							6	1	1	4	4	16
Rodriguez,Rafael											0	0
Rodriguez,Sean										3	0	3
Rodriguez,Wandy							2	2	7	9	16	36
Roenicke,Josh										0	1	1
Rogers,Esmil											0	0
Rohlinger,Ryan										0	0	0
Rolen,Scott	76	18	29	26	24	35	5	21	11	11	17	273
Rollins,Jimmy		1	20	17	18	24	21	25	28	24	19	197
Romero,Alex										1	2	3
Romero,J.C.	1	0	1	14	3	8	5	0	8	7	1	48
Romero,Niuman											0	0
Romero,Ricky											10	10
Romo,Sergio										4	4	8
Rosa,Carlos										0	1	1
Rosales,Adam										0	3	3
Rosales,Leo										2	2	4
Rosario,Francisco									0	0		0
Ross,Cody				1		0	6	10	16	16		49
Ross,David				1	4	2	3	13	7	5	6	41
Rowand,Aaron			5	7	6	20	18	7	21	14	15	113
Rowland-Smith,Ryan									2	9	7	18
Ruiz,Carlos								2	13	6	13	34
Ruiz,Randy										2	3	5
Rundles,Rich										1	0	1
Runzler,Dan											1	1
Rupe,Josh								1	2	3	0	6
Rusch,Glendon	10	11	6	7	0	10	6	0		3	0	53
Russell,Adam										2	1	3
Ryal,Rusty											2	2
Ryan,B.J.	2	2	3	3	6	11	14	19	0	10	0	70
Ryan,Brendan									5	2	14	21
Ryan,Dusty										3	1	4
Rzepczynski,Marc											4	4
Sabathia,CC			12	13	13	11	12	15	24	23	18	141
Sadler,Billy								0		2	0	2
Sadowski,Ryan											1	1
Saito,Takashi								18	17	9	6	50
Salazar,Jeff								2	4	3	0	9
Salazar,Óscar				1						3	7	11
Saltalamacchia,J									5	6	6	17
Samardzija,Jeff										3	0	3
Sammons,Clint									0	0	0	0
Sampson,Chris								4	5	7	3	19
Sanches,Brian								0	0	0	6	6
Sanchez,Anibal								10	1	0	5	16
Sanchez,Duaner				0	0	6	7	6	4	0		23
Sanchez,Freddy				0	1	0	12	23	21	11	13	81
Sanchez,Gaby										1	1	2
Sanchez,Jonathan								2	0	6	7	15
Sandoval,Freddy										0	0	0
Sandoval,Pablo										6	27	33
Santana,Ervin							6	12	3	19	6	46
Santana,Johan		2	2	10	16	26	23	24	17	21	14	155
Santiago,Ramon			4	5	0	0	1	2	6	7		25
Santos,Omir									0	0	7	7
Sardinha,Dane				0		0				1	1	2
Sarfate,Dennis								0	2	4	1	7
Saunders,Joe							0	4	7	18	11	40
Saunders,Michael											1	1
Scales,Bobby											2	2
Schafer,Jordan											2	2
Scherzer,Max										4	9	13
Schierholtz,Nate									2	3	8	13
Schilling,Curt	123	16	24	24	15	21	4	15	10			252
Schlereth,Daniel											0	0
Schlichting,Travis											0	0
Schmidt,Jason	34	1	9	10	23	19	9	15	0	0		120
Schneider,Brian		1	2	7	13	17	16	9	11	10	4	90
Schoeneweis,Scott	1	6	9	5	3	4	6	6	2	4	0	46
Schumaker,Skip							0	0	7	16	18	41
Scott,Luke							0	11	11	11	11	44
Scutaro,Marco				0	2	11	11	11	8	15	21	79

WIN SHARES BY YEAR

Player	<00	00	01	02	03	04	05	06	07	08	09	Career
Seay,Bobby		0		1	2	0	0	6	3	6		18
Segovia,Zack									0	0		0
Sheets,Ben			6	8	10	21	11	7	10	15		88
Sheffield,Gary	215	31	30	26	34	30	31	4	16	5	8	430
Shell,Steven										6	0	6
Shelton,Chris						0	13	8	1	0		22
Sherrill,George						1	2	3	8	7	13	34
Shields,James							6	12	15	11		44
Shields,Scot			2	6	12	11	13	11	8	8	0	71
Shoppach,Kelly							0	3	7	14	7	31
Shouse,Brian	0			0	6	6	2	3	5	6	2	30
Silva,Carlos			7	5	14	14	2	11	0	0		53
Silva,Walter										1		1
Simon,Alfredo										0	0	0
Sipp,Tony											3	3
Sizemore,Grady						5	24	24	29	26	13	121
Slaten,Doug								1	4	1	0	6
Slowey,Kevin									3	10	5	18
Smith,Chris										0	2	2
Smith,Jason		0	0	0	2	1	3	2	0	0		8
Smith,Joe									3	6	2	11
Smith,Seth									1	3	14	18
Smoltz,John	181		8	17	16	16	19	15	14	2	1	289
Snell,Ian						0	1	8	11	2	5	27
Snider,Travis										3	4	7
Snyder,Chris						2	4	7	16	15	3	47
Sonnanstine,Andy									3	10	0	13
Soria,Joakim									13	17	12	42
Soriano,Alfonso	0	0	16	28	27	16	16	26	20	16	10	175
Soriano,Rafael			1	7	0	1	7	9	2	12		39
Sosa,Jorge				2	5	3	14	2	6	0		32
Soto,Geovany							0	0	3	21	8	32
Sowers,Jeremy								7	0	2	3	12
Span,Denard										16	21	37
Speier,Justin	1	7	5	7	8	7	7	6	7	2	2	59
Speier,Ryan								2		2	3	7
Spilborghs,Ryan							0	3	9	8	7	27
Springer,Russ	20	3	0		0	1	3	5	8	6	3	49
Stairs,Matt	61	10	11	7	12	11	14	7	13	6	3	155
Stammen,Craig											3	3
Stansberry,Craig									0	1	0	1
Stark,Denny	0		0	10	2	0					0	12
Stauffer,Tim							0	1	0		3	4
Stavinoha,Nick										0	1	1
Stetter,Mitch									1	3	4	8
Stevens,Jeff											0	0
Stewart,Ian									1	9	11	21
Stokes,Brian								1	0	3	4	8
Stoner,Tobi											1	1
Street,Huston							16	14	10	10	15	65
Strop,Pedro										0	0	0
Stubbs,Drew											5	5
Stults,Eric								1	1	2	2	6
Sullivan,Cory							10	6	4	0	4	24
Suppan,Jeff	19	12	12	9	13	9	13	12	9	5	2	115
Sutton,Drew											3	3
Suzuki,Ichiro			36	26	23	27	22	24	33	19	28	238
Suzuki,Kurt									7	17	17	41
Swarzak,Anthony											0	0
Sweeney,Mike	33	26	18	18	14	14	16	5	5	3	6	158
Sweeney,Ryan								0	0	12	12	24
Swindle,R.J.										0	0	0
Swisher,Nick						1	12	20	18	12	18	81
Switzer,Jon					0		0	2	0		0	2
Taguchi,So			1	3	6	12	6	9	1	0		38
Takahashi,Ken											2	2
Tallet,Brian				2	0		0	4	4	5	4	19
Tankersley,Taylor								5	4	0	0	9
Taschner,Jack							3	0	2	2	1	8
Tatis,Fernando	35	11	2	6	1			2		13	8	78
Tatum,Craig											1	1
Tavarez,Julian	26	10	6	2	10	9	6	5	4	1	1	80
Taveras,Willy						0	13	13	11	6	5	48

WIN SHARES BY YEAR

Player	<00	00	01	02	03	04	05	06	07	08	09	Career
Taylor,Graham											0	0
Tazawa,Junichi											0	0
Teagarden,Taylor										4	3	7
Teahen,Mark							9	18	15	11	9	62
Teixeira,Mark					12	24	33	21	25	28	26	169
Tejada,Miguel	28	23	25	32	26	28	26	23	14	14	22	261
Tejeda,Robinson							5	4	0	3	6	18
Thames,Marcus				0	0	6	1	11	6	7	4	35
Thatcher,Joe									2	0	3	5
Thayer,Dale											0	0
Theriot,Ryan							0	6	11	16	17	50
Thole,Josh											2	2
Thomas,Clete										3	7	10
Thome,Jim	141	20	31	33	29	20	4	25	21	17	11	352
Thompson,Brad							5	5	4	3	2	19
Thompson,Rich									0	0	1	1
Thornton,Matt						2	1	7	4	10	12	36
Thurston,Joe			1	0	0		0			0	5	6
Tillman,Chris											2	2
Todd,Jesse											0	0
Tolbert,Matt										3	5	8
Tomko,Brett	25	5	1	6	6	10	8	5	1	1	4	72
Toregas,Wyatt											1	1
Torrealba,Yorvit			1	4	7	4	4	6	6	4	9	45
Torres,Andres				0	0	0	0				8	8
Torres,Carlos											0	0
Towers,Josh			6	0	5	6	13	0	2	0		32
Towles,J.R.									3	2	0	5
Traber,Billy				3			0	1	0	0		4
Tracy,Andy		5	0		0					0	1	6
Tracy,Chad						11	19	14	6	4	3	57
Treanor,Matt						1	2	5	6	5	0	19
Troncoso,Ramon										2	8	10
Tuiasosopo,Matt										0	0	0
Tulowitzki,Troy								1	24	9	24	58
Turner,Justin											0	0
Uehara,Koji											4	4
Uggla,Dan								23	16	24	18	81
Upton,B.J.						4		2	22	23	13	64
Upton,Justin									1	8	19	28
Uribe,Juan			7	10	9	18	17	11	13	11	13	109
Utley,Chase					5	8	25	27	28	30	32	155
Valbuena,Luis										1	6	7
Valdez,Luis											0	0
Valdez,Merkin				0						2	1	3
Valdez,Wilson					1	2		2			1	6
Valverde,Jose					11	3	13	4	14	14	11	70
Van Every,Jonathan										1	1	2
VandenHurk,Rick									0	0	3	3
Vargas,Claudio					7	3	6	7	5	2	4	34
Vargas,Jason							4	1	0		3	8
Varitek,Jason	17	7	8	12	16	18	18	7	14	8	7	132
Vasquez,Esmerling											3	3
Vasquez,Virgil										0	0	0
Vazquez,Javier	8	14	21	13	21	9	12	11	18	11	16	154
Vazquez,Ramon			0	14	10	1	1	1	6	10	3	46
Veal,Donnie											0	0
Velazquez,Gil										0	0	0
Velez,Eugenio									1	4	6	11
Venable,Will										3	8	11
Veras,Jose								1	1	5	2	9
Verlander,Justin							0	15	16	8	21	60
Victorino,Shane				0			1	11	11	20	22	65
Villanueva,Carlos								4	8	6	2	20
Villone,Ron	20	5	3	2	5	6	5	3	2	2	2	55
Viola,Pedro											0	0
Vizcaino,Luis	0	0	2	8	1	6	6	7	6	2	1	39
Vizquel,Omar	138	16	12	21	5	18	20	20	12	5	6	273
Volquez,Edinson							0	0	2	16	2	20
Volstad,Chris										7	4	11
Votto,Joey									3	19	24	46
Waddell,Jason											0	0
Wade,Cory										7	1	8

Player	<00	00	01	02	03	04	05	06	07	08	09	Career
Waechter,Doug					3	1	3	0		4	0	11
Wagner,Billy	50	1	13	16	19	10	18	14	12	10	2	165
Wagner,Ryan					3	2	1	1	0			7
Wainwright,Adam							0	9	13	11	21	54
Wakefield,Tim	70	5	11	15	12	8	15	7	10	10	8	171
Walker,Jamie	2		4	6	6	4	5	8	0	0		35
Walker,Neil											0	0
Walker,Tyler			0			4	7	3	3	4	3	24
Walters,P.J.											0	0
Wang,Chien-Ming							7	16	15	7	0	45
Washburn,Jarrod	7	7	15	18	9	8	14	7	10	5	14	114
Waters,Chris										2	0	2
Weathers,David	18	7	10	7	8	5	8	10	13	6	4	96
Weaver,Jeff	7	12	13	14	2	11	13	3	1		5	81
Weaver,Jered								14	12	11	17	54
Webb,Brandon					17	11	17	20	22	21	0	108
Webb,Ryan											1	1
Weeks,Rickie						0	9	10	14	16	7	56
Wellemeyer,Todd					0	1	0	4	4	12	0	21
Wells,Kip	3	2	6	13	15	6	3	0	2	1	2	53
Wells,Randy										1	13	14
Wells,Vernon	1	0	3	18	26	13	20	24	15	15	8	143
Werth,Jayson				1	1	11	9		13	17	26	78
West,Sean											4	4
Westbrook,Jake		0	2	1	6	15	8	13	9	3		57
Wheeler,Dan	1	1	0		3	3	10	12	4	12	6	52
Whisler,Wes										0		0
White,Sean									1		8	9
Whitesell,Josh										0	2	2
Whiteside,Eli							0				3	3
Wieters,Matt											9	9
Wigginton,Ty				3	14	10	4	13	11	14	4	73
Williams,Randy					0	1					1	2
Willingham,Josh						0	0	14	19	13	11	57
Willis,Dontrelle					14	9	22	13	7	0	0	65
Willits,Reggie								1	14	1	0	16
Wilson,Bobby										0	0	0
Wilson,Brian								1	5	9	15	30
Wilson,C.J.							0	3	9	2	11	25
Wilson,Jack			5	12	12	22	14	12	19	7	9	112
Wilson,Josh								0		3	3	6
Wilson,Vance	0	0	1	5	7	5	3	5				26
Winn,Randy	9	2	10	23	21	17	22	13	16	19	16	168
Wise,DeWayne		0	1		3		0	0		2	2	8
Wolf,Randy	4	13	11	15	12	6	4	2	5	7	14	93
Wolfe,Brian									4	2	0	6
Wood,Brandon									0	2	0	2
Wood,Kerry	14	7	13	12	18	9	4	2	2	12	6	99
Wood,Tim											2	2
Woodward,Chris	0	2	1	10	9	4	4	3	1		1	35
Wright,David						9	26	30	34	27	20	146
Wright,Jamey	23	9	7	2	2	5	4	4	5	3	4	68
Wright,Wesley										3	1	4
Wuertz,Mike						2	6	4	6	3	10	31
Yabuta,Yasuhiko										1	0	1
Yates,Tyler							0	3	2	3	0	8
Youkilis,Kevin						8	3	22	20	27	28	108
Young,Chris						2	10	12	12	5	1	42
Young,Chris B.								2	14	17	8	41
Young,Delmon								2	17	13	7	39
Young,Delwyn								0	2	1	8	11
Young,Dmitri	31	14	13	5	19	8	9	2	16	2		119
Young,Michael		0	7	11	22	25	29	26	23	20	17	180
Young Jr.,Eric											0	0
Zambrano,Carlos			0	5	18	20	18	17	16	16	10	120
Zaun,Gregg	21	9	4	2	2	11	14	8	9	8	7	95
Zavada,Clay											4	4
Ziegler,Brad										12	7	19
Zimmerman,Ryan							2	24	20	9	21	76
Zimmermann,Jordan											3	3
Zito,Barry		9	15	25	18	12	13	17	8	5	10	132
Zobrist,Ben								2	1	8	27	38
Zumaya,Joel								12	3	1	2	18

Instant Replay Analysis

Major League Baseball introduced instant replay late in the summer of 2008. Umpires were instructed to consult instant replay on disputable home run calls to determine whether the ball left the playing field, was fair or foul, or was interfered with by a fan. In just over one year (parts of two seasons), instant replay has been used 65 times. Twenty-two calls have been overturned.

The chart below summarizes the results. About a third of all plays reviewed have been overturned. That's hugely significant, especially when we keep in mind that these are limited to home runs calls.

The next page provides the details of each and every instant replay review in 2008 and 2009.

Instant Replay Summary

Season	Instant Replays	Calls Overturned	Percentage
2008	7	2	29%
2009	58	20	34%
Totals	65	22	34%

Instant Replay History

Date	Matchup	Pitcher	Hitter	Inning	Outs	Men On	Score	Initial Ruling	Video Ruling
9/3/2008	NYA@TB	Troy Percival	Alex Rodriguez	9	2	1	6-3	HR	HR
9/9/2008	PIT@HOU	Jesse Chavez	Hunter Pence	6	2	2	8-2	2B	2B
9/19/2008	MIN@TB	Boof Bonser	Carlos Pena	4	2	2	6-0	Fan Int	HR
9/23/2008	CIN@HOU	Chris Sampson	Joey Votto	7	2	1	2-1	1B	1B
9/24/2008	LAA@SEA	Felix Hernandez	Vladimir Guerrero	5	1	0	2-2	Foul	Foul
9/26/2008	WAS@PHI	Joe Blanton	Kory Casto	6	2	0	3-7	HR	HR
9/26/2008	LAN@SF	Scott Proctor	Bengie Molina	6	1	1	0-2	1B	HR
4/19/2009	CLE@NYA	Jensen Lewis	Jorge Posada	7	1	1	2-3	HR	HR
4/22/2009	OAK@NYA	CC Sabathia	Kurt Suzuki	2	0	2	0-0	HR	HR
4/24/2009	SF@ARI	Tim Lincecum	Eric Byrnes	3	2	0	0-1	2B	2B
4/25/2009	SEA@LAA	Carlos Silva	Gary Matthews Jr.	3	0	0	0-3	Fan Int	Fan Int
4/29/2009	FLA@NYN	Josh Johnson	Fernando Tatis	6	0	0	2-2	HR	HR
5/13/2009	FLA@MIL	Braden Looper	Ross Gload	6	2	1	5-8	HR	Foul
5/13/2009	STL@PIT	Joel Pineiro	Adam LaRoche	1	2	1	0-0	HR	2B
5/23/2009	TEX@HOU	Scott Feldman	Miguel Tejada	1	1	0	0-0	HR	HR
5/23/2009	NYN@BOS	Jonathan Papelbon	Omir Santos	9	2	1	1-2	2B	HR
5/24/2009	NYN@BOS	Tim Redding	Kevin Youkilis	5	0	0	3-5	Foul	Foul
5/25/2009	WAS@NYN	John Lannan	Gary Sheffield	6	0	2	1-1	HR	HR
5/27/2009	WAS@NYN	Jordan Zimmermann	Daniel Murphy	6	0	1	3-3	2B	2B
5/28/2009	TB@CLE	Jensen Lewis	Willy Aybar	6	1	0	0-2	HR	HR
6/3/2009	BAL@SEA	Jason Vargas	Aubrey Huff	1	2	1	0-0	HR	Foul
6/4/2009	BOS@DET	Tim Wakefield	Jeff Larish	6	1	1	3-6	Foul	Foul
6/6/2009	TEX@BOS	Derek Holland	Mike Lowell	2	1	0	0-0	2B	HR
6/9/2009	SEA@BAL	Jason Vargas	Melvin Mora	1	2	1	1-0	HR	Fan Int
6/9/2009	LAA@TB	James Shields	Howie Kendrick	5	0	0	2-0	3B	3B
6/10/2009	PIT@ATL	Jeff Karstens	Brian McCann	6	2	1	0-2	2B	2B
6/13/2009	CIN@KC	Bronson Arroyo	Billy Butler	4	0	0	5-3	Foul	Foul
6/19/2009	MIL@DET	Braden Looper	Dusty Ryan	4	2	1	3-4	HR	2B
6/19/2009	MIL@DET	Braden Looper	Miguel Cabrera	3	2	0	2-3	HR	HR
6/21/2009	LAN@LAA	John Lackey	James Loney	8	2	1	2-0	HR	HR
6/25/2009	PHI@TB	Jack Taschner	Pat Burrell	7	2	1	10-4	GR 2B	GR 2B
7/1/2009	SEA@NYA	Jarrod Washburn	Melky Cabrera	5	1	0	1-1	HR	HR
7/3/2009	HOU@SF	Felipe Paulino	Travis Ishikawa	2	2	2	6-0	2B	HR
7/6/2009	PIT@HOU	Virgil Vasquez	Geoff Blum	1	2	2	0-0	3B	3B
7/12/2009	WAS@HOU	Jordan Zimmermann	Carlos Lee	4	0	1	1-0	Foul	Foul
7/17/2009	LAA@OAK	Trevor Cahill	Kendry Morales	2	1	0	0-0	HR	HR
7/19/2009	MIN@TEX	Francisco Liriano	Andruw Jones	4	1	0	1-3	HR	Foul
7/20/2009	CIN@LAN	Jason Schmidt	Willy Taveras	1	0	0	0-0	3B	3B
7/22/2009	MIL@PIT	Jeff Suppan	Ryan Doumit	3	1	0	4-2	2B	HR
7/29/2009	WAS@MIL	Garrett Mock	Ryan Braun	3	1	1	0-4	HR	3B
7/29/2009	PHI@ARI	Tyler Walker	Gerardo Parra	8	0	0	3-0	2B	2B
7/31/2009	BOS@BAL	John Smoltz	Nolan Reimold	3	1	1	1-3	HR	HR
8/2/2009	LAA@MIN	Shane Loux	Joe Mauer	8	2	0	4-13	2B	2B
8/10/2009	CHN@COL	Esmailin Caridad	Troy Tulowitzki	2	2	3	4-0	Foul	Foul
8/11/2009	PHI@CHN	Angel Guzman	Carlos Ruiz	9	2	0	3-2	HR	Foul
8/11/2009	TOR@NYA	Jesse Carlson	Jorge Posada	8	0	0	4-4	HR	HR
8/14/2009	NYA@SEA	R. Rowland-Smith	Jorge Posada	2	0	0	0-2	2B	2B
8/16/2009	HOU@MIL	Braden Looper	Hunter Pence	6	1	0	4-2	HR	Foul
8/20/2009	MIN@TEX	Bobby Keppel	Michael Young	6	1	1	7-1	2B	2B
8/25/2009	DET@LAA	John Lackey	Curtis Granderson	7	0	0	3-3	3B	3B
8/25/2009	TEX@NYA	Kevin Millwood	Robinson Cano	4	0	0	4-7	HR	HR
8/26/2009	OAK@SEA	Luke French	Jack Cust	6	1	0	3-4	Foul	Video
8/28/2009	OAK@LAA	Craig Breslow	Kendry Morales	6	2	1	1-6	Foul	Foul
8/28/2009	NYN@CHN	Pat Misch	Aramis Ramirez	6	0	0	1-1	Foul	Foul
8/31/2009	PIT@CIN	Paul Maholm	Brandon Phillips	5	0	0	4-0	HR	Foul
9/5/2009	NYA@TOR	Andy Pettitte	Randy Ruiz	2	0	0	0-1	HR	Foul
9/10/2009	ATL@HOU	Derek Lowe	Lance Berkman	3	1	2	1-6	HR	HR
9/10/2009	DET@KC	Eddie Bonine	Alberto Callaspo	8	1	0	6-4	HR	HR
9/12/2009	SEA@TEX	Brandon Morrow	Chris Davis	5	0	0	2-5	HR	GR 2B
9/22/2009	SF@ARI	Matt Cain	Gerardo Parra	3	1	1	5-4	HR	2B
9/23/2009	SF@ARI	Jonathan Sanchez	Rusty Ryal	6	1	1	0-3	3B	3B
9/27/2009	SD@ARI	Edward Mujica	Chad Tracy	6	1	0	2-3	HR	HR
9/29/2009	ARI@SF	Jonathan Sanchez	Ryan Roberts	4	2	0	1-2	HR	GR 2B
9/30/2009	NYN@WAS	John Lannan	Jeff Francoeur	2	0	1	0-0	2B	2B
9/30/2009	HOU@PHI	Pedro Martinez	J.R. Towles	2	0	0	1-1	2B	HR

What Happened to the Young Talent Inventory?

Bill James

For the last two years we have included in these pages something called the "Young Talent Inventory." I have decided that the Young Talent Inventory does not really belong in this book, and we have decided to move it to the *Bill James Gold Mine,* which is another book that we do which comes out toward spring.

There are three reasons why the Young Talent Inventory does not belong in this book. First, this is a book of facts, as opposed to a book of analysis that is in any way speculative. We try to make a record of the season, and we try to include information that has never been seen before, and we try to pull that together as quickly as we can so that we can make it available to you while the breath of the season still hangs in the air.

But "Who has the most young talent?" is not really an objective question. We have tried to *make* it an objective question, but…it isn't. It is question requiring judgment. This is not a book of judgments; this is a book of facts.

Second, the work process necessary for this book is not compatible with the needs of the Young Talent Inventory. This book is pulled together at a breakneck pace in the ten days following the end of the regular season. There is not a lot of room here for contemplation and review—and wouldn't be, even if that was all we were trying to do.

But a question like "Who has more young talent, Cleveland or Minnesota?" is a question requiring some pondering. You need to look at your answer and ask, "Is that reasonable, and if not, what can we do to improve it?" We have a method to study this question as objectively as we can, but that method needs to evolve over time. We were not doing justice to that process by slapping the data out as quickly as we can without time to reflect or make adjustments.

Third, the issue of which team owns the most talent is a forward-looking question, the sort of thing that one asks in the spring, as the season is getting underway: Who owns the future?

Of course baseball fans care about the future of their franchise as much in the fall as they do in the spring; I'm not suggesting that they don't. But I think it's a question that is more naturally asked in a spring annual than in a fall summary, and we're going to move it over there where it belongs. I hope you understand.

Hitter Projections

Bill James

Johnny Carson, in the thirty years that he ruled late-night television, used to do a bit called "Carnac" or "Carnac the Magnificent". Carnac was a mystic and seer who knew the answers to questions before the questions were even asked, but it was a transparent charade, which was really just a way of telling jokes backward. That is, rather than asking "What is the difference between Brad Lidge and a serial arsonist?" and then saying "Red pinstripes", he would hold the envelope to his temple and say "Red pinstripes", then open the envelope and read the "question".

This is rather like Carnac. We are in the business of projecting next year's performance, but our pose as prophets is a transparent charade, by which we don't really intend to fool anyone.   And, to ensure that we don't fool anyone, let us begin by looking back at some of last season's projections. We had projected that Eric Chavez would play in 144 games and hit 25 homers, driving in 87 runs. He missed those numbers by. . .well, all of them:

Eric Chavez

	G	AB	R	H	D	T	HR	RBI	BB	SO	SB	Avg	Slg
Actual	8	30	0	3	1	0	0	1	1	7	0	100	133
Projected	144	555	80	143	34	1	25	87	67	117	4	258	458

That was our worst projection of the 2009 Handbook, but only because one can't do much worse.   We did almost as poorly on our projections for Jed Lowrie, Troy Glaus and Joaquin Arias.

Jed Lowrie

	G	AB	R	H	D	T	HR	RBI	BB	SO	SB	Avg	Slg
Actual	32	68	5	10	2	0	2	11	6	20	0	147	265
Projected	148	544	79	150	37	5	10	83	76	114	3	276	417

Troy Glaus

	G	AB	R	H	D	T	HR	RBI	BB	SO	SB	Avg	Slg
Actual	14	29	2	5	2	0	0	2	3	8	0	172	241
Projected	148	539	83	140	29	1	31	97	87	123	1	260	490

Joaquin Arias

	G	AB	R	H	D	T	HR	RBI	BB	SO	SB	Avg	Slg
Actual	3	8	0	0	0	0	0	0	0	3	0	0	0
Projected	138	415	49	116	17	7	5	39	16	48	21	280	390

Those were our four worst projections for 2009, all of which amounted to projecting playing time for players who didn't actually play. Those kind of problems are magnified by a policy that I personally defend, but which most of the people here at BIS don't actually like. I always argue that when a player *might* have playing time, we should project that he *will* have playing time.

It is always my argument that we have no chance of figuring out, in October, 2009, who will get playing time in 2010. We can foresee the broad strokes of that, but we have no chance of guessing right on the small brushwork. We make these projections before the free agent signings, before the trades, before the Arizona Fall League, before spring training. We cannot see through the haze that all of that creates, and we shouldn't try.

What we should do is try to answer this question: If this player plays, how will he play? If Joshua Bell opens the 2010 season as the Baltimore Orioles third baseman, what will he hit? That's the question we should be focused on. Whether Bell will or will not get a chance to play next season, when his chance might come. . .we don't have a fair chance to get that one right. Our job is to figure out how good he will be, when and if his ticket arrives. So sometimes we wind up projecting playing time for players like Joaquin Arias, who then don't play. That's my fault; that's my decision.

Those aren't the only times we miss, of course. Sometimes we project that a player will play, and he does play, but we're just totally wrong about his performance. Like this:

Chris Davis

	G	AB	R	H	D	T	HR	RBI	BB	SO	SB	Avg	Slg
Actual	113	391	48	93	15	1	21	59	24	150	0	238	442
Projected	158	566	107	171	42	3	40	118	43	147	8	302	599

I'm not sure why we had Davis projected to hit .302; that probably wasn't too bright. The 40 homers, I can see; the .302 average, not sure where that came from. But we missed on some other players:

Kelly Johnson

	G	AB	R	H	D	T	HR	RBI	BB	SO	SB	Avg	Slg
Actual	106	303	47	68	20	3	8	29	32	54	7	224	389
Projected	139	518	84	147	34	6	15	67	63	101	10	284	459

Geovany Soto

	G	AB	R	H	D	T	HR	RBI	BB	SO	SB	Avg	Slg
Actual	102	331	27	72	19	1	11	47	50	77	1	218	381
Projected	141	515	71	151	35	1	23	89	62	118	0	293	499

Jay Bruce

	G	AB	R	H	D	T	HR	RBI	BB	SO	SB	Avg	Slg
Actual	101	345	47	77	15	2	22	58	38	75	3	223	470
Projected	159	587	94	174	30	4	35	90	46	145	12	296	540

Garrett Atkins

	G	AB	R	H	D	T	HR	RBI	BB	SO	SB	Avg	Slg
Actual	126	354	37	80	12	1	9	48	41	58	0	226	342
Projected	158	617	90	183	41	1	22	105	57	95	1	297	473

Do you know what's interesting about those four players? They all had *better* strikeout/walk ratios than we had projected—but dramatically less production. Of course, some players also play dramatically *better* than we had projected. Like Scott Podsednik and Russell Branyan:

Russell Branyan

	G	AB	R	H	D	T	HR	RBI	BB	SO	SB	Avg	Slg
Actual	116	431	64	108	21	1	31	76	58	149	2	251	520
Projected	46	122	17	29	7	0	8	20	18	47	1	238	492

Scott Podsednik

	G	AB	R	H	D	T	HR	RBI	BB	SO	SB	Avg	Slg
Actual	132	537	75	163	25	6	7	48	39	74	30	304	412
Projected	69	155	22	41	8	1	1	12	15	27	11	265	348

Ben Zobrist switched power numbers with David Wright:

Ben Zobrist

	G	AB	R	H	D	T	HR	RBI	BB	SO	SB	Avg	Slg
Actual	152	501	91	149	28	7	27	91	91	104	17	297	543
Projected	95	345	53	92	18	3	12	41	48	59	9	267	441

David Wright

	G	AB	R	H	D	T	HR	RBI	BB	SO	SB	Avg	Slg
Actual	144	535	88	164	39	3	10	72	74	140	27	307	447
Projected	160	618	113	192	46	2	33	120	89	116	17	311	552

While Aaron Hill stole the power from Adrian Beltre:

Aaron Hill

	G	AB	R	H	D	T	HR	RBI	BB	SO	SB	Avg	Slg
Actual	158	682	103	195	37	0	36	108	42	98	6	286	499
Projected	126	463	62	132	32	2	9	57	38	62	5	285	421

Adrian Beltre

	G	AB	R	H	D	T	HR	RBI	BB	SO	SB	Avg	Slg
Actual	111	449	54	119	27	0	8	44	19	74	13	265	379
Projected	153	605	82	165	36	2	27	92	47	104	8	273	473

OK, we are often wrong; I wanted to make sure that you got that point. We are not seers or mystics. We just basically predict that players will continue to do well what they have done well in the past. When they do, we're right, and when they don't, we're wrong.

But in any season, the vast majority of players play in a manner that seems a natural extension of what they had done before. When that happens, our projection should be reasonably accurate. As, for example, Evan Longoria, Mark Teixeira, Adam LaRoche and Orlando Hudson:

Evan Longoria

	G	AB	R	H	D	T	HR	RBI	BB	SO	SB	Avg	Slg
Actual	157	584	100	164	44	0	33	113	72	140	9	281	526
Projected	154	599	102	168	39	1	37	116	69	142	9	280	534

Mark Teixeira

	G	AB	R	H	D	T	HR	RBI	BB	SO	SB	Avg	Slg
Actual	156	609	103	178	43	3	39	122	81	114	2	292	565
Projected	154	589	102	176	41	2	36	121	89	110	2	299	559

Adam LaRoche

	G	AB	R	H	D	T	HR	RBI	BB	SO	SB	Avg	Slg
Actual	150	555	78	154	38	2	25	83	69	142	2	277	488
Projected	151	551	76	149	40	1	26	91	60	135	1	270	488

Orlando Hudson

	G	AB	R	H	D	T	HR	RBI	BB	SO	SB	Avg	Slg
Actual	149	551	74	156	35	6	9	62	62	99	8	283	417
Projected	140	533	71	151	32	4	11	59	55	85	6	283	420

We had projected that Mike Lowell would drive in 75 runs, and he did:

Mike Lowell

	G	AB	R	H	D	T	HR	RBI	BB	SO	SB	Avg	Slg
Actual	119	445	54	129	29	1	17	75	33	61	2	290	474
Projected	128	462	59	128	31	0	16	75	42	64	2	277	448

We had projected that Yunel Escobar would hit .300, but he hit only .299:

Yunel Escobar

	G	AB	R	H	D	T	HR	RBI	BB	SO	SB	Avg	Slg
Actual	141	528	89	158	26	2	14	76	57	62	5	299	436
Projected	141	533	78	160	30	2	9	63	60	66	5	300	415

We missed Mike Fontenot's batting average by a wide margin, but we had projected that he would hit 9 homers and drive in 43 runs, and he did:

Mike Fontenot

	G	AB	R	H	D	T	HR	RBI	BB	SO	SB	Avg	Slg
Actual	135	377	38	89	22	2	9	43	35	83	4	236	377
Projected	118	358	54	103	24	3	9	43	41	65	4	288	447

We projected that Freddy Sanchez would hit .293, and he did. We had projected that Scott Hairston would hit .265, and he did:

Freddy Sanchez

	G	AB	R	H	D	T	HR	RBI	BB	SO	SB	Avg	Slg
Actual	111	457	56	134	29	3	7	41	22	76	5	293	416
Projected	148	557	73	163	36	2	8	62	29	64	1	293	408

Scott Hairston

	G	AB	R	H	D	T	HR	RBI	BB	SO	SB	Avg	Slg
Actual	116	430	50	114	27	2	17	64	25	83	11	265	456
Projected	121	385	56	102	22	3	19	48	35	84	3	265	486

We projected that Mike Cameron would hit 32 doubles, 3 triples and 24 homers, and he did:

Mike Cameron

	G	AB	R	H	D	T	HR	RBI	BB	SO	SB	Avg	Slg
Actual	149	544	78	136	32	3	24	70	75	156	7	250	452
Projected	145	558	82	132	32	3	24	80	67	173	18	237	434

Despite their up-and-down seasons we had good projections for Mark Teahen, Nelson Cruz and Jeff Francoeur:

Mark Teahan

	G	AB	R	H	D	T	HR	RBI	BB	SO	SB	Avg	Slg
Actual	144	524	69	142	34	1	12	50	37	123	8	271	408
Projected	139	494	67	135	31	5	12	61	50	113	6	273	429

Nelson Cruz

	G	AB	R	H	D	T	HR	RBI	BB	SO	SB	Avg	Slg
Actual	128	462	75	120	21	1	33	76	49	118	20	260	524
Projected	124	443	74	123	25	2	28	84	50	106	18	278	533

Jeff Francoeur

	G	AB	R	H	D	T	HR	RBI	BB	SO	SB	Avg	Slg
Actual	157	593	72	166	32	4	15	76	23	92	6	280	423
Projected	139	496	65	135	29	2	16	76	30	93	2	272	435

And Matt Holliday:

Matt Holliday

	G	AB	R	H	D	T	HR	RBI	BB	SO	SB	Avg	Slg
Actual	156	581	94	182	39	3	24	109	72	101	14	313	515
Projected	154	605	111	192	43	4	29	108	66	116	19	317	545

We had good projections for Juan Pierre and Andruw Jones:

Andruw Jones

	G	AB	R	H	D	T	HR	RBI	BB	SO	SB	Avg	Slg
Actual	82	281	43	60	18	0	17	43	45	72	5	214	459
Projected	101	301	45	70	14	1	16	50	37	80	2	233	445

Juan Pierre

	G	AB	R	H	D	T	HR	RBI	BB	SO	SB	Avg	Slg
Actual	145	380	57	117	16	8	0	31	27	27	30	308	392
Projected	117	394	54	115	14	4	1	26	23	24	34	292	355

These projections have been marinated for weeks on Funk and Wagnalls porch. We've been doing this for almost twenty years now, and, in our mystical and borderline divine manner, we have not yet learned to miss them all.

Is that all, moose breath?

2010 Hitter Projections

Hitter	Team	Age	G	AB	H	2B	3B	HR	R	RBI	RC	RC27	BB	SO	SB	CS	SB%	Avg	OBP	Slg	OPS
Abreu,Bobby	LAA	36	157	606	173	38	2	18	103	101	106	6.24	101	127	25	9	.74	.285	.389	.444	.833
Alfonzo,Eliezer	SD	31	64	189	49	10	0	7	19	25	23	4.27	6	48	1	0	1.00	.259	.286	.423	.709
Allen,Brandon	Ari	24	122	398	108	23	3	19	59	60	65	5.79	40	87	6	2	.75	.271	.338	.485	.823
Alonso,Yonder	Cin	23	94	258	72	27	0	6	26	32	42	5.84	32	36	3	1	.75	.279	.359	.453	.812
Anderson,Brian	Bos	28	84	161	39	9	0	6	22	18	20	4.19	14	40	2	2	.50	.242	.311	.410	.721
Anderson,Garret	Atl	38	129	447	124	25	1	13	51	67	60	4.81	24	68	2	1	.67	.277	.316	.425	.741
Anderson,Josh	KC	27	81	188	52	7	2	1	25	14	22	4.09	10	26	16	4	.80	.277	.317	.351	.668
Andino,Robert	Bal	26	77	176	42	8	1	3	21	14	17	3.23	12	39	5	3	.62	.239	.287	.347	.634
Andrus,Elvis	Tex	21	155	499	138	19	6	6	77	49	65	4.56	40	79	41	10	.80	.277	.335	.375	.710
Ankiel,Rick	StL	30	118	375	95	19	1	18	53	59	52	4.79	29	87	3	2	.60	.253	.310	.453	.764
Arencibia,JP	Tor	24	114	383	86	24	1	17	44	53	41	3.59	15	96	0	0	.00	.225	.254	.426	.679
Atkins,Garrett	Col	30	131	435	124	27	1	14	60	70	68	5.68	43	68	1	0	1.00	.285	.353	.448	.802
Aubrey,Michael	Bal	28	68	200	54	14	0	5	20	27	26	4.63	12	23	1	0	1.00	.270	.311	.415	.726
Aurilia,Rich	SF	38	71	152	39	7	0	4	17	19	18	4.14	11	25	0	0	.00	.257	.311	.382	.693
Avila,Alex	Det	23	57	168	43	11	0	7	25	28	26	5.37	25	39	1	1	.50	.256	.352	.446	.799
Aviles,Mike	KC	29	120	435	121	25	3	10	56	51	56	4.59	20	56	7	3	.70	.278	.310	.418	.728
Aybar,Erick	LAA	26	139	520	151	25	6	6	75	57	67	4.61	28	55	18	9	.67	.290	.330	.396	.726
Aybar,Willy	TB	27	85	217	56	12	0	7	25	29	29	4.65	24	32	1	1	.50	.258	.340	.410	.750
Baker,Jeff	ChC	29	114	322	90	21	2	11	45	47	50	5.58	27	72	2	1	.67	.280	.337	.460	.797
Baker,John	Fla	29	118	422	113	27	1	9	58	56	57	4.78	45	94	1	1	.50	.268	.341	.400	.742
Baldelli,Rocco	Bos	28	69	178	47	9	1	7	26	25	24	4.73	11	42	2	1	.67	.264	.321	.444	.765
Balentien,Wladimir	Cin	25	70	160	39	9	0	7	23	22	22	4.69	17	40	2	1	.67	.244	.316	.431	.748
Barajas,Rod	Tor	34	114	366	85	20	0	14	41	52	40	3.70	20	67	0	0	.00	.232	.278	.402	.679
Bard,Josh	Was	32	84	232	56	15	0	4	21	27	26	3.84	23	41	0	0	.00	.241	.313	.358	.670
Barmes,Clint	Col	31	134	474	123	29	2	14	61	51	57	4.15	23	88	9	6	.60	.259	.301	.418	.719
Bartlett,Jason	TB	30	146	540	157	31	4	8	82	54	78	5.17	48	89	24	9	.73	.291	.355	.407	.763
Barton,Daric	Oak	24	79	205	52	14	1	5	32	27	29	4.90	31	33	1	1	.50	.254	.357	.405	.762
Bautista,Jose	Tor	29	121	369	89	21	1	13	51	48	49	4.52	48	90	3	2	.60	.241	.335	.409	.744
Bay,Jason	Bos	31	153	560	150	32	2	32	99	103	104	6.53	88	159	11	4	.73	.268	.374	.504	.878
Beckham,Gordon	CWS	23	155	576	166	44	1	21	93	96	97	6.08	59	89	10	5	.67	.288	.360	.477	.838
Bell,Joshua	Bal	23	91	347	100	21	2	11	51	61	58	6.06	45	71	2	2	.50	.288	.370	.455	.825
Belliard,Ronnie	LAD	35	132	438	116	28	1	12	53	55	58	4.65	35	83	3	2	.60	.265	.322	.416	.738
Beltran,Carlos	NYM	33	136	522	147	33	2	24	92	91	97	6.64	76	88	17	5	.77	.282	.375	.490	.865
Beltre,Adrian	Sea	31	131	483	130	29	1	17	61	68	67	4.88	32	82	10	4	.71	.269	.321	.439	.760
Berkman,Lance	Hou	34	153	554	157	35	1	31	96	104	115	7.46	109	118	8	4	.67	.283	.406	.518	.924
Betancourt,Yuniesky	KC	28	144	497	134	29	4	7	55	51	57	4.05	19	44	5	3	.62	.270	.298	.386	.684
Blake,Casey	LAD	36	149	517	133	29	2	18	72	68	72	4.85	54	124	3	2	.60	.257	.337	.426	.762
Blalock,Hank	Tex	29	102	337	88	20	1	15	47	51	49	5.10	27	72	2	1	.67	.261	.320	.460	.780
Blanco,Andres	ChC	26	53	172	44	8	1	2	18	15	18	3.60	10	20	3	2	.60	.256	.301	.349	.649
Blanco,Henry	SD	38	82	228	51	11	0	6	22	23	23	3.38	20	52	0	0	.00	.224	.286	.351	.637
Blanks,Kyle	SD	23	142	524	145	23	3	25	79	93	89	6.07	66	140	3	2	.60	.277	.362	.475	.837
Bloomquist,Willie	KC	32	91	212	55	6	1	2	29	16	22	3.55	16	38	11	4	.73	.259	.314	.325	.640
Blum,Geoff	Hou	37	113	306	72	15	1	7	30	36	32	3.56	24	52	0	0	.00	.235	.297	.359	.657
Bonifacio,Emilio	Fla	25	90	231	62	8	3	1	33	15	26	3.89	17	43	12	5	.71	.268	.321	.342	.663
Borbon,Julio	Tex	24	136	522	161	17	6	5	85	47	78	5.42	39	61	42	13	.76	.308	.358	.404	.762
Bourn,Michael	Hou	27	150	575	156	20	8	5	91	37	76	4.57	60	121	54	13	.81	.271	.341	.360	.701
Bradley,Milton	ChC	32	133	467	129	25	1	18	74	64	79	6.02	75	113	5	3	.62	.276	.384	.450	.834
Brantley,Michael	Cle	23	130	526	141	21	1	4	77	43	65	4.27	59	55	48	11	.81	.268	.342	.335	.676
Branyan,Russell	Sea	34	112	412	98	21	1	27	56	67	67	5.53	57	155	2	1	.67	.238	.336	.490	.826
Braun,Ryan	Mil	26	154	615	194	42	6	39	112	119	135	8.22	53	112	17	6	.74	.315	.378	.593	.972
Brignac,Reid	TB	24	104	294	76	19	2	7	37	33	36	4.24	20	57	5	3	.62	.259	.306	.408	.714
Bruce,Jay	Cin	23	152	574	157	29	4	38	92	95	103	6.33	56	126	10	6	.62	.274	.340	.537	.877
Bruntlett,Eric	Phi	32	73	109	24	5	0	1	14	9	9	2.69	11	22	4	2	.67	.220	.303	.294	.597
Buck,John	KC	29	106	355	82	21	1	12	39	50	40	3.80	28	95	1	1	.50	.231	.295	.397	.692
Buck,Travis	Oak	26	60	161	41	10	1	4	21	19	21	4.51	16	31	2	1	.67	.255	.330	.404	.733
Burrell,Pat	TB	33	119	346	82	17	1	17	46	59	54	5.32	62	100	1	0	1.00	.237	.356	.439	.795
Burriss,Emmanuel	SF	25	65	140	36	4	1	1	16	10	14	3.37	10	16	9	4	.69	.257	.320	.321	.642
Buscher,Brian	Min	29	73	174	45	8	0	4	20	22	22	4.40	20	31	1	1	.50	.259	.338	.374	.712
Butler,Billy	KC	24	142	508	151	38	1	17	67	81	87	6.34	50	72	1	0	1.00	.297	.361	.476	.838
Byrd,Marlon	Tex	32	120	480	134	30	2	14	66	64	69	5.13	37	90	7	4	.64	.279	.340	.438	.777
Byrnes,Eric	Ari	34	74	205	51	12	1	7	28	25	26	4.31	15	31	7	3	.70	.249	.316	.420	.735
Cabrera,Asdrubal	Cle	24	157	582	171	41	3	9	96	74	88	5.46	56	95	19	8	.70	.294	.358	.421	.779
Cabrera,Everth	SD	23	145	545	146	29	11	3	90	44	74	4.68	67	117	37	12	.76	.268	.353	.378	.731
Cabrera,Melky	NYY	25	144	471	131	23	2	11	63	62	65	4.91	42	60	10	4	.71	.278	.341	.406	.747
Cabrera,Miguel	Det	27	160	617	196	43	2	36	101	124	137	8.42	73	118	5	2	.71	.318	.394	.569	.963
Cabrera,Orlando	Min	35	160	653	179	38	1	9	85	71	80	4.34	45	72	14	5	.74	.274	.323	.377	.700
Callaspo,Alberto	KC	27	145	529	152	31	5	8	69	57	75	5.15	46	40	3	2	.60	.287	.345	.410	.756
Cameron,Mike	Mil	37	149	561	133	32	3	23	79	74	77	4.62	71	171	11	5	.69	.237	.328	.428	.756
Cano,Robinson	NYY	27	161	624	193	46	3	20	89	87	104	6.23	32	69	4	3	.57	.309	.347	.489	.836
Cantu,Jorge	Fla	28	139	546	151	39	1	18	67	87	79	5.19	37	87	2	1	.67	.277	.328	.451	.779
Cardenas,Adrian	Oak	22	141	458	120	32	2	3	56	55	53	4.02	43	65	8	5	.62	.262	.325	.360	.686
Carp,Mike	Sea	24	92	284	73	15	1	8	37	36	39	4.81	37	63	0	0	.00	.257	.345	.401	.746
Carroll,Brett	Fla	27	77	147	37	9	1	5	20	20	19	4.49	11	34	0	0	.00	.252	.313	.429	.741
Carroll,Jamey	Cle	36	106	226	59	9	1	1	36	18	24	3.69	24	43	3	2	.60	.261	.343	.323	.666
Casilla,Alexi	Min	25	93	279	72	10	2	2	38	24	30	3.66	25	39	15	6	.71	.258	.324	.330	.653
Castillo,Luis	NYM	34	132	465	131	13	2	2	69	34	57	4.35	58	54	16	7	.70	.282	.363	.331	.694
Castro,Jason	Hou	23	97	359	95	15	2	3	46	36	40	3.91	32	54	3	2	.60	.265	.325	.343	.667
Castro,Ramon	CWS	34	60	163	38	9	0	8	19	25	22	4.58	17	43	0	0	.00	.233	.306	.436	.741
Catalanotto,Frank	Mil	36	50	110	30	8	1	2	14	12	16	5.20	10	14	1	0	1.00	.273	.360	.418	.778
Cedeno,Ronny	Pit	27	125	370	94	15	3	9	44	41	42	3.91	22	72	6	3	.67	.254	.299	.384	.683

470

2010 Hitter Projections

Hitter	Team	Age	G	AB	H	2B	3B	HR	R	RBI	RC	RC27	BB	SO	SB	CS	SB%	Avg	OBP	Slg	OPS
Cervelli,Francisco	NYY	24	58	161	45	8	0	3	20	19	20	4.48	11	27	0	0	.00	.280	.326	.385	.711
Chavez,Endy	Sea	32	75	145	39	6	1	1	18	11	16	3.85	10	16	5	2	.71	.269	.316	.345	.661
Chavez,Eric	Oak	32	88	337	84	20	1	15	46	50	50	5.12	41	72	3	1	.75	.249	.332	.448	.781
Chavez,Raul	Tor	37	64	170	40	8	0	2	14	17	14	2.80	7	22	0	0	.00	.235	.266	.318	.583
Choo,Shin-Soo	Cle	27	156	583	171	36	4	19	95	86	103	6.39	77	135	20	7	.74	.293	.383	.467	.850
Church,Ryan	Atl	31	124	409	111	28	1	11	54	57	59	5.10	41	85	5	3	.62	.271	.342	.425	.768
Coghlan,Chris	Fla	25	147	548	170	37	6	10	92	66	96	6.48	64	74	20	7	.74	.310	.385	.454	.840
Colvin,Tyler	ChC	24	52	125	33	6	1	4	16	17	16	4.47	7	24	2	1	.67	.264	.303	.424	.727
Cora,Alex	NYM	34	53	175	43	7	1	1	19	13	16	3.10	13	19	3	2	.60	.246	.323	.314	.637
Coste,Chris	Hou	37	74	191	48	10	0	4	18	23	21	3.82	13	36	0	0	.00	.251	.309	.366	.676
Counsell,Craig	Mil	39	127	342	84	15	2	3	45	25	37	3.70	42	51	4	2	.67	.246	.337	.327	.664
Crawford,Carl	TB	28	140	528	156	24	8	12	82	62	82	5.57	36	84	41	11	.79	.295	.346	.439	.786
Crede,Joe	Min	32	93	285	69	15	0	13	35	42	36	4.33	21	44	0	0	.00	.242	.303	.432	.735
Crisp,Coco	KC	30	113	386	106	22	3	7	59	40	53	4.78	38	57	20	8	.71	.275	.341	.402	.743
Crosby,Bobby	Oak	30	73	175	42	10	1	4	23	20	20	3.88	16	33	2	1	.67	.240	.311	.377	.688
Crowe,Trevor	Cle	26	93	311	81	18	2	3	46	30	38	4.17	35	55	17	7	.71	.260	.335	.360	.695
Cruz,Nelson	Tex	29	145	542	154	29	1	36	89	98	103	6.75	58	130	21	9	.70	.284	.354	.541	.895
Cuddyer,Michael	Min	31	132	473	129	29	4	20	74	72	77	5.79	49	96	5	2	.71	.273	.347	.478	.825
Cust,Jack	Oak	31	141	450	114	20	0	25	75	72	86	6.17	95	153	2	1	.67	.253	.385	.464	.849
Damon,Johnny	NYY	36	149	565	157	31	2	17	99	70	87	5.48	66	93	16	5	.76	.278	.355	.430	.786
Davis,Chris	Tex	24	128	494	141	29	2	30	80	91	90	6.61	42	146	2	1	.67	.285	.343	.534	.877
Davis,Rajai	Oak	29	138	496	141	27	4	4	74	44	65	4.53	37	77	50	18	.74	.284	.339	.379	.718
DeJesus,David	KC	30	147	554	158	32	5	11	82	65	80	5.19	53	83	6	5	.55	.285	.358	.421	.779
Delgado,Carlos	NYM	38	123	411	108	24	1	23	61	79	71	6.09	54	95	1	0	1.00	.263	.361	.494	.855
DeRosa,Mark	StL	35	140	507	132	27	1	17	76	71	69	4.76	51	115	3	2	.60	.260	.335	.418	.753
Desmond,Ian	Was	24	145	518	146	33	3	13	66	52	77	5.25	44	107	25	9	.74	.282	.338	.432	.771
Diaz,Matt	Atl	32	122	325	90	20	2	10	43	46	53	5.99	21	65	8	4	.67	.305	.358	.471	.829
Diaz,Robinzon	Pit	26	54	143	39	7	0	2	11	16	16	4.00	5	10	1	0	1.00	.273	.307	.364	.670
Dickerson,Chris	Cin	28	89	254	70	12	3	7	38	28	41	5.64	38	71	14	5	.74	.276	.372	.429	.801
Dobbs,Greg	Phi	31	104	199	55	10	1	6	24	28	27	4.84	13	33	2	1	.67	.276	.324	.427	.751
Doumit,Ryan	Pit	29	111	403	115	28	1	15	57	62	63	5.65	29	65	4	2	.67	.285	.341	.471	.812
Drew,J.D.	Bos	34	142	498	134	30	3	22	90	76	90	6.39	91	119	3	2	.60	.269	.385	.474	.859
Drew,Stephen	Ari	27	151	585	161	35	10	17	80	71	89	5.42	52	92	5	3	.62	.275	.335	.456	.792
Dukes,Elijah	Was	26	107	346	91	19	3	12	50	55	53	5.28	49	68	9	6	.60	.263	.359	.439	.799
Duncan,Chris	Bos	29	81	197	52	13	1	8	27	31	32	5.74	28	47	0	0	.00	.264	.356	.462	.817
Dunn,Adam	Was	30	159	562	141	30	0	40	94	103	112	6.90	121	183	3	1	.75	.251	.389	.518	.907
Dye,Jermaine	CWS	36	152	571	149	30	1	31	85	92	90	5.53	57	123	2	1	.67	.261	.333	.480	.813
Eckstein,David	SD	35	128	444	120	21	1	3	57	35	49	3.91	34	40	4	2	.67	.270	.337	.342	.680
Ellis,Mark	Oak	32	122	439	113	24	1	11	60	53	54	4.25	38	66	8	4	.67	.257	.324	.392	.715
Ellsbury,Jacoby	Bos	26	157	635	192	32	8	9	106	62	101	5.75	52	73	64	14	.82	.302	.360	.420	.780
Encarnacion,Edwin	Tor	27	129	452	117	28	1	21	64	69	70	5.40	50	91	3	2	.60	.259	.343	.465	.808
Erstad,Darin	Hou	36	73	119	29	6	0	1	15	12	11	3.14	8	24	1	1	.50	.244	.297	.319	.616
Escobar,Alcides	Mil	23	141	504	145	22	4	5	75	48	64	4.49	28	77	42	12	.78	.288	.326	.377	.703
Escobar,Yunel	Atl	27	144	539	163	30	2	12	84	70	86	5.88	61	62	5	4	.56	.302	.381	.432	.813
Ethier,Andre	LAD	28	156	560	161	39	4	24	85	89	100	6.45	64	103	5	4	.56	.288	.368	.500	.868
Everett,Adam	Det	33	97	272	64	14	1	3	33	28	25	3.10	18	46	4	2	.67	.235	.293	.327	.620
Feliz,Pedro	Phi	35	151	573	145	29	2	17	61	80	68	4.13	34	80	0	0	.00	.253	.296	.400	.696
Fielder,Prince	Mil	26	161	601	172	37	2	44	103	124	132	7.96	96	135	3	2	.60	.286	.393	.574	.967
Fields,Josh	CWS	27	80	234	60	12	1	10	33	35	35	5.17	28	69	4	2	.67	.256	.338	.444	.783
Figgins,Chone	LAA	32	154	578	165	25	5	5	97	51	81	4.92	76	105	37	15	.71	.285	.369	.372	.741
Flores,Jesus	Was	25	116	431	114	22	2	13	48	75	57	4.68	35	105	0	0	.00	.265	.323	.415	.738
Flowers,Tyler	CWS	24	67	273	75	17	1	12	40	32	46	6.01	32	85	2	1	.67	.275	.353	.476	.829
Fontenot,Mike	ChC	30	131	359	98	23	2	8	48	42	51	5.04	37	69	4	2	.67	.273	.343	.415	.758
Fowler,Dexter	Col	24	135	451	130	32	9	6	79	43	76	5.95	66	104	28	11	.72	.288	.380	.439	.819
Fox,Jake	ChC	27	78	218	62	16	1	13	33	42	40	6.62	16	44	2	1	.67	.284	.339	.546	.885
Francisco,Ben	Phi	28	124	379	102	26	1	12	54	46	55	5.07	35	70	12	5	.71	.269	.339	.438	.777
Francoeur,Jeff	NYM	26	154	588	162	35	3	18	75	87	79	4.79	30	101	5	3	.62	.276	.318	.437	.755
Frazier,Todd	Cin	24	151	507	141	45	1	17	61	69	79	5.51	44	78	9	7	.56	.278	.336	.471	.807
Fukudome,Kosuke	ChC	33	147	520	138	39	3	13	76	61	80	5.37	79	120	7	5	.58	.265	.365	.427	.792
Fuld,Sam	ChC	28	65	115	30	6	1	1	17	9	14	4.18	14	11	5	2	.71	.261	.346	.357	.703
Furcal,Rafael	LAD	32	139	583	162	28	4	10	94	50	79	4.80	60	83	16	7	.70	.278	.346	.391	.737
Gamel,Mat	Mil	24	124	455	126	28	3	17	65	73	74	5.81	53	142	3	2	.60	.277	.354	.464	.817
Garciaparra,Nomar	Oak	36	60	170	47	10	0	5	22	24	23	4.82	12	20	1	1	.50	.276	.332	.424	.755
Gardner,Brett	NYY	26	104	325	90	11	6	3	63	28	49	5.24	45	58	36	8	.82	.277	.368	.375	.744
Garko,Ryan	SF	29	130	419	118	22	1	16	53	69	65	5.61	37	64	0	0	.00	.282	.357	.453	.810
Gerut,Jody	Mil	32	78	162	42	9	1	5	23	20	21	4.48	14	25	3	2	.60	.259	.326	.420	.746
Getz,Chris	CWS	26	99	364	98	16	2	4	49	33	45	4.30	36	45	20	6	.77	.269	.340	.357	.697
Giambi,Jason	Col	39	71	244	56	10	0	14	37	44	39	5.39	49	65	0	0	.00	.230	.384	.443	.826
Giles,Brian	SD	39	92	292	77	17	1	7	40	36	43	5.18	47	36	2	1	.67	.264	.371	.401	.772
Glaus,Troy	StL	33	147	529	131	27	1	28	79	91	86	5.59	86	131	2	2	.50	.248	.356	.461	.817
Gload,Ross	Fla	34	99	228	64	13	1	5	28	29	31	4.88	16	29	1	1	.50	.281	.333	.412	.746
Gomes,Jonny	Cin	29	103	278	68	17	1	16	40	44	43	5.25	30	89	6	3	.67	.245	.331	.486	.817
Gomez,Carlos	Min	24	140	427	111	21	5	6	64	44	49	3.91	27	90	26	10	.72	.260	.310	.375	.685
Gonzalez,Adrian	SD	28	161	614	171	37	2	35	97	106	117	6.65	87	127	1	0	1.00	.279	.372	.516	.888
Gonzalez,Alberto	Was	27	87	219	58	12	2	2	25	24	24	3.85	13	22	1	1	.50	.265	.312	.365	.677
Gonzalez,Alex	Bos	33	80	230	57	14	0	6	25	28	26	3.89	14	42	1	1	.50	.248	.305	.387	.692
Gonzalez,Carlos	Col	24	143	515	144	35	7	19	78	73	83	5.69	41	107	18	8	.69	.280	.334	.485	.819
Gonzalez,Edgar	SD	32	63	112	30	6	0	3	13	13	15	4.70	11	22	1	1	.50	.268	.344	.402	.746
Gordon,Alex	KC	26	150	536	146	38	2	20	86	76	88	5.81	67	121	12	4	.75	.272	.359	.463	.821
Granderson,Curtis	Det	29	157	615	169	30	11	27	106	76	106	6.10	71	140	17	6	.74	.275	.353	.491	.844
Green,Nick	Bos	31	69	158	39	8	0	4	19	18	17	3.68	11	38	1	1	.50	.247	.312	.373	.686

2010 Hitter Projections

Hitter	Team	Age	G	AB	H	2B	3B	HR	R	RBI	RC	RC27	BB	SO	SB	CS	SB%	Avg	OBP	Slg	OPS
Greene,Khalil	StL	30	66	163	39	10	1	6	20	22	20	4.16	11	35	1	1	.50	.239	.307	.423	.731
Greene,Tyler	StL	26	71	208	52	9	1	6	31	20	25	4.09	15	53	13	3	.81	.250	.307	.389	.696
Griffey Jr.,Ken	Sea	40	83	250	58	12	0	11	30	36	34	4.60	36	52	0	0	.00	.232	.333	.412	.745
Gross,Gabe	TB	30	117	276	68	17	1	8	36	34	38	4.70	39	71	4	2	.67	.246	.342	.402	.744
Guerrero,Vladimir	LAA	35	135	508	155	29	1	24	77	88	93	6.79	46	70	5	3	.62	.305	.369	.508	.876
Guillen,Carlos	Det	34	123	444	124	26	3	13	67	63	69	5.54	54	82	5	4	.56	.279	.361	.439	.800
Guillen,Jose	KC	34	115	392	103	20	1	15	48	60	52	4.66	24	74	1	1	.50	.263	.323	.434	.757
Gutierrez,Franklin	Sea	27	151	556	154	34	2	17	88	67	81	5.16	46	114	14	6	.70	.277	.336	.437	.773
Guzman,Cristian	Was	32	138	550	155	26	5	7	73	49	65	4.24	23	72	5	4	.56	.282	.313	.385	.698
Guzman,Jesus	SF	26	149	544	155	27	3	15	70	74	78	5.19	41	98	2	2	.50	.285	.335	.428	.763
Gwynn,Tony	SD	27	88	212	56	8	2	1	29	14	24	3.90	22	32	10	4	.71	.264	.336	.335	.671
Hafner,Travis	Cle	33	98	309	85	20	0	16	48	55	57	6.62	49	68	0	0	.00	.275	.385	.495	.880
Hairston,Jerry	NYY	34	109	299	78	18	1	6	44	30	37	4.28	25	43	7	4	.64	.261	.328	.388	.716
Hairston,Scott	Oak	30	130	450	122	27	3	20	60	60	69	5.40	34	87	8	4	.67	.271	.325	.478	.803
Hall,Bill	Sea	30	88	218	51	15	1	7	27	27	26	4.00	19	69	3	2	.60	.234	.298	.408	.707
Hamilton,Josh	Tex	29	131	501	147	29	3	23	75	91	89	6.46	48	101	11	4	.73	.293	.359	.501	.860
Hanigan,Ryan	Cin	29	92	314	87	14	1	4	35	27	41	4.70	40	38	0	0	.00	.277	.361	.366	.727
Hannahan,Jack	Sea	30	90	219	53	13	0	4	25	25	25	3.89	28	56	1	1	.50	.242	.331	.356	.687
Hardy,J.J.	Mil	27	141	528	134	28	2	19	70	68	71	4.69	50	92	1	0	1.00	.254	.320	.422	.742
Harris,Brendan	Min	29	103	377	103	24	1	7	47	43	49	4.63	30	68	1	1	.50	.273	.332	.398	.730
Harris,Willie	Was	32	110	264	65	13	2	5	42	22	33	4.21	37	52	10	5	.67	.246	.348	.367	.715
Hart,Corey	Mil	28	143	533	145	37	5	19	78	76	81	5.33	43	110	16	7	.70	.272	.332	.467	.799
Hawpe,Brad	Col	31	151	543	152	36	3	26	79	97	101	6.70	81	153	1	1	.50	.280	.375	.501	.876
Headley,Chase	SD	26	149	528	150	34	3	16	72	72	87	5.94	63	129	8	3	.73	.284	.365	.455	.819
Helms,Wes	Fla	34	110	230	59	13	1	5	22	30	27	4.11	16	58	0	0	.00	.257	.316	.387	.703
Helton,Todd	Col	36	140	506	154	37	1	15	78	74	98	7.24	93	74	0	0	.00	.304	.415	.470	.886
Hermida,Jeremy	Fla	26	152	554	148	30	2	20	77	73	86	5.47	75	135	7	3	.70	.267	.360	.437	.796
Hernandez,Anderson	NYM	27	91	252	62	10	2	2	29	20	24	3.23	18	42	6	3	.67	.246	.296	.325	.622
Hernandez,Ramon	Cin	34	120	435	113	22	1	13	46	64	56	4.51	39	60	1	1	.50	.260	.328	.405	.732
Heyward,Jason	Atl	20	146	542	164	27	5	17	86	78	94	6.40	59	64	11	4	.73	.303	.371	.465	.836
Hill,Aaron	Tor	28	138	540	153	35	1	20	78	76	83	5.55	40	78	5	2	.71	.283	.337	.463	.800
Hill,Koyie	ChC	31	77	218	51	13	0	4	23	24	23	3.58	19	52	1	0	1.00	.234	.295	.349	.644
Hinske,Eric	NYY	32	60	154	38	10	0	6	23	21	22	4.89	20	40	2	1	.67	.247	.348	.429	.777
Hoffpauir,Micah	ChC	30	74	156	43	10	1	7	22	28	25	5.70	12	27	1	1	.50	.276	.331	.487	.819
Holliday,Matt	StL	30	155	605	191	43	3	27	105	109	123	7.61	66	112	14	6	.70	.316	.391	.531	.922
Howard,Ryan	Phi	30	160	609	169	33	2	48	103	143	129	7.59	87	197	5	2	.71	.278	.372	.575	.947
Hudson,Orlando	LAD	32	145	550	154	33	4	10	71	61	79	5.15	59	96	7	3	.70	.280	.353	.409	.762
Huff,Aubrey	Det	33	148	521	139	31	1	20	66	79	76	5.16	49	83	1	1	.50	.267	.334	.445	.780
Hundley,Nick	SD	26	84	264	60	14	1	10	30	38	31	3.93	25	64	3	1	.75	.227	.297	.402	.698
Hunter,Torii	LAA	34	146	556	151	33	1	24	82	92	85	5.36	48	113	16	7	.70	.272	.335	.464	.799
Iannetta,Chris	Col	27	113	386	100	23	3	20	58	68	68	6.18	60	92	0	0	.00	.259	.370	.490	.860
Ibanez,Raul	Phi	38	152	589	159	34	2	26	86	96	93	5.60	60	124	3	2	.60	.270	.340	.467	.807
Infante,Omar	Atl	28	84	263	73	14	2	4	33	30	34	4.60	20	40	3	2	.60	.278	.331	.392	.723
Inge,Brandon	Det	33	150	528	119	23	2	20	63	71	61	3.86	52	153	3	2	.60	.225	.307	.390	.697
Ishikawa,Travis	SF	26	130	360	95	19	2	13	50	56	52	5.06	37	85	3	2	.60	.264	.336	.436	.772
Iwamura,Akinori	TB	31	128	504	146	28	5	4	76	40	72	5.14	60	95	12	6	.67	.290	.367	.389	.756
Izturis,Cesar	Bal	30	126	387	100	16	2	1	40	28	37	3.28	22	34	11	6	.65	.258	.303	.318	.621
Izturis,Maicer	LAA	29	124	446	126	25	3	6	70	56	61	4.87	43	48	14	6	.70	.283	.348	.392	.741
Jackson,Austin	NYY	23	97	282	83	15	3	4	40	37	42	5.38	27	65	14	4	.78	.294	.356	.411	.767
Jackson,Conor	Ari	28	135	463	132	31	2	12	66	69	74	5.74	57	54	9	4	.69	.285	.368	.438	.807
Jacobs,Mike	KC	29	108	320	79	20	1	15	38	50	45	4.85	27	88	0	0	.00	.247	.307	.456	.764
Janish,Paul	Cin	27	77	188	42	12	0	2	22	15	17	3.01	18	32	2	1	.67	.223	.301	.319	.621
Jaramillo,Jason	Pit	27	72	235	60	13	0	4	24	26	27	4.01	22	40	1	0	1.00	.255	.319	.362	.681
Jennings,Desmond	TB	23	120	423	119	20	7	9	76	51	71	5.55	55	55	39	6	.87	.281	.364	.426	.790
Jeter,Derek	NYY	36	156	631	200	31	2	15	103	72	108	6.41	64	99	20	7	.74	.317	.388	.444	.832
Johjima,Kenji	Sea	34	107	354	90	19	0	11	36	40	40	3.91	17	37	2	2	.50	.254	.307	.401	.708
Johnson,Chris	Hou	25	116	346	92	18	2	11	38	39	44	4.49	17	78	2	1	.67	.266	.300	.425	.725
Johnson,Kelly	Atl	28	139	485	133	31	5	14	78	62	76	5.54	58	88	10	5	.67	.274	.354	.445	.799
Johnson,Nick	Fla	31	124	426	118	29	1	12	67	62	75	6.29	91	83	2	2	.50	.277	.414	.434	.849
Johnson,Reed	ChC	33	108	342	93	19	1	7	50	39	42	4.33	22	66	4	3	.57	.272	.336	.395	.731
Johnson,Rob	Sea	27	75	221	52	13	1	3	21	20	22	3.35	17	41	3	2	.60	.235	.293	.344	.637
Jones,Adam	Bal	24	154	571	162	29	5	22	95	83	88	5.51	40	115	13	6	.68	.284	.336	.468	.804
Jones,Andruw	Tex	33	77	203	47	10	0	11	30	34	29	4.80	27	53	2	1	.67	.232	.336	.443	.780
Jones,Chipper	Atl	38	134	459	136	27	1	21	78	78	93	7.46	86	81	3	1	.75	.296	.408	.497	.905
Jones,Garrett	Pit	29	151	549	149	35	2	25	78	88	87	5.57	48	109	14	6	.70	.271	.330	.479	.809
Joyce,Matt	TB	25	120	375	97	27	3	17	59	60	62	5.70	49	92	10	5	.67	.259	.346	.483	.829
Kapler,Gabe	TB	34	101	252	66	17	1	7	37	34	34	4.68	23	47	4	3	.57	.262	.326	.421	.747
Kearns,Austin	Was	30	84	224	55	13	1	7	32	31	31	4.74	31	54	1	1	.50	.246	.355	.406	.761
Kemp,Matt	LAD	25	153	573	178	32	6	23	99	91	107	6.87	47	122	32	10	.76	.311	.365	.508	.873
Kendall,Jason	Mil	36	128	409	104	19	1	2	43	35	41	3.46	37	44	5	3	.62	.254	.338	.320	.659
Kendrick,Howie	LAA	26	124	467	144	34	3	11	70	68	73	5.77	21	76	14	6	.70	.308	.343	.465	.808
Kennedy,Adam	Oak	34	121	389	105	20	1	6	47	40	47	4.23	32	63	11	5	.69	.270	.332	.373	.705
Keppinger,Jeff	Hou	30	115	367	107	19	2	5	44	35	50	4.98	30	26	1	1	.50	.292	.348	.395	.743
Kinsler,Ian	Tex	28	145	575	158	36	3	27	106	84	98	6.01	60	82	28	7	.80	.275	.348	.489	.837
Konerko,Paul	CWS	34	148	539	143	27	0	29	74	90	89	5.84	67	96	1	0	1.00	.265	.354	.477	.831
Kotchman,Casey	Bos	27	122	372	101	25	1	9	45	53	52	4.97	36	37	1	1	.50	.272	.342	.417	.759
Kotsay,Mark	CWS	34	78	209	56	12	1	3	23	23	25	4.19	17	24	2	2	.50	.268	.326	.378	.704
Kouzmanoff,Kevin	SD	28	144	512	141	32	2	20	59	84	74	5.17	29	95	1	1	.50	.275	.327	.463	.790
Kubel,Jason	Min	28	145	490	139	33	3	23	72	88	87	6.43	52	97	1	1	.50	.284	.354	.504	.858
Laird,Gerald	Det	30	124	444	111	25	2	8	60	48	50	3.87	37	85	5	3	.62	.250	.315	.369	.684
Langerhans,Ryan	Sea	30	84	175	44	11	1	5	27	22	25	4.89	25	48	3	2	.60	.251	.351	.411	.763

472

2010 Hitter Projections

Hitter	Team	Age	G	AB	H	2B	3B	HR	R	RBI	RC	RC27	BB	SO	SB	CS	SB%	Avg	OBP	Slg	OPS
LaPorta,Matt	Cle	25	121	451	120	29	1	20	70	68	70	5.47	44	82	3	2	.60	.266	.334	.468	.802
LaRoche,Adam	Atl	30	152	571	155	42	1	26	79	91	96	5.99	66	143	1	1	.50	.271	.348	.485	.833
LaRoche,Andy	Pit	26	150	523	133	28	2	15	71	69	70	4.64	63	81	4	2	.67	.254	.338	.402	.739
LaRue,Jason	StL	36	55	125	27	6	0	4	13	15	12	3.18	10	32	1	0	1.00	.216	.315	.360	.675
Lee,Carlos	Hou	34	152	587	172	36	0	29	79	107	102	6.34	49	61	6	3	.67	.293	.351	.503	.853
Lee,Derrek	ChC	34	153	595	173	40	2	30	94	98	115	7.05	79	127	5	2	.71	.291	.378	.516	.894
Lewis,Fred	SF	29	125	376	102	21	5	7	62	34	54	5.01	44	91	13	6	.68	.271	.351	.410	.760
Lind,Adam	Tor	26	153	590	180	43	2	31	90	113	116	7.34	52	107	2	1	.67	.305	.364	.542	.907
Loney,James	LAD	26	145	507	149	29	3	13	64	78	80	5.76	51	61	5	3	.62	.294	.360	.440	.799
Longoria,Evan	TB	24	157	595	171	42	1	37	106	120	120	7.32	73	134	9	2	.82	.287	.370	.548	.918
Lopez,Felipe	Mil	30	151	565	159	31	3	10	79	58	79	4.99	60	104	10	6	.62	.281	.352	.400	.752
Lopez,Jose	Sea	26	154	580	160	37	2	19	72	85	78	4.81	24	66	3	2	.60	.276	.310	.445	.755
Loretta,Mark	LAD	38	83	176	48	9	0	2	20	18	21	4.23	17	19	1	1	.50	.273	.350	.358	.708
Lowell,Mike	Bos	36	138	529	147	35	1	19	66	84	81	5.50	46	74	2	1	.67	.278	.339	.456	.795
Lowrie,Jed	Bos	26	129	384	100	35	3	9	55	59	59	5.38	53	80	2	1	.67	.260	.350	.438	.788
Ludwick,Ryan	StL	31	149	511	138	31	1	26	77	93	82	5.67	48	129	3	3	.50	.270	.339	.487	.826
Lugo,Julio	StL	34	97	320	83	17	2	4	41	31	38	4.10	32	58	11	4	.73	.259	.332	.363	.695
Maier,Mitch	KC	28	101	293	78	17	2	5	38	32	37	4.41	25	50	7	3	.70	.266	.328	.389	.717
Markakis,Nick	Bal	26	161	630	189	47	2	21	101	103	113	6.60	72	103	8	4	.67	.300	.374	.481	.855
Marson,Lou	Cle	24	49	150	42	9	0	1	20	16	20	4.77	22	32	2	1	.67	.280	.372	.360	.732
Marte,Andy	Cle	26	65	155	40	10	1	6	19	24	22	4.97	13	29	1	0	1.00	.258	.320	.452	.771
Martin,Russell	LAD	27	146	533	145	28	1	12	80	71	77	5.07	78	83	13	7	.65	.272	.372	.396	.768
Martinez,Fernando	NYM	21	121	448	116	29	3	13	58	53	58	4.49	30	84	8	4	.67	.259	.308	.424	.732
Martinez,Victor	Bos	31	150	560	167	36	0	19	78	97	97	6.42	67	74	1	0	1.00	.298	.377	.464	.841
Mathis,Jeff	LAA	27	85	238	52	12	1	6	30	20	24	3.34	21	61	2	1	.67	.218	.287	.353	.640
Matsui,Hideki	NYY	36	139	507	143	27	1	23	75	88	87	6.20	65	81	1	1	.50	.282	.367	.475	.842
Matsui,Kaz	Hou	34	125	445	117	24	2	8	60	40	54	4.22	33	82	16	5	.76	.263	.317	.380	.696
Matthews Jr.,Gary	LAA	35	124	403	101	23	2	9	55	48	50	4.26	44	91	6	3	.67	.251	.327	.385	.712
Mauer,Joe	Min	27	144	542	181	36	3	22	104	100	121	8.67	81	61	4	2	.67	.334	.422	.531	.954
Maxwell,Justin	Was	26	69	203	47	6	2	7	34	23	26	4.20	28	63	17	5	.77	.232	.328	.384	.712
Maybin,Cameron	Fla	23	127	426	122	23	6	10	69	47	68	5.72	50	108	14	5	.74	.286	.363	.439	.802
McCann,Brian	Atl	26	142	522	152	41	1	24	69	100	95	6.64	54	78	4	2	.67	.291	.362	.511	.874
McCutchen,Andrew	Pit	23	152	563	158	31	7	13	90	61	87	5.45	62	90	31	10	.76	.281	.353	.430	.783
McDonald,Darnell	Cin	31	65	174	47	11	1	4	22	20	23	4.64	13	30	6	2	.75	.270	.321	.414	.735
McDonald,John	Tor	35	60	145	34	6	0	2	16	12	12	2.79	5	21	1	1	.50	.234	.270	.317	.587
McGehee,Casey	Mil	27	125	492	134	30	1	15	63	76	69	5.01	41	86	0	0	.00	.272	.328	.429	.757
McLouth,Nate	Atl	28	148	528	139	34	2	20	93	67	82	5.41	61	97	19	5	.79	.263	.348	.449	.797
Michaels,Jason	Hou	34	87	155	38	9	0	4	21	20	19	4.19	17	37	1	1	.50	.245	.328	.381	.708
Miles,Aaron	ChC	33	51	124	34	6	1	1	15	10	14	4.00	7	15	2	1	.67	.274	.318	.363	.681
Millar,Kevin	Tor	38	75	190	46	11	0	6	24	24	25	4.51	24	37	0	0	.00	.242	.342	.395	.737
Milledge,Lastings	Pit	25	147	516	146	30	2	11	66	60	70	4.78	38	94	22	11	.67	.283	.340	.413	.753
Molina,Bengie	SF	35	140	627	142	25	0	18	47	83	65	4.39	18	62	0	0	.00	.269	.299	.419	.718
Molina,Jose	NYY	35	67	147	34	7	0	2	14	13	13	2.99	9	33	0	0	.00	.231	.285	.320	.605
Molina,Yadier	StL	27	136	485	135	24	0	7	42	59	61	4.49	44	41	5	3	.62	.278	.343	.371	.714
Montero,Miguel	Ari	26	132	472	130	30	1	18	63	69	73	5.53	47	82	1	1	.50	.275	.344	.458	.801
Mora,Melvin	Bal	28	131	456	123	22	0	14	61	61	61	4.72	40	71	4	3	.57	.270	.341	.410	.751
Morales,Jose	Min	27	110	323	95	19	1	3	35	30	44	5.00	29	46	1	1	.50	.294	.352	.387	.739
Morales,Kendry	LAA	27	153	572	168	38	1	29	80	98	99	6.32	40	97	2	3	.40	.294	.341	.516	.857
Morgan,Nyjer	Was	29	153	599	181	23	6	3	94	44	80	4.73	45	88	52	22	.70	.302	.356	.376	.732
Morneau,Justin	Min	29	154	588	166	37	2	31	91	115	108	6.65	71	96	0	0	.00	.282	.363	.510	.873
Morrison,Logan	Fla	22	50	145	39	10	1	4	24	23	26	6.26	32	25	5	2	.71	.269	.401	.434	.836
Moss,Brandon	Pit	26	101	271	73	20	2	7	36	37	40	5.23	27	63	2	1	.67	.269	.340	.435	.775
Murphy,Daniel	NYM	25	98	271	77	21	2	7	38	39	42	5.57	25	35	3	2	.60	.284	.345	.454	.798
Murphy,David	Tex	28	129	460	125	31	3	15	65	65	70	5.37	47	89	8	4	.67	.272	.339	.450	.789
Nady,Xavier	NYY	31	124	424	121	25	1	17	54	65	66	5.64	28	85	2	1	.67	.285	.337	.469	.806
Napoli,Mike	LAA	28	115	395	105	21	1	24	68	69	70	6.21	54	103	5	3	.62	.266	.361	.506	.868
Navarro,Dioner	TB	26	110	338	86	17	0	7	38	37	38	3.89	27	43	3	2	.60	.254	.315	.367	.682
Nieves,Wil	Was	32	74	187	47	8	1	2	17	17	18	3.34	10	29	1	0	1.00	.251	.293	.337	.630
Nix,Jayson	CWS	27	90	247	60	13	0	8	33	27	30	4.11	21	49	9	3	.75	.243	.307	.393	.700
Nix,Laynce	Cin	29	85	214	55	13	1	10	30	34	30	4.88	15	53	1	1	.50	.257	.309	.467	.776
Ojeda,Augie	Ari	35	95	242	57	11	1	1	31	18	23	3.22	27	24	2	1	.67	.236	.322	.302	.624
Olivo,Miguel	KC	31	119	433	103	21	2	18	49	60	48	3.75	18	130	6	3	.67	.238	.275	.420	.695
Ordonez,Magglio	Det	36	141	515	160	32	1	17	70	84	91	6.63	52	74	2	2	.50	.311	.376	.476	.852
Ortiz,David	Bos	34	138	484	128	34	1	29	79	99	92	6.72	77	112	0	0	.00	.264	.369	.519	.887
Overbay,Lyle	Tor	33	140	460	123	34	1	15	60	63	73	5.63	65	100	1	0	1.00	.267	.359	.443	.803
Pagan,Angel	NYM	28	101	334	93	18	6	5	48	32	46	4.84	27	56	12	6	.67	.278	.332	.413	.746
Parra,Gerardo	Ari	23	132	502	149	24	9	8	70	64	74	5.31	41	79	13	9	.59	.297	.351	.428	.779
Patterson,Eric	Oak	27	65	250	68	14	3	5	39	28	36	5.01	24	48	20	5	.80	.272	.336	.412	.748
Paulino,Ronny	Fla	29	85	257	71	14	1	7	28	32	36	5.01	23	47	1	1	.50	.276	.338	.420	.758
Pearce,Steve	Pit	27	70	180	47	14	1	6	23	28	26	5.01	17	32	3	2	.60	.261	.328	.450	.778
Pedroia,Dustin	Bos	26	156	623	191	50	2	15	109	75	109	6.47	66	43	16	6	.73	.307	.378	.465	.843
Pena,Brayan	KC	28	82	272	78	17	1	6	30	32	38	5.04	18	25	3	2	.60	.287	.331	.423	.754
Pena,Carlos	TB	32	148	530	127	27	1	36	88	99	93	5.97	93	176	3	2	.60	.240	.360	.498	.858
Pena,Ramiro	NYY	24	56	103	26	4	1	1	13	8	11	3.67	9	18	3	1	.75	.252	.313	.340	.652
Pence,Hunter	Hou	27	155	601	175	35	6	28	85	89	105	6.29	53	107	13	8	.62	.291	.351	.509	.860
Pennington,Cliff	Oak	26	60	207	52	10	1	2	29	18	25	4.09	26	33	13	4	.76	.251	.338	.338	.676
Peralta,Jhonny	Cle	28	146	531	143	33	2	15	74	72	75	5.01	50	124	1	1	.50	.269	.336	.424	.759
Perez,Fernando	TB	27	102	252	69	11	4	3	44	18	35	4.74	31	76	23	9	.72	.274	.353	.385	.738
Phillips,Brandon	Cin	29	155	613	165	32	3	21	85	81	85	4.85	43	91	22	8	.73	.269	.322	.434	.756
Pie,Felix	Bal	25	143	345	94	18	4	11	53	42	49	4.98	27	71	7	5	.58	.272	.325	.443	.769
Pierre,Juan	LAD	32	131	409	119	15	4	1	56	27	49	4.22	25	27	30	12	.71	.291	.342	.355	.697

473

2010 Hitter Projections

Hitter	Team	Age	G	AB	H	2B	3B	HR	R	RBI	RC	RC27	BB	SO	SB	CS	SB%	Avg	OBP	Slg	OPS
Pierzynski,A.J.	CWS	33	140	527	149	28	1	14	61	62	69	4.73	24	64	1	1	.50	.283	.323	.419	.742
Podsednik,Scott	CWS	34	110	324	89	17	2	3	45	26	40	4.28	29	50	17	8	.68	.275	.340	.367	.707
Polanco,Placido	Det	34	153	621	184	32	2	10	89	67	84	4.96	36	46	6	3	.67	.296	.343	.403	.745
Posada,Jorge	NYY	38	116	420	116	26	0	18	59	74	72	6.14	60	104	1	1	.50	.276	.372	.467	.839
Posey,Buster	SF	23	131	474	128	25	3	11	57	54	64	4.81	43	86	0	0	.00	.270	.331	.405	.736
Powell,Landon	Oak	28	50	180	41	7	0	8	25	30	23	4.30	25	43	0	0	.00	.228	.322	.400	.722
Prado,Martin	Atl	26	122	423	128	29	2	7	60	47	64	5.60	35	50	2	2	.50	.303	.357	.430	.788
Pujols,Albert	StL	30	158	579	193	45	1	44	121	129	162	10.77	106	63	11	5	.69	.333	.443	.642	1.085
Punto,Nick	Min	32	114	328	80	14	2	1	44	26	34	3.49	42	63	12	5	.71	.244	.330	.308	.638
Quentin,Carlos	CWS	27	146	542	147	36	2	30	92	97	95	6.22	59	77	5	2	.71	.271	.356	.511	.867
Quinlan,Robb	LAA	33	50	105	29	5	0	2	12	12	12	4.05	6	19	1	1	.50	.276	.321	.381	.702
Quintero,Humberto	Hou	30	71	173	43	10	0	3	15	18	17	3.40	7	30	0	0	.00	.249	.286	.358	.644
Raburn,Ryan	Det	29	133	439	121	25	3	22	74	73	75	6.04	48	100	10	5	.67	.276	.348	.497	.845
Ramirez,Alexei	CWS	28	147	527	150	19	2	18	75	78	76	5.16	42	58	12	6	.67	.285	.339	.431	.769
Ramirez,Aramis	ChC	32	132	506	148	32	1	26	76	97	92	6.66	49	74	2	1	.67	.292	.364	.514	.878
Ramirez,Hanley	Fla	26	156	615	194	44	5	27	117	86	127	7.64	69	109	31	11	.74	.315	.391	.535	.926
Ramirez,Manny	LAD	38	140	514	152	32	1	30	88	101	110	7.90	88	118	1	0	1.00	.296	.406	.537	.943
Rasmus,Colby	StL	23	147	471	119	26	2	18	75	55	65	4.76	47	91	8	3	.73	.253	.323	.431	.754
Redmond,Mike	Min	39	40	120	33	6	0	0	10	12	12	3.59	7	14	0	0	.00	.275	.331	.325	.656
Reed,Jeremy	NYM	29	71	104	28	6	1	1	12	10	13	4.39	9	15	1	1	.50	.269	.333	.375	.708
Reimold,Nolan	Bal	26	152	538	157	34	2	29	82	84	105	7.07	68	102	13	5	.72	.292	.373	.524	.898
Renteria,Edgar	SF	34	138	507	140	28	1	8	69	59	65	4.56	44	76	8	4	.67	.276	.335	.383	.718
Reyes,Jose	NYM	27	159	684	195	35	14	14	113	67	107	5.51	62	83	57	16	.78	.285	.345	.439	.784
Reynolds,Mark	Ari	26	153	559	150	32	3	40	103	107	108	6.73	72	191	18	8	.69	.268	.356	.551	.907
Rios,Alex	CWS	29	149	564	157	36	5	16	79	73	83	5.21	41	102	21	7	.75	.278	.332	.445	.777
Rivera,Juan	LAA	31	138	529	149	30	0	23	69	87	81	5.54	36	62	0	0	.00	.282	.329	.469	.797
Roberts,Brian	Bal	32	159	630	177	47	3	12	103	65	98	5.50	78	108	30	10	.75	.281	.361	.422	.783
Roberts,Ryan	Ari	29	125	411	113	24	3	11	54	47	63	5.41	51	77	12	5	.71	.275	.356	.428	.785
Rodriguez,Alex	NYY	34	145	544	160	26	1	37	104	113	117	7.82	84	125	15	5	.75	.294	.400	.550	.950
Rodriguez,Ivan	Tex	38	113	353	94	20	1	8	42	40	42	4.20	16	72	2	1	.67	.266	.302	.397	.698
Rodriguez,Luis	SD	30	95	244	62	13	1	2	27	20	27	3.84	28	21	1	1	.50	.254	.331	.340	.671
Rodriguez,Sean	TB	25	100	327	80	17	3	18	58	53	50	5.20	37	94	7	3	.70	.245	.323	.480	.803
Rolen,Scott	Cin	35	127	482	134	35	1	14	72	75	74	5.48	52	74	5	3	.62	.278	.357	.442	.799
Rollins,Jimmy	Phi	31	155	650	176	40	6	19	104	71	94	5.06	51	73	33	9	.79	.271	.328	.438	.766
Romero,Alex	Ari	26	72	135	37	8	1	1	15	15	16	4.16	9	15	3	2	.60	.274	.324	.370	.695
Rosales,Adam	Cin	27	81	219	57	13	2	7	32	25	30	4.76	20	40	3	2	.60	.260	.331	.434	.764
Ross,Cody	Fla	29	146	510	137	33	2	23	70	80	77	5.32	37	106	5	3	.62	.269	.324	.476	.801
Ross,David	Atl	33	62	147	35	7	0	7	18	20	21	4.88	20	40	0	0	.00	.238	.333	.429	.762
Rowand,Aaron	SF	32	154	574	153	31	1	17	74	72	75	4.60	38	134	5	3	.62	.267	.327	.423	.751
Ruiz,Carlos	Phi	31	118	358	93	24	1	9	43	47	49	4.77	43	41	3	2	.60	.260	.344	.408	.752
Ruiz,Randy	Tor	32	55	180	53	13	0	9	26	31	32	6.55	14	45	0	0	.00	.294	.352	.517	.869
Ryal,Rusty	Ari	27	50	118	31	8	1	4	15	15	16	4.73	8	26	1	1	.50	.263	.315	.449	.764
Ryan,Brendan	StL	28	146	452	121	21	4	4	65	33	51	3.92	31	62	16	7	.70	.268	.319	.358	.677
Salazar,Oscar	SD	32	88	246	72	16	1	9	31	40	40	5.94	18	33	1	1	.50	.293	.341	.476	.817
Salome,Angel	Mil	24	85	240	71	15	1	6	30	39	37	5.69	18	45	1	0	1.00	.296	.345	.442	.787
Saltalamacchia,Jarrod	Tex	25	121	447	113	24	1	15	60	59	60	4.67	50	130	0	0	.00	.253	.329	.412	.741
Sanchez,Freddy	SF	32	138	539	155	35	2	8	67	56	71	4.78	29	76	4	2	.67	.288	.329	.404	.733
Sanchez,Gaby	Fla	26	101	362	101	22	0	15	49	59	60	5.91	44	53	7	3	.70	.279	.357	.464	.821
Sandoval,Pablo	SF	23	153	556	182	45	4	24	86	97	116	8.00	46	70	4	3	.57	.327	.382	.552	.934
Santana,Carlos	Cle	24	128	503	136	25	1	16	85	90	75	5.28	67	98	2	2	.50	.270	.356	.419	.776
Santiago,Ramon	Det	30	106	330	80	13	2	6	42	33	34	3.51	24	56	4	2	.67	.242	.302	.348	.650
Santos,Omir	NYM	29	90	268	69	12	0	5	25	32	28	3.66	14	44	0	0	.00	.257	.297	.358	.655
Saunders,Michael	Sea	23	101	364	97	17	4	10	58	35	49	4.67	31	94	12	6	.67	.266	.324	.418	.742
Schafer,Jordan	Atl	23	63	197	47	10	1	5	26	20	25	4.25	30	63	6	3	.67	.239	.339	.376	.715
Schierholtz,Nate	SF	26	93	257	74	17	3	7	33	33	38	5.34	13	41	4	2	.67	.288	.325	.459	.784
Schneider,Brian	NYM	33	84	239	58	12	0	5	20	30	27	3.88	27	36	0	0	.00	.243	.325	.356	.680
Schumaker,Skip	StL	30	150	510	151	28	2	5	72	39	70	5.04	45	59	4	2	.67	.296	.353	.388	.741
Scott,Luke	Bal	32	142	463	120	29	2	24	64	76	76	5.74	56	109	1	1	.50	.259	.342	.486	.828
Scutaro,Marco	Tor	34	147	549	145	30	2	10	79	57	72	4.59	68	76	9	4	.69	.264	.347	.381	.728
Sheffield,Gary	NYM	41	122	401	100	17	0	16	58	60	57	4.88	58	68	6	3	.67	.249	.351	.411	.763
Shoppach,Kelly	Cle	30	113	381	95	25	0	19	57	61	56	5.09	39	125	0	0	.00	.249	.333	.465	.798
Sizemore,Grady	Cle	27	144	574	156	35	6	25	101	78	101	6.16	79	123	21	8	.72	.272	.369	.484	.853
Smith,Seth	Col	27	119	351	101	25	3	13	52	51	62	6.40	40	60	5	2	.71	.288	.362	.487	.849
Smoak,Justin	Tex	23	108	365	100	20	0	10	48	45	57	5.59	64	75	0	0	.00	.274	.382	.411	.793
Snider,Travis	Tor	22	141	527	145	35	1	26	82	90	92	6.21	65	159	4	3	.57	.275	.357	.493	.850
Snyder,Chris	Ari	29	78	225	53	14	0	9	28	34	32	4.84	34	54	0	0	.00	.236	.344	.418	.761
Soriano,Alfonso	ChC	34	133	567	149	35	1	30	85	77	87	5.33	43	137	15	6	.71	.263	.320	.487	.807
Soto,Geovany	ChC	27	135	473	129	31	1	20	58	79	80	6.05	63	106	1	0	1.00	.273	.361	.469	.830
Span,Denard	Min	26	145	553	166	20	8	7	94	63	83	5.40	63	86	25	13	.66	.300	.377	.403	.780
Spilborghs,Ryan	Col	30	116	310	90	21	2	8	48	43	50	5.78	34	58	8	5	.62	.290	.362	.448	.811
Stanton,Michael	Fla	20	65	162	37	8	1	9	26	28	22	4.58	16	55	1	0	1.00	.228	.298	.457	.755
Stewart,Ian	Col	25	147	475	121	29	4	24	77	76	76	5.52	54	131	8	4	.67	.255	.336	.484	.820
Stubbs,Drew	Cin	25	152	544	145	30	2	11	76	51	75	4.73	57	136	51	13	.80	.267	.336	.390	.726
Sullivan,Cory	NYM	30	64	122	35	7	1	1	16	11	16	4.73	10	18	3	1	.75	.287	.346	.385	.731
Suzuki,Ichiro	Sea	36	157	658	210	23	4	9	95	50	99	5.64	43	73	27	8	.77	.319	.365	.407	.772
Suzuki,Kurt	Oak	26	146	549	151	34	1	13	70	76	74	4.80	42	61	6	3	.67	.275	.334	.412	.746
Sweeney,Mike	Sea	36	74	200	55	12	0	7	23	31	29	5.20	17	25	0	0	.00	.275	.344	.440	.784
Sweeney,Ryan	Oak	25	134	476	138	26	2	8	65	57	66	5.00	43	66	7	5	.58	.290	.347	.403	.755
Swisher,Nick	NYY	29	150	507	125	32	1	26	85	80	85	5.77	90	131	1	1	.50	.247	.365	.467	.833
Tabata,Jose	Pit	21	62	161	44	9	0	2	22	16	19	4.12	12	21	6	3	.67	.273	.324	.366	.690
Tatis,Fernando	NYM	35	91	242	63	13	1	7	29	33	32	4.62	22	48	3	1	.75	.260	.335	.409	.744

2010 Hitter Projections

Hitter	Team	Age	G	AB	H	2B	3B	HR	R	RBI	RC	RC27	BB	SO	SB	CS	SB%	Avg	OBP	Slg	OPS
Taveras,Willy	Cin	28	92	277	75	9	1	1	40	14	29	3.64	16	43	20	5	.80	.271	.322	.321	.643
Taylor,Michael	Phi	24	87	249	71	13	2	9	39	44	41	5.89	25	40	11	3	.79	.285	.350	.462	.812
Teagarden,Taylor	Tex	26	69	206	48	11	1	9	28	27	26	4.28	19	71	0	0	.00	.233	.301	.427	.728
Teahen,Mark	KC	28	147	533	144	34	4	13	71	62	75	4.97	49	124	7	3	.70	.270	.336	.422	.758
Teixeira,Mark	NYY	30	156	596	179	42	2	36	101	121	129	8.02	84	113	2	1	.67	.300	.395	.559	.953
Tejada,Miguel	Hou	36	157	622	186	37	1	18	84	91	92	5.45	32	62	4	3	.57	.299	.342	.449	.791
Thames,Marcus	Det	33	94	256	62	12	1	15	36	40	37	4.96	25	72	0	0	.00	.242	.312	.473	.785
Theriot,Ryan	ChC	30	156	599	170	26	3	4	84	50	75	4.44	60	79	21	10	.68	.284	.352	.357	.709
Thomas,Clete	Det	26	85	227	59	14	2	5	34	26	32	4.84	27	57	11	4	.73	.260	.341	.405	.746
Thome,Jim	LAD	39	132	441	108	20	0	29	73	84	80	6.25	88	146	0	0	.00	.245	.374	.488	.862
Thurston,Joe	StL	30	83	196	52	11	1	2	24	18	22	3.89	15	29	4	3	.57	.265	.321	.362	.683
Tolbert,Matt	Min	28	79	216	57	11	2	2	31	22	25	4.01	17	32	7	3	.70	.264	.318	.361	.679
Torrealba,Yorvit	Col	31	75	253	64	15	1	4	27	32	28	3.83	20	49	1	1	.50	.253	.315	.368	.683
Torres,Andres	SF	32	87	292	77	12	5	6	45	25	39	4.59	29	75	14	6	.70	.264	.330	.401	.731
Tracy,Chad	Ari	30	84	203	56	14	1	6	25	28	30	5.31	17	33	1	0	1.00	.276	.338	.443	.781
Tulowitzki,Troy	Col	25	146	556	162	32	5	27	99	89	103	6.63	66	98	15	10	.60	.291	.371	.513	.883
Uggla,Dan	Fla	30	157	596	150	36	2	30	97	90	94	5.46	78	162	3	2	.60	.252	.345	.470	.815
Upton,B.J.	TB	25	142	507	135	30	3	13	81	59	75	5.04	67	136	39	15	.72	.266	.354	.414	.768
Upton,Justin	Ari	22	148	564	165	34	9	28	93	90	111	7.09	68	142	19	8	.70	.293	.371	.534	.904
Uribe,Juan	SF	31	124	385	98	22	2	13	47	51	48	4.32	24	78	2	2	.50	.255	.302	.423	.725
Utley,Chase	Phi	31	157	604	175	39	3	30	111	104	115	6.91	73	114	17	4	.81	.290	.384	.513	.897
Valbuena,Luis	Cle	24	103	366	94	21	2	9	53	36	47	4.43	36	70	7	4	.64	.257	.323	.399	.722
Valencia,Daniel	Min	25	131	438	121	33	3	12	66	57	63	5.17	30	78	0	0	.00	.276	.323	.447	.770
Varitek,Jason	Bos	38	95	253	58	13	0	9	29	34	31	4.13	34	69	0	0	.00	.229	.332	.387	.720
Vazquez,Ramon	Pit	33	84	178	43	9	1	2	22	17	20	3.82	23	41	1	1	.50	.242	.332	.337	.669
Velez,Eugenio	SF	28	82	206	56	11	0	2	30	20	26	4.17	13	33	14	6	.70	.272	.310	.393	.702
Venable,Will	SD	27	120	395	99	18	2	13	53	48	50	4.36	34	95	7	2	.78	.251	.313	.405	.718
Victorino,Shane	Phi	29	154	591	167	30	7	12	95	59	84	5.04	48	77	24	9	.73	.283	.343	.418	.761
Vizquel,Omar	Tex	43	70	185	45	7	1	1	19	15	18	3.30	17	22	4	2	.67	.243	.314	.308	.622
Votto,Joey	Cin	26	137	502	156	37	1	27	80	90	109	8.10	70	100	7	4	.64	.311	.397	.550	.947
Wallace,Brett	Oak	23	128	504	140	24	0	17	69	57	71	5.06	40	106	1	1	.50	.278	.331	.427	.757
Weeks,Rickie	Mil	27	114	425	110	23	5	16	80	48	67	5.44	56	100	14	5	.74	.259	.357	.449	.807
Wells,Vernon	Tor	31	144	549	149	33	2	19	77	77	79	5.07	43	75	11	5	.69	.271	.327	.443	.769
Werth,Jayson	Phl	31	149	510	137	25	2	28	86	88	92	6.33	76	145	17	5	.77	.269	.369	.490	.859
Whitesell,Josh	Ari	28	46	105	28	6	0	4	13	17	16	5.40	15	26	0	0	.00	.267	.364	.438	.802
Wieters,Matt	Bal	24	148	547	170	29	3	20	75	92	101	6.97	61	112	0	0	.00	.311	.381	.484	.865
Wigginton,Ty	Bal	32	122	400	109	23	1	15	49	53	58	5.15	31	70	2	2	.50	.273	.333	.448	.780
Willingham,Josh	Was	31	140	500	130	32	2	25	77	78	84	5.86	70	122	4	3	.57	.260	.363	.482	.845
Wilson,Jack	Sea	32	127	462	123	25	2	6	50	43	52	3.96	27	55	3	2	.60	.266	.311	.368	.679
Wilson,Josh	Sea	29	82	223	55	13	1	3	25	21	23	3.52	16	40	4	2	.67	.247	.303	.354	.657
Winn,Randy	SF	36	140	489	135	30	2	7	61	50	64	4.64	41	81	13	5	.72	.276	.337	.389	.726
Wise,DeWayne	CWS	32	85	194	49	10	2	6	27	21	23	4.01	10	36	8	4	.67	.253	.296	.418	.714
Wright,David	NYM	27	156	599	181	45	2	23	100	99	118	7.20	86	134	24	8	.75	.302	.393	.499	.892
Youkilis,Kevin	Bos	31	149	557	161	42	1	23	98	95	105	6.84	85	128	6	3	.67	.289	.394	.492	.885
Young Jr.,Eric	Col	25	45	146	40	7	2	2	25	9	19	4.41	14	24	12	6	.67	.274	.338	.390	.728
Young,Chris	Ari	26	151	560	137	39	4	25	84	73	84	5.09	65	142	17	6	.74	.245	.326	.463	.789
Young,Delmon	Min	24	129	455	135	24	2	12	60	67	65	5.22	20	87	8	4	.67	.297	.332	.437	.769
Young,Delwyn	Pit	28	120	351	95	24	1	9	43	45	48	4.86	27	79	2	1	.67	.271	.325	.422	.746
Young,Michael	Tex	33	152	616	184	37	2	16	88	80	96	5.74	49	104	8	3	.73	.299	.352	.443	.796
Zaun,Gregg	TB	39	88	244	58	13	0	7	29	29	30	4.19	33	44	0	0	.00	.238	.333	.377	.710
Zimmerman,Ryan	Was	25	149	593	171	42	3	28	97	98	107	6.56	62	110	3	2	.60	.288	.358	.511	.869
Zobrist,Ben	TB	29	153	509	143	28	5	23	86	75	96	6.71	84	93	15	6	.71	.281	.385	.491	.876

Pitcher Projections

Bill James

Projecting stats for pitchers is very different from projecting batting stats for players, and I will give you a couple of data points to illustrate the difference. For hitters, last year there were 8 batters whose batting averages we projected exactly right (to three decimals) and 54 players whose batting averages we projected correctly within ten points of the actual average.   For pitchers, on the other hand, there were no pitchers whose ERAs we projected correctly (to two decimals), and only 14 pitchers for whom we were within ten points.

The difference between pitchers' records and batters' records as they are traditionally presented is the difference between elemental and summary statistics. The most prominent parts of a hitter's record are the elements of his performance—the hits, the home runs, RBI, doubles, triples.   Batting average, which is a step away from an elemental record, is merely one step away; it is a contrast of two simple elements.

The most prominent parts of a pitcher's record, on the other hand, are not the elements but the summary stats—wins, losses, saves and ERA.   The batter's record is event-oriented; the pitcher's record is result-oriented.   Runs allowed result from combinations of events. . .what we are referring to here as combinations of elements.   An ERA is a summary of how effective the pitcher has been, and as such dozens of factors play into ERA—the pitcher's ground ball tendency, for example, and the quality of the double play combination behind him.   Everything the pitcher does feeds into his ERA—and a great many things that are done not by him but by the defense behind him.   Wins and Losses are an even more distant summary, a summary not merely of the pitcher's performance but of the performance of the team when he was pitching.   It's a small picture/big picture thing.   The pitcher's record is Big Picture; the batter's record is details.

In the last thirty years we have gained a vastly better understanding of how the details relate to the big picture, how the elements combine to form the results.   I am making this point because in a few years it will be lost.   The baseball fans of a generation ago—and the managers, and the general managers— did not have a good understanding of how singles, doubles, triples, homers, walks, strikeouts, home runs, balls in play and fielding performance combined to form runs, or how runs combined to form wins.   As people grow up understanding that, as that knowledge works its way ever more deeply into our culture, people will at some point cease to understand that these relationships are not obvious and were not always apparent.

As we have gained this understanding, two things have happened. First, we have learned to construct summary or result-oriented records for batters. OPS is a summary stat. Runs Created is a summary stat. And second, we have learned to focus much more on the raw elements of the pitcher's performance, and to understand the distortions that make the summary stats (ERA and won-lost record) less reliable than we once believed them to be.

Projecting pitcher performance is much different than projecting batter performance because projecting summaries is much different than projecting elements. Projecting the elements of performance accurately requires knowledge, understanding, hard work and luck. Projecting the summaries accurately requires luck, knowledge, luck, understanding, luck, hard work, and some extra luck.

We used to believe that pitching performance was much, much less predictable than batter performance. This is probably still true; pitching performance probably is much less predictable than batter performance, due to injuries and other factors. However, we were over-estimating the difference because we were contrasting summary projections with elemental projections. In this section last year we didn't project any pitcher's strikeouts and walks exactly correctly, but let's look at a few of them. We had projected that Chad Billingsley would have 189 strikeouts and 84 walks. It was actually 179 and 86:

Chad Billingsley

	G	IP	W	L	Pct	H	HR	SO	BB	ERA	Sv
Actual	33	196	12	11	.522	173	17	179	86	4.03	0
Projected	33	193	12	9	.571	174	17	189	84	3.69	0

We had projected that John Lackey would have 141 strikeouts and 51 walks:

John Lackey

	G	IP	W	L	Pct	H	HR	SO	BB	ERA	Sv
Actual	27	176	11	8	.579	177	17	139	47	3.83	0
Projected	26	175	11	9	.550	175	17	141	51	3.81	0

We had projected that Carsten Sabathia would have 205 strikeouts, 70 walks, and that his closer would be at 66 and 12:

CC Sabathia

	G	IP	W	L	Pct	H	HR	SO	BB	ERA	Sv
Actual	34	230	19	8	.704	197	18	197	67	3.37	0
Projected	34	240	16	10	.615	226	21	205	70	3.48	0

Mariano Rivera

	G	IP	W	L	Pct	H	HR	SO	BB	ERA	Sv
Actual	66	66	3	3	.500	48	7	72	12	1.76	44
Projected	61	70	5	2	.714	56	3	66	12	2.07	43

We had projected that King Felix would have 188 strikeouts, 74 walks:

Felix Hernandez

	G	IP	W	L	Pct	H	HR	SO	BB	ERA	Sv
Actual	34	239	19	5	.792	200	15	217	71	2.49	0
Projected	31	205	11	12	.478	202	19	188	74	3.86	0

Let us pause there for a moment.   If you focus on the summary categories, one could not describe this as an accurate projection.   We were 314 points off on his winning percentage, and 137 points off on ERA.   Those are mammoth discrepancies. But if you focus on the elements of performance, you can see that our projection is. . .well, I'll stop short of calling it "accurate", but it has its points. A similar case is Cleveland Closer Kerry Wood:

Kerry Wood

	G	IP	W	L	Pct	H	HR	SO	BB	ERA	Sv
Actual	58	55	3	3	.500	48	7	63	28	4.25	20
Projected	62	66	5	3	.625	53	7	74	28	3.51	33

Kerry Wood signed a big-dollar contract with Cleveland in the winter, and, because of some things that went wrong early in the season, was perceived as having a disastrous season.   But actually, if you focus on the whole season, and if you focus on the elements of his performance rather than the summary, he did about what he could have been expected to do.   We had projected 74 strikeouts in 66 innings; it was actually 11 fewer strikeouts in 11 fewer innings.   And there are other pitchers whose 2009 projections we can look back upon without regret:

Roy Halladay

	G	IP	W	L	Pct	H	HR	SO	BB	ERA	Sv
Actual	32	239	17	10	.630	234	22	208	35	2.79	0
Projected	32	241	17	10	.630	228	18	172	44	3.18	0

Dan Haren

	G	IP	W	L	Pct	H	HR	SO	BB	ERA	Sv
Actual	33	229	14	10	.583	192	27	223	38	3.14	0
Projected	32	210	14	10	.583	206	23	174	47	3.59	0

John Danks

	G	IP	W	L	Pct	H	HR	SO	BB	ERA	Sv
Actual	32	200	13	11	.542	184	28	149	73	3.77	0
Projected	33	201	12	11	.522	191	24	173	72	4.00	0

Erik Bedard

	G	IP	W	L	Pct	H	HR	SO	BB	ERA	Sv
Actual	15	83	5	3	.625	65	8	90	34	2.82	0
Projected	16	89	5	5	.500	82	8	86	35	3.72	0

Aaron Cook

	G	IP	W	L	Pct	H	HR	SO	BB	ERA	Sv
Actual	27	158	11	6	.647	175	19	78	47	4.16	0
Projected	29	182	11	10	.524	209	14	74	51	4.34	0

Barry Zito

	G	IP	W	L	Pct	H	HR	SO	BB	ERA	Sv
Actual	33	192	10	13	.435	179	21	154	81	4.03	0
Projected	31	197	10	12	.455	184	22	139	84	3.94	0

Luke Hochevar

	G	IP	W	L	Pct	H	HR	SO	BB	ERA	Sv
Actual	25	143	7	13	.350	167	23	106	46	6.55	0
Projected	26	146	6	10	.375	163	20	100	52	4.95	0

Yovani Gallardo

	G	IP	W	L	Pct	H	HR	SO	BB	ERA	Sv
Actual	30	186	13	12	.520	150	21	204	94	3.73	0
Projected	31	196	13	9	.591	179	13	201	76	3.61	0

Gavin Floyd

	G	IP	W	L	Pct	H	HR	SO	BB	ERA	Sv
Actual	30	193	11	11	.500	178	21	163	59	4.06	0
Projected	33	217	12	12	.500	215	34	157	87	4.00	0

Huston Street

	G	IP	W	L	Pct	H	HR	SO	BB	ERA	Sv
Actual	64	62	4	1	.800	43	7	70	13	3.06	35
Projected	61	70	5	3	.625	56	5	71	21	2.90	28

Of course, I wouldn't want you to think that that is our normal level of accuracy. It isn't. Sometimes a pitcher gets hurt, and when that happens our projections for him are knocked into a cocked hat:

Brandon Webb

	G	IP	W	L	Pct	H	HR	SO	BB	ERA	Sv
Actual	1	4	0	0	.000	6	2	2	2	13.50	0
Projected	32	222	15	9	.625	204	14	176	71	3.37	0

Jesse Litsch

	G	IP	W	L	Pct	H	HR	SO	BB	ERA	Sv
Actual	2	9	0	1	.000	14	4	8	1	9.00	0
Projected	27	180	9	11	.450	190	21	108	45	4.06	0

Jeremy Bonderman

	G	IP	W	L	Pct	H	HR	SO	BB	ERA	Sv
Actual	8	10	0	1	.000	16	4	5	8	8.71	0
Projected	24	150	8	8	.500	157	17	123	51	4.23	0

Daisuke Matsuzaka

	G	IP	W	L	Pct	H	HR	SO	BB	ERA	Sv
Actual	12	59	4	6	.400	81	10	54	30	5.76	0
Projected	30	184	12	8	.600	160	17	174	77	3.58	0

Chien-Ming Wang

	G	IP	W	L	Pct	H	HR	SO	BB	ERA	Sv
Actual	12	42	1	6	.143	66	7	29	19	9.64	0
Projected	30	200	13	9	.591	208	11	92	58	3.70	0

Archaic expression there, "knocked into a cocked hat". I only used it in an effort to distract you from our miserable performance in projecting these pitchers. Sometimes pitchers also perform much, much *better* than we had anticipated. Usually—but not always—this happens when they are returning from an injury:

Chris Carpenter

	G	IP	W	L	Pct	H	HR	SO	BB	ERA	Sv
Actual	28	193	17	4	.810	156	7	144	38	2.24	0
Projected	8	45	3	2	.600	42	4	36	11	3.34	0

Carl Pavano

	G	IP	W	L	Pct	H	HR	SO	BB	ERA	Sv
Actual	33	199	14	12	.538	235	26	147	39	5.10	0
Projected	14	69	4	4	.500	76	7	43	17	4.22	0

Adam Wainwright

	G	IP	W	L	Pct	H	HR	SO	BB	ERA	Sv
Actual	34	233	19	8	.704	216	17	212	66	2.63	0
Projected	25	150	9	7	.562	152	13	110	45	3.80	0

Justin Verlander

	G	IP	W	L	Pct	H	HR	SO	BB	ERA	Sv
Actual	35	240	19	9	.679	219	20	269	63	3.45	0
Projected	30	182	11	9	.550	173	18	147	68	3.87	0

David Aardsma

	G	IP	W	L	Pct	H	HR	SO	BB	ERA	Sv
Actual	73	71	3	6	.333	49	4	80	34	2.52	38
Projected	36	38	2	2	.500	37	5	36	22	4.81	0

Sometimes a change of performance in one area leads to a change in the summary:

Ryan Franklin

	G	IP	W	L	Pct	H	HR	SO	BB	ERA	Sv
Actual	62	61	4	3	.571	49	2	44	24	1.92	38
Projected	71	79	4	5	.444	83	11	42	24	4.36	2

One thing the Cardinals do brilliantly is to tinker with the pitcher's role and his pitch selection, often leading to dramatic changes in performance. The Cardinals apparently realized that Franklin was giving up home runs on his slider and giving up home runs when he was tired. The moved him from starter to relief and replaced his slider with a cut fastball, leading to a dramatic reduction in home runs allowed, leading to a new level of performance. Although in that case, since

Franklin had been the Cardinals' closer the second half of 2008, I really don't know why we projected him to have only two saves in 2009. . .apparently we just weren't paying quite as much attention as we should have been.

A similar thing with Brian Fuentes: I really can't understand *why* we projected him to have only four saves in 2009:

Brian Fuentes

	G	IP	W	L	Pct	H	HR	SO	BB	ERA	Sv
Actual	65	55	1	5	.167	53	6	46	24	3.93	48
Projected	63	62	5	2	.714	50	6	70	25	3.43	4

That must have been one of those end-of-the season things, maybe? Our process looks at the role that a relief pitcher is in at the end of the season, and projects his performance based on that, along with many other factors. We must have concluded, somehow, that Fuentes would not be a closer in 2009. It's embarrassing to look back on, but. . .these things happen. The rest of the projection is good; the "role" projection is inexplicable, even remembering that this projection was printed months before Fuentes signed with the Angels.

There are a lot of ways we can go wrong. We didn't realize that Oliver Perez would begin aiming pitches at outer space:

Oliver Perez

	G	IP	W	L	Pct	H	HR	SO	BB	ERA	Sv
Actual	14	66	3	4	.429	69	12	62	58	6.82	0
Projected	34	204	11	12	.478	186	31	205	109	4.53	0

Or that Daniel Cabrera would begin aiming even more pitches at outer space:

Daniel Cabrera

	G	IP	W	L	Pct	H	HR	SO	BB	ERA	Sv
Actual	15	51	0	6	.000	59	4	23	42	6.00	0
Projected	25	141	7	9	.438	141	15	108	78	4.85	0

We lack the ability to foresee these things. Actually, we lack the ability to foresee *anything;* we just project forward based on the assumption that everything is normal. As long as everything is normal, we do good. When it's not, we struggle.

2010 Pitcher Projections

Pitcher	Team	Age	G	GS	IP	H	HR	BB	SO	HB	W	L	Pct	Sv	BR/9	ERA
Aardsma,David	Sea	28	69	0	69	62	7	37	68	2	3	4	.429	27	13.2	4.17
Aceves,Alfredo	NYY	27	44	0	76	71	10	17	58	8	5	3	.625	0	11.4	3.55
Acosta,Manny	Atl	29	35	0	37	35	4	23	31	2	2	2	.500	0	14.6	4.62
Adams,Mike	SD	31	43	0	46	39	4	16	47	0	3	2	.600	0	10.8	2.93
Affeldt,Jeremy	SF	31	78	0	64	60	6	29	50	2	3	4	.429	0	12.8	3.94
Albaladejo,Jonathan	NYY	27	30	0	30	29	4	9	23	2	2	1	.667	0	12	3.60
Albers,Matt	Bal	27	57	0	64	69	6	30	46	3	3	4	.429	0	14.3	4.92
Anderson,Brett	Oak	22	30	30	189	187	21	49	172	8	11	10	.524	0	11.6	3.76
Arias,Alberto	Hou	26	33	0	33	36	2	14	24	3	2	2	.500	0	14.5	4.64
Arredondo,Jose	LAA	26	47	0	54	49	5	25	51	0	3	3	.500	0	12.3	3.67
Arroyo,Bronson	Cin	33	33	33	210	215	28	62	144	10	11	12	.478	0	12.3	4.11
Ascanio,Jose	Pit	25	28	0	31	31	3	12	29	3	2	2	.500	0	13.4	4.35
Baez,Danys	Bal	32	62	0	70	65	8	28	47	6	4	4	.500	0	12.7	3.99
Bailey,Andrew	Oak	26	60	0	72	58	6	29	71	5	5	3	.625	29	11.5	3.13
Bailey,Homer	Cin	24	29	29	170	177	20	79	140	14	8	11	.421	0	14.3	4.87
Baker,Scott	Min	28	32	32	200	204	25	47	156	5	12	10	.545	0	11.5	3.83
Balester,Collin	Was	24	11	11	47	54	6	18	32	5	2	3	.400	0	14.7	5.36
Balfour,Grant	TB	32	74	0	63	46	5	31	79	1	5	2	.714	4	11.1	2.86
Bannister,Brian	KC	29	23	23	134	142	16	41	83	5	6	8	.429	0	12.6	4.23
Bard,Daniel	Bos	25	57	0	53	40	5	25	70	1	4	2	.667	0	11.2	3.06
Bass,Brian	Bal	28	48	0	84	99	10	32	51	5	4	6	.400	0	14.6	5.25
Batista,Miguel	Sea	39	53	0	67	73	7	30	42	2	3	5	.375	4	14.1	4.84
Bazardo,Yorman	Hou	25	19	3	36	44	5	14	21	4	1	3	.250	0	15.5	5.75
Beckett,Josh	Bos	30	33	33	221	208	24	64	206	8	15	9	.625	0	11.4	3.62
Bedard,Erik	Sea	31	15	15	88	78	8	35	87	3	5	5	.500	0	11.9	3.58
Beimel,Joe	Col	33	72	0	51	53	3	21	30	1	3	2	.600	0	13.2	3.88
Belisario,Ronald	LAD	27	71	0	69	65	6	32	55	4	4	4	.500	0	13.2	4.04
Belisle,Matt	Col	30	25	0	34	39	4	9	23	2	2	2	.500	0	13.2	4.50
Bell,Heath	SD	32	75	0	77	65	4	24	81	1	5	4	.556	43	10.5	2.69
Bennett,Jeff	TB	30	37	0	42	45	4	21	28	4	2	3	.400	0	15	4.93
Benoit,Joaquin	Tex	32	45	0	50	45	6	24	47	2	3	3	.500	0	12.8	3.96
Bergesen,Brad	Bal	24	27	27	168	182	15	39	85	18	10	9	.526	0	12.8	4.18
Bergmann,Jason	Was	28	73	0	60	59	8	24	48	2	3	4	.429	0	12.8	4.35
Berken,Jason	Bal	26	29	29	146	171	17	50	99	18	6	10	.375	0	14.7	5.36
Betancourt,Rafael	Col	35	70	0	60	51	6	16	60	0	5	2	.714	2	10	2.70
Billingsley,Chad	LAD	25	32	30	185	165	16	81	177	6	12	8	.600	0	12.3	3.65
Blackburn,Nick	Min	28	33	33	203	232	22	42	103	6	11	12	.478	0	12.4	4.26
Blanton,Joe	Phi	29	32	32	213	225	23	61	136	6	13	11	.542	0	12.3	4.06
Blevins,Jerry	Oak	26	31	0	38	36	3	11	38	1	2	2	.500	0	11.4	3.08
Boggs,Mitchell	StL	26	22	10	75	85	7	36	50	9	3	5	.375	0	15.6	5.40
Bonderman,Jeremy	Det	27	30	30	185	198	23	63	149	6	9	11	.450	0	13	4.43
Bonine,Eddie	Det	29	12	6	48	56	6	10	24	6	2	3	.400	0	13.5	4.88
Bonser,Boof	Min	28	15	15	65	71	10	23	56	1	3	4	.429	0	13.2	4.71
Bowden,Michael	Bos	23	25	15	130	137	14	46	100	18	7	8	.467	0	13.9	4.71
Boyer,Blaine	Ari	28	49	0	57	63	4	27	45	4	3	4	.429	0	14.8	4.74
Braden,Dallas	Oak	26	25	25	170	179	16	54	124	7	9	10	.474	0	12.7	4.08
Bradford,Chad	TB	35	60	0	40	44	2	11	22	2	2	2	.500	0	12.8	3.83
Breslow,Craig	Oak	29	72	0	77	68	6	32	69	3	5	4	.556	0	12	3.39
Broxton,Jonathan	LAD	26	76	0	80	59	4	31	104	2	6	3	.667	40	10.4	2.36
Bruney,Brian	NYY	28	52	0	50	45	5	34	48	3	3	3	.500	0	14.8	4.68
Buchholz,Clay	Bos	25	27	27	161	150	17	63	155	12	10	8	.556	0	12.6	3.91
Buchholz,Taylor	Col	28	26	0	31	31	4	9	22	1	2	1	.667	0	11.9	3.77
Buckner,Billy	Ari	26	16	15	94	103	10	37	69	9	4	6	.400	0	14.3	4.98
Buehrle,Mark	CWS	31	33	33	216	232	25	48	122	5	12	12	.500	0	11.9	3.96
Bulger,Jason	LAA	31	60	0	60	50	4	29	74	2	4	3	.571	0	12.2	3.30
Burke,Greg	SD	27	46	0	46	43	4	15	44	1	3	2	.600	0	11.5	3.33
Burnett,A.J.	NYY	33	35	35	223	205	23	90	217	11	15	10	.600	0	12.3	3.75
Burnett,Sean	Was	27	65	0	49	54	5	25	27	2	2	3	.400	0	14.9	5.14
Burns,Mike	Mil	31	19	8	58	65	9	14	42	5	3	4	.429	0	13	4.66
Burton,Jared	Cin	29	57	0	64	61	5	27	54	3	4	3	.571	0	12.8	3.80
Bush,David	Mil	30	21	20	107	112	16	27	74	9	6	6	.500	0	12.4	4.29
Byrd,Paul	Bos	39	14	12	68	80	10	12	33	2	4	4	.500	0	12.4	4.63
Byrdak,Tim	Hou	36	85	0	68	59	9	37	67	2	4	4	.500	0	13	4.24
Cabrera,Daniel	Ari	29	16	6	42	43	5	25	31	3	2	3	.400	0	15.2	5.14
Cahill,Trevor	Oak	22	31	31	185	189	25	78	104	8	8	13	.381	0	13.4	4.62
Cain,Matt	SF	25	33	33	225	194	21	80	194	6	14	11	.560	0	11.2	3.36
Calero,Kiko	Fla	35	66	0	64	54	5	30	67	1	4	3	.571	0	12	3.38
Camp,Shawn	Tor	34	50	0	70	78	7	21	52	5	3	4	.429	0	13.4	4.50
Campillo,Jorge	Atl	31	36	21	142	149	14	39	95	3	9	7	.562	0	12.1	3.93
Capps,Matt	Pit	26	55	0	57	56	7	11	45	2	3	3	.500	30	10.9	3.47
Caridad,Esmailin	ChC	26	27	0	39	39	6	13	30	7	2	3	.400	0	13.6	4.85
Carlson,Jesse	Tor	29	71	0	67	67	7	21	59	4	4	4	.500	0	12.4	3.90
Carmona,Fausto	Cle	26	28	28	152	162	15	59	96	11	7	9	.438	0	13.7	4.56
Carpenter,Chris	StL	35	28	28	195	169	13	42	154	7	16	6	.727	0	10.1	2.95
Carrasco,Carlos	Cle	23	10	10	45	48	6	19	40	6	2	3	.400	0	14.6	5.20
Carrasco,D.J.	CWS	33	44	0	90	103	8	36	59	5	4	6	.400	0	14.4	4.90
Casilla,Santiago	Oak	29	45	0	51	50	5	24	50	3	2	3	.400	0	13.6	4.41
Cecil,Brett	Tor	23	19	18	98	103	10	40	85	15	4	7	.364	0	14.5	4.87
Chamberlain,Joba	NYY	24	33	33	176	167	18	77	190	9	11	8	.579	0	12.9	3.94
Chavez,Jesse	Pit	26	73	0	72	79	9	28	59	1	3	5	.375	0	13.5	4.75

484

2010 Pitcher Projections

PLAYER			HOW MUCH			WHAT HE WILL GIVE UP					THE RESULTS					
Pitcher	Team	Age	G	GS	IP	H	HR	BB	SO	HB	W	L	Pct	Sv	BR/9	ERA
Chen,Bruce	KC	33	23	9	78	81	14	29	56	5	3	6	.333	0	13.3	4.96
Clippard,Tyler	Was	25	62	0	91	85	13	45	84	8	4	6	.400	0	13.6	4.55
Coffey,Todd	Mil	29	81	0	87	96	10	26	66	4	4	5	.444	0	13	4.45
Coke,Phil	NYY	27	70	0	56	53	6	20	52	6	4	3	.571	1	12.7	3.86
Colon,Bartolo	CWS	37	6	6	31	33	5	9	21	1	2	2	.500	0	12.5	4.35
Colon,Roman	KC	30	50	0	63	73	9	24	42	3	2	5	.286	0	14.3	5.43
Condrey,Clay	Phi	34	41	0	39	45	3	12	21	2	2	2	.500	0	13.6	4.62
Contreras,Jose	Col	38	20	12	70	72	8	26	50	4	4	4	.500	0	13.1	4.37
Cook,Aaron	Col	31	28	28	164	186	14	47	69	5	9	9	.500	0	13.1	4.34
Cordero,Francisco	Cin	35	72	0	100	86	6	43	108	3	6	5	.545	37	11.9	3.15
Cormier,Lance	TB	29	57	0	72	82	8	31	42	1	3	5	.375	0	14.2	5.00
Corpas,Manny	Col	27	65	0	67	68	5	16	49	2	5	3	.625	4	11.6	3.49
Correia,Kevin	SD	29	33	33	217	225	23	81	156	7	11	13	.458	0	13	4.23
Crain,Jesse	Min	28	68	0	69	67	6	27	50	3	4	4	.500	0	12.7	3.91
Cruz,Juan	KC	31	29	0	35	30	3	18	37	3	2	2	.500	0	13.1	3.86
Cueto,Johnny	Cin	24	30	30	174	172	26	60	155	15	9	10	.474	0	12.8	4.40
Daley,Matt	Col	28	68	0	58	54	7	20	53	2	4	3	.571	0	11.8	3.57
Danks,John	CWS	25	33	33	206	209	29	75	168	5	11	12	.478	0	12.6	4.33
Davies,Kyle	KC	26	22	22	126	135	15	60	91	7	5	9	.357	0	14.4	5.07
Davis,Doug	Ari	34	34	34	202	207	21	93	153	5	11	12	.478	0	13.6	4.46
Davis,Wade	TB	24	26	26	151	146	14	65	134	22	8	9	.471	0	13.9	4.35
de la Rosa,Jorge	Col	29	33	33	194	200	22	94	174	9	10	11	.476	0	14.1	4.73
Delcarmen,Manny	Bos	28	63	0	58	54	4	27	54	2	4	3	.571	0	12.9	3.72
Dempster,Ryan	ChC	33	30	30	195	183	18	81	167	6	12	10	.545	0	12.5	3.83
Dessens,Elmer	NYM	39	30	0	35	37	4	11	22	1	2	2	.500	0	12.6	4.11
Devine,Joey	Oak	26	50	0	44	33	2	22	55	3	3	2	.000	0	11.9	2.86
Dickey,R.A.	Min	35	21	0	37	43	5	14	22	2	1	3	.250	0	14.4	6.36
DiFelice,Mark	Mil	33	53	0	43	39	5	9	40	3	3	2	.600	0	10.7	3.14
DiNardo,Lenny	KC	30	10	10	43	52	4	16	28	4	2	3	.400	0	15.1	5.23
Donnelly,Brendan	Fla	38	41	0	36	33	3	13	33	2	2	2	.500	2	12	3.50
Dotel,Octavio	CWS	36	57	0	64	53	0	28	80	3	4	3	.571	0	11.8	3.66
Downs,Scott	Tor	34	55	0	54	52	5	19	45	2	3	3	.500	16	12.2	3.07
Duchscherer,Justin	Oak	32	23	23	161	131	13	38	113	8	10	6	.625	0	10.5	3.16
Duensing,Brian	Min	27	32	16	134	153	14	41	86	14	6	9	.400	0	14	4.84
Duke,Zach	Pit	27	31	31	206	244	20	62	104	5	9	14	.391	0	13.2	4.54
Dumatrait,Phil	Pit	28	40	0	38	42	5	20	24	1	1	3	.250	0	14.9	5.45
Durbin,Chad	Phi	32	53	0	66	66	9	29	48	4	3	4	.429	0	13.5	4.50
Eaton,Adam	Col	32	12	4	36	41	5	13	24	3	2	2	.500	0	14.2	5.25
Embree,Alan	Col	40	60	0	45	45	5	15	37	1	3	2	.600	0	12.2	3.80
Eveland,Dana	Oak	26	15	9	48	52	4	22	37	4	2	3	.400	0	14.6	4.69
Eyre,Scott	Phi	38	44	0	31	29	3	15	29	1	2	2	.500	0	13.1	4.06
Eyre,Willie	Tex	31	35	0	35	36	3	14	23	2	2	2	.500	0	13.4	4.11
Farnsworth,Kyle	KC	34	40	0	40	38	6	17	42	1	2	3	.400	0	12.6	4.28
Feldman,Scott	Tex	27	32	32	195	194	20	73	113	11	11	11	.500	0	12.8	4.06
Feliciano,Pedro	NYM	33	87	0	57	52	5	23	53	3	3	3	.500	0	12.3	3.63
Figueroa,Nelson	NYM	36	15	6	53	56	6	18	40	6	2	3	.400	0	13.6	4.58
Fisher,Carlos	Cin	27	43	0	59	60	5	28	53	2	3	4	.429	0	13.7	4.42
Fister,Doug	Sea	26	21	19	122	142	14	31	88	13	5	9	.357	0	13.7	4.87
Floyd,Gavin	CWS	27	30	30	190	196	27	72	144	10	9	12	.429	0	13.2	4.59
Fogg,Josh	Col	33	25	2	54	61	8	19	28	4	3	3	.500	0	14	5.17
Francis,Jeff	Col	29	26	26	157	171	19	52	109	7	9	9	.500	0	13.2	4.59
Francisco,Frank	Tex	30	58	0	57	45	5	25	65	2	4	2	.667	30	11.4	3.00
Franklin,Ryan	StL	37	62	0	61	62	8	19	33	2	4	3	.571	17	12.2	4.13
Frasor,Jason	Tor	32	58	0	58	51	5	25	55	2	4	3	.571	1	12.1	3.41
French,Luke	Sea	24	19	16	91	102	11	33	57	12	3	7	.300	0	14.5	5.14
Fuentes,Brian	LAA	34	66	0	56	47	5	23	60	5	4	2	.667	40	12.1	3.38
Fulchino,Jeff	Hou	30	73	0	93	102	9	41	71	6	4	6	.400	0	14.4	4.94
Galarraga,Armando	Det	28	27	19	117	119	18	47	86	7	6	7	.462	0	13.3	4.62
Gallagher,Sean	SD	24	35	4	40	39	3	21	36	3	2	3	.400	0	14.2	4.50
Gallardo,Yovani	Mil	24	31	31	186	157	17	84	205	5	12	8	.600	0	11.9	3.53
Garcia,Freddy	CWS	34	17	17	112	116	15	31	81	4	6	6	.500	0	12.1	4.18
Garland,Jon	LAD	30	33	33	216	235	25	64	109	6	12	12	.500	0	12.7	4.33
Garza,Matt	TB	26	31	31	201	193	20	73	175	9	12	10	.545	0	12.3	3.85
Gaudin,Chad	NYY	27	35	16	138	141	14	60	111	6	8	7	.533	0	13.5	4.30
Geer,Josh	SD	27	23	23	137	150	18	34	81	14	6	9	.400	0	13	4.53
Gervacio,Sammy	Hou	25	56	0	42	38	5	18	49	0	2	2	.500	0	12	3.64
Gonzalez,Edgar	Oak	27	15	5	45	52	6	14	30	4	2	3	.400	0	14	5.00
Gonzalez,Gio	Oak	24	22	22	155	145	21	86	168	13	6	11	.353	0	14.2	4.76
Gonzalez,Mike	Atl	32	79	0	78	62	6	34	92	4	6	3	.667	5	11.5	3.12
Gorzelanny,Tom	ChC	27	29	14	81	80	7	32	64	5	5	4	.556	0	13	4.11
Gosling,Mike	Cle	29	19	0	32	38	4	14	27	1	1	2	.333	0	14.9	5.63
Grabow,John	ChC	31	78	0	72	67	7	34	61	2	4	4	.500	0	12.9	4.00
Gray,Jeff	Oak	28	42	0	50	55	4	14	35	2	2	3	.400	0	12.8	4.14
Green,Sean	NYM	31	79	0	69	68	3	35	51	5	4	4	.500	0	14.1	4.04
Gregerson,Luke	SD	26	81	0	82	69	5	32	92	2	6	3	.667	4	11.3	2.96
Gregg,Kevin	ChC	32	67	0	65	58	7	27	60	3	4	3	.571	4	12.2	3.60
Greinke,Zack	KC	26	33	33	225	211	21	57	209	7	13	12	.520	0	11	3.32
Grilli,Jason	Tex	33	45	0	37	38	3	17	28	2	2	2	.500	0	13.9	4.38
Guerrier,Matt	Min	31	77	0	75	72	9	23	51	2	5	4	.556	0	11.6	3.72
Guthrie,Jeremy	Bal	31	33	33	216	223	29	73	137	10	12	12	.500	0	12.8	4.38
Gutierrez,Juan	Ari	26	63	0	68	74	7	27	54	5	3	4	.429	4	14	4.76

485

2010 Pitcher Projections

Pitcher	Team	Age	G	GS	IP	H	HR	BB	SO	HB	W	L	Pct	Sv	BR/9	ERA
Guzman,Angel	ChC	28	50	0	58	55	6	25	53	4	3	3	.500	0	13	4.03
Haeger,Charlie	LAD	26	12	6	38	38	5	19	27	4	2	2	.500	0	14.4	4.97
Halladay,Roy	Tor	33	33	33	240	232	19	42	179	7	17	10	.630	0	10.5	3.23
Hamels,Cole	Phi	26	33	33	210	193	27	53	195	3	15	9	.625	0	10.7	3.43
Hammel,Jason	Col	27	32	32	182	200	20	63	144	8	10	10	.500	0	13.4	4.55
Hampton,Mike	Hou	37	14	14	76	85	8	30	41	2	3	5	.375	0	13.9	4.74
Hanrahan,Joel	Pit	28	64	0	64	64	8	36	60	2	3	4	.429	0	14.3	4.78
Hanson,Tommy	Atl	23	32	32	191	149	18	71	206	22	14	7	.667	0	11.4	3.30
Happ,J.A.	Phi	27	31	31	188	182	25	77	171	12	10	11	.476	0	13	4.31
Harang,Aaron	Cin	32	32	32	211	222	30	57	179	6	11	12	.478	0	12.2	4.18
Harden,Rich	ChC	28	24	24	135	107	14	59	147	4	10	5	.667	0	11.3	3.33
Haren,Dan	Ari	29	33	33	221	209	25	47	191	6	16	9	.640	0	10.7	3.38
Harrison,Matt	Tex	24	20	20	119	138	12	41	73	7	6	8	.429	0	14.1	4.92
Hart,Kevin	Pit	27	23	21	120	120	14	53	104	10	5	8	.385	0	13.7	4.58
Hawkins,LaTroy	Hou	37	62	0	63	61	6	17	45	1	4	3	.571	0	11.3	3.29
Hawksworth,Blake	StL	27	43	0	54	59	7	20	38	6	3	3	.500	0	14.2	5.00
Heilman,Aaron	ChC	31	66	0	72	66	8	31	63	4	4	4	.500	0	12.6	3.88
Hendrickson,Mark	Bal	36	55	2	65	75	8	19	37	1	3	4	.429	0	13.2	4.71
Herges,Matt	Col	40	28	0	31	33	3	11	21	1	2	2	.500	0	13.1	4.06
Hernandez,David	Bal	25	27	27	135	133	22	63	133	18	6	9	.400	0	14.3	5.07
Hernandez,Felix	Sea	24	35	35	235	213	19	79	216	7	14	12	.538	0	11.5	3.37
Hernandez,Livan	Was	35	31	31	186	218	23	61	103	4	8	13	.381	0	13.7	4.98
Herrera,Daniel Ray	Cin	25	70	0	61	58	5	22	53	2	4	3	.571	0	12.1	3.54
Hochevar,Luke	KC	26	29	29	171	191	23	58	121	12	7	12	.368	0	13.7	4.95
Hoffman,Trevor	Mil	42	61	0	63	52	5	14	57	1	4	3	.571	39	9.6	2.43
Howell,J.P.	TB	27	75	0	72	69	9	30	72	4	4	4	.500	6	12.9	4.13
Howry,Bob	SF	36	64	0	68	65	8	18	54	2	4	3	.571	0	11.2	3.44
Hudson,Tim	Atl	34	24	24	146	147	11	41	89	6	10	6	.625	0	12	3.64
Huff,David	Cle	25	24	24	143	150	17	45	106	15	7	9	.438	0	13.2	4.47
Hughes,Phil	NYY	24	61	12	121	110	10	41	122	7	9	5	.643	2	11.8	3.27
Hunter,Tommy	Tex	23	28	28	170	191	22	49	103	17	8	11	.421	0	13.6	4.82
Jackson,Edwin	Det	26	33	33	218	232	28	95	155	5	10	14	.417	0	13.7	4.75
Jackson,Steven	Pit	28	53	0	58	65	6	25	46	1	2	4	.333	0	14.1	4.81
Jakubauskas,Chris	Sea	31	29	4	68	66	7	22	46	5	4	4	.500	0	12.3	3.84
Janssen,Casey	Tor	28	33	2	41	46	4	11	26	2	2	2	.500	0	13	4.39
Jenks,Bobby	CWS	29	50	0	54	47	4	18	50	2	4	2	.667	30	11.2	3.00
Jennings,Jason	Tex	31	33	0	42	46	5	19	28	1	2	3	.400	0	14.1	5.14
Jepsen,Kevin	LAA	25	51	0	52	53	4	27	49	0	3	3	.500	2	13.8	4.33
Jimenez,Ubaldo	Col	26	33	33	210	195	17	102	182	11	13	10	.565	0	13.2	3.94
Johnson,Jim	Bal	27	63	0	68	77	7	27	46	5	3	4	.429	4	14.4	5.03
Johnson,Josh	Fla	26	33	33	206	199	13	72	181	6	14	9	.609	0	12.1	3.63
Johnson,Randy	SF	46	18	8	54	50	7	13	51	2	3	3	.500	0	10.8	3.67
Jurrjens,Jair	Atl	24	34	34	210	204	16	75	153	4	14	9	.609	0	12.1	3.69
Karstens,Jeff	Pit	27	38	11	87	95	11	28	57	3	4	6	.400	0	13	4.55
Kazmir,Scott	LAA	26	29	29	173	160	18	76	176	6	10	9	.526	0	12.6	3.90
Kendrick,Kyle	Phi	25	14	4	47	53	5	14	21	5	2	3	.400	0	13.8	4.60
Kensing,Logan	Was	27	36	0	41	40	6	20	38	2	2	3	.400	0	13.6	4.61
Keppel,Bobby	Min	28	54	0	78	98	9	29	40	8	3	6	.333	0	15.6	5.88
Kershaw,Clayton	LAD	22	31	31	180	140	11	91	188	6	13	7	.650	0	11.8	3.25
Kilby,Brad	Oak	27	21	2	34	28	3	13	35	0	2	2	.500	0	10.9	2.91
Kuo,Hong-Chih	LAD	28	53	0	48	40	3	20	56	2	4	2	.667	0	11.6	3.00
Kuroda,Hiroki	LAD	35	22	21	128	127	16	35	85	1	8	6	.571	0	11.5	3.80
Lackey,John	LAA	31	30	30	208	207	21	60	166	11	13	10	.565	0	12	3.81
Laffey,Aaron	Cle	25	28	25	157	183	12	60	92	12	7	11	.389	0	14.6	4.99
Lannan,John	Was	25	32	32	199	200	21	73	101	7	11	11	.500	0	12.7	4.03
League,Brandon	Tor	27	67	0	77	82	7	27	61	6	4	5	.444	0	13.4	4.32
LeBlanc,Wade	SD	25	22	22	127	119	19	44	110	17	6	8	.429	0	12.8	4.32
Lee,Cliff	Phi	31	32	32	222	228	21	60	168	7	14	11	.560	0	12	3.81
Lehr,Justin	Cin	32	20	20	123	132	15	43	74	10	6	8	.429	0	13.5	4.68
Lester,Jon	Bos	26	31	31	206	200	19	80	184	6	13	10	.565	0	12.5	3.84
Lewis,Jensen	Cle	26	50	0	74	68	9	31	75	3	4	4	.500	0	12.4	3.89
Lidge,Brad	Phi	33	69	0	60	51	6	28	78	4	4	3	.571	28	12.4	3.60
Lilly,Ted	ChC	34	25	25	170	155	24	56	144	4	11	8	.579	0	11.4	3.76
Lincecum,Tim	SF	26	31	31	228	176	12	80	261	6	18	7	.720	0	10.3	2.80
Lindstrom,Matt	Fla	30	58	0	51	55	4	25	44	3	3	3	.500	26	14.6	4.76
Linebrink,Scott	CWS	33	55	0	58	56	8	20	50	1	3	3	.500	0	11.9	3.88
Liriano,Francisco	Min	26	35	11	125	116	13	46	128	7	8	6	.571	0	12.2	3.67
Litsch,Jesse	Tor	25	15	15	75	80	9	18	46	5	4	4	.500	0	12.4	4.20
Lohse,Kyle	StL	31	24	22	118	128	14	36	72	5	6	7	.462	0	12.9	4.35
Looper,Braden	Mil	35	34	34	201	220	28	59	108	7	10	12	.455	0	12.8	4.52
Loux,Shane	LAA	30	17	3	49	61	4	16	22	7	2	3	.400	0	15.4	5.51
Lowe,Derek	Atl	37	34	34	193	211	16	55	110	4	12	9	.571	0	12.6	4.06
Lowe,Mark	Sea	27	77	0	88	86	8	38	77	2	4	5	.444	1	12.9	3.99
Lyon,Brandon	Det	30	68	0	82	82	7	26	54	1	5	4	.556	8	12	3.73
MacDougal,Mike	Was	33	67	0	67	66	4	39	59	3	3	4	.429	4	14.5	4.43
Madson,Ryan	Phi	29	77	0	79	80	8	24	66	4	5	4	.556	2	12.3	3.87
Mahay,Ron	Min	39	59	0	48	48	6	22	40	1	2	3	.400	0	13.3	4.50
Maholm,Paul	Pit	28	29	29	197	212	19	66	126	8	9	12	.429	0	13.1	4.29
Maine,John	NYM	29	27	27	168	153	20	73	137	5	9	9	.500	0	12.4	3.86
Maloney,Matt	Cin	26	9	9	55	56	8	15	49	6	3	3	.500	0	12.6	4.42
Manship,Jeff	Min	25	21	10	63	73	5	22	42	10	3	4	.429	0	15	5.00

2010 Pitcher Projections

PLAYER			HOW MUCH			WHAT HE WILL GIVE UP					THE RESULTS					
Pitcher	Team	Age	G	GS	IP	H	HR	BB	SO	HB	W	L	Pct	Sv	BR/9	ERA
Marcum,Shaun	Tor	28	22	22	120	116	19	37	99	6	6	7	.462	0	11.9	4.05
Marmol,Carlos	ChC	27	74	0	73	52	6	45	84	7	5	3	.625	34	12.8	3.45
Marquis,Jason	Col	31	32	32	202	209	22	77	110	9	12	11	.522	0	13.1	4.37
Marshall,Sean	ChC	27	51	6	71	70	8	27	53	3	4	4	.500	0	12.7	4.06
Marte,Damaso	NYY	35	61	0	43	37	4	20	46	2	3	2	.600	0	12.3	3.56
Martin,J.D.	Was	27	29	29	177	182	19	44	125	20	10	10	.500	0	12.5	4.07
Martinez,Joe	SF	27	14	10	56	60	3	16	38	9	3	3	.500	0	13.7	4.18
Martinez,Pedro	Phi	38	17	17	89	82	11	23	88	5	6	4	.600	0	11.1	3.54
Martic,Shairon	Was	23	7	7	43	48	6	17	26	5	2	3	.400	0	14.7	5.23
Masset,Nick	Cin	28	86	0	84	94	9	36	63	3	4	6	.400	0	14.1	4.82
Masterson,Justin	Cle	25	30	30	171	161	14	74	151	14	10	9	.526	0	13.1	4.00
Mathis,Doug	Tex	27	29	1	46	54	4	15	30	4	2	3	.400	0	14.3	4.89
Matsuzaka,Daisuke	Bos	29	32	32	195	184	21	83	184	10	12	10	.545	0	12.8	4.02
Mazzaro,Vin	Oak	23	17	17	91	94	6	30	65	11	4	6	.400	0	13.4	4.05
McCarthy,Brandon	Tex	26	26	26	162	158	22	59	123	8	9	9	.500	0	12.5	4.11
McClellan,Kyle	StL	26	65	0	66	62	5	27	52	2	4	3	.571	1	12.4	3.68
McClung,Seth	Mil	29	24	1	36	35	4	21	30	2	2	2	.500	0	14.5	4.75
McCutchen,Daniel	Pit	27	12	12	73	78	10	18	54	10	3	5	.375	0	13.1	4.56
McDonald,James	LAD	25	54	2	74	62	8	33	75	10	5	4	.556	0	12.8	3.77
McGowan,Dustin	Tor	28	17	17	80	79	7	33	68	3	4	5	.444	0	12.9	4.05
Meche,Gil	KC	31	27	27	153	157	18	60	115	3	7	10	.412	0	12.9	4.29
Medders,Brandon	SF	30	60	0	74	73	8	36	58	2	4	5	.444	0	13.5	4.38
Medlen,Kris	Atl	24	47	2	75	71	5	25	80	8	5	3	.625	0	12.5	3.60
Meek,Evan	Pit	27	29	0	32	30	2	18	28	0	2	2	.500	0	13.5	3.94
Meredith,Cla	Bal	27	67	0	70	76	5	20	49	2	4	4	.500	0	12.6	3.99
Meyer,Dan	Fla	28	65	0	56	57	7	26	44	4	3	2	.600	0	11	4.08
Mijares,Jose	Min	25	79	0	70	58	9	34	67	2	4	4	.500	0	12.1	3.60
Miller,Andrew	Fla	25	27	20	109	113	8	63	92	8	5	7	.417	0	15.2	4.87
Miller,Justin	SF	32	36	0	43	41	5	21	37	1	2	3	.400	0	13.2	4.40
Miller,Trever	StL	37	74	0	46	40	5	18	45	4	3	2	.600	0	12.1	3.72
Millwood,Kevin	Tex	35	29	29	175	190	19	55	126	7	9	10	.474	0	13	4.37
Miner,Zach	Det	28	57	4	101	108	9	47	65	3	6	6	.455	0	14.1	4.63
Misch,Pat	NYM	28	40	4	56	63	7	16	38	4	3	4	.429	0	13.3	4.66
Mitre,Sergio	NYY	29	15	6	45	54	5	13	29	4	2	3	.400	0	14.2	5.00
Mock,Garrett	Was	27	31	25	143	158	14	59	122	12	6	10	.375	0	14.4	4.91
Moehler,Brian	Hou	38	30	30	163	197	21	47	89	5	7	11	.389	0	13.7	5.08
Morales,Franklin	Col	24	57	1	58	56	6	33	43	7	3	4	.429	4	15.4	5.30
Morrow,Brandon	Sea	25	25	25	135	112	13	79	131	8	7	8	.467	0	13.3	3.93
Mortensen,Clayton	Oak	25	12	12	57	65	8	25	39	10	2	5	.286	0	15.8	5.84
Morton,Charlie	Pit	26	23	23	136	134	8	57	102	12	7	8	.467	0	13.4	3.97
Mota,Guillermo	LAD	36	53	0	55	50	6	21	44	2	4	3	.571	0	11.9	3.60
Motte,Jason	StL	28	65	0	56	49	6	24	68	2	4	3	.571	0	12.1	3.54
Moyer,Jamie	Phi	47	29	19	154	165	22	43	91	7	8	9	.471	0	12.6	4.38
Moylan,Peter	Atl	31	86	0	78	71	4	37	63	5	5	3	.625	0	13	3.58
Mujica,Edward	SD	26	61	8	103	112	13	25	88	1	5	6	.455	0	12.1	4.11
Mulvey,Kevin	Ari	25	13	8	47	50	4	17	35	6	2	3	.400	0	14	4.60
Myers,Brett	Phi	29	27	27	171	172	27	59	147	7	9	10	.474	0	12.5	4.37
Narveson,Chris	Mil	28	28	8	78	77	11	34	65	7	4	5	.444	0	13.0	4.70
Nathan,Joe	Min	35	71	0	75	51	5	23	90	2	6	3	.667	43	9.1	1.92
Neshek,Pat	Min	29	40	0	35	27	5	10	42	1	3	1	.750	0	9.8	2.57
Niemann,Jeff	TB	27	32	32	202	203	25	78	171	19	10	12	.455	0	13.4	4.46
Niese,Jonathon	NYM	23	20	20	118	122	10	43	101	18	6	8	.429	0	14	4.50
Nieve,Fernando	NYM	27	20	11	71	75	11	31	61	5	3	5	.375	0	14.1	5.07
Nippert,Dustin	Tex	29	30	5	88	91	10	39	72	5	4	5	.444	0	13.8	4.70
Nolasco,Ricky	Fla	27	32	32	205	207	27	52	189	8	13	10	.565	0	11.7	3.86
Norris,Bud	Hou	25	20	19	107	110	11	50	104	17	5	7	.417	0	14.9	5.05
Nunez,Leo	Fla	26	71	0	67	64	10	23	51	3	4	3	.571	9	12.1	4.03
O'Day,Darren	Tex	27	69	0	60	55	4	20	50	4	4	3	.571	5	11.8	3.45
O'Flaherty,Eric	Atl	25	75	0	60	62	3	24	48	6	4	3	.571	0	13.8	4.20
Ohka,Tomo	Cle	34	20	4	76	88	14	21	42	6	3	5	.375	0	13.6	5.33
Ohlendorf,Ross	Pit	27	26	26	167	191	23	50	118	9	7	12	.368	0	13.5	4.90
Okajima,Hideki	Bos	34	65	0	58	51	6	19	53	1	4	2	.667	0	11	3.26
Oliver,Darren	LAA	39	65	0	78	79	8	24	54	4	5	4	.556	0	12.3	3.92
Olsen,Scott	Was	26	22	22	121	131	18	50	91	3	5	8	.385	0	13.7	4.98
Olson,Garrett	Sea	26	29	5	57	59	8	27	44	4	2	4	.333	0	14.2	4.89
Ortiz,Russ	Hou	36	11	6	43	47	5	22	27	2	2	3	.400	0	14.9	5.23
Oswalt,Roy	Hou	32	33	33	205	205	18	48	159	8	13	10	.565	0	11.5	3.60
Owings,Micah	Cin	27	23	11	85	86	11	37	60	7	4	5	.444	0	13.8	4.66
Padilla,Vicente	LAD	32	26	24	141	149	18	51	97	10	7	8	.467	0	13.4	4.66
Palmer,Matt	LAA	31	45	8	114	119	12	49	80	12	6	7	.462	0	14.2	4.74
Papelbon,Jonathan	Bos	29	62	0	68	53	5	18	75	3	5	3	.625	41	9.8	2.38
Park,Chan Ho	Phi	37	43	3	66	74	10	27	51	4	3	4	.429	0	14.3	5.32
Parnell,Bobby	NYM	25	58	1	59	64	6	30	46	7	2	4	.333	0	15.4	5.34
Parra,Manny	Mil	27	28	28	147	158	13	67	130	4	7	9	.438	0	14	4.59
Paulino,Felipe	Hou	26	24	24	130	142	17	62	118	7	5	9	.357	0	14.6	5.19
Pavano,Carl	Min	34	32	32	200	227	25	45	132	10	10	12	.455	0	12.7	4.46
Peavy,Jake	CWS	29	33	33	215	181	19	69	217	7	16	8	.667	0	10.8	3.18
Pelfrey,Mike	NYM	26	31	31	194	211	15	74	122	13	9	12	.429	0	13.8	4.45
Pena,Tony	CWS	28	74	0	76	76	7	21	56	3	5	4	.556	0	11.8	3.67
Penny,Brad	SF	32	29	29	182	191	18	57	123	5	10	11	.476	0	12.5	4.01
Perez,Chris	Cle	24	61	0	63	46	7	37	76	5	4	3	.571	0	12.6	3.57

2010 Pitcher Projections

Pitcher	Team	Age	G	GS	IP	H	HR	BB	SO	HB	W	L	Pct	Sv	BR/9	ERA
Perez,Oliver	NYM	28	28	28	173	158	26	100	170	9	8	11	.421	0	13.9	4.73
Perez,Rafael	Cle	28	59	0	58	58	5	20	51	2	3	3	.500	1	12.4	3.72
Perkins,Glen	Min	27	12	10	56	63	8	20	38	2	3	4	.429	0	13.7	4.82
Petit,Yusmeiro	Ari	25	35	10	105	108	19	30	84	4	6	6	.500	0	12.2	4.37
Pettitte,Andy	NYY	38	31	31	198	210	19	59	150	3	13	9	.591	0	12.4	3.91
Pineiro,Joel	StL	31	33	33	205	224	22	53	118	7	12	11	.522	0	12.5	4.17
Pinto,Renyel	Fla	27	79	0	68	59	6	44	66	5	4	4	.500	0	14.3	4.37
Porcello,Rick	Det	21	34	34	195	205	26	59	105	3	10	11	.476	0	12.3	4.25
Price,David	TB	24	30	30	180	166	24	78	157	18	10	10	.500	0	13.1	4.30
Purcey,David	Tor	28	10	10	58	61	6	31	52	7	2	4	.333	0	15.4	5.12
Putz,J.J.	NYM	33	52	0	54	45	4	20	55	2	4	2	.667	0	11.2	3.00
Qualls,Chad	Ari	31	48	0	50	48	5	13	41	3	3	2	.600	39	11.5	3.42
Ramirez,Ramon	Bos	28	71	0	73	68	7	31	63	2	5	3	.625	0	12.5	3.82
Rauch,Jon	Min	31	74	0	72	68	8	22	59	1	5	3	.625	0	11.4	3.50
Ray,Chris	Bal	28	56	0	55	52	7	24	51	2	3	3	.500	0	12.8	4.09
Redding,Tim	NYM	32	38	20	156	171	22	59	104	5	7	11	.389	0	13.6	4.85
Reyes,Dennys	StL	33	74	0	46	44	3	22	38	2	3	2	.600	0	13.3	3.91
Rhodes,Arthur	Cin	40	64	0	53	45	3	21	52	1	4	2	.667	0	11.4	2.89
Richard,Clayton	SD	26	30	30	166	167	15	58	115	11	9	10	.474	0	12.8	4.01
Richmond,Scott	Tor	30	28	26	145	152	26	53	124	12	6	10	.375	0	13.5	5.03
Rincon,Juan	Col	31	30	0	36	35	3	16	33	1	2	2	.500	0	13	4.00
Rivera,Mariano	NYY	40	65	0	68	55	4	12	66	3	5	2	.714	44	9.3	2.12
Rivera,Saul	Was	32	43	0	59	64	3	26	42	2	3	4	.429	0	14	4.42
Robertson,David	NYY	25	46	0	45	34	2	23	63	0	4	1	.800	0	11.4	2.60
Robertson,Nate	Det	32	23	19	103	115	14	37	70	3	5	7	.417	0	13.5	4.89
Rodney,Fernando	Det	33	79	0	85	76	8	45	81	5	5	5	.500	30	13.3	4.02
Rodriguez,Francisco	NYM	28	69	0	64	47	5	30	79	1	4	3	.571	42	11	2.67
Rodriguez,Rafael	LAA	25	17	0	30	36	4	11	19	1	1	2	.333	0	14.4	5.40
Rodriguez,Wandy	Hou	31	33	33	212	214	24	75	179	8	11	12	.478	0	12.6	4.12
Roenicke,Josh	Tor	27	30	0	42	40	2	18	46	1	3	2	.600	0	12.6	3.64
Romero,J.C.	Phi	34	42	0	35	30	3	21	28	3	2	2	.500	0	13.9	4.11
Romero,Ricky	Tor	25	30	30	190	217	20	96	147	18	7	14	.333	0	15.7	5.59
Romo,Sergio	SF	27	57	0	44	34	2	12	48	2	4	1	.800	0	9.8	2.25
Rosa,Carlos	KC	25	32	0	41	44	4	17	34	3	2	3	.400	3	14	4.61
Rosales,Leo	Ari	29	38	0	47	46	5	17	34	1	3	2	.600	0	12.3	3.83
Rowland-Smith,Ryan	Sea	27	25	25	167	161	15	62	127	10	9	10	.474	0	12.6	3.88
Sabathia,CC	NYY	29	34	34	238	224	20	67	202	8	18	9	.667	0	11.3	3.40
Saito,Takashi	Bos	40	56	0	60	52	5	18	62	4	5	2	.714	0	11.1	3.00
Samardzija,Jeff	ChC	25	20	4	43	46	7	19	32	6	2	3	.400	0	14.9	5.44
Sampson,Chris	Hou	32	32	0	35	38	4	7	18	1	2	2	.500	0	11.8	3.86
Sanches,Brian	Fla	31	57	0	75	73	10	29	75	4	4	4	.500	0	12.7	4.20
Sanchez,Anibal	Fla	26	21	21	118	118	12	55	99	7	6	7	.462	0	13.7	4.42
Sanchez,Jonathan	SF	27	33	31	184	162	18	94	196	9	10	10	.500	0	13	3.91
Santana,Ervin	LAA	27	29	27	183	187	24	57	152	10	10	10	.500	0	12.5	4.23
Santana,Johan	NYM	31	33	33	225	188	26	57	224	4	17	8	.680	0	10	3.08
Sarfate,Dennis	Bal	29	45	0	42	41	5	28	42	3	2	3	.400	0	15.4	5.36
Saunders,Joe	LAA	29	29	29	178	186	21	56	110	4	10	10	.500	0	12.4	4.15
Scherzer,Max	Ari	25	30	30	180	163	16	74	194	15	11	9	.550	0	12.6	3.80
Schoeneweis,Scott	Ari	36	53	0	31	32	4	13	20	2	2	2	.500	0	13.6	4.65
Seay,Bobby	Det	32	64	0	48	47	3	18	40	3	3	2	.600	0	12.8	3.75
Sherrill,George	LAD	33	77	0	74	58	5	33	77	2	6	3	.667	2	11.3	2.92
Shields,James	TB	28	32	32	220	224	27	49	178	8	14	11	.560	0	11.5	3.80
Shields,Scot	LAA	34	62	0	60	52	5	23	56	2	4	2	.667	2	11.6	3.15
Shouse,Brian	TB	41	57	0	33	33	3	11	21	2	2	2	.500	0	12.5	3.82
Silva,Carlos	Sea	31	22	10	78	96	10	15	32	3	3	6	.333	0	13.2	4.85
Sipp,Tony	Cle	26	46	0	35	29	4	17	44	0	2	2	.500	0	11.8	3.34
Slowey,Kevin	Min	26	30	30	190	201	25	32	152	6	11	10	.524	0	11.3	3.84
Smith,Chris	Mil	29	37	0	47	53	7	14	36	3	2	3	.400	0	13.4	4.98
Smith,Joe	Cle	26	32	0	32	30	2	15	28	2	2	2	.500	0	13.2	3.94
Smoltz,John	StL	43	10	10	50	48	5	11	45	1	3	2	.600	0	10.8	3.42
Snell,Ian	Sea	28	30	30	169	175	18	75	137	5	7	11	.389	0	13.6	4.47
Sonnanstine,Andy	TB	27	21	13	77	87	10	18	54	3	4	5	.444	0	12.6	4.44
Soria,Joakim	KC	26	50	0	62	47	4	18	69	3	4	3	.571	32	9.9	2.32
Soriano,Rafael	Atl	30	81	0	79	57	8	25	90	3	6	3	.667	34	9.7	2.39
Sosa,Jorge	Was	33	35	0	45	47	6	20	32	1	2	3	.400	0	13.6	4.60
Sowers,Jeremy	Cle	26	27	27	150	167	15	48	81	8	7	9	.438	0	13.4	4.44
Springer,Russ	TB	41	78	0	58	52	7	18	53	2	4	3	.571	0	11.2	3.41
Stammen,Craig	Was	26	20	20	120	131	13	33	64	12	6	8	.429	0	13.2	4.50
Stauffer,Tim	SD	28	21	21	114	124	13	39	78	6	5	7	.417	0	13.3	4.58
Stetter,Mitch	Mil	29	65	0	39	33	3	19	39	3	2	2	.500	0	12.7	3.69
Stokes,Brian	NYM	30	59	0	61	66	6	25	42	5	3	4	.429	0	14.2	4.72
Street,Huston	Col	26	56	0	57	45	5	15	60	1	4	2	.667	31	9.6	2.37
Stults,Eric	LAD	30	6	6	32	36	4	12	25	3	1	2	.333	0	14.3	5.06
Suppan,Jeff	Mil	35	28	28	152	175	20	54	81	7	7	10	.412	0	14	5.09
Swarzak,Anthony	Min	24	12	12	50	57	6	17	34	7	2	3	.400	0	14.6	5.22
Tallet,Brian	Tor	32	50	3	85	86	9	36	63	4	4	5	.444	0	13.3	4.34
Tejeda,Robinson	KC	28	37	12	106	95	11	63	96	6	5	7	.417	0	13.9	4.33
Thatcher,Joe	SD	28	70	0	56	52	3	19	62	2	4	3	.571	0	11.7	3.21
Thompson,Brad	StL	28	31	4	64	71	8	18	30	6	3	4	.429	0	13.4	4.64
Thornton,Matt	CWS	33	73	0	81	70	7	33	86	2	5	4	.556	4	11.7	3.33
Tillman,Chris	Bal	22	22	22	123	126	15	50	116	20	6	8	.429	0	14.3	4.90

2010 Pitcher Projections

Pitcher	Team	Age	G	GS	IP	H	HR	BB	SO	HB	W	L	Pct	Sv	BR/9	ERA
Todd,Jesse	Cle	24	37	0	42	39	5	13	38	4	2	2	.500	0	12	3.86
Tomko,Brett	Oak	37	35	2	45	49	6	13	30	1	2	3	.400	0	12.6	4.40
Torres,Carlos	CWS	27	14	8	48	47	4	24	46	6	2	3	.400	0	14.4	4.50
Troncoso,Ramon	LAD	27	71	0	72	74	3	30	53	3	4	4	.500	0	13.4	3.88
Uehara,Koji	Bal	35	25	25	143	145	17	39	123	1	9	7	.688	2	9.6	4.22
Valdez,Merkin	SF	28	45	0	43	44	4	25	36	2	2	3	.400	0	14.9	5.02
Valverde,Jose	Hou	32	60	0	67	54	7	27	78	2	4	4	.500	38	11.1	3.22
VandenHurk,Rick	Fla	25	22	22	121	113	17	52	120	13	7	7	.500	0	13.2	4.30
Vargas,Claudio	Mil	32	58	0	66	69	10	24	49	3	3	4	.429	0	13.1	4.77
Vargas,Jason	Sea	27	23	8	74	82	11	28	56	4	3	5	.375	0	13.9	4.99
Vasquez,Esmerling	Ari	26	55	0	54	51	5	31	43	6	3	3	.500	0	14.7	4.67
Vasquez,Virgil	Pit	28	18	5	46	54	8	12	31	6	2	3	.400	0	14.1	5.48
Vazquez,Javier	Atl	33	31	31	215	205	26	52	204	7	15	9	.625	0	11.1	3.60
Veras,Jose	Cle	29	39	0	44	39	5	21	44	3	2	2	.500	0	12.9	4.09
Verlander,Justin	Det	27	35	35	235	219	22	76	215	13	15	11	.577	0	11.8	3.64
Villanueva,Carlos	Mil	26	60	10	110	106	16	39	95	3	6	6	.500	0	12.1	4.09
Villone,Ron	Was	40	71	0	54	51	5	29	44	3	3	3	.500	0	13.8	4.33
Volquez,Edinson	Cin	26	16	16	90	78	9	47	89	5	5	5	.500	0	13	4.00
Volstad,Chris	Fla	23	30	30	167	172	18	63	110	11	9	9	.500	0	13.3	4.37
Wagner,Billy	Bos	38	55	0	62	45	5	17	75	2	6	1	.857	0	9.3	2.18
Wainwright,Adam	StL	28	34	34	225	222	18	66	178	7	15	10	.600	0	11.8	3.64
Wakefield,Tim	Bos	43	16	16	96	93	12	33	62	6	6	5	.545	0	12.4	4.03
Walker,Tyler	Phi	34	44	0	48	45	6	17	40	1	3	2	.600	0	11.8	3.75
Wang,Chien-Ming	NYY	30	6	6	35	38	2	10	17	1	2	2	.500	0	12.6	3.86
Washburn,Jarrod	Det	35	25	25	152	150	19	45	86	6	8	8	.500	0	12.3	4.09
Weathers,David	Mil	40	72	0	70	66	8	30	49	0	1	4	.500	0	12.7	3.99
Weaver,Jeff	LAD	33	28	6	77	80	11	22	51	6	4	5	.444	0	13.7	5.03
Weaver,Jered	LAA	27	33	33	218	210	25	64	185	5	14	10	.583	0	11.5	3.67
Webb,Brandon	Ari	31	28	28	180	166	12	58	143	7	13	7	.650	0	11.6	3.40
Webb,Ryan	SD	24	50	0	46	54	6	17	34	5	2	3	.400	0	14.9	5.48
Wellemeyer,Todd	StL	31	22	12	79	82	10	38	58	3	4	5	.444	0	14	4.78
Wells,Kip	Cin	33	30	14	106	111	12	49	77	7	5	7	.417	0	14.2	4.84
Wells,Randy	ChC	27	30	30	188	194	20	60	147	14	10	10	.500	0	12.8	4.18
Wheeler,Dan	TB	32	71	0	59	50	8	17	52	1	4	2	.667	0	10.4	3.05
White,Sean	Sea	29	43	0	56	65	4	22	29	6	2	4	.333	0	14.9	4.98
Williams,Randy	CWS	34	47	0	34	35	5	16	31	1	1	2	.333	0	13.8	5.03
Wilson,Brian	SF	28	68	0	75	63	4	35	78	3	4	4	.500	41	12.1	3.24
Wilson,C.J.	Tex	29	78	0	78	72	7	36	76	6	5	4	.556	0	13.2	3.92
Wolf,Randy	LAD	33	34	34	200	191	24	67	159	9	12	10	.545	0	12	3.87
Wood,Kerry	Cle	33	56	0	56	47	6	24	62	4	4	3	.571	27	12.1	3.54
Wright,Jamey	KC	35	68	0	83	89	8	40	50	6	3	6	.333	0	14.6	4.88
Wright,Wesley	Hou	25	53	0	52	49	7	33	56	2	2	4	.333	0	14.5	4.85
Wuertz,Mike	Oak	31	65	0	74	60	7	31	84	0	5	3	.625	5	11.1	3.04
Young,Chris	SD	31	18	18	101	84	12	41	87	3	6	5	.545	0	11.4	3.48
Zambrano,Carlos	ChC	29	29	29	180	155	15	80	151	9	12	8	.600	0	12.2	3.60
Ziegler,Brad	Oak	30	70	0	75	78	4	23	49	2	4	4	.500	5	12.4	3.60
Zito,Barry	SF	32	33	33	196	184	22	83	140	7	11	11	.500	0	12.6	3.95
Zumaya,Joel	Det	25	32	0	36	30	3	21	30	1	2	2	.500	0	13	3.75

Career Targets

This section is designed to give probabilities on players achieving important career milestones. The method (formerly under the name of "The Favorite Toy") was developed by Bill James and takes into account a player's age and performance level in predicting the probability that he will accumulate certain career stats. A detailed explanation of how the system works can be found in the glossary.

Hats off to Randy Johnson, who notched career win number 300 this past season. Looking to next year, Alex Rodriguez should surpass 600 home runs by the All-Star Break, while one more healthy, productive year from slugger Jim Thome might just be enough to propel him into the top 10 home run hitters of all-time.

Other developments in the last year:

- Jose Reyes was listed on several hit charts last year and had a 27% chance to reach 1,000 stolen bases. With his injury he drops to 0% and is no longer on any chart.

-A-Rod, despite his injury (obviously less severe than Reyes), remains healthy in several areas: 87% chance of hitting 700 home runs, 40% chance to break the home run record, 34% chance to break the RBI record.

-Albert Pujols' monster season improves his chances in reaching 700 home runs (from 19 to 30%) and in breaking the doubles record (from 12 to 20%).

-Tim Lincecum remains baseball's most likely no-hit pitcher (but drops from 28 to 25%).

3,000 Hits	
% chance to reach milestone	
Jeter,Derek	96%
Rodriguez,Alex	89%
Damon,Johnny	46%
Pujols,Albert	44%
Cabrera,Miguel	36%
Suzuki,Ichiro	31%
Guerrero,Vladimir	26%
Rollins,Jimmy	25%
Ramirez,Hanley	24%
Tejada,Miguel	23%
Crawford,Carl	22%
Renteria,Edgar	22%
Anderson,Garret	21%
Cano,Robinson	21%
Wright,David	20%
Markakis,Nick	19%
Rodriguez,Ivan	19%
Young,Michael	18%
Griffey Jr.,Ken	17%
Abreu,Bobby	17%
Ramirez,Manny	17%
Pedroia,Dustin	17%
Lee,Carlos	14%
Lopez,Jose	14%
Cabrera,Orlando	13%
Braun,Ryan	13%
Beltre,Adrian	13%
Fielder,Prince	12%
Jones,Chipper	12%
Teixeira,Mark	11%
Zimmerman,Ryan	11%
Polanco,Placido	11%
Francoeur,Jeff	11%
Holliday,Matt	11%
Lee,Derrek	10%
Kemp,Matt	9%
Helton,Todd	8%
Roberts,Brian	7%
Ordonez,Magglio	7%
Rios,Alex	5%
Wells,Vernon	5%
Young,Delmon	4%
Butler,Billy	4%
Gonzalez,Adrian	4%
Lopez,Felipe	4%
Peralta,Jhonny	4%
Loney,James	3%
Morneau,Justin	3%
Sizemore,Grady	2%
Pierre,Juan	2%

Career Targets

762 Home Runs
% chance to break record

Rodriguez,Alex	40%
Pujols,Albert	18%
Fielder,Prince	10%
Dunn,Adam	7%
Howard,Ryan	6%
Cabrera,Miguel	< 1%

2,298 RBI
% chance to break record

Rodriguez,Alex	34%
Pujols,Albert	18%
Cabrera,Miguel	9%
Fielder,Prince	7%
Howard,Ryan	6%
Teixeira,Mark	1%

2,296 Runs Scored
% chance to break record

Rodriguez,Alex	22%
Pujols,Albert	9%
Ramirez,Hanley	3%

4,257 Hits
% chance to break record

Cabrera,Miguel	< 1%

900 Home Runs
% chance to reach milestone

Rodriguez,Alex	< 1%
Pujols,Albert	< 1%

2,000 RBI
% chance to reach milestone

Rodriguez,Alex	92%
Ramirez,Manny	52%
Pujols,Albert	40%
Cabrera,Miguel	23%
Fielder,Prince	18%
Howard,Ryan	18%
Teixeira,Mark	14%
Griffey Jr.,Ken	9%
Morneau,Justin	7%
Dunn,Adam	5%

6,857 Total Bases
% chance to break record

Pujols,Albert	14%
Rodriguez,Alex	10%
Cabrera,Miguel	6%
Fielder,Prince	2%

4,000 Hits
% chance to reach milestone

Jeter,Derek	6%
Cabrera,Miguel	5%
Pujols,Albert	3%
Ramirez,Hanley	< 1%

800 Home Runs
% chance to reach milestone

Rodriguez,Alex	24%
Pujols,Albert	12%
Fielder,Prince	7%
Dunn,Adam	2%
Howard,Ryan	2%

600 Home Runs
% chance to reach milestone

Griffey Jr.,Ken	done
Rodriguez,Alex	99%
Thome,Jim	96%
Ramirez,Manny	67%
Pujols,Albert	64%
Dunn,Adam	39%
Fielder,Prince	32%
Howard,Ryan	30%
Cabrera,Miguel	22%
Teixeira,Mark	14%

793 Doubles
% chance to break record

Pujols,Albert	20%
Pedroia,Dustin	14%
Markakis,Nick	11%
Roberts,Brian	10%
Cano,Robinson	7%
Wright,David	7%
Ramirez,Hanley	5%
Rollins,Jimmy	5%
Cabrera,Miguel	2%
Butler,Billy	2%

Most Likely No-Hitter
% chance to reach milestone

Lincecum,Tim	25%
Kershaw,Clayton	23%
Harden,Rich	21%
Verlander,Justin	20%
Gallardo,Yovani	19%
Lester,Jon	18%
Greinke,Zack	17%
Sanchez,Jonathan	15%
de la Rosa,Jorge	15%
Vazquez,Javier	15%

700 Home Runs
% chance to reach milestone

Rodriguez,Alex	87%
Pujols,Albert	30%
Fielder,Prince	17%
Dunn,Adam	16%
Howard,Ryan	13%
Cabrera,Miguel	7%
Teixeira,Mark	< 1%

500 Home Runs
% chance to reach milestone

Griffey Jr.,Ken	done
Rodriguez,Alex	done
Thome,Jim	done
Ramirez,Manny	done
Sheffield,Gary	done
Delgado,Carlos	96%
Pujols,Albert	91%
Dunn,Adam	87%
Howard,Ryan	58%
Fielder,Prince	57%

1,000 Stolen Bases
% chance to reach milestone

Crawford,Carl	5%

Pitchers on Course
For 300 Wins

Bill James

Name	2009 Age	R/L	W	L	EWL	Momentum	Chance
Roy Halladay	32	R	148	76	16.0	.889	.33
CC Sabathia	28	L	136	81	16.2	.863	.23
Dan Haren	20	R	79	02	14.3	.904	.21
Jamie Moyer	46	L	258	195	10.6	.670	.20
Andy Pettitte	37	L	229	135	12.5	.742	.18
Javier Vazquez	32	R	142	139	14.4	.851	.17
Justin Verlander	26	R	65	43	17.1	.823	.07
Cliff Lee	30	L	90	52	13.8	.794	.03
Derek Lowe	36	R	141	117	12.1	.744	.02
Josh Beckett	29	R	106	68	14.9	.742	.02
Bronson Arroyo	32	R	86	83	12.4	.792	.02
Mark Buehrle	30	L	135	97	11.0	.759	.02
A.J. Burnett	32	R	100	85	13.1	.737	.01
Barry Zito	31	L	133	106	10.2	.751	.01
Roy Oswalt	31	R	137	70	10.0	.746	.01
Chris Carpenter	34	R	117	74	11.2	.738	.01
Kevin Millwood	34	R	155	121	10.7	.670	.01
Jason Marquis	30	R	94	83	11.7	.726	.00
Jon Garland	29	R	117	102	10.3	.727	.00
Tim Wakefield	42	R	189	162	8.8	.620	.00
Livan Hernandez	34	R	156	151	9.0	.673	.00
Randy Wolf	32	L	101	85	10.4	.696	.00
Joel Pineiro	30	R	87	79	10.5	.639	.00

Note: EWL = Established Win Level

As of the end of the 2009 season no pitcher seems likely to emerge as a solid 300-win candidate for the next several seasons. The two pitchers who are well-positioned to emerge as 300-win candidates in about five years, if they can continue to pitch well, are Roy Halladay and CC Sabathia.

Dan Haren does well in our calculation (above) because Haren has made every start and pitched 200-plus innings a year for several years, which is characteristic of pitchers who last a long time.

It is likely that one or two pitchers now active will eventually win 300 games.

Baseball Glossary

% Inherited Scored
The percentage of inherited baserunners a relief pitcher allows to score.

% Pitches Taken
The percentage of pitches that a batter does not swing at out of the total number of pitches thrown to him.

1st Batter Average
The Batting Average that a relief pitcher allows to the first batter he faces when he enters a game.

1st Batter OBP
The On-Base Percentage that a relief pitcher allows to the first batter he faces when he enters a game.

1st to 3rd (Baserunning)
"Moved" is the number of times a runner goes from 1st base to 3rd base on a SINGLE. "Chances" are the number of times a runner is on 1st base and a batter is credited with a SINGLE.

1st to Home (Baserunning)
"Moved" is the number of times a runner goes from 1st base to home on a DOUBLE. "Chances" are the number of times a runner is on 1st base and a batter is credited with a DOUBLE.

2nd to Home (Baserunning)
"Moved" is the number of times a runner goes from 2nd base to home on a SINGLE. "Chances" are the number of times a runner is on 2nd base and a batter is credited with a SINGLE.

Active Career Batting Leaders
A list of batting leaders among active (appearing in the most recent season) players. An active player is eligible when he meets the minimum requirements for the following categories:

> 1,000 At Bats—Batting Average, On-Base Percentage, Slugging Average, At Bats Per HR, At Bats Per GDP, At Bats Per RBI, Strikeout to Walk Ratio
> 100 Stolen Base Attempts—Stolen Base Success Percentage

Active Career Pitching Leaders
A list of pitching leaders among active (appearing in the most recent season) players. An active player is eligible when he meets the minimum requirements for the following categories:

750 Innings Pitched—Earned Run Average, Opponent Batting Average, all "Per 9 Innings" categories, Strikeout to Walk Ratio
250 Games Started—Complete Game Frequency
100 Decisions—Win-Loss Percentage

AVG Allowed ScPos
The Batting Average allowed by a pitcher while pitching with runners in scoring position.

AVG Bases Loaded
The Batting Average of a hitter while batting with the bases loaded.

Base Taken
A player is credited with a Base Taken whenever he moves up a base on a Wild Pitch, Passed Ball, Balk, Sacrifice Fly (other than the runner who scores), or Defensive Indifference.

Batting Average
Hits divided by at bats.

Blown Save
When a relief pitcher enters a game in a Save Situation (see definition for Save Situation) and allows the other team to score the tying or go-ahead run.

Bomb (Intentional Walk)
An Intentional Walk blows up (Bombs) when the next batter after the intentional walk does not ground into a double play and subsequently more than one run scores in the inning.

BR Gain (Baserunning)
BR Gain (or Loss if a negative number) is the total of all the types of extra baserunning advances minus the (triple) penalty for all the BR Outs compared with what would be expected based on the MLB averages.

BR Outs (Baserunning)
BR Outs include the sum of Outs Advancing, Doubled Offs, and when a runner is tagged out on the bases when another runner moves up on a Wild Pitch, Passed Ball, or scores on a Sacrifice Fly.

BS Win
A Blown Save Win is a "win" credited to a reliever who has blown a save opportunity.

Career Targets
This method, once called the Favorite Toy, is a way to estimate the probability that a player will achieve a specific career goal. In this example, 3,000 hits will be used. The four components of the formula are Needed Hits, Years Remaining, Established Hit Level and Projected Remaining Hits.

Needed Hits. This is the number of Hits (or any statistic) that a player needs to reach a desired goal.

Years Remaining. This is the estimated number of years remaining in the player's career. It is determined using the player's age (on June 30th of the previous year; use 2009 when making the calculation after the 2009 season is complete). The formula is (42 - age) divided by two. This means a player who is 20 years old will have 11 remaining seasons, a player who is 25 years old will have 8.5 remaining seasons and a player who is 35 years old will have 3.5 remaining seasons. If the player is a catcher, then multiply his remaining seasons by .7. If a player is older than 39 (the Years Remaining calculation yields less than 1.5), consult the player's statistics for the most recent year. If the player either had 100 Hits or an Offensive Winning Percentage of .500 or greater, then the player will have 1.0 remaining seasons. If the player has both, he has 1.5 remaining seasons. If he has neither, he has .5 remaining seasons.

Established Hit Level. The Established Hit Level is a weighted average of the player's hits over the past three seasons. To calculate the Established Hit Level after the 2009 season is complete, add 2007 Hits, (2008 Hits multiplied by two) and (2009 Hits multiplied by three), then divide by six. If the Established Hit Level is less than 75% of the most recent performance (2009 Hits in this case), then the Established Hit Level is equal to .75 times the most recent performance.

Projected Remaining Hits. This is calculated by multiplying Years Remaining by the Established Hit Level.

The probability of achieving the specified goal is found by dividing Projected Remaining Hits by Needed Hits, then subtracting .5. The maximum that any player has of achieving a goal is .97 raised to the power of (Need Hits / Established Hit Level). This prevents the possibility of a player reaching a goal from being higher than 100 percent, which is impossible.

Catcher's ERA
The ERA for a catcher is equal to the ERA of pitchers pitching while the catcher is playing behind the plate. It is calculated exactly like ERA for pitchers. Take the number of earned runs allowed while the catcher is playing, multiply it by 9 and then divide it by the total number of defensive innings that the catcher was behind the plate.

Cheap Win
A starting pitcher who wins the game with a game score under 50 gets credit for a cheap win. See Game Score.

Clean Outing
A Clean Outing is a game in which the reliever is not charged with a run (earned or otherwise) AND does not allow an inherited runner to score.

Cleanup Slugging Average
The Slugging Average of a batter when he bats in the cleanup spot, or fourth, in the batting order.

Close and Late

A situation in a game that is very similar to a Save Situation. The following requirements are necessary for a Close and Late game:

1. The game is in the seventh inning or later AND
2. The batting team is either leading by one run or tied OR
3. The tying run is on base, at bat, or on deck.

Component ERA (ERC)

A statistic that estimates what a pitcher's ERA should have been, based on his pitching performance. The ERC formula is calculated as follows:

1. Subtract the pitcher's Home Runs Allowed from his Hits Allowed.
2. Multiply Step 1 by 1.255.
3. Multiply his Home Runs Allowed by four.
4. Add Steps 2 and 3 together.
5. Multiply Step 4 by .89.
6. Add his Walks and Hit Batsmen.
7. Multiply Step 6 by .475.
8. Add Steps 5 and 7 together.

This yields the pitcher's total base estimate (PTB), which is:

$$PTB = 0.89 \times (1.255 \times (H - HR) + 4 \times HR) + 0.475 \times (BB + HB)$$

For those pitchers for whom there is intentional walk data, use this formula instead:

$$PTB = 0.89 \times (1.255 \times (H - HR) + 4 \times HR) + 0.56 \times (BB + HB - IBB)$$

9. Add Hits and Walks and Hit Batsmen.
10. Multiply Step 9 by PTB.
11. Divide Step 10 by Batters Facing Pitcher. If BFP data is unavailable, approximate it by multiplying Innings Pitched by 2.9, then adding Step 9.
12. Multiply Step 11 by 9.
13. Divide Step 12 by Innings Pitched.
14. Subtract .56 from Step 13.

This is the pitcher's ERC, which is:

$$\frac{(H + BB + HB) \times PTB}{BFP \times IP} \times 9 - 0.56$$

If the result after Step 13 is less than 2.24, adjust the formula as follows:

$$\frac{(H + BB + HB) \times PTB}{BFP \times IP} \times 9 \times 0.75$$

498

Consecutive Days
A count of how many times the pitcher was used after having pitched on the previous day or (in a few cases) in an earlier game on the same day.

Defensive Runs Saved (Runs Saved, for short) is the innovative metric introduced by John Dewan in *The Fielding Bible—Volume II*. The Runs Saved value indicates how many runs a player saved or hurt his team in the field compared to the average player at his position. A player near zero Runs Saved is about average; a positive number of runs saved indicates above-average defense, below-average fielders post negative Runs Saved totals. There are eight components of Runs Saved:

Plus Minus Runs Saved (all positions except Catcher)
    2009 Leader: Chone Figgins (30)
Earned Runs Saved (Catchers)
    2009 Leader: Jason Varitek (8)
Stolen Base Runs Saved (Catchers)
    2009 Leader: Kenji Johjima (9)
Stolen Base Runs Saved (Pitchers)
    2009 Leaders: Buehrle/Kershaw/Verlander (4)
Bunt Runs Saved (Corner Infielders)
    2009 Leaders: Nick Johnson and Adrian Gonzalez (3)
Double Play Runs Saved (Middle Infielders)
    2009 Leaders: Placido Polanco and Ian Kinsler (5)
Outfield Arm Runs Saved (Outfielders)
    2009 Leader: Adam Jones (12)
Home Run Saving Catch Runs Saved (Outfielders)
    2009 Leader: Adam Jones (6)

Double Play %
Successful Double Plays divided by the number of Double Play opportunities. This statistic includes both the fielder who started the play and the pivot man.

Double Play Opportunity
A fielder is considered to have a double play opportunity when a ground ball is hit with a runner on first base and less than 2 outs and that fielder is involved in the play. This is used to calculate Double Play % and Pivot %.

Doubled Off
A runner is Doubled Off when he is out for failing to get back to his base before he, or the base, is tagged after a ball hit in the air is caught.

Early Entry
A count of the number of times the reliever entered the game in the sixth inning or earlier.

Earned Run Average
The number of earned runs that a pitcher surrenders per nine innings that he pitches. It is calculated by multiplying the total earned runs allowed by nine and dividing by the total number of innings pitched.

Easy Save

This label is used to separate Saves by difficulty level (Easy or Tough). A Save is considered Easy if the relief pitcher enters the game, pitches one inning or less, and the first batter he faces does not at least represent the tying run.

Fielding Percentage

The percentage of plays a player makes in the field without making an error out of the total number of opportunities. It is calculated by adding (Putouts plus Assists) and dividing by (Putouts plus Assists plus Errors).

Games Finished

The relief pitcher who is in the game for each team when the game ends is credited with a Game Finished.

Game Score

To determine the starting pitcher's Game Score:
Start with 50.
Add 1 point for each out recorded by the starting pitcher.
Add 2 points for each inning the pitcher completes after the fourth inning.
Add 1 point for each strikeout.
Subtract 2 points for each hit allowed.
Subtract 4 points for each earned run allowed.
Subtract 2 points for an unearned run.
Subtract 1 point for each walk.

GDP

Grounded into Double Play

GDP Opportunity

This is a situation where the batter has a chance to ground into a double play. It occurs with at least a runner on first base and less than two outs.

Ground / Fly Ratio (Grd/Fly, GB/FB)

Calculated for both batters and pitchers. For batters, it is the number of groundballs hit divided by the number of flyballs hit. For pitchers, it is exactly the same but uses the number of groundballs and flyballs allowed. Every fair batted ball is included except for bunts and line drives.

Hold

A relief pitcher is given a Hold anytime he enters the game in a Save Situation (see definition for Save Situation), records one out or more, and exits the game without giving up the lead. If the pitcher finishes the game, then he will only earn credit for a Save. He cannot receive credit for both a Hold and a Save.

Holds Adjusted Saves Percentage (same as Save/Hold Percentage)

Holds plus Saves divided by Holds plus Saves Opportunities.

Inherited Runner

When a relief pitcher enters the game, any runner who was on base at the time is considered an Inherited Runner.

Isolated Power

Slugging Average minus Batting Average.

K/BB Ratio

Strikeouts divided by Walks.

Leadoff On-Base Percentage

The On-Base Percentage of a batter when he bats leadoff, or first, in the batting order.

Leverage Index

Leverage is the amount of swing in the possible change in win probability, compared to the average swing in all situations. The average swing value, by definition, is indexed to 1.00.

If the score of the game is 12-0 or 14-1 the possible changes in win probability will be very close to negligible. Whether the pitcher gives up a home run or gets a double play ball, doesn't really change the outcome of the game. There won't be much swing in either direction for the probability of the win. But in the late innings of a close game, the change in win probability among the various events will have rather wild swings. With a runner on first, two outs, down by one, and in the bottom of the ninth, the game can hinge on one swing of that bat. A home run and an out will both end the game, but with different outcomes for the teams involved. The Leverage Index we use (LI) was developed at the website Tangotiger.net, and compiled at the website Fangraphs.com.

Long Outing

A Long Outing is one in which the starting pitcher throws more than 110 pitches. Prior to 2002, we used 120 pitches as the cutoff in the Manager's Record section.

Long Save

A Long Save is when the pitcher credited with a save pitches more than one inning.

Manufactured Runs

1) A run that scores without a hit, or a run on which the only hit(s) is/are infield hits, is always scored as a Manufactured Run.
2) A run which is driven in by a home run is never scored a Manufactured Run, under any circumstance.
3) A run which is driven in by a double or a triple is scored as a Manufactured Run only if *two* of the four bases result from advancing on one of these four acts: a sacrifice bunt, a stolen base, a hit and run, or a bunt single.
4) Otherwise, a run is considered to be a Manufactured Run if two of the four bases do not result from the runner being forced along by a walk, a hit batsman, or a safe hit reaching the outfield.
5) A forceout or fielder's choice which does not improve the position of the base runners should not be counted as contributing toward a Manufactured Run.   Advancing on a

forceout or a fielder's choice DOES count toward a manufactured run, if the play is one which improves the position of the baserunners.

6) A base "gained" on a double play does not count as a contribution to a Manufactured Run. A run scored on a double play is a Manufactured Run only if two of the OTHER bases are not attributable to forced advancement.

Not Good Outcome (Intentional Walk)

A Not Good Outcome (NG) for an Intentional Walk occurs when one run scored in the inning after the intentional walk (and the next batter after the intentional walk did not ground into a double play).

Offensive Winning Percentage (OWP)

A player's Offensive Winning Percentage is the winning percentage of a hypothetical team which has an offense consisting of nine of that player, and pitching and defense which is average for the player's league. It is calculated by taking the square of RC/27 (see the definition for Runs Created per 27 Outs), dividing it by the sum of the square of RC/27 and the square of the average runs scored per game in the league.

On-Base Percentage

(Hits plus Walks plus Hit by Pitcher) divided by (At Bats plus Walks plus Hit by Pitcher plus Sacrifice Flies).

$$\frac{H + BB + HBP}{AB + BB + HBP + SF}$$

Opponent Batting Average

Hits Allowed divided by (Batters Faced minus Walks minus Hit Batsmen minus Sacrifice Hits minus Sacrifice Flies minus Catcher's Interference).

$$\frac{H}{BFP - BB - HBP - SH - SF - CI}$$

Opposition OPS

The OPS of the hitters facing the pitcher.

Out Advancing

A runner is out advancing when he is tagged out attempting to score from 2nd base on a single or from 1st base on a double, or attempting to go from 1st base to 3rd base on a single.

PA*

Used in the denominator for the calculation of On-Base Percentage. It is calculated by subtracting (Sacrifice Hits plus Times Reached Base on Defensive Interference) from Plate Appearances (see definition for Plate Appearances).

Park Index

The Park Index of a given ballpark is the amount that the ballpark influences a given statistic. The following is a calculation of a park index using runs as the statistic:

    1.Add Runs and Opponent Runs in home games.
    2.Add At Bats and Opponent At Bats in home games. (If At Bats are unavailable, use home games.)
    3.Divide Step 1 by Step 2.
    4.Add Runs and Opponent Runs in road games.
    5.Add At Bats and Opponent At Bats in road games. (If At Bats are unavailable, use road games.)
    6.Divide Step 4 by Step 5.
    7.Divide Step 3 by Step 6.
    8.Multiply Step 7 by 100.

An index of 100 means the park is completely neutral and does not influence the particular statistic at all. A park index of 112 for runs indicates that teams score 12 percent more runs in this ballpark than a neutral park. A park index of 92 for runs means that teams tend to score 8 percent fewer runs in this ballpark than a neutral park.

PCS (Pitchers' Caught Stealing)
The number of runners officially scored as Caught Stealing where the pitcher initiated the play. The normal Caught Stealing is when a runner is out attempting to steal a base but the play was initiated by the catcher. PCS plays are often referred to as pickoffs, but differ when the runner breaks towards the next base as opposed to returning to the base he was currently on. Pickoffs occur when the pitcher throws to a base that a runner is leading from, and the runner is out attempting to return to that base. Pickoffs are not an official statistic.

Pitches per PA
The total number of pitches a hitter sees divided by his total Plate Appearances.

Pivot %
Successful Double Plays turned by pivot man divided by the number of Double Play opportunities with that pivot man involved.

Plate Appearances
At Bats plus Total Walks plus Hit By Pitcher plus Sacrifice Hits plus Sacrifice Flies plus Times Reached on Defensive Interference.

Platoon Advantage %
Platoon Advantage % is the percentage of players in the starting lineup who have the platoon advantage (i.e. bats right against a left-handed pitcher or bats left against a right-hander) against the starting pitcher; e.g. if the opposing starting pitcher is right handed and the batting team has six left-handed batters in its lineup, the platoon advantage for that game would be 67%.

Plus/Minus System
The Plus/Minus System is a method for evaluating defensive play on batted balls. It is made possible by a game scoring system in which each batted ball is rated for type (line drive, grounder, etc.), velocity within its type (hard, medium or soft), and location on the

field. A player gets credit (a "plus" number) if he makes a play that at least one other player at his position missed during the season and he loses credit (a "minus" number") if he misses a play that at least one player made. The size of the credits are proportional to the percentage of times all players make the play. All plays for each player at his position are summed to get his total plus/minus for the season. A total of zero would be average and any other number would approximate how many plays more or less the player made than the average player at the position for the number of chances the player had to field batted balls.

Power/Speed Number
A single number that reflects a combination of power and speed. To achieve a high Power/Speed Number, a player must score high in both power and speed. To calculate the Power/Speed Number, multiply Home Runs by Stolen Bases by two, and divide by the sum of Home Runs and Stolen Bases.

$$\frac{2 \times HR \times SB}{HR + SB}$$

PPO (Pitcher Pickoff)
The number of baserunners thrown out when a pitcher throws to a base with a leading baserunner, and the runner is tagged out attempting to return to the base. PPO is not an official statistic and does not count toward Caught Stealing totals.

Quality Start
A game where the starting pitcher pitches for at least six innings and allows no more than three earned runs.

Quality Start Percentage
Quality Starts divided by Games Started (see the definition for Quality Start).

Quick Hooks
Used in the Manager's Record. For Quick Hooks and Slow Hooks a score is calculated for each game that is the sum of the number of Pitches plus 10 times the number of Runs Allowed. The bottom 25% of scores in the league are considered to be Quick Hooks.

Range Factor
The number of Successful Chances (Putouts plus Assists) times nine divided by the number of Defensive Innings Played. The average for a player at each position in 2009:
      Second Base: 4.81
      Third Base: 2.62
      Shortstop: 4.37
      Left Field: 2.02
      Center Field: 2.66
      Right Field: 2.10

RBI %

The percentage of all potential runs driven in by a certain hitter. Simply put, it's RBIs divided by RBI Opportunities. An RBI Opportunity is any runner on base when the hitter steps up to the plate. We also count the hitter himself, as he can drive in a runner with no one on base via the solo home run. Here's the full formula:

A = Runs Batted In
B = Men On Base + Plate Appearances – Walks – Hit By Pitch – Reaches on Catcher's Interference + C
C = Walks, Hit By Pitch, or Reaches on Catcher's Interference with the bases loaded (resulting in a Run Batted In)

Regular Saves
Any save which does not meet the definition either of an Easy Save or a Tough Save is a "Regular" Save.

Run Support Per 9 IP
The total number of runs scored by a pitcher's team while he is in the game multiplied by nine and divided by total Innings Pitched.

Runs Created
"Runs Created" is an estimate of the number of a team's runs which are created by each individual hitter. The Cincinnati Reds scored 820 runs last year, let us say. How many of those were created by Joey Votto? How many by Brandon Phillips? How many by Jay Bruce?

There are many different formulas for estimating runs created. . .did you want the one that involves swinging a dead cat in the cemetery under a full moon? Yeah, I don't blame you. . .worm-eaten persimmons are so hard to find in the modern world.

This is the one we use now; it is complicated enough. First, there is an "A" Factor in the formula, a "B" Factor, and a "C" factor. The "A" Factor, which represents the number of times the hitter is on base, is Hits, Plus Walks, Plus Hit Batsmen, Minus Caught Stealing, Minus Grounded Into Double Play. The "B" Factor, which represents the hitter's ability to advance other runners, is 1.125 times the player's Singles, plus 1.69 times his Doubles, plus 3.02 times his Triples, plus 3.73 times his Home Runs, plus .29 times his Walks and Hit Batsmen, not counting intentional walks, plus .492 times Sacrifice Hits, Sacrifice Flies and Stolen Bases, minus .04 times Strikeouts. The "C" Factor, which represents opportunities, is At Bats, Plus Walks, Plus Hit By Pitch, Plus Sacrifice Hits, Plus Sacrifice Flies.

Having made these initial calculations of the A, B and C factors, we then change the "A" factor to "A plus 2.4 times C".

We change the "B" factor to "B plus 3 times C".

We change the "C" factor to "9 times C".

Multiply A times B, divide by then new C ("9 times C"), and subtract .90 times by the original C.

This is our first, temporary estimate of the player's runs created. We what we have done here is to ask these questions:

1. How many runs would a team probably score that consisted of eight "ordinary" type of hitters, plus this particular hitter?
2. How many of those runs would be created by the eight ordinary type of hitters?
3. What is the difference-and thus, how many runs did our player create?

To estimate this, we have placed our player in the context of eight hitters with a .300 on base percentage (2.4 divided by 8) and a .375 advancement percentage (3 divided by 8). For each trip through the batting order, the eight ordinary-type hitters would produce 9/10 of a run (2.4 times 3, divided by 8). The "9" in the denominator is eight ordinary hitters plus our man. The "-.9" being subtracted at the end is the runs created by the "ordinary" hitters. In essence, we have placed the hitter in a neutral solution, measured the neutral solution without our hitter, measured it with our hitter, and then estimated the contribution of this hitter as being the difference between the two.

We're not quite done. After that, we adjust the player's runs created estimate for his performance in two "run-sensitive" situations. Suppose that a player whose overall batting average is .250 has batted 100 times with runners in scoring position, and has gone 30-for-100. That's five hits better than expected, 30 hits where we would have expected 25. His team will score an extra five runs because he has done that, and so we increase the player's runs created estimate by five runs. If the player has hit poorly with runners in scoring position, we decrease it by the shortfall in the same way.

Suppose that a player has batted 250 times with runners on base, 250 times with the bases empty, and that he has hit 20 home runs overall. We would expect him to have hit 10 with men on base, 10 with the bases empty, right?

Suppose that he didn't. Suppose that he hit 12 with the bases empty, 8 with men on base. His team would score two runs less than expected because he did this, and we would thus penalize him two runs for the shortfall.

This is our second runs created estimate-the player's runs created, adjusted for his batting performance in run-sensitive situations.

Suppose, however, that we figure the runs created for all of the individuals on a team, and we add them up, and it doesn't match the runs actually scored by the team? What if the formulas say that the team should have scored 800 runs, but they actually scored 820?

Then obviously, the formulas missed. We're trying to measure the runs ACTUALLY created by each hitter as best we can, in the real world, not the theoretical impact of some combination of singles, doubles, triples and walks. If the actual number is different than the estimates, we have to adjust the estimates to fit the facts. In this case-820 runs scored with only 800 runs created-we would multiply each runs created estimate by 820/800, or 1.025. Then we round it off to an integer, and that's the player's estimated runs created.

Let go of that cat, Arthur.   Heck, the moon isn't full for three weeks, anyway.

Runs Created per 27 Outs (RC/27)

This statistic estimates the number of runs per game that a team made up of nine of the same player would score. To calculate RC/27, multiply Runs Created by league outs per team game, divide the result by outs made by the player (the sum of at bats plus sacrifice hits plus sacrifice flies plus caught stealing plus grounded into double plays, minus hits). The formula written out is:

$$\frac{\dfrac{RC \times 3 \times LgIP}{2 \times LgG}}{AB - H + SH + SF + CS + GDP}$$

Save Opportunities

The sum of Saves and Blown Saves (see Save Situation).

Save/Hold Percentage (same as Holds Adjusted/Saves Percentage)

The sum of Saves and Holds, divided by the sum of Saves, Holds, and Blown Saves.

For several years we figured "Save Percentage", which is simply Saves divided by Save Opportunities, and this stat has some currency in the game. But the Save Percentage severely discriminates against middle relievers, who have no real chance to be credited with the Save, since they will be taken out of the game and replaced by the Closer even if they throw 110 miles an hour and strike out everybody they see. Middle relievers typically have Save Percentages of zero, even if they pitch well. The Save/Hold Percentage is a much more realistic evaluation of a pitcher's success in Save situations.

Save Percentage

A pitcher's Saves divided by the total number of Save Situations he faces (see definition for Save Situation).

Save Situation

A relief pitcher is in a Save Situation when he enters the game with his team in the lead, has the opportunity to finish the game, is not the winning pitcher of record at the time, and meets any one of the three following conditions:

> 1.The pitcher's team is leading by no more than three runs and the pitcher has the chance to pitch for at least one inning,
> OR
> 2.The pitcher enters the game with the potential tying run on base, at bat, or on deck,
> OR
> 3.The pitcher pitches three or more effective innings regardless of the lead. The determination of a save in this situation is made by the official scorer.

It is not possible to have more than one save credited to a single team in a game.

SB Gain (Baserunning)

Stolen Base attempts must be successful greater than about two thirds of the time to have a positive result on the number of runs scored. SB gain is therefore the number of bases stolen minus two times the number of caught stealing (SB Gain = SB - 2CS). For example, a runner steals 30 bases and is caught stealing 7 times. His SB Gain would be 30 - 2*7 = +16. Another runner steals 10 bases and is caught stealing 6 times. His SB Gain (actually a loss) would be 10 - 2*6 = -2.

SB Success Percentage

Stolen Bases divided by the number of Stolen Base attempts (Stolen Bases plus Caught Stealing).

$$\frac{SB}{SB + CS}$$

Secondary Average

A number meant to reflect everything else except for batting average. A player will have a high Secondary Average if he hits for power, takes walks and steals bases. It is calculated with the following formula:

$$\frac{TB - H + BB + SB}{AB}$$

Similarity Score

A number which reflects the similarity between two different statistical lines, either for a player or for a team. A score of 1,000 means that the statistical lines are identical.

Slow Hooks

Used in the Manager's Record. For Quick Hooks and Slow Hooks a score is calculated for each game that is the sum of the number of Pitches plus 10 times the number of Runs Allowed. The top 25% of scores in the league are considered to be Slow Hooks.

Slugging Average

Total Bases divided by At Bats.

$$\frac{TB}{AB}$$

Speed Score

Speed Score is a number which evaluates how fast a player is. To calculate the Speed Score, start with the player's statistics over the last two seasons combined. A value will be found for each of the following six categories and will be combined for a final score at the end:

1.Stolen Base Percentage. The value of this category is:

$$\left(\frac{SB+3}{SB+CS+7} - 0.4\right) \times 20$$

2.Frequency of Stolen Base Attempts. The value of this category is:

$$\frac{\sqrt{\dfrac{SB+CS}{Singles+BB+HBP}}}{0.07}$$

3.Percentage of Triples. This is calculated by taking the percentage of triples out of the number of balls put in play. To get the percentage, use this formula:

$$\frac{3B}{AB-HR-SO}$$

From this assign an integer from 0 to 10, based on the following chart:

Less than .001	0
.001 - .0023	1
.0023 - .0039	2
.0039 - .0058	3
.0058 - .0080	4
.0080 - .0105	5
.0105 - .013	6
.013 - .0158	7
.0158 - .0189	8
.0189 - .0223	9
.0223 or more	10

4. Runs Scored Percentage. This is calculated by taking the percentage of times the player scores a run out of the number of times the player is on base. To get the percentage, use this formula:

$$\frac{\left(\dfrac{R-HR}{H+HBP+BB-HR} - 0.1\right)}{0.04}$$

5. Grounded Into Double Play Frequency. To get the frequency, use this formula:

$$\frac{0.055 - \left(\dfrac{GIDP}{AB-HR-SO}\right)}{0.005}$$

6. Range Factor. The value of this category depends on the players position:

Catcher—1
First Baseman—2

Designated Hitter—1.5
Second Baseman—1.25 x Range Factor
Third Baseman—1.51 x Range Factor
Shortstop—1.52 x Range Factor
Outfield—3 x Range Factor

For an explanation on Range Factor, consult the definition in this glossary. Remember to figure range factors over a two-year period.

If any category value is greater than 10, then reduce it to 10. If any value is less than zero, then increase the value to zero. All category values must fall within the zero to 10 range. The Speed Score is then calculated by discarding the lowest of the six values, and taking the average of the remaining five.

Total Bases
Hits plus Doubles plus (2 times Triples) plus (3 times Home Runs).

$$H + 2B + (2 \times 3B) + (3 \times HR)$$

Tough Loss
A starting pitcher who loses the game with a game score over 50 gets credit for a tough loss. See Game Score.

Tough Save
This label is used to separate Saves by difficulty level (Easy or Tough). A Save is considered Tough if the relief pitcher enters the game with the tying run on base.

Win Probability
The probability of a team winning the game determined at any time during the game based on the score, inning, outs and base situation.

Winning Percentage
Wins divided by (Wins plus Losses).

Baseball Info Solutions

What will box scores look like in a hundred years? What did they look like a century ago? Whatever the difference, it can almost be entirely attributed to advances in baseball statistics analysis.

But analysis alone is not responsible for the prevalence of advanced statistics now in broadcasts and bar-room arguments across the world; you need to have high quality, innovative data or you may draw the wrong conclusions. Baseball Info Solutions has been supplying top notch, timely, and in-depth baseball data to its customers since 2002.

BIS collects a statistical snapshot of every important moment of ever Major League Baseball game with the most advanced technology, resulting in a database that includes traditional data, pitch-by-pitch data, and defensive positioning data. The company also has the highest quality pitch charting data available anywhere, including pitch type, location, and velocity.

BIS provides comprehensive services to about half of the 30 Major League Baseball teams, as well as many sports agents, media, fantasy services, game companies and private individuals.

John Dewan, the principal owner of BIS, has been on the cutting edge of baseball analysis for over 20 years. His experience goes all the way back to his days as Executive Director of Project Scoresheet, the Bill James-led effort that pioneered the new wave of baseball statistics that are now common terminology.

President Steve Moyer brings nearly 20 years of baseball industry experience to BIS. His hands-on, can do business demeanor helps set BIS apart from its competition.

The rest of the BIS team includes former professional and collegiate baseball players as well as programming and database management experts. Over the last five seasons, BIS has more than tripled its full-time staff.

BIS continues to grow within the industry while emphasizing personal attention to its customers. This focus on personal attention is evidenced by the fact that if you contact the office with an inquiry you may very well find yourself speaking directly to the company president.

To contact BIS:

Baseball Info Solutions
41 S. 2nd Street
Coplay, PA 18037
610-261-2370
www.baseballinfosolutions.com

Notes

Notes

Notes

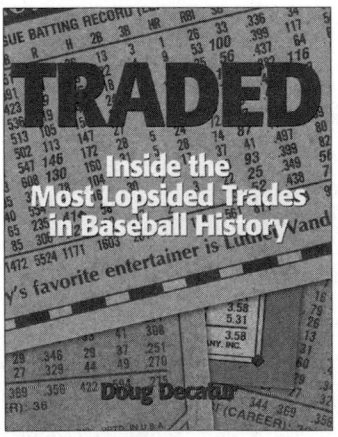